THE
ALL ENGLAND
LAW REPORTS
1981

Volume 1

Editor
PETER HUTCHESSON LL M
Barrister, New Zealand

Assistant Editor
BROOK WATSON
of Lincoln's Inn, Barrister
and of the New South Wales Bar

Consulting Editor
WENDY SHOCKETT
of Gray's Inn, Barrister

London
BUTTERWORTHS

ENGLAND: Butterworth & Co (Publishers) Ltd
                London: 88 Kingsway, WC2B 6AB

AUSTRALIA: Butterworths Pty Ltd
                Sydney: 586 Pacific Highway, Chatswood, NSW 2067
                Also at Melbourne, Brisbane, Adelaide and Perth

CANADA: Butterworth & Co (Canada) Ltd
                Toronto: 2265 Midland Avenue, Scarborough, M1P 4S1

NEW ZEALAND: Butterworths of New Zealand Ltd
                Wellington: 33–35 Cumberland Place

SOUTH AFRICA: Butterworth & Co (South Africa) (Pty) Ltd
                Durban: 152–154 Gale Street

USA: Butterworth & Co (Publishers) Inc
                Boston: 10 Tower Office Park, Woburn, Mass 01801

©

Butterworth & Co (Publishers) Ltd

1981

ISBN 0 406 85140 9

Typeset by CCC, printed and bound in Great Britain by William Clowes (Beccles) Limited, Beccles and
London

House of Lords

The Lord High Chancellor: Lord Hailsham of St Marylebone

Lords of Appeal in Ordinary

Lord Wilberforce
Lord Diplock
Lord Edmund-Davies
Lord Fraser of Tullybelton
Lord Russell of Killowen

Lord Keith of Kinkel
Lord Scarman
Lord Roskill
Lord Bridge of Harwich

Court of Appeal

The Lord High Chancellor

The Lord Chief Justice of England: Lord Lane

The Master of the Rolls: Lord Denning

The President of the Family Division: Sir John Lewis Arnold

Lords Justices of Appeal

Sir Denys Burton Buckley
(retired 6th February 1981)
Sir John Frederick Eustace Stephenson
Sir Frederick Horace Lawton
Sir Roger Fray Greenwood Ormrod
Sir Sebag Shaw
Sir George Stanley Waller
Sir James Roualeyn Hovell-Thurlow-
Cumming-Bruce
Sir Edward Walter Eveleigh
Sir Henry Vivian Brandon

Sir Sydney William Templeman
Sir John Francis Donaldson
Sir John Anson Brightman
Sir Desmond James Conrad Ackner
Sir Robin Horace Walford Dunn
Sir Peter Raymond Oliver
Sir Tasker Watkins VC
Sir Patrick McCarthy O'Connor
Sir William Hugh Griffiths
Sir Michael John Fox
(appointed 9th February 1981)

Chancery Division

The Lord High Chancellor

The Vice-Chancellor: Sir Robert Edgar Megarry

Sir John Patrick Graham
  (retired 26th January 1981)
Sir Peter Harry Batson Woodroffe Foster
Sir John Norman Keates Whitford
Sir Ernest Irvine Goulding
Sir Raymond Henry Walton
Sir Michael John Fox
  (appointed Lord Justice of Appeal,
    9th February 1981)

Sir Christopher John Slade
Sir Nicolas Christopher Henry Browne-
  Wilkinson
Sir John Evelyn Vinelott
Sir George Brian Hugh Dillon
Sir Martin Charles Nourse
Sir Douglas William Falconer
  (appointed 27th January 1981)
Sir Jean-Pierre Frank Eugene Warner
  (appointed 3rd March 1981)

Queen's Bench Division

The Lord Chief Justice of England

Sir Alan Abraham Mocatta
Sir John Thompson
Sir Helenus Patrick Joseph Milmo
Sir Joseph Donaldson Cantley
Sir Hugh Eames Park
Sir Stephen Chapman
Sir Bernard Caulfield
Sir Hilary Gwynne Talbot
Sir William Lloyd Mars-Jones
Sir Ralph Kilner Brown
Sir Phillip Wien
Sir Peter Henry Rowley Bristow
Sir Hugh Harry Valentine Forbes
Sir Robert Hugh Mais
Sir Neil Lawson
Sir David Powell Croom-Johnson
Sir John Raymond Phillips
Sir Leslie Kenneth Edward Boreham
Sir John Douglas May
Sir Michael Robert Emanuel Kerr
Sir Alfred William Michael Davies
Sir John Dexter Stocker
Sir Kenneth George Illtyd Jones
Sir Haydn Tudor Evans
Sir Peter Richard Pain

Sir Kenneth Graham Jupp
Sir Robert Lionel Archibald Goff
Sir Stephen Brown
Sir Gordon Slynn
  (appointed as an Advocate-General at the Court
    of Justice of the European Communities,
    1st March 1981)
Sir Roger Jocelyn Parker
Sir Ralph Brian Gibson
Sir Walter Derek Thornley Hodgson
Sir James Peter Comyn
Sir Anthony John Leslie Lloyd
Sir Frederick Maurice Drake
Sir Brian Thomas Neill
Sir Roderick Philip Smith
Sir Michael John Mustill
Sir Barry Cross Sheen
Sir David Bruce McNeill
Sir Harry Kenneth Woolf
Sir Thomas Patrick Russell
Sir Peter Edlin Webster
Sir Thomas Henry Bingham
Sir Iain Derek Laing Glidewell
Sir Henry Albert Skinner
Sir Peter Murray Taylor

Family Division

The President of the Family Division

Sir John Brinsmead Latey
Sir Alfred Kenneth Hollings
Sir Charles Trevor Reeve
Sir Francis Brooks Purchas
Dame Rose Heilbron
Sir Brian Drex Bush
Sir Alfred John Balcombe
Sir John Kember Wood

Sir Ronald Gough Waterhouse
Sir John Gervase Kensington Sheldon
Sir Thomas Michael Eastham
Dame Margaret Myfanwy Wood Booth
Sir Christopher James Saunders French
Sir Anthony Leslie Julian Lincoln
Dame Ann Elizabeth Oldfield Butler-Sloss
Sir Anthony Bruce Ewbank

CITATION

These reports are cited thus:

[1981] 1 All ER

REFERENCES

These reports contain references to the following major works of legal reference described in the manner indicated below.

Halsbury's Laws of England

The reference 35 Halsbury's Laws (3rd Edn) 366, para 524, refers to paragraph 524 on page 366 of volume 35 of the third edition, and the reference 26 Halsbury's Laws (4th Edn) para 577 refers to paragraph 577 on page 296 of volume 26 of the fourth edition of Halsbury's Laws of England.

Halsbury's Statutes of England

The reference 5 Halsbury's Statutes (3rd Edn) 302 refers to page 302 of volume 5 of the third edition of Halsbury's Statutes of England.

English and Empire Digest

References are to the replacement volumes (including reissue volumes) of the Digest, and to the continuation volumes of the replacement volumes.

The reference 44 Digest (Repl) 144, 1240, refers to case number 1240 on page 144 of Digest Replacement Volume 44.

The reference 28(1) Digest (Reissue) 167, 507, refers to case number 507 on page 167 of Digest Replacement Volume 28(1) Reissue.

The reference Digest (Cont Vol D) 571, 678b, refers to case number 678b on page 571 of Digest Continuation Volume D.

Halsbury's Statutory Instruments

The reference 12 Halsbury's Statutory Instruments (Third Reissue) 125 refers to page 125 of the third reissue of volume 12 of Halsbury's Statutory Instruments; references to subsequent reissues are similar.

CORRIGENDA

[1980] 3 All ER
p 840. **Re Furse (deceased).** Counsel for the Crown: read '*Donald Rattee QC* and *Peter Gibson*' instead of as printed.
p 913. **R v Sheppard.** Line *b* 2: between the words 'care' and 'whenever' insert the following, 'but they might be quite able to understand that they must obtain medical care'.

[1981] 1 All ER
p 54. **R v Bolton Supplementary Benefits Appeal Tribunal, ex parte Fordham.** Solicitors: for '*Treasury Solicitor*' substitute '*Solicitor to the Department of Health and Social Security*'.
p 100. **Green v Green (Barclays Bank Ltd, third party).** Solicitors for the husband: should read '*Hill & Perks*, Norwich'.
p 379. **Property Discount Corpn Ltd v Lyon Group Ltd.** Line *a* 5: dates of hearing and judgment should read 29th, 30th, 31st July 1980.
p 652. **A/S Awilco v Fulvia SpA di Navigazione.** Line *f* 2: dates of hearing and judgment should read 19th, 20th January, 19th February 1981.
p 660. **Laws v Florinplace Ltd.** Line *d* 4: for 'danger' read 'damage'.
p 754. **R v Lands Tribunal, ex parte City of London Corpn.** Counsel for the corporation: after '*Bernard Marder QC*' add 'and *Jeremy Sullivan*'.

Cases reported in volume 1

Re Jones (deceased)

b FAMILY DIVISION
ARNOLD P
17th JULY 1980

Will – Soldier's or mariner's privileged will – Actual military service – Soldier on patrol during armed and clandestine insurrection – Terrorist activities in Northern Ireland – Wills Act 1837, s 11.

c

The deceased was a soldier serving in Northern Ireland in 1978 at a time of armed and clandestine insurrection against the government. His unit was stationed in Northern Ireland as part of the armed forces deployed there at the request of the civil authorities to assist in the maintenance of law and order. While on patrol the deceased was shot and
d mortally wounded by an unknown gunman. En route to the hospital he stated to an officer and warrant officer of his battalion, 'If I don't make it, make sure Anne gets all my stuff.' Anne was his fiancée. The deceased died the next day. Under a written will made previously the deceased had left everything to his mother. On a summons taken out by the fiancée applying for the deceased's oral declaration to be admitted as his last will and testament on the basis that it was a privileged will under s 11ᵃ of the Wills Act 1837 the
e question arose whether the deceased had been 'in actual military service' at the time of making the declaration and was therefore entitled to make a nuncupative will.

Held – Whether the deceased was in actual military service for the purposes of s 11 of the 1837 Act depended on the nature of the activities of the deceased and the unit or force to which he was attached, and not on the character of the opposing operations. The fact
f that there was not a state of war or that the enemy was not a uniformed force engaged in regular warfare or an insurgent force organised on conventional lines was irrelevant in deciding whether the deceased was in actual military service. Nor was it relevant whether the deceased's military service took place in the context of a foreign expedition or invasion or a local insurrection. On the facts the deceased had clearly been in actual military service at the time of making the declaration and it would therefore be admitted
g as a valid nuncupative will (see p 3 b to d and p 5 j to p 6 b, post).

In the Will of Anderson (1958) 75 WN (NSW) 334 followed.

Shearman v Pyke (1724) 3 Curt at 539, *Drummond v Parish* (1843) 3 Curt 522, *In the goods of Tweedale* (1874) LR 3 P & D 204 and *Re Booth* [1926] All ER Rep 594 considered.

Notes
h For applications for orders admitting to proof nuncupative wills, see 17 Halsbury's Laws (4th Edn) para 841, and for cases on the subject, see 39 Digest (Repl) 400–403, 209–242.

For the Wills Act 1837, s 11, see 39 Halsbury's Statutes (3rd Edn) 862.

Cases referred to in judgment
Anderson, In the Will of (1958) 75 WN (NSW) 334.
j *Booth, Re, Booth v Booth* [1926] P 118, [1926] All ER Rep 594, 95 LJP 64, 135 LT 229, 48 Digest (Repl) 200, *1771*.

---

a Section 11 provides: 'Provided always, that any soldier being in actual military service, or any mariner or seaman being at sea, may dispose of his personal estate as he might have done before the making of this Act.'

Drummond v Parish (1843) 3 Curt 522, 7 Jur 538, 163 ER 812, 44 Digest (Repl) 204, *155.*
Reference under s 48A of the Criminal Appeal (Northern Ireland) Act 1968 (No 1 of 1975) **a**
    [1976] 2 All ER 937, [1976] NI 169, sub nom *Attorney General for Northern Ireland's*
    Reference (No 1 of 1975) [1977] AC 105, [1976] 3 WLR 235, HL, Digest (Cont Vol E)
    575, *941.
Shearman v Pyke (1724) referred to 3 Curt at 539, 163 ER at 818.
Tweedale, In the goods of (1874) LR 3 P & D 204, 44 LJP & M 35, 31 LT 799, 39 JP 152, 39
    Digest (Repl) 408, 276.   **b**
Wingham, Re, Andrews v Wingham [1948] 2 All ER 908, [1949] P 187, [1949] LJR 695, CA,
    39 Digest (Repl) 403, 237.

Probate action

By a summons Anne Mary Mannering applied for an order that the oral declaration of
the deceased, David Anthony Jones, be admitted to proof as his last will and testament on   **c**
the ground that it was a privileged will under s 11 of the Wills Act 1837. Mr Registrar
Holloway heard the application on 24th April 1979 and referred the matter to the High
Court on the question whether the deceased was in actual military service at the time of
the declaration. The sole beneficiary of the deceased's personal estate either on intestacy
or under an earlier will was the deceased's mother. The facts are set out in the judgment.

C P L Braham for the applicant.   **d**
John Mummery for the Attorney General as amicus curiae.
The deceased's mother did not appear.

ARNOLD P. This is an application in connection with an alleged will of David
Anthony Jones deceased, who was killed in Northern Ireland while on a military patrol
on 16th March 1978. He was fired on by unknown hands and died on the following   **e**
day. He was in the company of an officer and a warrant officer of his battalion, and to
those two men he made a declaration, and it was in these words: 'If I don't make it,' he
said, 'make sure Anne gets all my stuff.' Anne was his fiancée, Anne Mary Newport as
she then was, Anne Mannering as she has now become; and it is plain enough that if that
was an effective will it was one which contained a universal bequest of personalty in
favour of Anne. The question whether it was an effective will depends on whether there   **f**
extended to the deceased the privilege afforded by s 11 of the Wills Act 1837 to make a
nuncupative will in the form of an oral testamentary declaration, and in accordance with
the language of the section, that depends on whether the right view is that the deceased
was at the time of making that testamentary declaration in actual military service.

The evidence in the case includes this authoritative statement emanating from an
officer of the Ministry of Defence that in 1969 a request was made by the Northern   **g**
Ireland authorities for the deployment of the armed forces to assist the civil power in the
maintenance of law and order in Northern Ireland; and it was in pursuance of that
request that the deceased's unit was deployed in that province. The background was
something which was conveniently described by Lord Diplock in the House of Lords in
Reference under s 48A of the Criminal Appeal (Northern Ireland) Act 1968 (No 1 of 1975)
[1976] 2 All ER 937 at 946, [1977] AC 105 at 136 in the course of his speech: **h**

> 'In some parts of the province there has existed for some years now a state of
> armed and clandestinely organised insurrection against the lawful government of
> Her Majesty by persons seeking to gain political ends by violent means, that is by
> committing murder and other crimes of violence against persons and property.'

Now the doubt which has arisen in this case, and which has made the summons
necessary, arises from this general circumstance: that for the most part in cases which   **j**
have been held in the case of soldiers to come within the ambit of the statutory privilege
to which I have referred the background has been the existence or the impending
existence or the recent existence of something which may conventionally be described
as a war, in the sense of hostilities between two sovereign governments where the

a deceased in question has been in the service of one of them. That is not a state of affairs which can accurately be characterised as identical with or similar to that which prevails in Northern Ireland. The question therefore was posed whether the state of affairs which does prevail in Northern Ireland is such that a military participant in the aid to the civil power which is and was being afforded there was in a state of actual military service.

b In the Court of Appeal in *Re Wingham* [1948] 2 All ER 908, [1949] P 187 Bucknill and Denning LJJ, among the members of the court, gave consideration to the meaning of the words 'actual military service'. There emerges from that authority in my judgment this: that there may be equated with that description that of active military operations; that it must be predicated that the deceased was in service at the time that he made his will; that that service was active and of its character military.

c In this case, the person who would be entitled either on intestacy or on the basis of an earlier will to the personal estate of the deceased, if the will in question is not effective as a nuncupatory will, is the deceased's mother who for understandable reasons has chosen to take no part in the litigation, with the consequence that I have had the advantage of the assistance on the instructions of the Treasury Solicitor of counsel as amicus curiae. His submission has been that the answer to those questions is to be derived from a consideration of all the circumstances of the case and to be decided as a matter of fact.

d With that view of the matter, I wholeheartedly agree. There is ample material in the authorities for saying that this or that or the other circumstance is not by itself decisive one way or the other, and that it is the concatenation of circumstances, the totality of the relevant environment which has to be looked at in order to decide the question.

There have been a very large number of cases in which the question has to be answered against the background of a war, as that phrase is ordinarily understood. Those cases have all turned on the extent to which it could fairly be said that at the actual moment e of the alleged testamentary act the deceased was already embarked on activities in connection with that war, or whether at that moment he had ceased to be engaged in activities connected with that war, or in other cases whether his intrinsic connection with the prosecution of that war was sufficiently intimate to justify the view that he was engaged in actual military service.

Those cases help me in my judgment only to the extent that they demonstrate a f consistent view of the courts that in the interpretation of this section, and its predecessor section, the right view is the expansive view, that is, the view that if there be a doubt it should be resolved in favour of the validation rather than the invalidation of the alleged testamentary act. But there have been other cases in which either there has been an absence of what could ordinarily be referred to as a war, or the state of the facts has not been spelled out sufficiently to enable one to form any real conclusion on that matter and g it is really to those cases which one must look for guidance in the circumstances of the present case.

The statute which was the predecessor of the Wills Act 1837 in this manifestation was the Statute of Frauds (29 Car 2 c 3 (1677)) passed in the reign of Charles II, and s 23 dealt with a similar subject matter. The earliest case in which any relevant matter has had consideration was a case, not itself reported, which was referred to in *Drummond v Parrish* h (1843) 3 Curt 522, 163 ER 812. The decision in that case is of no great interest or importance to what I have to decide. But there were two matters within it in the judgment in the Prerogative Court of Canterbury of Sir Herbert Jenner Fust which do help. One was a citation from a very old book called Swinburne (Part 1, s 13, p 95), and Sir Herbert Jenner Fust's comment on that book was that it was one which undoubtedly the court would consider a very high authority. The citation is concerned with the j distinction between military operations and garrison duty (to use broad and not very precisely defined terms) which had of course a relevance to the question whether the deceased was or was not on actual military service. The contrast that Swinburne makes is this: when describing those on garrison duty, he describes them thus:

'. . . they be such as lie safely in some castle, or place of defence, or besieged by the enemy, only in readiness to be employed in case of invasion or rebellion, and then they do not enjoy these military privileges, [Swinburne then goes on to look at those who do, and he says this:] or else they be such as are in expedition or actual service of wars, and such are privileged, at least during the time of their expedition, whether they be employed by land or by water, and whether they be horsemen or footmen.'

(See 3 Curt 522 at 538, 163 ER 812 at 817–818.)

It is quite plain that what the author is there doing is describing within those two descriptions collectively the totality of those whose position has to be considered; and therefore it is plain that when they proceed on expedition or actual service of wars in the course of their employment in case of invasion or rebellion he regards them as coming within the privileged class. So that one can derive from that that the repulsion of an invasion on which they proceed from their garrison place, their castle or place of defence, or the suppression of a rebellion for which purpose they likewise proceed, in the view of that learned author would put them into the privileged class. So one finds at any rate a strong indication at this stage that the suppression of a rebellion is the sort of expedition or actual service of wars which creates the privilege. This is borne out by a reference a little later on in the judgment of Sir Herbert Jenner Fust when he proceeds to rely on and describe the case of *Shearman v Pyke* (1724) (see 3 Curt 522 at 539, 163 ER 812 at 818), whether in the Prerogative Court or in Doctors Commons does not appear with any clarity, but I think it was in the Prerogative Court at Canterbury. It was a case therefore which had been decided under the Statute of Frauds, s 23, the predecessor section to that of the Wills Act. It is not necessary to deal with the case at very great length. It concerned a cook who was a soldier in the service of the East India Company and attached in his culinary capacity to one Governor Pike of St Helena. In 1719 the governor with the cook in attendance left St Helena to proceed to Bencoolen, a place in India. But when they got as far as Batavia they were informed that the factory at Bencoolen was cut off by the natives, and so they proceeded, presumably not alone, to Bencoolen to re-establish the factory. And that service completed they returned to some intermediate place on the journey called Moco Moro where unfortunately the cook died. It was held in the event that that expedition to relieve the cut-off factory at Bencoolen, which had not been completed when the cook died on the way back, was an occasion of actual military service with the consequence that an informal will of the cook was upheld.

It is true to say, I think, that the state of affairs in which a factory is cut off by the natives could be part of an incident of conventional war, but it seems to be much more likely that it was a description of some sort of insurrection. At least this is significant: that no consideration seems to have been given to the question whether it was the one or the other in the course of the adjudication to the effect that its relief was the subject of actual military service; so that at least that case suggests that provided there is service, provided that it is military, and provided that it is active, it is not of consequence whether its purpose is to fight off a foreign enemy or to suppress a rebellious group of subjects.

That is the first case which is relevant to a consideration of the nature of the background against which the service requires to be performed. The next case, which has the same sort of utility, is *In the Goods of Tweedale* (1874) LR 3 P & D 204. It concerned a testator who was an officer at the relevant time in the 8th Regiment Bengal Calvalry. What had happened was this. In 1842 some disturbances broke out in the district of Bundelcund in India, and evidently from the report in British India, and a field force was put together for the purpose of suppressing the disturbances. The testator was engaged with his regiment as part of that field force. Sir James Hannen said (at 206):

'This will is not attested but it is proved to have been made whilst the deceased was in actual military service on an expedition which was employed in suppressing disturbances in the Bundelcund district.'

So that he regarded the suppression of insurrection, or disturbances within the ambit of *a* the area of government, but contrary to the ordinances of that government, as a matter of actual military service where the military were called out to suppress them. The operation was quite local. The field force proceeded from its station in India to the scene of the trouble, and that was in the eyes of Sir James Hannen the engaging in actual military service.

A less clear case, but one pointing in the same direction, is *Re Booth* [1926] P 118, [1926] All ER Rep 594. That concerned an officer of the 46th Regiment who, when

b stationed at Gibraltar in 1882, had been posted with his regiment to Egypt; immediately before embarkation he had made a testamentary declaration, and the question in the case was whether that was an effective nuncupatory will. The point which was argued was not whether the service on which he was about to embark was actual military service but whether the occasion on which he had made his will was sufficiently proximate to that service to justify the conclusion that he was already engaged on it. Nevertheless, it is the

c fact that it was regarded, the service in question, as being actual military service for the relevant purpose; and I have been given as part of the evidence an official description of what happened in the Egyptian campaign of 1882. The Khedive of Egypt, who was to an extent subject to the Ottoman Empire of the Sultan, had to face an insurrection led by one Arabi Pasha, and in pursuance of certain existing international engagements, as they are called in a letter written by the Secretary of State for War to Sir Garnet Wolseley who

d was in charge of the expedition, the British government went to the assistance of the Khedive to suppress that insurrection. It was very plainly an expedition in aid of the civil power, not the British civil power, it is true, but the civil power in authority in Egypt, for the purpose of assisting it to suppress an insurrection. The instructions to Sir Garnet included specifically an instruction that while he was at liberty to make any military settlement (military convention, as it is called) he was not to engage in any act of political

e settlement. There again the conception of actual military service as including the suppression of an insurrection is present.

That is really the extent of what one can derive from English authority; but there is the nearest of all cases to the present in an Australian decision, *In the Will of Anderson* (1958) 75 WN (NSW) 334. That concerned the death in action of a soldier in the Australian contingent made available for the assistance of the government of the

f Federation of Malaya to suppress what is described in the report as 'armed and organized aggression and violence against the Government and the people of Malaya designed to overthrow the Government by force'. This was the terrorist activity which prevailed in and about the year 1956, when the deceased was killed; and the very question which arises in this case, how far what is conventionally called and regarded as a state of war is necessary to the exercise of the jurisdiction, was considered by the judge, albeit on an

g unopposed application supporting the nuncupative will. Myers J said (at 335):

> 'In the present case there was no state of war and it is difficult to see how there could have been, for there was no nation or state with which a state of war could have been proclaimed to exist, but in all other respects there was no difference between the situation of a member of this force and that of a member of any
h military force in time of war. In my opinion the deceased was in actual military service and it would be unreasonable to hold otherwise.'

That decision is valuable persuasive authority which in my judgment is not distinguishable in any material particular from that which I have to decide.

When the deceased in the present case was ordered to go out on his patrol, the fatal patrol, he was obliged, by the conditions of his service in accordance with the discipline

j which prevailed in his military unit, so to do. That the service was military, that the service was active, seems to me to be beyond contest. The fact that the enemy was not a uniformed force engaged in regular warfare, or even an insurgent force organised on conventional military lines, but rather a conjuration of clandestine assassins and arsonists, cannot in my judgment affect any of those questions and I have no hesitation in pronouncing for this will as a valid nuncupative will. It is not the state of the opponent,

or the character of the opponent's operations, in my judgment, which affect the answers
to the questions which arise. They must be answered by reference to the activities of the *a*
deceased and those with whom he is associated; and it is nihil ad rem in relation to the
answers to the questions whether there is service, whether it is active and whether it is
military that the context in which it occurs is that of foreign expedition, foreign
invasion, or local insurrection.

Order accordingly.   *b*

Solicitors: *Wright, Atkinson & Pearson*, Keighley (for the applicant); *Treasury Solicitor.*

Bebe Chua   Barrister.

Spectrum Investment Co and another v   *c*
Holmes

CHANCERY DIVISION
BROWNE-WILKINSON J
12th, 13th, 16th, 17th, 18th JUNE, 9th JULY 1980   *d*

*Land registration – Effect of registration on legal estate – Possessory title – Leaseholds –
Registration of title acquired by squatter by adverse possession – Whether squatter's registered
title defeasible by surrender of lease by documentary lessee to freeholder – Whether surrender by
documentary lessee after removal of his title from register a valid surrender of lease – Whether
'transfer' of registered land including surrender – Land Registration Act 1925, ss 21(1), 69(4),* **e**
75(3).

The freehold interest in a house was registered in 1901. By a lease dated 24th December
1902 the freeholder granted a lease of the house for 99 years from 25th December 1902
to the leaseholder who registered the leasehold interest. In 1939 the leaseholder granted
a tenancy of the house to Mrs H who lived there with her daughter, the defendant. Mrs *f*
H paid the rent to the leaseholder's agent until 1944. In that year the leaseholder
assigned the lease to Mrs D who was then registered as the leasehold proprietor. After
the assignment tenders of rent by Mrs H were refused and the last payment by her of, or
on account of, rent was made in 1944. Mrs H died in 1951 and the defendant stayed on
in possession of the house without paying rent. In 1957 a company acquired the
freehold of the house and was registered as the freehold proprietor with a possessory *g*
title. By 1963 the defendant had acquired a possessory title to the house under the
Limitation Act 1939 as against the leaseholder, Mrs D, by 12 years adverse possession. In
March 1968 the defendant applied under s 75(2)[a] of the Land Registration Act 1925 to
be registered as the leasehold proprietor of the house. Notice of the application was
served on Mrs D's solicitors but they took no action and, in June 1968, the defendant was
registered as the leasehold proprietor with a possessory title, pursuant to s 75(3) of the *h*
1925 Act, and the title under which Mrs D was registered was closed. In 1975 the
company's registration was altered to registration as freehold proprietor with an absolute
title. The company and Mrs D then discovered that the defendant had been registered
as the leasehold proprietor and in May 1975 entered into a transaction intended to defeat
the defendant's title, by which Mrs D purported to surrender to the company her
leasehold interest comprised in the title which had been closed in 1968. The company, *j*
on the basis that the freehold and leasehold interests had merged as the result of the
surrender, then applied to the county court for possession of the house and mesne
profits. Those proceedings were stood over for a decision on the question of title to the
house raised in an originating summons issued by the company against the defendant

---

a   Section 75 is set out at p 11 *d* to *g*, post

a seeking, inter alia, rectification of the register by deletion of the defendant's title and declarations that the defendant had no rights under the lease and was a trespasser. At the hearing of the summons the company contended that the 1925 Act merely provided machinery for proving title and transferring land and did not affect a party's substantive rights under the general law, and that, since the company had obtained a surrender of the lease from the documentary lessee, Mrs D, it had a right to possession as against the defendant by virtue of s 11[b] of the 1925 Act. The defendant contended that

b notwithstanding the surrender by Mrs D she had a good right against the company, by virtue of the registration of her title, to remain in possession of the house until the expiry of the lease.

Held – (1) The registration of the defendant as the leasehold proprietor had the effect, by virtue of s 69(1)[c] of the 1925 Act, of vesting the legal term of the lease in her as against Mrs D because, by virtue of s 69(4)[d] of that Act, the registered leasehold estate could only

c be disposed of in accordance with the Act, namely by a 'transfer' under s 21(1)[e] of that Act by the registered proprietor, and since a transfer included a surrender that requirement extended to Mrs D's purported surrender. Accordingly, since Mrs D was not the registered proprietor at the date of the surrender and since, in any event, that surrender had not been effected by a registered disposition, the surrender was invalid and the

d company's claim therefore failed in limine (see p 12 *f* to p 13 *d* and p 15 *e f*, post).

(2) Mrs D was not entitled to rectification of the register to delete the defendant's title and reinstate her own title as the registered leaseholder, because the defendant as a squatter with 12 years' adverse possession against the documentary lessee (Mrs D) had acquired the title to the registered leasehold estate under the Limitation Act 1939 and was entitled, under s 75(3) of the 1925 Act, to be registered as the proprietor of the

e documentary lessee's registered estate, ie as proprietor of the lease. Accordingly, the defendant had been correctly registered as the proprietor of the lease (see p 14 *f* to p 15 *a* and *e*, post).

(3) The consequence of registration of a squatter's rights under s 75 of the 1925 Act was that those rights could not be defeated by a subsequent surrender of the lease between the documentary lessee and the freeholder. That meant that a squatter's rights over registered land differed from the rights he would have in respect of unregistered land

f since in the latter case the documentary lessee could effectively surrender the legal term to the freeholder to cause a merger. Accordingly, the company could not claim under s 11 of the 1925 Act to be entitled to any estate, right or interest in the house as against the defendant until the lease expired (see p 15 *b* and *d*, post); *Williams & Glyn's Bank Ltd v Boland* [1980] 2 All ER 408 applied; *Fairweather v St Marylebone Property Co Ltd* [1962] 2 All ER 288 distinguished.

g Semble. During the period preceding registration of a squatter's rights under the 1925 Act, both the documentary lessee, as the registered proprietor of the lease, and the freeholder can deal with the legal estate without reference to a squatter's rights (see p 15 *c*, post); dicta of Lord Radcliffe in *Fairweather v St Marylebone Property Co Ltd* [1962] 2 All ER at 296 and of Sir John Pennycuick in *Jessamine Investment Co v Schwartz* [1976] 3 All

h ER at 530 considered.

Notes

For registration where title acquired by possession, and for the effect of registration where the registered land is leasehold, see 26 Halsbury's Laws (4th Edn) paras 962–963, 984.

For authorised dealings with registered land, see ibid para 986.

j ───────────────────────────────

b   Section 11 is set out at p 11 *j*, post
c   Section 69(1) is set out at p 12 *c*, post
d   Section 69(4) is set out at p 12 *h*, post
e   Section 21(1), so far as material, provides: 'Where the registered land is a leasehold interest the proprietor may, in the prescribed manner, transfer the registered estate in the land or any part thereof . . .'

For the Land Registration Act 1925, ss 11, 21, 69, 75, see 27 Halsbury's Statutes (3rd
Edn) 793, 803, 842, 850.   *a*

Cases referred to in judgment
Fairweather v St Marylebone Property Co Ltd [1962] 2 All ER 288, [1963] AC 510, [1962]
    2 WLR 1020, HL, 32 Digest (Repl) 563, 1549.
Jessamine Investment Co v Schwartz [1976] 3 All ER 521, [1978] QB 264, [1977] 2 WLR
    145, 33 P & CR 346, CA, 32 Digest (Reissue) 636, 4666.   *b*
Williams & Glyn's Bank Ltd v Boland [1980] 2 All ER 408, [1980] 3 WLR 138, HL.

Originating summons
By an originating summons dated 11th January 1979 the plaintiff, Spectrum Investment
Co ('Spectrum'), sought as against the defendant, Mary Holmes, who was registered at the
Land Registry under title NGL 65073 as the proprietor of the leasehold interest under a
lease dated 24th December 1902 of premises known as 43 Mount Pleasant Lane, London   *c*
E5, (i) an order that the whole of the entry on the land register under title NGL 65073
be deleted, (ii) an order that the charges register of title NGL 55216, being the title of the
freehold interest in the premises, be rectified by the deletion of entry 2 which referred
to the lease of 1902 and Miss Holmes's registered title, (iii) a declaration that Miss Holmes
had no rights under the lease, and (iv) a declaration that since 7th May 1977 Miss Holmes
had been a trespasser in the premises or alternatively that she was a statutory tenant of the *d*
premises. Pursuant to leave granted by Browne-Wilkinson J during the course of the
trial, Louisa David ('Mrs David'), to whom the lease of 24th December 1902 had been
assigned in 1944, was added as co-plaintiff. The facts are set out in the judgment.

Romie Tager for Spectrum and Mrs David.
Arthur W H Charles for Miss Holmes.   *e*
                                                                      Cur adv vult

9th July. **BROWNE-WILKINSON J** read the following judgment: This case concerns
the rights of the defendant (Miss Holmes) in a house, 43 Mount Pleasant Lane, Hackney,
London ('the house'). The plaintiff, Spectrum Investment Co ('Spectrum') is registered at
the Land Registry as proprietor of the freehold with title absolute. Miss Holmes is in *f*
possession and claims to be entitled to remain in possession on two alternative grounds:
first, she claims on the ground that she is registered at the Land Registry as proprietor
(with possessory title) of a long leasehold interest which does not expire until the year
2001; alternatively, she claims as a tenant protected by the Rent Acts. As will emerge,
this case is primarily concerned with the first of those grounds.
      The material facts are as follows. The freehold interest was first registered on 20th *g*
September 1901. By a lease dated 24th December 1902 the freeholder granted a lease of
the house for 99 years from 25th December 1902 at a rent of £7 per annum. That
leasehold interest was registered on 2nd January 1903 and subsequently became vested
in a Miss Kelsey.
      In 1939 Miss Kelsey granted an oral monthly tenancy to a Mrs Holmes at a rent of
£4 13s 4d per month. Mrs Holmes lived there with her daughter, the defendant Miss *h*
Holmes, and paid the rent to Miss Kelsey's agent until 1944. In 1944 Miss Kelsey
assigned the lease to a Mrs David, who was registered as proprietor of the lease under title
LN 66166. Miss Kelsey told Mrs Holmes to pay the rent in future to a firm of solicitors,
Messrs Gale & Phelps. Mrs Holmes tried to do this but the tender of rent was refused.
She made some efforts to find out to whom she should pay the rent, but without
success. The last payment of rent by Mrs Holmes was in 1944. In 1947 the local *j*
authority, having carried out certain works to the house, required Mrs Holmes to pay the
rent to them under the Public Health (London) Act 1936. The last of such payments was
made in 1951.
      In 1951 Mrs Holmes died. No grant has been taken to her estate, but Miss Holmes
stayed in possession. Spectrum concede that, were it not for Miss Holmes's claim to be

in possession as registered proprietor of the lease, Miss Holmes is entitled to protection
a under the Rent Acts as successor to her mother. In 1957 Spectrum acquired the freehold
interest in the house and was registered as proprietor. It is common ground that by 1963
at the latest, 12 years having expired since the last payment of, or on account of, rent,
Miss Holmes had acquired a title to the house by adverse possession as against Mrs David,
the leaseholder, but not as against Spectrum, the freeholder. On 19th March 1968 Miss
Holmes applied to be registered at the Land Registry as proprietor of the leasehold
b interest. Notice of this application was given by the Land Registry to Messrs Gale &
Phelps as solicitors for Mrs David, but they took no action. In June 1968 the Land
Registry gave effect to Miss Holmes's application as follows: (a) they closed the registration
of the leasehold title LN 66166 on which Mrs David was registered as proprietor; (b) they
opened a new registration of the leasehold title under title NGL 65073 on which Miss
Holmes was shown as being registered on 19th March 1968 as first proprietor with
c possessory title of the leasehold interest. The property register describes the property
registered as 'The leasehold land known as 43 Mount Pleasant Lane, Hackney'. It then
goes on, under a cross-heading 'Short particulars of lease under which the land is held', to
give a description of the lease dated 24th December 1902.

Until 1975 the freehold title had itself only been a possessory title, but on 28th April
1975 Spectrum was registered as freehold proprietor with absolute title. There appeared
d on the land certificate a reference to Miss Holmes's title to the lease registered under title
NGL 65073. Either for this or for some other reason, at this stage Spectrum and Mrs
David woke up and started to take action.

It appears that Mrs David is a wealthy lady who during the war departed to the West
Country and ignored her properties. For some unexplained reason, neither she nor
Messrs Gale & Phelps (who were in fact her solicitors throughout) seem to have taken any
e normally prudent steps to safeguard her position. She is a member of the family who are
the shareholders in Spectrum. Messrs Gale & Phelps are the solicitors for Spectrum
also. A Mr Galinski is related to Mrs David, a director of Spectrum, and was also a
solicitor with Messrs Gale & Phelps.

Having discovered Miss Holmes's claim to a possessory title, Mrs David and Spectrum
entered into a transaction which was quite frankly admitted to be a device designed to
f defeat Miss Holmes's claim. On 7th May 1975 Mrs David executed a deed of surrender.
It reads as follows:

'H.M. Land Registry. Registration Acts 1926 & 1966. County of Greater
London. Title No. 66166. Property 13 Mount Pleasant Lane, Hackney. The 7th
Day of May 1975. IN CONSIDERATION of the Release hereinafter contained I LOUISA
DAVID called "the Lessee") as Beneficial Owner HEREBY SURRENDER AND RELEASE TO
g SPECTRUM INVESTMENT COMPANY (an Unlimited Liability Company formerly known
as Spectrum Investment Company Limited) of 220 Stamford Hill London N16
(hereinafter called "the Reversioner") the land comprised in the title above referred
to for all the unexpired residue of the term granted by the registered Lease to the
intent that the said term of years shall forthwith be merged and extinguished
absolutely in the reversion thereof registered under Title Number: LN 155216 of
h which the Reversioner is the Registered Proprietor AND the Reversioner in
consideration of the premises HEREBY RELEASES AND DISCHARGES the Lessee from all
and singular the covenants agreements and conditions contained in the registered
Lease and on the part of the Lessee to be paid performed and observed and from all
liability in respect thereof and from all claims demands expenses or proceedings in
respect of any breach or non-performance or non-observance of the said covenants
j agreements and conditions arising thereunder.'

The deed is executed by Mrs David and by Spectrum.

It is to be noted that the document purports to be a surrender of a lease registered in
the Land Registry under title LN 66166. At that date there was no such title number, it
having been closed in 1968.

It is Spectrum's case that the surrender by Mrs David was effective to merge the leasehold interest in the freehold interest and that, accordingly Spectrum, as freeholder, *a* is now entitled to possession against Miss Holmes. For this proposition Spectrum relies on the decision of the House of Lords in *Fairweather v St Marylebone Property Co Ltd* [1962] 2 All ER 288, [1963] AC 510. Moreover Spectrum alleges that Miss Holmes, having been in possession of the house under the possessory title to the lease, can no longer claim any protection under the Rent Acts. I pause only to point out that if Spectrum is right on both of these points the law will have achieved a result worthy of *b* Catch 22. Miss Holmes and her mother, having tried to pay the rent but been unable to find anyone to take it due to the landlord's shortcomings, have got into a position in which the defaulting landlord and her associated family company are able to evict Miss Holmes from her home, which could not have happened if the landlord had arranged for someone to receive the rent.

Having executed the surrender, Spectrum applied to the county court claiming *c* possession and mesne profits. Miss Holmes has tendered arrears of rent due under the lease but this has been refused. The county court proceedings have been stood over to enable the questions of title to be decided in these proceedings in the High Court.

By this originating summons Spectrum claims (1) rectification of the register by deleting the whole of Miss Holmes's possessory title to the lease and references to that title on the freehold register, (2) a declaration that Miss Holmes has no right under the *d* lease, and (3) a declaration that she is a trespasser or, alternatively, a statutory tenant.

In the course of the hearing before me Spectrum's case has been somewhat modified. First, Spectrum by its counsel has said that Spectrum will not in any event seek to evict Miss Holmes from the house, but, if successful on all points, will grant her a tenancy at a fair rent to be agreed. Second, whilst reserving the right to renew the claim in the Court of Appeal, Spectrum concedes that before me their claim to a declaration that Miss *e* Holmes is not even a statutory tenant is decided against them by the decision of the Court of Appeal in *Jessamine Investment Co v Schwartz* [1976] 3 All ER 521, [1978] QB 264 (another case in which Mrs David's strange management of her properties raised problems for her tenants).

Therefore, in the event, the only point that I have to decide is whether, notwithstanding the purported surrender of the lease, Miss Holmes has a good right against the freeholder *f* to remain in possession until the expiry of the lease by reason of her possessory title as against Mrs David.

I will first consider the Limitation Act 1939 as it applies to a case such as this, where the freeholder has granted a lease to X ('the documentary lessee') and Y ('the squatter') has been in adverse possession for upwards of 12 years. It is common ground that in such a case the squatter acquires no rights against the freeholder under the 1939 Act, since the *g* freeholder's right of action to recover possession does not accrue until the termination of the lease. But under ss 4(3) and 9 of the 1939 Act the right of the documentary lessee to recover possession from the squatter is barred. Section 16 of the 1939 Act reads as follows:

'Subject to the provisions of section seven of this Act and of section seventy-five *h* of the Land Registration Act, 1925, at the expiration of the period prescribed by this Act for any person to bring an action to recover land (including a redemption action) or an action to enforce an advowson, the title of that person to the land or advowson shall be extinguished.'

The impact of that section in a case where leasehold land is not registered is now established by the decision of the House of Lords in the *Fairweather* case. The facts of *j* that case are for all material purposes incapable of being distinguished from the facts in the present case, ie the right of action of the documentary lessee against the squatter was barred, but the documentary lessee had subsequently surrendered the lease to the freeholder. The House of Lords held that the freeholder was entitled to recover possession from the squatter.

Spectrum claims that the same result should follow in this case, notwithstanding that
a in this case both the freehold and the leasehold interest are registered at the Land
Registry. It is therefore important to analyse exactly what was decided by the House of
Lords in the *Fairweather* case.

The House of Lords held that the effect of the Limitation Act 1939 is not to vest the
lease in the squatter by a form of Parliamentary conveyance. Although by s 16 of the Act
the title of the documentary lessee is 'extinguished', that extinguishment operates only
b as against the squatter; the interest is not extinguished for all purposes. In particular, as
between the freeholder and the documentary lessee, the documentary lessee remains the
tenant and there is privity of estate between them: the documentary lessee continues to
hold the term of years and the estate in it granted by the lease. It follows that,
notwithstanding that the documentary lessee's rights against the squatter are barred, the
documentary lessee as holder of the legal estate in the term can effectively surrender the
c term to the freeholder so as to cause a merger. Thereafter the freeholder is entitled to
recover possession from the squatter by virtue of the freeholder's unincumbered interest
in the property.

Against that background I turn to the provisions of the Land Registration Act 1925
dealing with title acquired by adverse possession. It will be remembered that s 16 of the
Limitation Act 1939 is expressly made subject to the provisions of s 75 of the Land
d Registration Act 1925. Section 75 provides as follows:

'(1) The Limitation Acts shall apply to registered land in the same manner and to
the same extent as those Acts apply to land not registered, except that where, if the
land were not registered, the estate of the person registered as proprietor would be
extinguished, such estate shall not be extinguished but shall be deemed to be held
by the proprietor for the time being in trust for the person who, by virtue of the said
e Acts, has acquired title against any proprietor, but without prejudice to the estates
and interests of any other person interested in the land whose estate or interest is not
extinguished by those Acts.

'(2) Any person claiming to have acquired a title under the Limitation Acts to a
registered estate in the land may apply to be registered as proprietor thereof.

'(3) The registrar shall, on being satisfied as to the applicant's title, enter the
f applicant as proprietor either with absolute, good leasehold, qualified, or possessory
title, as the case may require, but without prejudice to any estate or interest
protected by any entry on the register which may not have been extinguished under
the Limitation Acts, and such registration shall, subject as aforesaid, have the same
effect as the registration of a first proprietor; but the proprietor or the applicant or
any other person interested may apply to the court for the determination of any
g question arising under this section.

'(5) Rules may be made for applying (subject to any necessary modifications) the
provisions of this section to cases where an easement, right or privilege has been
acquired by prescription.'

If (as in the present case) the squatter is registered under s 75(3) as first proprietor with
h possessory title of leasehold land, there are important sections stating the effect of such
registration. Section 11 of the 1925 Act reads as follows:

'Where the registered land is a leasehold interest, the registration of a person as
first proprietor thereof with a possessory title shall not affect or prejudice the
enforcement of any estate, right, or interest (whether in respect of the lessor's title
or otherwise) adverse to or in derogation of the title of such first registered
j proprietor, and subsisting or capable of arising at the time of the registration of such
proprietor; but, save as aforesaid, shall have the same effect as registration with an
absolute title.'

Therefore one has to find what is the effect of being registered with an absolute title.
That is provided for by s 9, which reads as follows:

'Where the registered land is a leasehold interest, the registration under this Act
of any person as first proprietor thereof with an absolute title shall be deemed to vest   *a*
in such person the possession of the leasehold interest described, with all implied or
expressed rights, privileges, and appurtenances attached to such interest, subject to
the following obligations, rights, and interests, that is to say,—(a) Subject to all
implied and express covenants, obligations, and liabilities incident to the registered
land . . . but free from all other estates and interests whatsoever, including estates
and interests of His Majesty.'   *b*

Section 69(1) then provides as follows:

'The proprietor of land (whether he was registered before or after the
commencement of this Act) shall be deemed to have vested in him without any
conveyance, where the registered land is freehold, the legal estate in fee simple in
possession, and where the registered land is leasehold the legal term created by the   *c*
registered lease, but subject to the overriding interests, if any, including any
mortgage term or charge by way of legal mortgage created by or under the Law of
Property Act, 1925, or this Act or otherwise which has priority to the registered
estate.'

I can now shortly state the contentions of Spectrum. Spectrum submits that the Land   *d*
Registration Act 1925 introduces mere machinery for proving title to and transferring
land and does not affect the substantive rights which parties enjoy under the general
law. Accordingly it is said that the rights of Spectrum (as established by *Fairweather v St
Marylebone Property Co Ltd* [1962] 2 All ER 288, [1963] AC 510) must be reflected in the
provisions of the Land Registration Act 1925 and are preserved by the words in s 11
which expressly provide that registration with possessory title 'shall not affect or prejudice   *e*
the enforcement of any estate, right, or interest (whether in respect of the lessor's title or
otherwise) adverse to or in derogation of' the proprietor with possessory title. So, it is
said, having obtained a surrender of the lease from Mrs David, Spectrum's right to
possession as against Miss Holmes is preserved.

There is in my judgment a short answer to the claim by Spectrum. Accepting for the
moment the broad proposition that the Land Registration Act 1925 was not intended to   *f*
alter substantive rights, it undoubtedly was intended to alter the manner in which such
rights were to be established and transferred. The surrender by Mrs David to Spectrum
is the linchpin of Spectrum's claim. But in my judgment that surrender has not been
affected by the only means authorised by the 1925 Act for the disposal of a registered
leasehold interest by act of the parties.

At the date of the alleged surrender the lease was registered under title NGL 65073 in   *g*
the name of Miss Holmes. Mrs David was not registered as proprietor, her title LN 66166
having been taken off the register. By virtue of s 69(1) of the 1925 Act the effect of the
registration of Miss Holmes as proprietor of the lease was, as against Mrs David, to vest
the term or deem it to be vested in Miss Holmes.

Section 69(4) of the 1925 Act provides as follows:
                                                                                          h
'The estate for the time being vested in the proprietor shall only be capable of
being disposed of or dealt with by him in manner authorised by this Act.'

In my judgment the effect of these provisions is that, so long as Miss Holmes is
registered as proprietor of the lease, only she can dispose of it. Moreover, by virtue of
ss 21 and 22, even Miss Holmes can only do so by a registered disposition. Accordingly   *j*
in my judgment there has, as yet, been no valid surrender of the lease and Spectrum's
claim fails in limine.

Counsel for Spectrum sought to avoid this result by saying that a surrender was not a
registrable disposition and referred me to s 46 of the 1925 Act. This argument does not
meet the point that Mrs David was not registered as proprietor when she purported to

a   surrender the lease. But, even if she had been, in my judgment the surrender would have had to be effected by a registered disposition. Section 69(4) makes it clear that even a registered proprietor only has power to deal with any estate vested in him in the manner authorised by the Act. The only powers of disposition are those conferred by s 21 of the Act which authorises the transfer of the registered estate. In my judgment the word 'transfer' in this section must include surrendering the term, otherwise the Act does not authorise a surrender. Any disposition under s 21 has to be completed by

b   registration: see s 22. Section 46, on which counsel for Spectrum relied, merely directs the registrar to note on the register the determination of the lease, however that occurs, which will include determination by effluxion of time or operation of law. Section 46 does not purport to lay down the ways in which the determination can be effected by disposition of one of the parties.

   Counsel for Spectrum submitted further that there ought to have been two registered

c   titles to the lease, of which Mrs David was the proprietor of one and Miss Holmes was the proprietor of the other. This suggestion seems to have no warrant in any provision of the Act and in my judgment runs contrary to the whole scheme of the Act, which is intended to ensure that there shall be one title for any interest in registered land and anyone dealing with that land can treat the registered proprietor of that interest as the owner of that interest.

d   For these reasons, in my judgment there has, as yet, been no surrender of the term by Mrs David to Spectrum. Therefore, Spectrum's claim fails since, so long as the term exists, it has no immediate right to possession.

   However, in order to determine the real issue between the parties I gave leave for Mrs David to be joined as co-plaintiff. If she is entitled to rectification of the register, she may thereafter be able to execute the necessary registered surrender and, if she can, Spectrum's

e   claim to possession would be unanswerable.

   Counsel's submissions for Miss Holmes were very far-reaching. He submitted that the whole scheme of the Land Registration Act 1925 shows that the position of the squatter on registered land is totally different from that of a squatter on unregistered land as laid down by the House of Lords in *Fairweather v St Marylebone Property Co Ltd*. He submits that s 75(2) makes it clear that the squatter who has obtained title against the

f   documentary lessee is entitled to apply to be registered as proprietor of the documentary lessee's registered estate in the land, ie as proprietor of the lease itself. Section 73(3) then requires the registrar, if satisfied of the facts, to effect such registration. Accordingly it is said that what was done in the present case was quite correct: Miss Holmes is rightly registered as proprietor of the lease itself. As a result, it is said, the legal term of years is vested in Miss Holmes by a Parliamentary conveyance contained in s 69 of the Act. By

g   virtue of ss 9 and 11 of the Act Miss Holmes as registered proprietor is deemed to have vested in her the possession of the leasehold interest, subject to the express and implied obligations in the lease and subject to any rights of the freeholder adverse to her interest. Therefore, her counsel submits, the scheme of the Act is to produce exactly the result which the House of Lords held was not the result in relation to unregistered land, namely to make the squatter the successor in title to the documentary lessee by

h   Parliamentary conveyance, the squatter taking subject to and with the benefit of the covenants in the lease.

   This is a formidable and far-reaching submission. But, on the other side, I was strongly impressed with authority suggesting that squatters rights were the same over both registered and unregistered land. In *Fairweather v St Marylebone Property Co Ltd* it emerged at a late stage in the proceedings that the land there in question was registered

j   land. The squatter was not registered as proprietor of the lease, but contended that the provisions of s 75(1) of the 1925 Act (which makes the documentary lessee as registered proprietor a trustee for the squatter) prevented the documentary lessee from surrendering the term to the freeholder. It was not proved at what date the documentary lessee was registered, and on that ground it was held that s 75 had no application. But Lord Radcliffe said ([1962] 2 All ER 288 at 296, [1963] AC 510 at 542):

'I do not think therefore that the appellant can succeed on this point. I only wish
to add that at present I am not at all satisfied that s. 75(1) does create a trust interest
in the squatter of the kind that one would expect from the words used. So to hold
would raise difficulties which I do not now explore; and the trust of the dispossessed
owner's title under sub-s. (1) must somehow be reconciled with the provision under
sub-s. (2) for the squatter to apply to register his own title, which would presumably
be his independent possessory title acquired by the adverse possession.'

See also per Lord Denning ([1962] 2 All ER 288 at 299, [1963] AC 510 at 548).

To similar effect are the remarks of Sir John Pennycuick in *Jessamine Investment Co v
Schwartz* [1976] 3 All ER 521 at 530, [1978] QB 264 at 275:

'I should be very reluctant to introduce a substantive distinction in the application
of a provision of the Limitation Act 1939 to registered land and unregistered land
respectively, based on what is plainly a conveyancing device designed to adapt that
provision to the former class of land.'

Although these are obiter dicta, they are obviously of some weight in supporting the
contention that the position of a squatter does not vary according to whether the land is
registered or unregistered.

Finally, the words of s 75(1) itself state that the Limitation Acts shall apply to registered
land 'in the same manner and to the same extent' as it applies to unregistered land, and
then goes on to state exceptions.

On the other hand, I take into account the recent decision of the House of Lords in
Williams & Glyn's Bank Ltd v Boland [1980] 2 All ER 408, [1980] 3 WLR 138 which shows
that, if the words of the Land Registration Act 1925 are clear, they are to be given their
natural meaning and not distorted so as to seek to produce uniformity in the substantive
law as between registered and unregistered land.

I therefore approach this question on the basis that one would expect that substantive
legal rights would be the same whether the land is registered or unregistered but that
clear words in the 1925 Act must be given their natural meaning even if this leads to a
divergence.

I do not find it necessary to reach any conclusion on the far-reaching propositions
which counsel for Miss Holmes put forward, since I think that I can decide this case on
quite a narrow ground, leaving it to others to resolve the more fundamental questions.
In my judgment, if Mrs David is to succeed in any claim to have Miss Holmes deleted
from the register as proprietor of the lease, she (Mrs David) must show at least that the
registration of Miss Holmes was not a mandatory requirement of the provisions of the
1925 Act. It is clear from the references in s 75(3) that s 75 applies to leasehold
interest. Under s 75(3) the registrar is under a mandatory duty to register the squatter
on the application made by the squatter under sub-s (2) if the registrar is satisfied as to the
squatter's title. For what does the squatter make application? I will read s 75(2) again:
'Any person claiming to have acquired a title under the Limitation Acts to a registered
estate in the land may apply to be registered as proprietor thereof.' To my mind the
words are clear and unequivocal: the squatter claims to have acquired a title to 'a
registered estate in the land' (ie the leasehold interest) and applies to be registered as a
proprietor '*thereof*' (my emphasis). Therefore, under s 75(2), references to the squatter
having acquired title to a registered estate must include the rights which under the
Limitation Act 1939 the squatter acquires in relation to leasehold interests. Subsection
(2) then refers to the squatter applying to be registered as proprietor 'thereof'. This word
can, in my judgment, only refer back to the registered estate in the land against which
the squatter has acquired title under the 1939 Act, ie the leasehold interest. The clear
words of the Act therefore seem to require that, once the 12 years have run, the squatter
is entitled to be registered as proprietor of the lease itself, and is bound to be so registered
if he applies for registration. It follows that in my judgment Miss Holmes (as the
squatter) is correctly registered as proprietor of the lease itself in accordance with the

clear requirements of s 75 of the 1925 Act. If that is right, Mrs David cannot be entitled
a to rectification of the register as against Miss Holmes, and she can therefore never get
into a position in which she is competent to surrender the lease to Spectrum.

I am conscious that in so deciding I am reaching a conclusion which produces at least
a limited divergence between squatter's rights over registered and unregistered land.
Once the squatter is rightly registered as proprietor under s 75(3) the documentary lessee
and the freeholder can no longer defeat the squatter's rights by a surrender. But I am not
b deciding anything as to the position during the period between the date when the
squatter obtains his title by adverse possession and the date on which he obtains
registration of it. This is the period covered by sub-s (1) of s 75 which is the subsection
on which Lord Radcliffe ([1962] 2 All ER 288 at 296, [1963] AC 510 at 542) and Sir John
Pennycuick ([1976] 3 All ER 521 at 530, [1978] QB 264 at 275) were commenting. It
may well be, as their dicta suggest, that during the period preceding any registration of
c the squatter's rights, the documentary lessee (as registered proprietor of the lease) and the
freeholder can deal with the legal estate with reference to a person whose rights are not
recorded on the register. But once the Act provides for registration of the squatter's title,
it must in my judgment follow that the squatter's rights (once registered) cannot be
overridden. The difference between registered and unregistered land in this respect is an
inevitable consequence of the fact that the Land Registration Act 1925 provides for
d registration of the squatter as proprietor and that registered proprietors have rights.

I can summarise my conclusions as follows. (a) Spectrum cannot, under s 11 of the
1925 Act, have any estate right or interest adverse to or in derogation of the title of Miss
Holmes (as registered proprietor of the lease with possessory title) unless and until the
lease has come to an end. (b) The lease has not come to an end by virtue of the purported
surrender of 7th May 1975, since at that date the leasehold interest was registered land
e and the surrender was not made in accordance with the provisions of the Act. (c) Mrs
David is not entitled to rectification of the register reinstating her as registered proprietor
of the lease, since Miss Holmes is registered in accordance with the mandatory
requirements of s 75 of the Act. Therefore, (d) Mrs David can never surrender the term
so as to merge it in the freehold, and accordingly Spectrum cannot become entitled to
possession by reason of such a surrender.

f In these circumstances it is not necessary for me to consider the argument that, in
exercising my discretion whether or not to rectify the register, I should not in any event
order rectification against Miss Holmes, the registered proprietor in possession, at the suit
of those whose disregard of their own property interest has led to Miss Holmes's
registration.

I therefore dismiss the claim by Spectrum.

g
Summons dismissed.

Solicitors: *Gale & Phelps* (for Spectrum and Mrs David); *G Houghton & Son* (for Miss
Holmes).

Hazel Hartman   Barrister.

Re C B (a minor)

COURT OF APPEAL, CIVIL DIVISION
ORMROD AND BRIDGE LJJ
22nd MAY 1980

Ward of court – Care and control – Factors to be considered – Child in voluntary care of local
authority – Application by local authority to make child a ward of court and for order committing
care and control to local authority – Effect of making child in voluntary care a ward of court and
committing care to local authority – Local authority placing child with suitable long-term foster
parents after period with foster mother – Natural mother a defendant to wardship proceedings
– Natural mother wishing child to be transferred back to foster mother – Whether local authority
required to establish that exceptional circumstances existed making it impracticable or undesirable
for child to be under natural mother's care or whether sole criterion the child's best interests –
Family Law Reform Act 1969, s 7(2).

In October 1977 an illegitimate child then aged 8 or 9 months who had been left by her
17-year-old mother in the care of the child's grandmother was taken into voluntary care
by the local authority with the mother's consent. The local authority placed the child
with a short-term foster mother, Mrs R, who provided a good home for her. The mother
occasionally visited the child. In April 1978 she married a man who was not the father
of the child and told the local authority that she wanted the child back. The local
authority was not satisfied with the mother's proposed arrangements for the child and
decided to make her a ward of court. Accordingly, the local authority, as plaintiff, took
out an originating summons, dated 26th May 1978, to which the mother was the
defendant, asking (i) that the child remain a ward of court during her minority and (ii)
that care and control of her be committed to the local authority. An interim order was
made granting care and control to the local authority and the child remained with Mrs
R. The mother visited the child in June 1978 but thereafter did not see her again until
January 1979, which was the last time she saw her. Consequently the child did not form
any relationship with the mother, and both she and the child's father were strangers to
her. In February 1979 the local authority decided that the situation at Mrs R's home was
disturbing for the child and that she should be transferred to long-term foster parents.
On 28th September, without referring the matter to the court, the local authority
transferred the child from Mrs R to the new foster parents who were eminently suitable
and with whom the child was forming a secure relationship. Mrs R was distressed at the
transfer. The court was informed of the change in the foster parents on 11th October.
The mother, who had left her husband, went back to live with the child's father and
wanted the child to be returned to Mrs R, who was therefore made second defendant to
the originating summons. The local authority's view was that the child should remain
in the care of the new foster parents. The judge, however, having ordered that the child
should remain a ward of court, ordered that the mother should have care and control of
her, since he thought that the matter was governed by s 7(2)[a] of the Family Law Reform
Act 1969 and he found that there were no 'exceptional circumstances making it
impracticable or undesirable', within that subsection, for the child to be under the
mother's care so as to justify an order under that subsection committing the child to the
care of the local authority. The local authority appealed.

Held – Section 7(2) of the 1969 Act was enacted to give the court the same powers to
make an order committing a child to the care of a local authority in wardship proceedings

---

a   Section 7(2) is set out at p 23 e f, post

between parents or between a parent and a third party as it had under s 43(1)[b] of the Matrimonial Causes Act 1973. However, where a local authority had itself initiated wardship proceedings in regard to a child in voluntary care and applied for care and control of the child, s 7(2) did not apply and the court had an unfettered jurisdiction to decide in its discretion the question of care and control according to the paramount interests of the child. It followed that the judge had erred in law in deciding the issue of care and control by considering whether the local authority had made out a case for care and control being committed to it under s 7(2). The real issue was whether it was in the child's best interests that she should be in the care and control of her natural parents or in the care of control of either the new foster parents or Mrs R. On the evidence before the court it would be contrary to the child's interests to hand her over to the natural parents, notwithstanding the ties of blood, since they were complete strangers to her, and, as between the new foster parents and Mrs R, it was in the child's interests that care and control should remain in the new foster parents. The appeal would therefore be allowed (see p 22 *j*, p 23 *c* and *h* to p 24 *a* and *f* to p 25 *e* and *j* to p 26 *g*, post).

J v C [1969] 1 All ER 788 applied.

Per Ormrod LJ. When a serious dispute arises about the welfare of a child in the voluntary care of a local authority it is to the advantage of the local authority and the other parties concerned to resort to the ward of court procedure. However, where in wardship proceedings by a local authority the court makes an order committing the child to the care and control of the local authority, that is not a care order under the children legislation although it has some similar effects to a care order, and whilst the court's order committing care and control to the local authority gives the local authority powers over the child the exercise of those powers is always subject to the court's supervision over the child as a ward of court. Accordingly, the local authority should not make any major change in the child's way of life without obtaining the approval of the court (see p 20 *a* and p 24 *a* to *f*, post).

Per Bridge LJ. Section 7(2) of the 1969 Act does not indicate an a priori preference for giving the care of a child to natural parents as against anybody else (see p 25 *j*, post).

Notes

For the courts' powers in respect of the care of a ward, see 24 Halsbury's Laws (4th Edn) paras 595–596, and for cases on jurisdiction of court over wards of court, see 28(2) Digest (Reissue) 911–916, 2220–2258.

For the Family Law Reform Act 1969, s 7, see 17 Halsbury's Statutes (3rd Edn) 797.

Case referred to in judgments

J v C [1969] 1 All ER 788, [1970] AC 668, [1969] 2 WLR 540, HL, 28(2) Digest (Reissue) 800, 1230.

Interlocutory appeal

By an originating summons dated 26th May 1978 the first plaintiff, the London Borough of Tower Hamlets ('the local authority'), claimed against the first defendant, the mother of a minor, (i) that the minor remain a ward of court during her minority or until further order and (ii) that the care and control of the minor be committed to the local authority. On 15th June 1978 Mr Registrar Kenworthy made a preliminary order granting interim care and control of the minor to the local authority until the hearing of

---

b   Section 43(1), so far as material, provides: 'Where the court has jurisdiction by virtue of this Part of this Act to make an order for the custody of a child and it appears to the court that there are exceptional circumstances making it impracticable or undesirable for the child to be entrusted to either of the parties to the marriage or to any other individual, the court may if it thinks fit make an order committing the care of the child to [a local authority]; and thereupon Part II of the Children Act 1948 (which relates to the treatment of children in the care of a local authority) shall, subject to the provisions of this section, apply as if the child had been received by the local authority into their care under section 1 of that Act.'

the summons. By an order dated 21st November 1979 the former foster mother of the minor, Mrs R, was added as second defendant to the summons. On 8th May 1980 Bush J in open court gave judgment on the summons ordering that wardship of the minor should continue and that the mother should have care and control of the minor. By notice of appeal dated 12th May 1980 the local authority appealed against the order giving care and control to the mother. On the same date the Court of Appeal stayed execution of the judge's order pending the hearing of the appeal. On the hearing of the appeal on 22nd May the present foster parents of the minor were added as second and third plaintiffs, and as appellants, on the summons. The facts are set out in the judgment of Ormrod LJ.

Shirley Ritchie QC and *Mhairi McNab* for the local authority.
Anita M Ryan for the present foster parents.
Lionel Swift QC and *Pamela Scriven* for the mother.
Brian Capstick QC and *Elizabeth Szwed* for Mrs R.

ORMROD LJ. This is an appeal by the local authority in wardship proceedings concerning a little girl whom I will call Claire. It is a very sensitive case and one which should be reported in such a way as to avoid identifying the child or any of the persons concerned in the case because it would be extremely sad if any of them were subjected to any kind of publicity to add to the distresses that they have already suffered in this case one way and another.

It is an important case from the point of view of local authorities, because it raises at least two points under the wardship jurisdiction which require to be made clear, and I will come to them in due course.

At the beginning of the appeal, counsel for the present foster parents of the child applied for them to be joined as appellants, or plaintiffs in the originating summons and appellants in this court. We decided that it was most desirable that they should be joined, and in fact had that application not been made it is probable that the court itself would have suggested it.

At present, for obvious reasons, they have been described in the application by their Christian names, but it seems to me, subject to anything that counsel may subsequently say, that so far as the court record itself is concerned, their surnames must appear on the court record. There is no necessity, as I see it at present, for any document or any copies of these documents to be circulated. It would be quite enough if the court record shows their true names because they must be capable of being identified in the event of any subsequent application.

Before I come to deal with the important points, I will give a brief summary of the facts. The judge, in his judgment, summarised them in great detail. This child was born on 23rd January 1977, so she is 3½ years now. She was the illegitimate child of her mother, who was then only 17, she herself having been born on 20th January 1960. She had had a very turbulent life herself and had been in care, and had had experience of a good deal of difficulty and violence in her own family. She had school problems which led to her being put into care.

She became pregnant as a result of intercourse with the father of this child, and when her pregnancy was discovered these two, who were then very, very young, ceased to see one another. She was living with her mother, and her mother was living with another man who, it is said, was a violent person.

This girl, not surprisingly with her background and faced with this child, was in a very difficult position. It is said that she often went out, not surprisingly at her age, leaving the child in the care of her mother, and her situation in her mother's home was obviously one of great stress and difficulty. So much so, that when the child was about 3 months old, she left home, taking the child with her, and went to stay with friends for a while, a matter of some two or three months. She then moved back into her mother's house.

a But on 23rd October 1977 (the child was then about 8 or 9 months old) she left the child altogether in the care of her own mother, that is the child's grandmother. In a matter of a few days, less than a week later, the grandmother asked for the child to be taken into voluntary care by the local authority. The local authority were able to contact the mother and she agreed.

So on 31st October 1977 Claire was placed with a lady who has been referred to throughout this case as Mrs R, that is the first foster mother. Mrs R was one of the local
b authority's short-term foster parents whom they used with great success from time to time and on whom they relied. She was a divorced lady with three children who were teenagers; her three children were at that time aged 16, 13 and 11, and she had one other foster child with her who was, we are told, about the same age as Claire. There is no doubt whatever that Mrs R made an admirable home for this baby, and she is certainly entitled to every credit for what she did for this child, and no one could have anything
c but sympathy for her in what later happened.

It is the fate of foster mothers to become attached to their foster children; that is what they are there for; and for the foster children to become fond of the foster mothers. Then sooner or later, and so often, a break has to be made, with all the distress and trauma which is inevitable in that situation.

It was contemplated by both Mrs R and the local authority that the child's stay with
d her would be essentially a short-term fostering. The local authority have other people whom they call 'long-term' foster parents and whom they choose, I suppose, on some rather different basis than they choose the 'short-term' foster parents.

In the early stages the mother occasionally visited the child; counsel who has appeared for the local authority in this court gave us six dates between 7th November 1977 and 25th May 1978, but it is said, and one can well understand it (and certainly would not
e make any criticism of it) that the mother found these visits distressing.

In April 1978, the mother married a man, not the father or the putative father of the child, and went to live with him with his parents. At that stage, very soon after the marriage, the mother indicated that she wanted Claire back. As the child was in voluntary care, subject only to giving the necessary 28 days' notice because the child had been in care so long, the mother would, prima facie, be entitled to have had the child
f back. But she did not give the 28 days' notice, so that the local authority's care under the Children Act 1948 continued.

A social worker, Mr Gilding, who was in charge of the case and who (everyone agrees) was a very experienced person had become anxious about the situation which had developed. The mother then was pregnant with another child; the local authority did not know anything about her new husband and they did not know anything about the
g accommodation or what arrangements she could possibly make for Claire if Claire ceased to be in their legal care.

So in those circumstances, faced with the difficulties which local authorities have to contend with in this area of their duties, owing to the difficulties of the legislation which they have to operate, it was decided that the right thing, in the interests of Claire, was to make the child a ward of court. The object of doing that is to fill a serious gap in the local
h authorities' powers where children are concerned, when a period of voluntary care looks as if it is going to be brought to an end by the withdrawal of the consent of the relevant parent. This produces a situation of great difficulty for the local authorities; they have obviously a very important and serious duty to the child in such cases, and it is all too easy to see how the interests of the child may clash with the wishes of the parent.

So the local authority's social workers in this case, and we all should recognise this, are
j in an invidious position: great responsibility, great moral responsibility but, as some would say, inadequate legal powers, to discharge those responsibilities. And so it has become customary, or perhaps not 'customary' but quite frequent, for the local authorities nowadays to resort to the ward of court procedure to help them over their difficulties. This court has never said, and I hope never will say, anything to discourage that practice.

It has always seemed to me that when a serious dispute arises about the welfare of a child *a*
it is asking too much for the social workers to be made to be judges as well as social
workers in these cases, and that it is to the advantage of all parties, including the local
authority, to resort to the court in order that a judge may take the responsibility for the
decision.

So that was what was decided to be done and on 26th May 1978 the originating
summons was issued, and the matter came before Mr Registrar Kenworthy on 15th June
1978 for directions and a preliminary order. He directed that the mother file an affidavit *b*
within 28 days, and made an order granting what is called interim care and control to the
local authority. I will come back to that later.

At that stage the mother instructed solicitors and they entered an appearance on her
behalf, but no affidavit was filed by her and thereafter she seems to have lost touch with
her solicitors. About the same time, that is in July 1978, she left her husband and
returned to live with her mother; but she did not get in contact with her solicitors and *c*
they did not seem to be able to find her, with the result that in October 1978 they applied
for their legal aid certificate to be discharged because they could not get instructions, and
that was done.

In June 1978 the mother did pay a visit to this child, but thereafter she did not see the
child again throughout 1978. Also about the same time, that is July 1978, the long-term
problem of Claire was coming to the surface so far as the local authority social workers *d*
were concerned. Mr Gilding, who was in charge of the case, was beginning to think of
long-term fostering for this child, with a view ultimately to adoption, on the footing that
the mother had in fact dropped out of the child's life altogether, or almost out of the
child's life.

At that time, Mrs R, the short-term foster mother, was anxious that some such step
should be taken, but at that moment, most tragically for all concerned in this case, the *e*
Tower Hamlets social workers' strike began. It is not for this court to make any
comment on that, except to note its consequences. The strike continued from August
1978 until June 1979, a very long time in the lives of the children who were in the charge
of the social workers in Tower Hamlets. But, very conscientiously, Mr Gilding, in spite
of the strike, paid a visit to see how this child was going on.

In January 1979 the mother did pay another visit to the child, but that was the last *f*
time that she had seen this child. It is not clear why she did not visit; there seems to have
been no physical difficulty and no obstruction put in her way by Mrs R, but she did
not. She said to the judge that it was a matter which caused her great distress and she
found it difficult to do. I think that all of us can understand that aspect of it, and it is
certainly no part of the court's duty to criticise her in any way at all. It is a mistake, I
think, in these cases for parties to criticise one another as to what they did or did not do *g*
in relation to the people concerned. The only relevant question is: what effect did the
conduct have on the child?

The effect it had on the child, of course, is obvious. The child has never formed any
kind of relationship with her mother, so that from the point of view of the child the
mother is a stranger. Parents may have some sense of blood ties, but the one thing that
a 3-year old child does not have is any sense of a blood tie to an absent mother or father. *h*

Without any criticism of the mother, she has brought about a situation, so far as this
little girl is concerned, which is unalterable and which the court has to deal with as best
it can. It is part of the facts and its significance is to be assessed in terms of its effects on
the child now and in the future.

In February 1979 Mr Gilding paid his unofficial visit, and there is doubt that he was,
as he said, alarmed by what he found. The situation had changed with regard to Mrs R *j*
in an important way. She had formed an association with a man of more or less, I think,
her own age but not at all in good health, who had parted from his wife and who had two
children who were aged 12 and 9. He and the two children had moved into Mrs R's
house, and about the same time, I think, her eldest daughter left the house; she moved

out but I do not suggest anything wrong in her leaving. There is no doubt Mr Gilding
a found the situation there in Mrs R's house disturbing.

In June 1979 there were discussions about this, that is, when the strike ended, and Mr
Gilding was in a position to take action. The situation was that he felt the household was
overcrowded. It is true that head counting made them only one more than they had
been in the past.

Neither Mrs R nor her cohabitee were in good health (not to any significant extent I
b think) but what disturbed Mr Gilding was the child. He thought her attitude had
changed and he described her as 'clinging to Mrs R, banging her head and rocking about'
and generally Mr Gilding was disturbed by what he found.

It is always difficult to describe why an experienced person like Mr Gilding is disturbed
by what he finds, and it may be that a description of the child's behaviour is not all that
convincing to a court, but the court should I think take note of the fact that a very
c experienced social worker was seriously disturbed by what he found.

At that stage, according to Mr Gilding (I think it may have been in issue), he saw the
mother and there was a discussion about the possibility of adoption, and arrangements
were made for the mother to see an adoption officer. Unfortunately, the mother again
at this stage, I think, was pregnant, and on 26th June she was seen when she was in
hospital. She was living in temporary council accommodation with her child, who had
d been born (another little girl) on 5th December 1978. At that stage the mother agreed
that she was not in a position to take over Claire, but she would not agree to an adoption,
as she was perfectly entitled not to do.

But meanwhile the social workers involved had come to the conclusion that in those
circumstances long-term arrangements would have to be made for Claire. They did not
think that Mrs R was in a position to provide long-term fostering care for the child, or
e perhaps not able to do it satisfactorily. At any rate they came to the conclusion, and there
was the usual conference on the matter, that a move of this child was necessary.

Mrs R was told about this and, as one can understand, she was extremely upset. The
child had been with her so long that obviously they had each become very fond of each
other, and a break could be nothing but painful on both sides. Not surprisingly, her
cohabitee was very upset and angry, but Mrs R did her best to help and there is no doubt
f she did honestly try her best, in spite of the distress which this caused her.

Attempts were made, at that stage, to get in touch with the mother, but they were not
successful. The judge said that he did not think sufficient effort had been made by the
local authority; he thought that they could have got in touch with the mother if they had
tried harder.

So on 28th September 1979 Claire was transferred to her new foster parents, that is, the
g persons who we have just given leave to join in these proceedings, and she has been with
those new foster parents since 28th September 1979.

At this stage, on 3rd October, both the mother and, I think, Mrs R were distressed and
upset about this change and they both went to see one of the social workers, a Mrs Hill.
The mother asked to see Claire although at that stage she did not give any clear indication
that she was going to ask for the child back. What the local authority did not do was to
h tell the court, the registrar, of this proposed change before it was made, and the judge, in
my view rightly, criticised the local authority for failing to take that step because it is
fundamental in wardship jurisdiction that no serious change in the arrangements for a
ward should be made without reference to the court. It is true that this wardship had not
proceeded further than the preliminary stages, but there is no doubt that in law the duty
of the local authority was to inform the court and obtain the sanction of the registrar to
j make the move. It would almost certainly have given the mother an opportunity to
make representations, and it would have given Mrs R, too, an opportunity to make
representations to the court, if either or both of them wished to do so.

The local authority did inform the court, on 11th October 1979, by letter, of the
change, but that was after it had happened and it was too late then to take any active step.

About the same time, some time in October, the mother seems to have got into touch again with the child's father, and the two of them went to see Mr Gilding. What she was a wanting at that stage is not very clear. Mr Gilding said she did not want the child herself but wanted the child returned to Mrs R, and indicated that she was prepared to fight all and sundry at that stage over the child.

Mrs R, by this time, had taken advice, and she applied on 8th November to intervene in the proceedings, and on 22nd November she was joined as a defendant in the proceedings by the registrar, who ordered a welfare officer's report. Thereafter, the b father and mother seem to have seen a lot of one another and in March or April 1980 they went to live together and they are at present living together, though they have not been together very long.

It was in that state of affairs that the matter came before Bush J whose order is the subject matter of this appeal. Having heard the evidence and having had the advantage of hearing all the social workers concerned and having an extremely full and detailed c welfare report, Bush J made an order that the care of Claire should be transferred to her mother. That order was a few days later stayed by this court pending appeal, and now the appeal comes on before us.

The local authority are the first plaintiff; the present foster parents are the second and third plaintiffs/appellants; the first defendant/respondent is the mother and the second defendant/respondent is Mrs R. d

Now on the facts of the case, the position is quite simple. Stated baldly, they are these. This child has known one stable home up to September 1979, and only one stable home and that is with Mrs R. The mother is a virtual stranger to her; the father is a total stranger to her. But since September 1979 she has begun to make, and it appears from all the evidence, particularly the welfare report and the short affidavit which has been filed today by the foster parents, is making, a successful relationship with her present e foster parents. There she is alone with no other children; they are described as eminently suitable foster parents. It is obvious from reading their brief affidavits that they are sensitive and responsible and reliable people, and from the evidence (such as it is and it is strong from the welfare officer and from the present foster parents themselves) that the child is extremely well placed with them and is forming a secure relationship with them.

So the judge, in practice, had three possible alternative solutions to this problem: one f was to leave the child where she is with the present foster parents: another to send her back to her pseudo-mother, her mother substitute, Mrs R; and the third was to hand her over to her own mother.

The indications for the first, that is leaving the child where she is with the present foster parents, are first, that she has settled down with them; second, that they are in a position to offer her the very highest standard of care; and, third, that any further g changes in this child's life are bound to add to her intense insecurity and are bound to be very upsetting to her, if not in the short-term then in the long-term. There are all sorts of psychological problems which might or might not arise from sending her back or moving her away from the present foster parents.

The attraction of Mrs R, of course, is that the child is going back to an environment with which she is familiar and where she might feel equally secure. But against that, the h court has to bear in mind the views of the social workers concerned that this arrangement was not going to be viable in the long-term and might have to be changed later, but it was clearly an alternative which was a practical alternative.

The third proposition that Claire should be handed over to her own mother and father, although emotionally attractive, in my judgment has very little to support it. It is absolutely vital in these cases that we look at reality and look at it through the eyes of j the child. It is clear that the child would be grossly disturbed by being handed over to yet a third couple and a third couple with whom she has had no contact at all, although she may have some vague memory of her mother. So it would require, I think, a very, very strong case to justify taking this child of three and handing her over to total strangers simply because they are her blood mother and blood father.

Now the judge did not, as I see it, approach the case in the way in which I have just
a indicated. In his judgment, having set out very fairly the facts, he said:

> 'This decision does not turn on the relative merits of John and Margaret [the
> present foster parents] and the mother in the ideal parents stakes. No doubt the
> mother would come off second best, particularly as she has not been given a chance
> to show what she can do with Claire. The question turns on whether the local
> *b* authority has shown that it is undesirable that the child should be or continue to be
> under the care of either of her parents. The court must look at the totality of the
> circumstances, bearing in mind that Parliament intended that children should
> remain with their parents if at all possible, and bearing in mind also, that the
> welfare of a child is the paramount consideration.'

With respect to the judge I think he was wrong and misdirected himself there in that
c passage because the decision *does* turn on what he called 'the relative merits of John and
Margaret and the mother in the ideal parents stakes'.

It may be that the judge was confused by the form of the relief which was sought by
the originating summons. In it the local authority asked, first, that the child should
remain a ward of court during her minority or until further order, and, second, that the
care and control of the minor should be committed to them. As I have already said, the
d registrar made an order for interim care and control to the local authority. It seems to
have got into the mind of the judge that the whole case was dominated and controlled
by s 7(2) of the Family Law Reform Act 1969. That subsection, which is in identical
terms with the corresponding provision in the Matrimonial Causes Act 1973, s 43(1),
reads:

e > 'Where it appears to the court that there are exceptional circumstances making it
> impracticable or undesirable for a ward of court to be, or continue to be, under the
> care of either of his parents or of any other individual the court may, if it thinks fit,
> make an order committing the care of the ward to a local authority; and thereupon
> Part II of the Children Act 1948 (which relates to the treatment of children in the
> care of a local authority) shall, subject to the next following subsection, apply as if
f > the child had been received by the local authority into their care under section 1 of
> that Act.'

That is the section which the judge treated as controlling the whole of the case. So,
instead of considering who was going to look after this child and considering, as he ought
to have done, what the welfare of the child as the paramount consideration required, he
g was led to consider whether or not there were exceptional circumstances making it
'impracticable or undesirable' for the ward to be under the care of either of her parents.
He treated the matter as one of law. He felt that he had to find first that the
circumstances were exceptional and second he had to decide whether it was impracticable
or undesirable for the ward to continue to be in the care of either of her parents or any
other individual. In fact, of course, s 7(2) of the 1969 Act never applied at all in this case
h because at all times the proposal of the local authority was that the child should remain
in the care of the present foster parents, that is 'another individual' within s 7(2). Nor is
it at all difficult, in a case like this, to find exceptional circumstances. No one, I venture
to think, would dream of making an order committing the care of a ward to a local
authority unless the circumstances were exceptional. Nor would they contemplate
doing it unless it was the only practical solution open to the court at the time.

j It was a mistake to treat this case as if it was an s 7(2) case because the local authority
were the plaintiffs. This is the first point to be made so far as the wardship jurisdiction
is concerned. It is an unfettered jurisdiction to place the ward in the care and control of
any person who can best look after him or her.

Ever since *J v C* [1969] 1 All ER 788, [1970] AC 668, the principles are absolutely clear:
the court in its discretion must decide what the paramount interests of the child require.

It is not concerned with allocating blame or adjusting rival claims. It has to make a decision sufficiently difficult in all conscience, but the decision it has to make is what is *a* in the best interests of this child at this stage.

Looking as far ahead as is possible to look, and making as wise a decision about the child's future as it is possible for the court to make, if the court thinks that it would be desirable in the interests of the child to make an order committing the child to the care and control of the local authority, so be it. But it is not a care order under the children legislation; it is an order which has some similar effects in the sense that the local *b* authority has powers over the child and is entitled to exercise them, but subject always to the court's supervision.

Now so far as wardship is concerned, this should be said at the outset I think, and I say it with sympathy for local authorities and social workers because I know the difficulties under which they work, but when a child is made a ward of court it means what it says. The child is a ward of the court and it is for the court to decide all the serious issues *c* relating to the child. That is why in orders made in the wardship jurisdiction the court never grants custody to anybody. It used to be said in the old days that the court 'retained custody in itself', which was only a form of words to emphasise the fact that the court remains in control of the child, and it grants care and control to somebody, that is to look after the child in the ordinary day-to-day way, and, although I do not want to make too much of this, if the child is a ward of the court in that sense, it is only reasonable that the *d* persons who have the actual control of the child under the order of the court should not make any major change in the child's way of life without getting the approval of the court. This may be an inconvenience, but this case illustrates very well how important it is to observe these sometimes tiresome routine rules because there is no doubt that the whole course of this case would have been different if the matter had come before the court in, say, August or September 1979 before the change to new foster parents was *e* made.

I am most anxious to emphasise that once the child is a ward of the court the major decisions relating to that child are for the court to take. That is equally the case whether the care and control is granted to either parent or to some other individual or to a local authority.

The judge unfortunately did not approach the matter, I think, in the right way. He *f* was side-tracked by considering whether he had the necessary jurisdiction under s 7(2) of the 1969 Act. But in this case the local authority were themselves the plaintiffs in the originating summons asking for 'care and control', not for an order under s 7(2). Had he had the present foster parents before him as parties, I do not think that this error would have crept in. The result is that, with respect to the judge, the conclusion is inescapable that he exercised his discretion on an entirely wrong basis. He did not, at any stage, *g* compare the mother's proposals with the present foster parents' proposals for the child. He did not weigh one against the other and make an assessment of the advantages to the child in regard to one course or the other, in the short-term or the long-term. He was almost wholly concerned with deciding whether the local authority had made out their case under s 7(2), but, as I have already said, if a local authority takes the initiative of making a child a ward I do not think that s 7(2) comes into the case at all. Section 7(2) *h* was passed to give the court power in proceedings between parents, or between a parent and a third party, to make an order committing the child to the care of the local authority, or to make it clear that the court, in wardship proceedings, had the same powers as it has under the Matrimonial Causes Act 1973.

That being the case, it is for this court to exercise its discretion on the material as it is before it. From what I have said already, it is obvious what view I take. To my mind, *j* it would be entirely wrong and contrary to this child's best interests to hand her over to her natural parents who, as I have said before, are total strangers to her. If they were not her natural parents, no one could imagine for a moment making such an order. So the real issue is whether she should be in the care and control of her present foster parents, or whether she should go back to Mrs R.

I hope I have said enough to make it plain to Mrs R that I feel very sorry for and
a sympathetic towards her. She has had a tragic experience with this child, but once the
break has been made between her and the child it would be wrong, in my view, to try
to go back, unless there was some pretty powerful indication that that would be the best
course. If the present foster parents were not able to get on terms with the child, or the
child was fretting for Mrs R, then there might have been a strong case for saying that she
should go back to Mrs R; but the evidence is really all the other way. Although the
b trauma of that break from Mrs R is going to be with this child, I should think for a very
long time indeed, it has been incurred, but I think it is going to be possible to repair that
damage. It may well be that, the step having been taken, it has been taken for the best
(I am not suggesting for a moment that the child would be better off with Mrs R than she
will be with her present foster parents). I do not however think it is possible to say that
it will be in her interests to try to go backwards in her development, and in view of the
c admirable reports as to the present foster parents, the proposed adopters, contained in the
welfare officer's report, I think that the right course is to follow the strong
recommendation of the welfare officer, not only because it is made by the welfare officer,
but because it seems to me to be plain and good commonsense, looked at from the point
of view of this child.

I would like to finish where I began by saying that what we are concerned with is the
d child's future. We are not concerned with the natural parents' position. We have to
judge the situation as it is at the moment, no matter how it has come about, and answer
the question: where does the future of this child best lie? I answer that without any
hesitation by saying: with her present foster parents.

In those circumstances, I would allow the appeal and make the order in that form.

e **BRIDGE LJ.** I agree. In the proceedings below, this case, as it seems to me, was
bedevilled by the attention which was directed to and the proposition derived from s 7(2)
of the Family Law Reform Act 1969. The judge said of that section:

> '. . . the section emphasises that if at all possible it is the intention of Parliament
> that parents should not lose their children to the care of local authorities except for
> *f* good cause and in exceptional circumstances. [Then, in a passage which has already
> been referred to by Ormrod LJ, he said:] The court must look at the totality of the
> circumstances bearing in mind that Parliament intended that children should
> remain with their parents if at all possible.'

Those two propositions, thought to be derived from s 7(2), seem to me to have dominated
g the judge's approach to this whole problem.

Now the situation with which s 7(2) is dealing is a situation where it is impracticable
or undesirable for a ward of court to be under the care of either of his parents or any other
individual, and I emphasise those concluding words, 'or any other individual', and once
that is appreciated it becomes apparent that s 7(2) had nothing whatever to do with this
case. No one could possibly have suggested that it was either impracticable or undesirable
h in this case for Claire to continue in the custody either of the present foster parents or to
be returned to the custody of Mrs R, the previous foster parent, or of the natural parents.

The reason why s 7(2) seems to have loomed so large was that by what seems to have
been a purely procedural accident the present foster parents were not parties before the
court, so it was the local authority who, in form, were applying for an order to be made
in their favour. But in substance, nobody could have been in any doubt that the issue
j was whether the little girl should be in the care of her natural parents, or one or other of
the sets of foster parents who were 'other individuals' within the meaning of s 7(2).

In fact, s 7(2) indicates no parliamentary a priori preference for giving the care of a
child to natural parents as against giving it to anybody else. The paramount consideration
in a simple case like this, and the sole consideration, is what will best serve the welfare of
the child. Once the misapprehension derived from s 7(2) is cleared out of the way, and

the case is approached on the basis of what will best serve the welfare of this little girl of now just over 3 years old, the solution to the problem to my mind stands out so as to be *a* unmistakable.

Here is a little girl who, in her short life, has already been disturbed by a number of traumatic experiences. Now for the last eight months she has been in what, from all accounts, appears to be an ideal home, in the care of the present foster parents of whom the welfare officer in her report speaks in glowing terms. From the evidence before us, it is apparent that signs of disturbed behaviour which were apparent when the child first *b* went to them are greatly improved, and that in the eight months she has been with them the present foster parents and the little girl have formed extremely strong bonds of mutual affection. So strongly did the welfare officer feel about the matter that she concluded her report by saying: 'I feel that it would be disastrous for Claire to be uprooted yet again and for the fine progress which John and Margaret [they are the present foster parents] have made with her be interrupted.' *c*

Against this background, when one considers the possibility of the child being returned to the care of her natural mother and father, it seems to me clear that that would be a course which would not serve the welfare of the child. As Ormrod LJ has pointed out, the father is a total stranger to the little girl, and the mother, through no fault of her own but inescapably in fact, has now become a virtual stranger. If one were to ask the question whether it would be in the interests of this child at the impressionable *d* age of just over three to be removed yet again from the home where she has settled and to be transferred to total strangers who were not related to her by blood, the answer would be so obvious that one would laugh the suggestion out of court.

The sole argument before this court, and the argument which misled the trial judge, as I think, is the argument that the tie of blood in some way supersedes other considerations and determines what the child's future must be unless there is some *e* overwhelming consideration to the contrary.

Accordingly, I reach, without hesitation, the conclusion that the judge's order was erroneous. I think the question whether the child should stay with the present foster parents or return to Mrs R, where she was for so long, is a much more difficult question, but on that the judge came to the conclusion that, if it were not for the involvement of the natural mother, the balance of the decision would be to leave the child with the *f* present foster parents rather than risk returning her to Mrs R, and he explained what he thought the risk involved in that course would be. So for the reasons he gave, and for the reasons given in the judgment of Ormrod LJ, I agree that the decision should be to leave the child with the present foster parents rather than to return her to Mrs R.

I accordingly agree that this appeal should be allowed and I agree with the order proposed by Ormrod LJ. *g*

Appeal allowed; care and control to the present foster parents; supervision order to the local authority. Leave to appeal to the House of Lords refused.

Solicitors: *H D Cook* (for the local authority); *Denton Hall & Burgin* (for the present foster parents); *Breeze, Benton & Co* (for the mother); *Alexander Johnson* (for Mrs R).

Bebe Chua   Barrister.

a   # Lewis v North Devon District Council

QUEEN'S BENCH DIVISION
WOOLF J
15th SEPTEMBER, 6th OCTOBER 1980

b   *Housing – Homeless person – Person becoming homeless intentionally – Family unit – Effect on family unit of husband becoming homeless intentionally – Application by wife – Applicant living with man in house provided by his employer – Man voluntarily giving up job and couple being required to vacate house – Man's application for accommodation rejected because he became homeless intentionally – Applicant making separate application for accommodation for herself and man – Whether rejection of man's application a good ground for rejection of applicant's*
c   *application – Whether applicant becoming homeless intentionally because she acquiesced in man leaving job – Housing (Homeless Persons) Act 1977, s 17.*

The applicant, a married woman, lived with a farm worker (who was not her husband) and a child of her marriage as a family in a house provided by the man's employer. The man became unhappy in his job and left it, with the result that the couple were forced
d   to vacate the house. When an application by the man to the local housing authority for accommodation under the Housing (Homeless Persons) Act 1977 for himself and the applicant was refused on the ground that by giving up his job he had become homeless intentionally, the applicant made an application in her name. She made it clear in her application that the man and her child were members of her household and would share any accommodation provided. The housing authority refused her application on the
e   ground that, by acquiescing in the man's decision to leave his job knowing that they would then have to vacate the house provided by his employer, she had herself become homeless intentionally. The applicant applied for judicial review of the authority's decision, contending that, in deciding whether she had become homeless intentionally within the meaning of that term in s 17[a] of the 1977 Act, it was her conduct alone which ought to be considered by the housing authority. The authority contended that where
f   one member of a family unit became homeless intentionally the whole family was to be treated as being homeless intentionally, with the result that rejection of an application by one member of the family because of intentional homelessness was sufficient reason to reject any further application by another member on behalf of the family. The authority submitted that if the position were otherwise a husband could make the family homeless intentionally and then the wife could successfully apply for accommodation under the
g   1977 Act.

Held – On the true construction of s 17 of the 1977 Act a woman who lived with a man who became homeless intentionally was not necessarily barred by his conduct or by the fact that he might benefit undeservingly if she were given accommodation from being entitled to the relief available under that Act to a person who had not become homeless
h   intentionally. However, since the policy of the 1977 Act required a housing authority to consider the family unit as a whole, it was entitled to take into account the conduct of other members of the family and could assume, in the absence of contrary evidence, that the applicant was a party to that conduct. Since the housing authority had concluded that the applicant had acquiesced in the decision by the man she was living with to become homeless intentionally by giving up his job, it was entitled to take the view that
j   the applicant had herself become homeless intentionally. The application would accordingly be dismissed (see p 31 *a* and *e* to p 32 *e*, post).

---

a   Section 17 is set out at p 30 *f* to *j*, post

Notes

For a housing authority's duties to a homeless person, see 22 Halsbury's Laws (4th Edn) *a* para 513.

For the Housing (Homeless Persons) Act 1977, s 17, see 47 Halsbury's Statutes (3rd Edn) 330.

Application for judicial review

By notice of motion dated 2nd September 1980 Julie Pauline Lewis applied with the *b* leave of the vacation judge granted on 1st September 1980, for (i) a declaration that she had not become homeless intentionally within the meaning of s 17 of the Housing (Homeless Persons) Act 1977, (ii) an order of certiorari to quash the decision to that effect made by the North Devon District Council ('the housing authority') on 9th July 1980, and (iii) an order of mandamus directed to the council requiring it to secure that accommodation was available or, alternatively, did not cease to be available for her *c* occupation. The motion was heard in chambers during the vacation and judgment was delivered in open court. The facts are set out in the judgment.

Anthony Puttick for Mrs Lewis.
David H Fletcher for the housing authority.

Cur adv vult *d*

6th October. **WOOLF J** read the following judgment: This case concerns an application by Mrs Julie Pauline Lewis for judicial review in respect of a decision by the North Devon District Council that Mrs Lewis had become homeless intentionally for the purposes of the Housing (Homeless Persons) Act 1977. Under that Act, if it is satisfied that an *e* applicant had become homeless intentionally, the duties of the housing authority are more restricted than they would otherwise be.

The case involves consideration of the effect on an application under the Act of a previous application by a person who has been living with the applicant as man and wife, where the housing authority, in respect of the previous application, has lawfully come to a conclusion that the other person had become homeless intentionally, and the applicant *f* intends to go on living with that other person in any accommodation provided by the authority. This is a question of general application and one in respect of which both parties invited me to give judgment in open court although, as the application was heard during the vacation, it was dealt with in chambers.

The housing authority argues that the whole scheme of the Act is to look at the family unit and to provide accommodation for that unit and it was the manifest intention of *g* Parliament that where one member of that family unit is homeless intentionally the family unit should be treated as homeless intentionally. The result of that approach is that where a man and woman are living together as man and wife the housing authority is entitled to reject an application by the woman merely because there has been a previous application by the man and it has found that that man became homeless intentionally.

Mrs Lewis, on the other hand, contends that it is her conduct and her conduct alone *h* which should be considered and that it is wrong to take into account any previous decision in respect of the man with whom she is living. On this approach, in this case, the housing authority's decision should at least be quashed as a decision which was wholly unreasonable, or as one which could only be reached on the basis of the housing authority wrongfully taking into account the conduct of the man with whom Mrs Lewis *j* is living.

The facts can be stated briefly as follows. Mrs Lewis had married on 25th August 1976, but in January 1979 she became separated from her husband, from whom she is now seeking a divorce on the grounds of his adultery. At the relevant time she had two children, one of whom is four and the other just three. In February 1979 she formed an

association with a Mr Hopkins, with whom she still lives. In August 1979 Mr Hopkins
a took employment as a farm labourer and was provided with a farmhouse to enable him
to perform his duties, and he lived at the farmhouse with Mrs Lewis and one of her
children.

Mr Hopkins was not happy in the job but according to Mrs Lewis she encouraged him
to stay. But the situation got worse and on 8th November 1979 Mr Hopkins told her
that he intended to give in his notice that day, and he was so unhappy and disappointed
b about the job that, Mrs Lewis says, 'his mind was firmly made up to leave and I could not
have changed it'.

As a result of giving in his notice, the owner of the farm required possession of the
farmhouse and eventually brought proceedings against Mr Hopkins which resulted in
possession of the farmhouse being obtained on 6th March 1980. Mrs Lewis was then
two months pregnant with Mr Hopkins's child.
c An application under the 1977 Act was made by Mr Hopkins but the housing
authority considered that both he and Mrs Lewis were intentionally homeless because
Mr Hopkins had voluntarily given up his job. The family were, however, provided with
temporary accommodation.

On 23rd May Mr Hopkins and Mrs Lewis sought orders in the Barnstaple County
Court restraining the housing authority from withdrawing temporary accommodation
d and a declaration that the council had misdirected itself in finding that they were
intentionally homeless. Those proceedings were dismissed after the facts had been fully
investigated by his Honour Judge Goodall. In giving his judgment, however, the judge
said (according to the note which is before me):

e 'Whether even though Mr Hopkins has no redress in action the question arises
whether Mrs Lewis had redress. At first sight no one could suggest that she has
made herself intentionally homeless. She was not employed by Mrs Bruton and did
not give notice. It is clear that discrimination between husband and wife or man
and common law wife creates appalling problems with the administration of the
1977 Act, problems I doubt Parliament considered. The only duty owed by the
local authority under s 4 of the Act is to a person who has applied to them for
f accommodation. Evidence on this point is scanty. It is clear Mr Hopkins was the
applicant even though his wife accompanied him to the housing department.
Evidence comes from Mr Cook [the housing assistant] that he saw the plaintiffs on
10th March when they visited the Civic Centre. He spoke to Mr Hopkins and
considered it as an application by the household and treated them as a whole
family. This is illustrated from the application form. The applicant is stated to be
Mr Hopkins; Mrs Lewis is listed in members of the household. The form which Mr
g Cook filled in at the time the plaintiffs visited him shows only one applicant, Mr
Hopkins. There is no suggestion that Mrs Lewis wanted a place on her own. There
is no suggestion that she was an applicant. It is not necessary for me to decide this
awkward question of what would happen if she made an application on her own
count. I am only concerned with the duty owed by the North Devon District
h Council to Mr Hopkins and for the reasons stated they are not in breach of duty. If
ever there were a deserving case where a man had made himself intentionally
homeless, then this is it. For example, often in cases of intentional homelessness a
couple come from elsewhere to take a job in a hotel and are trying to be given the
sack by carrying out their duties poorly. They then apply to the local authority for
housing. South Devon are well aware of the situation. However, here is a hard-
j working, deserving man who has always worked and had a reason for giving his
notice. An employer should not keep an employee dangling at the end of a string.
It is hard that he should be disqualified from the provisions of the Act. From the
dates it is clear that Mr Hopkins had no notice that a child was on the way when he
gave up his employment. However, in conclusion, it is easy for a judge not faced
with housing on a limited budget to come to such conclusions. No doubt this point

did not escape the North Devon District Council. I must say this is the worst
possible time to be without accommodation in Devon and it is the hardest case I
have yet had to determine. Nevertheless the action fails.'

Because of what was said by the judge Mrs Lewis made a fresh application for
accommodation under the Act. That application showed her child and Mr Hopkins as
members of her household and it is clear that it was intended that Mr Hopkins should
share accommodation which was provided under the Act.

Having investigated the application a letter dated 11th July was written to Mrs Lewis
by the solicitor to the council which begins as follows:

'Housing (Homeless Persons) Act 1977: Application No: Ho349
'Following enquiries made by Officers of my Department into your application
under the above Act, I write to inform you that the Council considers that you have
become homeless intentionally for the following reason:—You rendered yourself
and your dependants intentionally homeless within the meaning of Section 17 of
the Act in that you acquiesced in your common law husband's decision to terminate
his employment at Limeslake Farm, knowing that the accommodation which you,
your common law husband and your dependants occupied, was tied to your
common law husband's employment and that by terminating his employment,
you, your common law husband and your dependants' right to remain in occupation
ceased.'

It was that decision which gave rise to these proceedings.

In support of their approach, the housing authority contends that an absurd position
would be created if a husband or a man living with a woman could intentionally make
the family homeless and then the wife or woman concerned could make an application
and, because she, rather than he, makes the application, the family would be treated
differently from the way it would have been treated if he made the application. This
would result in his obtaining benefits under the Act which it was never intended that he
should receive because he had rendered himself intentionally homeless.

The test whether a person is intentionally homeless or not is contained in s 17. That
section provides:

'(1) Subject to subsection (3) below, for the purposes of this Act a person becomes
homeless intentionally if he deliberately does or fails to do anything in consequence
of which he ceases to occupy accommodation which is available for his occupation
and which it would have been reasonable for him to continue to occupy.
'(2) Subject to subsection (3) below, for the purposes of this Act a person becomes
threatened with homelessness intentionally if he deliberately does or fails to do
anything the likely result of which is that he will be forced to leave accommodation
which is available for his occupation and which it would have been reasonable for
him to continue to occupy.
'(3) An act or omission in good faith on the part of a person who was unaware of
any relevant fact is not to be treated as deliberate for the purposes of subsection (1)
or (2) above.
'(4) Regard may be had, in determining for the purposes of subsections (1) and
(2) above whether it would have been reasonable for a person to continue to occupy
accommodation, to the general circumstances prevailing in relation to housing in
the area of the housing authority to whom he applied for accommodation or for
assistance in obtaining accommodation.'

Section 4 makes it clear that it is not for the applicant to show that he did not become
homeless intentionally; it is for the housing authority, as a result of its inquiries, to satisfy
itself that the applicant became homeless or was threatened with homelessness
intentionally.

Homelessness is defined in s 1(1):

'A person is homeless ... if there is no accommodation—(a) which he, together
with any other person who normally resides with him as a member of his family or

in circumstances in which the housing authority consider it reasonable for that

a person to reside with him—(i) is entitled to occupy . . .'

That definition and a number of other provisions of the Act make it clear that in looking into an application under the Act the housing authority has to have regard to what I will loosely describe as the family unit. I draw attention to ss 2(1)(*a*) and (*c*), 2(2), 5(1)(*a*)(i) and (ii), and 16. Of those sections I will read only s 16 which says:

b   'For the purposes of this Act accommodation is only available for a person's occupation if it is available for occupation both by him and by any other person who might reasonably be expected to reside with him and any reference in this Act to securing accommodation for a person's occupation shall be construed accordingly.'

Those provisions make it clear that it is the policy of the Act to keep families together where possible. Such a policy is not surprising in an Act of Parliament passed in 1977.

c   As it is to the family unit that the housing authority is to have regard, it would be readily understandable if Parliament had provided expressly that the application should be made by the family unit and the question should be whether or not the family should be regarded as having become homeless intentionally. However, as is conceded on behalf of the housing authority, there are no express words which provide that where a man and a woman are living together, if one of the couple became homeless intentionally,

d the other should be treated as being homeless intentionally. The Act does not place any express limitation on who can make an application or how many applications can be made.

The main argument on behalf of the housing authority was that s 17 must be read as though it provided that, for the purposes of the Act, a person becomes homeless if he, or a person who resides with him or who could reasonably have been expected to reside

e with him, became homeless intentionally. Such a construction of s 17, in my view, is not possible. It is inconsistent with the wording of s 17 as a whole.

Clearly Parliament could have chosen to treat a woman who lived with a man who had become homeless intentionally as though she was tainted by his conduct. This would have been hard on her but would have avoided his obtaining benefits to which he was not entitled in his own right. Alternatively Parliament could have adopted the approach

f that, albeit the man was undeserving, because the woman was not herself homeless intentionally, he was to benefit because she was entitled to the additional rights of a person who was not homeless intentionally and she could only obtain those rights if he benefited as well. The literal wording of s 17 indicates that it was the second alternative that Parliament intended and such a result is not so wholly unreasonable that I feel compelled to read into the Act words which are not there so as to arrive at the opposite

g conclusion.

This construction does not mean that a housing authority should close its eyes to the conduct of the other members of the family. On the contrary, in my view, the fact that the Act requires consideration of the family unit as a whole indicates that it would be perfectly proper in the ordinary case for the housing authority to look at the family as a whole and assume, in the absence of material which indicates to the contrary, where the

h conduct of one member of the family was such that he should be regarded as having become homeless intentionally, that that was conduct to which the other members of the family were a party.

So, for example, where the husband is a tenant and gives notice in circumstances where he is properly to be regarded as having become homeless intentionally, the wife, even though she was not the tenant and she did not give the notice, can be regarded in

j the same way. In normal circumstances this would be treated as a joint decision. If, however, at the end of the day, because of material put before the housing authority by the wife, the housing authority is not satisfied that she was a party to the decision, it would have to regard her as not having become homeless intentionally.

In argument the housing authority drew my attention to the difficulties which could arise in cases where the husband spent the rent on drink. If the wife acquiesced to his doing this then it seems to me it would be proper to regard her, as well as him, as having become homeless intentionally. She had failed to do something the likely result of *a* which failure would be that she would be forced to leave the accommodation which was available for her occupation as provided by s 17. If, on the other hand, she had done what she could to prevent the husband spending his money on drink instead of the rent then she had not failed to do anything and it would not be right to regard her as having become homeless intentionally.

Turning therefore to the facts of this case, the finding of the housing authority stated *b* that Mrs Lewis had acquiesced in Mr Hopkins's decision to terminate his employment knowing the accommodation was tied to Mr Hopkins's employment. Having come to that conclusion it was perfectly proper to take the view that Mrs Lewis was herself intentionally homeless.

It was argued on behalf of Mrs Lewis, before me, that the housing authority could not reasonably come to a conclusion that she had acquiesced in this decision of Mr *c* Hopkins. However, on the material before the authority, I do not regard that contention as being right. There was ample material before the housing authority on which it could come to the conclusion which it did, and the decision which the housing authority came to in this case, which I regard as being perfectly proper, indicates that perhaps the difficulties, which the housing authority fear might be caused by what I regard as the proper construction of s 17, are not quite as great as it fears. *d*

Because the housing authority approached the matter properly by looking at Mrs Lewis's conduct, this application must be dismissed.

Application dismissed.

Solicitors: *Bischoff & Co*, agents for *Harding, Rootham & Stallard*, Barnstaple (for Mrs Lewis); *J G Bradley* (for the housing authority). *e*

K Mydeen Esq   Barrister.

FFF Estates Ltd v London Borough of   *f*
Hackney

COURT OF APPEAL, CIVIL DIVISION
STEPHENSON, ACKNER LJJ AND DAME ELIZABETH LANE
3rd, 4th, 7th, 8th, 9th, 25th JULY 1980

g

Housing – Improvement notice – Dwelling without one or more of the standard amenities – House divided into two dwellings but occupants sharing standard amenities – Whether dwellings 'without' standard amenities – Housing Act 1974, s 89(1)(b).

Housing – Improvement notice – Dwelling capable of improvement to full standard at reasonable expense – House divided into two dwellings occupied by sitting tenants – Improvement notice *h* *served on landlord – House in present state valued at less than £6,000 with tenants and more than £14,000 with vacant possession – Estimated cost of improvements £16,500 – Value of house if improvements carried out less than £8,000 with sitting tenants and more than £18,000 with vacant possession – Whether effect of sitting tenants on market value to be taken into account in deciding whether house could be improved at 'reasonable' expense – Whether dwellings capable of improvement at 'reasonable expense' – Housing Act 1974, s 89(3)(c).* *j*

The landlords owned a house which was divided into two dwellings, one of which was let under a controlled tenancy and the other under a regulated tenancy. Neither dwelling was self-contained because the tenants had to share a bathroom and toilet. In June 1977 the landlords informed the tenants that they intended to convert the house into self-

contained flats and in October instructed architects. In April 1978 the local authority
a notified the landlords under s 89ᵃ of the Housing Act 1974 that representations had been
made by the tenants that they were without the standard amenities (ie an internal
lavatory, bath and handbasin with hot and cold water) and that the landlords refused to
provide those amenities. The authority asked the landlords to advise the local authority
within 14 days whether they intended to improve the premises to the required
standard. The landlords did not reply, so in June 1978 the local authority sent the
b landlords provisional improvement notices under Part VIII of the 1974 Act. The local
authority attempted unsuccessfully to arrange meetings with the landlords and to contact
the landlords' architects to discuss proposals in respect of the improvement of the
premises. The landlords instead applied for planning permission and improvement
grants. On 8th February 1979 the local authority served on the landlords improvement
notices under s 89 in respect of each dwelling requiring the landlords to instal those
c standard amenities that were lacking. The landlords appealed under s 91ᵇ of the Act
against the notices, contending that they were invalid because neither dwelling was
'without one or more of the standard amenities' within the meaning of s 89(1)(b), and
that the local authority had failed to satisfy themselves before serving the notices as they
were required to do by s 89 (i) that the dwellings were without one or more of the
standard amenities, (ii) that the dwellings were capable of improvement at reasonable
d expense to the full standard and were unlikely to be so improved unless the local
authority exercised their powers under s 89, or (iii) that there were satisfactory housing
arrangements for the tenants during the period when the improvements were being
carried out. Alternatively, the landlords contended that the notices should be quashed
under s 91(2)(a) because it was not practicable to comply with the notices at reasonable
expense. At the hearing there was evidence that the house in its present state, with
e sitting tenants, was worth £5,000–£6,000 and with vacant possession £14,000–£15,000,
that the cost of carrying out the improvements listed in the notices was approximately
£18,000, that the landlords would get an improvement grant of £750 in respect of each
dwelling, and that if the work was carried out the value of the house would be £7,000–
£8,000 with sitting tenants and £18,000–£20,000 with vacant possession. The judge
allowed the appeal on the grounds that (i) neither dwelling was 'without one or more of
f the standard amenities' because, for the purposes of s 89, the standard amenities did not
have to be exclusive to one particular dwelling but could be shared, (ii) it was not possible
to improve either dwelling to the full standard at reasonable expense because the value
of the dwelling with the sitting tenants after improvement would be only about half the
cost of the work, (iii) there was every likelihood that the dwellings would be improved
to the full standard without the local authority exercising their powers under s 89, (iv)
g the local authority could not be satisfied about the housing arrangements for the tenants
during the period of improvement because, as the authority conceded, the arrangements
were not set out in a written agreement signed by the landlords or the authority as
required by s 86(2)ᶜ, and (v) the local authority could not rely on the power contained in
s 91(7) which enabled the court to validate an invalid notice, because the landlords would
be substantially prejudiced by the fact that the authority had not satisfied themselves of
h the matters of which they were required to be satisfied. The local authority appealed
contending, inter alia, that the judge was wrong to take the value of the property with
sitting tenants as the appropriate value when determining whether the property could
be improved at reasonable expense and that he should have had regard to the possibility
of the landlords obtaining vacant possession and the value of the house with vacant
possession.

j **Held** – (1) In the context of s 89(1)(b) of the 1974 Act 'a dwelling which is without one
or more of the standard amenities' meant a dwelling where the standard amenities were

---

a   Section 89, so far as material, is set out at p 37 b to g, post
b   Section 91, so far as material, is set out at p 38 b to e, post
c   Section 86 is set out at p 38 j to p 39 b, post

not provided for the exclusive use of the occupants. Accordingly, as the tenants of the two dwellings were sharing a bathroom and lavatory, each dwelling was without the *a* standard amenities and the judge had been wrong to hold that they were not without those amenities (see p 43 *c d* and p 44 *c* to *e*, post).

(2) On the evidence before it the local authority were entitled to decide that they were satisfied for the purposes of s 89 that the dwellings were unlikely to be improved unless they exercised their powers under that section (see p 48 *h* to p 49 *b*, post).

(3) Although the local authority had failed to comply with s 89(6)(*b*), in that they had *b* not executed written agreements as required by s 86(2) in respect of the arrangements for housing the tenants during the period when the improvements were being carried out, the improvement notices could have been confirmed by the court under s 91(7) because the interests of the landlords had not been substantially prejudiced, the agreements had been signed by the tenants and only needed to be signed by the local authority and there was evidence that the authority were prepared to sign them (see p 49 *e* to *h*, post).   *c*

(4) However, the appeal would be dismissed because there were no grounds for interfering with the judge's conclusion that the house could not be improved at reasonable expense to the standard required by the local authority. In determining, for the purposes of s 89(3)(*c*), whether a dwelling could be improved at reasonable expense, the court was required to take a realistic approach to the value of the dwelling as a saleable asset in the hands of the landlord, and therefore to have regard to the presence *d* of tenants and other rights of continuing occupation and the effect they had on the market value. On the evidence the judge was entitled to conclude that the expenditure which the local authority required the landlords to make in improving the dwellings was unreasonable (see p 44 *e f*, p 48 *d* to *f* and p 49 *h*, post); *Harrington v Croydon Corpn* [1967] 3 All ER 929 and *Hillbank Properties Ltd v London Borough of Hackney* [1978] 3 All ER 343 considered.   *e*

Notes

For the power of a local authority to serve improvement notices with respect to dwellings outside general improvement areas and housing action areas, see 22 Halsbury's Laws (4th Edn) paras 636 to 638.

For the Housing Act 1974, ss 86, 89, 91, see 44 Halsbury's Statutes (3rd Edn) 491, 494, *f* 496.

Cases referred to in judgment

Baker v Turner [1950] 1 All ER 834, [1950] AC 401, HL, 31(2) Digest (Reissue) 1010, 8033.

De Rothschild v Wing Rural District Council [1967] 1 All ER 597, [1967] 1 WLR 470, 131 JP 241, 65 LGR 203, CA, Digest (Cont Vol C) 420, 19*b*.   *g*

Dudlow Estates Ltd v Sefton Metropolitan Borough Council (1978) 249 Estates Gazette 1271.

Ellis and Ruislip-Northwood Urban District Council, Re [1920] 1 KB 343, 88 LJKB 1258, 122 LT 98, 83 JP 273, 17 LGR 607, CA, 45 Digest (Repl) 369, 166.

Ellis Copp & Co v Richmond upon Thames London Borough (1976) 245 Estates Gazette 931.

Goodrich v Paisner [1956] 2 All ER 176, [1957] AC 65, [1956] 2 WLR 1053, HL, 31(2) Digest (Reissue) 1010, 8034.   *h*

Harrington v Croydon Corpn [1967] 3 All ER 929, [1968] 1 QB 856, [1968] 2 WLR 67, 66 LGR 95, CA, Digest (Cont Vol C) 421, 36*Aa*.

Hillbank Properties Ltd v London Borough of Hackney [1978] 3 All ER 343, [1978] QB 998, [1978] 3 WLR 260, 76 LGR 677, CA, Digest (Cont Vol E) 247, 9*b*.

Inworth Property Co Ltd v Southwark London Borough Council (1977) 76 LGR 263, 34 P & CR 186, CA, Digest (Cont Vol E) 247, 9*a*.   *j*

Llewellyn v Hinson, Llewellyn v Christmas [1948] 2 All ER 95, [1948] 2 KB 385, [1949] LJR 291, CA, 31(2) Digest (Reissue) 1010, 8030.

Miller v Emcer Products Ltd [1956] 1 All ER 237, [1956] Ch 304, [1956] 2 WLR 267, CA, 31(1) Digest (Reissue) 350, 2764.

Victoria Square Property Co Ltd v London Borough of Southwark [1978] 2 All ER 281, [1978]

a   1 WLR 463, 142 JP 514, 76 LGR 349, 34 P & CR 275, [1978] RVR 10, CA, Digest (Cont
Vol E) 248, 57Aa.

Cases also cited
Heywood v Mallalieu (1883) 25 Ch D 357.
McPhail v London Borough of Islington [1970] 1 All ER 1004, [1970] 2 QB 197, CA.
Railway Assessment Authority v Great Western Railway Co [1947] 2 All ER 794, [1948] AC
b   234, HL.

Appeal
The London Borough of Hackney ('the council') appealed against the judgment of his
Honour Judge Willis given on 18th January 1980 in the Shoreditch County Court
allowing the appeals of FFF Estates Ltd ('the landlords') under s 91 of the Housing Act
1974 against two improvement notices dated 8th February 1979 served by the council on
c   the landlords under s 89 of the 1974 Act in respect of two dwellings at 43 Burma Road,
Stoke Newington, London N16, owned by the landlords, which required the landlords
to carry out certain works specified in the notices to bring the premises up to full
standard, and ordering the notices to be quashed. The facts are set out in the judgment
of the court.

d   *David Keene QC* and *William Birtles* for the council.
John Bowyer for the landlords.

Cur adv vult

25th July. **STEPHENSON LJ** read the following judgment of the court: FFF Estates
Ltd ('the landlords') are the owners of a dwelling house at 43 Burma Road, Stoke
e   Newington. The London Borough of Hackney ('the council') on 8th February 1979
served on the landlords two improvement notices under s 89 of the Housing Act 1974 in
respect of two dwellings into which no 43 was divided. On 18th January 1980 in the
Shoreditch County Court his Honour Judge Willis allowed an appeal by the landlords
under s 91 of the Act and quashed the notices. The council appeal to this court.
The appeal raises a number of points. The first two are of some general importance for
f   the construction and application of the Act and for the circumstances in which local
authorities may exercise their powers of compulsory improvement.
Number 43 has four floors. The basement and ground floor comprise four rooms and
a kitchen and are let to a Mrs Horton under a controlled tenancy. She has lived there
with her son for more than 15 years. The first and second floors comprise five rooms and
a kitchen and are let to a Mrs Wilkins under a regulated tenancy. She has lived there
g   with her husband for more than 15 years. These two dwellings are not self-contained.
There is only one bathroom, on the half landing between the ground and first floors,
with bath and hand basin and hot and cold water, the hot water supplied from a water
heater in Mrs Wilkins's kitchen. There are two water closets, one on the ground floor
and the other outside in the back yard. The bathroom and the inside water closet are
shared by the Hortons and the Wilkinses.
h   In the early part of 1977 Mrs Horton made a complaint of some sort to the council, as
a result of which Mr Brydson, their environmental health officer, inspected the premises,
considered some action necessary and eventually decided to act under s 89 of the 1974
Act. The landlords, whether with knowledge of the council's inspection or not (there
was no evidence about it), had on 15th June 1977 informed both Mrs Horton and Mrs
Wilkins that they intended to convert no 43 into self-contained flats. On 15th October
j   1977 they instructed an architect; on 10th and 19th July 1978 they applied to the council
for planning permission and an improvement grant respectively.
While the landlords were taking this action, the council were not idle. Mr Brydson
had visited both tenants at no 43 and obtained their signatures on 9th February 1978 and
14th March 1978 to standard forms making representations that their dwellings were
without the standard amenities of, in Mrs Horton's case, an internal water closet, and

bath and hand basin with hot and cold water and, in Mrs Wilkins' case, a water closet, and that the landlords had indicated to them that they would not provide those amenities voluntarily.

On 25th April 1978 the council sent to the landlords a notification of those representations under s 89 of the Act and requested them to let the council know in 14 days whether they were prepared to improve the premises to the standard requested. The landlords did not reply. On 8th June Mr Brydson then laid certain estimates before the council with a recommendation that authority be given for the service of provisional notices under s 89(4)(a) of the Act, and authority was given. On 23rd June 1978 the council sent the landlords provisional improvement notices under Part VIII of the Act with a letter inviting them to attend a meeting of the health and consumer protection sub-committee on 17th July, at which proposals in respect of the improvement of no 43 would be considered, and to meet senior officers of the council on 4th July to discuss any points they would like clarified before the sub-committee meeting. The landlords did not attend either meeting, but they wrote on 3rd July that they had decided a year ago to carry out their own improvements, were intending to apply for grants and would wish the notices to remain in abeyance.

After receipt of the landlords' application for an improvement grant the council had some difficulty in getting answers to their letters to the landlords' architect. In February 1979 the landlords changed their architect and acted thereafter through their manager, Mr Bard. On 8th February 1979 the council served on the landlords the improvement notices which are the subject of this appeal. On 20th February 1979 the landlords gave notice of appeal to the county court, and on 30th March 1979 the council granted them planning permission. Their application for an improvement grant has not yet been determined. Their appeal was heard by the judge on 21st September and 19th, 20th and 23rd November 1979 and allowed, as already mentioned, on 18th January 1980.

The two improvement notices are in due form. The first is addressed to the landlords as the person having control of the basement and ground-floor dwelling at no 43. It reads:

'TAKE NOTICE that—

'(1) the Hackney London Borough Council having on the 23rd June 1978 served a provisional notice under Section 89(3) of the Housing Act, 1974, have taken into consideration all such representations as were made on or before 17th July 1978, being the date given in the said provisional notice for discussion of the Council's proposals for the said dwelling;

'(2) the Council are satisfied—(a) that the dwelling is capable of improvement at reasonable expense to the (full) standard, and (b) that, having regard to all the circumstances, the dwelling ought to be improved to the said standard and is unlikely to be so improved unless the Council exercise their powers under section 89 of the Housing Act, 1974.

'(3) the Council, in pursuance of section 89(5) of the Housing Act, 1974 hereby require you to carry out, within twelve months from the date when this notice becomes operative, the works specified in the schedule to this notice, being works which, in the opinion of the Council, are required to improve the dwelling to the said standard.

'A copy of this notice is being served on the tenant and on every other person who, to the Council's knowledge, is an owner, lessee or mortgagee of the dwelling.

'*Amenities Required*

'(i) a fixed bath or shower;

'(ii) a hot and cold water supply at a fixed bath or shower;

'(iii) a wash hand basin;

'(iv) a hot and cold water supply at a wash hand basin;

'(v) an internal water closet.

'(see schedule attached)

'Estimated Cost: £5,411.'

Attached to that is a considerable schedule.

a   The second notice is addressed to the landlords as the person having control of the first and second floor dwelling and differs only in the schedule of amenities required ('An internal water closet') and the estimated cost ('£4,303').

To see why the judge quashed these apparently valid notices it is necessary to examine some of the provisions of Part VIII of the 1974 Act before considering the landlords' grounds of appeal to the judge and his reasons for quashing the notices.

b   Part VIII deals with compulsory improvement of dwellings. Sections 85 to 88 deal with dwellings in general improvement areas and housing action areas; s 89 deals with dwellings outside those areas. It provides:

'(1) An occupying tenant of a dwelling which—(a) is not in a general improvement area or a housing action area, and (b) is without one or more of the standard amenities, whether or not it is also in a state of disrepair, and (c) was provided (by
c   erection or by the conversion of a building already in existence) before 3rd October 1961, may make representations in writing to the local authority for the area in which the dwelling is situated with a view to the exercise by the authority of their powers under this section . . .

'(3) If, on taking the representations into consideration, the local authority are satisfied—(a) that the person making the representation is an occupying tenant of
d   the dwelling in question, and (b) that the provisions of paragraphs (a) to (c) of subsection (1) above apply in relation to the dwelling, and (c) that the dwelling is capable at reasonable expense of improvement to the full standard or, failing that, to the reduced standard, and (d) that, having regard to all the circumstances, the dwelling ought to be improved to the full standard or, as the case may be, to the reduced standard, and that it is unlikely that it will be so improved unless the local
e   authority exercise their powers under this section, the following provisions of this section shall apply . . .

'(5) Subject to subsection (6) below, in any case where—(a) representations have been made to a local authority under subsection (1) above, and (b) as a result of those representations, a provisional notice has been served by virtue of subsection (4)(a) above, the local authority may, at any time before the expiry of the period of 12
f   months beginning with the date on which the representations were received by them, serve an improvement notice on the person having control of the dwelling; and subsection (4) of section 88 above shall apply as it applies in relation to an improvement notice served by virtue of subsection (1) of that section.

'(6) Before serving an improvement notice in respect of a dwelling by virtue of subsection (5) above, a local authority shall satisfy themselves—(a) that the provisions
g   of paragraphs (b) to (d) of subsection (3) above still apply in relation to the dwelling; and (b) that the housing arrangements are satisfactory or that no housing arrangements are required or that the occupying tenant has unreasonably refused to enter into any housing arrangements . . .'

On appeal the judge took a point not taken by the landlords that these tenants might not have made the representations which they signed, but he made no finding that they
h   had not. Counsel for the landlords sought, in a respondent's notice which we gave him leave to put in, to take the point that they had not made the necessary representations. But the council were given no opportunity to call evidence on that matter and we refused to allow counsel for the landlords to raise it in this court. It is not disputed that these dwellings were provided before 3rd October 1961 and are not in a general improvement area or in a housing action area. So four conditions remain to be satisfied. (1) The
j   dwellings must be without one or more of the standard amenities: s 89(1)(b). (2) They must be capable at reasonable expense of improvement to the full standard: s 89(3)(c). (3) The council must be satisfied that, having regard to all the circumstances, they ought to be improved to the full standard: s 89(3)(d). (4) The council must be satisfied that housing arrangements are satisfactory for the tenants: s 89(6)(b).

Section 90 contains general provisions as to improvement notices:

'(1) Subject to the following provisions of this section, a notice under this section (in this Part of this Act referred to as an "improvement notice") shall— (a) specify the works which in the opinion of the local authority are required to improve the dwelling to the full standard or, as the case may be, to the reduced standard . . .'

Section 91 provides for appeals:

'(1) Within 6 weeks from the service on the person having control of the dwelling of an improvement notice, that person, the occupying tenant (if any) of the dwelling or any other person having an estate or interest in the dwelling may appeal to the county court against the improvement notice in accordance with the following provisions of this section. '(2) Subject to subsection (3) below, the grounds on which an appeal may be brought under this section are all or any of the following—(a) that it is not practicable to comply with the requirements of the improvement notice at reasonable expense; (b) that the local authority have refused unreasonably to approve the execution of alternative works, or that the works specified in the notice are otherwise unreasonable in character or extent . . . (d) that the dwelling is not, or is no longer, without one or more of the standard amenities . . . (g) that the improvement notice is invalid on the ground that any requirement of this Part of this Act has not been complied with or on the ground of some informality, defect or error in or in connection with the improvement notice . . . '(4) Subject to the following provisions of this section, on an appeal under this section the court may make such order either confirming or quashing or varying the improvement notice as the court thinks fit . . . '(7) In so far as an appeal under this section is based on the ground that the improvement notice is invalid, the court shall confirm the improvement notice unless satisfied that the interests of the appellant have been substantially prejudiced by the facts relied on by him.'

The meaning of some of the expressions used in these provisions of the Act calls for clear definition, in particular the expression 'standard amenities'. The call takes long to answer and the answer is far from clear. Section 129 is the general interpretation section and defines 'dwelling' as follows:

'"dwelling" means a building or part of a building occupied or intended to be occupied as a separate dwelling together with any yard, garden, outhouses and appurtenances belonging to or usually enjoyed with that building or part.'

Part VIII has, however, its own interpretation section, s 104, where are to be found a number of definitions:

'"improvement notice" means a notice under section 90 above';

'"provisional notice" means a notice under section 85(2) above';

'"housing arrangements" has the meaning assigned to it by section 86 above';

'"standard amenities" has the same meaning as in Part VII of this Act';

'"the full standard" has the same meaning as it has for the purposes of section 66 of this Act (intermediate grants)';

'"the reduced standard" has the same meaning as it has for the purposes of section 66 of this Act (intermediate grants).'

It is unnecessary to pursue notices into ss 90 and 85(2) but s 86 must be read for 'housing arrangements' and the quest for 'standard amenities' must be carried into Part VII and s 58, and into Sch 6; and 'full standard' must be hunted down in s 66 in the same part. Section 86 provides:

'(1) In this Part of this Act "housing arrangements", in relation to a dwelling falling within section 85(1) above, means arrangements falling within subsection a (2) below and making provision for the housing of an occupying tenant of the dwelling and his household—(a) during the period when improvement works are being carried out, or (b) after the completion of those works, or (c) during that period and after completion of those works, and for any matters incidental or ancillary thereto.

'(2) The arrangements referred to in subsection (1) above are arrangements contained in a written agreement to which the occupying tenant and either or both b of his landlord and the local authority concerned are parties.'

Section 58 is in these terms:

'(1) Subject to subsection (2) below, the "standard amenities" for the purposes of this Part of this Act are the amenities which are described in the first column of Part I of Schedule 6 to this Act and which conform to such of the provisions of Part II of c that Schedule as are applicable.

'(2) The Secretary of State may by order vary the provisions of Schedule 6 to this Act and any such order may contain such transitional or other supplemental provisions as appear to the Secretary of State to be expedient.'

Schedule 6 is as follows (omitting maximum eligible amounts):

d 'STANDARD AMENITIES

PART I

LIST OF AMENITIES AND MAXIMUM ELIGIBLE AMOUNTS

Description of Amenity

'A fixed bath or shower
e 'A hot and cold water supply at a fixed bath or shower
'A wash-hand basin
'A hot and cold water supply at a wash-hand basin
'A sink
'A hot and cold water supply at a sink
'A water closet

f 'PART II

'PROVISIONS APPLICABLE TO CERTAIN AMENITIES

'1. Except as provided by paragraph 2 below, a fixed bath or shower must be in a bathroom.

2. If it is not reasonably practicable for the fixed bath or shower to be in a g bathroom but it is reasonably practicable for it to be provided with a hot and cold water supply it need not be in a bathroom but may be in any part of the dwelling which is not a bedroom.

3. The water closet must, if reasonably practicable, be in, and accessible from within, the dwelling or, where the dwelling is part of a larger building, in such a position in that building as to be readily accessible from the dwelling.'

h Section 66 provides:

'(1) A local authority shall not approve an application for an intermediate grant unless they are satisfied that, on completion of the relevant works, the dwelling or, as the case may be, each of the dwellings to which the application relates will attain the full standard or, if any of subsections (3) to (5) below applies, the reduced j standard.

'(2) For the purposes of this section a dwelling shall be taken to attain the full standard if the following conditions are fulfilled with respect to it, namely—(a) that it is provided with all the standard amenities for the exclusive use of its occupants . . .

'(3) Where an application for an intermediate grant contains a statement, and the local authority are satisfied, that it is not practicable at reasonable expense for the dwelling to which the application relates to be provided with all the standard amenities, they shall dispense with the condition in paragraph (a) of subsection (2) above unless they are satisfied that the dwelling is, or forms part of, a house or building in respect of which they could, by a notice under section 15 of the Housing Act 1961, require the execution of such works as are referred to in subsection (1) of that section . . .

'(6) If, in relation to any dwelling, a local authority by virtue of subsection (3), subsection (4) or subsection (5) above dispense, in whole or in part, with any of the conditions in paragraphs (a) to (d) of subsection (2) above or vary the condition in paragraph (e) of that subsection, then for the purposes of this section the dwelling concerned shall be taken to attain the reduced standard if, subject to any such dispensation, or variation, the conditions in subsection (2) above are fulfilled with respect to it.'

The landlords challenged the validity of the notices before the judge on three grounds:

'1. . . . that the dwellings are neither of them without one or more of the standard amenities [under s 91(2)(d)].

'2. That [the council] failed before serving the said notices, to satisfy themselves [of five things, ie non-compliance under s 91(2)(g)]: (a) that the dwellings were without one or more of the standard amenities; or (b) that the dwellings were capable of improvement at reasonable expense to the full standard or to the reduced standard; or (c) that, having regard to all the circumstances, the dwellings ought to be improved to the full standard or to the reduced standard; or (d) that, having regard to all the circumstances, the dwellings were unlikely to be so improved unless the [council] exercised their powers under Section 89 of the Housing Act 1974; or (e) that there were satisfactory housing arrangements.

'3. That it is not practicable to comply with the requirements of the Improvement Notices at reasonable expense [under s 91(2)(a)].'

In his comprehensive and carefully considered judgment the judge found as follows. (1) Neither dwelling was without standard amenities because each had the use of them. The standard amenities did not have to be exclusive to the occupants of one particular dwelling; they could be shared. (2) Neither dwelling could be said to be improved to the full standard at reasonable expense because the value of the dwellings with the sitting tenants after the work of improvement was carried out would be only about half the cost of the work. (3) Although the council could properly be satisfied that the dwellings ought to be improved up to the full standard there was every likelihood that the dwellings would be so improved without the council exercising their powers under s 89. (4) The council could not have been satisfied about the housing arrangements because, as was conceded, there was no agreement sufficient to comply with the Act. (5) The council could not rely on s 91(7) of the Act to validate the notices because the landlords would be substantially prejudiced by having to carry out the improvements required by notices served without the council being satisfied of matters of which the Act said they must be satisfied.

The council contend in this court that in reaching each of these five conclusions the judge erred or misdirected himself in law.

The first question we consider is: was the judge wrong in interpreting in its context the phrase in s 89(1)(b) 'a dwelling which is without . . . the standard amenities' to mean a dwelling without the shared use of these basic facilities, as counsel in opening the council's appeal called them? Or does it mean a dwelling without the exclusive use by its occupants of these amenities?

When is a dwelling 'without' a standard amenity such as a fixed bath, a wash-hand basin or a water closet? Taking the words in their ordinary sense they seem ambiguous. A dwelling, in this case part of a building occupied as a separate dwelling, may be without a water closet if it has no internal water closet or no water closet for the exclusive use of its occupants; or it may be without a water closet if it does not have the use with *a* the occupants of other dwellings of a water closet, either by access to an outside water closet or by a right to share the use of a water closet inside or outside the dwelling. Section 89(1)(b) does not speak of a dwelling which is without *the use of* a standard amenity nor does it speak of a dwelling without *the exclusive use* of a standard amenity; but it might mean either when it speaks of a dwelling without an amenity. It is true that a dwelling 'with' an amenity means usually a dwelling with the exclusive use of it. If you buy a house with a bathroom, you are cheated if the house contains no bathroom but you

b have to go to someone else's property to find one for your use. If you rent a room with a bath, you ask for your money back if you have to leave your room to get to a bath used by the occupants of other rooms. But the word 'amenity' still connotes in a statute what Scrutton LJ thought it did on its first appearance in the Housing, Town Planning etc Act 1909: 'pleasant circumstances or features, advantages': see *Re Ellis and Ruislip-Northwood Urban District Council* [1920] 1 KB 343 at 370. It suggests in connection with a dwelling

c or building something to be enjoyed with it, a right in the nature of an easement, and even if the occupying tenant of a dwelling *with* a water closet would naturally mean a tenant occupying a dwelling with the exclusive use of a water closet, it does not follow that the occupying tenant of a dwelling *without* a water closet would mean only a tenant occupying a dwelling without such exclusive use.

Does the 1974 Act resolve this ambiguity? The Housing Act 1964 resolved it by an

d unequivocal definition. Part II of that Act introduced compulsory improvement of dwellings to provide standard amenities for dwellings without one or more of them: see ss 14(1) and 19(1), the forerunners of ss 85(1) and 89(1) of the 1974 Act. Section 43 of the 1964 Act provided:

'(1) Subject to this section, in this Part of this Act "the standard amenities", in relation to a dwelling, mean the following amenities provided for the exclusive use

e of the occupants of the dwelling, that is—(a) a fixed bath or shower, which, subject to subsection (2) of this section, is to be in a bathroom; (b) a wash-hand basin; (c) a hot and cold water supply at a fixed bath or shower, which, if reasonably practicable, is to be in a bathroom; (d) a hot and cold water supply at a wash-hand basin; (e) a hot and cold water supply at a sink; (f) a water closet; and (g) satisfactory facilities for storing food.

f '(2) The fixed bath or shower mentioned in paragraph (a) above may, if it is not reasonably practicable for it to be provided in a bathroom, but it is reasonably practicable for it to be provided with a hot and cold water supply, be in a part of the dwelling which is not a bathroom or bedroom.

'(3) The water closet mentioned in paragraph (f) above must, if reasonably practicable, be in, and readily accessible from, the dwelling or, if that is not

g reasonably practicable, in such a position in the curtilage of the dwelling, or where the dwelling is part of a larger building, in that building, as to be readily accessible from the dwelling.

'(4) In relation to a dwelling which is without one or more of the standard amenities, references in this Part of this Act to the improvement of the dwelling to the full standard are references to the carrying out of works to provide the dwelling

h with those of the standard amenities which it does not have.'

Part VIII of the 1974 Act has its own definition in s 104, which gives standard amenities in Part VIII the same meaning as in Part VII. Part VII's definition section, s 84, gives them the meaning assigned by s 58 unless the context otherwise requires. Section 58 says they are the amenities described in Sch 6. When at last we reach Sch 6 we find the equivalent of what was listed in s 43 of the 1964 Act, but we look in vain for anything

j corresponding to the explanatory words of s 43 'provided for the exclusive use of the occupants of the dwelling'.

The omission of those words inevitably supports both the landlords' submission that Parliament deliberately left them out and the judge's view that Parliament intended that the use of shared amenities should take dwellings out of the scope of Part VIII of the 1974 Act. But Parliament has not left out of the Act all reference to exclusive use. Section 104

gives 'full standard' and 'reduced standard' the same meaning as they have for the
purposes of s 66, unless the context otherwise requires. That section makes approval of *a*
applications for immediate grants conditional on the dwelling attaining a particular
standard and sub-s (2) provides (I read it again):

'For the purposes of this section a dwelling shall be taken to attain the full
standard if the following conditions are fulfilled with respect to it, namely—(a) that
it is provided with all the standard amenities for the exclusive use of its occupants . . .'
b

So a dwelling must be provided with standard amenities for the exclusive use of its
occupants if they are to qualify for the financial assistance towards works of improvement,
repair and conversion with which Part VII of the Act is concerned. Has Parliament
required the same qualification for compulsory improvement with which Part VIII is
concerned by the roundabout, not to say devious, method of cross-references through
which the courts, to say nothing of landlords, tenants and local authorities, are dragged *c*
by these statutory provisions?

The judge answered that question No, considering that Parts VII and VIII were dealing
with two different things. He went on to say:

'Part VII is providing for the financial assistance which the landlord could obtain
by means of an improvement grant and it is not surprising that he should be
required to provide standard amenities for the exclusive use of his tenants in order *d*
to get it. Part VIII is dealing with the compulsory improvement of dwellings as
distinct from their voluntary improvement. It might be said, that if one does not
have to have standard amenities for the occupants' exclusive use then there will be
few cases in which s 89 can be of use. I hope that I am allowed to use my own
knowledge of the area in question, having sat in this court for nearly twenty years,
if I say that often I have come across cases where a dwelling has no bath either *e*
because there is none in the house or because the only bath is in exclusive use of
another tenant. Equally I have met the case where the only washing facility for a
tenant was hot water from a kettle poured into a sink. Also I have met the case
where there is only one water closet in a house with several tenants. These are
typical cases where the standard amenities are not provided and the council could
properly serve the notice under s 89 requiring the landlord to provide the standard *f*
amenities for exclusive use of the occupant. Mr Callender [counsel for the landlords]
pointed out that, though it was true that under the 1964 Act an improvement
notice would require the provision of standard amenities for exclusive use of the
occupant, yet the council had no power to require the landlord to do any repairs.
He therefore argued that as Parliament had now given such a power to a council it
was not surprising that no longer was exclusive use of the standard amenities *g*
required. This may well be but I prefer to rest my judgment on the following
points. Nowhere is the phrase "exclusive use" used in relation to the definition of
standard amenities. It is only used in connection with the attainment of the full
standard in s 66 but it does not mean the council can serve an improvement notice
when there is no exclusive use of the standard amenities but all are provided. The
power to serve an improvement notice requiring the landlord to improve up to the *h*
full standard and therefore as s 66 makes clear, provide standard amenities for
tenants' exclusive use, arises only when one or more of the standard amenities are
missing. The result therefore is that I find that the first ground of appeal succeeds
and I find that the improvement notices are invalid as neither dwelling is without
one or more of the standard amenities.'

j
One criticism justly made of that passage by counsel for the council is that 'the case
where there is only one water closet in a house with several tenants', would not be a case
in which s 89 would be of no use but on the contrary a case within s 89 on the judge's
construction of it. If shared water closets are outside s 89 they are outside whether shared
between the occupants of two dwellings, as here, or shared between several tenants, it

may be occupants of three or more dwellings. Our attention was called to the provisions
a   in earlier legislation for securing, among other matters, water supply and sanitary
conveniences in Part II of the Housing Act 1957 (ss 4 and 9, as amended by s 72 of the
Housing Act 1969) and in Part II of the Housing Act 1961 (ss 15, 19 and 21) and for
maintaining standards in houses in multiple occupation in Part II of the 1961 Act (those
sections) and Part II of the Housing Act 1964 (ss 67 and 69) and Part IV of the Housing
Act 1969 (ss 58 and 59).

b   We cannot find in these provisions any clear pointer for or against the judge's view
that shared standard amenities are enough to preserve a dwelling from compulsory
improvement by a local authority. His view would still leave some dwellings where
standard amenities were not there to be shared, but completely absent, for the council to
improve by the exercise of their powers under Part VIII of the Act. But the history of this
housing legislation does show, as might be expected, a policy of increasing the range of
c   premises subject to improvement powers, and of raising housing standards, which the
judge's interpretation of the 1974 Act would to some extent reverse. Parliament might
have decided in 1974 that it had gone too far in 1964, and for reasons of economy or
practical difficulty or shortage of building labour and materials or local government staff
might have narrowed the areas of compulsory improvement and deprived occupants of
dwellings of rights to call for improvements which they had enjoyed for a decade. But
d   that legislative intent would, in our judgment, require clear expression. It is improbable
that it would be expressed by the repeal of Part II of the 1964 Act by s 130(4) and Sch 15
of the 1974 Act and the enactment of the provisions in Parts VII and VIII of the later Act
to which we have referred.

We were pressed by the submission for the landlords that to require a bathroom for
every dwelling consisting of a single room would be to set an inconceivably high
e   standard. But, as was pointed out for the council, the position was the same under the
1964 Act and the danger of setting too high a standard is mitigated by the provisions as
to reasonable expense (ss 89(3)(c) and 91(2)(a)) and unreasonable refusal to approve
alternative work or specifying work unreasonable in character or extent (s 91(2)(b)). It
would also be unlikely that, as counsel for the landlords contended, Parliament had set
different standards under s 89(1)(a) and (3)(b) and under s 89(1)(c) and required a local
f   authority to be satisfied that a dwelling lacked a water closet shared or unshared but that
it could be provided at reasonable expense with a water closet for the exclusive use of its
occupants: the authority cannot act on an occupying tenant's representation if he shares
a water closet but if he has no water closet and no use of one the authority can require his
landlord to provide him with one for his exclusive use. Furthermore, on the landlords'
interpretation, accepted by the judge, the authority can pay an improvement grant
g   under Part VII to improve the dwelling by supplying its occupants with a bath for their
exclusive use, but they cannot act under Part VIII on the occupants' representation that
they have the use of a bath but not the exclusive use of it.

We would require clear indications in the statute to be satisfied that Parts VII and VIII
are dealing with such different things that these consequences follow. Each side relied
on the language of s 129(1), the council for its reference to occupation 'as a separate
h   dwelling', the landlords for its reference to 'appurtenances'. The landlords submitted
that the right of one of these tenants to use the other's bath or water closet was an
easement or other right appurtenant to the dwelling she occupied, within s 62 of the Law
of Property Act 1925 and the decision of this court in *Miller v Emcer Products Ltd* [1956]
1 All ER 237, [1956] Ch 304, and so an appurtenance belonging to or usually enjoyed
with her part of no 43. Both the council and the landlords sought assistance from the
j   construction put on the words 'let as a separate dwelling' and the right to share the use
of rooms including water closets in such cases as *Llewellyn v Hinson* [1948] 2 All ER 95 at
96, [1948] 2 KB 385 at 391 per Asquith LJ, *Baker v Turner* [1950] 1 All ER 834 at 853,
[1950] AC 401 at 437 per Lord Reid, and *Goodrich v Paisner* [1956] 2 All ER 176, [1957]
AC 65.

We do not find any real help in these authorities. The question we have to determine is not answered by considering what rights might pass on a conveyance by implication of law or what joint use might defeat the protection given by the Rent Acts to a tenant *a* of premises which would otherwise be protected.

Each side relied also on the language of Part II of Sch 6. It was argued that para 2 favoured the council's interpretation because its language presupposed the amenity of a bath being in the dwelling and therefore exclusively used by its occupants; para 3 the landlords' interpretation because its language indicated that the amenity of a water closet might be outside the dwelling and in a larger building and therefore naturally shared *b* with other occupants of the larger building. These paragraphs appear to point to different answers to the question we have to consider, but they repeat the repealed Sch 1 to the 1969 Act which in its turn is derived from s 43(2) and (3) of the 1964 Act. Both those subsections refer back to s 43(1) and to the fixed bath or shower and the water closet which have expressly to be provided for the exclusive use of the occupants of the dwelling. We can only attach a wider meaning to the same words in Sch 6 of the 1974 *c* Act if we regard the omission of the express reference to a provision containing the requirement of exclusive use as deliberate. So we are back where we started.

On the whole we have come to the conclusion, in spite of the difficulties which are created by the devious directions given by the Act and which give strength to counsel for the landlords' formidable argument, that the standard amenities referred to throughout Parts VII and VIII of this Act are standard amenities provided for the exclusive use of the *d* occupants of a dwelling, and the context of s 89 does not require the phrase to mean anything else or the expression 'without one or more' of them to mean 'without the use of one or more' of them. When 'all the standard amenities' have just been stated to be provided for the exclusive use of a dwelling's occupants they are naturally repeated in shorthand as 'all the standard amenities': see s 61(3)(a) and (4)(a); s 66(2)(a) and (3). But it needs a long look back to regard the expression in s 89(1)(b) as shorthand for the *e* expression in s 66(2)(a). Such in effect we are driven to hold it is, however, by the considerations already set out.

We are therefore of opinion that the landlords cannot succeed on the first point.

On the second point, however, the learned judge was, in our judgment, right and the appeal must accordingly fail.

The judge accepted the values given in evidence by Mr Bard, the landlords' manager, *f* which he thought was supported by the evidence of Mr Edmunds, the council's valuer. Mr Bard's evidence was that the house 'in its present state with tenants' was worth £5,000 to £6,000. He did not value the two parts separately. But he valued the cost of the work scheduled in the improvement notices separately at £8,000 and £6,000, exclusive of decorations which he estimated at about £3,000. The value of the house, again with tenants, if the work were carried out, he put at £7,000 to £8,000. The landlords would *g* have to go to the bank, where they already had an overdraft, unless they received a large sum of money, and they would have to pay interest on a loan from the bank at 19% per annum or if they could pay for the improvements out of capital they would lose 15% per annum income on it. The judge disregarded the costs of redecoration as not referable to carrying out the improvements and the cost of borrowing because he had no evidence of the financial state of the landlords. He took into account the grants of £750 for each *h* dwelling which, according to the evidence of Mr Willis, the council's surveyor, the landlords would receive.

On these figures the judge was clearly entitled to come to the conclusion that no 43 could not be improved as the council required at reasonable expense unless he was wrong to take the value 'with tenants' or to have regard to the presence of sitting tenants exclusive of all other factors, including the possibility that they might leave the house in *j* the future. To spend £18,000 at least, which would only increase its value from £5,000 or £6,000 to £7,000 or £8,000, would be manifestly unreasonable, allowing for the improvement grant of £1,500 and leaving out of account such matters as the cost of redecoration and borrowing which, with professional fees for supervising the work, are alleged by the landlords in a respondent's notice to have been wrongly disregarded.

But the council contend in their notice of appeal that the judge was wrong in taking
a the value of the property with a sitting tenant and in not applying the test laid down by
this court in *Hillbank Properties Ltd v London Borough of Hackney* [1978] 3 All ER 343,
[1978] QB 998. Mr Bard's own figures for the value of the house with vacant possession
were: in its present state before the work of improvement was carried out £14,000 to
£15,000; after improvement £18,000 to £20,000. It might be argued that on those
figures and that basis of valuation an expenditure of £18,000 might be unreasonable, but
b we shall assume that it might be reasonable and consider the test to which the notice of
appeal refers and counsel's submissions for the council on it.

It is right to say that neither before the judge nor before this court was the argument
confined to a simple contrast between sitting tenant value and vacant possession value.
The judge was alive to the possibility of the 'mean figure' between the two being taken,
which on Mr Bard's evidence, was £13,250 and was conceded to favour the landlords'
c case that the expense of achieving that figure would not be reasonable. He was asked to
consider and did consider the *Hillbank Properties* case and two other authorities, after
which he reached his conclusion that the value (£7,000 to £8,000) after the cost of the
work (£18,000 less £1,500 grant = £16,500) would have only been about one half of the
cost of the work.

The first of these authorities was *Harrington v Croydon Corpn* [1967] 3 All ER 929,
d [1968] 1 QB 856. There this court had to consider s 27(2)(a) of the 1964 Act. Section 27
provided for appeals against improvement notices in substantially the same terms as s 91
of the 1974 Act. Salmon LJ said ([1967] 3 All ER 929 at 935, [1968] 1 QB 856 at 869):

> 'The next point taken on behalf of the landlord is taken under s. 27(2)(a): "That
> it is not practicable to comply with the requirements of the improvement notice at
> reasonable expense, regard being had to the estimated cost of the works and the
> *e* value which it is estimated that the dwelling or other premises will have when the
> works are completed." The words "reasonable expense" cannot be construed in
> vacuo. They must mean an expense reasonable to those called on to bear it. In the
> present case that is the landlord. In considering whether or not the required
> improvement is putting her to reasonable expense, the section requires that regard
> shall be had "to the estimated cost of the works and the value which it is estimated
> *f* that the dwelling will have when the works are completed". Those words, however,
> are not exhaustive; these are only two factors, important ones, which have to be
> taken into account in considering the reasonableness of the expense. There is
> another factor which to my mind is important, and that is that, under s 46 of the
> Act of 1964, the landlord will qualify for a grant of fifty per cent. of the cost of
> carrying out the work. It is impossible to leave that factor out of account from any
> *g* realistic point of view.'

Salmon LJ later continued:

> 'The question then arises as to the meaning of the words "the value which it is
> estimated that the dwelling will have when the works are completed". It was
> *h* vigorously argued on behalf of the local authority that the value when the work is
> completed is the value with vacant possession. I am wholly unable to accept that
> argument. It seems to me that the value must be the price which the saleable
> interests in the dwelling would fetch on the open market as between a willing buyer
> and a willing seller at the moment when the works are completed. The only person
> with any saleable interest in this dwelling is the landlord, and her interest is the
> *j* freehold interest.'

On the same provision, s 27(2)(a), Willmer LJ said ([1967] 3 All ER 929 at 941, [1968] 1
QB 856 at 879):

> 'The question immediately arises, however, expense reasonable to whom?—and
> in connection with that, bearing in mind that one of the factors to be considered is

the value which it is estimated the dwelling will have when the work has been completed, value to whom? Is it the hypothetical value of the dwelling with vacant possession, or is it the actual value to the present owner subject to the existing controlled tenancy? If, as I have already suggested, it is right to pay regard to the needs of the actual existing tenants in deciding whether the work required is unreasonable in character or extent under s. 27(2)(b), I think that it must be equally right to have regard to the existence of the tenants, and to the fact that this is a controlled tenancy, in determining the question of value under s. 27(2)(a). In that connexion I would venture to agree with the remark of the judge that this view is very much supported by the concluding words of s. 27(2)(a), which require the value to be ascertained "at the time when the works are completed", and not at some possibly hypothetical date in the future. It would, in my judgment, be quite unreal to attempt to assess the value of the premises for the purpose of applying s. 27(2)(a) on the hypothetical basis of vacant possession. After all, the ground of appeal provided in s. 27(2)(a) is inserted for the benefit of the person on whom the improvement notice is served, and it seems to me that the question to be determined must be determined on the basis of the expense to him or her of the works required, and on the basis of the value to him or her which the dwelling will have when the works are completed.'

We, like the judge, were referred to two subsequent decisions of this court, in neither of which was *Harrington's* case referred to and in the first of which this court allowed an appeal from a decision of this learned judge which quashed improvement notices served by this council.

In *Hillbank Properties Ltd v London Borough of Hackney* the court had to consider the validity of notices served under s 9(1A) of the Housing Act 1957. Lord Denning MR held that in s 39(1) of that Act the value which it is estimated that the house will have when the works are completed under s 9(1A) was, for policy reasons, 'primarily the value with vacant possession'; that would be the value which the judge should consider under s 9(1A) 'in many cases', or at any rate 'a value approaching it', or even 'a midway value' (see [1978] 3 All ER 343 at 348–349, [1978] QB 998 at 1007–1008). Geoffrey Lane LJ said ([1978] 3 All ER 343 at 352–353, [1978] QB 998 at 1013–1014):

'Again, are the local authority not permitted to take into account when deciding whether or not to serve the notice the fact that the cost of repairs far exceeds the value of the house? The chief environmental health officer said in evidence: "If my office reported that the costs of works was out of all proportion to benefit to the tenant from the work and because of the age of the property, I would not recommend this matter to the committee." So he is saying that he would at least take cost compared with benefit to the tenant into consideration at that stage. I agree with him on this point. The absence from s 9(1A) of the conditional sentence found in s 9(1) and the fact that there is no section applicable to s 9(1A) which corresponds with s 39 is not to my mind an oblique method of restricting the discretion of the local authority or of the county court judge. It is due to the fact that s 9(1A) was an afterthought. Had it been part of the original 1957 Act the inference might well have been different. Accordingly there is no fetter (apart from admissibility and relevance) on those matters which the local authority or the judge can take into account. The estimated cost of the required repairs compared with the value of the premises is obviously an important consideration: see *Victoria Square Property Co Ltd v London Borough of Southwark* [1978] 2 All ER 281 at 291, [1978] 1 WLR 463 at 474 per Bridge LJ. But it is at this point that one runs into difficulties. There are in the present cases, as there usually will be, two different house values for comparison. The "sitting tenant" value, which is less than the cost of the repairs, and the "vacant possession" value, which is a great deal more. The reasonableness or otherwise of the local authority's notice to repair may largely depend on which of those two values one selects for purposes of comparison. It may

a
be that evidence is available to show that the tenancy is unlikely to come to an end in the foreseeable future, in which case the owners should adduce it; it may be that there is evidence to the contrary, in which case the local authority should do the same. If there is no evidence one way or the other, as was the case here, what is the judge to do? It seems to me that in such a case it is wrong to take either the tenanted value or the vacant possession value, without qualification, as the standard of comparison. In those circumstances any disparity between the cost of repairs and

b
the value of the property will have much less weight, because one of the figures is necessarily imponderable. It may be that the judge will come to the conclusion that the true value of the house is too uncertain to enable him to base any conclusion on it at all. It may be that he will take the mean figure between the two extremes, which in this case would have been about £5,750. I feel the judge here was in error. Although he did properly set out the various values which had been ascribed

c
to the houses he does not seem to have considered the possibility that the owners might in the near future make a handsome profit by getting vacant possession. He seems to have assumed, without any evidential basis, that the tenants were there to stay. It may be helpful to mention one or two other matters which may be taken into consideration by the judge in considering appeals under this section. Owner-occupation would in most cases be a powerful argument against allowing a notice

d
to repair. The financial means of the owner where the premises are tenanted is of marginal significance, if any. In the present case such evidence of the owners' means as there was, was given, not by an officer of the property companies themselves but by an employee of the owners' estate agents. That was probably hearsay and certainly valueless. If the owner in these circumstances is not prepared to adduce proper evidence as to means through a witness who is in a position to

e
meet questions asked in cross-examination then the wealth or indigence of the owner should be disregarded.'

In *Dudlow Estates Ltd v Sefton Metropolitan Borough Council* (1978) 249 Estates Gazette 1271 the court dismissed an appeal against the quashing of a demolition order under s 17(1) of the 1957 Act when the house could be made fit for habitation at reasonable
f
expense. The judge gave his decision on the basis that he could only consider the value of the lease with a sitting tenant. After quoting the judgment of Geoffrey Lane LJ in the *Hillbank Properties* case, Browne LJ said (at 1277):

'As I understand it, what Geoffrey Lane LJ is saying there is really in substance what Megaw LJ said in the course of the argument, that when one is talking about value one is talking about open market value, and that when you are considering
g
open market value you must consider all the factors which would influence the mind of the willing seller and the willing purchaser; and obviously the possibility of getting vacant possession and the strength of that possibility is one of such factors.'

Megaw LJ said (at 1277–1278):

h
'The other matter on which I desire to say something is that the learned judge in his judgment in the present case adopted the basis that he had to look at the question posed in section 39(1) on the assumption that the house had in it a sitting tenant; and, as I understand it, that was the basis on which he did approach his decision. The view which I take on that matter is that which was expressed in the decision of this court in *Inworth Property Co Ltd v Southwark London Borough Council* (1977) 76
j
LGR 263. As is set out in the headnote in that case, this court there decided that "value" in section 39(1) of the Housing Act 1957 meant "open market value". In the assessment of the open market value, those facts and future possibilities, including facts and future possibilities as to a sitting, protected tenant, would be relevant— which would be likely to be relevant in the minds of a willing buyer and of a willing seller in negotiating for the purchase and sale of the property. It is unnecessary in

this case to go further into that matter, for the reasons given by Browne LJ. But, like him, I take the view that the manner in which Geoffrey Lane LJ dealt with the *a* question in his judgment in *Hillbank Properties Ltd v Hackney London Borough Council* ([1978] 3 All ER 343 at 352–353, [1978] QB 998 at 1013–1014) is, if I may say so with great respect, entirely correct.'

On these authorities counsel submitted on behalf of the council that the court (and the council) in determining what expense is reasonable should not look exclusively at the *b* value of the property, that when it does look at it, as it must, although not expressly required to by the Act, it must regard the sitting tenants not as the only factor but as a factor and vacant possession as a factor, together with other factors such as the resulting benefits to the tenants and the public interest in improvement of the property. He contended that the judge did look only to the sitting tenant value and had no regard to the possibility of the landlords obtaining vacant possession, whereas he should have looked at those other factors, including additionally if not primarily, the value with *c* vacant possession and the possibility of the landlords' obtaining it.

We are by no means satisfied that Mr Bard's lower figures did exclude the possibility, which seems to have been fairly remote, of the landlords obtaining vacant possession, or that the judge in accepting them was guilty of the same error. The evidence was that no 43 had been bought at auction in 1975 for £5,000 (when these tenants were already in *d* occupation) and it was Mr Edmunds's evidence that property companies (like the landlords) buy on the 'hope' value of vacant possession and the landlords paid too much for this property in 1975. The authorities appear to agree in requiring the court to make a realistic approach to the value of dwelling houses as a saleable asset in the hands of the landlord when considering the reasonableness of the expense required to improve them, and therefore to have regard to the presence of tenants and their rights of continued occupation and the effect that they have on the market value. This the judge appears to *e* have done and we agree with his conclusion that on the evidence which he was entitled to accept the expenditure which the council required the landlords to make in improving these dwellings was unreasonable.

We do not think that on the facts of this case any question of benefit to the tenants or the public arises. And we find it unnecessary to consider the matters raised in the respondent's notice. There is authority for the proposition that the costs of decoration *f* and financing the cost of improvement should be considered: *Ellis Copp & Co v Richmond upon Thames London Borough* (1976) 245 Estates Gazette 931 at 934. But it is not clear whether all the figures given are for market value of the premises in full decorative repair; the evidence as to the landlords' financial position was to a large extent speculative and secondhand; and there was no clear evidence about professional fees except that they would have to be paid, perhaps at 10%. *g*

In view of our conclusion on this point in the landlords' favour it is unnecessary to express an opinion on the two remaining points raised by the council. But they have been well argued and we can add that we have difficulty in accepting the judge's view of them and we would decide both in the council's favour.

In our opinion the council could have been lawfully satisfied under s 89(3)(d) that the dwellings were unlikely to be improved unless they exercised their powers under the *h* section. The judge expressed his views in this way:

'Assuming that there was material before the committee on 23rd June 1978, the date of the provisional improvement notice, that the landlords were unlikely to improve the dwelling, it is perfectly clear to my mind that the council could not have been satisfied that the provisions in the second part of sub-s (3)(d) still applied *j* when the improvement notice was served. Since these applications have been made by the landlords there was every likelihood that the dwellings would be improved. The council as far as I can see disregarded the applications of which it must have had constructive knowledge, or in fact it never applied its mind at all to the requirements of sub-s (6).'

There was no positive evidence that the council's sub-committee had the landlords'
a applications in mind on 17th July 1978; but the course of their correspondence with the
landlords since March 1977, which we have summarised, affords material on which the
council could have been satisfied that improvement notices were necessary, and material
which we would not assume they ignored. We find support for the council's pessimism
about the landlords' intentions in their failure to claim, in reliance on s 91(2)(*b*), that the
council had unreasonably refused to let them carry out the alternative work of
b conversion.

Differing as we respectfully do from the judge's opinion that the council had not
complied with the requirement of s 89(3)(*d*), we do not have to decide whether the
council can pray in aid s 91(7) to save the notices from invalidity on this ground. If that
requirement had not been complied with, we would agree with the judge that the
interests of the landlords would have been substantially prejudiced by being required to
c spend £18,000 on work they did not want to do instead of spending £17,000 on the
work which they wanted to do.

The reverse is true of the last point, when there was a clear failure to comply with a
requirement of Part VIII in fact and an equally clear absence of substantial prejudice to
the landlords' interests in consequence.

The first question is whether the council satisfied themselves or could have satisfied
d themselves that the housing arrangements were satisfactory. That is a necessary
condition before an improvement notice can be served: see s 89(6)(*b*). These arrangements
are 'arrangements contained in a written agreement to which the occupying tenant and
either or both of his landlord and the local authority concerned are parties' and 'making
provision for the housing of an occupying tenant of the dwelling and his
household . . . during the period when improvement works are being carried out . . .':
e see s 86(1) and (2). It was conceded before the judge that there was no written agreement
to satisfy s 86(2). So that requirement had not been complied with.

However, there were written agreements signed by the occupying tenants and
complying with s 86 in every particular except that they were not signed by the landlords
or the council. And Mr Brydson gave unchallenged evidence that they would be signed
by the council if the landlords' appeal to the judge failed.

f The second question is whether the notices should nevertheless be confirmed under
s 91(7).

The judge regarded the absence of satisfactory concluded housing arrangements as a
matter which had merit and was therefore not covered by s 91(7). And he relied on a
dictum of Danckwerts LJ in *De Rothschild v Wing Rural District Council* [1967] 1 All ER
597 at 600, [1967] 1 WLR 470 at 473 on the corresponding provision in s 27(3) of the
g 1964 Act that it was 'intended . . . to deal with cases which have no merits at all'. He also
had no doubt that the landlords would suffer substantial prejudice. We do not have to
consider how far this subsection is restricted to technical matters because we feel bound
to differ from the judge's opinion that the landlords have been substantially prejudiced
by the fact that the council had not yet executed the written agreements before serving
the notices already executed by the tenants. If there was any doubt about the council's
h executing the agreements it could have been removed by an adjournment or an
undertaking.

The appeal will be dismissed and the judgment below affirmed on the ground that it
was not practicable to comply with the requirements in the improvement notices at
reasonable expense.

j *Appeal dismissed. Both appellants' and respondents' applications for leave to appeal to the House
of Lords refused.*

Solicitors: *R A Benge* (for the local authority); *Arthur W Kemp* (for the landlords).

Mary Rose Plummer   Barrister.

R v Bolton Supplementary Benefits Appeal Tribunal, ex parte Fordham

COURT OF APPEAL, CIVIL DIVISION

LORD DENNING MR, WALLER AND DUNN LJJ

30th JUNE 1980

Supplementary benefit – Calculation of benefit – Deduction of resources from requirements – Calculation of resources – Monthly wages paid in middle of each month, half in arrear, half in advance – At time of November payment applicant on strike – Part of November payment constituting payment in advance covering period on strike – Employer informing applicant he would have to repay that part of payment at some future date – Applicant applying for benefit for wife and children for period up to middle of December – Whether applicant entitled to benefit – Whether 'resources' up to middle of December including part of the November payment liable to be repaid – Supplementary Benefits Act 1976, Sch 1, Part III.

The applicant, a fireman employed by a local authority, was paid two weeks in arrear and two weeks in advance on the 15th day of each calendar month. The applicant and other firemen went on strike on 14th November 1977 and remained on strike until 16th January 1978. On 15th November 1977 the applicant was paid a full month's wages, and was thus paid two weeks in advance in respect of a period when he was on strike. On 30th November the local authority informed the applicant that at some future unspecified date he would have to repay that part of the payment. The applicant applied for supplementary benefit for his wife and children for the period 1st to 15th December 1977. The Supplementary Benefits Commission and the Supplementary Benefits Appeal Tribunal decided that he was not entitled to benefit for that period because the whole of the payment made to him on 15th November had to be taken into account as his resources up to 15th December, even though that part of it paid in advance was repayable at some future date, and accordingly he had sufficient resources up to 15th December to meet his family's requirements. The applicant appealed, seeking an order of certiorari to quash the tribunal's decision, on the ground that the part of the payment made on 15th November which was repayable was not part of his resources. The judge upheld that contention and quashed the tribunal's decision. The commission appealed.

Held – Under the Supplementary Benefits Act 1976, Sch 1, Part III, the resources of an applicant for supplementary benefit had to be assessed on a weekly basis by taking into account the applicant's weekly earnings and requirements for the period in question. The payment made to the applicant on 15th November was to be treated as his resources for each of the next four weeks, that is until 15th December when the next payment of wages was due, and the fact that at some indeterminate future date he would have to repay part of that payment could not prevent the whole of the payment made on 15th November constituting his resources for the period from then until 15th December. Since those resources covered his weekly requirements it followed that he was not entitled to supplementary benefit during that period. Accordingly the appeal would be allowed and the decision of the commission restored (see p 52 *d e h j*, p 53 *c* to *f* and p 54 *c* to *h*, post).

Dictum of Lord Denning MR in *R v Preston Supplementary Benefits Appeal Tribunal, ex parte Moore* [1975] 2 All ER at 812 applied.

Notes

For calculating social security benefits, see Supplement to 27 Halsbury's Laws (3rd Edn) para 947A.

For the Supplementary Benefits Act 1976, Sch 1, Part III, see 46 Halsbury's Statutes (3rd Edn) 1083.

Cases referred to in judgments

a R v Manchester Supplementary Benefits Appeal Tribunal, ex parte Riley [1979] 2 All ER 1, [1979] 1 WLR 426, Digest (Cont Vol E) 447, 94Ab(iii).

R v Preston Supplementary Benefits Appeal Tribunal, ex parte Moore, R v Sheffield Supplementary Benefits Appeal Tribunal, ex parte Shine [1975] 2 All ER 807, [1975] 1 WLR 624, CA, Digest (Cont Vol D) 711, 94Ac.

b **Cases also cited**

Goddard v Minister of Housing and Local Government [1958] 3 All ER 482, 10 P & CR 28.

R v Barnsley Supplementary Benefits Appeal Tribunal, ex parte Atkinson [1977] 3 All ER 1031, [1977] 1 WLR 917, CA.

R v West London Supplementary Benefits Appeal Tribunal, ex parte Taylor [1975] 2 All ER 790, [1975] 1 WLR 1048, DC.

c **Appeal**

This was an appeal by the Supplementary Benefits Commission against the judgment of Sheen J given on 24th November 1978 whereby he granted an order of certiorari to the applicant, Michael Roy Fordham, a fire officer employed by the Greater Manchester Council, quashing a decision of the Bolton Supplementary Benefits Appeal Tribunal

d dated 10th January 1978 upholding the decision of the commission refusing to grant the applicant supplementary benefit for his wife and two children for the period 1st December to 15th December 1977. The grounds of the appeal were that the judge erred in law (i) in concluding that two of the four weeks' wages which the applicant received on 15th November 1977, which were wages in advance, were not resources for the purposes of the Supplementary Benefits Act 1976 because (a) the applicant was on strike

e for the two weeks to which the wages related and they were not capital, earnings or other income specified in Part III of Sch 1 to the Act, (b) the applicant was under an obligation to repay the two weeks' wages by deductions from his salary after he returned to work and, (c) if the wages were earned they were to be attributed to those months (in 1978) when they were deducted from his salary after he returned to work; (ii) in not holding that wages could be resources if they were available to the recipient as the means of

f support irrespective of whether they had been earned or had to be repaid. The facts are set out in the judgment of Lord Denning MR.

Simon Brown for the commission.
John Hoggett for Mr Fordham.

g **LORD DENNING MR.** This case raises one of the burning questions today. When men come out on strike, how much supplementary benefit ought to be paid for their wives and children?

In November 1977 all the firemen in England came out on strike. In particular 1,800 firemen employed by the Greater Manchester Council. They came out on strike on 14th November 1977; and remained out until 16th January 1978. That is two months.

h Under s 8 of the Supplementary Benefits Act 1976, when a man comes out on strike, his own requirements are to be disregarded: but not the requirements of his wife and children.

In this case the Greater Manchester Council pay their firemen in a strange way. It is their practice to pay them for any one calendar month on the 15th day of that month. So the applicant in this case, Mr Fordham, received his net salary for the whole month of November on 15th November. It came to £261. That was expected to carry him on to

j the 15th of the next month, in this case 15th December.

As I said, the firemen came out on strike on 14th November. This meant that half of the £261 had been paid to Mr Fordham for the first fortnight in November when he had been working, and half for the second fortnight when he was out on strike. Mr Fordham says that the Supplementary Benefits Commission ought not to have regard to the

payment for the second fortnight. He says that it was not part of his resources because
he would have to pay it back.   *a*

The Supplementary Benefits Commission and the Supplementary Benefits Appeal
Tribunal decided against him. But the judge below found for him. Now there is an
appeal to us.

Under the 1976 Act, when a man applies for supplementary benefit, account has to be
taken as to his 'resources' and as to his 'requirements'. If his resources are such that they
cover his requirements, he does not get supplementary benefit.   *b*

In this case it appears true that the £261 (which Mr Fordham was paid on 15th
November) meant that he had sufficient resources to carry him on until 15th
December. That would have been his next pay day if he had not been on strike. The
Supplementary Benefits Commission say that that sum should be taken as Mr Fordham's
resources for the period up to 15th December. If that is so, he had sufficient resources to
meet the requirements of his wife and children: and he is not entitled to claim   *c*
supplementary benefit for them.

On the other hand, Mr Fordham says that that argument is wrong: because he will
have to repay £125 of that sum, because he was out on strike during the last fortnight of
November. So that £125 ought not to be taken into account in assessing his resources.

Reading through the Supplementary Benefits Act 1976, it seems to me that the answer
is to be found by remembering that the applicant's position has to be assessed on a weekly *d*
basis. Under para 1(2)(a) of Sch 1 to the Act, his weekly requirements are calculated
taking into account his weekly earnings. Payment of supplementary benefit is made on
a weekly basis. The whole system is run on a weekly basis. When one takes that into
account, it goes a long way towards solving the question in this case: because for the four
weeks from 15th November 1977 until 15th December 1977 Mr Fordham's weekly
resources were £61 a week. That sum exceeded his weekly requirements. So he did not   *e*
qualify for supplementary benefit over that period.

It is true that in due course Mr Fordham would have to repay £125 of the £261. That
was made clear on 30th November 1977 when the county treasurer wrote to all the
firemen involved in the dispute:

> '. . . members of the Service who were paid to 30th November 1977, in advance   *f*
> on 15th November under the calendar monthly pay arrangements, should be
> advised that any overpayment will be recovered from salary at some future date.'

That date would depend on the length of the strike and internal arrangements.

At the time when the tribunal heard the case there was no evidence of any repayment
having been made by Mr Fordham at all. But we have been told what happened. When   *g*
the firemen went back to work on 16th January 1978 they were entitled to be paid for
the second fortnight of January. But they received no pay for that fortnight at all. The
council said that they had already been paid for the second fortnight in November, when
they were on strike. So no pay was due. Nevertheless, although no salary was payable
for that fortnight, to avoid any hardship the council lent each man £200 to go on with.
Then from March or April onwards £20 a month was deducted from their salary in   *h*
repayment of the loan.

The point is whether those repayments should be set against the £125 he received in
November 1977. It seems to me that they are not relevant to the weekly position. When
the weekly requirements and resources were being assessed in November 1977 no one
knew what was going to happen in the future. No one knew how long the strike would
last; whether Mr Fordham would remain in the employment of the council or not; or on *j*
what date or to what extent the refund would be made. It was so uncertain that no one
could properly take that into account in considering what the weekly resources and
requirements were.

A parallel point was considered by this court in *R v Preston Supplementary Benefits
Appeal Tribunal, ex parte Moore* [1975] 2 All ER 807 at 812, [1975] 1 WLR 624 at 630,

where I said:

a

'Again his earnings are to be calculated at a weekly sum, even though they are paid monthly or quarterly. Suppose he is paid monthly in advance. He may spend it all in the first day or two in buying a new stove or a suit of clothes. Yet his resources during the whole of that month are to be taken as the weekly equivalent. Suppose he is paid monthly in arrear, he has no actual resources in the first month and he is not to be regarded as notionally having them; but thereafter

b

he has resources which are to be calculated at a weekly sum, and when he leaves at the end of the last month, he has a month's pay in hand as his resources for the following month.'

That passage, especially the last sentence, was adopted by Sheen J in the recent case of *R v Manchester Supplementary Benefits Appeal Tribunal, ex parte Riley* [1979] 2 All ER 1,

c [1979] 1 WLR 426.

So it seems to me that the payment to Mr Fordham on 15th November 1977 of £261 was a payment which was to last him for the next four weeks. It could be calculated in his resources for the next four weeks until 15th December. Those being his resources, they covered his requirements. Therefore he was not entitled to supplementary benefit for his wife and children during that time.

d Looking at the case as a whole, it seems to me that the decision of the Supplementary Benefits Commission, which was followed by the tribunal, was correct. I take a different view from the judge. He seemed to think that Mr Fordham's obligation to repay meant that he had not earned anything during the relevant period, and that he had not had any payment in advance, and the like. I take a different view because of the indefinite, uncertain and almost unforeseeable obligation to refund the money. It was so far ahead

e that it would not affect the immediate resources available to Mr Fordham.

I would be in favour of allowing the appeal and restoring the decision of the tribunal.

WALLER LJ. I agree. Lord Denning MR has already set out the facts in this case. The section with which we are primarily concerned is s 1(1) of the Supplementary Benefits

f Act 1976, which says: '... every person in Great Britain ... whose resources are insufficient to meet his requirements shall be entitled to benefit' as thereinafter follows.

It was submitted on behalf of Mr Fordham that that part of the payment which was attributable to work which should have been done after the strike had started was not income and was not earnings because it had to be repaid. The factual position, as I see it, was that, when a month's wages were paid on 15th November, they related to the period

g of two weeks which had already elapsed and were a payment covering the two weeks immediately following 15th November. In the ordinary way, when the employee continued to work, there would be no obligation for repayment because the work would be done, the work which covered the second half of that payment. But the argument is that, because the strike started on that very day, the 14th, thereafter the second half of the payment had to be repaid and therefore was no longer to be regarded as a resource.

h Lord Denning MR has drawn attention to the letter from the Greater Manchester Council which said that members of the service who were paid to 30th November in advance on 15th November under the calendar monthly pay arrangements 'should be advised that any overpayment will be recovered from salary at some future date'. So notice was then given that at some future date there would have to be a repayment. It is because of that that it is submitted on behalf of the commission that the money was no

j longer a resource.

The sum was clearly not capital; and therefore, as it seems to me, it was income of some sort. The division in the various sections of the 1976 Act appears to be a division between income and capital, and there is no other possibility. The calculation is set out in Sch 1 to the Act. Part II is the calculation of requirements and Part III is the calculation of resources. There are several paragraphs in Part III which indicate that resources can be of a great variety of kinds. Paragraph 21 deals with net weekly earnings. Then para 27 says this:

> 'Any resources not specified in the foregoing provisions of this Schedule may be treated as reduced by such amount (if any) as may be reasonable in the circumstances of the case.'

A very wide provision indeed. Then para 28 deals with resources deliberately abandoned and para 29 deals with discretionary trusts. So it is clear from the whole of that part of Sch 1 that those things which can be income in some way or another are of a very great variety. Furthermore it is clear that the specific parts of that schedule are not all embracing.

The judge, when dealing with the question of whether this was capital or not, said that it was a misuse of language to describe the money as capital. He said in his judgment: 'It was paid as income. It represented two weeks' salary paid in advance. It did not change its character with each day the strike lasted.' In my opinion the judge was quite right in that statement. Where he was in error, in my view, was in coming to the conclusion that in some way that indicated that this should not be treated as a resource. In my view, it can properly be said that, when the payment was made on 15th November, it was a resource for each of the next four weeks, that is until the next payment was made on 15th December. It remained income, albeit that there was an obligation to repay at some future date when the strike was over. It remained as a resource for each of the next four weeks. It started as a resource for each of those four weeks, and the fact of a strike with a consequential obligation to repay at some future date did not alter the fact that it was a resource for each of the four weeks.

In those circumstances, I also agree that this appeal should be allowed and the decision of the tribunal restored.

DUNN LJ. I agree. In refusing the application for supplementary benefit, the supplementary benefits officer said this:

> 'Mr Fordham receives his earnings from his employer two weeks in arrears and two weeks in advance. Although he did not subsequently work for the money paid for the period 15 November to 30 November, he nevertheless received it under the terms of his employment. Therefore it is regarded as available to him, together with the two weeks earned, for living expenses. Since the total amount received is the equivalent of one month's wages he is not entitled to benefit until 15 December 1977.'

That seems to me to be a clear and entirely accurate statement of the position, and I agree that the appeal tribunal were right in holding that those sums paid as wages should be treated as a resource.

The Supplementary Benefits Commission were dealing with the period from 1st to 15th December, and only with that period. Mr Fordham had received wages covering that period. The fact that at some indeterminate future date those wages were to be repaid does not prevent them constituting resources available to Mr Fordham to meet his requirements during the relevant supplementary benefits period.

I too would allow the appeal and restore the decision of the tribunal.

Appeal allowed; decision of Supplementary Benefits Appeal Tribunal restored.

Solicitors: *Solicitor to the Department of Health and Social Security; Brian Thompson & Partners* (for Mr Fordham).

Sumra Green   Barrister.

a
Vervaeke v Smith (Messina and Attorney General intervening)

FAMILY DIVISION

WATERHOUSE J

20th, 21st, 22nd MARCH, 8th MAY 1979

b

COURT OF APPEAL, CIVIL DIVISION

ARNOLD P, CUMMING-BRUCE AND EVELEIGH LJJ

10th, 11th, 13th, 14th MARCH, 19th, 20th MAY, 8th JULY 1980

Marriage – Validity – Declaration – Foreign nullity decree – Jurisdiction to grant declaration
c *that decree effective in England for purpose of establishing validity of subsequent marriage –*
Discretion in exercise of jurisdiction – Discretion where foreign decree entitled to recognition
under binding international convention – Petitioner entitled to claim real estate in England if
subsequent marriage valid – Petitioner seeking declaration that foreign decree declaring earlier
marriage to respondent invalid entitled to recognition – Respondent but not petitioner resident in
England at date of petition – Whether petitioner entitled to declaration under rules of court that
d *foreign decree entitled to recognition – Whether jurisdiction to grant declaration – Whether if*
jurisdiction court having discretion in matter and should exercise discretion by refusing
declaration on ground that petitioner could claim declaration of validity of subsequent marriage
under matrimonial causes legislation – Matrimonial Causes Act 1973, s 45(1) – RSC Ord 15,
r 16.

e *Conflict of laws – Foreign judgment – Recognition by English courts – Foreign nullity decree –*
Marriage celebrated in England – Previous decision of English court that marriage valid under
English law – Previous decision based on petitioner's consent to marriage – Foreign decree based
on ground that marriage a sham although consented to – That ground not raised in English
proceedings – Whether foreign decree entitled to recognition by English court – Whether
convention for reciprocal enforcement of judgments in civil matters applying to case – Whether
f *recognition under convention excluded because of lack of jurisdiction of foreign court or because*
foreign decree contrary to English public policy or because subject matter of decree res judicata
– Whether decree entitled to recognition under legislation relating to reciprocal enforcement of
foreign judgments – Foreign Judgments (Reciprocal Enforcement) Act 1933, s 8(1) – Reciprocal
Enforcement of Foreign Judgments (Belgium) Order in Council 1936 (SR & O 1936 No 1169),
Sch, art 3(1)(a)(c)(d).

g In 1954 the petitioner, who was born in Belgium and resided there until 1954, went
through a ceremony of marriage in London with the respondent, who was a domiciled
Englishman. On 12th March 1970 the petitioner went through another ceremony of
marriage in Italy with M who died that day leaving real property in England. If the
petitioner's marriage to M was valid she was entitled to a share in that property. By a
petition dated 29th May 1970 in the Family Division of the High Court, the petitioner
h prayed for a declaration that her marriage to the respondent was null and void on the
ground that she had not consented to it because she was ignorant of the true nature of the
ceremony. A member of M's family intervened in the proceedings to contest the relief
claimed. On 7th May 1971 Ormrod J[a] dismissed the petition on the ground that the
petitioner knew that the 1954 ceremony was a marriage ceremony and had consented to
it. On 6th December 1971 the petitioner, who had returned to Belgium in May 1970
j and been resident there for 18 months, began proceedings in a Belgian court seeking a
declaration that the 1954 marriage was a nullity ab initio on the alternative pleas that (i)
she had not consented to the marriage through ignorance of the true nature of the
ceremony or (ii) it was a mock marriage, or mere formality, not accompanied by the

_____

a   See *Messina v Smith* [1971] 2 All ER 1046

parties' intention to cohabit, and was contracted solely to enable the petitioner to acquire British nationality and avoid deportation from England. In the Belgian proceedings the *a* respondent admitted the second plea. The intervener again intervened to oppose the relief claimed, on the grounds that the matter was res judicata by virtue of Ormrod J's decision and that the validity of the 1954 marriage was governed by English law and therefore the same conclusion would be reached in the Belgian court as was reached by Ormrod J. On 7th March 1972 the petitioner's appeal to the English Court of Appeal from Ormrod J's decision was dismissed by consent. On 9th June 1972 the Belgian court *b* decreed that the 1954 marriage ,was void ab initio on the ground that, although the parties had consented to it, it was a mock marriage not intended to constitute a lifelong community between them and, as such, was invalid under Belgian law. The court rejected the petitioner's plea of lack of consent to the marriage. The intervener appealed to a Belgian appeal court which on 27th April 1973 dismissed the appeal, holding that the plea of lack of consent to the marriage was barred by the res judicata afforded by *c* Ormrod J's decision, but that the plea of a mock marriage was not res judicata since it was not argued before Ormrod J. The court accordingly upheld the latter plea, thus rendering the marriage invalid under Belgian law. By a petition in the Family Division of the High Court dated 7th September 1973 ('the first current petition') the petitioner sought as against the respondent a declaration under RSC Ord 15, r 16[b] that the Belgian decree was entitled to recognition in the English courts and by a further petition ('the second *d* current petition') the petitioner sought under s 45(1)[c] of the Matrimonial Causes Act 1973 a declaration that her marriage to M was valid and subsisting at the date of his death. Members of M's family intervened in both petitions to oppose the relief claimed in them. On 8th May 1979 Waterhouse J dismissed both petitions holding (i) in respect of the first current petition that, although the court had jurisdiction to make the declaration sought by it because at the date of the petition the respondent was resident *e* in England, the court also had a discretion whether to exercise the jurisdiction, and, in view of the specific procedure under s 45 of the 1973 Act and in all the circumstances, the court would exercise its discretion by refusing to grant a declaration under Ord 15, r 16, and (ii) in respect of the second current petition that, although the parties were agreed that recognition of the Belgian decree in England (which was a necessary step in the relief claimed in the second petition) was governed by a 1934 convention[d] between Belgium *f* and the United Kingdom for the mutual recognition of judgments in civil matters, under art 3(1)(d)[e] of the convention the Belgian decree was excepted from recognition in England because it was in respect of a cause of action which at the date of the decree, and as between the same parties, formed the subject of another judgment, ie that of Ormrod J, which was recognised under English law as final and conclusive. The petitioner appealed, contending, in the alternative, that the Belgian decree was entitled to *g* recognition in the United Kingdom under s 8[f] of the Foreign Judgments (Reciprocal Enforcement) Act 1933.

---

b   Rule 16 provides: 'No action or other proceeding shall be open to objection on the ground that a merely declaratory judgment or order is sought thereby, and the Court may make binding declarations of right whether or not any consequential relief is or could be claimed.'

c   Section 45(1), so far as material, is set out at p 68 *j*, post   *h*

d   See the Reciprocal Enforcement of Foreign Judgments (Belgium) Order in Council 1936, SR & O 1936 No 1169, Sch

e   Article 3, so far as material, is set out at p 73 *b*, post

f   Section 8, so far as material, provides:

    '(1) Subject to the provisions of this section, a judgment to which Part I of this Act applies or would have applied if a sum of money had been payable thereunder, whether it can be registered or not, and whether, if it can be registered, it is registered or not, shall be recognised in any court *j* in the United Kingdom as conclusive between the parties thereto in all proceedings founded on the same cause of action and may be relied on by way of defence or counterclaim in any such proceedings.

    '(2) This section shall not apply in the case of any judgment ... (b) where the judgment has not been registered, it is shown (whether it could have been registered or not) that if it had been registered the registration thereof would have been set aside on an application for that purpose on some ground other than one of the grounds specified in paragraph (a) of this subsection ...'

Held – The appeal would be dismissed for the following reasons—

a　(1) Under English rules of private international law the court had jurisdiction under RSC Ord 15, r 16 to grant a declaration that a foreign nullity decree was effective if the respondent to the petition was resident in England at the date of the petition. However, even where the court was obliged by an international convention to recognise the foreign decree, exercise of the jurisdiction under Ord 15, r 16 still remained in the discretion of the court so that it was not obliged to make a declaration under that rule
b　recognising the foreign decree. Since the purpose of the relief claimed in the first current petition was to establish the validity of the petitioner's marriage with M, and since that could be achieved by a declaration of validity of the marriage under s 45 of the 1973 Act (which would be subject to the special safeguards in s 45(6) and (7) and r 109 of the Matrimonial Causes Rules 1977), that was a valid reason for exercising the discretion by refusing to make a declaration under Ord 15, r 16, since that would ensure that the
c　petitioner would submit to the procedure prescribed by s 45. Accordingly, the first current petition would be dismissed (see p 87 a b, p 90 e and p 91 a, post).

(2) Under English rules of private international law the validity of the 1954 marriage fell to be determined by reference to English law as the lex loci celebrationis, and since there was a judgment of the English court, ie Ormrod J's decision, deciding that the 1954 marriage was valid under English law, the Belgian decree, which decided by reference to foreign law that the 1954 marriage was invalid, could not be recognised by the English
d　courts unless recognition of the decree was required by statute or an instrument having statutory force (see p 87 d to f and p 90 e and j, post); *Sottomayor v De Barros* [1874–80] All ER Rep 97 and *Ogden v Ogden* [1904–7] All ER Rep 86 followed.

(3) Assuming that the 1934 convention applied to a matrimonial case such as the petitioner's (Cumming-Bruce and Eveleigh LJJ doubting that it did), so that the convention governed recognition of the Belgian decree, the decree was excepted from
e　recognition under the exception specified in art 3(1)(d) of the convention because the decree was in respect of a cause of action which at the date it was given formed the subject of another judgment (ie the judgment of Ormrod J) between the same parties which was recognised under English law as being final and conclusive, for the cause of action before Ormrod J and that before the Belgian courts was the same, namely a claim
f　to a declaration that the 1954 marriage was void, even though the petitioner had not raised before Ormrod J the point she had raised in the Belgian courts, namely that the marriage was invalid under Belgian law because the parties had consented to a mock and not a real marriage. However, the decree was not excepted from recognition under art 3(1)(a) on the ground of lack of jurisdiction in the Belgian courts, because the jurisdiction of those courts was recognised under English rules of private international law since the
g　petitioner was living in Belgium and had a real and substantial connection with that country at the date she had invoked the jurisdiction of the Belgian courts. Nor was the decree excepted from recognition under art 3(1)(c) as being contrary to English public policy merely because it was based on a concept offensive to English propriety, namely that a marriage was invalid where the parties, though consenting to it, did not intend it to constitute a real marriage (see p 88 b to p 89 e and p 90 e and j, post); *Law v Gustin*
h　[1976] 1 All ER 113 and *Perrini v Perrini* [1979] 2 All ER 323 approved.

(4) Furthermore, assuming that the 1933 Act also applied to judgments in a matrimonial case such as the petitioner's (Cumming-Bruce and Eveleigh LJJ doubting that it did), so that the Belgian decree came within the ambit of recognition under s 8 of that Act, the decree was excluded from recognition in the United Kingdom by virtue of s 8(2) of the Act because, had the decree been registered in the United Kingdom, an
j　English court would have exercised its discretion under s 4(1)(b)[g] of the Act to set aside the registration since the matter in dispute in the Belgian proceedings had, previously to the date of the judgments in the Belgian courts, been the subject of a final and conclusive

---

g　Section 4(1), so far as material, provides: 'On an application in that behalf duly made by any party against whom a registered judgment may be enforced, the registration of the judgment . . . (b) may be set aside if the registering court is satisfied that the matter in dispute in the proceedings in the original court had previously to the date of the judgment in the original court been the subject of a final and conclusive judgment by a court having jurisdiction in the matter.'

judgment by a court having jurisdiction in the matter, ie that of Ormrod J, and the
Belgian decree was based on foreign law in a context in which the English court would *a*
have recognised English law as governing the case (see p 90 *b* to *e* and *j*, post).

(5) It followed that there was no basis for holding that the Belgian decree was binding
on the English court or that the 1954 marriage was invalid, and since the invalidity of
that marriage was a necessary step in the relief sought in the second current petition, that
petition also would be dismissed (see p 90 *d e* and *j*, post).

Per Arnold P. (1) Semble. Estoppel per rem judicatam arising under art 3(1)(*d*) of the *b*
1934 convention applies not only to the point on which an English court was previously
required by the parties to form an opinion and pronounce judgment, but to every point
which properly belonged to the subject of that litigation and which might with
reasonable diligence have been brought forward in it (see p 89 *c*, post); *Henderson v
Henderson* [1843–60] All ER Rep 378 applied.

(2) A judgment given in matrimonial proceedings is a judgment given in civil *c*
proceedings within s 11(1) of the 1933 Act and is therefore to be recognised under and
subject to the provisions of s 8 of that Act (see p 89 *j* to p 90 *a*, post).

Notes

For recognition of foreign decrees of nullity of marriage, see 8 Halsbury's Laws (4th Edn) *d*
paras 500–502, and for cases on the subject, see 11 Digest (Reissue) 557–560, *1232–1246.*

For declarations as to status, see 8 Halsbury's Laws (4th Edn) para 503.

For the validity of a marriage celebrated in England where one party is domiciled in
England and the other party is domiciled elsewhere, see ibid para 466.

For the Foreign Judgments (Reciprocal Enforcement) Act 1933, ss 4, 8, see 6 Halsbury's
Statutes (3rd Edn) 368, 372. *e*

For the Matrimonial Causes Act 1973, s 45, see 43 ibid 594.

Cases referred to in judgments

Abate v Cauvin (formerly Abate otherwise Cauvin) [1961] 1 All ER 569, [1961] P 29, [1961]
    2 WLR 221, 11 Digest (Reissue) 558, *1237.* *f*
Adams v Adams (Attorney General intervening) [1970] 3 All ER 572, [1971] P 188, [1970]
    3 WLR 934, 11 Digest (Reissue) 553, *1231.*
Aldrich v Attorney General [1968] 1 All ER 345, [1968] P 281, [1968] 2 WLR 413, 32
    Digest (Reissue) 24, *168.*
Aldridge (otherwise Foster) v Aldridge 1954 SC 58, 1954 SLT 84, 11 Digest (Reissue) 544,
    *771. *g*
Armytage v Armytage [1898] P 178, [1895–9] All ER Rep 377, 67 LJP 90, 78 LT 689, 11
    Digest (Reissue) 535, *1150.*
Black-Clawson International Ltd v Papierwerke Waldhof-Aschaffenburg AG [1975] 1 All ER
    810, [1975] AC 591, [1975] 2 WLR 513, [1975] 2 Lloyd's Rep 11, HL, Digest (Cont Vol
    D) 108, *1591a.*
Bright v Bright [1953] 2 All ER 939, [1954] P 270, [1953] 3 WLR 659, 117 JP 529, 27(1) *h*
    Digest (Reissue) 490, *3542.*
Capon, Re, Capon and O'Brien v McLay (1965) 49 DLR (2d) 675, [1965] 2 OR 83, 11 Digest
    (Reissue) 385, **196.*
Carl-Zeiss-Stiftung v Rayner and Keeler Ltd (No 2) [1966] 2 All ER 536, [1967] 1 AC 853,
    [1966] 3 WLR 125, [1967] RPC 497, HL, 22 Digest (Reissue) 158, *1328.*
Collett v Collett (1843) 3 Curt 726, 2 Notes of Cases 504, 7 Jur 1164, 163 ER 881, 27(2) *j*
    Digest (Reissue) 628, *4634.*
Collett (otherwise Sakazova) v Collett [1967] 2 All ER 426, [1968] P 482, [1967] 3 WLR 280,
    11 Digest (Reissue) 521, *1080.*
Conradi v Conradi, Worrall and Way (1868) LR 1 P & D 514, 37 LJP & M 55, 18 LT 659,
    27(1) Digest (Reissue) 414, *3023.*

De Reneville v De Reneville [1948] 1 All ER 56, [1948] P 100, [1948] LJR 1761, CA, 11
a   Digest (Reissue) 542, *1182*.

Eneogwe v Eneogwe (1976) 120 Sol Jo 300, CA.

Formosa v Formosa [1962] 3 All ER 419, sub nom *Gray (otherwise Formosa) v Formosa*
[1963] P 259, [1962] 3 WLR 1246, CA, 11 Digest (Reissue) 559, *1245*.

Garthwaite v Garthwaite [1964] 2 All ER 233, [1964] P 356, [1964] 2 WLR 1108, CA, 11
Digest (Reissue) 348, *31*.

b *Graham v Graham* [1923] P 31, [1922] All ER Rep 149, 92 LJP 26, 128 LT 639, 11 Digest
(Reissue) 535, *1152*.

Har-Shefi v Har-Shefi [1953] 1 All ER 783, [1953] P 161, [1953] 2 WLR 690, CA, 11 Digest
(Reissue) 538, *1165*.

Hayward v Hayward [1961] 1 All ER 236, [1961] P 152, [1961] 2 WLR 993, 27(1) Digest
(Reissue) 492, *3549*.

c *Henderson v Henderson* (1843) 3 Hare 100, [1843–60] All ER Rep 378, 1 LTOS 410, 67 ER
313, 21 Digest (Repl) 244, *306*.

Indyka v Indyka [1967] 2 All ER 689, [1969] 1 AC 33, [1967] 3 WLR 510, HL, 11 Digest
(Reissue) 551, *1224*.

Kassim (otherwise Widmann) v Kassim (otherwise Hassim) (Carl and Dickson cited) [1962] 3 All
ER 426, [1962] P 224, [1962] 3 WLR 865, 11 Digest (Reissue) 505, *987*.

d *Kelly (otherwise Hyams) v Kelly* (1932) 148 LT 143, 27(1) Digest (Reissue) 32, *150*.

Kenward v Kenward [1950] 2 All ER 297, [1951] P 124, CA; *rvsg* [1949] 2 All ER 959,
[1950] P 71, 11 Digest (Reissue) 511, *1015*.

Law v Gustin (formerly Law) [1976] 1 All ER 113, [1976] Fam 155, [1975] 3 WLR 843,
Digest (Cont Vol E) 95, *1243a*.

Leon v Leon [1966] 3 All ER 820, [1967] P 275, [1966] 3 WLR 1164, 11 Digest (Reissue)
e   524, *1100*.

Lindsay v Lindsay [1934] P 162, [1934] All ER Rep 149, 103 LJP 100, 151 LT 283, 27(2)
Digest (Reissue) 826, *6609*.

Magnier v Magnier (1968) 112 Sol Jo 233, 11 Digest (Reissue) 539, *1172*.

Mansell v Mansell [1966] 2 All ER 391, [1967] P 306, [1967] 3 WLR 328, 11 Digest
(Reissue) 550, *1220*.

f *Mehta (otherwise Kohn) v Mehta* [1945] 2 All ER 690, 174 LT 63, 11 Digest (Reissue) 502,
971.

Merker v Merker [1962] 3 All ER 928, [1963] P 283, [1962] 3 WLR 1389, 11 Digest
(Reissue) 516, *1048*.

Messina (formerly Smith otherwise Vervaeke) v Smith (Messina intervening) [1971] 2 All ER
1046, [1971] P 322, [1971] 3 WLR 118, 11 Digest (Reissue) 549, *1217*.

g *Meyer v Meyer* [1971] 1 All ER 378, sub nom *Re Meyer* [1971] P 298, [1971] 2 WLR 401,
11 Digest (Reissue) 562, *1260*.

Miles v Chilton (falsely calling herself Miles) (1849) 1 Rob Eccl 684, 6 Notes of Cases 636, 163
ER 1178, 27(2) Digest (Reissue) 601, *4354*.

Ogden v Ogden [1908] P 46, [1904–7] All ER Rep 86, 77 LJP 34, 97 LT 827, CA, 11 Digest
(Reissue) 384, *275*.

h *Orlandi v Castelli* 1961 SC 113, 27(1) Digest (Reissue) 66, **200*.

Pemberton v Hughes [1899] 1 Ch 781, 68 LJ Ch 281, 80 LT 369, CA, 11 Digest (Reissue)
561, *1259*.

Perrini v Perrini [1979] 2 All ER 323, [1979] Fam 84, [1979] 2 WLR 472, Digest (Cont Vol
E) 95, *1243b*.

Porter v Porter [1971] 2 All ER 1037, [1971] P 282, [1971] 3 WLR 73, 27(2) Digest
j   (Reissue) 829, *6628*.

Postnikoff v Popoff (falsely called Postinikoff) (1964) 46 DLR (2d) 403, 48 WWR 685, 27(1)
Digest (Reissue) 42, **146*.

Quazi v Quazi [1979] 3 All ER 897, [1979] 3 WLR 833, HL, Digest (Cont Vol E) 97, *1277b*.

Qureshi v Qureshi [1971] 1 All ER 325, [1972] Fam 173, [1971] 2 WLR 518, 11 Digest
(Reissue) 565, *1275*.

Raeburn v Raeburn (1928) 138 LT 672, 11 Digest (Reissue) 536, *1153*.

Ramsey-Fairfax (otherwise Scott-Gibson) v Ramsey-Fairfax [1955] 3 All ER 695, [1956] P 115, **a**
[1955] 3 WLR 849, CA, 11 Digest (Reissue) 539, *1170*.

Ross Smith v Ross Smith (otherwise Radford) [1962] 1 All ER 344, [1963] AC 280, [1962] 2
WLR 388, HL, 11 Digest (Reissue) 540, *1178*.

Rowe v Rowe [1979] 2 All ER 1123, [1980] Fam 47, [1979] 3 WLR 101, CA, Digest (Cont
Vol E) 264, *6628a*.

Russ (otherwise De Wade) v Russ and Russ (otherwise Geffers) (1962) 106 Sol Jo 632, 11 Digest **b**
(Reissue) 539, *1171*.

Salvesen (or von Lorang) v Austrian Property Administrator [1927] AC 641, [1927] All ER
Rep 78, 96 LJPC 105, 137 LT 571, HL, 11 Digest (Reissue) 541, *1180*.

Silver (otherwise Kraft) v Silver [1955] 2 All ER 614, [1955] 1 WLR 728, 27(1) Digest
(Reissue) 30, *141*.

Sim v Sim [1944] 2 All ER 344, [1944] P 87, 113 LJP 72, 171 LT 257, 11 Digest (Reissue) **c**
536, *1155*.

Sinclair (formerly Steinbock) v Sinclair (formerly Steinbock) [1967] 3 All ER 882, [1968] P
189, [1967] 3 WLR 1540, [1967] RA 345, CA; *rvsg* [1967] 1 All ER 905, [1967] 2 WLR
1487, 11 Digest (Reissue) 536, *1157*.

Sottomayor v De Barros (1877) 2 PD 81; *on appeal* (1877) 3 PD 1, [1874–80] All ER Rep 94,
47 LJP 23, 37 LT 415, CA; *further proceedings* (1879) 5 PD 94, [1874–80] All ER Rep **d**
97, 49 LJP 1, 41 LT 281, 11 Digest (Reissue) 512, *1019*.

Thompson v Thompson [1957] 1 All ER 161, [1957] P 19, [1957] 2 WLR 138, CA, 27(1)
Digest (Reissue) 491, *3543*.

Torok v Torok [1973] 3 All ER 101, [1973] 1 WLR 1066, Digest (Cont Vol D) 434, *7590a*.

Travers v Holley and Holley [1953] 2 All ER 794, [1953] P 246, [1953] 3 WLR 507, CA, 11
Digest (Reissue) 523, *1099*.
e

Varanand v Varanand (1964) 108 Sol Jo 693, 11 Digest (Reissue) 566, *1278*.

White (otherwise Bennett) v White [1937] 1 All ER 708, [1937] P 111, 106 LJP 49, 156 LT
422, 11 Digest (Reissue) 542, *1185*.

Wilkins v Wilkins [1896] P 108, 65 LJP 55, 74 LT 62, CA, 27(2) Digest (Reissue) 802, *6426*.

Woodland v Woodland (otherwise Belin or Barton) [1928] P 169, 97 LJP 92, 139 LT 262,
27(2) Digest (Reissue) 736, *5774*.
f

Petitions

By a petition dated 7th September 1973 the petitioner, Marie Therese Rachelle Vervaeke,
formerly Messina, sought a declaration under RSC Ord 15, r 16 that a decree of a Belgian
court, the Kortrijk (West Flanders) County Court dated 9th June 1972, declaring that her **g**
marriage to the respondent, William George Smith, celebrated in London on 11th
August 1954, was absolutely void ab initio, which was upheld in the Ghent Court of
Appeal on 27th April 1973, was entitled to recognition in England. The underlying
object of the petition was to establish the validity of the petitioner's marriage on 12th
March 1970, in Italy, to Eugenio Messina who died on the same date leaving estate in
England to which the petitioner was entitled if her marriage to him was valid. A brother **h**
of Eugenio Messina, Salvatore Messina, intervened in the petition denying that the
decree of the Kortrijk court was entitled to recognition in England. By order dated 20th
March 1979 Waterhouse J gave leave for the Attorney General to be joined as a party to
the proceedings. By another order dated 22nd March 1979 Waterhouse J adjourned the
petition and granted the petitioner leave to file a further petition under s 45 of the
Matrimonial Causes Act 1973 and ordered that the further petition be consolidated with
the petition dated 7th September 1973. On 20th April 1979 the petitioner filed a further **j**
petition, under s 45, in which she asserted that the decree of the Kortrijk court and the
judgment of the Ghent Court of Appeal validly declared that her marriage to the
respondent was null and void ab initio and were entitled to recognition in England, and
that her marriage to Eugenio Messina was a lawful and subsisting marriage at the date of

a his death, and prayed for a declaration that her marriage to Eugenio Messina was valid and subsisting at the date of his death. Salvatore Messina having died, his brother Attilio Messina was substituted as intervener in the petition dated 7th September 1973 with effect from 30th August 1977. Attilio Messina also intervened in the petition dated 20th April 1979 on behalf of all those interested in Eugenio Messina's estate on the footing that the petitioner's marriage to him was invalid. The respondent took no part in the proceedings after the service on him of the first petition, and he died on 2nd August

b 1978. The facts are set out in the judgment.

Joseph Jackson QC and *Mathew Thorpe* for the petitioner.
Bruce Holroyd Pearce QC and *J J Davis* for the intervener.
Anthony Ewbank QC and *Nicholas Wilson* for the Attorney General.

Cur adv vult

c
8th May. **WATERHOUSE J** read the following judgment: The petitioner in this case, who is a native of Belgium, had the misfortune, as it now appears to her, to go through a form of ceremony of marriage with one William George Smith, now deceased ('the respondent'), at Paddington Register Office on 11th August 1954. A primary purpose of the ceremony was to enable her to acquire British nationality in order to remain in

d England whilst carrying on her trade of prostitution without fear of deportation. An additional object was to enable her to acquire a British passport so that she could travel freely between England and the Continent. The advantages of the status conferred on her by the ceremony of marriage have long since ceased to be of any substantial benefit to her; they have become outweighed heavily by the disadvantages. In consequence, her attempts to divest herself of the status have occupied the attention of the courts of three

e countries, England, Belgium and Italy.
    The first application now before me is contained in a petition dated 7th September 1973 in which the petitioner prays for a declaration by this court under RSC Ord 15, r 16, that a decree of the Kortrijk County Court in the Province of West Flanders, Belgium, pronouncing that the petitioner's 1954 marriage was 'absolutely invalid ab initio', is entitled to be recognised. The underlying purpose of the application is to establish that

f she is entitled to be recognised in England as the lawful widow of Eugenio Messina with whom she went through a form of ceremony of marriage on 12th March 1970 in San Remo. When the petitioner abandoned prostitution in London in or about 1965, she went to live in San Remo with Eugenio Messina, who had been released in 1960 from a long term of imprisonment in Belgium for offences connected with prostitution. He died during the evening of the day of the marriage ceremony, leaving a substantial estate

g in Italy, England and elsewhere. The English estate includes two freehold houses and a long leasehold house in London; the total value was assessed at more than £100,000 in 1970, and the value now may be twice that amount. Not surprisingly, therefore, the petitioner's application has been opposed by the brothers of Eugenio Messina on behalf of themselves and other members of the Messina family who have an interest in the estate. Letters of administration in respect of the English estate were granted to two

h brothers, Salvatore and Attilio Messina, by Mr Registrar Kenworthy on 19th June 1973; a caveat was entered on behalf of the petitioner in September 1973; and grants ad colligenda bona have been made since. In the present proceedings it was Salvatore Messina who was given leave initially to intervene, but he has since died and he has been replaced as intervener by Attilio Messina with effect from 30th August 1977.
    In the course of the unavoidably interrupted hearing of the petitioner's first application

j in June and July 1978, it became apparent to me that this might well be a case in which she should have proceeded by way of a petition pursuant to the provisions of s 45 of the Matrimonial Causes Act 1973 for a declaration as to the validity of her marriage to Eugenio Messina. This provisional view was reinforced by the submissions made on behalf of the intervener Attilio Messina by his counsel, who invited me to dismiss the first application on that and other grounds. Counsel's submissions generally raised important questions of jurisdiction and public policy and I thought it right, therefore, to invite the Queen's Proctor to consider the position in consultation with the Attorney *a* General, bearing in mind the statutory right of the Attorney General to be heard in any proceedings under s 45.

In the result the Attorney General has sought leave, which I have granted, to intervene in the proceedings on the petitioner's first application. Furthermore, in the light of the submissions on behalf of the Attorney General, of which the petitioner was given advance notice, counsel on her behalf has applied for leave to file a second application, *b* now contained in a petition dated 20th April 1979, by which she seeks a declaration under s 45 that the marriage celebrated on 12th March 1970 between the petitioner and Eugenio Messina was a valid and subsisting marriage at the date of the death of Eugenio Messina. In these second proceedings the Attorney General is a necessary party, and I have given leave to Attilio Messina to intervene again on behalf of all the members of the Messina family who may have an interest in the outcome. I need not repeat the *c* consequential directions that I gave on 22nd March 1979 on the petitioner's undertaking to file the second petition. It is sufficient for me to say that I dispensed with service on an alleged illegitimate son of Eugenio Messina because it is not necessary for him to be represented separately from Attilio Messina on the relevant issues before me; that I ordered that the two petitions should be consolidated; and that I dispensed with the service of further pleadings in view of the full arguments addressed to me. The *d* procedural requirements of s 45 and the rules have now been complied with and, by consent, I am able to deal with all the issues raised by both petitions. I should add that I have been assisted greatly by the submissions made by counsel on behalf of the Attorney General on all the issues.

e

History of the nullity proceedings in England, Belgium and Italy

The petitioner was initially successful here in obtaining a declaration of nullity in respect of the 1954 marriage, which was granted by his Honour Judge Forrest QC in an undefended suit on 23rd June 1970. Although she was then resident in Belgium, she petitioned on the basis that the marriage ceremony had taken place here; and the address of Smith, the respondent, was unknown to her when she filed the petition. The ground *f* on which the declaration was made was that the petitioner had not consented to the marriage because she was at all material times ignorant of the nature of the contract which she had been induced to enter into. An additional allegation that she had been subject to duress was rejected by the judge.

Before the decree was made absolute, Salvatore Messina, who had learnt of the proceedings by chance, was given leave to intervene in the suit to show cause why the *g* decree should not be made absolute, and the Queen's Proctor also intervened to show cause. As a result of the Queen's Proctor's inquiries, the petitioner learnt that the respondent had been married in Shanghai before the last war to a Russian woman who had obtained a divorce from him in June 1946 in Las Vegas, Nevada. The petitioner therefore filed a further petition, which was amended on 24th November 1970, praying for a declaration of nullity on the ground that the respondent did not have the capacity *h* to marry her in 1954 because his previous marriage had not been validly dissolved or annulled and his Russian wife was still alive. By this time the respondent's address was known because he had entered an appearance in the first suit, and the petitioner relied on the fact that he resided in England to found the jurisdiction of the court. The case came on for hearing before Ormrod J early in 1971 and he gave judgment on 7th May 1971. In relation to the first petition, he allowed both interventions, set aside the decree nisi, *j* and dismissed the petition with costs; and he dismissed the further petition, with costs in favour of Salvatore Messina, who had intervened in that suit also. The judge's judgment is reported as *Messina v Smith* [1971] 2 All ER 1046, [1971] P 322 and I have before me a full transcript, which includes the detailed consideration by Ormrod J of the evidence in relation to the first petition that is omitted in the reports (see [1971] 2 All ER 1046 at 1050, [1971] P 322 at 329).

Notices of appeal were served in respect of both the orders but the appeals were
a discontinued by the petitioner by notice dated 6th March 1972, and they were dismissed
by the Court of Appeal the following day.

Meanwhile, on 6th December 1971, whilst her English appeal was still pending, the
petitioner had begun proceedings in the court of first instance, or county court, in
Kortrijk in Belgium, again praying for a declaration of nullity. Her pleaded case was that
the 1954 marriage had taken place without her consent. In support of this, she alleged
b again that she had been ignorant of the true nature of the ceremony but she relied also
on allegations that she had not intended to contract a marriage with the respondent and
had never lived with him.

The respondent appeared by a solicitor in the Belgian proceedings and served a
pleading in which he admitted that the marriage ceremony was purely a formality and
was gone through solely for the purpose of obtaining British nationality for the petitioner
c in order to prevent her from being deported from the United Kingdom. The pleading
added: 'The very last purpose of this formality was living together, and immediately
after the ceremony the parties parted for good.' By way of prayer, it was said that the
respondent would conform to the wisdom of the court. In a later pleading he said that
he accepted 'the authority ratione loci' of the court.

As in the English proceedings, Salvatore Messina intervened to oppose the petitioner's
d claim. He prayed in aid the English decision, asserted that English law governed the
validity of the marriage, and impugned the petitioner's motives in seeking a declaration
of nullity.

The judgment of the three judges sitting in the Kotrijk court was given on 9th June
1972. They ruled that the intervention by Salvatore Messina was admissible but rejected
his arguments against the petitioner's claim. The court did not refer in its judgment to
e the question whether it was a court of competent jurisdiction, presumably because this
had been conceded by Smith and not argued by the intervener. In the absence of any
objection, the court would assume jurisdiction on the basis that the petitioner was
resident within its district, having resumed residence there by 21st May 1970 (see arts
636 and 638 of the Belgian Judicial Code). The court rejected the petitioner's claim in so
far as it was based on her alleged ignorance of the nature of the 1954 marriage
f ceremony. It held that it was not bound by the principle of res judicata because the
judgment of Ormrod J had not altered the status of persons, but it adopted, for the
purpose of its own decision, the findings of that judge. On the new part of the petitioner's
case, however, the Belgian judges held that the essential validity of the marriage or its
substratum was governed by the personal laws of the parties, that is by the law of each
party's antenuptual nationality, and that the marriage was invalid ab initio because s 146
g of the Belgian Civil Code provides that no marriage exists where there is no consent. In
this context it was said in the judgment that the findings of fact made by Ormrod J
showed that the petitioner and the respondent had agreed to bar any community of life
whatsoever, that they were never housed together, and that they never lived as husband
and wife. Accordingly, it was said, the consensus had been infected by lack of will,
namely the absence of a real consensus.

h   Salvatore Messina appealed against this decision to the Court of Appeal in Ghent, and
the decision of that court was given on 27th April 1973, after hearing the parties and the
public prosecutor. The decision of the lower court was affirmed. Dealing with the ratio
decidendi of the judgment of the Kortrijk court, the Court of Appeal said:

       'In consequence the consent they (the parties) both gave was not the consent to a
       marriage but a beguiling gesture meant to reach an aim completely unconnected to
j   the marriage bonds. The consent to a marriage belongs to the fundamental
       conditions. These conditions and also the sanctions applied to them by the law are
       determined by the personal law of each party or, with reference to the first defendant
       who was of Belgian nationality, by the Belgian law.'

After referring to the provisions of s 146 of the Civil Code, the judgment continued
(in the words of the translation with which I have been supplied):

'As the parties delusively indulged in a marriage ceremony without in fact really consenting to a marriage, they behaved against public policy. The disturbance of public order, the protection of what belongs to the essence of a real marriage and of human dignity, exact that such a sham marriage be declared invalid.'

It followed that, in the view of the Court of Appeal in Ghent, the Belgian court was not bound by the decision of Ormrod J in this country; and the Court of Appeal held that, in any event, Ormrod J had not been asked to consider the complete absence of consent to the marriage in the relevant sense argued before the Kortrijk court.

In order to complete the history of the petitioner's proceedings I should mention that she brought a civil action in Genoa in 1974 to obtain a declaration of the validity in the Italian Republic of the decision by the Court of Appeal in Ghent. The decision of the Court of Appeal of Genoa was given on 15th July 1976 in proceedings in which the respondent did not appear but Salvatore Messina was represented. The Court of Appeal granted the declaration prayed for and ordered that it should be endorsed on the registers of the civil status of the Commune of San Remo at the foot of the deed of marriage contracted between the petitioner and Eugenio Messina. In a short judgment the court held (inter alia) that the Belgian court was of competent jurisdiction according to Italian law, that its judgment was final according to Belgian law and not contrary to any Italian judgment or to Italian jurisdiction, and that it did not include any provision contrary to Italian public order. The threat of proceedings in Italy against the petitioner for bigamy has presumably, therefore, receded for the time being, but I have been told that an appeal against the Genoa decision is being pursued.

[His Lordship then considered the domicile, residence and nationality of the petitioner and respondent and found that at all material times the respondent was domiciled in England. The petitioner was born in Belgium with Belgian nationality. She resided there, in Deerlijk, until 1954 when she came to England. On 23rd September 1954 she was registered as a citizen of the United Kingdom and Colonies and shortly after obtained a British passport which she held at least until June 1970. Since May 1970 she had resided in Belgium, at Deerlijk until September 1976 and thereafter at Costrozebeke. She had retained her Belgian domicile of origin until the 1954 marriage and that domicile had revived on her return to Belgium in 1970 with the intention to remain there permanently. In December 1971, when she began the proceedings in the Kortrijk court, it was at least doubtful whether, according to Belgian law, she had reacquired Belgian nationality validly. His Lordship continued:]

Jurisdiction under RSC Ord 15, r 16

The power of the court to grant a declaration that a foreign nullity decree is effective in this country is now well established. The material provisions are contained in RSC Ord 15, r 16, which is general in its terms; and examples of its application in the case of foreign nullity decrees are to be found in *Abate v Cauvin* [1961] 1 All ER 569, [1961] P 29 and *Merker v Merker* [1962] 3 All ER 928, [1963] P 283.

The jurisdiction of the court to make such a declaration if either party to the purported marriage is not domiciled here is less clear. According to Dicey and Morris on the Conflict of Laws (9th Edn, 1973, p 372, r 51) the English court has jurisdiction only if, at the date of the institution of the proceedings, the petitioner is domiciled in England or both parties are resident in England. In this case the first petition for a declaration was dated 7th September 1973 and the petitioner was then resident in Belgium. Furthermore, she was domiciled in England only if her marriage to the respondent was a valid and subsisting marriage. She asserts, however, that this marriage was void ab initio and the court cannot, therefore, in the present case found its jurisdiction on her dependent domicile. This problem arose in rather different circumstances in *Garthwaite v Garthwaite* [1964] 2 All ER 233, [1964] P 356, when a wife sought a declaration that her marriage was valid and subsisting. Her difficulty was that, when she presented her petition seeking this declaration, her husband was domiciled in New York. The Court of Appeal

held that it had no jurisdiction to grant the declaration, and Willmer LJ said ([1964] 2 All
a ER 233 at 236, [1964] P 356 at 379);

'Accordingly, if, as the wife asserts, her marriage is still subsisting, her domicil is
that of her husband, i.e., New York State. It follows on well established principles
that, if this case is properly to be regarded as one falling within the matrimonial
jurisdiction of the High Court, the wife by her very assertion deprives the court of
b jurisdiction to entertain the suit.'

The alternative basis of the English court's jurisdiction, namely residence of both
parties here, is accepted by the editor of Cheshire's Private International Law (9th Edn,
1974, pp 425–426), and is founded on the decision of Simon P in *Qureshi v Qureshi* [1971]
1 All ER 325, [1972] Fam 173. In that case, commenting on the judgments in *Garthwaite
v Garthwaite* Simon P said ([1971] 1 All ER 325 at 340, [1972] Fam 173 at 193–194):

c
'*Garthwaite v Garthwaite* in reality decides that (in addition to jurisdiction based
on domicil) the court has power to make a declaration under RSC Ord 15, r 16, in
such circumstances as would have given the English ecclesiastical courts in their
totality before 1857 jurisdiction to accord matrimonial relief—in particular to grant
a decree of restitution of conjugal rights. I respectfully concur with this view of the
d decision: see per Willmer, Danckwerts and Diplock LJJ (see [1964] 2 All ER 233 at
239–40, 240, 247, [1964] P 356 at 383–385, 385, 397). In *Har-Shefi v Har-Shefi*
([1953] 1 All ER 783 at 790, [1955] P 161 at 174) Hodson LJ agreed with Barnard
J ([1952] 2 All ER 821) that petitions in nullity were analogous to declarations under
RSC Ord 25, r 5 (now RSC Ord 15, r 16), and thought that jurisdiction in respect of
each should be decided on the same principles. The ecclesiastical courts before 1857
had jurisdiction to entertain suits for marital relief if both parties were, at the date
e of commencement of proceedings, resident in the territorial area over which the
court exercised jurisdiction. The High Court still has jurisdiction to entertain a suit
for nullity, judicial separation or restitution of conjugal rights where the parties are
resident in England at the commencement of proceedings.'

It followed, in Simon P's view, that each party in the *Qureshi* case was entitled to the
f declaration sought because they had been resident in England at the commencement of,
and throughout, the proceedings; and he based his decision on that ground.
In the present case, counsel on behalf of the petitioner, has invited me to hold that the
court has jurisdiction to grant the declaration sought under RSC Ord 15, r 16, because
the respondent to the first petition was resident here when the proceedings were begun.
In his submissions to me, counsel adopted the view expressed in Rayden on Divorce
g (13th Edn, 1979, vol 1, p 75), that the bases of the jurisdiction are akin to those for nullity
of marriage. Jurisdiction in nullity is now governed by s 5(3) of the Domicile and
Matrimonial Proceedings Act 1973, which provides, inter alia, that the court shall have
jurisdiction to entertain the proceedings if either of the parties was habitually resident in
England and Wales throughout the period of one year ending with the date when the
proceedings were begun. The provisions of s 5(3), which came into force on 1st January
h 1974, nearly four months after the first petition for a declaration was presented, replaced
the common law rules and the earlier provisions of s 40 of the Matrimonial Causes Act
1965, as amended by s 7(2) of the Nullity of Marriage Act 1971, which was the legislation
in force in September 1973. However, the jurisdiction of the English court to annul a
marriage, if the respondent was resident in England at the commencement of the
proceedings, was well established before 1973 and was derived from the jurisdiction of
j the ecclesiastical courts. Thus, in *Ramsey-Fairfax v Ramsey-Fairfax* [1955] 3 All ER 695
at 696, [1956] P 115 at 132 (a case in which both parties were resident in England but
domiciled in Scotland) Denning LJ said:

'It is clear that the ecclesiastical courts based their jurisdiction in cases of nullity
on residence, not on domicil. If the defendant to a petition was resident within the

local jurisdiction of the court, then the court had jurisdiction to determine it. So
here in this case.'   *a*

See also the argument of counsel ([1956] P 115 at 129).

The old cases on residence were considered again by the House of Lords in *Ross Smith
v Ross Smith* [1962] 1 All ER 344, [1963] AC 280 in which there was very full argument
about the basis of the jurisdiction of the ecclesiastical courts in nullity suits (see, for
example, the account of that jurisdiction given by counsel for the appellant ([1963] AC   *b*
280 at 282)). The case itself turned on the question whether the fact that the marriage
had been celebrated in England was a sufficient basis for the court's jurisdiction in a suit
in which the marriage was alleged to be voidable. It was accepted, however, that
residence of the respondent was a proper foundation for jurisdiction: see the speeches of
Lord Reid, Lord Morris and Lord Hodson ([1962] 1 All ER 344 at 355, 363, 367, 369,
[1963] AC 280 at 304, 317, 323, 325).   *c*

Again, in *Garthwaite v Garthwaite* [1964] 2 All ER 233 at 243, [1964] P 356 at 390
Diplock LJ confirmed the rule derived from the ecclesiastical courts that residence of the
respondent in England was sufficient. There appear to be comparatively few reported
cases of nullity in which jurisdiction has been founded solely on that ground but
Scarman J did so in *Russ v Russ and Russ* (1962) 106 Sol Jo 632 (see also *Magnier v Magnier*
(1968) 112 Sol Jo 233 and the Scottish decision in *Aldridge (otherwise Foster) v Aldridge* *d*
1954 SC 58).

A similar rule has been applied in suits for judicial separation. A recent example of its
application is to be found in *Sinclair v Sinclair* [1967] 3 All ER 882, [1968] P 189. In that
case the wife petitioner was resident in England but this was not directly relevant to the
issue as to jurisdiction. The crucial argument in the Court of Appeal was whether there
was evidence to justify a finding that the respondent was resident here at the   *e*
commencement of the proceedings. Willmer LJ said ([1967] 3 All ER 882 at 886, [1968]
P 189 at 213):

> 'It is not in issue that pursuant to the practice of the old ecclesiastical courts
> (which was preserved by s. 22 of the Matrimonial Causes Act, 1857, and since 1925
> by s. 32 of the Supreme Court of Judicature (Consolidation) Act, 1925) jurisdiction   *f*
> in respect of proceedings for judicial separation may be founded on the husband's
> residence in this country.'

See also per Russell LJ and Scarman J ([1967] 3 All ER 882 at 892, 898, [1968] P 189 at
222, 232).   *g*

In the earlier case of *Sim v Sim* [1944] 2 All ER 344, [1944] P 87 Pilcher J founded
jurisdiction on the residence of the respondent in England, when both parties were
domiciled in Scotland and the wife petitioner was resident there. After reviewing the
authorities and the opinions of textbook writers, Pilcher J said ([1944] 2 All ER 344 at
348, [1944] P 87 at 94):

h

> 'In this case the party against whom relief is sought, namely, the husband, is
> resident in this country. I was satisfied on the evidence called at the hearing of the
> issue before me that but for his refusal to receive his wife in his Newcastle house she
> would have come and lived with him at Newcastle, in which case the husband and
> wife would both have been physically resident within the jurisdiction. I am not
> satisfied that the ecclesiastical courts attached any importance to the actual residence *j*
> within the jurisdiction of a wife seeking relief against her husband, and I see no
> reason why this court, acting on principles which conform to the principles acted on
> by the ecclesiastical courts, should attach any importance in a suit for judicial
> separation to the actual residence of a wife who has herself invoked the process of
> the court and so submitted to its jurisdiction.'

I respectfully agree.

In the light of this analysis of the authorities I am compelled, with some diffidence, to disagree with the opinions expressed in Dicey and Morris on the Conflict of Laws (9th Edn, 1973, p 372, r 51) and Cheshire's Private International Law (9th Edn, 1974, pp 425–426) as to the basis of the court's jurisdiction under RSC Ord 15, r 16. It seems clear that the true basis of jurisdiction, other than domicile, is residence of the respondent in this country; and that rule is unaffected by any of the recent statutory provisions to which I have referred earlier in this part of my judgment.

A particular problem which has arisen in the present case is that the respondent died on 2nd August 1978, nearly five years after the first petition for a declaration was presented. However, his death does not oust the jurisdiction of the court. The material date for determining jurisdiction is that when the proceedings were commenced: in this case in relation to the first petition, it is 7th September 1973. This point was dealt with by Ormrod J at first instance in *Sinclair v Sinclair* [1967] 1 All ER 905 at 908, [1968] P 189 at 200 as follows:

> 'The crucial date and stage of the suit for this purpose is, in my judgment, the inception of the suit, which means, in our current practice, the date on which the petition is filed. This must follow if the principles of the ecclesiastical courts are the foundation on which this jurisdiction depends. The Statute of Citations prohibited the citation of a person who was not inhabiting or dwelling within the diocese. DR. LUSHINGTON in *Collett* v. *Collett* ((1843) 3 Curt 726, 163 ER 881) specifically based jurisdiction on this statute. GORELL BARNES, J., in *Armytage* v. *Armytage* ([1898] P 178 at 194, [1895–9] All ER Rep 377 at 384), which is the locus classicus on this topic, said: "In my opinion, if the parties had a matrimonial home, but were not domiciled within the jurisdiction of an ecclesiastical court, that court would have interfered, if the parties were within the jurisdiction at the commencement of the suit, to protect the injured party against the other party in respect of the adultery or cruelty of the latter, and I can find no authority for the suggestion made by the husband's counsel that such interference could be limited to cases where the offence complained of was committed within the jurisdiction." *Graham* v. *Graham* ([1923] P 31, [1922] All ER Rep 149) and *Raeburn* v. *Raeburn* ((1928) 138 LT 672) are to the same effect.'

The correctness of that ruling was confirmed by the Court of Appeal, although the court reached a different conclusion from the trial judge on the facts of the case. A similar point had been decided in relation to divorce proceedings in *Leon v Leon* [1966] 3 All ER 820, [1967] P 275 and *Mansell v Mansell* [1966] 2 All ER 391, [1967] P 306, and the decisions of Baker and Cumming-Bruce JJ respectively in those cases were to similar effect.

I should add finally on this point that there is nothing in RSC Ord 15, r 16 to fetter the power of the court to make a declaration as prayed by the petitioner in this case when the other party to the disputed marriage is dead. A declaration that a German decree of divorce was void was made by Bagnall J in *Meyer v Meyer* [1971] 1 All ER 378, [1971] P 298 some five years after the death of the husband, and it was not suggested on behalf of the Queen's Proctor in that case that the death ousted the jurisdiction of the court.

Accordingly, I hold that the court has jurisdiction under the English rules of private international law to make the declaration for which the Petitioner prays in her first petition.

The discretion of the court under RSC Ord 15, r 16

As I said at the outset of this judgment, the underlying purpose of the petitioner in presenting both petitions before me is to establish that she is entitled to be recognised in England as the lawful widow of Eugenio Messina so that she will be entitled to a share in his estate. In other words, she seeks to establish here, for the purpose that I have stated, the validity of her marriage to Eugenio Messina on 12th March 1970 in San Remo. She has been quite straightforward in accepting that this is her objective. When I asked her counsel whether there was any other purpose behind the proceedings, he was instructed *a* to say that the petitioner did have an emotional, as well as a practical, desire that her Messina marriage should be recognised here because of her regard for Eugenio Messina, but I am unable to accept that assertion in the light of all her personal circumstances and the history generally.

In view of the petitioner's objective in the proceedings, it is necessary for me to consider at this stage of my judgment the nature of any discretion that the court has in *b* relation to the grant of a declaration under RSC Ord 15, r 16, and the principles on which any such discretion should be exercised.

I would have thought that it was clear beyond argument from the wording of r 16 that the court's power is discretionary, but counsel has argued on behalf of the petitioner that there is no relevant discretion in the present case. He says that the case, in relation to the first petition, is not about the validity of the Messina marriage: it is simply about the *c* recognition of the decree of a foreign court of competent jurisdiction. From that premise he goes on to submit that the court is bound by the terms of art 3 of the convention between Belgium and Great Britain and Northern Ireland for the Reciprocal Enforcement of Judgements in Civil and Commercial Matters dated 2nd May 1934 ('the Anglo-Belgian convention'), which has been duly ratified.

Article 3(1) provides in effect that a judgment in civil and commercial matters given *d* by any superior court in Belgium or England and executory in the country of the original court, although still open to proceedings by way of opposition, appeal or setting aside shall, in the courts of the territory of the other, be recognised in all cases where no objection to the judgment can be established on any of the grounds specified in the subparagraphs that follow. Article 3(3) further provides that—

'The recognition of a judgment under paragraph (1) of this Article means that *e* such judgment shall be treated as conclusive as to the matter thereby adjudicated upon in any further action as between the parties and as to such matter shall constitute a defence against further action between them in respect of the same cause of action.'

f
Counsel for the petitioner argues, therefore, that, if the prescribed conditions for recognition of a Belgian decree are fulfilled, the English court has no discretion to refuse a declaration that the decree is to be recognised.

In my judgment this argument fails to distinguish between entitlement to recognition of a particular decree under the Anglo-Belgian convention and the right of a litigant to a declaration to that effect under RSC Ord 15, r 16. The distinction between an *g* entitlement in law in relation to a specific subject matter and the right of a litigant to a declaration as to that entitlement is a very familiar one and does not need elaboration here. The court has evolved rules governing the exercise in many and varied circumstances of its discretion to make binding declarations, and I can see nothing in the provisions of the Anglo-Belgian convention that can have the effect of removing that discretion (see per Scarman J in *Varanand v Varanand* (1964) 108 Sol Jo 693). *h*

The problem that I have to face here is that Parliament has provided a specific procedure for determination of the very question that is crucial to the petitioner's objective, namely whether or not her marriage to Eugenio Messina should be recognised as valid in England. The material provisions of s 45(1) of the Matrimonial Causes Act 1973, replacing s 39(1) of the 1965 Act, are that—

j
'Any person who is a British subject, or whose right to be deemed a British subject depends wholly or in part on his legitimacy or on the validity of any marriage, may . . . if he claims any real or personal estate situate in England and Wales, apply by petition to the High Court for a decree declaring . . . that his own marriage was a valid marriage.'

In the present case it is now common ground that the petitioner is a British subject;
a that her status as such is independent of the validity of any marriage; that she claims real
and/or personal estate here; and that she is entitled to petition for a decree declaring that
her marriage to Eugenio Messina was a valid marriage. Moreover, there is now before
me, belatedly, a second petition praying for a declaration pursuant to the provisions of
s 45. On behalf of the petitioner, however, counsel presses her case for a declaration on
the prayer of the first petition.

b   There are a number of decisions on the effect of the provisions of s 39 of the 1965 Act
that are material to the exercise of my discretion in the present case. In *Kassim v Kassim*
[1962] 3 All ER 426 at 432, [1962] P 224 at 233 Ormrod J pointed out the different
sources of the general, but discretionary, jurisdiction of the court to grant declarations
under the earlier provisions of what was then RSC Ord 25, r 5, and the statutory
jurisdiction in nullity exercised under s 21 of the Supreme Court of Judicature
c (Consolidation) Act 1925. He went on to say ([1962] 3 All ER 426 at 432, [1962] P 244
at 234):

> 'In cases such as the present, therefore, where a declaration is sought that a
> marriage is void ab initio there is no need to invoke the provisions of R.S.C. Ord. 25,
> r. 5, and indeed, in my judgment, there is no room for the operation of the rule in
> this class of case. The jurisdiction of this court to deal with marriages void ab initio
d   exists quite independently of the Rules of the Supreme Court and unlike that
> jurisdiction is not a matter of discretion.'

The problem came before Ormrod J in a different form in two cases reported in
1968. The first was *Collett (otherwise Sakazova) v Collett* [1967] 2 All ER 426, [1968] P 482
in which there were alternative prayers for a decree of nullity or a declaration, in effect
e under RSC Ord 15, r 16, that the marriage was valid. Having rejected the prayer for a
decree of nullity, Ormrod J said in relation to the alternative prayer ([1967] 2 All ER 426
at 431–432, [1968] P 482 at 493–494):

> 'This prayer (as it appeared in the original petition), is clearly an attempt to invoke
> the jurisdiction of the court to make declaratory judgments under R.S.C. Ord. 15,
f   r. 16. The question arises, however, whether, in view of the Matrimonial Causes
> Act 1965, s. 39, this court can, or ought to, exercise this jurisdiction under the Rules
> of the Supreme Court in a case which is covered by that section. The point is of
> some importance because under s. 39 of the Act of 1965 and r. 74 of the Matrimonial
> Causes Rules, 1957 a special code of procedure is laid down which was not followed
> in this case. Section 39, which was formerly s. 17 of the Matrimonial Causes Act,
g   1950, applies primarily, but not exclusively, to petitions for declarations of
> legitimacy. Under sub-s. (1), it is provided that: "Any person who is a British
> subject ... may, if he is domiciled in England or Northern Ireland ... apply by
> petition to the court for a decree declaring that ... his own marriage was a valid
> marriage." These provisions cover in all respects the present wife and the present
> petition. By s. 39(6), all such petitions must be delivered to the Attorney-General,
h   and by r. 74 the petitioner must apply to the registrar for directions as to what
> parties shall be served with the petition. These are important safeguards, because
> the rights of third parties may be adversely affected by a declaration that a marriage
> is valid and, consequentially, that the children of the marriage are legitimate.
> Accordingly, if the court were to exercise the jurisdiction under the Rules of the
> Supreme Court and declare a marriage valid, it would enable a petitioner to obtain
j   what might be, in effect, a declaration of legitimacy of his or her children without
> complying with the requirements of s. 39 (6) and of r. 74.'

After referring to *Kassim v Kassim* Ormrod J continued:

> 'In the present case I have come to the same conclusion, namely, that in cases
> covered by s. 39 the court must proceed under, and in accordance with, that

section. The reasons for so holding, which I have already outlined, are at least as, if
not more, compelling than those in *Kassim* v. *Kassim*.'   *a*

The further case was *Aldrich v Attorney General* [1968] 1 All ER 345, [1968] P 281 in
which the petitioner sought declarations as to the validity of his marriage and as to the
legitimacy of his daughter. The petition in its original form was brought under the
provisions of RSC Ord 15, r 16, but the petitioner was within the terms of s 39 of the
1965 Act in relation to his prayer for a declaration that his marriage was valid and this
was granted after the Attorney General had been joined. However, Ormrod J refused a   *b*
declaration as to the legitimacy of the child. After reciting the provisions of s 21 of the
Supreme Court of Judicature Act 1925, he said ([1968] 1 All ER 345 at 350, [1968] P 281
at 293–294):

> 'The effect of this section on the present case is clearly of the greatest
> importance. Paragraph (*b*) lays down in express terms that the court shall have such   *c*
> jurisdiction with respect to declarations of legitimacy "as is hereinafter in this Act
> provided". This is, of course, a reference to s 188 of the Act of 1925 which became,
> with minor amendments, s 17 of the Matrimonial Causes Act, 1950, and s 39 of the
> Act of 1965. I find it quite impossible to construe this section as meaning that the
> court has also a jurisdiction to grant declarations of legitimacy under the Rules of
> the Supreme Court. If this were the effect of the rule it would be inconsistent with   *d*
> the section. Moreover, the section itself is subsequent in date to the rule, and it is
> not a mere re-enactment of a provision in an earlier Act. In my judgment, the
> principle "expressio unius est exclusio alterius" must apply, with the result that the
> jurisdiction of the court in this connexion is limited to cases falling within the
> provisions of s 39 of the Act of 1965.'

The latest reported decision on the application of s 21(*b*) of the 1925 Act to which I   *e*
have been referred is *Eneogwe v Eneogwe* (1976) 120 Sol Jo 300, in which case the Court
of Appeal approved the decisions in *Collett v Collett* and *Aldrich v Attorney General*. An
appeal against the grant of a declaration under RSC Ord 15, r 16 of the validity of a
Nigerian marriage was allowed on the ground that the court had no jurisdiction to make
the declaration.

Counsel for the petitioner has argued forcefully in the present case that the decisions   *f*
to which I have referred turn essentially on the construction of s 21(*b*) of the 1925 Act
and that they are irrelevant here because the first petition merely seeks a declaration as
to the validity of a foreign decree pursuant to the provisions of RSC Ord 15, r 16. For this
purpose, it is said to be immaterial whether the court's jurisdiction stems from s 21(*a*) of
the 1925 Act and the jurisdiction of the ecclesiastical court or from enactments which
came into force after the Matrimonial Causes Act 1873 (see, in this connection, *Har-Shefi*   *g*
v Har-Shefi [1953] 1 All ER 783, [1953] P 161). In support of his argument counsel for
the petitioner has prayed in aid a passage in Dr P M North's the Private International Law
of Matrimonial Causes in the British Isles and the Republic of Ireland (1977, p 85). The
passage reads:

> 'Declaratory judgments in the sphere of annulment of marriage raise a number   *h*
> of problems. There is no doubt that the court has power under R.S.C., O. 15, r. 16
> to grant a declaration as to the validity of a foreign nullity decree, i.e. whether such
> a decree will be recognised in England. The situation is different if the validity of
> a marriage falls for initial consideration before an English court. In that case the
> recognition of a foreign nullity decree is not in issue. The one question is whether
> the marriage is to be regarded as valid under the English rules of private   *j*
> international law.'

I confess that I do not find these comments of Dr North of assistance in the present case
because he does not appear to have been considering the problems that arise when the
validity of a second marriage depends on recognition of a foreign nullity decree in

respect of a first marriage. In deciding how to exercise my discretion in the instant case
I have to return to first principles and, in applying them, I accept the submission on
behalf of both interveners that the dicta and decision in the line of cases beginning with
Kassim v Kassim are relevant guides.

When the court is asked to pronounce a declaratory judgment it is always right for it
to consider both the purpose and the likely effect of the declaration that is sought. Here,
there is no dispute about the purpose. The petitioner hopes, by means of a declaration
that the Belgian nullity decree is entitled to be recognised here, to take an important step
forward towards establishing the validity of her Messina marriage and her ultimate goal
of securing a share in the English estate of Eugenio Messina. The effect of the declaration
prayed for would be less than clear; there could still be potential issues to be resolved,
including the question whether the English court could give full retrospective effect to
the Belgian decree so as to validate the Messina marriage in English law and the relevance
of public policy in relation to the validity of that marriage and the right of succession to
immovable property in England.

In the light of what I have said, I am firmly persuaded that it would be wrong for me
to grant a declaration under RSC Ord 15, r 16 in this case, even if other necessary
conditions for such a declaration were fulfilled. In the first place, I consider that, if a
specific procedure is prescribed by statute to enable a litigant to achieve a precise purpose
in defined circumstances that exist in the relevant case, the court should not enable the
litigant to invoke an alternative and less direct discretionary procedure, unless there is a
persuasive reason for doing so. In particular, I do not consider that the court should
make a declaratory judgment under RSC Ord 15, r 16 in such circumstances when the
effect would be to enable the litigant, merely by the choice of the declaration sought, to
circumvent a specific statutory procedure designed for the determination of the
underlying issue. In the present case no reason, so far as I am aware, and certainly no
persuasive reason, has been advanced for proceeding under RSC Ord 15, r 16 rather than
under s 45 of the Matrimonial Causes Act 1973. It is possible that at one stage the
petitioner may have had doubts about her continuing status as a British subject or may
have been apprehensive about relying on it to found the jurisdiction of the court, but
neither of these points has been argued on her behalf before me.

Second, even if the general principle that I have just stated may be criticised on the
ground that it is too wide, it should apply in my judgment in cases where the specific and
relevant procedure is that provided by s 45 of the Matrimonial Causes Act 1973: see also
rr 109 to 112 of the Matrimonial Causes Rules 1977, SI 1977 No 344. That section and
the rules are designed to ensure that the public interest is fully considered and that all
persons with a proper interest in the application shall be joined as parties to the
proceedings if they wish. The requirement of notice to the Attorney General is
mandatory; he has to be a respondent on the hearing of the application and in any
subsequent proceedings relating thereto; and the court has to give directions relating to
other parties. Further, if any proposed petitioner has any doubt about his status as a
British subject for the purpose of the section, he may apply to the High Court for a decree
declaring his right to be deemed a British subject. These provisions were drawn attention
to by Ormrod J in *Collett v Collett* and they underline the undesirability of permitting a
litigant to petition by an alternative procedure without the statutory safeguards. In this
case the inappropriateness of proceeding under RSC Ord 15, r 16 has been illustrated by
the unavoidable delay that has occurred since the early hearings because I thought it
necessary to invite the Queen's Proctor to consult with the Attorney General about the
issues raised by the first petition and the procedural implications. There does not appear
to be any provision enabling the Queen's Proctor to intervene in proceedings for a
declaration, and it has been necessary for me to give leave to the Attorney General to
intervene on the hearing of the first petition: see *Adams v Adams (Attorney General
intervening)* [1970] 3 All ER 572 at 576–577, [1971] P 188 at 197–198.

A third reason for refusing to exercise my discretion to grant a declaration under RSC
Ord 15, r 16 in the instant case is that it raises questions of public policy that should be

considered, if they have to be decided, in their full and proper context. The nub of this case is the disputed validity of the petitioner's marriage to Eugenio Messina, and *a* recognition of her Belgian decree of nullity is, or may be, only one of the issues that the court must decide ultimately. It would be wrong, therefore, in my judgment, for the court to permit the petitioner to divide the case up into separate compartments for her own convenience when there are wide questions of public importance to be considered.

Fourth, this is a case in which there has already been litigation, including appeals, in the courts of three countries, and representatives of the Messina family have felt *b* compelled to intervene on each occasion. Whatever the merits of their present case may be, they have the right to submit that it is the petitioner's duty to put the effective issue before the court now by means of the most appropriate procedure so that finality can be achieved at the minimum expense to the parties and with the maximum speed. This argument is, of course, relevant to the question of costs but I regard it as material also to the exercise of my discretion. I can see no justification for a protracted hearing in pursuit *c* of the limited declaration prayed for in the first petition.

For all these reasons, therefore, my decision is that the prayer of the first petition for a declaration should be rejected.

The issues that arise on the second petition   *d*

As I have indicated earlier in this judgment, it is common ground that the petitioner is entitled to petition under s 45 of the Matrimonial Causes Act 1973 for a declaration that her marriage to Eugenio Messina in San Remo on 12th March 1970 was a valid marriage. This she has now done by her petition dated 20th April 1979 and all the necessary parties are before the court. The respondent was, of course, dead when the petition was presented, but this does not affect the validity of the proceedings and it has *e* not been suggested to me that it is necessary for either his estate or his next of kin to be represented in the particular circumstances of the case.

According to the English rules of private international law, the petitioner's capacity to marry in 1970 was governed by the law of her ante-nuptial domicile. If her 1954 marriage to the respondent was a valid marriage, her domicile in March 1970 was her dependent domicile, namely England, as I have already found. If, however, her 1954 *f* marriage was void ab initio, she had acquired by 1970 a domicile of choice in Italy. The validity of the petitioner's marriage to Eugenio Messina turns, therefore, on the validity in March 1970, according to English law, in the widest sense, of the 1954 marriage here.

The only proceedings in England that are relevant now to this question were those before Ormrod J in 1971 (see [1971] 2 All ER 1046, [1971] P 322) and the subsequent abandoned appeals against his rejection of the prayers of both her petitions for nullity. *g* In English law, therefore, as the position was in March 1970, the 1954 marriage was valid, and there has been no English decision to alter that position. If that remains the position, the petitioner did not have the capacity, according to the law of her domicile, to contract a valid marriage to Messina in March 1970. In Belgium, however, she obtained a declaration on 9th June 1972 from the Kortrijk County Court that the 1954 marriage was invalid ab initio, and this decision was affirmed by the Court of Appeal in *h* Ghent on 27th April 1973. What then is the effect of the Belgian decree on the capacity of the petitioner to marry in March 1970 according to the English rules of private international law?

It is clear that as a first step towards answering this question, I have to consider whether the Belgian decree should be recognised by the English court. If the question is answered in favour of the petitioner, it will be necessary to consider the precise extent to which the *j* decree should be recognised and the impact of such recognition on the petitioner's capacity to marry in March 1970.

It is agreed between the parties to the present proceedings that recognition here of Belgian decrees is now governed by the provisions of the Anglo-Belgian convention to which I have already referred. I have summarised earlier in this judgment the general

effect of the provisions of art 3 and I need not repeat the summary here. What I now
a have to consider is whether any of the specific exceptions particularised in art 3(1) to the
general rule of mutual recognition apply in the present case. The relevant exceptions
are:

> '(a) In the case in question the jurisdiction of the original court is not recognised
> under the rules of Private International Law with regard to jurisdiction observed by
b > the court applied to . . .
> '(c) The judgment is one which is contrary to the public policy of the country of
> the court applied to;
> '(d) The judgment is in respect of a cause of action which had already at the date
> when it was given, as between the same parties, formed the subject of another
> judgment which is recognised under the law of the court applied to as final and
> conclusive . . .'
c

I will consider each of these exceptions in turn in the order (a), (d), (c).

*Is the Kortrijk County Court to be recognised as a court of competent jurisdiction
under the English rules of private international law?*

　　As I have said earlier, the judgment of the three judges sitting in the Kortrijk County
d Court did not refer to the question whether it was a court of competent jurisdiction,
presumably because this had been conceded on behalf of the respondent and had not
been challenged on behalf of the intervener, Salvatore Messina. According to Professor
Francis Rigaux, the expert in Belgian law who gave evidence on behalf of the petitioner
before me, the relevant provision of the Belgian Judicial Code is art 638, which provides
that—

e

> 'Where the various grounds contained in this part of the Code are insufficient to
> determine the competence of the Belgian courts over foreigners, the plaintiff may
> bring the action before the judge of the place where he himself has his domicile or
> place of residence.'

　　This is subject to the provisions of art 636 but I need not read the translation of that
f article here. As for the definition of domicile or place of residence for this purpose, art 36
defines it as the place where a person is registered on the register of population:
registration is, therefore, decisive.

　　In the present case the petitioner was registered from 21st May 1970 as resident at
Deerlijk within the jurisdiction of the Kortrijk court and she remained resident and
registered continuously thereafter at all relevant times. Thus, she had been resident for
g just over 18 months within that court's jurisdiction when she presented her petition for
nullity there on 6th December 1971.

　　On her behalf, counsel now submits that the Kortrijk court was of competent
jurisdiction according to the English rules of private international law on four grounds,
listed in the order of counsel's preference as follows: (1) that the petitioner was domiciled
in Belgium; (2) that she had a real and substantial connection with Belgium; (3) that she
h was of Belgian nationality; and (4) that she was habitually resident in Belgium.

　　Counsel on behalf of the intervener disputes each of these grounds and urges me to
hold that the Belgian decree should not be recognised because the parties were neither
domiciled nor resident there at the commencement of the proceedings and remained
domiciled in England according to English law. However, counsel on behalf of the
Attorney General invites me to accept the jurisdiction of the Belgian court because the
j petitioner had been resident in Belgium for more than a year when her proceedings there
began. He suggests also that the facts that the petitioner was living in Belgium and had
a real and substantial connection with Belgium may be a sufficient alternative basis for
accepting the Belgian jurisdiction, although the Attorney General has reserved his
position as to the correctness of the decision of Bagnall J in *Law v Gustin* [1976] 1 All ER
113, [1976] Fam 155.

A convenient starting place for consideration of the problem is the present English statutory provisions governing domestic jurisdiction in nullity, which are contained in *a* s 5(3) of the Domicile and Matrimonial Proceedings Act 1973, which came into force on 1st January 1974. They are as follows:

> 'The Court shall have jurisdiction to entertain proceedings for nullity of marriage if (and only if) either of the parties to the marriage—(*a*) is domiciled in England and Wales on the date when the proceedings are begun; or (*b*) was habitually resident in England and Wales throughout the period of one year ending with that date; or (*c*) *b* died before that date and either—(i) was at death domiciled in England and Wales, or (ii) had been habitually resident in England and Wales throughout the period of one year ending with the date of death.'

It is to be noted that apart from the special provisions of sub-para (*c*), the provisions are identical with those governing proceedings for divorce or judicial separation and closely *c* similar to those for proceedings for death to be presumed and a marriage to be dissolved.

In the field of recognition of foreign nullity decrees there are no provisions similar to those contained in the Recognition of Divorces and Legal Separations Act 1971. That Act, which came into force on 1st January 1972, followed in time the decision of the House of Lords in *Indyka v Indyka* [1967] 2 All ER 689, [1969] 1 AC 33. The main relevant provisions are contained in s 3 and are to the effect that the validity of an *d* overseas divorce or legal separation is to be recognised if either spouse was habitually resident in, or a national of, that country at the date of the institution of the proceedings in the country in which the decree was obtained. There is also a provision that the reference to habitual residence is to be deemed to include a reference to domicile in relation to countries the law of which uses the concept of domicile as a ground of jurisdiction in matters of divorce or legal separation. *e*

In my judgment it is right for me to look to the speeches delivered in *Indyka v Indyka* for guidance in determining the present jurisdictional issue and I consider that the guidance to be found there is fully sufficient to decide it. Counsel for the intervener submits that this is an incorrect approach because the House of Lords in that case was dealing only with the validity of a foreign divorce decree, and he argues that different considerations are relevant in relation to a nullity decree, which may have retrospective *f* effect. I am unable to accept this argument for a number of reasons. In the first place, I can find nothing in the speeches in *Indyka v Indyka* to suggest that similar reasoning would be inapplicable to the recognition of foreign nullity decrees. Second, although there is substance in the point that a nullity decree may have wider effects than a divorce decree, the English approach to jurisdiction in nullity has been relatively lax in comparison with that adopted in divorce. The history of this difference of approach is *g* outlined and explained in the Law Commission's published working paper (Law Com No 38 (1971)) and need not be repeated here. At pp 8 and 9 of the paper, the authors discussed the differences between void and voidable marriages and the effect of the Nullity of Marriage Act 1971 and then went on to say (at para 11):

> 'But these differences between the two types of nullity seem to us to be irrelevant *h* for the purpose of determining whether the English courts should have jurisdiction. That, as we have said, should depend on whether the parties have a sufficient connection with England for it to be proper for the English Courts to make a decree. That connection cannot, as we see it, reasonably differ according to whether the decree is retrospective or prospective, declaratory or operative. And, as the essential consequences of any nullity decree are identical with those of a divorce, *j* the connection ought, in our view, to be the same as that required to afford jurisdiction in divorce.'

I respectfully agree; and the Law Commission's specific recommendations were embodied in the Domicile and Matrimonial Proceedings Act 1973. I can see no basis, therefore, as a matter of general principle and apart from statutory provisions, for

adopting more stringent tests in relation to the recognition of foreign nullity decrees
a than would be applied to divorce decrees; and no authority has been cited to me to
compel me to do so. On the contrary, the principle enunciated by Lord Wilberforce in
Indyka v Indyka was applied by Bagnall J in *Law v Gustin* to recognition of a foreign nullity
decree, although he expressed some doubt as to the precise test to be applied. More
recently, Baker P in *Perrini v Perrini* [1979] 2 All ER 323, [1979] Fam 84 expressly agreed
with the decision of Bagnall J in applying the principles of *Indyka v Indyka* to a decree of
b nullity.

The effect of *Indyka v Indyka* was analysed by Ormrod J in his judgment in the present
petitioner's English nullity suit (see [1971] 2 All ER 1046 at 1051–1057, [1971] P 322 at
331–337). The judge had to consider the validity of a Nevada divorce obtained by the
respondent's first wife. In view of what Ormrod J said in his judgment, I am reluctant
to embark on further citations from the speeches in *Indyka v Indyka*, but it is necessary for
c me to do so because of their relevance to the present petitioner's own different
circumstances in December 1971. I begin with Lord Reid ([1967] 2 All ER 689 at 702–
703, [1969] 1 AC 33 at 68):

d 'I think that the need would best be met by reviving the old conception of the
matrimonial home and by holding that, if the court where that home is grants a
decree of divorce, we should recognise that decree. In this matter I can see no good
reason for making any distinction between the husband and the wife. If we
recognise a decree granted to the one, we ought equally to recognise a decree
granted to the other; but if the husband leaves the matrimonial home and the wife
remains within the same jurisdiction I think that we should recognise a decree
granted to her by the court of that jurisdiction. I find much more difficulty in
accepting the view that if a wife parts from her husband and goes to live by herself
e in a new jurisdiction, her residence there, whether for three years or any other
period, must necessarily be accepted as sufficient to require us to recognise a decree
granted to her. It would certainly be reasonable that, where such a wife is habitually
resident within that jurisdiction and has no present intention of leaving it, we
should recognise a decree granted to her there; but I do not wish to go further than
that without fuller consideration in an appropriate case.'

f Lord Morris said ([1967) 2 All ER 689 at 707, [1969] 1 AC 33 at 75–76):

'Even if the decision in *Travers v. Holley* ([1953] 2 All ER 794, [1953] P 246) was
new law, I would consider that it was both reasonable and desirable. If a deserted
wife may obtain a decree in England under the conditions laid down in 1937 (and
now contained in s. 40 (1) (a) of the Act of 1965) it seems to me to be reasonable to
g recognise a decree granted in another country in the exercise of a comparable
jurisdiction. So also if jurisdiction is exercised in England on the basis of three
years' residence by a wife if the conditions of s. 40 (1) (b) are satisfied, it seems to me
to be reasonable to recognise a decree granted to a wife in another country that
accepts jurisdiction in similar circumstances. These significant statutory exceptions
to the rules which previously adhered so closely to domicil as the basis and the only
h basis for jurisdiction would seem to justify, if not to require, recognition of decrees
of dissolution granted in another country in the exercise of a jurisdiction similar to
or, I would say, substantially similar to, that exercised by the court in England. I
would, therefore, approve the decision in *Travers v. Holley*. Nor do I see any reason
why after the passing of the Law Reform (Miscellaneous Provisions) Act, 1949, our
courts should not recognise the decree of the Czech court on the basis that though
j made before December, 1949, it was made by the court of a country in which the
wife had been ordinarily resident for three years. The issue which the judge tried
in the present case was whether the husband had been free to marry in March,
1959. In my view, he was free to marry because after December, 1949, our courts
were entitled to treat the Czech decree of January, 1949, as having dissolved the
husband's first marriage.'

Lord Pearce also expressed approval of the ground of recognition accorded by *Travers v Holley* and went on to say ([1967] 2 All ER 689 at 717, [1969] 1 AC 33 at 90–91):   *a*

> 'On the facts of the present case I accept the view of the majority of the Court of Appeal ([1966] 3 All ER 583, [1967] P 233) that the marriage in 1959 was good although the Czechoslovakian divorce was granted in 1949, a few months before this country extended its jurisdiction by allowing resident wives to obtain divorce in our courts. The ground of recognition rests not on any exact measure of our own jurisdiction, but on the wider ground of public policy in which our own jurisdiction *b* is a most important element. The facts which made it right for our courts to have wider jurisdiction and give wider recognition existed at the date of the Czech decree, even though those facts did not until a few months later result in the statute by which this country took wider jurisdiction. When once the appreciation of these facts has been brought home to our courts by Parliamentary extension of their jurisdiction, their recognition should be retrospective. Also, if our courts were *c* asked in 1959, at the date of the marriage, whether the husband was free to remarry, how could public policy tolerate the answer, "No, because, although we have for ten years been ourselves taking similar jurisdiction in such a case as this, we did not start to do so until a few months after the date of the Czechoslovakian decree"? In my opinion the question whether a foreign decree should be recognised should be answered by the court in the light of its present policy, regardless (within reason) of *d* when the decree was granted.'

Lord Wilberforce put the matter rather differently when he said ([1967] 2 All ER 689 at 727, [1969] 1 AC 33 at 105):

> 'How far should this relaxation go? In my opinion, it would be in accordance *e* with the developments that I have mentioned and with the trend of legislation— mainly our own but also that of other countries with similar social systems—to recognise divorces given to wives by the courts of their residence wherever a real and substantial connexion is shown between the petitioner and the country, or territory, exercising jurisdiction. I use these expressions so as to enable the courts, who must decide each case, to consider both the length and quality of the residence *f* and to take into account such other factors as nationality which may reinforce the connexion. Equally they would enable the courts (as they habitually do without difficulty) to reject residence of passage or residence, to use the descriptive expression of the older cases, resorted to by persons who properly should seek relief here for the purpose of obtaining relief which our courts would not give.'

Later he commented on *Travers v Holley* as follows ([1967] 2 All ER 689 at 727–728, *g* [1969] 1 AC 33 at 106–107):

> '... I am unwilling to accept either that the law as to recognition of foreign divorce (still less other) jurisdiction must be a mirror image of our own law or that the pace of recognition must be geared to the haphazard movement of our legislative process. There is no reason why this should be so, for the courts' decisions as regards *h* recognition are shaped by considerations of policy which may differ from those which influence Parliament in changing the domestic law. Moreover, as a matter of history, it is the law as to recognition which has led and that as to domestic jurisdiction which has followed, and Parliament, by refraining from legislating as to recognition (as with minor exceptions it has done) must be taken to have approved this divergence. So I would not regard the *Travers v. Holley* rule as *j* amounting to more than a general working principle that changes in domestic jurisdiction should be taken into account by the courts in decisions as to what foreign decrees they will recognise. If the principles of recognition of foreign decrees of divorce are placed on the more general basis which I have suggested (rather than being governed by the quasi-mathematical application in reverse of

domestic legislation) I have no fears that uncertainty will be introduced into the

a law. The courts are well able to perform the task of examining the reality of the connexion between the resident petitioner wife and the jurisdiction invoked, bearing in mind, but not being rigidly bound by, the developments of domestic jurisdiction. In so acting, I am convinced that they are more likely to reach just, and to avoid artificial, results.'

b Finally, for the sake of completeness, I should refer to the paragraph from the speech of Lord Pearson which reads as follows ([1967] 2 All ER 689 at 731, [1969] 1 AC 33 at 111):

'It seems to me that, subject to appropriate limitations, a divorce granted in another country on the basis of nationality or on the basis of domicil (whether according to English case law or according to a less exacting definition) should be recognised as valid in England. Also if the law of the other country concerned

c enables a wife living apart from her husband to retain or acquire a separate qualification of nationality or domicil for the purpose of suing for divorce, and the jurisdiction has been exercised on the basis of that qualification, that would not, normally at any rate, be a reason for refusing recognition.'

Lord Pearson expressed the view that there was difficulty about recognising the
d validity in England of divorces granted in other countries on the basis merely of residential qualifications but he approved the *Travers v Holley* principle and concluded ([1967] 2 All ER 689 at 731, [1969] 1 AC 33 at 113):

'Such recognition should be given on two grounds. First, the *Travers v. Holley and Holley* principle should be applied as mentioned above. Secondly, the divorce was granted in Czechoslovakia on the basis of the wife's proved Czechoslovakian
e nationality, and there was no lack of real and substantial connexion with Czechoslovakia.'

In the light of these speeches I am satisfied that I should hold that the Belgian court was a court of competent jurisdiction in the present case. By December 1971 the petitioner had been habitually resident in Belgium for over 18 months; and, on the majority view
f in *Indyka v Indyka* it is right to apply the *Travers v Holley* principle now, even though the Domicile and Matrimonial Proceedings Act 1973 did not come into force until just over two years after the commencement of the Belgian proceedings. Moreover, on a wider basis, the petitioner was habitually resident in Belgium in December 1971, with no present intention of leaving it, and she was a person with a real and substantial connection with that country. Although I have expressed doubts as to the validity of her allegedly
g retained Belgian nationality, she had been a Belgian national for the first 24 years of her life, she had lived more than half her life there and all her family connections were with Deerlijk. She fulfilled amply, therefore, the qualifications suggested in each of the speeches in *Indyka v Indyka*, other than Belgian domicile in the English sense and possibly Belgian nationality.

It follows that it is unnecessary for me to make any finding on the additional argument
h for the petitioner that the Belgian court had jurisdiction on the basis of her independent domicile in Belgium in 1971 because she was asserting that the 1954 marriage was void ab initio. Counsel for the petitioner has submitted that recognition should be accorded on this basis in view of the assumption by the English court of jurisdiction in like circumstances (see *White v White* [1937] 1 All ER 708, [1937] P 111 and *De Reneville v De Reneville* [1948] 1 All ER 56, [1948] P 100); and he has referred to a decision of the
j Ontario Court of Appeal, *Re Capon, Capon and O'Brien v McLay* (1965) 49 DLR (2d) 675 in which a Nevada decree of nullity was recognised on this ground. It would be unwise of me to venture into this unattractive maze (see, e g, Dicey and Morris on the Conflict of Laws (9th Edn, 1973, p 367)) and I am glad not to do so. I am comforted by the thought that the argument may now be obsolescent in view of the abolition in English law of a wife's dependent domicile since January 1974.

Was the Belgian judgment given in respect of a cause of action which had already, at the date when it was given, as between the parties, formed the subject of a decision by Ormrod J in Messina v Smith which is recognised under English law as final and conclusive?   *a*

The question whether the English rules of estoppel apply in matrimonial cases has been much debated in the past and the debate continues. In the present case, counsel on behalf of the Attorney General rightly concedes that the decision of Ormrod J in *Messina v Smith* [1971] 2 All ER 1046, [1971] P 322 was not a decision in rem, but he argues that, *b* in the terms of art 3(1)(d) of the Anglo-Belgian convention, the decision was nevertheless final and conclusive. He submits, firstly, that Ormrod J was deciding the issue of the validity of the petitioner's 1954 marriage, and that the petitioner could and should have raised before him the issue that she subsequently raised in the Belgian proceedings, namely the absence of an intention by the parties to the marriage ceremony to cohabit. Counsel for the Attorney General suggests that, because she failed to do so, the rule of *c* estoppel applies and Ormrod J's decision is to be recognised as final and conclusive under English law. In this connection counsel points to the concluding words of the judgment of Ormrod J where he said ([1971] 2 All ER 1046 at 1059, [1971] P 322 at 339): 'Mr Smith, therefore, was free to marry the petitioner in this case on 11th August 1954 and that marriage is a valid marriage.'

Alternatively, and more narrowly, counsel for the Attorney General argues that the *d* decision of Ormrod J was final and conclusive in England on the material issue, namely lack of consent to the marriage. This issue was dealt with very fully in the part of the judgment that is not reported and it is useful to read here what Ormrod J said:

'My conclusion, therefore, on this part of the case is that the petitioner did in fact know at the time of the ceremony on 11th August 1954 that it was a marriage *e* ceremony, and that the purpose of it was to enable her to obtain British nationality and a British passport. In my judgment that is sufficient to dispose of her case on the first petition. It may well be that in the years which followed she did wonder from time to time whether it was a "real" marriage and asked the Messina brothers whether she was "really" married, and was told not to worry about it and that it was only a "paper" marriage. In one sense it was an unreal marriage in that it was never *f* intended that the normal relationship of husband and wife should be established between Mr Smith and herself. But this cannnot affect the question which I have to determine, namely, whether the marriage was, in law, a valid marriage. Where a man and a woman consent to marry one another in a formal ceremony, conducted in accordance with the formalities required by law, knowing that it is a marriage ceremony, it is immaterial that they do not intend to live together as man and *g* wife. It is, of course, quite otherwise where one of the parties believes that the ceremony is something different, for example a formal betrothal ceremony as in *Kelly v Kelly* (1932) 148 LT 143 and the cases there referred to, or as in *Mehta v Mehta* [1945] 2 All ER 690, a ceremony of religious conversion. In such cases the essence of marriage, the mutual exchange of consents accompanied by the formalities requried by law, is missing and such marriages are, therefore, void or perhaps *h* voidable. On the other hand, if the parties exchange consents to marry with due formality, intending to acquire the status of married persons it is immaterial that they intend the marriage to take effect in some limited way or that one or both of them may have been mistaken about, or unaware of, some of the incidents of the status which they have created. To hold otherwise would impair the effect of the whole system of law regulating marriages in this country, and gravely diminish the *j* value of the system of registration of marriages on which so much depends in a modern community. Lord Merrivale P in *Kelly v Kelly* said (at 144): "In a country like ours, where the marriage status is of very great consequence and where the enforcement of marriage laws is a matter of great public concern, it would be intolerable if the marriage law could be played with by people who thought fit to a go to a register office and subsequently, after some change of mind, to affirm that it was not a marriage because they did not so regard it." See also the observations of Hodson J in *Way v Way* [1949] 2 All ER 959, [1950] P 71 approved by the Court of Appeal in *Kenward v Kenward* [1950] 2 All ER 297, [1951] P 124 and *Silver v Silver* [1955] 2 All ER 614, [1955] 1 WLR 728. In these circumstances it is unnecessary, and, indeed, inappropriate to consider the submissions which counsel have made on the hypothesis that the petitioner did not know that the ceremony was a marriage

b ceremony. The question whether in such circumstances the marriage is void or voidable, or whether it can be approbated, or whether some species of estoppel can operate to prevent its validity being attacked, must wait for another day. But, out of respect to the able and interesting arguments which have been addressed to me, I would make one general observation. The concept of marriage seems to be evolving from status towards contract, in accordance with Maine's generalisation,

c and recent changes in the law relating to divorce and matrimonial property may mark an acceleration of this process but it is not yet by any means complete. At this stage, therefore, the task of reconciling concepts arising from the law of contract, which are second nature to all common lawyers, with an institution which has not yet detached itself from its ancient roots in the quite different system of the canon law, is bound to be extremely difficult, particularly where words such as "consent"

d are common to both systems, but may have different implications in each.'

   In response to the arguments on behalf of the Attorney General, counsel for the petitioner says that Ormrod J was not asked to declare the 1954 marriage valid and could not do so. He says further that an invalid marriage cannot be converted into a valid marriage by operation of the rules of estoppel, and he cites in support of his argument

e the judgment of Phillimore J in *Hayward v Hayward* [1961] 1 All ER 236, [1961] P 152; see also the decision of the British Columbia Supreme Court in *Postnikoff v Popoff* (1964) 46 DLR (2d) 403 at 410, in which Wilson CJSC said: 'I do not think that a marriage can be established by estoppel.' In his second main submission, counsel for the petitioner said that it is not accepted on behalf of the petitioner that Ormrod J would have been bound to ignore Belgian law or that the petitioner would necessarily have failed if the

f issue as to a sham marriage had been argued before him. Third, it is said that the petitioner was entitled to choose her forum to argue the latter issue: see *Torok v Torok* [1973] 3 All ER 101, [1973] 1 WLR 1066. Finally, counsel submits that both the cause of action and the issues before Ormrod J were different from those before the Belgian court: the causes of action in England were the respondent's alleged bigamy, lack of knowledge by the petitioner of the nature of the ceremony and duress, whereas the cause

g of action in Belgium was a sham marriage. Although consent in a broad sense was in issue before both courts, it was a different classification or aspect of consent that was before the Belgian court.

   I do not think that it would be right to apply art 3(1)(d) of the Anglo-Belgian convention on the basis that Ormrod J made a binding declaration of the validity of the 1954 marriage. It is true that he did say in his judgment that the marriage was valid.

h In saying this, however, he was merely recognising what had been said in a quite general sense by Viscount Dunedin in *Salvesen (or von Lorang) v Austrian Property Administrator* [1927] AC 641 at 662, [1927] All ER Rep 78 at 86, that is: 'The judgment in a nullity case decrees either a status of marriage or a status of celibacy.' It is clear from what I have said earlier in this judgment that Ormrod J in *Messina v Smith* was fully aware that a binding declaration as to the validity of the 1954 marriage could only be made in other

j proceedings.
   One of the difficulties in considering the application of estoppel in the field of nullity is the uncertain status of the decision of the Court of Appeal in the bigamy case of *Wilkins v Wilkins* [1896] P 108 and that of Hill J in *Woodland v Woodland* [1928] P 169. These decisions were criticised by Phillimore J in *Hayward v Hayward* and he expressed a preference for the line of cases stemming from *Miles v Chilton* (1849) 1 Rob Eccl 684. A

helpful discussion of the history of these cases and of the conflict, by Mr Dimitri Tolstoy QC is to be found in his article published in 1968 (84 LQR 245). Most recently there has *a* been reference to the judgment in *Hayward* in *Rowe v Rowe* [1979] 2 All ER 1123, [1980] Fam 47. In the latter case, both Orr LJ and Sir Stanley Rees referred to *Hayward* because it had been prayed in aid in argument on behalf of the Official Solicitor. However, *Rowe* was a case of issue estoppel rather than cause of action estoppel, and the major effect of it is that the decision in *Lindsay v Lindsay* [1934] P 162, [1934] All ER Rep 149 has been disapproved. It does not appear that the correctness and limits of the decision in *Hayward* *b* were directly in point but, in view of the approving references to that decision, it would be unsafe for me to base my decision in the present case on the authority of *Wilkins* and *Woodland*, and I do not regard it as necessary to do so. I will confine myself, therefore, to two comments on *Hayward* that are relevant for my purposes. The first is that, according to the later section of the judgment, the issue of estoppel did not truly arise (see [1961] 1 All ER 236 at 243, [1961] P 152 at 161) and the factual background of the case *c* was very different from the present one. Secondly, I do not consider that the concept of a marriage void ipso jure or void ab initio, in the sense that a bigamous marriage is void, can usefully be applied to consideration of the Smith marriage in English law in the widest sense. One has only to read the passage in the judgment of Ormrod J in *Smith v Messina* that I have just quoted to see how inappropriate the analogy of a bigamous marriage would be. *d*

Approaching this case from first principles, I think that it is useful to begin with the statement of Denning LJ in *Thompson v Thompson* [1957] 1 All ER 161 at 165, [1957] P 19 at 29. It reads:

'The question in this case is, however, whether those ordinary principles do apply to the Divorce Division. The answer is, I think, that they do apply, but subject to the important qualification that it is the statutory duty of the Divorce Court to *e* inquire into the truth of a petition—and of any countercharge—which is properly before it, and no doctrine of estoppel by res judicata can abrogate that duty of the court. The situation has been neatly summarised by saying that in the Divorce Court "estoppels bind the parties but do not bind the court": but this is perhaps a little too abbreviated. The full proposition is that, once an issue of a matrimonial offence has been litigated between the parties and decided by a competent court, *f* neither party can claim as of right to re-open the issue and litigate it all over again if the other party objects (that is what is meant by saying that estoppels bind the parties): but the Divorce Court has the right, and indeed the duty in a proper case, to re-open the issue, or to allow either party to re-open it, despite the objection of the other party (that is what is meant by saying that estoppels do not bind the court). Whether the Divorce Court should re-open the issue depends on the circumstances. *g* If the court is satisfied that there has already been a full and proper inquiry in the previous litigation, it will often hold that it is not necessary to hold another inquiry all over again. But if the court is not so satisfied, it has a right and a duty to inquire into it afresh. If the court does decide to re-open the matter, then there is no longer any estoppel on either party. Each can go into the matter afresh.' *h*

Much of the discussion in the cases of the application of estoppel in the matrimonial jurisdiction has turned on the inquisitorial function of the court in that jurisdiction; but, if reliance on an issue estoppel does not interfere with any inquisitorial function of the court, the ordinary rules as to issue estoppel will apply even in the matrimonial jurisdiction (see, e g, *Conradi v Conradi* (1868) LR 1 P & D 514). Moreover, in general, in cases where the estoppel merely has the effect of preventing a party who was unsuccessful *j* in the first litigation from bringing forward the allegation again in later proceedings, it may rarely conflict with any inquisitorial function (see, e g, *Bright v Bright* [1953] 2 All ER 939, [1954] P 270).

I am unable to accept in the present case that reliance on estoppel between the parties to the first English proceedings in relation to the issue of consent to the marriage in a subsequent English proceedings would conflict with any inquisitorial function of the court. That function in nullity derives from the principles on which the ecclesiastical courts acted prior to the Matrimonial Causes Act 1857, whereas the duty to inquire in divorce is now defined by s 1(3) of the Matrimonial Causes Act 1973; but the effect is substantially the same in both jurisdictions. There is no conflict of public policy here of the kind that frequently arises when estoppel is considered in relation to ancillary proceedings (see per Ormrod J in *Porter v Porter* [1971] 2 All ER 1037 at 1039, [1971] P

b 282 at 284). If there is conflict at all, I consider that the balance of advantage rests heavily in favour of the application of estoppel if the rules, properly interpreted, may be applied.

In the present case the court is concerned with cause of action estoppel rather than issue estoppel, to use the helpful distinction that has been developed in recent times. The relevant cause of action before Ormrod J was lack of consent, of which the petitioner's lack of knowledge of the nature of the ceremony and the alleged duress to which she was

c subject (an allegation that was eventually abandoned) were merely facets or issues. It was for this reason that Ormrod J dealt with the issue of consent so fully in his judgment. Again, before the Belgian court the cause of action was lack of consent and the decision of the court was founded on a statutory provision dealing with consent in the most general terms. Article 146 of the Belgian Civil Code reads, in translation:

d 'No marriage exists where there is no consent. The absence of any consent, which is an essential element to a marriage, results in the marriage being absolutely void, a claim which may be invoked by either of the two parties.'

The alleged lack of intention to cohabit was merely a facet or issue to be considered in deciding whether or not there was consent.

It follows that I am unable to accept counsel for the petitioner's submission that the

e Belgian court was concerned with a distinct and separate cause of action. I have, of course, considered carefully counsel's own suggested classification of the different aspects of consent in his book on the Formation and Annulment of Marriage (2nd Edn, 1969, pp 274–305) and the structure of English nullity law both before and since the enactment of the Nullity of Marriage Act 1971. Equally, I have in mind the continuing debate as to the correctness of Dicey and Morris's rule (Conflict of Laws (9th Edn, 1973, p 275, r

f 35)) which states:

'No marriage is (it seems) valid if by either party's domicile one party does not consent to marry the other.'

It is sufficient for me to say that consideration of the structure strengthens, in my judgment, rather than weakens the conclusion that the petitioner's relevant cause of

g action in both England and Belgium was the same, namely, the absence of consent to marry.

In deciding whether or not cause of action estoppel applies in the present case I have to decide whether the petitioner could and should have raised the sham marriage issue on the basis of Belgian law in the proceedings before Ormrod J. It is necessary, therefore, for me to refer to the oft-quoted dictum of Wigram V-C in *Henderson v Henderson* (1843)

h 3 Hare 100 at 115, [1843–60] All ER Rep 378 at 381–382:

'The plea of *res judicata* applies, except in special cases, not only to points upon which the Court was actually required by the parties to form an opinion and pronounce a judgment, but to every point which properly belonged to the subject of the litigation and which the parties, exercising reasonable diligence, might have brought forward at the time.'

j This dictum has been criticised in some of the recent cases. Thus, Orr LJ said in *Rowe v Rowe* that it was too widely stated and Lord Wilberforce in *Carl-Zeiss-Stiftung v Rayner and Keeler Ltd (No 2)* [1966] 2 All ER 536 at 584, [1967] 1 AC 853 at 965 said of it that it was a decision of a colonial court and a simple example of a cause of action estoppel. However, in that case Lord Wilberforce was concerned with the limits of issue estoppel

rather than cause of action estoppel; and, in the same case, Lord Upjohn said in relation
to cause of action estoppel ([1966] 2 All ER 536 at 572, [1967] 1 AC 853 at 946):   *a*

'Res judicata itself has two branches: (a) Cause of action estoppel—that is where
the cause of action in the second case has already been determined in the first. To
such a case the observations of WIGRAM, V.-C., in *Henderson v. Henderson* apply in
their full rigour. These observations have been so often approved in your Lordships'
House that I will not repeat them.'

b

I am fully satisfied that the *Henderson v Henderson* principle should be applied in the
present case, whether or not its application should be restricted in other cases. All the
material facts were before the English court; the reality of the marriage in the light of
those facts was considered fully by Ormrod J; all that was lacking was an argument on
behalf of the petitioner, on the basis of the law of her ante-nuptual domicile, that the
marriage was void for lack of an intention by the parties to cohabit and a decision on that   *c*
argument was fundamental to the judgment given on the question of consent.
Furthermore, the nature of the argument must have been in the minds of some, at least,
of the petitioner's legal advisers because her Belgian petition was filed whilst an appeal to
the Court of Appeal here was still pending.

I do not regard my conclusion as in conflict with *Torok v Torok* or as infringing in any
way the principle that the English court will not, in general, go behind the judgment of   *d*
a foreign court and consider its reasoning (see, e g, *Pemberton v Hughes* [1899] 1 Ch 781).
Here, I am concerned with the strict application of art 3(1)(d) and the rules of res judicata
in English Law. I have sought to give the words 'cause of action' in that article an
interpretation that is appropriate in the sphere of nullity and that conforms with English
decisions in the field of res judicata; and it matters not, in my judgment, that many of
those decisions postdate the Anglo-Belgian convention.

e

Finally on the interpretation of art 3(1)(d), it has not been suggested in argument
before me that there was any relevant difference in the parties before the Belgian court
and those before the English court. The proceedings in England and Belgium were
between the petitioner, Smith and Salvatore Messina, and the role of the public
prosecutor in the Belgian proceedings was similar to that of amicus curiae. As Professor
Rigaux explained in his evidence before me, the public prosecutor would not initiate   *f*
proceedings in Belgium to annul a sham marriage where the purpose of the marriage
was the acquisition by a Belgian of foreign nationality because the question of Belgian
public policy would not be involved in those circumstances.

Before leaving this part of the case, I should say that I do not consider that it would be
appropriate for me to speculate as to what conclusion Ormrod J might have reached, if
the argument based on Belgian law had been put to him, or as to what might have   *g*
happened in the event of an appeal. Substantial argument has been addressed to me on
this question on behalf of each of the parties to the present proceedings but I do not
consider that it is either necessary or desirable for me to prolong this judgment by
comment on Dicey and Morris's rr 34 and 35 (Conflict of Laws (9th Edn, 1973, p 275))
in relation to consent or on the relevance and applicability of the much criticised rule in
Sottomayer v de Barros (No 2) (1879) 5 PD 94, [1874–90] All ER Rep 97.   *h*

The question of public policy

In view of my conclusion on the application of art 3(1)(d) of the Anglo-Belgian
convention it is clear that the petitioner's second petition must be dismissed. If her
Belgian decree is not entitled to be recognised, and the question of her consent to the   *j*
marriage is res judicata in English law, there can be no basis for a finding that her
marriage to Eugenio Messina is valid in English law. The application of art 3(1)(c) of the
Anglo-Belgian convention raises separate and difficult questions, and I do not think that
it would be helpful for me to attempt to resolve them in the present circumstances. If
the case proceeds further, an appellate court will not require further findings from me.

a In so far as Belgian law may be relevant, however, I should say that I found Professor Rigaux to be an impressive and authoritative witness. In the course of the interrupted hearings of the case, considerable argument has been addressed to me on the issue of English public policy and its relevance to recognition of the Belgian decree. I will, therefore, say something briefly about the nature of the argument in deference to the submissions of counsel, before concluding this judgment.

There is clearly a direct conflict of policy between the English courts and the Belgian *b* courts in relation to the validity of a marriage between parties who do not intend to cohabit. The Belgian approach, and that of a number of other countries, is that it is contrary to its public policy that a foreigner should be permitted to obtain the benefit of its nationality by going through a ceremony of marriage with one of its nationals when there is no intention by the parties to cohabit. This approach has been developed in a number of European decided cases, to which Professor Rigaux has referred (see also *c* Jackson, Formation and Annulment of Marriage (2nd Edn, 1969, p 292); and in Belgium it has evolved in judicial decisions on art 146 of the Civil Code, which I have read earlier, rather than in any more specific statutory provision. The same rule is applied where a Belgian national marries a foreigner with a view to acquiring a foreign nationality, but in that case public policy is not involved.

In England our rules have been developed from a different starting point. We have *d* emphasised the sanctity of the marriage bond freely entered into with due formality and have not been prepared to accept that private reservations nullify the consequences that flow from the marriage ceremony. On this point I would not wish to add to what Ormrod J has said in *Messina v Smith.*

The fact that this conflict exists does not lead inevitably to the conclusion that to recognise the Belgian decree in the present case would offend against English public *e* policy. What is decisive is the criterion of policy which is to be applied to recognition of a foreign decree. In the present case, counsel for the petitioner argues that the test is simply whether the Belgian decree offends English notions of substantial justice. He says with force that the application of public policy in this field should not now be extended: in relation to the recognition of foreign decrees, particularly those of neighbouring European countries, the categories of grounds of non-recognition based on public policy *f* should be regarded as closed, or virtually closed. In his submission the Maltese cases, such as *Formosa v Formosa* [1962] 3 All ER 419, [1963] P 259, are in a special compartment and have no relevance.

I agree with counsel that, at least on a narrow view, the concept of a marriage being void because the parties do not intend to cohabit might not be regarded as offending English notions of substantial justice. It is a concept recognised in a number of highly *g* civilised countries (see, eg, the Scottish decision in *Orlandi v Castelli* 1941 SC 113) and might be said to be analogous to impotence and wilful refusal to consummate in relation to the validity of marriage. In my opinion, however, counsel's argument does not dispose of the public policy issue. One aspect of it, which was touched upon in the judgment of Ormrod LJ in *Quazi v Quazi* [1979] 3 All ER 897, [1979] 3 WLR 833 is whether the interpretation of public policy is to be restricted in the way that counsel *h* suggests. The wording of art 3(1)(c) of the Anglo-Belgian convention is similar to that now to be found in s 8(2)(b) of the Recognition of Divorces and Legal Separations Act 1971. It remains to be decided hereafter whether 'public policy' in both statutory provisions embraces a wider notion than that of substantial justice in English eyes. If it is akin to the French concept of 'ordre publique', it may have wider connotations.

In the present case it has been argued on behalf of the Attorney General and the *j* Messina family that English public policy dictates that the Belgian decree should not be recognised. Part of the argument against recognition has been based on the history of the petitioner's conduct and intentions from 1954 onwards, to which I have referred in sufficient detail at the outset of this judgment; and counsel for the intervener has included in his argument a suggestion that the petitioner's approbation of the Smith marriage should be regarded as a bar to both her present petitions. It is suggested that to grant the declarations prayed for would offend English views of substantial justice in the light of the petitioner's conduct; and that she should not be enabled, therefore, to establish a right to immovable property in England by the avenue of recognition of the foreign decree.   *a*

On a wider basis counsel for the Attorney General has argued that it is contrary to the public policy of all civilised countries that foreign prostitutes and other undesirable aliens should make use of the marriage laws to contract sham marriages in order to obtain a nationality with a view to enabling them to pursue criminal activities and avoid deportation. He suggests that this view is reflected specifically in the marriage law of   *b* Belgium and some other countries in the particular way that I have indicated, whereas in England the question remains one of public policy because there is no specific provision in our marriage laws dealing with the point. Our marriage laws, in general, refuse to allow parties to a sham marriage of the relevant kind to avoid it. Counsel for the Attorney General argues, therefore, that it would be contrary to English public policy   *c* to allow the parties to obtain elsewhere a release recognised here when such a release could not be obtained by the parties in this country.

For my part, I doubt whether the application of public policy in this case should be decided by reference to the petitioner's conduct as a prostitute, her avoidance of deportation or the manner in which she has conducted the various phases of her nullity proceedings. There is, however, the crucial wider issue that arises from the differing   *d* attitudes of the English and Belgian courts to sham marriages generally; and my instinct suggests that the application of public policy may have to be decided ultimately on the basis of our different rules for the acquisition by a spouse of British nationality. The different British approach to acquisition of nationality is well illustrated here by the fact that the petitioner will remain a British national unless and until she is divested of that status by a separate procedure, whether or not her Smith marriage is declared or   *e* recognised to be void ab initio. The rationale of the Belgian view would appear, therefore, to be inapplicable in this country; and, in Belgium itself, the acquisition by a Belgian national of a foreign nationality does not raise directly any question of public policy for its courts.

Petitions dismissed.   *f*

Solicitors: *Theodore Goddard & Co* (for the petitioner); *Lieberman Leigh & Co* (for the intervener); *Official Solicitor.*

Georgina Chambers   Barrister.

   g

Appeal
The petitioner appealed to the Court of Appeal.

Joseph Jackson QC and *Mathew Thorpe QC* for the petitioner.
Ian Karsten for the intervener.
Anthony Hollis QC and *Nicholas Wilson* for the Attorney General.   *h*

Cur adv vult

8th July. The following judgments were read.

ARNOLD P. The petitioner was born in Belgium with a domicile of origin there and   *j* on 11th August 1954 went through a ceremony of marriage in London with the respondent who was a domiciled Englishman. There was an issue before the judge whether the petitioner retained her domicile of origin up to the date of this ceremony. The judge decided that she did, and no issue has been raised before this court on that matter.

On 12th March 1970 the petitioner went through a ceremony of marriage at San
a Remo, Italy, with Eugenio Messina who died on the same date, leaving estate including
landed estate in England to which or to a share in which the petitioner is entitled only if
her marriage to Eugenio Messina was valid.

The petitioner, in proceedings commenced in the Family Division by petition dated
29th May 1970, claimed a declaration of nullity on the ground that she did not effectively
consent to the 1954 ceremony as a marriage ceremony through various causes of
b ignorance, misunderstanding and duress. In that proceeding there intervened Salvatore
Messina, a brother of Eugenio, and a person claiming to be entitled to, or to a share in,
the estate of Eugenio Messina if the latter's purported marriage to the petitioner was
invalid.

On 7th May 1971 the petition was dismissed by Ormrod J (see [1971] 2 All ER 1046,
[1971] P 322) who held that the petitioner did know that the 1954 ceremony was a
c marriage ceremony and that she had consented to it. On the same date, Ormrod J
dismissed a further petition for nullity dated 6th November 1970 which had been filed
by the petitioner, claiming that the 1954 marriage was bigamous on the ground that a
previous marriage of the respondent had not been dissolved, a matter which requires no
further mention in this judgment. The petitioner appealed from those dismissals but on
7th March 1972 her appeal was dismissed by consent.

d On 6th December 1971 the petitioner started proceedings in the court of first instance
at Kortrijk, Belgium, claiming a declaration that the marriage contracted between herself
and the respondent on 11th August 1954 was nullified ab initio. The grounds which she
put forward were in the alternative, first, that she never intended to contract a marriage
with the respondent at all or, second, that the marriage contracted with the respondent
was only a mock marriage, purely a formality, unaccompanied by any intention to live
e together and contracted for the purpose of her acquiring British nationality in order to
avoid being deported from England. In those proceedings the respondent admitted the
allegations put forward in the petitioner's second alternative plea. Salvatore Messina
intervened in the Kortrijk proceedings to dispute the relief claimed, on the alternative
grounds that the matter had already been decided by the judgment of Ormrod J, or that
the matter fell to be decided in accordance with English law with the same conclusion as
f that which Ormrod J had reached.

The Kortrijk court on 9th June 1972 gave judgment for the relief claimed by the
petitioner. In so doing, they rejected the intervener's claim that the judgment of
Ormrod J constituted a res judicata, on the ground that Belgian law recognised for the
purposes of res judicata only those foreign judgments which alter the status of persons,
and not those which refused so to do; they rejected the petitioner's plea that she had not
g consented to the ceremony of her marriage to the respondent through any want of
knowledge, but upheld her plea based on the allegation of a mock marriage, saying that
a marriage is valid in Belgian law only if each of the parties satisfies the conditions which
their personal status imposes, namely, in the case of the petitioner, an intention to form
a community of life.

Salvatore Messina appealed from this decision to the Court of Appeal at Ghent on 30th
h August 1972. On 27th April 1973 the Court of Appeal at Ghent dismissed the appeal.
It held that the ground advanced by the petitioner of a want of consent through lack of
knowledge was barred by the res judicata afforded by Ormrod J's judgment, but that this
res judicata did not extend to the mock marriage point, because that had not been argued
before Ormrod J, and they upheld the latter point because consent to such a marriage did
not amount to a real consent and in the absence of such a consent the marriage did not
j exist according to Belgian law. There has been no appeal from the decision of the Court
of Appeal at Ghent. In so far as it is relevant to consider the ratio decidendi of the Belgian
courts it must, in my view, be the ratio adopted by the Court of Appeal in Ghent rather
than that adopted by the court of first instance at Kortrijk which demands consideration.

By a petition in the Family Division dated 7th September 1973 the petitioner claimed
a declaration that the decree of the Kortrijk court was entitled to be recognised. Again

Salvatore Messina intervened. He denied that the Kortrijk decree was entitled to
recognition, and relied on the decision of Ormrod J as conclusively determinate of the   *a*
validity of the marriage of the petitioner and the respondent, saying that the petitioner
was estopped from challenging that validity. He further denied the competence of the
Kortrijk court, and disputed the recognition of the Kortrijk decree on the ground that it
was based on Belgian public policy which was contrary to English public policy on the
same matter. He also put forward the assertions that the marriage between the petitioner
and the respondent was contracted on the basis of English law and that the petitioner,   *b*
having approbated that marriage, was not entitled to the relief claimed.

In the course of the hearing of that petition before Waterhouse J, the question arose
whether the relief claimed could or would be granted by the court, having regard to the
discretionary nature of the jurisdiction to grant declarations under RSC Ord 15, r 16, and
the existence of a specific jurisdiction under s 45 of the Matrimonial Causes Act 1973 to
grant declarations of the validity of a petitioner's marriage, in the light of the   *c*
circumstance that the underlying object of the petitioner was to establish the validity of
her marriage to Eugenio Messina. As a result the petitioner asked for, and was granted
by order dated 22nd March 1979, leave to file a further petition under s 45, and for the
consolidation of that petition when filed with the pending cause, which had been
commenced by the petition dated 7th September 1973.

The new petition was filed on 20th April 1979 and in it the petitioner asserted that the   *d*
decree of the Kortrijk court and the judgment of the Court of Appeal of Ghent were a
valid decree and judgment declaring the ceremony of marriage to the respondent null
and void ab initio, and were entitled to recognition in this country, and further asserted
that her marriage to Eugenio Messina was a lawful marriage subsisting at his death.

Salvatore Messina having died, Attilio Messina was substituted for him as intervener
in the petition dated 7th September 1973, with effect from the 30th August 1977, and   *e*
Attilio Messina intervened also in the petition dated 20th April 1979 on behalf, in each
case, of all those interested in the estate of Eugenio Messina, on the footing that the
latter's marriage to the petitioner was invalid.

Waterhouse J delivered judgment in both petitions on 8th May 1979 and dismissed
them both. He noticed the respondent's British nationality throughout his life and held
him to have had an English domicile at the date of his marriage to the petitioner on 11th   *f*
August 1954. He referred to the petitioner having lived in England for about nine years
after the date of that marriage, carrying on the trade of a prostitute, with many
convictions in that trade. He held that she had applied in September 1954 for registration
as a citizen of the United Kingdom and Colonies, in reliance on having married such a
citizen, and was duly registered as a citizen on 23rd September 1954, and that she had
shortly afterwards obtained, and thereafter until at least June 1970 held, a British   *g*
passport which was renewed in 1965 on her representation that she had retained her
citizenship. He held that the petitioner had retained her Belgian domicile until her
marriage to the respondent.

Waterhouse J held that the court had jurisdiction to make the declaration sought
by the first current petition because the respondent was resident in England at the date
of the petition, but that he had a discretion whether or not to exercise that jurisdiction   *h*
and in that discretion he decided not to do so. He accordingly dismissed the first
petition.

In my view, the judge was quite right to take this course. There is no doubt that the
purpose of the petitioner in seeking the declaration which she sought by the first petition
was that of establishing the validity of her marriage to Eugenio Messina. There is no
doubt that the procedure under s 45 of the Matrimonial Causes Act 1973 was available   *j*
to her for that purpose. There is no doubt that the jurisdiction to grant declarations
under RSC Ord 15, r 16 is, in general, a discretionary jurisdiction. It is argued on behalf
of the petitioner that if, as is her claim, the court is obliged by a convention having
binding force to give recognition to the Belgian decree this involves an obligation to
make a declaration giving such recognition under RSC Ord 15, r 16, so that in the

relevant context the jurisdiction ceases to be discretionary. I do not think that this is
a so. Any such obligation to afford recognition is, in my judgment, limited to the
affording of such recognition by whatever may be the due process of law. The
jurisdiction therefore, in my view, remains discretionary. Having regard to the special
safeguards and provisions applicable to the obtaining of a declaration of validity of
marriage under s 45 imposed by s 45(6) and (7) and r 109 of the Matrimonial Causes
Rules 1977, SI 1977 No 344, it seems to me to be an entirely valid ground for exercising
b the discretion against making under RSC Ord 15, r 16 a declaration designed to achieve
a purpose which could be achieved by s 45, that the court will thereby ensure submission
to the special safeguards and provisions to which I have referred.

Waterhouse J approached the question whether relief should be granted on the second
petition on the basis of an agreement between the parties that the recognition of Belgian
decrees in this country was governed by the provisions of the convention dated 2nd May
c 1934 between Belgium and Great Britain and Northern Ireland for the reciprocal
enforcement of judgments in civil and commercial matters (see the Reciprocal
Enforcement of Foreign Judgments (Belgium) Order in Council 1936, SR & O 1936 No
1169, Sch).

Before considering the terms of that convention, it is relevant to observe that in this
court the validity of the marriage between the petitioner and the respondent falls to be
d determined by reference to English law. The petitioner had a Belgian domicile
immediately before marriage, and the respondent an English domicile. In those
circumstances, according to declared law binding on this court, the lex loci celebrationis,
that is the law of England, applies to determine the validity of the marriage (see
Sottomayor v De Barros (1877) 2 PD 81; (1879) 5 PD 94, [1874–80] All ER Rep 97, and
Ogden v Ogden [1908] P 46, [1904–7] All ER Rep 86). In a situation in which there is a
e judgment of the High Court of this country deciding the matter according to English
law in one sense, and a judgment of a foreign court deciding the matter by reference to
foreign law in an opposite sense, there can in my judgment be nothing in the common
law of this country to require a subsequent court here, recognising that English law
applies, to give recognition to the foreign judgment in preference to the English
judgment. Thus it is only if recognition is required by statute or by an instrument
f having statutory force that the opposite result will follow.

The question of recognition of the Belgian decrees in this case was decisive in the
judge's approach to the question raised by the second petition because all the parties
approached the matter on the basis that the validity of the petitioner's marriage to
Eugenio Messina turned on the validity in March 1970 according to English law,
including English private international law, of the 1954 marriage. It was not pleaded,
g nor was it argued, either before Waterhouse J or in this court, that the validity of the
1970 marriage was governed by Italian law, nor was there any evidence of Italian law to
indicate whether it would accord retrospectivity to the Belgian decree which it has now
recognised or whether, if it did not, it would, by the application of the doctrine of renvoi,
whether based on the lex loci celebrationis or on the husband's nationality or otherwise,
have resorted to the English law for its conclusion as to the validity of the marriage
h between the petitioner and the respondent.

The convention provides in art 3(1) that judgments in civil and commercial matters
given by any such court as the court at Kortrijk or the court at Ghent shall, in the courts
of the territory of the other party, in casu the courts of this country, be recognised in all
cases where no objection to the judgment can be established on any of the enumerated
grounds, which include:

j
    '(a) In the case in question the jurisdiction of the original court is not recognised
    under the rules of Private International Law with regard to jurisdiction observed by
    the court applied to . . .
    '(c) The judgment is one which is contrary to the public policy of the country of
    the court applied to;

'(d) The judgment is in respect of a cause of action which had already at the date
when it was given, as between the same parties, formed the subject of another
judgment which is recognised under the law of the court applied to as final and
conclusive . . .'

In this court some reference was made to the question whether a matrimonial matter
such as that arising in the present case is comprehended within the description of civil
and commercial matters so as to make art 3 of the convention applicable at all, but in
view of the fact that in art 4(3)(a) it was thought necessary to exclude from the operation
of art 4(1) judgments in matters of family law or status, in my view, in the absence of any
comparable exclusion in art 3, the correct conclusion is that art 3 is apt to extend to
matrimonial matters.

Waterhouse J held, as regards exception (a), that the Kortrijk court was to be recognised
as a court of competent jurisdiction under the English rules of private international
law. He considered this matter principally against the background provided by the fact
that the petitioner was, at the date of her invocation of the Belgian jurisdiction, living in
Belgium and had a real and substantial connection with that country and, in reliance on
the decision of *Indyka v Indyka* [1967] 2 All ER 689, [1969] 1 AC 33 and the extension of
the principle of that decision from divorce to nullity by *Law v Gustin* [1976] 1 All ER 113,
[1976] Fam 155 and *Perrini v Perrini* [1979] 2 All ER 323, [1979] Fam 84, held that the
Belgian court was of competent jurisdiction. In my view *Law v Gustin* and *Perrini v
Perrini* were decided correctly and I come to the same conclusion as Waterhouse J for the
same reason.

The question of public policy, mentioned in the exception in art 3(1)(c) has been
argued in this court under a number of heads. It has been suggested that the Belgian
judgment was one which was contrary to the public policy of this country because of the
conduct of the petitioner in having relied on the valid existence of the marriage which
she sought to have declared void for the acquisition of British nationality and the
protection which that afforded to her from the deportation which might otherwise have
ensued as a consequence of her multifarious convictions. As regards this head of
argument it does not seem to me possible to reject recognition of a foreign decree on the
ground of public policy merely because the person who obtained that decree has behaved
with impropriety in relation to the subject matter of the decree; rather must any such
ground of rejection be based on the intrinsic character of the decree or of the foreign law
applied in it as being offensive to some principle of policy favoured in this country. It is
however also argued that these conditions are fulfilled since, it is said, the impugning of
the validity of a marriage on the ground that the parties consenting to it did not intend
that it would constitute any real marital relationship is contradictory of the policy of this
country which regards as unacceptable the uncertainty which would flow from the
possibility that a marriage, apparently valid according to all external appearance, could
be invalid because of some secret reservation. Certainly such a conception is entirely
foreign to English law, but I am not persuaded that it is so offensive to English
conceptions of propriety as to justify the view that a foreign judgment based on it must
be refused recognition as contravening the public policy of this country. In my
judgment therefore, exception (c) does not operate.

Exception (d) involves a conception closely akin to the English doctrine of estoppel per
rem judicatam but it is not a provision which makes that doctrine applicable to the
question to be decided. The language of the exception raises a number of issues which
in my judgment require to be examined in relation to the terms by which they are
raised. It is not in doubt that the judgment of the Belgian court was a judgment between
the same parties as were parties to the decision of Ormrod J, and it is not in doubt that the
latter is recognised in English law as final and conclusive. The question is whether
the Belgian judgment was in respect of a cause of action which formed the subject of the
judgment of Ormrod J. The cause of action before Ormrod J was the claim of the
petitioner to a declaration that the marriage celebrated between her and the respondent

was null and void, and the cause of action in the petition to the Kortrijk court was the
a petitioner's claim to a declaration that the same marriage was nullified ab initio. Thus
described, it appears to me that the two causes of action are the same. It is true that, in
deciding whether or not to grant the declaration asked for, the English court did not have
to consider the question whether the petitioner's consent to a purely formal marriage was
in truth a consent at all but was able to confine its attention to the question whether the
petitioner in fact consented to the marriage such as it was and was able to refuse the
b declaration on the ground, decided by the Belgian court in the same sense, that she had
so consented. This does not however, in my judgment, make the cause of action a
different cause of action and I do not consider it necessary to come to a conclusion as to
the extent to which the doctrine of *Henderson v Henderson* (1843) 3 Hare 100, [1843–60]
All ER Rep 378 operates in relation to such a case as this. If it were necessary so to do, my
conclusion would be that that principle does operate so as to apply the estoppel not only
c to the point on which the court was required by the parties to form an opinion and
pronounce a judgment, but to every point which properly belonged to the subject of the
litigation and which might with reasonable diligence have been brought forward. In
Carl-Zeiss-Stiftung v Rayner and Keeler Ltd (No 2) [1966] 2 All ER 536 at 572, [1967] 1 AC
853 at 946 Lord Upjohn said that the observations in *Henderson v Henderson* applied in
their full rigour to cause of action estoppel and, if that were the matter under
d consideration as distinct from an analogous provision in a convention of binding
statutory force, my view would be that that dictum should be applied so as to
comprehend within the estoppel the point which might have been brought forward by
the petitioner before Ormrod J, that Belgian law should be applied to the validity of the
marriage between the petitioner and the respondent and that this should have been
declared void for want of a consent to a real marriage. In my judgment therefore
e exception (*d*) operates to take the case out of the ambit of art 3 of the convention, so that
if this is the instrument governing the recognition of the Belgian decree, it would not
operate to require any such recognition.

In this court there has been some resiling from the agreement that the convention
rules the matter of recognition, and alternative arguments have been presented on the
provisions of the Foreign Judgments (Reciprocal Enforcement) Act 1933. Part I of that
f Act has no direct application to the recognition of foreign judgments; that subject is dealt
with in s 8 which is not framed so as to yield up its meaning easily or quickly. It provides
by sub-s (1) that a judgment to which Part I of the Act applies, or would have applied if
a sum of money had been payable thereunder, whether it can be registered or not, and
whether, if it can be registered, it is registered or not, is to be recognised in any court in
the United Kingdom as conclusive between the parties thereto in all proceedings founded
g on the same cause of action. Part I applies to any judgment of a superior court of a
foreign country if it is final and conclusive as between the parties thereto and there is
payable thereunder a sum of money (of a non-fiscal and non-penal nature), and it is given
after the coming into operation of the order in council directing that Part I shall extend
to the foreign country concerned (see s 1(2)). The order in council (SR & O 1936 No
1169) extending the Act to Belgium came into operation on 26th November 1936. Since
h the requirement that a sum of money should be payable thereunder is eliminated for
recognition purposes by the language of s 8(1), which also makes it irrelevant to consider
registrability, all that is needed to require a judgment to be recognised in the terms of
that section is, in my judgment, that it shall be of a superior court and final and
conclusive as between the parties thereto. If the Belgian decree was a judgment within
the meaning of the Act, it is therefore to be recognised under and subject to the
j provisions of s 8. A judgment is defined in s 11(1) as meaning a judgment given in any
civil proceedings, and a question has arisen whether civil proceedings extend to embrace
matrimonial proceedings. However, by s 11(2) the expression 'action in personam' is to
be deemed not to include matrimonial proceedings. This phrase occurs only in s 4(2) of
the Act in a context in which the deemed exclusion would be altogether unnecessary if
a judgment did not comprehend a judgment in matrimonial proceedings, and, in my

view therefore, the Belgian decree comes within the ambit of recognition under s 8. Section 8(2) excludes from the operation of the section any judgment which has not been registered but in respect of which it is shown that if it had been registered the registration would have been set aside on an application for that purpose on some ground other than the altogether irrelevant ground specified in s 8(2)(a). The setting aside of registered judgments is dealt with in s 4(1) of the Act, and that subsection provides, under para (b), that the registration of a judgment may be set aside if the registering court is satisfied that the matter in dispute in the proceedings in the original court had previously to the date of the judgment in that court been the subject of a final and conclusive judgment by a court having jurisdiction in the matter. In my judgment the matter in dispute in the proceedings in Kortrijk and Ghent (the original court for the purposes of s 4(1)) was the subject of Ormrod J's judgment, namely the question of the right to have the marriage between the petitioner and the respondent declared void, and accordingly in my view the registration of the Belgian decree if registrable could have been set aside under s 4(1)(b) of the Act. Moreover, in my judgment the discretion imported into the jurisdiction to set aside the registration by the use of the permissive 'may' would have been exercised so as to set it aside because an English court in exercising that discretion would be moved so to do by the circumstance that the registered judgment was based on foreign law in a context in which the English court recognised English law as governing the case and English law had been the basis of the previous conflicting English decision.

Accordingly in my judgment there is no basis for holding that the Belgian decree is binding on the English court or that the 1954 marriage between the petitioner and the respondent was invalid. Since this conclusion is a necessary step in the direction of the relief sought on the second petition, that must fail. I would therefore dismiss the appeal.

CUMMING-BRUCE LJ. I have had the advantage of considering the judgment that Eveleigh LJ is about to deliver. I agree with the judgment just delivered by Arnold P, subject to the qualification expressed by Eveleigh LJ.

EVELEIGH LJ. I am doubtful whether the Foreign Judgments (Reciprocal Enforcement) Act 1933 or the 1934 convention apply to matrimonial cases such as this. In *Black-Clawson International Ltd v Papierwerke Waldhof-Aschaffenburg AG* [1975] 1 All ER 810 at 817, [1975] AC 591 at 617 Lord Reid said, referring to the Act:

> 'It is said that the effect of these obscure words in s 8(1) is to make the section apply to all judgments which would come within the terms of s 1(2) if condition (b) were omitted. Besides the fact that this would be a very odd way of bringing in another section of the Act that cannot be right. If (b) is omitted then s 1(2) would apply to every kind of judgment including judgments on status, family matters and in rem. No one suggests that s 8 was meant to deal with them.'

The fact that matrimonial causes are mentioned in the Act and convention can be explained on the basis that money judgments in matrimonial causes are envisaged.

Also I would need further argument before deciding that the principle in *Henderson v Henderson* (1843) 3 Hare 100, [1843–60] All ER Rep 378 applies to this kind of case.

The validity of the marriage between the petitioner and the respondent, as Arnold P has said, falls to be determined by reference to English law (see *Ogden v Ogden* [1908] P 46, [1904–7] All ER Rep 86). We have had no evidence as to Italian law and the Belgian decree. I agree that it is only if recognition is required by statute or instrument having statutory force that the foreign judgment will be recognised in preference to the English judgment. Assuming, without so deciding, that the Act and the convention apply, I agree for the reasons stated in the judgment of Arnold P that there is no basis for holding the Belgian decree as binding on the English court or that the 1954 marriage is invalid.

a I also agree with what Arnold P has said in relation to RSC Ord 15, r 16. I too, therefore, would dismiss this appeal.

Appeal dismissed. Leave to appeal to the House of Lords.

Solicitors: *Theodore Goddard & Co* (for the petitioner); *Lieberman, Leigh & Co* (for the intervener); *Treasury Solicitor.*

b
                                                    Sumra Green   Barrister.

Plummer v P W Wilkins & Son Ltd

c QUEEN'S BENCH DIVISION
LATEY J
10th, 11th, 12th JUNE, 6th JULY 1980

Damages – Personal injury – Loss of earnings – Deduction of supplementary allowance paid after unemployment benefit ceasing – Whether supplementary allowance deductible from damages
d *awarded for plaintiff's loss of earnings.*

The plaintiff, a self-employed ceiling fixer, was injured when a trestle on which he was working collapsed because of the defendant's admitted negligence. The injury proved to be disabling and the plaintiff became unemployed. He received unemployment benefit and, when that ceased, a supplementary allowance under the Supplementary Benefit Act 1966. On the issue of quantum at the trial the defendant contended that both the
e unemployment benefit and the supplementary allowance amounting to £3,424 were deductible from the special damages for loss of earnings.

Held – Payments of supplementary allowance, like unemployment benefit, were deductible from the special damages awarded to a plaintiff for loss of earnings, since both
f benefits were similar in character in that qualifying recipients were entitled to them as of right, and if the supplementary allowance payments were not deducted the plaintiff would be in a better position than if he had not been injured (see p 93 *j* to p 94 *a* and p 95 *d* to *h*, post).

Dictum of Pearson LJ in *Parsons v BNM Laboratories Ltd* [1963] 2 All ER at 684 and *Nabi v British Leyland (UK) Ltd* [1980] 1 All ER 667 applied.

Dicta of Lord Reid in *Parry v Cleaver* [1969] 1 All ER at 558, 562 considered.
g *Foxley v Olton* [1964] 3 All ER 248 and *Basnett v J & A Jackson Ltd* [1976] ICR 63 not followed.

Notes
For deduction for benefits received and receivable in assessing damages in tort, see 12
h Halsbury's Laws (4th Edn) para 1152, and for cases on the subject, see 17 Digest (Reissue) 87–90, 32–46.

Cases referred in judgment
Basnett v J & A Jackson Ltd [1976] ICR 63, Digest (Cont Vol E) 418, 894*f*(i).
Cackett v Earl (1976) Times, 15th October.
j *Elridge v Videtta* (1964) 108 Sol Jo 137, 36(1) Digest (Reissue) 325, *1325.*
Foxley v Olton [1964] 3 All ER 248, [1965] 2 QB 306, [1964] 3 WLR 1155, 36(1) Digest (Reissue) 325, *1323.*
Nabi v British Leyland (UK) Ltd [1980] 1 All ER 667, [1980] 1 WLR 529, CA.
Parry v Cleaver [1969] 1 All ER 555, [1970] AC 1, [1969] 2 WLR 821, [1969] 1 Lloyd's Rep 183, HL, 36(1) Digest (Reissue) 320, *1295.*

Parsons v BNM Laboratories Ltd [1963] 2 All ER 658, [1964] 1 QB 95, [1963] 2 WLR 1273,
  [1963] TR 183, 42 ATC 200, CA, 17 Digest (Reissue) 90, 45.   *a*
Shaw v Cape Insulation Co Ltd (18th July 1977, unreported) QBD at Manchester.

Action

By a writ dated 6th December 1976 the plaintiff, Eddy Hardwick Plummer, claimed
against the defendant, P W Wilkins & Son Ltd, damages for personal injury arising from
the negligence or breach of statutory duty of the defendant, its servants or agents. The   *b*
defendant admitted liability. The question arose whether payments of supplementary
allowance made to the plaintiff who became unemployed as a result of the injury were
deductible from the special damages for loss of earnings. The facts are set out in the
judgment.

Colin F Sara for the plaintiff.
W R H Crowther QC and *Stephen Archer* for the defendant.   *c*

Cur adv vult

8th July.   **LATEY J** read the following judgment: This is an action for damages for
personal injury. The plaintiff, for much of his life, has been a skilled carpenter and joiner *d*
employed by others. In 1965 he set up his own business specialising in ceiling fixing.
New materials and new systems were being introduced. He did well, and, what was just
as important to him as his financial success, he was his own master.

On 5th March 1975 came the accident which caused the injury to his shoulder and
which has given rise to this action. A trestle platform, erected by the defendant, from
which he was working, collapsed. There is no need to go into more detail: liability is *e*
accepted by the defendant. He fell and injured his shoulder. The injury did not at first
appear serious. It turned out to be serious and disabling. He cannot raise his arm above
shoulder level and this continues to be so although a variety of treatments, including
surgery, have been carried out. It has meant the end of his business, that is his livelihood,
since 1975.

There are three heads of damages: first, special damages, that is what he has lost to *f*
date; second, general damages, that is to say compensation for pain, suffering and loss of
amenity since the accident to the present, and in the future; third, loss of earnings in the
future. I took time after the end of the hearing to consider my judgment for this reason:
after the accident the plaintiff received unemployment benefit for the statutory period.
When that expired he began to receive, and has continued to receive, supplementary
allowance under the Ministry of Social Security Act 1966 (the Supplementary Benefit Act *g*
1966). The defendant claims that the amounts, both of unemployment benefit and
supplementary allowance, which the plaintiff has received should be deducted from the
compensation which he would otherwise be entitled to.

For the plaintiff, it is accepted that as the law stands the amount of the unemployment
benefit must be deducted, because in *Nabi v British Leyland (UK) Ltd* [1980] 1 All ER 667,
[1980] 1 WLR 529 the Court of Appeal has so laid down, though in that case the Court *h*
of Appeal so held because it was bound by precedent but said that the matter should be
considered by the House of Lords. Counsel for the plaintiff informed me that inquiries
had been made and that there was not going to be an appeal in that case to the House of
Lords. He said that were it open to him he would argue that that decision, and earlier
cases which the Court of Appeal had felt bound to follow, were wrongly decided and that
unemployment benefit should not be deducted. But the Court of Appeal has never been *j*
called on to decide whether supplementary allowance, and its predecessor national
assistance, should or should not be deducted. That question has fallen to be considered
at first instance in the High Court. It has been differently decided by different judges.
Unfortunately, in some of these cases there is a report only of the conclusion and not of
the reasons.

a   In this case the amount of supplementary allowance is a substantial amount, £3,424, and whether or not it should be deducted from the damages to which the plaintiff would otherwise be entitled is of importance both to him and the defendant. Counsel have advanced their arguments on the point fully and helpfully and I think it is convenient to decide that matter first. It is unfortunate that it has not been decided by the Court of Appeal so that all concerned know where they stand. Counsel think, I suspect rightly, that in many cases the amount at stake is not sufficient to justify the expense of an
b   appeal. They further think that in the aggregate of cases over a year a large amount of money is at stake. As already mentioned, in *Nabi's* case the Court of Appeal gave a clear indication that the question whether or not unemployment benefit should be deducted should be considered by the House of Lords. After hearing the full and careful arguments by counsel in the instant case and the review of such authorities as there are, one hopes that there will soon be a suitable case taken to the House of Lords for a decision
c   both as to unemployment benefit and supplementary allowance in this context, so that the existing judicial doubts and dichotomy may be resolved.

      In *Parsons v BNM Laboratories Ltd* [1963] 2 All ER 658, [1964] 1 QB 95 the question for present purposes was whether the damages should be reduced by the amount of unemployment benefit which the plaintiff had received. The Court of Appeal held that they should. Pearson LJ posed the question in this form ([1963] 2 All ER 658 at 682,
d   [1964] 1 QB 95 at 141):

      'Are the sums of unemployment benefit received by the plaintiff to be brought into account in reduction of the damages for wrongful dismissal, or are they too remote to be brought into account for this purpose?'

      The answer to that question is in these terms ([1963] 2 All ER 658 at 684, [1964] 1 QB
e   95 at 143–144):

      'The common-sense answer is that of course it is not too remote. It is not "completely collateral". The dismissal caused the plaintiff to become unemployed, and therefore entitled, as a matter of general right under the system of state insurance and not by virtue of any private insurance policy of his own, to receive unemployment benefit. The effect of the dismissal was not to deprive him of all
f   income but to reduce his income by substituting unemployment benefit for his salary. It would be unrealistic to disregard the unemployment benefit, because to do so would confer on the plaintiff ... a fortuitous windfall in addition to compensation.'

      In this context is there any real distinction to be drawn between unemployment benefit, which ceases after the prescribed period has expired, and supplementary
g   allowance, or its predecessor, national assistance, which begins after unemployment benefit ceases? Were the matter at large, my view would have been, and anticipating is, that there is no valid distinction, but other judges have reached the contrary view. In *Eldridge v Videtta* (1964) 108 Sol Jo 137, Veale J held that national assistance benefit should not be deducted from the special damages. The report is a very short one. The case was decided on 3rd February 1964. Whether Veale J was referred to the decision of
h   the Court of Appeal in *Parsons's* case does not appear. He is reported as saying that no authority justifying the deduction of national assistance benefit had been cited to him. Such a deduction appeared to be wrong in principle and he was not prepared to make it.

      In *Foxley v Olton* [1964] 3 All ER 248 at 250, [1965] 2 QB 306 at 312 John Stephenson J held that national assistance grants were not deductible from the damages. He
j   observed: 'It is difficult to draw the line between what is too remote and what is not remote enough, and between the collateral and the completely collateral.' He held that the national assistance grants were too collateral and remote because of the discretionary nature of those grants. It is to be observed that unlike national assistance grants, supplementary allowances are not discretionary. A qualifying recipient is entitled to them as of right. Anticipating my own concluded view, unemployment benefit is

receivable as of right. Provided the claimant is otherwise qualified, as this plaintiff has been, he is entitled to supplementary allowances as of right. If unemployment benefit *a* is a deduction from damages, how can supplementary benefit not be? I can see no grounds for distinguishing one from the other in this context.

In *Parry v Cleaver* [1969] 1 All ER 555, [1970] AC 1 the plaintiff was a police constable. He had made compulsory contributions to a police pension fund which entitled him as of right to a pension on being discharged from the force for disablement. He was severely injured by a motor car driven negligently by the defendant *b* and he was discharged owing to disablement resulting from his injuries. The House of Lords, by a majority of three to two, held that the police pension should be ignored in assessing the damages under the head of financial loss. In his speech Lord Reid said ([1969] 1 All ER 555 at 558, [1970] AC 1 at 14):

> 'It would be revolting to the ordinary man's sense of justice, and therefore contrary to public policy, that the sufferer should have his damages reduced so that *c* he would gain nothing from the benevolence of his friends or relations or of the public at large, and that the only gainer would be the wrongdoer. We do not have to decide in this case whether these consideration also apply to public benevolence in the shape of various uncovenanted benefits from the welfare state, but it may be thought that Parliament did not intend them to be for the benefit of the wrongdoer.'

After referring to *Foxley v Olton* and *Eldridge v Videtta*, he said ([1969] 1 All ER 555 at *d* 562–563, [1970] AC 1 at 19):

> 'I find it difficult to draw a distinction between unemployment benefit and national assistance. The former could be regarded as a combination of insurance and national benevolence while the insurance element is absent from the latter. But there are here other considerations besides those with which I have dealt. There has *e* been no full argument about them and I do not propose to express any concluded opinion on this matter.'

Those dicta of Lord Reid were obiter, but coming from such a source they of course merit the most careful consideration and it is on the tenor of them that counsel for the plaintiff founds the main thrust of his argument.

In *Basnett v J & A Jackson Ltd* [1976] ICR 63 the plaintiff was made redundant and *f* received a redundancy payment. He further received unemployment benefit and, after that, supplementary benefit. The defendant accepted that the plaintiff was wrongly dismissed and most of the judgment is devoted to the argument whether or not the redundancy payment should be deducted from the damages. It was not apparently drawn to Crichton J's attention that, while national assistance grants were discretionary, supplementary benefit allowances are not. Crichton J followed what John Stephenson J *g* said in *Foxley v Olton* and held that the amount of the supplementary benefits should not be deducted from the damages.

In *Cackett v Earl* (1976) Times, 15th October the report merely records that Milmo J in a claim for damages for personal injuries held that unemployment benefit, industrial rehabilitation allowance and supplement benefits must all be deducted. Part of Hollings *h* J's judgment in *Shaw v Cape Insulation Co Ltd* (18th July 1977, unreported) is quoted in *Nabi v British Leyland (UK) Ltd* [1980] 1 All ER 667 at 675, [1980] 1 WLR 529 at 537–538. Hollings J held that unemployment benefit should be deducted but that supplementary benefits should not. In the passage quoted he said that he would quote briefly his reasons for the distinction but the statement of those reasons is not quoted. *Nabi v British Leyland (UK) Ltd* was concerned only with the question whether *j* unemployment benefit should be deducted, and in their judgment their Lordships expressed no view about supplementary benefit allowances.

Those are the authorities to which counsel referred. Counsel for the plaintiff contended that a distinction might be made on the ground that there are contributions from both employer and employee in the nature of insurance in the case of

unemployment benefit, whereas supplementary benefits are not directly linked to any
a contribution made by employer and employee. Yes, says counsel for the defendant, but
supplementary benefits come from public funds to which both plaintiff and defendant
contribute as taxpayers. Counsel for the plaintiff accepted realistically that it is difficult
to distinguish between unemployment benefit and supplementary benefit in any way
which can matter in this context. His main argument was along these lines: Lord Reid's
observations in *Parry v Cleaver* suggest that, were the deductibility of unemployment
b benefit, national assistance, supplementary benefits, payments from public benevolence
to be considered in the House of Lords, the decision would probably be that they should
not be deducted. There are similar indications, he says, in the judgment of the Court of
Appeal in *Nabi's* case. Accepting, as he must, that at the levels of a court of first instance
and of the Court of Appeal unemployment benefit must be deducted, there is no such
binding decision regarding supplementary allowance, and so, he argues, the court can
c and should follow the indications of Lord Reid and the Court of Appeal and not deduct
supplementary allowances; and of course he urges that other judges have taken this view,
though one, Milmo J, has not. I cannot myself accept this argument. Lord Reid's
indications are no more than indications and he points out that the matter was not fully
argued in the House. In *Nabi's* case the Court of Appeal goes no further than suggesting
that the point is ripe for decision by the House of Lords, as no doubt it is, in view of the
d dichotomy which has developed.

At first instance, if one kind of benefit, unemployment, must be deducted so, in my
opinion, must the other, supplementary, unless the character of the one is different from
the other in the relevant context of damages. I have been unable to discern any such
difference in character explained in the reported cases, nor have counsel in the instant
case been able to suggest any. Indeed, in my respectful opinion, there was no such
e difference of character between unemployment benefit and national assistance. To
adopt the words of Pearson LJ in *Parsons's* case, 'neither is too remote or completely
collateral'. Moreover after hearing counsel's very full and careful arguments I am by no
means persuaded that it is probable that the House of Lords would decide that these
payments of either kind should not be deducted. Leaving aside exemplary damages to
which essentially different considerations apply, the purpose of damages is to compensate
f the victim for what he has suffered and lost as a result of the tortious act of the
tortfeasor. It is not to fine the tortfeasor; it is not to put the victim in a better position
than he would have been had there been no tortious act; it is to put him in the same
position he would have been in had there been no tortious act. Unless the payments
concerned are deducted, he would be in a better position than if there had been no
tortious act. I add, parenthetically, that very different considerations apply in the case of
g a pension or charitable gifts or the like. As counsel for the defendant cogently put it,
'Would it be unfair to the plaintiff to deduct these payments?' Not in the slightest.
From one source or another he has received all the compensation to which he is entitled
to put him in the position he would have been had the accident not occurred. Is it unfair
to him not to confer on him a windfall profit? Why should he receive double
compensation?

h For these reasons, in my judgment, the payments of supplementary allowance as well
as those of unemployment benefit should be deducted from the otherwise agreed figure
of special damages. Parenthetically, I suppose yet another and perhaps wholly acceptable
solution might be for the tortfeasor to pay the full amount and, when the amounts were
met, the benefits to be repaid to public funds. But that would require legislation.

Next there are general damages, compensation for pain, suffering and loss of amenity.
j It is not necessary to review in detail the medical history which is set out in the agreed
reports. It is true, as counsel for the defendant says, that the results in this plaintiff's
private and personal life are not of the most serious kind. It is also true, as counsel for the
plaintiff says, that the restrictions on his activities are far from trivial. In particular he is,
and has always been, very close to his sons, 16 and 13 years of age now, and 11 and 7 at
the time of the accident. He taught them to swim, and until the injury they spent much

of their spare time swimming together. He has not been able, and will not be able, to do this or to enjoy other robust physical activities with them. In other respects he has been *a* and will continue to be somewhat restricted. The plaintiff is an intelligent man and will understand that reflecting pain, suffering and loss of amenity in terms of money cannot but be a largely artificial exercise. There is no, and cannot be any, scientific or arithmetical basis. All one can do is to draw on the experience of the courts over the years, remember that no two cases are ever identical, not overlook the changed value of money and try to reach a figure which is fair to both plaintiff and defendant. *b* Approaching this case in that way I have reached the sum of £5,000 under this head.

Finally, there is future loss of earnings. The plaintiff was aged 57 last February. He is a man who enjoyed work. He had a six-week course at an assessment centre and was advised that he was fit only for clerical work or sub-clerical or other light work not involving lifting or stretching upwards. He registered at the labour exchange and has attended every fortnight at the job centre. He has taken English and writing classes and *c* done a good deal of writing, including three plays, one of which he has sent to the BBC. He has had no luck with them yet. He has had one poem published and his future is encouraging. As well as attending the job centre he has watched the advertisements in the local newspaper and kept his eyes and ears open. He has not been able to find employment. It is far from easy for him at his age with the disablement and in the present conditions to find employment which he can manage. At Easter he did find a *d* part-time job directing traffic in a car park for one afternoon a week, and this he continues to do. He is not a man who enjoys idleness and he would have taken work if he could have found work which he could manage. The impression I am left with is that there is still a real possibility that he will find work, or some work, at some time, but that is not a strong probability and should only be reflected to a modest extent. Counsel I think are right in their suggestion that the most convenient method of taking this into *e* account in this case would be in fixing the multiplier rather than the multiplicand. Taking this factor into account along with the others I have reached 4½ years as the multiplier. So that the multiplicand, at the figure agreed, on the hypothesis that he earns nothing, will be multiplied by 4½. I will ask counsel to agree the arithmetic under this head and the earlier head of special damages. Then of course, there is interest.

f

Judgment for the plaintiff in the total sum of £27,206·70 with interest of £3,845.

Solicitors: *James Mason, Tucker & Son*, Newton Abbott (for the plaintiff); *Ashford, Penny & Harward*, Exeter (for the defendant).

K Mydeen Esq   Barrister.

Green v Green (Barclays Bank Ltd, third party)

FAMILY DIVISION

EASTHAM J

3rd OCTOBER 1980

Divorce – Financial provision – Avoidance of transaction intended to prevent or reduce financial relief – Power of court when making order setting aside transaction to give consequential directions for giving effect to order – Grounds of matrimonial home conveyed to third party – Third party giving charge to bank as security for advances – Whether if conveyance void court could give directions setting aside charge – Matrimonial Causes Act 1973, s 37(3)(4).

The husband and wife's matrimonial home, a large house with extensive grounds, was in their joint names. They sold 10½ acres of the grounds for £20,000 to an Isle of Man company which charged the land to a bank as security for certain advances. The wife received no part of the £20,000 paid by the company. The marriage broke down and after the divorce the wife claimed financial relief against the husband. The wife also applied to have the conveyance to the company set aside under s 37[a] of the Matrimonial Causes Act 1973 and gave notice to the bank to that effect. At the hearing of her application she contended, inter alia, that the charge was invalid ab initio because of certain irregularities between the company and the bank, but conceded that she could not directly attack the charge. She submitted, however, that if the court found that the conveyance could be successfully attacked under s 37(1) and (2) as against the husband it could, on making an order setting aside the conveyance, give directions setting aside or reducing the charge because s 37(3) gave the court an absolute discretion to 'give such consequential directions as it thinks fit for giving effect to the order (including directions requiring the making of any payments or the disposal of any property)'.

Held – The court could not set aside or reduce the charge under s 37(3) of the 1973 Act because—

(1) On the true construction of s 37(3), the court's power to give directions was restricted to giving directions requiring, for example, the repayment of any money which had been paid under the conveyance which had been set aside, and was not wide enough to enable it to give directions such as those sought by the wife (see p 99 c to f and j to p 100 a, post).

(2) Furthermore, if the wife's submissions were correct, the bank would be deprived of the defence provided by s 37(4) that the disposition had been made for valuable consideration without notice of any intention to defeat the wife's claim which it would be able to rely on if it were possible for proceedings to be brought against it under s 37(1) and (2) (see p 99 d to f, post).

Notes

For the avoidance of transactions intended to prevent or reduce financial relief, see 13 Halsbury's Laws (4th Edn) paras 1154–1156, and for cases on the subject, see 27(2) Digest (Reissue) 849, 6770–6774.

For the Matrimonial Causes Act 1973, s 37, see 43 Halsbury's Statutes (3rd Edn) 584.

Case cited

Whittingham v Whittingham (National Westminster Bank Ltd intervening) [1978] 3 All ER 805, [1979] Fam 9, CA.

---

a   Section 37, so far as material, is set out at p 98 *j* and p 99 *b c*, post

Ruling

On 9th July 1980 Felicity Jane Green ('the wife') applied, in the course of proceedings *a* claiming financial relief against Peter John Green ('the husband'), for an order under s 37 of the Matrimonial Causes Act 1973 setting aside a conveyance, dated 28th December 1977, whereby the husband and wife had jointly conveyed 10½ acres of the grounds of the matrimonial home to Green Farms Ltd ('the company') for £20,000. On 21st September 1978 the company had charged the 10½ acres to Barclays Bank Ltd as security for certain advances. The wife gave the bank notice of her application to have the *b* conveyance set aside. The bank asked the court to determine a point of law relating to s 37. The issue was heard in chambers but judgment was given by Eastham J in open court. The facts are set out in the judgment.

Joseph Jackson QC and *Bruce Blair* for the wife.
Margaret Puxon and *J Akast* for the husband.   *c*
Michael Oppenheimer for the bank.

EASTHAM J. At the request of Barclays Bank Ltd, which is interested in these proceedings in a manner which I will describe later, and without objection by the other parties to this litigation, I have been asked to determine a point of law relating to s 37 of *d* the Matrimonial Causes Act 1973.

The former wife (whom I shall call 'the wife' hereafter), Mrs Felicity Jane Green, is in these proceedings claiming financial relief against her former husband, Mr Peter John Green ('the husband'). Before the breakdown of the marriage, the matrimonial home was a very large and pleasant property called Shotesham House, near Norwich in Norfolk. The present value of that house, with the grounds which existed during the *e* marriage, is £165,000, that being an agreed valuation. That property was in the joint names, and still is in the joint names, of the husband and wife.

On 28th December 1977 the husband and wife conveyed approximately 10½ acres of the grounds of that house to a company called Green Farms Ltd, which is not an English company (it is an Isle of Man company), for a consideration of £20,000. The wife received no part of that sum. The wife contends in these proceedings that she was *f* induced to enter into that conveyance partly because of her fear of her former husband and partly because she was told it was a necessary transaction in order to avoid taxation.

The value of the house without those 10½ acres of land is somewhere between £75,000 and £80,000. In the proceedings before me there is an application at the instance of the wife to set aside that conveyance under s 37 of the 1973 Act.

After that conveyance, namely on 21st September 1978, the Isle of Man company, *g* Green Farms Ltd, charged those 10½ acres to Barclays Bank Ltd, and the bank, in respect of that security and other security, has advanced to the company sums in excess of £60,000. Notice has been given to the bank of the application by the wife to set aside the conveyance under s 37 of the 1973 Act, and it attends here by counsel.

It is conceded and accepted by counsel for the wife that it is not possible, having regard to the wording of s 37(1) and (2), for the wife to attack the charge between the Isle of Man *h* company and the bank under those subsections. If it were possible, the bank would be able to avail itself of the defence set out in sub-s (4) of the section, which provides that a disposition which would otherwise be reviewable ceases to be reviewable if it was made for valuable consideration—

> 'to a person who, at the time of the disposition, acted in relation to it in good faith *j* and without notice of any intention on the part of the other party to defeat the applicant's claim for financial relief.'

But in these proceedings counsel for the wife says, first of all, that, as a result of irregularities between the company and the bank and violations of the provisions of the

articles of association and as a result of defective minutes, the charge, in his submission,
a was invalid ab initio; secondly and more importantly, as a legal point he submits that,
even though the wife cannot under the provisions of s 37(1) and (2) make a direct attack
on the charge, if I come to the conclusion that the conveyance which preceded the charge
can be successfully attacked under s 37(1) and (2) as against the husband, then under the
provisions of sub-s (3) I can under an absolute discretion, as he submits, vested in me give
directions to give effect to the order setting aside the conveyance which would include
b setting aside the charge or reducing it, if I thought right.
    Subsection (3) reads as follows:

> 'Where the court makes an order under subsection (2)(*b*) or (*c*) above setting aside
> a disposition it shall give such consequential directions as it thinks fit for giving
> effect to the order (including directions requiring the making of any payments or
c the disposal of any property).'

    Counsel submits that those are very wide words and that they are not confined to any
particular property but extend to any property. Counsel for the bank says, first of all,
that he disagrees with the submission of counsel for the wife that the subsection is in
wide terms, and he lays particular emphasis on the words 'consequential directions',
d submitting that that restricts very largely or entirely the subsection to directions
requiring, for example, the repayment of any money which had been paid under the
conveyance which had been set aside.
    He also submits that, if the submissions of counsel for the wife are correct, it would
deprive his client, the bank, entirely of the statutory defence set out in sub-s (4) which it
could rely on if it were possible for the proceedings to be brought against the bank under
e s 37(1) and (2).
    I have been asked to decide the point of law because it has been submitted to me that
it may save a good deal of inquiry into facts if the bank's submissions are correct. I have
come to the conclusion that the submissions of counsel for the bank are correct and that
I have no discretion or power under sub-s (3) to attack the charge under the provisions of
that subsection.
f   That, however, does not end the matter, because by virtue of s 43 of the Supreme
Court of Judicature (Consolidation) Act 1925 it is provided that:

> 'The High Court . . . in the exercise of the jurisdiction vested in [it] by this Act,
> shall, in every cause or matter pending before the court, grant, either absolutely or
> on such terms and conditions as the court thinks just, all such remedies whatsoever
g as any of the parties thereto may appear to be entitled to in respect of any legal or
> equitable claim properly brought forward by them in the cause or matter, so that,
> as far as possible, all matters in controversy between the parties may be completely
> and finally determined, and all multiplicity of legal proceedings concerning any of
> those matters avoided.'

h   In relation to the first submission of counsel for the wife, namely that the charge was
invalid ab initio, quite clearly that argument must lie outside the scope of s 37, and in
relation to that matter, without objection from the bank, I have already directed that
points of claim setting out the grounds of the alleged invalidity shall be served on the
bank by Monday. It seems to me, having regard to the provisions of that section and
having regard to the fact that it may be that the bank has continued to advance money
j after having full knowledge of the wife's claims against her former husband and to get
rid of all matters in controversy between the parties, I should also in relation to the
second line of argument direct that, within a time to be discussed with counsel, points of
claim should be served setting out the grounds on which it is contended that the charge
should be reduced, partially or entirely, as a result of conduct or misconduct on the part
of the bank. But on the point raised by the bank I am quite satisfied for myself that I

cannot do as the wife requests me to do, attack the charge under the provisions of sub-s
(3) of s 37 of the 1973 Act.

a

Ruling accordingly.

Solicitors: *Mills & Reeve*, Norwich (for the wife); *Hill & Perks*, Norwich (for the husband);
Durrant Piesse (for the bank).

b

Bebe Chua   Barrister.

W v A (child: surname)

COURT OF APPEAL, CIVIL DIVISION
LAWTON, BRIDGE AND DUNN LJJ
24th JULY 1980

c

*Minor – Change of surname – Divorce of parents – Proper approach by court to decision to
change surname – Parents divorced and each remarried – Parents having joint custody of
children and mother having care and control – Father agreeing to mother and children going out
of jurisdiction with mother's second husband provided mother gave undertaking that children
would continue to use father's surname – Mother and children wishing second husband's surname
to be used by children – Change of surname a matter of importance to be decided by reference to
child's best interests in the circumstances – Whether judge right not to attach decisive importance
to children's wishes – Guardianship of Minors Act 1971, s 1.*

d

e

The mother and father were married in 1966 and had two children, a boy and a girl. The
mother left the matrimonial home with the children in 1971. Subsequently both
parents were divorced and each remarried. They were granted joint custody of the
children with the mother being granted care and control and the father reasonable
access. The mother's second husband was an Australian and wished to return to
Australia with the mother and the children. The mother applied to the court for leave
to take the children out of the jurisdiction. The father, who was a responsible parent
who played a part in the childrens' lives, agreed to the children being taken to Australia
provided the wife gave an undertaking that the children would continue to use his
surname. The mother wished the children to use her second husband's surname and the
children, who were by then aged 12 and 14, also wished to use his name and told the
judge so when they saw him in his room. The judge however ruled that the children
were to continue to use the father's surname because, in the judge's view, to change a
child's surname after its parents were divorced was a matter of importance, and because
little regard could be paid to the children's view on the matter since it reflected the
mother's view. The mother appealed from the ruling on the grounds that the judge had
erred in law and that he should have given more weight to the children's wishes.

f

g

h

Held – A decision on changing a child's surname after the divorce of its parents was to
be treated by the court as a matter of importance which was to be decided, in accordance
with s 1[a] of the Guardianship of Minors Act 1971, by reference to what was in the best
interests of the child's welfare in the particular circumstances, that being the first and

---

a   Section 1, so far as material, provides: 'Where in any proceedings before any court (whether or not
a court as defined in section 15 of this Act)—(a) the custody or upbringing of a minor . . . is in
question, the court, in deciding that question, shall regard the welfare of the minor as the first and
paramount consideration, and shall not take into consideration whether from any other point of
view the claim of the father in respect of such custody, upbringing, administration or application
is superior to that of the mother, or the claim of the mother is superior to that of the father.'

j

paramount consideration. Accordingly, the judge had adopted the correct approach in making his ruling and, further, was right not to attach decisive importance to the views of the children. The appeal would therefore be dismissed (see p 104 *f* to *j*, p 105 *c* and *f* to *j* and p 106 *a* to *f*, post).

Re W G (1976) 6 Fam Law 210 followed.

Dicta of Stamp and Ormrod LJJ in *R (BM) v R (DN)* [1978] 2 All ER at 37–39 considered.

Dictum of Ormrod LJ in *D v B (otherwise D)* [1979] 1 All ER at 100 not followed.

Notes

For the determination by the court of questions affecting the welfare of a minor where his parents disagree on the matter, see 24 Halsbury's Laws (4th Edn) para 512.

For the Guardianship of Minors Act 1971, s 1, see 41 Halsbury's Statutes (3rd Edn) 762.

Cases referred to in judgments

D v B (otherwise D) (child: surname) [1979] 1 All ER 92, [1979] Fam 38, [1978] 3 WLR 573, CA, Digest (Cont Vol E) 443, *38(i)*.

J v C [1969] 1 All ER 788, [1970] AC 668, [1969] 2 WLR 540, HL, 28(2) Digest (Reissue) 800, *1230*.

L v F (1978) Times, 1st August.

R (BM) v R (DN) (child: surname) [1978] 2 All ER 33, [1977] 1 WLR 1256, CA, Digest (Cont Vol E) 444, *386*.

W G, Re (1976) 6 Fam Law 210, [1976] Court of Appeal Transcript 164.

Appeal

This was an appeal by the mother, pursuant to leave granted by his Honour Judge Hutton on 20th June 1980, from an order made by the judge on 3rd June 1980 that the mother must continue the use by the children of the marriage of the surname of their father, and seeking an order that she might change their surnames to that of the mother's second husband. The grounds of the appeal were (i) that the judge failed to give sufficient weight to the children's wishes and (ii) that he erred in law because he did not pay sufficient regard to previous decisions of the Court of Appeal. The facts are set out in the judgment of Dunn LJ.

Lester Boothman for the mother.
The father did not appear.

DUNN LJ delivered the first judgment at the invitation of Lawton LJ. This is an appeal from an order of his Honour Judge Hutton made on 3rd June 1980 and amended on 20th June whereby in effect he ordered that two children should continue to use their father's surname. The mother appeals against that order. The father has not been represented on the appeal, although it is clear from the letter from his solicitors that he opposes any variation of the order. I say that the effect of the order was that the children's surname should not be changed because, in form, it was an application by the mother to be released from an undertaking to that effect which she gave to the judge as a condition of being allowed to take both children permanently out of the jurisdiction to Australia.

The father had originally opposed her application to take the children to Australia but eventually agreed, subject to seven undertakings being given by the mother, the last of which was, by reason of the ruling of the court, to continue the use by the children of their surname which I shall call 'A'. That was the only matter which was in contention before the judge, namely whether the children should continue, when they went to Australia, to be called A or whether they should be allowed to change their names to the name of the mother's second husband, which I shall call 'W'.

The background to the case can be stated quite shortly. The parents were married in 1966. The father was and is a farmer, farming near Tewkesbury in Gloucestershire, and his father was a farmer. The two children were born, Stephen on 19th July 1968 and Julie on 1st April 1970. In September 1971 the mother left the matrimonial home with the two children, and an order was made under the Guardianship of Minors Act 1971 whereby joint custody was granted to both parents with care and control to the mother and reasonable access to the father. That 'reasonable access' continued down to the time that the mother and the children went to Australia, which was earlier this month.

Both the parents subsequently remarried, there having been a decree nisi on 24th April 1974 under s 1(2)(d) of the Matrimonial Causes Act 1973. The father has two sons by his second marriage. The mother married an Australian who was over here temporarily, and there is a little girl of that marriage born in 1978. The mother's second husband desiring to return to Australia, application was made for leave to be granted for the children to leave the jurisdiction permanently.

When the question of the change of name came before the judge, he was faced with the dilemma that there are two apparently conflicting lines of authority in this court on the question of changing children's surnames. The first is that the change of a child's surname is an important matter, not to be undertaken lightly. The second is that the change of a child's surname is a comparatively unimportant matter. The judge, faced with the choice between those two lines of authority, opted for the first. The primary grounds of this appeal is that in so doing he erred in law.

It is necessary, accordingly, to look at the various decided cases which have been very helpfully cited to us by counsel for the mother who, if I may say so, has conducted this appeal with great ability and also with great responsibility, having no opponent.

The first case to which he referred was Re W G (1976) 6 Fam Law 210. That was a case in which the issue whether or not the child's surname should be changed was the very question which the court had to decide. There was evidence before the trial judge, Faulks J, from the headmistress of the children's school that it was administratively convenient that their names should be changed to the name of their stepfather. Faulks J accepted that view and made an order giving leave for a deed poll to be registered changing their names. The Court of Appeal reversed the judge's order and Cairns LJ is reported as saying (6 Fam Law 210):

'It was, of course, important to bear in mind all the way through . . . that it was in the paramount interests of the child with which their Lordships were concerned. It had not been suggested on either side here that the court should approach a decision in the case from any other point of view. But his Lordship thought it important that it should be realised that the mere fact that there had been a divorce, that the mother had remarried and had custody of the child and had a name different from that of the child, was not sufficient reason for changing the child's surname . . . The courts recognise the importance of maintaining a link with the father, unless he had ceased to have an interest in the child or there were some grounds, having regard to his character and behaviour, which made it undesirable for him to have access to the child at all. It must greatly tend to create difficulties in the relations between a father and a child if the child ceased to bear the father's name.'

The other two members of the court agreed.

There followed R (BM) v R (DN) (child: surname) [1978] 2 All ER 33, [1977] 1 WLR 1256, also in the Court of Appeal. It is I think important to have regard to what the issue which fell to be determined in that case was and what the facts of the matter were. The facts of the matter were that the mother had left the father and four children and had gone to live with a soldier. About two years after she left she obtained a decree nisi and she obtained custody of all the children. The youngest child, C, was unhappy with her and the soldier, and returned to live with the father. The issue in R v R was whether the custody of C should be granted to the mother who, by that time, had been living for some time with the soldier and the other three children, or whether C should remain with the father. The question of change of name only arose in this way: there was evidence that the three older children living in the army camp with the mother and the soldier, Sergeant W, were known in the camp as W and this was used by those representing the father as an indication that W would try to eliminate the father from the lives of the children and usurp his position. Stamp LJ made this very clear. He said this ([1978] 2 All ER 33 at 37, [1977] 1 WLR 1256 at 1259):

> 'I think it is convenient to mention that the point was made by counsel for the father in the course of his submissions in this court that the judge might not have been aware at that point or had it present to his mind at that point in his judgment that the three elder children, now in the camp where they are, are known officially by the surname of W, and it was suggested that this rather tended to counter the judge's findings that Sergeant W would always be ready to remind the children that he was not their real father, and a good deal of play was made by counsel for the father regarding this change in the way the children are known in the camp. I am bound to say I do not think that the fact that the three elder children are known as W now in Bovington camp really signifies anything as regards the characters of Sergeant W and the mother. I think that too much attention is paid to these matters of names of children, the names by which they are known, on some occasions at least, and it must be most convenient that they should be known as W in the camp in which they are being brought up where Sergeant W is the head of the family.'

I think it is important to read that last sentence in its context and not to take it out of its context as suggesting the laying down of any general proposition as to changes of name.

Ormrod LJ in his judgment, referred to the change of name as a peripheral matter, and no doubt in the facts and circumstances of that case it was a peripheral matter. He went on to make certain general observations as to the question of changing the surnames of children and emphasised the embarrassment for the school authorities if children are not known by the same name as their mother. Those observations were clearly, in my view, obiter. They were not necessary for the decision of the case and they should not be regarded as other than comments on the factual situation which arose in that case. They were in any event inconsistent with *Re W G*.

The second case which was cited by counsel for the mother in support of what he submitted was the proper approach to the question of changing children's names was *D v B (otherwise D) (child: surname)* [1979] 1 All ER 92, [1979] Fam 38. That again was a case which was decided by Stamp and Ormrod LJJ. The facts of the matter were somewhat complicated. The child in question was born after the mother had left the father and had gone to live with another man. The mother took the name of the other man. She registered the birth of the child in that man's name, but on the registration form declared that her husband was the father, and she refused him access. The father then issued a summons seeking access and asked for an order that the register of births should be altered so as to show the child's name as being his name, and also asked for a rectification of a deed poll which had been executed by the mother, by which she assumed the other man's surname for herself and any children of hers.

The case came before Lane J who ordered access to the father, ordered that the mother should take all necessary steps to ensure that the deed poll and the register of births should be amended, and also ordered that until the child reached the age of 18, the mother should not let him be known by any other surname than that of the father without the father's consent.

The mother failed to carry out the judge's order, the father applied for directions, and the judge, on that application, directed the mother to execute a statutory declaration and a fresh deed poll and attached a penal notice to the order. It was against that order that the mother appealed.

It appears from the report that, in the course of the appeal, the father consented to the child being known by the mother's name. As it is put in the headnote ([1979] Fam 38 at 39)

> '... the father having consented, that part of the order of December 1976 requiring the mother not to allow the child to be known by any other surname than

that of the father, would be varied to enable the child to be known by the mother's
new surname.'   *a*

So that, so far as this court was concerned, the question whether or not the child should
be known by the father's surname or should be known by the surname which the
mother had assumed was not in issue. This is clear from the judgment when Ormrod LJ
said ([1979] 1 All ER 92 at 94, [1979] Fam 38 at 42):

> 'The substantive issue in the case was whether or not the father should have access *b*
> to a very young boy. The formalistic issues rotate round the question of the name
> by which this boy is to be known, and it is a great pity that these issues have come
> to overshadow the real issue of substance, which in fact has been resolved by an
> earlier decision of the judge.'

The Court of Appeal upheld the judge's order as to access, but they varied the order
because of some technical provision of the Enrolment of Deeds (Change of Names) *c*
Regulations 1949, SI 1949 No 316, and also of the Registration of Births, Deaths and
Marriages Regulations 1968, SI 1968 No 2049. At the end of his judgment Ormrod LJ
made some general observations about applications to change names, and they may
perhaps be summarised by reading shortly from the end of his judgment ([1979] 1 All
ER 92 at 100, [1979] Fam 38 at 50):
                                                                                                   d
> 'She had changed her own name to B by deed poll so that she could say, "Now I
> am properly known as B", and she had registered the child in the name of B so that
> she could say, "But the child's real name is B", and one can understand that the
> father's tactics should direct an attack on those two points. It is bad enough for him
> that both of them have proved abortive. But neither of them is real. What is real
> is that the father and the child should know one another, that the child should, in *e*
> course of time, come to recognise the fact that D is his natural father, and so long as
> that is understood, names are really of little importance, and they only become
> important when they become a casus belli between the parents.'

Once again in my view that last sentence was not necessary for the decision of the
issues before the court in that case and the dicta were obiter. But I go further than *f*
that. Assuming that they were necessary for the decision of the case, they are in direct
contradiction with what was said in this court by Cairns LJ in Re W G (1976) 6 Fam Law
210 and speaking for myself, with the greatest respect to Ormrod LJ, I do not agree with
his dicta.

A useful footnote to the authorities was provided by Latey J in L v F (1978) Times, 1st
August. Once again in that case the direct issue which the judge had to decide was the
question whether the mother should or should not be allowed to change her children's *g*
surname to that of her new husband, and Latey J referred to the two decisions to which
I have just referred, and also to the decision in Re W G.

He is reported as saying this:

> 'Until the two recent decisions expressed by Lord Justice Stamp and Lord Justice
> Ormrod the prevailing view, enunciated in In re W G and which had never been *h*
> questioned, was that on the failure of a marriage a decision to change children's
> surnames should never be taken unilaterally and that unless parents were in
> agreement a decision about it should be approached by the court as a matter of real
> importance. [Pausing there for one moment, I agree with every word of that. The
> judge went on:] The fact that one approach had been evolved over many years and
> the other had only recently been expressed did not mean that either should *j*
> automatically be accepted as correct. One had to make a fresh appraisal. His
> Lordship had reached the opinion that the approach expressed by Lord Justice
> Cairns in In re W G was the correct one. The court was concerned with cases where
> the parents were in disagreement. A marriage could be dissolved but not
> parenthood. The parents in most cases continued to play an important role in their

children's emotional lives and development. From the point of view of the children's best interests it was essential that the parents' feelings should be taken very carefully, and anxiously into consideration.'

Then the judge referred to the character of the father and the fact that, as in this case, he was a responsible father who had played a part in the children's lives, and also to psychiatric evidence which is often called in this type of case and which the judge had before him in *L v F*. In regard to it he said this:

'A very distinguished child psychiatrist had given evidence that, when they grew older, children were often greatly concerned with their biological origin. How then could one accept that a change of name was of little importance to the children? His Lordship could not. In one case a change might be of benefit to them. In another it might injure them. Surely it was an important decision?'

How then does the law stand with regard to the approach by courts in applications for change of a surname? As in all cases concerning the future of children whether they be custody, access, education or, as in this case, the change of a child's name, s 1 of the Guardianship of Minors Act 1971 requires that the court shall regard 'the welfare of the [child] as the first and paramount consideration'. Those words were construed by Lord MacDermott in *J v C* [1969] 1 All ER 788 at 820–821, [1970] AC 668 at 710 in the following well-known passage:

'Reading these words in their ordinary significance, and relating them to the various classes of proceedings which the section has already mentioned, it seems to me that they must mean more than that the child's welfare is to be treated as the top item in a list of items relevant to the matter in question. I think they connote a process whereby, when all the relevant facts, relationships, claims and wishes of parents, risks, choices and other circumstances are taken into account and weighed, the course to be followed will be that which is most in the interests of the child's welfare as that term has now to be understood. That is the first consideration because it is of first importance and the paramount consideration because it rules on or determines the course to be followed.'

That is the first and paramount consideration which must be in the judge's mind. When considering the question of a change of name, that is to be regarded as an important matter (see Cairns LJ in *Re W G*). It is a matter for the discretion of the individual judge hearing the case, seeing the witnesses, seeing the parents, possibly seeing the children, to decide whether or not it is in the interests of the child in the particular circumstances of the case that his surname should or should not be changed; and the judge will take into account all the circumstances of the case, including no doubt where appropriate any embarrassment which may be caused to the child by not changing his name and, on the other hand, the long-term interests of the child, the importance of maintaining the child's links with his paternal family, and the stability or otherwise of the mother's remarriage. I only mention those as typical examples of the kinds of considerations which arise in these cases, but the judge will take into account all the relevant circumstances in the particular case before him.

Now how did the judge in this case approach the matter? He approached the matter by preferring the approach of Cairns LJ in *Re W G* to the approach in the obiter dicta in *R v R* and *D v B* (*otherwise D*), and in my judgment in taking that course he was right.

Certain detailed criticisms have been made of his reasons for refusing to allow the mother to change the surname of these children. First and foremost it is said that he did not pay sufficient regard to the express wishes of the children themselves. The judge saw the children in his room and has recorded that Stephen had said that because of difficulties at school and because there were no relatives of his father in Australia he wanted to be called W, and the little girl Julie agreed. The judge dealt with this in one or two sentences. He said: 'I think they are too young to express a view on what is a fairly drastic

step. I pay little regard to their views, which are views that largely reflect the mother's
views.'

In my judgment this court could not possibly go behind that. The judge, experienced
in these matters, would know that children are suggestible at this age and that inevitably,
having spent the whole of their lives with their mother, they would be likely to reflect
their mother's views, and that is not to make any criticisms of the mother or suggest that
she put words into their mouths. But they would naturally be anxious not to offend her,
and they would no doubt know that it was her wish that they should change their
surname.

Speaking for myself, I think the judge was entirely right not to attach decisive
importance to the views of two young children of 12 and 10 who were about to embark
on the excitement of going to Australia with their mother and their new stepfather.

Other criticisms were made of the judge. It was said that there were positive
advantages to these children in changing their surname. They were about to make a
fresh start in a new country and it would be an advantage to them to go out as a united
family. A change of name, it was said, would not make much difference to the father
because the children would be at the other end of the world and he has two sons by his
second marriage, so the name of A will survive in Gloucestershire. It is also said that,
when they get older, if the children wished to change their name back to A they could
always do so.

I have no doubt that the judge had all these matters in mind and there is nothing in
his reasons, in his short judgment, which leads me to suppose that he did not. On the
contrary, it seems to me that the judge approached this matter entirely rightly. It was a
matter for his discretion. I cannot see that this court can possibly interfere with that
discretion and, speaking for myself, I should have come to the same conclusion as did the
judge.

For these reasons, I would dismiss this appeal.

BRIDGE LJ. I too would dismiss this appeal for all the reasons given in the judgment
of Dunn LJ, with which I am in complete agreement.

LAWTON LJ. I too am in complete agreement with the judgment of Dunn LJ. That
means that this appeal is dismissed.

Appeal dismissed.

Solicitors: *Sharples & Co*, Bristol (for the mother).

Bebe Chua   Barrister.

a Adeoso (otherwise Ametepe) v Adeoso

COURT OF APPEAL, CIVIL DIVISION
ORMROD LJ AND DAME ELIZABETH LANE
14th, 15th JULY 1980

b *Injunction – Exclusion of party from matrimonial home – County court – Man and woman who are living with each other in the same household as husband and wife – Parties living in small flat – Parties' relationship breaking down but parties continuing to live in flat in separate rooms, without speaking to each other – Whether parties living 'in the same household as husband and wife' – Whether court having jurisdiction to entertain application for injunction – Domestic Violence and Matrimonial Proceedings Act 1976, s 1(2).*

c From 1976 the applicant and the respondent lived together as man and wife. Although they were not married the applicant took the respondent's name. In May 1977 they became joint tenants of a council flat consisting of one bedroom, a sitting room, a kitchen and bathroom. Their relationship broke down and, although they continued to live in the flat, from 1979 they slept in separate rooms and communicated only by notes. From d January 1980 the applicant stopped cooking and washing for the respondent. In April 1980 the applicant applied for injunctions restraining the respondent from molesting the applicant and excluding him from the flat pursuant to s 1(1)^a of the Domestic Violence and Matrimonial Proceedings Act 1976. The judge ruled that by analogy with the authorities on desertion by a spouse the parties had severed their living arrangements and were living apart in separate households even though they were living in the same e house and that therefore the court had no jurisdiction to entertain the application because the parties were not, in the circumstances, 'living with each other in the same household as husband and wife' within s 1(2)^b of the 1976 Act. The applicant appealed.

Held – On the true construction of s 1(2) of the 1976 Act the jurisdiction of the county court to grant an injunction under s 1(1) of the Act extended to a man and woman who f were living with each other in the same household 'as if' they were husband and wife. On an objective view the parties were living together in the flat as if they were husband and wife, their relationship being comparable to a marriage in the last stages of breakdown. Furthermore, the mere fact that the parties had severed their living arrangements did not mean that they were living in different households, and, having regard to the shared facilities and the size of the flat, the parties were living 'in the same g household' for the purposes of s 1(2). The judge therefore had jurisdiction under s 1(2) to entertain the application, and the case would be remitted to the county court to be heard on the merits (see p 109 b d and p 110 d to j, post).

Dicta of Lord Denning MR and of Viscount Dilhorne in *Davis v Johnson* [1978] 1 All ER at 850, 1145 applied.

Per Curiam. The cases on desertion have no application to the situations with which h the 1976 Act is concerned (see p 109 d to f and p 110 j, post).

Notes
For the jurisdiction of the county court to grant matrimonial injunctions, see Supplement to 13 Halsbury's Laws (4th Edn) para 1228A.

---

j a Section 1(1), so far as material, provides: 'Without prejudice to the jurisdiction of the High Court, on an application by a party to a marriage a county court shall have jurisdiction to grant an injunction containing one or more of the following provisions, namely,—(a) a provision restraining the other party to the marriage from molesting the applicant ... (c) a provision excluding the other party from the matrimonial home or a part of the matrimonial home or from a specified area in which the matrimonial home is included ...'
   b Section 1(2) is set out at p 108 f, post

For the Domestic Violence and Matrimonial Proceedings Act 1976, s 1, sec 46
Halsbury's Statutes (3rd Edn) 714.

Cases referred to in judgments

B v B [1978] 1 All ER 821, [1978] Fam 26, [1978] 2 WLR 160, CA, Digest (Cont Vol E)
297, 7683Cc.
Davis v Johnson [1978] 1 All ER 1132, [1979] AC 264, [1978] 2 WLR 553, HL; *affg* [1978]
1 All ER 841, [1979] AC 264, [1978] 2 WLR 182, CA, Digest (Cont Vol E) 279, 7683Ce.
McLean v Nugent [1979] Court of Appeal Transcript 490.

Appeal

By an originating application dated 22nd April 1980 the applicant, Juliana Esive Adeoso
(also known as Juliana Esive Ametepe) applied for an order under the Domestic Violence
and Matrimonial Proceedings Act 1976 that the respondent, Ebenezer Olakunle Adeoso,
be restrained from assaulting, molesting or otherwise interfering with her, and that he
leave the property at 51 Southwold Road, London E5 where the applicant and the
respondent had been living since May 1977. On 16th May 1980 his Honour Judge
Willis, in the Shoreditch County Court, dismissed the application on the ground that he
had no jurisdiction under s 1(2) of the 1976 Act to entertain it because in the
circumstances the applicant and the respondent were not living with each other in the
same household as husband and wife within s 1(2) of the Act. The applicant appealed.
The facts are set out in the judgment of Ormrod LJ.

Robert Glancy for the applicant.
Peter Higginson for the respondent.

ORMROD LJ. This is an appeal by Miss or Mrs Adeoso against a judgment by his
Honour Judge Willis in the Shoreditch County Court on 16th May 1980 by which he
dismissed an application by her against Mr Adeoso for an injunction turning him out of
a council flat which they hold as joint tenants.

The case raises again the question of construction of s 1(2) of the Domestic Violence
and Matrimonial Proceedings Act 1976 which, just to remind ourselves, reads as follows:

'Subsection (1) above shall apply to a man and a woman who are living with each
other in the same household as husband and wife as it applies to the parties to a
marriage and any reference to the matrimonial home shall be construed accordingly.'

The point that is taken in this case by counsel for the respondent is that the parties
were not living as man and wife in the same household. It is necessary, therefore, to give
a brief summary of the facts. These parties have been living together on a sexual footing
certainly since the middle of 1976, or earlier, probably earlier. According to the
respondent's affidavit, he had a council flat in 77 Hendle House, London E8 and, at some
time between 1974, when he met the applicant, and May 1977, when the Hackney
Council moved them both from 77 Hendle House to 51 Southwold Road, they began
living together as man and wife. They are and have been joint tenants of this council flat
at 51 Southwold Road since May 1977. The flat consists of one bedroom, a sitting room,
kitchen and bathroom.

The relationship has become more and more unhappy in recent years, and it
culminated in the applicant applying for an order turning the respondent out of the
flat. The date of her application was 22nd April 1980. She swore two affidavits in
support of that application alleging violence, saying that there had been no sexual
intercourse between them since December 1978 and that they had been sleeping in
separate rooms, he on the floor in the sitting room and she in the bedroom, since July
1979. There was an act of violence on Christmas Day and New Year's Eve 1979 which
precipitated these proceedings. That is roughly the background.

In the course of her oral evidence the applicant took the matter a little further. She *a* said that she had ceased to cook for the respondent in January 1980 and stopped washing his clothes, but she added, and this I cannot help thinking is rather significant, that they had been living together for three years but, because there was no child, the respondent told her that she must go. That seems to throw a flood of light on the real relationship between the parties, and it turns out that she had been told, apparently, that she could not have children. They continued to share the electricity, gas and the rent between them. They have not been on speaking terms, at least since some time last year,

b communicating by notes; and she or he keeps the door locked, whoever is in charge of the lock. So that is the state of the relationship. In other words, in ordinary human terms, the relationship is exactly comparable to a marriage which is in the last stages of break-up.

It was submitted to the judge below that they could not be said, in those circumstances, to be a man and woman who are living with each other in the same household as

c husband and wife, and the judge accepted that submission and ruled that he had no jurisdiction. He accepted, of course (as he must) that, if they had actually been married, there was no question about his jurisdiction. Section 1(1) plainly provides for that; but it was said that owing to the difficult drafting of s 1(2), on the present facts there is no jurisdiction.

It would be plainly absurd, in the circumstances, to hold that there was no

d jurisdiction. These two have been living as man and wife to all intents and purposes for at least three years. She has taken his name and, to anyone looking at them from outside, there can be no doubt whatever that they were and are apparently living together as husband and wife. The judge, I think, attached, with respect, too much importance to the old cases about desertion and was thinking in terms of those old cases which held that it was possible for a spouse to desert the other while living in closest possible contiguity

e in the same house, if they succeeded in severing the cooking and washing arrangements and so on. I do not, for my part, think that those cases have any application to the present situation. They were invented by a succession of judges to get over the impossible position where a couple had ceased to communicate altogether but neither could leave because they had no alternative accommodation; and so a certain amount of stretching of the law had to be done. I see no useful purpose in reviving those cases and that

f doctrine in this present situation.

Counsel for the applicant has drawn attention to the relevant passages in the authorities which I will just briefly mention. The first is to be found in the judgment of Lord Denning MR in *Davis v Johnson* [1978] 1 All ER 841 at 850, [1979] AC 264 at 275. There Lord Denning MR was concerned with the words 'are living' in sub-s (3) and he said:

g 'The judges in *B v B* [1978] 1 All ER 821, [1978] Fam 26 felt difficulty with the words "are living with each other in the same household". They felt that on the literal meaning of the words they must be living with each other at the time when the woman applies to the court. They realised that in most cases the woman would have already left the house at the time when she makes her application. So the literal meaning would deprive the subsection of much of its effect. To my mind these words do not present any difficulty. They are used to denote the relationship

h between the parties before the incident which gives rise to the application. If they were then living together in the same household as husband and wife, that is enough.'

Counsel for the applicant referred us also to a passage in the judgment of Baker P, which I do not think I need read; and then the other passage, which is perhaps the more

j important one, is to be found in Viscount Dilhorne's speech in the House of Lords in *Davis v Johnson* [1978] 1 All ER 1132 at 1145, [1979] AC 317 at 334 where he said:

'Our task is to give effect to the intention of Parliament if that can be seen from the language of the statute. Here the language is clear and unambiguous and Parliament's intention apparent. Unmarried persons living together in the same

household as husband and wife are for the purposes of s 1(1) to be treated as if they
were married. The unmarried woman to whom sub-s (2) applies is to have the same *a*
rights as a married woman. A county court judge in the exercise of his discretion
can grant an injunction excluding a husband from the home or requiring him to
permit her to enter and remain there whether or not she has been subjected to or
threatened with violence or molestation.'

Then he continued on those lines.

In *Maclean v Nugent* [1979] Court of Appeal Transcript 490, in dealing with this point *b*
I said:

'In my judgment the test, as it emerges from the passages I have cited, depends
essentially on the existence at some time of a relationship which is that of "a man
and a woman living together as man and wife". In other words, if the evidence
shows that they have been living together as man and wife, they are, within limits *c*
which are not easy to define, to be treated as though they were married at that
time. The question of fact which arises, of course, in such a situation will be: when
has that relationship come to an end? How long after it comes to an end is a party
entitled to take advantage of sub-s (2)?'

Then I went on to deal with the facts in that case, which were very much more extreme
than these, because the plaintiff, or the applicant, in *McLean v Nugent* had been parted *d*
from the respondent for a long time.

I think, for my part, that we have to read s 1(2) of the 1976 Act simply as if it read:
'Subsection (1) shall apply to a man and woman who are living with each other in the
same household as if they were husband and wife.' That makes some sense of it because
these two people are clearly living in the same household as if they were husband and
wife. For my part, I would deprecate any nice attempts to dissect households and ask the *e*
question and try to answer it: 'Are these two people living in the same household?' In
practical terms you cannot live in a two-room flat with another person without living in
the same household. You have to share the lavatory, share the kitchen, share the
bathroom and take great care not to fall over one another in most of these cases; and it
would be quite artificial to suggest that two people living at arm's length in such a
situation, from which they cannot escape by reason of the housing difficulties, are to be *f*
said to be living in two separate households. Of course, if this were a large household and
they were middle-class persons, no doubt one could live upstairs and the other could live
downstairs; one of them could improvise some cooking facilities and one use the kitchen,
and so on. There would, of course, then come a stage when one could say: 'Well, they
really have separated their households.' But, on the facts of this case, it would be totally
artificial, in my judgment, to say that they succeeded in separating themselves into two *g*
individual households. They obviously have not.

In those circumstances, it is plain that these two people have been living together as
man and wife for a period of years and have deliberately arranged their lives so; and that
they are now at the stage when the relationship is breaking down. Ultimately, somebody
will have to deal with the joint tenancy. At the moment, both of them are completely
boxed in. There is no way either of them can get out of this situation without an order *h*
of the court. It is only by getting an order of the court that they have any chance, as I
understand it, of getting rehoused; so that it would be a great unkindness to both of
them to decline jurisdiction.

In my judgment, the judge was wrong. He had jurisdiction to entertain this
application. In those circumstances I would allow the appeal and send the case back to
the county court for the application to be heard on its merits. *j*

DAME ELIZABETH LANE. I agree and I would add only this; and I add it, perhaps,
for the comfort of the respondent. There was no determination by the county court
judge as to the facts which the applicant alleged as regards violence and so forth, and the

judge, in rejecting her application for the order sought, was careful to look at the facts
a from her point of view. When the case is remitted for rehearing, then both sides will be
heard and, if the respondent is in a position to show that the applicant's allegations
against him are false, doubtless she will fail to obtain her order.

Appeal allowed.

b Solicitors: M Wernick & Co (for the applicant); *Peter Kingshill* (for the respondent).

Avtar S Virdi Esq   Barrister.

c # Macarthys Ltd v Smith
(Case 129/79)

COURT OF JUSTICE OF THE EUROPEAN COMMUNITIES
JUDGES KUTSCHER (PRESIDENT), O'KEEFFE, TOUFFAIT (PRESIDENTS OF CHAMBERS), MERTENS DE
d WILMARS, PESCATORE, LORD MACKENZIE STUART, BOSCO, KOOPMANS, DUE
30th JANUARY, 28th FEBRUARY, 27th MARCH 1980

COURT OF APPEAL, CIVIL DIVISION
LORD DENNING MR, LAWTON AND CUMMING-BRUCE LJJ
17th APRIL 1980

e
*Employment – Equality of treatment of men and women – Like work – Comparison of woman's
work with duties of former male employee – Substantial interval between respective employments
– Whether comparison restricted to comparing woman's work with that of man in
contemporaneous employment – Equal Pay Act 1970 (as amended by the Sex Discrimination Act
1975), s 1(2)(a)(i) – EEC Treaty, art 119.*

f
*Costs – Order for costs – Action concerned with construction of legislation – United Kingdom law
inconsistent with EEC law – Litigant arguing case on basis of meaning of United Kingdom law
– Whether litigant required to have regard to EEC law – Whether litigant required to pay costs
of action when United Kingdom law on which he relied is struck down as being inconsistent with
EEC law.*

g
The employers employed a man to manage their stockroom and paid him £60 a week.
He left their employment and 4½ months later they appointed the applicant, a woman,
to manage the stockroom in his place at a wage of only £50 a week. The applicant
claimed that she was entitled to equal pay by virtue of s 1(2)(a)(i)[a] of the Equal Pay Act

h *a* Section 1, so far as material, provides:
      '(1) If the terms of a contract under which a woman is employed at an establishment in Great
      Britain do not include (directly or by reference to a collective agreement or otherwise) an equality
      clause they shall be deemed to include one.
      '(2) An equality clause is a provision which relates to terms (whether concerned with pay or not)
      of a contract under which a woman is employed (the "woman's contract"), and has the effect that—
j   (a) where the woman is employed on like work with a man in the same employment—(i) if (apart
      from the equality clause) any term of the woman's contract is or becomes less favourable to the
      woman than a term of a similar kind in the contract under which that man is employed, that term
      of the woman's contract shall be treated as so modified as not to be less favourable, and (ii) if (apart
      from the equality clause) at any time the woman's contract does not include a term corresponding
      to a term benefiting that man included in the contract under which he is employed, the woman's
      contract shall be treated as including such a term . . .'

1970. An industrial tribunal found in her favour on the grounds that she was employed on like or broadly similar work to that of her male predecessor and it was only because *a* she was a woman that she was paid less. The Employment Appeal Tribunal ([1978] 2 All ER 746) dismissed an appeal by the employers. The employers appealed to the Court of Appeal ([1979] 3 All ER 325), which held that the 1970 Act did not prevent an employer from paying a female employee less than a male employee who had been previously employed to do the same job. However, because of a doubt about the ambit of art 119*b* of the EEC Treaty and because the court was bound by s 2(1)*c* of the European *b* Communities Act 1972 to give effect to the provisions of the EEC Treaty in priority to a United Kingdom statute, the court decided to stay the proceedings and refer to the Court of Justice of the European Communities the question of the true interpretation of art 119. The applicant submitted that in order to discover whether there was discrimination comparison should be made not merely with a person who was previously employed to do the work in question but also with a hypothetical male worker.   *c*

Held (by the Court of Justice of the European Communities) – (1) A court was required under art 119 of the EEC Treaty to ensure equal pay in so far as that could be achieved by the simple application of the criteria of equal work and equal pay contained in the article. The scope of the concept of 'equal work' in the article was essentially qualitative in character and was exclusively concerned with the nature of the services provided and *d* could not be restricted by the introduction of a requirement of contemporaneity. It followed that the principle of equal pay for equal work was not confined to situations in which men and women were contemporaneously doing equal work for the same employer. Accordingly the applicant was entitled to equal pay even though she had been employed after the man had left, provided, as a matter of fact, that there were no other reasons unconnected with the sex of the employee for treating them differently *e* (see p 118 *h* to p 119 *c* and *j*, post).

(2) A court could not, however, under art 119 alone, be required to make a comparison with a hypothetical male worker, because, for that to be effective, there would have to be comparative studies of the industry concerned according to criteria elaborated in implementing legislation by the Community and by the member states. It followed that, in cases of actual discrimination falling within the scope of the direct application of *f* art 119, comparisons were confined to parallels which could be drawn on the basis of concrete appraisals of the work actually performed by employees of different sex within the same establishment or service (see p 119 *d* to *g*, post); *Defrenne v Sabena* p 122, post, applied.

Accordingly, **Held** (by the Court of Appeal) – The employers' appeal would be dismissed *g* (see p 120 *j* and p 121 *c* to *e*, post).

Per the Court of Appeal. Since the 1972 Act has made EEC law part of United Kingdom law, and since EEC law takes priority over inconsistent United Kingdom law, a litigant is obliged to look at both EEC law and United Kingdom law, and if he loses his case he should pay the costs of the litigation in the normal way (see p 120 *g h* and p 121 *b* to *e*, post).   *h*

Decision of the Employment Appeal Tribunal [1978] 2 All ER 746 affirmed.

b Article 119, so far as material, provides: 'Each Member State shall during the first stage ensure and subsequently maintain the application of the principle that men and women should receive equal pay for equal work . . .'

c Section 2(1) provides: 'All such rights, powers, liabilities, obligations and restrictions from time to time created or arising by or under the Treaties, and all such remedies and procedures from time *i* to time provided for by or under the Treaties, as in accordance with the Treaties are without further enactment to be given legal effect or used in the United Kingdom shall be recognised and available in law, and be enforced, allowed and followed accordingly; and the expression "enforceable Community right" and similar expressions shall be read as referring to one to which this subsection applies.'

Notes

For equal treatment of men and women as regards terms and conditions of employment, see 16 Halsbury's Laws (4th Edn) para 767.

For the legal consequences of accession to the EEC Treaty, see 39A Halsbury's Laws (3rd Edn) para 7.

For the Equal Pay Act 1970, s 1 (as amended by the Sex Discrimination Act 1975), see 45 Halsbury's Statutes (3rd Edn) 290.

For the European Communities Act 1972, s 2, see 42 ibid 80.

For the EEC Treaty, art 119, see 42A ibid 779.

Case cited

Defrenne v Sabena Case 43/75 p 122, post, [1976] ECR 455, [1976] ICR 547, [1976] 2 CMLR 98, CJEC.

Reference

The Court of Appeal, Civil Division referred certain questions (set out at p 118 *d* to *f*, post) as to the interpretation of art 119 of the EEC Treaty to the Court of Justice of the European Communities for a preliminary ruling under art 177 of the treaty. The questions arose as a result of the hearing by the Court of Appeal (Lord Denning MR, Lawton and Cumming-Bruce LJJ) ([1979] 3 All ER 325) of an appeal by Macarthys Ltd ('the employers') against the decision of the Employment Appeal Tribunal (Phillips J, Mr E Alderton and Mrs A L Taylor) ([1978] 2 All ER 746, [1978] 1 WLR 849) dated 14th December 1977 dismissing their appeal against the decision of an industrial tribunal (chairman Mr H A Harris) sitting in London on 28th April 1977 allowing the complaint of the applicant, Mrs Wendy Smith, that she was entitled to equal pay commensurate with that paid by the employers to her male predecessor. The United Kingdom and the Commission of the European Communities submitted observations to the European court. The facts are set out in the opinion of the Advocate-General.

Anthony Lester QC for the applicant.
Henry Brooke for the United Kingdom.
Armando Toledano-Laredo and *Michael Beloff* for the Commission.
The employers were not represented.

28th February. **The Advocate-General (F Capotorti)** delivered the following opinion: The English company Macarthys Ltd ('the employers'), who are wholesale dealers in pharmaceutical products, paid in 1974 and 1975 a weekly wage of £60 to a Mr McCullough, who was the manager of one of their warehouses. On 1st March 1976, after that post of warehouse manager had been vacant for more than four months, the applicant, Mrs Wendy Smith, was employed to fill it at a weekly wage of £50. Thereafter, relying on the English legislation on equal pay (the Equal Pay Act 1970), Mrs Smith applied to an industrial tribunal in London for an order that, by virtue of that Act, she was entitled to the same salary as that which had been received by her predecessor.

By a decision of 27th June 1977 the tribunal, although finding that the applicant's duties were not identical to those of her predecessor (in particular, in contrast to the latter, she was not responsible for the maintenance of vehicles), held that her work was 'broadly similar', within the meaning of s 1(4) of the 1970 Act, to that previously performed by Mr McCullough. It accordingly decided that the applicant's remuneration should have been calculated on the same basis as that adopted for calculating Mr McCullough's salary, particularly as the applicant did not have available the assistance of the two assistant warehouse managers which her predecessor had had.

That decision was upheld by the appellate tribunal in employment disputes, the Employment Appeal Tribunal ([1978] 2 All ER 746, [1978] 1 WLR 849) although it recognised that to do so it was necessary to go beyond a strict construction of the 1970 Act, which restricts the right of equality of treatment to the case of contemporaneous employment with the same firm of men and women whose actual duties (and not the abstract title of the post held) are to be compared. According to the Employment Appeal Tribunal, it appeared necessary to go beyond a strict construction of the 1970 Act in order to avoid the unjust results which would otherwise arise and to avoid, moreover, incompatibility with the Community principle of equal pay for workers of both sexes for 'equal work' laid down in art 119 of the EEC Treaty.

On further appeal to the Court of Appeal, the employers prayed in aid the literal wording of the 1970 Act while counsel for the applicant advanced the need to interpret the national law in accordance with Community law and referred not only to art 119 of the EEC Treaty but also to art 1 of EEC Council Directive 75/117 of 10th February 1975 on the approximation of the laws of the member states relating to the application of the principle of equal pay for men and women. According to the latter provision—

> 'The principle of equal pay for men and women outlined in Article 119 of the Treaty . . . means, for the same work *or for work to which equal value is attributed*, the elimination of all discrimination on grounds of sex with regard to all aspects and conditions of remuneration.' (Emphasis mine.)

By order of 25th July 1979, the Court of Appeal in London referred to this court four questions on the interpretation of the Community legislation with a view to establishing whether the principle of equal pay must apply in a situation of the kind in which the applicant found herself (see [1979] 3 All ER 325 at 336, [1979] 1 WLR 1189).

The Court of Appeal asks, first, whether the principle of equal pay for men and women for 'equal work', referred to in art 119 of the EEC Treaty and art 1 of EEC Council Directive 75/117, is confined to cases in which the men and women concerned are contemporaneously engaged on equal work within the same undertaking.

A restriction on the application of the principle of art 119 in the sense indicated by that question is not warranted by the wording of that provision which confines itself to laying down, as a condition for its application, similarity in the services rendered, without in fact mentioning any criterion of contemporaneity. In addition, *Defrenne v Sabena* p 122, post, in holding art 119 to be directly applicable, refers to the case 'where men and women receive unequal pay for equal work carried out in the same establishment' without requiring contemporaneity in the work in question (see p 134, post).

Nor is the restriction mentioned justified by the objectives of art 119. As is clearly stated in *Defrenne v Sabena* (see p 133, post)—

> 'Article 119 pursues a double aim. First, in the light of the different stages of the development of social legislation in the various member states, the aim of art 119 is to avoid a situation in which undertakings established in states which have actually implemented the principle of equal pay suffer a competitive disadvantage in intra-Community competition as compared with undertakings established in states which have not yet eliminated discrimination against women workers as regards pay. Second, this provision forms part of the social objectives of the Community, which is not merely an economic union but is at the same time intended, by common action, to ensure social progress and seek the constant improvement of the living and working conditions of their peoples, as is emphasised by the preamble to the EEC Treaty.'

The Commission has correctly pointed out that if an undertaking could, by replacing its male employees with female employees, by that fact alone pay lower wages that would result in its having an unfair competitive advantage over undertakings which contemporaneously employ men and women to carry out the work in question. Further, if the only reason for a difference in the level of remuneration for the same work performed for the same undertaking at different times was the difference in sex, female workers would be unjustly discriminated against and placed at a disadvantage in comparison with male workers, which would be manifestly contrary to the social objectives of the legislation in question.

The United Kingdom government submitted in the course of these proceedings that, in order to apply the principle contained in art 119 to equal work performed at different times, it would be necessary to adopt legislation defining the limitative criteria in terms of time and the appropriate reference period for the comparison. In the absence of such details art 119 could not apply to work carried out at different times. In support of that proposition the United Kingdom government referred to the distinction drawn by the court, once again in *Defrenne v Sabena* (see p 134, post), between—

'first, direct and overt discrimination which may be identified solely with the aid of the criteria based on equal work and equal pay referred to by the article in question, and, second, indirect and disguised discrimination which can only be identified by reference to more explicit implementing provisions of a Community or national character.'

However, what led the court to make that distinction and to hold that art 119 had no direct effect in regard to the second type of discrimination was, above all, the existence of cases in which it is impossible to compare the work of men and women, as occurs, for example, when discrimination takes place not simply within the same establishment but in relation to whole sectors of industry which are characterised by exclusively or predominantly female employment, not to speak of the disguised discrimination which arises by virtue of restrictions on access by women to certain posts or levels of employment. Direct comparability between the functions performed by employees of both sexes for the same undertaking is not, on the other hand, prevented by the fact that the services are rendered at different times; and detailed legislation is surely not necessary to enable a court to establish whether work is 'equal' within the meaning of the first paragraph of art 119.

In order to make such an assessment it is necessary only that there be ascertained, in each individual case, certain matters of fact, namely whether the tasks performed by workers of both sexes are comparable. That manifestly comes within the field of the direct application of art 119, as is made clear by the *Defrenne v Sabena* judgment (see paras 16 to 18 of the decision, pp 133–134, post).

Difficulties may arise in a case where the period of time which has elapsed between the two periods of employment in question is such as to render a comparison between the two remunerations not reasonably possible, given the change in general economic conditions and, especially, the particular conditions of the employer. The adoption of a more restrictive incomes policy may also affect earnings from one day to the next. But in cases of that kind the difference in treatment would have an objective justification in the changing general or particular economic conditions just mentioned; there would thus be no longer any ground for speaking of unjustified and arbitrary discrimination in pay between men and women employees. All depends, even in this regard, on the ascertainment of the facts, which is the task of the national tribunal. It is permissible to suppose, for example, that an undertaking wishing to show that it was constrained by economic circumstances to pay a woman employee less than the man who preceded her in the same post will rely on facts relating to the general level of wages inside, and possibly outside, the undertaking. I would note incidentally that, in the present case, the court making the reference held that no facts other than the lower remuneration paid to the applicant in comparison with her predecessor and the almost total identity of the tasks entrusted to both of them were to be taken into account.

These considerations lead me to hold that the principle of equal pay without discrimination on grounds of sex for equal work for the same undertaking (contained in art 119 of the EEC Treaty) may not be restricted to cases in which the work is contemporaneously carried out by male and female workers.

In the second question, which is dependent on a negative answer to the first, the Court of Appeal asks whether the principle of equal pay may be relied on by a worker who shows that she receives less pay than would have been received by a man doing equal work for the same undertaking, assuming a man were appointed to her post, or than had actually been received by a male worker who had been employed previously and who had been doing equal work for the same undertaking.

In my opinion, an affirmative answer is the logical and necessary consequence to the reply given to the preceding question. The method of making a hypothetical comparison between the wage paid to a female worker and that which *would have been* paid to a male worker, had he held her position, gave rise to debate in the course of the proceedings. However, such a comparison is undoubtedly possible when there is a means of referring to wages normally paid or offered to male workers for equal work within the same undertaking.

I have already observed that there are grounds for reliance on art 119 where the reason for the difference in treatment lies in the difference in sex. That means that a mere finding of a difference in treatment, to the detriment of a female worker, with respect to the remuneration which a man has already received, or could have received, for the same work within the same undertaking can represent at the most a mere presumption of unlawful discrimination.

Apart from the possibility already mentioned where the difference in treatment arises from changes in the general or particular economic conditions, there is also the specific case where the difference in wage levels as regards a woman who has actually taken the position of a man may be caused by the personal circumstances of the workers in question, as may arise when the man taken as a basis of comparison has a greater length of service than the woman in question. In truth, such a situation would justify differing wages even in a case of contemporaneous employment.

Another specific case is that in which the management of the undertaking considers it proper to classify differently certain tasks previously carried out by a male worker which, from the point of view of their grading, had been overrated. Here, too, the factual problem is that of ascertaining whether the alleged overgrading existed; and the tribunal charged with investigating the facts must resolve the issue by resorting to objective terms of reference (such as the position in other undertakings in the same line of business or the level of grading provided for in collective agreements). What is important is that the lower wage should be due to circumstances other than the sex of the workers. It is for the undertaking accused of discrimination in pay to raise the defence that that state of affairs is brought about by circumstances of that nature; and, of course, the most persuasive proof will be provided by showing that the reduction in salary would also have affected a man if he had been employed instead of a woman in succession to another male employee.

In the third question, which, in its turn, presupposes an affirmative answer to that just considered, the national court inquires whether that answer is 'dependent' on the provisions of art 1 of EEC Council Directive 75/117.

I had occasion earlier to refer to the content of that article. It is clear that it is closely linked to art 119 of the EEC Treaty; but more precisely, its purpose is to implement art 119 and also to supplement it by going beyond the case of 'equal work', to which the concept of 'work to which equal value is attributed' is related (thereby taking up the provisions of art 2 of the Equal Remuneration Convention) (International Labour Organisation Convention no 100 (Geneva, 29th June 1951, TS 88 (1972), Cmnd 5039)). Thus it is only in relation to that innovative aspect of art 1 of the directive that there can be any point in inquiring whether the answer to the issue raised by the second question is dependent on that article rather than on art 119 alone. And it appears to me to be clear that the answer must be in the negative; indeed, it was on the basis of art 119 alone that I concluded that the principle of equal pay must not be confined to contemporaneous work performed by a man and a woman working within the same undertaking. In other words, that view is not influenced in the least by the fact that today, as a result of the 1975 directive, the principle in question extends to two jobs to which equal value is attributed; irrespective of that extension, and even if the extension had not occurred, the view which I have adopted would be tenable (and, in my opinion, well founded).

In the present case, the English tribunal of first instance, and, at least by implication, that of second instance also, considered that the applicant's work was 'broadly similar', and that her services were 'broadly comparable', to that of the previous warehouse manager. That led those tribunals to hold that s 1(4) of the 1970 Act applied, thereby surmounting, as I stated at the outset, the restriction in the legislation whereby only two jobs performed contemporaneously could be regarded as comparable. The wording of the first question put by the Court of Appeal, to which the second is linked, also reflects this. It is well settled that the assessment of whether the two jobs to be compared are identical or similar is a matter for the tribunal having jurisdiction as to the substance of the case. I think that all that may be added, in general terms, is that the approach adopted in EEC Council Directive 75/117, in the sense of interpreting and implementing art 119 of the EEC Treaty in a broad manner, warrants a liberal construction of the expression 'equal work' used in that provision. Accordingly, in my opinion, that phrase is to be construed in such a manner as to include two jobs which display a high degree of similarity the one to the other, even if there is not total identity between them.

The negative reply which I thus propose to give to the third question deprives of content the fourth and final question framed by the Court of Appeal to cover the sole eventuality of an affirmative answer to question 3.

In conclusion, I would suggest that the court, in answering the questions referred to it for a preliminary ruling by the Court of Appeal should rule that:

1. the application of the principle of equal pay for equal work without discrimination on grounds of sex contained in art 119 of the EEC Treaty is not confined solely to cases where men and women employed by the same undertaking are contemporaneously engaged on that employment;

2. the above-mentioned principle is equally valid in cases where a female worker can show that she received from her employer a lesser remuneration than that which a male worker had previously received or that which he would have received if he had been contemporaneously engaged in the same undertaking and on the same work, provided always that there is no objective justification for the difference in treatment on grounds other than the difference in sex;

3. in the case of 'equal work' (which includes two jobs having a high degree of similarity) the affirmative answers to the preceding questions are based on art 119 of the EEC Treaty and are not dependent on the provisions of art 1 of EEC Council Directive 75/117.

27th March. **THE COURT OF JUSTICE** delivered its judgment which, having summarised the facts, procedure and submissions of the parties, dealt with the law as follows:

1. By order of 25th July 1979, received at the Court of Justice on 10th August 1979, the Court of Appeal in London referred to the court for a preliminary ruling under art 177 of the EEC Treaty four questions concerning the interpretation of art 119 of the EEC Treaty and art 1 of EEC Council Directive 75/117 of 10th February 1975 on the approximation of the laws of the member states relating to the application of the principle of equal pay for men and women (OJ L45, 19.2.1975, p 19).

2. It appears from the file that the respondent in the main action, Mrs Wendy Smith ('the applicant'), was employed as from 1st March 1976 by Macarthys Ltd ('the employers'), wholesale dealers in pharmaceutical products, as a warehouse manageress at a weekly salary of £50. She complains of discrimination in pay because her predecessor, a man, whose post she took up after an interval of four months, received a salary of £60 per week.

3. The applicant brought proceedings before an industrial tribunal on the basis of the Equal Pay Act 1970. By its decision of 27th June 1977 that tribunal held that the applicant was employed on like work with her predecessor and ordered the employers to pay the applicant a salary equal to his salary.

4. The employers appealed to the Employment Appeal Tribunal, which dismissed the appeal by its judgment of 14th December 1977 ([1978] 2 All ER 746, [1978] 1 WLR

849). That judgment, which was based, as was the decision of the industrial tribunal, on the 1970 Act, made reference also to art 119 of the EEC Treaty and to the judgment of the Court of Justice in *Defrenne v Sabena* p 122, post, which was concerned with the interpretation of that provision.

5. A further appeal was brought before the Court of Appeal by the employers. The employers contended that, according to its natural and ordinary meaning, the 1970 Act makes it impermissible for a woman to compare her situation with that of a man formerly in the employment of the same employer. In their submission, such an interpretation would not be inconsistent with the principle of equal pay for men and women laid down in art 119 of the EEC Treaty.

6. For her part, the applicant contended that the employers' interpretation was contrary to art 119 of the treaty and to art 1 of the directive in that the principle of equal pay for equal work is not confined to situations in which men and women are contemporaneously doing equal work for their employer but that, on the contrary, that principle also applies where a worker can show that she receives less pay in respect of her employment than she would have received if she were a man doing equal work for the employer or than had been received by a male worker who had been employed prior to her period of employment and who had been doing equal work for her employer.

7. In order to decide the dispute the Court of Appeal formulated four questions worded as follows (see [1979] 3 All ER 325 at 336, [1979] 1 WLR 1189):

'(1) Is the principle of equal pay for equal work, contained in art 119 of the EEC Treaty and art 1 of the EEC Council Directive of 10th February 1975 (75/117/EEC), confined to situations in which men and women are contemporaneously doing equal work for their employer?

'(2) If the answer to question (1) is in the negative, does the principle apply where a worker can show that she receives less pay in respect of her employment from her employer (a) than she would have received if she were a man doing equal work for the employer or (b) than had been received by a male worker who had been employed prior to her period of employment and who had been doing equal work for the employer?

'(3) If the answer to question (2)(a) or (b) is in the affirmative, is that answer dependent on the provisions of art 1 of the directive?

'(4) If the answer to question (3) is in the affirmative, is art 1 of the directive directly applicable in member states?'

8. It follows from the wording of these questions, as much as from the reasons given in the order making the reference, that the questions relating to the effect of EEC Council Directive 75/117 and to the interpretation of art 1 thereof only arise if the application of art 119 of the EEC Treaty should not permit the issue raised in the proceedings to be resolved. It is therefore appropriate to consider first how art 119 is to be interpreted having regard to the legal situation in which the dispute has its origin.

The interpretation of art 119 of the EEC Treaty

9. According to the first paragraph of art 119 the member states are obliged to ensure and maintain 'the application of the principle that men and women should receive equal pay for equal work'.

10. As the court indicated in *Defrenne v Sabena*, that provision applies directly, and without the need for more detailed implementing measures on the part of the Community or the member states, to all forms of direct and overt discrimination which may be identified solely with the aid of the criteria of equal work and equal pay referred to by the article in question. Among the forms of discrimination which may be thus judicially identified, the court mentioned in particular cases where men and women receive unequal pay for equal work carried out in the same establishment or service.

11. In such a situation the decisive test lies in establishing whether there is a difference in treatment between a man and a woman performing 'equal work' within the meaning

of art 119. The scope of that concept, which is entirely qualitative in character in that it is exclusively concerned with the nature of the services in question, may not be restricted by the introduction of a requirement of contemporaneity.

12. It must be acknowledged, however, that, as the Employment Appeal Tribunal properly recognised, it cannot be ruled out that a difference in pay between two workers occupying the same post but at different periods in time may be explained by the operation of factors which are unconnected with any discrimination on grounds of sex. That is a question of fact which it is for the court or tribunal to decide.

13. Thus the answer to the first question should be that the principle that men and women should receive equal pay for equal work, enshrined in art 119 of the EEC Treaty, is not confined to situations in which men and women are contemporaneously doing equal work for the same employer.

14. The second question put by the Court of Appeal and expressed in terms of alternatives concerns the framework within which the existence of possible discrimination in pay may be established. This question is intended to enable the court to rule on a submission made by the applicant and developed by her before the Court of Justice to the effect that a woman may claim not only the salary received by a man who previously did the same work for her employer but also, more generally, the salary to which she would be entitled were she a man, even in the absence of any man who was concurrently performing, or had previously performed, similar work. The applicant defined this term of comparison by reference to the concept of what she described as 'a hypothetical male worker'.

15. It is clear that the latter proposition, which is the subject of question (2)(a), is to be classed as indirect and disguised discrimination, the identification of which, as the court explained in *Defrenne v Sabena*, implies comparative studies of entire branches of industry and therefore requires, as a prerequisite, the elaboration by the Community and national legislative bodies of criteria of assessment. From that it follows that, in cases of actual discrimination falling within the scope of the direct application of art 119, comparisons are confined to parallels which may be drawn on the basis of concrete appraisals of the work actually performed by employees of different sex within the same establishment or service.

16. The answer to the second question should therefore be that the principle of equal pay enshrined in art 119 applies to the case where it is established that, having regard to the nature of her services, a woman has received less pay than a man who was employed prior to the woman's period of employment and who did equal work for the employer.

17. From the foregoing it appears that the dispute brought before the national court may be decided within the framework of an interpretation of art 119 of the EEC Treaty alone. In those circumstances it is unnecessary to answer the questions submitted in so far as they relate to the effect and to the interpretation of EEC Council Directive 75/117.

Costs

18. The costs incurred by the government of the United Kingdom and by the Commission of the European Communities, which have submitted observations to the court, are not recoverable. As these proceedings are, in so far as the parties to the main action are concerned, in the nature of a step in the action pending before the Court of Appeal in London, the decision as to costs is a matter for that court.

On those grounds, the court, in answer to the questions referred to it by the Court of Appeal, Civil Division, of the Supreme Court of Judicature by order of 25th July 1979, hereby rules: (1) the principle that men and women should receive equal pay for equal work, enshrined in art 119 of the EEC Treaty, is not confined to situations in which men and women are contemporaneously doing equal work for the same employer; (2) the principle of equal pay enshrined in art 119 applies to the case where it is established that, having regard to the nature of her services, a woman has received less pay than a man who was employed prior to the woman's period of employment and who did equal work for the employer.

Agents: *John L Williams* (for the applicant); *A D Preston*, Treasury Solicitor's Department (for the United Kingdom); *Stanley Crossick* (for the Commission).

Andrew Durand Esq   Barrister.

Appeal

Following the receipt by the Court of Appeal, Civil Division of the answers to the questions referred by it to the Court of Justice of the European Communities the employers conceded that they had no alternative but to submit to judgment in the appeal.

R L Turner for the employers.
Anthony Lester QC and *C R McConnell* for the applicant.

LORD DENNING MR. Although this application is only about costs, I will say a word about it; because it is of public importance.

The applicant, Mrs Wendy Smith, was employed by wholesale dealers in pharmaceutical products. She was paid a salary of £50 a week. She discovered that a man (who had left) had previously been performing her task. He had been paid £60 a week. She took proceedings under our English statute, the Equal Pay Act 1970 (as amended by the Sex Discrimination Act 1975). She claimed that her pay should be equal to his. An objection was taken that her application was bad in point of law, because our English statute did not apply in the case of successive employment, and it only applied when the man and the woman were employed together at the same time contemporaneously.

That point was argued before this court. The majority of the court held that the objection was well founded. They interpreted it as meaning that the equal pay provisions only applied when the man and the woman were employed at the same time contemporaneously. But then the point arose: what was the position under Community law? We were referred to art 119 of the EEC Treaty. The Court of Justice of the European Communities sitting at Luxembourg had decided that art 119 of the treaty was directly applicable in the national courts of each country. It was submitted that under art 119 there was no requirement that the man and the woman should be employed contemporaneously at the same time, and that, under that article, the woman was entitled to equal pay even though the man had left before she joined and the woman had taken his job afterwards.

The majority of this court felt that art 119 was uncertain. So this court referred the problem to the European Court at Luxembourg. We have now been provided with the decision of that court. It is important now to declare, and it must be made plain, that the provisions of art 119 of the EEC Treaty take priority over anything in our English statute on equal pay which is inconsistent with art 119. That priority is given by our own law. It is given by the European Communities Act 1972 itself. Community law is now part of our law; and, whenever there is any inconsistency, Community law has priority. It is not supplanting English law. It is part of our law which overrides any other part which is inconsistent with it. I turn therefore to the decision given by the European Court. The answer they gave was that the man and the woman need not be employed at the same time. The woman is entitled to equal pay for equal work, even when the woman is employed after the man has left. That interpretation must now be given by all the courts in England. It will apply in this case and in any such case hereafter.

Applying it in this case, the applicant was right. Although she was employed subsequently to the man, she was entitled to be paid the same as the man. She was entitled to be paid not £50, but £60. That is the result of the Community law as applied to our present law. So that must be the decision.

The appeal that the employers brought to this court must therefore be dismissed.

The argument before us today was as to costs. It was argued before us that at the hearing before the tribunals, and indeed before this court, the employers were entitled

to look solely to our English statute on equal pay. It was said that, in that statute, our
a parliamentary draftsmen thought they were carrying out, and intended to carry out, the
provisions of the EEC Treaty. So much so that, before the European Court at
Luxembourg, the United Kingdom government argued that, in order for the woman to
be entitled to equal pay, her employment had to be contemporaneous. Accordingly the
employers said that they were entitled to go by the English statute, and not the EEC
Treaty, and so the costs should not fall on them of the appeal to this court.

b   The answer is this: the employers had no right to look at our English statute alone.
They ought throughout to have looked at the EEC Treaty as well. Community law is
part of our law by our own statute, the European Communities Act 1972. In applying
it, we should regard it in the same way as if we found an inconsistency between two
English Acts of Parliament; and the court had to decide which had to be given priority.
In such a case the party who loses has to pay the costs. So it seems to me that the
c employers should pay all the costs of the appeal to this court.

     I may say that the applicant, or those behind her, do not ask for the costs of the
reference to Luxembourg. That is a special arrangement which applies in this particular
case, although it may not apply in other cases. All we are concerned with today are the
costs in this court. In my judgment, the appeal should be dismissed with the costs in this
court to be paid by the unsuccessful appellants, the employers.

d **LAWTON LJ.** I agree.

CUMMING-BRUCE LJ. I agree. I would only add a word in view of the fact that
counsel for the applicant has drawn the attention of this court to the existence of a note
by Professor Hood Phillips in the Law Quarterly Review ((1980) 96 LQR 31) which
e apparently expressed the view that the decision of this court has created a doubt about
the constitutional position arising from a conflict between an English statute and
European law. In my view there is no real room for doubt, and, if anything that I said
in my judgment has given rise to doubt which is based on misunderstanding, I repeat
what I said on the last occasion, that 'If the terms of the Treaty are adjudged in
Luxembourg to be inconsistent with the provisions of the Equal Pay Act 1970, European
f law will prevail over that municipal legislation'. I went on to say this: 'But such a
judgment in Luxembourg cannot affect the meaning of the English statute' (see [1979]
3 All ER 325 at 335–336).

     Perhaps I expressed myself a little too widely there. The majority in this court took
the view that there was no ambiguity about the words of the Equal Pay Act 1970 which
we had to construe; and, as there was no ambiguity, the majority took the view that it
g was not appropriate, according to English canons of construction, to look outside the
statute at art 119 as an aid to construction. In my view that was clearly right, but I would
make it clear that had I been of the view that there was an ambiguity in the English
statute, I would have taken the view that it was appropriate to look at art 119 in order to
assist in resolving the ambiguity.

     I only add those words because of the doubt which has arisen in the article in the Law
h Quarterly Review.

Appeal dismissed.

Solicitors: *Baileys, Shaw & Gillett* (for the employers); *John L Williams* (for the applicant).

                                  Sumra Green   Barrister.

Note
Defrenne v Sabena
(Case 43/75)

COURT OF JUSTICE OF THE EUROPEAN COMMUNITIES

JUDGES LECOURT (PRESIDENT), KUTSCHER, O'KEEFFE (PRESIDENTS OF CHAMBERS), DONNER,
MERTENS DE WILMARS, PESCATORE AND SØRENSON

3rd DECEMBER 1975, 10th MARCH, 8th APRIL 1976

European Economic Community – Treaty provisions – Direct application in member states – Social policy – Equal pay for equal work – Member states obliged to ensure and maintain principle of equal pay for equal work – Member state failing to enact legislation giving effect to obligation – Whether national courts having duty to give effect to obligation in private proceedings between employee and employer – EEC Treaty, art 119.

In October 1963 the plaintiff was promoted to the post of air hostess by her employer, the defendant. It was conceded that a female air hostess performed the same work as a male cabin steward but until 1st February 1966 the plaintiff's rate of pay as an air hostess was less than that of a male cabin steward. In that year the employer introduced equal pay in anticipation of Belgian equal pay legislation, which came into force in October 1967. The plaintiff retired at the beginning of 1968 and in March claimed damages from her employer for wrongfully failing to pay her at the same rate as a male cabin steward between 15th February 1963 and 1st February 1966. The claim did not relate to any period before 15th February 1963 because of Belgium's five-year limitation period. The basis of the plaintiff's claim was that art 119[a] of the EEC Treaty gave her an enforceable right to equal pay as from 1st January 1962 and that therefore her employer's disregard of that right rendered it liable to compensate her for her loss. The defendant's submission that it was only obliged to comply with Belgian law and that the obligation imposed by art 119 was imposed, if at all, on the state of Belgium was upheld by the Tribunal du travail, Brussels. On appeal, the Cour du travail, Brussels stayed the proceedings and referred to the Court of Justice of the European Communities the question whether art 119 had introduced directly into the national law of each member state the principle of equal pay, and, if so, from what date.

Held – Article 119 of the EEC Treaty could be invoked directly by an employee against his employer for the following reasons—

(1) A fundamental obligation imposed on a member state by the EEC Treaty bound all the organs of that state, the judiciary as well as the legislature. In so far as a court using the techniques of legal analysis could give effect to a fundamental obligation imposed by the Treaty, then it was required to do so. Where the legislature of a member state failed to enact the necessary legislation to carry out such an obligation by the date laid down in the Treaty, the courts, in so far as it was possible, were themselves obliged to execute the obligation at the request of a person concerned in litigation between private parties (see p 134 *d e* and *j* to p 135 *d*, post).

(2) The obligation in art 119 that member states should introduce and subsequently maintain the application of the principle that men and women should receive equal pay for equal work by 31st December 1961 was a fundamental obligation. In so far as it could, without further legislation, be enforced by the courts in litigation between employer and employee it was required to be so enforced. A distinction was, however,

---

[a] Article 119, so far as material, provides: 'Each Member State shall during the first stage ensure and subsequently maintain the application of the principle that men and women should receive equal pay for equal work . . .'

to be drawn between direct and overt discrimination on the one hand and indirect or
a disguised discrimination on the other, both of which had to be removed to comply with
art 119. The courts, without further clarification, were capable of identifying overt
discrimination using the criteria in the Treaty. However, the prohibition of indirect or
disguised discrimination might require further implementing legislation before it could
give rise to justiciable issues. The courts were capable of giving and obliged to give a
remedy to a person aggrieved by discrimination contained in legislative provisions or
b collective labour agreements or by discrimination occurring in the same establishment
or service (see p 134 *a* to *f*, p 135 *e f*, p 136 *f* to *j*, p 137 *b* to *e* and p 138 *c* to *f*, post).

(3) Since employers had been given the impression by the Commission of the
European Communities and the member states themselves that discriminatory practices
could be maintained until prohibited by national law, considerations of legal certainty
required the court, as an exceptional measure, to declare the law for the future only
c except for those who had already commenced proceedings (see p 137 *g* to p 138 *a* and *f*,
post).

Notes
For the right of men and women under the EEC Treaty to receive equal pay for equal
work, see 16 Halsbury's Laws (4th Edn) para 521.
d For the EEC Treaty, art 119, see 42A Halsbury's Statutes (3rd Edn) 779.

Cases cited
Airola (Jeanne) v EC Commission Case 21/74 [1975] ECR 221, CJEC.
Alfons Lütticke GmbH v Hauptzollamt Saarlouis Case 57/65 [1966] ECR 205, [1971] CMLR
674, CJEC.
Defrenne (Gabrielle) v Belgian State Case 80/70 [1971] ECR 445, [1974] 1 CMLR 494, CJEC.
e *EC Commission v Italian Republic* Case 39/72 [1973] ECR 101, [1973] CMLR 439, CJEC.
Firma Fink-Frucht GmbH v Hauptzollamt München-Landsbergerstrasse Case 27/67 [1968]
ECR 223, [1968] CMLR 187, CJEC.
Firma-Molkerei-Zentrale Westfalen/Lippe GmbH v Hauptzollamt Paderborn Case 28/67 [1968]
ECR 143, [1968] CMLR 187, CJEC.
Internationale Handelsgesellschaft mbH v Einfuhr- und Vorratsstelle für Getreide und
f *Futtermittel* Case 11/70 [1970] ECR 1125, [1972] CMLR 255, CJEC.
Pubblico Ministero v Flavia Manghera Case 59/75 [1976] ECR 91, [1976] 1 CMLR 557,
CJEC.
Reyners (Jean) v Belgian State Case 2/74 [1974] ECR 631, [1974] 2 CMLR 305, CJEC.
Sabbatini (Luisa), née Bertoni v European Parliament Case 20/71 [1972] ECR 345, [1972]
CMLR 945, CJEC.
g *van Binsbergen (Johannes Henricus Maria) v Bestuur van de Bedrijfsvereniging voor de*
Metaalnijverheid Case 33/74 [1974] ECR 1299, [1975] 1 CMLR 298, CJEC.
Van Duyn v The Home Office (No 2) Case 41/74 [1975] 3 All ER 190, [1975] Ch 358, [1975]
2 WLR 760, [1974] ECR 1337, [1975] 1 CMLR 1, CJEC, Digest (Cont Vol D) 317, 4.
Walrave (BNO) and LJN Koch v Association Union Cycliste Internationale, Koninklijke
Nederlandsche Wielren Unie and Federacion Española Ciclismo Case 36/74 [1974] ECR
h 1405, [1975] 1 CMLR 320, CJEC.

Reference
Following proceedings commenced in the Tribunal du travail, Brussels by Gabrielle
Defrenne against Société Anonyme Belge de Navigation Aérienne (Sabena) and on appeal
in the Cour du travail, Brussels, the latter court by judgment of 23rd April 1975 referred
j two questions (set out at p 125 *b* to *d*, post) concerning the interpretation of art 119 of the
EEC Treaty to the Court of Justice of the European Communities for a preliminary
ruling under art 177 of the Treaty. The United Kingdom and Ireland submitted
observations to the European court. The language of the case was French. The facts are
set out in the opinion of the Advocate-General, which has been translated from the
Italian.

Marie-Thérèse Cuvelliez (of the Brussels Bar) for Miss Defrenne.
Philippe de Keyser (of the Brussels Bar) for Sabena.
Peter Scott (of the Bar of England and Wales) for the United Kingdom.
The Chief State Solicitor of Ireland (*Liam T Lysaght*) for Ireland.
Marie-Josée Jonczy, Legal Adviser to the EC Commission, for the Commission.

10th March. **The Advocate-General (A Trabucchi)** delivered the following opinion: Mr President, Members of the Court, after the solemn declarations made by the heads of state and of government in Paris in 1972 on the importance of the social aspects of European integration, here we have a private individual, a female worker, who succeeds in obtaining from her national court a reference for a preliminary ruling on the interpretation of the provision in the EEC Treaty which establishes the principle of equal treatment for men and women in the field of employment. A reference which in itself is of very modest financial importance provides an opportunity for this court to clarify certain aspects of the protection which fundamental rights are entitled to receive within the framework of the Community structure.

This is the second reference for a preliminary ruling which bears the name of Miss G Defrenne, a former air hostess of Sabena (the Société Anonyme Belge de Navigation Aérienne).

Engaged on 10th December 1951 as a 'trainee air hostess' she proceeded, on 1 October 1963, under a new contract, to discharge the responsibilities appropriate to the category of 'cabin steward, air hostess/principal cabin attendant'. Earlier, on 15th March 1963, Sabena and the workers' trade unions concluded a collective agreement which could not be made binding by a royal decree and which, in fact, has never been binding. In conformity with the collective contract, a clause was inserted in the individual contract of the person concerned providing that the contract of women members of the cabin crew was in all cases to cease automatically on completion of 40 years of age. This clause was applied to Miss Defrenne on 15th February 1968.

Under the terms of her contract, she received a grant equivalent to one year's salary. Miss Defrenne then took two actions.

On 9th February 1970 she applied to the Belgian Conseil d'Etat for annulment of the Royal Decree of 3rd November which, for civil aviation crew, laid down special rules governing the acquisition of the right to a pension and special procedures for implementation of Royal Decree No 50 of 24th October 1967 concerning retirement pensions and survivors' pensions for employed persons, on the basis of which her pension had been calculated.

Giving a preliminary ruling on a reference made to it by the Belgian court, this court, in its judgment of 25th May 1971, ruled that a retirement pension established within the framework of a social security scheme laid down by legislation does not constitute consideration which the worker receives indirectly in respect of his employment from his employer within the meaning of art 119 of the EEC Treaty (see *Defrenne v Belgian State* [1971] ECR 445).

At the same time, on 13th March 1968, Miss Defrenne brought proceedings against Sabena before the Tribunal du travail, Brussels, claiming compensation for the injury she alleged she had suffered owing to the fact that: (1) the salary paid to her during the period between 15th February 1963 and 1st February 1966 was FB 12,716 less than that to which a male 'steward' with the same seniority would have been entitled; (2) she was entitled to a severance grant of FB 166,138; (3) she ought to have been recognised as entitled to a higher pension, up to a maximum of FB 334,000.

In its judgment on 17th December 1970, the Tribunal du travail, Brussels, dismissed all three heads of claim without recourse to art 177 of the EEC Treaty.

On 11th April 1971 Miss Defrenne thereupon brought an appeal before the Court du travail, Brussels. Finally, on 23rd April 1975, that court found that only the first head of claim required interpretation of art 119 of the treaty and thereupon referred to this court the questions which we must now consider.

In spite of the opinion to the contrary expressed by the Auditeur Général, the Cour du travail dismissed the applications relating to the injury which Miss Defrenne claims to have suffered, in connection with pension and grant as a result of the difference in previous salary and the difference in pensionable age respectively compared with her male colleagues.

Arrears were claimed only with effect from 15th February 1963 because of the five-year limitation rule provided for under art 2277 of the Belgian Civil Code. The reason why the claim does not extend beyond 1st February 1966 is that, with effect from that date, Sabena, of its own accord, placed 'hostesses' and 'stewards' on the same basic rates of pay.

The questions referred to the Court are in the following terms: (1) does art 119 of the EEC Treaty introduce directly into the national law of each member state of the European Community the principle that men and women should receive equal pay for equal work and does it therefore, independently of any national provision, entitle workers to institute proceedings before national courts in order to ensure its observance, and if so as from what date? (2) has art 119 become applicable in the internal law of the member states by virtue of measures adopted by the authorities of the European Economic Community (if so, which, and as from what date?) or must the national legislature be regarded as alone competent in this matter?

Article 119 is not a complete innovation: it must be viewed both in the light of internationally recognised principles and in the light of the EEC Treaty.

At international level art 119 is the extension, the 'European translation', of the International Labour Organisation convention concerning equal remuneration for men and women workers for work of equal value (ILO Convention no 100 (Geneva, 29th June 1951, TS 88 (1972), Cmnd 5039)). The convention has now been ratified by all the member states of the EEC although some of them ratified it after the entry into force of the EEC Treaty (the Netherlands in 1971 and Ireland in 1974). Belgium, however, had already ratified it on 23rd May 1952. The convention, which came into force a year later, on 23rd May 1953, is accordingly applicable in all the member states although not with effect from the same date. The question whether it is or is not 'self-executing' has no bearing on the interpretation to be placed in Community law on the provision of art 119 of the EEC Treaty which is, essentially, its counterpart.

In the EEC Treaty art 119 appears in Chapter 1 (Social Provisions) of Title III (Social Policy) of Part Three (Policy of the Community).

It embodies an objective consonant with that laid down in the preamble to the treaty and subsequently expressed more precisely in art 117, which recognises 'the need to promote improved working conditions and an improved standard of living for workers, so as to make possible their harmonisation while the improvement is being maintained'. Obviously, this harmonisation can be achieved only if the standard of living and working conditions, in particular those relating to pay, are harmonised not only as between the member states but also within each state and, again, as between men and women.

As Mr Advocate-General Dutheillet de Lamothe said in *Defrenne v Belgian State* [1971] ECR 445 at 455, art 119 has a double objective:

> '... a social objective ... since it leads all the countries of the Community to accept the principle of a basically social nature raised by the ILO Convention; but an economic objective, too, for in creating an obstacle to any attempt at "social dumping" by means of the use of female labour less well paid than male labour, it helped to achieve one of the fundamental objectives of the common market, the establishment of a system ensuring that "competition is not distorted".'

Confirmation of this view is provided both by the 'preparatory documents' and by the subsequent attitudes adopted by the member states.

The authors of the ECSC Treaty provided that the Community should 'progressively bring about conditions which will of themselves ensure the most rational distribution of production at the highest possible level of productivity' (see art 2). In much clearer terms, the authors of the EEC Treaty declared (about twenty years ago) that 'spontaneous' harmonisation of rates of pay as a result of action by the trade unions and of the progressive establishment of the Common Market must be completed by special action on the part of the governments.

This brings us to the wording of art 119. The first paragraph reads as follows:

'Each Member State shall during the first stage ensure and subsequently maintain the application of the principle that men and women should receive equal pay for equal work.'

The principle quoted was, therefore, due to be put into operation before the end of the first stage, namely before 1st January 1962.

The treaty forms a single entity; it is impossible to lay emphasis on some of its provisions and ignore others without upsetting the balance of the whole. Thus, in order to prevent any delay whatsoever affecting social policy pending transition to the second stage, the Commission addressed to member states and, through them, to all the authorities competent to determine rates of pay, a recommendation, dated 20th July 1960, in which it reminded them of the need to fulfil the obligation imposed by art 119 and indicated the means whereby this aim could be achieved. But, because, subsequently, the member states considered that they were not in a position to comply with the prescribed time limit, the 'conference of member states' adopted, on 30th December 1961, a resolution on art 119 in which a fresh timetable was laid down for the phasing out of differences of treatment and laid down 31st December 1964 as the date by which all discrimination must be abolished.

It should be noted that both the recommendation and the resolution emphasise the need for the member states to establish, in their own national legal systems, a means of redress of which women can avail themselves in the event of an infringement of art 119. This would appear to indicate that, in the view of the Commission and of the member states, art 119 was not 'self executing'.

This leads us to the heart of the matter and to the question, which we must now consider, whether art 119 constitutes a provision having direct effect.

Under the criteria established by the case law of this court, a Community provision produces direct effects so as to confer on individuals the right to enforce it in the courts, provided that it is clear and sufficiently precise in its content, does not contain any reservation and is complete in itself in the sense that its application by national courts does not require the adoption of any subsequent measure of implementation either by the states or the Community.

Let us consider whether, viewed in the light of the context and spirit of the treaty, the character and content of art 119 satisfy these conditions.

The provision in question places every member state under the unconditional obligation to ensure during the first stage, and subsequently to maintain, the application of the principle that men and women should receive equal pay for equal work.

Although the form of words used, 'principle that men and women should receive equal pay', may seem too vague and the meaning of the word 'principle' itself not to be very specific, the purpose of the rule is nevertheless clear: to prohibit any discrimination to the detriment of women with regard to pay.

It can be argued that, even though art 119 defines the concept of pay for the purposes of equality, the definition given of it is not so complete as to exclude all doubt about the precise meaning of the rule. Under the case law of the court, however, the fact that the concepts relied on in a provision require interpretation by the national court, which may, inter alia, avail itself of the procedure in art 177 of the treaty, constitutes no obstacle to recognition of its direct effect (see *Firma Fink-Frucht GmbH v Hauptzollamt München-Landsbergerstrasse* [1968] ECR 223 and *Van Duyn v The Home Office (No 2)* [1975] 3 All ER 190, [1975] Ch 358).

Again, with regard to the definition of the concept of 'equal work', which is in any case
partly described in the third paragraph of art 119 (which, in addition to using the term
'same work' for work at piece rates, also refers to pay for work at time rates as 'the same
for the same job'), there is no need to exaggerate its importance in applying the article.
It has been rightly observed that art 119—

> 'does not try to determine when men and women are doing the same work but
> only to ensure that the sex of the worker is in no way taken into account in decisions
> on pay. Whether the work is the same or different is a question of fact to be
> determined in every individual case in accordance with the responsibilities assigned
> to each person concerned and must not be the subject of an a priori decision any
> more than there is an a priori decision that two men placed on the same rate of pay
> perform the same work.'

(See Levi Sandri, Commentario CEE, vol 2, p 956.)

The conclusion may therefore be drawn that, as regards the abolition, in connection
with pay, of all discrimination based on sex, art 119 imposes an obligation which is clear,
precise and unconditional. It must, however, be emphasised that art 119 does not
provide for, or rather does not always necessarily provide for, all possible implications of
the principle of equal pay for men and women in its fullest sense. The application of the
principle to situations other than those referred to in the aforesaid article (cases where the
'same work', namely identical work, is performed) lies, without doubt, outside the
context in which the question of the direct applicability of the rule can arise and more
properly falls within the field of social policy the definition and application of which
primarily depend on the initiative and co-ordinating action of the Community executive
and of the member states.

The obligation imposed on the member states, to which the rule is formally addressed,
consists of an obligation to act subject to a specific time limit (the end of the first stage).
As we know, by the resolution of 31st December 1961 the member states determined
to extend the time limit for full application of the principle of equal pay until 31st
December 1964. As the validity and effect of that act must be established I must point
out that in form it constitutes an agreement reached between the representatives of the
member states meeting in Council; as for its effect, it specifies the substance of art 119 by
laying down the methods and the timetable to be followed in implementing it.

As in the case of the ruling given in *Pubblico Ministero v Manghera* [1976] ECR 91
concerning a resolution on another subject, there can be no doubt that the resolution is
powerless to amend the treaty by replacing the clear provision in art 119 in respect of the
time limit therein provided.

The resolution must, therefore, be regarded as an essentially political act expressing
the states' concern to solve the problems arising from implementation of art 119. It does
not constitute an independent source of obligations for the states; such obligations stem
exclusively from the article of the treaty. The wording of the provision under
consideration certainly implies action by the states to put the obligation which they have
assumed into full effect.

In view of this the question arises whether art 119 possesses the completeness which
a provision is required to have in order to be recognised as having direct effect.

From the precedents established by this court it is clear that an article of the treaty does
not cease to have direct effect merely because it imposes on the states an obligation to act,
provided that the obligation is expressed clearly and unconditionally, its tenor is precise
and no real discretion is left to the member states with respect to the application of the
provision (see, for example, *Alfons Lütticke GmbH v Hauptzollamt Saarlouis* [1966] ECR
205).

Apart from cases where work which is not identical has to be established as being of
equal value, which could undoubtedly give rise to fairly complicated assessments on the
part, in the first place, of the legislature, the application of art 119 does not necessarily
require the adoption of implementing legislation in circumstances (which, in this case,

are exclusively the concern of the court making the reference) where work which is undoubtedly identical is differently rewarded on grounds of sex.

Difficulties might, of course, be involved in the concept of 'pay'. Those who drafted art 119 tried to define this concept. Repeating, on this point word for word the text of art 1(*a*) of the ILO convention[1], art 119 provides:

'... "pay" means the ordinary basic or minimum wage or salary and any other consideration, whether in cash or in kind, which the worker receives, directly or indirectly, in respect of his employment from his employer ...'

Despite this clarification, it will, in my opinion, frequently be necessary to interpret the concept of pay and especially that of 'any other consideration'. The court did this in the first *Defrenne* case and, in respect of the treatment of dependants, in *Sabbatini v European Parliament* [1972] ECR 345.

Nevertheless, it seems clear to me that the ordinary basic wage or salary as set out in the salary table or scales must be treated as pay and that if, in the event, there is found to be discrimination solely on grounds of sex, this constitutes one of the conditions for application of art 119. All that I need add is that, as is observed by the court making the reference, the difference of FB 12,716 is due to the difference in the 'basic salary scales' applicable to men and women and not to supplementary perquisites, whether direct or indirect, in cash, or in kind, such as 'flight bonuses' or 'cabin bar takings'.

On this point, too, therefore, I consider that there is nothing standing in the way of the direct applicability of art 119 in a case such as that on which the national court is called on to rule.

But another question arises. In contrast to the other articles of the EEC Treaty which the court has hitherto declared to have immediate effect and which are concerned with matters on which there is a direct legal relationship between the state and its subjects (customs or taxation law and the right of establishment), art 119, despite the fact that it is restricted to imposing an obligation on the states, is primarily concerned with the relationship between individuals. The discrimination which the provision sets out to prohibit will, in the majority of cases, consist of discriminatory action by a private undertaking against women workers.

The state directly intervenes in the fixing of rates of pay only in the public sector; in the private sector, on the other hand, pay rates are largely left to be fixed by agreement between the independent parties to the contract. The national authorities might not, therefore, be in a position, on the basis of this provision alone, forthwith to impose the principle of equal pay. To this end it would be necessary to adopt appropriate national legislation.

For these reasons, the intervener governments have argued that the provision under consideration does no more than impose a direct obligation on the member states alone and that it cannot create rights and duties in the case of individuals.

A subsidiary argument contended for by the representative of the Commission is to the effect that, from a purely technical standpoint, art 119 could enable individuals to bring an action which, although admissible, would be upheld only if it were based on discrimination for which, as the employer, the state was responsible or, at least, on systems of payment directly fixed by the national legislative or executive authorities in the country concerned.

The above-mentioned arguments seem to me to misconceive the principles of the Community legal order which have been developed by case law covering more than twenty years.

To begin with, if we were able to accept that the provision is directly applicable only

---

1   Translator's note: But not of the English text of the convention, which, so far as material, provides: '... "remuneration" includes the ordinary, basic or minimum wage or salary and any additional emoluments whatsoever payable directly or indirectly, whether in cash or in kind, by the employer to the worker and arising out of the worker's employment ...'

against public employers this would, as was emphasised by the agent of the Irish
a Government, constitute fresh and unacceptable discrimination between the public and
private sectors. The legal status of Sabena and its relationship with the Belgian State
have, therefore, no relevance to the present dispute.

It should also be borne in mind that, under settled and well-known precedents
established by this court, even provisions addressed to the states alone are, in certain
conditions, capable of creating individual rights which the national courts can and must
b protect.

The decisive factor in determining what the effects of a Community provision are in
national law is not the identity of those to whom it is addressed but its nature, which the
court defines on the basis of 'the spirit, the general scheme and the wording' of the
provision itself.

The object of art 119 is, within a specified time, to abolish discrimination of any kind
c in fixing rates of pay and, moreover, not only discrimination created by the laws or
regulations of the member states but also discrimination produced by collective
agreements or individual contracts of employment.

It follows that the obligation to observe the principle of equality is imposed not only
on the states, inasmuch as the determination of the pay of government servants is
concerned, but, provided that the requirement stated in the provision is sufficiently clear
d and precise in meaning to enable it to apply in relation to third parties, it also has effects
in the field left to trade union organisations and individuals in which to conclude their
collective or individual contracts. This is due entirely to the provision of the EEC Treaty,
regardless of other implementing provisions adopted to this end by the state.

When requested to give a ruling on a private 'regulation' adopted by an international
sporting organisation, the court stated in *Walrave v Association Union Cycliste Internationale*
e [1974] ECR 1405 that both art 59 and art 48 prohibit not only discrimination which has
its origin in acts of a public authority but also those arising from 'rules of any other
nature aimed at regulating in a collective manner gainful employment and the provision
of services'. The attainment of the fundamental objectives of the EEC Treaty would in
fact be compromised in the absence of 'the abolition of . . . obstacles resulting from the
exercise of their legal autonomy by associations or organizations which do not come
f under public law'.

It is true that, in contrast to the free movement of persons, the principle of equal pay
is not included amongst the fundamental objectives of the EEC Treaty but its attainment
is of exceptional importance as a step towards 'economic and social progress' and in
achieving the 'constant improvement of the living and working conditions . . .' (see the
preamble to the treaty).

g I therefore feel able to conclude that the principle of equal pay, which by its very
nature is of direct concern to individuals, is, within the limits which I have indicated
above, capable of producing direct effects in respect of such individuals and enables them
to rely on it in the national courts without the need for it to be subject to adoption of
relevant legislative measures by the states.

Of course, the adoption of administrative or even penal sanctions could only reinforce
h the direct effectiveness of Community laws and would for this reason be particularly
favourable, but the main sanction is the inapplicability of national law or of any other
kind of act, public or private, which conflicts with directly applicable Community law.

Consequently, where previous national legislation or regulations have been repealed
or amended only by implication through the automatic incorporation of Community
laws within the national legal system, or where the contracting parties maintain in force
j collective or individual contracts which conflict with Community legislation, it is not
necessary, for an acknowledgment of the direct effectiveness of the latter, for those
national provisions to be formally harmonised with the Community laws concerned in
order that all concerned may be made aware of the change and any uncertainty as to the
law in force may be removed. Here, too, formal harmonisation would, without doubt,
be of great value, but any doubts, assuming there are any, may be removed by the use of

art 177 of the EEC Treaty; the danger that this court would be overwhelmed with requests for 'clarification' is an argument worthy of consideration only on grounds of expediency.

Accordingly, for the purposes of art 119, there is a very simple and effective method of moving against a discrimination; it is enough for the national courts to declare null and void any clause in an individual or collective contract which conflicts with that article. Here again, however, we must define the precise meaning of the words 'null and void'. Notwithstanding the axiom 'no nullity save as provided for by the law', the nullity to which I refer is based on public policy and thus takes priority over any individual provision of the law. On the question of pay, nullity means that the rate of pay provided for by the clause which is void is automatically replaced by the higher rate of pay granted to male workers.

There is nothing new in this. The courts in various member states have, even in the face of opposition from management and workers, and even in the absence of implementing legislation, so acted in order to give effect to the principles of equal treatment enshrined in the constitutions of the countries concerned.

The court has, moreover, recognised other provisions of the EEC Treaty as having direct effect, although they raised much greater problems (see, for example, art 95(1) of the EEC Treaty which is the subject of the judgment in *Alfons Lütticke GmbH v Hauptzollamt Saarlouis* [1966] ECR 205).

It is no more difficult for the national court to disallow a discriminatory contractual agreement than to disallow a national law which is incompatible with the EEC Treaty or to award compensation to an individual who has suffered damage as the result of such a law.

Furthermore, in interpreting art 119, the court cannot overlook the fact that the principle of equal treatment is enshrined in the legal system of member states, the majority of which have erected it into a principle formally underwritten by the constitution itself. In *Internationale Handelsgesellschaft mbH v Einfuhr- und Vorratsstelle für Getreide und Futtermittel* [1970] ECR 1125 at 1134 the court stated that respect for fundamental rights forms an integral part of the general principles of law and that the protection of such rights within the Community can and must be inspired by the constitutional traditions common to the member states. In view of this it seems to me that the prohibition of all discrimination based on sex (particularly on the subject of pay) protects a right which must be regarded as fundamental in the Community legal order as it is elsewhere.

In cases where discrimination was based on the criterion of mere residence or nationality (see *van Binsbergen v Bestuur van de Bedrijfsvereniging voor de Metaalnijverheid* [1974] ECR 1299 and *Reyners v Belgian State* [1974] ECR 631) the court declared any discrimination based on residence or nationality to be contrary to the EEC Treaty. I propose that the court should extend the principle of these decisions to discrimination based solely on considerations of sex, as the court has already done in the case of Community dependants (see *Sabbatini v European Parliament* [1972] ECR 345 at 351 and *Airola v EC Commission* [1975] ECR 221 at 228).

To summarise my comments, at this point, let me say that the words in art 119, 'Each Member State (shall ... ensure)', taken from ILO Convention no 100 and which are explained by the fact that the putting into effect of art 119 requires, on the part of the authorities of the member states (and of the so-called 'social partners', namely the employers, the workers and their respective organisations), constant action in order to ensure that the realisation of the principle is not placed in jeopardy even in the event of a technological development or a change in economic policy, have nevertheless a much deeper significance in the EEC Treaty; the words refer not only to the member state as a sovereign body bound by an international treaty, as was also the case under ILO Convention no 100 but, in addition, all the competent authorities of the state, including the courts, which have a duty to apply the provisions of the EEC Treaty.

It is true that application of the concepts of 'pay' and of 'work' may give rise to

difficulty but it is equally true that 'the fulfilment of [the obligation] had to be made
a easier by . . . the implementation of a programme of progressive measures' (see *Reyners
v Belgian State* [1974] ECR 631 at 651).

Undoubtedly, action by the member states and by the Community institutions in the
form of legislation, regulations or administrative measures is essential for the reason that,
if the principle of equal treatment were to apply only to pay in the strict sense of the
word or to absolutely identical work, the practical effect of art 119 would be rather
b small. This gives the member states and the Community institutions enormous scope in
taking action to put into effect the principle of non-discrimination laid down in art 119
without having to rely on its direct applicability.

Discrimination against women is, in fact, often disguised by the pay structure, the
classification or description of work and the special character of labour in certain spheres,
not to mention inequalities due to job training or promotion systems and general
c working conditions. The list of studies and investigations carried out at Community
level in order to make the principle of equal treatment fully effective is an impressive
one.

Furthermore, on 10th February 1975, the Council adopted under art 100 a directive
(75/117), submitted to it by the Commission in 14th November 1973, on the
approximation of the laws of the member states relating to the application of the
d principle of equal pay for men and women 'for the same work or for work to which equal
value is attributed'. The purpose of the directive was to ensure smooth and effective
application of the principle of equal pay and indicated in general terms certain measures
which would provide minimum protection, in particular through judicial process. The
member states were given a year, ending in February 1976, to comply with the directive
and three years, ending in February 1978, to report to the Commission on its
e application. The directive did not, however, avail to amend the original scope of art
119. All that can be said is that, as no one disputes, provisions adopted under art 100
(approximation of laws) can help to make more effective application of art 119.

I can now bring the considerations I have mentioned to bear on the national law which
raised doubts in the minds of the Cour du travail, Brussels.

Article 14 of Royal Decree No 40 of 24th October 1967, promulgated in
f implementation of the Law of 31st March 1967 on economic recovery, reads as follows:

> 'In accordance with Article 119 of the Treaty establishing the European Economic
> Community, ratified by the Law of 2 December 1957, any woman worker may
> institute proceedings before the relevant court for the application of the principle
> that men and women should receive equal pay for equal work.'

g The court which has referred the matter to the Court of Justice for a preliminary
ruling seems, therefore, to take the view, in conformity with the explanatory
memorandum to the decree, that women workers have the right to bring proceedings to
compel the employer to comply with 'individual rights arising from the principle of
equal treatment' only with effect from 1st January 1968, the date when Royal Decree No
40 came into force (see art 30 thereof).

h But the fact that, in order to make art 119 more effective, the Belgian authorities
deemed it necessary to make express provision for women workers to take legal action
in no way implies that, without that provision, the principle in art 119 would not have
created and did not create individual rights and that analogous rights exist solely because
and from the date when national law recognised the principle.

The measure adopted by the Belgian authorities has no effect whatsoever on the
j meaning of art 119; if we accept that, at least within certain limits, art 119 is directly
effective as from the end of the first stage, we must recognise that the nationals of the
original member states were and are able to avail themselves of it from that date, subject
to the laws governing application to the courts for redress and to the law of limitation
affecting that right.

It is true that in Belgium, the King 'regularly' refuses to give the force of law to collective contracts which conflict with the principle contained in art 119. But, since the collective contract between Sabena and its employees could not be subject to review by the King, the obstacle consisting of the 'independent wishes of employers and employed' and of the 'freedom to negotiate and enter into collective contracts' could not be surmounted in this way. If there were anything discriminatory in the contract and if there were a desire to remove it, this could only be done by the use, in the words of the explanatory memorandum, of a 'legal fiction'. But this fiction does not require the consent of national law; it is merely the legal translation into national law of 'the direct effect' of the Community provision to be applied.

In my opinion, therefore, a royal decree is not necessary in a case such as the present one. The principle embodied in art 119 of the EEC Treaty was not introduced into the Belgian legal system by the royal decree in question but by the law ratifying the EEC Treaty, which was approved on 2nd December 1957.

Under the case law of this court, the methods adopted for implementation of a Community provision cannot jeopardise its uniform application:

'. . . all methods of implementation are contrary to the Treaty which would have the result of creating an obstacle to the direct effect of Community regulations and of jeopardizing their simultaneous and uniform application in the whole of the Community.'

(See *EC Commission v Italian Republic* [1973] ECR 101 at 114.) The national provision in question may have value for the future but it could not affect the substance of the principle embodied in art 119.

Finally, I feel justified in reaching the following conclusion: with effect from 1st January 1962 a woman worker in the six original member states could, purely on the basis of art 119, bring proceedings against any infringement whatever of the principle embodied in the article. The validity of the action would depend on the meaning attributed to the concepts of 'pay' and of 'equal work'.

A final argument against the 'direct effect' of art 119 is put forward by the governments of the United Kingdom and of the Irish Republic, both of whom appear to be peculiarly sensitive to what might be called the 'cost of the operation'.

Arguments of this kind, however pressing on grounds of expediency, have no relevance in law. This court did not deem it necessary to alter its interpretation of art 95 which, in Germany, resulted in a large number of applications and created difficulties for the fiscal courts. The court declared: 'This argument is not by itself of such a nature as to call in question the correctness of that interpretation' (*Firma Molkerei-Zentrale Westfalen/Lippe GmbH v Hauptzollamt Paderborn* [1968] ECR 143 at 153).

On the other hand, in view of the fact that art 119 is recognised as having direct effect solely in respect of pay, properly so called, representing consideration for 'equal work', the financial consequences should not reach too high a level, having regard to the effects of limitation in the various member states.

For the foregoing reasons I am of the opinion that the court should rule as follows: inasmuch as art 119 of the EEC Treaty is concerned with pay in the strict sense of the word and with work which is not merely similar but is the same, the article has, with effect from 1st January 1962, introduced into the national law of the original member states of the Community the principle of equal pay for men and women, and has by itself directly conferred rights on the workers concerned, which national courts must protect; such protection is not subject to prior adoption of rules for its implementation either by the states or by the Community.

8th April. **THE COURT OF JUSTICE** delivered its judgment which, having summarised the facts, procedure and submissions of the parties, dealt with the law as follows:

1. By a judgment of 23rd April 1975, received at the court registry on 2nd May 1975, the Cour du travail, Brussels, referred to the court under art 177 of the EEC Treaty two

questions concerning the effect and implementation of art 119 of the treaty regarding the principle that men and women should receive equal pay for equal work.

2. These questions arose within the context of an action between an air hostess and her employer, Sabena, concerning compensation claimed by the applicant in the main action on the ground that, between 15th February 1963 and 1st February 1966, she suffered as a female worker discrimination in terms of pay as compared with male colleagues who were doing the same work as 'cabin steward'.

3. According to the judgment containing the reference, the parties agree that the work of an air hostess is identical to that of a cabin steward and in these circumstances the existence of discrimination in pay to the detriment of the air hostess during the period in question is not disputed.

The first question (direct effect of art 119)

4. The first question asks whether art 119 of the EEC Treaty introduces—

'directly into the national law of each member state of the European Community the principle that men and women should receive equal pay for equal work and does it therefore, independently of any national provision, entitle workers to institute proceedings before national courts in order to ensure its observance?'

5. If the answer to this question is in the affirmative, the question further inquires as from what date this effect must be recognised.

6. The reply to the final part of the first question will therefore be given with the reply to the second question.

7. The question of the direct effect of art 119 must be considered in the light of the nature of the principle of equal pay, the aim of this provision and its place in the scheme of the EEC Treaty.

8. Article 119 pursues a double aim.

9. First, in the light of the different stages of the development of social legislation in the various member states, the aim of art 119 is to avoid a situation in which undertakings established in states which have actually implemented the principle of equal pay suffer a competitive disadvantage in intra-Community competition as compared with undertakings established in states which have not yet eliminated discrimination against women workers as regards pay.

10. Second, this provision forms part of the social objectives of the Community, which is not merely an economic union but is at the same time intended, by common action, to ensure social progress and seek the constant improvement of the living and working conditions of their peoples, as is emphasised by the preamble to the EEC Treaty.

11. This aim is accentuated by the insertion of art 119 into the body of a chapter devoted to social policy whose preliminary provision, art 117, marks 'the need to promote improved working conditions and an improved standard of living for workers, so as to make possible their harmonisation while the improvement is being maintained'.

12. This double aim, which is at once economic and social, shows that the principle of equal pay forms part of the foundations of the Community.

13. Furthermore, this explains why the EEC Treaty has provided for the complete implementation of this principle by the end of the first stage of the transitional period.

14. Therefore, in interpreting this provision, it is impossible to base any argument on the dilatoriness and resistance which have delayed the actual implementation of this basic principle in certain member states.

15. In particular, since art 119 appears in the context of the harmonisation of working conditions while the improvement is being maintained, the objection that the terms of this article may be observed in other ways than by raising the lowest salaries may be set aside.

16. Under the terms of the first paragraph of art 119, the member states are bound to ensure and maintain 'the application of the principle that men and women should receive equal pay for equal work'.

17. The second and third paragraphs of the same article add a certain number of details concerning the concepts of pay and work referred to in the first paragraph.

18. For the purposes of the implementation of these provisions a distinction must be drawn within the whole area of application of art 119 between, first, direct and overt discrimination which may be identified solely with the aid of the criteria based on equal work and equal pay referred to by the article in question and, second, indirect and disguised discrimination which can only be identified by reference to more explicit implementing provisions of a Community or national character.

19. It is impossible not to recognise that the complete implementation of the aim pursued by art 119, by means of the elimination of all discrimination, direct or indirect, between men and women workers, not only as regards individual undertakings but also entire branches of industry and even of the economic system as a whole, may in certain cases involve the elaboration of criteria whose implementation necessitates the taking of appropriate measures at Community and national level.

20. This view is all the more essential in the light of the fact that the Community measures on this question, to which reference will be made in answer to the second question, implement art 119 from the point of view of extending the narrow criterion of 'equal work', in accordance in particular with the provisions of Convention no 100 on equal pay concluded by the International Labour Organisation in 1951 (Geneva, 29th June 1951, TS 88 (1972), Cmnd 5039), art 2 of which establishes the principle of equal pay for work 'of equal value'.

21. Among the forms of direct discrimination which may be identified solely by reference to the criteria laid down by art 119 must be included in particular those which have their origin in legislative provisions or in collective labour agreements and which may be detected on the basis of a purely legal analysis of the situation.

22. This applies even more in cases where men and women receive unequal pay for equal work carried out in the same establishment or service, whether public or private.

23. As is shown by the very findings of the judgment making the reference, in such a situation the court is in a position to establish all the facts which enable it to decide whether a woman worker is receiving lower pay than a male worker performing the same tasks.

24. In such a situation, at least, art 119 is directly applicable and may thus give rise to individual rights which the courts must protect.

25. Furthermore, as regards equal work, as a general rule, the national legislative provisions adopted for the implementation of the principle of equal pay as a rule merely reproduce the substance of the terms of art 119 as regards the direct forms of discrimination.

26. Belgian legislation provides a particularly apposite illustration of this point, since art 14 of Royal Decree No 40 of 24th October 1967 on the employment of women merely sets out the right of any female worker to institute proceedings before the relevant court for the application of the principle of equal pay set out in art 119 and simply refers to that article.

27. The terms of art 119 cannot be relied on to invalidate this conclusion.

28. First of all, it is impossible to put forward an argument against its direct effect based on the use in this article of the word 'principle', since, in the language of the treaty, this term is specifically used in order to indicate the fundamental nature of certain provisions, as is shown, for example, by the heading of the first part of the treaty which is devoted to 'Principles' and by art 113, according to which the commercial policy of the Community is to be based on 'uniform principles'.

29. If this concept were to be attenuated to the point of reducing it to the level of a vague declaration, the very foundations of the Community and the coherence of its external relations would be indirectly affected.

30. It is also impossible to put forward arguments based on the fact that art 119 only refers expressly to 'member states'.

31. Indeed, as the court has already found in other contexts, the fact that certain

a provisions of the treaty are formally addressed to the member states does not prevent rights from being conferred at the same time on any individual who has an interest in the performance of the duties thus laid down.

32. The very wording of art 119 shows that it imposes on states a duty to bring about a specific result to be mandatorily achieved within a fixed period.

33. The effectiveness of this provision cannot be affected by the fact that the duty imposed by the treaty has not been discharged by certain member states and that the b joint institutions have not reacted sufficiently energetically against this failure to act.

34. To accept the contrary view would be to risk raising the violation of the right to the status of a principle of interpretation, a position the adoption of which would not be consistent with the task assigned to the Court of Justice by art 164 of the treaty.

35. Finally, in its reference to 'member states', art 119 is alluding to those states in the exercise of all those of their functions which may usefully contribute to the c implementation of the principle of equal pay.

36. Thus, contrary to the statements made in the course of the proceedings, this provision is far from merely referring the matter to the powers of the national legislative authorities.

37. Therefore, the reference to 'member states' in art 119 cannot be interpreted as excluding the intervention of the courts in direct application of the treaty.

d 38. Furthermore, it is not possible to sustain any objection that the application by national courts of the principle of equal pay would amount to modifying independent agreements concluded privately or in the sphere of industrial relations such as individual contracts and collective labour agreements.

39. In fact, since art 119 is mandatory in nature, the prohibition on discrimination between men and women not only applies to the action of public authorities, but also e extends to all agreements which are intended to regulate paid labour collectively, as well as to contracts between individuals.

40. The reply to the first question must therefore be that the principle of equal pay contained in art 119 may be relied on before the national courts and that these courts have a duty to ensure the protection of the rights which this provision vests in individuals, in particular as regards those types of discrimination arising directly from legislative f provisions or collective labour agreements, as well as in cases in which men and women receive unequal pay for equal work which is carried out in the same establishment or service, whether private or public.

The second question (implementation of art 119 and powers of the Community and of the member states)

g 41. The second question asks whether art 119 has become 'applicable in the internal law of the member states by virtue of measures adopted by the authorities of the European Economic Community', or whether the national legislature must 'be regarded as alone competent in this matter'.

42. In accordance with what has been set out above, it is appropriate to join to this question the problem of the date from which art 119 must be regarded as having direct h effect.

43. In the light of all these problems it is first necessary to establish the chronological order of the measures taken on a Community level to ensure the implementation of the provision whose interpretation is requested.

44. Article 119 itself provides that the application of the principle of equal pay was to be uniformly ensured by the end of the first stage of the transitional period at the latest.

j 45. The information supplied by the Commission reveals the existence of important differences and discrepancies between the various states in the implementation of this principle.

46. Although, in certain member states, the principle had already largely been put into practice before the entry into force of the treaty, either by means of express constitutional and legislative provisions or by social practices established by collective

labour agreements, in other states its full implementation has suffered prolonged delays.

47. In the light of this situation, on 30th December 1961, the eve of the expiry of the time limit fixed by art 119, the member states adopted a resolution concerning the harmonisation of rates of pay of men and women which was intended to provide further details concerning certain aspects of the material content of the principle of equal pay, while delaying its implementation according to a plan spread over a period of time.

48. Under the terms of that resolution all discrimination, both direct and indirect, was to have been completely eliminated by 31st December 1964.

49. The information provided by the Commission shows that several of the original member states have failed to observe the terms of that resolution and that, for this reason, within the context of the tasks entrusted to it by art 155 of the treaty, the Commission was led to bring together the representatives of the governments and the two sides of industry in order to study the situation and to agree on the measures necessary to ensure progress towards the full attainment of the objective laid down in art 119.

50. This led to the drawing up of successive reports on the situation in the original member states, the most recent of which, dated 18th July 1973, recapitulates all the facts.

51. In the conclusion to that report the Commission announced its intention to initiate proceedings under art 169 of the treaty, for failure to take the requisite action, against those of the member states who had not by that date discharged the obligations imposed by art 119, although this warning was not followed by any further action.

52. After similar exchanges with the competent authorities in the new member states the Commission stated in its report dated 17th July 1974 that, as regards those states, art 119 had been fully applicable since 1st January 1973 and that from that date the position of those states was the same as that of the original member states.

53. For its part, in order to hasten the full implementation of art 119, the Council on 10th February 1975 adopted Directive 75/117 on the approximation of the laws of the member states relating to the application of the principle of equal pay for men and women (OJ L45, 19.2.1975, p 19).

54. This directive provides further details regarding certain aspects of the material scope of art 119 and also adopts various provisions whose essential purpose is to improve the legal protection of workers who may be wronged by failure to apply the principle of equal pay laid down by art 119.

55. Article 8 of this directive allows the member states a period of one year to put into force the appropriate laws, regulations and administrative provisions.

56. It follows from the express terms of art 119 that the application of the principle that men and women should receive equal pay was to be fully secured and irreversible at the end of the first stage of the transitional period, that is, by 1st January 1962.

57. Without prejudice to its possible effects as regards encouraging and accelerating the full implementation of art 119, the resolution of the member states of 30th December 1961 was ineffective to make any valid modification of the time limit fixed by the treaty.

58. In fact, apart from any specific provisions, the treaty can only be modified by means of the amendment procedure carried out in accordance with art 236.

59. Moreover, it follows from the foregoing that, in the absence of transitional provisions, the principle contained in art 119 has been fully effective in the new member states since the entry into force of the Treaty of Accession, that is, since 1st January 1973.

60. It was not possible for this legal situation to be modified by Directive 75/117, which was adopted on the basis of art 100 dealing with the approximation of laws and was intended to encourage the proper implementation of art 119 by means of a series of measures to be taken on the national level, in order, in particular, to eliminate indirect forms of discrimination, but was unable to reduce the effectiveness of that article or modify its temporal effect.

61. Although art 119 is expressly addressed to the member states in that it imposes on them a duty to ensure, within a given period, and subsequently to maintain the application of the principle of equal pay, that duty assumed by the states does not exclude competence in this matter on the part of the Community.

62. On the contrary, the existence of competence on the part of the Community is shown by the fact that art 119 sets out one of the 'social policy' objectives of the treaty which form the subject of Title III, which itself appears in Part Three of the treaty dealing with the 'Policy of the Community'.

63. In the absence of any express reference in art 119 to the possible action to be taken by the Community for the purposes of implementing the social policy, it is appropriate to refer to the general scheme of the treaty and to the courses of action for which it provided, such as those laid down in arts 100, 155 and, where appropriate, 235.

64. As has been shown in the reply to the first question, no implementing provision, whether adopted by the institutions of the Community or by the national authorities, could adversely affect the direct effect of art 119.

65. The reply to the second question should therefore be that the application of art 119 was to have been fully secured by the original member states as from 1st January 1962, the beginning of the second stage of the transitional period, and by the new member states as from 1st January 1973, the date of entry into force of the Treaty of Accession.

66. The first of these time limits was not modified by the resolution of the member states of 30th December 1961.

67. As indicated in reply to the first question, EEC Council Directive 75/117 does not prejudice the direct effect of art 119 and the period fixed by that directive for compliance therewith does not affect the time limits laid down by art 119 of the EEC Treaty and the Treaty of Accession.

68. Even in the areas in which art 119 has no direct effect, that provision cannot be interpreted as reserving to the national legislature exclusive power to implement the principle of equal pay since, to the extent to which such implementation is necessary, it may be relieved by a combination of Community and national measures.

The temporal effect of this judgment

69. The governments of Ireland and the United Kingdom have drawn the court's attention to the possible economic consequences of attributing direct effect to the provisions of art 119, on the ground that such a decision might, in many branches of economic life, result in the introduction of claims dating back to the time at which such effect came into existence.

70. In view of the large number of people concerned, such claims, which undertakings could not have foreseen, might seriously affect the financial situation of such undertakings and even drive some of them to bankruptcy.

71. Although the practical consequences of any judicial decision must be carefully taken into account, it would be impossible to go so far as to diminish the objectivity of the law and compromise its future application on the ground of the possible repercussions which might result, as regards the past, from such a judicial decision.

72. However, in the light of the conduct of several of the member states and the views adopted by the Commission and repeatedly brought to the notice of the circles concerned, it is appropriate to take exceptionally into account the fact that, over a prolonged period, the parties concerned have been led to continue with practices which were contrary to art 119, although not yet prohibited under their national law.

73. The fact that, in spite of the warnings given, the Commission did not initiate proceedings under art 169 against the member states concerned on grounds of failure to fulfil an obligation was likely to consolidate the incorrect impression as to the effects of art 119.

74. In these circumstances, it is appropriate to determine that, as the general level at which pay would have been fixed cannot be known, important considerations of legal certainty affecting all the interests involved, both public and private, make it impossible in principle to reopen the question as regards the past.

75. Therefore, the direct effect of art 119 cannot be relied on in order to support

claims concerning pay periods prior to the date of this judgment, except as regards those workers who have already brought legal proceedings or made an equivalent claim.

Costs

76. The costs incurred by the Commission of the European Communities, which has submitted observations to the court, are not recoverable.

77. As these proceedings are, in so far as the parties to the main action are concerned, in the nature of a step in the action pending before the Cour du travail, Brussels, the decision as to costs is a matter for that court.

On those grounds, the court, in answer to the questions referred to it by the Cour du travail, Brussels, by judgment dated 23rd April 1975 hereby rules: (1) the principle that men and women should receive equal pay, which is laid down by art 119, may be relied on before the national courts. These courts have a duty to ensure the protection of the rights which that provision vests in individuals, in particular in the case of those forms of discrimination which have their origin in legislative provisions or collective labour agreements, as well as where men and women receive unequal pay for equal work which is carried out in the same establishment or service, whether private or public; (2) the application of art 119 was to have been fully secured by the original member states as from 1st January 1962, the beginning of the second stage of the transitional period, and by the new member states as from 1st January 1973, the date of entry into force of the Treaty of Accession. The first of these time limits was not modified by the resolution of the member states of 30th December 1961; (3) EEC Council Directive 75/117 does not prejudice the direct effect of art 119 and the period fixed by that directive for compliance therewith does not affect the time limits laid down by art 119 of the EEC Treaty and the Treaty of Accession; (4) even in the areas in which art 119 has no direct effect, that provision cannot be interpreted as reserving to the national legislature exclusive power to implement the principle of equal pay since, to the extent to which such implementation is necessary, it may be achieved by a combination of Community and national provisions; (5) except as regards those workers who have already brought legal proceedings or made an equivalent claim, the direct effect of art 119 cannot be relied on in order to support claims concerning pay periods prior to the date of this judgment.

Andrew Durand Esq   Barrister.

a
R v Post Office, ex parte Association of Scientific, Technical and Managerial Staffs

COURT OF APPEAL, CIVIL DIVISION
LORD DENNING MR, CUMMING-BRUCE AND ACKNER LJJ
18th, 21st JULY 1980

b

Trade union – Recognition – Statutory duty – Refusal of recognition by Post Office – Whether breach of statutory duty – Post Office Act 1969, Sch 1, para 11(1).

When carrying out its statutory duty under para 11(1)[a] of Sch 1 to the Post Office Act 1969 to 'seek consultation with any organisation appearing to it to be appropriate' for the
c settlement of the terms and conditions of employment of Post Office employees, the Post Office does not have an absolute discretion to decide which organisations it will consult. The Post Office is required to consider whether a particular organisation is appropriate to be consulted but if it decides fairly and reasonably that a particular organisation is not appropriate because it would lead to separate negotiations with different trade unions on the same issues the courts will not interfere with that exercise
d of its discretion (see p 141 *h j* and p 142 *a* to *c* and *e* to *h*, post).

Dictum of Brightman J in *Gallagher v Post Office* [1970] 3 All ER at 720 disapproved.

Notes
For the Post Office Act 1969, Sch 1, para 11, see 25 Halsbury's Statutes (3rd Edn) 545.

e ### Cases referred to in judgments
Associated Provincial Picture Houses Ltd v Wednesbury Corpn [1947] 2 All ER 680, [1948] 1 KB 223, [1948] LJR 190, 177 LT 641, 122 JP 55, 45 LGR 635, CA, 45 Digest (Repl) 215, 189.
Gallagher v Post Office [1970] 3 All ER 712, Digest (Cont Vol C) 802, 7a.

f ### Appeal
This was an appeal by the Telephone Contract Officers' Section ('the TCO Section') of the Association of Scientific, Technical and Managerial Staffs against an order of the Divisional Court of the Queen's Bench Division (Donaldson LJ and Mustill J) dated 14th July 1980 refusing its application for judicial review by way of (i) a declaration that it was an appropriate organisation with which the Post Office had a duty to seek consultation
g within the meaning and for the purposes of para 11(1) of Sch 1 to the Post Office Act 1969 in respect of sales representatives employed by the Post Office, and (ii) an order of mandamus directed to the Post Office ordering it to seek consultation with the TCO Section for the purposes specified in para 11(1). The facts are set out in the judgment of Lord Denning MR.

h R J *Harvey* QC and Andrew *Thompson* for the TCO Section.
John *Newey* QC and Andrew *Collins* for the Post Office.

LORD DENNING MR. The Post Office is one of the largest organisations in the country. We are told that it employs 434,000 people. It is larger than all the armed forces put together, the army, the navy and the air force.
j   Today we have to consider a recognition dispute. It is whether the Post Office should recognise a group of their employees (1,000 sales representatives) who have recently become members of a big union, the Association of Scientific, Technical and Managerial

---

a   Paragraph 11(1), so far as material, is set out at p 141 *a b*, post

Staffs (ASTMS). The Post Office has decided that it is not appropriate to recognise that union. So the ASTMS has brought these proceedings against the Post Office. It says that *a* it is the duty of the Post Office to seek consultation with the ASTMS.

Before I read the Act, I must give a short history. The Post Office was for many years a government department. In 1969 it became a nationalised corporation. There are proposals for reorganisation in the future.

Since the 1920s there have been about a thousand men (sales representatives) who go around offering equipment for sale. They formed themselves into a body called the *b* Telephone Contracts Officers' Association (TCOA). Whilst that₁ association was in existence, it was an independent union. It negotiated with the Post Office on its members' terms and conditions of employment, and so forth.

When the Post Office was reorganised in 1969, there were about 18 trade unions representing various classes of employees of the Post Office. Each of these unions negotiated with the Post Office authorities. In 1969 they combined together to form a *c* council which was called the Council of Post Office Unions. This council negotiated in some matters with the Post Office on behalf of all the trade unions in the council; but each negotiated separately in some respects.

That went on for some years; but, as everyone in industry knows, it is very undesirable to have a large number of small unions negotiating on behalf of small groups of men. I will read what Mr Heatherington, the Post Office's Director of Industrial Relations, said *d* in his affidavit:

'The Post Office believes it important that collective bargaining arrangements should avoid so far as possible a multiplicity of bargaining units and pay review dates which can lead to complex and prolonged negotiations and encourage "leap-frogging" pay claims by the various unions.'

e

The experience of the Post Office is the experience of industry generally. So the policy throughout from 1969 has been gradually to limit the number of trade unions, by mergers and the like, so that there can be a better structure for collective bargaining, not only as to pay, and so forth, but as to grades. One of the important things in industry is to put employees in their proper grades, so as to see that they are paid according to their grades, and the like. That policy of the Post Office was agreed to by the Council of Post *f* Office Unions. In pursuance of that objective, for years there were negotiations whereby the small TCOA would merge with one of the other Post Office unions, the Association of Post Office Executives. That had 23,000 members. Those negotiations were going forward until the end of 1979. Then a surprise was sprung on all the people in the Post Office who were engaged in the negotiations, because out of the blue a big outside union (the ASTMS) came in.

g

We do not know the details of the negotiations between the TCOA and the ASTMS, but we know the result of them. A ballot was taken of the 1,000 men in the TCOA whether they wanted to become a section of the ASTMS. About 80% of the men filled in their ballot papers. The number voting in favour of the transfer to the ASTMS was 739, and the number voting against was 40. So the overwhelming majority voted to join the ASTMS as a section of it. That was put into operation on 28th January 1980. So the *h* TCOA ceased to be an independent trade union on its own within the Post Office. It became a section of the big outside union, the ASTMS.

The Post Office was greatly upset. So was the Council of Post Office Unions. They said that they would not have anything to do with the ASTMS or the section. The Post Office decided that, as the members of the TCOA had joined the ASTMS as a section, they could not afford it recognition. It would not allow its representatives time off, and the like, for *j* union activities. So, in effect, the Post Office ceased to recognise the TCOA now it had become a section of the ASTMS.

Faced with that expulsion, if I may put it that way, the ASTMS, on behalf of its new section, brought proceedings in the Divisional Court. It said that the Post Office was

acting unlawfully and contrary to its duty as prescribed in para 11(1) of Sch 1 to the Post
a Office Act 1969. That provides:

> 'Except so far as the Post Office is satisfied that adequate machinery exists for
> achieving the purposes of this paragraph . . . it shall be the duty of the Post Office to
> seek consultation with any organisation appearing to it to be appropriate with a
> view to the conclusion between it and that organisation of such agreements as
> appear to the parties to be desirable with respect to the establishment and
b > maintenance . . . of machinery for—(a) the settlement by negotiation of terms and
> conditions of employment of persons employed by the Post Office . . . (b) the
> promotion and encouragement of measures affecting efficiency . . .'

So the issue was joined. On behalf of the section of the ASTMS counsel before us has
said that it is certainly an 'appropriate' organisation within that sub-paragraph, and it
c ought to have been recognised, because it is virtually the selfsame organisation as the one
which has existed for the last six years. He said that the same 1,000 men are members;
it is the same organisation; it has the same officers; and it makes the same independent
decisions, and the like, as it always has done. The difference is that it has become a
section of the ASTMS. He submitted that that should not disqualify it from being an
'appropriate' organisation. He said that the effect of the Post Office's decision now is that
d these 1,000 men are left unrepresented by any organisation; and that cannot be right.
He said that in those circumstances it must be right for the Post Office to recognise the
organisation as appropriate, even though it is now a section of the ASTMS.

That argument sounded attractive in the first instance. But one has to consider the
size of the Post Office and the problems facing it. I would stress that the organisation has
to appear to the Post Office to be 'appropriate' in respect of a lot of other things. Such as
e '. . . the settlement by negotiation of terms and conditions of employment of persons
employed by the Post Office'. That may involve restructuring of the grading system.
There is also 'the promotion and encouragement of measures affecting efficiency'. The
Post Office says that far more efficiency can be obtained when there are only a few unions
within the Post Office, which are members of the Council of Post Office Unions. That
council can negotiate on one level with the Post Office without the intrusion of an
f outside body like the ASTMS. The Post Office pointed out that, if it was to recognise this
section of the ASTMS, in future it would have to negotiate with two sets of people: on the
one hand the Council of Post Office Unions, and on the other hand with this section of
ASTMS separately, because this section is not a member of the council. If it had to have
separate negotiations, there would be a danger of disagreement, and a danger of 'leap-
frogging'. As soon as one grade arrived at a settlement, another grade would say, 'We
g ought to go higher', and the like. The Post Office, in these circumstances, says: 'If we are
to reach pay settlements sensibly, if we are to achieve the restructuring of grading
sensibly, and if we are to carry out the objectives of recognition, we should consult with
the Council of Post Office Unions and not have the intrusion of an outside body. This
section, although nominally independent, will be under the umbrella of the ASTMS; and
they will bring undesirable pressures to bear on our negotiations with our own people.'
h That seems to me an approach which cannot be faulted. The Post Office is doing its
duty. It has to seek consultation with organisations which appear to be appropriate with
those objectives in view. It takes the view, honestly and in good faith and, it seems to
me, on reasonable grounds, that this section of the ASTMS is not appropriate for the
purpose. I cannot see any fault in its reasoning in coming to its decision, either by taking
into account things it ought not to have taken into account or failing to take into account
j things that it should.

There has only been one previous case on this section. It is Gallagher v Post Office [1970]
3 All ER 712. In a way that was a stronger case than this one, because the Post Office did
not consult with the men who were in its own guild. It only consulted with the Union
of Post Office Workers. That decision was upheld by Brightman J. I need not go into the

details of it, except to say that it is agreed on all hands that the judge put it too high when he said the Post Office had an absolute discretion in these matters. He put it too high *a* when he said that the duty was no more than a duty to seek consultation with such appropriate organisations as it shall think fit to consult (see [1970] 3 All ER 712 at 720). That is not quite the right test. The requirement is that the Post Office must consider the appropriateness of the organisation. It did consider it fairly and reasonably and found it was not appropriate.

No fault can be found with the decision of the Post Office in this matter. I would agree *b* with the view of the Divisional Court, and dismiss the appeal.

CUMMING-BRUCE LJ. I agree. The function of this court in these proceedings is restricted to deciding whether the Post Office is in breach of para 11(1) of Sch 1 to the Post Office Act 1969; and, as Lord Denning MR stated during the course of argument, in discharge of that function, the case which is most relevant as a guide is *Associated* *c* *Provinical Picture Houses Ltd v Wednesbury Corpn* [1947] 2 All ER 680, [1948] 1 KB 223.

On first hearing counsel on behalf of the section of ASTMS, it seemed a natural construction of the phrases 'appearing to it to be appropriate' that it must apply to a body which has for years been recognised and which has sat at the negotiating table with the Post Office for more than a generation, and against whose negotiators nobody has raised any kind of criticism. As counsel put it, if these people are not appropriate, who are *d* appropriate? But it will not do. The meaning of the phrase is to be collected partly by reference to the objectives contemplated in the sub-paragraph. When one looks to see what the organisation is appropriate for, it is 'with a view to the conclusion . . . of such agreements as appear to the parties to be desirable with respect to the establishment and maintenance . . . of machinery for', and then three purposes of the machinery are set out; and it is immediately plain in my view that the meaning of 'appropriate' can only be *e* discovered by looking at the objectives for which the machinery has been designed.

Taking that view of the approach to the construction of para 11(1), I have no doubt that the meaning proposed by counsel on behalf of the section of ASTMS is too narrow a meaning and a meaning which is not apt for clothing the Post Office with powers that the sub-paragraph contemplated.

For the reasons stated by Lord Denning MR, I agree that the appeal should be *f* dismissed.

ACKNER LJ. I also agree. On the facts recounted by Lord Denning MR the Post Office is entitled to reach the conclusion that it would be a retrograde step to recognise a union from outside the Post Office to represent and perpetuate a single grade which constituted a minority staff within the relevant range of the recently negotiated common *g* pay spine, and which like many other grades forms part of a much larger restructured bargaining unit. It was entitled to conclude that such recognition would fragment, complicate and conflict with its system of consultation, negotiation and participation, and would therefore be detrimental to orderly and effective collective bargaining. It was thus entitled to reach the conclusion that the ASTMS (TCO Section) was not an appropriate organisation with which to seek consultation. *h*

For the reasons given by Lord Denning MR and Cumming-Bruce LJ, I also agree that this appeal should be dismissed.

Appeal dismissed. Leave to appeal to the House of Lords refused.

Solicitors: *Robin Thompson & Partners* (for the TCO Section); *Saul Rothstein* (for the Post Office).

Sumra Green   Barrister.

a

Castanho v Brown & Root (UK) Ltd and another

HOUSE OF LORDS

LORD WILBERFORCE, LORD DIPLOCK, LORD KEITH OF KINKEL, LORD SCARMAN AND LORD BRIDGE
OF HARWICH

b 20th, 21st, 22nd, 23rd OCTOBER, 4th DECEMBER 1980

*Practice – Discontinuance of action – Discontinuance by plaintiff – Action brought in England
claiming damages for personal injuries – Defendant ordered to make interim payments on
admitting liability – Plaintiff commencing action in America in hope of getting higher damages –
Plaintiff purporting to discontinue English action – Defendant applying for order to strike out*
c *notice of discontinuance and for injunction to restrain plaintiff continuing proceedings in America
and commencing other proceedings there or elsewhere – Whether notice of discontinuance should
be struck out – Whether injunction should be granted – RSC Ord 21, r 2(1).*

The plaintiff, a Portuguese citizen residing in Portugal, was employed by the second
defendant, a Panamanian company, as an oiler on one of its ships. In February 1977 he
d sustained serious personal injuries in an accident on board the ship while it was in an
English port. In September 1977 he brought an action in England against the first
defendant, a British company which provided shore services for the ship, and the second
defendant claiming damages for personal injuries. Both the first and second defendants
were part of a large Texan group of companies. In March 1978 a consent order was made
requiring the second defendant to make an interim payment of damages and in June the
e second defendant admitted liability. During 1978 the plaintiff was approached by a firm
of American lawyers who pressed him to enforce his claim in America (where the
damages would probably be much greater) and to retain them on a contingency fee
basis. His English solicitors, although aware that American proceedings were likely,
obtained a further interim payment, making a total of £27,250, on a summons in
December 1978. On 7th February 1979 an action was begun on the plaintiff's behalf in
f a state court in Texas claiming damages for the plaintiff's injuries against five companies
of the Texan group, including the parent company and the first and second defendants.
The following day the plaintiff, his English solicitors and the American lawyers agreed
that the plaintiff should prosecute his claim in America, leaving the English action in
being in case the American action failed. The defendants, wishing to have the action
decided in England, moved in the Texan court to set aside or stay the American action
g and, on 30th April, delivered a defence in the English action formally admitting
liability. The following day they issued a summons for directions and a summons for an
injunction restraining the plaintiff from prosecuting or continuing proceedings in
America. In order to prevent the defendants obtaining the injunction the plaintiff, on
14th May 1979, gave notice of discontinuance of the English action, relying on RSC Ord
21, r 2(1)[a] which entitled a plaintiff to give notice of discontinuance without leave within
h 14 days of service of a defence. On 6th June, on the hearing of the defendants' summons
for directions, it was directed that it should be treated as an application by the defendants
to strike out the plaintiff's notice of discontinuance and was adjourned. Because the
plaintiff's American advisers considered that a federal court was less likely to decline
jurisdiction than the state court, on 18th July the plaintiff commenced an action in a
federal court in Texas claiming compensatory and punitive damages and abandoned the
j state proceedings the following day by entering a nonsuit. The defendants applied in the

---

a Rule 2(1), so far as material, provides: 'The plaintiff in an action begun by writ may, without the
leave of the Court, discontinue the action, or withdraw any particular claim made by him therein,
as against any or all of the defendants at any time not later than 14 days after service of the defence
on him . . .'

federal court to stay the new action. On 19th November on the hearing of the
summonses in the English action the judge ([1980] 1 All ER 689) struck out the notice   *a*
of discontinuance (thus causing the English action to remain in being) on the ground
that it would be an abuse of the process of the court if the plaintiff were to discontinue
the English action without leave (even though under RSC Ord 21, r 2 leave was not
required) in order to improve his position in the American proceedings while remaining
free to commence a fresh action in England if those proceedings failed. The judge also
granted the injunction sought by the defendants. The plaintiff appealed to the Court of   *b*
Appeal ([1980] 3 All ER 72) which allowed his appeal, restored his notice of
discontinuance and discharged the injunction. The defendants appealed to the House of
Lords.

Held – (1) Termination of legal process such as a notice of discontinuance, like any other
step in the process, could be used by a party to obtain a collateral advantage which it   *c*
would be unjust for him to retain and could therefore be prevented by the court under
its inherent jurisdiction to prevent an abuse of the process of the court. Thus, even
though under the Rules of the Supreme Court leave was not required to discontinue the
action, the judge had jurisdiction to strike it out and leave the English action in being if
the notice of discontinuance amounted to an abuse of the process of the court. On the
facts, the judge was right to strike out the plaintiff's notice of discontinuance because, if   *d*
leave had been required, it was inconceivable that the court would have allowed a
plaintiff who had secured interim payments and an admission of liability by proceeding
in an English court to discontinue his action in order to improve his chances in a foreign
suit without being put on terms, which could well include not only repayment of the
moneys received but also an undertaking not to issue a second writ in England.
However, on the basis that the English action was still in being, the court then had to   *e*
decide whether the plaintiff should be allowed to proceed in America or be required to
continue proceeding in England. In the circumstances, the court would grant the
plaintiff leave to discontinue the English action (see p 146 *a* to *c*, p 148 *e* to *j* and p 152
e f and *j*, post).
     (2) Although an injunction restraining proceedings in a foreign jurisdiction could be
granted whenever it was appropriate to avoid injustice, in seeking an injunction the   *f*
defendants were required to show both that the English court was a forum to which they
were amenable and in which justice could be done between the parties at substantially
less inconvenience and expense than in Texas, and also that an injunction would not
deprive the plaintiff of a legitimate personal or juridical advantage available to him in
Texas. The prospect of higher damages in Texas was a legitimate personal or juridical
advantage available to the plaintiff, and, furthermore, the balance of convenience came   *g*
down clearly in the plaintiff's favour since the Texas court was as natural and proper a
forum as England, the interim payments could be repaid and the admission of liability
obtained in the English action was not a significant factor because it was clear beyond
doubt that the accident was caused by the negligence of a servant of the defendants. In
the circumstances the Court of Appeal was right to discharge the injunction. The appeal
would be dismissed but with the substitution of an order for discontinuance of the action   *h*
for the order upholding the notice of discontinuance (see p 146 *a* to *c*, p 149 *h*, p 150 *f* to
p 151 *b* and p 152 *a* to *g* and *j*, post); *The Atlantic Star* [1973] 2 All ER 175 and *MacShannon
v Rockware Glass Ltd* [1978] 1 All ER 625 applied.
     Per Curiam. It is a question of fact to be determined in the light of the particular
circumstances of the case whether a party who is suing abroad has a sufficient connection
with England to justify the granting of an injunction restraining him from proceeding   *j*
with his foreign suit (see p 146 *a* to *c*, p 150 *b c* and p 152 *j*, post); *The Tropaioforos (No 2)*
[1962] 1 Lloyd's Rep 410 approved.
     Decision of the Court of Appeal [1980] 3 All ER 72 varied.

Notes
For the discontinuance of an action, see 30 Halsbury's Laws (3rd Edn) 409, para 770, and
for cases on the subject, see 51 Digest (Repl) 570–574, 2036–2080.

RSC Ord 21, r 2(2A), which was inserted by RSC (Amendment No 2) 1980, SI 1980 No 1010, and which came into force on 1st October 1980, provides that a party in whose favour an interim payment has been ordered, in accordance with RSC Ord 29, r 11 (as substituted by the same amending rules), may not discontinue any action or counterclaim, or withdraw any particular claim therein, except with the leave of the High Court or the consent of all the other parties.

Cases referred to in opinions

Atlantic Star, The, The Atlantic Star (Owners) v The Bona Spes (Owners) [1973] 2 All ER 175, [1974] AC 436, [1973] 2 WLR 795, [1973] 2 Lloyd's Rep 197, HL, 11 Digest (Reissue) 645, *1777*.

Birkett v James [1977] 2 All ER 801, [1978] AC 297, [1977] 3 WLR 38, HL, Digest (Cont Vol E) 666, *2698b*.

Bushby v Munday (1821) 5 Madd 297, [1814–23] All ER Rep 304, 56 ER 908, 11 Digest (Reissue) 639, *1731*.

Christiansborg, The (1885) 10 PD 141, 54 LJP 84, 53 LT 612, 5 Asp MLC 491, CA, 11 Digest (Reissue) 645, *1774*.

Ellerman Lines Ltd v Read [1928] 2 KB 144, [1928] All ER Rep 415, 97 LJKB 366, 138 LT 625, 17 Asp MLC 421, 33 Com Cas 219, CA, 11 Digest (Reissue) 602, *1478*.

Hagen, The [1908] P 189, [1908–10] All ER Rep 21, 77 LJP 124, 98 LT 891, 11 Asp MLC 66, CA, 50 Digest (Repl) 337, *657*.

Janera, The [1928] P 55, [1927] All ER Rep 490, 97 LJP 58, 138 LT 557, 17 Asp MLC 416, 11 Digest (Reissue) 643, *1767*.

Liddell's Settlement Trusts, Re [1936] 1 All ER 239, [1936] Ch 365, 105 LJ Ch 161, 154 LT 558, CA, 28(2) Digest (Reissue) 921, *2299*.

MacShannon v Rockware Glass Ltd [1978] 1 All ER 625, [1978] AC 795, [1978] 2 WLR 362, HL, Digest (Cont Vol E) 99, *1691a*.

Portarlington (Lord) v Soulby (1834) 3 My & K 104, [1824–34] All ER Rep 610, 40 ER 40, LC, 11 Digest (Reissue) 637, *1715*.

St Pierre v South American Stores (Gath and Chaves) Ltd [1936] 1 KB 382, [1935] All ER Rep 408, 105 LJKB 436, 154 LT 546, CA, 11 Digest (Reissue) 399, *392*.

Siskina (Cargo owners) v Distos Compania Naviera SA, The Siskina [1977] 3 All ER 803, [1979] AC 210, [1977] 3 WLR 818, [1978] 1 Lloyd's Rep 1, HL, Digest (Cont Vol E) 660, *782a*.

Tropaioforos, The, (No 2) [1962] 1 Lloyd's Rep 410.

Appeal

The first and second defendants, Brown & Root (UK) Ltd and Jackson Marine SA, appealed by leave of the Court of Appeal against a decision of that court (Shaw and Brandon LJJ, Lord Denning MR dissenting) dated 22nd April 1980 ([1980] 3 All ER 72, [1980] 1 WLR 833) allowing an appeal by the plaintiff, Inocencio Fernando Castanho, against an order made by Parker J on 19th November ([1980] 1 All ER 689, [1980] 1 WLR 833) whereby the judge struck out the plaintiff's notice of discontinuance dated 14th May 1979 and granted the defendants an injunction perpetually restraining him from commencing or causing to be commenced or continuing or prosecuting any further or other proceedings in the United States of America or elsewhere against the defendants or certain of their associated companies or any of them directed to obtaining damages for personal injuries sustained by the plaintiff as a result of an accident which occurred on 11th February 1977 on board the ship American Moon at Great Yarmouth, Norfolk. The Court of Appeal restored the plaintiff's notice of discontinuance of his action in England and discharged the injunction which the judge had granted, thus allowing the plaintiff to proceed in America. The facts are set out in the opinion of Lord Scarman.

Viscount Bledisloe QC, Timothy Walker and *Michael Lerego* for the defendants.
John Melville Williams QC, George Newman and *John Hendy* for the plaintiff.

Their Lordships took time for consideration.

4th December. The following opinions were delivered.

LORD WILBERFORCE. My Lords, I have had the benefit of reading in advance a draft of the speech to be delivered by my noble and learned friend Lord Scarman. I agree with it and with the order which he proposes for dismissing the appeal.

LORD DIPLOCK. My Lords, I have had the advantage of reading in draft the speech of my noble and learned friend Lord Scarman, with which I agree. For the reasons he has given I too would dismiss the appeal.

LORD KEITH OF KINKEL. My Lords, I have had the benefit of reading in advance the speech to be delivered by my noble and learned friend Lord Scarman. I agree that for the reasons which he gives the appeal should be dismissed and an order made in the terms which he proposes.

LORD SCARMAN. My Lords, this is an appeal by the defendants from an order of the Court of Appeal ([1980] 3 All ER 72, [1980] 1 WLR 833), with the leave of that court, whereby, allowing the plaintiff's appeal from Parker J ([1980] 1 All ER 689, [1980] 1 WLR 833), the court restored the plaintiff's notice of discontinuance of his action in England and discharged an injunction which Parker J had granted restraining the plaintiff from proceeding with his claim in America. Put shortly, Parker J required the plaintiff to proceed in England; the Court of Appeal allowed him to proceed in America.

The respondent, the plaintiff in the suit, is a citizen of Portugal, and resides in that country. The first-named appellant is a British company; the second named is a Panamanian company; the two companies are the defendants in suit. It will assist clarity if I refer to the respondent as the plaintiff and to the two appellants as the first and second defendants.

On 11th February 1977 the plaintiff in the course of his employment by the second defendants sustained very serious injuries in an accident on board the American Moon while that ship lay in the harbour of Great Yarmouth. The ship was owned by the second defendant which is a subsidiary of Jackson Marine Corpn ('JMC'), a company incorporated in Texas, USA. JMC carried on a world-wide business, using for the purpose a group of companies which it owns and controls. The group includes the two defendants as well as many other companies, some of which feature in the story of the case.

As a result of the accident the plaintiff was paralysed from the neck downwards. On 29th September 1977 he brought suit in England by issuing a writ claiming damages for personal injuries. The appeal arises out of that suit, in which the plaintiff has, so far, obtained two interim payments totalling £27,250 and an admission of liability by the second defendant. On 14th May 1979 the plaintiff gave notice to discontinue the suit. He did so without seeking the leave of the court, in reliance on RSC Ord 21, r 2 which allows notice to be given without leave at any time up to the expiry of 14 days after service of defence. He discontinued because he had decided, on advice, to sue for damages in the United States of America. The reason for his decision was the prospect of a very much greater recovery there than here.

Before he discontinued his English suit, the plaintiff had begun proceedings in Texas. He was approached by United States attorneys during the summer of 1978. His English solicitors had learnt of the approach and knew that American proceedings were likely before they issued the summons which led to the order for the second interim payment, one of £20,000. The defendants became aware of the plaintiff's intention on, or before, 7th February 1979 when an action was begun on his behalf in a Texan state court in which he claimed damages for the injuries he had sustained in the accident. On the following day, 8th February 1979, it would appear final agreement was reached between the plaintiff and his American and British advisers. His strategy was now clear. He would prosecute his American action, leaving the English action in being in case he should fail in America.

The defendants' reaction to his decision to sue in America was understandable and predictable, bearing in mind how much more they stood to lose if he proceeded there. They moved to set aside, or stay, the American proceedings, and did all they could to move along the English proceedings. On 30th April they delivered a defence in the English action; and on 1st May they issued two summonses, one for directions and the other for an injunction to restrain the plaintiff from prosecuting or continuing proceedings in the USA.

Meanwhile there were certain developments in the American courts. The defendants to the action in the Texan state court were five JMC companies, amongst them JMC itself and the two defendants. In the face of strenuous efforts made by the defence to stay or set aside these proceedings, the plaintiff's advisers decided to switch from the state to the federal court. They believed (apparently) that the federal court was less likely to decline jurisdiction or stay proceedings. Accordingly, the state proceedings were abandoned by entering a nonsuit; and on 18th July 1979 they began an action on behalf of the plaintiff in the District Court for Eastern Texas, to which three JMC companies were made defendants. This number included JMC itself and the second defendant, but not the first defendant. The defendants applied to stay this action in the district court but no decision on their application had been reached when in October 1979 the two summonses in the English action reached Parker J in chambers.

The judge in chambers had before him two applications, one (on the summons for directions) to strike out the notice of discontinuance and the other for the injunction. He made the two orders sought, delivering a judgment in open court. He held that the notice of discontinuance was in the circumstances an abuse of the process of the court and struck it out. Having so held, he had no difficulty in deciding, indeed, it was conceded, that he had jurisdiction to grant the injunction; and, in the exercise of his discretion, he granted it.

The Court of Appeal by a majority (Shaw and Brandon LJJ, Lord Denning MR dissenting) allowed an appeal against both orders. They also acceded to an application by the defendants to stay proceedings on a second protective writ which the plaintiff had issued on 8th February 1980, to which the defendants were the same as in the United States federal suit. The purpose of this writ was to take care of the possibility of failure in the American courts.

This second writ was a wise precaution. On 14th February 1980 the United States District Court did dismiss the application by the defence to dismiss the federal action. But your Lordships have been told that on 7th November 1980 the United States Court of Appeals for the Fifth Circuit ordered a stay 'until further order' of the federal action in response to a petition by the defendants for a writ of mandamus directed to the District Council to stay the action. The respondent to the petition was given 20 days to reply.

My Lords, no necessity arises to consider this further step by the defendants in the American litigation. The question for the House is not whether the United States action should be stayed but whether the plaintiff should be restrained by an order of the English court from proceeding in America. If the United States court does impose a stay, the plaintiff will, of course, have the right to apply, in the changed circumstances, to the English court for removal of the stay on his 'protective writ'. The defendants could not successfully resist such an application, if they had themselves succeeded in staying the United States action, on the ground, no doubt, that the proper forum is the English court.

The question in the appeal is, therefore, whether the plaintiff should be restrained by the English court from pursuing his claim for damages in the American courts. It is a question of great importance to the parties. In the American courts the plaintiff claims punitive as well as compensatory damages ($5m compensation, and 'at least' $10m punitive or exemplary). In England he has no claim for punitive damages, and the scale of compensatory damages is much less. It is conceded that, had he begun in Texas in the first place, the English courts would not grant an injunction to restrain him from continuing there. The defendants base their case on the fact that he started in England, on the advantages he has won from them in the litigation which ensued here, and on the disadvantages, in the circumstances which have arisen, of their being sued in America.

The first issue is whether the notice of discontinuance can be struck out, and, if it can, whether it should be. It is accepted that under the Rules of the Supreme Court as they were in 1979 (for they have now been amended to take care of the situation which arises when interim payments have been made: see RSC (Amendment No 2) 1980, SI 1980 No 1010, r 4), the plaintiff, notwithstanding the two interim payments and the admission of liability, could discontinue without leave, if he did so not later than 14 days after service of defence. Lord Denning MR was, however, prepared to hold that our courts can, by the device of statutory interpretation, repair the omission in the unamended RSC Ord 21, r 2 to provide for the case in which interim payments had been ordered and made before the expiry of the time limit. 'I fear', he said, 'that the draftsmen of interim payments forgot all about notices of discontinuance. Interim payments are quite inconsistent with a right to discontinue without leave' (see [1980] 3 All ER 72 at 80, [1980] 1 WLR 833 at 854). Interim payments were made possible by the Administration of Justice Act 1969 s 20, and introduced into the law in 1970 by RSC Ord 29, rr 12 to 17. Like Lord Denning MR, I have no doubt that the failure to amend the rule relating to notice of discontinuance was a casus omissus. But I do not agree that it is an omission which the courts can make good by reading into the rule a provision that leave is needed when the rule expressly said it was not. Unless, therefore, it is possible to treat a notice of discontinuance without leave which complies with the Rules of the Supreme Court as an abuse of process (which is what Parker J did), the notice cannot be struck out.

In the Court of Appeal, Lord Denning MR was prepared so to hold (see [1980] 3 All ER 72 at 80, [1980] 1 WLR 833 at 855). Brandon LJ expressed no opinion. Shaw LJ, however, held that it was not possible. It seemed to him 'an inversion of logic to speak of an act which purports to terminate a process as being an abuse of that process' (see [1980] 3 All ER 72 at 88, [1980] 1 WLR 833 at 864). I am not sensitive to the logical difficulty. Even if it be illogical (and I do not think it is) to treat the termination of legal process as an act which can be an abuse of that process, principle requires that the illogicality be overridden, if justice requires. The court has inherent power to prevent a party from obtaining by the use of its process a collateral advantage which it would be unjust for him to retain; and termination of process can, like any other step in the process, be so used. I agree, therefore, with Parker J and Lord Denning MR that service of a notice of discontinuance without leave, though it complies with the rules, can be an abuse of the process of the court.

Was it, then, in the circumstances of this case, an abuse? In my judgment, it was. A sensible test is that which both the judge and Lord Denning MR applied. Suppose leave had been required (as it would have been, if the notice had been served 24 hours later), would the court have granted unconditional leave? It is inconceivable that the court would have allowed a plaintiff, who had secured interim payments and an admission of liability by proceeding in the English court, to discontinue his action in order to improve his chances in a foreign suit without being put on terms, which could well include not only repayment of the moneys received but an undertaking not to issue a second writ in England.

The notice being an abuse of process, Parker J was right, in my judgment, to strike it out. It does not, however, follow that the court may not thereafter give the plaintiff leave on terms to discontinue. Because he reached the conclusion that he should restrain the plaintiff from proceeding with his claim in America, the judge, logically and appropriately, made no order staying or discontinuing the English action. But, had he refused the injunction, it would have been necessary for him to consider what he ought to do with the English action on the basis that the American action was proceeding. This he never did, for the situation did not, on his judgment, arise.

In the Court of Appeal no majority ratio decidendi emerged. Lord Denning MR, though he preferred a declaration to an injunction, agreed with the judge. Shaw LJ based his judgment on lack of jurisdiction; as the English action had been ended, in his view, by the notice of discontinuance, the court had no jurisdiction to grant an injunction. Brandon LJ assuming without deciding that there was jurisdiction, concluded (implicitly rather than expressly) that the judge had erred in the exercise of his discretion, and gave detailed reasons why in his view no injunction ought to have been granted.

In this welter of judicial differences it becomes necessary for your Lordships' House to trace a clear path based on accepted principle. And, since the crux of the appeal is whether the plaintiff should be allowed to proceed in America, I would answer this question before considering the future of the English proceedings.

Injunction, being an equitable remedy, operates in personam. It has been used to order parties amenable to the court's jurisdiction 'to take, or to omit to take, any steps and proceedings in any other court of justice whether in this country or in a foreign country': Leach V-C in *Bushby v Munday* (1821) 5 Madd 297 at 307, [1814–23] All ER Rep 304 at 306. The English court, as Leach V-C went on to say, 'does not pretend to any interference with the other court; it acts upon the defendant by punishment for his contempt in his disobedience to the order of the court'. The jurisdiction, which has been frequently exercised since 1821, was reviewed by the Court of Appeal in *Ellerman Lines Ltd v Read* [1928] 2 KB 144, [1928] All ER Rep 415. Scrutton LJ in that case quoted with approval a passage from the judgment of Lord Brougham LC in *Lord Portarlington v Soulby* (1834) 3 Myl & K 104 at 107, [1824–34] All ER Rep 610 at 611, where Lord Brougham LC affirmed that 'the injunction was not directed to the foreign Court, but to the party within the jurisdiction here'. I would not, however, leave *Ellerman's* case without a reference to the warning of Eve J ([1928] 2 KB 144 at 158, [1928] All ER Rep 415 at 422): 'No doubt, the jurisdiction is to be exercised with caution . . .'

The considerable case law to which your Lordships have been referred does not, in terms, express any limitation on the sorts of cases in which it may be appropriate to exercise the jurisdiction. Counsel for the plaintiff, however, submitted that it is to be found to have been exercised only in two classes of cases: (1) 'lis alibi pendens', where the object is to prevent harassment (he cited as examples *The Christiansborg* (1885) 10 PD 141, with especial reference to the judgment of Baggallay LJ (at 152–153), *The Hagen* [1908] P 189 at 202, [1908–10] All ER Rep 21 at 26 and *The Janera* [1928] P 55, [1927] All ER Rep 490); and (2) where there is a right justiciable in England, which the court seeks to protect. In support of his second class, counsel cited a passage from the speech of Lord Diplock in *The Siskina* [1977] 3 All ER 803 at 824, [1979] AC 210 at 256:

> 'A right to obtain an interlocutory injunction is not a cause of action . . . It is dependent on there being a pre-existing cause of action against the defendant arising out of an invasion, actual or threatened, by him of a legal or equitable right of the plaintiff for the enforcement of which the defendant is amenable to the jurisdiction of the court.'

No doubt, in practice, most cases fall within one or other of these two classes. But the width and flexibility of equity are not to be undermined by categorisation. Caution in the exercise of the jurisdiction is certainly needed; but the way in which the judges have expressed themselves from 1821 onwards amply supports the view for which the defendants contend that the injunction can be granted against a party properly before the court, where it is appropriate to avoid injustice.

The plaintiff went home to Portugal after his accident (in fact, on 1st November 1977), where he has ever since remained. He is neither a British subject nor resident in England. But he has sued in England, where he has agents, ie the solicitors acting for him, and his cause of action arose in England. Is this a sufficient connection with England to enable an English court to grant an injunction against him? The question might be of some difficulty if this House were in agreement with the view expressed by Shaw LJ that the action in which the injunction is sought had been terminated by notice of discontinuance before it was granted. The point was considered by Megaw J in *The Tropaioforos (No 2)* [1962] 1 Lloyd's Rep 410, where it was sought to discharge an injunction restraining a party from proceeding in a foreign court after the English proceedings had come to an end. Counsel for the applicant in that case submitted that an English court has no jurisdiction to restrain a foreigner who is not resident here (and who has no assets against which an order could be enforced) from instituting or continuing proceedings in a foreign court, unless this would constitute an abuse of the process of the English court (see [1962] 1 Lloyd's Rep 410 at 416). The point does not arise for decision, if your Lordships refuse to accept, as I do, that the English action in the present case had come to an end before the injunction was granted. But, if I may respectfully express an opinion, I would think that the approach of Megaw J in *The Tropaioforos* was correct in principle, namely that it is a question of fact to be determined in the light of the particular circumstances of the case whether one who is suing abroad has sufficient connection with England to justify the granting of an injunction restraining him from proceeding with his foreign suit. In that case the existence of a contract was held to have provided the connnection.

There remains the point that to grant an injunction in the circumstances of this case against the plaintiff would be useless, a mere brutum fulmen. The answer was given succinctly by the Court of Appeal in *Re Liddell's Settlement Trusts* [1936] Ch 365, Romer LJ observing that (at 374) 'It is not the habit of this Court in considering whether or not it will make an order to contemplate the possibility that it will not be obeyed', and Slesser LJ (at 373): 'We are not to assume that the lady will necessarily disobey the court' (cf [1936] 1 All ER Rep 239 at 248 and 247).

I turn to consider what criteria should govern the exercise of the court's discretion to impose a stay or grant an injunction. It is unnecessary now to examine the earlier case law. The principle is the same whether the remedy sought is a stay of English proceedings or a restraint on foreign proceedings. The modern statement of the law is to be found in the majority speeches in *The Atlantic Star* [1973] 2 All ER 175, [1974] AC 436. It had been thought that the criteria for staying (or restraining) proceedings were twofold: (1) that to allow the proceedings to continue would be oppressive or vexatious, and (2) that to stay (or restrain) them would not cause injustice to the plaintiff (see Scott LJ in *St Pierre v South American Stores (Gath and Chaves) Ltd* [1936] 1 KB 382 at 398, [1935] All ER Rep 408 at 414). In *The Atlantic Star* this House, while refusing to go as far as the Scottish doctrine of forum non conveniens, extended and reformulated the criteria, treating the epithets 'vexatious' and 'oppressive' as illustrating but not confining the jurisdiction. Lord Wilberforce put it in this way. The 'critical equation', he said, was between 'any advantage to the plaintiff' and 'any disadvantage to the defendant'. Though this is essentially a matter for the court's discretion, it is possible, he said, to 'make explicit' some elements. He then went on ([1973] 2 All ER 175 at 194, [1974] AC 436 at 468–469):

> 'The cases say that the advantage must not be "fanciful"—that "a substantial advantage" is enough . . . A bona fide advantage to a plaintiff is a solid weight in the scale, often a decisive weight, but not always so. Then the disadvantage to the defendant: to be taken into account at all this must be serious, more than the mere disadvantage of multiple suits . . . I think too that there must be a relative element in assessing both advantage and disadvantage—*relative to the individual circumstances of the plaintiff and defendant*.' (Emphasis mine.)

In *MacShannon v Rockware Glass Ltd* [1978] 1 All ER 625 at 630, [1978] AC 795 at 812 Lord Diplock interpreted the majority speeches in *The Atlantic Star* as an invitation to drop the use of the words 'vexatious' and 'oppressive' (an invitation which I gladly accept) and formulated his distillation of principle in words which are now very familiar:

> 'In order to justify a stay two conditions must be satisfied, one positive and the other negative: (a) the defendant must satisfy the court that there is another forum to whose jurisdiction he is amenable in which justice can be done between the

parties at substantially less inconvenience or expense, and (b) the stay must not deprive the plaintiff of a legitimate personal or juridical advantage which would be available to him if he invoked the jurisdiction of the English court.'

Transposed into the context of the present case, this formulation means that to justify the grant of an injunction the defendants must show (a) that the English court is a forum to whose jurisdiction they are amenable in which justice can be done at substantially less inconvenience and expense, *and* (b) that the injunction must not deprive the plaintiff of a legitimate personal or juridical advantage which would be available to him if he invoked the American jurisdiction.

The formula is not, however, to be construed as a statute. No time should be spent in speculating what is meant by 'legitimate'. It, like the whole of the context, is but a guide to solving in the particular circumstances of the case the 'critical equation' between advantage to the plaintiff and disadvantage to the defendants.

No question arises on (a). I will assume that justice can be done in the English proceedings at substantially less expense to the defendants. The balance of convenience is, however, less heavily tipped against them, Texas being their headquarters. Parker J directed himself correctly as to the applicable law, founding himself on the *MacShannon* formulation and dealing with (b) at length. The challenge that is made to his decision is that, in exercising his discretion to grant the injunction, he wrongly analysed the relevant factors, giving weight to something which he ought not to have taken into account and failing to give weight to something which he ought to have taken into account: see *Birkett v James* [1977] 2 All ER 801 at 804, [1978] AC 297 at 317 per Lord Diplock. It is, indeed, submitted that Parker J's exercise of his discretion was plainly wrong, a submission which Brandon LJ must have accepted, since he embarked on his own analysis of the factors relevant to discretion.

The attack on Parker J's exercise of discretion stands or falls on a consideration of one paragraph in his judgment ([1980] 1 All ER 689 at 699–700, [1980] 1 WLR 833 at 846–847).

Having acknowledged that the prospect of higher damages in America can be a legitimate advantage for a plaintiff, he gives two reasons for considering the advantage to be of little weight in this case. First, he instances a situation in which two plaintiffs 'suffering identical personal injuries' sue in England but one sues also in Texas because his defendant has an office and assets there. Parker J considers it would be unjust to allow the second plaintiff to recover more in Texas than the first can recover in England. But this example, on which he heavily relies for his conclusion, is an irrelevancy. The criterion, as was emphasised in *The Atlantic Star*, is the critical equation between the advantage to the plaintiff and the disadvantage to the defendant, but not, as Parker J assumes, a comparison between different plaintiffs in their separate claims against different defendants. Parker J, though he pays lip service to the principle that he must do justice *between* the parties, relies in this instance on a comparison not between them but with others. He ignores 'the relative element' of which Lord Wilberforce spoke in *The Atlantic Star*.

Second, he treats as 'the question of real importance' whether the plaintiff is likely to obtain a lower award in England than he would in the country where he lives, ie Portugal. There being no evidence that an English award would be treated as unjustly low in Portugal, he considers the prospect of a higher recovery in Texas to be 'of little weight'. I reject the reasoning and its relevance. The fact that the plaintiff can sue in Texas defendants who have an office and substantial assets in Texas and that under the law there he has the legitimate personal and juridical advantage of the prospect of a much greater recovery than if he were to sue in England cannot be discarded as of little weight merely because an English award would not be regarded as unjustly low in Portugal. The discretion is not to be exercised on such a comparison, even if there were (which there was not) any evidence to guide the judge's speculation as to the Portuguese possibilities. The balance is between the English and the American proceedings; the relative elements of plaintiff's advantage and defendant's disadvantage in each have to be weighed. The balance is not to be confused by uncertain legal, social and economic elements arising outside the two sets of litigation.

It is, therefore, open to this House to review the exercise of the judge's discretion. My Lords, on this aspect of the case I find the judgment of Brandon LJ convincing. He found that to restrain the plaintiff from proceeding in Texas would deprive him of a legitimate personal or juridical advantage. I agree. If he had been advised early enough to sue the JMC group in Texas first, they could not have compelled him to sue in England. The only additional expense incurred by the defendants as a result of the plaintiff suing first in England has been that of legal costs, which are recoverable by the defendants. Texas is as natural and proper a forum for suing a group of Texan-based companies as England, even though England, as the scene of the accident, is also a natural and proper forum. The interim payments can be repaid, if (which appears improbable) the defendants want repayment. The admission of liability obtained in the English action, which could in some cases be a significant factor, is not in this case, for as Brandon LJ said ([1980] 3 All ER 72 at 93, [1980] 1 WLR 833 at 870) 'it is clear beyond doubt that [the accident] was caused by negligence of the ship's chief engineer'. Finally, there is the possible injustice to the defendants that, if the Texan court should decline jurisdiction, the plaintiff can start afresh here; but the court can safeguard the defendants either by putting the plaintiff on terms or by staying whatever English action is in being. For the reasons which Brandon LJ gives I agree with his conclusion 'that the balance comes down clearly in the plaintiff's favour'.

My conclusion is, therefore, that the Court of Appeal was right to discharge the injunction, but that the judge was right to strike out the notice of discontinuance. The plaintiff has, therefore, succeeded in persuading the English courts that he should be allowed to continue with his American proceedings. What, then, is to be done with the English action? Had the plaintiff sought leave to discontinue, as he should have done and now, under the amended rules of court, would have to do, the logical course for the court would have been to give leave to discontinue on such terms as to costs, repayment of interim payments and future proceedings in England as the defendants might seek and the court think just. Costs are provided for; the defendants, for sound tactical reasons, are not asking for the interim payments back or any other terms, and the House can give leave, pursuant to RSC Ord 21, r 3(1) to discontinue the first action and maintain the stay on the second protective writ. Accordingly, I would vary the order of the Court of Appeal by substituting an order for discontinuance of the action for the Court of Appeal's order upholding the notice of discontinuance. Subject to that variation, I would dismiss the appeal.

Much time was spent below on evidence and argument on the propriety of the conduct of the American attorneys of the plaintiff. They certainly approached him with the object, in which they were successful, of persuading him to sue in America; and they will receive for themselves the substantial benefit of a fee on a contingency basis, 40% of the damages recovered, nothing if he fails. The agreement they reached with him was said to contain terms unethical by the standards of the American Bar, though it is conceded a contingency-fee basis is itself acceptable, and common practice.

I venture to suggest, my Lords, that these matters are for the American authorities, and not for your Lordships' House. They have no place in the 'critical equation' which is fundamental to the proper exercise of the discretion in this case.

As far as costs are concerned, I would leave undisturbed the Court of Appeal's order and give the plaintiff his costs in your Lordships' House. In substance he is the victor.

LORD BRIDGE OF HARWICH. My Lords, I have had the advantage of reading in draft the speech of my noble and learned friend Lord Scarman. I agree with it and with the order he proposes for dismissing the appeal.

Appeal dismissed. Order appealed from affirmed, with variation that notice of discontinuance restored therein be struck out and in lieu thereof the plaintiff's action against the defendants in the United Kingdom be discontinued.

Solicitors: *Clyde & Co* (for the defendants); *B M Birnberg & Co* (for the plaintiff).

Mary Rose Plummer   Barrister.

Midland Bank Trust Co Ltd and another v Green and another

HOUSE OF LORDS,
LORD WILBERFORCE, LORD EDMUND-DAVIES, LORD FRASER OF TULLYBELTON, LORD RUSSELL OF KILLOWEN AND LORD BRIDGE OF HARWICH
4th, 5th, 6th NOVEMBER, 11th DECEMBER 1980

Land charge – Failure to register – Estate contract – Contract void against purchaser of legal estate for money or money's worth – Purchaser – Sale of land by husband to wife for consideration substantially less than real value of land – Transaction executed for ulterior motive of defeating option to purchase land – Option not registered – Whether wife a 'purchaser' of the legal estate for money or money's worth – Whether option binding on her – Land Charges Act 1925, ss 13(2), 20(8).

In 1961 a father, who was the owner of a 300-acre farm, granted his son, who was the tenant of the farm, an option to purchase it at the price of £75 an acre, the option to be effective for 10 years. The option was not registered under the Land Charges Act 1925. By a conveyance dated 17th August 1967 the father conveyed the legal estate in the farm, then worth some £40,000, to his wife for the sum of £500, the purpose of the conveyance being to defeat the son's option. In October 1967 the son discovered the existence of the conveyance when he gave notice exercising the option. Neither the father nor the mother complied with the son's notice. The mother died in 1968. In 1970 the son commenced an action against his father and the executors of his mother's estate claiming, inter alia, a declaration that the option was binding on his mother's estate and specific performance of the option. The defendants pleaded in their defence that the conveyance to the mother was a bona fide sale, that the mother was a 'purchaser of [the] legal estate for money or money's worth' for the purposes of s 13(2)[a] of the 1925 Act since she had taken an interest in land 'for valuable consideration' for the purposes of s 20(8)[b], and that therefore the unregistered option was void as against her under s 13(2). The judge ([1978] 3 All ER 555) held that the conveyance had effected a genuine passing of the legal estate for money or money's worth, notwithstanding either the inadequacy of the consideration or the ulterior motive behind the conveyance, and had therefore rendered the son's option void. On appeal, the Court of Appeal ([1979] 3 All ER 28) reversed his decision, holding that the consideration provided by the mother was grossly inadequate and a sham, and granted the relief sought by the son. The surviving executor of the mother's estate appealed to the House of Lords.

Held – The appeal would be allowed for the following reasons—
(1) A purchaser of a legal estate who claimed the protection of s 13(2) of the 1925 Act against an unregistered land charge was not required to show that he had no notice of the charge or that he had otherwise acted in 'good faith', since the requirement of acting in

---

a   Section 13(2), so far as material, is set out at p 156 *f g*, post
b   Section 20(8), so far as material, is set out at p 156 *h*, post

good faith had been deliberately omitted from the section and accordingly avoided the necessity of inquiring into the purchaser's motives and state of mind (see p 158 *a* to *d* and *g* and p 160 *a* to *d*, post); *Re Monolithic Building Co* [1914–15] All ER Rep 249 considered.

(2) For the purposes of s 20(8) of the 1925 Act 'valuable consideration' included a nominal consideration and a purchaser who provided merely nominal consideration for the purchase of a legal estate was accordingly not barred from the protection afforded to him by s 13(2) against an unregistered land charge merely because the consideration provided by him may not have been adequate. Thus even if the £500 provided by the mother was only nominal consideration (which was doubtful) it was nevertheless valuable consideration (see p 159 *c* to p 160 *d*, post).

(3) On the clear wording of ss 13(2) and 20(8) the mother had taken the fee simple interest in the farm for valuable consideration and was accordingly a purchaser of a legal estate for money or money's worth. The son's unregistered option was therefore void as against her (see p 156 *h j*, p 159 *j* and p 160 *a* to *d*, post).

Decision of the Court of Appeal [1979] 3 All ER 28 reversed.

Notes

For the effect of unregistered estate contracts and for the position of purchasers in relation to unregistered land options, see 26 Halsbury's Laws (4th Edn) paras 743, 750.

For the Land Charges Act 1925, ss 13, 20, see 27 Halsbury's Statutes (3rd Edn) 706, 714.

As from 29th January 1973 ss 13(2) and 20(8) of the 1925 Act have been replaced by ss 4(5) and (6) and the definition of 'purchaser' in s 17(1) of the Land Charges Act 1972.

Cases referred to in opinions

Berwick & Co v Price [1905] 1 Ch 632, 74 LJ Ch 249, 92 LT 110, 20 Digest (Repl) 332, 652.

Greaves v Tofield (1880) 14 Ch D 563, 50 LJ Ch 118, 43 LT 100, CA, 35 Digest (Repl) 314, 303.

Grey v Inland Revenue Comrs [1959] 3 All ER 603, [1960] AC 1, [1959] 3 WLR 759, [1959] TR 311, 38 ATC 313, HL, 39 Digest (Repl) 333, 723.

Le Neve v Le Neve (1747) 3 Atk 646, Amb 436, 1 Ves Sen 64, 26 ER 1172, 20 Digest (Repl) 335, 669.

Monolithic Building Co, Re, Tacon v Monolithic Building Co [1915] 1 Ch 643, [1914–15] All ER Rep 249, 84 LJ Ch 441, 112 LT 619, CA, 44 Digest (Repl) 272, 996.

Oliver v Hinton [1899] 2 Ch 264, 68 LJ Ch 583, 81 LT 212, CA, 20 Digest (Repl) 340, 696.

Pilcher v Rawlins (1872) LR 7 Ch App 259, 41 LJ Ch 485, 25 LT 921, LC and LJJ, 20 Digest (Repl) 314, 529.

Taylor v London and County Banking Co, London and County Banking Co v Nixon [1901] 2 Ch 231, 70 LJ Ch 477, 84 LT 397, CA, 20 Digest (Repl) 324, 613.

Appeal

By a writ and statement of claim dated 27th January 1970 and subsequently amended the plaintiff, Thomas Geoffrey Green, claimed against the defendants, Walter Stanley Green personally and as executor of his wife, Evelyne Green deceased, and Robert Derek Green as executor of Evelyne Green deceased, (1) a declaration that an option to purchase a property known as Gravel Hill Farm, Thornton-le-Moor, Lincolnshire, granted by Walter Stanley Green to Thomas Geoffrey Green was binding on the estate of Evelyne Green, (2) specific performance of the contract arising out of the option and the notice exercising it dated 6th October 1967, (3) all necessary accounts and inquiries, (4) damages in lieu of or in addition to specific performance, and (5) damages for conspiracy. On Walter Stanley Green's death his executrix, Beryl Rosalie Kemp, carried on the action as a defendant by an order to carry on dated 19th January 1973, but she failed to comply with an order for discovery and her defence was struck out by order dated 7th October 1975. On Thomas Geoffrey Green's death his personal representatives, Midland Bank Trust Co Ltd and Margaret Ann Green, carried on the action as plaintiffs by an order to carry on dated 16th November 1973. The action accordingly came on for trial before Oliver J as a claim by the plaintiffs as executors of Thomas Geoffrey Green against the defendants Beryl Rosalie Kemp and Robert Derek Green, representing respectively the estates of Walter Stanley Green and Evelyne Green. As against Walter Stanley Green's estate the action was undefended. On 21st October 1977 Oliver J ([1978] 3 All ER 555, [1980] Ch 590) dismissed the action against the defendant Robert Derek Green, the surviving executor of Evelyne Green, and as against the defendant Beryl Rosalie Kemp directed an inquiry as to damages. The plaintiffs appealed against the dismissal of the action as against the defendant Robert Derek Green. On 11th April 1979 the Court of Appeal (Lord Denning MR and Eveleigh LJ, Sir Stanley Rees dissenting) ([1979] 3 All ER 28, [1980] Ch 590) reversed Oliver J's decision. The defendant Robert Derek Green appealed to the House of Lords pursuant to leave granted by the Court of Appeal. The facts are set out in the opinion of Lord Wilberforce.

L H Hoffmann QC and *Gavin Lightman QC* for the appellant.
Jonathan Parker QC and *M Walters* for the respondents.

Their Lordships took time for consideration.

11th December. The following opinions were delivered.

LORD WILBERFORCE. My Lords, this appeal relates to a 300-acre farm in Lincolnshire called Gravel Hill Farm. It was owned by Walter Stanley Green ('Walter') and, since 1954, it was let to his son Thomas Geoffrey Green ('Geoffrey') who farmed it as tenant. Walter owned another large farm which he farmed jointly with another son, Robert Derek Green ('Robert'), the appellant. In 1960 Walter sold this other farm to Robert at £75 per acre.

On 24th March 1961 Walter granted to Geoffrey an option to purchase Gravel Hill Farm, also at £75 per acre. The option was granted for the consideration of £1, and so was contractually binding on Walter. It was to remain open for ten years. It seems that the reason why this transaction was entered into, rather than one of sale to Geoffrey, was to save estate duty on Walter's death. This option was, in legal terms, an estate contract and so a legal charge, class C, within the meaning of the Land Charges Act 1925. The correct and statutory method for protection of such an option is by means of entering it in the register of land charges maintained under the Act. If so registered, the option would have been enforceable, not only (contractually) against Walter, but against any purchaser of the farm. The option was not registered, a failure which inevitably called in question the responsibility of Geoffrey's solicitor. To anticipate, Geoffrey in fact brought proceedings against his solicitor which have been settled for a considerable sum, payable if the present appeal succeeds.

In 1967 there appears to have been some family disagreement. We do not know the nature of it, or the merits. I am not prepared to assume, in the absence of any evidence, that either side was in the wrong. All we know is that Walter formed the intention, contrary to what he had planned in 1961, to defeat Geoffrey's option and to make Gravel Hill Farm available for the family. He instructed solicitors to prepare a conveyance of it to his wife Evelyne; this the solicitors did after verifying that the option was not registered as a land charge.

On or about 17th August 1967 Walter executed a conveyance of Gravel Hill Farm to Evelyne for a consideration of £500. The judge found that this sum was paid by Evelyne to Walter. It was of course far less than the value of the farm, which was then worth about £40,000. The conveyance was also a breach of contract by Walter for which Walter or his estate was liable to Geoffrey in damages.

Later, Evelyne made a will in which she left the farm, subject to Walter's life interest, to her five children, including Geoffrey. On 5th September 1967 Geoffrey, who had learnt of the conveyance, caused the option to be registered as an estate contract, and on 6th October 1967 gave notice exercising the option. Finally, on 27th January 1970, Geoffrey issued a writ against Walter and Evelyne's executors (she had died in 1968) claiming that the option was still binding, specific performance of the contract arising from its exercise and damages. This was later amended so as to claim damages for conspiracy by Walter and Evelyne.

Most of the principals involved in the above transactions are dead. The place of Geoffrey is taken by the present respondents as his executors; that of Evelyne by the appellant, as her sole surviving executor; the place of Walter was taken by Beryl Rosalie Kemp as his executrix, but her defence was struck out by order dated 7th October 1975. The issue therefore effectively is between the appellant, as representing the estate of Evelyne, and the respondents, as representing the estate of Geoffrey.

The trial took place before Oliver J in 1977. A number of issues arose which are no longer relevant. The learned judge ([1978] 3 All ER 555, [1980] Ch 590), in an admirable judgment with which I wholly agree, decided: (i) that the sale and conveyance to Evelyne was not a sham and was a genuine sale by the vendor to a 'purchaser', as defined by the Land Charges Act 1925 for money or money's worth, and accordingly that the option was not specifically enforceable; (ii) that Walter's estate had no answer to a claim for damages, and that an inquiry as to damages must be made; (iii) that any claim for damages against the estate of Evelyne was statute-barred by virtue of the Law Reform (Miscellaneous Provisions) Act 1934.

An appeal was brought to the Court of Appeal ([1979] 3 All ER 28, [1980] Ch 590) which, by a majority, reversed the judge's decision on point (i), and declared the option specifically enforceable. The ground of this decision appears to have been that the sale in 1967 was not for 'money or money's worth', within the meaning of s 13 of the 1925 Act. In addition Lord Denning MR was prepared to hold that the protection of the Act was not available in a case of fraud, meaning thereby 'any dishonest dealing done so as to deprive unwary innocents of their rightful dues'. The respondents, however, did not seek to support this except to the extent that they relied on lack of good faith on the part of Evelyne.

My Lords, s 13(2) of the 1925 Act reads as follows:

'A land charge of Class B, Class C or Class D, created or arising after the commencement of this Act, shall (except as hereinafter provided) be void as against a purchaser of the land charged therewith . . . unless the land charge is registered in the appropriate register before the completion of the purchase: Provided that, as respects a land charge of Class D and an estate contract created or entered into after the commencement of this Act, this subsection only applies in favour of a purchaser of a legal estate for money or money's worth.'

As regards the word 'purchaser' s 20(8) of the same Act reads: '"Purchaser" means any person . . . who, for valuable consideration, takes any interest in land . . .'

Thus the case appears to be a plain one. The 'estate contract', which by definition (s 11) includes an option of purchase, was entered into after 1st January 1926; Evelyne took an interest (in fee simple) in the land 'for valuable consideration', so was a 'purchaser'; she was a purchaser for money, namely £500; the option was not registered before the completion of the purchase. It is therefore void as against her.

In my opinion this appearance is also the reality. The case is plain; the Act is clear and definite. Intended as it was to provide a simple and understandable system for the protection of title to land, it should not be read down or glossed; to do so would destroy the usefulness of the Act. Any temptation to remould the Act to meet the facts of the present case, on the supposition that it is a hard one and that justice requires it, is, for me at least, removed by the consideration that the Act itself provides a simple and effective protection for persons in Geoffrey's position, viz by registration.

The respondents submitted two arguments as to the interpretation of s 13(2): the one sought to introduce into it a requirement that the purchaser should be 'in good faith'; the other related to the words 'in money or money's worth'.

The argument as to good faith fell into three parts: first, that 'good faith' was something required of a 'purchaser' before 1926; second, that this requirement was preserved by the 1925 legislation and in particular by s 13(2) of the Land Charges Act 1925. If these points could be made good, it would then have to be decided whether the purchaser (Evelyne) was in 'good faith' on the facts of the case.

My Lords, the character in the law known as the bona fide (good faith) purchaser for value without notice was the creation of equity. In order to affect a purchaser for value of a legal estate with some equity or equitable interest, equity fastened on his conscience and the composite expression was used to epitomise the circumstances in which equity would, or rather would not, do so. I think that it would generally be true to say that the words 'in good faith' related to the existence of notice. Equity, in other words, required not only absence of notice, but genuine and honest absence of notice. As the law developed, this requirement became crystallised in the doctrine of constructive notice which assumed a statutory form in the Conveyancing Act 1882, s 3. But, and so far I would be willing to accompany the respondents, it would be a mistake to suppose that the requirement of good faith extended only to the matter of notice, or that when notice came to be regulated by statute the requirement of good faith became obsolete. Equity still retained its interest in, and power over, the purchaser's conscience. The classic judgment of James LJ in *Pilcher v Rawlins* (1872) LR 7 Ch App 259 at 269 is clear authority that it did: good faith there is stated as a separate test which may have to be passed even though absence of notice is proved. And there are references in cases subsequent to 1882 which confirm the proposition that honesty or bona fides remained something which might be inquired into (see *Berwick & Co v Price* [1905] 1 Ch 632 at 639, *Taylor v London and County Banking Co* [1901] 2 Ch 231 at 256 and *Oliver v Hinton* [1899] 2 Ch 264 at 273).

But did this requirement, or test, pass into the property legislation of 1925? My Lords, I do not think it safe to seek the answer to this question by means of a general assertion that the property legislation of 1922 to 1925 was not intended to alter the law, or not intended to alter it in a particular field, such as that relating to purchases of legal estates. All the 1925 Acts, and their precursors, were drafted with the utmost care, and their wording, certainly where this is apparently clear, has to be accorded firm respect. As was pointed out in *Grey v Inland Revenue Comrs* [1959] 3 All ER 603, [1960] AC 1, the 1922 to 1924 Acts effected massive changes in the law affecting property and the House, in consequence, was persuaded to give to a plain word ('disposition') its plain meaning, and not to narrow it by reference to its antecedents. Certainly that case should firmly discourage us from muddying clear waters. I accept that there is merit in looking at the corpus as a whole in order to produce if possible a consistent scheme. But there are limits to the possibilities of this process; for example it cannot eliminate the difference between registered and unregistered land, or the respective charges on them.

As to the requirement of 'good faith' we are faced with a situation of some perplexity. The expression 'good faith' appears in the Law of Property Act 1925 definition of 'purchaser' ('a purchaser in good faith for valuable consideration'): s 205(1)(xxi); in the Settled Land Act 1925, s 117(1)(xxi) (ditto); in the Administration of Estates Act 1925, s 55(1)(xviii) ('"purchaser" means a lessee, mortgagee or other person who in good faith acquires an interest in property for valuable consideration') and in the Land Registration Act 1925, s 3(xxi), which does not however, as the other Acts do, include a reference to nominal consideration. So there is certainly some indication of an intention to carry the concept of 'good faith' into much of the 1925 code. What then do we find in the Land Charges Act 1925? We were taken along a scholarly peregrination through the numerous Acts antecedent to the final codification and consolidation in 1925: the Land Charges Registration and Searches Act 1888, the Law of Property Act 1922, particularly Sch 7, the Law of Property (Amendment) Act 1924 as well as the

Yorkshire and Middlesex Deeds Registration Acts. But I think, with genuine respect for an interesting argument, that such solution as there is of the problem under consideration must be sought in the terms of the various 1925 Acts themselves. So far as concerns the Land Charges Act 1925, the definition of 'purchaser' quoted above does not mention 'good faith' at all. 'Good faith' did not appear in the original Act of 1888, or in the extension made to that Act by the 1922 Act, Sch 7, or in the 1924 Act, Sch 6. It should be a secure assumption that the definition of 'purchaser for value' which is found in s 4 of the 1888 Act ('. . . person who for valuable consideration takes any interest in land') together with the limitation which is now the proviso to s 13(2) of the 1925 Act, introduced in 1922, was intended to be carried forward into the 1925 Act. The expression 'good faith' appears nowhere in the antecedents. To write the words in, from the examples of contemporaneous Acts, would be bold. It becomes impossible when it is seen that the words appear in ss 3(1) and 7(1) of the 1925 Act, in each case in a proviso very similar, in structure, to the relevant proviso in s 13(2). If canons of constructions have any validity at all, they must lead to the conclusion that the omission in s 13(2) was deliberate.

My Lords, I recognise that the inquiring mind may put the question: why should there be an omission of the requirement of good faith in this particular context? I do not think there should be much doubt about the answer. Addition of a requirement that the purchaser should be in good faith would bring with it the necessity of inquiring into the purchaser's motives and state of mind. The present case is a good example of the difficulties which would exist. If the position was simply that the purchaser had notice of the option, and decided nevertheless to buy the land, relying on the absence of notification, nobody could contend that she would be lacking in good faith. She would merely be taking advantage of a situation, which the law has provided, and the addition of a profit motive could not create an absence of good faith. But suppose, and this is the respondents' argument, the purchaser's motive is to defeat the option, does this make any difference? Any advantage to oneself seems necessarily to involve a disadvantage for another; to make the validity of the purchase depend on which aspect of the transaction was prevalent in the purchaser's mind seems to create distinctions equally difficult to analyse in law as to establish in fact; avarice and malice may be distinct sins, but in human conduct they are liable to be intertwined. The problem becomes even more acute if one supposes a mixture of motives. Suppose, and this may not be far from the truth, that the purchaser's motives were in part to take the farm from Geoffrey and in part to distribute it between Geoffrey and his brothers and sisters, but not at all to obtain any benefit for herself, is this acting in 'good faith' or not? Should family feeling be denied a protection afforded to simple greed? To eliminate the necessity for inquiries of this kind may well have been part of the legislative intention. Certainly there is here no argument for departing, violently, from the wording of the Act.

Before leaving this part of the case, I must comment on *Re Monolithic Building Co* [1915] 1 Ch 643, [1914–15] All ER Rep 249, which was discussed in the Court of Appeal. That was a case arising under s 93 of the Companies (Consolidation) Act 1908, which made an unregistered mortgage void against any creditor of the company. The defendant Jenkins was a managing director of the company, and clearly had notice of the first unregistered mortgage; he himself subsequently took and registered a mortgage debenture and claimed priority over the unregistered mortgage. It was held by the Court of Appeal, first, that this was not a case of fraud ('. . . it is not fraud to take advantage of legal rights, the existence of which may be taken to be known to both parties': see [1915] 1 Ch 643 at 663, [1914–15] All ER Rep 249 at 251 per Lord Cozens-Hardy MR), and, second, that s 93 of the Act was clear in its terms, should be applied according to its plain meaning, and should not be weakened by infusion of equitable doctrines applied by the courts during the nineteenth century. The judgment of Lord Cozens-Hardy MR contains a valuable critique of the well-known cases of *Le Neve v Le Neve* (1747) 3 Atk 646, 26 ER 1172 and *Greaves v Tofield* (1880) 14 Ch D 563, arising under the Middlesex Registry Act 1708 and other enactments, which had led the judges to import equitable doctrines into cases of priority arising under those Acts, and establishes that the principles of those cases should not be applied to modern Acts of Parliament.

My Lords, I fail to see how this authority can be invoked in support of the respondents' argument, or of the judgments of the majority of the Court of Appeal. So far from supporting them, it is strongly the other way. It disposes, for the future, of the old arguments based, ultimately, on *Le Neve v Le Neve* for reading equitable doctrines (as to notice etc) into modern Acts of Parliament; it makes it clear that it is not 'fraud' to rely on legal rights conferred by Act of Parliament; it confirms the validity of interpreting clear enactments as to registration and priority according to their tenor.

The judgment of Phillimore LJ does indeed contain a passage which appears to favour application of the principle of *Le Neve v Le Neve*, and to make a distinction between a transaction designed to obtain an advantage, and one designed to defeat a prior (unregistered) interest (see [1915] 1 Ch 643 at 669, [1914–15] All ER Rep 249 at 254–255). But, as I have explained, this distinction is unreal and unworkable, this whole passage is impossible to reconcile with the views of the other members of the Court of Appeal in the case and I respectfully consider that it is not good law.

My Lords, I can deal more shortly with the respondents' second argument. It relates to the consideration for the purchase. The argument is that the protection of s 13(2) of the Land Charges Act 1925 does not extend to a purchaser who has provided only a nominal consideration and that £500 is nominal. A variation of this was the argument accepted by the Court of Appeal that the consideration must be 'adequate', an expression of transparent difficulty. The answer to both contentions lies in the language of the subsection. The word 'purchaser', by definition (s 20(8)), means one who provides valuable consideration, a term of art which precludes any inquiry as to adequacy. This definition is, of course, subject to the context. The proviso to s 13(2) requires money or money's worth to be provided, the purpose of this being to exclude the consideration of marriage. There is nothing here which suggests, or admits of, the introduction of a further requirement that the money must not be nominal.

The argument for this requirement is based on the Law of Property Act 1925 which, in s 205(1)(xxi) defining 'purchaser' provides that 'valuable consideration' includes marriage but does not include a 'nominal consideration in money'. The Land Charges Act 1925 contains no definition of 'valuable consideration', so it is said to be necessary to have resort to the Law of Property Act definition; thus 'nominal consideration in money' is excluded. An indication that this is intended is said to be provided by s 199(1)(i). I cannot accept this. The fallacy lies in supposing that the Acts (either of them) set out to define 'valuable consideration'; they do not: they define 'purchaser', and they define the word differently (see the first part of the argument). 'Valuable consideration' requires no definition; it is an expression denoting an advantage conferred or detriment suffered. What each Act does is, for its own purposes, to exclude some things from this general expression: the Law of Property Act includes marriage but not a nominal sum in money; the Land Charges Act excludes marriage but allows 'money or money's worth'. There is no coincidence between these two, no link by reference or necessary logic between them. Section 199(1)(i), by referring to the Land Charges Act 1925, necessarily incorporates, for the purposes of this provision, the definition of 'purchaser' in the latter Act, for it is only against such a 'purchaser' that an instrument is void under that Act. It cannot be read as incorporating the Law of Property Act definition into the Land Charges Act. As I have pointed out the land charges legislation has contained its own definition since 1888, carried through, with the addition of the reference to 'money or money's worth', into 1925. To exclude a nominal sum of money from s 13(2) of the Land Charges Act 1925 would be to rewrite the section.

This conclusion makes it unnecessary to determine whether £500 is a nominal sum of money or not. But I must say that for my part I should have great difficulty in so holding. 'Nominal consideration' and a 'nominal sum' in the law appear to me, as terms of art, to refer to a sum or consideration which can be mentioned as consideration but is not necessarily paid. To equate 'nominal' with 'inadequate' or even 'grossly inadequate' would embark the law on inquiries which I cannot think were contemplated by Parliament.

I would allow the appeal.

LORD EDMUND-DAVIES. My Lords, for the reasons indicated in the speech of my noble and learned friend Lord Wilberforce, which I have had the advantage of reading in draft, I would allow this appeal.

LORD FRASER OF TULLYBELTON. My Lords, I have had the advantage of reading in draft the speech of my noble and learned friend Lord Wilberforce. I agree with it, and for the reasons that he gives I too would allow this appeal.

LORD RUSSELL OF KILLOWEN. My Lords, I entirely concur in the reasoning of my noble and learned friend Lord Wilberforce and cannot usefully add to it. Accordingly I agree that this appeal must be allowed.

LORD BRIDGE OF HARWICH. My Lords, I have had the advantage of reading in draft the speech of my noble and learned friend Lord Wilberforce. I agree with it and for the reasons he gives I too would allow the appeal.

Appeal allowed. Order appealed from reversed and order of Oliver J restored.

Solicitors: *Simmons & Simmons*, agents for *Roythorne & Co*, Spalding (for the appellant); *Sidney Torrance & Co*, agents for *J Levi & Co*, Leeds (for the respondents).

Mary Rose Plummer   Barrister.

National Carriers Ltd v Panalpina (Northern) Ltd

HOUSE OF LORDS

LORD HAILSHAM OF ST MARYLEBONE LC, LORD WILBERFORCE, LORD SIMON OF GLAISDALE, LORD RUSSELL OF KILLOWEN AND LORD ROSKILL

6th, 7th, 8th OCTOBER, 11th DECEMBER 1980

Contract – Frustration – Change of circumstances – Lease – Lease of warehouse – Access to warehouse closed by local authority – Whether lease frustrated.

The appellants leased a warehouse from the respondents for a term of 10 years from 1st January 1974 at an annual rent of £6,500 for the first five years and £13,300 for the second five years. In May 1979 the local authority closed the street giving the only access to the warehouse because of the dangerous condition of a building opposite the warehouse. Because the dangerous building was listed as being of special architectural or historical interest the local authority were required to apply to the Secretary of State for consent to demolish it. After holding a local inquiry the Secretary of State gave his consent in March 1980, and it was envisaged by the local authority that the demolition would be completed and the street reopened in January 1981. The closure of the street prevented the appellants from using the warehouse for the only purpose contemplated by the lease, viz as a warehouse, and from May 1979 they stopped paying rent. In July 1979 the respondents brought an action against the appellants claiming payment of two quarterly instalments due under the lease, and shortly afterwards issued a summons for summary judgment under RSC Ord 14 for the sums claimed in the writ. The appellants by their defence contended that they were not liable to pay the rent because the lease was frustrated by the closure of the street giving access to the warehouse. The master gave judgment for the respondents on the Ord 14 summons and his decision was affirmed by the judge on the ground that he was bound by authority to hold that the doctrine of frustration could not apply to a lease. The appellants appealed directly to the House of Lords.

Held – (1) (Lord Russell dubitante) The doctrine of frustration was capable of applying to an executed lease of land so as to bring the lease to an end if a frustrating event (ie an event such that no substantial use, permitted by the lease and in the contemplation of the parties, remained possible to the lessee) occurred during the currency of the term. Furthermore there was no class of lease to which the doctrine was inherently inapplicable. However, the circumstances in which the doctrine of frustration could apply to a lease of land were exceedingly rare (see p 167 a b, p 168 b, p 169 e f, p 170 e h j, p 171 b to d and h, p 172 e, p 173 a to c, p 176 b to f and h j, p 177 c, p 179 b to p 180 a and c d, p 181 c, p 182 c, p 186 a e, p 187 b j and p 188 d to g, post); *Cricklewood Property and Investment Trust Ltd v Leightons Investment Trust Ltd* [1945] 1 All ER 252 considered.

(2) Although by the time access to the warehouse was restored the appellants would have lost two out of ten years' use of the warehouse and their business would have been severely disrupted, the closure of access to the warehouse was not sufficiently grave to amount to a frustrating event since there would be a further three years of the lease remaining after access was re-established. In view of the fact that the obligation to pay rent under the lease was otherwise unconditional (except in the case of fire) the appellants had no defence to the action and the appeal would be dismissed (see p 163 d e, p 166 f g, p 169 g, p 173 g to j, p 180 g to p 181 a, p 182 d to f and h j and p 188 f g, post).

Notes

For the ambit of the doctrine of frustration, see 9 Halsbury's Laws (4th Edn) para 452, and for cases on its application to leases, see 12 Digest (Reissue) 504–505, 3506–3511.

Cases referred to in opinions

Admiral Shipping Co Ltd v Weidner, Hopkins & Co [1916] 1 KB 429, 85 LJKB 409, 114 LT
171; rvsd [1917] 1 KB 222, 86 LJKB 336, 115 LT 812, 12 Asp MLC 539, 22 Com Cas
154, CA, 12 Digest (Reissue) 483, 3430.

Bank Line Ltd v Arthur Capel & Co [1919] AC 435, [1918–19] All ER Rep 504, 88 LJKB
211, 120 LT 129, 14 Asp MLC 370, HL, 12 Digest (Reissue) 490, 3461.

Blane Steamships Ltd v Minister of Transport [1951] 2 KB 965, [1951] 2 Lloyd's Rep 155,
CA, 12 Digest (Reissue) 476, 3403.

Cricklewood Property and Investment Trust Ltd v Leightons Investment Trust Ltd [1945] 1 All
ER 252, [1945] AC 221, 114 LJKB 110, 172 LT 140, HL; affg [1943] 2 All ER 97,
[1943] KB 493, 112 LJKB 438, 169 LT 116, CA; affg [1942] 2 All ER 580, [1943] KB
493, 112 LJKB 83, 167 LT 348, 12 Digest (Reissue) 505, 3509.

Cusack-Smith v London Corpn [1956] 1 WLR 1368, 31(2) Digest (Reissue) 898, 7436.

Davis Contractors Ltd v Fareham Urban District Council [1956] 2 All ER 145, [1956] AC 696,
[1956] 3 WLR 37, 54 LGR 289, HL, 12 Digest (Reissue) 507, 3518.

Denman v Brise [1948] 2 All ER 141, [1949] 1 KB 22, [1948] LJR 1388, CA, 31(2) Digest
(Reissue) 1005, 8011.

Denny, Mott & Dickson Ltd v James B Fraser & Co Ltd [1944] 1 All ER 678, [1944] AC 265,
113 LJPC 37, 171 LT 345, HL, 12 Digest (Reissue) 500, 3495.

Embiricos v Sydney Reid & Co [1914] 3 KB 45, [1914–15] All ER Rep 185, 83 LJKB 1348,
111 LT 291, 12 Asp MLC 513, 19 Com Cas 263, 12 Digest (Reissue) 487, 3451.

Firth v Halloran (1926) 38 CLR 261, 12 Digest (Reissue) 505, *1849.

Highway Properties Ltd v Kelly, Douglas & Co Ltd (1971) 17 DLR (3d) 710.

Hirji Mulji v Cheong Yue Steamship Co Ltd [1926] AC 497, [1926] All ER Rep 51, 95 LJPC
121, 134 LT 737, 17 Asp MLC 8, 31 Com Cas 199, PC, 12 Digest (Reissue) 482, 3427.

Jackson v Union Marine Insurance Co Ltd (1874) LR 10 CP 125, [1874–80] All ER Rep 317,
44 LJCP 27, 31 LT 789, 2 Asp MLC 435, Ex Ch, 12 Digest (Reissue) 484, 3435.

Krell v Henry [1903] 2 KB 740, [1900–3] All ER Rep 20, 72 LJKB 794, 89 LT 328, CA, 12
Digest (Reissue) 481, 3422.

Liverpool City Council v Irwin [1976] 2 All ER 39, [1977] AC 239, [1976] 2 WLR 562, 74
LGR 392, 32 P & CR 43, HL, Digest (Cont Vol E) 366, 4870a.

London and Northern Estates Co v Schlesinger [1916] 1 KB 20, [1914–15] All ER Rep 593,
85 LJKB 369, 114 LT 74, 31(1) Digest (Reissue) 22, 14.

Matthey v Curling [1922] 2 AC 180, [1922] All ER Rep 1, 91 LJKB 593, 127 LT 247, HL,
12 Digest (Reissue) 504, 3508.

Paradine v Jane (1647) Aleyn 26, Sty 47, [1558–1774] All ER Rep 172, 82 ER 897, 12
Digest (Reissue) 459, 3322.

Port Line Ltd v Ben Line Steamers Ltd [1958] 1 All ER 787, [1958] 2 QB 146, [1958] 2 WLR
551, [1958] 1 Lloyd's Rep 290, 41 Digest (Repl) 175, 175.

Rom Securities Ltd v Rogers (Holdings) Ltd (1967) 205 Estates Gazette 427.

Tamplin (FA) Steamship Co Ltd v Anglo-Mexican Petroleum Products Co Ltd [1916] 2 AC 397,
[1916–17] All ER Rep 104, 85 LJKB 1389, 115 LT 315, 13 Asp MLC 467, HL, 12
Digest (Reissue) 489, 3457.

Tatem (WJ) Ltd v Gamboa [1938] 3 All ER 135, [1939] 1 KB 132, 108 LJKB 34, 160 LT 159,
19 Asp MLC 216, 43 Com Cas 343, 12 Digest (Reissue) 459, 3321.

Tay Salmon Fisheries Co Ltd v Speedie 1929 SC 593, 31(1) Digest (Reissue) 171, *484.

Taylor v Caldwell (1863) 3 B & S 826, [1861–73] All ER Rep 24, 2 New Rep 198, 32 LJQB
164, 8 LT 356, 27 JP 710, 122 ER 309, 12 Digest (Reissue) 460, 3329.

Tsakiroglou & Co Ltd v Noblee & Thorl GmbH [1961] 2 All ER 179, [1962] AC 93, [1961]
2 WLR 633, [1961] 1 Lloyd's Rep 329, HL, 12 Digest (Reissue) 497, 3488.

Walsh v Lonsdale (1882) 21 Ch D 9, 52 LJ Ch 2, 46 LT 858, CA, 31(1) Digest (Reissue) 77,
594.

Whitehall Court Ltd v Ettlinger [1920] 1 KB 680, [1918–19] All ER Rep 229, 89 LJKB 126,
122 LT 540, 12 Digest (Reissue) 504, 3507.

Appeal

By a writ issued on 9th July 1979 the plaintiffs, National Carriers Ltd, claimed against the defendants, Panalpina (Northern) Ltd, payment of the sum of £5,115.38 in respect of rent due under a lease dated 12th July 1974 made between the plaintiffs as landlords and the defendants as tenants. On 15th August 1979 the plaintiffs issued a summons under RSC Ord 14 for judgment for the sum claimed in the writ and statement of claim. The defendants' sole ground of defence to the claim for rent was that in the events which had happened the lease was frustrated. On 20th September Master Waldman gave judgment for the plaintiffs on the summons and on 16th October Sheen J dismissed the defendants' appeal against that judgment on the ground that he was bound by the decision of the Court of Appeal in *Leightons Investment Trust Ltd v Cricklewood Property and Investment Trust Ltd* [1943] 2 All ER 97, [1943] KB 493 to hold that a lease of land was not capable of discharge by frustration. Pursuant to a certificate granted by the judge under s 12 of the Administration of Justice Act 1969 and with the leave of the House granted on 5th December 1979 the defendants appealed directly to the House of Lords. The facts are set out in the opinion of Lord Hailsham of St Marylebone LC.

Anthony Scrivener QC, Mark Lowe and *M Rose* for the appellants.
Gerald Godfrey QC and *Edwin Prince* for the respondents.

Their Lordships took time for consideration.

11th December. The following opinions were delivered.

LORD HAILSHAM OF ST MARYLEBONE LC. My Lords, we are all agreed that this appeal from decisions of Master Waldman and Sheen J refusing leave to defend under RSC Ord 14 fails on the facts for the reasons given by my noble and learned friends to which personally I have nothing to add. The appellants have failed to raise a triable issue.

Nevertheless, though they arrive in your Lordships' House by an unusual route, the proceeding do raise an interesting and important general question of principle relating to the extent and nature of the law of frustration which has long been debated and which, since the matter has reached this stage and has been fully argued, should now be decided by your Lordships' House.

This question is the applicability of the law of frustration to leases and agreements for a lease. The question is discussed at length in *Cricklewood Property and Investment Trust Ltd v Leighton's Investment Trust Ltd* [1945] 1 All ER 252, [1945] AC 221 by the decision of which in the Court of Appeal ([1943] 2 All ER 97, [1943] KB 493 at 496), Master Waldman and Sheen J rightly considered themselves bound, with the result that, in dismissing the appeal from Master Waldman, Sheen J gave his certificate under s 12 of the Administration of Justice Act 1969, and so, for the first time in my experience, an Ord 14 summons bypasses the Court of Appeal and 'leapfrogs' directly to the Appellate Committee of the House of Lords.

Before I reach a discussion of the point of law it is necessary that I fill in the factual background. This illustrates the curious and sometimes unexpected results which can ensue from the present vogue of listing industrial buildings as part of our national heritage. Kingston Street, Hull is a continuation of English Street (of which, originally, it may have been part) and terminates by running perpendicularly into a T-junction with Railway Street. Before it reaches this end, it crosses more or less at right angles an intersection with Commercial Road and Manor House Street. Hereinafter, when I speak of Kingston Street, I shall be referring solely to that section of it between this intersection and the T-junction with Railway Street. Although it is now, it would seem, a public highway for all types of traffic, it may well be that at one time it was the private property of a railway company, since otherwise it is difficult to explain the 'demise' (sic) of a private right of way along it by the lessors of the property about to be described.

Kingston Street is bounded on both sides by warehouses and on part of one side by a railway shed. At one side of it, at the point nearest the intersection, is a derelict and ruinous Victorian warehouse which at some time has become, under the laws for the conservation of our national heritage, a 'listed building' which means that it cannot be demolished without the consent of the Secretary of State for the Environment, and that, if the demolition is objected to by local conservationists (as in fact happened), this consent will not be granted without the holding of a public local inquiry. Even assuming a result favourable to demolition the total process is likely to last a year. In the events which have happened, the process is not yet complete, but, on the material before us, is likely to be concluded by the end of December 1980 or the beginning of January 1981. By that time it will have lasted about twenty months.

Since, in course of time, the Victorian warehouse became dangerous as well as derelict it evidently presented problems of safety to the City Council of Hull. In 1978 they placed a restriction order on Kingston Street, and on 16th May 1979 they closed it altogether to vehicular traffic. It was not made altogether clear to us under what powers they acted, but the closure was subsequently confirmed and continued by the Secretary of State, and, at the present, access to Kingston Street is not merely prohibited to vehicles, but rendered physically impossible by the erection across it by the local authority of a fenced barrier. This will not be removed until the demolition process is completed at the end of 1980 or the beginning of 1981.

Opposite the ruinous listed building there is another warehouse, more or less triangular in shape, the only access to which (except perhaps on foot) is via a loading bay in Kingston Street. The consequence of the application for demolition, and the subsequent proceedings, has been that, from 16th May 1979 until the time when the barriers are finally removed and the prohibition order lifted, this triangular warehouse has been rendered totally useless for the one purpose, that of a commercial warehouse, for which alone it is fitted, and for which alone, by the terms of the contract between the parties, it may be lawfully used.

In 1974 the triangular warehouse had become the subject of a demise between the plaintiffs/respondents to these proceedings, the lessors, and the defendants/appellants. This demise was contained in a lease dated 12th July 1974 and was expressed to run for ten years from 1st January 1974. The terms of the lease, most of which are not unusual in documents of this kind, contained, inter alia, a covenant to pay an annual rent (£6,500 for the first five years, and for the second five years subsequently increased by agreement in accordance with a formula contained in cl 4(1) of the lease to £13,300) payable in advance by four quarterly instalments. The present proceedings, commenced by writ dated 9th July 1979, are for the payment of £5,115·38 being the two quarterly instalments due on 1st April and 1st July 1979. There is no dispute between the parties as to the amount of this sum, or, subject to the defence of frustration hereinafter to be mentioned, of the liability of the appellants to pay it.

The lease also contained obligations by the tenant to pay rates, to repair, to pay a rateable proportion of the expense of cleaning and maintaining the sewers, roads etc, to insure at full value in the joint names of landlord and tenant, to paint, to yield up in good and substantial repair at the end of the tenancy, not to assign or sublet, alter, or to utilise otherwise than for the purpose of a warehouse without the written consent of the landlord, and other matters. The landlord's covenants included an express covenant of quiet enjoyment. There were special provisions for the suspension of the obligation to pay rent and for the termination of the tenancy at the option of the landlord in case of destruction by fire, and provisions for re-entry by the landlord in case of breach of covenant, or on six months notice, if the premises were required for the proper operation of British Railways (with whom the respondents are associated).

The sole defence raised by the appellants to their obligation to pay rent was that, by reason of the events described above, the lease had become frustrated and was therefore wholly at an end. By their printed case each party raised two questions for your Lordships' decision. The first is the broad question of principle, viz whether the doctrine of frustration can ever apply to determine a lease, and the second, of particular application, whether even if the doctrine can on occasion apply, there is here a triable issue whether it does apply to the lease between the parties in the circumstances described. In the event of both questions being determined in favour of the appellants, your Lordships, if allowing the appeal, would have no option but to return the case for trial at first instance, with the possible result that, after a lapse of two years, it might reappear in your Lordships' list for a second hearing. In any event, unless some guidance is given on the first issue, sooner or later argument would have to be directed to it in some later proceeding. It is therefore perhaps as well that, although dismissing the appeal on the second question, we thought it right to hear the first fully argued on both sides. We are doubly indebted to counsel for the appellants, who, though aware that he had not succeeded, nevertheless stayed to deliver an admirably concise reply to the forceful arguments on the point of principle helpfully presented on behalf of the respondents.

The doctrine of frustration is of comparatively recent development. The general rule of common law, laid down as early as 1647 in *Paradine v Jane* (1647) Aleyn 26, [1558–1774] All ER Rep 172, is that the performance of absolute promises is not excused by supervening impossibility of performance. *Paradine v Jane* itself, a case arising out of the civil war, was, like the present, an action of debt based on a covenant to pay rent contained in a lease. But, since the doctrine of frustration had not at that stage come into existence, the argument turned solely on the absolute and unconditional nature of the promise to pay the rent, and the applicability to the estate in land created by the demise of any such doctrine did not arise.

It is generally accepted that the doctrine of frustration has its roots in the decision of the Court of Queen's Bench given by Blackburn J in *Taylor v Caldwell* (1863) 3 B & S 826, [1861–73] All ER Rep 24. In that case, the parties to the contract had used terms appropriate to the relationship of landlord and tenant describing the money payment as 'rent' and the transaction as a 'letting'. But, after analysing the facts, Blackburn J decided that the true nature of the transaction was not one of landlord and tenant but one of licensor and licensee. He then added, cryptically, the words: 'Nothing, however, in our opinion depends on this' (see 3 B & S 826 at 832, [1861–73] All ER Rep 24 at 26). I am inclined to think that by these words he was in effect taking the view which I myself am about to express, but, as counsel for the respondents firmly pointed out when I put the point to him in argument, they are capable of a more neutral meaning, viz, that since the question of demise did not arise in the case before the court, it did not call for decision. I am content to assume, though I am inclined to the contrary view, that this is right.

At least five theories of the basis of the doctrine of frustration have been put forward at various times, and, since the theoretical basis of the doctrine is clearly relevant to the point under discussion, I enumerate them here. The first is the 'implied term', or 'implied condition', theory on which Blackburn J plainly relied in *Taylor v Caldwell* as applying to the facts of the case before him. To these it is admirably suited. The weakness, it seems to me, of the implied term theory is that it raises once more the spectral figure of the officious bystander intruding on the parties at the moment of agreement. In the present case, had the officious bystander pointed out to the parties in July 1974 the danger of carrying on the business of a commercial warehouse opposite a listed building of doubtful stability and asked them what they would do in the event of a temporary closure of Kingston Street pending a public local inquiry into a proposal for demolition after the lease had been running for over five years, I have not the least idea what they would have said, or whether either would have entered into the lease at all. In *Embiricos v Sydney Reid & Co* [1914] 3 KB 45 at 54, [1914–15] All ER Rep 185 at 188 Scrutton J appears to make the estimate of what constitutes a frustrating event something to be ascertained only at the time when the parties to a contract are called on to make up their minds, and this I would think, to be right, both as to the inconclusiveness of hindsight which Scrutton J had primarily in mind and as to the inappropriateness of the intrusion of an officious bystander immediately prior to the conclusion of the agreement.

Counsel for the respondents sought to argue that *Taylor v Caldwell* could have as easily been decided on the basis of a total failure of consideration. This is the second of the five theories. But *Taylor v Caldwell* was clearly not so decided, and in any event many, if not most, cases of frustration which have followed *Taylor v Caldwell* have occurred during the currency of a contract partly executed on both sides, when no question of total failure of consideration can possibly arise.

In *Hirji Mulji v Cheong Yue Steamship Co Ltd* [1926] AC 497 at 510, [1926] All ER Rep 51 at 59 Lord Sumner seems to have formulated the doctrine as a 'device [sic] by which the rules as to absolute contracts are reconciled with a special exception which justice demands', and Lord Wright in *Denny, Mott & Dickson Ltd v James B Fraser & Co Ltd* [1944] 1 All ER 678 at 683, [1944] AC 265 at 275 seems to prefer this formulation to the implied condition view. The weakness of the formulation, however, if the implied condition theory, with which Lord Sumner coupled it, be rejected is that, though it admirably expresses the purpose of the doctrine, it does not provide it with any theoretical basis at all.

Hirji Mulji v Cheong Yue Steamship Co Ltd is, it seems to me, really an example of the more sophisticated theory of 'frustration of the adventure' or 'foundation of the contract' formulation, said to have originated with *Jackson v Union Marine Insurance Co Ltd* (1874) LR 10 CP 125, [1874–80] All ER Rep 317; cf also eg per Goddard J in *W J Tatem Ltd v Gamboa* [1938] 3 All ER 135 at 144, [1939] 1 KB 132 at 138. This, of course, leaves open the question of what is, in any given case, the foundation of the contract or what is 'fundamental' to it, or what is the 'adventure'. Another theory, of which the parent may have been Earl Loreburn in *F A Tamplin Steamship Co Ltd v Anglo-Mexican Petroleum Co* [1916] 2 AC 397, [1916–17] All ER Rep 104, is that the doctrine is based on the answer to the question, 'What, in fact, was the true meaning of the contract?' (see [1916] 2 AC 397 at 404, [1916–17] All ER Rep 104 at 108). This is the 'construction theory'. In *Davis Contractors Ltd v Fareham Urban District Council* [1956] 2 All ER 145 at 160, [1956] AC 696 at 729 Lord Radcliffe put the matter thus, and it is the formulation I personally prefer:

'. . . frustration occurs whenever the law recognises that, without default of either party, a contractual obligation has become incapable of being performed because the circumstances in which performance is called for would render it a thing radically different from that which was undertaken by the contract. Non haec in foedera veni. It was not this that I promised to do.'

Incidentally, it may be partly because I look at frustration from this point of view that I find myself so much in agreement with my noble and learned friends that the appellants here have failed to raise any triable issue as to frustration by the purely temporary, though prolonged, and in 1979 indefinite, interruption, then expected to last about a year, in the access to the demised premises. In all fairness, however, I must say that my approach to the question involves me in the view that whether a supervening event is a frustrating event or not is, in a wide variety of cases, a question of degree, and therefore to some extent at least of fact, where in your Lordships' House in *Tsakiroglou & Co Ltd v Noblee & Thorl GmbH* [1961] 2 All ER 179, [1962] AC 93 the question is treated as one at least involving a question of law, or, at best, a question of mixed law and fact. For a discussion of the apparent inconsistency of this view with the verdict of the jury in *Jackson v Union Marine Insurance Co Ltd* (1874) LR 10 CP 125, [1874–80] All ER Rep 317, see Professor Treitel's treatise on the Law of Contract (5th Edn, 1979, p 671), when the author suggests that the reconciliation may lie in the distinction between primary and secondary facts now developing as the result of the disappearance of the civil jury.

This discussion brings me to the central point at issue in this case, which, in my view, is whether or not there is anything in the nature of an executed lease which prevents the doctrine of frustration, however formulated, applying to the subsisting relationship between the parties. That the point is open in this House is clear from the difference of opinion expressed in the *Cricklewood* case between Lord Russell and Lord Goddard on the one hand, who answered the question affirmatively, and Viscount Simon LC and Lord Wright on the other, who answered it negatively, with Lord Porter reserving his opinion until the point arose definitively for consideration. The point, though one of principle, is a narrow one. It is the difference immortalised in HMS Pinafore between 'never' and 'hardly ever', since both Viscount Simon LC and Lord Wright clearly conceded that, though they thought the doctrine applicable in principle to leases, the cases in which it could properly be applied must be extremely rare.

With the view of Viscount Simon LC and Lord Wright I respectfully agree. It is clear from what I have said already that, with Lord Radcliffe in the passage I have cited, I regard these cases as a sub-species of the class of case which comes so regularly before the courts, as to which of two innocent parties must bear the loss as the result of circumstances for which neither is at all to blame. Apart from Law Reform (Frustrated Contracts) Act 1943, the doctrine of frustration brings the whole contract to an end, and in the present case, apart from any adjustment under that Act and any statutory right to compensation under the closure order, the effect of frustration, had it been applicable, would have been to throw the whole burden of interruption for 20 months on the landlord, deprived as he would be of all his rent, and imposed, as he would have, on his shoulders the whole danger of destruction by fire and the burden of reletting after the interruption. As it is, with the same qualification as to possible compensation, the tenant has to pay the entire rent during the period of interruption without any part the premises being usable at all, together with the burden (such as it may be) of the performance of the other tenant's covenants which include covenants to insure and repair. These are no light matters.

I approach the question first via the authorities, mainly catalogued in the report of the *Cricklewood* case at first instance ([1942] 2 All ER 580, [1943] KB 493) and in the Court of Appeal ([1943] 2 All ER 97, [1943] KB 493 at 496). I need not analyse these in detail, but, your Lordships having done so in the course of argument, I must say that, although they all tend in that direction, they do not and they never did afford the court compelling authority for the proposition advanced. The point was not argued at all in front of Asquith J, and in the very short judgment of the Court of Appeal the three cases cited, *London and Northern Estates Co v Schlesinger* [1916] 1 KB 20, [1914–15] All ER Rep 593, *Whitehall Court Ltd v Ettlinger* [1920] 1 KB 680, [1918–19] All ER Rep 229 and *Matthey v Curling* [1922] 2 AC 180, [1922] All ER Rep 1, do not, I believe, on analysis constitute authority for the proposition. The most that can be said is that, as Lord Goddard said, the view that frustration did not apply to leases was widely held in the profession at the time and that Lord Atkinson in *Matthey v Curling* [1922] 2 AC 180 at 233, 237, [1922] All ER Rep 1 at 8, 10 gave expression to the view that *Whitehall Court v Ettlinger* was rightly decided. I agree here with what Viscount Simon LC said on this in the *Cricklewood* case [1945] 1 All ER 252 at 257, [1945] AC 221 at 231, and I would add that what was decided both in *Whitehall Court* and *London and Northern Estates* was no more than that the legal estate created by a lease was not destroyed by wartime requisition and that such requisition was not an eviction by title paramount. In the Court of Appeal I do not find that Bankes LJ or Younger LJ were unequivocal on the present point at issue (see [1922] 2 AC 180 at 185, 210), and I note that Younger LJ committed himself to the now untenable proposition that the doctrine of frustration was not to be extended. Atkin LJ (who dissented) gave (at 199–200) important reasons for rejecting the 'never' principle and in *Cricklewood* [1945] 1 All ER 252 at 256, [1945] AC 221 at 230 Viscount Simon LC expressly approved the crucial paragraph in Atkin LJ's judgment in support of the 'hardly ever' doctrine. Before us there was some discussion in argument of American cases, especially the liquor saloon cases based on prohibition, in some of which at least the frustration doctrine was applied to leases. We were also referred to the opinion of Laskin J in Canada in *Highway Properties Ltd v Kelly, Douglas & Co Ltd* (1971) 17 DLR (3d) 710 at 721, and that of Isaacs J in the Australian case of *Firth v Halloran* (1926) 38 CLR 261 at 269 (where, however, he appears to have differed from his colleagues), all of which favour the 'hardly ever' doctrine. Reference was also made to textbook authority. Megarry and Wade (Law of Real Property (4th Edn, 1975)) tend to the 'never' view, but run into fairly heavy weather when they discuss the possible destruction of a flat on the higher floors of a tenement building (see p 675). Professor Treitel (Law of Contract, 5th Edn, 1979, p 669), after referring to *Cusack-Smith v London Corpn* [1956] 1 WLR at 1368, which in turn relied on *Denman v Brise* [1948] 2 All ER 141 esp at 143, [1949] 1 KB 22 esp at 26 (the only case where frustration appears to have been advanced on behalf of a landlord), comes to the conclusion that the 'never' position is only open to review at the level of the House of Lords but concludes that the 'hardly ever' view is intrinsically preferable. This also appears to be the opinion of the American writers Williston and Corbin and in England of Cheshire and Fifoot.

I conclude that the matter is not decided by authority and that the question is open to your Lordships to decide on principle. In my view your Lordships ought now so to decide it. Is there anything in principle which ought to prevent a lease from ever being frustrated? I think there is not. In favour of the opposite opinion, the difference in principle between real and chattel property was strongly urged. But I find it difficult to accept this, once it has been decided, as has long been the case, that time and demise charters even of the largest ships and of considerable duration can in principle be frustrated. This was sufficiently well established by 1943 to make these charters worthy of an express exception on an exception in the Law Reform (Frustrated Contracts) Act 1943, s 2(5), and since then the Suez cases have supervened. There would be something anomalous in the light of what has been going on recently in the Shatt al-Arab to draw a distinction between a leased oil tank and a demise-chartered oil tanker. Other anomalies would follow if the absolute principle were to be applied to leases. Goff J appears to have found no difficulty in applying frustration to an agreement for a lease (which creates an equitable estate in the land capable of being specifically enforced and thereby converted into a legal estate operating as from the beginning of the equitable interest): see *Rom Securities Ltd v Rogers (Holdings) Ltd* (1968) 205 Estates Gazette 427. Personally I find the absurdities postulated by Megarry and Wade (Law of Real Property, 4th Edn, 1975, p 675) in the case of the destruction by fire of the upper flat of a tenement building (already referred to) unacceptable if the 'never' doctrine were rigidly applied, and I am attracted by Professor Treitel's argument (Law of Contract, 5th Edn, 1979, p 669) of the inequitable contrast between a contract for the provision of holiday accommodation which amounted to a licence, and thus subject to the rule in *Taylor v Caldwell*, and a similar contract amounting to a short lease. Clearly the contrast would be accentuated if Goff J's view be accepted as to the applicability of the doctrine to agreements for a lease (see above).

I accept of course that systems of developed land law draw a vital distinction between land, which is relatively permanent, and other types of property, which are relatively perishable. But one can overdo the contrast. Coastal erosion as well as the 'vast convulsion of nature' postulated by Viscount Simon LC in the *Cricklewood* case [1945] 1 All ER 252 at 255–256, [1945] AC 221 at 229 can, even in this island, cause houses, gardens, even villages and their churches to fall into the North Sea, and, although the law of property in Scotland is different, as may be seen from *Tay Salmon Fisheries Co Ltd v Speedie* 1929 SC 593, whole estates can there, as Lord President Clyde points out (at 600), be overblown with sand for centuries and so fall subject to the rei interitus doctrine of the civil law. In *Taylor v Caldwell* (1863) 3 B & S 826 at 834, [1861–73] All ER Rep 24 at 27 itself Blackburn J, after referring to the Digest (lib XLV, title 1) on the subject of 'obligatio de certo corpore' on which in part he founds his new doctrine, expressly says:

'. . . no doubt the propriety, one might almost say the necessity, of the implied condition is more obvious when the contract relates to a living animal, whether man or brute, than when it relates to some inanimate thing (*such as in the present case a theatre*) [emphasis mine] the existence of which is not so obviously precarious as that of the live animal, but the principle is adopted in the Civil law as applicable to every obligation of which the subject is a certain thing.'

He then refers to Pothier, Traité des Obligations (partie 3, ch 6, art 3, § 668) in support of his contention.

No doubt a long lease, say for example one for 999 years, is almost exactly identical with the freehold for this purpose, and therefore subject to the ordinary law regarding the incidence of risk (recognised as regards chattels in s 7 of the former Sale of Goods Act 1893). But there is no difference between chattels in this respect and real property except in degree. Long term speculations and investments are in general less easily frustrated than short term adventures and a lease for 999 years must be in the longer class. I find myself persuaded by the argument presented by Atkin LJ in his dissenting judgment in *Matthey v Curling* [1922] 2 AC 180 at 199–200 and quoted with approval by Viscount Simon LC in the *Cricklewood* case [1945] 1 All ER 252 at 256, [1945] AC 221 at 230. In that passage Atkin LJ said:

> '... it does not appear to me conclusive against the application to a lease of the doctrine of frustration that the lease, in addition to containing contractual terms, grants a term of years. Seeing that the instrument as a rule expressly provides for the lease being determined at the option of the lessor upon the happening of certain specified events, I see no logical absurdity in implying a term that it shall be determined absolutely on the happening of other events—namely, those which in an ordinary contract work a frustration.'

I pause here only to observe that, in the instant case, the lease gave the lessor a contingent right of determination in case of destruction by fire or in a case of a need for the use of the premises in connection with the railways, and to point out that in the War Damage Acts the lessee was given a statutory right, albeit different in kind from the doctrine of frustration, to disclaim a current lease on the happening of other events as the result of enemy action.

In the result, I come down on the side of the 'hardly ever' school of thought. No doubt the circumstances in which the doctrine can apply to leases are, to quote Viscount Simon LC in the *Cricklewood* case [1945] 1 All ER 252 at 257, [1945] AC 221 at 231, 'exceedingly rare'. Lord Wright appears to have thought the same, whilst adhering to the view that there are cases in which frustration can apply (see [1945] 1 All ER 252 at 263, [1945] AC 221 at 241). But, as he said in the same passage: 'The doctrine of frustration is modern and flexible and is not subject to being constricted by an arbitrary formula.' To this school of thought I respectfully adhere. Like Lord Wright, I am struck by the fact that there appears to be no reported English case where a lease has ever been held to have been frustrated. I hope this fact will act as a suitable deterrent to the litigious, eager to make legal history by being first in this field. But I am comforted by the reflexion of the authority referred to in the Compleat Angler (pt i, ch 5) on the subject of strawberries: 'Doubtless God could have made a better berry, but doubtless God never did.' I only append to this observation of nature the comment that it does not follow from these premises that He never will, and, if it does not follow, an assumption that He never will becomes exceedingly rash.

In the event my opinion is that the appeal should be dismissed with costs.

LORD WILBERFORCE. My Lords, there are two questions for decision in this appeal: (a) whether the doctrine of frustration can apply to a lease so as to bring it to an end if a frustrating event occurs; (b) whether, if so, in the circumstances the existing lease between the respondents and the appellants has been determined.

The lease was dated 12th July 1974. The respondents as landlords let to the appellants as tenants a purpose-built warehouse in Hull for a term of ten years from 1st January 1974. The rent was £6,500 a year during the first five years, and for the remainder was to be the open-market rent of the demised premises let as a warehouse. In fact this was fixed at £13,300.

There was a covenant by the tenants not without the landlords' consent to use the premises for any purpose than that of warehousing in connection with the tenants' business, or to assign, underlet or part with possession.

There was only one access to the warehouse, along a street called Kingston Street. This would appear to be a public highway, but the landlords purported to grant a right of way along it for all purposes connected with the occupation of the premises. On 16th May 1979 the city council made an order under s 12(1) of the Road Traffic Regulation Act 1967 closing Kingston Street for use with or without a vehicle. This was done because another warehouse, of the Victorian period and style, abutting on the street was in a dangerous condition. Because it was a listed building there were conservationist objections against its demolition. The order was, it appears, renewed by the Secretary of State, under the same Act on 15th August 1979 and again, purportedly, but with questionable validity, by the council's engineer under s 25 of the Public Health Act 1961. We must assume, at this stage, that all these acts of closure were valid and legal. I shall refer further to this matter when dealing with the second question.

Because of this closure, which made the warehouse unusable for the only purpose for which it could be used under the lease, the appellants contended that the lease was frustrated, so that rent ceased to be payable. In an action for rent due, followed by a summons for summary judgment under RSC Ord 14 the master, upheld by the judge, held that the defence of frustration was not available as a matter of law. That the doctrine of frustration was not available to determine a lease had in fact been decided by the Court of Appeal in *Leighton's Investment Trust Ltd v Cricklewood Property and Investment Trust Ltd* [1943] 2 All ER 97, [1943] KB 493. An appeal was brought to this House but, on the question of law, their Lordships were divided, two Lords holding that the doctrine could be applied, two that it could not, and the fifth expressing no opinion. The House unanimously held, on the facts, that frustration had not occurred. The point is therefore open for decision.

My Lords, the arguments for and against application of this doctrine are fully and cogently put in the rival speeches in the *Cricklewood* case, for its possible application by Viscount Simon LC and Lord Wright, against by Lord Russell and Lord Goddard. I can therefore give fairly briefly the reasons which have persuaded me, on the whole, that the former ought to be preferred.

1. The doctrine of frustration of contracts made its appearance in English law in answer to the proposition, which since *Paradine v Jane* (1647) Aleyn 26, [1558–1774] All ER Rep 172 had held the field, that an obligation expressed in absolute and unqualified terms, such as an obligation to pay rent, had to be performed and could not be excused by supervening circumstances. Since *Taylor v Caldwell* (1863) 3 B & S 826, [1861–73] All ER Rep 24 it has been applied generally over the whole field of contract.

2. Various theories have been expressed as to its justification in law: as a device by which the rules as to absolute contracts are reconciled with a special exception which justice demands, as an implied term, as a matter of construction of the contract, as related to removal of the foundation of the contract, as a total failure of consideration. It is not necessary to attempt selection of any one of these as the true basis; my own view would be that they shade into one another and that a choice between them is a choice of what is most appropriate to the particular contract under consideration. One could see, in relation to the present contract, that it could provisionally be said to be appropriate to refer to an implied term, in view of the grant of the right of way, or to removal of the foundation of the contract, viz use as a warehouse. In any event, the doctrine can now be stated generally as part of the law of contract; as all judicially evolved doctrines it is, and ought to be, flexible and capable of new applications.

3. In view of this generality, the onus, in my opinion, lies on those who assert that the doctrine can *never* apply to leases. They have at once to face the argument that it has been held to apply to demise charters of ships (and presumably by analogy could apply to hirings of other chattels) and to licences for use (see *Krell v Henry* [1903] 2 KB 740, [1900–3] All ER Rep 20 and other Coronation cases). So why not to leases of land? To place leases of land beyond a firm line of exclusion seems to involve anomalies, to invite fine distinctions, or at least to produce perplexities. How, for example, is one to deal with agreements for leases? Refusal ever to apply the doctrine to leases of land must be based on some firm legal principle which cannot be departed from (compare art 62 of the Vienna Convention on the Law of Treaties 1969 (Cmnd 4818) which excludes boundary disputes from the analogous doctrine in international law).

4. Two arguments only by way of principle have been suggested. The first is that a lease is more than a contract: it conveys an estate in land. This must be linked to the fact

that the English law of frustration, unlike its continental counterparts, requires, when it
a applies, not merely adjustment of the contract, but its termination. But this argument,
by itself, is incomplete as a justification for denying that frustration is possible. The
argument must continue by a proposition that an estate in land once granted cannot be
divested, which, as Viscount Simon LC pointed out, begs the whole question.

It was pointed out, however, by Atkin LJ in *Matthey v Curling* [1922] 2 AC 180 at 199–
200, in a passage later approved by Viscount Simon LC, that as a lease can be determined,
b according to its terms, on the happening of certain specified events, there is nothing
illogical in implying a term that it should be determined on the happening of other
events, namely, those which in an ordinary contract work a frustration. It has indeed
been held, with reference to an agreement for a lease, that this can be put an end to
through implication of a term (see *Rom Securities Ltd v Rogers (Holdings) Ltd* (1967) 205
Estates Gazette 427 per Goff J). So why, in the present case, for example, should an actual
c lease not be determinable by implication of a term? If so, it could hardly be suggested
that a lease was not capable of frustration even though the theory of frustration had
shifted to another basis.

In the second place, if the argument is to have any reality, it must be possible to say
that frustration of leases cannot occur because in any event the tenant will have that
which he bargained for, namely, the leasehold estate. Certainly this may be so in many
d cases, let us say most cases. Examples are *London and Northern Estates Co v Schlesinger*
[1916] 1 KB 20, [1914–15] All ER Rep 593, where what was frustrated (viz the right of
personal occupation) was not at the root of the contract, and requisitioning cases, e g
Whitehall Court Ltd v Ettlinger [1920] 1 KB 680, [1918–19] All ER Rep 229, where again
the tenant was left with something he could use. But there may also be cases where this
is not so. A man may desire possession and use of land or buildings for, and only for,
e some purpose in view and mutually contemplated. Why is it an answer, when he claims
that this purpose is 'frustrated' to say that he has an estate if that estate is unusable and
unsaleable? In such a case the lease, or the conferring of an estate, is a subsidiary means
to an end, not an aim or end of itself. This possible situation is figured, in fact, by
Viscount Simon LC in the *Cricklewood* case.

The second argument of principle is that on a lease the risk passes to the lessee, as on
f a sale it passes to the purchaser (see per Lord Goddard in the *Cricklewood* case). But the
two situations are not parallel. Whether the risk, or any risk, passes to the lessee depends
on the terms of the lease; it is not uncommon, indeed, for some risks (of fire or
destruction) to be specifically allocated. So in the case of unspecified risks, which may be
thought to have been mutually contemplated, or capable of being contemplated by
reasonable men, why should not the court decide on whom the risks are to lie? And if
g it can do this and find that a particular risk falls on the lessor, the consequence may follow
that on the risk eventuating the lessee is released from his obligation.

To provide examples, as of a 999-year lease during which a frustrating event occurs, or
of those in decided cases (see above), to show that in such cases frustration will not occur
is insufficient as argument. These examples may be correct; they may cover most, at
least most normal, cases. But the proposition is that there can be no case outside them
h and that I am unable to accept.

5. I find the experience in the United States of America instructive. It is clear that in
the common law jurisdictions of that country, the doctrine of frustration has developed
and is still developing. It has been applied, inter alia, in connection with Prohibition and
leases of liquor saloons, to leases. Yet neither of the well-known commentators, Williston
or Corbin, sees any doctrinal objection to this. I quote one passage from Corbin on
j Contracts (1951, vol 6, para 1356):

'In modern cases, there has been a tendency to treat a lease as a contract instead of
a conveyance, although in fact it is both at once. The older allocation of risks does
not now always seem just. Many short-term leases have been made, in which the
purpose of the lessee was to conduct a liquor saloon, a purpose known to the lessor

and one which gave to the premises a large part of its rental value. There followed the enactment of a . . . prohibitory law preventing the use of the premises for the expected purpose. The prohibition law does not make it impossible or illegal for the lessee to keep his promise to pay the rent . . . but it frustrates his purpose of using the premises for a liquor saloon in the reasonable hope of pecuniary profit. If the terms of the lease are such that the lessee is restricted to this one use, it has been held in a considerable number of cases that his duty to pay rent is discharged.'

Williston is to a similar effect, where it is pointed out that termination of a lease by frustration is more difficult to establish than termination of a mere contract (Contracts (3rd Edn, 1978, para 1955)).

There is a similar indication in Canada. In *Highway Properties Ltd v Kelly, Douglas & Co Ltd* (1971) 17 DLR (3d) 710 the Supreme Court had to consider the extent to which the contractual doctrine of wrongful repudiation could be applied to a lease, the argument being that the landlord was limited to remedies given by the law of property. In an instructive judgment Laskin J said (at 721):

'It is no longer sensible to pretend that a commercial lease, such as the one before this Court, is simply a conveyance and not also a contract. It is equally untenable to persist in denying resort to the full armoury of remedies ordinarily available to redress repudiation of covenants, merely because the covenants may be associated with an estate in land.'

So, here is a route opened by common law jurisdictions, by which the result of frustration of leases may be attained. This may be wide, or narrow, or indeed very narrow; that we need not decide in advance. But it would be wrong to erect a total barrier inscribed 'You shall not pass'.

6. I can deal briefly with the authorities: they are one way (against application of the doctrine), they are partial. They decide that particular sets of facts do not amount to frustrating events. A judgment often quoted is that of Lush J in *Schlesinger's* case [1916] 1 KB 20, [1914–15] All ER Rep 593 where a lessee was unable to occupy the rented premises because he was an alien enemy. Lush J said ([1916] 1 KB 20 at 24; cf [1914–15] All ER Rep 593 at 595):

'As the contract could be performed without his personal residence, the fact that his personal residence was prohibited by the Order did not make the performance of the contract impossible. But there is, I think, a further answer to the contention. It is not correct to speak of this tenancy agreement as a contract and nothing more. A term of years was created by it and vested in the appellant, and I can see no reason for saying that because this Order disqualified him from personally residing in the flat it affected the chattel interest which was vested in him by virtue of the agreement.'

There is nothing to disagree with here, the argument may indeed by valid in many or most cases of leases. It is not expressed as one which must apply to all.

The reasoning of this House in *Matthey v Curling* [1922] 2 AC 180, [1922] All ER Rep 1 is not 'clear' or any authority that the doctrine of frustration does not apply to a lease (see per Lord Wright in the *Cricklewood* case [1945] 1 All ER 252 at 256, [1945] AC 221 at 230). It was not until the *Cricklewood* case that the argument was put on principle and fully explored. The governing decision (of the Court of Appeal) was summary, unargued and based on previous cases which will not bear the weight of a generalisation. I think that the movement of the law of contract is away from a rigid theory of autonomy towards the discovery, or I do not hesitate to say imposition, by the courts of just solutions, which can be ascribed to reasonable men in the position of the parties.

It is said that to admit the possibility of frustration of leases will lead to increased litigation. Be it so, if that is the route to justice. But, even if the principle is admitted, hopeless claims can always be stopped at an early stage, if the facts manifestly cannot

support a case of frustration. The present may be an example. In my opinion, therefore,
a though such cases may be rare, the doctrine of frustration is capable of application to
leases of land. It must be so applied with proper regard to the fact that a lease, ie a grant
of a legal estate, is involved. The court must consider whether any term is to be implied
which would determine the lease in the event which has happened and/or ascertain the
foundation of the agreement and decide whether this still exists in the light of the terms
of the lease, the surrounding circumstances and any special rules which apply to leases or
b to the particular lease in question. If the 'frustrating event' occurs during the currency
of the lease it will be appropriate to consider the Law Reform (Frustrated Contracts) Act
1943.

I now come to the second question, which is whether on the facts of the case the
appellants should be given leave to defend the action: can they establish that there is a
triable issue? I have already summarised the terms of the lease. At first sight, it would
c appear to my mind that the case might be one for possible frustration. But examination
of the facts leads to a negative conclusion. The circumstances which it is claimed amount
to a frustrating event are proved by affidavit evidence supplemented and brought up to
date by other documents. They are as follows. The first order closing Kingston Street
was made on 16th May 1979 to take effect from 18th May. The lease had then 4 years
6½ months to run. In his affidavit sworn on 20th September 1979 the appellants' solicitor
d stated that it was likely that 'well over a year' would have elapsed before a decision could
be made as regards the listed Victorian warehouse opposite the appellants' premises, the
condition of which made the closure necessary. The town clerk of the City of Kingston-
upon-Hull had written on 7th August that it was probably unlikely that the matter could
be resolved 'within the next year'. It appears that a local inquiry was held into the future
of the listed warehouse, and the Secretary of State on 20th March 1980 approved the
e inspector's report and granted consent for its demolition. On 30th September 1980 the
town clerk informed the lessors that the estimated date for completion of the demolition
was 'sometime in late December 1980 or early January 1981'. I think it is accepted that
the reopening of Kingston Street would immediately follow.

So the position is that the parties to the lease contemplated, when Kingston Street was
first closed, that the closure would probably last for a year or a little longer. In fact it
f seems likely to have lasted for just over eighteen months. Assuming that the street is
reopened in January 1981, the lease will have three more years to run.

My Lords, no doubt, even with this limited interruption the appellants' business will
have been severely dislocated. They will have had to move goods from the warehouse
before the closure and to acquire alternative accommodation. After reopening the
reverse process must take place. But this does not approach the gravity of a frustrating
g event. Out of ten years they will have lost under two years of use; there will be nearly
three years left after the interruption has ceased. This is a case, similar to others, where
the likely continuance of the term after the interruption makes it impossible for the
lessee to contend that the lease has been brought to an end. The obligation to pay rent
under the lease is unconditional, with a sole exception for the case of fire, as to which the
lease provides for a suspension of the obligation. No provision is made for suspension in
h any other case; the obligation remains. I am of opinion therefore that the lessees have no
defence to the action for rent, that leave to defend should not be given and that the appeal
must be dismissed.

LORD SIMON OF GLAISDALE. My Lords, by a lease dated 12th July 1974 the
respondents as landlords let to the appellants (who carry on business of warehousing) as
j tenants premises which were described in the lease as 'warehouse premises . . . comprising
warehouse no. 2'. Included in the demise was 'a right of way for purposes connected
with the occupation of the said premises . . .'; this was along a road called Kingston Street,
the only road giving access to the premises. The lease was for ten years as from 1st
January 1974 at a rent of £6,500 during the first five years of the term; as for the
remainder, a rent review clause provided that 'the yearly rent payable during the last 5

years of the said term . . . shall be the fair yearly rent of the said premises let in the open
market for the purpose of a warehouse at the commencement of such period', being a
determinable by arbitration in default of agreement. The landlords' reservation of
services was subject to compensation to the tenants for disturbance of the tenants'
business. Amongst other tenants' covenants (mostly common form) were the following
(cl 2):

'(5) To insure and keep insured the said premises to the full value thereof . . . in
the joint names of the Landlord and the Tenant against loss or damage by fire and b
such other risks as may from time to time be required by the Landlord . . .
'(13) Not to do or omit to do or suffer to be done or omitted to be done in or upon
the said premises any act or thing which will render any increased or extra premium
payable for the insurance of the said premises or any adjoining property of the
Landlord . . . provided always that the tenant's business of warehousing to be carried
on upon the premises shall not constitute any such act or thing as is referred to in c
this clause and the tenant shall not be liable in respect of any increased premiums
by virtue of activities in accordance with the ordinary course of such business . . .
'(15) Not without the consent in writing of the Landlord to use the said premises
or any part thereof or permit or suffer the same to be used for any other purpose
than that of warehousing in connection with the Tenant's business and in particular
that they shall not be used for residential purposes or for any person to sleep thereon d
or in any manner which would constitute a change of use under the Town &
Country Planning Acts . . .
'(17) That no act or thing which shall or may be or become a nuisance [etc] to the
Landlord or the Landlord's tenants [etc] shall be done upon the said premises or any
part thereof save that any activities properly carried on in the ordinary course of the
tenant's business shall not constitute a breach of this clause . . . e
'(20) Not to use or permit or suffer to be used the said premises or any part
thereof as a factory or workshop . . .'

By cl 3 the landlords covenanted in usual terms for the tenants' quiet enjoyment of the
premises during the term.
Clause 4(1) is the rent review clause. Clause 4(2) deals with destruction or damage by f
fire. It provides for abatement of the rent pending reinstatement, and for the landlords'
right to determine the tenancy in the event of complete destruction or substantial
damage by fire of the demised premises or the landlords' adjoining property. Clause 4(3)
provides for the landlords' right to determine in the event of the premises being 'required
in connection with the proper operation of the British Railways undertaking and Part III
of the Landlord and Tenant Act 1954 shall not apply'. g
The rent review clause was in fact operated so that the yearly rent for the last five years
of the term was agreed to be £13,300.
The lease makes it clear that the parties contemplated that the demised premises,
which were purpose-built as a warehouse, should be used as such throughout the term;
rent was geared to this use; and no other use was contemplated.
The demised warehouse has a loading bay and large doors at the entrance from h
Kingston Street. Immediately opposite stood a large derelict Victorian warehouse, a
building listed by the Department of the Environment. The Kingston-upon-Hull City
Council believed that building to be a dangerous structure; and they applied to the
Secretary of State for the Environment for listed-building consent to demolish it; this
must have been some time between April 1978 and July 1979. Demolition was opposed
by a number of conservation groups; and at the time the evidence was filed (September j
1979) the Secretary of State was to appoint a public inquiry into the matter. In April
1978 the City Council made an order under s 12(1) of the Road Traffic Regulation Act
1967, as amended, restricting the passage of vehicular and pedestrian traffic in Kingston
Street. On 16th May 1979 the city council made a further order, this time closing
Kingston Street to all vehicular and pedestrian traffic from 18th May 1979. The order of

16th May 1979 was continued by order of the Secretary of State for the Environment; and it was still effective when the evidence was filed. No question turns on the vires of these orders. There being no other form of access to the demised premises than along Kingston Street, the closure of that street made it impossible for the appellants to continue to use the demised premises as a warehouse; nor have they used it for any other purpose.

An affidavit sworn on behalf of the appellants deposed the opinion that in those circumstances well over a year would elapse between application for listed-building consent and the ministerial decision. An exhibited letter from the town clerk of 7th August 1979 stated that 'it is probably unlikely that the matter can be resolved within the next year'. From evidence placed before your Lordships it appears that a public inquiry had been held in the meantime, that demolition of the derelict warehouse was sanctioned and that on 30th September 1980 the town clerk informed the respondents that the estimated date for demolition was late December 1980 or early January 1981. The appellants apparently accept that Kingston Street would thereupon be again open to all traffic.

The appellants ceased to pay rent to the respondents as from 18th May 1979, the date of total closure of the highway. By a writ issued on 9th July 1979 the respondents demanded the rent which would have been due under the lease in the sum of £5,115·38. On 27th July the appellants filed a defence claiming that by reason of the closure of Kingston Street the lease had been frustrated on 18th May 1979, and they counterclaimed a declaration that the lease had been discharged by frustration. On 20th September 1979 Master Waldman heard the respondents' summons for summary judgment under RSC Ord 14. He was bound by authority (*Leightons Investment Trust Ltd v Cricklewood Property and Investment Trust Ltd* [1943] 2 All ER 97, [1943] KB 493; *Denman v Brise* [1949] 1 KB 22) to hold that the submission that a lease could be discharged by frustration was not open to the appellants to argue to any court below your Lordships' House (see *Cricklewood Property and Investment Trust Ltd v Leightons Investment Trust Ltd* [1945] All ER 252, [1945] AC 221). The appellants appealed from the order of the learned master. Sheen J, being similarly bound by such authority, by consent dismissed the appeal; and, since the Court of Appeal would also be similarly bound, he granted the appellants a certificate under s 12 of the Administration of Justice Act 1969 (leapfrogging). An Appeal Committee of your Lordships' House in due course gave leave to appeal.

The appeal raises three questions. (1) Is the doctrine of frustration inherently incapable of application to a lease? (2) If not inherently and generally inapplicable to leases, is the doctrine of frustration capable of applying to this lease in particular? (3) If Yes, have the appellants demonstrated a triable issue that this lease has been discharged by frustration?

Unless the appellants can demonstrate that the answer to (1) is No, and to (2) and (3) Yes, the respondents are entitled to summary judgment, and the appeal must be dismissed.

I. Frustration of a contract takes place when there supervenes an event (without default of either party and for which the contract makes no sufficient provision) which so significantly changes the nature (not merely the expense or onerousness) of the outstanding contractual rights and/or obligations from what the parties could reasonably have contemplated at the time of its execution that it would be unjust to hold them to the literal sense of its stipulations in the new circumstances; in such case the law declares both parties to be discharged from further performance.

Whether the doctrine can apply to a lease is of more than academic interest, considerable though that is. In the *Cricklewood Property* case Viscount Simon LC, who favoured the extension of the doctrine to leaseholds, nevertheless considered it likely to be limited to cases where 'some vast convulsion of nature swallowed up the property altogether, or buried it in the depths of the sea' (see [1945] 1 All ER 252 at 256, [1945] AC 221 at 229). But I think this puts the matter too catastrophically, even in the case of a long lease. There are several places on the coast of England where sea erosion has undermined a cliff causing property of the top of the cliff to be totally lost for occupation; obviously occupation of a dwelling house is something significantly different in nature from its aqualung contemplation after it has suffered a sea change. And in the case of a short lease something other than such natural disaster (the sort of occurrence, for example, that has been held to be the frustrating event in a charterparty) might in practice have a similar effect on parties to a lease. Take the case of a demise-chartered oil tanker lying alongside an oil storage tank leased for a similar term, and an explosion destroying both together.

The question is entirely open in your Lordships' House, as was recognised in the *Cricklewood Property* case. In my view a lease is not inherently unsusceptible to the application of the doctrine of frustration.

In the first place, the doctrine has been developed by the law as an expedient to escape from injustice where such would result from enforcement of a contract in its literal terms after a significant change in circumstances. As Lord Sumner said, giving the opinion of a strong Privy Council in *Hirji Mulji v Cheong Yue Steamship Co Ltd* [1926] AC 497 at 510, [1926] All ER Rep 51 at 59: 'It is really a device, by which the rules as to absolute contracts are reconciled with a special exception which justice demands.' Justice might make a similar demand as to the absolute terms of a lease.

Secondly, in the words of Lord Wright in the *Cricklewood Property* case [1945] 1 All ER 252 at 263, [1945] AC 221 at 241: 'The doctrine of frustration is modern and flexible and is not subject to being constricted by an arbitrary formula.' It is therefore on the face of it apt to vindicate justice wherever owing to relevant supervening circumstances the enforcement of any contractual arrangement in its literal terms would produce injustice.

Thirdly, the law should if possible be founded on comprehensive principles: compartmentalism, particularly if producing anomaly, leads to the injustice of different results in fundamentally analogous circumstances. To deny the extension of the doctrine of frustration to leaseholds produces a number of undesirable anomalies. It is true that theoretically it would create an anomalous distinction between the conveyance of a freehold interest and of a leasehold of, say, 999 years. But it would be only in exceptional circumstances that a lease for as long as 999 years would in fact be susceptible of frustration. On the other hand, to deny the application of the doctrine would create an anomalous distinction between the charter of a ship by demise (see *Blane Steamships Ltd v Minister of Transport* [1951] 2 KB 965; the Law Reform (Frustrated Contracts) Act 1943, s 2(5)(a)) and a demise of land; compare, for example, a short lease of an oil storage tank and a demise charter for the same term of an oil tanker of a peculiar class to serve such a storage tank, and a supervening event then frustrating the demise charter and equally affecting the use of the oil storage tank. Again, a time charter has much in common with a service tenancy of furnished accommodation. Then there would be the distinction between a lease and other chattel interests, say, under a hire-purchase agreement. But most striking of all is the fact that the doctrine of frustration undoubtedly applies to a licence to occupy land: see, e g, *Krell v Henry* [1903] 2 KB 740, [1900–3] All ER Rep 20 and the other Coronation cases. However, the distinction between a licence and a lease is notoriously difficult to draw, and, when it comes to the application of a doctrine imported to secure justice, even more difficult to justify. The point is well put by Treitel, Law of Contract (5th Edn, 1979, pp 669–670). I am clearly of opinion that the balance of anomaly indicates that the doctrine of frustration should be applied to a lease. Moreover, I shall venture to refer later to the effect of an agreement to grant a lease operating to create an equitable term of years; if, as would seem to be the case, the doctrine of frustration applies to such an agreement, there would be yet another anomaly.

Fourthly, a number of theories have been advanced to clothe the doctrine of frustration in juristic respectability, the two most in favour being the 'implied term theory' (which was potent in the development of the doctrine and which still provides a satisfactory explanation of many cases) and the 'theory of a radical change in obligation' or 'construction theory' (which appears to be the one most generally accepted today). My noble and learned friends who have preceded me have enumerated the various theories;

and the matter is discussed in Chitty on Contracts (23rd Edn, 1968, vol 1, pp 585–592). Of all the theories put forward the only one, I think, incompatible with the application of the doctrine to a lease is that which explains it as based on a total failure of consideration. Though such may be a feature of some cases of frustration, it is plainly inadequate as an exhaustive explanation: there are many cases of frustration where the contract has been partly executed. (I shall deal later with the argument that 'the foundation of the contract' in a lease is the conveyance of the term of years, which is accomplished once for all and can never be destroyed.)

Fifthly, a lease may be prematurely determined in a considerable variety of circumstances. Perhaps forfeiture by denial of title is the most relevant (though now largely of historical interest), since it depended on a rule of law extraneous to any term of the lease or to agreement of the parties whereby the lease was prematurely discharged. I can see no reason why a rule of law should not similarly declare that a lease is automatically discharged on the happening of a frustrating event.

Sixthly, it seems that authorities in some other common law jurisdictions have felt no inherent difficulty in applying the doctrine of frustration to a lease. This appears especially in the American cases on the frustration of leases of premises to sell liquor by the advent of constitutional Prohibition (see Corbin on Contracts (1951, vol 6, p 338ff) for a general discussion and pp 388–390 for a discussion of the Prohibition cases in particular). Corbin's summary (p 391) has relevance to such a lease as is under your Lordships' instant consideration:

> 'If there was one principal use contemplated by the lessee, known to the lessor, and one that played a large part in fixing rental value, a governmental prohibition or prevention of that use has been held to discharge the lessee from his duty to pay the rent. It is otherwise if other substantial uses, permitted by the lease and in the contemplation of the parties, remain possible to the lessee.'

(See also the passage quoted by my noble and learned friend Lord Wilberforce.) Then there is the judgment of Isaacs J in *Firth v Halloran* (1926) 38 CLR 261 at 269. Less directly in point, but important and relevant for its general reasoning, is the judgment of the Canadian Supreme Court delivered by Laskin J in *Highway Properties Ltd v Kelly, Douglas & Co Ltd* (1971) 17 DLR (3d) 710, holding that the contractual doctrine of repudiation, with its remedies independent of the landlord/tenant relationship, is applicable to a lease.

Lastly, then, from Laskin J's judgment (at 721): 'It is no longer sensible to pretend that a commercial lease . . . is simply a conveyance and not also a contract.' The doctrine of frustration, no less than the doctrine of repudiation, is applicable to a contract. It must therefore be determined whether there is anything in a lease-as-conveyance which repels the doctrine of frustration inherent in the lease-as-contract, outweighing the demands of justice, of consistency, of juristic theory accounting for the doctrine, of analogy and of authoritative opinion in other common law jurisdictions.

I therefore turn to consider the arguments to the contrary. Counsel for the respondents advanced six arguments of principle against the extension of the doctrine of frustration to a lease. Several would, it seems to me, apply equally to a licence to occupy land and/or to the charter of a ship, both unquestionably susceptible of frustration. I shall consider the others along with the arguments collected from the speeches of Lord Russell and Lord Goddard in the *Cricklewood Property* case. The arguments are, I think, fourfold. (1) The lease itself is the 'venture' or 'undertaking' on which the parties have embarked. In so far as the lease is contractual, the 'foundation' of the contract is the transfer of the landlord's possession of the demised property for a term of years in return for rent; that happens once for all on the execution of the lease; so that its contractual 'foundation' is never destroyed. (2) The lease is more than a contract: it creates a legal estate or interest in land; and, added counsel for the respondents, it operates in rem. (3) The contractual obligations in a lease are merely incidental to the relationship of landlord and tenant.

(4) On the conveyance the 'risk' of unforeseen events passes to the lessee, as it does to the purchaser of land.

I presume to think that the third proposition adds nothing to the first two, from which it necessarily follows if they are valid. As for the lease itself being the 'venture' or 'undertaking' the same might be said of a licence or of a demise charter. So, too, it may be said that the 'foundation' of a demise charter is that the shipowner parts with his possession of the demised property for a term of years in return for hire. In truth, 'venture', 'undertaking' and 'foundation' are picturesque or metaphorical terms; though useful in illuminating the doctrine, they are too vague to be safe for juristic analysis. The real questions, in my respectful submission, are the second and fourth, namely, whether the fact that a legal estate or interest in land has been created makes a lease inherently unsusceptible of the application of the doctrine of frustration, and that the risk of what might otherwise be a frustrating event passes irrevocably to the lessee on execution of the lease.

As for the significance of the creation of a legal estate or interest in land, it is convenient to note at this stage the case of an agreement to grant a lease. This can operate to create an equitable term of years (see *Walsh v Lonsdale* (1882) 21 Ch D 9). Cheshire's Modern Law of Real Property (12th Edn, 1976, p 388) states specifically: 'An *equitable* term of years may pass to the person who holds under a contract for a lease' (author's italics). See also Megarry and Wade, Law of Real Property (4th Edn, 1975, pp 625ff). So take the case of an agreement to grant a lease of a house on a clifftop which, before execution of any lease, collapses into the sea. It was conceded that equity would not grant specific performance at the suit of the prospective lessor, the subject matter having disappeared. Nor, since the subject matter of the agreement cannot now be delivered, could he recover damages for breach of contract. Nor could any obligation to pay rent be enforced, since rent is payable under the lease, which will not now be decreed. Faced with this situation, counsel for the respondents gave two alternative answers: first, the doctrine of frustration is not applicable to an agreement for a lease; and, second, if it is, it does not apply after the conveyance. But in the postulated case no conveyance follows; and in any case the second answer is a mere reiteration of the general conclusion (which is in question) that the doctrine of frustration does not apply to a lease. As for the first alternative, the situation involves that the agreement for a lease has been frustrated de facto, it cannot be further performed and neither party has any obligation to or remedy against the other. It would be ridiculous for the law to close its eyes to the reality of this situation or to refuse it its proper name. Moreover, an agreement to grant a lease is certainly an interest in land; it is registrable as an estate contract class C (iv): see the Land Charges Act 1925, s 10; the Land Charges Act 1972, s 2(4). So here we have the case of an agreement being effectually discharged by frustration notwithstanding that it has created an estate or interest in land, albeit equitable. The rule can hardly depend on whether the estate or interest in land is legal or equitable: no one has so suggested; and it would constitute an even more absurd anomaly than those to which I have ventured already to refer.

I cite *Denny, Mott & Dickson Ltd v James B Fraser & Co Ltd* [1944] 1 All ER 678, [1944] AC 265 with some hesitation, since your Lordships did not have the benefit of adversary argument on it. But it was a case where both a contract to grant a lease (which may have operated as a lease) and an option to purchase land were held to be frustrated. It is true that they were part of a larger agreement including trading arrangements which had been frustrated; but I do not think that this can affect the force of the decision as regards the frustration of the contract for a lease (or the lease) and of the option. It is also true that it was a Scottish appeal; but Lord Macmillan stated that the incidence of the Scots doctrine of frustration was the same as the English (though the consequences might be different) (see [1944] 1 All ER 678 at 681, [1944] AC 265 at 271–272); and none of their Lordships indicated that the decision depended on any peculiar rule of Scots land law.

Again, although *Rom Securities Ltd v Rogers (Holdings) Ltd* (1967) 205 Estates Gazette 427 was cited to your Lordships, no argument was developed on it. Goff J was faced with an agreement for a lease entered into on the unexpressed assumption that relevant planning permission would be granted, whereas in the event it was refused. Though the learned judge 'was far from satisfied that the doctrine of frustration could not be applied to an agreement for a lease' at least before entry into possession, in fact he held that the agreement was discharged under an implied term that this should be the effect if planning permission was refused, that is, he applied a similar line of reasoning to that of Blackburn J, giving the judgment of the Court of Queen's Bench, in *Taylor v Caldwell* (1863) 3 B & S 826, [1861–73] All ER Rep 24, the fons et origo of the modern doctrine of frustration. In my view *Rom Securities* was a case of frustration.

I can for myself see nothing about the fact of creation of an estate or interest in land which repels the doctrine of frustration. It cannot be that land, being relatively indestructable, is different from other subject matter of agreement; that would perhaps make a lease so much the less likely to be frustrated in fact, but would not constitute inherent repugnance to the doctrine. In any case, we are concerned with legal interests in the land rather than the land itself. It cannot be because a lease operates in rem; so, for example, does a contract for seamen's wages, since that gives rise to a maritime lien, yet can presumably like other contracts for personal services be frustrated by ill-health or death. Moreover, the criterion of operation in rem hardly matches counsel's first submission on agreements for a lease, which operate in personam. It cannot be because, once vested, a lease cannot be divested except by agreement of the parties. That would be to beg the question; if frustration applies, it can be so divested. Moreover, as I have tried to demonstrate, quite apart from frustration it can be so divested by operation of law in the doctrine of denial of title. And, as my noble and learned friend Lord Wilberforce has pointed out, there is nothing illogical in implying a term in a lease that it shall be discharged on the occurrence of a frustrating event. Nor, finally, is it realistic to argue that on execution of the lease the lessee got all that he bargained for. The reality is that this lessee, for example, bargained, not for a term of years, but for the use of a warehouse owned by the lessor, just as a demise charterer bargains for the use of this ship.

I turn, then, to the second main contention, namely, that the risk of unforeseen mischance passes irrevocably to the lessee at the moment of conveyance. This, too, begs the question whether the doctrine of frustration applies to leaseholds. If it does, such risk does not pass in all circumstances. Moreover, the sale of land is a false analogy. A fully executed contract cannot be frustrated; and a sale of land is characteristically such a contract. But a lease is partly executory: rights and obligations remain outstanding on both sides throughout its currency. Even a partly executed contract is susceptible of frustration in so far as it remains executory; there are many such cases in the books.

As for the authorities, I have had the advantage of reading in draft the speeches of my noble and learned friends who have preceded me and of my noble and learned friend Lord Roskill. I agree with, and beg to adopt, their analyses and conclusions. I would only add a comment on *Paradine v Jane* (1647) Aleyn 26, [1558–1774] All ER Rep 172, since that seems to be the starting point of those who deny the applicability of the doctrine of frustration to leases. But it did not turn at all on the fact that a leasehold was in question. It went on the then prevalent rule of the law of contract that when a party—

> 'by his own contract creates a duty or charge upon himself, he is bound to make it good, if he may, notwithstanding any accident by inevitable necessity, because he might have provided against it by his contract.'

A rule in such terms can hardly stand since the development of the doctrine of frustration.

My conclusion on the first issue is therefore that the doctrine of frustration is in principle applicable to leases.

II. Counsel for the appellants claimed that this was a 'commercial lease', a class at any rate to which the doctrine of frustration is applicable. In a sense every lease is commercial in so far as it is a matter of business between landlord and tenant. On the other hand, a lease and its subject matter may be more or less closely connected with commerce, trade or industry. The answer which I ventured to propose to the first issue facing your

Lordships indicates my view that there is no class of lease to which the doctrine is inherently inapplicable. But, as with any other agreement, the terms and subject matter of a lease will affect the circumstances in which it might be frustrated. The more commercial the character of an agreement, the more various are the circumstances in which it is liable to frustration.

In a lease, as in a licence or a demise charter, the length of the unexpired term will be a potent factor. So too, as the American cases show, will be any stipulations about, particularly restrictions on, user. In the instant case the lease was for a short term, and had only about 4½ years to run at the time of the alleged frustrating event, the closure of Kingston Street. The demised premises were a purpose-built warehouse, and both parties contemplated its use as a warehouse throughout the term. This use, in Corbin's words, 'played a large part in fixing rental value', as the rent review clause shows. After the closure of Kingston Street it could no longer be used as a warehouse. No 'other substantial use, permitted by the lease and in the contemplation of the parties,' remained possible to the lessee.

Therefore, although I do not think that there is any definable class of lease which is specifically susceptible of frustration, the facts of the case as I have summarised them in the previous paragraph indicate that this lease is very much the sort that might be frustrated in the circumstances that have occurred.

III. The question therefore arises whether the appellants have demonstrated a triable issue that the lease has been frustrated. The matter must be considered as it appeared at the time when the frustrating event is alleged to have happened. Commercial men must be entitled to act on reasonable commercial probabilities at the time they are called on to make up their minds (see *Embiricos v Sydney Reid & Co* [1914] 3 KB 45 at 54, [1914–15] All ER Rep 185 at 188 per Scrutton J). What we know has in fact happened is, however, available as an aid to determine the reasonable probabilities at the time when decision was called for (see *Denny, Mott & Dickson Ltd v James B Fraser & Co Ltd* [1944] 1 All ER 678 at 685, [1944] AC 265 at 277–278 per Lord Wright).

Favourably to the appellants' case, the road would remain closed for 'well over a year' from application for listed-building consent to demolition. Still more favourable is that it will in fact remain closed for some twenty months.

The appellants were undoubtedly put to considerable expense and inconvenience. But that is not enough. Whenever the performance of a contract is interrupted by a supervening event, the initial judgment is quantitative: what relation does the likely period of interruption bear to the outstanding period for performance? But this must ultimately be translated into qualitative terms: in the light of the quantitative computation and of all other relevant factors (from which I would not entirely exclude executed performance) would outstanding performance in accordance with the literal terms of the contract differ so significantly from what the parties reasonably contemplated at the time of execution that it would be unjust to insist on compliance with those literal terms? In the instant case, at the most favourable to the appellants' contention, they could, at the time the road was closed, look forward to pristine enjoyment of the warehouse for about two-thirds of the remaining currency of the lease. The interruption would be only one-sixth of the total term. Judging by the drastic increase in rent under the rent review clause (more than doubled), it seems likely that the appellants' occupation towards the end of the first quinquennium must have been on terms very favourable to them. The parties can hardly have contemplated that the fire risk expressly provided for was the only possible source of interruption of the business of the warehouse: some possible interruption from some cause or other cannot have been beyond the reasonable contemplation of the parties. Weighing all the relevant factors, I do not think that the appellants have demonstrated a triable issue that the closure of the road so significantly changed the nature of the outstanding rights and obligations under the lease from what the parties could reasonably have contemplated at the time of its execution that it would be unjust to hold them to the literal sense of its stipulations.

It follows that in my judgment the appellants fail on the third issue; and I would therefore dismiss the appeal.

I would, however, presume to suggest that consideration should be given to whether the English doctrine of frustration could be made more flexible in relation to leases. The Law Reform (Frustrated Contracts) Act 1943 seems unlikely to vouchsafe justice in all cases. As often as not there will be an all or nothing situation, the entire loss caused by the frustrating event falling exclusively on one party, whereas justice might require the burden to be shared. Nor is this situation confined to leases.

LORD RUSSELL OF KILLOWEN. My Lords, I am prepared to accept that the termination of a lease may be involved in the frustration of a commercial adventure when, as merely incidental to the overall commercial adventure and a subordinate factor, a lease has been granted. To that extent at least I accept that there may be frustration of a lease, and that the second answer of the Pinafore's captain on the subject of mal de mer is to be preferred to his first.

But the instant case is in no way such a case. It is simply a lease of the land with the building on it. I cannot accept that it is to the point to say that the use to which it was assumed and intended that the building on the demised land was to be put was commercial. That does not bring the lease into the field of a commercial adventure, so as for that reason to bring it within the scope of frustration. The only adventure was the granting and acceptance of a demise of the land, as in the case of any lease, at a rent.

Land is of its nature different from a chattel, however small the plot and however large the chattel. A leasehold interest is described as a chattel real, but that distinction touched only on questions of descent and inheritance. Originally perhaps sounding only in contract or covenant it has long since come to man's estate as a legal estate in land, indeed now one of the only two.

Land has in general a quality of indestructibility lacking in any chattel. Under a grant of the freehold estate in the fee simple the land passes as to its surface and below its surface, and the airspace above, subject to exclusions, e g of minerals, though 'flying' freeholds require special consideration. Under the grant of the leasehold interest the land similarly passes for its duration, subject to the ability to determine that duration by either the lessor or the lessee according to the terms of the lease. And I remark at this stage that I cannot see the force in the suggestion that, because according to its terms the lease may in certain circumstances be determined otherwise than by the expiry of its term, there can be no objection to its determination by application of the doctrine of frustration.

Another distinction between the nature of land and of chattels is that in certain situations, riparian or by the seashore, there may be accretion to the land and therefore to the site comprised in the lease. A vessel under a so-called time charter demise can only acquire barnacles.

It is my understanding of the law that the purchaser of land, whether for a freehold or a leasehold interest, takes the risk that it may be or may turn out to be less suitable or quite unsuitable for the purpose he has in mind, unless the vendor or lessor has taken on himself by warranty or otherwise some liability in that event. A freehold purchaser cannot in that event, after completion, return the land and ask for his money back, though in an appropriate case he might be able to resist specific performance while the contract remained outstanding. So also in the case of a lease for which a premium has been paid in addition to rent, the lessee cannot require repayment of the premium and refuse to pay the rent; nor where there is no premium can he refuse to pay the covenanted rent.

Under the bargain between lessor and lessee the land for the term has passed from the lessor to the lessee, with all its advantages and disadvantages. In the instant case a disadvantage existed, or rather supervened, in that access to the building preventing its use for any purpose was blocked by administrative action which we must assume was legally permitted, and for which we were not told that any compensation could be claimed. If a principle of achieving justice be anywhere at the root of the principle of frustration, I ask myself why should justice require that a useless site be returned to the lessor rather than remain the property of the lessee? (It is not suggested that a just solution can be achieved by somehow sharing the bad luck between lessor and lessee by, for example, a reduction of rent.)

I would reserve consideration of cases of physical destruction of flying leaseholds and of the total disappearance of the site comprised in the lease into the sea so that it no longer existed in the form of a piece of terra firma and could not be the subject of re-entry or forfeiture. In that last case I would not need the intervention of any court to say that the term of years could not outlast the disappearance of its subject matter: the site would no longer have a freeholder lessor, and the obligation to pay rent, which issues out of the land, could not survive its substitution by the waves of the North Sea.

It will be sufficiently seen from what I have said that I am not able to go so far as do your Lordships on the potential applicability of the doctrine of frustration to leases, and would with minor qualification adhere to the views expressed in the *Cricklewood* case in this House by Lord Russell and Lord Goddard. These views expressed, as Lord Goddard said, the general view taken of the law by the profession, and there has been some statutory recognition of that view in giving relief to lessees where war damage had made the building on the leased site useless for its purpose as a dwelling house. In the instant case I would have denied a case of frustration even if the closing of the access to the site had followed only a year after the commencement of the lease and were to last for the whole of its remaining duration.

Having regard to the powerful expressions of opinion of the others of your Lordships, I do not think that any useful purpose would be served by elaboration on my part.

I am, on the assumption that in general your Lordships are correct, entirely in agreement with the view that on the facts of this case, as now known, the appellants do not establish a triable issue of frustration, and accordingly I concur in the view that this appeal must be dismissed. I trust that those advising lessees will mark well the 'hardly ever' approach, and that litigation will be little encouraged by this cautious departure from what may previously have been thought to be the law.

LORD ROSKILL. My Lords, the appellants are the lessees of a warehouse in Kingston Street, Hull, of which the respondents are the lessors. Their lease was dated 12th July 1974 and its term was ten years from 1st January 1974. It therefore expires on 31st December 1983. It is beyond question that since 18th May 1979 the appellants have been deprived of the beneficial use of the warehouse by the closure of Kingston Street both for vehicles and pedestrians, but their possession of the warehouse under the demise from the respondents has in no way been disturbed. It is not necessary in this appeal to consider precisely the powers under which the closure order was finally made, on which the information before your Lordships' House was regrettably sparse. It can be assumed that that order was lawfully made and is still in force. The cause of the closure was the unsafe condition of a derelict Victorian warehouse opposite. That warehouse is now being demolished with permission and the recent correspondence placed before your Lordships shows that that demolition should be complete by the end of 1980 or the beginning of 1981. If this prediction proves accurate, the appellants will once again have the necessary access to their warehouse and its beneficial use will once again be available to them. On the basis of those dates the appellants will have lost their beneficial use for about 20 months. There was at the time of the first closure order just over 4½ years of the term of ten years unexpired and there will be some three years remaining when the beneficial use is likely to be restored.

The respondents have claimed rent throughout the period of closure. The obligation to pay rent is, it is said, absolute and unqualified and the risk of loss of beneficial use falls on the lessees. The appellants refused to pay. They claimed that their obligation to pay rent had come to an end because of frustration brought about by the closure of Kingston Street and the denial to them of the beneficial use of the warehouse. The respondents issued a writ on 9th July 1979 in respect of rent due on 1st April and 1st July 1979. Your Lordships were told that there was no dispute on figures and if the appellants are liable the sum due is that claimed. I would only observe that on any view of this case I find it difficult to see what defence there could be to the claim for rent due on 1st April 1979 since the event relied on for excusing liability, namely the street closure order, did not take effect until 18th May 1979 and under the lease rent was payable in advance. But if the appellants be right they would have a defence to the claim for rent for the quarter beginning 1st July 1979.

The respondents sought judgment under RSC Ord 14. The learned master gave judgment for the amount claimed. The appellants appealed to the judge in chambers, Sheen J. That learned judge rightly dismissed the appeal on 16th October 1979. Your Lordships were told that he did so without giving a reasoned judgment because he was bound by the decision of the Court of Appeal in *Leightons Investment Trust Ltd v Cricklewood Property and Investment Trust Ltd* [1943] 2 All ER 97, [1943] KB 493 that as a matter of law the doctrine of frustration could not apply to a lease. Accordingly there could be no defence to the respondents' claim. The learned judge was clearly bound by that decision as the Court of Appeal would have been had the present appeal first proceeded to that court.

The learned judge then certified under s 12 of the Administration of Justice Act 1969 that a point of law of general public importance was involved in respect of which he was bound by a decision of the Court of Appeal and accordingly gave the appellants a certificate for leave to present a petition of appeal to your Lordships' House. That petition your Lordships subsequently granted. The course so adopted, very naturally in the circumstances, has had the result that this important and long debated question of law (namely, can a lease ever be frustrated?) comes before your Lordships for decision in Ord 14 proceedings without your Lordships having the benefit of judgments of the trial judge or of the Court of Appeal and on facts the supply of which has certainly been economical.

My Lords, this question was last before your Lordships' House some 35 years ago on appeal in the *Cricklewood* case [1945] 1 All ER 252, [1945] AC 221. There were then sitting in your Lordships' House Viscount Simon LC, the second Lord Russell, Lord Wright, Lord Porter and Lord Goddard. All their Lordships were agreed that if the doctrine of frustration could apply to a lease it did not apply to the building lease in question. But on the issue now before your Lordships there was a sharp division of opinion, Viscount Simon LC and Lord Wright taking the view that the doctrine could apply to a lease, albeit extremely rarely, and Lord Russell and Lord Goddard emphatically taking the view that it could never apply to a lease. Lord Porter declined to express a view, leaving the point to be decided when it arose for decision. My Lords, some 35 years later the point does arise for decision. In the interval there has been much debate and much learning which view should prevail.

One thing at least is plain. This question has never yet been the subject of direct decision in your Lordships' House. My Lords, what is now called the doctrine of frustration was first evolved during the nineteenth century when notwithstanding the express language in which the parties had concluded their bargain the courts declined in the event which occurred to hold them to the strict letter of that bargain. *Taylor v Caldwell* (1863) 3 B & S 826, [1861–73] All ER Rep 24 is perhaps the most famous mid-nineteenth century case, in which the relevant principle was laid down by Blackburn J giving the judgment of the Court of Queen's Bench. The dispute in that case arose under a document which was expressed in the language of the lease but which was held to be a licence. There was no demise of the premises. But the licensee was relieved of his obligation to pay 'rent' because of the fire which destroyed the premises and so made performance impossible. One can find what might be called anticipatory traces of the doctrine enunciated in *Taylor v Caldwell* in some of the earlier nineteenth century cases, principally in relation to contracts of personal service made impossible of performance by death or illness, but no useful purpose would be presently served by reviewing them. What is important is not what happened before *Taylor v Caldwell* but what happened thereafter.

The doctrine evolved slowly, especially in the field of commercial law. It was invoked in the Coronation cases. As late as *Matthey v Curling* [1922] 2 AC 180 at 210, Younger LJ said in the Court of Appeal that the doctrine of frustration was not one to be extended, a view much falsified in the event. It is interesting to observe, in view of the respondents' insistence that the doctrine had no application to a lease, that for a while it was thought that the doctrine had no application to the ordinary form of time charterparty under which no possession passes to the time charterer. In *Admiral Shipping Co Ltd v Weidner, Hopkins & Co* [1916] 1 KB 429 as experienced a judge as Bailhache J expressed the view that this was so and some support for his view can be found in the speech of Lord Parker in *F A Tamplin Steamship Co Ltd v Anglo-Mexican Petroleum Products Co Ltd* [1916] 2 AC 397 at 424–425, [1916–17] All ER Rep 104 at 119. But your Lordships' House in *Bank Line Ltd v Arthur Capel & Co* [1919] AC 435, [1918–19] All ER Rep 504 determined the law beyond all doubt, that such a time charterparty could be determined by frustration if the facts of the particular case justified that conclusion. That decision did not, however, expressly at least, embrace a charter by demise where possession passes to the demise charterer and counsel for the respondents was able to show that as recently as *Blane Steamships Ltd v Minister of Transport* [1951] 2 KB 965 at 975 counsel for the appellants were able on the strength of the *Cricklewood* case to argue (albeit wholly unsuccessfully) that the doctrine had no application to a charter by demise. It is now clear beyond question that the doctrine applies to time charters by demise as well as to other forms of time or voyage charterparties.

My Lords, I mention these matters for three purposes: first to show how gradually but also how extensively the doctrine has developed; second to show how, whenever attempts have been made to exclude the application of the doctrine to particular classes of contract, such attempts, though sometimes initially successful, have in the end uniformly failed; and third, albeit I hope without unnecessary reference to a mass of decided cases, many in your Lordships' House, the doctrine has at any rate in the last half century and indeed during and since the 1914–18 war been flexible, to be applied whenever the inherent justice of a particular case requires its application. The extension in recent years of government interference in ordinary business affairs, inflation, sudden outbreaks of war in different parts of the world, are all recent examples of circumstances in which the doctrine has been invoked, sometimes with success, sometimes without. Indeed the doctrine has been described as a 'device' for doing justice between the parties when they themselves have failed either wholly or sufficiently to provide for the particular event or events which have happened. The doctrine is principally concerned with the incidence of risk: who must take the risk of the happening of a particular event, especially when the parties have not made any or any sufficient provision for the happening of that event. When the doctrine is successfully invoked it is because in the event which has happened the law imposes a solution casting the incidence of that risk on one party or the other as the circumstances of the particular case may require, having regard to the express provisions of the contract into which the parties have entered. The doctrine is no arbitrary dispensing power to be exercised at the subjective whim of the judge by whom the issue has to be determined. Frustration if it occurs operates automatically. Its operation does not depend on the action or inaction of the parties. It is to be invoked or not to be invoked by reference only to the particular contract before the court and the facts of the particular case said to justify the invocation of the doctrine.

My Lords, I think it can at the present time be safely said that, leases and tenancy agreements apart, there is no class of contract in relation to which the doctrine could not be successfully invoked if the particular case justified its implication, however slow and however hesitant the common law may have been in developing the doctrine thus far. Clearly it is likely to be able to be more successfully invoked in some classes of cases than others, for example, where the requisition of a ship under time charter which is likely to outlast the remaining period of the charter (see, e g, *Bank Line Ltd v Arthur Capel & Co*), though not if the requisition is likely to be short in its duration (see *Port Line Ltd v Ben Line Steamers Ltd* [1958] 1 All ER 787, [1958] 2 QB 146). It will not often (if at all) be able to be successfully invoked by a seller of goods who is likely to invoke it on a rising market merely because the mode of performance contemplated when the contract was made proves impossible but some other and, according to the tribunal of fact, not fundamentally different but more expensive mode of performance remains available: see *Tsakiroglou & Co Ltd v Noblee and Thorl GmbH* [1961] 2 All ER 179, [1962] AC 93 and the other Suez cases.

If, therefore, this doctrine, developed as it has pragmatically and empirically, has advanced thus far by the last quarter of the twentieth century, I ask what the reasons are in principle why it should not now be held capable of embracing leases and tenancy agreements. Some of the reasons are certainly formidable and have undoubtedly attracted weighty support in your Lordships' House from the second Lord Russell and Lord Goddard. First it is said that the lessee has secured full consideration for his covenant to pay rent, namely the conveyance of the leasehold interest for the relevant term of years with all the attendant benefits and burdens. Then it is said that it is a basic principle of land, law not now to be disturbed in your Lordships' House which has prevailed both in relation to the conveyance of freeholds and leases, that the incidence of the risk of accidents passes to the purchaser or lessee. Then it is said, quite correctly, that a lease creates an estate in land and third parties may acquire rights thereunder so that to apply the doctrine of frustration would or might destroy the interests of third parties against their wishes. It is also said that it is the lease and therefore the estate in land which is the adventure and that the attached contractual conditions are but ancillary provisions to that estate in land.

But there are also formidable arguments the other way. The law should not be compartmentalised. In principle a common law doctrine ought not to be held capable of applying only in one field of contract but not in another. To preserve the dichotomy between leases on the one hand and other types of contract on the other can undoubtedly create anomalies. Thus if a ship is demise chartered for the purpose of storing oil and explodes without fault of either party, the demise charter would clearly be frustrated. If the same demise charterer also leases an adjacent shore installation for the same purpose and the same explosion destroys that installation along with the demise-chartered ship, rent for that storage installation would remain payable in full for the unexpired period of the lease though liability for demise charter hire had ceased on the frustration of the demise charterparty.

My Lords, another consideration is surely this. There are many reported cases in recent years, especially in connection with attempts to avoid the operation of the Rent Acts, where disputes have arisen whether a particular agreement is a lease or tenancy agreement on the one hand or a licence on the other. Such cases often turn on narrow distinctions. But it is difficult to justify a state of the law which would uphold the application of the doctrine of frustration where the agreement is held to be a licence but would deny the application of that doctrine where the agreement is held to be a lease or tenancy agreement. In so stating I have not lost sight of the contrary anomaly to which my noble and learned friend Lord Russell drew attention during the argument and which could in theory arise if the appellants' submissions are allowed to prevail; for their submission would deny the invocation of the doctrine where the conveyance was of a freehold but would allow its invocation, at least in legal theory if not in reality, if the conveyance were only of a lease for 999 years. Yet another consideration which is relevant is this. However much weight one may give to the fact that a lease creates an estate in land in favour of the lessee, in truth it is by no means always in that estate in land in which the lessee is interested. In many cases he is interested only in the accompanying contractual right to use that which is demised to him by the lease, and the estate in land which he acquires has little or no meaning for him. In Professor Treitel's book on Contract (5th Edn, 1979, pp 669–670) the learned author mentions the case of a cottage leased for a period as a holiday home. In many such cases the holiday-maker's rights are not only a licence to use but include a demise with the concomitant right to exclusive possession. The holiday-maker acquires an estate in land. But that, my Lords, has little meaning for him. He acquires that estate in land, it is true, but only in order to enjoy for a while that exclusive right to the demised premises for his holiday. I find it difficult to see why in principle such a lease should be incapable of being frustrated if the facts justify that result, especially as the doctrine would clearly be applicable had the holiday-maker's rights derived from a licence and not from a lease.

My Lords, if your Lordships are now to say that a lease can never be frustrated, it must be for some reason of policy. I unreservedly accept that hitherto whenever the argument that a lease can be frustrated has been advanced, that argument has failed. In passing it is interesting to note that, although all members of your Lordships' House thought otherwise, Asquith J, the trial judge in the *Cricklewood* case, would have held the building lease there in question to be frustrated had he felt free to hold that the doctrine was capable of application to leases.

My Lords, in a matter of this kind while it is right for your Lordships to look back to the past, it is surely more important to look forward and consider what rule of law should henceforth prevail. Historic considerations alone cannot justify the preservation of a rule if that rule has ceased to serve any useful purpose and is unlikely to serve any useful purpose in the years immediately ahead.

One submission in favour of preserving the old rule was that to hold that the doctrine is applicable to leases would encourage unmeritorious litigation by lessees denying liability for rent which was plainly due. This is the not unfamiliar 'floodgates' argument invariably advanced whenever it is suggested that the law might be changed. My Lords, such an argument should have little appeal. If a defence of frustration be plainly unarguable, it will always be open to the master or judge in chambers so to hold and to give summary judgment for the lessors on the ground that the lessees have failed to show any arguable defence. I respectfully agree with Viscount Simon LC and Lord Wright in the *Cricklewood* case that the cases in which the doctrine will be able to be successfully invoked are likely to be rare, most frequently though not necessarily exclusively where the alleged frustrating event is of a catastrophic character. If that be so the 'floodgates' argument ceases to have any weight.

Your Lordships were referred to a decision of Goff J in *Rom Securities Ltd v Rogers (Holdings) Ltd* (1967) 205 Estates Gazette 427, in which that learned judge expressed himself as far from satisfied that the doctrine of frustration could not be applied to an agreement for a lease. My Lords, if that view be right, as I think it is, and the doctrine is applicable to an agreement for a lease, I find it difficult to see why a different view should apply in the case of a lease because in the latter case there has been a demise whereas in the former there has not; equity presumes that to have been done which should be done.

Thus far, my Lords, I have sought to examine the crucial question on principle and without detailed regard to the many authorities to which your Lordships have referred. The three principal English cases relied on by the respondents are *London and Northern Estates Co Ltd v Schlesinger* [1916] 1 KB 20, [1914–15] All ER Rep 593, *Whitehall Court Ltd v Ettlinger* [1920] 1 KB 680, [1918–19] All ER Rep 229 and *Matthey v Curling* [1922] 2 AC 180, [1922] All ER Rep 1. In the first of these cases Lush J stated as a ground for denying the applicability of the doctrine that a term of years has been created by the agreement in question (see [1916] 1 KB 20 at 24, [1914–15] All ER Rep 593 at 595), but the decision was plainly right on the true construction of the lease and the facts of that case. The lease properly construed did not contemplate only personal residence by the defendant. Similarly *Whitehall Court Ltd v Ettlinger* was rightly decided on the true construction of the lease and the particular facts of that case. Like Lord Wright in the *Cricklewood* case I do not regard the passage in the judgment of Lord Reading CJ (be it noted that it was an extempore judgment) as holding that a lease is incapable of frustration (see [1920] 1 KB 680 at 685, [1918–19] All ER Rep 229 at 231).

My Lords, I think counsel for the respondents was right in saying that the genesis of the suggestion that a lease is capable of frustration lies in the dissenting judgment of Atkin LJ in the Court of Appeal in *Matthey v Curling* [1922] AC 180 at 199–200. I have

read and reread the speeches in your Lordships' House. I am clearly of the view that the
a   majority of your Lordships' House though disagreeing with that dissenting judgment
were deciding that case (a singularly harsh decision from the tenant's point of view) by
reference to the particular lease and the particular facts of the case. I do not think that
decision in any way assists the determination of the present question. Nor, with respect,
is any assistance to be gained from the Scottish case of *Tay Salmon Fisheries Co Ltd v Speedie*
1929 SC 593 which was decided under a system of law different in the crucial respect
b   from that applicable to *Matthey v Curling*. In my judgment the Court of Appeal in the
Cricklewood case was wrong in asserting categorically that those three English cases to
which I have referred were decisive in favour of the proposition that the doctrine of
frustration had no application to a lease, even though in the first there is a dictum to that
effect. I find myself in respectful agreement with what Viscount Simon LC and Lord
Wright said with regard to those three cases.

c   Your Lordships were referred to certain United States authorities collected in Williston
on Contracts (3rd Edn, 1978, vol 18, para 1955). Clearly there are United States decisions
(none it seems of the highest authority) both ways. Many of these cases arose from the
Eighteenth Amendment and its effect on leases of premises entered into solely for the
sale of liquor. I respectfully doubt whether much help is to be gained from such
decisions. It is however interesting to observe that Professor Corbin in his work on
d   Contracts (1951, vol 6, para 1356, p 387) takes the view that the argument in favour of
the non-applicability of the doctrine of frustration based on the view that the lessee had
assumed the risk 'has long since ceased to be convincing', adding: 'Whether the
frustration of the tenant's purposes operates in discharge of his duty depends upon all the
circumstances, especially upon the extent of that frustration and the prevailing practices
of men in like cases.'

e   Your Lordships were helpfully referred to one Canadian and one Australian decision,
the former of the Supreme Court of Canada, the latter of the High Court of Australia.
In the former, *Highway Properties Ltd v Kelly, Douglas & Co Ltd* (1971) 17 DLR (3d) 710
at 721, Laskin J, delivering the judgment of the Supreme Court, said:

> 'There are some general considerations that support the view that I would take.
> It is no longer sensible to pretend that a commercial lease, such as the one before this
f   > Court, is simply a conveyance and not also a contract. It is equally untenable to
> persist in denying resort to the full armoury of remedies ordinarily available to
> redress repudiation of covenants, merely because the covenants may be associated
> with an estate in land.'

In the latter case, *Firth v Halloran* (1926) 38 CLR 261 at 269, Isaacs J, though agreeing
g   with other members of the court in holding that in a particular case there was no
frustration, said:

> 'I do not agree that, because the contractual obligation relied on by the plaintiff
> is created by an instrument of lease, the doctrine of frustration is necessarily
> excluded. The nature of the relation of landlord and tenant, the history of the
> doctrine of frustration, its inherent meaning and the judicial determination of
h   > relevant cases would lead me to reject so sweeping a rule. Nor do I think the
> consequences of terminating the relation of landlord and tenant any more
> extraordinary than that of terminating any other legal relation which by hypothesis
> is expressly and impliedly created on a mutual and fundamental basis of existence
> or continuance which fails at a given point.'

j   It is, however, right to say that he alone of the members of the High Court of Australia
took that view and certainly two other members of that court agreed with the court
below in holding that the doctrine had no application to a lease.
My Lords, I do not find anything in these writings and decisions which affords a
compelling reason for maintaining the view that the doctrine is inapplicable to leases.
The inclination of these writings and decisions is to my mind the other way. The learned

authors of Megarry and Wade's Law of Real Property (4th Edn, 1975, p 674), not surprisingly in view of the difference of opinion in the *Cricklewood* case, treat the question as open.

My Lords, I do not find it necessary to examine in detail the jurisprudential foundation on which the doctrine of frustration supposedly rests. At least five theories have been advanced at different times: see the speech of Lord Wilberforce in *Liverpool City Council v Irwin* [1976] 2 All ER 39 at 43, [1977] AC 239 at 253–254. At one time without doubt the implied term theory found most favour, and there is high authority in its support. But weighty judicial opinion has since moved away from that view. What is sometimes called the construction theory has found greater favour. But my Lords, if I may respectfully say so, I think the most satisfactory explanation of the doctrine is that given by Lord Radcliffe in *Davis Contractors Ltd v Fareham Urban District Council* [1956] 2 All ER 145 at 159–160, [1956] AC 696 at 728. There must have been by reason of some supervening event some such fundamental change of circumstances as to enable the court to say, 'This was not the bargain which these parties made and their bargain must be treated as at an end', a view which Lord Radcliffe himself tersely summarised in a quotation of five words from the Aeneid: 'Non haec in foedera veni.' Since in such a case the crucial question must be answered as one of law (see the decision of your Lordships' House in the *Tsakiroglou* case) by reference to the particular contract which the parties made and to the particular facts of the case in question, there is, I venture to think, little difference between Lord Radcliffe's view and the so-called construction theory.

My Lords, it follows that on the question of principle, I find it impossible to justify compartmentalisation of the law or to agree that the doctrine of frustration applies to every type of contract save a lease. I can see no logical difference between frustration of a demise charterparty and frustration of a lease. In principle the doctrine should be equally capable of universal application in all contractual arrangements. I therefore find myself in respectful agreement with the reasoning of Viscount Simon LC and Lord Wright and in respectful disagreement with the views of the second Lord Russell and Lord Goddard in the *Cricklewood* case.

But to hold that the doctrine is capable of applying to leases does not mean that it should be readily applied. Viscount Simon LC and Lord Wright both indicated in the *Cricklewood* case some of the limitations to which the invocation of the doctrine would be subject. I respectfully agree with what was there said but I do not think any useful purpose would presently be served by attempting to categorise those cases where the doctrine might be successfully invoked and those where it might not. Circumstances must always vary infinitely. I am, however, clearly of the view in common with all your Lordships that the doctrine cannot possibly be invoked in the present case for the reasons given by my noble and learned friend Lord Wilberforce. I would therefore dismiss this appeal with costs.

Appeal dismissed.

Solicitors: *Samuel Tonkin & Co*, agents for *Carrick, Carr & Garwood*, Hull (for the appellants); *Bower, Cotton & Bower*, agents for *Simpson, Curtis & Co*, Leeds (for the respondents).

Mary Rose Plummer   Barrister.

a

Chinn v Collins (Inspector of Taxes)

HOUSE OF LORDS

LORD WILBERFORCE, VISCOUNT DILHORNE, LORD FRASER OF TULLYBELTON, LORD RUSSELL OF KILLOWEN AND LORD ROSKILL

28th, 29th, 30th JULY, 11th DECEMBER 1980

b

Capital gains tax – Settlement – Tax avoidance scheme – Related transactions – Trustees exercising power to appoint trust property to beneficiary contingently on his surviving period of three days from date of appointment – On same date beneficiary assigning to foreign company for consideration his contingent interest in property – By contract made on same date beneficiary agreeing to purchase property from foreign company – Beneficiary surviving three-day period and scheme completed by transfer of property to him by foreign company – Whether scheme an arrangement under which beneficiary became absolutely entitled to property – Whether beneficiary chargeable to tax on gain arising from deemed disposal of property – Finance Act 1965, s 42(2)(7).

c

By a settlement dated 24th February 1960 the settlor settled a small number of ordinary shares of 5s each in L Ltd on trusts under which the trustees had power, with the consent of the settlor during his lifetime, to appoint the trust fund in favour of, inter alios, his two sons, A and S. Subject to such appointment the trust fund was to be held on discretionary trusts for a class consisting of A, S, their spouses and their issue. There were four original trustees of the settlement, all of whom were resident in England. In the course of time further shares in L Ltd were brought into the settlement and in 1969 the trust fund included 370,100 shares in L Ltd. The settlor wished those shares to be appointed to A and S without incurring any liability to capital gains tax and, accordingly, took the following steps pursuant to a tax avoidance scheme. On 31st March 1969 a Guernsey company and five of its directors were appointed to be trustees of the settlement in place of three of the original trustees. Subsequently the administration of the settlement was transferred to Guernsey. Neither the Guernsey company nor any of its directors was resident or ordinarily resident in the United Kingdom. By a deed of appointment dated 28th October 1969 the trustees of the settlement, with the settlor's consent, appointed 184,500 shares in L Ltd in favour of A absolutely, contingently on his surviving a period of three days from the date of the appointment. By a deed of assignment, also dated 28th October, A assigned his contingent interest in the shares to a Jersey company, R Ltd, which was not resident in the United Kingdom. In consideration of the assignment, R Ltd covenanted to pay to A on 1st November £352,705 and took out insurance against his death before 28th November. On 28th October R Ltd drew a cheque for £352,705 without sufficient funds in its bank account to meet the cheque. On the same day R Ltd and A executed an agreement whereby R Ltd agreed to sell and A agreed to buy 184,500 shares in L Ltd free from all liens, charges or encumbrances for £355,162. Completion of the agreement was to take place on 1st November and time was to be of the essence of the contract. After 1st November the nominee company in whose name the trust holding of 370,100 shares in L Ltd was registered was given notice that 184,500 of those shares were beneficially owned by A. The Crown assessed A to capital gains tax on the footing (i) that, from the moment the trustees had appointed the 184,500 shares to him, he had become entitled to them in equity, that the supervening sale by him of his contingent interest in the shares to R Ltd and the agreement to repurchase those shares from R Ltd did not affect that equitable interest, that, therefore, when he survived the period of three days from 28th October, he became absolutely entitled to those shares as against the trustees of the settlement and that, since he was resident and ordinarily resident in the United Kingdom, the gains accruing to the trustees by virtue of the deemed disposal under s 25(3) of the Finance Act 1965 and on which they would have been chargeable to capital gains tax had they been

d

e

f

g

h

j

domiciled and resident in the United Kingdom fell, under s 42(2)ᵃ of that Act to be
treated as accruing to him, or, alternatively, (ii) that the scheme was an 'arrangement' and *a*
therefore a 'settlement' within s 42(7) of the 1965 Act, that A was the beneficiary under
the arrangement and that the trustees' gain should therefore be apportioned to him and
not to R Ltd.   The Special Commissioners determined that the scheme was an
'arrangement' for the purposes of s 42(7) and that A was the beneficiary under the
arrangement, and upheld the assessment.   The judge dismissed A's appeal ([1978] 1 All
ER 65), holding (i) that the assignment and the contract to sell the shares were *b*
interdependent and conditional one on the other and that on the true construction of
both the documents A became on 1st November the beneficiary absolutely entitled to the
shares as against the trustees and (ii) that the events which took place between the
appointment of the new trustees on 31st March 1969 and the final transfer of the shares
to A under the contract to sell were part of an arrangement for the purposes of s 42(7) and
that the settlor and trustees of the arrangement were the settlor and trustees of the 1960 *c*
settlement and that the beneficiary under the arrangement was A.   The Court of Appeal
allowed A's appeal ([1979] 2 All ER 529), holding (i) that since the share sale agreement
was a contract for the sale of 184,500 unspecified shares in L Ltd, or, alternatively, was
a contract for which, in the event of a breach, damages only and not specific performance
would be the appropriate remedy, A had not acquired an equitable interest in any
particular share in L Ltd and, therefore, was not a beneficiary under the settlement *d*
within s 42(2) in respect of the 184,500 shares on 1st November 1969 when the
contingent interest vested and (ii) that the scheme did not involve any act of bounty by
anyone and consequently could not constitute a 'settlement' within s 42(7).   The Crown
appealed.

Held – The appeal would be allowed for the following reasons— *e*
   (1) Looking at the scheme as a whole and the legal form and nature of the transactions
carried out, it was clear that, by a chain of transactions set in motion on 31st March 1969
or, effectively, on 28th October 1969 and intended to be carried through without further
action (since the Guernsey company, on instructions from A and R Ltd, had, as trustee
of the settlement, the power, the duty and the money to complete the scheme as from
28th October 1969), the 184,500 shares previously held by the settlement were intended *f*
to vest in A.   Although the share sale agreement did not identify the shares to be sold to
A as being the settlement shares, there could have been no question of R Ltd going into
the market in order to buy 184,500 shares in L Ltd since (a) it had no money to do so and
there was no certainty that it could have acquired so considerable a block at the quoted
market price, still less deliver them by the covenanted date, and (b) if by some
inconceivable means it had acquired such shares it would have been landed with two *g*
parcels of 184,500 shares, only one of which A had agreed to repurchase and for the other
of which it could not have paid on the covenanted date.   Furthermore, the legal title to
the shares was at all times vested in a nominee for the Guernsey company, and dealings
relating to the equitable interest in them required no formality; as soon as there was an
agreement for their sale accompanied or followed by payment of the price, the equitable
title passed at once to the purchaser, viz A, and all that was needed to perfect his title was *h*
notice to the trustees or the nominee, which notice both had at all material times.   It
followed, therefore, that the trustees were bound to transfer the shares to A immediately
the interests vested on 1st November 1969, and that A was the beneficiary, under the
settlement, as regards the shares, and accordingly, liable to capital gains tax under s 42(2)
of the 1965 Act on the gains accruing to the trustees (see p 194 *g* to p 195 *c* and *e f*, p 196
c to *e* and *g* to *j*, p 197 *b c*, p 199 *c* to *e* and *g* to *j*, p 200 *a* and p 201 *a* and *d*, post); dictum *j*
of Lord Wilberforce in *Inland Revenue Comrs v Plummer* [1979] 3 All ER at 779 applied.
   (2) Furthermore, the circumstance that A obtained, on the execution of the deed of
appointment, a contingent interest, likely to become vested after three days, in 184, 500

---

a   Section 42, so far as material, is set out at p 192 *a* to *d*, post.

shares could not be regarded otherwise than as an act of bounty in his favour, and that, taken together with the sale and repurchase, made it an arrangement which constituted a settlement, within s 42(7) of the 1965 Act. On that ground also A was liable to capital gains tax under s 42(2) (see p 195 *j* to p 196 *a* to *e*, p 197 *c*, p 200 *h* to p 201 *a* and *d*, post); *Inland Revenue Comrs v Plummer* [1979] 3 All ER 775 applied.

Per Curiam. If an agreement can only be carried out in one way, it is superfluous to mention that one way specifically in the agreement: the parties are presumed to intend it (see p 195 *d*, p 196 *d*, p 197 *b* and p 199 *j*, post).

Quaere. Whether it is sufficient for the purposes of s 42(2) of the 1965 Act for a beneficiary to be a beneficiary under the settlement at any time during the year of assessment in which the chargeable gain accrued (see p 195 *fg*, p 196 *d*, p 197 *c* and p 201 *b* to *d*, post).

Decision of the Court of Appeal [1979] 2 All ER 529 reversed.

Notes

For the liability of United Kingdom beneficiaries to capital gains tax in respect of gains accruing to the trustees of a non-resident trust, see 5 Halsbury's Laws (4th Edn) para 113.

For the Finance Act 1965, ss 25, 42, see 34 Halsbury's Statutes (3rd Edn), 884, 912.

Section 42 was replaced by the Capital Gains Tax Act 1979, s 17, with effect from 6th April 1979.

Cases referred to in opinions

Inland Revenue Comrs v Church Comrs for England [1976] 2 All ER 1037, [1977] AC 329, [1976] 3 WLR 214, [1976] STC 339, 50 Tax Cas 516, [1976] TR 187, HL, Digest (Cont Vol E) 289, 866c.
Inland Revenue Comrs v Payne, Inland Revenue Comrs v Gunner (1941) 23 Tax Cas 610, 110 LJKB 328, CA, 28(1) Digest (Reissue) 419, 1522.
Inland Revenue Comrs v Plummer [1979] 3 All ER 775, [1980] AC 896, [1979] 3 WLR 689, [1979] STC 793, HL, Digest (Cont Vol E) 290, 866d.
Tiller v Atlantic Coast Line Railroad Co (1943) 318 US 54.

Cases also cited

Chamberlain v Inland Revenue Comrs [1943] 2 All ER 200, 25 Tax Cas 317, HL.
Duncust v Albrecht (1841) 12 Sim 189, 59 ER 1104.
Eilbeck (Inspector of Taxes) v Rawling [1980] 2 All ER 12, [1980] STC 192, CA.
Inland Revenue Comrs v Morton 1941 SC 467, 24 Tax Cas 254.
Inland Revenue Comrs v Pay (1955) 36 Tax Cas 109.
Inland Revenue Comrs v Prince-Smith [1943] 1 All ER 434, 25 Tax Cas 84.
Khatijabai Jiwa Hasham v Zenab D/O Chandu Nansi, Widow and Executrix of Haji Gulam Hussein Harji (deceased) [1958] 3 All ER 719, [1960] AC 316, PC.

Appeal

The Crown appealed against the decision of the Court of Appeal (Buckley, Goff and Shaw LJJ) ([1979] 2 All ER 529, [1979] Ch 447, [1979] STC 332) on 2nd February 1979 allowing an appeal of the taxpayer, Anthony Elliot Chinn ('Anthony'), against the decision of Templeman J ([1978] 1 All ER 65, [1977] STC 468) on 20th July 1977 dismissing the taxpayer's appeal by way of case stated from the determination of the Special Commissioners whereby an assessment to capital gains tax made on the taxpayer for the year 1969–70 under s 42(2) of the Finance Act 1965 was upheld. The facts are set out in the opinion of Lord Wilberforce.

D C Potter QC and *R W Ham* for Anthony.
D J Nicholls QC and *Peter Gibson* for the Crown.

Their Lordships took time for consideration.

Viscount Dilhorne died on 7th September 1980.

11th December. The following opinions were delivered.

LORD WILBERFORCE. My Lords, this case involves consideration of s 42 of the Finance Act 1965, the Act which introduced the capital gains tax. For convenience I cite the relevant portions of this section:

'(1) This section applies as respects chargeable gains accruing to the trustees of a settlement if the trustees are not resident and not ordinarily resident in the United Kingdom, and if the settlor, or one of the settlors, is domiciled and either resident or ordinarily resident in the United Kingdom, or was domiciled and either resident or ordinarily resident in the United Kingdom when he made his settlement.

'(2) Any beneficiary under the settlement who is domiciled and either resident or ordinarily resident in the United Kingdom during any year of assessment shall be treated for the purposes of this Part of this Act as if an apportioned part of the amount, if any, on which the trustees would have been chargeable to capital gains tax under section 20(4) of this Act, if domiciled and either resident or ordinarily resident in the United Kingdom in that year of assessment, had been chargeable gains accruing to the beneficiary in that year of assessment; and for the purposes of this section any such amount shall be apportioned in such manner as is just and reasonable between persons having interests in the settled property, whether the interest be a life interest or an interest in reversion, and so that the chargeable gain is apportioned, as near as may be, according to the respective values of those interests, disregarding in the case of a defeasible interest the possibility of defeasance . . .

'(7) In this section "settlement" and "settlor" have the same meanings as in Chapter III of Part XVIII of the Income Tax Act 1952 and "settled property" shall be construed accordingly.'

The question is as to the application of these provisions to a scheme admittedly devised to avoid a substantial charge to the tax. It is necessary to describe it in detail.

The antecedents of the scheme

On 24th February 1960 Mr Norman N Chinn, father of the taxpayer ('Anthony'), made a settlement for the benefit of his family. All that it is necessary to know about it is that it contained an overriding power, exercisable by the trustees with the consent of the settlor, to appoint capital in favour of all or any of the settlor's sons Anthony and Steven and their respective wives, widows and issue. The settlor had also power to appoint new trustees. In October 1969 the trustees held 370,100 ordinary shares in Lex Garages Ltd (out of a total issued ordinary capital of 4,111,068 shares). Lex was a public company whose shares were quoted on the London Stock Exchange. These shares had risen considerably in value since acquisition and so carried a potential liability to capital gains tax on any disposal. It was the settlor's desire that (approximately) one-half of the shares should be vested in each of Anthony and Steven absolutely. In February 1969 the settlor consulted a solicitor about means of mitigating the liability to tax, was advised by him of a 'contingent interest scheme' operated by N M Rothschild & Sons ('Rothschilds'), and instructed him to proceed with such a scheme subject to counsel's advice.

Preparation

On 31st March 1969 the settlor appointed, in the place of the existing trustees who were resident in the United Kingdom, a Guernsey company controlled by Rothschilds called N M Rothschild & Sons (CI) Ltd ('NMR(CI)'), two directors of that company resident in Guernsey and one English resident trustee. The administration of the trusts of the settlement passed shortly afterward to Guernsey. This operation clearly brought the case within s 42(1) quoted above. The settlor then instructed the solicitor to implement the 'contingent interest scheme'. As applied to the settlor's requirements it involved, after the appointment of foreign trustees, the creation of contingent interests in the shares for Anthony and Steven to vest in three days, the purchase of these contingent interests by a Channel Island Rothschilds subsidiary, and, on the vesting of the interest, repurchase of the shares by Anthony and Steven with money obtained by them from the sale of their contingent interest; the end result would be that each of Anthony and Steven would acquire approximately one-half of the Lex shares held by the trustees. It was expected that no capital gains tax would be payable on the disposals involved.

Implementation of the scheme

The series of operations to be carried out and the documents to be used were, in accordance with Rothschilds' practice, all prepared in advance and there was a precise timetable for each step. This technique has become normal in tax avoidance schemes. On 28th October 1969 the trustees of the settlement with the consent of the settlor executed a deed of appointment of two funds each of 184,500 Lex shares in favour of Anthony and Steven contingently on surviving three days. Anthony and Steven, and the solicitor, flew to Jersey and, also on 28th October, Anthony and Steven offered to sell to a company called Rozel Holdings Ltd ('Rozel') their contingent interests for, in each case, £352,705 payable on 1st November 1969. Rozel was a Jersey company with an issued capital of £150 owned by Rothschilds. On the same day Anthony and Steven executed deeds of assignment to Rozel of their contingent interests in consideration of covenants by Rozel to pay the said sums on 1st November 1969. Before they executed these deeds, Rozel handed to Anthony and Steven cheques, postdated to 1st November 1969, for £352,705 drawn on Rozel's account with Lloyds Bank, Jersey, and Anthony and Steven immediately handed these cheques to NMR(CI) for the credit of accounts recently opened with NMR(CI). Rozel did not have sufficient credit balance with Lloyds Bank to meet these cheques.

At the same meeting each of Anthony and Steven executed an agreement to purchase from Rozel 184,500 Lex shares for £355,162, completion to take place on 1st November 1969, and time to be of the essence of the contract. Still on the same day (28th October 1969) Anthony and Steven each gave letters to NMR(CI) instructing it on 1st November 1969 to debit their respective accounts to pay £355,162 10s to Rozel, and each gave NMR(CI) cheques for approximately £200 to complete the financing. Neither Anthony nor Steven had any credit with NMR(CI) apart from the (uncleared) cheques for £352,705 above-mentioned and apart from a small sum sufficient to pay the difference between the sale price and the purchase consideration. The figure of £355,162 10s was equal to the middle market price for 184,500 shares at the close of business on 27th October 1969 on the London Stock Exchange. The figure of £352,705 was based on that middle market price, less a negotiated discount sufficient to give Rozel its profit. These figures had been agreed in advance between the solicitor and Rothschilds. In due course the cheques mentioned were cleared by cross-entries arranged between the banks. The trustees' holding of 370,100 Lex shares was at all material times registered in the name of a nominee for NMR(CI) and after 1st November 1969 advice was given to the nominee that 184,500 belonged to each of Anthony and Steven.

There were also arrangements, made by Rozel, to insure against the risk of Anthony or Steven dying within the three-day period, but I think that these are neutral as regards the issues now arising, and that what might have happened as regards the shares if Anthony or Steven had so died throws no light on what did happen when, in fact, they survived.

It is undisputed that the sale of the contingent interests, taken alone, brought about no charge to capital gains tax. But the Crown claims that tax is due on three alternative bases. It is sufficient for the Crown to succeed on any one of these.

1. It is claimed, in the first place, that the transactions are caught by the initial words of s 42(2) because each of Anthony and Steven (I shall confine myself to Anthony to whom this appeal relates) were 'beneficiaries under the settlement' in respect of 184,500 settlement shares. Anthony, on the other hand, contends that it was Rozel that, on 1st November 1969, became beneficially entitled to these shares, and, being neither resident

nor ordinarily resident in the United Kingdom, was not liable to capital gains tax. The latter contention can only be valid, in my opinion, if the chain of operations set in motion on 28th October 1969 can be arrested on 1st November when the contingent interests were vested. It is said that on the documents, which it is not suggested were shams, it can and should be so arrested.

In this context it is necessary to look at the findings of the Special Commissioners. They had narrated first, before making their formal findings, that in essence the scheme was that NMR(CI) would procure and finance the purchase by Rozel of contingent interests in Lex shares which Anthony and Steven would acquire by virtue of appointments to be made by the trustees of the settlement. On the vesting of those interests three days later, Anthony and Steven would repurchase the Lex shares with the money received from a sale of their contingent interests. They went on to find that ([1978] 1 All ER 65 at 73–74, [1977] STC 468 at 476–477)—

> 'There was a single scheme which was planned from the outset with the object of vesting one half of 369,000 Lex shares in each of [Anthony and Steven] absolutely without incurring liability to capital gains tax ... There was never any possibility that [Anthony and Steven] and Rozel would complete the sale (stage (ii) above) and not go on to execute and eventually complete the purchase (stage (iii) above), for that would have defeated the financial arrangements previously made and finally worked out on 28 October. Rozel was paid to participate in the purchase and sale for a pre-arranged fee. It was at all times intended that Rozel would sell the Lex shares it would acquire on 1 November to [Anthony and Steven]. If, immediately after the execution of the assignments (stage (ii)), news had come by telephone of some calamity which would halve the value of the shares, it is unthinkable that Rothschild's would have allowed [Anthony and Steven] to refuse to proceed with the purchase at the price the basis for which had been arranged, and equally unthinkable that they would have attempted to do so.'

In relation to pre-arranged, predrafted, tax avoidance schemes I may repeat what I said in *Inland Revenue Comrs v Plummer* ([1979] 3 All ER 775 at 779, [1980] AC 896 at 907, [1979] STC 793 at 797):

> 'The plan now involved was explained by the brokers in great detail, and its intended accomplishment set out, with timetables, in almost military precision. This (as I ventured to suggest in *Inland Revenue Comrs v Church Comrs for England* [1976] 2 All ER 1037, [1977] AC 329, [1976] STC 339) entitles and requires us to look at the plan as a whole. It does not entitle us to disregard the legal form and nature of the transactions carried out.'

In this case the plan as a whole, by a chain of transactions set in motion on 31st March 1969, or, effectively, on 28th October 1969, and intended to be carried through without further action, called for the vesting in Anthony of 184,500 Lex shares previously held by the settlement. I have said 'without further action' because NMR(CI) had, on instructions from Anthony and from Rozel, and as trustees of the settlement, the power, the duty and the money to complete the scheme as from 28th October 1969. The machinery had been started, and would follow out its instructions without further human initiative.

As regards the shares, it is clear that it was never the intention of Anthony, or of Rozel, that these should be purchased or held by Rozel: Anthony would never have agreed to assign his contingent interest unless he had established that he would get the shares on 1st November if he survived; Rozel would never have agreed to acquire the contingent interest (for £352,705 which it could not find) unless it had established that Anthony would buy the shares on 1st November for £355,162 10s: its only interest was in earning the small sum of £2,457 10s for its services.

It is contended by Anthony that, even granted the interdependence of the transaction of sale and purchase, there is nothing to show that the 184,500 shares acquired by him were the shares previously held in the settlement. The contract it was said referred merely to the purchase of the specified number of shares and not to any particular shares. Reliance was placed on the agreement of 28th October 1969 in which the shares to be sold by Rozel were described as 'One hundred and eighty-four Thousand Five Hundred (184,500) Ordinary Shares of Five shillings (5/-) each of Lex Garages Limited' without the addition of any words identifying these shares with the settlement shares. I regard this argument as wholly unreal.

It was of course clear that there could be no question of Rozel going into the market in order to buy 184,500 shares in Lex. It had no money with which to do so, and there could be no certainty that it could have acquired so considerable a block at the quoted market price, still less deliver them on 1st November 1969, which date was of the essence of the contract. If by some inconceivable means it did, it would be landed with two parcels of 184,500 shares, only one of which Anthony had agreed to repurchase, for the other of which it could not pay on the settlement date. So the mutual intention can only have been that the shares to be sold to Anthony should be settlement shares, and since the transaction could only be carried out in this way, there was no need to specify in the sale agreement that the shares should come from this source. If an agreement can only be carried out in one way, it is superfluous to mention that one way specifically in the agreement: the parties are presumed to intend it.

Then Anthony contended that, granted the identity of the shares sold with the settlement shares, he could not be regarded as a beneficiary in respect of them because he could not get specific performance of the agreement. This was said to be because the law of Guernsey does not recognise specific performance. It may be open to argument whether this is so or not, and whether in any case specific performance could be obtained in England. But in my opinion the whole contention is misconceived. The legal title to the shares was at all times vested in a nominee for NMR(CI), and dealings related to the equitable interest in these required no formality. As soon as there was an agreement for their sale accompanied or followed by payment of the price, the equitable title passed at once to the purchaser, viz Anthony, and all that was needed to perfect his title was notice to the trustees or the nominee, which notice both had at all material times. Consequently, the trustees were bound to transfer the shares to Anthony immediately the interests vested on 1st November 1969, and Anthony was the beneficiary, under the settlement, as regards the shares.

2. The second contention for the Crown was founded on the terms of s 42(2) quoted above. It is said that it is sufficient for the purposes of this subsection for a beneficiary to be a beneficiary under the settlement at any time during the year of assessment in which the chargeable gain accrues. Since Anthony was such a beneficiary by virtue of the appointment, and even if thereafter Rozel became the beneficiary, the charge attaches. Support for this argument was drawn from other provisions in the Finance Act 1965. This argument was not raised in either court below and appears not to have been put forward in any previous case. For this reason, and because I am not satisfied that the consequences of its success have been fully explored, I prefer to reserve my opinion on it for another occasion.

3. The Crown's third contention arises out of the definition of 'settlement' in s 42(7). This incorporates the extension of the word to include any 'arrangement'. The scheme as a whole, it is said, constituted an arrangement, under which Anthony was a beneficiary. The word 'arrangement' is wide in scope, and may include a combination, or series, of transactions some of which may be for consideration or of a commercial character (see *Inland Revenue Comrs v Payne* (1941) 23 Tax Cas 610). In *Inland Revenue Comrs v Plummer* [1979] 3 All ER 775, [1980] AC 896, [1979] STC 793 it was decided, in order to place some limitation on the extent of the word, that there must be an element of bounty in the transaction, a conception admittedly not without its difficulty. In this case I have no difficulty in finding this test satisfied. It was part, an essential part, of the arrangement that interests under the settlement should be appointed to Anthony (and Steven). This was done on 28th October 1969. Before that date, the interest of each son

was liable to be overridden by an exercise of the power of appointment, which might wholly exclude him; after that date each son had a contingent interest, likely to become vested after three days, in 184,500 shares. I fail to see how this can be regarded otherwise than as an act of bounty in their favour, and that, taken together with the sale and repurchase, makes an arrangement. If it be said that there must be an act of bounty of the settlor and that the latter had fully divested himself of his settled property when he made the settlement, I would reply that his bounty was at that point incomplete, and became completed only when an appointment was made, thereby, as it were, filling in the names of his intended beneficiaries. If one looks at the whole scheme more broadly, Anthony and Steven at the end of it became entitled to shares worth over £350,000 for which they had not provided consideration (other than the small amount of Rozel's commission) and this was brought about by the action of the settlor and of the trustees. If the word 'arrangement' does not cover this, its presence in the definition is hard to appreciate.

I hold therefore that the Crown succeeds on each of the two points I have considered, and consequently that the appeal should be allowed.

LORD FRASER OF TULLYBELTON. My Lords, I have found the questions in this appeal more difficult than my noble and learned friends Lord Wilberforce and Lord Roskill have done, but, having had the benefit of reading their speeches in draft, I now agree with their reasoning and with their conclusions that the first and third issues should be answered in favour of the Crown. Like my noble and learned friends I, too, reserve my opinion on the second issue, viz whether it is sufficient for the purpose of s 42(2) for a beneficiary to be such at any time during the year of assessment.

I would allow the appeal.

LORD RUSSELL OF KILLOWEN. My Lords, I must admit that I have found the solution of this appeal one of great difficulty. I am in the end persuaded that the appeal should be allowed.

The fact that the purpose of the scheme was that the sons should become each beneficially entitled to an aliquot portion 184500/370100 of the settled funds without suffering capital gains tax does not of course mean that it must fail in that purpose, nor even that it ought to fail. As always in matters of taxation the question involved is the applicability of legislation to the methods adopted in carrying out the scheme.

There were in this case (I refer for convenience only to the son Anthony), as it seems to me, two matters of crucial importance. The first is that on 28th October the record on the turntable which was switched on contained the whole story from beginning to end, and there was no provision for switching it off half way. The second is that having regard to the scheme as a whole I find it quite unreal to construe the agreement by Anthony to purchase from Rozel and Rozel to sell (in which agreement time was of the essence) 184,500 shares in Lex as anything other than to repurchase the aliquot interest in the settled funds which had been the subject of the contingent appointment on its expected maturing to an absolute interest.

It is true that, on 28th October Rozel became by assignment entitled under the settlement to Anthony's contingent aliquot share. But that entitlement was qualified and restricted by the contemporaneously accepted obligation to reinstate Anthony as entitled absolutely thereto on its maturing into an absolute interest. There was here no question of specific performance. Throughout the parties were concerned with equitable interests in the aliquot share. The transactions were not 'sham' in the sense that what was said in the documents was not intended. But what was said and intended had the effect which I have summarised above.

It is said that, if Anthony had died within the three days, Rozel would have not become entitled to the aliquot appointed share, having only acquired a contingent interest which had failed to mature. In such case on the documents Rozel it is said would have had to pay the £352,000-odd to Anthony's estate and would on the construction of

the share sale agreement have been obliged to acquire in the market 184,500 Lex shares
with the help of the insurance moneys and sell to Anthony's estate for £355,000-odd.
The situation which might have arisen had Anthony prematurely died, which
incidentally on analysis of the pros and cons of the possible transactions in that event
suggests that some aspects or consequences may not have been fully thought out, does
not persuade me to a view other than that the share sale agreement, in the expected
events which happened, related to the aliquot interest of Anthony under the settlement
on its maturing into an absolute interest.

On the above basis I find myself in agreement with the conclusion of my noble and
learned friend Lord Wilberforce that the first of the three contentions advanced by the
Crown is correct, and that on that ground this appeal should be allowed.

On the third point of the Crown, the 'arrangement' point, I am also in agreement that
it succeeds. But on the second point of the Crown, the new point, I too would prefer to
express no present opinion.

Accordingly I too would allow this appeal.

LORD ROSKILL. My Lords, the issue for determination in this appeal is whether a
tax avoidance scheme, known as 'the contingent interest scheme', the architects of which
seemingly were Rothschilds, successfully achieved its avowed purpose enabling Anthony
Chinn ('Anthony') and his brother Steven Chinn ('Steven') to avoid liability for large
sums claimed by the Crown in capital gains tax. Only Anthony's case was argued before
your Lordships' House, it being common ground that Steven's case was indistinguishable
and must be governed by whatever result was reached in Anthony's appeal.

My Lords, this case has given rise to a remarkable, but perhaps not surprising,
difference of judicial opinion. The Special Commissioners held that the scheme did not
achieve its objective. Templeman J agreed. Anthony's, and therefore Steven's, appeal
against the assessments respectively made on them, accordingly failed. But the Court of
Appeal (Buckley, Goff and Shaw LJJ) disagreed. Both Buckley and Goff LJJ delivered
elaborate judgments differing strongly from the views expressed by Templeman J. Shaw
LJ did not, however, deliver a separate judgment. From those judgments of the Court
of Appeal, and with the leave of that court, the Crown appealed to your Lordships'
House.

My Lords, the story starts with a settlement made by Mr Chinn senior ('the settlor'),
the father of Anthony and Steven, on 24th February 1960. The settlor was at that time
the owner of a very large block of 5s ordinary shares in Lex Garages Ltd ('Lex'). The
settlor in due course transferred to the trustees of this settlement 370,100 of those
ordinary shares, some 9% of the total issued ordinary share capital of Lex, a public
company with its shares quoted on the London Stock Exchange. Until 31st March 1969
the trustees of the settlement all resided in this country. The value of the Lex shares in
the settlement had greatly increased since the settlement was created in 1960.

The settlement contained an overriding power of appointment exercisable by the
trustees with the consent of the settlor in favour, inter alios, of Anthony and Steven. It
also gave the settlor power to appoint new trustees.

Between 1960, when the settlement was created, and 1969, when the scheme with
which your Lordships are concerned was put into effect, capital gains tax was imposed by
Part III of the Finance Act 1965. That Act by s 19 provided for such tax to be charged
'in respect of capital gains, that is to say, chargeable gains computed in accordance with
this Act and accruing to a person on the disposal of assets'. If, therefore, the trustees were
to exercise their overriding power of appointment with, of course, the consent of the
settlor in favour of Anthony or Steven, or of both, in respect of all or any of the Lex shares
then held by them on the trusts of the settlement, there would, or at least might, have
been a 'disposal of assets', attracting capital gains tax, which on the then value of these
shares was likely to be onerous.

Not unnaturally the trustees and the settlor were anxious that Anthony and Steven
should acquire some or all of these Lex shares absolutely, but, if possible, without

incurring any liability to capital gains tax. The Special Commissioners found that from the outset, by which they clearly meant early in 1969, there was a 'single scheme', I venture to stress those last two words, which was planned with the object of vesting a large number of the relevant Lex shares in Anthony and Steven absolutely without incurring their liability to capital gains tax (see [1978] 1 All ER 65 at 73, [1977] STC 468 at 476).

The successive steps which this single scheme involved are very clearly summarised in the stated case and in the judgments in the courts below. They are fully related in the speech of my noble and learned friend Lord Wilberforce and are summarised in the judgment of Buckley LJ in the Court of Appeal ([1979] 2 All ER 529 at 531–533, [1979] Ch 447 at 454–456, [1979] STC 332 at 334–336). They require no further repetition by me.

But to those statements I would add these further considerations. First, legal title to all the Lex ordinary shares in question was, at all material times, vested in Old Court Ltd, a Rothschilds company, as nominee for NMR(CI), after that latter company became one of the non-resident trustees of the 1960 settlement. Second, none of these shares ever physically left London but at all times remained in the possession of their legal owners. Third, the various interests in the shares which were or purported to be the subject of the several transactions with which your Lordships are now concerned were equitable interests and, in the first instance, only contingent equitable interests.

Templeman J held that as a result of these several transactions the beneficiary who, on 1st November 1969 when the contingent interest vested, became as against the trustees absolutely entitled to the 184,500 settlement shares comprised in the appointment was Anthony, who, being resident and ordinarily resident in the United Kingdom, was liable under s 42(2) of the Finance Act 1965 to pay the capital gains tax which became, therefore, payable under s 25(3) of that Act. This was the principal ground on which Templeman J decided the appeal in favour of the Crown. It was with this conclusion that the Court of Appeal all disagreed, holding that Anthony was not such a beneficiary.

The first question, as I have already indicated, is therefore whether Anthony was a beneficiary under the settlement so as to be liable to capital gains tax under s 42(2). The second question argued in the courts below was whether, by reason of the definition of settlement in s 42(7) and the consequent importation into s 42 of the provisions of s 411(2) of the Income Tax Act 1952, this settlement was an 'arrangement' within that subsection. This question was argued third before your Lordships since the Crown sought and obtained from your Lordships leave to make a new submission based on s 42(2) of the Finance Act 1965 which had not been argued below, and on which therefore your Lordships have not had the benefit of the views of the learned judge and of the Court of Appeal. This new submission was argued second before your Lordships, but in view of the conclusion I have reached on the two main issues argued below I shall deal first with those issues.

My Lords, on the first issue the difference of opinion between Templeman J and the Court of Appeal, though fundamental, in my judgment turns on a somewhat narrow point of the interpretation of the relevant documents and of the facts found in the stated case. Templeman J emphatically took the view that the shares which ultimately Anthony acquired from Rozel on 1st November 1969 on the performance of the last of the acts which this single scheme involved were the same shares as those Anthony's contingent interest in which Rozel had previously agreed to purchase from him, the trustees having already exercised their power of appointment in Anthony's favour, contingent on his surviving for three days from 28th October 1969. That in the event the interest in the shares which actually passed from Anthony to Rozel and back to Anthony was an interest in the same shares throughout is beyond question. But the crucial issue is whether the numerous complex documents to which this tax avoidance scheme gave birth necessarily involved that this should be so. The view which appealed to Buckley LJ was that the scheme involved no appointment of any specific shares to Anthony, and that the share sale agreement was—

'a straightforward agreement for sale and purchase of 184,500 Lex ordinary shares without reference to the provenance of the subject-matter. On the face of these documents I can see no justification for saying that the share sale agreement was a contract for the sale and purchase of particular shares to which Rozel would become entitled under the settlement and appointment.'

(See [1979] 2 All ER 529 at 535, [1979] Ch 447 at 458–459, [1979] STC 332 at 338.) Goff LJ took the same view (see [1979] 2 All ER 529 at 542, [1979] Ch 447 at 467, [1979] STC 332 at 345).

Before your Lordships this conclusion was further supported by the existence of the life policy on Anthony's life lest he did not survive the requisite three days, which was a prerequisite for the completion of the scheme. The money payable under that policy, in the event of Anthony's premature death, could, it was submitted, have been available for the purchase by Rozel of the same number of Lex ordinary shares on the market.

It is entirely correct, as the Court of Appeal emphasised, that the shares which were the subject of the successive transactions which this single scheme involved were never specifically identified by number in any relevant document. They were identified in those documents solely by description. My Lords, I do not find this surprising since there was never any intention of the shares themselves being physically the subject of any transaction. As I have already mentioned, legal title to all the shares held by the trustees remained in Old Court Ltd; the shares themselves were at all times physically in London. The transactions involved the transfers of equitable or of contingent equitable interests only. Certainly the share sale agreement, if read in isolation from all the other documents and the factual background against which these transactions fall to be considered, is, on its face, a contract only for the sale and purchase of a stated number of shares of a particular description and class.

But, my Lords, with profound respect to those who have taken a different view, I find it impossible to construe the share sale agreement in isolation from its companion documents and from the factual background, especially in view of the finding that this was a single scheme. In the courts below there was much argument whether in English law specific performance would have been ordered of the relevant obligations. Before your Lordships this submission was barely touched on by learned counsel, but it was suggested that, if the relevant documents, and especially the share sale agreement, on their true construction were not dealing with the same specific shares throughout, the share sale agreement could be rectified so as to give effect to what was said to have been, on the evidence, the clear prior common intention of all parties to the various documents. My Lords, I find it unnecessary to consider problems of specific performance or of rectification, for I do not think either arises. The question is one of construction. If it had been permissible to ask any of the parties by reference to what block of shares they were dealing throughout their answer must be to the same 184,500 of the larger number of Lex ordinary shares comprised in the settlement. But I do not find it necessary to go outside the relevant documents to reach the same answer as a matter of the true construction of those documents. I have not in reaching this conclusion lost sight of the point made on the policy of life insurance. But I find it impossible to think, having regard to the narrow time limits involved, that the parties can ever have contemplated that the proceeds of this policy should be used to purchase the same number of shares on the open market which might subsequently be tendered to Anthony's personal representatives in fulfilment of Rozel's obligations under that share sale agreement. This number of shares has represented a not unsubstantial proportion of the total issued share capital of Lex and it was never envisaged that immediate control of those shares should ever pass from members of the Chinn family. The clear intention was that the beneficial interest in the actual shares in question should pass from the trustees to Anthony.

My Lords, on the first question I might have contented myself by saying that I am in complete agreement with the speech of my noble and learned friend Lord Wilberforce and with the judgment of Templeman J. But in deference to those who have taken a different view I have thought it right to set out my own reasons for my conclusions.

I turn to deal briefly with the question argued third before your Lordships, and second in the courts below. Strictly, in view of the conclusion on the first question, it is not necessary to deal with this further question. But I think your Lordships should do so as the matter was fully debated in argument.

My Lords, was this settlement an 'arrangement' within s 411(2) of the Income Tax Act 1952, which as already stated, is incorporated into the Finance Act 1965 by s 42(7) of that statute? Templeman J held that it was such an arrangement, dealing with this question only briefly at the end of his judgment. The Court of Appeal who dealt with this question much more elaborately held that it was not.

In *Inland Revenue Comrs v Plummer* [1979] 3 All ER 775, [1980] AC 896, [1979] STC 793 your Lordships have recently had to consider the problem to which this section gives rise. On the authorities as they now stand it seems clear that if the particular transaction is a commercial transaction devoid of any element of what has been called 'bounty' it is not within the section and the majority of your Lordships in *Plummer's* case accepted that the transaction there in question escaped as being a commercial transaction without the necessary element of 'bounty'.

My Lords, the relevant authorities go back long before s 411 was placed on the statute book and first arose out of one of the statutory predecessors of that section. Those authorities are collected in the judgment of Buckley LJ in the present case ([1979] 2 All ER 529 at 539, [1979] Ch 447 at 463–464, [1979] STC 332 at 342), and in your Lordships' judgments in *Plummer's* case and no useful purpose will be served by a further review of them.

My Lords, the sole question here is whether there was the requisite element of 'bounty' in this transaction so as to make it an 'arrangement' within this subsection. It was argued for Anthony that the settlor's 'bounty' had been exhausted in 1960 when he created the settlement and that there was no exercise of 'bounty' by the trustees as they possessed no beneficial interest in respect of which they could be bountiful. This was the view which appealed to the Court of Appeal.

My Lords, I would venture to point out that the word 'bounty' appears nowhere in the statute. It is not a word of definition. It is a judicial gloss on the statute descriptive of those classes of cases which are caught by the section in contrast to those which are not. The courts must, I think, be extremely careful not to interpret this descriptive word too rigidly. I would recall some sapient observations of Frankfurter J in *Tiller v Atlantic Coast Line Railroad Co* (1943) 318 US 54 at 68:

'A phrase begins life as a literary expression; its felicity leads to its lazy repetition; and repetition soon establishes it as a legal formula, undiscriminatingly used to express different and sometimes contradictory ideas.'

What the cases have sought to do is to distinguish between those cases where the recipient has in return for that benefit which he has received accepted some obligation which he has to perform, either before receiving the benefit or at some stated time thereafter, and those cases where the recipient benefits without any assumption by him of any correlative obligation. In *Plummer's* case the transaction in question was for consideration. Under this scheme there was an appointment without consideration. Anthony was among the objects of the 1960 settlement but before the power of appointment was exercised there was no absolute certainty, however strong the probability, that Anthony would receive any of the shares held by the trustees. In my judgment there was a very real 'bounty' conferred when the trustees with the settlor's consent exercised the power of appointment in question in Anthony's favour. As counsel for the Crown put it, when the power of appointment was exercised a blank was filled in the original settlement which left blank how the final distribution of the trust's assets was to be made. That in my judgment was a clear act of 'bounty'.

It follows that on this question as on the first, I find myself in complete agreement with Templeman J and in respectful disagreement with the Court of Appeal.

For those reasons, therefore, I would allow the appeal and restore the judgment of Templeman J confirming the determination of the Special Commissioners.

My Lords, there remains the third question, argued second before your Lordships, which your Lordships gave leave to raise for the first time in your Lordships' House. The Crown's submissions arose under s 42(2) and ran thus. If the 1960 settlement was a settlement within the subsection as it was submitted it clearly was, then in order to be a 'beneficiary' under that settlement all that was necessary was that that description should be satisfied *at some time* during the relevant year of assessment. That which would then fall to be apportioned is that part of the amount to which the trustees would have been chargeable if domiciled in the United Kingdom.

The contrary submission, stated briefly, was that the liability under the subsection arose only at the time the chargeable gain accrued, and support for this submission was sought from s 42(3)(a). But it was pointed out for the Crown that this submission involved writing into the subsection words such as 'at the time the chargeable gain accrued'; such words were present in s 41(5) and therefore there was no justification for writing these words into s 42(2) where they did not appear.

My Lords, I have thought it right briefly to record the rival submissions. The question is novel and to my mind difficult. It is not necessary to decide it in this appeal and I think your Lordships should leave it for decision until it is necessary to decide it. In the result I would allow the appeal by the Crown with costs here and below.

Appeal allowed.

Solicitors: *Solicitor of Inland Revenue ; Berwin Leighton* (for the taxpayer).

Rengan Krishnan Esq   Barrister.

Re Woodhams (deceased)
Lloyds Bank Ltd v London College of Music and others

CHANCERY DIVISION
VINELOTT J
8th MAY, 23rd JULY 1980

Charity – Cy-près doctrine – General charitable intention – Method of determining general charitable intention – Will – Particular charitable purpose expressed in will impracticable – Gifts of residue to music colleges for music scholarships for orphans from named charitable homes – Adequate public grants available for musical education of such orphans – Colleges considering it impractical to restrict scholarships as required by will – Colleges only prepared to accept gift if restriction removed – Whether gift failing to take effect ab initio – Whether restriction on scholarships essential part of testator's scheme – Whether testator showing general charitable intention to further music by founding scholarships.

The testator was a musician and teacher of music. By his will made on 2nd November 1956 he left a number of small legacies to individuals, two of which showed a charitable intention to benefit orphans' homes, namely Dr Barnardo's or the Church of England Children's Society homes. The will then directed that the residue, on the expiration of a life interest, was to be divided between two colleges of music with which the testator had long been connected, to be used by them to found annual scholarships 'for the complete musical education of a promising boy who is an absolute orphan and only of British Nationality and Birth from any one of the Dr Barnardo's Homes or the Church of England Children's Society Homes'. The testator died in November 1968 and at the date of his death the amount of his residuary estate was sufficient to finance an annual scholarship at each college in accordance with the terms of the will. Neither college was prepared, however, to accept the bequest when it fell due because in their view, having regard to the decrease in the number of orphans and the adequacy of public grants to educate those that had musical ability, it would be impractical to restrict the scholarships as required by the terms of the will. The colleges were however prepared to accept the bequest if it could be used to provide scholarships for any boys of British nationality and birth to complete their musical education. The testator's executor and trustee sought the determination of the court whether the residuary bequests to the colleges failed altogether because the colleges had refused to accept them on the terms of the will or whether, if the bequests failed for impracticability, they could be applied cy-près under a scheme. The next of kin entitled under an intestacy of the residue contended that the terms of the will showed that, apart from the specific legacies to individuals, the testator intended to devote his estate to further two charitable objects, namely music and the welfare of orphans cared for by the named homes, and to delete the requirement that the bequests should be used to found scholarships for orphans from the named homes would frustrate the testator's intention.

Held – (1) The jurisdiction of the court to direct a scheme for carrying out the trusts of a charitable gift in a will which would otherwise fail for impracticability was founded on the fact that, although the will directed the mode of applying the gift and therefore gave it for a particular charitable purpose, it was nevertheless possible to say that on the true construction of the will, and notwithstanding the form in which the gift was expressed, there was a paramount intention on the part of the testator to give the property for a general charitable purpose, so that if it were impracticable to give effect to the particular purpose expressed the court could, by a scheme, apply the property for the general charitable purpose. The distinction to be drawn was between, on the one hand, the case where the scheme prescribed by the will could be regarded as the mode by which a general charitable purpose was to be effected, in which case the mode was not the substance of the gift, and, on the other, the case where no part of the scheme in the will could be disregarded as inessential without frustrating the testator's intention. One way to determine that question was to ask whether a modification of the scheme in the will to enable the gift to be carried into effect at the relevant time would frustrate the testator's intention as disclosed in the will, interpreted in the light of any admissible evidence of surrounding circumstances (see p 209 *e* to p 210 *d* and *h j*, post); dicta of Lord Eldon LC in *Mills v Farmer* (1815) 19 Ves at 486, of Lindley LJ in *Re Rymer* [1891–4] All ER Rep at 334, of Parker J in *Re Wilson* [1911–13] All ER Rep at 1102–1103, of Younger LJ in *Re Willis* [1921] 1 Ch at 54, of Dixon and Evatt JJ in *Attorney General for New South Wales v Perpetual Trustee Co Ltd* (1940) 63 CLR at 227 and of Buckley J in *Re Lysaght (deceased)* [1965] 2 All ER at 892–893 applied.

(2) On the true construction of the will the intention to be discerned from the bequest of the residue was twofold: to further musical education and to do so by founding scholarships at the two colleges. Although the testator had chosen orphans from the named homes as those most likely to need assistance with musical education, it was not an essential part of his scheme that the scholarships should be restricted to them, and, that being so, that part of the scheme or mode of achieving the testator's charitable purpose could be modified by the court without frustrating his intention. Accordingly the trusts of the residue did not fail, since at the date of the testator's will the trusts could have been carried into effect by a modification of the trust of each moiety by deleting the restriction of the scholarships to orphans from the named homes. It followed that the court would declare that the residuary estate be applied cy-près under a scheme to be settled (see p 212 *c* to *e*, post).

Notes

For impracticable charitable gifts, see 5 Halsbury's Laws (4th Edn) para 649.
  For the consequences of failure of stated objects, see ibid paras 653–657.
  For the jurisdiction of the court to make schemes cy-près, see ibid para 700.
  For cases on conditional gifts, see 8(1) Digest (Reissue) 356–357, 368–370, 866–872, 976–982. For cases on application of the cy-près doctrine, see ibid 400–402, 1350–1371.

Cases referred to in judgment

Attorney General for New South Wales v Perpetual Trustee Co Ltd (1940) 63 CLR 209, 14 ALJ 122, 46 ALR 209, 8(1) Digest (Reissue) 405, *610.
Biscoe v Jackson (1887) 35 Ch D 460, 56 LJ Ch 540, 56 LT 753, CA, 8(1) Digest (Reissue) 404, 1382.
Crowe (deceased), Re, National Westminster Bank Ltd v Balfour (3rd October 1979, unreported).
Dalziel, Re, Midland Bank Executor and Trustee Co Ltd v St Bartholomew's Hospital [1943] 2 All ER 656, [1943] Ch 277, 112 LJ Ch 353, 169 LT 168, 8(1) Digest (Reissue) 294, 366.
Lysaght (deceased), Re, Hill v Royal College of Surgeons of England [1965] 2 All ER 888, [1966] Ch 191, [1965] 3 WLR 391, 8(1) Digest (Reissue) 369, 982.
Mills v Farmer (1815) 19 Ves 483, 1 Mer 55, 34 ER 595, 8(1) Digest (Reissue) 410, 1423.
Mitchell's Will Trusts, Re, Jago v Attorney General (1966) 110 Sol Jo 291, 8(1) Digest (Reissue) 247, 61.
Monk, Re, Giffen v Wedd [1927] 2 Ch 197, 96 LJ Ch 296, 137 LT 4, CA, 8(1) Digest (Reissue) 251, 79.
Packe, Re, Sanders v Attorney General [1918] 1 Ch 437, 87 LJ Ch 300, 118 LT 693, 8(1) Digest (Reissue) 386, 1148.
Rymer, Re, Rymer v Stanfield [1895] 1 Ch 19, [1891–4] All ER Rep 328, 64 LJ Ch 86, 71 LT 590, 12 R 22, CA, 8(1) Digest (Reissue) 352, 840.
Tacon (deceased), Re, Public Trustee v Tacon [1958] 1 All ER 163, [1958] Ch 447, [1958] 2 WLR 66, CA, 8(1) Digest (Reissue) 402, 1371.

Willis, Re, Shaw v Willis [1921] 1 Ch 44, 90 LJ Ch 94, 124 LT 290, CA, 8(1) Digest (Reissue) 411, *1432*.
Wilson, Re, Twentyman v Simpson [1913] 1 Ch 314, [1911–13] All ER Rep 1101, 82 LJ Ch 161, 108 LT 321, 8(1) Digest (Reissue) 356, 869.

Adjourned summons

By an originating summons dated 6th September 1978, as amended, the plaintiff, Lloyds Bank Ltd, the sole executor and trustee of a will dated 2nd November 1956 made by the testator, Herbert George Woodhams deceased, who died on 18th November 1968, applied for: (1) the determination whether on the true construction of the will and in the events which had happened the trusts of the testator's residuary estate declared in the will, which were to take effect from and after the death of Helen Amy Dear, were valid and effectual so that the first and second defendants, the London College of Music and the Tonic Sol-fa Association Ltd, were each entitled to receive and give good receipt for a moiety of the residuary estate, or whether the trusts were invalid for impracticability or otherwise; (2) if the trusts were invalid, the determination whether the property thereby affected fell to be applied cy-près or was subject to the trusts affecting the property if there was an intestacy; (3) if necessary, an order that a scheme be directed for the application of the testator's residuary estate; (4) a direction that the third defendant, Henry George Payne, be appointed to represent for the purposes of the application the persons entitled to property in respect of which the testator died intestate; and (5) if and so far as necessary, administration of the testator's estate. The Attorney General was the fourth defendant to the summons. The facts are set out in the judgment.

John Weeks for the bank.
Robert Ham for the first and second defendants.
Charles Turnbull for the third defendant.
John Mummery for the Attorney General.

Cur adv vult

23rd July.   **VINELOTT J** read the following judgment: The testator, Herbert George Woodhams, died on 18th November 1968. His will, which he made on 2nd November 1956, was proved on 17th January 1969 by Lloyds Bank Ltd (which I will call 'the bank'), the sole executor and trustee named therein. In his will the testator described himself as 'Musician and Teacher of Music'. By cl 4 of his will he gave a number of small pecuniary and some very detailed specific legacies; there were 21 pecuniary and specific legacies in all. Some were given on charitable trusts and have been relied on as throwing light on the questions before me, which relate to the testator's residuary estate.

They are as follows. First, by para (a) of cl 4 the testator gave £200 to the vicar and churchwardens of the church where he should hold the appointment as organist and choirmaster at his death to be spent in the purchase of a piece of furniture which was to bear a tablet with an inscription commemorating him and his family. Secondly, by para (b) he gave the bank £200 conditionally on his holding the appointment of organist at a church at the time of his death on trust to invest the same and pay the income to the vicar and churchwardens of the church to be applied by them for charitable purposes for the benefit of the parish, so long as the vicar and churchwardens should out of the income provide an annual tea and entertainment for the choirboys, with a gift over to a charity to be selected by his trustee (but with preference for Dr Barnardo's Homes) in the event that the vicar and churchwardens should fail to provide an annual tea and entertainment. Thirdly, by para (c) he gave to the London College of Music of Great Marlborough Street his textbooks on musical subjects and his pianoforte music for use in their library and his licentiate and other certificates to be hung in the college building; and he gave his licentiate cap, gown, and hood for use by a deserving male student taking the licentiate for the pianoforte. Fourthly, by para (d) he gave to the Curwen Memorial

College (Tonic Sol-fa College of Music), 9 Queensborough Terrace, his pianoforte, his textbooks on tonic sol-fa and his licentiate and membership certificates, expressing the wish that they should be hung in the college building, and he gave his licentiate hood for the use of a deserving male student for the licentiate for singing; and he gave his copies of services, cantatas, and oratorios for use in the college library. Lastly, by para (u) he gave to the bank £300 on trust to invest the same and to pay the income to the vicar and churchwardens of the church where he should hold the appointment of organist and choirmaster at his death to be applied for charitable purposes, and he directed that the trust should continue for so long as the vicar and churchwardens should 'out of the said income' keep in good order and repair a family grave, keeping the lettering on the gravestones legible and that on failure to observe these conditions the gift should determine and the fund be paid and transferred to a charitable institution selected by the trustee with a preference for Dr Barnardo's Homes or the Church of England Children's Society.

The validity of both of the trusts of the income of this last legacy and of the gift over must be open to serious doubt: see *Re Dalziel* [1943] 2 All ER 656, [1943] Ch 277. There may also be a question whether the provision of a tea and entertainment for choirboys is a charitable purpose, and if it is not whether the trusts of income in para (b) and the gift over in that paragraph are not also void. The validity of these gifts is not one of the questions raised in the originating summons. The amount of the legacies would hardly support the cost of deciding these questions, even if the income were sufficient to maintain the family grave and provide tea and entertainment for the choir. But reliance is placed on the identity of the institutions named as beneficiaries under the gifts over.

The testator gave his residuary estate on usual administrative trusts and directed that the income of the net residue (defined as 'the Trust fund') should be paid to one Helen Amy Dear. Clause 7 reads as follows:

'AFTER the death of the said Helen Amy Dear as to both capital and income to divide the same (IN EQUAL SHARES) between the LONDON COLLEGE OF MUSIC Great Marlborough Street London W.1. and the CURWEN MEMORIAL COLLEGE (Tonic Sol-fa College of Music) 9 Queensborough Terrace Bayswater London W.2. and at each College TO FOUND A SCHOLARSHIP TO BE KNOWN AS THE HERBERT G. WOODHAM'S SCHOLARSHIP for the complete musical education of a promising boy who is an absolute orphan and only of British Nationality and Birth from any one of the Dr. Barnardo's Homes or The Church of England Children's Society Homes at the London College of Music to enable such boy to be educated for the Teacher's Licentiate Diploma in Pianoforte playing and at the Curwen Memorial College for the Associate and Licentiate Diploma (singing) in both notations (music and tonic sol-fa) one boy to each college annually and in each case when the boys have taken their respective Diploma to have the right to state that they are Herbert G. Woodhams' Scholars the selection of boys in each case must rest with the college Authorities.'

The testator made a codicil to his will dated 6th October 1961 whereby after revoking a small pecuniary legacy he confirmed his will.

The gross value of the testator's estate was sworn for the purposes of probate at £12,712. After payment or satisfaction of funeral and testamentary expenses and death duties, and specific and pecuniary legacies, the net residue amounted to £11,437. Helen Amy Dear died on 2nd November 1973. No death duties were payable on her death. At her death the value of the trust fund did not differ significantly from its value at the testator's death. It is now worth approximately £15,700.

The London College of Music was founded in 1887 and incorporated in 1939. It has at all material times provided full-time courses in musical education. It also holds examinations for its own diplomas. One diploma awarded is the licentiate teachers diploma in a musical subject including the pianoforte. The course leading to the diploma is of two or three years' duration. There is evidence in an affidavit by Mr John

Paul Pelham Burn, the warden of the London College, and in correspondence between the London College and the Treasury Solicitor, exhibited to an affidavit filed on behalf of the Attorney General, which is sufficient to justify the inference that in the circumstances known or foreseeable at the death of the testator a half-share of his residuary estate would probably have sufficed at the time when it might have been expected to fall into possession, to found a scholarship which could have been administered by the London College strictly in accordance with the terms of the will.

So far no difficulty arises. However, the London College have made it clear that they would not have been willing to accept the bequest of a half-share of the testator's residuary estate at or at any time after the testator's death if the college would thereby have become bound to use the bequest to found and administer a scholarship to be awarded strictly in accordance with the directions in the testator's will. While the London College would have been and would now be prepared to accept the bequest and to found and administer a scholarship to assist a male of British nationality and birth to study for the teacher's licentiate diploma in the pianoforte, it would not then have been willing and is not now willing to found and administer such a scholarship if subject to a further condition restricting it to absolute orphans coming from one of Dr Barnardo's homes or the Church of England Children's Society homes. The reason given in Mr Burn's affidavit and in correspondence with the Treasury Solicitor, as elaborated in argument by counsel for the London College, is that in the post-war world there has been a decrease in the number of absolute orphans brought up in those homes and at the same time an increase in public moneys available for the musical education of promising boys. Local authority grants are mandatory for the college's school music courses and discretionary in the case of the professional courses; but even in the field of discretionary grants an absolute orphan from one of the named homes, who proved to have musical ability, would be a strong candidate for a grant. The advantage to the London College of a scholarship to be awarded by it would be to enable the college to make a discretionary award to a promising boy who did not qualify for a full grant or who for some other reason might not be able to complete his course without assistance. In these circumstances, the London College feel that the creation of a scholarship strictly in accordance with the conditions in the testator's will would create problems which would more than outweigh any practical benefit which might be derived from it.

The position of the institute described as the Curwen Memorial College (Tonic Sol-fa College of Music) is more complex. At the dates of the will, the codicil, and the testator's death there was in existence a company originally called the Tonic Sol-fa College which later changed its name to the Tonic Sol-fa College of Music and which I will call 'the old Tonic Sol-fa College'. It had been founded in 1863 and incorporated in 1875. Its purpose was to propagate the method of teaching music devised and advocated in the writings of a Mr John Curwen. The testator was a long-standing member of the council of the old Tonic Sol-fa College. After the war the old Tonic Sol-fa College carried on its activities under the name 'the Curwen Memorial College', the name of the old Tonic Sol-fa College carrying, it was thought, an old-fashioned image. The Curwen Memorial College has never had any separate existence. There can be no doubt that the old Tonic Sol-fa College is the body described by the testator as 'the Curwen Memorial College (the Tonic Sol-fa College of Music)'.

The activities of the old Tonic Sol-fa College included the holding of examinations and the awarding of certificates, scholarships, and diplomas. It also held subsidised summer schools for students. In 1950 or thereabouts the council decided that it would try to accommodate full-time students, but this project was not a success. The old Tonic Sol-fa College ceased to provide regular tuition for an enrolled student body in 1966, that is after the testator made his codicil but before his death. The old Tonic Sol-fa College finally abandoned the project of providing a full-time musical education in 1970 and in 1971 it formally resolved that 'General Musical Teaching at the College will cease as from the end of the present term (July, 1971)'. However, returning to the position at the testator's death, an affidavit has been filed on behalf of the defendant, the Tonic Sol-fa

Association Ltd (which, as I shall later explain, has taken over the assets of the old Tonic Sol-fa College), by one Bernard Rainbow, the chairman of the association and formerly for many years the chairman of the old Tonic Sol-fa College. Mr Rainbow's evidence is that at the testator's death the old Tonic Sol-fa College, under the name of the Curwen Memorial College, could have provided a complete musical education, including tuition in a wide variety of instrumental playing, singing, harmony, counterpoint, and sight-singing by means of the conventional and the tonic sol-fa notations, though that education would have been provided on the basis of individual teaching or coaching and not to a full-time enrolled student body, and that at that time the old Tonic Sol-fa College still examined for and awarded (to cite from the will) 'the Associate and Licentiate Diploma (singing) in both notations (music and tonic sol-fa)'. The evidence of Mr Rainbow, as amplified in correspondence between the Treasury Solicitor and the solicitors for the association, and as elaborated by counsel for the association, is that in the light of the circumstances known or reasonably foreseeable at the testator's death the old Tonic Sol-fa College would have expected that a half-share of the testator's residuary estate when it fell into possession would be sufficient to found a scholarship which could then have been administered by the old Tonic Sol-fa College in accordance with all the conditions in the testator's will. However, like the London College, the old Tonic Sol-fa College would not then or at any time thereafter have been willing to accept the bequest on terms that it should be used to found a scholarship confined to applicants who were absolute orphans from one of Dr Barnardo's homes or the Church of England Children's Society homes, though it would have accepted the bequest and have founded and administered a scholarship to be awarded to a promising boy of British nationality and birth.

In 1975 the defendant association was incorporated and in 1976 the old Tonic Sol-fa College was dissolved and its assets transferred to the association. The association carries on two activities. First, under the name 'the Curwen Institute' it organises and disseminates a new tonic sol-fa method of music teaching using a new notation recommended by a working party set up by the old Tonic Sol-fa College. Secondly, it continues under the name 'the Tonic Sol-fa College' to cater for the needs of those who wish to continue to use the old notation. Although the old college ceased to provide any general musical education in 1971 the association has revived the summer schools which were one of the original and central features of the old Tonic Sol-fa College activities. A summer school was started under the name of the Curwen Institute in conjunction with the Britten Pears School of Advanced Musical Studies at Snape in 1979. These developments are, of course, irrelevant to the question which I have to decide, which is whether the bequest of a half-share of the testator's residuary estate failed to take effect ab initio. They are relevant to the further question as to the way in which that moiety should be applied if a cy-près application is possible. The association propose that a half-share of the residuary estate be used to endow the summer schools so as to enable free places to be made available, preference being given to suitable candidates presented by Dr Barnardo's Homes and the Church of England Children's Society homes.

It is clear that the testator intended that on the death of Helen Amy Dear a half-share of his residuary estate should be transferred to each of the London College and the old Tonic Sol-fa College and intended that the scholarships which he wanted to provide should be founded and administered by the London College and the old Tonic Sol-fa College and by no one else. Thus each bequest was, in effect, conditional on the London College and the old Tonic Sol-fa College (as the case may be) being willing to accept the bequest as trustee on trust to found a scholarship in accordance with the terms of the will. The willingness of the London College or the old Tonic Sol-fa College to accept the bequest on those terms must, of course, be determined at the date of the testator's death when the bequest first vested in interest and in the light of circumstances and reasonable expectations at that time (see *Re Tacon* *(deceased)* [1958] 1 All ER 163, [1958] Ch 447). The question which I have to decide is whether the fact that each of the London College and the old Tonic Sol-fa College would have refused to accept a reversionary interest in a half-share of the residuary estate on terms that they would be bound when the interest fell into possession to found and administer scholarships restricted to absolute orphans from one of the named homes has the consequence that the residuary gifts fails altogether.

A similar question (but without the complication of an intervening life interest) arose in *Re Lysaght (deceased)* [1965] 2 All ER 888, [1966] Ch 191. In that case a testatrix gave a legacy to the Royal College of Surgeons on trust to apply the income in establishing and maintaining scholarships of a specified amount tenable for a term of one to five years. She set out detailed conditions restricting the class of persons to whom studentships might be awarded and governing the courses of study to be followed by the holders of studentships and conferred wide discretions on the council of the college to revoke studentships and to call on students for reports. One of the qualifications was that a student must be 'a British born subject and not of the Jewish or Roman Catholic faith'. The college refused to accept the bequest if it bound them to restrict the class of persons amongst whom it might award studentships to those who were not of the Jewish or Roman Catholic faith. The college was willing to accept the bequest if that restriction was deleted. Buckley J held that the court could, by way of a scheme, modify the terms of the trust by deleting that restriction. In reaching this conclusion he made some general observations as to the meaning of the 'general charitable intent' which has to be shown before the court can modify the terms of a charitable gift which would otherwise fail for impracticability. He took the example of four imaginary testators ([1965] 2 All ER 888 at 892–893, [1966] Ch 191 at 201–202):

'The first bequeaths a fund for charitable purposes generally, the second for the relief of poverty, the third for the relief of poverty in the parish of "X", the fourth for the relief of a particular class of poor (for example, of a particular faith or of a particular age group) in the parish of "X". Each of them couples with his bequest an indication of a particular manner in which the gift should be carried into effect, say, by paying the fares of poor persons travelling by rail from the village of "X" to the town of "Y" to obtain medical advice and attention. Between the dates of the wills and of the deaths of the four testators the railway between "X" and "Y" is closed, so that it becomes impossible for anyone to travel by rail from one to the other. In each case the court must consider whether it was an essential part of the testator's intention that his benefaction should be carried into effect in all respects in the particular manner indicated and no other, or whether his true intention was, in the first case to make a gift for charitable purposes without qualification; in the second, to relieve poverty; in the third, to relieve poverty in the parish of "X"; and in the fourth, to relieve the poverty of the particular class of persons in the parish of "X"; the specification of a particular mode of giving effect to such intention being merely an indication of a desire on his part in this respect (see the well known passage in the judgment of PARKER, J., in *Re Wilson, Twentyman v. Simpson* ([1913] 1 Ch 314 at 320–321, [1911–13] All ER Rep 1101 at 1102–1103). If on the true construction of any of the wills the latter is the true view, the court will, if it can, carry the testator's true intention into effect in some other way cy-près to the impracticable method indicated by the testator. In so doing the court is not departing from the testator's intention but giving effect to his true paramount intention. Such an intention is called a general charitable intention. It is not general in the sense of being unqualified in any way or as being confined only to some general head of charity. It is general in contrast with the particular charitable intention which would have been shown by any of the four supposed testators who on the true construction of his will intended to benefit poor people by paying their railway fares when travelling by rail between "X" and "Y" to obtain medical advice and attention and in no other way. Such a general intention would not avail if the court could find no practical or legal method of giving effect to it—if, for instance, it could be shown in respect of the bequest of the fourth testator that at the relevant time there were no poor people of the particular class specified in his will to be found in the parish of "X" and there were no reasonable likelihood of there being any such at any foreseeable time in the future. The question would then arise whether the testator's true intention was restricted to benefiting this particular class of poor people or whether he had some yet more general charitable intent to which the court could give effect.

'A general charitable intention, then, may be said to be a paramount intention on the part of a donor to effect some charitable purpose which the court can find a method of putting into operation, notwithstanding that it is impracticable to give effect to some direction by the donor which is not an essential part of his true intention—not, that is to say, part of his paramount intention.

'In contrast, a particular charitable intention exists where the donor means his charitable disposition to take effect if, but only if, it can be carried into effect in a particular specified way, for example, in connexion with a particular school to be established at a particular place (*Re Wilson, Twentyman* v. *Simpson*), or by establishing a home in a particular house (*Re Packe, Sanders* v. *A.-G.* ([1918] 1 Ch 437)).'

This passage is criticised in Tudor on Charities (6th Edn, 1967, pp 247–248). After referring to the penultimate paragraph of the passage I have cited, the editors say:

'It is suggested, with diffidence, that this formulation does not accord with the usual understanding of a "general charitable intention" discussed above. Furthermore, there would seem to be a considerable difficulty, in view of the detailed provisions in the will, in the way of the construction which was made; and it is respectfully suggested that the learned judge's view of the will was, as a matter of construction, erroneous. Although a "liberal spirit" may perhaps in some circumstances be commendable, it should not be applied in such a way as to defeat a testator's intention.'

That criticism is, I think, ill founded. In a well-known passage in *Re Wilson* [1913] 1 Ch 314 at 320–321, [1911–13] All ER Rep 1101 at 1102–1103 Parker J stresses that the jurisdiction of the court to direct a scheme for the carrying out of the trusts of a charitable gift which has otherwise failed through impracticability is founded on the fact that—

'the gift is given for a particular charitable purpose, but it is possible, taking the will as a whole, to say that, notwithstanding the form of the gift, the paramount intention, according to the true construction of the will, is to give the property in the first instance for a general charitable purpose rather than a particular charitable purpose . . .'

But in earlier cases what is stressed is the distinction between, on the one hand, the case where the scheme prescribed by a testator can be regarded as the mode by which a charitable purpose is to be carried into effect and where 'the court does not hold that the mode is of the substance of the legacy; but will effectuate the gift to charity, as the substance' (see per Lord Eldon LC in *Mills v Farmer* (1815) 19 Ves 483 at 486, 34 ER 595 at 596); and, on the other hand, the case where no part of the scheme prescribed by the testator can be disregarded as inessential without frustrating the testator's evident intention. The distinction was explained by Lindley LJ in *Re Rymer* [1895] 1 Ch 19 at 35, [1891–4] All ER Rep 328 at 334 in these terms: '. . . you have to consider whether the mode of attaining the object is machinery or not, or whether the mode is not the substance of the gift.' And in *Re Willis, Shaw v Willis* [1921] 1 Ch 44 at 54 Younger LJ, in a passage cited by Buckley J in *Re Lysaght* [1965] 2 All ER 888 at 893, [1966] Ch 191 at 203, expresses the principle in these terms:

'The problem which in this case we have to solve is to say by which of two different principles the construction of this gift has to be controlled. The first of these principles is that if a testator has manifested a general intention to give to charity, whether in general terms or to charities of a defined character or quality, the failure of the particular mode in which the charitable intention is to be effectuated shall not imperil the charitable gift. If the substantial intention is charitable the court will substitute some other mode of carrying it into effect. The other principle, which I paraphrase from the judgment of Kay J. in *Biscoe* v. *Jackson* ((1887) 35 Ch D 460 at 463) is this. If on the proper construction of the will the mode of application is such an essential part of the gift that you cannot distinguish any general purpose of charity, but are obliged to say that the prescribed mode of doing a charitable act is the only one the testator intended or at all contemplated, then the court cannot, if that mode fails, apply the money cy-pres.'

The distinction between these two categories of cases is expressed in the joint judgment of two very distinguished Australian judges, Dixon and Evatt JJ, in *Attorney General for New South Wales v Perpetual Trustee Co Ltd* (1940) 63 CLR 209 at 225 as a distinction—

'. . . between, on the one hand, cases in which every element in the description of the trust is indispensable to the validity and operation of the disposition and, on the other hand, cases where a further and more general purpose is disclosed as the true and substantial object of the trust, which may therefore be carried into effect at the expense of some part of the particular directions given by the trust instrument.'

These are, of course, all different ways of expressing the same distinction. I have referred to what Sargant LJ once called 'the long bead-roll of cases on the subject' (see *Re Monk* [1927] 2 Ch 197 at 212), to which some recent cases have been added, because if the well-known passage in the judgment of Parker J in *Re Wilson* [1913] 1 Ch 314 at 320–321, [1911–13] All ER Rep 1101 at 1102–1103 which I have cited is read in isolation, it may mislead the reader into looking at the testator's will or at the document by which a disposition of property on charitable trusts is made to see whether there can be discovered a paramount or dominant charitable purpose served by the specific directions made by the testator or settlor. To search for such a paramount or dominant charitable purpose or intention is in many cases to follow a will-o'-the-wisp. Of course, there are cases where a particular disposition is prefaced by general words which state expressly the object which the testator or settlor desires to achieve and make it clear that the particular scheme prescribed is only a means of achieving that more general end. Such cases are rare. In most cases the charitable intention can only be inferred from the particular scheme directed by the testator or settlor. And as was pointed out by Dixon and Evatt JJ in the joint judgment in *Attorney General for New South Wales v Perpetual Trustee Co Ltd* 63 CLR 209 at 227 to which I have referred:

'The construction of the language in which the trust is expressed seldom contributes much towards a solution. More is to be gained by examination of the nature of the charitable trust itself and what is involved in the author's plan or project.'

Dixon and Evatt JJ also observe (at 225) that the distinction 'however clear in conception, has proved anything but easy of application'. As I see it one way of approaching the question whether a prescribed scheme or project which has proved impracticable is the only way of furthering a desirable purpose that the testator or settlor contemplated or intended is to ask whether a modification of that scheme or project, which would enable it to be carried into effect at the relevant time, is one which would frustrate the intention of the testator or settlor as disclosed by the will or trust instrument interpreted in the light of any admissible evidence of surrounding circumstances. Two cases where such an interpretation would have frustrated the testator's intention may serve to illustrate this. In *Re Mitchell's Will Trusts* (1966) 110 Sol Jo 291, a testator gave a three-quarters share of her residuary estate in reversion after a life interest on trust to be applied 'to the providing of four beds in the Barnsley Beckett Hospital for the use of injured workmen from the Mitchell Main and Darfield Main Collieries', to be known by the names of four members of the Mitchell family. At her death the income of three-quarters of her residuary estate was insufficient to maintain four beds at the hospital. At the date of her will and at the date of her death the hospital had a scheme for the naming of cots and beds in perpetuity in return for gifts of stated amounts, the money given being invested and applied for the general purposes of the hospital. There was evidence that, assuming that four beds had been reserved exclusively for injured workmen in the Main Collieries, the beds would have been very much under used; that the hospital committee would not have accepted the gift if it required them to set aside the four beds for the exclusive use of men from the named collieries and that they could not or would not have accepted the gift if it required them to guarantee that, even if no beds were set aside exclusively for the workmen, up to four beds would always be available. Cross J held that the gift failed. There the gift could not be construed as a gift for the benefit of the hospital alone; to treat it as a mere endowment of the hospital would have frustrated the testator's evident intention to benefit miners from the named pits. Equally the gift could not be construed as a gift for the benefit of miners from the named pits, otherwise than by the provision of special facilities in the named hospital. It is clear from the judgment of Cross J that he did not take the view that the scheme prescribed by the testatrix could not be modified in any particular. He said (at 292):

> 'Had the evidence been that, although the hospital would not provide four beds for the exclusive use of the workmen, it would nevertheless guarantee that there would always be four beds available, the position might be different . . .'

But any modification of the terms of the gift which would have made the scheme practicable would have frustrated the testatrix's intention to benefit workmen from the named pits and to do so by the provision of special facilities at the named hospital.

In *Re Crowe (deceased)* (3rd October 1979, unreported) a testatrix gave her residuary estate on trust to arrange for—

> '. . . the creation of a scholarship at the Royal Naval School for Officers' Daughters . . . to be used for the best student, (such student must be a Naval Officer's daughter) in the Spanish and Russian languages in memory of my father . . .'

Slade J construed the gift as a gift to provide a single scholarship, such scholarship to be awarded in both Spanish and Russian. The school did not teach Russian and was not willing to provide a course at or outside the school. On the construction of the will adopted by Slade J the foundation of a scholarship in Spanish alone, or in Spanish and some language other than Russian, or the creation of a scholarship in Spanish and Russian otherwise than for pupils at the named school, would equally have frustrated the testatrix's intention. No modification was possible which would have made the gift practicable without frustrating her evident intention.

On the other side of the line stands *Attorney General for New South Wales v Perpetual Trustee Co Ltd* (1940) 63 CLR 209. In that case a testatrix whose home was a farming property known as 'Milly Milly' gave it on trust to be used as a training farm for orphan lads in Australia. The farm was too small, the plant was too old-fashioned, and the income would not have sufficed to meet the expenses of the supervisory staff needed. It was held by the majority of the High Court of Australia that the intention that 'Milly Milly' should be the actual place of training was not an essential part of the gift, so that the property could be sold and the proceeds applied for the purpose of training Australian orphan boys in farming without frustrating her intention.

Returning to the residuary gift in the instant case counsel who argued the case for intestacy on behalf of the representative next of kin, stressed that apart from small legacies to individuals and gifts designed to perpetuate his own and his family's reputation the testator devoted his whole estate to the furtherance of two charitable objects, namely music and the welfare of orphans cared for by Dr Barnardo's or the

Church of England Children's Society homes. He pointed out that the gifts over of the legacies settled or purportedly settled by cl 4, paras (b) and (u) of the will were in favour of or with a preference for those bodies. Thus, said counsel, the gifts of the two half-shares of the residuary estate are designed to further two ends: first, the activities of the London College and the old Tonic Sol-fa College, and, second, the welfare of orphans brought up in one of Dr Barnardo's or the Church of England Children's Society homes. To delete the requirement that persons to whom scholarships might be awarded should be absolute orphans from one of these homes would be to frustrate the testator's intention as surely as to transfer either bequest to some body other than the London College or the old Tonic Sol-fa College.

I do not take that view. The testator has in cl 7 of his will set out in very considerable and, in view of the modest value of his estate and the indefinite duration of the trusts, somewhat excessive detail a scheme for the foundation of scholarships. But as I see it the intention which can be discerned from the bequest is twofold. The testator wanted to further musical education and to do so by means of founding scholarships at colleges with which he had a long and, as is apparent from paras (c) and (d) of cl 4 of the will, a valued connection. He chose absolute orphans from homes run by well-known charities as those most likely to need assistance. But it was not, as I see it, an essential part of this scheme that the scholarships should be so restricted, whatever needs might present themselves in changed circumstances. That being so, that part of the scheme or mode of achieving a charitable purpose can be modified without frustrating his intention.

In my judgment, therefore, the trusts of residue do not fail. At the date of the testator's will the trusts could have been carried into effect by a modification of the trust of each moiety, deleting the restriction to absolute orphans from the named homes. There have been further changes of circumstances as regards the old Tonic Sol-fa College since the testator's death and a more radical scheme may be required. I will therefore refer to the Charity Commissioners the settlement of a scheme.

Declaration that residuary estate be applied cy-près.

Solicitors: *Latter & Willett*, Bromley (for the bank); *Norton, Rose, Botterell & Roche* (for the first and second defendants); *Warmingtons & Hasties* (for the third defendant); *Treasury Solicitor*.

Jacqueline Metcalfe   Barrister.

Cadbury Schweppes Pty Ltd and others v Pub Squash Co Pty Ltd

PRIVY COUNCIL

LORD WILBERFORCE, LORD EDMUND-DAVIES, LORD FRASER OF TULLYBELTON, LORD SCARMAN AND LORD ROSKILL

23rd, 24th, 26th, 30th JUNE, 1st JULY, 13th OCTOBER 1980

Passing off – Descriptive material – Imitation of advertising campaign for and get-up of goods – Slogans and themes made familiar to market in radio and television advertising campaign – Whether plaintiff acquiring an intangible property right in advertised descriptions – Test to be applied.

In 1974 the appellants began marketing in Australia a lemon flavoured soft drink called 'Solo'. The soft drink was sold mainly in cans similar to those used for beer and was presented as an alternative to beer. The cans had a distinctive colour and a medallion device similar to that which was common on beer cans. The marketing of Solo was accompanied by an intensive national television and radio advertising campaign emphasising Solo as a drink associated with rugged masculine endeavour and evoking memories of the sort of squash drink hotels and bars used to make in the past. The campaign, which, with a short break in 1974, continued until 1977, had a remarkable impact. By early 1975 Solo was selling well. In 1975 the respondent launched a similar product called 'Pub Squash'. Pub Squash was sold in cans of the same type and colour as those in which Solo was put up and they also had a medallion device on their label. The marketing of Pub Squash was accompanied by a similar but more modest television campaign which also used the theme of masculine endeavour. In 1976 the appellants noticed a 15% drop in the sales of Solo which they believed had caused by the advent of Pub Squash and the manner in which the respondent had deliberately taken advantage of the appellants' advertising campaign for Solo. The appellants accordingly brought proceedings against the respondent claiming, inter alia, damages or an account of profits and an injunction in respect of the passing off of Pub Squash as Solo. The Supreme Court of New South Wales dismissed the appellants' claim on the ground that the respondent had sufficiently distinguished its goods from those of the appellants' and that although the respondent had deliberately taken advantage of the appellants' advertising campaign it had not misrepresented its goods as those of the appellants'. The appellants appealed to the Privy Council.

Held – (1) The tort of passing off was not anchored to the name or trade mark of a product or business but was wide enough to encompass other descriptive material, such as slogans or visual images associated with a plaintiff's product by means of an advertising campaign, if that material had become part of the goodwill of the plaintiff's product, the test of which was whether the plaintiff had acquired an intangible property right for his product by virtue of the product deriving from the advertising a distinctive character recognised by the market, and in applying that test the court had to bear in mind the balance to be maintained between the protection of plaintiff's investment in his product and the protection of free competition (see p 218 *f* to *j*, p 223 *a* to *c* and p 224 *b*, post); *Hornsby Building Information Centre Pty Ltd v Sydney Building Information Centre Pty Ltd* (1978) 52 ALJR 392 and *Erven Warnink BV v J Townend & Sons (Hull) Ltd* [1979] 2 All ER 927 applied.

(2) On the facts, the judge was entitled to find that the two themes used by the appellants in their radio and television advertising campaign, although descriptive of the type of product advertised, had never become a distinguishing feature of the product or generally associated with it, and that although the respondent in promoting Pub Squash had deliberately taken advantage of the appellants' advertising campaign for Solo the

consuming public were not deceived or misled by either the get-up, the formula or the advertising of Pub Squash into thinking that Pub Squash was the appellants' product. The judge was consequently entitled to conclude that the appellants had not established a cause of action in tort for passing off against the respondent, and it followed therefore that the appeal would be dismissed (see p 218 *j* to p 219 *a*, p 220 *g h*, p 221 *h*, p 222 *c* to p 223 *c* and p 224 *b*, post).

Notes
For the nature of the legal right to prevent the use of a trade mark, get-up and description, see 38 Halsbury's Law (3rd Edn) 593, para 995, and for cases on the subject of advertising, see 46 Digest (Repl) 276, *1803–1806*.

Cases referred to in judgment
Chemical Corpn of America v Anheuser-Busch Inc (1962) 306 F 2d 433.
Cheney Bros v Doris Silk Corpn (1929) 35 F 2d 279.
Erven Warnink BV v J Townend & Sons (Hull) Ltd [1979] 2 All ER 927, [1979] AC 731, [1979] 3 WLR 68, HL, Digest (Cont Vol E) 630, *1494a*.
Felton v Mulligan (1971) 124 CLR 367, HC of Aust.
Goya Ltd v Gala of London Ltd (1952) 69 RPC 188.
Hornsby Building Information Centre Pty Ltd v Sydney Building Information Centre Pty Ltd (1978) 52 ALJR 392, HC of Aust.
Howe Scale Co v Wyckoff, Seamans & Benedict (1905) 198 US 118.
International News Service v Associated Press (1918) 248 US 215.
Kark (Norman) Publications Ltd v Odhams Press Ltd [1962] RPC 163.
Leather Cloth Co Ltd v American Leather Cloth Co Ltd (1865) 11 HL Cas 523, 6 New Rep 209, 35 LJ Ch 53, 12 LT 742, 29 JP 675, 11 Jur NS 513, 11 ER 1435, HL, 46 Digest (Repl) 121, *737*.
Office Cleaning Services Ltd v Westminster Window and General Cleaners Ltd (1946) 63 RPC 39.
Perry v Truefitt (1842) 6 Beav 66, 49 ER 749, 46 Digest (Repl) 251, *1627*.
Reddaway v Banham [1896] AC 199, [1895–9] All ER Rep 133, 65 LJQB 381, 74 LT 289, 13 RPC 218, HL, 46 Digest (Repl) 221, *1454*.
Saville Perfumery Ltd v June Perfect Ltd (1941) 58 RPC 147, HL.
Slazenger & Sons v Feltham & Co (1889) 6 RPC 531, CA, 46 Digest (Repl) 258, *1669*.
Spalding (AG) & Bros v A W Gamage Ltd (1915) 84 LJ Ch 449, 113 LT 198, 32 RPC 273, HL, 46 Digest (Repl) 204, *1362*.
Tavener Rutledge Ltd v Specters Ltd [1959] RPC 83; *affd* [1959] RPC 355, CA.
Victoria Park Racing and Recreation Grounds Co Ltd v Taylor (1937) 58 CLR 479, HC of Aust.

Appeal
Cadbury Schweppes Pty Ltd, Tarax Drinks Holdings Ltd, Tarax Drinks Pty Ltd and Tarax Pty Ltd appealed pursuant to final leave to appeal granted by the Supreme Court of New South Wales, Equity Division, on 24th November 1978 and entered on 8th November 1979 against the judgment of the Supreme Court of New South Wales, Equity Division (Powell J) pronounced on 8th August 1978 dismissing their claim against the respondent, Pub Squash Co Pty Ltd, formerly Passiona Marketers Pty Ltd, for damages or an account of profits and an injunction in respect of the passing off by the respondent as and for a soft drink manufactured and sold by the appellants under the name of 'Solo' of a similar soft drink manufactured and sold by the respondent under the name of 'Pub Squash', and the expungement from the register of the respondent's 'Pub Squash' trade mark, or, alternatively, unfair trading. The facts are set out in the judgment of the Board.

L J Priestley QC and *P G Hely* (both of the New South Wales Bar) for the appellants.
C J Bannon QC and *S M P Reeves* (both of the New South Wales Bar) for the respondent.

LORD SCARMAN. Two questions arise in this appeal from the Supreme Court of New South Wales, Equity Division. One, which goes to the merits of the dispute, is whether the appellants, who are the plaintiffs in the suit, have established a cause of action in tort against the respondent. The tort alleged is that which is known to lawyers as passing off one's own goods as the goods of another. The second question is whether Her Majesty in Council has jurisdiction to entertain the appeal. The trial judge, Powell J, found against the appellants on the first question. He did not consider, nor was it any part of his duty to consider, the second question; for it could not arise until the appellants sought leave to appeal to Her Majesty in Council. Counsel, for reasons which will later emerge, developed the case on the merits before they turned to the question of jurisdiction. It will be convenient for their Lordships to take the same course.

The history
    The full story is well and, as counsel admit, accurately told by Powell J. Their Lordships, therefore, extract from his narrative only the critical events. The appellants are members of the Cadbury Schweppes Australian group of companies. The respondent company, which was incorporated in 1973, came under the control of a Mr P R Brooks in 1974, when he acquired its shares. Originally Langeath Pty Ltd, the respondent company changed its name, when Mr Brooks acquired control, to Passiona Marketers Pty Ltd. In 1976 there was another change of name to Pub Squash Co Pty Ltd.
    In 1973 Cadbury Schweppes decided on a new strategy to increase their share of the market in soft drinks in Australia. They would develop a new product to compete with Coca-Cola. It was to be of a different flavour from Cola. They selected as their product a lemon squash, which the trial judge described as 'a type of soft drink commonly accepted in hotels and licensed clubs and restaurants as an occasional alternative to beer'. It was to be presented as a man's drink, fit for, and a favourite with, rugged masculine adventurers. The advertising campaign was to stress its masculinity and at the same time to awake happy memories of the sort of squash hotels and bars in the past used to make. The two themes of manliness and pubs were reflected in the name of the product and its get-up. They named it 'Solo' and designed a medallion type of label very similar to the labels on beer sold in Australia. It was to be put up in cans and bottles, but especially cans, for which they chose a distinctive greenish yellow colour.
    A major feature in launching the new product was a television and radio advertising campaign. Their Lordships would not seek to better the trial judge's description of this campaign.
    They (ie the commercials) were, he said, as follows:
        '(i) *Television commercial.* The bulk of this commercial was devoted to action shots (accompanied by dramatic background music) of a rugged lone male canoeist shooting the rapids in a single kayak, attention being focused on the potential dangers, such as rocky outcrops, bends, eddies and the like, on the run down the rapids. At the conclusion of the run, the canoeist pushes his kayak ashore. He then reaches into a portable icebox and, having taken out and opened a can of "Solo", gulps it down. While he is drinking, a "voice-over" announcer says: "You've never tasted a lemon drink like 'Solo' before . . . unless it was one of those great lemon squashes that pubs used to make . . . extra tang . . . not too many bubbles . . ." As he drinks, the canoeist spills some of the liquid down his chin. He finishes his drink with a smile and wipes his chin with the back of his hand. The "voice-over" announcer says, and, as well, there is flashed on the screen, the words: "'Solo', a man's drink."
        '(ii) *Radio commercials.* Although the first two radio commercials were not precisely identified, it seems that they were in or to the following effect: (A) "You hear the sound first . . . the hairs on the back of your neck rise. And you're into the white water. It's not so much the rocks you see that bother ya. It's the ones ya can't see. You've only a thin skin of fibreglass under you and no time to think. Just react. And all the time you're building up a 'Solo' thirst. 'Solo' lemon. With all the

tang of those great lemon squashes that pubs used to make. 'Solo' lemon. A man's drink." (B) "Remember those lemon squashes the pubs used to make? Dry, hard extra tang. Today, Tarax have captured that true lemon squash in 'Solo'. 'Solo' is the lemon drink you can quaff straight down without too many bubbles getting in the way of your thirst. Just like the lemon squashes you remember. 'Solo' lemon. A man's drink".'

The initial launch was in Victoria and Queensland during the summer months of 1974. Television and radio advertising began in the two states in December 1973 and continued, with a break in January, until the end of May 1974. It was backed up by a drive to introduce the product to supermarkets, hotels and other retail outlets. The advertising material used in the drive included such descriptions as: 'Great product, research proven, just like the old pub squash.'

By the end of May or June in 1974 the limited initial launch was considered a success and it was decided to launch the product nation-wide in the coming spring.

Radio advertising was resumed in July 1974 and television advertising in September when the product went on sale. Again, by way of back-up, there was the distribution of advertising material to the trade. The cost of the advertising represented a very substantial investment in the product; television and radio advertising in 1974 alone cost some $300,000. As the national campaign developed, the theme of the lone male adventurer was further elaborated. Viewers were introduced to a lone sailor fighting his way through boiling surf in a catamaran, and two virile men battling it out in a squash court. Lone masculine endeavour was the theme supporting the name 'Solo'. Meanwhile the 'audio' in television and the radio broadcasts maintained the other theme, nostalgia for 'those great lemon squashes the pubs used to make'.

The product sold well. The advertising programme continued throughout 1975, television costing over $400,000 and radio over $160,000 in that year. New rugged men arrived on television, amongst others, a big-game fisherman, a horse breaker and wrestlers. The nostalgic pub squash theme continued to sound in the ears of viewers and listeners. The trial judge summed up the success of the campaign in these words:

'... the impact of this advertising campaign, and, in particular, of the television advertising campaign, appears to have been quite remarkable. Nearly every witness who was called, whether by the [appellants] or the [respondent], recalled the television advertisements, particularly the first, and the incident of the canoeist spilling some of the drink down his chin, and many recalled the slogans "a great squash like the pubs used to make" and "a man's drink", although not all the witnesses associated the former slogan with "Solo".'

Advertising 'Solo' continued along the same lines in 1976 and 1977; but in September 1976 the pub motif disappeared, sound as well as vision now concentrating on 'a man's drink' and the word 'Solo'.

On 8th April 1975 the respondent launched on the market its product 'Pub Squash'. Full-scale production did not, however, begin until June 1975. A television advertising programme, modest when compared with that of the appellants, began at the end of April. Its theme was, as was that for 'Solo', heroically masculine ('The Million Dollar Man') and the audio was similarly nostalgic, the hero after his endeavours ripping into a Pub Lemon Soda Squash. The label on the product was of a medallion type on which the name 'Pub Squash' appeared in bold red letters. The cans in which it was sold were of the same size and the same shade of yellow as those in which 'Solo' was put up. On 6th May 1975 the respondent applied to register its 'Pub Squash' label as a trade mark; and on 6th September 1976 it was registered in class 32 no B286,987.

The competition from 'Pub Squash' and certain other lemon squashes which entered the market in 1975 had its effect on the sale of 'Solo'. They were 15% lower in 1976 than they had been in 1975.

The appellants believed, and the belief was not unreasonable, that the advent of 'Pub Squash', timed as it was to take advantage of their advertising campaign, put up in not dissimilar cans, and accompanied by its own advertising campaign stressing its high favour with stalwart men and evoking the memory of the pub squashes of the past, was a substantial cause of the drop in the sale of 'Solo'. On 1st June 1977 they instituted these proceedings, claiming damages or an account of profits and an injunction in respect of passing off, and the expungement from the register of the respondent's 'Pub Squash' trade mark. By a later amendment they added a claim in respect of unfair trading.

The appeal on the merits

It is unnecessary to explore the law in any depth, because it is now accepted by both sides that the issue in the case is whether in promoting its product the respondent so confused or deceived the market that it passed its product off as the product of the appellants. Nevertheless the case presents one feature which is not to be found in the earlier case law. The passing off of which the appellants complain depends to a large extent on the deliberate adoption by the respondent of an advertising campaign based on themes and slogans closely related to those which the appellants had developed and made familiar to the market in the radio and television advertising of their product. Does confusion or deception, if it be shown to arise from such an advertising campaign, amount to a passing off? To answer the question it is necessary to consider the modern character of the tort.

In *Erven Warnink BV v J Townend & Sons (Hull) Ltd* [1979] 2 All ER 927, [1979] AC 731 (the advocaat case) the House of Lords formulated, so far as the law of England is concerned, the modern principle which governs the tortious liability compendiously described as 'passing off'. The facts of that case bear no resemblance to the present case, but the declarations of principle to be found in the speeches of Lord Diplock and Lord Fraser are of general application.

Lord Diplock found a rational basis for the modern tort in the speech of Lord Parker in *A G Spalding & Bros v A W Gamage Ltd* (1915) 84 LJ Ch 449 at 450, where he identified the right protected by the tort as the 'property in the business or goodwill likely to be injured by the misrepresentation'. The significance of the *Spalding* case Lord Diplock found to lie—

> 'in its recognition that misrepresenting one's own goods as the goods of someone else was not a separate genus of actionable wrong but a particular species of wrong included in a wider genus of which a premonitory hint had been given by Lord Herschell in *Reddaway v Banham* [1896] AC 199 at 211, [1895–9] All ER Rep 133 at 140 when, in speaking of the deceptive use of a descriptive term, he said: "I am unable to see why a man should be allowed *in this way more than in any other* to deceive purchasers into the belief that they are getting what they are not, and thus to filch the business of a rival".' (Lord Diplock's emphasis.)

(See [1979] 2 All ER 927 at 932, [1979] AC 731 at 741.)

Lord Fraser stated the principle as being that—

> 'the plaintiff is entitled to protect his right of property in the goodwill attached to a name which is *distinctive* of a product or class of products sold by him in the course of his business.' (My emphasis.)

(See [1979] 2 All ER 927 at 943, [1979] AC 731 at 755.)

The advocaat case was all about a name. But Lord Fraser did not, any more than did Lord Diplock, limit the principle to the misappropriation of a name. He cited with approval, as also had Lord Diplock, Lord Herschell's speech in *Reddaway v Banham* [1896] AC 199, [1895–9] All ER Rep 133 and quoted a passage ([1896] AC 199 at 209, [1895–9] All ER Rep 133 at 139) where Lord Herschell approved the now classic dictum of Lord Kingsdown in *Leather Cloth Co Ltd v American Leather Cloth Co Ltd* (1865) 11 HL Cas 523 at 528, 11 ER 1435 at 1438 to the effect that—

> 'The fundamental rule is, that one man has no right to put off his goods for sale as the goods of a rival trader, and he cannot, therefore (in the language of Lord

Langdale, in the case of *Perry* v. *Truefitt* ((1845) 6 Beav 66 at 73, 49 ER 749 at 752), be allowed to use names, marks, letters, *or other indicia,* by which he may induce purchasers to believe that the goods which he is selling are the manufacture of another person.' (My emphasis.)

In *Hornsby Building Information Centre Pty Ltd v Sydney Building Information Centre Pty Ltd* (1978) 52 ALJR 392 the High Court of Australia stated the principle in similar terms. Again the case was about a name but Stephen J, with whom Barwick CJ agreed, formulated the principle in terms which allow of its applicability to 'other indicia' than the name of the product. But he also sounded a warning as to its application in cases where the descriptive material which the defendant has misappropriated is also applicable to 'other like businesses'.

Stephen J, after referring to the principle that the tort of passing off is essentially an infringement of the 'plaintiff's intangible property rights' in the goodwill attaching to his product, went on to say (at 396–397):

'There is a price to be paid for the advantages flowing from the possession of an eloquently descriptive trade name. Because it is descriptive it is equally applicable to any business of a like kind, its very descriptiveness ensures that it is not distinctive of any particular business and hence its application to other like businesses will not ordinarily mislead the public. In cases of passing off, where it is the wrongful appropriation of the reputation of another or that of his goods that is in question, a plaintiff which uses descriptive words in its trade name will find that quite small differences in a competitor's trade name will render the latter immune from action—*Office Cleaning Services Ltd.* v. *Westminster Window and General Cleaners Ltd.* ((1946) 63 RPC 39 at 42, per Lord Simonds). As his Lordship said (at 43), the possibility of blunders by members of the public will always be present when names consist of descriptive words—"So long as descriptive words are used by two traders as part of their respective trade names, it is possible that some members of the public will be confused whatever the differentiating words may be." The risk of confusion must be accepted, to do otherwise is to give to one who appropriates to himself descriptive words an unfair monopoly in those words and might even deter others from pursuing the occupation which the words describe.'

He is discussing a name; but what he says about a name may with equal force be applied to other descriptive material, if it has given to a product (or business) a distinctive character.

The width of the principle now authoritatively recognised by the High Court of Australia and the House of Lords is, therefore, such that the tort is no longer anchored, as in its early nineteenth century formulation, to the name or trade mark of a product or business. It is wide enough to encompass other descriptive material, such as slogans or visual images, which radio, television or newspaper advertising campaigns can lead the market to associate with a plaintiff's product, provided always that such descriptive material has become part of the goodwill of the product. And the test is whether the product has derived from the advertising a distinctive character which the market recognises.

But competition must remain free; and competition is safeguarded by the necessity for the plaintiff to prove that he has built up an 'intangible property right' in the advertised descriptions of his product, or, in other words, that he has succeeded by such methods in giving his product a distinctive character accepted by the market. A defendant, however, does no wrong by entering a market created by another and there competing with its creator. The line may be difficult to draw; but, unless it is drawn, competition will be stifled. The test applied by Powell J in the instant case was to inquire whether the consuming public was confused or misled by the get-up, the formula or the advertising of the respondent's product into thinking that it was the appellants' product. And he held on the facts that the public was not deceived. Their Lordships do not think that his approach in law (save in one respect, as will later appear) to the central problem of the case can be faulted. The real question in the appeal is, therefore, one of fact, whether the judge erred in the inferences he drew from the admitted primary facts.

The appellants' alternative case of unfair trading irrespective of whether the market was deceived or confused into mistaking the respondent's product for that of the appellants' need not be considered by the Board, since the appellants now restrict themselves to a case based on such confusion. For such a case to succeed it would be necessary to show that the law of Australia has developed a tort of unfair competition along the lines suggested in the well-known decision of the United States Supreme Court, *International News Service v Associated Press* (1918) 248 US 215 at 241–242, in which Pitney J, delivering the majority opinion, said:

> 'It is said that the elements of unfair competition are lacking because there is no attempt by defendant to palm off its goods as those of the complainant, characteristic of the most familiar, if not the most typical, cases of unfair competition: *Howe Scale Co. v. Wyckoff, Seamans & Benedict* ((1905) 198 US 118 at 140). But we cannot concede that the right to equitable relief is confined to that class of cases. In the present case the fraud upon complainant's rights is more direct and obvious. Regarding news matter as the mere material from which these two competing parties are endeavoring to make money, and treating it, therefore, as *quasi* property for the purposes of their business because they are both selling it as such, defendant's conduct differs from the ordinary case of unfair competition in trade principally in this that, instead of selling its own goods as those of complainant, it substitutes misappropriation in the place of misrepresentation, and sells complainant's goods as its own.'

The development of such a tort has not escaped judicial criticism in the USA itself (eg Learned Hand J in *Cheney Bros v Doris Silk Corpn* (1929) 35 F 2d 279). It has also been criticised in Australia: see *Victoria Park Racing and Recreation Grounds Co Ltd v Taylor* (1937) 58 CLR 479, and, in particular, the criticism offered by Dixon J (at 508–509). Their Lordships prefer to express no opinion on it in a case such as the present where the facts do not require that it be considered.

The hearing before Powell J occupied some 26 days. Sixty-four witnesses gave evidence, some thirty of whom spoke to the issue of confusion between the two products. As always in a passing-off action the ultimately critical question was one of fact. The critical question in this case proved to be: were customers, or potential customers, led by the similarities in the get-up and advertising of the two products into believing that 'Pub Squash' was the appellants' product? Or, if no deception be proved, was there a real probability of deception? The trial judge addressed himself to this question of fact first when considering the claim in 'passing off', and second when stating his conclusions on the alternative claim of unfair trading. In respect of passing off, he asked himself whether the respondent did sufficiently distinguish its product from 'Solo'. He answered the question as follows:

> '. . . it can readily be seen that they are different. This, however, is not necessarily enough, for one must take into account the nature of the marketplace and the habits of ordinary purchasers (see, for example, *Saville Perfumery Ltd v June Perfect Ltd* (1941) 58 RPC 147 at 174–175 and *Tavener Rutledge Ltd v Specters Ltd* [1959] RPC 83 at 88–89). As I have pointed out earlier, it is not uncommon, albeit that it is not the universal practice, both in supermarkets, and in mixed businesses and milk bars which have self-selection display refrigerators for products such as "Solo" and "Pub Squash" to be displayed alongside each other; and in those cases in which they are not, they are, nonetheless displayed in close proximity to each other. Further, as I have pointed out, the purchase of a soft drink is often a casual transaction. These

two features of the market seem to explain most, if not all, of the cases of incorrect selection of which evidence has been given . . . But, even accepting, as I do, that by reason of the nature of the marketplace and of the habits of purchasers, mistakes are likely to, and do, in fact, occur, the evidence would seem to demonstrate that in most, although not all, cases in which there has initially been a wrong selection by a customer, or the wrong product has been offered by the shopkeeper, the error has been recognised before the purchase has been completed . . . This being so, it seems to me that the [respondent] has sufficiently differentiated its product from that of the [appellants'].'

This answer, it is true, related to the effect of get-up as a cause of confusion and was not addressed to the problems of the advertising campaign. Nor, when he gave it, was the judge directing his attention, let alone making any findings, on the conduct of Mr Brooks or any of the other officers of the respondent company in the marketing of its product.

When, however, he came to consider the claim of unfair trading, he examined in detail, and made a number of adverse findings on, their conduct in the development and marketing of 'Pub Squash'. He stated his findings and conclusion on this aspect of the case in a remarkable passage which, because it is the key to a full understanding of his judgment, their Lordships quote in full:

'(vii) *Conclusion.* From what I have written above it will appear that it is my view that, as from a time being no later than the later part of August 1974, the defendant, having by means of one or more of its officers become aware of the successful launch of "Solo" in Victoria and of the sale of "Solo" in southern New South Wales, and, thus, appreciating that in all probability the Victorian "launch" would be followed by a large-scale "launch" of "Solo" on the New South Wales market, set out in a deliberate and calculated fashion to take advantage of the [appellants'] past efforts in developing "Solo" and of the [appellants'] past and anticipated future efforts in developing a market for a product such as "Solo", and that, in particular, the [respondent], by its officers, sought to copy or to approximate the formula for "Solo", and chose a product name and package for the [respondents'] proposed product derived from, and intended to gain the benefit of, the [appellants'] past and anticipated advertising campaign and the [appellants'] package for their product. Notwithstanding these findings, it is my view, as I have earlier indicated, that, as the facts, as I have earlier found them, do not reveal any relevant misrepresentation on the part of the [respondent] as to its goods, the [appellants] have not made out a case for relief based on the expanded concept of passing off or on unfair trading.'

Put very shortly, the learned trial judge concluded that there was no 'relevant misrepresentation', no deception or probability of deception. The competition developed by the respondent and its officers took advantage of the appellants' promotion of their own product but never went so far as to suggest that 'Pub Squash' was the product of the appellants, or merely another name for 'Solo'. It might have been expected that he would have inferred from these findings the existence of confusion and the fact of deception; but after a long trial and a detailed examination of the evidence he refused to take the step of drawing the inference. His decision, taken very deliberately and with full awarenesss of what the respondent and its officers did in promoting their product, is, whether right or wrong, entitled to the greatest respect.

Counsel for the appellants accepted that the issue of deception was crucial. In submitting that the judge fell into error, he sought to rely on three points. He submitted, first, that the judge misled himself by the way in which he 'compartmentalised' his judgment, second, that he misled himself by an error of law as to the relevant date for establishing the necessary goodwill or reputation of the appellants' product, and, third that his conclusion was contrary to his primary findings of fact.

First, the 'compartmentalisation' point. The appellants' submission may be summarised as follows. Counsel attributed the error, into which, on his submission, the judge fell, to the structure of the judgment. The judge, as their Lordships have already noted, dealt with the cause of action in passing off first. At that stage he made no findings as to the conduct of the respondent's officers, Mr Brooks and his colleagues. He found that there was no 'relevant misrepresentation on the part of the [respondent] as to its goods' without considering the respondent's intentions. But intention is relevant. Having found no misrepresentation, he then considered the case of unfair trading. He now found as a fact that the respondent set out deliberately to take advantage of the appellants' efforts to develop the market for 'Solo'; but this was of no consequence, since he had already found no deception or misrepresentation. Had the learned judge appreciated that the case must be considered as a whole, and not in separate compartments, he would have had regard to the respondent's intention in determining whether there was deception or the probability of deception; and, had he done so, only one conclusion was possible, namely, that the respondent was passing off its goods as the goods of the appellants.

This is a formidable submission.

Where an intention to deceive is found, it is not difficult for the court to infer that the intention has been, or in all probability will be, effective: see *Slazenger & Sons v Feltham & Co* (1889) 6 RPC 531 at 538 per Lindley LJ. But in dealing with the issue of deception the learned judge directed himself correctly and made the comment, which is also good law, that—

> 'the court must be on its guard against finding fraud *merely* because there has been an imitation of another's goods, get-up, method of trading or trading style (see, for example, *Goya Ltd v Gala of London Ltd* (1952) 69 RPC 188).' (Powell J's emphasis.)

After a very careful consideration of the judgment as a whole, their Lordships do not think that in the arrangement of the subject matter of his judgment the judge allowed himself to overlook the importance, subject to safeguards, of a defendant's intention when deciding the issue of deception.

Once it is accepted that the judge was not unmindful of the respondent's deliberate purpose (as he found) to take advantage of the appellants' efforts to develop 'Solo', the finding of 'no deception' can be seen to be very weighty, for he has reached it notwithstanding his view of the respondent's purpose. But it is also necessary to bear in mind the nature of the purpose found by the judge. He found that the respondent did sufficiently distinguish its goods from those of the appellants. The intention was not to pass off the respondent's goods as those of the appellants but to take advantage of the market developed by the advertising campaign for 'Solo'. Unless it can be shown that in so doing the respondent infringed 'the [appellants'] intangible property rights' in the goodwill attaching to their product, there is no tort, for such infringement is the foundation of the tort: see Stephen J in *Hornsby Building Information Centre Pty Ltd v Sydney Building Information Centre Pty Ltd.*

In their Lordships' view, therefore, the first submission fails. And, once the conclusion is reached that the judge did not allow the structure of his judgment to mislead him, the submission recoils on itself. The finding of the judge becomes, by its rejection, immensely strengthened.

The second submission is less formidable. The judge, it is conceded, misdirected himself in holding that the relevant date for determining whether a plaintiff has established the necessary goodwill or reputation of his product is the date of the commencement of the proceedings (ie 1st June 1977). The relevant date is, in law, the date of the commencement of the conduct complained of, ie 8th April 1975, when the respondent began to market 'Pub Squash': see *Norman Kark Publications Ltd v Odhams Press Ltd* [1962] RPC 163. Despite his error, the learned judge did direct his mind to the facts as they were in 'the early months of 1975'. He found that by then 'Solo' had attained a significant level of recognition and acceptance in the market and went on to consider, and make findings on, 'the nature and extent of the goodwill and reputation which

"Solo" had, *by early 1975*, attained, and which it thereafter maintained' (my emphasis). This submission, therefore, fails.

Their Lordships now turn to the main attack on the judge's conclusion. His primary findings, which the appellants accept, should, it is submitted, have led him to conclude that there was confusion amongst buyers and deception by the respondent.

The judge's analysis of the nature of the good will or distinctive reputation which 'Solo' had acquired by April 1975 cannot, in their Lordships' view, be challenged. The reputation he found to be that of—

> 'a lemon squash type of soft drink, marketed under the name of "Solo", packaged, principally in yellow cans bearing a rounded-like or medallion-like device ... and widely advertised on television by advertisements featuring a rugged masculine figure.'

He was not, however, persuaded that *any of the variants* on the phrase 'those great old squashes like the pubs used to make' and 'a man's drink' were generally associated with 'Solo'. He based his negative conclusion on his understanding of the evidence of 'the confusion witnesses', especially those members of the consuming public, who were called, and on his view of the nature and effect of the advertisements for 'Solo', of which he said that he—

> 'had regard to two particular types ... namely the fact that television is principally a visual medium so that the "audio" tends to have less impact than the visual image, and, secondly, the fact that, no matter what variation be worked on it, the phrase "those great old squashes the pubs used to make" is essentially descriptive of the *type* of product advertised; it does not, of itself, *identify*, or denote the origin of, the product being advertised (cf the slogan in issue in *Chemical Corpn of America v Anheuser-Busch Inc* (1962) 306 F 2d 433).' (Powell J's emphasis.)

The appellants' challenge is to the negative conclusion. In their Lordships' opinion, it fails to displace either the judge's inference, based on his analysis of the nature of the market in which the two products were sold, or his finding that the advertising of 'Pub Squash', intended though it was to win a share of the market from its competitor 'Solo', led to no significant confusion or deception. He accepted that on occasions there was confusion at the point of sale; but he found, and there was plenty of evidence on which he could find, that the confusion was almost always corrected before the moment of sale. Such confusion as there was arose, in his view, from the casual attitude of many purchasers in the market to the product offered and not from any failure of the respondent sufficiently to distinguish its product from 'Solo'.

He found that 'the principal, if not the only, part of the market in which the wrong product has been selected or given, is in relation to cans'. He saw the two cans; he refused to hold that, because 'Solo' became known as being sold in yellow cans, it 'thereby became entitled to a monopoly' of sale or that the mere fact the respondent adopted a yellow can for its product dictated a finding of 'passing off'. He was unable, on the evidence, to find that the consuming public associated yellow cans only with 'Solo'.

Nevertheless, the judge recognised that the similarity in size and shape of can (which was a stock size and shape in the trade) and in colour made it 'incumbent' on the respondent to distinguish its package from that of 'Solo'. He looked at the cans and commented that 'it can readily be seen that they are different' and then proceeded to analyse the market and the effect of such confusion as there was in the way already described.

When the judge turned to consider the effect of the radio and television advertising, he rejected the submission that either of the two themes used in these media had become the property of the appellants' in the sense in which the word 'property' is used in this class of case. They were descriptive of the product (perhaps even 'eloquently descriptive'), but they never became a distinguishing feature. There was ample evidence to support his rejection of this submission, and their Lordships are in no position to substitute for his assessment of the effect of the 'Solo' advertising campaign a different assessment or to challenge his analysis of the market, ie the character of the buying public.

In reaching his conclusion of fact that the respondent had 'sufficiently' distinguished its product from 'Solo', the judge had not only to conduct an elaborate and detailed analysis of the evidence, which he certainly did, but to bear in mind the necessity in this branch of the law of the balance to be maintained between the protection of a plaintiff's investment in his product and the protection of free competition. It is only if a plaintiff can establish that a defendant has invaded his 'intangible property right' in his product by misappropriating descriptions which have become recognised by the market as distinctive of the product that the law will permit competition to be restricted. Any other approach would encourage monopoly. The new, small man would increasingly find his entry into an existing market obstructed by the large traders already well known as operating in it.

For these reasons their Lordships are of the opinion that the appeal fails, even if it be competent, the question to which they now turn.

The question of jurisdiction

By their statement of claim the appellants raised a question of federal law, ie the validity or otherwise of the respondent's registered trade mark, and sought the expungement of the trade mark from the register. Powell J, though a state judge, undoubtedly possessed the necessary federal jurisdiction to deal with the trade mark question: and, if he did so, no appeal would lie to Her Majesty in Council. Final appeal in such a case would lie only to the High Court of Australia: see s 39(2) of the Judiciary Act 1903–1973. The only exception would be if the High Court itself should certify (which in this case it has not done) that the question is one which ought to be determined by Her Majesty in Council: see s 74 of the Constitution. The respondent submits that the judge was exercising his federal jurisdiction that no appeal lies, therefore, to Her Majesty in Council. The judge ruled, it is submitted, on the question *even though he did not expressly deal with it.*

The propositions of constitutional law, to which their Lordships have briefly referred, are, of course, not in dispute: nor is it disputed that the trade mark question was raised on the pleadings. But the appellants say that the question was not litigated at trial and that, by consent, the judge confined himself to the issue of liability, which the judge clearly understood to be that of passing off. The federal question was, therefore, it is submitted, not adjudicated on; on the contrary, the judge confined himself to the issue of passing off, which was within his state jurisdiction.

The very late appearance of the point strongly suggests that neither the parties nor the judge regarded the trial as directed to any issue other than that of passing off. If the point were going to be raised, the time to raise it was when the appellants sought leave to appeal. But the respondent did not raise it until it lodged its written case. The point has no merits and, were it not one of jurisdiction, would be rejected out of hand.

But, since it goes to the competence of the Board to entertain the appeal, the submission of the respondent must be considered. The issue is whether, the trade mark question having been raised and never abandoned, the trial judge must be held to have been exercising his federal jurisdiction when dealing with the case. The submission that he must be held to have been doing so largely rested on the decision of the High Court in *Felton v Mulligan* (1971) 124 CLR 367, and in particular on the following passage in the judgment of Barwick CJ (at 374):

'The critical question in the case is whether the defence did involve the exercise of federal jurisdiction by the Supreme Court. It would do so if the matter before the Supreme Court became or involved by reason of the defence raised to the applicant's claim, either wholly or partly a matter arising under a law made by the [federal] Parliament . . . Further the matter arising under a law of the Parliament will have arisen if the suit could have been disposed of by deciding the matter, whether or not the suit was so disposed of ... It is of course not enough that a law made by the Parliament must be construed in the course of the decision of the case. There must be a matter arising under a law of the Parliament.'

In their Lordships' view the question is one of legal policy which is pre-eminently a matter for the High Court to determine. Their Lordships would not, therefore, express an opinion unless it were necessary for a decision in the appeal. In the present case the necessity does not arise.

For the reasons given in considering the appellants' claim based on passing off their Lordships are able to advise Her Majesty that the appeal be dismissed without having to rule on the point so belatedly raised by the respondent as to its competence. Accordingly, they humbly advise Her Majesty that the appeal be dismissed with costs.

Appeal dismissed.

Solicitors: *Stephenson Harwood* (for the appellants); *Slaughter & May* (for the respondent).

Mary Rose Plummer   Barrister.

Practice Note

FAMILY DIVISION

Injunction – Exclusion of party from matrimonial home – County court – Time limit on operation of injunction – Time limit not to exceed three months in normal cases – Where danger to applicant still possible at end of three months application may be made to extend duration of injunction – Domestic Violence and Matrimonial Proceedings Act 1976, s 1(1)(c).

The police are holding some thousands of orders containing a power of arrest made under s 1(1)(c) of the Domestic Violence and Matrimonial Proceedings Act 1976. Experience has shown that the police are rarely called on to take action on an injunction which is more than three months old, and the requirement that they should retain indefinitely the orders containing a power of arrest imposes an unnecessary burden on them.

The Practice Note dated 21st July 1978 ([1978] 2 All ER 1056, [1978] 1 WLR 1123) recommended that consideration be given to imposing a time limit of three months on injunctions excluding a party from a matrimonial home or a specified area.

To assist in easing the burdens of the police and in enabling them to concentrate on the cases where action may be required, judges should consider, at the time a power of arrest is attached to an injunction, for what period of time this sanction is likely to be required. Unless a judge is satisfied that a longer period is necessary in a particular case, the period should not exceed three months. In those few cases where danger to the applicant is still reasonably apprehended towards the expiry of the three months, application may be made to the court to extend the duration of the injunction.

Issued by the President with the concurrence of the Lord Chancellor.

R L BAYNE-POWELL
Senior Registrar.

22nd December 1980

Choice Investments Ltd v Jeromnimon
(Midland Bank Ltd, garnishee)

COURT OF APPEAL, CIVIL DIVISION
LORD DENNING MR, BRIGHTMAN AND GRIFFITHS LJJ
24th, 27th OCTOBER, 6th NOVEMBER 1980

Execution – Garnishee order – Debts owing or accruing from third party to judgment debtor – Sum standing to debtor's credit in deposit account – Foreign currency – Whether amount in foreign currency in deposit account constituting a 'debt' – Whether amount in foreign currency attachable to satisfy judgment given in sterling – Administration of Justice Act 1956, s 38(1) – County Courts Act 1959, s 143(1).

Since in respect of a sum payable in England in foreign currency English courts can give judgment for it in that foreign currency, it follows that a sum in foreign currency standing to the credit of a judgment debtor in the jurisdiction in a deposit account in a bank is a 'debt' for the purposes of s 38(1)^a of the Administration of Justice Act 1956 and s 143(1)^b of the County Courts Act 1959, and is attachable accordingly in garnishee proceedings notwithstanding that the judgment or order for payment has been given or made in sterling (see p 226 g, p 227 e to j, p 228 a b and p 229 b c, post).

Miliangos v George Frank (Textiles) Ltd [1975] 3 All ER 801 applied.

Observations on the method by which a bank may comply with a garnishee order where the sum credited in a deposit account is in foreign currency (see p 228 b to p 229 b, post).

Notes

For the attachment of a bank account by a garnishee order, see 17 Halsbury's Laws (4th Edn) para 530, and for cases on the subject, see 21 Digest (Repl) 713–747, 2144–2347.

For the Administration of Justice Act 1956, s 38, see 18 Halsbury's Statutes (3rd Edn) 24.

For the County Courts Act 1959, s 143, see 7 ibid 396.

Cases referred to in judgments

Joachimson v Swiss Bank Corpn [1921] 3 KB 110, [1921] All ER Rep 92, 90 LJKB 973, 125 LT 338, 26 Com Cas 196, CA, 21 Digest (Repl) 742, 2302.

Miliangos v George Frank (Textiles) Ltd [1975] 3 All ER 801, [1976] AC 443, [1975] 3 WLR 758, [1976] 1 Lloyd's Rep 201, HL, Digest (Cont Vol D) 691, 64c.

Pritchard v Westminster Bank Ltd (Westminster Bank Ltd, garnishee) [1969] 1 All ER 999, [1969] 1 WLR 547, CA, Digest (Cont Vol C) 342, 2159a.

Rainbow v Moorgate Properties Ltd [1975] 2 All ER 821, [1975] 1 WLR 788, CA, Digest (Cont Vol D) 323, 2453a.

Richardson v Richardson [1927] P 228, 96 LJP 125, 137 LT 492, 21 Digest (Repl) 718, 2186.

United Railways of Havana and Regla Warehouses Ltd, Re [1960] 2 All ER 332, [1961] AC 1007, [1960] 2 WLR 969, HL, 11 Digest (Reissue) 489, 919.

---

a   Section 38(1) provides: 'A sum standing to the credit of a person in a deposit account in a bank shall, for the purposes of the jurisdiction of the High Court to attach debts for the purpose of satisfying judgments or orders for the payment of money, be deemed to be a sum due or accruing to that person and, subject to rules of court, shall be attachable accordingly, notwithstanding that any of the following conditions applicable to the account, that is to say—(a) any condition that notice is required before any money is withdrawn; (b) any condition that a personal application must be made before any money is withdrawn; (c) any condition that a deposit book must be produced before any money is withdrawn; or (d) any other condition prescribed by rules of court, has not been satisfied.'

b   Section 143(1) makes like provision in respect of county courts

Appeal

Midland Bank Ltd appealed with the judge's leave against a garnishee order nisi made by his Honour Judge Curtis-Raleigh in the Bloomsbury and Marylebone County Court on 24th July 1980 whereby it was ordered that the bank should exchange into sterling and thereafter attach such sum in any foreign currency or currencies standing to the credit of the judgment debtor, Gregory Jeromnimon, as would satisfy the judgment of £982·16 judgment debt and £52·00 costs obtained by the judgment creditor, Choice Investments Ltd, on 28th March 1980. The facts are set out in the judgment of Lord Denning MR.

George Newman for the bank.
Diana Faber for the judgment creditor.
The judgment debtor did not appear.

Cur adv vult

6th October. The following judgments were read.

LORD DENNING MR. The facts in this case are simple but they raise an important point about foreign currencies.

A gentleman, Mr Jeromnimon, who lives in a London suburb, owed a company called Choice Investments Ltd the sum of £982·16 in sterling. He did not pay. So the company sued him in the Clerkenwell County Court. On 17th January 1980 the company recovered judgment against him for £982·16 for debt and £52·00 for costs, making in all £1,034·16. Still he did not pay. The company discovered that he had a banking account at the Midland Bank in Wigmore Street in which sums were held to his credit. So on 28th March 1980 the company got a garnishee order nisi against the bank by which the sums to his credit were attached to answer the judgment. It then turned out that he had three acounts at the bank with credit balances as follows: (i) current account, £44·45; (ii) sterling seven-day notice deposit, £4·68, with accrued interest of £4·27; (iii) United States dollars seven-day notice deposit, $2,358·55, with $166·04 accrued interest.

No difficulty arose about the two small sterling accounts. But a difficulty arises about the sum in US dollars. Under the rules and statutes which allow attachments, only 'debts' can be attached. Until recently a debt owing in foreign currency was not regarded as a 'debt' which could be attached. If it was not paid, it gave rise only to an action for 'damages' for breach of contract; and that could not be attached: see *Richardson v Richardson* [1927] P 228 and *Re United Railways of Havana and Regla Warehouses Ltd* [1960] 2 All ER 332 at 356, [1961] AC 1007 at 1069.

The question is as to the effect of recent decisions. It is now settled that, if a sum is payable in this country in a foreign currency, the courts here can give judgment for that sum in that foreign currency. Is that sum a 'debt' which is capable of being attached? In order to understand the problem, I will first explain what is meant by 'attaching' a debt. It is a mode of execution which was introduced by s 61 of the Common Law Procedure Act 1854, since repealed under the Statute Law Revision Act 1883 and replaced by RSC Ord 49, r 1. It always applied to money held by a bank for its customer on current account: see *Joachimson v Swiss Bank Corpn* [1921] 3 KB 110 at 121, 131, [1921] All ER Rep 92 at 97, 102. It has been extended now by statute to money held by a bank on deposit account. The relevant statutory provisions are in s 38 of the Administration of Justice Act 1956 and s 143 of the County Courts Act 1959, which are too long to set out here. Those who wish can refer to them.

Garnishee

The word 'garnishee' is derived from the Norman-French. It denotes one who is required to 'garnish', that is, to furnish, a creditor with the money to pay off a debt. A simple instance will suffice. A creditor is owed £100 by a debtor. The debtor does not pay. The creditor gets judgment against him for the £100. Still the debtor does not pay. The creditor then discovers that the debtor is a customer of a bank and has £150 at his bank. The creditor can get a 'garnishee' order against the bank by which the bank is required to pay into court or direct to the creditor, out of its customer's £150, the £100 which he owes to the creditor.

There are two steps in the process. The first is a garnishee order *nisi*. Nisi is Norman-French. It means 'unless'. It is an order on the bank to pay the £100 to the judgment creditor or into court within a stated time *unless* there is some sufficient reason why the bank should not do so. Such reason may exist if the bank disputes its indebtedness to the customer for one reason or other. Or if payment to this creditor might be unfair by preferring him to other creditors: see *Pritchard v Westminster Bank Ltd* [1969] 1 All ER 999, [1969] 1 WLR 547 and *Rainbow v Moorgate Properties Ltd* [1975] 2 All ER 821, [1975] 1 WLR 788. If no sufficient reason appears, the garnishee order is made *absolute*, to pay to the judgment creditor, or into court, whichever is the more appropriate. On making the payment, the bank gets a good discharge from its indebtedness to its own customer, just as if he himself directed the bank to pay it. If it is a deposit on seven days' notice, the order nisi operates as the notice.

As soon as the garnishee order nisi is served on the bank, it operates as an injunction. It prevents the bank from paying the money to its customer until the garnishee order is made absolute, or is discharged, as the case may be. It binds the debt in the hands of the garnishee, that is, creates a charge in favour of the judgment creditor: see *Joachimson v Swiss Bank Corpn* [1921] 3 KB 110 at 131, [1921] All ER Rep 92 at 102, per Atkin LJ. The money at the bank is then said to be 'attached', again derived from Norman-French. But the 'attachment' is not an order to pay. It only freezes the sum in the hands of the bank until the order is made absolute or is discharged. It is only when the order is made absolute that the bank is liable to pay.

The application of the statutes

Taking the words of the statutes, it seems to me that the sum of $2,358·55 was a 'sum sterling' standing to the credit of Mr Jeromnimon in a deposit account. True it was in US dollars, but it was still a 'sum' standing to his credit. It was, I think, also a 'debt', because judgment could be given for it in US dollars as a debt. No one was aware of this until the law was so declared by this court and the House of Lords in the line of cases culminating in *Miliangos v George Frank (Textiles) Ltd* [1975] 3 All ER 801, [1976] AC 443. But the decision in *Miliangos* was, I think, retrospective. Every decision of the House in its judicial capacity is retrospective. It declares what the law is and always has been. The House of Lords has no jurisdiction to change the law. It can hold that a previous decision was wrong and can be departed from, but not that it was right up till now and can be changed for the future. At any rate, not unless it makes it clear that it is doing a piece of 'prospective overruling'. There was no such reservation in the *Miliangos* case. In my opinion, therefore, when the House held in 1975 that judgment could be given for a debt in a foreign currency, it held that that was the law of the land, and that it was, and always had been, the law of the land, but the judges had never before appreciated it. So, right from the time in 1854, when attachment of debts was introduced, a sum owing in foreign currency by a person within the jurisdiction here was a 'debt' which could be attached, though no one had ever thought so before, and the courts had previously held the contrary.

In the statute about bank deposits, there is a provision that the attachment is 'subject to rules of court', but no rules of court have been made to govern this practice in regard to our present problem. So there is nothing to detract from the force of the statutes themselves. There is nothing to which the attachment is subject. There is in the High Court a practice direction (see [1976] 1 All ER 669, [1976] 1 WLR 83) in which the masters suggest the practice to be followed when the English courts give judgments in foreign currency. But that direction has no statutory force. In any case, it applies only to judgments in foreign currency, not to third parties who owe debts in foreign currency.

So we are left with the wording of the statutes. These enable the High Court and the county courts 'to attach debts for the purpose of satisfying judgments or orders'. In my opinion the word 'debts' covers sums in this country payable in a foreign currency. So they cover the sum of $2,358·55 in this case. This is a very desirable state of the law, especially now that exchange controls have been removed. Otherwise a debtor, who owes to his creditor a debt payable in sterling (but who has a credit in sterling at his bank) could always avoid execution by the simple device of changing his credit at the bank out of sterling into a foreign currency. That cannot be allowed. It must be possible to attach a debt payable here in a foreign currency, for the purpose of satisfying an English sterling judgment.

The remaining point is the machinery by which it is done. It seems to me that, as soon as the garnishee order nisi is served on the bank, it operates to 'freeze' the sum in the hands of the bank, in this way. The bank must, as soon as reasonably practicable, in the ordinary course of business, put a 'stop order' on the requisite amount of US dollars. It should be such a number of dollars which if realised, at the time of the stop order, would realise the amount of the sterling judgment, at the buying rate of sterling ruling at the time of the stop order. The bank should *not* make a transfer into sterling at that stage. But, if and when the garnishee order is made absolute, the bank should exchange that stopped amount from dollars into sterling, so far as is necessary to meet the sterling judgment debt, and pay over that amount to the judgment creditor. But if and so far as the stopped amount (owing to exchange fluctuations) is more than enough to meet the judgment debt, the bank must release the balance from the stop and have it available for its customer on demand.

I see no reason why this machinery should prejudice the bank in any way. As soon as they can reasonably do so, after being served with the garnishee order nisi, they should telephone the exchange department and ascertain the buying rate of exchange at that moment. They should calculate the dollar equivalent of the sterling judgment, and put a stop order preventing those dollars from being taken out of the customer's account. I will call them the 'stopped dollars'. They should then wait to see if the order is made absolute. If it is, on receipt of the order absolute, they should realise the 'stopped dollars' to pay sterling. If the amount is not sufficient to satisfy the whole of the judgment debt, they must pay over the whole to the judgment creditor. If it is more than sufficient, they should only realise so many of the 'stopped dollars' as is sufficient to satisfy the judgment debt, and return the balance of the dollars for the benefit of their customer. The procedure was well summarised in a proposal submitted by counsel for the bank: (1) so soon as reasonably practicable after the time of service of the order nisi, the bank shall ascertain, at its then normal buying rate of exchange against sterling, the amount of the foreign currency balance of the judgment debtor as would, if converted at that rate, produce an amount equal to the sterling judgment debt and costs, and that amount of foreign currency as ascertained shall be attached; (2) so soon as reasonably practicable after service of the order absolute, the bank shall purchase, at its then normal buying rate of exchange against sterling, the attached amount of foreign currency, or so much thereof as will by the application of that rate produce the sterling judgment debt and costs, and pay the same into court or to the judgment creditor.

To which I would add an addendum suggested by Griffiths LJ. When the garnishee order is made absolute, its wording should be adapted to meet this procedure. Suppose the garnishee order nisi addressed to the bank was to pay a debt and costs of £1,000, it should not then be made absolute in the same form because, if this was done, the order to the bank might order them to pay a greater sum than the attached amount of foreign currency would realise. The order absolute should express the bank's obligation as an obligation to pay the sterling equivalent of the attached amount of currency or the judgment debt and costs whichever be the lesser. This paragraph should therefore be added: (3) in order that the garnishee order absolute should express the obligation of the bank under the foregoing procedure, the bank should inform the court of the amount of foreign currency attached and the rate of exchange used by the bank. When the order is made absolute, it should order the bank to pay the sterling equivalent of the foreign currency attached or the amount of the judgment debt and costs, whichever be the lesser.

Conclusion

The principles invoked in this case will require adaptation to meet other cases. For instance, the judgment creditor may have a judgment in Swiss francs, and then find that his debtor has a credit at the bank in US dollars. I see no reason why a garnishee order nisi should not be made to attach so many US dollars as would be needed to meet the judgment. Adaptation may need to be made when the debtor has a sum owing to him by a shipping company or an insurance company, and not to a bank. These adaptations can and should be made. Suffice it that the general principle is that a sterling judgment creditor can attach a sum which is payable in a foreign currency, so as to make it available to meet the judgment debt.

Brightman LJ cannot be here this morning, but he authorises me to say that he agrees with the judgment which I have just read.

GRIFFITHS LJ. I also agree with the judgment of Lord Denning MR.

Appeal allowed. Garnishee order affirmed with variations.

Solicitors: *Coward Chance* (for the bank); *Michael Votsis & Co* (for the judgment creditor).

Frances Rustin   Barrister.

R v National Insurance Commissioner, ex parte Warry

QUEEN'S BENCH DIVISION
DONALDSON LJ AND MUSTILL J
23rd JULY 1980

National insurance – Benefit – Disqualification – Persons undergoing imprisonment or detention in legal custody – Claim for benefit in respect of period when claimant was serving prison sentence in Irish Republic – Whether claimant disqualified for receiving benefit while imprisoned abroad – National Insurance Act 1965, s 49(1)(b).

The claimant, an Irish national living in England, was sentenced by a court in the Republic of Ireland to a term of 12 months' imprisonment in Ireland in respect of a criminal offence committed there. During his imprisonment in Ireland he suffered from sickness and spent some time in hospital. On release from prison he applied in England for sickness benefit for the whole period of his imprisonment. His claim was rejected by the insurance officer and by the insurance tribunal on the ground that he was disqualified for receiving benefit under s 49(1)(b)[a] of the National Insurance Act 1965 during the period of his imprisonment. The claimant appealed to a national insurance commissioner who held that he was not disqualified under s 49(1)(b) because a person was disqualified from receiving benefit under s 49(1)(b) for any period during which he was 'undergoing imprisonment or detention in legal custody' only where the imprisonment or detention was in Great Britain, since a person was disqualified for receiving benefit for any period he was abroad under s 49(1)(a) and therefore it was not necessary under s 49(1)(b) to consider imprisonment abroad. The commissioner further held that by virtue of European Community legislation s 49(1)(a) could not apply to disqualify the applicant as an EEC national for receiving benefit. The insurance officer applied for an order of certiorari to quash the commissioner's decision.

Held – Section 49(1)(a) and (b) of the 1965 Act dealt with disparate disqualifications. On the plain meaning of s 49(1)(b) the disqualification therein referred to imprisonment or

---

a   Section 49(1) is set out at p 231 *a*, post

detention anywhere in the world. It followed that the commissioner's decision was wrong, and the court would, pursuant to RSC Ord 53, r 9(4)[b], quash it and remit the matter to the commissioner with a direction to reconsider it (see p 231 j to p 232 a and f to h, post).

Notes

For disqualification for receiving benefit, see Supplement to 27 Halsbury's Laws (3rd Edn) para 1352A.

For the National Insurance Act 1965, s 49, see 23 Halsbury's Statutes (3rd Edn) 312.

Section 49(1) of the 1965 Act has been replaced by s 82(5) of the Social Security Act 1975.

Application for judicial review

By a notice of motion Christine Margaret Warry, an insurance officer, applied for an order of certiorari to quash a decision of the National Insurance Commissioner (Mr J G Monroe) dated 14th December 1978 that Patrick Christopher Kenny was not by reason of his imprisonment in the Republic of Ireland disqualified for receiving sickness or invalidity benefit for the inclusive period 29th June 1973 to 27th March 1974 and that sickness benefit or, as the case might be, invalidity benefit was payable to him for that period. The grounds of the application were that the commissioner erred in law in not concluding that s 49(1)(b) of the National Insurance Act 1965 disqualified Mr Kenny from benefit because, on the true interpretation of s 49(1)(b), it disqualified a person for receiving benefit when undergoing imprisonment or detention in legal custody outside Great Britain as well as in Great Britain and the exceptions contained in reg 11 of the Social Security (General Benefit) Regulations 1970, SI 1970 No 1981, did not apply to Mr Kenny so that it was not necessary to consider the impact of EEC legislation on those regulations. The facts are set out in the judgment of Donaldson LJ.

Simon D Brown for the insurance officer.
Michael Howard as amicus curiae.
Mr Kenny did not appear.

DONALDSON LJ. In this case application is made for judicial review, on behalf of an insurance officer of the Department of Health and Social Security. She seeks to quash the decision of the National Insurance Commissioner in connection with a claim for sickness benefit.

Mr Patrick Kenny, as his name implies, is an Irish national. He claimed sickness benefit in respect of a period when he was in fact in custody in Ireland. The circumstances in which he came to be in that predicament were these. He had been sentenced for an offence of common assault, the sentence including a provision that he was not to go within a stated distance of his wife's home. He had gone from Great Britain to the Republic and breached that condition. He was arrested and incarcerated for a period of 12 months. He had been suffering from sickness, and, apart from the fact that he was in prison in the Republic of Ireland, would have been entitled to sickness benefit. His claim was rejected by the insurance officer in reliance on s 49(1) of the National Insurance Act 1965 (since re-enacted in s 82(5) of the Social Security Act 1975).

Mr Kenny appealed to the insurance tribunal where he lost, and he then appealed to a National Insurance Commissioner where he was triumphantly successful, and it is the insurance officer who now seeks judicial review.

As I say, this question turns in the first instance on s 49(1) of the National Insurance Act 1965, which is in these terms:

---

b　　Rule 9(4) provides: 'Where the relief sought is an order of certiorari and the Court is satisfied that there are grounds for quashing the decision to which the application relates, the Court may, in addition to quashing it, remit the matter to the court, tribunal or authority concerned with a direction to reconsider it and reach a decision in accordance with the findings of the Court.'

'Except where regulations otherwise provide, a person shall be disqualified for receiving any benefit, and an increase of benefit shall not be payable in respect of any person as the beneficiary's wife or husband, for any period during which that person—(a) is absent from Great Britain; or (b) is undergoing imprisonment or detention in legal custody.'

Subsection (2) provides:

'Regulations may provide for the suspension of payment to or in respect of any person during any such period as aforesaid of benefit which is excepted from the operation of subsection (1) of this section or which is payable otherwise than in respect of that period.'

Regulations were in fact made, and they are contained in the Social Security (General Benefit) Regulations 1970, SI 1970 No 1981. We have been concerned with reg 11, which is the regulation contemplated by s 49(1). Regulation 11 is somewhat lengthy but it provides that s 49(1) shall not operate to disqualify a person for receiving certain benefits or allowances in specified circumstances, none of which has any application to Mr Kenny.

The argument which succeeded before the National Insurance Commissioner was that there was a problem in the application of this section to Mr Kenny's case because of European Economic Community legislation. Community legislation prohibits discrimination in the social services against a national of the EEC other than a national of what might be described as the host nation. In other words, you may not discriminate against nationals of other nations of the EEC although you may be able to discriminate against your own nationals. What is being said by Mr Kenny is that there was a measure of discrimination against the Irish and other members of the EEC, because, when one looks at reg 11 read with s 49(1)(b), one finds that in the context of reg 11(4), for example—

'"penalty" means a sentence of imprisonment, borstal training, or detention under section 53 of the Children and Young Persons Act 1933, or under section 57 of the Children and Young Persons (Scotland) Act 1937, or under section 1(4) of the Criminal Justice (Scotland) Act 1963, or an order for detention in a detention centre . . .'

The terminology is that of Great Britain, so that there is a blanket disqualification for those undergoing imprisonment coupled with exceptions which are peculiarly apt to apply to the native English, Welsh and Scots, and that this is discriminatory.

The way in which the National Insurance Commissioner dealt with the matter was this. He came to the conclusion that there was in fact no discrimination because on the true construction of s 49(1)(b) its reference to 'undergoing imprisonment or detention in legal custody' was confined to detention in Great Britain. Accordingly Mr Kenny was not disqualified because his imprisonment was not within Great Britain, and the EEC regulations prevented reliance on s 49(1)(a) and the fact that he was absent from Great Britain.

The National Insurance Commissioner came to that conclusion for two reasons. First, he concluded that there would be no point in the section referring to imprisonment abroad since, as written, it disqualified people for benefit by the very fact that they were abroad. Second, he thought that there were problems involved in the operation of the section if it included imprisonment abroad, because it is accepted by all concerned that imprisonment means criminal imprisonment, and it would be necessary to examine the law of the nation where the claimant was imprisoned; and perhaps under different systems of law it would be very difficult to decide whether the imprisonment was criminal imprisonment or whether it was not.

For my part, I would be unable to accept either of those reasons, although I accept the force of them, because, as it seems to me, all that is happening here is that Parliament has in mind two entirely disparate disqualifications which it has set out seriatim and there is no reason at all why Parliament should be presumed to have removed, by an implied term, an overlap between the two provisions. I would give s 49(1)(*b*) the plain meaning of the words, namely, that somebody is undergoing imprisonment or detention in legal custody anywhere in the world.

The commissioner, having reached the conclusion that Mr Kenny was not disqualified under s 49(1), did not have to go on to consider the question of whether there was discrimination, but he did express the view that, if the section is to be construed as I would construe it, Mr Kenny would succeed on that ground. What he said was this. Community law would regard parts of the scheme as discriminatory. I would accept, at any rate for present purposes, that there is discrimination in this scheme because it is much more likely that native-born British people will be able to escape under the exceptions than that foreigners will be able to do so. He goes on to say that there are various ways in which discrimination can be dealt with consistently with Community law. The first is to apply a 'blue pencil', and he has given very serious and careful thought to whether it is possible to apply a blue pencil to these regulations and came to the conclusion that it was not. Again I have not, I confess, considered whether it is possible to do this, but I am quite prepared to accept that it is not possible to do so. He then goes on to say that the next possibility is to strike out the whole of reg 11, and I agree that is the next possibility. He says that, if you do that, you introduce an entirely different scheme and one which Parliament did not contemplate. Therefore, it cannot be done, and one is left with the only other possibility, which, in obedience to Community legislation, is to strike out s 49(1) as well, or perhaps the relevant part of it. I am unable to agree with him on that.

It seems to me that there is no objection to striking out the regulation and that one would indeed do that in an appropriate case. It does not arise in this case. It does not help Mr Kenny one way or the other. It would leave the exclusion under s 49(1) because, while it is quite correct (as counsel appearing as amicus curiae said) that Parliament contemplated that regulations would be made, and no doubt the executive putting forward the Bill for the consideration of Parliament was very certain that they would be made, we as a court have to look at the statute. The statute does not make it a precondition to the operation of this section that there shall be any regulations. It says: 'Except where regulations otherwise provide . . .' It does not say that a person shall be disqualified for receiving benefit in accordance with such provisions or exceptions as the Secretary of State shall provide by regulation or anything of that sort. In no way is this section on its wording contingent on regulations being made. It follows that in no way can it be contingent on regulations which are made continuing in full force and effect. Their striking out by Community legislation cannot defeat the operation of s 49(1).

Accordingly, for the reasons which I have sought to express, I would respectfully differ from the National Insurance Commissioner and would grant whatever is the appropriate remedy. It may be certiorari. We can discuss that in a moment.

I would not, however, like to part with this case without expressing my gratitude to counsel who has appeared as amicus curiae and has given us every possible assistance in understanding this rather tangled skein of the proceedings and of course my usual thanks to counsel for the insurance officer for the economy of his argument.

MUSTILL J. I agree.

Order of certiorari; matter remitted to commissioner under RSC Ord 53, r 9(4).

Solicitors: *Solicitor, Department of Health and Social Security* (for the insurance officer); *Treasury Solicitor.*

N P Metcalfe Esq   Barrister.

Re Gibson's Settlement Trusts
Mellors and another v Gibson and others

CHANCERY DIVISION

SIR ROBERT MEGARRY V-C SITTING WITH CHIEF MASTER MATTHEWS AND MR MONTGOMERY
CAMPBELL AS ASSESSORS

26th, 27th MARCH, 13th MAY 1980

Costs – Taxation – Costs of and incidental to application – Application by plaintiffs for directions as to what steps if any they should take to implement an undertaking – Judge awarding defendants their costs of and incidental to plaintiffs' application – Whether judge's order referring only to costs incurred by defendants after issue of summons or including costs of preparatory work – RSC Ord 62, r 28(4).

Costs – Taxation – Review of taxation – Stating of decisions on objections and reasons therefor – Reason for taxing officer's decisions on objections to be properly stated – RSC Ord 62, r 34(4).

In 1965 the settlor, a married man with two children, established a settlement creating wide discretionary trusts and giving the trustees a wide special power of appointment which they exercised by making a revocable appointment of the whole of the trust fund in favour of the children, contingent on their attaining the age of 25. Subsequently, when the settlor and his wife became estranged, it was proposed that instead of the wife claiming in the ensuing divorce proceedings a lump sum payment for the children the revocable appointment under the trust should be replaced by an irrevocable appointment in favour of the children of a substantial part of the trust fund. As time was required to consider the tax implications of the proposal, the trustees on 7th June 1974 gave an undertaking that by 31st December 1974 they would enter into such deed or agreement as was necessary to cause the sum of £50,000 to be appointed absolutely to each child, contingently on each of them attaining the age of 25. The tax position still being uncertain on 31st December 1974, the trustees did not comply with the terms of the undertaking by that date. Various schemes for implementing the undertaking were drafted and on 4th December 1975 a draft appointment, prepared by the trustees, was sent to the children's solicitors. The solicitors objected to the draft on the grounds that it did not satisfy the undertaking because it provided for assets to be appointed which would be worth £50,000 when each child attained the age of 25 instead of appointing to each child assets worth £50,000 at the time of the appointment. The views of the trustees and the children's solicitors remained irreconcilable, and on 29th March 1976 the trustees made an irrevocable appointment in favour of the children on the basis of the draft appointment. Because of continuing objections by the children's solicitors, the trustees issued an originating summons on 3rd December 1976 seeking the court's directions as to what steps, if any, they ought to take in implementing the undertaking. The defendants to the summons were the settlor's two children, acting by their mother, who was appointed their guardian ad litem on 3rd February 1977, and the children of the settlor's sister, who were objects of the power in the settlement. The judge dismissed the summons on the ground that the undertaking was invalid because it fettered the trustees' discretion, and ordered, inter alia, that the defendants' 'costs of and incidental to the said application' be taxed on the common fund basis. On taxation a principal clerk allowed (1) the settlor's children's claim for costs for work done from December 1974 (ie the date of the failure to implement the undertaking), (2) 90 hours of solicitors' time, charged at the rate of £20 per hour, spent in collating evidence and documents preparatory to drawing up briefs to counsel, and (3) a mark-up of 100% in respect of the general care and conduct of the proceedings. The children of the settlor's sister objected, contending, inter alia, that costs should not be allowed for work done prior to the issue of the summons, or, at the earliest, prior to December 1975 when the dispute on the interpretation of the trustees' undertaking arose. On a review of the taxation, the master dismissed their objection to category (1) but, without giving his reason for doing so, allowed their objection to category (2) and reduced the number of hours allowed to 20. Although in the course of his answers to the objections he said that he considered a mark-up of two-thirds reasonable, he in fact disallowed the objection to (3) and allowed a mark-up of 100% because he calculated that the net costs were £982, then rounded that up to £1,000, added two-thirds, making £1,666, and then increased that figure to £2,000, which he stated was a 'fair and reasonable' sum. The four defendants applied for a review of the taxation.

Held – (1) The master was right to disallow the objection to the date from which the costs could be allowed because—

(a) costs which were otherwise recoverable in respect of work done prior to the issue of a writ or originating summons were not to be disallowed merely because they were incurred before action brought. Under RSC Ord 62, r 28(4), on a taxation on the common fund basis 'a reasonable amount in respect of all costs reasonably incurred' was permitted, and the judge's order allowing the defendants the 'costs of and incidental to the said application' included costs reasonably incurred both in the litigation and in the preparation for it. In the circumstances the taxing officer was entitled to go back to December 1974 and include in the costs to be taxed all the costs that were, in his opinion, reasonably incurred for the purpose of the litigation as it came to be framed by the trustees (see p 237 j, p 238 g to p 239 b, p 240 a to g and p 241 a b, post); *Société Anonyme Pêcheries Ostendaises v Merchants Marine Insurance Co* [1928] All ER Rep 174 and *Frankenburg v Famous Lasky Film Service Ltd* [1930] All ER Rep 364 considered; *Re Fahy's Will Trusts* [1962] 1 All ER 73 disapproved;

(b) the fact that the guardian ad litem for the settlor's children was not appointed until 3rd February 1977 did not prevent costs which were incurred before that date from being included in the costs to be taxed. A guardian ad litem when appointed could adopt work previously done for the benefit of the minors, if that work appeared to be of value in the litigation, and the court would readily assume that that had been done (see p 241 d e, post).

(2) However, the taxation could not stand as regards the second and third objections because the master had not complied with RSC Ord 62, r 34(4), which required a taxing officer, on a review of taxation, to state, on request, the reason for his decision and any special facts or circumstances relevant to it. In relation to the objection as to the number of hours, the taxing master had given no reason, and that which he had given in relation to the mark-up was inadequate. His answers were required fairly to reveal to those who were reasonably skilled in such matters the process of reasoning whereby the objection in question was allowed or disallowed, together, where appropriate, with a statement of the matters in question that were taken into account or disregarded in the process. In the circumstances the court would not order a further taxation of the disputed items but would adjourn the matter into chambers for further consideration of the facts by the judge and assessors (see p 241 j, p 242 j and p 243 b to j, post); *Eaves v Eaves and Powell* [1955] 3 All ER 849 applied; *Re Eastwood* [1974] 3 All ER 603 considered.

Notes

For taxation of costs generally, see 36 Halsbury's Laws (3rd Edn) 158–167, paras 209–222.

Cases referred to in judgment

Department of Health and Social Security v Envoy Farmers Ltd [1976] 2 All ER 173, [1976] 1 WLR 1018, [1976] ICR 573, Digest (Cont Vol E) 444, 3d.

Eastwood (deceased), Re, Lloyds Bank Ltd v Eastwood [1974] 3 All ER 603, [1975] Ch 112, [1974] 3 WLR 454, CA, Digest (Cont Vol D) 845, 1281a.

Eaves v Eaves and Powell [1955] 3 All ER 849, [1956] P 154, [1955] 3 WLR 984, 27(2) Digest (Reissue) 768, 6135.

Fahy's Will Trusts, Re, McKnight v Fahy [1962] 1 All ER 73, [1962] 1 WLR 17, 51 Digest (Repl) 900, 4512.

Frankenburg v Famous Lasky Film Service Ltd [1931] 1 Ch 428, [1930] All ER Rep 364, 100 LJKB 187, 144 LT 534, CA, 51 Digest (Repl) 932, 4727.

Llewellin, Re, Llewellin v Williams (1887) 37 Ch D 317, 57 LJ Ch 316, 58 LT 152, 47 Digest (Repl) 309, 2780.

Société Anonyme Pêcheries Ostendaises v Merchants Marine Insurance Co [1928] 1 KB 750, [1928] All ER Rep 174, 97 LJKB 445, 138 LT 532, 17 Asp MLC 404, CA, 51 Digest (Repl) 931, 4724.

Wright v Bennett [1948] 1 All ER 410, [1948] 1 KB 601, [1948] LJR 1019, CA, 51 Digest (Repl) 842, 3958.

Review of taxation

On 21st November 1979 Master Razzall disallowed two objections ('objections 1 and 3') by the objectors who were the third and fourth defendants in proceedings instituted by the trustees of a settlement dated 31st March 1965, to the taxation, by his principal clerk, Mr Burroughs, of the costs of the first and second defendants in the proceedings, but allowed a third objection ('objection 2'), with the result that the sum of £3,800 allowed by the principal clerk was reduced to £2,000. By a summons dated 5th December 1979 the objectors applied for an order that their three objections be allowed. By a summons dated 7th December 1979 the first and second defendants applied for an order that the taxation of their costs be reviewed and that objection 2 be disallowed and that the sum of £4,557 originally claimed by them or alternatively the sum of £3,800 allowed by the principal clerk or such other sum as the judge thought fit be substituted for the sum of £2,000 allowed by Master Razzall. The summonses were heard in chambers but leave was given to report the judgment, which was delivered in open court. The facts are set out in the judgment.

Kenneth Farrow for the objectors.
W R Stewart Smith for the first and second defendants.

Cur adv vult

13th May. **SIR ROBERT MEGARRY V-C** read the following judgment: These summonses for review of taxation raise questions about the extent to which costs can be allowed for work done prior to the issue of the writ or originating summons. I am delivering judgment in open court on the points of principle involved, though on the detailed application of those principles to the facts of the case I shall give my decision in chambers. The originating summons in this case was issued on 3rd December 1976, and an order dismissing the summons was made by Whitford J on 16th January 1978. The dispute arose under a settlement dated 31st March 1965 which created wide discretionary trusts and gave the trustees a wide special power of appointment. At the centre of the dispute is a somewhat remarkable undertaking under seal given by the trustees of the settlement on 7th June 1974. I do not propose to go into the details of the trusts and other matters affecting the family, but I must say enough to make the decision on costs intelligible.

The settlor, a wealthy man, became estranged from his wife. There were two children of the family, and the trustees of the settlement had exercised their powers under the settlement to make a revocable appointment of the whole of the trust fund in favour of the two children, contingently on their attaining the age of 25 years. When in 1973 a divorce was proposed, it was suggested that out of the trust fund, worth some £300,000, the revocable appointment should be replaced by an irrevocable appointment to the two children of a substantial part of the fund; and the proposal became a proposal for the appointment of £50,000 to each child, contingently on attaining the age of 25 years. By the time this was agreed, it had become known that the government intended to introduce the tax now known as capital transfer tax; and it was generally agreed that time had to be allowed to consider the proposed new legislation in order that the sums of £50,000 could be provided in the manner which, from a taxation point of view, *a* would be most beneficial to all concerned.

In order to do this, the undertaking under seal of 7th June 1974 was executed by the two trustees. It was a simple undertaking with the wife, the mother of the two children, that the trustees—

'... will by 31st December 1974 enter into such Deed or Agreement as is necessary to cause the sum of £50,000 ... to be appointed absolutely to each of the *b* [two children] contingent only upon each of them attaining the age of twenty five.'

The fact that this appointment was plainly open to the objection that it fettered the trustees in the exercise of their discretionary powers seems to have escaped the notice of everyone.

On this footing, the wife allowed the husband's petition for divorce to proceed *c* without being defended, and no claim for any lump sum payment for the children was made. A decree nisi was in fact granted on 4th June 1974, three days before the undertaking was executed. Unhappily, there were other matrimonial proceedings between husband and wife, though I need not pursue these. As is well known, there were delays in introducing capital transfer tax, and 31st December 1974, the date by which the undertaking should have been performed, came and went before the final *d* shape of the tax was known. Various schemes for implementing the undertaking were drafted by Revenue and Chancery counsel, and then, on 4th December 1975, a draft appointment prepared by one of the trustees (they were solicitors) was sent to the children's solicitors. On 24th December 1975 the children's solicitors replied, taking the objection that the draft appointment did not satisfy the undertaking, in that instead of appointing to each child assets then worth £50,000, it provided only for assets to be *e* appointed to each child which would be worth £50,000 when that child attained the age of 25 years. I pause only to say that as the argument on costs developed, December 1974 and December 1975 emerged as rival dates back to which appropriate items for costs could be taken if one could go back further than the issue of the originating summons on 3rd December 1976.

After the divergence of opinion in December 1975, the views of the trustees and the *f* children's solicitors remained irreconcilable. On 29th March 1976 the trustees made an irrevocable appointment in favour of the two children on the basis for which the trustees contended. On the basis for which the children contended, this appointment was of less than the amount required by the undertaking, so that some further appointment ought to be made. Finally, on 3rd December 1976 the trustees issued the originating summons which has given rise to the taxation. The summons could, of course, have asked the *g* simple question of construction which was in dispute, namely whether under the undertaking the sum of £50,000 to which each child was entitled meant a present £50,000 or merely £50,000 when the child was 25 years old. Instead, the originating summons sought—

'Directions as to what steps (if any) the plaintiffs ought to take as trustees of the said settlement in implementation of or otherwise in relation to an undertaking *h* given by them under seal and dated 7th June 1974 ...';

and apart from making the usual precautionary request for further or other relief, and seeking an order for costs, that was all.

When the originating summons was heard, the objection that the undertaking was invalid, as fettering the trustees' discretion, duly emerged. This disposed of the case, and *j* the originating summons was dismissed, though I was told that the judge indicated that the children's construction of the undertaking was right and the trustees' construction wrong. A résumé of the judgment which is included in the papers makes it plain that this was so. The two children were the first and second defendants to the summons, acting by the wife as their guardian ad litem. The only other defendants, the third and the fourth, were children of the husband's sister; they were objects of the power in the settlement. The order provided for the taxation of the costs of and incidental to the application of the plaintiffs, the trustees, and also, on the common fund basis, 'the costs of and incidental to the said Application of the Defendants'. The taxation now in dispute is that of the costs of the first and second defendants; and I shall call them simply 'the defendants'.

The bill of costs brought in by the defendants claims under item 26, as 'Instructions for hearing', the sum of £4,557. By consent, the bill was taxed by a principal clerk; and on 11th May 1979 he taxed this item down to £3,800. On 25th May the third and fourth defendants (whom I may now call 'the objectors') carried in four objections to this item as thus taxed. The fourth of these, relating to counsel's fees, is no longer in issue; the other three are. The first, and most substantial, may be called 'the date objection'. This objection was:

'The Taxing Officer was wrong in holding that the costs stemmed from the date of the failure to implement the undertaking given by the Trustees and that the Bill should allowably include work dating back to December 1974.'

It was submitted that the costs 'of and incidental to' the application to the court 'should only date from the issue of the Originating Summons', so that the costs in the bill should have commenced only in December 1976. The answer of the defendants, dated 11th June 1979, was that the taxing officer had been correct in allowing costs for work done from December 1974, on the basis that the originating summons was concerned solely with matters arising out of the execution of the undertaking; and they relied on two decisions of the Court of Appeal, *Société Anonyme Pêcheries Ostendaises v Merchants Marine Insurance Co* [1928] 1 KB 750, [1928] All ER Rep 174 and *Frankenburg v Famous Lasky Film Service Ltd* [1931] 1 Ch 428, [1930] All ER Rep 364. For brevity, I shall call these the *Pêcheries* case and the *Frankenburg* case respectively. Master Razzall, the taxing master, disallowed this objection, and in his answers to the objections, dated 21st November 1979, adopted the defendants' answers on this point.

The master also disallowed the third objection, but he allowed the second objection relating to the number of hours spent on the case. I shall leave details of these objections and the figures until later; but the upshot of the master's consideration of the objections was that the £3,800 fixed by the principal clerk was reduced to £2,000. After the master had given his answers to the objections, the two summonses to review the taxation were issued, the objectors' on 5th December and the defendants' on 7th December. Put shortly, the objectors sought to have their second objection allowed, whereas the defendants sought to have their original £4,557 restored, or, in default, the £3,800 which had been fixed by the principal clerk.

I shall leave the second and third objections for the present, and return to the date objection. In the course of his submissions on behalf of the objectors, counsel did at one stage seek to contend that on the facts of this case no costs incurred prior to the issue of the originating summons could be allowed to the defendants; but he accepted that in some cases costs incurred prior to the commencement of the proceedings were allowable. By the time the argument had proceeded any distance, I think he felt obliged to accept that the real issue lay between December 1974, when the undertaking was broken, and December 1975, when the dispute on interpretation arose, and that December 1976, when the originating summons was issued, had scant prospects of success.

In considering this question, both on principle and in relation to the authorities, I think that I should take matters by stages.

(1) On an order for taxation of costs, costs that otherwise would be recoverable are not to be disallowed by reason only that they were incurred before action brought. This is carried by the *Pêcheries* case, where the order was for party and party costs, and also by the *Frankenburg* case, where the costs were on the basis which was then known as the solicitor

and client basis, but is now called the common fund basis. I shall say more about these cases in due course.

(2) If the order for costs is not for costs simpliciter, but for the costs 'of and incidental to' the proceedings (and this is the language of the order in the present case), the words 'incidental to' extend rather than reduce the ambit of the order. It is true that in *Re Fahy's Will Trusts* [1962] 1 All ER 73, [1962] 1 WLR 17 it was held at first instance that in an order for the taxation on a common fund basis of the costs 'of and incidental to the negotiations leading up to this order', the words 'and incidental to' confined the costs to those which were consequent upon the negotiations, and excluded those incurred before negotiations commenced. In that case, however, no cases were cited in argument, and the judge was told that there was no authority on the meaning of the words 'and incidental to', and what they added to 'costs' in an order for costs.

I find great difficulty in seeing on what basis it can be said that the addition of these words drives out the right to antecedent costs which the *Pêcheries* and *Frankenburg* cases established. The words seem to me to be words of extension rather than words of restriction. The litigant is to have the costs 'of' the proceedings and also the costs 'incidental to' the proceedings. The phrase cannot include the costs 'of' the proceedings only if they are also 'incidental to' them. The Chief Taxing Master (Master Matthews), who, with Mr Montgomery Campbell, sat with me as an assessor, referred me to *Re Llewellin* (1887) 37 Ch D 317, a case on the application of capital money under the Settled Land Act 1882. By s 21(x), such money may be applied in payment of costs, charges, and expenses 'of or incidental to' the exercise of powers under the Act; and Stirling J (at 326) considered the force to be given to the words 'incidental to'. He said that they meant that in addition to the costs, charges and expenses which 'directly and necessarily' arose out of the exercise of powers under the Act, the words included those which were incurred 'casually or incidentally in the course of that exercise'. In *Department of Health and Social Security v Envoy Farmers Ltd* [1976] 2 All ER 173 at 175, [1976] 1 WLR 1018 at 1021 Jupp J, in considering the words 'incidental to' in relation to costs, adopted a dictionary definition that a thing was 'incidental' if it occurred 'in subordinate conjunction with something else'. However, *Wright v Bennett* [1948] 1 All ER 410, [1948] 1 KB 601 provides a warning that it is important to identify the something else to which the thing is incidental. The cost of documents used on an appeal cannot be brought within the costs 'of and incidental to' the appeal if they were prepared for use in the lower court, and so are the costs of and incidental to the proceedings in that lower court, and not the appellate court.

Counsel for the objectors understandably did not seek to rely on *Re Fahy's Will Trusts* [1962] 1 All ER 73, [1962] 1 WLR 17. He did point out that it concerned negotiations, and that although one person could litigate, it took at least two to negotiate. This, however, does not seem to carry matters much further, for I do not see why costs should not be incurred as part of the preparations for negotiations, and as incidental to them, just as they may be incurred as part of the preparations for litigation. However, he accepted that the decision was inconsistent with decisions of the Court of Appeal which were not cited; and in this I think that he was right. For myself, I would regard *Re Fahy's Will Trusts* as a decision that should not be followed.

(3) The power to award 'the costs of and incidental to all proceedings in the Supreme Court' is conferred by the Supreme Court of Judicature (Consolidation) Act 1925, s 50(1); and these words are echoed by RSC Ord 62, r 2(4) which provides that the power is to be exercised 'subject to and in accordance with this Order'. By r 28(2), on a party and party taxation there are to be allowed 'all such costs as were necessary or proper for the attainment of justice or for enforcing or defending the rights of the party whose costs are being taxed'. By r 28(4), on a taxation on the common fund basis, 'being a more generous basis than that provided for by paragraph (2)', there is to be allowed 'a reasonable amount in respect of all costs reasonably incurred', and para (2) does not apply. I think that from the setting in which this provision occurs, it is plain enough that the words 'costs reasonably incurred' refer to 'the costs of and incidental to' the proceedings in

question. However reasonably incurred, costs which are neither costs 'of' the proceedings nor costs 'incidental to' them cannot be awarded under the order for costs. It is thus important to identify the proceedings. This involves not only taking the correct stage of the proceedings, as is shown by *Wright v Bennett*, but also determining the nature of those proceedings. Only when it is seen what is being claimed can it be seen what the proceedings are to which the costs relate. In this case, the proceedings consisted of the application by the trustees for the directions of the court that I have set out. This perhaps seems obvious; but I think that it is of some importance to make it explicit.

(4) It is not very easy to extract from the authorities the principles which are to be applied in the case of costs incurred before action brought. In the *Pêcheries* case, a trawler had been lost at sea, and the dispute was about the collection of evidence from the master and crew of the vessel prior to the issue of a writ claiming recovery on an insurance policy on the vessel. Later the action was settled, on terms that the insurers paid the plaintiffs their taxed costs. Lord Hanworth MR referred to costs for 'materials ultimately proving of use and service in the action' (see [1928] 1 KB 750 at 757, [1928] All ER Rep 174 at 176). Atkin LJ quoted the words now in RSC Ord 62, r 28(2) as to what is proper for the attainment of justice, and spoke of the taxing master considering the probability of the defendant disputing liability (see [1928] 1 KB 750 at 763, [1928] All ER Rep 174 at 179). It would, indeed, be most unfortunate if the costs of obtaining evidence while it was fresh after an accident could not be allowed, even if litigation seemed probable, merely because no writ had then been issued. Lawrence LJ abstained from resolving the point, but did not differ from the decision that the taxing master had a discretion to allow the costs of collecting the evidence (see [1928] 1 KB 750 at 765, [1928] All ER Rep 174 at 180).

In the *Frankenburg* case, the plaintiff feared that a proposed demolition and reconstruction of the defendants' neighbouring building would injure his ancient lights, and so he instructed solicitors and had elevations and plans of the neighbouring premises prepared. Negotiations for a settlement failed, the plaintiff issued a writ, and ultimately the case was compromised on terms that the defendants should pay the plaintiff the damages found due on an inquiry, and also his solicitor and client costs. The dispute was as to the plaintiff's costs incurred before he issued his writ. Lord Hanworth MR made it clear that in his view the plaintiff's case began not merely when the writ was issued, but before (see [1931] 1 Ch 428 at 435, [1930] All ER Rep 364 at 367). He reiterated the views that he had expressed in the *Pêcheries* case, repeating his words about materials which ultimately proved of use and service in the action (see [1931] 1 Ch 428 at 436, [1930] All ER Rep 364 at 367–368). However, he explained this in terms of being 'relevant to some of the issues which had to be tried and in respect of which justice was sought'. Further on he referred to costs 'which may be fairly attributable to the conduct of the defendants and thus within the costs which it was contemplated would have to be paid by the defendants'. There were thus three strands of reasoning, that of proving of use and service in the action, that of relevance to an issue, and that of attributability to the defendants' conduct. Lawrence LJ referred to the concept of use and service in the action, and made it plain that even if the immediate purpose of obtaining materials was to see whether to sue, the taxing master could allow costs which he considered to have been properly incurred in obtaining materials which would be useful to the plaintiff at the trial (see [1931] 1 Ch 428 at 440–441, [1930] All ER Rep 364 at 369). Slesser LJ simply agreed with both judgments.

(5) Obviously the test cannot be simply whether the materials in question proved in fact to be of use in the action, for otherwise when a case is settled before trial (as it was in both the *Pêcheries* case and the *Frankenburg* case) it would often not be possible to say with any certainty which materials had been or would have been of use in the action. Nor would it be right to penalise the successful litigant for obtaining materials which appeared likely to be of use in the action but which, in the event, were never used because the other party did not contest the point. Whatever may be the position on a party and party taxation, if the taxation is on the common fund basis I think that one

must go back to the words 'costs reasonably incurred'; and, as I have said, I think that this must mean the costs of and incidental to the proceedings in question. Neither the fact that at the time when the costs were incurred no writ or originating summons had been issued, nor the fact that the immediate object in incurring the costs was to ascertain the prospective litigant's chances of success, will per se suffice to exclude the costs from being regarded as part of the costs of the litigation that ensues. Of course, if there is no litigation there are no costs of litigation. But if the dispute ripens into litigation, the question then arises how far the ambit of the costs is affected by the shape that the litigation takes.

(6) It is obvious that the matters disputed before a writ or originating summons is issued, and the matters raised by the writ or originating summons, and by any pleadings and affidavits, may differ considerably from each other. A wide-ranging series of disputed matters may be followed by a writ or originating summons which raises only a few of the issues; or a narrow dispute may be followed by proceedings which seek to resolve wider issues as well. How far does the ambit of the litigation extend or restrict the matters occurring before the issue of the writ or originating summons which may be included in the taxed costs on the common fund basis?

If the proceedings are framed narrowly, then I cannot see how antecedent disputes which bear no real relation to the subject of the litigation could be regarded as being part of the costs of the proceedings. On the other hand, if these disputes are in some degree relevant to the proceedings as ultimately constituted, and the other party's attitude made it reasonable to apprehend that the litigation would include them, then I cannot see why the taxing master should not be able to include these costs among those which he considers to have been 'reasonably incurred'.

The converse case, that of a narrow area of dispute followed by widely-framed proceedings, seems to me to be somewhat different. If a prospective litigant goes into a number of matters outside the immediate area of dispute, but he then finds that these matters fall within the widely-framed scope of his adversary's proceedings, it seems to me that those proceedings will almost of necessity make the costs of these matters part of the costs of the proceedings, subject always, of course, to the taxing master considering the costs to have been reasonably incurred. Even though the acts, when done, could not fairly be considered to be related in any real way to what was then in dispute, they will have subsequently been made part of the litigation; and if the costs of what was then done were costs reasonably incurred in relation to what subsequently became defined as the matters in dispute, it seems to me that the taxing master may properly allow them. There is a kind of legitimation by subsequent litigation. Of course, if it is made clear between the parties, whether by the pleadings or otherwise, that what is widely framed is nevertheless only to be fought on a narrow point, that may, from the time that it is done, have the practical effect of narrowing widely-framed proceedings.

With that, I return to the facts of this case. The originating summons is indeed in wide terms. Furthermore, it is directly related to the undertaking of the trustees dated 7th June 1974. It asks what steps (if any) the trustees as such ought to take in implementation of, or otherwise in relation to, the undertaking. An affidavit dated 4th March 1977 by one of the trustees opens up the whole course of dealings in relation to the settlement, the undertakings, the revocable appointment, the irrevocable appointment and the anxieties as to tax liability. It can indeed be said (and counsel for the objectors said it) that the mere failure to comply with the undertaking by 31st December 1974 was not in itself a matter of dispute: all concerned were waiting to see the form that capital transfer tax would take, and to find the fiscally least burdensome way of carrying out the undertaking. Yet the unresolved question between those concerned was how the undertaking should, belatedly, be carried out. It has not been suggested that there was anything which made it explicit that nothing would be in issue at the hearing save the date at which each child's £50,000 was to be ascertained; and the terms of the affidavit that I have just mentioned plainly suggested the contrary.

There are obvious complications in making the proper attributions of the various letters and other documents, and all the telephone conversations and attendances, and so on. Matrimonial disputes were being dealt with at the same time, and many matters call for some form of apportionment between what was the subject of the litigation and what was not. But in my judgment, subject to all proper attributions and apportionments, the taxing master was perfectly entitled to go back to 31st December 1974, the last date for compliance with the undertaking, and include in the costs to be taxed all costs that in his opinion were reasonably incurred for the purpose of the litigation as it came to be framed by the trustees. In short, I think that the taxing master was right to disallow the date objection.

On this branch of the case there was one other point. Counsel for the objectors contended that as the defendants were both minors, litigating by their guardian ad litem, no costs incurred before their guardian ad litem was appointed (which I was told was on 3rd February 1977) could be included in the costs to be taxed. The costs incurred by the wife before she became the guardian ad litem of the defendants were incurred in her personal capacity, and her subsequent change of capacity did nothing to make those costs part of the costs of the proceedings: for minors, the rule was 'No guardian ad litem, no costs'. When asked why a guardian ad litem, when appointed, could not adopt work previously done for the benefit of the minors, taking the benefit of it and shouldering the burden, counsel for the objectors could give me no intelligible reason.

I do not think that there is anything in the point. I do not see why a guardian ad litem should not adopt work already done if that work appears to be of value in the litigation; and if the guardian ad litem does this, I cannot see why he or she should not be liable, as such, for the value of the work so adopted, or why the court should not readily assume that this has been done. This contention fails.

I can at last turn from the first of the objections to the taxation, the date objection, to the second. In the bill there was an item for 90 hours of a partner's time for collating evidence and documents preparatory to drawing briefs to counsel. The objection was that the figure was arbitrary and unsupported by attendance notes and notes of time spent, and that the taxing officer was wrong to allow it merely because the trustees could not disprove the estimate. The defendants' answer was that time sheets and attendance records, together with correspondence and documents, had been produced, and that the time included time spent on looking up statutes and case law and dealing with matters raised by the trustees in correspondence. The defendants also said that the taxing officer had invited the objectors' solicitors to state how long they and the trustees' solicitors had spent on the matter, and to produce their attendance notes and time sheets for the purpose of comparison, but that they had been unable to do this.

The taxing master allowed this objection and reduced the 90 hours to 20. His answers to the objections omit any heading for this objection, objection 2, but under the heading 'Objection 1', there appear some words which might be in point. They run: 'I retaxed item 26. I asked where this item began in the bill and was informed by the Solicitors supporting the bill that it started at the foot of page 9'. The answers then turn to totals and percentages which I shall mention in due course.

As an explanation of how 90 hours came to be reduced to 20 hours, this answer seems almost valueless. As the taxing master had adopted the defendants' answer on the first objection, to the effect that the taxing master had been correct in allowing for work done from December 1974, the reduction cannot have been made on the footing that some of the work had been done at too early a period. Presumably, then, there were other grounds for disallowing over three-quarters of the time claimed: but what were they? The silence of the taxing master's answer is carried to the point not only of giving no reasons for the reduction, but also of not stating what the reduction was. This has to be gathered from page 10 of the bill, where opposite the typed claim for 90 hours there appears, in what the Chief Taxing Master told me was Master Razzall's handwriting, a notation indicating 20 hours, together with the sum of £400, inappropriately entered in the VAT column.

It is not easy either to attack or to defend the figure of 20 hours without any indication of the taxing master's reasons for adopting it. A perusal of the documents in the case suggests that while 90 hours may have been too generous, 20 hours is substantially less than is just. Counsel for the defendants sought to sustain the 90 hours, while counsel for the objectors tried to uphold the 20 hours: but everyone was in the dark because the taxing master had given no reasons. At this stage I shall say no more on this point; but I shall have to return to it.

With that, I come to the third objection. This relates to the 'mark-up', the usual name for the element in the gross sum charged which is appropriate to the words 'the general care and conduct of the proceedings' which appear in para (j) of the note to items 26 and 27 in App 2 to RSC Ord 62. This mark-up is normally expressed as a fraction or percentage. I understand that it is often 50%, and that in appropriate cases it may be considerably more. In the defendants' bill the mark-up was 100%. The taxing master reduced it to the fraction two-thirds, and the objectors contended that this was still excessive. It should, they said, be reduced to 60%, since £20 per hour had been allowed for the partner's time. This, said counsel for the objectors, was at the top end of the range at the time, namely in the period 1974 to 1977; and he cited Re Eastwood [1974] 3 All ER 603 at 607, [1975] Ch 112 at 131 as supporting his contention that the mark-up should be less if the hourly rate is high. The defendants, on the other hand, contended that a mark-up of at least 100% was fully justified; and they said that on a review of taxation 100% ought to be allowed. I may say at once that it soon became common ground that there was no real issue on the objectors' contention that two-thirds should be reduced to 60%: towards the end counsel for the objectors, on instructions, realistically accepted that the only issue under this head was as between two-thirds and 100% or some intermediate figure.

Under the heading 'Objection 3', all that the taxing master said in his answers was: 'I consider 2/3rds mark-up to be reasonable and disallow this objection'. However, under the previous heading of objection 1, but in the part of it which had plainly gone beyond that objection, the taxing master said that his breakdown was set out in the bill, and that he made the net costs £982 '... which I called £1,000 ... to which I added 2/3rds, making £1,666 ... I increased this to £2,000 ... which I consider fair and reasonable. The charging rate claimed was £20 ... an hour plus 2/3rds.' As I have mentioned, he then stated, under the objection 3 heading, that he considered a two-thirds mark-up to be reasonable.

I am quite unable to understand the reasoning of this. The rounding up of £982 to £1,000 seems reasonable enough; but to increase this to £2,000 is obviously to make an increase of 100%, and not of a mere two-thirds. I do not think that an increase from £1,666 to £2,000 can fairly be called a rounding up. For one thing it is an increase of over 20% and goes far beyond any process that could properly be called a rounding up; there are earlier points after £1,666 that could be called 'rounded' before reaching £2,000. Further, there had already been one rounding up; and if at each stage of the calculation there were to be a rounding up, it would not be long before the cumulative roundings would match and overtop the starting figure. A round up on a round up may not be void; but it deserves critical scrutiny.

The question, then, is what is to be done. On an application to a judge for the review of a taxation RSC Ord 62, r 35(4) provides that the judge 'may exercise all such powers and discretion as are vested in the taxing officer in relation to the subject matter of the application'; and under r 35(6), the judge 'may make such order as the circumstances require', including the remission of the items in question to the same or another taxing officer for taxation. One thing seems quite plain, and that is that the taxation cannot stand as regards the second and third objections, dealing with the dispute as to 90 hours or 20 hours, and the dispute whether the mark-up should be two-thirds or 100%. In the one case no reasoning has been put forward, and in the other case such reasoning as there is seems insupportable. In the process of investigating the second objection, it seems inescapable that the whole of the documents will have to be examined to discover the proper number of hours. In doing that, it is obviously sensible that the material examined should be considered in the light of this judgment on the first point, namely the extent to which what was done before the originating summons was issued falls within what I have said about the 'costs reasonably incurred'. The taxing master, of course, did not have the advantage of being able to consider this; and although in my judgment he was perfectly right in disallowing the objectors' contention that nothing prior to the issue of the originating summons should be allowed, the date is far from being the only consideration.

It would, of course, be possible to order a further taxation of the disputed items by the same or another taxing master. However, after hearing this case strenuously argued for a day and a half in the light of the documents, I think that the assessors and I have a knowledge of the issues which would make it preferable, and save in time and costs, for the matter to be dealt with as a whole at this stage without ordering any further taxation. Accordingly, the suggestion was made on the second day of the hearing that the assessors should undertake the task of examining the papers under all three heads with a view to advising me of the proper sums to allow, and that then, having considered their advice and the documents, I should myself determine the proper sums to be allowed. I am glad to say that both counsel appeared to consider this to be a suitable course to take; and in my view it is plainly the right one, though of course burdensome, particularly to the assessors. Accordingly, this has been done.

Before I turn to my conclusions on this review, however, duty compels me to deal with one further matter. RSC Ord 62, r 34(4) requires a taxing officer who has reviewed a taxation to state, on request, 'the reasons for his decision on the review, and any special facts or circumstances relevant to it'. The duty to give reasons is plainly most important. The reasons are needed initially to enable the unsuccessful party to decide whether to carry matters further. If he does bring the taxation before a judge for review, the reasons are needed to enable the parties to know the propositions they have to attack or defend, and also to enable the judge to understand why the taxing officer did what he did. All this, of course, is obvious. As Sachs J once emphasised, the duty of the taxing officer is to make a full statement of all his reasons, and this duty may well entail stating specifically whether or not a matter complained of was taken into account. Sachs J also pointed out that 'a taxing officer is not entitled to take cover, so to speak, under an omnibus statement that he has taken "all relevant circumstances" into account'; see *Eaves v Eaves* [1955] 3 All ER 849 at 851, [1956] P 154 at 156–157. The same applies to a mere statement that the taxing officer considers something to be 'reasonable' or 'fair and reasonable'. To say 'My reasons for holding that the costs were "reasonably incurred" within r 28(4) are that I thought them to be fair and reasonable' is to give no reason at all. A bare assertion in terms of the proposition itself is no more a reason than the once familiar 'Because I tell you to'.

I appreciate that the task of taxing officers is burdensome, and that the press of detailed work may sometimes make it difficult for them to do more than express their reasons somewhat concisely. I am certainly not saying that there is any duty for them to write lengthy and detailed expositions of their thoughts, or that such expositions would be desirable. The question is whether their answers will fairly reveal to those who are reasonably skilled in these matters the process of reasoning whereby the objection in question was allowed or disallowed, together, where appropriate, with a statement of the matters in question that were taken into account or disregarded in the process; and in most cases it should be possible to do this with reasonable brevity, without descending into prolixity. In this case, after making all possible allowances, I feel obliged to say that in my judgment the taxing master's answers were perfunctory, and fell much below the minimum standard of explicitness and cogency that litigants and judges alike are entitled to expect. I hope indeed that in this respect this case is exceptional, and will remain so.

That said, I shall now adjourn into chambers in order to state the detailed results of the review by the assessors.

[The Vice-Chancellor gave leave to report that in chambers he accepted the advice of the assessors in toto, and determined the amount of item 26 in the bill in the sum of £3,000, in place of the claim for £4,557, the principal clerk's £3,800, and the taxing master's £2,000.]

Order accordingly.

Solicitors: *Sharpe Pritchard & Co* (for the objectors); *Hall Brydon,* Manchester (for the defendants).

Azza M Abdallah   Barrister.

Chokolingo v Attorney General of Trinidad and Tobago

PRIVY COUNCIL

LORD DIPLOCK, LORD EDMUND-DAVIES, LORD KEITH OF KINKEL, LORD SCARMAN AND LORD ROSKILL

14th july, 13th october 1980

Constitutional law – Constitution – Separation of powers – Separation of legislative and judicial powers – Westminster-style constitution – Function of judiciary – Declaration and interpretation of what law is by judiciary.

Trinidad and Tobago – Constitutional law – Human rights and freedoms – Right not to be deprived of liberty otherwise than by due process of law – Due process of law – Redress – Committal for contempt of court – Appellant admitting contempt of court and being sentenced to imprisonment – Appellant not appealing – Appellant later claiming that he had been imprisoned otherwise than by due process of law because judge had wrongly interpreted law – Whether appellant committed according to due process of law – Whether appellant entitled to exercise parallel remedies – Constitution of Trinidad and Tobago 1962 (SI 1962 No 1875, Sch 2), ss 1(a), 6(1).

In 1972 a newspaper published a short story written by the appellant, who was the editor of the newspaper, which, under the guise of fiction, suggested that the judiciary in Trinidad and Tobago was corrupt. The Trinidad and Tobago Law Society applied to have the appellant committed for contempt of court and at his trial the appellant, on the advice of his counsel, admitted that the story was a contempt and unreservedly apologised. The judge held that the appellant's story 'scandalised the court' and thereby amounted to a criminal contempt of court. He sentenced the appellant to 21 days' imprisonment. The appellant did not appeal and served his sentence. In 1975 the appellant applied for a declaration under s 6(1)[a] of the Constitution of Trinidad and Tobago that his committal was unconstitutional and void because it contravened his right under s 1(a)[b] of the Constitution not to be deprived of his liberty 'except by due process of law'. The appellant contended that the offence of scandalising the court was obsolete and not known to the common law in force in Trinidad when the Constitution came into force and that therefore the trial judge in committing him for that offence had not imprisoned him according to due process of law. The appellant's application was

---

a   Section 6(1) provides: 'For the removal of doubts it is hereby declared that if any person alleges that any of the provisions of the foregoing sections or section of this Constitution has been, is being, or is likely to be contravened in relation to him, then, without prejudice to any other action with respect to the same matter which is lawfully available, that person may apply to the High Court for redress.'

b   Section 1(a), so far as material, is set out at p 246 f, post

dismissed both at first instance and by the Court of Appeal. The appellant appealed to the Privy Council.

Held – The appeal would be dismissed for the following reasons—

(1) Under the constitution of an independent member of the Commonwealth having a Westminster-style constitution based on the separation of powers, it was the function of the judiciary alone to interpret the law, whether it was written law made by the legislative power or unwritten law (such as the common law and doctrines of equity) incorporated into the legal system by the constitution. It followed that where the decision of a court was final, either because there was no right of appeal or because neither party had exercised his right of appeal, the law was that which the court interpreted and declared the law to be when reaching its decision, and if a person was imprisoned according to the law as so interpreted and declared he was imprisoned according to 'due process of law', however erroneous that interpretation and declaration might be. Accordingly even if the trial judge had been in error in deciding that scandalising the court amounted to a criminal contempt the appellant had not thereby been denied due process of law for the purposes of s 1(a) of the Constitution (see p 247 j to p 248 h and p 249 c, post); *Maharaj v Attorney General of Trinidad and Tobago (No 2)* [1978] 2 All ER 670 explained.

(2) It would be irrational and would subvert the rule of law, which the Constitution was declared to enshrine, if the appellant were to be allowed to apply under s 6(1) for a declaration that he had been denied due process of law because the judge had wrongly interpreted and declared what the law was, since that would amount to the appellant having parallel and collateral remedies with respect to the same matter, namely a direct appeal and an application under s 6(1), which could lead to conflicting decisions (see p 248 h to p 249 a and c, post).

Notes

For the Constitution of Trinidad and Tobago, see 6 Halsbury's Laws (4th Edn) para 1009.

Cases referred to in judgment

Ambard v Attorney General for Trinidad and Tobago [1936] 1 All ER 704, [1936] AC 322, 105 LJPC 72, 154 LT 616, PC, 16 Digest (Repl) 22, 161.

Maharaj v Attorney General of Trinidad and Tobago (No 2) [1978] 2 All ER 670, [1979] AC 385, [1978] 2 WLR 902, PC, Digest (Cont Vol E) 49, 563a.

Appeal

Patrick Chokolingo appealed with the leave of the Court of Appeal of the Supreme Court of Judicature of Trinidad and Tobago against the dismissal on 28th December 1978 by the Court of Appeal (Hyatali CJ, Corbin and Kelsick JJA) of his appeal against the judgment of Cross J on 28th April 1975 dismissing his application by notice of motion dated 31st January 1975 claiming redress against the Attorney General, under s 6 of the Constitution of Trinidad and Tobago 1962, for contravention of his rights under s 1 of the Constitution. The facts are set out in the judgment of the Board.

David Turner-Samuels QC and *Stephen Sedley* for the appellant.
The Solicitor General of Trinidad and Tobago (Jean Permanand) and *George Newman* for the Attorney General.

LORD DIPLOCK. On 26th May 1972 there was published in a newspaper, 'The Bomb', of which the appellant was the editor, what was described as a 'Short Story by P. David Lincott' entitled 'The Judge's Wife'. P David Lincott was a nom de plume of the appellant, who was the author of the story. It was written in the vernacular current in Trinidad and purported to be an account by a servant recently dismissed from a judge's household of the way in which the judge and his wife and, it was suggested, his fellow judges habitually conducted themselves. A box heading to the story accurately summarised its contents: 'The old domestic was bent on exposing bribery, corruption and fraud in the household.'

The Trinidad and Tobago Law Society took the view that, under a thin disguise of fiction, this was an attack on the probity of the judiciary of Trinidad and Tobago as a whole. It charged them with corruption and was calculated to undermine the authority of the courts and public confidence in the administration of justice.

The society, which is incorporated by an Act of Parliament, applied to the High Court for an order for committal of the appellant and the publisher of the newspaper for contempt of court. At the hearing of the application by Hassanali J, the appellant was represented by both senior and junior counsel. After certain preliminary objections to the form of the proceedings had been overruled by the judge, the appellant filed an affidavit in which he stated that he had been advised that the short story amounted to a contempt of court for which he unreservedly apologised. His counsel also conceded that the publication of the so-called short story was a criminal contempt.

On 17th July 1972 Hassanali J held the appellant and the publisher of 'The Bomb' guilty of contempt of court and ordered the appellant to be imprisoned for 21 days, of which he in fact served 12, the remainder having been remitted by the Crown. He and the publisher, who was fined $500, were also ordered to pay the costs of the Law Society.

In 1972 no appeal lay to the Court of Appeal from committal by the High Court for contempt. An appeal lay directly to Her Majesty in Council by special leave of this Board (see *Ambard v Attorney General for Trinidad and Tobago* [1936] 1 All ER 704, [1936] AC 322); but no such leave was sought by the appellant, no doubt in view of what in effect had been a plea of guilty on his part.

Two and a half years later, on 31st January 1975, the appellant sought to resurrect the matter by applying to the High Court, under s 6(1) of the Constitution of Trinidad and Tobago, for declarations that the order of Hassanali J for his committal was unconstitutional and void and that his subsequent imprisonment under that order was in breach of the human rights and fundamental freedoms guaranteed to him by s 1(a), (i) and (k) of the Constitution, viz:

> '(a) the right of the individual to life, liberty, security of the person and enjoyment of property, and the right not to be deprived thereof except by due process of law ...
> '(i) freedom of thought and expression ...
> '(k) freedom of the press.'

Against the Trinidad and Tobago Law Society who were (mistakenly) made respondents to the application, he also claimed damages for wrongful imprisonment and repayment of the costs of the contempt proceedings in 1972, which he had been ordered to pay. Notice of this application was given to the Attorney General as is required by s 13 of the Supreme Court of Judicature Act 1962, but he was not made the respondent to the application, as he should have been.

The application came on for hearing before Cross J in March and April 1975, some three years before the judgment of this Board in *Maharaj v Attorney General of Trinidad and Tobago (No 2)* [1978] 2 All ER 670, [1979] AC 385 had been delivered. Cross J took the view that, on an application under s 6 of the Constitution, it was incumbent on him to reopen the whole question of whether the appellant had been guilty of criminal contempt of court in 1972, notwithstanding the unappealed judgment to that effect of Hassanali J and the concession made at the hearing before that judge by the appellant's own counsel that the appellant had been guilty of contempt. Cross J accordingly proceeded to consider the various grounds on which the appellant's counsel relied for their submission that Hassanali J had erred in law in holding the appellant guilty. Of these the only ground to which their Lordships need refer is a submission that, whatever may have formerly been the law, 'scandalising the court' by a scurrilous attack on the judiciary as a whole, impugning their probity and accusing them of corruption was no longer capable of amounting to a criminal contempt of court in Trinidad and Tobago.

Cross J, after a careful survey of the authorities from English and other Commonwealth jurisdictions, rejected this and the other submissions that had been made on behalf of the appellant and dismissed the application.

From this dismissal of his application, the appellant appealed to the Court of Appeal. The effective hearing of the appeal took place in October 1978, after the judgment of this Board in *Maharaj v Attorney General of Trinidad and Tobago (No 2)* had been reported. At the hearing the appellant's counsel expressly abandoned any claim that his rights under s 1(*i*) or (*k*) had been infringed; reliance was placed solely on s 1(*a*). All three members of the Court (Hyatali CJ, Corbin and Kelsick JJA) held that the only grounds on which the appellant's application under s 6 of the Constitution was based consisted of allegations of errors of substantive law in the original judgment of Hassanali J or mere irregularities in procedure; and that nothing that was alleged was capable of amounting to a failure to observe one of the fundamental rules of natural justice. Applying what was said in the majority judgment in *Maharaj v Attorney General of Trinidad and Tobago (No 2)* (the minority judgment was more restrictive of the scope of s 1(*a*)) the Court of Appeal held that such errors, even if they were established, were not capable of constituting an infringement of the appellant's right, under s 1(*a*), not to be deprived of his liberty except by due process of law.

All three appellate judges, however, did go on to consider whether Hassanali J had made an error in substantive law in holding that scandalising the court, in the way that the so-called story complained of did, amounted to a criminal contempt of court. All three were of opinion that his judgment to this effect was correct, though Kelsick JA was of opinion that the proper procedure for dealing with this kind of contempt was by criminal prosecution rather than by the summary procedure that had in fact been adopted by the Law Society. Kelsick JA's opinion on this matter was not shared by the majority of the Court of Appeal; nor has it been relied on before this Board. Even if it were right, it would at most amount to a mere irregularity of procedure which, as this Board pointed out in *Maharaj v Attorney General of Trinidad and Tobago (No 2)* [1978] 2 All ER 670 at 679, [1979] AC 385 at 399, does not of itself constitute an infringement of rights protected by s 1(*a*) unless it involves a failure to observe one of the fundamental rules of natural justice. There was no such failure here. The appellant had been fully informed of the charges against him in the contempt proceedings in 1972; he had ample opportunity to prepare his defence. He was represented at the hearing by both senior and junior counsel; it was on their advice that, in effect, he pleaded guilty to the charge.

The appellant exercised his right under s 82(1)(*c*) of the Constitution to appeal to the Judicial Committee of the Privy Council from the decision of the Court of Appeal and by leave of this Board the Attorney General was substituted for the Law Society as respondent, so that the application under s 6(1) should be properly constituted.

In dismissing the appellant's application under s 6(1) the Court of Appeal relied on the statement by this Board in *Maharaj v Attorney General of Trinidad and Tobago (No 2)* [1978] 2 All ER 670 at 679, [1979] AC 385 at 399:

> '... no human right or fundamental freedom recognised by Chapter 1 of the Constitution is contravened by a judgment or order that is wrong and liable to be set aside on appeal for an error of fact or substantive law, even where the error has resulted in a person's serving a sentence of imprisonment. The remedy for errors of these kinds is to appeal to a higher court. Where there is no higher court to appeal to then none can say that there was error.'

It may be that technically this statement was obiter, but, as the context indicates, it was the subject of careful deliberation by the Board in the light of the judgments of Hyatali CJ and Corbin JA in the Court of Appeal and the minority judgment in the Judicial Committee itself.

The arguments addressed to their Lordships in the instant appeal, however, call for some expansion of that statement. Under a constitution on the Westminster model, like that of Trinidad and Tobago, which is based on the separation of powers, while it is an exercise of the legislative power of the state to make the written law, it is an exercise of the judicial power of the state, and consequently a function of the judiciary alone, to interpret the written law when made and to declare the law where it still remains unwritten, ie the English common law and doctrines of equity as incorporated in the law of Trinidad and Tobago by s 12 of the Supreme Court of Judicature Act 1962. So when in Chapter 1 the Constitution of Trinidad and Tobago speaks of 'law' it is speaking of the law of Trinidad and Tobago as interpreted or declared by the judges in the exercise of the judicial power of the state.

The normal way in which this interpretative and declaratory function is exercised is by judges sitting in courts of justice for the purpose of deciding disputes between parties to litigation (whether civil or criminal), which involves the application to the particular facts of the case of the law of Trinidad and Tobago that is relevant to the determination of their rights and obligations. It is fundamental to the administration of justice under a constitution which claims to enshrine the rule of law (preamble, paras (d) and (e)) that if between the parties to the litigation the decision of that court is final (either because there is no right of appeal to a higher court or because neither party has availed himself of an existing right of appeal) the relevant law as interpreted by the judge in reaching the court's decision *is* the 'law' so far as the entitlement of the parties to 'due process of law' under s 1(a) and the 'protection of the law' under s 1(b) are concerned. Their Lordships repeat what was said in *Maharaj v Attorney General for Trinidad and Tobago (No 2)*. The fundamental human right guaranteed by s 1(a) and (b), and s 2, of the Constitution is not to a legal system which is infallible but to one which is fair.

It was argued on behalf of the appellant that, if he could persuade the Board that, because it had become obsolete long before 1962, no such offence as 'scandalising the court' was known to the common law in force in Trinidad at the commencement of the Constitution, this would entitle the appellant to redress under s 6 for his having been imprisoned by the state for exercising his constitutional rights of freedom of expression and freedom of the press. But giving a separate label to what Hassanali J held in the contempt proceedings to be a species of the genus of offences known as 'contempt of court' does not, in their Lordships' view, assist the appellant. 'Scandalising the court' is a convenient way of describing a publication which, although it does not relate to any specific case either past or pending or any specific judge, is a scurrilous attack on the judiciary as a whole, which is calculated to undermine the authority of the courts and public confidence in the administration of justice. Even if it were possible to persuade their Lordships that publication of written matter which has these characteristics no longer constituted a criminal contempt of court in Trinidad and Tobago in 1972, it would merely show that the judge had made an error of substantive law as to a necessary ingredient of the genus of common law offences which constitute contempt of court. In their Lordships' view there is no difference in principle behind this kind of error and a misinterpretation by a judge, in the course of an ordinary criminal trial, of the words of the Act of Parliament creating the offence with which the accused is charged. If the former is open to collateral attack by application to the High Court under s 6(1) of the Constitution so must the latter be.

Acceptance of the appellant's argument would have the consequence that in every criminal case in which a person who had been convicted alleged that the judge had made any error of substantive law as to the necessary characteristics of the offence there would be parallel remedies available to him: one by appeal to the Court of Appeal, the other by originating application under s 6(1) of the Constitution to the High Court with further rights of appeal to the Court of Appeal and to the Judicial Committee. These parallel remedies would be also cumulative since the right to apply for redress under s 6(1) is stated to be 'without prejudice to any other action with respect to the same matter which is lawfully available'. The convicted person having exercised unsuccessfully his right of appeal to a higher court, the Court of Appeal, he could nevertheless launch a collateral attack (it may be years later) on a judgment that the Court of Appeal had upheld, by making an application for redress under s 6(1) to a court of co-ordinate jurisdiction, the

High Court. To give to Chapter I of the Constitution an interpretation which would lead to this result would, in their Lordships' view, be quite irrational and subversive of the rule of law which it is a declared purpose of the Constitution to enshrine.

For the sake of completeness their Lordships will deal briefly with the other argument addressed to them on behalf of the appellant. It was that he had been convicted by Hassanali J without there being any evidence that he had committed an offence and that accordingly his conviction was not obtained by 'due process of law'. But this, on analysis, is only another way of saying that the judge made an error of substantive law in holding that to constitute a criminal contempt of court it is not necessary that a publication attacking the judiciary should refer to a specific case or to a specific judge. The publication of the issue of 'The Bomb' containing the so-called short story 'The Judge's Wife' was proved, the appellant's authorship was admitted. The only fact of which evidence was missing was one which on Hassanali J's view of the substantive law was unnecessary, viz that the short story related to a specific case or a specific judge.

The application under s 6(1) was misconceived.

The appeal must be dismissed with costs.

Appeal dismissed.

Solicitors: *Ingledew, Brown, Bennisson & Garrett* (for the appellant); *Charles Russell & Co* (for the respondent).

Sumra Green   Barrister.

R v Crown Court at Reading, ex parte Malik and another

QUEEN'S BENCH DIVISION

DONALDSON LJ AND MCNEILL J

14th OCTOBER, 6th NOVEMBER 1980

Criminal law – Bail – Crown Court – Jurisdiction to grant bail – Application for bail refused by High Court – Further application to Crown Court for bail – Whether Crown Court having jurisdiction to grant bail – RSC Ord 79, r 9(12).

The applicants, who had been charged with certain criminal offences and remanded in custody by the justices, applied to the High Court for bail but their applications were refused. Shortly afterwards they were committed to the Crown Court for trial and applied to that court for bail. The Crown Court judge held that as they had already been refused bail by a High Court judge he had no jurisdiction to entertain their application because by virtue of RSC Ord 79, r 9(12)[a] if an applicant to the High Court in any criminal proceedings was refused bail by a judge in chambers he was not entitled to make a fresh application for bail to 'any other judge' or to a Divisional Court. On an application by the applicants to the Divisional Court for a judicial review of the Crown Court judge's decision,

Held – The jurisdiction of the Crown Court and that of the High Court in relation to the granting of bail were distinct and different. RSC Ord 79, r 9(12) related exclusively to the jurisdiction of the High Court which was exercisable only by the judge in chambers and the reference to 'any other judge' was merely a reference to any other judge in the High Court to indicate that the judge in chambers had exclusive jurisdiction in the High

---

a   Rule 9(12) is set out at p 251 *g*, post

Court to grant bail. Rule 9(12) was not a bar to the exercise by a Crown Court judge of the Crown Court's jurisdiction in respect of bail and once an accused person had been committed to the Crown Court for trial, a Crown Court judge had jurisdiction under s 13(4)[b] of the Courts Act 1971, to grant bail. It followed that the Crown Court judge should have considered the applicants' applications for bail on their merits, but since they had been convicted and sentenced in the meantime no order would be made (see p 251 j and p 252 g to p 253 a and g, post).

Per Curiam. Although the Crown Court Rules 1971 contain no provision equivalent to RSC Ord 79, r 9(12), it should not be thought that simultaneous or immediately consecutive applications for bail can be made to more than one Crown Court judge. The jurisdiction is that of the Crown Court and not of the individual judges exercising that jurisdiction. An accused person, however, can make a fresh application to the Crown Court for bail if circumstances change. Furthermore r 9(12) does not prevent a judge of the High Court from hearing an application for bail after an application by the same person has been refused by a judge of the Crown Court, since the High Court judge can hear the application under the court's inherent jurisdiction (see p 253 b and d to f, post).

Notes
For the Courts Act 1971, s 13, see 41 Halsbury's Statutes (3rd Edn) 300.

Cases referred to in judgment
Hastings, Re [1958] 1 All ER 707, [1958] 1 WLR 372, 122 JP 283, 42 Cr App R 132, DC, 14(2) Digest (Reissue) 666, 5453.
Hastings, Re (No 2) [1958] 3 All ER 625, [1959] 1 QB 358, [1958] 3 WLR 768, 123 JP 79, 43 Cr App R 47, 16 Digest (Repl) 293, 649.
Hastings, Re (No 3) [1959] 1 All ER 698, [1959] Ch 368, [1959] 2 WLR 434, 123 JP 366; *affd* [1959] 3 All ER 221, [1959] 1 WLR 807, 123 JP 502, CA, 16 Digest (Repl) 293, 650.
Kray, Re, Re Kray, Re Smith [1965] 1 All ER 710, [1965] Ch 736, [1965] 2 WLR 626, 49 Cr App R 164, 14(1) Digest (Reissue) 243, 1764.
R v Nottingham Justices, ex parte Davies [1980] 2 All ER 775, [1980] 3 WLR 15, 71 Cr App R 178, DC.

Application for judicial review
On 28th August 1980 his Honour Judge Blomefield, sitting in the Crown Court at Reading, declined to entertain an application for bail by Liaquat Ali Malik and Tariq Mohammed Malik, who were in custody at HM Prison, Oxford. By notice of motion, dated 19th September 1980, the applicants sought a judicial review of his decision in the following form: an order of mandamus directing the Crown Court to exercise the jurisdiction conferred by the Courts Act 1971 to hear and adjudicate on the application for bail. The facts are set out in the judgment of the court.

Christopher Smith for the applicants.
The Crown was not represented.

Cur adv vult

6th November. **DONALDSON LJ** read the following judgment of the court: On 28th August, 1980, the applicants applied for bail to his Honour Judge Blomefield sitting at the Crown Court at Reading. The judge declined to entertain the application, holding that he had no jurisdiction. The applicants then applied to this court for judicial review. The matter would have been treated as one of urgency, but for the fact that within a short time of Judge Blomefield's decision the applicants were tried, convicted and sentenced. We understand that a probation order was made in each case.

---

b   Section 13(4), so far as material, is set out at p 251 j to p 252 b, post

Although the matter is thus of only academic interest to the applicants, the point taken by the judge is of general importance and we have, therefore, heard full argument and taken time to consider our judgment.

The background facts giving rise to these applications can be stated briefly. The applicants were arrested and charged with criminal offences. They were brought before the Windsor justices who on more than one occasion remanded them in custody. If the applicants were unrepresented on any of these occasions, the justices were bound by s 5(6) of the Bail Act 1976 to inform them that they might apply to the High Court for bail.

That is just what the applicants did. Their application by summons was heard by Peter Pain J in the High Court on 24th July 1980. The police objected to bail on the grounds that there was still one prosecution witness to be interviewed and that they feared that there might be interference with witnesses. These are grounds on which bail can properly be withheld in accordance with s 4 of and para 2 of Sch 1 to the 1976 Act. Peter Pain J refused the application, saying that he was unable to grant bail 'until committal'.

On 6th August 1980 the applicants were committed to the Crown Court for trial. The justices declined to hear an application for bail on that occasion, holding that there had been no change of circumstances. In passing, we would have thought that there had been a very clear change of circumstances, namely that the prosecution had by then completed its investigations and that the applicants had been committed for trial. Although there may be exceptional cases, as a general rule the moment of committal for trial must, in our judgment, be an occasion on which an accused person is entitled to have his right to bail fully reviewed. In any particular case, the eligibility of the accused for bail may or may not have improved, but it is almost inevitable that there will have been a change in circumstances. For example, the court will be in a much better position to assess 'the nature and seriousness of the offence . . .' (see para 9(a) of Sch 1 to the 1976 Act). In addition the strength of the prosecution case can for the first time be fully assessed, both by the committing court and by the accused himself. This can be very material in considering the likelihood that the accused may 'fail to surrender to custody . . .' (see para 2(a) of Sch 1 to the 1976 Act).

If an accused person is unrepresented when he is committed for trial, justices are obliged by s 5(6)(a) of the 1976 Act to inform him that he may apply for bail to the High Court *or to the Crown Court*. Clearly this information was given to the applicants either by the justices or by their legal advisers and they in fact applied to the Crown Court.

The reason which Judge Blomefield gave for refusing to examine the merits of the applicants' claim to bail was that he considered himself deprived of jurisdiction by RSC Ord 79, r 9(12) which is in the following terms:

'If an applicant to the High Court in any criminal proceedings is refused bail by a judge in chambers, the applicant shall not be entitled to make a fresh application for bail to any other judge or to a Divisional Court.'

We assume that he read the words 'any other judge' as applying to him.

This decision, if correct, would make nonsense of s 5(6)(a) of the 1976 Act. As we have pointed out, justices have a duty on committal to inform the unrepresented defendant of his right to apply for bail to the High Court or the Crown Court. But if the judge is right, there is no such right of application to the Crown Court if a previous application for bail had been refused by a judge of the High Court.

The jurisdictions of the Crown Court and of the High Court in respect of bail are distinct and different. Section 13(4) of the Courts Act 1971 confers power on the Crown Court to grant bail in the following terms:

'The Crown Court may [grant bail to] any person—(a) who has been committed in custody for appearance before the Crown Court, or (b) who is in custody pursuant to a sentence imposed by a magistrates' court, and who has appealed to the Crown

Court against his conviction or sentence, or (c) who is in the custody of the Crown Court pending the disposal of his case by the Crown Court, or (d) who, after the decision of his case by the Crown Court, has applied to the Crown Court for the statement of a case for the High Court on that decision, or (e) who has applied to the High Court for an order of certiorari to remove proceedings in the Crown Court in his case into the High Court, or has applied to the High Court for leave to make such an application . . .'

Thus the jurisdiction of the Crown Court arises only after the magistrates have convicted and sentenced the accused who is appealing to the Crown Court, or after the magistrates have committed him to the Crown Court for trial or sentence, or after a voluntary bill of indictment has been preferred.

On the other hand, the power of the High Court to grant bail exists both before and after committal. It arises from its inherent jurisdiction and from s 22(1) of the Criminal Justice Act 1967, as amended, which provides:

'Where [a magistrates' court] withholds bail in criminal proceedings or imposes conditions in granting bail in criminal proceedings the High Court may grant bail or vary the conditions.'

Section 22(5) expressly preserves the inherent jurisdiction.

The judge's decision is also inconsistent with the provisions of r 18(1) of the Crown Court Rules 1971, SI 1971 No 1292, as amended by the Crown Court (Amendment) Act Rules 1978, SI 1978 No 439. Rule 18(1) provides:

'Every person who makes an application to the Crown Court relating to bail shall inform the Court of *any earlier application to the High Court or the Crown Court* relating to bail in the course of the same proceedings.'

We have emphasised the material words.

If the judge were right, the very fact that an application for bail is made to the Crown Court implies that no previous application has been made to the High Court and the reference to the High Court is otiose. Moreover, the rule contains no suggestion that a previous application to the High Court deprives the Crown Court of jurisdiction. Indeed, it appears to treat previous applications to the High Court and Crown Court on an equal footing.

However, in our judgment, the judge's decision was not correct. The jurisdictions of the Crown Court and of the High Court in relation to the granting of bail remain quite distinct, notwithstanding that judges of the High Court are empowered to exercise the jurisdiction and powers of the Crown Court and, when so doing, are judges of the Crown Court (see s 4(2) of the Courts Act 1971). Order 79, r 9(12) relates exclusively to the jurisdiction of the High Court.

The origin of this rule is clear. There was at one time a widespread belief that the jurisdiction of the High Court to grant bail was not that of the High Court as such, but of the individual judges of that court. The logical consequence would be that the decision of one judge to refuse bail would not preclude another judge from entertaining the same application immediately thereafter or perhaps even simultaneously. This belief should not have survived the decisions of *Re Hastings* [1958] 1 All ER 707, [1958] 1 WLR 372, *Re Hastings (No 2)* [1958] 3 All ER 625, [1959] 1 QB 358 and *Re Hastings (No 3)* [1959] 1 All ER 698, [1959] Ch 368 at least in relation to applications made in term time. However, it was resurrected in *Re Kray* [1965] 1 All ER 710, [1965] 1 Ch 736. Order 79, r 9(12) was made in order to put the matter beyond doubt. It was also designed to affirm that the jurisdiction of the High Court was that of the court rather than of the individual judges and that it was exercisable only by the judge in chambers. It may avoid further difficulties if we point out that the words 'any other judge' in the sentence 'The applicant shall not be entitled to make a fresh application for bail to any other judge' refer to the judge in chambers and not to the particular judge who considered the earlier application or applications.

Order 79, r 9(12) was not an obstacle to the exercise by Judge Blomefield of the Crown Court's jurisdiction; he should have considered the applicants' claims to bail on their merits.

Four further things should perhaps be said. The first is that although the Crown Court Rules contain no provision which is equivalent to RSC Ord 79, r 9(12), it should not be thought that simultaneous or immediately consecutive applications for bail can be made to more than one Crown Court judge. The jurisdiction is that of the Crown Court and not of the individual judges exercising that jurisdiction. It may be that it would be better if the Crown Court Rules made this clear. At present there is only a practice direction from Lord Widgery CJ ([1971] 3 All ER 829 at 832, [1971] 1 WLR 1535 at 1538) in the following terms:

> '15. (i) Where a person gives notice in writing to the Crown Court that he wishes to apply for bail, and requests that the Official Solicitor shall act for him in the application, the application shall be heard by a Crown Court judge in London.
>
> '(ii) All other applications shall be heard at the location of the Crown Court where the proceedings in respect of which the application for bail arises, took place or are due to take place.'

This does not cover the point in question here.

Second, the decision of this court in *R v Nottingham Justices, ex parte Davies* [1980] 2 All ER 775, [1980] 3 WLR 15 (the right of an applicant to make a fresh application for bail on a change of circumstances) in terms refers only to applications for bail which are made to the magistrates' court. However, the same principles apply to applications to the Crown Court.

Third, a judge of the High Court may, under the inherent jurisdiction, hear an application for bail after an application by the same person has been refused by a judge of the Crown Court and Ord 79, r 9(12) is no bar.

Fourth, there may be some confusion as to the theoretical position of the judge in chambers when considering applications for bail from prisoners who are subject to the jurisdiction of the Crown Court. If the application under para 15(i) of the Practice Direction ([1971] 3 All ER 829, [1971] 1 WLR 1535) comes through the Official Solicitor, it seems that the judge is likely to be acting as a 'Crown Court judge in London', whereas in all other cases including other cases which come through the Official Solicitor he is probably acting as a judge of the High Court. This is of no practical importance in terms of the success or failure of the application. The judge who considers the application will in fact be a High Court judge and accordingly he will have no cause to consider in which capacity the application comes before him. But the position is certainly untidy.

As the applicants no longer need the relief which they originally sought, there will be no order on these applications.

No order.

Solicitors: *C R Thomas & Son*, Maidenhead (for the applicants).

April Weiss   Barrister.

Re Laceward Ltd

CHANCERY DIVISION
SLADE J
14th OCTOBER 1980

Solicitor – Costs – Non-contentious business – Recovery – Proceedings to recover costs for non-contentious business – Whether winding-up proceedings in respect of debt for costs for non-contentious business constituting 'proceedings to recover costs on a bill for non-contentious business' – Solicitors' Remuneration Order 1972 (SI 1972 No 1139), art 3(2).

Company – Compulsory winding up – Petition by creditor – Disputed debt – Solicitor's costs – Petition based on bill of costs in advance of taxation – Whether petition based on disputed debt.

On the true construction of art 3(2)[a] of the Solicitors' Remuneration Order 1972 'proceedings to recover costs on a bill for non-contentious business' include not only proceedings where costs are specifically claimed but also winding-up proceedings where the petition has been presented by a solicitor for the purpose of recovering costs. Accordingly, before a winding-up petition is presented by a solicitor to recover costs for work done for a company, the solicitor is required by art 3(2) to inform the company of its right to have the costs taxed (see p 256 a to e, post).

Since there is no certainty prior to taxation of a solicitor's bill of costs that all or any specific part of the debt asserted thereby will be found truly due to the solicitor, a petition to wind up a company in respect of a claim under a solicitor's bill of costs in advance of taxation is based on a debt disputed bona fide on substantial grounds, and in accordance with the practice of the court should not be allowed (see p 256 e to h, post).

Notes

For remuneration of solicitors for non-contentious business, see Supplement to Halsbury's Laws (3rd Edn) para 160A, and for cases on the subject, see 43 Digest (Repl) 256–273, 2717–2870.

For restrictions on the presentation of a petition to wind up a company for a debt, see 7 Halsbury's Laws (4th Edn) para 1004, and for cases on the subject, see 10 Digest (Reissue) 933–935, 5436–5468.

For the Solicitors' Remuneration Order 1972, art 3, see 20 Halsbury's Statutory Instruments (Third Reissue) 278.

Cases referred to in judgment

Clement-Davis v Inter GSA (1979) 123 Sol Jo 505, CA, Digest (Cont Vol E) 567, 1612a.

North Bucks Furniture Depositories Ltd, Re [1939] 2 All ER 549, [1939] Ch 690, 108 LJ Ch 275, 160 LT 523, 103 JP 207, 37 LGR 371, [1938–39] B & CR 122, 10 Digest (Reissue) 937, 5488.

Petition

By a petition dated 23rd May 1980 William F Prior & Co (a firm) sought the winding up of Laceward Ltd, a private company limited by shares and incorporated under the Companies Act 1948, in respect of an unpaid debt of £642·44 for work done by the petitioners as solicitors for the company. The facts are set out in the judgment.

J D Martineau for the petitioners.
Michael Todd for the company.

---

a　Article 3(2), so far as material, is set out at p 255 d, post

SLADE J. This is a petition by which a firm of solicitors seek the usual compulsory winding-up order in respect of the company concerned. The petition is founded on an alleged debt arising in consideration of work done by the petitioners for the company, as solicitors, between October 1977 and April 1978. It is common ground that the work in question was non-contentious business.

Article 2 of the Solicitors' Remuneration Order 1972, SI 1972 No 1139, provides that a solicitor's remuneration for non-contentious business should be such sum as might be 'fair and reasonable having regard to all the circumstances of the case'. The article then proceeds to list a number of particular matters which should be taken into account in this context.

Article 3 provides:

'(1) Without prejudice to the provisions of sections 69, 70 and 71 of the Solicitors Act 1957 (which relate to taxation of costs) the client may require the solicitor to obtain a certificate from The Law Society stating that in their opinion the sum charged is fair and reasonable or, as the case may be, what other sum would be fair and reasonable, and in the absence of taxation the sum stated in the certificate, if less than that charged, shall be the sum payable by the client.

'(2) Before the solicitor brings proceedings to recover costs on a bill for non-contentious business he must, unless the costs have been taxed, have informed the client in writing—(i) of his right under paragraph (1) of this article to require the solicitor to obtain a certificate from The Law Society, and (ii) of the provisions of the Solicitors Act 1957 relating to taxation of costs . . .'

Article 5(1) provides:

'After the expiry of one month from the delivery of any bill for non-contentious business a solicitor may charge interest on the amount of the bill (including any disbursements) at a rate not exceeding the rate for the time being payable on judgment debts, so, however, that before interest may be charged the client must have been given the information required by article 3(2) of this Order.'

I have been told that, notwithstanding the passing of the Solicitors Act 1974, the relevant provisions of the 1972 order remain in full force and effect.

Though other points have been taken by the company in evidence in answer to this petition, a preliminary point has been taken on its behalf in reliance on the provisions of the 1972 order, with which this judgment is concerned.

It is common ground that before the petition was presented, the relevant costs had not been taxed and the petitioners had never informed the company in writing of its right under art 3(1) of the 1972 order to require the petitioners to obtain a certificate from the Law Society. In these circumstances counsel for the company has put forward substantially two propositions as reasons why this petition should be dismissed in limine. First, he has submitted, the petition constitutes 'proceedings to recover costs on a bill for non-contentious business', within the meaning of art 3(2) of the 1972 order. In these circumstances, he has submitted, since the requisite information had not been given to the company before the petition was presented, the petition was premature and constituted an abuse of the process of the court, as infringing art 3(2).

Further or alternatively, counsel has submitted that the petitioners have no locus standi to present this petition in their purported capacity as creditors, in that the alleged debt is bona fide disputed on substantial grounds. The company accepts that almost certainly some moneys are due to the petitioners, but asserts that, in advance of the taxation of the relevant costs which it now seeks, it does not know what the true sum is. It submits that the sum should be ascertained on a taxation of the petitioners' bills and that, since it has never been informed of its right to taxation before presentation of the petition, the petition is misconceived and oppressive.

The correctness or otherwise of counsel's first submission depends on the true construction of the phrase 'proceedings to recover costs on a bill for non-contentious business' in art 3(2) of the 1972 order. Counsel for the petitioners submitted that this phrase should be construed narrowly, in such manner as to include only those proceedings in which recovery of costs is specifically sought. For this reason, he submitted that a winding-up petition (such as the present) would not fall within the ambit of the phrase. Counsel for the company, on the other hand, substantially submitted that the phrase is wide enough to include not only proceedings where costs are specifically claimed but also proceedings such as the present, whose obvious purpose is to recover as much of the relevant costs as may prove possible.

I think that the narrow construction put forward on behalf of the petitioners is certainly an arguable one. On balance, however, I prefer the construction propounded by the company, which seems to me to be justifiable not only by reference to the wording of art 3(2) but also by reference to what one must assume was the intention of the makers of the rules. I take it to have been their clear intention that a client, or former client, should not be subjected to proceedings of any kind by a solicitor in respect of costs for non-contentious work until the solicitor had informed him of his rights under art 3(1). Furthermore, it would appear from the decision of the Court of Appeal in *Clement-Davis v Inter GSA* (1979) 123 Sol Jo 505 that the court will expect the relevant information to have been given to the client in an explicit manner before it will treat the client as having been given the information required by art 3(2). That was a case relating to a solicitor's claim for interest, so that it was governed by art 5(1) of the 1972 order read in conjunction with art 3(2).

On these grounds alone, therefore, I would be prepared to hold that the presentation of this petition was in violation of art 3(2) and that the petition should accordingly be dismissed. In case my conclusion on this point is wrong, however, I think I should briefly refer to counsel's second point for the company.

It is the well-established practice of this court to refuse to allow petitions for the winding up of companies brought at the suit of alleged creditors whose debts are disputed bona fide on substantial grounds. It has been said in several reported cases that the procedure of a winding-up petition is not an appropriate course by which to attempt to resolve such a dispute. In the present case, following the presentation of the petition, the company, I am told, took advice from new solicitors, who advised it of its rights under the 1972 order, of which it was previously unaware. The company then indicated to the petitioners its desire to rely on these rights and to have a taxation of its costs. Before such taxation takes place there is no certainty whatever whether all or any specific part of the debt alleged by the petition will be found truly due to the petitioners. In these circumstances, it seems to me that, in the events which have happened, the alleged debt on which the petition is founded is manifestly disputed on bona fide and substantial grounds.

Counsel for the petitioners pointed out that the request for taxation had not been made at the time when the petition was presented. But, at best, this point would in my judgment only avail the petitioners in respect of the costs of the petition arising before the point had been taken on behalf of the company, and I do not think that, in all the circumstances, it even avails the petitioners to this extent. In my judgment, the case is one where the debt is truly disputed on grounds which cannot be said to be insubstantial.

Counsel for the petitioners referred me to the decision of Crossman J in *Re North Bucks Furniture Depositories Ltd* [1939] 2 All ER 549, [1939] Ch 690 in which it was held that a local authority to which unpaid rates were due was a creditor within s 170 of the Companies Act 1929 and entitled to present a petition, after having issued a distress warrant and recovered nothing thereby. This decision, that a creditor-debtor relationship existed, was reached, as counsel pointed out, even though Crossman J recognised that an action by a local authority to recover unpaid arrears of rates would not lie, the proper recovery being by way of distress. In my judgment, however, the decision is of no real assistance to the petitioners in the present case. On the facts of *Re North Bucks Furniture Depositories Ltd*, I think it clear that a presently owing debt of an ascertained sum existed in favour of the petitioners, even though one particular remedy for enforcing that debt, namely an action for payment, might not have been available to them.

In the present case, as I have indicated, there is no clearly ascertained sum in respect of which the petitioners have a claim to be creditors in advance of a taxation. Correspondingly, in my judgment, they have no locus standi to present a petition on this second, alternative ground. For this reason also, I therefore find that the petition must be dismissed and I order accordingly.

Petition dismissed.

Solicitors: *William F Prior & Co* (for the petitioners); *Mendoza Segal* (for the company).

Jacqueline Metcalfe   Barrister.

Chatterton v Gerson and another

QUEEN'S BENCH DIVISION
BRISTOW J
21st, 22nd, 23rd, 24th, 25th, 31st JANUARY 1980

Medical practitioner – Trespass to the person – Consent to operation – Operation on patient without consent – Vitiation of patient's consent – Doctor explaining nature of operation in broad terms to patient – Whether lack of real consent by patient to operation.

Medical practitioner – Negligence – Test of liability – Risk of misfortune inherent in treatment proposed by doctor – Doctor's duty to warn of inherent risk of misfortune.

Following a hernia operation the plaintiff suffered chronic and intractable pain in the area surrounding the operation scar. She was referred to the defendant who was a specialist in the treatment of chronic intractable pain. The defendant operated on the plaintiff by injecting a solution near the spinal cord with the object of destroying pain conducting nerves which served the scar area. Although the defendant could not remember what he told the plaintiff prior to the operation, it was his practice to explain to patients that the form of treatment used would involve numbness at the site of the pain and a larger surrounding area and might involve temporary loss of muscle power. The plaintiff's recollection was that although the defendant told her of the method of pain blocking treatment he intended to use she was not warned of the prospect of numbness and possible loss of muscle power. After the operation by the defendant the plaintiff's pain was temporarily relieved but she experienced numbness in her right leg. After two months the pain returned and the defendant operated on the plaintiff by administering a second spinal injection. The defendant did not warn the plaintiff a second time of the possible side effects since he considered the second operation involved no more risk than the first. The second operation was unsuccessful and failed to relieve the pain. The plaintiff also found that her right leg was completely numb, which considerably impaired her mobility. The plaintiff claimed damages from the defendant alleging that he had not given her an explanation of the operations and their implications so that she could make an informed decision whether to risk them, and that the defendant (i) had committed a trespass to her person since her consent to the operations was vitiated by the lack of prior explanation and (ii) had been negligent in not giving an explanation as he was required to do as part of his duty to treat a patient with the degree of professional skill and care expected of a reasonably skilled medical practitioner.

Held – The plaintiff's action would be dismissed for the following reasons—
   (1) In an action against a medical practitioner for trespass to the person based on alleged lack of consent to the treatment administered by the practitioner the patient had

to show that there had been a lack of real consent. Furthermore, once the patient had been informed in broad terms of the nature of the intended treatment and had given his consent the patient could not then say that there had been a lack of real consent. Since the plaintiff had been under no illusion as to the general nature of the operations performed by the defendant, there had been no lack of real consent on her part and her claim for trespass to the person would be dismissed (see p 264 j, p 265 d to h and p 267 c, post).

(2) A doctor was required, as part of his duty of care to his patient, to explain what he intended to do, and the implications involved, in the way in which a responsible doctor in similar circumstances would have done, and if there was a real risk of misfortune inherent in the procedure, however well it was carried out, the doctor's duty was to warn of the risk of such misfortune. On the facts, the defendant had carried out his duty to inform the plaintiff of the implications of the operation, and since the numbness in her leg was not a foreseeable risk of the operation the defendant was not under a duty to warn the plaintiff of that possibility. In any event, even if the defendant had failed in his duty to warn the plaintiff of the implications inherent in the second operation, the plaintiff had not proved that if she had been properly informed she would have refused to undergo the operation and the risks involved (see p 262 g h, p 265 j to p 266 a and e to p 267 c, post).

Notes

For the civil liability of medical practitioners and hospital authorities, see 30 Halsbury's Laws (4th Edn) paras 34–40, and for cases on the subject, see 33 Digest (Repl) 525–535, 53–112.

For the duty to exercise the special skill required in the practice of a profession, see 34 Halsbury's Laws (4th Edn) para 12, and for cases on the degree of skill or knowledge required of a medical practitioner, see 33 Digest (Repl) 526, 65–74.

For the classification of trespass to the person, see 38 Halsbury's Laws (3rd Edn) 760, para 1251, and for cases on the subject, see 46 Digest (Repl) 415–417, 581–601.

Cases referred to in judgment

Bolam v Friern Hospital Management Committee [1957] 2 All ER 118, [1957] 1 WLR 582, 33 Digest (Repl) 527, 81.
Hatcher v Black (1954) Times, 2nd July
Reibl v Hughes (1978) 21 OR (2d) 14, 89 DLR (3d) 112, Ont CA, Digest (Cont Vol E) 401, *100b.
Stoffberg v Elliot [1923] CPD 148, 46 Digest (Repl) 417, *600.

Action

By a writ issued on 22nd July 1976 the plaintiff, Elizabeth Chatterton, claimed against the defendants, Gary Raymond Gerson and the East Sussex Area Health Authority, damages for injury and loss occasioned to the plaintiff by the assault and/or negligence and/or breach of duty on the part of the first defendant as the consultant anaesthetist at the Royal Sussex County Hospital and/or as agent of the second defendant and on the part of the servants or agents of the second defendant between August 1974 and June 1975. The facts are set out in the judgment.

Ian Kennedy QC and Roderick Adams for the plaintiff.
Roy Beldam QC and Nicholas Underhill for the defendants.

Cur adv vult

31st January. **BRISTOW J** read the following judgment:
1 Miss Chatterton

For many years Elizabeth Chatterton and her twin sister ran kennels near Shoreham. Then, after her sister had found a late vocation for nursing, Miss Chatterton took up work as a 'universal aunt', looking after other people and their families in times of their need for periods of not more than six weeks at a stretch. There are no records of the time she put in on this work, but it is agreed that it was probably 40 weeks at most per year and it is agreed that she would in the early 1970s have received in the order of £28 per week clear, and had she still been operating would now have been receiving in the order of £48 per week clear.

2 The hernia operation

In 1973 she went into hospital at Shoreham under the care of Mr Arthur as consultant surgeon for attention to varicose veins in her legs. After dealing with her right leg Mr Arthur decided that a small congenital inguinal hernia on that side ought to be repaired. Miss Chatterton with reluctance accepted his advice to that effect. On 21st February 1974 a nylon darn repair was carried out by Mr King. She was then aged 55 and had been in good health and living an active happy life.

Unhappily her ileo-inguinal nerve was trapped in the repair. By 21st March she was suffering from very severe pain at the operation site in her right groin, and her family doctor, Dr Riddle, sent her back to hospital where Mr Arthur's team injected local anaesthetic and steroid. This did not take away the pain. On 25th March Mr King explored the wound, found a trapped nerve, and cut it. This was unsuccessful and did not relieve her pain. On 24th April Mr Arthur re-explored the wound but this also was unsuccessful.

3 Dr Gerson

On 16th May 1974 Mr Arthur wrote to Dr Gerson, consultant anaesthetist to the Brighton Hospital Group, who runs a pain clinic at the Royal Sussex County Hospital, as follows:

'Dear Dr. Gerson,
'I would be grateful if you could have a look at this patient for me. She had a hernia repair at this hospital recently and following operation developed hyperaesthesia in the region of the medial end of the scar. We thought this was due to trapping of the ileo-inguinal nerve in the repair. Re-exploration was carried out and nerve filaments divided. She was improved very temporarily but then her symptoms recurred. We re-explored the wound once again and the skin was lifted over a very wide area, cutting the ileo-hypogastric nerve and also the femoral branch of the genito femoral. All was well for two weeks but she has now returned again with extreme pain and hyperaesthesia in the area, just above the wound. I am really at a loss as to what more I can do for her but wonder if you would possibly be able to help her.
'With many thanks and kind regards . . .'

Dr Gerson is a specialist in the treatment of chronic intractable pain, a subject which he has studied in Sweden and in Boston, Massachusetts, as well as in England. The establishment of clinics for this purpose is relatively new in the United Kingdom and there are few. Dr Gerson established the Royal Sussex County Hospital clinic in 1970, and in December 1975 published a paper on the management of chronic intractable pain. In the section on 'Principles of Management', having dealt with the problem of diagnosis, he wrote:

'At this stage it should be possible to offer treatment. In some cases therapy may carry a risk of complications, the advantages and disadvantages of any line of treatment should be put to the patient so that he may choose. The vast majority of patients with severe pain are willing to risk considerable side effects if there is a hope of relief. However, it is still necessary to be explicit about these; a patient who for example, has not had the numbness associated with the use of neurolytic agents explained to him in advance may feel aggrieved when it occurs. Such complications are important, but it is even more important to see the advantages of any successful procedure in the context of a patient's ability to lead a more normal life with complete or relative freedom from severe pain, and the reduction, or absence, of the need for potent analgesics with all their disadvantages.'

4. Intrathecal pain block injection

One of the available forms of treatment for pain from, in, and around incisions, pain that is associated with nerve injury, the class of pain from which Miss Chatterton was suffering as a result of her hernia operation, is to block the sensory nerve which transmits the pain signals from the scar site to the brain by an intrathecal injection, ie the injection into the space containing the spinal cord surrounded by spinal fluid, of a solution of phenol and glycerine at the level of the nerve roots which serve the area in which the scar tissue is situated. The strength of solution is designed to allow destruction of the pain conducting fibres, which are the most thinly insulated, with the minimum damage to the adjacent sensation conducting fibres which are more thickly insulated; but it is a necessary concomitant of the relief from pain that the injection will produce numbness in the area of the scar more extensive than around the scar tissue itself.

The relative situations of the sensory nerves and the motor nerves, which are even more thickly insulated, and the position in which the patient is placed during the injection, ensures that if the operation is properly carried out there is no risk of damage to the motor nerves by the phenol solution. During injection sensation in the area intended to be affected is carefully monitored so that no more fluid is injected than is necessary to produce the desired result. The viscosity of the fluid is such that it remains fixed against the nerve fibres where it is injected. Although the gap between the dura mater and the spinal cord into which the fluid is injected is in the order of 2 mm only, if the operation is properly carried out there is no risk of damage to the cord by the needle.

The operation for nerve block by the intrathecal injection of phenol solution, even if it at first relieves pain, does not always produce lasting relief. The affected nerve may to some extent regenerate or its pain transmission function may be taken over by adjacent nerves. Numbness may decrease and pain return. A repeat operation may be necessary. Even that may not achieve the desired result. The whole procedure is designed only for the relief of chronic intractable pain, pain the patient finds unendurable, where the only available alternative is ever increasing doses of narcotic drugs with all the disastrous effects which that will bring. It is a treatment of last resort; so much so that, while Dr Gerson and others think it right to try it on patients suffering from pain other than that caused by terminal cancer, there are many distinguished doctors who while respecting this view would not themselves use the treatment except for terminal cancer patients. Some would not use it at all.

5 The first pain block

It is not suggested in this case that it was negligent of Dr Gerson to use this treatment, as he did, to try to relieve Miss Chatterton from the chronic intractable pain in respect of which Mr Arthur had called in his help. Nor is it suggested that he was in any way negligent in his performance of the injections which he gave. Her pain was such that she could not bear the touch of clothing on the scar site, had to have a cradle over it in bed, and could bear to wear nothing other than a loose cotton dress to cover the affected area.

Following Mr Arthur's letter of 16th May 1974 Miss Chatterton went to see Dr Gerson at the pain clinic on 3rd June. On 4th June Dr Gerson wrote to Mr Arthur:

> 'Thank you for asking me to see this lady who has severe pain and hypersensitivity in the right groin following a right herniorrhaphy operation and two subsequent re-explorations. On examination she has an area of hyperaesthesia above the lateral end of the scar. As a provisional diagnostic procedure I infiltrated the area with Marcaine in adrenaline solution and I will see her again next week.'

She saw him again on 10th June and he reported to Mr Arthur on 11th June:

> 'I saw Miss Chatterton again and she informed me that the local infiltration which I performed last week lasted for about 36 hours. I repeated the block again today but if you do not get an extension in duration of the analgesia I will put her down to have an intrathecal phenol injection in order to block the sensory pathways involved on the right side.'

She saw him again on 17th June and he reported to Dr Riddle, her family doctor, again on that day:

'The last local infiltration which I performed on this lady had an effect for 2½ days. I will continue to see her in my outpatients doing further local blocks pending the intrathecal phenol block for which she is on my waiting list.'

Dr Riddle replied on 21st June:

'My thanks to you for your letter of the 17th June telling me that you had again seen the above named and further infiltrated the very troublesome neuralgia. This is a most unusual and unfortunate happening following her hernia repair and as she is a very pleasant and sensible person I do hope that you will be able to help.'

She saw Dr Gerson again on 24th June and 8th and 15th July for repeat local injections at the scar site. Dr Riddle's letter of 5th July reflects the urgency of the situation. He wrote:

'This lady is certainly having a very trying time and your local infiltration only seems to give her a bare 48 hours relief. I was called to see her during the week when she told me that she had felt somewhat faint on the Tuesday and that sickness and diarrhoea had occurred. When I saw her on Thursday, the latter appeared to have abated and with a normal temperature and pulse I could find little to account for her upset. It may well have been a food disturbance, but at the same time I thought you ought to know lest this should have been some complication of your treatment. I gather she is to be admitted for your proposed caudal block shortly.'

The gravity is also reflected in Dr Gerson's replies keeping Dr Riddle in the picture. On 14th August Dr Gerson carried out an intrathecal phenol solution block injection at the interspace between nos 9 and 10 thoracic vertebrae, the appropriate site for the interruption of the pain conducting sensory nerve roots serving the scar site. Miss Chatterton stayed in the short stay ward overnight and went home next morning. She found the procedure unpleasant and suffered from the sort of headache which often follows a lumbar puncture. The pain from the scar site was for the time being relieved. Dr Gerson saw her on 19th August and reported to Dr Riddle and Mr Arthur:

'I saw Miss Chatterton again today. I am pleased to say that she has no more pain in the region of her herniorrhaphy scar. On examination there is analgesia to pinprick from thoracic 11 to lumbar 1 on the right side. She has had a headache following the lumbar puncture but I have told her that this should disappear within the next week or so. I do not think that I need to see her again unless she has any further problems.'

It was not until Dr Riddle wrote to Dr Gerson two months later that it had become clear that the pain relief afforded by the operation would be temporary.

6   What explanation was given before the first intrathecal injection?

It was Dr Gerson's regular practice to explain to patients when he intended to try to help by intrathecal phenol solution injection all about the process. His practice was to tell them that he hoped to relieve their pain by interrupting the nerve along which it was signalled to the brain, that this would involve numbness in the area from which the pain signals had been transmitted, numbness over an area larger than the pain source itself, and might involve temporary loss of muscle power. Sister Welch who worked with him at the clinic from 1973 says that he was very meticulous about his explanations. Neither she nor Dr Gerson pretend now to remember what he said to Miss Chatterton on the occasions in the summer of 1974 preceding the first intrathecal injection. Both remembered her very well as a charming, sensible, intelligent woman who did not make a fuss but complained, as Sister Welch remembers it, of desperate pain. There is no apparent reason why in Miss Chatterton's case Dr Gerson should have departed from his normal practice and not acted in accordance with the advice shortly to be published in his paper.

Miss Chatterton's recollection is that after the initial local injections at the scar site he told her about his pain block method and that it had been perfected in Boston, Massachusetts. It would be done under local anaesthetic and would not take very long. If you block the nerve which sends the pain message the brain does not receive it and so you do not have a pain. Dr Gerson told her what the clinic was all about. She does not remember him saying that the blocking injection would be near the spine. Her recollection is that he did not say she would have numbness and might have some muscle weakness. Is her evidence in this respect reliable? I have no doubt that she and all the other witnesses in this case have been entirely honest in their evidence, but that does not of itself mean that I can rely on her evidence that Dr Gerson did not explain that she would get numbness and possibly some muscle weakness as a result of the intrathecal block.

In the correspondence which followed the first operation there is no complaint by Dr Riddle that the numbness which she mentions on 24th October was unexpected or a matter of complaint by Miss Chatterton. Nor is there any complaint to that effect in Dr Riddle's letter of 16th January 1975 to Mr Crymble, the neurosurgeon whose advice was sought, though the numbness is referred to as an effect of the injection which was by then wearing off. Nor was there any such complaint in Dr Riddle's letter of 3rd July 1975 to Dr Gerson, which was as follows:

'Thank you for your further letter of the 24th June regarding the above-named unfortunate lady. I wrote to Dr. Quin straight away and, as you had kindly spoken to him, she has already had her appointment, and I gather is commencing physiotherapy and rehabilitation daily treatment. Her condition is really quite alarming and it is most disappointing in that although she is numb from the lower rib margin on the right side down to the foot, she is again experiencing quite severe pain in the original area round the scar. I suppose one can only wait and see what degree of recovery will take place from this motor weakness, after which I wonder if Mr. Crymble and his neurosurgical unit would be able to help.'

It was not until the indorsement on the writ in this action, issued on 22nd July 1976, as amended on 8th June 1978, that the averment of assault, which is based on a lack of proper explanation vitiating Miss Chatterton's consent to the intrathecal injections, first appears on our scene.

I am sure that if Miss Chatterton had not been told by Dr Gerson that she would get an area of numbness not confined to the scar site as a necessary concomitant of the interruption of the nerve passing the pain signals, she would have said both to Dr Gerson and Dr Riddle that she had not been told she would get the numbness she experienced following the first operation, and that Dr Riddle would have raised the matter with Dr Gerson if she had raised it with him.

I have come to the conclusion that on the balance of probability Dr Gerson did give his usual explanation about the intrathecal phenol solution nerve block and its implications of numbness instead of pain plus a possibility of slight muscle weakness, and that Miss Chatterton's recollection is wrong; and on the evidence before me I so find.

7 The second pain block

Miss Chatterton was naturally disappointed in November to find the pain beginning to come back. She had found the intrathecal injection procedure painful and unpleasant. Dr Gerson saw her again on 26th November 1974 and reported to Dr Riddle:

'I saw Miss Chatterton again today and although she is getting far less pain than she had before my injections, she is still getting some discomfort in the region of the scar and the muscles around it. On examination she still has analgesia to pinprick from T9 to L1 on the right side and I therefore think there is little to be gained by any further nerve block. I will see her again in three months time.'

This can have been little comfort to her, and her sisters were anxious about her condition. On 16th January 1975 Dr Riddle wrote to Mr Crymble, a well-respected neurosurgeon at Haywards Heath, giving the history of her condition since the hernia operation, and describing her present condition as follows:

'In June Dr. Gerson gave her repeated injections of local anaesthetic which again gave only short-lasting relief and in September he proceeded to an intrathecal phenol injection. Following this Miss Chatterton complained of headache for some little time and was numb below the knee up to the L1 on the right side. The pain was completely relieved and she was able to again wear normal clothing. However, by November of last year the effect of this was apparently wearing off in that the anaesthesia had come up to mid-thigh but still remained about rib margin level on the right side. The sad thing was that the painful sensitivity was again reappearing, this time mainly in and above the scar for some 2 or 3 inches. That is the position we are in today and again she is finding it difficult to wear clothing in contact with her pelvis. Dr Gerson who saw her again some weeks ago, thought the condition was reasonably satisfactory but that he would in all probability have to resort to a further intrathecal injection later. Miss Chatterton and her family are becoming a little apprehensive about this and she herself is somewhat depressed and despondent at this long continued post-operative misery. She is needing no less than eight Distalgesic tablets daily together with Mogadon etc. at night. I should be grateful to have your advice . . .'

Mr Crymble saw Miss Chatterton and advised her that she should continue to see Dr Gerson in the hope that he could give her permanent relief. He so informed Dr Gerson by letter dated 10th February 1975 saying that he would be willing to step back into the scene if Dr Gerson wished it. A copy of the letter was sent to Dr Riddle. Dr Gerson saw Miss Chatterton again on 25th February, found that there had been some shrinkage of the numb area, and put her down for a repeat intrathecal block.

It is Dr Gerson's opinion, borne out by his experience, that a repeat intrathecal block involves no more risk to the patient of unintended or adverse consequences than a first operation. There is no evidence to suggest that he is wrong. Because he is of this opinion, when he discussed with Miss Chatterton whether she should have a repeat of the operation carried out in the previous August, he says he would not have again given the explanation, including reference to numbness and possible slight muscle weakness, which it was his custom to give when first discussing treatment by intrathecal block with a patient. His recollection is that he told her simply that the second operation would be a repeat of the first and she knew what to expect. Miss Chatterton's recollection is to the same effect.

Miss Chatterton, though no doubt not enthusiastic about the prospect of a repeat intrathecal block, had now experienced the problems of winter in relation to pain such that she could not bear underclothes or wool near her scar, and was, I am satisfied, desperately anxious that the pain should be relieved if possible.

On 11th June 1975 Miss Chatterton had the second intrathecal phenol solution nerve block operation. She says that during the injection she experienced sudden instantaneous acute pain and said: 'You've struck me like lightning.' Dr Gerson said: 'Where?' She said: 'From the groin to the big toe.' And he said: 'I've struck the motor nerve.' Sister Welch, who was present, says that during the operation nothing unusual happened. If it had it would have been Dr Gerson's duty to record it. There is no record. Dr Gerson says he does not remember anything special being said by Miss Chatterton and certainly did not say he had struck a motor nerve. He says he could not have done so because of the position of the motor nerve. I am satisfied as a result of the expert evidence of the subsequent examination of the motor nerve supply to Miss Chatterton's right leg that she has sustained no damage to the motor nerve, and I am satisfied that her account of this, which she clearly now believes to be the truth, is entirely unreliable and results from trying to rationalise the cause of the grievous disability which followed the second intrathecal block operation.

8 *The aftermath*

Next morning when Miss Chatterton was discharged from the short stay ward at the clinic in which she had again spent the night she found that she had no sensation in her right leg and foot. Dr Riddle came to see her and recorded that she was numb from the lower chest right down the right side to her foot, and there was 'some muscular weakness of right leg unfortunately'. On 23rd June she saw Dr Gerson again. He had noted: 'No sensation right leg. Still getting pain left groin. Can flex and extend right knee but with reduced power. No movement right foot or ankle.' He advised physiotherapy, and reported to Dr Riddle. On 1st July Dr Riddle recorded no power in her leg and that pain occurred round the scar.

The outcome has been that Miss Chatterton still experiences acute agony if she knows that something is touching the scar area, cannot in consequence tolerate clothing in contact with it, and cannot feel her right leg. She is a brave and sensible person and in spite of these very grave handicaps can, as I was able to see, get about to some extent, with a stick, though she is very unsteady. She still has to wear loose cotton dresses.

To the distinguished anaesthetists and neurosurgeons who have examined her for the purposes of this action she has presented a confusing picture. Electrical tests have shown that the motor nerve supply to her leg is undamaged. As I understand their evidence, the signs from which you conclude whether there is any and what organic lesion to account for the loss of sensation in and lack of knowledge of position of the foot and lower leg are equivocal. There is now no organic explanation of the fact that she still experiences pain in the scar area because when she cannot see that it is being touched she does not feel the touch or feel pain. Whether or not there is an organic explanation for the fact that she still experiences pain from the scar area and lacks sensation, and so knowledge of the position of her lower leg and foot, these difficulties are perfectly real to Miss Chatterton and amount to a grave disability. On her behalf it is not sought to attribute the continued pain from the scar area to any act or omission by Dr Gerson. It is the condition of her right leg which is laid at his door. Mr Currie, consultant neurosurgeon at St Bartholomew's Hospital called as expert witness on her behalf, summed up the end result in this way: 'Her main problem is that she still has the pain she started with. Now she has also got her dud right leg, but it is not so bad as if she had an artificial leg.'

9 *The claim*

As I have said, there is no claim that Dr Gerson was negligent either in embarking on treatment of Miss Chatterton's chronic intractable pain by intrathecal phenol solution injection or in the performance of either of the operations which he carried out. The claim against him is put in two ways: (i) that her consent to operation was vitiated by lack of explanation of what the procedure was and what its implications were, so that she gave no real consent and the operation was in law a trespass to her person, that is, a battery; and (ii) that Dr Gerson was under a duty, as part of his obligation to treat his patient with the degree of professional skill and care to be expected of a reasonably skilled practitioner having regard to the state of the art at the time in question, to give Miss Chatterton such an explanation of the nature and implications of the proposed operation that she could come to an informed decision on whether she wanted to have it or would prefer to go on living with the pain which it was intended to relieve; that such explanation as he gave was in breach of that duty; that if he had performed that duty she would have chosen not to have the operation; and that therefore the unhappy consequences resulting from the operation, however wisely recommended and skilfully performed it may have been, are damage to Miss Chatterton which flows from Dr Gerson's breach of duty and for which he is responsible.

10 *Trespass to the person and consent*

It is clear law that in any context in which consent of the injured party is a defence to what would otherwise be a crime or a civil wrong, the consent must be real. Where, for example, a woman's consent to sexual intercourse is obtained by fraud, her apparent consent is no defence to a charge of rape. It is not difficult to state the principle or to appreciate its good sense. As so often, the problem lies in its application.

No English authority was cited before me of the application of the principle in the context of consent to the interference with bodily integrity by medical or surgical treatment. In *Reibl v Hughes* (1978) 21 OR (2d) 14, which was an action based on negligence by failure to inform the patient of the risk in surgery involving the carotid artery, the Ontario Court of Appeal said that the trial judge was wrong in injecting the issue, Was it a battery? into the case pleaded and presented in negligence. The majority of the court, having referred to the United States cases on what is there called the 'doctrine of informed consent', decided that the action of 'battery' seemed quite inappropriate to cases in which the doctor has acted in good faith, and in the interests of the patient, but in doing so has been negligent in failing to disclose a risk inherent in the recommended treatment. They reversed the finding of battery. I am told that that decision is now under appeal.

In *Stoffberg v Elliot* [1923] CPD 148 Watermeyer J, in his summing up to the jury in an action of assault in this context, directed them that consent to such surgical and medical treatment as the doctors might think necessary is not to be implied simply from the fact of going to hospital. There it was admitted that express consent to the operation should have been obtained but was not, due to oversight.

In my judgment what the court has to do in each case is to look at all the circumstances and say, 'Was there a real consent?' I think justice requires that in order to vitiate the reality of consent there must be a greater failure of communication between doctor and patient than that involved in a breach of duty if the claim is based on negligence. When the claim is based on negligence the plaintiff must prove not only the breach of duty to inform but that had the duty not been broken she would not have chosen to have the operation. Where the claim is based on trespass to the person, once it is shown that the consent is unreal, then what the plaintiff would have decided if she had been given the information which would have prevented vitiation of the reality of her consent is irrelevant.

In my judgment once the patient is informed in broad terms of the nature of the procedure which is intended, and gives her consent, that consent is real, and the cause of the action on which to base a claim for failure to go into risks and implications is negligence, not trespass. Of course, if information is withheld in bad faith, the consent will be vitiated by fraud. Of course, if by some accident, as in a case in the 1940s in the Salford Hundred Court, where a boy was admitted to hospital for tonsilectomy and due to administrative error was circumcised instead, trespass would be the appropriate cause of action against the doctor, though he was as much the victim of the error as the boy. But in my judgment it would be very much against the interests of justice if actions which are really based on a failure by the doctor to perform his duty adequately to inform were pleaded in trespass.

In this case in my judgment even taking Miss Chatterton's evidence at its face value she was under no illusion as to the general nature of what an intrathecal injection of phenol solution nerve block would be, and in the case of each injection her consent was not unreal. I should add that getting the patient to sign a pro forma expressing consent to undergo the operation 'the effect and nature of which have been explained to me', as was done here in each case, should be a valuable reminder to everyone of the need for explanation and consent. But it would be no defence to an action based on trespass to the person if no explanation had in fact been given. The consent would have been expressed in form only, not in reality.

11 Negligence

The duty of the doctor is to explain what he intends to do, and its implications, in the way a careful and responsible doctor in similar circumstances would have done: see *Bolam v Friern Hospital Management Committee* [1957] 2 All ER 118, [1957] 1 WLR 582 per McNair J and *Hatcher v Black* (1954) Times, 2nd July per Denning LJ sitting as an additional judge of the Queen's Bench Division.

I am satisfied that Dr Gerson told Miss Chatterton what an intrathecal phenol solution injection nerve block was all about. I am satisfied that he told her that the concomitant of relief from pain would be numbness not confined to the scar but in the area served by the sensory nerves the injection would be intended to block, and that she might suffer from slight muscle weakness. Ought he to have done more?

The evidence before me on this was that of Dr Gerson himself, of Dr Mehta, an anaesthetist expert in pain relief, who would not have used the procedure except in a patient suffering from cancer pain, Mr Currie, consultant neurosurgeon at St Bartholomew's Hospital, who has used these procedures for the relief of intractable pain but confines his operations to the lumbar region where the insertion of the needle involves less risk than higher up, and Dr Bodley, a consultant anaesthetist, who would not have undertaken the procedure anyway, taking a gloomy view of it.

Dr Mehta, if he had been talked into using the procedure as a last resort on someone suffering from chronic intractable pain other than that caused by terminal cancer, would have told the patient that there might be more loss of sensation than she would expect; that there might be loss of bladder control, though he agreed that at the level at which Miss Chatterton's injections were given it would be very unlikely; and there might be some muscle weakness. He would not have anticipated an effect on the leg from which Miss Chatterton subsequently suffered, and would not have warned her of the possibility of any such thing. Mr Currie, apart from saying that the higher up the spine the injection is to be given the more closely you have to think about what warning to give, did not help on this aspect of the case. Dr Bodley would not have used this procedure anyway, but helped by saying that the risks involved in an anaesthetic given by the same means but without the use of phenol solution involves about as much danger as crossing Oxford Street, so that he would not volunteer any warning of risk in that case. None of these three, however distinguished, could really help over the adequacy of the explanation which as I have held Dr Gerson gave Miss Chatterton before the first operation, which he alone of those called thought right to do.

In my judgment there is no obligation on the doctor to canvass with the patient anything other than the inherent implications of the particular operation he intends to carry out. He is certainly under no obligation to say that if he operates incompetently he will do damage. The fundamental assumption is that he knows his job and will do it properly. But he ought to warn of what may happen by misfortune however well the operation is done, if there is a real risk of a misfortune inherent in the procedure, as there was in the surgery to the carotid artery in the Canadian case of *Reibl v Hughes*. In what he says any good doctor has to take into account the personality of the patient, the likelihood of the misfortune, and what in the way of warning is for the particular patient's welfare.

I am not satisfied that Dr Gerson fell short of his duty to tell Miss Chatterton of the implications of this operation, properly carried out. At the level at which he gave the injection there was on the evidence no real risk of damage to bladder control, and it is clear that the bladder difficulty of which Miss Chatterton now complains was wholly independent of the injections. There was no risk of significant damage to the motor nerves. There was no foreseeable risk that her leg and foot would be deprived of sensation or control, nor am I satisfied that anything done in the course of the second injection caused that result. In my judgment, on the expert evidence here, that may be functional, just as the continuance of her scar pain is functional. The certain and intended result of the injections was to replace the pain at which they were aimed by numbness, numbness over an area larger than the scar area itself. This I am satisfied she was told before the first injection. Before the second injection she knew what to expect and in my judgment there was no need to spell it out again.

In my judgment the fact is that it is the lack of sensation in the leg and foot, which Dr Mehta would not have anticipated or warned of as a possibility, and the failure of the second injection to relieve her pain which very naturally are Miss Chatterton's causes for complaint. As a result of the second injection there is no organic cause left for the pain still being there. The condition of her leg and foot was not a possibility inherent in the operation of which Dr Gerson should have warned her. Accordingly the claim of negligence fails.

I should add that if I had thought that Dr Gerson had failed in his duty to inform her of the implications inherent in the second injection, I would not have been satisfied that if properly informed Miss Chatterton would have chosen not to have it. The whole picture on the evidence is of a lady desperate for pain relief, who has just been advised by Mr Crymble to let Dr Gerson try again. When asked what she would have done she said that she would have refused because she knew her family was opposed to the second operation, because she knew how much it hurt and what it was like, and because she still had the pain and was beginning to learn to put up with it. She did not say she would have refused because the numbness following the first injection was unacceptable, or that she was not prepared to risk slight muscle weakness again. In my judgment the reasons which she did mention would all have been equally cogent whether she had been told again what she had been told before the first injection or not.

12 Conclusion

Accordingly the action fails and must be dismissed.

Judgment for the defendants.

Solicitors: *Chapman & Wilson*, Brighton (for the plaintiff); *Hempsons* (for the defendant).

K Mydeen Esq   Barrister.

Whitehouse v Jordan and another

HOUSE OF LORDS

LORD WILBERFORCE, LORD EDMUND-DAVIES, LORD FRASER OF TULLYBELTON, LORD RUSSELL OF KILLOWEN AND LORD BRIDGE OF HARWICH

27th, 28th, 29th, 30th OCTOBER, 3rd NOVEMBER, 17th DECEMBER 1980

Medical practitioner – Negligence – Test of liability – Error of judgment – Hospital registrar testing forceps delivery – Registrar pulling fetus several times with obstetric forceps – Baby born with brain damage – Whether error of clinical judgment amounting to negligence – Whether doctor negligent.

Appeal – Evidence – Finding of fact of trial judge – Inference from finding of fact – Whether appellate court entitled to substitute own inference from finding of fact.

The defendant, a senior hospital registrar, took charge of the plaintiff's delivery as a baby after the mother had been in labour for a considerable time. The notes made by the consultant professor in charge of the hospital maternity unit identified the pregnancy as likely to be difficult and noted that a 'trial of forceps' delivery would have to be tried before proceeding to delivery by Caesarian section. Trial of forceps was a tentative procedure requiring delicate handling of the baby with forceps and a continuous review of the baby's progress down the birth canal, with the obligation to stop traction if it appeared that the delivery could not proceed without risk. Having examined the mother and read the professor's notes, the defendant embarked on a trial of forceps delivery. He pulled on the baby six times with the forceps coincident with the mother's contractions, but when there was no movement on the fifth and sixth pulls he decided, some 25 minutes after the commencement of the trial of forceps, to abandon that procedure and to proceed to a Caesarian section. He then quickly and competently delivered the plaintiff by Caesarian section. The plaintiff was found soon after the delivery to have sustained severe brain damage due to asphyxia. Acting by his mother as next friend he claimed damages for negligence against the defendant alleging that he had pulled too long and too hard on the plaintiff's head in carrying out the trial of forceps and thereby caused the brain damage. At the trial the mother gave evidence that she was 'lifted off' the bed by the application of the forceps and although that description of what happened was rejected by the judge as being clinically impossible, on the suggestion of an expert witness he interpreted it to mean that the forceps were applied with such force that she was pulled towards the bottom of the bed in a manner inconsistent with a properly carried out trial of forceps. The defendant gave evidence that when there was no progress on the fifth pull of the forceps he pulled once more to see if he could ease the head past what might have been only a minimal obstruction but as there was no further progress he decided to proceed to Caesarian section and he had easily pushed the head slightly upwards to effect the Caesarian section. He denied that the head was wedged or stuck prior to the Caesarian section. The judge interpreted his evidence to mean that he had pulled too long and too hard, causing the head to become wedged or stuck. There was also in evidence a report made by the consultant professor shortly after the delivery, from clinical notes and after discussion with the defendant, the tenor of which was that the mother had received correct and skilled treatment and that no blame attached to anyone for the plaintiff's condition. However, in the report the professor referred three times to 'disimpaction' of the head prior to the Caesarian section. At the trial the professor gave evidence that he had used that term as meaning no more than that a gentle push of the head up the birth canal was needed before proceeding to the Caesarian section. There was no unanimity of opinion among the other medical experts as to the meaning of the term 'impacted' or whether it meant that there had been excessive or unprofessional traction with the forceps. The evidence of the medical experts made it clear, however, that the amount of force to be properly used in a trial of forceps was a matter of clinical judgment, although there should be no attempt to pull the fetus past a bony obstruction, and if the head became so stuck as to cause asphyxia excessive force had been used. The judge inferred from the professor's use of the term 'disimpacted' that the plaintiff's head had become so firmly wedged or stuck in the birth canal as to indicate that excessive force had been used in the trial of forceps. The judge found that the brain damage probably occurred during the trial of forceps. From his interpretation of the mother's evidence, the defendant's evidence and the professor's report the judge concluded that in carrying out the trial of forceps the defendant had pulled too long and too hard with the forceps so that the plaintiff's head had become wedged or stuck, that in so doing or in getting the head unwedged or unstuck he had caused the plaintiff's asphyxia, and that in so using the forceps he had fallen below the standard of skill expected from the ordinary competent specialist and had therefore been negligent. The judge accordingly awarded the plaintiff substantial damages. The defendant appealed. The Court of Appeal ([1980] 1 All ER 650) reversed the judge's decision on the grounds that (i) if the judge's finding that the defendant pulled too long and too hard with the forceps during the trial of forceps was accepted, that amounted only to an error of clinical judgment and as such was not negligence in law, and (ii) in any event the court was entitled to, and would, reverse that finding because it was based on an unjustified interpretation of the evidence. The plaintiff appealed to the House of Lords.

Held – Although the view of the trial judge (who had seen and heard the witnesses) as to the weight to be given to their evidence was always entitled to great respect, where his decision on an issue of fact was an inference drawn from the primary facts and depended on the evidentiary value he gave to the witnesses' evidence and not on their credibility and demeanour, an appellate court was just as well placed as the trial judge to determine the proper inference to be drawn and was entitled to form its own opinion thereon. Since the judge's conclusion of fact that the defendant had pulled too long and too hard with the forceps was primarily an inference from the primary facts, no issue of credibility was involved. Accordingly, his conclusion was open to reassessment by the appellate court and it was entitled to find that the evidence did not justify the inference that the defendant negligently pulled too hard and too long with the forceps. It followed that the Court of Appeal was entitled to reject the judge's finding of negligence. The appeal would therefore be dismissed (see p 270 g h, p 273 e to g, p 274 g, p 275 a h j, p 276 a b, p 278 j, p 280 f to h, p 281 d to f, p 282 f to h, p 283 d to g, p 284 g h, p 285 a to e, p 286 c to e, p 287 j and p 288 f h, post).

The Hontestroom [1927] AC 37 and *Powell v Streatham Manor Nursing Home* [1935] All ER Rep 58 applied.

Per Lord Edmund-Davies, Lord Fraser and Lord Russell. To say that a surgeon has committed an error of clinical judgment is wholly ambiguous and does not indicate whether he has been negligent, for while some errors of clinical judgment may be completely consistent with the due exercise of professional skill, other acts or omissions in the course of exercising clinical judgment may be so glaringly below proper standards as to make a finding of negligence inevitable. The test whether a surgeon has been negligent is whether he has failed to measure up in any respect, whether in clinical judgment or otherwise, to the standard of the ordinary skilled surgeon exercising and professing to have the special skill of a surgeon (see p 276 h to p 277 c, p 281 b c and p 284 j, post); dictum of McNair J in *Bolam v Friern Hospital Management Committee* [1957] 2 All ER 118 at 121 approved.

Per Lord Wilberforce and Lord Fraser. While some degree of consultation between experts and legal advisers is entirely proper, it is necessary that expert evidence presented to the court should be, and should be seen to be, the independent product of the expert, uninfluenced as to form or content by the exigencies of litigation (see p 276 a b and p 284 h, post).

Decision of the Court of Appeal [1980] 1 All ER 650 affirmed.

Notes

For the duty to exercise the special skill required in the practice of a profession, see 34 Halsbury's Laws (4th Edn) para 12, and for cases on the degree of skill or knowledge required of a medical practitioner, see 33 Digest (Repl) 526, 65–74.

Cases referred to in opinions

Bland v Ross, The Julia (1860) 14 Moo PCC 210, Lush 224, 15 ER 284, PC, 1(1) Digest (Reissue) 386, 2696.
Bolam v Friern Hospital Management Committee [1957] 2 All ER 118, [1957] 1 WLR 582, 33 Digest (Repl) 527, 81.
Chin Keow v Government of Malaysia [1967] 1 WLR 813, PC, Digest (Cont Vol C) 666, 81a.
Clarke v Edinburgh and District Tramways Co 1919 SC (HL) 35.
Glannibanta, The (1876) 1 PD 283, sub nom *The Transit* 34 LT 934, 2 Char Pr Cas 18, 3 Asp MLC 233, CA, 1(1) Digest (Reissue) 385, 2689.
Hontestroom (Owners) v Owners of Steamship Sagaporack, Owners of Steamship Hontestroom v Owners of Steamship Durham Castle [1927] AC 37, 95 LJP 153, 136 LT 33, 17 Asp MLC 123, HL, 51 Digest (Repl) 815, 3712.
Powell v Streatham Manor Nursing Home [1935] AC 243, [1935] All ER Rep 58, 104 LJKB 304, 152 LT 563, HL, 51 Digest (Repl) 816, 3720.

Appeal

By a writ dated 14th December 1972 the plaintiff, Stuart Charles Whitehouse, an infant suing by his father and next friend Victor Edward Whitehouse, claimed damages against Joseph Alan Jordan and Professor H C McLaren, respectively a senior registrar and consultant professor of obstetrics at Queen Elizabeth Hospital, Edgbaston, Birmingham, and the West Midlands Regional Health Authority for personal injuries sustained on or about 7th January 1970 in the course of his birth at the Queen Elizabeth Hospital, Edgbaston, Birmingham. By notice of discontinuance dated 31st March 1976 the plaintiff discontinued his action against the second defendant, Professor McLaren. On 26th September 1976 Eileen Whitehouse, the plaintiff's mother, was substituted as his next friend. At the trial of the action Bush J gave judgment on 1st December 1978 for damages against the first and third defendants in the sum of £100,000. On 5th December 1979 the Court of Appeal (Lord Denning MR and Lawton LJ, Donaldson LJ dissenting) ([1980] 1 All ER 650) reversed his decision and refused leave to appeal. The plaintiff appealed by leave of the House of Lords granted on 21st February 1980. The facts are set out in the opinion of Lord Wilberforce.

Michael Wright QC and *Desmond Perrett* for the plaintiff.
Ian Kennedy QC, Bernard Hargrove QC and *R Warne* for the defendants.

Their Lordships took time for consideration.

17th December. The following opinions were delivered.

LORD WILBERFORCE. My Lords, Stuart Whitehouse is a boy now aged ten; he was born on 7th January 1970, with severe brain damage. In these circumstances, tragic for him and for his mother, this action has been brought, by his mother as next friend, in which he claims that the damage to his brain was caused by the professional negligence of Mr J A Jordan who was senior registrar at the hospital at Birmingham where the birth took place. There were originally also claims against Professor McLaren, the consultant in charge of the maternity unit to which Mr Jordan belonged, and also against the hospital on its own account. But these have disappeared and the hospital, more exactly the West Midlands Regional Health Authority, remains in the case only as vicariously responsible for any liability which may be established against Mr Jordan.

A large number of claims have been made since the event most of which have now been eliminated or withdrawn. The negligence ultimately charged aginst Mr Jordan is that in the course of carrying out a 'trial of forceps delivery', he pulled too long and too strongly on the child's head, thereby causing the brain damage. The trial judge, after a trial of 11 days in which eminent medical experts were called on each side, and numerous issues were canvassed, reached the conclusion which he expressed in a most careful judgment, that the plaintiff had made good his case: he awarded £100,000 damages. His decision was reversed by a majority of the Court of Appeal (Lord Denning MR and Lawton LJ, Donaldson LJ dissenting) ([1980] 1 All ER 650) which refused leave to appeal to this House. Leave was, however, granted by an Appeal Committee. The essential and very difficult question therefore has to be faced whether, on a pure question of fact, the Court of Appeal was justified in reversing the decision of the trial judge.

My Lords, I need not elaborate on the principles of law which have to be applied. First, it is necessary, in order to establish liability of, and to obtain an award of compensation against, a doctor or a hospital that there has been negligence in law. There is in this field no liability without proof of fault. Secondly, there are strict limitations on the power of an appeal court to reverse the decision of the judge on an issue of fact. These have been well and clearly stated, notably by Lord Sumner in *The Hontestroom* [1927] AC 37 and by the Court of Appeal in *The Glannibanta* (1876) 1 PD 283 at 287. The Court of Appeal had them fully in mind. The main reason why, in the absence of an error of law, the judgment of the trial judge calls for the utmost respect, is that he has seen and heard the witnesses, often, as in this case, including the rival parties (the mother and Mr Jordan). The strength of this consideration will vary from case to case according as conclusions have to be reached as to credibility, or based on demeanour. In the present case they exist but are not compelling. A view had to be and was expressed as to the credibility of the mother; she was, generally, found to be incapable, in the understandable circumstances, of giving reliably precise evidence, but there remains a question whether, though what she said was unacceptable, something of evidentiary value can be extracted from it. On this I consider that the Court of Appeal was entitled to form an opinion. As to the evidence of Mr Jordan, no question of credibility arose; there was no doubt that he was telling the truth as he saw it. The judge did not express disbelief of his account; what he did was to appraise it in relation to such other evidence as was available; this he was entitled to do, but the Court of Appeal, while bound to attach great weight to the judge's views, was able to evaluate it for itself. Thirdly, there was the evidence of Professor McLaren. I think that his demeanour in the witness box must have had an influence on the judge's views, and this calls for complete respect. But as I shall hope to show, the ultimate conclusion to be drawn depends much more on the setting in which his evidence was given, and the relation which it must be thought to have to the events which occurred. Lastly, there were the expert witnesses. The judge was entitled to be impressed by the way in which each of them gave evidence, but he gave no indication how this factor balanced out. In the end, as to the standard of skill to be expected of Mr Jordan, there was little difference of opinion; such as there was related to what they respectively thought Mr Jordan had actually done. This brings us back to the primary issue, as to what really happened in the critical 25 minutes.

The appeal brought out, very clearly to my mind, that the issue does not depend on the endless refinements (for example on the meaning of 'impactation') of the experts, but on one issue: what, if any, evidence of negligence was provided by (a) the evidence of the mother, (b) the report and evidence of Professor McLaren, (c) the evidence of Mr Jordan? Unfortunately the solution of this issue remains one of immense difficulty.

Mr Jordan was at the time a senior registrar, of near consultant status, esteemed by his professional colleagues. There is no question but that he brought the utmost care to bear on Mrs Whitehouse's labour and delivery. If he was negligent at all, this consisted in a departure, in an anxious situation, from a standard accepted by the profession at the time. Put very briefly, it was said to lie in continuing traction with the forceps after an obstruction had been encountered so that the baby's head became 'impacted'. I shall not explain this word at this stage. It is obvious that the error, if error there was, lay centrally in the area of the exercise of expert judgment and experienced operation. Mr Jordan was a member of the obstetrical unit at the hospital headed by Professor McLaren, which had a high reputation; Professor McLaren himself was a distinguished obstetrician, unfortunately ill at the time of the birth.

Mrs Whitehouse was accepted as 30 years of age; this was her first baby. She was small, only 4ft 10½in in height. She was a difficult, nervous and at times aggressive patient. She was unable, or refused, to agree to vaginal examination during her pregnancy, or to have a lateral X-ray taken, though urged to do so by Professor McLaren. These processes would have helped to discover the exact shape of the pelvis. It is fair to say that when Mr Jordan came on the scene he was not greatly handicapped by this, because Mrs Whitehouse was at that time under epidural anaesthetic, and he was able to examine her vaginally. However, he had not the advantage of accurate measurements of the pelvis or of the ischial spines.

I need say little about the prenatal history of the case. It is fully told in the judgments of the trial judge and Lord Denning MR. The mother was seen by a number of doctors in the course of her pregnancy including Professor McLaren and Mr Jordan. I do not think that any criticism can be made of what they did. She was identified clearly as likely to be a difficult case; on 31st December 1969 Professor McLaren recorded that he thought the outlet was tight and that a trial of labour would be needed. This means that labour would be permitted to start and to proceed under close supervision in order to see whether the head could, with safety, proceed down the birth canal.

Mrs Whitehouse was admitted to the hospital at 0200 hrs on 6th January 1970, her membranes having ruptured shortly before. The vertex was recorded as engaged at 0230, and this was confirmed by Mr Kelly, of consultant status, at 1000 hrs. He noted 'fair sized baby'.

So at this point we have a small woman, anxious and distressed, awaiting a baby, for her on the large side, with the head in a favourable position and engaged in the pelvis; noted as being probably a case for 'trial of labour'. At 1130 she was given an epidural anaesthetic which would prevent her from feeling pain and probably from sensation below the waist.

At 1830 she was seen by Dr Skinner. He examined her vaginally and abdominally. He reported 'vertex engaged, fetal heart satisfactory . . . pelvis seems adequate'.

Now comes the period critical for this case. At 2330 Mr Jordan, who was not on duty, came to talk to Dr Skinner. On his radio communicator the latter was told that Mrs Whitehouse was fully dilated. Dr Skinner thought that this was the case for a more senior man than he, and Mr Jordan agreed to go; he saw her at 2330 and examined her abdominally and vaginally. He read the notes on the case, which, as the above summary shows, informed him precisely of what he had to deal with; a difficult case calling for great care.

He made a detailed note which I need not copy in full. It gave all the necessary medical details. Against 'pelvis' he wrote 'small gynaecoid' (ie of appropriate female shape) and then 'Normal delivery out of the question'.

He decided to embark on a trial of forceps and did so at 2345. The full expression for this is 'trial of forceps delivery' which, as the evidence showed beyond doubt, means the operator tries to see whether with the use of forceps a delivery per vaginam is possible. This involves two things, first tentative and delicate handling at least at the start; second the necessity of continuously reviewing progress with the obligation to stop traction if it appears that the delivery per vaginam cannot be proceeded with without risk. Then delivery will take place by Caesarian section.

Two things must be said at this stage. First, though for the plaintiff it was at one time otherwise contended, the decision to try for vaginal delivery rather than go at once to a Caesarian section was unquestionably the right and correct procedure, in order to avoid if possible the risk to the mother inevitably involved in section. Secondly, for the plaintiff an attempt was made to draw a line between trial of forceps, on the one hand, and delivery by forceps on the other hand, and to make a case that Mr Jordan was, unjustifiably, proceeding to the latter. This, to my mind, completely failed. There is no such clear-cut distinction. A trial of forceps (delivery) is what it says: it is an attempt at delivery accompanied by the two special conditions I have mentioned. There can be no doubt that this is what Mr Jordan was attempting. I take what happened from his notes. Under 'summary of reasons for operation' he wrote: 'Trial of forceps under epidural anaesthetic. Lower segment Caesarian section under G.A.' Then:

> '(1) Forceps begun at 23.45, 6 1 70. Head rotated to OA [occiput anterior] with Kiellands—no problem. [Kiellands is a kind of forceps used by some operators to rotate the head. This procedure was correct]. A very tight fit. No episiotomy [cutting of the perineum]. After pulling with 5 or 6 contractions, it was obvious that vaginal delivery would be too traumatic—so Caesarian section.'

He then recorded the Caesarian which everyone agrees was impeccably performed in two minutes. He noted 'no apparent (vaginal) trauma'. To complete the history, the baby, extracted apparently unharmed, was handed over to the paediatricians, found apnoeic, and made to breathe after 35 minutes, by which time irretrievable brain damage had occurred.

Here, with one possible exception, is a record of a birth carried out with all correct procedures, with, as unhappily occurs in the best managed hospitals and the best medical care, tragic results. The possible exception lies in the reference in Mr Jordan's own report to 'pulling with 5 or 6 contractions'. Did Mr Jordan pass the limits of professional competence either in continuing traction too long, or in pulling too hard? That is the whole issue. As direct evidence from persons present there was evidence of Mr Jordan, Mrs Whitehouse and Dr Skinner. There was no ward sister present and the two attending midwives could not be traced. As indirect evidence there was a report from Professor McLaren made to the hospital administrator some time between 22nd January and 10th March 1970, based on his reading of the notes, a conference with Mr Jordan, and his own experience. On top of this there was expert evidence on each side as to what Mr Jordan ought to have done, and as to the correctness of what he did. What is clear is that, in a trial of forceps, the operator should not attempt to pull past an obstruction, or at least not past a bony obstruction. Did Mr Jordan do this?

My Lords, at this point it is vital to recall that we are not here entitled to retry the case. We have indeed read almost the whole of the transcribed evidence. But it is not for us to say how we would have decided the case at trial. What we can properly do is to examine the judge's findings and to reach a conclusion, difficult though this may be, whether they can reasonably be supported on the evidence, recognising his advantages and, as fairly as we can, his difficulties, and whether the Court of Appeal was justified in reversing them.

One point must be put out of the way: was whatever occurred at the birth causative of the brain damage, in itself a very difficult question? The baby was apparently undamaged at birth: brain damage does occur for no ascertainable reason, and in normal births. Many alternatives were considered. The judge was able to find and did so that the probability was that the damage occurred between 2345 and 0010 on 6th–7th January, ie during the period in which the forceps were used. Whether I, or any other judge, would have reached the same conclusion is not here or there: the finding had evidence to support it and cannot be disturbed. It does not of itself, of course, prove that the damage arose from lack of skill; that is a point which must be independently decided.

There were three critical pieces of evidence.

First, there was the evidence of the mother, in the abstract the best person to know exactly what happened. In the concrete, the situation was otherwise. She had been in labour for nearly 24 hours; recorded as distressed; there had been vomiting; she was, for understandable reasons connected with her family, intensely anxious and tense; she was in a condition of lack of confidence in the medical procedure. She was under epidural anaesthetic, so inhibited from feeling, unless very imprecisely, what was going on. In these conditions she testified as follows: '[When the forceps were applied] It felt like a deadened electric shock that lifted my hips off the table, up off the bed.' This is also what she told the eminent professors who on this basis prepared their report for the plaintiff. But the judge, inevitably, did not accept this. No witness regarded it as possible: any traction must have been downwards. Dr Skinner, who was standing by her side the whole time, said that nothing like this occurred: he would have seen it and remembered it 'for its fantasticness'. With all allowance for professional loyalty this evidence is too strong to be totally discounted. But, though rejecting this account, the judge did make some use of it: he said 'it could be that she was pulled towards the bottom of the delivery bed *depending on the amount of force used*' (emphasis mine). But this does not prove that excessive force *was* used, and that is what is required. Again, in the crucial conclusory part of his judgment he says:

> 'Though Mrs Whitehouse's description of what occurred to her when the forceps were applied may not be exact in its clinical detail, I believe her, in so far as her description can be taken to be understood as a pulling of her toward the bottom of the delivery bed in a manner and with such force as to be inconsistent with a trial of forceps properly carried out.'

But I must agree with the majority of the Court of Appeal that I cannot accept this as a defensible finding. A process by which, after rejecting the account given by a witness, and it was more than inexact 'in clinical detail', that account is reconstructed so as to be evidence not of a general character, but of a precise and critical degree of traction supposed to differ from what would have been quite proper, seems to me with all respect to be illegitimate. If excessive traction is otherwise proved, her evidence might be consistent with that, but it cannot be used itself as evidence of that excess. I think that the Court of Appeal was quite right to discard this finding. In this they were unanimous.

The next piece of evidence consists of Mr Jordan's own testimony. He was examined and cross-examined at length. In his judgment the judge made comparatively little reference to this evidence, relying much more heavily on the secondhand evidence of Professor McLaren. For myself, I would regard Mr Jordan's firsthand account of the matter as of cardinal importance. Parts of it, indeed, may be regarded as the most solid evidence against him. I have anxiously considered it with the reservations proper in a case when a man is defending himself against a serious claim. The tenor of it, read as a whole, was that this was a very tight fit, that with the very first few pulls, made (correctly) with the contractions, some progress was made. With the fifth pull he realised that he was not making progress; he tried once more to see if he could ease the head past what might be minimal obstruction. Failing this, he thought that delivery per vaginam, though possible, would be too traumatic and that a Caesarian section was needed. With a view to this he eased the head slightly upwards with the forceps.

The attack on this was really twofold. First, it was to say that Mr Jordan pulled too hard. There was no direct evidence of this except that of the mother which I have already discussed. Dr Skinner, though I accept that not too much weight can be placed on his description, said that he had never ever (sic) seen Mr Jordan violently pull forceps in his life.

Then, and this was the critical point, it was said that Mr Jordan tried to pull past a bony obstruction, which would be contrary to the best medical practice, and got the head 'wedged' or 'stuck' or 'impacted'. In his judgment the judge quoted this passage:

> 'Q. Perhaps I should end by asking you this: did you try to pull past any bony
> part? A. My trial by forceps was to overcome what may be minimal obstruction so
> one did, as it were, pass the level of the ischial spines.
> 'Q. The question was not well phrased. Did you try to pull despite them? A.
> No.'

The judge's comment on it is that 'perhaps some clue was given by [it]'.

But if the first answer is somewhat obscure, the second is a plain denial that he tried
to pull despite (ie over any resistance of) the ischial spines.

I would compare with this his final answer given in reply to the learned judge:

> '*Bush J*. Mr Jordan, on that aspect of it that you have been talking about, what was
> it that made you believe that to continue the traction might be harmful to the
> baby? A. Because one is aware from the very nature of the forceps delivery that
> there is some resistance, and the aim of a trial of forceps is to ease the baby past
> whatever resistance there may be, whether it is the pelvic floor or the side walls of
> the pelvis, and you pull slowly and tentatively and then you form an impression
> that to continue with that rate of progress may take too long, or too much traction,
> and I think that is all.'

Other passages exist to the same effect. And what I think Mr Jordan is trying to explain
is that, in a trial of forceps, the operator, who has to work on feel, and instinct, and
experience, is by the nature of things always working against resistance, just because of
the narrowness and irregular shape of the birth canal. This he has to do, with of course
care, and a margin of safety. What he must not do, and what Mr Jordan denies that he
did, was to pull past a bony obstruction: then he must stop.

This leads on to the issue of whether the head was 'stuck' or 'wedged'. So far as Mr
Jordan is concerned he firmly denied that it ever was. It would not, without risk, go any
further, but that was all. At the end he was able without difficulty to push it back up a
little in preparation for the Caesarian. I think it is possible to carry this point further.
Sir John Dewhurst, Professor at Queen Charlotte's Hospital and at Chelsea Hospital for
Women, and the author of an important book, Integrated Obstetrics, gave evidence *after*
Mr Jordan and *after* hearing the latter's evidence, an advantage not possessed by the
plaintiff's witnesses. He found nothing wrong in the procedure which Mr Jordan had
followed, including the resort to five or six pulls.

I reach the conclusion, then, that here too the Court of Appeal, particularly Lawton LJ,
was justified in taking, contrary to the view of the judge, Mr Jordan's evidence as
evidence that he did not get the head wedged or stuck.

So finally there is Professor McLaren's report and evidence, on which the judge placed
much reliance. I have explained that his report was prepared on the basis of the hospital
notes and conference with Mr Jordan. It is therefore evidence against Mr Jordan, to the
extent, and only to the extent, that it may be taken to incorporate Mr Jordan's account
at the time to his superior. It must be borne in mind that it was written in order to
answer a long letter of complaints by Mr Whitehouse as to the conduct of the birth, one
of his complaints relating to the pulls exerted by Mr Jordan. The tenor of the report was
to maintain that Mrs Whitehouse had received correct and skilled treatment and that no
blame attached to anyone for the sad result which followed. Though this was the
purpose of the report it was said that nevertheless it 'let the cat out of the bag' in two
respects revelatory of a failure of skill by Mr Jordan.

In a critical passage he wrote:

> 'A trial of forceps was carried out under epidural anaesthesia the head rotating
> with ease with Kiellands forceps. Descent, however, did not follow traction and *in
> the interest of the child* the head was disimpacted prior to speedy delivery by Caesarian
> section. However, there was need to switch from epidural to general anaesthetic for
> section.' (Professor McLaren's emphasis.)

The first point is easily disposed of. 'Descent did not follow traction' is clearly a statement referring to the whole of the process and is merely saying that the traction did not extract the baby. It cannot be read as saying, as for the plaintiff it was sought to say, that no movement whatever took place. It leads to no conclusion.

The second point is more difficult. It relates to the word 'disimpacted'. This involves, it is said, that the head was 'impacted', and 'impacted' means 'wedged or stuck'. This proves therefore that Mr Jordan pulled too hard. It should be noted that a copy of this report was sent to Mr Jordan who did not comment on the word; he must therefore, it is said, be taken to have agreed with it.

Many hours of evidence were devoted to this word. Professor McLaren himself tried to explain it away: he should not have used it, he did not mean to convey that the head required to be 'unstuck' or that it was stuck. He pointed out, justly, that the report referred to 'a tentative attempt at forceps', 'the accepted obstetrical technique of tentative trial of forceps' and 'satisfactory trial of labour'. All of this was inconsistent with getting the head 'wedged'. But what he did mean by the word, used three times?

There was no unanimity among the experts as to the meaning of the word 'impacted'. The dictionary meaning is (Steadman's Medical Dictionary (23rd Edn, 1976)): 'Denoting a fetus that, because of its large size or narrowing of the pelvic canal, has become wedged and incapable of spontaneous advance or recession.' No reference here, be it noted, to the result of force.

Sir John Stallworthy did not disagree with this. Sir John Peel said:

> 'I think that an impacted head is one that does not move either up or down without further force or exertion being applied. Either with forceps in pulling it down or the fingers pulling it up.'

Sir John Dewhurst said:

> 'It is not a term I use in my medical practice, no. I think it is capable of being used in various ways. I suppose perhaps one reason why I never use it is impaction in the sense solidly wedged has almost disappeared from medical practice in this country.'

Dame Josephine Barnes said: 'I mean the head is in a position where it cannot go any further on.' So there is no unanimity, or even balance of opinion, that impaction is something which occurs from or is evidence of excessive or unprofessional pulling. It is a condition which may arise from many causes.

The learned judge's conclusion was: 'I find it difficult to accept Professor McLaren's explanation of his use of the word "impacted"'; and this was a critical finding against Mr Jordan. But with respect I think that the mass of medical evidence had led him to focus on an inessential question. The argument was not about the meaning of a word, but about what Mr Jordan did. Mr Jordan gave a complete and detailed account of what he did. He proceeded to the point when the baby would go no further. He denied that it was 'stuck'. He said that he easily pushed it up. All of this was consistent with sound medical practice, and with a possible use of the terminology. If Professor McLaren had thought, after discussing the case with Mr Jordan, that something had gone wrong, and that the head had become wedged through excessive force, it is incredible that, in the context of a wholly disculpatory report, he would have used a word meaning 'wedged by force' without some explanation. It is quite simple to suppose that the word was used to refer to the routine action in preparation for Caesarian section.

In my opinion, the Court of Appeal was justified in concluding that this, together with the evidence of Mrs Whitehouse which formed the main pillars of the judgment, was not nearly of sufficient strength to lead to a finding of professional negligence.

My Lords, I could, but will not, comment on other aspects of the evidence. I am, for myself, not happy about the manner in which the judge used the evidence about the fetal heart beat; I understand that others of your Lordships may enlarge on this point. At the end of it all, on the single issue whether during the critical half hour Mr Jordan departed from his own high standard of professional competence, I find the judgments of Lord Denning MR and Lawton LJ convincing, and, appreciative as I am, as were the members of the Court of Appeal, of the judge's care and clarity, I must agree that this is a case where an appeal court can and should interfere.

One final word. I have to say that I feel some concern as to the manner in which part of the expert evidence called for the plaintiff came to be organised. This matter was discussed in the Court of Appeal and commented on by Lord Denning MR. While some degree of consultation between experts and legal advisers is entirely proper, it is necessary that expert evidence presented to the court should be, and should be seen to be, the independent product of the expert, uninfluenced as to form or content by the exigencies of litigation. To the extent that it is not, the evidence is likely to be not only incorrect but self defeating.

I would dismiss the appeal.

LORD EDMUND-DAVIES. My Lords, I have wrestled long and hard over this appeal. The evidence at the trial occupied 11 days, and the judgment delivered 10 days later by Bush J is a model of clarity and care. But the fact that this award of £100,000 to the grossly disabled infant plaintiff was reversed by a majority at the conclusion of a four-day hearing in the Court of Appeal and that the appeal to this House occupied five days should serve to demonstrate that difficult issues are involved.

I gratefully adopt the narrative of salient facts prepared by my noble and learned friend Lord Wilberforce, and I shall add little to it. There arose an acute conflict on many points and between both lay and expert witnesses. It has long been settled law that, when the decision of a trial judge is based substantially on his assessment of the quality and credibility of witnesses, an appellate court 'must, in order to reverse, not merely entertain doubts whether the decision below is right, but be convinced that it is wrong' (see *Bland v Ross, The Julia* (1860) 14 Moo PCC 210 at 235, 15 ER 284 at 293 per Lord Kingsdown). And that is so irrespective of whether or not the trial judge made any observation with regard to credibility (*Clarke v Edinburgh and District Tramways Co* 1919 SC (HL) 35 at 36 per Lord Shaw).

Certain important matters are not in doubt. The first (as the learned judge himself stressed) is that the delivery of a brain-damaged baby does not necessarily connote negligence by anyone, for such a misfortune can inexplicably occur in circumstances where there are no grounds for suspecting any lack of proper skill. Again, although the obdurate attitude of Mrs Whitehouse during her pregnancy had created a lack of information regarding the dimensions of her birth canal, before Mr Jordan started even an exploratory pull on the fetus he contemporaneously noted that he was confronted by 'a very tight fit', a situation which Dame Josephine Barnes described as 'certainly a high risk case' and one which Sir John Dewhurst said would have occasioned him 'considerable concern'. On the other hand, it was unchallenged that Mr Jordan was right to use forceps, for, although vaginal delivery by contraction alone was out of the question, it was inadvisable to proceed directly to Caesarian section.

The principal questions calling for decision are: (a) in what manner did Mr Jordan use the forceps? and (b) was that manner consistent with the degree of skill which a member of his profession is required by law to exercise? Surprising though it is at this late stage in the development of the law of negligence, counsel for Mr Jordan persisted in submitting that his client should be completely exculpated were the answer to question (b), 'Well, at the worst he was guilty of an error of clinical judgment'. My Lords, it is high time that the unacceptability of such an answer be finally exposed. To say that a surgeon committed an error of clinical judgment is wholly ambiguous, for, while some such errors may be completely consistent with the due exercise of professional skill, other acts or omissions in the course of exercising 'clinical judgment' may be so glaringly below proper standards as to make a finding of negligence inevitable. Indeed, I should have regarded this as a truism were it not that, despite the exposure of the 'false antithesis' by Donaldson LJ in his dissenting judgment in the Court of Appeal, counsel for the defendants adhered to it before your Lordships.

But doctors and surgeons fall into no special category, and, to avoid any future disputation of a similar kind, I would have it accepted that the true doctrine was enunciated, and by no means for the first time, by McNair J in *Bolam v Friern Hospital Management Committee* [1957] 2 All ER 118 at 121, [1957] 1 WLR 582 at 586 in the following words, which were applied by the Privy Council in *Chin Keow v Government of Malaysia* [1967] 1 WLR 813:

> '... where you get a situation which involves the use of some special skill or competence, then the test as to whether there has been negligence or not is not the test of the man on the top of a Clapham omnibus becauses he has not got this special skill. The test is the standard of the ordinary skilled man exercising and professing to have that special skill.'

If a surgeon fails to measure up to that standard in *any* respect ('clinical judgment' or otherwise), he has been negligent and should be so adjudged.

Mr Jordan said that, in the situation confronting him, he embarked on a trial of forceps, its object being to establish whether there was any disproportion or obstruction in the birth canal sufficient to put at risk a vaginal delivery. Trial by forceps needs to be carried out gently and tentatively, 'progress being observed when reasonable traction is exerted', as Sir John Dewhurst, a defence witness, put it. If progress is achieved, the process of pulling with contractions, opening the forceps when a contraction ceases, then applying them again with the next contraction continues until (in Mr Jordan's words) 'such time as the baby was delivered or (as in this case) it became apparent that further attempt at delivery may be unwise'. He accepted that during the trial of forceps the surgeon is *not* embarking on a delivery, but merely exploring the possibility of vaginal delivery being achieved, and that—

> 'Before undertaking mid-forceps delivery, the physician's clinical judgment must permit him to conclude unequivocally that he can in fact deliver the baby safely per vaginam, and that this method of delivery placed less risk to the mother and baby than Caesarian section.'

How far had Mr Jordan proceeded before he abandoned the notion of a vaginal delivery and decided on a Caesarian section? He said he had pulled with five or six contractions, and formed the view that the head was making satisfactory progress after the first four pulls. There came a fifth pull with possibly no 'movement'. When asked, 'What conceivable factor can there be which would stop you on the fifth?', his significant reply was 'The spines', ie the ischia. A little later he said: 'If I got difficulty on the fifth, then I would confirm it on the sixth.' Asked how in such circumstances he could justify pulling yet once more, Mr Jordan answered:

> 'What one wants to know is, is there at this particular moment, and this is the crucial part as far as the trial of forceps is concerned, or would this little extra pressure or traction deliver this head past the bony obstruction or not? In these circumstances, realising that this was the point at which the decision had to be made finally, as to continue or go back, it is justified to see whether or not a little more, a little extra traction with other contractions, would be enough to overcome the resistance one is feeling.'

That answer has to be considered in the light of the directive in a work prepared by Sir John Dewhurst that: '*No obstruction below the head.* This is an absolute rule. The head should never be pulled past an area of obstruction. Caesarian section is indicated.'

Mr Jordan insisted that the trial of forceps terminated at the stage when the factor of the *safety* of the baby arose, although he entertained no doubt that vaginal delivery could have been achieved. As to this, and the case generally, the conclusion of the learned judge was expressed in this way:

> 'I am doubtful whether Mr Jordan was in fact undertaking a trial of forceps, as opposed to an attempt at vaginal delivery which failed, and in the course of which the baby was wedged, stuck, or jammed, and which on anyone's view of the matter would be unjustified. However, in any event, if it were a trial of forceps then he

pulled too hard and too long, so that the fetus became wedged or stuck. In getting it wedged or stuck, or unwedged or unstuck, Mr Jordan caused asphyxia which in its turn caused the cerebral palsy. In this respect Mr Jordan fell below the very high standard of professional competence that the law requires of him.'

In the light of the conflicting evidence, is that a conclusion to which the experienced trial judge was entitled to arrive? With the single exception of Dame Josephine Barnes, the medical witnesses on both sides agree that, as the judge put it—

'. . . if in fact the trial of forceps proceeded to the lengths where the fetal head was wedged or stuck and had to be unwedged or unstuck with the use of force, then unprofessional force would have been used, both in getting it wedged and in having to unwedge it.'

His observations on this cardinal issue began with the evidence given by the mother, and he dealt with it in this way:

'According to Mrs Whitehouse, when the forceps were applied, "It felt like a deadened electric shock that lifted my hips off the table", and she described her buttocks and hips as being lifted off the table. This cannot be an accurate description, since the pull is downwards, but it could be that she was pulled towards the bottom of the delivery bed, depending on the amount of force used. She was a little woman and it would be a question of degree whether this indicated in itself the use of excessive force.'

When Sir John Stallworthy, a plaintiff's witness, was cross-examined to establish that the mother would not be lifted off the bed, he said:

'What very frequently happens, and I would have thought (I don't know) what probably happened from her description was with the forceps she was pulled down to the end of the bed. She is a small woman and it was a big baby, and it would have been perfectly reasonable with an ordinary, successful forceps delivery for this to have happened.'

But two comments on that evidence are called for. (1) We are not here concerned with an accomplished forceps delivery, but with what was described as a trial of forceps which was abandoned at a stage when it was still open to Mr Jordan to change his mind and proceed to a Caesarian section. (2) Dr Skinner, who was standing nearby in the operating theatre when the baby was delivered, said that Mr Jordan never went further than trial of forceps. He added that there was no violent pulling, and spoke of the 'fantasticness' of the allegation of Mrs Whitehouse being lifted off the bed. That does not in terms negative a *downward* pull, but it controverts the use of force beyond that customary in a trial of forceps.

Regarding this important matter the learned judge said:

'Though Mrs Whitehouse's description of what occurred to her when the forceps were applied may not be exact in its clinical detail, I believe her, in so far as her description can be taken to be understood as a pulling of her toward the bottom of the delivery bed in a manner and with such force as to be inconsistent with a trial of forceps properly carried out.'

My Lords, I have some difficulty in following how anything in Mrs Whitehouse's testimony could be 'understood' in the sense adopted by the learned judge. She was the only witness who in direct terms spoke adversely of the degree of force exerted by Mr Jordan, and he had found her unreliable in several respects. Once more the learned judge rejected her evidence, this time in relation to what happened when the forceps were applied. In its place he 'believed' an account which, while to a degree in conformity with what Sir John Stallworthy said *could* happen in forceps delivery, was one which she herself did not advance. It was accordingly not such a finding as an appellate court, lacking the judge's advantage of seeing and hearing the witnesses, is normally obliged to leave undisturbed. It was in truth a finding without an evidential basis.

I turn to consider another matter which undoubtedly operated powerfully on the judge's mind, and which, indeed, he described as 'perhaps the strongest piece of evidence that something untoward was done . . .' It has perplexed me perhaps more than any other part of this worrying case, and I entertain no strong conviction even now that I have reached the right conclusion about it. I have in mind the report prepared by Professor McLaren, head of the unit and himself a defendant to these proceedings until they were discontinued against him in March 1976. He drafted the report after discussions with Mr Jordan which began a few days after the baby was delivered. Each knew that Mrs Whitehouse was very upset and angry, and on 22nd January 1970 there arrived a letter from her husband making grave complaints against the unit staff. The hospital administrator therefore called for a report, and this led to discussions on points which both the professor and Mr Jordan realised were of 'the utmost importance'. It was in the light of these discussions and the hospital notes that Professor McLaren prepared his undated report, and, in due course, showed it to Mr Jordan before submitting it to the hospital administrator on 10th March. Judging from the time factor, accordingly, it does not appear to have been hastily prepared. It can, I think, be fairly described as in some respects an odd document for a person with the professional experience and sophistication of Professor McLaren to have prepared, and for Mr Jordan, in his turn, to have passed without amendment. Certainly one can well understand the learned judge being very troubled by it. But, having said that, what is beyond doubt is that the report set out to be wholly exculpatory of Mr Jordan and of the entire hospital staff. Thus, it refers to 'this well-conducted trial of labour of forceps', to Mrs Whitehouse's 'first-class obstetric care', and it concluded: 'We accept no criticism or implication that in terms of being humane, or in technical skills, we neglected Mrs Whitehouse.' Yet the learned judge found it possible to conclude that the report was actually confirmatory of the charge of negligence made against Mr Jordan, and this mainly on the strength of the inclusion therein of the following observations. (1) 'A trial of forceps was carried out under epidural anaesthesia . . . *Descent, however, did not follow traction*, and *in the interest of the child the head was disimpacted* prior to speedy delivery by Caesarian Section'. (2) In relation to the fetus having sustained a cerebral haemorrhage, 'It could be that a congenital weakness of a blood vessel existed, *so that the fixing of the head in the pelvis and its disimpaction* for Caesarian Section led to a leaking of blood in the skull'. (3) 'Possibly at Caesarian Section *the disimpaction of the head* was critical and cerebral haemorrhage followed.' (My emphasis in each case.)

For my part, I cannot attach significance to the observation that 'Descent . . . did not follow traction', as it is the plaintiff's own case that descent to a point there certainly was. But at the trial, in the Court of Appeal, and again in this House many hours were spent considering the much more important matter of the threefold use of the word 'disimpaction'. Is 'impaction' its converse and what situation or action does each word connote? Mr Jordan himself, in common with several of the expert witnesses, accepted as accurate the Steadman's Medical Dictionary (23rd Edn, 1976) meaning of 'impacted' as 'Denoting a fetus that, because of its large size or narrowing of the pelvic canal, has become wedged and incapable of spontaneous advance or recession.'

Professor McLaren, too, accepted that it had the generally accepted meaning of 'stuck', but he averred that his repeated use of 'disimpaction' had no relation to unsticking or unwedging, or fixation or any state of immovability. He apologised for his misuse of language and explained that in his vocabulary 'disimpaction' involves no more than a gentle pushing of the head upwards with one finger before proceeding to a Caesarian section.

My Lords, the point is important in the light of the expert evidence supportive of the view that, if the head of the fetus had become so stuck as to cause asphyxia, excessive force had been used. I remain mystified why, in the drafting of what was known to be an extremely important report, its author should have used in the sense claimed by him a variant of the word 'impaction' which in medical science has such a different meaning, and why Mr Jordan (who was familiar with that accepted meaning) should have allowed 'disimpaction' to go forward without comment.

I could well understand the McLaren report taking the form it did were the version of events then intended to be advanced that Mr Jordan had gone past the trial of forceps stage and had decided on vaginal delivery, that he had proceeded with proper skill to implement that decision up to the stage when he could with safety go no further and therefore turned to Caesarian section, and that the misfortune which occurred did not arise from any negligence on his part. But the defence presented to the judge was that Mr Jordan never went beyond a trial of forceps. It is true that, if all goes well, there may be no clear line of demarcation between trial of forceps and actual delivery by forceps, the one merging into the other. But that is not to say that there does not arise, however fleetingly, a stage when the operator has to consider whether he can safely go further. At one time, however, Mr Jordan referred in evidence to his 'attempt at forceps delivery, followed by Caesarian section', and in his pleaded defence it was expressly admitted that he 'attempted but abandoned a forceps delivery and then proceeded to deliver the plaintiff by Caesarian section', an admission which his counsel told this House was due to an oversight and should not have been made. It could well be that it was on the basis of such material that the learned trial judge expressed himself as 'doubtful whether Mr Jordan was in fact undertaking a trial of forceps, as opposed to an attempt at vaginal delivery which failed . . . '

But the point is a fine one, and it should not of itself lead to the condemnation of the defendant. In his dissenting judgment, Donaldson LJ concluded that the evidence of Mrs Whitehouse being 'pulled down towards the bottom of the bed, in the sense that her body was moved' could not be right, and he added ([1980] 1 All ER 650 at 666):

> 'But, having said that, I still have to decide whether the judge's conclusion was wrong, and I am not satisfied that it was. Reading the judgment as a whole, it seems to me that Mrs Whitehouse's evidence was treated as no more than consistent with, or, at most, confirmatory of Professor McLaren's report, and that even if Bush J had put her evidence on one side, he would still have reached the same conclusion.'

If that is right, as with respect it seems to be, the outcome of these proceedings was regarded by the learned judge as finally turning on the use of one word. I dare say that at times even greater issues have turned on less. But that word cannot properly be considered out of context, and I again stress that the whole drift of the lengthy McLaren report was that the Whitehouse baby had been delivered in accordance with the highest professional standards. Such being the setting, to hold that the threefold use of 'disimpaction' should be regarded as establishing that the complete opposite was the truth is, in my judgment, to impose on it an excessive and unsupportable burden.

Such, at least, is my conclusion about this distressing case. It has evidently caused me greater difficulty than it has any of my noble and learned brethren. But I have at last found myself impelled and compelled to hold that, despite the great care and ability manifested by the learned judge, there was lacking the evidence needed to uphold his basic finding that Mr Jordan 'pulled too hard and too long, so that the fetus became stuck'. I therefore concur in holding that the appeal should be dismissed.

LORD FRASER OF TULLYBELTON. My Lords, this is an action of damages for professional negligence against a senior registrar at Birmingham Maternity Hospital. After a long trial, the learned judge held negligence established against the registrar, but the Court of Appeal by a majority (Lord Denning MR and Lawton LJ, Donaldson LJ dissenting) ([1980] 1 All ER 650) reversed his decision. They did so not because they considered that the learned trial judge had misstated the relevant law. Clearly he did not; he said, rightly in my opinion, that negligence for the purposes of this case meant 'a failure . . . to exercise the standard of skill expected from the ordinary competent specialist having regard to the experience and expertise that specialist holds himself out as possessing'. He added the proviso that the skill and expertise to be considered were those applying in 1969 to 1970. Although that statement was not criticised in the Court of Appeal, Lord Denning MR did criticise a later sentence in the judgment because, in his view, it suggested that the law made no allowance for errors of judgment by a professional man. Referring to medical men, Lord Denning MR said ([1980] 1 All ER 650 at 658): 'If they are to be found liable [sc for negligence] whenever they do not effect a cure, or whenever anything untoward happens, it would do a great disservice to the profession itself.' That is undoubtedly correct, but he went on to say this: 'We must say, and say firmly, that, in a professional man an error of judgment is not negligent.' Having regard to the context, I think that Lord Denning MR must have meant to say that an error of judgment 'is not *necessarily* negligent'. But in my respectful opinion, the statement as it stands is not an accurate statement of the law. Merely to describe something as an error of judgment tells us nothing about whether it is negligent or not. The true position is that an error of judgment may, or may not, be negligent; it depends on the nature of the error. If it is one that would not have been made by a reasonably competent professional man professing to have the standard and type of skill that the defendant held himself out as having, and acting with ordinary care, then it is negligent. If, on the other hand, it is an error that a man, acting with ordinary care, might have made, then it is not negligence.

The main reason why the Court of Appeal reversed the judge's decision was that they differed from him on the facts. The question therefore is whether the Court of Appeal was entitled to reverse the judge's decision on a pure question of fact. The view of the judge who saw and heard the witnesses as to the weight to be given to their evidence is always entitled to great respect. We were reminded particularly of dicta to that effect in *The Hontestroom* [1927] AC 37 and *Powell v Streatham Manor Nursing Home* [1935] AC 243, [1935] All ER Rep 58, and there is other high authority to the same effect. But in this case, unlike cases such as *Powell* and *The Hontestroom*, no direct issue of credibility arises. It is not suggested that any witness, or body of witnesses, was giving dishonest evidence. The only witness whose reliability is seriously in question is Mrs Whitehouse, the mother of the plaintiff, and I shall refer to the critical part of her evidence in a moment. Apart from her evidence, the important facts are almost entirely inferences from the primary facts, and in determining what inferences should properly be drawn, an appellate court is just as well placed as the trial judge. Accordingly this is a case where the judge's decision on fact is more open to be reassessed by an appellate court than it often is.

The learned judge expressed his conclusion as to the primary facts which had been established with admirable clarity and conciseness, as follows:

> 'On the balance of probabilities I have come to the conclusion, firstly that the damage to the brain of Stuart [the infant plaintiff] was not the result of inherent maldevelopment, and secondly that asphyxia or anoxia caused the brain damage, and thirdly that the asphyxia itself was caused by some event between 2345 and 0025 hrs, that is between the commencement of the trial of forceps and the delivery of the child by Caesarian section.'

That passage in the judgment is immediately followed by a repetition of the caution, to be found elsewhere in the judgment, that such damage may be caused by the violent event of birth itself and 'may occur without professional fault on the part of those having the care and management of the patient'. So the learned judge was evidently on his guard against treating this case as a case of res ipsa loquitur.

He then turned to consider what evidence there was on the vital question of whether 'unprofessional force', by which he evidently meant excessive force, had been applied by Mr Jordan when using forceps. He relied firstly on the evidence of Mrs Whitehouse herself, and secondly on what he regarded as 'perhaps the strongest piece of evidence that something untoward was done', namely the report by Professor McLaren who was the head of department in which Mr Jordan worked, and who himself was a distinguished obstetrician. Professor McLaren was ill at the time and was not present at the birth. Thirdly, the learned judge relied on the evidence of Mr Jordan, the first defendant. I must consider these pieces of evidence.

The evidence of Mrs Whitehouse was that when Mr Jordan pulled on the forceps she had 'felt something like a deadened electric shock that lifted my hips off the table'. All the medical evidence was that Mrs Whitehouse was not, and could not have been, lifted up off the table by pulling on the forceps because the traction would have been in a downward direction. The judge rejected Mrs Whitehouse's account of what had occurred as being mistaken. He had already rejected her evidence on several points relating to her treatment in the earlier stages of pregnancy. So far as this matter is concerned, it is not surprising that she was mistaken considering her condition at the time to which she was referring. She had been without sleep, according to her own account, for 40 hours by this time. She had not had any food because she had been vomiting, and as she put it herself 'I was at the end of the line really'. Above all the lower part of her body was under epidural anaesthetic which meant that it was largely without sensation. But the judge, having rejected Mrs Whitehouse's account, went on to accept an interpretation of it suggested by Sir John Stallworthy, one of the medical experts who gave evidence on behalf of the plaintiff. He said that he interpreted Mrs Whithouse's evidence as meaning that she had been pulled down off the bed and then lifted back on to it by the medical staff. That interpretation was never put to Mr Jordan or to the other medical witness who had been present at the time (Dr Skinner) although Dr Skinner was asked about Mrs Whitehouse's original account of being lifted up off the bed and denied that any such thing had occurred. It would be natural for Dr Skinner to feel professional and personal loyalty towards Mr Jordan, who was his superior and also his friend, and who had taken charge of the delivery because Dr Skinner felt that it was beyond his competence. I would therefore have been prepared to discount his evidence to some extent if it had stood alone, but the learned judge does not indicate any doubt about its reliability, and so far as it goes it is entirely consistent with the evidence of the medical experts as to the impossibility of Mrs Whitehouse's account. The learned judge's conclusion about Mrs Whitehouse's evidence on this matter was expressed thus:

> 'Though Mrs Whitehouse's description of what occurred to her when the forceps were applied may not be exact in its clinical detail, I believe her, in so far as her description can be taken to be understood as a pulling of her toward the bottom of the delivery bed in a manner and with such force as to be inconsistent with a trial of forceps properly carried out.'

In my opinion that conclusion contains two serious flaws, either of which would be enough to make it unacceptable. Firstly, I do not consider that it is permissible to accept Mrs Whitehouse's evidence 'in so far as' her description can be taken to mean something different from what she said, and something which was not tested by a cross-examination of the witnesses, including the defendant and Dr Skinner, who could have confirmed or denied it. I agree with Lawton LJ who said ([1980] 1 All ER 650 at 660):

> 'In Lord Sumner's words in the *The Hontestroom* [1927] AC 37 at 47 the trial judge in this case "palpably misused his advantage" in having seen and heard the mother. These advantages could not be used, as the trial judge used them, to turn an account of what had happened which physically could not have taken place, into one which could.'

Secondly, even if the interpretation of Mrs Whitehouse's evidence were correct, it would not by itself indicate that the degree of force used was excessive and inconsistent with a trial of forceps delivery properly carried out.

I come now to Professor McLaren's report. This was written in answer to a request from the hospital administrator for information. It was based partly on the clinical notes and partly on oral discussion with Mr Jordan, and it was shown to Mr Jordan before being sent (by Mr Jordan) to the administrator. It can, therefore, be regarded as having been accepted by Mr Jordan and as having possible evidential value against him. There was one word in the report on which the learned judge particularly relied for drawing an inference unfavourable to Mr Jordan. That was the word 'disimpacted'. It was used, as the judge pointed out, no less than three times in the report. Probably the most significant use was the following sentence which is quoted in the judgment: 'Descent, however did not follow traction and *in the interest of the child* the head was disimpacted prior to speedy delivery by Caesarian section' (Professor McLaren's emphasis). The importance attached to the word by the judge arose in this way. He said: 'For something to be disimpacted it must first have been impacted', and he relied on a definition of the word 'impacted' in relation to a fetus given in Steadman's Medical Dictionary (23rd Edn, 1976) as follows: 'Denoting a fetus that, because of its large size or narrowing of the pelvic canal, has become wedged and incapable of spontaneous advance or recession.' That definition was accepted by several of the medical experts, though not by all of them, and the learned judge considered that, if the head was impacted, that indicated that it had become tightly stuck or wedged between parts of the bony structure of the pelvis and that it had been pulled by forceps too long or too hard. I do not think that the latter part of his conclusion was justified. Professor McLaren in his evidence apologised for using the word. He said that it was not a good word but it was one that he was accustomed to use, though he did not intend it to suggest that there had been such wedging and one needed a lot of force to push the head up again before embarking on Caesarian section. It seems that Professor McLaren's apologetic evidence made an unfavourable impression on the judge and his finding on the matter was expressed thus: 'It is with regret that I find it difficult to accept Professor McLaren's explanation of his use of the word "impacted".' I have tried to make proper allowance for the importance to be attached to the judge's view on this matter but I have reached the opinion that the Court of Appeal was entitled to differ from it for these reasons. Firstly, the conclusion of the professor's report was to the effect that Mrs Whitehouse had received excellent care while in the hospital, and in particular he said that there was no evidence that she had anything but 'first class obstetric care'. That conclusion would have been impossible if the obstetrician concerned, Mr Jordan, had employed forceps with excessive force, and it is therefore very unlikely that the Professor used the word 'disimpacted' in a sense intended to imply that such force had been used. It is also unlikely that Mr Jordan would have passed the report, containing that word, without objection if he had understood the word in that sense. Secondly, the medical evidence as a whole showed that the word is used with various shades of meaning, and it does not necessarily mean that the fetus is so firmly wedged or stuck as to require much force to dislodge it. The medical evidence showed also that the exact degree of force which could properly be used was a matter for expert judgment by a skilled obstetrician and might vary considerably according to circumstances. Thirdly (and in my opinion of considerable importance), when the two witnesses who gave evidence for the plaintiff were preparing their joint report (or rather approving the joint report which was, rather surprisingly, 'settled' for them by counsel), they did not emphasise Professor McLaren's reference to 'disimpaction'; if it was really so fatal to the defendant's case as the learned judge seems to have thought, one would have expected them to fasten on it at once. It seems to me, therefore, that he attached too much importance to it.

Apart from the use of that one word, the learned judge evidently regarded Professor McLaren's report as a whole as indicating that the defendant had pulled too hard and too long. That may have been partly because he treated the expression 'descent did not follow traction' as meaning that the fetus did not descend at all as a result of traction. That meaning was urged on us in argument, but I do not accept it because if *no* descent took place, ie if the fetus did not move downwards at all as a result of traction, the impaction (whatever be the exact meaning of the word) could not have been caused by the traction. I read the expression as meaning what Mr Jordan said it meant, that descent did not continue to the extent of delivery. So read, the statement is correct but throws no light on the question we are considering. I think much of the importance attached by the learned judge to the report was due to the statement it contained that 'after a reasonable *attempt at delivery* by forceps a Caesarian section was carried out' (my emphasis). The significance of the words emphasised is that a distinction was drawn by the medical witnesses between a *trial* of forceps delivery (generally abbreviated to a trial of forceps) and an *attempted* forceps delivery. The former should be very tentative and gentle. The latter, in which stronger traction is permissible, should never be embarked on unless the physician's clinical judgment permits him to conclude unequivocally that he can deliver the patient safely per vaginam. Mr Jordan in his evidence was insistent that he never got beyond the trial stage and that the fact of his having used five or six pulls did not indicate the contrary. He did not profess to remember every detail of what he had done, and his evidence was based on the clinical notes and on his usual practice, but he was quite clear about what he must have done. He said that, taking six pulls as the total, he must have made some progress until the fifth pull. The fifth pull made no progress and the sixth pull would have confirmed that no further progress was possible consistent with safety. The learned judge did not in terms reject that evidence nor did he express any reservation about Mr Jordan's evidence as a whole. What he said, in the decisive paragraph of his judgment, was this:

'In all these circumstances I am doubtful whether Mr Jordan was in fact undertaking a trial of forceps as opposed to an attempt at vaginal delivery which failed, and in the course of which the baby was wedged, stuck or jammed, and which on anyone's view of the matter would be unjustified. However, in any event if it were a trial of forceps then he pulled too hard and too long so that the fetus became wedged or stuck. In getting it wedged or stuck, or unwedged or unstuck, Mr Jordan caused asphyxia which in turn caused the cerebral palsy. In this respect Mr Jordan fell below the very high standard of professional competence that the law requires of him.'

It seems to me with respect that the learned judge was seeking to draw too sharp a line between a trial of forceps delivery and an attempted forceps delivery. The former, if it makes progress, will merge into the latter, and may be carried on to a complete delivery. Whether Mr Jordan ever moved from the trial stage to the attempted delivery stage is really a question of words; the important issue is whether there was evidence that, in the learned judge's words, 'he pulled too hard and too long so that the fetus became wedged or stuck'. He himself denied that it ever became wedged or stuck, and I have already explained why I do not think that Professor McLaren's use of the word 'impacted' means stuck. The evidence which seems to come nearest to convicting him of negligence in this respect is his own. He explained, what after all is obvious, that the purpose of pulling with forceps is to overcome resistance to the descent of the fetus down the natal canal and that after the fifth pull he would have to make a decision whether to continue, and whether a 'a little extra pressure or traction [would] deliver this head past that bony obstruction or not'. It was argued that that passage in Mr Jordan's evidence, and some other passages to the like effect, showed that he was willing to pull too hard. But the trial judge does not seem to have thought so, and nor do I. The mere fact that he pulled five or six times is no indication of how hard he pulled. After he had finished the trial of forceps he pushed the fetal head upwards to facilitate removal of the fetus by Caesarian section, but that again does not indicate that it had become wedged; it is a normal preliminary to Caesarian section, as Dame Josephine Barnes explained. In these circumstances there was in my opinion no sufficient evidence to justify a finding that he had been negligent.

I would therefore dismiss the appeal.

I respectfully agree with the observations of my noble and learned friend Lord Wilberforce in the final paragraph of his speech about his concern as to the manner in which part of the expert evidence for the plaintiff was organised.

LORD RUSSELL OF KILLOWEN. My Lords, I wish at the outset to emphasise one matter. Some passages in the Court of Appeal might suggest that if a doctor makes an error of judgment he cannot be found guilty of negligence. This must be wrong. An error of judgment is not per se incompatible with negligence, as Donaldson LJ pointed out. I would accept the phrase 'a mere error of judgment' if the impact of the word 'mere' is to indicate that not all errors of judgment show a lapse from the standard of skill and care required to be exercised to avoid a charge of negligence.

The details of this case and the reasons for dismissing this appeal have been so fully canvassed by my noble and learned friends that there is but little that I can add, without tedious repetition, in saying that I agree to that dismissal. As has been pointed out, and as Sir John Stallworthy accepted, there was no indication from the fetal heartbeats that during the trial of forceps delivery the fetus was in any way distressed. They were normal.

The learned judge, in a passage quoted by your Lordships, which came immediately before his conclusion of negligence by Mr Jordan, in that he pulled too long and too hard, inferred from evidence given by the mother that she was physically pulled down the bed. This I think was quite without justification on the basis of her evidence which did not point to that at all. It was not permissible to erect a theory of what she might have said but did not say, and base a conclusion of negligence at least in part on that theory. It may be that the judge borrowed the theory from medical evidence given on behalf of the plaintiff; but the medical experts were no more entitled than the judge to read the mother's rejected evidence as intended to mean something totally different. As has been pointed out it was never suggested to Mr Jordan that his activities pulled the mother towards him. As to the report written by Professor McLaren (and shown to Mr Jordan) two points were sought to be made. The first was its statement that descent did not follow traction; I see nothing in this: it means not that no progress at all resulted from the trial of forceps delivery but that there was no delivery by forceps. The second was the reference to disimpaction. Much evidence was given as to the meaning of disimpaction and impaction, and what was involved in 'stuck' and 'wedged'. All these words are words of degree. 'Impacted' may simply mean that the fetus is unable to move either way spontaneously, and some assistance is required. The mere fact that some assisstance was required to 'disimpact' cannot show negligence; if it did, the joint medical report would not merely have mentioned disimpaction but would surely have said that it proved negligence.

My Lords, I also would dismiss this appeal.

LORD BRIDGE OF HARWICH. My Lords, at 25 minutes past midnight on 7th January 1970 the appellant was born at the Birmingham Maternity Hospital. The mother had been in labour since the early hours of the 6th. The possibility of a difficult birth had been anticipated by the medical authorities at the hospital responsible for her case. By 11.30 pm on the 6th, the mother was fully dilated. From that point onwards the first respondent, now a consultant obstetrician, then a senior registrar in Professor McLaren's unit at the hospital, was in charge of the operation of delivering the child. He concluded from his examination of the mother that a normal delivery was out of the question. At 11.45 pm he proceeded to undertake a 'trial of forceps'. In the light of this trial he decided that delivery per vaginam would be too traumatic for the mother and the child. Accordingly he proceeded to effect delivery by Caesarian section. The child was found to have sustained severe brain damage.

Bush J, the trial judge, made a finding, which is not challenged, that the brain damage to the plaintiff was caused by anoxia occurring at some time between the beginning of the trial of forceps and the delivery of the child. This might seem to the layman to suggest some improper use of the forceps, but any such suggestion is emphatically refuted by the evidence. It is common ground that a child may, in the course of an apparently normal birth, suffer anoxia for which no specific cause can be assigned and certainly that the mere fact of anoxia occurring when it did in the course of the plaintiff's birth affords no evidence whatsoever of fault on the part of the first defendant.

The judge's finding of negligence against the first defendant (on which the vicarious liability of the hospital authority in turn depends) is based on a finding that in using the forceps 'he pulled too hard and too long so that the fetus became wedged or stuck' and that 'in getting it wedged or stuck, or unwedged or unstuck' the first defendant caused the anoxia which occasioned the brain damage. In the light of the direction the judge had given himself early in his judgment in defining the criterion to be applied to decide whether the first defendant was negligent (a direction which I do not criticise) this finding must be understood as implying that the first defendant applied traction to the fetus with the forceps which both in strength and duration exceeded what any competent obstetrician of the status of senior registrar would have regarded as the permissible limits in carrying out the procedure of a trial of forceps. The judge's decision in favour of the plaintiff having been reversed by a majority in the Court of Appeal, the sole question, as it seems to me, which your Lordships' House has to decide is whether the judge's finding that the first defendant applied excessive traction to the fetus in the sense indicated above can be supported on the evidence.

My Lords, I recognise that this is a question of pure fact and that in the realm of fact, as the authorities repeatedly emphasise, the advantages which the judge derives from seeing and hearing the witnesses must always be respected by an appellate court. At the same time the importance of the part played by those advantages in assisting the judge to any particular conclusion of fact varies through a wide spectrum from, at one end, a straight conflict of primary fact between witnesses, where credibility is crucial and the appellate court can hardly ever interfere, to, at the other end, an inference from undisputed primary facts, where the appellate court is in just as good a position as the trial judge to make the decision. It has been strongly urged, on behalf of the plaintiff, that in this case the judge's assessment of the reliability of the witnesses, particularly of the first defendant himself and of his superior at the Birmingham Maternity Hospital, Professor McLaren, was of such critical importance to his decision as to render it unassailable and this view prevailed with Donaldson LJ, who dissented in the Court of Appeal, even though he in terms rejected one of the judge's subordinate findings on which his ultimate conclusion depended. At first blush I was much attracted to this view of the case but a close scrutiny of the judge's analysis of the evidence and of the particular features of the evidence on which he relied in support of his finding of negligence persuades me that that finding was not justified. I will consider in turn the four main aspects of the evidence on which the judge based his conclusion.

1. *The mother's evidence.* The mother gave evidence emphatically that when the forceps were applied she was lifted up from the bed. Everyone accepted that this was impossible. Any pulling on the forceps is downward. The plaintiff's expert witnesses canvassed the possibility that the mother might have been pulled off the end of the bed and lifted back on to it. This was denied by Dr Skinner, a witness who was present at the birth, and the suggestion was never even put to the first defendant in cross-examination. The mother's evidence at every other point where it was in controversy had been rejected by the judge. At the time of the trial of forceps she had been in labour for many hours and was under an epidural anaesthetic. Yet the judge said of her:

> 'Though Mrs Whitehouse's description of what occurred to her when the forceps were applied may not be exact in its clinical detail, I believe her, in so far as her description can be taken to be understood as a pulling of her toward the bottom of the delivery bed in a manner and with such force as to be inconsistent with a trial of forceps properly carried out.'

Counsel for the plaintiff has not sought to support this part of the judge's judgment and it was rejected by all three members of the Court of Appeal. I agree with them. The mother's evidence could not be understood in the sense suggested and was manifestly incapable of affording any reliable indication of the degree of force applied with the forceps by the first defendant.

2. *Professor McLaren's report.* Following complaints by the plaintiff's parents to the hospital administrator, Professor McLaren, as head of the unit responsible, prepared a report on the circumstances of the plaintiff's birth. This was based in part on the hospital records, in part on discussion with the first defendant. In its express terms the report was wholly favourable to the first defendant. In his summary Professor McLaren said:

> 'Finally an expert obstetrician in my team undertook the accepted obstetrical technique of tentative trial of forceps. After a reasonable attempt at delivery by

forceps a Caesarian section was carried out. The baby, alas, was seriously affected by this well conducted trial of labour and forceps.'

In expressing his opinion he added:

'My own view is that both Mr and Mrs Whitehouse are naturally very distressed although there is no evidence that she had anything but first class obstetric care. We can appreciate the letter from Mr Whitehouse of 22.1.70 but we accept no criticism or implication that in terms of being humane, or in technical skills, we neglected Mrs Whitehouse.'

Despite these passages the judge described the report as 'perhaps the strongest piece of evidence that something untoward was done'. He based this view on the use more than once in the report of the word 'disimpaction' to describe the action of the first defendant, having decided to abandon the trial of forceps and proceed to Caesarian section, in pushing the head of the fetus upwards with the forceps to facilitate delivery by Caesarian section.

It was common ground that a trial of forceps is a tentative procedure to discover whether the baby's head can pass safely through the mother's pelvis. The obstetrician must proceed gently and not attempt actual delivery unless and until he is satisfied that there is no such bony disproportion between head and pelvis as to present a risk of injury to the baby. Of course, if no significant obstruction is encountered, the trial of forceps will merge into an actual forceps delivery.

Against this background a great deal of evidence was given by the expert witnesses on both sides as to the significance, in relation to the conduct of a trial of forceps, of the fact of the fetus becoming 'stuck' or 'wedged' in the course of it. A definition of 'impacted' from Steadman's Medical Dictionary (23rd Edn, 1976) as 'Denoting a fetus that, because of its large size or narrowing of the pelvic canal, has become wedged and incapable of spontaneous advance or recession' was canvassed with the witnesses.

Now it will be apparent that in any context the words 'stuck' or 'wedged' are imprecise. An object may be lightly or tightly stuck or wedged. The degree of force required to free it may be great or small. I can find nothing in the expert evidence to suggest that in an obstetric context the words as applied to a fetus described as 'stuck' or 'wedged' in the pelvic canal do not suffer from the same imprecision. If 'impacted' is synonymous with 'wedged' the same consideration must apply.

The judge, however, has drawn the inference from Professor McLaren's use of the word 'disimpaction' that the fetus had become so firmly wedged as to indicate that a degree of force must have been used by the first defendant in producing that result which was clearly excessive in a trial of forceps. He rejected Professor McLaren's explanation that he meant no more by 'disimpaction' than what could be achieved by gently pushing the head of the fetus up out of the pelvic cavity with one finger.

If Professor McLaren used the word 'disimpaction' *intending* it to bear the meaning the judge attributed to it, the implications are twofold. First, Professor McLaren must have appreciated from what the first defendant told him that the trial of forceps had been misconducted and had ended in disaster; it would follow from this that the exculpatory passages in the report were a dishonest attempt to whitewash a subordinate. But, secondly, it also reveals Professor McLaren as not only a knave but a fool who attempts a whitewash in one part of his report but gives the game away in another part.

I find it impossible to suppose that the judge appreciated these far-reaching implications of the significance he was attaching to a single word in the professor's report or that, if he had done so, he would have been prepared to stigmatise the witness in such a manner.

3. *The fetal heart rate.* The defendants relied at the trial, in support of their case that the trial of forceps was not the cause of the appellant's anoxia, on readings of the fetal heart rate during the trial of forceps being within normal limits. At 11.35 pm the rate was 140. At 11.45 pm, when the trial of forceps began, it was 130. It was the same five minutes later. At 12.10 am when the trial of forceps concluded it was 120. After the

delivery of the baby at 12.25 am the rate had fallen to 100 or below. After referring to this evidence the judge commented: 'Though all these readings save the one at 100 or below are within normal limits, there is here a steady drop indicating to my mind that something was wrong.' I take this comment to indicate that the judge not only rejected the evidence that the readings during the trial of forceps were inconsistent with anoxia being caused at that stage but also regarded the fall from 140 before the trial began to 120 when it concluded as affording some support for the contrary view. That view, however, was not expressed by any of the expert witnesses and indeed is contrary to all the expert evidence on the subject.

4. *The number of pulls.* The first defendant had recorded in his operation notes: 'After pulling with five or six contractions it was obvious that vaginal delivery would be too traumatic.' He accepted in evidence that he had probably exerted six pulls coincident with the mother's uterine contractions. The effect of his evidence was that, so far as he could remember or reconstruct the occasion, the first pull was extremely tentative and produced no movement. Thereafter, the next three pulls achieved some progress, the last two none. Having encountered difficulty on the fifth pull, he pulled once more to see whether a little extra traction would overcome the resistance he was feeling, but it did not. Sir John Peel, an expert witness called for the plaintiff, had based his criticism of the first defendant in part on the recorded note of five or six pulls but had said that it was 'difficult to be dogmatic' about this.

The judge refers to this issue in the following passage:

'Sir John Peel, while conceding that the number of pulls may depend on the progress being made, has said that he cannot understand why it should have needed five or six pulls to test whether delivery per vaginam was possible. Mr Jordan's answer to this is, as I have related above, that until say the fifth pull he was making progress. If, as I have found, the head was engaged it would not have all that far to go before the widest part of the head was at the ischial spines, and I share Sir John Peel's doubt.'

The judge added a reference to two cryptic answers given in re-examination by the first defendant, but I refrain from quoting these because I confess that I do not follow what significance the judge attached to them.

This is perhaps the most difficult part of the case, but I am satisfied that the criticism of the first defendant for exerting six pulls, qualified as it was, could not by itself sustain a finding of negligence against him.

As regards the evidence of the first defendant, the judge records that, according to him, there was nothing unusual that occurred from the commencement of the trial of forceps to the delivery of the child. I appreciate, of course, that the judge's finding involves, by necessary implication, a rejection of this evidence. It is trite to observe, however, that rejection of a defendant's denial provides no material to establish the positive case sought to be made against him. On the other hand, if the judge had construed anything in the first defendant's evidence as amounting to an admission of fault on his own part (which the cryptic answers referred to above certainly did not provide), he would surely have made this abundantly clear and put it in the forefront of his reasons for making a finding of negligence against him.

In the result I can find no sufficient foundation for this finding and would accordingly dismiss the appeal.

Appeal dismissed.

Solicitors: *Keene Marsland & Co*, agents for *Roper & Co*, Birmingham (for the plaintiff); *Hempsons* (for the defendants).

Mary Rose Plummer   Barrister.

Bremer Vulkan Schiffbau Und Maschinenfabrik v South India Shipping Corpn

HOUSE OF LORDS

LORD DIPLOCK, LORD EDMUND-DAVIES, LORD FRASER OF TULLYBELTON, LORD RUSSELL OF KILLOWEN AND LORD SCARMAN

10th, 11th, 12th, 13th, 17th NOVEMBER 1980, 22nd JANUARY 1981

Arbitration – Practice – Want of prosecution – Injunction restraining claimant from proceeding with arbitration – Claimant's delay prejudicing fair hearing and just result – Claimant's conduct such that it would justify dismissal of claim for want of prosecution if it were an action at law – Whether implied term in contract to arbitrate that claimant not to be so dilatory as to frustrate purpose of contract – Whether breach of that term a repudiation of contract entitling respondent to rescind – Whether respondent's right to rescind and right to fair hearing can be protected by injunction – Whether court empowered under inherent jurisdiction to issue injunction restraining claimant.

In August 1964 a German shipbuilding company agreed to build five bulk carriers for an Indian shipowning company. The contract, although governed by German law, provided for disputes or differences to be referred to arbitration in London in accordance with the Arbitration Act 1950. Delivery of the vessels was completed in December 1966. Disputes arose between the parties both shortly after delivery and later regarding alleged defects in the construction of the vessels. The parties attempted to reach an amicable settlement up until April 1971 when the shipowners gave notice to the builders that they intended to refer the disputes to arbitration. In January 1972 the parties appointed a London arbitrator and in April agreed a procedure by which the owners were to deliver a full statement of claim to which the builders would reply raising specific defences. When further alleged defects were raised in 1973 and 1975 the parties agreed that they should be included in the owners' claim. The owners delivered long and detailed points of claim in April 1976. Neither party applied to the arbitrator for directions and nothing further happened until the builders issued a writ in 1977 seeking an injunction restraining the owners from proceeding with the arbitration because of their alleged dilatoriness from the time the arbitrator was appointed. The judge ([1979] 3 All ER 194) found that the owners had been guilty of delay making it impossible for the builders to marshal the evidence necessary for a proper hearing, and held that the court had power to grant an injunction restraining a claimant from proceeding further with an arbitration if his conduct was such that if the case was an action at law the action would be dismissed for want of prosecution, since such conduct amounted to a repudiatory breach of an implied term in the arbitration agreement that each party would reasonably endeavour to bring the matter to a speedy conclusion. The judge granted the injunction sought. On appeal, the Court of Appeal ([1980] 1 All ER 420) affirmed that decision on the ground that a term was to be implied in the arbitration agreement imposing a duty on a claimant not to be so dilatory that a fair hearing or just result could no longer be obtained thus causing the whole purpose of the agreement to be frustrated. The shipowners appealed to the House of Lords.

Held (Lord Fraser and Lord Scarman dissenting) – A court did not have jurisdiction to dismiss a claim in an arbitration for want of prosecution or to grant an injunction restraining a claimant from proceeding with the arbitration if he has been guilty of inordinate and inexcusable delay. An arbitration was not sufficiently analogous to an action at law for the jurisdiction to dismiss an action for want of prosecution to be applied mutatis mutandis to an arbitration, since the court's jurisdiction to dismiss an action was derived from its inherent jurisdiction whereas the jurisdiction to supervise the conduct of an arbitration was confined to the statutory powers contained in the Arbitration Acts 1950 and 1979. Furthermore, submission to a private arbitration was consensual and voluntary by both parties, unlike an action where the defendant was obliged to submit to the jurisdiction of the court, and the duty on the parties to an arbitration not to be dilatory was a mutual contractual obligation. If therefore one party was dilatory the other party was under a duty to apply to the arbitrator for directions with a view to keeping the arbitration moving, and, applying the principle that the law only assisted the vigilant, it was not open to a respondent to sit back while the claimant did nothing and then found on the claimant's delay as a reason for asking for the claim to be dismissed. Since the shipbuilders had not applied to the arbitrator for directions and had been content to allow the shipowners voluntarily to prepare the points of claim, they were as much in breach of the contractual obligation to proceed with the arbitration with despatch as were the shipowners in being dilatory in delivering the points of claim. Neither party was entitled to rely on the other's breach as bringing the arbitration to an end. Moreover, in the circumstances the shipbuilders, as the party seeking the injunction restraining the shipowners from proceeding with the arbitration, did not have a legal or equitable right that required protection. The appeal would accordingly be allowed (see p 294 b, p 295 b c e, p 296 b to e h, p 297 c d, p 299 e to j, p 301 a f g, p 302 g to j and p 307 c, post).

Crawford v A E A Prowting Ltd [1972] 1 All ER 1199 approved.

Allen v Sir Alfred McAlpine & Sons Ltd [1968] 1 All ER 543 distinguished.

Per Lord Diplock, Lord Edmund-Davies and Lord Russell. An arbitrator has power to fix a date of hearing and make an ex parte award in favour of the respondent if the claimant fails to appear, or to debar the claimant from raising a claim of which he has failed to give adequate notice to the respondent in breach of the arbitrator's directions (see p 302 b c f and p 307 c, post).

Decision of the Court of Appeal [1980] 1 All ER 420 reversed.

Notes

For the court's power to restrain arbitration proceedings by injunction, see 2 Halsbury's Laws (4th Edn) para 518, for an arbitrator's powers generally, see ibid para 577, and for cases on restraint of arbitration by injunction, see 3 Digest (Reissue) 95–98, 484–500.

For dismissal of actions for want of prosecution, see 30 Halsbury's Laws (3rd Edn) 410, para 771.

Section 5 of the Arbitration Act 1979 which came into force on 1st August 1979 and applies to all arbitrations commenced after that date and to arbitrations commenced before that date if the parties have agreed that it should do so (in which case the Act applies from 1st August 1979 or the date of the agreement, whichever is the later) provides that, if any party to an arbitration fails within the time specified or a reasonable time to comply with an order made by an arbitrator, then on the application of the arbitrator or a party the High Court may authorise the arbitrator to proceed with the arbitration in default of appearance or any other act by the party.

Cases referred to in opinions

Allen v Sir Alfred McAlpine & Sons Ltd, Bostic v Bermondsey and Southwark Group Hospital Management Committee, Sternberg v Hammond [1968] 1 All ER 543, [1968] 2 QB 229, [1968] 2 WLR 366, CA, Digest (Cont Vol C) 1091, 2262b.

Angelic Grace, The, Japan Line Ltd v Aggeliki Charis Compania Maritima SA [1980] 1 Lloyd's Rep 288, CA.

Beddow v Beddow (1878) 9 Ch D 89, 47 LJ Ch 588, 3 Digest (Reissue) 97, 495.

Birkett v James [1977] 2 All ER 801, [1978] AC 297, [1977] 3 WLR 38, HL, Digest (Cont Vol E) 666, 2698b.

Congimex v Continental Grain Export Corpn [1979] 2 Lloyd's Rep 246, CA.

Crawford v A E A Prowting Ltd [1972] 1 All ER 1199, [1973] QB 1, [1972] 2 WLR 749, 3 Digest (Reissue) 116, *637.*

Czarnikow v Roth, Schmidt & Co [1922] 2 KB 478, 92 LJKB 81, 127 LT 824, 28 Com Cas 29, CA, 3 Digest (Reissue) 178, *1082.*

Glasgow and South-Western Railway Co v Boyd and Forrest 1918 SC (HL) 14.

Heyman v Darwins Ltd [1942] 1 All ER 337, [1942] AC 356, 111 LJKB 241, 166 LT 306, HL, 3 Digest (Reissue) 88, *453.*

Kent v Elstob (1802) 3 East 18, [1775–1802] All ER Rep 637, 102 ER 502, 3 Digest (Reissue) 250, *1643.*

Kitts v Moore [1895] 1 QB 253, 64 LJ Ch 152, 74 LT 676, 12 R 43, CA, 3 Digest (Reissue) 96, *488.*

Malmesbury Railway Co v Budd (1876) 2 Ch D 113, 45 LJ Ch 271, 3 Digest (Reissue) 97, *494.*

Moorcock, The (1889) 14 PD 64, [1886–90] All ER Rep 530, 58 LJP 73, 60 LT 654, CA, 12 Digest (Reissue) 751, *5395.*

North London Railway Co v Great Northern Railway Co (1883) 11 QBD 30, 52 LJQB 380, 48 LT 695, CA, 3 Digest (Reissue) 95, *485.*

Photo Production Ltd v Securicor Transport Ltd [1980] 1 All ER 556, [1980] AC 827, [1980] 2 WLR 283, [1980] 1 Lloyd's Rep 545, HL.

Pickering v Cape Town Railway Co (1865) LR 1 Eq 84, 13 LT 357, 570, V-C and LC, 3 Digest (Reissue) 97, *493.*

R v Disputes Committee of National Joint Council for the Craft of Dental Technicians, ex parte Neate [1953] 1 All ER 327, [1953] 1 QB 704, [1953] 2 WLR 342, DC, 3 Digest (Reissue) 152, *874.*

R v Northumberland Compensation Appeal Tribunal, ex parte Shaw [1952] 1 All ER 122, [1952] 1 KB 338, 116 JP 54, 50 LGR 193, 2 P & CR 361, CA, 30 Digest (Reissue) 267, *742.*

Scott v Avery (1856) 5 HL Cas 811, [1843–60] All ER Rep 1, 25 LJ Ex 308, 28 LTOS 207, 2 Jur NS 815, 10 ER 1121, HL, 3 Digest (Reissue) 57, *305.*

Siskina, The, Owners of cargo lately laden on board the vessel Siskina v Distos Compania Naviera SA [1977] 3 All ER 803, [1979] AC 210, [1977] 3 WLR 818, [1978] 1 Lloyd's Rep 1, HL, Digest (Cont Vol E) 660, *782a.*

Unione Stearinerie Lanza and Weiner, Re an arbitration between [1917] 2 KB 558, 117 LT 337, sub nom *Lanza v Weiner* 86 LJKB 1236, 3 Digest (Reissue) 327, *2252.*

Interlocutory appeal and cross-appeal

By a writ issued on 25th April 1977 the plaintiffs, Bremer Vulkan Schiffbau Und Maschinenfabrik ('Bremer Vulkan'), a body corporate of West Germany, sought as against the defendants, South India Shipping Corpn Ltd ('South India'), a body corporate of India, (i) an injunction restraining South India by themselves or their agents from proceeding with, pursuing or taking any further step in a reference to arbitration in which South India were the claimants and Bremer Vulkan were the respondents, commenced pursuant to an arbitration clause in a contract between the parties dated 6th August 1964 and in which the Rt Hon Sir Gordon Willmer was appointed sole arbitrator by an agreement dated 7th January 1972, or (ii) alternatively, a declaration that the arbitrator had power to make and issue a final award in the reference dismissing South India's claim on the grounds only that they had failed to prosecute their claims in the reference with diligence and had been guilty of gross and inexcusable delay causing serious prejudice to Bremer Vulkan and/or that the dispute could not fairly be tried at the likely time of hearing. On 10th April 1979 Donaldson J ([1979] 3 All ER 194, [1979] 3 WLR 471) granted the injunction sought and also held that an arbitrator had the power referred to in the alternative claim. South India appealed. On 23rd November 1979 the Court of Appeal (Lord Denning MR, Roskill and Cumming-Bruce LJJ) ([1980] 1 All ER 420, [1980] 2 WLR 905) dismissed the appeal from Donaldson J's grant of an injunction but held that the arbitrator did not have the power referred to in the alternative claim. South India appealed to the House of Lords with leave of the Court of Appeal. Bremer Vulkan cross-appealed on the issue raised by the alternative claim. The facts are set out in the opinion of Lord Diplock.

Anthony Evans QC and *Giles Caldin* for South India.
Kenneth Rokison QC and *David Grace* for Bremer Vulkan.

Their Lordships took time for consideration.

22nd January. The following opinions were delivered.

LORD DIPLOCK. My Lords, this case concerns an arbitration clause contained in a shipbuilding contract dated 6th August 1964 for the construction of five bulk carriers. The shipbuilders ('Bremer Vulkan'), who are respondents to this appeal, are a German company and their shipyard at which the vessels were built was in Germany. The purchasers ('South India'), who are appellants in the appeal, are incorporated in India where their principal place of business is situated. It was expressly provided by the contract that it was to be governed by German law. The only connection that the whole transaction had with England was that the contract contained an arbitration clause couched in the widest terms providing that any 'dispute or difference shall be referred to Arbitration in London within the meaning of the English Arbitration Act 1950, and the rules, regulations, etc., of the said Act shall solely apply'.

The five vessels were delivered over a period of some thirteen months, between 4th November 1965 and 3rd December 1966. The contract provided for a guarantee period of 12 months after delivery, so the last of these periods expired on 3rd December 1967. A number of complaints in respect of alleged defects in each of the five vessels were notified by South India to Bremer Vulkan during the respective guarantee periods. Some of these were rectified and others were disputed. The parties hoped to reach an amicable settlement and on 13th October 1967 they agreed in writing not to have recourse to arbitration for the time being. Efforts to reach an amicable settlement continued until the autumn of 1969. In the meantime, in July 1969, South India complained to Bremer Vulkan that cracks had appeared in the cylinder heads in respect of which they claimed damages for breach of the shipbuilding contract. Bremer Vulkan by letter of 3rd September 1969 rejected this claim both on the merits and on the ground that having regard to the guarantee periods of 12 months from delivery of each vessel this claim and any other claims first notified to them after the expiry of the relevant 12-month period were time-barred under German law. In May 1970 South India wrote to Bremer Vulkan a long letter summarising their various claims under 15 heads and suggesting a further meeting. This meeting was postponed from time to time by agreement between the parties. It ultimately took place in April 1971, but no settlement was reached as Bremer Vulkan intended to rely on their defence that under German law the bulk of the claims were time-barred. South India then gave notice to Bremer Vulkan of their intention to refer the disputes between them to arbitration and invited Bremer Vulkan to concur in the appointment of an arbitrator. Discussion followed between the parties' solicitors whether the terms of reference to the arbitrator should provide for him to hear the time-bar point as a preliminary issue. In the result it was not until January 1972 that there was appointed as sole arbitrator Sir Gordon Willmer, who had retired from the Court of Appeal some three years previously. His notice of appointment referred, without particularising them, to disputes having arisen between the parties under and concerning the shipbuilding agreement and that Bremer Vulkan's time-bar point should be determined in the arbitration.

No application was made to the arbitrator for a preliminary appointment. Instead, in April 1972 it was agreed between the parties, both of whom were represented by London solicitors very experienced in commercial arbitration, that South India should deliver 'a full Statement of Claim' so that Bremer Vulkan could plead the time-bar defence to specific claims to which they contended this defence applied.

Later in 1972 South India claimed that structural defects had been discovered in the stern frames of the vessels and in May 1973 it was agreed between the parties that claims in respect of these alleged defects should be added to the points of claim in the current arbitration without the need for any further formal submission. A similar agreement was reached in April 1975 in respect of an alleged defect in a collision bulkhead which was discovered in November 1974 as a result of an explosion on one of the vessels. In the result the points of claim, which together with its accompanying schedules, is a very long and detailed document, was not delivered until 23rd April 1976.

No application for directions had been made by either party to the arbitrator. The notice of his appointment couched in the broad terms that I have mentioned was all that he received and all he ever knew about the arbitration until the proceedings in which this appeal is brought appeared in the law reports.

The court proceedings were started by Bremer Vulkan on 25th April 1977 in the High Court by writ claiming in the alternative (1) an injunction restraining South India from proceeding with the arbitration or (2) a declaration that the arbitrator had power to dismiss South India's claim for want of prosecution. The case was tried on affidavit, without pleadings, in the Commercial Court by Donaldson J, although not until nearly two years later in March 1979. It was heard together with another action between different parties which raised similar points of law. Donaldson J ([1979] 3 All ER 194, [1979] 3 WLR 471) granted Bremer Vulkan the injunction sought. South India's appeal to the Court of Appeal (Lord Denning MR, Roskill and Cumming-Bruce LJJ) ([1980] 1 All ER 420, [1980] 2 WLR 905) was dismissed on 23rd November 1979.

My Lords, this summary and timetable of events makes it evident that the disputes between the parties that give rise to this appeal have been dealt with in a most dilatory way at all three stages: (1) from the expiry of the guarantee periods in 1966–67 to the appointment of the arbitrator in January 1972; (2) from his appointment to the issue of the writ by Bremer Vulkan in April 1977; and (3) from the issue of the writ to the hearing of the action at first instance in March 1979. It is, however, common ground that your Lordships are concerned only with the delay at the second stage from January 1972 to April 1977, and in particular the delay between the nomination of the arbitrator and the delivery of the full points of claim in April 1976. That is because the basis on which the action was argued and decided in the courts below was that the High Court had the same discretionary power to enjoin a dilatory claimant from proceeding with an English arbitration at the behest of a respondent who had passively endured the delay as it had to dismiss for want of prosecution an action brought by a dilatory plaintiff in the High Court. Though this was the effect of the conclusion reached alike by Donaldson J and all three members of the Court of Appeal the trains of reasoning by which each came to this conclusion were not identical. All, however, were at one in holding that to justify the court in granting such an injunction in cases where there has been no application to the arbitrator for directions the principles (first stated by the Court of Appeal in *Allen v Sir Alfred McAlpine & Sons Ltd* [1968] 1 All ER 543, [1968] 2 QB 229 and approved by this House in *Birkett v James* [1977] 2 All ER 801, [1978] AC 297) applicable to the exercise of the court's discretion to dismiss a plaintiff's action in the High Court for want of prosecution would apply mutatis mutandis to the exercise of the court's discretion to enjoin a claimant from proceeding further with an arbitration.

On the application of these principles to the facts of the instant case, Donaldson J and the Court of Appeal were also at one in holding that the delay by South India as claimant in proceeding with the arbitration during the period between the appointment of the arbitrator and the delivery, more than four years later, of the detailed points of claim was so inordinate and inexcusable and had given rise to so substantial a risk that a fair trial of the issues could not be had that *if the arbitration had been an action* it ought to have been dismissed for want of prosecution. It was on this ground that the injunction was granted and upheld.

My Lords, an injunction is a discretionary remedy, and if the analogy between dismissing an action in the High Court for want of prosecution and granting an injunction to restrain a claimant from proceeding with a pending arbitration is sound, I apprehend that your Lordships, having regard to what was said on this topic in *Birkett v James*, would not think it right to review the facts yourselves with a view to considering whether either collectively or individually your Lordships would have exercised the discretion in the same way as the learned judge. The question that lies at the heart of this appeal is whether that analogy is sound in law. For my part I think that it is not and that nothing that had happened had given the judge jurisdiction to grant the injunction that he did.

Much reliance was placed by counsel for Bremer Vulkan on the similarity of what he called 'this kind of arbitration' to an ordinary heavy action in the Commercial Court. No doubt where heavy claims for damages under a shipbuilding contract are the subject matter of a reference to English arbitration before a legal arbitrator familiar with the procedure of English courts, and the parties are represented in the arbitration by English solicitors and counsel, the way in which the proceedings in the arbitration are in fact conducted, except that they are not held in public or in wigs and gowns, will show considerable resemblances to the way in which an action to enforce a similar claim would be conducted in the Commercial Court. The method of trial when it comes to the hearing will be substantially the same. So, it is suggested on behalf of Bremer Vulkan, by agreeing to an English arbitration clause the parties to the contract are, in practical reality, doing no more than to make a choice between one trier of fact, the arbitrator, and another trier of fact, the commercial judge, by whom, in the absence of such clause, the case would fall to be decided. There is no reason, they submit, why the consequences of delay in prosecuting the claim before one trier of fact should not be the same as before the other; what is good for English High Court actions is good for English arbitrations.

My Lords, in the instant case that was not the choice between the parties when they decided to adopt the English arbitration clause. Their contract was governed by German law; it was made between an Indian corporation and a German company; it was to be performed in Germany; the English courts would have no jurisdiction to entertain an action brought by South India for breaches of that contract. What the parties have done is to substitute a remedy by English arbitration not for a remedy by action in the English courts but for a remedy by action in a German court or, possibly, some other foreign court. So this superficially attractive way of putting the argument breaks down on the facts of the instant case. In my view, it also fails on a broader ground. There are a whole variety of procedures used in arbitrations for the resolution of disputes between the parties. Most of them do not reflect at all closely the pattern of procedure in an action in the High Court. In many there is no oral hearing or oral evidence; in some physical inspection by the arbitrator of the subject matter of the dispute is substituted for any other kind of hearing. If the analogy between the court's jurisdiction to dismiss an action for want of prosecution and its jurisdiction to grant an injunction to restrain a claimant from proceeding with a reference under an English arbitration clause is sound in law, it must be applicable to all arbitrations under such a clause and not merely to those in which the actual dispute between the parties that is referred to arbitration is of a kind where it is likely (although not certain, for this will lie within the arbitrator's discretion) that the proceedings will follow much the same pattern as they would in an action in the High Court.

Donaldson J recognised that the analogy between action and arbitration which he regarded as justifying the court in granting an injunction to restrain further proceedings in an arbitration by reason of the claimant's delay applied to all kinds of arbitration with the possible exception of quality arbitrations of what he called the 'look-sniff' variety. He based his analogy between English action and English arbitration on the broad ground that the procedures in both were 'adversarial' in character. The Court of Appeal accepted that analogy and there is nothing in their judgments to suggest that it called for any restriction on the kind of arbitration in which the court had power to intervene by injunction.

My Lords, to test the soundness of this analogy in my view calls for a closer legal analysis than this (1) of the respective sources of the jurisdiction of the High Court (a) to dismiss for want of prosecution an action that is pending before it and (b) to prohibit further proceedings in an arbitration pending before a duly qualified arbitrator, and (2) of the differences between action at law and arbitration as ways of resolving disputes between private parties as to their contractual rights.

The High Court's power to dismiss a pending action for want of prosecution is but an instance of a general power to control its own procedure so as to prevent its being used to achieve injustice. Such a power is inherent in its constitutional function as a court of justice. Every civilised system of government requires that the state should make available to all its citizens a means for the just and peaceful settlement of disputes between them as to their respective legal rights. The means provided are courts of justice to which every citizen has a constitutional right of access in the role of plaintiff to obtain the remedy to which he claims to be entitled in consequence of an alleged breach of his legal or equitable rights by some other citizen, the defendant. Whether or not to avail himself of this right of access to the court lies exclusively within the plaintiff's choice; if he chooses to do so, the defendant has no option in the matter; his subjection to the jurisdiction of the court is compulsory. So, it would stultify the constitutional role of the High Court as a court of justice if it were not armed with power to prevent its process being misused in such a way as to diminish its capability of arriving at a just decision of the dispute.

The power to dismiss a pending action for want of prosecution in cases where to allow the action to continue would involve a substantial risk that justice could not be done is thus properly described as an 'inherent power' the exercise of which is within the 'inherent jurisdiction' of the High Court. It would I think be conducive to legal clarity if the use of these two expressions were confined to the doing by the court of acts which it needs must have power to do in order to maintain its character as a court of justice.

The supervisory jurisdiction that the High Court exercises over the way in which inferior courts and tribunals conduct their proceedings on which Lord Denning MR and Cumming-Bruce LJ relied as one source of its jurisdiction to prohibit further proceedings in an arbitration is not inherent in its character as a court of justice; it is statutory. True it is that, in typical English fashion, the supervisory jurisdiction over inferior tribunals that is vested in the High Court by statute is that which was vested in or capable of being exercised by the superior courts of common law, principally the Court of Queen's Bench, before the Supreme Court of Judicature Act 1873; so one must look to see over what inferior courts or tribunals the Court of Queen's Bench did assert a supervisory jurisdiction. The procedure by which it exercised this jurisdiction until the very recent change in the Rules of the Supreme Court was by the issue of the prerogative writs (certiorari, prohibition, mandamus etc) or the making of orders of the like nature, although there existed too at common law the confessedly anomalous jurisdiction to set aside an award of private arbitrators for error of law on its face: see *Kent v Elstob* (1802) 3 East 18, [1775–1802] All ER Rep 637 and *R v Northumberland Compensation Appeal Tribunal, ex parte Shaw* [1952] 1 All ER 122 at 129, [1952] 1 KB 338 at 351 per Denning LJ. This jurisdiction, however, was not directed to controlling the procedure followed in the arbitration but was concerned only with the written award resulting from it. So one must start by inquiring whether during the centuries-long history of English arbitration there are any instances of the Court of Queen's Bench before 1873 or the High Court thereafter asserting a jurisdiction to control the conduct of a consensual private arbitration by the issue of prerogative writs or orders.

My Lords, in *R v National Joint Council for the Craft of Dental Technicians (Disputes Committee), ex parte Neate* [1953] 1 All ER 327, [1953] 1 QB 704 it was stated by Lord Goddard CJ, whose knowledge of the history of the common law was profound, that there were no such instances; and none has been drawn to the attention of this House. In that case it was held by the Divisional Court that the general supervisory jurisdiction of the High Court over the proceedings of inferior courts and tribunals extended only to 'bodies on whom Parliament has conferred statutory powers and duties which, when exercised, may lead to the detriment of subjects who may have to submit to their jurisdiction' (see [1953] 1 QB 704 at 708; cf [1953] 1 All ER 327). These bodies would include arbitrators appointed to conduct a statutory arbitration to whose jurisdiction parties to a particular kind of dispute are compelled to refer it for determination, but they do not include arbitrators appointed pursuant to private arbitration agreements. In relation to private arbitrations the jurisdiction of the High Court to supervise the conduct of the arbitration is confined to exercising the powers conferred on it by the Arbitration Acts 1950 and 1979 (though the latter Act does not apply to the arbitration in the instant case). The reason for this distinction is that the jurisdiction of an inferior court or statutory tribunal or arbitrator over the person who wishes to resist the claim is compulsory whereas the jurisdiction of an arbitrator over both parties to a private arbitration agreement is consensual only. As Lord Goddard CJ, in the case that I have cited, said of such an arbitrator ([1953] 1 QB 704 at 708):

> 'in one sense he is the antithesis of a court. A person goes to arbitration because he does not want to go to the court. Therefore, he sets up his own private judge to decide the case, but the arbitrator is not deciding it as a judge, he is deciding it as an arbitrator, and procedural rights and all matters relating to procedure are to be found in the Arbitration Act, 1950.' [now the Arbitration Acts 1950 and 1979].

I find myself unable to accept as well founded the general proposition by Lord Denning MR that 'the High Court has an inherent jurisdiction to supervise the conduct of arbitrators. It is not confined to statutory powers'. That such a general supervisory power was vested in the High Court had never been asserted until the judgment of the Court of Appeal delivered in June 1979 in *The Angelic Grace* [1980] 1 Lloyd's Rep 288, where, although in the result it was not acted on, the claim that it exists is to be found in the judgment of Lord Denning MR himself. It does not appear that *R v National Joint Council for the Craft of Dental Technicians (Disputes Committee), ex parte Neate* had been cited to the court in *The Angelic Grace* and the authorities relied on for the proposition were statements made obiter by Lord Denning MR's predecessor, Jessel MR, in two judgments at first instance delivered shortly after the passing of the Supreme Court of Judicature Act 1873 and before the passing of the Arbitration Act 1889. These were *Malmesbury Railway Co v Budd* (1876) 2 Ch D 113 and *Beddow v Beddow* (1878) 9 Ch D 89. Both were about the jurisdiction of the newly-created High Court to grant an injunction to restrain an arbitrator, who was disqualified by bias, from proceeding with the arbitration. I shall revert to these two cases when I come, as I shall do shortly, to consider the extent to which the statutory jurisdiction under s 45 of the Supreme Court of Judicature (Consolidation) Act 1925 to grant injunctions empowers the court to intervene by injunction in the conduct of arbitrations. For the moment I confine myself to rejecting the notion that the High Court has a general supervisory power over the conduct of arbitrations more extensive than those that are conferred on it by the Arbitration Acts; nor do I suppose that the assertion of such an open-ended power of intervention in the conduct of consensual private arbitration would be likely to encourage resort to London arbitration under contracts between foreigners which have no other connection with this country than the arbitration clause itself.

I turn next to the general jurisdiction of the High Court to grant injunctions as an alternative source of its power to control the conduct in an arbitration of the parties to it or the arbitrator. As recently as 1977, this House, in *The Siskina* [1977] 3 All ER 803, [1979] AC 210, had occasion to confirm as a matter of ratio decidendi the well-established law that the jurisdiction of the High Court to grant injunctions, whether interlocutory or final, was confined to injunctions granted for the enforcement or protection of some legal or equitable right. In doing so, this House expressly approved the judgment of

Cotton LJ in *North London Railway Co v Great Northern Railway Co* (1883) 11 QBD 30. That was a case in which both Cotton and Brett LJJ discussed several pronouncements, made by Jessel MR in earlier cases at first instance, which to an ingenuous reader might suggest that a judge had an almost unfettered discretion to grant injunctions whenever he thought it would be convenient to do so. The Court of Appeal in that case, however, found themselves able to explain away those statements by putting on them a somewhat strained gloss to the effect that they meant no more than that the court had jurisdiction to grant an injunction *for the enforcement or protection of a legal or equitable right* when it was just and convenient so to do. The pronouncements of Jessel MR, the generality of which was cut down in this way, included those to be found in *Malmesbury Railway Co v Budd* and *Beddow v Beddow*, and those cases thereafter ceased to be authority for the existence of any wider jurisdiction than that.

So in the instant case one must look for some legal or equitable right of Bremer Vulkan to be enforced or protected; and the only sources of this right that there can be are the arbitration clause included in the shipbuilding agreement of 6th August 1964 and appointment in January 1972 of Sir Gordon Willmer as arbitrator in respect of all disputes under and concerning that agreement that existed between the parties at that date.

The arbitration clause constitutes a self-contained contract collateral or ancillary to the shipbuilding agreement itself: see *Heyman v Darwins Ltd* [1942] 1 All ER 337, [1942] AC 356. It expressly incorporates, by reference, 'the rules, regulations, etc, of the [Arbitration Act 1950]', many of whose sections deal with various provisions that are deemed to be contained or included in every arbitration agreement unless a contrary intention is expressed therein. Of these the most important for present purposes is s 12(1), which deals with the duties of the parties during the course of the reference. This statutory incorporation into all English arbitration agreements of so many implied terms unless they have been expressly excluded does not rule out the possibility that terms additional to these are to be read into the arbitration agreement by necessary implication, though it makes somewhat less likely the need to do so. For example, in addition to those terms that are spelt out expressly, the Act itself, in s 24(1), recognises by implication the right of each party to an arbitration agreement to have the dispute decided by an arbitrator who is impartial, and, for the protection of that right, to obtain an injunction to restrain the other party from proceeding with the reference before an arbitrator who has been shown to be biased. The concept of 'arbitration' as a method of settling disputes carries with it by necessary implication that the person appointed as arbitrator to decide the dispute shall be and remain throughout free from all bias for or against any of the parties; and it was in enforcement of this right that injunctions had been sought in *Malmesbury Railway Co v Budd* and *Beddow v Beddow*.

I would accept that the unperformed primary obligations of the parties under an arbitration agreement, like other contracts, may be brought to an end by frustration, or at the election of one party where there has been a repudiatory breach of that agreement by the other party. (I speak of repudiatory breach as covering both what I described in *Photo Production Ltd v Securicor Transport Ltd* [1980] 1 All ER 556, [1980] AC 827 as 'fundamental breach' and 'breach of condition'.) I would also accept that when, on the commission of such a breach, the party to an arbitration agreement who is not in default has lawfully elected to bring to an end the unperformed primary obligations of both parties to continue with the arbitration up to the issue of an award the High Court has jurisdiction, in protection of that party's legal right to do so, to grant him an injunction to restrain the other party from proceeding further with the arbitration. The reason for such an injunction is to prevent his being harassed by the making of a purported award against him which on the face of it will be enforceable against him in England and many foreign countries, thus forcing him to incur the costs of resisting its enforcement.

This is the reason for those injunctions which have hitherto been granted in two types of cases. The first is where one party claims that the arbitration agreement relied on was void or voidable ab initio (eg for fraud, mistake, ultra vires or want of authority). The leading case is *Kitts v Moore* [1895] 1 QB 253. This type of case is to be distinguished from cases where the arbitration agreement itself is not impeached but one party claims that no dispute has arisen under it. Whether there is a dispute or not is a matter to be decided by the arbitrator, and no injunction will be granted. *North London Railway Co v Great Northern Railway Co* was such a case; so was *R v National Joint Council for the Craft of Dental Technicians (Disputes Committee), ex parte Neate.* The second type of case in which injunctions have been granted is where the arbitrator is or has become disqualified by reason of bias. Here, if the arbitration agreement is restricted to the submission of an identified existing dispute to a named arbitrator, the agreement is frustrated if the arbitrator turns out not to be impartial; while if the arbitration agreement is contained in a clause that forms part of a wider contract and provides for all future disputes arising under that contract to be referred to arbitration the reference of any such dispute to a biased arbitrator is a breach of the contractual obligation to refer the dispute to arbitration. *Malmesbury Railway Co v Budd* and *Beddow v Beddow* provide examples of the former kind of arbitration agreement; in the instant case we are concerned with the latter: the arbitration agreement was contained in a clause of a wider contract, the shipbuilding agreement. But there is no previous reported case in which the court has granted an injunction to restrain a party from proceeding with an arbitration under either type of arbitration agreement on the ground that he has committed a repudiatory breach of the arbitration agreement in the course of those proceedings before they have been terminated by the issue of an award.

My Lords, in the instant case the shipbuilding agreement, apart from the arbitration clause, had ceased to be executory; the time for performance of the parties' primary obligations under it was past. The arbitration clause on the other hand would continue to remain executory so long as there were outstanding any disputes between the parties as to the existence or extent of their secondary obligations under the other clauses of the shipbuilding agreement. The collateral agreement contained in the arbitration clause does not fit readily into a classification of contracts that are synallagmatic on the one hand or unilateral or 'If' contracts on the other. It is an agreement between the parties as to what each of them will do if and whenever there occurs an event of a particular kind.

The event is one that either party can initiate by asserting against the other a claim under or concerning the shipbuilding agreement which they have not been able to settle by agreement. In that event, each is obliged to join with the other in referring the claim to arbitration and to abide by the arbitrator's award. The arbitration clause itself creates no obligation on either party to do or refrain from doing anything unless and until the event occurs, and even then the mutual obligations that arise are in relation to the particular claim that constitutes the event. The primary obligations of both parties that arise then are contractual, whether express, or implied by statute or included by necessary implication in the arbitration clause. Breach of any of them would give rise to a general secondary obligation to pay compensation (damages), though this may well be nominal; but if the breach were such as to deprive the other party of substantially the whole benefit which it was the intention of the parties he should obtain from the mutual performance by both parties of their primary obligations in relation to the reference of the particular dispute to arbitration, ie what in an ordinary synallagmatic contract would be a repudiatory breach, I see no ground in principle why the party not in breach should not be entitled to elect to put an end to all primary obligations to proceed with the reference then remaining unperformed on his part and on the part of the party in default, and, in appropriate cases, to obtain an injunction to restrain the party in default from continuing with the reference to arbitration of that particular dispute.

It was this principle that Donaldson J and Roskill LJ (with whom Cumming-Bruce LJ also agreed) purported to invoke in the instant case. They held that the arbitration agreement, indeed all arbitration agreements, were subject to an implied term of which they held that South India was in repudiatory breach. They stated the implied term in somewhat different ways, but when applied to the facts of the instant case the effect of both was the same, viz the claimant in an arbitration who is guilty of such delay in proceeding with the arbitration as would justify the High Court in dismissing the proceedings for want of prosecution if the arbitration were an action commits a repudiatory breach of the contract to refer the disputes to arbitration. Donaldson J was inclined to treat it as a fundamental breach of an innominate implied term 'that each party will use reasonable endeavours to bring the matter to a speedy conclusion'; whereas the implied term dealing with claimants proceeding timeously that was favoured by Roskill LJ required them only to avoid such delay as would justify the High Court in dismissing the proceedings for want of prosecution if it had occurred in an action; and the breach of this implied term would be repudiatory because it was a breach of condition.

Common to both ways of putting it is an assumption that an obligation to bring the arbitration to a conclusion with reasonable dispatch is incumbent on the claimant only, except where the next step in the procedure to be taken by either party is one which no one but the respondent is capable of taking. Even though there are available to the respondent effective means of requiring the claimant to put an end to any delay that is detrimental to the respondent, and sanctions for the claimant's non-compliance, the assumption is that the respondent is entitled to remain entirely passive and wait until the detriment is so great as to amount to a repudiatory breach of the agreement to refer.

This notable departure from the maxim vigilantibus non dormientibus jura subveniunt is introduced into the implied term as a consequence of the decision of the Court of Appeal in *Allen v Sir Alfred McAlpine & Sons Ltd* [1968] 1 All ER 543, [1968] 2 QB 229, which was treated by Donaldson J and Roskill LJ as applicable by analogy to arbitrations; but in my view the differences both conceptual and procedural between actions and private arbitrations make any such analogy fallacious.

My Lords, I have already drawn attention to a fundamental difference between action at law and arbitration. The submission of the defendant to the jurisdiction of the High Court to determine a dispute that has arisen between him and the plaintiff is compulsory. If he wants to resist the claim he has no other choice. The plaintiff has a choice whether or not to bring an action in a court of law to enforce a disputed claim against the defendant, but if he does want to enforce it the only forum in which he can do so is a court of law, unless he and the defendant mutually agree to submit their dispute about the plaintiff's claim for determination in some other way. As plaintiff and defendant in an action the parties assume no contractual obligations to one another as to what each must do in the course of the proceedings: their respective obligations as to procedure are imposed on them by the rules and practice of the court. In contrast to this, the submission of a dispute to arbitration under a private arbitration agreement is purely voluntary by both claimant and respondent. Where the arbitration agreement is in a clause forming part of a wider contract and provides for the reference to arbitration of all future disputes arising under or concerning the contract, neither party knows when the agreement is entered into whether he will be claimant or respondent in disputes to which the arbitration agreement will apply. If it creates any contractual obligation to proceed with reasonable dispatch in all future arbitrations held pursuant to the clause (and I will consider later what that obligation is) the obligation is, in my view, mutual: it obliges each party to co-operate with the other in taking appropriate steps to keep the procedure in the arbitration moving, whether he happens to be the claimant or the respondent in the particular dispute.

Another fundamental difference between an action and an arbitration where, as in the instant case, the arbitration agreement does not expressly contain or incorporate by reference specific procedural rules is that in an action the successive steps to be taken by each party and the timetable for taking them are prescribed by the rules and practice of the court, and, as was pointed out in *Allen v Sir Alfred McAlpine & Sons Ltd* [1968] 1 All ER 543 at 552, [1968] 2 QB 229 at 254, it is an underlying principle of civil litigation in the English courts that the court takes no action in it of its own motion but only on the application of one or other of the parties to the litigation, whereas in an arbitration there is no fixed pattern of procedure: what steps are to be taken by each party in a particular arbitration and the timetable which each party must observe are matters to be determined by the arbitrator. In requiring particular steps to be taken by any party he is entitled to act not only on the application of a party to the arbitration but also on his own initiative; but he is not under any duty to do the latter, for in the absence of any application he is justified in assuming that *both* parties are satisfied with the way in which the proceedings leading up to his making an award are progressing.

My Lords, up to the 1960s, the High Court had applied the maxim vigilantibus non dormientibus jura subveniunt to applications by defendants to dismiss an action for want of prosecution. The practice was that an action would not be dismissed for this reason on the application of a defendant, unless he had previously obtained from the court a peremptory order requiring the plaintiff to take within a specified time the next step in the procedure that was incumbent on him under the rules of court and the plaintiff had not complied with the order, or had given reasonable notice to the plaintiff of his intention to apply for the dismissal of the action if the plaintiff did not take that step within a limited time. In the 1960s, however, largely as a result of legal aid, this practice had proved inadequate to prevent such inordinate delay by solicitors acting for plaintiffs in bringing actions on for trial that, because memories would have faded and witnesses would have become unavailable, there was substantial risk that at the hearing the court would be unable to do justice. The mischief which the Court of Appeal sought to cure by the abandonment of the maxim about vigilantes in the case of applications for dismissal for want of prosecution is described in the judgments in *Allen v Sir Alfred McAlpine & Sons Ltd*. The change in practice was instituted primarily to protect the interests of plaintiffs who had the misfortune to be represented by negligent solicitors, rather than in the interests of defendants, who already had adequate powers under the rules and practice of the court to compel the plaintiff to proceed (through his solicitors) with reasonable dispatch. But, for the reasons given in *Allen v Sir Alfred McAlpine & Sons Ltd*, it was seldom in the defendant's interest to have resort to those powers, since long delay was more likely to operate to the detriment of the plaintiff on whom the onus of proof would lie at a belated trial, and any interlocutory proceeding initiated by the defendant would add to his costs, which would be irrecoverable against an unsuccessful legally-aided plaintiff. It was generally in the defendant's interest to let sleeping dogs lie. So the Court of Appeal, of which I was then a member, had to devise some other sanction against negligent dilatoriness on the part of solicitors for plaintiffs. This it did by dismissing the action for want of prosecution, notwithstanding that the defendant had let sleeping dogs lie, if the delay had become so inordinate and inexcusable that there was a substantial risk that justice between the parties could not be done at the trial and, as was later decided by this House in *Birkett v James* [1977] 2 All ER 801, [1978] AC 297, the delay had also extended beyond the end of the limitation period for the cause of action. On the dismissal of the action against the defendant, a right of action by the plaintiff in negligence against his dilatory solicitor would be substituted for his former right of action against the defendant. That the change in practice was introduced mainly for the protection of plaintiffs against the negligence of their own solicitors is underlined by the fact that in *Allen v Sir Alfred McAlpine & Sons Ltd* both Salmon LJ and I expressed the opinion that a likelihood that the plaintiff's solicitor would not be in a financial position to satisfy a judgment for damages for negligence was a matter to be taken into consideration by the court in deciding whether or not to dismiss the action; and, although I myself on further consideration in *Birkett v James* felt compelled to recant on this point, this does not affect the identification of the mischief which the Court of Appeal in *Allen v Sir Alfred McAlpine & Sons Ltd* was seeking to cure.

The mischief which was the cause of the change in the practice of the High Court brought about by the guidelines laid down by the Court of Appeal in *Allen v Sir Alfred McAlpine & Sons Ltd* arose because the Rules of the Supreme Court, by leaving the initiative to the defendant to take steps to compel a dilatory plaintiff to get on with the preparations for trial, had proved inadequate to prevent the risk of injustice being caused by neglect by solicitors for plaintiffs of their duty to their clients to bring actions on for trial with reasonable promptitude. These rules do not apply to private arbitrations, nor does the resulting mischief for which the Court of Appeal, by departing from the principle expressed in the maxim about vigilantes, intended to provide a remedy. Like Bridge J in *Crawford v A E A Prowting Ltd* [1972] 1 All ER 1199, [1973] QB 1, I see no justification for extending to private arbitrations a similar exception to that principle.

I turn then to consider what the mutual obligations of the parties are in a private arbitration. By appointing a sole arbitrator pursuant to a private arbitration agreement which does not specify expressly or by reference any particular procedural rules, the parties make the arbitrator the master of the procedure to be followed in the arbitration. Apart from a few statutory requirements under the Arbitration Act 1950, which are not relevant to the instant case, he has a complete discretion to determine how the arbitration is to be conducted from the time of his appointment to the time of his award, so long as the procedure he adopts does not offend the rules of natural justice. The contractual obligation which the parties assume to one another in relation to the procedure to be followed in the arbitration unless a contrary intention is expressed in the arbitration agreement is that which is stated in s 12(1) of the Act, viz:

'... parties to the reference, and all persons claiming through them respectively, shall, subject to any legal objection, submit to be examined by the arbitrator or umpire, on oath or affirmation, in relation to the matters in dispute, and shall, subject as aforesaid, produce before the arbitrator or umpire all documents within their possession or power respectively which may be required or called for, *and do all other things which during the proceedings on the reference the arbitrator or umpire may require.*'

No doubt in some arbitrations of a kind with which those who act on behalf of the parties in the conduct of the arbitration are familiar both claimant and respondent may carry out voluntarily some or all of the preliminary steps needed to prepare the matter for the hearing by the arbitrator, and do so without seeking and obtaining any prior direction from him; but, if what is done voluntarily by way of preparation is done so tardily that it threatens to delay the hearing to a date when there will be a substantial risk that justice cannot be done, it is in my view a necessary implication from their having agreed that the arbitrator shall resolve their dispute that both parties, respondent as well as claimant, are under a mutual obligation to one another to join in applying to the arbitrator for appropriate directions to put an end to the delay. Even if an application to the arbitrator for directions in such circumstances were a matter of right only and not, as I think it is, a mutual obligation, it provides a remedy to the party who thinks that the proceedings are not progressing fast enough voluntarily, which renders unnecessary the implication in the arbitration agreement of any such term as was suggested by Donaldson J or Roskill LJ.

My Lords, it was objected on behalf of Bremer Vulkan that this remedy was ineffectual in arbitrations started before 1st August 1979, to which s 5 of the Arbitration Act 1979 did not apply, because before that Act there were no sanctions that could be imposed for failure to comply with the arbitrator's directions as to the time within which a party must take a step preparatory to the hearing, such as delivering points of claim or defence or giving discovery. Your Lordships were invited to imagine a claimant who defied the arbitrator's direction putting a time limit within which points of claim must be delivered.

My first comment on this is that in the instant case it did not happen. If Bremer Vulkan had applied at any time to the arbitrator for directions as to the various steps to be taken and fixing what he regarded as a reasonable time within which each step was to be taken, there is no reason to suppose that South India would not have complied with his directions.

In any event, however, I do not accept that the arbitrator would be wholly impotent in the face of such defiance. In *Crawford v A E A Prowting Ltd* there had been no disobedience to any direction made by the arbitrator. Bridge J held that in those

circumstances the arbitrator had no power to strike out the arbitration proceedings and
dismiss the claim for want of prosecution; but that learned judge did go on to indicate,
though only obiter, that, if the arbitrator were to give a peremptory direction requiring
the claimant to give proper particulars of his claims within a limited time failing which
the arbitrator would proceed to a hearing at which the claimant, if he appeared, would
be debarred from tendering evidence of any claim of which he had not given the
required particulars, the arbitrator would have jurisdiction at such hearing to make an
award in favour of the respondent dismissing the claimant's claims in the dispute
referred to him. In the instant case, Donaldson J was of opinion that an arbitrator had
power, before the 1979 Act, to dismiss a claim for want of prosecution without having
given any previous directions as to steps to be taken by the claimant and without the
need to make an award in favour of the respondent. The Court of Appeal did not agree
with him; neither do I in so far as he was of opinion that an arbitrator could dismiss a
claim for want of prosecution instead of carrying out the procedure leading to an award
in favour of the respondent that had been suggested by Bridge J. Section 5 of the
Arbitration Act 1979, which enables an arbitrator to obtain from the High Court a
power, inter alia, to dismiss a claim for want of prosecution in the event of non-
compliance with an order made by him, even where the exercise of such a power would
be contrary to an express term of the arbitration agreement, does not 'derogate from any
powers conferred on an arbitrator or umpire, whether by an arbitration agreement or
otherwise'. So the section does not take away any pre-existing power of an arbitrator,
although, no doubt, in arbitrations to which the new Act does apply it will avoid all risk
of any possible charge of misconduct being made against him in the future if he proceeds
under s 5.

My Lords, arbitrators have in the past often exercised the power to make an award ex
parte against a respondent who failed to appear at the time and place fixed for the
hearing, and, if he did appear, to debar him from raising a defence of which, in breach
of the arbitrator's directions, he had failed to give to the claimant adequate and timely
notice. The power of arbitrators to refuse to allow a new defence to be raised for the first
time at the hearing where they thought that it would not be fair to allow this to be done
was recently upheld by the Court of Appeal in *Congimex v Continental Grain Export Corpn*
[1979] 2 Lloyd's Rep 246. In agreement with Bridge J, I see no reason why an arbitrator
should not have the like power to fix a date for the hearing and to make an award ex parte
in favour of the respondent when the claimant has failed to appear at the time and place
so fixed, and likewise, if he has appeared, to debar the claimant from raising any claim
of which, in breach of the arbitrator's directions, he has failed to give the respondent
adequate and timely notice.

In the instant case, however, as in *Crawford v A E A Prowting Ltd*, the respondents,
Bremer Vulkan, were content to allow the claimants, South India, to carry out voluntarily
the preparation of detailed points of claim. They never made an application for directions
to the arbitrator and none were made by him. For failure to apply for such directions
before so much time had elapsed that there was a risk that a fair trial of the dispute would
not be possible, both claimant and respondent were in my view in breach of their
contractual obligations to one another; and neither can rely on the other's breach as
giving him a right to treat the primary obligations of each to continue with the reference
as brought to an end. Respondents in private arbitrations are not entitled to let sleeping
dogs lie and then complain that they did not bark.

I would allow this appeal.

LORD EDMUND-DAVIES. My Lords, I have had the advantage of reading in draft
the seminal speech of my noble and learned friend Lord Diplock. For the reasons he
gives I am for allowing this appeal. I desire to add that I have found it irksome that the
appeal has been conducted on the basis that, were we here concerned not with arbitration
proceedings but with a civil action, it is beyond doubt that the court would have been
justified in dismissing the action on the ground that the plaintiff's inordinate and

inexcusable delay had rendered a fair trial impossible. The nonchalant behaviour of the respondent shipbuilders over the years, despite intimations from the appellant shipowners of fresh complaints (their quiescence obviously deriving from complete reliance on what they regarded as an irrefragable time bar) creates a substantial doubt in my mind that it would follow as night does the day that an order dismissing the claim for want of prosecution would be the appellants' for the mere asking. The notion that a defendant may always safely indulge in 'letting sleeping dogs lie' is not wholly without its dangers, not the least being that prolonged and complete inactivity may cast doubt on the acceptability of his assertion of prejudice occasioned by the plaintiff's delay. But we are enjoined to have no regard to any such considerations in the present case, and, having given expression to my doubts, I have naturally (albeit reluctantly) proceeded on the basis of the prescribed assumption in arriving at my conclusion that the appeal should be allowed.

LORD FRASER OF TULLYBELTON. My Lords, this appeal is concerned with the question whether the court has jurisdiction to restrain a claimant, by injunction, from pursuing a claim in an arbitration after he has been guilty of such inordinate and inexcusable delay that a fair hearing is no longer possible. The facts are summarised by my noble and learned friends Lord Diplock and Lord Scarman and I need not repeat them.

In April 1977 the respondents served the writ in the present proceedings alleging that they had been prejudiced by the appellants' delay in lodging their claim and claiming an injunction restraining the appellants from proceeding with the arbitration or, alternatively, a declaration that the arbitrator had power to make a final award dismissing the claim on the ground that the appellants had been guilty of gross and inexcusable delay causing serious prejudice to the respondents. Donaldson J, in the Commercial Court concluded ([1979] 3 All ER 194 at 209, [1979] 3 WLR 471 at 485) that 'the delay in delivering the points of claim was both inordinate and inexcusable and, further, that no significant part of the delay was induced by the conduct of the builders [respondents in the appeal]'. He went on to find that the respondents had thereby suffered serious prejudice in two ways and he granted the injunction claimed. He also held that an arbitrator had the power referred to in the alternative claim. The Court of Appeal (Lord Denning MR, Roskill and Cumming-Bruce LJJ) ([1980] 1 All ER 420, [1980] 2 WLR 905) dismissed an appeal from Donaldson J's grant of an injunction but they held that the arbitrator did not have the power referred to in the alternative claim. We must, I think, accept the concurring findings of the Commercial Court and the Court of Appeal that the delay was such as to prevent a fair hearing, and that if the claim had been made in an action it would have been dismissed for want of prosecution. That, of course, leaves open the questions of whether the court has jurisdiction to grant an injunction and, if so, whether it ought to grant one in the circumstances.

It is convenient to consider first whether an arbitrator himself has power to dismiss a claim for want of prosecution and to make an award to that effect. Before the proceedings in the action now under appeal, that question appears to have been decided in only one reported case, *Crawford v A E A Prowting Ltd* [1972] 1 All ER 1199, [1973] 1 QB 1, where Bridge J held that an arbitrator had no power to dismiss on this ground. When the present case was before Donaldson J he took the opposite view and held that the arbitrator did have such power, but the Court of Appeal held that his view was erroneous. In the Court of Appeal some reliance was placed on the decision of the Divisional Court in *Re an arbitration between Unione Stearinerie Lanza and Weiner* [1917] 2 KB 558 to the effect that an arbitrator had no power to order security for costs. In that case, which had not been cited to Donaldson J, Lord Reading CJ said that the provisions of the Arbitration Act 1889 obliging parties to a reference to 'do all other things which during the proceedings on the reference the arbitrators or umpire may require' did not invest arbitrators with the powers of a judge, such as power to commit for contempt and to issue a writ of attachment for default in compliance with an order made by him.

Roskill LJ examined the history of arbitrations in England and I gratefully adopt his reasoning and agree with the conclusion of all the members of the Court of Appeal that arbitrators do not have power to dismiss for want of prosecution.

I do not think it can make any difference whether an arbitrator purports to dismiss a claim for want of prosecution in so many words, or reaches the same result indirectly, by making a peremptory order for the plaintiff to lodge his claim by a certain day and then, if the claimant fails to obey the order, refusing to hear him. There seems to be no authority as to the arbitrator's power in these circumstances. Section 12(1) of the Arbitration Act 1950 imposes an obligation on the parties to a reference to obey the arbitrator's orders (in terms virtually identical with those of the 1889 Act mentioned above), but it does not expressly confer any power on the arbitrator to apply sanctions for disobedience, and, having regard to the decision in *Stearinerie*, I do not think they can be implied. Moreover s 12(6) of the 1950 Act provides that the High Court shall have power for the purpose of a reference to make orders in respect of, inter alia, discovery of documents, and it seems to me that, notwithstanding the proviso to sub-s (6), the reason for conferring the power on the High Court must be that it is not already vested in the arbitrator. An even stronger implication to the same effect emerges from s 5 of the Arbitration Act 1979, although that Act does not apply to the arbitration in the present case which began in 1972. I consider therefore that an arbitrator does not have power to refuse to hear a party who has failed to obey a peremptory order for lodging a claim.

In fact no peremptory order was sought or made in this case, and part of the argument for the appellants was that it would have been essential for such an order to have been made by the arbitrator and disobeyed by the claimant before the claim could be dismissed by the court. If that is right, it would mean that the respondent in an arbitration, who believes that the claimant's delay had been such as to prevent the possibility of a fair trial, would have to ask the arbitrator to make an order on the claimant for lodging his claim by a specified date, while hoping that the order would be disobeyed so as to leave the way open for sanctions to be imposed. Why should the respondent be obliged to seek an order for something which would be directly contrary to his interests? It seems unreasonable. The argument in favour of requiring some such procedure depends, as I understand it, on the view that a reference to arbitration, because it is contractual, differs fundamentally from litigation, particularly in respect that both parties to an arbitration have an obligation to avoid unreasonable delay. The result is said to be that, if the respondent in an arbitration remains inactive while the claimant delays to make his formal claim, he, the respondent, is not entitled to found on the delay as a reason for asking for dismissal of the claim. I recognise that an argument on these lines is acceptable to the majority of my noble and learned friends who heard this appeal, but I regret that I cannot agree with it. The contractual element in an arbitration such as the present, which depends on an agreement made before any dispute had arisen, consists, in my opinion, of the choice of the tribunal which is to come in place of the court that would otherwise have had jurisdiction, in this case presumably a German court. The choice of an English arbitration as the tribunal would probably imply that the rules of the English Arbitration Act 1950 would apply to the procedure, but in this case the matter is put beyond doubt by a provision to that effect in the arbitration clause. Once the tribunal has been chosen, I agree with Donaldson J and with Roskill LJ that proceedings in the arbitration, like those in litigation, are in most cases, and certainly in the present case, adversarial in character. It is therefore for each party to act in what he conceives to be his own interest, subject of course to any agreement on procedure that may have been made between them, and to the relevant statutory provisions including the obligation to obey orders made by the arbitrator. But, if no order is made, the respondent in an arbitration, like the defendant in an action, is in my opinion entitled to sit back and await a formal claim. In the words used by Donaldson J, he is entitled to let sleeping dogs lie. If the sleep lasts long enough and he is prejudiced thereby, he may seek a remedy for the delay.

The fact that, but for the arbitration clause, the court which would have had jurisdiction in this case would have been a foreign court seems to me immaterial. If, by English law, an injunction may be granted by the English court against proceeding with an English arbitration in which there has been inordinate and inexcusable delay in presenting the claim, resulting in serious prejudice to the respondent, then it must be for the English court to decide in any particular case whether that sort of delay and that result has occurred. In reaching its decision, the court will naturally have regard to its own practice as a guide, when the arbitration is analogous to a litigation, but I agree with my noble and learned friend Lord Scarman that the analogy must not be taken too far. The decision will ultimately depend on whether the party who is not responsible for the delay has suffered, or is likely to suffer, such serious prejudice that a fair trial is not possible. The same principle will apply to all types of arbitration. In the present case both parties were represented in the arbitration proceedings by solicitors and counsel, and both assumed that a formal statement of claim and answers analogous to pleadings in court would be required. The analogy of proceedings in court was therefore appropriate. But in a simple case, which might be dealt with by the arbitrator's inspecting goods without any formal hearing, the analogy would not be appropriate and a much shorter delay might prevent the possibility of a fair trial (for instance if perishable goods were involved).

If the arbitrator does not have power to dismiss for want of prosecution then, unless the court has power to restrain the arbitration by injunction, there is no means of preventing its proceeding even if the delay has been such as to preclude the possibility of a fair trial. If that were indeed the position I would agree with Roskill LJ that it would reveal a lamentable gap in English jurisprudence. But I do not think that such a gap exists. It is well established, and is not disputed by the appellants, that the court has jurisdiction to grant injunctions against proceeding with arbitrations in two cases. One is where the arbitrator has been guilty of misconduct, or has become unqualified: see *Beddow v Beddow* (1878) 9 Ch D 89. The other is where the validity or the application of the contract of arbitration is denied or 'impeached' by one party: see *Kitts v Moore* [1895] 1 QB 253. The real question is whether these two types of case are unique in being the only types in which an injunction can be pronounced, or, as I think, are examples of the application of a more general principle. The principle which underlay the decision in *Beddow* was explained in *North London Railway Co v Great Northern Railway Co* (1883) 11 QBD 30 at 40 by Cotton LJ who said:

'In *Beddow v. Beddow* (9 Ch D 89 at 93) [Jessel MR] granted an injunction to restrain an arbitrator from going on, and he uses there this language: "In my opinion, having regard to those two Acts of Parliament, I have unlimited power to grant an injunction in any case where it would be right or just to do so; and what is right or just must be decided, not by the caprice of the judge, but according to sufficient legal reasons or on settled legal principles." He means that if there is either a legal or an equitable right which is being interfered with, or which the Court is called upon to protect, and the circumstances do not render it inconvenient or unadvisable to interfere, but render it convenient and advisable to interfere, the Court may protect that right by giving the remedy which previously would not have been given, namely, an injunction, and in that case what he did was to interfere where an arbitrator was acting corruptly in the exercise of his jurisdiction under the reference.'

That shows that Cotton LJ regarded the injunction granted against an arbitration proceeding in *Beddow* not as something unique or very special, but as an ordinary exercise of the court's power and duty to protect legal rights. Cotton LJ did not define the right which was being interfered with, but he must have had in mind the right to a fair trial, which includes the right to have the reference determined by an impartial arbitrator, or, more accurately, the right not to be harassed by an arbitration before a tribunal that was not impartial. I regard the latter formulation of the right as more accurate, and more relevant, because it is only a right so formulated that would be directly protected by an injunction.

In the *North London Railway* case itself, an injunction was refused because the Court of Appeal (Brett and Cotton LJJ) held that no legal right of the plaintiff would be interfered with if the defendant went on with an arbitration before an arbitrator who had no jurisdiction in the matter, so that any award would be futile. Whether that view of the facts be right or wrong, and I am bound to say that I doubt whether it would be accepted in similar circumstances today, the principle is clear and is still applicable to the power of the court under the Supreme Court of Judicature (Consolidation) Act 1925. The *North London Railway* case has been recently referred to with approval in *The Siskina* [1977] 3 All ER 803 at 824, [1979] AC 210 at 256, by Lord Diplock who said that—

> 'the High Court has no power to grant an interlocutory injunction except in protection or assertion of some legal or equitable right which it has jurisdiction to enforce by final judgment . . .'

I fully accept that principle as applying in the present case and I will return to it.

Before doing so I wish to mention a decision which, if it is good law in England, demonstrates that misconduct and impeachment are not the only grounds for an injunction. It is a decision of this House in *Glasgow and South-Western Railway Co v Boyd and Forrest* 1918 SC (HL) 14, where the House upheld the grant of an interdict against proceeding with an arbitration on matters which, as they held, were res judicata. The appeal came from Scotland, and there was no argument on the question of jurisdiction to grant an interdict, but it seems unlikely that the English Law Lords who were present, Lord Finlay LC, Lord Parmoor and Lord Atkinson, would not have raised a question if they had entertained any doubt about the jurisdiction of the English court in similar circumstances. I think therefore that the case may be regarded as giving some support to the view that the English courts have jurisdiction to grant injunctions to protect the right of a party not to be harassed by an arbitration that would in the end be futile. Before parting with the case I observe that the House discriminated between those issues which were res judicata and those which were not; interdict was pronounced only in respect of the former. That would dispose of the suggestion made in argument before us that an injunction must relate to the whole reference.

It follows that the decision in the instant appeal depends on whether, if the arbitration were now allowed to proceed, it would infringe a legal or equitable right of the respondents. In my opinion it would. It would infringe their right to a fair trial, just as an arbitration before an arbitrator who was not impartial would do; more accurately, it would infringe their right not to be harassed by arbitration proceedings which cannot lead to a fair trial. The source of this right may be contractual, arising from the contract to refer, or it may be imposed by law as a rule of natural justice. The former view was taken by Donaldson J and it was also, I think, the preferred view of Roskill LJ. But Lord Denning MR regarded the right as correlative to a duty which was imposed by law, and not by any application of the *Moorcock* principle of implied terms (see *The Moorcock* (1889) 14 PD 64, [1886–90] All ER Rep 530), and Roskill LJ thought that there was 'also' such a right in addition to the contractual right. Cumming-Bruce LJ agreed with both Lord Denning MR and Roskill LJ so he cannot have regarded the difference between them as important. For my part, I would rest my opinion in favour of the respondents in this appeal on the principle that they have an equitable right not to be harassed by arbitration proceedings which cannot result in a fair trial. I do not think it is necessary to rely on any implied term in the arbitration contract, and I would prefer to avoid the difficulty of defining exactly what term is to be implied.

In my opinion the court, in granting an injunction to restrain an arbitrator from proceeding, is not exercising a supervisory jurisdiction of the same sort as it exercises over inferior tribunals by the issue of prerogative writs. The contrast between the prerogative writs and an injunction was referred to in *Pickering v Cape Town Railway Co* (1865) LR 1 Eq 84 at 87 by Page Wood V-C when he said:

> 'We have nothing in this Court in the nature of a writ of prohibition authorizing the Court to proceed against an arbitrator, and the only jurisdiction that exists to stop the proceedings before arbitration is founded upon the conduct of the parties.'

The same contrast was drawn by Lord Goddard CJ in the course of argument in *R v National Joint Council for the Craft of Dental Technicians (Disputes Committee), ex parte Neate* [1953] 1 QB 704 at 706 when he said:

'It would be revolutionary if this court were to grant an application for these writs [certiorari and prohibition] to issue to a private arbitrator. These writs issue from a superior court to an inferior court. These gentlemen are not entrusted by law with any functions at all. They have simply been given certain rights by the parties to the indenture. The proper course to take would be to move for an injunction.'

My Lords, for these reasons as well as for the reasons explained by my noble and learned friend Lord Scarman, with which I agree, I would dismiss this appeal.

LORD RUSSELL OF KILLOWEN. My Lords, this appeal has been very fully discussed in the speech of my noble and learned friend Lord Diplock. I find it convincing, and I also would allow this appeal.

LORD SCARMAN. My Lords, the specific question raised by the appeal is whether the High Court may properly grant an injunction to restrain a party from proceeding with an arbitration, notwithstanding that there has been a valid agreement to refer and no misconduct, unfitness or other disqualification of the arbitrator. The ground on which the respondents seek relief by injunction is excessive and prejudicial delay in the conduct of the proceedings by the appellants, who are the claimants in the arbitration. The delay, it is said, has denied the respondents their right to a fair arbitration, a right which it is accepted that the law recognises. The trial judge granted the injunction, and the Court of Appeal upheld his decision. The appeal to the House is by leave of the Court of Appeal.

There is no earlier case like this in the books. There are cases, but not many, in which the court has by injunction restrained arbitration proceedings. They were cases in which either the agreement to refer was, or could in the circumstances be treated as, invalid or there was misconduct, unfitness or incompetence displayed by the arbitrator. The present case falls to be decided under the law as it was before the coming into force of the Arbitration Act 1979; but your Lordships' decision is not thereby rendered of merely academic interest.

The Act does not, save perhaps incidentally by excluding some rights which previously existed, limit the injunctive power of the High Court, though its provisions, of which s 5 is of particular relevance, are bound to have a marked effect on the exercise of the court's discretion. For, if an arbitrator has power, or may be given power by the court, to remedy or prevent injustice occurring in the arbitration proceedings, it will be less likely that the grant of an injunction by a court would be a just or convenient course.

There is also a cross-appeal, whereby the respondents seek to restore the ruling of the trial judge, Donaldson J, that an arbitrator has power to dismiss a claim for want of prosecution.

Their basic case, of course, is to resist the appeal, submitting that, whether or not an arbitrator had (under the pre-1979 law) this power, the High Court certainly had power to restrain an arbitration on the ground of excessive and prejudicial delay. It is obvious that, if an arbitrator did have the power to dismiss, the occasions for the exercise of the court's power to restrain would be few. The respondents, if need be, are, however, prepared to contend that, in the present case where neither party went near the arbitrator after his appointment and where (as they submit) responsibility for delay was on the claimants, the court may, and should, intervene to restrain the arbitration without prior recourse to the arbitrator, if the delay be excessive and destructive of the possibility of a fair arbitration. It will be convenient, therefore, to consider the powers of an arbitrator in the course of dealing with the appeal.

It will be convenient to consider first the jurisdiction of the High Court to grant an injunction. There is no distinction to be drawn, so far as jurisdiction is concerned, between an interlocutory and a final injunction. A recent restatement of principle is to be found in the speech of Lord Diplock in *The Siskina* [1977] 3 All ER 803 at 824, [1979] AC 210 at 256 where he said that—

> 'the High Court has no power to grant an interlocutory injunction except in protection or assertion of some legal or equitable right which it has jurisdiction to enforce by final judgment . . .'

This formulation was based on the decision of the Court of Appeal in *North London Railway Co v Great Northern Railway Co* (1883) 11 QBD 30, which, on this point, is now to be treated as having been approved by the House.

The *North London Railway* case was one in which an order of the Queen's Bench granting an injunction to restrain a party from proceeding with an arbitration was discharged by the Court of Appeal. There was a valid arbitration agreement between the parties but the party seeking the injunction contended that the subject matter of the dispute was not within it. If he were right, the continuance of the arbitration would have been futile and vexatious. But the Court of Appeal considered that, as Brett LJ put it (at 36), 'the fact of the appellants going on with that futile arbitration is no legal injury'.

Like my noble and learned friend Lord Fraser and Lord Denning MR, I do not believe that the proposition that no legal injury can arise from the futility and vexation of the arbitration process would be accepted today, and I do not accept it. But the ratio decidendi of the case is certainly accepted law. The case resolved a doubt, which had arisen in the years following the Supreme Court of Judicature Act 1873, as to the extent of the power conferred on the High Court by s 25(8) of that Act, now re-enacted in s 45 of the Supreme Court of Judicature (Consolidation) Act 1925. In short, the Court of Appeal decided that the section was to be construed as procedural in its purpose and effect. The section does not extend the power of the court to cases where there is no legal or equitable right to be protected. It enables the court, where there is a legal right, to 'grant an injunction where it is just or convenient to do so for the purpose of protecting or asserting the legal rights of the parties' (see 11 QBD 30 at 39 per Cotton LJ).

It is necessary, therefore, to discover whether, if the arbitration proceedings in the present case continue, the respondents will suffer a legal injury, and then to determine whether the judge erred in exercising his discretion to grant an injunction protecting them from such injury.

First, the facts. The appellants are shipowners. The respondents are shipbuilders, and in August 1964 agreed to build five bulk carriers for the appellants. The contract was governed by German law but disputes were to be referred to arbitration in London. The contract included a guarantee clause whereby the respondents agreed to rectify defects appearing within twelve months of delivery. The last of the five ships was delivered on 3rd December 1966. The last guarantee period, therefore, expired on 3rd December 1967.

The appellants claim that very serious defects have appeared in the ships. The claim is resisted on the facts and in law, the principal legal defence being the contention that under German law the claim became time-barred six months after the end of the guarantee period, ie on 3rd May 1967.

I now take up the story in the words of Donaldson J ([1979] 3 All ER 194 at 204, [1979] 3 WLR 471 at 483):

> 'The arbitration proceedings in fact began in January 1972, over five years after the last vessel was delivered. Points of claim were served in April 1976, over nine years after that delivery. These proceedings, which were begun a year later in April 1977 have only been heard in March 1979, over 12 years from the delivery of the last vessel and nearly 15 years from the time when the contract was concluded. Clearly some explanation is called for, not only from the parties, but also from the court.'

After a full investigation of the facts which included the correspondence between the parties' solicitors he concluded 'that the delay [by the appellants] in delivering the points of claim was both inordinate and inexcusable and, further, that no significant part of the delay was induced by the conduct of the [respondents]' (see [1979] 3 All ER 194 at 209, [1979] 3 WLR 471 at 485). He further found that the delay had caused the respondents serious prejudice in two ways: first, in the loss of witnesses by reason of death, retirement or having left the respondents' employment; and, second, in the effect of the delay on the ability of the respondents to collect the necessary evidence to ensure that justice is done. The learned judge concluded: 'I am satisfied that if the proceedings had been pursued by action, I should have dismissed them for want of prosecution' (see [1979] 3 All ER 194 at 209, [1979] 3 WLR 471 at 486). The Court of Appeal concurred in his findings of fact and also accepted as relevant the analogy of litigation. The analogy is, of course, open to challenge in this House. But I do not think that the findings of fact can properly be challenged. Even if I were disposed to differ, which I am not, I would not disturb them. I accept, therefore, that the appellants have been guilty of delay which has made it impossible for the respondents to collect the evidence necessary to ensure that justice can be done at the hearing of the arbitration. I also accept that the respondents were not guilty of any acts which contributed to the delay; but I treat as open to decision by your Lordships' House the question whether the respondents could and should, by seeking the directions of the arbitrator, have ended the delay before it became excessive and prejudicial.

The appellants' case can be summarised in two sentences. No relevant comparison is to be made between litigation and arbitration. And, where parties agree to refer their dispute (or disputes) to arbitration, they mutually bind themselves by contract to use the arbitration process to prevent the mischief of delay. Clearly the submission assumes the existence of effective powers in the arbitrator to overcome or prevent delay. It also raises a question as to the scope of the principle, which has been slowly gaining strength in English law ever since the enactment of the Common Law Procedure Act 1854 and has been dramatically extended by the 1979 Act, that, where the parties have agreed on arbitration, they take it with all its faults.

My Lords, I will deal at once within the scope of this principle. Though it has been extended in the modern law, it is not of universal application. It has not yet achieved such supremacy as totally to oust the power of the High Court to remedy or prevent injustice in the arbitration process.

The principle yielded in the past to a measure of judicial control and review of the arbitration process; and this remains true of most arbitrations even after the coming into force of the 1979 Act. This power of the court has been exercised in many ways: for example, review of awards (limited, changed, regulated, but not discarded by the new Act), removal of arbitrators where their impartiality, fitness or competence is impugned, the grant of injunctions to restrain arbitration proceedings where the arbitrator has been shown to be unfit or incompetent. Such landmarks in the law as the Common Law Procedure Act 1854, *Scott v Avery* (1856) 5 HL Cas 811, [1843–60] All ER Rep 1, *Beddow v Beddow* (1878) 9 Ch D 89 where an injunction to restrain an arbitration was granted, *Czarnikow v Roth, Schmidt & Co* [1922] 2 KB 478, [1922] All ER Rep 45 and the 1979 Act itself bear witness to the importance attached in the various branches of our arbitration law to a measure of judicial control and review. Though the jurisdiction of the courts may now be ousted in those international arbitrations where the new Act allows an exclusion agreement, it remains a vital, if no longer universal, principle of the law that the courts will act to prevent injustice arising in arbitration proceedings where it is necessary so to do.

I therefore agree with my noble and learned friend Lord Fraser and with Lord Denning MR that the courts retain such a power save where excluded by statute and that parties to arbitration have a right to a fair arbitration. If the right can be protected within the arbitral process, as in most cases under the 1979 Act it will be, the courts will not intervene, for neither justice nor convenience will require so drastic a step. If the right be excluded by statute, as well it may be under an exclusion agreement rendered lawful by the new Act, there will be no legal right for the court to protect.

What then is the nature of the right? In practice, I do not think it matters whether it be treated as one of natural justice which the courts in the exercise of a supervisory power will enforce, if need be, or as arising from an implied term of the arbitration contract. Whether the agreed process be a 'look-sniff' commodity arbitration, or an award on documents submitted without a hearing, or an award reached after a full-dress hearing with pleadings, discovery and evidence, the right is fundamental. But since the question has arisen and differing answers have been given, I will state my view. The right does not depend on contract, and cannot be excluded by contract, save where statute allows its exclusion, as it may be that the 1979 Act does in certain cases (though I reserve my opinion on the point). The right arises from the judicial element inherent in the arbitration process which is a process for reaching a decision where parties have not themselves resolved their difference. Nevertheless in most cases, and this is such a case, the right is implicit in the contract, and, if infringed, may be enforced as a right given by the contract. And, with respect, I do not see *R v National Joint Council for the Craft of Dental Technicians (Disputes Committee), ex parte Neate* [1953] 1 All ER 327, [1953] 1 QB 704 as an authority inconsistent with such a supervisory power. In that case the Divisional Court, though holding that the prerogative writs (or orders) would not go to a private arbitrator, did not rule out the possibility of injunction (see Lord Goddard CJ's intervention ([1953] 1 QB 704 at 706)). Since, however, I accept the analysis which enabled the judges below to deal with this case as one of contractual rights and duties, I say no more as to the general power of the High Court to prevent injustice in this field, save to express agreement with Lord Denning MR and my noble and learned friend Lord Fraser. The existence of such a power, associated as it is with the requirements of natural justice in any adversarial process, remains, subject to the statutory law regulating arbitrations, a powerful weapon for justice in the armoury of the law, even though the occasions for its use will be few and far between.

I turn now to consider the contractual position. Where parties agree to refer present or future differences to arbitration, they enter into a contract, an implied term of which is that each has a right to a fair arbitration. The implication arises necessarily from the nature and purpose of their agreement, which is to submit their dispute (or disputes) to the arbitrament of an independent and impartial arbitrator of their choice. I do not understand the appellants to challenge the existence of the term. Such a contract is often to be found as an arbitration clause in a commercial, industrial or other type of contract. Where so found it is, in strict analysis, a separate contract, ancillary to the main contract: see *Heyman v Darwins Ltd* [1942] 1 All ER 337, [1942] AC 356. It follows that obstruction of the right will be a breach of contract and may be a repudiatory breach, and that frustration of the right, ie conduct of a party making the fair arbitration of a dispute impossible, will be a repudiatory breach at least of the agreement to refer that dispute to arbitration.

These general propositions were, as I understand their judgments, accepted by the judge and the Court of Appeal, notwithstanding that in the refinement of their reasons by way of response to the detailed arguments addressed to them by counsel they expressed themselves in different ways. After all, they were considering a specific case in which it was alleged that the claimant's delay had made a fair arbitration impossible. It was natural therefore to formulate the term by reference to delay. But it matters not whether in the context of delay it be formulated as an obligation implicitly accepted by a party, if he finds himself the claimant in the proceedings, to use his best endeavours to move the arbitration along, which was the view of Donaldson J, or whether it be formulated as a term imposing a duty on parties not to be guilty of frustrating delay, as Roskill LJ accepted, or whether there are mutual obligations, as Lord Denning MR thought, namely a duty on the claimant to proceed with reasonable dispatch and a duty on the respondent not to baulk the claimant by devious manoeuvres. Cumming-Bruce LJ found it possible to agree with the formulations of both Lord Denning MR and Roskill LJ. I think he was right to perceive and accept their basic consistency. In a contract of arbitration I accept that there are mutual obligations to be implied into the parties' agreement not to obstruct or frustrate the purpose of the agreement, ie a fair arbitration to be conducted in accordance with the terms of their agreement.

Unless, therefore, the breach is by the terms of the parties' contract itself to be referred to arbitration, a remedy for its breach may be sought in the courts. In the case of a non-repudiatory breach this will depend on the true construction of the arbitration clause. But, if, as is alleged in the present case, the breach consists of a frustrating delay, it discharges the aggrieved party from further performance of his agreement to refer. If he chooses then to sue in the courts, he will be able to show the infringement of a legal right entitling him to damages; and, if he can show that the defendant is persisting in a course of action, ie proceeding with the arbitration, which is a continuing infringement of the right, the court may grant him an injunction restraining the claimant from pursuing this course of conduct, if it thinks it just and convenient so to do. The injunction will be issued to avert legal injury and to protect a legal right.

My Lords, I believe these propositions constitute the basis of principle on which the present case is to be decided. As I understand it, this was the view of the very experienced judges below. And I would add that, on their findings, justice and convenience would appear to require that the respondents, their contractual right having been infringed, be granted the injunction if they are to be protected from the harassment of a vexatious, expensive, time-consuming and futile arbitration.

But, before reaching a conclusion, the formidable submissions of the appellants have to be considered. The first is that no relevant comparison is to be made between litigation and arbitration. It was argued, and, as I understand it, a majority of your Lordships accept, that the analogy is misleading. Litigation, it is submitted, is a compulsory process available as of right to anyone who issues a writ; it is not to be compared with the process of arbitration, which arises from consent and is conducted according to terms agreed, expressly or impliedly, by the parties. Arbitration is, of course, subject to a measure of statutory control; but this control in no way detracts from the essentially contractual nature of arbitration. My Lords, all this is true. But arbitration, while consensual, is also an adversarial process. There is a dispute, the parties having failed to settle their difference by negotiation. Though they choose a tribunal, agree its procedure and agree to accept its award as final, the process is adversarial. Embedded in the adversarial process is a right that each party shall have a fair hearing, that each should have a fair opportunity of presenting and developing his case. In this respect, there is a comparability between litigation and arbitration. In each delay can mean justice denied. And the analogy is not falsified because of the wide variation of types of arbitration. Whether the arbitration be 'look-sniff' or a full-scale hearing with counsel and solicitors, the right to a fair arbitration remains. An unfair arbitral process makes no sense either in law or in fact. It is a contradiction which it is inconceivable that the law would tolerate or the parties select.

But the analogy must not be taken too far. It does not follow that, because a court may protect a party from abuse of its own process in a lawsuit, it has the same power in connection with arbitration proceedings. I do not understand the judges below to have fallen into this trap. They used the analogy not to introduce the decision of *Allen v Sir Alfred McAlpine & Sons Ltd* [1968] 1 All ER 543, [1968] 2 QB 229 into the law of arbitration but as a strong indication that arbitrators or the court (or, as Donaldson J was disposed to hold, both) have a power to prevent injustice arising from a party's delays in the proceedings. Though arbitration is consensual and litigation compulsory in so far as the respondent (or defendant) is concerned, both are judicial processes of an adversarial character. The analogy, taken thus far, is therefore helpful; and I reject the submission that the judges erred in making use of it for the purpose of showing the need for such a power to reside either in the arbitrator or the court.

I pass now to the most powerful submission made by the appellants, that the respondents should have sought to prevent delay by applying to the arbitrator for directions. The judges below considered very carefully the pre-1979 powers of an arbitrator to deal with delay, and concluded that, though he could exercise influence, he had no sanction other than to make a final award on the merits of the dispute. I respectfully adopt the analysis of the law on this point to be found in the judgment of Roskill LJ. Like him, I attach importance to para 57 of the Commercial Court Committee's Report on Arbitration (Cmnd 7284 (1978)) as a correct description of the mischief which s 5 of the 1979 Act was enacted to remove. I think, therefore, that the judge and the Court of Appeal were justified in their conclusion that, the arbitrator having in the circumstances no effective power to protect the respondents from the legal injury of an unfair arbitration, the mere fact of his appointment did not exclude the power of the court.

But the point remains that the respondents, pursuant to s 12(1) of the Arbitration Act 1950, could have applied to the arbitrator for directions, and that an order by him for the delivery of points of claim within a time limit, though backed by no sanction, might have galvanised the appellants into action before their dilatoriness had caused the respondents serious prejudice. This is, I think, the most formidable argument available to the appellants. I reject it because of the adversarial nature of the arbitration process. I accept that parties to an agreement to refer may expressly agree that each, whether he be claimant or respondent, will use his best endeavours, by application to the arbitrator or otherwise, to move the arbitration along. But in the absence of express agreement to do so it can hardly be said that a party who finds himself a respondent in an adversarial process has implicitly agreed to move along the claim being made against him. Certainly a term might well be implied, as suggested by Lord Denning MR, that, if a party to the agreement finds himself respondent to a claim, he will not by devious manoeuvres seek to baulk the claim: but no more.

I reject, therefore, the appellants' submissions. The respondents have been denied by the appellants' delay their right to an arbitration in which justice can be done. Whether the denial be viewed as a denial of natural justice or a fundamental breach of contract, it constitutes a legal injury from which the court may grant relief by injunction to restrain the appellants from proceeding with the arbitration. I would, therefore, dismiss the appeal. In doing so, I wish at the same time to express my concurrence with the speech delivered by my noble and learned friend Lord Fraser.

As I understand that the majority of your Lordships take a different view it is incumbent on me to express an opinion on the respondents' cross-appeal. Under the law as it was before the 1979 Act I can find no justification for the view that an arbitrator had power to dismiss an arbitration for want of prosecution. His power was limited to making an award on the merits. The nearest he could get to a dismissal on grounds of delay would have been to fix a day for hearing and make an award on the merits based on whatever evidential material was then available to him. I agree with Roskill LJ on this point and do not think it necessary to elaborate further my reasons. I would dismiss the cross-appeal.

Appeal allowed. Order appealed from reversed and injunction discharged. Cross-appeal dismissed.

Solicitors: *Richards, Butler & Co* (for South India); *Norton, Rose, Botterell & Roche* (for Bremer Vulkan).

Mary Rose Plummer   Barrister.

Melon and others v Hector Powe Ltd

HOUSE OF LORDS

LORD DIPLOCK, LORD ELWYN-JONES, LORD EDMUND-DAVIES, LORD FRASER OF TULLYBELTON AND LORD KEITH OF KINKEL

8th OCTOBER, 6th NOVEMBER 1980

Redundancy – Dismissal by reason of redundancy – Change of ownership of business – Distinction between transfer of business or part of business and transfer of assets – Employer transferring one of two factories and plant therein to new owner – New owner taking over contracts of employment of employees – Employees engaged in same sort of work as before – New owner guaranteed orders from employer for period of 7 months – Guaranteed orders constituting only two-thirds of new owner's business – Remaining third of business coming from new owner's own customers – Whether transfer of 'part of ... business' – Whether employer liable to make redundancy payments to employees – Redundancy Payments Act 1965, s 13(1)(a).

The appellants were a company of multiple tailors who had two factories, one at Dagenham and the other at Blantyre, in which they manufactured men's suits, mainly made to measure. From 1974 onwards the demand for such suits fell, and the appellants arranged to manufacture ready-made suits for an associate company, W. In 1976 there was a further decline in business, and eventually the appellants contracted with an unconnected company, E, that the latter would take over the Blantyre factory on 17th January 1977. The contract provided, inter alia, (i) that E would offer the entire workforce, except the general manager, contracts of employment on terms not less favourable than they had enjoyed with the appellants, on condition that the offer was accepted, which it duly was, by at least 90% of the employees, (ii) that the lease of the Blantyre factory would be assigned to E and the plant and machinery in it would be sold to E, (iii) that E would take over and complete the work in progress, and (iv) that the appellants would order for themselves and W 475 ready-made suits a week until 31st August 1977. Pursuant to the contract E took over the factory and practically all the appellants' employees, including the respondents, who worked there. Their contracts of employment with the appellants were terminated on 17th January 1977, but they carried on working in the same factory, on the same machines and in many cases doing the same sort of work, on no less favourable terms under new contracts with E. For the period from 17th January until 31st August 1977 70% of the factory's output was devoted to work for the appellants and the remaining 30% was devoted to work for other customers of E's. The respondents claimed redundancy payments from the appellants on the ground that they had been dismissed on 17th January 1977 by reason of redundancy. The appellants resisted the claims, contending that on that date there had been 'a change ... in the ownership ... of a part of [the] business' in which the respondents were employed, within s 13(1)(a)[a] of the Redundancy Payments Act 1965, and that since the respondents had been re-employed on no less favourable terms under new contracts of employment with E they were not, by virtue of s 13(2) of the 1965 Act, to be taken to have been dismissed. The respondents contended that the change which occurred on 17th January 1977 was merely a transfer of certain assets, consisting mainly of the factory and its machinery, which were the means of carrying on the business, and not a transfer of any part of the business itself.

Held – The essential distinction between the transfer of a business, or part of a business, and a transfer of physical assets, was that in the former case the business was transferred as a going concern, so that the business remained the same business but in different hands, whereas in the latter case the assets were transferred to the new owner to be used

---

a Section 13, so far as material, is set out at p 315 *j* to p 316 *b*, post

in whatever business he chose. In the latter case individual employees might continue to do the same work in the same environment and might not appreciate that they were working in a different business, but that would not affect the true position if on consideration of the whole circumstances the new operation was a different business. If the factory at Blantyre had been solely devoted to making suits for W and if it had been transferred to E with a view to their continuing that work, that might well have amounted to a transfer of part of the appellants' business. However, after E took over the factory they operated it for a different business, and the appellants' guarantee to order 475 suits a week was merely a temporary expedient to help E through the initial stages of starting up their business at Blantyre. It followed that there had not been a transfer of part of the appellants' business, within s 13(1)(a) of the 1965 Act, and that, accordingly, the respondents had been dismissed by reason of redundancy (see p 314 j, p 315 a and p 317 g to p 318 c and f g, post).

Dictum of Lord Denning MR in *Lloyd v Brassey* [1969] 1 All ER at 384 applied.

Per Curiam. A change in the ownership of a part of a business will seldom occur except when that part is to some extent separate and severable from the rest of the business, either geographically or by reference to the products or in some other way (see p 314 j, p 315 a and p 318 a and f g, post).

Notes

For what constitutes a change of ownership of a business for purposes of redundancy, see 16 Halsbury's Laws (4th Edn) para 679.

For the Redundancy Payments Act 1965, s 13, see 12 Halsbury's Statutes (3rd Edn) 249.

As from 1st November 1978 s 13 of the 1965 Act has been replaced by s 94 of the Employment Protection (Consolidation) Act 1978.

Case referred to in opinions

Lloyd v Brassey [1969] 1 All ER 382, [1969] 2 QB 98, [1969] 2 WLR 310, 5 KIR 393, 4 ITR 100, CA, Digest (Cont Vol C) 692, 816Afd.

Appeal

Hector Powe Ltd appealed against the interlocutor dated 14th November 1979 of the First Division of the Court of Session (the Lord President (Emslie), Lord Cameron, Lord Stott and Lord Dunpark) allowing the appeal of the respondents, Clara Melon, Robert McDonald and Marion McMillan, against the decision of the Employment Appeal Tribunal (Lord McDonald, Dr J S Flanders and Mr E Humphries) sitting in Glasgow on 1st February 1978 whereby it allowed the appellants' appeal against the decision of an industrial tribunal (chairman Mr G V McLaughlin) dated 9th September 1977 whereby it held that the respondents were entitled to redundancy payments from the appellants. The facts are set out in the opinion of Lord Fraser.

Denis R M Henry QC and *Bruce Reynolds* for the appellants.
John Murray QC and *Robert Black* (both of the Scottish Bar) for the respondents.

Their Lordships took time for consideration.

6th November. The following opinions were delivered.

LORD DIPLOCK. My Lords, I have had the advantage of reading in draft the speech prepared by my noble and learned friend Lord Fraser, with which I agree. I therefore would dismiss the appeal.

LORD ELWYN-JONES. My Lords, I have had the advantage of reading in draft the speech prepared by my noble and learned friend Lord Fraser, with which I agree. I therefore would dismiss the appeal.

LORD EDMUND-DAVIES. My Lords, I have had the advantage of reading in draft the speech prepared by my noble and learned friend Lord Fraser, and I cannot usefully add to it. For the reasons he gives, I would concur in dismissing this appeal.

LORD FRASER OF TULLYBELTON. My Lords, the appellants are a well-known company of multiple tailors. Until 17th January 1977 they had two factories, one at Dagenham and the other at Blantyre, in which they manufactured men's suits, mainly made to measure. From about 1974 onwards, the demand for made to measure suits fell, and eventually the appellants contracted with another company, called Executex Manufacturing Ltd, that they (Executex) would take over the Blantyre factory on 17th January 1977. One term of the contract was that Executex would offer the entire workforce, except the general manager, contracts of employment on terms not less favourable than they had enjoyed with the appellants. The transfer was conditional on that offer being accepted by at least 90% of the employees. It was duly accepted, and on 17th January Executex took over the factory and practically all the appellants' employees who worked there, including the three respondents. Their cases are typical of about 120 former employees of the appellants, whose claims will follow the decision in this appeal. Their contracts of employment with the appellants were terminated on 17th January, but they carried on working in the same factory, on the same machines and in many cases doing the same sort of work, on no less favourable terms under new contracts with Executex.

The respondents claimed redundancy payments from the appellants on the ground that they had been dismissed on 17th January by reason of redundancy. The appellants resisted the claims, and contended that by virtue of the Redundancy Payments Act 1965, s 13, read with s 3(2), the respondents should not be taken to have been dismissed. The scheme of the 1965 Act is that where an employee, who has been continuously employed for the requisite qualifying period of two years, is dismissed by his employer by reason of redundancy, he is entitled to receive a redundancy payment calculated by reference to the length of his period of employment. Dismissal is defined by s 3(1) of the Act, and by s 3(2) certain circumstances are specified in which an employee shall not be taken to have been dismissed for the purpose of claiming a redundancy payment. One such circumstance is a case where the employee's contract of employment is renewed, or he is re-engaged by the same employer under a new contract of employment, on terms that are not in essence different from the terms of his previous contract. Section 13 of the 1965 Act provides that s 3(2) shall apply in a similar way, mutatis mutandis, where a change occurs in the ownership of a business or of a part of a business, and the new owner renews the employee's contract of employment on terms not less favourable than he had before. The employee is then not to be taken to be dismissed, and he is accordingly not entitled to a redundancy payment from his previous employer, but his period of employment with the previous employer is, so to speak, carried forward and counts as a period of employment with the new employer, and the change of employment does not break the continuity of his period of employment. The effect is that, when s 13 applies, the employee gets one redundancy payment in respect of his entire service, if he is made redundant by his new employer, and, when s 13 does not apply, he gets two redundancy payments, one from his new employer, if employed by him for long enough, and one from his former employer in respect of the separate period of service with him.

The particular provisions on which this appeal turns are those of s 13(1) and (2) of the 1965 Act which are as follows:

'(1) The provisions of this section shall have effect where—(a) a change occurs (whether by virtue of a sale or other disposition or by operation of law) in the ownership of a business for the purposes of which a person is employed, *or of a part of such a business*, and (b) in connection with that change the person by whom the employee is employed immediately before the change occurs (in this section referred to as "the previous owner") terminates the employee's contract of employment, whether by notice or without notice. [My emphasis.]

'(2) If, by agreement with the employee, the person who immediately after the change occurs is the owner of the business or of the part of the business in question, as the case may be (in this section referred to as "the new owner") renews the employee's contract of employment (with the substitution of the new owner for the previous owner) or re-engages him under a new contract of employment, section 3(2) of this Act shall have effect as if the renewal or re-engagement had been a renewal or re-engagement by the previous owner (without any substitution of the new owner for the previous owner).'

I need not quote s 3(2), the effect of which I have already described. Section 3(2) had been replaced at the relevant date by a new s 3(3) as set out in Sch 16, para 3, to the Employment Protection Act 1975, but there is no relevant difference between the original subsection and the new one and as all references in the courts below have been to the original subsection I shall continue to refer to it. I should only add that ss 3 and 13 of the 1965 Act have now been superseded by ss 84 and 94 respectively of the Employment Protection (Consolidation) Act 1978.

The question in the appeal turns on the application of the words 'or of a part of such a business' which I have emphasised in s 13(1)(a) above. The appellants' contention is that on 17th January 1977 there was a change in the ownership of a part of their business in the sense of the paragraph and therefore that the respondents are not to be taken to have been dismissed, and are not entitled to redundancy payments from them. The respondents contend that the change which occurred on that date was merely a transfer of certain assets, consisting mainly of the factory and its machinery, which were the means of carrying on the business, but not a transfer of any part of the business itself. The only question is which of those views should prevail. The industrial tribunal decided that no part of the appellants' business had been transferred, that is, it decided in favour of the respondents. On appeal, the Employment Appeal Tribunal reversed that decision. The First Division of the Court of Session allowed the appeal from the Employment Appeal Tribunal and restored the decision of the industrial tribunal. The reasons for that decision are set out in the opinion of the Lord President (Emslie) in which Lord Cameron, Lord Stott and Lord Dunpark concurred.

It is common ground that the appeal from the industrial tribunal to the Employment Appeal Tribunal and thence to the courts is open only on a question of law. The appellate tribunals are therefore only entitled to interfere with the decision of the industrial tribunal if the appellants can succeed in showing, as they seek to do, that it has either misdirected itself in law or reached a decision which no reasonable tribunal, directing itself properly on the law, could have reached (or that it has gone fundamentally wrong in certain other respects, none of which is here alleged). The fact that the appellate tribunal would have reached a different conclusion on the facts is not a sufficient ground for allowing an appeal.

The facts found by the industrial tribunal may be summarised as follows. The appellants operate retail shops throughout the United Kingdom, supplying mainly made to measure men's suits. The suits were made at their factories at Dagenham and Blantyre. There had been some redundancies in 1974 owing to falling demand, and, when further redundancies were threatened in autumn 1976, they obtained from the Department of Trade a temporary employment subsidy in order to avoid such redundancies. From about October 1976 they also contracted with an associated company, Willerbys, which like the appellants were part of the GUS Group, to supply ready-made suits to their order on what is called the 'cut, make and trim' (CMT) basis. Before the takeover on 17th January all the cloth used at Blantyre to produce suits for the appellants' own shops was supplied from Dagenham, mostly from stocks held there belonging to the appellants, but the cloth used for the Willerbys suits was supplied by Willerbys. The allocation of orders between Dagenham and Blantyre was decided on at

Dagenham. Blantyre did no work for outside customers, apart from Willerbys. Separate accounts were kept for the operations at Blantyre. In spite of the arrangements made with Willerbys, demand continued to fall and the appellants arranged to transfer the factory at Blantyre to Executex. They are not part of the GUS Group. The detailed terms of the arrangement for the transfer were set out in a missive offer made by the appellants' solicitors to Executex's solicitors, and in accordance with the arrangement the appellants assigned to Executex the lease of the Blantyre factory and sold them the plant and machinery in the factory as detailed in an elaborate schedule. Executex took over all work in progress and undertook to complete it. They also took over practically the whole workforce as already mentioned. The appellants guaranteed to order for themselves and Willerbys 475 CMT suits each week until 31st August 1977, and during the period from 17th January until 31st August about 70% of the production of the factory was devoted to that work. The other 30% was devoted to doing CMT work for other customers of Executex and to making a small quantity of ready-made jackets for other customers by another method called 'engineering'. The following finding by the industrial tribunal seems to me to be of some significance in considering the question before us:

'It is fair to say, therefore, that the factory at Blantyre, before the take-over by Executex, was employed solely in providing garments for sale by the [appellants] and their associated company [Willerbys]. After the take-over, however, a different situation prevailed at Blantyre. Executex made garments of a different quality from those made by [the appellants]. They are in business to manufacture garments on a C.M.T. basis for whatever customers they can attract.'

My Lords, it is clear from the findings of the industrial tribunal that there were some factors pointing towards this transaction being a change of ownership of part of the appellants' business, and other factors pointing towards its being a mere change of ownership of particular assets. The decision between those two views was one of fact and degree for the industrial tribunal, as it must be in all, or almost all, such cases. The industrial tribunal addressed itself, in my opinion, to the proper question; it expressed itself thus:

'We must look at the true nature of the transaction and try to make up our minds whether or not it truly represented a transfer of a business, or part of a business, or whether it was a convenient method whereby [the appellants] could dispose of their assets and commitments at Blantyre.'

Counsel for the appellants argued that there were no factors which could have been taken to show that this was a mere sale of assets. I cannot agree. One such factor was the difference between the business of the appellants and that of Executex which I have already mentioned and which the industrial tribunal said had impressed it. Another was the absence of any transfer to Executex of the right to use the appellants' name or of any general transfer of assets and liabilities. There was ample material on which the industrial tribunal was entitled to take the view it did that the Blantyre factory was not transferred to Executex as a going concern. No doubt it was open to the tribunal to have taken the opposite view, but that is nothing to the point.

The appeal must, therefore, fail unless it can be shown that the industrial tribunal made some error of law in reaching its decision. It is said to have erred by applying the wrong test in asking itself whether this was a transfer of a going concern. I do not agree. It seems to me that the essential distinction between the transfer of a business, or part of a business, and a transfer of physical assets, is that in the former case the business is transferred as a going concern, 'so that the business remains the same business but in different hands' (if I may quote from Lord Denning MR in *Lloyd v Brassey* [1969] 1 All ER 382 at 384, [1969] 2 QB 98 at 103 in a passsage quoted by the industrial tribunal), whereas in the latter case the assets are transferred to the new owner to be used in whatever business he chooses. Individual employees may continue to do the same work in the same environment and they may not appreciate that they are working in a different business, but that may be the true position on consideration of the whole circumstances. A change in the ownership of a part of a business will, I think, seldom occur except when that part is to some extent separate and severable from the rest of the business, either geographically or by reference to the products, or in some other way. In the present case, if the factory at Blantyre had been solely devoted to making suits for Willerbys, and if it had been transferred to Executex with a view to their continuing the same work, that might well have been a transfer of part of the appellants' business, especially if the transfer had been accompanied by an undertaking by the appellants not to compete with them for Willerbys' work. But that is not what happened. After Executex took over the factory they operated it for a different business, and the appellants' guarantee to order 475 suits per week was merely a temporary expedient to help Executex through the initial stages of starting up their business there.

Much of the criticism of the industrial tribunal's reasoning was concentrated on one passage which runs as follows:

'It is true that [the appellants'] manufacturing capacity comprised two factories, one at Dagenham and one at Blantyre. We could not, however, see how part of that manufacturing capacity could be sold as a going concern. This is the test proposed in nearly all the cases referred to above. The factory at Blantyre was not what we would describe as a going concern. It was an integral part of the manufacturing side of [the appellants'] organisation.'

It was argued for the appellants that that was a misdirection because it was a finding of law that there could not be a change of ownership of part of a business in any case where the owner had integrated his manufacturing capacity into more than one factory. I do not read the passage in that way. In my opinion it was simply a statement of the tribunal's conclusion on the facts of this case and I agree with the Lord President that that appears from the detailed reasons with which the tribunal followed the statement that I have quoted.

In my opinion none of the criticisms of the industrial tribunal's decision succeeds. I am entirely in agreement with the opinion of the Lord President and in my opinion the appeal fails.

I would dismiss the appeal. Expenses in the Court of Session have already been dealt with in the First Division's interlocutor of 14th November 1979. The appellants must pay the respondents' costs of the appeal to this House.

LORD KEITH OF KINKEL. My Lords, I agree with the speech of my noble and learned friend Lord Fraser which I have had the opportunity of reading in draft and to which I cannot usefully add anything. I, too, would dismiss the appeal.

Appeal dismissed.

Solicitors: *Paisner & Co* (for the appellants); *Campbell, Hooper Wright & Supperstone,* agents for *Courtney, Crawford & Co*, Edinburgh (for the respondents).

Mary Rose Plummer   Barrister.

Prasad v The Queen

PRIVY COUNCIL
LORD HAILSHAM OF ST MARYLEBONE LC, LORD DIPLOCK, LORD EDMUND-DAVIES, LORD RUSSELL OF KILLOWEN AND LORD ROSKILL
13th, 14th OCTOBER, 17th NOVEMBER 1980

Criminal evidence – Admissions and confessions – Answers and statements to police – Voluntary statement – Duress and fabrication of confession alleged by accused on voire dire – Whether question whether confession made voluntarily a matter for jury.

The accused was charged in Fiji with the murder of his father. At the beginning of his trial, which in accordance with Fijian practice was before a judge and assessors and not a judge and jury, the prosecution intimated that it would be relying solely on a confession which it claimed the accused had made. On a voire dire before the judge alone, the accused challenged the admissibility of the confession, alleging that it was a complete fabrication and that he had been forced to sign it by the police. The judge, who was the ultimate decider of fact as well as law, ruled that the confession was voluntary and admissible. In his summing up to the assessors, whose function was to help him in making up his mind as the sole decider of fact, the judge told them that they did not have to be satisfied whether the confession was voluntary but merely had to consider whether the accused had made the statement and whether it was true. But he did go on to point out that if they thought that the accused had been forced to make the confession they might think that that was a very good reason for it not to be true. The assessors were unanimously of the opinion that the accused was guilty. The judge agreed and the accused was convicted. The accused appealed to the Fiji Court of Appeal, contending that there were errors in the judge's summing up and, in particular, that he had not sufficiently stressed to the assessors the danger of convicting on the evidence of a confession alone. The Fiji Court of Appeal dismissed the appeal, holding that the judge had correctly stated the law and that his summing up on the confession and the weight to be attached to it when taken as a whole was adequate. The accused appealed to the Privy Council, relying on a recent English Court of Appeal authority which he submitted established that it was for a jury to decide whether a confession which had been admitted on a voire dire was voluntary.

Held – (1) As the mode of trial in England was different from that in Fiji, the directions which a judge in Fiji was required to give in his summing up to the assessors were not necessarily the same as those which a judge in England was required to give in his summing up to a jury (see p 321 *e f*, post).

(2) There was no rule of law that the question whether a confession was voluntary was to be decided by a jury. However, in assessing the probative value of a confession a jury should take into consideration all the circumstances in which it was made, including allegations of force, if those allegations were thought to be true. In the circumstances there was nothing to justify the Board re-examining the sufficiency of the judge's summing up in respect of the reliability of the confession, because taken as a whole his summing up satisfied the basic requirements of justice and there were no grounds for interfering with the Fiji Court of Appeal's decision. Accordingly the appeal would be dismissed (see p 322 *f* to *j* and p 323 *d*, post); *Ibrahim v R* [1914–15] All ER Rep 874 and *Chan Wai-Keung v R* [1967] 1 All ER 948 followed; dictum of Waller LJ in *R v McCarthy* (1980) 70 Cr App R at 272 explained.

Per Curiam. Courts of appeal composed of judges more familiar with local conditions and social attitudes than members of the Board can hope to be are in a better position than the Board to assess the likely effect of any misdirection or irregularity on a jury or other deciders of fact in a criminal case (see p 321 *d*, post).

Notes
For the duty of the trial judge as regards questions of admissibility of confessions, see 11
Halsbury's Laws (4th Edn) para 413, and for cases on admissible confessions, see 14(2)
Digest (Reissue) 562–565, 4578–4601.
For the judicature of Fiji, see 6 Halsbury's Laws (4th Edn) para 947.

Cases referred to in judgment
Chan Wai-Keung v R [1967] 1 All ER 948, [1967] 2 AC 160, [1967] 2 WLR 552, 51 Cr App
R 257, PC, Digest (Cont Vol C) 210, 4448e.
Deeming, Ex parte [1892] AC 422, PC, 8(2) Digest (Reissue) 835, 820.
Dillet, Re (1887) 12 App Cas 459, 56 LT 615, 16 Cox CC 241, PC, 8(2) Digest (Reissue)
835, 817.
Ibrahim v R [1914] AC 599, [1914–15] All ER Rep 874, 83 LJPC 185, 111 LT 20, 24 Cox
CC 174, PC, 14(2) Digest (Reissue) 562, 4583.
Macrea, Ex parte [1893] AC 346, 69 LT 734, 17 Cox CC 702, PC, 8(2) Digest (Reissue)
836, 829.
R v Bertrand (1867) LR 1 PC 520, 4 Moo PC CNS 460, 16 LT 752, 31 JP 531, 10 Cox CC
618, 16 ER 391, sub nom *Attorney General of New South Wales v Bertrand* 35 LJPC 51,
PC, 8(2) Digest (Reissue) 817, 642.
R v Burgess [1968] 2 All ER 54n, [1968] 2 QB 112, [1968] 2 WLR 1209, 132 JP 314, 52
Cr App R 258, CA, Digest (Cont Vol C) 211, 4448g.
R v McCarthy (1980) 70 Cr App R 270, CA.
Riel v R (1885) 10 App Cas 675, 55 LJPC 28, 54 LT 339, 16 Cox CC 48, PC, 8(2) Digest
(Reissue) 685, 139.

Appeal
Ragho Prasad appealed, pursuant to special leave granted on 30th March 1979, against
the judgment of the Fiji Court of Appeal, Criminal Division (Gould V-P, Marsack and
Henry JJA) dated 22nd July 1977 dismissing his appeal against his conviction by the
Supreme Court of Fiji, Western Division, sitting at Lautoka (Stuart J and five assessors)
dated 1st December 1976 of murdering his father, Ram Autar Rao, and his sentence to
life imprisonment. The facts are set out in the judgment of the Board.

Anthony Scrivenor QC and *Nigel Murray* for the appellant.
George Newman for the Crown.

LORD DIPLOCK. At a trial in the Supreme Court of Fiji, held before Stuart J and
five assessors, the appellant was convicted of murdering his father, and sentenced to life
imprisonment. He appealed to the Fiji Court of Appeal against his conviction, on the
ground of various alleged errors and other defects in the judge's summing up to
the assessors, whose unanimous opinion, with which the judge concurred, was that
the appellant was guilty of murder.

The Court of Appeal gave thorough and detailed consideration to these criticisms.
They are dealt with in the judgment of the court delivered by Gould V-P who concluded
by saying:

'We have expressed some criticism of the summing up but do not consider, in the
light of the whole, that the learned judge went beyond permissible limits in
permitting his opinions of some facts to be seen, and do not find any of the other
criticisms urged by counsel are justified to such an extent as would induce us to
allow the appeal.'

The practice of the Judicial Committee in the exercise of its appellate jurisdiction in
criminal matters was authoritatively stated by Lord Sumner in *Ibrahim v R* [1914] AC 599
at 614–615. The practice remains unchanged, and the whole passage bears repetition:

'. . . Leave to appeal is not granted "except where some clear departure from the requirements of justice" exists: *Riel* v. *Reg.* ((1885) 10 App Cas 675); nor unless "by a disregard of the forms of legal process, or by some violation of the principles of natural justice or otherwise, substantial and grave injustice has been done": *Dillet's Case* ((1887) 12 App Cas 459). It is true that these are cases of applications for special leave to appeal, but the Board has repeatedly treated applications for leave to appeal and the hearing of criminal appeals as being upon the same footing: *Riel's Case* ; *Ex parte Deeming* ([1892] AC 422). The Board cannot give leave to appeal where the grounds suggested could not sustain the appeal itself; and, conversely, it cannot allow an appeal on grounds that would not have sufficed for the grant of permission to bring it. Misdirection, as such, even irregularity as such, will not suffice: *Ex parte Macrea* ([1893] AC 346). There must be something which, in the particular case, deprives the accused of the substance of fair trial and the protection of the law, or which, in general, tends to divert the due and orderly administration of the law into a new course, which may be drawn into an evil precedent in future: *Reg.* v. *Bertrand* ((1867) LR 1 PC 520).'

To this their Lordships would only add that courts of appeal composed of judges more familiar than members of this Board can hope to be with local conditions and social attitudes are in a better position than their Lordships to assess the likely effect of any misdirection or irregularity upon a jury or other deciders of fact in a criminal case. This is all the more so where, as in Fiji, the mode of trial is not the same as in England or Scotland. There is no jury; the trial is before a judge and assessors to the number of not less than four in capital cases. The judge sums up to them; each then states his individual opinion as to the guilt of the accused; although permitted to consult with one another they are not obliged to do so; and the ultimate decider of fact (as well as law) is the judge himself who need not conform to the opinions of the assessors, even though they be unanimous, if he thinks that their opinions are wrong. The field of comment on evidence that is proper to a judge in summing up to a jury in a trial in which they are collectively the exclusive deciders of fact is not necessarily the same as in summing up to assessors whose function it is to help the judge in making up his own mind as the sole ultimate determiner of fact.

Adherence to their settled practice, as described in *Ibrahim v R* [1914] AC 599, makes it unnecessary in the instant case for their Lordships to do more than state in bare outline the case against the appellant, of which a full account is to be found in the judgment of the Court of Appeal.

On 27th July 1976 there had been a party attended by members of an extended Hindu family of which the deceased, the father of the appellant, was the head. It was held at premises in the compound where most of the extended family lived to celebrate the completion of the cane harvest by one of the appellant's brothers. The appellant, the deceased and some eight others were present, including one called Jai Raj. The deceased had left the party before it ended in order to go home to bed. His body was discovered some time later near a toilet in the compound. He had received some thirteen cuts from a sharp instrument of which four were very severe and were the cause of his death.

For reasons into which it is unnecessary to enter the only evidence of the appellant's guilt that was available at his trial was a confession. If he had made it and it was true, it was conclusive of his guilt. The prosecution's case was that he had made it to a police inspector when he had been confronted with Jai Raj who had said to the appellant: 'When grandfather went to sleep, after some time when the dogs started barking, you went and came back after 10 to 15 minutes.'

When asked by the inspector if what Jai Raj had said was true, the appellant replied:

'Yes, sir, now, this is true. My brother Sohan Lal said to get rid of this problem. My father went towards the house. A little after, I went and I was annoyed and struck him with a knife.'

'Q. How many times did you strike with a knife? A. Three or four times.
'Q. What did you do with the knife? A. I kept the knife at home after washing
it and the police took it from me.'

This dialogue was recorded in the inspector's notebook and initialled by the appellant.

At the trial the admissibility of this confession was challenged on a voire dire before
the judge in the absence of the assessors. The appellant gave evidence on oath. He
alleged that what purported to be recorded in the note book was a complete fabrication;
he had never said it, it had never been read over to him: he had been forced to initial it
as a result of violence inflicted on him by the police. The judge disbelieved the appellant's
evidence on the voire dire. He held the confession to be voluntary and admitted it in
evidence. At the trial in the presence of the assessors, the appellant again gave evidence
on oath and made the same sort of allegations of fabrication and violence as he had made
on the voire dire. Nevertheless the assessors were unanimous in their opinion that he
was guilty beyond reasonable doubt, and so was the learned judge.

Of the complaints made in the Court of Appeal about the judge's summing up, it was
sought on behalf of the appellant to reargue two before this Board.

The first was that the judge did not sufficiently stress to the assessors the danger of
convicting on the evidence of the confession alone. Having admitted the confession on
the voire dire he instructed the assessors:

'It was suggested to you that you have to be satisfied that the confession is
voluntary, but that is not so. All you have to consider is whether the accused made
that statement and whether it is true.'

He went on, however, to point out that if they thought that the appellant had been
forced to make it they might think it was a very good reason why it was not true. The
Court of Appeal were of opinion that the first sentence in the passage that their Lordships
have reproduced verbatim correctly stated the law as laid down by this Board in *Chan
Wai-Keung v R* [1967] 1 All ER 948, [1967] 2 AC 160, and that the summing up on the
confession and the weight to be attached to it when taken as a whole was adequate.
Before their Lordships, however, it was contended that, since the decision of the Fiji
Court of Appeal in the instant case, the Court of Appeal in England had decided in *R v
McCarthy* (1980) 70 Cr App R 270 that the question whether a confession that had been
admitted on the voire dire was voluntary was for the jury to decide.

Their Lordships have considered the passage in *McCarthy* that was relied on. It
consists of the few words emphasised hereunder in a single sentence of the judgment (at
272):

'If he [sc the judge] allows the evidence to be given, then it is for the jury to
consider whether or not there was an inducement *and whether or not it was voluntary*
and it is for the jury, after a proper direction, to assess its probative value . . .'

Looked at in their context the words emphasised may be equivocal, but the authorities
cited for the proposition are *Chan Wai-Keung* itself and *R v Burgess* [1968] 2 All ER 54,
[1968] 2 QB 112, a decision of the Court of Appeal of England in which *Chan Wai-Keung*
was followed and applied. In their Lordships' view all that the words emphasised should
be understood to mean is that the jury should take into consideration all the circumstances
in which a confession was made, including allegations of force, if it thinks they may be
true, in assessing the probative value of a confession.

So, in their Lordships' view, there is no fresh authority in this particular field of
criminal law that would justify this Board in re-examining the sufficiency of the
summing up as respects the reliability of the confession, since this is a matter that was
peculiarly the province of the Fiji Court of Appeal.

The same applies to the criticisms advanced against the way in which the judge in his
summing up permitted his own views of the credibility of the appellant and of other
witnesses to become apparent to the assessors.

Finally, their Lordships must deal briefly with a point on which they have not had the benefit of the views of the Fiji Court of Appeal, for the point was not taken before them. At an early stage in his summing up, when he was in the course of narrating how the prosecution put its case, the learned judge mentioned that it alleged that when the appellant rejoined the family party after 10 to 15 minutes' absence (during which he was alleged to have killed his father) he had changed his clothes. Jai Raj had in fact said this but not in the presence of the appellant. That Jai Raj had so informed the police inspector at a previous interview was extracted from the inspector in the course of cross-examination on behalf of the appellant. It was, however, hearsay and did not constitute evidence to which the deciders of fact were entitled to have regard in determining the guilt of the accused. Apart from this passing reference the judge never mentioned the changing of clothes again. He never suggested that there was any evidence that the appellant had changed his clothes. He emphasised to the assessors that the only evidence against the appellant was the alleged confession; and the only subsequent reference that he made to the clothes of the appellant was to suggest to the assessors that it did not help at all in determining whether or not the confession was true.

In their Lordships' view there is nothing in this fresh point. They are fortified in this view by the fact that despite what had obviously been a meticulous analysis of each sentence in the summing up, it had never occurred to anyone to take the point in the notices of appeal (original and supplementary) to the Court of Appeal or at the hearing in that Court or even in the appellant's written case before this Board. It was advanced for the first time at the oral hearing.

Their Lordships will, accordingly, humbly advise Her Majesty that this appeal must be dismissed.

Appeal dismissed.

Solicitors: *Philip Conway, Thomas & Co* (for the appellant); *Charles Russell & Co* (for the Crown).

Sumra Green   Barrister.

Practice Direction

FAMILY DIVISION

Affidavit – Filing – Family Division – Time for filing – Cause or matter for which hearing date fixed – Affidavit or other document to be lodged not less than 14 days before appointed hearing date.

1. Where, in any cause or matter proceeding in the Principal Registry, a party wishes to file an affidavit or other document in connection with an application for which a hearing date has been fixed, the affidavit or other document must be lodged in the Principal Registry *not less than 14 clear days* before the appointed hearing date.

2. Where insufficient time remains before the hearing date to lodge the affidavit or other document as required by (1) above, it should be retained and handed to the clerk to the registrar, or associate in attendance on the judge, before whom the application is to be heard immediately before the hearing. Service should be effected on the opposing party in the normal way.

3. The Practice Direction of 31st October 1972 ([1972] 3 All ER 910, [1972] 1 WLR 1519) is amended by substituting '14 days' for 'eight days' and the Registrar's Direction of 24th July 1956 (not reported) is amended by substituting '14 days' for '7 days'.

R L BAYNE-POWELL
Senior Registrar.

12th January 1981

ACT Construction Ltd v Customs and Excise Commissioners

COURT OF APPEAL, CIVIL DIVISION

LORD DENNING MR, BRANDON AND ACKNER LJJ

7th, 8th, 9th OCTOBER 1980

Value added tax – Zero-rating – Building works – Work of repair or maintenance – Underpinning of defective foundations – Existing foundations damaged by subsidence – Building company constructing additional foundations and leaving original foundations unaltered – Whether work carried out by company 'maintenance' – Finance Act 1972, Sch 4, Group 8, item 2, note 2.

A company carried out work on the foundations of a number of buildings which had been damaged by subsidence. The original foundations did not comply with modern building regulations and the work of correcting the subsidence could not be carried out merely by repairing or replacing the original foundations. The company therefore constructed additional foundations to underpin the buildings, leaving the original foundations unaltered. The company was assessed to value added tax in respect of the work done on the basis that it was work of 'maintenance' within note 2[a] to Group 8 of Sch 4 to the Finance Act 1972 and therefore excluded from being a supply 'in the course of the . . . alteration' of a building within item 2[b] of Group 8. A value added tax tribunal upheld the assessment, holding that the work done was 'maintenance' because 'maintenance' extended to improvements by substitution. The judge ([1979] 2 All ER 691) reversed the tribunal's decision, holding that work which substantially and significantly altered the building was not 'maintenance' within note 2. The Crown appealed.

Held – The expression 'maintenance' in note 2 to Group 8 of Sch 4 to the 1972 Act was to be given its ordinary and natural meaning, and what maintenance meant was a question of law for the court to decide. Having regard to its nature, scale and effect, the work done by the company was entirely new work, involving a radical and fundamental alteration to the construction of the building. Such work clearly was not capable of being maintenance in the ordinary and natural meaning of that word and the appeal would accordingly be dismissed (see p 327 g h, p 328 b and g, p 329 a b d to f and h j, p 330 a to e and p 331 b and d to g, post). Dictum of Sachs LJ in *Brew Brothers Ltd v Snax (Ross) Ltd* [1970] 1 All ER at 602, *British Railways Board v Customs and Excise Comrs* [1977] 2 All ER 873 and *Pearlman v Keepers and Governors of Harrow School* [1979] 1 All ER 365 applied. Dictum of Neill J in *Customs and Excise Comrs v Morrison Dunbar Ltd* [1979] STC at 413 disapproved.

Decision of Drake J [1979] 2 All ER 691 affirmed.

Notes

For zero-rating of supplies in connection with the construction and alteration of buildings, see 12 Halsbury's Laws (4th Edn) para 912.

For the Finance Act 1972, s 12, Sch 4, Group 8, see 42 Halsbury's Statutes (3rd Edn) 219, but note that with effect from 4th September 1978 Sch 4 to the 1972 Act was substituted by the Value Added Tax (Consolidation) Order 1978, SI 1978 No 1064, art 3 and Sch 1.

---

a   Note 2, so far as material, is set out at p 330 *j*, post

b   Item 2 is set out at p 330 *g*, post

Cases referred to in judgments

Brew Brothers Ltd v Snax (Ross) Ltd [1970] 1 All ER 587, [1970] 1 QB 612, [1969] 3 WLR 657, 20 P & CR 829, CA, 31(2) Digest (Reissue) 615, 5001.

British Railways Board v Customs and Excise Comrs [1977] 2 All ER 873, [1977] 1 WLR 588, [1977] STC 221, [1977] TR 79, CA, Digest (Cont Vol E) 511, 961a.

Customs and Excise Comrs v Morrison Dunbar Ltd [1979] STC 406, [1978] TR 267, Digest (Cont Vol E) 512, 961c.

Davies v Customs and Excise Comrs [1976] VATTR 205.

Pearlman v Keepers and Governors of Harrow School [1979] 1 All ER 365, [1979] QB 56, [1978] 3 WLR 736, 38 P & CR 136, CA, Digest (Cont Vol E) 125, 4476a.

Racal Communications Ltd, Re [1980] 2 All ER 634, [1980] 3 WLR 181, HL.

Cases also cited

Lister v Lane [1893] 2 QB 212, [1891–4] All ER Rep 388, CA.

Lurcott v Wakely [1911] 1 KB 905, [1911–13] All ER Rep 41, CA.

Ravenseft Properties Ltd v Davstone (Holdings) Ltd [1979] 1 All ER 929, [1980] QB 12.

Sotheby v Grundy [1947] 2 All ER 761.

Appeal

The Customs and Excise Commissioners appealed against an order of Drake J ([1979] 2 All ER 691, [1979] STC 358) allowing an appeal by the taxpayer, ACT Construction Ltd ('ACT'), against the decision of a value added tax tribunal (chairman Neil Elles Esq) sitting in London given on 8th August 1978 whereby an assessment to value added tax in the sum of £1,072·44 made by the commissioners on ACT was upheld. The facts are set out in the judgment of Lord Denning MR.

Michael Beloff for ACT.
Simon D Brown for the Crown.

LORD DENNING MR. The question is this: when the foundations of a house are insufficient and contractors are employed to remedy the insufficiency by inserting a concrete beam (underpinning the house) is the work liable for value added tax or not? Or, in technical language, is it zero-rated or positive-rated? It depends on whether the work of underpinning comes within the description of 'repair or maintenance'. If it comes within that description, it is positive-rated. If it does not come within that description, then it is zero-rated.

That is the point in this case. But we have discussed other points which are important to the building industry, such as: is the insertion of a damp-proof course zero-rated or positive-rated? Is the insertion of double-glazing instead of single-glazing zero-rated or positive-rated? If you put a tiled roof instead of a thatched roof, is that zero-rated or positive-rated? In all these cases it depends on the words, 'Is it repair or maintenance?' If it is work of repair or maintenance, then it is positive-rated. If it is not work of repair or maintenance, then it is zero-rated.

The Finance Act 1972 imposed value added tax from 1973 onwards. The tax is under the care and management of the Commissioners of Customs and Excise, not the Inland Revenue. Section 12 says that certain supplies and services are to be zero-rated. They are set out in a schedule. In it there are groups which have been up-dated by the Value Added Tax (Consolidation) Order 1976, SI 1976 No 128. So we have to look at that order and the schedules to it to see whether any supplies or services are zero-rated or not.

The particular group which applies to this case is Group 8 'Construction of Buildings, Etc'. One of the items which is to be zero-rated is item 2:

'The supply, in the course of the construction, alteration or demolition of any building or of any civil engineering work, of any services . . .'

I will stop there because there is a note to that item, which says: 'Item 2 does not include—(a) any work of repair or maintenance . . .' So the construction or alteration of building work is zero-rated, but not any work of repair or maintenance.

I now turn to our particular problem. In the 1930s many houses were built in which the foundations were too shallow. (Such foundations would not be allowed under the modern regulations.) Builders in the 1930s did not realise that they were putting in foundations which were too shallow. The result was that during the drought of 1976 there was subsidence, especially in houses built on clay soil. There was movement in the structure of the houses. Cracks appeared. The houses were unsafe.

To remedy this, some wise owners had their foundations underpinned, not only of houses that had already been affected, but also of houses which might be affected. They had their houses underpinned, even though movement had not yet started.

One of the firms which specialised in underpinning work was ACT Construction Ltd ('ACT'). Their method was to leave the shallow foundation in place, but a foot or two underneath it they would put a big concrete beam, with pillars sunk in the earth to hold it, so as to hold up the older foundation. It was not an actual raft, but an underlying structure. It had to be done in short stages. It was a specialist job.

ACT took advice whether this work should be zero-rated or not. They were advised that it was zero-rated. On 18th October 1977 they gave this quotation for the underpinning of a house:

'. . . our fixed price quotation for the works are as follows:—Provide 1·2 m deep reinforced concrete footing to all elevations of property . . . For the sum of £7271·00 . . . rated ZERO.'

That was the quotation they gave. It was no doubt accepted by the householder, and the work was done on that footing.

Now the Crown says that ACT were wrong, and that the work should be positive-rated. Value added tax has been assessed at £1,072·44. ACT had to pay that sum. But they ask that it should be returned to them as the work should have been zero-rated.

The matter was discussed with insurance assessors. They wrote to the commissioners on 3rd September 1977, saying:

'We have been advised by certain underpinning contractors that their local VAT offices have given different rulings in that underpinning is to be treated as alterations or new works and therefore zero rated.'

So it seems that different rulings were given by various value added tax offices.

The commissioners said that they had already given a ruling on the matter. They issued a booklet as far back as 1975. It was Notice 715. It had a blue cover. So I will call it the blue booklet. It gives examples of work which is zero-rated, and examples of work which is positive-rated. Para 4(a) says: 'The following are examples of work which is **positive-rated** as repair or maintenance . . . Shoring up and underpinning buildings . . .'

In further correspondence the commissioners said in a letter of 9th January 1978:

'The meaning of the word "maintenance" which we accept is the one adopted in the VAT Tribunal case of T G Davies ([1976] VATTR 205 at 213). The Tribunal in the decision defined maintenance as "the keeping of something in proper order before the thing falls out of condition". When underpinning of buildings is undertaken to prevent the building falling into disrepair, we regard this as work of maintenance and therefore subject to a positive rate of VAT.'

On 6th April 1978 they said: '. . . we have already given our ruling that underpinning of buildings following subsidence is chargeable with VAT, as indeed is clearly stated in Public Notice 715 paragraph 4(a).' So there is the head office of the Customs and Excise making it as plain as can be that in their view the work of underpinning is positive-rated and not zero-rated.

This matter being of so much importance to the industry, ACT appealed to a value added tax tribunal. The tribunal gave a considered judgment. They expressed sympathy for the contractors because they had consulted their accountants and had been told that it was not work of repair or maintenance, but the tribunal felt driven to the conclusion that it was maintenance and was positive-rated. This is the crucial passage in the decision of the tribunal: 'We adopt the definition of "maintenance" set out in the decision of the London Tribunal in *Davies v Customs and Excise Comrs*.' As that is the definition on which they rested, I will read it:

'The third question is whether or not the supplies under consideration amounted to "work of repair or maintenance" so as to be excluded from items 2 and 3 of Group 8 by para (a) of Note (2) thereto. We were not greatly assisted during the hearing by the quotation of authorities on the meaning to be given to these words. In our view "repair" means the restoration to a sound condition after injury or decay; in its ordinary context it indicates the putting back into good condition of something that, having been in a good condition, has fallen into a bad condition. The word "maintenance" in the context of "work of repair or maintenance" is harder to define. We think it extends to the keeping of something in proper order before the thing falls out of condition. It does not, in our opinion, exclude improvements. In performing works of maintenance on a building, the householder may substitute for one article a reasonable improvement thereto. For example, in "maintaining" a house in relation to its central heating, a householder may substitute an oil-fired boiler for a coal-fired boiler. So, in our view, one may maintain something by ensuring that it remains in the same good condition, or by improving it. But each case must be considered individually, an improvement may or may not be "maintenance".'

Applying that definition, the tribunal in this case held that underpinning was not 'repair' but that it was 'maintenance', and therefore positive-rated.

ACT appealed to the judge. Drake J ([1979] 2 All ER 691, [1979] STC 358) reversed the tribunal's decision. He disagreed with the test of 'maintenance' as propounded by the tribunal. He considered a number of cases of landlord and tenant on repair or maintenance. He said that he could not give an exhaustive definition, but he was inclined to see whether the work had changed the character of the building so that it became something different. Applying that test, he held that this was not 'maintenance'. He also said that on the ordinary meaning of the word the underpinning of the house was not 'maintenance'. It should be zero-rated. The Crown appeals to this court. It comes down to the construction of the few words in the schedule.

First, I would like to mention the word 'alteration' in the opening sentence. Neill J, in *Customs and Excise Comrs v Morrison Dunbar Ltd* [1979] STC 406 at 413, said: '... that the alteration to which item 2 applies is an alteration *of the building* and therefore one which involves some structural alteration' (Neill J's emphasis). I am afraid I cannot share that view. I do not think that the word 'structural' should be inserted. It seems to me that 'alteration' means any alteration of a building whether it is structural or not. But nothing depends on it in this case. Clearly the work of underpinning was an 'alteration'.

I agree with the judge, and with the tribunal, that underpinning was not 'repair'. I understand that in one or two of the houses cracks had to be plastered over, or work had to be done on the actual defects that then appeared. That would be 'repair', and that would be positive-rated. But the work with which we are concerned was the underpinning, putting the concrete beam underneath the foundations. That is not 'repair'.

The great contest in the case is whether it is 'maintenance' or not. Counsel for the Crown said that the question whether a particular work is 'maintenance' or not is a matter on which two opinions can easily be held without either being unreasonable at all. Quite reasonably one person might say that underpinning is 'maintenance'. Another person might equally reasonably say that it is not 'maintenance'. So he said there is a band in which either view is reasonable. He said that in such a case the courts should not interfere with the decision of a tribunal, whichever way it decided. He said the courts should not interfere with the decision of a tribunal unless it was right outside the band of reasonableness, so unreasonable that no reasonable man could come to that conclusion. He sought to find some support for this argument in some observations of Lord Diplock in the recent case of *Re Racal Communications Ltd* [1980] 2 All ER 634 at 639, [1980] 3 WLR 181 at 187–188. But I cannot accept that submission. Once you have the primary facts established, as you have here, about the underpinning, then the question whether the work comes within the word 'maintenance' or not is a question of law for the judges to decide. Brandon and Ackner LJJ pointed out that in hundreds of arbitrations in the City of London the arbitrators state their findings of fact and then ask the court whether on the true construction of the document (the charterparty or whatever it may be) they came to the right conclusion. In everyday practice, once the primary facts are found, the interpretation of a word is a question of law for the judges to decide.

Many a time we have expressly so held. We so held in a value added tax case, *British Railways Board v Customs and Excise Comrs* [1977] 2 All ER 873, [1977] STC 221; and we so held in an analogous case not involving value added tax but structural alterations, *Pearlman v Keepers and Governors of Harrow School* [1979] 1 All ER 365, [1979] QB 56. With regard to the latter case, I would say that the whole court were unanimous in thinking that the county court judge below was wrong in his construction of the words 'structural alterations', and that accordingly he had made a mistake of law. The only ground on which Geoffrey Lane LJ dissented was that he thought it was an error within their jurisdiction which was not subject to correction. But, on whether it was a point of law, Geoffrey Lane LJ agreed with the rest of us.

I would add that this is especially important in work which is repetitive, and frequently arising, as in this case of underpinning. Throughout the industry it is essential that the contractors and their employers should know whether the work is to be positive-rated or zero-rated. It would be intolerable if one tribunal were to give one view and another tribunal were to give another view, and that no one could decide between them. You would have different rulings in relation to similar work in different parts of the country, according to which tribunal happened to be hearing the case. That cannot be right. I would ask: if there are two tribunals giving different decisions, what are the commissioners to do? Are they to be the arbitrators between the differing views? I hope not. Tax gatherers should not be judges in their own cases. Surely not. When a definite ruling is needed for the guidance of builders and customers everywhere, it must be for the courts of law to give a definite and final ruling as to the meaning of a word such as 'maintenance'.

So I will turn to the meaning of the word 'maintenance'. Was this underpinning maintenance? 'Repair' and 'maintenance' are used in conjunction throughout the industry, and in the landlord and tenant cases. In the context of repair and maintenance to buildings, they are used every day. They are ordinary English words. Judges have tried from time to time to define them. They do the best they can. Always in relation to the particular case in hand. To my mind, definitions are not much help. I go by the observations made by Sachs LJ on this line of cases in *Brew Brothers Ltd v Snax (Ross) Ltd* [1970] 1 All ER 587 at 602, [1970] 1 QB 612 at 640. That was a case about a bulging wall, and the question was about a covenant for repair and maintenance:

'In the course of their submissions counsel referred to a number of varying phrases which had been used by judges in an endeavour to express the distinction between the end-product of work which constituted repair and that of work which did not. They included "improvement", "important improvement", "different in kind", "different in character", "different in substance", "different in nature", "a new and different thing", and just "something different". . . . I doubt whether there is any definition—certainly not any general definition—which satisfactorily covers the above distinctions; nor will I attempt to provide one . . . [The question is] whether, on a fair interpretation of those terms in relation to that state, the requisite work can fairly be termed repair.'

I would look at this case in that way. I ask myself what would an ordinary reasonable man say if he was asked, 'Look at this work of underpinning this house at a cost of £7,000 or more. Is that repairing the house? Is it maintaining the house?' I am sure he would say, 'Certainly not. I know what to "repair" a house is. If a window is broken, or one of the stairs is broken, that is "repair". I also know what "maintaining it" is. It has to be painted from time to time. It has to be cleaned. It has to be kept in good condition. That is "maintenance". But underpinning a house, that is not "maintenance".'

A word about the blue book. If I were asked, 'Is putting in a damp course to a house which has never had one "repair" or "maintenance"?', I would agree with the commissioners that it is not maintenance. It should be zero-rated. If I were asked, 'If you are installing double-glazing for the first time, is that maintenance or is it not?', I would say it is clearly not maintenance. It should be zero-rated. So also if you are putting fixed cupboards in the house. It is 'alteration', but it is not 'maintenance'. I would agree with the commissioners on all those items. But, when I turn the page and find the things which are said to be positive-rated, I do not agree with some of these. They say that 'Shoring up and underpinning buildings' is maintenance. I do not agree. Take this case. It cost over £7,000 to underpin this building. That is not maintenance. Take an old wall which has to be kept up by making buttresses. That is not maintenance. Then again: 'Replacing one type of roof by another, e.g. slates by tiles.' The commissioners say that that is maintenance. I do not think so. It is an alteration which is far more than 'maintenance' requires.

I have given those illustrations to show the problems which do arise in this particular Act. For myself, I think that each case has to be decided as it comes up according to the ordinary meaning which the ordinary man would give to these words. As each case is decided, the courts will build up a body of law so that people will know whether or not the work is zero-rated or positive-rated. In some respects the blue book gives good guidance. In other respects it does not. So far as the law is concerned, the ultimate decision must rest with the judges and not with the tribunals whether these cases, which occur time after time, are zero-rated or positive-rated.

In the result I come to the same conclusion as Drake J. I think that this was not maintenance. It was an alteration to a building, and under the provisions it should be zero-rated. I would therefore dismiss this appeal.

BRANDON LJ. The question of law which appears to me to arise in this case is this: is the work of underpinning which the value added tax tribunal found was done to the building concerned capable of coming within the expression 'maintenance' contained in note 2 to Group 8 in the Value Added Tax (Consolidation) Order 1976? I limit the question in that way because it has been conceded on behalf of the Crown that the work is not capable of coming within the other word, 'repair', also contained in note 2.

If the work concerned is capable of coming within the expression 'maintenance' in note 2, the decision whether it does or not is a decision of fact for the value added tax tribunal. This court, which only has power to hear an appeal on a question of law, cannot interfere even though it would have decided the question of fact differently itself. If the work concerned is not capable of coming within the expression 'maintenance' in note 2, the decision of the value added tax tribunal that it did so was wrong in law, and this court has both the power and the duty to set it aside.

It is possible to take up two extreme positions on the meaning of the expression 'maintenance' in note 2. One extreme position is to say that, if the work done involves an improvement to the building, it can never be maintenance. The other extreme position is to say that, if the work has the purpose of remedying an existing defect in the building or preventing a future defect from developing, it must always be maintenance.

In my view, neither of these extreme positions is correct. The expression 'maintenance' should be given its ordinary and natural meaning. In regard to the first extreme position, there may well be cases where the work done, although it involves some degree of improvement (for instance, because of the use of modern or better materials or methods), is nevertheless maintenance in the ordinary and natural meaning of that word. For example, if metal gutters, which are liable to decay in time, are replaced with plastic gutters which are not liable to decay however long they remain there, that is an improvement to the building, but I would still regard that work as maintenance. With regard to the second extreme position, there may well be cases where, although the purpose of the work is to remedy existing or to prevent future defects in the building, it is nevertheless not within the expression 'maintenance' in the ordinary and natural meaning of that word. For example, if a building has a flat roof which leaks continuously and the owner decides to replace the flat roof with a pitched roof so as to eliminate that defect, then, although that work was designed to eliminate a defect, it would not in my view be maintenance in the ordinary and natural meaning of that word.

In the present case the work done was not done to any existing part of the building; it was entirely new work. It involved a radical and fundamental alteration to the construction of the building as it had been before. It involved an extension of the existing building in a downward direction. Such work in my view is not capable of coming within the expression 'maintenance' in the ordinary and natural meaning of that word. It is conceded that, if that is right, then the work was work of alteration within the meaning of that expression in item 2 of Group 8 and is accordingly zero-rated.

For the reasons which I have given, I agree with the decision of Drake J that the value added tax tribunal was wrong in law and their decision should be set aside on that ground.

I would dismiss the appeal.

ACKNER LJ. I agree. To my mind this appeal raises a short question of law, viz whether on the true construction of the relevant section of and schedule to the Finance Act 1972, as applied to the undisputed facts in this case, there was a zero-rated supply of service. Value added tax was imposed by the Finance Act 1972. Section 12 provides that the supply of certain specified goods and services shall be treated as a taxable supply, and yet no tax shall be charged on those goods and services. The goods and services which are zero-rated are specified in Sch 4 to the Act, and it is Group 8 of that schedule, which is headed 'Construction of Buildings, Etc', with which we are concerned. Item 2 is the relevant one, and that reads:

> 'The supply, in the course of the construction, alteration or demolition of any building or of any civil engineering work, of any services other than the services of an architect, surveyor or any person acting as consultant or in a supervisory capacity.'

I agree with Lord Denning MR that the word 'alterations' has no limit placed on it. The particular item to my mind covers the three phases in the life of the building: its birth, namely its construction; its continued existence; and, finally, its demolition. I therefore repectfully do not agree with the decision of Neill J in *Customs and Excise Comrs v Morrison Dunbar Ltd* [1979] STC 406 at 413, but I accept that that part of this judgment is not necessary for the decision in this case. What occurred here was clearly structural alterations.

Section 46 is an odd provision because it provides that Sch 4 should be interpreted in accordance with the notes contained in the schedule; and the relevant note, which is note 2, provides: 'Item 2 does not include—(a) any work of repair or maintenance . . .' The issue therefore is: was the alteration, which is the subject matter of this appeal, properly described as work of maintenance, it being accepted that that tribunal reached the correct conclusion that it was not work of repair?

The agreed facts are very short. I take them from the tribunal's decision. The underpinning was properly defined as being 'New and permanent support for an existing structure so as to increase the load-bearing capacity of a building'. It consisted in the construction of an additional foundation to a structure which already existed. The method adopted by ACT improved its load-bearing capacity by the construction of a further foundation beneath an existing foundation. No work was carried out on the existing foundations.

I have no hesitation in concluding, having regard to the nature, scale and effect of this work, that it was not work of maintenance in the ordinarily accepted sense of that word. On the agreed facts it is easy to imagine the substance of the expert advice which ACT would have given to the building owners. They would have said, in effect, 'It is useless to try and carry out any work on the existing foundations of these houses. You would only be throwing good money after bad. You need to put in an entirely new foundation.'

Counsel for the Crown submits that, if you carry out work which is designed to safeguard the building from future deterioration, that is maintenance. I cannot accept that such a test could be conclusive. I respectfully agree with the example referred to by Brandon LJ in relation to the pitched roof which takes the place of a flat roof. Equally, the first-time provision of a damp proof course, which the commissioners in their own booklet accept is not maintenance. I think there is force in counsel's submissions for the Crown that, without entering into the realms of definition, maintenance *generally* involves the following characteristics: firstly, an element of repetition, because the object is to keep the building in the condition in which it started; secondly, that the work is generally speaking foreseeable, whereas this was dramatically unforeseeable; thirdly, again generally speaking, that the work is of a minor character and habitual, although naturally there are exceptions as in the case of roof works; fourthly, that generally speaking in maintenance one does not add something substantial which is new; and, lastly, that you do not in ordinary maintenance make a substantial improvement to that which you maintain. Significantly, here it is not the omission of any one of those characteristics which is of particular importance: it is the omission of all those characteristics.

The landlord and tenant authorities seem clearly to establish that the provision of an entirely new foundation cannot be considered as work of maintenance. In none of those cases was there any attempt to construe the word 'maintain' in other than its ordinary sense. The learned judge correctly placed some reliance on those cases, although he properly said that caution is required because of the fact that landlord and tenant cases are dealing with positive obligations on the tenants and involve on occasions consideration of the condition of the premises in question at the date of the demise.

I too would affirm the decision of Drake J and accordingly dismiss this appeal.

Appeal dismissed. Leave to appeal to the House of Lords refused.

Solicitors: *Solicitor for the Customs and Excise; Herbert Smith & Co* (for ACT).

Frances Rustin   Barrister.

R v Lambie

COURT OF APPEAL, CRIMINAL DIVISION
CUMMING-BRUCE LJ, STOCKER AND SMITH JJ
30th JUNE, 30th JULY 1980

Criminal law – Obtaining pecuniary advantage by deception – Deception – Implied representation – Credit card transaction – Payment guaranteed by bank which issued credit card – Retailer not concerned with card holder's credit standing at bank – Whether card holder who used card when over credit limit imposed by bank obtaining pecuniary advantage by deception – Theft Act 1968, s 16(1).

The appellant obtained a credit card from a bank giving her credit facilities up to a limit of £200. The bank entered into contracts with retailers prepared to accept the card for the purchase of goods, by which the bank guaranteed payment of any purchase up to £50 made with the credit card provided the retailer complied with certain conditions relating to the validity of the card. The appellant, when well over her credit limit of £200, purchased goods for £10·35 from a shop using her credit card. The shop complied with the conditions for a credit card purchase and, since the amount involved was less than the amount for which special authorisation was required from the bank, made no inquiry of the bank as to the appellant's credit standing. The appellant was charged with obtaining a pecuniary advantage by deception contrary to s 16(1)[a] of the Theft Act 1968. At her trial the shop assistant who made the sale gave evidence that, although she regarded the state of the appellant's account with the bank as irrelevant, she would not have completed the transaction had she known the appellant had been using the credit card in a way which she (the appellant) was not entitled to use it, and also that, provided the credit card appeared valid, she would normally conclude a credit card transaction by going through the prescribed procedure without inquiring whether the person presenting the card had authority to use it. In his summing up the judge asked the jury whether the shop assistant had relied on the presentation of an apparently valid credit card as being due authority within the appellant's credit limit at that time to use the card. The jury returned a verdict of guilty and the appellant was convicted. On an appeal by the appellant the questions arose whether there was evidence of a false representation to the shop assistant and, if there was, whether there was evidence on which the jury could have found that the shop assistant had been induced to rely on that representation.

Held – (1) Since the shop assistant had made it clear that she would not have completed the credit card transaction had she known that the appellant had been using the credit card in an unauthorised way, it followed that as a matter of law there was evidence on which the jury could have found that the appellant had made a representation that she was authorised by the bank to use her credit card. By its verdict the jury had found that the appellant had made such a representation and that it was false (see p 337 *c*, post); *Metropolitan Police Comr v Charles* [1976] 3 All ER 112 applied.

(2) However, by its contract with the bank the shop had bought from the bank the right to sell goods to a card holder such as the appellant without regard to whether the card holder was complying with his or her contract with the bank. In those circumstances the evidence of the shop assistant that, provided a credit card appeared valid, she would normally go through the prescribed procedure without inquiry as to the customer's authority to use the card was not evidence which could found a verdict that necessarily involved a finding of fact that the shop assistant had been induced by a false representation that the appellant's credit standing at the bank gave her authority to use the credit card.

---

a Section 16(1) provides: 'A person who by any deception dishonestly obtains for himself or another any pecuniary advantage shall on conviction on indictment be liable to imprisonment for a term not exceeding five years.'

Since it was necessary, in order to obtain a conviction under s 16(1) of the 1968 Act, to show that the person to whom the representation was made had acted or relied on that representation, it followed that the appeal would be allowed and the conviction quashed (see p 334 *j* to p 335 *a* and p 339 *h j* to p 340 *a*, post).

Notes

For obtaining a pecuniary advantage by deception, see 11 Halsbury's Laws (4th Edn) para 1279, and for cases on the subject, see 15 Digest (Reissue) 1387–1391, *12,138–12,152.*
For the Theft Act 1968, s 16, see 8 Halsbury's Statutes (3rd Edn) 793.

Cases referred to in judgment

Director of Public Prosecutions v Ray [1973] 3 All ER 131, [1974] AC 370, [1973] 3 WLR 359, 136 JP 744, 58 Cr App R 130, HL, 15 Digest (Reissue) 1390, *12,149.*
London and Globe Finance Corpn Ltd, Re [1903] 1 Ch 728, [1900–3] All ER Rep 891, 72 LJ Ch 368, 88 LT 194, 10 Mans 198, 15 Digest (Reissue) 1332, *11,509.*
Metropolitan Police Comr v Charles [1976] 3 All ER 112, [1977] AC 177, [1976] 3 WLR 431, 140 JP 531, 63 Cr App R 252, HL; *affg* [1976] 1 All ER 659, [1976] 1 WLR 248, CA, 15 Digest (Reissue) 1390, *12,150.*
R v Kovacs [1974] 1 All ER 1236, [1974] 1 WLR 370, 138 JP 425, 58 Cr App R 412, CA, 15 Digest (Reissue) 1390, *12,148.*

Case also cited

R v Laverty [1970] 3 All ER 432, CA.

Appeal

Shiralee Ann Lambie appealed by leave of the single judge, Park J against her conviction in the Crown Court at Bedford before his Honour Judge Counsell of obtaining a pecuniary advantage by deception contrary to s 16(1) of the Theft Act 1968. The facts are set out in the judgment of the court.

John Plumstead (assigned by the Registrar of Criminal Appeals) for the appellant.
Michael Pert for the Crown.

Cur adv vult

30th July. **CUMMING-BRUCE LJ** read the following judgment of the court: On 10th August 1979 in the Crown Court at Bedford the appellant was arraigned on an indictment with three counts. She pleaded guilty to an offence of being carried in a conveyance taken without authority (count 3). She pleaded not guilty to two counts laid under s 16(1) of the Theft Act 1968. In the first count she was charged as follows:

'STATEMENT OF OFFENCE
'Obtaining a pecuniary advantage by deception contrary to Section 16(1) of the Theft Act 1968.

'PARTICULARS OF OFFENCE
'Shiralee Ann Lambie on the 5th day of December, 1977 dishonestly obtained for herself a pecuniary advantage namely the evasion of a debt for which she made herself liable by deception namely by false representations that she was authorised to use a Barclaycard . . . to obtain goods to the value of £9·70.'

The jury acquitted her on this count.

She was charged in the second count with an exactly similar offence, save that the date alleged was 15th December and the value of the goods was £10·35. The jury convicted on this count. She now appeals to this court.

The perfected grounds of appeal raise the question of the nature of the representation made by one who uses a credit card, and the question whether the deception (if any) operated on the mind of the shop assistant who sold the goods so as to induce her to sell them on credit. These problems have not arisen for consideration in this court in the context of a credit card transaction. In *Metropolitan Police Comr v Charles* [1976] 1 All

ER 659, [1976] 1 WLR 248; *affd* [1976] 3 All ER 112, [1977] AC 177 this court and the House of Lords considered a series of dishonest cheque card transactions.

Counsel for the appellant submits that on the evidence relevant to count 2 in the instant case (i) there was no evidence on which the jury could find, in relation to count 2, that the appellant made any representation that she was authorised by the bank to use her credit card and (ii) there was no evidence on which the jury could find that the shop assistant was induced to act on that representation. He submits that the legal relationships between bank, credit card holder and retailer are different from those that exist in a cheque card transaction, and that this case should be distinguished from the situation that existed in *Metropolitan Police Comr v Charles*.

At the trial, the evidence for the prosecution consisted of unchallenged statements and exhibits put in before the committing magistrates and depositions taken before them. This evidence was read to the jury. No evidence was called on behalf of the defence.

The evidence related to four areas of primary fact: (i) the contractual relations of the bank with the appellant and with the shops concerned with counts 1 and 2; (ii) the history of the appellant's transactions on her account with the bank; (iii) the events when the appellant bought the goods on 5th December from a shop called Braggins (count 1) and when she bought goods on 5th December from a shop called Mothercare (count 2); and (iv) the admissions by the accused to the police. Though this appeal is only concerned with the conviction on count 2, it is necessary to refer to evidence relevant to count 1, because the summing up of the learned judge cannot otherwise be properly understood.

(1) In April 1978 the appellant applied to the Barclaycard branch of Barclays Bank for a credit card. The bank agreed to grant her credit facilities up to a limit of £200. They gave her a Barclaycard, whereby the bank guaranteed to pay on her credit account up to the sum of £50 on any single transaction by which the appellant bought goods from a retailer with whom the bank had entered into an agreement relating to sales to purchasers who presented a Barclaycard. Such shops were guaranteed payment of Barclaycard vouchers. The course of dealing between the bank and the appellant provided for the posting of a monthly statement to the appellant at the address which she had given. The statement showed the then state of her account with the bank. The credit limit continued unless and until another limit was agreed.

Barclays had entered into contracts with retailers, and at all materials times had contracts with the two shops named in counts 1 and 2. The terms of those contracts were not strictly or comprehensively proved, but their general effect was described by a Barclays Bank investigator who had access to the records held by the Barclaycard organisation. The bank agreed to pay the shop the sums shown on a voucher signed by the credit card holder, provided that five simple conditions were complied with by the retailer. These conditions were (i) that a voucher was properly completed, (ii) that the card presented was current in date, (iii) that the card did not appear on the current 'stop list', (iv) that the shop checked the signature of the customer with the specimen signature on the card, and (v) that either the transaction was individually checked and authorised by Barclaycard or the transaction fell within 'the floor limit' of the shop.

The last condition was explained as follows. The bank agree with retailers that any transaction above a certain figure will be individually reported to the bank, who retain power to authorise or refuse payment. In the case of Mothercare, the shop concerned in count 2, the 'floor limit' was agreed at £70. But on any single Barclaycard transaction less than £70 at Mothercare the bank agreed to pay the sum shown on the voucher without requiring or expecting any inquiry from the shop as to the state of the customer's account with the bank.

The object and effect of the contracts entered into between Barclays and the retailers was to relieve the retailer of any concern with the state of the cardholder's account with the bank, provided that the 'floor limit' was not exceeded. On the contract between the bank and the retailer, the retailer agreed to pay to the bank a commission in order to enjoy the bank's guarantee of payment of vouchers made out by the retailer in compliance with the five conditions, and the convenience of being able to trade with Barclaycardholders without any regard to the question whether the customer is overdrawn on her Barclays Bank account, provided only that the 'shop limit' is not exceeded. Both the witness from the bank and the shop assistant concerned in count 2 agreed that, if the shop carried out its business in accordance with the five conditions, it received something as good as cash. Barclaycard made their profits in two ways: by charging the shops commission for the security which the Barclaycard transactions provide, and by charging customers on the money forwarded by Barclaycard. No cheque is drawn by the customer, who simply presents a Barclaycard and signs the voucher on which the shop assistant has entered particulars of the transactions.

(2) The appellant, then 18 years of age, received her Barclaycard in April 1978 and until November used it without exceeding her agreed credit limit of £200. The bank sent her monthly statements showing the state of her account. On the statement dated 14th November she was in debit of £140·38. She then rapidly carried out a series of transactions with the result that when she used the card in the shop called Braggins (count 1) on 5th December she owed the bank £553·20. The 'shop limit' agreed between the bank and Braggins was £30. The appellant used her card to buy goods for £9·70, so there was no occasion for Braggins to concern themselves with the customer's credit. The shop assistant concerned was Mrs Walker. She said: 'At the time of the transaction I considered the purchaser authorised to use the card. As far as I was concerned, the transaction was quite straightforward.' On this count the jury acquitted, probably because the jury were not sure that it was proved that by 5th December the appellant was already dishonest.

The appellant continued to use her card, without taking any step to reduce her debit balance at the bank. She had given up her job. She had no money save what she procured by use of her Barclaycard. By 13th December her debit balance as recorded in Barclaycard records had risen to £921·61. Before 15th December she knew that Barclays were trying to get in touch with her, so she changed her address without telling the bank where they could find her, and went on using the card, largely to buy for her lover whatever he wanted, and to provide herself and him with means of livelihood.

(3) Against this background she carried out the transaction the subject of the count 2 with which alone this appeal is concerned. She bought goods in Mothercare for £10·35. She produced her Barclaycard to Miss Rounding, the shop assistant. The 'floor limit' agreed between Barclays and Mothercare was £70, so there was no reason for Miss Rounding to concern herself with the appellant's credit standing with the bank. Miss Rounding checked the 'stop list'. The appellant's name was not on it. The appellant signed the voucher. Miss Rounding compared the signature with that on the card and delivered the goods. The voucher was duly dispatched by Mothercare to Barclays, and Barclays paid up, presumably less the commission that had been agreed. Miss Rounding described her state of mind. Her evidence about it is so important that we quote what she said in cross-examination and re-examination:

'If someone came into the shop and wanted to buy something for cash I wouldn't go through with the transaction unless they produced the cash. It is a company rule that management have to deal with Barclaycard transactions. The procedure already outlined is all part of the company policy. The company rules exist because of the company's agreement with Barclaycard. If I follow the rules because of the agreement it means that Barclaycard will pay my company anything up to £70. As far as I know it is a private agreement with Barclaycard and Mothercare. The floor limit of £70 is not something that Mothercare advertise. It is a confidential thing only known by management and staff that are authorised to accept Barclaycard at Mothercare. Provided I check everything including my stop list a Barclaycard voucher for under £70 is as good as cash. By looking at Barclaycard one cannot tell a person's own credit limit. I have no means of telling whether a person can afford the goods or not. If a Barclaycard matches up to all checks I don't give a second thought whether the person can afford the goods. As far as I am concerned once the transaction is done whatever dealing the customer has with Barclaycard is their own business. If someone comes to me and buys a pram for cash I am not concerned how they are going to pay the next week's housekeeping. I am only concerned that my store gets paid. I can only remember this particular transaction because someone came and asked me about it after it had taken place. All Barclaycard means to me is that if I check things properly we will in due course get the cash. I would not be popular with my shop if I asked people buying things if they could really afford them. It is not my business or the shop's business if someone goes into debt to buy goods from me. I cannot remember thinking on this occasion anything else other than it was a normal transaction as good as cash. I did all the things necessary to get paid by Barclaycard in this case. I would expect the shop to be paid after such a transaction. From my experience I or my shop is not any more worried about accepting a Barclaycard as accepting the same number of pound notes. If someone came into the shop and offered pound notes for a maternity garment there would be no problem with that transaction. If someone comes in and pays with a Barclaycard I scrutinise that card. I check to see if the card is date valid and also the two signatures. If for any reason there was something unusual I would not go through with the transaction. Provided everything was normal with the card the transaction would go through normally and I would hand over the goods. I would not worry what went on between the customer and Barclaycard.'

(4) Later on 15th December the appellant gave her Barclaycard to her mother, who returned it to the bank. The Barclaycard organisation had begun inquiries about her on 6th December. They never instituted any criminal proceedings. At some stage they made some arrangement with the appellant for repayment of her debt, and at the date of the committal proceedings she had repaid them by four instalments of £10, in respect of a debt then amounting to some £1,700. On 12th January she was arrested when she was a passenger in a car stolen by her lover. She then disclosed to the police that she was in trouble because she owed Barclays Bank £1,000. On that date and the next she told the police how she had been using the card, and signed two statements in which she admitted that she went on using the card although she knew that she should not have done so. She said that she was not using the card honestly, but that she wanted to pay the money back when she could get a job.

On these facts there was ample evidence that on 15th December she knew that she was acting dishonestly in using the card. The two questions raised by this appeal are whether on the facts there was evidence of a false representation to the shop assistant at Mothercare, and evidence on which the jury could find that Miss Rounding was induced to rely on the false representation.

In a cheque card transaction the bank authorises its customer to identify himself to a seller of goods or services by presenting a card stating the number of his account with the bank and displaying his signature. The bank offers to the seller a guarantee to pay a cheque drawn by the buyer, provided certain simple conditions of identification and comparison of signatures are fulfilled. It is clear that this court was troubled by the submission that there was no necessity, in order to give business efficacy to the transaction, that there should be any collateral representation implied on the part of the drawer of the cheque who presents the cheque and the card as to the state of his account with the bank or as to his authority to draw on that account. Further, this court was inclined to regard with favour the submission that there was no basis for an inference that any such representation operated on the mind of the recipient of the cheque as an inducement persuading him to accept it, because he relied exclusively on the bank's undertaking embodied in the cheque card. But this court held that it was bound by the earlier decision of the court in *R v Kovacs* [1974] 1 All ER 1236, [1974] 1 WLR 370. The House of Lords in *Metropolitan Police Comr v Charles* [1976] 3 All ER 112, [1977] AC 177 analysed the representations implied by the action of the purchaser. Their Lordships held that the purchaser acted as agent of the bank in presenting the cheque card, whereby the bank gave the guarantee to the seller that the cheques drawn by the purchaser would be met up to the limit of £30 on each cheque that he drew.

The House held that on drawing the cheque backed by the card the drawer impliedly represented that he was authorised by the bank to give the guarantee on the bank's behalf, as stated on the face of the cheque card, but that authority was conditional on the drawer's account with the bank being in credit or within his agreed borrowing limit. On the question of inducement the House held that the evidence of the representee could lead to an inference that he was induced by the deception because he believed the representation that the drawer of the cheque was then authorised as agent of the bank to use the card. The witness had made it clear that, although he regarded the state of the drawer's account with the bank as irrelevant, he would not have accepted the cheques if he had known that the accused was using his cheque book and cheque card 'in a way in which he was not allowed or entitled to use them'.

In our view, the ratio of the decision in *Metropolitan Police Comr v Charles* establishes as a matter of law that on the evidence the jury could find that the appellant had made a representation that she was authorised by the bank to use her credit card. The learned judge correctly explained to the jury the law on that implied representation, and the jury by their verdict held that she made the representation and that it was false. It is the question of inducement that gives rise to difficulty. Was there evidence on which the jury could find that the false representation induced Mothercare to sell her the goods on the credit given by the bank to the appellant and the guarantee given by the bank to Mothercare that the bank would pay the price of the goods?

There has been much discussion by distinguished academic criminal lawyers about the effect and implications of the speeches in the House of Lords in *Charles* on the inducement which has to be proved in a charge of an offence under s 16 of the Theft Act 1968 in a cheque card transaction. We have considered the powerful argument propounded by Professor J C Smith in his commentary on *Charles* ([1977] Crim LR 615), and in his textbook, The Law of Theft (4th Edn, 1979, para 158). In *Charles* the representee gave evidence that he accepted the cheque because he did not know that the accused had no authority to use the card. Professor Smith points out that that is by no means the same thing as a belief that he had authority to use it. So the argument runs that *Charles* is a special and unusual case because the ratio does not apply to what Professor Smith describes as 'the typical case' where the representee is indifferent whether the cardholder had authority or not. In that situation he argues that there is no inducement, because the only reason that the cheque is usually accepted is because the conditions on the cheque card were satisfied, and for no other reason. Professor Glanville Williams expresses the same view in his Textbook of Criminal Law (1978, pp 846–847):

> 'If the creditor is an ordinary mortal who simply goes by the words on the cheque card, then the court ought to hold that no offence is committed . . .'

He adds that no offence is likely to be committed against s 16 of the 1968 Act in a dishonest credit card transaction, because most sellers could not honestly say that they regarded the position between the buyer and the credit company as of any importance to them.

We are impressed by the analysis of the relation between the deception and obtaining made by Professor Griew in his textbook entitled The Theft Acts 1968 and 1978 (3rd Edn, 1978, pp 95–96 at paras 6-20 to 6-28). We quote paras 6-21 and 6-22.

> 'The effect of representation on P's mind.
>
> '6-21   (i) *What state of mind must the representation induce?* "To deceive is, I apprehend, to induce a man to believe that a thing is true which is false." This well-known statement by Buckley J. in *Re London and Globe Finance Corporation* ([1903] 1 Ch 728 at 732, [1900–3] All ER Rep 891 at 893) was cited with approval in *D.P.P. v. Ray* ([1973] 3 All ER 131, [1974] AC 370). It appears at first sight to state the obvious and to require no elaboration. Yet there is, on reflection, a good deal of uncertainty attaching to the notion of "believing that a thing is true"; and there has been no judicial consideration of what amounts to "believing" for this purpose. It is submitted that, if indeed "believing" is an appropriate word in this context, it should not be understood only in the sense of firmly accepting the truth of the

statement in question. The deception offences can hardly be limited to cases in which P is induced to hold a strong positive belief. P may be well-aware he does not know D, that there are rogues and liars abroad and that D may be one of them. He may act "on the strength" of D's assertion and in reliance upon it, but without any positive sense either believing or disbelieving it. If D is lying, P is surely "deceived" for the purpose of section 15. It may in fact be better to abandon the word "believe" and say that to deceive is to induce a man to act in reliance upon a false representation.

'6-22 It is further submitted that this view is consistent with the decision of the House of Lords in *Commissioner of Police for the Metropolis* v. *Charles* ([1976] 3 All ER 112, [1977] AC 177). P accepted D's cheques because they were backed by a cheque card. He would not have done so if he had known that D had no authority to use the card. D's conviction under section 16 of obtaining a pecuniary advantage by deception was upheld. It is quite clear from the evidence that P was at best agnostic on the question of D's right to use the cheque card. Their lordships, in asserting that P "believed" that D was authorised to use it, must, on the facts, have been using "belief" to stand for ignorance of the truth plus reliance on the representation of authority; firm acceptance of the truth of that representation was not in question. The situation in a cheque card case is peculiar in that P stands to lose nothing if D's assertion is untrue; the bank will certainly pay. But this is merely the particular reason why in such a case P is prepared to act without a positive belief in the representation. When in any other situation he acts in reliance on D's representation, he may or may not be aware that he is taking a risk as to its truth. It is submitted that in either case, if the representation is untrue, he is "deceived".'

In our view, this analysis is helpful and correct, and the opposite view expressed by Professor Smith and Professor Glanville Williams is explained by their different understanding of the kind of belief which has to be proved for the purpose of establishing that a false representation induced the action of the representee. The analysis of the problem by Professor Griew was made in relation to offences against s 15 of the 1968 Act, but it applies equally for the purposes of s 16 of that Act.

So we approach consideration of the evidence of Miss Rounding, and the way in which the learned judge presented the question of inducement to the jury in relation to count 2. In order to understand it, it is necessary to consider also the way in which the learned judge put the issue of inducement to the jury, by considering his summing up on count 1 as well as count 2. On 5th December the shop assistant at Braggins' shop had followed the same procedure as that described by Miss Rounding at Mothercare. We quote from the summing up:

'Is it dishonest conduct on the part of the defendant on any particular presentation in relation to the transactions involved? Did it affect the mind of the shop assistant who knew that she was going to get paid or that the shop would be paid in the end? The assistant said: "I would have no reservation in accepting a Barclaycard for payment." She would if the signature differed on the documents she has to complete in accordance with the procedure she has to follow, but she does not say to the customer: "Are you over your limit?" She does not even know what the limit is. A card presented in this way is accepted at its face value. You will have to consider whether that face value is a representation in itself that all the conditions, including the condition as to the limit allowance, in this case one of £200, are being complied with and acted on by the shop assistant, without that knowledge as to the cash limit imposed or the credit limit imposed, who allows the goods, in good faith, to be taken away with the knowledge that she will eventually be paid. The shop assistant said: "Over £30 we ring up and ask authorisation. The card itself, under £30, is evidence that that is what it is good for." You can buy goods up to £30, going through the proper procedure which the shop assistant has to go through. She checks that the signatures are the same. Mrs Walker said: "At the time of this transaction I considered the purchaser authorised to use the card. As far as I was concerned, the transaction was quite straightforward. If there had been anything untoward we would have got the manager, seized the card and telephoned Barclaycard." She later said: "Under the limit of £30 Barclaycard will pay regardless. The steps taken for transactions under £30 is to satisfy myself that the card is in date, the voucher is filled in correctly and the signatures are the same." She thought that the person was authorised, that is, she thought that she was the holder of this card. You will have to consider, members of the jury, was this part of the dishonesty in the defendant's mind? Was this presentation of the Barclaycard in that manner a deception on the store assistant where the defendant (and this is a matter for you to judge) may have the knowledge that she was well over her credit limit, nevertheless was getting the benefit of the use of the Barclaycard presented, although the store was paid eventually by Barclaycard, the debt still remains and has, therefore, been evaded as at that date?'

Having thus dealt with the question of the alleged inducement on count 1, the judge came to the evidence of Miss Rounding in relation to the count now under appeal:

'The transaction on 15th December, count 2, is in similar vein. I must remind you directly of the evidence of Miss Rounding. This was at Mothercare in Luton. She said: "If someone came into the shop and gave me a Barclaycard and I found the number to be on the 'stop list' I would not go through with the transaction. Provided the card appears to be valid I would normally proceed with the transaction." Is that a reliance by her, Miss Rounding of Mothercare, on the presentation of the card as being due authority within the limits as at that time as with count 1?'

It is to be observed that Mrs Walker had given evidence: 'At the time of the transaction I considered the purchaser authorised to use the card. As far as I was concerned, the transaction was quite straightforward.' This evidence may be compared with that of Miss Rounding, that provided the card appeared to be valid she would normally proceed with the transaction, and that having gone through the prescribed procedure she concluded the transaction. Miss Rounding made it perfectly plain that she regarded the state of the customer's credit with Barclays as nothing to do with her. It was not her business to inquire. And it appears from the evidence of Mr Fishwick, the witness from Barclays, that, if Miss Rounding had for some extraordinary reason rung up Barclays to inquire about the appellant's credit standing, the bank would have refused to disclose anything about it.

Using the test of belief suggested by Professor Griew, was it proved that Miss Rounding was induced by false representation in the sense that she acted 'on the strength' of its truth?

We would pay tribute to the lucidity with which the learned judge presented to the jury the law which the House of Lords had declared in relation to deception in a cheque card transaction. If that analysis can be applied to this credit card deception, the summing up is faultless. But, in our view, there is a relevant distinction between the situation described in *Metropolitan Police Comr v Charles* and the situation devised by Barclays Bank for transactions involving use of their credit cards. By their contract with the bank, Mothercare had bought from the bank the right to sell goods to Barclaycard holders without regard to the question whether the customer was complying with the terms of the contract between the customer and the bank. By her evidence Miss Rounding made it perfectly plain that she made no assumption about the appellant's credit standing at the bank. As she said: 'The company rules exist because of the company's agreement with Barclaycard.' The flaw in the logic is, in our view, demonstrated by the way in which the judge put the question of the inducement of Miss Rounding to the jury:

'Is that a reliance by her, Miss Rounding of Mothercare, on the presentation of the card as being due authority *within the limits as at that time* as with count 1?'

In our view, the evidence of Miss Rounding could not found a verdict that necessarily involved a finding of fact that Miss Rounding was induced by a false representation that the appellant's credit standing at the bank gave her authority to use the card.

For those reasons we allow the appeal.

The court has reached this conclusion with some hesitation and with reluctance. Hesitation, lest the court has fallen into the same error into which another Division of this court fell in *Metropolitan Police Comr v Charles*. Reluctance, because the dishonest deception of the appellant was manifest. If we are right, Barclays Bank has by its contractual arrangements opened a gateway to fraud, which may have for the bank such commercial advantages that the bank has no great incentive to make a change in their contracts. If this is the case, Parliament may decide to frame legislation specifically to deal with the credit card fraud.

Appeal allowed; conviction on count 2 quashed.

The court refused leave to appeal to the House of Lords but certified, under s 33(2) of the Criminal Appeal Act 1968, that the following point of law of general public importance was involved in the decision: whether, in view of the proved differences between a cheque card transaction and a credit card transaction, the court was right in distinguishing the case from that of Metropolitan Police Comr v Charles on the issue of inducement.

6th November. The Appeal Committee of the House of Lords allowed a petition by the Crown for leave to appeal.

Solicitors: *David Picton & Co*, St Albans.

Sepala Munasinghe Esq   Barrister.

Santiren Shipping Ltd v Unimarine SA
The Chrysovalandou-Dyo

QUEEN'S BENCH DIVISION
MOCATTA J
6th, 7th, 8th, 19th MAY 1980

Shipping – Time charterparty – Hire – Equitable set-off – Charterer's contractual right to deduct from hire claims for bunkers on redelivery and slow speed – Whether deduction required to be precise and accurate – Whether deduction of amount subsequently proved to be excessive constituting non-payment of hire – Whether reasonable assessment made in good faith sufficient – Whether absence of express finding in special case that deductions were reasonable and made in good faith invalidating deductions.

Shipping – Time charterparty – Hire – Lien for non-payment of hire – Exercise of lien – Charterparty entitling owner to exercise lien on cargo for amounts due under charter – Uncertainty whether cargo belonging to charterer or to third party – Bill of lading incorporating charterparty – Charterer ordering vessel to port of discharge – Owner threatening to withdraw vessel for non-payment of hire but ordering her to anchor off port of discharge – Owner purporting to exercise lien while vessel at anchorage – Whether lien properly exercised – Whether lien applicable to cargo – Whether denial of possession – Whether lien exercisable at anchorage or only at place of discharge in port.

By a time charter dated 5th July 1978 the charterers hired the owners' vessel to carry a cargo from the Philippines to the Persian Gulf. The charterparty included the following terms: (i) by cl 5 that hire was payable 15 days in advance at the specified rate but in respect of the last half month the 'approximate amount' of hire was payable and if it did not cover the actual hire up to redelivery the balance was payable day by day as it became due; (ii) that failure to make punctual and regular payment of hire entitled the owners to withdraw the vessel subject to giving the charterers notice of failure to pay and time to rectify the breach; (iii) that the captain of the vessel was to be under the charterers' orders and directions; (iv) by cl 18 that the owners were to have a lien on all cargoes and sub-freights for any amounts due under the charterparty; (v) by cl 56 that in the event of failure to comply with the speed warranty the charterers were to have the right to deduct from the hire due an amount 'equivalent to' time lost and/or the cost of any extra fuels consumed; and (vi) that the charterers were also to be entitled to deduct from the final payment of hire an amount in respect of the 'estimated' bunkers remaining on board on redelivery based on the prices per ton stated in the charterparty. The vessel was delivered on 18th July 1978. It loaded a cargo and proceeded to the Persian Gulf. The bill of lading in respect of the cargo incorporated the terms of the charter. On 22nd August the vessel anchored at Bandar Shahpur, the port of discharge originally nominated by the charterers. The charterers duly paid the hire up to 1st September 1978. On 1st September they nominated Dubai as the port of discharge and ordered the vessel to go there to discharge. The charterers also estimated that 13th September 1978 would be the redelivery date, and arranged for a remittance of hire to the owners of $11,864, being nine days' hire from 1st to 10th September less deductions for loss due to breach of the speed warranty and for the estimated bunkers on redelivery. The owners alleged that the deductions were improper, and they claimed hire to 13th September and threatened to withdraw the vessel unless the charterers paid additional hire. However, they allowed the vessel to proceed to Dubai and to anchor off Dubai anchorage, which she did on 3rd September, but instructed the master not to communicate with the charterers. Despite an injunction obtained by the charterers in the High Court restraining the owners from withdrawing the vessel, the owners ordered the vessel to remain at the anchorage off Dubai and stated that they were exercising their lien on the cargo under the terms of the charter. On 11th September they informed the charterers that they would continue to exercise the lien unless the charterers paid a further sum of hire. On 21st September the charterers paid further hire and the owners ordered the vessel into Dubai to discharge. On 1st October discharge was completed and the vessel was redelivered to the owners. The dispute regarding the amount of hire payable from 1st September went to arbitration. The owners contended that the vessel was on hire from 1st to 22nd September and that the hire paid on 1st September fell short of the hire due on that date, entitling them to exercise their lien under cl 18 of the charter. The charterers contended that in breach of the charter they were deprived of the use of the vessel from 3rd to 22nd September and that no further hire was payable on 1st September. The arbitrator found, inter alia, that on 1st September the charterers should have paid hire down to 13th September, the estimated redelivery date, so that there was a shortfall of three days' hire, that they had over-deducted in respect of the breach of speed warranty, although on previous occasions they had under-deducted for breach of warranty, and that there was a 'small shortfall' because the charterers had overestimated by $1,500 the amount payable for bunkers on redelivery. Accordingly, the arbitrator found that the charterers owed a further sum of hire on 1st September. He further held that the owners were entitled to exercise their lien over the cargo under the charter and that the lien was exercisable while the vessel was anchored off Dubai. The findings did not make it clear whether the cargo belonged to the charterers or to third parties. The award was stated as a special case raising for the court's decision the question of how much hire was payable for the period 1st to 22nd September. At the hearing of the special case the owners contended that further hire was payable on 1st September in respect of the over-deduction for breach of the speed warranty, the overestimate of the amount payable for bunkers on redelivery and the three days' shortfall of hire, and that they were entitled to exercise a lien over the cargo for non-payment of that hire. The charterers contended (i) that no further hire was payable on 1st September and (ii) that even if further hire was due on 1st September the owners were not entitled to exercise a lien under cl 18 because there was no demand for, or denial of possession of, the cargo and the lien was not exercisable until the vessel was at a discharging place in the port of discharge.

Held – (1) The amount set off under the equitable right in cl 56 of the charter to set off any loss caused by breach of the speed warranty against hire due did not have to be an accurate assessment of the loss but merely a reasonable assessment made in good faith, even though that might exceed what was subsequently proved to be an accurate assessment of the loss. Similarly, the amount deducted from hire for bunkers on redelivery did not have to be a precise estimate but merely a reasonable estimate made in good faith. Furthermore, the fact that the arbitrator had not made express findings that the deductions made by the charterers on 1st September were reasonable assessments made in good faith did not preclude the charterers from relying on the deductions as being valid under the charter since, having regard to the fact that the charterers had on previous occasions made an underestimate and to the fact that the expression of the arbitrator's findings did not suggest that he thought the charterers had acted unreasonably or in bad faith, the court was entitled to infer that the deductions were reasonable assessments made in good faith, and thereby to supplement the special case. Accordingly, the deductions made on 1st September, though overestimates, were valid deductions and did not constitute an underpayment of hire (see p 346 d to j, post); dicta of Lord Denning MR in *Federal Commerce and Navigation Ltd v Molena Alpha Inc, The Nanfri* [1978] 3 All ER at 1078 followed and of Goff LJ at 1083–1084 not followed.

(2) However, the shortfall of three days' hire, ie for 11th, 12th and 13th September, in the payment made on 1st September was an unjustified underpayment since the charterers had stated that 13th September was the estimated redelivery date, and payment of hire down to 10th September only could not be said to be an 'approximate' amount of the hire payable on 1st September for the last half month, within cl 5 of the charter (see p 346 j to p 347 a, post).

(3) The owners had properly exercised their lien under cl 18 of the charter because there had been a denial of possession of the cargo by virtue of the fact that, on 1st September, the charterers had ordered the master to go to Dubai to discharge there and subsequently the owners had ordered him merely to anchor off Dubai and not to communicate with the charterers. Furthermore, it was not a condition precedent to the exercise of the lien that the vessel should be at a discharging place in the port of discharge and accordingly the lien was exercisable at the anchorage off Dubai. Moreover, the lien applied to the cargo even if it did not belong to the charterers, since the bill of lading incorporated the terms of the charterparty (see p 347 g h, post); *Steelwood Carriers Inc of Monrovia, Liberia v Evimeria Compania Naviera SA of Panama, The Agios Giorgis* [1976] 2 Lloyd's Rep 192 and *International Bulk Carriers (Beirut) SARL v Evlogia Shipping Co SA, The Mihalios Xilas* [1978] 2 Lloyd's Rep 186 distinguished.

Notes

For the payment of hire under a time charter, see 35 Halsbury's Laws (3rd Edn) 281, para 423.

For shipowner's lien by express contract, see ibid 471–472, paras 671–672.

Cases referred to in judgment

Aegnoussiotis Shipping Corpn of Monrovia v A/S Kristian Jebsens Rederi of Bergen, The Aegnoussiotis [1977] 1 Lloyd's Rep 268, Digest (Cont Vol E) 546, 482b(i).

Federal Commerce and Navigation Ltd v Molena Alpha Inc, The Nanfri, The Benfri, The Lorfri [1978] 3 All ER 1066, [1978] QB 927, [1978] 3 WLR 309, CA; *affd in part* [1979] 1 All ER 307, [1979] AC 757, [1978] 3 WLR 991, [1979] 1 Lloyd's Rep 201, HL, Digest (Cont Vol E) 109, 3036a.

International Bulk Carriers (Beirut) SARL v Evlogia Shipping Co SA, The Mihalios Xilas [1978] 2 Lloyd's Rep 186, Digest (Cont Vol E) 547, 535a.

Steelwood Carriers Inc of Monrovia, Liberia v Evimeria Compania Naviera SA of Panama, The Agios Giorgis [1976] 2 Lloyds Rep 192, Digest (Cont Vol E) 546, 482c.

Universal Cargo Carriers Corpn v Citati (No 2) [1958] 2 All ER 563, [1958] 2 QB 254, [1958] 3 WLR 109, [1958] 2 Lloyd's Rep 17, CA, 3 Digest (Reissue) 187, 1133.

Award in form of special case

By a final award in the form of a special case stated by Mr Donald Davies as the sole arbitrator in a dispute between the charterers of the vessel Chrysovalandou-Dyo, Unimarine SA, and the owners of the vessel, Santiren Shipping Ltd, the arbitrator awarded, subject to the court's decision, that in respect of the period 1st to 22nd September 1978 the charterers owed the owners hire amounting to $37,053·69, and that the owners were entitled under the charterparty to exercise, and did exercise, a lien for that amount. The question of law raised in the special case for the court's decision was whether on the facts found by the arbitrator and on the true construction of the charterparty any and, if so, how much hire was payable by the charterers in respect of the period 1st to 22nd September 1978. The facts are set out in the judgment.

Bruce Reynolds for the charterers.
Angus Glennie for the owners.

Cur adv vult

19th May. **MOCATTA J** read the following judgment: This is a special case stated by Mr Donald Davies as sole arbitrator in a dispute between the charterers of a Cypriot vessel called the Chrysovalandou-Dyo and her owners, arising under a time charter dated 5th July 1978 on the New York Produce Exchange form. The contract was for a 'time charter trip' from the Philippines to the Persian Gulf. The vessel was delivered on 18th July 1978, loaded a cargo of cement at Iligan and proceeded to the Persian Gulf via Singapore. Her cargo was eventually discharged at Dubai, discharge being completed on 1st October, on which date she was redelivered.

Subject to the decision of the court, the arbitrator awarded that in respect of the period from 1st to 22nd September the owners were entitled to a further payment of $US40,210·60, but this figure, subject to the question of liability, has been corrected by agreement between the parties to $US37,053·69. The charterers contend that in breach of the charter they were deprived of the use of the vessel from 1415 hrs on 3rd September, when she anchored somewhere off Dubai, until 0610 hrs on 22nd September when she left the anchorage for the port. They argue that on the facts found and the true construction of various clauses in the charter nothing is due from them to the owners and that on balance a small sum is owing to them by the owners. The form of the special case is such that should I differ from the conclusion reached by the arbitrator the award must, in default of agreement between the parties, be remitted to him to make a final award in accordance with my decisions on the points at issue.

The case falls into two parts. The first concerns whether after a payment by the charterers on 1st September there was an amount due to the owners under the charter, and the second whether, if there was, the owners were entitled under cl 18 to and did exercise a lien for such amount.

In the preamble to the charter the vessel was described as being capable at all times of steaming, fully laden, under good weather conditions at about 13½ knots on a consumption of about 20 tons of fuel oil plus 2 tons of gas oil. This speed warranty was breached both on the first leg of the voyage, namely from Iligan to Singapore, and on the second, from Singapore to Bandar Shahpur, at the head of the Persian Gulf, where she anchored on 22nd August. It seems as if the charterers had intended that she should discharge there, but on 1st September the charterers ordered her to Dubai, near the entrance to the Gulf, to discharge. Clause 56 of the charter provided that in the event of failure to comply with the speed warranty the charterers should have the right to deduct from hire an amount equivalent to the time lost and/or the cost of any extra fuels consumed.

Another relevant clause about permissible deductions from hire was cl 31, which provided:

'Owners to take over and pay for bunkers remaining on board at time of redelivery but sufficient to reach nearest bunkering port ... Charterers have the right to deduct from final full hire payment estimated bunkers on redelivery.'

The prices per ton of fuel and gas oil were then stated.

Clause 4 provided that hire should be paid at the rate of $US2,700 daily every 15 days on and from the date of delivery and at the same rate until the hour of her redelivery, whilst cl 5, after stating that payment of hire was to be made in London every 15 days in advance, provided that for the last half month or part of the same the approximate amount of hire should be paid and should that not cover the actual time, hire should 'be paid for the balance day by day, as it becomes due'. The clause concluded that failing the punctual and regular payment of the hire the owners should be at liberty to withdraw the vessel from the service of the charterers. This right of withdrawal was, however, subject to cl 33 which provided that the owners should give notice of failure by the charterers to pay hire and that the owners should not be entitled to withdraw the vessel unless and until the charterers failed to rectify the breach within two working banking days.

Finally I will set out two short but very relevant extracts from cll 8 and 18. The first is: 'The Captain (although appointed by the Owners), shall be under the orders and directions of the Charterers as regards employment and agency . . .' The second is: 'That the Owners shall have a lien upon all cargoes, and all sub-freights for any amounts due under this Charter . . .'

The first two payments of hire in advance were duly made, but two days before the third payment was due on 17th August the charterers informed the owners that on the basis that the port of discharge, though not settled, would be Bahrain, and the estimated date of delivery 29th August, they calculated that no further payment of hire would be due after allowing for estimated bunkers on redelivery and $7,934·59 as a deduction for the vessel's slow speed from Iligan to Singapore. It was found in the special case that in fact the charterers were entitled to the larger deduction of $10,415·96 in respect of the slow speed on the first leg of the voyage from Iligan.

I have already stated that the vessel was in fact first ordered to Bandar Shahpur where she anchored on 22nd August and remained waiting orders. On 29th August the charterers arranged a hire remittance to cover 15 days from 17th August to 1st September less the speed claim already mentioned and an estimate in respect of bunkers on redelivery. There was what is described as a small shortfall in this payment as the charterers made an overestimate of the allowance for bunkers on redelivery, which did not take place until 1st October, of $1,500. But the charterers, in view of the size of the speed claim as later assessed, could have deducted a further $2,481·37 in respect thereof.

On 31st August the owners reminded the charterers that a further 15 days' hire was due on the next day. The charterers replied by nominating Dubai as the port of discharge with a redelivery date of 13th September and arranged a remittance of $11,864·67 based on hire for nine days (1st to 10th September) less $11,220·33 in respect of a speed claim for the passage from Singapore to Bandar Shahpur.

It was found that the charterers were entitled to deduct only $6,969·69 for this speed claim and so over-deducted on 1st September $4,250·64. It was also found that they should have paid hire for the period until 13th September so that there was a shortfall of three days' hire ($8,100) in this respect.

In para 11 of the special case it was found that there was a minimum shortfall of hire on 1st September amounting to $11,369·27 made up by $8,100 for three days' hire, plus $4,250·64 for the excess of speed claim, plus $1,500 overestimate for bunkers on redelivery, less $2,481·37.

Various other communications passed on 1st September. The owners complained about alleged improper deductions from hire and proposed that it should be paid to 13th September. Unless there were additional payments the owners warned that they would not order the vessel to Dubai. In the afternoon the charterers ordered the master to proceed to Dubai. In the evening of 1st September the owners advised the charterers that the vessel was being withdrawn from the charterers, but early on 2nd September they ordered the master to proceed to Dubai, which he did shortly thereafter, anchoring off Dubai at 1415 hrs on 3rd September. However, the master made no communication with the charterers, on the owners' instructions, until 9th September, save for a short communication on 2nd September that he was proceeding to anchor off Dubai anchorage. Finally on the evening of 1st September the owners advised the charterers that their vessel was being withdrawn.

Telex altercations followed between the parties, the owners threatening to sell the cargo, whilst the charterers stated that the vessel was off-hire since the evening of 1st September. On 6th September the charterers obtained an ex parte injunction from the High Court restraining the owners from withdrawing the vessel from the service of the charterers, which was renewed on 8th September.

On 9th September the charterers informed the master of the terms of the injunction and instructed him to proceed to Dubai for discharge. The owners, however, ordered the vessel to remain at the same anchorage since a lien was being exercised on the cargo under cl 18 of the charter. The owners on 11th September telexed to the charterers that a sum of $54,935·33 was due to them and that unless the charterers paid or secured this the lien would continue to be exercised on the cargo.

What is described as a state of deadlock continued until 21st September when, after a payment of nearly $15,000 to the owners, the vessel was ordered to proceed into Dubai for discharge. She left the anchorage on 0610 hrs on 21st September, completed discharge on 1st October and was redelivered later on that day.

The first question to be decided is whether on 1st September there was, after the payment of $11,864·67 made on that day, an amount due from the charterers. If there was, then subject to the giving of the necessary notice under cl 33 and but for the High Court injunction, the owners would have been entitled to withdraw the vessel. Similarly if money was due, the provisions of cl 18 as to a lien, on which the owners rely, would be applicable.

There were three headings under which the owners submitted that there was money due on 1st September, namely (i) the over-deduction in respect of the speed warranty, amounting to $1,269·27, namely the over-deduction made in respect of the voyage from Singapore to Bandar Shahpur, less the remaining credit in respect of the under-deduction made in respect of the first leg of the voyage, (ii) the overestimate of the amount payable in respect of bunkers on redelivery of $1,500, and (iii) the alleged shortfall of three days' hire amounting to $8,100.

As regards heading (i), counsel for the charterers accepted that he could not rely on cl 56 as negativing the over-deduction in respect of the speed warranty, since the charterers had deducted slightly more than that clause entitled them to do. However, he submitted on the authority of *Federal Commerce and Navigation Ltd v Molena Alpha Inc, The Nanfri* [1978] 3 All ER 1066, [1978] QB 927, in the Court of Appeal, that he had a right of equitable set-off by reducing hire pro tanto provided that the amount deducted was an honest and reasonable assessment. Whilst cl 56 gave the right to deduct it is clear that a correct deduction depends on a close examination of log-books and, if necessary, weather reports, as the full text of that clause indicates. Further, in para 8 of the special case mention is made of the speed claim being 'later assessed', that is to say at some time after 15th and 29th August. Apart from what was said in *The Nanfri*, it would seem prima facie very difficult and distinctly hazardous, because of the risk of the vessel being withdrawn if an over-deduction were made, to make use of the right to deduct given by cl 56 until considerably after the passage of the vessel in question.

In *The Nanfri*, which concerned a six-year time charter, with hire payable half monthly in advance, provision was made by cl 11 for deductions from hire in respect of speed reduction due to defect or breakdown in hull, machinery or equipment. The deductions were to be for time so lost and the cost of any extra fuel consumed. The majority of the Court of Appeal held that the doctrine of equitable set-off applied to hire due under a time charter, which was thus distinguished from freight under a voyage charter. Lord Denning MR said ([1978] 3 All ER 1066 at 1078, [1978] QB 927 at 975):

> 'If the charterer quantifies his loss by a reasonable assessment made in good faith, and deducts the sum quantified, then he is not in default. The shipowner cannot

withdraw his vessel on account of non-payment of hire nor hold him guilty at that
point of any breach of contract. If it subsequently turns out that he has deducted
too much, the shipowner can of course recover the balance. But that is all.'

Goff LJ agreed that the defence of equitable set-off was available against a claim for time
charter hire, though he differed from Lord Denning MR on one aspect of the matter. He
said, referring to equitable set-off ([1978] 3 All ER 1066 at 1083–1084, [1978] QB 927 at
982):

> '... this defence by its nature is such that it must be open to the charterer to set
> it up before ascertainment, not merely as a means of preventing the owner obtaining
> judgment or, at any rate, execution, but also as an immediate answer to his liability
> to pay hire otherwise due.'

He then said, differing from Lord Denning MR:

> 'Of course he acts at his peril and, if he is wrong, he will enable the owner to
> determine the charterparty if he is willing for his part to act at his peril the other
> way.'

I accordingly have to decide as between the contrasting opinions of Lord Denning MR
and Goff LJ whether the equitable set-off, in order to be valid, must be an accurate figure
or whether it is sufficient if the set-off is 'a reasonable assessment made in good faith',
though in excess of what can ultimately be justified on subsequent information and an
unhurried scrutiny of the full facts as later known. Kerr J clearly favoured Lord Denning
MR's view; it is what he called 'the half-way position' (see [1978] QB 927 at 948). With
respect to the contrary view taken by Goff LJ, I would follow Lord Denning MR's view,
which seems to me to be in accord with what commercial considerations demand. The
time charter contains a withdrawal clause applying in the event of failure to pay punctual
and regular payment of hire, the stringency of which is only lessened by the notice
provision of cl 33. At the same time by cl 35 it permits the charterers to deduct owners'
disbursements from hire against presentation of vouchers or telexed breakdown of
estimated disbursements and cl 56 deals with deductions from hire in respect of the
speed warranty. These two entitlements would be of little value if, despite being made
reasonably and in good faith, they could not be relied on if by error they were too large.

Counsel for the owners then submitted that counsel for the charterers could not rely
on *The Nanfri* because there were no express findings in the special case that the
deductions for (i) and (ii) were reasonable assessments made bona fide. This is true, but
the court is entitled to draw an inevitable inference of fact to supplement a special case
if the circumstances so justify: see Russell on Arbitration (19th Edn, 1979, p 304) and
Universal Cargo Carriers Corpn v Citati (No 2) [1958] 2 All ER 563 at 565–566, [1958] 2 QB
254 at 262–263. Here, in para 5 of the award the charterers were found to have made a
smaller deduction in respect of slow speed than they were entitled to, and again in para
8 it is found that they could on 29th August have deducted a further sum. It is true that
they over-deducted for slow speed in respect of the payment on 1st September, but the
inferences to be drawn from these findings to my mind indicate reasonable and bona fide
behaviour. Similarly when one looks at the way in which the special case deals with the
$1,500 in respect of bunkers on redelivery one is led to the same conclusion. Firstly cl 31
of the charter provided that the charterers were to have the right to deduct the 'estimated'
bunkers on redelivery at the prices set out. It would be difficult to make a precise
estimate. Secondly, in para 8 of the award it is said that there was 'a small shortfall in that
the Charterers over estimated the bunkers on redelivery'. This language is quite
inconsistent with behaviour which was thought unreasonable or not in good faith.

There remains the shortfall of three days' hire amounting to $8,100, being the hire
due for 11th, 12th and 13th September, the latter being the estimated date of
redelivery. Clause 5 provided that the hire should be made every 15 days in advance 'and
for the last half month or part of same the approximate amount of hire', with the extra
provision that should this not cover the actual time used, hire was to be paid for the

balance day by day. Counsel for the charterers submitted that 'approximate' permitted a conservative estimate to be supplemented as necessary by daily 'topping up' until redelivery. I cannot accept this argument. The charterers themselves had on 31st August nominated Dubai with a redelivery date of 13th September. I do not think payment down to and including 10th September is, in those circumstances, the approximate amount of hire due down to and including 13th September. Accordingly I am of the opinion that on 1st September there was an underpayment of hire, which the charterers cannot justify or defend.

I next turn to the question whether the owners can justify their conduct, having been enjoined by order of the High Court from withdrawing their vessel, on the grounds that they were exercising a lien on the cargo under cl 18 of the charter. It is quite clear from *Steelwood Carriers Inc of Monrovia v Evimeria Compania Naviera SA, The Agios Giorgis* [1976] 2 Lloyd's Rep 192, and *Aegnoussiotis Shipping Corpn v A/S Kristian Jebsens Rederei, The Aegnoussiotis* [1977] 1 Lloyd's Rep 268, that a temporary withdrawal of the vessel was not justified under the withdrawal clause, cl 5. The crucial question is whether the owners' conduct was consistent with the proper exercise of a lien on cargo under the words in cl 18: 'That the Owners shall have a lien upon all cargoes, and all sub-freights for any amounts due under this Charter . . .' The arbitrator has found that the owners were entitled to exercise a lien on the cargo and that such a lien can be exercised when a vessel is lying off the port of discharge. He also found that there was no exercising of a lien, expressly or by way of inference, until the charterers made application for an injunction. He has allowed three days as a period for off-hire or damages between 3rd and 6th September, but otherwise held that the vessel was on hire for the whole period from 1st to 22nd September.

On this somewhat difficult question of lien, counsel drew my attention to the different views expressed by Donaldson J in *The Aegnoussiotis* [1977] 1 Lloyd's Rep 268 at 276, and by myself in the earlier case of *The Agios Giorgis* [1976] 2 Lloyd's Rep 192 at 204. In each of those cases, as in the present one, cl 18 provided 'That the Owners shall have a lien upon all cargoes, and all sub-freights for any amounts due under this Charter . . .' This clause differs from the comparable clause in the Baltime form of time charter where there is a qualification in relation to the lien to the effect that the shipowner is only vested with it over cargo belonging to the time charterer. I took the view in *The Agios Giorgis* that cl 18 could not give the owners the right to detain cargo not belonging to the charterers and on which no freight was owing to the owners. It is uncertain on the findings in the present case whether the cargo did belong to the charterers. However I did remark in *The Agios Giorgis* that there was no finding that the bills of lading contained any clause rendering the cargo shipped under them subject to the charterparty lien. There is, however, a finding that the bill of lading covering the goods in question incorporated the terms and conditions of the charterparty and the only charterparty which these words could have incorporated was the one under the provisions of which the dispute arose, the arbitration was held and the special case was stated. I consider the clause in the bill of lading mentioned differentiates the *Agios Giorgis* case and my reasoning in it from the present case. Accordingly if the lien was on the facts properly exercised, it applied to the cargo here by reason of the incorporating clause in the bill of lading and it is unnecessary to come to a conclusion on the different reasoning in the two cases cited.

Was the lien properly exercised? A lien operates as a defence available to one in possession of a claimant's goods who is entitled at common law or by contract to retain possession until he is paid what he is owed. Here the owners rely on their contractual right to a lien given by cl 18.

Counsel for the charterers argued that under cl 8 the master was under the orders and direction of the charterers as regards employment, that he was ordered on 31st August or 1st September to go to Dubai to discharge and that the most that he did was to proceed down the Persian Gulf and anchor off Dubai anchorage on 2nd September. The owners do not seem to have notified the charterers that they were exercising a lien until 11th September. Counsel for the charterers submitted that this was just a stratagem adopted to avoid the effect of the injunction granted by the High Court preventing the withdrawal of the vessel. He cited a passage from the judgment of Donaldson J in *International Bulk Carriers (Beirut) SARL v Evlogia Shipping Co SA, The Mihalios Xilas* [1978] 2 Lloyd's Rep 186, where a vessel that had loaded at Casablanca put into Augusta for bunkers and remained there for three days because the owners were in default in not having paid a month's hire in escrow or for fuel on board on delivery under the time charter. The owners' defence to the charterers' claim for hire or damages for the ship's delay in Augusta was that of lien. Donaldson J said (at 191):

> 'I do not think that a shipowner can usually be said to be exercising a lien on cargo simply by refusing to carry it further. The essence of the exercise of a lien is the denial of possession of the cargo to someone who wants it. No one wanted the cargo in Augusta and the owners were not denying possession of it to anyone.'

Counsel for the charterers further submitted that for a lien to be exercised there must be a demand for possession and that a shipowner's lien could not be exercised unless the vessel was at a discharging spot, whether wharf or buoy.

Whilst counsel for the charterers presented his argument very attractively, he failed to convince me that he was right on the facts of this case. The owners had been told to go to Dubai to discharge, which differentiates the case from *The Mihalios Xilas*. No authority was cited for the proposition that a vessel had to be at a discharging spot in a port as a condition precedent to the exercise of a lien. To require this might involve unnecessary expense and in certain cases cause congestion in the port. I think counsel for the owners was right in his submission that the requirements for which counsel for the charterers argued before a lien could be exercised would seriously limit the commercial value of a lien on cargo granted by a clause in a charter. The argument that counsel for the charterers advanced that demand for possession was necessary before delivery could justifiably be refused on the basis of a lien was met by the fact that the master had been ordered to Dubai to discharge.

In the result I uphold the conclusions reached by the arbitrator in relation to the lien. The precise question of law for the decision of the court is:

> 'Whether on the facts found and on the true construction of the Charterparty:— Any, and if so, how much hire is payable by the Charterers in respect of all, or any of, the period from September 1 to September 22.'

I was not requested or expected by either counsel to do the necessary arithmetic. The arbitrator has disallowed hire for three days between 3rd and 6th September since he found there was no exercising of a lien, expressly or by way of inference, until the charterers applied for their injunction on 6th September, by which time the charterers knew, or should reasonably have known, that the owners were not willing to discharge the cargo. Subject to this deduction, which was not challenged, I agree with the arbitrator that the vessel was on hire from 1st to 22nd September. I accordingly uphold the award, subject to the correction of the figures in para 2, as agreed by counsel, from $40,210·00 to $37,053·69.

Award, subject to agreed correction, upheld.

Solicitors: *Holman, Fenwick & William* (for the owners); *Lloyd, Denby, Neal, Jones & Maynard* (for the charterers).

K Mydeen Esq   Barrister.

Chappell and another v Mehta

COURT OF APPEAL, CIVIL DIVISION
LAWTON, TEMPLEMAN AND O'CONNOR LJJ
4th, 5th NOVEMBER 1980

Costs – Taxation – Solicitor – Withdrawal and redelivery of bill – Jurisdiction of court to permit – Six bills delivered by solicitor – Counsel's fees not included in bills – Bills disputed by client – Bills taxed and final certificate issued – Whether court should allow solicitor to withdraw bills and issue new bills including counsel's fees.

The defendant was a party to five actions which were due to be heard in January 1979. In December 1978 he retained the plaintiff firm of solicitors to act for him and instructed them to brief counsel. Because the solicitors would become personally liable for counsel's fees once the brief was delivered and the fees agreed, they obtained from the defendant a substantial sum of money on account of counsel's fees. Counsel subsequently advised the defendant that he had no prospect of success in his litigation. As a result of that advice the defendant decided to settle three of the actions and fight the other two, which he lost. The defendant expressed dissatisfaction with counsel to the solicitors and instructed them not to pay counsel's fees. The defendant then instructed them to take steps to see whether there was any prospect of a successful appeal and the solicitors instructed different counsel to advise. Thereafter the solicitors delivered six bills of costs to the defendant, who disputed them. None of the bills included counsel's fees. In due course the costs were taxed and a final certificate was issued by the master. On the certificate the sums which the defendant had paid to the solicitors on account of counsel's fees were shown as being due to the defendant, since they had not been paid. The solicitors then realised that they had not dealt with counsel's fees and the work done in respect of the defendant's instructions about an appeal and they therefore applied to the court by summons for liberty to withdraw their six bills and deliver a new bill. The judge granted them leave and ordered that the certificate of taxation should be set aside. The defendant appealed, contending that the court had no jurisdiction to allow a solicitor to withdraw a taxed bill of costs and present a new bill.

Held – Although as a general rule a solicitor was required to deliver a bill of costs which was final, and in the interests of his client would not be allowed to amend a bill once it was delivered, if there were special circumstances the court had jurisdiction to allow a solicitor to withdraw a bill. Since there was no evidence that the solicitors had been negligent or had tried to deceive the court and since it would be unjust if the court were to allow the defendant to assert that the solicitors were responsible for counsel's fees and that he was not, it was clearly a case where it was appropriate for the court to allow the solicitors to withdraw the bills and present a new one. The appeal would accordingly be dismissed (see p 351 *h* to p 352 *c* and *eg*, post).

Re a Solicitor, re Taxation of Costs [1943] 1 All ER 157 applied.

Notes

For withdrawal of a bill of costs delivered by a solicitor to his client and the substitution of a new bill, see 36 Halsbury's Laws (3rd Edn) 136, para 85, and for cases on the subject, see 43 Digest (Repl) 174–177, *1619–1648*.

Cases referred to in judgments

Solicitor, Re a, re Taxation of Costs [1943] 1 All ER 157, [1943] Ch 48, 112 LJ Ch 73, 168 LT 127, 43 Digest (Repl) 176, *1640*.
Thomas (Peter) & Co v Smith (2nd May 1932, unreported), CA.

Interlocutory appeal

The defendant, Jal Pirojsha Mehta, appealed against the judgment of his Honour Judge Hawser QC sitting as a judge of the High Court on 1st November 1979 whereby he ordered (i) that the certificates of taxation issued by Master Berkeley on 20th June 1979 pursuant to an order of Master Creightmore made on 28th March 1979 should be set aside and (ii) that the plaintiffs, Denis Chappell and Philip Englefield, carrying on practice as Boyce, Evans & Sheppard, solicitors, should have leave to withdraw the bills of costs dated 18th and 28th December 1978, 4th, 15th and 23rd January and 14th February 1979 delivered by them to the defendant in relation to work done by the plaintiffs as solicitors for the defendant in connection with certain High Court actions brought by the defendant. The facts are set out in the judgment of Lawton LJ.

The defendant appeared in person.
Robert Owen for the plaintiffs.

LAWTON LJ. This is an appeal by the defendant to an originating summons, which was taken out by a firm of solicitors, the partners of whom are the plaintiffs. As a result of that originating summons by a reserved judgment delivered on 1st November 1979 his Honour Judge Hawser QC ordered that the certificate of taxation issued by Master Berkeley and dated 20th June 1979 pursuant to an order of Master Creightmore made on 28th March 1979 in certain proceedings should be set aside and that the plaintiffs should have leave to withdraw bills of costs delivered by them to the defendant which were dated 18th and 28th December 1978, 4th, 15th and 23rd January and 14th February 1979. Those bills related to work done by the plaintiffs as solicitors for the defendant in connection with certain actions brought by the defendant in the High Court of Justice. The order went on to provide that the plaintiffs within seven days should deliver a new bill of costs to cover all matters which they desired to have dealt with; and it was also ordered that within 28 days thereafter a new bill of costs should be referred to a taxing master for taxation under the Solicitors Act 1974. There was no order as to costs.

The problem in this appeal, which has been obscured by the defendant's unfamiliarity with the law, can be stated shortly. When solicitors deliver bills of costs which do not cover all the work they have done and all disbursements they have made, and those bills of costs are taxed, can they subsequently apply to the court for leave to withdraw those bills and deliver a new bill which covers all the work they have done and all the disbursements which they have made?

The defendant was a party to no less than five actions which were due to be heard in January 1979. In December 1978 he decided to change his solicitors, and he retained the plaintiff firm. He is a man not without experience of litigation, and he seems to have come to some kind of arrangement with the plaintiffs whereby they were to deliver him weekly bills showing what work they had done.

As the actions were due to be tried in January 1979, in December 1978 it was clearly necessary for counsel to be instructed as quickly as possible. The defendant had his own ideas who junior counsel should be, and he also decided that leading counsel should be briefed. The solicitors sensibly pointed out that if they were going to brief counsel for the purposes of this litigation they would have to be put in funds, because following the usual practice of the legal profession once they delivered briefs to counsel and had agreed what counsel's fees would be they themselves would become personally liable to pay the fees. The defendant would have known this. Before the litigation started he handed over to the solicitors a substantial sum of money on account of counsel's fees; leading counsel's brief fee had been fixed at £1,000 and junior counsel's fee at £500. The defendant had consultations and conferences with counsel. It appears from the judgment of Judge Hawser that counsel advised him that he had no prospects of success in his litigation. No doubt as a result of that advice, he decided to settle three of the actions and to fight two of them. Counsel's advice turned out to be correct, because he lost the two actions.

Perhaps because of his lack of success, but there may have been other reasons with which we are not concerned, he expressed to the solicitors dissatisfaction with counsel. He had a number of complaints against them which the solicitors were urged to bring to the attention of the Professional Conduct Committee of the Bar Council. The solicitors did not share his views about counsel, according to Judge Hawser's finding, and nothing was done. The defendant's complaints about counsel are not a matter with which we are concerned in any way at all. Because of his dissatisfaction with counsel and the results of the litigation, by February 1979 the defendant had come to the conclusion that he did not want to pay counsel. He gave the solicitors instructions to that effect, overlooking the fact that by this time, on his instructions, the solicitors had incurred liabilities which they had personally to discharge to counsel. About the same time he requested the solicitors to do no more work except on his specific instructions. But what in fact happened was that having been dissatisfied with the results of his litigation he instructed the solicitors to take steps to see whether there was any prospect of a successful appeal. The solicitors did as they were told, and they briefed different counsel to advise the defendant. For some reason the defendant seems to have taken the view that because there was not a specific agreement that they should do this work and all that had happened was that he had told them to do it he was not liable to pay them for what they had done.

The next relevant events were as follows. The solicitors had delivered six bills of costs. The defendant disputed them. The result was that they had to go to taxation. The matter first came before Master Creightmore because the solicitors took the point, which subsequently turned out to be a bad one, that they had agreed a fixed fee of so many pounds per hour for work done, and in those circumstances under the Solicitors Act 1974 they were entitled to be paid the fixed fee that they had agreed and there was no room for taxation of their bill. That did not meet with Master Creightmore's approval, and the result was he ordered that the matter should be referred to Master Berkeley for taxation, and in due course these six bills were taxed. The final certificate was drawn on 20th June 1979. None of these bills related to counsel's fees. After proceedings for taxation had started the plaintiffs woke up to the fact that they had to deal with counsel's fees and with the work they had done in respect of the defendant's instructions about a possible appeal. As a result they delivered a new bill which was dated 7th June 1979. In that bill they asked to be paid a comparatively modest sum for the work they had done advising about an appeal, namely £96·25, but they also asked to be paid a sum of £2,716·20 in respect of the fees due to counsel in the litigation, and fees paid to another member of the Bar in respect of the appeal. The defendant took up the attitude that, as they had already presented six bills and Master Creightmore had made an order that those six bills should be taxed, the plaintiffs had no right to deliver any other bills. On 20th June 1979 Master Berkeley taxed the six bills and issued a final certificate. As a result of that certificate the defendant issued a writ of fi fa which was executed in the solicitors' offices, because on the certificate the sums which he had paid to the solicitors on account of counsel's fees had inevitably, as they had not been paid, been shown as being due to the defendant. This goaded the plaintiffs into action, and there were complicated proceedings before first Master Jacob and then before Judge Hawser as to what the legal position was.

In general solicitors should deliver bills which are final bills, and they are not usually allowed to amend their bills once they have delivered them. This is in the interests of the clients, and the courts have always taken a strict view about solicitors' responsibilities to their clients. But there is clearly jurisdiction for the court in special circumstances to allow solicitors to withdraw their bills. It is for the court to decide whether special circumstances arise. If the solicitors have acted honestly then maybe they should be allowed to have their original bills withdrawn.

In this case the defendant has alleged that the solicitors acted negligently and he said they tried to deceive the court, for which there is not a shred of evidence. In fact the evidence all goes the other way. From first to last they have revealed to the court at all stages what the situation was. If there is any doubt about the jurisdiction of the court it is dissipated by the judgment of Uthwatt J in *Re a Solicitor* [1943] 1 All ER 157, [1943] Ch 48. The learned judge there said ([1943] Ch 48 at 49; cf [1943] 1 All ER 157 at 158):

> '... there is undoubtedly jurisdiction in the court to allow a solicitor to withdraw a bill and to deliver a fresh bill. There are old authorities to that effect, and recently the Court of Appeal, in *Peter Thomas & Co. v. Smith* (unreported, 2nd May 1932), exercised that power in circumstances which, so far as can be gathered from the only available material, were exceedingly like those of the present case.'

Uthwatt J went on to stress that what should be done would depend on the facts of each case.

Now the facts of this case were very special indeed. The defendant had put the solicitors in funds to brief counsel; they had briefed counsel; they had incurred liabilities to counsel; and it would be most unjust if the court now should allow the defendant to say that he was not to be responsible for counsel's fees and the solicitors were. If there ever was a case where it was appropriate for the court to allow a solicitor to withdraw bills of costs and present a new bill this is it.

The defendant has taken the point that up to the present time as far as we know and he knows the solicitors still have not paid counsel's fees. Assuming that to be so it makes no difference, because all that Judge Hawser ordered was that they should deliver a new bill and that it should be taxed within 28 days. When it is taxed the plaintiffs will have to comply with the normal rules, and as I understand them they will not be allowed to charge the defendant in respect of counsels' fees unless they can show that they have paid their fees; and that is what they will have to do. It is not a matter which justifies this court in interfering with the discretion of Judge Hawser. It follows therefore that there is nothing in this appeal; it is a pity that it was ever brought. For my part I readily understand why the learned judge adjudged that there should be no costs to the defendant, even though on one part of the case, namely the plaintiffs' submission that Master Creightmore was wrong in adjudging that the first set of bills could be taxed, failed. This undoubtedly was a case where the defendant was taking advantage of what he thought was a technicality which would enable him to avoid having to pay counsel and leaving the solicitors to do it.

Finally for my part I would like to say that it is manifest from the reserved judgment which Judge Hawser delivered that he took great care over this case. He went into it in depth, and for my part I found it was a most helpful judgment for which I am personally very grateful indeed.

I would dismiss this appeal.

TEMPLEMAN LJ. I agree.

O'CONNOR LJ. I agree.

Appeal dismissed. The sum of £2,888 in court to be paid out to the plaintiffs on their undertaking to discharge counsel's fees.

Solicitors: *Boyce, Evans & Sheppard* (for the plaintiffs).

                                          Mary Rose Plummer   Barrister.

Allen v Gulf Oil Refining Ltd

HOUSE OF LORDS

LORD WILBERFORCE, LORD DIPLOCK, LORD EDMUND-DAVIES, LORD KEITH OF KINKEL AND LORD ROSKILL

1st, 2nd, 3rd DECEMBER 1980, 29th JANUARY 1981

Nuisance – Defence – Statutory authority – Action for damages for nuisance arising out of construction and operation of oil refinery – Statute authorising oil company to acquire land compulsorily for construction of oil refinery – Oil company authorised to construct certain works and to construct and use certain subsidiary works in connection with refinery – Whether oil company able to rely on defence of statutory authority in action for nuisance – Gulf Oil Refining Act 1965 (c xxiv), ss 5, 15, 16.

By the Gulf Oil Refining Act 1965, an oil company ('Gulf Oil') were authorised to construct certain works in connection with an oil refinery they intended to establish at Milford Haven. The preamble to the Act recited that 'it is essential that further facilities for the importation of crude oil and petroleum products and for their refinement should be made available', and s 5 gave Gulf Oil power to acquire compulsorily land near Milford Haven 'for the purposes of [works authorised by s 15 of the Act] or for the construction of a refinery'. Section 15 authorised the construction of certain jetties and a branch railway line outside the boundary of the land. Section 16(1) authorised Gulf Oil to 'construct . . . and use' for the purposes of or in connection with the works authorised by s 15 certain subsidiary works, including, inter alia, railways, sidings etc. Section 16(3) provided for Gulf Oil to make reasonable compensation for any damage caused by the exercise of the power conferred by s 16(1). In 1967 Gulf Oil built a large oil refinery on the land referred to in the Act and which they had compulsorily acquired for the purpose, and constructed various jetties and railways in connection with it. The plaintiff, who lived in the near neighbourhood of the refinery, brought an action for damages or compensation against Gulf Oil, alleging that the operation of the refinery was a nuisance or alternatively that Gulf Oil were guilty of negligence in the method of construction and operation of the refinery. Gulf Oil resisted the claim by a plea of statutory authority. On a preliminary issue the judge ordered that Gulf Oil could rely on the 1965 Act as having authorised the construction and operation of the oil refinery. The plaintiff appealed to the Court of Appeal ([1979] 3 All ER 1008) which reversed the judge's decision. Gulf Oil appealed to the House of Lords.

Held (Lord Keith dissenting) – The preamble to the 1965 Act clearly showed that Parliament intended that a refinery, and not merely specifically authorised works such as jetties and railway lines, would be constructed on the land to be acquired, and such authority to construct a refinery expressly or impliedly carried with it authority to operate a refinery when constructed. It followed that Gulf Oil were entitled to statutory immunity in respect of any nuisance which was an inevitable result of constructing and operating on the site a refinery (but not necessarily inevitably resulting from the refinery in fact constructed) which conformed with Parliament's intention. Being a matter of defence, the fact that the nuisance was an inevitable result of a refinery on that site was a matter for Gulf Oil to prove. However, to the extent that the actual nuisance caused by the refinery in fact constructed exceeded the nuisance which inevitably resulted from any refinery on that site, the statutory immunity would not apply and Gulf Oil would be liable to the plaintiff. The appeal would therefore be allowed (see p 356 g and j to p 357 b and g to p 358 f, p 359 f and j to p 360 b and p 365 f to j, post).

Metropolitan Asylum District Managers v Hill [1881–5] All ER Rep 536 and *Manchester Corpn v Farnworth* [1929] All ER Rep 90 considered.

Decision of the Court of Appeal [1979] 3 All ER 1008 reversed.

Notes

For the defence of statutory authority in actions for nuisance and negligence, see 3
Halsbury's Laws (3rd Edn) 690–696, paras 1330–1337, and for cases on the subject, se
38 Digest (Repl) 13, 34–41, 49, 173–212.

Cases referred to in opinions

Altrincham Union Assessment Committee v Cheshire Lines Committee (1885) 15 QBD 597, 5(
JP 85, CA, 44 Digest (Repl) 338, *1738*.

Edgington, Bishop and Withy v Swindon Corpn [1938] 4 All ER 57, [1939] 1 KB 86, 10ξ
LJKB 51, 159 LT 550, 102 JP 473, 36 LGR 650, 38 Digest (Repl) 11, *41*.

Geddis v Proprietors of the Bann Reservoir (1878) 3 App Cas 430, HL, 38 Digest (Repl) 16
64.

Hammersmith and City Railway Co v Brand (1869) LR 4 HL 171, [1861–73] All ER Rep 60·
38 LJQB 265, 21 LT 238, 34 JP 36, HL, 38 Digest (Repl) 15, *59*.

London, Brighton and South Coast Railway Co v Truman (1885) 11 App Cas 45, [1881–5] A)
ER Rep 134, 55 LJ Ch 354, 54 LT 250, 50 JP 388, HL, 38 Digest (Repl) 41, *212*.

Manchester Corpn v Farnworth [1930] AC 171, [1929] All ER Rep 90, 99 LJKB 83, 94 J)
62, 27 LGR 709, 142 LT 145, HL, 38 Digest (Repl) 38, *193*.

Metropolitan Asylum District Managers v Hill (1881) 6 App Cas 193, [1881–5] All Reᵖ
536, 50 LJQB 353, 44 LT 653, 45 JP 664, HL, 36(1) Digest (Reissue) 250, *887*.

R v Pease (1832) 4 B & Ad 30, [1824–34] All ER Rep 579, 1 Nev & MKB 690, 1 Nev &
MMC 535, 2 LJMC 26, 110 ER 366, 38 Digest (Repl) 39, *205*.

Sturges v Bridgman (1879) 11 Ch D 852, 48 LJ Ch 785, 41 LT 219, 43 JP 716, CA, 36(1̾
Digest (Reissue) 407, *32*.

Vaughan v Taff Vale Railway Co (1860) 5 H & N 679, [1843–60] All ER Rep 474, 29 LJ Ex
247, 2 LT 394, 24 JP 453, 6 Jur NS 899, 157 ER 1351, Ex Ch, 38 Digest (Repl) 13, *54*.

Interlocutory appeal

By writ issued on 13th February 1975 in the Haverfordwest District Registry and
amended pursuant to an order of the district registrar dated 22nd May 1975, the
respondent, Elsie May Allen, the occupier of premises at 20 Alban Crescent in the village
of Waterston commenced an action against the appellants, Gulf Oil Refining Ltd, for the
nuisance alleged to be caused by the operation of an oil refinery constructed by the
appellants in 1967 at Waterston, near Milford Haven in the County of Dyfed. By a
statement of claim served on 19th February 1975 and amended pursuant to an order of
the district registrar dated 10th June 1976 the respondent alleged nuisance, the particulars
of which were noxious odours, vibration, offensive noise levels, excessive flames from
burning waste gases, causing consequent ill-health, and fear of an explosion. Further and
in the alternative, the respondent alleged negligence in the construction and/or operation
of the refinery and claimed that by reason of nuisance and negligence, she and her family
had sustained personal injury, damage and expense. The respondent sought an
injunction that the appellants forthwith desist from the acts of nuisance and negligence,
and damages. By their defence served on 19th April 1975 and re-served as amended on
1st October 1976 the appellants denied nuisance, negligence, personal injury, loss or
damage, and further or in the alternative pleaded that if any of the matters referred to in
the statement of claim otherwise constituted a nuisance, the construction and operation
of the refinery were and continued to be authorised by the Gulf Oil Refining Act 1965
(c xxiv) and they relied on the defence of statutory authority. On a summons for
directions the respondent sought an order for determination of a preliminary point of
law before trial of the action on the question whether the appellants could rely on the
defence of statutory authority. The appellants appealed against the registrar's order and
on 23rd May 1977 Kerr J in chambers dismissed their appeal, but, on an undertaking
being given by the respondent's counsel that if the appellants were held to be entitled to
rely on the defence of statutory authority the respondent would not proceed with the
allegation of negligence, varied the registrar's order by ordering that the question 'Can

[the appellants] rely on the Gulf Oil Refining Act 1965 as having authorised the construction and operation of an oil refinery at Waterston, Milford Haven in the County of Dyfed?' be tried as a preliminary issue. On 4th May 1978 May J tried the preliminary issue and gave judgment for the appellants. The respondent appealed. On 27th June 1979 the Court of Appeal (Lord Denning MR and Cumming-Bruce LJ) ([1979] 3 All ER 1008, [1980] QB 156) allowed the appeal. The appellants appealed to the House of Lords by leave of the Court of Appeal. The facts are set out in the opinion of Lord Wilberforce.

Charles Sparrow QC, Francis Ferris and *John Henty* for the appellants.
John Davies QC and *Gordon Langley* for the respondent.

Their Lordships took time for consideration.

29th January. The following opinions were delivered.

LORD WILBERFORCE. My Lords, this action is brought by an inhabitant of the small village of Waterston, in the County of Dyfed, complaining that the appellants, a branch of a multinational oil company, are committing a common law nuisance through the construction and operation of an oil refinery. Many other persons have brought similar actions. The appellants have installed this refinery on land immediately adjoining the village and extending over more than 400 acres; it consists of a vast complex of jetties on Milford Haven harbour, where the largest oil tankers can deliver crude oil, refining plant, pipes, pumping apparatus, storage tanks, a petrochemical plant, and a private railway with sidings which passes close to the village before connecting with the main British Railways line. It is alleged by the respondent, but not yet proved, that the operation of the refinery causes a nuisance by smell, noise and vibration, and at this point in the action it must be assumed (but remains a matter of assumption only) that the allegation is true.

My Lords, I and others of your Lordships have protested against the procedure of bringing, except in clear and simple cases, points of law for preliminary decision. The procedure indeed exists and is sometimes useful. In other cases, and this is frequently so where they reach this House, they do not serve the cause of justice. The present is such an example. The question as originally framed was clearly inept. It was recast by Kerr J into an improved form. But both judges in the Court of Appeal (Lord Denning MR and Cumming-Bruce LJ) ([1979] 3 All ER 1008, [1980] QB 156) found it either unintelligible or unanswerable; so I believe do some at least of your Lordships. The fact is that the result of the case must depend on the impact of detailed and complex findings of fact on principles of law which are themselves flexible. There are too many variables to admit of a clear-cut solution in advance.

The question as framed by Kerr J reads: 'Can [the appellants] rely on the Gulf Oil Refining Act 1965 as having authorised the construction and operation of an oil refinery at Waterston . . .' In this House both sides accepted that this is incomplete and they have endeavoured to recast, or at least to expand, it. I quote from the respondent's printed case:

> 'The issue arising in this appeal is whether the Appellants, Gulf Oil Refining Limited ("Gulf") can rely on the Gulf Oil Refining Act, 1965 ("the Act") as having authorised the construction and operation of an oil refinery at Waterston, Milford Haven in the County of Dyfed. Gulf seek to rely on the Act as providing the defence of "statutory authority" to [the respondent's] claims for nuisance aris␣ ␣ut of the operation of the refinery in fact constructed and operated by ␣␣␣ Waterston. Gulf contends, in effect, that by reason of the Act any ␣␣␣ nuisance caused by the construction or operation of the refinery must ␣ [the respondent] without compensation.'

The appellants' formulation is much to the same effect. I think that thes␣

your Lordships a workable indication of what is needed. That must be in the form of a direction of law on which the judge who is to try the case can proceed.

The case, as a matter of law, depends on the construction of the 1965 Act.

We are here in the well-charted field of statutory authority. It is now well settled that where Parliament by express direction or by necessary implication has authorised the construction and use of an undertaking or works, that carries with it an authority to do what is authorised with immunity from any action based on nuisance. The right of action is taken away (see *Hammersmith and City Railway Co v Brand* (1869) LR 4 HL 171 at 215, [1861–73] All ER Rep 60 at 72 per Lord Cairns). To this there is made the qualification, or condition, that the statutory powers are exercised without 'negligence', that word here being used in a special sense so as to require the undertaker, as a condition of obtaining immunity from action, to carry out the work and conduct the operation with all reasonable regard and care for the interests of other persons (see *Geddis v Proprietors of the Bann Reservoir* (1878) 3 App Cas 430 at 455 per Lord Blackburn). It is within the same principle that immunity from action is withheld where the terms of the statute are permissive only, in which case the powers conferred must be exercised in strict conformity with private rights (see *Metropolitan Asylum District Managers v Hill* (1881) 6 App Cas 193, [1881–5] All ER Rep 536).

What then is the scope of the statutory authority conferred in this case? The Act was a private Act, promoted by the appellants, no doubt mainly in their own commercial interests. In order to establish their projected refinery with its ancillary facilities (jetties, railway lines etc), and to acquire the necessary land, they had to seek the assistance of Parliament. And so they necessarily had to satisfy Parliament that the powers they were seeking were in the interest of the public to whom Parliament is responsible. The case they undertook to make, which they had to prove, and which, as the passing of the Act shows, they did prove, is shown by the preamble. This recites 'increasing public demand for [the appellant's parent company's] products in the United Kingdom' and that 'it is *essential* that further facilities for the importation of crude oil and petroleum products and *for their refinement* should be made available' (emphasis supplied). It proceeds to recite the intention of the appellants to establish a refinery at Llanstadwell, that it was expedient that in connection therewith the appellants should be empowered to construct works including jetties for the accommodation of vessels (including large tankers) and for the reception from such vessels of crude oil and petroleum products for the proposed refinery and for conveying oil and petroleum products therefrom, that it was expedient for the appellants to be empowered to acquire lands, and that plans showing the lands which may be taken or used compulsorily under the powers of the Act for the purposes thereof had been deposited.

My Lords, all of this shows most clearly that Parliament considered it in the public interest that a *refinery*, not merely the works (jetties etc), should be constructed, and constructed on lands at Llanstadwell to be compulsorily acquired.

To show how this intention was to be carried out I need only quote s 5:

'(1) Subject to the provisions of this Act, the Company may enter upon, take and use such of the lands delineated on the deposited plans and described in the deposited book of reference as it may require for the purposes of the authorised works or *for the construction of a refinery* in the parish of Llanstadwell in the rural district of Haverfordwest in the county of Pembroke or for the purposes ancillary thereto or connected therewith.

'(2) The powers of compulsory acquisition of land under this section shall cease after the expiration of three years from the 1st October, 1965.'

The lands in question were the specific lands, about 450 acres in extent, shown with precise detail in the deposited plans.

I cannot but regard this as an authority, whether it should be called express or by necessary implication may be a matter of preference, but an authority to construct and operate *a refinery* on the lands to be acquired, a refinery moreover which should be commensurate with the facilities for unloading offered by the jetties (for large tankers), with the size of the lands to be acquired, and with the discharging facilities to be provided by the railway lines. I emphasise the words *a refinery* by way of distinction from *the refinery* because no authority was given or sought except in the indefinite form. But that there was authority to construct and operate *a refinery* seems to me indisputable.

The respondent's contention against this is a curious one. She points to the sections (mainly s 15) dealing with works; these specify in great detail what is to be carried out, in the way of construction of jetties and of railway lines. Here, she says, is plain statutory authority of the kind conferred in the well-known cases concerned with railways. By contrast there is no authority to construct or operate a refinery, not even by implication. There is nothing but power to acquire lands. The construction of the refinery is left entirely to the promoters; there is no specification of the size or nature of the refinery, they have 'carte blanche' and therefore the intention must be that they must construct it with regard to private rights. The case is similar, she says, to that of *Metropolitan Asylum District Managers v Hill*. This argument has remarkable consequences. It follows that if the respondent, or any other person, can establish a nuisance, he or she is entitled (subject only to a precarious appeal to Lord Cairns's Act (the Chancery Amendment Act 1858)) to an injunction. This may make it impossible for the refinery to be operated; that in turn would leave the appellants as the owners and occupiers of a large area of land which they have compulsorily acquired under the authority of the 1965 Act for the purpose of a refinery, and which, in accordance with well-known principles, they could not use for any other purpose. Such consequences must be accepted if they clearly flow from the terms of the Act.

But I must say that I find the construction which would give rise to this result to be not only far from clear but a most artificial reading of the enactment. It is true, and at one time I was impressed by the point, that, by contrast with the detailed specification given to the 'works', by description, plans, levels etc, the Act conspicuously does not define or specify the refinery even in general terms, and this might appear to support an argument that this was left altogether outside the Parliamentary authority. But I think that it was answered by the case in this House of *Manchester Corpn v Farnworth* [1930] AC 171, [1929] All ER Rep 90. In that case the statutory authority was simply, in general terms, for the erection of a generating station, without specification, but nevertheless it was held that, subject to the 'negligence' exception, the usual rule applied (see particularly per Viscount Dunedin [1930] AC 171 at 183, [1929] All ER Rep 90 at 95). There could be 'no action for nuisance caused by the making or doing of that thing [ie the thing authorised] if the nuisance is the inevitable result of the making or doing so authorised'. That, in my opinion, describes the situation in the present case. It is true that the 1965 Act does not, as did the relevant Act considered in the *Manchester Corpn* case (the Manchester Corporation Act 1914 (4 & 5 Geo 5 c cxlvi)), confer express authority to use or operate any refinery which might be installed on the site, but the preamble refers to 'refinement', ie operation of the refinery, and authority to construct must in this case carry authority to refine. The two cases are entirely parallel.

If I am right on this point, the position as regards the action would be as follows. The respondent alleges a nuisance, by smell, noise, vibration etc. The facts regarding these matters are for her to prove. It is then for the appellants to show, if they can, that it was impossible to construct and operate a refinery on the site, conforming with Parliament's intention, without creating the nuisance alleged, or at least a nuisance. Involved in this issue would be the point discussed by Cumming-Bruce LJ in the Court of Appeal, that the establishment of an oil refinery etc was bound to involve some alteration of the environment and so of the standard of amenity and comfort which neighbouring occupiers might expect. To the extent that the environment has been changed from that of a peaceful unpolluted countryside to an industrial complex (as to which different standards apply: see *Sturges v Bridgman* (1879) 11 Ch D 852) Parliament must be taken to have authorised it. So far, I venture to think, the matter is not open to doubt. But in my opinion the statutory authority extends beyond merely authorising a change in the environment and an alteration of standard. It confers immunity against proceedings for any nuisance which can be shown (the burden of so showing being on the appellants) to be the inevitable result of erecting a refinery on the site, not, I repeat, the existing refinery, but any refinery, however carefully and with however great a regard for the interest of adjoining occupiers it is sited, constructed and operated. To the extent and only to the extent that the actual nuisance (if any) caused by the actual refinery and its operation exceeds that for which immunity is conferred, the plaintiff has a remedy.

For myself I would respond in this sense to the question asked, rather than in the purely negative sense favoured by the Court of Appeal, and to that extent I would allow the appeal.

LORD DIPLOCK. My Lords, I have had the advantage of reading in advance the speech of my noble and learned friend Lord Wilberforce. I agree with it; so there is very little that I would seek to add.

The question is one of statutory construction: does the Gulf Oil Refining Act 1965 by necessary implication authorise the company to operate on the land that it was authorised to acquire compulsorily an oil refinery on a scale commensurate with the area of that land and the provision to be made for jetties in Milford Haven for the reception at the refinery of crude oil and petroleum products brought there by large tankers?

I cannot think that this depends on the presence or absence of an express authority to 'use' the refinery as well as to construct it. Parliament can hardly be supposed to have intended the refinery to be nothing more than a visual adornment to the landscape in an area of natural beauty. Clearly the intention of Parliament was that the refinery was to be operated as such; and it is perhaps relevant to observe that in *Metropolitan Asylum District Managers v Hill* (1881) 6 App Cas 193, [1881–5] All ER Rep 536 all three members of this House who took part in the decision would apparently have reached the conclusion that the nuisance caused by the smallpox hospital could not have been the subject of an action if the hospital had been built on a site which the managers had been granted power by Act of Parliament to acquire compulsorily for that specific purpose.

LORD EDMUND-DAVIES. My Lords, the preliminary question of law now calling for consideration derives from the plea of statutory authority advanced by the appellants in these proceedings. Although not strictly in the nature of a test action, they are likely to have a significant impact on the 52 other actions of a similar kind instituted against the appellants which have been stayed pending the outcome of this interlocutory stage.

The essence of the plea was summarised in the following words of Viscount Dunedin in *Manchester Corpn v Farnworth* [1930] AC 171 at 183, [1929] All ER Rep 90 at 95:

'When Parliament has authorized a certain thing to be made or done in a certain place, there can be no action for nuisance caused by the making or doing of that thing if the nuisance is the inevitable result of the making or doing so authorized. The onus of proving that the result is inevitable is on those who wish to escape liability for nuisance.'

The circumstances of the case have been set out in the speech of my noble and learned friend Lord Wilberforce and the preliminary question of law, as revised by Kerr J, is worded in this way:

'Can [the appellants] rely on the Gulf Oil Refining Act 1965 as having authorised the construction and operation of an oil refinery at Waterston, Milford Haven in the County of Dyfed?'

At this interlocutory stage is it exceedingly difficult and, indeed, impossible to give a categorical and final answer to that question. For an effective plea of 'statutory authority' presupposes the absence of any relevant negligence by the appellants. As yet there has been no trial to determine whether the working of the refinery, which began operation in 1967, does constitute *any* nuisance (inevitable or avoidable), or whether the appellants have been guilty of negligence. Those issues are in themselves capable of having considerable legal and factual complexity. The burden will be on the plaintiff to prove nuisance or negligence, arising from the construction or operation of the refinery. On the other hand, it would be for the defendant to establish that any proved nuisance was wholly unavoidable, and this quite regardless of the expense which might necessarily be involved in its avoidance, whereas he will clear himself of negligence if at the end of the day it emerges that any discomfort suffered by the plaintiff arose despite his exercise of *reasonable* care. It follows that an affirmative answer now given to the prescribed question of law can only be tentative, for it might emerge from the facts that the only possible conclusion was that the plea of 'statutory authority' was *not*, after all, available to the defendant. But, despite the ultimate uncertainty, this House is nevertheless called on to consider and answer the question as best it can.

The task involves interpreting the Gulf Oil Refining Act 1965 (c xxiv), and that exercise has already been performed in the speech of my noble and learned friend Lord Wilberforce in a manner with which I am in respectful agreement. I should add that, in so concluding, I have derived considerable assistance from the admirable judgment of May J, and I propose to restrict myself to brief remarks on some of the salient points of the case.

1. Bearing in mind always that this private Act must be construed strictly against its promoters wherever there is any doubt as to its meaning, its preamble makes clear that the paramount object of the project was the construction and operation ('in the public interest') of a refinery on the acquired land 'in order to meet the increasing public demand'.

2. Under the Act the appellants could '*take and use*' the 450 acres of land they were thereby empowered to acquire compulsorily *only* 'for the purpose of the authorised works or for the construction of a refinery ... or for purposes ancillary thereto or connected therewith' (see s 5(1)).

3. In the light of the foregoing, no significance should be attached to the fact that, whereas the Act made express provision for the nature, scale and layout of the 'authorised works' (see s 15), no such detailed provision was made in respect of the refinery which was to be constructed. In my judgment, it was nevertheless a necessary implication of the Act that the appellants were thereby authorised to construct and operate the refinery which they in fact later constructed and operated (see *London, Brighton and South Coast Railway Co v Truman* (1885) 11 App Cas 45, [1881–5] All ER Rep 134); and in acting as they did the appellants took and used the land for the sole purposes for which a power of compulsory acquisition had been conferred on them.

4. The respondent understandably places strong reliance on the absence from the Act of any provision for the payment of compensation for any damage caused by the construction or operation of the refinery or by the exercise of the powers conferred by s 15, and this particularly as s 16(3) made express provision for compensation in respect of damage caused by the exercise of powers conferred by that section in relation to 'subsidiary works'. But the works contemplated and authorised by the two sections are basically different, those covered by s 16 of their very nature necessarily affecting proprietorial and other rights of outside bodies, and it would be inconceivable that provision for compensation would not be made in respect of damage done in their cases.

The general legal approach unquestionably is that the absence of compensation clauses from an Act conferring powers affords an important indication that the Act was not intended to authorise interference with private rights: see *Metropolitan Asylum District Managers v Hill* (1881) 6 App Cas 193 at 203, [1881–5] All ER Rep 536 at 540, and the other cases cited in 1 Halsbury's Laws (4th Edn) para 196. But the indication is not conclusive (see *Edgington, Bishop and Withy v Swindon Corpn* [1938] 4 All ER 57, [1939] 1 KB 86), and if the correct view (as I believe it to be) is that in 1965 Parliament, in part expressly and in part impliedly, authorised the construction and use of the Waterston refinery, that carries with it immunity from liability for nuisance inevitably and without negligence arising therefrom (see *Hammersmith and City Railway Co v Brand* (1869) LR 4 HL 171 at 215ff, [1861–73] All ER Rep 60 at 72ff per Lord Cairns).

My Lords, I respectfully adopt the ipsissima verba of May J in saying that 'I have come to the conclusion that it would be totally artificial to say that this 1965 Act did not "authorise" the erection of this refinery within the ambit of the defence of statutory authority . . . to actions in nuisance'. I would therefore allow the appeal, and the trial will presumably now proceed on the issues of (1) nuisance ('inevitable' or otherwise) and (2) negligence.

LORD KEITH OF KINKEL. My Lords, this appeal is concerned with the correct answer to a question of law which, following an application by the respondent, was by an order of Kerr J dated 23rd May 1977, formulated by him and directed to be tried as a preliminary issue.

The question is in these terms:

> 'Can [the appellants] rely on the Gulf Oil Refining Act 1965 as having authorised the construction and operation of an oil refinery at Waterston, Milford Haven in the county of Dyfed?'

The wording of the question has been subjected to some criticism, but there is common ground between the parties as to the issue which it is thereby sought to raise and determine. That issue is whether the 1965 Act affords the appellants a good defence against the respondent's action for common law nuisance arising from the normal operation of a refinery on the site in question, on the assumption that the creation of a nuisance is a necessary incident of such operation, not avoidable by any reasonable measures which might be taken by the appellants. An undertaking has been given on behalf of the respondent that, if that issue is decided in her favour, she will not pursue the allegation contained in her pleadings that a nuisance has been created by negligence on the part of the appellants.

The issue was decided in the appellants' favour by May J but on 27th June 1979 the Court of Appeal (Lord Denning MR and Cumming-Bruce LJ) ([1979] 3 All ER 1008, [1980] QB 156) reversed his decision. The appellants now appeal to this House.

The defence on which the appellants rely is commonly known as that of 'statutory authority'. Its availability in appropriate circumstances was established by a series of nineteenth century cases concerned with the operation of railways under statutory powers, of which the best known are *R v Pease* (1832) 4 B & Ad 30, [1824–34] All ER Rep 579 and *Vaughan v Taff Vale Railway Co* (1860) 5 H & N 679, [1843–60] All ER Rep 474. The correctness of these decisions was affirmed by this House in *Hammersmith and City Railway Co v Brand* (1869) LR 4 HL 171, [1861–73] All ER Rep 60. The majority of the consulted judges had expressed the view that these cases were wrongly decided. Bramwell B had founded on the absence in the Railway Clauses Act of any express provision conferring power on the railway company to use locomotives so as to be a nuisance to their neighbours. Lord Chelmsford said (LR 4 HL 171 at 202, [1861–73] All ER Rep 60 at 65):

> 'With great respect to the learned Baron, we do not expect to find words in an Act of Parliament expressly authorizing an individual or a company to commit a nuisance or to do damage to a neighbour. The 86th section gives power to the company to use and employ locomotive engines, and if such locomotives cannot possibly be used without occasioning vibration and consequent injury to neighbouring houses, upon the principle of law that "*Cuicunque aliquis quid concedit concedere videtur et id sine quo res ipsa esse non potuit*", it must be taken that power is given to cause that vibration without liability to an action. The right given to use the locomotive would otherwise be nugatory, as each time a train passed upon the line and shook the houses in the neighbourhood actions might be brought by their

owners, which would soon put a stop to the use of the railway. I therefore think, notwithstanding the respect to which every opinion of Mr Baron *Bramwell* is entitled, that the cases of *Rex* v. *Pease* and *Vaughan* v. *The Taff Vale Railway Company* were rightly decided.'

Geddis v *Proprietors of the Bann Reservoir* (1878) 3 App Cas 430 established that the authority of Parliament to construct and use certain works does not relieve the undertakers from the obligation to take due care that their operations do not cause injury to neighbouring proprietors. So the defence of statutory authority, the application of which has been extended to a wide field of industrial activities, does not avail against a claim that the creation of a nuisance has been brought about by negligence. In *Manchester Corpn v Farnworth* [1930] AC 171 at 183, [1929] All ER Rep 90 at 95 Viscount Dunedin said:

'When Parliament has authorized a certain thing to be made or done in a certain place, there can be no action for nuisance caused by the making or doing of that thing if the nuisance is the inevitable result of the making or doing so authorized. The onus of proving that the result is inevitable is on those who wish to escape liability for nuisance, but the criterion of inevitability is not what is theoretically possible but what is possible according to the state of scientific knowledge at the time, having also in view a certain common sense appreciation, which cannot be rigidly defined, of practical feasibility in view of situation and of expense.'

For the purpose of disposing of the preliminary issue which I have described, it is to be assumed that the respondent's averments about the existence of a nuisance emanating from the appellants' refinery are true, and also that the nuisance would be the inevitable result, in the sense of Viscount Dunedin's words, of operating, not the refinery which the appellants have actually built, but such a refinery as must reasonably be regarded as having been in the contemplation of Parliament when it passed the Gulf Oil Refining Act 1965.

The question whether on these assumptions the defence of statutory authority is available to the appellants turns on the ascertainment, on a proper construction of the 1965 Act, of the extent of the authorisation thereby granted to the appellants by Parliament. The Act is divided into four parts. Part I is headed 'Preliminary'. Section 3 incorporates with certain exceptions the Lands Clauses Acts, the Railways Clauses Consolidation Act 1845 and·the Harbours Clauses Act 1847. Among the excluded sections of the 1845 Act is s 86, which makes lawful the use of locomotive engines and carriages and wagons to be drawn thereby. Section 4 contains a number of definitions including that of 'the authorised works' as meaning 'the works authorised by section 15 (Power to construct works) of this Act'. Part II, starting with s 5, is headed 'Lands'. Section 5(1) provides:

'Subject to the provisions of this Act, the Company may enter upon, take and use such of the lands delineated on the deposited plans and described in the deposited book of reference as it may require for the purposes of the authorised works or for the construction of a refinery in the parish of Llanstadwell in the rural district of Haverfordwest in the county of Pembroke or for purposes ancillary thereto or connected therewith.'

Section 7(1) provides:

'The Company may, instead of acquiring any land that it is authorised to acquire compulsorily under this Act, acquire compulsorily such easements and rights over or in the land as it may require for the purpose of constructing, using, maintaining, renewing or removing the works authorised by this Act or for the purpose of obtaining access to the works or for the purpose of doing any other thing necessary in connection with the works or for the construction of a refinery.'

The remainder of Part II deals with a number of ancillary provisions, such as power to expedite entry, power to enter for survey or valuation and power to stop up roads and footpaths. Part III, headed 'Works', consisting of ss 15 to 32, contains a number of detailed provisions relating to construction of certain specific works according to deposited plans and sections. The works comprise a main approach jetty and two jetty heads in Milford Haven intended for the berthing of tankers, and also a single track railway, 2½ miles in length, connecting the refinery site to the British Rail line at a specified point. Section 15(1) provides that the appellants 'may construct' these works. Section 16(1) provides that the appellants, 'for the purposes of or in connection with the authorised works' and within 'the limits of deviation', may 'construct or place and maintain and use' a very large number of specified facilities, including 'buildings, engines, pumps, machinery . . . railways . . . junctions, sidings', and also temporarily or permanently 'use . . . alter or otherwise interfere with' such things as 'drains, sewers . . . electric, gas, water and other pipes'; the appellants are further empowered to 'raise, sink or otherwise alter the position of any of the steps, areas, cellars, windows and pipes or spouts belonging to any house or building'. By s 16(3) it is provided that in the exercise of these powers the appellants 'shall cause as little detriment and inconvenience as the circumstances permit to any person and shall make reasonable compensation for any damage caused by the exercise of such powers'. Part IV, headed 'Miscellaneous' and comprising ss 33 to 57, includes provisions governing the appellants' status as a pier authority, and also a number of saving and protective provisions including, in s 55, a saving for town and country planning legislation.

Examination of the provisions of the Act shows that those relating to the 'authorised works', which do not include the construction of any refinery, are elaborate and reasonably precise. These provisions were necessary to enable the appellants to do things, which they would otherwise have no right to do, in particular to interfere with the tidal waters of Milford Haven. In connection with the authorised works and ancillary operations the Act confers certain rights to compensation on persons who may be affected thereby. The precise ambit of these rights is not altogether clear, but need not for present purposes be investigated.

So far as the construction of a refinery is concerned, the Act does no more than confer on the appellants for that purpose power to acquire compulsorily certain specified lands. Such power of acquisition also extends to lands acquired for the construction of the authorised works. As an alternative to compulsory purchase, the appellants are by s 7(1) given power to acquire compulsorily such easements or other rights over the specified land as may be required for construction purposes and also, in the case of the authorised works but not as regards any refinery, for the purpose of using, maintaining, renewing or removing the works. It is apparent that the Act touches very lightly on the matter of construction of a refinery. No specification or detail of any kind is given of the refinery which the appellants propose to construct. It is of some significance that the preamble to the Act, to which I have not so far alluded, does no more in relation to the refinery than say that the appellants intend to establish one in the parish of Llanstadwell. The powers which the preamble represents as being expedient in the public interest to be conferred on the appellants are related only to the construction of the authorised works, to the acquisition of land and to the constitution of the appellants as a pier authority. Nothing is said about any power specifically related to the refinery as such. It is true that the preamble recites that it is essential that further facilities for the importation of crude oil and petroleum products and for their refinement should be made available in the United Kingdom, but this is related merely to the purpose of meeting the increasing public demand for 'its', ie the appellants', products in the United Kingdom. It is apparent that the Act is directed to furthering the appellants' own business interests in the United Kingdom, though of course Parliament would not have conferred on the appellants the powers therein contained unless satisfied that it was in the public interest to do so.

In construing a private Act of this kind it is necessary to keep the contra proferentem rule firmly in mind:

'In the case of a private Act, which is obtained by persons for their own benefit, you construe more strictly provisions which they allege to be in their favour, because the persons who obtain a private Act ought to take care that it is so worded that that which they desire to obtain for themselves is plainly stated in it.'

See *Altrincham Union Assessment Committee v Cheshire Lines Committee* (1885) 15 QBD 597 at 603 per Lord Esher MR.

It is the duty of those promoting private Acts to make plain the precise extent to which they propose to derogate from the common law rights of those who may be affected by their proposals. It will not do to slip through Parliament provisions which do not on the face of them express reasonably clearly the intention to take away the rights of others, with a view to subsequently relying on them as having had that effect. In order to check any such tendency, it is essential that any doubtful provision of the kind in question should be most strictly construed.

In the present case it is s 5(1) of the Act which is principally founded on as having the result contended for, s 7(1) also being to some extent prayed in aid. It is said that Parliament, having by s 5(1) authorised the appellants to acquire compulsorily and use certain specified lands for the construction of a refinery, must by necessary implication be taken to have authorised the operation of a refinery commensurate in size and scale with the extent of the designated site. Any nuisance which is the inevitable result of operating such a refinery is accordingly not actionable.

My Lords, I am unable to accept that view of the effect of s 5(1). It is true that the burden of establishing that Parliament intended to take away the private right of individuals may be discharged by showing that such intention appears either from express words or by necessary implication: see *Metropolitan Asylum District Managers v Hill* (1881) 6 App Cas 193 at 208, [1881–5] All ER Rep 536 at 543 per Lord Blackburn. I cannot, however, find any necessary implication of such intention in a provision the operative purpose and effect of which merely is to confer powers of compulsory purchase. Any compulsory purchase powers, whether conferred by Parliament directly or under statutorily delegated authority, must be conferred for a specific purpose. I do not consider that the mere mention of that purpose in the conferment of the powers is sufficient in itself to infer an intention to authorise any particular activity on the acquired lands which might infringe the rights of others. The position would have been different if s 5(1) had specifically authorised the appellants to use a refinery on the site in question. Thus in *Manchester Corpn v Farnworth* s 36(1)(a) of the Manchester Corporation Act 1914 (4 & 5 Geo 5 c cxlvi) gave the corporation authority to 'construct, maintain, alter, improve, enlarge, extend, renew, work and use' on the site described 'a station for generating electricity'. It was held that the corporation were liable only for such nuisance as could not be prevented by the use of due diligence. In the passage quoted above, Viscount Dunedin referred to there being no action for inevitable nuisance caused by the 'making or doing' of a certain thing which Parliament has authorised to be made or done in a certain place. The making of a certain thing is different from the doing of a certain thing. If in that case Parliament had not specifically authorised the corporation 'to work and use' the power station, it does not appear that their doing so would have been protected in any way.

The defence of statutory authority is well known. The appellants here may reasonably be taken to have access to the best legal advice in connection with the promotion of their private Act. The precedents show clearly the route to be taken in order to avoid any doubt about its availability. The appellants failed to include in their Act reference to authority to operate, work or use a refinery. If they had done so, Parliament might well have insisted on provisions for compensation. Applying the principles of construction to which I have alluded, I am not prepared to hold that s 5(1) is susceptible of the necessary implication contended for by the appellants.

My Lords, for these reasons I would dismiss the appeal.

LORD ROSKILL. My Lords, as my noble and learned friend Lord Wilberforce states, your Lordships' House has often protested against the procedure of inviting courts to determine points of law on assumed facts. The preliminary point procedure can in certain classes of case be invoked to achieve the desirable aim both of economy and simplicity. But cases in which invocation is desirable are few. Sometimes a single issue of law can be isolated from the other issues in a particular case, whether of fact or of law, and its decision may be finally determinative of the case as a whole. Sometimes facts can be agreed and the sole issue is one of law. But the present is not a case in which this procedure ought ever to have been adopted for the reasons stated by my noble and learned friend. The question posed was, in its original form, hopeless. In spite of the valiant attempt by Kerr J to improve it, I doubt whether the question could ever have been cast into a satisfactory form. Both parties, however, invited your Lordships' House to treat the question for decision as that stated in virtually identical terms in para 1 of their respective cases, namely, whether the appellants can rely on the Gulf Oil Refining Act 1965 (c xxiv) as having authorised the construction and operation of an oil refinery at Waterston, Milford Haven, thereby affording to the appellants the defence commonly known as 'statutory authority' against a common law action for nuisance.

My Lords, in common with all your Lordships, I agree that this should be treated as the question to be answered. But I hope that your Lordships' agreement so to treat it will not encourage others to invoke the preliminary point procedure in unsuitable cases, or lead those whose task it is to decide whether or not the trial of preliminary points should be ordered to be other than extremely cautious before acceding to pleas for the making of such orders as a result of attractively advanced submissions founded on pleas of supposed economy.

My Lords, the answer to the question depends on the true construction of the Gulf Oil Refining Act 1965. The most important sections are ss 5, 7 and 15. The Act itself was a private Act, no doubt promoted by the appellants in their own commercial interests. But Parliament must, I think, be taken to have accepted that the construction of a refinery, such as was proposed, was also in the public interest for the third recital asserts that—

> 'in order to meet the increasing public demand for its [ie the appellants' parent company's] products in the United Kingdom, it is essential that further facilities for the importation of crude oil and petroleum products and for their refinement should be made available in the United Kingdom,'

while the fifth recital, after recording the appellants' intention 'to establish a refinery' continues—

> 'it is expedient in the public interest that in connection therewith the Company [ie the appellants] should be empowered to construct the works authorised by this Act including jetties in the waters of Milford Haven and on the foreshore thereof . . .'

and the tenth recital refers to a deposit of plans and sections showing (inter alia) 'the lands which may be taken or used compulsorily under the powers of this Act for the purposes thereof'.

My Lords, for a period of over one hundred and fifty years the principles on which statutes such as the 1965 Act have to be construed have been considered and authoritatively determined by your Lordships' House. Where Parliament by express words or necessary implication authorises the construction or use of an undertaking, that authorisation is necessarily accompanied by immunity from any action based on nuisance. The underlying philosophy plainly is that the greater public interest arising from the construction and use of undertakings such as railways must take precedence over the private rights of owners and occupiers of neighbouring lands not to have their common law rights infringed by what would otherwise be actionable nuisance. In short, the lesser private right must yield to the greater public interest.

My Lords, the many authorities are reviewed in the judgments in the courts below and in the speeches of your Lordships, and no useful purpose will be served by further review of them by me. But the immunity to which I have just referred is not unqualified or unlimited. The statutory undertaker must in return for the rights and privileges which he has thus obtained exercise his powers without negligence, a word which has been interpreted as meaning reasonable regard for the interests of others.

My Lords, the principal argument for the respondent has been that the 1965 Act did not authorise the construction of a refinery. It authorised, it was said, the construction of the works specified in s 15, for example, the jetties and the railway, but so far as any refinery was concerned, its construction was facilitated by permitting the compulsory acquisition of large tracts of land but nowhere is there to be found in the statute any express authority for its construction. Therefore, the argument ran, the principles derived from the decided cases had no application to any nuisance arising from the operation of any refinery built, for the construction of such a refinery was not, unlike the works referred to in s 15, 'authorised'.

Learned counsel for the respondent, if I understood him correctly, ultimately accepted that there would be the relevant conferment of immunity in relation to works specifically authorised by s 15, so that nuisance created by (for example) the erection of jetties and possible consequential interference with tidal flow affecting the rights of neighbouring owners and occupiers of land could not be the subject of action at common law.

My Lords, I confess that for some time I was impressed by the apparent contrast in the 1965 Act between the works authorised by s 15, and the absence of express authority for the construction of a refinery as well as by the absence of any express abrogation in the statute of the common law rights of others. But, on further reflection as to the second of these points, the decided cases show that the absence of express abrogation of the rights of others in the relevant statute is of itself no reason for denying the immunity sought if from the language of the statute as a whole it is plain that the carrying on of the undertaking on the one hand and the unrestricted private rights of neighbouring landowners on the other could not have been intended to co-exist.

As to the first of these points, the respondent's argument leads to a most curious, and as I venture to think, illogical result. If the argument be sound, then, subject only to the provisions of Lord Cairns's Act (the Chancery Amendment Act 1858), the respondent on proof of the existence of nuisance or nuisances pleaded would be entitled to an injunction. Such an injunction would be likely to make the operation of a refinery impossible and thus wholly defeat the very purpose for which the 1965 Act was passed, a purpose which the recitals describe as 'essential'.

My Lords, I cannot, with all respect to those who have taken a different view, think that this conclusion can be correct. In the result I find myself in complete and respectful agreement with the speech of my noble and learned friend Lord Wilberforce.

My Lords, I do not think the question raised even as interpreted by your Lordships is susceptible of a monosyllabic answer. In agreement with my noble and learned friend I think it should be answered in the form of a direction to the trial judge by whom this action will ultimately fall to be tried, if it goes to trial, as to the law to be applied by him to the facts as he finds them to be. I think that direction should be in the form stated in the penultimate paragraph of my noble and learned friend's speech.

I would therefore allow the appeal and answer the question as my noble and learned friend suggests.

Appeal allowed. Order appealed from set aside and declaration that the appellants may rely on the Gulf Oil Refining Act 1965 as a defence in any proceedings for nuisance but only so far as the nuisance can be shown to be the inevitable result of erecting and operating a refinery.

Solicitors: *Hextall Erskine & Co*, agents for *Cartwrights*, Bristol (for the appellants); *Calow Easton*, agents for *Price & Kelway*, Milford Haven (for the respondent).

Mary Rose Plummer   Barrister.

Attorney General's Reference (No 1 of 1980)

COURT OF APPEAL, CRIMINAL DIVISION

LORD LANE CJ, STOCKER AND GLIDEWELL JJ

3rd, 24th OCTOBER 1980

Criminal law – False accounting – Document made or required for an accounting purpose – Falsification of loan proposal form – Whether proposal form a 'document made or required for [an] accounting purpose' – Theft Act 1968, s 17(1)(a).

The accused, a trader in domestic appliances, gave to householders personal loan proposal forms addressed to a finance company to enable them to borrow money from the company to pay for the appliances. In order to ensure that the proposals would be accepted by the company, he advised some of the householders to give false particulars on their proposal forms. The proposal forms when received by the company were considered and accepted. The accused was charged, inter alia, with falsifying a document required for an accounting purpose contrary to s 17(1)(a)[a] of the Theft Act 1968. At the end of the prosecution case the trial judge directed the jury to acquit the accused, ruling that the proposal form in question was used for an accounting purpose when the loan had been accepted by the company, but that at the time it was falsified it was not 'made or required' for an accounting purpose within s 17(1)(a). On a reference by the Attorney General for the opinion of the Court of Appeal under s 36 of the Criminal Justice Act 1972,

Held – The words 'made or required' in s 17(1)(a) of the 1968 Act indicated that a distinction was to be drawn between a document made specifically for the purpose of accounting and one made for some other purpose but which was required for an accounting purpose. Thus a document might fall within the ambit of s 17 if it was made for some purpose other than an accounting purpose but was required for an accounting purpose as a subsidiary consideration. Although in the circumstances each borrower had made the document for the purpose of having his loan proposal considered by the company, at the same time that document might have been required by the company in due course for an accounting purpose, even though when considered by the company the proposal might have been rejected. It followed that the trial judge was wrong in the conclusions which he reached (see p 369 *b* to *e*, post).

Per Curiam. (1) The moment at which a duty to account arises has no relevance to the question whether the document is or is not required for an accounting purpose (see p 369 *a b*, post).

(2) Although a document is required for an accounting purpose as to part and is

---

a   Section 17(1), so far as material, is set out at p 368 *e*, post

falsified as to part, the fact that the two parts are not the same does not exonerate the person responsible for the falsification where the document constitutes one entire document (see p 369 *f*, post).

Notes

For false accounting, see 11 Halsbury's Laws (4th Edn) para 1280, and for cases on the subject, see 15 Digest (Reissue) 1334, *11,512–11,519*.

For the Theft Act 1968, s 17, see 8 Halsbury's Statutes (3rd Edn) 793.

For the Criminal Justice Act 1972, s 36, see 42 ibid 129.

Case referred to in judgment

R v Mallett [1978] 3 All ER 10, [1978] 1 WLR 820, 142 JP 528, 67 Cr App R 239, CA, Digest (Cont Vol E) 159, *11,515a*.

Reference

This was a reference by the Attorney General, under s 36 of the Criminal Justice Act 1972, for the opinion of the Court of Appeal on a point of law arising in a case where the accused had been acquitted on the direction of the trial judge on an indictment containing, inter alia, two counts charging the accused with an offence contrary to s 17(1)(*a*) of the Theft Act 1968. The terms of the reference and the facts are set out in the judgment of the court.

David Tudor Price for the Attorney General.
David Jeffreys as amicus curiae.

Cur adv vult

24th October. **LORD LANE CJ** read the following judgment of the court: This is a reference by the Attorney General under the provisions of s 36 of the Criminal Justice Act 1972. The reference is in these terms:

> 'Whether a person who dishonestly falsifies a personal loan proposal form in material particulars which he sends thereafter to a Finance Company, and which they use in their accounting process, falsifies a document "required for any accounting purpose" contrary to Section 17(1)(*a*) of the Theft Act 1968.'

The facts of the case are as follows. The accused man was engaged at the material times in selling domestic appliances to householders. For that purpose, he gave to householders personal loan proposal forms addressed to a finance company to enable the householders to borrow money to pay for the appliances. So that the proposals would be accepted by the finance company, he advised some of the householders to give false particulars on their proposal forms. Two examples were proved. In the first, the householder, at the suggestion of the accused, understated the number of his dependants and falsely stated that he had no outstanding instalment commitments. In the second, the householder was induced by the accused man similarly to understate the number of his dependants and to state falsely that he had a National Savings Bank account.

The proposal forms when received by the finance company were considered and accepted. The information set out on the reverse side of the forms was used by the company to make up its accounts on a computer. The relevant forms were exhibited at the trial and were similar to each other. They are headed with the name of the finance company and are entitled 'Personal Loan Proposal Form'. There then follows a section entitled 'Particulars of Proposer', the particulars to be supplied including the name and address of the proposer, his nationality, personal details of his marital and family circumstances, including the number of his dependants, his employer's name and address and other personal details. Also included in this section on the form is a space in which the proposer is required to state the details of other hire-purchase commitments then existing. It was this section of the form which contained the false answers in the present case. The next section requires details of the house in which the equipment is to be installed, including any relevant mortgage details. Finally, the form on its face contains a section 'For office use only' in which the finance company would enter the details needed to be fed into their computer. At the bottom is a space designated 'Signature of witness'. At the head of the reverse side of the forms is a request signed by the proposer and addressed to the finance company requesting the loan 'for the purpose described below' and certifying the truth of the particulars given. Beneath this request is a section in which the purpose for which the loan is required is stated. Then there follow details of the cash price of the equipment and the amount of the initial payment, the amount of the advance, the interest charged and the total sum due and the number of the monthly instalments by which the loan is to be paid and the amount repayable on each instalment. Finally, there are blank forms for direct debit authority and promissory note.

The accused was charged in four counts. Two of these are immaterial to this reference. The remaining two give rise to the question posed in this reference; they were in similar terms and each charged the accused with an offence under s 17(1)(a) of the Theft Act 1968. The particulars of each count allege that he had dishonestly, with a view to gain for himself or his company, falsified the personal loan proposal form specified, being a document required for the accounts of the finance company.

The trial judge ruled that the proposal form was used for an accounting purpose when the loan had been accepted by the finance company, but that at the time that it was falsified it was not 'made or required for any accounting purpose' within the meaning of the section.

The question at issue is therefore whether or not the proposal forms were documents required for an accounting purpose within the meaning of s 17(1)(a). The relevant parts of the section read as follows:

> 'Where a person dishonestly, with a view to gain for himself or another, or with intent to cause loss to another—(a) . . . falsifies any . . . document made or required for any accounting purpose . . .'

The judge ruled that the proposal forms in question were not documents made or required for an accounting purpose and expressed his ruling in the following terms:

> 'I find it a great help, as always, to look at the document itself and it is headed "Personal Loan Proposal Form", and then there are set out particulars of the proposer and it is those particulars which are alleged to be false in this case. It is true that over the page the purpose for which the loan is required is set out and the amount of the loan, the amount of the interest and the amount of the monthly instalments are all set out, but the point is made broadly that on the face of it this document is not made or required for an accounting purpose. If the proposal were accepted (and it was in this case), there is evidence for the jury that the proposal form is used for an accounting purpose because once the proposal form is accepted, various parts of the form are filled up on the front of the form and it is used for what the witness called "computer input". So undoubtedly if the proposal is accepted the form is used for an accounting purpose and material is put on the face of the form . . . Right until the moment that the proposal is accepted, the borrower would be under no duty whatever to account; that would only arise after the proposal were accepted. In my opinion it would be a misuse of the words of the statute to refer to it as a document made or required for any accounting purpose. In my view the highest that the evidence goes is that this document was for use in an accounting process, but there was no duty of any sort to account until after the proposal was accepted and ceased to be a proposal . . . I have come to the conclusion that there is no evidence on which a jury could find that this was a document made or required for any accounting purpose.'

The judge based his conclusion, so it seems, on two grounds: (1) that the document was not required for an accounting purpose until after it had been received and considered by the finance company and after the decision had been reached to grant a loan; and (2) that there was no duty to account until after this decision had been made.

As to the second ground, it does not seem to us that the moment at which any duty to account arose had any relevance to the question of whether the document was or was not required for an accounting purpose.

As to the first ground, it is to be observed that s 17(1)(a) in using the words 'made or required' indicates that there is a distinction to be drawn between a document made specifically for the purpose of accounting and one made for some other purpose but which is required for an accounting purpose. Thus it is apparent that a document may fall within the ambit of the section if it is made for some purpose other than an accounting purpose but is required for an accounting purpose as a subsidiary consideration.

In the present circumstances the borrower would be making the document for the purpose of his loan proposal to be considered, whereas, at the same time, the document might be 'required' by the finance company for an accounting purpose. Can it be said that the document is so required when the proposal may on consideration by the company be rejected? We think it can. The purpose, or at any rate one of the purposes, of the figures on the reverse side of the form was in due course to provide the necessary information for the computer.

The fact that the necessity might not arise in the event does not, it seems to us, mean that the information was not required in the first instance for the eventual accounting purpose. One can imagine the conversation: 'What do you need this for?' Answer: 'We need it for our computer accounting system in the event of the proposal being accepted.'

For these reasons we think that the learned judge was wrong in the conclusions which he reached.

The other point argued before us was this: that the part of the form which was falsified (that is the obverse side) was not in any way required for an accounting purpose. It was only the reverse side which was material for accounting, and consequently no offence was committed. We do not think that the words of the section permit of that interpretation. This was one entire document; it was as to part required for an accounting purpose; it was as to part falsified. The fact that these two parts were not the same does not exonerate the man who was responsible for the falsification. Indeed, the reverse side containing the figures also carries the borrower's signature and declaration.

We were referred to *R v Mallett* [1978] 3 All ER 10, [1978] 1 WLR 820, but the question we have to decide was not debated in that case and we do not think the judgment helps our decision.

It follows from what we have said that much will turn in a case of this sort on the precise nature and content of the proposal form in question. In giving the answer Yes to the question posed in the Attorney General's reference, we add the proviso that the answer might well be different were the form which has been falsified to be materially different from that which we are considering here.

Determination accordingly.

Solicitors: *Director of Public Prosecutions; Treasury Solicitor.*

N P Metcalfe Esq   Barrister.

R v Kelly and others

COURT OF APPEAL, CRIMINAL DIVISION
LORD LANE CJ, STOCKER AND GLIDEWELL JJ
7th, 24th OCTOBER 1980

Criminal law – Jurisdiction – Ship – Foreign ship on high seas – Offence of criminal damage committed by British subject on board foreign ship on high seas – Whether English courts having jurisdiction to try offender – Whether offender 'belonging' to foreign ship on which he was a passenger – Merchant Shipping Act 1894, s 686(1).

The appellants, who were British subjects, damaged or destroyed various fittings on a Danish ship on which they were travelling as passengers between Denmark and England. The ship was on the high seas at the time. The appellants were later charged with criminal damage, contrary to s 1(1) of the Criminal Damage Act 1971, and, notwithstanding that the offences occurred on a foreign ship on the high seas, were tried and convicted in the Crown Court on the basis that the court had jurisdiction under s 686(1)ᵈ of the Merchant Shipping Act 1894 to try them because they were each a British subject charged with having committed an offence 'on board [a] foreign ship to which he [did] not belong'. They appealed, contending (i) that the acts committed by them were not offences triable by an English court because at common law extra-territorial jurisdiction on the high seas was confined to British ships and there was no express provision in the 1971 Act extending that Act so as to apply to British subjects on board foreign ships, and (ii) that the appellants 'belonged' to the ship and that therefore s 686(1) did not apply.

Held – The appeals would be dismissed for the following reasons—

(1) Section 686(1) of the 1894 Act conferred on English courts extra-territorial jurisdiction additional to the common law Admiralty jurisdiction and to the extra-territorial jurisdiction given by specific statutes. Accordingly, the jurisdiction conferred on English courts by s 686(1) extended to any offence against English law committed by a British subject on board a foreign ship on the high seas (see p 373 *b* to *d* and p 374 *c*, post).

(2) A person 'belonged to' a ship, in the ordinary meaning of that phrase when used in the context of s 686(1), if he had a reasonably permanent attachment to it, as for example by being a member of the crew or a person who was on the ship for a substantial period of time for some other purpose, but a person who was a passenger and was only on the ship for the duration of a short voyage did not 'belong' to the ship. The appellants had therefore been on board a foreign ship to which they did not belong at the time the offences were committed and thus came within the ambit of s 686(1) (see p 374 *a* to *c*, post); *The Fusilier* (1865) Brown & Lush 341 considered.

Notes

For offences on the high seas, see 11 Halsbury's Laws (4th Edn) para 78, and for cases on the subject, see 14(1) Digest (Reissue) 158–161, 1103–1132.

For jurisdiction in respect of crimes committed out of England, see 11 Halsbury's Laws (4th Edn) para 87, and for cases on the subject, see 14(1) Digest (Reissue) 161–162, 1133–1139.

For the Merchant Shipping Act 1894, s 686, see 31 Halsbury's Statutes (3rd Edn) 383.

For the Criminal Damage Act 1971, s 1, see 41 ibid 409.

Cases referred to in judgment

Fusilier, The (1865) 3 Moo PCCNS 51, Brown & Lush 341, 5 New Rep 453, 12 LT 186, 11 Jur NS 289, 2 Mar LC 177, 167 ER 391, PC, 1(1) Digest (Reissue) 388, 2716.

a   Section 686(1) is set out at p 371 *g h*, post

R v Liverpool Justices, ex parte Molyneux [1972] 2 All ER 471, [1972] 2 QB 384, [1972] 2 WLR 1033, [1972] 1 Lloyd's Rep 367, 136 JP 477, DC, 14(1) Digest (Reissue), 159, 1118.

Sarpedon, The Cargo ex (1877) 3 PD 28, 37 LT 505, 3 Asp MLC 509, 42 Digest (Repl) 970, 7594.

Appeals

William Robert Kelly, David James Murphy and Stephen Paul Avison appealed against their conviction in the Crown Court at Newcastle upon Tyne on 18th October 1979 before his Honour Judge Stroyan QC on charges of causing criminal damage on the high seas contrary to s 1(1) of the Criminal Damage Act 1971. The facts are set out in the judgment of the court.

Robin Stewart QC and *C S A Rich* (assigned by the Registrar of Criminal Appeals) for the appellants.
David Robson QC and *Neil Jones* for the Crown.

Cur adv vult

24th October. **GLIDEWELL J** read the following judgment of the court: On 16th October 1979 these three appellants appeared at the Crown Court at Newcastle upon Tyne before his Honour Judge Stroyan QC to answer an indictment containing counts alleging criminal damage to or the destruction of the property of another, contrary to s 1(1) of the Criminal Damage Act 1971. In summary, the facts alleged by the prosecution, which all the appellants admitted, were that on 24th November 1978 these three young men, who are all British subjects, were travelling from Esbjerg in Denmark to North Shields as passengers on board the mv Winston Churchill, a vessel which despite its name is owned by a Danish company called DFDS. During the course of the voyage, whilst on the high seas, each of the appellants committed acts of vandalism which damaged or destroyed various fittings in the ship. These acts formed the subject of the various charges against them.

Before the appellants were arraigned their counsel on their behalf demurred to the indictment. The argument advanced was that, since each count in the indictment specifically alleged in the particulars that the offences had been committed in a foreign vessel on the high seas, the Crown Court at Newcastle upon Tyne had no jurisdiction to try or take any cognisance of the indictment. By analogy, it was argued that no other court in England or Wales would have jurisdiction.

In answer, the Crown relied on s 686(1) of the Merchant Shipping Act 1894, which provides:

'Where any person, being a British subject, is charged with having committed any offence on board any British ship on the high seas or in any foreign port or harbour or on board any foreign ship to which he does not belong, or, not being a British subject, is charged with having committed any offence on board any British ship on the high seas, and that person is found within the jurisdiction of any court in Her Majesty's dominions, which would have had cognizance of the offence if it had been committed on board a British ship within the limits of its ordinary jurisdiction, that court shall have jurisdiction to try the offence as if it had been so committed.'

The matter was dealt with as a preliminary issue, a sensible and convenient course. At the conclusion of the argument the judge delivered a reserved judgment in which he rejected the contentions advanced by the appellants and ruled that the Crown Court had jurisdiction to try the alleged offences. The appellants, while reserving their right to challenge that ruling by way of appeal, then entered pleas of guilty to certain of the counts.

The appellants Kelly and Murphy were sentenced to undertake 100 hours' community service, and the appellant Avison 120 hours'; in addition, each of them was ordered to pay £300 compensation. All three appellants now appeal to this court against their convictions, on the same issue of law as they raised in the Crown Court. We have granted the appellants Murphy and Avison extensions of time to enter their appeals. We have had the benefit of clear and concise arguments on both sides to which we wish to pay tribute.

Before the judge in the Crown Court, the appellants' submissions were supported by a variety of arguments. In this court counsel for all three appellants has restricted himself to two of these arguments, which he expresses in the following propositions: first, an act which, if committed in England, would be an offence under the Criminal Damage Act 1971, is not an offence triable by an English court if it is committed by a British subject on a foreign ship on the high seas; second, if that is wrong, a passenger on such a ship is 'a person belonging to the ship' and thus does not come within s 686(1) of the Merchant Shipping Act 1894.

We will consider each of these propositions in turn. In his argument in relation to the first proposition, counsel for the appellants puts before us the following general principles. (1) At common law acts constituting indictable offences which are committed on a British ship on the high seas are within the jurisdiction of the Admiral, and this is so whether the actor is a British or a foreign subject. (2) At common law acts committed on a foreign ship outside territorial waters are not within the jurisdiction of the English courts. Such acts can come within the jurisdiction only as the result of some express statutory provision. (3) There is a general presumption against extra-territorial criminality. (4) The Criminal Damage Act 1971 contains no words which purport to extend the normal territorial ambit of the Act. (5) Thus it follows that, unless there is some other express statutory provision which extends English criminal law generally or the Criminal Damage Act 1971 in particular so as to apply to British subjects on foreign ships, the acts committed by the appellants do not constitute offences against English law.

As we have said, the Crown relies on s 686(1) of the Merchant Shipping Act 1894, and in particular the words in the subsection, 'Where any person, being a British subject, is charged with having committed any offence . . . on board any foreign ship to which he does not belong . . .'

Counsel for the appellants argues, and we agree, that this subsection does not create offences where none would otherwise exist. Its purpose is to deal with the jurisdiction of the courts. Section 21 of the Merchant Shipping Acts Amendment Act 1855, the predecessor of s 686 of the 1894 Act, dealt only with the two cases of British subjects charged with offences committed on British ships on the high seas or in foreign ports or harbours, and foreign subjects charged with offences committed on British ships on the high seas. Counsel for the appellants argues that, since such offences were already within the jurisdiction of the Admiral, s 21 of the 1855 Act did no more than provide competent courts of jurisdiction. Thus, he says, the 'British subjects on foreign ships' provision, which s 686 of the 1894 Act added, should not be construed as having a wider impact.

Counsel for the appellant summarises his argument by saying that it is unclear what is meant by 'an offence' within s 686. He submits that the words should be interpreted as meaning only those acts which, by statute, are specifically made offences against English law and triable in England although committed abroad, for example, homicide by a British subject, which is dealt with in the Offences against the Person Act 1861, s 9, offences against the Foreign Enlistment Act 1870, and bigamy, again dealt with in the Offences against the Person Act 1861, s 57.

Counsel for the Crown, on the other hand, submits that the words in the section, 'an offence', mean an act which is an offence against English law. The reason, he argues, why there has been no decision of the courts on the meaning of these words in the section is that the words themselves are so clear.

The only recent decision on s 686 of the 1894 Act to which we were referred is *R v Liverpool Justices, ex parte Molyneux* [1972] 2 All ER 471, [1972] 2 QB 384. In that case a

British seaman, on a British ship in dock in Nassau in The Bahamas, stole a case of whisky from the ship's cargo. On the ship's return to Liverpool he was charged with theft before the Liverpool magistrates and convicted, reliance being placed on s 686 as giving the court jurisdiction. The Divisional Court held that the court had jurisdiction under s 686. However, it was not argued that theft was not 'an offence' within s 686. The argument was that Nassau in The Bahamas is not a 'foreign port' and that a ship in dock there cannot be said to be 'on the high seas'. Thus the decision does not greatly assist us in the present case.

We think that counsel for the Crown is correct in his submission. In our judgment the words 'any offence' in s 686(1) of the 1894 Act mean an offence against English law. The subsection thus embraces all such offences, and gives jurisdiction to the courts in this country to try such an offence if it is shown to have been committed by a British subject on a foreign ship on the high seas. The effect of the specific statutory provisions to which counsel for the appellants refers us, for example, s 9 of the Offences against the Person Act 1861, is not to restrict the jurisdiction of the English courts to deal with offences committed outside England to those particular offences. Section 686 of the 1894 Act gives the English courts extra-territorial jurisdiction which is additional to the common law Admiralty jurisdiction and to the jurisdiction given by those specific provisions.

We turn, therefore, to consider counsel for the appellants' second proposition, that the appellants did 'belong to' the ship on which they were travelling, and thus were not within the subsection. Counsel for the appellants submits that not only the master and the crew but also the passengers 'belong to' a ship. On this part of his submissions, he relies on the decision in *The Fusilier* (1865) Brown & Lush 341, 167 ER 391. That case concerned a claim for salvage under s 458 of the Merchant Shipping Act 1854, the material part of which provided that, when a ship was stranded within the territorial waters of the United Kingdom and services were rendered by any person 'in saving the lives of the persons belonging to the ship', salvage was payable by the owners of the ship to the persons rendering the services.

It was argued that passengers on a ship stranded in a gale were not 'persons belonging to the ship' within the meaning of that section. Dr Lushington held that they were. He relied on 'the reason of the thing', saying in effect that common humanity required the section to be construed in a way that encouraged the saving of life as well as the salvaging of the ship and its cargo, for which salvage would admittedly be payable. His decision was upheld by the Privy Council, though it seems that the point was argued only faintly, if at all, before the Judicial Committee. The decision was followed in the later case of *The Cargo ex Sarpedon* (1877) 3 PD 28.

Counsel for the appellants argues with force that the same construction should be placed on the words 'belong to the ship' wherever they occur in the Merchant Shipping Acts, and that we should follow the decision in *The Fusilier*. Counsel for the Crown, on the other hand, argues that, where a long statute deals with several different subjects in separate parts, it may be proper to construe words in one sense when they are used in one part of the Act and in a different sense in another part. He points out that, if the argument for the appellants is correct, only a limited range of persons on a ship do not belong to it: pilots, customs officers and perhaps stowaways. The 'British subject on a foreign ship' provision in s 686 must, he says, have been intended to have a far wider application than this.

We note that s 458 of the 1854 Act was replaced in the 1894 Act by a group of sections of which the first, s 544, applies to salvage payable for saving life. Neither that section nor s 545 or s 546 contain the words 'belong to' the ship. Thus, whatever meaning is given to the words 'does not belong' in s 686, that meaning will not be inconsistent with ss 544 to 546. The phrase 'belonging to the vessel' is, however, used in s 511 of the 1894 Act, a section in Part IX which deals with 'Wreck and Salvage', dealing with the duties of the receiver of wrecks. That section, however, specifically refers to such persons as 'shipwrecked persons', which may well give a wider meaning than the words otherwise have.

While we acknowledge the force of counsel for the appellants' argument, we must seek to give the words in s 686 'on board any foreign ship to which he does not belong' their ordinary meaning in the context in which they are used. In the context of this section, it is our view that those persons 'belong to' a vessel who have some reasonably permanent attachment to it. Understood in this sense, the phrase is wide enough to include not only the master and crew but persons who are on the ship for a substantial period of time for some other purpose, for example, scientists or engineers engaged in exploration or survey. The words do not, however, include persons who are passengers on a passenger ferry and are only on the ship for the duration of a short voyage. We therefore conclude that the appellants did not 'belong to' the mv Winston Churchill when they committed the offences with which they were charged.

It follows that we agree with the decision of the learned judge on both the points which were argued before us. For these reasons the appeals are dismissed.

Appeals dismissed.

Solicitors: *D E Brown*, Newcastle upon Tyne (for the Crown).

N P Metcalfe Esq   Barrister.

R v Austin and others

COURT OF APPEAL, CRIMINAL DIVISION
WATKINS LJ, PURCHAS AND TUDOR EVANS JJ
24th JULY 1980

Criminal law – Child stealing – Defence – Persons claiming right to possession of child not liable to prosecution – Father hiring accused to take child out of mother's possession – Accused aiding and abetting father to take child out of mother's possession by force – Whether accused entitled to immunity from prosecution – Offences against the Person Act 1861, s 56.

A husband, who was living apart from his wife, employed a firm of inquiry agents, of which W was a member, to find his wife and their three year old child. After the firm had done so, the husband instructed W to recover the child, who was in the lawful possession of the wife. W enlisted the services of A, T and F, and the four of them lay in wait, with the husband, for the wife and child. The husband forcibly snatched the child from the wife and then he and the others made off. W, A, T and F were charged with, and convicted of, child stealing, contrary to s 56[a] of the Offences against the Person Act 1861. They appealed, contending that although they had deliberately aided and abetted the husband, they were not guilty of the offence charged because the husband had not been acting 'unlawfully' within the meaning of s 56 and had committed no offence, or, alternatively, even if he had been acting unlawfully, they were entitled to immunity from prosecution under the proviso to s 56 since they were the agents of a 'person who . . . claimed [a] right to the possession of such child'.

Held – (1) On the true construction of s 56 of the 1861 Act the word 'unlawfully' meant 'without lawful excuse' and on the evidence the husband had committed the offence of child stealing, but, as he was the father of the child and as such could properly claim a right to possession of her, he was protected from prosecution by the proviso to s 56 (see p 378 *a* to *d*, post); *R v Prince* [1874–80] All ER Rep 881 applied.

(2) The proviso to s 56 only protected from prosecution a person, such as the father and mother of the child or a guardian, who had a legitimate right to, or interest in, the

---

a   Section 56, so far as material, is set out at p 377 *b*, post

possession of the child and did not protect paid hirelings who aided and abetted a parent to take a child by force out of the possession of the other parent. It followed that the appellants had been properly convicted (see p 378 e to j, post).

Notes

For the offence of child stealing, see 11 Halsbury's Laws (4th Edn) 1243, and for cases on the subject, see 15 Digest (Reissue) 1237–1238, 10,553–10,559.

For the Offences against the Person Act 1861, s 56, see 8 Halsbury's Statutes (3rd Edn) 166.

Case referred to in judgment

R v Prince (1875) LR 2 CCR 154, [1874–80] All ER Rep 881, 44 LJMC 122, 32 LT 700, 39 JP 676, 13 Cox CC 138, CCR, 14(1) Digest (Reissue) 31, 123.

Appeals

On 17th January 1979 in the Crown Court at Winchester before Park J Christopher Timothy John Austin, Ian Douglas Withers, Leeland Alexander Fieldsend and Barry Ronald Trigwell were convicted of child stealing, contrary to s 56 of the Offences against the Person Act 1861, and fined. They each appealed against conviction. The facts are set out in the judgment of the court.

M Kalisher (assigned by the Registrar for Criminal Appeals) for the appellants.
John Sparkes QC and Christopher Gardner for the Crown.

WATKINS LJ delivered the following judgment of the court: This is a disturbing case. On 17th January 1979 in the Crown Court at Winchester the appellants, Austin, Withers, Fieldsend and Trigwell whose ages range from 24 to 39 years, all pleaded guilty to child stealing. They did so at the conclusion of the Crown's case during a trial before Park J who had been invited to, and did, rule on submissions of counsel for the appellants, who now appeal against their convictions. The submissions were to the effect that they could not in law, on facts which were not in dispute, be guilty of the offence charged, which was founded on the provisions of s 56 of the Offences against the Person Act 1861.

This case is obviously of importance to parents and children. From some of the submissions made to this court we have the impression it is commonly understood that when parents have been separated one parent may against the will of the other take away by force a child or the children of the family. That notion if it exists needs to be dispelled.

Mrs Janice King when she was a single woman went from her home in this country to the United States of America. She took up employment there. She met a United States citizen named Robert King, whom she married. They did not get on. On 30th June 1975 she gave birth to a female child by him. The child became known as Lara. In March of the following year Mrs King came to England ostensibly to attend a wedding. Within a matter of a few weeks she decided not to return to the United States. She consulted solicitors with the object of obtaining a divorce. Before those proceedings commenced the solicitors issued an originating summons for an order granting her custody of the child. On the issue of that summons Lara became a ward of court. Mr King came to this country and took out a similar summons. The Official Solicitor was appointed guardian ad litem of Lara. Thereafter he had the right and duty to act in the best interests of the child in any proceedings which affected her. He was content that interim care and control, although there was no order to that effect, should for all practical purposes remain with Mrs King, who was living at that time near Winchester.

King was, not unnaturally, concerned at having lost his child so he sought relief from a court in the State of Maryland where he lives. On 29th October 1976 that court ordered that he should have the care and control of the child. Mrs King was acquainted with the terms of that order. It was of no effect here since it could not be enforced in this country and Mrs King would not and did not obey its terms. That court in May 1977 declared her to be in contempt for failing to surrender the care and control of the child to her husband. It also issued a warrant for her arrest. That warrant could not be executed outside the United States, and perhaps not outside Maryland.

King therefore decided to resort to other and far less desirable means of regaining possession of his child. He became acquainted with a firm of inquiry agents in this country known as Nationwide Investigations. He asked this firm, of which Withers is a member, to find his wife and child. In late July 1977 Withers found the wife and child. Thereupon King engaged him to take Lara out of the possession of her mother for a fee of £2,000. Withers was aware of the orders of the court in Maryland. He was informed that there was no order affecting the child made by any court in this country. He planned an operation which apparently required the services of no less than three other husky warriors, namely, the other three appellants, Austin, Fieldsend and Trigwell.

They all went off in a number of motor cars to Winchester. They spent the night in a hotel, no doubt going through the plan so that they would be sure of its details. King was with them, so that by now five men were ready to spring on the unsuspecting Mrs King. On 2nd August, at about 4.15 pm, she was walking along a street, pushing a perambulator. Lara was in it. Along came a number of cars, in which were King, Withers and Fieldsend, Austin and Trigwell. The leading car came alongside Mrs King. Out of it jumped her husband. He seized the child, bundling her into the car whilst pushing his wife aside. The car was then driven off at high speed. Mrs King was beside herself; she was hysterical. Who came to her assistance? None other than Austin and Trigwell. The car they were riding in came up alongside her and stopped; they offered her assistance. She wanted to be driven to a telephone box so that she could speak to a policeman. They offered to take her to such a place. They did so but so slowly that Mrs King suspected that they had something to do with what had happened to her child. How right she was. She was dropped off. The cars sped towards Heathrow Airport. There was a change of motor cars. Meanwhile Mrs King was telephoning the police, and the police were putting out messages over their inter-communication system. An alert policeman on motor cycle patrol happened to note the registration number of the car in which Austin and Trigwell were riding. Mrs King had taken a careful note of it and had given it to the police. The motor cyclist gave chase. By now Austin and Trigwell had split up and were in two different but identical motor cars. The police stopped two cars, and apprehended the four appellants. King outdistanced the police. After all, a motor cycle is no match for an aeroplane. He was soon on his way by air to Dublin and from there to the United States.

Withers gave wholly false and misleading information to put the police off the scent of King. In the course of an interview in which he revealed himself to be untrustworthy and in many respects untruthful, he informed the police that this was about the 53rd time he had been involved in snatching a child by force from one parent on behalf of the other.

Time went by. Mrs King and her husband were divorced on his petition in the United States. She could not tolerate being parted from her child, so she went to the United States. She still lives and works there. She has obtained an order of access to her child, so that the family are to that extent reunited.

Nothing can excuse the reason why King enlisted the services of Nationwide Investigations, or the quite appalling way in which each one of the members of that firm behaved in assisting him to take the child away from her mother. But that does not automatically mean that any one of them is guilty of child stealing.

At the close of the case for the Crown in the Crown Court at Winchester counsel for the appellants, to whom we are extremely indebted for his restrained, able and frank submissions to us, made a number of concessions on behalf of the appellants. He has repeated them to this court. They are: (1) that each of these appellants aided and abetted King in taking Lara away from the possession of her mother; and (2) that the child was taken by King by the use of force on the mother and on the child. It was also conceded that they all knew the child was in the lawful possession of the mother, since there was no order in this country which affected her right to that at the material time and the order of the American court could not affect it in any practical way. It was also admitted that they had the intention to deprive the mother of possession of the child.

Having regard to those admissions and the background of this affair, one looks at s 56 of the 1861 Act which provides:

'Whosoever shall unlawfully ... by force ... take away ... any child under the age of fourteen years, with intent to deprive any parent ... of the possession of such child ... shall be liable, at the discretion of the court ... to be imprisoned: Provided, that no person who shall have claimed any right to the possession of such child, or shall be the mother or shall have claimed to be the father of an illegitimate child, shall be liable to be prosecuted by virtue hereof on account of the getting possession of such child ...'

It is submitted that there are two questions relevant to the issue of whether the appellants were rightly convicted: (1) did King commit an offence under s 56, bearing in mind that he assaulted his wife and when taking the child away the child too, and (2) if King committed an offence under s 56, does it follow that the appellants are also guilty of that offence? Furthermore, suppose King had been indicted and found not guilty by reason only of being able to take advantage of the proviso, could the appellants have escaped conviction in that way too?

It is argued that the mother and the father were equally entitled in law to custody of the child. Whilst this is not disputed by counsel for the Crown, who has assisted us greatly, he reminded us of the rights and obligations of the Official Solicitor.

But counsel for the appellants submits that, although the mother had actual possession of the child with the consent of the Official Solicitor, the father had a right to regain possession of the child at will, and to do almost anything including the use of violence on the mother with the assistance of a gang of men to achieve this without being guilty of an offence under s 56. It is an alarming proposition, which requires and has had our careful consideration.

It is argued that what was done did not infringe the provisions of s 56 since no one committed an independent unlawful act. King might have been convicted of conspiracy or of an assault on his wife had he been proceeded against. One of the appellants might have been convicted of perverting the course of justice; but these offences would not have proved that King behaved unlawfully in taking away the child. He had a right to take his child away. The mind boggles at what might happen if that be right. We could easily descend into a state of almost complete anarchy in domestic affairs if that is a permissible interpretation of s 56. Parliament surely could not have contemplated so extraordinary a state of affairs, namely the assertion of a right to possession of a child by the use of violence.

Counsel for the Crown submits that if a father snatches his child away from the mother by the use of force and has no lawful excuse for using that means to obtain possession of the child he is guilty of an offence. It would be difficult to envisage what lawful excuse there could be for the use of violence in such a circumstance.

In considering the meaning of the word 'unlawfully' assistance can be derived from *R v Prince* (1875) LR 2 CCR 154, [1874–80] All ER Rep 88. In that case there had been a conviction under s 55 of the 1861 Act of unlawfully taking an unmarried girl under the age of 16 out of the possession and against the will of her father. The principal issue was whether the defendant knew that at the relevant time the girl was under the age of 16 years. The decision turned on the meanings of the word 'unlawfully' as used in s 55. In the course of his judgment Denman J said (LR 2 CCR 154 at 178, [1874–80] All ER Rep 881 at 895–896):

'Bearing in mind the previous enactments relating to the abduction of girls under sixteen, 4 & 5 Phil. & Mary, c. 8 [the Abduction Act 1557], s. 2, and the general course of the decisions upon those enactments, and upon the present statute, and looking at the mischief intended to be guarded against, it appears to me reasonably clear that the word "unlawfully", in the true sense in which it was used, is fully satisfied by holding that it is equivalent to the words "without lawful excuse" using those words as equivalent to "without such an excuse as being proved would be a complete legal justification for the act, even where all the facts constituting the offence exist".'

In our judgment, that construction of the word 'unlawfully' can properly be applied to the identical word as used in s 56 of the 1861 Act. Therefore a parent who seeks, especially when there is no order of a court in existence affecting the ordinary common law right of possession of parents to a child, to take away that child from the other parent by force will inevitably commit the offence of child stealing under s 56, unless it be shown that at the time there was lawful excuse for the use of the force as a means of taking the child away. Accordingly, apart from the proviso, King on the known facts could have had no defence if charged with this offence.

Undoubtedly King could properly have claimed a right of possession to the child and so have gained the protection of the proviso. What would have been the effect of that? The effect would have been that, although he had committed the offence of child stealing, because he was the child's father and could claim a right to possession of the child he would not have been prosecuted. It is submitted on the appellants' behalf that the proviso also protects a class of persons wide enough to include those who aid a person such as the father of the child in gaining possession of his child by force. They become his agents for the purpose. Many persons have from time to time the temporary possession of a child as agents of parents. Why are they not protected to the same extent as parents when regaining possession as agents of parents?

In our view the only sensible construction of the proviso allows of its protection being granted to a small class of persons only, which includes the father and the mother of the child, whether the child be legitimate or illegitimate, or a guardian appointed by a testamentary document, or by an order conferring the status of guardianship, or a person to whom is granted an order conferring some form of care, control, custody or access. We can think of no other who could claim exemption from prosecution by reason of the proviso.

What of these appellants? They had no good reason for doing what they did. They had no right to assert, and no interest in, the possession of the child. They were the paid hirelings of King to aid him in the commission of a criminal offence, namely stealing a child, and with him they committed it as aiders and abettors. While King may shelter behind the proviso, there is no room there for them. Parliament in its wisdom undoubtedly decided that the mischiefs of matrimonial discord which are unhappily so widespread should not give rise to wholesale criminal prosecutions arising out of disputes about children, about who should have possession and control of them. That and that alone is the reason for the existence of the proviso to s 56. Thus, as we have said, its application is confined to the select class of persons we have endeavoured to define.

It should be clearly understood that those such as these appellants who aid a father or a mother to take possession of a child from the other parent, and who do so by the use of force as aiders and abettors to it, commit the offence of child stealing, and that they are not immune from prosecution.

This was a wicked example of aiding and abetting the commission of the offence, child stealing. In the judgment of this court, the appellants are extremely fortunate that the trial judge treated them so mercifully by the sentences he imposed. This kind of activity must be condemned and those who are tempted to engage in it should be deterred from doing so.

Appeals dismissed.

Solicitors: *Treasury Solicitor.*

Sepala Munasinghe Esq   Barrister.

Property Discount Corpn Ltd v Lyon Group Ltd and another

COURT OF APPEAL, CIVIL DIVISION
BUCKLEY, TEMPLEMAN AND BRIGHTMAN LJJ
29th, 30th, 31st JULY 1980

Land – Interest in land – Creation – Agreement for lease – Building agreement providing for grant of lease by owner to developer on completion of buildings – Developer granting plaintiff equitable mortgage of his interest under agreement – Mortgage including covenant to execute legal mortgage of lease granted under building agreement – Equitable charge registered under companies legislation but not under land charges legislation – Owner granting lease to developer – Whether mortgage creating equitable charge enforceable against assignee of lease from developer – Whether mortgage creating single charge on developer's interest under building agreement – Whether mortgage creating separate charge on developer's covenant to execute legal mortgage of lease.

Company – Charge – Registration – Equitable charge affecting land – Charge registered under companies legislation in name of company creating charge but not registered under land charges legislation – Whether registration under companies legislation effective as registration under land charges legislation – Whether purchaser for value of land affected by notice of charge even though not registered in name of estate owner – Land Charges Act 1925, s 10(5) – Companies Act 1948, s 95(1) – Land Charges Act 1972, s 3(7).

W Ltd, which owned the freehold of an industrial site, decided to develop it and entered into a building agreement with L Ltd dated 27th February 1968 for the erection of buildings on the site by L Ltd. The work was to be completed within five years, and pending completion L Ltd was to be tenant at will of the site until each building was completed, when W Ltd was to grant L Ltd a long lease of that part of the site. L Ltd arranged to borrow money by instalments from the plaintiff to finance the development and on 31st July 1968 executed a mortgage to secure the loan. Under the terms of the mortgage L Ltd assigned to the plaintiff by way of equitable charge all its interest under the building agreement and the benefit thereof. The mortgage contained a covenant by L Ltd to execute a legal mortgage in favour of the plaintiff over any lease of the site granted to it while money remained due under the mortgage. On 12th August 1968 particulars of the mortgage were registered under s 95[a] of the Companies Act 1948 in the name of L Ltd but the mortgage was never registered under the Land Charges Act 1925. L Ltd erected two buildings on parts of the site, and, pursuant to the building agreement, W Ltd granted L Ltd leases of those parts of the site. Although money remained due under the equitable mortgage, a legal mortgage of the leases was not executed in favour of the plaintiff. In January 1973 L Ltd assigned one of the leases to one of the defendants. In July, after the Land Charges Act 1972, which superseded the 1925 Act, had come into force, L Ltd assigned the other lease to the other defendant. Money still remained due from L Ltd to the plaintiff under the mortgage and in 1975 the plaintiff began proceedings to enforce the mortgage against both defendants. In the

___

a   Section 95, so far as material, provides:
    '(1) Subject to the provisions of this Part of this Act, every charge created after the fixed date by a company registered in England and being a charge to which this section applies shall, so far as any security on the company's property or undertaking is conferred thereby, be void . . . unless the prescribed particulars of the charge together with the instrument, if any, by which the charge is created or evidenced, are delivered to or received by the registrar of companies for registration in manner required by this Act within twenty-one days after the date of its creation . . .
    '(2) This section applies to . . . (d) a charge on land, wherever situate, or any interest therein . . .
    '(10) In this Part of this Act—(a) the expression "charge" includes mortgage . . .'

course of those proceedings one of the defendants issued a summons for the trial of the preliminary issue whether on the agreed facts the defendants' interests under the leases were subject to the equitable mortgage. At the trial of that issue the plaintiff contended that the mortgage created a single equitable charge on the land, namely a charge on the whole of L Ltd's interest under the building agreement, including L Ltd's right to be granted leases, that, although that was a charge which was registrable under s 10(1) of the Land Charges Act 1925 and had not been registered thereunder, the registration of the charge under s 95 of the 1948 Act was, by virtue of s 10(5)[b] of the 1925 Act, sufficient registration in place of registration under the 1925 Act, and accordingly, that the registration under s 95 was binding on the defendants' interests under the leases. The defendants contended that the mortgage conferred two separate securities on the plaintiff, namely a charge on L Ltd's chose in action entitling it to require the grant of leases by W Ltd and a charge on L Ltd's covenant to execute a legal mortgage in favour of the plaintiff. Since the first charge, although registerable under s 95, had become spent on the grant of the leases by W Ltd, and since the second was not registrable under s 95 and had not been registered, as it could have been, under the 1925 Act, the registration under s 95 fell to be ignored. The defendants further contended that, in any event, registration under s 95 would not have effected registration under the 1925 Act because it was not registration in the name of the estate owner. The judge ([1980] 1 All ER 334) held that the defendants' interests were subject to the equitable charge which was created by the mortgage. The defendants appealed.

Held – The appeal would be dismissed for the following reasons—

(1) The mortgage from L Ltd conferred on the plaintiff a single continuing equitable charge on a single subject matter, namely L Ltd's conditional right to be granted leases by W Ltd and on those leases as and when they were granted, and that charge was an equitable interest in land (see p 384 b to d, p 385 c to e g h and p 386 a, post).

(2) The registration of the plaintiff's charge under s 95 of the 1948 Act was, by virtue of s 10(5) of the 1925 Act, sufficient registration in place of registration under the 1925 Act even though the s 95 registration was against the name of the company affected (ie L Ltd) and not, as s 10(2) of the 1925 Act and s 3(1)[c] of the 1972 Act required, against the name of the estate owner whose land was affected (ie W Ltd), since on the true construction of s 10(5) (which was repeated in s 3(7) of the 1972 Act) the provision for registration under s 95 to operate in lieu of registration under the 1925 Act was not confined to a case where the s 95 registration was in fact against the name of the estate owner because registration under s 95 had effect as if there had been registration under the 1925 Act against the name of the estate owner. Since the material provisions of the 1925 Act were repeated in s 3 of the 1972 Act, it followed that both defendants were bound by the registration of the charge under s 95 (see p 385 a to e g h and p 386 a, post).

Decision of Goulding J [1980] 1 All ER 334 affirmed.

Notes

For registration of a charge by a company and for the effect of such registration under the Land Charges Act 1972, see 7 Halsbury's Laws (4th Edn) para 862 and for cases on the subject, see 10 Digest (Reissue) 857–868, 4946–4994.

For the Land Charges Act 1925, s 10, see 27 Halsbury's Statutes (3rd Edn) 696.

---

b   Section 10(5), so far as material, is set out at p 383 a, post
c   Section 3, so far as material, provides:
    '(1) A land charge shall be registered in the name of the estate owner whose estate is intended to be affected . . .
    '(7) In the case of a land charge for securing money created by a company before 1st January 1970 or so created at any time as a floating charge, registration under [inter alia, s 95 of the Companies Act 1948] shall be sufficient in place of registration under this Act, and shall have effect as if the land charge had been registered under this Act . . .'

For the Companies Act 1948, s 95, see 5 ibid 189.
For the Land Charges Act 1972, s 3, see 42 ibid 1600.

Cases referred to in judgments

Barrett v Hilton Developments Ltd [1974] 3 All ER 944, [1975] Ch 237, [1974] 3 WLR 545.
    29 P & CR 300, CA, Digest (Cont Vol D) 756, 926cb.

Jackson and Bassford Ltd, Re [1906] 2 Ch 467, 75 LJ Ch 697, 95 LT 292, 13 Mans 306, 10
    Digest (Reissue) 818, 4720.

Williams v Burlington Investments Ltd (1977) 121 Sol Jo 424, HL.

Appeals

J H Fenner & Co (Holdings) Ltd ('Fenner') and ITT Distributors Ltd ('ITT'), the second
and third defendants respectively in proceedings commenced by originating summons
dated 25th September 1975 by the plaintiffs, Property Discount Corpn Ltd ('Property
Discount'), for the enforcement of an equitable mortgage, appealed against so much of
the judgment of Goulding J ([1980] 1 All ER 334) given on 31st July 1979 as declared
that the interest of Fenner under a lease dated 15th December 1969 and the interest of
ITT under a lease dated 7th November 1969 were subject to the equitable mortgage. The
facts are set out in the judgment of Brightman LJ.

Richard Scott QC and *Benjamin Levy* for Fenner and ITT.
Donald Rattee QC and *R E Pearce* for Property Discount.

BRIGHTMAN LJ delivered the first judgment at the invitation of Buckley LJ. This
is an appeal from a decision of Goulding J ([1980] 1 All ER 334). The dispute is between
an equitable mortgagee and assignees of the mortgagor. The issue is whether the
assignees took subject to or free from the mortgage. The mortgage was registered under
s 95 of the Companies Act 1948, but not under the Land Charges Act 1925. The matter
came before the judge on an agreed statement of facts and copies of the relevant
documents. The facts are fully set out in his judgment and I do not therefore intend to
repeat them, but to confine myself to a brief summary necessary to enable my judgment
to be, I hope, understood.

    In 1968 Western Ground Rents Ltd owned the freehold of a six-acre industrial site in
Cardiff. It decided to develop the site through a company which later became known as
Lyon Group Ltd. For this purpose it entered into a building agreement with Lyon
Group Ltd dated 27th February 1968. By cl 2 of the building agreement, Lyon Group
agreed to erect industrial buildings according to plans and specifications to be approved
by the surveyor of Western Ground Rents. The work was to be completed within five
years. Pending completion Lyon Group was to be a tenant at will. As and when each
building was completed, Western Ground Rents was to grant to Lyon Group or its
nominee a long lease of that part of the site. As part of the financing, Lyon Group
arranged to borrow money by instalments from Property Discount Corpn Ltd. In order
to secure the loan, Lyon Group executed a mortgage deed, dated 31st July 1968, in favour
of Property Discount. By cl 1 of that deed, Lyon Group assigned to Property Discount
by way of equitable charge all the interest of Lyon Group under the building agreement
and the benefit thereof, as security for the money to be advanced.

    Clause 3(e) of the 1968 mortgage provided that if any lease should be granted to Lyon
Group of the site or any part thereof while any money remained owing on the mortgage,
Lyon Group would forthwith execute a proper legal mortgage in favour of Property
Discount of the land comprised in such lease, to secure all the money for the time being
remaining due under the mortgage deed.

    On 12th August 1968 the mortgage was registered under s 95 of the Companies Act
1948. No registration was effected under the Land Charges Act 1925. Lyon Group
proceeded to erect buildings on the site. Two of the buildings came to be identified as
'unit 7' and 'unit 8'.

On 15th December 1969 Western Ground Rents executed a lease of unit 8 in favour of Lyon Group pursuant to its obligation under the building agreement. Lyon Group, in circumstances which are not known to us, did not execute a legal mortgage of unit 8 as required by cl 3(e) of the 1968 mortgage.

On 22nd January 1973 Lyon Group assigned to J H Fenner & Co (Holdings) Ltd, for value, the benefit of the lease of unit 8. That assignment is not before us, but I think it is accepted that it contained nothing that is material for present purposes. I shall deal later with the lease of unit 7 and the assignment thereof to a company called ITT Distributors Ltd.

Money secured by the 1968 mortgage remains due from Lyon Group to Property Discount. Proceedings were begun in 1975 by Property Discount against Lyon Group, Fenner and ITT. In the course of those proceedings ITT issued a summons for the trial of a preliminary issue, whether on the basis of an agreed statement of facts and the documents, the interests of Fenner and ITT under the leases were subject to the charge created by the 1968 mortgage notwithstanding the absence of any registration under the Land Charges Act 1925. Goulding J decided this issue in favour of Property Discount. Fenner and ITT now appeal. The arguments in the court below seem to have been, for the most part, the same as those submitted to us in this court. I think it would be simpler to explain first the argument of the respondents, Property Discount. I shall still confine myself only to unit 8.

The argument is as follows. Clause 1 of the 1968 mortgage was expressed to create an equitable charge over the whole interest of Lyon Group under the building agreement and the benefit thereof. That interest and benefit included the right of Lyon Group to occupy the site for the purpose of putting up the buildings, and the right of Lyon Group to a lease of each building as and when completed. Therefore, when the lease of unit 8 was executed, that lease became in equity subject to the charge created by the 1968 mortgage. The charge, which was equitable throughout, attached automatically to the lease when granted. The 1968 mortgage created a land charge which was registrable as a class C land charge under s 10(1) of the Land Charges Act 1925, though it was not in fact so registered. Section 10(1) provides, so far as material:

> 'The following classes of charges on, or obligations affecting, land may be registered as land charges in the register of land charges, namely . . . Class C:—A mortgage charge or obligation affecting land of any of the following kinds . . . (iii) Any other equitable charge, which is not secured by a deposit of documents relating to the legal estate affected and does not arise or affect an interest arising under a trust for sale or a settlement and is not included in any other class of land charge (in this Act called "a general equitable charge") . . .'

The 1968 mortgage created a charge. That charge was a land charge within the meaning of the Act because it was a charge on land, namely a charge on the interest of Lyon Group in the six-acre site under the terms of the building agreement. 'Land' is widely defined by s 20 of the Land Charges Act 1925; it includes—

> 'land of any tenure, and mines and minerals, whether or not severed from the surface, buildings or parts of buildings . . . and other corporeal hereditaments . . . and . . . incorporeal hereditaments, and an easement, right, privilege or benefit in, over or derived from land . . .'

Section 13(2) of the Land Charges Act 1925 contains the sanction for failure to register. It provides that a land charge of, inter alia, class C shall be void as against a purchaser of the land charged therewith unless the land charge is registered in the appropriate register before the completion of the purchase. Under s 20 'purchaser' means a person who for valuable consideration takes any interest in land. Fenner was such a purchaser. However, the omission to register under the Land Charges Act 1925 does not avoid the charge as against Property Discount; the charge is saved, it is submitted, by s 10(5) of the Land Charges Act 1925 which, so far as is material for present purposes, reads:

> 'In the case of a land charge for securing money, created by a company . . . registration under [s 95 of the Companies Act 1948] shall be sufficient in place of registration under this Act, and shall have effect as if the land charge had been registered under this Act.'

The words I have omitted in reading the subsection were words inserted by the Law of Property Act 1969, but in my view they have no relevance to the argument that we have to consider.

The 1968 mortgage, it was submitted, created a land charge for securing money. The charge was created by a company and it was duly registered under s 95 of the 1948 Act, which applies, inter alia, to a charge on land wherever situate or any interest therein, excluding a rent charge. In the result, it was argued, registration of the land charge created by the 1968 mortgage under s 95 of the 1948 Act was sufficient in place of registration under the Land Charges Act 1925, and has effect as if the land charge had been registered under the Land Charges Act 1925. It therefore binds the interest of Fenner in unit 8, notwithstanding that Fenner was a purchaser of the lease for valuable consideration.

The arguments of counsel for Fenner and ITT against the validity of the charge are deployed from two directions. The attack stems, first, from a careful analysis of the effect of the 1968 mortgage, and, second, from what is said to be the true construction and effect of s 10(5) of the Land Charges Act 1925. The first attack is based on the proposition that the 1968 mortgage does not contain one single security consisting of a charge on all the interest of Lyon Group under the building agreement. The subject matter of the charge, it was said, varies from time to time as the development of the site progresses, as buildings are completed and leases are granted. This variation of the subject matter of the charge leads to inevitable changes from time to time in the registrations necessary in order to preserve the priority of Property Discount as mortgagee. Counsel for Fenner and ITT submitted that on a true analysis the 1968 mortgage contained, first, an assignment by way of charge of the contractual right of Lyon Group to be given a lease of each part of the site on the completion of a building; and, second, a covenant by Lyon Group to grant a legal mortgage of each lease as and when it was granted. The 1968 mortgage, it was said, did not, either at the date of execution or at the date of registration under s 95 of the 1948 Act, create any charge on the leasehold interest of Lyon Group in unit 8 because that leasehold interest was not in existence at those times. The only land charge which qualified for registration under s 95 of the 1948 Act on 12th August 1968, which was the date of registration, was the *contractual right* of Lyon Group to be granted a lease on the future completion of the building. The effect of the execution of the lease of unit 8 was, inevitably, to discharge Western Ground Rents' obligation under the building agreement to grant such a lease, and thus the charge of Lyon Group's contractual right quoad unit 8 necessarily disappeared at that stage. All that was then left to Property Discount quoad unit 8 was the benefit of the covenant of Lyon Group to execute a legal mortgage over the lease which had been granted. It cannot possibly be said that that covenant at the date of the 1968 mortgage created a charge on the lease, because the lease was not then in existence.

Reliance was placed on the observations of Buckley J in *Re Jackson and Bassford Ltd* [1906] 2 Ch 467 at 477 to the effect that an agreement that in some future circumstances a security shall in the future be created, does not create any present security which qualifies for registration under the predecessor of s 95 of the 1948 Act. Reference was also made to *Williams v Burlington Investments Ltd* (1977) 121 Sol Jo 424, decided by the House of Lords. The covenant to execute a legal mortgage was not registerable under s 95 of the 1948 Act; it was a contract to create a legal estate, and therefore fell to be registered as an estate contract under class C(iv) of the Land Charges Act 1925, s 95 of the 1948 Act having no relevance to that contract. In the result, the registration under s 95 falls to be ignored for present purposes and the sanction imposed by s 13(2) of the Land Charges Act 1925 applies. Accordingly Fenner is left with the lease of unit 8, free from any charge.

Goulding J rejected that argument for a reason which he stated quite shortly as follows. Indeed, I do not think it is susceptible of much elaboration. He said ([1980] 1 All ER 334 at 339):

'When Lyon expressly assigned by way of equitable charge to the plaintiff all Lyon's interest under the building agreement, and the benefit thereof, it gave the plaintiff, in my judgment, a single continuing equitable charge that operated (as between Lyon and the plaintiff) both on Lyon's chose in action enforceable against Western Ground Rents Ltd and on each term of years as granted to Lyon, the leases being in truth the only real benefit of the building agreement to Lyon. The covenant to execute legal mortgages I regard as an ancillary or supplementary provision, though no doubt sufficient of itself to constitute an equitable charge if it stood alone.'

I agree. In my view the 1968 mortgage contained a charge on one single subject matter, namely the conditional right of Lyon Group to be granted leases, and on such leases as and when granted. That was a single subject matter, subjected to a single charge. I intend no disrespect to counsel for Fenner and ITT if I describe his able arguments on this aspect of the case as artificial, and as introducing a subtlety which I think would be more apt to confuse the system of registration of charges than to contribute to any rational scheme of registration, and I would accede to his submissions with great regret.

I turn to what I think, as did Goulding J, is the real problem in this case. If the 1968 mortgage had been registered as a general equitable charge, as it could have been and certainly ought to have been in the absence of any registration under s 95 of the Companies Act 1948, it would have been registrable against, and only against, Western Ground Rents. This follows from s 10(2) of the Land Charges Act 1925 which, so far as material for present purposes, provides that a land charge shall be registered in the name of the estate owner whose estate is intended to be affected. Registration against the name of a subsequent estate owner is ineffective: *Barrett v Hilton Developments Ltd* [1974] 3 All ER 944, [1975] Ch 237. Under s 20 of the Land Charges Act 1925, 'estate owner' means, by reference to the Law of Property Act 1925, the owner of a legal estate. The only owner of the legal estate in the six-acre site at the date of the 1968 mortgage and at the date of registration under s 95 of the 1948 Act, was Western Ground Rents. The registration under s 95, however, was necessarily against Lyon Group.

The question therefore arises whether registration of a land charge under s 95 against company X can, on the true construction of s 10(5) of the Land Charges Act 1925, be regarded as an effective substitute for registration under the Land Charges Act in the name of Y. The obvious purpose of s 10(2) of the Land Charges Act 1925 was to avoid the necessity of double registration, as indeed is said by the editors of both the 1932 and the 1972 editions of Wolstenholme and Cherry in their commentaries on the subsection (see Conveyancing Statutes, 12th and 13th Edns). There could, however, be no double registration in a case where the company creating the charge on the land is not the estate owner, because the registration names under the two Acts would in that case be different. It might be considered a somewhat odd result if registration under the Companies Act 1948 against X absolved an encumbrancer from registration under the Land Charges Act 1925 against Y under the guise of avoiding the necessity for double registration. It is possible to construct cases in which a system of substituted registration so applied could work a real injustice, as was demonstrated during the course of argument, though I think that the likelihood of any such case of injustice would be fairly remote.

I was at one time disposed to think, on general principles of logic, that s 10(5) of the 1925 Act must somehow be confined to a case where the registration under the Companies Act 1948 is against the same name as the registration would be if done under the Land Charges Act 1925. If that were so in the present case, the appeal of Fenner must succeed, for Property Discount would then have no escape route from the penalty of invalidity imposed by s 13(2) of the Land Charges Act 1925. I have, however, in the end come to the conclusion, as did Goulding J, that the argument must be rejected. The wording of s 10(5) is too clear, however illogical the result may seem on the facts of the present case. The Companies Act registration is to be sufficient. It is to be sufficient in place of registration under the Land Charges Act. It is to have effect as if the land charge had been registered under the Land Charges Act. As the only registration which could have been validly effected under the Land Charges Act at the date of the registration under the Companies Act was registration against the name of Western Ground Rents, it follows, in my view, that the registration whose place is taken by the s 95 registration must be registration against the name of Western Ground Rents, and the same effect is to follow as if there had in fact been such a registration.

In the result, therefore, I accept in toto the argument of counsel for Property Discount, which I sought to summarise at the start of my judgment, and I would dismiss the appeal of Fenner.

The facts in the ITT case differ only to the extent that the assignment of the lease by Lyon Group of unit 7 took place after the date when the Land Charges Act 1972 superseded the Land Charges Act 1925, namely in January 1973. The provisions of the land charges legislation which apply in the ITT case are therefore those of the 1972 Act, but such provisions repeated the 1925 legislation in all material respects.

I would therefore also dismiss the appeal of ITT.

TEMPLEMAN LJ. I agree, and I cannot see that there is any great harm done in the result.

The assignee in 1973 of a 99 year lease granted in 1969 should have taken the precaution of investigating the title of the landlord and the title of the lessee. Investigation of the title of a lessee company will routinely include a search in the Companies Registry to see if there are any entries under s 95 of the Companies Act 1948. Such a search in the present case would have disclosed the mortgage entered into by Lyon Group; the fact that the mortgage preceded the grant of the lease would not, in view of the possibility of the existence of a relevant floating charge, absolve the assignee from inquiring into the terms of the mortgage and from then satisfying himself that the property comprised in the lease had been released from the equitable charge contained in the mortgage. It is hardly possible to conceive of instances in which a proper investigation of title would not have disclosed the s 95 entry.

For the reasons given by Brightman LJ, I agree that the appeals should be dismissed.

BUCKLEY LJ. I also entirely agree with the judgment that Brightman LJ has delivered.

Before the judge in the court below it was treated as common ground that an equitable charge on an equitable interest in land would fall within class C (iii) of s 10(1) of the Land Charges Act 1925 as an equitable charge described in that paragraph. Initially counsel for Fenner and ITT, in the course of his argument in this court, sought to depart from that concession, if it was a concession, in the court below and to contend that only an equitable charge on a legal estate in land could fall within class C(iii). However, in the course of his argument in this court he abandoned that point and accepted that para (iii) is apt to extend to an equitable charge on an equitable interest in land.

I have nothing to add to the reasoning of the judgment delivered by Brightman LJ and

I agree that, for the reasons which he has given, these appeals fail and should be dismissed.

Appeals dismissed. Leave to appeal to the House of Lords refused.

Solicitors: *Barlow, Lyde & Gilbert* (for Fenner); *Slaughter & May* (for ITT), *Linklaters & Paines* (for Property Discount).

Diana Brahams   Barrister.

Chester v Buckingham Travel Ltd

CHANCERY DIVISION
FOSTER J
1st, 14th, 15th, 16th, 17th, 30th JULY 1980

Landlord and tenant – Covenant – Usual covenants – Determination by court – Meaning in open contract as distinct from agreement to assign existing lease – Evidence on which court determines usual covenants – Open contract made in 1971 for grant by landlord to tenant of lease of garage and workshop in residential area of London – Draft lease settled by conveyancing counsel of court because parties failing to agree terms of lease – Landlord objecting to draft lease and wishing to insert further tenant's covenants and to enlarge proviso for re-entry – Matter referred to court – Whether landlord wishing to insert 'usual covenants' in lease – Whether 'usual covenants' in open contract more limited than in agreement to assign lease.

On 14th April 1975 the court ordered specific performance by the landlords of an agreement made in 1971 to grant the tenant a lease of a garage and workshop in a residential area of London for a term of approximately 14 years, and further ordered that if the parties could not agree the terms of the lease it was to be settled by conveyancing counsel of the court. The landlords submitted a draft lease to the tenant which was not acceptable to him because, he alleged, it contained unusual covenants. Accordingly conveyancing counsel was instructed to settle a draft lease, but that lease was not acceptable to the landlords who wished to have inserted in the lease seven further covenants by the tenant and to enlarge the landlords' proviso for re-entry. Pursuant to RSC Ord 31, r 6 the matter was referred back to the court. The questions in issue were (i) whether the usual covenants in an open contract, like the one in question, were more limited than the usual covenants in an agreement to assign an existing lease, (ii) what the expression 'usual covenants' meant and on what evidence they were to be determined by the court, and (iii) whether the clauses which the landlords wished to insert were usual covenants in 1971 in a lease of the kind in question.

Held – (1) The test to be applied by the court in determining what were or were not usual covenants (in addition to the 'usual covenants' in the technical sense always inserted by the court viz covenants by the lessee to pay rent, to pay taxes except where expressly made payable by the lessor, to keep and deliver up the premises in repair and to allow the lessor to enter and view the state of repair of the premises, and a covenant by the lessor for quiet enjoyment) was the same for both an open contract and an agreement to assign an existing lease, that test being that determination of the usual covenants was a question of fact to be decided by looking at the nature of the premises, their situation, the purpose for which they were being let, the length of the term, the evidence of conveyancers and the books of precedents. Furthermore, in deciding what was a usual covenant the court was not implying a term into the lease but merely, in the case of an assignment, deciding whether the existing lease included an unusual covenant which should have been disclosed and, in an open contract, deciding what covenants were to be inserted, and therefore the cases on the implication of terms into an agreement were irrelevant (see p 389 *e* to p 390 *b d e* and *g* to *j*, post); *Hampshire v Wickens* (1878) 7 Ch D 555 and *Flexman v Corbett* [1930] All ER Rep 420 applied.

(2) Applying the relevant test, the court would give judgment on which of the clauses put forward by the landlords were in 1971 usual covenants in a lease of a garage and workshop in the area in which the premises in question were situated and were therefore to be inserted in the lease (see p 391 *e* to p 394 *e*, post).

Notes

For usual and unusual covenants, see 23 Halsbury's Laws (3rd Edn) 442–444, paras 1044, 1045, and for cases on usual covenants, see 31(1) Digest (Reissue) 339–344, 2669–2720.

Cases referred to in judgment

Allen v Smith [1924] 2 Ch 308, 93 LJ Ch 538, 131 LT 667, 40 Digest (Repl) 145, *1113*.

Bennett v Womack (1828) 7 B & C 627, 3 C & P 96, 6 LJOSKB 175, 108 ER 856, 31(1) Digest (Reissue) 340, *2672*.

Brookes v Drysdale (1877) 3 CPD 52, 37 LT 467, 31(1) Digest (Reissue) 325, *2579*.

Church v Brown (1808) 15 Ves 258, [1803–13] All ER Rep 440, 33 ER 752, LC, 31(1) Digest (Reissue) 339, *2670*.

Flexman v Corbett [1930] 1 Ch 672, [1930] All ER Rep 420, 99 LJ Ch 370, 143 LT 464, 31(1) Digest (Reissue) 340, *2673*.

Hampshire v Wickens (1878) 7 Ch D 555, 47 LJ Ch 243, 38 LT 408, 31(1) Digest (Reissue) 340, *2680*.

Henderson v Hay (1792) 3 Bro CC 632, 29 ER 738, 31(1) Digest (Reissue) 341, *2682*.

Liverpool City Council v Irwin [1976] 2 All ER 39, [1977] AC 239, [1976] 2 WLR 562, 74 LGR 392, 32 P & CR 43, HL, Digest (Cont Vol E) 366, *4870a*.

Moorcock, The (1889) 14 PD 64, [1886–90] All ER Rep 530, 58 LJP 73, 60 LT 654, 6 Asp MLC 373, HL, 12 Digest (Reissue) 751, *5395*.

Shirlaw v Southern Foundries (1926) Ltd [1939] 2 All ER 113, [1939] 2 KB 206, 108 LJKB 747, 160 LT 353, CA; *affd sub nom Southern Foundries (1926) Ltd v Shirlaw* [1940] 2 All ER 445, [1940] AC 701, 109 LJKB 461, 164 LT 251, HL, 9 Digest (Reissue) 569, *3406*.

Cases also cited

Anderton and Milner's Contract, Re (1890) 45 Ch D 476.

Bishop v Taylor & Co (1891) 60 LJQB 556, DC.

Blakesley v Whieldon (1841) 1 Hare 176, 66 ER 996.

Charalambous v Ktori [1972] 3 All ER 701, [1972] 1 WLR 951.

Doe d Marquis of Bute v Guest (1846) 15 M & W 160, 153 ER 804.

Hodgkinson v Crowe (1875) LR 10 Ch App 622.

Hyde v Warden (1877) 3 Ex D 72, CA.

Jones v Jones (1803) 12 Ves 186, 33 ER 71.

Lander and Bagley's Contract, Re [1892] 3 Ch 41.

Van v Corpe (1834) 3 My & K 269, 40 ER 102.

Vere v Loveden (1806) 12 Ves 179, 33 ER 69.

Wilbraham v Livesey (1854) 18 Beav 206, 52 ER 81.

Objection under RSC Ord 31, r 6

In an action brought by the plaintiff, Jack Chester, against the defendants, Buckingham Travel Ltd, for specific performance of an agreement dated 25th March 1971 to let commercial premises at 18–20 Danvers Street, London SW3 to the plaintiff for a term of 14 years at an annual rent exclusive of rates of £6,000, Foster J on 14th April 1975 granted the plaintiff specific performance of the agreement for so much of the term of 14 years as the defendants under their headlease were able to grant, and ordered, pursuant to RSC Ord 31, r 5, that if the parties could not agree the terms of the lease the matter should be referred to a conveyancing counsel of the court to settle a draft lease. On 2nd April 1979 conveyancing counsel settled a draft lease which was acceptable to the plaintiff but not to the defendants who wished to have further covenants by the plaintiff and an enlarged proviso for re-entry included in the lease. The matter was referred back to Foster J under RSC Ord 31, r 6, the issue before him being whether the clauses which the defendants wished to have inserted in the lease were 'usual covenants'. The facts are set out in the judgment.

Vivian Chapman for the plaintiff.
C P F Rimer for the defendants.

Cur adv vult

30th July. **FOSTER J** read the following judgment: In this case, I am concerned with what are the so-called 'usual covenants' to be inserted in a lease.

As long ago as 25th March 1971, the defendants agreed to let to the plaintiff certain premises at 18–20 Danvers Street, Chelsea, London SW3, for a period of 14 years at an annual rent of £6,000, exclusive of rates. The actual agreement, which was signed by both parties, was in these terms: it was between J Chester Esq, of West Tower, Little Gaddesden, Berkhamsted and Buckingham Travel Ltd:

'1. It is agreed that the garage-workshops situated at 18/20 Danvers Street, London, S.W.3. are let by Buckingham Travel Ltd to J. Chester Esq., for a period of 14 years at the annual rental of £6,000, exclusive of rates, the rent to be paid quarterly in advance on quarterdays as from 25th March 1971.
'2. It is further agreed that pending completion of a lease contract between the two parties, J. Chester Esq. will take immediate possession of the leased premises.
'3. Both parties will, at the same time, come to a separate agreement as to the stock and equipment contained in the premises leased, which Buckingham Travel Ltd will sell to J. Chester Esq. for cash at prices to be mutually agreed.
'4. It is further agreed that provided their agreement is first sought and obtained, such members of the staff as are at present employed in the leased garage-workshops by Buckingham Travel Ltd will be re-employed by J. Chester Esq. at rates of pay not lower than those at present obtaining.
'Signed in London on March 25th, 1971 . . .'

Both the defendants and the plaintiff signed it.

In 1972, the plaintiff sued the defendants for specific performance of that agreement and the defendants defended that action and, in the alternative, counterclaimed for the agreement to be rectified in respect of four clauses. I heard the case as long ago as April 1975 and gave judgment on 14th April 1975. During the case, the defendants dropped the claim that the plaintiff was only a licensee and not a lessee but proceeded on their counterclaim that the agreement should be rectified to include four terms: (a) that there should be a rent review clause at five and ten years, (b) that there should be a fully repairing covenant, (c) that the plaintiff should pay a proportion of the insurance premiums, and (d) that there should be a covenant restricting the user of the premises to that of garage workshops.

On 14th April 1975 I granted the plaintiff specific performance of the agreement and dismissed the counterclaim. At the date of the agreement on 25th March 1971, the defendants were holding over under a previous lease and they were not granted a new lease until 21st May 1971. This new lease granted the defendants a lease of 14 years from 24th June 1970 so that the defendants were unable to grant to the plaintiff a term of 14 years from 25th March 1971. But, the plaintiff was prepared to take the term (a little over 13 years) which the defendants could grant. It is common ground that the plaintiff, on 25th March 1971, had no knowledge of the contents of the lease of 21st May 1971 or of any of the covenants contained in it. In my order of 14th April 1975, it was provided that the agreement of 25th March 1971 should be specifically performed and carried into execution but only in respect of so much of the term of 14 years specified in the agreement, as the defendants under the headlease dated 21st May 1971 were enabled to grant. The parties were agreed that the term should not be for the whole term but should have a reversion of say less one day. The order went on to order '. . . such lease to be settled by one of the conveyancing counsel to the Court in case the parties differ'.

Further litigation ensued between the parties as to what land was to be included in the agreement and on 28th April 1977 Lord Grantchester QC, sitting as a deputy High Court judge of the Chancery Division, decided what land was to be incorporated in the lease. The defendants' solicitors accordingly submitted a draft lease to the plaintiff's solicitor which was unacceptable to them as it was said that it contained several covenants which were not usual. Accordingly, instructions were delivered to Mr John Bradburn, then one of the conveyancing counsel to the court, and on 2nd April 1979 he settled a draft lease. This draft is acceptable to the plaintiff but the defendants wish to have some further clauses added to this draft lease and under RSC Ord 31, rr 5 and 6, it is possible, if a party is not satisfied with a document produced by counsel, have the matter referred back to the judge. It is in these circumstances that the matter comes before me.

The questions which face me can, I think, be stated as follows. (1) Is there any distinction between cases where there is an assignment of an existing lease and cases where there is an open contract as in this case? (2) What did the expression 'usual covenant' mean in 1971 and on what evidence should the court act? (3) What individual covenants which the defendants seek to have inserted should I allow to be inserted?

Assignments and open contracts

Counsel for the plaintiff submitted that the usual covenants were much more limited in open contracts than where there is an agreement to assign a lease, which it is said contains the usual covenants. No less than 22 cases were cited to me and I confess I find that nowhere is any distinction made between the two. The test to be applied seems to be the same in each case. It is well settled that in the technical sense, the term 'usual covenant' is limited to those which are set out clearly in the judgment of Jessel MR in *Hampshire v Wickens* (1878) 7 Ch D 555 at 561–562 where he said this:

'Usual covenants may vary in different generations. The law declares what are usual covenants according to the then knowledge of mankind. Lord Eldon, in *Church* v. *Brown* ((1808) 15 Ves 258 at 264, [1803–1813] All ER Rep 440 at 442) puts it thus: "Before the case of *Henderson* v. *Hay* ((1792) 3 Bro CC 632, 29 ER 738) therefore, upon an agreement to grant a lease with nothing more than proper covenants, I should have said they were to be such covenants as were just as well known in such leases as the usual covenants under an agreement to convey an estate." Now what is well known at one time may not be well known at another time, so that you cannot say that usual covenants never change. I have therefore looked at the last edition of *Davidson*'s Precedents in Conveyancing (2nd Edn, 1864, vol 5, pt 1, pp 48–49) to see whether the usage is said to have changed. He says "The result of the authorities appear to be that in a case where the agreement is silent as to the particular covenants to be inserted in the lease, and provides merely for the lease containing 'usual covenants', or, which is the same thing, in an open agreement without any reference to the covenants, and there are no special circumstances justifying the introduction of other covenants, the following are the only ones which either party can insist upon, namely, Covenants by the lessee 1. To pay rent. 2. To pay taxes, except such are expressly payable by the landlord. 3. To keep and deliver up the premises in repair, and 4. To allow the lessor to enter and view the state of repair. And the usual qualified covenant by the lessor for quiet enjoyment by the lessee." When he refers to "special circumstances" he means peculiar to a particular trade, as for example, in leases of public-houses, where the brewers have their own forms of leases, the "usual covenants" would mean the covenants always inserted in the leases of certain brewers. There is no mention of any other "usual covenants", and as nothing in this case has been lost for want of industry on the part of the counsel who have argued it, I am justified in saying that there is nothing in any text-book or book of precedents to shew that a covenant not to assign is a usual covenant. I am therefore of opinion that it is not a usual covenant, and I dismiss the action with costs.'

I reiterate that in this case also there has been nothing which has been lost for want of industry on the part of the counsel who have argued it.

In *Flexman v Corbett* [1930] 1 Ch 672 at 680–681, [1930] All ER Rep 420 at 425, Maugham J said:

'I will only add that my view that the question is one of fact is supported by the authority of *Bennett* v. *Womack* ((1828) 7 B & C 627, 108 ER 756) and *Hampshire* v. *Wickens* ((1878) 7 Ch D 555) and . . . *Allen* v. *Smith* ([1924] 2 Ch 308). I might also add the case of *Brookes* v. *Drysdale* ((1877) 3 CPD 52) in which it was held that a condition that assignments or under-leases shall be registered by the lessor's solicitor and the fee paid to him, was not a usual covenant.'

Of the four cases there cited, the first and fourth were assignment cases and the second and third were open contract cases. In my judgment, there is no distinction between the two and the test as to what is or what is not a usual covenant is the same in both.

Meaning of usual covenants

If, in the agreement, these are not defined or not even mentioned, the court inserts them and the usual covenants in the technical sense are always included. For the defendants, it was submitted that 'usual' means occurring in ordinary use: see per Maugham J in *Flexman v Corbett* [1930] 1 Ch 672 at 678, [1930] All ER Rep 420 at 423. For the plaintiff it was submitted that for a covenant to be usual it must pass the test of what the court will imply into an agreement. Counsel put his submission in this way: in an open contract for the grant of a lease there is an implied term that the lease should contain usual and proper covenants, that is the usual covenants in the strict sense, together with such other covenants that on the particular facts of the case the party must have impliedly intended the lease to contain. He referred me to three cases: (a) *The Moorcock* (1889) 14 PD 64, [1886–90] All ER Rep 530 (the business efficacy test); (b) *Shirlaw v Southern Foundries (1926) Ltd* [1939] 2 All ER 113, [1939] 2 KB 206 (the officious bystander test); and (c) *Liverpool City Council v Irwin* [1976] 2 All ER 39, [1977] AC 239 (the necessary implication test). In my judgment, these cases deal with quite another subject, namely, what the court will imply into a formal document. But when the court has to decide what is a usual covenant it is not implying anything into a document but merely deciding, in an assignment case, whether the existing lease includes an unusual covenant which should have been disclosed and in an open contract case, what covenants should be inserted. In my judgment, the cases where the court implies something are irrelevant and I reject the plaintiff's submission. I only have to decide what covenants which are usual should be included in the lease.

Usual covenants in 1971

In coming to a conclusion on this question, in my judgment, it is a question of fact to be determined by the court, not necessarily on the view of conveyancing counsel but by looking at the nature of the premises, their situation, the purpose for which they are being let, the length of the term, the evidence of conveyancers and the books of precedents. In *Flexman v Corbett* Maugham J said ([1930] 1 Ch 672 at 678–679, [1930] All ER Rep 420 at 423–424):

'I think it right to express my opinion, after having heard and considered all the numerous authorities which have been cited to me, that the question whether particular covenants are usual covenants is a question of fact, and that the decision of the Court on that point must depend upon the admissible evidence given before the Court in relation to that question. I think that it is proper to take the evidence of conveyancers and others familiar with the practice in reference to leases and that it is also permissible to examine books of precedents. It is permissible to obtain evidence with regard to the practice in the particular district in which the premises in question are situated. I would add that in my view it is a complete mistake to suppose that the usual covenants in regard to a lease, for instance, of a country house are necessarily usual covenants in regard to the lease of a London residence, and I would add that it seems to me that it may very well be that what is usual in Mayfair or Bayswater is not usual at all in some other part of London such, for instance, as Whitechapel. Further, in my opinion, "usual" in this sense means no more than "occurring in ordinary use", and I think that it is an error to suppose that the Court is entitled to hold that a particular covenant is not usual because it may be established that there are some few cases in which that covenant is not used. If it is established that (to put a strong case) in nine cases out of ten the covenant would be found in a lease of premises of that nature for that purpose and in that district, I think that the Court is bound to hold that the covenant is usual. The Court must bear in mind here the ultimate question which is being decided, which is whether the form of the covenant is such as to constitute a defect in the subject-matter of the contract: and if it were established that the lease is in the form in which it would be anticipated as being in the great majority of cases, having regard to the nature of the property and to the place where it is situated and to the purposes for which the premises are to be used, it does not seem to me reasonable to say that there is a defect in the subject-matter of the contract.'

In this case, the premises are situated in Chelsea, in a predominantly residential area, and the premises are part of a complex of properties consisting of (1) the plaintiff's premises, (2) a garage, (3) a yard, and (4) four residential flats. The term is under 14 years but may, of course, be extended as business premises by statute. I was quoted three precedents and I had before me an affidavit filed on behalf of the defendants by Mr M J Woodrow, a solicitor since 1959, who is second senior partner out of nine in the property department of Norton, Rose, Botterell and Roche and who has, during the last 15 to 20 years, had considerable experience of commercial leases in London, acting for both landlords and tenants.

What extra covenants should be inserted in the draft lease, if any?
The defendants asked the court to insert a further seven covenants and to enlarge the proviso for re-entry. I refer to the covenants as numbered in the defendants' draft lease.

1. The first is para 2(13), which is in these terms:

    'Not without previous written consent of the landlords in any way to alter the plan height elevation or appearance of the demised premises or of any part thereof or to cut or injure any of the party or other walls or the principal or bearing timbers iron steel or any supports of the demised premises except for the purpose of making good any defects thereof or to erect or place any building or erection upon the demised premises or any part thereof additional to the building and existing at the date hereof.'

I was referred to cl 2(7) of a precedent of a lease of premises for the purpose of a garage and petrol filling station, contained in the Encyclopaedia of Forms and Precedents (4th Edn, vol 12, form 10:2, cl 2(7), p 1006) which has a similar, though simpler, clause. Mr Woodrow, in his affidavit, says:

    'Prohibition of alteration of a building in a qualified or absolute form is a very usual covenant in modern commercial leases and in the context of the building we are dealing with, and the full repairing covenants imposed, I think it reasonable that some control should be retained by the Defendants.'

It must be remembered that there are other users and the lease is a short one. In my judgment, this is a usual covenant in 1971, provided that the clause contains a provision that the landlords' consent should not be unreasonably withheld.

2. Clause 2(14) reads as follows:

> 'Not to stop-up darken or obstruct any window or light belonging to the demised premises or any adjoining buildings now or hereafter belonging to the landlords nor knowingly permit any encroachment or easements to be acquired against or upon the premises and in case any window light opening doorway path passage drain or other encroachment or easement shall be opened or made or attempted to be opened made or acquired upon receiving notice to give immediate notice thereof to the landlords and at the request and cost of the landlords to take and do all such proceedings acts and things and to carry out all such works as may be reasonably required or deemed proper for preventing any such encroachment or the acquisition of any easement and if the tenant shall omit or neglect to take do or carry out all or any such things as aforesaid to permit the landlords or the superior landlords with or without workmen to enter upon the demised premises and to take do or carry out the same and on demand pay to the landlords the whole or such part as the landlords' agents may certify as fairly payable by the tenant of the costs of any such proceedings acts things or works.'

Mr Woodrow said that it is a normal clause to find in a modern commercial lease and could be particularly important here with common access and differing users on the site. At one stage in the negotiation the plaintiff was minded to agree that the clause should be inserted. In my judgment, this was a usual covenant in 1971 and should be inserted.

3. Clause 2(15) reads:

> 'Not to use or permit or suffer the demised premises to be used otherwise than as garage/workshops in connection with the tenant's business.'

It was pointed out that in the agreement itself, not only was there a reference to garage/workshops but there was a clause providing that the plaintiff should employ such members of the staff as are at present employed in the leased garage/workshops by the defendants. Mr Woodrow said that it is now entirely usual to find in commercial leases a clause restricting the user of premises and certainly the covenant is to be found in the precedent book: see the Encylopaedia of Forms and Precedents (4th Edn, vol 12, form 10:2, cl 2(15), p 1007 and form 9:1, cl 3(7), p 883). But these contain the words 'not without the consent of the landlords', to which, I think, should be added the words 'such consent not to be unreasonably withheld'. If these words were inserted and the last six words deleted, I think that such covenant would be a usual one and ought to be inserted.

4. Clause 2(17). Only the last two lines of the clause, namely, 'Not to hold or permit or suffer to be held any sale by auction on the demised premises or any part thereof', are now sought by the defendants to be inserted. Mr Woodrow, in his evidence, says that such a clause is not essential. I agree with him and, although it is to be found in the Encyclopaedia of Forms and Precedents (4th Edn, vol 12, form 10:2, cl 2(18), p 1008) I do not think that it is a usual covenant and it should not be inserted.

5. Clause 2(21). This is a long clause but the defendants only seek to have inserted the first seven lines which read as follows:

> 'Not to do or permit or suffer to be done on any part of the demised premises any act or thing which may grow to be a nuisance annoyance disturbance or discomfort to the landlords or the superior landlords or any tenant of the landlords or to the owner or occupier of any premises in the neighbourhood . . .'

and the rest of the clause they do not now seek to have inserted. Mr Woodrow says in his affidavit: 'I would certainly regard such a clause as usual in commercial leases these days and relevant to a lease of a garage.' I would regard it as usual provided the words 'or discomfort' and the words 'or the superior landlords' and the words 'or to the owner or occupier of any premises in the neighbourhood' are deleted and 'or' is inserted between 'annoyance' and 'disturbance'.

6. Clause 2(24) and (25). These subclauses seem to me to stand or fall together. Clause 2(24) reads:

'Not to assign under-let part with possession or occupation of the demised premises or any part thereof except with the prior written consent of the landlords and the superior landlords, such consent, not (in the case of the landlords) to be unreasonably withheld.'

Clause 2(25) reads:

'To procure that every permitted under-lessee of the demised premises shall covenant with the landlords to observe and perform the covenants on the part of the tenant herein contained (except the covenant to pay the rents hereby reserved) and covenant not to assign under-let or part with possession or occupation of the property comprised in any such under-lease, except with the prior written consent of the landlords and the superior landlords, such consent (in the case of the landlords), not to be unreasonably withheld.'

Mr Woodrow says that it is entirely common for provisions governing alienation to be inserted in commercial leases these days, although those clauses differ considerably from lease to lease. Such covenants are to be found in the precedent books (see the Encyclopaedia of Forms and Precedents (4th Edn, vol 12, form 10:2, cl 2(12), p 1007 and form 9:1, cl 3(15), p 885) but they differ considerably and it cannot, I think, be said that these particular covenants are usual. In my judgment, they should not be inserted and particularly in view of the decision in *Hampshire v Wickens* (1878) 7 Ch D 555.

7. Clause 2(30). This reads:

'To pay all costs charges and expenses (including legal costs and surveyors' fees) incurred by the landlords (or the superior landlords) for the purpose of or incidental to the preparation or service of any notice under sections 146 and 147 of the Law of Property Act, 1925 (or any statutory modification thereof) notwithstanding that the forfeiture may be avoided otherwise than by relief granted by the Court . . .'

and the defendants do not seek now to have inserted the last four lines. Mr Woodrow's evidence falls far short of what is required and in view of the decision of Eve J in *Allen v Smith* [1924] 2 Ch 308 where he held that such a covenant was not usual, I do not think it should be included.

The proviso for re-entry.

Clause 4 of the defendants' lease reads as follows:

'If the rent hereby reserved or any part thereof shall remain unpaid for 21 days after becoming payable (whether formally demanded or not) or if any of the covenants on the tenant's part herein contained shall not be performed or observed or if the tenant shall have a receiving order in bankruptcy made against him or if the tenant shall make any assignment or composition for the benefit of his creditors or suffer any distress or process of execution to be levied upon his goods or (being a corporation) shall enter into liquidation whether voluntarily or by the Court (otherwise than for the purposes of reconstruction or amalgamation) then and in any of the said cases it shall be lawful for the landlords at any time thereafter to re-enter upon the demised premises or upon any part thereof in the name of the whole and thereupon this demise shall absolutely determine but without prejudice to any right of action of the landlords in respect of any antecedent breach or non-observance of the tenant's covenants and conditions herein contained.'

The defendants do not now seek to have inserted sub-cll (2), (3), (4) and (5) of the proviso in cl 4. In conveyancing counsel's draft the power of re-entry is limited to non-payment of rent and does not include the power of re-entry if there is a breach of covenant. In *Flexman v Corbett* [1930] 1 Ch 672 at 682, [1930] All ER Rep 420 at 425 Maugham J said:

'I do not think that the evidence in this case is sufficient to enable me to express the opinion that the proviso for re-entry [and he was dealing with the re-entry for breach of covenant] is in the usual form, although I think that, even with regard to the proviso for re-entry, the matter is one which might usefully and properly be reconsidered in the light of modern evidence at some future time.'

In this case, the right of re-entry in the defendants' draft lease includes the right of re-entry on breach of any of the covenants in the lease. I confess, until I read conveyancing counsel's draft I, myself, had never seen a right of re-entry in a lease limited to non-payment of rent only. Every precedent contains a right of re-entry for breach of covenant and I have no doubt that it was usual in 1971. On the other hand, this clause seeks a right of re-entry if the tenant has a receiving order in bankruptcy made against him and other matters in regard to insolvency. In my judgment, these provisions are far too wide. I think that the proviso should be inserted with the deletion of the words 'or if the tenant shall have a receiving order . . .' down to and including the words '. . . then and in any of the said cases'. In view of what I have held, I will discuss with counsel the form of the order which I shall make.

Order that parties execute a lease in the terms of a draft to be settled by counsel for the defendants and agreed by counsel for the plaintiff.

Solicitors: *Carlson & Co* (for the plaintiff); *A Banks & Co* (for the defendants).

Jacqueline Metcalfe   Barrister.

Page v Freight Hire (Tank Haulage) Ltd

EMPLOYMENT APPEAL TRIBUNAL
SLYNN J, MISS J W COLLERSON AND MR R THOMAS
3rd NOVEMBER 1980

Employment – Discrimination against a woman – Acts done under statutory authority – Discrimination in the interests of safety – Employers refusing to allow woman driver to transport chemicals for safety reasons – Whether employers guilty of discrimination – Whether employers' action reasonable in order to comply with health and safety legislation – Health and Safety at Work etc Act 1974, s 2 – Sex Discrimination Act 1975, s 51(1).

The complainant, a 23-year old woman, was employed as a lorry driver by a firm of carriers engaged in the transport of chemicals between various chemical plants. The employers, acting on the instructions of the manufacturers of the chemicals, refused to allow the complainant to transport a particular chemical which was potentially harmful to women of child-bearing age. The complainant made a complaint to an industrial tribunal that she had been unfairly discriminated against contrary to s 1 of the Sex Discrimination Act 1975. The tribunal held that the employers had discriminated against the complainant but, since they had done so in the interests of safety, there was no breach of the statute. The complainant appealed to the Employment Appeal Tribunal.

Held – The fact that discriminatory action by an employer was taken in the interests of safety did not of itself provide the employer with a defence to a complaint of unlawful discrimination under the 1975 Act. However, if the employer's action was necessary in order to comply with another, earlier statute, the employer was then protected by s 51(1)^a of the 1975 Act. Since the employers were under a statutory duty, by virtue of s 2^b of the Health and Safety at Work etc Act 1974, to ensure, so far as reasonably practicable, the health, safety and welfare of their employees, which included, in particular, ensuring safety and absence of risks to health in the use, handling, storage and transport of substances, they were, in the circumstances, entitled to take the view that the only way they could comply with s 2 of the 1974 Act was to refuse to allow the complainant to transport a chemical which was potentially dangerous to her. The employers were accordingly protected by s 51(1) of the 1975 Act and the appeal would be dismissed (see p 397 f to j, p 398 f g, p 399 h j and p 400 c, post).

Peake v Automotive Products Ltd [1978] 1 All ER 106 and *Ministry of Defence v Jeremiah* [1979] 3 All ER 833 considered.

Notes

For sex discrimination generally and for discrimination against employees, see 16 Halsbury's Laws (4th Edn) paras 771:2 and 771:5.

For the Health and Safety at Work etc Act 1974, s 2, see 44 Halsbury's Statutes (3rd Edn) 1087.

For the Sex Discrimination Act 1975, s 51, see 45 ibid 261.

Cases referred to in judgment

Greig v Community Industry [1979] ICR 356, [1979] IRLR 158, EAT.
Ministry of Defence v Jeremiah [1979] 3 All ER 833, [1980] QB 87, [1979] 3 WLR 857, [1979] IRLR 436, CA, Digest (Cont Vol E) 408, 72Ac(i).
Peake v Automotive Products Ltd [1978] 1 All ER 106, [1978] QB 233, [1977] 3 WLR 853, [1977] ICR 968, CA, Digest (Cont Vol E) 407, 72Aa.
Shields v E Coomes (Holdings) Ltd [1979] 1 All ER 456, [1978] 1 WLR 1408, [1978] ICR 1159, [1978] IRLR 263, CA, Digest (Cont Vol E) 409, 72Af.

Appeal

Jacqueline Dawn Page appealed against the decision of an industrial tribunal (chairman Mr J H Bloom) sitting at Middlesbrough on 26th March 1980 dismissing her complaint against her employers, Freight Hire (Tank Haulage) Ltd, that they had discriminated against her contrary to s 1 of the Sex Discrimination Act 1975. The Equal Opportunities Commission applied to the appeal tribunal to make submissions and were invited to do so with the consent of the parties. The facts are set out in the judgment of the appeal tribunal.

Tim Hirst for Mrs Page.
Stephen Duffield for the employers.
Michael Beloff for the Equal Opportunities Commission.

SLYNN J delivered the following judgment of the appeal tribunal: Mrs Page was employed by Freight Hire (Tank Haulage) Ltd as a heavy goods vehicle driver. She is approximately 23 years of age. When she began to work for the employers it appears that she concentrated mainly on the driving of vehicles for relatively short routes. She worked on a regular basis from, approximately, June 1979 until September 1979, when, because of a shortage of work, her contract of employment was terminated.

Subsequently, she was asked to work on a casual daily basis, to drive when there was

---

a   Section 51(1), so far as material, is set out at p 397 *j*, post
b   Section 2, so far as material, is set out at p 398 *a b*, post

a need for her services. On 5th October 1979 she was told that one of the drivers employed on a regular basis had broken his leg, and she was asked to come on a casual daily basis but more frequently than she had in the past. One of the jobs that she was asked to do involved hauling chemicals between chemical plants in the Cleveland area; one of those was a chemical called dimethylformamide ('DMF') which is made by ICI Ltd.

On 17th October 1979 Mrs Page took a load of DMF from one of the ICI petrochemical works. Two days later, a senior manager from the Petrochemicals Division of ICI Ltd telephoned Mrs Lewis, the wife of the managing director of the employers, to say that because of the danger to women of child-bearing age Mrs Page must not be used on the haulage of that product again. Accordingly, the employers decided that they would not let her drive the vehicle which was carrying DMF.

She apparently said initially that she had been dismissed. She brought a claim alleging that there had been discrimination against her contrary to s 1 of the Sex Discrimination Act 1975. The industrial tribunal which heard the case decided that she had not been dismissed but that she had been told that she would not be allowed to carry this particular chemical and, as a result, she had decided that she no longer wished to be employed by the employers. The tribunal found that in an interview with Mr Lewis she had made her position very clear; she had said that she knew of the dangers of DMF but that she was prepared both to accept them and to provide the employers with some form of indemnity.

The industrial tribunal concluded that there had been discrimination against her on the ground of her sex. They found that she was refused the opportunity of delivering this chemical because she was a woman, and that a male employee would have been allowed to continue carrying DMF. However, they took the view, on the basis of what was said in *Peake v Automotive Products Ltd* [1978] 1 All ER 106, [1978] QB 233, that it was an answer for an employer to show that what had been done was done in the interests of safety or in the interests of good administration. They decided that what the Court of Appeal had held there was not affected by the decision of the Court of Appeal in *Ministry of Defence v Jeremiah* [1979] 3 All ER 833, [1980] QB 87, and they were satisfied that what had been done here was in the interests of safety and that, accordingly, although there was discrimination there was here no breach of the statute.

The danger which was referred to with regard to this particular chemical was the subject matter of a certain amount of evidence before the tribunal. A document had been issued by ICI, headed with the name of the chemical, which referred to a number of precautions which ought to be taken by those concerned in the handling of the material. In addition, there was another document which bore the same title and referred to a number of hazards to personnel which were possible health risks. Some of those could have affected both men and women, ie loss of appetite, intestinal disorders, the possible effect on the liver, the stomach and the kidneys. The document also contained this statement: 'Recent publications have suggested that there may be an embryotoxic effect at levels of exposure greater than the Threshold Limit Value.' That was said to be 10 parts per million in this particular product. It went on:

'Precautionary measures must therefore be rigorously applied when women of child bearing age are likely to be exposed to the material. Regular monitoring of the atmosphere is essential.'

Mrs Page admitted that she did know of the dangers before she began to carry this material in the middle of October 1979. It was her view, on what she had been told about this product, that it was potentially harmful to women of child-bearing age. It appears, from the evidence which she gave, that she may have thought that this was capable of producing sterility in a woman. Evidence was given by a Mr Wilkinson as to what he understood the position to be. He had been a driver but was employed as a fitter. He said that he knew that if the vapour of this chemical was absorbed it could make one sterile. He thought that it affected men and women, that both were at risk of sterility.

Quite clearly the only evidence which was before the tribunal on which they could place any reliance was that contained in the second document to which we have referred. That indicates, not so much that there was a danger of sterility, but that there may be an effect on the fetus of a pregnant woman, that the dangerous effects of this particular chemical do not affect men.

But the issue really arose because of the telephone call from the manager of ICI to which we have referred. On the evidence of Mrs Lewis it is quite clear that she said that he had told her that, because of the danger to women of child-bearing age, Mrs Page must not be used on the haulage of the product again. Mr Lewis's own evidence was, perhaps, not quite so specific. He said, from the notes of evidence taken by the chairman, that he was told that ICI did not allow women to come into contact with DMF. The note taken by the solicitor for Mrs Page in this case, which we have been invited to look at with the consent of both parties, is that Mr Lewis was not told by his wife specifically that ICI were banning women from driving. It is, however, quite clear that Mrs Lewis was saying that she had been told that they must not use Mrs Page to drive the vehicles which carried this particular chemical.

On this appeal, counsel for Mrs Page has submitted that the tribunal were quite wrong in deciding that considerations of safety were an answer to the allegations of discrimination, that, once the tribunal had found that there was discrimination, that really was the end of the case. He submits that the tribunal were wrong to say that the statements of the Court of Appeal in *Peake v Automotive Products Ltd* still stood; they have been affected by the decision in *Ministry of Defence v Jeremiah*.

If one turns to the decision in *Peake v Automotive Products Ltd* it is plain that Lord Denning MR (with whom, as we understand it, both the other judges, but particularly Goff LJ, agreed) was saying that arrangements which are made in the interests of safety or of good administration are not infringements of the law, even though they may be more favourable to women than to men, or, conversely, more favourable to men than to women. When one comes to the decision in *Ministry of Defence v Jeremiah* Lord Denning MR, in his judgment, referred to the fact that good administrative arrangements and safety had been put forward as answers in the *Peake* case. But he went on to say that that reason, so far as it related to good administration, should no longer be regarded as a ground to substantiate the decision. In our judgment, Lord Denning MR was saying that not only good administration but also the interests of safety were no longer to be put forward as a justification for what was otherwise discrimination on the grounds of sex.

Brandon LJ did not express any view either way about the matter. Accordingly, he is not to be taken as agreeing with Lord Denning MR.

Brightman LJ did not expressly refer to the decision in the *Peake* case, or to what effect the decision in the *Jeremiah* case was intended to have on what had been said there. He did say this ([1979] 3 All ER 833 at 840, [1980] QB 87 at 103): 'The question is whether the employer's solicitude towards female workers is unlawful under the Sex Discrimination Act. I think it is.' He then went on to deal with the section. Reading his judgment as a whole, it seems to us that he was in substance intending to agree with Lord Denning MR in regarding the two reasons which were put forward in the *Peake* case as being a sufficient answer.

It seems to us that in this legislation, as has been said on an earlier occasion by Bridge LJ in *Shields v E Coomes (Holdings) Ltd* [1979] 1 All ER 456, [1978] 1 WLR 1408 (which is referred to in *Greig v Community Industry* [1979] ICR 356 at 360), that the exceptions to the provisions which define what is a breach of the Sex Discrimination Act 1975 are to be found only in the sections of the Act itself, in particular, s 7. It would seem to us, therefore, that this tribunal did err in regarding the interests of safety in itself as an answer to the case once they had found that there was discrimination.

But that is not the end of the case. Section 51(1) of the 1975 Act provides as follows:

'Nothing in Parts II to IV shall render unlawful any act done by a person if it was necessary for him to do it in order to comply with a requirement—(a) of an Act passed before this Act . . .'

The rest of the subsection is not relevant for present purposes.

The one Act which was in existence before the 1975 Act was passed was the Health and Safety at Work etc Act 1974 which provides, in s 2:

'(1) It shall be the duty of every employer to ensure, so far as is reasonably practicable, the health, safety and welfare at work of all his employees.

'(2) Without prejudice to the generality of an employer's duty under the preceding subsection, the matters to which that duty extends include in particular ... (b) arrangements for ensuring, so far as is reasonably practicable, safety and absence of risks to health in connection with the use, handling, storage and transport of articles and substances ...'

In this case it is submitted on behalf of Mrs Page that there was insufficient evidence here of the sort of hazard which could possibly justify the barring of her from driving a vehicle which carried this particular chemical. That view is supported by counsel who has appeared on behalf of the Equal Opportunities Commission and whom, with the consent of both parties, we invited to make submissions to us following a practice which had previously (we are told) been followed in the Court of Appeal when the Equal Opportunities Commission desired to put submissions before the court on a question arising under the 1975 Act. We felt it was right to accede to the application of the Equal Opportunities Commission that they should make submissions today, in particular because of the provisions of s 55 of the 1975 Act which impose on the commission statutory duties dealing with health and safety.

Counsel for the Equal Opportunities Commission and, indeed, counsel for Mrs Page have submitted that the proper approach here is to ask oneself: was it necessary for the employer to do what he did in order to comply with the requirements of the Health and Safety at Work etc Act 1974? Counsel for the commission submits that, as a matter of principle, it has to be shown that there is no other way of protecting a woman (or a man, in a case where a man is involved) other than by debarring her (or him) from taking up a job. He says that, when the matter is considered as a whole, the conclusion must inexorably lead to a need to debar the individual from doing the job, otherwise it cannot be said that it is necessary for the purposes of satisfying the requirements of the 1974 Act.

It seems to us that it is clearly right that it is not an answer, under s 51(1) of the 1975 Act, for an employer to say: 'There was a risk, and, accordingly, I am not going to allow you, a woman [or, in the appropriate case, you, a man] to do this particular job because you, a woman [or, if there is such a case, you, a man], are particularly vulnerable to risk because of your sex.' It is important to consider all the circumstances of the case, to consider the risk involved and the measures which it can be said are reasonably necessary to eliminate the risk. It may well be that the wishes of the person whom it is desired to protect give a factor. Here it was said that Mrs Page did not want to have a child and did not anticipate becoming pregnant, as she was divorced. We accept that the individual's wishes may be a factor to be looked at, although, in our judgment, where the risk is to the woman, of sterility, or to the fetus, whether actually in existence or likely to come into existence in the future, these wishes cannot be a conclusive factor.

We feel that counsel for the commission has put the matter too high. It does not seem to us that an employer, in order to satisfy the test of s 51 of the 1975 Act (read with s 2 of the 1974 Act), has to show that inexorably this was the only method available to him. It is to be remembered that the duty is to ensure, so far as is reasonably practicable, the health, safety and welfare at work of employees. It seems to us that there may well be cases where one course (which is suggested as being sufficient) may leave open some doubt whether it is going to achieve the desired level of protection. In such a case it may well be that an employer is complying with the requirements of the legislation if, in all the circumstances, he thinks it right not to allow an employee, for his (or her) own protection or safety, to do the particular job at all.

It is said here that the matter was not gone into in the kind of detail which was called for on the part of the employer, or alternatively that the tribunal itself should have gone into the matter in much greater detail. It is, as we have said on many occasions, for the tribunal to probe into the facts and material before them to see whether there is discrimination or not. But it does not seem to us that, once discrimination is established, it really is for the tribunal itself (as has been suggested here) to ensure that all the scientific information which might be relevant is brought before the tribunal. The tribunal has to decide the matter on the evidence which is there.

The question in this case is whether we can be satisfied, firstly, what the attitude of this tribunal would have been on the facts which they found had s 51 of the 1975 Act been specifically in mind, and, secondly, whether those facts are sufficient, on the material before the tribunal, to justify the reliance of the employers on s 51. If one looked simply at the second document to which we have referred, it might be that the employers would not satisfy that burden, because there it is said: 'Precautionary measures must be rigorously applied when women of child-bearing age are likely to be exposed to the material.' But that was not the whole of the material before the tribunal. The employers gave evidence of this very clear warning, indeed, direction, from ICI, the manufacturers of the substance, that a woman of child-bearing age could not with safety be concerned with the transport of this particular chemical. It seems to us that, on that direction from the manufacturers, and with that warning, the employers prima facie were entitled to say: 'Well, the only way in which we can ensure, so far as is reasonably practicable, the safety of this woman is not to allow her to drive a vehicle which is carrying this particular chemical, even if she is going to drive other vehicles.' If there had been material which suggested that this was an act of excessive caution on the part of the employers, that it really was being used as a device to prevent Mrs Page from being employed, then the situation would be very different. But it would appear here that, on the material, this tribunal was very concerned with the question of safety; its members attached great importance to what they described as 'the arrangement dictated by ICI'. Although they put it on the basis of the *Peake* case, it seems quite plain that, had they had their attentions drawn to s 51 of the 1975 Act and to the provisions in detail of the Health and Safety at Work etc Act 1974, they would have concluded that what was done was necessary in order for the company to comply with a requirement of the 1974 Act on the information which the company had before them at that particular time. Since there was no evidence to suggest that any other course was a sufficient form of protection for Mrs Page (who was clearly still potentially of child-bearing age despite the fact that she was, at the time, divorced) it seems to us that the tribunal must have come to that particular conclusion.

It is said by counsel, on behalf of the employers, that in any event there is no finding by the tribunal that Mrs Page had suffered a detriment. Accordingly, he says that, if we be wrong on the view to which we have come on the first two points, in any event Mrs Page must fail. He says that all the tribunal decided was that there had been discrimination contrary to s 1 of the 1975 Act in that she was treated less favourably than a man would have been treated. But he says that that is not enough: it is essential, for a claim of this kind to succeed, that one of the paragraphs of s 6 of the 1975 Act should be satisfied. The only one that was relevant here was s 6(2)(b), namely, the subjecting of Mrs Page to 'any other detriment'. He says that in the absence of a finding of a detriment the matter is concluded against her.

Even assuming that what has to be done, in a case of this kind, is a balancing of the detriment against the advantages which flow from it, it seems to us that (although the matter is not expressly dealt with) this tribunal was quite clearly intending to decide here that there had been a subjecting to a detriment, that, when they read ss 1 and 6 of the Act together and then said that they were satisfied that there had been discrimination on the ground of sex, they were intending to include the finding of a detriment, as well as a finding under s 1 of the 1975 Act. Accordingly, we do not accept the submissions put forward on behalf of the company on that second point. We consider that the tribunal came to the right conclusion, albeit on a different basis from that at which we have arrived.

It is important to bear in mind that we are here dealing with a case where the only evidence on which reliance can be placed was that there was a danger of embryotoxic effects at certain levels of exposure. This is not a case (despite the evidence given by Mr Wilkinson) where the tribunal had to decide what would happen if both men and women were subjected to the same kind of risk and the employers had decided that it was more desirable to protect the woman than to protect the man; wholly different considerations would arise in that kind of case. Here we are not concerned with a situation where a man's ability to procreate is involved; and it does not seem to us to be material in any way that both men and women were liable to be affected by this chemical in other ways, ie in relation to their digestive organs, their liver and so on. That is a very different matter; and the only relevant aspect of the case is that with which we have been concerned.

Accordingly, in all the circumstances, it seems to us that this is not a case which we need to remit to an industrial tribunal. The evidence was such that this tribunal would have come to the same conclusion, for the reasons the industrial tribunal gave, but on the basis of s 51 of the 1975 Act rather than of what was said in *Peake v Automotive Products Ltd*.

The appeal is, accordingly, dismissed.

Appeal dismissed.

Solicitors: *Alex Lauriston & Son*, Middlesbrough (for Mrs Page); *Frank Gibbon*, Hartlepool (for the employees); *J A Lakin* (for the Equal Opportunities Commission).

K Mydeen Esq   Barrister.

Practice Direction

FAMILY DIVISION

Case stated – Family Division – Appeals relating to affiliation proceedings and appeals from magistrates' courts – Application for appeal to be heard by single judge outside London – Procedure – RSC Ord 56, rr 4A, 5 (as amended by RSC (Amendment No 4) 1980 (SI 1980 No 2000), r 9(2)).

The President has issued the following Practice Direction with the concurrence of the Lord Chancellor.

With effect from 12th January 1981, RSC Ord 56, rr 4A and 5 are amended so that appeals by case stated in any of the types of proceedings therein set out are taken by a single judge as a general rule and only by a Divisional Court of the Family Division if the court so directs (see RSC (Amendment No 4) 1980, SI 1980 No 2000, r 9 (2)).

The rules require that all relevant papers be lodged in the Principal Registry of the Family Division, but there is no requirement in the rules that the single judge must be a single judge sitting in London. Accordingly, any party wishing the appeal to be heard and determined by a single judge outside London should apply to the President for a direction to this effect. The application should be made by letter addressed to the Clerk of the Rules. Where such a direction is given, the Clerk of the Rules will inform the appellant of the relevant divorce town and will refer the papers to the listing officer of the appropriate circuit office for a date of hearing to be fixed and notified to the appellant.

R L Bayne-Powell
Senior Registrar.

22nd January 1981

Manley v Law Society and others

QUEEN'S BENCH DIVISION
BRISTOW J
8th, 9th, 10th OCTOBER 1980

COURT OF APPEAL, CIVIL DIVISION
LORD DENNING MR, ORMROD AND O'CONNOR LJJ
25th, 26th, 27th NOVEMBER, 16th DECEMBER 1980

Legal aid – Charge on property recovered for deficiency of costs – Property recovered or preserved in proceedings – Compromise of proceedings – Terms of compromise designed to avoid charge attaching to sum accepted by plaintiff in settlement of action – Action by legally-aided plaintiff for breach of contract arising out of defendant's refusal to exploit his invention – Plaintiff incurring debts in developing invention – Under terms of compromise defendants paying sum to parties' solicitors in settlement of action – Solicitors buying plaintiff's debts for defendants and paying balance to plaintiff – Terms of compromise disclosed to court and Law Society and embodied in consent order – Whether charge attaching to whole sum paid by defendants to solicitors or only to balance paid over to plaintiff – Whether amount provided by defendants property recovered for plaintiff's benefit – Legal Aid Act 1974, s 9(6)(7).

The plaintiff, who was legally aided, brought an action against a company for damages for breach of contract in refusing to exploit his invention. In view of the uncertain outcome of the action and the heavy costs already incurred and likely to be incurred by both parties, the parties attempted to negotiate a compromise. In the course of those negotiations the company indicated that it was prepared to offer the plaintiff £40,000 in settlement. The plaintiff's solicitors estimated that their costs incurred on his behalf amounted to £25,000 but agreed to limit them to £17,000. Those costs were payable by the legal aid fund under s 10(1)[a] of the Legal Aid Act 1974. By virtue of s 9(6) and (7)[b] of the 1974 Act the fund would have a charge for that amount on the £40,000 if it was accepted by the plaintiff, but the plaintiff would not then be left sufficient to meet his debts incurred in developing his invention. The parties' legal advisers therefore devised a scheme of compromise under which the £40,000 was to be paid to the parties' solicitors jointly and out of that sum they, acting as the company's agents, were to buy the plaintiff's debts for the company, which would then write them off. The balance, if any, after expenses were deducted was to be paid to the plaintiff, although, in fact, the plaintiff's debts were likely to exhaust the bulk of the £40,000. It was thought that because the plaintiff would not recover the £40,000 under the compromise but merely the right to have the terms of the compromise enforced, the fund's charge would attach only to the balance (if any) paid to the plaintiff and that his solicitors could recover their costs from the fund. The Law Society was informed of the terms of the compromise, and when the action came on for trial the judge also was informed together with the reasons for it, and he embodied its terms in a consent order. The company paid the £40,000 to the parties' solicitors under the terms of the order. By an originating summons the plaintiff sought a declaration that the £40,000 paid to the parties' solicitors under the terms of the consent order was not charged to the Law Society under s 9(6) and (7). The Law Society contended that the statutory charge attached to the £40,000 because (i) that sum, rather than the balance to be paid to the plaintiff, was the 'property . . . recovered . . . for him in the proceedings' under the compromise, within s 9(6) and (7), and (ii) the compromise scheme should be disregarded as being merely a fiction or device designed to defeat the statutory charge. The judge made the declaration sought, on the grounds

---

a   Section 10(1), so far as material, is set out at p 409 d, post
b   Section 9(6) and (7) is set out at p 413 b to d, post

that the compromise, which had been arrived at by the parties acting with complete candour and honesty, was not a fiction merely because it was intended to defeat the fund's charge, and all that the plaintiff had 'recovered' under the compromise was the right to have his debts discharged and to be paid the balance of the £40,000, if any, rather than the £40,000 itself. The Law Society appealed. At the hearing of the appeal the plaintiff submitted that the court ought to have regard merely to the words of the compromise and their legal effect.

Held – The appeal would be allowed for the following reasons—

(1) Looking, as the court was bound to do, at the reality of the compromise, which was that the plaintiff had obtained the right to have his debts paid at his request and as he specified and was thus in effective control of the distribution of the £40,000 provided by the company and was the sole beneficiary of it, the £40,000 was property 'recovered for him' within s 9(6) and (7) of the 1974 Act since it was property recovered for his benefit and (per Ormrod and O'Connor LJJ) that was supported by the fact that reg 18(4)(a)^c of the Legal Aid (General) Regulations 1971 showed that the legal aid fund's charge extended to property recovered for a plaintiff's benefit (see p 410 b to e, p 411 d e, p 413 d e, p 414 d to j, p 415 b and p 416 c to h, post); *Inland Revenue Comrs v Duke of Westminster* [1935] All ER Rep 259 not followed.

(2) (Per Lord Denning MR) Alternatively, the plaintiff's solicitors having intentionally deprived the legal aid fund of a charge which would have allowed the fund to recoup the payment made to the solicitors in respect of costs, the solicitors were precluded in equity from making any claim on the fund for those costs since they would otherwise be taking advantage of a condition they had themselves brought about (see p 411 b to e and j, post).

Observations on the responsibility of legal advisers in the conduct of an action for a legally-aided person (see p 411 e to j and p 412 a to j, post).

Notes

For charges for the benefit of the legal aid fund on property recovered or preserved, see 30 Halsbury's Laws (3rd Edn) 506–507, paras 940–941.

For the Legal Aid Act 1974, s 9, see 44 Halsbury's Statutes (3rd Edn) 1048.

For the Legal Aid (General) Regulations 1971, reg 18, see 5 Halsbury's Statutory Instruments (Fourth Reissue) 346.

Cases referred to in judgments

Customs and Excise Comrs v Pools Finance (1937) Ltd [1952] 1 All ER 775, CA, 39 Digest (Repl) 352, 840.

Griffiths (Inspector of Taxes) v J P Harrison (Watford) Ltd [1962] 1 All ER 909, [1963] AC 1, [1962] 2 WLR 909, 41 ATC 36, 40 Tax Cas 292, HL, 28(1) Digest (Reissue) 49, 203.

Hanlon v Law Society [1980] 1 All ER 763, [1980] 2 WLR 756, CA; *on appeal* [1980] 2 All ER 199, [1980] 2 WLR 792, HL.

Hope, The (1883) 8 PD 144, 52 LJP 63, 49 LT 158, 5 Asp MLC 126, CA, 43 Digest (Repl) 308, 3231.

Inland Revenue Comrs v Duke of Westminster [1936] AC 1, [1935] All ER Rep 259, 104 LJKB 383, 153 LT 223, 19 Tax Cas 510, HL, 28(1) Digest (Reissue) 507, 1845.

Margetson and Jones, Re [1897] 2 Ch 314, 66 LJ Ch 619, 76 LT 805, 43 Digest (Repl) 307, 3218.

New Zealand Shipping Co Ltd v Société des Ateliers et Chantiers de France [1919] AC 1, [1918–19] All ER Rep 552, 87 LJKB 746, 118 LT 731, 14 Asp MLC 291, HL, 7 Digest (Reissue) 324, 2210.

Welsh v Hole (1779) 1 Doug KB 238, 99 ER 155, 43 Digest (Repl) 309, 3245.

Cases also cited

Barker v St Quintin (1844) 12 M & W 441, 152 ER 1270.

Brunsdon v Allard (1859) 2 E & E 19, 121 ER 8.

Bryant, Ex parte (1815) 1 Madd 49, 56 ER 19.

---

c   Regulation 18(4), so far as material, is set out at p 416 *f g*, post

Cadogan v Cadogan [1977] 3 All ER 831, [1977] 1 WLR 1041, CA.
Dunthorne v Bunbury (1888) 24 LR Ir 6.
Foxon v Gascoigne (1874) LR 9 Ch App 654, LJJ.
Fuld, In the estate of (No 4) [1967] 2 All ER 649, [1968] P 727.
Harrison v Cornwall Minerals Railway Co (1884) 53 LJ Ch 596.
Harrison v Harrison (1888) 13 PD 180, CA.
Neill v Glacier Metal Co Ltd [1963] 3 All ER 477, [1965] 1 QB 16.
Pinkerton v Easton (1873) LR 16 Eq 490, LC.
Price v Crouch (1891) 60 LJQB 767.
Rolli's Will Trusts, Re, Calvocoressi v Rodocanachi [1963] 3 All ER 940, [1964] Ch 288.
Ross v Buxton (1889) 42 Ch D 190.
Shaw v Neale (1858) 6 HL Cas 581, 10 ER 1422, HL.
Slater v Mayor of Sunderland (1864) 33 LJQB 37.
Sullivan v Pearson, Re, ex parte Morrison (1868) LR 4 QB 153.
Till v Till [1974] 1 All ER 1096, [1974] QB 558, CA.
Twynham v Porter (1870) LR 11 Eq 181.
White v Pearce (1849) 7 Hare 276, 68 ER 113.

Originating summons

By an originating summons dated 15th June 1979 Dr David Michael John Picton Manley sought as against the Law Society a declaration that the fund of £40,000 paid to Messrs Coward Chance and Messrs Kennedys, solicitors, agents for Marconi International Marine Co Ltd ('Marconi'), the defendants in an action brought by Dr Manley for damages for breach of contract, under the terms of a consent order made in the action on 3rd October 1978 did not stand and never had stood charged for the benefit of the legal aid fund under s 9(6) and (7) of the Legal Aid Act 1974. Marconi were added as second defendants pursuant to the order of Master Lubock dated 24th April 1980. The facts are set out in the judgment.

Jack Hames QC and *Peter Flint* for Dr Manley.
Duncan Matheson for the Law Society.
Marconi were not represented.

BRISTOW J. Dr David Manley is an inventor. He invented a shallow water echo sounder for large ships and entered into an agreement with Marconi International Marine Co Ltd ('Marconi') for its exploitation. He and his corporate alter ego incurred heavy expenditure, met by borrowing, in the development of his invention. Marconi refused to exploit it on the ground that it did not meet the requirements of the agreement. Dr Manley brought an action for damages for breach of contract against Marconi. He applied for and obtained a legal aid certificate for the purpose and prosecuted his action throughout as an assisted person.

The essence of the legal aid scheme in this country is that an assisted person who brings an action shall have the same services of solicitors and counsel as he would have if he were not an assisted person and that the costs of those services, subject to his own contribution, which is assessed according to his means, will be paid by the Law Society, to whom his solicitors render the bill they would otherwise have rendered to him, out of the legal aid fund of public money which the Law Society administers. If any fruits accrue to the assisted person as a result of his litigation then those fruits are available to the Law Society to meet the assisted person's solicitor's bill or to recoup them for meeting the assisted person's solicitor's bill, and the machinery by which they are made available is a statutory first charge on them in favour of the Law Society. The solicitor of a litigant not assisted under the legal aid scheme has since the time of Lord Mansfield had the right to apply to the court, of which he is an officer, for an order that the fruits of litigation conducted by him for his client shall be charged in his favour to meet his costs and the court has a discretion to make an order to that effect, an order enforceable by effective remedies.

As can be seen from the many reported cases, that discretion was freely exercised by the court to protect its officers, the basis of the jurisdiction being that it is in the public interest that the courts should have the assistance of solicitors and counsel in order to do justice to those who have to come before the courts to resolve their disputes which they are unable to resolve for themselves. There is a common thread which runs through all the cases that the discretion will be exercised not simply where a solicitor is at risk of not recovering his costs but where he is at risk of not recovering his costs by reason of a 'dirty trick'. Sometimes in the cases the word used to describe the dirty trick is 'fraud', sometimes it is 'collusion', sometimes it is 'cheating' and sometimes the facts are described without any opprobrious label at all. But the common denominator in all the cases cited to me (and I am told by counsel, as you would expect, that it is the common denominator of the many cases on the subject which he did not cite) is the presence of a 'dirty trick' of one sort or another. That, in my judgment, is a factor which leads the court in its discretion to charge the fruit of the litigation in favour of the solicitor, and to give effect to the charge.

The charge on the fruits of litigation of an assisted person in favour of the Law Society and the remedies to enforce the charge are creatures of statute, are not discretionary and have nothing to do with 'dirty tricks'. The provisions are to be found in s 9 of the Legal Aid Act 1974. Subsection (6) provides as follows:

> 'Except so far as regulations otherwise provide, any sums remaining unpaid on account of a person's contribution to the legal aid fund in respect of any proceedings and, if the total contribution is less than the net liability of that fund on his account, a sum equal to the deficiency shall be a first charge for the benefit of the legal aid fund on any property (wherever situated) which is recovered or preserved for him in the proceedings.'

Subsection (7) provides:

> 'The reference in subsection (6) above to property recovered or preserved for any person shall include his rights under any compromise arrived at to avoid or bring to an end the proceedings and any sums recovered by virtue of an order for costs made in his favour in the proceedings (not being sums payable into the legal aid fund under section 8 above).'

These provisions imposing and dealing with the ambit of the charge are reinforced by reg 19 of the Legal Aid (General) Regulations 1971, SI 1971 No 62, which provides, under para (1):

> 'Any charge on property recovered or preserved for an assisted person arising under section 3(4) of the Act shall vest in The Law Society.'

Paragraph (2) deals with enforcement. Paragraph (3) deals with the charges affecting land. Paragraph (4) provides:

> 'Subject to the provisions of the Land Charges Act 1925, all conveyances and acts done to defeat, or operating to defeat, such charge shall, except in the case of a conveyance to a bona fide purchaser for value without notice, be void as against The Law Society.'

As was inevitable from the nature of Dr Manley's action, very heavy costs were incurred by both sides in the preparation of the case for trial, and the ultimate outcome was uncertain. As any sensible person would in the circumstances, the parties and their advisers before trial thought in terms of compromise. Negotiations took place, and Dr Manley's solicitors and counsel ascertained that Marconi were prepared to pay Dr Manley £40,000. No doubt this was in part to be rid of the continuing cost and uncertainty of the litigation, especially because of the difficulty in the case brought by an assisted person of a defendant getting any significant contribution to his costs if he wins. But I am told, and readily accept, that Marconi felt a moral obligation to Dr Manley in respect to the debts incurred in the development of his invention.

Dr Manley and his advisers then considered whether £40,000 was acceptable or whether it would be an acceptable risk to refuse and go forward to trial, with the additional costs which would be involved and no certainty of success at any rate to the extent of more than £40,000 or indeed at all. Kennedys, Dr Manley's solicitors, then estimated what that bill would be for the costs involved to date, and the figure they gave was £25,000. So the amount payable under the statutory charge in favour of the Law Society which would immediately attach if Dr Manley accepted £40,000 in satisfaction of his claim would be £25,000. Dr Manley found that the amount of his debts was such that the balance of the £40,000 would not be sufficient to save him from bankruptcy, so that from his point of view there was nothing to lose by taking the risk of refusing the £40,000 and taking the risk of losing his action.

But solicitors and counsel for an assisted person have a duty not only to their client, not only to the court, but also to the legal aid fund, and it would be a breach of that duty to continue to act for an assisted person who was unreasonably pursuing a course of action likely to be detrimental to the fund. Dr Manley's advisers took the view that on their assessment of the prospects of success in the action the probable detriment to the fund, if Dr Manley went on to trial, would be very great and that it would not only be in the interests of their client Dr Manley but also in the interests of the fund itself if a way could be found of compromising the action at the figure which Marconi were prepared to provide which would not involve so much of the fruit of the litigation going to the fund that Dr Manley would be bankrupt anyway.

The scheme which Dr Manley's advisers devised, which was acceptable to Dr Manley and to which solicitors and counsel on the other side were prepared to agree, was this. The £40,000 was to be paid to Kennedys and to Coward Chance, Marconi's solicitors, jointly. The solicitors were to be Marconi's agents for the purpose of buying for Marconi the debts incurred in developing the invention.

Marconi were then to write off the debts. The solicitors were to reimburse themselves from the expenses properly incurred in the conduct of the operation out of the £40,000. If there was any balance they were to pay it to Dr Manley.

The result, of course, would be that the only money in Dr Manley's hands to satisfy the Law Society's statutory charge in favour of the fund would be such balance as might be paid to him after the purchase of the debts out of the £40,000 paid to the solicitors by Marconi and after they had deducted their expenses. So Dr Manley's advisers put the area secretary of the Law Society in the picture. The compromise was arrived at very shortly before the action was to come on and the Law Society had very little time to consider what action it could or should take. Nevertheless, it was informed of what was being done and had the opportunity to apply to the court to stop it. It did not do so, as is perfectly understandable having regard to the time scale involved.

On 3rd October 1978 Dr Manley's action was called on before Tudor Evans J. Dr Manley's counsel explained the terms of the compromise and the reasons for the compromise fully to the judge and a consent order was then made embodying its terms. Marconi paid the £40,000 to the solicitors. The Law Society claimed that the statutory charge had attached to the £40,000. Kennedys ultimately undertook that their bill to be defrayed by the Law Society would not exceed £17,000, and that sum therefore is all that the statutory charge is there to protect, and the solicitors are presently holding that sum inviolate.

In that state of affairs Dr Manley on 15th June 1979 issued an originating summons claiming a declaration that the £40,000 paid by Marconi to the solicitors under the terms of the consent order is not charged to the Law Society by s 9(6) and (7) of the 1974 Act. The Law Society says that the statutory charge attaches to the £40,000 because (i) it is the £40,000 which is the property which is recovered for Dr Manley in the proceedings; it is his money; (ii) the form of settlement is a fiction; the truth of the matter is that Dr Manley recovered £40,000 in respect of damages and costs; the scheme embodied in the terms of settlement is a 'dirty trick' and the court should disregard it and look at the reality.

Counsel for the Law Society, as I would expect, expressly disclaimed any intention by his clients to attack Dr Manley's counsel, or Kennedys, or Coward Chance, on the basis that any of them had taken part in a 'dirty trick' or that the solicitors, having been paid the £40,000, would apply it in any way other than the way in which the consent order requires them to do. In my judgment, this immediately disposes of the second limb of the Law Society's case. It is, in my judgment, not enough to make the scheme of the compromise a fiction, or a 'dirty trick' which the court will not allow to defeat the statutory charge, that the object of the exercise was to defeat the effect of the charge. You cannot hunt the 'dirty trick' line when you say, as counsel for the Law Society does, that Dr Manley's advisers and both firms of solicitors have acted with complete candour and honesty. If you are doing a 'dirty trick' you would be unlikely to tell the judge all about it in asking him to make a consent order, and if you did it is unlikely that the order would be made.

Then what was the property recovered for Dr Manley in the action to which by reason of s 9(6) of the 1974 Act the charge in favour of the Law Society attaches? Certainly the fruit of the compromise was worth £40,000 to Dr Manley. But, in my judgment, it does not follow that £40,000 was what he recovered as fruits of the action. In my judgment, the results of the compromise embodied in the consent order was that he acquired the right to have his debts discharged by the machinery which the compromise provided and the right to be paid any balance remaining. In my judgment, the effect of s 9(6) and (7) is that it is that right, and not the £40,000, to which, for better or for worse, this charge attaches. This result, in my judgment, is produced by the plain words of the Act and the facts of this case. That being so, the provisions of reg 19(4) do not affect this problem. It is not what has happened since the charge attached which is the subject matter of attack.

I am told that, when the debts have been bought, out of the £40,000 there is likely to be nothing left, let alone £17,000; so that the charge which the statute imposes will probably produce nothing. Whether the legal aid fund will be better or worse off than it would have been had the action been fought to the bitter end is a matter of speculation; but, for better or worse, the impact of the statutory provisions on the facts of this case is, in my judgment, that the charge in favour of the Law Society did not attach to the £40,000 paid by Marconi to the solicitors, and I make the declaration accordingly.

There is one further complication in this matter. I am told that, in the course of the solicitors buying off a major liability, land which was charged to secure that liability has now been freed from its incumbrance. Counsel for the Law Society wishes to argue that that land is available just as any balance after payment of the debts would be available, to meet the liability imposed by the charge. This was something raised this morning on the third day of the hearing and it obviously calls for an investigation of fact about what happened. There may be a number of complications of which counsel for the Law Society is not aware. Having asked counsel for Dr Manley what his view of the situation was, he very candidly says that he is not in a position to argue that there may not be a case to be made that that land might be available to discharge the obligations to the Law Society under the charge which has attached to Dr Manley's rights.

In those circumstances, it seems to me that the right way to deal with the problem is to adjourn this summons for that matter to be considered further by both parties, and, if they come to the conclusion that the proposition either is or is not well founded, no doubt they will act accordingly; or they may, having investigated the facts, be unable to agree on it, in which case the summons should be restored and the matter can be decided. It might be that even if they were unable to agree they might conclude that a compromise was the right answer.

As far as I can see, there would not be any point in this case in making an order for costs because the Law Society, with the utmost propriety, has given Dr Manley a legal aid certificate for the purposes of these proceedings, and it seems that they are paying the cost of both sides anyway.

Declaration in terms sought by summons.

K Mydeen Esq　　Barrister.

Appeal

The Law Society appealed to the Court of Appeal.

Duncan Matheson for the Law Society.
Jack Hames QC and *Peter Flint* for Dr Manley.
Marconi were not represented.

Cur adv vult

16th December. The following judgments were read.

LORD DENNING MR. Some ten years ago David Manley invented an 'echo sounder' by which large ships could tell if they were getting into shallow water. He got the Marconi International Marine Co Ltd interested in it. They agreed to exploit it if it came up to their requirements. But it failed to come up to their requirements. So they refused to go on with it. He alleged that they were guilty of a breach of contract. He claimed damages, huge damages because of the loss of profit that he said he would have made. He also claimed to be reimbursed the money he had spent in developing his echo sounder. It came to £30,000 or more. He borrowed it from the banks and charged his house as security for it.

David Manley had no money of his own to bring an action. So he applied for legal aid and got it. His contribution to the costs was only £100 payable by 11 monthly instalments of £8.35. He started an action in 1972 against Marconi. The interlocutory stage took six years. Marconi paid £8,000 into court. I do not suppose for one moment that they considered themselves under any liability to David Manley; but they wanted to get rid of a case in which they would get no costs even if they won, because David Manley was legally aided. David Manley refused to take out the £8,000. So the proceedings went on until the case was ready for trial. It was fixed to start on 3rd October 1978, and was estimated to last for 30 days.

The action was, however, settled. Marconi were ready to pay £40,000 to get rid of it altogether, rather than incur that expense in fighting the case of 30 days against a legally-aided plaintiff. But here is the crux of the case. David Manley was not agreeable to settle for £40,000, if that money was to be paid straight to his solicitors. David Manley was himself already insolvent. He had bankruptcy notices outstanding against him, but they were being held over pending the action. He owed at least £30,000 or more to his creditors. In addition, his own solicitors estimated their own costs on his behalf to be in the region of £25,000, for which the legal aid fund would have a charge on the £40,000 if paid over to him or his solicitors. The legal aid fund would have to insist on their charge, and take it out of the £40,000: see *Hanlon v Law Society* [1980] 2 All ER 199 at 210–211, [1980] 2 WLR 756 at 802–803. So there would be only £15,000 left for David Manley, and he would remain, as he says in his affidavit, 'in a bankrupt situation'.

The pressure brought by David Manley

So David Manley (with the backing of his solicitors and counsel) said to himself: 'I will only settle for £40,000 if that money is used first to pay off my creditors [of £30,000 or more], and then any balance [of £10,000 or less] can go to my solicitors, as a contribution to their costs, and they can get the rest of their costs from the legal aid fund.' Marconi said: 'We don't mind how you deal with the £40,000 as long as you accept that sum in settlement of the action.'

David Manley brought this pressure to bear on all concerned. He said to them in effect: 'Unless things can be settled on these lines, I insist on the action going on for trial for the 30 days, and that will put Marconi and the legal aid fund to enormous expense in costs.'

Faced with this problem, David Manley's legal advisers put their thinking caps on and brought forward a solution which was eventually agreed between the counsel and solicitors for both sides.

Terms simplified

1. Marconi to pay £40,000 into a joint account in the names of Kennedys (the solicitors for David Manley) and Coward Chance (the solicitors for Marconi). Then those two firms were to hold the £40,000 *as agents* for Marconi.

2. Kennedys (as agents for Marconi) were to negotiate with the creditors of David Manley and to pay them off, out of the £40,000 in the joint account belonging to Marconi. But in those negotiations Kennedys were not to disclose to the creditors that the money was coming from the account of Marconi. The creditors might then be induced to accept less than their full amount.

3. The payment off of the creditors should be made in the form of a purchase by Marconi of the debts which David Manley owed to the creditors. The creditors were to assign to Kennedys (as undisclosed agents for Marconi) the benefit of the debts. But Marconi undertook not to enforce the debts against David Manley.

4. After the payment off of the creditors, then if there was any balance left of the £40,000 it was to be paid to Kennedys (as David Manley's solicitors) as a contribution to his costs. On that being done, all claims of David Manley against Marconi were to be extinguished.

The information to the Law Society

The legal advisers thought that those terms would deprive the legal aid fund of their charge. They thought that Kennedys would not have 'recovered' the £40,000 for David Manley. They would only have 'recovered' for David Manley the right to have the terms enforced. That was only a chose in action which was worth little or nothing in money. It only sufficed to keep him out of bankruptcy. The legal advisers thought that Kennedys could still recover their costs from the legal aid fund, despite having deprived it of the charge. Their justification for this advice was that, by settling on these terms, they would save the legal aid fund all the expense of a 30-day trial.

But the legal advisers felt that they ought to tell the Law Society about the terms of settlement and get their opinion on it. I must say that it was a very rushed affair. The case was due to start on the morning of Tuesday, 3rd October 1978. It was only the day before, at 9.30 am on Monday, 2nd October 1978, that counsel for David Manley telephoned the offices of the area secretary of the Law Society. He outlined the proposed terms of settlement and said he thought that the charge would not apply to the £40,000. The reply was that, in the opinion of the legal aid fund, the charge would apply. Later that day there were further discussions. In the result the legal aid fund felt itself unable to commit itself on such short notice to any firm view, and that counsel must exercise his own judgment on the right course to follow.

I must say that I think the Law Society acted with complete propriety. It could not possibly be expected, at such short notice, and on such meagre information, to look into this complicated matter and express any view on it.

The settlement is announced

On the morning of Tuesday, 3rd October 1971, the case of *Manley v Marconi International Marine Co Ltd* was in the list for hearing. As soon as it was called on counsel for David Manley rose and made a short explanation. He asked for a consent order in the Tomlin form. The judge did not approve or disapprove. The terms were set out in a schedule to the order. It was all over in 19 minutes.

The follow-up

On 17th October 1978 Marconi paid the £40,000 into the joint account. David Manley's debts have been found to be, not £30,000, but £40,000. So if the terms of settlement were implemented, the whole of the £40,000 would be used up in 'purchasing' David Manley's debts. But the terms of settlement have been held up. The reason is because the legal aid fund are liable to pay Kennedys their costs of the action against Marconi, when taxed on a legal aid taxation. Kennedys put their costs at £25,000, but they have agreed to limit them to £17,000. The legal aid fund say that they have a charge on the £40,000 for that £17,000. Kennedys dispute it. They say that the legal aid fund have no such charge. These proceedings have been brought to resolve the issue. Pending the decision, the £17,000 has been retained in the joint account. The remaining £23,000 has been used, or will be used, to pay off some of David Manley's debts. In particular £20,000 of it has been used to pay a debt to a bank and release some land which was given by David Manley to the bank as security.

The issue

Kennedys say that the £40,000 is not subject to the statutory charge. They say that the whole of the £40,000 should be used to clear off David Manley's debts, as far as possible, and that Kennedys themselves should be paid their own costs (fixed at £17,000) by the legal aid fund. The legal aid fund admit that they are liable to pay Kennedys the £17,000, but claim to recoup themselves out of the £40,000, because they have a statutory charge on it or alternatively they have an equitable claim to it.

The statutory provisions

The clause which gives Kennedys their right to have their costs paid is s 10(1) of the Legal Aid Act 1974, which says:

> '. . . a solicitor who has acted for a person receiving legal aid shall be paid for so acting out of the legal aid fund, and any fees paid to counsel for so acting shall be paid out of that fund.'

The provision which gives the statutory charge is s 9(6) which says (omitting unnecessary words) that the net liability of the fund to the solicitor 'shall be a first charge for the benefit of the legal aid fund on any property (wherever situated) which is recovered or preserved for him in the proceedings'.

But when there is a compromise (as happened here) there comes into play s 9(7) which says:

> 'The reference in subsection (6) above to property recovered or preserved for any person shall include his rights under any compromise arrived at to avoid or bring to an end the proceedings . . .'

The judge's ruling

The judge pinned his faith on s 9(7). There was here a compromise arrived at so as to bring to an end the proceedings. The charge was on 'his rights under the compromise'. The judge said that David Manley—

> 'acquired the right to have his debts discharged by the machinery which the compromise provided and the right to be paid any balance remaining . . . it is that right, and not the £40,000, to which, for better or for worse, this charge attaches.'

Good faith

Everyone accepted that, in making this compromise, all the legal advisers acted honestly and in good faith and with the desire to act fairly by the legal aid fund. That is why they told the area committee about it before they concluded it. They say that, if they had not settled the case on these terms, it would have gone on for 30 days, at a great expense to the legal aid fund. So it was, they say, to the advantage of the legal aid fund to do this. They were entitled, they say, to draw up the terms of settlement, so as to express the rights of David Manley under the compromise, as being (a right to have his debts discharged) a chose in action and not the £40,000. They say that the written terms should be given their legal effect just as were the terms of the covenants in *Inland Revenue Comrs v Duke of Westminster* [1936] AC 1, [1935] All ER Rep 259.

The truth of the transaction

I can see the force of that argument. The judge accepted it. But I think it is erroneous. This case comes under another and better principle which I stated simply in *Customs and Excise Comrs v Pools Finance (1937) Ltd* [1952] 1 All ER 775 at 780: '[The parties] cannot assert that black is white and expect the courts to believe it.' It is the same as that which Lord Reid and I applied in *Griffiths (Inspector of Taxes) v J P Harrison (Watford) Ltd* [1962] 1 All ER 909 at 914, 917, [1963] AC 1 at 14–15, 20. The court should always look for the truth of the transaction. It should not let itself be deceived by the strategems of lawyers, or accountants. It should not allow them to pull the wool over its eyes. It should not allow them to dress up a transaction in clothes that do not belong to it.

Now the plain truth of this transaction is that the £40,000 was to be used to pay off David Manley's debts. Kennedys were to supply particulars of his debts. They were to negotiate the payment without disclosing that they were acting for anyone else but David Manley. The payment off was to be described as a 'purchase' of David Manley's debts, but the purchaser (Marconi) undertook not to enforce his purchase against David Manley. So, although it was in form a 'purchase', it was in fact a payment off of the creditors, by David Manley's solicitor, on the best terms that he could arrange, on the appearance that he was acting for David Manley.

To my mind, once we pull aside the curtain of words, and the supposed rights, the truth is that this £40,000 was to be used to pay off David Manley's debts at his request. It is, therefore, the subject of the statutory charge in favour of the legal aid fund. When money is paid to a party, or at his request to his creditors, it is plainly recovered 'for him' within s 9(6). The legal aid fund has, therefore, a charge for the £17,000 costs on the money in the joint account. It should be paid out to the fund. The fund should pay it to the solicitors. But the fund should pay nothing out of its own pocket.

Other provisions

If I am wrong, however, in looking behind the curtain, if the transaction is to be taken at its face value, then I doubt whether it would be defeated by the other provisions which were put before us.

Regulation 19(4) of the Legal Aid (General) Regulations 1971, SI 1971 No 62, may not help. If the charge is only on the chose in action, the settlement does not defeat it.

Regulation 18(3)(b) may not help. The £40,000 was not received by David Manley's solicitor as his solicitor, but as agent for Marconi.

Regulation 18(4)(a) may not help because the first charge would be on the chose in action and not on the £40,000.

Equity

Counsel for the Law Society referred us to a very interesting line of cases on a solicitor's lien. A typical instance is when a man is owed £100 by another. He goes to a solicitor who issues proceedings. If the defendant settles the action by paying £75 to the plaintiff's solicitor, then the solicitor has a lien on the £75 for his costs. These amount to £25. So that the plaintiff only receives £50 clear. Now, suppose the plaintiff, behind the back of his solicitor, goes to the defendant and agrees to take £70 in settlement, and spends it all in riotous living. The settlement is binding. The solicitor has been deprived of his lien for costs. Has he any recourse against the defendant? It is clear that if the defendant had notice of the solicitor's lien, and made the agreement with the plaintiff collusively so as to deprive the solicitor of his lien, then the solicitor can recover from the defendant his costs of £25. That is clear from a series of cases from *Welsh v Hole* (1779) 1 Doug KB 238, 99 ER 155, to *Re Margetson and Jones* [1897] 2 Ch 314. But there is a question as to what constitutes 'collusion' for this purpose. On this point I am content to go by the observation of Brett MR in *The Hope* (1883) 8 PD 144 at 145–146: '... the plaintiffs' solicitors must shew that both the plaintiffs and the defendants entered into the compromise with the intention of depriving them of their lien.'

Those cases do not apply directly to our present case. David Manley's solicitors had no lien for their costs. They looked to the legal aid fund for payment of them. The legal aid fund had no lien for costs. They had only a charge on any property when it was 'recovered'. Marconi had no intention to defeat the legal aid fund. They left everything to Kennedys to arrange.

Now, although those cases do not directly apply, I am of opinion that the principle of them does. It is clear beyond doubt that the object of David Manley and his solicitors was to deprive the legal aid fund of any charge on the £40,000. That was the be-all and end-all of this elaborate transaction. The solicitors wanted to make the legal aid fund pay all their costs, and at the same time deprive the legal aid fund of any charge in respect of those costs. I do not think they should be permitted to succeed in this. I do not think the settlement itself can be set aside. It has gone too far to do that. But I think that equity can intervene so as to hold that, if and in so far as the solicitors have intentionally deprived the legal aid fund of a charge on their costs, they are themselves precluded from making any claim on the legal aid fund for those costs. It is a very old principle laid down by Lord Coke (Co Litt 206b) that a man shall not be allowed to take advantage of a condition that he himself has brought about: see *New Zealand Shipping Co Ltd v Société des Ateliers et Chantiers de France* [1919] AC 1 at 8, [1918–19] All ER Rep 552 at 536 per Lord Finlay LC.

Conclusion

My conclusion is that the £17,000 now in the joint account should be released to the legal aid fund, because the fund has a charge on it to secure the costs of £17,000 which the legal aid fund has to pay to the solicitor for David Manley. Alternatively, if the £17,000 is released to the solicitors, they are precluded in equity from recovering anything from the legal aid fund. In short, the solicitors get the £17,000, but the legal aid fund pay nothing.

In parting from this case I cannot forbear from saying that I think the legal advisers of David Manley were ill-advised to try and circumvent the statutory charge. Either the settlement at £40,000 was good or it was bad, on the merits of the action itself. If it was good, it should have been accepted without any manipulation of the destination of the £40,000. If it was bad, it should have been rejected. It was quite wrong for David Manley to say: 'You must go ahead with the action unless my creditors are paid off.' That was a quite inadmissible threat by a legally-aided person, who was not paying the costs of going on. It was most unfair to put the defendants to all the great expense of contesting the case. If the £40,000 was reasonable on the merits of the case, and David Manley refused to accept it, his refusal should have been reported to the area committee for them to decide whether his certificate should be continued or not.

This case brings out vividly the responsibility which attaches to legal advisers who conduct an action for a legally-aided person. They must remember that they are funded at the expense of the state, and that they are putting the defendant (who is not legally aided) to a great deal of worry and expense in contesting the case, defendants who will not recover any of their costs even if they win. This puts the legal advisers for the plaintiff in an extremely strong bargaining position. There is inequality of bargaining power. They should not abuse it at the expense of the defendants. Nor should they abuse it at the expense of the legal aid fund. Whenever the question of a settlement comes up, the legal advisers for the plaintiff should consider any offer on the merits of the case itself, just as if they were acting for a private client of moderate means, not one who is wealthy enough to go to any expense, nor one who is very much in debt already, against a defendant who is also of moderate means and will get an order for costs against the plaintiff if he wins. Once a figure is reached which is reasonable, they should settle the case at that figure. They should not try and manipulate its destination so as to avoid the statutory charge. In particular they should not make the sum payable to the creditors of the plaintiff or to anyone else other than the plaintiff. If they should do so, they will find, as in this case, they will incur the displeasure of the court, which will see that their manipulations do not succeed.

I would allow the appeal accordingly.

ORMROD LJ. It is right to say at the outset of this judgment that I accept unreservedly that counsel for Dr Manley and those who helped him to draw up the terms of the compromise agreement believed that they were acting in the best interests of all concerned, including that of the Law Society as administrators of the legal aid fund. On the other hand, I think that they misapprehended the position of the Law Society.

The situation as they saw it was that Dr Manley had reasonable grounds for pursuing his claim for very substantial damages against Marconi International Marine Co Ltd, the defendants, but that the action, which was estimated to last for six weeks, and which would involve heavy costs, particularly in respect of expert witnesses, might very well fail in the end. The consequences would be that Dr Manley could recover nothing and a very heavy liability in respect of his costs would fall on the legal aid fund.

Marconi were prepared to offer £40,000 in full settlement of all Dr Manley's claims and costs, but Dr Manley, who was under a threat of bankruptcy, insisted on his outstanding debts being paid out of this sum, which would not be enough to meet both his debts and his costs to date. It was assumed, erroneously in my opinion, that Dr Manley was in a position, vis-à-vis the Law Society, to insist on going on with his action unless he received a sufficient proportion of the sum of £40,000 to clear his debts. Consequently, it would be to the advantage of the Law Society in the long run if terms of compromise could be so arranged that no effective charge in favour of the Law Society under s 9(6) and (7) of the Legal Aid Act 1974 fell on the sum of £40,000. The Law Society would be compensated by the substantial savings in costs if the action did not proceed to judgment. This assumes that Dr Manley was in control of the situation. In my opinion he was not.

Under the Legal Aid (General) Regulations 1971, reg 12(3) and (6), the area committee could have discharged Dr Manley's legal aid certificate from such date as they considered appropriate if they considered:

'(i) the assisted person no longer [had] reasonable grounds ... for taking, defending or being a party to the proceedings; or (ii) the assisted person [had] required ... the proceedings to be conducted unreasonably so as to incur an unjustifiable expense to the fund; or (iii) it [was] unreasonable in the particular circumstances that the assisted person should continue to receive legal aid.'

This, and many other provisions of the legal aid scheme, show that, although the scheme is designed to interfere as little as possible with the traditional relationship between counsel and solicitors and client, and is administered in such a way as to keep interference to a minimum, nonetheless it has altered these relationships in important, and sometimes subtle, ways. The existence of the legal aid fund has introduced a third party into what was formerly a one-to-one relationship, and this new relationship is governed by the Legal Aid Act 1974 and the regulations made under it. It was, in my opinion, the duty of Dr Manley's solicitors to inform and consult the area committee of the Law Society before entering, on Dr Manley's behalf, into the compromise agreement of 3rd October 1978. Some attempt was made on 2nd October by counsel for Dr Manley to consult the officers of the area committee, but they were given a wholly inadequate time in which to consider the complex and difficult issues involved. In retrospect at least, it is difficult to appreciate the reasons for the apparent urgency.

The extent to which the position of solicitors and counsel has been changed by the introduction of legal aid is shown by the facts of this case. Had Dr Manley not been an assisted person, the terms of compromise would have been inconceivable, unless his solicitors were prepared to forgo their lien or charge on the £40,000. Had they refused to do so, they would have declined to continue to act for Dr Manley until he had put them in funds.

Counsel for Dr Manley submitted that all rights and obligations relating to the legal aid fund are statutory in origin and must be found in the Legal Aid Act 1974 or in the regulations made under it. They are, therefore, dependent on the construction of the relevant statutory provisions. I accept that submission, from which it follows that the rules of common law or equity affecting the rights of solicitors are relevant only in so far as they may throw light on the true construction of the relevant provisions in the Act or the regulations. The answer to the question raised in the originating summons in this case, therefore, depends, first, on the construction of s 9(6) and (7) of the 1974 Act, which create the Law Society's statutory charge on the proceeds of the litigation as security for the costs of the assisted person which ultimately fall on the fund and, second, on the true construction of the written agreement of compromise dated 3rd October 1978.

Subsections (6) and (7) of s 9 are in these terms:

'(6) Except so far as regulations otherwise provide, any sums remaining unpaid on account of a person's contribution to the legal aid fund in respect of any proceedings and, if the total contribution is less than the net liability of that fund on his account, a sum equal to the deficiency shall be a first charge for the benefit of the legal aid fund on any property (wherever situated) which is recovered or preserved for him in the proceedings.

'(7) The reference in subsection (6) above to property recovered or preserved for any person shall include his rights under any compromise arrived at to avoid or bring to an end the proceedings and any sums recovered by virtue of an order for costs made in his favour in the proceedings (not being sums payable into the legal aid fund under section 8 above).'

The crucial words for present purposes in sub-s (6) are 'any property (wherever situated) which is recovered or preserved for him in the proceedings'. Subsection (7) extends sub-s (6) to 'rights under [a] compromise', but does not restrict the charge to such rights. This is made clear by the use of the word 'include' in sub-s (7).

Counsel for Dr Manley submitted that the property recovered for Dr Manley under the compromise was limited to the bundle of rights or choses in action which he acquired, ie a right to compel Marconi to pay £40,000 to their agents, the respective firms of solicitors for the parties, a right to require Marconi to purchase such of his debts for up to £40,000 as he chose, a right to insist on Marconi not enforcing such debts against him, and so on. This is property in one sense, but it is valueless to support the Law Society's charge as security for the costs paid on Dr Manley's behalf. Counsel for the Law Society argued that the statutory charge attached to so much of the £40,000 as was required to meet the net liability of the legal aid fund, after deducting any contribution paid by Dr Manley as a term of his legal aid certificate.

The submission of counsel for Dr Manley requires that the word 'property' be construed in the sense in which lawyers use it as a term of art; counsel for the Law Society urged that it should be given its ordinary meaning in the English language.

This question was fully considered (though in a different context) by the House of Lords in *Hanlon v Law Society* [1980] 2 All ER 199, [1980] 2 WLR 756. Lord Scarman and Lord Lowry favoured the broader construction. Lord Scarman said ([1980] 2 All ER 199 at 214, [1980] 2 WLR 756 at 806):

'The subsection must be construed so that in matrimonial as in other proceedings the legal aid fund has the security of its charge. The words "recovered or preserved" are apt to cover ordinary civil litigation in which a plaintiff recovers or a defendant preserves an asset; but they are not so apt to cover a transfer of property ordered by a court in the exercise of its discretion under ss 24 and 25 of the Matrimonial Causes Act 1973. Nevertheless, they can be read as covering such an order without any very great distortion of their ordinary meaning. A woman who obtains an order transferring to her the matrimonial home will be seen, by herself and by others, to have "got" the house; and it is not difficult to construe "property recovered" as property obtained.'

Lord Lowry said ([1980] 2 All ER 199 at 216, [1980] 2 WLR 756 at 809):

'The purpose, after all, of creating a charge on property is to give the legal aid fund or the solicitor, as the case may be, a security, if the assisted person or the client has gained financially as a result of the proceedings; the way in which that result has been achieved should not matter.'

Lord Simon, however, thought a liberal approach to construction was not appropriate 'in a measure imposing a charge for a social service' (see [1980] 2 All ER 199 at 206, [1980] 2 WLR 756 at 796). It is, however, clear on the facts of that case that the House of Lords did not adopt the strict legal meaning of the word 'property' or of 'recovered', but instead came to the conclusion that Mrs Hanlon had substantially recovered the whole of the former matrimonial home to which, accordingly, the statutory charge attached.

In reaching their conclusion, the House of Lords held that it was permissible to look at the regulations made under the Legal Aid Act 1974 as an aid to the construction of the Act itself (see in particular per Lord Lowry [1980] 2 All ER 199 at 218ff, [1980] 2 WLR 756 at 811ff). There is one regulation which is useful in the present case, namely reg 18(4)(*a*) of the Legal Aid (General) Regulations 1971, which reads:

'Where in any proceedings to which an assisted person is a party—(*a*) an order or agreement is made providing for the recovery or preservation of property for the benefit of the assisted person and, by virtue of the Act, there is a first charge on the property for the benefit of the fund . . .'

This is a clear indication that the statutory charge is not limited to property recovered by the assisted person but extends to property recovered for his benefit.

In my judgment, therefore, the court should adopt the broader approach and construe the phrase 'property recovered or preserved' for the assisted person as including property recovered for his benefit, looking at the reality of the matter rather than concentrating exclusively on the form of the transaction, particularly when the court is concerned with a compromise. Judgments deal in realities; compromises provide scope for an infinite variety of forms, limited only by the ingenuity of the draftsman. It would be wrong, in my view, to extend the formalistic approach adopted in Revenue cases, e g *Inland Revenue Comrs v Duke of Westminster* [1936] AC 1, [1935] All ER Rep 259, to other branches of the law.

I now turn to consider the terms of the compromise as finally agreed. The concept underlying it is in the last degree artificial. There could be no conceivable reason, or at least there is no evidence at all of any reason, why Marconi should wish to purchase unspecified debts from unspecified creditors of Dr Manley at his option. Still less when they undertake not to enforce them against Dr Manley. There can equally be no sensible reason why Dr Manley's solicitors should be involved in the purchase of such debts, or why they should be made joint agents of Marconi with Marconi's solicitors except to avoid receipt of the £40,000 by Dr Manley's solicitors which would have instantly brought reg 18(3)(*b*) of the 1971 regulations into force, and require them to pay over to the Law Society any sum so received. In my view the compromise was expressed in this form solely for the benefit of Dr Manley, in order that the whole sum of £40,000 would be available to him to pay his debts and nothing would be available to the Law Society as security for their costs. In truth and in fact, Dr Manley was clearly in effective control of the distribution of this fund and was the sole beneficiary of it.

I would, therefore, hold that the statutory charge attached to the fund of £40,000 to the extent necessary to cover the net liability of the Law Society for Dr Manley's costs.

On this view of the case the only remaining question is that of enforcement of the statutory charge, but fortunately a sum of £17,500 has been retained by the solicitors at the insistence of the Law Society, pending the outcome of this appeal, which is sufficient to cover the net liability of the legal aid fund. So this problem does not arise. Had it been necessary to consider it, as the learned judge in the court below felt obliged to do, the line of cases cited to us by counsel for the Law Society dealing with solicitors' liens and charges might have been helpful. They show the lengths to which the court has been prepared to go in its equitable jurisdiction to protect solicitors who have been deprived of their lien or charge under the Solicitors Acts. An analogous situation might have arisen in this case if the whole of the £40,000 had been put out of reach of the statutory charge, eg by a simple agreement that Marconi would pay Dr Manley's debts direct to the creditors up to a total of £40,000. It is unnecessary to say more than this. There is no case in the books in which a solicitor who has been a party to such an arrangement which deprives himself of his own lien or charge has recovered his costs from a third party. That is not, however, to say that a solicitor for an assisted party puts his costs at risk if he is a party to a compromise in which the other party, for reasons of his own, offers terms which do not include the payment of money or the transfer of property, but some other less tangible form of benefit to the assisted person.

I too would allow this appeal.

O'CONNOR LJ. This case is concerned with legal aid in civil proceedings. Where a person qualifies for legal aid, solicitors and counsel act for him but are paid by the legal aid fund. The Legal Aid Act 1974 gives to the fund a first charge on all property recovered or preserved for the assisted person in the proceedings. These provisions cause no difficulty in any case where the assisted person loses the case. They can be troublesome where the assisted person wins his case and very often raise serious problems when a compromise is under discussion.

The present case is a classic example of the compromise difficulty. The plaintiff is an inventor who alleged that the defendants, Marconi, were in breach of a contract to exploit his invention. The matter was highly technical and the damages claimed for loss of royalties on worldwide sales of very expensive equipment were large. The case was due to start on 3rd October 1978 and the parties estimated that the hearing would take thirty days. This is very expensive litigation. The defendants knew that, if they succeeded, they would have to pay their own costs and, if they lost, in addition they would have to pay to the plaintiff both damages and costs. That was a situation which was ripe for compromise.

The plaintiff gave firm instructions. He had incurred debts in producing a working prototype of his invention of the order of £30,000 although no accurate figure was known on 3rd October 1978. His creditors were threatening to make him bankrupt. He said that so long as Marconi paid enough to pay his debts he was content; if not, the case must go on. Negotiations took place and Marconi made a final offer of £40,000 inclusive of costs to be rid of the litigation at that time. Counsel leading for the plaintiff asked his solicitors for an estimate of their costs to date and got the answer £25,000. It was obvious that if the legal aid charge attached to this money there would not be enough to discharge the plaintiff's debts.

Leading counsel certainly, and possibly others of the plaintiff's legal advisers, did not take a rosy view of the plaintiff's chances of success in this litigation. They calculated that if the trial ran for the estimated 30 days the plaintiff's costs would rise to £60,000. Marconi would pay no more. So it was that they decided to devise a scheme so as to avoid the charge to the legal aid fund. The scheme proposed would leave any balance of £40,000 after payment of the plaintiff's debts available for the legal aid fund, and as at 3rd October this was thought to be of the order of £10,000. The legal aid fund was being asked to buy a potential liability of £60,000 for £15,000.

The scheme devised was simple. Marconi were to pay £40,000 into an account in the joint names of the plaintiff's and defendant's solicitors who were declared to be agents for Marconi for this purpose. The plaintiff's solicitors as undisclosed agents for Marconi were to buy the plaintiff's debts for Marconi. Marconi undertook not to have recourse to the plaintiff for such debts. The solicitors were to recover their own charges for this work from the £40,000. Thereafter if there was any money left it would be paid to the plaintiff's solicitors who would hold it for the legal aid fund.

On 2nd October the Law Society was told of the scheme on the telephone and asked to approve it and to agree not to claim the legal aid fund charge against the £40,000. This the Law Society would not and did not do. On 3rd October 1978 the case was settled on the terms of the scheme now embodied in a Tomlin order. It was fully mentioned in open court to the judge. It is not and never has been suggested that the plaintiff's legal advisers acted other than openly and in good faith believing that they were acting in the best interests of their client and the legal aid fund.

The Law Society claimed the charge on the fund of £40,000. The plaintiff's solicitors quantified their costs and agreed to limit their claim against the fund to £17,000. That sum is held pending the outcome of these proceedings; the balance was released for the purposes of this scheme. The plaintiff commenced these proceedings against the Law Society by originating summons asking for a declaration that the fund of £40,000 'does not stand and never has stood charged for the benefit of the legal aid fund under and by virtue of the provisions and for the purposes of the Legal Aid Act 1974'.

The case was heard by Bristow J who gave judgment on 10th October 1980 in favour of the plaintiff and made the declaration prayed for. The Law Society appeals to this court.

The Law Society contends that on the true construction of the compromise agreement the fund of £40,000 was 'property . . . recovered or preserved for [the plaintiff] in the proceedings' within the meaning of s 9(6) of the Legal Aid Act 1974. The crucial words are 'property . . . recovered or preserved *for him*'. That the £40,000 was a fruit of this litigation is beyond doubt, but not all fruits of litigation are 'property recovered'. Counsel leading on behalf of the plaintiff submits that the property recovered in this case was the right to force Marconi to carry out the terms of compromise which included a contingent right to any balance of the £40,000 that might remain, and he submitted that that was the property to which the charge attached. I cannot agree. Under the terms of the compromise the plaintiff had the right to specify which of his debts were to be discharged out of the £40,000. Marconi had no interest in what debts the plaintiff chose to have paid off. The provision in the compromise making the plaintiff's solicitors the undisclosed agents of Marconi was solely for the benefit of the plaintiff in the hope that his debts could be 'bought' for less than their book value. I do not think that there can be any doubt that the £40,000 was property recovered for the benefit of the plaintiff. Can it be said that nevertheless it is not recovered 'for him'? I think not and I am fortified in that view when I look at reg 18(4)(*a*) of the Legal Aid (General) Regulations 1971:

> 'Where in any proceedings to which an assisted person is a party—(*a*) an order or agreement is made providing for the recovery or preservation of property for the benefit of the assisted person and, by virtue of the Act, there is a first charge on the property for the benefit of the fund . . . The Law Society may take such proceedings in its own name as may be necessary to enforce or give effect to such an order or agreement.'

For these reasons I hold that the £40,000 was property recovered for the plaintiff and the charge in favour of the legal aid fund attaches.

In the present case no problem of enforcement arises and I do not wish to add anything of my own to what Lord Denning MR and Ormrod LJ have said were the position to be that the money had all gone, save that I agree with them.

I too would allow the appeal.

Appeal allowed. Declaration made in terms sought.

Solicitors: *Collyer-Bristow* (for the Law Society); *Kennedys* (for Dr Manley).

Sumra Green   Barrister.

British Steel Corpn v Granada Television Ltd

CHANCERY DIVISION
SIR ROBERT MEGARRY V-C
11th, 12th, 13th, 14th MARCH, 2nd APRIL 1980

COURT OF APPEAL, CIVIL DIVISION
LORD DENNING MR, TEMPLEMAN AND WATKINS LJJ
18th, 21st, 22nd, 23rd, 24th APRIL, 7th MAY 1980

HOUSE OF LORDS
LORD WILBERFORCE, VISCOUNT DILHORNE, LORD SALMON, LORD FRASER OF TULLYBELTON AND
LORD RUSSELL OF KILLOWEN
14th, 15th, 16th, 17th, 21st, 22nd, 30th JULY, 7th NOVEMBER 1980

Evidence – Privilege – Press – Television authority – Source of information – Whether privileged from disclosure.

Evidence – Privilege – Confidential relationships – Journalist and source of information – Discretion of court to order disclosure of identity of informant in public interest – Whether defendant privileged from disclosing informant's identity on grounds of self-incrimination.

Discovery – Privilege – Identity of informant – Informant wrongfully passing plaintiff's confidential documents to defendant for publication – Plaintiff bringing action against defendant to discover informant's identity – Whether defendant should be ordered to disclose informant's identity.

In January 1980, during a national steel strike by British Steel Corpn ('BSC') employees, a television company ('Granada') decided to broadcast a programme on the strike. A few days before the programme Granada received copies of 250 secret and confidential documents from BSC's files relating to internal actions and discussions at a high level within BSC and between BSC and the government. The documents were received unsolicited from an unofficial source, who was clearly someone inside BSC who had access to them, and showed possible mismanagement within BSC. Granada used 27 of them in their programme. The informant was not revealed, in accordance with a promise by Granada to him that his identity would not be disclosed. BSC brought proceedings against Granada seeking, inter alia, an order that Granada disclose the identity of the informant. BSC contended that it was necessary for them to know the identity of the informant in order to prevent further misuse of BSC documents, possibly by an injunction, and to remove the suspicion directed at those of their staff who had access to the documents. On the hearing of the motion, the judge ordered Granada to disclose the identity of the informant, and that order was upheld by the Court of Appeal. Granada appealed to the House of Lords, contending (i) that BSC were not entitled to obtain the name of the informant by what was in substance an action for discovery because, inter alia, newspapers and broadcasting authorities were in a special position regarding being compelled to disclose information, as was illustrated by the 'newspaper rule' which protected newspapers from the requirement that a defendant in a libel action should disclose the source of his information on discovery, (ii) that disclosure could not be ordered against Granada because it was not required to assist either existing or intended proceedings against the informant, there being no evidence that BSC would bring an action against him, (iii) that disclosure of the identity of the informant by Granada would tend to incriminate them, and (iv) that the court ought to exercise its discretion by refusing to order such disclosure because of the public interest that the public should be informed about the steel strike and BSC's conduct of their affairs.

Held (Lord Salmon dissenting) – The appeal would be dismissed for the following reasons—

(1) Although the courts had an inherent wish to respect the confidentiality of information obtained as the result of a particular relationship, including the relationship between a journalist and his sources, journalists and the information media had no immunity based on public interest protecting them from the obligation to disclose their sources of information in court if such disclosure was necessary in the interests of justice. The 'newspaper rule' was confined to libel actions and did not extend to actions based on breach of confidence and hence did not operate to confer on newspapers and broadcasting authorities a general immunity from disclosure of their sources (see p 455 *f g*, p 456 *b c j*, p 457 *d*, p 458 *h*, p 463 *e f*, p 465 *b* to *f*, p 476 *a* to *e*, p 477 *b j*, p 478 *g h*, p 481 *d* and p 482 *b*, post); *McGuinness v Attorney General of Victoria* (1940) 63 CLR 73, *Attorney General v Clough* [1963] 1 All ER 420 and *Attorney General v Mulholland* [1963] 1 All ER 767 applied.

(2) BSC were prima facie entitled to an order that Granada disclose the identity of their informant because—

(a) in becoming involved in their informant's tortious act in removing the documents from BSC without authority, Granada would have been under a duty to assist BSC by disclosing the identity of the wrongdoer even if they had been involved through no fault of their own, and a fortiori they were under such a duty having used the documents for their own purposes while knowing their removal to have been unauthorised (see p 457 *g h*, p 466 *j*, p 467 *a b*, p 476 *g h*, p 481 *d* and p 482 *b*, post); *Norwich Pharmacal Co v Customs and Excise Comrs* [1973] 2 All ER 943 applied;

(b) BSC were not seeking discovery for the mere gratification of curiosity but had suffered a wrong for which they had a real and unsatisfied claim against the informant and could not bring any proceedings against him until Granada revealed his identity. The conditions for granting the remedy sought therefore existed (see p 459 *a* and *g* to *j*, p 467 *a b*, p 479 *e f*, p 481 *d* and p 482 *b*, post).

(3) Granada were not able to rely on the defence that disclosure of the informant's identity might tend to incriminate them because even if there was a real and appreciable risk of Granada being prosecuted for the offences of handling stolen goods and conspiracy to defraud by infringing BSC's copyright in the documents, the disclosure of the informant's identity would not strengthen the case against Granada since Granada had already stated in evidence all the matters which might disclose an offence and (per Lord Russell) the disclosure of a name by Granada which might lead to further inquiries and further evidence did not amount to Granada incriminating itself by its own evidence. Neither could Granada claim privilege under the 'iniquity rule' because the documents had not revealed any iniquity or misconduct by BSC (see p 455 *h j*, p 460 *c* to *e*, p 462 *h* to p 463 *a*, p 479 *g h*, p 481 *d* and p 482 *a b*, post).

(4) If BSC were to be confined to their remedy against Granada and denied the opportunity of a remedy against the informant there would be a significant denial of justice, and the strong public interest in doing justice outweighed any public interest that the public should be informed about the steel strike. The balance of the court's discretion whether to order disclosure of the source came down strongly in BSC's favour (see p 460 *b* to *d*, p 467 *b d e*, p 478 *f g*, p 479 *f g*, p 480 *g* to p 481 *a d g* to *j* and p 482 *b*, post).

Notes

For actions for discovery, see 13 Halsbury's Laws (4th Edn) para 18, and for cases on the subject, see 18 Digest (Reissue) 8, *16–23*.

For privilege from disclosure of confidential documents, see 17 Halsbury's Laws (4th Edn) para 237, and for cases on the subject of press privileges, see 22 Digest (Reissue) 459, *4587–4588*.

For privilege on the grounds of self-incrimination, see 17 Halsbury's Laws (4th Edn) para 240, and for cases on the subject, see 22 Digest (Reissue) 435, *4318–4336*.

Cases referred to in judgments and opinions

Abernethy v Hutchinson (1825) 1 H & Tw 28, 3 LJOS Ch 209, 47 ER 1313, LC, 13 Digest (Reissue) 66, *633*.

Adam v Fisher (1914) 110 LT 537, 30 TLR 288, CA, 18 Digest (Reissue) 205, *1622*.

Advocate, HM v Airs 1975 JC 64.

Albert (Prince) v Strange (1849) 1 Mac & G 25, 1 H & Tw 1, 18 LJ Ch 120, 12 LTOS 441, 13 Jur 109, 41 ER 1171, LC, 13 Digest (Reissue) 76, *686*.

Annesley v Earl of Anglesea (1743) 17 State Tr 1139, 22 Digest (Reissue) 447, *4449*.

Anton Piller KG v Manufacturing Processes Ltd [1976] 1 All ER 779, [1976] Ch 55, [1976] 2 WLR 162, [1976] Ch 55, CA, Digest (Cont Vol E) 338, *1238b*.

Attorney General v Clough [1963] 1 All ER 420, [1963] 1 QB 773, [1963] 2 WLR 343, 22 Digest (Reissue) 459, *4587*.

Attorney General v Mulholland, Attorney General v Foster [1963] 1 All ER 767, [1963] 2 QB 477, [1963] 2 WLR 658, CA, 22 Digest (Reissue) 459, *4588*.

Baker v F & F Investment (1972) 470 F 2d 778.

Branzburg v Hayes (1972) 408 US 665.

Brill v Television Service One [1976] 1 NZLR 683.

Broadcasting Corpn of New Zealand v Alex Harvey Industries Ltd [1980] 1 NZLR 163.

Buchanan, Re (1964) 65 SR (NSW) 9.

Cardale v Watkins (1820) 5 Madd 18, 56 ER 801, 18 Digest (Reissue) 12, *48*.

Colonial Government v Tatham (1902) 23 Natal LR 153.

Cunningham v Duncan and Jamieson (1889) 16 R (Ct of Sess) 383.

D v National Society for the Prevention of Cruelty to Children [1977] 1 All ER 589, [1978] AC 171, [1977] 2 WLR 201, HL, Digest (Cont Vol E) 185, *1301b*.

Democratic National Committee v McCord (1973) 356 F Supp 1394.

Duport Steels Ltd v Sirs [1980] 1 All ER 529, [1980] 1 WLR 142, [1980] ICR 161, CA and HL.

Elliott v Garrett [1902] 1 KB 870, 71 LJKB 415, 86 LT 441, CA, 18 Digest (Reissue) 211, *1656*.

Express Newspapers Ltd v MacShane [1980] 1 All ER 65, [1980] AC 672, [1980] 2 WLR 89, [1980] ICR 42, HL.

Garland v Torre (1958) 250 F 2d 545.

Gartside v Outram (1856) 26 LJ Ch 113, 28 LTOS 120, 3 Jur NS 39, 18 Digest (Reissue) 129, *984*.

Genese, Re, ex parte Gilbert (1886) 3 Moir 223, CA, 22 Digest (Reissue) 434, *4316*.

Georgius v Oxford University Press (Delegates) [1949] 1 All ER 342, [1949] 1 KB 729, [1949] LJR 454, CA, 18 Digest (Reissue) 206, *1624*.

Hennessy v Wright (No 2) (1888) 24 QBD 445n, CA, 18 Digest (Reissue) 205, *1618*.

Hillman's Airways Ltd v SA d'Editions Aéronautiques Internationales [1934] 2 KB 356, 103 LJKB 670, 151 LT 451, 18 Digest (Reissue) 203, *1604*.

Hope v Brash [1897] 2 QB 188, [1895–9] All ER Rep 343, 66 LJQB 653, 76 LT 823, CA, 18 Digest (Reissue) 71, *500*.

Ibrahim v R [1914] AC 599, [1914–15] All ER Rep 874, 83 LJPC 185, 111 LT 20, 24 Cox CC 174, PC, 14(2) Digest (Reissue) 562, *4583*.

Initial Services Ltd v Putterill [1967] 3 All ER 145, [1968] 1 QB 396, [1967] 3 WLR 1032, CA, 28(2) Digest (Repl) 1087, *907*.

Isbey v New Zealand Broadcasting Corpn (No 2) [1975] 2 NZLR 237.

Lawson v Odhams Press Ltd [1948] 2 All ER 717, [1949] 1 KB 129, [1949] LJR 685, CA, 18 Digest (Reissue) 206, *1623*.

Lennard's Carrying Co Ltd v Asiatic Petroleum Co Ltd [1915] AC 705, [1914–15] All ER Rep 280, 84 LJKB 1281, 113 LT 195, 13 Asp MLC 81, HL; *affg* sub nom *Asiatic Petroleum Co Ltd v Lennard's Carrying Co Ltd* [1914] 1 KB 419, CA, 41 Digest (Repl) 295, *1073*.

Loose v Williamson [1978] 3 All ER 89, [1978] 1 WLR 639, Digest (Cont Vol E) 180, *16a*.

Lyle-Samuel v Odhams Ltd [1920] 1 KB 135, [1918–19] All ER Rep 779, 88 LJKB 1161, 122 LT 57, CA, 18 Digest (Reissue) 207, *1626*.

Maass v Gas Light and Coke Co [1911] 2 KB 543, 80 LJKB 1313, 104 LT 767, CA, 18 Digest (Reissue) 215, 1691.

Manenti v Melbourne and Metropolitan Tramways Board [1954] VLR 115.

Marks v Beyfus (1890) 25 QBD 494, 59 LJQB 479, 63 LT 733, 55 JP 182, 17 Cox CC 196, CA, 22 Digest (Reissue) 432, 4297.

McGuinness v Attorney General of Victoria (1940) 63 CLR 73, 14 ALJ 38, 46 ALR 110, 18 Digest (Reissue) 208, *1035.

Morris v Crown Office [1970] 1 All ER 1079, [1970] 2 QB 114, [1970] 2 WLR 792, CA, 14(2) Digest (Reissue) 695, 5830.

Norwich Pharmacal Co v Customs and Excise Comrs [1973] 2 All ER 943, [1974] AC 133, [1973] 3 WLR 164, [1974] RPC 101, HL, 18 Digest (Reissue) 8, 23.

Ocli Optical Coatings Ltd v Spectron Optical Coatings Ltd [1980] FSR 227, CA.

Orr v Diaper (1876) 4 Ch D 92, 46 LJ Ch 41, 35 LT 468, 18 Digest (Reissue) 8, 16.

Parnell v Walter (1890) 24 QBD 441, 59 LJQB 125, 62 LT 75, 54 JP 311, DC, 18 Digest (Reissue) 205, 1619.

Plymouth Mutual Co-operative and Industrial Society Ltd v Traders' Publishing Association Ltd [1906] 1 KB 403, 75 LJKB 259, 94 LT 258, CA, 18 Digest (Reissue) 205, 1621.

Post v Toledo, Cincinnati and St Louis Railroad Co (1887) 11 NE Rep 540, Massachusetts SC.

R v Armagh Justices (1883) 18 ILTR 2.

R v Boyes (1861) 1 B & S 311, [1861–73] All ER Rep 172, 30 LJQB 301, 5 LT 147, 25 JP 789, 7 Jur NS 1158, 9 Cox CC 32, 121 ER 730, 22 Digest (Reissue) 433, 4314.

R v Garbett (1847) 2 Car & Kir 474, 1 Den 236, 9 LTOS 51, 13 JP 602, 2 Cox CC 448, 175 ER 196, CCR, 22 Digest (Reissue) 439, 4372.

R v Hall (1776) 2 Wm Bl 1110, 96 ER 655, 14(1) Digest (Reissue) 242, 1750.

R v Slaney (1832) 5 C & P 212, 172 ER 944, NP, 22 Digest (Reissue) 214, 1804.

RCA Corpn v Reddingtons Rare Records [1975] 1 All ER 38, [1974] 1 WLR 1445, [1975] RPC 95, Digest (Cont Vol D) 277, 63a.

Rank Film Distributors Ltd v Video Information Centre [1980] 2 All ER 273, [1980] 3 WLR 487, CA.

Reynolds, Re, ex parte Reynolds (1882) 20 Ch D 294, 51 LJ Ch 756, 46 LT 508, 46 JP 533, 15 Cox CC 108, CA, 22 Digest (Reissue) 434, 4315.

Rogers v Secretary of State for the Home Department, Gaming Board for Great Britain v Rogers [1972] 2 All ER 1057, [1973] AC 388, [1972] 3 WLR 279, 136 JP 574, HL; affg in part sub nom R v Lewes Justices, ex parte the Gaming Board of Great Britain, R v Lewes Justices, ex parte the Secretary of State for the Home Department [1971] 2 All ER 1126, [1972] 1 QB 232, [1971] 2 WLR 1466, 135 JP 442, Digest (Cont Vol D) 267, 2835c.

Science Research Council v Nassé, BL Cars Ltd (formerly Leyland Cars Ltd) v Vyas [1979] 3 All ER 673, [1980] AC 1028, [1979] 3 WLR 762, [1979] ICR 921, HL, Digest (Cont Vol E) 186, 1301d.

Scott v Comr of Police for the Metropolis [1974] 3 All ER 1032, [1975] AC 819, [1974] 3 WLR 741, 139 JP 121, 60 Cr App R 124, 15 Digest (Reissue) 1401, 12,272.

Senior v Holdsworth [1975] 2 All ER 1009, [1976] QB 23, [1975] 2 WLR 987, CA, Digest (Cont Vol D) 326, 4588a.

Short v Mercier (1851) 3 Mac & G 205, 20 LJ Ch 289, 16 LTOS 453, 18 LTOS 266, 15 Jur 93, 42 ER 239, LC, 18 Digest (Reissue) 177, 1421.

South Suburban Co-operative Society Ltd v Orum and Croydon Advertiser Ltd [1937] 3 All ER 133, [1937] 2 KB 690, 106 LJKB 555, 157 LT 93, CA, 18 Digest (Reissue) 212, 1667.

Tesco Supermarkets Ltd v Natrass [1971] 2 All ER 127, [1972] AC 153, [1971] 2 WLR 1166, 135 JP 289, 69 LGR 403, HL, Digest (Cont Vol D) 991, 1142a.

Triplex Safety Glass Co Ltd v Lancegay Safety Glass (1934) Ltd [1939] 2 All ER 613, [1939] 2 KB 395, 108 LJKB 762, 160 LT 595, CA, 18 Digest (Reissue) 245, 1933.

Upmann v Elkan (1871) LR 12 Eq 140, 40 LJ Ch 475, 24 LT 896; affd (1871) LR 7 Ch App 130, 41 LJ Ch 246, 25 LT 813, 36 JP 295, LC, 28(2) Digest (Reissue) 1157, 1589.

Westinghouse Electric Corpn Uranium Contract Litigation MDL Docket No 235 (No 2) [1977] 3 All ER 717, [1978] AC 547, [1977] 3 WLR 492, CA; on appeal sub nom Rio Tinto Zinc Corpn v Westinghouse Electric Corpn, RTZ Services Ltd v Westinghouse Electric Corpn

[1978] 1 All ER 434, [1978] AC 547, [1978] 2 WLR 81, HL, Digest (Cont Vol E) 222, 7114a.
Woodward v Hutchins [1977] 2 All ER 751, [1977] 1 WLR 760, CA, Digest (Cont Vol E) 338, 907a.

Cases also cited

Attorney General v Jonathan Cape Ltd [1975] 3 All ER 684, [1976] QB 752.
Attorney General v North Metropolitan Tramways Co [1892] 3 Ch 70; affd (1895) 72 LT 340, CA.
Beloff v Pressdram Ltd [1973] 1 All ER 241.
Brayley v Associated Newspapers Group Ltd (1976) Times, 4th July.
Burmah Oil Co Ltd v Bank of England [1979] 3 All ER 700, [1980] AC 1090, HL.
Conway v Rimmer [1968] 1 All ER 874, [1968] AC 910, HL.
Crompton (Alfred) Amusement Machines Ltd v Customs and Excise Comrs (No 2) [1973] 2 All ER 1169, [1974] AC 405, HL.
Distillers Co (Biochemicals) Ltd v Times Newspapers Ltd [1975] 1 All ER 41, [1975] QB 613.
Dixon v Enoch (1872) LR 13 Eq 394.
Fraser v Evans [1969] 1 All ER 8, [1969] 1 QB 349, CA.
Hesperides Hotels v Muftizade [1978] 2 All ER 1168, [1979] AC 508, HL.
Morgan v Morgan [1977] 2 All ER 515, [1977] Fam 122.
Neville v Dominion of Canada News Co Ltd [1915] 3 KB 556, [1914–15] All ER Rep 979, CA.
R v John Jones [1974] ICR 310, CA.
Rice v Connolly [1966] 2 All ER 649, [1966] 2 QB 414, DC.
Riddick v Thames Board Mills Ltd [1977] 3 All ER 677, [1977] QB 881, CA.
Verrier v Director of Public Prosecutions [1966] 3 All ER 568, [1967] 2 AC 195, HL.
X (a minor) (wardship: restriction on publication), Re [1975] 1 All ER 697, [1975] Fam 47, CA.

Motion

By a writ dated 6th February 1980 the plaintiffs, British Steel Corpn ('BSC'), sought as against the defendants, Granada Television Ltd ('Granada'), (1) an injunction to restrain Granada from (a) making use of any confidential information being the property of BSC for any purpose whatsoever, (b) infringing BSC's copyright in their internal documents, (c) converting to their own use infringing copies of the works subject to such copyrights and (d) otherwise converting to their own use or unlawfully interfering with BSC's property, (2) an order for delivery up of all documents and other articles containing any such confidential information which were in Granada's possession, power, custody or control, (3) an order for delivery up of all infringing copies of the copyright works particularised under para (1)(b) and delivery up of all other documents the property of BSC which were in Granada's possession, power, custody or control, and (4) an inquiry as to what damage BSC had suffered by reason of Granada's breach of confidence in making use of such confidential information and/or infringment of copyright and/or conversion and/or detention and unlawful interference with BSC's property or, at BSC's option, an account of profits and the payment of all sums found due to BSC on making such an inquiry or taking an account, together with interest thereon. On 7th March 1980 BSC amended the writ to seek an order that Granada make and serve on BSC's solicitors an affidavit setting forth the names of all persons responsible for supplying Granada with, or who had offered to supply them with, the documents or other articles which were the subject of the orders prayed for under paras (2) and (3) of the original writ. By a notice of motion in the action dated 6th March 1980 BSC moved the Chancery Division of the High Court for an order that Granada forthwith make and serve on BSC's solicitors an affidavit setting forth the names of all persons responsible for supplying Granada with or who had offered to supply them with documents being the property of BSC or with any copies thereof. The facts are set out in the judgment.

Leonard Hoffmann QC and David Kitchin for BSC.
Alexander Irvine QC, J E Camp and Patrick Moloney for Granada.

2nd April. **SIR ROBERT MEGARRY V-C** read the following judgment: The
essential facts in this motion are relatively simple, though I cannot say the same for the
law. The plaintiffs, British Steel Corpn (which I shall call 'BSC'), seek an order that the
defendants, Granada Television Ltd (which I shall call 'Granada'), should forthwith make
and serve on BSC's solicitors an affidavit setting forth the names of all persons responsible
for supplying Granada with documents owned by BSC, or any copies thereof, and the
names of all persons who have offered to supply Granada with such documents. The
motion arises out of a television programme transmitted by Granada on Monday, 4th
February 1980, in the 'World in Action' series produced by Granada. That programme
was directed towards the strike of steel workers which had existed since the beginning of
the year, mainly in relation to the pay of workers employed by BSC. The programme
consisted of a variety of videotaped material, including a number of quotations from
statements made by the Secretary of State for Industry, Sir Keith Joseph, and others, brief
interviews with a trade union official, a picket, and a member of a strike committee, a
number of comments by the reporter conducting the programme, and finally an
interview with Sir Charles Villiers, the chairman of BSC, by the reporter. Many points
were mentioned, but the main thrust of the programme seemed to be to advance the
view that what was responsible for BSC's difficulties was not just the low productivity of
the steel workers to which BSC had referred, but also poor management by those
responsible for running BSC, and intervention by the Government. That, of course, did
not appear to be a view to which Sir Charles subscribed.

During the programme (a recording of which was, by agreement, shown to me in
court), the documents obtained from BSC played a substantial part. The programme was
entitled 'The Steel Papers'; there were various references to the documents; and there
were a number of views of some of them. Both by sound and sight it was made plain
that the documents were secret documents, not intended for publication; there were a
number of shots showing documents with 'Secret' stamped on them in large letters.
Extensive quotations from a number of the documents were read out. A transcript of
the programme has been put in evidence, and this shows that not far short of one half of
the programme consisted of quotations from these documents, with the reporter's
connective comments; the rest of the programme was split between rather less than a
quarter for the opening quotations that were in the public domain, and nearly a third for
the interview with Sir Charles.

It is common ground that BSC never consented to the documents being given to
Granada or being used by them in any way. On 5th February, the day after the
programme was broadcast, BSC sent Granada a telex stating that the documents were
highly confidential, and that publication of them was a breach of confidence and a breach
of BSC's copyright in them. BSC demanded undertakings in wide terms against any
publication or reproduction of the documents, and also that Granada would return the
documents forthwith to BSC. Granada would not give these undertakings, and so on 6th
February BSC issued the writ and a notice of motion; and on the same day Oliver J
granted an ex parte injunction restraining the publication or reproduction of the
documents. After correspondence between solicitors, the documents were delivered to
BSC's solicitors on 28th February. On examination, it was discovered that many of the
documents had been mutilated by cutting off corners on which numerals probably
appeared, or by tearing or cutting off parts of documents on which manuscript comments
may have appeared, or by otherwise making it difficult or impossible to identify which
particular copy of a duplicated document it was that had come into Granada's possession.
I have inspected some samples of the two large boxfuls of papers which were thus
returned to BSC; and some of them are documents which appear to have been ripped in
two and then repaired with transparent adhesive tape. BSC's request to be informed of the
identity of the person who supplied these documents to Granada was not complied with.

It was in these circumstances that on 6th March BSC issued the notice of motion that
is now before me, and amended the writ to match. As I have mentioned, the only relief

claimed is for an affidavit setting out the names of all persons responsible for supplying Granada with BSC's documents or any copies of them, or who offered to supply them. The basis of the application is the decision of the House of Lords in *Norwich Pharmacal Co v Customs and Excise Comrs* [1973] 2 All ER 943, [1974] AC 133. Put shortly, the decision is to the effect that a person who becomes involved in the tortious acts of others, even if innocently, is under a duty to assist a person who is injured by those acts by giving him full information by way of discovery and disclosing the identity of the tortfeasor. Such an action may be brought even though the plaintiff has no other cause of action, and seeks no other relief, though it cannot be brought against someone who is not involved in the wrongdoing beyond being a mere witness or having some relevant document in his possession. The action is a descendant of the old bill of discovery in Chancery. Under the auxiliary jurisdiction, equity used to aid litigants in the courts of law, as well as litigants in equity, by compelling discovery; the courts of law had no means of doing this. But in addition to this process, which has now long been part of the ordinary process of litigation, there was a procedure whereby a would-be plaintiff could bring a bill of discovery in equity in order to find out who was the proper person to bring his action against; and it is this process which led to the *Norwich Pharmacal* case.

In that case, the owners of a patent for a chemical compound found that their patent was being infringed by illicit importations of the compound which had been manufactured abroad. The owners sued the Commissioners of Customs and Excise for discovery of the documents which would show who were the importers, and the commissioners not only disputed the plaintiffs' rights to bring such an action, but also contended that public policy precluded the making of the order. The House of Lords rejected these defences, and held that the action should succeed.

Now in the motion before me, there was no real issue on the *Norwich Pharmacal* case. On behalf of Granada, counsel did not dispute that the documents had reached Granada as a result of wrongful acts by a person or persons unknown to BSC, nor did he suggest that Granada had received them in ignorance of any wrongdoing. He accepted the inevitable conclusion that Granada had known very well that they were receiving and using documents in contravention of BSC's rights. The indorsement on the writ bases BSC's claim on breach of confidence, breach of copyright and conversion; and it seems plain that these claims are well founded. I do not think that this conclusion is affected by the statement in the affidavit of Mr Boulton, the head of current affairs programmes for Granada, that Granada were firmly of the view that they received the documents in circumstances 'not involving any dishonesty or criminal conduct'. Counsel for Granada did stress, however, that Granada did not solicit the documents, or make any agreement about them, and that no money or benefit in kind was sought or paid or given in return for the documents; and I see no reason to question Mr Boulton's assertion that this was the case. The documents, he said, were volunteered by a 'source' with 'a keen sense of indignation about the dealings between BSC and the Government before and during the strike'. He also said that a firm promise was made to the 'source' that no step would be taken that might reveal or risk the disclosure of the 'source's' identity.

It is difficult to see what meaning is to be ascribed to the word 'honesty' if it is to be applied to the conduct of an employee who has access to his employers' confidences and is receiving his pay from them, and yet at the same time is secretly removing highly confidential documents from his employers and passing them to third parties so as to enable them to criticise the employers in public. It would be more frank to describe this as 'dishonesty in what is claimed to be a worthy cause'. However, I do not think that I need to go into this further. Nor do I need to discuss in any detail the conduct of Granada in receiving the documents, making use of them, and then, after some delay, returning them to BSC in a mutilated state. Counsel prudently refrained from advancing any contention that Granada had been entitled to do what they did; and he accepted that at the lowest the documents must have been obtained in breach of confidence, and said that there might well be a foundation for bringing criminal charges. This, of course, sharply distinguishes Granada from the Commissioners of Customs and Excise in the *Norwich Pharmacal* case, for the commissioners' involvement with the wrongdoers there was entirely innocent. All counsel's efforts were directed towards establishing that Granada should not be ordered to disclose to BSC the names of those who supplied Granada with the documents or offered to supply them. In this, he relied on two main propositions. The first and most complex was that the court had a discretion to refuse to order disclosure where disclosure would be in breach of some ethical or social value, and that the confidential relationship between newspapers or other media of information and their sources of information was an ethical or social value which the court ought to protect by refusing to order any disclosure. The second proposition was simply that Granada were protected against the demand for disclosure by the privilege against self-crimination. I propose to consider this second point first.

The privilege against self-crimination did not emerge as a possible defence until Mr Boulton's affidavit, sworn the day before the hearing began, had put forward the material on which it is based. He said that 'there is a real risk that if Granada were to identify its source then, with BSC in its present mood, criminal proceedings might result against both the source and Granada'. No contention that this privilege protected Granada appears to have been advanced previously in the interchanges between solicitors or otherwise. This plea committed counsel for Granada to a somewhat delicate balancing act. The words I have just quoted come from a sentence which began with the assertion by Mr Boulton that I previously mentioned, stating that Granada were firmly of the view that they had received the documents in circumstances 'not involving any dishonesty or criminal conduct'. Despite that, counsel had to establish that Granada had reasonable grounds for believing, and did believe, that if they disclosed the source of the documents, there would be a 'real and appreciable danger' that 'in the ordinary course of things', and under 'the ordinary operation of law', they would be prosecuted for some criminal offence: see *R v Boyes* (1861) 1 B & S 311 at 330, [1861–73] All ER Rep 172 at 174, approved in *Re Reynolds* (1882) 20 Ch D 294. The latter case makes it plain that the privilege against self-crimination can be invoked only by someone who does so in good faith for his own protection, and not for some ulterior purpose: it is a privilege against self-crimination, and not a privilege against the incrimination of others, or for the protection of them or their property. Thus in *R v Armagh Justices* (1883) 18 ILTR 2, a woman who refused to testify that a publican had sold her a naggin of whiskey out of hours was held not to have been entitled to do so, the reason, I think, being that her refusal was made to protect not herself but the publican.

Counsel for Granada also faced the problem of identifying the crimes for which Granada feared prosecution if they revealed their sources of information. What was it that they feared, despite their firm view of their own innocence? A prosecution for handling stolen goods or any other offence under the Theft Act 1968 did not help Granada much, as by s 31 the privilege does not apply to civil proceedings of the nature mentioned in the section (including the recovery of property), though any statements or admissions made in consequence cannot be used in evidence in a prosecution: I put it shortly. So counsel for Granada addressed himself to conspiracy to steal and conspiracy to defraud. He relied on the Criminal Law Act 1977, ss 1(1), 5(1), as showing that apart from conspiracy to defraud, conspiracy at common law had been replaced by the offence of conspiracy under that Act, so that conspiracy to steal could not come within the Theft Act 1968, and so escaped s 31. The result was the same for conspiracy to defraud, he said, for although it still existed at common law, it too was not an offence within the Theft Act 1968. Counsel for Granada also cited *Scott v Comr of Police for the Metropolis* [1974] 3 All ER 1032, [1975] AC 819 as showing that it was an offence to conspire to contravene the Copyright Act 1956, s 21. He further relied on *Rank Film Distributers Ltd v Video Information Centre* [1980] 2 All ER 273, [1980] 3 WLR 487 a decision of the Court of Appeal.

The whole essence of the *Rank* case was copyright. The case against the defendants was that they were making and selling illicit copies of copyright films, transposed on to magnetic tape. An Anton Piller order was made ex parte against them, and this included provisions requiring them to answer interrogatories and give discovery of documents which would disclose the names of those who supplied them with the films, and also those to whom the defendants supplied the illicit copies. Over the dissent of Lord Denning MR, the majority held that these provisions of the order should be deleted from it because, if the information was given, it would tend to criminate the defendants of an offence under the Copyright Act 1956, s 21. The offences thus created are summary offences punishable on a first conviction with a fine not exceeding £50, a sum which must be trivial in relation to the huge profits which appear to be obtainable from this copying. For the illicit copier, s 21 of the 1956 Act is indeed a blessing, a blessing which must be envied by those who infringe patents or trade marks and cannot claim any corresponding immunity from disclosure under an Anton Piller order because there is nothing to make the infringements criminal. However, in the *Rank* case the privilege was also claimed in relation to conspiracy to contravene s 21 of the 1956 Act as well as conspiracy to defraud, and it may be that at any rate some of those who infringe patents or trade marks will find some comfort under the latter head. I forbear to explore this last point.

The *Rank* case, however, did not long stand alone; for within a fortnight it was considered by another division of the Court of Appeal in *Ocli Optical Coatings Ltd v Spectron Optical Coatings Ltd* [1980] FSR 227. This too was a case of an Anton Piller order, made in relation to the manufacture and sale of vacuum-deposited thin film coatings used for optical and electrical purposes, and particularly in relation to computers. The contention was that the defendant company was using confidential information of the plaintiffs, obtained and disclosed in breach of confidence by other defendants. At first instance, the judge applied the *Rank* case and excluded from the order those parts which required the defendants to disclose the names and addresses of the persons who had supplied the defendants with copies of documents or information derived from the plaintiffs' intellectual property, as well as the names of those to whom these had been supplied. The same was done in relation to an application for an order requiring the disclosure of the whereabouts of documents and other articles infringing the plaintiffs' rights. However, on appeal it was held that if any criminal proceedings were taken, they would almost certainly be proceedings under the Theft Act 1968, and not under the Copyright Act 1956, s 21. On the footing that there was no real or appreciable risk for apprehending prosecution under s 21, the court accordingly restored the portions of the Anton Piller order which the judge had omitted, and so required the defendants to make disclosure. In the case before me, it has not been contended that there is any apprehension of peril under s 21 which would arise from Granada revealing the source of the documents; any case under the section exists without this. But the *Ocli* case is important, I think, in making it clear that in this field the court will look at the realities and disregard the theoretical.

Counsel for Granada also contended that the privilege entitled a person to refuse to provide any information which might be used as a step towards obtaining any evidence against him relating to the commission of an offence. For this he relied on *R v Slaney* (1832) 5 C & P 213. I do not think that that case supports so wide a proposition. True, it makes it plain that the privilege is not confined to questions which will in fact criminate the witness, but extends to those which tend to criminate him; for otherwise the questions might go from one thing to another, without any direct crimination, and yet enough would be elicited to found a charge against him. In that case, concerning criminal libels, the privilege did not prevent the witness from being required to say whether he knew who had written a defamatory document; but it did allow him to refuse to say who it was, since it might be himself. This seems to me to fall far short of counsel for Granada's wide proposition. It appears to me to be one thing to say, 'To answer this question would tend to incriminate me', and another to say, 'To answer this question might lead to a train of inquiry which, if pursued, might lead to some evidence which, if adduced, might tend to criminate me'. If the privilege extended that far, a witness who was guilty of a gang affray which had nothing to do with the case in which he is testifying could refuse to say who any of his friends were, since to identify them might lead to those who could give evidence against him, if he were charged with making an affray.

However that may be, in this case I cannot see any reality in the fear of a charge of conspiracy. There is not the slightest evidence of any conspiracy. Indeed, Granada's explicit evidence is that the documents were volunteered, and reached them without any prior agreement or solicitation by them. If a question is put to a witness which itself indicates some jeopardy to him if he answers it one way, then that will normally support the privilege. But if there is nothing in the question or anything else to indicate anything save an innocent question, the court must be satisfied from some other source of the tendency to criminate: see *Re Genese, ex parte Gilbert* (1886) 3 Morr 223 at 226–227, per Lord Esher MR. He can claim the privilege if he 'states circumstances consistent on the face of them with the existence of the peril alleged, and which also render it extremely probable': *Short v Mercier* (1851) 3 Mac & G 205 at 217, per Lord Truro LC. The words 'extremely probable' relate to the existence of the risk, and not to whether a prosecution will in fact be brought; for the latter, all that is required is an appreciable chance: see *Rio Tinto Zinc Corpn v Westinghouse Electric Corpn* [1977] 3 All ER 717 at 728, [1978] AC 547 at 581 per Shaw LJ; and see per Lord Denning MR at [1977] 3 All ER 717 at 721, [1978] AC 547 at 574 and approved per Viscount Dilhorne at [1978] 1 All ER 434 at 457, [1978] AC 547 at 627. What is there in this case to show that there is any real risk of Granada being liable to be prosecuted for any offence save under the Theft Act 1968, which for this purpose counsel for Granada accepted was of no avail to Granada? Counsel was reduced to contending that if the identity of the person who delivered the documents was disclosed, that person might falsely allege against Granada that there had been a prior conspiracy. In this world, I suppose, almost anything *might* happen: but it seems quite impossible to regard such a wild and speculative surmise as being a fear or apprehension with any substance in it. The whole edifice which counsel laboured to erect seemed to me to rest on wholly exiguous foundations of evidence, and to be a last-minute make-weight devoid of reality. Accordingly I reject this contention.

I turn to the second main head, that of Granada's claim that the court has a discretionary power to refuse to order disclosure, and that this ought to be exercised in this case. Counsel put before me at the outset of his address 11 propositions. At my request, he helpfully reduced these to typescript on day 2 in a slightly amended form, which on day 3 he subjected to some small but significant further amendments. At the heart of these propositions was the contention that it was in the public interest that the media of information, whether newspapers, television or otherwise, should normally not be forced to disclose their sources of information, for otherwise much of the information would cease to flow to them, and they would be disabled from doing their beneficial work.

Before I turn to the manifold authorities that were put before me, I should mention that I attempted to persuade counsel for Granada to identify those who were entitled to the benefit of this special position. On the footing that it extends to newspapers and television companies and their staff, does it apply to freelance journalists or freelance television reporters, obtaining information in the hope of persuading a newspaper or television company to buy the results? Does it apply to an author gathering material for a book for which he hopes to find a publisher? Does it apply to a crank or a busybody preparing a pamphlet that he will publish at this own expense? What of manufacturers or advertising agents engaged in market research? Does it apply even to newspapers and television companies and their staffs if the material is being gathered for some article or programme which is intended merely to entertain and not to expose some evil or wrong? I asked these questions because it seemed to me that the answers might help in identifying the basis on which the alleged exemption rests. Is it, indeed, an exemption for newspapers and television companies and members of their staffs, whatever they do, or is it an exemption which depends on the person concerned being engaged in some investigations in what he believes to be the public good? If one takes the cant phrase 'investigative journalism', does the emphasis lie on the first word or the second?

My endeavours were unsuccessful, in that for the most part counsel could not be tempted to give me any specific answers to my questions; in the main he rested on the authorities that he put before me. However, it was plain that the general thrust of his contentions was that the court had to balance the public interests involved both for and against disclosure. On this footing, I think that the basic answer to my questions might be a contention that information that is used with a serious purpose has a greater weight in the scales than information which is used for other purposes or not at all. There would thus be a sliding scale, as it were, and so there would be no need to lay down categories of persons or purposes.

I think that I should take the matter by stages. First, there has been no contention that the exemption has been recognised as amounting to a privilege which, as of right, entitles a person to refuse to testify or disclose matters, such as the privilege which enables a client to exclude confidences between him and his solicitor and counsel. That, I think, clearly appears from two cases arising out of the inquiry in 1962 and 1963, usually known as the Vassall Inquiry, namely, *Attorney General v Clough* [1963] 1 All ER 420, [1963] 1 QB 773 and *Attorney General v Mulholland* [1963] 1 All ER 767, [1963] 2 QB 477: see especially the latter case, per Lord Denning MR ([1963] 1 All ER 767 at 771, [1963] 2 QB 477 at 489). In these cases, journalists giving evidence were held to have no immunity from answering proper questions which required them to disclose their sources. The whole question is not one of rights, but of how far the court has a discretion, and of the factors that should be weighed in exercising that discretion.

Second, in some respects newspapers were for a long while undoubtedly treated as being in a special position as regards being forced to disclose their sources of information. A practice grew up that in libel cases the courts would normally not compel a newspaper, prior to the trial of the action, to disclose the source of its information. The rule, which was applied to interrogatories in *Hennessy v Wright (No 2)* (1888) 24 QBD 445n, was applied to discovery of documents in *Hope v Brash* [1897] 2 QB 188, [1895–9] All ER Rep 343, to a trade periodical in *Plymouth Mutual Co-operative and Industrial Society Ltd v Traders' Publishing Association Ltd* [1906] 1 KB 403, to an action for malicious prosecution in *Maass v Gas Light and Coke Co* [1911] 2 KB 543, and, a little surprisingly, to a defendant who was an MP in *Adam v Fisher* (1914) 30 TLR 288; but it was withheld from the writer of a letter in a newspaper as regards the source of his information in *South Suburban Co-operative Society Ltd v Orum* [1937] 3 All ER 133, [1937] 2 KB 690: see also *Lyle-Samuel v Odhams Ltd* [1920] 1 KB 135, [1918–19] All ER Rep 779.

Running through the cases there are two strands of reasoning for the rule, one that the process of discovery ought not to be used for the ulterior purpose of enabling the plaintiff to discover the name of someone against whom he could bring another action, and the other that there was some public interest in not requiring defendants in the position of newspapers to disclose their sources of information. At the same time, it is abundantly clear that the matter was one of discretion: disclosure should not be compelled without sufficient cause. A further stage was reached when in 1949 the rule which now stands as RSC Ord 82, r 6, was introduced. This applies to all defendants in defamation, whether newspapers or otherwise, and it lays down a flat prohibition and is not merely discretionary; yet it is confined to interrogatories, and to the defences of fair comment or publication on a privileged occasion. Presumably the extension to everybody, in a strengthened form, of part of the rule which applied to newspapers has not taken away the benefits of the rest of the rule from newspapers. It should be observed, however, that the rule is one which was applied at the interlocutory stage, and not at the trial. I think that it is important to distinguish between, first, the interlocutory stage; second, evidence at the trial; and, third, the relief claimed in the action. To this I shall have to return.

With that, I come to counsel for Granada's propositions. I think that they may be summarised in this way. His first two propositions are at the heart of his argument, and I will set them out verbatim in a moment. The other nine are, I think, mainly reasons for supporting the first two propositions, or amplifications of particular parts of those propositions; and although of course I have considered them and given them, I hope, due weight, I shall not reproduce them here. The first two propositions are as follows: the words in square brackets in the first were added by counsel on day 3 by way of amendment, and I have divided the second into two sub-propositions for ease of reference:

'1. There is a recognised discretion in the courts to exclude evidence, or to abstain from requiring the disclosure of evidence (by way of discovery or interrogatories), which should be exercised when considerations of [a recognised] public interest and policy, in the circumstances of the particular case, outweigh the interests of the party desiring the evidence to be given or disclosed.

'2(1). The categories of public interest are not closed; and (2) the courts will refuse to order disclosure where (a) disclosure would be in breach of some ethical or social value and (b) on balance, that interest is best served by refusing to order disclosure.'

The most fundamental question lies in the first part of the first proposition. I say nothing about criminal cases; but is it true that in civil cases the court has a recognised discretion to exclude relevant evidence? I have no doubt whatever that a judge may and sometimes should discourage the adduction of evidence that he considers to be unfair or objectionable in some way; but does he have the power, as a matter of law, to refuse to admit it? The question probably does not arise often; counsel, knowing that the decision of the case lies with the judge in all save the few cases that are heard with a jury, will usually have the forensic sense not to press a judge with evidence which the judge finds objectionable. Where there is a jury, there is some Australian authority which suggests that the judge cannot exclude admissible evidence, though he may well warn the jury about it in suitable terms (see *Manenti v Melbourne and Metropolitan Tramways Board* [1954] VLR 115); and again counsel may exercise forensic prudence. Lord Sumner and at least some members of a strong Board of the Judicial Committee seem to have thought that relevant evidence which a judge could have excluded in a criminal case could not be excluded in a civil case: *Ibrahim v R* [1914] AC 599 at 610, [1914–15] All ER Rep 874 at 878.

As against that, there is the statement in para 1 of the 16th Report of the Law Reform Committee on Privilege in Civil Proceedings (Cmnd 3472, 1967). This refers to the law restricting the categories of privilege to the minimum, but according to the judge—

'a wide discretion to permit a witness, whether a party to the proceedings or not, to refuse to disclose information where disclosure would be a breach of some ethical or social value and non-disclosure would be unlikely to result in serious injustice in the particular case in which it is claimed.'

For the existence of the 'wide discretion', *Attorney General v Clough* and *Attorney General v Mulholland* are cited; and in the latter case Donovan LJ [1963] 1 All ER 767 at 772, [1963] 2 QB 477 at 492 undoubtedly expressed the view that the judge has an ultimate discretion not to order a witness to answer a question if to do so would do more harm than good. Danckwerts LJ simply expressed his agreement; and this may have related to what Donovan LJ said on this point and not merely to the main decision, which was that the journalists did not have any privilege which allowed them to refuse to answer proper questions. However, in *Re Buchanan* (1964) 65 SR (NSW) 9, the Supreme Court of New South Wales, sitting in banco, treated this as relating only to the relevance and propriety of the question, so that if the judge's conclusion is that the question is both relevant and proper, he has no further discretion to excuse the witness from answering. In other words, the question is not one of balancing a relevant and proper question against the strength of the objections to answering it, but one of merely scrutinising the question for relevance and propriety.

The proposition of the Law Reform Committee was much discussed in what is the most important authority on the subject, *D v National Society for the Prevention of Cruelty to Children* [1977] 1 All ER 589, [1978] AC 171. The issue there arose in an action against the NSPCC, as I shall call it, in which the plaintiff claimed damages against the NSPCC and also disclosure of their documents which would reveal the identity of the informant who had made unfounded complaints against her. The main issue was whether the rule of public policy which excludes evidence of the sources of information of the police (save where required to establish innocence in a criminal trial) should be extended to the sources of information of the NSPCC, a body which has statutory authority to bring proceedings concerning the welfare of children, in cases of alleged neglect or ill-treatment of children. All save Lord Edmund-Davies, who rested his decision on discretion, held that the immunity from disclosure should be extended in this way.

On the proposition in the Law Reform Committee's report that I have mentioned, Lord Hailsham ([1977] 1 All ER 589 at 602, [1978] AC 171 at 227) accepted that the proposition did represent the practice that existed in 1967, though that was different from the position some 35 years earlier; and Lord Kilbrandon ([1977] 1 All ER 589 at 615, [1978] AC 171 at 242) simply expressed his entire agreement with Lord Hailsham's reasoning and conclusion. Lord Simon, on the other hand, was critical of the proposition, and took the view ([1977] 1 All ER 589 at 613, [1978] AC 171 at 239) that although the judge could exert considerable moral authority to dissuade counsel from pressing a question, 'if it comes to the forensic crunch . . . it must be law, not discretion, which is in command'. As I understand his speech, he did not accept that the judge has a general discretionary power to permit a witness to refuse to answer a proper question. Lord Edmund-Davies ([1977] 1 All ER 589 at 616, [1978] AC 171 at 243) also had misgivings about Lord Hailsham's treatment of the proposition of the Law Reform Committee, though in the end he formulated a proposition ([1977] 1 All ER 589 at 617, [1978] AC 171 at 245) which has a number of resemblances to the committee's proposition, and also certain differences. Put shortly, Lord Edmund-Davies considered that the court had a discretion to uphold a refusal to disclose relevant evidence where a confidential relationship exists, where disclosure would be in breach of some ethical or social value involving the public interest, and where on balance the public interest would be better served by excluding such evidence. Lord Diplock, who delivered the leading speech, and was a signatory of the report of the Law Reform Committee, did not mention the report.

In that state of affairs, the only conclusion that I can reach is that, on balance, the prevailing view is that in civil cases the judge does have some discretionary power to exclude evidence that would otherwise be admissible. I say that with some hesitation, as I too was a signatory of the Law Reform Committee's report; and preconceptions may distort judgment. One thing that clearly emerges from the NSPCC case is the re-affirmation of the view that a mere promise of confidentiality will not, without more, protect a communication from disclosure (see also Science Research Council v Nassé [1979] 3 All ER 673, [1980] AC 1028). What matters is the public interest, and something must be found to countervail the strong public interest of getting the truth out in the administration of justice. Yet although not enough per se, a promise of confidence may strongly support a countervailing public interest. Another thing that emerges is that the categories of public interest are not closed. That is involved in the decision itself, in that the protection long accorded to police informers was extended by analogy to informers of the NSPCC; but there are also express statements to that effect (see, for example, [1977] 1 All ER 589 at 605, [1978] AC 171 at 230).

A third matter that emerges from the NSPCC case is the rejection of what was called the 'broad submission' in favour of the 'narrow submission'. The broad submission may be summarised as being to the effect that if there is a claim that the public interest would be served by withholding disclosure, the duty of the court is to weigh the alleged public interest against the public interest in uncovering the truth in the process of litigation, and to rule according to the way the balance tilts. This was unanimously rejected. Lord Diplock's rejection may have been mainly or wholly based on the unwisdom of deciding a case on a broad principle when a narrow principle suffices (see [1977] 1 All ER 589 at 596, [1978] AC 171 at 220), but I think the other members of the House rejected it on its merits, or perhaps I should say its demerits: (see [1977] 1 All ER 589 at 600, 614, 615, 616, [1978] AC 171 at 225, 240, 242, 243). I need not elaborate on Lord Hailsham's series of questions which expose the problems if all courts were committed to the general process of weighing up the conflicting claims over an undefined field in each individual case.

In the present case, the importance of this lies in the fact that in its general form, counsel for Granada's first proposition was in substance a restatement of the broad submission that the *NSPCC* case had rejected. His amendment, inserting the words 'a recognised' in front of 'public interest', was needed to carry him past the barrier of the *NSPCC* case. This, however, as counsel pointed out on behalf of BSC, then wrought havoc on para 2 of the second proposition; for this, instead of basing itself on a recognised public interest, sought to invoke broad and indefinite concepts of ethical and social values. Throughout this case, as well as other cases, there is always the difficulty of the protean meaning of the phrase 'public interest' when used by itself. I use it, of course, not in the sense of something which catches the interest of the public out of curiosity or amusement or astonishment, but in the sense of something which is of serious concern and benefit to the public. The phrase 'recognised public interest' thus refers to a public interest in the latter sense which has become recognised as such. Has there arisen a recognised public interest in the press and television companies not being obliged to disclose their sources of information, and, if not, ought such an interest now to be recognised?

Before I attempt to answer that question, there is another factor that I should mention, one which did not appear in counsel for Granada's 11 propositions, and one about which little was said in argument; and it distinguishes this case from many of those cited. That is that this is a case in which the relief sought appears to be equitable relief, descended from the bill of discovery in equity; and the general rule is that equitable relief is discretionary. In the *Norwich Pharmacal* case, I think that it was recognised that the relief was discretionary (see [1973] 2 All ER 943 at 949, 954, 961–962, 969–970, 976, [1974] AC 133 at 176, 182, 190, 199, 206), though I have not found any explicit ascription of this to the equitable nature of the remedy. Even if one says that ordinary discovery as part of the process of litigation has shed its equitable nature because it is now regulated by rules of court, that leaves untouched an action in which the substantive relief sought is or includes an order disclosing the names of certain persons. Such an action seems to me to be just as much an action for equitable relief as an action for specific performance or an injunction. If that is right, then the significance is that the court is called on to exercise the wide general jurisdiction to consider all the relevant factors of the case in deciding whether the discretion ought to be exercised in favour of granting the relief. That question would not be the narrower one of weighing matters of public interest or policy.

I feel some hesitation on this matter, for two reasons. First, though touched on in argument, it was not explored in any detail; and I hesitated to incur the delay involved in restoring the case for further argument, especially when the press of other work had made it impossible for me to prepare this judgment as soon as I had hoped. Second, as I have already mentioned, part of the plaintiff's claim in the *NSPCC* case, as set out in her statement of claim, was a direct claim for discovery which appears to be of the *Norwich Pharmacal* type. The case arose at the interlocutory stage, on whether there should be what may be called orthodox discovery; but, as Lord Diplock pointed out ([1977] 1 All ER 589 at 595–596, [1978] AC 171 at 219), the judge's reasoning at the interlocutory stage would also rule out discovery as part of the substantive relief. Yet despite this linkage between the interlocutory order and the final relief, no question appears to have arisen as to the discretionary nature of the substantive remedy of discovery. In those circumstances I think that I should consider the question of discretion in both its narrower and its wider aspects.

The first question, I think, is whether there is a recognised public interest in the press not being required to disclose their sources of information. For brevity, I shall in general speak only of the press, on the footing that what applies to the press applies also to those who provide the public with television programmes: see, for example, *Isbey v New Zealand Broadcasting Corpn (No 2)* [1975] 2 NZLR 237, *Brill v Television Service One* [1976] 1 NZLR 683. Where it is desirable to do so, I shall mention television separately. There is no difficulty in accepting that much information is given to the press under a pledge of confidentiality, and that some sources of that information would 'dry up' if that confidentiality were not to be preserved. Equally I would accept that in many cases the press has exposed wrongdoings which otherwise might have remained concealed for a long time or for ever. Furthermore, I can see no possible grounds for refusing to accept the proposition that it is in the public interest to preserve the liberty of the press. That liberty does not, of course, mean that the press is free to do with impunity whatever it chooses; but, speaking generally, it does mean that the press is free to publish what it wishes without prior censorship, and that what it publishes is then subject only to the ordinary law of the land. I also accept that it is in the interests of the public that there should be a regular supply of reliable news.

Given all that, has it been established that there is a recognised public interest in the press being entitled to refuse to disclose the source of its information; and, if not, ought there to be? Counsel for Granada contended that the first of these propositions was established by the special position that had long been accorded to the press in defamation actions at the interlocutory stage, by the *Clough* and *Mulholland* cases, and by a dictum of Lord Scarman in *Express Newspapers Ltd v MacShane* [1980] 1 All ER 65 at 78, [1980] AC 672 at 693.

I shall turn to the *Express Newspapers* case in due course; but as for the other authorities, I do not think that they carry the point. The interlocutory stage, directed to shaping the proceedings for the trial, certainly does not determine the law to be applied at the trial: see *Attorney General v Clough* [1963] 1 All ER 420 at 426, [1963] 1 QB 773 at 790, per Lord Parker CJ. At this stage, interrogatories are very much a matter of discretion for the master or judge; and, in exercising this discretion, the master or judge is entitled to take the view that, as in the public interest a rule of practice has grown up against requiring the interlocutory disclosure of a newspaper's sources, the interrogatories should be disallowed: see *Lawson v Odhams Press Ltd* [1948] 2 All ER 717, [1949] 1 KB 129 and *Georgius v Oxford University Press* [1949] 1 All ER 342, [1949] 1 KB 729. But that is very far from saying that the courts have held that there is a recognised public interest to this effect at the trial. In *Attorney General v Clough* [1963] 1 All ER 420 at 427–428, [1963] 1 QB 773 at 792, Lord Parker CJ, after rejecting the contention that the confidential relationship between the press and its informants had crystallised into a class of privilege known to the law, went on to say that he conceived it to remain open to the court to say that in the special circumstances of a particular case public policy did demand that the journalist should be immune. That, however, falls far short of saying that there is a recognised public interest and policy for the press; indeed, it tends to negate any such recognition by emphasising the special circumstances of a particular case.

The dictum of Lord Scarman in the *MacShane* case, even taken in isolation, offered little enough comfort to counsel for Granada. Lord Scarman said ([1980] 1 All ER 65 at 78, [1980] AC 672 at 693):

'The question is: if industrial action poses a substantial threat to a defined public interest, eg the freedom of the Press and the right of the public to be informed, is the threat a factor which the court should properly put into the balance together with the other relevant factors when asked to grant an interlocutory injunction restraining the industrial action?'

Taken in its context, the dictum seems to me to help counsel for Granada not at all. The subject matter of the case was the ambit of the famous statutory formula 'in . . . furtherance of a trade dispute' as conferring immunity from liability in tort in a case of 'secondary blacking'. The reference to 'the freedom of the press and the right of the public to be informed' as 'a defined public interest' had nothing to do with any immunity of the press from disclosing its sources, but concerned the ability of the press to publish newspapers, and the ability of the public to buy them when published and so obtain information from them. In those circumstances, I do not see how the words 'a defined public interest' as applied to freedom to publish and purchase newspapers can fairly be transmuted into 'a recognised public interest' in the press not being required to disclose its sources.

Doing the best that I can with the authorities put before me, I have failed to find anything which I can regard as establishing the 'recognised public interest' for which counsel contends. Indeed, the authorities seem to me to point the other way. I may add that I have considered *Senior v Holdsworth* [1975] 2 All ER 1009, [1976] QB 23, which concerned a witness summons to a television company to produce all the film which its team had taken of a 'pop' festival, whether transmitted or not. The summons was set aside as being so wide as to be oppressive; but there were various dicta concerning the rights of the press and television companies which were cited to me. I have considered these, of course, but I do not think that they add much of any relevance to the other authorities. I certainly do not think that they give any real assistance to Granada.

I therefore turn to the question whether such an interest ought to be established by the courts. The *NSPCC* case strongly indicates that in these matters development normally proceeds through evolution by extension of recognised principles, or by analogy to them: see [1977] 1 All ER 589 at 600, 609, 614, 615, [1978] AC 171 at 225, 235, 241, 242; *Science Research Council v Nassé* [1979] 3 All ER 673 at 680, 685, 686, 692, 696–697, [1980] AC 1028 at 1067, 1072–1073, 1081, 1086–1087). Thus the rule for police informers was extended to those who informed the NSPCC. I do not say that there can never be a new category: but in deciding whether to recognise any claimant, the principles to be deduced from the settled law will provide guidance. Indeed, there is high authority for saying that only by analogy can any extension be made: see the *Nassé* case [1979] 3 All ER 673 at 692, [1980] AC 1028 at 1081.

In the present case it is far from easy to see on what principle it ought to be declared that there is a recognised public interest and policy in protecting press sources against disclosure. As I have said, the press has often exposed wrongdoings which otherwise might have remained hidden. In that sense, and to that extent, the press no doubt is promoting a public benefit. But unlike the police or the NSPCC, whose major function is to prevent wrongdoing and take remedial action when it occurs, these activities are but a minor part of the usual functions of the press. The press seeks, not always successfully, to make money by providing the public with a particular form of useful service. In the press, news predominates over entertainment, though of course I do not suggest that news cannot be made entertaining, or that the balance between news and entertainment will not vary considerably from day to day and between one newspaper and another. With television, entertainment predominates over news. But however much or little these generalisations may be accepted, it cannot be disputed that the so-called 'investigative journalism' occupies but a small part of the space in the press and the time of the television programmes. No doubt a striking piece of investigative journalism assists in selling newspapers and in attracting the public to watch commercial television programmes, thereby encouraging advertisers. If such journalism damped sales and repelled viewers, or perhaps if it merely stood neutral, it is unlikely that it would be undertaken. After all, it costs money; and although no doubt there are a number of instances of crusading zeal which would seek to ignore financial discouragement, there must be some limits. All this, it seems to me, is very different from the police and the NSPCC.

There is a further consideration. It has not been suggested that the press or television companies have been accorded any legal duties or powers in carrying out investigations and making exposures. For the police there is a duty, and for the NSPCC there is a statutory power: but for the press and television companies there appears to be nothing save the exercise of their free choice. They can do as much or as little as they wish. At most, there could, I suppose, be said to be a self-imposed duty; and such a duty seems to be a slender foundation for extending to them the rule for the police and the NSPCC.

It may be said that investigative journalism is by no means always beneficial to the public. There have been instances of the exposure of scandals which in the event have turned out to be no scandals at all, but only the prelude to expensive claims for defamation. There have been instances, too, where the fair conduct of criminal trials has been impaired by the publication of information from which the jury was being shielded. None could say that there was any public advantage in the publication of the unjustified libels or in bringing unfairness to criminal trials. There have also been instances of grave and unwarranted invasions of privacy. These matters, however, do not seem to me to be of any great relevance to what I have to decide. The police and the

NSPCC are by no means immune from making mistakes. Sometimes prosecutions are brought that turn out to be unfounded, and sometimes investigations are made that prove to be based on false information, as in the *NSPCC* case itself; yet these blemishes do not deprive the police or the NSPCC of their special position. I would readily assume that for the press and television the balance lies much on the credit side, and that their activities in this field are in the main beneficial to the public. Yet there is an important difference, as it seems to me, in that whereas the police and the NSPCC are wholly devoted to activities which are plainly in the public interest, without being impelled by any profit motive or considerations of mere newsworthiness, the same cannot be said of the press or television companies.

In one sense, of course, the activities of any organisation which makes useful goods or provides useful services, and gives employment to many, may be said to be in the public interest; and the same may be said of those who provide entertainment, for nobody would want life to be grey and cheerless. In this sense, the press and television are plainly included. But I do not think that in the sphere with which I am concerned the phrase 'public interest' is used in so wide and general a sense. Instead, I think that there must be something in the nature of a compelling demand for the services in question in order that the life of the community may be carried on in a civilised manner. Crimes must be prevented or detected, children must be protected, national security must be preserved, and justice must be done. It is at least highly desirable, too, that there should be a regular supply of reliable news; but I do not think that investigative journalism can claim so high a place.

As the *NSPCC* case shows, a duty to do such things is not essential, though no doubt it helps. The press is not to be excluded from this category merely because it investigates or exposes under none save a self-imposed duty. But it stands outside because I cannot see that the function that the press discharges is one in which there is any sufficient public interest and policy which requires the confidentiality of its sources to be preserved at a trial. Certainly there is no statutory recognition of its position in these matters such as the NSPCC was accorded when it was given power to take proceedings for the protection of children. I would therefore hold that there is no recognised public interest and policy for the press and television as claimed by counsel for Granada.

Let me suppose that this is wrong, and that there is the recognised public interest and policy for the press and television for which counsel contends, and that I ought to weigh this against the interest involved in requiring a disclosure of sources. One of counsel's subsidiary propositions, in its amended form, was that there was 'no reported case in England in which the private interest of the plaintiff has been held to override the public interest in protecting the media's sources of information'. The words 'in England' were inserted in order to allow for *Re Buchanan*, to which I have already referred. The proposition, which puts the plaintiff's private interest in apposition to the public interest, seems to me to be plainly fallacious in its formulation. The plaintiff's 'private interest' seems to me to be a misdescription for the paramount public interest that in litigation all relevant evidence should be available to the court. However private the interest that the plaintiff seeks to protect, the real balance is between the public interest in justice being done, and whatever public interest there is in protecting the media's sources of information. I do not think that authority for this need be cited, though if authority be required, it may be found in the *NSPCC* and the *Nassé* cases, and elsewhere.

Now in this case, BSC are not seeking to discover Granada's sources as part of some other claim: the action is a direct action simply to discover the sources. Discovery of the sources is not merely a means to an end; it is the end itself. The evidence of Mr Siddons, a director of the secretariat of BSC, is that inquiries have been made to discover the person or persons responsible for removing the documents; and these inevitably have created an unpleasant atmosphere among BSC's employees, particularly at their head office. A cloud hangs over a number of people, many of who must be entirely innocent. Inevitably there must be suspicion and uncertainty about whether there will be any further disclosures of confidential information, and to whom. On behalf of Granada, Mr Boulton asserts that it is plain 'that BSC have embarked on a punitive expedition'. That may or may not be so; but punishment apart, I think that any organisation, including Granada itself, would want to take precautions against any further disclosures of information which is considered to be confidential, and against placing any further confidential information in the power of an undiscovered employee who has committed a grave breach of confidence. As well as being unpleasant, such an atmosphere is plainly likely to militate against efficiency.

If, contrary to my opinion, I have to weigh Granada's claim to a public interest in preserving confidentiality against the public interest in full disclosure being made in litigation, I feel no hesitation in holding that the balance comes down on the side of disclosure. There is no other way in which BSC can obtain the information, and they plainly need it to protect themselves against a real peril. To deny them this information would be a denial of justice to plaintiffs who clearly have been seriously wronged. Even at the interlocutory stage, if the fair disposal of a case cannot be achieved without ordering discovery, then as a last resort discovery will be ordered: see the *Nassé* case [1979] 3 All ER 673 at 681, [1980] AC 1028 at 1067, per Lord Wilberforce, commenting on the use of the term 'balancing'.

Finally, there is the question of a *Norwich Pharmacal* order as an equitable remedy. If it is right to consider such an order as being discretionary, like the generality of equitable remedies, then it is necessary to consider all proper questions which may affect the exercise of the discretion, and not merely questions of the public interest. I do not think that damages would be an adequate remedy. They would be very difficult to assess, and I cannot see how any sum that would be likely to be awarded could adequately recompense BSC for the continuing injury done to them by leaving in their midst an undiscovered and undiscoverable employee who has been guilty of so grave a breach of confidence. Nor can Granada claim to be in the state of innocence that the Commissioners of Customs and Excise were in the *Norwich Pharmacal* case. Granada received a large number of documents which they knew were confidential and had been illicitly brought to them; they used them for a critical television programme, making considerable play of their secrecy, and doubtless taking full advantage of the public's curiosity about things secret; and when at last they returned them, they mutilated them, knowing full well that they had no right to do so. From first to last BSC has done nothing to injure or provoke Granada. In those circumstances, the contention that BSC should drop it all and let bygones be bygones almost took my breath away. Such a phrase can have no application where all the injury is on one side. I have never heard of a quid non pro quo.

In the result, if the general discretion applicable to equitable remedies has to be exercised in this case, I would unhesitatingly exercise it in favour of BSC. I can see nothing in Granada's claim to preserve confidentiality which comes near to countervailing BSC's claim to the relief which they seek. It is indeed trite that there is no confidentiality in iniquity; and Granada's participation in the breach of confidence, if nothing worse, was flagrant. The case is one not of the exposure of iniquity, but of exposure by iniquity, and of exploiting the fruits of wrongdoing. What Granada are saying is that, although they have knowingly and publicly infringed BSC's confidences, they are entitled to maintain the confidentiality that they promised their dishonest source of information. I say nothing about Granada's right to remain silent about information honestly supplied: that does not arise.

One point that I should add is that although in form this is merely a motion, it was rightly accepted on all hands that if the order sought by BSC was made, that would dispose of everything of any real substance in the action, save only the question of damages, if BSC chose to pursue this. Thus although the proceedings were in form interlocutory, they were treated on both sides as if they were in substance final for the purposes of the relief claimed. What has once been disclosed cannot be subsequently undisclosed.

As this judgment is of some length and complexity, it may be of assistance if I try to summarise the main points. Here, as elsewhere, I use the term 'press' as including television companies.

(1) Granada are not protected against having to disclose the identity of their source of

information by any privilege against self-crimination, because there is no real peril of Granada incriminating themselves by making the disclosure. (2) Granada have no absolute privilege against disclosing the source of their information, and they have rightly not sought to contend that they have any such absolute privilege. (3) There has long been a practice, which may have ripened into a rule of law, that at the interlocutory stage the press will normally not be required to disclose their sources of information: but this does not apply at the trial of the action. (4) It is not yet entirely clear whether the court has a discretion after the interlocutory stage to exclude relevant evidence and so to exempt the press from disclosing their sources of information, or whether there is merely a discretion to discourage rather than exclude. The prevailing balance seems to be in favour of the former of these two views, though I can see much force in the latter. (5) If there is a discretion to exclude, it does not exist in the wide form of requiring the court in each case to balance the advantages of exclusion against the disadvantages, regarded from the point of view of the public interest. What is required is that there should be shown to be considerations of a recognised public interest which support exclusion sufficiently strongly to outweigh the recognised public interest that all relevant and proper evidence should be available at the trial. (6) No public interest in the press not being forced to disclose their sources of information at the trial has yet been recognised; and there are insufficient grounds for holding that such an interest ought to exist. (7) If, contrary to my view, there is or ought to be such an interest, then in this case I do not consider that it outweighs the public interest in enforcing BSC's legal claim to be given the information that they seek. (8) If BSC's claim to disclosure is to be treated as a claim to equitable relief lying in the discretion of the court on general grounds, then I think that the balance of those general grounds lies firmly in favour of granting the remedy. (9) Although in form this is a motion and not the trial of the action, I think that the parties were right to treat it as being in substance the trial of the action for the purpose of the relief claimed in the motion.

In the result, for the reasons that I have given, I hold that this motion succeeds. The precise form of order will be for discussion.

Order in terms of notice of motion; order not to be operative until 15 days from the date of judgment. Leave to appeal.

Azza M Abdallah   Barrister.

Interlocutory appeal

Granada appealed to the Court of Appeal.

Alexander Irvine QC and *Patrick Moloney* for Granada.
Leonard Hoffmann QC and *David Kitchin* for BSC.

Cur adv vult

7th May. The following judgments were read.

LORD DENNING MR. The 'steel papers' were highly confidential. Granada Television used them in a programme which contained severe criticism of the British Steel Corpn. The question is: can Granada be compelled to disclose their source of information?

All of us remember the steel strike at the beginning of 1980. It is described in my judgment in *Duport Steels Ltd v Sirs* [1980] 1 All ER 529 at 534–535, [1980] 1 WLR 142 at 148–149. The men employed by the British Steel Corpn came out on strike for higher wages. On the face of it, the dispute was between the workers and the management. But it developed into a confrontation between the trade union and the government. The media gave the dispute full coverage. Each side went on the air to give its point of view. There was a battle in which each sought to get the support of public opinion.

Much might be said in this case against the conduct of the unnamed informer and against Granada for the programme which they put on the air. But I feel that we should for the moment look on the facts as they appeared to the unnamed informer and Granada. A good deal of it is surmise, but that is inevitable, seeing that the unnamed informer has not come forward to put his case.

The viewpoint of the unnamed informer

The unnamed informer was probably a man in the uppermost levels of the British Steel Corpn. Either in the offices of the board of the corporation or in the offices of the chief executive. He had access to all the confidential papers—reports, memoranda, minutes, even those which were most secret. He knew all about the dealings between the corporation and the government before and during the strike. He was indignant about them. He thought that the corporation itself was not free from blame, owing to its poor management record. He also thought that the government were to blame because the corporation would have been prepared to make an offer to the men which they would have accepted, but it was blocked by the government. He thought the public ought to know this. So he determined to tell the Granada Television people. He went through the confidential papers in his office. He sorted them out. He picked out the most telling parts. He took them to Granada. Two hundred and fifty sheets of them. This was a grave breach of confidence on his part. It was quite inexcusable. But I think we should assume that he did it not out of malice, nor to make money out of it, but out of a keen sense of indignation. He asked no money. Nor any other benefit. He did it because he thought the public ought to know.

The viewpoint of Granada

When Granada read the papers, they were most interested. At the first glance they were very confidential. Many of them were marked 'Secret'. Granada thought that the papers might be useful to put in a programme. They gave a firm assurance to the unnamed informer that no step would be taken that might reveal or risk the disclosure of his identity. They regarded it 'as a basic ethic of the journalists' profession that the identity of sources must be protected'.

What use should be made of these steel papers, as they were called? It was considered by the head of current affairs at Granada Television, Mr David Boulton. He asked the programme editors and the producer to go through the steel papers and assess their content and import. He got their assessment. He decided that there were a number of points which were of considerable public interest that should be ventilated. Especially as the British Steel Corpn was a public corporation accountable to Parliament. He thought that the disclosure of the documents could legitimately be regarded as a public duty. He felt, however, that the co-operation of the British Steel Corpn should be sought. The corporation should be advised that Granada had the documents: and Sir Charles Villiers, the chairman of the corporation, should be invited to take part in a programme. Mr Boulton says that their purpose was to make a fair presentation and to afford the corporation ample opportunity to explain and answer the points which arose from the documents.

The implementation of the plan

The implementation of the plan was left by Granada to Mr Segaller, the producer. He got into touch with Mr Melvin, the press officer of the corporation. It was arranged that Sir Charles should give an interview on television. It was to be prerecorded on the afternoon of Monday, 4th February 1980. It was to be used as part of a programme on 'The World in Action' at 8.30 pm that day. It was to be broadcast countrywide on the whole of the Independent Television network.

One thing is unfortunate. Granada left it very late before they warned the corporation that they had possession of these confidential papers. It was not until 4 pm on Sunday, 3rd February. Mr Segaller the producer then telephoned Mr Melvin the press officer of the steel corporation, and said: 'We have come into possession of some of the corporation's documents which we intend to use in the World in Action programme.' Mr Melvin said: 'What are they? Let me have a list of them. I cannot do anything until I know what they are.' Six hours later, at 10 o'clock that Sunday evening, Mr Segaller telephoned Mr Melvin at his home. He read out a list of 27 headings such as 'Extract' from this report or that, without giving any details of their contents. Mr Melvin was worried. He thought that the documents must have been obtained improperly. He asked: 'How did you get hold of these? Where did you get them from?' The producer replied: 'Obviously we cannot tell you that.'

That was about 10.00 pm on the Sunday night. But Mr Segaller must have worked late that night. He set to work there and then on a letter. He dated it that day, Sunday, 3rd February 1980 in Manchester. He had it ready by first thing on Monday morning. Then he sent it by air messenger to London. This is what it said:

'3rd February 1980.
'I enclose a draft outline of the contents of the World in Action programme to be recorded and transmitted today [that would be Monday, 4th February], for the information of Sir Charles Villiers before the interview we have agreed to record. This outline includes details of BSC internal papers of which copies have been passed to us in the past few days, and to which the programme will refer. These documents, and the filmed material in the programme, form the basis for the areas of questioning detailed on another sheet, also enclosed. I think you will find that the programme's full script will stick very closely to the outline, and the questions to be put in the interview will reflect the programme material very straightforwardly. I look forward to speaking to you again later this morning [that is the Monday] to confirm arrangements for Sir Charles's interview in either Manchester or London.'

Note, as I said, 'to-day' and 'this morning' must mean Monday, 4th February 1980.

The enclosures were three pages outlining the programme and referring to some of the steel papers, specifying this or that report or memorandum but not the particular part of it which was to be used.

That letter arrived at the corporation's office in Grosvenor Place, London, on the Monday. Not long before Sir Charles and Mr Melvin had to leave on the train for Manchester. They took it with them and read it, I expect, on the train. As soon as they got to the Granada office, Mr Segaller, the producer, gave Sir Charles a full script of the whole programme. Granada had evidently got the programme all prepared, all extracts from the steel papers photographed, all words spoken, all on video tape, covering 20 minutes of viewing time, with only another seven minutes to be filled by the interview with Sir Charles. That was to be transmitted unedited.

Sir Charles protested, he says, about their possession of the steel papers. They say that he did not protest. But whether he did so or not, there was certainly no consent on his part to their using them. At any rate, Sir Charles was interviewed. It did take seven minutes. We have seen the whole programme as it was sent out, and we have the script of it. At the outset (before interviewing Sir Charles) the commentator made full play with the steel papers. He said:

'Last week a number of documents came into the possession of World in Action. They are letters, memos and internal reports from the BSC. They were drawn up over the last five years and none of them was ever intended for publication. Tonight we examine these papers and the new light they appear to throw on the corporation strategy and the government's declared policy of non-intervention.'

Then the commentator goes on, time after time, to say that 'the BSC documents received by World in Action' show this, that or the other. Sometimes it was to show poor management on the part of the corporation. At other times it was to show that there had been 'back-door government intervention' which had produced or prolonged the strike. The programme showed extracts from the steel papers to support these suggestions.

Eventually, when the time came for Sir Charles to be interviewed, the commentator said: 'The strike is now in its sixth week. Here to discuss the implications of the steel papers is Sir Charles Villiers, chairman of BSC.' Then the commentator takes Sir Charles to task. He does it with all the skill of an expert cross-examiner who has all the papers at hand with which to confound the witness. Such questions as: 'Were not your decisions "a direct result of Government policy"?' 'Surely it is a government intervention?' 'Your bankers are the government and therefore the government are essentially controlling your policy-making.' Then there was this illuminating interchange about the documents:

> 'Several documents have your officials and executives referring to the fact that they have to consult the government on this and on that. Does that not make it sound a little strange when Sir Keith Joseph says he is not intervening in the steel dispute?'
> *Sir Charles*: 'I don't know what documents you're referring to and we shall see perhaps before very long.'

On several occasions the commentator interrupted Sir Charles and did not let him finish his answer. It reminded me of the many occasions when I have had to rebuke an advocate, saying: 'Please let him finish his answer.'

In short, the commentator was making the case which the unnamed informer had made, using the steel papers to confound the British Steel Corpn and the government and Sir Charles himself.

As soon as Sir Charles finished his seven minutes, he went off to catch his train back to London. There were newspaper reporters waiting. He had, of course, to be cautious with them. They asked him: 'Was it unfair?' He answered: 'It was not a totally unfair programme.' They asked: 'Was it accurate?' He answered: 'Most of the programme was accurate, but there are one or two things which were screwed up.'

Next day the Daily Mail gave its impression of the programme, reading it as putting the blame on the government, with a big headline: 'Sir Keith "blocked a pay offer to steel men".' But also putting the blame on the corporation:

> 'BSC chiefs knew strike was on the way—TV probe.
> 'Secret British Steel Corporation documents show that BSC bosses apparently knew last summer that Government cash restrictions would cause a strike . . . It was alleged that the Corporation was preparing for a 14 per cent pay rise for the steelmen—which would have averted the strike—but were prevented by Industry Secretary Sir Keith Joseph from putting it on the table.'

The demand for the papers

The corporation were most disturbed. On the Tuesday morning, 5th February, the director of their legal services sent a telex to the managing director of Granada:

> 'The BSC documents are the property of BSC, are highly confidential, and BSC owns the copyright in all these documents. I do not know how you obtained possession of the BSC documents. However, you certainly did not receive the BSC documents with the consent or approval or knowledge of BSC. In the circumstances your possession of the BSC documents is unlawful. Your publication of the BSC documents is a breach of confidence and a breach of copyright.'

He demanded undertakings from Granada including an undertaking to deliver up to BSC forthwith the BSC documents and any copies thereof in the possession of Granada.

On the next day, 6th February, the corporation issued a writ against Granada, claiming an injunction and an order for delivering up the documents. This was followed by correspondence between solicitors. By a letter of 27th February Granada agreed to submit to injunctions and to make no further use of the documents. Furthermore, they agreed to deposit the documents in the joint custody of the two firms of solicitors. The solicitors for Granada also adumbrated their defence in these words:

'It is right to put on record that our clients' decision to use the documents and to make the television programme arose from a firm conviction on their part that there were matters of urgent and important public interest that needed to be ventilated following relevations contained within the documents. It is also right to say that no payment of any kind was made by our clients or anyone on their behalf in respect of the documents.'

The state of the papers

On the next day the papers were delivered into joint custody and inspected on behalf of the corporation. They were then found to have been tampered with so as not to give any clue to the identity of the unnamed informer. For instance, each copy of a secret document was issued with a number so as to show to whom it had been handed, such as 'Secret Copy No 12'. The number '12' was cut off. There were not many such clues, but such as they were, they were cut off. No doubt Granada did this so as to implement their promise to the unnamed informer that they would do nothing to disclose his identity.

The corporation's solicitors were so astonished by this discovery that they at once protested. They demanded to know 'when and by whom the documents were mutilated' and 'the identity' of the informer. When this information was not forthcoming, they amended the writ claiming an order on Granada to make an affidavit setting forth the names of all persons responsible for supplying them with the documents.

I must say that I regard this tampering with the documents as a most serious matter. These documents were the property of the British Steel Corpn beyond all question. They were the very subject of a pending action by the corporation against Granada. They were the most important evidence in the case. To destroy them, or any part of them, is just as bad as the obstruction of a witness. Just as it is a contempt of court to obstruct oral evidence by preventing a witness from attending the hearing (see *R v Hall* (1776) 2 Wm Bl 1110, 96 ER 655) so also is it a contempt of court to obstruct documentary evidence by destroying or defacing a piece of paper which is of importance in a pending action. Counsel for Granada tried to draw a distinction between destroying evidence and destroying the subject matter. But that is a distinction without a difference. It is no excuse to say that it was done with a good motive, such as to protect the source of the information, or, as I would say, to conceal the identity of the informer. Whatever the motive, it is a contempt of court deliberately to mutilate a document which is likely to be called for in a pending action. Let me assume for the moment that it may be privileged or protected from disclosure. That can be discussed later. But what is not permissible is deliberately to mutilate it with the intent that it should not be available if called for.

The law

This brings me to the law. I will first dispose of two points raised by counsel for Granada.

First: no doubt *Norwich Pharmacal Co v Customs and Excise Comrs* [1973] 2 All ER 943, 1974] AC 133 opened a new chapter in our law. It enables a person, who has been injured by wrongdoing, to bring an action to discover the name of the wrongdoer. Counsel for Granada suggested that this was limited to cases where the injured person desired to *sue* the wrongdoer. I see no reason why it should be so limited. The same procedure should be available when he desires to obtain redress against the wrongdoer, or to protect himself against further wrongdoing.

Second: it was suggested that Granada might avoid disclosing the identity by pleading the privilege against self-incrimination. The simple answer is that in these courts, as in the United States, the privilege is not available to a corporation. It has no body to be kicked or soul to be damned. The public interest lies much more in making corporations disclose their misdeeds than in giving them this shield of privilege.

This clears the decks for the great question in the case: ought Granada to be compelled to disclose their source of information? This lies, I believe, in balancing the public interests as we have done in all our recent cases, such as *D v National Society for the Prevention of Cruelty to Children* [1977] 1 All ER 589, [1978] AC 171 and *Science Research Council v Nassé* [1978] 3 All ER 1196, [1979] 1 QB 144. This I proceed to do.

The cases in England

For well over 100 years it has been a settled rule that, when a plaintiff sues a newspaper for damages for libel, the newspaper will not be compelled to disclose its source of information: at any rate in answer to interrogatories administered in interlocutory proceedings before trial. We have looked at all the reported cases such *Hennessy v Wright (No 2)* (1888) 24 QBD 445n, *Hope v Brash* [1897] 2 QB 188, [1895–9] All ER Rep 343, *Plymouth Mutual Co-operative and Industrial Society Ltd v Traders' Publishing Association Ltd* [1906] 1 KB 403, *Lyle-Samuel v Odhams Ltd* [1920] 1 KB 135, [1918–19] All ER Rep 779 and *Georgius v Oxford University* [1949] 1 All ER 342, [1949] 1 KB 429. Sometimes this is put as a rule of practice, on the ground that it is not necessary at the interlocutory stage to discover the name of the informant. At other times it is put as a rule of law, on the ground that the plaintiff has an adequate remedy in damages against the newspaper and that it is not in the public interest that the name of the informant should be disclosed, else the sources of information would dry up. But, whichever way it is put, the court has never in any of our cases compelled a newspaper to disclose the name of its informant. Save in the leading case of *Attorney General v Mulholland* [1963] 1 All ER 767, [1963] 2 QB 477 where on balance the public interest in compelling disclosure outweighed the public interest in protecting the sources of information.

The cases in the United States of America

The problem has been much considered in the United States of America. The cases show the courts there striking a balance between the various public interests. On the one hand the importance of the press not being compelled to disclose their sources of information. On the other hand the importance that a private individual should have redress for wrongs done to him. Neither interest overrides the other. Each case depends on its own facts. Three cases are instructive.

In 1958 the New York Herald Tribune published an article which was highly defamatory of the actress Judy Garland. The article was written by a columnist Marie Torre who said in it that she had got her information from an executive of a broadcasting network. Judy Garland tried all possible ways of discovering the name of the informant, but without success. She sued the columnist and asked for the name of the informant. The question 'went to the heart of' Judy Garland's case. The court ordered the columnist to disclose the name: see *Garland v Torre* (1958) 250 F 2d 545.

In 1962 the Saturday Evening Post published an article which exposed the wrongdoing of unscrupulous real estate speculators, especially in discriminating against blacks. The article was written by a journalist who got his information from an anonymous real estate agent in Chicago. The blacks brought a class action and asked the court to compel the journalist to disclose his source of information. The court refused. It said (see *Baker v F & F Investment* (1972) 470 F 2d 778 at 785): 'The public interest in non-disclosure of journalists' confidential news sources will often be weightier than the private interest in compelled disclosure.'

In 1972 there was a break-in at the Watergate offices of the Democratic National Committee. Journalists made a close investigation so as to ascertain whether the highest levels of government were involved. They got confidential information from a broad range of sources. They were subpoenaed so as to give evidence about their sources of information. The court set aside the supoenas saying (see *Democratic National Committee v McCord* (1973) 356 F Supp 1394 at 1396): 'What is involved here is the right of the press to gather and publish, and that of the public to receive news, from widespread, diverse and ofttimes confidential sources.' Then the court expressed its full accord with the language of Powell J in the Supreme Court of the United States in *Branzberg v Hayes*

(1972) 408 US 665 at 710: 'The balance of these vital constitutional and societal interests on a case-by-case basis accords with the tried and traditional way of adjudicating such questions.'

The resulting principle

After studying the cases it seems to me that the courts are reaching towards this principle: the public has a right of access to information which is of public concern and of which the public ought to know. The newspapers are the agents, so to speak, of the public to collect that information and to tell the public of it. In support of this right of access, the newspapers should not in general be compelled to disclose their sources of information. Neither by means of discovery before trial. Nor by questions or cross-examination at the trial. Nor by subpoena. The reason is because, if they were compelled to disclose their sources, they would soon be bereft of information which they ought to have. Their sources would dry up. Wrongdoing would not be disclosed. Charlatans would not be exposed. Unfairness would go unremedied. Misdeeds in the corridors of power, in companies or in government departments would never be known. Investigative journalism has proved itself as a valuable adjunct of the freedom of the press. Notably in the Watergate exposure in the United States and the Poulson exposure in this country. It should not be unduly hampered or restricted by the law. Much of the information gathered by the press has been imparted to the informant in confidence. He is guilty of a breach of confidence in telling it to the press. But this is not a reason why his name should be disclosed. Otherwise much information that ought to be made public will never be made known. Likewise with documents. They may infringe copyright. But that is no reason for compelling their disclosure, if by so doing it would mean disclosing the name of the informant. In all these cases the plaintiff has his remedy in damages against the newspaper, or sometimes an injunction, and that should suffice. It may be for libel. It may be for breach of copyright. It may be for infringement of privacy. The courts will always be ready to grant an injunction to restrain a publication which is an infringement of privacy. That was well shown when Mr Strange published drawings which Queen Victoria made for her private amusement: see *Prince Albert v Strange* (1849) 1 Mac & G 25, 41 ER 1171. So let the plaintiff sue the newspaper, without getting the name of their informant. I know that in some cases it might be relevant and useful, in the interests of justice, for a plaintiff to get to know the name of the newspaper's informant, so as to prove malice, for instance, but the plaintiff will have to forego this advantage in deference to the interest which the public has in seeing that newspapers should not be compelled to disclose their sources of information.

Nevertheless, this principle is not absolute. The journalist has no privilege by which he can claim, as of right, to refuse to disclose the name. There may be exceptional cases in which, on balancing the various interests, the court decides that the name should be disclosed. Such as in *Garland v Torre* in the United States and *Attorney General v Mulholland* here. Have we any scales by which to hold the balance? Have we any yardstick by which to determine which cases are exceptional? It seems to me that the rule (by which a newspaper should not be compelled to disclose its source of information) is granted to a newspaper on condition that it acts with a due sense of responsibility. In order to be deserving of freedom, the press must show itself worthy of it. A free press must be a responsible press. The power of the press is great. It must not abuse its power. If a newspaper should act irresponsibly, then it forfeits its claim to protect its sources of information.

To show what I mean by irresponsibly, let me give some examples. If a newspaper gets hold of an untrustworthy informant and uses his information unfairly to the detriment of innocent people, then it should not be at liberty to conceal his identity. If it pays money to an informant so as to buy scandal, and publishes it, then again it abuses its freedom. It should not be at liberty to conceal the source. But, if it gets hold of a trustworthy informant who gives information of which the public ought to know, then, even though it originated in confidence, the newspaper may well be held to act with a due sense of responsibility in publishing it. It should not be compelled to divulge its source. All that I have said applies equally to television. The like principles apply to them.

Applying the principles

I have been much troubled whether Granada acted with a due sense of responsibility. Many things they did are disturbing. Not so much in the decision to use the information in the public interest, but in the way they went about it. True it is that they did not pay any money to the unnamed informer. If they had, if they had bought his disloyalty with a bribe, it would have put them out of court at once. At any rate out of this court. But they did something equally irresponsible. They made an unfair use of this confidential information. Counsel for Granada admitted that if it was 'blatantly unfair' they might have to disclose the name. I think it was. It is most unfortunate that they left it so late to tell British Steel Corpn: and they did not give Sir Charles any opportunity to see the script before he got to the studio. I have also described the conduct of the interview by the commentator. It speaks for itself. It was deplorable. Added to this, their tampering with the papers was disgraceful. In those circumstances I hold that Granada did not act with a due sense of responsibility. If earlier warnings had been given, I would have expected the corporation to have moved for an injunction, which they might have got, and the programme would never have been shown. I cannot think it right that their want of responsibility should enable them to make this damaging attack on the corporation and on the government. They behaved so badly that they have forfeited the protection which the law normally gives to newspapers and broadcasters. This protection is given only on condition that they do not abuse their power. Here Granada have abused it. They should be compelled to discover the source of their information.

I would dismiss the appeal.

TEMPLEMAN LJ. British Steel Corpn ('BSC') sought, and Sir Robert Megarry V-C granted, a mandatory injunction directing Granada to identify the BSC employee who provided Granada with BSC documents which were the property of BSC. The employee acted in breach of his contractual duty to BSC in handing over the documents to Granada and thereby, in further breach of his contractual duty, disclosed to Granada information confidential to BSC. Granada appreciated that the employee was acting in breach of his duty to BSC. The employee was promised that his identity would not be revealed. After studying the documents, Granada used the documents in Granada's television programme and thereby knowingly acted in breach of their duty in tort to BSC.

It has long been the law that one wrongdoer may be compelled by the victim to disclose the identity of another wrongdoer where their offences are connected: see *Norwich Pharmacal Co v Customs and Excise Comrs* [1973] 2 All ER 943 at 948–949, [1974] AC 133 at 175. The decision in the *Norwich Pharmacal* case established that an innocent person who becomes involved in the actions of a wrongdoer may also be ordered to disclose the identity of the wrongdoer provided that disclosure is necessary to enable the victim to take proceedings against the wrongdoer. In the words of Viscount Dilhorne ([1973] 2 All ER 943 at 960, [1974] AC 133 at 188): '. . . a discovery can be granted against a person who is not a mere witness to discover, the fact of some wrongdoing being established, who is responsible for it.'

Lord Kilbrandon ([1973] 2 All ER 943 at 975, [1974] AC 133 at 205) adopted the words of Beaumont AJ in *Colonial Government v Tatham* (1902) 23 Natal LR 153 at 159:

> 'The principle which underlies the jurisdiction which the law gives to Courts of Equity in cases of this nature, is that where discovery is absolutely necessary in order to enable a party to proceed with a *bona fide* claim, it is the duty of the Court to assist with the administration of justice by granting an order for discovery, unless some well-founded objection exists against the exercise of such jurisdiction.'

BSC must first establish wrongdoing. An employee who discloses information confidential to his employer is guilty of wrongdoing unless the information relates to misconduct on the part of the employer. In *Initial Services Ltd v Putterill* [1967] 3 All ER 145 at 148, [1968] 1 QB 396 at 405 Lord Denning MR agreed that in the employment of every servant there is imposed by law an implied obligation that he will not disclose information or documents which he has received in confidence. Lord Denning MR nevertheless commented that this obligation is subject to exceptions and is not binding on the servant where the master has been guilty of misconduct of such a nature that it ought in the public interest to be discovered. Thus the servant who conveys to a journalist information which discloses that the employer has been guilty of crime or fraud or misconduct which ought to be laid bare in the public interest does not commit a breach of duty and the journalist may safely promise to conceal the identity of the servant.

Granada do not suggest that BSC were guilty of misconduct which released the employee from his duty of confidentiality or justified a promise of secrecy or justified Granada's use of BSC's documents and confidential information. Granada admit that BSC have established wrongdoing by their employee followed by wrongdoing on the part of Granada.

BSC must secondly establish that they are concerned to obtain discovery in order that they may not be denied justice. In the *Norwich Pharmacal* case the court assisted the victim of the wrongdoing to ascertain the identity of the wrongdoer in order that the victim might institute legal proceedings against the wrongdoer. In the present case it was argued by Granada that BSC have no intention of taking legal proceedings against their employee but only intend to dismiss or reprimand or harass the employee. In my judgment the principle of the *Norwich Pharmacal* case applies whether or not the victim intends to pursue action in the courts against the wrongdoer provided that the existence of a cause of action is established and the victim cannot otherwise obtain justice. The remedy of discovery is intended in the final analysis to enable justice to be done. Justice can be achieved against an erring employee in a variety of ways and a plaintiff may obtain an order for discovery provided he shows that he is genuinely seeking lawful redress of a wrong and cannot otherwise obtain redress. In the present case BSC state that they will not finally determine whether to take legal proceedings or whether to dismiss the employee or whether to obtain redress in some other lawful manner until they have considered the identity, status and excuses of the employee. The disclosure of the identity of the disloyal employee will by itself protect BSC and their innocent employees now and for the future and is essential if BSC are to redress the wrong.

In the third place BSC must establish that discovery by Granada of the identity of the employee is necessary. On behalf of Granada it was submitted that BSC obtained and abandoned a sufficient remedy against Granada in damages for the consequences of the wrongdoing by the employee and by Granada. It was submitted that BSC suffered little harm from the television programme and that BSC should not be allowed to pursue their employee. In my judgment the remedy of BSC against Granada in damages in the present instance is irrelevant and plainly inadequate. BSC need to establish the identity of their employee because innocent employees are under suspicion, because free and frank discussions between members of the staff of BSC are inhibited and because further wrongdoing either by the present disloyal employee or by other employees tempted to be disloyal in the future must be prevented and will be prevented if and only if the identity of the wrongdoer is disclosed. Granada do not suggest that BSC have any practicable method of discovering the identity of their employee save the method of obtaining an order of the court that Granada shall reveal his or her identity.

Thus BSC are entitled to an order for discovery of the identity of their employee unless, in the words of Lord Reid in the *Norwich Pharmacal* case [1973] 2 All ER 943 at 949, [1974] AC 133 at 175, 'there is some consideration of public policy which prevents that'. In the *Norwich Pharmacal* case Lord Reid proceeded to weigh the requirements of justice against the considerations put forward for justifying non-disclosure. The consideration put forward in the *Norwich Pharmacal* case was that there was a public interest in protecting the confidentiality of information given to the customs authorities by importers because the information was given by compulsion of statute and because importers would cease to give full and candid information to the customs authorities if those authorities could be compelled to reveal that information to the court and to third parties. The reasons advanced in the *Norwich Pharmacal* case for resisting discovery were judged by the House of Lords to be insufficient.

In *D v National Society for the Prevention of Cruelty to Children* [1977] 1 All ER 589, [1978] AC 171, however, the NSPCC successfully resisted an order for the discovery of an informant who inaccurately alleged that the plaintiff had ill-treated a child. Discovery was refused because information regarding child cruelty would not be forthcoming if the NSPCC were obliged to reveal the names of their informants and it was in the public interest that such information should be supplied to the NSPCC. Lord Diplock said ([1977] 1 All ER 589 at 594, [1978] AC 171 at 218):

'The private promise ... must yield to the general public interest that in the administration of justice truth will out, unless by reason of the character of the information or the relationship of the recipient of the information to the informant a more important public interest is served by protecting the information or the identity of the informant from disclosure in a court of law.'

In the present case the public interest claimed by Granada is an interest in securing that informants are not deterred by the possibility of disclosure from providing the press and other media with information relating to matters of general interest.

Counsel for Granada relied on the authorities which he said established the existence of a public policy immunity from the remedy of discovery enjoyed by the media for the purpose of ensuring that the public received full information on matters of public concern. Counsel relied in particular on authorities which establish a settled rule of practice or rule of law that newspapers in libel actions are entitled, save in special and undefined circumstances, to decline to reveal their sources of information.

In *Hennessy v Wright (No 2)* (1890) 24 QBD 445n an interrogatory demanding the name of the newspaper's informant was disallowed because the question was not asked bona fide for the purposes of the libel action against the newspaper. A similar reason was given in *Parnell v Walter* (1890) 24 QBD 441. Neither of these cases assists counsel. But in *Adam v Fisher* (1914) 30 TLR 288 Buckley LJ suggested two reasons for the practice of disallowing discovery and interrogatories directed to ascertaining the source of information of a newspaper libel. One reason, he suggested, might be that 'a newspaper stood in such a position that it was not desirable on grounds of public interest that the name of a newspaper's informant should be disclosed'. In *Lyle-Samuel v Odhams* [1920] 1 KB 135, [1918–19] All ER Rep 779 the reason suggested by Buckley LJ in *Adam v Fisher* was not received with any enthusiasm, but the immunity of a newspaper from disclosing its source in a libel action save in undefined special circumstances was recognised. In *South Suburban Co-operative Society v Orum* [1937] 3 All ER 133, [1937] 2 KB 690 it was decided that the immunity of the press did not extend to protecting a defendant to a libel action who was the writer or contributor to the newspaper but not a journalist from disclosing the source of his information. In *Georgius v Oxford University Press* [1949] 1 All ER 342 at 343, [1949] 1 KB 729 at 733 Denning LJ said that in a libel action it was not necessary to find out the name of a newspaper's informant in order to do justice to the plaintiff and that the remedy of the plaintiff against the newspaper should be sufficient. I agree. Such a remedy enables a plaintiff to vindicate his reputation and recover adequate damages unless the newspaper is impecunious. In the present case BSC's remedy against Granada is insufficient for the reasons I have indicated. In *Isbey v New Zealand Broadcasting Corpn (No 2)* [1975] 2 NZLR 237 at 238 Cooke J, now a member of the Court of Appeal of New Zealand, held that the 'practice or principle of common law ... that in an action against the proprietor of a newspaper ... interrogatories will not be allowed as to the name of the person who wrote the alleged libel or supplied the information on which it was founded' applied in New Zealand and extended to television and radio broadcasting. He added (at 239) that—

'while no doubt there are no small number of instances in which the ferreting out and publication of material by news media serves no true public interest, and may do little more than titillate the palate of consumers and cause distress to persons referred to, there is another category of cases in which it clearly is in the public interest that the news media should undertake the responsibility of investigation provided, of course, that they do so with appreciation that it is indeed a responsibility.'

In my judgment these authorities support the submission of counsel for Granada that there is a public interest in upholding the claim of the media to immunity from disclosing their sources of information, but sound a word of warning as to the ground for claiming and granting immunity.

A similar approach is to be found in the authorities dealing with the refusal of journalists to reveal their sources to the tribunal of inquiry appointed to inquire into breaches of security in connection with spying offences committed by Vassall. In *Attorney General v Clough* [1963] 1 All ER 420 at 425, [1963] 1 QB 773 at 778 Lord Parker CJ referred to classes of communication which had been recognised as privileged and continued:

'In the rest of a vast area, it must be for the court to ascertain what public policy demands. If, in the circumstances of any particular case, it became clear that public policy demanded a recognition of some claim to privilege, then it would be the duty of this court to give due effect to public policy and recognise the claim.'

But he concluded ([1963] 1 All ER 420 at 427–428, [1963] 1 QB 773 at 792):

'. . . in regard to the press, the law has not developed and crystallised the confidential relationship in which they stand to an informant into one of the classes of privilege known to the law [but] it still, as I conceive it, would remain open to this court to say in the special circumstances of any particular case that public policy did demand that the journalist should be immune. . .'

Similarly in *Attorney General v Mulholland* [1963] 1 All ER 767 at 771, [1963] 2 QB 477 at 489–490 Lord Denning MR commented that:

'A judge is the person entrusted, on behalf of the community, to weigh these conflicting interests—to weigh on the one hand the respect due to confidence in the profession and on the other hand the ultimate interest of the community in justice being done. . . If the judge determines that the journalist must answer, then no privilege will avail him to refuse.'

These authorities also support counsel for Granada's submission that there is a public interest in upholding the claim of the media to immunity from disclosing their sources but the authorities also establish that the immunity is not absolute and must be weighed against the interests of the community that justice shall not be denied.

Counsel for BSC submitted that on principle and on authority, whenever there was a conflict between public policy in securing justice and public policy in upholding the immunity of the media from disclosing their sources, that conflict must always be resolved by ordering disclosure. In the present case, he submitted, BSC cannot obtain justice without disclosure of the name of their employee. Counsel relied on the speech of Lord Wilberforce in *Science Research Council v Nassé* [1979] 3 All ER 673 at 681, [1980] AC 1028 at 1067 where Lord Wilberforce referred to authorities, including *Attorney General v Mulholland* and *Attorney General v Clough*, as examples 'of cases where the courts have recognised that confidences, particularly those of third persons, ought, if possible, in the interests of justice, to be respected'. He explained that—

'the process is to consider fairly the strength and value of the interest of preserving confidentiality and the damage which may be caused by breaking it; then to consider whether the objective, to dispose fairly of the case, can be achieved without doing so, and only in a last resort to order discovery, subject if need be to protective measures.'

Counsel for BSC submitted that justice cannot be achieved in the present case without disclosure and therefore that the claim by Granada to immunity from discovery cannot prevail. The *Norwich Pharmacal* case itself however recognised that the remedy of discovery would not be granted, in the words of Lord Reid ([1973] 2 All ER 943, at 949, [1974] AC 133 at 175) to which I have referred, until after weighing 'the requirements of justice . . . against considerations put forward justifying non-disclosure'. In the *NSPCC* case the order for discovery was refused although the plaintiff's chances of success in her action against the NSPCC were thereby diminished and she was unable to institute proceedings against the NSPCC's informant. In the *NSPCC* case public policy considerations which protect the anonymity of police informers (see *Marks v Beyfus* (1890) 25 QBD 494) and protect the anonymity of the informants to the Gaming Board (see *Rogers v Secretary of State for the Home Department* [1972] 2 All ER 1057, [1973] AC 388) were extended by analogy to protect the anonymity of informants to the NSPCC in an action for discovery. In my judgment public policy considerations may also in a proper case protect the anonymity of sources of information to the media in an action for discovery, albeit that an injured plaintiff may be hampered or frustrated in his quest for justice.

The considerations which the authorities disclose and which confer on newspapers immunity from discovery of their sources of information in libel actions, save in special circumstances and which were acknowledged in the Vassall Tribunal case, support the view, which also seems to me to be the correct view in principle, that there is a recognised public interest in the immunity of the media from disclosing their sources and that immunity must apply not only in libel actions and other actions directed to obtaining an injunction, damages or other direct relief from the media but also to actions directed solely to the discovery of a wrongdoer.

The authorities also disclose that the immunity of the media from discovery of their sources of information is not absolute and it follows that there will be cases where the media give to an informant a promise of secrecy which the media will be unable to honour. If the media were given power to extend and honour pledges of secrecy in every case then that power would amount to a general exemption for the media from the law of the land and in particular from the law which, pursuant to the *Norwich Pharmacal* case, requires the identity of a wrongdoer to be revealed. Such a general exemption is inconsistent with the authorities, is not sustainable in principle and is not claimed by counsel for Granada.

It was said that if Granada are obliged to disclose in the present well publicised proceedings the identity of the employee who provided the BSC documents, then sources of information will cease to be available to the media and the media will be unable to discharge their duty of keeping the public informed on matters of public interest. I do not believe that result will follow. There will always be informants who, for good reason or bad, confide in the media. Those who for good reason disclose facts which the public are entitled to know, such as facts relating to corruption or misconduct, are fully protected against discovery.

In the result the question in the present case is whether Granada's claim to the public policy immunity of the media from disclosing their sources of information ought to prevail over BSC's claim that justice must be done.

When the court is called on to balance the public interest in the attainment of justice against the public interest in the media protecting their sources, the result must inevitably depend on the facts of each case. In my judgment the court will strive to uphold the immunity of the media against discovery provided the media do not misuse information which they ought not to have received. Some information is not confidential and the media may use such information and conceal its source. Some information claimed to be confidential discloses misconduct and the media may use such information and conceal its source. Some information which is truly confidential may be communicated to the media and then the media may be allowed to conceal the source provided the confidence is respected. But if the media receive truly confidential information they cannot expect both to conceal the source and disclose the information in breach of confidence unless there are strong reasons to justify publication. If, for example, the information discloses facts rather than confidences, or if there is an overwhelming reason to justify publication or if the information is not damaging or embarrassing, or if the reasons advanced by the plaintiff for discovering the source are not cogent, the media may be allowed both to publish the information and conceal the source.

The media should have less difficulty in making decisions about confidential information than they experience in making decisions about publishing statements which may be libellous. The media do not lack legal advisers. The newspaper libel actions are to be distinguished for present purposes because newspapers do not make statements unless they believe them to be true and fair comment, plaintiffs can obtain adequate redress from the newspapers if they are not justified in their belief, and informants may have committed no wrong. Similarly in the NSPCC case there was no conscious wrongdoing by the NSPCC and no evidence of conscious wrongdoing by their informant. The striking features of this case are that Granada knew full well that the BSC employee had no right to hand over the BSC documents and Granada knew full well that they had no right to publish extracts and confidential information from those documents.

As a general rule, the court should not, in my judgment, allow the media knowingly to break the law, civil or criminal, and claim the immunity. The media should not be allowed to exploit the immunity by promising a wrongdoer concealment so that he may break the law with impunity or by rewarding a wrongdoer with a promise that the media will conceal his guilt, when the wrongdoing is committed with the object and is successful in achieving the object of enabling the media in turn to break the law provided they are successful in evading an injunction and are willing to pay damages. There is no acceptable public interest in upholding the secrecy of unlawful communications made for the purposes of unlawful publication.

In the present case Granada deliberately broke the common law by publishing information confidential to BSC and still Granada claim the immunity of concealing their source. BSC satisfy me that it is damaging to BSC, unfair to the employees of BSC, and undesirable in the public interest that any employee of BSC and Granada should behave in the way they have, leaving the employee undetected and still apparently a trusted employee, enjoying his pay and earning his pension. The employee broke his contractual duty to BSC in order that Granada might act in breach of their duty to BSC. Whether the employee would have acted in breach of his duty to BSC if he had not expected or had not been promised concealment by Granada will never be known. Granada argue that BSC are a public corporation and should have no secrets. But discussions between members of the staff of BSC about difficult decisions or management problems are truly confidential and it was unfair for Granada to publish many of the extracts from the BSC papers which found their way into Granada's television programme. If information is truly confidential it does not cease to be confidential merely because it relates to matters of public interest. In the present case the BSC documents and the contents of those documents which were quoted by Granada were truly confidential albeit that they related to matters of public concern and Granada were not entitled to conceal the source and break the confidence.

For the sake of imparting dramatic impact to a topical television programme, Granada knowingly succumbed to the temptation unlawfully to use confidential material unlawfully obtained. No principle of public policy or freedom of the press or freedom of information or journalistic ethics justifies resistance in these circumstances to BSC's claim to discover from Granada the identity of BSC's employee who broke his promise to BSC, enabled Granada to breach their duty to BSC and now shelters behind Granada's promise of concealment.

In addition to their defence based on the claim of the media to keep secret the sources of information Granada submitted two further alternative defences to the present proceedings. It was suggested that BSC acquiesced in the use made by Granada of the BSC documents. The evidence filed by Granada demonstrates that BSC were lured by Granada into taking part in the television programme but does not establish acquiescence. In the alternative Granada submit that they should not be ordered to reveal the identity of the BSC employee because to do so might involve Granada in self-incrimination. Granada accept the apparent inconsistency between their submission that they are entitled to conceal the identity of the BSC employee by claiming an immunity based on public policy and their submission that they are entitled to conceal his identity by claiming the immunity which is afforded to those apprehensive of criminal proceedings. I do not believe there is substance in Granada's fear that a crime is more likely to be charged against them if they reveal the name of the relevant BSC employee. Granada have already confessed their part in the events which led to their misuse of the BSC documents. The disclosure of the name of the individual who provided the ammunition which enabled Granada to concentrate their fire on BSC cannot increase the liability, civil or criminal, of Granada for pulling the trigger.

Sir Robert Megarry V-C ordered Granada to disclose the name of the employee of BSC and, for the reasons I have indicated, I would dismiss the appeal.

WATKINS LJ. It is I believe well founded on ample legal authority that newspapers and television and broadcasting authorities and their servants are in principle immune from disclosing their confidential sources of information. This principle has been applied in a number of cases before courts and tribunals, some of which have achieved public prominence. The public can be said to approve of it. It is in their interest to do so. It is, therefore, a public interest immunity.

The immunity whenever and wherever asserted in legal proceedings, civil and criminal, must not be regarded as one of the species of privilege to which the courts will pay a unique respect. This is especially so whenever questions arise affecting admissibility of evidence or the duty or obligation of anybody either to answer questions or produce documents of evidential or other essential value for a just conclusion of proceedings to ensue.

It can never be said too often that a just conclusion to proceedings means that justice having been seen to be done has in fact and in law been done.

A question of the kind to which I allude may arise from the commencement of proceedings at any stage up to and including the final hearing of them. If the response to the question whenever it is raised is that 'press immunity', as I shall call it, from disclosure of a confidential source is claimed, the court is entitled, as it thinks fit, either to rule on or to adjourn consideration of it to some later and more appropriate occasion. This procedure is subject, I think, to only one exception, by which I mean that provided for in libel actions by RSC Ord 82, r 6.

The argument, very forcibly presented on behalf of Granada, that the practice followed in libel actions preceding the making of r 6 is of general application fails to acknowledge the altogether special nature of the issues in those actions, in contrast to those which arise in a widely varied range of others. Furthermore, it ignores the vital need which arises from time to time for one party to obtain from the other information which is properly required at a stage prior to the hearing of the action in which they have joined and for the purpose of it.

It seems to me that the notion of confining a question going to the identity of a source of confidential information, which is that asked in the present case, to the hearing of the action is an unacceptable challenge to the court's right and duty to do what is just whenever and howsoever it is called on and decides to settle an issue between the parties before it.

Whenever the issue is settled the determination of it will inevitably flow from the exercise of the court's discretion in the circumstances obtaining to uphold or to deny the claim to press immunity. I am convinced that this claim should be sparingly denied. Those who, in an all-embracing word I shall call journalists, go about the business of seeking information on behalf of newspapers and television and broadcasting authorities perform a public service which is crucial to the maintenance of a free and well-informed society.

If legal constraints are needlessly placed on the activities of journalists, they will tend to become undesirably circumspect about their methods of seeking knowledge. Sources of it will be inhibited from passing on what they believe the public ought to know through fear of losing their anonymity. The promise of confidentiality going from journalist to source may become untrustworthy. This state of affairs must not arise. If it does, it would react intolerably against the public interest.

On the other hand the journalist must know that he, like everyone else, must live and work within the law of the land. If he does not and a claim is brought which the court will entertain to cause him to disclose his source of information these consequences are, in my opinion, likely to follow:

(1) If he commits a crime in concert with his source when obtaining information, even if this be done to expose iniquity about which the public ought to know, his claim to press immunity should be denied him.

(2) If he commits a civil wrong by using confidential information to which there is no public right of access from a source whom he knows has obtained it in breach of his contract of employment with an employer against whom no iniquity is alleged, his claim to press immunity will be very unlikely to succeed in the face of competing public interest, that of doing justice to the wronged employer especially.

(3) If he commits a like civil wrong for the purpose of exposing the employer's iniquity which, in the public interest, should be revealed, his claim to press immunity should be granted.

I should add that save in very rare and exceptional circumstances it is impossible to foresee a claim for disclosure which a court would entertain being brought by anybody whose iniquity has been exposed.

Whenever the claim for press immunity falls for consideration it is a weighty matter. Whether it is outweighed by other interests, including notably the public interest in the doing of justice and among other things the preservation of state secrets, the court in its discretion will decide. Whether it does this by what is called simply a balancing of interests is debatable. With respect, I prefer the process of the exercise of discretion described by Lord Wilberforce in *Science Research Council v Nassé* [1979] 3 All ER 673 at 681, [1980] AC 1028 at 1067:

'It is sometimes said that in taking this element into account, the court has to perform a balancing process. The metaphor is one well worn in the law, but I doubt if it is more than a rough metaphor. Balancing can only take place between commensurables. But here the process is to consider fairly the strength and value of the interest in preserving confidentiality and the damage which may be caused by breaking it; then to consider whether the objective, to dispose fairly of the case, can be achieved without doing so, and only in a last resort to order discovery, subject if need be to protective measures. This is a more complex process than merely using the scales: it is an exercise in judicial judgment.'

If in the exercise of judicial judgment it be found that doing justice can be reconciled with preserving press immunity the problem resolves itself and the immunity should be granted. That relatively simple solution is not available to Granada. A reconciliation of doing justice and of conceding press immunity is impossible of achievement in the face of the facts outlined by Lord Denning MR.

There is no doubt that BSC have suffered a wrong for which they are entitled to redress. They seek no more than any other employer would in reacting to the loss and unlawful use being made of their confidential documents. And I suspect that there are few employers, in substantial undertakings at any rate, who would fail to react as BSC have done.

Their motives and behaviour in this rather shabby affair are beyond reproach. The same regrettably cannot be said of Granada, one or two at least of whose servants displayed an attitude to the rights of property of others which is discreditable to put it mildly.

In their writ BSC claimed from Granada the delivery up to them of all the documents taken away by their servant and among other things an injunction restraining them from unlawfully interfering with those documents meanwhile. There could have been only one reason for BSC seeking that injunction, as I have no doubt Granada when they received the writ quickly appreciated. It was that BSC knew the documents would, if not interfered with, carry tell-tale signs which would enable them on inspection to discover the identity of their servant who had given them to Granada. So Granada before handing the documents over mutilated them so as effectively to erase the tell-tale signs. Whether this was done before or after BSC warned Granada against such action as that is not known to this court. Either way it was a gross interference with BSC's rights of property which, since no iniquity on the part of BSC is and could not have been alleged, was in my judgment totally unjustifiable granted that Granada's concern for press immunity prompted their wrongful action.

By this action they were taking the law into their own hands. They were attempting to pre-empt the court's determination of very important issues involving handing over of documents in combination with, as Granada must have known, disclosure of their confidential source.

Leading counsel, who argued Granada's case with skill, resourcefulness and refreshing frankness, argued that there never was an issue about the return of the documents. That depends on what documents are in contemplation, the documents as handed to Granada or the same documents as mutilated by them. If Granada intended to hand over the documents in the condition in which they received them (it has not been suggested that 'the source' removed the tell-tale signs) there would have been no issue. Since they did not do that, there was and is an issue about the proper handing over of documents which has yet to be resolved.

One further observation on this aspect of the matter is of significance if not relevance. In removing the tell-tale signs Granada left open to themselves the choice of either paying the penalty for refusing to obey an order of the court to reveal the identity of the source or to obey it. The penalty on a limited company for a refusal is limited to the payment of a fine.

By their act of mutilation of the documents alone Granada are in my judgment disentitled to immunity. It constituted a gross interference with BSC's rights of property.

Such a conclusion can conceivably be supported by directly likening the mutilation of the documents to an attempt by him or those who did it to obstruct the course of justice. To act in that way is, in a civil as well as in a criminal action, a contempt of court. In *Morris v Crown Office* [1970] 1 All ER 1079 at 1081, [1970] 2 QB 114 at 122 Lord Denning MR stated: 'The course of justice must not be deflected or interfered with. Those who strike at it strike at the very foundations of our society.'

Counsel for Granada contended that because Granada have not disobeyed an order of the court and the documents themselves are not the subject matter of BSC's motion Granada have not in any way obstructed nor attempted to obstruct the course of justice. That this is an unattractive argument is easily demonstrated.

On 7th March 1980 BSC by order amended their writ so as to include the relief sought in the motion before this court. What prompted them to seek leave to do this was the mutilated state of their documents when these were returned to them on the 28th February. Furthermore, the bundle of these documents as delivered was, so BSC say, probably with justification, incomplete. There were two or more documents missing. They have yet to be recovered from the appellants.

The mutilation of some documents and the probable retention by Granada of others was designed to thwart discovery of the identity of 'the source' by BSC in the event of Granada by order releasing to them all the documents in the state in which they had received them. Thus the court has been effectively prevented from determining BSC's claim for an injunction to restrain Granada from unlawfully interfering with their property and very likely also from effectively ordering Granada to hand over all BSC's documents received by them.

I have no doubt that BSC were entitled to both the injunction and to the order and that the circumstances which have denied them these forms of relief would on close scrutiny in contempt proceedings almost certainly be found to reveal an obstruction of the course of justice. Were it not for this obstruction these proceedings would not have come about.

Granada have indisputably not disobeyed any order of the court. But they anticipated being placed in the position of some day having to decide whether to obey an order embarrassing to them. The documents are not the subject matter of the motion in that an order for the recovery of them is being sought, but what unlawfully happened to them produced the motion. Moreover in the disposal of the motion what happpened to them is a matter of significance in the judicial process of exercising a discretion to compel or not to compel Granada to reveal their source.

I desire finally to speak of the issue of self-incrimination without being influenced one way or the other by its late appearance in Granada's defensive screen.

What do Granada have to fear from their source when and if he is forced into the light of day? That is the question. What can he say to their detriment which has not already been made known by them? Is their claim to having received the documents in circumstances which did not involve dishonesty or criminal conduct suspect? They would surely prefer this court to believe that it is not.

The only crime which, according to counsel, Granada fear they could be placed in jeopardy of being found guilty of committing is conspiracy to defraud. The particulars of the offence could be he suggests 'using documents in violation of the BSC's proprietary rights' or something akin to that.

On the supposition that those particulars of an agreement could amount to a criminal conspiracy nothing more needs to be known than Granada have already revealed to form a prima facie case of guilt against them. The source is not required. He is the person unknown with whom they conspired. Nobody can be shielded from answering questions at any stage of proceedings because to do so would have a tendency to incriminate when he or they have already laid bare the facts of criminality. The element of dishonesty within the crime of fraud is found to exist if it does as a matter of legitimate inference from those facts. It is difficult to envisage how the source could damage Granada in this respect.

This consideration of self-incrimination does not stand alone. There are two other relevant matters which demand attention. They are as follows:

(1) There is no doubt that a limited company can be indicted for conspiracy. But the circumstances in which this can be done must be within those indicated by Lord Reid in *Tesco Ltd v Nattrass* [1971] 2 All ER 127 at 132, [1972] AC 153 at 171. He said:

'Normally the board of directors, the managing director and perhaps other superior officers of a company carry out the functions of management and speak and act as the company. Their subordinates do not. They carry out orders from above and it can make no difference that they are given some measure of discretion. But the board of directors may delegate some part of their functions of management giving to their delegate full discretion to act independently of instructions from them. I see no difficulty in holding that they have thereby put such a delegate in their place so that within the scope of the delegation he can act as the company. It may not always be easy to draw the line but there are cases in which the line must be drawn. *Lennard's case* [1915] AC 705, [1914–15] All ER Rep 280 was one of them.'

I should be surprised if any of those servants of Granada who have taken any part whatsoever in the acceptance and the use made of the documents could be said to be acting 'as the company' so as to expose it to be charged with conspiracy.

(2) Agreements which are intended to result in the use of documents in violation of the proprietorial rights of someone who owns the documents and who is not party to the agreement are not universally recognised as criminal conspiracies. There is a reputable body of opinion which would not regard agreements of this kind as criminal.

To what extent if at all Granada have been sensitive to these two matters I do not know. If they were in their minds when the decision was taken to rely on the defence of self-incrimination their influence should have been strong enough to resist the temptation to do so.

In my view this claimed protection against self-incrimination, although plausibly presented, does not and could not reasonably be said to have arisen from genuine apprehensions of prosecution for a criminal offence. If it was, it was without foundation.

The submission of counsel for BSC that an order to disclose Granada's source is appropriate in the circumstances of this case is to my mind irresistible.

I agree with Lord Denning MR and Templeman LJ. I too would dismiss this appeal.

Appeal dismissed. Seven days for discovery of informants. Application for leave to appeal to the House of Lords refused. Stay of execution of order until House of Lords decide application for leave to appeal. If leave to appeal granted, stay to continue until appeal heard.

Frances Rustin   Barrister.

Appeal

Granada appealed to the House of Lords pursuant to leave granted by the House on 5th July 1980.

Patrick Neill QC, Alexander Irvine QC and *Patrick Moloney* for Granada.
Leonard Hoffmann QC and *David Kitchin* for BSC.

Their Lordships took time for consideration.

30th July. Their Lordships made the following announcements.

LORD WILBERFORCE. My Lords, after consideration of the arguments in this case I have reached the conclusion that this appeal must be dismissed. My detailed reasons for that opinion I will incorporate in a speech which will at a later date be available in print.

VISCOUNT DILHORNE. My Lords, for reasons which will be made known in due course, I too would dismiss this appeal.

LORD SALMON. My Lords, I understand that my noble and learned friends Lord Fraser and Lord Russell have reached the same decision as my noble and learned friends Lord Wilberforce and Viscount Dilhorne. It follows that the decision at which I shall arrive, whatever it may be, cannot affect the result of this appeal. The hearing which lasted about six days finished only a week ago. I regret that I am not prepared to come to any final decision before I have had more time to reflect on the many authorities and documents and the arguments which were put before us.

LORD FRASER OF TULLYBELTON. My Lords, I have reached the opinion that this appeal should be dismissed, and I shall incorporate my reasons in due course in a written speech.

LORD RUSSELL OF KILLOWEN. My Lords, for reasons which I will in due course give in writing, I am of opinion that this appeal should be dismissed.

Viscount Dilhorne died on 7th September 1980.

7th November. The following written opinions were given.

LORD WILBERFORCE. My Lords, on 4th February 1980 the appellants, Granada Television Ltd ('Granada'), broadcast on a national television network a current affairs programme devoted to the steel strike. This strike, of the workers in the nationalised steel industry, had started in January 1980 and was one of great concern to the government and to the public. The programme, which lasted about half an hour and a replay of which we have seen, showed on the screen, and quoted from, a number of secret or confidential documents the property of the respondents, British Steel Corpn ('BSC'), a nationalised undertaking, and a good deal was made of the achievement of Granada in securing these documents, called 'The Steel Papers', for public discussion. The revelation of them, irrespective of their contents, was no doubt intended to, and did, impart a dramatic effect to the programme. In addition, there was an appearance by the chairman of BSC, Sir Charles Villiers, who had put to him, and answered, some questions based on the papers.

The 'steel papers' used in the programme were some 27 documents out of 250 or thereabouts which had been delivered to Granada on 28th January 1980 by a person, then unknown, who must have been an employee or former employee of BSC and whose work entitled him or her to have access to highly classified documents. There is no doubt that many of them were confidential, indeed very confidential, relating as they did to internal action and discussions at a high level within BSC, and with the government, to financial and commercial facts which BSC had not made public, and to other matters concerned with productivity and industrial relations. Quite clearly the person concerned had no right, and Granada knew he had no right, to hand them over and in doing so he may well have been guilty of an act of theft.

The documents were delivered to a representative of Granada without, it is said, any previous appointment with Granada, and Granada says that no inducement or payment was made in connection with them. We have, naturally, no knowledge of the source's motives and no right, or need, to speculate about them. The representative gave to the source a promise, on behalf of Granada, that no step would be taken that might reveal or risk disclosure of the source's identity.

This appeal raises the question whether in these proceedings brought by BSC Granada can or should be ordered to disclose the identity of the source. Before considering it I must describe the procedure which has been followed by BSC and the present status of the litigation.

On 6th February 1980 (I omit various communications which had taken place between BSC and Granada which raise matters still in controversy) BSC issued against Granada a writ and notice of motion claiming an injunction against further breaches of confidence and copyright, an order for delivery up of the documents and copies thereof, an inquiry as to damages, and an account of profits. On the same day BSC applied for and obtained an ex parte injunction restraining Granada from further publication or reproduction of the documents.

On 28th February 1980 (ie after the programme had been broadcast) by agreement between solicitors Granada purported to deliver the documents to the solicitors for BSC. On examination of them it was found that they were incomplete, portions having been cut out. Granada admits that this was done, on 27th February, because it was thought that marks on the documents might reveal or risk revelation of the identity of the source. Whatever the reason, this mutilation of documents, which were undoubtedly BSC's property and which they were incontestably entitled to recover, was a clear and deliberate violation of BSC's rights. Granada's present argument seems necessarily to involve that they were entitled to mutilate the documents in order to protect the source.

On 6th March 1980 BSC amended their notice of motion and their writ so as to claim an order that Granada make and serve on BSC's solicitors an affidavit setting forth the names of all persons responsible for supplying Granada with the documents. BSC contended, and their counsel at the hearing strongly stressed this point, that it was important for them to ascertain who this person was in order to prevent further misuse by him of BSC documents and in order to dispel the cloud of suspicion hanging over those of its staff who might have handed the documents over. This immediately raised the issue whether Granada can be compelled by judicial process to reveal the source of their information.

The motion came before Sir Robert Megarry V-C on 11th March. He decided that no public interest in the media not being forced to disclose their sources of information at the trial of an action had yet been recognised and that there were insufficient grounds for holding that such an interest ought to exist. In so far as the case was one for the balancing of public interests, or for the exercise of discretion, he held that the interest of BSC in having the identity of the source disclosed should prevail. He also held that Granada were not protected against disclosure on the ground of possible self-incrimination. He ordered that Granada should forthwith state on affidavit the names of the persons responsible for supplying them with the documents. On this decision it was agreed, and so ordered, that the motion should be treated as the trial of the action. BSC indicated that they would not pursue any claim for damages. They were awarded the costs of the action.

The Court of Appeal, on appeal by Granada, heard the appeal on 15th April. They upheld the decision of the Vice-Chancellor. Lord Denning MR held that there was a public interest in seeing that newspapers should not be compelled to disclose their sources of information. This principle, however, was not absolute: it is granted on condition that the newspaper acts with a due sense of responsibility. His Lordship, after examining the conduct of Granada, held that they had not so acted: they had made an unfair use of confidential information in leaving it so late to tell BSC that the papers were to be used, in the conduct of the interview with Sir Charles Villiers and in their mutilation of the papers.

Templeman LJ undertook to balance the public interest in the attainment of justice against the public interest in the media preserving their sources. He held that no principles of public policy justified resistance to BSC's claim to discover the identity of BSC's employee who broke his promise to BSC and enabled Granada to breach their duty to BSC. He also rejected the defence based on possible self-incrimination. Watkins LJ opened his judgment with a general proposition that the media are in principle immune from disclosing their confidential sources of information. He later held however that this principle could be and was outweighed by other competing interests. The Court of Appeal gave Granada seven days to disclose the source.

So all the learned judges so far have decided in favour of disclosure of the source. Granada's final appeal was to this House. The hearing took place in July 1980, having been expedited at the request of BSC, when the decision was announced. I now give the reasons which, on the arguments then heard, induced me to suggest dismissal of the appeal. Before coming to what I regard as the crucial point for disposal of the case I would make some general observations.

First, there were appeals, made in vigorous tones to such broad principles as the freedom of the press, the right to a free flow of information, the public's right to know. In Granada's printed case we find quotations from pronouncements of Sheridan in Parliament and from declarations of eminent judges in cases where the freedom of the press might be involved. I too would be glad to be counted among those whose voice had been raised in favour of this great national possession, a free press; who indeed would not? But this case does not touch on the freedom of the press even at its periphery. Freedom of the press imports, generally, freedom to publish without precensorship, subject always to the laws relating to libel, official secrets, sedition and other recognised inhibitions. It is not necessary to define the concept more closely, for it is clear and *not disputed by Granada*, that BSC could, if they had acted in time, have obtained from the courts an injunction against publishing or reproducing any of the contents of the documents. I quote from Granada's printed case: 'such an injunction [restraining Granada's use of the documents] would certainly have been granted.' This position was maintained by counsel at the bar. In other words, Granada do not make the case that they had the right to publish. The question before us, as to disclosure of the source, is another question altogether.

Then there is the alleged right to a free flow of information, or the right to know. Your Lordships will perceive without any demonstration from me that use of the word 'right' here will not conduce to an understanding of the legal position. As to a free flow of information, it may be said that, in a general sense, it is in the public interest that this should be maintained and not curtailed. Investigatory journalism too in some cases may bring benefits to the public. But, granting this, one is a long way from establishing a right which the law will recognise in a particular case. Before then it is necessary to take account of the legitimate interest which others may have in limiting disclosure of information of a particular kind. I shall return to this point later. As to an alleged 'right to know', it must be clear that except in a totally open society (if any such exists) limitations on this not only exist but are considerable, whether one is concerned with the operations of government, or of business, one's neighbours' affairs or indeed any other activity. To keep to the concrete, as regards BSC, the conduct of its affairs and the disclosures and reports which have to be made are, as one would expect of a public body, regulated by statute, now by the Iron and Steel Act 1975. The legitimate interest of the public in knowing about its affairs is given effect to through information which there is a statutory duty to publish and through reports to the Secretary of State who is responsible to Parliament. That some of the internal activities of BSC at particular times are of interest to the public there can be no doubt. But there is a wide difference between what is interesting to the public and what it is in the public interest to make known.

Third, as to information obtained in confidence, and the legal duty, which may arise, to disclose it to a court of justice, the position is clear. Courts have an inherent wish to respect this confidence, whether it arises between doctor and patient, priest and penitent, banker and customer, between persons giving testimonials to employees, or in other relationships. A relationship of confidence between a journalist and his source is in no different category; nothing in this case involves or will involve any principle that such confidence is not something to be respected. But in all these cases the court may have to decide, in particular circumstances, that the interest in preserving this confidence is outweighed by other interests to which the law attaches importance. The only question in this appeal is whether the present is such a case.

One final point. There is an important exception to the limitations which may exist on the right of the media to reveal information otherwise restricted. That is based on what is commonly known as the 'iniquity rule'. It extends in fact beyond 'iniquity' to misconduct generally (see *Initial Services Ltd v Putterill* [1967] 3 All ER 145, [1968] 1 QB 396). It is recognised that, in cases where misconduct exists, publication may legitimately be made even if disclosure involves a breach of confidence such as would normally justify a prohibition against disclosure. It must be emphasised that we are not in this field in the present case; giving the widest extension to the expression 'iniquity' nothing within it is alleged in the present case. The most that it is said the papers reveal is mismanagement and government intervention. Granada has never contended that it had a right to publish in order to reveal 'iniquity'.

So the question is, and remains, whether the court, at the instance of BSC, would compel disclosure of the source. This in turn involves the questions (a) whether BSC can obtain this relief by the procedure adopted in this case, (b) whether, if so, any balancing of the public interest and considerations on either side is required and if so with what result. In addition, we have to consider (c) whether Granada can refuse to disclose on the ground that to do so might incriminate them.

Granada's main argument in this House was directed to points (a) and (c) above, that is to say, largely of a technical character. They are none the worse for that, but they do bring out the limitations of the reasons we are required to give.

I now come more particularly to the law relevant to this case. I start with the proposition that the media of information, and journalists who write or contribute for them, have no immunity based on public interest which protects them from the obligation to disclose in a court of law their sources of information, when such disclosure is necessary in the interest of justice. No such claim has ever been allowed in our courts, and such attempts as have been made to assert such an immunity have failed. A claim for immunity was made before the Parnell Commission in 1889 and flatly rejected by Hannen P sitting with two other judges. In the two cases arising out of the Vassall inquiry, in which the usual argument was strongly put that if disclosure were ordered in such cases the sources of information would dry up, the claim was firmly repelled. In *Attorney General v Clough* [1963] 1 All ER 420 at 425, [1963] 1 QB 773 at 788 Lord Parker CJ expressed the clear opinion that no such immunity had been recognised or existed. In *Attorney General v Mulholland* [1963] 1 All ER 767, [1963] 2 QB 477 a similar claim in respect of communications between journalists and sources of information was rejected by the Court of Appeal. Lord Denning MR in a classic passage said ([1963] 1 All ER 767 at 770–771, [1963] 2 QB 477 at 489–490):

'Then it is said ... that, however relevant these questions were and however proper to be answered for the purpose of the inquiry, a journalist has a privilege by law entitling him to refuse to give his sources of information ... It seems to me that the journalists put the matter much too high. The only profession that I know which is given a privilege from disclosing information to a court of law is the legal profession, and then it is not the privilege of the lawyer but of his client. Take the clergyman, the banker or the medical man. None of these is entitled to refuse to answer when directed to by a judge. Let me not be mistaken. The judge will respect the confidences which each member of these honourable professions receives in the course of it, and will not direct him to answer unless not only it is relevant but also it is a proper and, indeed, necessary question in the course of justice to be put and answered. A judge is the person entrusted, on behalf of the community, to weigh these conflicting interests—to weigh on the one hand the respect due to confidence in the profession and on the other hand the ultimate interest of the community in justice being done or, in the case of a tribunal such as this, in a proper investigation being made into these serious allegations. If the judge determines that the journalist must answer, then no privilege will avail him to refuse.'

In *McGuinness v Attorney General of Victoria* (1940) 63 CLR 73, a case concerned with a tribunal of inquiry into allegations of bribery, a claim to immunity for a journalist was made and rejected by the High Court of Australia. A memorable judgment was given by Dixon J rejecting the claim, and dealing also with the so-called 'newspaper rule'. Passages from this judgment are cited by my noble and learned friend Viscount Dilhorne, and I shall not repeat them, but venture to emphasise their force.

All these authorities (and there is none the other way before this case) came down firmly against immunity for the press or for journalists. To contend that, in principle, journalists enjoy immunity from the obligation to disclose which may however be withheld in exceptional cases is, in my opinion, a complete reversal of the rule so strongly affirmed.

It is said that *Clough* and *Mulholland* were exceptional in that disclosure was ordered because the security of the state required it. But I do not think that these cases can be disposed of in this way. The tribunal certified merely that the questions were relevant and the two cases based their decision on relevancy. So too with *McGuinness*. Considerations as to security arose, if at all, with reference to the court's ultimate discretion. That the court has such a discretion I accept and I shall consider it in due course.

The only support for reversal of this rule is to be found, at least by implication, in some passages in the judgments of the Court of Appeal in this present case. But these must be read in the light of their decision, on the whole matter, that disclosure should be ordered. I do not think that Lord Denning MR should be understood as departing from his judgment in *Mulholland* and from every reported case. Such a reversal would place journalists (how defined?) in a favoured and unique position as compared with priest-confessors, doctors, bankers and other recipients of confidential information and would assimilate them to the police in relation to informers. I can find nothing to encourage such a departure even with the qualifications sought to be introduced to the general principle asserted.

Lord Denning MR's judgment in *Mulholland* makes two further points. First, that it is not for the media alone to be the judges of the public interest. That is the task of the courts. Second, the qualification is made, and strongly stated by Lord Denning MR, that disclosure must be necessary to enable justice to be done. The same point is made by Dixon J (63 CLR 73 at 102–103). The existing position in law is therefore, in my view, not open to doubt. Indeed I am surprised that it should be thought open to question at this time.

Then as to procedure. The present proceedings, now that all other claims against Granada have been disposed of, are simply for an order that Granada disclose the identity of the person who handed over the documents. This form of action is based on the ancient bill of discovery in equity which has been given new life by the decision of this House in *Norwich Pharmacal Co v Customs and Excise Comrs* [1973] 2 All ER 943, [1974] AC 133, since followed in a number of cases (eg *RCA Corpn v Reddingtons Rare Records* [1975] 1 All ER 38, [1974] 1 WLR 1445 and *Loose v Williamson* [1978] 3 All ER 89, [1978] 1 WLR 639).

That case had itself followed other decisions of which the most important, subsequent to the Supreme Court of Judicature Act 1873, was *Orr v Diaper* (1876) 4 Ch D 92. In that, and in earlier cases, the plaintiff seeking discovery had a cause of action against the immediate defendant, and wished to obtain the name of a third party with a view either to joining him in the proceedings or to bringing a separate action. In the *Norwich Pharmacal* case it was held that the remedy extended to a case where the plaintiff had no direct cause of action against the immediate defendant. Here, of course, he has.

Their Lordships, after an extensive review of previous authorities, expressed the principle in very general terms (see [1973] 2 All ER 943 at 948, [1974] AC 133 at 175 per Lord Reid):

'... if through no fault of his own a person gets mixed up in the tortious acts of others so as to facilitate their wrongdoing he may incur no personal liability but he comes under a duty to assist the person ... wronged by ... disclosing the identity of the wrongdoers.'

The words 'through no fault of his own' relate of course to that actual case; the present is a fortiori. So on the face of it the plaintiffs are entitled to the remedy.

But leading counsel for Granada argued that the remedy of, in effect, a bill of discovery ought not to be applied to a case such as the present. His grounds were, I think, as follows. Historically there is no case of such an action having been brought against a newspaper, or in a breach of confidence case. Yet, in the eighteenth and nineteenth centuries many opportunities must have arisen for doing so, if the action lay. The press was, then as now, eager to publish any information, the more sensational the better, which it had obtained from confidential sources, and, then as now, breaches of confidence or leaks were of common occurrence. The failure or abstinence to invoke such proceedings must, it is said, be taken to reflect an opinio juris that no such proceedings could be brought. That they could not be brought is supported by some positive indications, in decided cases and in statutes.

First, in the well-known case of *Abernethy v Hutchinson* (1825) 1 H & Tw 28 at 34, 37, 47 ER 1313 at 1315, 1316, concerned with the unauthorised publication of notes of a surgeon's lectures, Lord Eldon LC is reported as saying that he had no right to require the defendants (the publishers) to inform how they had acquired the material. Lord Eldon LC must, of course, have been well aware of the existence and scope of a bill of discovery and if, while knowing of its existence, he thought that it was limited to certain cases, or that it did not apply to certain cases, he would surely have said so. It seems more reasonable to attribute what he said to the absence of any such bill from the proceedings before him. There would indeed have been little interest for Mr Abernethy in suing one of his pupils; what he was concerned with was to prevent the publication of the lectures.

Then, in the equally well-known case of *Prince Albert v Strange* (1849) 1 H & Tw 1, 47 ER 1302, another case of breach of confidence, there was no consideration of the possibility of a bill of discovery. One would not expect there to be. The whole question was as to the Prince's right to restrain publication of unpublished etchings and of a catalogue which listed some made by Queen Victoria. It was clear enough that the etchings had either been surreptitiously taken from the private apartments, or obtained from one Brown. No further investigation of the precise means of abstraction was called for or would have served any purpose.

Second, in support of the proposition that a bill of discovery was never thought to be available against a newspaper, leading counsel for Granada relied on the Stamp Duties on Newspapers Act 1836 (re-enacted by the Newspapers, Printers and Reading Rooms Repeal Act 1869). This specifically enabled a bill of discovery to be filed in order to discover the name of the printer, publisher or proprietor of a newspaper. The fact that specific legislation was thought necessary for this purpose demonstrated, he said, that the general remedy was not available. The wording of the enactment is, however, in my opinion against him. The relevant section (s 19) starts with the words 'If any person shall file any bill in any court for the discovery of the name etc' and goes on to provide that the bill shall not be demurrable and that the defendant shall be compellable to answer. This, to my mind, supports rather than negatives the possibility of filing a bill of discovery against a newspaper, and suggests that the purpose was to remove the privilege against self-incrimination. I think that this is confirmed by the judgment of Du Parcq J in *Hillman's Airways Ltd v SA d'Editions Aéronautiques Internationales* [1934] 2 KB 356 at 359.

Third, leading counsel for Granada relied on the so-called 'newspaper rule' which protects newspapers, and by analogy broadcasting companies (see *Broadcasting Corpn of New Zealand v Alex Harvey Industries* [1980] 1 NZLR 163 referred to below), against being compelled to disclose their sources through interrogatories. Much reliance was placed on this rule as showing that newspapers have, in the law, been treated as a special case. I had prepared an examination in detail of this 'rule' and of the authorities that related to it; since doing so I have had the benefit of reading a draft of the speech prepared by my noble and learned friend, Lord Fraser. I am entirely content to accept his argument and to express agreement with his conclusion that the rule is of no help to us here. This is not an action for libel or slander; it is based on breach of confidence. The argument that a plaintiff by proceeding to trial against the defaming newspaper is likely to get all the relief he needs, and therefore does not need to sue the source, cannot be transferred to breach of confidence cases. The interest in fact works strongly the other way. The claim against the newspaper may be of little value (it is so here) whereas the weightier claim by far may be against the employee. And if the test is to see whether, at the trial, the plaintiff has got, against the newspaper, all that he may reasonably require and, only if he has not, to force disclosure so that he may sue the source, this test is certainly satisfied. Any proceedings against Granada have in effect been terminated; the motion has been treated as the trial of the action. Little enough has been gained: a partial return of the documents and some costs. There is nothing more to be obtained against

Granada. But BSC still have a real unsatisfied claim against the source, to deprive them of which would require justification.

In the end, although many of the supporting points made by counsel for Granada can be, as I think, answered, the case against use of the *Norwich Pharmacal* procedure still seems to be formidable. Though perhaps rather technical and procedural, it still appeared to me to be the strongest weapon in Granada's armoury. But in the end I am not persuaded that we ought to deny BSC their remedy. The cases are indecisive and only support an argument a silentio; the statute seems to have been passed for a different purpose. Abstinence from using this weapon hitherto can be explained by the fact that it is only exceptionally that the aggrieved person would have, and could demonstrate, a real interest in suing the source. If the present is such a case (and I think it is), it is to that extent exceptional, and decision on it would not open floodgates to actions against newspapers, still less support any general argument that the confidence existing between journalists and their sources is something which the courts will not respect, still less stifle investigation. To succeed in proceedings aimed at compelling disclosure the plaintiff will always have to satisfy the court that he has a real grievance, even after suing the newspaper, which, in the interest of justice, he ought to be allowed to pursue, and that this ought, in the particular case, to outweigh whatever public interest there may be in preserving the confidence. It is possible that, if the plaintiff succeeds here, fewer 'leaks' will occur, though that must be speculation. But I do not think that judicially we are able to place a value on this. 'Leaks' may vary all the way from mere gossip or scandal to matters of national or international importance. A general proposition that leaks should be encouraged, or at least not discouraged, cannot be made without weighing the detriments in loss of mutual confidence and co-operation which they involve. The public interest involved in individual leaks can be taken account of and weighed by the court in deciding whether to grant the remedy in a particular case.

There remains one further argument, again of a technical character. It is said that the relief, being in the nature of discovery, can only be granted in aid of some existing proceedings, or at the most in aid of intended proceedings. This is supported by the admirably brief authority of *Cardale v Watkins* (1820) 5 Madd 18, 56 ER 801. But there may be a middle ground between the 'mere gratification of curiosity' which is discountenanced and 'in aid of some other proceeding either pending or intended' which is permitted. Here it is claimed that BSC desire to known the identity of the source, not for any actual proceedings (there are and could be none until a name is disclosed), nor for any intended proceedings; their purpose it is said is only to be able to dismiss the employee and/or to deprive him of his pension. Now I would be prepared if necessary to hold that, given a cause of action, an intention to seek redress, by court action or otherwise, would be enough, and there is support fot this: see *Norwich Pharmacal* [1973] 2 All ER 943 at 960, [1974] AC 133 at 188 per Viscount Dilhorne and *Post v Toledo, Cincinnati and St Louis Railroad Co* (1887) 11 NE Rep 540. But in any event I find that this argument fails on the facts. Clearly BSC had a cause of action against the source. They cannot identify it unless Granada reveal the name. Their representative stated on affidavit that BSC wished to prevent further disclosures. This might involve proceedings for an injunction. BSC have been put to expense by reasons of the source's tortious action. They have not renounced any intention to proceed against him for damages; the suggestion that their only intention was to dismiss him is an assertion of Granada and nothing more. The conditions for the granting of the remedy therefore exist.

I come then to the final and critical point. The remedy (being equitable) is discretionary. Although, as I have said, the media, and journalists, have no immunity, it remains true that there may be an element of public interest in protecting the revelation of the source. This appears from the speeches in *Norwich Pharmacal* (see per Lord Reid, Lord Morris, Viscount Dilhorne and Lord Cross [1973] 2 All ER 943 at 948–949, 954, 960, 969, [1974] AC 133 at 175, 182, 188, 199), and from the judgments of the New Zealand Court of Appeal on the 'newspaper rule' (see *Broadcasting Corpn of New Zealand v Alex Harvey Industries Ltd* [1980] 1 NZLR 163). The court ought not to compel confidences bona fide given to be breached unless necessary in the interests of justice (see *Science Research Council v Nassé* [1979] 3 All ER 673, [1980] AC 1028). There is a public interest in the free flow of information, the strength of which will vary from case to case. In some cases it may be very weak; in others it may be very strong. The court must take this into account. How ought the discretion which the court undoubtedly has to be exercised in this case? Sir Robert Megarry V-C considered this and exercised it in favour of BSC. I would, for myself, give somewhat greater weight to the public interest element involved in preserving, qua the relevant information, the confidence under which it was obtained than he did. But I think that even so the balance was strongly in BSC's favour. They suffered a grievous wrong, in which Granada themselves became involved, not innocently, but with active participation. To confine BSC to its remedy against Granada and to deny them the opportunity of a remedy against the source would be a significant denial of justice. Granada had, on their side, and I recognise this, the public interest that people should be informed about the steel strike, of the attitude of BSC, and perhaps that of the government towards settling the strike. But there is no 'iniquity' here, no misconduct to be revealed. The courts, to revert to Lord Denning MR's formulation in *Mulholland*, had to form their opinion whether the strong public interest in favour of doing justice and against denying it was outweighed by the perfectly real considerations that Granada put forward. I have reached the conclusion that it was not.

Finally, as to the risk of self-incrimination, I agree with the courts below in rejecting this argument. I understand that others of your Lordships will expand on the point, but with all respect to counsel's well-developed argument, I shall simply express my agreement with the judgment of Templeman LJ on this point.

For these reasons I was in favour of dismissing the appeal.

VISCOUNT DILHORNE[1]. My Lords, Mr Boulton, the head of current affairs at Granada Television, in his affidavit of 10th March 1980 stated that a few days before the date on which it had been decided to televise a 'World in Action' programme on the steel industry, someone delivered to Granada documents which were the property of British Steel Corpn ('BSC'). This, he swore, was done without any prior agreement and not as the result of any solicitation on the part of Granada. Their unexpected receipt must have come as manna from heaven to the producer of the programme which was then built around them and was called 'The Steel Papers'.

Granada promised the donor of the documents that no step would be taken that might reveal or risk the disclosure of his identity. They must have known that he had no right to give them the papers and that they had no right to use them. There were some 250 documents, most, if not all, of which were highly confidential. Some had the word 'secret' stamped on them in large letters.

After their receipt on 28th January 1980 Mr Boulton says that he went through them and decided 'that there were a number of important points arising from them which were of considerable public interest'. It is not, of course, the case that publication of material however interesting to the public is necessarily in the public interest.

Five days after their receipt, during the night of Sunday 3rd February the producer of the programme spoke to Mr Melvin of BSC on the telephone and gave him a list of 27 documents of BSC's which it was proposed to use in the broadcast which was to take place the following evening. This was the first intimation that BSC had that documents of theirs were in the possession of Granada. It was not until some time later that BSC discovered that Granada had some 250 documents of theirs. The next day, 4th February, BSC received from Granada an outline of the contents of the World in Action programme it was proposed to televise that evening. That outline included 'details of BSC internal papers of which copies have been passed to us [Granada] in the past few days, and to which the programme will refer'.

---

1   His Lordship's opinion was completed before his death on 7th September 1980

We were shown what was broadcast. On a table a number of documents marked 'secret' were displayed and selected extracts from some of them were shown. The documents did not reveal, and the contrary has not been suggested, the commission of any crime or any iniquity on the part of BSC. At most they show mismanagement, that it was wrong to put the whole blame for the state of the industry on low productivity on the part of the workers and that it was not true that there had been no government intervention.

After the broadcast BSC demanded a number of undertakings from Granada. These were not forthcoming and on 6th February BSC issued a writ claiming, inter alia, delivery up to them of their documents held by Granada. About 250 were then delivered up. Many of them had been mutilated by cutting off anything on them which might have led to the identification of the person who gave them to Granada. It was not suggested that Granada had any right to do this.

In March 1980 the writ was amended to include a claim for an order that Granada should disclose the names of those who supplied the documents to them. On 2nd April Sir Robert Megarry V-C made such an order. Granada appealed to the Court of Appeal without success and from there to this House.

We were asked to give and we gave a speedy hearing to the appeal. At the conclusion of the argument we were pressed to give our decision without delay and we have done so. We have now to state our reasons for our decision.

I think that I should begin by emphasising that this case, despite the resounding rhetoric so liberally employed since our decision was announced, does not affect the freedom of the press. That freedom, the exercise of which is, of course, subject to the rule of law and abuse of which may be held to be wrongful and even criminal, eg the publication of an obscene libel, cannot be in any way affected by our decision. What is said is that ordering the disclosure by Granada of the name of the person who gave them the documents will deter others from 'leaking' information to the press through fear that their names may be disclosed, and that there is a public interest in the free flow of information to the press which will be restricted, if not stopped, if the identity of the donor of the documents is disclosed. This public interest in the free flow of information involves the conclusion that there is a public interest in the leakage of confidential information to the press. My Lords, it must not be forgotten that there is a well-recognised public interest in the preservation of privacy and confidentiality. If there be a public interest in the free flow of information and the continuance of leaks to the press, then it will not infrequently be the case that there will be a conflict of public interests.

Granada have not asserted that they had any right to use BSC's confidential documents. They do not dispute that, if BSC had sought an injunction to restrain them from using the documents in their programme, they would have had no answer to that claim. Nor have they sought to justify the conduct of the person who gave them the documents. All that Mr Boulton has had to say about that is that the individual concerned, whose identity we were told Mr Boulton did not know, 'apparently gave them out of a keen sense of indignation about the dealings between BSC and the government before and during the strike'. If that was his reason, it explains but does not justify his conduct. There are times when a breach of confidence by an employee is and can be justified, as, for instance, when it reveals some iniquity or crime, but it was not suggested that it could be in this case.

Granada do not dispute that BSC have suffered a wrong at the hands of the donor of the documents and at their hands but they say that they cannot be compelled to give his name. If this was right, it would mean that BSC would be left without a remedy for the wrong inflicted on them. They said they could not themselves trace him and, until he is identified, they may still be employing an untrustworthy and disloyal employee and suspicion will continue to attach to those other employees who in the course of their duty saw these confidential papers.

Granada based their refusal to disclose the name on two grounds. First, they contended that newspapers and broadcasting companies, the 'media', are in a privileged position under the law of England and cannot lawfully be ordered to state the source of any information that comes into their possession. Second, they say that it is a well-recognised and established rule of law that a man cannot be compelled to incriminate himself and that if they gave the name of the man who gave them the documents it would tend to incriminate them.

I propose to consider this second contention first.

In *Re Westinghouse Electric Corpn Uranium Contract Litigation MDL Docket No 235 (No 2)* [1977] 3 All ER 717 at 721, [1978] AC 547 at 574 Lord Denning MR in the Court of Appeal said:

'No one is bound to furnish evidence against himself. It [the common law] says: "If a witness claims the protection of the court, on the ground that the answer would tend to incriminate himself and there appears reasonable ground to believe that it would do so, he is not compellable to answer": see *R v Edmund Garbett* (1847) 1 Den 236 at 257–258 decided by nine judges after two arguments.'

Lord Denning MR went on to say that if the court thinks that he has no reasonable ground for that belief it will overrule that objection and compel him to answer, but if it appears that a witness is at risk of furnishing evidence against himself if he answers 'then "great latitude should be allowed to him in judging for himself the effect of any particular question"' (see *R v Boyes* (1861) 1 B & S 311 at 330, 121 ER 730 at 738). He went on to say that there must be a real and appreciable risk of proceedings being taken against him.

With these observations, I expressed my agreement (see [1978] 1 All ER 434 at 457, [1978] AC 547 at 627), and the rule applies to a company just as it does to an individual (see *Triplex Safety Glass Co Ltd v Lancegaye Safety Glass (1934) Ltd* [1939] 2 All ER 613, [1939] 2 KB 395).

Counsel for Granada submitted that there was a real and appreciable risk of Granada being prosecuted for two offences, handling stolen goods, contrary to s 22 of the Theft Act 1968, and conspiracy to defraud by infringing BSC's copyright in the documents. He laid most stress on the possibility of a prosecution for handling. For such a prosecution to succeed, it would have to be proved that Granada dishonestly received the documents knowing them to have been stolen and that involves proof that the person who gave them to Granada was a thief, that is to say, had dishonestly appropriated property of BSC with the intention of permanently depriving BSC of it. It was not suggested that the person who took the documents had any right to do so, and prima facie in taking them he acted dishonestly. It was not suggested that they were merely loaned to Granada, and it may well be that a prima facie case of theft might be established. Granada must have known that the giver of these confidential documents had no right to dispose of them by handing them to Granada and that they had no right to use them. Did they dishonestly receive them? Mr Boulton in his affidavit swore that Granada were 'firmly of the view that [they] received the documents in circumstances not involving any dishonesty or criminal conduct'. Despite this assertion I am prepared to accept Granada's counsel's submission that there was a real and appreciable risk of Granada being prosecuted for handling stolen goods.

If it be the case that there was such a risk, would the disclosure of the name of the supplier render whatever case there might be against Granada any stronger? I do not see that it could and so I conclude that disclosure of the name would not tend to incriminate Granada of this offence.

The charge of conspiracy to defraud would presumably involve proof of an agreement between the supplier of the documents and Granada that the copyright in them should be infringed by their use on television. Though they must have been given with the intention that Granada should make some use of them, I can see difficulty in establishing any agreement that they should be used in that way. But if there was a real and appreciable risk of prosecution for this offence, how is the case strengthened by the disclosure of the supplier's identity? I do not see that it can be.

In my view Granada's claim that disclosure of the name would tend to incriminate them should be rejected.

I now turn to the other ground advanced by Granada.

The contention that the media cannot be required to disclose the source of information it has received was based on the long established rule, conveniently called 'the newspaper rule' that in libel actions against newspapers interrogatories directed to discovering the source of information are not permitted. In *Adam v Fisher* (1914) 30 TLR 288 Buckley LJ said that it seemed to him that two answers might be given to the question why in this respect newspapers were treated differently from others. One was that it might be assumed that the object of such interrogatories was to get the name of the informant in order to sue him, and that was improper, and the other was that disclosure of the informant's identity was not in the public interest. He said that in *Plymouth Mutual Co-operative Society and Industrial Society Ltd v Traders' Publishing Association* [1906] 1 KB 403 Vaughan Williams LJ seemed to have thought that the privilege of not having to answer such interrogatories might be raised in matters interesting to a number of the public. In *Lyle-Samuel v Odhams Ltd* [1920] 1 KB 135 at 141, [1918–19] All ER Rep 779 at 782 Bankes LJ referred to these observations of Buckley LJ and said that it was not necessary to discuss the rule or the wisdom of it for it was well established. While he accepted its existence, Scrutton LJ clearly did not like it.

Implementing a recommendation of the Porter Committee on the Law of Defamation in 1948 (Cmd 7536), RSC Ord 31, r 1A (now RSC Ord 82, r6) was made forbidding interrogatories as to a defendant's sources of information or grounds of belief in all actions for libel and slander where fair comment or publication on a privileged occasion was pleaded. The committee thought that such interrogatories added considerably to the cost of litigation, imposed considerable hardship on a defendant and were seldom of any practical value.

Whether the newspaper rule originated for those reasons and not on grounds of public interest, it is not necessary to consider. What is important is that that rule only applied to interlocutory proceedings in actions for libel and slander. No case was cited to us in which it had been held that the proprietors and editors of newspapers were not compellable at a trial to disclose the source of their information if the interests of justice required it and in none of the cases cited was any support to be found for the contention that newspapers enjoyed such a privileged position.

The claim to such a privilege seems first to have been advanced by the editor of The Times before the Parnell Commission. Hannen P who was a member of the commission said that there was no such privilege. In Australia the editor of a newspaper called to give evidence before a Royal Commission claimed that he could not be compelled to disclose the source of information confidentially obtained. He asserted that he would not be compellable to do so at the trial of an action. The High Court of Australia held that no privilege attached to proprietors of newspapers, editors and writers which entitled them to refuse to disclose at a trial their sources of information (see *McGuinness v Attorney General of Victoria* (1940) 63 CLR 73). In an illuminating judgment, which is so relevant to the present case that I propose to quote from it at some length, Dixon J said (at 102–103):

'No one doubts that editors and journalists are at times made the repositories of special confidences which, from motives of interest as well as of honour, they would preserve from public disclosure, if it were possible. But the law was faced at a comparatively early stage of the growth of the rules of evidence with the question how to resolve the inevitable conflict between the necessity of discovering the truth in the interests of justice on the one hand and on the other the obligation of secrecy or confidence which an individual called upon to testify may in good faith have undertaken to a party or other person. Except in a few relations where paramount considerations of general policy appeared to require that there should be a special privilege, such as husband and wife, attorney and client . . . an inflexible rule was

established that no obligation of honour, no duties of non-disclosure arising from
the nature of a pursuit or calling, could stand in the way of the imperative necessity
of revealing the truth in the witness box. Claims have been made from time to
time for the protection of confidences to trustees, agents, bankers, and clerks,
amongst others, and they have all been rejected.'

He went on to say (at 104–105):

'. . . although all authority is against the existence of any rule of evidence under
which an editor or journalist is protected when called as a witness on the trial of an
action from the necessity of deposing to the source of the information contained in
his publication or to statements made in confidence to him in the exercise of his
calling, yet a special exception is made in favour of publishers, proprietors and
editors of newspapers as defendants in actions of libel from the general rule that
discovery by affidavit of documents and answers to interrogatories must be made of
all relevant matters. By a long line of cases a practice is recognized of refusing to
compel such a defendant to disclose the name of the writer of an article complained
of as a libel or of the sources of information he has relied upon . . . The cases are
collected in *Lyle-Samuel* v. *Odhams Ltd* ([1920] 1 KB 135, [1918–19] All ER Rep 779)
and *South Suburban Co-operative Society Ltd* v. *Orum* ([1937] 3 All ER 133, [1937] 2 KB
690) which are the latest authorities upon the application of the rule. The appellant
stands upon these decisions and says that they disclose a development which, in
reason and logic, should not stop at discovery, but should supply a general
justification for withholding the names of contributors and the sources of
information at all stages of any legal proceeding. The answer is that it is not a rule
of evidence but a practice of refusing in an action of libel against the publisher, &c.,
of a newspaper to compel discovery of the name of his informants. It "rests not on
a principle of privilege but on the limitations of discovery", to quote the comment
of Professor *Wigmore*, who expresses himself somewhat strongly against the
pretensions to a privilege on the part of journalists (*Treatise on Evidence* (2nd Edn, vol
5, § 2286, n 7)). In my opinion the existence of the practice and the reasons on
which it is based can form no ground for holding that a lawful excuse existed for the
appellant's refusal to answer as to his sources of information. Lawful excuse means
a reason or excuse recognized by law as sufficient justification for a failure or refusal
to produce documents or answer questions.'

No such claim to privilege was advanced before the Bank Rate Tribunal though, if my
recollection is correct, it might well have been. Before the Vassall Tribunal it was, and
three journalists having refused to disclose their sources were proceeded against for
contempt. Two appealed to the Court of Appeal and one argument then put forward as
summarised by Lord Denning MR in *Attorney General v Mulholland* [1963] 1 All ER 767
at 770–771, [1963] 2 QB 477 at 489–490 was similar to that advanced in this case. Lord
Denning MR said:

'Then it is said . . . that, however relevant these questions were and however
proper to be answered for the purpose of the inquiry, a journalist has a privilege by
law entitling him to refuse to give his sources of information. The journalist puts
forward as his justification the pursuit of truth. It is in the public interest, he says,
that he should obtain information in confidence and publish it to the world at large,
for, by so doing he brings to the public notice that which they should know. He can
expose wrongdoing and neglect of duty which would otherwise go unremedied.
He cannot get this information, he says, unless he keeps the source of it secret. The
mouths of his informants will be closed to him if it is known that their identity will
be disclosed. So he claims to be entitled to publish all his information without ever
being under any obligation, even when directed by the court or a judge, to disclose
whence he got it. It seems to me that the journalists put the matter much too
high. The only profession that I know which is given a privilege from disclosing
information to a court of law is the legal profession, and then it is not the privilege

of the lawyer but of his client. Take the clergyman, the banker or the medical man. None of these is entitled to refuse to answer when directed to by a judge. Let me not be mistaken. The judge will respect the confidences which each member of these honourable professions receives in the course of it, and will not direct him to answer unless not only it is relevant but also it is a proper and, indeed, necessary question in the course of justice to be put and answered . . . If the judge determines that the journalist must answer, then no privilege will avail him to refuse.'

In that case the claim to privilege was rejected as it was by Lord Parker CJ in *Attorney General v Clough* [1963] 1 All ER 420, [1963] 1 QB 773 in relation to the third journalist. In the light of these authorities the legal position can, I think, be summarised as follows. Save in respect of the administration of interrogatories in libel and slander actions, newspapers have never been held to enjoy the privilege of not being compellable to disclose the sources of their information. Every time that that claim has been put forward it has been rejected. Since 1949 newspapers no longer receive any special treatment with regard to interrogatories.

The present action is in substance an action for discovery. Although the question which has now to be decided came before Sir Robert Megarry V-C on an interlocutory motion, no other relief than an order for the disclosure of the identity of Granada's informants is now sought.

If it is the case, as in my view it is, that in law newspapers are not entitled to any privilege at a trial, before a Royal Commission or before a tribunal set up under the Tribunals of Inquiry (Evidence) Act 1921 with regard to the disclosure of the names of informants, I can find no satisfactory basis for concluding that they are entitled to any exceptional treatment in respect of an action for discovery. If an order could properly be made against an individual unconnected with the media for the disclosure of the donor's identity if the documents had been given to him, then in my opinion such an order can properly be made against Granada. Conversely if no such order could be made against such an individual, it cannot be made against Granada.

In *Norwich Pharmacal Co v Customs and Excise Comrs* [1973] 2 All ER 943, [1974] AC 133 the Customs and Excise knew from documents lodged with them who were the importers of a substance called furazolidone. Norwich Pharmacal were the owners of the patent relating to that chemical. None of the importations of it were licensed by Norwich Pharmacal and in relation to the majority, if not all, of them the importations constituted an infringement of their patent. Unless Norwich Pharmacal could secure disclosure by the Customs and Excise of the identity of the importers, they could not take any steps to protect their patent for, unless they obtained that information from the Customs and Excise, they could not identify the wrongdoers. They started proceedings against the Customs and Excise and, though other claims were indorsed on the writ, it was agreed at the trial before Graham J that the proceedings could be treated as an action for discovery of the identity of the importers.

In this House three questions had to be decided. First, could the respondents, the Customs and Excise, who were not themselves wrongdoers, be ordered to disclose the names of the importers who, the validity of the patent being admitted, were wrongdoers; second, in the exercise of the discretion vested in the court, should they be ordered to do so; and third, were the respondents prohibited from disclosing that information?

The House answered the first two questions in the affirmative and the third in the negative.

While it is not necessary to refer to the cases then considered, I think that the following passages from the speeches can usefully be cited. Lord Reid said ([1973] 2 All ER 943 at 948, [1974] AC 133 at 174):

'So discovery to find the identity of a wrongdoer is available against anyone against whom the plaintiff has a cause of action in relation to the same wrong. It is not available against a person who has no other connection with the wrong than that he was a spectator or has some documents relating to it in his possession. But the respondents are in an intermediate position. Their conduct was entirely innocent; it was in execution of their statutory duty. But without certain action on their part the infringements could never have been committed. Does this involvement in the matter make a difference?'

He thought that the observations of Lord Romilly MR and Lord Hatherley LC in *Upmann v Elkan* (1871) LR 12 Eq 140 at 145, LR 7 Ch App 130 at 133 pointed to—

'a very reasonable principle that if through no fault of his own a person gets mixed up in the tortious acts of others so as to facilitate their wrongdoing he may incur no personal liability but he comes under a duty to assist the person who has been wronged by giving him full information and disclosing the identity of the wrongdoers.'

Lord Morris said ([1973] 2 All ER 943 at 951, [1974] AC 133 at 178):

'It is not suggested that in ordinary circumstances a court would require someone to impart to another some information which he may happen to have and which the latter would wish to have for the purpose of bringing some proceedings. At the very least the person possessing the information would have to have become actually involved (or actively concerned) in some transactions or arrangements as a result of which he has acquired the information.'

He posed the question ([1973] 2 All ER 943 at 952, [1974] AC 133 at 179) whether there was any reason in that case—

'why the court, in the interests of justice, and in the absence of any real doubt that certain wrongdoers are enjoying a quite fortuitous protection, should not authorise and require the [commissioners] to disclose the names,'

and he cited ([1973] 2 All ER 943 at 953, [1974] AC 133 at 180–181) with approval the words of Hall V-C in *Orr v Diaper* (1876) 4 Ch D 92 at 96:

'In this case the Plaintiffs do not know, and cannot discover, who the persons are who have invaded their rights, and who may be said to have abstracted their property. Their proceedings have come to a deadlock, and it would be a denial of justice if means could not be found in this Court to assist the Plaintiffs.'

I said ([1973] 2 All ER 943 at 960, [1974] AC 133 at 188) that it was far too late to challenge the decision in *Orr v Diaper* and that that case decided that discovery can be granted against a person who is not a mere witness to discover, the fact of some wrongdoing being established, who was responsible for it and that it mattered not whether his involvement was innocent and in ignorance of the wrongdoing.

Lord Cross thought that the right to discovery depended on the relation between the defendant to the action for discovery and the persons the disclosure of whose names was sought. He said ([1973] 2 All ER 943 at 968, [1974] AC 133 at 197):

'In cases such as *Upmann v Elkan* and *Orr v Diaper* the relation was that of persons engaged by the tortfeasor to deal with the goods in question and who in the course of doing so unwittingly facilitated the commission of the tort. In my judgment no sensible distinction can be drawn ... between the position of the respondent commissioners and the position of Diaper or Messrs Elkan or St Katherine's Dock Co.'

Lord Kilbrandon too was of the opinion that the commissioners were in such a relation to the importers as to entitle the plaintiffs to demand from them the names of the infringers.

These passages show that the House was unanimous in thinking that an action for discovery would lie against an innocent person involved in the tortious acts of another and that an order could properly be made requiring him to name the wrongdoers.

In the present case the person who took the documents and gave them to Granada was clearly a wrongdoer, if not a thief. Granada can scarcely claim to come within the category of innocent persons for they must have known that the taker of the documents had no right to give them to them and they maintained that they were liable to prosecution. Their relationship to the taker of the documents was in my opinion such as to impose on them the duty to disclose that persons's identity for, we were told and it was not disputed, without such disclosure BSC would have been unable to secure any redress for the wrong they had suffered at the hands of the taker. Sir Robert Megarry V-C was in my opinion right in the interests of justice to exercise his discretion in favour of making the order.

My Lords, we were told more than once of the dire consequences which, it was said, were likely to follow if disclosure was ordered. The sources of information for the media would, it was said, dry up to the great injury to the public interest. These consequences do not appear to have followed from the decisions in 1963 to which I have referred and which established that journalists did not enjoy any privileged position with regard to disclosure of their sources. I find it difficult to accept that those consequences will follow from the decision in this case which follows those decisions.

It is not in every case that a journalist will be ordered to disclose his source. There must have been some wrongdoing in which the journalist has become involved and, where that is established, a judge must be satisfied that the interests of justice require him to exercise his discretion in favour of making such an order.

If in a case such as this, where the taker of the documents had no right to take them, where he was clearly a wrongdoer and where Granada were involved in handling the documents and used them when they had no right to do so, no order for the discovery of the identity of the wrongdoer could be made with the result that BSC could not obtain redress for the wrong they had suffered at the hands of the taker, there would be a denial of justice to BSC and the gap in the law would constitute a charter for wrongdoers such as the taker of the documents in this case.

For these reasons in my opinion the appeal failed.

LORD SALMON. My Lords, a free press is one of the pillars of freedom in this and indeed in any other democratic country. Granada Televison Ltd ('Granada') report news throughout the whole of this country and can properly be regarded as part of the press. A free press reports matters of general public importance, and cannot, in law, be under any obligation, save in exceptional circumstances, to disclose the identity of the persons who supply it with the information appearing in its reports.

It has been accepted for over a hundred years that if this immunity did not exist, the press's sources of information would dry up and the public would be deprived of being informed of many matters of great public importance; this should not be allowed in any free country.

British Steel Corpn ('BSC') are no ordinary industrial undertaking. They have no shareholders; they are a nationalised industry. If they operate at a profit, it benefits the nation. If they operate at a serious loss, it causes serious harm to the nation and may threaten its whole economy. Last year BSC lost £700m and were lent this sum by the nation, interest free. In the present year, BSC considered that they would reduce their loss to £450m; and the nation agreed to lend, interest free, that sum but no more. The nation had also lent BSC £3 billion to provide themselves with the finest machinery and equipment in existence, in order to enable them to equal their foreign competitors. Their chief competitors are in Germany and Japan, whose steel industries produce large profits. BSC had acquired their new machinery and equipment prior to the losses which I have mentioned. It still takes two British workmen to produce the amount of steel which is produced by one workman in West Germany.

It is not surprising that the public should wish, and indeed are morally entitled, to know how it is that BSC are in such a parlous condition. Is it due to bad management, or to government interference, or to the trade unions' actions or to some other reasons?

A man whom I shall call 'the unnamed source of information' and who was thought to be a man in a high executive post in BSC apparently had copies of many of the corporation's confidential documents (reports, memoranda and minutes) including those which were marked 'most secret'. There is no evidence that he stole any of these copies. The probability, in my opinion, is that they were given to him by BSC. There is certainly no evidence that they were not. He selected 250 sheets of these papers and took them to Granada on Monday, 28th January 1980. It seems to me to be obvious that he was convinced that the contents of these papers would (a) reveal the faults of management and other reasons which had put BSC into such an appalling financial position and (b) help to stop the rot.

In my opinion, he considered that it was his public duty to make the contents of those documents available to the public because the immense sums of money which were being lost were being lost by the public. It has certainly never been suggested that what he did was out of malice or that he would have accepted even a penny for what he had done. In my opinion, he believed that his duty to help to reveal the contents of the documents to the public was far greater than his duty to BSC to keep the public in the dark. I certainly do not believe that in these circumstances it is fair to describe him as a traitor.

If an ordinary company had not been nationalised and found itself in a parlous condition similar to that of BSC's, the shareholders would exercise their rights to have a full investigation made and to be informed of all the mistakes which had caused the company to be in such a parlous state. That is why the unnamed source of information was in an entirely different position from that of a company executive. The shareholders have the power to call for the relevant documents and to discover the faults which are causing them to lose their money. In the case of a nationalised industry there are no shareholders, and its losses are borne by the public which does not have anything like the same safeguards as shareholders.

When Granada were brought these copy papers (the originals of which have always been in the possession of BSC) they recognised at once that they were marked 'confidential' or 'secret', and they were asked by and promised the unnamed source of information that his identity would not be revealed.

Granada also considered, rightly in my view, that if any of these papers exposed the faults and mistakes which were causing the immense losses made by BSC, it would be Granada's public duty to disclose the contents of those papers to the public.

Granada had already arranged that a large part of their programme 'The World in Action' which was to be televised throughout this country on Monday, 4th February 1980 at 8.30 p m should be devoted to the BSC's affairs.

On 29th January Granada, by telephone, invited Sir Charles Villiers, the chairman of BSC, to take part in the programme to be televised on 4th February. He accepted. He had not been told of the 250 papers which Granada had received the previous day because Granada had had no time in which to examine those papers.

Granada then made a long and very careful examination of the 250 papers left with them. This examination took up most of the week starting 28th January 1980. It was not until Sunday morning, 3rd February 1980 that Granada had finally selected 27 out of the 250 confidential and secret papers, extracts from which revealed a great deal about the BSC business, the serious faults and mistakes of their management, their low productivity, the strike then still going on, BSC's connection with the government and their failure to staunch the immense losses they were then making.

On Sunday evening there were a number of telephone conversations between BSC and Granada in which Granada told BSC of the details of the 27 documents to be used, and read a complete list of those documents to BSC. There can be no doubt that BSC, who had the originals of these documents, must have known they were all marked 'confidential' or 'secret'.

BSC could have applied, ex parte, on the morning of 4th February for an interim injunction to prohibit those documents from being used by Granada; and that injunction might have been temporarily granted. This does not mean that later, when Granada were heard, the interim injunction would have remained alive.

The chairman of BSC appears to have been satisfied that he could deal effectively with any points that might be made against BSC and himself from the documents; the public might have been alarmed had it discovered that Granada had kept from them the contents of those documents written by BSC about their own business affairs.

We have read the text of the television programme which started at 8.30 p m on 4th February and we have also seen and heard the television programme itself. It stated the alleged serious mistakes of management, low productivity, government interference, the strike, etc, and quotations were made from the confidential papers to which I have referred. In my view, the conduct of the commentator did not deserve any adverse criticism; and this also appears to have been the view of Sir Charles Villiers. Sir Charles Villiers who came into the programme during its last seven minutes seems to me to have acquitted himself quite well and, in my opinion, he certainly was not treated unfairly. He said that the only direction BSC had had from the government was 'that our cash limit is £700m for the current year and £450m for next year, and within that we have to live'. On leaving the studio he was asked by waiting newspaper reporters whether the programme was unfair. To which he replied: 'It was not a totally unfair programme. We got a pretty fair hearing. I did not learn anything I did not already know . . . Most of the programme was accurate, but there are one or two things which were screwed up.'

On 6th February, BSC issued a writ against Granada claiming an injunction that Granada should make no further use of the documents received by them from the unnamed source of information, an order that Granada should give up those documents, and an inquiry as to what damage BSC had suffered by reason of Granada's use of the documents and the alleged infringement of copyright and conversion and detention of BSC's documents.

Following correspondence between the parties' respective solicitors, Granada agreed to submit to the injunction claimed by BSC and to deposit the documents in the joint custody of their own and BSC's solicitors. I would point out that at this stage, BSC had not made any claim against Granada to supply them with the name of whoever it was who had brought the confidential and secret papers to Granada. It may be that this was because BSC had learnt that the law had, for very good reason, made the press immune, save in the rarest circumstances, from having to identify the source from which it had obtained news of great public importance. This is a point to which I shall return later.

I am also inclined to think that BSC recognised that in all the circumstances to which I have referred there was no real chance of any substantial damages being awarded to BSC against Granada or the source; and that all that BSC were really anxious to achieve was to discover the identity of the source of information; and this discovery might be made by obtaining, in their pristine state, the copy documents delivered to Granada by the source, since they would bear some number or mark which would disclose the identity of the source. The demand for the delivery up of these documents in their pristine state would amount, amongst other things, to asking Granada to identify the source. Granada eliminated these numbers or marks from the documents because they recognised that they were immune, certainly at that stage, from identifying the source of the news which was of great public importance. Thereupon BSC amended their claim by demanding that Granada identify the source from which they obtained the confidential documents.

This became and has remained the sole issue between BSC and Granada, because BSC abandoned all their other claims against Granada in the course of the hearing before Sir Robert Megarry V-C. The action therefore became solely an action for discovery. In *McGuinness v Attorney General for Victoria* (1940) 63 CLR 73 at 104 Dixon J said:

'But although all authority is against the existence of any rule of evidence under which an editor or journalist is protected when called as a witness on the trial of an action from the necessity of deposing to the source of the information contained in his publication . . . yet a special exception is made in favour of publishers, proprietors and editors of newspapers as defendants in actions of libel from the general rule that discovery by affidavit of documents and answer to interrogatories must be made of all relevant matters. By a long line of cases a practice is recognized of refusing to compel such a defendant to disclose the name of the writer of an article complained of as a libel or of the sources of information he has relied upon.'

I do not think that when Dixon J referred to the necessity of a witness when giving evidence deposing to the source of the information he meant that there was any such necessity unless the identity of the source was plainly relevant to an issue in the case in question.

I recognise that the long line of cases recited by my noble and learned friend Lord Fraser which laid down 'the newspaper rule' that the press cannot be obliged to disclose its source of information on discovery were all cases of libel. This, I think, is because the vast majority of the litigation in which the press has ever been concerned consists of libel actions. I cannot imagine any reason why the newspaper rule should be confined to libel actions. In the present case, passages about the management of BSC in the papers which Granada quoted on 4th February 1980 are, in my view, clearly defamatory. BSC could have sued for libel to which there might very well have been a defence of justification, so they wisely chose a different form of action as they were entitled to do; and they have now altered it into an action solely for discovery, a very ancient form of action which for a long time has been a rarity. Since, in an action against the press, the press cannot be obliged to identify its source of information on discovery in that action, it would be absurd if the plaintiff could overcome that rule by bringing a separate action for discovery. For the reasons I have indicated I am of the opinion that in an action against the press for discovery the plaintiff cannot and never could obtain, and never has obtained, from the defendant his source of information.

Before leaving this point, I would refer to *Broadcasting Corpn of New Zealand v Alex Harvey Industries Ltd* [1980] 1 NZLR 163. In that case there was a claim based on slander of goods in addition to a claim for defamation, and Woodhouse J said (at 166–167):

> 'Does the newspaper rule apply to the one cause of action as well as the other? The answer is to be found, in my opinion, upon the general purpose of the rule, based as it is on public interest rather than the private purposes of the news media. And I do not think there can be any reason of public policy or of logic or of fairness for drawing a distinction. The rule itself is not really concerned with the form of litigation but with supporting a proper flow of information for use by the news media.'

I agree with Woodhouse J that 'the newspaper rule' is not confined to libel or any other form of action.

Woodhouse J and each of the other two judges in the New Zealand Court of Appeal then went on to disagree with the decision of the Court of Appeal in the present case. I agree with them.

Lord Denning MR very carefully examined the cases in England and in the USA relevant to the question whether ought Granada to disclose their source of information.

Save for *Garland v Torre* (1958) 250 F 2d 545 which in my view is hardly relevant, I agree with those cases (which I need not repeat) and from which Lord Denning MR drew a principle (see p 441, ante) with most of which I also respectfully agree and wish to recite (see p 441, ante):

> 'After studying the cases it seems to me that the courts are reaching towards this principle: the public has a right of access to information which is of public concern and of which the public ought to know. The newspapers are the agents, so to speak, of the public to collect that information and to tell the public of it. In support of this right of access, the newspapers should not in general be compelled to disclose their sources of information. Neither by means of discovery before trial. Nor by

questions or cross-examination at the trial. [I would add 'save in exceptional circumstances'.] Nor by subpoena. The reason is because, if they were compelled to disclose their sources, they would soon be bereft of information which they ought to have. Their sources would dry up. Wrongdoing would not be disclosed. Charlatans would not be exposed. Unfairness would go unremedied. Misdeeds [and I would add 'serious faults and mistakes'] in the corridors of power, in companies or in government departments would never be known. Investigative journalism has proved itself as a valuable adjunct of the freedom of the press . . . It should not be unduly hampered or restricted by the law. Much of the information gathered by the press has been imparted to the informant in confidence. He is guilty of a breach of confidence in telling it to the press. But this is not a reason why his name should be disclosed. Otherwise much information that ought to be made public will never be made known. Likewise with documents. They may infringe copyright. But that is no reason for compelling their disclosure, if by so doing it would mean disclosing the name of the informant. In all these cases the plaintiff has his remedy in damages against the newspaper, or sometimes an injunction, and that should suffice. It may be for libel. It may be for breach of copyright. It may be for infringement of privacy . . . So let the plaintiff sue the newspaper, without getting the name of their informant.'

My Lords, I have no doubt that the words 'the public has a right of access to information which is of public concern and of which the public ought to know' do not embrace any information which may be of interest to the public, but are confined to information which it is in the public interest to make known.

Attorney General v Clough [1963] 1 All ER 420, [1963] 1 QB 773 and *Attorney General v Mulholland* [1963] 1 All ER 767, [1963] 2 QB 477 are the only two cases in which the press has ever been ordered by our courts to name its source of information; and this was in order to protect the security of the state. Lord Radcliffe who was chairman of the tribunal of inquiry stated on behalf of himself and his two colleagues that it was imperative for the safety of the state that the press should disclose the identity of its informants.

These cases, which have nothing to do with discovery, arose out of the Vassall Tribunal of Inquiry in 1962 under the Tribunals of Inquiry (Evidence) Act 1921. The Report of the Royal Commission on Tribunals of Inquiry dated 1st November 1966 (Cmnd 3121) recommended in para 27 that inquiries under the 1921 Act should be confined to 'matters of vital public importance concerning which there is something in the nature of a nation-wide crisis of confidence'. The report, which was later agreed by the government, cited the Vassall Inquiry as being a typical example of such a case. The Attorney General stated, correctly, in the *Clough* case [1963] 1 QB 773 at 780 that this inquiry was set up, amongst other things, 'to deal with the safety and security of the state, the activities of a most dangerous spy, and the conduct of the Ministers of the Crown of officers of Her Majesty's services and of civil servants'. There was a nation-wide crisis of confidence about all these matters. It is certainly not surprising that the courts considered that the man who had informed the journalists of what they had reported in the press would probably be able to give and, if so, ought to have given the tribunal evidence about the matters to which I have referred; and therefore the journalists should have given the tribunal their informant's name.

In the *Mulholland* case [1963] 1 All ER 767 at 769, [1963] 2 QB 477 at 486, Lord Denning MR said:

'It appears that allegations were made in some newspapers which reflected gravely on persons in high places and on naval officers and civil servants in the Admiralty. The articles clearly imported that there had been neglect of duty on their part in not discovering a spy who was in their midst . . . If well founded, the security arrangements at the Admiralty needed complete overhaul and those at fault would have to pay the penalty for their neglect.'

Lord Denning MR went on to say, in effect, that the journalists knew only what they had been told by their informant and that it was therefore essential that they should disclose his name so that he could be called as a witness before the tribunal to enable the tribunal 'to see whether [his evidence] is such as to implicate or exculpate those concerned at the Admiralty' (see [1963] 1 All ER 767 at 770, [1963] 2 QB 477 at 488). Donovan LJ said ([1963] 1 All ER 767 at 772–773, [1963] 2 QB 477 at 492–493):

> 'I add a few words only about the need for some residual discretion in the court of trial in a case where a journalist is asked in the course of the trial for the source of his information . . . In the present case, where the ultimate matter at stake is the safety of the community, I agree that no such consideration as I have mentioned, calling for the exercise of a discretion in favour of the appellants, arises, and that accordingly their appeals fail . . .'

My Lords, I confess, with the greatest respect, that I cannot understand how it can be erroneous to hold that in *Clough* and *Mulholland* the disclosure of the identity of the journalists' informant was ordered because the security of the state required it.

It seems to me that the principles which Lord Denning MR has laid down in the present case and with which I agree and the many authorities which he has cited in support of those principles, if they are as correct as I believe them to be, make it wrong to dismiss this appeal.

Lord Denning MR however states that a newspaper's (and therefore Granada's) immunity to disclose the source of its informants exists only if it acts with a due sense of responsibility. Responsibility in this context is difficult to define. Accordingly, Lord Denning MR said, to show what he meant by irresponsibility (see pp 441–442, ante): '. . . let me give some examples.' He gives three examples. The first two are examples of irresponsibility but they certainly have no resemblance to the present case. The third example is an example of responsibility, which seems to me to be exactly like the present case. Lord Denning MR goes on to say: 'I have been much troubled whether Granada acted with a due sense of responsibility. Many things they did are disturbing. Not so much in the decision to use the information in the public interest, but in the way they went about it.'

If, as I believe, Granada obviously gave the information in the public interest, I cannot think how they went about it could oblige them to disclose their source of information to BSC. I cannot agree with the finding that Granada did not act with a due sense of responsibility. This finding was based on the following supposed facts: (a) Granada 'left it so late to tell BSC', (b) 'they did not give Sir Charles any opportunity to see the script before he got to the studio', (c) 'the conduct of the interview by the commentator was deplorable', and (d) the 'tampering with the papers was disgraceful'.

I have already dealt with these suggestions. I do not think that (a) and (b) are of any real importance; and for the reasons I have already given I do not agree with (c) and (d). It follows that, in my opinion, Granada did nothing to deprive themselves of their immunity to identify the source of the information which they disclosed in the public interest.

I will now deal with the different grounds relied on by the other members of the Court of Appeal to support the findings of Sir Robert Megarry V-C. With very great respect, I consider that those grounds are based on a fallacy, namely that the press's immunity from revealing its sources of information is confined to cases in which the press publishes information that a plaintiff has been 'guilty of crime or fraud or misconduct which ought to be laid bare in the public interest'.

No doubt crime, fraud or misconduct should be laid bare in the public interest; and these, of course, did not occur in BSC. There was however much else, even more important in all the circumstances, which called aloud to be revealed in the public interest. I have already stated the most important of these matters at the beginning of this speech. I should perhaps add that there was also 'example after example of failure to meet targets because of mechanical breakdown and design faults', 'the lateness and inaccuracy of export documentation . . . which must be costing the corporation . . .

almost certainly millions of pounds' and 'errors of estimation up to £200m'. I consider it was the moral duty of Granada to lay all these matters before the public on whose shoulders the losses fell, so that a decision would be taken as to how the mistakes causing the parlous conditions of BSC could be remedied. Since Granada's programme at 8.30 p m on 4th February 1980, no doubt much has been done to put BSC on the road to recovery. We know, for one thing, that an American industrialist of the highest standing is now chairman of BSC in place of Sir Charles Villiers who has retired. True it is that the new chairman is receiving what in our country are considered to be exceptionally large emoluments; that however would hardly matter should he be able to stop the losses of hundreds of millions of pounds which BSC have suffered this year and last, and then to transform these losses into reasonable profits.

I do not agree that BSC have established wrongdoing by their employee (Granada's source of information) followed by wrongdoing on the part of Granada. Nor do I agree that Granada admitted any such things.

BSC relied very strongly on *Norwich Pharmacal Co v Customs and Excise Comrs* [1973] 2 All ER 943, [1974] AC 133 in support of their amendment of the claim demanding the identity of Granada's source of information, ie the person who brought 250 papers to Granada. If, in the *Norwich Pharmacal* case, the Customs had been the press or part of it, I think that that case might have been of help to BSC; it is however plain that the Customs have no similarity to the press and that accordingly the *Norwich Pharmacal* case brings no assistance to BSC.

Pharmacal were the owners of a patent for a chemical compound called furazolidone which is widely used. Thirty consignments of it were imported for sale into the United Kingdom between 1960 and 1970. Pharmacal had not licensed any of the importers of those consignments to sell them in the United Kingdom or anywhere else; and accordingly the importers were tortiously infringing the Pharmacal patent and cheating them. Pharmacal could not identify any of the importers. The Customs however could, since the importers' names and addresses appeared in their records. Unless the Customs gave Pharmacal the names of the importers, Pharmacal would have no means of protecting themselves against the importers in question or of obtaining any redress from the importers for their wrongdoing. Your Lordships decided that—

> 'if through no fault of his own a person gets mixed up in the tortious acts of others so as to facilitate their wrongdoing . . . he comes under a duty to assist the person . . . wronged by . . . disclosing the identity of the wrongdoers'.

(See [1973] 2 All ER 943 at 948, [1974] AC 133 at 175 per Lord Reid.)

The Customs had argued that it would be contrary to public policy or public interest to compel them to pass on to Pharmacal or to the courts the names of the importers. This was because the importers had been compelled by statute to give their names to the Customs, and also because they might cease to give full and candid information to the Customs if their names were to be made known. This was a bad argument but symptomatic of the line normally taken by civil servants in one department to refuse to pass on any information they receive to anyone, even to any other department to which it would be most helpful. For example, the Board of Inland Revenue sometimes discover, for certain, that a taxpayer is most corrupt and has been distributing enormous bribes or has been stealing large sums of money. None of this information is ever passed on to the Director of Public Prosecutions and indeed the bribes are allowed to be treated as tax deductible expenses.

The Customs without any reason for suspecting that the importers were bringing furazolidone into this country for the purpose of cheating Pharmacal allowed them to do so. The Customs by giving Pharmacal the names of the importers could not be doing anything which could prejudice themselves or the public. The *Norwich Pharmacal* case, in my view, has no relevance to the present appeal.

Templeman LJ after reviewing all the authorities cited to the Court of Appeal, *other* than *Attorney-General v Clough* and *Attorney-General v Mulholland* says (see p 445, ante):

'In my judgment these authorities support the submission of counsel for Granada that there is a public interest in upholding the claim of the media to immunity from disclosing their sources of information, but sound a word of warning as to the ground for claiming and granting immunity.'

I agree with him and need not weary your Lordships by reciting any of those authorities. Templeman LJ then goes on to deal with *Attorney General v Clough* and *Attorney General v Mulholland*. He does so however without referring to the fact that in those cases the courts refused the press immunity from disclosing their sources chiefly on the ground that the disclosure of those sources was necessary to protect the security of the nation; nor did he notice that those were the only two cases in which our courts have ever held that the press should disclose its sources. I agree with Watkins LJ when he said (see p 448, ante): 'It is I believe well founded on ample legal authority that newspapers and television . . . are in principle immune from disclosing their confidential sources of information'; but I cannot agree with the grounds on which he dismissed the appeal.

Templeman LJ disagrees with the principle which I have already recited and which in my view has been accepted by the courts and acted on for over a hundred years. I consider this principle to be the very basis of the freedom of the press and accordingly a bastion of the freedom of man.

We do not know whether the man who considered it was his duty to take the papers to Granada did so on his own or whether he represented other members of the higher executive. I should think there was probably considerable disagreement amongst the higher executive about what BSC were to do to rescue their life. I also think that it is unlikely that there was only one who was determined that justice demanded that the public should be informed of the disastrous state of BSC's business as revealed in the papers given to Granada. Assuming however, that the man who gave those papers to Granada was doing so on his own and in breach of confidence, for the reasons I have already stated this would not have destroyed Granada's immunity from revealing his name to BSC or anyone else.

Counsel for BSC relied strongly on the speech of Lord Wilberforce in *Science Research Council v Nassé, BL Cars Ltd (formerly Leyland Cars) v Vyas* [1979] 3 All ER 673 at 681, [1980] AC 1028 at 1067. Templeman and Watkins LJJ accepted that that authority strongly supported counsel's very able arguments on behalf of BSC. I do not agree. The *Nassé* and *Vyas* cases are certainly of great importance. They concerned certain recent statutes which had given redress to anyone who suffered unlawful discrimination on account of sex, race or trade union activities. They raised the question: what right has an employee, complaining of unlawful discrimination, to obtain an order against his employer for the production of documents which contain confidential information? These documents were mostly reports of the record, ability and experience of complainants and of their competitors for promotion or a change of job. A perusal of those documents might well in many cases reveal important evidence whether there had or had not been discrimination. There were five speeches by your Lordships, each of them allowing the appeal. I venture to quote a short passage in my speech ([1979] 3 All ER 673 at 684, [1980] AC 1028 at 1071) which I do not think was challenged in any of the other speeches:

'If the tribunal is satisfied that it is necessary to order certain documents to be disclosed and inspected in order fairly to dispose of the proceedings, then, in my opinion, the law requires that such an order should be made; and the fact that the documents are confidential is irrelevant. The law has always recognised that it is of the greatest importance from the point of view of public policy that proceedings in the courts or before the tribunals shall be fairly disposed of. This, no doubt, is why the law has never accorded privilege against discovery and inspection of confidental documents which are necessary for fairly disposing of the proceedings.'

With respect, I do not think that the *Nassé* or *Vyas* cases had anything to do with the case we are now considering. Those cases, like the *Norwich Pharmacal* case, had not the slightest link with this or any other case concerning the immunity of the press to reveal its sources of information save in the exceptionally rare cases to which I have referred. This immunity has nothing to do with confidentiality, whether between the press and the source, or the source and his employer. It rests solely on the authorities to which I have referred and the principle of justice that the public shall not be unreasonably deprived by a free press of information of great public importance.

It was argued on behalf of Granada that BSC acquiesced in the use by Granada of the BSC documents. Sir Charles Villiers attended the television programme knowing that the BSC documents were to be used. He was present when they were used and then made no complaint of their use. Neither did he, after the conclusion of the programme, make any complaint of their use when he spoke to a number of the reporters who were asking him if the programme had been fair, to which he made the replies which I have already mentioned. I think that this could be regarded as acquiescence, but I do not attach very much importance to it.

I attach still less importance to the defence based on self-incrimination. Indeed, I am surprised that it was argued on behalf of Granada.

My Lords, it is, I imagine, apparent from what I have said that I have the misfortune to disagree with your Lordships. The immunity of the press to reveal its sources of information save in exceptional circumstances is in the public interest, and has been so accepted by the courts for so long that I consider it is wrong now to sweep this immunity away. The press has been deprived of this immunity only twice, namely in the *Clough* and *Mulholland* cases. And the exceptional circumstances in each of those cases were that the security of the nation required that the press's source of information must be revealed. Certainly no such circumstances appear in the present case. I do not say that national security will necessarily always be the only special circumstances but it is the only one which has been effective until now. Moreover, there are no circumstances in this case which have ever before deprived or ever should deprive the press of its immunity against revealing its sources of information. The freedom of the press depends on this immunity. Were it to disappear so would the sources from which its information is obtained; and the public would be deprived of much of the information to which the public of a free nation is entitled.

My Lords, I would allow the appeal.

LORD FRASER OF TULLYBELTON. My Lords, the question in this appeal is whether the appellants ('Granada') can be compelled in these proceedings to disclose the identity of the person or persons who handed over to them a bundle of about 250 confidential documents belonging to the respondents ('BSC'). The documents contained information relating to the internal management of BSC which was used by Granada in a television programme on 4th February 1980 in a current affairs series called 'World in Action'. The programme was of topical interest because it was broadcast during a national steel strike by BSC employees. It was generally critical of BSC's management, and the leaked information was said to show that the management was to blame for inefficiency for which BSC were seeking to blame the trade unions. At the end of the programme Sir Charles Villiers, the head of BSC, was interviewed and dealt with some of the points raised. Whether the programme damaged BSC will be of a matter of opinion, but BSC's real complaint is that the occurrence of the leak has shown that they have a disloyal employee with access to confidential information, that their efforts to identify him have created an unpleasant atmosphere of suspicion among their employees, especially at head office, and that they need to know the name of the traitor in order to clear the air. In answer to that, Granada say that they received the information in confidence and promised the informant that they would not disclose his identity. They say that, if they are compelled to break their promise and disclose the informant's name, the flow of information to the press will tend to dry up, and that that would be contrary to public interest which lies in having a free flow of information to the press. The decision will affect all the news media including television, sound broadcasting, newspapers and individual journalists, and I shall refer to them collectively as 'the press'.

Consideration of the legal position starts from the proposition that a witness is not as a general rule entitled to withhold relevant admissible evidence in court, merely on the ground that it will disclose information which is confidential. The reason is that the public interest in the administration of justice requires such information to be disclosed, and is deemed to prevail over any public interest in preserving confidentiality. The courts will try to avoid forcing witnesses to commit breaches of confidentiality, and will not do so if the information can be obtained from another source or if it is not essential. But if it is essential, or at least if it 'will serve a useful purpose in relation to the proceedings in hand' (see *Attorney General v Mulholland* [1963] 1 All ER 767 at 772, [1963] 2 QB 477 at 492 per Donovan LJ) disclosure will be ordered. The law to that effect is well established. It is subject to exception in a very few cases where, in the public interest, immunity from disclosure has been recognised by law on grounds which were recently considered in this House in *D v National Society for the Prevention of Cruelty to Children* [1977] 1 All ER 589, [1978] AC 171. These exceptions include disclosure of information affecting the security of the state, and information as to the identity of police informers and of informers to the NSPCC, but they do not include information imparted in confidence by patients to their doctors or penitents to their priests or informers to journalists and the news media: see *Attorney General v Clough* [1963] 1 All ER 420, [1963] 1 QB 773, *Attorney General v Mulholland*, [1963] 1 All ER 767, [1963] 2 QB 477 and *HM Advocate v Airs* 1975 JC 64 at 70. That general position was not disputed on behalf of Granada. Their argument was directed to the more limited proposition that disclosure either could not, as a matter of law, or should not, in the exercise of judicial discretion, be ordered in the present proceedings. It is therefore necessary to consider the procedural position.

When the proceedings began BSC were seeking an injunction against Granada from making further use of the leaked documents and for delivery up of the documents. These matters have now been disposed of and the only live issue (which was added by amendment) is whether an order should be made for disclosure of the informant's name. Such an order was made in *Norwich Pharmacal Co v Customs and Excise Comrs* [1973] 2 All ER 943, [1974] AC 133. In that case Lord Reid said ([1973] 2 All ER 943 at 948, [1974] AC 133 at 175):

> '[The authorities] seem to me to point to a very reasonable principle that if through no fault of his own a person gets mixed up in the tortious acts of others so as to facilitate their wrongdoing he may incur no personal liability but he comes under a duty to assist the person who has been wronged by giving him full information *and disclosing the identity of the wrongdoers*.' (My emphasis.)

Unless that principle is excluded in the circumstances of the present case, it would apply very aptly to Granada, who clearly became mixed up in what must have been the tortious act of the person who removed, and probably stole, confidential documents from BSC Granada could not even be said to have become mixed up 'through no fault of their own' as they received the documents from the informant knowing what they were and used them for their own purposes. Their position is therefore weaker than that of defendants who become involved in ignorance of the true position, as in the *Norwich Pharmacal* case and in the earlier cases of *Upmann v Elkan* (1871) LR 12 Eq 140, LR 7 Ch App 130, and *Orr v Diaper* (1876) 4 Ch D 92, in both of which the defendants were innocent importers or shippers of goods marked with counterfeit trade marks, or brand marks. Nevertheless it is said that Granada, as an organ of the press, have no duty to assist by disclosing the name of their source in proceedings such as the present, even if the plaintiff cannot otherwise discover the name of the wrongdoer who has invaded his rights.

The claim of the press to be in a special position is rested on two grounds. The first is the so-called newspaper rule, the effect of which was described thus by Bankes LJ in *Lyle-Samuel v Odhams Ltd* [1920] 1 KB 135 at 143, [1918–19] All ER Rep 779 at 783:

'All I say is that this is an action of libel against the publishers of a newspaper, that it is well established that in the case of newspapers there is an exception to the rule requiring a defendant to disclose the source of his information where he pleads either privilege or fair comment.'

I would make the following comments on the newspaper rule.

1. The rule applied only to libel actions. It has recently been extended in *Broadcasting Corpn of New Zealand v Alex Harvey Industries Ltd* [1980] 1 NZLR 163 to slander of title, but the present case has nothing to do with libel or slander of title.

2. The rule applied only at the interlocutory stage of discovery. The reasons for the rule are obscure as judges have often pointed out: see, e g, per Scrutton LJ in *Lyle-Samuel v Odhams Ltd* [1920] 1 KB 135 at 144, [1918–19] All ER Rep 779 at 783 and per Scott LJ in *South Suburban Co-operative Society v Orum and Croydon Advertiser Ltd* [1937] 3 All ER 133 at 137, [1937] 2 KB 690 at 703. It has sometimes been held that the name of the informant was irrelevant: see *Parnell v Walter* (1890) 24 QBD 441 and *Adam v Fisher* (1914) 30 TLR 288. But that reason cannot apply in a case where the defendant pleads privilege: see *Elliott v Garrett* [1902] 1 KB 870 and *Lyle-Samuel v Odhams Ltd*. I agree with Lord Hailsham that the rule must have been based on public policy: see *D v National Society for the Prevention of Cruelty to Children* [1977] 1 All ER 589 at 603, [1978] AC 171 at 228. The reasons of public policy, and the limits of the rule, were explained by Dixon J in the Australian case of *McGuinness v Attorney General for Victoria* (1940) 63 CLR 73 at 104 when he said:

'But although all authority is against the existence of any rule of evidence under which an editor or journalist is protected when called as a witness on the trial of an action from the necessity of deposing to the source of the information contained in his publication or to statements made in confidence to him in the exercise of his calling, yet a special exception is made in favour of publishers, proprietors and editors of newspapers as defendants in actions of libel from the general rule that discovery by affidavit of documents and answers to interrogatories must be made of all relevant matters. By a long line of cases a practice is recognized of refusing to compel such a defendant to disclose the name of the writer of an article complained of as a libel or of the sources of information he has relied upon. The foundation of the rule is the special position of those publishing and conducting newspapers, who accept responsibility for and are liable in respect of the matter contained in their journals, and the desirability of protecting those who contribute to their columns from the consequences of unnecessary disclosure of their identity. The cases are collected in *Lyle-Samuel v. Odhams Ltd* and *South Suburban Co-operative Society Ltd v. Orum*, which are the latest authorities upon the application of the rule. The appellant stands upon these decision and says that they disclose a development which, in reason and logic, should not stop at discovery, but should supply a general justification for withholding the names of contributors and the sources of information at all stages of any legal proceeding. The answer is that it is not a rule of evidence but a practice of refusing in an action of libel against the publisher, &c., of a newspaper to compel discovery of the name of his informants. It "rests not on a principle of privilege but on the limitations of discovery". . . .'

3. Since 1949 the rules of court have applied the same rule to all defendants (see now RSC Ord 82, r 6), so that there is no longer a separate newspaper rule on discovery which could be relied on to justify giving special treatment to the press as a defence to a *Norwich Pharmacal* type of order.

4. The limits of the rule are uncertain. It applied to a newspaper and to a journalist in the full-time employment of a newspaper: see *Lawson v Odhams Press Ltd* [1948] 2 All ER 717, [1949] 1 KB 129. It did not apply to the writer of a libellous letter to a

newspaper: see *South Suburban Co-operative Society Ltd v Orum and Croydon Advertiser Ltd* [1937] 3 All ER 133, [1937] 2 KB 690. What is not clear is whether it applied to a freelance journalist or to the writer of a pamphlet or broadsheet or of the many other kinds of publication which impart useful information to the public. For instance, it is uncertain whether Crockford's Clerical Directory counts as a newspaper for this purpose: see *Georgius v Oxford University Press* [1949] 1 All ER 342, [1949] 1 KB 729. In the American Supreme Court case of *Branzburg v Hayes* (1972) 408 US 665 at 705 the majority opinion pointed out the difficulty of defining the categories of newsmen who would qualify for any special privilege to be accorded to the press and they said this:

'The informative function asserted by representatives of the organized press in the present cases is also performed by lecturers, political pollsters, novelists, academic researchers, and dramatists. Almost any author may quite accurately assert that he is contributing to the flow of information to the public, that he relies on confidential sources of information, and that these sources will be silenced if he is forced to make disclosures before a grand jury.'

I would be reluctant to support a rule whose boundaries are so ill defined.

5. The rule has repeatedly been said to be subject to possible exceptions (see, e g, *Hope v Brash* [1897] 2 QB 188 at 192, [1895–9] All ER Rep 343 at 345 per A L Smith LJ) although there seems to be no reported case in England where the exception has been held to apply. Indeed in the *Broadcasting Corpn of New Zealand* case, Woodhouse J thought that the rule should now be regarded as absolute. But the Scottish case of *Cunningham v Duncan and Jamieson* (1889) 16 R (Ct of Sess) 383 seems to be an example of such an exception. The newspaper rule was not mentioned by name in the judgments, and as a matter of procedure it could not be exactly applied in Scotland, but the rule was in effect recognised by Lord Mure (at 388) who said there was a 'general rule . . . that the editor of a newspaper, where he takes the responsibility for anonymous correspondence published in his paper, is not bound to disclose the author'. Nevertheless, in the special circumstances of that case, the court allowed a diligence to recover, before the trial, the manuscripts of letters to a newspaper. The special circumstances were that, according to the pursuer's averments, the letters, which had been published under pseudonyms and appeared to have been written by members of the public, had really been written or procured to be written by the publishers of the newspaper as part of a systematic plan to discredit the pursuer. If the newspaper rule were otherwise applicable, I think the circumstances of the present appeal might well be within the exception because refusal to order disclosure of the informant's name will probably deprive BSC of any effective remedy for a wrong they have suffered. Even if they could quantify damage done to them by the fact of disclosure having occurred, any award of damages against Granada would not provide a remedy for the continuing lack of mutual confidence within their staff.

For these reasons I do not regard the newspaper rule as providing a good reason why a *Norwich Pharmacal* order should not be made against the press in a case such as the present. The second, and more formidable, reason relied on by Granada is that discovery has never been used against the press in this way although it is well known that leaks of information have often occurred. We were referred to an interesting historical survey of political leaks to the press in England in the eighteenth and nineteenth centuries: see Aspinall, Politics and the Press 1780 to 1850 (1973, p 192). Some of the leaks mentioned in that work were thought at the time to have been made by persons in very high places. In one case in 1797 Canning, who was then Under-Secretary of State for Foreign Affairs, suspected that the King himself was responsible. In such circumstances it is easy to see that it may have been thought that action in the courts to compel disclosure of the source would have led to scandal and publicity even more damaging than the leaks. I think that is probably the explanation, at least in some cases, why no attempt to compel disclosure was made. But there may also have been a belief that the courts had no power to compel disclosure of sources, either by the press or by any other defendant. Thus in *Abernethy v Hutchinson* (1825) 1 H & Tw 28, 47 ER 1313, where the proprietors of the Lancet had published lectures delivered orally by the plaintiff professor to his students, Lord Eldon LC granted an injunction against further publication but he said that the court had no right to compel the defendants to disclose the source of information which had evidently been given to them in breach of confidence. But the point does not appear to have been argued, and in any event it does not seem that the identity of the informant was material for the action. The same is true in *Prince Albert v Strange* (1849) 1 H & Tw 1, 47 ER 1302 where the plaintiff sought and obtained an injunction against the defendant's publishing etchings by himself and Queen Victoria which had been obtained in breach of confidence, but made no attempt to obtain discovery of the name of the person who had handed over the etchings to the defendant. I therefore conclude that the absence of precedents for the use of discovery for this purpose against the press, or indeed against any other defendants, while certainly striking, can be readily explained otherwise than on the ground that discovery was not available as a remedy.

A separate argument against making a *Norwich Pharmacal* order in this case was that such an order, it was said, could not be made against any defendant in the absence of evidence that it was required for the purpose of bringing an action against the informant. It is true that in most of the cases referred to in the speeches in the *Norwich Pharmacal* case the plaintiff intended to bring proceedings against the source, but no authority was cited to us showing that such an intention was essential to obtain discovery. In *Cardale v Watkins* (1820) 5 Madd 18, 56 ER 801 Leach V-C did indeed say that discovery would not be given for the mere gratification of curiosity but in aid of some other proceeding either pending or intended. In the present case discovery is certainly not sought for the mere gratification of curiosity: it is sought for the vindication of BSC's rights, and I do not think it matters whether separate proceedings are required for that purpose or not. That view is supported by American authority in *Post v Toledo, Cincinnati and St Louis Railroad Co* (1887) 11 NE Rep 540 at 547 where Field J said that a plaintiff can obtain discovery if he has a cause of action against the informant whether or not he intends to raise proceedings. In the present case it is clear that BSC do have a cause of action against the informant who has disclosed confidential information of theirs. I agree with Templeman LJ in the Court of Appeal that discovery ought to be available to ascertain the wrongdoer when it is necessary to enable justice to be done.

In my opinion therefore there is no reason in principle why discovery cannot be ordered, and the question of whether it should be ordered is one for the discretion of the court. Sir Robert Megarry V-C held that, if the matter was one for his discretion, he would unhesitantly exercise it in favour of ordering disclosure, and his decision was upheld in the Court of Appeal. I entirely agree. I have particularly in mind the fact that the informant had committed a wrong against a third party (BSC) by supplying the information, and no attempt was made to justify it. The information did not reveal criminal conduct or anything that could be described as iniquity by BSC. If it had done so, its disclosure would have been justified and not wrongful: 'there is no confidence as to the disclosure of iniquity' (see *Gartside v Outram* (1856) 26 LJ Ch 113). If it had disclosed iniquity, Granada's appeal might well have succeeded. As to what is covered by the word iniquity in this context I find guidance in *Initial Services Ltd v Putterill* [1967] 3 All ER 145, [1968] 1 QB 396 where the facts were not altogether unlike those in the present case. The sales manager of the plaintiff company resigned his appointment and when he left he took with him a number of documents belonging to the company which he handed to a newspaper. The newspaper published an article based on the information in the documents. The defendants pleaded that the disclosures were justified because they showed, inter alia, that the company had failed to register an agreement to which s 6 of the Restrictive Trade Practices Act 1956 applied and had sent out a circular which gave a misleading explanation of its reasons for increasing its charges. Cusack J, and on appeal the Court of Appeal, refused to strike out the defence. Lord Denning MR said ([1967] 3 All ER 145 at 148, [1968] 1 QB 396 at 405):

'Suppose a master tells his servant: "I am going to falsify these sale notes and deceive the customers. You are not to say anything about it to anyone." If the master thereafter falsifies the sale notes, the servant is entitled to say: "I am not going to stay any longer in the service of a man who does such a thing. I will leave him and report it to the customers." It was so held in *Gartside* v. *Outram*. Counsel suggested that this exception was confined to cases where the master has been "guilty of a crime or fraud"; but I do not think it is so limited. It extends to any misconduct of such a nature that it ought in the public interest to be disclosed to others . . . The exception should extend to crimes, frauds and misdeeds, both those actually committed as well as those in contemplation, provided always—and this is essential—that the disclosure is justified in the public interest. The reason is because "no private obligations can dispense with that universal one which lies on every member of the society to discover every design which may be formed, contrary to the laws of the society, to destroy the public welfare." See *Annesley* v. *Earl of Anglesea* ((1743) 17 State Tr 1139 at 1223–1246).'

Salmon LJ spoke to the same effect.

Woodward v Hutchins [1977] 2 All ER 751, [1977] 1 WLR 760 was a case where the Court of Appeal refused an injunction against publication of confidential information about a pop group. Lord Denning MR said ([1977] 2 All ER 751 at 754, [1977] 1 WLR 760 at 763–764):

'If a group of this kind seek publicity which is to their advantage, it seems to me that they cannot complain if a servant or employee of theirs afterwards discloses the truth about them. If the image which they fostered was not a true image, it is in the public interest that it should be corrected. In these cases of confidential information it is a question of balancing the public interest in maintaining the confidence against the public interest in knowing the truth.'

The affidavits lodged on behalf of Granada in this appeal seem to hint at making the sort of case referred to by Lord Denning MR in *Woodward*, but no such case was attempted to be made in argument. On the contrary, it was accepted by Granada that publication could have been prevented if an injunction had been applied for before publication. The scope of the iniquity rule is therefore not in issue in this appeal, and the existence of the rule should protect the press from being ordered to disclose the identity of their source in any case where the behaviour of the source has been justified. The result of the appeal, so far as that rule is concerned, will be to show that the final decision on whether confidential information discloses such iniquity as to justify its publication must be made by the courts and not by the press.

The answer to the question therefore seems to me to involve weighing up the public interest for and against publication. The balance does not in my opinion depend on the use made of the leaked information by the appellants in this particular case. Anyone who hands over to the press a bundle of confidential documents belonging to someone else must surely expect, and intend, that, if they contain information of topical interest, it will be published in some form. The informer's motives are, in my opinion, irrelevant. It is said, and I am willing to accept, that in this case the informant neither asked for nor received any money, or other reward, but that he acted out of a keen sense of indignation about the dealings between BSC and the government before and during the strike. No doubt there is a public interest in maintaining the free flow of information to the press, and therefore against obstructing informers. But there is also I think a very strong public interest in preserving confidentiality within any organisation, in order that it can operate efficiently, and also be free from suspicion that it is harbouring disloyal employees. There is no difference in this respect betwen a public corporation like BSC and an ordinary company. Both have to disclose certain information about their activities; BSC report to the minister who lays their report before Parliament (see the Iron and Steel Act 1975, s 5), while a company reports to the shareholders and to the public.

Unauthorised disclosure of confidential information about either is equally liable to damage efficiency and morale. In the present case I am of opinion that the public interest in preserving confidentiality should prevail, and I would dismiss the appeal.

As regards Granada's mutilation of the documents before returning them to BSC, by cutting off marks which they thought might tend to identify the source, their behaviour was reprehensible but not directly relevant to the issues in this appeal.

The argument that Granada run a real risk of being prosecuted for handling stolen goods or for conspiracy to defraud seems to me, if I may say so without disrespect to the persuasive way in which it was presented, to be far-fetched. In any event, I agree with my noble and learned friend Viscount Dilhorne, whose recent death we now deplore, that disclosure of the informant's name would not tend to incriminate Granada in his offences.

I would dismiss the appeal.

LORD RUSSELL OF KILLOWEN. My Lords, I concurred at the time of the decision with the opinion then expressed by the majority of your Lordships that this appeal failed, stating that I would later express in writing my reasons for that concurrence.

I have since had the advantage of reading the written reasons of my noble and learned friend Lord Wilberforce with which I am in agreement and which deal so fully with the facts and the law that I refrain from repetition. I would however seek to stress some salient points in the hope of dispelling misunderstandings (or misgivings) that have since the decision been expressed.

The first such point. Granada, rightly in my opinion, agreed that they had no right in law to make the use which they did of the abstracted documents; indeed Granada expressly asserted that had BSC moved quickly enough an injunction against such use must have been granted. Granada did not contend that publication was justified by a public interest in a free flow of information.

The second such point. Since Granada had no such right, let alone freedom, in law this case has not even marginal connection with any concept of 'the freedom of the press'.

The third such point was the situation in which BSC found themselves. In their organisation was someone with access to important secret or otherwise confidential papers who was prepared (for reasons which may have seemed good to him or her but did not involve revelation of what has been referred to compendiously as 'iniquity') to commit a gross breach of the trust and confidence necessarily reposed in him, and who might be so prepared on some future occasion should he see fit. BSC had endeavoured to pinpoint the miscreant but had failed. No imagination is needed to appreciate that that failure must have led to an atmosphere of suspicion between management and staff and between members of management and of staff, and must have been profoundly disturbing to staff relations and the conduct of business. A grave injustice had been done to BSC by the 'source', and Granada by tampering with the BSC documents before their return with a view to preventing his identification had contrived (or at least sought) to prolong (or perpetuate) that grave injustice.

My Lords, in general terms I recognise a public interest in the free flow of information, and that there may be some obstruction to that flow if a source is not entitled in law to rely on an undertaking by a journalist to treat the identity of the source as confidential to him. But where, as here, the undertaking results in or would perpetuate the gross wrong and injustice done to BSC, to accede to such contention would indeed encourage the doing of injustice. I cannot accept that the public interest in the prevention of injustice is here negatived by any public interest in a free flow of information.

I have, my Lords, also had the advantage of reading the reasons prepared by my noble and learned friend Viscount Dilhorne before his recent and greatly to be lamented death. As will be seen they march with those of Lord Wilberforce. The latter however did not deal in detail with a suggestion by Granada that identification by Granada of the source might tend to incriminate Granada. I find this suggestion to be wholly without foundation. Save as a matter of quite improbable speculation Granada have already stated in their evidence all the matters which might (or might not) disclose an offence by Granada. Viscount Dilhorne has answered this contention in his reasons, and I agree with him. It seems to me that to give a name, the giving of which might (speculatively) lead to further inquiries and further evidence, is not to incriminate oneself by one's own evidence.

Since writing these reasons for dismissal of this appeal I have also had the advantage of reading the reasons of my noble and learned friend Lord Fraser. It will be seen that I am also in agreement with his reasons.

Appeal dismissed.

Solicitors: *Goodman, Derrick & Co* (for Granada); *Clifford-Turner* (for BSC).

Mary Rose Plummer   Barrister.

Alpha Trading Ltd v Dunnshaw-Patten Ltd

COURT OF APPEAL, CIVIL DIVISION
LAWTON, BRANDON AND TEMPLEMAN LJJ
10th, 11th NOVEMBER 1980

Agent – Commission – Loss of commission – Damages – Agent prevented from earning commission – Wilful default of principal – Breach of implied term in agency contract – Agent introducing buyer to principal – Contract concluded between buyer and principal – Principal breaking contract with buyer and purchase price not becoming payable – Whether implied term in agency contract that principal would not break contract with buyer – Whether agent remaining entitled to commission or damages.

The plaintiffs and the defendants were international traders who entered into a contract whereby in consideration of the plaintiffs introducing to the defendants a buyer for 10,000 tonnes of cement at $49·50 per tonne the defendants agreed to pay the plaintiffs commission on the sale at the rate of $1·50 per tonne and also to make certain other payments. The plaintiffs duly introduced a buyer for the cement and the defendants and the buyer entered into a contract for the quantity and at the price envisaged. The buyer opened a letter of credit and the defendants provided the buyer with a 3% performance bond but, the defendants later being unable or unwilling to provide the cement, the contract of sale was never implemented and the buyer was released from its obligation to pay the purchase price. The plaintiffs claimed to be entitled to be paid the commission agreed under the agency contract or, alternatively, damages for breach of an implied term in the agency contract that the defendants would not break their contract with the buyer and thereby deprive the plaintiffs of the commission. The defendants denied that any term was to be implied in the agency contract and contended that the commission only became payable if the purchase price became payable, and since it had not they were not liable for the commission. The judge rejected the plaintiffs' direct claim for commission but held that there was an implied term in the agency contract that the defendants would not break their contract with the buyer and that the plaintiffs were entitled to damages for breach of that implied term. The defendants appealed.

Held – Where a principal and an agent agreed that in return for the agent introducing a buyer to the principal the agent would receive commission on any contract concluded between the principal and the buyer, and a contract was in fact concluded between the principal and the buyer as a result of the agent's mediation, then in order to give business efficacy to the agency contract a term would be implied in it that the principal would not commit a breach of the contract with the buyer which would deprive the agent of his commission. It followed that the plaintiffs were entitled to damages and that the appeal would be dismissed (see p 486 *b* and *j* to p 487 *b*, p 489 *h* to p 490 *f*, p 491 *a b e* and *h* to p 492 *a g* to *j* and p 493 *b c*, post).

Dictum of Lord Wright in *Luxor (Eastbourne) Ltd v Cooper* [1941] 1 All ER at 61 followed.

L French & Co Ltd v Leeston Shipping Co Ltd [1922] All ER Rep 314 distinguished.

Notes

For the recovery of damages by an agent wrongfully prevented from earning remuneration, see 1 Halsbury's Laws (4th Edn) para 805, and for cases on the subject, see 1(2) Digest (Reissue) 700–704, 4668–4687.

Cases referred to in judgments

British and Beningtons Ltd v North Western Cachar Tea Co Ltd [1923] AC 48, [1922] All ER Rep 224, 92 LJKB 62, 128 LT 422, 28 Com Cas 265, 13 Ll L Rep 67, HL, 12 Digest (Reissue) 440, 3185.

French (L) & Co Ltd v Leeston Shipping Co Ltd [1922] 1 AC 451, [1922] All ER Rep 314, 91 LJKB 655, 127 LT 169, 15 Asp MLC 544, 27 Com Cas 257, HL, 1(2) Digest (Reissue) 706, 4705.

Grogan v Smith (1890) 7 TLR 132, CA, 1(2) Digest (Reissue) 717, 4735.

James v Smith [1931] 2 KB 317n, 100 LJKB 585n, 145 LT 457n, CA, 1(2) Digest (Reissue) 712, 4721.

Kahn v Aircraft Industries Corpn Ltd [1937] 3 All ER 476, CA, 1(2) Digest (Reissue) 701, 4673.

Lott v Outhwaite (1893) 10 TLR 76, CA, 1(2) Digest (Reissue) 719, 4742.

Luxor (Eastbourne) Ltd v Cooper [1941] 1 All ER 33, [1941] AC 108, 110 LJKB 131, 164 LT 313, 46 Com Cas 120, HL, 1(2) Digest (Repl) 701, 4675.

McCallum v Hicks [1950] 1 All ER 864, [1950] 2 KB 271, CA, 1(2) Digest (Reissue) 703, 4683.

Martin v Perry and Daw [1931] 2 KB 310, [1931] All ER Rep 110, 100 LJKB 582, 145 LT 455, 1(2) Digest (Reissue) 712, 4724.

Nosotti v Auerbach (1899) 15 TLR 140, CA, 1(2) Digest (Reissue) 706, 4704.

Peacock v Freeman (1888) 4 TLR 541, CA, 1(2) Digest (Reissue) 705, 4700.

Reed (Dennis) Ltd v Goody [1950] 1 All ER 919, [1950] 2 KB 277, CA, 1(2) Digest (Reissue) 709, 4709.

Roberts v Bury Improvement Comrs (1870) LR 5 CP 310, 39 LJCP 120, 22 LT 132, 34 JP 821, Ex Ch, 7 Digest (Reissue) 341, 2260.

Trollope (George) & Sons v Martyn Brothers [1934] 2 KB 436, 103 LJKB 634, 152 LT 88, 40 Com Cas 53, CA, 1(2) Digest (Reissue) 700, 4669.

Vulcan Car Agency Ltd v Fiat Motors Ltd (1915) 32 TLR 73, 1(2) Digest (Reissue) 704, 4692.

Cases also cited

Houlder (Howard) & Partners Ltd v Manx Isles Steamship Co Ltd [1923] 1 KB 110, [1922] All ER Rep 579.

Roberts v Barnard (1884) Cab & El 336.

Appeal

The defendants, Dunnshaw-Patten Ltd, appealed against the judgment of Mocatta J given on 30th November 1979 awarding the plaintiffs, Alpha Trading Ltd, damages in their action against the defendants to recover agency commission of $US25,833, or alternatively damages of an equivalent amount for being prevented from recovering such commission. The facts are set out in the judgment of Brandon LJ.

Christopher Smith for the defendants.
Patrick Milmo for the plaintiffs.

BRANDON LJ delivered the first judgment at the invitation of Lawton LJ. This is an appeal by the defendants from a judgment of Mocatta J given in the Commercial Court on 30th November 1979.

The action was brought by the plaintiffs to recover agency commission, or alternatively damages of an equivalent amount for being prevented by the defendants from receiving such commission. The learned judge found for the defendants on their claim for damages, and gave them judgment for $US25,000, with interest of $4,504·11, and costs. The defendants now appeal against that judgment, asking that it be set aside and that the plaintiffs' claim be dismissed.

Both the plaintiffs and the defendants carry on business as international merchants and dealers. The representative of the plaintiffs who was concerned in the material transactions was a Mr Brodie. His opposite number on the defendants' side was a Mr Marchant Lane.

Early in January 1978 the plaintiffs were aware that a Dutch company called Mueller International BV were interested in purchasing about 10,000 metric tons of cement at a price of $49·50 per ton c and f Bandar Shahpur or Khorramshahr in Iran.

Mr Brodie was acting for the plaintiffs in the matter and first contemplated that the plaintiffs would buy the cement themselves, either from the defendants or from other suppliers, and would then resell it to Mueller at a profit.

Early in January 1978 certain telexes were exchanged between the plaintiffs and the defendants on that basis, namely that the plaintiffs would buy the cement from the defendants. Subsequently, however, Mr Brodie decided that it would be more convenient and more profitable if the cement were sold direct by the defendants to Mueller through the agency of the plaintiffs. In particular, this form of transaction would avoid the necessity of two letters of credit and two performance bonds. The basis of such transaction would be that the profit which the plaintiffs would have made on a resale would be covered by the defendants, in consideration of the plaintiffs introducing Mueller to them as buyers, paying the plaintiffs commission on the sale and also making certain other payments in connection with the demurrage payable at the port of discharge.

The defendants were agreeable to this new arrangement and negotiations took place between them in January and February 1978, mainly by telex but also in part by telephone conversations between Mr Brodie and Mr Marchant Lane. Simultaneously, further negotiations took place by telex between the defendants and Mueller in relation to a contract of sale between them of which the plaintiffs were kept informed.

In the upshot, two contracts were made. First, there was a contract for the sale of 10,000 metric tons of cement, c and f Bandar Shahpur, between the defendants and Mueller. Second, there was an agency contract between the plaintiffs and the defendants under which the plaintiffs were to be remunerated for introducing Mueller to the defendants as buyers. This remuneration was divided into three parts. First, the plaintiffs were to receive a commission of $1·50 per metric ton of the cement sold. Second, they were to receive 25% of the demurrage, namely 40 cents per metric ton per day, payable by Mueller to the defendants in respect of the first ten days of unloading. Third, the plaintiffs were to be paid half the difference, amounting to 5 cents per metric ton, between the rate of demurrage payable by the defendants to the shipowners and that payable by Mueller to the defendants after the first ten days of unloading had expired.

The terms of the telexes in which this agreement was reached are to some extent important. The terms which I have referred to were expressed in somewhat different language as regards the demurrage during the first ten days of unloading. The term was expressed in this way: 'Value of ten days free time to be held at our disposal.' Again, with regard to the commission, the words were: '$1·50 per metric ton commission to be held at our disposal.' Those expressions were repeated in a later telex at the time when the contract was finally concluded.

The contract between Mueller and the defendants provided, among other things, that Mueller should open a letter of credit for the price of the cement and that the defendants should provide Mueller with a 3% performance bond. These two obligations on either side were duly carried out, but the contract of sale was never implemented by the defendants. The precise cause of the defendants' failure to perform the contract was not proved in evidence. There was evidence which showed that the defendants had met a claim made against them by Mueller by forfeiting the performance bond and paying a further sum of £21,000. The only reasonable inference from this is that the defendants were either unwilling or unable to perform the contract and, accordingly, defaulted on it. Following this default in the performance of the contract by the defendants, the plaintiffs claimed that they were entitled, despite such default, to be paid the remuneration agreed under the agency contract. The defendants rejected that claim, and the present action was brought by the plaintiffs against the defendants in consequence.

The plaintiffs put their case in their point of claim in two ways. The first way they put it is set out in paras 4, 5, 6 and 7. In para 4, they said: 'The said remuneration was due to the Plaintiffs upon mutual performance of the contract between Mueller and the Defendants'. Then, in para 5:

'It was an implied term of the said agreement between the Plaintiffs and the Defendants that the Defendants would do or cause to be done everything necessary to perform the contract with Mueller and/or would not do anything to prevent the Plaintiffs from earning the remuneration described in paragraph 3 above.'

In para 6 the plaintiffs pleaded that the contract had been concluded between the defendants and Mueller. In para 7 they alleged that, in breach of the said implied term, the defendants failed to ship or arrange shipment of the said cement to Mueller. They went on to claim, by way of damages, the remuneration that they would have received had the contract of sale been performed by the defendants. That was, as I say, the first way that the plaintiffs put their case. It can be described as the case based on an implied term of the agency contract.

In para 8, they tried as an alternative what might be described as 'rather a long shot'. They pleaded:

'Alternative to the contentions set out in paragraphs 4, 5 and 7 above pursuant to the said agreement the Plaintiffs were entitled to the remuneration described in paragraph 3 above, amounting to $25,833, upon the Defendants entering into the contract with Mueller as described in paragraph 6 above . . .'

That alternative claim can be described as the direct claim for remuneration under the contract as compared with the other claim for damages for breach of an implied term of the contract.

The learned judge dealt with these claims in reverse order. He began by rejecting the direct claim for commission, which was made in para 8 of the points of claim. He said:

'If one has regard to the terms of the agency agreement, it seems clear that commission could not have been due on the making of the contract. The repeated reference in the telexes . . . of "to be held at our disposal" indicate very clearly that payment was to be forthcoming from Mueller's letter of credit. Whilst it is true that no claim is made in the points of claim for the half share of the difference between 35 cents demurrage and 40 cents, which could clearly not have been ascertained until after discharge, this cannot affect the clear inference to be drawn from the other terms that the plaintiffs had no right to or expectation of their commission until the defendants had been paid under the letter of credit and were thus in a position "to hold" the appropriate amounts for the plaintiffs.'

I am not sure whether the learned judge is right in saying that in the points of claim no claim had been made for the half share of the difference between 35 cents demurrage and 40 cents, for in the amended points of claim there is an amendment making just that claim. Whatever may be the position about that, however, the judge's conclusion is clear, namely that, having regard to the terms of the telexes in which the agency agreement was made, or by which it was evidenced, it was the intention of the parties that commission should only become payable when the contract had been performed, and the letter of credit had been drawn on.

The learned judge then directed his attention to what in the pleadings was the first way in which the plaintiffs put their case, namely on the basis of damages for breach of an implied term. On that part of the case he concluded that there was an implied term that, once the defendants had entered into a contract with Mueller, they would not break it and thereby deprive the plaintiffs of the remuneration to which, if the contract had been performed, they would have been entitled.

In reaching that conclusion, the learned judge evidently relied very much on certain observations made by Lord Wright in *Luxor (Eastbourne) Ltd v Cooper* [1941] 1 All ER 33, [1941] AC 108. That was a case concerned with an estate agent. The headnote reads ([1941] AC 108):

> 'Where an agent is promised a commission only if he brings about the sale which he is endeavouring to effect there is no room for an implied term that the principal will not dispose of the property himself or through other channels or otherwise act so as to prevent the agent earning his commission. Dissenting judgment of Scrutton L.J. in *Trollope and Sons* v. *Martyn Brothers* ([1934] 2 KB 436) approved.'

The actual decision, as appears from that headnote, was that, in the case of an estate agent, the law will not imply a term that the principal will not dispose of the property himself or through other channels. The House of Lords did not need to consider whether, after an agent had introduced a purchaser to someone who wanted to sell, and a concluded contract had then been made, there would be any term implied to protect the agent in that situation.

Lord Wright in his speech made an extensive examination of the situation arising in contracts of this kind, particularly in the field of estate agency. There are two passages in his speech which bear on the situation which we have in this case. He said ([1941] 1 All ER 33 at 55–56, [1941] AC 108 at 141–142):

> 'However, it is necessary to reserve certain eventualities in which an agent may be entitled to damages where there is a failure to complete even under a contract like one in this case. For instance, if the negotiations between the vendor and the purchaser have been duly concluded and a binding executory agreement has been achieved, different considerations may arise. The vendor is then no longer free to dispose of his property. Though the sale is not completed, the property in equity has passed from him to the purchaser. If he refuses to complete he would be guilty of a breach of agreement *vis-à-vis* the purchaser. I think, as at present advised, that it ought then to be held that he is also in breach of his contract with the commission agent—that is, of some term which can properly be implied. However, that question and possibly some other questions do not arise in this case and may be reserved.'

Lord Wright referred to the dissenting judgment of Scrutton LJ in *Martyn*'s case, and to the expression 'wrongful act' which had been used by Scrutton LJ in that judgment. He said ([1941] 1 All ER 33 at 61, [1941] AC 108 at 149–150):

> 'I take it that SCRUTTON, L.J., meant an act which was wrongful under the contract between the appellants and the respondents. There could be no wrongful act as between the employer and the prospective purchaser in breaking off the negotiations while they were going on "subject to contract", and no wrongful act thereby, in my opinion, as between the appellants and the respondents, for the reasons I have attempted to state. It may well be, as I have already stated, that, as soon as a binding executory contract is effected between the employer and the purchaser, a different state of things arises. The property is transferred in equity, and the seller can be specifically ordered to complete. The agent may then fairly claim that he is entitled

to his commission, or at least to substantial damages, and, as at present advised, I think that a term of that nature may be implied in the contract. It cannot have been contemplated that, when a binding contract with the purchaser has been made on the agent's mediation, the principal can, as between himself and the agent, break that contract without breaking his contract with the agent. I understand that this was the view of SCRUTTON, L.J., and, though the question does not arise in this case, I am, as at present advised, in agreement with it. In that case, it may fairly be said that the employer prevented the fulfilment of the condition, and was in default under the commission agreement just as much as under the agreement of sale. While the matter is still in negotiation, however, it is a different matter.'

The researches of counsel have been unable to find any case in which those observations of Lord Wright were applied as a matter of decision. This seems to me somewhat surprising considering the length of time that has elapsed since Lord Wright made those observations. What I would have expected to be the likelihood is that some such question as we presently have before us would have arisen in commercial contracts. The position, therefore, is that this court is not bound by any decision which is directly on the point.

Counsel for the defendants submitted that the observations of Lord Wright in *Luxor (Eastbourne) Ltd v Cooper* which I have read were obiter, that they were erroneous and should not be followed by this court. In support of that contention, he relied in the main on another case in the House of Lords, *L French & Co Ltd v Leeston Shipping Co Ltd* [1922] 1 AC 451, [1922] All ER Rep 314.

The headnote of that case reads ([1922] 1 AC 451):

'Shipbrokers employed to effect a charter of a steamship procured a charter for eighteen months, but after four months of the charter had run the owner sold the vessel to the charterers and the charterparty was cancelled. The charterparty provided for payment of a commission of $2\frac{1}{2}$ per cent. on the hire paid and earned under the said charterparty and on any continuation thereof. In an action by the brokers to recover commission for the remainder of the charter period:—*Held*, that it was not an implied term of the contract that the shipowners should not agree to put an end to the charterparty by the sale of the ship to the charterers, and the action failed.'

It was urged on us by counsel for the defendants that the reasoning applied by the House of Lords in that case led, inevitably, to the conclusion that no term of the kind alleged by the plaintiffs should be implied in the present case. He pointed out that it could be said in that charterparty case, and was indeed said on behalf of the defendants, that as a result of the contract being concluded the agent had, in a sense, a vested interest in the performance of the contract. It could be said that by selling the ship and bringing the charterparty to an end the shipowners were doing an act, quite deliberately, which deprived the agent of the commission which he would have had if the ship had not been sold. That argument certainly carries great force. It is, however, to be observed that in that case there was no breach by the agent's employer of his contract with the third party. All that was done was done by agreement. What really happened was that the shipowner disposed of his property in a way that he desired to do with the consequences that the charterparty came to an end.

Counsel for the plaintiffs put his case in two ways. He said, first of all, that there were special circumstances in this case which would justify the court in implying the kind of term which he relied on even if it might not be right to do so in the generality of agency agreements. In this connection he said that what had originally been contemplated in this case was a transaction under which the plaintiffs bought the cement from the defendants and resold it to Mueller thereby gaining a profit, the difference in the two prices. He said that the fact that there had been substituted for that transaction a different kind of transaction, namely an agency contract, did not make any difference to the true position. Since in the first case a breach by the defendants of their contract to sell to the plaintiffs would have resulted in a legitimate claim for damages, so ought there to be a legitimate claim for damages when in the revised type of transaction the defendants failed to perform their contract with Mueller.

For myself I do not think that any great importance should be attached to the circumstance that a different kind of transaction had been contemplated originally from that into which the parties ultimately entered. It seems to me to be no more than a matter of history. I would not think that it would be right to imply a term into the agency contract, because of that history, which, apart from that history, it would not be right to imply. I would approach the matter more generally by considering whether the observations made by Lord Wright in *Luxor (Eastbourne) Ltd v Cooper*, on which the learned judge based his decision, should be followed by this court or not, because it seems to me that those observations, although made in a case involving estate agency, are capable of being applied, and if correct should be applied, to contracts of agency in general.

In his speech in *Luxor (Eastbourne) Ltd v Cooper*, Lord Wright expressly approved the dissenting judgment of Scrutton LJ in *George Trollope & Sons v Martyn Brothers* [1934] 2 KB 436. I think it would be helpful to read part of that dissenting judgment. Scrutton LJ said (at 445–446):

> 'The decisions of the Court of Appeal reported only in the Times Law Reports seem to me either to support, or not to contradict the view I have taken. In *Peacock v. Freeman* ((1888) 4 TLR 541) the Court declined to give the auctioneer any commission, other than the commission agreed, if no sale took place, and the Master of the Rolls said that to give the agent any further right there must be a default on the part of the employer, something contrary to the contract, something wrong done, and there the contract with the purchaser entitled the vendor to do what he did. In *Grogan v. Smith* ((1890) 7 TLR 132) there never was any binding contract with the purchaser, and therefore the agent recovered no commission. In *Lott v. Outhwaite* ((1893) 10 TLR 76) there was an agreement to pay commission if a sale was completed, and the sale was not completed because the purchaser had not the money to complete; obviously it followed that the agent got no commission. I do not see how Lindley L.J.'s statement that the agent could have earned commission if the vendor had been in default helps the matter, until "default" has been defined. Lindley L.J. refused compensation on a quantum meruit, though part of the property had been sold. Lastly, in *Nosotti v. Auerbach* ((1899) 15 TLR 140), it was held that where there was a contract of sale to give possession in a reasonable time, and the vendor refused to give such possession, the agent was entitled to recover commission. There the vendor broke his contract with the purchaser and was clearly in default.'

The next case which was cited to us by counsel for the plaintiffs in support of his argument was *Dennis Reed Ltd v Goody* [1950] 1 All ER 919, [1950] 2 KB 277. That case was, again, an estate agency case, and the decision of the court, as appears from the headnote ([1950] 2 KB 277), was:

> '. . . as the person introduced had withdrawn from the negotiations before any binding contract had been made, and the defendants had never been in default, the plaintiffs had not introduced a person "ready, able and willing to purchase" within the meaning of the contract of agency, and were therefore not entitled to commission.'

That was the actual decision. The passage in the judgment of Denning LJ on which counsel for the plaintiffs relied must be regarded, I think, as obiter. It is, nevertheless, entitled to careful consideration and respect. Denning LJ said ([1950] 1 All ER 919 at 923, [1950] 2 KB 277 at 285):

'Some confusion has arisen because of the undoubted fact that, once there is a binding contract for sale, the vendor cannot withdraw from it except at the risk of having to pay the agent his commission. This has led some people to suppose that commission is payable as soon as a contract is signed, and I said so myself in *McCallum* v. *Hicks* ([1950] 1 All ER 864 at 866, [1950] 2 KB 271 at 275). This, however, is not correct. The reason why the vendor is liable in such a case is because, once he repudiates the contract, the purchaser is no longer bound to do any more towards completion, and the vendor cannot rely on the non-completion in order to avoid payment of commission, because it is due to his own fault: see *Roberts* v. *Bury Improvement Comrs.* ((1870) LR 5 CP 310) and *Luxor (Eastbourne) Ltd.* v. *Cooper* ([1941] 1 All ER 33 at 45, 55–56, [1941] AC 108 at 126, 142) *per* LORD RUSSELL OF KILLOWEN and *per* LORD WRIGHT. If, however, the vendor could show that the purchaser would not, in any event, have been able or willing to complete, he would not be liable for commission: see *British and Benningtons Ltd.* v. *North Western Cachar Tea Co.* ([1923] AC 48 at 72, [1922] All ER Rep 224 at 234) *per* LORD SUMNER. When it is not the vendor, but the purchaser, who withdraws, the case is entirely different, for, even though a binding contract has been made, nevertheless, if the purchaser is unable or unwilling to complete, the agent is not entitled to his commission: see *James* v. *Smith* ([1931] 2 KB 317n at 322) *per* ATKIN, L.J., and *Martin* v. *Perry & Daw* ([1931] 2 KB 310, [1931] All ER Rep 110). The vendor is not bound to bring an action for specific performance or for damages simply to enable the agent to get commission. If, however, the vendor does get his money, he would probably be liable to pay the commission out of it. It only remains to add that, when no binding contract has been made, the vendor can himself withdraw at any time without being liable to pay commission: see *Luxor (Eastbourne) Ltd.* v. *Cooper.*'

It seems that Denning LJ considered that there would be a liability to the agent if the agent's employer failed to perform or defaulted on his contract with the third party. It seems to me that that passage is in line with what Scrutton LJ said in *Martyn's* case and what Lord Wright said in *Luxor (Eastbourne) Ltd* v *Cooper*.

We were referred to certain earlier cases by counsel for the plaintiffs, but I do not think it is necessary that I should cite them. I say that primarily because it seems to me that the whole law relating to these matters was reviewed by the House of Lords in *Luxor (Eastbourne) Ltd* v *Cooper* in 1941, and no great advantage is gained by going back before that date.

Were it not for the decision of the House of Lords in *L French & Co Ltd* v *Leeston Shipping Co Ltd* ([1922] 1 AC 451, [1922] All ER Rep 314), I do not think I should hesitate long before following the observations of Lord Wright in *Luxor (Eastbourne) Ltd* v *Cooper* which I read. The reputation of Lord Wright as a commercial lawyer is one of the greatest. Anything he has said after a very careful consideration of the whole law of agency contracts merits the greatest respect and consideration. However, there is a difficulty in reconciling what Lord Wright said in *Luxor (Eastbourne) Ltd* v *Cooper* with what the House of Lords said in *L French & Co Ltd* v *Leeston Shipping Co Ltd*. The latter case appears to involve the concept that an agent, who has been employed by a person to assist him to enter into a contract with a third party and has reserved for himself a benefit from that contract, has no remedy if, for some reason or other, the person who employed him brings the contract to an end.

I am fully conscious of the difficulty presented by the *Leeston Shipping Co* case, but I do not think that it is applicable to a case of the kind which we have here. The true basis of the *Leeston Shipping Co* case, as I understand it, is that a person is free to deal with his property as he chooses, and a person is entitled either to carry on his business or give up carrying on his business as he wishes. It would not be right, therefore, to imply in a contract between him and an agent a term that he should not be free to deal with his property as he chooses, or should not be able to continue or to give up his business as he wishes. That seems to me quite a different proposition from saying that, when an agent has introduced a buyer to a seller and a contract has been made between the seller and the buyer with a benefit reserved to the agent under an agency contract, the seller is entitled to break his contract with the buyer without being under any liability to the agent for the loss which the agent thereby suffers.

In my judgment, the reasoning underlying the observations of Lord Wright in *Luxor* (*Eastbourne*) *Ltd v Cooper* which I have read is sound and sensible reasoning, and is fully applicable to a case of this kind.

There is no question here of denying the defendants' freedom to deal with their own property as they choose. There is no question of denying them freedom either to continue their business or not to continue it as they wish. This was what one might call a 'one-off' transaction. The defendants were introduced by the plaintiffs to a buyer of cement. It was in the contemplation of the plaintiffs that the defendants would make a contract of sale with that buyer. The defendants did make a contract of sale with that buyer on the basis that, if the contract was performed, the agent would receive substantial remuneration. The only reason the contract was not performed was that the defendants were either unwilling or unable to perform it.

It seems to me that, in a case of that kind, it is right for the court to imply a term that the defendants will not fail to perform their contract with the buyer so as to deprive the agent of the remuneration due to him under the agency contract.

Various tests have been propounded from time to time with regard to the implication of terms in a contract. The officious bystander is one of the tests which has been used. It seems to me that the officious bystander, looking over the shoulders of Mr Brodie and Mr Marchant Lane, as they made the contract which they did, and asking himself whether the defendants could make a contract with Muellers and then break it without incurring any liability to the plaintiffs, would have answered, 'No, that cannot be what is intended. It must be intended that, if they make the contract, after having had the buyer introduced to them, they will perform it and enable the agent to earn his remuneration.'

For the reasons that I have given, I am of the opinion that the learned judge was right in the view which he took that the plaintiffs' case based on an implied term of the contract succeeded.

I would uphold the learned judge's judgment and dismiss this appeal.

TEMPLEMAN LJ. The plaintiff agents contracted to provide, and did provide, for the defendant vendors a purchaser for 10,000 metric tons of cement at $49·50 per ton in consideration of the vendors agreeing to pay the agents' commission of $1·50 per ton out of the purchase price. The vendors entered into the stipulated contract with the purchaser, but the purchase price was never paid because the vendors, in breach of their contract with the purchaser, failed to supply the cement and thereby released the purchaser from its obligation to pay the purchase price.

The agents claim damages on the grounds that the vendors are in breach of an implied term in the contract between the agents and the vendors, an implied term that the vendors would perform their contract with the purchaser so as to become entitled to the purchase price out of which the commission was to be paid.

The vendors deny that any term is to be implied. By repudiating their contract with the purchaser, they painlessly released themselves from their contract with the agents.

Counsel for the defendant vendors submitted that there was no room or necessity for any implied term. The commission was only payable out of the purchase price paid by the purchaser. The purchase price was never paid. Therefore, the commission never became payable.

In the present case, the agents performed their part of their bargain with the vendors by providing a purchaser who was ready and willing to contract with the vendors. The vendors utilised and took advantage of the services provided by the agents by entering into a contract with the purchaser on terms acceptable to the vendors and, no doubt, designed and intended by the vendors to produce a profit for themselves.

In my judgment, it is necessary to imply a term to prevent the vendors from making use of the agents' services without being under any liability to the agents to ensure, so far as the vendors were concerned, that the agents then received the stipulated reward for the agents' services, which were supplied to and utilised by the vendors. An agent does not provide services and agree to accept and postpone payment for his services restricted to the purchase price on terms that the vendor, who accepts, exploits and makes use of the agent's services, is free to deprive the agent of the reward promised for the services of the agent if the vendor thinks fit to do so. If there was no implied term in the present case, the vendors could have sold their cement to the purchaser provided by the agents if the market price of cement went down, thus increasing the benefit of the contract with the purchaser so far as the vendors were concerned.

On the other hand, if the market price of cement remained stable or went up, the vendors were free in the absence of an implied term to sell to a third party, to repudiate their contract with the purchaser furnished by the agents, and in the result would be $1·50 per tonne better off at the expense of the agents.

If the vendors are right, they were entitled to keep $1·50 per tonne in their pocket by selling to a third party while retaining power to complete their contract with the purchaser provided by the agents, if that contract in the event yielded the vendors a higher rate of profit than any available contract with a third party. In other words, the agents' commission depended on the vendors not discovering that it was worth their while to break their contract with the agents' purchaser and thereby deprive the agent of the commission which was earned by the services provided by the agent and exploited and utilised by the vendors.

In my judgment, it is necessary to imply a term which prevents a vendor, in these circumstances, from playing a dirty trick on the agent with impunity after making use of the services provided by that agent in order to secure the very position and safety of the vendor. It is necessary to imply a term which prevents the vendor from acting unreasonably to the possible gain of the vendor and the loss of the agent. In my judgment, the term properly to be implied in the present circumstance is that the vendors will not deprive the agents of their commission by committing a breach of the contract between the vendors and the purchaser which releases the purchaser from its obligation to pay the purchase price.

Counsel for the defendants relied on *Luxor (Eastbourne) Ltd v Cooper* [1941] 1 All ER 33, [1941] AC 108. In that case the House of Lords held that a promise to pay a commission on completion of a sale did not imply an obligation on the vendor to enter into any contract for sale. The position would have been different if the vendor, as in the present case, not only received the benefit of the agent's work in finding a purchaser but also made use of the agent's services by entering into a contract which bound that purchaser for the benefit of the vendor on terms acceptable to and dictated by the vendor.

Lord Wright said that the result is different 'if the negotiations between the vendor and the purchaser have been duly concluded and a binding executory agreement has been achieved' (see [1941] 1 All ER 33 at 55, [1941] AC 108 at 142). It is true that he then refers to specific performance which was relevant to the facts in the *Luxor* case, which dealt with real property. For myself, I can see no sensible distinction between an agency contract relating to the sale of real property and other agency contracts for present purposes.

Similarly, Lord Wright said that different considerations would apply if a contract had been entered into. He said, in particular ([1941] 1 All ER 33 at 61, [1941] AC 108 at 150):

'It cannot have been contemplated that, when a binding contract with the purchaser has been made on the agent's mediation, the principal can, as between himself and the agent, break that contract without breaking his contract with the agent.'

Adapting those words to the present circumstances, it cannot have been contemplated that when a binding contract with the purchaser had been made on the agents' mediation, the vendors, as principals, could as between themselves and the agents break that contract with the purchaser without breaking their contract with the agents.

The result which I have reached is consistent with the dicta of Lord Wright in the *Luxor* case, and also with the decision of Rowlatt J in *Vulcan Car Agency Ltd v Fiat Motors Ltd* (1915) 32 TLR 73. The result is also consistent with the dissenting judgment of Scrutton LJ, later upheld by the House of Lords, in *George Trollope & Sons v Martyn Brothers* [1934] 2 KB 436 at 445–446, and with the observations of Denning LJ in *Dennis Reed Ltd v Goody* [1950] 1 All ER 919 at 923, [1950] 2 KB 277 at 285.

Counsel for the defendants relied on the decision of the House of Lords in *L French & Co Ltd v Leeston Shipping Co Ltd* [1922] 1 AC 451, [1922] All ER Rep 314. In that case shipowners had agreed to pay an agent commission on the monthly hire charge payable during an 18-month charterparty. After four months the shipowners sold the vessel to the charterers whereupon the charterparty automatically came to an end. The agents claimed commission for the remaining 14 months of the charterparty period. Lord Buckmaster said that the agent could only succeed if the court implied a term in the contract between the shipowners and the agents that the shipowners would not terminate the charterparty under any circumstances by agreement (see [1922] 1 AC 451 at 454, [1922] All ER Rep 314 at 315). Lord Sumner said that the implied term which was sought created an obligation, virtually, that the shipowner would not sell his own ship during the charter term (see [1922] 1 AC 451 at 456, [1922] All ER Rep 314 at 316). All their Lordships refused to imply any term and the agent's claim failed. Both Lord Buckmaster and Lord Dunedin expressed the view that different considerations might apply if, in the words of Lord Buckmaster—

'the destruction of the position upon which the right to commission arose was expressly effected by the person bound to pay the commission for the purpose of relieving himself from liability for payment.'

(See [1922] 1 AC 451 at 455, [1922] All ER Rep 314 at 316.)

There are difficulties in this concept which I feel involves analysing the motives, possibly the mixed motives, of actions taken by principals which result in commissions not being payable.

In *Kahn v Aircraft Industries Corpn Ltd* [1937] 3 All ER 476 at 482 Slesser LJ referred to the decision in *L French & Co v Leeston Shipping Co* as one of a line of authorities which establish that the court will not imply an obligation on any principal to go on conducting his business in order to enable the agent to earn his commission.

In my judgment, *L French & Co v Leeston Shipping Co*, where the principal did not commit any breach of any contract procured by the agent and where the suggested implied term would have created an intolerable burden for the principal, has no application to the present case.

In the present case, I can see no uncertainty, no difficulty and no hardship in implying a term that, if the principal enters into a contract with a third party procured by the agents, then the principal agrees that he will not deprive the agent of his commission by committing a breach of the contract which releases the third party from his obligation to pay the purchase price which is the sole agreed source of the agent's commission.

In my judgment, it is necessary to imply a term in the present case because no agent would agree and no principal would attempt to insist that the principal should be able to take the benefit of the agent's work and the advantages of the contract with the third party and yet retain the right to defeat the agent's claim for commission by breaking his contractual obligations to the third party.

I would dismiss the appeal.

LAWTON LJ. I agree with both the judgments which have been delivered. The point of this appeal, in my opinion, can be expressed in one sentence. Is the implied term relied on by the plaintiffs such as is necessary to give the transaction business efficacy?

The life of an agent in commerce is a precarious one. He is like the groom who takes a horse to the water-trough. He may get his principal to the negotiating table but when he gets there there is nothing he can do to make the principal sign, any more than the groom can make the horse drink. This has been recognised by the law by the decision in *Luxor (Eastbourne) Ltd v Cooper* [1941] 1 All ER 33, [1941] AC 108.

Once the signing has been done, the agent is in a different position altogether, because by that time the principal has accepted the benefit of the agent's work. In those circumstances, he ought not to be allowed to resile from his obligations to the agent. As a matter of business efficacy, if principals in that sort of situation could behave in the way described by Templeman LJ in his judgment, agents would not work for them. In other words, the whole relationship of principal and agent depends on the principal accepting his obligations to the agent once the agent has done his work and the principal has accepted the benefit of it.

I, too, would dismiss the appeal.

Appeal dismissed.

Solicitors: *Ashurst, Morris, Crisp & Co* (for the defendants); *Lucien A Isaacs & Co* (for the plaintiffs).

Mary Rose Plummer   Barrister.

Attorney General's Reference (No 2 of 1980)

COURT OF APPEAL, CRIMINAL DIVISION
LORD LANE CJ, STOCKER AND GLIDEWELL JJ
3rd, 24th OCTOBER 1980

Criminal law – Forgery – Forgery of document made evidence by law – Written statement of witness – Police officer forging witness's statement and later tendering it in evidence to magistrates' court – Whether officer forging document 'made evidence by law' – Whether officer uttering forged document made evidence by law when tendering statement in evidence – Forgery Act 1913, ss 3(3)(g), 6(1).

A police officer in charge of a summary prosecution forged a written statement of a witness's evidence because he had forgotten to approach the witness for a statement. At the hearing the officer handed the statement to the clerk of the magistrates' court as a written statement he was tendering under s 9(1)[a] of the Criminal Justice Act 1967. Under s 9(2) of that Act certain conditions had to be satisfied before the statement was admissible in evidence. On the basis that the statement was genuine the clerk properly received it in evidence. The officer later admitted that the statement had not been made or signed by the witness and was charged with forging, with intent to deceive, a document which was made evidence by law, contrary to s 3(3)(g)[b] of the Forgery Act 1913, and with uttering such a document, contrary to s 6(1)[c] of the 1913 Act. At his trial the judge ruled that there was no case to go to the jury because (i) at the time the statement was forged it was not 'evidence by law' within s 3(3)(g) since it only became

---

a   Section 9, so far as material, is set out at p 495 e, post
b   Section 3(3), so far as material, is set out at p 495 d, post
c   Section 6(1), so far as material, provides: 'Every person who utters any forged document . . . shall be guilty of an offence and on conviction thereof shall be liable to the same punishment as if he himself had forged the document . . .'

'evidence' when it was received in evidence by the magistrates' court, and (ii) the statement was uttered, at the latest, when it was tendered to the court by the officer and at that moment it had not been received in evidence, and therefore no offence under s 6(1) of the 1913 Act had been committed. On a reference by the Attorney-General to the court for its opinion on the meaning of s 3(3)(g) of the 1913 Act, it was submitted by the officer that documents 'made evidence by law' for the purpose of s 3(3)(g) were confined to documents which at all stages of their existence were admissible in evidence (eg the Official Gazette) and that documents which were made admissible only if certain conditions were fulfilled were excluded since they had no status as 'evidence' within s 3(3)(g) until those conditions were fulfilled.

Held – (1) The expression 'made evidence by law' in s 3(3)(g) of the 1913 Act described the class of document which was covered by s 3(3)(g) and not the moment when, by reception in evidence, a document in that class was made 'evidence'. Accordingly, s 3(3)(g) covered forgery of any document which would become evidence in law if tendered in evidence in proceedings in accordance with the statutory provisions relating to it, and was not confined to the forgery of such a document after it had become 'evidence' in the sense of being properly received in evidence (see p 496 j to p 497 g, post).

(2) It followed that a person who with intent to deceive forged a written statement which was later tendered as evidence to a magistrates' court under s 9 of the 1967 Act committed an offence under s 3(3)(g) of the 1913 Act, and that when he tendered the statement to the court he uttered a forged document made evidence by law, contrary to s 6(1) of the 1913 Act (see p 497 g, post).

Notes

For forgery of legal documents, see 11 Halsbury's Laws (4th Edn) para 1359, for uttering forged documents, see ibid, para 1368, and for cases on forgery of legal documents and on uttering, see 15 Digest (Reissue) 1486, 1487, 1490–1494, 13,246–13,253, 13,284–13,325.

For the Forgery Act 1913, ss 3, 6, see 8 Halsbury's Statutes (3rd Edn) 261, 264.

For the Criminal Justice Act 1967, s 9, see ibid 585.

Reference

This was a reference by the Attorney General under s 36 of the Criminal Justice Act 1972 asking for the opinion of the Court of Appeal, Criminal Division, on two points of law under the Forgery Act 1913. The points of law are set out in the judgment.

David Tudor Price for the Attorney General.
Peter Digney for the respondent.

Cur adv vult

24th October. **STOCKER J** read the following judgment of the court: This is a reference by the Attorney General under the provisions of s 36 of the Criminal Justice Act 1972, a proceeding whereby the Attorney General can institute steps for the testing of a direction on a principle of law decided in the Crown Court which seems to have been wrongly decided and which may be in danger of reproduction in later cases if not corrected.

This case concerns the tendering as evidence at the trial of an accused person before a magistrates' court of a statement pursuant to s 9 of the Criminal Justice Act 1967. The statement had not been made or signed by the person by whom it was purported to have been made and signed but had been written and signed by the police officer tendering it. The judge at the trial of that officer for forgery and uttering a forged document ruled that there was no case to go to the jury under s 3(3)(g) of the Forgery Act 1913 since the document only became evidence when tendered to the court, and at the time of the forgery had not achieved the status of 'a document which is made evidence by law' and ruled that accordingly there was no evidence under s 6(1) that a forged document had been uttered.

The point of law which this court has been asked to decide has been stated in the reference in the following terms: (a) whether a person who with intent to deceive forges a written statement which is later tendered to a magistrates' court under s 9 of the Criminal Justice Act 1967 commits an offence under s 3(3)(g) of the Forgery Act 1913 of forging a document which is made evidence by law; (b) whether a person who knowingly hands to the court a forged written statement which he is tendering under s 9 of the Criminal Justice Act 1967 commits an offence under s 6(1) of the Forgery Act 1913 of uttering a forged document which is made evidence by law.

The facts as set out in the reference are as follows. (i) The accused man who was a police officer was in charge of a summary prosecution. (ii) At the hearing of this prosecution in open court he handed to the clerk of the court a written statement which he was tendering under the provisions of s 9 of the Criminal Justice Act 1967 with the consent of the defence. (iii) The court received the statement in evidence. (iv) The accused later admitted that the purported witness had neither made the statement nor signed it. (v) The matters contained in the statement were capable of proof by two witnesses but the accused stated that because he had forgotten to approach them by the date of the trial he wrote the purported statement to cover up his omission.

The police officer concerned was charged on an indictment containing two counts: first, forgery contrary to s 3(3)(g) of the Forgery Act 1913; second, uttering such document contrary to s6(1) thereof.

The 1913 Act, by s 3(3), makes it an offence to forge 'the following documents . . . with intent to defraud or deceive . . . (g) . . . any document which is made evidence by law . . .' It was not disputed that the document tendered, if genuine, was properly admitted in evidence in accordance with s 9 of the Criminal Justice Act 1967, which states:

> '(1) In any criminal proceedings . . . a written statement by any person shall, if such of the conditions mentioned in the next following subsection as are applicable are satisfied, be admissible as evidence to the like extent as oral evidence to the like effect by that person.'

It is unnecessary for the purpose of this judgment to recite in detail the conditions referred to in sub-s (1) save to observe that sub-s (2) states the form and necessary contents of the statement and requires that before the hearing at which it is tendered a copy shall be served on each of the other parties to the proceedings and that no objection to it being tendered in evidence is received from any party within seven days. Subsection (3) sets out further procedural requirements which must be fulfilled before that statement can be admitted. Subsection (4) confers power on parties to the proceedings or the court of its own motion to require the person who made the statement to give oral evidence notwithstanding that the statement is admissible in evidence, all requirements having been fulfilled.

The judge's ruling was in these terms:

> 'What was the nature of that written statement at the time it was so falsely, on the evidence, dishonestly prepared or forged by the accused? At this stage it was no more than a witness statement, or purported to be a witness statement made by the witness. At the time it was forged it was not, on any view, a document made evidence by law.'

The judge continued later:

> 'When was the uttering? In my view it must be, at the latest, the tendering of the statement to be used in evidence. It is right that it was subsequently read, but that was the administrative process of dealing with it after it had been accepted in evidence. At the moment of tendering it was not a document made evidence by law and it could not be until it had been accepted in evidence.'

Counsel for the respondent in his submissions to this court supported this part of the judge's ruling quoted above on the same grounds that he had advanced to the trial judge when advocating such a ruling.

His first submission was that s 9 of the 1967 Act did not make the document itself evidence but only its contents and that properly construed the words in s 9(1) 'shall be admissible to the like extent as oral evidence to the like effect by that person' meant that the document was the medium through which the evidence of the matter contained in the statement would be put before the court. He supported this construction of the section by the contention that in practice statements under s 9 were not put in evidence but were read either wholly or in part to the court. This court, while accepting that the reading of statements rather than their being put in evidence as documents may be common practice in the Crown Court, doubts whether in the magistrates' court this is a universal practice. In any event, such practice does not assist in the construction of s 9 of the 1967 Act, the wording of which states in terms which seem unequivocal, 'a written statement by a person . . . shall be admissible as evidence'. The trial judge rejected counsel's contention and held that the written statement itself was made evidence by the Act. We agree with this part of his ruling and do not propose further to consider it.

Counsel's second submission, which was accepted as correct by the trial judge and is the basis of his ruling, the correctness of which this court has been asked to consider, was that the document itself when made and forged is not at that stage evidence at all or admissible as such. It becomes evidence under the Act if, and only if, the requirements of s 9(2), (3) and (4) of the 1967 Act have been complied with and the document had been tendered to the court as evidence. He argued that until these requirements were fulfilled, the document was simply a document and not evidence at all, either under the Criminal Justice Act 1967 or in any other sense and thus could not be the subject of forgery under s 3(3)(g) of the Forgery Act 1913 since it was not at the time at which the 'forgery' took place a document 'made evidence by law'. In support of this submission he sought to draw a distinction between certain classes of documents made evidence under certain other statutes and statements tendered under the 1967 Act. It is manifest that in 1913, when the Forgery Act became law, statements under s 9 of the Criminal Justice Act 1967 could not have been in contemplation and he sought to argue that the documents which at that date might have been tendered which were the subject matter of s 3(3)(g) were documents which the relevant statutes relating to them made 'evidence' in the sense that they were themselves evidence at all stages and did not require any conditions to be fulfilled as a prerequisite of their admissibility. He submitted that the proper formula to apply in reaching the decision whether a document was or was not 'evidence' for the purpose of s 9 of the Criminal Justice Act 1967, and if forged for the purpose of conviction under s 3(3)(g) of the Forgery Act 1913, was: does anything remain to be done before the document can be admitted in evidence?

He submitted that documents made evidence by statute prior to 1913 and which were accordingly documents 'made evidence by law' had the characteristic that nothing remained to be done to render them admissible. He cited a number of Acts and documents made evidence under them such as s 1 of the Evidence Act 1845, s 7 of the Evidence Act 1851 and such documents as the Official Gazette, which were themselves evidence of the proclamation, order or regulations published therein. His contention was that the definition of documents 'made evidence by law' for the purpose of s 3(3)(g) of the Forgery Act 1913 was confined to such documents and excluded documents which were admissible only on the performance of certain conditions, for the reason already stated that, at the time they were forged they were no more than statements and had no status as evidence.

In our view the judge's ruling and the arguments advanced in support of it are erroneous and should be rejected. We accept that there are classes of documents which by statute are themselves 'evidence' proving the facts contained in them on production without further formality, such as certificates of birth or marriage (covered by s 3(2)(a) of the 1913 Act), Queen's Printers' copies of statutes or other official orders, but these, too, in our view become 'evidence' only when tendered as such to the appropriate court or other tribunal. If the judge's ruling and counsel's argument in support of it are correct, even this class of document would not be capable of being forged until tendered in evidence (subject to specific statutory enactments regarding this). Nor do we accept as valid counsel's formula that documents within the ambit of s 3(3)(g) are confined to documents which require nothing further to be done before they can be admitted, since, for example, the Bankers' Books Evidence Act 1879, which renders a copy of an entry in a banker's book receivable as evidence, prescribes a number of requirements and formalities to be fulfilled before an entry in a banker's book is so receivable, with the consequence that if the judge's ruling and counsel's argument are correct, no false copy of such entry would support a conviction under s 3(3)(g) of the 1913 Act until it was tendered in evidence, nor could it be uttered until after it was so received. We cite these examples in support of our view that the judge's ruling renders impossible in every or almost every case any conviction under s 3(3)(g) of the Forgery Act 1913 unless the forgery takes place after the document is received as evidence.

This rather startling consequence is not necessarily conclusive of the point in issue but in our view stems from a misconstruction of the meaning of the word 'evidence' in s 3(3) of the 1913 Act. In our view no 'evidence' can exist, be it documentary, oral or in the form of an exhibit, until it is received as such in proceedings in which it is evidence of the fact then in issue. It seems contrary to the manifest intention of the 1913 Act to confine offences under s 3(3)(g) to documents after they have become evidence in that sense.

We think it so improbable that the draftsman of s 3(3)(g) of the 1913 Act had in mind that the subject matter of that section should be forgery after the document had been tendered in evidence that any conclusion which confines the subject matter of this section to that situation can be regarded as fanciful. On this basis the judge's ruling would for practical purposes deprive this subsection of all subject matter.

In our judgment, on its proper construction, s 3(3)(g) is concerned with documents which if made and tendered in accordance with the provisions and conditions of the relevant Act become documents 'made evidence by law' and it is the forgery of such class of documents which is the subject matter of this subsection. Thus the phrase 'document which is made evidence by law' is descriptive of a class of document, and is not descriptive of the moment when its reception in evidence renders it 'evidence'.

Consequently any person commits an offence under s 3(3)(g) of the Forgery Act 1913 if he, with intent to defraud or deceive, forges any document which if made and tendered in evidence in accordance with the terms and conditions of the relevant statute relating thereto, will become a document made evidence by law.

For these reasons, in our view, the ruling of the judge on this point was wrong and we would answer each question posed in the reference in the affirmative and will so advise the Attorney General.

Determination accordingly.

Solicitors: *Director of Public Prosecutions*; *Bertram White & Co*, Epsom (for the respondent).

N P Metcalfe Esq   Barrister.

Armar Shipping Co Ltd v Caisse Algérienne d'Assurance et de Réassurance
The Armar

COURT OF APPEAL, CIVIL DIVISION
MEGAW, EVELEIGH AND OLIVER LJJ
17th, 18th, 31st JULY 1980

Conflict of laws – Contract – Proper law of contract – Average bond – Lloyd's average bond executed in Algeria between Cyprian shipowner and Algerian insurers – Bond not stating law governing contract – Parties having no connection with England – Shipowner having right under bill of lading to nominate venue for adjustment of general average – Shipowner arranging for adjustment in London – Time for determining proper law of contract – Whether designation of London under bill of lading making English law proper law of bond – Whether bond having floating proper law until determined retrospectively by subsequent events.

Practice – Service out of the jurisdiction – Action on contract governed by English law – Proper law of contract – Claim in respect of general average contribution – Lloyd's average bond executed in Algeria between Cyprian shipowner and Algerian insurers – Bond not stating law governing contract – Parties having no connection with England – Shipowner having right under bill of lading to nominate venue for adjustment of general average – Shipowner arranging for adjustment in London – Shipowners claiming against insurers in England – Whether designation of London under bill of lading making English law the proper law of the contract under the bond – Whether court having jurisdiction to grant shipowner leave to serve notice of writ out of the jurisdiction on the insurers – RSC Ord 11, r 1(1)(f)(iii).

The plaintiffs, a Cyprian ship-owning company, chartered a vessel on a time charter to a Cuban company for the carriage of a cargo of two consignments of sugar from Cuba to Spain and Algeria. The charterparty provided for arbitration and the settlement and adjustment of general average in London, but the terms of the charterparty were not incorporated into the bills of lading for the two consignments. Instead the bills of lading provided for the adjustment of general average at a port or place chosen by the plaintiffs. During the course of the voyage the vessel grounded off a Spanish port and the plaintiffs incurred expenditure of a general average nature in order to be able to complete the voyage. Following discharge of the Spanish consignment the vessel proceeded to Algeria where the Algerian consignees and the defendants, an Algerian company who were the consignees' insurers, executed a Lloyd's average bond at the plaintiffs' request. Under the terms of the bond, which was in English, the consignees agreed to pay the plaintiffs the general average charges found to be payable on their consignment. The bond contained a reservation in French reserving to the defendants 'the right to discuss both the principles of general average and the amounts of the contribution'. The bond did not state the law which was to govern the contract; nor did it incorporate the bill of lading or contain provision for London arbitration or for submission to the jurisdiction of the English courts. The plaintiffs then arranged for general average to be adjusted in London, that being their choice of venue under the bill of lading. The defendants were found to be liable to pay the plaintiffs £52,420 on the adjustment but they refused to pay. The plaintiffs issued a writ in England against the defendants claiming the amount due and obtained leave under RSC Ord 11, r 1(1)[a] to serve notice of the writ on the defendants in Algeria. On an application by the defendants to set aside the order granting leave, on the grounds that they were not parties to the bill of lading and that the bond was not a contract which was either expressly or impliedly governed by English

---

a   Rule 1(1), so far as material, is set out at p 500 a b, post

law within Ord 11, r 1(1)(*f*)(iii), the judge held that the bond was impliedly governed by English law and refused to exercise his discretion to set aside the order. The judge decided that the bond could be regarded as having a floating proper law until the plaintiffs' choice of venue for the adjustment fixed the proper law as English law, notwithstanding that the proper law was thereby determined by an event occurring after the contract had been made. On appeal,

Held – Because a contract was required to have a proper law at the time it was made in order that disputes which might arise immediately following the formation of the contract could be settled, the proper law of a contract was that law attaching to it at the time it was made. It followed that the proper law could not be determined retrospectively by an event which at the time the contract was made was merely an uncertain event in the future. Nor could the contract float in an absence of law until the proper law was determined, nor could it change from one country to another on the happening of subsequent events. The choice of London by the plaintiffs as the venue for the adjustment of general average therefore had no relevance in determining the proper law of the bond and, since there were no other factors making English law the legal system with which the bond had the closest and most real connection, the court did not have jurisdiction to grant leave for service of notice of the writ out of the jurisdiction on the defendants. The appeal would accordingly be allowed (see p 504 *g* to p 505 *d* and *g* to *j*, post).

Notes
For an inferred choice of law and for time for determining intention of parties, see 8 Halsbury's Laws (4th Edn) paras 585, 590, and for cases on the subjects, see 11 Digest (Reissue) 458–468, 760–800.

For leave to serve writ out of jurisdiction, see 30 Halsbury's Laws (3rd Edn) 323–326, paras 588–589, and for cases on the subject, see 50 Digest (Repl) 336–338, 652–663.

Cases cited
Compagnie d'Armement Maritime SA v Compagnie Tunisienne de Navigation SA [1970] 3 All ER 71, [1971] AC 572, HL.
Rossano v Manufacturers Life Insurance Co Ltd [1962] 2 All ER 214, [1963] 2 QB 352.
Schothorst and Schuitema v Franz Dauter GmbH, The Nimrod [1973] 2 Lloyd's Rep 91.

Interlocutory appeal
By a writ dated 8th October 1979 the plaintiffs, Armar Shipping Co Ltd, of Cyprus, brought an action against the defendants, Caisse Algérienne d'Assurance et de Réassurance, of Algeria, claiming general average contributions in accordance with a statement of general average prepared by adjusters in London on 14th February 1977 in which general average expenditures and sacrifices arising from the stranding of the mv Armar off Santander, Spain, on 17th April 1974 were apportioned between the parties pursuant to an agreement contained in a Lloyd's average bond signed by the parties on 24th May 1974. On 5th October 1979 Robert Goff J gave the plaintiffs leave under RSC Ord 11, r 1 to issue the writ and to serve notice of it on the defendants in Algeria. The defendants appealed to the judge in chambers to set aside that order. On 2nd April 1980 Mustill J dismissed the appeal. The defendants appealed to the Court of Appeal. The facts are set out in the judgment of Megaw LJ.

Peregrin Simon for the defendants.
Stewart Boyd for the plaintiffs.

Cur adv vult

31st July. The following judgments were read.

MEGAW LJ. This appeal from an order of Mustill J of 2nd April 1980 is concerned with the question whether leave should be given to the plaintiffs, a shipowning company in Cyprus, to serve notice of a writ out of the jurisdiction on the intended defendants, an Algerian company. Mustill J granted leave. The defendants (I shall for brevity omit the word 'intended') appeal to this court.

The issue arises on RSC Ord 11, r 1(1)(*f*)(iii). Leave may be given to serve out of the jurisdiction, under that paragraph, where the action is brought on a contract which 'is by its terms, or by implication, governed by English law'. The contract here in question is contained in a Lloyd's average bond which was signed on behalf of the plaintiffs and the defendants on 24th May 1974.

The plaintiffs own a vessel, the Armar. By a charterparty dated 6th February 1973 they chartered the Armar for 20 months to a Cuban company, Empresa Cubana de Fletes. The charterparty included a London arbitration clause and a provision that general average would be settled and adjusted in London according to the York-Antwerp Rules 1950. It is agreed that those charterparty provisions do not affect the issue with which we are concerned. Perhaps unusually, the charterparty terms were not incorporated into the bill of lading contract, to which I shall refer hereafter. We, therefore, do not have to consider what the decision should have been in the present case if the charterparty terms had been incorporated.

Under the charterparty, a cargo of sugar was shipped at Havana for carriage to Santander in Spain and to Mostaganem in Algeria. There were, of course, separate bills of lading for the parcels of cargo destined to these different destinations. The bill of lading which was before the court was that of the parcel destined to Mostaganem. Mustill J was prepared to hold that, apart from quantity and destination, there would be no material difference in the terms of the two contracts of carriage, if and in so far as those terms might be relevant to the issue which he had to decide.

A question was raised before us in the submissions on behalf of the defendants as to the proper law of the bill of lading contract. It would seem that this had not been raised in the arguments before Mustill J. I do not know what the answer to that question would be; but I do not think that it matters for the decision of the present issue. No one suggests that it is English law.

As I have said, the bill of lading did not incorporate the charterparty terms. The only part of the bill of lading contract which, on the submissions, might be relevant is the first paragraph of cl 10. It reads:

> 'General average shall be adjusted, stated and settled, according to York-Antwerp Rules 1950, except Rule XXII thereof, at such port or place as may be selected by the Carrier. Matters not provided for by these rules to be adjusted, stated and settled according to the laws and usages at such port or place as may be selected by the carrier.'

'The carrier' in this provision is the plaintiff shipowner.

On the face of the bill of lading, against 'Consignee', appear the words 'To order'; and then, against the printed words 'Notify (if consigned to shipper's order)', were typed the initials ONACO, with an address in Algeria. It is not in dispute that ONACO are to be regarded as the consignees and, at the relevant time, the owners of the parcel of sugar as purchasers, directly or indirectly from the shippers, even though no indorsement appears on the copy of the bill of lading before the court. They obtained their title, as purchasers, by transfer to them of the bill of lading.

During the voyage, on 17th April 1974, the vessel grounded off Santander. It is asserted by the owners, the plaintiffs, that they incurred sacrifices and expenditures of a general average nature, in order to enable the voyage to be completed. The parcel destined to Santander was discharged at that port. The vessel went on to Mostaganem.

At Mostaganem, before the cargo was delivered to ONACO and, no doubt, as a condition of the plaintiffs not exercising a lien in respect of a claim for general average contribution, a Lloyd's average bond was signed on 24th May 1974. It was signed by the master on behalf of the shipowners, the plaintiffs. In the schedule, which contains columns in which are identified (i) the number of the bill of lading, (ii) the description and quantity of cargo and (iii) the signature and address of consignees, the consignees were shown as ONACO; but the signature, verifying a rubber stamp bearing the name of the defendant company, was that of the defendant company. No doubt they are insurers of ONACO. It is not disputed that the defendants became parties to the contract contained in the Lloyd's average bond. Over their stamp and signature there were typed, in the French language, words of reservation as follows: 'Sous Réserve de discuter tant les principes de l'avarie commune que le taux de la contribution.'

The Lloyd's average bond is a printed form with its title 'Lloyd's Average Bond' in large print at the top. The first paragraph of the bond reads as follows:

'AN AGREEMENT made this   day of   19   BETWEEN ARMAR SHIPPING CO OF FAMAGUSTA, CYPRUS, Owner of the ship or vessel called the ARMAR of the first part and the several Persons whose names or Firms are set and subscribed hereto being respectively consignees of Cargo on board the said Ship of the second part WHEREAS the said Ship lately arrived in the Port of   on a voyage from   and it is alleged that during such voyage the Vessel met with a casualty and sustained damage and loss and that sacrifices were made and expenditure incurred which may form a Charge on the Cargo or some part thereof or be the subject of a salvage and/or a general average contribution but the same cannot be immediately ascertained and in the meantime it is desirable that the Cargo shall be delivered NOW THEREFORE THESE PRESENTS WITNESS and the said Owner in consideration of the agreement of the parties hereto of the second part hereinafter contained hereby agrees with the respective parties hereto of the second part that he will deliver to them respectively or to their order respectively their respective consignments particulars whereof are contained in the Schedule hereto on payment of the freight payable on delivery if any and the said parties hereto of the second part in consideration of the said Agreement of the said Owner for themselves severally and respectively and not the one for the others of them hereby agree with the said Owner that they will pay to the said Owner of the said Ship the proper and respective proportion of any salvage and/or general average and/or particular and/or other charges which may be chargeable upon their respective consignments particulars whereof are contained in the Schedule hereto or to which the Shippers or Owners of such consignments may be liable to contribute in respect of such damage loss sacrifice or expenditure and the said parties hereto of the second part further promise and agree forthwith to furnish to the Owner of the said Ship a correct account and particulars of the value of the goods delivered to them respectively in order that any such salvage and/or general average and/or particular and/or other charges may be ascertained and adjusted in the usual manner.'

The second and third paragraphs contain provisions, which were not brought into operation in this case, for the deposit by the consignees of security in joint names. Nothing, therefore, turns in this case on the fact that those paragraphs contain the word 'trustees', which in other circumstances might have some bearing on an issue as to the proper law of the contract.

The Lloyd's average bond contains no express provision as to the law which is to govern the contract contained therein; nor is there any provision for arbitration in London or for submission to the jurisdiction of the English courts, which, if such provision had been included, would, in English private international law, almost inevitably have made such an agreement governed by English law. In this respect, the Lloyd's average bond differs significantly from two other standard forms of agreement bearing the name of Lloyd's: the Lloyd's standard form of salvage agreement 'no cure—no pay', and the Lloyd's general average bond and guarantee, settlement of claims abroad. The texts of these forms are set out in British Shipping Laws, vol 7, Law of General Average and the York-Antwerp Rules (10th Edn, 1975, appendix 3, at paras 1068–1084, 1085–1090). In their text, in contrast with the standard form with which we are concerned, there are provisions which might be said to point, at least strongly, to English law as being the intended proper law.

After the Lloyd's average bond was signed (how long after we do not know) the plaintiffs arranged for general average to be adjusted in London. That, vis-à-vis a bill of lading holder, the plaintiffs were contractually entitled to do by virtue of cl 10 of the bill of lading. The resulting adjustment was published in London on 14th February 1977. It showed that a contribution was due to the shipowners, the plaintiffs, from cargo. On the basis of that adjustment, the defendants presumably having refused to pay, the plaintiffs issued a writ in England, claiming against the defendants the sum of £52,420·18 as the contributions in general average which the defendants were liable to pay by reason of their promise contained in the Lloyd's average bond. We are told that the defendants' refusal to pay is based on their contention that the event which gave rise to the general average sacrifice and expenditure was due to the fault of the plaintiff shipowners. By virtue of r D of the York/Antwerp rules that would not be a matter which would be considered by the average adjusters. But it could provide a defence to the claim on the adjustment or a counterclaim. What is 'fault' may, as a matter of law, be decided differently in different systems of law.

Leave to serve notice of that writ out of the jurisdiction was granted by Robert Goff J on 5th October 1979. The defendants applied to set aside that order. Mustill J declined to set aside the order. By his judgment of 2nd April 1980 he held that the contract between the plaintiffs and the defendants contained in the Lloyd's average bond was, by implication, governed by English law; therefore RSC Ord 11, r 1(1)(f)(iii) permitted the grant of leave to serve notice on the defendants out of the jurisdiction. The learned judge rejected the further submission on behalf of the defendants that, even if English law were the proper law of the contract, he should exercise his discretion against granting leave.

The defendants appeal on both points. I say at once that, if I had come to the conclusion that the learned judge was right in holding that English law is the governing law of the contract, I should have seen no ground for interfering with his view as to the proper exercise of the discretion.

The defendants are not parties to the bill of lading contract. If the plaintiffs had sued ONACO, as being parties to the contract, on the average adjustment, and if ONACO had objected to the grant of leave to serve them outside the jurisdiction, different considerations would have arisen. That does not arise here. The defendants are not contractually bound by cl 10 of the bill of lading contract. They have not agreed with the plaintiffs, as a matter of contract between them, that the plaintiffs may decide where any average adjustment, arising out of the bill of lading voyage, is to take place and that the law of that place, so chosen, will apply.

What, then, is the proper law of the contract contained in the Lloyd's average bond? For on the answer to that question, by reason of the provisions of RSC Ord 11, r 1(1)(f)(iii), the question whether the English court has jurisdiction depends. It is a contract made in Algeria, between a Cyprian shipowner and two Algerian companies. It is in the English language, though the defendants' signature is conditioned by a reservation in the French language. It provides for the delivery of a cargo of sugar shipped in Cuba, under a bill of lading the proper law of which is not English law, in a ship flying, I imagine, the flag of Cyprus, at a port in Algeria, consequent on the abandonment of a lien which would have been exercisable there, against the payment in that Algerian port of freight, if any, due on the cargo, and against the promise of the consignee and the defendant, the consignee's insurer, to pay the proper proportion of any general average charges which might be payable on the particular consignment of cargo. Where is there scope for implication that English law governs that contract? Can it be suggested that the intention of the parties is to be inferred that English law shall govern? See Dicey and Morris on the Conflict of Laws (9th Edn, 1973, r 142(2)). Can it be fairly asserted that the transaction has its closest and most real connection with English law? See sub-r (3).

Mustill J did not place any weight on the use of the English language. I think that in the circumstances that is right. Amongst other considerations the English language is, if I may use the phrase, the lingua franca of commerce; it is the language of the United States of America; and, in the present case, the contractual document included a reservation in the French language inserted at the instance of the defendants. Counsel for the plaintiffs before us sought to place some reliance on the use of the word 'Lloyd's' in the heading of the contract form. I do not regard that as a matter of great significance, especially when one observes the absence from this standard form of the indications of English law as the governing law which are to be found in the other two Lloyd's standard forms to which I have referred.

The only way in which, as I see it, an attractive or persuasive argument can be adduced in support of English law as the governing law, by implication, of this contract is the way in which Mustill J, if I may say so, both attractively and persuasively stated the argument which he thought it right to accept. That argument is founded on the basis that an important factor (the plaintiffs say it is a decisive factor) is the place where the average is to be adjusted. If the Lloyd's average bond had provided, expressly or by clear and unambiguous implication, that the general average adjustment was to take place in London, I should have thought that that might well have been decisive. But this contract, in my opinion, did not so provide, either expressly or by clear implication.

In an affidavit on behalf of the plaintiffs it is stated:

'London is an important international centre for the adjustment of General Average. [That fact may unhesitatingly be accepted.] Algeria has no internationally recognised average adjusters. London is the most commonly chosen centre for adjustments where the General Average is connected with Europe or the Mediterranean.'

But whether or not it would be chosen in a particular case would obviously depend on many factors affecting the particular case. It is accepted that London is by no means the only possible choice of venue for general average adjustment in respect of a casualty such as gave rise to this claim. General average adjustments are, we are told, by no means uncommonly carried out in, for example, Germany, Belgium and the United States of America. No doubt individual shipowners, where it rests with them, or their insurers, have their own individual preferences.

Mustill J accepted that 'if this had been an ordinary contract, there would have been strong grounds for arguing that the system of law with which the contract had the closest connection was the law of Algeria'. But he did not regard this as an ordinary contract. As I understand it, his reasons for regarding it as being out of the ordinary were that it contemplated an adjustment of general average; as the defendants' obligation to pay under the contract (apart from any initial payment of freight due) was an obligation to pay the amount of general average chargeable on the consignment, so assessed, the place of the average adjustment became the paramount consideration in ascertaining the proper law of the contract contained in the Lloyd's average bond; and, ultimately, in this particular case London was the venue for general average adjustment chosen by the carriers, the plaintiffs, who, so far as the bill of lading contract was concerned, had the contractual option so to decide.

The learned judge accepted that the defendants, not having been parties to the bill of lading, 'cannot be fixed beyond doubt with notice of the terms of the bill of lading'. Counsel for the plaintiffs accepted, before us, that he could not contend that the defendants were to be treated in this commercial sphere as being affected with constructive notice of those terms. Mustill J said:

'But they [the defendants] must at least be taken to have foreseen that there would be a contract of carriage between the persons liable to contribute and the shipowners, and that this contract might stipulate for a place of adjustment other than Algiers, and expressly or by inference provide for a law to govern the adjustment which was not the law of the state of Algeria.'

Subject to a caveat as to the words 'at least', I should not be disposed to quarrel with the inference which the learned judge there states. However, stress must be laid, as counsel for the defendants rightly contends, on the word 'might'. But, in my opinion, if it rests there, it falls short, and far short, of establishing that English law is the law with which this 'transaction' has the closest and most real connection. It is no more than this: that the average adjustment *might* take place in England, and that, if so, this would not be inconsistent with the terms of the bill of lading contract, as between the plaintiffs and ONACO, who were the defendants' assured. That does not, in my judgment, satisfy the standard, the strict standard, which the courts of this country should maintain in examining a claim for the assertion of this extra-territorial jurisdiction.

The learned judge then went on to say:

> 'It seems to me that in the particular circumstances of this case, where there was a contract of carriage to which ONACO were parties and where pursuant to that contract English law became the law of the adjustment, and hence the law governing the liability of ONACO to make contribution in general average, and where the defendants took on a primary obligation to pay the sum assessed as the amount for which contribution was to be made, it can properly be said that English law is the system of law with which the bond is most closely concerned.'

With very great respect, the only additional matter added in that sentence is the fact that 'English law became the law of the adjustment'. That is a reference to the fact that at some unknown date, after the contract with which we are concerned, contained in the Lloyd's average bond, had been made, the plaintiffs, as 'carriers' under the bill of lading contract, decided that the average adjustment should take place in London. Whether, and if so when, that decision was made or when it was notified to ONACO, or to the defendants, we know not. But, at least, it was something which took place after the contract, the proper law of which we are seeking to ascertain, had already been made and had, almost certainly, already been executed in part.

The learned judge, as one would expect, had not overlooked the possible difficulty which arises in bringing in as a factor for ascertaining the proper law of a contract an event which has happened after the contract was made. However, Mustill J came to the conclusion, for reasons which he expounded attractively in the following paragraph of his judgment, that 'the proper law can be regarded as "floating" until such time as the exercise of a choice by the carriers had the effect of fixing both governing laws at the same time'. (The other governing law to which the judge referred is, I assume, the governing law of the average adjustment provisions in the bill of lading contract, introduced by cl 10.)

But can this really be so? Counsel for the defendants submits, with what seems to me to be unanswerable legal logic, that there must be a proper law of any contract, a governing law, at the time of the making of that contract. If, as is the case here, at the time when the contract was made, the question remained undecided whether the average adjustment was to be in England or in the United States or in Germany or somewhere else, then the fact that it was subsequently decided by one of the parties that the venue should be England cannot be a relevant factor in the ascertainment of the proper law at an earlier date. As a matter of legal logic, I find insuperable difficulty in seeing by what system of law you are to decide what, if any, is the legal effect of an event which occurs when a contract is already in existence with no proper law, but, instead, with a 'floating' non-law.

But in my opinion the difficulty goes beyond mere technicality or legal logic. Under the terms of this Lloyd's average bond contract, things had to be done by the parties forthwith and disputes under the contract might well, as a matter of commercial reality, arise forthwith. For example, there might be an immediate dispute whether freight was payable, or, if so, how much freight. There might be a dispute whether the shipowner had duly delivered the right cargo, in the right amount, or at the right time, to the right person. Those disputes, if they were to arise, would be disputes under the terms of this contract, involving, it may be, questions as to the construction and effect of those contractual terms. It cannot be that the contract has to be treated as being anarchic, as having no governing law which the court, taking jurisdiction in respect of such a dispute under the contract, would apply in deciding the dispute. There must be a governing law from the outset, not a floating absence of law, continuing to float until the carrier, unilaterally, makes a decision.

The governing law cannot fall to be decided, retrospectively, by reference to an event which was an uncertain event in the future at the time when obligations under the contract had already been undertaken, had fallen to be performed and had been performed. Nor is it, I think, an attractive, or a possible, concept of English private international law that the governing law, initially being, say, the law of Algeria, should thereafter change into the law of England.

If, as I believe, the fact of the carriers' subsequent designation of England as the place of the general average adjustment cannot operate to crystallise a theretofore 'floating' proper law (or to fill the gap of a theretofore non-existent proper law), the most that can be said in this case is that, when the contract was made, there was a possibility that English law might be the place of the general average adjustment. But that, as I have said, cannot, in my opinion, have the effect of making English law the governing law of the contract.

Nothing else in the facts and circumstances of the present case appears to be sufficient to have that effect, or to make the English system of law the system with which this transaction had the closest and most real connection.

I would add that in the earlier part of his judgment Mustill J made a very helpful analysis of what he described as the 'three groups of issues' which may arise. He said that 'it does not follow that all three groups are governed by the same system of law'. By this, I think, he meant that, if, for example, the proper law of the Lloyd's average bond contract were English law, that would by no means necessarily mean that the English court would apply English domestic law to all the different types of issue which might arise by way of dispute under the contract. The English court, applying English law including the English principles of private international law, might, for example, apply the proper law (whatever it may be) of the bill of lading contract in respect of any issues which involved the interpretation of that contract for purposes relevant to the decision of the dispute under the Lloyd's average bond contract. But I am confident that the learned judge was not, for one moment, intending to suggest that, on the question whether, for the purposes of RSC Ord 11, r 1(1)(f)(iii), the Lloyd's average bond contract was to be treated as governed by English law, the court might properly reach different decisions according to the nature of the particular dispute under that contract which it might be anticipated would fall to be decided if the court assumed jurisdiction. If it were possible, or permissible, to conceive that the contract might have different governing laws according to which particular contractual provision was relevant to the particular dispute under the contract, then I should say, without hesitation, that the English court could not properly treat the contract in question (for it must be the whole contract as a single entity) as governed by English law for the purposes of asserting extra-territorial jurisdiction. Accordingly, on that hypothesis (which I think is an unreal one, at least in this case) the court should refuse jurisdiction.

I would allow this appeal and set aside the order for leave to serve notice of the writ out of the jurisdiction.

EVELEIGH LJ. I agree.

OLIVER LJ. I agree.

Appeal allowed. Leave to appeal to House of Lords refused.

Solicitors: *Ince & Co* (for the defendants); *Elborne Mitchell & Co* (for the plaintiffs).

Mary Rose Plummer   Barrister.

Wicks v Firth (Inspector of Taxes)
Johnson v Firth (Inspector of Taxes)

CHANCERY DIVISION
GOULDING J
4th, 5th, 6th NOVEMBER 1980

Income tax – Emoluments from office or employment – Benefits derived by directors and higher-paid employees from employment – Scholarship awarded to employee's child by employer – Whether award emolument from parent's employment – Income and Corporation Taxes Act 1970, s 375(1) – Finance Act 1976, s 61(1).

In 1977 ICI Ltd, a large public company, established an educational trust for the award of scholarships to children of employees of ICI or nominated subsidiaries of ICI for full-time study at university or comparable institutions. The award of the scholarships was at the discretion of the trustees. The taxpayers were higher-paid employees of ICI who were assessed to income tax in 1978–79 under Sch E on scholarships awarded by the trustees to their children. Each assessment was made under s 61(1)[d] of the Finance Act 1976 on the basis that as a person 'employed in . . . higher-paid employment' there had 'by reason of his employment [been] provided for him, or . . . members of his family . . . [a] benefit'. The taxpayers appealed against the assessments, contending that s 375(1)[b] of the Income and Corporation Taxes Act 1970 which exempted 'income arising from a scholarship' applied in their case. The Crown contended that for the purposes of s 61 of the 1976 Act the charge was on the 'cash equivalent of a benefit', and that it was impossible to equate that with 'Income arising from a scholarship' within s 375(1) of the 1970 Act, for, although the two might be the same in amount, they were different in character, and that, accordingly, s 375(1) could not confer exemption on a charge which arose under s 61. The Special Commissioners dismissed the taxpayers' appeal holding that the charge under s 61 of the 1976 Act was on the cash equivalent of the benefit provided, which was to be treated as an emolument, and that a notional sum so treated was not 'income arising from a scholarship' within s 375(1) of the 1970 Act. The taxpayers appealed.

Held – The scheme of assessing the cash equivalent of benefits under s 61 of the 1976 Act was aimed generally at benefits given not in cash but in kind, and was not intended to nullify or impair the unqualified exemption from tax conferred by s 375(1) of the 1970 Act on income arising from a scholarship. Furthermore, the provision in s 375(1) that 'no account shall be taken of [income arising from a scholarship] in computing the amount of income for income tax purposes' was not restricted to computing the income of the scholarship holder. It followed that the taxpayers were not liable under s 61(1) of the 1976 Act to tax on the income arising from their children's scholarship awards. The appeals would, therefore, be allowed (see p 519 *d* to *f* and p 520 *a b* and *d*, post).

Notes
For the taxation of benefits received by reason of employment, see 23 Halsbury's Laws (4th Edn) paras 694–696.

For scholarship income, see ibid para 1077.

For the Income and Corporation Taxes Act 1970, s 375, see 33 Halsbury's Statutes (3rd Edn) 490.

For the Finance Act 1976, s 61, see 46 ibid 1672.

---

a Section 61(1), so far as material, is set out at p 516 *c*, post
b Section 375(1) is set out at p 517 *d*, post

Case referred to in judgment

Mapp (Inspector of Taxes) v Oram [1969] 3 All ER 215, [1970] AC 362, [1969] 3 WLR 557, 45 Tax Cas 651, 48 ATC 270, [1969] TR 267, HL, 28(1) Digest (Reissue) 448, *1606*.

Cases also cited

Barty-King v Minister of Defence [1979] 2 All ER 80, [1979] STC 218.
Brumby (Inspector of Taxes) v Milner [1976] 3 All ER 636, [1976] 1 WLR 1096, [1976] STC 534, HL.
Comrs for the General Purposes of Income Tax for the City of London v Gibbs [1942] 1 All ER 415, [1942] AC 402, 24 Tax Cas 221, HL.
Hochstrasser (Inspector of Taxes) v Mayes [1959] 3 All ER 817, [1960] AC 376, 38 Tax Cas 673, HL.
Hughes (Inspector of Taxes) v Bank of New Zealand [1938] 1 All ER 778, [1938] AC 366, 21 Tax Cas 472, HL.
Inland Revenue Comrs v Educational Grants Association [1967] 2 All ER 893, [1967] Ch 993, 44 Tax Cas 93, CA.

Cases stated

Wicks v Firth (Inspector of Taxes)

1. At a meeting of the Commissioners for the Special Purposes of the Income Tax Acts held on 6th, 7th and 8th February 1980, Malcolm James Wicks ('Mr Wicks') appealed against an assessment to income tax under Sch E for the year 1978–79 in the sum of £11,413.

2. Shortly stated the question for decision was whether Mr Wicks was liable to income tax in respect of an award made to his son from the Imperial Chemical Industries Educational Trust ('the educational trust').

3. At the same time the commissioners heard an appeal by Mr Maurice Johnson ('Mr Johnson') against an assessment to income tax under Sch E in respect of an award to his daughter from the educational trust.

4. The decision which the commissioners gave in writing on 8th April and which was appended to the case as a schedule covered the appeals of both Mr Wicks and Mr Johnson.

5. The witnesses who gave evidence before the commissioners were listed in para 4 of the decision.

[Paragraph 6 listed the documents proved or admitted before the commissioners.]

7. The decision set out the facts that the commissioners found admitted or proved (paras 5 and 6) and the contentions of the parties.

8. The following cases were referred to before the commissioners: *Brumby (Inspector of Taxes) v Milner* [1976] 3 All ER 636, [1976] STC 534, HL; *Duport Steels Ltd v Sirs* [1980] 1 All ER 529, [1980] 1 WLR 142, CA and HL; *Hochstrasser v Mayes* [1959] 3 All ER 817, [1960] AC 376, 38 Tax Cas 673, HL; *Rendell v Went (Inspector of Taxes)* [1964] 2 All ER 464, 41 Tax Cas 642, HL; *Vestey v Inland Revenue Comrs (Nos 1 and 2)* [1979] 3 All ER 976, [1980] AC 1148 [1980] STC 10, HL.

9. Mr Wicks immediately after the determination of the appeal declared his dissatisfaction therewith as being erroneous in point of law and on 9th April 1980 required the commissioners to state a case for the opinion of the High Court pursuant to s 56 of the Taxes Management Act 1970.

10. The questions of law for the opinion of the court were: (1) whether there was evidence before the commissioners on which they could find the facts that they did and, if so, (2) whether on the basis of those facts their decision was correct in law.

Johnson v Firth (Inspector of Taxes)

1. At a meeting of the Commissioners for the Special Purposes of the Income Tax Acts held on 6th, 7th and 8th February 1980, Maurice Johnson ('Mr Johnson') appealed against an assessment to income tax under Sch E for the year 1978–79 in the sum of £10,168.

2. At the same time the commissioners heard an appeal against an assessment to income tax under Sch E made on Mr Wicks.

3. In the event the written decision, which covered both appeals, was in favour of the Crown and the commissioners confirmed the assessments accordingly.

4. Both Mr Johnson and Mr Wicks duly expressed dissatisfaction after the determination of the appeals and in due course required the commissioners to state cases for the opinion of the court in their respective appeals pursuant to s 56 of the Taxes Management Act 1970.

5. The commissioners stated a case with reference to their decision on Mr Wicks's appeal setting out the relevant facts relating to both appeals, their decision thereon and the questions on which the opinion of the court was required. To save repetition and expense they did not set them out again.

Decision

1. These are two separate appeals—one by Mr Wicks and the other by Mr Johnson. Mr Wicks and Mr Johnson are together called 'the taxpayers' and by agreement their appeals were heard together. The taxpayers are and at all material times were employees of Imperial Chemical Industries Ltd ('ICI') and, put shortly, the question for our decision is whether the taxpayers are liable to income tax under Sch E for the year 1978–79 in respect of awards made to their children from the Imperial Chemical Industries Educational Trust ('the Educational Trust').

2. It has been agreed that these two appeals should be regarded as a test case in the sense that the outcome will determine the Inland Revenue's policy regarding the large number of other ICI employees whose children have received or may in the future receive similar awards.

3. Both leading and junior counsel appeared for the taxpayers. The inspector of taxes was represented by Mr A Wheaten of the Office of the Inland Revenue Solicitor.

4. The following witnesses gave evidence before us: Dr Trevor Cawdor Thomas, Vice-Chancellor of Liverpool University from 1970 to 1976 and at all material times chairman of the trustees ('the Trustees') of the Educational Trust; Sir Roy Marshall, Secretary General of the Committee of Vice-Chancellors and Principals of the United Kingdom Universities ('CVCP') from 1974 to 1979 and since then Vice-Chancellor of Hull University; James Ferguson Mitchell, an employee of ICI from 1953 to March 1977 and since that date secretary of the Educational Trust; Mrs Dian Kaye Huddart, who at the material time was a personnel officer at ICI Head Office, Millbank, London; Miss Gwendoline Irene Evans, who was employed by the personnel department of ICI specifically to prepare schedules of particulars (which were presented before us) of awards made from the Educational Trust in the academic year 1978–79; Martin Wicks ('Martin'), son of Mr Wicks and an undergraduate at King's College, Cambridge; the taxpayers.

The facts

5. The following facts (taken from a statement of agreed facts) were admitted before us. (1) By a deed ('the trust deed') dated 13th January 1977 ICI established the Educational Trust. The initial trust fund comprised £15,000 which ICI on that day transferred to the Educational Trust, and this was augmented by subsequent payments, again made by ICI, as follows:—26th January 1977, £735,000; 1st September 1977, £800,000; 20th July 1978, £700,000; 31st August 1978, £200,000; 27th June 1979, £800,000. Apart from these payments no other contributions as such have been made to the Educational Trust, although other substantial sums have been received by way of deposit interest. This interest amounted to (in round figures) £28,000 for the period 13th January 1977 to 30th September 1977, £33,000 for the year to 30th September 1978 and £71,000 for the year to 30th September 1979, totalling in all £132,000 (these figures are all gross before deduction of income tax). [Further particulars are set out in paragraph 6 below.] (2) Under the trust deed the trustees are directed to exercise their discretion in paying what the trust deed terms scholarships to such of the class of beneficiaries as they think fit.

Scholarships are limited (by cl 4) to awards only in respect of full-time instruction at a university or other comparable establishment of further education, with preference to be given to undergraduate courses. The class of beneficiaries is defined (by cl 1(3)) to mean the children of all employees and officers of the settlor (that is to say ICI) and certain nominated subsidiaries of ICI. Children for this purpose includes adopted children, step-children and illegitimate children. It is expressly provided (by cl 4(5)) that once a scholarship has been awarded to a beneficiary it remains payable normally even if he or she ceases to be a beneficiary as a result of the parent's ceasing to be employed by ICI (or one of the nominated subsidiaries). It is further provided that such an individual (even though technically no longer a beneficiary) remains eligible for some future awards. (3) The trustees awarded 2,072 scholarships for the academic year 1976–77, 2,533 scholarships for the academic year 1977–78, and 2,683 scholarships for the academic year 1978–79. No issue arises as to any of the scholarships awarded in the academic years 1976–77 and 1977–78, because until 14th June 1978 the Inland Revenue accepted that scholarship awards of this type were exempted from income tax by s 375 of the Income and Corporation Taxes Act 1970. By a press release issued on that date the Inland Revenue announced that henceforth they would regard the cost of providing such scholarship awards as being a benefit in kind taxable (in the case of directors and higher-paid employees) under s 61 of the Finance Act 1976. The press release included the following paragraphs:

'3. The Revenue will not, however, contend that there is a benefit giving rise to liability under Section 61 where there is only a fortuitous connection between the identity of the recipient of the scholarship and his parent's employment, for example, where a firm sets up a scheme for awarding scholarships which is open to all, but where one of the successful candidates happens to be the child of a higher-paid employee of that firm.

'4. The new practice will be applied to income from scholarships awarded on or after [14th June 1978] but not to income from existing awards.'

(4) In November 1978 the trustees awarded a scholarship of £600 to Martin and a scholarship of £460 to Christine Johnson ('Christine'), daughter of Mr Johnson. Christine was about to start her first year at Newcastle University reading medicine, and Martin was about to start his first year at King's College, Cambridge reading natural sciences. In the tax year 1978–79 (with which we are concerned) the emoluments of both taxpayers exceeded the threshold of the 'higher-paid' employment for the purposes of s 61. (5) On 13th July 1979 an income tax assessment for the year 1978–79 was made on Mr Wicks in respect of his emoluments from ICI. This assessment included the sum of £600 for Martin's Scholarship, which is described in the assessment as 'Benefits—ICI Educational Trust'. On 17th August 1979 an assessment for the year 1978–79 was made on Mr Johnson in respect of his emoluments from ICI. This assessment included the sum of £460 for Christine's scholarship, which is described in the assessment as 'ICI Ltd. Educational Trust'.

'6. As a result of the oral and documentary evidence produced before us, we find the following further facts proved. (1) Dr Thomas and Sir Roy Marshall gave evidence to the effect that many students at universities and colleges suffered hardship (which could affect both their health and their studies) if their financial resources for living expenses were limited to the amount of the grant that they actually received from local education authorities ('LEAs')—parents often failed to pay the full amount of the assessed parental contribution—and that the Educational Trust fulfilled a valuable educational and social purpose. We fully accept their evidence. (2) Sir Roy Marshall also gave evidence to the effect that the awards from the Educational Trust were scholarships, as that word is normally understood among educationalists. Mr Wheaten accepted on behalf of the inspector of taxes for the purposes of these appeals that the awards were scholarships. (3) Dr Thomas and Mr Mitchell gave evidence in considerable detail about the criteria used by the trustees in making awards and the mechanics by which candidates applied for and received awards. For the purposes of these proceedings we can summarise the evidence, which we fully accept, as follows:

(A) *Selection of scholars*

The trustees in deciding whether to make an award were in no way influenced by the position of the applicant's parent vis-à-vis his employer. The only criteria were whether the applicant was eligible under the terms of the trust deed and whether his educational attainments were such that he had been accepted for a course which in accordance with the trust deed the trustees had determined as eligible for awards. Indeed, when the question whether the award should be renewed for a subsequent year came before the trustees they would not know whether his parent was still an employee of ICI (or one of its nominated subsidiaries, as the case might be). Broadly speaking, however, awards were made to all eligible applicants for eligible courses. We inferred that ICI had made and would continue to make (if the present appeals were to succeed) sufficient contributions to the Educational Trust to enable the trustees to continue their existing policy in this respect.

(B) *Selection of courses*

Clause 4(1) to (3) of the trust deed is in the following terms:

'4. (1) A Scholarship shall be awarded to a Beneficiary only in respect of his or her full-time instruction at a university or such other comparable establishment of further education as the Trustees may determine. The Trustees shall give preference in their award of Scholarships to Beneficiaries who are or will be following instruction leading to a first university degree or comparable diploma but shall not be precluded in exceptional circumstances from awarding Scholarships in respect of post-graduate courses. (2) The Trustees may upon awarding a Scholarship to a Beneficiary prescribe such terms and conditions attached to the holding of the Scholarship as they may think fit. (3) No Scholarship shall be awarded to a Beneficiary unless:—(a) the beneficiary qualifies or has qualified for the award of some other scholarship exhibition bursary grant or other similar educational endowment on grounds of academic merit only not awarded by the Trustees in respect of the particular educational establishment where he or she attends or intends to attend; or (b) the Beneficiary has been accepted for admission by a university or other comparable establishment of further education for instruction leading to a first university degree or comparable diploma; or (c) the Trustees after considering any information concerning the academic ability of the Beneficiary as is available to them and after examining or interviewing the Beneficiary (which examination or interview may in exceptional circumstances be dispensed with) determine in their absolute discretion that the Beneficiary has sufficient academic ability to merit the award of a Scholarship.'

The trustees determined as eligible courses for 1978–79 those that were either: (a) designated by the Department of Education and Science ('DES') as qualifying for awards by LEAs or (b) supported by the Department of Health and Social Security and which required of the applicant the attainment of an academic standard equivalent to that required of an applicant for a course designated by DES. They considered courses individually, however, and, exceptionally, might accept as eligible other courses, eg, for a second first degree as where an applicant who had graduated as a BSc wanted to qualify as a doctor or where the applicant's education had suffered as a consequence of exceptional hardship.

(C) *Amount of award*

The award consisted of a basic award which might, according to the merits of the case, be supplemented by a merit award.

(i) *The basic award*

The trustees fixed the basic award with the general object of closing the gap between the national maximum amount of maintenance awards made by LEAs (£1,100 per annum for the academic year 1978–79) and the LEA maintenance award actually made. Their aim was that the gap should be no greater than £300. If, which was rare, a student had a scholarship from another source, that would be taken into account. Parental contributions were not taken into account.

(ii) *The merit award*

The basic award might be supplemented by a merit award of variable amount. This was based, broadly, on the scholar's academic performance. For the first year's award, it would normally depend on the results of his GCE A Level examination and for later years on a report from his university or college.

(D) *Machinery*

Applicants for awards usually learned about the Educational Trust from their parents, who knew of the scheme from internal publicity in ICI (eg notice boards) and who would obtain application forms from ICI personnel officers. After the applicant had made his application, his parent had no further standing in the matter and the trustees dealt only with the applicant himself and, if he was successful, sent him the cheque: they would refuse to tell the parent of the amount of any award to his child. No award would be made until the trustees had seen a copy of the letter stating the amount of the LEA's award to the applicant. The scheme of awards was sufficiently flexible to meet special circumstances and special hardship. (4) We summarise below the income and expenditure accounts of the Educational Trust for the period ended 30th September 1977 and the years ended 30th September 1978 and 30th September 1979:

	13.1.77 to 30.9.77	Year ended 30.9.78	Year ended 30.9.79
	£	£	£
Payments received from ICI	1,550,000	900,000	800,000
Deposit interest received	28,482	32,657	70,960
	1,578,482	932,657	870,960
Less income tax	11,332	9,484	29,088
	1,567,150	923,173	841,872
Less expenses (Secretary's salary, wages, services etc)	18,609	25,558	29,219
	1,548,541	897,615	812,653
Less awards for academic years 1976–77, 1977–78 and 1978–79 respectively	617,994	824,144	823,933
Accumulated surplus [deficit] of income for period	930,547	73,471	[11,280]
Surplus brought forward	—	930,547	1,004,018
	930,547	1,004,018	992,738

(5) The trustees' award to Martin for his first year at university was £600—a basic award of £400 and a merit award of £200 (based on 4 grade As in his A-Levels): his LEA maintenance grant for the year was £409. Mr Wicks did not reduce his assessed parental contribution as a result of the award to Martin; when the trustees came to consider renewing Martin's award for the academic year 1979–80, they continued the basic award but, having taken account of his college report, did not renew the merit award. (6) The

award to Christine for her first year was £460—a basic award of £260 and a merit award of £200 (based on 4 grade As in her A-levels): her LEA maintenance grant was £542. Mr Johnson did not cut down his assessed parental contribution as a result of the award. Christine had an outstanding college report (coming first with distinction in a class of 130 students) and the trustees increased her merit award for 1979–80 while continuing her basic award.

The contentions

7. (1) The primary contention of counsel for the taxpayers was that even assuming that all the conditions were satisfied for the application of s 61 of the Finance Act 1976, the taxpayers were exempt from any tax charge thereunder by virtue of s 375 of the Income and Corporation Taxes Act 1970. The requirement in the last few lines of s 61(1) that 'an amount equal to whatever is the cash equivalent of the benefit' is to be treated as an emolument of the employment and chargeable to income tax under Sch E was another way of saying that it should be treated as taxable income. It was 'income arising from a scholarship held by a person receiving full time instruction at a university, college, school or other educational establishment' within the meaning of s 375(1) and was accordingly exempt from income tax under that subsection and no account was to be taken of such income in computing the amount of income of the scholar's parents for income tax purposes; (2) that in the alternative, counsel for the taxpayers contended that, as the benefit was provided not for the taxpayers themselves but for their children, it could only be brought within the scope of s 61(1) via ss 72(3) and 63(2), so that to pin a charge on an employee of ICI, the inspector of taxes had to show that the benefit was provided at the cost of ICI. Here the source of the award was a trust fund. However, the benefit had not been provided at the cost of the trustees. Moreover, it was impossible to find out from what particular source any particular payment to Martin or Christine came—from the original fund or from the income from it. Unless the Inland Revenue could say with precision how the tax claim was to be quantified it must fail: it was not for the courts to come to their aid; and (3) that the appeal should succeed in principle and the assessments should be reduced by the sum of £600 in the case of Mr Wicks and by the sum of £460 in the case of Mr Johnson.

8. It was contended for the Crown: (1) that the awards to Martin and Christine were benefits within the meaning of s 61(2) not only for them but also for their respective parents; (2) that on the facts there was a close link between ICI, the Educational Trust and ICI's employees. The inference was that the purpose of the trust was to confer benefits on the employees. Accordingly, the benefit of the awards was provided by reason of the employment. In this connection reference was made to *Rendell v Went (Inspector of Taxes)* [1964] 2 All ER 464, [1964] 1 WLR 655, 41 Tax Cas 642 and *Brumby (Inspector of Taxes) v Milner* [1976] 3 All ER 636, [1976] 1 WLR 1096, [1976] STC 534; (3) that if he was wrong on (2), such provision was deemed to have been made by virtue of s 72(3); (4) that accordingly the amount equal to whatever was the cash equivalent of the benefit was chargeable to income tax under s 61(1); (5) that the expense incurred in or in connection with the provision of the benefit was incurred both by ICI and by the trustees. There was only one lot of expenses but ICI were the paymasters and the trustees handed out the money after deduction of expenses. In the present cases the cost of the provision of the benefit was the actual amount paid to the child—£600 to Martin, £460 to Christine; (6) that the charge under s 61 of the 1976 Act is on the 'cash equivalent of a benefit' (which by s 63 is 'an amount equal to the cost of the benefit'). It was impossible to equate that with 'income arising from a scholarship' (which was the amount the scholar receives) within the meaning of s 375 of the Income and Corporation Taxes Act 1970. The two might be the same in amount but were different in character. Neither leg of s 375(1) could confer exemption on a charge which arose under s 61; and (7) that the assessments should be confirmed.

9. *Conclusion*

(1) Chapter II of Part III of the Finance Act 1976 sets out to extend the scope of the liability for tax imposed on a director or a higher-paid employee (both hereinafter referred to for convenience as 'employee') in respect of fringe benefits. Previously a charge to tax arose if a company incurred expense in the provision of a benefit for such an employee. Under s 61 an employee is chargeable if by reason of his employment he receives a benefit—it matters not from whom. (2) Moreover, if the benefit is provided by his employer, it will be deemed to be received by the employee by reason of his employment whether or not intended to be received as a reward or in return for his services. (3) At the receiving end liability extends to any benefit provided for a member of the employee's family or household. (4) Four ingredients of the charge can thus be identified, of which one of (i) and (ii) and one of (iii) and (iv) at least must be present: (i) receipt of a benefit by the employee, or (ii) by a member of his family, including a child whether or not any longer dependent on him, and (iii) a causal link between employment and benefit or (iv) provision of the benefit by his employer with or without such link. (5) The question who is the provider of a particular benefit is to be answered by asking at whose cost was it provided. (6) For good measure it has been argued before us on behalf of the Crown that in these proceedings all four ingredients were present. In the case of Mr Wicks it is said that Mr Wicks himself received a benefit and that Martin received a benefit, that ICI provided the benefit and that the trustees provided the benefit, that the benefit was received by reason of Mr Wicks' employment and that it matters not whether or not it was so received since it was provided at the cost of ICI. (7) That Martin received a benefit is common ground and not in dispute. (8) The evidence before us does not support the suggestion that Mr Wicks received any financial benefit from Martin's award. Mr Wicks was under no legal obligation to finance Martin at Cambridge. Martin's award made no difference to his moral obligation to make a parental contribution. He paid what he would have paid to Martin in any event, sufficient to bring Martin's resources together with his LEA grant, up to the recommended level. We find that no benefit was received by Mr Wicks. (9) It seems to us that Martin's benefit was provided by ICI. It was ICI which each year put the trustees in funds to make awards. To say that the awards were paid or provided at the cost of the trustees appears to us to be a wholly inaccurate use of language. The function of the trustees was to select recipients of awards provided at the cost of ICI. Each year it cost ICI the sum which ICI contributed to the fund to provide the awards paid out of the fund in that year. To the extent to which what ICI paid into the fund in the year was in excess of the awards paid out, the cost was in part attributable to awards paid out in subsequent years. We see no reason to distinguish the income of the trust fund from the capital in identifying the source. (10) The benefit which Mr Wicks must be deemed to have received must also be deemed to have been received by reason of his employment because provided by ICI. There was no evidence before us to establish that the benefit was in fact received by Mr Wicks by reason of his employment. Reliance was placed on behalf of the Crown on the circumstance that Martin was and could only be selected as the recipient of an award because he was the son of an ICI employee. But that, as it seems to us, falls short of establishing that the reason for Martin's award was his father's employment. It was for the Revenue to establish a causal link between Mr Wicks' employment and Martin's award. They have not done so. Martin received his award because he was selected by the trustees as a person having the necessary qualifications. One of those qualifications was that when he first applied for an award, his father was an ICI employee. We have not been told and do not know why ICI established the fund or contributed to it each year save as appears from the terms of the trust deed. We do not infer that ICI's purpose was to remunerate its employees or to add an additional perquisite to their emoluments. (11) Since, however, we hold that within the meaning of the statute the benefit was provided at the cost of ICI, what purpose ICI had is immaterial. (12) As ingredients (ii) and (iv) to which we have referred in sub-para (4) above are present, we decide the first issue (see sub-para (6)) in principle in favour of the inspector

of taxes. (13) It seems to us that the proper proportion of the cost incurred by ICI in making its contribution to the fund in a particular year to be attributed to Martin's award is the same proportion of the whole as Martin's award bears to the aggregate of the awards paid out in that year. We do not have to decide this point, however, as it is common ground in these appeals that the actual amounts of the awards to Martin and Christine should be taken as the measure of any liability under s 61. (14) As to the second issue—whether the scholarship exemption applies—we find, first, so far as it may be relevant, that Martin's scholarship was not in itself income. It was neither an annual payment taxable under Case III nor, contrary to the suggestion advanced on the Revenue's behalf, such an annual profit or gain as is taxable under Case VI. But nor was the cost of providing the scholarship incurred by ICI, of itself, income. The charge under s 61 is on the cash equivalent of the benefit provided, not on the benefit itself. The cash equivalent is not of itself income but is to be treated as an emolument. A notional sum so treated is not, in our judgment, covered by the words 'income arising from a scholarship'. That a wholly laudable attempt to assist young people of promise in their university careers may to some extent be frustrated or discouraged may well be a matter for regret, but regret as it seems to us is not a factor in what we have to decide, whether Martin's award was provided at the cost of ICI. If it was, and we find the conclusion inescapable on the language use in the statute, liability follows unless the expense incurred in providing the award was itself income arising from the award. But the expense of providing a benefit cannot itself be income arising from what is provided: the charge under s 61 is quite separate and distinct from the benefit the provision of which is the occasion of the charge. (15) What is said about Martin's award applies equally to Christine's. (16) The appeals fail in principle and we confirm the assessments. (17) This decision does not, of course, cover awards from the Educational Trust to children of parents employed not by ICI but by one of its nominated subsidiaries.

F Heyworth Talbot QC and *Graham Aaronson* for the taxpayers.
Robert Carnwath for the Crown.

GOULDING J. I have before me two appeals by taxpayers from decisions of the Special Commissioners given in favour of the Crown. Both taxpayers are in the employment of Imperial Chemical Industries Ltd, which I shall refer to by the well-known abbreviation of 'ICI'. The subject matter of the appeals is the taxation of certain scholarships, coming from a fund known as the ICI Educational Trust, which was set up in 1977 by ICI, in cases where the scholarship is given to the child or dependant of a director or of what is known in the legislation as 'a higher-paid employee' of ICI.

The trust, as I have said, was established in 1977. It is constituted under a trust deed dated 13th January. The initial trust fund mentioned in the deed is £15,000, but it has been subsequently augmented by very large payments, all made by ICI. The Special Commissioners found that at the date with which they were concerned no other contributions had been made to the fund, although it had of course received additions by way of interest on money awaiting use.

I am content to take from the case stated by the Special Commissioners, without reading the deed, a sufficient indication of its character. They say:

'Under the Trust Deed the Trustees are directed to exercise their discretion in paying what the Trust Deed terms Scholarships to such of the class of beneficiaries as they think fit. Scholarships are limited . . . to awards only in respect of full-time instruction at a university or other comparable establishment of further education, with preference to be given to undergraduate courses.'

The class of beneficiaries is defined under the deed to mean the children of all employees and officers of ICI and of certain nominated subsidiaries of ICI. 'Children' for this purpose includes adopted children, stepchildren and illegitimate children. It is expressly provided by the deed that once a scholarship has been awarded to a beneficiary it remains payable normally even if he or she ceases to be a beneficiary as a result of the parent employee ceasing to be employed by ICI or one of the nominated subsidiaries. It is further provided that such an individual remains eligible for certain future awards. The trustees, according to the case stated, have been awarding scholarships regularly since the foundation of the trust at the rate of something over 2,000 in each academic year.

The facts as regards the particular cases before the court are these. A son of one of the taxpayers received in November 1978 from the trustees the award of a scholarship of £600. He was about to start his first year at King's College, Cambridge, reading natural sciences. Subsequently, when the trustees came to consider the renewal of the award for a second academic year, they continued a part of the £600, namely what they called a basic award of £400, but did not renew the additional £200, which was originally described as a merit award, because of the contents of his college report.

The other case is that of a daughter of the other taxpayer. She also, in November 1978, was about to start her university career, in her case reading medicine at the University of Newcastle. Her initial award was £460, consisting of a basic award of £260 and a merit award of £200, the merit award, as in the boy's case, being based on her previous record, particularly her A levels. However, the lady, when she completed her first year at college, had a quite exceptionally distinguished report, and so in her case, not only was the basic award continued for a second year but the merit award was also continued and, indeed, increased.

In both cases income tax assessments for the year 1978–79 were made on the respective fathers of the scholarship holders, that is on the two taxpayers, in respect of their emoluments from ICI, and in each case a figure was included as a benefit from the ICI Educational Trust, the figure being that of the first year's scholarship award, £600 in the case of the boy's father, £460 as regards the girl's father. The Special Commissioners received oral as well as documentary evidence of the practice of the trustees in exercising their discretion under the trust deed. They accepted evidence that the trust fulfilled a valuable educational and social purpose in helping to bridge the gap between the financial resources available to university students and their real needs for money sufficient to get the maximum benefit from the university.

Evidence was also given (at considerable length, I am told) about the selection of candidates by the trustees. The Special Commissioners found these facts:

> 'The trustees in deciding whether to make an award were in no way influenced by the position of the applicant's parent vis-à-vis his employer. The only criteria were whether the applicant was eligible under the terms of the trust deed and whether his educational attainments were such that he had been accepted for a course which in accordance with the trust deed the trustees had determined as eligible for awards. Indeed, when the question whether the award should be renewed for a subsequent year came before the trustees they would not know whether his parent was still an employee of ICI (or one of its nominated subsidiaries, as the case might be). Broadly speaking, however, awards were made to all eligible applicants for eligible courses.'

The Special Commissioners 'inferred that ICI had made and would continue to make (if the present appeals were to succeed) sufficient contributions to the Educational Trust to enable the trustees to continue their existing policy in this respect'.

The Special Commissioners also found that applicants for awards usually learned about the trust from their parents, who knew of the scheme from notice boards and other publicity inside ICI and obtained their application forms from ICI's personnel officers. Then the Special Commissioners said this:

> 'After the applicant had made his application, his parent had no further standing in the matter and the trustees dealt only with the applicant himself and, if he was successful, sent him the cheque: they would refuse to tell the parent of the amount

of any award to his child. No award would be made until the trustees had seen a copy of the letter stating the amount of the LEA's award to the applicant. The scheme of awards was sufficiently flexible to meet special circumstances and special hardship.'

Such being, in outline, the facts of the case as found by the Special Commissioners, I now turn to the legislation under which the Crown has assessed the two taxpayers in respect of the sums here in question. It is s 61 of the Finance Act 1976, the first subsection of which I will now read, though, as will appear in a moment, it is necessary in order to understand it to look at several other subsections in the same Act. Section 61(1) of the 1976 Act reads (I omit certain immaterial words at the beginning):

'... where in any year a person is employed in director's or higher-paid employment and—(a) by reason of his employment there is provided for him, or for others being members of his family or household, any benefit to which this section applies; and (b) the cost of providing the benefit is not (apart from this section) chargeable to tax as his income, there is to be treated as emoluments of the employment, and accordingly chargeable to income tax under Schedule E, an amount equal to whatever is the cash equivalent of the benefit.'

The phrase 'director's or higher-paid employment' is defined in s 69(1) of the Act, subject to certain qualifications, as employment as a director of a company or employment with emoluments at a particular rate per year or more, the figure having been modified from time to time. It was originally £5,000; it was £7,500 in the year 1978–79; and it was subsequently raised to £8,500. There is no question in this case as to the meaning of the term: it is accepted that both the taxpayers are in 'director's or higher-paid employment'.

Then, para (a) of s 61(1) starts off with the words 'by reason of his employment there is provided' a benefit. The phrase 'by reason of his employment' has an extended meaning, because in s 72(3) of the Act we find this:

'For the purpose of this Chapter, all sums paid to an employee by his employer in respect of expenses, and all such provision as is mentioned in this Chapter which is made for an employee, or for members of his family or household, by his employer, are deemed to be paid to or made for him or them by reason of his employment.'

Thus, a benefit is material for the purposes of s 61 if it is either, on a proper construction of the words, provided by reason of the taxpayer's employment or in fact provided by his employer. Either of those alternatives, which of course must often coincide, will bring the benefit within s 61.

The next phrase explained is 'members of his family or household', benefits to whom are to rank in the same way as benefits to the employee himself. That is explained in s 72(4), which is in these terms: 'References to members of a person's family or household are to his spouse, his sons and daughters and their spouses, his parents and his servants, dependants and guests.'

Then there is a provision in s 61(3) to identify the person who provides the benefit. That says: 'For the purposes of this section and sections 62 and 63 below, the persons providing a benefit are those at whose cost the provision is made.'

'Benefit' receives a highly extended meaning by sub-s (2) of s 61, which (as amended) reads:

'The benefits to which this section applies are accommodation (other than living accommodation), entertainment, domestic or other services, and other benefits and facilities of whatsoever nature (whether or not similar to any of those mentioned above in this subsection), excluding however those taxable under ss 64 to 68 below in this Chapter, and subject to the exceptions provided for by the next following section.'

The subsection thus makes a number of special exceptions, but it is not necessary for me to go through them here.

Finally, in order to understand what s 61 is doing it is necessary to see what is meant by the phrase 'the cash equivalent of the benefit', because at the end of the first subsection what is to be chargeable to tax under Sch E is 'an amount equal to whatever is the cash equivalent of the benefit'. That is defined in s 63(1), which reads: 'The cash equivalent of any benefit chargeable to tax under section 61 above is an amount equal to the cost of the benefit, less so much (if any) of it as is made good by the employee to those providing the benefit.'

Both counsel for the taxpayers, made, I think, five alternative points in answer to the claim by the Crown under s 61 of the 1976 Act. I can deal with the matter most conveniently if I enumerate the five points at once and afterwards return to two of them which require further observations not convenient to make in a short survey. The first point, and, in the submission of counsel for the taxpayers, at any rate, the primary or main point, was that the claim is answered by a specific exemption relating to scholarship income contained in s 375 of the Income and Corporation Taxes Act 1970. It is necessary for me to read only the first two subsections of the three in s 375:

> '(1) Income arising from a scholarship held by a person receiving full-time instruction at a university, college, school or other educational establishment shall be exempt from income tax, and no account shall be taken of any such income in computing the amount of income for income tax purposes.
> '(2) In this section "scholarship" includes an exhibition, bursary or any other similar educational endowment.'

That, as I have said, was counsel's primary submission for the taxpayers, and I shall return in a moment to deal with it in detail.

The second point was that when one looks at the provisions of s 61 of the 1976 Act and the neighbouring ancillary sections one sees that the emphasis is entirely on benefits in kind, and they are not apt to cover cash payments such as that made by the trustees to the children of the two taxpayers. It is pointed out that there is a long enumeration of benefits in kind in s 61(2), which I have read, and that s 62, which I have not read, contains exceptions relating to different species of benefit in kind. It is also submitted that the very words of charge, if you read the definition of 'cash equivalent' back into s 61(1) (that is, tax is chargeable on 'an amount equal to whatever is an amount equal to the cost of the benefit, less so much (if any) of it as is made good by the employee'), are really only sensible in relation to benefits in kind, and not in cash.

I may say at once that I have not been persuaded by that submission. The words 'of whatsoever nature (whether or not similar to any of those mentioned above in this subsection)' are to my mind too strong to admit of the inference which I have been invited to draw. It is also not immaterial, I think, that one of the specific exceptions in s 62, namely in sub-s (6) thereof, is a benefit consisting in the provision of a pension, annuity or the like on the employee's death or retirement. At least that makes it clear that, but for the words of exception, provisions for future cash sums would be within the scope of s 61, thereby making it all the harder, I think, to limit the words 'benefits and facilities of whatsoever nature' by reference to what has gone before. Accordingly, without further ado I can reject that second submission.

The third point is this. The taxpayers challenge the assertion of the Crown that the scholarships (or the benefit of the scholarships, if preferred) have been provided by reason of the taxpayers' employment. That, of course, requires two propositions to be made good: first, that on the proper construction of the words in the statute the benefits were not in fact provided by reason of the employment; and, second, bearing in mind the extended provision in s 72(3), that the provision was not in fact made by ICI. It is said that, on the one hand, the employment of the parent was a necessary qualification for the child, as was, on the other, the attainment by the child of a sufficient academic standing to benefit from or be eligible for a university or college course. But those are qualifications. The benefits, it is submitted, were *provided* by reason of the decision of the trustees as an independent act, quite independent, as the Special Commissioners have found, of ICI, in the exercise of their fiduciary discretion under the trust deed. It is contended, secondly, on a consideration of the same facts, that the provision was made not by ICI but by the trustees out of the trust fund under their sole control. Those submissions raise matters of difficulty on the interpretation of the Finance Act 1976 and I leave them for the moment.

The fourth point is really conceived, I think, as a reductio ad absurdum. The Finance Act 1976 inserted a fresh version of s 15 into the Taxes Management Act 1970. That is the section which requires employers to make returns to the inspector of taxes relating to their employees; and in its revised form it provides also for returns to state, in respect of an employee, whether any benefits have been provided 'for him (or for any other person) by reason of his employment, such as may give rise to charges to tax under', among other provisions, ss 61 to 68 of the Finance Act 1976. Various details may be required; and there is also provision for the inspector to require information from any person who appears to him to have been concerned 'in providing benefits to or in respect of employees of another'.

I need not go into detail, but counsel for the taxpayers submitted, putting it shortly, that when one looks at that section and also at the general machinery for obtaining information for the purposes of assessment to income tax, the charge introduced under s 61 is simply unworkable if construed so widely as to bring in the scholarship payments made, not by an employer but by the trustees, not to an employee but to the child of an employee, in the present case. He says that without information that they perhaps could not get, it would be impossible for employees to make correct returns of their own income; it would be impossible for employers to comply with their statutory obligations because they would be required to have knowledge in the possession of people like the trustees in the present case, whom they might not be able to compel to disclose the facts; and s 61 would present, it may be, an impossible task to the officers of the Inland Revenue themselves.

That submission is another that I can dispose of shortly. I am not convinced by it. It is of course possible that, in spite of the endeavour of Parliament to extend the field of s 15 of the Taxes Management Act 1970, to dimensions commensurate with the new legislation in the Finance Act 1976, great difficulties will arise in particular cases, both for the taxpayer and for the Crown. Nevertheless, such difficulties cannot to my mind affect the construction of the Act to such an extent as to curtail the natural meaning of the terms employed in s 61 and its appended ancillary sections.

I can likewise dismiss shortly the fifth and last of the points made on behalf of the taxpayers, as I understood them. That again is an appeal to possible difficulty in the application of the 1976 legislation if given the wide construction favoured by the Crown. The particular difficulty emphasised was that a payment might be made to an individual who had a double qualification, so that two or more employees of the same employer might be assessable. For example, the child of one employee of ICI might be the dependant of another, or might be the wife of a child of the other. In those cases, who is to be assessed, or is there to be a double charge to tax? It is even conceivable that a director or higher-paid employee might himself be a scholar under the educational trust. Those are interesting and difficult problems which may or may not arise in practice, but, once again, I do not think they are any answer to the proper construction of the charging section itself.

After that survey I return to what was described on behalf of the taxpayers as the primary submission, that based on the exemption contained in s 375(1) of the Income and Corporation Taxes Act 1970. It has two limbs. The first says that 'Income arising from a scholarship held by a person receiving full-time instruction at a university, college, school or other educational establishment shall be exempt from income tax'; and the second limb is that 'no account shall be taken of any such income in computing the amount of income for income tax purposes'. Both limbs were relied on by counsel for the taxpayers, and both have been debated at some length. On the first limb, that income arising from a scholarship should be exempt, it is not disputed that the awards under the ICI Educational Trust are scholarships; nor is it disputed for the purposes of these cases that the sums received by the taxpayers' children are income arising from a scholarship.

In their decision the Special Commissioners relied on the distinction between the income received by the scholarship holder and the cash equivalent which is to be taxed as emoluments of the parent employee under s 61 of the Finance Act 1976. They said this:

'The charge under s 61 is on the cash equivalent of the benefit provided, not on the benefit itself. The cash equivalent is not of itself income but is to be treated as an emolument. A notional sum so treated is not, in our judgment, covered by the words "income arising from a scholarship".'

I think that at one time I should have found that reasoning more conclusive than I do at present. I think there is no doubt that, perhaps under continental influences, in recent years the court, in interpreting recent statutes, has tended to be less literal and to look a little more at the purposes of a particular enactment, as disclosed by the words of the enactment itself.

Considered in that way, although I do not find the point free of difficulty, I cannot think that Parliament, without giving an express indication, intended in effect to nullify or impair an unqualified exemption of this kind of scholarship income under s 375 by introducing, in relation to a very much wider class of benefit, a scheme of assessing notional sums, that scheme (which is really in the nature of machinery) being necessary because in general the benefits aimed at are given not in cash but in kind. Accordingly, although I see the force of the distinction drawn by the Special Commissioners between a purely notional sum and actual income, when one looks at the purposes of s 375 in giving an exemption and at the reason for introducing the fiction of a notional sum in s 61 of the later Act, I do not think it would be right to infer that the generality of the exemption was impaired. Accordingly, it seems to me that on the first limb the taxpayers should succeed.

I now turn to the second limb. There are really two points, I think, on that. When the Act says that no account shall be taken of income arising from the scholarship in computing the amount of income for income tax purposes, does it relate only to the scholarship holder or does it forbid the taking of scholarship income into account in computing any taxpayer's income? The main argument about that for the Crown was that if s 375(1) receives such a construction that its latter part is not limited to the income of the scholarship holder, then the proviso to s 10(5) of the 1970 Act would be otiose. Of course, one hesitates to make inferences of that kind from a consolidation statute drawn from many sources, but any such objection was removed when it was shown that both the present s 10(5) and the present s 375 are derived from the same original statute; namely the Finance Act 1920.

However, a similar argument was developed before the Court of Appeal in *Mapp (Inspector of Taxes) v Oram* [1969] 3 All ER 215, [1970] AC 362, 45 Tax Cas 651 and it was not found persuasive by any of the members of the court, divided though they were on the result of the appeal in that case. It afterwards went to the House of Lords, but the particular argument was not, as I understand it, used there, so no further light can be found in the speeches of their Lordships. There is, I think, no other sufficient ground for curtailing the literal breadth of the second limb, so I decline to limit it to the income of the scholarship holder himself.

The other point is directed to the words 'computing the amount of income for income tax purposes'. The relevant computation, as it seems to me, of the amount of income for income tax purposes is of the emoluments taxable under Sch E of the scholarship holder's parent. Counsel for the Crown submitted that in making that computation you do not take account of the scholarship income: it is only taken into account, if it is proper to use such words at all, at the earlier stage of ascertaining the relevant benefit received by the child of an employee from his employer which is afterwards converted into a cash equivalent by the 1976 Act, the cash equivalent but nothing else entering into the computation of the amount of income for income tax purposes. That, I think, is too narrow an interpretation. Trying to use words in their ordinary sense, it seems to me that account has been taken in the present case of the income arising from the taxpayers' children's scholarships in computing the amount of the taxpayers' respective emoluments for income tax under Sch E. Accordingly, in my judgment, they succeed on the second limb of s 375(1) as well as on the first.

That leaves the third point, as I called it in my general survey, which relates to the construction of the provisions in s 61 and also s 72 of the 1976 Act, requiring the relevant benefits to be provided by reason of the employment of the taxpayer. As I said, those questions are difficult. They apply not only to scholarships but to the whole field of operation of s 61. It would not assist an appellate court, if this case should go further, to know what was my opinion on these pure matters of law. Accordingly, though I must not be thought in any way ungrateful or discourteous in regard to the excellent arguments I heard on both sides, I think it better that I should not give any judgment on that question; I have found in favour of the taxpayers' main contention, that they can rely on the specific exemption in s 375 of the Income and Corporation Taxes Act 1970. Accordingly, in my judgment, both appeals must be allowed.

Appeals allowed.

Solicitors: *V O White* (for the taxpayers); *Solicitor of Inland Revenue.*

Edwina Epstein   Barrister.

R v Croydon Justices, ex parte Lefore Holdings Ltd

COURT OF APPEAL, CIVIL DIVISION
LAWTON AND WALLER LJJ
19th MARCH 1980

Case stated – Application to state a case – Identification of question for opinion of High Court – Compliance with requirement to identify question – Application to state a case not specifically identifying question – Only one issue in dispute before magistrates – Whether question sufficiently identified – Magistrates' Court Rules 1968 (SI 1968 No 1920), r 65(1).

A rating authority took out a summons for the issue of a distress warrant against the applicants in respect of their occupation of some waste ground. When the summons came on for hearing the applicants contended that the land had not been of some use, value or benefit to them and that accordingly there had been no rateable occupation. The only contested issue was whether the evidence called by the applicants, which was not disputed by the rating authority, showed that the applicants had not been in rateable occupation of the land. The magistrates found that the applicants had had, or could have had, beneficial use of the land and issued a distress warrant. The applicants applied, within the 21 days prescribed by the Magistrates' Courts Act 1952, s 87[a], to the magistrates 'to state and sign a case setting forth the facts and grounds of such your determination including evidence upon which the Justices made their findings of fact for the opinion thereon of the ... High Court'. On the day on which the 21-day period expired the magistrates' clerk wrote to the applicants asking them to identify, as required

_____
a   Section 87, so far as material, is set out at p 523 *f*, post

by r 65[b] of the Magistrates' Courts Rules 1968, the question or questions of law or jurisdiction on which the opinion of the High Court was sought. There was a delay in the delivery of the letter, and the applicants replied some days later, stating that there had been only the one finding of fact and that they contended that it could not be supported by the evidence. The magistrates decided that there had not been any proper identification of the issue in the application, as required by r 65, and refused to state a case. The Divisional Court refused the applicants leave to apply for a judicial review of the magistrates' refusal to state a case. The applicants appealed to the Court of Appeal.

Held – Since the only contested issue at the hearing before the magistrates was whether the evidence called by the applicants had shown any rateable occupation, and since the application to the magistrates to state a case referred specifically to the evidence on which they had made their findings of fact, it followed that the magistrates had been alerted to what was in issue and that they could, without further information, have stated a case on the application. There was, accordingly, substantial compliance with the requirement of r 65(1) of the 1968 rules that the applicant should identify the question of law on which the opinion of the High Court was sought. The appeal would therefore be allowed (see p 525 b to j, post).

Notes
For applications to magistrates to state a case, see 29 Halsbury's Laws (4th Edn) para 478, and for cases on the subject, see 33 Digest (Repl) 315, 1394–1401.

For the Magistrates' Courts Act 1952, s 87, see 21 Halsbury's Statutes (3rd Edn) 258.

For the Magistrates' Courts Rules 1968, r 65, see 13 Halsbury's Statutory Instruments (Third Reissue) 63.

As from a day to be appointed s 87 of the 1952 Act is to be replaced by s 111 of the Magistrates' Courts Act 1980.

Cases referred to in judgments
Coney v Choyce [1975] 1 All ER 979, [1975] 1 WLR 422, Digest (Cont Vol D) 288, *103fa.*
Howard v Bodington (1877) 2 PD 203, 42 JP 6, 44 Digest (Repl) 304, *1340.*
R v Industrial Injuries Comr, ex parte Amalgamated Engineering Union [1966] 1 All ER 97, [1966] 2 QB 21, [1966] 2 WLR 91, CA, Digest (Cont Vol B) 216, *3768a.*

Case also cited
Michael v Gowland [1977] 2 All ER 328, [1977] 1 WLR 296, DC.

Interlocutory appeal
Lefore Holdings Ltd appealed against the refusal of the Divisional Court of the Queen's Bench Division (Lord Widgery CJ, Eveleigh LJ and Swanwick J) on 2nd October 1979 to grant leave to apply for an order of mandamus directed to the justices for the London Borough of Croydon requiring them to state a case for the opinion of the High Court in respect of their decision at Croydon Magistrates' Court on 22nd November 1978. The facts are set out in the judgment of Lawton LJ.

Graham Clarke for the applicants.
Simon D Brown as amicus curiae.

LAWTON LJ. On 2nd October 1979 the applicants applied to the Queen's Bench Divisional Court for leave to apply for a judicial review with the object of obtaining a mandamus against the Croydon justices. That application was refused; the same day, they appealed against the refusal to this court. This court heard that application ex parte and granted leave to apply. We have been informed by counsel for the applicants that on

---

b   Rule 65 is set out at p 524 *c*, post

the occasion of the refusal the court directed that the motion in respect of which leave was required should be heard by this court. This court clearly has jurisdiction to hear a motion in those circumstances, having regard to its own decision in *R v Industrial Injuries Comr, ex parte Amalgamated Engineering Union* [1966] 1 All ER 97, [1966] 2 QB 21.

The matter arises out of an application for a distress warrant against the applicants in respect of their rateable occupation of some waste ground at the rear of premises in Croydon. The allegation was that they had been in rateable occupation of that waste ground for approximately a year, namely from September 1977 to September 1978. The applicants claimed that they had not been in rateable occupation. When the summonses came on for hearing in the magistrates' court at Croydon on 18th October 1978 they appeared by counsel and called evidence to show that they had not been in rateable occupation. We have been informed, and accept for the purposes of this motion, that that evidence was not contested.

There was a subsidiary point in the case, namely if they had been in rateable occupation, when had such occupation come to an end? We have been informed, and it seems to be a fact, that the rating authority accepted that the occupation, if there were any, had come to an end on 8th May 1978 when the National Westminster Bank took over the piece of waste ground as tenants of the London Borough of Croydon.

At the end of the hearing on 18th October 1978 the chairman of the bench said that it would be necessary to consult their senior clerk who had not been in court when the case was being heard, and as a result the case would be adjourned. The adjournment was until 22nd November 1978. On that day the chairman of the bench announced the finding of the magistrates that the applicants had had, or could have had, beneficial use of the land in question, and that as a result of the concession made by the rating authority the magistrates had decided to issue a distress warrant in the sum of £240·26 together with costs at £3·11.

The applicants were aggrieved by that finding and as a result, by a notice dated 8th December 1978, they applied to the magistrates to state a case. Their contention, so we have been told, was that the applicants had not at any material time been in possession of land which was of some use, value or benefit to them, and that there was no evidence before the magistrates on which they could so find. Accordingly, so the submission went, there had been no rateable occupation.

We have been told, and again we accept for the purposes of this motion, that at the hearing on 18th October the only contested issue was whether the evidence called by the applicants, and not disputed by the rating authority, had shown any rateable occupation. It is against that background that we have to consider the application for a case to be stated.

The relevant parts of the application are these:

> 'Now [the applicants] being dissatisfied and aggrieved with your determination upon the hearing of the said information, as being wrong in law, hereby, pursuant to the provision of the Magistrates Courts Act 1952, s. 87, apply to you to state and sign a case setting forth the facts and grounds of such your determination including evidence upon which the Justices made their findings of fact for the opinion thereon of the Queen's Bench Division of the High Court of Justice.'

We have been told by counsel for the applicants that whoever drafted that notice did so using a precedent in Oke's Magisterial Formulist (19th Edn, 1979, pp 131–132) and the precedent followed was numbered 41. That precedent is not as helpful as the one which is set out in Stone's Justices' Manual (112th Edn, 1980, vol 3, p 6174) numbered 194. If the applicants' advisers had followed the precedent no 194 in Stone, it is doubtful whether this application would now be before the court.

The time in which the application had to be made, under the provisions of s 87 of the Magistrates' Courts Act 1952, as amended by the Criminal Law Act 1977, was 21 days. That period expired on 13th December 1978. On that day the magistrates' clerk wrote to the applicants' solicitors in these terms:

'Dear Sirs,

'Further to your letter of the 8th December enclosing an Application to State Case please identify the question or questions of law or jurisdiction on which the opinion of the High Court is sought in accordance with r 65 of the Magistrates' Courts Rules 1968.'

That letter seems to have been posted during the Christmas period, and as a result there was some delay in delivery. It was answered on 10th January 1979 in these terms:

'It is our understanding that there was only one major finding of fact, namely, that [the applicants] had beneficial use or could have had beneficial use of the ground in question as a car park and it is that finding of fact which it is claimed cannot be supported by the evidence before the Court.'

The clerk to the magistrates seems to have consulted the magistrates and to have given them advice and as a result the magistrates decided that there had not been any proper identification of the issue in the application to state a case as is required by r 65 of the Magistrates' Courts Rules 1968, SI 1968 No 1920. It was because of that refusal that the applicants applied to the Divisional Court for a judicial review.

The problems which have arisen in this case are as follows. First, was the application dated 8th December 1978 one which complied with s 87 of the Magistrates' Courts Act 1952, as amended? Second, did it comply with r 65 of the 1965 rules? Third, if it did not comply with r 65, were those rules mandatory or directory? If they were mandatory, any defects in the application dated 8th December 1978 could not be rectified. If they were directory and not mandatory, they might, subject to the discretion of the court, be rectified by subsequent addition or amendment.

It is necessary now to look at the terms of the relevant statutes and rules. Section 87 of the Magistrates' Courts Act 1952, as amended, reads as follows:

'(1) Any person who was a party to any proceeding before a magistrates' court or is aggrieved by the conviction, order, determination or other proceeding of the court may question the proceeding on the ground that it is wrong in law or is in excess of jurisdiction by applying to the justices composing the court to state a case for the opinion of the High Court on the question of law or jurisdiction involved... (2) An application under the preceding subsection shall be made within twenty-one days after the day on which the decision of the magistrates' court was given...'

It is clear, in our judgment, that the provisions of sub-s (2) are mandatory. There is no power in the Magistrates' Courts Act 1952 to extend the time in which an application can be made. It follows, therefore, that if what purports to be an application in law does not amount to an application no new application can be made after 21 days.

The first problem, therefore, in this case is whether the application made on 8th December 1978 was an application for the purposes of s 87 of the 1952 Act. If it were such an application, the next problem is whether it complied with r 65 of the Magistrates' Courts Rules 1968 as amended by the Magistrates' Courts (Amendment) (No 2) Rules 1975, SI 1975 No 518. The 1968 rules dealt with cases stated. Rule 65 of those rules was in these terms:

'An application under section 87(1) of the [1952] Act shall be made in writing and shall be delivered to the clerk of the magistrates' court whose decision is questioned or sent to him by post.'

There were difficulties about the application of that rule. Those difficulties arose in this way: applicants for a case stated were not bound and in general did not state the point on which they wanted the magistrates to state a case. This could lead to the magistrates wasting a good deal of effort in reviewing the whole of a case when only one aspect of it was in issue. Secondly, time was wasted by the practice which had existed for many years, up to 1975, whereby normally the applicant for a case drafted it, submitted it to the respondent, who then either agreed or disagreed with the draft. There was a good deal of coming and going of the draft between the applicant and the respondent, and it was only after the pair of them had agreed the draft that it was sent to the magistrates' clerk for the magistrates' approval. All this took time, and as there were considerable delays in the hearing of applications before the Queen's Bench Divisional Court it was thought that the procedure ought to be made tighter so that these delays could be obviated.

It is against that background that we come to consider the changes which were made by the Magistrates' Courts (Amendment) (No 2) Rules 1975. Rule 2 provides as follows:

> 'For rules 65 to 68 of the Magistrates' Courts Rules 1968, as amended, there shall be substituted the following rules:—"*Application to state case*   65—(1) An application under section 87(1) of the Act shall be made in writing and signed by or on behalf of the applicant and shall identify the question or questions of law or jurisdiction on which the opinion of the High Court is sought. (2) Where one of the questions on which the opinion of the High Court is sought is whether there was evidence on which the magistrates' court could come to its decision, the particular finding of fact made by the magistrates' court which it is claimed cannot be supported by the evidence before the magistrates' court shall be specified in such application. (3) Any such application shall be sent to the clerk of the magistrates' court whose decision is questioned . . ."'

Then comes r 65A, and the substance of that rule (which I need not set out in detail) is that for the future magistrates' clerks are to prepare the first draft, and the old practice of letting the applicant prepare the first draft is to come to an end.

One of the problems which arises in this case is whether the provisions of r 65, as amended, are mandatory or directory. Counsel for the applicants has submitted that they are directory. They are essentially procedural; their object is to ensure that justice is done but done quickly, and that there is no reason to think that Parliament intended, when approving those rules, that people should be shut out from the seat of justice merely because of some failure to observe one of the technical provisions of the rules.

On the other hand, counsel who has appeared as amicus has called our attention to the fact that in 1975 Parliament approved a change in the existing practice and put in its place a more stringent set of rules, the object of which was to speed up the administration of justice. He submitted, and in my view rightly submitted, that the intention of Parliament must not be overridden by any elasticity which this court, on merely equitable grounds, might seek to apply in circumstances such as arise in this case.

For my part I accept that this court should be chary about relaxing what appear to be the strict provisions of the 1975 rules. Nevertheless, as was pointed out by Lord Penzance many years ago in *Howard v Bodington* (1877) 2 PD 203 at 211, the whole scope and purpose of the enactment must be considered and one must assess 'the importance of the provision that has been disregarded, and the relation of that provision to the general object intended to be secured by the Act'.

Now the 'general object intended to be secured' by the change in the law was the speeding up of justice. It was not to curtail the opportunities for doing justice.

I have to bear in mind that all sorts and manner of persons come before the magistrates' courts; some may be worldly wise, some may have the benefit of expert legal advice, some may not be worldly wise; others may have the advice of inexperienced lawyers. It would be a sad state of affairs if, in matters which are mostly penal and often include cases which involve the liberty of the subject, a mere failure to comply with a procedural rule should in all circumstances keep an applicant away from the seat of justice.

It seems to me, therefore, that the scope of these amended rules and, to use the words of *Bodington*'s case, 'the importance of the provision that has been disregarded, and the relation of that provision to the general object intended' by the change of the rules should be kept in mind. Justice has to be done to applicants who may not be familiar with the technicalities of the law. Each case, of course, has to be looked at on its merits, and in my judgment the court cannot begin to waive the strict provisions of the law unless there has been, to use Templeman J's phrase in *Coney v Choyce* [1975] 1 All ER 979 at 990, [1975] 1 WLR 422 at 434, a 'substantial compliance with the regulations'.

The problem, therefore, for this court as I see it is to ask whether the application dated 8th December 1978 complied substantially with r 65 as amended. The rule allows an applicant to raise a question whether there was evidence on which the magistrates' court could come to its decision, and then it goes on:

> '. . . the particular finding of fact made by the magistrates' court which it is claimed cannot be supported by the evidence before the magistrates' court shall be specified in such application.'

The problem arises in this case whether the application of 8th December did identify the kind of point on which the magistrates' case was to be founded. It referred specifically to the evidence on which the magistrates made their finding of fact, and that, in my judgment, to a clerk to the magistrates would have indicated at that date that what the applicants wanted to argue in the High Court was that on the only evidence before the magistrates the rating authority had not shown that they were in rateable occupation of this waste land. There could not have been any other question on which the magistrates were being asked to state a case, because that was the only question at the hearing. In those circumstances, the magistrates were alerted to what was in issue, and they could, without further information, have stated a case on that application.

There were unnecessary words in the application, but once again, the clerk to the magistrates would have appreciated (and I am sure that he did) that those unnecessary words did not take the application any further and would be unlikely to confuse them because there was no issue in the case other than that relating to the evidence about rateable occupation. So there was a substantial compliance, in my judgment, with the rule, and the subsequent events and correspondence clarified the matter for the magistrates.

Accordingly, I would hold that the magistrates should be ordered to state a case.

WALLER LJ. I entirely agree. I would only add this, that we are told that at the hearing before the magistrates every fact was agreed except the ingredients of rateable occupation, and the only witness called was a witness called on behalf of the applicants. When the distress warrant was ordered to be issued, they were aggrieved and they served the notice that Lawton LJ has already quoted.

The fact that there was only one witness and only one point before the magistrates must have indicated clearly, when the notice was received, what the particular point was; and indeed, when one looks at the affidavit of the magistrates, there appears this paragraph:

> 'We appreciated that rateable occupation contained four ingredients, namely, (i) actual occupation or possession; (ii) this must be exclusive to the applicants; (iii) this must also be of value or benefit to the applicant; (iv) the period must not be too transient. Item No. (iv) did not cause difficulty, but we wished to give items (i) to (iii) more detailed consideration than was possible during the time remaining to us on the 18th October and we therefore adjourned the hearing.'

We are told by counsel that items (i) and (ii) were conceded, so there only was the one point, namely item (iii): were they satisfied that it was of value? Indeed, the phrase in Stone's Justices' Manual (12th Edn, 1980, vol 2, p 3547) is 'of use or value or benefit to the [applicant]', and accordingly that underlines the point that there could only be one possible interpretation of the notice which Lawton LJ has quoted.

Appeal allowed.

Solicitors: *W G R Saunders & Son* (for the applicants); *Treasury Solicitor.*

Frances Rustin   Barrister.

Vibroplant Ltd v Holland (Inspector of Taxes)

CHANCERY DIVISION
DILLON J
15th, 16th JULY 1980

Income tax – Capital allowances – Industrial building or structure – Factory – Building used for subjecting goods or materials to a process – Plant hire operator's depots used for repair and maintenance of equipment hired out – Whether building a 'factory or other similar premises' or used for subjecting goods or materials to a 'process' – Capital Allowances Act 1968, s 7(1)(a)(e).

The taxpayer carried on business as a plant hire operator. Between hirings to customers the plant was returned to one of the taxpayer's depots to be cleaned, serviced and, if necessary, repaired. Each depot had the facilities and equipment to undertake that work. The taxpayer claimed initial and writing-down allowances under ss 1 and 2 of the Capital Allowances Act 1968 in respect of buildings at the depots on the basis that they were 'industrial buildings' within the meaning of s 7(1)(a) or (e)[a] of the 1968 Act. The Special Commissioners disallowed the claim and the taxpayer appealed, contending that the buildings were industrial buildings since they were used for the purposes of the taxpayer's trade of hiring plant, that the cost of servicing and repair was a substantial part of the cost of carrying on that trade and that the buildings were a 'factory or other similar premises' within s 7(1)(a) or were used for the 'subjection of goods or materials to [a] process' within s 7(1)(e). The Crown contended (i) that the buildings were not industrial buildings since the taxpayer's trade was not that of repairing and servicing plant, (ii) that the use of the buildings was, therefore, only ancillary to the taxpayer's trade and (iii) that the buildings were not factories or other similar premises and were not used for the manufacture of goods or materials or the subjection of goods or materials to a process.

Held – For the purposes of s 7(1)(a) of the 1968 Act a 'factory or other similar premises' was a building used for the manufacture of goods, while for the purposes of s 7(1)(c) of that Act a 'process' connoted a substantial measure of uniformity of treatment or system of treatment. Accordingly, since nothing was made by the taxpayer in the buildings, and since each item of plant was treated individually according to its particular needs or defects, it could not be said either that the buildings were factories or similar premises within s 7(1)(a) or that the items were subjected to a process within s 7(1)(e). It followed therefore that the buildings were not industrial buildings or structures within s 7(1) and that the taxpayer was not entitled to initial and writing-down allowances. The appeal would accordingly be dismissed (see p 531 f to h and p 532 c d g, post).

Ellerker (Inspector of Taxes) v Union Cold Storage Co Ltd [1939] 1 All ER 23, *Inland Revenue Comrs v Leith Harbour and Docks Comrs* 1942 SC 101 and *Kilmarnock Equitable Co-operative Society Ltd v Inland Revenue Comrs* (1966) 42 Tax Cas 675 followed.

Notes

For the general definition of 'industrial building or structure', see 23 Halsbury's Laws (4th Edn) para 397.

For the Capital Allowances Act 1968, ss 1, 2, 7, see 34 Halsbury's Statutes (3rd Edn) 1041, 1042, 1050.

Cases referred to in judgment

Buckingham (Inspector of Taxes) v Securitas Properties Ltd [1980] STC 166, [1980] 1 WLR 380.

---

a   Section 7(1), so far as material, is set out at p 530 j, post

*Ellerker (Inspector of Taxes) v Union Cold Storage Co Ltd, Thomas Borthwick & Sons Ltd v
Compton (Inspector of Taxes)* [1939] 1 All ER 23, 22 Tax Cas 195.
Inland Revenue Comrs v Leith Harbour and Docks Comrs 1942 SC 101, 24 Tax Cas 118, 28(1)
Digest (Reissue) 221, *739.
Kilmarnock Equitable Co-operative Society Ltd v Inland Revenue Comrs (1966) 42 Tax Cas 675,
45 ATC 205, [1966] TR 185, 1966 SLT 224, 28(1) Digest (Reissue) 535, *1294.

Cases also cited

Blunson (Inspector of Taxes) v West Midlands Gas Board (1951) 33 Tax Cas 315.
Inland Revenue Comrs v Lambhill Ironworks 1950 SC 331, 31 Tax Cas 393.

Case stated

1. At a meeting of the Commissioners for the Special Purposes of the Income Tax Acts
held on 8th February 1978 Vibroplant Ltd ('Vibroplant') appealed against an assessment
to corporation tax in the sum of £420,000 for the accounting period ended 31st March
1974.
2. Shortly stated the question for decision was whether in computing the profits of
Vibroplant for corporation tax purposes for the accounting period Vibroplant was
entitled to initial and writing-down allowances under ss 1 and 2 of the Capital Allowances
Act 1968 in respect of certain buildings on the basis that these buildings were industrial
buildings within one or other of paras (*a*), (*e*) or (*f*)(ii) of s 7 of that Act.
3. Mr Roy Clinning, the secretary and financial director of Vibroplant, gave evidence
before the commissioners.
[Paragraph 4 listed the documents proved admitted before the commissioners.]
5. As a result of the evidence both oral and documentary adduced before the
commissioners they found the following facts proved or admitted. (a) Vibroplant was a
company incorporated under the Companies Act 1948, whose registered office (which
was also its head office from which the main body of the administrative staff operated)
was situated at Prospect Road, Starbeck, Harrogate in the County of North Yorkshire. In
the accounting period under appeal Vibroplant carried on the trade of plant hire operators
from its head office. It had 21 depots situated throughout England, Wales and
Scotland. (b) Each depot consisted of a storage area which was open and which was used
for the storage of plant awaiting hire or repair and had, in addition, building structures
on it where the repairs and refurbishing were carried out and in respect of which the
allowances in issue in the appeal were claimed. Each depot had substantial repair
facilities as it was Vibroplant's policy to maintain its own plant in a high state of repair
to prolong its useful life. The repair facilities were used to clean, service and repair each
item of plant after it had been returned from a hiring. Each depot had all the facilities
necessary to undertake all but some 3% or 4% of this work. Some items of plant were so
badly damaged while out on hire that they had to be virtually rebuilt. Most of the
necessary spare parts were provided from the ample stores carried by the depots, or by
'cannibalising' from broken down pieces of equipment. In a few cases a part was
specially made, lathes being available to enable this to be done, and occasionally an item
of plant was modified for a special purpose. In addition to a lathe, each depot was
equipped with welding plant, a machine for compressing metal with a weight of up to
60 tons, hoists, battery chargers, cutting benches, drilling equipment, power tools,
inspection pits, spraying equipment for repainting, steam cleaning equipment, work
benches and presses. No services were provided for cleaning, servicing or repairing plant
belonging to anyone else nor did Vibroplant hold itself out as prepared to accept, nor did
it accept, orders for such work. Vibroplant's standard hiring agreement provided, in
particular, that the hiring agreement covered the customer for normal wear and tear but
in the case of damage caused by misuse of the plant an additional charge was made. In
the year ended 31st March 1974 such additional charges amounted to some £116,000
out of a total turnover of over £4,900,000. Vibroplant had a fleet of vehicles at each
depot for the delivery of plant to and its collection from customers, and these vehicles

were also maintained at the depots. Vibroplant's vehicles used by directors and employees were also maintained at the depots. (c) Besides the repair facilities each building complex contained office space for the manager and his staff; in no case did this exceed 10% of the floor area of the building. After initial paperwork on hirings, all subsequent documentation and in particular the handling of all accounts was dealt with at Vibroplant's head office in Harrogate. The office part of the building was the only part open to the public. Whilst the managers of each depot were not forbidden to agree hirings any such agreement made by them was subject to contract. The terms and conditions of all hirings, all price structures and questions of policy were determined at the head office and all binding hiring agreements, and correspondence relating thereto, emanated from that office. (d) A typical depot was that at Washington, County Durham. The site had an area of some 157,970 square feet on which there was a building of 13,290 square feet, of which the workshop covered 12,496 square feet and the offices 794 square feet. The total number of employees was 30, of whom 20 were employed in the workshop, six were drivers and there was an office staff of four. (e) Vibroplant's accounts for the two years ended 31st March 1973 and 1974 showed, respectively, a turnover of £3,414,065 and £4,913,666, charges for damage to items hired, in addition to the normal hire charge, of £87,673 and £116,114, the cost of repairs, spares and general expenses, £358,401 and £627,422, the cost of wages £640,737 and £913,922, and motor expenses £152,436 and £203,980.

6. It was contended on behalf of Vibroplant: (a) that each building at the depots which had buildings was an 'industrial building or structure' which fell within the definition in s 7(1) of the 1968 Act because (i) it was in use for the purposes of a trade or part of the trade carried on therein, being the repair of vehicles hired out, and consisted of premises similar to a mill, and s 7(1)(a) of the 1968 Act therefore applied, (ii) alternatively, it was in use for the purposes of a trade or part of a trade being the repair of vehicles hired out which consisted in the subjection of goods or materials to a process, and s 7(1)(e) therefore applied, (iii) alternatively, it was in use for the purposes of a trade or part of a trade which consisted in the storage of goods or materials which were to be subjected, in the course of that trade or part of that trade, to a process, and s 7(1)(f)(ii) therefore applied, and (b) that Vibroplant was, therefore, entitled to initial and writing-down allowances under ss 1 and 2 of the 1968 Act in respect of the buildings.

7. It was contended by the Crown: (a) that Vibroplant's trade was that of plant hire operators, (b) that that trade was conducted from the head office in Harrogate, (c) that the alleged industrial buildings were premises used only for the maintenance, repair and refurbishing of the plant and vehicles which Vibroplant hired out or otherwise used in the trade, (d) that the use of these buildings was ancillary to the trade and did not constitute a separate trade or part of a trade within s 7(2) but provided facilities to enable Vibroplant to carry on its trade, (e) that the buildings did not fall within the category of buildings or structures within s 7(1) and so were not industrial buildings or structures, and (f) that the capital expenditure on the construction of the buildings did not qualify for initial or writing-down allowances within s 1 or s 2.

8. The following cases were cited to the commissioners: *Blunson (Inspector of Taxes) v West Midlands Gas Board* (1951) 33 Tax Cas 315; *Bourne (Inspector of Taxes) v Norwich Crematorium Ltd* [1967] 2 All ER 576, [1967] 1 WLR 691, 44 Tax Cas 164; *Dale v Johnson Brothers* (1951) 32 Tax Cas 487; *Ellerker (Inspector of Taxes) v Union Cold Storage Co Ltd* [1939] 1 All ER 23, 22 Tax Cas 195; *Inland Revenue Comrs v Lambhill Ironworks* 1950 SC 331, 31 Tax Cas 393; *Inland Revenue Comrs v Leith Harbour and Docks Comrs* 1942 SC 101, 24 Tax Cas 118; *Kilmarnock Equitable Co-operative Society Ltd v Inland Revenue Comrs* (1966) 42 Tax Cas 675; *Ricketts v Colquhoun (Inspector of Taxes)* [1926] AC 1, 10 Tax Cas 118, HL.

9. The commissioners who heard the appeal took time to consider their decision and gave it in writing on 13th March 1978 as follows:

'[Counsel for Vibroplant] contended that each building at the depots which had one was a building in use for the purposes of a trade or part of a trade carried on in the building and that having regard to the activities carried on in that building it was similar to a mill and so fell within paragraph (a) of section 7 of the 1968 Act. [The Crown] contended that Vibroplant's trade of plant hire operators was not carried on in any of the buildings and that they did not therefore qualify as industrial buildings. We accept [the Crown's] contention. It is true, as is conceded by [the Crown], that all the activities carried on in the buildings were for the purposes of Vibroplant's trade. That trade, however, was not carried on in any of the buildings. Vibroplant merely repaired and maintained its plant and fleet of vehicles in those buildings. It also there maintained the vehicles used by directors and employees and the accounts produced in evidence before us draw no distinction between expenses under this head and the expense of repairing and maintaining Vibroplant's plant and fleet of delivery vehicles. Had Vibroplant's trade been that of a repairer or maintainer of plant and vehicles the requirement as to the carrying on of a trade would have been satisfied but such was not its trade. Those activities of repair and maintenance, in our view, although substantial, were subordinate to and not part of Vibroplant's trade. [Counsel for Vibroplant] sought to gain support from *Ellerker v Union Cold Storage Co Ltd* [1939] 1 All ER 23, 22 Tax Cas 195 and *Inland Revenue Comrs v Leith Harbour and Docks Comrs* 1942 SC 101, 24 Tax Cas 118. He contended that the successful taxpayer in each of those cases carried on a trade which consisted of providing a service to its customers, and that Vibroplant did the same in the present case and was equally entitled to succeed in its claim. In our view, however, these cases are distinguishable inasmuch as in each of them the activities in the relevant building (viz refrigeration and cold storage of meat in the one case, and the unloading from ships and the maintenance in good condition of grain in the other) comprised or was an integral part of the trade which the taxpayer carried on for its customers. Per contra, in the present case the activities carried on in the buildings were not carried on for Vibroplant's customers; they were necessary to put Vibroplant in a position to carry on its plant hire trade; they themselves did not constitute that trade or part of that trade.

'Should however, the true view be that Vibroplant's trade, or part of it, was carried on in each of the buildings we hold that none of the buildings was similar to a mill. [Counsel for Vibroplant] submitted that each building was so similar because what was done in it was to subject plant to a treatment or process viz that of cleaning, maintenance and repair, (which involved in some cases the manufacture of spare parts or the virtual rebuilding of an item of plant). He relied primarily on the judgment of Macnaghten J in the *Union Cold Storage* case where each storage building was held to be similar to a mill because goods were treated or processed in it by means of machinery provided for the purpose. In deciding what amounted to treatment or process in this context, of the many cases cited to us we derived most assistance from the observations in *Kilmarnock Equitable Co-operative Society Ltd v Inland Revenue Comrs* (1966) 42 Tax Cas 675 at 685 and in particular from those of Lord Cameron who said that a process was an application of a method of manufacture or adaptation of goods or materials towards a particular use, purpose or end. In that case the activity in question was the subjection of crude coal to a purifying process which made it fit for sale. [Counsel for Vibroplant] contended that the cleaning, maintenance and repair of plant by Vibroplant involved the subjection of that plant to a treatment or process. We are, however, unable to accept that submission. In the course of cleaning, maintenance and repair each item of plant was given individual attention, the precise nature of which depended on the extent of the damage suffered, by contrast with the treatment applied in the *Union Cold Storage*, the *Leith Harbour and Docks* and the *Kilmarnock* cases. The plant was essentially the same both before and after being cleaned, maintained and repaired and it would not, in our view, accord with the ordinary use of language to say that cleaning, maintaining and repairing involved treatment or processing analogous to what goes on in a mill.

'We therefore hold that the buildings do not fall within paragraph (a) of section 7(1) of the 1968 Act.

'[Counsel for Vibroplant] contended that if paragraph (*a*) did not apply then either paragraph (*e*) or paragraph (*f*)(ii) applied though he frankly admitted that he could not press too hard for (*f*)(ii). In order to come within (*e*) it must be shown, in this case, that the buildings were in use for a trade consisting in the subjection of goods or materials to any process. We reject this contention for the reasons given in connection with paragraph (*a*) viz that Vibroplant's plant was not subjected to any process and that even if it was such subjection was not its trade or part of its trade. We reject the contention for (*f*)(ii) because the storage of goods was, in our view, clearly not Vibroplant's trade or any part of it.

'We therefore dismiss the appeal and increase the assessment to the agreed sum of £474,757.'

10. Vibroplant immediately after the determination of the appeal declared dissatisfaction therewith as being erroneous in point of law and on 21st March 1978 required the commissioners to state a case for the opinion of the High Court pursuant to s 56 of the Taxes Management Act 1970.

11. The question for the opinion of the court was whether the commissioners' decision in para 9 above was correct in law.

Stewart Bates QC and *Michael Musgrave* for Vibroplant.
David Woolley QC and *Robert Carnwath* for the Crown.

DILLON J. This is an appeal by the taxpayer company, Vibroplant Ltd, against a decision of the Special Commissioners. Vibroplant carries on the business of plant hire operators. The business involves hiring out a wide range of articles to customers. The articles include such things as tractors, fork-lift trucks, generating sets, concrete mixers, air compressors, dumpers, compressed air tools and vibrating rollers.

For the purposes of that business Vibroplant has a head office in Yorkshire and 21 depots spread around England and Scotland. At 20 of these depots buildings or structures have been erected which are used for the repair and refurbishing of the plant which is to be let out on hire. I shall come to the details of what is done later. A depot at Washington, County Durham, has been taken as typical. The point which the Special Commissioners had to decide was whether Vibroplant was entitled to capital allowances in respect of these buildings, and the Special Commissioners decided that Vibroplant was not so entitled.

The right to capital allowances now depends on the Capital Allowances Act 1968. Section 1(1) of that Act provides:

'... where a person incurs capital expenditure on the construction of a building or structure which is to be an industrial building or structure occupied for the purposes of a trade carried on [as there mentioned], there shall be made to the person who incurred the expenditure ... "an initial allowance". ...'

Section 2 provides that where a person is entitled to an interest in a building or structure and the building or structure is an industrial building or structure, a writing-down allowance shall be made to him. The key words are 'industrial building or structure', and the nub of this case is whether these buildings at Vibroplant's depots are industrial buildings or structures.

That term is defined by s 7 of the 1968 Act. Section 7 sets out a number of detailed matters, but it is not necessary to read all of them. Keeping only to those on which Vibroplant's case has been founded, I read the section as follows:

'(1) ... "industrial building or structure" means a building or structure in use—
(*a*) for the purposes of a trade carried on in a mill, factory or other similar premises, or ... (*e*) for the purposes of a trade which consists in the manufacture of goods or materials or the subjection of goods or materials to any process ...'

The detailed findings of the Special Commissioners in relation to these depots are as follows:

'Each depot consisted of a storage area which was open and which was used for the storage of plant awaiting hire or repair and had, in addition, building structures upon it where the repairs and refurbishing were carried out and in respect of which the allowances in issue in this appeal are claimed. Each depot had substantial repair facilities as it was Vibroplant's policy to maintain its own plant in a high state of repair to prolong its useful life. The repair facilities were used to clean, service and repair each item of plant after it had been returned from a hiring. Each depot had all the facilities necessary to undertake all but some 3 or 4% of this work. Some items of plant were so badly damaged while out on hire that they had to be virtually rebuilt. Most of the necessary spare parts were provided from the ample stores carried by the depots, or by "cannibalising" from broken down pieces of equipment. In a few cases a part was specially made, lathes being available to enable this to be done, and occasionally an item of plant was modified for a special purpose. In addition to a lathe, each depot was equipped with welding plant, a machine for compressing metal with a weight of up to 60 tons, hoists, battery chargers, cutting benches, drilling equipment, power tools, inspection pits, spraying equipment for repainting, steam cleaning equipment, work benches and presses. No services were provided for cleaning, servicing or repairing plant belonging to anyone else nor did Vibroplant hold itself out as prepared to accept, nor did it accept, orders for such work. [Then, the findings also include the finding:] Vibroplant had a fleet of vehicles at each depot for the delivery of plant to, and its collection from customers, and these vehicles were also maintained at the depots. Vibroplant's vehicles used by directors and employees were also maintained at the depots.'

Counsel for Vibroplant submits in relation to s 7(1)(a) that the buildings on the depots were used 'for the purposes of a trade carried on in a ... factory or other similar premises'; he does not claim that they were used 'for the purposes of a trade carried on in a mill ... or other similar premises'. However, on the authorities, the term 'factory', used in its ordinary sense, means a building used for the making of something. In *Ellerker (Inspector of Taxes) v Union Cold Storage Co Ltd* [1939] 1 All ER 23 at 27–28, 22 Tax Cas 195 at 208, in which the phrase under consideration was 'mills, factories or other similar premises', Macnaghten J said, firstly: '... since the words "mills" and "factories" are ordinary English words, they must be construed in their ordinary and natural sense.' He then went on to say: 'I take it that a factory is a building used for the manufacture of goods and equipped with machinery, and that the word is generally understood in that sense. It is a building where goods are made.'

Again, in *Inland Revenue Comrs v Leith Harbour and Docks Comrs* 1942 SC 101, 24 Tax Cas 118, where again the phrase under consideration was 'mills, factories or other similar premises', Lord Normand, after referring to a finding of the commissioners that certain grain elevators 'are similar to factories in all but this, that they do not make anything', said 1942 SC 101 at 109, 24 Tax Cas 118 at 123: 'The finding that the elevators are similar to factories is self-destructive, because the characteristic property of a factory is that it makes something.' So, in my judgment, Vibroplant cannot make out a claim under s 7(1)(a) that these buildings are in use 'for the purposes of a trade carried on in a ... factory or other similar premises'.

I therefore turn to s 7(1)(e), and the contention here is that the buildings are in use 'for the purposes of a trade which consists in ... the subjection of goods or materials to any process'. Counsel for Vibroplant points out that under s 7(2) of the 1968 Act, the provisions of sub-s (1) are to apply 'in relation to a part of a trade or undertaking as they apply in relation to a trade or undertaking'.

The Special Commissioners decided the case against Vibroplant on two grounds. The first ground was that Vibroplant's trade of plant hire operators was not carried on in any of the buildings, and that they therefore did not qualify as industrial buildings. They concluded that the activities carried on in the buildings were not carried on for Vibroplant's customers; they were necessary to put Vibroplant in a position to carry on its plant hire trade, but they did not themselves constitute that trade or part of that trade. The second ground of decision was that the treatment provided in the buildings did not involve the subjection of the articles being treated to any 'process', and they said: 'In the course of cleaning, maintenance and repair each item of plant was given individual attention, the precise nature of which depended on the extent of the damage suffered, by contrast with the treatment applied . . .'

Counsel for the Crown has argued that the first finding of the commissioners should stand as a finding of fact. I am very doubtful about that because it is a finding essentially geared to the interpretation of the section as a matter of law, and I see very great force in counsel's argument for Vibroplant that what it is doing in these buildings in servicing and repairing the plant it wishes to hire out is an essential part of its business of plant hire operators; it is a part of its trade, and a part which consists, if he is right on other grounds, in the subjection of goods to a process. But I do not need to express any final view on that, because I think the Special Commissioners are right on their second ground.

The essence of the treatment which is provided in these buildings is that it is individual for the particular defects or needs of a particular piece of plant; each item is treated individually. By contrast, in my view, 'process' connotes a substantial measure of uniformity of treatment or system of treatment. I note that a dictionary definition of 'process' in the Shorter Oxford English Dictionary, which was cited by Slade J in *Buckingham (Inspector of Taxes) v Securitas Properties Ltd* [1980] STC 166 at 173, [1980] 1 WLR 380 at 386 is: 'a continuous and regular action or succession of actions, taking place or carried on in definite manner; a continuous (natural or artificial) operation or series of operations.'

That is in line with the views expressed by all the members of the Court of Session in *Kilmarnock Equitable Co-operative Society Ltd v Inland Revenue Comrs* (1966) 42 Tax Cas 675, where what was in question was a process for breaking up coal, separating it from dross and packing it into bags for distribution. It is also in line with the process under consideration in the *Leith Harbour and Docks Comrs* case 1942 SC 101, 24 Tax Cas 118, which was concerned with grain elevators, and the process involved in a cold storage plant which had to be considered in *Ellerker (Inspector of Taxes) v Union Cold Storage Co Ltd* [1939] 1 All ER 23, 22 Tax Cas 195.

It seems to me that an ordinary garage where cars are serviced and repaired according to their particular requirements does not involve subjecting goods or materials to any process. Similarly, a doctor's surgery where individuals are treated for their individual ailments does not involve the subjection of people to any process. Therefore, in my judgment, Vibroplant fails to establish that these buildings are industrial buildings or structures within the meaning of s 7. The decision of the Special Commissioners was correct, and this appeal fails.

Appeal dismissed.

Solicitors: *Kirbys*, Harrogate (for Vibroplant); *Solicitor of Inland Revenue*.

Edwina Epstein   Barrister.

Cane v Jones and others

CHANCERY DIVISION
MICHAEL WHEELER QC SITTING AS A DEPUTY JUDGE OF THE HIGH COURT
27th, 28th, 29th, 30th NOVEMBER, 19th DECEMBER 1979

Company – Articles of association – Alteration – Agreement by all the corporators to alter articles – Signatories to agreement not meeting together to sign agreement and not signing in each other's presence – Agreement to remove chairman's casting vote – Family company – Shares in company equally divided between two opposed sides of family – Whether agreement of all corporators effective to alter articles – Whether special resolution at general meeting required for alteration of company's articles – Companies Act 1948, s 10(1).

A family company was incorporated in 1946 by two brothers, P and H, who were the only directors of the company. The company's issued share capital was held as to one half by P's side of the family, in the joint names of his children (the first and second defendants), and as to the other half by H's side of the family, in the name of the trustees of a trust of which H's daughter, the plaintiff, was the sole beneficiary. The company's articles of association provided that P and H should be life directors, that the chairman of directors should be elected by the directors and that the chairman should have a casting vote at board and general meetings. By an agreement made in March 1967 between the then shareholders, who were the first and second defendants of the one part and the trustees of the plaintiff's trust of the other, it was agreed that the chairman of the company should not exercise a casting vote and that in the event of an equality of votes at a meeting the parties to the agreement should appoint an independent chairman. The parties to the agreement did not meet together to sign it nor did they sign it in the presence of each other. In August 1967 the trust came to an end and the plaintiff became the registered holder of half the issued share capital. The two sides of the family fell out and P's side claimed that P was the chairman of the company and that by the articles he had a casting vote. The plaintiff, for H's side, claimed that the 1967 agreement had altered the articles and that P, if he was the chairman, no longer had a casting vote. She brought an action against the first and second defendants and P seeking, inter alia, a declaration that the chairman was not entitled to a second or casting vote at any company meeting. The first defendant and P contended that by virtue of s 10(1)*ᵃ* and s 141(2)*ᵇ* of the Companies Act 1948 the articles of a company could only be altered by a special resolution passed at a general meeting and, accordingly, that the 1967 agreement had not altered the company's articles.

Held – It was a basic principle of company law that all the corporators of a company acting together could do anything which was intra vires the company. Section 10(1) of the 1948 Act did not undermine that principle but merely laid down the procedure whereby some only of the shareholders of a company could validly alter the articles. Since the 1967 agreement, though not drafted as a resolution and though not signed by the signatories in each other's presence, represented a meeting of all the shareholders' minds, and since a meeting of shareholders' minds was the essence of a general meeting and the passing of a resolution, the 1967 agreement was effective to override the articles in regard to the casting vote of the chairman, and accordingly restricted the use of the chairman's vote (see p 539 g h, p 540 a b h j and p 544 b, post).

Dicta of Younger LJ in *Re Express Engineering Works Ltd* [1920] 1 Ch at 471, of Astbury J in *Parker and Cooper Ltd v Reading* [1926] All ER Rep at 328 and of Buckley LJ in *Re Duomatic Ltd* [1969] 1 All ER at 168 applied.

---

a   Section 10(1) is set out at p 538 *c d*, post
b   Section 141(2) is set out at p 538 *e* to *g*, post

Re Oxted Motor Co Ltd [1921] All ER Rep 646 and *Re Moorgate Mercantile Holdings Ltd* [1980] 1 All ER 40 considered.
Re Pearce Duff & Co Ltd [1960] 3 All ER 222 doubted.

Notes

For alteration of articles, see 7 Halsbury's Laws (4th Edn) para 452, and for cases on the subject, see 9 Digest (Reissue) 612–614, 3652–3662.

For the Companies Act 1948, ss 10, 141, see 5 Halsbury's Statutes (3rd Edn) 128, 223.

Cases referred to in judgment

Consolidated Nickel Mines Ltd, Re [1914] 1 Ch 883, 83 LJ Ch 760, 111 LT 243, 21 Mans 273, 9 Digest (Reissue) 481, 2866.

Duomatic Ltd, Re [1969] 1 All ER 161, [1969] 2 Ch 365, [1969] 2 WLR 114, 9 Digest (Reissue) 483, 2879.

Express Engineering Works Ltd, Re [1920] 1 Ch 466, 89 LJ Ch 379, 122 LT 790, CA, 9 Digest (Reissue) 557, 3331.

MacDougall v Gardiner (1875) 1 Ch D 13, 45 LJ Ch 27, 33 LT 521, CA, 9 Digest (Reissue) 641, 3842.

Moorgate Mercantile Holdings Ltd, Re [1980] 1 All ER 40, [1980] 1 WLR 227.

Newman (George) & Co, Re [1895] 1 Ch 674, 64 LJ Ch 407, 72 LT 697, 2 Mans 267, 12 R 228, CA, 9 Digest (Reissue) 177, 1086.

Oxted Motor Co, Re [1921] 3 KB 32, [1921] All ER Rep 646, 90 LJKB 1145, 126 LT 56, [1921] B & CR 155, DC, 9 Digest (Reissue) 620, 3701.

Parker and Cooper Ltd v Reading [1926] Ch 975, [1926] All ER Rep 323, 96 LJ Ch 23, 136 LT 117, 9 Digest (Reissue) 515, 3076.

Pearce Duff & Co Ltd, Re [1960] 3 All ER 222, [1960] 1 WLR 1014, 9 Digest (Reissue) 639, 3830.

Wenlock (Baroness) v River Dee Co (1883) 36 Ch D 675n, 57 LT 402n, CA; *affd* (1885) 10 App Cas 354, 54 LJQB 577, 53 LT 62, 49 JP 773, HL, 10 Digest (Reissue) 795, 4583.

Cases also cited

Bentley-Stevens v Jones [1974] 2 All ER 653, [1974] 1 WLR 638.
Beswick v Beswick [1967] 2 All ER 1197, [1968] AC 68, HL.
Browne v La Trinidad (1887) 37 Ch D 1, CA.
Cotter v National Union of Seamen [1927] 2 Ch 58, [1929] All ER Rep 342, CA.
Dunlop Pneumatic Tyre Co Ltd v Selfridge & Co Ltd [1915] AC 847, [1914–15] All ER Rep 833, HL.
Foster v Foster [1916] 1 Ch 532, [1916–17] All ER Rep 856.

Action

The plaintiff, Mrs Gillian Mary Cane, the registered holder of half the issued shares in a family company, Kingsway Petrol Station Ltd ('the company'), by writ dated 22nd February 1977 issued against Ronald Vivien Courtney ('Ronald') and Maureen Heather Jones ('Heather'), the first and second defendants, in whose joint names the remaining half of the company's issued shares were registered, and against Percival Charles Jones ('Percy'), their father, the third defendant, and the company, claimed the following declarations: (1) that Percy and his brother Harold Courtney Jones ('Harold') were the only directors of the company, (2) that certain heads of agreement in a document signed on 27th September 1975 were void and of no effect so far as they purported either to reconstitute the company's board of directors, or alter its articles of association or amend the provisions of an agreement made in March 1967, (3) that the proceedings of a meeting on 27th September 1976 purporting to be a meeting of the company's directors were a nullity, (4) that the proceedings at meetings on 31st December 1976 so far as they purported to be an annual general meeting of the company and an extraordinary general meeting of the company were a nullity, (5) that at any agreed meeting of the company, in the case of an equality of votes, whether on a show of hands or on a poll, the chairman of the meeting was not entitled to a second or casting vote, and (6) that the proceedings at meetings on 26th January 1977 so far as they purported to constitute a directors' meeting of the company and an extraordinary general meeting were a nullity. The plaintiff also claimed an injunction restraining Ronald from acting or holding himself out as a director of the company and an injunction restraining the company whether by it directors, servants, agents or otherwise from acting on any resolutions declared to be void. The facts are set in the judgment.

Oliver Weaver for the plaintiff.
Robin Pitts for the first and third defendants.
The second defendant did not appear.
The company took no part in the proceedings.

Cur adv vult

19th December. **MICHAEL WHEELER QC** read the following judgment: This action concerns a dispute in a family company, called Kingsway Petrol Station Ltd ('the company'). The family is the Jones family and I will briefly refer to the family tree. In doing so I shall adopt for convenience the method adopted by counsel of referring to them (if they will forgive me) by their Christian names. There are two brothers, Percy and Harold Jones (Harold is sometimes called 'Nick'). Percy has a son, Ronald and a daughter, Maureen Heather (more usually referred to as 'Heather') who is now Mrs Fooks. Harold has a daughter, Gillian, who is Mrs Cane. Gillian is the plaintiff in this action. Ronald and Percy are the first and third defendants. Heather is the second defendant, who has entered an appearance but has not been represented at the hearing, and the company is the fourth defendant, which has taken no part at all, for reasons which will become apparent in the course of this judgment.

The company was incorporated on 21st June 1946 under the Companies Act 1929, and its articles mainly adopt the 1929 Table A. It was formed by Percy and Harold and they are named in the articles as life directors. It has a present issued capital of £30,000 in 30,000 fully-paid £1 shares, and at all material times 15,000 of these shares have been registered in the joint names of Ronald and Heather. It is now common ground (although initially it was in dispute) that since August 1967 the remaining 15,000 shares have been registered in the name of Gillian (the plaintiff) on a transfer from Mr T J Williams and Mr J A Fooks. They were the trustees of a family trust of which Gillian was sole beneficiary and to which she had become absolutely entitled. Mr T J Williams is a solicitor and a family friend of Harold's. Mr Fooks is the company's secretary and Heather's husband. The position, therefore, is that half the share capital is held by what I might call Percy's side (in the shape of Ronald and Heather as joint holders) and the other half is held by Harold's side (initially by Messrs Williams and Fooks and more recently by Gillian).

I will refer briefly to one or two other provisions in the articles. Article 13 provides that there be up to six directors. Article 14 provides for the two life directors, namely Percy and Harold, who do not retire by rotation. All other directors do and regs 73 to 77 of the 1929 Table A apply to the company. The regulations relating to the chairman are of importance: the company's articles incorporate four regulations of the 1929 Table A, namely reg 84, under which the chairman of directors is to be elected by the directors (I shall have to refer to that again later); reg 81, where the chairman of directors has a casting vote at board meetings; reg 47, where the chairman of the board presides at general meetings; and reg 50, where the chairman has a casting vote at general meetings. It will be seen at once that if these articles are still in force in a company where the shares are held fifty-fifty, the position of the chairman of directors could be crucial. That is really what this action is all about. The two sides of the family have fallen out.

The plaintiff (Harold's side) claims that by virtue of an agreement entered into between all the shareholders in March 1967 (ie Ronald and Heather as joint holders on the one hand and Mr Williams and Mr Fooks as joint holders on the other) the chairman has ceased to be entitled to exercise a casting vote; or, alternatively, that there is currently no chairman, so that on either view there is complete deadlock.

The first and third defendants (Percy's side) claim that the original articles are still in force, unaltered, and that in any event Gillian, not being a party to the March 1967 agreement, cannot enforce it, and that, on the facts, Percy is currently the chairman so that Percy's side have control.

Counsel for the plaintiff accepts that if Percy is chairman with a casting vote, the plaintiff must fail because in that event all the acts complained of are capable of ratification and that, on the principles laid down in *Macdougall v Gardiner* (1875) 1 Ch D 13 the court will not interfere. I agree with him.

It is common ground that there were from time to time other directors who were liable to retire by rotation. It is also common ground that owing to successive failures to hold annual general meetings the directors who should have retired by rotation in due course automatically ceased to be directors on the principles recognised in *Re Consolidated Nickel Mines* [1914] 1 Ch 883. In particular it is common ground that although Ronald was for a time a director, he too ceased to hold office at the latest by 31st December 1978, on the same principle.

The position now is therefore that both sides agree that Percy and Harold are the only two directors. Percy's side claim that *he* is the chairman with the casting vote, but Harold's side claim that there is no chairman's casting vote, or alternatively that there is no chairman.

I should add that the issues have been simplified because in the course of the hearing before me both sides (very properly) abandoned contentions which clearly were not supported by the evidence.

With this introduction, I can now go straight to the shareholders' agreement of March 1967 to which I have already briefly referred ('the 1967 agreement'). It is common ground that it was made in March 1967 although the copy in the agreed bundle is not in fact dated. It reads as follows:

'THIS AGREEMENT is made the   day of [March] One thousand nine hundred and sixty [seven] BETWEEN [Ronald] and [Heather] of the first part [Mr Fooks] and [Mr Williams] (as trustees for the Deed of Settlement in favour of [Gillian]) of the second part and [Mr Fooks] and [Mr Simons] of the third part WHEREAS this Agreement is supplemental to an Agreement (hereinafter called "the said Agreement") bearing even date herewith and made between [the various people there named] AND WHEREAS at the time of entering into the said Agreement it was agreed by and between the parties thereto to enter into this Agreement also NOW THIS AGREEMENT made in pursuance of the said agreement and in consideration of the premises WITNESSETH as follows:—

'1. THE Chairman of Kingsway Petrol Station Limited shall not exercise any casting vote as Chairman and in the event of an equality of votes occurring it is agreed by and between the parties hereto that an independent Chairman shall be appointed by them and in default of agreement upon such appointment the same shall be made by the President of the Institute of Chartered Accountants

'2. [Harold] and [Percy] shall continue as Directors of Kingsway Petrol Station Limited and shall be paid Directors' Fees of Five Hundred Pounds per annum each and in addition shall be paid a salary of Two Thousand Pounds each or such lesser sums as they the said [Harold] and [Percy] shall both mutually agree upon provided that either the said [Harold] or the said [Percy] may renounce their respective salaries or a part or parts thereof in favour of a member or members of their respective families but so that in the aggregate the fees and salaries paid to one family shall in no way exceed those paid to the other family

'3. UPON the death of either the said [Harold] and/or [Percy] the parties hereto shall cause Kingsway Petrol Station Limited to enter into an agreement to pay their wives Dulcie Jones and Joan Jones a Pension of One Thousand Pounds per annum each for and during their respective lives or until their remarriage

'4. [Ronald] and [Mr Fooks] shall be paid by Kingsway Petrol Station Limited [and another company which I need not bother with] a salary based upon and according to the time and services rendered to those Companies by them due regard being paid to the fact that they will be following full time employment by the new Company

'5. THE parties hereto shall cause Kingsway Petrol Station Limited and [the other company] to pay out Sixty per cent of their respective net incomes and profits by way of Dividends unless the Shareholders shall otherwise agree

'6. IT IS HEREBY DECLARED that the parties hereto shall where the context so admits include their respective successors in title to all or any of the Shares in Kingsway Petrol Station Limited and [the other company] and all references to those Companies shall include any successors or assignees thereof howsoever and whatsoever

'7. THE parties hereto hereby jointly and severally agree to do any act matter or thing necessary to carry into effect the terms of this Agreement and also to execute any documents necessary or required to carry out the terms hereof and also to cause the said Companies to do any such act matter or thing to carry out the terms hereof'

The other agreement referred to in the 1967 agreement provided for the reorganisation of a company called S W B Ltd. It is unnecessary for me to go through the terms of that agreement. It is sufficient to say that cl 1 of the 1967 agreement was the quid pro quo for Harold's side agreeing to the reorganisation of S W B Ltd.

Now as to the arguments about the effect of the 1967 agreement. Counsel for the plaintiff contends that it operated as an alteration of the articles on what was conveniently called in argument 'the *Duomatic* principle' based on *Re Duomatic Ltd* [1969] 1 All ER 161, [1969] 2 Ch 365, and the principle is, I think, conveniently summarised in a short passage in the judgment of Buckley J in that case ([1969] 1 All ER 161 at 168, [1969] 2 Ch 365 at 373) where he says:

'... I proceed on the basis that where it can be shown that all shareholders who have a right to attend and vote at a general meeting of the company assent to some matter which a general meeting of the company could carry into effect, that assent is as binding as a resolution in general meeting would be.'

Applying that principle to the present case, counsel for the plaintiff says that the agreement of all the shareholders embodied in the 1967 agreement had the effect, so far as requisite, of overriding the articles. In other words, it operated to deprive the chairman for the time being of the right to use his casting vote except, perhaps, in so far as an independent chairman contemplated by cl 1 might need to do. I should add here that it is quite clear that Percy, who was actually chairman of the company at the time, was well aware of the terms of the 1967 agreement.

For the first and third defendants, counsel has two answers to counsel's argument for the plaintiff: first, that on its true interpretation in relation to a special or extraordinary resolution the *Duomatic* principle only applies if there has been (i) a resolution and (ii) a meeting; and that here he says, with some truth, there was neither a resolution nor a meeting of the four shareholders; second, he stresses that the agreement does not in terms purport to alter the articles at all: it rests, he says, solely in contract and Gillian, not being a party, cannot take either the benefit or the burden of the agreement.

On the first of these two arguments, counsel for the first and third defendants helpfully reminded me of the line of cases in which the effect of the unanimous consent of the corporators has been considered, starting with *Baroness Wenlock v River Dee Co* (1883) 36 Ch D 675n. I do not propose to refer to all these cases in detail but, for the record, I will list them. The other cases are *Re George Newman & Co* [1895] 1 Ch 674.

Then there is *Re Express Engineering Works Ltd* [1920] 1 Ch 466, *Re Oxted Motor Co Ltd* [1921] 3 KB 32, [1921] All ER Rep 646, *Parker and Cooper Ltd v Reading* [1926] Ch 975, [1926] All ER Rep 323, *Re Pearce Duff & Co Ltd* [1960] 3 All ER 222, [1960] 1 WLR 1014, *Re Duomatic*, to which I have already referred, and finally a decision of Slade J in *Re Moorgate Mercantile Holdings Ltd* [1980] 1 All ER 40, [1980] 1 WLR 227.

Counsel for the first and third defendants pointed out, correctly, that of these cases only three were concerned with special or extraordinary resolutions, namely *Re Pearce Duff & Co Ltd*, and *Re Moorgate Mercantile Holdings Ltd* (both of which were concerned with special resolutions) and *Re Oxted Motor Co Ltd* (which was concerned with an extraordinary resolution). All the rest were concerned with matters which, if capable of ratification at all, could have been validated by ordinary resolutions.

The starting point of counsel for the first and third defendants is s 10 of the Companies Act 1948 which provides for the alteration of articles by special resolution; and from that he goes on to s 141, mentioning sub-ss (1) and (2) and including the particular proviso, laying down how special and extraordinary resolutions are to be passed. First of all s 10:

> '(1) Subject to the provisions of this Act and to the conditions contained in its memorandum, a company may by special resolution alter or add to its articles.
> '(2) Any alteration or addition so made in the articles shall, subject to the provisions of this Act, be as valid as if originally contained therein, and be subject in like manner to alteration by special resolution.'

Then s 141:

> '(1) A resolution shall be an extraordinary resolution when it has been passed by a majority of not less than three fourths of such members as, being entitled so to do, vote in person or, where proxies are allowed, by proxy, at a general meeting of which notice specifying the intention to propose the resolution as an extraordinary resolution has been duly given.
> '(2) A resolution shall be a special resolution when it has been passed by such a majority as is required for the passing of an extraordinary resolution and at a general meeting of which not less than twenty-one days' notice, specifying the intention to propose the resolution as a special resolution, has been duly given: Provided that, if it is so agreed by a majority in number of the members having the right to attend and vote at any such meeting, being a majority together holding not less than ninety-five per cent. in nominal value of the shares giving that right, or, in the case of a company not having a share capital, together representing not less than ninety-five per cent. of the total voting rights at that meeting of all the members, a resolution may be proposed and passed as a special resolution at a meeting of which less than twenty-one days' notice has been given . . .'

Thus, says counsel for the first and third defendants, you can only alter the articles by special resolution. That is his first argument. Secondly, a special resolution must be passed at a meeting; thirdly, here there was neither a resolution nor a meeting.

Re Pearce Duff & Co Ltd, he says, does not help counsel for the plaintiff because in that case there had been a resolution and a meeting: and all that was later cured by the unanimous (but separate) consents of the shareholders was a defect in the consent to short notice under the proviso to s 141(2).

Re Moorgate Mercantile Holdings Ltd was concerned with the extent to which, if at all, a resolution which is to be proposed as a special resolution could be amended at the meeting, and its relevance for present purposes lies solely in the fact that Slade J referred to *Re Pearce Duff & Co Ltd* and *Re Duomatic Ltd* (and also to s 143(4) of the Act to which I too shall refer in a moment) and stated that the proposition which he had laid down earlier in his judgment for the amendment of special resolutions might be subject to modification where the members unanimously agreed to waive the requirements of notice.

Re Oxted Motor Co Ltd was a case of an extraordinary resolution for voluntary winding up. There were only two shareholders, who were also the two directors. They met and passed a resolution that the company be wound up and they signed a minute to that effect; but no notice to propose the resolution as an extraordinary resolution had ever been given. The Court of Appeal upheld the resolution on the ground that it was competent for the shareholders of the company acting together to waive the formalities required by what is now s 141(1) of the 1948 Act.

In *Re Pearce Duff & Co Ltd* (which was a petition to confirm a reduction of capital) Buckley J, after referring to *Re Oxted Motor Co Ltd* and also to *Parker and Cooper Ltd v Reading* as showing that in certain circumstances all the corporators, if they agree, can bind the company, continued ([1960] 3 All ER 222 at 224, [1960] 1 WLR 1014 at 1017):

> 'Those cases relate to a rather different subject-matter from that which I have to consider, because I have to consider not whether these resolutions bound the company as special resolutions but whether any shareholder could now say that the resolutions were not properly passed as valid special resolutions. Having regard to the one hundred per cent. consent which has been obtained to the resolutions being treated as valid and to the fact that the petition has been presented on that footing, I do not think that this court ought to hear, or be ready to hear, any of the shareholders to say that those resolutions were not validly passed. In those circumstances the case being a rather exceptional one, I am entitled to regard this special resolution as sufficient basis for the reduction which the court is asked to confirm; and accordingly, being satisfied by the evidence of excess of wants, I will confirm the reduction . . .'

It is with very great diffidence that I venture to criticise the reasoning of so distinguished a judge in a short extempore judgment delivered, I notice, on the last Monday of the 1960 Trinity Term. But with great respect to Buckley J the problem he was faced with surely was not whether any shareholder could *object* that the resolutions had not been passed as valid special resolutions but whether as a matter of law they *had* been validly so passed, because unless he had before him a validly passed special resolution he had no jurisdiction to confirm the desired reduction of capital: see ss 66(2) and 67(1) of the 1948 Act. I do not think, therefore, that I can regard the *Pearce Duff* decision as concluding the point which I have to consider.

The first of counsel's two arguments for the first and third defendants (namely that there must be a 'resolution' and a 'meeting') does not appear to have been raised in any of the three reported cases which were concerned with special or extraordinary resolutions. But it is not an argument to which I would readily accede because in my judgment it would create a wholly artificial and unnecessary distinction between those powers which can, and those which cannot, be validly exercised by all the corporators acting together.

For my part I venture to differ from counsel for the first and third defendants on the first limb of his argument, namely that articles can *only* be altered by special resolution. In my judgment, s 10 of the Act is merely laying down a procedure whereby *some only* of the shareholders can validly alter the articles; and, if, as I believe to be the case, it is a basic principle of company law that all the corporators, acting together, can do anything which is intra vires the company, then I see nothing in s 10 to undermine this principle. I accept that the principle requires all the corporators to 'act together'; but with regard to this I respectfully adopt what Astbury J said in *Parker and Cooper Ltd v Reading* [1926] Ch 975 at 984, [1926] All ER Rep 323 at 328:

> 'Now the view I take of both these decisions [those were in *Re Express Engineering Works Ltd* and *Re George Newman & Co*] is that where the transaction is intra vires and honest, and especially if it is for the benefit of the company, it cannot be upset if the assent of all the corporators is given to it. I do not think it matters in the least whether that assent is given at different times or simultaneously.'

See also per Younger LJ in *Re Express Engineering Works Ltd* [1920] 1 Ch 466 at 471 and the passage from the judgment of Buckley J in *Re Duomatic Ltd* [1969] 1 All ER 161 at 168, [1969] 2 Ch 365 at 373 which I have read earlier in this judgment.

I should add that the evidence in the case before me is that the 1967 agreement was signed by 'the two sides' (if I may call them that) separately and that they did not meet together, however informally, for the purpose of signing the document. But it is clear beyond doubt that the agreement did represent a meeting of minds which is, after all, the essence of a meeting and the passing of a resolution.

Some light is also, I think, thrown on the problem by s 143(4) of the 1948 Act. Section 143 deals with the forwarding to the Registrar of Companies of copies of every resolution or agreement to which the section applies, and sub-s (4) reads as follows:

> 'This section shall apply to—(*a*) special resolutions; (*b*) extraordinary resolutions; (*c*) resolutions which have been agreed to by all the members of a company, but which, if not so agreed to, would not have been effective for their purpose unless, as the case may be, they had been passed as special resolutions or as extraordinary resolutions; (*d*) resolutions or agreements which have been agreed to by all the members of some class of shareholders but which, if not so agreed to, would not have been effective for their purpose unless they had been passed by some particular majority or otherwise in some particular manner, and all resolutions or agreements which effectively bind all the members of any class of shareholders though not agreed to by all those members . . .'

Paragraph (*c*) thus appears to recognise that you can have a resolution, at least, which has been agreed to by all the members and is as effective as a special or extraordinary resolution would have been, but, as counsel for the first and third defendants was quick to point out, para (*c*) says nothing about 'agreements' in contrast to para (*d*) which refers to resolutions or agreements which have been agreed to by all members of some class of shareholders. I should say in passing that I think the reference in para (*d*) to 'resolutions or agreements' stems directly from reg 4 of Part 1 of the 1948 Table A, which, dealing with class meetings, provides briefly as follows:

> 'If at any time the share capital is divided into different classes of shares, the rights attached to any class (unless otherwise provided by the terms of issue of the shares of that class) may, whether or not the company is being wound up, be varied with the consent in writing of the holders of three-fourths of the issued shares of that class, or with the sanction of an extraordinary resolution passed at a separate general meeting of the holders of the shares of the class,'

so that you have either a consent which might be termed an agreement or a resolution.

I cannot regard this difference in drafting between paras (*c*) and (*d*) of s 143(4) as fatal to the basic argument. It may be, as counsel for the plaintiff suggested, that a document which is framed as an agreement can be treated as a 'resolution' for the purposes of para (*c*). (I should add in passing that a copy of the 1967 agreement was never, as far as I am aware, sent to the Registrar of Companies for registration.) It may be that there is a gap in the registration requirements of s 143. But be that as it may, the fact that the 1967 agreement was drafted as an agreement and not as a resolution, and that the four signatories did not sign in each other's presence does not in my view prevent that agreement overriding pro tanto, and so far as necessary, the, articles of the company; in my judgment counsel for the first and third defendants' first argument fails and unless he can show that the 1967 agreement has been superseded, the chairman of the company has no casting vote at board or general meetings.

In view of my conclusion on the first argument of counsel for the first and third defendants it is not strictly necessary to consider his second argument that the 1967 agreement does not purport to alter the articles and that its force and effect rest solely in contract so as to preclude Gillian (the plaintiff) from relying on it since she did not sign it.

I shall take this argument quite shortly. In the first place it is in my view significant

that although in 1967 Percy and Harold were clearly still the dominant figures in the
company, it was the four *shareholders* who signed the agreement, thus underlining the
nature and purpose of the agreement. Nor do I think that cl 7 (under which the parties
agreed to do whatever was necessary to carry the agreement into effect) is inconsistent
with this view, having regard, for example, to the terms of cl 3 under which, on the
death of Harold or Percy, the parties were to procure the company concerned to enter
into agreements to pay their widows a pension each.

Moreover, I am by no means certain that even if regarded as a contract the plaintiff
would be out of court on the privity of contract argument. Messrs Williams and Fooks
were, and were recorded as, acting as her trustees. Clause 6 declares that the parties to the
agreement are to include their successors in title to all or any of the shares in the
company: and I see a good deal of force in counsel's argument for the plaintiff that
the combination of these factors was sufficient to enable the plaintiff to take the benefit
of the agreement when, on the termination of her trust, the 15,000 shares were
transferred to her by Mr Williams and Mr Fooks: and that she would therefore require
Mr Fooks and Mr Williams (although Mr Williams, of course, is now dead) to enforce the
agreement on her behalf.

However, in the circumstances, it is unnecessary to express a concluded opinion on
this point and I do not do so.

I can now move forward in time to 27th September 1975. On that day Harold, Percy,
Ronald and Mr Williams signed a document entitled 'Heads of Agreement providing for
arrangements within SWB Ltd and Kingsway Petrol Station Ltd and ancillary matters'.
It is to be observed that Gillian did not sign this document, although she was, of course,
by that time the registered holder of her 15,000 shares.

I refer to these heads of agreement ('the 1975 heads') because they purport to affect the
composition of the board of the company and also the chairman's casting vote. I do not
propose to read the whole of the 1975 heads since only three clauses are, I think, strictly
relevant, namely: cl 3: 'The Board of Kingsway Petrol Station Limited will be changed
forthwith so that the following persons only will be directors: [Ronald, Percy and
Harold.]'; cl 4: '[Ronald] will be appointed Chairman of each of the above companies
[that was Kingsway Petrol Station Ltd and SWB Ltd] with a second vote in the event of
a tie on voting in any situation.'; cl 5: 'The Articles of Association of each of the above
companies will be changed insofar as is necessary to achieve the above.'

It must be remembered that at the date of the 1975 heads neither Harold nor Percy
were shareholders in the company at all. Ronald was, of course, joint holder of the
15,000 shares held by Percy's side and cl 6(C) of the 1975 heads provided that Ronald
would enter into an agreement with Gillian to acquire her shares in the company, such
agreement to be a mutual option exercisable within a four to six year period.

Counsel for the first and third defendants relied on the 1975 heads in the following
way. Accepting (as he does) that Ronald is now no longer a director of the company
(because of the *Consolidated Nickel Mines* principle), he nevertheless argues, as I understand
it, (i) that the 1975 heads are binding on the signatories, (ii) that those signatories include
the two existing directors of the company (Harold and Percy), (iii) that as such directors
they have power under art 15 to appoint an additional director, (iv) that the 1975 heads
are specifically enforceable and (v) that I ought to regard Ronald as entitled to require
Percy and Harold to appoint Ronald as additional director. (Counsel for the first and
third defendants does not, of course, worry about a casting vote in these circumstances
because, if he can get Ronald on the board, Ronald and Percy would side together and
thus outvote Harold.)

I should add that a good deal of time was taken up in evidence in trying to establish the
allegation that Harold, in signing the 1975 heads, bound Gillian, either because he had
some general or specific prior authority to do so or because she subsequently ratified it.
I do not propose to review the evidence on this aspect in any detail. Gillian's evidence in
particular was very confused. Suffice it to say that I am entirely satisfied that as a matter
of law Gillian was *not* bound by the 1975 heads. It may well be that Harold and Mr

Williams thought that the 1975 heads were in Gillian's interest: it may also be that
Harold felt certain that Gillian would do whatever he wanted. And Mr Fulwell, solicitor
to Percy and Ronald, who actually drafted the 1975 heads, told me that he considered the
agreement to be binding on Gillian. But in my view he was wrong. The parties took a
risk in not getting the 1975 heads signed by Gillian: she never did sign them; nor in my
judgment did she either authorise or ratify them; and they are not binding on her.

As to the specific performance argument of counsel for the first and third defendants,
I would merely point out (i) that his case as pleaded does not contain any claim for
specific performance, (ii) that the 1975 heads are already more than four years old, (iii)
that if specific performance were required it would have to be of the whole of the 1975
heads and not part only (and I do not know whether this is even practicable), and (iv) that
specific performance is in any event an equitable remedy. In short the argument is not
open on the pleadings, has not been seriously argued before me and is in my view at best
highly suspect.

There remains counsel's last point for the first and third defendants, namely that of the
two present directors, ie Percy and Harold, Percy is in fact the chairman.

This of course will only help him if, contrary to the view which I have expressed as to
the effect of the 1967 agreement, the chairman *has* a casting vote. It is necessary at this
point to refer again to the manner in which under the 1929 Table A, reg 84 a chairman
is appointed:

> 'The directors may elect a chairman of their meetings and determine the period
> for which he is to hold office; but if no such chairman is elected, or if, at any
> meeting the chairman is not present within five minutes after the time appointed
> for holding the same, the directors present may choose one of their number to be
> chairman of the meeting.'

It is common ground that for a number of years, possibly up to the 1967 agreement,
Percy was chairman. By 27th September 1976 (at a board meeting) a resolution was
purportedly passed instructing the secretary to implement cl 3 of the 1975 heads (that
the board was to consist only of Ronald, Percy and Harold). But that meeting was in law
a nullity because it was attended only by Percy and Ronald and Ronald was not (and this
is common ground) a director at that time. (Nothing was said in the minutes about
implementing cl 4 (that Ronald was to be chairman with a casting vote).)

At the annual general meeting held on 31st December 1976 the minutes record that
Mr Williams and Mrs Jones (Harold's wife) questioned whether or not Percy had resigned
as chairman of the company and that neither of them accepted Ronald as chairman.
(This annual general meeting was ineffective because only one shareholder (Ronald) was
personally present so that there was no quorum.)

At a board meeting held immediately after this annual general meeting, at which
Ronald is shown as chairman Mr Williams and Mrs Jones again objected to Ronald acting
as chairman and questioned whether Percy 'had ever handed over the chairmanship to
Ronald'.

Despite this at a board meeting on 26th January 1977 at which Percy, Harold and
Ronald were all present, Ronald was again shown as chairman and a letter from Gillian's
solicitors was produced in which they advised that as a result of the 1967 agreement the
only directors were Harold and Percy and that the chairman would not have a casting
vote.

At a board meeting on 25th February 1977 (ie three days after the issue of the writ in
these proceedings) Ronald is again shown as chairman, Percy and Harold also being
present, and Harold asked for his objections to the position of Ronald as chairman and
director to be recorded.

On 8th August 1977 there was another board meeting (the first minutes prepared by
Mr Watson, the new secretary). All three gentlemen were present, none named as
chairman, and the minutes were in fact signed by Percy.

On 16th August 1977, at a board meeting, all three were present and the minutes record: 'It was unanimously agreed that Mr. P. C. Jones be Chairman *for this meeting.*' That was why Percy had signed the minutes of the previous board meeting. Counsel for the plaintiff accepts that at this meeting a resolution was validly passed which had the effect of appointing Ronald an additional director. It was also resolved to hold the annual general meeting on 14th September 1977 and (by a majority of two to one against Harold) that Ronald 'should be Chairman of that meeting'.

On 31st August 1977 there was an extraordinary general meeting to increase the company's capital. Ronald was shown as chairman. Ronald was for the resolution and Gillian voted against. Ronald as chairman purported to use his casting vote. Gillian objected and says she does not accept that Ronald was in fact chairman of the meeting.

Ronald also took the chair at a board meeting held on the same day.

On 14th September 1977 there was a board meeting at which all three were present and Percy was shown as chairman. Minute 3 reads as follows: 'R. V. C. Jones proposed that P. C. Jones be elected Chairman of the Directors. This was accepted by H. C. Jones on condition that no casting vote be used. This was not accepted, but notwithstanding the proposal was carried unanimously.' I find that slightly difficult to understand.

At an *extraordinary general meeting* held on the same day Percy was shown as chairman and purported to use his casting vote, and Harold asked that his objection to this be minuted.

Again on the same day there was an *annual general meeting* and Percy was in the chair. The resolution to re-elect Ronald a director was purportedly carried by the use of Percy's casting vote.

At a *board meeting* on 27th September 1977 (when all three were present) Percy was shown as chairman, and Harold asked for the minutes of the last board meeting 'to be amended to show Percy as acting temporary chairman': but this was not done.

At a *board meeting* on 29th March 1978 (*Harold was not present*) Percy proposed that 'in accordance with the Agreement he had signed in September 1975 [the 1975 heads] he should invite Ronald to take the chair. Ronald agreed and the meeting continued under his chairmanship'.

This meeting was not properly called (and there is no doubt about this) because notice of it had not been given to Harold.

The only other board or general meeting held in 1978 was a board meeting on 6th December 1978. Percy and Ronald were the only two there: there is no record of either of them acting as chairman.

It is common ground (as I have already mentioned) that Ronald ceased to be a director on 31st December 1978.

I have referred to the meetings recorded in the company's minute book in some detail because counsel for the first and third defendants claims that, properly analysed, Percy has never lawfully ceased to be chairman and that the purported appointment of Ronald at the board meeting on 29th March 1978 was a nullity because the meeting had been improperly called. (It is slightly ironic that counsel should be relying on the failure of his clients to give proper notice of the board meeting to Harold.) Therefore, he says, if Ronald was not validly appointed, Percy did not effectively resign.

I find it difficult to accept this argument. True that under the 1929 Table A, reg 84 'the directors' may 'elect a chairman of their meetings and determine the period for which he is to hold office': but the first point I would make is that there is no evidence whatsoever before me of anyone ever having been appointed chairman of the board for any specific period. Moreover, there is nothing in reg 84 which requires any specific formality for a chairman of the board to resign that office. In view of this, I have, as it seems to me, to look at the factual history and decide, in the light of that, what those concerned must be taken as having decided. I would also add that one of the most striking features of this case has been the almost total failure of all concerned to observe the simplest requirements of company law.

In the light of these considerations, and of the confused and confusing attitudes which the various dramatis personae adopted from time to time, I do not feel justified in concluding that there is, or has been for some considerable time, any effective agreement between Percy and Harold that the former should be chairman: or that the original situation, when Percy was admittedly chairman, should be perpetuated or restored.

It follows, therefore, in my judgment that even if I am wrong in holding that the 1967 agreement has effectively put the chairman's casting vote in baulk, there is, on the facts of this case, at present no chairman who could effectively exercise that casting vote.

I have accordingly reached the conclusion (a) that the 1967 agreement was and is effective to restrict the use of the chairman's casting vote and (b) that if I am wrong in that conclusion and if the chairman has a casting vote, nevertheless there is currently no chairman.

These conclusions give me no satisfaction nor, may I add, would it have afforded me any satisfaction to have reached a contrary conclusion that Percy's side were in control by virtue only of the casting vote. It seems to me that, unless the parties can pull themselves together and arrive at some practical solution of their family squabble, the company is doomed to one thing and one thing only, namely liquidation and it may be compulsory liquidation and further waste of money.

As I have said, the conclusions I have reached, even if only one of those main conclusions is correct, means that this is a deadlocked company, and I do not, as at present advised, see any prospect (unless the parties can manage to live together) of the company being able to continue effectively in business.

I can quite appreciate there may be monetary difficulties in one side buying the other out, but if that is so it seems to me that both sides have only one sensible course open to them and that is to combine together to put the company into voluntary liquidation and realise this undertaking for the best possible price in the interests of both sides of the family.

Declaration accordingly.

Solicitors: *Rye, Naylor & Leman*, agents for *Meade-King & Co*, Bristol (for the plaintiff); *Fulwell & Partners*, Bristol (for the first and third defendants).

Hazel Hartman   Barrister.

Royal College of Nursing of the United Kingdom v Department of Health and Social Security

QUEEN'S BENCH DIVISION
WOOLF J
24th, 31st JULY 1980

COURT OF APPEAL, CIVIL DIVISION
LORD DENNING MR, BRIGHTMAN LJ AND SIR GEORGE BAKER
27th, 28th, 29th OCTOBER, 7th NOVEMBER 1980

HOUSE OF LORDS
LORD WILBERFORCE, LORD DIPLOCK, LORD EDMUND-DAVIES, LORD KEITH OF KINKEL AND LORD ROSKILL
8th, 9th DECEMBER 1980, 5th FEBRUARY 1981

Criminal law – Abortion – Defence – Termination of pregnancy by registered medical practitioner – Termination by medical induction – Doctor initiating process of induction – Nurses performing operative acts of termination under doctor's instructions – Doctor not present but on call – Normal hospital practice for nurses to carry out treatment in doctor's absence but under his instructions – Whether participating nurses involved in unlawful acts – Whether doctor required to carry out entire process – Whether termination by induction according to normal procedure amounting to termination 'by a registered medical practitioner' – Offences against the Person Act 1861, ss 58, 59 – Abortion Act 1967, s 1(1).

Prior to 1967 it was an offence under ss 58 and 59[a] of the Offences against the Person Act 1861 for any person, including doctors and nurses, unlawfully to use any means to procure the miscarriage of a woman. However, a doctor who carried out an abortion to save a pregnant woman's life or because the consequence of the continuation of the pregnancy would make her 'a physical or mental wreck' apparently had a defence at common law to a charge under s 58 or s 59 of the 1861 Act. In 1967 s 1(1)[b] of the Abortion Act 1967 enacted that no offence was committed 'when a pregnancy [was] terminated by a registered medical practitioner' in specified circumstances. The Act further provided, by s 1(3), that 'any treatment for the termination of pregnancy' was to be carried out in a national health service hospital or an approved clinic. In 1972 surgical methods of carrying out abortions in hospitals were replaced by the medical induction method which involved pumping a chemical fluid into the mother's womb to induce premature labour. There were two stages in medical induction, the first being the insertion of a catheter into the womb and the second the administration of the fluid into the womb via the catheter by means of a pump or drip apparatus. The first stage was carried out by a doctor and the second by nurses under the doctor's instructions but in his absence, although he would be on call. The causative factor in inducing labour and thus in terminating the pregnancy was the administration of the fluid, which was done by the nurses and not the doctor. The Department of Health and Social Security issued a circular to the nursing profession stating that no offence was committed by nurses who terminated a pregnancy by medical induction if a doctor decided on the termination, initiated it and remained responsible throughout for its overall conduct and control. The department took the view that in such circumstances the pregnancy was 'terminated by a registered medical practitioner' within s 1(1) of the 1967 Act. The Royal College of

---

a   Section 58 is set out at p 567 *c d*, post. Section 59 deals with supplying abortifacients and
      instruments for use in unlawful abortions
b   Section 1 is set out at p 568 *e* to *j*, post

Nursing disputed that view, and sought a declaration as against the department that the advice in the circular was wrong and that the acts carried out by nurses in terminating pregnancies by medical induction contravened s 58 of the 1861 Act. The judge held that the department's advice did not involve the performance of unlawful acts by nurses, and granted the department a declaration to that effect. The college appealed to the Court of Appeal which reversed the judge's decision, holding that the whole process of medical induction had to be carried out by a doctor and not merely under a doctor's instructions if it was to come within s 1(1) of the 1967 Act. The department appealed to the House of Lords.

Held (Lord Wilberforce and Lord Edmund-Davies dissenting) – The 1967 Act was to be construed in the light of the fact that it was intended to amend and clarify the unsatisfactory and uncertain state of the law previously existing and in the light of the policy of the Act, which was to broaden the grounds on which abortions might lawfully be obtained and to ensure that abortions were carried out with proper skill in hygienic conditions in ordinary hospitals as part of ordinary medical care and in accordance with normal hospital practice in which tasks forming part of the treatment were entrusted as appropriate to nurses and other members of the staff under the instructions of the doctor in charge of the treatment. Accordingly, provided a doctor prescribed the treatment for the termination of a pregnancy, remained in charge and accepted responsibility throughout, and the treatment was carried out in accordance with his directions, the pregnancy was 'terminated by a registered medical practitioner' for the purposes of the 1967 Act and any person taking part in the termination was entitled to the protection afforded by s 1(1). The appeal would therefore be allowed (see p 567 b, p 568 j to p 569 a and e to p 570 c, p 574 j to p 575 a, p 575 c to j and p 577 f to j and p 578 a, post).

Notes

For lawful medical termination of pregnancy, see 30 Halsbury's Laws (4th Edn) para 44.

For unlawfully procuring an abortion, see 11 ibid paras 1191–1194, and for cases on the subject, see 15 Digest (Reissue) 1199–1202, 10,294–10,314.

For the Offences against the Person Act 1861, ss 58, 59, see 8 Halsbury's Statutes (3rd Edn) 168.

For the Abortion Act 1967, s 1, see ibid 682.

Cases referred to in judgments and opinions

Brutus v Cozens [1972] 2 All ER 1297, [1973] AC 854, [1972] 3 WLR 521, 136 JP 636, 56 Cr App R 799, HL, 15 Digest (Reissue) 910, 7807.

Gouriet v Union of Post Office Workers [1977] 3 All ER 70, [1978] AC 435, [1977] 3 WLR 300, 141 JP 552, HL, Digest (Cont Vol E) 168, 3776a.

Imperial Tobacco Co Ltd v Attorney General [1980] 1 All ER 866, [1980] 2 WLR 466, HL.

Luke v Inland Revenue Comrs [1963] 1 All ER 655, [1963] AC 557, [1963] 2 WLR 559, [1963] TR 21, 42 ATC 21, 1963 SLT 129, 40 Tax Cas 630, 1963 SC (HL) 65, HL, Digest (Cont Vol A) 888, 1020a.

Paton v Trustees of BPAS [1978] 2 All ER 987, [1979] QB 276, [1978] 3 WLR 687, 142 JP 497, Digest (Cont Vol E) 277, 7564a.

R v Bourne [1938] 3 All ER 615, [1939] 1 KB 687, 108 LJKB 471, CCA, 15 Digest (Reissue) 1201, 10,310.

R v Hollis and Blakeman (1873) 28 LT 455, 37 JP 582, 12 Cox CC 463, CCR, 15 Digest (Reissue) 1200, 10,302.

R v Marlow (1964) 49 Cr App R 49, 15 Digest (Reissue) 1201, 10,307.

R v Newton and Stungo [1958] Crim LR 469.

Stock v Frank Jones (Tipton) Ltd [1978] 1 All ER 948, [1978] 1 WLR 231, [1978] ICR 347, HL, Digest (Cont Vol E) 620, 1560a.

Vickers Sons & Maxim Ltd v Evans [1910] AC 444, 79 LJKB 954, 103 LT 292, HL.

Western Bank Ltd v Schindler [1976] 2 All ER 393, [1977] Ch 1, [1976] 3 WLR 341, 32 P & CR 352, CA, Digest (Cont Vol E) 440, 1467a.

Originating summons

By an originating summons dated 27th June 1980 the plaintiffs, the Royal College of Nursing of the United Kingdom, sought as against the defendants, the Department of Health and Social Security, a declaration that the statement as to the legality of the role of the nurse in termination of pregnancy by medical induction and the statement as to procedures that might be performed by an appropriately skilled nurse or midwife, contained in Annexes A and B to a letter dated 21st February 1980 from Dame Phyllis Friend and Sir Henry Yellowlees acting on behalf of the department, issued to regional and area medical officers and regional, area and district nursing officers, was wrong in law and that acts carried out by nurses and midwives in performance of the termination of pregnancies as set out in Annex B contravened the law relating to abortion. In the course of argument the Solicitor General, appearing on behalf of the department, intimated that, although there was no formal cross-claim by the department, if the matter was decided adversely to the college he would seek a declaration in favour of the department that the advice contained in the letter of 21st February 1980 and the annexes thereto did not involve the performance of unlawful acts by members of the college. The facts are set out in the judgment of Woolf J.

Michael Spencer for the Royal College of Nursing.
The Solicitor General (Sir Ian Percival QC) and *Simon D Brown* for the department.

Cur adv vult

31st July. **WOOLF J** read the following judgment: The Royal College of Nursing of the United Kingdom has brought these proceedings in order to obtain clarification as to the role which nurses can lawfully play in termination of pregnancy by medical induction.

The college is an association of nurses incorporated by royal charter and its objects are, inter alia, to further nursing as a profession, to raise standards of nursing care of the sick and infirm, and to represent and protect the professional interests of, among others, enrolled and registered nurses. In furtherance of its objects the college provides for its members advice as to proper nursing practice, including advice as to the law which is relevant to nursing practice. It also, through the Commercial Union Insurance Co, provides nurses with indemnity insurance to protect them from liability for negligence in the performance of their duties.

The reason that the college has commenced these proceedings is that it differs from the Department of Health and Social Security as to what activities it is lawful for nurses to perform in relation to the termination of pregnancy by medical induction.

In order to understand the nature of the dispute between the department and the college it is necessary at the outset to consider the relevant statutory provisions which are contained in three Acts of Parliament. The earliest Act is the Offences against the Person Act 1861. Section 58 of that Act, so far as material, provides:

'. . . whosoever, with Intent to procure the Miscarriage of any Woman, whether she be or be not with Child, shall unlawfully administer to her or cause to be taken by her any Poison or other noxious Thing, or shall unlawfully use any Instrument or other Means whatsoever with the like Intent, shall be guilty of Felony . . .'

Section 59 deals with the unlawful supplying or procuring of any poison or other noxious thing or any instrument or thing whatsoever knowing that the same is intended to be unlawfully used or employed with intent to procure the miscarriage of any woman, whether she be or not be with child.

The second Act is the Infant Life (Preservation) Act 1929, which created the offence of child destruction in relation to a child capable of being born alive. The significant feature of that offence, which was contained in s 1 of the Act, was that it was subject to a proviso—

'that no person shall be found guilty of an offence under this section unless it is proved the act which caused the death of the child was not done in good faith for the purpose only of preserving the life of the mother.'

The third Act was the Abortion Act 1967, which was an Act to amend and clarify the law relating to termination of pregnancy by registered medical practitioners. For present purposes the most important section is s 1. The relevant parts of that section provide:

'(1) Subject to the provisions of this section, a person shall not be guilty of an offence under the law relating to abortion when a pregnancy is terminated by a registered medical practitioner if two registered medical practitioners are of the opinion, formed in good faith—(a) that the continuance of the pregnancy would involve risk to the life of the pregnant woman, or of injury to the physical or mental health of the pregnant woman or any existing children of her family, greater than if the pregnancy were terminated; or (b) that there is a substantial risk that if the child were born it would suffer from such physical or mental abnormalities as to be seriously handicapped . . .

'(3) . . . any treatment for the termination of pregnancy must be carried out in a hospital . . . or in a place for the time being approved . . . by . . . the Secretary of State.

'(4) Subsection (3) of this section, and so much of subsection (1) as relates to the opinion of two registered medical practitioners, shall not apply to the termination of a pregnancy by a registered medical practitioner in a case where he is of the opinion, formed in good faith, that the termination is immediately necessary to save the life or to prevent grave permanent injury to the physical or mental health of the pregnant woman.'

It will be noted that the defence provided by s 1(1) of the 1967 Act only applies when 'pregnancy is terminated by a registered medical practitioner'. At the time when that Act was passed the normal method of termination adopted by medical practitioners involved surgical intervention. Where surgical intervention is the method of termination of pregnancy adopted, no difficulty has arisen as to whether or not the termination is by a registered medical practitioner as required by the Act. However, in recent times there has been increasing reliance on medical methods of induction. These involve the use of prostaglandins or other abortifacients to induce labour and hence the termination of pregnancy. In this country two methods of medical induction are used for termination of pregnancy, one being the intra-amniotic process and the other being the extra-amniotic process. As the intra-amniotic procedure is itself invariably carried out by registered medical practitioners, this method does not give rise to substantial difficulties in relation to the 1967 Act. However, in the case of the extra-amniotic process the registered medical practitioner initiates the process by inserting a catheter through which the prostaglandin solution is to be administered to the patient, but the subsequent steps in the process are either in whole or in part carried out by nurses who will sometimes be responsible for connecting the prostin pump to the catheter so that the abortifacients can be fed into the patient and will monitor progress of the process which lasts on average about 18 hours and can last up to 30 hours. The statement agreed between the parties as to the clinical background describes the situation as follows:

'In the medical induction process the causative factor in inducing the labour and hence the termination of pregnancy is the effect of the administration of prostaglandin and/or oxytocin and not any mechanical effect from the insertion of the catheter or cannula. In that the nurse does, on the instructions of the doctor, commence or augment the flow of prostaglandin or oxytocin, and even sometimes effect the connection between the already inserted catheter and the prostin pump and the already intravenous cannula and the oxytocin infusion, her role in the process does include acts which have, and are intended to have, an abortifacient effect. Such acts are however always carried out in accordance with the specific instructions of the registered medical practitioner.'

In performing the role described in the agreed statement in relation to inducing an abortion, the registered medical practitioner and the nurse perform the same roles that they do in relation to a normal birth where labour has to be induced by medical means. It cannot therefore be suggested that the nurse is not fully qualified from a professional point of view to perform the role which she is called on to perform in relation to abortions. Nor does any issue arise as to any conscientious objection which a nurse may have to being involved in the process. The right of conscientious objection is fully recognised in s 4 of the 1967 Act which provides that (apart from cases of necessity) no person shall be under any duty, whether by contract or by any statutory or other legal requirement, to participate in any treatment authorised by the Act to which he has a conscientious objection. The problem is confined to whether the nurse's role as described in the agreed statement is such that it prevents reliance on the defence provided by s 1(1) of the 1967 Act.

The problem came to light as a result of the recent 'abortive' proposals to amend the law as to abortion. Apparently in considering the attitude the college should adopt to the amendment of the law, the college's attention was drawn to the role of the nurses as set out in the agreed statement and this caused the college to take legal advice which was to the effect that the present practice was unlawful. Apparently the view of the college was shared by certain of the health authorities and in December 1979 the college issued a memorandum setting out the advice which stated:

'It has been brought to the attention of the RCN that in some instances nurses are administering Prostaglandins and related drugs to effect a medical abortion. In the RCN's view a nurse would be contravening the Abortion Act and is therefore advised that only a registered medical practitioner should administer Prostaglandins. This includes "topping up" once the infusion has commenced.'

The reaction of the Department of Health and Social Security to this was to circulate the letter of 21st February 1980 and two annexes. The letter is in the following terms:

'In the past ten years, medical induction methods have generally been employed when it is considered necessary to carry out a termination in the middle trimester of pregnancy under the terms of the Abortion Act 1967. These methods have largely replaced hysterotomy and other surgical procedures which carry a greater risk to the patient. We know that doubts have recently been expressed about the legal position of a nurse, midwife, or other person who is not medically qualified, who assists with a medical induction termination, even though she may be acting on the instructions of the doctor and performing duties that are generally undertaken by nurses and others in accordance with accepted professional practice. Legal advice has been taken on this complex issue, and is fully explained in Annex A to this letter. Consequential guidance on professional practice is given in Annex B. Taken together, the Annexes indicate that provided the registered medical practitioner personally decides upon and initiates the process of medical induction, and throughout remains responsible for it, it is not necessary for him personally to perform each and every action which is needed for the treatment to achieve its intended objective. In this context the guidance given in HC(76)9—the Addition of Drugs to Intravenous Infusion—and HC(77)22—the Extending Role of the Clinical Nurse, Legal Implications and Training Requirements—is relevant. Health Authorities and proprietors of private nursing homes approved under the Abortion Act 1967 should observe the requirements and qualifications noted in the Annexes to the letter, and should ensure that policy in relation to the duties that may be undertaken by nurses and midwives is clearly understood. In relation to those with conscientious objections, it is important to point out that this letter in no way affects the rights of any person under Section 4 of the 1967 Act to refuse (save in the circumstances postulated in subsection (2) of that Section) to participate in any treatment under the Act. Where the recent doubts mentioned at the beginning of this letter have led to restrictions on the part a nurse, midwife, or other person who is not a registered medical practitioner may play in the termination of pregnancy by medical induction methods, any such restrictions should now be reviewed in the light of this letter.'

The letter was signed by Dame Phyllis Friend, the chief nursing officer, and Dr H Yellowlees, chief medical officer. It is not necessary for me to read the annexes in full. It will suffice if I point out that they refer to the relevant parts of the Act and that Annex A states:

'From this it can be seen that one of the requirements of the 1967 Act is that the pregnancy be terminated by a registered medical practitioner and that where the requirements of the 1967 Act are satisfied the protection of that Act applies to any person participating and not just to the registered medical practitioner.'

And then there is a passage in these terms:

'The various medical induction processes differ from the surgical process in that the process of terminating the pregnancy takes place over a much longer period of time, and that (with the exception of the intra amniotic process which is always carried out by a registered medical practitioner) some of the acts necessary to bring about the termination are carried out not by a registered medical practitioner personally but by persons without medical qualifications acting on his instructions and often without his presence. Moreover some of these acts are acts which in themselves are capable of terminating the pregnancy (for example the connection to the patient of a "prostin pump" or the substitution of a full for an empty bottle of abortifacient fluid). However, the Secretary of State is advised that the termination can properly be said to have been termination by the registered medical practitioner provided it is decided upon by him, initiated by him, and that he remains throughout responsible for its overall conduct and control in the sense that any actions needed to bring it to conclusion are done by appropriately skilled staff acting on his specific instructions but not necessarily in his presence. Whether any such actions have an abortifacient effect or render the process of termination irreversible is irrelevant. From which it follows, for example, that, if the other requirements of the 1967 Act are satisfied, a nurse or midwife will be within the protection of that Act in carrying out actions which in conformity with accepted professional practice she is instructed to do by the registered medical practitioner responsible for the termination, including acts which in themselves may have an abortifacient effect or which could be said to render the process irreversible.'

There then follows Annex B. I do not propose to read any part of that annex because it is accepted that that annex sets out in clear terms the respective roles of the nursing staff and the registered medical practitioner in the light of the interpretation of the law adopted by the department.

Although the view expressed by the department as to the legal position in its letter of 21st February 1980 was in accordance with the advice that the department had received from the law officers, the college were firmly of the opinion that the department's advice was wrong. In March 1980 the college issued a circular on nurses and abortion which concluded by saying that the Royal College of Nursing reiterated its view that nurses would be contravening the 1967 Act if they administered prostaglandins and related drugs to procure an abortion and were therefore advised that only a registered medical practitioner should administer prostaglandins. This includes 'topping up' once the infusion has commenced.

There followed correspondence between the department and the college which led to a letter of 11th June 1980 being written to the solicitor to the department by the college's solicitor. This letter recites the desire of the college that the position should be clarified and that their membership should not be caught between, on the one hand, having to refuse to do work that otherwise they would have no objection to carrying out and which they are contractually obliged to perform, and, on the other hand, carrying out acts which their professional organisation has told them are unlawful and for which they cannot and do not enjoy the benefit of professional indemnity insurance in respect of negligence which the college provides. The letter asked for an undertaking from the department that it would withdraw its advice and as this undertaking was not forthcoming these proceedings were commenced.

The first question that arises in the proceedings is whether or not the college or department has locus standi to bring the proceedings. I refer to both the college and the department because, although there has been no formal cross-claim by the department, the Solicitor General, on behalf of the department, intimated in the course of argument that if I decide the matter adversely to the college he would seek a declaration in favour of the department. Neither the college nor the department desires to take any points as to the jurisdiction of the court to grant a declaration. Both recognise that not only would it be in the interests of nurses and the department that the law should be clarified but that it would also be in the interests of the public since a result of the present difference of views between the college and the department is that doctors, being deprived of the assistance of nursing staff, are unable to use the medical induction method of termination and instead are having either to use surgical methods which are less satisfactory, or to decline to assist patients whom they would otherwise be prepared to help.

However, questions of locus standi cannot be overcome by consent of the parties and therefore the Solicitor General addressed me on this question. He referred me to the recent decision of the House of Lords in *Imperial Tobacco Co Ltd v Attorney General* [1980] 1 All ER 866, [1980] 2 WLR 466. That case made it clear that it was not a proper exercise of judicial discretion for a civil court to grant a defendant in criminal proceedings a declaration that the facts alleged by a prosecution did not, in law, prove an offence charged, because to make such a declaration would be to usurp the function of the criminal courts. The present case is clearly distinguishable from that case. First of all there is no question of existing criminal proceedings in this case. Furthermore, the issue is not confined to whether the nurses would be committing a criminal offence if they followed the recommendations of the department. As is pointed out in the evidence, the case raises questions as to what duties a nurse should be prepared to perform for her employers and her right to be indemnified by the policy of insurance which the college provides for her. I see nothing therefore inconsistent with the speeches in the House of Lords in the *Imperial Tobacco* case in my granting a declaration in this case.

There is, however, also the problem whether the parties are not in the same position as Mr Gouriet was in *Gouriet v Union of Post Office Workers* [1977] 3 All ER 70, [1978] AC 435. Are they seeking to ask the court to declare public rights? If so, the court has only jurisdiction to grant a declaration at the suit of the Attorney General. As to this, I think the Solicitor General is right in saying that this case is, and should be regarded as, exceptional because of the special responsibilities that the college has in providing not only advice but also insurance for its members, and the relationship between the department and the nurses, many of whom are employed by bodies acting under the supervision of the department. I therefore conclude that I have jurisdiction.

However, I would emphasise that, in my view, it would have been much better if in this type of case proceedings were brought by way of judicial review under RSC Ord 53, when the court has the same power to grant a declaration. By proceeding by a different route, in a case which is appropriate to be dealt with under Ord 53, the safeguard of the requirement of obtaining leave to proceed under Ord 53 is circumvented. If it had not been for the great urgency for a decision in this case, I would have inquired into that matter in this case and could have felt it right not to proceed with the hearing and, as a matter of discretion, required the parties to proceed under Ord 53. If the procedure of seeking judicial review had been adopted at the outset it would not have caused delay. On the contrary, because an application can be made forthwith to the court and directions made on the application for leave, it is frequently possible to have the matter heard more quickly using the procedure by way of judicial review than is possible proceeding by originating summons. The fact that the court could have given directions for a very early hearing on the application for leave is not the only advantage of proceeding under Ord 53. Under Ord 53, because the jurisdiction is the same as that which previously existed on an application for prerogative writ, the requirement as to locus standi is more liberal than that in inter partes proceedings: see Lord Wilberforce in the *Gouriet* case [1977] 3 All ER 70 at 84, [1978] AC 435 at 482. However because of the urgency I will proceed to consider the merits of this dispute between the college and the department.

The extent of that dispute is limited because the college accepts that the letter of 21st February 1980 and the annexes cannot be criticised if the advice which they contain is lawful. The effect of the advice is correctly summarised in the letter of 21st February 1980 as being to—

> 'indicate that provided the registered medical practitioner personally decides upon and initiates the process of medical induction, and throughout remains responsible for it, it is not necessary for him personally to perform each and every action which is needed for the treatment to achieve its intended objective.'

Counsel for the college contends that that advice is wrong because the annexes clearly require the nurse to participate in the treatment and this contravenes the clear meaning of the words in s 1 of the 1967 Act that the termination should be by a registered medical practitioner. He correctly says that it is agreed that the causative factor inducing labour and hence the termination of pregnancy is the administration of the drugs, and these are, in fact, administered by the nurse and so she must be terminating the pregnancy. Counsel points out that if what Parliament intended was that there should be a defence if a pregnancy is terminated under the supervision of a registered medical practitioner, it would have been easy for this to be stated. However, this is not what s 1(1) of the 1967 Act provides. He referred me to a series of statutes which indicated how Parliament, when it wants to, can use language designed to extend the protection in a manner which would, if it had been incorporated in the 1967 Act, have clearly protected the nurses in their role proposed by the department. The absence of any such clear protection indicates that Parliament did not intend there to be a defence in such circumstances. Although counsel recognises that the result of the college's interpretation is, in effect, to make terminations of pregnancy by medical induction impracticable since registered medical practitioners do not have the time to be present throughout the process which lasts, on average, 18 hours, and can last up to 30 hours, he says this is due to the fact that the 1967 Act was not designed to deal with abortions by this method and if a change in the law is required to cover the advances made in medical science since the Act was passed, particularly in an area as sensitive as abortion, it is for Parliament to legislate and not the courts.

The Solicitor General, on the other hand, contends that looking at the Act as a whole, while it was not drafted with modern methods of abortion in mind, the ordinary meaning of the words used in the Act in their context are sufficiently wide to avoid nurses acting unlawfully if they follow the guidance laid down by the department.

The critical words in s 1(1) are 'terminated by a registered medical practitioner'. If those words are narrowly construed, the result could be that where a registered medical practitioner, complying with the conditions of s 1, sought to terminate a pregnancy, he would not be guilty of an offence under s 58 of the 1861 Act if the mother was with child and he terminated the pregnancy, but would be guilty of an offence if, contrary to his expectation, the mother was not in fact pregnant, it being irrelevant to the commission of an offence under s 58 whether the mother is with child or not. Such a result cannot have been intended by Parliament. Again, the college, which contends for the narrow interpretation, submits that if there is any intervention by a non-registered medical practitioner in the process which is causative of termination of the pregnancy, the defence is not available. Again, I do not believe this can be what Parliament intended, bearing in mind that even in the case of surgical methods of terminating pregnancy there would be expected to be a medical team consisting partly of doctors and partly of nurses involved.

The reason why the words 'terminated by a registered medical practitioner' do not have such narrow effect is because they refer to the treatment of termination by a registered medical practitioner and are not confined to the fact of termination. That this is the right approach is not disputed by counsel for the college. He, correctly in my view, accepts that s 1(3), s 3(1)(c) and in particular s 4(1) of the 1967 Act lead to this conclusion. Taking s 4(1), it provides that no person shall be under any duty etc 'to participate in any treatment authorised by this Act to which he has a conscientious objection'. The only treatment authorised by the Act is that referred to in s 1(1), namely what I have described as treatment for the termination of pregnancy.

The question which therefore arises as to the advice given by the department is whether that advice constitutes treatment for termination of pregnancy by a registered medical practitioner. When this question is posed, I conclude, without any doubt at all, that although a nurse may play a large part in the process the treatment is still by a registered medical practitioner. No doubt the time is not far ahead when a pregnancy can be terminated merely by the patient taking a pill. If in such circumstances the doctor, having examined the patient, decides that it is a case where in accordance with s 1 the pregnancy should be terminated, and he complies with the other conditions of s 1, then the fact that the pill may be handed to the patient by the nurse rather than the doctor so that the patient can take the pill will not mean that the treatment is not that of the doctor. If such a patient was asked who is treating her she would say the doctor, and the nurse would be assisting the doctor in the treatment. So in the case of the procedure laid down by the department, this makes it clear that the registered medical practitioner must decide on the termination; the process must be initiated by him, and he must remain throughout responsible for its overall conduct and control in the sense that any actions needed to bring it to a conclusion are done by appropriately skilled staff acting on his specific instructions, but not necessarily in his presence, though he or another registered medical practitioner must be available to be called if required. I can see no reason for interpreting the provision of s 1(1) of the 1967 Act so narrowly that if anyone other than the registered medical practitioner participates in the treatment the defence is not available. As long as it is initiated and strictly controlled by the registered medical practitioner, it is treatment for termination of pregnancy, which the parties agree is the proper test to be applied under s 1 by the registered medical practitioner.

I therefore refuse the application of the college and am prepared to grant a declaration to the department that the advice contained in the letter of 21st February 1980 and the annexes thereto, does not involve the performance of unlawful acts by members of the college.

Finally, I should make it clear that although counsel for the college indicated that the college's position was a neutral one and that the college merely sought clarification as to the law he has argued the matter ably, fully and with vigour.

Summons dismissed. Declaration that advice contained in letter of 21st February and annexes thereto did not involve the performance of unlawful acts by members of the college.

K Mydeen Esq   Barrister.

Appeal

The Royal College of Nursing appealed to the Court of Appeal.

Michael Spencer for the Royal College of Nursing.
The Solicitor General (Sir Ian Percival QC), Simon D Brown and *Stephen Aitchison* for the department.

Cur adv vult

7th November. The following judgments were read.

LORD DENNING MR. Abortion is a controversial subject. The question for us today is this: when a pregnancy is terminated by medical induction, who should do the actual act of termination? Should it be done by a doctor? Or can he leave it to the nurses? The Royal College of Nursing say that the doctor should do the actual act himself and not leave it to the nurses. The Department of Health take a different view. They say that a doctor can initiate the process and then go off and do other things, so long as he is 'on call'. The controversy is so acute that it has come before us for decision.

Throughout the discussion I am going to speak of the unborn child. The old common lawyers spoke of a child en ventre sa mère. Doctors speak of it as the fetus. In simple English it is an unborn child inside the mother's womb. Such a child was protected by the criminal law almost to the same extent as a new-born baby. If anyone terminated the pregnancy, and thus destroyed the unborn child, he or she was guilty of a felony and was liable to be kept in penal servitude for life (see the Offences against the Person Act 1861), unless it was done to save the life of the mother (see *R v Bourne* [1938] 3 All ER 615, [1939] 1 KB 687). Likewise anyone who assisted or participated in the abortion was guilty, including the mother herself. I have tried several cases of 'backstreet abortions', where the mother died or was made seriously ill. I have passed severe sentences of imprisonment for the offence.

The Abortion Act 1967

The approach to the subject was revolutionised by the Abortion Act 1967. It legalised abortion if it was done so as to avoid risk to the mother's health, physical or mental. This has been interpreted by some medical practitioners so loosely that abortion has become obtainable virtually on demand. Whenever a woman has an unwanted pregnancy, there are doctors who will say it involves a risk to her mental health. But the Act contains some safeguards. It provided that, in order for the abortion to be lawful, it was subject to three conditions. (1) The woman had to get two doctors to give a certificate. (2) The abortion had to be done in hospital. (3) The pregnancy had to be 'terminated by a registered medical practitioner'. It is this last condition which comes up for consideration today. It arises because of the advance in medical science.

The material words of the 1967 Act, in s 1(1), are that '. . . a person shall not be guilty of an offence under the law relating to abortion when a pregnancy is terminated by a registered medical practitioner . . .'

At the time that the Act was passed, and for five years afterwards, there was no difficulty of interpretation. All abortions then, at any rate when the mother was three months pregnant or more, were done by surgical methods. The knife with the cutting edge was operated by a registered medical practitioner. He used it to remove the unborn child. The knife was never handled by a nurse. She was not a registered medical practitioner.

Medical induction

Since 1972 a new method has been used. It is called medical induction. It does not involve a knife. It started quite simply in ordinary full-time births, so as to induce labour a few hours early, to save the mother the stress of waiting, or for the convenience of doctors and staff. But it is now becoming much used to effect abortions, when the mother is pregnant for three months or more. It is done by pumping a chemical fluid into the mother's womb. It is called prostaglandin. This fluid so affects the muscles and shape of the mother's inside that it forces her into labour prematurely, so that the unborn child is expelled from the body, usually dead, but sometimes at the point of death.

There are two distinct stages in this process. The first stage is done by a doctor, a registered medical practitioner. The mother is taken from the ward to the operating theatre. She is given a general anaesthetic. The doctor inserts a fine catheter into her body so as to reach a particular part of her womb. But no fluid is pumped into her at that stage. She is then taken back to the ward. She is left there until she recovers from the anaesthetic. The doctor writes out a few notes telling the nurse what to do. He then goes off, saying, 'Give me a call if there is any difficulty'.

The second stage is done by the nurses. When the mother comes round from the anaesthetic, they get a flexible tube and connect up the catheter to a pump which is electrically driven; or to a dripping device. They then get the special fluid called prostaglandin. They have to see that it is of the right concentration. They have it in a bottle, and pump the fluid into the woman's body. They have to regulate the dose and control the intake, by speed and amount, as occasion requires. If need be, they have to get another bottle. They have to watch the woman and note her reactions; and take such steps as occasion requires. Labour is induced. The unborn child is expelled from the woman's body. The process may take 18 hours, or even up to 30 hours. If the unborn child is not expelled by that time, the process is stopped. The child is allowed to live on, to await normal delivery later.

Here I would stop for a moment to point out that the first stage (done by the doctor) does nothing to terminate the pregnancy. The insertion of the catheter is only a preparatory act. It is the second stage (done by the nurses) which terminates the pregnancy. There is an agreed statement of facts which shows that the causative factor is the administration of prostaglandin. This is the way in which it is put:

'It will be appreciated that in the medical induction process the causative factor in inducing the labour and hence the termination of pregnancy is the effect of the administration of prostaglandin and/or oxytocin and not any mechanical effect from the insertion of the catheter or cannula. In that the nurse does, on the instructions of the doctor, commence or augment the flow of prostaglandin or oxytocin, and even sometimes effect the connection between the already inserted catheter and the prostin pump and the already intravenous cannula and the oxytocin infusion, her role in the process does include acts which have, and are intended to have, an abortifacient effect.'

To take a parallel from the removal of an appendix. The anaesthetist makes all the preparations, but the removal is done by the surgeon himself. So here, the doctor makes the preparations (inserting the catheter) but the pregnancy is terminated by the act, the continuous act, done by the nurses from the moment that they start the pump or the drip to the moment when the baby is expelled.

The Royal College's objection

I can quite understand that many nurses dislike having anything to do with these abortions. It is a soul-destroying task. The nurses are young women who are dedicated by their profession and training to do all they can to preserve life. Yet here they are called on to destroy it. It is true that the statute gives them an escape clause. They can refuse to participate in any treatment to which they have a 'conscientious objection': see s 4 of the 1967 Act. But the report of Dame Elizabeth Lane and her colleagues (Report of the Committee on the Working of the Abortion Act (vol 2, Cmnd 5579-I (1974)) shows that many nurses do not take advantage of this 'escape clause': because it means that other nurses will have to do this heart-rending task; and they feel it may be held against them by their superiors. So they take part in it, much against their will (see paras 321 to 374 of the Lane report).

It is against this background that the Royal College of Nursing ask the question: is it lawful for nurses to be called on to terminate pregnancy in this way? The Royal College say No, it is not lawful; it is not a nurse's job to terminate a pregnancy. The Department of Health and Social Security say Yes, it is lawful. They have issued a circular in which they presume to lay down the law for the whole of the medical profession. They say that it is no offence if the pregnancy is terminated by a suitably qualified person in accordance with the written instructions of a registered medical practitioner. This is the wording of the circular:

> 'However, the Secretary of State is advised that the termination can properly be said to have been terminated by the registered medical practitioner provided it is decided upon by him, initiated by him, and that he remains throughout responsible for its overall conduct and control in the sense that any actions needed to bring it to conclusion are done by appropriately skilled staff acting on his specific instructions but *not necessarily in his presence.*'

Note those words 'not necessarily in his presence'. They are crucial.

The interpretation of the 1967 Act

The lawfulness depends on the true interpretation of the statute; but, before going into it, I would say a word or two about the approach to it.

(i) Abortion is a subject on which many people feel strongly. In both directions. Many are for it. Many against it. Some object to it as the destruction of life. Others favour it as the right of the woman. Emotions run so high on both sides that I feel that we as judges must go by the very words of the statute, without stretching it one way or the other, and writing nothing in which is not there.

(ii) Another thing to remember is that the statute is directed to the medical profession, to the doctors and nurses who have to implement it. It is they who have to read it and to act on it. They will read it, not as lawyers, but as laymen. So we should interpret it as they would.

(iii) If there should ever be a case in the courts, the decision would ultimately be that of a jury. Suppose that during the process the mother died or became seriously ill, owing to the nurse's negligence in administering the wrong chemical fluid, and the nurse was prosecuted under the 1861 Act for unlawfully administering to her a noxious thing or using other means with intent to procure her miscarriage. The nurse would have no defence unless the pregnancy was 'terminated by a registered medical practitioner'. Those are simple English words which should be left to a jury to apply, without the judge attempting to put his own gloss on them: see *Brutus v Cozens* [1972] 2 All ER 1297 at 1299, [1973] AC 854 at 861. I should expect the jury to say that the pregnancy was not terminated by a registered medical practitioner but by a nurse.

(iv) If in such a case there were a claim for damages, the nurse might not be covered by insurance because she would not be engaged in 'nursing professional services acceptable to the Royal College of Nursing'.

(v) Statutes can be divided into two categories. In the first category Parliament has expressly said 'by a registered medical practitioner or by a person acting in accordance with the directions of any such practitioner', or words to that effect: see the Radioactive Substances Act 1948, s 3(1)(a); the Therapeutic Substances Act 1956, s 9(1)(a); the Drugs (Prevention of Misuse) Act 1964, s 1(2)(g); the Medicines Act 1968, s 58(2)(b); the Tattooing of Minors Act 1969, s 1. In the second category Parliament has deliberately confined it: 'by a fully registered medical practitioner' omitting any such words as 'or by his direction': see the Human Tissue Act 1961, s 1(4). This statute is in the second category.

(vi) Woolf J tested the statute by supposing that a registered medical practitioner performed an abortion operation on a woman whom he believed to be pregnant but who was not so in fact. The 1967 Act would give him no defence to a charge under the 1861 Act. That is such a fanciful instance that I do not think it throws any light on the true construction of this statute.

(vii) The Solicitor General emphasised the word 'treatment' in ss 1(3), 3(1)(a) and (c) and 4(1). He suggested that s 1(1) should be read as if it said that a person should not be guilty of an offence 'when the treatment (for termination of a pregnancy) is by a registered medical practitioner'. He submitted that, whenever the registered medical practitioner did what the Department of Health advised, it satisfied the statute, because the treatment, being initiated by him and done under his instructions, was 'by' him. I cannot accept this interpretation. I think the word 'treatment' in those sections means 'the actual act of terminating the pregnancy'. When the medical induction method is used, this means the continuous act of administering prostaglandin from the moment it is started until the unborn child is expelled from the mother's body. This continuous act must be done by the doctor personally. It is not sufficient that it is done by a nurse when he is not present.

Conclusion

Stress was laid by the Solicitor General on the effect of this ruling. The process of medical induction can take from 18 to 30 hours. No doctor can be expected to be present all that time. He must leave it to the nurses: or not use the method at all. If he is not allowed to leave it to the nurses, the result will be *either* that there will be fewer abortions *or* that the doctor will have to use the surgical method with its extra hazards. This may be so. But I do not think this warrants us departing from the statute. The Royal College of Nursing have advised their nurses that under the statute they should not themselves terminate a pregnancy. If the doctor advises it, he should do it himself, and not call on the nurses to do it.

I think that the Royal College are quite right. If the Department of Health want the nurses to terminate a pregnancy, the Minister should go to Parliament and get the statute altered. He should ask them to amend it by adding the words 'or by a suitably qualified person in accordance with the written instructions of a registered medical practitioner'. I doubt whether Parliament would accept the amendment. It is too controversial. At any rate, that is the way to amend the law and not by means of a departmental circular.

I would allow the appeal accordingly.

BRIGHTMAN LJ. The order appealed from is a declaration that the advice contained in the department's letter and in the annexes thereto does not involve the performance of unlawful acts by nurses or midwives. Counsel have agreed that the only relevant part of the letter and annexes is Annex B. This annex is divided into 'A. Procedures which must be carried out by a registered medical practitioner' and 'B. Procedures that may be performed by an appropriately skilled nurse or midwife'.

The criminal offences with which we are concerned are defined by ss 58 and 59 of the Offences against the Person Act 1861. These sections are introduced by the cross-heading 'Attempts to procure Abortion'. Section 58, so far as relevant for present purposes, enacts that a criminal offence is committed by a person who, 'with intent to procure the miscarriage of any woman, whether she be or be not with child, shall unlawfully administer to her ... any poison or other noxious thing'. Section 59 enacts that a criminal offence is committed by a person who 'shall unlawfully supply ... any poison or other noxious thing ... knowing that the same is intended to be unlawfully used etc'.

The Abortion Act 1967 qualifies the earlier statute by enacting that a person shall not be guilty of an offence under s 58 or s 59 of the 1861 Act, or any rule of law relating to the procurement of abortion, if certain conditions are fulfilled. There are three conditions. They are expressed as follows (leaving aside certain modifications which apply to visiting forces etc):

Condition 1—'when a pregnancy is terminated by a registered medical practitioner';

Condition 2—'if two registered medical practitioners are of the opinion, formed in good faith ... that [put shortly, the abortion is necessary]';

Condition 3—'[provided that] any treatment for the termination of pregnancy must be carried out in a [National Health Service] hospital or in a place for the time being approved ... by the ... Minister'.

Both counsel agreed, in my view correctly, that a proper way to test the position was to assume that an abortion is carried out in a national health service hospital or other approved nursing home in such a way as to involve the maximum nurse or midwife participation which is envisaged by Annex B; then to consider whether, if an abortion be so carried out, the nurse or midwife will be able, by virtue of s 1 of the Abortion Act 1967, to plead successfully that he or she is not guilty of an offence under the 1861 Act. In a given case this would be a question of fact for the jury. However, counsel agreed, in my view correctly, that the declaration appealed from would be rightly made if, but only if, it can be said that, were an abortion to be so performed, the trial judge would be bound to direct an acquittal.

I first turn to consider what steps are taken in the course of an abortion by medical induction, and how the abortion would be carried out in a hospital or approved nursing home if performed with the 'maximum nurse participation' contemplated by Annex B (I include participation by a midwife).

The steps which are taken, or may be taken, in the case of extra-amniotic medical induction for termination of pregnancy are as follows. For this purpose I rely on para 5 of the 'Agreed statement as to clinical background'. Some of the steps described overlap in point of time.

Step 1. A catheter is passed via the cervix into the potential space between the wall of the womb and the amniotic sac.

Step 2. The catheter is attached to an electrically driven pump. This pump controls the rate at which the carrier solution containing prostaglandin is propelled from a syringe and through the catheter. The purpose of the prostaglandin solution is to separate the sac from the womb.

Alternative step 2. In place of a prostin pump, the catheter may be linked to a gravity feed drip apparatus.

Step 3. The electric pump is started by a switch, or the drip apparatus is opened by turning a valve.

Step 4. A cannula is inserted into a vein. Its function will be to introduce into the bloodstream by gravity a carrier solution containing oxytocin and thus promote uterine contractions. This step requires some qualification. First, the cannula may already be in position, having been inserted for pre-medication purposes. Second, this infusion is sometimes introduced only where there is delay in the start of the induced labour.

Step 5. The oxytocin drip feed is connected to the cannula.

Step 6. The patient's condition is continuously monitored, including quarterly or half hourly records of pulse, blood pressure, strength, duration and frequency of uterine contractions and blood-loss. If a gravity drip is used for the prostaglandin infusion, the drip rate must be constantly monitored.

Step 7. The syringes or infusion bottles are replaced or replenished as necessary during the operation.

Step 8. The concentration and flow rates of both the prostaglandin solution and the oxytocin solution are adjusted as necessary during the operation.

Step 9. If the fetus has not been aborted after the lapse of 30 hours, the treatment is discontinued. There is a failure rate of 1% to 2%. The average lapse of time is 18 hours.

In a case in which there is 'maximum nurse participation' as contemplated by Annex B, the roles of registered medical practitioner ('doctor') and nurse will be as follows:

Step 1. The doctor inserts the catheter into the womb, but does not pass fluid through it.

Step 2. The nurse attaches the catheter to the pump, or to the gravity feed drip apparatus.

Step 3. The nurse switches on the pump or turns the feed drip valve, in order to administer the prostaglandin infusion to the patient.

Step 4. The doctor inserts the cannula into the vein, but does not pass fluid through it.

Step 5. The nurse links up the oxytocin drip feed, in order to administer the infusion to the patient.

Step 6. The monitoring of the patient, and the monitoring of the drip rate, are carried out by the nurse.

Step 7. The nurse replaces or replenishes the syringe and infusion bottle as necessary in order to administer the correct quantities of the infusions.

Step 8. The nurse adjusts the flow rates of both the infusions.

Step 9. The nurse discontinues the treatment, either because the fetus has been discharged, or because the allotted period has elapsed and the operation has failed.

As regards all the steps, the nurse performs her part in accordance with the instructions of the doctor, which will be written instructions in all important respects. In the case supposed of 'maximum nurse participation' the doctor will be on call; however, it is implicit in Annex B that he may not in fact be called, and therefore he may be absent throughout except for steps 1 and 4 (insertion of catheter and cannula).

The question now to be asked, against the background described, is whether in such a case the pregnancy has been 'terminated by a registered medical practitioner'.

During the course of argument considerable discussion was directed to the identification of the precise act or acts which ought to be regarded as 'terminating the pregnancy' and whether the operation would be outside the 1967 Act just because the finger of the nurse rather than the finger of the doctor presses the switch which activates the electrical circuit that operates the pump, or turns the valve of the feed drip. Fanciful examples were conjured up of extreme cases: suppose the doctor is present in the operating theatre or ward for every second of the operation and supervises it throughout but makes use of the nurse's skill to carry out important steps under his watchful eye; does the Act intend that an offence is committed? These examples are not in my view helpful. We have to consider only the procedure set out in Annex B and decide whether that procedure, not some other procedure, is or is not within the 1967 Act.

There was discussion as to whether s 1 of the Act should receive a broad construction or a narrow construction. Emphasis was placed on the fact that the section only exempts from criminality an occasion when a pregnancy 'is terminated', and therefore would not exempt from criminality the 2% of cases where an abortion is attempted but fails; or the case where an abortion is attempted but no pregnancy is terminated because it turns out, as may happen, that the woman is not pregnant. It was pointed out that, although the opening words of s 1 use the formula 'a pregnancy is terminated', sub-s (3), and also s 3(1)(a), refer to *'the treatment'* for termination of the pregnancy, and s 4(1) refers to '*treatment* authorised by this Act'. It was submitted that where s 1(1) refers to a 'pregnancy being terminated' by a doctor, it is in reality referring to 'the treatment' for termination of a pregnancy being 'carried out by' a doctor.

I am disposed to accept this last submission and to read s 1(1) as meaning that a person shall not be guilty of an offence under the law relating to abortion 'when *treatment for* termination of a pregnancy *is carried out by*' a registered medical practitioner. Such a construction does not in my opinion involve adding any words at all to the statute. I think it is what the section means on its true construction in the context in which the words are found. It is a construction which removes the apparent absurdity which would arise if, for example, the operation did not succeed in terminating the pregnancy; or if the woman proved not to be with child; or if the operation were carried out under the constant, immediate and whole-time supervision of the doctor who allowed a nurse to do some of the 'mechanical' acts in his presence and under his immediate eye.

Having attempted to construe the Act, I hope correctly, I must apply such construction to the facts supposed in Annex B on the basis of 'maximum nurse participation'. It will be recalled that in the case supposed, the doctor inserts the catheter into the womb and also inserts the cannula into the vein but is then free to leave and does leave the operating theatre or ward before any infusions are administered, and he does not necessarily return unless specifically recalled. In my opinion it would be a misuse of language to describe such a termination of a pregnancy as done 'by' a registered medical practitioner, or to describe such a treatment for termination of a pregnancy as 'carried out by' a registered medical practitioner, however detailed and precise the written instructions given by the registered medical practitioner to the nurse. It would not be far removed from the nurse carrying out the operation from detailed instructions in a textbook. The true analysis is that the doctor *has provided the nurse with the means* to terminate the pregnancy, not that the doctor has terminated the pregnancy.

I decline to express a view as to precisely what does or does not need to be done by, or to be personally and immediately supervised by, the doctor in order to satisfy the stringent requirements of s 1. It is not the function of the court to decide how close to dangerous waters it is possible to sail without actually being shipwrecked.

For the reasons which I have endeavoured to express, I think that this appeal ought to be allowed.

SIR GEORGE BAKER. The parts played by a nurse in the medical induction methods for terminating a pregnancy are set out in the 'Agreed statement as to clinical background', the vital words in para 5(7) of which have already been read by Lord Denning MR. The acts which she performs or may perform, as, for example, connecting the catheter to the prostin pump, starting the pump to enable the prostaglandin solution to be propelled into the uterine cavity, replacing an empty syringe, initiating and controlling an intravenous infusion of oxytocin, are each and all administering a noxious thing, namely the prostaglandin and/or oxytocin, with intent to procure miscarriage and so within the Offences against the Person Act 1861, s 58. That there is an administration is unarguable, and that an abortifacient is a noxious thing has been the law for at least a century, for in *R v Hollis and Blakeman* (1873) Cox CC 463 at 467 Bramwell B said: 'A noxious thing within the statute means a thing that will produce the effect mentioned in the statute—that is, a miscarriage'; and more recently Brabin J, after reviewing the authorities, said: 'If the substance, in the quantity taken or by its nature, is an abortifacient, it cannot be suggested . . . that it is anything but a noxious thing': see *R v Marlow* (1964) 49 Cr App R 49 at 54.

Such acts of administration by the nurse are in direct contrast to those other things done by the nurse which are not 'administering', such as monitoring the patient's vital signs and keeping records as described in the agreed facts. But s 58 of the 1861 Act further requires that for an offence to be committed the noxious thing must be administered unlawfully, and the department contends that everything the nurse does in the process of producing the miscarriage, and in particular acts which amount to administering a noxious thing, are lawful if the provisions of s 1 of the Abortion Act 1967 are satisfied.

It is of primary importance to have clearly in mind what the 1967 Act says. Its long title is: 'An Act to amend and clarify the law relating to termination of pregnancy by registered medical practitioners', and the marginal note to s 1 is 'medical termination of pregnancy'. The section provides:

'. . . a person [the protection is not limited to nurses] shall not be guilty of an offence under the law relating to abortion when a pregnancy is terminated by a registered medical practitioner if two registered medical practitioners are of the opinion in good faith etc.'

In an emergency the requirement of the opinion of two registered medical practitioners is unnecessary (s 1(4)), but again there must be 'the termination of a pregnancy by a registered medical practitioner'. The words 'terminated by a registered medical practitioner' are by themselves clear and unambiguous. The operative act or acts which have or are intended to have an abortifacient effect must be done by or performed or carried out by a registered medical practitioner. But the department says that the words should not be read literally for that would 'defeat the obvious intention of the legislation and . . . produce a wholly unreasonable result' (per Lord Reid in *Luke v Inland Revenue Comrs* [1963] 1 All ER 655 at 664, [1963] AC 557 at 577 quoted by Buckley LJ in *Western Bank Ltd v Schindler* [1976] 2 All ER 393 at 399, [1977] Ch 1 at 13). They should on the contrary be read as meaning that if the treatment for the termination of a pregnancy is by a registered medical practitioner then no offence is committed by the nurse (or person) who administers abortifacients or does any other act with intent to procure the miscarriage.

On 21st February 1980 a letter was sent by the department signed by the chief nursing officer and the chief medical officer with a wide distribution which included regional, area and district nursing officers under the heading 'Termination of pregnancy by medical induction: The role of the nurse or midwife and others who are not registered medical practitioners', which in two annexes gave guidance on professional practice. The first half of the final paragraph of Annex A has already been read by Lord Denning MR. It continues:

> 'Whether any such actions have an abortifacient effect or render the process of termination irreversible is irrelevant. From which it follows, for example, that, if the other requirements of the 1967 Act are satisfied, a nurse or midwife will be within the protection of that Act in carrying out actions which in conformity with accepted professional practice she is instructed to do by the registered medical practitioner responsible for the termination, including acts which in themselves may have an abortifacient effect or which could be said to render the process irreversible.'

Annex B sets out the procedures which must be carried out by a registered medical practitioner such as giving specific or precise instructions on some matters, written instructions on others, and that he or another registered medical practitioner must be on call, and those which may be performed by an appropriately skilled nurse or midwife when the registered medical practitioner acting in accordance with these directions gives the orders. In short this direction or guidance, and, indeed the basic argument of the department, seems to me to be that not only doctors' acts but also doctors' orders will satisfy s 1(1) of the Abortion Act 1967.

Much has been said about the apparent anomalies of the strict or literal interpretation of s 1(1), that there is no defence for doctors or any person if (a) there is no pregnancy, or (b) the pregnancy is not terminated, but with the wider 'doctors' orders' interpretation the nurse would apparently be committing an offence under s 58 if she failed to follow or misinterpreted the instructions of the doctor or indeed, if possibly unknown to her, the prerequisite opinions of the two registered medical practitioners had not been formed in good faith.

The department's case necessitates s 1(1) being read as meaning: '. . . if two registered medical practitioners are of the opinion, formed in good faith' etc then provided that the 'treatment for termination of the pregnancy [is] carried out in a hospital vested in the Minister . . . or in a place for the time being' approved etc 'a person *participating or assisting in that treatment* and who would otherwise be guilty of an offence under the law relating to abortion as defined in this Act shall not be guilty of such an offence when *the treatment* is by a registered medical practitioner.'

The word 'treatment' appears in three other subsections of the Abortion Act 1967.

1. Section 1(3) provides:

> 'Except as provided by subsection (4) of this section [the emergency subsection] any treatment for the termination of pregnancy must be carried out in a hospital . . .', etc.

This provision seems to me to be much wider than and in direct contrast to the words 'terminated by'. In my opinion 'treatment' includes all that happens before the abortifacient is administered (or an instrument used), the nursing, as distinct from acts of administration during the administration or use and care after the termination, and cannot be a guide to the interpretation of s 1(1).

2. In the 'Application of [the] Act to visiting forces', s 3(1) reads:

> 'In relation to the termination of a pregnancy in a case where the following conditions are satisfied that is to say—(a) the treatment for termination of the pregnancy was carried out in a hospital controlled by [visiting forces]; (b) the

pregnant woman had at the time of the treatment a relevant association with [visiting forces]; (c) the treatment was carried out by a registered medical practitioner or a person who at the time of the treatment was a member of [the visiting force] appointed as a medical practitioner for [that visiting force] by the proper authorities of [that visiting force] . . .'

In paras (a) and (b) 'treatment' is in direct contrast to the opening words 'in relation to the termination of a pregnancy'. Termination takes place during and is a part of treatment. At first sight para (c) '. . . treatment . . . carried out by a registered medical practitioner' gives some support to the liberal construction of s 1(1), but (i) it also is governed by the words 'in relation to the termination of a pregnancy', (ii) it is for the application of the Act to a visiting force, and (iii) the provision is to give the visiting force the utmost freedom to arrange its own medical affairs within the ambit of our law.

3. Finally, in the conscience section, s 4(1) provides: '. . . no person shall be under a duty . . . to participate in any treatment authorised by this Act to which he has a conscientious objection.' This does not assist, for if administration of an abortifacient or use of an instrument by a nurse on doctor's orders has not been authorised by the Act, she cannot be under a duty to participate.

Under the Abortion Regulations 1968, SI 1968 No 390, which the Minister of Health is required to make by s 2 of the 1967 Act, a certificate of the opinion of two registered medical practitioners must be given 'before the commencement of the treatment for the termination of the pregnancy to which it relates' (see reg 3(2)). So too must the opinion that 'termination is immediately necessary to save . . . life etc' under s 1(4) of the Act, but if impracticable it may be given after the termination (see reg 3(3)).

Under reg 4 notices have to be given by the 'operating practitioner', that is 'any practitioner who terminates a pregnancy . . . within 7 days of the termination', not, be it noted, within seven days of the treatment after termination.

In my opinion there is nothing in the Act or regulations to indicate that the intention of Parliament was other than that clearly expressed in the simple words 'when a pregnancy is terminated by a registered medical practitioner'. They are words which have to be understood by ordinary mortals in legislation on a topic which can arouse great emotions (see *Paton v Trustees of BPAS* [1978] 2 All ER 987 at 989, [1979] QB 276 at 278). Maybe Parliament never had in mind abortions by medical induction which, as the Ministry letter indicates, has been employed in the past ten years; maybe a decision that it can be done only by a registered medical practitioner and not by a nurse on doctor's orders in any causative respect will result in a safe and easy method being less used with consequent hardship or even greater danger to pregnant women. I do not know. Even if so, it is not for judges 'to read words into an Act of Parliament unless clear reason for it is to be found within the four corners of the Act itself' (per Lord Loreburn LC in *Vickers Sons & Maxim Ltd v Evans* [1910] AC 444 at 445, cited by Viscount Dilhorne in *Stock v Frank Jones (Tipton) Ltd* [1978] 1 All ER 948 at 951, [1978] 1 WLR 231 at 235). Nor is a judge entitled to read an Act differently from what it says simply because he thinks Parliament would have so provided had the situation been envisaged at that time. In the words of Lord Simon in *Stock v Frank Jones (Tipton) Ltd* [1978] 1 All ER 948 at 953, [1978] 1 WLR 231 at 237:

'. . . in a society living under the rule of law citizens are entitled to regulate their conduct according to what a statute has said rather than by what it was meant to say or by what it would have otherwise said if a newly considered situation had been envisaged.'

There is no manifest absurdity; on the contrary the provision is clear and understandable. If the intention had been to make lawful the acts of persons participating in or carrying out the termination of a pregnancy on doctors' orders that could have been expressly stated either as the department suggests the section should be read, or by some other appropriate words: see the Radioactive Substances Act 1948, s 3(1)(a), '. . . a person acting in accordance with the directions of a designated general medical practitioner'; or the Tattooing of Minors Act 1969, s 1, '... performed for medical reasons by a duly qualified medical practitioner or a person working under his direction'.

The Abortion Act 1967 requires the termination to be by the operative acts of the registered medical practitioner himself; his orders are not enough. I too would allow the appeal.

Appeal allowed with costs in Court of Appeal and below. Leave to appeal to the House of Lords granted on terms that order for costs not be disturbed and that no costs be asked for in the House against the Royal College of Nursing.

Sumra Green   Barrister.

Appeal

The department appealed to the House of Lords.

The Solicitor General (Sir Ian Percival QC), Simon D Brown and *Stephen Aitcheson* for the department.
Michael Spencer and *Caroline Moore* for the Royal College of Nursing.

LORD WILBERFORCE. Their Lordships appreciate the urgency of this matter and think it right in the interests of the health service to announce their decision now. They will be reporting to the House that the appeal should be allowed and the decision of Woolf J be restored. This is an unusual course and it is not to be taken as a precedent.

5th February. The following written opinions were given.

LORD WILBERFORCE. My Lords, on 27th October 1967 Parliament passed the Abortion Act 1967. Its long title describes it as an Act 'to amend and clarify the law *relating to termination of pregnancy by registered medical practitioners*'.

Before the Act was passed it was an offence (sc felony) for *any person* with intent to procure the miscarriage of any woman, whether she be or be not with child, unlawfully to administer to her or cause to be taken by her any poison or other noxious thing or unlawfully to use any instrument or other means whatsoever with the like intent (see the Offences against the Person Act 1861, s 58). Further, the Infant Life (Preservation) Act 1929 created the offence of child destruction in relation to a child capable of being born alive. These provisions thus affected not only doctors, but nurses, midwives, pharmacists and others; they were in operation in 1967, subject only to the defence judicially given to the doctor in *R v Bourne* [1938] 3 All ER 615, [1939] 1 KB 687.

Section 1 of the 1967 Act created a new defence, available to any person who might be liable under the existing law. It is available (i) *'when a pregnancy is terminated by a registered medical practitioner'* (these are the words of the Act), (ii) when certain other conditions are satisfied, including the expressed opinion of two registered medical practitioners as to the risks (specified in paras (a) and (b)) to mother, or child, or existing children, and the requirement that the treatment for the termination of pregnancy must be carried out in a national health service hospital or other approved place. The present case turns on the meaning to be given to condition (i).

The issue relates to a non-surgical procedure of medical induction by the use of a drug called prostaglandin. This operates on the mother's muscles so as to cause contractions (similar to those arising in normal labour) which expel the fetus from the womb. It is used during the second trimester. The question has been raised by the Royal College of Nursing as to the participation of nurses in this treatment, particularly since nurses can be called on (subject to objections of conscience which are rarely invoked) to carry it out. They have felt, and express grave concern as to the legality of doing so and seek a declaration, that a circular issued by the Department of Health and Social Security, asserting the lawfulness of the nurses' participation, is wrong in law.

There is an agreed statement as to the nature of this treatment and the part in it played by the doctors and the nurses or midwives. Naturally this may vary somewhat from hospital to hospital, but, for the purpose of the present proceedings, the assumption has to be made of maximum nurse participation, ie that the nurse does everything which the doctor is not required to do. If that is not illegal, participation of a lesser degree must be permissible.

1. The first step is for a thin catheter to be inserted via the cervix into the womb so as to arrive at, or create, a space between the wall of the womb and the amniotic sac containing the fetus. This is necessarily done by a doctor. It may, sometimes, of itself bring on an abortion, in which case no problem arises: the pregnancy will have been terminated by the doctor. If it does not, all subsequent steps except no 4 may be carried out by a nurse or midwife. The significant steps are as follows (I am indebted to Brightman LJ for their presentation):

2. The catheter (ie the end emerging from the vagina) is attached, probably via another tube, to a pump or to a gravity feed apparatus. The function of the pump or apparatus is to propel or feed the prostaglandin through the catheter into the womb. The necessary prostaglandin infusion is provided and put into the apparatus.

*3. The pump is switched on, or the drip valve is turned, thus causing the prostaglandin to enter the womb.

4. The doctor inserts a cannula into a vein.

*5. An oxytocin drip feed is linked up with the cannula. The necessary oxytocin (a drug designed to help the contractions) is supplied for the feed.

6. The patient's vital signs are monitored; so is the rate of drip or flow.

*7. The flow rates of both infusions are, as necessary, adjusted.

*8. Fresh supplies of both infusions are added as necessary.

9. The treatment is discontinued after discharge of the fetus, or expiry of a fixed period (normally 30 hours) after which the operation is considered to have failed.

The only steps in this process which can be considered to have a direct effect leading to abortion (abortifacient steps) are those asterisked. They are all carried out by the nurse, or midwife. As the agreed statement records 'the causative factor in inducing . . . the termination of pregnancy is the effect of the administration of prostaglandin and/or oxytocin and not any mechanical effect from the insertion of the catheter or cannula'.

All the above steps 2 to 9 are carried out in accordance with the doctor's instructions, which should, as regards important matters, be in writing. The doctor will moreover be on call, but may in fact never be called.

On these facts the question has to be answered: has the pregnancy been terminated by the doctor; or has it been terminated by the nurse; or has it been terminated by doctor and nurse? I am not surprised that the nurses feel anxiety as to this.

In attempting to answer it, I start from the point that in 1967, the date of the Act, the only methods used to produce abortions were surgical methods; of these there were several varieties, well enough known. One of these was by intra-amniotic injection, ie the direct injection of glucose or saline solutions into the amniotic sac. It was not ideal or, it appears, widely used. Parliament must have been aware of these methods and cannot have had in mind a process where abortifacient agents were administered by nurses. They did not exist. Parliament's concern must have been to prevent existing methods being carried out by unqualified persons and to insist that they should be carried out by doctors. For these reasons Parliament no doubt used the words, in s 1(1), 'termination of pregnancy by a registered medical practitioner'.

Extra-amniotic administration of prostaglandin was first reported in 1971, and was soon found to have advantages. It involves, or admits, as shown above, direct and significant participation by nurses in the abortifacient steps. Is it covered by the critical words?

In interpreting an Act of Parliament it is proper, and indeed necessary, to have regard to the state of affairs existing, and known by Parliament to be existing, at the time. It is a fair presumption that Parliament's policy or intention is directed to that state of affairs. Leaving aside cases of omission by inadvertence, this being not such a case when a new state of affairs, or a fresh set of facts bearing on policy, comes into existence, the courts have to consider whether they fall within the parliamentary intention. They may be held to do so if they fall within the same genus of facts as those to which the expressed policy has been formulated. They may also be held to do so if there can be detected a clear purpose in the legislation which can only be fulfilled if the extension is made. How liberally these principles may be applied must depend on the nature of the enactment, and the strictness or otherwise of the words in which it has been expressed. The courts should be less willing to extend expressed meanings if it is clear that the Act in question was designed to be restrictive or circumscribed in its operation rather than liberal or permissive. They will be much less willing to do so where the new subject matter is different in kind or dimension from that for which the legislation was passed. In any event there is one course which the courts cannot take under the law of this country: they cannot fill gaps; they cannot by asking the question, 'What would Parliament have done in this current case, not being one in contemplation, if the facts had been before it?', attempt themselves to supply the answer, if the answer is not to be found in the terms of the Act itself.

In my opinion this Act should be construed with caution. It is dealing with a controversial subject involving moral and social judgments on which opinions strongly differ. It is, if ever an Act was, one for interpreting in the spirit that only that which Parliament has authorised on a fair reading of the relevant sections should be held to be within it. The new (post-1967) method of medical induction is clearly not just a fresh species or example of something already authorised. The Act is not one for 'purposive' or 'liberal' or 'equitable' construction. This is a case where the courts must hold that anything beyond the legislature's fairly expressed authority should be left for Parliament's fresh consideration.

Having regard particularly to the Act's antecedents and the state of affairs existing in 1967, which involved surgical action requiring to be confined to termination by doctors alone, I am unable to read the words 'pregnancy terminated by a registered medical practitioner' as extended or extensible to cover cases where other persons, whether nurses, or midwives, or even lay persons, play a significant part in the process of termination. That a process in which they do so may be reliable, and an improvement on existing surgical methods, may well be the case, we do not in fact even know this. It may be desirable that doctors' time should be spared from directly participating in all the stages of the abortifacient process; it may be (though there are very many hospitals and nursing homes in the United Kingdom, not all with the same high standards) that nurses, midwives etc may be relied on to carry out the doctor's instructions accurately and well. It may be that doctors, though not present, may always be available on call. All this may, though with some reservation, be granted, but is beside the point. With nurse, etc, participation, to the degree mentioned, a new dimension has been introduced; this should not be sanctioned by judicial decision, but only by Parliament after proper consideration of the implications and necessary safeguards.

The department contend that the Act is framed in sufficiently wide terms to authorise what they say is lawful.

Their contention, or that which they were willing to accept as their contention during argument, was that the words 'pregnancy is terminated by a registered medical practitioner' means 'pregnancy is terminated by treatment of a registered medical practitioner in accordance with recognised medical practice'. But, with all respect, this is not construction: it is rewriting. And, moreover, it does not achieve its objective. I could perhaps agree that a reference to treatment could fairly be held to be implied; no doubt treatment is necessary. But I do not see that this alone carries the matter any further: it must still be treatment by the registered medical practitioner. The additional words, on the other hand, greatly extend the enactment, and it is they which are supposed to introduce nurse participation. But I cannot see that they do this. For a nurse to engage in abortifacient acts cannot, when first undertaken, be in accordance with recognised practice, when it is the legality of the practice that is in question. Nor can the recognised practice (if such there is, though the agreed statements do not say so) by which nurses connect up drips to supply glucose or other life-giving or preserving substances cover connecting up drips etc giving substances designed to destroy life, for that is what they are. The added words may well cover the provision of swabs, bandages or the handing up of instruments; that would only be common sense. They cannot be used as cover for a dimensional extension of the Act.

The argument for the department is carried even further than this, for it is said that the words 'when a pregnancy is terminated by a registered medical practitioner' mean 'when treatment for the termination of pregnancy is carried out by a registered medical practitioner'. This is said to be necessary in order to cover the supposed cases where the treatment is unsuccessful, or where there is no pregnancy at all. The latter hypothesis I regard as fanciful; the former, if it was Parliament's contemplation at all in 1967 (for failures under post-1967 methods are not in point), cannot be covered by any reasonable reading of the words. Termination is one thing; attempted and unsuccessful termination wholly another. I cannot be persuaded to embark on a radical reconstruction of the Act by reference to a fanciful hypothesis or an improbable casus omissus.

It is significant, as Lord Denning MR has pointed out, that recognised language exists and has been used, when it is desired that something shall be done by doctors with nurse participation. This takes the form 'by a registered medical practitioner or by a person acting in accordance with the directions of any such practitioner'. This language has been used in four Acts of Parliament (listed by Lord Denning MR), three of them prior to the 1967 Act, all concerned with the administration of substances, drugs or medicines which may have an impact on the human body. It has not been used, surely deliberately, in the present Act. We ought to assume that Parliament knew what it was doing when it omitted to use them.

In conclusion, I am of opinion that the development of prostaglandin induction methods invites, and indeed merits, the attention of Parliament. It has justly given rise to perplexity in the nursing profession. I doubt whether this will be allayed when it is seen that a majority of the judges who have considered the problem share their views. On this appeal I agree with the judgments in the Court of Appeal that an extension of the 1967 Act so as to include all persons, including nurses, involved in the administration of prostaglandin is not something which ought to, or can, be effected by judicial decision. I would dismiss the appeal.

LORD DIPLOCK. My Lords, this appeal arises out of a difference of opinion between the Royal College of Nursing of the United Kingdom and the Department of Health and Social Security about the true construction of the Abortion Act 1967, and, in particular, whether it renders lawful the part played by hospital nurses in the treatment for terminating pregnancies by a method known as medical induction. This comparatively modern method, which was unknown as a means of bringing about an abortion at the time of the passing of the Act, has come into increasing use for terminating pregnancies in the second trimester (ie between the 12th and 24th weeks), when it presents less risk to the patient than those methods more exclusively surgical in character that were formerly employed. The treatment takes considerably longer than the purely surgical methods; the average duration is 18 hours with a maximum of 30 hours and the part played by nurses in the treatment is of greater importance as well as longer than when a purely surgical method is employed.

The Abortion Act 1967 which it falls to this House to construe is described in its long title as 'An Act to amend and clarify the law relating to termination of pregnancy by registered medical practitioners'. The legalisation of abortion, at any rate in circumstances in which the termination of the pregnancy is not essential in order to save the mother's life, is a subject on which strong moral and religious convictions are held; and these convictions straddle the normal party political lines. That, no doubt, is why the Act, which incorporates a 'conscience clause' that I shall be quoting later, started its parliamentary life as a private member's Bill and, maybe for that reason, it lacks that style and consistency of draftsmanship both internal to the Act itself and in relation to other statutes which one would expect to find in legislation that had its origin in the office of parliamentary counsel.

Whatever may be the technical imperfections of its draftsmanship, however, its purpose in my view becomes clear if one starts by considering what was the state of the law relating to abortion before the passing of the Act, what was the mischief that required amendment, and in what respects was the existing law unclear.

The Abortion Act 1967 applies to England and to Scotland; but your Lordships are not concerned with Scotland in the instant case. In England the 'law relating to abortion' which it was the purpose of the Act to amend and clarify, is defined in s 6 of the Act itself as meaning 'sections 58 and 59 of the Offences against the Person Act 1861'. The relevant section, which it is desirable to set out verbatim, is s 58. (Section 59 deals with supplying abortifacients and instruments for use in unlawful abortions.) Section 58 provides:

> 'Every Woman, being with Child, who, with Intent to procure her own Miscarriage, shall unlawfully administer to herself any Poison or other noxious Thing, or shall unlawfully use any Instrument or other Means whatsoever with the like Intent, and whosoever, with Intent to procure the Miscarriage of any Woman, whether she be or be not with Child, shall unlawfully administer to her or cause to be taken by her any Poison or other noxious Thing, or shall unlawfully use any Instrument or other Means whatsoever with the like Intent, shall be guilty of Felony, and being convicted thereof shall be liable to be kept in Penal Servitude for Life.'

An offence under the section is committed whether the woman was in fact pregnant or not, and, if pregnant, whether or not the attempt to terminate it was in fact successful. The section on the face of it draws no distinction between terminations of pregnancies carried out on the advice of medically-qualified gynaecologists or obstetricians and those 'back-street abortions' that figured so commonly in the calendars of assizes in the days when I was trying crime; but the requirement that in order to constitute the offence the abortifacient must be administered or the instrument used 'unlawfully', indicated that there might be circumstances in which it would be lawful to bring about an abortion.

It had long been generally accepted that abortion was lawful where it was necessary to save the pregnant woman's life; but what circumstances, if any, short of this, legitimised termination of a pregnancy does not appear to have attracted judicial notice until, in 1938, the matter was put to a sagaciously selected test by Mr Aleck Bourne, a well-known obstetrical surgeon at St Mary's Hospital, London. He there performed an abortion on a 14-year old girl who was seven weeks pregnant as a consequence of being the victim of a particularly brutal rape. He invited prosecution for having done so. The evidence at his trial was that if the girl had been allowed to bear the child she would 'be likely to have become a mental wreck'.

The summing up by Macnaghten J in *R v Bourne* [1938] 3 All ER 615, [1939] 1 KB 687 resulted in an acquittal. So the correctness of his statement of the law did not undergo examination by any higher authority. It still remained in 1967 the only judicial pronouncement on the subject. No disrespect is intended to that eminent judge and former head of my old chambers if I say that his reputation is founded more on his sturdy common sense than on his lucidity of legal exposition. Certainly his summing up, directed as it was to the highly exceptional facts of the particular case, left plenty of loose ends and ample scope for clarification. For instance, his primary ruling was that the onus lay on the Crown to satisfy the jury that the defendant did not procure the miscarriage of the woman in good faith for the purpose only of 'preserving her life' but this requirement he suggested to the jury they were entitled to regard as satisfied if the probable consequence of the continuance of the pregnancy would be to 'make the woman a physical or mental wreck', a vivid phrase borrowed from one of the witnesses but unfortunately lacking in precision. The learned judge would appear to have regarded the defence as confined to registered medical practitioners, and there is a passage in his summing up which suggests that it is available only where the doctor's opinion as to the probable dire consequences of the continuance of the pregnancy was not only held bona fide but also based on reasonable grounds and adequate knowledge, an objective test which it would be for the jury to determine whether, on the evidence adduced before them, it was satisfied or not.

Such then was the unsatisfactory and uncertain state of the law that the Abortion Act 1967 was intended to amend and clarify. What the Act sets out to do is to provide an exhaustive statement of the circumstances in which treatment for the termination of a pregnancy may be carried out lawfully. That the statement, which is contained in s 1, is intended to be exhaustive appears from s 5(2):

> 'For the purposes of the law relating to abortion, anything done with intent to procure the miscarriage of a woman is unlawfully done unless authorised by section 1 of this Act.'

This sets aside the interpretation placed by Macnaghten J in *R v Bourne* on the word 'unlawfully' in ss 58 and 59 of the Offences against the Person Act 1861.

The 'conscience clause' which I have already mentioned is also worth citing before coming to the crucial provisions of s 1. It is s 4(1) and so far as is relevant for the present purposes it reads:

> '. . . no person shall be under any duty, whether by contract or by any statutory or other legal requirement, to participate in any treatment authorised by this Act to which he has a conscientious objection . . .'

Section 1 itself needs to be set out in extenso:

> '(1) Subject to the provisions of this section, a person shall not be guilty of an offence under the law relating to abortion when a pregnancy is terminated by a registered medical practitioner if two registered medical practitioners are of the opinion, formed in good faith—(*a*) that the continuance of the pregnancy would involve risk to the life of the pregnant woman, or of injury to the physical or mental health of the pregnant woman or any existing children of her family, greater than if the pregnancy were terminated; or (*b*) that there is a substantial risk that if the child were born it would suffer from such physical or mental abnormalities as to be seriously handicapped.
>
> '(2) In determining whether the continuance of a pregnancy would involve such risk of injury to health as is mentioned in paragraph (*a*) of subsection (1) of this section, account may be taken of the pregnant woman's actual or reasonably foreseeable environment.
>
> '(3) Except as provided by subsection (4) of this section, any treatment for the termination of pregnancy must be carried out in a hospital vested in the Minister of Health or the Secretary of State under the National Health Service Acts, or in a place for the time being approved for the purposes of this section by the said Minister or the Secretary of State.
>
> '(4) Subsection (3) of this section, and so much of subsection (1) as relates to the opinion, of two registered medical practitioners, shall not apply to the termination of a pregnancy by a registered medical practitioner in a case where he is of the opinion, formed in good faith, that the termination is immediately necessary to save the life or to prevent grave permanent injury to the physical or mental health of the pregnant woman.'

My Lords, the wording and structure of the section are far from elegant, but the policy of the Act, it seems to me, is clear. There are two aspects to it: the first is to broaden the grounds on which abortions may be lawfully obtained; the second is to ensure that the abortion is carried out with all proper skill and in hygienic conditions. Subsection (1) which deals with the termination of pregnancies other than in cases of dire emergency consists of a conditional sentence of which a protasis, which is a condition precedent to be satisfied in order to make the abortion lawful at all, is stated last: 'if two registered medical practitioners are of the opinion etc'. It is this part of the subsection which defines the circumstances which qualify a woman to have pregnancy terminated lawfully. They are much broader than the circumstances stated in *R v Bourne*; and, since they depend on comparative risks of injury to the physical or mental health of the pregnant woman or existing children of the family and to the possibility of abnormalities in the yet unborn child, they are matters of expert medical opinion. The Act leaves them to be decided not by the jury on expert evidence after the event, as in *R v Bourne*, but in advance by two registered medical practitioners whose opinion as to the existence of the required circumstances, if formed in good faith and duly certified under s 2(a), renders treatment for the termination of the pregnancy lawful if it is carried out in accordance with the requirements of the Act.

I have spoken of the requirements of the Act as to the way in which 'treatment for the termination of the pregnancy' is to be carried out rather than using the word 'termination' or 'terminated' by itself, for the draftsman appears to use the longer and the shorter expressions indiscriminately, as is shown by a comparison between sub-ss (1) and (3) of s 1, and by the reference in the conscience clause to 'treatment authorised by this Act'. Furthermore, if 'termination' or 'terminated' meant only the event of miscarriage and not the whole treatment undertaken with that object in mind, lack of success, which apparently occurs in 1% to 2% of cases, would make all who had taken part in the unsuccessful treatment guilty of an offence under s 58 or s 59 of the Offences against the Person Act 1861. This cannot have been the intention of Parliament.

The requirement of the Act as to the way in which the treatment is to be carried out, which in my view throws most light on the second aspect of its policy and the true construction of the phrase in sub-s (1) of s 1 which lies at the root of the dispute between the parties to this appeal, is the requirement in sub-s (3) that, except in cases of dire emergency, the treatment must be carried out in a national health service hospital (or private clinic specifically approved for that purpose by the minister). It is in my view evident that, in providing that treatment for termination of pregnancies should take place in ordinary hospitals Parliament contemplated that (conscientious objections apart) like other hospital treatment, it would be undertaken as a team effort in which, acting on the instructions of the doctor in charge of the treatment, junior doctors, nurses, para-medical and other members of the hospital staff would each do those things forming part of the whole treatment which it would be in accordance with accepted medical practice to entrust to a member of the staff possessed of their respective qualifications and experience.

Subsection (1) although it is expressed to apply only 'when a pregnancy is terminated by a registered medical practitioner' (the subordinate clause that although introduced by 'when' is another protasis and has caused the differences of judical opinion in the instant case) also appears to contemplate treatment that is in the nature of a team effort and to extend its protection to all those who play a part in it. The exoneration from guilt is not confined to the registered medical practitioner by whom a pregnancy is terminated, it extends to any person who takes part in the treatment for its termination.

What limitation on this exoneration is imposed by the qualifying phrase, 'when a pregnancy is terminated by a registered medical practitioner'? In my opinion, in the context of the Act, what it requires is that a registered medical practitioner, whom I will refer to as a doctor, should accept responsibility for all stages of the treatment for the termination of the pregnancy. The particular method to be used should be decided by the doctor in charge of the treatment for termination of the pregnancy; he should carry out any physical acts, forming part of the treatment, that in accordance with accepted medical practice are done only by qualified medical practitioners, and should give specific instructions as to the carrying out of such parts of the treatment as in accordance with accepted medical practice are carried out by nurses or other members of the hospital staff without medical qualifications. To each of them, the doctor, or his substitute, should be available to be consulted or called on for assistance from beginning to end of the treatment. In other words, the doctor need not do everything with his own hands; the requirements of the subsection are satisfied when the treatment for termination of a pregnancy is one prescribed by a registered medical practitioner carried out in accordance with his directions and of which a registered medical practitioner remains in charge throughout.

My noble and learned friend Lord Wilberforce has described the successive steps taken in the treatment for termination of pregnancies in the third trimester by medical induction; and the parts played by registered medical practitioners and nurses respectively in the carrying out of the treatment. This treatment satisfies the interpretation that I have placed on the requirements of s 1 of the Act. I would accordingly allow the appeal and restore the declaration made by Woolf J.

LORD EDMUND-DAVIES. My Lords, this House is presently concerned with the task of interpreting the Abortion Act 1967, and of applying the interpretation to the termination of pregnancy by a certain type of medical induction. It is well known that the Act was the outcome of a private member's Bill dealing with a highly controversial topic and, as enacted, it is the product of considerable compromise between violently opposed and emotionally charged views. In its preamble it is described as an Act 'to amend and clarify the law relating to termination of pregnancy by registered medical practitioners', and, far from simply enlarging the existing abortion facilities, in the true spirit of compromise it both relaxed and restricted the existing law.

Before turning to the 1967 Act, reference must be made to the still-extant s 58 of the Offences against the Person Act 1861, which provides as follows:

> 'Every Woman, being with Child, who, with Intent to procure her own Miscarriage, shall unlawfully administer to herself any Poison or other noxious Thing, or shall unlawfully use any Instrument or other Means whatsoever with the like Intent, and whosoever, with Intent to procure the Miscarriage of any Woman, whether she be or be not with Child, shall unlawfully administer to her or cause to be taken by her any Poison or other noxious Thing, or shall unlawfully use any Instrument or other Means whatsoever with the like Intent . . . shall be liable to [imprisonment] for Life.'

Section 1 of the Abortion Act 1967 is in these terms:

> '(1) Subject to the provisions of this section, a person shall not be guilty of an offence under the law relating to abortion when a pregnancy is terminated by a registered medical practitioner if two registered medical practitioners are of the opinion, formed in good faith—(a) that the continuance of the pregnancy would involve risk to the life of the pregnant woman, or of injury to the physical or mental health of the pregnant woman or any existing children of her family, greater than if the pregnancy were terminated; or (b) that there is a substantial risk that if the child were born it would suffer from such physical or mental abnormalities as to be seriously handicapped.
>
> '(2) In determining whether the continuance of a pregnancy would involve such risk of injury to health as is mentioned in paragraph (a) of subsection (1) of this section, account may be taken of the pregnant woman's actual or reasonably foreseeable environment.
>
> '(3) Except as provided by subsection (4) of this section, any treatment for the termination of pregnancy must be carried out in a hospital vested in the Minister of Health or the Secretary of State under the National Health Service Acts, or in a place for the time being approved for the purposes of this section by the said Minister or the Secretary of State.

'(4) Subsection (3) of this section, and so much of subsection (1) as relates to the opinion of two registered medical practitioners, shall not apply to the termination of a pregnancy by a registered medical practitioner in a case where he is of the opinion, formed in good faith, that the termination is immediately necessary to save the life or to prevent grave permanent injury to the physical or mental health of the pregnant woman.'

Although no reference to an act done 'for the purpose only of preserving the life of the mother' appears in the 1861 Act, it does appear in the Infant Life (Preservation) Act 1929, s 1. And in *R v Bourne* [1938] 3 All ER 615, [1939] 1 KB 687 Macnaghten J expressed the view that it represented the common law and should be read into the earlier Act by reason of the inclusion of the adverb 'unlawfully' in s 58. In that case a surgeon had aborted a girl who had been shockingly raped and, although there was no immediate danger to her life, he claimed that she would have become a physical and mental wreck had her pregnancy been allowed to continue. Directing the jury on a charge of contravening s 58, the learned judge said of 'preserving the life of the mother' that the words—

'ought to be construed in a reasonable sense, and, if the doctor is of opinion, on reasonable grounds and with adequate knowledge, that the probable consequence of the continuance of the pregnancy will be to make the woman a physical or mental wreck, the jury are quite entitled to take the view that the doctor, who, in those circumstances, and in that honest belief, operates, is operating for the purpose of preserving the life of the woman.'

(See [1938] 3 All ER 615 at 619, [1939] 1 KB 687 at 693–694.)

Following the acquittal in that case, the courts did not closely scrutinise the evidence of danger to life itself: see, for example, *R v Newton and Stungo* [1958] Crim LR 469 where, on a s 58 charge of unlawfully using an instrument, Ashworth J directed the jury that—

'"Such use of an instrument is unlawful unless the use is made in good faith for the purpose of preserving the life *or health* of the woman." When I say health I mean not only her physical health but also her mental health.'

My Lords, such was the law and practice when the Abortion Act reached the statute book in 1967, s 6 thereof providing that the phrase 'the law relating to abortion' used in ss 1(1) and 5(2) thereof means 'sections 58 and 59 of the Offences against the Person Act 1861, and any rule of law relating to the procurement of abortion'. And s 5(2) itself provided:

'For the purposes of the law relating to abortion, anything done with intent to procure the miscarriage of a woman is unlawfully done unless authorised by section 1 of this Act.'

Details of the termination of pregnancy by administering prostaglandin are the subject of a helpful agreed statement prepared by the parties to this litigation. This has been examined in the speech of my noble and learned friend Lord Wilberforce, and it is sufficient for me to say that the Royal College of Nursing, while adopting a neutral role, were and remain deeply disturbed as to the legality of the marked degree of participation by nurses in the challenged method of induction and therefore sought clarification and guidance from the court. They must ruefully regard such judicial illumination as has hitherto been vouchsafed them, Woolf J pronouncing 'without any doubt at all' that the prostaglandin procedure is permissible within the terms of s 1 of the 1967 Act, while the Court of Appeal unanimously held that it is not, Lord Denning MR declaring emphatically that 'the continuous act of administering prostaglandin from the moment it is started until the unborn child is expelled from the mother's body . . . must be done by the doctor personally. It is not sufficient that it is done by a nurse when he is not present.' (See p 557, ante.)

My Lords, I have already commented that it would be quite wrong to regard the 1967 Act as wholly permissive in character, for it both restricted and amplified the existing abortion law. It amplified 'the law relating to abortion' as declared in R v Bourne by extending it in s 1(1)(a) to cases where—

'the continuance of the pregnancy would involve risk to the . . . physical or mental health of . . . any existing children of [the pregnant woman's] family, greater than if the pregnancy were terminated . . .'

and in s 1(1)(b) by including the case of—

'substantial risk that if the *child* were born it would suffer from such physical or mental abnormalities as to be seriously handicapped.'

On the other hand, the Act also restricted the *Bourne* law in several ways. The pregnancy must now be terminated 'by a registered medical practitioner', and this even if, in the words of s 1(4), '. . . the termination is immediately necessary to save the life or to prevent grave permanent injury to the physical or mental health of the pregnant woman', whereas *Bourne* imposed no such restriction in the cases predicated, and a qualified doctor who was not a registered medical practitioner could have invoked the decision in that case. And, save in those circumstances of urgency, abortive treatment is required under the Act to be carried out in such premises as are designated in ss 1(3) and 3. Again, in the forefront is the requirement in s 1(1) of the opinion of two doctors that the risks indicated in para (a) or para (b) are involved if pregnancy were allowed to go full term. And a further practical (though not legal) restriction was imposed by the requirement under s 2 that the—

'registered medical practitioner who terminated a pregnancy [must] give notice of the termination and such other information relating to the termination as may be . . . prescribed.'

My Lords, the opening words of s 1(1) are clear and simple, clear to understand and simple to apply to the only abortive methods professionally accepted in 1967 when the Act was passed. Save in grave emergency, only a qualified doctor or surgeon could then lawfully perform the orthodox surgical acts, and the statute could have had no other person in mind. Then should s 1 be interpreted differently now that abortive methods undreamt of in 1967 have since been discovered and become widely applied? The answer must be that its simple words must not be distorted in order to bring under the statutory umbrella medical procedures to which they cannot properly be applied, however desirable such an extension may be thought to be. The extra-amniotic procedure first reported in 1971 has already been described by my noble and learned friend Lord Wilberforce, and it is sufficient for my present purpose to quote merely the final paragraph of the 'Agreed statement as to clinical background':

'It will be appreciated that in the medical induction process the causative factor in inducing the labour and hence the termination of pregnancy is the effect of the administration of prostaglandin and/or oxytocin and not any mechanical effect from the insertion of the catheter or cannula. In that the nurse does, on the instructions of the doctor, commence or augment the flow of prostaglandin or oxytocin, and even sometimes effect the connection between the already inserted catheter and the prostin pump and the already intravenous cannula and the oxytocin infusion, her role in the process does include acts which have, and are intended to have, an abortifacient effect. Such acts are, however, always carried out in accordance with the specific instructions of the registered medical practitioner.'

In my judgment, it is quite impossible to regard an abortion resulting from such procedure as one 'terminated by a registered medical practitioner', for the acts indispensable to termination are in many such cases performed not by the doctor but by the nurses over a long period of hours after the doctor last saw the pregnant woman.

And, despite the claims of the Solicitor General that he sought simply to give the statutory words 'their plain and ordinary meaning', he substantially departed from that approach by submitting that they should be read as meaning 'terminated by treatment for the termination of pregnancy carried out by a registered medical practitioner in accordance with recognised medical practice'. My Lords, this is redrafting with a vengeance. And, even were it permissible, it would still remain to consider what *part* the doctor played in the treatment, in order to ensure that it was not so remote from the termination as to make it impossible to say in any realistic sense that it was he who terminated the pregnancy. I am in respectful agreement with Brightman LJ, who said of the extra-amniotic procedure (see pp 559–560, ante):

> '... it would be a misuse of language ... to describe such a treatment for termination of a pregnancy as "carried out by" a registered medical practitioner, however detailed and precise the written instructions given by the registered medical practitioner to the nurse ... The true analysis is that the doctor *has provided the nurse with the means* to terminate the pregnancy, not that the doctor has terminated the pregnancy.' (Brightman LJ's emphasis.)

It is true that the word 'treatment' is to be found in several places in the Act, and that the phrase 'treatment of the termination of pregnancy' appears both in s 1(3) and in s 3(1), but both are significantly different from the language of s 1(1). And, had Parliament been minded to legislate on the lines which the appellants submit was its aim, Lord Denning MR demonstrated by reference to several earlier statutes in the medical field that the legislature had ready to hand suitable words which would have rendered unnecessary any such expansive interpretation as that favoured in the present instance by the Solicitor General.

My Lords, at the end of the day the appellants were driven to rely on a submission that, were s 1(1) given its literal meaning, such absurd consequences would follow that a liberal construction is unavoidable if the 1967 Act is to serve a useful purpose. In the foreground was the submission that, were a termination of pregnancy embarked on when (as it turned out) the woman was not pregnant, the Act would afford no defence to a doctor prosecuted under the 1861 Act. And it was secondly urged that he would be equally defenceless even where he personally treated a pregnant woman throughout if, for some reason, the procedure was interrupted and the pregnancy not terminated. I have respectfully to say that in my judgment it is these objections which are themselves absurd. Lawful termination under the Act predicates the personal services of a doctor operating in s 1(3) premises and armed with the opinion of two medical practitioners. But where termination is nevertheless not achieved the appellants invite this House to contemplate the doctor and his nursing staff being prosecuted under s 58 of the 1861 Act, the charge being, of course, not the unlawful termination of pregnancy (for ex hypothesi there was *no* termination) but one of unlawfully administering a noxious thing or unlawfully using an instrument with intent to procure miscarriage. And on *that* charge unlawfulness has still to be established and the prosecution would assuredly fail. For the circumstances predicated themselves establish the absence of any mens rea in instituting the abortive treatment, and its initial lawfulness could not be rendered unlawful either by the discovery that the woman was not in fact pregnant or by non-completion of the abortive treatment. Were it otherwise, the unavoidable conclusion is that doctors and nurses could in such cases be convicted of what in essence would be the extraordinary crime of attempting to do a *lawful* act.

My Lords, it was after drafting the foregoing that I happened on the following passage in Smith and Hogan's Criminal Law (4th Edn, 1978, p 346) which I now gratefully adopt, for it could not be more apposite:

> '... the legalisation of an abortion must include the steps which are taken towards it. Are we really to say that these are criminal until the operation is complete, when they are retrospectively authorised, or alternatively that they are lawful until the

operation is discontinued or the woman is discovered not to be pregnant when, retrospectively, they become unlawful? When the conditions of the Act are otherwise satisfied, it is submitted that [the doctor] is not unlawfully administering, etc., and that this is so whether the pregnancy be actually terminated or not.'

I am in this way fortified in my conclusion that the 'absurdities' on which the Solicitor General relies are in reality non-existent and that there is no reason for not giving the specific words of s 1 of the 1967 Act their plain and ordinary meaning. Doing just that, the prostaglandin treatment presently adopted requires the nursing staff to participate unlawfully in procedures necessitating their personally performing over a period of several hours a series of acts calculated to bring about a termination of pregnancy. This they cannot lawfully do, and in my judgment the Royal College of Nursing were entitled to a declaration in those terms.

My Lords, I express no view regarding this result, save that I believe it to be inevitable on the facts of the case, and this despite my awareness that several thousand extra-amniotic terminations are now performed annually. If it is sought to render such medical induction lawful, the task must be performed by Parliament. But under the present law it is a registered medical practitioner who must terminate pregnancy. I would therefore affirm the unanimous view of the Court of Appeal and dismiss this appeal.

LORD KEITH OF KINKEL. My Lords, this appeal is concerned with the question whether s 1(1) of the Abortion Act 1967 applies, so as to relieve the participants from criminal liability, to the procedures normally followed in operating a modern technique for inducing abortion by medical means.

The technique, which has been evolved and become common practice over the past ten years for the purpose of terminating pregnancy during the third trimester, is considered in medical circles to involve less risk to the patient than does surgical intervention. The details of the procedure have been fully described in the judgments of the courts below. Its main feature is the introduction via a catheter into the interspace between the amniotic sac and the wall of the uterus of an abortifacient drug called prostaglandin. The purpose of this is to induce uterine contractions which in most cases, but not in all, result in the expulsion of the fetus after a period of between 18 and 30 hours. The process is assisted by the introduction into the blood stream, via a cannula inserted in a vein, of another drug called oxytocin. Responsibility for deciding on and putting the procedure into operation rests with a registered medical practitioner who himself inserts the catheter and the cannula. The attachment of the catheter and the cannula to a supply of prostaglandin and of oxytocin respectively and the initiation and regulation of the flow of these drugs are carried out by a nurse under the written instructions of the doctor, who is not normally present at those stages. He or a colleague is, however, available on call throughout.

Section 1(1) of the 1967 Act can operate to relieve a person from guilt of an offence under the law relating to abortion only 'when a pregnancy is terminated by a registered medical practitioner'. Certain other conditions must also be satisfied, but no question about these arises in the present case. The sole issue is whether the words I have quoted cover the situation where abortion has been brought about as a result of the procedure under consideration.

The argument for the Royal College of Nursing is, in essence, that the words of the subsection do not apply because the pregnancy has not been terminated by any registered medical practitioner but by the nurse who did the act or acts which directly resulted in the administration to the pregnant woman of the abortifacient drugs.

In my opinion this argument involves placing an unduly restricted and unintended meaning on the words 'when a pregnancy is terminated'. It seems to me that these words, in their context, are not referring to the mere physical occurrence of termination. The sidenote to s 1 is 'Medical termination of pregnancy'. 'Termination of pregnancy' is an expression commonly used, perhaps rather more by medical people than by laymen, to describe in neutral and unemotive terms the bringing about of an abortion. So used, it is capable of covering the whole process designed to lead to that result, and in my view it does so in the present context. Other provisions of the Act make it clear that termination of pregnancy is envisaged as being a process of treatment. Section 1(3) provides that, subject to an exception for cases of emergency, 'treatment for the termination of pregnancy' must be carried out in a national health service hospital or a place for the time being approved by the minister. There are similar references to treatment for the termination of pregnancy in s 3, which governs the application of the Act to visiting forces. Then by s 4(1) it is provided that no person shall be under any duty 'to participate in any treatment authorised by this Act to which he has a conscientious objection'. This appears clearly to recognise that what is authorised by s 1(1) in relation to the termination of pregnancy is a process of treatment leading to that result. Section 5(2) is also of some importance. It provides:

> 'For the purposes of the law relating to abortion, anything done with intent to procure the miscarriage of a woman is unlawfully done unless authorised by section 1 of this Act.'

This indicates a contemplation that a wide range of acts done when a pregnancy is terminated under the given conditions are authorised by s 1, and leads to the inference that, since all that s 1 in terms authorises is the termination of pregnancy by a registered medical practitioner, all such acts must be embraced in the termination.

Given that the termination of pregnancy under contemplation in s 1(1) includes the whole process of treatment involved therein, it remains to consider whether, on the facts of this case, the termination can properly be regarded as being 'by a registered medical practitioner'. In my opinion this question is to be answered affirmatively. The doctor has responsibility for the whole process and is in charge of it throughout. It is he who decides that it is to be carried out. He personally performs essential parts of it which are such as to necessitate the application of his particular skill. The nurse's actions are done under his direct written instructions. In the circumstances I find it impossible to hold that the doctor's role is other than that of a principal, and I think he would be very surprised to hear that the nurse was the principal and he himself only an accessory. It is true that it is the nurse's action which leads directly to the introduction of abortifacient drugs into the system of the patient, but that action is done in a ministerial capacity and on the doctor's orders. Even if it were right to regard the nurse as a principal, it seems to me inevitable that the doctor should also be so regarded. If both the doctor and the nurse were principals, the provisions of the subsection would be still satisfied, because the pregnancy would have been terminated by the doctor notwithstanding that it had also been terminated by the nurse.

I therefore conclude that termination of pregnancy by means of the procedures under consideration is authorised by the terms of s 1(1). This conclusion is the more satisfactory as it appears to me to be fully in accordance with that part of the policy and purpose of the Act which was directed to securing that socially acceptable abortions should be carried out under the safest conditions attainable. One may also feel some relief that it is unnecessary to reach a decision involving that the very large numbers of medical practitioners and others who have participated in the relevant procedures over several years past should now be revealed as guilty of criminal offences.

My Lords, for these reasons I would allow the appeal, and restore the declaration granted by Woolf J.

LORD ROSKILL. My Lords, the long title of the Abortion Act 1967 is 'An Act to amend and clarify the law relating to the termination of pregnancy by registered medical practitioners'. The Royal College of Nursing accepted before your Lordships' House that the 1967 Act had a social purpose, namely the making of abortions available more freely and without infringement of the criminal law but subject always to the conditions of that Act being satisfied. But Parliament sought to achieve that admitted social purpose not as in the case of some social reforms by expressly creating some positive entitlement on the part of members of the public to that which the statute sought to achieve but by enacting in s 1(1) that 'a person' (not, be it noted, simply 'a registered medical practitioner') should 'not be guilty of an offence under the law relating to abortion' provided that certain other conditions were satisfied. 'The law relating to abortion' was defined in s 6 as meaning 'sections 58 and 59 of the Offences against the Person Act 1861, and any rule of law relating to the procurement of abortion'. Thus the scheme of the 1967 Act was to exempt from the sanctions of the criminal law imposed principally by the 1861 Act on those who carried out or attempted to carry out abortions those, but only those, who carried them out in a manner which satisfied all the requirements of the 1967 Act.

My Lords, the question which now requires determination by your Lordships' House arises because of the development by the medical profession of the termination of pregnancy by the extra-amniotic process, a process not developed or indeed in use when the 1967 Act became law. The details of the extra-amniotic process and its development will be found in the 'Agreed statement as to clinical background' which the parties conveniently made available to the courts below and in the agreed addition to that statement which was further agreed by the parties for the purposes of the instant appeal.

In his judgment in the Court of Appeal Brightman LJ analysed the successive steps in the case of extra-amniotic medical induction for the termination of pregnancies under nine steps and on the basis of what was called 'maximum nurse participation' in that process and further detailed under each of those nine steps those which required action by the doctor and those which required action only by the nurse (see pp 558–559 ante). I gratefully adopt, without repetition, what Brightman LJ there states. It will be observed that of those nine steps the doctor is only positively involved in performing two, the first and the fourth. The remainder are all performed by the nurse. The first step in which the doctor is personally involved is the insertion of the catheter into the womb. The fourth is the insertion of the cannula into the vein but no fluid is then passed by the doctor through the cannula. Thereafter every positive step is taken by the nurse up to and including the ninth step which occurs when the nurse discontinues the treatment either because the fetus has been discharged or because the allotted period has elapsed and the operation has failed. But it must be emphasised that every step taken by the nurse will be in accordance with the instructions of the doctor and those will be written instructions in all important respects. Though the insertion of the catheter into the womb by the doctor can have an abortifacient effect, the intention of the entirety of the process is that the abortion shall be achieved by the administration of the fluids by the nurse.

On those facts, which I have summarised (they will be found more fully detailed in the judgments of the courts below) the crucial issue is whether 'a pregnancy is terminated by a registered medical practitioner' assuming, as of course I do for present purposes, that the other prerequisites of s 1(1) of the 1967 Act are also satisfied. If a narrow meaning is given to the phrase I have just quoted, then it is the nurse and not the doctor who terminates the pregnancy. If that be right the doctor and the nurse are each guilty of a separate offence against the 1861 Act, the nurse because she is carrying out an abortion when she is not a doctor and the doctor because he is attempting to carry out an abortion when he engages in the first step which is not authorised by the 1967 Act. In addition, he is aiding and abetting the nurse's offence and both, and maybe others as well, are guilty of conspiracy to infringe the 1861 Act. This is the position which the Royal College of Nursing feared might arise and which led them to institute the present proceedings on behalf of the nursing profession in order that the question whether or not their profession are, in these circumstances, entitled to the protection of the 1967 Act might be finally determined. If the construction placed on the 1967 Act by the majority of the Court of Appeal (Lord Denning MR and Sir George Baker) is correct, then the College's fears are indeed well founded.

The department, on the other hand, contend for a wider construction of the 1967 Act. It was this wider construction which found favour both with Woolf J and with Brightman LJ. It was this view of the law for which the department had contended,

under legal advice, in a letter dated 25th February 1980, the circulation of which led to
the institution of the present proceedings. The difference of view between Woolf J and
Brightman LJ arose only on the facts since Brightman LJ felt that the actual termination
of the pregnancy by the nurse could not legitimately be described as 'termination by a
registered medical practitioner'. Brightman LJ summarised his view by saying that 'the
doctor has provided the nurse with the means to terminate the pregnancy, not that the
doctor has terminated the pregnancy' (see p 560, ante).

Counsel for the Royal College of Nursing did not shrink from the anomalies which
would necessarily flow from the acceptance of his submission and the construction
adopted by the majority of the Court of Appeal. There was, he said, only a limited
qualification engrafted on an otherwise unchanged criminal law and in 1967 Parliament
had legislated by reference to the surgical techniques of abortion as they then were and
not for other techniques of abortion as they might subsequently be evolved. Pressed to
say whether a new method must not be adopted which involved less risk to the patient,
he replied that any such new method would only be lawful if the doctor were present
throughout, a view which would seemingly make unrealistic demands on medical
manpower since no one suggested that each of the seven steps taken by the nurse, to
which I have already referred, was not well within the capacity of someone possessed of
the qualifications and experience which such a nurse would necessarily possess.

My Lords, I read and reread the 1967 Act to see if I can discern in its provisions any
consistent pattern in the use of the phrase 'a pregnancy is terminated' or 'termination of
a pregnancy' on the one hand and 'treatment for the termination of a pregnancy' on the
other hand. One finds the former phrase in s 1(1) and (1)(a), the latter in s 1(3), the
former in ss 1(4) and s 2(1)(b) and the latter in s 3(1)(a) and (c). Most important to my
mind is s 4, which is the conscientious objection section. This section in two places refers
to 'participate in treatment' in the context of conscientious objection. If one construes s 4
in conjunction with s 1(1), as surely one should do in order to determine to what it is that
conscientious objection is permitted, it seems to me that s 4 strongly supports the wider
construction of s 1(1). It was suggested that acceptance of the department's submission
involved rewriting that subsection so as to add words which are not to be found in the
language of the subsection. My Lords, with great respect to that submission, I do not
agree. If one construes the words 'when a pregnancy is terminated by a registered
medical practitioner' in s 1(1) as embracing the case where the 'treatment for the
termination of a pregnancy is carried out under the control of a doctor in accordance
with ordinary current medical practice' I think one is reading 'termination of pregnancy'
and 'treatment for termination of pregnancy' as virtually synonymous and as I think
Parliament must have intended they should be read. Such a construction avoids a
number of anomalies as, for example, where there is no pregnancy or where the extra-
amniotic process fails to achieve its objective within the normal limits of time set for its
operation. This is, I think, the view which appealed to Woolf J and to Brightman LJ and
I find myself in respectful agreement with that view. But with respect I am unable to
share Brightman LJ's view on the facts. I think that the successive steps taken by a nurse
in carrying out the extra-amniotic process are fully protected provided that the entirety
of the treatment for the termination of the pregnancy and her participation in it is at all
times under the control of the doctor even though the doctor is not present throughout
the entirety of the treatment.

My Lords, I have reached this conclusion simply as a matter of the construction of the
1967 Act. But, as I have already pointed out, Parliament has achieved whatever reforms
the 1967 Act did achieve by engrafting qualifications on the criminal law principally as
enacted in the 1861 Act. If the Royal College of Nursing's contentions and the views of
the majority of the Court of Appeal are correct and one envisages a doctor and a nurse on
trial on indictment for offences or attempted offences against the 1861 Act, the trial
judge would be bound at least to tell the jury that if they found the facts as Brightman
LJ described them in his judgment they might find it difficult to see what verdicts other
than verdicts of guilty they could properly return even though such a trial judge might
properly shrink from telling them that it was positively their duty in those circumstances

to convict. Either direction would, I apprehend, be given with reluctance and acted on, if at all, with dismay.

My Lords, it was common ground that if the appeal succeeded the proper declaration was that granted to the appellants by Woolf J. Since in my opinion the appeal should succeed it follows that I would allow the appeal and grant the same declaration as was granted by that learned judge.

Appeal allowed. Declaration granted by Woolf J restored.

Solicitors: *Treasury Solicitor*; *M J Scrivenger* (for the Royal College of Nursing).

Mary Rose Plummer   Barrister.

Gammell v Wilson and others
Furness and another v B & S Massey Ltd

HOUSE OF LORDS

LORD DIPLOCK, LORD EDMUND-DAVIES, LORD FRASER OF TULLYBELTON, LORD RUSSELL OF KILLOWEN AND LORD SCARMAN

18th, 19th, 24th NOVEMBER 1980, 5th FEBRUARY 1981

Damages – Personal injuries – Action for benefit of deceased's estate – Whether damages recoverable in respect of loss of earnings in lost years – Basis on which damages if recoverable to be assessed – Law Reform (Miscellaneous Provisions) Act 1934, s 1(2)(c).

The plaintiffs in two separate actions were the parents of two young men who had been killed in accidents as the result of the negligence of the respective defendants. Both deceased died intestate and the plaintiffs were therefore the administrators of their estates. In both actions the plaintiffs claimed damages against the defendants under (i) the Fatal Accidents Act 1976 (or in the second action, the Fatal Accidents Acts 1846 to 1959) on behalf of themselves as dependants and (ii) the Law Reform (Miscellaneous Provisions) Act 1934 on behalf of the deceased's estate.

In the first case, the plaintiff's 15-year old son was killed in a road accident. He had started working and had a career planned. The defendants admitted liability and the only issue was the quantum of damages. For the purpose of the 1976 Act, the trial judge assessed the dependencies of the plaintiff and his wife at £250 and £1,750 respectively and, on the claim under the 1934 Act, awarded the plaintiff damages totalling £9,335, which included £1,750 for loss of expectation of life, and £6,656 for the son's loss of future earnings during the years of life lost to him because of the defendants' negligence ('the lost years'), on the basis that the son would have earned £416 a year net after deduction of living expenses to which the judge applied a multiplier of 16 years. An appeal by the defendants against the award under the 1934 Act was dismissed by the Court of Appeal ([1980] 2 All ER 557). The defendants appealed to the House of Lords.

In the second case, the plaintiffs' 22-year old son was killed in the course of his employment. The defendants, his employers, admitted liability subject to contributory negligence of 10%. For the purposes of the fatal accident claim the trial judge assessed the dependencies of the plaintiffs at £2,028 and, on the claim under the 1934 Act, awarded damages which included £17,275 (less 10%) for loss of earnings during the lost years. The defendants appealed to the House of Lords.

In each case, because the award to the estate under the 1934 Act exceeded that under the Fatal Accidents Acts, no award was made in respect of the fatal accident claim, in accordance with the rule that in assessing loss of dependency under the Fatal Accidents Acts the court was required to take into account any benefit accruing to a dependant from the deceased's estate. At the hearing of the appeals the respective defendants contended that in a claim under the 1934 Act a deceased's estate was not entitled to recover damages for the deceased's loss of earnings during the lost years because the cause of action for such earnings was a 'gain to the estate' while the loss of the earnings was a 'loss to the estate' and that therefore, in accordance with the requirement of s 1(2)(c)[a] of the 1934 Act that damages under the Act were to be 'calculated without reference to any loss or gain to [the] estate consequent on [the deceased's] death', such damages were to be ignored in the assessment of damages awarded to the estate. The defendants further contended that in any event, even if such damages could be awarded under the 1934 Act, the amounts awarded were excessive.

Held – The appeals would be dismissed for the following reasons—

(1) On the true construction of s 1(2)(c) of the 1934 Act the restriction on an estate recovering or being deprived of a 'loss or gain to [the] estate' consequent on a person's death applied only to a loss or gain directly consequent on the death and not to a loss or gain resulting from a right to recover damages which vested in the deceased immediately before his death and which then passed to the beneficiaries of his estate, whether they were his dependants or not. That construction, coupled with the principle that a cause of action for loss of earnings in the lost years vested in the deceased before he died (and in the case of instantaneous death vested in him immediately before he died) meant that the estate was not precluded by s 1(2)(c) from recovering damages for the deceased's loss of earnings during the lost years in a claim under the 1934 Act. Accordingly, even though it produced a result which was neither sensible nor just, the House was constrained to hold that the plaintiffs were entitled to the damages awarded for the lost years despite the fact that those damages far exceeded the amount to which they were entitled under the 1976 Act as dependants (see p 581 c, p 584 d f g i, p 586 g h, p 588 c to j, p 590 f to j, p 592 c d f g and p 593 b c, post); *Rose v Ford* [1937] 3 All ER 359 and *Pickett v British Rail Engineering Ltd* [1979] 1 All ER 774 applied.

(2) On the principle that damages for loss of earnings in the lost years should be fair compensation for the loss suffered by the deceased in his lifetime, there was no room for conventional award. Accordingly, the court was required to make the best estimate it could on the evidence available, which was what the trial judge in each case had done. The awards would therefore not be disturbed (see p 581 c to f, p587 j, p 588 b to e h j, p 590 h j, p 593 d to g and p 594 f h, post).

Per Curiam. The law in England and Wales relating to damages for death recoverable by the estate of a deceased is neither sensible nor just, but it is so well established that change can only be brought about by legislation, a good model for which would be the Damages (Scotland) Act 1976 (see p 583 h, p 587 d to f, p 588 d h, p 590 g, p 592 b c and p 595 d e, post).

Decision of the Court of Appeal in *Gammell v Wilson* [1980] 2 All ER 557 affirmed.

Notes

For damages for loss of future earnings under the Law Reform (Miscellaneous Provisions) Act 1934, s 1, see 12 Halsbury's Laws (4th Edn) para 1154.

For the Law Reform (Miscellaneous Provisions) Act 1934, s 1, see 13 Halsbury's Statutes (3rd Edn) 115.

Cases referred to in opinions

Benham v Gambling [1941] 1 All ER 7, [1941] AC 157, 110 LJKB 49, 164 LT 290, HL, 36(1) Digest (Reissue) 383, 1544.

Flint v Lovell [1935] 1 KB 354, [1934] All ER Rep 200, 104 LJKB 199, 152 LT 231, CA, 36(1) Digest (Reissue) 317, 1276.

Kandalla v British Airways Board (formerly British European Airways Corpn) [1980] 1 All ER 341, [1980] 2 WLR 730.

Oliver v Ashman [1961] 3 All ER 323, [1962] 2 QB 210, [1961] 3 WLR 669, CA, 36(1) Digest (Reissue) 313, 1267.

Pickett v British Rail Engineering Ltd [1979] 1 All ER 774, [1980] AC 136, [1978] 3 WLR 955, [1979] 1 Lloyd's Rep 519, HL, Digest (Cont Vol E) 459, 1314b.

---

a   Section 1(2), so far as material, is set out at p 585 a, post

Quirk v Thomas [1916] 1 KB 516, 85 LJKB 519, 114 LT 308, CA, 17 Digest (Reissue) 122, 220.

Rose v Ford [1937] 3 All ER 359, [1937] AC 826, 106 LJKB 576, 157 LT 174, HL, 36(1) Digest (Reissue) 382, *1530*.

Appeals

Gammell v Wilson and another

By a writ issued on 18th October 1977 the plaintiff, James Gammell, brought an action against the defendants, Reginald Wilson and Swift & Co Ltd, claiming damages under the Fatal Accidents Act 1976 and the Law Reform (Miscellaneous Provisions) Act 1934, in respect of the death of his son, Edward James Gammell, on 3rd September 1976 in a road accident caused by the first defendant's negligence for which the second defendants were vicariously liable. The defendants admitted liability but disputed the quantum of damages. On 27th July 1979 Mr B A Hytner QC, sitting as a deputy judge of the High Court, gave judgment for the plaintiff under the 1934 Act for damages in the sum of £9,335·04 on the basis of £6,656 damages for loss of future earnings, £584·04 special damages plus £40 interest thereon, and £1,750 damages for loss of expectation of life plus £305 interest thereon. The judge made no award under the 1976 Act on the basis that the claim under that Act was eliminated by the amount of the award under the 1934 Act. The defendants appealed against the amount awarded under the 1934 Act, on the grounds (1) that the judge was wrong in law and misdirected himself in awarding any sum by way of damages under the Act in respect of lost earnings during the years of life lost to the son because of the defendants' negligence ('the lost years'), (2) alternatively, that the sum awarded for the lost years by the judge was excessive, (3) that the sum awarded in respect of a memorial or gravestone for the son was excessive, and (4) that the sum awarded in respect of loss of expectation of life was excessive. On 1st April 1980 the Court of Appeal (Brandon LJ and Sir David Cairns, Megaw LJ dissenting) ([1980] 2 All ER 557, [1980] 3 WLR 591) allowed the appeal in respect of damages for loss of expectation of life and reduced the element of damages to £1,250, but (Megaw LJ concurring) dismissed the appeal in respect of the other two elements of the award. As the total award under the 1934 Act was in excess of the sums recoverable under the 1976 Act no award was made under that Act, and accordingly the plaintiff was awarded a sum of £8,745 damages (the interest payable on the general damages being reduced to £215). The defendants appealed to the House of Lords with the leave of the Court of Appeal. The appeal was confined to the award of £6,656 in respect of the loss of earnings during the lost years. The facts are set out in the opinion of Lord Scarman.

Furness and another v B & S Massey Ltd

By a writ issued on 15th April 1977 and statement of claim amended pursuant to an order of Tudor Evans J on 14th November 1979 the plaintiffs, Marian Furness and Edward Furness, as administrators of the estate of their son, Kevin Furness deceased, brought an action against the defendants, B & S Massey Ltd, claiming damages under the Fatal Accidents Acts 1846 to 1959 and the Law Reform (Miscellaneous Provisions) Act 1934 in respect of their son's death on 31st August 1976 in an accident at the premises of the defendants during the course of his employment with them caused by the defendants' negligence and breach of statutory duty. Liability was not in issue. The parties agreed that the deceased was 10% to blame for the accident. On 20th December 1979 Tudor Evans J gave judgment for the plaintiffs for damages under the 1934 Act in the sum of £1,350 for loss of expectation of life, £273 agreed funeral expenses, and £15,547 for loss of earnings which the deceased would have earned during the years lost to him by his premature death ('the lost years'), those sums being 90% of the value of their claims. As the total award under the 1934 Act was far in excess of the sum recoverable under the Fatal Accidents Acts, ie £1,825, no award was made under those Acts, the damages thereunder being absorbed by the award of damages under the 1934 Act. The judge therefore awarded the plaintiffs a total sum of £17,170 plus £924 interest. The plaintiffs were awarded damages in respect of the lost years because the judge considered that he was required to do so by virtue of the decision of the House of Lords in *Pickett v British Rail Engineering Ltd* [1979] 1 All ER 774, [1980] AC 136. Pursuant to a certificate granted by the judge under s 12 of the Administration of Justice Act 1969 and with the leave of the House granted on 5th March 1980 the defendants appealed directly to the House of Lords against the award of damages in respect of the lost years. Since the appeal raised the same point as that considered in *Gammell v Wilson* the appeals were heard together. The facts are set out in the opinion of Lord Scarman.

Piers Ashworth QC and *William Gage* for Mr Wilson and Swift & Co Ltd.
Lionel Swift QC and *Christopher Sumner* for Mr Gammell.
Piers Ashworth QC and *J Rowe* for B & S Massey Ltd.
Richard Clegg QC and *Janet Smith* for Mr and Mrs Furness.

Their Lordships took time for consideration.

5th February. The following opinions were delivered.

LORD DIPLOCK. My Lords, I understand your Lordships to be at one in holding that both of these appeals must be dismissed. I am of the same opinion, reluctantly, because I do not think that this outcome is either sensible or just.

On the answer to the question of construction of s 1(2)(c) of the Law Reform (Miscellaneous Provisions) Act 1934, I find myself in agreement with your Lordships' acceptance of the interpretation placed on it by the majority of the Court of Appeal in *Gammell v Wilson* [1980] 2 All ER 557, [1980] 3 WLR 591. On the question whether this House would be justified in interfering with the damages awarded by the trial judge in either of the cases I agree with your Lordships that we should not. Where the deceased is as young as in these two cases (15 and 22 years respectively) the law requires the judge to indulge in what can be no better than the merest speculation about what might have happened to the deceased during a normal working lifespan if he had not been prematurely killed. Although I think that the award in *Furness v B & S Massey Ltd* was so high as to approach the borderline at which an appellate court would be justified in interfering even in so speculative an assessment, I nevertheless consider that it falls short of crossing it.

In England today the law about damages for death has been developed partly by Parliament through legislation now consolidated in the Fatal Accidents Act 1976, and partly by judicial decisions arrived at on a case to case basis. This has its dangers, for the facts presented by what turns out to be a landmark case may make the legal principle therein stated appear beguilingly simple of application. But this may be falsified by subsequent experience. In the result the law of damages for death has, in my view, reached a state for which I can see no social, moral or logical justification. The first judicial step down the slippery slope that led into a morass from which I think that only Parliament can now extricate us was taken by the Court of Appeal in *Flint v Lovell* [1935] 1 KB 354, [1934] All ER Rep 200, where it was held that a wealthy and previously healthy living plaintiff aged 69 years whose lifespan was likely to be shortened by some five or six years by the injury he had sustained could recover under the head of 'loss of expectation of life' an unidentified part of a total sum of £4,000 awarded as general damages. To draw up in hard cash a balance sheet in which the joys and pleasures of life which the victim would have experienced during 'the lost years' are weighed against its suffering and sorrows led to such divergences in assessment as between one case and another that ultimately this House in *Benham v Gambling* [1941] 1 All ER 7, [1941] AC 157 felt constrained to hold that this element in damages for personal injuries in all but the most exceptional cases should be limited to a moderate arbitrary sum to be awarded regardless of the particular circumstances of the plaintiff or the number of years that it was estimated he had lost. Whatever logic might have justified awarding damages on a compensatory basis for loss of expectation of life, it vanished with the decision in *Benham v Gambling*.

It might have been supposed that an award of damages for loss of expectation of life took into account on the credit side the satisfaction of earning money by one's work. In *Oliver v Ashman* [1961] 3 All ER 323, [1962] 2 QB 210 the Court of Appeal drew this conclusion and held that earnings lost during the lost years were not recoverable as an additional item of damages. So far as living plaintiffs were concerned, it looked by 1968 as if the law as to the assessment of damages to be awarded for 'the lost years', after a temporary aberration between *Flint v Lovell* and *Benham v Gambling*, presented no insuperable difficulties, however lacking in strict logical justification it might be.

And so the law for living plaintiffs as to the recovery of damages for the lost years remained until the decision of this House in *Pickett v British Rail Engineering Ltd* [1979] 1 All ER 774, [1980] AC 136. If the plaintiff died after he had recovered judgment his cause of action merged in the judgment and the judgment debt became an asset which formed part of his estate; but, so long as the old rule actio personalis moritur cum persona applied, if he died from his injuries before he had brought his action and recovered judgment, his own cause of action lapsed and where he left a widow or dependent relatives who had looked to him for their support it was replaced by a statutory cause of action for their benefit under the Fatal Accidents Acts 1846 to 1908. The damages recoverable under these Acts were purely compensatory and were assessed according to the jury's estimate of the economic loss which the dependants had suffered and would continue to suffer in consequence of the withdrawal of the deceased's support. It was not until the passing of the Law Reform (Miscellaneous Provisions) Act 1934 that the personal representative of the deceased had a cause of action for loss to the deceased's estate resulting from his premature death.

Section 1 of the 1934 Act by abolishing the maxim actio personalis moritur cum persona enabled damages suffered by the deceased before his death under the three heads, loss of earnings, pain and suffering and loss of expectation of life, to be recovered for the benefit of his estate in an action brought after his death. The Act did not deprive the deceased's dependants of their statutory cause of action under the Fatal Accidents Acts, but in the usual case, in which it was the deceased's dependants who succeeded beneficially to his estate, this seldom involved any duplication of the damages recoverable, since the financial benefit accruing to the dependants from the estate fell to be deducted from the compensation for loss of dependency awarded to them under the Fatal Accidents Acts. Since damages for loss of expectation of life had become a moderate conventional sum and pain and suffering and loss of earnings were suffered only up to the time of death, it was not often that, in cases of fatal injuries, the damages under the 1934 Act exceeded the amount of the dependency.

The amount by which the estate of the deceased was increased by damages awarded under the 1934 Act would not, however, be deductible from the damages awarded under the Fatal Accidents Acts, except in the case of beneficiaries under the deceased's estate who were dependent relatives. This seems to have occurred very seldom, and where it did the sums involved in bequests to non-dependent beneficiaries were relatively small. There would, however, be an anomaly that would offend one's sense of justice, if a living plaintiff, after having obtained a judgment in his favour which took no account of what he would have earned in the lost years, died shortly after from the injuries which he had sustained. His cause of action would have merged in the judgment and, although I know of no direct authority on the point, it has always been regarded as too clear to brook of argument that the merger of this cause of action carries with it the merger of any cause of action by his dependants under the Fatal Accidents Acts, however great and prolonged their dependency might have been expected to be. At best his dependants could be compensated for their loss of his future support to the extent to which his estate had been augmented by the damages awarded to him; and they would be deprived even of this compensation unless they were the beneficial successors to his estate. The anomaly is not one that was likely to be brought to the attention of the court directly as a matter of decision; but it did arise in *Pickett v British Rail Engineering Ltd*, because the deceased before his death had obtained a judgment in his lifetime for damages for personal injuries which, in accordance with the rule in *Oliver v Ashman*, did not include any

compensation for his potential earnings during the lost years. An appeal launched in his
lifetime against this judgment was carried on after his death by his dependent widow as
administratrix of his estate. The deceased in that case was aged 53 at the date of the
trial. But for the injury (an industrial disease) in respect of which he sued he could have
expected to continue working for another 12 years until the normal retirement age of
65. As a result of the injury his expectation of life was estimated to be reduced to one
year, an estimate which events proved to have been accurate. So he lost 11 years during
when he would have been earning good wages out of which he would have maintained
his wife.

If the deceased had died before judgment in his action had been entered his widow
would have had her cause of action under the Fatal Accidents Acts. This would have
enabled her to recover the value of the provision that he would have made for her needs
out of his earnings during those 11 'lost years'. But because he died after the judgment
his dependent widow was deprived of that cause of action, and the general damages for
pain and suffering recoverable on behalf of his estate, of which she was the sole
beneficiary, fell considerably short of the sum that she would have been likely to recover
under the Fatal Accidents Acts as the amount of the dependency if that cause of action
had remained open to her.

Here was an obvious injustice which this House remedied by overruling *Oliver v
Ashman* and holding that a living plaintiff could recover damages for loss of earnings
during the lost years, but that in assessing the measure of such damages there should be
deducted from the total earnings the amount that he would have spent out of those
earnings on his own living expenses and pleasures since these would represent an expense
that would be saved in consequence of his death. In the case of a married man of middle
age and of a settled pattern of life, which was the case of Mr Pickett, the effect of this
deduction is to leave a net figure which represents the amount which he would have
spent on providing for his wife and any other dependants, together with any savings that
he might have set aside out of his income. If one ignores the savings element, which in
most cases would be likely to be small, this net figure is substantially the same as the
damages that would have been recoverable by the widow under the Fatal Accidents Acts:
it represents the dependency. So, in the particular case of Mr Pickett's widow the result
was to do substantial justice.

My Lords, if the only victims of fatal accidents were middle-aged married men in
steady employment living their lives according to a well-settled pattern that would have
been unlikely to change if they had lived on uninjured, the assessment of damages for
loss of earnings during the lost years may not involve what can only be matters of purest
speculation. But, as the instant appeals demonstrate and so do other unreported cases
which have been drawn to the attention of this House, in cases where there is no such
settled pattern (and this must be so in a high proportion of cases of fatal injuries) the
judge is faced with a task that is so purely one of guesswork that it is not susceptible of
solution by the judicial process. Guesses by different judges are likely to differ widely,
yet no one can say that one is right and another wrong.

Where Parliament has intervened by passing the Fatal Accidents Acts, the law relating
to damages for death recoverable by dependants is sensible and just with the possible
exception of the case of widows who have remarried or become engaged to do so by the
time the action is heard. I join with your Lordships in thinking that it is too late for
anything short of legislation to bring the like sense and justice to the law relating to
damages for death recoverable by the estate of the deceased.

LORD EDMUND-DAVIES. My Lords, in *Pickett v British Rail Engineering Ltd* [1979]
1 All ER 774, [1980] AC 136 this House found itself ineluctably driven to hold that an
injured plaintiff whose working life had been shortened as a result of the defendant's
negligence was entitled to be compensated for any loss of earnings during the period ('the
lost years') when, but for his injuries, he would have been likely to continue at work. In
these two appeals we are confronted by a situation different in an important respect from
that in *Pickett*. For, whereas there the plaintiff had instituted proceedings and actually

recovered judgment during his lifetime, in the present appeals the respective plaintiffs are administrators of the estates of deceased persons who were killed either instantaneously or very shortly after being involved in accidents attributable to the defendants' negligence.

The facts are summarised in the speech of my noble and learned friend Lord Scarman and I need not add to his narrative. In each case the plaintiffs are also the parents of the deceased (each of whom died intestate) and they sue (1) under the Fatal Accidents Act 1976 on behalf of themselves as dependants and (2) under the Law Reform (Miscellaneous Provisions) Act 1934 on behalf of the deceased's estate. No question arises as to the awards under the former, but, in relation to the 1934 Act awards for the 'lost years' of £6,656 in the *Gammell* case and £15,547 in the *Furness* case, two questions are raised by these appeals. (A) Does an action lie to recover such damages, seeing that the injured party died without having instituted legal proceedings? (B) If an action does lie, on what basis should damages for the 'lost years' be assessed? The submission in each of the two cases is that both points were incorrectly disposed of by the respective trial judges and by the majority of the Court of Appeal in *Gammell*. I turn to consider these questions.

(A) *Does the action lie?*

My Lords, subject to what must later be said about sub-s (2)(*c*) of s 1 of the Law Reform (Miscellaneous Provisions) Act 1934, in my judgment an affirmative answer to that question is obligatory in the light of the decisions of this House in *Rose v Ford* [1937] 3 All ER 359, [1937] AC 826 and *Pickett*. For it is impossible to distinguish in legal principle between a claim in respect of shortened expectation of life on the one hand and in respect of shortened expectation of *working* life on the other. And in *Rose v Ford* [1937] 3 All ER 359 at 365–366, [1937] AC 826 at 839 Lord Russell said:

> 'I am of the opinion that, if a person's expectation of life is curtailed, he is necessarily deprived of something of value, and that, if that loss to him is occasioned by the negligence of another, that other is liable to him in damages for the loss. That cause of action was vested in the deceased before and when she died, and, by virtue of the Act of 1934, it survives for the benefit of her estate. It is no new cause of action created by that Act; it is a cause of action existing independently of the Act, which by the Act is preserved from the extinction which the death of the deceased would otherwise have brought about.'

That passage must equally be applicable in its entirety to a claim in respect of the 'lost years' resulting from cutting short a person's *working* life, and, as Holroyd Pearce LJ said in *Oliver v Ashman* [1961] 3 All ER 323 at 330, [1962] 2 QB 210 at 227–228, it leaves 'no room for distinguishing between a claim brought by a living plaintiff and a claim brought on behalf of a dead plaintiff in respect of the loss of earnings during the years of which he has been deprived'. In an earlier passage ([1961] 3 All ER 323 at 329–330, [1962] 2 QB 210 at 227) Holroyd Pearce LJ recalled that in *Rose v Ford* [1937] 3 All ER 359 at 363, [1937] AC 826 at 835 Lord Atkin had rhetorically asked, 'Can the damages include a calculation of loss of income which the deceased would have received during normal expectation of life but would not have saved so as to increase his estate?', and commented: 'Those words seem by implication to suggest that he could at least claim such sums as he would have saved during the lost years.' This is in line with the view expressed by Lord Scarman in *Pickett* [1979] 1 All ER 774 at 798, [1980] AC 136 at 171 that, as to the lost years, '. . . a plaintiff (or his estate) should not recover more than that which would have remained at his disposal after meeting his living expenses'.

The decision in *Pickett* was carefully analysed by Megaw LJ in the course of his dissenting judgment in *Gammell*. I respectfully agree with him that there did not emerge therefrom 'in obiter dicta a clear consensus that the earnings of the lost years should equally be recoverable in a Law Reform Act claim as in a claim brought by the victim himself'. But the search for obiter dicta is in my judgment unnecessary, for the interaction of *Pickett* itself and s 1(1) of the 1934 Act surely leads to the inevitable conclusion that a claim for the lost years does lie in each of these two cases.

Indeed the appellants in both cases accept that this would be so were it not for the provision in s 1(2)(c) of the 1934 Act that—

> 'where the death . . . has been caused by the act or omission which gives rise to the cause of action, [the damages recoverable for the benefit of the estate of the victim] shall be calculated without reference to any loss or gain to his estate consequent on his death, except that a sum in respect of funeral expenses may be included.'

The appellants submit that this provision is fatal to the claim made in relation to the 'lost years' in each case. The contrary view was expressed in the *Furness* case by Tudor Evans J, who held that such cause of action was vested in the deceased the instant before he died and that the loss was accordingly consequent not on the death but on the tortious act of the wrongdoer. And the majority of the Court of Appeal reached a similar conclusion in *Gammell*.

My Lords, the general nature of the wording of s 1 of the 1934 Act is important, providing as it does ('subject to the provisions of this section') for the survival of *all* causes of action vested in the deceased. What follows by way of exception to the general rule should be restrictively interpreted, lest that generality be largely or completely nullified. It deals simply with the calculation of the damages exigible in relation to an established cause of action, and in *Rose v Ford* [1937] 3 All ER 359 at 363, [1937] AC 826 at 835 Lord Atkin said:

> 'I can see the possibility of discussion in the provision of sect. (2)(c) that the damages "shall be calculated without reference to any loss or gain to his estate consequent on his death". Plainly this does not mean that his estate is not to gain by the award of any damages at all, for this would be absurd.'

Lord Wright, referring specifically to s 1(2)(c), described it as 'especially significant because it particularises certain classes of losses and gains', and added ([1937] 3 All ER 359 at 368, [1937] AC 826 at 842):

> 'It presupposes that damages may, in general, be calculated where death has been caused by the wrong, but excludes from the calculation losses or gains to the estate consequent on the death. I need not examine the full scope of this proviso, which is not directly material in this appeal. Obvious instances of what are referred to are such items as, on the one side, insurance moneys falling due on death, and, on the other, annuities ceasing on death. These are irrelevant to the question of what damages can survive, because the dead man could neither have collected such gains nor experienced such losses. They are subsequent to, and only remotely, for present purposes, connected with, his death . . . The claim now in question is, by contrast, one for personal injuries suffered by the deceased girl while alive.'

And so, too, are the claims made under the 1934 Act in each of the two cases now being considered. Fully cognisant of s 1(2)(c), Lord Wright regarded it as having no impingement on the claim there being advanced.

But there has been some discussion over the years whether Lord Wright was correct in citing annuities ceasing on death as falling within s 1(2)(c), Megaw LJ, for example, commenting that such a loss '*would* have been an element in the damages recoverable by a plaintiff bringing an action on his own account, who was able to show a shortened expectation of life', and concluding that if Lord Wright's example was correctly chosen, '. . . it must, as I see it, follow that the loss of income in the lost years must also not be taken into account' (see [1980] 2 All ER 557 at 565, [1980] 3 WLR 591 at 600).

If this indeed be the logical conclusion, it must, in my judgment, be held that Lord Wright was erroneous in citing annuities ceasing on death as illustrating a 'loss' within s 1(2)(c). For, with the solitary exception of funeral expenses, the section creates *no* new cause of action and deals only with those vested in the deceased at the time of his death, and sub-s (2) provides that, even though such causes of action survive by virtue of sub-s (1), the quantum of damages otherwise recoverable thereunder are in certain instances to be reduced from those recoverable by a living plaintiff. It is an awkwardly phrased subsection, and para (c) in particular could have been more clearly expressed; it may have been drafted in a hurry, Acton J having given judgment in *Flint v Lovell* [1935] 1 KB 354, [1934] All ER Rep 200 on 13th May 1934, and the Act receiving the royal assent on 25th July. Paragraph (a) deals with exemplary damages, such as may be recovered by a living plaintiff to penalise outrageous conduct by a defendant and so rehabilitate the plaintiff's good name; but if the injured party has died there is no merit in penalising the defendant merely to increase the estate of the deceased. Paragraph (b) dealt with breach of promise of marriage, which could well result in loss of money spent in preparation for the marriage; and under s 1(1) this could have been recovered even though the death of the injured party had supervened. But, although, until the Law Reform (Miscellaneous Provisions) Act 1970, s 1 abolished the cause of action, exemplary damages could be recovered 'in respect of the personal injury to the plaintiff occasioned by the personal conduct of the defendant' (see *Quirk v Thomas* [1916] 1 KB 516 at 527 per Swinfen Eady LJ), the 1934 Act by sub-s (2)(b) in effect rendered such damages irrecoverable after the death of the injured party. Subsection (2)(c) is more complicated. But its effect, in my judgment, is that the fact that death has occurred as a result of the defendant's wrongful act is *not* to increase or reduce such damages as would have been recoverable by the plaintiff when alive. As Chapman helpfully commented (Statutes on the Law of Tort (1962, p 6)):

> '(i) If a person is killed as a result of negligent driving of a motor-car, it may happen that enormous damage is caused to his estate by reason of the fact that death duties become payable which would have been avoided had he survived for another month, a week, or day. The *loss* to the estate on that account is to be ignored. (ii) By reason of a person's death on a particular day there may be enormous benefit to his estate as a result of the operation of family settlements. The benefit to the estate on that account is to be ignored.'

But Megaw LJ, drawing what he regarded as an essential distinction between loss of earnings before death and after death, said ([1980] 2 All ER 557 at 566, [1980] 3 WLR 591 at 601):

> 'If the victim has survived for, say, six months or a year, but has died before action brought or before judgment in an action brought by him, any loss of earnings caused by his injuries up to the date of death is recoverable as a part of the damages in the Law Reform Act action. For they are a loss antecedent to, but in no way caused by, or "consequent on" his death. But the loss of earnings thereafter is consequent on his death. Hence it is excluded by s 1(2)(c).'

I respectfully disagree. Just as Lord Russell observed in *Rose v Ford* [1937] 3 All ER 359 at 365, [1937] AC 826 at 838 that damages for shortened expectation of life '... are not for loss to the estate consequent on the death, but for loss to a living person consequent on the wrongful act of the defendant', so also damages for cutting short a man's working life (the 'lost years') are in no sense 'consequent on the death'. Sir Noël Hutton QC has rightly observed that 'The relevance of the death is purely evidentiary as providing conclusive proof that the deceased's expectation of life has been curtailed ...' ((1961) 24 Mod LR at 25). Such, in effect, was the majority conclusion in the Court of Appeal, and I have respectfully to say that I find it the only acceptable conclusion.

There seems little room for doubt that inspiring and underlying the resistance to giving an affirmative answer to what I have labelled question (A) are considerations of policy. For example, it is claimed that, if compensation for the lost years are recovered by dependants in excess of their Fatal Accidents Acts claims, they will gain what Griffiths J somewhat derogatorily described in *Kandalla v British Airways Board* [1980] 1 All ER 341 at 349, [1980] 2 WLR 730 at 739 as a 'windfall', and added:

> 'The damages will, of course, almost always be paid by insurance companies, but the ability to pay such damages will have to be passed on to the general public through increased premiums; so it is the public who will be paying these extra

damages which appear to me to breach the underlying basis on which damages are
assessed, namely that they should be fair compensation for the loss sustained.'

But, my Lords, such 'windfalls' have not appeared inadvertently on the legal
landscape. On the contrary, the legislature had them clearly in contemplation when it
provided by s 1(5) of the 1934 Act that—

'The rights conferred by this Act for the benefit of the estates of deceased persons
shall be in addition to and not in derogation of any rights conferred on the
dependants of deceased persons by the Fatal Accidents Acts, 1846 to 1908 . . .'

It has further been objected that the deceased may by his testamentary disposition
have left his estate, wholly or in part, away from his dependants, with the result that, in
the words of Griffiths J ([1980] 1 All ER 341 at 349, [1980] 2 WLR 730 at 738)—

'Not only will the estate be able to recover the full value of the sums he spent on
his dependants, but the dependants will also be able to recover the like sum under
the Fatal Accidents Acts.'

It is in the light of such criticisms as these that the attention of this House was drawn
to the express provision in s 2(3) of the Damages (Scotland) Act 1976 that—

'There shall not be transmitted to the executor of a deceased person any right to
damages . . . (b) by way of compensation for patrimonial loss attributable to any
period after the deceased's death . . .'

But, despite the view expressed by Megaw LJ that in England and Wales such a provision
had been effectively anticipated by s 1(2)(c) of the 1934 Act and that 'legislation on the
point would not be necessary to achieve the desirable result that English and Scottish law
should conform in this respect', I have already indicated my own respectful view that the
law of this country remains different.

And, in relation to the complaint that the decisions of the Court of Appeal and Tudor
Evans J impose additional and unfair liability on the wrongdoer, it is just as well to recall
the anticipatory words of Lord Atkin many years ago in *Rose v Ford* [1937] 3 All ER 359
at 363, [1937] AC 826 at 835:

'I . . . see no difficulty as to the alleged duplication of damages under the Act of
1934 and the Fatal Accidents Acts. If those who benefit under the last-mentioned
Acts also benefit under the will or intestacy of the deceased personally, their damages
under those Acts will be affected. If they do not, there seems no reason why an
increase to the deceased's estate in which they take no share should affect the
measure of damages to which they are entitled under the Act.'

My Lords, I would answer question (A) in the affirmative.

(B). *On what basis should damages for the 'lost years' be assessed?*

My Lords, the assessment of compensation for the 'lost years' rests on no special basis
of its own and it proceeds on no peculiar principle. It may present unusual difficulties,
but the task itself is the ordinary one of arriving at a fair figure to compensate the estate
of the deceased for a loss of a particular kind sustained by him in his lifetime at the hands
of the defendant. But the appellants in *Gammell* submit that there was *no* evidence from
which Deputy Judge Hytner QC could have assessed and awarded any damages in respect
of the 'lost years', and that, whereas he made an award of £6,656 under that head, 'in the
absence of any cogent evidence of substantial savings the court can and should award no
more than a modest conventional sum'. Such material as was available to the learned
judge was admittedly meagre, but it was there to be weighed up. The amount of the
award consequently arrived at was unanimously upheld in the Court of Appeal, and in
my judgment it should not be interfered with by this House.

In the *Furness* case, it is objected that any damages awarded to the estate of a deceased
person for the lost years amount not to fair compensation but to a windfall, whether or

not the deceased leaves dependants. But castigation of 1934 Act damages as a 'windfall' is no justification for denying them in toto. More cogent is the further criticism that 'any assessment is at best speculative, usually pure guesswork, and where there is any basis for making a calculation such a basis is frequently unreal'. It is true that the task confronting Tudor Evans J was difficult, but, even so, there was available to him the sort of exiguous material which frequently has to be dealt with in the courts. And, if I may say so, in doing his valiant best he had the inestimable advantage of vast experience in coping with difficulties of the very kind that arose in *Furness*. On general principles, this House will interfere only where an assessment of damages is perverse or it appears from the amount awarded that it was arrived at on an incorrect principle. I take leave to doubt that I should have awarded the plaintiffs in *Furness* as high a sum as £15,547 for the 'lost years'. But here again I see no error in principle, and, while counselling moderation in assessing such claims so as to reflect the high degree of speculation inevitably involved, I am not prepared to hold that the award calls for adjustment.

My Lords, in the result I would dismiss the appeal in each of these cases.

LORD FRASER OF TULLYBELTON. My Lords, I have had the advantage of reading in draft the speeches prepared by my noble and learned friends Lord Diplock and Lord Scarman, and I agree with them. Under the existing legislation, and following the decision of this House in *Pickett v British Rail Engineering Ltd* [1979] 1 All ER 774, [1980] AC 136, there is, in my opinion, no escape from dismissing both these appeals, but, like Lord Diplock, I regard the result as neither sensible nor just.

It is, no doubt, just and sensible that, where the death of the family breadwinner is caused by the negligence of some other person, that person should be liable to compensate the deceased's dependants for the injury which they have suffered from the death. The main element of injury will normally be loss of support. Such compensation is provided for by the Fatal Accidents Act 1976. But it seems to me difficult to justify a law whereby the deceased's estate, which may pass to persons or institutions in no way dependent on him for support, can recover damages for loss of earnings, or other income, which he would probably have received during the 'lost years'. It is particularly difficult to justify the law in cases such as the present, in each of which the deceased was a young man with no established earning capacity or settled pattern of life. In such cases it is hardly possible to make a reasonable estimate of his probable earnings during the 'lost years' and it is, I think, quite impossible to take the further step of making a reasonable estimate of the free balance that would have been available above the cost of maintaining himself throughout the 'lost years', and the amount of that free balance is the relevant figure for calculating damages. The process of assessing damages in such cases is so extremely uncertain that it can hardly be dignified with the name of calculation: it is little more than speculation. Yet that is the process which the courts are obliged to carry out at present.

In my opinion, the unhappy state into which this part of the law of England has fallen can now only be corrected by legislation on lines similar to that recently enacted for Scotland, for much the same reason, in the Damages (Scotland) Act 1976: see ss 2(3)(b) and 9.

The amount of damages awarded in both these cases seems to me high, but having regard to the uncertain basis of assessment which I have mentioned I do not feel able to say that they proceed on any error of principle. I would therefore not interfere with them.

I would dismiss both appeals.

LORD RUSSELL OF KILLOWEN. My Lords, these appeals involve the next step after *Pickett v British Rail Engineering Ltd* [1979] 1 All ER 774, [1980] AC 136 in this House. In that case it was decided that when, as a result of a personal injury to X due to the fault of another, the term of the life of X was shortened X was entitled to claim in his damages compensation for financial benefits (in that case earnings) which would have come to him during the 'lost years', less what he might have been expected to spend on himself. I ventured to dissent for reasons which I gave briefly, being of opinion that if such an advance were to be made it were better for it to be done by legislation rather than by a judicial decision, one which was perhaps induced by consideration of the fact that, otherwise, dependants of X, he having pursued his claim to judgment, would not have a Fatal Accidents Act claim, which claim would have brought such lost future earnings into calculation. *Pickett* was not a case of survival on death of a cause of action, and the Law Reform (Miscellaneous Provisions) Act 1934 was not in point.

Misliking, as I did, the decision in *Pickett* and drawing as I did attention to possible repercussions beyond the question of earnings in the lost years, I did not then envisage the problems that would be raised by it under the 1934 Act.

In both these cases the death of X was caused by the wrongful act or omission of the defendant, substantially instantaneously. One was aged 15, the other 22. The personal representatives in each case sued, claiming damages on behalf of the estate for the wrong done to the deceased, and also under the Fatal Accidents Act on behalf of the dependants. In order to claim on behalf of the estate reliance had to be placed on the 1934 Act, which reversed the principle that a personal action did not survive the death of the injured person.

Section 1(1) of the 1934 Act provided that (subject to the provisions of s 1) on the death of X all causes of action vested in him shall survive for the benefit of his estate, but excluding causes of action for defamation or seduction etc, not now material. Subsection (2) deals with the damages recoverable for the benefit of the estate where a cause of action survives under sub-s (1) for the benefit of the estate. It is in the following terms:

'Where a cause of action survives as aforesaid for the benefit of the estate of a deceased person, the damages recoverable for the benefit of the estate of that person:—(a) shall not include any exemplary damages; (b) in the case of a breach of promise to marry shall be limited to such damage, if any, to the estate of that person as flows from the breach of promise to marry; (c) where the death of that person has been caused by the act or omission which gives rise to the cause of action, shall be calculated without reference to any loss or gain to his estate consequent on his death, except that a sum in respect of funeral expenses may be included.'

In each of these cases there was undoubtedly a cause of action against the wrongdoer vested in the deceased in his life, even though only momentarily prior to his death, and under sub-s (1) that cause of action survived for the benefit of his estate. His personal representatives could, prima facie, by standing in his shoes claim such damages as he, had he survived, could have claimed as flowing from the cause of action; and under the decision in *Pickett* part of those damages would fall to be assessed in respect of the financial disappointments involved in the 'lost years'. So the short point is whether sub-s (2)(c) excluded what might be labelled '*Pickett* damages' from a claim brought for the benefit of the deceased's estate.

The structure of sub-s (2) is to be noted. It deals with a case of a cause of action surviving for the benefit of a dead man's estate and affects in terms the damages recoverable for the benefit of that estate. The cause of action survives, but the quantum of damages is not under paras (a) and (b) to be the same as would have been recoverable by the deceased person pursuing to judgment on the cause of action in his lifetime. By para (a), if he would have been entitled to exemplary damages, such damages are not to be 'included' in the damages recoverable for the benefit of his estate. By para (b) (now repealed by the Law Reform (Miscellaneous Provisions) Act 1970, s 7 and Schedule) in a case of breach of promise to marry the damages recoverable for the benefit of the estate of the deceased person are limited to such damage (if any) to the estate of the deceased as flows from the breach of promise, and I would suppose this to be intended to limit the damages to net financial outlay by the plaintiff incurred on the faith of the promise but for which his (or her) estate would have been greater, and to exclude damages that might have been based on matters such as injured feelings.

Paragraph (c) is somewhat different in construction. It deals with a particular case when the death of X was caused by the wrong which constituted the relevant cause of action which under sub-s (1) survives for the benefit of the estate of X. In such case para (c) states how the damages recoverable for the benefit of the estate of X are to be calculated: they are to be 'calculated without reference to any loss or gain to his estate consequent on his death, except that a sum in respect of funeral expenses may be included'. What is involved in this phrase? What, so to speak, is it getting at? There is no indication to be got from paras (a) and (b); they have their own reasons, logical or not.

In para (c) we are dealing with a case in which a wrongdoing to X has not only harmed him but has even caused his death, in one sense the greatest harm that could be done to him. It is perhaps simple to say that two heads of damages normally involved (though I think regrettably) in death by a wrongdoing are excluded by para (c) from the calculation of damages, viz (i) damages for loss of expectation of life and (ii) damages in respect of financial benefits which would have accrued during the lost years leaving it for the estate to claim damages (in an appropriate case) for loss of earnings before death, expenses of treatment, pain and suffering, all of which would have, if recovered, swollen the estate, as would indeed damages under (i) and (ii) above if recovered in his life by X.

But the difficulty arises in two ways. (1) Why should the legislature have so tempered the wind to the wrongdoer albeit it has done so to some extent by paras (a) and (b); and (2) more importantly, it is not only loss but also gain to the estate consequent on the wrongfully induced death that is excluded from the calculation of damages. The impression is gained of balance sheet (perhaps rather a profit and loss account) being drawn up. What *gain* to the estate consequent on the death is in mind? The immediate example that springs to the mind is life insurance. There may be others which by the general law a wrongdoer cannot plead in reduction of the damages which he must pay. I find it impossible to think of any *gain* to the estate of X consequent on his death which could be set against the liability of the wrongdoer for his responsibility for the cause of action other than one under the general law.

This in my opinion throws a conclusive light on the reference, in the calculation, to loss consequent on the death. I accept the suggestion that it refers to liabilities of the estate which arise only because it is the estate of a deceased person under the general law.

Accordingly, I am of opinion that the damages recoverable for the benefit of the estates in both these cases include damages which he could have recovered if living in respect of the lost years. I would therefore dismiss these appeals.

My Lords, I regret these decisions. I think that the law has gone astray by excessive refinement of theory. I would welcome legislation which overruled in the future the results of the decision in *Pickett*, and its extension in cases such as the present, which since *Pickett* has led to almost grotesque embodiment of estimates, or rather guesses. That might be combined with legislation which in some way prevented respondents being barred from a Fatal Accidents Act claim by the fact that the deceased pursued his claim to judgment.

For good measure I may add that I do not favour a system which embodies a 'conventional' (or any) figure being awarded for loss of expectation of life.

So far as concerns quantum of damages in respect of the 'lost years' claims for the benefit of the estates, I am quite unable to assert that they were either right or wrong.

Accordingly I would dismiss both appeals.

LORD SCARMAN. My Lords, I also would dismiss these appeals.

In *Gammell v Wilson* [1980] 2 All ER 557, [1980] 3 WLR 591 the defendants appeal, with the leave of the Court of Appeal, from an order of the Court of Appeal dismissing their appeal from part of a judgment given by Mr B A Hytner QC sitting as a deputy judge of the High Court. In *Furness v Massey* the defendants appeal direct from part of a judgment given by Tudor Evans J. The judge granted his certificate under s 12(1) of the Administration of Justice Act 1969, and the House gave leave to appeal.

The two appeals were heard together, since they raise the same two questions of law. First, when the victim of an accident, for which the defendant is legally responsible, has died before action brought or judgment recovered, does the cause of action, which he would have had, if he had lived, for damages for the loss of earnings during 'the lost years', survive for the benefit of his estate? It is a question of construction of s 1(2)(c) of the Law Reform (Miscellaneous Provisions) Act 1934. Second, if it does, what is the correct approach in law to the assessment of such damages? The appellants in each appeal also contend that the assessment of the trial judge was in any event excessive. The third point will require separate consideration of the two cases.

The appeals are a natural, even an inevitable, consequence of the House's decision in *Pickett v British Rail Engineering Ltd* [1979] 1 All ER 774, [1980] AC 136. Ruling that a living plaintiff is entitled to such damages, the House was not called on in *Pickett's* case to construe s 1(2)(c) of the Law Reform Act. Nor was the House faced with any very difficult problem in the assessment of damages, for Mr Pickett was 53 years of age at the time of trial, a family man whose expectations for the future, had not his injuries supervened, were reasonably clear. But in these two appeals the facts are very different. In the *Gammell* case a boy, aged 15, was killed in a road accident, suit being brought by his father under the Fatal Accidents Act 1976 for his and his mother's benefit as dependants, and under the Law Reform (Miscellaneous Provisions) Act 1934 for the benefit of the boy's estate. In the *Furness* case a young man, aged 22, unmarried, was killed at work, suit being brought by his parents under the 1976 Act for their benefit as dependants and under the 1934 Act for his estate. In each case the deceased died intestate.

Section 1(2)(c) of the 1934 Act

The relevant provisions of s 1 of the 1934 Act are the following:

'(1) Subject to the provisions of this section, on the death of any person after the commencement of this Act all causes of action subsisting against or vested in him shall survive against, or, as the case may be, for the benefit of, his estate. Provided that this subsection shall not apply to causes of action for defamation or seduction or for inducing one spouse to leave or remain apart from the other or to claims under section one hundred and eighty-nine of the Supreme Court of Judicature (Consolidation) Act, 1925, for damages on the ground of adultery.

'(2) Where a cause of action survives as aforesaid for the benefit of the estate of a deceased person, the damages recoverable for the benefit of the estate of that person:—(a) shall not include any exemplary damages; (b) in the case of a breach of promise to marry shall be limited to such damage, if any, to the estate of that person as flows from the breach of promise to marry; (c) where the death of that person has been caused by the act or omission which gives rise to the cause of action, shall be calculated without reference to any loss or gain to his estate consequent on his death, except that a sum in respect of funeral expenses may be included ...

'(5) The rights conferred by this Act for the benefit of the estates of deceased persons shall be in addition to and not in derogation of any rights conferred on the dependants of deceased persons by the Fatal Accidents Acts, 1846 to 1908 ...'

(Section 1 has since been amended by the Law Reform (Miscellaneous Provisions) Act 1970, s 7 and Schedule.)

Subsection (5) has some general significance. It makes clear that the rights which under the Act survive for the benefit of the estate are additional to, not a substitution for, the rights conferred on dependants by the fatal accidents legislation. In dealing, therefore, with a 'law reform' claim, the court has no regard to what dependants can claim under the Fatal Accidents Act. The converse is, however, not true. In assessing the loss of a dependency under the fatal accidents legislation the courts have always had regard to the benefits accruing to the dependants from the estate of the deceased. In most fatal accident cases, the dependants will, of course, be the beneficiaries of the estate. In such cases there will be no 'double recovery', by which is meant no recovery both by the estate and the dependants of damages calculated by reference to the lost earnings of the lost years; for the dependants' claim will be reduced or extinguished (subject to certain exceptions) by the benefits they receive from the estate. But, if the deceased has made a will leaving his estate, or a substantial part of it, to other than his dependants, both the estate and the dependants will have a claim.

This element of advantage gained by beneficiaries of the estate who are not dependants of the deceased has been described by judges, and others, as a 'windfall'. It arises because the estate's claim is additional to, and not in derogation of, the rights of the dependants. If, which many believe, it is a mischief which should be removed from our law, legislation will be needed. A model is to hand in the Damages (Scotland) Act 1976, which recognises the right of a living pursuer to damages for the lost years but refuses it to the estate of one who has died before suing his claim to judgment: see ss 2(3) and 9.

Section 1(1) of the 1934 Act creates no cause of action, but provides only for the survival of an existing cause of action. I agree with your Lordships in thinking that in the light of *Pickett's* case it is not possible to sustain any view of the law other than that the cause of action for damages for the lost years vests in the deceased when he is injured, and, if he be killed instantaneously, immediately before his death. The reasoning of *Rose v Ford* [1937] 3 All ER 359, [1937] AC 826 is as applicable to a 'lost years' case as to the case of general damages for shortened expectation of life; and I respectfully adopt what my noble and learned friend Lord Edmund-Davies has said on the point.

Under s 1(1), therefore, the cause of action survives for the benefit of the estate unless sub-s (2) provides otherwise. Paragraphs (*a*) and (*b*) of the subsection do make irrecoverable by the estate certain categories of damage which a living plaintiff could recover. Paragraph (*c*) has a different purpose: it provides a method of calculating damages where the victim's death was itself caused by the act or omission which gave rise to the cause of action. No account is to be taken of 'any loss or gain to his estate' except for funeral expenses met out of the estate.

In the course of his closely argued dissenting judgment in *Gammell's* case Megaw LJ concluded that, as damages for the lost earnings of the lost years are in respect of a loss 'consequent on' the death, they are irrecoverable by the estate. His approach to s 1(2)(*c*) was that it must be interpreted as excluding from recovery by the estate damages which would have been recoverable by the deceased if he had not died. He interpreted para (*c*) as being comparable with paras (*a*) and (*b*).

The majority, Brandon LJ and Sir David Cairns, interpreted s 1(2)(*c*) in the opposite sense. 'Loss to his estate consequent on his death' was not, in their view, to be construed as including any loss in respect of which a right to recover damages was already vested in the deceased immediately before his death.

Such authority as there is supports the majority view. Some members of this House, albeit obiter, did consider the problem of s 1(2)(*c*) in *Rose v Ford*. Lord Atkin said of the subsection: 'Plainly this does not mean that his estate is not to gain by the award of any damages at all, for this would be absurd' (see [1937] 3 All ER 359 at 363, [1937] AC 826 at 835). Lord Wright, in the passage quoted by my noble and learned friend Lord Edmund-Davies, read the subsection as requiring to be excluded from the calculation only those items of loss or gain to the estate which the dead man, had he lived, could neither have experienced nor collected ([1937] 3 All ER 359 at 368, [1937] AC 826 at 842). His instance of a gain ('insurance moneys falling due on death') is a good illustration, even though his instance of a loss ('annuities ceasing on death') is not; for that loss, like the loss of the earnings of the lost years, is to be attributed to the years lost by reason of the injury sustained and is, therefore, part of the cause of action which vested in the deceased before his death. Nevertheless, there are losses to an estate consequent on death which could never arise as losses to the deceased during his lifetime. Brandon LJ, who listed some of them, also made the telling point that, were it not for the express exception in s 1(2)(*c*) itself, funeral expenses would be such a loss.

It may be, as Brandon LJ and Sir David Cairns suggested, that sub-s (2)(*c*) was introduced into s 1 ex abundanti cautela. Certainly, if construed as limited to gains or losses *to the estate* as distinct from gains or losses to the deceased which survive for the benefit of the estate, it is consistent with the principle declared in sub-s (1), viz that, subject to the section, 'all causes of action' shall survive. If Megaw LJ be correct in construing it as excluding losses suffered by the deceased when injured but arising after death, it would constitute a substantial erosion of the rights surviving for the benefit of his estate after his death. If there be two possible interpretations of sub-s (2)(c), I have no doubt that, the purpose of the section being to eliminate almost totally from the law the effect of the ancient rule actio personalis moritur cum persona, the correct interpretation is that which would tend to further, rather than to limit, that purpose. I would expect to find, as in paras (a) and (b), express limitations clearly formulated. But I do not think that, on a proper consideration of the language of s 1(2)(c), the choice arises. Its careful drafting so as to distinguish its effect from the purely exclusionary paras (a) and (b) of the subsection leaves no room for doubt. In my view, therefore, the words 'loss or gain to his estate consequent on his death' mean in the context of the section a loss or gain *to the estate* consequent on death and do not cover a loss or gain capable of being suffered or collected by the deceased before his death.

Assessment of the damages

The correct approach in law to the assessment of damages in these cases presents, my Lords, no difficulty, though the assessment itself often will. The principle must be that the damages should be fair compensation for the loss suffered by the deceased in his lifetime. The appellants in *Gammell's* case were disposed to argue, by analogy with damages for loss of expectation of life, that, in the absence of cogent evidence of loss, the award should be a modest conventional sum. There is no room for a 'conventional' award in a case of alleged loss of earnings of the lost years. The loss is pecuniary. As such, it must be shown, on the facts found, to be at least capable of being estimated. If sufficient facts are established to enable the court to avoid the fancies of speculation, even though not enabling it to reach mathematical certainty, the court must make the best estimate it can. In civil litigation it is the balance of probabilities which matters. In the case of a young child, the lost years of earning capacity will ordinarily be so distant that assessment is mere speculation. No estimate being possible, no award, not even a 'conventional' award, should ordinarily be made. Even so, there will be exceptions: a child television star, cut short in her prime at the age of five, might have a claim; it would depend on the evidence. A teenage boy or girl, however, as in *Gammell's* case may well be able to show either actual employment or real prospects, in either of which situation there will be an assessable claim. In the case of a young man, already in employment (as was young Mr Furness), one would expect to find evidence on which a fair estimate of loss can be made. A man, well-established in life, like Mr Pickett, will have no difficulty. But in all cases it is a matter of evidence and a reasonable estimate based on it.

The problem in these cases, which has troubled the judges since the decision in *Pickett's* case, has been the calculation of the annual loss before applying the mutiplier (ie the estimated number of lost working years accepted as reasonable in the case). My Lords, the principle has been settled by the speeches in this House in *Pickett's* case. The loss to the estate is what the deceased would have been likely to have available to save, spend or distribute after meeting the cost of his living at a standard which his job and career prospects at time of death would suggest he was reasonably likely to achieve. Subtle mathematical calculations, based as they must be on events or contingencies of a life which he will not live, are out of place; the judge must make the best estimate based on the known facts and his prospects at time of death. The principle was stated by Lord Wilberforce in *Pickett's* case [1979] 1 All ER 774 at 781–782, [1980] AC 136 at 150–151:

'The judgments, further, bring out an important ingredient, which I would accept, namely that the amount to be recovered in respect of earnings in the "lost" years should be after deduction of an estimated sum to represent the victim's probable living expenses during those years. I think that this is right because the basis, in principle, for recovery lies in the interest which he has in making provision for dependants and others, and this he would do out of his surplus. There is the additional merit of bringing awards under this head into line with what could be *a* recovered under the Fatal Accidents Acts.'

I turn now to consider whether there was error by the judge in the assessment of damages in either case. First, *Gammell's* case. The learned deputy judge directed himself correctly in law, quoting the relevant passages from the speeches in *Pickett's* case. It was urged that the factual basis, on which he proceeded, was too exiguous to enable a *b* reasonable assessment to be made. I do not agree. The boy was 15. His father is of the Romany blood, uneducated and illiterate. His mother is a well-educated woman who, as a witness, impressed the judge. She knew her boy and was confident he would make his way in the world. He never went to school, but his mother taught him his three Rs. At 14 (the year before he died) he began work. When he died, he was earning £20 a week from the sort of work he, with his Romany background, was well placed to find *c* (fruit picking, scrap dealing and road surfacing). He was saving up for a van in order to follow the career of an antique dealer (in the footsteps of an uncle). When he died, his future was not merely matter for speculation: he had made a start, was in work and had won the confidence of his sensible mother, who had herself educated him.

The judge took a multiplier of 16 for the lost years, a 'surplus' (on Lord Wilberforce's formula) of £8 per week, and assessed the value of the claim for lost earnings of the lost *d* years at £6,656. No exception can be taken to the multiplier. The £8 per week, however, was said to be a figure picked out of the sky. It was not. It was based on the circumstances known to the judge. I do not believe that a sensible parent (like his mother) would have rated his prospects as nil or as substantially lower than the judge did. The only question which the House has to consider is whether, on the facts found, it was an unreasonable estimate, ie so excessive as to justify its reduction by an appellate *e* court. For myself, I think it was a moderate and reasonable estimate; but, even if I considered it high, it is not so high as to justify the House's intervention.

The award of £6,656 is to be compared with the damages of £3,184 which the judge assessed as the value of his parents' dependency claim under the Fatal Accidents Act. Since he died intestate, they will receive the total damages of £9,090 (less expenses) awarded the estate, which will be more than sufficient to extinguish their Fatal Accidents *f* claim.

In *Furness's* case the learned judge assessed the total damages under the 1934 Act at £19,106 and awarded the estate 90% of the total (having found a degree of contributory negligence). He assessed the damages under the Fatal Accidents Acts at £2,028, to 90% of which the parents would have been entitled had not their claim been extinguished by the benefits they will get from the damages awarded to their son's estate.

He assessed damages for the lost years at £17,275. This is a high figure but it cannot *g* be said either that the judge erred in principle in reaching it or that it is so high that it must be wrong. In the course of a careful and detailed judgment the judge directed himself in law in accordance with the speeches in *Pickett's* case. He had a more extended factual basis for his assessment than had the judge in *Gammell's* case. At the time of his death young Mr Furness was in steady employment. He was active and healthy. He was *h* living at home, enjoying the full life of a young man with plenty of pleasant things to do and no commitments. The judge estimated, on the basis of his earnings up to his death, that for the future he would have earned £4,063 a year net. He had a substantial body of evidence relating to his way of life on which he could assess his probable living expenses both for the immediate future and in the longer term. He put it thus: 'I think he would have spent two-thirds of his income when at home and three-quarters after he *j* had left home.' Finally, on the basis of a normal life expectancy, he applied a multiplier of 16.

It was not suggested that this very experienced judge had departed from the principle and practice of the courts. The true case for the appellants was that the resultant figure of £17,275 was excessive; and the contrast with the value of the parents' dependency (assessed at £2,028) was emphasised. If the law allows damages for the lost years, as since *Pickett's* case it certainly does, there is nothing excessive in a figure of £17,000 for an active and healthy young man in steady employment struck down in the early days of his working life.

My Lords, there is some disquiet expressed by judges, and understandably felt by insurers, about two aspects of the law: the 'double recovery' now possible in some cases, and the very great discrepancy which can arise, as happened in the *Furness* case, between the damages recoverable by the estate for the lost years and the damages recoverable by the dependants under the Fatal Accidents Act. Each of these possibilities may well be a mischief; certainly, a law which allows the discrepancy to arise wears the appearance of anomaly, and is unlikely to be understood or acceptable.

The logical, but socially unattractive, way of reforming the law would be to repeal the Fatal Accidents Act, now that the rule actio personalis moritur cum persona has itself belatedly perished. This would leave recovery to the estate; and the dependants would look, as in a family where the breadwinner is not tortiously killed, to him (or her) for their support during life and on death. They would have the final safeguard of the Inheritance (Provision for Family and Dependants) Act 1975. But the protection of the fatal accidents legislation has been with us for so long that I doubt whether its repeal would be welcomed. If, therefore, the law is anomalous (and it certainly bears hardly on insurers and ultimately the premium-paying public), the way forward would appear to be that adopted by Parliament for Scotland. The Damages (Scotland) Act 1976 appears to work well; and the Royal Commission on Civil Liability and Compensation for Personal Injury (Cmnd 7054–I, ch 12, para 437) recommends its adoption in English law. The denial of damages to the estate, but not to a living plaintiff, is the denial of a right vested in the estate; but social and financial circumstances, as well as the legal situation, of which the Fatal Accidents Act is now an integral part, suggest that, though illogical, this is the reform which is needed.

Appeals dismissed.

Solicitors: *Mawby Barrie & Scott*, agents for *Gardner & Croft*, Canterbury (for Mr Wilson and Swift & Co Ltd); *Furley, Page, Fielding & Pembrook*, Canterbury (for Mr Gammell); *Hextall, Erskine & Co*, agents for *Stanley Evans, Oates & Co*, Manchester (for B & S Massey Ltd); *Brian Thompson*, Manchester (for Mr and Mrs Furness).

Mary Rose Plummer   Barrister.

Note
R v Crown Court at Ipswich, ex parte Baldwin

QUEEN'S BENCH DIVISION
DONALDSON LJ AND MCNEILL J
21st OCTOBER 1980

Crown Court – Appeal from Crown Court – Appeal to Divisional Court – Mode of appeal – Case stated or application for judicial review – Application for judicial review inappropriate in cases involving complicated findings of fact by Crown Court – Courts Act 1971, s 10(3)(5).

Notes

For the jurisdiction of the High Court in relation to Crown Court proceedings, see 10 Halsbury's Laws (4th Edn) para 870.

For the Courts Act 1971, s 10, see 41 Halsbury's Statutes (3rd Edn) 298.

Application for judicial review

Richard James Baldwin applied, with the leave of the Divisional Court of the Queen's Bench Division granted on 30th July 1979, for judicial review of the decision of the Crown Court at Ipswich before his Honour Judge Richards sitting with justices on 30th May 1979 whereby it dismissed the applicant's appeal against sentence and orders made on 15th January 1979 in the Felixstowe Magistrates' Court in respect of an offence of using a motor vehicle without a vehicle excise licence on 6th March 1978 contrary to s 8 of the Vehicles (Excise) Act 1971. The Department of Transport was the respondent to the application. The case is reported only on the question of the mode of appeal to the Divisional Court from decisions of the Crown Court.

John Chapman for the applicant.
John Laws for the respondent.

DONALDSON LJ outlined the facts of the case, so far as they were known to the court, and continued: This is therefore a classic case in which the court needs information from the justices.

It is against that background that I turn to s 10 of the Courts Act 1971 which deals with the jurisdiction of this court in respect of Crown Court proceedings. The section does not apply to a judgment or other decision relating to trial on indictment, so in other words what the section is concerned with is what used to be the old quarter sessions jurisdiction which is now assumed by the Crown Court.

Section 10 has two subsections which are difficult to reconcile:

'(3) The decision shall be questioned by applying to the Crown Court to have a case stated by the Crown Court for the opinion of the High Court . . .

'(5) In relation to the jurisdiction of the Crown Court, other than its jurisdiction in matters relating to trial on indictment, the High Court shall have all such jurisdiction to make orders of mandamus, prohibition or certiorari as the High Court possesses in relation to the jurisdiction of an inferior court . . .'

Those two subsections can only be reconciled if the word 'shall' in sub-s (3) is not to be treated as mandatory but as directory in some sense. The section has to be operated; sense has to be made of it; and for my part I would read it as authorising the bringing of proceedings either by case stated or by judicial review, whichever is the most convenient in the circumstances. But quite clearly in circumstances such as this it is much more convenient that it should be brought by case stated because then we can get at the facts.

But in this case unfortunately, when the matter came before this court in July 1979, this point was not discussed, and so it has come forward on a judicial review basis with completely inadequate evidence. It is too late now to send it back to the learned judge and ask him to state a case, too late I think even to send it back and ask him to swear an affidavit giving his reasons. It would impose an undue strain on his memory, even if, which I am quite prepared to concede, his memory is a great deal better than mine for cases tried two years ago.

I think in the circumstances that the only proper course to adopt is to set this decision aside and to send it back to the Crown Court with a direction that the matter be reheard. The learned judge may well think it would be more satisfactory that it should be reheard by somebody else who can approach the matter afresh. Their decision may be the same as this decision or it may be different. At all events the applicant will know that he has had justice. At the moment he may well have had justice but he has grounds for wondering whether he has.

McNEILL J, after outlining the facts, concluded: I agree entirely with the order which Donaldson LJ proposes and, as will have been clear from what I said at the outset, in a case such as this which bristles with factual difficulties the only convenient and proper way to get it before the Divisional Court is by case stated and not by way of application for judicial review.

Order of certiorari granted; decision of the Crown Court quashed. Case sent back to the Crown Court with a direction that it be reheard by a different judge.

Solicitors: *Keene, Marsland & Co* (for the applicant); *Treasury Solicitor.*

Sepala Munasinghe Esq   Barrister.

McCartney v McCartney

FAMILY DIVISION
ARNOLD P AND EWBANK J
21st JULY 1980

Husband and wife – Summary proceedings – Protection of party to marriage or child of family – Order excluding respondent from matrimonial home – Danger of physical injury to applicant – Wife applying for protection and exclusion orders – Husband not giving evidence but submitting that wife's evidence disclosed no case to answer – Magistrates deciding that wife not in immediate danger of physical injury and refusing to make exclusion order – Magistrates nevertheless making protection order and attaching power of arrest – Whether exclusion order can be made only if danger of physical injury – Whether power of arrest should be attached to protection order if there is no immediate danger of physical injury – Whether magistrates entitled to determine complaint without hearing evidence from both sides – Domestic Proceedings and Magistrates' Courts Act 1978, ss 16(2)(3), 18(1).

On 22nd May 1980 the wife applied to a magistrates' court under s 16(2)[a] of the Domestic Proceedings and Magistrates' Courts Act 1978 for an order restraining her

---

a   Section 16, so far as material, provides:
    '... (2) Where on an application for an order under this section the court is satisfied that the respondent has used, or threatened to use, violence against the person of the applicant or a child of the family and that it is necessary for the protection of the applicant or a child of the family that an order should be made under this subsection, the court may make one or both of the following orders, that is to say—(a) an order that the respondent shall not use, or threaten to use, violence against the person of the applicant; (b) an order that the respondent shall not use, or threaten to use, violence against the person of a child of the family.
    '(3) Where on an application for an order under this section the court is satisfied—(a) that the respondent has used violence against the person of the applicant or a child of the family, or (b) that the respondent has threatened to use violence against the person of the applicant or a child of the family and has used violence against some other person ... and that the applicant or a child of the

(Continued on p 598)

husband from using or threatening to use violence against her or the children of the family, and for an order under s 16(3) excluding the husband from the matrimonial home. At the hearing the wife gave evidence of a number of assaults by the husband, the last of which occurred on 15th January 1980, and called supporting evidence. The wife also said that she had no complaint about the husband's behaviour since 15th January. At the conclusion of the wife's case the husband's solicitor submitted that there was no case to answer under s 16(3) because the evidence did not establish that the wife or children were 'in danger of being physically injured' as required by s 16(3). Because of the submission the husband did not give evidence. The magistrates accepted the submission and decided that, since there had been no act of violence since 15th January and the husband's behaviour since then had been good, there was no evidence of 'immediate danger' of physical injury and therefore the wife and children were not 'in danger' of being physically injured within s 16(3). Accordingly, the magistrates refused to make an order under s 16(3), but, for the general protection of the wife and to enable the parties to live peacefully in the same household, they made an order under s 16(2)(a) and (b) and attached to it, pursuant to s 18(1)[b] of the 1968 Act, a power of arrest for breach of the order. The wife appealed against the refusal to make an order under s 16(3) excluding the husband from the matrimonial home.

Held – The appeal would be allowed and the case remitted to the magistrates for further hearing, for the following reasons—

(1) The magistrates were wrong to take the view that the danger of which they were to be satisfied before they could make an order under s 16(3) of the 1978 Act excluding the husband from the matrimonial home should be immediate. However, having taken that view and having also found that there was no immediate danger of physical injury to the wife and children, it was inconsistent of them to attach a power of arrest to the order made under s 16(2), because under s 18(1) of the 1978 Act the court had to be satisfied that the respondent had physically injured the applicant or a child of the family and was 'likely to do so again' before they could attach a power of arrest to an order under s 16. That inconsistency alone was sufficient for the court to conclude that the magistrates had erred in law (see p 599 g to j and p 600 c d and f to h, post).

(2) Furthermore, the magistrates were wrong to decide the complaint without hearing evidence from both sides, and were wrong to make an order under s 16(2) to which a power of arrest was attached, which involved a finding that there was future danger of physical injury by the husband, without hearing evidence from him (see p 599 j and p 600 c d and h, post).

Per Arnold P. 'Danger' of physical injury within s 16(3) means danger objectively observable by the magistrates and not that which the complainant subjectively believes to exist (see p 600 e f, post).

Notes
For the power of a magistrates' court to make an order excluding a party to a marriage from the matrimonial home, see Supplement to 13 Halsbury's Laws (4th Edn) para 1288B.

For the Domestic Proceedings and Magistrates' Courts Act 1978, ss 16, 18, see 48 Halsbury's Statutes (3rd Edn) 761, 764.

Appeal
Irene McCartney ('the wife') applied to Gateshead Magistrates' Court for a protection

(Continued from p 597)

family is in danger of being physically injured by the respondent . . . the court may make . . . (i) an order requiring the respondent to leave the matrimonial home . . . '

b   Section 18(1), so far as material, provides: 'Where a magistrates' court makes an order under section 16 of this Act which provides that the respondent—(a) shall not use violence against the person of the applicant, or (b) shall not use violence against a child of the family . . . the court may, if it is satisfied that the respondent has physically injured the applicant or a child of the family and considers that he is likely to do so again, attach a power of arrest to the order.'

order under s 16(2) and an exclusion order under s 16(3) of the Domestic Proceedings and Magistrates' Courts Act 1978 against the respondent, Kenneth McCartney ('the husband'). On 22nd May 1980 the magistrates refused to make an exclusion order under s 16(3) but made a protection order under s 16(2) and attached to it, pursuant to s 18(1) of the Act, a power of arrest. The wife appealed to the Divisional Court of the Family Division against the refusal to make an order under s 16(3) on the ground that there was evidence before the magistrates on which they should have exercised their discretion to grant that order. The facts are set out in the judgment of Ewbank J.

Peter Wright for the mother.
Brian Forster for the husband.

EWBANK J delivered the first judgment at the invitation of Arnold P. This is an appeal by the wife against an order made by the Gateshead magistrates on 22nd May 1980 when they granted her an order under s 16(2) of the Domestic Proceedings and Magistrates' Courts Act 1978 that her husband should not use or threaten to use violence against her or against the two children of the family, a girl who is nearly 15, and a boy who is nearly 14. At the same time the magistrates refused a further application made by her for an order under s 16(3) of the 1978 Act that he should be ordered to leave the matrimonial home.

At the hearing before the magistrates the wife gave evidence of a number of assaults culminating in an assault on 15th January 1980, and she called supporting evidence. At the end of the wife's case the solicitor on behalf of the husband submitted that there was no case to answer under s 16(3), that is on the application for the husband to be evicted. The conditions required under s 16(2) and s 16(3) are different. For an order under s 16(2) that a respondent shall not use or threaten to use violence, the applicant has to prove that the respondent has used or threatened to use violence and that it is necessary for her protection or the protection of a child of the family that an order should be made. The conditions for an order under s 16(3) include that the applicant or the child is 'in danger of being physically injured'. The magistrates, having heard that submission, took the view that, because there had been no act of violence since 15th January 1980 and because the wife had in evidence described her husband as being very good since then, the conditions under s 16(3) had not been met. They felt, however, as they say in their reasons, that for the general protection of the wife and in order to enable the parties to live in the same household fairly peacefully they would grant an order under s 16(2), · although they granted that reluctantly because of the accepted good behaviour of the husband. They considered, as they put it at the end of their reasons, that the provisions for an order under s 16(3) seemed, as indeed they are, much stricter and that under that subsection an immediate danger is required. The subsection itself uses the word 'danger', without any qualification and in my judgment it is a mistake to add other words to the terms of this statute; I think the magistrates were probably wrong in insisting that an immediate danger was a requirement of the statute. However, having decided that there was no immediate danger, and having rejected the wife's application for an order for eviction, they then went on to make an order under s 18 of the Act and attached a power of arrest to the family protection order they were making under s 16(2). Under s 18 the power of arrest can only be made if the court is satisfied the respondent has physically injured the applicant or a child of the family and considers that he is likely to do so again.

For my part I consider that the granting of a power of arrest is inconsistent with the finding under s 16(3) that the wife and children were not in danger of being physically injured. I consider that the inconsistency shown by the addition of the power of arrest is sufficient for this court to come to the conclusion that the magistrates must at some stage have adopted the wrong test.

A further point arises in this case. The magistrates never heard the evidence of the husband because of the submission of no case. In general it is very unwise in this type of case to decide and dismiss a complaint without hearing both sides. The law on this aspect is, in my judgment, well set out in Rayden on Divorce (13th Edn, 1979, p 1219) where it is said:

'The desirability of hearing both sides is especially true in behaviour cases, where it is very important to get the whole atmosphere from both sides, and the power to dismiss a complaint at the conclusion of the complainant's case should only be exercised in exceptional cases as, for example, where no credence can be given to the complainant's evidence, or where it is crystal clear that the complainant has no case in law. It has been said there are very few matrimonial cases in which justice can be done without hearing both sides. A distinction must be drawn between a submission at the end of the complainant's case that there is no case to answer as a matter of law, and a submission at that stage that the complainant's case should be rejected on the merits.'

In the present case, where there was evidence of violence prior to 15th January and violence on 15th January 1980, evidence of such a nature that the magistrates were prepared to make an order for the protection of the wife and children, it was, in my judgment, unwise of the magistrates to consider the submission and to make any finding whether there was a danger of physical injury by the husband in the future without hearing his evidence. I would accordingly allow this appeal and order a rehearing or a continuance of the hearing which has taken place.

ARNOLD P. I agree, and particularly I agree with what has fallen from Ewbank J in relation to the unwisdom of magistrates in matrimonial disputes where the issue of conduct arises of accepting a submission of no case to answer on the evidence as distinct from some point of law.

It can well be said that what Ewbank J has pointed out as an error in regarding danger as having to be immediate danger to satisfy the requirements of s 16(3) arose because the complaint that was made by the wife was made expressly on the ground that in view of the husband's recent conduct she believed that she was in immediate danger of further physical injury. Of course, one does not want to elevate summonses in magistrates' courts to the degree of exigency which attends pleadings in the High Court, but it is easy to see why the magistrates approached the matter in this way. It is worth pointing out that the complaint was poorly phrased in two respects. In the first place it seems to me that whatever may be the precise application of the requirements of s 16(3), subjective belief by a complainant is not one of them. If there is to be demonstrated a danger, such as is mentioned in the last part of s 16(3), it must in my judgment be an objectively observable danger, one which the magistrates think to exist and not one which the complainant thinks to exist. Further, I can see no justification for saying that a danger to qualify for that section must be an imminent danger, and I share with Ewbank J the greatest difficulty in seeing how the magistrates can on the one hand validly have decided for the purposes of the power of arrest that the conditions of s 18 were fulfilled, including the condition that the husband was likely to do so again (ie cause physical injury), to use the language of that section, with their decision on the submission that the wife was not in danger of being physically injured.

I agree with the order proposed; the case should go back to the magistrates with a direction to continue the hearing, but against the background that, just as they are obliged to reconsider the conclusion which they reached under s 16 on the submission, they must equally be at liberty to reconsider the conclusion which they reached under s 18 in attaching the power of arrest. It would be most unwise for us to say any more at this stage since, as we understand, there is pending tomorrow a proceeding consequent on the exercise or purported exercise of the power of arrest at which matters posterior in time to those which the magistrates had to consider will fall to be considered by the Bench.

Appeal allowed. Case remitted to magistrates for further hearing.

Solicitors: *Rooks, Rider & Co*, agents for *Thomas Magnay & Co*, Gateshead (for the wife); *Ward Bowie*, agents for *Basil P Mellon & Co*, Gateshead (for the husband).

Bebe Chua   Barrister.

R v Slough Borough Council, ex parte London Borough of Ealing and other appeals

QUEEN'S BENCH DIVISION
LORD LANE CJ AND COMYN J
17th JULY 1980

COURT OF APPEAL, CIVIL DIVISION
LORD DENNING MR, SHAW AND TEMPLEMAN LJJ
1st, 2nd, 19th DECEMBER 1980

Housing – Homeless person – Duty of housing authority to provide accommodation – Responsibility between housing authorities – Notifying authority deciding that applicant had local connection with area of notified authority – Notified authority previously deciding that applicant intentionally homeless – Notifying authority deciding that applicant unintentionally homeless – Notifying authority seeking to transfer to notified authority consequent duty to accommodate applicant indefinitely – Whether notified authority bound by notifying authority's subsequent finding – Whether notified authority required to accommodate applicant indefinitely – Housing (Homeless Persons) Act 1977, ss 4(5), 5(3).

Housing – Homeless person – Duty of housing authority to provide accommodation – Responsibility between housing authorities – Dispute – Reference to arbitration – Scope of arbitrator's jurisdiction – Whether jurisdiction limited to determining questions relating to local connection of applicant with another housing authority's area – Whether arbitrator precluded from determining whether applicant homeless intentionally – Housing (Homeless Persons) Act 1977, s 5(7).

Housing – Homeless person – Duty of housing authority to provide accommodation – Person becoming homeless intentionally – Finding of intentional homelessness by authority – Validity of finding – When finding may be impugned – Housing (Homeless Persons) Act 1977, s 17(1).

Two families, the L family and the J family (an unmarried mother and her children), lived for some years in council houses in the borough of Slough. Slough borough council ('Slough') evicted the L family from their council house for non-payment of rent, and evicted Miss J because of justified complaints by neighbours of her conduct. When Miss J moved to another council house in Slough, the council again evicted her because she was a trespasser. Mr L and Miss J applied as homeless persons to Slough for accommodation under the Housing (Homeless Persons) Act 1977. As required by that Act Slough made inquiries and decided that the L family and Miss J had become homeless intentionally. On that basis Slough's responsibility under the Act was limited to securing temporary accommodation for each family. The L family went to live with friends in the borough of Hillingdon but because of the consequent gross overcrowding the Hillingdon borough council ('Hillingdon') required them to leave the house. The L family then applied to Hillingdon for accommodation under the Act. In the case of Miss J, Slough fulfilled its duty by providing her with accommodation for two weeks in a guesthouse in the borough of Ealing. Towards the end of that time Miss J applied for accommodation under the Act to the Ealing borough council ('Ealing'). Hillingdon and Ealing, as required by the Act, made their own inquiries about the L family and Miss J respectively, and, though not purporting to set aside Slough's decision that both families had become intentionally homeless, determined that both families had become homeless unintentionally. On that basis Hillingdon and Ealing were under a duty, by virtue of s 4(5)[a] of the 1977 Act, to house them indefinitely unless, under s 5[b] of that Act, they

---

a   Section 4(5) is set out at p 605 h, post
b   Section 5, so far as material, is set out at p 606 a to e, post

could pass that duty over to Slough as the local authority with whom the families had a local connection. Since both families had resided in Slough for some years, Hillingdon and Ealing ('the notifying authorities') respectively notified Slough ('the notified authority'), under s 5(1), that each family had a local connection with Slough and no local connection with Hillingdon or Ealing. If that was in fact the case, Slough then came under a duty under s 5(3) to house the families indefinitely. Slough, however, contended that the families were intentionally homeless and that therefore Hillingdon and Ealing were not under the duty contained in s 4(5) to house them indefinitely and could not pass on that duty to Slough under s 5. The disputes between the councils were referred to separate arbitrations under s 5(7) of the 1977 Act and the Housing (Homeless Persons) (Appropriate Arrangements) Order 1978, the question for determination in each case being whether s 5(3) or s 5(5) was applicable, ie whether by reason of local connection with the area of Slough the duty to house the families fell on Slough. Although requested by Slough to do so, the arbitrators declined to determine whether the families had become intentionally homeless, on the ground that they had no jurisdiction to do so. In each case the arbitrator determined that the family had a local connection with Slough by reason of residence and had no local connection with Hillingdon or Ealing, and that Slough was under the duty in s 5(3) to house the families. Slough applied to the Divisional Court for an order of certiorari to quash the arbitrators' decisions on the grounds (i) that Hillingdon and Ealing were not under a duty to house the families indefinitely under s 4(5), and had erred in law in notifying Slough under s 5, and (ii) the arbitrators ought to have considered whether the families were intentionally homeless. The Divisional Court held that under s 5(7) of the Act and the 1978 order the only issue the arbitrators could determine was whether s 5 applied and that accordingly the disputes had been properly determined by the arbitrators. The court declined to decide whether Slough was bound by the decisions of Hillingdon and Ealing that the families were unintentionally homeless. Slough appealed, contending that although it did not seek to challenge the decisions of Hillingdon and Ealing on the ground of unreasonableness or bad faith, nevertheless Hillingdon and Ealing were not entitled under the Act to override or replace Slough's decision that the families were intentionally homeless.

Held – (1) Under the 1977 Act each local authority to whom a homeless person applied for accommodation was required to make its own inquiries about the homelessness of that person and to form its own view whether the homelessness was intentional or unintentional within the meaning of the Act, and was required to act according to that view. Furthermore, every authority applied to was entitled, if the circumstances warranted it, to form the opinion that a different authority was the one with whom the applicant had a local connection. It followed that, although Slough had been entitled to find that the respective families had become homeless intentionally (Lord Denning MR doubting that the families had), Hillingdon and Ealing were required to make their own inquiries when the respective families applied to them for accommodation, and were entitled to decide that the families were unintentionally homeless, and were then entitled to pass on to Slough the duty falling on them under s 4(5) because of the families' local connection with Slough (see p 613 g to j, p 616 a to d and p 618 b c, post).

(2) (Per Shaw and Templeman LJJ) Furthermore, under s 5 of the 1977 Act the only questions which could be determined by an arbitrator were those in dispute under s 5, which were essentially questions relating to the local connection of the applicant with another authority, and an arbitrator had no jurisdiction to determine the question under s 4 of the Act of whether a person was intentionally homeless (see p 615 d, and p 618 f to h, post).

(3) It followed that Hillingdon and Ealing had acted within their powers and that Slough was bound to accept their findings that the respective families were unintentionally homeless, and, having been properly notified by Hillingdon and Ealing under s 5(1), Slough was under the duty in s 5(3) to house the families indefinitely. Accordingly the appeals would be dismissed (see p 613 j, p 614 a to d, p 616 d to f and p 618 c to e and h, post).

Per Shaw LJ. (1) The 1977 Act does not restrict a homeless person's choice of the authority to which he can apply for accommodation, and the decision as to venue is his (see p 614 j to p 615 a, post).

(2) The concept of intentional homelessness is subjective, and accordingly an authority's decision on the matter can only be impeached on the ground that no reasonable authority acting reasonably in the discharge of its functions could have reached that decision (see p 615 e to h, post).

Per Templeman LJ. If an appeal from a finding of intentional homelessness is desirable, Parliament should provide appropriate machinery for the purpose. If an appeal procedure is not desirable, one local authority should not be entitled to reverse the decision of another local authority without assuming responsibility for the accommodation of the homeless person in question (see p 617 j, post).

Notes

For a housing authority's duties to a homeless person, and the responsibility of other housing authorities, see 22 Halsbury's Laws (4th Edn) paras 513–514.

For the Housing (Homeless Persons) Act 1977, ss 4, 5, 17, see 47 Halsbury's Statutes (3rd Edn) 318, 319, 330.

Cases referred to in judgments

Associated Provincial Picture Houses Ltd v Wednesbury Corpn [1947] 2 All ER 680, [1948] 1 KB 223, [1948] LJR 190, 177 LT 641, 112 JP 55, 45 LGR 635, CA, 45 Digest (Repl) 214, 186.

De Falco v Crawley Borough Council [1980] 1 All ER 913, [1980] QB 460, [1980] 2 WLR 664, 78 LGR 180, CA.

Delahaye v Oswestry Borough Council (1980) Times, 29th July.

Cases also cited

Brown (Christopher) Ltd v Genossenschaft Oesterreichischer Waldbesitzer Holzwirtschaftsbetriebe Registrierte GmbH [1953] 2 All ER 1039, [1954] 1 QB 8.

Tyson v Kerrier District Council [1980] 3 All ER 313, [1980] 1 WLR 1205, CA.

Smith v Martin [1925] 1 KB 745, [1925] All ER Rep 510, CA.

Applications for judicial review

R v Slough Borough Council, ex parte London Borough of Ealing

By a notice of motion dated 7th March 1980 the London Borough of Ealing ('Ealing council') applied for judicial review by way of mandamus directed to Slough Borough Council ('Slough council') requiring it as housing authority for the borough of Slough to fulfil its duty under the Housing (Homeless Persons) Act 1977 by securing accommodation within its area for Miss Patricia Jack and her child Jonathan Jack, then residing in the Ealing area, and damages against Slough council for the cost of providing accommodation in the Ealing area for Miss Jack and her child. The grounds for the relief sought were (i) that pursuant to ss 4(5) and 5(3) and (4) of the Housing (Homeless Persons) Act 1977, and a determination on 5th January 1980 of a referee appointed under the Housing (Homeless Persons) (Appropriate Arrangements) Order 1978, SI 1978 No 69, Slough council as the notified authority under the 1977 Act was under a duty to secure that accommodation became available for occupation by Miss Jack and her child who qualified as homeless persons, and had refused and continued to refuse to perform that duty, and (ii) that Ealing council had provided and continued to provide accommodation for Miss Jack and her child and had thereby suffered loss and damage. The facts are set out in the judgment of Lord Lane CJ.

R v Slough Borough Council, ex parte Jack

By a notice of motion dated 4th July 1980 Miss Jack applied for an order of mandamus directed to Slough council requiring it to secure that accommodation became available for her occupation, and for Deionne Jack and Jonathan Jack as persons who might reasonably be expected to reside with her, and claimed damages, on the grounds that Slough council on 5th January 1980 became subject to a duty under s 5(3) of the 1977 Act to secure that accommodation became available for her occupation and in breach of that duty had failed and refused to secure accommodation for her and in consequence Miss Jack had suffered loss and damage. The facts are set out in the judgment of Lord Lane CJ.

R v London Borough of Ealing and Jack, ex parte Slough Borough Council

By a notice of motion dated 24th April 1980 Slough council applied for (i) an order of certiorari to remove into the High Court and quash a decision of an arbitrator dated 5th January 1980 whereby he held that Miss Jack had a local connection with the borough of Slough by reason of residence and that Slough council was therefore under a duty to provide housing for her and her family by virtue of s 5(3) of the 1977 Act, (ii) alternatively, an order of mandamus requiring the arbitrator forthwith to hear the arbitration referred to him under the 1978 Order relating to a dispute between Slough council and Ealing council concerning the legal duty to provide housing for Miss Jack and her family and to decide the jurisdictional question whether or not Ealing council failed to take into account the relevant consideration that Miss Jack was intentionally homeless as defined by s 17 of the 1977 Act, and to provide an opportunity of a formal hearing at which Slough and Ealing councils respectively could put forward oral representations. The facts are set out in the judgment of Lord Lane CJ.

R v London Borough of Hillingdon and Lynch, ex parte
Slough Borough Council

By a notice of motion dated 10th October 1979 Slough council applied for (i) an order of certiorari to move into the High Court to quash a decision of an arbitrator dated 23rd April 1979 whereby he held that Mr John Lynch and Mrs Florence Lynch had a local connection with Slough council by reason of residence and that Slough council was therefore under a duty to house them by virtue of s 5(3) of the 1977 Act, or (ii) alternatively an order of mandamus requiring the arbitrator forthwith to hear the arbitration referred to him under the 1978 Order relating to a dispute between Slough council and the London Borough of Hillingdon ('Hillingdon council') concerning the legal duty to provide housing for Mr and Mrs Lynch and to decide the jurisdictional question whether Hillingdon council failed to take into account the relevant consideration that Mr and Mrs Lynch were intentionally homeless as defined by s 17 of the 1977 Act, and to provide the opportunity of a formal hearing at which Slough and Hillingdon councils could put forward oral representations. The facts are set in the judgment of Lord Lane CJ.

Anthony Scrivener QC and *William Birtles* for Slough council.
Konrad Schiemann QC and *Patrick Clarkson* for Ealing council.
David Fletcher for Hillingdon council.
Joseph Harper and *John Howell* for Miss Jack and Mr and Mrs Lynch.

LORD LANE CJ. This hearing involves a number of different applications to the court which all arise out of the provisions of the Housing (Homeless Persons) Act 1977. There are proceedings instituted by Slough borough council ('Slough council'), there are proceedings instituted by the London Borough of Ealing ('Ealing council') and there are proceedings instituted by Miss Patricia Jack.

The nature of the applications, briefly speaking, is this. The Slough council applications involve a Mr and Mrs Lynch. Those comprise an application for certiorari to quash the decision of an arbitrator; alternatively, an order of mandamus that the arbitrator should be ordered to consider the jurisdictional question, if I may call it that, of intentional homelessness, and in the second alternative, a further application on the basis that the arbitrator can consider the jurisdictional point. The next application is that by Slough council in respect of what may be called the Miss Jack case, and there they are seeking exactly the same remedies as they were in the Lynch case. Ealing council are asking for an order of mandamus directed to the Slough council and are also claiming damages. Finally, Miss Jack is claiming an order of mandamus directed to the Slough council and also general damages, among other things, for the 21 months she has been spending in temporary accommodation.

The first matter to consider is the structure of the 1977 Act. It is not an easy Act to understand, as will become apparent very shortly. Section 1 deals with homeless persons and persons threatened with homelessness generally. It defines its terms and sets out, I need not read it, what is meant by a person being homeless. Section 2 deals with the question of priority need for accommodation, the priority in these circumstances being a term of art which applies to certain categories of people. Miss Jack in this case is a priority case, and so are the Lynches. It is not necessary for that section to be read in detail.

Section 3 deals with preliminary duties of housing authorities in cases of possible homelessness and it reads as follows:

'(1) If—(a) a person applies to a housing authority for accommodation or for assistance in obtaining accommodation, and (b) the authority have reason to believe that he may be homeless or threatened with homelessness, the authority shall make appropriate inquiries.

'(2) In subsection (1) above "appropriate inquiries" means—(a) such inquiries as are necessary to satisfy the authority whether the person who applied to them is homeless or threatened with homelessness, and (b) if the authority are satisfied that he is homeless or threatened with homelessness, any further inquiries necessary to satisfy them—(i) whether he has a priority need, and (ii) whether he became homeless or threatened with homelessness intentionally.

'(3) If the authority think fit, they may also make inquiries as to whether the person who applied to them has a local connection with the area of another housing authority.

'(4) If the authority have reason to believe that the person who applied to them may be homeless and have a priority need, they shall secure that accommodation is made available for his occupation pending any decision which they may make as a result of their inquiries (irrespective of any local connection he may have with the area of another housing authority).'

Section 4 deals with the duties of housing authorities to homeless persons and persons threatened with homelessness. Section 4(1) reads as follows:

'If a housing authority are satisfied, as a result of inquiries under section 3 above, that a person who has applied to them for accommodation or for assistance in obtaining accommodation is homeless or threatened with homelessness, they shall be subject to a duty towards him under this section.'

Then it sets out the different permutations of fact which may affect them as to their duties. It is s 4(5) which is material here, and is as follows:

'Where—(a) they are satisfied—(i) that he is homeless, and (ii) that he has a priority need, but (b) they are not satisfied that he became homeless intentionally, their duty, subject to section 5 below, is to secure that accommodation becomes available for his occupation.'

Then set out are the duties which fall upon a local authority in these circumstances.

Then we come to s 5 which has been the centre of the argument in this case. It is headed 'Responsibility as between housing authorities'. May I remark in passing that counsel on behalf of Slough council draws the court's attention to the use of the word 'responsibility' in that section, as opposed to the use of the word 'duties' in the two preceding sections, ss 3 and 4.

The terms of s 5 read as follows:

'(1) A housing authority are not subject to a duty under section 4(5) above—(a) if they are of the opinion—(i) that neither the person who applied to them for accommodation or for assistance in obtaining accommodation nor any person who might reasonably be expected to reside with him has a local connection with their area, and (ii) that the person who so applied or a person who might reasonably be expected to reside with him has a local connection with another housing authority's area, and (iii) that neither the person who so applied nor any person who might reasonably be expected to reside with him will run the risk of domestic violence in that housing authority's area, and (b) if they notify that authority—(i) that the application has been made, and (ii) that they are of the opinion specified in paragraph (a) above.

'(2) In this Act "notifying authority" means a housing authority who give a notification under subsection (1) above and "notified authority" means a housing authority who receive such a notification.

'(3) It shall be the duty of the notified authority to secure that accommodation becomes available for occupation by the person to whom the notification relates if neither he nor any person who might reasonably be expected to reside with him has a local connection with the area of the notifying authority but the conditions specified in subsection (4) below are satisfied . . .

'(7) Any question which falls to be determined under this section shall be determined by agreement between the notifying authority and the notified authority or, in default of such agreement, in accordance with the appropriate arrangements . . .'

We shall have to examine what the 'appropriate arrangements' are in a moment.

The next section to which it is necessary to refer is s 8, and s 8(3) runs as follows:

'If they notify him that their decision is that he has a priority need, they shall at the same time notify him—(a) of their decision on the question whether he became homeless or threatened with homelessness intentionally, and (b) whether they have notified or propose to notify any other housing authority that his application has been made.'

That of course is the duty cast on the notifying authority to make known their decision to the applicant.

Section 9 in effect urges co-operation between the authorities which unhappily has not been successful here. Section 12 relates to guidelines to authorities, which I need not deal with.

Section 17 deals with persons intentionally homeless or threatened with homelessness and is important, and must be read:

'(1) Subject to subsection (3) below, for the purposes of this Act a person becomes homeless intentionally if he deliberately does or fails to do anything in consequence of which he ceases to occupy accommodation which is available for his occupation and which it would have been reasonable for him to continue to occupy.

'(2) Subject to subsection (3) below, for the purposes of this Act a person becomes threatened with homelessness intentionally if he deliberately does or fails to do anything the likely result of which is that he will be forced to leave accommodation which is available for his occupation and which it would have been reasonable for him to continue to occupy.

'(3) An act or omission in good faith on the part of a person who was unaware of any relevant fact is not to be treated as deliberate for the purposes of subsection (1) or (2) above.

'(4) Regard may be had, in determining for the purposes of subsections (1) and (2) above whether it would have been reasonable for a person to continue to occupy accommodation, to the general circumstances prevailing in relation to housing in the area of the housing authority to whom he applied for accommodation or for assistance in obtaining accommodation.'

So much for the terms of the Act.

The circumstances of the two cases, because they are in essence two cases, the Lynch case and the Miss Jack case, were these. I am now giving a brief summary of the facts, which is not to be taken as wholly accurate. In the case of the Lynches, the Slough council had them as tenants. According to their records at any rate, there was a history of rent arrears going right back to 1971. Those arrears are I think in dispute. Nevertheless, that was the council's belief. A suspended possession order was made against the Lynches, and the warrant was eventually executed on 30th September 1975. Mr Lynch suffers from severe disability. The Lynches were then rehoused in low-rent property. They were in receipt of social security payments, but for one reason or another, it is alleged, whether truthfully or not one does not know, that they failed to pay the rent. On 11th November 1976 a suspended possession order was made when it was alleged that £924 arrears of rent were outstanding. On 12th April 1977 the possession warrant was executed. They had to vacate the council house and they then spent short periods in various houses in the district.

On 5th December 1977 Mr Lynch applied to the Slough council under the 1977 Act. Slough council came to the determination that under the Act the Lynches were intentionally homeless and the Lynch family were so notified.

The Lynches then moved to the Hillingdon area, to a house in Ruislip. Unfortunately their arrival at this particular house caused the premises to become statutorily overcrowded, and they were eventually required, by the friends who were putting them up, to leave. They were then housed temporarily by the Hillingdon council, to whom they made application, Hillingdon having come to the conclusion that the Lynches were homeless, but not intentionally homeless. So under the provisions of the Act which I have read, that is s 5, Hillingdon council notified Slough council that here they had people who were not intentionally homeless; people who plainly had connections with Slough. As to that there was no dispute. In fact they had no proper connection with Hillingdon. Slough council on the other hand maintained that the Lynches were intentionally homeless. There you have battle lines drawn up between two local authorities.

It is now necessary to turn to the provisions for these matters to be referred to arbitration, because that was the next step in the Lynch story. I turn to the Housing (Homeless Persons) (Appropriate Arrangements) Order 1978, SI 1978 No 69. There are set out in the schedule to the order the nature of the panel of persons who may be appointed as arbitrators, the proper officers for the implementation of the rules of the order, or determination by the person agreed on by the local authorities and the report by the authorities to the proper officer. I will read para 4 of the schedule, 'Report to proper officer', which I read:

'(1) If—(a) at the end of the period of 21 days mentioned in sub-paragraph 3 above—(i) any such question as is mentioned in that sub-paragraph has not been determined by agreement between the notifying authority and the notified authority, and (ii) those authorities have not made arrangements for that question to be determined as provided in paragraph 3 above; or (b) before the end of that period both those authorities have agreed that they will be unable either—(i) to determine that question by agreement, or (ii) to make arrangements for that question to be determined as provided in that paragraph before the end of that period, the notifying authority shall, and the notified authority may, report that fact in writing to the person who is, under paragraph 2 above, the proper officer for the purposes of this paragraph in relation to the authority making the report.

'(2) A report under sub-paragraph (1) above—(a) shall identify the notifying authority, the notified authority, and the person to whom the notification under section 5(1) of the Act relates, and (b) subject to sub-paragraph (3) below, shall contain either—(i) a statement, agreed by both those authorities, that the question which they have not determined by agreement is the question whether subsection (3) or (5) of section 5 of the Act applies to that person, or (ii) a statement, agreed by both those authorities, setting out the particular question or questions falling to be determined under that section which they have not determined by agreement.

'(3) If a report under sub-paragraph (1) above does not contain a statement falling within sub-paragraph (2)(b) above, it shall be deemed to contain a statement falling within sub-paragraph (2)(b)(i) above.'

All that highly complicated matter, so far as this case is concerned, means in simple English is this: if there is no statement agreed by both the parties and sent to the arbitrator, then it shall be deemed that a statement has been agreed by both the parties that the question which they had not determined by agreement was the question whether sub-s (3) or sub-s (5) of s 5 of the 1977 Act applies. Consequently in the absence of an agreement, the matter to be determined by the arbitrator is whether s 5(3) or s 5(5) applies, and sub-ss (3) and (5) are these: whether it is the notifying authority who, so to speak, has to foot the bill or whether it is the notified authority who has to foot the bill.

What happened after that, so far as the Lynches were concerned, was as follows. The matter was referred to the arbitrator. Slough council urged the arbitrator to determine whether the family was intentionally homeless or not. The arbitrator refused to determine that matter. He felt under no obligation to do so and indeed that he had no power to do so. The arbitrator determined the local connection issue, which was the only issue still alive, in favour of Hillingdon council, as indeed he had to, because the evidence was all one way, and he made an order under s 5(3), namely that Slough council was the authority which would have to accommodate this family. Therefore Slough council are under a duty to house the Lynch family.

The determination was as follows:

'For the purposes of determining the question referred to me by the proper officers, I find (i) that Mr. and Mrs. Lynch and the family have a local connection with the Borough of Slough by reason of residence; and (ii) that neither Mr. Lynch nor the other members of the family have a local connection with Hillingdon; and that (iii) sub-section (3) of section 5 applies to the Lynch family; (iv) neither of the conditions mentioned in sub-section (4) is relevant in this case.'

Slough council challenges the decision of the arbitrator and suggests that the arbitrator was bound in the circumstances of this case to consider the question of whether there was intentional homelessness or not.

The situation with regard to Miss Jack's case again may not be entirely accurate, but is sufficiently so for the purposes of this judgment. She suffered, so it is said, from rent arrears, although this is disputed. Also, according to Slough council, she was the subject of complaints from neighbours. By an affidavit which has only recently seen the light of day, she suggests that the complaints by the neighbours were unjustified; she was the subject of racialist interference from her neighbours, she being coloured and the neighbours being white. Whatever the truth behind these matters may be, the fact is that she was served with a notice to quit her council house within the jurisdiction of the Slough housing authority on 16th September 1977. On 16th February 1978 there was an order for possession, which was not enforced. A warrant for possession was obtained and eviction was arranged for 22nd May 1978. She then lodged in another council house but the tenant of that house was prohibited from having lodgers. The tenant apparently left the house in September 1978. Miss Jack and her young child were remaining unlawfully in that house on their own. On 29th September 1978 there was an order for possession made against her. Slough council then determined that she was intentionally homeless.

Once again one gets a similar situation as happened in the Lynch case. They found her temporary accommodation in Ealing. Hence the intervention of the Ealing council. That accommodation ceased to be available to Miss Jack in September or November 1978. Ealing council thereupon notified Slough council that the family was homeless and not intentionally homeless and a dispute between the two authorities on the question of intentional homelessness arose. Once again arbitration proceedings were instituted and once again the arbitrator was invited to decide the question of intentional homelessness. He declined to do so and he determined in the end, really without the assistance of any argument from Slough council, that the Slough council was under a duty to house Miss Jack and her child; hence the application to this court.

There are certain other documents at which it is necessary to look. First of all the agreement on procedures. This is a document to which, I am told, Slough council was a party. It is an agreement entered into by a number of local authorities as to the referrals of the homeless. It was it seems a domestic attempt to solve some of the difficulties posed by the Act so as to prevent the necessity of the sort of litigation on which we are engaged at the moment.

It is interesting to see, for what it is worth, paragraph 3.3 which reads as follows:

'All inquiries having been completed the Act contains no provision for the notified authority to challenge the receiving authority's decision that the applicant is homeless, not intentionally homeless and in priority need. Should the notified authority produce fresh evidence as to the facts of the case, the receiving authority's duty is to reconsider its decision in the light of these new facts.'

In this case of course the notified authority is Slough council.

That is a reading of the Act which does not bind this court, and probably does not bind anyone. But it is interesting to note that it is not the contention which is being put forward by Slough council in this case. Indeed it is diametrically opposed to that contention.

The point taken by counsel for Slough council is that the arbitrator was not in a position to, and could not properly, determine whether s 5(3) or s 5(5) of the Act applied to Miss Jack or the Lynch family, as the case may be, and thus could not decide whether the burden of finding accommodation for Miss Jack or the Lynches falls on the Ealing or Hillingdon councils on the one hand or Slough council on the other, without first determining whether Ealing council was entitled to be satisfied when Miss Jack claimed to be homeless in their area after having had to leave the guest house in Ealing where she had been accommodated by Slough, that her homelessness was not intentional. Counsel submits that although the strict wording of the Act, at least at first blush, appears to be against him, such a heavy responsibility lies on the local authority under ss 1 to 4 of the Act that it would be grossly unfair, and cannot have been Parliament's intention, that the local authority should have the duty thrust on it with no chance of investigation and no say in the matter as to whether, in the light of their knowledge, the person could properly be said to be intentionally homeless. He points to certain matters in the Act, which, he says, support that indication. He points to a matter already mentioned, namely the use of the word 'responsibility' in s 5 as opposed to 'duties' in ss 3 and 4. He suggests, in the light of those matters, and particularly the hardship which would exist if a local authority was to be bound to provide accommodation as far as the foreseeable future goes for a person whose circumstances that authority has no power to examine, that Slough council ought to be allowed to re-examine the question of intentional homelessness or otherwise, and also the arbitrator ought to be allowed, and indeed is bound, he submits, to examine the question of whether the notifying authority properly came to the conclusion that the applicant was not intentionally homeless.

He submits that that is the only way to make sense of the Act. The only way to make sense of it is to interpret it as meaning that Slough council are not bound by Ealing council's decision or Hillingdon council's decision and also that the arbitrator has jurisdiction to determine the question of intentional homelessness or otherwise. He submits that s 17(4) of the Act really indicates that that contention is true.

Whilst agreeing that hardship results from the contention of Hillingdon and Ealing councils, nevertheless I have come to the conclusion, eventually without very much doubt, that on a reading of the Act as a whole, the contentions of Ealing and Hillingdon councils are correct. If we look at s 4(5) of the Act, the question is: were the local authority satisfied? It is not suggested here that there was no evidence on which they could not be so satisfied. It is not the situation of *Associated Provincial Picture Houses Ltd v Wednesbury Corpn* [1947] 2 All ER 680, [1948] 1 KB 223. Consequently all that has to happen is the state of being satisfied on the part of the notifying authority, and that is the end of that part of the matter. The prerequisite, as counsel for Ealing council puts it, is not the absolute state of the facts, but the satisfaction of the local authority that a certain set of facts exist. That is what we have here.

Having determined that, and there having been without doubt evidence on which they could come to that conclusion, we turn to s 5(7) of the 1977 Act:

'Any question which falls to be determined under this section shall be determined by agreement between the notifying authority and the notified authority or, in default of such agreement, in accordance with the appropriate arrangements.'

That section deals with disputes under s 5, that is responsibilities between housing authorities, and does not deal with disputes under s 4, namely questions of intentional homelessness or otherwise.

Finally I repeat the part of my judgment earlier which related to the provisions of the 1978 order and particularly para 4(2)(b)(ii) of the schedule to the 1978 order which, as I have already indicated, seems to me to limit, and limit in terms, the ambit of the arbitrator from going outside that very narrow issue, namely the question of the application of s 5(3) or s 5(5). The arbitrator is not entitled to go outside the strict terms of his reference. It seems to me really that the submission of counsel for Slough council would entail that he would be bound to go outside those terms. In those circumstances I do not think that counsel's contentions are correct.

There is nothing more that needs to be said, save this. We were invited by counsel for Slough council to determine whether the notified authority, that is Slough council in the present case, is bound by the decision of the notifying authority, Ealing council in one case and Hillingdon council in the other. I do not myself feel it is necessary to go into that question. We would require more detailed argument than those which have been directed to us and I would prefer and do leave that question open for decision on another day. It is sufficient to say that, so far as these various applications are concerned, Slough council fails.

COMYN J. I entirely agree. There are only two matters I want to deal with. First, I consider that Slough council fails in limine here and does so for two reasons: one is, for the reason given by Lord Lane CJ, that it did not fall on the arbitrator to decide whether there was intentional homelessness or not; the second is that Slough council would not submit a case of its own on this matter. The case therefore went before the arbitrator on the footing only of the case put by the other side.

The second matter is this. This is not an easy Act to interpret and construe. Would that it were, especially when it is dealing with such an important problem as homelessness. I express a fervent hope that it will not be allowed to give rise to the sort of running battles which occurred 150 years ago with regard to paupers, itinerants and the inmates of work houses.

Lord Lane CJ has made it clear that there is no appeal of any kind under this Act save as is provided in s 5, and s 5(7) confines the arbitration to that section. If we look at s 5(1), it speaks of a housing authority being of the opinion in (a) and of notifying the authority in (b); these cannot be the subject matter of arbitration. So arbitration must lie deeper in the section and it lies, in my view, clearly in sub-ss (3) and (5) only.

For these reasons I consider that Slough council fail in the whole of this virtually consolidated matter.

Declaration in favour of Ealing council and Miss Jack that Slough council was under a statutory duty to house Miss Jack. Damages to be assessed. Declaration in favour of Hillingdon council that Slough council was under a statutory duty to house Mr and Mrs Lynch. Applications of Slough council dismissed.

N P Metcalfe Esq   Barrister.

Appeals

Slough council appealed to the Court of Appeal.

Anthony Scrivener QC and *William Birtles* for Slough council.
Konrad Schiemann QC and *Patrick Clarkson* for Ealing council.
David Fletcher for Hillingdon council.
Joseph Harper and *John Howell* for Miss Jack and Mr and Mrs Lynch.

Cur adv vult

19th December. The following judgments were read.

LORD DENNING MR. Under the Housing (Homeless Persons) Act 1977 each local authority is under a statutory duty to house the homeless persons in its area. This case raises the question: what is to happen when a person who is homeless in one housing area moves, or is moved, to another housing area and becomes homeless there? One or other local authority is bound to house him. Which is it? To us old folk this is a repeat performance of the disputes under the Poor Law 200 years ago. In those days each parish was responsible for the relief of those who were poor and unable to work. When a poor man moved from one parish to another, the question arose: which parish was responsible? The disputes, Blackstone tells us, 'created an infinity of expensive law-suits between contending neighbourhoods, concerning those settlements and removals': see 1 Bl Com 362. Many of the cases that came before Lord Mansfield were settlement cases. History tends to repeat itself. If our present cases are anything to go by, we are in for another dose of the same medicine.

Here we have two families who were settled in the borough of Slough. They had been there for years. Each family had a council house. But each behaved deplorably. So badly that the council had to evict them. Each moved to a different area. They claimed to be homeless in the new area. But the housing authorities in those new areas did not want them. They tried to return them to Slough. But Slough council refused to have them back. All was set for a game of battledore and shuttlecock, with the homeless the shuttlecock and the housing authorities wielding the battledore. But instead they resorted to arbitration. This got them nowhere. So they resorted to the courts. Now I go to the details.

Patricia Jack

Patricia Jack is a coloured woman, aged 26. She is unmarried and has three children. The two older ones (a girl aged 8 and a girl of 5½) are in the care of the local authority. They have been put out with foster parents. The youngest (a boy aged 2) is with his mother.

In 1973 she was the tenant of a council house at Slough, 60 Lancaster Avenue. She often had men in the house. The neighbours complained of her conduct. So the Slough council in 1976 moved her into another council house at Slough, 10 Marish Court. She took in lodgers. She behaved so badly there that her neighbours complained about her. Eight of them signed a petition to the council. The council investigated the position. They found that the complaints were justified. They gave Miss Jack notice to quit on 16th September 1977. They went to the county court and got an order for possession. If she had behaved properly, the council would not have enforced it. But she still behaved so badly that on 22nd April 1978 her neighbours wrote this letter to the council:

> 'We are writing to inform you that as from this day, 22nd April 1978, we, Mrs. Rockell, Mrs. Wallis and Mrs. Newport are withholding our rent until we can get the tenants of 10 Marish Court evicted. We have had the police in again and Mrs. Rockell has been assaulted. We have, as you know, already been to court in connection with these people before. We have also written to the social security people to inform them that they have got at least five lodgers. This letter is a formal complaint. We will seek our solicitor's advice about holding the rent for us. We have been threatened with our lives in front of the police. We hope this letter receives your utmost attention.'

The council themselves got a warrant for possession on that and evicted Miss Jack and her baby son. She then went to another council house in Slough of which a Mrs Richardson was the tenant. It was at 271 Humber Way, Langley, Slough. She became a lodger there, quite contrary to the terms of the tenancy. Mrs Richardson left that house. Miss Jack and her son remained in it, without any licence or permission at all. The council got an order for her eviction. So she was turned out. But then she made a complete come-back on the council. She made application to them for accommodation as she was homeless. This put the council in an appalling dilemma. If she was homeless *unintentionally*, they were bound to house her indefinitely themselves, presumably to find her another council house, where she would again harass the neighbours. But if she was homeless *intentionally*, they were only bound to house her for a short time, such as bed and breakfast accommodation for a couple of weeks, so as to enable her to find accommodation for herself: see *De Falco v Crawley Borough Council* [1980] 1 All ER 913 at 919, [1980] 2 WLR 664 at 671.

Faced with this dilemma, the Slough council found that she was homeless *intentionally*. It was, I should have thought, a debatable point. Many people would have thought that Miss Jack's conduct, however deplorable, was not 'deliberate' in the sense required by s 17(1) of the 1977 Act. She did not deliberately do anything to get herself turned out. But the Slough council found that she had. And their finding has not been challenged. So I take it that it was correct. Finding that she was homeless *intentionally*, they were only bound to provide accommodation for her for a short time. They had none available in Slough at all. So they arranged with a guest house in Ealing to take her, bed and breakfast accommodation, for two weeks. They got a taxi, bundled her and her baby into it, took her the fifteen miles to the Ealing guest house, and paid for their accommodation there for a fortnight from 16th to 30th October 1978.

I expect that Miss Jack by this time knew all about the duty of the local authority to house the homeless. So, just before the fortnight was up, she went along to the Ealing housing authority and applied for accommodation. The Ealing council made all the inquiries they thought appropriate. In the result they took a different view from the Slough council. They found that she was homeless *unintentionally*. This was a legitimate finding which was made quite honestly. It is not challenged. This finding left them with the duty to house her themselves indefinitely (see s 4(5) of the 1977 Act), unless they could pass on the obligation to Slough under s 5(3) of the Act. This they claimed to be able to do. It is obvious that Miss Jack had a local connection with Slough, but none with Ealing. So they had a good chance of passing on the responsibility to Slough.

The Lynch family

John and Florence Lynch are husband and wife. There are three children of the family (two of Mrs Lynch's by a former husband, and one by Mr Lynch).

They had a council house at 74 Priory Road, Slough, but fell into arrears with their rent. In 1972 the council got an order for possession and payment of arrears of £151·74. They did not keep up the instalments. So the order for possession was executed on 30th September 1975. The rent was £6·66 a week. The arrears were £701·33. They were housed by the Slough council for a month. They were then granted a fresh tenancy of another council house, 104 Abbey Street, Slough, at a low rent of £2·89 a week. They did not pay this rent either. So another eviction order was made. It was executed on 12th April 1977. The arrears were £924·06.

After being evicted, the Lynch family lived rough or in bed and breakfast accommodation for some eight months. But then on 5th December 1977 John Lynch applied again to the Slough council for accommodation, as they were homeless. This again placed the Slough council in an appalling dilemma. They had no accommodation available for them. They asked themselves: 'How can we be expected to find accommodation for these people who never pay their rent?' The Slough council found that the Lynch family was homeless *intentionally*. Again I should think their finding was debatable. Their non-payment of rent was deplorable, but it may not have been 'deliberate', in the sense required by s 17(1). The family did not do it deliberately so as to get turned out. But the Slough council found that they had. And their finding has not been challenged. So I take it to be correct. So finding, the Slough council declined to provide the family with any more accommodation.

Getting no help from Slough, the Lynch family then moved to the London Borough of Hillingdon. They went to stay with friends at 17 Breakspear Road, Ruislip. But they did not last long. There was not enough room for them in the house. It became grossly overcrowded. The Hillingdon council insisted on their leaving. The Lynch family agreed to leave, but made application to the Hillingdon council to house them. The Hillingdon council made all the inquiries they thought appropriate. They took a different view from the Slough council. They found that the Lynch family were homeless *unintentionally*. This was a perfectly legitimate finding. It left the Hillingdon council with the duty to house the Lynch family indefinitely (see s 4(5) of the Act) unless they could pass on the obligation to Slough under s 5(3). This they claimed to do. It is obvious that the Lynch family had a local connection with Slough, but not with Hillingdon. So Hillingdon had a good chance of passing on the responsibility to Slough.

The law

I do not propose to analyse in detail the various sections of the 1977 Act. That would be much too tedious. I take Miss Jack's case, but the same applies to the Lynch family.

First, the Slough council were entitled to find that Miss Jack was intentionally homeless when she was removed by them from Slough into the Ealing area. But that finding was not binding on Ealing. The Ealing council were entitled to make their own inquiries and they were entitled to come to their own conclusion. They were entitled to find that Miss Jack was unintentionally homeless, even though this meant contradicting the Slough finding.

Second, if the finding of Ealing stopped there, it would mean that Ealing was bound to house Miss Jack and her baby indefinitely under s 4(5) of the Act.

But, third, Ealing was entitled to pass on *that* obligation to Slough. That follows because Miss Jack had a local connection with Slough and none with Ealing. So Ealing was the 'notifying authority' and Slough the 'notified authority' within s 5.

Fourth, on being so notified, Slough came under a duty 'to secure that accommodation becomes available for occupation by the person to whom the notification relates': see s 5(3). That is the selfsame duty as is imposed by s 4(5) in the selfsame words 'to secure that accommodation becomes available for his occupation'. It is Slough's duty to secure that accommodation is available for him indefinitely, and not merely for a short time.

Fifth, this means that Slough are bound to accept the finding of Ealing that the homelessness of Miss Jack was unintentional.

Conclusion

Each of these two families was, by long residence in Slough, the responsibility of the Slough council. Each family behaved deplorably and the Slough council were quite right to evict them from their council homes. But I am afraid that, under this statute, the Slough council cannot get rid of them by evicting them. So long as they were in Slough, each could come back at once, say they are homeless, and demand to be housed again by the Slough council indefinitely. It is an intolerable burden to put on the Slough council, and worse still on the people of the neighbourhood who have to put up with them. Yet the statute will have it so.

In these two cases the Slough council hoped that, by moving them, or getting them to move, to adjoining areas, they might shift the responsibility onto the adjoining local authorities. But Slough's efforts have not succeeded. The adjoining local authorities can turn round and say to Slough: 'They are your responsibility. Not ours. You must have them back. You must house them indefinitely, not us.'

As it happens, pending this litigation, the two families have been housed in Ealing and Hillingdon respectively at the expense of those councils. Now that we have decided that it was the responsibility of Slough to house them, Slough must bear that expense and repay Ealing and Hillingdon.

I would dismiss the appeals, accordingly.

SHAW LJ (read by Templeman LJ). These appeals pose questions as to the interpretation and operation of the Housing (Homeless Persons) Act 1977. The individual histories which give rise to these appeals have been recounted in the judgment of Lord Denning MR and I do not dwell on them but come at once to the law and the scheme devised by the Act.

The opening words of its preamble state that it is 'An Act to make further provision as to the functions of local authorities with regard to persons who are homeless'. As would be expected from this introduction, s 1 defines the circumstances in which, for the purposes of the Act, persons are to be regarded as being homeless.

Having established the category of persons to whom the Act applies, ss 3 and 4 describe the duties imposed on housing authorities in regard to homeless persons. By s 19 a 'housing authority' is identified in England and Wales as a local authority. The incidence and allocation of these duties is determined, at any rate in the first instance, by an application by a person to a local authority for assistance in obtaining accommodation (see s 3). When such an application is made, the local authority to whom it is made must, if they have reason to believe the applicant is homeless or is threatened with homelessness, make inquiries of the nature described in the section. These are directed to ascertaining whether the authority can be satisfied that the applicant is homeless; and, if they are so satisfied, whether the authority can be further satisfied that either the applicant has a priority need (as defined in s 2) or is intentionally homeless (as defined in s 17).

If the authority are satisfied under the first head, they are bound to do something to assist the applicant. The extent of that obligation will however be more or less according to whether the authority is further satisfied that the applicant has a priority need and further, whether or not the applicant is intentionally homeless (see s 4).

Where the authority are *not* satisfied that the applicant has a priority need or where they *are* satisfied that the applicant became homeless intentionally, the obligation cast on the local authority to whom the application was made is to provide assistance in regard to accommodation of a transitory or temporary kind (see s 4(2) and (3)).

On the other hand, where the local authority *are* satisfied that the applicant is homeless and has a priority need but are *not* satisfied that the applicant became homeless intentionally, it is incumbent on them to secure that accommodation becomes available for his occupation (see s 4(5)). This is the most ample obligation imposed by the Act. It must fall initially on the authority to whom the applicant directs his application.

Nowhere in the Act is there any provision which restricts a homeless person in his choice of the authority to which he desires to direct his application. The decision as to venue is his.

Where the situation thereafter revealed by the inquiries which the authority has to make under s 3 is such as to impose no more than the short-term assistance called for under s 4(2) or s 4(3), the fact that the applicant had no previous connection with the area of the authority is of no great consequence. The burden they are called on to assume is not a lasting one and involves relatively little cost.

If, however, the continuing burden contemplated by s 4(5) falls on an authority to whose locality the applicant has previously been a stranger, it is open to that authority to consider whether the applicant has a local connection with the area of another housing authority. Should they form the opinion that such is indeed the case, they may notify that other authority accordingly. The authority thus notified will then have to assume the burden which otherwise would have rested on the authority to whom the application which set this process in motion was made (s 5). There are certain reservations, the more important and significant one for the purposes of the present appeals being that the authority notified may dispute the applicant's local connection with that authority on which the purported transfer of the duty to house is founded. If such a dispute arises, s 5(7) and (8) provides that appropriate arrangements shall be made to determine any question arising under s 5. Such arrangements have been made and they take the form of a reference to arbitration (see the Housing (Homeless Persons) (Appropriate Arrangements) Order 1978, SI 1978 No 69). It is only what may give rise to dispute under the section that is within the scope of such an arbitration, and essentially this is the question of local connection.

As I have said already, where in the course of the procedure under ss 3, 4 and 5 an authority have to be satisfied of any matter under s 3 or s 4, or may form an opinion under s 5, it is the authority to whom the application which touched off *that* procedure is made who have to be so satisfied or may form the relevant opinion.

Of course the 'satisfaction' called for in relation to the specified matters must be honestly and reasonably arrived at. Subject to this requirement and to the resolution of any dispute as to 'local connection', any decision in this connection made by a housing authority can only be impeached, if at all, on the ground that no reasonable authority acting reasonably in the discharge of its functions could have reached that decision. Unless and until the relevant authority's decisions in those regards are nullified on such a basis, they remain effective and operative. Accordingly, in those situations which give rise to the maximum burden under the impact of s 4(5), the machinery of s 5 provides for a lateral shift of that burden to the authority with whom the applicant has a local connection affirmed by reference to arbitration if this issue is in dispute.

The present conflict arises because when Miss Jack and the Lynches respectively applied to Slough council ('Slough'), that authority, having made inquiry as required under s 3, came to the conclusion that they were satisfied in regard to both the applicants that they were 'intentionally homeless'. Section 17 of the Act in its four subsections seeks, for the purposes of the Act, to define this concept, but it remains an elusive one. There may be cases where different minds may reasonably come to different conclusions in this regard on the same facts. Where the facts are not precisely the same because the situation is examined at different times, there is even more room for diversity of view.

In each of the cases when the respective applications were made to Slough, that authority formed the view that they were satisfied that the respective applicants became homeless intentionally. Slough accordingly were under a duty to provide only limited assistance as required by s 4(2) and s 4(3). Having discharged the duties thus defined, they regarded themselves as free of any further responsibility in the case of Miss Jack, who had been what can be described as an undesirable tenant, and also in the case of the Lynches, whom it might be difficult to regard as desirable tenants.

One can understand the mortification of a local authority who have, as they believe, disposed of applicants whom they considered to be intentionally homeless, when those same persons reappear as local obligations once more, *and* on the s 4(5) full burden basis, by way of the merry-go-round set up under s 5.

Slough complain that Ealing and Hillingdon have acted on their respective views in a way which overrides or purports to supersede the view on which Slough had acted and which was antecedent to the view of Ealing or of Hillingdon.

This is based on a misconception. Neither Ealing nor Hillingdon has purported to set aside the conclusion formed by Slough. Each of them was required by the Act to make their own inquiries and to form their own view as to what they revealed; and each was bound to act on their view, for that view was the operative view on which their respective responsibilities fell to be determined.

That Miss Jack and the Lynches are back with Slough is not the result of their having had a second bite at the cherry as did the applicant in *Delahaye v Oswestry Borough Council* (1980) Times, 27th July, for they did not renew their application to Slough. As the law stands under the 1977 Act, the merry-go-round can be boarded at different points by application to different local authorities. Each is under a duty to make its own assessment after due inquiry of the factors involved, including homelessness. Each is entitled if the circumstances warrant it to form the opinion that a different authority is the one with which the applicant has a local connection; and is empowered on that ground to seek to bring about the lateral shift of responsibility where the duty to provide accommodation appears to the authority to whom application was made to arise under s 4(5).

In my judgment both in the case of Ealing and of Hillingdon the local authority has acted within the powers and has sought properly to discharge the duties arising from the 1977 Act. It is not difficult to understand that different and conflicting ideas may be reached as to intentional homelessness. It may sometimes, no doubt, be thought that the inquiries which led to the view which is formed may have the appearance of being perfunctory or casual. It matters not so long as the process and the outcome considered together are bona fide and could be justified as reasonable in all the circumstances. If this be so, those views prevail. There is no suggestion of bad faith in the present cases and there has been no challenge on the ground that the decisions of Ealing and of Hillingdon were such as could not reasonably have been reached.

It follows, in my judgment, that the appeals of Slough must fail and should be dismissed. The cross-appeal claiming expenses incurred by Miss Jack as the result of the attitude taken up by Slough must in consequence succeed and I would, though not with any marked enthusiasm, allow it accordingly.

TEMPLEMAN LJ. Miss Jack became the tenant of 60 Lancaster Avenue, Slough, a council house, in about 1973. Following complaints from neighbours which the Slough Borough Council ('Slough') found to be justified, Miss Jack was transferred to another council property, 10 Marish Court, Slough, in about 1976.

Following complaints from neighbours and the accumulation of substantial rent arrears, Slough obtained a court order for possession against Miss Jack on 16th February 1978 but Slough announced that they would not enforce the order provided Miss Jack did not cause further disturbance to her neighbours.

Following further complaints from neighbours which Slough found to be justified, the order for possession was enforced against Miss Jack on 22nd May 1978.

Miss Jack then moved into 271 Humber Way, Langley, as a lodger without the knowledge or consent of Slough. The tenant of that council house property moved out, Miss Jack was found to be in occupation as a trespasser and Slough obtained a possession order against Miss Jack on 29th September 1978.

On 9th October 1978 Miss Jack applied to Slough for accommodation under the Housing (Homeless Persons) Act 1977. Section 17(1) provides that—

'. . . a person becomes homeless intentionally if he deliberately does or fails to do anything in consequence of which he ceases to occupy accommodation which is *a*   available for his occupation and which it would have been reasonable for him to continue to occupy.'

On 10th October 1978 a sub-committee of the Slough council housing committee, acting under delegated powers, was satisfied that Miss Jack's homelessness was intentional being attributable to her conduct which resulted in her eviction from 10 Marish Court. The conclusion reached by Slough that they were satisfied that Miss Jack's homelessness was intentional cannot be challenged on this appeal.

b   As a result of that decision, Slough by s 4(3) of the Act became under a duty to Miss Jack to secure that accommodation was made available for her occupation for such period as Slough considered would give her a reasonable opportunity of herself securing accommodation for her occupation. On 11th October 1978 Slough complied with that duty by offering bed and breakfast accommodation to Miss Jack for a period of 14 days at an address in Ealing. Miss Jack took up that offer on 16th October 1978.

c   On 26th October 1978 Miss Jack applied to the Ealing Borough Council ('Ealing') for accommodation under the Housing (Homeless Persons) Act 1977.

As a result of Miss Jack's application, it became the duty of Ealing to make appropriate inquiries under s 3 of the Act. Those inquiries established to the satisfaction of Ealing, and it is not disputed, that Miss Jack was homeless or threatened with homelessness, that she had a priority need, that she had no local connection with Ealing but that she had a

d   local connection with Slough. Ealing notified Slough, pursuant to s 5 of the Act, that Miss Jack had a local connection with Slough but none with Ealing.

As a further result of Miss Jack's application to Ealing, it became the duty of Ealing under s 3 of the Act to make inquiries to satisfy themselves whether Miss Jack had become homeless or threatened with homelessness intentionally. If Ealing was so

e   satisfied, it was the duty of Ealing under s 4(3) to secure that accommodation was made available for Miss Jack for such period as Ealing considered would give her a reasonable opportunity of herself securing accommodation for her occupation. If Ealing were not satisfied that Miss Jack's homelessness was intentional, it would become the duty of Slough under s 5(3) of the Act to secure that accommodation became available for occupation by Miss Jack.

f   Ealing decided that they were not satisfied that Miss Jack had become homeless intentionally. That decision was reached by a management officer of the homeless families unit of the housing department of Ealing council. That management officer, of undisclosed experience and qualifications, interviewed Miss Jack, telephoned a welfare officer at Slough council, and without more ado and in the blithe belief that she had in her own words 'heard the two sides of the case' came to the conclusion that Miss Jack was 'not threatened with homelessness intentionally because she was evicted from 271

g   Humber Way, Langley, where she had entered by leave of the then tenant'. In a subsequent statement Ealing's chief solicitor asserted that after Miss Jack had been placed in bed and breakfast accommodation in Ealing she could not be blamed for the ensuing homelessness that followed after Slough ceased paying for such accommodation and that Ealing was therefore of the opinion that Miss Jack's homelessness was unintentional. In that same statement Ealing's chief solicitor asserted that, on the strength of Ealing's

h   opinion, there is a duty on Slough to secure accommodation for Miss Jack. The conclusion reached by Ealing that they were not satisfied that Miss Jack's homelessness was intentional cannot be challenged on this appeal.

In my judgment it is lamentable that Ealing should be able to reverse the decision of Slough that Miss Jack's homelessness was intentional while at the same time Ealing disclaim responsibility for providing accommodation for Miss Jack. If an appeal from a

j   finding of intentional homelessness is desirable, Parliament should provide an appropriate machinery for this purpose. If an appeal procedure is not desirable, one local authority should not be entitled to reverse another local authority without assuming responsibility for the accommodation of the homeless person in question.

In my judgment it is equally lamentable that Ealing should have reached a decision which contradicted that of Slough and imposed an onerous burden on Slough to the detriment of other persons in need of accommodation in Slough in the casual and irresponsible manner set forth in the affidavit of the management officer in these proceedings.

However we must take the Act as we find it. Section 3 required Ealing to make such inquiries as were necessary to satisfy Ealing whether Miss Jack had become homeless or was threatened with homelessness intentionally. By s 4(5) when Ealing were not satisfied that Miss Jack became homeless intentionally, their duty, subject to s 5, was to secure that accommodation became available for the occupation of Miss Jack. But by s 5(3) when Ealing, the notifying authority, notified Slough, the notified authority, that Ealing were of the opinion that Miss Jack had a local connection with Slough and no local connection with Ealing and that Miss Jack ran no risk of domestic violence in the Slough area, then it became 'the duty of the notified authority to secure that accommodation becomes available for occupation by the person to whom the notification relates'.

The effect of the Act is that Slough are bound by Ealing's decision that Ealing were not satisfied that Miss Jack's homelessness was intentional. Counsel on behalf of Slough struggled manfully to escape the express provisions of the Act but finally submitted that Slough are not under a duty to provide accommodation pursuant to s 5(3) until Miss Jack impliedly applies to Slough for accommodation and that when that implied application is made Slough can then treat the implied application as an application under s 3 and proceed to decide whether Slough are satisfied that Miss Jack's homelessness is intentional. In my judgment the Act does not permit or contemplate a third decision by Slough which could reverse the second decision of Ealing which on the true construction of the Act reversed the first decision of Slough.

Section 5(7) of the Act provides that—

'any question which falls to be determined under [the] section shall be determined by agreement between the notifying authority and the notified authority or, in default of such agreement, in accordance with the appropriate arrangements.'

Those appropriate arrangements amount to arbitration (see the Housing (Homeless Persons) (Appropriate Arrangements) Order 1978, SI 1978 No 69). Counsel on behalf of Slough argued that one question which fell to be determined was whether Miss Jack was homeless intentionally or not. In my judgment the only questions which fall to be determined under s 5 are questions which are in doubt under that section, in particular questions which arise as to the local connection of an applicant for housing accommodation. Once these and allied questions arising under the section have been determined against the notified authority, then s 5(3) provides in clear and express terms that it shall be the duty of the notified authority to secure accommodation for the person to whom the notification relates. Section 5 does not come into operation at all unless and until the notifying authority have carried out their duty under s 4 and are not satisfied that the applicant became homeless intentionally. There is no machinery for the arbitrator or anyone else to decide that the notifying authority were satisfied that the applicant became homeless intentionally or that the notifying authority ought reasonably to have been satisfied that the applicant became homeless intentionally.

In the result the appeal must be dismissed, and for similar reasons the other appeals before this court must also be dismissed.

Appeals dismissed. Leave to appeal to the House of Lords refused.

Solicitors: *Dawson & Co*, agents for *Maurice F Hulks*, Slough (for Slough Borough Council); *Sharpe, Pritchard & Co*, agents for *N L Green*, Ealing (for London Borough of Ealing); *John Douglas* (for Miss Jack); *Roger Smith* (for Mr and Mrs Lynch); *J A Kosky*, Uxbridge (for London Borough of Hillingdon).

Sumra Green   Barrister.

a
GMS Syndicate Ltd v Gary Elliott Ltd and others

CHANCERY DIVISION
NOURSE J
11th, 14th, 15th, 16th, 17th, 18th, 21st, 22nd, 23rd JULY, 23rd OCTOBER 1980

b
Landlord and tenant – Relief against forfeiture – Immoral user of premises – Court's discretion to grant relief – Extent – Lease of ground floor and basement – Sublease of basement – Lessee and sublessee both guilty of permitting basement to be used for immoral purposes – Whether court able to restrict order for possession to basement of demised premises only – Law of Property Act 1925, s 146.

c
The plaintiff company owned a building consisting of six floors, the top four of which were let to residential tenants. By a lease dated 2nd April 1969 it demised the ground floor and basement to the first defendant (which ran a chain of retail men's clothing shops) for a term expiring on 25th March 1981. The lease contained a covenant by the first defendant not to permit anything to be done on the premises which might be or *d* become an annoyance, inconvenience or nuisance to the plaintiff or occupiers of any adjoining or neighbouring property and a covenant not to allow the premises or any part of them to be used for any immoral purpose. The plaintiff as lessor had a right to re-enter the premises or any part of them in the event of the first defendant failing to observe any of the covenants. The basement was sublet, with the plaintiff's consent, to the second and third defendants for use as a health club for a term until 30th June 1977 and on *e* identical covenants to those in the headlease. By a deed executed on 23rd December 1974 the second and third defendants covenanted with the first defendant, and also with the plaintiff, to perform the covenants in the sublease as from that date and 'thenceforth during the residue of the term granted by the sublease'. After their contractual term expired on 30th June 1977, the second and third defendants held over under Part II of the Landlord and Tenant Act 1954. In 1979 the plaintiff brought an action against the *f* defendants claiming (i) as against the first defendant forfeiture of the headlease on the ground that the first defendant had allowed the basement to be used for immoral purposes between July 1978 and June 1979 and had permitted a business to be carried on there which was an annoyance, inconvenience or nuisance to the plaintiff and to the occupiers of the adjoining and neighbouring properties, and (ii) as against the second and third defendants possession of the basement on similar grounds and damages for breach *g* of the direct covenant with the plaintiff contained in the deed of 23rd December 1974. The defendants denied the allegations and claimed relief against forfeiture under s 146[a] of the Law of Property Act 1925. The judge found on the evidence that the second defendant had allowed the basement to be used for immoral purposes between July 1978 and June 1979, that the first defendant although knowing of the immoral user had not taken reasonable steps to prevent it from continuing, and that the presence of the second *h* and third defendants' business had caused annoyance, inconvenience and nuisance to the plaintiff's residential tenants.

Held – (1) Having regard to the finding that the basement had been allowed to be used for immoral purposes, the plaintiff was prima facie entitled to judgment against the first defendant for possession, and that necessarily involved forfeiture of the second and third *j* defendants' sublease of the basement (see p 623 g h, post).

(2) On the true construction of the deed of 23rd December 1974 the second and third defendants' obligation to the plaintiff to observe the covenants 'thenceforth during the residue of the tenancy granted by the sublease' meant that the obligation did not expire at the end of their contractual term on 30th June 1977 but continued, by virtue of s 24(1) of the 1954 Act, while they held over under Part II of that Act. Accordingly the plaintiff

---
a Section 146, so far as material, is set out at p 625 *f*, post

was entitled to damages from them for breach of covenant (see p 624 *f* to *j* and p 627 *a b*, post).

(3) Relief against forfeiture would not be granted to the second and third defendants because it was the practice of the court not to grant relief where a breach of covenant involved immoral user, unless there were very exceptional circumstances and there were no such circumstances so far as the second and third defendants were concerned (see p 624 *j*, post); *Central Estates (Belgravia) Ltd v Woolgar (No 2)* [1972] 3 All ER 610 applied.

(4) The court could however grant the first defendant relief against forfeiture in respect of the ground floor, although it was only part of the premises comprised in the headlease, because the ground floor was physically separated from the basement and capable of being distinctly let and enjoyed and the breaches complained of were confined to the basement. Since the plaintiff's main aim in the proceedings was to have the second and third defendants removed from the basement and since it had no objection to the first defendant remaining in possession of the ground floor, the court would therefore grant relief to the first defendant by restricting the order for possession to the basement only (see p 626 *f* to *h* and p 627 *a b*, post); *Dumpor's Case* (1603) 4 Co Rep 119b applied.

Notes

For relief against forfeiture, see 23 Halsbury's Laws (3rd Edn) 674–683, paras 1400–1411, and for cases on the subject, see 31(2) Digest (Reissue) 827–834, 6863–6906.

For the Law of Property Act 1925, s 146, see 27 Halsbury's Statutes (3rd Edn) 563.

For the Landlord and Tenant Act 1954, s 24, see 18 ibid 557.

Cases referred to in judgment

Berton v Alliance Economic Investment Co [1922] 1 KB 742, 91 LJKB 748, 127 LT 422, CA; subsequent proceedings [1923] All ER Rep 539, 92 LJKB 750, 129 LT 76, 87 JP 85, 21 LGR 403, CA, 31(1) Digest (Reissue) 385, 3076.

Borthwick-Norton v Dougherty [1950] WN 481, 94 Sol Jo 706, 31(2) Digest (Reissue) 829, 6872.

Bowser v Colby (1841) 1 Hare 109, [1835–42] All ER Rep 478, 11 LJ Ch 132, 5 Jur 1178, 66 ER 969, 31(2) Digest (Reissue) 680, 5578.

Central Estates (Belgravia) Ltd v Woolgar (No 2) [1972] 3 All ER 610, [1972] 1 WLR 1048, 24 P & CR 103, CA, 31(2) Digest (Reissue) 828, 6866.

Cornish v Brook Green Laundry Ltd [1959] 1 All ER 373, [1959] 1 QB 394, [1959] 2 WLR 215, CA, 31(2) Digest (Reissue) 967, 7800.

Dendy v Evans [1910] 1 KB 263, [1908–10] All ER Rep 589, 79 LJKB 121, 102 LT 4, CA, 31(2) Digest (Reissue) 810, 6715.

Dumpor's Case (1603) 4 Co Rep 119b, 76 ER 1110, sub nom *Dumper v Syms* Cro Eliz 815, 31(2) Digest (Reissue) 708, 5808.

Cases also cited

Atkin v Rose [1923] 1 Ch 522.

Baynton v Morgan (1888) 22 QBD 74.

Bleachers' Association Ltd's Leases, Re, Weinbergs Weatherproofs Ltd v Radcliffe Paper Mill Co Ltd [1957] 3 All ER 663, [1958] Ch 437.

Evans v Vaughan (1825) 4 B & C 261, 107 ER 1056.

Fairclough v Berliner [1931] 1 Ch 60, [1930] All ER Rep 170.

Glass v Kencakes Ltd [1964] 3 All ER 807, [1966] 1 QB 611.

Great Western Railway Co v Smith (1875) 2 Ch D 235, CA.

Holme v Brunskill (1877) 3 QBD 495.

Junction Estates v Cope (1974) 27 P & CR 482.

Knight's Case (1588) 5 Co Rep 54b, [1558–1774] All ER Rep 347, 77 ER 137.

Love v Pares (1810) 13 East 80, 104 ER 297.

R v De Munck [1918] 1 KB 638, [1918–19] All ER Rep 499, CCA.

Sefton v Tophams Ltd [1966] 1 All ER 1039, [1967] 1 AC 50, HL.
a *Singleton v Ellison* [1895] 1 QB 607.
Skelton (William) & Son Ltd v Harrison and Pinder Ltd [1975] 1 All ER 182, [1975] QB 361.
Walker's Case (1587) 3 Co Rep 22a, 76 ER 676.

Action

By a writ issued on 4th September 1979 the plaintiff, GMS Syndicate Ltd, brought an
b action against the first defendant, Gary Elliott Ltd, to whom the plaintiff had, by a lease
dated 2nd April 1969, demised the ground floor and basement of 125 Queensway,
London W2, until 25th March 1981, and the second and third defendants, Napleandra
Ruparel and Yvonne Ruparel, to whom the basement of 125 Queensway had been sublet
until 30th June 1977 with the consent of the plaintiff. The plaintiff claimed as against
each of the defendants possession of the demised premises and damages for breach of
c covenant against the second and third defendants. The defendants served defences and
counterclaims in which they either denied, or did not admit, the allegations made in the
writ, and each claimed, so far as was necessary, relief against forfeiture under s 146 of the
Law of Property Act 1925. The facts are set out in the judgment.

Anthony G Bompas for the plaintiff.
d *Robert Pryor* for the first defendant.
Richard Moshi for the second and third defendants.

Cur adv vult

23rd October. **NOURSE J** read the following judgment: This is a forfeiture action based
primarily on the alleged immoral user of basement premises known as the Queensway
e Health Club at 125 Queensway, London W2. Those premises are used as a sauna bath,
gymnasium and health club. The plaintiff, GMS Syndicate Ltd, is the freehold owner of
125 Queensway. The first defendant, Gary Elliott Ltd, is the lessee of the ground floor and
basement. The second and third defendants, Napleandra Ruparel and his wife, Yvonne
Ruparel, are the sublessees of the basement, and the proprietors, through the medium of
a private company, of the Queensway Health Club.
f 125 Queensway is built on six floors including the basement. The upper floors are let
to residential tenants of the plaintiff. The tenants of the third and fourth floors are Mr
and Mrs Joseph Ralph, who have been there since 1946. Their daughter, Miss Kathleen
Ralph, was the tenant of the second floor flat from June 1968 until September 1977. The
tenants of the first floor flat are Mr and Mrs Eric McGregor, who have been there since
1947.
g By a lease dated 2nd April 1969 the plaintiff demised to the first defendant the ground
floor and the basement for a term of twelve and a quarter years from 25th December
1968. That term will expire on 25th March, 1981. Clause 3 of the lease contains covenants
by the first defendant in the following terms:

'(14) Not to do or suffer or permit to be done or suffered on the premises
anything which may be or become an annoyance inconvenience or nuisance to the
h Lessors or the other owners or occupiers of any adjoining or neighbouring property
or to the neighbourhood or which may infringe any legislation for the time being
in force.
'(15) Not to carry on or permit upon the premises or any part thereof any noisy
or dangerous trade business manufacture or occupation or any nuisance nor use the
same or allow the same to be used for any illegal or immoral purpose . . .'

j The lease contains a common form proviso for re-entry on non-payment of rent or on
failure or neglect by the first defendant to perform or observe any of the covenants,
conditions or agreements on its part therein contained.
The first defendant runs a chain of retail men's clothing shops under the name of 'Lord
John'. By the end of 1969 the first defendant had made arrangements, with the consent

of the plaintiff, to sublet the basement to a Mr Silvalingham and a Mr Roberts for use as a sauna bath, gymnasium and health club until September 1972, that being the period *a* covered by a planning permission which had been obtained for that use. Those arrangements were put into effect by an agreement dated 29th December 1969 and were continued after an extension of the planning permission until 30th June 1977 had been granted in August 1972. The continuation was effected by a supplemental agreement dated 30th January 1974, by which the first defendant agreed to let, and Mr Silvalingham and Mr Roberts agreed to take, the basement premises for a further term commencing *b* on 1st September 1972 and expiring on 30th June 1977. That agreement incorporated (by reference to the earlier agreement of 29th December 1969) covenants on the part of Mr Silvalingham and Mr Roberts in all respects identical to the covenants on the part of the first defendant contained in cl 3(14) and (15) of the headlease to which I have already referred.

By an assignment dated 23rd December 1974 Mr Silvalingham and Mr Roberts *c* assigned to the second and third defendants, Mr and Mrs Ruparel, the benefit of the agreement of 30th January 1974. On the same day the plaintiff, the first defendant, Mr Silvalingham and Mr Roberts and Mr and Mrs Ruparel executed a deed whereby, first, the plaintiff and the first defendant granted their consents to the assignment to Mr and Mrs Ruparel and, secondly, Mr and Mrs Ruparel covenanted with the first defendant, and as a separate covenant with the plaintiff, that as from the date of the assignment 'and *d* thenceforth during the residue of the term granted by the Underlease as extended by the Supplemental tenancy agreement' they would pay the rent thereby reserved and observe and perform the covenants and conditions on the part of the sublessees therein contained. There was therefore a direct covenant by Mr and Mrs Ruparel with the plaintiff to observe and perform, amongst others, first, the covenant against annoyance, inconvenience and so forth and, secondly, the covenant against illegal or immoral user *e* incorporated in the agreement of 30th January 1974. One of the questions in these proceedings is whether that direct covenant expired with the contractual term on 30th June 1977 or whether it continues while Mr and Mrs Ruparel hold over (as they now do) under Part II of the Landlord and Tenant Act 1954. They have been able to do that because in September 1978 an appeal by them against the Westminster City Council's refusal to extend the planning permission for the continued use of the basement as a *f* sauna bath, gymnasium and health club was allowed.

I have already said that the plaintiff's action is based primarily on the alleged immoral user of the Queensway Health Club. I must now state that and the other alleged causes of complaint in greater detail. First, the plaintiff alleges that since in or about July 1978 Mr and Mrs Ruparel have allowed the basement to be used for illegal and immoral purposes and in particular that they have employed as masseuses on the premises women *g* who for reward commit lewd and immoral practices at the behest of customers of the business. Second, the plaintiff alleges that the business carried on by Mr and Mrs Ruparel in the basement has become an annoyance, inconvenience and nuisance to the plaintiff and the occupiers of adjoining and neighbouring property, in particular the plaintiff's residential tenants at 125 Queensway, and the plaintiff says that the business has been so conducted as to encourage persons to attend at the premises seeking women with whom *h* to perform lewd or immoral practices. The plaintiff says that Mr and Mrs Ruparel have thereby brought the basement and the building as a whole into disrepute and, further or alternatively, have caused persons seeking disreputable services to attend at and loiter near the building so causing nuisance and giving offence to the plaintiff and its residential tenants. The plaintiff alleges that in these two respects Mr and Mrs Ruparel have been in breach of the direct covenant with the plaintiff contained in the deed of 23rd *j* December 1974 and for that the plaintiff claims damages. However, its principal claim is against the first defendant for forfeiture of the headlease on the grounds that the first defendant also has allowed the basement to be used for illegal and immoral purposes and that it has suffered or permitted a business to be carried on in the basement which is an annoyance, inconvenience or nuisance to the plaintiff and to the occupiers of the

adjoining and neighbouring property. In this connection, the plaintiff alleges that on or
before 1st August 1978 the first defendant had become aware of the matters of which the
plaintiff complains in relation to the use of the basement but that it has nevertheless
failed and neglected to take any sufficient steps against Mr and Mrs Ruparel. If the
plaintiff succeeds in its claim for forfeiture of the headlease then, subject to any question
of relief, it will follow that Mr and Mrs Ruparel's subtenancy will be forfeited as well.
I should at this stage say that the plaintiff's primary objective is to get Mr and Mrs
Ruparel out of the basement. If it succeeds in that it will be less concerned with its claim
against them for breach of the direct covenant in the deed of 23rd December 1974.

The defendants either deny, or do not admit, that the matters complained of have
taken place. Further, they say that if they have, they have not allowed or suffered or
permitted them to happen. They each, so far as may be necessary, claim relief against
forfeiture.

[His Lordship then considered the facts and evidence in detail and found that the
basement had been used for immoral purposes. His Lordship then considered the
plaintiff's allegation that the second defendant knew or ought to have known of the
immoral user, that he abstained from taking reasonable steps to prevent it when it was
within his power to do so and that he thereby 'allowed' the premises to be so used,
according to the test adumbrated by Atkin LJ in *Berton v Alliance Economic Investment Co
Ltd* [1922] 1 KB 742 at 759. His Lordship stated that, having considered all the evidence
on the question, and in particular that of the second defendant himself, he was satisfied
that the second defendant either knew that indecent and immoral acts were being
committed on the premises or that he had shut his eyes to whether they were being
committed or not. His Lordship concluded that in all the circumstances the second
defendant had allowed the premises to be used for immoral purposes between July 1978
and June 1979. His Lordship continued:]

I deal next with the question whether the first defendant allowed the premises to be
used for immoral purposes. Shortly after the planning inquiry in July 1978 the plaintiff's
advisers sent the first defendant a copy of the written report of a visit by Mr Price, a
private investigator, to the premises on 14th July. In all material respects that report was
to the same effect as the evidence given by Mr Price in these proceedings. I need not deal
in detail with what the first defendant did or did not do after receiving that report,
because it is clear that it did not take reasonable steps to prevent the immoral user from
continuing. Indeed counsel for the first defendant, while making no concession on the
point, found it difficult to argue the contrary. The facts are that it accepted rent from Mr
and Mrs Ruparel after serving the notice under s 146 of the Law of Property Act 1925 in
December 1978. It did not serve a fresh notice. It did not take forfeiture proceedings
against the second and third defendants. In my judgment, the first defendant ought to
have taken those steps. Since it did not do so it is clear that it too allowed the premises
to be used for immoral purposes.

On that footing and, subject to questions of relief, the plaintiff is entitled to judgment
for possession against the first defendant. That will necessarily involve the forfeiture of
the second and third defendants' subtenancy of the basement. That means that the
plaintiff's secondary claim based on annoyance, inconvenience and nuisance becomes of
less importance, but I must nevertheless deal with it as shortly as I can in relation to the
plaintiff's claim against the second and third defendants under the direct covenant
contained in the deed of 23rd December 1974.

Counsel for the plaintiff emphasised that as against the second and third defendants
this claim is not based on their having allowed or permitted or suffered something to
happen. Clause 2(14) of the agreement dated 29th December 1969, when suitably
abstracted for present purposes, requires the lessees not to do on the premises anything
which may be or become an annoyance, inconvenience or nuisance to the plaintiff or the
other owners or occupiers of any adjoining or neighbouring property and so forth.
Counsel for the plaintiff, assuming at this stage that the second and third defendants are
still liable under the direct covenant contained in the deed of 23rd December 1974, says

that they are in breach of this covenant because they have carried on on the premises a business which has become an annoyance, inconvenience and a nuisance to the plaintiff and its residential tenants of the upper parts of the building. As to this, evidence was given by Mr McGregor, Mr and Mrs Ralph, and also Miss Kathleen Ralph. Without going into great detail, I am entirely satisfied on the evidence that the presence of the second and third defendants' business in the basement has caused annoyance and inconvenience and has been a nuisance to the plaintiff's residential tenants above. Many incidents were described in evidence. In particular, evidence was given of men ringing the doorbells to the flats late into the night on frequent occasions, and asking if the sauna was open or whether massage was available and even explicitly asking for sexual intercourse. Mrs Ralph gave evidence that this request was made to her on one occasion in respect of a named woman in terms which were so offensive to her that she asked to be allowed to write them down on a piece of paper. Then there was ample evidence that the tenants and their visitors had been subjected to various forms of importunity and insult from persons standing in or outside the common entrance passageway which leads from the front door both to the stairs down to the basement and the stairs up to the flats. On one occasion Mrs Ralph, who is an elderly lady, was prevented from going down the passageway by two youths, one of whom threatened her in a way which frightened her badly. In general I have every sympathy with the tenants in respect of their complaints on these matters and I am quite satisfied that the events which they described were the direct result of the presence of the second and third defendants' business in the basement.

The convenient course will be for me to deal next with the question whether the direct covenant by the second and third defendants with the plaintiff contained in the deed of 23rd December 1974 expired with the contractual term on 30th June 1977, or whether it continues while the second and third defendants hold over under Part II of the Landlord and Tenant Act 1954. As I have said, the material words are 'and thenceforth during the residue of the term granted by the Underlease as extended by the Supplemental tenancy agreement'. On one reading of those words it certainly might be said that the covenant expired with the contractual term, on the ground that that and no more was the term granted by the agreement of 29th December 1969, as extended by that of 30th January 1974. But it seems to me that such a reading ignores the effect of s 24(1) of the 1954 Act, which provides that a tenancy to which Part II applies shall not come to an end unless terminated in accordance with the provisions of Part II. It is now well established that this means that the term granted by the tenancy continues by way of a statutory extension and with a statutory variation as to the mode of determination: see, for example, *Cornish v Brook Green Laundry Ltd* [1959] 1 All ER 373 at 383, [1959] 1 QB 394 at 409. In the circumstances, it seems to me that the term granted by the first agreement as extended by the second is still subsisting, albeit that it has been further extended by the 1954 Act. It is still the same term. On that footing, it seems to me that the better reading of the material words in the direct covenant is to construe the obligation as continuing so long as the second and third defendants hold over under Part II of the 1954 Act. And I am fortified in that conclusion by the knowledge that the rival construction would produce an anomalous state of affairs which cannot have been within the contemplation of the parties to the deed. It follows that the plaintiff's claim against the second and third defendants for damages for breach of the direct covenant in the two respects I have mentioned succeeds. I will deal with quantum at the end of this judgment.

I deal next with the question of relief against forfeiture. Taking it by stages, it is clear, first, that I cannot, or at least that I should not, grant relief to the second and third defendants. It is the established practice of the court not to grant relief in cases where the breach involves immoral user, save in very exceptional circumstances such as those which were considered in *Central Estates (Belgravia) Ltd v Woolgar (No 2)* [1972] 3 All ER 610, [1972] 1 WLR 1048. There are no such circumstances in the present case so far as the second and third defendants are concerned.

The position of the first defendant is more difficult. As I have said, the plaintiff's primary objective is to get the second and third defendants out of the basement. If the only way it can achieve that is to forfeit the headlease in toto, then that is what the plaintiff seeks. On the other hand, provided that the plaintiff can be sure of obtaining possession of the basement, it has said that it will not object to the first defendant remaining in possession of the ground floor. This has raised a novel and interesting question. Has the court got jurisdiction to grant relief against forfeiture in respect of part only of the property comprised in a lease?

I should start by saying that if the only way in which the plaintiff can get possession of the basement is to forfeit the headlease in toto, I would think it clear that this is not a case in which I ought to grant the first defendant relief: compare *Borthwick-Norton v Dougherty* [1950] WN 481. But if there is jurisdiction to grant partial relief, I would think it equally clear that I ought to do so. Indeed, since the plaintiff has said that it will not object to the first defendant remaining in possession of the ground floor, this is a question which has effectively been removed from my decision. I assume, of course, that the first defendant will be able to satisfy the plaintiff and the court that the plaintiff will not suffer in costs as a result of this action and that it will not be prejudiced in any material way by the severance of the ground floor from the basement. Accordingly, I turn to consider whether there is jurisdiction to grant partial relief. On this question, counsel for the plaintiff, being apprehensive that it might not be possible to grant such relief without at the same time procuring a surrender by the first defendant of the headlease so far as it concerns the basement, thus leaving the second and third defendants as direct tenants of the plaintiff, has argued against there being jurisdiction. Counsel for the first defendant has argued in favour. Counsel for the second and third defendants has argued against.

It is to be noted that s 146(2) of the Law of Property Act 1925, under which the first defendant's application is made, does not specify the nature of the relief which the court can grant. It says that—

> 'the court may grant or refuse relief, as the court, having regard to the proceedings and conduct of the parties under the foregoing provisions of this section, and to all the other circumstances, thinks fit . . .'

It appears from cases such as *Bowser v Colby* [1841] 1 Hare 109, [1835–42] All ER Rep 748 and *Dendy v Evans* [1910] 1 KB 263, [1908–10] All ER Rep 589 that regard will readily be had to the practice of the old Court of Chancery before the Landlord and Tenant Act 1730, when relief against forfeiture was exclusively a matter for that court. This is not of direct assistance in the present case. In those days relief was confined to cases of non-payment of rent, and since rent issues out of the property as a whole there could have been no question of relief in part. But it is, I think, important to notice that the Court of Chancery, acting in personam, either restrained the landlord from proceeding to take possession at law or, if he had already done so, required him to grant a new lease. Either result could have been achieved by the landlord of his own volition. The court did not seek to impose a result which could not have been arrived at by the landlord himself.

Relief against forfeiture was a process by which equity restricted a landlord from enforcing his rights at law. In my judgment it could not then, and cannot now, be granted so as to impose on the parties a legal relationship which could not have been procured by the act of the landlord. If, therefore, I am to grant partial relief in the present case I must first be satisfied that the plaintiff could, had it wished, have forfeited the lease so far as concerns the basement alone.

I start with the proviso for re-entry which is in common form and allows the plaintiff 'into and upon the premises or any part thereof in the name of the whole to re-enter'. It is therefore possible for the plaintiff to forfeit as to the whole by entering on part, but I do not read those words as restricting any right to forfeit as to part which is otherwise available to the plaintiff. As to that, my instinct was against the notion that a landlord can forfeit in part. But counsel for the first defendant referred me to *Dumpor's Case* (1603) 4 Co Rep 119b, 76 ER 1110 in which the Court of King's Bench established the once well known rule of common law that a licence to do an act in breach of a condition in a lease determined the condition. That rule was abolished by s 1 of the Law of Property Amendment Act 1859 (Lord St Leonard's Act), which (with amendments) is now s 143 of the Law of Property Act 1925, and it is possible that this has caused the 'divers points' which, as the report of *Dumpor's Case* says, were there 'debated and resolved' to be forgotten. One of them is treated in this way (4 Co Rep 119b at 120b, 76 ER 1110 at 1113):

> 'But it was agreed, that a condition may be apportioned in two cases. 1. By act in law. 2. By act and wrong of the lessee.'

Apportionment by act in law is then dealt with and the report proceeds as follows (4 Co Rep 119b at 120b, 76 ER 1110 at 1114):

> '2. By act and wrong of the lessee, as if the lessee makes a feoffment of part, or commits waste in part, and the lessor enters for the forfeiture, or recovers the place wasted, there, the rent and condition shall be apportioned, for none shall take advantage of his own wrong and the lessor shall not be prejudiced by the wrong of the lessee . . .'

Having considered this passage with very great care, I can only conclude that the Court of King's Bench were of the opinion that it was in certain circumstances possible for a landlord to forfeit in part. Although the words 'and the lessor enters for the forfeiture' do not expressly refer to an entry on part, it appears clear from the context as a whole that that is what they mean. Once that point is overcome, the whole passage is seen to contemplate forfeiture in part and a consequential apportionment of the rent and the conditions of the lease between the part taken by the landlord and that retained by the tenant. It is true that what was under consideration in that case was re-entry for breach of condition without an express power to re-enter. But I can see no distinction in principle between that and re-entry under a common form proviso such as that found in the present case. There being no express restriction on the right to re-enter on part, I conceive that that right must exist as much in the latter case as in the former.

In the circumstances, the researches of counsel having revealed no other authority either way, I think that I am entitled to treat *Dumpor's Case* as establishing that a landlord can in certain circumstances, such as those found in the present case, forfeit in part. Had it not been for that case I might have found some difficulty in acceding to the arguments of counsel for the first defendant on this point. But there it is, and it seems to me to be a perfectly respectable peg on which to hang a decision which I believe will produce a fair and workable result as between the plaintiff and the first defendant. I emphasise that I do not intend to go beyond the circumstances of the present case, where the two parts of the demised property are physically separated one from the other and are capable of being distinctly let and enjoyed, and where the breaches complained of were committed on one part of the property and on that part alone. I have not considered what would have happened if the circumstances had been different.

I therefore propose to grant the first defendant relief against forfeiture by restricting the order for possession to the basement. I will make that order against all three defendants. I have already indicated the matters on which I shall first wish to be satisfied in favour of the plaintiff and I will discuss those matters with counsel at the end of this judgment. I agree with counsel for the first defendant that the order for possession of the basement alone will not cause any conveyancing difficulties, because it is clear on the authorities that the apportionment of rent and any other questions consequential on the severance of the two parts of the property can, if necessary, be settled by the court. No doubt an attempt will first be made to settle those matters by agreement. I should add that I cannot see how the order which I propose to make could operate as a surrender by the first defendant of the headlease so far as it concerns the basement, with the consequences of which counsel for the plaintiff was apprehensive. A surrender could not be made without the concurrence of the first defendant. The order for possession of the basement is made in invitum as against the first defendant, which has claimed relief in respect of the whole and has only obtained it in part.

Finally, I return to the quantum of the damages which I should award the plaintiff for the second and third defendants' breaches of the direct covenant contained in the deed of 23rd December 1974. Having achieved its primary objective of getting the second and third defendants out of the basement, the plaintiff is less concerned with its claim against them for damages. I propose, therefore, to award a sum which makes every allowance in favour of the second and third defendants. The sum I award is £500.

Solicitors: *Collyer-Bristow* (for the plaintiff); *Bennetts* (for the first defendant); *Portner & Jaskel* (for the second and third defendants).

Hazel Hartman   Barrister.

Practice Direction

FAMILY DIVISION

Husband and wife – Maintenance – Failure to maintain – Application for relief – Practice – Application may be heard by registrar – Application for hearing date – Matrimonial Causes Act 1973, s 27 (as amended by the Domestic Proceedings and Magistrates' Courts Act 1978, s 63) – Matrimonial Causes Rules 1977 (SI 1977 No 344), rr 98, 99 (as substituted by the Matrimonial Causes (Amendment) Rules 1981 (SI 1981 No 5), r 2).

As from 1st February 1981 s 27 of the Matrimonial Causes Act 1973 is amended by the Domestic Proceedings and Magistrates' Court Act 1978 so as to provide that either party to a marriage may apply to the court for an order under that section that the other party has failed to provide reasonable maintenance for the applicant or has failed to provide, or to make a proper contribution towards, reasonable maintenance for any child of the family. The revised jurisdiction does not require that the failure should be wilful.

The Matrimonial Causes Rules 1977, SI 1977 No 344, have been amended accordingly, so as to provide, inter alia, that these applications may be dealt with by a registrar (see the Matrimonial Causes (Amendment) Rules 1981, SI 1981 No 5, r 2, substituting rr 98 and 99 of the 1977 rules).

In the Divorce Registry it will not be the practice to allocate a hearing date on the notice of the application which is served on the respondent. Application for a hearing date should be made by lodging form D270 as in any other application for financial provision in a matrimonial cause proceeding in this registry.

R L BAYNE-POWELL
Senior Registrar.

4th February 1981

Albert v Lavin

QUEEN'S BENCH DIVISION
DONALDSON LJ AND HODGSON J
17th, 27th NOVEMBER 1980

Criminal law – Assault – Self-defence – Mistaken belief that self-defence justified – Assault on police constable in execution of his duty – Accused restrained by off-duty police officer in plain clothes – Police officer informing accused that he was a policeman – Accused genuinely but unreasonably believing officer not a policeman – Accused continuing to hit officer in what he believed to be self-defence – Accused charged with assaulting police officer in execution of his duty – Whether accused required to have reasonable grounds for belief that self-defence justified.

The appellant caused a disturbance in a bus queue while attempting to board a bus. He was restrained by an off-duty police officer who was in plain clothes. A struggle ensued between the appellant and the officer, in the course of which the officer told the appellant that he was a police officer and threatened to arrest him. The police officer was unable to produce his warrant card because he was grappling with the appellant. The appellant continued to hit the officer and was arrested and charged with assaulting a police officer in the execution of his duty. At the hearing of the charge the magistrates found that the appellant had caused a breach of the peace, that the police officer had done everything he reasonably could to ensure that the appellant knew that he was a police officer and that although the appellant genuinely believed that the officer was not a policeman he had no reasonable grounds for that belief. The appellant was convicted and appealed, contending, inter alia, that his belief that he was being subjected to an unjustified assault because of his genuine, albeit mistaken, belief that the officer was not a policeman was a good defence to the charge. The appellant submitted that it was illogical that a person charged with assault could escape conviction if he showed that he mistakenly but unreasonably thought his victim was consenting or that his action was not unlawful, but not if he mistakenly but unreasonably thought that his victim had no right to detain him and that he was therefore justified in using self-defence.

Held – It was not a defence to a charge of assault that the accused honestly but mistakenly believed that his action was justified as being reasonable self-defence if there were no reasonable grounds for his belief. The appellant had therefore been rightly convicted and his appeal would be dismissed (see p 637 *d e*, p 639 *e* to *h* and p 640 *d e*, post).

    R v Weston (1879) 14 Cox CC 346, *R v Rose* (1884) 15 Cox CC 540, *Owens v HM Advocate* 1946 JC 119 and *R v Chisam* (1963) 47 Cr App R 130 followed.

    R v Smith (David Raymond) [1974] 1 All ER 632 and *Director of Public Prosecutions v Morgan* [1975] 2 All ER 347 considered.

    Per Donaldson LJ. An ill-founded but completely honest and genuine belief that the self-defence was justified removes all or much of the culpability in the offence of assault. It therefore provides powerful mitigation and in an appropriate case would justify a court granting an absolute discharge (see p 640 *d e*, post).

Notes

For assaulting a constable in the execution of his duty, see 11 Halsbury's Laws (4th Edn) para 962, and for cases on the subject, see 15 Digest (Reissue) 985–988, 8546–8566.

    For justified assault in self-defence, see 11 Halsbury's Laws (4th Edn) para 1217, and for a case on the subject, see 15 Digest (Reissue) 991, 8590.

Cases referred to in judgments

Director of Public Prosecutions v Morgan [1975] 2 All ER 347, [1976] AC 182, [1975] 2

WLR 913, 139 JP 476, 61 Cr App R 136, HL; *affg* [1975] 1 All ER 8, [1976] AC 182, [1975] 2 WLR 913, CA, 15 Digest (Reissue) 1212, *10,398*.

Hyam v Director of Public Prosecutions [1974] 2 All ER 41, [1975] AC 55, [1974] 2 WLR 607, 138 JP 374, 59 Cr App R 91, HL, 15 Digest (Reissue) 1110, *9325*.

King v Hodges [1974] Crim LR 424, DC.

Mancini v Director of Public Prosecutions [1941] 3 All ER 272, [1942] AC 1, 111 LJKB 84, 165 LT 353, 28 Cr App R 65, HL, 14(1) Digest (Reissue) 391, *3324*.

Owens v HM Advocate 1946 JC 119, 15 Digest (Reissue) 1172, *7495*.

Palmer v R [1971] 1 All ER 1077, [1971] AC 814, [1971] 2 WLR 831, 55 Cr App R 223, 16 WIR 499, PC, 15 Digest (Reissue) 1171, *9967*.

Piddington v Bates, Robson v Ribton-Turner [1960] 3 All ER 660, [1961] 1 WLR 162, DC, 15 Digest (Reissue) 910, *7809*.

R v Chisam (1963) 47 Cr App R 130, CCA, 15 Digest (Reissue) 1171, *9970*.

R v Fennell [1970] 3 All ER 215, [1971] 1 QB 428, [1970] 3 WLR 513, 134 JP 678, 54 Cr App R 451, CA, 15 Digest (Reissue) 988, *8568*.

R v King [1963] 3 All ER 561, [1964] 1 QB 285, [1963] 3 WLR 892, 48 Cr App R 17, CCA, 15 Digest (Reissue) 1029, *8927*.

R v Porritt [1961] 3 All ER 463, [1961] 1 WLR 1372, 125 JP 605, 45 Cr App R 348, CCA, 14(1) Digest (Reissue) 392, *3325*.

R v Rose (1884) 15 Cox CC 540, 15 Digest (Reissue) 1170, *9946*.

R v Smith (David Raymond) [1974] 1 All ER 632, [1974] QB 354, [1974] 3 WLR 20, 138 JP 236, 58 Cr App R 320, CA, 15 Digest (Reissue) 1439, *12,690*.

R v Steane [1947] 1 All ER 813, [1947] KB 997, [1947] LJR 969, 177 LT 122, 111 JP 337, 32 Cr App R 61, 45 LGR 484, CCA, 14(1) Digest (Reissue) 19, *52*.

R v Tolson (1889) 23 QBD 168, [1886–90] All ER Rep 26, 58 LJMC 97, 60 LT 899, 54 JP 420, 16 Cox CC 629, CCR, 15 Digest (Reissue) 1028, *8922*.

R v Weston (1879) 14 Cox CC 346, 15 Digest (Reissue) 1153, *9772*.

Sweet v Parsley [1969] 1 All ER 347, [1970] AC 132, [1969] 2 WLR 470, 133 JP 188, 53 Cr App R 221, HL 15 Digest (Reissue) 1084, *9179*.

Warner v Metropolitan Police Comr [1968] 2 All ER 356, [1969] 2 AC 256, [1968] 2 WLR 1303, 132 JP 328, 52 Cr App R 373, HL, 15 Digest (Reissue) 1069, *9156*.

Wilson v Inyang [1951] 2 All ER 237, [1951] 2 KB 799, 115 JP 411, 49 LGR 654, DC, 33 Digest (Repl) 543, *143*.

Cases also cited

Fagan v Metropolitan Police Comr [1968] 3 All ER 442, [1969] 1 QB 439, DC.

Kenlin v Gardiner [1966] 3 All ER 931, [1967] 2 QB 510, DC.

R v Venna [1975] 3 All ER 788, [1976] QB 421, CA.

Rice v Connolly [1966] 2 All ER 649, [1966] 2 QB 414, DC.

Case stated

This was a case stated by the magistrates for the Middlesex area of Greater London sitting at Brentford. On 12th June 1979 an information was preferred by the respondent, John Lavin, against the appellant, Cleve Albert, that he on 8th June 1979 at The Mall, Ealing, London W5, assaulted the respondent, a constable of the Metropolitan Police Force, in the execution of his duty contrary to s 51 of the Police Act 1964. The following facts were found. (a) On the afternoon of Friday, 8th June 1979 the appellant who at that time worked for the British Broadcasting Corpn at its office in White City left his work early at about 4 pm in order to go home because he was suffering from influenza. (b) The appellant's route home was by underground train to Ealing Broadway Station and a no 207 bus from The Mall to Southall. (c) At about 4.45 pm on that afternoon both the appellant and the respondent were standing in a queue at the bus stop for a no 207 bus, situated on the south side of The Mall in Ealing. Both the appellant and respondent were waiting for a no 207 bus. (d) The bus stop was used for buses other than those which served route 207. There was only provision for one queue. When a particular bus arrived at the bus stop it was necessary for those people in the queue who wished to board it to leave the queue and walk to it past those who were waiting for different buses. (e) The respondent was standing off-duty in plain clothes at the head of the queue. (f) When a no 207 bus arrived at the stop the appellant pushed past certain other people in the queue. Several people standing in the queue raised objection to the appellant's conduct and the respondent tried to obstruct the appellant's entry to the bus by standing in his way. (g) The appellant pushed past the respondent onto the first step of the bus turned and grabbed the respondent's lapel with his left hand and made to hit the respondent with his right hand. The respondent in order to protect himself pulled the appellant from the bus and away from the queue into an adjacent shop doorway. The appellant was highly excited and was trying to hit the respondent. (h) When the appellant had calmed down the respondent told him that he was a police officer and would arrest the appellant unless he stopped struggling. The appellant asked to see the respondent's warrant card but it was impossible for the respondent to show the appellant his warrant card because each had hold of the other's clothing. The appellant heard the respondent say that he was a policeman but did not believe him. (i) The appellant became excited once more and hit the respondent five or six times in the abdomen. Those blows formed the subject of the information. A struggle ensued and the respondent forced the appellant to the ground supine. (j) The respondent repeated to the appellant that he was a police officer and informed the appellant that he was being arrested for assaulting a constable in the execution of his duty. (k) The appellant was taken to Ealing police station and charged, whereupon he protested that he had not believed the respondent to be a constable until after he had been arrested. (l) If the appellant was unlawfully detained the blows which were the subject of this information amounted to use of no more force than was reasonable to effect his release from an unlawful detention. It was contended on behalf of the appellant that: (i) a constable's entitlement to take such steps, including the reasonable use of force to prevent in circumstances which he believed proper a breach of the peace which he reasonably believed to be about to take place was not without limit and did not extend to a power to detain without arrest; (ii) without valid arrest detention of a person against his will was never lawful; (iii) the appellant was unlawfully detained by the respondent and was entitled to use reasonable force in self-defence; (iv) therefore the respondent was not acting in the execution of his duty at the time of the blows which were the subject of the information; (v) if at the time of the blows which were the subject of the information the appellant believed that the respondent was not a constable he was entitled to resist what he honestly but wrongly believed to be unjustified assault and false imprisonment by the respondent. It was contended on behalf of the respondent that: (i) a police officer reasonably believing that a breach of the peace was about to take place was entitled to take such steps including the reasonable use of force to prevent it in circumstances which appeared to him to be proper; (ii) in that connection an entitlement to use reasonable force included an entitlement to do an act which would otherwise constitute an assault. Detention was a species of assault. In certain circumstances a police officer's entitlement to use reasonable force to prevent a breach of the peace which he reasonably believed to be about to take place included a power to detain without arrest; (iii) it was not necessary to prove that the accused knew that the officer was in the execution of his duty: the offence was not assaulting an officer knowing him to be in the execution of his duty but assaulting him being in the execution of his duty. The magistrates were of the opinion that: (i) because of the reactions of the other members of the bus queue when the appellant pushed past them the respondent had reasonably expected a breach of the peace to be about to take place and so he was entitled to use reasonable force to prevent that breach of the peace; (ii) accordingly the respondent was acting in the course of his duty when he obstructed the appellant's access to the bus; (iii) the appellant's reaction to the respondent's obstruction of his access to the bus, his excitable behaviour and his attempts to hit the respondent amounted to a breach of the peace; (iv) accordingly the respondent was still entitled to use reasonable force to prevent a breach of the peace. The magistrates accordingly convicted the appellant and conditionally discharged him for a period of one year. The questions for the opinion of the High Court were whether: (i) a constable who reasonably believed that a breach of the peace was about to take place was entitled to detain any person without arrest to prevent that breach of the peace in circumstances which appeared to him to be proper; (ii) a person being detained in the circumstances set out above but who did not accept that the person detaining him was a constable might be convicted of assault on a constable in the execution of his duty if he used no more force than was reasonably necessary to protect himself for what he mistakenly and without reasonable grounds believed to be an unjustified assault and false imprisonment.

Ronald J Walker for the appellant.
John L Reide for the respondent.

Cur adv vult

27th November. The following judgments were read.

HODGSON J (delivering the first judgment at the invitation of Donaldson LJ). This is an appeal by case stated from the decision of lay magistrates for the Middlesex area sitting at Brentford. The information preferred against the appellant charged him with assaulting the respondent, a police officer, in the execution of his duty, on 8th June 1979 at The Mall in Ealing.

The magistrates took no less than three days to hear this case lasting from the first hearing on 12th January 1979 to 6th November 1979 on which date they found the appellant guilty.

The facts of the case appear from the careful findings made by the magistrates. In June 1979 the appellant was working for the BBC in White City. On the afternoon of 8th June 1979 he left work early as he was ill. His route home was by way of underground to Ealing Broadway and thereafter by a no 207 bus from The Mall to Southall.

The respondent was also intending to travel from The Mall by no 207 bus. The bus stop which both had to use had provision for only one queue but was used for other buses as well as the no 207 buses. Consequently when a bus arrived it was necessary for those who intended to board a bus to walk along the queue, passing those intending passengers who were awaiting another bus.

The respondent was off duty and in plain clothes. He was standing at the front of the queue. The appellant was further down the queue. When a no 207 bus arrived the appellant pushed past other people in the queue. This caused resentment and several people in the queue objected to the appellant's conduct. The respondent tried to obstruct the appellant's entry to the bus by standing in his way.

The magistrates were of the opinion that the reactions of the other members of the queue caused the respondent reasonably to expect that a breach of the peace was about to take place and that he was entitled to use reasonable force to prevent that breach. He was, the magistrates found, acting in the course of his duty when he obstructed the appellant's access to the bus.

What happened next can charitably be attributed to the appellant's illness. He pushed past the respondent onto the first step of the bus, grabbed the lapel of the respondent's coat with his left hand and made to hit him with his right hand. In order to protect himself the respondent pulled the appellant from the bus and away from the queue into an adjacent shop doorway. During this time the appellant was highly excited and was trying to hit the respondent who, at that stage, had made no attempt to reveal his identity as a police officer.

The appellant then apparently calmed down somewhat but was still struggling. Each had hold of the other's clothing, and the respondent then told the appellant that he was a police officer and would arrest the appellant unless he stopped struggling. The appellant heard the respondent say he was a policeman and asked to see his warrant card, but because each had hold of the other's clothing it was impossible for the respondent to produce it. The appellant did not believe the respondent when he said he was a policeman. He became excited once more and hit the respondent five or six times in the abdomen. These were the blows which were the subject of the information. A struggle ensued and the respondent forced the appellant to the ground, repeated the fact that he was a police officer and told the appellant that he was being arrested for assaulting a constable in the execution of his duty.

The appellant was taken to Ealing police station and charged, whereupon he protested that he had not believed the respondent to be a constable until after he had been arrested.

The magistrates found that the appellant's reaction to the respondent's obstruction of his access to the bus, his excitable behaviour and his attempts to hit the respondent amounted to a continuing breach of the peace and that, accordingly, the respondent was entitled to use reasonable force to prevent a continuing breach of the peace by the appellant lasting up to the moment of his arrest.

They further found that the respondent had done everything a reasonable man could do in the circumstances to ensure that the appellant knew he was a constable. They accepted that the appellant genuinely believed that the respondent was not a constable but that he had no reasonable grounds for this belief. The appellant had, they found, no reasonable grounds for doubting that the respondent was a constable.

Finally the magistrates found that, if the appellant was being unlawfully detained by the respondent, the blows which were the subject of the information amounted to the use of no more force than was reasonable to effect his release from an unlawful detention.

On those findings of fact counsel, who has argued the appellant's case with skill and economy, submits that the conviction was wrong for two reasons. Firstly, he contends that the respondent unlawfully detained the appellant and that the appellant was entitled to use reasonable force to effect his release.

This argument is based on the well-established principle that to detain a man against his will without arresting him is an unlawful act and a serious interference with a citizen's liberty. It is said that the restraint placed on the appellant by the respondent amounted to a detention without arrest and was therefore unlawful, and that the appellant was therefore justified in his use of reasonable force. On the facts the respondent was clearly not intending to arrest the appellant when he was holding him in the shop doorway.

It is however clear law that a police officer, reasonably believing that a breach of the peace is about to take place, is entitled to take such steps as are necessary to prevent it, including the reasonable use of force: see *King v Hodges* [1974] Crim LR 424 and *Piddington v Bates* [1960] 3 All ER 660, [1961] 1 WLR 162. And if those steps include physical restraint of someone then that restraint is not an unlawful detention but a reasonable use of force. It is a question of fact and degree when a restraint has continued for so long that there must be either a release or an arrest, but on the facts found in this case it seems to me to be clear that that point had not been reached. Obviously where a constable is restraining someone to prevent a breach of the peace he must release (or arrest) him as soon as the restrained person no longer presents a danger to the peace. In this case the magistrates found that the appellant continued in breach of the peace up to the time when he assaulted the respondent.

The second argument presented to us by counsel is a much more difficult one. It is this. On the findings of fact made by the magistrates the appellant genuinely believed that the man restraining him was not a police constable, that if he had not been a police constable what he was doing to the appellant was a false imprisonment and assault, that the appellant would in the circumstances he believed to exist have been entitled to use reasonable force in self-defence, and that, of course, the magistrates found as a matter of fact that what he did would in those supposed circumstances have been reasonable.

The question which we are being asked to answer based on counsel's submission is this: whether a person being detained in the circumstances set out above but who does not accept that the person detaining him is a police constable may be convicted of an assault on a constable in the execution of his duty if he uses no more force than is reasonably necessary to protect himself for what he mistakenly and without reasonable grounds believes to be an unjustified assault and false imprisonment.

The short question is whether in the circumstances set out a person's belief (the added words 'honest' or 'genuine' may be useful emphasis but in fact add nothing) is of itself sufficient to render him not guilty or whether that belief must be reasonable belief or, which is the same thing, a belief based on reasonable grounds.

But, before I come to deal with this difficult question for which, surprisingly, no direct authority cited to or known to me provides an answer, I must make two things clear. First, it is not of course contended that it is necessary that the appellant should have known that the man he was hitting was a police officer before he could be guilty of assaulting a police officer in the execution of his duty. On the wording of s 51 of the Police Act 1964 it is now trite law that that is not so. What is in issue here is whether the appellant is guilty of an assault at all.

I turn now to deal with this most important question in this appeal. As I have said, there appears to be no reported instance of a man being convicted of an assault (or aggravated assault) when he acted, as he believed, in self-defence, but the belief was held to be unreasonable. However nearly all the authorities when considering self-defence require that a mistaken belief must be reasonable.

In *R v Weston* (1879) 14 Cox CC 346 at 351 Cockburn CJ, in directing the jury on the law relating to self-defence, said:

> '... if under such circumstances, the prisoner resorted to the gun in order to defend himself from serious violence, or under a reasonable apprehension of it, and so used it in necessary self-defence he would be justified.'

In *R v Rose* (1884) 15 Cox CC 540 Lopes J told the jury that they were entitled to acquit on the ground of self-defence only—

> 'if you think that at the time he [the defendant] fired that shot he honestly believed, and had reasonable grounds for the belief, that his mother's life was in imminent peril...'

In 10 Halsbury's Laws (3rd Edn) 721, para 1382 the rule (in relation to murder) was formulated thus:

> 'Where a forcible and violent felony is attempted upon the person of another, the party assaulted ... is entitled to repel force by force, and, if necessary, to kill the aggressor. There must be reasonable necessity for the killing, or at least an honest belief based upon reasonable grounds that there is such necessity...'

In *R v Chisam* (1963) 47 Cr App R 130 this statement of the law was expressly approved. That case held that, where a man is charged with the killing of another and alleges that the killing took place in defence of a relative or friend, in order that the defence of self-defence may be available, he must have believed that that relative or friend was in imminent danger and the belief must have been based on reasonable grounds. Reasonable grounds for such belief may, however, exist though they are founded on a genuine mistake of fact. In giving the judgment of the court Lord Parker CJ cited with approval a passage from the direction of the Lord Justice-General (Lord Normand) in *Owens v HM Advocate* 1946 JC 119 at 125:

> 'In our opinion self-defence is made out when it is established to the satisfaction of the jury that the panel believed that he was in imminent danger and that he held that belief on reasonable grounds. Grounds for such belief may exist though they are founded on a genuine mistake of fact.'

The requirement of reasonableness is also to be found in *R v Fennell* [1970] 3 All ER 215, [1971] 1 QB 428.

So far as self-defence is concerned the only dictum which recognises what may be called the subjective view which I have been able to find is *R v Porritt* [1961] 3 All ER 463, [1961] 1 WLR 1372. That was a case of capital murder and the point at issue was whether, where there was evidence of facts which could amount to provocation but that partial defence had not been raised, the issue should have been left to the jury. In giving the judgment of the Court of Criminal Appeal, Ashworth J said ([1961] 3 All ER 463 at 465, [1961] 1 WLR 1372 at 1375):

> 'At the trial it was conceded on behalf of the Crown that if the jury took the view that the firing was done in the honest belief that it was necessary for the protection of his stepfather, then the proper verdict was one of not guilty, and a similar concession was made in regard to the possibility of an honest belief that it was reasonably necessary to protect the house by shooting.'

It may be that the facts were thought to be so strong by the prosecution (the defendant was found guilty of capital murder by the jury) that they felt able to go further than they needed to in regard to self-defence. All that can be said is that Ashworth J did not say that the concessions had gone further than was necessary.

The rule that only a reasonable mistake may constitute a ground for the defence of self-defence has (both before and since *Director of Public Prosecutions v Morgan* [1975] 2 All ER 347, [1976] AC 182) been vigorously criticised (see Glanville Williams, Criminal Law— The General Part (2nd Edn, 1961, para 73, pp 208–209); Kenny, Outlines of Criminal Law (19th Edn, 1966, pp 59–60); Russell on Crime (12th Edn, 1964, pp 75–76); Smith and Hogan, Criminal Law (4th Edn, 1978, pp 328–329, 364–365)). Whilst *Morgan* was on its way from the Court of Appeal to the House of Lords, Professor Smith wrote a comment on the Court of Appeal decision in which he strongly contended for the subjective test (see [1975] Crim LR 40). Perhaps the most cogent recent criticism of the objective test is to be found in Professor Glanville Williams's Textbook of Criminal Law (1978, pp 451ff). He concludes a lengthy and extremely persuasive argument with the words: 'The law must be prepared, so far as it can do so, to look into the mind of the defendant and give him the benefit of the facts as they appeared to him.'

Counsel for the appellant has asked us to look again at the requirement of reasonableness in the light of the decision of the House of Lords in *Morgan*. Professor Glanville Williams warns that that decision is a formidable obstacle to any argument in favour of the subjective rule. He goes on to say, correctly:

> '... but here again it may be said that the question of *mens rea* in relation to defences was not before the House, it being held that the question of consent in rape was not a matter of defence but an ingredient of the offence.'

To find out what *Morgan* says directly about self-defence and mistaken belief, it is convenient to begin with the judgment of Bridge J in the Court of Appeal where he said ([1975] 1 All ER 8 at 14–15, [1976] AC 182 at 190–191):

> 'The relevant principles can perhaps be restated in the following propositions: 1. In all crimes the Crown has both the evidential and the probative burden of showing that the accused did the prohibited act, and where that act, according to the definition of the offence, is an act of volition, of showing that the act of the accused was voluntary. An obvious example of a crime where the evidential burden on the Crown is limited to these two elements is common assault. 2. Wherever the definition of a crime includes as one of its express ingredients a specific mental element both the evidential and the probative burden lie on the Crown with respect to that element. Typical examples are dishonesty in theft and knowledge or belief in handling. In seeking to rebut the Crown's case against him in reference to his state of mind the accused may and frequently does assert his mistaken belief in non-existent facts. Of course it is right that in this context the question whether there were reasonable grounds for the belief is only a factor for the jury's consideration in deciding whether the Crown has established the necessary mental element of the

crime. This is because the issue is already before the jury and no evidential burden
rests on the accused. The decision of the Divisional Court in *Wilson v Inyang* [1951]
2 All ER 237, [1951] 2 KB 799 is to be understood in the light of this principle. The
court there rejected the argument that an acquittal by a magistrate of a defendant
charged with an offence under s 40 of the Medical Act 1858 should be reversed on
appeal by case stated on the ground that the defendant had no reasonable ground for
his belief that he was entitled to call himself a "physician". Lord Goddard CJ said
([1951] 2 All ER 237 at 240, [1951] 2 KB 799 at 803): "If he has acted without any
reasonable ground and says: 'I had not properly inquired, and did not think this or
that,' that may be (and generally is) very good evidence that he is not acting
honestly. But it is only evidence." The Act, however, under which that prosecution
was brought required the prosecution to prove that the defendant acted "wilfully
and falsely". Inevitably, therefore, if this subjective mental element was not proved
the prosecution failed. 3. Where, however, the definition of the crime includes no
specific mental element beyond the intention to do the prohibited act, the accused
may show that though he did the prohibited act intentionally he lacked mens rea
because he mistakenly, but honestly and reasonably, believed facts which, if true,
would have made his act innocent. Here the evidential burden lies on the accused
but once evidence sufficient to raise the issue is before the jury the probative burden
lies on the Crown to negative the mistaken belief. The rationale of requiring
reasonable grounds for the mistaken belief must lie in the law's consideration that
a bald assertion of belief for which the accused can indicate no reasonable ground is
evidence of insufficient substance to raise any issue requiring the jury's
consideration. Thus, for example, a person charged with assault on a victim shown
to have been entirely passive throughout who said he had believed himself to be
under imminent threat of attack by the victim but could indicate no circumstance
giving cause for such a belief would not discharge the evidential burden of showing
a mistaken belief that he was acting lawfully in self-defence.'

In the House of Lords, Lord Hailsham cited the whole of this passage and continued
([1975] 2 All ER 347 at 360–362, [1976] AC 182 at 213–214):

'In the event Bridge J then went on to subsume rape under the third and not the
second heading and so to reach the conclusion ([1975] 1 All ER 8 at 15, [1976] AC
182 at 192): "The correct view, we think, is that, on proof of the fact of absence of
consent from circumstances which in the nature of the case must have come to the
notice of the defendant he may be presumed to have appreciated their significance,
and it is this presumption which casts on the defendant the evidential burden of
showing an honest and reasonable belief in consent before any issue as to his state of
mind can arise for the jury's consideration." He goes on to say that, once the
"evidential" burden is discharged the "probative burden" is cast once more on the
Crown. With due respect, though with one qualification there is something to be
said for the premises of this statement, I do not believe the conclusion follows. The
qualification I make to the premise is that I can see no reason why the class of case
to which his second proposition applies should be limited to cases where the mental
ingredient is limited to a "specific mental element" if, as appears to be the case, by
that is meant an "ulterior" intent within Smith and Hogan's definition of that term
(Criminal Law, 3rd Edn, 1973, p 47). I believe the law on this point to have been
correctly stated by Lord Goddard in *R v Steane* [1947] 1 All ER 813 at 816, [1947] KB
997 at 1004 when he said: ". . . if, on the totality of the evidence, there is room for
more than one view as to the intent of the prisoner, the jury should be directed that
it is for the prosecution to prove the intent to the jury's satisfaction, and if, on
review of the whole evidence, they either think the intent did not exist or they are
left in doubt as to the intent, the prisoner is entitled to be acquitted." That was
indeed, a case which involved a count where a specific, or, as Smith and Hogan call
it, an ulterior, intent was, and required to be, charged in the indictment. But, once

it be accepted that an intent of whatever description is an ingredient essential to the guilt of the accused I cannot myself see that any other direction can be logically acceptable. Otherwise a jury would in effect be told to find an intent where none existed or where none was proved to have existed. I cannot myself reconcile it with my conscience to sanction as part of the English law what I regard as logical impossibility, and, if there were any authority which, if accepted would compel me to do so, I would feel constrained to declare that it was not to be followed. However, for reasons which I will give, I do not see any need in the instant case for such desperate remedies. The beginning of wisdom in all the "mens rea" cases to which our attention was called is, as was pointed out by Stephen J in *R v Tolson* (1889) 23 QBD 168 at 185, [1886–90] All ER Rep 26 at 36, that "mens rea" means a number of quite different things in relation to different crimes. Sometimes it means an intention, eg in murder, "to kill or to inflict really serious injury". Sometimes it means a state of mind or knowledge, eg in receiving or handling goods "knowing them to be stolen". Sometimes it means both an intention and a state of mind, eg "Dishonestly and without a claim of right made in good faith with intent permanently to deprive the owner thereof". Sometimes it forms part of the essential ingredients of the crime without proof of which the prosecution, as it were, withers on the bough. Sometimes it is a matter, of which, though the "probative" burden may be on the Crown, normally the "evidential" burden may usually (though not always) rest on the defence, eg "self-defence" and "provocation" in murder, though it must be noted that if there is material making the issue a live one, the matter must be left to the jury even if the defence do not raise it. In statutory offences the range is even wider since, owing to the difficulty of proving a negative, Parliament quite often expressly puts the burden on the defendant to negative a guilty state (see per Lord Reid in *Sweet v Parsley* [1969] 1 All ER 347 at 351, [1970] AC 132 at 150) or inserts words like "fraudulently", "negligently", "knowingly", "wilfully", "maliciously", which import special types of guilty mind, or even imports them by implication by importing such word as "permit" (cf Lord Diplock in the same case ([1969] 1 All ER 347 at 361, [1970] AC 132 at 162)) or as in *Warner v Metropolitan Police Comr* [1968] 2 All ER 356, [1969] 2 AC 256 prohibit the "possession" of a particular substance, or, as in *Sweet v Parsley* itself, leaves the courts to decide whether a particular prohibition makes a new "absolute" offence or provides an escape by means of an honest, or an honest and reasonable belief. Moreover of course, a statute can, and often does, create an absolute offence without any degree of mens rea at all. It follows from this, surely, that it is logically impermissible, as the respondent sought to do in this case, to draw a necessary inference from decisions in relation to offences where mens rea means one thing, and cases where it means another, and in particular from decisions on the construction of statutes, whether these be related to bigamy, abduction or the possession of drugs, and decisions in relation to common law offences. It is equally impermissible to draw direct or necessary inferences from decisions where the mens rea is, or includes, a state of opinion, and cases where it is limited to intention (a distinction I referred to in *Hyam v Director of Public Prosecutions* [1974] 2 All ER 41, [1975] AC 55), or between cases where there is a special "defence", like self defence or provocation, and cases where the issue relates to the primary intention which the prosecution has to prove. Once one has accepted, what seems to me abundantly clear, that the prohibited act in rape is non-consensual sexual intercourse, and that the guilty state of mind is an intention to commit it, it seems to me to follow as a matter of inexorable logic that there is no room either for a "defence" of honest belief or mistake, or of a defence of honest and reasonable belief and mistake. Either the prosecution proves that the accused had the requisite intent, or it does not. In the former case it succeeds, and in the latter it fails. Since honest belief clearly negatives intent, the reasonableness or otherwise of that belief can only be evidence for or against the view that the belief and therefore the intent was actually held, and it matters not whether, to quote Bridge J in the passage cited above: "the definition of a crime includes no specific element beyond the prohibited act." If the mental element be primarily an intention and not a state of belief it comes within his second proposition and not his third. Any other view, as for insertion of the word "reasonable" can only have the effect of saying that a man intends something which he does not.'

It is clear from the passage I have cited that Lord Hailsham was accepting as good law the requirement of reasonableness in self-defence. Neither of the other two majority speeches referred to self-defence specifically but both the dissenting speeches did. Lord Edmund-Davies said ([1975] 2 All ER 347 at 378, [1976] AC 182 at 233): 'The law requires that reasonable grounds for believing that physical action in self-defence or defence of another is called for', and he cited four of the cases to which I have referred. Lord Simon said ([1975] 2 All ER 347 at 366, [1976] AC 182 at 219):

> '... Lord Edmund-Davies has cited the cases which exemplify the same rule operating in the common law doctrine of self-defence. Once the prosecution has discharged the burden of proving an actus reus of assault and (by inference therefrom or extrinsically) the necessary mens rea, the evidential burden shifts to the accused. He can discharge it by raising a case fit for the consideration of the jury that he believed in a state of affairs whereby the actus proved by the prosecution would not be reus. He may do this by showing that his conduct towards the victim was prompted by his belief that the victim was about to attack him, and that what he did was no more than was necessary for his own defence in the circumstances as he believed them to exist. But it is clear law that, in order to establish a defence in such circumstances, his belief must be based on reasonable grounds.'

It is clear from these citations that the majority of the House of Lords, albeit obiter, approved of the objective test in self-defence.

The reason why the House of Lords was able to reach the decision which it did in *Morgan* without overruling the authorities on self-defence was because they distinguished between the mens rea required for the basic or definitional elements of an offence and that required for a defence. It is said that the offence of assault requires an attack on a person (definitional element) but that the question whether the attack had to be made by the defendant in self-defence is a defence element, and the question of fault is not the same. It is this double test of a defendant's state of mind which has been the subject of vigorous academic criticism.

But counsel for the appellant submits that, despite the long line of authority some of which I have cited and the' obiter dicta in *Morgan*, the ratio decidendi itself of *Morgan* leads one, in respect of self-defence, to a different conclusion as to what the law is. The argument goes thus. He accepts that to decide, in respect of any offence, whether the objective or subjective test should be applied to mistake it is necessary first of all to see what the definitional elements of the offence are. Citing Archbold, Pleading, Evidence and Practice in Criminal Cases (40th Edn, 1979, para 2634) he submits that the definition of assault is the actual or intended use of unlawful force to another without that other's consent, and that, just as lack of consent is one of the essential ingredients, so the unlawfulness of the assault is another. Applying the reasoning in *Morgan*, he says that the intention which the prosecution has to prove in assault is an intention to use or threaten actual force unlawfully and without the consent of the victim. It follows that if a man believes that what he is doing is not unlawful it avails him just as much as if he believes that he has the consent of his victim.

The further contention is that to make the difference between the objective and subjective test of mistake depend on where the evidential burden lies is unreal and illogical. At the end of the evidence all the facts are before the tribunal of fact which has then to direct itself or be directed as to the burden of proof and (with few exceptions) in respect of common law offences that burden lies on the prosecution. It matters not where the evidence has come from nor whether any issue has been specifically raised; if it is an issue the resolution of which in the defendant's favour would be to his advantage it must be left to the jury (or magistrates must consider it): see *R v Porritt* [1961] 3 All ER 463, [1961] 1 WLR 1372.

Support for the contention that the question whether the subjective or objective test should be applied does not depend on where the evidential burden as to any issue lies can be found in the comparatively recent decision of the Court of Appeal, Criminal Division, in *R v Smith* [1974] 1 All ER 632, [1974] QB 354. In that case the court held that a person who damages property belonging to another has a defence to a charge under the Criminal Damage Act 1971 if he does so in the mistaken belief that the property is his own whether that belief is a justifiable one or not. That decision did not depend on the particular provisions of the 1971 Act but on a general principle of the criminal law ([1974] 1 All ER 632 at 636, [1974] QB 354 at 360):

> 'Applying the ordinary principles of mens rea, the intention and recklessness and the absence of lawful excuse required to constitute the offence have reference to property belonging to another.'

In his comment on the Court of Appeal decision on *Morgan*, Professor Smith writes ([1975] Crim LR at 43–44):

> 'The one clear decision requiring reasonable grounds among the cases cited is *King* ([1963] 3 All ER 561, [1964] 1 QB 285), where a conviction for bigamy was upheld because the accused did not have reasonable grounds for his belief. This, however, might be matched by the recent decision of the Court of Appeal in *Smith (D.R.)* ([1974] 1 All ER 632, [1974] QB 354) where it was held that a person who damages property belonging to another has a defence to a charge under the Criminal Damage Act 1971 if he does so in the honest but mistaken belief that the property is his own. The court stated, ". . . provided that the belief is honestly held it is irrelevant to consider whether or not it is a justifiable belief." It is very important to notice that this decision does not depend on the particular provisions of the Criminal Damage Act but on a general principle of the criminal law: "Applying the ordinary principles of *mens rea*, the intention and recklessness and the absence of lawful excuse required to constitute the offence have reference to property belonging to another." It is submitted that equally in the present case the intention or recklessness required have reference to sexual intercourse *without consent*. An intention to damage one's own property is not a *mens rea* under the Criminal Damage Act because the result intended is not an offence. Similarly an intention to have intercourse with a consenting woman is not *mens rea* because the result intended is not an offence. The ordinary principles of *mens rea* should certainly be no less applicable to the common law offence of rape than to the statutory offences of criminal damage. The court distinguished between cases where the evidential burden rests on the accused and those where it rests on the Crown. It is in the former class of case that it is for accused to show reasonable grounds for belief. This is inconsistent with *Smith (D.R.)*. Once the prosecution proved that the accused deliberately damaged property and that the property in fact belonged to another, they had made out a prima facie case and it was for the accused to introduce evidence (*i.e.* there was an evidential burden on him) that he believed that the property was his. According to the present case, he should therefore have had the burden of showing that this belief was based on reasonable grounds. Apart altogether from this case, however, it is respectfully submitted that the proposed distinction is unworkable. Although it is often stated the evidential burden of making out particular defences is on the accused, this, though a convenient generalisation, is not a rule of law. Whether there is an evidential burden on the accused depends on the course which the evidence takes in the particular case. The accused who wishes to set up the defence of provocation or self-defence will

normally have the evidential burden of doing so; but if facts emerge in the course of prosecution's own evidence which are capable of amounting to either of these defences (or indeed any other defence) then the defence in question must be left to the jury: *Mancini* v. *D.P.P.* ([1942] AC 1); *Palmer* v. *R.* ([1971] 1 All ER 1077, [1971] AC 814). The accused has incurred no evidential burden and, consequently, may have done nothing which could have satisfied such a burden had it existed. If the defence depends on a mistake of fact, is it really to be said that this must be a reasonable mistake if the accused introduced the evidence, but not if the prosecution introduced it? With respect, it is submitted that there is no connection between the incidence of the evidential burden and the question whether the mistake must be reasonable.'

I agree with the criticism voiced by Professor Smith in that passage and I do not think that the test whether the objective or subjective test of mistake applies can depend on where in respect of the relevant issue the evidential burden lies or may, in any particular case, lie.

But in my judgment counsel's ingenious argument for the appellant fails at an earlier stage. It does not seem to me that the element of unlawfulness can properly be regarded as part of the definitional elements of the offence. In defining a criminal offence the word 'unlawful' is surely tautologous and can add nothing to its essential ingredients. The requirement in the Criminal Damage Act 1971 that the property should be that of another is however clearly part of the definition of the statutory offence.

It seems to me that the law is that one has to distinguish between the mens rea required for the basic elements of the offence and that required for a defence. In the absence of express words in any offence created by statute (eg the Criminal Damage Act 1971, s 5) where the issue is whether a defence is made out then mistake avails a defendant nothing if it is an unreasonable (and therefore negligent) one. And, no matter how strange it may seem that a defendant charged with assault can escape conviction if he shows that he mistakenly but unreasonably thought his victim was consenting but not if he was in the same state of mind whether his victim had a right to detain him, that in my judgment is the law.

That being so this appeal fails, and I would answer the questions we are asked as follows. (1) A constable who reasonably believes that a breach of the peace is about to take place is entitled to restrain a person without arrest if such is necessary to prevent a breach of the peace. In answering that question I have intentionally used the word 'restrain' rather than 'detain'. In the circumstances of this case the two words mean the same. I have used 'restrain' to make it clear that I look on the restraint as being a step which the officer was entitled to take to prevent a breach of the peace and not as a detention primarily aimed at depriving a man of his liberty. (2) A person being restrained in the circumstances found by the magistrates to exist who does not accept that the person restraining him is a constable may be convicted of assault on a constable in the execution of his duty if he uses no more force than is reasonably necessary to protect himself from what he mistakenly and without reasonable grounds believes to be an unjustified assault and false imprisonment.

I would only add this. In *Morgan* Lord Edmund-Davies felt that he was constrained by authority to dismiss the appeal but he felt strongly that the law (as he would have held it to be) ought to be changed. However he thought that if change was to come it should be brought about by legislation. He referred to a passage from Smith and Hogan, Criminal Law (3rd Edn, 1973, p 150):

> 'It is now established by s. 8 of the Criminal Justice Act 1967 that a failure to foresee the material *results* of one's conduct is a defence whether reasonable or not. It is odd that a different rule should prevail with respect to circumstances, the more particularly since foresight of results frequently depends on knowledge of circumstances ... Such a distinction seems unjustifiable. Its existence points in

favour of a rule allowing as a defence any honest mistake which negatives *mens rea*, whether reasonable or not.'

In March 1980 the Criminal Law Revision Committee (of which Lord Edmund-Davies was, for many years, chairman) published its 14th report, Offences Against the Person (Cmnd 7844). The committee considered self-defence (paras 281–288). Their proposal is summarised in Part IX. It recommends adoption of the subjective test. Paragraph 72(a) reads:

'The Common Law defence of self-defence should be replaced by a statutory defence providing that a person may use such force as is reasonable in the circumstances as he believes them to be in the defence of himself or any other person, or in the defence of his property or that of any other person.'

Paragraph 72(e) reads:

'There should be a provision that, in considering whether the defendant believed he or another or his property or that of another was under attack, the presence or absence of reasonable grounds for such a belief is a matter to which the court or jury is to have regard in conjunction with any other relevant matters.'

DONALDSON LJ. I agree. On the law as it stands at the present it is no defence to a charge of assault that the accused honestly but mistakenly believed that circumstances existed which would have justified his action as being undertaken in reasonable self-defence unless there are reasonable grounds for that belief. However, an ill-founded but completely honest and genuine belief removes all or much of the culpability involved in the offence. It therefore provides powerful mitigation and in an appropriate case would justify a court granting an absolute discharge.

Appeal dismissed. The court refused leave to appeal but certified, under s 1(2) of the Administration of Justice Act 1960, that the following point of law of general public importance was involved in the decision: whether a person charged with an offence of assault may properly be convicted if the court finds that he acted in the belief that facts existed which if true would justify his conduct on the basis of self-defence but that there were in fact no reasonable grounds for so believing.

18th February 1981. The Appeal Committee of the House of Lords granted leave to appeal.

Solicitors: *Somers & Leyne* (for the appellant); *R E T Birch* (for the respondent).

Jacqueline Charles Barrister.

Megarity and others v Law Society
Gayway Linings Ltd v Law Society

HOUSE OF LORDS

LORD DIPLOCK, LORD SIMON OF GLAISDALE, LORD EDMUND-DAVIES, LORD SCARMAN AND LORD BRIDGE OF HARWICH

21st, 22nd JANUARY, 19th FEBRUARY 1981

Legal aid – Unassisted person's costs out of legal aid fund – Costs incurred by successful unassisted party – Costs incurred in proceedings between him and party receiving legal aid – Proceedings – Interlocutory appeal – Interlocutory appeal in action in Queen's Bench Division for damages for personal injuries – Interlocutory appeal by legally-aided plaintiff dismissed – Whether power to order payment of unassisted defendant's costs of appeal out of legal aid fund – Whether interlocutory appeal 'proceedings' in connection with which plaintiff receiving legal aid – Legal Aid Act 1974, s 13(1).

Legal aid – Unassisted person's costs out of legal aid fund – Costs incurred by successful unassisted party – Costs incurred in proceedings between him and party receiving legal aid – Costs incurred on appeal – District registrar entering judgment for plaintiff – Legally-aided defendant appealing unsuccessfully to judge in chambers – Whether judge in chambers acting as appellate court – Legal Aid Act 1974, s 13(3).

In two separate actions questions arose whether under the Legal Aid Act 1974 and the regulations made thereunder the costs of a successful unassisted party on an interlocutory appeal to the Court of Appeal or on appeal from a registrar to a judge in chambers could be ordered to be paid out of the legal aid fund.

In the first case the plaintiff was granted a legal aid certificate in respect of the entirety of his proceedings against the defendants in the Queen's Bench Division for damages for personal injuries. The defendants, who denied liability, were not legally aided. The defendants obtained from the judge in chambers an interlocutory order requiring the plaintiff to submit unconditionally to examination by the defendants' medical adviser. The legal aid committee authorised the plaintiff to appeal against the order but did not issue a separate legal aid certificate in respect of the appeal. The Court of Appeal dismissed the interlocutory appeal and ordered, pursuant to s 13(1)[a] of the 1974 Act, that the defendants' costs of the appeal be paid out of the legal aid fund, since in the court's opinion, it was just and equitable that they should be so paid. The Law Society objected to the order, contending that the Court of Appeal had no power under s 13(1) to make it because the 'proceedings' in connection with which the plaintiff was receiving legal aid, within s 13(1), were the whole action, and since the whole action had not then been decided it could not be said that on determination of the interlocutory appeal the 'proceedings [were] finally decided in favour of the unassisted party [the defendants]', within s 13(1), so as to empower the court to make an order for payment of the defendants' costs out of the legal aid fund. The Court of Appeal ([1980] 3 All ER 602) held that the interlocutory appeal was a separate proceeding which had been finally determined in the unassisted party's favour for the purposes of s 13(1) and ordered the defendants' costs on the interlocutory appeal to be paid out of the legal aid fund. The Law Society appealed to the House of Lords where it repeated its contentions before the Court of Appeal and further contended that, alternatively, if the Court of Appeal had jurisdiction to make the order, it ought to have exercised its discretion to refuse to make it since the plaintiff's means might eventually be enhanced by damages recovered by him in the action and, by virtue of s 13(2), that would have a bearing on whether the

---

a   Section 13 is set out at p 646 *c* to *g*, post

plaintiff himself or the legal aid fund should bear the defendants' costs of the interlocutory appeal.

In the second case the plaintiffs, who were not legally aided, brought an action against the defendant on four dishonoured bills of exchange. On an application by the plaintiffs the defence filed by the defendant was struck out and judgment was entered for the plaintiffs by a district registrar. The defendant then received legal aid to appeal to the judge in chambers against the registrar's order. The judge dismissed the defendant's appeal and on the plaintiffs' application their costs of the appeal were ordered to be paid out of the legal aid fund. The Law Society appealed to the Court of Appeal against that order contending that the judge in chambers was not acting as an appellate court from the registrar but as a court of first instance, since the judgment in the plaintiffs' favour was made by the High Court, of which the judge was a part, and the plaintiffs did not come within the category of unassisted litigants specified in s 13(3) who were entitled to have 'costs incurred in a court of first instance' paid out of the legal aid fund. The Court of Appeal dismissed the appeal and the Law Society appealed to the House of Lords.

Held – The Law Society's appeal in both cases would be dismissed for the following reasons—

(1) The philosophy of the 1974 Act (derived from the mischief which its predecessor, the Legal Aid Act 1964, was designed to mitigate) was that a legally-aided party to civil proceedings was allowed one unsuccessful attempt to prove his case at the expense, inter alia, of an unassisted opponent and if thereafter he made a further attempt by way of appeal to prove his case and was unsuccessful the costs of that further attempt were to be borne entirely by the legal aid fund if the appellate court considered it just and equitable that the fund should bear the costs of the successful unassisted party on the appeal; s 13 and the regulations made under s 14[b] of the 1974 Act were to be interpreted as giving effect to that philosophy. Since the reference to 'part only of [the] proceedings' in s 14(5) was a reference either to part of the period during which the proceedings were going on or to one issue out of several in a single action, proceedings in separate courts could not be 'part only of [the] proceedings' and the reference to 'separate proceedings' in s 14(1)(a) had to refer to proceedings in the same action in separate courts. Accordingly, on the true construction of s 14(1)(a) the regulations made thereunder provided, as s 14(1)(a) compelled them to do, for all proceedings on appeal to an appellate court to be treated as 'separate proceedings' from the proceedings in the court of first instance (see p 645, j to p 646 a, p 647 f, p 649 e f and p 652 a to c, post).

(2) It followed that the proceedings in the interlocutory appeal to the Court of Appeal in the first case were 'proceedings' which were separate from the whole action for the purposes of s 13(1), and since they had been 'finally determined' in favour of the unassisted defendants the Court of Appeal had been entitled to order that the defendants' costs of the appeal be paid out of the legal aid fund. Furthermore, if the interlocutory appeal was a separate proceeding which had been finally determined it could not later be taken into consideration when the costs of whole action were determined by the trial judge, and there was therefore no room for the Court of Appeal to exercise its discretion to refuse payment of the defendants' costs out of the legal aid fund on that ground (see p 650 e to j and p 652 a to c, post).

(3) Having regard to the respective functions performed by a registrar or master on the one hand and the judge in chambers on the other, rather than to their status in the hierarchy of courts, where an order by a registrar or master finally decided an action by entering judgment for a party to the action, the registrar or master was the court of first instance and the judge in chambers by whom the appeal, if any, was heard was an appellate court. Accordingly, in the second case the judge in chambers was entitled to order that the plaintiffs' costs of the appeal to him be paid out of the legal aid fund (see p 651 d to p 652 c, post).

---

b   Section 14 is set out at p 646 *g* to p 647 *d*, post

Decision of the Court of Appeal in *Megarity v D J Ryan & Sons Ltd (No 2)* [1980] 3 All ER 602 affirmed.

Notes

For the Legal Aid Act 1974, ss 13, 14, see 44 Halsbury's Statutes (3rd Edn) 1053, 1057.

As from 1st January 1981 the Legal Aid (General) Regulations 1971, SI 1971 No 62, and the Legal Aid (Costs of Successful Unassisted Parties) Regulations 1964, SI 1964 No 1276, have been replaced by the Legal Aid (General) Regulations 1980, SI 1980 No 1894.

Cases referred to in opinions

Mills v Mills [1963] 2 All ER 237, [1963] P 329, [1963] 2 WLR 831, CA, 50 Digest (Repl) 494, 1752.
Shiloh Spinners Ltd v Harding (No 2) [1973] 1 All ER 966, [1973] 1 WLR 518, HL, Digest (Cont Vol D) 1054, 1733f.

Appeals

Megarity and others v Law Society

In an action for personal injuries by the plaintiff, Brian Megarity, against the defendants, D J Ryan & Sons Ltd, the Court of Appeal (Roskill and Ormrod LJJ) ([1980] 2 All ER 832, [1980] 1 WLR 1237) on 13th March 1980 gave judgment for the defendants in an interlocutory appeal by the plaintiff against an order of Hollings J made on 4th February 1980 that all further proceedings in the action be stayed until the plaintiff submitted unconditionally to examination by the defendants' medical adviser. The plaintiff was legally aided but the defendants, being a body corporate, were not. At the conclusion of the interlocutory appeal the court ordered that, subject to any objection by the Law Society, the defendants' costs of the interlocutory appeal be paid by the legal aid fund. The Law Society objected to that order but the Court of Appeal (Roskill and Ormrod LJJ) (sub nom *Megarity v D J Ryan & Sons Ltd (No 2)* [1980] 3 All ER 602, [1980] 1 WLR 1318) held that the defendants' costs of the interlocutory appeal were to be paid out of the legal aid fund. The Law Society appealed to the House of Lords. The facts are set out in the opinion of Lord Diplock.

Gayway Linings Ltd v Law Society

In an action on four dishonoured bills of exchange brought by the plaintiffs, Gayway Linings Ltd, against the defendant, Mr Fred Toczek, judgment was entered for the plaintiffs in the Manchester District Registry by order of Mr District Registrar Lockett on 1st February 1979. On 27th March 1979 Eastham J in chambers dismissed an appeal by the defendant. The defendant was legally aided but the plaintiffs were not. The plaintiffs applied to have their costs on the appeal to Eastham J paid out of the legal aid fund and although that application was contested by the Law Society it was granted by Latey J on 22nd June 1979. The Law Society appealed to the Court of Appeal (Lord Denning MR, Shaw and Brandon LJJ) which dismissed the appeal on 22nd February 1980. The Law Society appealed to the House of Lords. The facts are set out in the opinion of Lord Diplock.

Duncan Matheson for the Law Society.
Michael Kershaw QC and *Michael Black* for Mr Megarity.
G W Wingate-Saul for D J Ryan & Sons Ltd.
R D Scholes for Gayway Linings Ltd.
Mr Toczek was not represented.

Their Lordships took time for consideration.

19th February. The following opinions were delivered.

LORD DIPLOCK. My Lords, these two appeals, which I shall refer to as *Megarity* and *Gayway Linings*, were heard together. They raise questions of great practical importance as to the power of courts exercising appellate functions to order that the costs of a successful party who has not received legal aid ('the unassisted party') shall be paid out of the legal aid fund.

At the times at which the orders for costs that are the subjects of these appeals were made, the relevant regulations that were in force under the Legal Aid Act 1974 were the Legal Aid (General) Regulations 1971, SI 1971 No 62, and the Legal Aid (Costs of Successful Unassisted Parties) Regulations 1964, SI 1964 No 1276. These have since been replaced by a single set of amended and consolidated regulations, the Legal Aid (General) Regulations 1980, SI 1980 No 1894, which came into operation on 1st January 1981. Although the new regulations incorporate amendments to some of the former regulations to which I shall find it necessary to refer specifically, it was conceded by the Law Society that those amendments, had they been in force when the orders appealed against were made, would not have affected the outcome of the proceedings in your Lordships' House. So far as I can judge from a careful perusal of the regulations now current, that concession was rightly made; so your Lordships' decisions in the instant cases as to the true construction of the Act and the regulations will govern also orders for costs of successful unassisted parties made under the Legal Aid (General) Regulations 1980.

The Legal Aid and Advice Act 1949

The purpose of the Legal Aid and Advice Act 1949, in its original form so far as it applied to legal aid in civil cases, was plain. It was that no one should be debarred by poverty from access to a court of law for the vindication of his legal rights. For simplicity of exposition I can confine myself to cases where proceedings are brought against or by a solvent unassisted party by or against an assisted party whose means are such that he is not required to make any contribution to the legal aid fund; for in each of the appeals that are now before this House the cases fall within this category.

Under the 1949 Act, if the assisted party were successful in civil proceedings brought by him as plaintiff the financial consequences to both parties as respects the costs of the litigation were substantially the same as if it had been conducted without legal aid; and little or no burden fell on the national exchequer, at any rate when, as was usually the case, the successful action was for damages. The unassisted loser was responsible for his own costs and in the ordinary course would be ordered to pay to the legal aid fund the party and party costs of the assisted winner. The assisted winner had to suffer a deduction from any amount recovered by him in the proceedings of the difference between the actual costs incurred by the legal aid fund on his behalf and the party and party costs received by the fund from the unassisted loser. Similarly if the assisted party were successful in civil proceedings brought against him as defendant the like consequences would follow, save that the legal aid fund would not be able to obtain reimbursement by the successful defendant of any difference between the actual costs incurred by the fund on his behalf and the party and party costs paid to the fund by the unsuccessful unassisted plaintiff. These financial consequences of success by assisted plaintiffs or defendants were broadly the same whether success was finally achieved in a court of first instance or an appellate court.

Where the assisted party was unsuccessful, however, the financial consequences to the unassisted party and to the national exchequer under the 1949 Act were very different from what they would have been if the litigation had been conducted without legal aid. The successful unassisted party, whether defendant or plaintiff, had to pay his own actual costs; he could not recover any part of them from the assisted party or from the legal aid fund; while the national exchequer, through the legal aid fund, paid all the costs of the unsuccessful assisted party. These consequences followed as respects the costs of proceedings not only in the court of first instance but also in any appellate court to which the case went before being finally decided. So where the assisted party was ultimately unsuccessful the costs of the litigation not only at first instance but also at any appellate stage, instead of falling on him, fell in part on the successful party and in part on public funds.

In most cases, leaving aside matrimonial proceedings, the assisted party would not have brought or defended the civil proceedings in which he was unsuccessful or carried them to appeal if he had not been granted legal aid to do so by the appropriate committee under the legal aid scheme, and the unassisted party would have been spared the expense of incurring legal costs in defending or asserting his own legal rights. The majority of civil cases, other than matrimonial causes, that were being brought with legal aid between 1949 and 1964 were claims for damages for personal injuries arising out of traffic accidents and accidents at work. The liability of the defendants in such actions was normally covered by insurance, so that the costs of defending them successfully were met out of the premium income of insurance companies and thus spread over the general body of their policy holders. Since legal aid could not be granted to a person to assert or dispute a claim in civil proceedings at first instance or on appeal unless the appropriate committee (composed of practising lawyers) were satisfied that he had reasonable grounds for doing so, Parliament may well have thought that the number of legally-aided actions of this kind that failed at first instance would not be large and, since personal injury actions generally turn on questions of fact, the number of appeals to an appellate court from an adverse judgment at first instance would be very small. So where insurance companies met the costs of successful unassisted defendants, no great social injustice would be done by leaving that burden where it lay instead of adding it to the unsuccessful assisted plaintiff's costs and meeting both from public funds.

Where, however, the successful unassisted party was himself of modest means and not protected by insurance, as was not infrequently the case in actions not concerned with personal injuries, his having to incur the costs of resisting an unsuccessful claim against him or of bringing an action to vindicate his own legal rights against resistance by an unsuccessful defendant, might, and before 1964 quite often did, cause him severe financial hardship, or even ruin.

So too the number of appeals by unsuccessful assisted parties from judgments given against them at first instance that were brought to the Court of Appeal only to be dismissed there was considerable, and a substantial proportion of them during the period up to 1964 appeared to the Court of Appeal, of which I myself was then a member, to be devoid of merit, with the result that not only the legal aid fund, whose appropriate committee had authorised the bringing of the appeal, but also the unassisted respondent had been compelled to incur substantial additional legal costs to no purpose.

These, as I well recall, were the two mischiefs that the Legal Aid Act 1964 was designed to mitigate.

The Legal Aid Act 1964

So far as concerns the hardship to a successful unassisted party of modest means the new Act mitigated the mischief by enabling the court by which the order for costs was made to transfer to the national exchequer through the legal aid fund the burden of costs incurred by him in resisting the assisted party's claim or asserting his own claim against a resisting assisted party. This the Act empowered the court to do if it were satisfied that the unassisted party would suffer severe financial hardship unless an order were made for payment of his costs out of the legal aid fund.

In addition to dealing with cases of severe financial hardship to successful unassisted parties arising from costs incurred by them in courts of first instance the Act dealt with the mischief of unjustified appeals. It drew a distinction between costs incurred by successful unassisted parties at first instance and costs incurred by them on appeal, regardless of the unassisted party's means. The 'philosophy' of the Act (if I may be forgiven this neologistic use) was to allow a legally-aided party to civil proceedings only one unsuccessful bite at the legal cherry at the expense, in part, of a successful unassisted party, and, in part, of the legal aid fund. If he was to be given a second bite in an appellate court and this was unsuccessful it was to be taken at the expense wholly of the legal aid fund if the appellate court considered that it was just and equitable to make an order for the payment of the successful unassisted person's costs in the appellate court out of the legal aid fund.

My Lords, the drafting of the 1964 Act, which gave effect to this philosophy, was highly elliptical. It took the first two sections only of the Act to deal with legal aid in England and Wales. These are reproduced in the selfsame terms in ss 13 and 14 of the Legal Aid Act 1974, the consolidation Act that is currently in force.

The Legal Aid Act 1974

Since I shall have to refer to most of the subsections of ss 13 and 14 of this Act in order to dispose of the two appeals before this House, it is convenient to set them out at this point verbatim:

'**13.**—(1) Where a party receives legal aid in connection with any proceedings between him and a party not receiving legal aid (in this and section 14 below referred to as "the unassisted party") and those proceedings are finally decided in favour of the unassisted party, the court by which the proceedings are so decided may, subject to the provisions of this section, make an order for the payment to the unassisted party out of the legal aid fund of the whole or any part of the costs incurred by him in those proceedings.

'(2) An order may be made under this section in respect of any costs if (and only if) the court is satisfied that it is just and equitable in all the circumstances that provision for those costs should be made out of public funds; and before making such an order the court shall in every case (whether or not application is made in that behalf) consider what orders should be made for costs against the party receiving legal aid and for determining his liability in respect of such costs.

'(3) Without prejudice to subsection (2) above, no order shall be made under this section in respect of costs incurred in a court of first instance, whether by that court or by any appellate court, unless—(a) the proceedings in the court of first instance were instituted by the party receiving legal aid; and (b) the court is satisfied that the unassisted party will suffer severe financial hardship unless the order is made.

'(4) An order under this section shall not be made by any court in respect of costs incurred by the unassisted party in any proceedings in which, apart from this section, no order would be made for the payment of his costs.

'(5) Without prejudice to any other provision restricting appeals from any court, no appeal shall lie against an order under this section, or a refusal to make such an order, except on a point of law.

'(6) In this section "costs" means costs as between party and party; but the costs in respect of which an order may be made under this section include the costs of applying for that order.

'(7) References in this section and section 14 below to legal aid include references to assistance by way of representation.

'**14.**—(1) Regulations may make provision—(a) for determining the proceedings which are or are not to be treated as separate proceedings for the purposes of section 13 above, or as having been instituted by the party receiving legal aid for the purposes of subsection (3)(a) of that section; (b) for modifying subsection (3)(b) of that section in its application to an unassisted party who is concerned in proceedings only in a fiduciary, representative or official capacity; and (c) for regulating the procedure to be followed in connection with orders under that section.

'(2) Regulations made by virtue of subsection (1)(c) above may in particular make provision—(a) for the reference of applications for orders under section 13 above, or of any question of fact relevant to such applications, for inquiry and report by a master, a registrar or a district registrar, as the case may be; (b) for the exercise by a master, a registrar or a district registrar of the powers under that section of a High Court judge or of a judge assigned to a county court district; (c) for enabling the Law Society to be heard in connection with any order under that section.

'(3) For the purposes of section 13 above proceedings shall be treated as finally decided in favour of the unassisted party—(a) if no appeal lies against the decision in his favour; (b) if an appeal lies against the decision with leave, and the time limited for applications for leave expires without leave being granted; or (c) if leave to appeal against the decision is granted or is not required, and no appeal is brought within the time limited for appeal; and where an appeal against the decision is brought out of time the court by which the appeal (or any further appeal in those proceedings) is determined may make an order for the repayment by the unassisted party to the legal aid fund of the whole or any part of any sum previously paid to him under that section in respect of those proceedings:

'(4) Where a court decides any proceedings in favour of the unassisted party and an appeal lies (with or without leave) against that decision, the court may, if it thinks fit, make or refuse to make an order under section 13 above forthwith, but any order so made shall not take effect—(a) where leave to appeal is required, unless the time limited for applications for leave to appeal expires without leave being granted; (b) where leave to appeal is granted or is not required, unless the time limited for appeal expires without an appeal being brought.

'(5) Where a party begins to receive legal aid in connection with any proceedings after those proceedings have been instituted, or ceases to receive legal aid before they are finally decided or otherwise receives legal aid in connection with part only of any proceedings, the reference in section 13(1) above to the costs incurred by the unassisted party in those proceedings shall be construed as a reference to so much of those costs as is attributable to that part.'

The appeal in *Megarity* turns on the meaning of 'those proceedings' where that expression first appears in s 13(1); and the appeal in *Gayway Linings* turns on the meaning of an 'appellate court' in s 13(3). *Megarity* concerns an order for the payment of the costs incurred by an unassisted defendant in resisting an unsuccessful interlocutory appeal to the Court of Appeal by an assisted plaintiff in an action for damages for personal injuries. *Gayway Linings* concerns an order for the payment of costs incurred by an unassisted plaintiff in resisting an unsuccessful appeal by an assisted defendant to a judge in chambers from an order of a district registrar striking out his defence to the plaintiff's claim on four bills of exchange and ordering judgment to be entered against him. The meaning of those expressions in s 13(1) and (3) of the 1974 Act is of an importance that is not confined to the two cases in which these appeals have been brought. That was why leave to appeal to this House was given; and, before giving further details of the actual facts in these two appeals, some preliminary exegesis of the sections is in my view appropriate to show how they give effect to what I have suggested was the philosophy of the 1964 Act.

The power of a court to award costs out of the legal aid fund to a successful unassisted party is conferred by s 13(1); but for a proper understanding of the nature and limits of the power so conferred the style of draftsmanship adopted compels frequent cross-reference to and fro between the various subsections of ss 13 and 14 and regulations made under the previous Acts consolidated by the 1974 Act and kept in operation by s 42(2).

My Lords, the proceeding to which s 13(1) applies are confined to proceedings in connection with which a party receives legal aid. This throws one back to ss 6 and 7 of the Act which confer a right to legal aid on parties to civil proceedings before the courts and tribunals specified in Sch 1 to the Act, if they can satisfy the statutory criteria as to financial means and as to the existence of reasonable grounds for taking, defending or being a party to those proceedings. Section 20(2)(a), which was formerly s 12(2) of the 1949 Act, authorises the Lord Chancellor to make regulations 'as to the proceedings which are or are not to be treated as distinct proceedings for the purposes of legal aid'; and I shall revert later to regulations made pursuant to this general power. But these cannot be determinative of what are or are not to be treated as 'separate proceedings' for the purposes of s 13(1), since s 14(1) confers a special power to make other regulations for that specific purpose, a difference to which the draftsman subtly draws attention by substituting the adjective 'separate' for 'distinct'.

To achieve the two purposes for which the 1964 Act was passed it was essential that proceedings before an appellate court in any action, cause or matter should be treated as separate proceedings in themselves for the purpose of determining the right of the unassisted party to costs out of the legal aid fund. This is done by s 13(3) which lays down different criteria to be applied when awarding costs to a successful unassisted party, depending on whether the costs were incurred in a court of first instance or an appellate court. In my opinion a regulation under s 14(1) which purported to determine that proceedings in a court of the first instance and proceedings on appeal to an appellate court in the same action were *not* separate proceedings would have been ultra vires; but the actual regulations made under s 14(1), on their true construction, in my view do nothing of the sort.

Sections 13 and 14 draw a distinction too between 'proceedings' simpliciter, the expression used in s 13(1), and 'part only of any proceedings' to which reference is made in s 14(5). This subsection makes it plain that the expression 'part' is not limited to cases where legal aid is received by the assisted party for part only of the period during which the proceedings are going on but refers also to cases where legal aid to the assisted party has been limited to one issue out of several in a single action, as in *Mills v Mills* [1963] 2 All ER 237, [1963] P 329, or has been limited to a particular step in proceedings, such as applying for an interlocutory injunction. That particular part of the proceedings may be finally decided by an unappealed refusal of the injunction but the proceedings as a whole continue and may well be finally decided in favour of the party who failed on the application for the interlocutory injunction.

Jurisdiction to make an order under s 13(1) awarding costs out of the legal fund to an unassisted party does not arise until the 'proceedings' are finally decided in favour of the unassisted party. Section 14(3) prevents this happening in a court of first instance until the time for appeal is past. So, where there is an appeal to an appellate court, the only court that *can* make an order under s 13(1) is the appellate court. This will be the first appellate court, if the appeal ends there, or, if the appeal is taken further, the final appellate court. No jurisdiction remains in the court of first instance to make such an order in respect of costs incurred in the proceedings before it; and s 13(3) plainly contemplates that, in that event, the order relating to the unassisted party's costs at first instance may be made by the appellate court by which the proceedings are finally decided. It was this consideration that led this House in *Shiloh Spinners Ltd v Hardin (No 2)* [1973] 1 All ER 966, [1973] 1 WLR 518 to hold that 'the costs incurred by him in those proceedings' referred to at the end of s 13(1) must have been intended by Parliament to include costs in the lower courts with which the appellate court has jurisdiction to deal in its own order for costs made on the appeal. Otherwise the manifest purpose of the Act would be thwarted.

Section 14(1)(a) is the regulation-making power to which I have already referred. The relevant power is to make provision 'for determining the proceedings which are or are not to be treated as separate proceedings for the purposes of section 13 above'. What are separate proceedings will determine which court it is that has finally decided the proceedings and as such has jurisdiction to make an order under s 13(1). Read in the context of the special provision made in s 14(5) for cases where the assisted party receives legal aid in connection with 'part only' of legal proceedings, I do not think that s 14(1)(a) authorises the making of regulations splitting a single action into several parts, either in a court of first instance or in an appellate court, and determining that each part shall be treated as separate proceedings for the purpose of s 13. This would conflict with the provisions of s 14(5). In those cases where the assisted party received legal aid in connection with part only of those proceedings that subsection leaves the sole jurisdiction to make the modified order under s 13(1) for which it provides with the court that finally decides the whole proceedings in favour of the unassisted party and only if it does so decide them, whereas an order splitting the whole proceedings in the court of first instance or those in the appellate court into several separate parts would have the result

of transferring the sole jurisdiction to make the order to whichever court, whether of
first instance or appellate, that finally decided a particular part in favour of the unassisted
party, even though the proceedings as a whole were finally decided in favour of the
assisted party and not of the unassisted party as is required by s 13(1).

The regulation originally under the 1964 Act in the exercise of the power conferred by
s 14(1)(a) was reg 2 of the Legal Aid (Costs of Successful Unassisted Parties) Regulations
1964. It was maintained in operation by s 42(2) of the Legal Aid Act 1974, and at the
relevant time was in the following terms:

> 'Any proceedings in respect of which a separate civil aid certificate could properly
> be issued under the General Regulations to a person receiving legal aid shall be
> treated as separate proceedings for the purposes of the Act.'

This throws one back to the Legal Aid (General) Regulations, of which the version in
force at the date of the making of reg 2 was that of 1962. The relevant regulation, reg
6 of the Legal Aid (General) Regulations 1962, was amended in 1971 and it was this
version that was maintained in force by s 42(2) of the Legal Aid Act 1974. Those
amendments, however, were not material to the questions involved in the instant
appeals, and it is sufficient for present purposes to set out the terms of reg 6 of the 1962
regulations:

> '(1) A certificate may be issued in respect of ... (b) the whole or part of—(i)
> proceedings in a court of first instance, or (ii) proceedings in an appellate court; but
> no certificate shall relate to proceedings (other than interlocutory appeals) both in a
> court of first instance and in an appellate court or to proceedings in more than one
> appellate court ...'

This regulation draws a distinction between three kinds of proceedings: those in a
court of first instance, those in a first appellate court, and those in a second appellate
court. While it is permissible to include interlocutory appeals to an appellate court in the
same certificate as that issued in respect of proceedings in a court of first instance, the
power to do so is permissive only and such interlocutory appeals may properly be the
subject of a separate certificate. So the regulations made under s 14(1) provide, as in my
view the Act compels them to do, that all proceedings on appeal to an appellate court in
any action, cause or matter are to be treated as separate proceedings from the proceedings
in the same action in the court of first instance from which the appeal is brought.

Regulation 6(1) also draws the distinction between the whole proceedings and parts of
proceedings that was reflected in s 2(5) of the 1964 Act, now reproduced in s 14(5) of the
1974 Act. Regulation 6(1) imposes no legal limitation on what parts of proceedings may
be made the subject of a separate civil aid certificate. In theory a separate certificate
might be issued for each distinct procedural step taken on a civil action, though practical
considerations would generally rule out dissection of proceedings in this way. Regulation
2 of the 1964 regulations speaks only of 'proceedings', not of 'parts of proceedings'. It
does not provide that a part of proceedings only in respect of which a civil aid certificate
could properly be issued is to be treated as separate proceedings for the purpose of s 13;
such separate status is restricted to proceedings treated as a whole. Any other construction
of the regulations would, in my opinion, render them ultra vires, and lead to results that
would be manifestly absurd.

I turn now to the application of the Act and regulations to what happened in the cases
of *Megarity* and of *Gayway Linings* respectively.

Megarity

Megarity, the party receiving legal aid, was the plaintiff in an action in the High Court
against his employers, D J Ryan & Sons Ltd, the unassisted party, as defendants. He
claimed damages for personal injuries received in the course of his employment as a
result of their negligence or breach of statutory duty. The defendants applied to the
district registrar for an order that Megarity should submit himself for examination by
the defendants' medical adviser. Megarity refused to do this except on condition that the
medical report on the examination be disclosed to him. The defendants applied to the

district registrar for an order that all further proceedings in the action should be stayed until Megarity submitted to the medical examination without any such condition attached to it. The district registrar refused to make the order sought by the defendants, but, on appeal from his decision to the judge in chambers, it was granted. From this order Megarity appealed, by leave of the judge, to the Court of Appeal, the civil aid certificate which had been issued to him, with a nil contribution, having been extended to cover the interlocutory appeal. The Court of Appeal ([1980] 2 All ER 832, [1980] 1 WLR 1237) dismissed the appeal, which it regarded as devoid of merit, and intimated its intention of making an order under s 13(1) of the 1974 Act for the payment out of the legal aid fund of the defendants' costs of the proceedings in the Court of Appeal.

In response to that intimation the Law Society duly appeared to resist the proposed order on the grounds that the Court of Appeal had no jurisdiction under s 13(1) to make the order or, if it had jurisdiction, it should, in the exercise of its discretion, refuse to make it. The rival arguments in the Court of Appeal on jurisdiction were, as they have been in your Lordships' House, on the one hand the contention by the Law Society that 'any proceedings' and 'those proceedings' in s 13(1) mean the whole lis between the parties in connection with any part of which a civil aid certificate has been issued, and on the other hand the contention by the defendants that the interlocutory appeal to the Court of Appeal was a separate proceeding. If the Law Society's contention were right, then 'those proceedings' had not been finally decided in favour of either party by the Court of Appeal's decision on an interlocutory matter; and, since those proceedings would continue, what was a condition precedent to the jurisdiction of the court to make an order under s 13(1) remained unfulfilled when the Court of Appeal made its order.

The Court of Appeal ([1980] 3 All ER 602, [1980] 1 WLR 1318) found itself unable to accept this argument. It took the view that on the true construction of the Act in the light of its manifest purpose an interlocutory appeal to the Court of Appeal constitutes separate proceedings for the purposes of s 13. The court referred to some previous cases under various sections of the Act but did not find those authorities helpful on the question of construction which it had to decide. I too have considered those cases and some others that were cited at the hearing in your Lordships' House and I too find them unhelpful and see no need to refer to them here.

For the reasons I have already stated at length I agree with the construction accepted by the Court of Appeal. In my opinion that court had jurisdiction to make the order that it did.

My Lords, the argument on discretion can be disposed of briefly. The defendants have been put to the expense of successfully resisting in the Court of Appeal an interlocutory appeal that it considered to be devoid of merit. It was submitted by the Law Society that the question of what order, if any, should be made under s 13 in respect of the costs of the interlocutory appeal should be remitted by the Court of Appeal to the judge of the High Court by whom the case will be tried to be dealt with at the conclusion of the trial. At the conclusion of the trial, it is suggested, Megarity's means might be enhanced by damages recovered by him in the action, and the judge would then be obliged by s 13(2) to take into account those enhanced means in deciding how liability for the costs of the interlocutory appeal should be apportioned between Megarity himself and the legal aid fund. The short answer to this is that, on the construction that I have placed on s 13(1), the interlocutory appeal was separate proceedings, the court that finally decided those proceedings was the Court of Appeal; it alone had jurisdiction to make an order for payment of those costs or any part of them out of the legal aid fund.

Accordingly I would dismiss the appeal in *Megarity*.

Gayway Linings

Gayway Linings Ltd, the unassisted party, were plaintiffs in an action brought against Mr Toczek, the defendant, for some £4,000 for principal and interest due on four dishonoured bills of exchange of which the defendant was a co-acceptor. A defence was put in on behalf of the defendant, who at that stage of the proceedings was not receiving legal aid. It simply said that he did not admit that he accepted the bills. Gayway Linings Ltd applied to the district registrar in Manchester for an order striking out the defence and entering judgment for Gayway Linings Ltd for the amount of the bills together with interest. The registrar made the order on 1st February 1979. On 6th February the defendant became a person receiving legal aid to appeal to the judge in chambers from that order of the registrar. Initially an emergency certificate was issued to him limited to all steps up to and including filing notice of appeal and obtaining counsel's opinion, but on 21st March the certificate was extended to the whole proceedings on the appeal. The appeal, which was obviously hopeless, was duly dismissed by Eastham J on 27th March, and Gayway Linings Ltd sought an order for payment of their costs of the appeal out of the legal aid fund. The Law Society was duly notified and appeared to oppose the making of the order. Its objection was heard before Latey J; he made the order for which Gayway Linings Ltd had asked. By leave of Latey J an appeal to the Court of Appeal was brought from his order as to costs. That appeal was dismissed by the Court of Appeal on 22nd February 1980.

The question of construction involved in this appeal is a short one. Is a judge in chambers in the High Court, when hearing an appeal from an order of a district registrar or Queen's Bench master ordering final judgment to be entered in the action, acting as a 'court of first instance' or an 'appellate court' within the meaning of s 13(3) of the 1974 Act? Or, put more briefly, do these expressions refer to the function that the court is performing in the particular proceedings or to its status in the hierarchy of courts?

My Lords, as Lord Denning MR pointed out in his judgment in the Court of Appeal, orders made by district registrars, like those of masters of the Queen's Bench Division and registrars of the Family Division ordering judgment to be entered for a party to an action, are orders that finally decide the action. They take effect as soon as they are made; the only way of setting them aside is by what is described in RSC Ord 58, r 1 as an 'appeal' to a judge in chambers, and such appeal does not even operate as a stay of proceedings on the judgment unless the court otherwise directs. So where a district registrar orders judgment in an action to be entered for an unassisted plaintiff and no appeal is brought against his order to the judge in chambers the registrar becomes the court by which the proceedings are finally decided in favour of the unassisted party. He is the court of first instance in those proceedings and if there is an appeal from his decision the judge in chambers by whom the appeal is determined is acting as an appellate court and not otherwise. I agree with the Court of Appeal that the expression 'appellate court' in s 13(3) should be taken to refer to the function that the court is performing. This is also the only view that is consistent with what I have earlier called the philosophy of the Act. When appealing from the registrar to the judge in chambers the assisted party is having a second bite at the legal cherry.

But for the appeal to the Court of Appeal in *Gayway Linings* the judge's order dismissing the defendant's appeal from the order of the district registrar would have been a final decision in favour of the unassisted party of the whole of the proceedings brought by him against a party receiving legal aid. The appeal was without any merit and the judge was entitled in his discretion to take the view that it was just and equitable that the legal aid fund should bear the costs of an unmeritorious appeal that would probably never have been brought had the defendant not been encouraged to do so by the financial provision for his costs to be made available from that fund. His contribution to his costs was assessed at nil.

Very different considerations are likely to apply to appeals to the judge in chambers from the ordinary run of interlocutory orders made by a registrar or Queen's Bench master which do not finally dispose of the action. Your Lordships have not had occasion in the instant appeals to consider these, and nothing that I have said should be taken as encouraging the making of orders under s 13(1) in respect of an unassisted party's costs in an appeal from the registrar or master to a judge in chambers from any other kind of interlocutory order than one that finally disposes of the action.

I would dismiss the appeal in *Gayway Linings* also.

LORD SIMON OF GLAISDALE. My Lords, I was privileged to read in draft the speech just delivered by my noble and learned friend on the Woolsack. I agree with it, and for the reasons which he gives I would dismiss both appeals.

LORD EDMUND-DAVIES. My Lords, I have had the advantage of reading in draft the speech prepared by my noble and learned friend Lord Diplock. I am in respectful agreement with it and therefore concur in holding that both appeals should be dismissed.

LORD SCARMAN. My Lords, I have had the advantage of reading in draft the speech of my noble and learned friend Lord Diplock. For the reasons he gives I also would dismiss these appeals.

LORD BRIDGE OF HARWICH. My Lords, I have had the advantage of reading in draft the speech delivered by my noble and learned friend Lord Diplock. I agree with it and for the reasons he gives I would dismiss both these appeals.

Appeals dismissed.

Solicitors: *David Edwards*, Secretary, Legal Aid (for the Law Society); *Whitehouse, Gibson & Alton* (for Mr Megarity); *Mackrell & Co* (for D J Ryan & Sons Ltd); *Barnett & Barnett* (for Gayway Linings Ltd).

Mary Rose Plummer   Barrister.

A/S Awilco v Fulvia SpA di Navigazione The Chikuma

HOUSE OF LORDS

LORD DIPLOCK, LORD SIMON OF GLAISDALE, LORD EDMUND-DAVIES, LORD SCARMAN AND LORD BRIDGE OF HARWICH

19th, 20th JANUARY, 19th FEBRUARY 1981

Shipping – Charterparty – Time charter – Payment of hire – Punctual payment – Unconditional right to immediate use of payment of hire – Charterers paying hire on due date by irrevocable transfer to owners' bank – Payment received by owners' bank on due date but not attracting interest for four days – Owners entitled on due date to withdraw amount paid subject to payment of four days' interest – Whether owners having unconditional right to immediate use of amount paid – Whether owners receiving equivalent of cash – Whether charterers making 'punctual payment'.

A time charterparty in the New York Produce Exchange form provided that in the event of the charterers failing to make 'punctual and regular payment of the hire' monthly in advance to the owners' bank in Genoa, Italy, the owners were to be entitled to withdraw the chartered vessel from the charterers. On 22nd January 1976 when the 81st monthly payment of $US68,863 was due the charterers' bank in Norway arranged for an Italian bank to make a credit transfer of the due hire to the owners' bank in Genoa. That was duly carried out on 22nd January by telex. However, although the transfer was irrevocable and the owners could on 22nd January have withdrawn the amount transferred, under Italian banking law interest on the amount transferred did not begin to run in favour of the owners' bank until 26th January and if the owners had withdrawn the amount on 22nd January they would have had to pay interest of between $70 and $100 to their bank. The owners decided that the hire had not been punctually paid and withdrew the vessel from the charterers who countered by claiming $3,000,000 damages from the owners. The dispute went to arbitration and the arbitrator decided that payment of the hire had been made on the due date. On appeal by a special case stated by the arbitrator the judge held that the transfer to the owners' bank had not given the owners the unconditional right to the immediate use of the funds transferred and that they were therefore entitled to withdraw the vessel. The Court of Appeal reversed his decision on the ground, inter alia, that the interest payable by the owners if they withdrew on the due date the funds transferred was merely a bank charge arising out of an inter-banking arrangement which did not affect the fact that the funds were available to the owners on the due date. The owners appealed to the House of Lords.

Held – Although the transfer of the due hire to the owners' bank was 'unconditional' in the sense that it was irrevocable and was neither subject to a condition precedent being fulfilled nor defeasible on the failure to fulfil a condition subsequent, nevertheless to comply with the requirement regarding punctual payment in the charterparty the transfer had to be unconditional in the sense of being unfettered or unrestricted, which it could only do if what the owners received was the equivalent of cash or as good as cash. Since the funds transferred could not be used immediately to earn interest and could only be withdrawn subject to payment of interest, the transfer was the equivalent of an overdraft facility rather than cash. Therefore, although the minor failure to comply with their contractual obligation produced what was apparently a harsh result for the charterers, the owners were entitled to withdraw the vessel, and their appeal would accordingly be allowed (see p 654 c to e, p 656 j to p 657 d and g to j and p 659 b, post).

Dicta of Edmund Davies and Megaw LJJ in *The Brimnes* [1974] 3 All ER at 98, 110 applied.

Dictum of Brandon J in *The Brimnes* [1973] 1 All ER at 782 explained.

Per Curiam. Where shipowners and charterers (who bargain at arm's length and neither class of whom has such a preponderance of bargaining power as to be in a position to oppress the other) embody in their contracts common form clauses, it is of overriding importance that their meaning and legal effect should be certain and well understood, and in construing such clauses the courts should aim to produce a result such that in any given situation both parties seeking legal advice as to their rights and obligations can expect the same clear and confident answer from their advisers and neither will be tempted to embark on long and expensive litigation in the belief that victory depends on winning the sympathy of the court (see p 654 c to e and p 658 j to p 659 a, post).

Notes

For stipulations as to hire in time charters, see 35 Halsbury's Laws (3rd Edn) 281, para 423, and for cases on the subject, see 41 Digest (Repl) 220–229, 472–539.

Cases referred to in opinions

Brimnes, The, Tenax SS Co Ltd v The Brimnes (Owners) [1973] 1 All ER 769, [1973] 1 WLR 386, [1972] 1 Lloyd's Rep 465; *affd* [1974] 3 All ER 88, [1975] QB 929, [1974] 3 WLR 613, [1974] 2 Lloyd's Rep 241, CA, Digest (Cont Vol D) 819, 482b.

Empresa Cubana de Fletes v Lagonisi Shipping Co Ltd, The Georgios C [1971] 1 All ER 193, [1971] 1 QB 488, [1971] 2 WLR 221, [1971] 1 Lloyd's Rep 7, CA, Digest (Cont Vol D) 819, 482a.

Mardorf Peach & Co Ltd v Attica Sea Carriers Corpn of Liberia, The Laconia [1977] 1 All ER 545, [1977] AC 850, [1977] 2 WLR 286, [1977] 1 Lloyd's Rep 315, HL, Digest (Cont Vol E) 547, 539d.

Nova Scotia Steel Co v Sutherland Steamship Co (1899) 5 Com Cas 106, 41 Digest (Repl) 229, 536.

Tankexpress A/S v Compagnie Financière Belge des Petroles SA, The Petrofina [1948] 2 All ER
939, [1949] AC 76, [1949] LJR 170, HL, 41 Digest (Repl) 221, 482.   *a*

Appeal
Fulvia SpA di Navigazione of Cagliari, Italy ('the owners') appealed against the judgment
of the Court of Appeal (Lord Denning MR, Waller and Dunn LJJ) on 4th June 1980
allowing the appeal of A/S Awilco of Oslo, Norway ('the charterers') against the judgment
of Robert Goff J on 23rd October 1978 whereby he held on an award stated in the form   *b*
of a special case by the arbitrator, Mr Donald Davies, that the owners were entitled to
withdraw the vessel Chikuma which was time chartered to the charterers on the ground
that the charterers had failed to make payment of hire in accordance with the
charterparty. The facts are set out in the opinion of Lord Bridge.

Christopher Staughton QC and *V V Veeder* for the owners.   *c*
Andrew Leggatt QC and *Roger Buckley QC* for the charterers.

Their Lordships took time for consideration.

19th February. The following opinions were delivered.
                                                                                          d
LORD DIPLOCK. My Lords, I have had the advantage of reading in draft the speech
prepared by my noble and learned friend Lord Bridge. For the reasons he has given I too
would allow the appeal.

LORD SIMON OF GLAISDALE. My Lords, I have had the privilege of reading in
draft the speech prepared by my noble and learned friend Lord Bridge. For the reasons   *e*
he has given I too would allow the appeal.

LORD EDMUND-DAVIES. My Lords, I am in respectful agreement with the
reasons advanced in the speech prepared by my noble and learned friend Lord Bridge, for
concluding that this appeal should be allowed.
                                                                                          f
LORD SCARMAN. My Lords, I have had the advantage of reading in draft the speech
to be delivered by my noble and learned friend Lord Bridge. For the reasons he gives I
would allow the appeal.

LORD BRIDGE OF HARWICH. My Lords, this appeal arises from a dispute under
the terms of a time charterparty in the New York Produce Exchange form to which at   *g*
the material time the appellants ('the owners') were parties as owners of the vessel
Chikuma and the respondents ('the charterers') as charterers. By cl 5 of the charterparty
payment of the hire was 'to be made . . . in cash in United States currency, monthly in
advance . . . otherwise failing the punctual and regular payment of the hire . . . the
Owners shall be at liberty to withdraw the vessel from the service of the Charterers . . .'
An addendum to the charterparty provided for all freights to be paid to the owners'   *h*
agents 'care of ISTITUTO BANCARIO SAN PAOLO DI TORINO—Sede di Genova' ('the owners'
bank').
    On 24th January 1976 the owners withdrew the vessel from the service of the
charterers on the ground that they had failed to pay the monthly instalment of hire due
on 22nd January. The charterers disputed the alleged failure and in due course claimed
damages for wrongful withdrawal of the ship. This claim was referred to arbitration by   *j*
Mr Donald Davies as sole arbitrator. On a preliminary issue he was requested by the
parties and agreed to state an interim award in the form of a special case on the
assumption that a monthly instalment of hire fell due on or before 22nd January 1976
in the sum of $68,863·84 (the amount of which was at one time, but may well now no
longer be, in issue).

Having set out his findings of primary fact, the arbitrator held that the charterers had paid the appropriate sum on the due date in accordance with the contract and that the owners were accordingly not entitled to withdraw the vessel when they did. This conclusion was reversed by Robert Goff J. On appeal by the charterers, the Court of Appeal (Lord Denning MR, Waller and Dunn LJJ) unanimously restored the decision of the arbitrator. The owners now appeal to your Lordships' House.

Before January 1976 monthly payments of hire had always been made punctually by credit transfer to the owners' bank. On 21st January 1976 the charterers instructed their Norwegian bank to make the required payment by credit transfer. On Thursday, 22nd January at 11.41 am, on instructions from the Norwegian bank, Credito Italiano, Genoa sent a telex to the owners' bank to the following effect: 'Pay without expenses for us USA $68,863·84 [by] order Christiania Bank OG Kredietkasse Oslo for account AS Awilco in favour SASDA SpA Account 16020 C/O yourgoodselves re: Chikuma Stop [We] telecover you value 26 through Chase Manhattan Bank New York account Yours of Turin Stop.'

This text is a translation from the original Italian of the telex but I have added in square brackets words which, it was agreed at the hearing of the appeal, produce a more accurate version than the English text used in the courts below, though I think nothing turns on this. I should add that this telex was not exhibited to the special case by the arbitrator, but it was agreed between the parties at the hearing before Robert Goff J that it should be treated as an exhibit. This was eminently sensible, for without seeing the telex it would be difficult to understand the arbitrator's crucial findings of fact which are set out in the following two paragraphs:

'4. By a telex message of 1141 on Thursday, January 22, there was a credit transfer to the Owners' bank of U.S. dollars 68,863·84 representing the 81st payment of hire. At about noon on the same day the said credit transfer became irrevocable under Italian banking law and practice and the funds representing the 81st payment of hire became available to the Owners' bank for payment to the Owners although interest on those funds would not begin to run in favour of the Owners' bank until Monday, January 26.

'5. On January 22, 1976, the Owners' bank credited the Owners' account with U.S. dollars 68,863·84 (representing the 81st payment of hire) and, under Italian banking law and practice, the Owners had the immediate use of the said sum even though interest on the sum would not begin to run in favour of the Owners until Monday, January 26. If the Owners had withdrawn the said sum from their bank on January 22 (which was not the case although they had the right so to do) they would probably have incurred a liability to their bank to pay interest on the sum until January 26.'

It is further found that, on the owners' instructions, the owners' bank recredited the amount of the transfer to Credito Italiano on 23rd January.

At the conclusion of his findings of fact, the arbitrator posed the question of law for the decision of the court (on the assumption to which I have referred earlier) in the following terms:

'Whether the Respondent Owners were entitled to withdraw the vessel on Saturday 24th January 1976 under Clause 5 of the charterparty dated 18th December 1968.'

Under the heading 'Award' the arbitrator wrote:

'Subject to the decision of the Court, I HOLD that:

'1. There was a payment to the Owners, by the Charterers, of U.S. dollars 68,863.84, on Thursday, January 22, 1976.

'2. On the assumption that hire in the above sum was due on January 22 the Owners were not entitled to withdraw the vessel on Saturday, January 24, 1976, under Clause 5 of the Charterparty.'

I have set out these extracts from the special case at some length in order to point to the conclusion, which seems to me inevitable, that the arbitrator was treating the question *a* he had to resolve, having found the relevant primary facts, as a pure question of law depending on the true construction of the contractual provision applicable. What he held in setting out his award did not purport to be other than a conclusion of law and, in particular, there is no indication in the case that, either on the basis of expert evidence or by applying his own knowledge as a very experienced commercial arbitrator, he was attaching to any of the contractual words any special technical meaning other than their *b* ordinary meaning.

This is a convenient point at which to make two general observations about the facts. First, the effect of the telex from Credito Italiano to the owners' bank seems, in the light of the arbitrator's findings in paras 4 and 5, to produce a situation, in accordance with Italian banking law and practice, which in the eyes of an English banker or lawyer, has some strikingly unusual features. It is a situation hardly likely to trouble the English *c* courts again unless as a result of a similar Italian inter-bank transaction. Second, if the owners are right, this is yet another instance of a clause such as cl 5 of the New York Produce Exchange form operating to produce what appears to be a harsh result. The unexpired term of the time charter must have been a valuable asset. The Court of Appeal was told that the charterers' claim for damages was $3,000,000. Yet their failure, if there was a failure, to comply with their obligation under cl 5 was obviously of a very *d* minor character.

My Lords, this is not the first time that cl 5 of the New York Produce Exchange form of charterparty has been before the courts. In giving his considered judgment in *The Brimnes* [1973] 1 All ER 769 at 782, [1973] 1 WLR 386 at 400 Brandon J said of this very clause:

> 'I consider first the meaning of payment in cash in cl 5 of the charterparty. In my *e* view these words must be interpreted against the background of modern commercial practice. So interpreted it seems to me that they cannot mean only payment in dollar bills or other legal tender of the USA. They must, as the shipowners contend, have a wider meaning, comprehending any commercially recognised method of transferring funds, the result of which is to give the transferee the unconditional right to the immediate use of the funds transferred.' *f*

In the instant case, the test enunciated in the last sentence of the passage quoted was adopted and applied both by Robert Goff J and by the Court of Appeal. But it led them to opposite conclusions. Robert Goff J said:.

> 'Here, the money took the form of a telex transfer and the telex transfer had attached to it, in my judgment, a condition embodied in the words "value 26". The *g* effect of that was that the transfer was conditional on interest not accruing on that money for the benefit of the transferee until a date later than the due date specified in the contract. I can see no escape from the conclusion that the effect of the imposition of that condition was to render it a payment which did not give the transferee the unconditional right to the immediate use of the funds transferred ... It is as though the cash was handed over the counter on the Thursday and at the time *h* of its transfer a condition was attached to it that, if it was made available to the beneficiary immediately, interest was to be payable until the Monday, and, if it was not made available to him immediately, interest would not accrue to him until the Monday ... In my judgment ... one cannot ignore the power of money to breed interest. To do so is to ignore an essential attribute of money itself.' *j*

All three members of the Court of Appeal reached the conclusion that the owners' right to the immediate use of the funds transferred was unconditional. They naturally expressed themselves in different terms, but I hope I fairly summarise their main grounds as follows: (1) that the last sentence of the telex containing the crucial words 'value 26' was an inter-banking arrangement which did not affect the rights of the owners; (2) that the arbitrator had found as a fact, or on a mixed question of fact and law, that the owners' right was unconditional and there was evidence to support such a finding; (3) that the stipulation as to interest imposed no true condition.

With respect, it seems to me clear that the first two grounds are unsound. As to the first, Credito Italiano, as sub-agents of the charterers, effected the transfer on terms which deferred the right of owners' bank to the enjoyment of the funds to 26th January. It was a plainly foreseeable consequence of the deferment that it would be, as it was, reflected in the terms which the owners' bank would be entitled to impose on the use of the funds by the owners between 22nd and 26th January. As to the second, the word 'unconditional' nowhere appears in the special case and, as I have pointed out earlier, the arbitrator treated the question he had to decide as a question of law depending on the construction of cl 5 of the charterparty.

The third ground depends on the interpretation of the word 'unconditional' in the context of the statement of principle by Brandon J in *The Brimnes* bearing in mind that it is not to be construed as if it were a statute. If the word is understood in its narrow, legal sense as meaning that the transferee's right to the use of the funds transferred is neither subject to the fulfilment of a condition precedent nor defeasible on failure to fulfil a condition subsequent, I can see that the owners' right in this case to the use of the funds on 22nd January could be described as unconditional. But Robert Goff J obviously understood it in a much wider and more liberal sense as equivalent to unfettered or unrestricted. I am bound to say that, before the argument in this appeal brought to light this ambiguity, it would never have occurred to me that Brandon J's formulation of the relevant principle was in any respect either inaccurate or inadequate. Now that the ambiguity is exposed, I have no doubt how it should be resolved. The underlying concept is surely this, that when payment is made to a bank otherwise than literally in cash, ie in dollar bills or other legal tender (which no one expects), there is no 'payment in cash' within the meaning of cl 5 unless what the creditor receives is the equivalent of cash, or as good as cash. This is supported both by the common sense of the matter and by the judgments in the Court of Appeal affirming the decision of Brandon J in *The Brimnes*. Edmund Davies LJ said [1974] 3 All ER 88 at 98, [1975] QB 929 at 948:

> 'But the shipowners' contention that the tendering of the commercial equivalent of cash would suffice found favour with the trial judge. In particular, he concluded that any transfer of funds to MGT for the credit of the shipowners' account so as to give them the unconditional right to the immediate use of the funds transferred was good payment. In my judgment, this was clearly right . . .'

Megaw LJ said ([1974] 3 All ER 88 at 110, [1975] QB 929 at 963):

> 'Whatever mode or process is used, "payment" is not achieved until the process has reached the stage that the creditor has received cash or that which he is prepared to treat as the equivalent of cash, or has a credit available on which, in the normal course of business or banking practice, he can draw, if he wishes, in the form of cash.'

The book entry made by the owners' bank on 22nd January in the owners' account was clearly not the equivalent of cash, nor was there any reason why the owners should have been prepared to treat it as the equivalent of cash. It could not be used to earn interest, e g by immediate transfer to a deposit account. It could only be drawn subject to a (probable) liability to pay interest. In substance it was the equivalent of an overdraft facility which the bank was bound to make available. I have put the word 'probable' in brackets because I attach no significance to its use in the arbitrator's finding. The finding of a probable liability to pay interest must connote a right in the owners' bank to charge interest, which is the decisive factor. It follows, in my view, that on 22nd January there was no 'payment in cash' by the charterers of the hire then assumed to be due and accordingly the owners, having refused to accept the credit as payment in accordance with cl 5, were entitled to withdraw the ship, as they did, on 24th January.

In the Court of Appeal it was calculated that the interest on the monthly instalment of hire from Thursday, 22nd January to Monday, 26th January would have been $70 or $100. This calculation encouraged Lord Denning MR to say:

> 'It seems to me that that trifling bank charge, if it had been exacted, would not have affected the nature of the payment which had already been made. The credit was available to the owners, in their bank, as from midday on Thursday, 22nd January. The owners had the full use of it. It was unconditional. The mere debiting of a trifling bank charge would not make it conditional.'

I do not know if the emphasis in this passage on the word 'trifling' was intended to invoke and apply the de minimis principle. It was not argued for the charterers before your Lordships that, if there was a failure to make punctual payment in cash under cl 5, the owners' right to withdraw the ship in consequence of that failure could be resisted on the ground that the failure was de minimis. Accordingly, it is unnecessary to decide in what circumstances, if ever, the de minimis principle could be invoked to excuse such a failure. It certainly could not in this case.

My Lords, earlier exercises of judicial ingenuity to mitigate the rigours of clauses in charterparties giving to shipowners a right to withdraw their ships on failure or default in payment of hire or freight have not had a happy history. One such was the decision of Bigham J in *Nova Scotia Steel Co Ltd v Sutherland Steam Shipping Co Ltd* (1899) 5 Com Cas 106. This was overruled by your Lordships' House in *Tankexpress A/S v Compagnie Financière Belge des Petroles SA* [1948] 2 All ER 939 at 946, [1949] AC 76 at 94–95: Lord Wright said:

> 'A *dictum* or decision of BIGHAM, J., in *Nova Scotia Steel Co. v. Sutherland Steam Shipping Co.*, has been relied on as an authority that a certain latitude was permissible so that payment made two days after the due date did not constitute a default in payment, but I cannot agree that so drastic a departure from the specific words of the charter can be supported. In that case the clause provided for regular and punctual payment. These adjectives, however, add nothing to the stringency of the simple and unqualified language in the charter before this House. I think that so much of BIGHAM, J.'s, judgment as conceded a latitude as to the date of payment is erroneous in law and should be overruled. The importance of this advance payment to be made by the charterers, is that it is the substance of the consideration given to the shipowner for the use and service of the ship and crew which the shipowner agrees to give. He is entitled to have the periodical payment as stipulated in advance of his performance so long as the charterparty continues. Hence the stringency of his right to cancel.'

Another such attempt was the decision of the Court of Appeal in *The Georgios C* [1971] 1 All ER 193, [1971] 1 QB 488, which gave rise to much difficulty and uncertainty until it was overruled by this House in *The Laconia* [1977] 1 All ER 545, [1977] AC 850. As Lord Salmon said ([1977] 1 All ER 545 at 558, [1977] AC 850 at 878):

> 'Certainty is of primary importance in all commercial transactions. I am afraid that ever since 1971 when *The Georgios C* was decided a great deal of doubt has been generated about the effect of clauses conferring the right on shipowners to withdraw their vessels when charterers fail to pay hire in accordance with the terms of the charterparties in the well-known New York Produce Exchange, Baltime and Shelltime forms. No such doubt existed between 1948 (when the *Tankexpress* case was decided) and 1971. My Lords, I hope that the doubts which have troubled the waters since 1971 will now be finally dispelled by this decision of your Lordships' House.'

It has often been pointed out that shipowners and charterers bargain at arm's length. Neither class has such a preponderance of bargaining power as to be in a position to oppress the other. They should be in a position to look after themselves by contracting only on terms which are acceptable to them. Where, as here, they embody in their contracts common form clauses, it is, to my mind, of overriding importance that their

meaning and legal effect should be certain and well understood. The ideal at which the
courts should aim, in construing such clauses, is to produce a result such that in any given
situation both parties seeking legal advice as to their rights and obligations can expect the
same clear and confident answer from their advisers and neither will be tempted to
embark on long and expensive litigation in the belief that victory depends on winning
the sympathy of the court. This ideal may never be fully attainable, but we shall
certainly never even approximate to it unless we strive to follow clear and consistent
principles and steadfastly refuse to be blown off course by the supposed merits of
individual cases.

I would allow the appeal, restore the order of Robert Goff J and order the respondents
to pay the appellants' costs in your Lordships' House and in the Court of Appeal.

Appeal allowed.

Solicitors: *Sinclair, Roche & Temperley* (for the respondents); *Richards, Butler & Co* (for the
appellants).

Mary Rose Plummer   Barrister.

Laws and others v Florinplace Ltd and another

CHANCERY DIVISION
VINELOTT J
5th, 6th NOVEMBER 1980

*Injunction – Nuisance – Interlocutory injunction – Sex shop – Defendant opening sex shop in
predominantly residential area – Residents contending that sex shop would attract undesirable
customers who would threaten ordinary family life of area – Residents also fearing adverse effect
of shop on property values – Whether appropriate case for grant of interlocutory injunction.*

In August 1980 a dress shop on the corner of two streets was purchased by the
defendants. The locality was an area which included residential accommodation in some
streets and restaurants, snack bars, food stores and so forth in others. In addition there
were a major railway terminal and a bus garage in the vicinity. On 13th September a
large illuminated sign, 2ft high and extending round the corner so as to be visible in both
streets, announced that a 'sex centre and cinema club' was to open in the shop. Cinema
seats were installed in the following week. The premises opened on 19th September.
Shortly afterwards signs were placed in the window stating 'Uncensored adult videos for
sale or available. Not for persons under 18. Inquire within without obligation' and
'Warning: These premises show explicit sex acts. If you are easily offended, please do not
enter. Persons under 18 years not admitted'. On 17th October the plaintiffs, the
residents of one of the streets, issued a writ seeking an injunction and damages against
the defendants and on the same day moved for an interlocutory injunction pending
trial. The plaintiffs described the area as having a marked and attractive village
atmosphere, and contended that the defendants' activities would attract undesirable
customers, who would threaten the ordinary enjoyment of family life in the street and
would be an embarrassment and potential danger to young persons, and in particular
young girls who might meet with indecent suggestions. They also put in evidence
suggesting that property values might suffer adversely if the defendants' activities were
allowed to continue. The defendants claimed that the plaintiffs' fears were exaggerated. They contended that their experience was that customers of such shops were well-
educated respectable normal individuals and put in an affidavit from a behavioural
psychotherapist who stated that persons likely to be customers were very often perfectly
normal and respectable citizens, who would tend to be discreet visiting the shop, and that
the material available in such shops could serve a very necessary educational function in

sexual matters, especially when used in a therapeutic context. They also filed evidence suggesting that the defendants' business would not significantly affect the value of the residential accommodation in the street. On the motion for an interlocutory injunction pending trial,

Held – (1) It was established law that cases of nuisance were not confined to cases where there was some physical emanation of a damaging kind from the defendant's premises which had occurred or was reasonably feared but extended to cases where the use made by the defendant of his property was such that, while not necessarily involving a breach of the criminal law, it was such an affront to the reasonable susceptibilities of ordinary men and women that the fact of its being carried on in such a way that its nature was apparent to neighbours and visitors constituted an interference with the reasonable domestic enjoyment of their property. In the circumstances, it was impossible to say that there was not at least a triable issue whether the existence of a business like that of the defendants', conducted so that the nature of the business was evident to residents of and visitors to the neighbourhood, was not a nuisance independently of any risk of attracting undesirable and potentially dangerous customers, and of any risk that the shop might in the future prove a plague spot which would be a source of infection in the neighbourhood. Furthermore, the fact that, however discreetly conducted, the business would in fact be the sale of hard pornography and would be a business deeply repugnant to the reasonable sensibilities of most ordinary men and women could not be disregarded (see p 665 c to e, p 666 e f and p 667 c, post); *Metropolitan Asylum District Managers v Hill* [1881–5] All ER Rep 536 and *Thompson-Schwab v Costaki* [1956] 1 All ER 652 applied.

(2) Since, on the one hand, the danger that might be suffered by the defendants by the grant of interim relief which was afterwards found to be unjustified was quantifiable and would be recoverable, and since, on the other hand, there were features which favoured the grant of interim relief, not the least of which was that the defendants' business operated near the boundary of the criminal law, the balance of convenience lay in favour of granting the interlocutory injunction sought by the plaintiffs. The injunction would, accordingly, be granted (see p 667 f to p 668 d, post).

Notes

For grounds for the grant of an injunction to restrain the continuance of a nuisance, see 34 Halsbury's Laws (4th Edn) para 386, and for cases on the subject, see 36(1) Digest (Reissue) 499–504, 725–772.

Cases referred to in judgment

American Cyanamid Co v Ethicon Ltd [1975] 1 All ER 504, [1975] AC 396, [1975] 2 WLR 316, 119 Sol Jo 136, [1975] RPC 531, Digest (Cont Vol D) 536, 152a.

Bradford Corpn v Pickles [1895] AC 587, [1895–9] All ER Rep 984, 64 LJ Ch 759, 73 LT 353, 60 JP 3, 36(1) Digest (Reissue) 412, 67.

Colls v Home and Colonial Stores Ltd [1904] AC 179, [1904–7] All ER Rep 5, 73 LJ Ch 484, 90 LT 687, 28(2) Digest (Reissue) 1124, 1229.

Cunard v Antifyre Ltd [1933] 1 KB 551, [1932] All ER Rep 558, 103 LJKB 321, 148 LT 287, 36(1) Digest (Reissue) 404, 10.

Metropolitan Asylum District Managers v Hill (1881) 6 App Cas 193, [1881–5] All ER Rep 536, 50 LJQB 353, 44 LT 653, 45 JP 664, 36(1) Digest (Reissue) 520, 887.

Sedleigh-Denfield v O'Callagan [1940] 3 All ER 349, [1940] AC 880, 164 LT 72, 36(1) Digest (Reissue) 486, 632.

Thompson-Schwab v Costaki [1956] 1 All ER 652, [1956] 1 WLR 335, 36(1) Digest (Reissue) 469, 464.

Cases also cited

Assagay Quarries (Pty) Ltd v Hobbs 1960 (4) SA 237.

Lyons (J) & Sons v Wilkins [1899] 1 Ch 255.

Poirier v Turkewich (1963) 42 DLR (2d) 259.
Pugliese v National Capital Commission (1977) 79 DLR (3d) 592.

Motion

By notice of motion dated 17th October 1980 the plaintiffs, John Grant McKenzie Laws, Sophie Susan Sydenham Cole Laws, Alick Pringle, Helen Pringle, Charles Paterson, Sarah Paterson, Myrtle May, Herbert Beech, Elizabeth Beech and John R H Garey, sought as against the defendants, Florinplace Ltd and Tomas Colin Hayes, an order that they and each of them be restrained by themselves, their servants or agents or otherwise howsoever from carrying on or causing or permitting to be carried on on the premises known as 89–90 Wilton Road, London SW1 the business or undertaking of a sex and video centre, a sex shop or any other business of a like or similar nature. The facts are set out in the judgment.

Richard Scott QC for the plaintiffs.
Roger Ellis for the defendants.

VINELOTT J. This is a motion brought by ten residents in Longmoore Street to restrain by interlocutory injunction the continued operation of a shop selling pornographic magazines, books and video films which has recently opened on the corner of Longmoore Street and Wilton Road in Pimlico. The first defendant, Florinplace Ltd, is the owner of the shop. The second defendant, Mr Hayes, is its controlling director.

Longmoore Street is a residential street in Pimlico, about a quarter of a mile or a little more from Victoria Station. It bisects a busy road, Wilton Road, which runs south-east from the station. If a visitor continues south-east down Wilton Road after the intersection with Longmoore Street he will reach, after a distance of some fifty to a hundred yards, another main road, Warwick Way, which again crosses and marks the end of Wilton Road. Retracing his footsteps and crossing again the intersection with Longmoore Street he will reach after a longer distance, some three or four hundred yards, another intersection called Gillingham Street. The part of Wilton Road which lies between Gillingham Street and Longmoore Street consists almost wholly of commercial properties of one kind or another, which serve to some extent the casual trade of people coming to and from the station. There are a number of restaurants and snack-bars, two public houses, food stores, a hairdresser and so forth. Further, most of the area between Longmoore Street and Gillingham Street on the south-west side of Wilton Road is taken up by a large London Transport Executive garage. But the part of Longmoore Street which lies to the south-west of Wilton Road is almost wholly residential. The houses are small terrace houses, built a hundred years or so ago for artisans. Three have been converted into small private hotels. The remainder are in private occupation. On the other side of Wilton Road, that is, the north-east half of Longmoore Street, a new sports complex built by the Westminster City Council is nearing completion. At the far end lies Tachbrook Street, where there is a street market and a large council residential estate. Nearby are the well-known residential squares, Eccleston and Warwick Squares.

Mr Laws, a barrister who lives there and who is the first-named plaintiff, has described this area, that is, the bottom half of Longmoore Street and the part of Wilton Road which lies between Longmoore Street and Warwick Way, as having a marked and attractive village atmosphere. That description is disputed by the defendants, who point to the proximity of Victoria Station, to the commercial nature of the part of Wilton Road which lies between Longmoore Street and Victoria Station, and more particularly to the existence on the north-east side of Wilton Road, near the intersection of Gillingham Street, of a bookshop described as an 'adult bookshop', the windows of which are blacked out, to the existence of a nearby stationers and newsagents which displays advertisements for, amongst other things, Swedish massage, and to the existence on the other side of Gillingham Street of a cinema which, it is said, displays films of the kind often described as 'soft pornography' and of a shop described as a 'sex shop'.

It is impossible, on affidavit evidence, to form any firm opinion whether Mr Laws's description is accurate or exaggerated, and it would be inappropriate that I should do so. That is a matter which will have to be decided at the trial. But on the evidence before me, including photographs which I have seen, the area seems at least to be a residential enclave, albeit in a commercially developed area, and it seems to me far from surprising that the residents of Longmoore Street should be the more anxious to ensure that the type of development to which the defendants have drawn attention should not be extended and engulf it.

Until August 1980 there was, on the south-east corner of Wilton Road and Longmoore Street, a dress shop called Jean Arden which had been there for many years. It comprised 89–90 Wilton Road. In August it changed hands. The gossip in the neighbourhood was that it was going to become a bookshop. On 13th September a large shop sign was erected, extending round the corner and so having a front both in Wilton Road and in Longmoore Street. On the Wilton Road frontage it read 'Victoria Sex Centre and Cinema Club' and on the Longmoore Street frontage 'Cinema Club'. These words were in black capitals on a white ground. The sign was two feet high and it was illuminated at night. During the following week cinema seats were installed in no 89.

The premises opened on 19th September. Shortly thereafter signs were put up in the shop window. One read: 'Uncensored adult videos for sale or available. Not for persons under 18. Inquire within without obligation.' The other read: 'Warning: These premises show explicit sex acts. If you are easily offended, please do not enter. Persons under 18 years not admitted.' Another sign indicated that the premises were open from 12 noon until 1 am from Monday to Saturday, and from 2 pm until 10 pm on Sunday. Later the shop sign was altered to read, on the Wilton Road frontage, 'Victoria Sex and Video Centre', and, on the Longmoore Street frontage, 'Video Centre'. It continues to be illuminated at night.

No planning permission had been obtained for the change of use of the premises to a cinema or video theatre. An enforcement notice was served by the local planning authority and on 6th or 7th October a three-day stop notice was served. On 17th October ten of the residents in Longmoore Street issued a writ claiming an injunction and damages and on the same day served notice of intention to move for an interlocutory injunction pending trial. That motion is now before me.

All the plaintiffs live in the part of Longmoore Street which lies south-west of Wilton Road. As I have said, Mr Laws is one of them. All of them live permanently in Longmoore Street. Two of them, a Mr and Mrs Beech, own a private hotel at no 21, but they live there with their young children. The plaintiffs comprise a large proportion, between one-third and one-half, of the residents in this part of Longmoore Street. Another house in this part of Longmoore Street was until recently owned by Mr Andrew Leggatt, a Queen's Counsel. He bought no 33 in June this year, primarily with a view to providing a base in London for his son and daughter, who are aged 22 and 19 respectively. He and his wife live at Woking. He bought it, he says, because he had satisfied himself before buying it that it was in a typical part of Pimlico and removed from the less salubrious area in the immediate vicinity of Victoria Station. He has transferred it to his son and daughter but planned, until recently, to spend a substantial sum on improving it for them. The recent developments have made him hold his hand. He is disinclined to spend any substantial sum on the house if the defendants' shop continues to carry on its trade. He takes the view, after seeking advice from estate agents, that the continuance of the defendants' business would severely injure the value of his property. He is also concerned that, as he says in his affidavit—

'there are attracted to the premises a number of men of sleazy and unprepossessing mien, of the very kind that might be expected to frequent them. I am even more concerned by the fact that the sex shop provides a meeting point close to our house for men of pornographic proclivities than I am by the offensive nature of the business itself.'

Mr Laws also expresses the fear that the defendants' activities will attract undesirable customers, who will threaten the ordinary enjoyment of family life in Longmoore Street, and will be an embarrassment and potential danger to young persons, in particular young girls who might meet with indecent suggestions. There is some, though admittedly cursory, evidence in Mr Laws's affidavit of one such incident. He says that he was told by a Mrs Walhurst, who lives in the street at no 30 with her husband and 7-year old son, that, and I cite, 'she was recently deliberately followed by a man who emerged from the Sex Centre'.

The plaintiffs have also put in evidence by Mr Trouw, an estate agent, who expresses the opinion that—

'there is a difference in character between Wilton Road to the north of Longmoore Street, which is commercially orientated towards customers generated by Victoria, and Wilton Road to the south of Longmoore Street, which is a mixture of residential homes and smaller shops designed to serve the immediate residential community.'

He expresses the opinion that property values and hotel custom in Longmoore Street may well suffer adversely if this sex shop is allowed to continue in its present position.

The second defendant, Mr Hayes, claims that this evidence is much exaggerated. He says that the cinema or video shows or displays were originally planned as ancillary to the sale of video films, and that he was therefore surprised to find that planning consent was necessary. He claims that since stop notices were served the activity of screening films and video tapes has ceased. The plaintiffs have put in evidence copies of the Evening Standard, advertising daily, until immediately before the hearing of this motion, the showing of what are described as 'adult movies' at the defendants' cinema club premises. Mr Hayes, through his counsel, explained that this arose because he inadvertently failed to cancel a 28-day booking for a daily advertisement. I find that explanation surprising. Although if, as Mr Hayes explains, the telephone at the premises was disconnected, so that customers who saw the advertisements could not telephone to inquire about the times of viewing and so forth, it is, none the less, to my mind surprising that that inadvertent advertisement did not come to the attention of those in charge of the defendants' premises through the arrival of customers who had read the advertisement. If they had done so the existence of the advertisement would have come to their knowledge and, on Mr Hayes's explanation, it would have been cancelled. However, that is a matter which may have to be more fully investigated at the trial.

Mr Hayes also claims that the notices which I have read were taken down before this action was commenced, and through his counsel he has offered extensive undertakings pending trial. They are: first, that he will not replace the notices which have been removed; second, that he will not screen films or video tapes, even if the planning consent which has been applied for is obtained; third, that the sign advertising the shop on the Longmoore Street frontage will be blacked out; fourth, that the shop will be open only between 12 noon and 9 pm on Monday to Saturday and not on Sunday; and last, that the words on the fascia now displayed will be altered from the present 'Victoria Sex and Video Centre' to 'Victoria Bookshop and Video Centre'. These undertakings were offered in the course of the hearing, after counsel had opened the plaintiffs' case, and are offered until the trial of the action.

In his evidence Mr Hayes, who claim to have considerable experience in operating shops of this kind, and therefore with their clientele, says, and I cite his affidavit:

'Although it may come as a surprise to the Deponents a sex bookshop attracts as the overwhelming majority of its customers persons who are far from being unprepossessing in appearance and strike those who run the shops as experienced and mature businessmen.'

He estimates that—

'Speaking from numerous years of experience without having done an actual numerical survey, at least 80 per cent of the customers of a sex bookshop, and this one in particular, could be described as constituting well-educated respectable normal individuals.'

He summarises this by saying:

'. . . the Deponents' aversion to the concept of the sex bookshop has allowed them to assume that the clientele are undesirable, without the slightest evidence in that behalf; whereas my experience of sex bookshops, coupled with the knowledge of the clientele of this particular bookshop, suggest quite the contrary.'

His evidence is also supported by the evidence of a behavioural psychotherapist, a Dr Sharpe, a director of the Institute of Behavioural Therapists, who says in his affidavit that in his professional judgment, based on his experience:

'Persons who feel the need for explicit sexual material of a visual type cannot fairly and properly be described as disturbed individuals on the fringe of society. I consider that such people are very often perfectly normal and respectable citizens.'

He concludes, in his affidavit:

'It is very common for people who wish to purchase visual material of explicit sexual conduct not to want their families and friends to know of their interest in this material. I consider this attitude as perfectly normal and understandable and it does not suggest that the individuals concerned are in a disturbed psychological state or that they are undesirable members of society. This very natural desire for secrecy implies that they would not want to be involved in any disturbance or other activity which would draw attention to them. Therefore the clientele of this type of shop tend to be discreet, quiet and inoffensive in their appearance. I also consider that explicit sexual material, whether of a visual or written kind, may serve a very necessary educational function in sexual matters, especially when used in a therapeutic context.'

There is also evidence filed on behalf of the defendants of an estate agent who stresses the features of the neighbourhood to which I have referred and who expresses the opinion that the existence of the defendants' business and the nature of that business would not significantly affect the value of the freehold residential accommodation in Longmoore Street.

Counsel for the plaintiffs put his case on two broad grounds. First, he submitted that the existence of a business of this kind, selling hard pornography, and selling it in such a way that the nature of the business would be apparent to those living in or visiting the area, is itself a nuisance, because the instinctive repugnance that would be felt by ordinary decent men and women, and the embarrassment that would be felt by visitors, would in itself constitute a material and unreasonable interference with the comfort and enjoyment of their property. Second, he said that the nature of the business was such that the plaintiffs are justified in fearing that it may become a plague spot, attracting undesirable customers, and with them others, such as prostitutes, who trade on those customers, and, in turn, criminals trading on the prostitutes. Further, some of the customers, it is suggested, may be of a kind who might molest young girls with indecent suggestions.

Counsel referred me to a well-known passage in the speech of Lord Wright in *Sedleigh-Denfield v O'Callagan* [1940] 3 All ER 349 at 364, [1940] AC 880 at 903:

'In *Cunard v. Antifyre, Ltd.* ([1933] 1 KB 551 at 557, [1932] All ER Rep 558 at 560), TALBOT, J., succinctly defined private nuisances as interferences by owners or occupiers of property with the use or enjoyment of neighbouring property. "Property" here means land, and should be amplified to include rights over it, or in connection with it. "Occupiers" may in certain cases be used with a special connotation. The ground of responsibility is the possession and control of the land from which the nuisance proceeds. The principle has been expressed in the maxim *sic utere tuo ut alienum non laedas*. This, like most maxims, is not only lacking in definiteness but is also inaccurate. An occupier may make in many ways a use of his land which causes damage to the neighbouring landowners and yet be free from liability. This may be illustrated by *Bradford Corpn.* v. *Pickles* ([1895] AC 587, [1895–9] All ER Rep 984). Even where he is liable for a nuisance, the redress may fall short of the damage, as, for instance, in *Colls* v. *Home & Colonial Stores, Ltd.* ([1904] AC 179, [1904–7] All ER Rep 5), where the interference was with enjoyment of light. A balance has to be maintained between the right of the occupier to do what he likes with his own and the right of his neighbour not to be interfered with. It is impossible to give any precise or universal formula, but it may broadly be said that a useful test is perhaps what is reasonable according to the ordinary usages of mankind living in society, or, more correctly, in a particular society. The forms which nuisance may take are protean. Certain classifications are possible, but many reported cases are no more than illustrations of particular matters of fact which have been held to be nuisances.'

Counsel stressed that cases of nuisance cannot be confined to cases where there is some physical emanation of a damaging kind from the defendants' premises which has occurred or is reasonably feared (such as the smallpox germs, the escape of which was feared in *Metropolitan Asylum District Managers v Hill* (1881) 6 App Cas 193, [1881–5] All ER Rep 536). The principle on which the court acts extends to cases where the use made by defendants of their property is such that, while not necessarily involving a breach of the criminal law, it is an affront to the reasonable susceptibilities of ordinary men and women and such an affront that the fact of its being carried on in a way that makes its nature apparent to neighbours and visitors constitutes an interference with the reasonable domestic enjoyment of their property. In this connection, he referred me to a decision of the Court of Appeal in *Thompson-Schwab v Costaki* [1956] 1 All ER 652, [1956] 1 WLR 335. There the plaintiffs owned property in Chesterfield Street in Mayfair. The first plaintiff owned property adjoining the defendants' property. He claimed that he lived at 13 Chesterfield Street with his family, including a young son and three young girls employed domestically, that Chesterfield Street, though not far distant from streets with an unsavoury reputation, remained a good class residential street, not affected by the activities of common prostitutes, that the two defendants had been carrying on business as prostitutes from 12 Chesterfield Street and that their activities seriously depreciated the value of his house and seriously interfered with the comfortable and convenient enjoyment of his house as a residence. He moved for an interlocutory injunction. That, of course, was before the test applicable to the grant of interlocutory relief had been clarified by the House of Lords in *American Cyanamid Co v Ethicon Ltd* [1975] 1 All ER 504, [1975] AC 396, and at a time when an applicant for interim relief had to satisfy the court that there was a probability that he would succeed in obtaining a permanent injunction at the trial. It was argued that the use of property for prostitution was incapable, in itself, of constituting a nuisance. As to that argument, Lord Evershed MR said ([1956] 1 All ER 652 at 654, [1956] 1 WLR 335 at 339):

'The case made for the plaintiffs shows to my mind at least a sufficient prima facie case to this effect, that the activities being conducted at No. 12 Chesterfield Street are not only open, but they are notorious and such as force themselves on the sense of sight at least of the residents in No. 13. The perambulations of the prostitutes and of their customers is something which is obvious, which is blatant, and which as I think the first plaintiff has shown prima facie to constitute not a mere hurt of his sensibilities as a fastidious man, but so as to constitute a sensible interference with the comfortable and convenient enjoyment of his residence where live with him his wife, his son and his servants.'

As I read this passage, in referring to the perambulations of prostitutes and their customers Lord Evershed MR did not have in mind the danger that the plaintiff might suffer material inconvenience by being accosted or the danger that criminals and other undesirable people might be attracted into the immediate neighbourhood. This observation was directed to his earlier observation that the use of the property for purposes of prostitution was open and notorious, so that the plaintiff could not but be aware of the nature of the activities carried on in the defendants' premises. The point is quite explicitly made in the judgment of Romer LJ [1956] 1 All ER 652 at 656, [1956] 1 WLR 335 at 341–342):

'The question then whether the plaintiffs have made out a case for the interference of this court by injunction is, as I have indicated, one of fact; and although the affidavit evidence which the plaintiffs have put in is not of a very elaborate description (and will no doubt receive further attention and be given in more detail at the trial) there is I think ample to lead to the conclusion that what these defendants have been doing in this house constitutes an actionable interference with the plaintiffs in the reasonable and ordinary enjoyment of their houses. As LORD EVERSHED, M.R., said, one of them at all events—indeed I think both of them—have young sons living there and their wives, and one of them has three young servants. One can well imagine the effect of what is going on in the house almost next door in one case and exactly next door in the other is likely to have on the minds of those young people. One can imagine also the feelings of visitors who come to the houses, or are invited to the houses, and all sorts of other considerations inevitably arise from the user to which the defendants have openly been putting the house to which they have resorted.'

There what is stressed is the knowledge by occupants and visitors of the open use of the defendants' property which, it is said, is in itself a material interference with the comfortable enjoyment of the plaintiffs' property.

It would, of course, be wrong that I should endeavour to form, far less express, any opinion whether the existence of a business such as that conducted by the defendants in the circumstances which I have outlined constitutes a nuisance. But, as I see it, it is impossible to say that there is not at least a triable issue whether the existence of a business of this kind, conducted in the way in which it was initially conducted, so that the nature of the business is evident to residents of, and visitors to, Longmoore Street, is not a nuisance independently of any risk of attracting undesirable and potentially dangerous customers, and of any risk that the shop may in the future prove a plague spot which will be a source of infection in the neighbourhood.

Counsel for the defendants was, I think, at least inclined to accept that there was a triable issue, whether the business as originally planned, comprising a cinema showing sexually explicit films, with the notices that I have described displayed on the outside, might not constitute a nuisance, at least in some areas, although, of course, his clients contend that even if such a business carried on in that way might constitute a nuisance in a quiet residential area it would not constitute a nuisance in an area so near to Victoria Station.

However, relying on the undertakings offered by the defendants, counsel submitted that the defendants' business, if carried on under the name of 'Victoria Bookshop and Video Centre', displayed on the Wilton Road frontage only, without displaying the offending notices, and between the hours of 12 noon and 9 pm only, could not constitute a nuisance because there would be nothing to draw the attention of the inhabitants or visitors to the nature of the material sold. He says that the second defendant is experienced in the trade carried on in these premises, and it is one which those experienced in the trade are anxious to carry on in a discreet way to meet their customers' needs for secrecy and anonymity.

As for the argument that the business would attract undesirable customers who might be an embarrassment or danger and that the premises would become a plague spot to which even more undesirable activities might spread, he relied on the evidence of the second defendant and of the behavioural psychotherapist that 80% of the customers appeared to be mature and normal men. He stressed the absence of any positive evidence that unbalanced or perverted men resorted to the shop, or of any actual molestation in the neighbourhood, and submitted that the plaintiffs' case, if sound, could and should have been supported by evidence that the consequences they say they fear have followed in other areas where similar shops have been established.

These arguments were forcibly developed by counsel in his able address, but I am not convinced that there is not a serious and triable issue whether the defendants' business, even if carried on subject to the undertakings which have been offered, would not constitute a nuisance. The business having started and having been advertised, it may well have acquired some reputation and, moreover, even if the name over the shop is altered to 'Victoria Bookshop and Video Centre', the way in which the business is conducted, with curtained windows and no outward display, with soft porn displayed on the shelves inside, the material truly for sale being concealed beneath the counter, may well suggest to any person with experience in the ways of the world the nature of the books and video cassettes that are being traded in. Further, I cannot disregard the fact that, however discreetly conducted, the business will in fact be the sale of hard pornography and will be a business deeply repugnant to the reasonable sensibilities of most ordinary men and women. If customers are to use the shop, it must be because the nature of the material sold will be evident from the name of the shop, coupled with its external appearance.

Lastly, the argument founded on the defendants' evidence as to the character of 80% of the customers, even if it transpires to be correct, means that there are a substantial number of others, 20%, some of whom may be, or are likely to be, persons who are unbalanced and perhaps perverted and who would be an embarrassment and might be a danger to visitors and residents. That risk is not, I think, one which can be easily brushed aside. There are, no doubt, wide differences even between medical and psychological experts whether pornography has a therapeutic effect or whether it may not act as a stimulus to acts which the subject would not otherwise have performed. This, and evidence as to experience in other neighbourhoods of the effect of opening businesses of this kind, are matters which will have to be fully explored at a trial. For the purposes of an interlocutory motion I do not think that these fears can be wholly disregarded.

I turn, therefore, to consider the balance of convenience. Counsel for the defendants accepted, rightly I think, that the damage that would be suffered by the defendants if an interlocutory injunction were granted, and if it were held at the trial that the plaintiffs were not entitled to injunctive relief, would not extend beyond the loss of profit which the defendants might otherwise have earned, and that the plaintiffs are persons from whom such damages, when assessed, would be recoverable. He submitted the loss of profit may be difficult to ascertain if the business is closed at a time when it has no record of profit on which an assessment can be based. I find that argument unconvincing. The defendants are, and assert that they are, experienced in this trade and there should be no real difficulty in estimating profits that might have been earned by reference to earnings in similar establishments. Further, this is not a case where the defendants will suffer irreparable and possibly unquantifiable damage to goodwill by the loss of the momentum in the promotion of a new business, the launching of which is delayed by an interim injunction.

On the one hand, therefore, it seems to me that the damage that might be suffered by the defendants by the grant of interim relief which is afterwards found to be unjustified is quantifiable and will be recoverable. On the other hand there are features which, to my mind, favour the grant of interim relief, notwithstanding the undertakings that have been offered. First, the plaintiffs know the nature of the business carried on. They have seen, as I have, some of the hard pornography which is purveyed, and they feel, to my mind reasonably, a profound repugnance at the possibility that such a trade will continue to be carried on on their very doorstep. I do not think I should lightly compel them to accept the continued existence of this trade, however discreetly conducted, until the trial. Second, there must be a danger that in such a small residential area, which is, as it were, perched insecurely on the edge of the environs of Victoria Station, the continued existence of this business will slowly and insensibly erode the quality of the immediate neighbourhood, even during the period betwen now and the trial.

Last, I am, I think, entitled to bear in mind that the business which the defendants carry on, and which will be stopped if an injunction is granted, is one which operates at least near the boundary of the criminal law. The material I have seen is, I think, patently capable of corrupting and depraving any ordinary member of the public into whose hands it might come. Some has been seized by the police and a prosecution is, I understand, pending. The defence, as I understand it, will be that those persons who resort to the shop and ask for the hidden material, and who are therefore the only persons likely to read, see or hear this material, are persons who are mature and aware of the nature of the material they are buying, and therefore unlikely to be corrupted or depraved by it. The question whether that is so or not will in due course be a question for a jury to decide, but I think I am entitled to weigh in the scales the fact that the trade that will be interrupted by an injunction is one of selling material of a kind which is, in the ordinary sense of the word, obscene, even though its sale may not involve the commission of a criminal offence, if the particular defence to which I have referred is ultimately established.

In the light of the undertakings that have been offered I do not find the question whether an interim injunction should be granted at all an easy one. A man should not be lightly prevented from carrying on a lawful trade and, in turn, the question whether this trade is a lawful one is one which will have to be decided, if at all, by another tribunal. But, weighing these factors as best I can, I have come to the conclusion that the plaintiffs are entitled to interim relief. Until the trial this trade should not, in my judgment, continue, and the shop sign and other forms of advertisement must cease.

Interim injunction granted in terms sought by plaintiffs.

Solicitors: *Bower, Cotton & Bower* (for the plaintiffs); *Cowan, Lipson, Rumney* (for the defendants).

Jacqueline Metcalfe   Barrister.

Post Office v Wallser

COURT OF APPEAL, CIVIL DIVISION
LAWTON, BRIDGE LJJ AND SIR DAVID CAIRNS
2nd, 3rd JULY 1980

Unfair dismissal – Right not be unfairly dismissed – Restriction on right where employee reaches normal retiring age or specified age – Normal retiring age – Determination – Employee's contract providing for compulsory retirement at 60 unless conditions relating to efficiency and health complied with – Evidence that majority of employees retained beyond age of 60 – Whether normal retiring age 60 – Whether employee unfairly dismissed because compulsorily retired at 60 – Trade Union and Labour Relations Act 1974, Sch 1, para 10(b).

The contractual terms applicable to the applicant's employment in the Post Office provided that he could be compulsorily retired at the age of 60 unless he complied with certain conditions relating to efficiency and physical fitness and there was no reason in the public interest against retaining him beyond the age of 60; they also required that before he reached 60 the Post Office should give preliminary consideration whether he should be retained after his sixtieth birthday. Before the applicant reached the age of 60 the Post Office considered his position and decided not to retain him after he reached 60. Accordingly they notified him by letter that he would be retired on the day prior to his sixtieth birthday. The applicant complained to an industrial tribunal that he had been unfairly dismissed. The Post Office contended that under para 10(b)ᵃ of Sch 1 to the

---

ᵃ   Paragraph 10, so far as material, is set out at p 672 *d*, post.

Trade Union and Labour Relations Act 1974 the tribunal had no jurisdiction to entertain the application because the applicant had attained the 'normal retiring age' for an employee holding his position in the Post Office, namely 60, before the effective date of termination of his employment. The tribunal found that the applicant had been unfairly dismissed. On appeal by the Post Office, the Employment Appeal Tribunal set aside that finding. The applicant appealed to the Court of Appeal, before which he adduced evidence that a substantial majority of men employed in the same work as he had been were retained beyond the age of 60. He therefore contended that there was no normal retiring age for employees holding the position he had held.

Held – The 'normal retiring age' within para 10(b) of Sch 1 to the 1974 Act was a matter of evidence and did not depend exclusively on the relevant contract of employment. However, where the terms of the contract of employment governed retirement age, that provided the best evidence for determining the normal retiring age and would prevail unless the contractual terms were effectively contradicted by other evidence. In the applicant's case the contractual terms provided for compulsory retirement at the age of 60 unless certain conditions were complied with, and the operation of that rule was not contradicted by the evidence adduced regarding retention after 60. Accordingly, the normal retiring age in regard to the applicant was 60. It followed that the appeal would be dismissed (see p 672 j to p 674 b, post).

Nothman v London Borough of Barnet [1979] 1 All ER 142 applied.

Notes

For an employee's exclusion from compensation for unfair dismissal because of age, see 16 Halsbury's Laws (4th Edn) para 620.

For the Trade Union and Labour Relations Act 1974, Sch 1, para 10, see 44 Halsbury's Statutes (3rd Edn) 1794.

As from 1st November 1978 para 10 of Sch 1 to the 1974 Act has been replaced by s 64(1) of the Employment Protection (Consolidation) Act 1978.

Cases referred to in judgments

Nothman v London Borough of Barnet [1979] 1 All ER 142, [1979] 1 WLR 67, [1979] ICR 111, 77 LGR 89, HL; *affg* [1978] 1 All ER 1243, [1978] 1 WLR 220, [1978] ICR 336, 76 LGR 617, CA, Digest (Cont Vol E) 625, *1575*.

Ord v Maidstone and District Hospital Management Committee [1974] 2 All ER 343, [1974] ICR 369, NIRC, Digest (Cont Vol D) 976, *1524cc*.

Appeal

This was an appeal by Mr Maurice Wallser against a judgment of the Employment Appeal Tribunal (Slynn J, Mrs D Lancaster and Mr J A Scouler) given on 4th December 1978 setting aside a finding of an industrial tribunal in London (chairman Mr F de F Stratton) that he had been unfairly dismissed. The facts are set out in the judgment of Lawton LJ.

Stephen Sedley for Mr Wallser.
Christopher Carr for the Post Office.

LAWTON LJ. This is an appeal by Mr Maurice Wallser against a judgment of the Employment Appeal Tribunal given on 4th December 1978, whereby a finding of an industrial tribunal given in his favour to the effect he had been unfairly dismissed by the Post Office was set aside. Mr Wallser, through counsel, has submitted that the Employment Appeal Tribunal erred in law in taking the course it did.

Mr Wallser was born on 17th December 1917; by 1973 he had become crippled by osteoarthritis in a knee. He was anxious to take up new employment. He went to a government retraining centre where he acquired skills as a technician which made him a possible person to be employed in the telecommunication branch of the Post Office.

He applied for a job with the Post Office, and after an interview he was taken on. He was told of his appointment by a letter from the Post Office dated 19th November 1973. *a* That letter offered him employment as a technician in the City area, beginning on 19th November 1973 and 'on the terms and conditions shown in this letter and in the enclosed formal statement and contract documents'. The last paragraph of the letter was as follows:

> 'You are not eligible because you are over 55 years of age, and are unable to qualify for a pension by normal retiring age, for membership of Section B of the *b* contributory part of the Post Staff superannuation scheme.'

Amongst the documents which were sent to him was one which was headed: 'Terms and conditions of full time employment', and the opening paragraph, under the heading 'General' said: 'You will be subject to the rules, notices, instructions and other directions issued from time to time in regard to your employment.' At the end of that letter there *c* were set out a number of references to 'standing instructions' of different kinds, and there was a cross heading which stated 'Retirement on age grounds'. There then followed what presumably were references to a number of Post Office handbooks and the like. A copy of one of them was not sent to Mr Wallser, but it was available to him, had he asked to see it once he took up his employment. That document set out in considerable detail the regulations of the telecommunications branch of the Post Office in relation to what *d* was called 'Retention'. The opening paragraph was in these terms:

> 'CONDITIONS OF RETENTION All fit and willing officers of all grades should be kept on for as long as is practicable, subject to the following conditions: 1.1: *Efficiency* The efficiency of all officers whom it is proposed to retain beyond 60 should be reviewed. Regular reviews of the efficiency of all officers retained beyond 60 should be carried out. Officers who no longer reach the acceptable level of efficiency *e* will be retired.'

Then there was another paragraph, para 1.3:

> '*Physical Fitness* In certain grades special standards of physical fitness are required. Officers who no longer fulfill these standards should not, of course, be retained beyond the age of 60.' *f*

The next paragraph, para 1.4, is as follows:

> '*Promotion necessity* Circumstances may arise in grades to which promotions are made in which some measure of compulsory retirement of officers over the age of 60 who are fully efficient and willing to remain may be made in accordance with the best interests of the public service.' *g*

Paragraph 5 had a sub-reference 'Compulsory retirement at or after age 60', and the body of the paragraph was in these words: 'Officers may be compulsorily retired on age grounds at or after the age of 60.'

There were numerous references in other sections of the instructions to the effect that retirement at 60 was a matter to be looked at, and in para 16 there were detailed *h* provisions as to the steps which were to be taken before a man reached the age of 60 to see whether it was in the Post Office's interest that he should be retained after the age of 60.

Paragraph 16.1 was the part which was referable to Mr Wallser, and it was in these terms:

> 'In addition to the arrangements described in 16 when an officer in a grade *j* represented by the Form EF [that is Mr Wallser's grade] and S DWC reaches 58, preliminary consideration should be given to whether he should be retained after his sixtieth birthday.'

Counsel for the Post Office has submitted that the effect of this document was to provide that men should retire at the age of 60 unless certain specified conditions applied to them. Counsel for Mr Wallser, on the other hand, has submitted that the effect of this document is to say that men shall be employed as long as they are efficient and physically capable, and that if they are not efficient or physically capable and/or the public interest requires it, they may be retired at 60. Counsel for the Post Office followed up his submission by saying that the overall effect of the document is to create a normal retiring age of 60. Counsel for Mr Wallser, on the other hand, says that is not so. All the document does is to say that in certain circumstances the Post Office may retire a man at 60. Which of those two submissions is right is of importance in this case.

Having accepted the offer of employment contained in the letter to which I have referred, Mr Wallser started work for the Post Office and gave satisfaction. His physical disability resulted from time to time in his not being able to work with a degree of regularity which he would have liked to have done, but as against that, when he did work, his work was found to be satisfactory.

In accordance with the terms of para 16.1 of the Retention Instructions to which I have referred, on 4th March 1976 he was interviewed with a view to seeing whether he should be kept on after the age of 60. A memorandum of that interview was made. It was before the industrial tribunal and was in these terms:

'Mr Wallser was interviewed in accordance with Area Instruction AI 12/75. He expressed a desire to stay after 60 years of age and he appreciates that this will be dependant upon his fitness and P.O. policy at that time. He was advised that his present performance of duty was considered satisfactory.'

When he approached the age of 60, the Post Office considered the position and decided not to retain him after his sixtieth birthday. That decision was made known to Mr Wallser in a letter dated 13th October 1977 which was in these terms:

'Dear Mr Wallser
'The question of your retention beyond your sixtieth birthday has been under consideration and I am sorry to tell you that because of your sick absence it has been decided to retire you on the day prior to your sixtieth birthday, 16th December 1977.'

He was then thanked for his services.

Mr Wallser was aggrieved by that decision and decided to appeal to an industrial tribunal on the grounds that he had been unfairly dismissed. His application was dated 10th January 1978. The Post Office put in an answer dated 1st February 1978. Under a heading as to the grounds on which they were resisting Mr Wallser's claim, the Post Office said this: 'The applicant had reached the age of 60 which is the normal retiring age within the Post Office.'

The Post Office applied to the industrial tribunal for that matter to be dealt with as a preliminary issue. The industrial tribunal agreed, and on 25th April 1978, an industrial tribunal sitting in London purported to deal with the preliminary issue. It did not have the benefit of the quality of legal representation which this court has enjoyed on the hearing of this appeal, and probably because of that lack of quality, the industrial tribunal, everyone now agrees, came to a conclusion which is unsupportable. It is unnecessary in my judgment to go into the details of its conclusion. It decided, although it had been told the Post Office wished their point to be dealt with as a preliminary issue, that Mr Wallser had been unfairly dismissed.

The Employment Appeal Tribunal set aside the actual finding of the industrial tribunal because of the unsupportable grounds on which it had been made, but considered the question whether, on such material as was before the industrial tribunal, the same result might have followed, and came to the conclusion that it would not.

It is now necessary for me to recount what evidence there was before the industrial tribunal. The only evidence given on behalf of Mr Wallser was his own testimony. He recounted the circumstances in which he had come to be employed. The Post Office put in the documents to which I have referred, together with others to which so far I have not referred. Neither side sought to prove what was the average age at which men employed in the telecommunications branch of the Post Office actually retired. Indeed, there were no figures produced to the Employment Appeal Tribunal.

After the decision of the Employment Appeal Tribunal, Mr Wallser's solicitors wrote to the Post Office asking for particulars of the ages at which men in the same grade as Mr Wallser, and employed in the same area, had retired. The information showed that a substantial majority of the men so employed were retained beyond the age of 60. For example, in 1975 two men were retired at 60 and seven were retained beyond 60; similar figures for 1976 were that one man was retired and eleven were retained; in 1977 three men were retired and eight were retained and in 1978 no one was retired and eighteen were retained. Counsel for Mr Wallser asked us to consider these figures. As the Post Office did not object, we agreed to do so.

The next problem is to consider what was the consequence of the evidence before the industrial tribunal and the additional evidence put before this court. The statutory basis for the Post Office's objection to the jurisdiction of the industrial tribunal at the material time is contained in para 10 of Sch 1 to the Trade Union and Labour Relations Act 1974. Those provisions have now been re-enacted in s 64 of the Employment Protection (Consolidation) Act 1978. The effect of para 10 was to provide that the right to bring a complaint of unfair dismissal under para 4 of Sch 1—

> 'does not apply to the dismissal of an employee from any employment if the employee . . . (b) on or before the effective date of termination attained the age which, in the undertaking in which he was employed, was the normal retiring age for an employee holding the position which he held, or, if a man, attained the age of sixty-five, or, if a woman, attained the age of sixty . . .'

As I have recounted, the Post Office were saying in this case that the normal retiring age for the Post Office was 60.

Before the industrial tribunal it was submitted on behalf of Mr Wallser that there was no such 'normal retiring age of 60' in the Post Office, so it follows that the first questions for consideration were: was there a 'normal retiring age'? If there was, what was it?

Before the decision of this court in the case of *Nothman v London Borough of Barnet* [1978] 1 All ER 1243, [1978] 1 WLR 220 there had been doubt as to how a court should approach the problem of a normal retiring age. In *Ord v Maidstone and District Hospital Management Committee* [1974] 2 All ER 343 at 346 Donaldson P had said: 'The ordinary meaning is "the age at which the employees concerned usually retire".' That concept was challenged in the *Nothman* case, and it was decided that the proper approach to this problem was as follows: that the word 'retiring' in the phrase 'the normal retiring age' was to be given the sense of 'must' or 'should'. That construction was set out in my judgment. Lord Denning MR in his judgment referred to what I had said to that effect in the course of argument and stated that he agreed with it. Eveleigh LJ started his judgment by saying, 'I agree'. (See [1978] 1 All ER 1243 at 1247, 1245, 1248, [1978] 1 WLR 220 at 229, 227, 230.) In this court counsel for Mr Wallser has not challenged the construction which was put on the words 'normal retiring age' as set out in the *Nothman* case. He could not have done so because the decision in *Nothman* went to the House of Lords (see [1979] 1 All ER 142, [1979] 1 WLR 67). The main point which was under discussion in the House of Lords was not the one which is under discussion in this case; but in the course of considering the Court of Appeal's decision in *Nothman* the House of Lords must be taken in my opinion to have approved of the construction which this court put on the words 'normal retiring age'.

It follows, therefore, that the problem we have to face in this case is: was there a normal retiring age in the sense that there was an age at which telecommunication branch employees either must or should retire? That seems to me to be a matter of evidence rather than a matter of contract. That was accepted by counsel on both sides. They agreed, however, that the best evidence as to what the 'normal retiring age' was would be provided by any contract or contractual documents which existed in any particular case. They also agreed that if there was no such evidence, or alternatively there was evidence which was to the opposite effect to what was disclosed by the contract or contractual documents, that evidence could be considered. I stress that point because the House of Lords, when considering *Nothman* did pay some attention to the contractual conditions of employment. Lord Salmon, in his speech, referred specifically to an employee whose conditions of employment specify a normal retiring age.

I am satisfied, as counsel seem to have been in this case, that the concept of a normal retiring age does not depend exclusively, or indeed at all, on the terms of a contract. It is a matter of evidence in respect of which contractual terms may be of the greatest importance. Indeed, as was pointed out by Sir David Cairns in the course of argument, in the majority of cases where there is a normal retiring age in a particular enterprise or in a particular industry, it is unlikely that such an age would be specified in a contract of employment.

It follows that we should look closely at the contract and contractual documents in this case. I stress 'contractual documents' because in this case there are a number of documents which were referred to in the letter offering Mr Wallser employment which did not become terms of the contract of employment at all. The Post Office did not give any contractual undertaking to employ Mr Wallser up to normal retiring age; indeed, the contract contains terms saying what notice he can be given to terminate his employment.

The contractual terms to which I have referred in my judgment indicate clearly that the employee, that is Mr Wallser, could expect to be retired at the age of 60 unless he had complied with the conditions relating to efficiency and physical fitness, and there were no factors of public interest operating against his retention in the public service. If that be so, it seems to me that the evidence was overwhelming in this case that the normal retiring age was 60, and that it is irrelevant that at the time when Mr Wallser was employed, namely between 1973 and 1977, a substantial majority of those who did reach the age of 60 were kept on because they complied with the conditions relating to efficiency and physical fitness.

Counsel for Mr Wallser submitted that if there was evidence that the policy of retiring at a particular age was generally disregarded, it could be said that there was not a policy. With that I agree, and counsel for the Post Office accepted that the mere existence of a rule does not prove that the rule operated if the evidence showed that it did not. But in this case such meagre evidence as we have, and it was all produced at a very late stage, seems to show that the rule was still complied with in the Post Office. In Mr Wallser's case that is shown clearly by the fact that para 16.1 was applied to him because when he reached the age of 58 he was interviewed with a view to seeing what should happen after the normal retiring age. As counsel pointed out, Mr Wallser seems to have accepted that he would have to go at 60 unless a specific decision was made to keep him on after the age of 60.

I would dismiss the appeal.

BRIDGE LJ. I agree. I agree with the broad proposition that the normal retiring age within the meaning of what is now s 64(1)(*b*) of the Employment Protection (Consolidation) Act 1978 is not necessarily to be discovered in the contract of employment of the group of workers with whom the court or tribunal is concerned, but it does seem to me that when contractual terms and conditions of employment do govern the age of retirement of the relevant group, those terms provide the best evidence which will prevail to determine what is the normal age of retirement, unless effectively contradicted by other evidence.

In the instant case, the relevant contractual terms provide for compulsory retirement of employees in the appellant's position at the age of 60, unless the Post Office decide to retain individual employees who comply with stringent criteria of efficiency and physical fitness and in whose case there is no reason in the public interest (such for instance as might be created by the necessity to contract or to reorganise a particular department of the Post Office, or the necessity to make way for others who are due for promotion), why that individual employee should not be retained beyond the age of 60.

Those terms and conditions of employment in my judgment, applying the test laid down by the Court of Appeal in the case of *Nothman v London Borough of Barnet* [1978] 1 All ER 1243, [1978] 1 WLR 220, clearly lead to the conclusion that the normal retiring age in Mr Wallser's case was the age of 60.

Accordingly I agree that the appeal should be dismissed.

SIR DAVID CAIRNS. I also agree the appeal should be dismissed for the reasons which have been given in the two judgments already delivered, to which I have nothing to add.

Appeal dismissed. Leave to appeal to the House of Lords refused.

Solicitors: *Willey, Hargrave & Co* (for Mr Wallser); *Saul Rothstein* (for the Post Office).

Bebe Chua   Barrister.

Howard v Department of National Savings

COURT OF APPEAL, CIVIL DIVISION

LORD DENNING MR, ACKNER AND GRIFFITHS LJJ

13th, 14th OCTOBER 1980

Unfair dismissal – Right not to be unfairly dismissed – Restriction on right where employee reaches normal retiring age or specified age – Normal retiring age – Determination – Normal retiring age depending on express or implied conditions of service – Conditions of service specifying minimum retirement age but permitting discretionary extension – Retirement age extended in many cases – Whether minimum retirement age the normal retiring age – Trade Union and Labour Relations Act 1974, Sch 1, para 10(b).

The applicant's employment in a department of the Civil Service was, in the letter appointing him to the department in 1959, expressly made subject to the establishment regulations and to the rules[a] applicable generally to civil servants. Those rules provided for the compulsory retirement of civil servants at the age of 60 although a civil servant could be kept on after that age at the discretion of the head of his department. The general rules also provided (in para 10442) that a civil servant who had not completed 20 years' service on reaching 60 'should' be allowed to continue until he completed 20 years' service or reached 65, whichever was the earlier, provided he was fit, efficient and wished to remain in employment. A special retirement provision relating to the applicant's department stated that officers who had not completed 20 years' service when they reached 60 'will' be allowed to stay on. That provision, which was introduced in 1970, was expressly made subject to review and, if necessary, alteration. The applicant reached the age of 60 in July 1976 by which date he had completed 17 years' service. The department conceded that he would normally have been allowed to stay on until he completed 20 years' service, but because of a Civil Service policy decision in 1977 to withdraw civil servants from the applicant's department by 31st March 1978 the department's special retirement provision was reviewed, and, in a circular issued by the department in 1977, it was stated that officers who had reached the age of 60 would not be allowed to continue in employment beyond 31st March 1978. A letter dated 15th

---

a   Formerly contained in 'Estacode' and now contained in the Civil Service Pay and Conditions of Service Code

March 1977 was sent to the applicant giving him 12 months' notice that his appointment
a would be terminated on 31st March 1978 on the grounds of redundancy. The applicant
claimed compensation for unfair dismissal pursuant to para 4(1)*b* of Sch 1 to the Trade
Union and Labour Relations Act 1974. The industrial tribunal dismissed the claim on
the ground that the applicant's 'normal retiring age', within para 10(*b*)*c* of Sch 1 to the
1974 Act, was the age of 60 under his conditions of service and since he had attained that
age before his employment was terminated on 31st March 1978 there was no jurisdiction
b to entertain his application. The applicant appealed to the Employment Appeal Tribunal
which upheld the industrial tribunal's decision. The applicant appealed to the Court of
Appeal, contending (i) that para 10442 of the general rules applicable to civil servants
meant that an employee who had not completed 20 years' service on reaching the age of
60 'must' be allowed to stay on until he completed 20 years' service or reached 65,
whichever was the earlier, and (ii) that on the true construction of the applicant's
c conditions of service there was no normal retiring age or alternatively, if there was, it was
not 60, because his contract of service did not automatically come to an end when he
reached 60 but continued thereafter and did so without the need for extension by mutual
agreement between him and his employers.

Held – The appeal would be dismissed for the following reasons—
d   (1) The 'normal retiring age' within para 10(*b*) of Sch 1 to the 1974 Act was to be
determined by looking at an employee's conditions of service, written or oral, or implied
by custom or practice. If those conditions of service specified an age at which the
employee could be compulsorily retired, that was the normal retiring age even though
he might be retained thereafter by mutual arrangement, and (per Ackner LJ) the question
to be asked was at what age an employee would have to retire if his service was not
e extended by mutual agreement, or, in a case where the contract did not come to an end
specifically on the intended retirement age, when he would have to retire if the employer
wished him to retire. It followed that the 'normal retiring age' was the minimum
retiring age, in the sense of being the earliest age at which an employer could
contractually impose retirement, even though there might be a practice for the majority
of employees holding the relevant position to retire much later (see p 679 *g h*, p 680 *e* to
f *j* and p 681 *a* and *d*, post); *Nothman v London Borough of Barnet* [1979] 1 All ER 142 and
Post Office v Wallser p 668, ante, applied; dicta of Lawton and Bridge LJJ in *Post Office v
Wallser* at p 673, ante, doubted.
    (2) Paragraph 10442 of the general rules applicable to civil servants did not alter the
fact that the minimum retiring age under the rules was 60, since the provision that civil
servants 'should' be allowed to continue beyond that age did not require their employer
g to allow them to continue. The effect of the 1977 circular was that the applicant's
department returned to the compulsory retirement age under the general rules, namely
60, and that was the applicant's normal retirement age for the purpose of para 10(*b*) of Sch
1 to the 1974 Act (see p 680 *c d* and p 681 *e*, post).

Notes
h For an employee's exclusion from compensation for unfair dismissal because of age, see
16 Halsbury's Laws (4th Edn) para 620.
    For the Trade Union and Labour Relations Act 1974, Sch 1, para 10, see 44 Halsbury's
Statutes (3rd Edn) 1794.
    As from 1st November 1978 para 10 of Sch 1 to the 1974 Act has been replaced by
s 64(1) of the Employment Protection (Consolidation) Act 1978.

j

---

b   Paragraph 4(1), so far as material, provides: 'In every employment to which this paragraph applies
    every employee shall have the right not to be unfairly dismissed by his employer, and the remedy
    of an employee so dismissed for breach of that right shall be by way of complaint to an industrial
    tribunal . . .'
c   Paragraph 10, so far as material, is set out at p 677 *g*, post

Cases referred to in judgments

Department of Health and Social Security v Randalls (4th July 1980, unreported), EAT.

Nothman v London Borough of Barnet [1978] 1 All ER 1243, [1978] 1 WLR 220, [1978] ICR 336, 76 LGR 617, CA; *affd* [1979] 1 All ER 142, [1979] 1 WLR 67, [1979] ICR 111, 77 LGR 89, HL, Digest (Cont Vol E) 625, *1575*.

Post Office v Wallser p 668, ante, CA.

Cases also cited

Government Communications Headquarters v Waite (22nd January 1980) unreported, EAT.

Ord v Maidstone and District Hospital Management Committee [1974] 2 All ER 343, [1974] ICR 369, NIRC.

Appeal

The applicant, Mr Ronald James Clarke Howard, complained to an industrial tribunal pursuant to para 4(1) of Sch 1 to the Trade Union and Labour Relations Act 1974, that he had been unfairly dismissed by his employers, the Department of National Savings. An industrial tribunal sitting at Ashford, Kent (chairman Mr B A Hepple) decided, on 12th December 1977, that at the material time the minimum age of compulsory retirement for officers in the department in the applicant's position was 60 under the establishment regulations and the rules and conditions applicable generally to civil servants (the Civil Service Pay and Conditions of Service Code) which were the conditions of service applicable to Mr Howard's employment by virtue of his letter of appointment dated 24th November 1958, that therefore 60 was the age at which an officer in the applicant's position would have to retire unless his service was extended by mutual agreement, that, applying *Nothman v London Borough of Barnet* [1978] 1 All ER 1243, [1978] 1 WLR 220, 60 was the 'normal retiring age' for an employee in the applicant's position within para 10(b) of Sch 1 to the 1974 Act, and that as the applicant's employment was terminated when he was aged 61 the tribunal, by virtue of the provisions of para 10(b), had no jurisdiction to entertain the application. Mr Howard appealed to the Employment Appeal Tribunal (Slynn J, Mr M L Clement Jones and Mr J D Hughes) which, by a judgment given on 23rd March 1979, dismissed the appeal and upheld the industrial tribunal's decision. Mr Howard appealed to the Court of Appeal. The grounds of the appeal were (1) that the appeal tribunal erred in law in holding that the normal retiring age in the Department of National Savings was 60 because it failed to take cognisance of (a) para 10442 of the Civil Service Pay and Conditions of Service Code providing that an officer who had not completed 20 years' service on reaching 60 should, provided he was fit, efficient and willing to remain in service, be allowed to continue in service until he had completed 20 years' service or had reached 65, whichever was earlier, (b) that Mr Howard had not completed 20 years' service or reached 65 when his employment was terminated, and (c) that the rules of the code were mandatory, and (2) that on the true construction of the words 'normal retiring age' in para 10(b) of Sch 1 to the 1974 Act and the contractual conditions of service relating to retirement applicable to Mr Howard, the appeal tribunal erred in holding (a) that there was a normal retiring age for an employee holding the position held by Mr Howard, and/or (b) that the normal retiring age for such an employee was 60. The facts are set out in the judgment of Lord Denning MR.

Alexander Irvine QC and *Elizabeth Slade* for Mr Howard.
Simon D Brown for the Department of National Savings.

LORD DENNING MR. This case will be of interest to those in the Civil Service, and elsewhere, who are approaching retirement age. Unlike me! To understand it, you must realise that, under the statute, when you are *compulsorily* retired, you are to be regarded as having been dismissed by your employers. The question of compensation depends on whether or not there is *a normal retiring age* for a man in your position. If there is a normal retiring age, let us say at 60, and you stay on at work afterwards, say till

63, you cannot claim for unfair dismissal. But if there is no normal retiring age, you can claim up till the age of 65.

The contest in this case is whether there was a normal retiring age for Mr Howard. He held a position with a National Savings Committee for many years. His rank was said to be rather equivalent to that of a higher executive officer in the Civil Service. He was *compulsorily* retired at the age of $61\frac{3}{4}$, that is $3\frac{1}{4}$ years short of 65. He claimed that, in the circumstances, it was equivalent to an unfair dismissal. But the department say that he cannot claim at all: because the normal retiring age for a man in his position is 60. That is the whole question in the case: was the normal retiring age for a man in his position age 60? In which case he cannot claim. Or was there no normal retiring age for a man in his position? In which case he can claim. That is the question. It has come before the industrial tribunal and before the Employment Appeal Tribunal, each of which held that the normal retiring age for Mr Howard was 60. And so each held that he cannot claim. Now there is an appeal to this court.

First, I will give Mr Howard's dates. He was born on 2nd July 1916. He joined the Civil Service on 5th January 1959, when he was 42. He was appointed to the National Savings Committee. In 1977 the department in which he was employed virtually closed down. He was then 61 years of age. Steps were taken to transfer as many employees as possible to other departments. But, so far as employees aged 60 or over were concerned, and Mr Howard was one of them, they were given notice that their employment would be determined in March 1978. This is the letter to him of 15th March 1977:

> 'It is with regret that I write to advise you that, because of the Government's decision to withdraw Civil Service support staff from the Voluntary Savings Movement, it will not be possible to retain mobile grades over the age of 60 beyond 31 March 1978. There will however be employment for you up to this date but I now give you 12 months' formal notice that your appointment will be terminated on grounds of redundancy on 31 March 1978 which will be regarded as your last day of service.'

That was the notice terminating his employment. He claims compensation for unfair dismissal. But he cannot succeed if the *normal retiring age* was 60, even though he went on working afterwards.

The statute and regulations

The right to compensation for unfair dismissal is given by para 4 of Sch 1 to the Trade Union and Labour Relations Act 1974. But para 10 of Sch 1 provides:

> '... paragraph 4 above does not apply to the dismissal of an employee from any employment if the employee ... (b) on or before the effective date of termination *attained the age which*, in the undertaking in which he was employed, *was the normal retiring age* for an employee holding the position which he held, or, if a man, attained the age of sixty-five, or, if a woman, attained the age of sixty ...'

The question is: what was the *normal retiring age* for a person holding the position which Mr Howard held?

The Civil Service generally

So far as the Civil Service generally is concerned, there are provisions dating back to 1952 which say that a person can be compulsorily retired at the age of 60. Thereafter he may be kept on but it is a matter entirely within the discretion of the head of the department. The 'minimum' retiring age, as it is put, is age 60 in the Civil Service as a whole; but a man can be retained afterwards at the discretion of the head of the department.

But there is a provision which would apply to people, like Mr Howard, who had not completed a full 20 years' service. At the time Mr Howard left, he had only served $19\frac{3}{4}$ years. I will read from the general Civil Service provisions:

'10442. Any officer who has not completed 20 years' reckonable service on
reaching age 60 should, provided he is fit, efficient and willing to remain in service,   *a*
be allowed to continue until he has completed 20 years' reckonable service or has
reached age 65, whichever is the earlier.'

The word 'should' has been canvassed before us. It was suggested that it means 'must'.
I do not agree. I think it means should *normally* be allowed. It still leaves the compulsory
retirement age at 60, with a potential extension.
                                                                                        b

Mr Howard's department

So far as Mr Howard's department is concerned, there was a special provision about
retirement (the Department of National Savings Retirement Policy Statement dated 7th
October 1970). It was introduced in 1970. It contemplated that several officers should
be called on to retire at the age of 60. But there was to be an exception under para 7(c)
of that document. This exception is very much relied on by Mr Howard. It was this: *c*

'Subject to reasonable efficiency and physical capacity any officer who would have
less than 20 years' reckoned service to his credit at age 60 *will* be allowed to stay on
until he has completed 20 years or reached age 65 whichever is the earlier.'

At the age of 60 Mr Howard had not completed 20 years' service at all. He had only
served about 17 years. The department agree that that provision did apply to him in   *d*
1970: and that, at that time, if he had served less than 20 years, he would have been
allowed to stay on until he had completed 20 years' service. But it is important to notice
that in the 1970 statement of retirement policy there is an overriding clause. It is para
13, which says:

'All the above arrangements are subject to review from time to time as occasion   *e*
may require and are specifically subject to alteration if general Civil Service rules
make that necessary.'

Some years later it was necessary to review the arrangement. It was necessary by the
year 1977. In that year a different policy was adopted whereby the staff of the National
Savings Committee were to be withdrawn and placed elsewhere. So in 1977 an   *f*
amendment was made. It was announced (by Department of National Savings circular
44/1977) that:

'In the new situation created by the decision to withdraw the staff of the National
Savings Committees by 31 March 1978, officers of the NSCs with the dispensation
provided in the DNS Agreement of 1970 [who] will by that date ... (5.4) [have]
reached age 60 (including those who are already 60) [will] be allowed to continue in   *g*
DNS employment up to 31 March 1978.'

What was the effect of this policy change? Did it mean that there was a return to the
compulsory retirement age of 60 with an allowable extension to 31st March 1978? Or,
as counsel for Mr Howard has contended before us, does it do away with the normal
retiring age of 60 for people like Mr Howard? In which case, it would mean that there   *h*
was no normal retiring age.

The law

It remains to consider the law on the matter, particularly the meaning of 'normal
retiring age'. There are several authorities about it. In the early days Donaldson P, when
he was sitting in the Industrial Relations Court, suggested that 'normal retiring age'   *j*
meant the *usual* age at which men retired. That has now been held to be incorrect. It
was departed from in *Nothman v London Borough of Barnet* in this court ([1978] 1 All ER
1243, [1978] 1 WLR 220; affirmed by the majority in the House of Lords [1979] 1 All
ER 142, [1979] 1 WLR 67). The contest there was whether there was a fixed age of
retirement for both men and women at the age of 65: or whether there was no normal

retiring age. The evidence showed that teachers up and down the country retired at varying times between ages 55 and 65. So you could not find any 'usual' retiring age. It was held by this court and by the House of Lords that the normal retiring age was that which was fixed by the conditions of the contract. Lord Salmon said in the House of Lords ([1979] 1 All ER 142 at 146, [1979] 1 WLR 67 at 72):

'... that paragraph [ie para 10(*b*) of Sch 1 of the Trade Union and Labour Relations Act 1974] sets up two different upper age limits for basically different classes of people, one for those who have a normal retiring age fixed by their *conditions of service* and the other for those who do not.' (My emphasis.)

Then the next question arises: what is the position when, as in many cases, there is an age at which a person *can* be retired compulsorily according to their contract, but which can be departed from at the discretion of the head of the department? For instance, a circuit judge can be retired compulsorily at age 72, but he may be allowed to stay on for another year or two. In *Nothman*'s case [1978] 1 All ER 1243 at 1247–1248, [1978] 1 WLR 220 at 229 Lawton LJ said:

'It follows that the normal retiring age of teachers employed by the authority is the age at which they would have to retire unless their service was extended by mutual agreement.'

That one sentence places stress on the age at which *they would have to retire* under their contract: unless their service was extended by mutual agreement.

That observation was applied by this court last July in *Post Office v Wallser* p 668, ante. The contract with the Post Office said: 'Officers may be compulsorily retired on age grounds at or after the age of 60.' That was a term of the contract. It was held that 60 was the normal retiring age. Evidence was brought before this court that a lot of people did not retire at the age of 60 in the Post Office. Hardly any people were retired compulsorily at the age of 60 from the years 1975 to 1978. Many were allowed to stay on some years longer. The court held that that evidence did not affect the position. People could be compulsorily retired at age 60. So 60 was the normal retiring age.

I find some of the observations in the judgments difficult to follow. Lawton LJ said (at p 673, ante): '... the concept of a normal retiring age does not depend exclusively, or indeed at all, on the terms of a contract.' Bridge LJ said that the normal retiring age is not necessarily to be discovered in the contract of employment (see p 673, ante).

It seems to me that those observations only apply when there is no term in the contract fixing the time of retirement. As I read the authorities, the normal retiring age is to be found by looking at the provisions of the contract. If they specify an age at which the man *can be compulsorily retired*, that is the normal retiring age: even though he may be retained thereafter by mutual arrangement. It would be the same if there was no express term in the contract but it was imported by custom and practice that a man could be compulsorily retired, say, at age 60.

But when there is nothing of that kind, nothing in the contract, or in custom and practice, then there is no 'normal retiring age' at all. You revert to the statutory age, 65 for men, 60 for women.

This ruling brings certainty into the law. It is fair enough. If a man is being retired at the age at which he can be compulsorily retired, he ought not to be able to complain of unfair dismissal. He is being retired at the allotted age which he understood when he entered the employment. In the same way as a circuit judge can be dismissed at the age of 72: or he may be allowed to stay on. But, if he is dismissed at the age of 72, he cannot claim for unfair dismissal. That seems to me to be the underlying notion of the statute.

We have had before us a very interesting and important judgment by the Employment Appeal Tribunal in a case which seems to be of general application throughout the Civil Service, *Department of Health and Social Security v Randalls* (unreported). It was only given on 4th July 1980: but the same point arises now. In that case Slynn J put it quite succinctly in a passage which I should like to read:

'Nor does the fact, relied upon by Mr Randalls, that many civil servants may be kept on beyond 60, affect the position. It will be very relevant to the question: what is the usual age of retirement? That is not now the test and it seems to us that the matter must, as we have said, be approached on the basis of the conditions of his employment. It is only if the conditions themselves do not make the position clear that it might be necessary to look to what happens in practice to see whether a condition of service is to be implied or has been established by conduct and practice over the years.'

The tribunal go on to say that they were satisfied that the normal retiring age appropriate to Mr Randalls was 60. That goes back to what I said in the very first part of this judgment: that, in the Civil Service, the minimum retiring age from the year 1952 has been 60. That is the age at which a civil servant could be compulsorily retired. Even though in many cases that is extended, it still remains the compulsory retiring age. Therefore, on the authorities, it is the normal retiring age. In the latest provision, para 10442, as I have indicated, the word 'should' ought not to be read as altering the fact that the normal retiring age is the age of 60.

Those are the general Civil Service provisions. They do not directly arise in this case. We are only concerned with one particular department, the National Savings Committee. For the reasons which I have given, it seems to me that the normal retiring age at the time when Mr Howard retired, that is, from 1976 onwards, was 60.

I would therefore uphold the decision of the tribunal and dismiss the appeal.

ACKNER LJ. *Nothman v London Borough of Barnet* [1978] 1 All ER 1243, [1978] 1 WLR 220, CA; [1979] 1 All ER 142, [1979] 1 WLR 67, HL, decides that 'normal retiring age' does not mean the usual or average retiring age as had previously been thought to be the case. The question to ask is: at what age would an employee have to retire unless his service was extended by mutual agreement?

It was submitted by counsel for Mr Howard in his powerful address to us, that in *Nothman's* case the contract automatically came to an end on the retiring age, but that here the contract does not come to an end at 60, but continues. Therefore there was no need for there to be any extension by mutual agreement when Mr Howard reached the age of 60. However, on the basis that the *Nothman* test is correct, and I must so treat it, that is too artificial a distinction. In a case where the contract, unlike the *Nothman* contract, does not come to an end specifically on the age intended to be the retiring age, one asks the question: when would he have to retire if the employers so wished? This means, perhaps surprisingly, that often the *normal* retiring age is the *minimum* retiring age in the sense that it is the earliest date at which there is a contractual liability to retire, even though in practice it may be that the vast majority of employees holding the relevant position retire much later.

In order to apply the *Nothman* test, it seems to me that you must look at the conditions of service (see in particular the speech by Lord Salmon cited by Lord Denning MR); because, if the employee does not have to retire at a given date, then there is no normal retiring age. The conditions of service may of course not only be in writing; the contract may be partly oral, partly in writing or wholly oral. Moreover, terms may have to be implied by reason, for instance, of a custom, or by virtue of some long-standing practice. But I too, like Lord Denning MR, am puzzled by the observations made by this court, to which he has made reference, in *Post Office v Wallser* p 668, ante.

Counsel for the Department of National Savings submits that, if a normal retiring age cannot be found in the contract, then there is no normal retiring age. On the basis of the authority of *Nothman*, I accept his submission, and I too would therefore dismiss this appeal for the reasons given by Lord Denning MR as well as for the reasons which I have set out above.

GRIFFITHS LJ. I agree that the normal retirement age must be ascertained by looking at the terms of the contract of service whether they be express or implied. If this matter were free from authority, I doubt if I should have construed 'normal retiring age' as the minimum retiring age in the sense of it being the earliest age at which an employer could impose compulsory retirement.

Suppose a contract provided both a minimum and a maximum retiring age, and the fact was that employees were in practice kept on until the maximum retiring age, why should not the maximum retiring age in those circumstances be considered to be the normal retiring age? It appears to me that ordinary use of language would drive one to the conclusion that the maximum retiring age was in those circumstances the normal retiring age. If against this practice, one employee finds himself singled out for compulsory retirement at the minimum retiring age, I can well understand him having a real sense of grievance and believing that he has been unfairly dismissed. Furthermore, although perhaps it is a somewhat unlikely contingency, counsel for Mr Howard points out that such a construction would enable an unscrupulous employer to evade the protection given to employees in the Act by inserting in the contract of service a wholly unrealistic minimum compulsory age of retirement.

It is, however, not free from authority. In *Nothman v London Borough of Barnet* [1978] 1 All ER 1243, [1978] 1 WLR 220, CA; [1979] 1 All ER 142, [1979] 1 WLR 67, HL, the normal retiring age was construed as the age at which an employee must retire if required to do so, and that decision was followed by this court in *Post Office v Wallser* p 668, ante. *Nothman v London Borough of Barnet* can be distinguished on its facts from the present case because in *Nothman* the contract provided for a fixed date of retirement, but I can find no such distinguishing feature in *Post Office v Wallser*; and I regard those two authorities of this court as conclusive on the main point which arises in this appeal.

I agree that the narrow construction of circular 44/1977 advanced by counsel for Mr Howard is not the correct one; and for the reasons given on that point by Lord Denning MR I agree that this appeal must be dismissed.

Appeal dismissed with costs not to be enforced without leave of the court. Leave to appeal to the House of Lords.

Solicitors: *Simmonds Church Rackham* (for Mr Howard); *Treasury Solicitor.*

Sumra Green   Barrister.

Cargill v Gotts

COURT OF APPEAL, CIVIL DIVISION

LAWTON, BRANDON AND TEMPLEMAN LJJ

12th, 13th, 14th NOVEMBER, 18th DECEMBER 1980

Easement – Water – Right to take water from source of supply in river authority area – Effect on easement of statutory restrictions on abstracting water from source of supply – Easement at common law to abstract water from pond in river for purposes of dominant tenement owner's farm at date statutory restrictions came into effect – Less than 1,000 gallons abstracted on any one occasion but aggregate amount abstracted exceeding 1,000 gallons – Whether statutory restrictions altering right to easement – Whether restrictions enforceable by servient tenement owner – Whether succession of abstractions on separate occasions constituting 'a series of operations' to abstract more than 1,000 gallons – Water Resources Act 1963, ss 23(1), 24(1).

Easement – Water rights – Prescription – Substantial increase in quantity of water abstracted during prescriptive period – Water abstracted from river by dominant tenement owner for farm purposes from 1928 onwards – From 1950s quantity abstracted substantially increased to spray crops – Whether increase in user barring right to easement by prescription.

The plaintiff had been in continuous occupation of a farm since 1928. From before that time water had been drawn from a pond in a nearby river for use on the farm, mainly for watering horses and cattle. From the 1950s the quantity of water abstracted from the pond by the plaintiff increased tenfold because it was used to spray crops as well as water cattle. In 1977 the defendant became the owner of the pond and took measures to prevent the plaintiff using it. The plaintiff brought an action seeking a declaration that he had an easement by prescription at common law or under statute to abstract water from the pond for the purposes of the farm, an injunction to restrain the defendant from preventing him from drawing water from the pond, and damages. At the trial of the action the defendant contended (i) that after 30th June 1965, when the prohibition on abstracting water from a river without a licence from the river authority imposed by s 23(1)[a] of the Water Resources Act 1963 came into effect, the plaintiff's abstraction of water from the pond had been illegal because he had not obtained a licence, and as he had not used the water as of right since 30th June 1965 the claim based on prescription failed, and (ii) that the user throughout the prescriptive period was not sufficiently certain and uniform to support a prescriptive right, having regard to the substantial increase in the quantity of water abstracted over the years. The plaintiff contended that by s 24(1)[b] of the 1963 Act he was exempted from the restrictions on abstracting water and from the requirement to obtain a licence because each abstraction did not exceed 1,000 gallons and '[did] not form part of a continuous operation, or of a series of operations, whereby in the aggregate more than one thousand gallons of water [were] abstracted'. The trial judge held ([1980] 2 All ER 49) that the 1963 Act did not confer any remedy on the defendant if the plaintiff failed to observe the statutory restrictions, and that in any event the plaintiff's abstraction of waters were not 'a series of operations' and he was therefore entitled under the Act to extract up to 1,000 gallons on each occasion he drew off water from the pond, and that he was entitled vis-à-vis the defendant to draw water from the pond because he had an easement by prescription. The judge granted the declaration and injunction sought and awarded the plaintiff £50 damages. The defendant appealed.

---

a   Section 23(1), so far as material, provides: 'Subject to the following provisions of this Part of this Act, as from [1st July 1965] no person shall abstract water from any source of supply in a river authority area, or cause or permit any other person so to abstract any water, except in pursuance of a licence under this Act granted by the river authority . . .'

b   Section 24(1), is set out at p 685 e, post

Held – (1) The plaintiff could not rely on the exception from statutory restrictions contained in s 24(1) of the 1963 Act because each abstraction of water from the pond by him formed 'part . . . of a series of operations' for the same purpose, namely the water requirements for the agricultural purposes of his farm. It followed that every abstraction of water by the plaintiff after 30th June 1965 had required a licence under s 23(1) and in the absence of a licence had been illegal. Since the court would not recognise an easement established by illegal activity, the plaintiff could not rely on any abstraction of water from the pond after 30th June 1965 to establish an easement by prescription (see p 685 *j* to p 686 *d*, p 688 *e* and p 690 *c d* and *g*, post).

(2) However, the plaintiff was able to assert 20 years' uninterrupted user of water from the pond for agricultural purposes prior to 1st July 1965 and had therefore established a prescriptive easement entitling him to draw water from the pond. The fact that there were fluctuations from time to time in the amount and application of the water drawn off attributable to changes in the type and method of farming on the plaintiff's farm did not destroy or alter the nature or character of the right asserted or the easement acquired, since the easement was a right to take water for farm purposes generally. Since the 1963 Act did not destroy easements already acquired, that easement remained although it could not be lawfully exercised without a licence from the river authority (see p 686 *e* and *j* to p 687 *f*, p 688 *c e*, p 689 *g* to p 690 *c* and *g*, post); dictum of Bovill CJ in *Williams v James* (1867) LR 2 CP at 580 and *British Railways Board v Glass* [1964] 3 All ER 418 applied; *Millington v Griffiths* (1874) 30 LT 65, *Hulley v Silversprings Bleaching and Dyeing Co Ltd* [1922] All ER Rep 683 and *Rugby Joint Water Board v Walters* [1966] 3 All ER 497 distinguished.

(3) Since the plaintiff had established that he was entitled to the easement claimed, a declaration would be made to that effect. However, because the plaintiff was not lawfully entitled to use the easement without a licence a further declaration would be made in terms of that restriction, and since he was not so entitled to use the easement the injunction restraining the defendant from preventing his using it was unnecessary and would be discharged. To that extent the appeal would be allowed (see p 688 *f g*, p 689 *f g* and p 690 *g*, post).

(4) As between the parties, the defendant had no right to exercise self-help to prevent the plaintiff contravening the 1963 Act since his remedy in that event was confined to reporting the matter to the appropriate authorities. Furthermore (Templeman LJ dissenting), although the plaintiff had, from 1st July 1965, been exercising his easement contrary to the 1963 Act, that did not prevent him from recovering damages against the defendant for interference with that right because the effect of s 135(8)(*c*)ᶜ of that Act was that restrictions imposed by the Act were a matter for the river authority and did not affect the rights of individuals vis-à-vis one another (see p 689 *b c* and p 690 *f g*, post).

Decision of H E Francis QC sitting as a deputy judge of the High Court [1980] 2 All ER 49 varied.

Notes

For easements relating to natural water courses, see 14 Halsbury's Laws (4th Edn) paras 194–195, for the nature of user for prescription at common law and under statute, see ibid paras 80–83, 104, and for cases on rights relating to pools, springs and waters, see 19 Digest (Repl) 176–177, 1187–1195.

For the Water Resources Act 1963, ss 23, 24, 135, see 39 Halsbury's Statutes (3rd Edn) 251, 252, 369.

Cases referred to in judgments

British Railways Board v Glass [1964] 3 All ER 418, [1965] Ch 538, [1964] 3 WLR 913, CA, Digest (Cont Vol B) 609, 410a.

Hulley v Silversprings Bleaching and Dyeing Co Ltd [1922] 2 Ch 268, [1922] All ER Rep 683, 91 LJ Ch 207, 126 LT 499, 86 JP 30, 19 Digest (Repl) 68, 380.

Millington v Griffiths (1874) 30 LT 65, 19 Digest (Repl) 172, 1147.

---

c   Section 135(8), so far as material, is set out at p 690 *e*, post

RPC Holdings Ltd v Rogers [1953] 1 All ER 1029, 19 Digest (Repl) 122, 757.

Rugby Joint Water Board v Walters [1966] 3 All ER 497, [1967] Ch 397, [1966] 3 WLR
934, 131 JP 10, Digest (Cont Vol B) 734, 92a.

Williams v James (1867) LR 2 CP 577, 36 LJCP 256, 16 LT 664, 19 Digest (Repl) 116, 714.

Woodhouse & Co Ltd v Kirkland (Derby) Ltd [1970] 2 All ER 587, [1970] 1 WLR 1185, 21
P & CR 534, Digest (Cont Vol C) 302, 215b.

Case also cited

Neaverson v Peterborough Rural District Council [1902] 1 Ch 557, CA.

Appeal

The plaintiff, David Cargill, brought an action against the defendant, Brown Gordon
Gotts, seeking (1) a declaration that he was entitled to draw water from the Mill Pond,
Gimingham, Norfolk as a legal right under s 2 of the Prescription Act 1832 appertaining
to the dominant tenement, (2) alternatively, a declaration that he was entitled to the
right to draw water from the pond as having been enjoyed by him and the possessors of
the dominant tenement for the time being through whom he claimed from time
immemorial and by virtue of a grant by deed by all necessary parties which had been
accidentally lost or destroyed, (3) an injunction restraining the defendant whether by
himself, his servants or agents or otherwise howsoever from preventing the plaintiff or
his servants or agents from drawing water from the pond and (4) damages. On 29th
October 1979 H E Francis QC sitting as a deputy judge of the High Court ([1980] 2 All
ER 49, [1980] 1 WLR 521) held that the plaintiff was entitled to a declaration that he had
an easement at common law to draw water from the pond, an injunction restraining the
defendant from preventing the exercise of the easement by the plaintiff and £50 damages
for interference with his right. The defendant appealed. The facts are set out in the
judgment of Templeman LJ.

John Knox QC and *Sonia Proudman* for the defendant.
Vivian Chapman for the plaintiff.

Cur adv vult

18th December. The following judgments were read.

TEMPLEMAN LJ (delivering the first judgment at the invitation of Lawton LJ). This
is an appeal from a decision of Mr H E Francis QC sitting as a deputy High Court judge
in the Chancery Division and delivered on 26th October 1979. The deputy judge held
that the plaintiff was entitled at common law to an easement to draw water from the
defendant's Mill Pond at Gimingham in Norfolk for the purpose of farming the plaintiff's
Grove Farm. The defendant appeals to this court.

The River Mun flows in a south-easterly direction from Clapham Dams and south of
Grove Farm under the highway which runs north and south through the village of
Gimingham. After crossing the highway, the river flows east to the sea at Mundesley.
West of the highway the river broadens to the Gimingham Mill Pond which is separated
from the highway by a narrow strip of land. The Mill Pond and the narrow strip of land
which allows access from the highway to the Mill Pond are owned by the defendant.
The plaintiff's Grove Farm comprises 400 acres and its southern boundary is 500 yards
from the defendant's Mill Pond.

Since before 1927 water was drawn from Mill Pond by a water cart for use on Grove
Farm, mainly for the purpose of watering horses and cattle. At first, the water cart
carried a barrel with a capacity variously estimated at between 50 and 100 gallons. The
water cart drew water from Mill Pond at intervals of time which varied according to the
seasons and according to the recollection of the witnesses from four times a week to two
or three times a day. In winter the Mill Pond was not used so much by Grove Farm
because sufficient water was available from another source. At threshing times and
possibly at other times water from Mill Pond was or may have been used to operate
steam-driven machinery on Grove Farm.

About 1942 the plaintiff began to use water from the Mill Pond to spray crops on Grove Farm. The water barrel was replaced by a tank which held 250 to 300 gallons. Crop spraying which was originally carried out in April and May was progressively extended and intensified. By 1953 crop spraying was described as a practice and, in the late 1950s, the 250-gallon tank was replaced by a 900-gallon tanker called a bowser. This was later augmented by a second tank of 500 gallons so that 1,400 gallons in all could be drawn from the Mill Pond by means of a pump attached to the bowser at any one time. Between the middle 1950s and 1977 the quantity of water abstracted by the plaintiff from the Mill Pond increased tenfold, but this increase was partly due to the fact that the plaintiff by 1977 was taking water not only for Grove Farm but for three other farms as well. Occasionally the plaintiff drew 4,000 gallons in a single day. In February 1977 the defendant forcibly prevented the plaintiff from drawing water from Mill Pond and, by the writ in these proceedings dated 6th December 1977, the plaintiff claimed a declaration that he was entitled to draw whatever water he required from the Mill Pond for the more convenient occupation of Grove Farm by virtue of the Prescription Act 1832 or, alternatively, by common law or, alternatively again, by the operation of the doctrine of lost modern grant. The plaintiff also claimed an injunction restraining the defendant from preventing the plaintiff from drawing water from Mill Pond and the plaintiff asked for damages. The defendant by his defence denied that the plaintiff had acquired any easement and further pleaded that, since 1st July 1965, the plaintiff had been prevented by the Water Resources Act 1963 from drawing water from Mill Pond.

By s 23(1) of the Water Resources Act 1963 and orders made under that Act, it became illegal on and after 1st July 1965, subject to certain exceptions, for any person to abstract water from any source of supply except in pursuance of a licence under the Act granted by the appropriate river authority. The Mill Pond is such a source.

Section 24(1) provides:

> 'The restriction imposed by [s 23(1)] does not apply to any abstraction of a quantity of water not exceeding one thousand gallons, if it does not form part of a continuous operation, or of a series of operations, whereby in the aggregate more than one thousand gallons of water are abstracted.'

By s 24(2) the restriction imposed by s 23(1) does not apply to any abstraction from an inland water by or on behalf of an occupier of land contiguous to that water at the place where the abstraction is effected, in so far as the water is abstracted for use on a holding consisting of that land and is abstracted for use on that holding for, inter alia, agricultural purposes other than spray irrigation. This exception does not avail the plaintiff because Grove Farm is not contiguous to Mill Pond.

By s 27 an application for a licence to abstract water may be made by the occupier of land contiguous to the supply or by anyone who has a right of access to the supply. The plaintiff had a right of access to Mill Pond if he acquired an easement before 1st July 1965, but he did not apply for a licence prior to these proceedings.

By s 33 where any person abstracted water from a source of supply at any time within a period of five years ending with 30th June 1965 he was, on application made to the river authority before 1st July 1965, entitled to a grant of a licence under the Act. The plaintiff was thus entitled to a licence of right under the Act, a licence which would have been limited to the amount of water and the purposes for which he had used the water from time to time during the preceding five years: see s 35. The plaintiff did not apply for a licence of right under the Act.

In the result, the plaintiff acted illegally on every occasion when he abstracted water from Mill Pond after 30th June 1965 unless he is entitled to the benefit of the exception contained in s 24(1) and can establish that, every time his bowser abstracted 1,000 gallons or less from Mill Pond, that abstraction did not 'form part of a continuous operation, or of a series of operations'. The deputy judge held that it was open to the plaintiff to abstract water from the Mill Pond consistently with the provisions of the 1963 Act provided he did not draw more than 1,000 gallons on any one occasion (see [1980] 2 All ER 49 at 54, [1980] 1 WLR 521 at 527).

I am unable to agree. If the plaintiff planned to abstract 10,000 gallons by ten instalments of 1,000 gallons for the purpose of filling a swimming pool, then clearly each abstraction would form part of a series of operations designed to fill the pool, whether the instalments were abstracted on the same day or on ten separate days or at irregular intervals. If the plaintiff planned to abstract as much water as was needed to fill and maintain a swimming pool and employed a 1,000-gallon tank for that purpose, again each abstraction would form part of a series of operations designed to fill and maintain the swimming pool, whether the capacity of the pool was known or not, whether the pool leaked at an unknown rate or not and whether or not the 1,000-gallon tank was filled once per day or on irregular days. Similarly, if the plaintiff planned to abstract 10,000 gallons to spray his crops or planned to abstract as much water as was necessary to spray his crops and employed a 1,000-gallon tank for that purpose, again each filling of the tank formed part of a series of operations designed to spray the crops. In my judgment, on the facts of the present case, each abstraction of water by the plaintiff formed part of a series of operations, the object of which was to help meet the water requirements of Grove Farm for agricultural purposes. Section 24(1) is not apt to authorise and was not intended to authorise any one person to abstract as much water as he pleases from any one source of supply provided only that each abstraction does not exceed 1,000 gallons.

I conclude that every abstraction of water by the plaintiff from Mill Pond after 30th June 1965 was illegal. It follows, in my judgment, that the plaintiff cannot rely on any abstraction of water carried out after 30th June 1965 in order to establish an easement by prescription. The court will not recognise an easement established by illegal activity.

The 1963 Act, however, does not contain any provision which destroys an easement already acquired. An easement of water acquired before 1st July 1965 may not lawfully be exercised without a licence, but does not cease to be an easement if a licence is not obtained; nor does it cease to be an easement until a licence has been obtained. The easement remains an easement but cannot be exercised without committing an offence under the Act.

If the plaintiff can establish that, before 1st July 1965, he acquired an easement to take water from Mill Pond, then he will be entitled to apply for a licence and, if he is granted a licence, may thereafter lawfully exercise the easement to the extent justified by the easement but subject to any limitations and provisions imposed by the terms of the licence or any modification or renewal of the licence from time to time.

The plaintiff claims that the evidence established that, before 1st July 1965, Grove Farm acquired by more than 20 years user the right to water from the Mill Pond for agricultural purposes. The deputy judge was right to declare that the plaintiff, as the owner of Grove Farm, is entitled at common law to an easement to draw water from Mill Pond for the purpose of farming Grove Farm.

The defendant claims that, down to 1953, the evidence only established user of water from Mill Pond to the extent of 300 gallons a day for the purpose of watering stock and operating steam machinery on Grove Farm. Between 1953 and 1965 the quantity of water abstracted was increased and the purpose for which the water was used was altered. The plaintiff cannot demonstrate 20 years definite and continuous user necessary to found any prescriptive right. Alternatively, if the plaintiff began to establish a separate easement to use water for crop spraying in 1953 that did not ripen into an easement before 1965 when the user became illegal. The argument is that the introduction of crop spraying made a substantial change in the rights claimed by the dominant tenement and imposed a substantial additional burden on the servient tenement.

In my judgment, it is a mistake to concentrate on gallonage and detailed user. When Grove Farm, in or before 1927, took 100 gallons from Mill Pond to water 100 bullocks, Grove Farm did not begin to acquire an easement to take 100 gallons to water 100 bullocks but began to assert a right which, after 20 years, ripened into an easement to take water from Mill Pond for the benefit of Grove Farm for all purposes according to the ordinary and reasonable use to which Grove Farm might be applied at the time when the right was and continued to be asserted.

To state the obvious, Grove Farm was and at all times remained a farm. The right to take water from Mill Pond was and at all times remained a right to take water for farm purposes. If bullocks were replaced by sheep, if pasture became arable, if beetroot was substituted for barley, the right asserted for the benefit of Grove Farm, provided that the right was asserted over the requisite period of 20 years, was a right to take water for farm purposes and that right did not cease to be asserted by fluctuations from time to time in the amount and application of the water, fluctuations which were attributable to changes in the type and method of farming currently pursued at Grove Farm. Water used for crop spraying is just as much used for agricultural purposes as water used for bullocks, and the fact that more water may be required for crop spraying than for watering bullocks is not sufficient to destroy or alter the nature of the right asserted or the easement acquired. The principle in relation to prescriptive rights of way was enunciated in *Williams v James* (1867) LR 2 CP 577 at 580 per Bovill CJ and applied in *RPC Holdings Ltd v Rogers* [1953] 1 All ER 1029. The principle is:

'When a right of way to a piece of land is proved, then that is, unless something appears to the contrary, a right of way for all purposes according to the ordinary and reasonable use to which that land might be applied at the time of the supposed grant.'

In my judgment, the same principle must apply to a right to take water. The right to take water for the benefit of Grove Farm is a right to take water for farming purposes, that being the ordinary and reasonable use to which Grove Farm has at all times been applied.

There may in other cases be some scientific developments which completely change the character of the right asserted. Thus in *Rugby Joint Water Board v Walters* [1966] 3 All ER 497, [1967] Ch 397 the right of a riparian owner to take water for ordinary purposes, including agricultural purposes, did not extend to taking 60,000 gallons a day for the purposes of spray irrigation. In the present case the improvement of farming methods by crop spraying and the quantity of water employed for that purpose do not jointly or separately amount to the assertion of a new right or the excessive exercise of an ancient right. On the evidence in this case, the right asserted in 1977 was no different from the right asserted in 1927, namely the right to use the water in Mill Pond for the agricultural purposes of Grove Farm. The introduction of crop spraying did not effect a radical change in the dominant tenement.

Counsel for the defendant referred to *Millington v Griffiths* (1874) 30 LT 65. In that case a prescriptive right to pollute was not established because, over the alleged prescription period, the amount of pollution had gone on increasing. If a plaintiff claims a prescriptive right to pollute a stream he must show that he has, for a 20 year period, asserted the right to introduce polluting material of a kind and quantity which produces the effect on the stream which he claims to be entitled to continue. No such principle applies or needs to be applied to a prescriptive right to take water from a stream if, as in the present case, the right claimed has no material effect on the stream. The defendant in the present case is not defending the stream; he is seeking, for understandable reasons, to prevent the plaintiff from introducing a vehicle on the defendant's property.

In *Hulley v Silversprings Bleaching and Dyeing Co Ltd* [1922] 2 Ch 268, [1922] All ER Rep 683 it was held that the progressive increase in plant in a mill which polluted water taken from a stream and in the volume of water subsequently polluted was destructive of that certainty and uniformity essential for the measurement and determination of the user by which the extent of the prescriptive right claimed was to be established. That is another pollution case in which the plaintiff could not establish the extent of the right which he had asserted for 20 years. It was not sufficient for him to show that he had put some polluting material in the stream throughout the 20-year period. He must justify the extent of the pollution which he was causing at the date of the proceedings. In the present case the plaintiff does not claim a prescriptive right to extract any particular volume of water from Mill Pond. He claims he has asserted for 20 years and more the right to take such water as he requires from Mill Pond for agricultural purposes connected with Grove Farm. Easements to take water, whether express or prescriptive, are rarely if ever defined by reference to quantity as well as or instead of by reference to the purposes for which the water may be abstracted.

A mere increase in the enjoyment of the right asserted does not throw into confusion the nature of the right asserted, nor does it destroy the right. Thus, in *British Railways Board v Glass* [1964] 3 All ER 418, [1965] Ch 538, the right asserted during the 20-year prescriptive period was a right of way to a field used from time to time as a caravan site. During the period the number of caravans on the site increased from 6 to 30. This did not prevent the owner of the field from obtaining a prescriptive right of way for caravans without limitation on numbers. There had been no change in the character of the dominant tenement. In the present case the increase from 300 gallons to a maximum of 4,000 gallons without any change in the character of the dominant tenement did not affect the nature or quality of the right asserted during the prescriptive period.

In *Woodhouse & Co Ltd v Kirkland (Derby) Ltd* [1970] 2 All ER 587, [1970] 1 WLR 1185 increased user, as distinct from user of a different kind or for a different purpose, did not affect or prejudice the acquisition of a prescriptive right of way. Plowman J refrained from considering 'whether an increase in user, if very great, can ever of itself amount to excessive user' (see [1970] 2 All ER 587 at 592, [1970] 1 WLR 1185 at 1192). It is equally unnecessary to decide the point in the present case because, in the circumstances, the increase in user cannot be described as being very great, measured, as it must be measured, by the effect of the user on the stream and on riparian owners.

In the result I agree with the deputy judge that the plaintiff is entitled at common law to an easement to draw water from the defendant's Mill Pond for the purpose of farming Grove Farm.

But, contrary to the views expressed by the deputy judge, I do not consider that it has been lawful for the plaintiff to exercise his rights since 1st July 1965.

I would accordingly declare that the plaintiff is entitled to the easement but also declare that it has not been lawful since 1st July 1965 and remains unlawful for the plaintiff to abstract water from Mill Pond for the purpose of farming Grove Farm except in pursuance of a licence under the Water Resources Act 1963 and in accordance with the provisions of such licence.

The deputy judge granted the plaintiff an injunction restraining the defendant from preventing the plaintiff from drawing water from Mill Pond in exercise of the plaintiff's easement. I do not consider that the injunction is now necessary or appropriate. So long as the plaintiff is not in possession of a licence and cannot lawfully exercise his easement, he will not draw water from Mill Pond. When the plaintiff obtains a licence the defendant will not, in view of the outcome of this appeal, seek to prevent the plaintiff from drawing water from Mill Pond.

The deputy judge also awarded the plaintiff £50 damages for interferences with his easement. Counsel for the plaintiff argued that the plaintiff remained entitled to damages because, by s 135(8) of the Water Resources Act 1963, the restrictions imposed by s 23 of the Act shall not be construed as derogating from any right of action or other remedy (whether civil or criminal) in proceedings instituted otherwise than under the Act. In my judgment, s 135(8) confirms, if such confirmation is necessary, that the plaintiff, despite the provisions of the Water Resources Act 1963, remains entitled to a declaration concerning the easement which he has proved at common law. But, though the plaintiff is entitled to the easement, he has not suffered damage from any interference with his exercise of the rights constituting that easement because such exercise was illegal at the time of the interference. In my judgment, the plaintiff does not suffer damage by being prevented from doing something which it was illegal for him to do.

It does not follow, as counsel for the defendant claimed, that the defendant was entitled forcibly to prevent the plaintiff from taking water from Mill Pond. Section 49

of the Water Resources Act 1963 provides that any person who contravenes s 23(1) shall
a be guilty of an offence and shall be liable on conviction on indictment or on summary
conviction to a fine. Section 118 provides that it shall be the duty of a river authority to
enforce the provisions of the Act in relation to the area of the authority and that no
proceedings for any offence under the Act shall be instituted except by a river authority
or by or with the consent of the Director of Public Prosecutions. Section 135(8) provides
that the restrictions imposed by s 23 shall not be construed as conferring a right of action
b in any civil proceedings in respect of any contravention of those restrictions. Counsel
submitted that the defendant, as the owner of Mill Pond, had the right to prevent any
illegality happening on his property and to exercise the right of self-help to prevent any
such illegality. In my judgment, as between the plaintiff and the defendant, the plaintiff
has the right to come onto the defendant's land and to take water from Mill Pond. If the
defendant knows or suspects that the plaintiff is committing an offence under the Water
c Resources Act 1963, the defendant may report the matter and make representations to
the relevant river authority or the Director of Public Prosecutions.

At a late stage of this appeal the defendant asked to amend his pleadings to allege that
the plaintiff was, in 1977, extracting water from Mill Pond not only for Grove Farm but
also for three other farms. This allegation corresponds with the evidence, but the
plaintiff never had the opportunity to demonstrate at the trial, if he could, that he had
d become entitled to a prescriptive right to take water for one or more of those three farms,
and, accordingly, I do not think the amendment should now be allowed.

At the trial, as between the plaintiff and the defendant, the sole real issue was whether
the plaintiff could establish an easement at common law to take water from Mill Pond
for the purposes of Grove Farm. On this issue the plaintiff succeeded below and
succeeded in this court. The defendant was never entitled to interfere with the exercise
e of this easement. It has not been established whether the defendant was entitled to
require the plaintiff to desist from taking water for the purposes of any farm other than
Grove Farm and the defendant only interfered with the plaintiff's rights in order to
prevent water being taken for Grove Farm. This interference was not justified. The
defendant attempted and failed to rely on the Water Resources Act 1963 to prove that the
plaintiff was not entitled to an easement for Grove Farm. The defendant has succeeded
f in this court in getting rid of an injunction which was, in my view, in any event
unnecessary once the court decided an easement existed.

I would declare that the plaintiff is entitled at common law to an easement to take
water from Mill Pond for the farming purposes of Grove Farm and I would add a
declaration that the plaintiff is only entitled to exercise his easement when he has
obtained a licence under the Water Resources Act 1963 and in accordance with the terms
g of that licence.

LAWTON LJ. I too am satisfied that before 1st July 1965, ie before the end of the
initial period for the purposes of s 23(1) of the Water Resources Act 1963, the plaintiff as
the owner of Grove Farm acquired by more than 20 years use the right to take water
from the Mill Pond for agricultural purposes on that farm. When, on or before 1927,
h water from the Mill Pond first came to be used on Grove Farm, it was for the needs of
that farm at that date. Those needs were principally for watering cattle and providing
water for steam-driven farm machinery such as a threshing machine. The probabilities
were, as counsel for the defendant accepted, that from time to time small quantities were
used for other farm purposes.

A farm's needs for water can change with the seasons, with changes in the demand for
j agricultural produce and with improvements in agricultural methods. What is wanted
in a dry summer may not be needed in a wet one. At one time it may be worthwhile
fattening store cattle on arable land which has been turned into pasture. A few years
later it may be more profitable to change from raising beef to growing corn, and when
this is done less water will be needed. Crop spraying is an example of the improvements
in agricultural methods which have come about since 1927. In those days farmers often

dressed their seed corn with chemicals which were reputed to deter birds, field mice and other rodents but they had few, if any, means of protecting their crops from insects and plant diseases. Now, by means of spraying, they can give their crops this kind of protection, but such spraying has to be done with water-based chemicals. When water is so used it is for a normal agricultural purpose just as in 1927 water was used on farms to generate steam in threshing machines. The fact that spraying is a new way of protecting growing crops whereas threshing machines are now more often seen in museums than on farms does not confine the user of the easement of water appertaining to Grove Farm to the purpose for which water was used in or about 1927 or to the quantities which were used before 1953, when large scale spraying started. The legal position would be different if water were used on Grove Farm for some abnormal agricultural purpose as might happen, for example, if part of the farm were turned into a trout hatchery. Whether a particular purpose was a normal or abnormal agricultural use would be a question of fact.

What has affected the use of this easement is the Water Resources Act 1963. I agree with Templeman LJ that the plaintiff will not be able to take advantage of the exception contained in s 24(1) by limiting each abstraction of water to 1,000 gallons or less. In the past he has sent his bowser to the Mill Pond for his farming purposes at Grove Farm. Each abstraction has been, or should have been, for such purposes and amounted to an operation with an end in view and it was always the same end, namely the agricultural purposes of that farm. It follows, in my judgment, that his abstractions since 1965 have formed part 'of a series of operations, whereby in the aggregate more than one thousand gallons of water [have been] abstracted'.

Although I agree generally with the reasoning in Templeman LJ's judgment I find myself unable to agree with him on the issue of damages. This is because of the unusual wording of s 135(8) which provides that—

> '. . . the restrictions imposed by sections 23 . . . shall not be construed as . . . (c) derogating from any right of action or other remedy (whether civil or criminal) in proceedings instituted otherwise than under this Act.'

These proceedings were by way of a civil action for nuisance. To deny the plaintiff a remedy in damages because his abstraction of water was prohibited by s 23 would be to run counter to the provision of s 135(8). The intention of Parliament appears to have been to leave the enforcement of the restrictions imposed by the Act entirely to the river authority concerned, leaving the rights of individuals as between themselves unchanged. It follows in my judgment that the award of £50 damages should stand. This may seem a strange result but I cannot find any other way of construing the Act.

BRANDON LJ. I agree in general with the judgment of Templeman LJ. With regard to the issue of damages, however, I agree with the different view expressed by Lawton LJ and with the reasons given by him for that view.

Appeal allowed to extent that the injunction ordered by the deputy judge be discharged. Declaration that the plaintiff is entitled to an easement to take water from Mill Pond for the farming purposes of Grove Farm and that he is only entitled to exercise that easement subject to his obtaining a licence under the Water Resources Act 1963. Remainder of appeal dismissed. Leave to appeal to the House of Lords refused.

Solicitors: *Collissons,* agents for *Keefe, Forman & Co,* Norwich (for the defendant); *Daynes, Chittock & Back,* Norwich (for the plaintiff).

Mary Rose Plummer   Barrister.

Stafford and another v Conti Commodity Services Ltd

QUEEN'S BENCH DIVISION (COMMERCIAL COURT)

MOCATTA J

13th, 14th, 15th, 16th, 17th, 20th, 21st, 22nd, 23rd OCTOBER 1980

Negligence – Professional person – Duty to exercise reasonable skill and care – Broker on commodities market – Broker carrying out 46 transactions for investor – Broker giving advice to investor but investor usually making own decision in regard to transactions – Transactions resulting in substantial losses – Whether broker negligent having regard to unpredictable nature of commodities market – Whether error of judgment amounting to negligence – Whether fact of losses establishing negligence by virtue of doctrine of res ipsa loquitur.

The plaintiff, an investor on the London commodities futures market, after discussions with the defendants, who were well-known brokers dealing on the market, gave them a substantial sum to invest on the market. There was no written agreement between the parties. Between January and August 1976 the defendants carried out 46 transactions on the market for the plaintiff. The defendants gave the plaintiff advice and brought to his notice different points of view regarding a proposed transaction but the plaintiff usually made his own decision and often rejected the defendants' advice. The commodities market was an unpredictable and rapidly changing market. The 46 transactions resulted in a loss of over £19,000, only ten of the transactions making a profit for the plaintiff. He brought an action for damages against the defendants alleging that in breach of the oral agreement between the parties they had negligently failed properly to advise on and handle the transactions. In the particulars of the claim the plaintiff relied on the losses incurred and the failure to realise profits as showing that there had been failure to exercise due care and diligence and thus, in effect, relied on the doctrine of res ipsa loquitur as establishing negligence.

Held – The action would be dismissed for the following reasons—

(1) An error of judgment in giving advice on the part of a broker dealing on an unpredictable market like the commodities market would not necessarily be negligence since, in relation to such a market, the broker could not always give correct advice. Furthermore, it would require very strong evidence to establish negligence against a broker on the commodities market in relation to an individual transaction. But, in any event, since the plaintiff usually made his own decisions, it was impossible to say that the losses had been caused by the defendants' bad advice (see p 697 *a b* and p 698 *f*, post); *Whitehouse v Jordan* [1980] 1 All ER 650 applied.

(2) Furthermore, losses made on such an unpredictable market as the commodities market could not of themselves provide evidence of negligence on the part of a broker, even if he had advised on both the purchase and sale in a transaction which produced a loss. Moreover, in the circumstances the transactions were not under the management of the defendants or their servants because the plaintiff often made his own decisions. It followed that the doctrine of res ipsa loquitur did not apply (see p 697 *c* and p 698 *d e*, post); dictum of Erle CJ in *Scott v London and St Katherine Docks Co* [1861–73] All ER Rep at 248 applied.

Notes

For the standard of care required in professions of particular skill, see 34 Halsbury's Laws (4th Edn) para 12, and for cases on the subject, see 36(1) Digest 49–50, 149–158.

Cases referred to in judgment

Hedley Byrne & Co Ltd v Heller & Partners Ltd [1963] 2 All ER 575, [1964] AC 465, [1963]
   3 WLR 101, [1963] 1 Lloyd's Rep 485, HL, 36(1) Digest (Reissue) 24, 84.
Scott v London and St Katherine Docks Co (1865) 3 H & C 596, 5 New Rep 420, [1861–73]
   All ER Rep 246, 34 LJ Ex 220, 13 LT 148, 11 Jur NS 204, 159 ER 665, 36(1) Digest
   (Reissue) 232, 916.
Whitehouse v Jordan [1980] 1 All ER 650, CA; *affd* p 267, ante, HL.

Action

By a writ issued on 7th July 1977 the plaintiffs, Patrick Joseph Stafford and Comstock
Ltd, claimed against the defendants, Conti Commodity Services Ltd, brokers dealing on
the London commodities futures markets, (inter alia) damages for negligence in failing
properly to handle the plaintiffs' investments on the London commodities market. The
facts are set out in the judgment.

Timothy W Sewell for the plaintiffs.
Angus Glennie for the defendants.

MOCATTA J. This is a somewhat unusual case of an investor in the commodities
future market suing his brokers for large sums of money.

The claim falls into two main parts. In the first case negligence against the defendants
is alleged by the plaintiffs, whether in contract or in tort, in relation to 46 transactions
opened and closed which, between January and August 1976, resulted in the loss of over
£19,000. The second part has to be divided into two halves; both concern actions taken
by the defendants allegedly without any authority from the plaintiffs. The first half
concerns the opening and closing of 14 transactions without any authority from the
plaintiffs, leading to a loss claimed at £8,314·75, and the second half of this part of the
case deals with the closing of 7 transactions without authority from the plaintiffs, leading
to total losses of something over £40,000. The transactions in the second part of the case
are all included in the 46 transactions in respect of which negligence is claimed under the
first part of the case.

It is agreed that the defendants had no authority to open or close transactions without
the plaintiffs' consent save only that the plaintiffs rely on two forms of stop loss agreement
under which the defendants, without specific authorisation, could sell or buy under
certain circumstances; indeed, were obliged to as a result of the agreement alleged. The
defendants deny ever having acted without the plaintiffs' authority. They further deny
that they entered into either form of stop loss agreement.

Although the arguments and evidence about the stop loss agreements took a
considerable time, in fact they turned out in the end not to be very material to the claim,
though the evidence about them may be of importance on the question of credibility.

Outstanding features of the case are that, first, there was no agreement in writing
between the parties setting out the terms on which trading was to take place by the
defendants on behalf of the plaintiffs. Second, there were no complaints in writing, at
any time, of the action taken by the brokers, or for that matter their inaction, despite the
fact that confirmation slips or contract notes were sent by the defendants to the plaintiffs
after each transaction. Third, there is nothing whatever in a short but careful solicitors'
correspondence before trial relating to a charge that the defendants at any time acted
without authority.

The first part of the case is covered in para 3 of the points of claim, which alleges that:

> 'The Defendants negligently and in breach of the said agreement failed properly
> to advise and handle the Plaintiffs' investments on the London Commodity Market,
> or at all, whereby the Plaintiffs suffered a loss of [as it was then put] £20,291·68p.'

The particulars were ultimately amended and agreed between the parties and amounted

in all to 46 items. When I say an item I mean the opening of a transaction and the closing
a of a transaction. The exact total of losses was £19,262·57.

The allegations in the second part of the case are contained in paras 4 and 5 of the
points of claim. Paragraph 4 alleges that 14 of the transactions listed in the particulars of
para 3 were both opened and closed without the knowledge or consent of the plaintiffs.
As regards para 5, this substantially alleges premature sales of transactions without
authority resulting in losses in the large sum I have already mentioned although the
b opening of these transactions was obviously well founded because, had they not been
closed as they were, large profits would have been made.

I should now give a very short description of the parties and of the chronology. There
are two plaintiffs in the case: Mr Stafford, the first plaintiff, and a company called
Comstock Ltd, the second plaintiff. Mr Stafford appeared to be a man, possibly in his
early forties, who was a name at Lloyd's and who had indulged in investment on the
c commodities futures market prior to coming into contact with the defendants. Those
dealings had been done through a local Dublin broker (Mr Stafford lives in Dublin). The
local broker had passed on Mr Stafford's orders to commodity brokers in London. The
plaintiff company is a company registered in Gibraltar, owned, to all intents and purposes,
by Mr Stafford and used by him in connection with his deals on the commodities futures
market. In future I will regard the two plaintiffs as one and will merely refer to them as
d 'the plaintiff'.

The defendants are a well-known company of brokers dealing on the commodities
futures markets. They are a subsidiary of the large Chicago firm, Continental Grain
Inc. The individual in their office in London who had most to do with the facts of this
case was a Mr Dobell; he was one of quite a number of persons, employed by the
defendants, called account executives. The managing director of the defendants' firm
e was a Mr Shama, who gave evidence. There were one or two directors, one of whom, Mr
Freemantle, is mentioned from time to time in the evidence though he was not called as
a witness.

Mr Dobell, in describing what his duties were and those of the defendants, his
employers, said that the defendants are commodities futures brokers looking after clients
who wished to invest money in the commodities futures markets and accepting orders
f from clients. A broker gives advice if asked for it but always with the reserve that he
does not know the answers.

The parties came into contact with each other because the defendants advertised in the
press. Mr Stafford saw their advertisement and read one of the publications which he
thought was an impressive analysis in depth on the subject under discussion. The result
of this was that there was an interview in London, either in November or December
g 1975, when Mr Stafford came over from Dublin and saw Mr Dobell. They had a
considerable discussion about trading in the commodities markets. The result of this
meeting, and on the evidence there was a little uncertainty whether there was a second
meeting, was that on 6th January 1976 Mr Stafford sent to Mr Dobell a cheque for
£10,000 to fund initial deals. Dealings then began. Indeed the first transaction was
opened on that very date, 6th January.

h They continued with considerable frequency until 18th May before there was a
pause. This arose from the fact, as I read the correspondence, that the funds available to
the defendants, belonging to the plaintiff, were running out or had run out. There is a
letter of 18th May from Mr Freemantle to Mr Stafford in which he says that he
understands from Mr Dobell that Mr Stafford was not prepared to remit further funds to
cover his open position in sugar and accordingly that had been liquidated. The letter
added: 'When the metal positions have reached maturity and are closed, you will find
j your account is in deficit.' The deficit was a very small one. It was notified to the
plaintiff by a letter, again from Mr Freemantle, of 11th June, saying that there was a debit
balance of £249·73 for which the defendants would appreciate the plaintiff's remittance.

Mr Stafford visited London on 8th July. He says that he made complaints then to Mr
Dobell about how his account had been managed and what Mr Dobell had been doing.

Mr Dobell did not agree with the plaintiff's version but quite apart from that, there was a problem in as much as there was prevailing at that time a strike in the Irish banks. The result was that if a debtor gave a creditor a cheque on an Irish bank the creditor could not clear the cheque pending the termination of the strike. I think that what happened was that on 8th July it had been decided by the defendants to give the plaintiff extended credit owing to the strike affecting the banks in Ireland. They typed out a letter, addressed to the defendants, for signature by Mr Stafford who signed that letter. In it he undertook to pay the defendants '. . . on demand all sums of money owing for margins, deposits or losses outstanding on my account as soon as banking facilities permit . . .'

Although, I suppose, it is possible to argue as to the true construction of that letter, that is to say whether it only applied to past transactions or whether it applied to future transactions, the letter seems to have been acted on on the basis that it applied to both and it was apparently extending unlimited credit to Mr Stafford. There was considerable confusion in the evidence about whether or not Mr Stafford gave, at that time, a cheque to the defendants which they were unable to use owing to the strike but locked away in their safe until the strike should be over or whether there was nothing save this letter of 8th July, signed by Mr Stafford, to support the extended credit given by the defendants. Mr Shama, the managing director, who had to approve the giving of credit, thought, though he was not certain about it after this interval of time, that a cheque was given and so did the defendants' accountant, a Mr Kundi. The matter is not of any very great importance. Thus, consequent on the granting of credit on those terms further dealings took place beginning on 8th July and continuing until 23rd August.

There is no doubt that Mr Stafford visited London on 27th September. There is clearly no doubt that he then saw Mr Shama and that he paid two cheques to the defendants, one of £6,500 on that date and one for £5,000 on 5th October. Those two cheques put him, at that time, in credit to the figure of £2,237·43. He then agreed with Mr Shama that Mr Shama might operate a discretionary account in his name with that money. Mr Shama did so and between 8th November 1976 when Mr Stafford signed a power of attorney and indemnity in favour of Mr Shama, and May 1977 Mr Shama made a profit on behalf of Mr Stafford, after deducting commission, of £1,948. He was thus able to return that sum, plus the £2,000 odd that I have already mentioned, to Mr Stafford at the closing of the discretionary account. So much for the chronology of what occurred.

Returning to the original meeting between Mr Stafford and Mr Dobell, Mr Stafford said, and I have no doubt that he was correct in this, that there was a wide discussion about various subjects in connection with dealing in futures on the commodity markets. It was recognised by Mr Stafford that the market was subject to very wide fluctuations. He accordingly suggested to Mr Dobell that it was important to have a stop loss provision of 10% to limit losses and also what was described, in short, as a 'trading' stop loss position involving the stop loss going up with the price of a commodity if the price did rise after purchase and then, if the price turned and fell, the stop loss would apply when the fall amounted to 10%.

It is perhaps of some significance that what I have called the 'trading' part of this suggested stop loss arrangement only appeared in para 2 of the points of claim when they were first amended. Originally that paragraph read:

> 'It was an express term of the agreement that the Defendants would not buy or sell any commodities on behalf of the Plaintiffs without [Mr Stafford's] prior approval. It was also an express term of the agreement that if the value of the commodity purchased dropped by 10% the commodity would be sold, thus limiting any loss to 10% on each transaction.'

When the points of claim were amended the latter part of that paragraph was altered to read:

> '. . . it was also an express term of the said agreement that if the value of a commodity purchased dropped by 10 per cent of its purchase price or having risen in value thereafter dropped by 10 per cent of that greater value that commodity

would be sold without further instructions, thus limiting any loss to 10 per cent of the original purchase price of the commodity comprised in each transaction.'

Whilst Mr Dobell was prepared to accept that there was mention of 10% as a figure to have regard to in relation to limiting losses as a result of fluctuations in the market, he strongly denied that there was any such agreement as regards stop losses in either form. That is either in a direct form or in the form of a trading stop loss agreement. Mr Dobell explained that the defendant company did make available to its clients a limited stop loss system of the direct type. He produced a form called an 'open order notice' which stated:

'We have this day entered in accordance with your instructions the following order for your account and risk. This order will be effective through the last business day of the current month unless it has been previously executed or cancelled by you.'

If filled in that form would indicate that a commodity was to be bought or sold at a particular figure, not at a percentage of some figure. The open order notice could be limited in its duration, it could not extend for more than a month without being renewed, but within a month it could either be for a specific period or 'good until cancelled'.

As regards the suggestion that there was an agreement that a stop loss arrangement should be operated on a percentage basis, Mr Dobell's evidence was that such a basis was impracticable and was never adopted. It involved the constant recalculation, having regard to the current price of the particular commodity, at any one moment during the course of the trading day. It also involved problems in connection with the limitations that different markets had on the size of fluctuations which were permitted. When I say that what I mean is that in one market it was not possible to deal at a figure of a fraction of a pound lower than a half and in another market it was possible to deal in pounds and 25p or quarters of a pound. A rigid application of the 10% rule would clearly not fit in with those market limitations. Apart from that matter Mr Dobell's evidence was that if a stop loss agreement was entered into on a percentage basis it afforded a dangerous opportunity in a violently changing market for a trader to challenge the brokers' conduct.

Mr Shama, the managing director, gave evidence about this, although he did not have any conversation about it with the plaintiff. Mr Shama was an impressive witness. He said that he did not think anybody on the floor of any of the exchanges would handle a stop loss order expressed as a percentage, quite apart from the minimum fluctuations varying between one market and another depending on the commodity, of 50p or 25p as already mentioned. He took as an example the price of cocoa at the time that he was giving evidence. He said that its price was then, per lot, £1,055·50. Of course it might not remain at that figure for more than a minute or two and no one would welcome having to calculate what 10% of that was and take the necessary action if the price had fallen by 10%. As regards a trading stop loss policy the position in practice would have been far more difficult because the order to the floor broker would have had to change constantly according to the movement of prices in the market and indeed it would, as Mr Shama put it, really involve having one man on the floor for every contract entered into by a client.

The practical probabilities therefore are strongly against Mr Stafford's evidence that there was any agreement about stop loss in either of the two forms mentioned, and I accept Mr Dobell's evidence that he never agreed to either form of stop loss policy. I would add that Mr Stafford did not avail himself of the stop loss facilities which the defendants were prepared to offer their clients by using the open notice which I have already mentioned.

As I have said earlier the existence or non-existence of either form of stop loss agreement is not of great moment to this case because probably only two transactions would have come within the scope of either form of stop loss agreement had there been one. The matter, however, does throw some light on the credibility of the witnesses. Save for any freedom or obligation on the broker to act under a stop loss agreement without consulting Mr Stafford, it is common ground that the defendants had no authority to buy or sell without his consent in the type of account which he was opening with them. There is, in fact, another type of account, called a discretionary account, under which the broker can act without reference to his client. It was that type of account, already mentioned, that Mr Shama operated, with some success, on behalf of Mr Stafford towards the end of 1976, and which was closed in May 1977 and achieved a modest profit of £1,948.

[His Lordship then reviewed the evidence regarding the 46 transactions and stated that it was important that it was common ground that confirmations or contract notes in respect of all 46 transactions were sent by the defendants to Mr Stafford and were received by Mr Stafford. It was also important that there were no written complaints by Mr Stafford to the defendants regarding the transactions and no mention in the plaintiff's solicitors' letters before action that the defendants had acted without authority. His Lordship continued:]

The plaintiff's case therefore fails on the allegations of acting without authority, that is to say the claims under paras 4 and 5 of the points of claim. That makes it unnecessary to consider the point of ratification made by counsel for the defendants based on the fact that the plaintiff paid all the amounts due on 27th September and 5th October and by doing so, with full knowledge of the transactions which Mr Dobell had carried out on his behalf, he impliedly ratified Mr Dobell's acts if they had been unauthorised originally. I doubt that there is very much to be said for the arguments for ratification were it necessary to go into them. Various schedules were put in about the question of what damages would be recoverable under paras 4 and 5 were I in the plaintiff's favour on the basis of fact. I need not go into these since I have held against him on the facts.

I now turn to the claim of negligence which occupied much less than half of the time of the action both as regards evidence and argument. The plaintiff, in the points of claim in para 3, alleges that:

'The Defendants negligently and in breach of the said agreement failed properly to advise and handle the Plaintiffs' investments . . .'

The plaintiff was asked for further and better particulars of this, stating:

'Of "the Defendants' negligence" . . . (1) Precisely the nature of the duty alleged and all facts and matters relied on as giving rise to such a duty, and (2) In relation to each of the transactions set out under the heading "Particulars", [in paragraph 3] in precisely what respects it is alleged in each case that the Defendants were in breach of any such duty.'

The answer given to that request for further and better particulars was:

'The Plaintiffs will rely upon the losses incurred in the said transactions and the failure to realise prospective profits therein as showing that the Defendants failed to exercise due care and diligence in the conduct of the Plaintiffs' affairs, and in particular to carry out its instructions under the agreement.'

In other words the plaintiffs were relying on res ipsa loquitur.

I think that counsel for the defendants was correct in submitting that this was a very strange allegation to make in relation to a notoriously wayward and erratic commodities futures market. The duty of the defendants was not in dispute between the parties. Counsel on both sides were prepared to accept what was said in Charlesworth on Negligence (6th Edn, 1977, para 1021) in relation to the liability of stockbrokers who, in this respect, it was agreed did not differ from commodity brokers:

'With regard to the customer, a stockbroker's duty lies in contract and not in tort and stockbrokers are liable for failing to use that skill and diligence which a reasonably competent and careful stockbroker would exercise.'

The paragraph continues that the principle in *Hedley Byrne & Co Ltd v Heller & Partners*

Ltd [1963] 2 All ER 575, [1964] AC 465 would apply were there no contract and were a
stockbroker negligently to give advice.

Counsel for the defendants submitted, plainly rightly in my judgment, that a broker
cannot always be right in the advice that he gives in relation to so wayward and rapidly
changing a market as the commodities futures market. An error of judgment, if there
be an error of judgment, is not necessarily negligent any more than has recently been
said in relation to an obstetrician in a very important case recently decided by the Court
of Appeal (*Whitehouse v Jordan* [1980] 1 All ER 650) which is now on its way up to the
House of Lords [see p 267, ante]. Furthermore, what is stated in that case is that the
hazards of childbirth are such that the fact that a child eventually is brought into this
world suffering from infirmities cannot by itself be relied on on the basis of the maxim
of res ipsa loquitur. Similarly, losses made on the commodity market do not of
themselves, in my judgment, provide evidence of negligence on the part of a broker,
even if he advised both parts of the particular transaction which produced the loss.

The plaintiff's case based on res ipsa loquitur is that there were 46 transactions over
eight months of which only 10 were profitable. In relation to the doctrine of res ipsa
loquitur, which was, in fact, what counsel for the plaintiff was obliged to rely on, counsel
for the defendants referred to Charlesworth on Negligence (6th Edn, 1977, para 268) and
the quotation in that paragraph, from Erle CJ, in the well-known case of *Scott v London
and St Katherine Docks Co* (1865) 3 H & C 596 at 600, [1861-73] All ER Rep 246 at 248 in
the following terms:

> 'There must be reasonable evidence of negligence. But, where the thing is shown
> to be under the management of the defendant, or his servants, and the accident is
> such as, in the ordinary course of things, does not happen if those who have the
> management use proper care, it affords reasonable evidence, in the absence of
> explanation by the defendant, that the accident arose from want of care.'

Counsel for the defendants submitted that neither of those principles really applied
here because the loss was not wholly under the control of the brokers. Mr Dobell
undoubtedly gave advice and expressed a wide range of views on the subject of various
different commodities but Mr Stafford had views of his own. According to Mr Dobell he
was impulsive and required holding back. Mr Stafford's own evidence as regards his
previous brokers in Dublin was that those brokers, or their London principals, would
make suggestions to him which he would either accept or reject. On this matter, about
the advice Mr Dobell gave and whether it was accepted or not, Mr Dobell said:
'Sometimes he followed my advice, sometimes he did not. I would say he did sometimes
do something contrary to my advice without any question', and then he went on to say
that on this account one had to hold him back rather than encourage him. He said later
on, particularly in relation I think to a transaction where, according to Mr Stafford, the
purchase was sanctioned by him but the sale was not, that he made the decision himself,
and he got advice not only from Mr Dobell but from other brokers. That Mr Dobell
knew because Mr Stafford made no secret of it. When counsel for the plaintiff put the
whole list to Mr Dobell, Mr Dobell said: 'I would say the result of his trading showed he
acted against my advice during the whole period though not, of course, on every single
transaction.' He continued, when he was being cross-examined on this particular topic,
that Mr Stafford did talk to other colleagues of Mr Dobell's as well as to other brokers and
that he spoke to Mr Dobell about four or five times a day. He was very strong on his own
ideas and what he wanted to do. Mr Dobell did not accept that Mr Stafford would not
enter into a transaction contrary to Mr Dobell's advice. Mr Dobell said: 'I say the account
acted badly because he took wrong decisions as to my advice and the advice he received
from others.' He accepted what counsel for the plaintiff put to him that had Mr Stafford
acted solely on Mr Dobell's advice throughout the period he would not have done so
badly as he did. His experience was that what happened in this case did not happen
during a period of six to eight months if a client acted on Mr Dobell's advice. Finally, in
re-examination, Mr Dobell said: 'You put all the points of view to the client; say it is

always a decision by the client and he would pick one of the views preferred. I might indicate my own preference.'

Counsel for the defendants referred to two specific examples of Mr Stafford acting contrary to Mr Dobell's advice. The first concerned items 7, 9 and 11 which were opened on Mr Dobell's advice; they related to silver and they were sales. But the decision to close the account when the price of silver went up and not down was Mr Stafford's decision, not Mr Dobell's. Mr Dobell's advice was to wait, though of course he admitted this might be wrong, but Mr Stafford wished to sell and so he did. Another example given concerned items 32 and 34, where Mr Stafford insisted on selling the sugar he purchased contrary to the advice given by the defendants. Accordingly, counsel for the defendants submitted, quite apart from any question of authority or guidance that can be obtained from reading the latest judgment in the Court of Appeal now going to the House of Lords in *Whitehouse v Jordan*, the position is not the type of situation to which the doctrine of res ipsa loquitur applies, for two reasons. First, the matter in question was not under the management of the defendant or his servants, to use the words of Erle CJ (in *Scott v London and St Katherine Docks Co* (1865) 3 H & C 596, [1861–73] All ER Rep 246), because Mr Stafford constantly made his own decisions. Second, losses in the ordinary course of things do occur even if proper care is used when one is dealing with transactions on the commodities futures market. It is quite impossible to say that the losses here were, on the evidence before me, caused by bad advice given by Mr Dobell inasmuch as so many decisions were Mr Stafford's. That Mr Dobell brought to Mr Stafford's notice various different opinions and would not hide from him any facts which he was able to obtain in relation to any of these particular commodities I am satisfied. I am also satisfied that with the best advice in the world, in such an unpredictable market as this, it would require exceedingly strong evidence from expert brokers in relation to individual transactions to establish negligence on the part of the defendants. Such negligence cannot, in my judgment, be established merely by relying on the doctrine of res ipsa loquitur which, in my judgment, has no application to the facts of this case.

If, in answer to the particulars requested the plaintiff had pointed out a number of transactions in which Mr Dobell had given advice which had turned out badly, it might have been possible for the defendants to have called evidence showing that other experienced and careful brokers would have given similar advice at the time. The fact that it turned out to be wrong would be no evidence that such persons were negligent. Accordingly, in my judgment, the plaintiff fails on the first part of his case as well as on the second part and the action is dismissed with costs.

Judgment for the defendants.

Solicitors: *Elborne, Mitchell & Co* (for the plaintiffs); *Thomas Cooper & Stibbard* (for the defendants).

K Mydeen Esq   Barrister.

Podbery v Peak and another

COURT OF APPEAL, CIVIL DIVISION
BUCKLEY, EVELEIGH AND OLIVER LJJ
10th NOVEMBER, 19th DECEMBER 1980

Court of Appeal – Jurisdiction – Appeal from Divisional Court – Bankruptcy proceedings – Appeal against refusal of Divisional Court to extend time for appealing from county court – Whether Divisional Court's refusal to extend time for appeal a 'decision' or 'order' – Whether Court of Appeal having jurisdiction to hear appeal against Divisional Court's refusal to extend time – Bankruptcy Act 1914, s 108(2) – Supreme Court of Judicature (Consolidation) Act 1925, s 27(1) – RSC Ord 3, r 5.

An order was made in the county court on the application of the trustee in bankruptcy of the husband for the sale of a house which was jointly owned by the husband and the wife. The time limit for appealing against that order having expired, the wife applied to the Divisional Court for an extension of time in which to appeal. The Divisional Court refused her application and she appealed to the Court of Appeal against that refusal. At the Court of Appeal hearing the question arose whether the Court of Appeal had jurisdiction to entertain an appeal against the refusal of the Divisional Court to extend the time for an appeal in bankruptcy proceedings from the county court. The wife contended (i) that RSC Ord 3, r 5ª by which the 'court may . . . extend the period within which a person is required . . . to do any act' gave the Court of Appeal jurisdiction, (ii) that the Divisional Court's refusal was a 'decision of the divisional court upon [an] appeal' within s 108(2)(a)ᵇ of the Bankruptcy Act 1914 and that therefore the Court of Appeal could give special leave to appeal, and (iii) that the Divisional Court's refusal was an 'order . . . made by the High Court' (and not an order on appeal from a county court) and as such there was a direct right of appeal to the Court of Appeal under s 108(2)(b) of the 1914 Act or s 27(1)ᶜ of the Supreme Court of Judicature (Consolidation) Act 1925.

Held – The appeal would be dismissed for the following reasons—

(1) The Court of Appeal did not have an original jurisdiction under RSC Ord 3, r 5 to extend the time for appealing to the Divisional Court since the Court of Appeal's power to extend time given by that rule applied only in relation to its own proceedings. Although the Court of Appeal did on occasion extend the time for proceedings in the High Court that resulted from a true exercise of its appellate jurisdiction, since once it had jurisdiction to hear and determine an appeal it was then empowered by s 27(1) of the 1925 Act to exercise the jurisdiction of the High Court. However an application for leave to appeal was not an appeal (see p 701 *f* to *j* and p 702 *a*, post).

(2) The Court of Appeal also had no jurisdiction under s 108(2)(a) of the 1914 Act to entertain the appeal because a refusal by the Divisional Court to extend the time for an appeal was not a 'decision . . . upon [an] appeal' for the purposes of s 108(2)(a), since a decision on an appeal only resulted if an appeal had been heard, and because the wife had been refused an extension of time it followed that no appeal had been heard (see p 701 *j* to p 702 *b* and p 703 *d*, post); *Re a debtor (No 20 of 1910)* [1911] 1 KB 841 considered.

(3) Nor did the Court of Appeal have jurisdiction under s 27(1) of the 1925 Act or s 108(2)(b) of the 1914 Act because the Divisional Court's refusal to extend the time was not an 'order' of the High Court for the purposes of either section; but even if it was there was no jurisdiction under s 108(2)(b) because it was an order on appeal from a county

---

a   Rule 5, so far as material, is set out at p 701 *d e*, post
b   Section 108(2) is set out at p 701 *a b*, post
c   Section 27(1), so far as material, is set out at p 701 *g h*, post

court and therefore excepted from the Court of Appeal's jurisdiction by s 108(2)(b) (see p 702 b, p 703 d e h and p 704 f to h, post); *Lane v Esdaile* [1891] AC 210 followed.

Notes

For appeals in bankruptcy matters from county courts, see 3 Halsbury's Laws (4th Edn) para 944, and for appeals from High Court judgments and orders in bankruptcy, see ibid para 945.

For the Bankruptcy Act 1914, s 108, see 3 Halsbury's Statutes (3rd Edn) 134.

For the Supreme Court of Judicature (Consolidation) Act 1925, s 27, see 7 ibid 588.

Cases referred to in judgment

Debtor (No 20 of 1910), Re a [1911] 1 KB 841, 80 LJKB 508, 104 LT 233, 18 Mans 107, CA, 4 Digest (Reissue) 570, 5016.

Lane v Esdaile [1891] AC 210, 64 LT 666, sub nom *Payne v Esdaile* 60 LJ Ch 644, HL; *on appeal from* (1889) 40 Ch D 520, 58 LJ Ch 265, 59 LT 910, CA, 51 Digest (Repl) 808, 3642.

Appeal

Mavis Daisy Podbery ('the wife') appealed by leave of the Court of Appeal given on 3rd November 1980 against an order of the Divisional Court of the Chancery Division (Goulding and Browne-Wilkinson JJ) dated 23rd October 1980 dismissing her application for leave to appeal out of time to that court against an order made by his Honour Judge Clover QC in the Oxford County Court on 10th March 1980 on the application of the respondent, Michael Frederick Ronald Peak, the trustee in bankruptcy of Alan Spencer Podbery ('the husband'), by which the circuit judge ordered the sale of the property known as 3 Cumnor Road, Farmoor, Oxfordshire, jointly owned by the wife and the husband, but postponed the sale for three months from the date of the order. At the hearing of the appeal the question was raised whether the Court of Appeal had jurisdiction to entertain an appeal against a refusal of the Divisional Court to extend the time for appealing to it. The facts are set out in the judgment of the court.

Leo Curran for the wife.
Anthony Clover for the respondent.

Cur adv vult

19th December. **EVELEIGH LJ** read the following judgment of the court: On 10th March 1980, in the Oxford County Court on the application of the trustee in bankruptcy, his Honour Judge Clover QC made an order for the sale of the property known as 3 Cumnor Road, Farmoor, Oxfordshire, but postponed the sale for three months from the date of the order. The property was jointly owned by the bankrupt and his wife. No notice of appeal was served, but on 5th August 1980 the wife gave notice of her intention to apply to the Divisional Court for an extension of time in which to appeal. On 23rd October the Divisional Court refused the application. The wife now appeals against that refusal pursuant to leave of this court given on 3rd November.

At the hearing of this appeal argument was first directed to the question whether the court had jurisdiction to entertain an appeal against the refusal of the Divisional Court to extend the time for appealing to it from the county court. The application was also considered on its merits de bene esse, and we decided that we ought not to interfere with the discretion of the Divisional Court even if we had jurisdiction to do so. This judgment is concerned with the first point, namely the jurisdiction to entertain the appeal.

Section 108 of the Bankruptcy Act 1914 reads as follows:

'(1) Every court having jurisdiction in bankruptcy under this Act may review, rescind or vary any order made by it under its bankruptcy jurisdiction.

'(2) Orders in bankruptcy matters shall, at the instance of any person aggrieved, be subject to appeal as follows:—(a) Where the order is made by a county court, an appeal shall lie to a divisional court of the High Court, of which the judge to whom bankruptcy business is for the time being assigned shall, for the purpose of hearing any such appeal, be a member. The decision of the divisional court upon any such appeal shall be final and conclusive, unless in any case the divisional court or the Court of Appeal sees fit to give special leave to appeal therefrom to the Court of Appeal, whose decision in any such case shall be final and conclusive; (b) Where the order (not being an order on appeal from a county court) is made by the High Court, an appeal shall lie to the Court of Appeal, and an appeal shall, with the leave of the Court of Appeal, but not otherwise, lie from the order of that court to the House of Lords . . .'

Rule 132 of the Bankruptcy Rules 1952, SI 1952 No 2113, provides:

'Subject to the foregoing Rules, the Rules of the Supreme Court relating to appeals to the Court of Appeal shall apply to appeals to the Appellate Court as if the expression "Appellate Court" were substituted for the expression "Court of Appeal" wherever it occurs in those Rules.'

By virtue of RSC Ord 55, r 1(3) and Ord 59, r 4(1)(b) the time for appeal is 21 days. However Ord 3, r 5(1) provides:

'The Court may, on such terms as it thinks just, by order extend or abridge the period within which a person is required or authorised by these rules, or by any judgment, order or direction, to do any act in any proceedings.'

Order 3, r 5(4) reads: 'In this rule references to the Court shall be construed as including references to the Court of Appeal.' The appellate court in the present case being the Divisional Court by virtue of s 108(2)(a), that court will be substituted for the expression 'Court of Appeal' by virtue of r 132 of the Bankruptcy Rules 1952; and by the further cross-reference in Ord 3, r 5(4) the Divisional Court is given power to extend the time for appeal.

It has been submitted that the Court of Appeal under Ord 3, r 5 has an original jurisdiction to extend the time for appealing to the Divisional Court. We do not agree. Order 3, r 5(4) is intended to give the Court of Appeal power to extend time in relation to its own proceedings. The technique of drafting by cross-reference has been used, but this does not give the Court of Appeal the same original power as that of the court to which the reference has been made. It is true that the Court of Appeal does extend the time for proceedings in the High Court. This however results from a true exercise of its appellate jurisdiction.

Section 27(1) of the Supreme Court of Judicature (Consolidation) Act 1925 reads:

'Subject as otherwise provided in this Act and to rules of court, the Court of Appeal shall have jurisdiction to hear and determine appeals from any judgment or order of the High Court, and for all the purposes of and incidental to the hearing and determination of any appeal, and the amendment, execution and enforcement of any judgment or order made thereon, the Court of Appeal shall have all the power, authority and jurisdiction of the High Court . . .'

Once the Court of Appeal has jurisdiction to hear and determine an appeal, it may then by virtue of this subsection exercise the jurisdiction of the High Court.

It was also sought to establish jurisdiction by virtue of s 108(2)(a) of the Bankruptcy Act 1914 on the grounds that the Divisional Court's refusal to extend the time for appeal from the county court came within the words 'The decision of the divisional court upon . . . [an] appeal'. In our opinion the refusal was not a decision on an appeal. In s 108(2)(b) we find the expression 'not being an order on appeal from a county court'. This is significant. The expression 'an order on appeal' is apt to cover any order made in the course of an appeal. A 'decision . . . upon [an] appeal', however, results from an appeal having been heard. In the present case there has been no hearing of 'any such appeal' as sub-s (2)(*a*) refers to, namely an appeal from an order made by the county court. An application for leave is not an appeal.

It is then said that the case falls within s 108(2)(*b*). It is submitted that the refusal was not an order on appeal from a county court and consequently this appeal falls directly within the subsection. We will in a moment consider whether a refusal to extend time is an order. If it is, however, in our opinion it is an order on appeal from a county court. The contrast between the expression 'decision . . . upon [an] appeal' and 'order on appeal' indicates that the latter is dealing with an order which is in the course of being appealed or which it is sought to challenge by an appeal.

The effect of s 27 of the Supreme Court of Judicature (Consolidation) Act 1925 must be considered. If the refusal is an order of the High Court, in our opinion s 27 would give a right of appeal. In the course of argument reference was made to s 31(1)(*b*) of the 1925 Act. That provides that no appeal shall lie 'from an order allowing an extension of time for appealing from a judgment or order'. It is argued that an order extending the time is clearly an order of the court and is so recognised by the above subsection in that it has been found necessary specifically to exclude a right of appeal when time has been extended. It is said that on the other hand the refusal of an extension of time has not been excluded, and that therefore an appeal will lie.

We have been referred to *Re a debtor* (*No 20 of 1910*) [1911] 1 KB 841. The Divisional Court had granted the debtor an extension of time for appealing to the Divisional Court against a receiving order made by the registrar of the county court. The petitioning creditors sought the leave of the Divisional Court to appeal to the Court of Appeal against the order extending the time, but the Divisional Court refused. The Court of Appeal, however, gave leave to appeal against the order extending the time, but when the appeal against the order extending the time came on for hearing a preliminary objection was taken that under s 1(1)(*a*) of the Supreme Court of Judicature (Procedure) Act 1894 it was not competent to the Court of Appeal to entertain the appeal. That Act provided that no appeal should lie from an order allowing an extension of time for appealing from a judgment or order. It was argued that the Bankruptcy Rules provided a complete code for the regulation of appeals in bankruptcy and that the 1894 Act did not apply. The Court of Appeal held that it did and that consequently, although they had given leave to appeal, the appeal itself from the order extending the time had to be dismissed as there was no jurisdiction to entertain it. On the authority of that case it is argued that in granting leave the court must have regarded the order extending time as a decision on an appeal because the matter fell within s 2 of the Bankruptcy Appeals (County Courts) Act 1884 which was, with an insignificant difference, in the same terms as s 108(2)(*a*) of the Bankruptcy Act 1914. The order granting an extension of time was, it is said, regarded as a decision on an appeal and, while it was ultimately decided that the appeal was not competent, this was the effect of s 1(1)(*a*) of the Supreme Court of Judicature (Procedure) Act 1894, which denied an appeal against an order granting an extension of time. There is no similar provision, it is submitted, denying an appeal against a refusal to extend time.

There is no report giving the reason why the Court of Appeal in that case granted leave in the first place. One does not know whether the matter was fully argued. We suspect that it was not, because we would have expected the 1894 Act to have been brought to the attention of the court, and that of itself would have been conclusive against the grant of leave. A clue may be found why leave was granted in the judgment of Buckley LJ. There he says (at 844):

> 'The order under appeal is one allowing an extension of time for appealing. By s. 104 of the Bankruptcy Act, 1883, that order was made appealable, because that Act says in so many words "an appeal shall lie" from every order. Subsequently in 1894 was passed the Judicature Act of that year, which provides that no appeal shall

lie from an order allowing an extension of time for appealing from a judgment or order.'

It would seem that Buckley LJ had in mind the words of s 104(2)(a) of the Bankruptcy Act 1883 as giving jurisdiction to entertain an appeal because the order extending the time, as opposed to a refusal, is within those words. However, s 104(2)(a) of that Act no longer applied to bankruptcy appeals from the county court. It was repealed by s 2 of the Bankruptcy Appeals (County Courts) Act 1884, which substituted a section similar to s 108(2)(a) of the 1914 Act. It may also be that the Court of Appeal treated the extension of time as an order within s 19 of the Supreme Court of Judicature Act 1873, which is similar in its terms to s 27 of the Supreme Court of Judicature (Consolidation) Act 1925. We certainly would not regard the fact that leave was granted in the first instance as authority on the words 'decision . . . upon [an] appeal'. Even though Cozens-Hardy MR does refer to s 2 of the Bankruptcy Appeals (County Courts) Act 1884, he does not consider whether a refusal of an extension of time is a decision on an appeal. We feel confident that the matter could not have been fully argued before the court until the hearing at which the preliminary objection was raised giving rise to the decision to which we have referred. Indeed, it was not argued before this court when leave was given. We therefore feel free to consider the meaning of 'decision . . . upon any such appeal' unaided by authority and conclude that it does not embrace a refusal of extension of time.

There remains, therefore, the question whether the refusal is an order of the court so that a right of appeal will exist by virtue of s 27(1) of the Supreme Court of Judicature (Consolidation) Act 1925. In our opinion, while various rulings of the court in interlocutory proceedings may be loosely called orders of the court, we do not think that the refusal of an extension of time is an order within the meaning of s 27. *Lane v Esdaile* [1891] AC 210 establishes this.

That case was concerned with RSC 1883, Ord 58, r 15 which provided:

'No appeal to the Court of Appeal from any interlocutory order, . . . shall, except by special leave of the Court of Appeal, be brought after the expiration of 21 days, and no other appeal shall, except by such leave, be brought after the expiration of one year.'

The Court of Appeal refused an application for special leave, 'making no order' (see (1888) 40 Ch D 520). The appellants appealed to the House of Lords. Section 3 of the Appellate Jurisdiction Act 1876 reads:

'Subject as in this Act mentioned an appeal shall lie to the House of Lords from any order or judgment of any of the courts following; that is to say, (1) Of Her Majesty's Court of Appeal in England; and (2) Of any Court in Scotland from which error or an appeal at or immediately before the commencement of this Act lay to the House of Lords by common law or by statute; and (3) Of any Court in Ireland from which error or an appeal at or immediately before the commencement of this Act lay to the House of Lords by common law or by statute.'

For the purpose of the present case we can see no material difference between those words and the words of s 27 of the Supreme Court of Judicature (Consolidation) Act 1925. The House of Lords dismissed the appeal, saying that the refusal to grant leave was not an order or judgment within the meaning of the Act. Lord Halsbury LC said ([1891] AC 210 at 211):

'The words used are "leave of the Court"; and although it may be that in some sense leave of the Court, whether it is given or withheld, becomes an order (that I will not stay to discuss), that is not the ordinary mode in which it would be described. It is to be something that is done by the order of the Court.'

Lord Herschel said (at 214):

'But then it was thought that there might be special circumstances in which the Court of Appeal might relax that rule and consider that, notwithstanding it, an appeal should be permitted. I think that the matter was intrusted, and intended to be intrusted, to their discretion; and that the exercise of a discretion of that sort intrusted to them is not, within the true meaning of the Appellate Jurisdiction Act, an order or judgment from which there can be an appeal.'

The House of Lords expressed the opinion that a limitation of time had been placed on the right of appeal so that a party might safely rely on the judgment and that there should not be an appeal after the time had expired, unless the Court of Appeal itself should permit an appeal to the House of Lords. Lord Halsbury LC said (at 212):

'Now just let us consider what that means, that an appeal shall not be given unless some particular body consents to its being given. Surely if that is intended as a check to unnecessary or frivolous appeals it becomes absolutely illusory if you can appeal from that decision or leave or whatever it is to be called itself. How could any Court of Review determine whether leave ought to be given or not without hearing and determining upon the hearing whether it was a fit case for an appeal? And if the intermediate court could enter and must enter upon that question, then the court which is the ultimate court of appeal must do so also.'

He went on to say that the result would be that the House of Lords would find itself considering the merits of an appeal in order to determine whether leave should have been granted when the intention of the legislature was to impose a check on appeals by requiring the leave of the Court of Appeal before the case could go to the House of Lords. Lord Field said (at 216):

'It seems to me that if your Lordships were to say now "We will give leave" and the Court of Appeal must enforce that, it would be imposing upon them the duty of giving a leave, as their leave, which they in their own judgment think ought not to be given.'

In our opinion the reasoning in that case applies mutatis mutandis to an appeal to the Court of Appeal against a refusal of the High Court to extend time. Although the present position is governed by RSC Ord 59, r 3(5), we do not think, in the way in which the time limit is today imposed by the Rules of the Supreme Court and the power to extend the time is now worded, that there is any material difference for the purpose of the present case between the relevant Rules of the Supreme Court with which we are concerned and RSC 1883, Ord 58, r 15.

When the time for appeal expires, there is an obstacle to the right of appeal which must be decisive unless the court orders its removal by extending the time. An extension of time involves a positive order of the court. It is not surprising, therefore, that the legislature should regard it as necessary to make specific reference to it when it decided that there should be no appeal against such an order. The fact that no mention is made of a decision to refuse an extension of time is explicable on the basis that such a refusal is not considered to be an order, and consequently does not come within s 27 at all.

Appeal dismissed.

Solicitors: *Darby & Son*, Oxford (for the wife); *Bower & Bowerman*, Bicester (for the respondent).

Mary Rose Plummer   Barrister.

Landau and another v Sloane

HOUSE OF LORDS

LORD WILBERFORCE, LORD FRASER OF TULLYBELTON, LORD RUSSELL OF KILLOWEN, LORD KEITH OF KINKEL AND LORD ROSKILL

21st, 22nd JANUARY, 19th FEBRUARY 1981

Rent restriction — Resident landlord — Death of landlord or transfer of landlord's interest inter vivos — Transitional period — Tenant having security of tenure during transitional period — Nature of tenancy at expiration of transitional period — Effect of notice to quit served and expiring during transitional period — Rent Act 1977, s 12(1), Sch 2, paras 1, 3.

In March 1978 a landlord let rooms on the ground floor of her house to a tenant on a weekly tenancy. By virtue of the Rent Act 1977, the tenancy was not a protected tenancy during the landlady's lifetime because she was a resident landlord. The landlady died on 11th August 1978 and her interest in the premises passed to her personal representatives. By para 1[a] of Sch 2 to the 1977 Act personal representatives were given a year ('the transitional period') during which they could leave a property without a resident landlord and not thereby break the condition as to continuity of residence. The landlady's personal representatives did not move in a new resident landlord during the year following her death but instead on 17th December 1978 served on the tenant a notice to quit which expired on 4th July 1979. The tenant refused to give up possession either on 4th July 1979 or on 11th August 1979 when the transitional period came to an end. The personal representatives applied to the court on 19th July 1979 for an order for possession. The tenant claimed that, as the personal representatives had not moved in a resident landlord during the transitional period, she had security of tenure because on 11th August 1979 she would become a statutory tenant within the meaning of the 1977 Act. On 7th November 1979 the judge made the possession order on the grounds that once the tenant's contractual tenancy had been determined on the expiry of the notice to quit she had ceased to be a tenant and had become a trespasser, and, although para 3[b] of Sch 2 to the 1977 Act precluded the court from making a possession order against her during the transitional period, that period had expired. The tenant appealed. The Court of Appeal ([1980] 2 All ER 539) allowed the appeal, holding that a tenant was not a trespasser during the transitional period if he remained in possession after the expiry of a notice to quit served on him by a non-resident landlord since he was in lawful possession by virtue of para 3 and his status at the end of the transitional period depended not on whether his contractual tenancy had been determined during that period but on whether the new landlord had taken advantage of that period to qualify as a resident landlord, and if the new landlord had not done so the tenant was protected by the 1977 Act and became a statutory tenant. The personal representatives appealed to the House of Lords. At the hearing of the appeal the tenant contended that the effect of para 3 was to introduce a standstill or 'wait and see' period to see whether a new resident landlord entered into occupation, and if he did not the tenant became a statutory tenant at the end of the transitional period.

Held (Lord Roskill dissenting) — On the true construction of para 3 of Sch 2 to the 1977 Act, during the transitional period, created by para 1 of that Schedule, following the death of a resident landlord the tenant was merely a person holding over without any right to do so while being temporarily protected from an order for possession by virtue of para 3. It followed that when that period of temporary protection came to an end on

---

a   Paragraph 1, so far as material, is set out at p 713 *d*, post
b   Paragraph 3 is set out at p 707 *g h*, post

the expiration of the transitional period, the personal representatives of the former landlord were entitled to an order for possession if they had served a notice to quit during the transitional period. The personal representatives were accordingly entitled to possession and their appeal would be allowed (see p 708 *c* to *f*, p 709 *j* to p 710 *b* and *g*, p 711 *d* to *j* and p 712 *a b*, post).

Decision of the Court of Appeal [1980] 2 All ER 539 reversed.

Notes

For tenancies where the landlord's interest belongs to a resident landlord, see Supplement to 23 Halsbury's Laws (3rd Edn) para 1523A.

For the Rent Act 1977, ss 2, 12, Sch 2, see 47 Halsbury's Statutes (3rd Edn) 396, 407, 562.

As from 28th November 1980, s 12 of and paras 1 and 3 of Sch 2 to the 1977 Act were amended by s 65 of the Housing Act 1980.

Appeal

Fay Lilian Landau and Peter Michael Neumann (the personal representatives of Miss M T Newman deceased) appealed by leave of the House of Lords granted on 7th May 1980 against the decision of the Court of Appeal (Stephenson, Bridge and Templeman LJJ) ([1980] 2 All ER 539, [1980] 3 WLR 197) on 17th March 1980 allowing an appeal by the respondent, Louisa Sloane, against an order made by his Honour Judge Leslie in the Bloomsbury and Marylebone County Court on 7th November 1979 whereby he ordered that the appellants were entitled to an order for possession of the ground floor flat at 35 Lyncroft Gardens, London NW6 and mesne profits and dismissed the respondent's counterclaim for a declaration that she was a statutory tenant of the premises. The facts are set out in the opinion of Lord Wilberforce.

Ronald Bernstein QC and *Paul Morgan* for the appellants.
Derek Wood QC and *Andrew Arden* for the respondent.

Their Lordships took time for consideration.

19th February. The following opinions were delivered.

LORD WILBERFORCE. My Lords, this appeal arises from a letting of a residential premises by a resident landlord, a matter regulated by the Rent Act 1977. On 4th March 1978 Miss M T Newman let rooms on the ground floor of her freehold house to the respondent on a weekly tenancy at a rent of £10 a week. Miss Newman herself lived, and continued to live until her death, on the first floor. She died on 11th August 1978 and the appellants are her executors. On 17th December 1978 they gave the respondent notice to quit with effect from 28th February 1979. The respondent applied to a rent tribunal which, on 21st March 1979, deferred the operation of the notice until 28th June 1979 but increased the rent to £15 a week exclusive of rates. The respondent unsuccessfully applied for a further deferral, so her contractual tenancy ran out on 4th July 1979. On 19th July 1979 (ie within the period of 12 months from the landlord's death) the appellants issued a summons claiming possession and mesne profits. This relief was granted on 7th November 1979 in the Bloomsbury and Marylebone County Court by his Honour Judge Leslie, but his decision was reversed by the Court of Appeal ([1980] 2 All ER 539, [1980] 3 WLR 197).

It is well known that before 1974 the basic division as regards residential tenancies was between those of unfurnished and those of furnished premises. The Rent Act 1974 altered the law so that furnished tenancies which previously had only a limited degree of protection became entitled to the full protection of rent legislation. On the other hand, lettings by resident landlords of part of a larger building (other than a purpose-built block of flats) were removed from full protection so long as the landlord remained resident; this was no doubt to encourage resident owners of houses with rooms to spare to let them, in the expectation that they could regain vacant possession on the expiry or termination of the tenancy.

a The Rent Act 1977, which governs the present case, has the following structure. By
s 1, a letting of a 'dwelling-house' which includes a part of a building, is a 'protected
tenancy'. By s 2, when a protected tenancy comes to an end, the tenant becomes a
'statutory tenant' so long as he occupies the dwelling house as his residence. Thus a
statutory tenancy arises and only arises by conversion from a protected tenancy, which
itself is contractual. The case of 'resident landlords' is an exception carved out of this
structure: it is dealt with by s 12 and Sch 2. Broadly, a tenancy of a 'dwelling-house' let
b by a resident landlord is not a protected tenancy, so long as the landlord continues to
reside in a part of the building. So, provided that this condition is satisfied, the landlord
may regain possession of the portion he has let. However, the letting is what is called a
'restricted contract' (see ss 19 and 20), which may attract the jurisdiction of a rent
tribunal.

The case when a resident landlord dies during the currency of a tenancy such as that
c with which we are concerned is dealt with in Sch 2. Since the requirement (in s 12(1))
that the landlord must remain resident until the termination of the contract cannot be
complied with if he is dead, the schedule introduces for the benefit of his estate a period
of 'disregard'. Paragraph 1(c) fixes this, in the case of personal representatives, as a period
of not more than 12 months from the date when the landlord's interest vested in them.
The purpose and effect of this is evidently to confer on the personal representatives the
d same remedies as regards the tenancy as would have been exercisable by the resident
landlord whose estate they represent, the period of non-residency by the personal
representatives being disregarded. The policy behind these provisions is reasonably
clear. First it is essential if the Act is to work, and if owners of houses are to be induced
to let rooms, that the owner should be able to regain possession of the portion let, so that
he can sell with vacant possession. His house is probably his major asset, and if he cannot
e sell it, at its full value, he will not let. The Act clearly allows him to do this, subject only
to the qualification that he must remain in residence until the tenancy comes to an end.

Second, and similarly, his personal representatives must be able to realise the house,
very likely, again, the most valuable asset in the estate. So, though in fact they may not
be resident, they are, by the process of 'disregard' treated as resident, if their testator was
resident. Consequently one could expect that they could serve a notice to quit (assuming
f that the contract allows this), regain possession and sell. Anything which prevents them
from doing this would be unjust to the estate of the landlord and confer an uncovenanted
benefit on the tenant. The argument for holding that this is the effect of the Act is thus
a very strong one; it was described by Bridge LJ as formidable and indeed as unanswerable
but for a provision to which he referred. He pointed out, rightly, that there is nothing
in Sch 2 which would, after the period of 'disregard', convert a tenancy such as that now
g in issue into a statutory tenancy.

The provision, and the only provision, which led Bridge LJ and the other members of
the Court of Appeal to a contrary conclusion was that contained in Sch 2, para 3, which
I quote:

> 'Throughout any period which, by virtue of paragraph 1 above, falls to be
> disregarded for the purpose of determining whether the condition in section 12(1)(c)
h > is fulfilled with respect to a tenancy, no order shall be made for possession of the
> dwelling-house subject to that tenancy, other than an order which might be made
> if that tenancy were or, as the case may be, had been a regulated tenancy.'

Whatever quality can be claimed for this paragraph, clarity is not one, either as to
wording or as to policy. The effect which the respondent attributes to it is this. It is, her
j counsel contended, to introduce, after the determination of the contractual tenancy, a
period of 'wait and see' until the period of disregard comes to an end, to 'wait and see'
whether a new resident landlord enters into occupation. If he does not, a statutory
tenancy arises; if he does, it does not.

There are two reasons which prevent me from accepting this. First it may produce an
unjust result, one which Parliament cannot have intended. It denies to the executors of
a resident landlord what would seem to be an undeniable right, to remove a tenant who

has no contractual right to stay on, in order to realise this valuable asset. All they can do, on this interpretation, is to introduce another resident landlord who can then take his own steps to determine the tenancy. But this might be severely depreciatory of the value, for who would pay a vacant possession price for a house part of which is occupied by a tenant, to remove whom will at the best involve delay (for a rent tribunal may be appealed to) and, at worst, litigation?

Second, it involves the erection of a considerable structure on this paragraph. It involves conferring on the tenant a statutory tenancy at the end of the period of disregard (if no new resident landlord comes in) although the paragraph does not say so, still less enter on the terms of the statutory tenancy as regards rent and otherwise. I find, in this connection, significant the very different and explicit language used elsewhere in the Act where it desires to create a statutory tenancy in notional circumstances: see Sch 24, paras 3(2) and 7. It has to be remembered that, by definition, a statutory tenancy arises only after a protected tenancy so that special and explicit provision is needed if a statutory tenancy is to arise in such a case as the present where there was no protected tenancy to precede it. I regard the words, in para 3 of Sch 2, that no order for possession may be made throughout the period of disregard as quite insufficient to achieve this; to my mind indeed they carry the contrary implication that an order can be made for possession after the period has ended, provided that there is no longer a contractual tenancy in existence.

Further, there remains the difficult question: what is the status of the tenant in the intermediate period between the termination of the contractual tenancy and the arising of the statutory tenancy? Bridge LJ tried to grapple with this problem. The solution which he arrived at was that there was a hybrid situation, partly a restricted contract, partly a statutory, or quasi-statutory, tenancy, each half of the hybrid attracting different jurisdictions. I find this prescription, logical no doubt if the hypothesis is right, most difficult to swallow. By contrast, I find no difficulty in the rival view (if the appellants are right) that the tenant is simply a person holding over without any right to do so against whom an order for possession cannot, temporarily and by virtue of the statute, be made.

I appreciate that it is not easy to offer a convincing alternative to the respondent's interpretation of the statute except that any alternative to so strange a result is likely to be preferable. But I simply read para 3 as doing what it says, namely giving, for a reason which seemed good to Parliament, an extra period of grace, corresponding to the executor's year, in a case where no new resident landlord has been introduced. Rent legislation is full of compromises, and this may be one. I prefer to interpret the paragraph as an unexplained concession, in the tenant's favour, to the intense convolutions and potential injustice of the respondent's contention.

One other line of argument deserves mention. It is pointed out, justly, that if the contractual tenancy extends beyond the executor's year the tenant will become protected, and so a statutory tenant. This is no doubt so, under the terms of the Act. But I do not see that this is an argument to giving the same benefit to a tenant whose tenancy determines in the executor's year. If anything, it creates an anomaly which requires correction; in fact it has partly been so corrected by the Housing Act 1980, s 65(5). It is also said that, in the latter case, a rent tribunal may be applied to and may extend the tenancy beyond the 12 months, in which case too the tenant would become statutory. Templeman LJ described this as a terrible power, with deterrent effect against the appellants' argument. With respect I do not find it so deterrent. The power of rent tribunals to alter contractual arrangements is inherent in the legislation; in many cases they may alter what would otherwise be the legal situation. But, as exemplified by the present case (where a second extension was refused), it must not be assumed that the rent tribunal will act so as seriously to affect legal rights: deliberately to do so would be an abuse of power; and if, as is likely, most cases before them are either of short periodic tenancies, or of fixed tenancies (in which case they cannot extend the period), it is not to be assumed that, with para 3 of Sch 1 and the Protection from Eviction Act 1977 available for the tenant, they will readily take action which would radically affect the landlords' rights.

My Lords, in the end, I think that the merits of the situation before us are not doubtful and that the legislation allows them to be given effect to. The judgment of Judge Leslie I find clear and reasonable. I would restore it and allow the appeal.

LORD FRASER OF TULLYBELTON. My Lords, the facts have already been set out by my noble and learned friend Lord Wilberforce, and I need not repeat them. I take up the narrative at 4th July 1979 on which date the notice to quit given by the appellants took effect, and the respondent's tenancy of the premises came to an end. That was within the period of 12 months after the death of the landlord, a period which falls to be 'disregarded' in determining whether the landlord has lived in the building 'at all times' since the tenancy was granted: see Sch 2, para 1(c) to the Rent Act 1977. It seems clear that the reason why Parliament has provided for disregarding that period is to allow reasonable time for the deceased landlord's personal representatives to administer his estate and to find a new (resident) landlord. If para 1 of Sch 2 stood alone, its effect would be that during the period of disregard the personal representatives would have the full rights of a resident landlord, notwithstanding that they were not actually resident. The difficulty is created by para 3 of Sch 2 which provides as follows:

'Throughout any period which, by virtue of paragraph 1 above, falls to be disregarded for the purpose of determining whether the condition in section 12(1)(c) is fulfilled with respect to a tenancy, no order shall be made for possession of the dwelling house subject to that tenancy, other than an order which might be made if that tenancy were or, as the case may be, had been a regulated tenancy.'

In searching for the effect of that puzzling paragraph it is I think helpful first to consider its underlying purpose. The argument for the respondent adopted and relied on the explanation suggested by Bridge LJ in the Court of Appeal which was that para 3 was intended to provide 'a standstill or "wait and see" period during which the new landlord has the option either to take up residence and retain the rights of a resident landlord as against the tenant, or to accept the tenant on the terms of a regulated tenancy' (see [1980] 2 All ER 539 at 545, [1980] 3 WLR 197 at 205). If the paragraph is read so as to give effect to that purpose, certain difficulties and complications arise, as Bridge LJ recognised. Nevertheless, I was at one time inclined to accept the argument, largely because I did not consider that there was any other explanation of the policy which was satisfactory. But I have come to think that the true policy behind para 3 is probably on the following lines. It is one thing to allow a landlord who is actually living in a building to exercise his full rights by obtaining an order for possession against the tenant (subject to a possible postponement by a rent tribunal). But it is another thing, which Parliament may have considered harsh, to allow personal representatives to exercise the full rights of the landlord to the extent of obtaining physical possession of the premises immediately after the contractual tenancy has ended, although they are not actually residing in the building. Their position might be sufficiently protected by preserving the right to obtain vacant possession (subject to possible postponement by a rent tribunal) at the end of the period of disregard, or earlier if the personal representatives or a new landlord, or a beneficiary under para 2, actually take up residence in the building before the end of that period. Some such explanation satisfies my mind as to the purpose of para 3 and it enables the paragraph to be fitted into the scheme of the Act without attributing to it a meaning wider than its words will naturally bear.

Paragraph 3 is indeed not without its obscurities. The provision that no order shall be made for possession of the dwelling house 'subject to that tenancy', if read literally, seems to refer to a dwelling house that is, at the time when the order is made, still subject to the tenancy. But I think, in agreement with his Honour Judge Leslie, that it must envisage that the tenancy has come to an end, otherwise the court could not make an order for possession. The effect of para 3, in light of the policy which I have suggested above, is limited to preventing the personal representatives from obtaining an order for possession during the disregard period. That is in fact all that the paragraph expressly states. In all other respects their rights are the same as those of a resident landlord. Accordingly, where a tenancy is (as in this case) a 'restricted' contract under s 20 of the Act, and where *a* it comes to an end during the period of disregard, the tenant, or more properly now the ex-tenant, is left with no relevant rights under the Act except the right not to have an order for possession made against him during the disregard period. It seems inappropriate to describe a person in that position as a trespasser, but I see no alternative.

The argument for the tenant which was accepted by the Court of Appeal involves reading into para 3 important implications which are not there expressed and leads to *b* difficulties and complications. It requires attention to be concentrated on the position at the end of the period of disregard. If at that time there is no resident landlord it was said that the tenant then becomes a statutory tenant, even if his contractual tenancy had already expired some time previously. But it is difficult to see how he can attain the status of statutory tenant in such circumstances. There is no provision in the Act that a tenant under a restricted tenancy is to become a statutory tenant immediately on the *c* expiry of the period of disregard if there is still no resident landlord. One would have expected such a provision in order to create an exception to the normal process envisaged by s 2(1) of the Act whereby a statutory tenancy occurs either (*a*) immediately after a protected tenancy or (*b*) by a succession to a protected tenant or a statutory tenant. It might be possible to regard the normal process under s 2(1) as not being the only possible process and to read para 3 as creating another route to the status of statutory tenant, *d* although it would be surprising, if that were the intention, that there is no express provision comparable to the elaborate provisions of paras 3 and 7 of Sch 24 for creating statutory tenancies in special cases. But the argument for the respondent raises the even more serious difficulty of finding a status for the former tenant under s 12 after his tenancy has come to an end and until the end of the period of disregard. In the circumstances of this case that period was between 4th July and 11th August 1979. If *e* this were merely a question of labels it would not be important. But, on the respondent's argument, she was neither a trespasser nor a full statutory tenant during that period and it is necessary to find some status by which her rights can be defined. One suggestion on behalf of the tenant was that her status could only be ascertained retrospectively and that, in the event that happened of there being no resident landlord at the end of the disregard period, it can now be seen that she was a protected tenant between 4th July and 11th *f* August 1979. An alternative suggestion was that adopted by Bridge LJ, namely that the tenancy was of a hybrid character during that period. But there is no statutory warrant for either of these views, each of which carries considerable legal implications, and requires one to read into para 3 more than I would be disposed to do unless driven by the most compelling reasons. I do not think we are so driven. I am therefore of opinion that para 3 should receive the comparatively limited effect that is expressly required by its *g* terms and that the contention of the appellants should succeed.

For these reasons I would allow the appeal.

LORD RUSSELL OF KILLOWEN. My Lords, the answer to this appeal must be mined from the complicated seams of the Rent Act 1977. The respondent became a tenant of a dwelling house part of a larger building, the other part of which was then *h* occupied by the landlord as her residence. Parliament in the hope and expectation of making available more rented accommodation introduced legislation which reduced the security of tenure of a tenant in such circumstances, by providing by s 12 of the Act that the tenancy should not be a protected tenancy at any time in the circumstances above mentioned if (subject to para 1 of Sch 2 to the Act) at all times since the tenancy was granted the interest of the landlord under the tenancy has belonged to a person who at *j* the time he owned that interest occupied as his residence another dwelling house also forming part of the building.

The landlord, whose legal personal representatives are the appellants, died. Thus a time arrived when, but for Sch 2, the circumstances ceased to be such that the respondent was debarred from having a protected tenancy by s 12.

Schedule 2, however, by para 1 provided that in those circumstances, in determining whether the required continuity of landlord's residence under s 12 was or was not fulfilled, a period of not more than 12 months from the time when the landlord's interest became vested in the personal representatives of the deceased as such, or in trustees as such, or in the probate judge, was to be disregarded.

Accordingly after the death of the resident landlord the respondent tenant was unable to assert that she had a protected tenancy: she had a restricted contractual tenancy which could be determined on due notice, though subject to an ability in the rent tribunal to postpone to a limited extent the operation of such a notice. If no step were taken by the appellants on behalf of the estate to determine the tenancy, and it remained in existence at the expiration of the 12-month period without a previous substitution of another resident landlord, it would then become a protected tenancy, and if then determined by notice would move to the status of a statutory tenancy.

If the landlord had given in her lifetime due notice to terminate the contractual tenancy, expiring during the 12-month period, the tenancy would have then expired, subject to an ability in a rent tribunal to postpone to some extent (because the tenancy was a restricted contract) the date of efficacy of the notice to determine. Similarly the appellant personal representatives of the deceased resident landlord had the ability after her death to determine the contractual tenancy on due notice. This they did, effective on a date within the 12-month disregard period; the effective date was extended by the rent tribunal to a date still within the 12-month period, and a further extension was refused.

The situation then was that the respondent had no longer any tenancy of the dwelling house: there was no tenancy which could blossom into a protected tenancy, which ex hypothesi is a contractual tenancy, still less was there a possibility of a statutory tenancy emerging, as it would have to, from a protected tenancy.

All this is clear, and indeed is not disputed by the respondent.

The contention for the respondent that she has security of tenure once the 12-month period has expired without the arrival of a substitute resident landlord is founded entirely on para 3 of Sch 2, which has already been quoted by my noble and learned friend Lord Wilberforce. (For present purposes the reference there to a regulated tenancy may be taken to refer to a protected tenancy or a statutory tenancy; s 18 and Sch 15 impose the familiar requirements for an order for possession to be made in such cases.) The provisions of para 3 in that regard underline the fact that from the due termination of the contractual tenancy during the 12-month period there was not thereafter during the remainder of that period a regulated tenancy in existence, ie either a protected tenancy or a statutory tenancy.

It appears to me that para 3 cannot be stretched to mean more than it says, or to intend greater protection to the former tenant than it says; nor do I see why it should. No order for possession is to be made, notwithstanding that the former tenant has no tenancy, either protected or statutory, until the expiration of the 12-month period (except on 'regulated tenancy' grounds). A breathing space, for some reason, is to be given to the former tenant, limited in time, and I would assume that that would end at its expiration.

The elaborate, and it seems to me, anomalous theory ('wait and see') erected by the Court of Appeal seems to result in a protected and statutory tenancy springing apparently simultaneously at the end of 12 months from the ashes of a former contractual, but determined, tenancy. Paragraph 3 cannot in my opinion bear that legislative weight.

It is said that during the relevant period the respondent could not have been a trespasser and protected from an order for possession. I do not find that a problem. She was temporarily protected from the consequences of her holding over, though still at risk if events occurred which would have put a regulated tenant (had she been that, which she was not) at risk.

For these reasons I would uphold the judgment of the county court judge and allow this appeal.

LORD KEITH OF KINKEL. My Lords, I have been unable to discover any satisfactory and rational explanation for the presence, in Sch 2 to the Rent Act 1977, of the provisions of para 3, except on the basis that the earlier 'disregard' provisions are intended to be operative only where the relevant periods constitute interruptions in otherwise continuous occupancy by a resident landlord. But that basis itself presents serious difficulties, in respect that the Act contains no provisions regulating the status of one whose contractual tenancy has come to an end in the course of a period which is potentially, but in the event turns out not to be, a period of disregard. In a situation of extreme obscurity, I am prepared to accept, with considerable hesitation, that, for the reasons given by those of your Lordships who have already spoken, the matter should be resolved in favour of the representatives of the former resident landlord, and accordingly to concur in the allowance of the appeal.

LORD ROSKILL. My Lords, this appeal raises a novel problem in relation to tenancies which are not 'protected' at the time they are granted because they are at that time excluded from the purview of s 1 of the Rent Act 1977 by reason of s 12 of that Act, which is concerned with the letting of a dwelling house by a resident landlord. That the problem is not only novel but one of difficulty is demonstrated by the fact that a very experienced circuit judge (his Honour Judge Leslie) in a judgment of admirable clarity decided the appellants' claim for possession in their favour. The Court of Appeal (Stephenson, Bridge and Templeman LJJ) ([1980] 2 All ER 539, [1980] 3 WLR 197) unanimously reversed that decision and decided the case in favour of the tenant. And unhappily I find myself unable to agree with the contrary view which commends itself to your Lordships.

My Lords, the facts are simple and one imagines not unusual. It is therefore perhaps permissible to regret that when the provisions of what became s 12 of and Sch 2 to the 1977 Act were first introduced by the Rent Act 1974 the legal consequences of those facts were not specifically or clearly provided for. Your Lordships were pressed with the submission that s 65 of the Housing Act 1980, by the changes therein wrought to s 12 of and Sch 2 to the 1977 Act, had for the future effectively reversed the instant decision of the Court of Appeal. All learned counsel agreed before your Lordships that this was so. I am content to assume this to be correct but I say no more about s 65 for, with respect, I regard the submission that your Lordships should consider the provisions of that section in determining the law as it was before that section was enacted as quite unsound in principle. The present appeal falls to be decided on the true construction of the relevant parts of the 1977 Act, as those parts stood at the time the relevant events took place. Those events, about which there was no dispute, are fully detailed in the judgments in the court below. They require no further repetition.

My Lords, the most relevant parts of the 1977 Act are ss 1, 2, 12, 17, 18, 19, 20 and 21 and Sch 2. Of those parts the most important are ss 1, 12 and 20 and Sch 2. For brevity I do not set those sections out for they are to be found in the judgments of the court below and in the speeches of some of your Lordships.

My Lords, the resident landlord, whose personal representative the appellants are, died on 11th August 1978. She had let the premises in question on 4th March 1978. At no time during the ensuing 12 months following the resident landlord's death was there a resident landlord. The respondent claims that on 11th August 1979 (the anniversary date of the resident landlord's death) she became a statutory tenant with the relevant protection which the 1977 Act accords to such tenants. The appellants challenge that submission and claim possession, saying that from the expiry of a properly given notice to quit, which was extended by the relevant rent tribunal until 14th July 1979, the respondent became a trespasser, protected from eviction only by para 3 of Sch 2 to the 1977 Act, a protection which ended on the anniversary date just mentioned, namely 11th August 1979.

My Lords, it is beyond question that, but for s 12 and Sch 2, the respondent's tenancy would have been a protected tenancy, and that protected tenancy would on due termination by proper notice to quit have become a statutory tenancy. But, in order to encourage landlords who lived in private dwelling houses to let part of those premises to tenants seeking accommodation, Parliament first in 1974 and later by s 12 of the 1977

Act provided that tenancies granted on and after 14th August 1974 should not be protected tenancies, subject to certain conditions, one of which was that the landlord must himself reside in another part of the building at the time the tenancy was granted. Another condition to be found in s 12(1)(c) was that—

> 'subject to paragraph 1 of Schedule 2 to this Act, *at all times* [my emphasis] since the tenancy was granted the interest of the landlord under the tenancy has belonged to a person who, at the time he owned that interest, occupied as his residence another dwelling-house which also formed part of that building.'

Schedule 2 is imported into s 12 by sub-s (4) of that section to 'supplement' that section.

Schedule 2, para 1 begins by making provision in connection with s 12(1)(c) for certain periods of time to be 'disregarded'. In other words, when considering whether there has been a resident landlord 'at all times' (see s 12(1)(c)) the several periods specified in Sch 2, para 1 are to be disregarded. Clearly some provision was required when a landlord died, for a dead landlord could not be a resident landlord, and it cannot have been intended that a tenant could suddenly at the moment of the death of a resident landlord acquire all the rights, first, of a protected and, later, of a statutory tenant. So far as death is concerned, para 1 of Sch 2 provides:

> 'In determining whether the condition in section 12(1)(c) of this Act is at any time fulfilled with respect to a tenancy, there shall be disregarded . . . (c) any period of not more than 12 months beginning with the date on which the interest of the landlord under the tenancy becomes, and during which it remains, vested—(i) in the personal representatives of a deceased person acting in that capacity . . .'

For present purposes, the further qualifications on s 12(1)(c) in para 1(c) of Sch 2, can be ignored. Thus the relevant 'period of disregard' in the instant appeal is 12 months. Hence the importance of the anniversary date, namely 11th August 1979.

Now it is clear from s 12 that, ignoring for the moment the complications which may arise by reason of the transmission of the resident landlord's interest by sale or by death, the resident landlord can regain possession when either the tenancy, if it be for a fixed term, expires by effluxion of time or, in the case of a periodic tenancy, when notice to quit is duly given and expires. The tenant not being a protected tenant does not in these circumstances become a statutory tenant. But, if the resident landlord dies, then the provisions of Sch 2, para 1(c) come into operation. The deceased resident landlord's personal representatives do not cease to qualify for the benefit of s 12(1) merely because during the 12 months immediately following the resident landlord's death there is no resident landlord. But equally Sch 2, para 3 provides that during any relevant period of 'disregard', subject to certain exceptions not presently relevant, no order for possession of the dwelling house in question should be made against the tenant.

But, my Lords, what is to happen at the end of the period of disregard if there is then no resident landlord? The appellants maintain that para 3 of Sch 2 is merely a standstill provision and that at the end of that period (provided of course that a valid notice to quit has by that time been given and expired) the tenant is without protection, and is a trespasser liable to eviction. Indeed it is contended that the tenant is a trespasser from the time of the expiry of that notice to quit but is saved from eviction only by para 3 of Sch 2.

The respondent, on the other hand, claims that on the expiry of the period of disregard if there is no resident landlord the tenancy then becomes a statutory tenancy. The exemption given by s 12 of the 1977 Act which protects a tenancy from being a protected tenancy is at an end because there is no resident landlord, and the period of disregard is at an end because the 12-month period has elapsed. The tenant, so the argument runs, was lawfully in possession until that moment and thereupon became a statutory tenant.

The appellants' reply to that contention is that nowhere in the 1977 Act is there any provision to be found that in such circumstances the tenant should become a statutory tenant, that no such provision can be implied into the statute, and that a statutory tenancy cannot in these circumstances arise because there is no immediately antecedent protected contractual tenancy.

My Lords, the rival contentions were powerfully advanced by all four learned counsel and I would like, in particular, to express my gratitude for the admirable argument of the learned junior counsel for the appellants.

My Lords, there is no doubt that there is no express provision that in the circumstances in question a tenant should become a statutory tenant. The crucial question to my mind is what effect must be given to para 3 of Sch 2. Must it be deduced from its provisions when read with the other provisions that the tenant was to become a statutory tenant in these circumstances, or is the right conclusion that it accords limited temporary protection only to the tenant, leaving the former resident landlord's personal representatives free to obtain possession as soon as that limited temporary protection has determined?

My Lords, I start consideration of this difficult problem from the fact that s 12 is an exception on the provisions of ss 1 and 2. The resident landlord is freed from the bonds of the 1977 Act and his right to sell the whole of his house (which may well be and perhaps usually will be his only capital asset) with vacant possession is not to be jeopardised by the fact that he, a resident landlord, has let part of his house to a tenant so long as the relevant conditions in s 12(1) are satisfied. This exception, to my mind, is a personal privilege to a resident landlord, a privilege which can be lost if those conditions are not at any time complied with. Those conditions, inter alia, require the presence of a resident landlord 'at all times' save only during any period of disregard. But, if at any time there is no resident landlord and there is also no relevant period of disregard running, then, it seems to me, the relevant conditions are not fulfilled and the privilege accorded by s 12 is lost.

It is forcibly argued against this view that this creates a statutory tenancy in favour of the tenant by reason of the resident landlord's death for which the statute makes no provision, that the purpose of this part of the legislation is to protect landlords rather than tenants, that para 3 of Sch 2 as drafted is an insufficiently strong foundation on which to engraft in favour of the tenant the rights of a statutory tenant when no express provision to this end is made, and that the result of this suggested construction is to deprive the personal representatives of the deceased resident landlord of the ability to sell the premises in question with vacant possession. Thus it is said the beneficiaries of the deceased resident landlord's estate are penalised.

My Lords, I think the solution must lie in determining the status of the tenant during the balance of the period of disregard after the expiry of the notice to quit. Is the tenant then a trespasser protected only from eviction by para 3 of Sch 2, or does the tenant, during that period, have a more positive status? This was the problem which the Court of Appeal solved by saying (pace Bridge LJ) that during that period the tenant had the attributes of a statutory tenant and would be subject to the rights and obligations of the now expired contractual tenancy. The learned Lord Justice described this tenancy as one of a hybrid character, and suggested that he might be called a quasi-statutory tenant.

My Lords, with profound respect to those who take the opposite view, I find it impossible to accept that para 3 of Sch 2 simply leaves the tenant as a trespasser protected from eviction but with no other rights. What the tenant would owe the landlord or his personal representatives during the balance of the period of disregard would, I think, be rent and not mesne profits. I think full effect can only be given to para 3 of Sch 2 along the lines suggested by Bridge LJ and for those reasons I would dismiss this appeal.

Appeal allowed. Order appealed from reversed and order of his Honour Judge Leslie of 7th November 1979 restored.

Solicitors: *Fay L Berman*, Brighton (for the appellants); *John Crosthwait* (for the respondent).

Mary Rose Plummer   Barrister.

Evans v London Hospital Medical College and others

QUEEN'S BENCH DIVISION
DRAKE J
3rd JULY, 25th SEPTEMBER 1980

Malicious prosecution – Action – Essentials to action for malicious prosecution – Setting law in motion – Pathologist preparing post-mortem report for police – Plaintiff charged with murder after report considered by Director of Public Prosecutions – Plaintiff subsequently acquitted when no evidence offered by prosecution – Whether pathologist setting law in motion – Whether plaintiff entitled to bring action for malicious prosecution against pathologist.

Action – Immunity from civil action – Witness – Privilege of witness in court of justice – Extent of immunity from civil action – Conduct or statements prior to proceedings being commenced – Accused charged with murder following pathologist's post-mortem report – Whether pathologist immune from action by accused in respect of negligence in preparing report.

At the request of the police the defendants, a pathologist and two toxicologists employed in the forensic medicine department of a hospital, carried out a post-mortem on the plaintiff's infant son shortly after the infant's death. In their report to the police which was submitted to the Director of Public Prosecutions, the defendants stated that they had found morphine in organs examined by them. The plaintiff was subsequently charged with the murder of her infant son by morphine poisoning. A pathologist engaged by the plaintiff found no morphine in other organs examined by him, from which he concluded that at the time of removal there could not have been morphine in the organs examined by the defendants and that they must have been contaminated with morphine following removal. When the report of the plaintiff's pathologist was referred to the defendants they did not retract or amend their own report. At the plaintiff's trial the prosecution offered no evidence against her and she was acquitted. The plaintiff brought an action against the defendants and the hospital claiming damages for negligence in conducting the post-mortem and preparing the report or, alternatively, for malicious prosecution arising from the fact that the defendants had made a false analysis and communicated it to the police and the Director of Public Prosecutions and had procured the plaintiff's arrest and prosecution. The defendants applied to a master to have the plaintiff's claim dismissed and the action struck out as disclosing no reasonable cause of action, on the grounds that (i) the claim for malicious prosecution failed because the defendants had not initiated the prosecution, and (ii) the defendants were entitled to rely on the immunity from civil action accorded to witnesses in criminal proceedings. The master struck out the action and the plaintiff appealed, contending that (i) she was entitled to proceed with the claim for malicious prosecution because the defendants had 'set the law in motion', and (ii) the defendants were not entitled to the immunity claimed because their negligence had occurred before the criminal proceedings were commenced.

Held – The appeal would be dismissed for the following reasons—

(1) The plaintiff had no claim against the defendants for malicious prosecution because the law had not been set in motion by the defendants but either by the police when they requested the defendants to prepare their report or by the police or the Director of Public Prosecutions when, on the strength of the report, the decision to prosecute was taken (see p 718 *h* to p 719 *b*, post).

(2) The defendants were also entitled to have both the claim in negligence and the claim for malicious prosecution dismissed because they were covered by the absolute immunity from any form of civil action conferred on a witness in criminal proceedings in respect of his evidence, since that immunity extended to cover conduct or statements

made prior to the commencement of proceedings if it could fairly be said to be part of the investigation of a crime or possible crime for the purpose of a prosecution or possible prosecution (see p 719 *e f h j*, p 720 *f* to *h* and p 721 *b* to *h*, post); *Marrinan v Vibart* [1962] 3 All ER 380 applied; *Saif Ali v Sydney Mitchell & Co (a firm)* [1978] 3 All ER 1033 distinguished.

Notes

For persons liable to an action for malicious prosecution, see 25 Halsbury's Laws (3rd Edn) 349–350, paras 684–685, and for cases on the subject, see 33 Digest (Repl) 391–392, 38–50.

For the immunity of a witness in respect of his evidence, see 17 Halsbury's Laws (4th Edn) para 261, and for a case on the subject, see 22 Digest (Reissue) 427, 4268.

Cases referred to in judgment

Marrinan v Vibart [1962] 3 All ER 380, [1963] 1 QB 528, [1962] 3 WLR 912, CA; *affg* [1962] 1 All ER 869, [1963] 1 QB 234, [1962] 2 WLR 862, 22 Digest (Reissue) 427, 4268.

Rees v Sinclair [1974] 1 NZLR 180, Digest (Cont Vol D) 59, *49Aa.

Saif Ali v Sydney Mitchell & Co (a firm) [1978] 3 All ER 1033, [1980] AC 198, [1978] 3 WLR 849, HL, Digest (Cont Vol E) 19, 4879.

Watson v M'Ewan, Watson v Jones [1905] AC 480, [1904–7] All ER Rep 1, 74 LJPC 151, 93 LT 489, 7 F 109, HL, 32 Digest (Reissue) 224, *1910*.

Interlocutory appeal

The plaintiff, Michelle Evans, appealed against the order of Master Warren dated 17th October 1978 striking out her claim against the defendants, London Hospital Medical College, Peter Vanezis, Ann Robinson and Anne Holder, and dismissing her claim against the defendants for damages for negligence and/or malicious prosecution, on the grounds that the statement of claim disclosed no reasonable cause of action. The appeal was heard in chambers but judgment was given by Drake J in open court. The facts are set out in the judgment.

Phillip Otton QC and *John Hunter* for the plaintiff.
Hugh Carlisle QC and *Timothy Briden* for the defendants.

Cur adv vult

25th September. **DRAKE J** read the following judgment: This is an appeal by the plaintiff from a decision of Master Warren, given as long ago as 17th October 1978, in which, on the application of the first, third and fourth defendants, he ordered that the plaintiff's statement of claim against them be struck out and the action dismissed on the grounds that it disclosed no reasonable cause of action. I was informed that the second defendant has not been served with any of the proceedings; therefore, save where I state otherwise, any references to 'the defendants' will exclude him. I am also concerned with a summons taken out by the plaintiff on 5th June 1980 whereby she applies for leave to amend the writ and statement of claim. The amendments proposed at the time that summons was taken out were altered in two respects during the hearing before me. The defendants did not oppose the proposed amendments as such but argued that even with such amendments the writ and statement of claim still show no reasonable cause of action. I was invited by counsel for the defendants to deal with the appeal and summons on the basis of the writ and statement of claim as proposed to be amended and to allow the amendments if, but only if, I considered that the pleadings as amended disclosed a reasonable cause of action against the defendants.

The plaintiff's claim indorsed on the writ is for—

'damages for injury and loss occasioned by the negligence of the Defendants and each of them in issuing inaccurate post-mortem and toxicological reports to the police and/or Director of Public Prosecutions whereby the Plaintiff was on or about the 13th July 1975 falsely charged with the murder of Jamie Evans.'

The proposed amendments added an alternative claim for malicious prosecution.

Jamie Evans was the five-month old son of the plaintiff and the facts alleged in the statement of claim may be summarised as follows. (i) The first defendant (which I will refer to as 'the hospital') provided, through its department of forensic medicine, post-mortem reports for the purpose of placing such reports before the police and the Director of Public Prosecutions ('the DPP'). The three individual defendants were employed by the hospital as lecturers in that department. (ii) On 7th July 1975 Jamie Evans died from a condition known as 'sudden infant death syndrome'. On the same day at Deptford Public Mortuary the second defendant carried out a post-mortem on the infant during which he removed from the body a number of organs and specimens which were sent to the third and fourth defendants for toxicological analysis. On 8th July at the hospital they carried out tests on these organs and specimens and purported to find in them concentrations of morphine. They reported their findings to the police and/or the DPP and to the second defendant, and on 5th August 1975 they made statements in accordance with the Criminal Justice Act 1967, ss 2 and 9, setting out the results of their analysis. On the same day the second defendant made a statement under the same statutory provisions in which he alleged that the infant's death had been caused by morphine poisoning. (iii) As a result of the reports made by the three individual defendants to the police and/or the DPP the plaintiff was arrested on 13th July 1975 and charged with the murder of her infant son by morphine poisoning. (iv) On 18th August 1975 the plaintiff's solicitors, through the DPP, informed the defendants (a) that further organs had been removed from the body of the infant by a pathologist (Professor Mant) acting for the plaintiff, and toxicological analysis had shown these organs to be free from morphine and (b) that it followed that it was not possible for there to have been any morphine in the organs removed by the second defendant on 7th July at the time of such removal because the morphine would have contaminated all the organs in the body. It also followed that the organs analysed by the third and fourth defendants must have become contaminated with morphine after they had been removed from the body and whilst they were in the care of the defendants. (v) On receipt of this information the defendants took no action to retract or amend the statements they had made on 5th August. (vi) On 16th February 1976 the plaintiff appeared at the Central Criminal Court on the charge of murder, but the prosecution offered no evidence against her and she was acquitted. However, because of the failure of the defendants to retract their statements or in any way indicate that they were unreliable in the light of Professor Mant's findings, the prosecution, whilst offering no evidence against the plaintiff, reaffirmed that the infant's death was due to morphine poisoning.

That is a summary of the facts alleged in the statement of claim. When addressing me counsel for the defendants invited me to consider a transcript of the proceedings at the Central Criminal Court to show what prosecuting counsel had then stated as the reasons why the prosecution still believed that the infant had died from morphine poisoning. He read out to me some of the transcript; but I declined to give any effect to it because it is well settled that in deciding whether a statement of claim discloses any reasonable cause of action the court should *not* consider any evidence. My decision is based solely on the allegations contained in the pleadings.

The statement of claim on the basis of those allegations alleges negligence. In its unamended form the allegations made against the second, third and fourth defendants are, summarised, (i) permitting the organs to become contaminated, (ii) failing to appreciate that the concentration of morphine revealed by analysis was so high that it was very unlikely that it could have existed in the infant whilst he was alive, and that it therefore got there by contamination, (iii) failing to act on the information given to them as a result of Professor Mant's examination, and (iv) failing to retract or amend their reports made to the police and/or the DPP or the written statements made on 5th August.

The allegations against the hospital are, summarised, (i) failing to act on the information given to them as a result of Professor Mant's examination, (ii) failing to set up an inquiry into the way in which the removed organs had become contaminated, (iii) failing to disclaim or withdraw the statements or reports made by the individual defendants to the police and/or the DPP and failing to ensure that the prosecution of the plaintiff did not proceed any further, and (iv) failing to ensure that the individual defendants carried out a proper analysis of the removed organs.

A proposed amendment would have the effect of making these allegations not only in respect of acts or omissions of the second, third and fourth defendants as servants or agents of the first defendant but against 'the Defendants their servants or agents' without identifying the servants or agents referred to; in other words it would cover the possible contamination of the infant's removed organs by anyone employed by or acting on behalf of the hospital. It would, for example, cover the possible contamination by a cleaner or porter who had no direct connection with the examination of the organs for the purpose of submitting a report to the police or the DPP. It is right to say that the particulars of negligence do not contain any suggestion that contamination occurred in this or indeed in any specified manner and the proposed amendment was only put forward during the hearing before me. An amendment proposed at the time the summons for leave to amend was issued would not have covered any negligence save that of 'the Defendants'.

A further proposed amendment made the alternative allegation of malicious prosecution by the defendants and each of them in that they made a false analysis and communicated it to the police and/or the DPP and procured the arrest and prosecution of the plaintiff. By way of malice the plaintiff relies on the allegations set out as particulars of negligence.

The defendants' successful application to the master to strike out the writ and statement of claim was made on the grounds that the defendants were at all times acting in the course of preparing evidence for a possible prosecution and for that reason were immune from any civil proceedings arising from such acts. This ground was relied on in the present hearing to give immunity from the additional cause of action in malicious prosecution as well as negligence; but it was further submitted that the statement of claim disclosed no basis for alleging malicious prosecution since the defendants had not initiated the prosecution but had merely passed on information to the police and/or the DPP. Counsel for the plaintiff, whilst conceding that the defendants had immunity in respect of negligence after the criminal proceedings had started, argued that the negligent acts or omissions relied on were prior to the prosecution being commenced. As to the malicious prosecution he submitted that it was because of the defendants' acts and omissions that the plaintiff had been charged and that the defendants, judged by their entire conduct, had in reality 'caused the law to be set in motion'.

I will deal first with the proposed amendment to claim damages for malicious prosecution, because it seems to me that this can be briefly disposed of.

As is said in Clerk and Lindsell on Torts (14th Edn, 1975, para 1887):

'To prosecute is to set the law in motion, and the law is only set in motion by an appeal to some person clothed with judicial authority in regard to the matter in question . . . If a charge is made to a police constable and he thereupon makes an arrest, the party making the charge, if liable at all, will be liable in an action for false imprisonment, on the ground that he has directed the arrest and therefore it is his own act and not the act of the law.'

In my judgment the statement of claim in the present case makes it clear that all that is alleged against the defendants is that they provided reports '. . . for the purpose of placing such reports before the police and/or the Director of Public Prosecutions'. It was for the police or the DPP (in reality, clearly for the DPP) to decide whether or not to prosecute and I think the proposed addition of a claim of malicious prosecution against the defendants or any of them is misconceived. That is sufficient to dispose of that proposed cause of action. However, I think there are other grounds for doubting whether the defendants can be said to have 'set the law in motion'. As I have just stated, the statement of claim avers that the hospital 'purported to provide . . . post-mortem investigation and reports . . . for the purpose of placing such reports before the police and the Director of Public Prosecutions'. When the second defendant carried out a post-mortem on the deceased infant he must have been requested by some other person, probably a police officer, so to do. In the circumstances it is certainly arguable that it was not the defendants who 'set the law in motion'.

The cause of action in negligence gives rise to more difficulty. The cases show clearly that a witness in criminal proceedings enjoys absolute immunity from any form of civil action in respect of evidence given by him during those proceedings, and, further, that such immunity extends to cover statements made by him in preparing a proof for trial or in a report to the DPP (see *Marrinan v Vibart* [1962] 1 All ER 869, [1963] 1 QB 234, applying *Watson v M'Ewan* [1905] AC 480, [1904–7] All ER Rep 1).

But how far does this absolute immunity extend to cover the acts or omissions of a witness or potential witness during the stage when they are collecting or considering material with a view to its *possible* use in criminal proceedings?

The decision of the Court of Appeal in *Marrinan v Vibart* does, it seems to me, make the position clear. In the leading judgment given by Sellers LJ with which the other two members of the court, Willmer and Diplock LJJ, agreed, he said ([1962] 3 All ER 380 at 383, [1963] 1 QB 528 at 535):

'Whatever form of action is sought to be derived from what was said or done in the course of judicial proceedings must suffer the same fate of being barred by the rule which protects witnesses in their evidence before the court *and in the preparation of the evidence which is to be so given*.' (Emphasis mine.)

Counsel for the plaintiff concedes that these words are apparently wide enough to make it difficult for the plaintiff to bring her claim in this action. But he seeks to overcome the difficulty on two grounds. First he says that 'the preparation of the evidence' applies only to preparing the statements or proof of evidence containing what the witness is expected to say at the trial. Second he argues that the alleged negligence of the defendants arose before the judicial process had started, and was in the course of the routine administrative inquiries which follow a death such as that of an infant in its cot.

I do not accept either of these arguments. I think it essential to keep in mind the reason for the immunity. Counsel suggests that the main reason is to prevent disgruntled convicted prisoners from seeking to have their cases retried in a civil suit. I think that that is undoubtedly one of the reasons for the existence of the immunity; but I think that the reason is in fact more broadly based than this. It was stated by Salmon J in his judgment at first instance in *Marrinan v Vibart* [1962] 1 All ER 869 at 871, [1963] 1 QB 234 at 237:

'This immunity exists for the benefit of the public, since the administration of justice would be greatly impeded if witnesses were to be in fear that any disgruntled or possibly impecunious persons against whom they gave evidence might subsequently involve them in costly litigation.'

The judgment of Salmon J was approved by all three members of the court on the subsequent appeal. It seems to me that this immunity would not achieve its object if limited to the giving of evidence in court and to the preparation only of the statements or proof of evidence given by the witness. Any disgruntled litigant or convicted person could circumvent the immunity by saying he was challenging the collection and preparation of the evidence, to be taken down as a statement or proof of evidence later, and *not* challenging the statement or proof itself. In other words he would seek to base his claim on things said or done by the witness at some time prior to the statement or proof being given by him.

In my opinion this would largely destroy the value of the immunity. Equally I think that it would open the way to convicted persons seeking to have their cases retried in the civil courts. An action could be brought alleging negligence against police officers in their investigations and the collection of evidence which at some later date resulted in criminal proceedings being commenced.

I think that the wide language used by the Court of Appeal in the *Marrinan* case, ie that the immunity 'protects witnesses in their evidence before the court and in the preparation of the evidence which is to be so given', was deliberately given in those very wide terms.

It remains, of course, a question to be decided on the facts of each case (or, in the present instance of an application to strike out, on the alleged facts) whether or not the negligent act or omission arose during the course of preparation of the evidence. In the present case I think it did arise during the course of preparing or collecting evidence.

Although the scope of the decision in *Marrinan v Vibart* may be clear it remains to consider to what extent if at all it has been narrowed by the more recent decision of the House of Lords in *Saif Ali v Sydney Mitchell & Co (a firm)* [1978] 3 All ER 1033, [1980] AC 198. That decision was concerned with the immunity from being sued enjoyed by a barrister or solicitor when engaged in the conduct of litigation.

The majority decision can conveniently be taken from the headnote ([1980] AC 198 at 199), so far as is relevant to the present case:

> '. . . that in principle those who undertook to give skilled advice were under a duty to take reasonable care and skill, and that a barrister's immunity from suit for negligence in respect of his conduct of litigation on the ground of public policy was an exception and applied only in the area to which it extended; that the immunity was not confined to what was done in court but included some pre-trial work, but that protection should not be given any wider application than was absolutely necessary in the interests of the administration of justice and each piece of pre-trial work had to be tested against the one rule, namely, that the protection existed only where the particular work was so intimately connected with the conduct of the cause in court that it could fairly be said to be a preliminary decision affecting the way that cause was to be conducted when it came to a hearing . . .'

It was further held that the same immunity attaches to a solicitor acting as an advocate in court as attaches to a barrister.

So, if the limits to the immunity enjoyed by a witness were in all respects similar to those of the advocate's immunity, then the test to be applied would be to consider whether the statement or conduct of the witness was so intimately connected with the conduct of the cause in court that it could fairly be said to be a preliminary decision affecting the way the case was to be conducted at the hearing. On that test the immunity would not cover all of the negligence alleged against these defendants, as at least some of it related to a time before any proceedings were in being. The post-mortem examination and toxicological analysis on some of the infant's organs were carried out as part of the investigations necessary to decide *whether* any prosecution should be brought. If it is possible to compare the position of a barrister to that of the defendants in this case I think it clear that the barrister would not be immune from being sued for negligence.

But although the immunity attaching to barristers exists for reasons of public policy, as does that attaching to witnesses, I think it clear that it is not identical. The immunity enjoyed by a witness does in fact protect everyone engaged in proceedings in court, not merely the witnesses, but the judge, counsel, jurors and the parties (see per Lord Wilberforce and Lord Diplock in *Saif Ali v Sydney Mitchell & Co* [1978] 3 All ER 1033 at 1038, 1044, [1980] AC 198 at 214, 222). The barrister's immunity from action in respect of his conduct of the litigation is a separate, even if in some ways related, branch of immunity. Public policy gives immunity to the barrister so that he may be free, without any fear of civil action, in his conduct of litigation; it is not, however, right that he should be given any wider immunity than is necessary for that purpose. The immunity given to a witness or potential witness is because—

'the administration of justice would be greatly impeded if witnesses were to be in fear that persons against whom they gave evidence might subsequently involve them in costly litigation.'

(See per Salmon J in *Marrinan v Vibart* [1962] 1 All ER 869 at 871, [1963] 1 QB 234 at 237.)

If this object is to be achieved I think it essential that the immunity given to a witness should also extend to cover statements he makes prior to the issue of a writ or commencement of a prosecution, provided that the statement is made for the purpose of a possible action or prosecution and at a time when a possible action or prosecution is being considered. In a large number of criminal cases the police have collected statements from witnesses before anyone is charged with an offence; indeed sometimes before it is known whether or not *any* criminal offence has been committed.

If immunity did not extend to such statements it would mean that the immunity attaching to the giving of evidence in court or the formal statements made in preparation for the court hearing could easily be outflanked and rendered of little use. For the same reason I think that the immunity must extend also to the acts of the witness in collecting or considering material on which he may later be called to give evidence. If it does not so extend then a convicted person could, for example, sue the police officers for the allegedly negligent manner in which they had investigated the crime, by complaining that they had wrongly assessed the evidential value of certain matters or had failed to interview possible witnesses whose evidence was thought by the accused to be favourable to him.

It is for these reasons that I think that the words used by the Court of Appeal in *Marrinan v Vibart*, that immunity protects witnesses in their evidence before the court and in the preparation of the evidence which is to be given, covers and was intended to cover the collection and analysis of material relevant to the offence or possible offence under investigation, and was not intended merely to cover the preparation of the witness's formal statement or proof of evidence.

Applying, to the immunity to be given to a witness, the test suggested by McCarthy P in the New Zealand Court of Appeal in *Rees v Sinclair* [1974] 1 NZLR 180 at 187 cited and approved by the majority of the House of Lords in *Saif Ali v Sydney Mitchell & Co,* I would alter it to apply it to the immunity attaching to a witness or possible witness in a criminal investigation, thus: 'The protection exists only where the statement or conduct is such that it can fairly be said to be part of the process of investigating a crime or a possible crime with a view to a prosecution or possible prosecution in respect of the matter being investigated.'

Applying this test to the present case I think it clear that the defendants and each of them were so engaged at the time when they were allegedly negligent in the different ways set out in the statement of claim as proposed to be amended. Accordingly I hold that they are protected by immunity and that no reasonable cause of action is shown against them. It follows that in my judgment this appeal against the master's order must be dismissed and I dismiss also the plaintiff's application for leave to amend.

As I have adjourned this summons into open court, at the request of counsel for the plaintiff and because I think the decision is one of interest beyond the interests of the parties themselves, I think it right to repeat that I have been required by the Rules of the Supreme Court to consider this matter entirely on the basis of allegations made by the plaintiff, without hearing or in any way considering whether these allegations could be supported by evidence. No negligence or wrongful conduct of any kind whatsoever has been proved against any of the defendants; and it has been made clear to me that were the action to go to trial these allegations would be very vigorously defended and strenuously denied.

Appeal dismissed.

Solicitors: *Sheratte, Caleb & Co* (for the plaintiff); *L Watmore & Co* (for the defendants).

K Mydeen Esq   Barrister.

R v Southampton Justices, ex parte Davies

QUEEN'S BENCH DIVISION
DONALDSON LJ AND FORBES J
4th, 7th NOVEMBER 1980

Magistrates – Fine – Committal to prison in default of payment – Maximum period of imprisonment – Committal for non-payment of several fines – Whether maximum period that applicable to aggregate of fines not paid or total of maxima applicable to individual fines – Magistrates' Courts Act 1952, s 64, Sch 3.

On 22nd January 1980 justices convicted the applicant of seven motoring offences and sentenced him to fines of £60, £25, £60, £15, £25, £25 and £25, respectively, which, with £10 costs, totalled £245. The £245 was not paid, and on 13th February on a means inquiry the applicant was committed to prison for a total of 95 days, the committal order being suspended on payment of £15 a week. The period of 95 days was made up of periods of 30 days, 7 days, 30 days, 7 days, 7 days, 7 days and 7 days made to run consecutively, being respectively the maximum periods of imprisonment in default of payment applicable under Sch 3[a] to the Magistrates' Courts Act 1952 for each of the fines imposed on the applicant. By 24th September it was clear that no further instalments were likely to be paid, the applicant having by then paid only £81·37. The justices' clerk applied the first £70 of that amount to cancel the first period of 30 days for non-payment of the £60 fine and the £10 costs. The balance of £11·37 was used to reduce the second period of 30 days by 6 days, £11·37 bearing the same relationship to £60 as does 6 days to 30 days. The justices then issued a warrant committing the applicant to prison for the balance of 59 days. The applicant applied for an order of certiorari to quash that order, contending that a term of imprisonment imposed for non-payment of a number of fines was subject to the maximum period specified in Sch 3 applicable to the aggregate of the fines imposed.

Held – It was clear from the terms of s 64[b] of the 1952 Act, under which the justices derived their power to commit a defaulter to prison, that where a warrant was issued for an outstanding sum the period for which the defaulter might be committed to prison was not to exceed the maximum for the aggregated sum found on the warrant. Furthermore, in fixing the consecutive sentences of imprisonment for the non-payment of the fines, the justices had still been imposing consecutive sentences and they should, in accordance with well-established principles, have considered the maximum period applicable to the aggregate of the sums outstanding. Accordingly, the court would issue an order of certiorari to quash the justices' order fixing the period of imprisonment at 59 days and would substitute therefor an order fixing the period at 30 days (see p 725 j to p 726 c, post).

R v Metropolitan Stipendiary Magistrate for South Westminster, ex parte Green [1977] 1 All ER 353 distinguished.

Per Curiam. Where justices think that separate periods of imprisonment for non-payment of separate fines ought to be fixed, separate warrants will have to be issued for each period. Such a course is not, however, to be encouraged, each case having to be decided on its own facts (see p 725 h and p 726 c, post).

Notes

For imprisonment for default in the payment of a fine, see 29 Halsbury's Laws (4th Edn) paras 454–455, 457, and for cases on the subject, see 33 Digest (Repl) 380–381, 1050–1958.

---

a   Schedule 3, so far as material, is set out at p 724 d to g, post
b   Section 64, so far as material, is set out at p 725 g, post

a   For the Magistrates' Courts Act 1952, s 64, Sch 3, see 21 Halsbury's Statutes (3rd Edn) 238, 295.

As from a day to be appointed s 64 of and Sch 3 to the 1952 Act are to be replaced by s 76 of and Sch 4 to the Magistrates' Courts Act 1980.

Case referred to in judgments

b   *R v Metropolitan Stipendiary Magistrate for South Westminster, ex parte Green* [1977] 1 All ER 353, 141 JP 151, DC, Digest (Cont Vol E) 399, 835c.

Case also cited

R v Clerkenwell Stipendiary Magistrate, ex parte Mays [1975] 1 All ER 65, [1975] 1 WLR 52, DC.

c   **Application for judicial review**

Neil Osborne Davies applied, with the leave of the Divisional Court of the Queen's Bench Division given on 27th October 1980, for an order of certiorari to quash the order of the Southampton Magistrates' Court dated 8th October 1980 committing the applicant to prison for a period of 59 days for default in payment of fines imposed by the Southampton justices on 21st January 1980. The facts are set out in the judgment of

d   Forbes J.

Peter J H Towler for the applicant.
The respondent was not represented.

Cur adv vult

e   7th November. The following judgments were read.

FORBES J (delivering the first judgment at the invitation of Donaldson LJ). In this case counsel moves on behalf of the applicant to bring up and quash an order of the Southampton justices committing him to prison for 59 days. The case raises a novel point about justices' powers to impose terms of imprisonment for non-payment of fines.

f   The facts are these. On 20th June 1979 the applicant appeared before the Southampton justices and was ordered to pay a total of £232·63 in respect of a fine, costs and compensation.

On 22nd January 1980 he appeared before the same justices in respect of a number of motoring offences. He was convicted of them and sentenced as follows: (1) driving without insurance, £60; (2) using a vehicle with a defective tyre, £25; (3) driving

g   without due care and attention, £60; (4) driving without L-plates, £15; (5) driving unsupervised, £25; (6) using a vehicle with defective brakes, £25; (7) using a vehicle with a defective tyre, £25.

In addition the justices disqualified him from driving, ordered him to pay £10 costs in respect of the first offence and made an instalment order for the payment of the total of £245 at the rate of £5 per week.

h   On 13th February 1980 the applicant appeared again before the same court on a means inquiry. At that date there was still outstanding £173·63 from the June 1979 order and the full sum of £245 from the January 1980 order. He was accordingly committed to prison by the magistrates for 30 days in respect of the amount outstanding on the earlier order and a total of 95 days in respect of the sum of £245. Each of these committal orders was suspended on payment of the sum of £15 a week, starting on 18th February

j   1980.

The period of 95 days was made up as follows: (1) £60 and costs: 30 days; (2) £25: 7 days; (3) £60: 30 days; (4) £15: 7 days; (5) £25: 7 days; (6) £25: 7 days; (7) £25: 7 days.

Each of these periods was made to run consecutively, making a total of 95 days. On 24th September 1980 it became clear to the justices' clerk's staff that the instalment payments, as a condition of which the justices had suspended his committal, had not been paid. Accordingly a warrant was issued for his committal to prison for 59 days, the balance of the total of 95 days. This period of 59 days was arrived at in a manner I shall *a* refer to in a moment. In fact before the warrant was executed the applicant of his own volition appeared before the Southampton justices on 8th October 1980 asking them to order that the warrant be withdrawn. The justices declined and the applicant was accordingly conveyed to prison on the authority of that warrant. The applicant in his affidavit suggests that the magistrates committed him to prison on that day, but it seems clear to me that the correct way of looking at what occurred on 8th October is as I have *b* set out.

By 24th September 1980 the applicant had in fact paid off the whole of the sum due under the June order and £81·37 towards the sum of £245 due for the convictions in January. The justices' clerk had applied that £81·37 to the outstanding sum of £245 in this way. The first £70 was applied to cancel the first period of 30 days for non-payment of the £60 fine and costs; the balance of £11·37 was used to reduce the second period of *c* 30 days, that is for offence no 3, by 6 days, because £11·37 bears the same relationship to £60 as does 6 days to 30 days.

It is now necessary to consider the provisions of Sch 3 to the Magistrates' Courts Act 1952, as amended by s 59 of the Criminal Law Act 1977. This schedule reads thus:

> '1. Subject to the following provisions of this Schedule, the periods set out in the second column of the following Table shall be the maximum periods applicable *d* respectively to the amounts set out opposite thereto, being amounts due at the time the imprisonment is imposed . . .'

There then follows a table starting with 'an amount not exceeding £25 . . 7 days. An amount exceeding £25 but not exceeding £50 . . 14 days. An amount exceeding £50 but not exceeding £200 . . 30 days' and finishing up with 'An amount exceeding *e* £5,000 . . 12 months'.

It will be seen that the periods of imprisonment fixed by the magistrates on 13th February 1980 were in fact the maxima permitted under this table. Paragraph 2 of Sch 3 to the 1952 Act reads:

> 'Where the amount due at the time imprisonment is imposed is so much of a sum adjudged to be paid by a summary conviction as remains due after part payment, *f* the maximum period applicable to the amount shall be the period applicable to the whole sum reduced by such number of days as bears to the total number of days therein the same proportion as the part paid bears to the whole sum: Provided that in calculating the reduction required under this paragraph any fraction of a day shall be left out of account and the maximum period shall not be reduced to less than five days.' *g*

Counsel's main argument for the applicant is that, when imposing terms of imprisonment under s 65(2) of the Magistrates' Courts Act 1952, Sch 3 to that Act must be read as if the justices in imposing a term of imprisonment for non-payment of fines were subject to the maxima applicable to the aggregate of the fines imposed. He says this is so for three main reasons. First, the application of the schedule produces anomalies if *h* it is not so construed. Second, the 1952 Act is a consolidating Act (except for amendments detailed by the Lord Chancellor to Parliament, and there are none relevant here); that its predecessor, the Summary Jurisdiction Act 1879, s 5, can be read as indicating that at any rate partial aggregation was intended by Parliament; and that therefore the 1952 Act provisions must be assumed to adopt the same approach as those of 1879. And, third, in any event the period of imprisonment ordered by the justices ran counter to well-established principles affecting the imposition of consecutive sentences, and, as there is *j* no appeal to the Crown Court against sentences of imprisonment imposed by the magistrates for non-payment of fines, the applicant is entitled to come to this court for redress under this procedure for judicial review.

Before turning to examine these contentions it would be as well to be clear about two

points. First, the powers of the justices are derived from ss 64 and 65 of the Magistrates'
a Courts Act 1952. Section 64(1) gives the power, where default is made in payment of
sums due by conviction or order, to issue a distress warrant or a warrant committing the
defaulter to prison. By s 64(3) the period for which a defaulter may be sent to prison is
limited to the appropriate maximum set out in Sch 3. Section 65(2) empowers the
justices to fix a term of imprisonment and postpone the issue of the warrant until such
time and on such conditions as the court thinks just. It is clear to me that on 13th
b February 1980 the justices here decided to fix the appropriate terms of imprisonment
and to postpone the issue of the warrant so long as the applicant paid £15 a week. This
they did under s 65(2) and it meant that on failing to pay the £15 in any one week the
warrant would then and there issue, unless of course before its issue the justices took
steps, as, say, on an application by the defaulter to stay the warrant. It is accordingly the
decision of the justices on 13th February 1980 which is before us and not their decision
c not to recall the warrant, assuming they had power to do so, on 8th October.

The second point is that there can be no doubt that it is competent for the justices to
impose consecutive terms of imprisonment in default of payment of fines imposed for
separate offences; this is clear from a perusal of s 108 of the 1952 Act. The broad effect
of sub-ss (1) and (2) of that section, as amended by the Criminal Law Act 1977, Sch 12,
is to impose overall maxima of 6 months and 12 months respectively for consecutive
d sentences in respect of summary offences triable either way which are tried summarily.
Section 108 (5) reads:

> 'For the purposes of this section a term of imprisonment shall be deemed to be
> imposed in respect of an offence if it is imposed as a sentence or in default of
> payment of a sum adjudged to be paid by the conviction . . .'

e Counsel for the applicant does not challenge that there is power to impose consecutive
sentences in respect of default in payment of fines imposed for two or more offences; he
says, as I have indicated, that Sch 3 must be read as involving maxima for the aggregate
of the sums unpaid and not for each of the constituent sums.

Counsel made his submissions with great skill and persuasiveness, and as a result I have
changed my original attitude to his application. But it is not necessary, I think, to
f consider his submissions in detail because I believe that there is another and more
fundamental objection to the course the justices adopted.

What the justices purported to do on 13th February 1980 was to fix a term of
imprisonment under s 65(2) and postpone the issue of the warrant. But these powers
themselves derive from s 64 of the 1952 Act. On turning to that section it will be seen
that under sub-s (1) where there is 'default . . . in paying a sum adjudged to be paid . . .
the court may . . . issue a warrant committing the defaulter to prison'. Subsection (3)
g brings in the maxima: 'The period for which a person may be committed to prison *under
such a warrant* . . . shall not . . . exceed the period applicable to the case under the Third
Schedule . . .'

It seems plain to me from these provisions that where a warrant is issued for an
outstanding sum the period must be no more than the maximum for the aggregated
h sum found on the warrant. If separate periods for non-payment for separate fines are to
be fixed, then separate warrants would have to be issued. In coming to this conclusion
I am not to be taken as encouraging the issue of many separate warrants where a number
of separate fines are outstanding. Each case will clearly have to be decided by the justices
on its own facts. In doing so they should, it seems to me, adopt the approach which
formed the subject matter of counsel's third and most eloquent submission for the
j applicant: the fixing of consecutive sentences of imprisonment for non-payment of fines
is still the imposition of consecutive sentences and as such is subject to certain well-
known principles. These include that, usually, consecutive sentences are inappropriate
where several offences arise out of the same incident, and that, even when they are
appropriate, the court should consider whether the totality of the sentence is not excessive
having regard to the totality of the criminal activity.

But, having said that, I have no doubt that in fixing the term of imprisonment for which the warrant was to issue the justices should have considered the maximum period applicable to the aggregate of the sums outstanding. We have not been shown the warrant but it is clear from the affidavit of the justices' clerk that in this case only one warrant for the total of 59 days' imprisonment was issued. Accordingly the maximum period in this case is 30 days. The order fixing the period of imprisonment at 59 days should therefore be quashed and there should be substituted an order fixing the period at 30 days.

Before leaving this case I should refer, because we have been referred to it, to *R v Metropolitan Stipendiary Magistrate for South Westminster, ex parte Green* [1977] 1 All ER 353. All I need say about it is that that was argued on wholly different submissions, namely, that s 108 of the 1952 Act prevented the magistrates from imposing terms of imprisonment of more than six months in the aggregate, and that the significance of the wording of s 64 was not brought to the court's attention.

DONALDSON LJ. I agree.

Application granted. Order of justices quashed and order fixing period of imprisonment at 30 days substituted therefor.

Solicitors: *Gregory, Rowcliffe & Co*, agents for *Abels*, Southampton (for the applicant).

April Weiss   Barrister.

Shemshadfard v Shemshadfard

FAMILY DIVISION
PURCHAS J
3rd, 4th, 19th MARCH 1980

Divorce – Stay of proceedings – Discretionary stay – Balance of fairness and convenience – Relevant factors – Remedies available in foreign court – Cultural background of parties – Iranian wife petitioning for divorce in England against Iranian husband on ground of unreasonable behaviour – Husband commencing divorce proceedings in Iran – Husband applying for stay of English proceedings – Wife having no rights or remedies against husband in Iran but likely to obtain divorce in England and financial provision out of husband's English assets – Whether balance of fairness and convenience making it appropriate to stay English proceedings until disposal of Iranian proceedings – Domicile and Matrimonial Proceedings Act 1973, s 5(6), Sch 1, para 9(2).

The husband and wife were Iranians who were married in Iran in 1974. It was a polygamous marriage, the wife being the third wife of the husband. The husband, a man of substance, decided to come to England with the wife and their young daughter and to settle the wife and daughter there, although he himself did not intend to leave Iran permanently. He bought a house and business in London and installed the wife as manageress of the business. He still maintained a home and his business in Iran. In 1979 the marriage broke down and in consequence the husband sold the London business. However, he retained the London house and the wife and daughter continued to live there, while he lived mainly in Iran. In August 1979 the wife commenced divorce proceedings in England on the ground of the husband's unreasonable behaviour. Her petition alleged, inter alia, that he had falsely accused her of adultery and prostitution, and also alleged physical violence by the husband. In January 1980 the husband issued a petition in Iran seeking a certificate of non-compatibility with the wife which under Iranian law would relieve him of any obligation to maintain the wife. On 8th February the husband applied to the English court under para 9(1)^d of Sch 1 to the Domicile and Matrimonial Proceedings Act 1973 for a stay of the wife's proceedings pending determination of the Iranian proceedings. On the hearing of the application the husband contended that he had discharged the burden on him of showing, within para 9(1)(b) of Sch 1, that the balance of fairness and convenience between the parties rendered it appropriate for the Iranian proceedings to be disposed of before further steps were taken in the English proceedings because (i) the husband spoke no English and the wife's English was limited and it would therefore be more expeditious and less expensive if the proceedings were conducted in their native language in Iran, (ii) if the husband defended the wife's petition he would have to incur expense in bringing witnesses from Iran to England, and (iii) the cultural background of the parties being Iranian it was inappropriate that an English court should deal with the wife's suit. The wife had no relatives in England but neither did she have any family in Iran with whom she could live, other than the husband. At the date of the application she was living a Western way of life and had departed considerably from her former Iranian cultural background. The wife submitted that the balance of fairness and convenience was in favour of the English proceedings being allowed to continue because the husband's sole object in asking for a stay was to force her back to Iran where she would have no remedies against him and where he could dispose of her and obtain custody of their daughter, whereas in the English proceedings she was likely to obtain a divorce and financial provision out of the husband's English assets which in turn might ensure the success of a pending application by her for permission to stay in England.

Held – The 'relevant factors' to be considered by the court under para 9(2) of Sch 1 to the 1973 Act, when considering the balance of fairness and convenience, were to be liberally defined. They included, where appropriate, the remedies which were available in the foreign court, including the possibility or otherwise of dissolution of the marriage there, provision for custody of children and ancillary matters, and the cultural background of the parties, although that was merely one element in the relevant factors. The balance of fairness and convenience between the parties was such that it was inappropriate to stay the English proceedings until disposal of the Iranian proceedings because (a) on the balance of convenience and expense of having witnesses either in England or Iran the burden on the wife in taking witnesses from England to Iran to support her allegations against the husband would be heavier than the burden on the husband in bringing witnesses from Iran to England, (b) it was probable that the husband would not defend the English proceedings in regard to the wife's allegations of unreasonable behaviour, (c) at the date of the application to stay, which was the relevant date for considering the question of fairness and convenience, the wife had acquired a Western culture, and (d) it was likely that the wife would not be able to pursue her remedies or protect her interests against the husband in the proceedings in Iran. It followed that the application to stay would be dismissed (see p 734 b to e and h to p 735 g and j, post).

Per Curiam. Since the power to stay proceedings in s 5(6)^b of the 1973 Act is expressed to be without prejudice to any power to stay which is exercisable apart from that Act, the power to stay under the 1973 Act is to be more liberally interpreted than the power to stay which was formerly only exercisable under s 41 of the Supreme Court of Judicature

---

a   Paragraph 9, so far as material, is set out at p 734 f to h, post

b   Section 5(6), so far as material, provides: 'Schedule 1 to this Act shall have effect as to the cases in which matrimonial proceedings in England and Wales are to be, or may be, stayed by the court where there are concurrent proceedings elsewhere in respect of the same marriage, and as to the other matters dealt with in that Schedule; but nothing in the Schedule . . . (b) prejudices any power to stay proceedings which is exercisable by the court apart from the Schedule.'

(Consolidation) Act 1925, and cases decided before the 1973 Act are to be considered in that light (see p 733 j, post); dictum of Lord Penzance in *Wilson v Wilson* (1872) LR 2 P *a* & D at 442 and *Sealey (otherwise Callan) v Callan* [1953] 1 All ER 942 considered.

Notes

For statutory staying of matrimonial proceedings, see 13 Halsbury's Laws (4th Edn) paras 896–899.

For the Domicile and Matrimonial Proceedings Act 1973, s 5, Sch 1, para 9, see 43 *b* Halsbury's Statutes (3rd Edn) 621, 630.

Cases referred to in judgment

Mytton v Mytton (1977) 7 Fam Law 244, CA.
Sealey (otherwise Callan) v Callan [1953] 1 All ER 942, [1953] P 135, [1953] 2 WLR 910,
  11 Digest (Reissue) 634, 1702. *c*
Wilson v Wilson (1872) LR 2 P & D 435, 41 LJP & M 74, 27 LT 351, 11 Digest (Repl) 525,
  1106.

Application to stay proceedings

On 14th August 1979 the wife, Nazy Shemshadfard, an Iranian, began divorce proceedings in England against the husband, Abbas Shemshadfard, also an Iranian. In *d* January 1980 the husband issued a petition in Iran seeking a certificate of non-compatibility with the wife for the purpose of a divorce. On 8th February 1980 the husband applied under the Domicile and Matrimonial Proceedings Act 1973, Sch 1, para 9 for a stay of the wife's proceedings pending determination of the proceedings in Iran. The facts are set out in the judgment.

Michael Irvine for the husband. *e*
H W Turcan for the wife.

Cur adv vult

19th March. **PURCHAS J** read the following judgment: This is an application under *f* the Domicile and Matrimonial Proceedings Act 1973 by the respondent, to whom I shall hereafter refer as 'the husband', to stay proceedings brought by the petitioner, to whom I shall hereafter refer as 'the wife'.

I heard oral evidence from both the husband and the wife. The husband speaks no English. Although the wife speaks a limited amount of English she also availed herself of the services of an interpreter. Notwithstanding the necessity for the use of the latter *g* I was able to come to clear conclusions on the limited area of disputed fact. During the course of the hearing counsel for the wife sought to establish elements of Iranian family law including that pertaining to the dissolution of marriage through the testimony of the wife. Objection was made to this by counsel for the husband on the basis that the wife was not properly qualified to deal with Iranian law. I permitted the evidence to be given de bene esse but have come to the conclusion that counsel's submission was correct *h* and I do not therefore take notice of the wife's views as to the detail of Iranian law. I must comment that she did not pretend to have any detailed information in any event.

The brief history as established by the evidence or agreed between the parties is as follows. The marriage took place on 9th March 1974 in Iran. It was a polygamous marriage. The wife was and is the third wife of the husband. It was, however, the wife's first and only marriage. Both parties are Iranian and at the time of the marriage were *j* living in Iran. There is one child who is the issue of this marriage, a daughter called Marjan, who was born on 1st January 1976. At the time of the marriage the wife was nearly 20 years of age. The husband was very much older.

The husband is a hairdresser. He owns a hairdressing business in Iran in which the wife had worked for about two years before the marriage. After the marriage the wife continued to work in the husband's business. The husband and wife lived in rented accommodation in Tehran together in due course with their child.

The two other wives are still alive and have families. The first wife, Sakineh Toliat, to whom the husband was married in 1934 has had four children by him. The second wife, Faroukh Ali Akbari, to whom the husband was married in 1960 has one child by him. The first wife and one of her children, a daughter, are living in this country in the same house as the wife and Marjan. The daughter will at least remain here until she has finished her studies. After that whether she or her mother will remain in England is in doubt. The second wife, Faroukh Ali Akbari, and her child have a home in Iran which is maintained by the husband and to which he has regularly returned during the wife's stay in England. This house was, of course, separate from the rented accommodation to which the husband and the wife went after the third marriage.

According to the evidence of the wife, which I accept, by the summer of 1977 at least one if not both of the other wives were causing trouble over the husband's living with her in separate accommodation in the manner I have described. The husband is clearly a man of substance. In order to avoid further difficulty of this sort he came with the wife and Marjan to England where he bought for cash a property in Kilburn. This property is said by the husband to be worth between £40,000 and £50,000. The wife suggests that it is worth more like £70,000. The husband also bought a hairdressing business in which he set up the wife as manageress. The husband, wife and Marjan arrived in England on 23rd August 1977. There has been some dispute as to the intentions of the various parties with regard to the length of their stay in England. I have no doubt that the husband is right when he says that he did not intend to leave Iran for ever. He maintained his business in Iran and between August 1977 and July 1979, when the marriage broke down, spent about half his time in England and half in Iran, if anything spending a little more time in Iran than in England. I am also satisfied that the husband's intention with regard to the wife was that she should settle more or less permanently in England whilst she remained his responsibility and whilst the hairdressing business continued to prosper. This was a satisfactory solution to the husband's domestic problems and a way in which he could keep all three of his wives contented. I am satisfied that if all had gone well the husband would have been himself content for the wife to remain in England for the foreseeable future and his daughter brought up in the English way of life at English schools.

Shortly after their arrival in England the husband arranged for the wife to attend evening classes in English at the Kilburn Polytechnic. These took place on three or four nights a week and were intended to last for six months. It was obviously in the husband's interest that the wife should learn to speak English if only to assist her in managing the hairdressing business. In the event the wife only stayed at the course for three of the six months. For the remaining three months the daughter of the first wife, to whom I have referred, attended the course. I accept that the reason for this was that, owing to the husband's return to Iran after three months, the wife had to cease attending night school in order to look after her daughter.

Things apparently went well for nearly two years. The husband was going backwards and forwards between Iran and the house at Kilburn while the wife remained permanently at Kilburn working in the husband's English hairdressing business. The hairdressing business in Iran also continued and the husband continued to maintain a home in Iran in which the second wife and her child were living.

Difficulties arose during the summer of 1979. There may be dispute between the parties as to the cause of the breakdown of the marriage. There is no dispute that during July, August and September 1979 the wife and her daughter were accommodated in a hotel run by the local authority for battered wives. Since October 1979 the wife and her daughter have been back in the house at Kilburn. The husband has been mainly in Iran.

After leaving the house in Kilburn the wife presented a petition dated 14th August 1979 seeking the dissolution of her marriage under s 1(2)(b) of the Matrimonial Causes Act 1973. There are a number of specific allegations on which she relies. I need only mention that one of them concerns false allegations of adultery and prostitution and a number of others set out complaints of physical violence of a severe degree.

I am satisfied that because of the breakdown of the marriage the husband sold his hairdressing business. He has not sold the house in which the wife, Marjan and the first wife and her daughter live.

The husband has issued proceedings in the courts in Iran. Exhibited to his affidavit are copies of his petition and a translation. The date of the issue of these proceedings may be important. I have studied the documents with such care as I can and must comment that a date stamp of January 1979 appears in more than one place. I have come to the conclusion that these date stamps are misleading. The contents of the document make it clear that the petition was issued during January 1980, not January 1979. The husband's petition seeks only a certificate of non-compatibility in the following terms:

'The principal has married with the defendant for four years, who has been living in England (the said address) for three years. She does not intend to return to Iran to live with her husband. Any action taken by friends and acquaintance and by the husband himself to make her come back to Iran to resume her usual living in accordance with social and moral rules of Iran but all attempts in this respect was in vain. As declared by her husband as well as the witnesses she prefers free living and western unrestrained living to holy and warm environment of family with Islamic rules. Therefore, kindly request you investigate the case and issue certificate of non-compatibility for divorce.'

This petition was issued in conjunction with a document the translated title of which was 'Notification sheet'. This calls on the wife to appear in the Private Civil Court, Branch 5 at 11 am on 25th February 1980 to answer a petition presented by the husband requesting the issue of 'a certificate of non-compatibility'. This is the extent of the proceedings which were issued in Iran by the husband some four or five months after the date of the wife's petition. The wife has taken no step in these proceedings and has not appeared in answer to the summons. I have no formal evidence that, apart from appearing to refute the allegations in the petition in Iran, any process by way of counterclaim or answer against the husband are available to her. I have no evidence about the effect of the certificate if it were granted.

The husband said that if the wife came with him to Iran he would sell the house in Kilburn but that if she did not want to come he would not want to sell the property. It was not certain whether the first wife would or would not stay in England but he accepted that the third wife definitely wished to stay in England. He frankly admitted that the reason why he did not wish for the divorce to be heard in England was that if this happened, 'She can take things from me in England and I do not want this'. Another answer which he gave in cross-examination which I accept reflected his views was 'Give me my child and I will go'. It must be remembered that this answer came via translation by the interpreter. The husband frankly disclosed his motive for bringing the application, namely to oblige his wife if possible to return to Iran, but, failing this, to be able to obtain a certificate of incompatibility in Iran which according to Iranian law would relieve him of any obligation to maintain or look after his wife. It is not clear to me how in such circumstances he would hope to obtain the custody of his daughter. On the other hand the husband said that if the wife came to Iran and lived with him as his wife he would give her everything that she wanted. Otherwise he would rely on his rights under Iranian law.

Reverting to the wife's position, on her arrival in England in August 1977 she was admitted, as disclosed on her passport, for the purposes of being a manageress in a hairdressing establishment. The permission to reside in England lasted six months and thereafter was renewed on the application of the husband for further six-month periods the last of which expired in July 1979. By the summer of 1979 the marriage had broken down. The wife's solicitors, realising that the husband would not make a further application for an extension of the permission to stay, themselves applied to the Home Office. Very properly in making this application they informed the Home Office of the breakdown of the marriage. The application was refused on the ground that the wife had no apparent means of financial support and would be a charge on the country. This decision was dated 24th September 1979. There was a right of appeal within fourteen days. A notice of appeal was dated 12th October 1979 which was a Friday but not received by the tribunal until the following Monday 15th October. In effect the notice of appeal was a week out of time. There has therefore to be an application to grant leave to extend the period for appeal before the appeal against the Home Office refusal can be heard. The Home Office have applied for this matter to be tried as a preliminary issue.

If the application to stay these proceedings succeeds then it is acknowledged by counsel for the wife that her application to appeal to the tribunal for permission to stay in this country will be virtually hopeless. If the application to stay the proceedings is refused then the appeal will be deferred until the divorce proceedings are concluded and it is known what provisions have been made by way of ancillary relief for the wife in the proceedings. It is therefore clear that the determination of this application cannot be deferred until after it is known whether or not the wife can remain in this country. On the other hand counsel for the husband submitted that he is entitled to rely on the tenuous position of the wife in this country. He submitted that it is by no means certain that the leave to appeal out of time will be granted by the tribunal. Counsel for the wife submitted that the tribunal would be virtually certain to allow an extension of time to appeal in the circumstances.

The wife in evidence said that when she came to England with her husband and child she thought she was going to stay in England for ever because 'we wanted to work here and live for ever'. This answer must be considered in context of a later answer which she gave, namely that if matters were satisfactory between her and her husband, had he wanted to return to Iran she would have returned with him. I am satisfied that whatever may have been the view of the husband when the wife came to England in August 1977 she thought she would be staying in this country at least for the foreseeable future if not permanently. She did not consider the possibility of her husband ceasing his business operations in England which were the cause of their coming to this country; but when faced with the hypothetical question 'What would have happened if, all being well, your husband had wished to return to Iran?' she gave the frank answer which I have mentioned.

The wife has, in fact, no alternative family unit in Iran to which she could return. Her parents are not alive. She was brought up by her cousin's daughter. This lady died some six years ago and her husband died a year before that. Her cousin had three sisters who are still alive and who are apparently living in Iran with their respective husbands and children; but I am not satisfied that there would be a convenient home with any of them to which the wife could return. The only option open to the wife is that of returning to her husband in Iran.

On the other hand the wife frankly admitted that she has no relations in England and that at the time she came here she knew no English nor did she know anything about the country. As a result of living here since the summer of 1977 she wishes to remain here. She does not want to return to Iran—

> 'because my country is a war country. I do not believe in my country, I am afraid to go back to Iran. If I went back to Iran to defend my husband's petition I would be very unlucky.'

The wife went on to say that she was afraid of what would happen if she returned to Iran because she did not believe her husband's expressed intentions because—

> 'we have not any good life in this country . . . I have no idea what will happen if I go back to Iran and do not return to my husband. It would be impossible for me to live separate and apart, I have no salary and money.'

The wife went on in fact to say that she did not want anything for herself, just for her daughter and that she wanted to be divorced from her husband. The daughter Marjan goes to a nursery school in England. She is very happy there and at school speaks English. In the home the mother and the daughter speak Iranian.

In these circumstances I must now turn to consider the impact of the provisions of the Act. I am indebted to forceful and skilful argument by counsel for each of the two parties in a case which is clearly not without difficulty. Counsel for the husband relied on part of the speech of Lord Penzance in *Wilson v Wilson* (1872) LR 2 P & D 435 at 442 cited by Davies J in *Sealey (otherwise Callan) v Callan* [1953] 1 All ER 942 at 946, [1953] P 135 at 141:

> 'It is the strong inclination of my own opinion that the only fair and satisfactory rule to adopt on this matter of jurisdiction is to insist upon the parties in all cases referring their matrimonial differences to the courts of the country in which they are domiciled. Different communities have different views and laws respecting matrimonial obligations, and a different estimate of the causes which should justify divorce. It is both just and reasonable, therefore, that the differences of married people should be adjusted in accordance with the laws of the community to which they belong, and dealt with by the tribunals which alone can administer those laws. An honest adherence to this principle, moreover, will preclude the scandal which arises when a man and woman are held to be man and wife in one country and strangers in another.'

Counsel for the husband also relied on a report of the judgment of Ormrod LJ in *Mytton v Mytton* (1977) 7 Fam Law 244 at 245:

> 'It was not, His Lordship thought, a very attractive exercise to compare the remedies offered by one jurisdiction with those offered by another. Nor was it very helpful in terms of fairness, because what was fair for one party may seem to have an equal and opposite effect on the other. But the section plainly contemplated, as the opening words showed, that there are two sets of properly constituted proceedings at the time when the application is made.'

Counsel for the husband contended that he had discharged the onus admittedly on him that the balance of fairness (including convenience) was such that it was appropriate for the proceedings in Iran to be disposed of before any further steps took place in this court. He relied on the following matters: (1) that the husband speaking no English and the wife's command of English being limited it would be clearly more expeditious and indeed less expensive for the proceedings between the parties to be conducted in Iranian; (2) that, although he could not be certain, it was not improbable that the husband would defend the wife's petition in England and would wish to bring witnesses from Iran for this purpose; (3) that as set out in his affidavit it would be embarrassing to the husband to have to leave his business in Iran unattended during the course of a hearing in this country; (4) that the culture and background of the parties was entirely Iranian and that it was inappropriate for the English court to deal with the wife's suit.

So far as the matter of being away from his business in Iran was concerned it is fair to counsel to record that he did not press this point with much appetite. This was a point made in the husband's affidavit but it did not impress me in view of the history of the husband spending long periods of time in England since the summer of 1977 and still operating his business in Tehran.

Counsel for the husband went so far as to say that the submissions made by counsel for the wife that she would have no remedies whatever in Iran and that her only hope of achieving any relief or support lay in proceedings in this country were not relevant to the question of fairness. Counsel for the husband relied for this on the extract from the judgment of Ormrod LJ to which I have already referred.

Counsel for the wife submitted that in considering the question of fairness I should have in mind the following matters: (1) that it was only fair that the wife should be allowed to demonstrate that she would and could be self-supporting in this country; (2) that she had been subjected to violence and had a petition which must succeed in all probability and under which she would be entitled to claim maintenance or other ancillary relief for herself and her daughter which would be produced from the admitted assets of the husband in this country, and that if she were not allowed to proceed with her suit and application for relief any realistic hope of her being able to stay in this country would be destroyed; (3) that the wife had clearly established a status for the purposes of the Act under s 5(2) and that, therefore, questions of domicile or intention permanently to remain in this country were not relevant to the question of status; (4) counsel relied on *Sealey (otherwise Callan) v Callan* ([1953] 1 All ER 942 at 950, [1953] P 135 at 149 per Davies J for the proposition that a stay would only be granted in very clear cases:

> 'In my judgment, on the authorities it requires a very strong case to persuade this court to prevent a party from proceeding, whether it be with an action at common law or a petition in this court, when this court has beyond question jurisdiction in the matter, on the ground that the defendant or the respondent in this court has either previously, as in some cases, or subsequently, as in the present case, started what for convenience I may call a cross-action or cross-petition in a foreign jurisdiction.'

Counsel further relied on the answer given by the wife that there was 'no law in Iran' and on the answer given by the husband 'Give me my daughter and I will go' and that the husband admitted that he was applying for a stay because under English law he would have to make provision for his wife. The husband's attitude is only logical if the husband was confident that under Iranian law he would not have to make provision for the wife. I have indicated earlier that I was against counsel for the wife in his efforts to adduce evidence of the laws of Iran. Counsel for the wife also invited me to take judicial knowledge of the fact that the recent regime in Iran had executed two prostitutes and to consider this in the context of the allegation in the wife's petition of false accusations of prostitution. As I indicated during the course of argument I was not able to accede to this invitation and I consider that counsel for the husband was right in saying that I should put from my mind any matters which had come to my knowledge in a secondhand way, that is through the channel of the news media.

Counsel for the wife further relied on the fact that the husband's sole object in asking for the stay was to force the wife back to Iran where she would have no remedies against him and where he could then dispose of her and obtain custody of his daughter. As to the absence of any formal evidence as to Iranian law counsel for the wife relied on the fact that the onus to justify the application was on the husband. Counsel for the husband submitted that he had established facts, eg language difficulties, expense and cultural background, sufficient to cause the burden to shift to the wife if she wished to rely on an absence of remedies in Iran.

It is of assistance to consider the circumstances in which the Act came to be passed. At the time when Lord Penzance delivered his speech, the sole basis of jurisdiction recognised by the English courts was domicile. By the Law Reform (Miscellaneous Provisions) Act 1949 'ordinary residence' by the petitioner immediately preceding the commencement of proceedings was introduced for the first time as a basis of jurisdiction. This was consolidated in the Matrimonial Causes Act 1950, s 18(1). When *Sealey (otherwise Callan) v Callen* was decided in 1953 the power of granting a stay was that granted by the Supreme Court of Judicature (Consolidation) Act 1925, s 41.

Under the provisions of the 1973 Act the wife is able to have a domicile separate from her husband. Besides this the Act reduced the qualifying period for ordinary residence to one year. In considering what reliance can be placed on previous authorities it must be remembered that whilst extending the jurisdiction of the court qua the wife in the manner I have just mentioned, Parliament saw fit to deal specifically with the question of the court's power to stay proceedings in s 5(6). This power to stay is given expressly without prejudice to any power to stay under the existing authority of the 1925 Act. The powers to grant a stay envisaged in the Act of 1973 must, therefore, be more liberally interpreted than the powers granted under the Act of 1925. Both the quotation from *Sealey* relied on by counsel for the wife and the quotation from Lord Penzance's speech must be read in the light of the extended jurisdiction granted to the court by the Act.

Considering the provisions of the 1973 Act generally, it is clear from s 5(2)(b) that Parliament envisaged that the courts in England would be dealing with cases in which not only one but both parties were domiciled elsewhere. This is of significance in view of the provisions in the Act for the first time enabling the wife to have a separate domicile of her own. In view of the findings of fact I have recorded earlier in this judgment I am by no means satisfied that the wife had not, on arrival in England in 1977, abandoned her domicile of origin and acquired a domicile of choice in England. It is, however, not necessary to consider this matter in further detail because the wife clearly qualifies by virtue of being ordinarily resident for one year under s 5(2)(b). In considering the balance of fairness, including convenience, the cultural background of the parties is merely an element, but no more than an element, amongst the number of factors which the court must consider in coming to its conclusion whether or not to grant a stay under the Act within the provisions of Sch 1.

I now turn to consider the submission of counsel for the husband based on the judgment of Ormrod LJ in *Mytton v Mytton*. Taken as it stands the quotation might appear to support the submission that the remedies or lack of remedies available to the wife in Iran were not relevant to the question of fairness as defined in para 9 of Sch 1 to the Act. With respect to counsel I think that he is straining the significance to be attached to that part of the judgment of Ormrod LJ. In one sense the question of comparing remedies is bound up with questions involving the culture and background of the parties and their domicile, all matters which formerly would determine in which jurisdiction matters relating to the marriage should be determined.

In *Mytton v Mytton* Ormrod LJ had said earlier in his judgment that in whatever court the parties proceeded the question of divorce would be a formality and that the real issue behind the application to stay was a question of ancillary relief. Whilst one of the husband's motives in the present case clearly was to prevent the wife obtaining financial relief, that is where the similarity between the issues in the case of *Mytton* and this case end. The issues in this case clearly involve much more than a comparison of the remedies by way of ancillary relief to which Ormrod LJ was referring.

The powers and duties to grant a stay imposed on the court are set out in Sch 1 to the 1973 Act. In this case I am concerned only with para 9 of Sch 1, namely discretionary stays. Paragraph 9(1) grants a discretionary power to stay proceedings where—

> 'it appears to the court (a) that any proceedings in respect of the marriage in question, or capable of affecting its validity or subsistence, are continuing in another jurisdiction; and (b) that the balance of fairness (including convenience) as between the parties to the marriage is such that it is appropriate for the proceedings in that jurisdiction to be disposed of before further steps are taken in the proceedings in the court or in those proceedings so far as they consist of a particular kind of matrimonial proceedings, the court may then, if it thinks fit, order that the proceedings be stayed . . . so far as they consist of proceedings of that kind.'

Paragraph 9(2) provides:

> 'In considering the balance of fairness and convenience for the purposes of sub-paragraph 1(b) above, the court shall have regard to all factors appearing to be relevant, including the convenience of witnesses and any delay or expense which may result from the proceedings being stayed, or not being stayed.'

There is no doubt that in the exercise of its discretion under these provisions the court must have regard to all relevant factors and that the area of this inquiry ought to be defined liberally. This must include, where relevant, the broad question of remedies including the possibility of the dissolution of the marriage itself and custody of children besides ancillary relief as matters of general fairness between the parties.

In considering the balance of fairness and convenience under para 9(2) of Sch 1 I have taken into account the convenience of conducting the proceedings in Iranian and the inconvenience of conducting them in English. This factor militates in favour of the husband. However, I am by no means satisfied that if the proceedings were allowed to continue in this court that the husband would, as he threatens at the moment, defend them as to the merits of the wife's allegations under s 1(2)(b) of the Matrimonial Causes

Act 1973. I must not, however, and do not, assume that he will not do so; nor should I try to prejudge this issue. I merely take into account the probability of such a course. It is difficult to envisage witnesses being brought from Iran to deal with matters that arose in this country but it is not beyond the bounds of possibility and I, therefore, bear that in mind. On the other hand if such a course were open to her under the laws in Iran and the wife decided to pursue her remedies based on the husband's ill-treatment of her whilst in this country in the Iranian courts, she would suffer a very heavy burden in having to take her witnesses from this country to Iran to support such an allegation. On the balance of convenience and expense so far as witnesses are concerned I am satisfied that a hearing in this country would be fairer and more convenient than one in Iran. If such a course were not open to the wife and she were merely able to defend the proceedings brought by the husband, then to deprive her of the opportunity of proceeding against him in these courts could not be fair even as between the parties.

So far as the cultural background of the parties is concerned I bear in mind that they are both Iranians and that the marriage, both as to the ceremony and as to its subsistence thereafter, was one of Iranian culture and background. I also bear in mind, however, that the wife, both by her own evidence and confirmed by the allegations made by the husband in his petition, has now espoused a Western culture of her own. In dealing with questions of fairness and convenience it is to the situation as it persists at the time of the application for a stay that I must consider these matters. Although the husband still clearly adheres to his Iranian culture and background I am satisfied that the wife has made considerable departures from those traditions under which she first entered marriage.

Finally, I am by no means satisfied that there is even a possibility of the wife being able to pursue her remedies or protect her interests in the proceedings as at present constituted in Iran. I do not have to have technical evidence as to the laws of Iran to come to this conclusion. I reach the conclusion without doubt by studying the husband's own affidavit and the exhibits thereto in conjunction with his evidence as outlined earlier in this judgment. In so far as the wife's evidence confirms the husband's view and my own assessment of the situation I accept it.

Taking all these matters into account in considering the balance of fairness and convenience as between the parties to the marriage I am not satisfied that it would be appropriate for the proceedings in Iran to be disposed of before further steps are taken in the proceedings in this court. Even if I had come to the conclusion in view of all the circumstances in the case I would not think fit to grant a stay if and in so far as that part of para 9 of Sch 1 relates to the exercise of my discretion.

At the end of the hearing before me I announced my decision and said that I would deliver a judgment in writing subsequently. Counsel for the husband made two applications to which I acceded. The first was that he should have leave to appeal. When I granted that leave he made a further application that I should extend the time for appealing so that it should run from the delivery of this judgment. I acceded to his second application. On reconsidering the matter during the preparation of this judgment I have come to the conclusion that I was wrong to have granted leave to appeal and that justice would be done if I accede only to counsel's second application, namely that the time for appealing should be extended to run from the date of the delivery of this judgment. This leaves ample time for him to consider this judgment and if he thinks fit to make an application to the Court of Appeal for leave to appeal.

Accordingly the application will be dismissed but the time for appealing will be extended so that it runs from today's date.

Application dismissed. Leave to appeal refused.

Solicitors: *Spilsbury & Co*, Kilburn (for the husband); *Alexander & Partners*, Willesden (for the wife).

Bebe Chua   Barrister.

Roome and another v Edwards (Inspector of Taxes)

HOUSE OF LORDS

LORD WILBERFORCE, LORD EDMUND-DAVIES, LORD RUSSELL OF KILLOWEN, LORD KEITH OF KINKEL
AND LORD ROSKILL

15th, 16th, 17th DECEMBER 1980, 5th FEBRUARY 1981

Capital gains tax – Settlement – Settled property – Trustees of settlement appointing part of trust fund of settlement to different beneficiaries under different trusts – Transfer of beneficial interests in residue of fund to two Cayman Islands companies – Replacement of trustees of original fund by Cayman Islands trustees – Beneficial interests assigned to Cayman Islands companies becoming vested in one company and that company becoming absolutely entitled as against Cayman Islands trustees – Whether separate settlement created in respect of appointed fund – Whether trustees of appointed fund assessable in respect of gains arising on disposal by Cayman Islands trustees – Finance Act 1965, s 25(1)(3)(11), Sch 10, para 12(1).

Under a settlement made in 1944 a trust fund ('the 1944 fund') was settled on trustees to hold the fund for the wife for life, then for the husband for life and thereafter for such of their issue as the husband and wife or survivor thereof should appoint. In October 1955 the wife and the husband executed a deed of appointment and release (i) irrevocably appointing a fund ('the appointed fund'), consisting of part of the 1944 settlement, in trust for one of their daughters absolutely when she reached the age of 25 and (ii) surrendering the wife's life interest in the investments making up the appointed fund. Thereafter the fund representing the balance of the 1944 settlement ('the main fund') and the appointed fund were administered separately, although they had common trustees until 1972. In 1972 the original trustees of the 1944 fund were replaced by trustees in the Cayman Islands and the husband and wife and their two daughters each assigned for substantial consideration their beneficial interests in the main fund to two Cayman Islands companies, one of which on 13th April assigned its reversionary interest to the other, so that for the purposes of a deemed disposal under s 25(3)ᵃ of the Finance Act 1965 the assignee company became absolutely entitled to the main fund. In consequence the taxpayers, who were the trustees of the appointed fund and were resident in the United Kingdom, were assessed to capital gains tax for the year 1972–73 on gains accruing to the Cayman Islands trustees on the basis that on 13th April the appointed fund and the main fund were subject to the same settlement and that therefore, under s 25(11) of, and Sch 10, para 12(1)ᵇ to, the 1965 Act, they and the Cayman Islands trustees together constituted a single body of trustees for the purpose of liability to capital gains tax. The Special Commissioners upheld the assessment. On appeal by the taxpayers the judge ([1979] STC 546) held that, although the main fund and the appointed fund constituted a single settlement and the trustees of both funds were to be regarded as a single body of trustees, tax could not be recovered from the taxpayers because para 12 could not make persons liable for any tax arising on the disposal of assets if they had no control over the assets. The Court of Appeal ([1980] 1 All ER 850) dismissed an appeal by the Crown, holding that the appointed fund by virtue of the 1955 appointment became, for the purposes of assessment, charge and payment of capital gains tax, comprised in a different settlement from the settlement of the main fund and, accordingly, the trustees of the appointed fund, who since 1972 were not the same persons as the trustees of the main fund, were not liable to tax in respect of the gain relating to the main fund. The Crown appealed to the House of Lords.

---

a   Section 25, so far as material, is set out at p 739 *a* to *d*, post

b   Paragraph 12(1) is set out at p 739 *e*, post

Held – The appeal would be allowed for the following reasons—

(1) The question whether a particular set of facts amounted to a 'settlement' was to be approached by asking what someone with knowledge of the legal context of the word under established doctrine and applying that knowledge in a practical and commonsense manner to the facts under examination would conclude. However, the mere existence of separate trusts applying to parts of settled property did not of itself give rise to separate settlements for the purposes of capital gains tax under the 1965 Act and, although part of a trust property might be vested in one set of trustees and part in another, under s 25(11) of that Act the whole of the property could still remain 'comprised in a settlement', ie a single settlement, even if each part was not held on identical trusts. On the facts, it was clear that the parties to the 1944 settlement and the 1955 appointment intended to treat the appointed fund as being held on the trusts of the 1944 settlement as added to and varied by the 1955 appointment. It followed, therefore, that on 13th April 1972 the taxpayers and the Cayman Islands trustees were the trustees of a single settlement (see p 739 j, p 740 c to e g h, p 741 c d g, p 742 d to g, p 743 b to f and p 744 e f, post).

(2) The words 'accruing to the trustees of a settlement' in para 12(1) of Sch 10 to the 1965 Act were not to be read otherwise than in the light of the situation produced by s 25(1) and (11). Thus when on 13th April 1972 the Cayman Islands assignee company became absolutely entitled to the trust property as against the Cayman Islands trustees there was a deemed disposal by the Cayman Islands trustees, and the taxpayers and the Cayman Islands trustees were to be treated as a single body of trustees. It followed that the gains arising on the deemed disposal accrued to that notional single body of trustees, and, since some of the trustees were resident or ordinarily resident in the United Kingdom, an assessment in respect of those gains could be made on any one or more of them resident or ordinarily resident in the United Kingdom (see p 742 b to g and p 743 h to p 744 c and e f, post).

Decision of the Court of Appeal [1980] 1 All ER 850 reversed.

Notes

For different sets of trustees treated as together constituting a single body of trustees, see 5 Halsbury's Laws (4th Edn) paras 116–117.

For capital gains tax in relation to settled property, see ibid paras 45–48.

For the Finance Act 1965, s 25 and Sch 10, para 12, see 34 Halsbury's Statutes (3rd Edn) 884, 470.

Section 25(1), (3) and (11) and Sch 10, para 12 were replaced by the Capital Gains Tax Act 1979, ss 52(1), 54(1), 52(3) and s 48 with effect from 6th April 1979.

Case referred to in opinions

Muir (or Williams) v Muir [1943] AC 468, 112 LJPC 39, HL.

Appeal

The Crown appealed against an order of the Court of Appeal (Buckley, Bridge and Templeman LJJ) ([1980] 1 All ER 850, [1980] Ch 425, [1980] STC 99) dated 30th November 1979 affirming on other grounds an order of Brightman J ([1979] 1 WLR 860, [1979] STC 546) made on 23rd February 1979 whereby on a case stated by the Commissioners for the Special Purposes of the Income Tax Acts (set out at [1979] STC 548–555), he allowed an appeal by the respondents, John Watford Roome and Thomas Graham Denne ('the taxpayers'), against the determination of the commissioners dismissing their appeal against the assessment to capital gains tax made on them for the year 1972–73. The facts are set out in the opinion of Lord Wilberforce.

D J Nicholls QC and *Peter Gibson* for the Crown.
D C Potter QC and *Robert Walker* for the taxpayers.

Their Lordships took time for consideration.

5th February. The following opinions were delivered.

LORD WILBERFORCE. My Lords, this is an appeal by the Crown in a case concerning capital gains tax. The relevant facts appear complicated but can be simplified to the following essentials. A full statement is to be found in the case stated by the Special Commissioners ((see [1979] STC 548–555).

On 24th March 1944 there was made a marriage settlement on the marriage of Captain and Mrs Lombard-Hobson. This was in a usual form, conferring a life interest on the wife followed by a protected life interest for her husband, a special power of appointment exercisable by the spouses jointly, or by the survivor, in favour of issue, and a trust, in default, for children at 21 or, if female, on marriage. There were a number of other powers and administrative provisions usual in marriage settlements.

There were two daughters of the marriage born in 1948 and 1951.

On 20th October 1955 (this event is critical) Captain and Mrs Lombard-Hobson exercised their joint power of appointment so that part of the settled property ('the 1955 fund') then worth about £13,000 should be held, subject to prior interests, in trust for the elder of the daughters on attaining 25, or if she died under 25 for her children. Mrs Lombard-Hobson also 'assigned and surrendered' her life interest to the trustees, but not so as to accelerate Captain Lombard-Hobson's expectant life interest. The trustees were to accumulate the interest of the fund with power to apply all accumulations for the daughter's benefit. Thereafter the trusts of the 1955 fund and of the remainder of the settled property ('the main fund') were administered separately, and separate accounts were kept and tax returns made. The present trustees of the 1955 fund ('the taxpayers') are the respondents, Mr Roome and Mr Denne. When Mr Denne was appointed, in 1972, as a separate trustee of the 1955 fund, together with Mr Roome, it was stated in the deed of appointment that this was done under s 37(1)(b) of the Trustee Act 1925. Mr Roome and Mr Denne have at all times been resident in the United Kingdom.

In 1972 some elaborate transactions took place, including an application to the court under the Variation of Trusts Act 1958. Only two are relevant for present purposes. (i) On 21st March 1972 two persons resident in the Cayman Islands were appointed trustees of the main fund, in place of the existing trustees who were then Mr Roome and a Mr Askew, and the assets of the main fund were vested in them. So there are now two sets of trustees, the taxpayers of the 1955 fund and the Cayman Islands trustees of the main fund. (ii) On 13th April 1972 a Cayman Islands company called Royal Oak Investments Ltd ('Royal Oak') became absolutely entitled to the main fund as against the trustees of the main fund. This brought about a 'deemed disposal' for the purposes of the capital gains tax of all the property vested in the trustees of the main fund, viz the Cayman Islands trustees. Among the assets to which Royal Oak became absolutely entitled as against the trustees of the main fund was a valuable property in Lincoln's Inn Fields, London, and it is mainly in respect of this that a claim for capital gains tax is made. The Crown is seeking to make good this claim against the taxpayers, who are trustees only of the 1955 fund.

There are two issues for decision. 1. Whether the taxpayers and the Cayman Islands trustees were on 13th April 1972 trustees of a single settlement for the purposes of the capital gains tax or whether the taxpayers are trustees of a separate settlement from the settlement of the main fund. 2. Whether, if there was a single settlement, a chargeable gain arising on the deemed disposal on 13th April 1972 accrued to all the trustees of the single settlement or only to the Cayman Islands trustees. If the former, the Crown could assess the taxpayers as residents in the United Kingdom in respect of this gain.

If the Crown is to succeed in the appeal, both of the above questions must be answered affirmatively; they were so answered by the Special Commissioners. On appeal to the High Court, Brightman J ([1979] STC 546) answered the first question Yes but the second question No. In the Court of Appeal ([1980] 1 All ER 850, [1980] Ch 425, [1980] STC 99), these answers were reversed, so that the taxpayers succeeded in both courts on different grounds.

There are a number of provisions in the Finance Act 1965 which have had to be examined. I think that those most relevant are the following (I cite them from the original 1965 Act, prior to amendment and consolidation). Section 25 provides:

'(1) In relation to settled property, the trustees of the settlement shall for the purposes of this Part of this Act be treated as being a single and continuing body of persons (distinct from the persons who may from time to time be the trustees), and that body shall be treated as being resident and ordinarily resident in the United Kingdom unless the general administration of the trusts is ordinarily carried on outside the United Kingdom and the trustees or a majority of them for the time being are not resident or not ordinarily resident in the United Kingdom ...

'(3) On the occasion when a person becomes absolutely entitled to any settled property as against the trustee all the assets forming part of the settled property to which he becomes so entitled shall be deemed to have been disposed of by the trustee, and immediately reacquired by him in his capacity as a trustee within section 22(5) of this Act, for a consideration equal to their market value ...

'(11) For the purposes of this section, where part of the property comprised in a settlement is vested in one trustee or set of trustees and part in another (and in particular where settled land within the meaning of the Settled Land Act 1925 is vested in the tenant for life and investments representing capital money are vested in the trustees of the settlement), they shall be treated as together constituting and, in so far as they act separately, as acting on behalf of a single body of trustees ...'

Schedule 10, para 12(1) provides:

'Capital gains tax chargeable in respect of chargeable gains accruing to the trustees of a settlement or capital gains tax due from the personal representatives of a deceased person may be assessed and charged on and in the name of any one or more of those trustees or personal representatives, but where an assessment is made in pursuance of this sub-paragraph otherwise than on all the trustees or all the personal representatives the persons assessed shall not include a person who is not resident or ordinarily resident in the United Kingdom.'

The first question. The Finance Act 1965 contains no definition of 'settlement'. As to 'settled property' s 45 merely states that the words mean, subject to sub-s (8) (concerned with unit trusts), any property held in trust other than property to which s 22(5) applies (property held by a nominee). So a 'settlement' must be a situation in which property is held in trust. But when is a settlement a separate settlement?

There are a number of obvious indicia which may help to show whether a settlement, or a settlement separate from another settlement, exists. One might expect to find separate and defined property, separate trusts, and separate trustees. One might also expect to find a separate disposition bringing the separate settlement into existence. These indicia may be helpful, but they are not decisive. For example, a single disposition, eg a will with a single set of trustees, may create what are clearly separate settlements, relating to different properties, in favour of different beneficiaries, and conversely separate trusts may arise in what is clearly a single settlement, eg when the settled property is divided into shares. There are so many possible combinations of fact that, even where these indicia or some of them are present, the answer may be doubtful, and may depend on an appreciation of them as a whole.

Since 'settlement' and 'trusts' are legal terms, which are also used by business men or laymen in a business or practical sense, I think that the question whether a particular set of facts amounts to a settlement should be approached by asking what a person, with knowledge of the legal context of the word under established doctrine and applying this knowledge in a practical and commonsense manner to the facts under examination, would conclude. To take two fairly typical cases. Many settlements contain powers to appoint a part or a proportion of the trust property to beneficiaries; some may also confer power to appoint separate trustees of the property so appointed, or such power may be conferred by law (see the Trustee Act 1925, s 37). It is established doctrine that the trusts declared by a document exercising a special power of appointment are to be read into the original settlement (see *Muir v Muir* [1943] AC 468). If such a power is exercised, whether or not separate trustees are appointed, I do not think that it would be natural for such a person as I have presupposed to say that a separate settlement had been created, still less so if it were found that provisions of the original settlement continued to apply to the appointed fund, or that the appointed fund were liable, in certain events, to fall back into the rest of the settled property. On the other hand, there may be a power to appoint and appropriate a part or portion of the trust property to beneficiaries and to settle it for their benefit. If such a power is exercised, the natural conclusion might be that a separate settlement was created, all the more so if a complete new set of trusts were declared as to the appropriated property, and if it could be said that the trusts of the original settlement ceased to apply to it. There can be many variations on these cases each of which will have to be judged on its facts.

There are indications in the Finance Act 1965 that this general conception is accepted and applied for purposes of capital gains tax and that the mere existence of separate trusts applying to parts of settled property does not of itself give rise to a separate settlement. Section 25(11) contemplates that part of trust property may be vested in one set of trustees and part in another but yet remain 'comprised in a settlement', ie a single settlement. I can see no reason why this should be confined to a case where each part is held on identical trusts. And sub-ss (4) and (12) contemplate that a life interest can subsist in a part of the property comprised in a settlement. Subsection (12) then treats that part as settled under a separate settlement but only for the purposes there stated, viz for the purposes of sub-ss (4) to (7) (these provisions have been later amended but this does not affect the argument). The inference must be that except for these limited purposes settled property held on separate trusts is not necessarily treated as held under separate settlements.

A further argument relates to the consequences which would follow if the mere fact of creating separate trusts over part of settled property were to cause that part to be held under a separate settlement. It would seem inescapable that in such a case there would be a deemed disposal under s 25(3) of that part in favour of the trustees of that part (even though they might be the same persons as the trustees of the original settlement, their personality being irrelevant under s 25(1)). This would give rise to a multitude of charges to capital gains tax and would in effect paralyse the working of settlements. The Court of Appeal, recognising this difficulty, sought to avoid it by an argument that, although for purposes of capital gains tax a new settlement might be created by the exercise of a special power of appointment, there would be no deemed disposal (under s 25(3)) unless the original settlement came to an end, which, as exemplified by the present case, it might not do. But I respectfully think that the second part of this argument refutes the first and that the two cannot live together. If the original settlement survives and continues to apply to the appointed part, it must follow that no separate settlement has been created.

Counsel for the taxpayers, I think, accepted the argument so far. He did not contend that the mere exercise of a special power of appointment over part of settled property brought about a separate settlement, or, as a consequence, a deemed disposition under s 25(3). He accepted that in so holding the Court of Appeal may have gone too far. What he relied on was the totality of the transaction which took place on 20th October 1955, when not only was the special power of appointment jointly exercised by the husband and wife, but the wife assigned and surrendered her life interest in the 1955 fund. This, he said, was (or rather would have been if executed after 1965) a disposition within the provisions of s 25(4) and, consequently or in any event, the creation of a separate trust.

As to this contention, it may be agreed that the assignment and surrender of the wife's life interest in the 1955 fund introduces an additional and relevant element, but it remains necessary to ask: is it decisive on the question whether a separate settlement was then made? This has still to be answered in the light of the tests indicated above.

Normally, a mere assignment or release of a life interest would not be thought of as creating a separate settlement; so no doubt one must look at the whole of the 1955 transaction. It seems in fact clear how the parties to the 1944 settlement and the 1955 appointment viewed the matter. In the first place, although the wife had divested herself of her life interest, it remained in existence for the purpose of enabling the trustees, during her life, to accumulate the income. The husband, moreover, retained his protected life interest in the whole of the 1944 settlement fund, including the 1955 fund. Then, when Mr Roome was appointed a new trustee on 22nd October 1959, he was appointed as trustee of the 1944 settlement for all the purposes of that settlement, an indication that the trusts of the 1944 settlement included those of the 1955 appointment; the same formula was used on 9th October 1961 when another new trustee was appointed. Again, when on 7th February 1972 separate trustees (the taxpayers) were appointed to the 1955 fund, it was recited in the deed of appointment that the 1955 fund was held by the then trustees of the 1944 settlement 'upon the trusts declared concerning the same by the Settlement and by the 1955 Appointment' and the taxpayers were appointed trustees of the 1944 settlement so far as regarded the appointed (ie 1955) fund. So the intention throughout seems clearly to have been to treat the 1955 fund as being held on the trusts of the 1944 settlement as added to and varied by the 1955 appointment.

It is true that the appointed fund from 1955 onwards was administered separately from the main trust fund, and that separate accounts were kept of it. The taxpayers relied strongly on this as indicating distinctness, or separation. They suggested further that to treat the fund as a separately settled fund would fit the framework of the capital gains tax legislation, in that gains and losses of the appointed fund (and also of course of the main fund) could be charged to that fund and not to any other part of the settled property. This led into what may be called a 'purposive' argument to the effect that, if a capital gains tax on trust property is to operate fairly and effectively, it is necessary to treat any part of that property which may be held on distinct trusts as held under a separate settlement. The concept of 'settlement' in the legislation was, counsel for the taxpayers suggested, merely a device for breaking up trusts into units, or packets, which will bear their own taxes on their gains, less losses. This argument was in substance accepted by the Court of Appeal. Now this might be a sensible prescription for a legislature minded to set up a capital gains tax. But it is not what the Act, on a reasonable construction (however purposefully orientated), has done. It has taken a simpler course: it has attached the liability to pay capital gains tax to the trustees of settlements, not to funds held on distinct trusts, and (in this in contrast to estate duty legislation) has not concerned itself with questions of incidence of the tax between beneficiaries or funds within a settlement.

I therefore cannot follow the Court of Appeal in this part of the argument. For the reasons I have given, in agreement with the judge, I reach the conclusion that the respondents and the Cayman Islands trustees were trustees of a single settlement.

The second issue. This has to be approached on the basis that, as decided on the first, there was a single settlement. It can be stated as follows: did the gain arising on the deemed disposal which took place on 13th April 1972 accrue to the Cayman Islands trustees as the actual trustees by whom the deemed disposal was made or to the Cayman Islands trustees and the taxpayers, treated as a notional single body of trustees? If the latter, since the majority were not resident or ordinarily resident outside the United Kingdom, an assessment could be made on any one or more of the trustees subject to the qualification that it could not be made on persons (viz the Cayman Islands trustees) who are not resident or ordinarily resident in the United Kingdom (see Finance Act 1965, Sch 10, para 12). Thus it could be made on the taxpayers.

The critical statutory provisions for this purpose are s 25(1) and (11) of Sch 10, para 12(1) to the 1965 Act, which I have already reproduced.

I have found greater difficulty on this point than I believe is felt by some of your Lordships. The dilemma is well expressed in the judgment of Brightman J. Like the learned judge I do not find it easy to relate the liability and assessment provisions in Sch 10, para 12(1) to those contained in s 25, and it does not seem to me at all clear that s 25(1), which introduces the concept of a single and continuing body of persons, is concerned with more than questions of residence and segregation of trustees as a body from the component individuals. The result of the Crown's argument that one set of trustees may be charged to the tax in respect of the transactions of another set over which they have no control does not appear attractive in principle, however little practical hardship may arise in some cases and indeed in the present case. However, I have to agree that the linguistic argument is a strong one in favour of the Crown. Section 25(11) cannot be read as limited to a case where property (vested in two sets of trustees) is held on identical trusts; the particular case given in parenthesis might be such a case, but sub-s (11) clearly extends beyond it. If so, it seems to produce the result, in this case, that the United Kingdom trustees and the Cayman Islands trustees are treated as a single body of trustees, a concept which has already been introduced in sub-s (1). Then it is necessary, for the purpose of establishing liability to apply Sch 10, para 12(1). Again it seems difficult to read the words 'accruing to the trustees of a settlement' otherwise than in the light of the situation produced by s 25(1) and (11) as analysed above.

Since the Court of Appeal and your Lordships regard it as clear that the analysis summarised above is correct and inescapable, I am not prepared to dissent from the conclusion that the Crown succeeds on this issue also.

The appeal must therefore be allowed.

LORD EDMUND-DAVIES. My Lords, I have had the advantage of reading in draft form the speech prepared by my noble and learned friend Lord Wilberforce. Like my Lord, I have found question 2 substantially more difficult to deal with than question 1, but I am nevertheless in respectful agreement with the manner in which both questions have been answered by him. I accordingly concur in allowing the appeal.

LORD RUSSELL OF KILLOWEN. My Lords, I have had the advantage of reading in advance the speech prepared by my noble and learned friend Lord Wilberforce. I agree with his view that both the points which arise for decision in this appeal fall to be decided in favour of the Crown, and on the second of those points without the hesitation felt by my noble and learned friend. Accordingly I too would allow this appeal.

LORD KEITH OF KINKEL. My Lords, I agree with the speech of my noble and learned friend Lord Wilberforce, which I have had the advantage of reading in draft and to which I cannot usefully add. Accordingly I too would allow the appeal.

LORD ROSKILL. My Lords, in this appeal your Lordships' House has to consider the efficacy of a scheme evolved for the purpose of avoiding liability for capital gains tax. There has been a remarkable difference of opinion in the courts below which have had to consider this problem. There were, it was common ground, two questions which had both to be answered in favour of the Crown before this appeal could succeed. The Special Commissioners decided both questions in favour of the Crown. Brightman J decided the first in favour of the Crown but the second in favour of the taxpayer. He therefore allowed the taxpayer's appeal. On the Crown's appeal to the Court of Appeal (Buckley, Bridge and Templeman LJJ) the learned Lords Justices dismissed the appeal but for the opposite reasons given by Brightman J, deciding the first question against the Crown but the second in their favour. Leave to appeal to your Lordships' House was given by the Court of Appeal.

My Lords, the relevant facts are so clearly stated in the judgment by Brightman J (see [1979] 1 WLR 860 at 862–864 [1979] STC 546 at 555–557) that no useful purpose will be served by further repetition of them. The first question is whether in 1955 a separate settlement was created when the special power of appointment was exercised. The answer to my mind must depend on the true construction of the 1955 deed itself. This deed is declared to be supplemental to the 1944 marriage settlement and to be made pursuant to the powers thereby conferred. The trusts of the 1955 appointment were not exhaustive. They could fail and would have failed if Mrs Robinson (as Jane became) were not to survive until she were 25 years of age. The husband expressly retained his protected reversionary life interest. I venture to think that if in 1955 anyone had been asked if the 1955 appointment constituted a separate settlement the answer must have been in the negative. Of course, at that time no one contemplated the imposition of capital gains tax. That was introduced ten years later by the Finance Act 1965. That Act contains no relevant definition of settlement and like Brightman J I do not find authorities on what have been held to be separate settlements for the purposes of other statutes of assistance in determining whether a particular document or particular documents do or do not create a separate settlement for the purposes of s 25 of the 1965 Act. Counsel for the Crown pressed on your Lordships, as part of his argument, a number of anomalies which would arise if the view taken by the Court of Appeal be correct. Though they thought otherwise, I see no escape from the conclusion that if the 1955 appointment created a separate settlement it involved a notional transfer of the relevant assets in the 1944 settlement to the new trustees and that there then would be a disposal from the old trustees to the new for the purposes of s 25(3). With profound respect to the contrary view of Templeman LJ (see [1980] 1 All ER 850 at 855, [1980] Ch 425 at 436, [1980] STC 99 at 104), I think the new trustees on this hypothesis would become absolutely entitled to the assets thus taken out of the 1944 settlement. Furthermore, on the view taken by the Court of Appeal I venture to ask, as did counsel for the Crown, how the acquisition cost to the new trustees is to be calculated. My Lords, on this part of the case I find the reasoning of Brightman J (see [1979] 1 WLR 860 at 867, [1979] STC 546 at 559–560) compelling and I would respectfully adopt it as my own. I think the right conclusion is that the main fund as it was called and the 1955 fund remain comprised in a single settlement at all times from 24th March 1944 until 13th April 1972 on which date it was agreed that Royal Oak became absolutely entitled to the main fund as against the Cayman Island trustees. It follows that on that last-mentioned date there was a deemed disposal by those trustees. I would, therefore, answer the first question in favour of the Crown.

I now turn to consider the second question on which the Court of Appeal agreed with the Crown but Brightman J had taken the contrary view. The Crown sought to make the taxpayers, the trustees of the 1955 fund, liable to the relevant capital gains tax payable on this deemed disposal. One argument advanced on behalf of the taxpayers was that it was clearly wrong and unjust to impose on one set of trustees liability for tax as a result of a disposal by another set of trustees over whom the former set had no control. At first sight this may seem strange. But the critical question is not whether the result is strange, or even unjust (in the present case I detected no relevant injustice whatever for in truth this was all part of the same scheme for avoiding capital gains tax), but on what the relevant provisions of the Finance Act 1965 provide should happen in such a contingency as this.

My Lords, the first thing to observe is that s 25(1) provides for the creation of a new and 'single and continuing body of persons (distinct from the persons who may from time to time be the trustees)' as the trustees of the settlement which is, of course, in the light of my conclusion on the first question the single settlement already referred to. Further s 25(1) provides that that single and continuing body is to be treated as resident and ordinarily resident in the United Kingdom subject to certain exceptions not presently relevant. There were, of course, at the material date two separate sets of trustees but because of s 25(1) those two sets are to be treated as a single and continuing body. Further, by reason of s 25(11) each set of trustees is to be treated as having acted on behalf of that single and continuing body which is ordinarily resident. With all respect to the argument of counsel for the taxpayers I find myself unable to construe s 25(11) as applying only to a case where there is a unity of beneficial interests. The language used seems to be deliberately wide and plain in its scope. That single and continuing body is treated as being resident and ordinarily resident in the United Kingdom and in my view must be so treated as at 13th April 1972.

Paragraph 12(1) of Sch 10 to the 1965 Act imposes liability for capital gains tax on the trustees. The paragraph charges their tax on any one or more of those trustees. In other words, each is and all are liable, subject to the safeguard that where the assessment is not made on all the trustees those trustees not resident or ordinarily resident in the United Kingdom cannot lawfully be assessed.

I think this was the view taken by Templeman LJ when he expressed disagreement with the conclusion of Brightman J on this issue saying, 'I find this argument impossible to sustain in view of the provisions of ss 25(1), 25(11) of and para 12(1) of Sch 10 to the 1965 Act' (see [1980] 1 All ER 850 at 856, [1980] Ch 425 at 437, [1980] STC 99 at 105). In common with Templeman LJ, I am of the view that the taxpayers were at the material time trustees in whom part of the property comprised in the settlement was vested and because of those statutory provisions ought to be treated with the trustees of the main fund as trustees of the settlement each of whom is liable for capital gains tax on the whole.

Your Lordships were strongly pressed with the submission that this conclusion would, or at any rate might, jeopardise trustees such as the taxpayers who had no legal control over the assets which were the subject of the deemed disposal. Your Lordships were assured that in the present case the taxpayers were properly and adequately protected by the beneficiaries in relation to any liability which might fall on them. My Lords, the short answer to this powerfully urged plea is surely this. Persons, whether professional men or not, who accept appointment as trustees of settlements such as these are clearly at risk under the 1965 Act and have only themselves to blame if they accept the obligations of trustees in these circumstances without ensuring that they are sufficiently and effectively protected whether by their beneficiaries or otherwise for fiscal or other liabilities which may fall on them personally as a result of the obligations which they had felt able to assume. In the result I have reached the same conclusion as did the Special Commissioners. Accordingly I would allow the Crown's appeal and restore the Special Commissioners' determination.

Appeal allowed.

Solicitors: *Solicitor of Inland Revenue; Withers* (for the taxpayers).

Rengan Krishnan Esq   Barrister.

Chanel Ltd v F W Woolworth & Co Ltd and others

CHANCERY DIVISION
FOSTER J
13th, 14th, 15th, 23rd OCTOBER 1980

COURT OF APPEAL, CIVIL DIVISION
BUCKLEY, SHAW AND OLIVER LJJ
3rd, 4th NOVEMBER 1980

Judgment – Order – Consent order – Interlocutory order – Setting aside – Grounds for setting aside interlocutory order – Defendants giving undertaking on hearing of interlocutory motion – Undertaking embodied in consent order until trial or further order – Point at issue subsequently decided by Court of Appeal in another case – Defendants applying to have undertaking discharged – Judge refusing to discharge undertaking and refusing leave to appeal – Whether defendants entitled to leave to appeal – Whether contractual effect of undertaking making it binding until trial – Whether defendants required to adduce grounds sufficient to set aside a contract – Whether acquisition of subsequent evidence and Court of Appeal decision justifying discharge of undertaking and rehearing of interlocutory motion.

The defendants imported and distributed to English retailers perfumes and toiletries originating from a United States company and bearing the name 'Chanel'. On 29th March 1979 the plaintiffs, an English company which was the registered holder of the 'Chanel' trade mark in the United Kingdom, commenced an action against the defendants for infringement of the mark and passing off, and obtained on an ex parte motion injunctions, inter alia, against the defendants. The defendants believed that their only defence was under EEC law and intended to raise that defence at the trial of the action. Accordingly, when the motion came on for hearing inter partes on 6th April they gave an undertaking that they would not until judgment in the action 'or until further order in the meantime' infringe the plaintiffs' trade marks or pass off products as the plaintiffs' products. The motion was then disposed of by consent and ordered to be stood over until the trial of the action. In May the defendants discovered from various company searches that the plaintiffs and the US company from which they acquired the goods were apparently part of the same group of companies. In November 1979 in another case[a] the Court of Appeal held that where a trade mark was developed as a house mark and was distinctive of a group of companies every company in the group was to be taken to have consented to other companies in the group using the mark. On the basis that that decision applied to their case, and that, together with the evidence acquired since the consent order on 6th April, it altered the legal position between the parties, the defendants applied to have the undertaking given by them on 6th April discharged. The judge refused to discharge the undertaking, on the grounds (i) that the consent order of 6th April had contractual effect and could not be set aside unless the defendants put forward grounds sufficient to set aside a contract, and (ii) that the defendants had not put forward sufficient evidence to establish that their case was covered by the Court of Appeal decision and the mere fact that there had been a change in the law subsequent to the undertaking being given was not a sufficient reason to set aside the consent order. The judge refused leave to appeal, and the defendants applied to the Court of Appeal for leave but also contended that leave to appeal was not required because the judge's refusal to discharge the consent order was analogous to the grant or refusal of an injunction from which leave to appeal was not required.

---

a   Revlon Inc v Cripps & Lee Ltd [1980] FSR 85

Held – (1) The judge's order refusing to discharge the consent order was not analogous to the grant or refusal of an injunction and therefore leave to appeal was required (see p 752 c d, post).

(2) Even assuming, as was probably the case, that the consent order had contractual force, an order or undertaking given to the court which was expressed to be 'until further order' impliedly gave the party bound by the order or undertaking the right to apply to the court to have it discharged or modified if there were good grounds for doing so, since the applicant was not applying to set aside or modify any contract implicit in the order or undertaking but merely exercising the implied right in accordance with the term of the contract that the undertaking should be binding only until judgment or further order (see p 751 d to f and p 752 d, post).

(3) However, the defendants would not be allowed to reopen the order made on 6th April 1979 since a party was not entitled to a rehearing of an interlocutory matter unless there had been some significant change of circumstances or he had become aware of facts which he could not reasonably have known or found out by the time of the original hearing. It had been open to the defendants at the hearing of the motion on 6th April 1979 to take the point subsequently decided by the Court of Appeal, even though that point had not then been decided, and to adduce evidence in support of it, and if they had asked for an adjournment for that purpose it would probably have been granted. It followed that since 6th April 1979 there had not been any change in the defendants' potential ability successfully to resist the plaintiffs' interlocutory motion that justified the court in discharging or modifying the undertaking given on 6th April. Accordingly, leave to appeal would be refused and the application dismissed (see p 751 g to p 752 d, post).

Notes

For setting aside a consent order, see 26 Halsbury's Laws (4th Edn) para 562, and for cases on the subject, see 51 Digest (Repl) 732–736, 3220–3245.

Cases referred to in judgment

American Cyanamid Co v Ethicon Ltd [1975] 1 All ER 504, [1975] AC 396, [1975] 2 WLR 316, [1975] RPC 513, HL, Digest (Cont Vol D) 537, 152a.

GCT (Management) Ltd v Laurie Marsh Group Ltd [1972] FSR 519, [1973] RPC 432, Digest (Cont Vol D) 1000, 2035c.

Purcell v F C Trigell Ltd (trading as Southern Window and General Cleaning Co) [1970] 3 All ER 671, [1971] 1 QB 358, [1970] 3 WLR 884, CA, Digest (Cont Vol C) 1095, 3232a.

Regent Oil Co Ltd v J T Leavesley (Litchfield) Ltd [1966] 2 All ER 454, [1966] 1 WLR 1210, Digest (Cont Vol B) 701, 130b.

Revlon Inc v Cripps & Lee Ltd [1980] FSR 85, CA.

Cases also cited

Attorney General v Tomline (1877) 7 Ch D 388.

B(GC) v B(BA) [1970] 1 All ER 913, sub nom *Brister v Brister* [1970] 1 WLR 664.

Dunhill (Alfred) Ltd v Sunoptic SA and Dunhill (C) [1979] FSR 337, CA.

Lonrho Ltd v Shell Petroleum Co Ltd [1980] QB 358, [1980] 2 WLR 367, CA; *affd* [1980] 1 WLR 627, HL.

Wenlock v Maloney [1965] 2 All ER 871, [1965] 1 WLR 1238, CA.

Motion

By notice of motion dated 5th June 1980 Three Pears Wholesale Cash and Carry Ltd, the second defendants in an action commenced on 29th March 1979 by the plaintiffs, Chanel Ltd, for alleged infringement of trade marks and passing off, sought to be released or discharged from undertakings they gave on 6th April 1979, on the hearing of an interlocutory motion in the action, not to (i) part with possession, power, custody or control or in any way deal with certain products not being the plaintiffs' products which bore the words or marks Chanel or Chanel No 5 or any words colourably similar, or (ii) otherwise infringe the plaintiffs' registered trade marks or otherwise pass off products not being the plaintiffs' products as or for the plaintiffs' products. The grounds of the motion were that the plaintiffs had no real prospect of obtaining at the trial of the action relief of the nature they sought, alternatively the balance of convenience was in favour of the discharge or release of the defendants' undertakings, and, in the further alternative, it was just and convenient that the defendants should be discharged or released from their undertakings. The facts are set out in the judgment.

T L G Cullen QC and *John Baldwin* for the second defendants.
Charles Sparrow QC and *Bruce Spalding* for the plaintiffs.

Cur adv vult

23rd October. **FOSTER J** read the following judgment: I have before me a motion which seeks to discharge an undertaking given by the second defendants by consent on the footing that there has been a change of law since that date. Before I go further I should say that both parties have relied to a very limited extent on delay. I have carefully examined the dates in this case but I do not think that the delays which have occurred are unusual in such a difficult action as the present. I therefore propose to disregard any question of delay in deciding this motion.

Chanel Ltd

This is an English company which sells in the United Kingdom and Ireland the well-known marks of perfumery, scent and sprays under the names Chanel No 5, Chanel No 19 and Chanel No 22. It is the registered holder of the trade mark in those countries. It discovered that the second defendants were importing from Belgium and selling to retailers similar products which had been imported into Belgium from the United States which were sold to it by Chanel Inc, a United States company. All of the distinctive marks were on both, the only difference being that on the back of the United States product it showed Chanel Inc New York, and the formula used which was necessary under United States law.

The parent company seems to be a Swiss company called Fibo AG. There is also another English company called Bourjeois Ltd, which is also a subsidiary of Fibo AG. It is not known who are the shareholders in the French company Chanel SA. There is another Swiss company Pamerco, but there is no information as to its shareholders either, and there is no information as to who are the shareholders in Chanel Inc, the United States company. It seems that the plaintiffs, Chanel Ltd, mainly market goods from France, and the United States company either purchases the goods from France or itself manufactures them. No doubt the interconnection between these companies and the degree of control exercised by whichever company is the parent will emerge at the trial.

The writ was issued on 29th March 1979 and on that date an Anton Piller order was obtained against the second defendants. These orders were served on the second defendants on 2nd April 1979, the goods being seized on 3rd April, and on 5th April the plaintiffs brought a motion for committal for breach of that order. The main motion came on for hearing on 6th April 1979 and a consent order was made on that date. On 24th April 1979 the motion for committal of the second defendants and two of their directors was heard and Walton J held that there was a contempt and ordered that the directors should pay the costs on an indemnity basis. The present position of the action is that it was set down for hearing on 15th September 1980 though there is still outstanding a request by the second defendant for further discovery. If the parties are willing to allow the action to float it could well be heard early in 1981 though if they wanted a date to be fixed a date could not be obtained before October or November 1981.

The present motion

On 6th April 1979, as I have said, a consent order was made in these terms:

'UPON MOTION for an Injunction this day made unto this Court by Counsel . . . AND
UPON READING the order dated 29th March 1979 AND the Plaintiffs and the
Defendants by their Counsel consenting to this Order [then there is the usual
undertaking as to damages and the order goes on:] AND the Defendants by their
Counsel undertaking until after Judgment in this Action or until further Order in
the meantime that they will not do (whether by their directors officers servants or
agents or any of them or otherwise howsoever) the following acts or either of them
that is to say (i) part with possession power custody or control of or in any way deal
with perfume eau de toilette eau de cologne bath oil bath powder and other
toiletries (hereinafter referred to as "products") not being the Plaintiffs' or any
cartons boxes or other packaging therefor not being the Plaintiffs' bearing on or in
relation thereto the words or marks Chanel or Chanel No 5 or any words or marks
colourably similar thereto (ii) otherwise infringe the plaintiffs' registered trade
marks [and the numbers of five are given] or any of them or otherwise pass off
products not being the Plaintiffs' as or for the Plaintiffs' AND the Defendants by their
Counsel undertaking until after Friday 13th April 1979 or until further Order in
the meantime that they will not do . . . the following act that is to say disclose
without the leave of the Plaintiffs the subject matter of this Action or the Plaintiffs'
interest herein to any person save for the purpose of obtaining legal advice THIS
COURT DOTH ORDER that the said Motion do stand to the trial of this Action'

The notice of motion for committal had not then been heard.

On 22nd November 1979 the Court of Appeal gave judgment in *Revlon Inc v Cripps
& Lee Ltd* [1980] FSR 85. The present motion by the second defendants is dated 5th June
1980 and came on for hearing on 10th June when it was stood over to be heard as a
motion by order on 13th October, when it came before me. The present motion is in
these terms:

'. . . by counsel on behalf of the Second Defendants for an order that the Second
defendants be released or discharged from their undertakings given to this Court on
6th April 1979 not to: [and then there is the two undertakings which they gave] ON
THE GROUNDS THAT the Plaintiffs have no real prospect of obtaining relief of such a
nature at the trial herein alternatively that the balance of convenience is in favour
of such discharge or release alternatively that it is just that there be such discharge
or release. AND FOR further or other relief AND FOR the costs . . .'

As I have said, the second defendants seek to have the consent order of 6th April set
aside pending the hearing of the action. Two questions arise: first, can a consent order
be set aside where there is no allegation that the order was made by fraud or by mistake
when it was made, and, second, does the effect of the *Revlon* decision mean that the
plaintiff company has no reasonable chance of succeeding at the hearing of the action?

The consent order

In *Purcell v F C Trigell Ltd* [1970] 3 All ER 671, [1971] 1 QB 358 the Court of Appeal
decided that a consent order could not be set aside even in an interlocutory matter unless
there were grounds which would justify the setting aside of a contract entered into with
knowledge of the material matter by a legally competent person (see per Winn LJ [1970]
3 All ER 671 at 676, [1971] 1 QB 358 at 365). In *GCT (Management) Ltd v Laurie Marsh
Group Ltd* [1973] RPC 432 an undertaking was offered by the defendant company until
judgment or further order and accepted by the plaintiffs. The plaintiffs brought a second
interlocutory motion as they said confusion between the names of the two cinemas was
still causing confusion. Whitford J said (at 434):

'The point of interlocutory relief is basically to protect the position of the plaintiffs
who fear that unless some interlocutory relief be granted to them they will suffer
damage and will not be adequately compensated in damages if they eventually
succeed in the action. When they made their first application the plaintiffs were in

fact prepared to accept that the possibility of serious damage pending the final determination of the action would be sufficiently obviated if they accepted the undertaking which the defendants offered, and they accepted the undertaking upon this basis. It seems to me that, in those circumstances, it would be wholly wrong for them now if perhaps they feel, or circumstances would appear to indicate, that they wrongly estimated what the result of the change of name would be, to reopen the matter.'

The second defendants rely on *Regent Oil Co Ltd v J T Leavesley (Lichfield) Ltd* [1966] 2 All ER 454, [1966] 1 WLR 1210. In that case the plaintiff was granted an injunction to restrain the defendant from breaking a solus agreement until a certain date and on that date the defendant consented to the injunction being extended to the trial. Meantime two decisions of the Court of Appeal had held that the doctrine of restraint of trade did have a place in commercial agreements which limited the restraint to a particular property, reversing a previous decision. The defendant company brought another motion to have the injunction discharged. This case was of course prior to the House of Lords decision in *American Cyanamid Co v Ethicon Ltd* [1975] 1 All ER 504, [1975] AC 396 and the test then was whether the plaintiff had made out a prima facie case for the continuance of the injunction. Stamp J said ([1966] 2 All ER 454 at 458, [1966] 1 WLR 1210 at 1216):

'For the reasons which I have given, if the plaintiff were today applying for interlocutory relief, I should be constrained reluctantly to refuse it, reluctantly because this court is reluctant, on an interlocutory application, not to hold a party bound to the very words of his covenant and I would have to hold that there ought not to be an injunction from today until the trial. Taking the view that I do that the plaintiff company has no built-in right to the continuance of the injunction it obtained, after it has become apparent that it was founded on a decision wrong in law, I ought, in my view, to discharge the injunction, and this I do.'

In that case the original injunction was not made by consent but the defendant consented to its continuing until trial. The point before me was never argued in that case. In the *Revlon* case all the facts were before the court and were adjudicated on. In the present case all the facts are by no means before the court and the consent order provided that there should be no hearing of the motion at all until trial. As I have said, the test is now different. It is: has the plaintiff any real prospect of succeeding in his claim for a permanent injunction at the trial? The defendants admit that their evidence is incomplete in attempting to prove what the actual Chanel group control in fact amounts to but says that the court should draw inferences to show that there is sufficient group control to bring it within the *Revlon* case. It is interesting to note that the House of Lords in refusing leave to appeal in the *Revlon* case said that it would be better if the action went for trial.

In my judgment I do not have proper evidence to decide whether the undertaking given should be now discharged as the plaintiffs have not answered the second defendants' evidence on this motion other than to answer the allegation of delay. The second defendants do not allege any mistake when the consent order was made. They rely on a subsequent change of the law. In my judgment a subsequent change of the law is insufficient to upset a consent order. Even if I am wrong in that and I should hear the motion on the evidence before the court, it is clearly insufficient in showing that the *Revlon* case completely covers the present case.

The Revlon decision

In my judgment there are many facts in the present case which would enable the plaintiffs to distinguish this case from the *Revlon* case. To mention just a few: (a) In that case the English company was not the registered holder of the trade mark as in the present case. (b) In the *Revlon* case the following words were on the register: 'The trade mark is to be used by the registered user in relation to the goods only so long as the registered proprietor and the registered user are controlled by Revlon Inc.' (c) On all the Revlon products sold in the United Kingdom were the words 'Revlon, New York, Paris and London'. In this case on the plaintiffs' products sold there are usually the words 'Chanel, Paris' and some have also the words 'Made in France'. On the United States products the words always used are 'Chanel Inc, New York, NY 10019'. (d) There is no specific evidence as to the control imposed on the English company by the French or any other company in the group.

In those circumstances I cannot conclude that the plaintiffs have any real prospect of succeeding in obtaining a permanent injunction at the trial. It follows that the motion fails and I propose to dismiss it.

Motion dismissed. Leave to appeal refused.

Application for leave to appeal
The second defendants applied to the Court of Appeal for leave to appeal.

T L G Cullen QC and *John Baldwin* for the second defendants.
Charles Sparrow QC and *Bruce Spalding* for the plaintiffs.

BUCKLEY LJ. This is an application by the second defendants for leave to appeal against the refusal by Foster J to discharge or modify an undertaking given by those defendants until judgment or further order in the following circumstances.

By their writ issued on 29th March 1979 the plaintiffs sued for relief of a normal character for alleged infringement of trade marks and alleged passing-off. They moved ex parte for interlocutory relief by way of an Anton Piller order and injunctions, and obtain ex parte relief on 29th March 1979. Before the motion came on inter partes the second defendants, Three Pears Wholesale Cash and Carry Ltd, believing that the only defence available to them was one under EEC law, felt constrained to give an undertaking until judgment or further order in the terms of the notice of motion. Accordingly, when the motion came before the court inter partes, the defendants tendered such an undertaking. The plaintiffs were content, on the defendants giving that undertaking, to their motion being stood over until the trial. Accordingly, on 6th April 1979, the motion was disposed of in that manner by consent, without its being opened to the court and without the evidence being read.

Subsequently, on 2nd to 10th May, the defendants made certain company searches. Those disclosed certain apparent organisational links between the plaintiff company and the other companies (which were in fact foreign companies) through whom the goods which are the subject matter of the alleged infringements and passings-off were acquired by the defendants. These links suggest that there may exist a group structure embracing both the plaintiff company and the foreign companies from or through whom the defendants acquired the goods. The defendants also discovered other evidence in the form of advertising material and the like, suggesting the existence of a group structure of that kind.

In November 1979 this court decided an appeal in *Revlon Inc v Cripps & Lee Ltd* [1980] FSR 85. In that case the plaintiff company formed part of a group of companies in which all save the parent company were wholly owned subsidiaries, or wholly owned sub-subsidiaries, of that parent company. The plaintiff company sued for passing-off Revlon goods manufactured in the United States of America by a Revlon company operating in the United States as Revlon goods manufactured in the United Kingdom by another Revlon company operating in the United Kingdom. This court held that the marks, or get-up, in that case had been developed as a house mark distinctive of the whole group and that every company in the group must be taken to have consented to the marks *a* being used by every other company of the group to designate the products so marked as products of the group as a whole.

The defendants in the present case contend that that decision threw a new light on the legal position of the parties in this case, and that this, in conjunction with the additional evidential material which they had acquired since they gave their undertaking, created a new state of affairs, in which they were entitled to ask the court to discharge the undertaking. They accordingly moved Foster J for such relief. The judge refused it on *b* two grounds: first, that the order of 6th April 1979 being a consent order, had contractual effect and could not be set aside unless there were grounds which would justify setting it aside as a contract (see *Purcell v F C Trigell Ltd* [1970] 3 All ER 671, [1971] 1 QB 358); and second that the evidence was insufficient to establish that the case was covered by the decision in *Revlon Inc v Cripps & Lee Ltd* [1980] FSR 85.

The defendants have submitted that the consent order, or rather the undertaking *c* associated with it, was only to bind the defendants until judgment or further order in the meantime. The plaintiffs contend that their motion was stood over until the trial in consideration of the undertaking, and that the defendants are contractually bound by it until the trial unless grounds are adduced for rescinding or modifying it, which would be effective grounds for rescinding or modifying a contract. I shall assume in the plaintiffs' favour, as I think is probably the case, that the consent order has contractual *d* force as between the parties. Nevertheless, it was a term of that contract that the undertaking should only bind the defendants until judgment or further order in the meantime.

In my judgment an order or an undertaking to the court expressed to be until further order, by implication gives a right to the party bound by the order or undertaking to apply to the court to have the order or undertaking discharged or modified if good *e* grounds for doing so are shown. Such an application is not an application to set aside or modify any contract implicit in the order or undertaking. It is an application in accordance with such contract, being an exercise of a right reserved by the contract to the party bound by the terms of the order or undertaking. Accordingly, with deference to Foster J, I take a different view from that which he took on his first ground for rejecting the defendants' application.

f When the motion for an injunction came before the judge inter partes, the defendants did not seek any adjournment to permit them to put in evidence in answer to the plaintiffs' evidence. They might then have asked for a sufficiently long adjournment to permit them to make the company searches which they made in May, and possibly to search for corroborative evidence in the form of advertising material and so forth, to build up a case for saying that a relevant group structure existed in this case. They did *g* not do so, probably because it had not then occurred to their advisers that evidence of this kind might assist them in accordance with the reasoning on which the *Revlon* decision was based. The fact that the *Revlon* decision had not then taken place is, in my view, no ground for saying that the defendants might not have succeeded in resisting the motion successfully on parallel reasoning. Let me assume (which I am not deciding) that the evidence now available would have enabled the defendants to succeed on those lines if *h* such evidence had been adduced before Foster J in April 1979 and they had resisted the motion on *Revlon* lines. Ought they to be allowed to reopen the matter six months later, having armed themselves with evidence which they could have obtained on the earlier occasion but failed to do so? In my judgment the answer should be No.

They, the defendants, are seeking a rehearing on evidence which, or much of which, so far as one can tell, they could have adduced on the earlier occasion if they had sought *j* an adequate adjournment, which they would probably have obtained. Even in interlocutory matters a party cannot fight over again a battle which has already been fought unless there has been some significant change of circumstances, or the party has become aware of facts which he could not reasonably have known, or found out, in time for the first encounter. The fact that he capitulated at the first encounter cannot improve a party's position. The *Revlon* point was open to the defendants in April 1979, notwithstanding that this court had not then decided that case. Some at least of the new evidence was readily available to them at that time.

In my judgment there has been no change, since 6th April 1979, in the potential ability of the defendants to resist the plaintiffs' motion successfully, sufficient to justify a court in discharging or modifying the undertaking which the defendants then offered and gave.

The defendants have contended that the order of the judge from which they seek leave to appeal is analogous to the grant or refusal of an injunction, being in effect a refusal to discharge an injunction or an undertaking having the same effect as an injunction. No leave is required to appeal from an order granting or refusing an injunction. So, they say, we should give leave in the present case.

I feel unable to accept this. The defendants freely offered their undertaking in April of 1979. They now seek to escape from it. The position, in my view, is not analogous to the grant or refusal of an injunction. Leave to appeal is required.

For the reasons I have indicated, I do not consider that this is a case in which we should give leave. I would consequently dismiss this motion.

SHAW LJ. I agree.

OLIVER LJ. I agree.

Application dismissed.

Solicitors: *Sharpe, Pritchard & Co*, agents for *Philip Baker, King & Co*, Birmingham (for the second defendants); *Wilkinson, Kimbers & Staddon* (for the plaintiffs).

Jacqueline Metcalfe   Barrister.

Practice Direction

CHANCERY DIVISION

Practice – Trial – Setting down action – Chancery Division – Setting down action for new trial – Setting down after time ordered has expired – Leave of court or consent of defendant no longer required – RSC Ord 3, r 6, Ord 34, r 2.

The following direction is made to bring the Chancery practice in line with the practice in the Queen's Bench Division as set out in the Practice Direction of 16th July 1979 ([1979] 3 All ER 193, [1979] 1 WLR 1040).

1. Subject to compliance with RSC Ord 3, r 6 (requirement of service of notice of intention to proceed after a year's delay), where applicable, the plaintiff need not obtain the leave of the court or the consent of the defendant or defendants, if there are more than one, before setting an action down for trial after the period fixed by an order under Ord 34, r 2(1).

2. The foregoing change in the practice in no way relieves the plaintiff of his obligation to set the action down for trial within the time fixed by the order of the court, and his failure to do so may entail the dismissal of the action for want of prosecution under Ord 34, r 2(2).

By direction of the Vice-Chancellor.

EDMUND HEWARD
Chief Master.

20th February 1981

R v Lands Tribunal, ex parte City of London Corpn

QUEEN'S BENCH DIVISION

HIS HONOUR JUDGE NEWEY QC SITTING AS A JUDGE OF THE HIGH COURT

10th, 11th, 18th NOVEMBER 1980

Lands Tribunal – Case stated – Decision – Final decision on point of law – Application for discovery at commencement of hearing of appeal – Dismissal of application – Application renewable later in proceedings if circumstances requiring it – Tribunal refusing to state case on determination of application for discovery – Whether determination a final 'decision' on a point of law – Lands Tribunal Act 1949, ss 1(3)(e), 3(4).

The City of London corporation appealed to the Lands Tribunal against assessments for rating of three public houses in the City made by a local valuation court. The corporation contended that a different method of assessment than that applied by the valuation court (involving closer examination of the profits of public houses) ought to be applied in the City of London. At the commencement of the hearing of the appeals the corporation applied under r 40 of the Lands Tribunal Rules 1975 for disclosure by the respondents (the owner/occupiers of the public houses and the valuation officer), prior to the hearing of the substantive issues, of certain documents including records of the deliveries of alcohol to the public houses and the owner/occupiers' profit and loss accounts. After hearing the parties' submissions the tribunal dismissed the application but indicated that, if discovery of the records of deliveries became necessary later in the proceedings, it would hear a further application for discovery. The tribunal also refused the corporation's request to state a case for the decision of the Court of Appeal pursuant to s 3(4)[a] of the Lands Tribunal Act 1949, on the ground that the determination of the application was not a 'decision' of the tribunal within s 3(4). The corporation applied for an order requiring the tribunal to state a case on the ground that the determination was a final decision on a point of law within s 3(4). The respondents submitted (i) that under s 1(3)(e)[b] of the 1949 Act only a determination by the tribunal on the question referred to it could be a final decision within s 3(4) and since the application for discovery was renewable the determination was not a final decision, and (ii) that the determination was one of fact and not of law.

Held – The tribunal would be ordered to state a case under s 3(4) of the 1949 Act for the following reasons—

(1) Since s 1(3)(e) of the 1949 Act conferred jurisdiction on the Lands Tribunal to decide not only the express question referred to it but also any interlocutory matters which arose during the course of the proceedings and the tribunal when granting or refusing an interlocutory application was making a final decision on that application, on its natural and ordinary meaning 'decision' in s 3(4) included a decision on an interlocutory matter. Moreover, such a construction of s 3(4) would, in most cases, be likely to avoid inconvenience and save costs. Accordingly, the tribunal could be required to state a case on an interlocutory matter, such as an application for discovery (see p 758 *a* to *c* and *e* to *j* and p 759 *a b*); *Norwich Rating Authority v Norwich Assessment Committee* [1941] 3 All ER 225 and *Becker v Marion City Corpn* [1977] AC 271 distinguished; dictum of Viscount Caldecote CJ in *Norwich Rating Authority v Norwich Assessment Committee* [1941] 3 All ER at 228 considered.

(2) The tribunal's determination, though involving considerations of fact, also involved questions of law, such as the relevance of the documents and whether they

---

a Section 3(4), so far as material, is set out at p 755 *j*, post

b Section 1(3), so far as material, is set out at p 757 *b*, post

could be withheld from disclosure on the ground of confidentiality. Accordingly the
determination was a decision on a point of law within s 3(4) (see p 759 *a b*, post).

Notes

For appeal by case stated from the Lands Tribunal to the Court of Appeal, see 8
Halsbury's Laws (4th Edn) para 248.

For the Lands Tribunal Act 1949, ss 1, 3, see 6 Halsbury's Statutes (3rd Edn) 191, 196.

For the Lands Tribunal Rules 1975, r 40, see 12 Halsbury's Statutory Instruments
(Fourth Reissue) 226.

As from 1st March 1981 r 40 of the 1975 rules was substituted by the Lands Tribunal
(Amendment) Rules 1981, SI 1981 No 105.

Cases referred to in judgment

Atkinson v United States Government [1969] 3 All ER 1317, [1971] AC 197, [1969] 3 WLR
1074, 134 JP 29, HL, 14(1) Digest (Reissue) 444, 3803.

Becker v Marion City Corpn [1977] AC 271, [1976] 2 WLR 728, 8 ALR 421, PC, Digest
(Cont Vol E) 51, 905a.

Magdalen College, Oxford v Howard (Valuation Officer) (1960) 7 RRC 123, CA.

Norwich Rating Authority v Norwich Assessment Committee [1941] 3 All ER 225, [1941] 2 KB
326, 111 LJKB 204, 165 LT 413, 105 JP 374, 39 LGR 332, DC, 38 Digest (Repl) 736,
1633.

Science Research Council v Nassé, BL Cars Ltd (formerly Leyland Cars) v Vyas [1979] 3 All ER
673, [1980] AC 1028, [1979] 3 WLR 762, [1979] ICR 921, HL, Digest (Cont Vol E)
186, 1301d.

Watney Mann Ltd v Langley [1963] 3 All ER 967, [1966] 1 QB 457, [1964] 2 WLR 858, 128
JP 97, 62 LGR 432, [1964] RVR 22, Digest (Cont Vol A) 1297, 1235a.

Motion

By a notice of motion dated 13th October 1980 issued pursuant to leave given on 10th
October by a Queen's Bench Divisional Court and a direction given by the court pursuant
to RSC Ord 53, r 5(2), the Mayor and Commonalty and Citizens of the City of London
('the corporation') applied to a single judge of the Queen's Bench Division for an order
that the Lands Tribunal (J H Emlyn Jones Esq FRICS) be required to state and sign a case
for the decision of the Court of Appeal pursuant to s 3(4) of the Lands Tribunal Act
1949. The first respondents to the motion were Watneys London Ltd and Goodhews
Ltd. The second respondent was the valuation officer. The facts are set out in the
judgment.

Bernard Marder QC for the corporation.
Gerald Moriarty QC and *Susan Hamilton* for the first respondents.
Alan A Fletcher for the valuation officer.

Cur adv vult

18th November. **HIS HONOUR JUDGE NEWEY QC** read the following
judgment: In 1973 entries were made in the rating valuation list for the City of London
in respect of three public houses, known as the Sir Christopher Wren, the Cock Tavern
and the Magogs. Subsequently proposals were made by the first respondents, Watneys
London Ltd and Goodhews Ltd, respectively owners and occupiers of the Sir Christopher
Wren, and by owners and occupiers of the other public houses, for reductions in the
assessments.

In 1978 the proposals came before divisions of the London Valuation Court, when
valuations which had been agreed between the valuers acting for the owners and
occupiers and the licensed property valuer, acting on behalf of Mr R Burrows, the
valuation officer for the City, were put forward and resulted in orders providing for
assessments which were substantially lower.

The Corporation of the City of London, which is the rating authority for the City, had
not been a party to any of the agreements between the valuers, and it appealed to the
Lands Tribunal against all three assessments. The assessments had been made in
accordance with what is known as the 'direct method' of assessing public houses,

described by Thompson J in *Watney Mann Ltd v Langley* [1963] 3 All ER 967, [1966] 1 QB

a 457; and the gist of the corporation's appeals is that other methods of assessment involving closer examination of a public house's profits is more appropriate in the City of London. A public house is often comparable with licensed restaurants and wine bars.

On 20th December 1979 Mr J H Emlyn Jones FRICS, a member of the Lands Tribunal, held an informal 'pre-trial review' to determine how the appeals should be heard. Neither at the pre-trial review nor by application to the registrar of the Lands Tribunal

b under r 45(1) of the Lands Tribunal Rules 1975, SI 1975 No 299, made under s 3(6) of the Lands Tribunal Act 1949 did the corporation apply for disclosure of documents under r 40 of the 1975 Rules. If the corporation had applied to the registrar and had then been refused, the corporation would have had a right of appeal to the president of the tribunal under r 45(8).

At the commencement of the hearing of the appeals by Mr Emlyn Jones, on 1st

c October 1980, counsel applied under r 40, on behalf of the corporation, that the tribunal should require the other parties to disclose certain documents, and it was agreed by all that the application should be dealt with as a preliminary issue. After reading an affidavit by Mr E C Payne, the valuer advising the corporation on licensed property matters, and hearing argument, Mr Emlyn Jones adjourned the hearing. On 7th October 1980 Mr Emlyn Jones issued a document, 15 pages long, refusing to order the production

d of any of the documents, save for some which the respondents had agreed to produce voluntarily; expressing the opinion that he had no power to state a case at that stage; and refusing a stay of the proceedings.

The documents in respect of which orders for discovery were refused, included the valuations which led to the existing list entries and the owners' and occupiers' records of deliveries of beer, wines and spirits, and their profit and loss accounts.

e Mr Emlyn Jones held that the original valuations were irrelevant. He was not prepared to reach a similar conclusion with regard to the other documents; and after quoting Lord Wilberforce in *Science Research Council v Nassé* [1979] 3 All ER 673 at 679, [1980] AC 1028 at 1065 stated that he had a discretion, in the exercise of which he had to weigh the balance of advantage between the parties and the degree of relevance.

Mr Emlyn Jones decided that the profit and loss accounts would not be of any real help

f to him, that he was not prepared to extend the information which a valuation officer reasonably requires to include profit and loss accounts, and that it would not be in the public interest to require traders to produce such confidential information. Mr Emlyn Jones expressed willingness to hear further argument as to records of deliveries if, later, detailed examination of return forms showed that answers were incomplete; and with that qualification he dismissed the application.

g Mr Emlyn Jones stated that while he appreciated that the ruling which he had given could be described as a decision, if every time the tribunal gave a ruling, for example, on the admissibility of evidence, an appeal arose, the consequences could be that there might be any number of appeals during the same case. He thought that he had not given a 'decision' within the meaning of the 1949 Act, but on a procedural matter arising during the course of the hearing.

h The corporation applied without delay to the Divisional Court of the Queen's Bench Division for leave to apply for an order that the Lands Tribunal should state and sign a case for the decision of the Court of Appeal. Leave to apply was granted with the result that this application came before me. The corporation also applied to the Divisional Court for a stay of proceedings in the Lands Tribunal which was also granted.

The provision in the Lands Tribunal Act 1949 which refers to the stating of a case is

j s 3(4), which, omitting the last part, reads:

'A decision of the Lands Tribunal shall be final: Provided that any person aggrieved by the decision as being erroneous in point of law may, within such time as may be limited by rules of court, require the tribunal to state and sign a case for the decision of the court . . .'

The time limited by RSC Order 61, r 1 is six weeks.

In order that Mr Emlyn Jones may be ordered to state a case, it is necessary therefore, that he should have made a decision which was final and that that decision should have *a* concerned law and not fact.

Dealing first with the question of what is a decision which is final within s 3(4) of the 1949 Act, all counsel agreed that it had never previously been considered directly by the courts.

Counsel for the corporation, however, referred me to three cases, the first two of which he relied on as being persuasive, and the third he sought to distinguish. The first case, *b* *Norwich Rating Authority v Norwich Assessment Committee* [1941] 3 All ER 225, [1941] 2 KB 326 had arisen under the Rating and Valuation Act 1925. In it the Recorder of Norwich had, after deciding as a preliminary point of law, that the method of valuation proposed by the rating authority was unlawful, dismissed its appeal. On the recorder stating a case for the opinion of the Divisional Court, the occupier objected on the grounds that the court would not entertain a case stated by quarter sessions unless the court's decision *c* would finally dispose of the matter in issue. The occupier argued that the recorder should have heard evidence and made an assessment before stating a case.

The Divisional Court held that it had jurisdiction to entertain the appeal by case stated. Viscount Caldecote CJ said that the rule for which the occupier contended 'was never more than a question of practice' (see [1941] 3 All ER 225 at 228, [1941] 2 KB 326 at 330). Tucker J said that, although the recorder had come to his decision on the basis *d* that the appellant's proposal was bad in law, he had 'nonetheless come to a determination' (see [1941] 3 All ER 225 at 230, [1941] 2 KB 326 at 332).

The second case was *Magdalen College, Oxford v Howard (Valuation Officer)* (1960) 7 RRC 123 in which the Lands Tribunal acting as arbitrator under a reference by consent under s 50 of the Local Government Act 1948 gave, at the request of the parties, an interim decision as to the appropriate method of rating colleges and then, on the *e* application of the valuation officer, stated a case. At the beginning of the argument the Court of Appeal raised the question whether an appeal lay to the court where the tribunal had acted as arbitrator, to which counsel for the valuation officer replied that the interim decision was a decision of the Lands Tribunal within s 3(4) of the Lands Tribunal Act 1949. Lord Evershed MR said (at 126) that he assumed 'for the purposes of this Judgment that that is so'. Lord Evershed MR's assumption related solely to the court's jurisdiction *f* where the tribunal was acting as arbitrator under the 1948 Act; the question of whether the court had jurisdiction when the decision was 'interim' was not raised.

The third case cited by counsel for the corporation, *Atkinson v United States Government* [1969] 3 All ER 1317, [1971] AC 197, was concerned with extradition proceedings. In it the House of Lords decided, inter alia, that s 87 of the Magistrates Courts Act 1952, which provides (omitting irrelevant words) that:

g

'Any person, who ... is aggrieved by the conviction, order, determination, or other proceeding of the court may question the proceeding on the ground that it is wrong in law ... by applying to the justices ... to state a case'

did not apply to committal proceedings, since they did not lead to a final decision. Lord Reid said ([1969] 3 All ER 1317 at 1324, [1971] AC 197 at 235): *h*

'... it frequently happens that a court has to make a decision in the course of the proceedings—e.g., whether certain evidence is admissible—but it cannot have been intended that the proceedings should be held up while a case on such a matter is stated and determined by the superior court.'

The basis of the decision was, however, that it was settled law under earlier Acts that *j* examining magistrates had no power to state a case and that since the 1952 Act was a consolidation statute there was a strong presumption that it did not alter the existing law.

Counsel for the corporation submitted that even if a decision did not dispose of the case before the tribunal, but was of an interlocutory nature, it could still be a final decision. He said that any other construction of s 3(4) could lead to great inconvenience

and waste of costs. In the present case, if as a result of a case being stated, the opinion of
a the Court of Appeal could be obtained, the tribunal and the parties would know how to
proceed. Otherwise the corporation would have to present its case before the tribunal as
best it could and afterwards ask for a case to be stated. If eventually the Court of Appeal
held that the corporation had been right about the documents, proceedings in the Lands
Tribunal would have to begin again, possibly before another member of the tribunal.

Counsel for the first respondents, the owners and occupiers, said that the Lands
b Tribunal's powers in the present case are derived solely from s 1(3)(e) of the 1949 Act,
which provides that there should be referred to and determined by the tribunal 'any
question on which, but for this provision, an appeal or reference to the county court
would or might be made by virtue of section sixty-two or eighty-seven of the Local
Government Act, 1948'. He said that only a determination by the tribunal of the
question referred and resulting in the giving of directions within s 77 of the General Rate
c Act 1969, could be a final decision within s 3(4). Counsel for the first respondents
conceded, however, that when the president of the tribunal has heard an appeal from the
registrar concerning an interlocutory matter under r 45(8), the president can be required
to state a case.

Counsel for the first respondents submitted that if rulings given during the course of
proceedings before the Lands Tribunal could be the subject of cases stated, the result
d would be likely to be long delays and waste of costs. He submitted that even if Mr
Emlyn Jones had given a decision, it was not final; for example he himself had stated that
he would reconsider disclosure of records of deliveries in certain circumstances.

Counsel for the valuation officer adopted the submissions of counsel for the first
respondent except that he said that the risk of inconvenience played little part in his case.
Counsel for the valuation officer submitted that a decision on an interlocutory matter
e such as discovery of documents, could not of its nature be a final decision because it could
always be renewed. He said that to be final, an order had to decide the rights of the
parties. He said that the words of s 31(5) of the Rating and Valuation Act 1925 involved
in the *Norwich Rating Authority* case were different from those in s 3(4) of the 1949 Act.
Counsel for the valuation officer cited *Becker v Marion City Corpn* [1977] AC 271, in
which the Privy Council, on an appeal from the Supreme Court of South Australia,
f decided that a decision that a plan did not comply with the requirements of planning
legislation, with the result that the appellant had not been able to have the proposals
considered, was a final order entitling her to appeal to the Privy Council without leave.

Counsel for the valuation officer said that the corporation was not entitled to have a
case stated, but that if the Lands Tribunal went wrong in law at any stage of its
proceedings, an application for judicial review of its conduct could be made. Counsel for
g the valuation officer further submitted that since s 6(6)(c) expressly provided that rules
might apply to the tribunal provisions of the Arbitration Acts and since r 38 had applied
some of them, including s 12 of the Arbitration Act 1950, the corporation could apply
under s 12(6)(b) of the 1950 Act to the High Court direct for an order for discovery.

Counsel's final submission for the valuation officer was that Parliament had by s 3(10)
of the 1949 Act expressly preserved to the rule-making body the ability to make rules
h conferring a right to require the stating of cases in circumstances in which official
arbitrators could have been required to state them as the result of various statutes existing
prior to 1949. The power had not been exercised, but it might be inferred from its
existence that Parliament had intended that any power to state a case under s 3(4) should
be limited and that any alternative power should be conferred by the rules.

In reply counsel for the corporation said that if the formula used in s 3(4) of the 1949
j Act had been the same as that used in s 31(5) of the Rating and Valuation Act 1925,
namely 'On the determination of an appeal under this section any party to the appeal
may, if dissatisfied with the decision of the court as being erroneous in point of law,
make an application [for] a case stated', it would have been much more difficult for him
to have contended that Mr Emlyn Jones's decision was final. Counsel for the corporation
agreed with counsel for the valuation officer that under s 12 of the Arbitration Act 1950,

a party to proceedings before the Lands Tribunal could apply to the High Court for discovery. He said that if I were against him he would immediately issue an originating summons and request me to hear it.

I think that s 1(3)(e) of the 1949 Act, when providing that certain questions should be referred to and determined by the Lands Tribunal, conferred jurisdiction on it, not merely to decide those express questions, but also others of an interlocutory nature arising during the course of the proceedings. The fact that r 45 made under the 1949 Act provides a method whereby the registrar may determine interlocutory applications subject to appeal to the president, does not take away the power of a member of the tribunal to make such decisions.

A member of the tribunal when granting or refusing an application made to him is, in my view, making a decision about it, which in ordinary language can only be described as final. The fact that it may be open to a party in changed circumstances to make a further application, for example as envisaged by Mr Emlyn Jones in the present case with regard to records of deliveries, does not prevent the decision on the application from being final.

If Parliament had intended that s 3(4) of the 1949 Act should be limited to decisions bringing the whole reference to an end, I would have expected it to have used a form of words similar to that in s 31(5) of the 1925 Act, or possibly included in the Act provisions of the type contained in the Planning Acts and in the Highways Acts.

The recorder's decision in the Norwich case had in fact determined the proceedings, but I think that Viscount Caldecote CJ's words are persuasive as indicating the court's willingness to consider interlocutory questions on case stated in suitable circumstances. I have not derived assistance from the Magdalen College case, nor from Atkinson's case. The latter was dealing with the construction of a particular statute and with matters very different from those in the present case. In Becker v Marion City Corpn the decision with regard to the plan had disposed of the whole case.

If on a proper construction of s 3(4) it does not provide a method of avoiding inconvenience, or if it gives rise to delays and to expense, the parties must bear the consequences. If, however, the meaning of the section is ambiguous, since Parliament is unlikely to have intended to create hardship, consequences likely to result from alternative constructions may, I think, be taken into account. In my view, to construe s 3(4) as giving a right to require a case to be stated is likely to save inconvenience and costs in most cases. If a party were to make repeated interlocutory applications and repeated requests for cases to be stated, the courts could deal with such conduct by refusing to stay proceedings before the tribunal and by appropriate orders as to costs.

The right of a party to obtain discovery by an order under the Arbitration Act 1950 is not, I think, a reason why a case should not be stated under s 3(4) particularly as an appeal lies in an interlocutory matter, admittedly with leave, from a single judge to the Court of Appeal. I attach no weight to the fact that rules could have provided for cases to be stated in situations where they could have been prior to 1949. Theoretically the rule makers may have thought that there was less need for such provision because a wide construction could be placed on s 3(4).

I think that counsel for the first respondents was right to concede that a party may require the president to state a case in relation to a decision under r 45, but I think that that right exists more generally.

In my judgment the natural and ordinary meaning of s 3(4) is that it includes decisions on interlocutory matters. If it be necessary to take into account inconvenience and other considerations to determine the intention of Parliament, I think that they point to the same construction. I find that Mr Emlyn Jones made a decision which was final.

As to the question of whether the decision related to law, counsel for the first respondents submitted that it did not, and referred in particular to Mr Emlyn Jones's statement that the profit and loss accounts would be of little help to him. Counsel for the valuation officer said that the corporation was only seeking the earlier valuation documents from the valuation officer and that Mr Emlyn Jones's decision that they were *a* not relevant was a decision of fact. Counsel for the corporation said that Mr Emlyn Jones's decision contains many decisions on law.

I have no doubt that while Mr Emlyn Jones's decision involved some considerations of fact and exercise of discretion, it also involved substantial questions of law, such as those relating to relevance and non-disclosure of documents because of confidentiality.

In the result I make an order requiring the Lands Tribunal to state a case for the Court of Appeal under s 3(4) of the 1949 Act.

b
Order accordingly.

Solicitors: *Stanley F Heather* (for the corporation); *B J S Stanfield* (for the first respondents); *Solicitor of Inland Revenue.*

c
K Mydeen Esq   Barrister.

d New Zealand Government Property Corpn v H M & S Ltd

QUEEN'S BENCH DIVISION
WOOLF J
e 29th, 30th, 31st OCTOBER 1980

Landlord and tenant – Lease – Fixtures – Fixtures annexed by tenant – Tenant's right to remove fixtures on surrender of lease – Surrender by operation of law – Lease expiring by effluxion of time and being replaced by new lease – Rent under new lease to be open market rental value – Whether tenant losing right to remove fixtures on surrender of lease – Whether rent to be assessed
f *without regard to tenant's fixtures.*

In 1952 the tenant purchased the leasehold of a theatre. In addition the tenant also purchased certain fixtures and fittings such as seats, curtains and carpets which had been installed by the previous tenant. The lease expired at the end of September 1970 and the tenancy continued by virtue of s 24 of the Landlord and Tenant Act 1954. On 1st July *g* 1971 the landlord and the tenant agreed the material terms of a new lease which was duly executed on 8th February 1973. The new lease contained a rent review clause by which the rent for the second seven years of the term was to be the 'open market rental value'. When the rent came to be reviewed in 1978, the parties failed to agree on a new rent and the question arose whether all or none of the fixtures or only those annexed prior to 1st July 1971 (the date when the parties agreed the terms of the new lease) were to be taken into account in fixing the open market rental value. The landlord contended *h* that when the original lease expired and the new lease was entered into the tenant lost the right it previously had during the currency of the original lease to remove the tenant's fixtures.

Held – Although a tenant's right to remove tenant's fixtures was lost if there was an *j* express surrender of a tenancy (even if it was followed by an express grant of a new lease), where a lease expired by effluxion of time and was replaced by a new lease between the same parties so that the original lease was surrendered by operation of law, and the original lease was silent and therefore neutral regarding the tenant's right to remove his fixtures, it was to be inferred that the parties did not intend that on the expiration of the original lease the tenant should give up his right to remove his fixtures. Accordingly the open market rental value of the premises was to be assessed without regard to any of the tenant's fixtures regardless of when they were annexed (see p 763 *b* to *e*, p 766 *j* and p 767 *f* to p 768 *d*, post).

Dictum of Parker J in *Leschallas v Woolf* [1908] 1 Ch at 653 applied.

Slough Picture Hall Co Ltd v Wade (1916) 32 TLR 542 distinguished.

Notes

For the effect of new lease on a tenant's right to remove fixtures, see 23 Halsbury's Laws (3rd Edn) 498, para 1134, and for cases on the subject, see 31(1) Digest (Reissue) 454, 3726–3728.

Cases referred to in judgment

Leschallas v Woolf [1908] 1 Ch 641, 77 LJ Ch 345, 98 LT 558, 31(1) Digest (Reissue) 459, 3763.

Poole's Case (1703) Holt KB 65, 1 Salk 368, 90 ER 934, 31(1) Digest (Reissue) 439, 3523.

Roberts, Re, ex parte Brook (1878) 10 Ch D 100, [1874–80] All ER Rep 1310, 48 LJ Bcy 22, 39 LT 458, 43 JP 53, 286, CA, 31(1) Digest (Reissue) 452, 3705.

Slough Picture Hall Co Ltd v Wade, Wilson v Nevile, Reid & Co Ltd (1916) 32 TLR 542, 31(1) Digest (Reissue) 450, 3692.

Smith v City Petroleum Co Ltd [1940] 1 All ER 260, 31(1) Digest (Reissue) 444, 3590.

Special case stated

By an interim award dated 24th August 1979 in the form of a special case stated by his Honour Judge Hawser QC as the sole arbitrator in a dispute between the New Zealand Government Property Corpn ('the landlord') and H M & S Ltd ('the tenant') over the open market rental value of the property known as Her Majesty's Theatre, Haymarket, London, leased by the tenant from the landlord for a term of 21 years from 1st October 1970, the arbitrator awarded, subject to the court's decision, that the rent was to be determined on the basis that only tenant's fixtures annexed after 1st July 1971 were to be disregarded in assessing the rent. The question of law raised in the special case for the court's decision was whether, on the assumption that the lease had ended and the tenant had vacated removing any tenant's fixtures he was lawfully entitled to remove, the rent was to be determined on the basis that on vacating the tenant removed (i) all his fixtures whenever annexed or (ii) such fixtures annexed by him after 1st July 1971 or (iii) no fixtures at all. The facts are set out in the judgment.

Ronald Bernstein QC and *Kirk Reynolds* for the tenant.
Raymond Sears QC and *Anthony Porten* for the landlord.

Cur adv vult

31st October. **WOOLF J** read the following judgment: The issue in this case is as to the effect of a surrender of a tenancy by operation of law on the grant of a new tenancy on the tenant's right to remove fixtures under the old tenancy. The issue comes before the court in somewhat unusual circumstances and by an abnormal route. The respondent is the tenant of Her Majesty's Theatre in the Haymarket and the claimant is the landlord. The respondent is the tenant under an underlease made on 8th February 1973, which I will call 'the new lease'. That new lease has a rent review clause which provided that the rent for the second seven years of the term was to be the open market rental value of the demised premises, and defined 'open market rental value' as—

'the annual rental value of the demised premises in the open market which might reasonably be demanded by a willing landlord on a lease for a term of years certain equivalent in length to the residue unexpired at the review date of the term of years hereby granted with vacant possession at the commencement of the term but upon the supposition (if not a fact) that the Lessee has complied with all the obligations as to repair and decoration . . . and there being disregarded (if applicable) those

a
matters set out in paragraphs (a) (b) and (c) of Section 34 of the Landlord and Tenant
Act 1954 . . .'

After the procedure for rent review prescribed in the new lease had been instituted,
the parties failed to agree on a new rent and they therefore entered into an agreement
dated 28th August 1978 whereby they referred their disputes and differences and all
matters of fact and law arising therein to the award of a circuit judge discharging the
b functions of an official referee.
On 24th August 1979 his Honour Judge Hawser QC made an interim award in the
form of a special case for the decision of this court, the judge sitting as an arbitrator
appointed by consent under s 11 of the Arbitration Act 1950 and RSC Ord 36. By the
interim award the judge gave answers to three questions as follows:

c
'Question 1. Is the open market rental value to be determined on the basis that the
lease has ended, that the tenant has vacated and that the tenant has removed any
tenant's fixtures that he could lawfully remove at the end of the term? Answer. Yes.
'Question 2. If the answer to Question 1 is Yes is the open market rental value to
be determined on the basis that upon vacating the tenant removed (a) all the said
fixtures whenever annexed or (b) such of the said fixtures as were annexed after 1st
July 1971 or (c) none of the said fixtures? Answer. (b).'

d
Then question 3 in an amended form:

'In respect of each of the said fixtures which added to the letting value of the
premises, is it to be treated as an improvement made immediately before 1st July
1971 or as an improvement made when it was annexed to the premises? Answer.
When it was annexed to the premises.'
e

Before me, the parties accepted that the judge's answer to question 1 is correct, and
most of the argument has turned on question 2. The reference to 1st July 1971 in
question 2(b) is because that was the date at which the parties agree they had agreed the
material terms for the grant of a new lease. Were it not for that agreement the critical
date, subject to the provisions of the 1954 Act, would be the date on which the new lease
f was made, namely 8th February 1973.
The reason why the answer to the second question is important in order to resolve the
issues between the parties is that prior to the new lease there had been an earlier lease of
the premises and the landlord contends that on the new lease being entered into the
tenant lost the right which previously existed during the currency of the old tenancy to
remove the tenant's fixtures. If, but only if, this was right would their value have to be
g taken into account in determining the increase of rent payable as a result of the review.
The old lease was made on 11th July 1899 between the Carlton Hotel Ltd as lessors and
Herbert Beerbohm Tree and Playhouse Ltd whereby, in consideration of the expense
incurred by the said Herbert Beerbohm Tree in erecting the theatre, the lessors, at the
request of the said Tree, demised the theatre to Playhouse Ltd for 72 years from 10th
October 1898 (less ten days) so that the term was due to expire at the end of September
h 1970. By an agreement dated 29th December 1952 G C Dobell & Co Ltd, being the then
lessees, agreed first to assign to the tenants H M & S Ltd the premises demised by the lease
for the residue of the term thereby created and second to sell to the tenants 'The fixtures
fittings carpets curtains seating and other contents and equipment as now in and about
the said Theatre and belonging to the Vendors' for the price of £30,000.
By the date on which the term granted by the underlease was due to expire, the
j freehold reversion had become vested in the landlord. The landlord in due course served
notice on the tenant to determine the old tenancy under s 25 of the Landlord and Tenant
Act 1954. The tenant served the appropriate counter-notice and commenced proceedings
in the Chancery Division for a new tenancy. Those proceedings were adjourned pending
negotiations between the parties which on 8th February 1973 resulted in the new lease.
The new lease was for a term of 21 years from 1st October 1970, that being the date the

term of the old lease expired, the old tenancy having been continued in the interim by
s 24 of the 1954 Act.

The new lease described the premises demised as—

'ALL THAT piece of land situate in the Parish of St. James in the said City of
Westminster and being on the west side of The Haymarket and the south side of
King Charles II Street Together with the buildings erected thereon and known as
Her Majesty's Theatre which land and buildings are delineated on the plan annexed
hereto and are thereon edged red and are hereinafter called "the demised premises".'

The new lease contained a covenant to repair which was in these terms:

'THE LESSEE . . . covenants . . . To put and keep the demised premises and the
appurtenances thereof including the Landlord's fixtures doors windows and window
frames and all fitting pipes and the sanitary and water apparatus and the painting
papering and decoration thereof in good and substantial repair and condition and
properly fitted up and decorated in a state in every respect fit for theatrical
representations of a high class character (damage by fire and other insured risks save
where the insurance moneys shall be irrecoverable in consequence of any act or
default of the Lessee only excepted).'

The tenant also covenanted—

'Not at any time during the said term to use the demised premises for any other
purposes than those of a Theatre used for the production of plays concerts [etc] . . .'

and covenanted—

'To yield up the demised premises with the fixtures and fittings and additions
thereto (tenants fixtures only excepted) at the expiration or sooner determination of
the said term in good and substantial repair and condition (Landlords fixtures and
fittings being duly renewed and replaced) in accordance with the several covenants
hereinbefore contained.'

There was also a collateral agreement dated 8th February 1973 whereby, in
consideration of the tenant having that day exchanged the new underlease and having
incurred or been about to incur substantial expenditure estimated as shown in the
schedule thereto, the tenant agreed to fulfil its repairing obligations under the lease and
the landlord agreed that it would during the first four years of the term grant to the
tenant in each of those years an allowance of £5,000 as a deduction from rent subject to
the production of certified receipts.

The schedule included items which would appear to be tenant's fixtures in normal
circumstances and subject to the questions in issue in this case.

The tenant has never sought to remove the tenant's fixtures which were attached to
the premises during the old tenancy. However, this does not affect the importance of the
answer given by the judge to the second question since in carrying out the hypothetical
exercises involved in fixing the rent, although those fixtures have not in fact been
removed, if they are still removable by the tenant they would have to be ignored in
fixing the increased rent. If they cannot be removed they would be treated as being
included in the demise and would have to be taken into account subject to the correct
answer to the third question, which I will deal with as a separate matter.

In considering the effect of surrender by operation of law of the old tenancy which was
continued under the 1954 Act, it is convenient to begin by stating certain general
principles which are not in dispute.

Tenant's fixtures are normally only removable by the tenant during the term and for
such longer period of possession which is (and I quote from Hill and Redman on the Law
of Landlord and Tenant (16th Edn, 1976, p 529) 'in such circumstances that he is entitled
still to consider himself as tenant'. So the right to remove continues while a business
tenancy is continued under the 1954 Act.

It is always open to the parties to make special provisions as to the right of removal, subject to such a special agreement not being inconsistent with rights of third parties.

There is a qualification to these general principles where the tenancy terminates in such circumstances that the tenant would not have time to remove fixtures. Then the right of removal continues for a reasonable time after the expiration of the term. I would refer in that connection to *Smith v City Petroleum Co Ltd* [1940] 1 All ER 260.

In accord with the general principles, if there is an express surrender of a tenancy by a tenant, the right to remove subject to the terms of the surrender ends with the surrender. Furthermore, I regard myself as being bound by the authorities to which I will have to refer hereafter to take the same view where there is an express surrender followed by an express grant of a new lease between the same parties of the same premises.

There is, however, no clear authority on what is to be the position where a tenancy comes to an end by normal effluxion of time and there is a new tenancy entered into immediately following the termination of the old tenancy. Where the tenant holds over as a yearly tenant, however, the position appears to be that the right to remove continues in accordance with the general principles which I have stated above.

Before turning to the authorities, it is right that I should make it clear that it is my view that the ordinary tenant, untutored in the intricacies of the law of landlord and tenant, would never expect that by taking a new tenancy he could, if nothing was said, lose the right, which could be of considerable value, to remove tenant's fixtures. In this respect I can see very real differences in practical terms between an express surrender and a surrender by operation of law. In the case of an express surrender which is silent about what is to happen to fixtures, I can well understand why the courts have taken the view that the tenant has given up all his rights to what is then part of the premises. Where, however, there is no express surrender, it seems to me the position is different because what the parties have in mind is the granting to the tenant new rights and not taking away old rights except in so far as they are inconsistent with the new rights. I mention this because it is clear from the reasoning set out in the case by the judge that he was influenced in giving the answer which he did to the second question by the fact that he regarded the authorities, as I do, as binding on him in respect of express surrender, and took the view that there was no logical basis for differentiating between the effect of an express surrender and of a surrender by the operation of law.

Turning to the authorities. I start with Foa's General Law of Landlord and Tenant (8th Edn, 1957, pp 706–707). I do so because counsel appearing on behalf of the tenant found this his most embarrassing hurdle because in fact he was one of the editors responsible for the relevant edition of this authoritative textbook. I refer first of all to para 1075:

> '*Tenant continuing in possession.*—The mere fact that the tenant retains possession of the demised premises after the expiration of his interest does not extend the period during which he may sever fixtures, even though the reason for his holding over is that his successor in the tenancy has failed to pay him an agreed price for them. And where the continuance in possession is under a new lease or agreement, his right to carry away the fixtures is determined, and he is in the same situation as if the landlord, being seised of the land together with the fixtures, had demised both to him; so that if a tenant taking a fresh lease of the demised premises wish to preserve his right to remove fixtures they must be made the subject of a special agreement. So, where the old lease has come to an end by surrender, the transaction being what is usually termed one of surrender and renewal; though where such a surrender is one by operation of law upon the taking of a new lease, it may, in certain circumstances, be inferred that what are surrendered and re-demised are, not the premises in their actual condition, but the premises *minus* the tenant's fixtures. But if nothing be said about the fixtures at all, there would seem to be no ground for drawing such an inference, and the general rule will not be displaced. It is thought, however, that the ordinary case where a tenant holds over by arrangement after the

expiration of a lease, and pays rent on a tenancy from year to year, is not a continuance in possession under a "new agreement" within the meaning of the above rule, and that the right to remove fixtures when he gives up possession being one of the terms of the lease applicable to his new holding, the special agreement here spoken of would be implied.'

And then para 1076:

'*Surrender or forfeiture.*—The general principle appears equally to apply (apart from cases of fresh holding) where the tenant by his own act puts an end to the term, as where it expires by effluxion of time; so that after a surrender, for instance, the tenant's right to sever fixtures is gone. In the case indeed of surrender, it has been said that the right does not survive the time when the agreement upon which it is founded is made: the tenant as from that time being in the same position as if he had contracted to sell his lease. Upon a forfeiture, in spite of a somewhat guarded *dictum* of the Court of Appeal, that possibly the tenant may have a reasonable time afterwards, when he remains in possession, to sever his fixtures, it has more than once been decided that he has no such right, and that a person claiming under him is in no better position than himself.'

The only part of the passages to which I have referred from which counsel for the tenant can get any comfort at all is the qualification which is made in respect of surrenders by operation of law that—

'it may, in certain circumstances, be inferred that what are surrendered and re-demised are, not the premises in their actual condition, but the premises *minus* the tenant's fixtures.'

However, that passage has to be read in conjunction with the following sentence which indicates that if nothing is said about fixtures at all there would be no ground for drawing such an inference.

The next textbook to which I shall refer is Hill and Redman on the Law of Landlord and Tenant (16th Edn, 1976, p 529, para 425):

'*Time for removal.*—Where fixtures are removable by a tenant he is only entitled to exercise this right during the term, and if he omits to do so they become the absolute property of the reversioner, save that if the tenant remains in possession after the term in such circumstances that he is entitled still to consider himself as tenant, his right to remove fixtures continues as long as this state of things lasts; and if he is a tenant holding on an uncertain tenancy, then his right to remove fixtures continues for a reasonable time after the determination of the tenancy. This rule applies in whatever manner the term comes to an end, whether by effluxion of time or by surrender or forfeiture; save that, in case of surrender or forfeiture, a third party, such as a mortgagee of the fixtures from the tenant, is entitled to a reasonable time within which to remove them. A tenant, who is entitled to remove fixtures under the stipulations of the lease, can remove them within a reasonable time after the determination of the term. From the principle that the tenant is not at liberty to remove fixtures after the determination of the term, including a determination by surrender, it follows that where there is a surrender, followed by the grant of a new lease to the same lessee, the new lease includes the former tenant's fixtures as part of the demised premises, and, in the absence of express stipulation, any right which he had to remove them is gone. Similarly, tenant's fixtures left by a former tenant do not become tenant's fixtures of the subsequent tenant.'

As I read that passage, there is not the same difficulty in the way of counsel for the tenant because that passage is at least open to the interpretation that it is referring to a situation where there is an express surrender followed by a regrant; and it is not dealing with the question of surrender by operation of law.

The third textbook is Woodfall on Landlord and Tenant (28th Edn, 1978, vol 1, p 678), and in relation to Woodfall I refer to paras 1–1572 and 1–1573. Without setting out the paragraphs in full in this judgment, it is sufficient if I draw particular attention to this statement in para 1–1573:

> 'On negotiating a renewal, a tenant must be careful to preserve his right to fixtures, for without some express stipulation he may lose his right of removal.'

It is right to say that with regard to Woodfall, like Hill and Redman, it does not expressly close the door to the right of removal continuing notwithstanding a surrender by operation of law, as opposed to an express surrender.

Counsel for the tenant took me through all the authorities which were relevant, which are cited in Foa, so as to support his contention that, in the case of a surrender by operation of law, it is still open to the court to take the view which he submitted was in accord with commercial realities of the situation, namely, that such a surrender does not automatically bring to an end the right of removal of tenant's fixtures. In the end, the result turns on two cases which I must now examine.

The first of those cases is *Leschallas v Woolf* [1908] 1 Ch 641. I do not think it is necessary to extend this judgment by reading the headnote. It will suffice if I indicate that that was a case where there were three parties involved, landlord, tenant and subtenant. The tenant surrendered and there was a new tenancy granted direct to the subtenant. The decision was one of Parker J and he said as follows (at 650–652):

> 'Assuming, however, that I am wrong in this, I will pass to the second point in the case . . . Now it seems to me that a tenant who contracts for the surrender of his lease to his landlord is in the same position as if he had contracted to sell the lease, and cannot as against the surrenderee, any more than he could as against a purchaser, remove fixtures which were upon the freehold at the date of the contract, even though they might be of the nature of tenant's or trade fixtures. No contract for the surrender of the lease would, however, affect his sub-tenants or alter their rights without their consent, though, if a sub-lessee stepped in and rightfully removed fixtures after such a contract to surrender, the lessee might be unable to complete the surrender which he had contracted to make, or might be bound to make compensation for breach of his contract. I also think that a contract to surrender a lease is a contract to surrender in possession free from sub-tenancies, and is not a contract to surrender subject to such sub-tenancies as may have been created by the surrenderor. This position appears to have been accepted by the solicitors for both parties . . . On the construction of the surrender I am of opinion that all fixtures are included in the premises surrendered. If, as I think is at any rate arguable, the defendant was a consenting party to this surrender, his tenancy would be determined thereby, and any right he might have to remove fixtures would be gone . . . The [subtenant] claims now, not only that he had the right to remove during those three days the fixtures which had been affixed by him to the freehold during his tenancy under [the former tenant], but that the right continued after the determination of such tenancy by the acceptance of a new tenancy under the agreement of August 7. It seems to me that there is no precise authority deciding that a tenant loses his right to remove tenant's fixtures by the surrender of his tenancy to, and the acceptance of a new tenancy from, his landlord. It is quite clear that he loses the right by a surrender alone, but it is said that this applies only when he ceases to be the tenant, and not to cases where the tenancy is merely surrendered in order that a new tenancy on the same or different terms may be created so that he does not go out of possession of the property at all. In my opinion, however, if the tenant upon the surrender of his lease in order that a new lease may be granted makes no stipulation to the contrary, he does lose his right to remove tenant's fixtures, for the surrender of the demised premises prima facie includes fixtures, and the subject of the new lease is prima facie what is surrendered in order to be re-demised.

Furthermore, it may well be that the value of the fixtures the right to remove which is thus abandoned is a material consideration in settling the terms of the new lease. The right to remove fixtures erected during the term is, I think, a right coupled with and dependent upon the termor's interest. Prima facie when this interest ceases the right is gone, though there are, no doubt, exceptional cases in which, where the termor has remained in possession after the expiration of his term under such circumstances that the period of such possession can be looked upon as a mere prolongation of the term, he has been allowed to exercise the right after the term is ended.'

Then he said that that seems to him to be the effect of a number of decisions, and added (at 652):

'The law on the subject is summed up more or less by Thesiger L.J. in *Ex parte Brook* ((1878) 10 Ch D 100 at 109, [1874–80] All ER Rep 1310 at 1313). I will read the following passage in his judgment: "The general presumption of law with reference to tenant's fixtures remaining affixed to the freehold when a term comes to an end is, that 'they become a gift in law to him in reversion,' and are, therefore, not removable (per Lord Holt in *Poole's Case* ((1703) Holt KB 65, 90 ER 934))".'

Pausing there, so far as an express surrender is concerned, it seems to me that that statement by Parker J is clearly binding on me and should be given effect to by me in coming to my conclusion about this case. In saying that it is binding on me I do have regard to the fact that that is a decision which has been referred to thereafter by the Court of Appeal, and by other courts, and has never been doubted as an expression of the law, subject to one matter which I will refer to hereafter in a later case. Parker J, quoting Thesiger LJ, later on went on to say this (at 653–654):

'"... But, however that may be, we are clearly of opinion that the case of a surrender of a lease by a tenant, while tenant's fixtures remain affixed to the freehold, does not, either upon principle or the authority of decided cases, give any right to the tenant subsequently to remove such fixtures. At the date of the surrender they form part of the freehold, and the law has no right to limit the effect of the surrender by excluding from it that which legally passes by it, and which has not been excluded from it by the bargain of the parties." Possibly, where the surrender is a surrender by operation of law upon the taking of a new lease, it may, under certain circumstances, be inferred that what is surrendered and re-demised is not the premises in their actual condition, but the premises minus the tenant's fixtures. Possibly also, parcel or no parcel being a question of fact, evidence might be admitted under this head. There may, too, be cases where the terms of the existing tenancy are varied only without the creation of a new tenancy: but in the present case I am of opinion that what [the tenant] contracted to surrender, and did surrender, included all fixtures; that what was agreed to be let to the defendant under the agreement of August 7, 1907, was what [the tenant] agreed to surrender, and subsequently did surrender; and that, by accepting the tenancy commencing on August 12, 1907, the defendant himself surrendered such tenancy as he might have had in the premises, and with it any right which he might have had to remove fixtures as an incident of the tenancy. This, indeed, seems to me to be the only conclusion consistent with the surrounding facts.'

So far as that second passage of the judgment of Parker J is concerned, and particularly his reference to surrenders by operation of law, it could be said, and said with justification, that that passage is in fact obiter. Nonetheless, I think it is right to approach this case on the basis that that passage should be regarded as setting out the appropriate approach to the law and one which I propose to adopt.

The next case to which I should refer is *Slough Picture Hall Co Ltd v Wade* (1916) 32 TLR 542. The facts of that case are complicated, and again I do not propose to read those facts or indeed read the headnote. Certain of the effects of the judgment can however be

understood from a passage which refers to the fact that on 14th April 1915 a series of
a events took place, the legal effect of which the judge, Scrutton J, said was of great
importance. He then referred to that series of events and went on (at 543):

> 'Both Wilson [the tenant] and his sublessee thus surrendered their interest in the
> premises to the landlords, who let to Mrs. Wade, who relet to the Picture Hall
> Company.'

b   What is being described in that passage is a situation whereby what was originally a
letting by a landlord to a tenant, and a letting by a tenant to a subtenant, is replaced by
a situation where the subtenant enters into a new agreement with a new tenant after the
original tenant has given up its tenancy. The judge refers to the case which I have just
cited, *Leschallas v Woolf*, and then recites what Parker J held, and goes on:

> 'I have come to the conclusion that this is a precise authority on the point before
c   me and I must follow it. Wilson must have surrendered his tenancy to the brewers
> when he sold his interest to Mrs. Wade and consented to her granting a tenancy to
> the Slough Picture Hall Company. The Picture Hall Company surrendered their
> sub-tenancy when they accepted a new sub-tenancy from Mrs. Wade, who had
> acquired her tenancy from the brewers. As a general rule fixtures cannot be
> removed after the end of the term except by express agreement. In cases where the
d   tenancy determines on an uncertain event, as in a lease for lives, the tenant may
> have a reasonable time to remove fixtures after the end of the last life. I have
> considered the suggestion of Mr. Justice Parker ([1908] 1 Ch 641 at 654) that
> "possibly where the surrender is by operation of law upon the taking of a new lease
> it may under certain circumstances be inferred that what is surrendered and
> redemised is not the premises in their actual condition, but the premises minus the
e   tenant's fixtures. Possibly also parcel or no parcel being a question of fact evidence
> might be admitted under this head." But in this case nothing was said about the
> fixtures at all, and I can find no ground for implying an exception out of the
> ordinary consequences of a surrender or for treating the premises demised to and
> sublet by Mrs. Wade as anything less than the whole premises.'

f   That case does create a difficulty from the tenant's point of view in this case, over and
above that created by the words of Parker J in the first case that I cited, because it indicates
that, on the facts before Scrutton J, he was not prepared to make an inference which
Parker J envisaged as a possibility. However, it is to be noted that there is a distinction
between that case and this in that, unlike this case, there was not in that case a
straightforward grant of a new tenancy which operated as the surrender of the earlier
g   tenancy, the new tenancy being between the same parties as the previous tenancy and,
although on different terms, in practical effect a continuation of the old tenancy.
    I propose now to approach this case relying on the same words as were considered by
Scrutton J from the judgment of Parker J. Basing myself on those words I have come to
the view that in this case there is a clear inference that it was not the tenant's intention
to give up its right to remove the fixtures. It is correct that the demise did not refer to
h   fixtures and the lease expressly reserved the right to remove tenant's fixtures at the end
of the term granted by the new lease without indicating that tenant's fixtures meant
other than tenant's fixtures attached to the premises after the commencement of that
lease. However, so far as old fixtures are concerned, while I would accept that the lease
can be regarded as being neutral, there is a firm inference, even in the case of a neutral
lease, that the tenant was not intending to give up the right to his old fixtures when he
j   enters into a new lease with the same landlord. If the parties turned their minds to the
question I feel confident that that is what they intended. If, not having turned their
minds to it, they had been asked I feel confident the parties would have agreed that the
tenant's rights should not be given up. Certainly that, in my view, would be the reaction
of an objective bystander. I do not regard the collateral agreement as being inconsistent
with this approach although I accept that there is a technical argument to be based on the
use of the word 'repair'.

I regard my view as being confirmed by the fact that in the long experience of counsel for the tenant in this field he has never seen a new lease which resulted in the surrender of an old lease by operation of law which contained any provision to protect a tenant's right to remove fixtures. The very experienced solicitors acting for the landlord were unable to find any lease for which they had been responsible which protected a tenant's rights in such circumstances. I cannot believe that the very many tenants, of whom those practitioners can speak, whose old tenancies must have been terminated by operation of law on the grant of a new tenancy, wanted to give up their right to remove the fixtures.

It may well be that there are leases where there is an express reference by the lawyers who were responsible for the drafting to what was to happen on the taking of a new lease. Such an express reference would indeed be desirable because, as I have already indicated so far as the effects of a surrender by operation of law is concerned on the right to remove fixtures, the law is certainly far from clear. The authorities do not deal with the matter precisely and, apart from Foa, the textbooks, so far as my investigations have revealed, and those of counsel who placed the relevant textbooks before me have revealed, do not deal with the matter in clear language.

It follows from what I have already said that, unlike the learned judge, I do not consider myself bound to follow alternative (b) in a situation as here where there is only a surrender by the operation of law, and not a surrender by express agreement. Accordingly, it follows that my answer to question 2 would be (a) instead of (b) which was the answer of the learned judge.

So far as question 3 is concerned, I can deal with the matter shortly, and I will do so by repeating as part of this judgment the reasons of the learned judge, on which I do not feel I can improve, for rejecting the tenant's contention that the limitation contained in s 34(2) of the 1954 Act on disregarding improvements made by the tenant ran for 21 years in the case of tenant's fixtures from the date on which the tenant's fixtures became irremovable and not 21 years from the date on which they were affixed. It follows that in respect of question 3, I would reject the tenant's contentions which were argued before me.

Order accordingly.

Solicitors: *Nicholson, Graham & Jones* (for the tenant); *Allen & Overy* (for the landlord).

K Mydeen Esq   Barrister.

R v National Insurance Commissioner, ex parte Connor

QUEEN'S BENCH DIVISION
LORD LANE CJ, GRIFFITHS AND WEBSTER JJ
2nd MAY 1980

National insurance – Benefit – Disqualification – Public policy – Widow's allowance – Claim by widow convicted of husband's manslaughter by stabbing – Jury's verdict showing killing to be deliberate and intentional act – Probation order passed on widow – Widow fulfilling conditions in social security legislation for claiming allowance – Whether widow entitled to allowance – Whether public policy applicable to claim for widow's allowance – Whether nature of crime such that entitlement to allowance not precluded by public policy – Social Security Act 1975, s 24(1).

The applicant's husband died from a stab wound inflicted by the applicant with a knife. The applicant was charged with the husband's murder and at her trial asserted that his death was an accident which occurred during a quarrel. On the direction of the trial judge the jury acquitted the applicant of murder but she was convicted of manslaughter, from which it was to be inferred, having regard to the judge's summing up, that the jury was satisfied that she had used the knife on the husband deliberately and intentionally. The judge placed her on probation for two years. The applicant applied for a widow's allowance under s 24(1)[a] of the Social Security Act 1975. Although she fulfilled all the conditions laid down in that Act for entitlement to the allowance, a local tribunal decided that public policy disentitled her from receiving the allowance. On appeal by the applicant, the Chief National Insurance Commissioner upheld the tribunal's decision. The applicant applied to the Divisional Court for an order of certiorari to quash the commissioner's decision on the grounds (i) that the rules of public policy did not apply to the 1975 Act because it was a self-contained code which alone regulated entitlement to benefit under the Act, and (ii) the circumstances of the manslaughter were such that public policy did not disentitle the applicant from claiming a widow's allowance.

Held – The application would be dismissed for the following reasons—
(1) Although the 1975 Act was a self-contained code it was to be applied subject to the rules of public policy. Accordingly, even though that Act did not specifically provide for a widow to be disentitled to a widow's allowance if she created her status of widowhood by killing her husband, the applicant's claim was subject to the rules of public policy (see p 773 j to p 774 a and p 774 j to p 775 b, post).
(2) Whether the rules of public policy applied to disentitle an applicant from an allowance depended on the nature of the crime committed rather than on the label the law attached to the crime, and where the line was to be drawn in applying public policy to a claimant who had committed a crime might be a difficult matter. However, since the applicant's act in causing her husband's death had been a deliberate, conscious and intentional act, public policy applied to disentitle her to a widow's allowance, even though only a probation order had been made in respect of the crime (see p 774 d e and p 774 h to p 775 b, post); dicta of Lord Denning MR and Salmon LJ in *Gray v Barr* [1971] 2 All ER at 956, 964 applied.

Notes
For widow's allowance, see 27 Halsbury's Laws (3rd Edn) 738, para 1332.
For the Social Security Act 1975, s 24, see 45 Halsbury's Statutes (3rd Edn) 1105.

---

a   Section 24(1) is set out at p 773 *a*, post

Cases referred to in judgments

Gray v Barr (Prudential Assurance Co Ltd, third party) [1971] 2 All ER 949, [1971] 2 QB **a**
554, [1971] 2 WLR 1334, [1971] 2 Lloyd's Rep 1, CA, 15 Digest (Reissue) 1140, 9649.
Hardy v Motor Insurers' Bureau [1964] 2 All ER 742, [1964] 2 QB 745, [1964] 3 WLR 433,
[1964] 1 Lloyd's Rep 397, CA, Digest (Cont Vol B) 462, 3703a.
James v British General Insurance Co Ltd [1927] 2 KB 311, [1927] All ER Rep 442, 96 LJKB
729, 137 LT 156, 27 Ll L Rep 328, 29 Digest (Repl) 517, 3629.
Tinline v White Cross Insurance Association Ltd [1921] 3 KB 327, 90 LJKB 1118, 125 LT 632, **b**
26 Com Cas 347, 15 Digest (Reissue) 1154, 9776.

Application for judicial review

Mrs Joanna Connor, a widow, applied pursuant to leave of the Divisional Court of the
Queen's Bench Division given on 4th October 1979 for an order of certiorari to quash the
decision of the Chief National Insurance Commissioner (R J A Temple QC) on 3rd May **c**
1979 (reported as Decision R(G) 2/79) dismissing the applicant's appeal against the
decision of the local tribunal at York that she was not entitled to a widow's allowance
under s 24 of the Social Security Act 1975 because her status as a widow was brought
about by her own unlawful act. The facts are set out in the judgment of Lord Lane CJ.
    The following is a summary of the Chief Commissioner's decision.
    The rule of public policy raised in bar to the applicant's claim was expressed by the **d**
maxim that no one should take benefit from his own wrong, expressed as 'ex turpi causa
non oritur actio'. Lord Wright MR in *Beresford v Royal Insurance Co Ltd* [1937] 2 All ER
243 at 254, [1937] 2 KB 197 at 219 said: 'The maxim itself, notwithstanding the dignity
of a learned language, is, like most maxims, lacking in precise definition. In these days,
there are many statutory offences which are the subject of the criminal law, and in that
sense are crimes, but which would, it seems, afford no moral justification for a court to **e**
apply the maxim. There are, likewise, some crimes of inadvertence which, it is true,
involve *mens rea* in the legal sense, but are not deliberate, or, as people would say,
intentional.'
    The statutory requirements concerning contributions and the de facto status of being
a widow under pensionable age had been met by the applicant. The basic question was
whether the Act, as a self-contained social security code which wholly regulated the **f**
benefit, was susceptible of the application of the principle expressed by the maxim. The
appeal was argued on the basis that it was. In *Cleaver v Mutual Reserve Fund Life
Association* [1892] 1 QB 147 at 156, [1891–4] All ER Rep 335 at 340 Fry LJ said: 'It appears
to me that no system of jurisprudence can with reason include amongst the rights which
it enforces rights directly resulting to the person asserting them from the crime of that
person. If no action can arise from fraud, it seems impossible to suppose that it can arise **g**
from felony or misdemeanour . . . This principle of public policy, like all such principles,
must be applied to all cases to which it can be applied without reference to the particular
character of the right asserted or the form of its assertion.' That had been applied in *Re
Sigsworth, Bedford v Bedford* [1935] Ch 89, [1934] All ER Rep 113, precluding benefit
under the trusts declared by the Administration of Estates Act 1925, s 46, notwithstanding
the positive and peremptory provisions of the statute. The commissioner concluded that **h**
the Act, providing for entitlement to and payment of the benefit, was nevertheless to be
read as subject to the rule of public policy. The commissioner was further of the view
that the benefit claimed attracted the operation of the rule, being a direct result of what
the applicant had done, ie a benefit directly following from her status as widow, which
she had acquired on her husband's death (see per Fry LJ in the passage in *Cleaver's* case
referred to above and per Devlin J in *St John Shipping Corpn v Joseph Rank Ltd* [1956] 3 All **j**
ER 683, [1957] 1 QB 267).
    Counsel for the applicant did not contend that cases of manslaughter as such did not
fall within the scope of the maxim. In *Re Hall's Estate, Hall v Knight and Baxter* [1914]
P 1, [1911–13] All ER Rep 381 it was held that *Cleaver's* case was sufficient authority for
holding that the rule applied; see also *Re Peacock, Midland Bank Executor & Trustee Co Ltd
v Peacock* [1957] 2 All ER 98, [1957] Ch 310.

It was submitted that the commissioner was entitled to, and should, consider the facts of the case and conclude that the death of the applicant's husband was an accident, or so close to an accidental death that the maxim should not apply to deprive the applicant of benefit. Mrs Morgan for the insurance officer agreed that that course was open to the commissioner, and that if he reached the conclusion that the death was an accident the maxim would not apply. The submission was based on *Gray v Barr (Prudential Assurance Co Ltd, third party)* [1971] 2 All ER 949, [1971] 2 QB 554, a case where, after acquittal of murder and manslaughter at the Central Criminal Court, the Court of Appeal held itself free to go behind the verdict to see whether the acquittal could be justified, and whether the facts, on his own story, established that the defendant was guilty of manslaughter. With some hesitation the commissioner adopted that course.

Accordingly the commissioner had read and perused the summing up by the trial judge. It was plain that the applicant had asserted from first to last that her husband's death had arisen out of what was an accident during the course of an episode described as a stupid quarrel. In evidence given to the commissioner she had described how the unfortunate death of her husband was brought about, but her evidence had not materially differed from or added to her previous explanations which, in much greater detail, were before the jury for their consideration, and to which the trial judge referred on more than one occasion. The issue whether the fatal blow was accidental or not was put to the jury who were directed that they could only convict if they were quite sure that the applicant's account of what happened was untrue. In the result, by a majority, the jury felt unable to accept the defence that the death was an accident. Having carefully considered the evidence the commissioner did not feel able to disagree with their view, and was unable to reach a conclusion which was other than that at which they arrived.

Accepting the verdict of the jury as correct and properly arrived at, the question arising was whether, in the circumstances of the case, the maxim was to be applied in bar of the claim. Counsel for the applicant referred the commissioner to a passage in the judgment of Salmon LJ in *Gray v Barr* [1971] 2 All ER 949 at 964, [1971] 2 QB 554 at 581. 'In particular, I am not deciding that a man who has committed manslaughter would, in any circumstances, be prevented from enforcing a contract of indemnity in respect of any liability he may have incurred for causing death or from inheriting under a will or on the intestacy of anyone whom he has killed. Manslaughter is a crime which varies infinitely in its seriousness. It may come very near to murder or amount to little more than inadvertence, although in the latter class of case the jury only rarely convicts.' Founding on that passage it was submitted that the case was a case of involuntary or accidental manslaughter, amounting to little more than inadvertence, and that having regard to the fact that probation, an unusual course, had been thought appropriate, it should not attract the operation of the rule of public policy to bar the claim to widow's benefit. In short, it was a submission that because there was no degree of moral culpability and because the manslaughter was not deserving of punishment, the rule should not apply in a case where there was no deliberate killing, and where ordinary people would not be shocked if the applicant succeeded in her claim. Mrs Morgan for the insurance officer on the other hand submitted that the commissioner ought to follow *Re Giles, Giles v Giles* [1971] 3 All ER 1141, [1972] Ch 544.

In that case, Pennycuick V-C had considered the case of a woman convicted of manslaughter by reason of diminished responsibility. He held that having been convicted of manslaughter she was disqualified from taking any benefit under the testator's (her husband's) will, or on intestacy, even though the sentence passed on her, which was detention for hospital treatment under s 60 of the Mental Health Act 1959, was remedial in nature, and not by way of punishment. The argument addressed to the commissioner was, in his opinion, essentially that which was addressed to Pennycuick V-C and rejected by him, saying ([1971] 3 All ER 1141 at 1145, [1972] Ch 544 at 522): '... neither the deserving of punishment nor carrying a degree of moral culpability has ever been a necessary ingredient of the crime the perpetrator of which is disqualified from benefiting under the will or intestacy of the person whom he has killed.'

The commissioner appreciated that public policy was a reflection of the current public conscience, and was not static. Pennycuick V-C accepted that the principles of public policy on which the courts act changed over the generations and the centuries. Nevertheless, he was not persuaded that there was any sufficient ground for qualifying the established rule in the manner in which counsel sought to qualify it: that could only be done by a higher tribunal. The remedial nature of the sentence in *Re Giles* was held an insufficient reason for the exclusion of the application of the rule, and the commissioner did not consider that putting the applicant on probation was of any greater persuasive effect.

The commissioner considered whether the applicant was in any better situation in her claim against public funds than she would have been in a claim to benefit from her late husband's will, or under his intestacy. In those situations she would, in the commissioner's opinion, have been held disqualified to benefit: see *Re Callaway, Callaway v Treasury Solicitor* [1956] 2 All ER 451, [1956] Ch 559, *Re Peacock, Midland Bank Executor and Trustee Co Ltd v Peacock* [1957] 2 All ER 98, [1957] Ch 310 and *Re Giles*. Conscious as he was of the observation of the trial judge in placing the applicant on probation, that she had suffered enough, the commissioner was unable to hold that the circumstances of the manslaughter were such that the rule of public policy should not be applied, and on such application her claim to benefit was, in his opinion, to be disallowed.

Finally, the commissioner dealt with the motor insurance cases, which were concerned with the compensation of third parties. He was referred to *Tinline v White Cross Insurance Association Ltd* [1921] 3 KB 327, *James v British General Insurance Co Ltd* [1927] 2 KB 311, [1927] All ER Rep 442 and *Hardy v Motor Insurer's Bureau* [1964] 2 All ER 742, [1964] 2 QB 745. The impact of those cases, not specifically referred to, was considered in *Re Giles* where it was held that nothing there said, in an entirely different sphere, modified the principle laid down in the sphere of succession on death. They were cases where, although a man could not be insured so as to be indemnified against his own crime, it had been found desirable that he should be put in funds to compensate his victim; as such they were cases sui generis and distinguishable from such a case as that with which the commissioner was concerned: see *Gray v Barr* [1971] 2 All ER 954 at 965, [1971] 2 QB 554 at 581 per Salmon LJ and *Re Giles*.

The commissioner's decision was that the claim for widow's allowance was not admissible and benefit was not payable because the applicant's entitlement, founded on her status as widow, directly resulted from the unlawful act of manslaughter, and public policy precluded her from taking benefit therefrom. The appeal was disallowed.

John Reddihough for the applicant.
Simon D Brown for the commissioner.

LORD LANE CJ. In this case, the applicant applies for judicial review directed to the Chief National Insurance Commissioner pursuant to leave granted to her on 4th October 1979.

The facts are out of the ordinary. On 4th May 1978 in the Crown Court at Leeds, in a trial before Smith J and a jury, the applicant was, on the direction of the judge, acquitted of murdering her husband but was convicted of the manslaughter of her husband, and was made the subject, with her consent, of a probation order for two years. He had met his death, to put it objectively, by reason of the fact that a knife held in the hand of the applicant had penetrated his chest, inflicting a wound on the periphery of the heart which caused him to die very shortly thereafter.

The reason why this matter comes before this court at all is that on 3rd January 1978 the applicant sought to obtain a widow's allowance under the provisions of the Social Security Act 1975. The relevant provisions of that Act are contained in s 24 and read as follows:

'(1) A woman who has been widowed shall be entitled to a widow's allowance at the weekly rate specified in relation thereto in Schedule 4, Part I, paragraph 5, if— (a) she was under pensionable age at the time when her late husband died, or he was then not entitled to a Category A retirement pension (section 28); and (b) her late husband satisfied the contribution condition for a widow's allowance specified in Schedule 3, Part I, paragraph 4 . . .'

There is no doubt that those two conditions were satisfied and that had the situation been a normal one she would have been entitled to the widow's allowance under that section.

Counsel for the applicant points out that nowhere in the wording of the Act is there any provision disentitling the widow to her widow's allowance by reason of the fact that she may have been responsible in some degree for her own widowhood. He also points out, perfectly correctly, that there are provisions elsewhere in the Act, and particularly in paras (a) to (c) of s 20(1), which do operate as a disqualification in certain circumstances to persons who are claiming benefits; for example, if a man becomes unemployed through his misconduct and that sort of thing, he is, under the provisions of that section, expressly disentitled to claim benefit. Nothing like that, says counsel for the applicant, is to be found in the case of a widow.

The basis on which the Chief National Insurance Commissioner came to the conclusion which he did, namely that the applicant was not entitled to the widow's allowance, was that in the circumstances of this case public policy decreed that the court would not entertain the application, and it is to that matter which this court must turn.

First of all, it is necessary to see what it was that the jury decided at Leeds. The direction to the jury by Smith J was a model of clarity and fairness. He was at great pains to put the matter as beneficially to the applicant as he possibly could, and there is no doubt about that. In the end, the issue for the jury was: were they satisfied so as to feel sure that what the applicant did was not accidental but was on purpose?

Let me read a passage from his direction in the summing up:

'Now, members of the jury, this is the crucial bit [then he quotes what the applicant said in her evidence]: "He was making noises like you do to children, 'Come, come.' I just turned and I told him not to be so stupid, and I pushed him forward; I just turned and pushed him away with both arms", and she demonstrated. "I still had the knife in my hand. I had no intention of striking him with the knife. We neither of us knew that he was injured. He was just standing and I went into the drawing room to get my keys, the front door keys. I couldn't find them. He called out, 'Come here darling, I'm cut.' I went. He was standing. He opened his shirt. I saw a very small cut. I said, 'I'll get a plaster.' He asked me to get a doctor." She went to telephone. The telephone was not connected through from the exchange in the administration block. She went to the block, and the rest of it we know all about from other witnesses. [Then the judge added this:] The question for you, members of the jury, is quite simply this: has the lady been lying when she gave that account? Because you could only convict her if you are quite sure that she has; and if she has told the truth, or you think it may be the truth, she is entitled to be acquitted. The only issue is whether what happened was done deliberately in order to hurt, or whether it happened accidentally, and from the start to the finish, from the very first moment she opened her mouth to the police, she has maintained it was an accident.'

There the jury are told in crystal clear terms what their task was. They came to the conclusion by a majority of ten to two that they were satisfied so as to feel sure that the applicant used that knife intentionally on her husband, and there is no doubt that what she did caused his death.

One turns to the two problems which counsel has placed before us. The first submission made is that because this particular Act with which we are concerned, the Social Security Act 1975, is, as he puts it, a self-contained modern Act the rules of public policy do not apply and that whatever may have happened, I think he is driven to submitting that nothing that the applicant did can alter her plain entitlement under the words of s 24 which I have read.

I do not accept that submission. The fact that there is no specific mention in the Act of disentitlement so far as a widow is concerned if she were to commit this sort of offence and so become a widow is merely an indication, as I see it, that the draftsman realised perfectly well that he was drawing this Act against the background of the law as it stood at the time.

The second proposition is that it is not every type of crime which operates so as to cause public policy to make the courts reject a claim.

I, for my part, would agree with that. Indeed there are dicta, particularly in *Gray v Barr* [1971] 2 All ER 954, [1971] 2 QB 554, which support that proposition, and in particular the judgment of Salmon LJ which reads ([1971] 2 All ER 954 at 964, [1971] 2 QB 554 at 581):

'Although public policy is rightly regarded as an unruly steed which should be cautiously ridden, I am confident that public policy undoubtedly requires that no one who threatens unlawful violence with a loaded gun [that was the case in *Gray v Barr*] should be allowed to enforce a claim for indemnity against any liability he may incur as a result of having so acted. I do not intend to lay down any wider proposition. In particular, I am not deciding that a man who has committed manslaughter would, in any circumstances, be prevented from enforcing a contract of indemnity in respect of any liability he may have incurred for causing death or from inheriting under a will or on the intestacy of anyone whom he has killed. Manslaughter is a crime which varies infinitely in its seriousness. It may come very near to murder or amount to little more than inadvertence, although in the latter class of case the jury only rarely convicts.'

I would respectfully agree with that dictum, and I would agree that in each case it is not the label which the law applies to the crime which has been committed but the nature of the crime itself which in the end will dictate whether public policy demands the court to drive the applicant from the seat of justice. Where that line is to be drawn may be a difficult matter to decide, but what this court has to determine is whether in the present case what this applicant did was sufficient to disentitle her to her remedy.

The judgment of Lord Denning MR in the same case does provide some assistance in determining where to draw the line. He says this ([1971] 2 All ER 954 at 956, [1971] 2 QB 554 at 568):

'Does this manslaughter mean that, as a matter of public policy, Mr Barr is not to be allowed to recover on the policy? In the category of manslaughter which is called "motor manslaughter", it is settled beyond question that the insured is entitled to recover: see *Tinline v White Cross Insurance Association Ltd* [1921] 3 KB 327; *James v British General Insurance Co Ltd* [1927] 2 KB 311, [1927] All ER Rep 442. But, in the category which is here in question, it is different. If his conduct is wilful and culpable, he is not entitled to recover: see *Hardy v Motor Insurers' Bureau* [1964] 2 All ER 742, [1964] 2 QB 745. I agree with [Geoffrey Lane J] when he said ([1970] 2 All ER 702 at 710, [1970] 2 QB 626 at 640): "The logical test, in my judgment, is whether the person seeking the indemnity was guilty of deliberate, intentional and unlawful violence, or threats of violence. If he was, and death resulted therefrom, then, however unintended the final death of the victim may have been, the court should not entertain the claim for indemnity."'

One turns then to see what it was that happened here. On the verdict of the jury it is plain that the applicant's act was a deliberate, conscious and intentional act. She was holding the knife in her hand and she deliberately thrust it into her husband's chest. It is not the same as discharging two barrels of a shotgun; no two situations will ever be the same. But, speaking for myself, I can see no distinction in principle between the situation in *Gray v Barr*, which was sufficient to disentitle the plaintiff to recover, and the situation here, which also to my mind disentitles the applicant to recover.

We have had the benefit of being able to read the very full judgment of the Chief National Insurance Commissioner in this case (reported as Decision R(G) 2/79). It was a reserved judgment. It sets out all the authorities. It is a model of clarity and scholarly exposition. For my part, I would be content to adopt the reasoning which the Chief Commissioner sets out in that judgment. For those reasons and for the reasons which I have endeavoured to explain myself in this short judgment, I would dismiss this application.

GRIFFITHS J. I agree.

WEBSTER J. I agree.

Application dismissed.

Solicitors: *Lawrence, Graham, Middleton Lewis,* agents for *Dibb, Lupton & Co,* Leeds (for the applicant); *Solicitor to the Department of Health and Social Security.*

Dilys Tausz   Barrister.

Procedure Direction

HOUSE OF LORDS

House of Lords – Parties to appeal – Death of party – Abatement of appeal – Petition for revivor – Explanatory affidavit.

The Appeal Committee of the House of Lords announces an amendment to Direction as to Procedure no 35(i) applicable to Civil Appeals (Form of Appeal, Directions as to Procedure and Standing Orders (the Blue Book, 1979), p 25):

Leave out 'in Appeals from England and Northern Ireland by a certified copy of the Order of the Court below making the persons named parties to the Cause, and, in Scottish Appeals, by a certified copy of the Confirmation of Executors' and insert 'by an affidavit explaining the circumstances in which the Petition for Revivor is being lodged'.

PETER HENDERSON
16th February 1981   Clerk of the Parliaments.

R v Secretary of State for the Home Department, ex parte Puttick

QUEEN'S BENCH DIVISION

DONALDSON LJ AND FORBES J

14th NOVEMBER 1980

Citizenship – United Kingdom citizenship – Entitlement – Entitlement of woman married to United Kingdom citizen – Effect of public policy – Valid marriage procured by woman's criminal acts – Woman applying to be registered as United Kingdom citizen – Applicant fulfilling requirements of legislation – Whether Secretary of State entitled to refuse registration as citizen on ground of public policy despite mandatory terms of legislation – British Nationality Act 1948, s 6(2).

The applicant was a German citizen who had committed serious crimes in Germany. She obtained entry into the United Kingdom on a false passport in the name of another German citizen and, using that name, went through a marriage ceremony with a United Kingdom citizen at a register office and signed the marriage certificate in that name. The German authorities discovered her real identity and began extradition proceedings. In order to avoid extradition the applicant applied to the Secretary of State in her real name for registration as a United Kingdom citizen under s 6(2)[a] of the British Nationality 1948 Act. The Secretary of State refused her application and on appeal the Court of Appeal refused to grant her leave to apply for judicial review of the Secretary of State's decision. The applicant then applied to the court for a declaration of the validity of her marriage. On the hearing of that application the court determined ([1979] 3 All ER 463) that the marriage was valid but exercised its discretion by refusing to make a declaration of validity. Subsequently the Secretary of State, although accepting the court's decision that the applicant's marriage was valid, affirmed his refusal to register her as a United Kingdom citizen unless the court directed otherwise. The applicant applied for an order of mandamus requiring him to register her as a United Kingdom citizen on the grounds that she fulfilled the express terms of s 6(2) for registration, she was not affected by any disqualifying provisions of the Act, and therefore she had an absolute entitlement to be registered under s 6(2) and her registration thereunder was mandatory. The Secretary of State submitted that, even though the applicant fulfilled the requirements of s 6(2), he was entitled in an exceptional case to refuse registration on the grounds of public policy.

Held – Where there was a statutory duty involving the recognition of some right, then, notwithstanding the mandatory nature of the terms imposing that duty, it was nevertheless subject to the limitation that the right would not be recognised if the entitlement to it had been obtained by criminal activity and (per Donaldson LJ) to the limitations implied by the principles of public policy accepted by the courts at the time when the statute was passed. It followed that the Secretary of State was not bound to give effect to an entitlement to registration under s 6(2) of the 1948 Act which had been directly obtained by criminal activity, because (per Donaldson LJ) it was well established when the 1948 Act was passed that public policy required the courts to refuse to assist a criminal to benefit from his crime. Since the applicant had achieved her marriage, and therefore her entitlement to registration under s 6(2), by the crimes of fraud, forgery and perjury, and could not claim to be entitled to registration without relying on her criminality, the Secretary of State was entitled, despite the mandatory terms of s 6(2), to refuse to register her as a United Kingdom citizen. The application for mandamus would therefore be dismissed (see p 780 *b*, p 781 *f* to *h* and p 782 *h* to p 783 *c*, post).

---

a   Section 6(2), so far as material, is set out at p 779 *a*, post

Dictum of Lord Atkin in *Beresford v Royal Insurance Co Ltd* [1938] 2 All ER at 607 and
a *R v National Insurance Comr, ex parte Connor* p 769, ante, applied.

Notes
For entitlement of a married woman to United Kingdom citizenship, see 4 Halsbury's
Laws (4th Edn) para 920.
For the British Nationality Act 1948, s 6, see 1 Halsbury's Statutes (3rd Edn) 868.

b
Cases referred to in judgments
Amicable Society v Bolland (1830) 4 Bli NS 194, 2 Dow & Cl 1, 5 ER 70, HL, 29 Digest
   (Repl) 400, 3009.
Beresford v Royal Insurance Co Ltd [1938] 2 All ER 602, [1938] AC 586, 107 LJKB 464, 158
   LT 459, HL, 29 Digest (Repl) 397, 2995.
c *Cleaver v Mutual Reserve Fund Life Association* [1892] 1 QB 147, [1891–4] All ER Rep 335,
   61 LJQB 128, 66 LT 220, 56 JP 180, CA, 48 Digest (Repl) 74, 535.
Gray v Barr (Prudential Assurance Co Ltd, third party) [1971] 2 All ER 949, [1971] 2 QB
   554, [1971] 2 WLR 1334, [1971] 2 Lloyd's Rep 1, CA, 15 Digest (Reissue) 1140, 9649.
Hardy v Motor Insurers' Bureau [1964] 2 All ER 742, [1964] 2 QB 745, [1964] 3 WLR 433,
   [1964] 1 Lloyd's Rep 397, CA, Digest (Cont Vol B) 462, 3703a.
d *James v British General Insurance Co Ltd* [1927] 2 KB 311, [1927] All ER Rep 442, 96 LJKB
   729, 137 LT 156, 27 Ll L Rep 328, 29 Digest (Repl) 517, 3629.
Puttick v Attorney General and Puttick [1979] 3 All ER 463, [1980] Fam 1, [1979] 3 WLR
   542, Digest (Cont Vol E) 255, 347a.
R v National Insurance Comr, ex parte Connor p 769, ante, DC.
Sigsworth, Re, Bedford v Bedford [1935] Ch 89, [1934] All ER Rep 113, 104 LJ Ch 46, 152
e LT 329, 48 Digest (Repl) 75, 539.
Tinline v White Cross Insurance Association Ltd [1921] 3 KB 327, 90 LJKB 1118, 125 LT 632,
   26 Com Cas 347, 15 Digest (Reissue) 1154, 9776.

Cases also cited
R v All Saints, Wigan (Churchwardens) (1876) 1 App Cas 611, HL.
f *R v Committee Men for South Holland Drainage* (1838) 8 Ad & El 429, 112 ER 904.
St John's Shipping Corpn v Joseph Rank Ltd [1956] 3 All ER 683, [1957] 1 QB 267.

Application for judicial review
Pursuant to the leave of the Divisional Court given on 5th June 1979 Astrid Puttick
(otherwise known as Anna Puttick) applied for an order of mandamus directed to the
g respondent, the Secretary of State for the Home Department, requiring him to register
her as a citizen of the United Kingdom and Colonies under the provisions of s 6(2) of the
British Nationality Act 1948. The grounds of the application were that, although Mrs
Puttick had made due application in the prescribed form under 6(2) of the 1948 Act for
registration as a citizen of the United Kingdom and Colonies, the Secretary of State had
declined to register her as such unless the court otherwise directed and in the premises
h had failed to register her notwithstanding the mandatory provision of s 6(2), whereas, by
virtue of s 6(2), she was entitled as of right to such registration. The facts are set out in
the judgment of Donaldson LJ.

David Turner-Samuels QC and *Owen Davies* for Mrs Puttick.
Simon D Brown for the Secretary of State.

j
DONALDSON LJ. Astrid Proll wishes to change her citizenship from that of Germany
to that of the United Kingdom. In May 1971 she had been arrested in Germany on a
number of serious criminal charges. In February 1974, after her trial had begun and
been adjourned because of her ill-health, she was released on bail. In breach of the
conditions of that bail, she went to Italy and then, in October 1974, came to this
country. For obvious reasons she did not use her own name. Instead she bought a

passport in the name of Senta Gretel Sauerbier. Using that passport she was given permission to enter and stay in this country until 6th February 1975.

One way of achieving United Kingdom citizenship is by marriage to a United Kingdom citizen, followed by registration under s 6 of the British Nationality Act 1948. In Astrid Proll's situation this was probably the only possible way of achieving her object. Accordingly she determined to marry Robin Puttick, a bachelor with whom she was acquainted. Astrid Proll was a spinster and, in the traditional sense, there was no 'just impediment' to the marriage. There were, however, several obstacles, all of which arose out of the fact that she had entered this country using Frau Sauerbier's passport. If Fraulein Proll were not to risk identification and deportation she had to be married as Frau Sauerbier. Accordingly, the licence to marry had to be obtained in that name and she had to satisfy the Registrar General that Frau Sauerbier's previous marriage had been dissolved. All this involved forgery and perjury, but the obstacles were surmounted and on 22nd January 1975, Astrid Proll went through a ceremony of marriage with Robin Puttick at a register office.

The next move was to obtain registration as a citizen of the United Kingdom and Colonies. Shortly after the ceremony Mrs Senta Puttick, as Astrid Proll then called herself, made the necessary application to the Secretary of State. She used 'Senta' as her first name, because that was the first name of Frau Sauerbier whose identity she was still using. I need say no more about this application than that it was withdrawn before the Secretary of State had reached any decision and that, if it had been granted, the registration and consequent citizenship of the United Kingdom and Colonies could thereafter have been cancelled by the Secretary of State under s 20(2) of the 1948 Act on the grounds that the registration had been obtained by means of fraud, false representation and the concealment of material facts.

There matters remained until October 1978, by which time the Federal German authorities had identified Mrs Puttick as Astrid Proll and were taking steps to secure her extradition. Mrs Puttick then made a new application for registration under s 6(2) of the Act in the name of Astrid Proll. The Secretary of State refused to register her as a citizen of this country and she sought the leave of this court to apply for judicial review of his decision. Leave was refused and Mrs Puttick appealed to the Court of Appeal. Leave was again refused, but it was suggested that the appropriate course was for Mrs Puttick to seek a declaration of the validity of her marriage pursuant to s 45 of the Matrimonial Causes Act 1973.

Mrs Puttick adopted this course and the matter was heard and determined by Baker P. His judgment is reported in *Puttick v Attorney General and Puttick* [1979] 3 All ER 463, [1980] Fam 1. Suffice it to say that Baker P found that Mrs Puttick's marriage to Robin Puttick was a valid marriage, but refused to make the declaration on two grounds. The first was that Mrs Puttick was not domiciled in the United Kingdom, this being an essential prequisite to the right to make application under s 45(1) of the 1973 Act. The other was that, under s 45(5), the court had a discretion whether to make such a declaration and that, in the circumstances of this application, it was inappropriate to do so. This judgment was delivered on 8th May 1979, and on 30th May the Secretary of State affirmed his refusal to register Mrs Puttick as a citizen of the United Kingdom and Colonies unless the court otherwise directed. Hence the present application for an order requiring the Secretary of State so to register Mrs Puttick.

Let me make two matters clear at once. First, in the light of the reasons in the judgment of Baker P, the Secretary of State now accepts as a matter of law and fact that Mrs Puttick's marriage was valid. Second, we are not concerned with the offences with which Mrs Puttick was charged before the German courts or with such of them as led to convictions. She was sentenced to a term of imprisonment, that term has been served and it is not suggested that these are relevant matters for our consideration.

Counsel for Mrs Puttick has no difficulty in bringing her within the express terms of s 6(2) of the 1948 Act, as amended by the Immigration Act 1971, for it is in the following terms:

a   '... a woman who has been married to a citizen of the United Kingdom and
      Colonies shall be entitled, on making application therefor to the Secretary of State
      in the prescribed manner, to be registered as a citizen of the United Kingdom and
      Colonies, whether or not she is of full age and capacity.'

Mrs Puttick has been married to such a citizen and she has made application in the
prescribed manner.

b   Counsel for the Secretary of State submits that in an exceptional case the Secretary of
State is entitled to refuse registration on grounds of public policy and that this is such a
case. He further submits that, even if the Secretary of State is not justified in refusing
registration, this court is entitled and perhaps bound on grounds of public policy to
refuse to order him to perform his statutory duty under the Act. It is these submissions
which lie at the heart of this dispute and which I must now consider.

c   I doubt whether this second submission can be justified. It is true, of course, that the
remedy of judicial review is discretionary, but any considerations of public policy which
inhibit the courts from requiring the Secretary of State to perform a duty imposed by
Parliament must equally provide some unexpressed limitation on the apparent extent of
that duty. To put it in another way, it would be more than a little surprising if
Parliament intended to legislate in a manner inconsistent with the principles of public
d   policy applied by the courts without making this intention clear by the use, for example,
of such a time hallowed formula as 'any rule of law to the contrary notwithstanding'.

In my judgment, the crucial issue is whether the first submission of counsel for the
Secretary of State is correct. In other words, what in the circumstances of Mrs Puttick's
application is the duty of the Secretary of State under s 6(2) of the Act?

There is much authority on the circumstances in which the courts will refuse to
enforce contractual rights on grounds of public policy, but I doubt whether this is
e   directly applicable where the right is conferred and the concomitant duty is imposed by
statute. Until this year, the nearest approach to grappling with that problem seems to
have been the judgment of Clauson J in *Re Sigsworth, Bedford v Bedford* [1935] Ch 89,
[1934] All ER Rep 113. There it was held that a sane murderer could not take any benefit
under trusts declared by s 46 of the Administration of Estates Act 1925 of the residuary
f   estate of his intestate victim. This decision is not binding on this court and may in any
event be distinguishable in that the statute created private rights without imposing any
public duty.

The problem was, however, directly faced by this court in *R v National Insurance Comr,
ex parte Connor* p 769, ante. Mrs Connor had been acquitted of the murder of her
husband, but found guilty of his manslaughter. She applied for a widow's allowance
under the Social Security Act 1975 but this was refused by the chief national insurance
g   commissioner on the grounds that it was contrary to public policy that she should benefit
from her own crime.

Counsel appearing for Mrs Connor made two main submissions. The first could be
applied mutatis mutandis to the present case. He submitted that the Social Security Act
1975 was a self-contained modern statute to which rules of public policy should not be
h   applied, particularly since it contained express provisions disqualifying persons from
obtaining benefit in specified circumstances. Mrs Connor's claim fell fairly and squarely
within the wording of s 24 of the 1975 Act which created an absolute entitlement and
was not affected by any disqualifying provisions. The same submission can be, and is,
made in the present case. Mrs Puttick's claim to registration as a citizen of the United
Kingdom and Colonies falls fairly and squarely within the wording of s 6(2) of the 1948
j   Act and, in the true and accurate form in which it is now presented, is not affected by any
disqualifying provisions such as those contained in s 20. Strictly speaking those
provisions do not disqualify, but inasmuch as they entitle the Secretary of State to deprive
a registered citizen of citizenship, they would justify him in refusing registration in
circumstances in which he would revoke any citizenship which was achieved by
registration.

Lord Lane CJ, in a judgment with which Griffiths and Webster JJ agreed, rejected this submission saying (see p 774, ante):

> 'I do not accept that submission. The fact that there is no specific mention in the Act of disentitlement so far as a widow is concerned if she were to commit this sort of offence and so become a widow is merely an indication, as I see it, that the draftsman realised perfectly well that he was drawing this Act against the background of the law as it stood at the time.'

This decision provides authority for the proposition that statutory duties which are in terms absolute may nevertheless be subject to implied limitations based on principles of public policy accepted by the courts at the time when the Act is passed.

The second submission made on behalf of Mrs Connor was that it is not every type of crime which operates so as to cause the national insurance commissioner (in that case) and the courts to reject a claim. On this Lord Lane CJ said (see pp 774–775, ante):

> 'I, for my part, would agree with that. Indeed there are dicta, particularly in *Gray v Barr* [1971] 2 All ER 954, [1971] 2 QB 554, which support that proposition, and in particular the judgment of Salmon LJ which reads ([1971] 2 All ER 954 at 964, [1971] 2 QB 554 at 581): "Although public policy is rightly regarded as an unruly steed which should be cautiously ridden, I am confident that public policy undoubtedly requires that no one who threatens unlawful violence with a loaded gun [that was the case in *Gray v Barr*] should be allowed to enforce a claim for indemnity against any liability he may incur as a result of having so acted. I do not intend to lay down any wider proposition. In particular, I am not deciding that a man who has committed manslaughter would, in any circumstances, be prevented from enforcing a contract of indemnity in respect of any liability he may have incurred for causing death or from inheriting under a will or on the intestacy of anyone whom he has killed. Manslaughter is a crime which varies infinitely in its seriousness. It may come very near to murder or amount to little more than inadvertence, although in the latter class of case the jury only rarely convicts." I would respectfully agree with that dictum, and I would agree that in each case it is not the label which the law applies to the crime which has been committed but the nature of the crime itself which in the end will dictate whether public policy demands the court to drive the applicant from the seat of justice. Where that line is to be drawn may be a difficult matter to decide, but what this court has to determine is whether in the present case what this applicant did was sufficient to disentitle her to her remedy. The judgment of Lord Denning MR in the same case does provide some assistance in determining where to draw the line. He says this ([1971] 2 All ER 954 at 956, [1971] 2 QB 554 at 568): "Does this manslaughter mean that, as a matter of public policy, Mr Barr is not to be allowed to recover on the policy? In the category of manslaughter which is called 'motor manslaughter', it is settled beyond question that the insured is entitled to recover: see *Tinline v White Cross Insurance Association Ltd* [1921] 3 KB 327; *James v British General Insurance Co Ltd* [1927] 2 KB 311, [1927] All ER Rep 442. But, in the category which is here in question, it is different. If his conduct is wilful and culpable, he is not entitled to recover: see *Hardy v Motor Insurers' Bureau* [1964] 2 All ER 742, [1964] 2 QB 745. I agree with [Geoffrey Lane J] when he said ([1970] 2 All ER 702 at 710, [1970] 2 QB 626 at 640): 'The logical test, in my judgment, is whether the person seeking the indemnity was guilty of deliberate, intentional and unlawful violence, or threats of violence. If he was, and death resulted therefrom, then, however unintended the final death of the victim may have been, the court should not entertain the claim for indemnity.'" One turns then to see what it was that happened here. On the verdict of the jury it is plain that the applicant's act was a deliberate, conscious and intentional act. She was holding the knife in her hand and she deliberately thrust it into her husband's chest. It is not the same as discharging two barrels of a shotgun; no two situations will ever be the same. But, speaking for myself, I can see

no distinction in principle between the situation in *Gray v Barr*, which was sufficient to disentitle the plaintiff to recover, and the situation here, which also to my mind disentitles the applicant to recover.'

This is not a homicide case and, to that extent, such authorities as *Cleaver v Mutual Reserve Fund Life Association* [1892] 1 QB 147, [1891–4] All ER Rep 335 and *Beresford v Royal Insurance Co Ltd* [1938] 2 All ER 602, [1938] AC 586 are not directly applicable. However, it is noteworthy that Lord Atkin in *Beresford's* case, with whom Lord Thankerton and Lord Russell agreed, did not limit the principle to homicide cases. He quoted with approval the general statement of law by Fry LJ in *Cleaver's* case [1892] 1 QB 147 at 156, [1891–4] All ER Rep 335 at 340:

'It appears to me that no system of jurisprudence can with reason include amongst the rights which it enforces rights directly resulting to the person asserting them from the crime of that person.'

Furthermore, Lord Atkin supported this general statement by reference to *Amicable Insurance Society v Bolland* (1830) 4 Bli NS 194, 5 ER 70 in which the claim owed its existence to forgery and the execution of the life assured for that crime. Later in his speech Lord Atkin stated the principle in these terms ([1938] 2 All ER 602 at 607, [1938] AC 586 at 598):

'I think that the principle is that a man is not to be allowed to have recourse to a Court of Justice to claim a benefit from his crime, whether under a contract or under a gift. No doubt the rule pays regard to the fact that to hold otherwise would in some cases offer an inducement to crime, or remove a restraint to crime, and that its effect is to act as a deterrent to crime. But, apart from these considerations, the absolute rule is that the courts will not recognise a benefit accruing to a criminal from his crime.'

Lord Macmillan in a separate speech which led to the same conclusion accepted that Beresford's claim gave rise to a conflict of principles of public policy. On the one hand it was an accepted principle that persons who entered into contractual arrangements should be required to fulfil them. On the other, it was an accepted principle that no court ought to assist a criminal to derive benefit from his crime.

For my part, I think that when the British Nationality Act 1948 was enacted it was well established that public policy required the courts to refuse to assist a criminal to benefit from his crime at least in serious cases and that Parliament must be deemed to have been aware of this. Against this background, and bearing in mind additionally that citizenship is not only a matter of private right but also of public status and concern, in my judgment, Parliament can never have intended that a woman should be entitled to claim registration as a citizen of the United Kingdom and Colonies on the basis of a marriage achieved only by the commission of serious crime. In this case Mrs Puttick's impersonation of Frau Sauerbier and the commission of the crime of perjury and forgery formed the foundation of her marriage to Robin Puttick and, in my judgment, disentitled her to rely on the right which she would otherwise have had to claim registration as a citizen of the United Kingdom and Colonies. I consider that the Secretary of State was fully justified in refusing Mrs Puttick's application for registration and accordingly she is not entitled to the relief for which she applies.

I would dismiss the application.

FORBES J. Astrid Puttick asks this court to order the Home Secretary to register her as a citizen of the United Kingdom and Colonies under s 6(2) of the British Nationality Act 1948. This subsection is, materially, in these terms:

'. . . a woman who has been married to a citizen of the United Kingdom and Colonies shall be entitled, on making application therefor to the Secretary of State in the prescribed manner, to be registered as a citizen of the United Kingdom and Colonies . . .'

On 22nd January 1975 she went through a form of marriage before a registrar, as
Donaldson LJ has related. She had assumed the identity of Senta Sauerbier, an actual *a*
person who lived in West Berlin.

Counsel on her behalf points out that the terms of the section are mandatory and says
that, as the Home Secretary now accepts that her marriage was valid, he has no option but
to register her as a citizen.

Counsel for the Home Secretary argues that he is not bound to register her for two
reasons, each of them concerned with the principle enshrined in the maxim ex turpi *b*
causa non oritur actio. The first is that however mandatory may be the terms of the
statute no person is entitled to any rights under it if the purported entitlement has been
procured by fraud; and the second is that the prerogative remedy of mandamus is
discretionary and the court should not allow an order to go in a case where the applicant
has to rely on an entitlement obtained by fraud.

The main authorities relied on are the passage from the judgment of Fry LJ in *Cleaver's* *c*
case to which Donaldson LJ has referred and the case of *Connor* in this court. For my part,
I think it important to distinguish three separate arguments: (1) that where a person, or
body, is charged by statute with a duty involving the recognition of some right, however
mandatory the terms imposing that duty, that person is not bound to recognise the right
if the entitlement to it has been obtained criminaliter; (2) that no court will allow itself
to be used to enforce rights the entitlement to which has been illegally obtained; (3) that *d*
the remedy of mandamus is a discretionary remedy.

Of these I do not think the last is applicable here. Unless there were some other
principle involved as well, I do not think this court would refuse to order the carrying
out of a clearly mandatory duty arising under a statute; the discretion of the court in this
field is ordinarily exercised in relation to delay or the existence of alternative remedies
and other matters of that kind. But it is important to distinguish all three principles. *e*

If the first of them is right, the Home Secretary himself can say that, despite the
mandatory terms of the statute, he is not bound to entertain this application for
registration. No doubt his action, or refusal to act, is reviewable in this court in
accordance with the usual principles involved in judicial review, but, subject to that, on
this argument the initial decision is the Home Secretary's. If the first is wrong, then the
Home Secretary can only rely on the second argument and ask this court not to use its *f*
powers to order him to register.

Neither of these two propositions is, as I understand it, seriously challenged by counsel
for Mrs Puttick. Instead he argues, on a number of grounds, that the principles do not
apply in this case. His first point is that the illegality complained of must be the direct
source of the relief sought. Thus he argues that the illegality had nothing to do with the
ceremony itself: Robin Puttick and Astrid Proll were in fact the people who went *g*
through this ceremony; they were in fact married and there is no illegality in the
marriage itself, the validity of which is now accepted by the Home Secretary. His second
point is that the entitlement arises out of status; and his third that the Mrs Puttick did
not obtain something to which she was not entitled; she was at all times entitled to be
married to Robin Puttick.

I think the answer to all these arguments is the same. The words of s 6(2) show that *h*
the entitlement accrues to a woman who 'has been married' to a United Kingdom
citizen. These words indicate to my mind that it is the fact of going through the
marriage ceremony, and, be it said, the status which that produces, which creates the
entitlement. But here the registrar who performed the ceremony was fraudulently
misled into believing that he was marrying Robin Puttick to someone called Sauerbier,
a divorced person of whose capacity to contract a second marriage he had satisfied *j*
himself, and whose father was called Eric Schulz, a machine engineer; that deception was
persisted in throughout the ceremony and indeed afterwards when Mrs Puttick signed
the marriage certificate as Senta Sauerbier. Further, when making her application in the
prescribed manner to the Home Secretary for registration she produced, as she had to,
this marriage certificate with its fraudulent entries and forged signature, and had to
explain in a covering letter the extent of her criminal activities. I therefore have no
doubt that it was her fraud and forgery which directly obtained for her the entitlement

she now seeks to enforce and that she cannot claim that entitlement without relying on
a her own criminality. I would reject her counsel's submissions.

To return to the two main arguments which I earlier set out, I have no doubt that the
case of *Connor* is conclusive of the first: the Home Secretary, like the insurance
commissioner, is not bound to give effect to an entitlement directly obtained by criminal
activity. In *Connor*, as in *Barr*, it was necessary to consider in addition the degree of
criminality involved. But this was due to the fact that there the entitlement arose on a
b death. That is not the case here and it is therefore unnecessary to be diverted in
argument by the niceties of the law of homicide. It is sufficient to consider whether the
entitlement was directly obtained by criminal activity. I conclude that it was, and that
therefore the Home Secretary, despite the mandatory terms of the statute, is competent
to refuse to register Mrs Puttick as a citizen. No valid reason for reviewing that decision
as a decision has been shown.

c The second of the arguments depends on the judgment of Fry LJ in *Cleaver's* case,
approved as it has been in a number of subsequent decisions. But in view of the
conclusion I have come to on the first proposition I think it unnecessary to consider the
second further.

I, too, would dismiss the application.

d *Application dismissed.*

Solicitors: *Seifert, Sedley & Co* (for Mrs Puttick); *Treasury Solicitor.*

Dilys Tausz   Barrister.

e

Beard v Beard

COURT OF APPEAL, CIVIL DIVISION
CUMMING-BRUCE, DUNN AND GRIFFITHS LJJ
f 5th NOVEMBER 1980

*Divorce – Custody – Care and control – Interim order – Emergency situation – Power to order
person given interim care and control to enter house where children living – Power to exclude
tenant of house during emergency if in children's interest – Mother and father divorced – Mother
having custody, care and control – Mother and children living in council house of which mother
sole tenant – Mother ill and away from home – Whether jurisdiction to give father interim care
g and control and to grant injunction restraining mother from entering house – Matrimonial
Causes Act 1973, s 42(1).*

When the parents' marriage broke down the mother and children left the matrimonial
home in about 1977 to live in a council house of which the mother was the sole tenant.
h The parents were divorced in 1979 and the mother was granted custody, care and control
of the children. The mother became ill and invited the father to live in the house with
the children while she was in hospital for treatment. When she came out of hospital she
returned home and for a short time both the mother and father lived in the house.
However, she found it impossible to live with him and after an incident on 27th August
1980 she became ill again and went back into hospital. She later discharged herself from
j hospital but did not return to the house because the father was living there. By an
application dated 28th August the father applied for an order restraining the mother
from entering the house. On 29th August the mother cross-applied for an injunction
restraining the father from entering the house and from interfering with her occupation
of it. When the applications came on for hearing in September, the father undertook to
issue a summons for the transfer of the custody of the children to himself. Pending the
hearing of that summons (which was not likely to be heard before December) the judge
had to deal with the emergency situation created by the mother's illness and absence

from the house, and to decide who should have interim care and control of the children
pending determination of the father's summons. The judge ordered, pursuant to s 42(1)[a] **a**
of the Matrimonial Causes Act 1973, that the father should have interim care and control
and granted him an injunction for three months or until the hearing of the father's
summons restraining the mother from entering the council house without the court's
leave or the father's prior authority, and dismissed the mother's application. The mother
appealed, contending that the judge did not have jurisdiction to make an order which
affected her right to occupy a house of which she was sole tenant.   **b**

Held – Where there was an emergency situation in regard to children of a family which
required the court to make an interim care and control order to deal with the situation
during the continuance of the emergency, the court had jurisdiction to order, for the
protection of the children, that the person given the interim care and control should have
the right to enter a house which was the children's home and to remain there during the **c**
emergency (unless the landlord intervened on the ground that his rights were infringed),
even though the tenant of the house objected. Furthermore, consequent on such an
order the court had power to order that during the emergency the tenant should not
return to the house if, in the court's view, his or her presence there would put the
children at risk. It followed that the court would affirm the judge's order and that the
appeal would be dismissed (see p 787 d to j, post).   **d**

Notes
For custody orders after divorce see 13 Halsbury's Laws (4th Edn) para 926.
    For the Matrimonial Causes Act 1973, s 42, see 43 Halsbury's Statutes (3rd Edn) 590.

Appeal   **e**
The mother and father were divorced in October 1979 and the mother was granted
custody, care and control of the four children of the marriage. She lived with them in
a council house of which she was the sole tenant. The mother became ill and had to go
into hospital and she invited the father to live in the house to look after the children.
Shortly afterwards, she returned to the house and lived there with the father and the
children. On 27th August 1980 after an incident at the house she went into hospital **f**
again. The father, by notice of application dated 28th August 1980, applied for an order
restraining her from molesting or interfering with him and the children, and restraining
her from entering the house other than with leave of the court or prior written authority
from the father or his solicitors. The mother, by notice dated 29th August, cross-applied
for an order requiring the father to leave the house and prohibiting him from calling at
or entering the house or in any way interfering with the mother's occupation of it. The **g**
mother discharged herself from hospital but did not return to the house. On 26th
September 1980 his Honour Judge Monier-Williams sitting as a judge of the High Court,
made an order giving interim care and control of the children to the father, on his
undertaking to file a summons for custody of the children, and granted him an
injunction restraining the mother until 26th December 1980 or the hearing of the
father's summons for custody, whichever was the earlier, from molesting or interfering **h**
with the father or the children and from entering or attempting to enter the house
without the court's leave or the prior authority of the father or his solicitors. The mother
appealed on the grounds (1) that the judge misdirected himself in holding that he had
jurisdiction to make an order restraining the mother from returning to the house
because it was a council house in her sole name which she had acquired after the
breakdown of the marriage and in which the parties had never lived as man and wife, **j**
(2) that the judge misdirected himself in holding he had jurisdiction to make an order
affecting the rights of occupation of a council house in the absence of any notice to the

---

a   Section 42(1), so far as material, provides: 'The court may make such order as it thinks fit for the
      custody and education of any child of the family who is under the age of eighteen—(*a*) in any
      proceedings for divorce . . . before or on granting a decree or at any time thereafter (whether, in
      the case of a decree of divorce . . . before or after the decree is made absolute) . . .'

local authority as landlord or any evidence from the local authority properly as to its intentions in the case, and (3) that the judge failed to take into account the evidence and wrongly rejected evidence that the mother was a fit and proper person to care for the children. The facts are set out in the judgment of Cumming-Bruce LJ.

Robert Sich for the mother.
J C J Tatham for the father.

CUMMING-BRUCE LJ. This is an appeal by a former wife and present mother against the order of his Honour Judge Monier-Williams when on 26th September 1980 it was ordered that, on the respondent father undertaking to file a summons for custody, the children of the family should remain in the care and control of the father. Also that the petitioner mother be restrained from returning to 20 Church Road, Pembury. There was to be reasonable access. A court welfare report was ordered. The injunction was to remain in force until 26th December 1980 or the hearing of the application for custody, whichever was to be the sooner. A supervision order was to continue in force. The mother's application that the father leave 20 Church Road and that he should not enter the property or interfere with the mother's occupation was dismissed.

In the circumstances that have arisen it is unnecessary to explain the facts save in the barest details. As custody proceedings are on foot and it is hoped to resolve them in a matter of weeks, the less that is said in this court about the merits of the respective cases for custody, care and control the better.

The parties were married in January 1964. They are now 36 and 31. There were four children. The eldest boy was born in March 1964 and the next son was born in 1965; then there is a boy born in 1970 and the youngest son was born in 1974. Proceedings for the dissolution of the marriage, which had been unhappy for some time, began in September 1975. An order was then made excluding the father from the then matrimonial home, 43 Church Road, which, we are told, was a council house. The judge found that from that time onwards the marriage was effectively at an end and the parties have not since lived together as husband and wife.

Eventually the dissolution proceedings were settled. The decree absolute was in October 1979 and after contested custody proceedings the mother was granted custody, care and control of all four children. About three years ago the mother moved into another council house, 20 Church Road, Pembury, of which she is the sole tenant. Of course she moved into that house with the children. That has been the children's home ever since.

It appears from the findings of the judge, who made an interim order for care and control in favour of the father, that in the summer of last year a crisis arose in the childrens' lives flowing, on the judge's findings, from a combination of two main factors. The mother had a major breakdown of health and had to resort to hospital treatment as an in-patient, leaving the children high and dry unless she made some other arrangements for their care, which she very properly did by inviting her former husband, the father, to come into her house at 20 Church Road and look after the children during her temporary absence. There was another factor which the judge dwelt on in his judgment: the mother had made friends with a young man whom she brought to live with her at 20 Church Road. The two elder boys did not get on with that young gentleman and there were alleged to have been features of his behaviour which gave rise to anxiety. The mother decided to give up the treatment being advised for her and she came back home and there was a short period when the mother and the father were living with the children under the same roof. On 27th August 1980 there was some trouble which the judge referred to and the mother went to hospital again but discharged herself. She had not before the judge's decision been back to live in the home.

The judge heard evidence and considered a welfare report of a kind on the subject of who should look after the children on an interim basis having regard to the emergency that had arisen as a result of the mother's apparent two successive breakdowns in health. It is perfectly clear from the judge's judgment that, and he says it in terms, all that he was deciding on 26th September was what to do for the children in the emergency that had arisen. He decided that it was not practicable for him to attempt to reopen the custody proceedings proper, if only because there was no such application at that time. The father gave an undertaking to issue a summons for variation of the existing custody order. The judge gave directions, it is clear from his order, for a welfare report and evidently contemplated that the custody proceedings would come on in December 1980, so that he was focusing his attention on the practical arrangements for the care of the children during the period that would elapse between 26th September and the determination of the custody proceedings, which, with any luck, it was anticipated would come on in December. That was all that the judge expressly was dealing with and he came to the conclusion that it was quite clear that during that tiding-over period until the custody proceedings could be launched and heard the father ought to look after the children.

I may say that meanwhile the mother is living in accommodation provided for her by her employers at her place of employment, which, we are told, is a caravan which is manifestly, unless it is a very exceptional caravan, not an ideal kind of accommodation as the winter approaches. She would like to come home of course.

Counsel for the mother has exercised characteristic judgment in the way in which he has handled this appeal. Having had a chance of reading the judge's very clear and emphatic findings of fact on the material then before him, counsel rightly did not seek any longer to challenge in this court the judge's decision that the interim care and control of the children should be confided to the father. That is the basis on which we now approach the appeal. The other ground of appeal raised questions that might, if it was necessary to grapple with them, give rise to some rather interesting and nice questions in relation to the power of the court under the Matrimonial Causes Act 1973 to intervene and interfere with the common law rights of the mother as tenant of a local authority and entitled thereby to occupation of her home, 20 Church Road, Pembury.

The question of jurisdiction was canvassed before the judge. The judge's approach was to exercise his powers under the Matrimonial Causes Act 1973 on an emergency basis for the protection of the children in the emergency that had arisen. In his findings of fact he explained what the emergency was and it is unnecessary for me to repeat it, save to say that it is not challenged in this court that there was an emergency in the lives of the children so that the judge had to deal with it. What the judge decided to do was, having regard to his powers conferred under the 1973 Act in relation to custody, care and control and protection of children, to make an order that the person to whom he confided interim care and control of the children should remain in the house, which was the childrens' home, in the absence of the mother and that he reached his decision because of the background history which showed quite clearly that it was no longer feasible for the former husband, the father, and the former wife, themselves, to attempt to live together in amity in 20 Church Road. That it was not practicable is demonstrated by the fact that the mother, on seeking to return to her home, has not I think suggested on a long term basis that it would be sensible for her former husband to be there too.

The judge heard in argument a discussion of cases which discussed the problems of transfer of property and considered also some obiter dicta in cases which did not actually have to decide the extent of the jurisdiction of the court when it is called on to interfere with the exercise of common law rights in order to exercise appropriately the power conferred for the protection and care of the children in the Matrimonial Causes Act 1973. It may be that after the custody proceedings have been concluded (one hopes in December) that some of those problems may arise. It is perfectly possible that they will not arise at all. There are all kinds of permutations and combinations. The mother may find that she is restored to the care and control of the children. Alternatively the father may find that the interim order for custody care and control made in September is translated into an order that he, for the immediately foreseeable period, is to be the custodian of the children with care and control. As the children are living in their mother's council house the local authority is closely involved and if there is a transfer of custody from mother to father it may very well be that it will be necessary for the parties to approach the local authority and invite the local authority to make up their minds whether to make any change in the present allocation of the council tenancy to the mother or not. What they will do it is pointless to speculate. The situation may not arise at all. But it may arise and the experience of courts has been that these problems where children are living in council property can only be satisfactorily resolved by means of close co-operation between the courts exercising the jurisdiction under the Matrimonial Causes Act 1973 and the local authority with a responsibility for housing the adults and the children. All those matters may fall for argument and decision after the custody proceedings have been decided. They are wholly hypothetical at the moment.

Counsel for the mother has expressed an anxiety that the judge in his judgment expressed himself in terms that might be interpreted by another judge as suggesting that the judge had formed a view about the jurisdiction of the court to interfere with the common law rights of the mother other than on an emergency basis to deal with an emergency situation facing the children. Having read the way in which the judge expressed himself, I find no reason for sharing counsel's apprehension, but I have such confidence in counsel's judgment that, if there really was absolutely no ground for apprehension, I would not expect him to have any anxiety at all and so I respect the fact that he has announced an anxiety. On reading the judgment, the passage that matters concludes with the sentence: 'The point that I have to consider is that I have to consider an emergency situation.' That sentence follows a passage in which the judge expressly shows that he is not looking beyond the present emergency and its resolution in the custody proceedings which will take place in or about December 1980. All that I say is this, for the removal of doubt: nothing in my judgment is to be interpreted as throwing any light at all on the question whether in any situation other than the emergency considered by the judge the court has jurisdiction to intervene for the protection of the children by making the orders that the judge made. In connection with those orders I state the following propositions. If children of a family are in an emergency which requires action on the part of the court for their protection, the court has power to decide whether, if there is no suitable person presently in care and control under an order of the court, to make an order for care and control of the children to protect them during the emergency. If, as on the facts in the instant case, the childrens' home is the home in which they have lived for some years which it would be quite wrong to disturb on an interim basis, then when the judge has made an order deciding who is the adult who should on an interim basis come into the childrens' lives to exercise care and control in the emergency, the court has power to order, for the protection of the children, that the person selected as the person appropriate for interim care and control shall have the right, on the order of the court, to enter the childrens' house (the house where the children are living) whether the council tenant agrees or not, and has jurisdiction for the period of the emergency to order that the interim custodian shall stay in the council house unless the local authority takes steps to intervene on the ground that the landlord's rights have been infringed, which appears to me an extremely outside chance. Consequential on such an order for the protection of children during the continuance of the emergency, the court has power to order the tenant not to return to the house in which she is a tenant if the court takes the view, as the judge decided in this case, that her presence in the home would put the children temporarily at risk.

For those reasons I would affirm the judge's order, having made it perfectly clear that this court, like the judge, has only been considering the temporary protection of the children during the continuance of an emergency situation. For those reasons I would dismiss this appeal.

DUNN LJ. I agree.

GRIFFITHS LJ. I also agree.

Appeal dismissed.

Solicitors: *Berry & Berry*, Tunbridge Wells (for the mother); *Cripps, Harries, Hall & Co*, Tunbridge Wells (for the father).

Avtar S Virdi Esq   Barrister.

R v Secretary of State for the Environment and another, ex parte Powis

COURT OF APPEAL, CIVIL DIVISION

STEPHENSON, DUNN LJJ AND SIR DAVID CAIRNS

22nd, 23rd, 27th, 28th, 29th OCTOBER, 6th NOVEMBER 1980

Landlord and tenant – Business premises – Change in use or occupation of property – Land requisite for public purposes – Requisite – Minister deciding that tenant's land reasonably necessary for local authority's purposes – Whether land 'requisite' for authority's purposes – Landlord and Tenant Act 1954, s 57(1).

Certiorari – Evidence – Fresh evidence – Judicial review – Categories of fresh evidence admissible on judicial review – Whether evidence admissible to show that minister misled by party's failure to present relevant evidence.

From 1964 the appellant carried on business as a car breaker and scrap metal dealer on one acre of land rented from a borough council. There were two other car breaker's yards in the locality. Following local government reorganisation in 1974 a county council took over the borough council's functions and became the appellant's landlord. In 1976 the county council decided to reduce the number of car breaker's yards in the locality and that the only car breaker's yard in the area should be located at another site. It invited tenders for the lease of the new site. The appellant submitted a tender but was unsuccessful. In July 1977 the council, as the landlord of the appellant's site, applied to the Secretary of State for the Environment for a certificate under s 57(1)[a] of the Landlord and Tenant Act 1954 that the site, being held by a local authority as landlord, was 'requisite for the purposes . . . of the authority' and that the use or occupation thereof be changed accordingly. The reason given by the council in its application was that the appellant's site was required for the storage of highways material. In August 1977 the Secretary of State issued the certificate, giving as his reasons for doing so the fact that the land was 'required' or wanted by the council and that he accepted the council's submission that there was no alternative site available. An application by the appellant to the Divisional Court for judicial review of the Secretary of State's certificate was refused. The appellant appealed, contending, inter alia, (i) that land was 'requisite' for a local authority's purposes only if it was necessary for the authority's purposes and the Secretary of State had misdirected himself in law as to the meaning of 'requisite', (ii) that there was no evidence put forward by the council to the Secretary of State that the appellant's land was in fact requisite for its purposes, and (iii) that the Divisional Court had been wrong to refuse to allow the appellant to produce fresh evidence showing that the Secretary of State had been misled by the failure of the council to put relevant evidence before him.

Held – The appeal would be dismissed for the following reasons—

(1) In the context of s 57(1) of the 1954 Act land did not have to be indispensable to a council but merely reasonably necessary for its purposes in order to be 'requisite'. Whether particular land was reasonably necessary was a matter of planning judgment based on the evidence before the Secretary of State. In respect of the appellant's site it was clear from the reasons given by the Secretary of State that, although he considered 'requisite' to mean merely 'genuinely required', he had gone on to consider whether the appellant's site was reasonably necessary for the council's purposes and had decided that it was (see p 795 *a b f* to *j*, p 796 *c d* and p 799 *f g*, post); dictum of Sachs LJ in *Coleen Properties Ltd v Minister of Housing and Local Government* [1971] 1 All ER at 1054 applied.

---

a   Section 57(1), so far as material, is set out at p 790 *f*, post

(2) Having regard to the fact that s 57 did not provide for an inquiry or other hearing to be held prior to the Secretary of State making his decision, he was entitled to weigh the statements submitted to him by the council and the appellant and to reach his decision on the material put before him. In those circumstances, the Secretary of State was not required to insist that the council submit detailed evidence in support of its submissions (see p 796 *h* to p 797 *a e f* and p 799 *f g*, post); dictum of Lord Denning MR in *Coleen Properties Ltd v Minister of Housing and Local Government* [1971] 1 All ER at 1053 distinguished.

(3) The categories of fresh evidence which was admissible on a judicial review were limited to (a) evidence to show what material was before the person making the decision, (b) evidence required to determine a jurisdictional or procedural error, and (c) evidence of misconduct by a party or the person making the decision. That limitation applied to proceedings for certiorari generally, whether to quash the decision of an inferior tribunal after a hearing or to quash the decision of a minister when there was no hearing. But fresh evidence was not admissible to show that the minister had been misled by the failure, short of fraud, of a party to put before him evidence which would probably have caused him to come to a different conclusion. There was nothing in the fresh evidence sought to be adduced by the appellant which brought it within the categories of evidence admissible on a judicial review and the Divisional Court was therefore right to exclude it (see p 797 *h* to p 798 *f* and p 799 *c* to *g*, post); *R v West Sussex Quarter Sessions* [1973] 3 All ER 289 and dicta of Lord Wilberforce and Lord Russell in *Secretary of State for Education v Metropolitan Borough of Tameside* [1976] 3 All ER at 685, 704 applied.

Notes

For the granting of a certificate under s 57 of the Landlord and Tenant Act 1954, see 23 Halsbury's Laws (3rd Edn) 903, para 1735.

For the Landlord and Tenant Act 1954, s 57, see 18 Halsbury's Statutes (3rd Edn) 594.

Cases referred to in judgment

Ashbridge Investments Ltd v Minister of Housing and Local Government [1965] 3 All ER 371, [1965] 1 WLR 1320, 129 JP 580, 63 LGR 400, CA, Digest (Cont Vol B) 336, *86c*.

Associated Provincial Picture Houses Ltd v Wednesbury Corpn [1947] 2 All ER 680, [1948] 1 KB 223, [1948] LJR 190, 117 LT 641, 112 JP 55, 45 LGR 635, CA, 45 Digest (Repl) 215, *189*.

Coleen Properties Ltd v Minister of Housing and Local Government [1971] 1 All ER 1049, [1971] 1 WLR 433, 135 JP 226, 69 LGR 175, 22 P & CR 417, [1971] RVR 489, CA, Digest (Cont Vol D) 387, *109a*.

R v West Sussex Quarter Sessions, ex parte Albert and Maud Johnson Trust Ltd [1973] 3 All ER 289, [1974] QB 24, [1973] 3 WLR 149, 137 JP 784, 71 LGR 379, CA, Digest (Cont Vol D) 268, *2897a*.

Robinson v Minister of Town and Country Planning [1947] 1 All ER 851, [1947] KB 702, [1947] LJR 1285, 117 LT 375, 111 JP 378, 45 LGR 497, CA, 45 Digest (Repl) 366, *158*.

Secretary of State for Education and Science v Metropolitan Borough of Tameside [1976] 3 All ER 665, [1977] AC 1014, [1976] 3 WLR 641, 75 LGR 190, CA and HL, Digest (Cont Vol E) 194, *33c*.

XL Fisheries Ltd v Leeds Corpn [1955] 2 All ER 875, [1955] 2 QB 636, [1955] 3 WLR 393, 119 JP 519, 31(2) Digest (Reissue) 949, *7742*.

Cases also cited

Attorney General of St Christopher, Nevis and Anguilla v Reynolds [1979] 3 All ER 129, [1980] 2 WLR 171, PC.

East Hampshire District Council v Secretary of State for Health and Social Security [1978] JPL 182.

Global Plant Ltd v Secretary of State for Health and Social Security [1971] 3 All ER 385, [1972] 1 QB 139.

R v London Borough of Hillingdon, ex parte Royco Homes Ltd [1974] 2 All ER 643, [1974] QB 720, DC.

Westminster Bank v Minister of Housing and Local Government [1970] 1 All ER 734, [1971] AC 508, HL.

Appeal

Arthur Glyn Powis appealed against the refusal of the Divisional Court of the Queen's Bench Division (Shaw LJ and Kilner Brown J) on 23rd May 1980 to grant his application for judicial review by way of an order of certiorari to bring up and quash a certificate granted to the Buckinghamshire County Council by the Secretary of State for the Environment under s 57(1) of the Landlord and Tenant Act 1954 that the use and occupation of a site at High Heavens Wood, Marlow Bottom, Buckinghamshire rented by the appellant from the council should be changed as being requisite for the council's purposes. The appellant also appealed against the Divisional Court's refusal to grant a declaration that the site was not requisite for the council's purposes. The facts are set out in the judgment of the court.

Richard Rougier QC and *R G Marshall-Andrews* for the appellant.
Simon D Brown for the Secretary of State.
Nicholas Huskinson for the county council.

Cur adv vult

6th November. **DUNN LJ** read the following judgment of the court: This is an appeal by leave from the refusal of the Divisional Court on judicial review to grant an order of certiorari to bring up and quash a certificate of the Secretary of State for the Environment given under s 57(1) of the Landlord and Tenant Act 1954.

The material provisions of s 57 are as follows:

'(1) Where the interest of the landlord or any superior landlord in the property comprised in any tenancy belongs to or is held . . . by a local authority . . . the Minister or Board in charge of any Government department may certify that it is requisite for the purposes of the first-mentioned department, or, as the case may be, of the authority . . . that the use or occupation of the property or a part thereof shall be changed by a specified date.

'(2) A certificate under the last foregoing subsection shall not be given unless the owner of the interest belonging or held as mentioned in the last foregoing subsection has given to the tenant a notice stating—(a) that the question of the giving of such a certificate is under consideration by the Minister or Board specified in the notice, and (b) that if within twenty-one days of the giving of the notice the tenant makes to that Minister or Board representations in writing with respect to that question, they will be considered before the question is determined, and if the tenant makes any such representations within the said twenty-one days the Minister or Board shall consider them before determining whether to give the certificate . . .'

Subsections (3) and (4) of s 57 provide in effect that the section has no immediate effect on the rights of a contractual tenant of business premises. But, once the contractual tenancy is validly determined by a landlord's notice under s 25 of the Act, then where a certificate has been given the tenant is precluded from applying for a new tenancy and the court has no power to grant the tenant a new tenancy expiring later than the date specified in the certificate. Section 59 of the Act provides for compensation to a tenant in respect of whose property a certificate has been given. Such compensation is in accordance with s 37 of the Act.

The result of these provisions is that business tenants of local authorities and other public bodies may be deprived by certificate under s 57 of the rights which they would otherwise have had of applying to the county court to obtain a new tenancy. They are deprived of the opportunity of testing in court any objection by the landlord under s 30 of the Act to a grant of a new tenancy, with the advantages of a public hearing, discovery of documents and cross-examination of witnesses. The decision under s 57 is a ministerial decision which can only be challenged in the courts on the well-established principles laid down in *Associated Provincial Picture Houses Ltd v Wednesbury Corpn* [1947] 2 All ER 680, [1948] 1 KB 223 and other similar cases. As Lord Evershed MR said in *XL Fisheries Ltd v Leeds Corpn* [1955] 2 All ER 875 at 880, [1955] 2 QB 636 at 648 the section confers certain particular privileges on public authorities.

The appellant is the tenant of about one acre of land at High Heavens Wood, Marlow Bottom, Buckinghamshire. He held originally under a lease from the High Wycombe borough council dated 1st June 1964. The lease comprised, in addition to the land, a right of way to afford access. It was a yearly tenancy determinable by a quarter's notice given by either party and the yearly rent was £5. Amongst the tenant's covenants there was a covenant 'not to use or permit the said piece of land to be used in connection with any trade or business other than that of breaking up derelict motor vehicles'. The demised site was immediately adjacent to a large rubbish tip owned by the borough council at High Heavens Wood and extending to some 64 acres. On 11th December 1972 a new lease in the same terms was entered into between the borough council and the appellant. The appellant also had an agreement with the borough council for the disposal of abandoned vehicles which had been removed by the borough council pursuant to their powers and duties under s 21(1) of the Civic Amenities Act 1967, and in addition he carried on a general business on the site of a car breaker and scrap metal dealer with the concurrence of the borough council. At that time there were two other traders, a Mr Jackman and a Mr Bowen carrying on similar businesses at different sites. Mr Jackman was a tenant of the borough council; Mr Bowen was not. As a result of the local government reorganisation in 1974 the Buckinghamshire County Council took over the relevant functions of the High Wycombe borough council. The agreement for the disposal of vehicles with the appellant was terminated and on 1st April 1974 the reversion of the lease vested in the county council and they then became the appellant's landlords.

On 4th August 1975 outline planning permission for 2½ acres of land immediately north of the refuse tip was granted by the county council to itself for use as a gipsy caravan site. This permission provides:

'a landscaping scheme shall be submitted to and approved by the County Council ... [including] the planting of trees and shrubs where necessary ... in order to preserve the amenities of the neighbourhood.'

The southern part of this site encroached on the northern part of the appellant's land. In fact the local authority did not use the northern part of the land because it was in other ownership and would have required a compulsory purchase order. So the limits of the caravan site were confined to the southern portion.

In March 1976 the county council as they were entitled to do also granted themselves planning permission for the erection of a refuse pulveriser and transfer station for the treatment of refuse and salvage at the High Heavens refuse tip. Final planning permission was granted on 23rd March 1976. The permission was subject to the following condition:

'The screen bank along the south side of the transfer station shall be completed and landscaped within one year of the station being brought into operation, and shall be constructed so as to effectively screen the buildings, treatment area, highway depot and car breaking areas from the south, and the trees shall be planted in the first planting season following completion of any section of the bank. The reasons for imposing the above conditions are: To minimise the effect that the development is likely to have on the amenities of the locality.'

It was not surprising that that condition was inserted because High Heavens Wood was scheduled as an area of outstanding natural beauty.

There was no other condition attached to the planning permission although, according to the county council in representations which they subsequently made to the Secretary of State, the planning permission was granted on the understanding that the area to be used for waste disposal purposes would be kept to the minimum, that the rest of the site would be restored to an agricultural use, and that the appearance of the waste disposal facility would be as tidy as the nature of the business would allow. Two banks of earth were erected by the county council to mark the southern limit of the refuse treatment area and to screen it from the south.

Thus the appellant's site was sandwiched between the proposed gipsy caravan site to the north and the refuse treatment area to the south. Meanwhile on 27th August 1975 the county council served notice on the appellant under s 25 of the Landlord and Tenant Act 1954. That notice stated that on the termination of the current tenancy the county council intended to demolish or reconstruct the whole or a substantial part of the premises or to carry out substantial work of construction on the whole or part of them, and that they could not reasonably do so without obtaining possession of the premises. This constituted reliance on s 30(1)(f) of the Act. The appellant did not serve a counter notice under s 26 but filed a defence alleging that the s 25 notice had been waived by subsequent acceptance of rent by the county council. The judge upheld that defence and gave judgment for the appellant on 5th May 1977. So the appellant still holds under the tenancy of 11th December 1972.

Certainly by 1976 the county council had decided to reduce the number of car breakers from three to one. They sent out invitations to tender for the lease of the site occupied by Mr Jackman, opposite the appellant's site to the west of the access road to the tip. The appellant duly tendered on 23rd July 1976 but his tender was not accepted. Mr Jackman also tendered but his tender was not accepted, and the successful tenderer was a Mr Powell. Mr Jackman had by then given up his site pursuant to a possession order against him in the county court on 30th October 1975. The third breaker, Mr Bowen, remained in occupation of his site just to the south of the appellant's site but he has now also given up his site and left the area.

In May 1977 shortly after the county court judgment the county council caused the appellant's telephone to be cut off at the site. We mention this because it is relied on as evidence of bad faith on the part of the county council. The appellant at once issued a writ in the Queen's Bench Division and obtained an interim injunction on 3rd June 1977 which was discharged on 16th June on undertakings by the county council in effect not to take any steps to remove the telephone. The appellant was granted his costs in any event.

On 15th July 1977 the county council applied to the Secretary of State for a certificate under s 57. The application was supported by reasons which were sent to the minister under a covering letter, although the county council at first refused to send their reasons to the appellant. However these were later sent to him by the Secretary of State. On 4th August the appellant submitted written representations to the minister and there were further representations and reasons by both parties including a report from a surveyor instructed by the appellant. All this material was put before the Secretary of State in writing.

The reasons given by the county council in support of their application were that the site was required (1) partly for a gipsy caravan site, (2) for a store for highways material and (3) for the erection of fencing round the pulveriser and transfer stations. The appellant having agreed to surrender the northern part of his site for incorporation into the gipsy caravan site, and the proposed fencing having been shown to be unnecessary, the only ground finally relied on by the county council was that the site was required for use as a store for highways materials.

On 7th August 1978 the Secretary of State issued his decision by letter. Paragraph 2 of that letter reads:

'The Secretary of State, having considered the representations of the [appellant], is satisfied that it is requisite for the purposes of the Council that the use and occupation of the property should be changed by 23 February 1979 and hereby certifies accordingly.'

On 31st October, in reply to a request by the appellant, the Secretary of State gave his reasons for his decision, although, as he said, he was not bound to do so. He set out the nature of the application, the submissions of both parties and his conclusion which is in the following terms:

'5. The Secretary of State carefully considered the submissions of both parties. It was noted that the pulveriser complex proposals had gone ahead, apparently without [the appellant's] land being required in connection with preparatory work for fencing, and account was taken of [the appellant's] willingness to give up part of his land for the proposed gypsy site. However, the evidence showed that only a very small area was required in connection with the fencing proposals and it was not accepted that the Council's decision not to proceed in accordance with the permission granted for a gypsy caravan site in 1975 indicated that they did not really require [the appellant's] land. The majority of [the appellant's] land was, in fact, required in connection with the Council's proposals for a highways materials store; and the Council's submission was accepted that the land was suitable for this purpose and that, whilst they did not necessarily have to show that this was the case, no alternative site was available, either within the area covered by planning permission or elsewhere. [The appellant's] personal reasons for opposing the grant of a certificate were taken into account but, on the evidence as a whole, the Secretary of State was satisfied that it was requisite for the purposes of the Council that the use or occupation of the land should be changed by the date specified in the certificate. He was satisfied that the Council genuinely intended to carry out their proposals, to which there was no obstacle such as a refusal of planning permission; and that the public need to repossess the land in question justified taking [the appellant's] tenancy out of the normal operation of the provisions of Part II of the 1954 Act.'

In summary form the case of the appellant may be put in this way. The county council had available a refuse tip extending to 64 acres. They had voluntarily reduced the available area of that tip to about 10 acres by using the southern part of the tip for forestry, which was a limitation not imposed on them by the planning permission of 23rd March 1976. But even with the remaining 10 acres there was ample room for the county council to store the highways materials for which less than one acre was needed. As Mr Bowen had given up his site the existing highways material store could remain in its present position without interfering with the activities of the county council in the refuse treatment area, and it was not necessary to use the appellant's site for the storage of highways materials. It was said that no reasonable Secretary of State could have come to any other conclusion.

It was submitted on behalf of the appellant that the history of the matter showed that the application of the county council was not made bona fide but for the purpose of evicting the appellant from his site for a purpose unconnected with the application, namely so that the appellant could not compete with Mr Powell, the successful tenderer on the site opposite.

Second, it was submitted that the Secretary of State misdirected himself in law as to the meaning of the words 'requisite for the purposes . . . of the [local] authority' in s 57(1). It was said that those words meant more than 'required' or 'reasonably required' and that the word 'requisite' was synonymous with 'necessary' or 'reasonably necessary' for the purposes of the county council. The Divisional Court held that the word 'requisite' meant 'required by circumstances' and it was submitted on behalf of the appellant that the Divisional Court having given that meaning to the word 'requisite' should have held that the minister had misdirected himself in the phraseology he used in para 5 of his letter of 31st October 1978.

Third, it was submitted that whether or not the use of the appellant's site was requisite or necessary for the purposes of the county council was a question of fact, not of planning policy, and that there was no evidence apart from the bald assertion of the county council to establish that fact. It was said that the Secretary of State should not have based his decision on that assertion. Reliance was placed on the decision of this court in *Coleen Properties Ltd v Minister of Housing and Local Government* [1971] 1 All ER 1049, [1971] 1 WLR 433. It was submitted that the Divisional Court in upholding the minister's decision on the evidence misdirected itself as to certain important issues of fact, and made findings of fact which were unsupported by the evidence.

It was finally submitted that the court should consider fresh evidence considered de bene esse by the Divisional Court, and that the Divisional Court was wrong to refuse to allow such evidence to be admitted on judicial review.

We were told that this was the first case in which the decision of a minister to give a certificate under s 57(1) has been the subject of judicial review, and we consider first the meaning of the word 'requisite' in the subsection. Taken by itself the natural and ordinary meaning of the word 'requisite' is 'required by circumstances' or 'necessary' as used in the Book of Common Prayer in the phrase 'to ask those things which are requisite and necessary as well for the body as the soul'. But it is said on behalf of the Secretary of State and the county council that a looser and more subjective meaning should be put on the word in the context of this particular Act of Parliament. It is said that in that context the word means 'reasonably wanted for a purpose which the local authority genuinely and bona fide intended to carry out'.

Section 57 appears in Part IV of the Act. Part II of the Act enables certain tenants of business premises to obtain new tenancies in certain cases. Some business tenancies, eg agricultural tenancies which are covered by other legislation, are excluded from Part II. The material sections of Part II are expressed to be subject to Part IV, which contains a group of sections giving any minister power to give a certificate in effect excluding the tenant from his rights under Part II. Different language is used in each of these sections as to the circumstances in which the minister may give a certificate of change of use. The words in sub-s (1) of s 57 are, as I have already quoted, 'requisite for the purposes of the first-mentioned department'. The words in sub-s (5) are that the minister 'may certify that it is necessary in the public interest . . .' In sub-s (7) are the words:

'Where the interest of the landlord . . . belongs to the National Trust the Minister of Works may certify that it is requisite for the purpose of securing that the property will as from a specified date be used or occupied in a manner better suited to the nature thereof . . .'

In s 58, which is concerned with 'Termination on special grounds of tenancies to which Part II applies', sub-s (1) provides that the minister may certify 'that for reasons of national security it is necessary that the use or occupation of the property should be discontinued or changed . . .'

Subsection (3) of that section provides:

'Where the landlord's interest . . . is held by statutory undertakers, nothing in this Act shall invalidate an agreement to the effect—(a) that where the Minister . . . certifies that possession of the property comprised in the tenancy or a part thereof is urgently required for carrying out repairs (whether on that property or elsewhere) which are needed for the proper operation of the landlord's undertaking, the tenancy may be terminated . . .'

Section 60, which deals with 'Special provisions as to premises provided under Distribution of Industry Acts', provides for cases where 'the board of Trade certify that it is necessary or expedient for achieving the objects of the said Acts that the use or occupation of the property should be changed . . .'

These different words were described by counsel in *XL Fisheries v Leeds Corpn* [1955] 2 QB 636 at 642 as 'a rising scale of urgency', and in this case by counsel for the county council as a 'hierarchy of terms', and it was submitted that the word 'requisite' comes low in the hierarchy and that it must mean something less than necessary. We accept that in

the context of Part IV of the Act the word 'requisite' should be given a less exacting
a meaning than 'necessary' in the sense of 'indispensable' and that the word 'necessary'
must be qualified so as to give effect to that. We would say that 'reasonably necessary'
was compatible both with the ordinary and natural meaning of the word 'requisite' and
the context of the section in which it appears in this part of the Act.

Little assistance is to be derived from the construction given by courts to the same
word used in other statutes. The only case which has been cited to us in which the word
b 'requisite' has been construed in anything like the present context was *Robinson v Minister
of Town and Country Planning* [1947] 1 All ER 851, [1947] KB 702, in which the word
'requisite' in s 1(1) of the Town and Country Planning Act 1944 fell to be construed.
Lord Greene MR said ([1947] 1 All ER 851 at 857, [1947] KB 702 at 713):

> 'The words "requisite" and "satisfactorily" clearly indicate that the question is one
> of opinion and policy, matters which are peculiarly for the Minister himself to
c > decide. No objective test is possible.'

It is important to observe the context in which the word 'requisite' appears in s 1(1) of the
Town and Country Planning Act 1944. The subsection provides:

> 'Where the Minister of Town and Country Planning . . . is satisfied that it is
> requisite, for the purpose of dealing satisfactorily with extensive war damage in the
d > area of a local planning authority, that a part or parts of their area, consisting of land
> shown to his satisfaction to have sustained war damage or of such land together with
> other land contiguous or adjacent thereto, should be laid out afresh and redeveloped
> as a whole, an order declaring . . . the land subject to compulsory purchase . . . may
> be made by the Minister . . .'

e The case affords little if any assistance as to the meaning of the word itself, though it is
valuable as to the nature of the minister's decision.

In *Coleen Properties Ltd v Minister of Housing and Local Government* the court had to
consider the words 'reasonably necessary' which is the meaning we have put on the word
'requisite'. Lord Denning MR described it as an inference of fact. Sachs LJ said this
([1971] 1 All ER 1049 at 1054, [1971] 1 WLR 433 at 439):

f > 'The question before [the minister] was not, to my mind, one of policy: it was in
> essence a question of fact that had to be established as a condition precedent to the
> exercise of the powers to take away the subject's property. It was no less a question
> of fact because it involved forming a judgment on matters on which expert opinion
> can and indeed ought to be given. (I rather doubt whether there is much material
> difference between the view I have just expressed and that of counsel for the
g > Minister who has argued that the question was simply a matter of planning
> judgment which had to be based on evidence.)'

We agree with the words of Sachs LJ which appear in brackets in the last sentence as
referable to this case. We think it matters not whether the decision of the minister is
described as one of opinion and planning policy or as forming a judgment on matters of
h fact and opinion. In either case the minister has to arrive at a value judgment based on
facts. If in arriving at that decision the minister asks himself the wrong question and so
errs in law, or if he takes into account matters he should not have taken into account or
fails to take into account matters he should have taken into account, or if there is no
evidence to support his decision so that it is contrary to all the evidence before him, then
the court can interfere with his conclusion.

j Did the minister err in law by putting the wrong meaning on the word 'requisite'?
If he did his decision cannot stand. The answer to this question depends on the terms of
the minister's reasons in his letter of 31st October 1978 and in particular para 5.
Although the minister used the word 'required' in three different places in that paragraph
in the sense of 'wanted', which is different from 'reasonably necessary', he ended the
paragraph in this way:

'. . . and the Council's submission was accepted that the land was suitable for this
purpose and that, whilst they did not necessarily have to show that this was the case,   *a*
no alternative site was available, either within the area covered by planning
permission or elsewhere. [The appellant's] personal reasons for opposing the grant
of a certificate were taken into account but, on the evidence as a whole, the Secretary
of State was satisfied that it was requisite for the purposes of the Council that the use
or occupation of the land should be changed by the date specified in the certificate.
He was satisfied that the Council genuinely intended to carry out their proposals, to   *b*
which there was no obstacle such as a refusal of planning permission; and that the
public need to repossess the land in question justified taking [the appellant's] tenancy
out of the normal operation of the provisions of Part II of the 1954 Act.'

What the minister was there saying was: 'I think that the word requisite means genuinely
required, but if I am wrong about that and if I have to consider whether alternative sites   *c*
were available so that I can be satisfied that the appellant's site was reasonably necessary
for the purposes of the county council, then I am satisfied that it was.'

Despite the submissions of counsel for the appellant there is nothing wrong in the
minister expressing himself in this way. It is a type of formula commonly used by
judges and we cannot find that the minister erred in law in using it.

But then it was said that the only evidence before the minister was the bald assertion   *d*
of the county council that no alternative sites were available and that accordingly the
appellant's site was reasonably necessary for their purposes. It was said that the minister
should not have acted on that bald assertion in the light of the evidence on behalf of the
appellant and especially the statement of the surveyor which was before him. It was said
that the county council made no attempt to put before the minister evidence of the
acreage required for each of their activities within the refuse treatment area, so as to   *e*
demonstrate that it was reasonably necessary for them to use the appellant's site for a
highways material store.

Reliance was placed on the statement of Lord Denning MR in *Coleen Properties Ltd v
Minister of Housing and Local Government* [1971] All ER 1049 at 1053, [1971] 1 WLR 433
at 437:

      f

'At any rate, I am quite clear that the mere ipse dixit of the local council is not
sufficient. There must be some evidence to support their assertion. And here there
was none.'

It is said that that statement exactly reflects the situation in this case in that the only
evidence before the minister was the ipse dixit of the county council. It is important to   *g*
see the facts of *Coleen Properties Ltd v Minister of Housing and Local Government*. There had
been a public inquiry. Evidence had been called before the inspector. Witnesses had
been examined and cross-examined. The inspector had made a report containing his
findings of fact, conclusions and recommendations. The minister reversed his
recommendations. There was no evidence on which he could do so except the statement
of the advocate for the local authority that the land was reasonably necessary for the   *h*
proposed redevelopment.

The situation here is quite different. Section 57(2) does not envisage an inquiry or
other hearing, and no inquiry or hearing was held. The tenant was entitled to make
representations in writing which he did. There is not even a provision in the subsection
for reasons to be given by the local authority although reasons were in fact given. And
there were counter-reasons and counter-representations by both parties. All this material   *j*
was before the minister and it amounted to considerably more material than was
envisaged by the subsection.

The nature of the material on which a minister is entitled to rely in reaching a decision
must depend on the statutory provisions and the circumstances of each case. It may well
be that where there is a public hearing the minister should not rely on bare assertions

unsupported by evidence. But where as here there was no public hearing, the minister
a must assess the submissions and reach his conclusion as best he can on the material put
before him. It is a matter for him to weigh the statements submitted to him and reach
his decision in accordance with them.

The minister summarised the submissions of the county council in para 3 of his letter
of 31st October 1978 in this way:

b   'The Council submitted that it was essential that the materials store be between
        the pulveriser complex and gypsy site for the pulveriser complex to remain secure
        and this would also facilitate use of the containers and the movement of vehicles in
        and around the pulveriser. An earth-bank screen was being constructed south of
        the transfer station and treatment area, in accordance with the planning consent,
        beyond which only forestry would be undertaken and the Council argued that, for
        that reason, the treatment area could not be moved further south. Because a
c   number of activities would be concentrated in the treatment area, it was stated to be
        impossible for highways materials to be stored there as well, and it was said to be
        impracticable to locate a highways depot on the far side of the waste disposal
        complex. The Council submitted that the depot at High Heavens Wood was used
        by Wycombe District Council, as agent authority for the County Council, to keep
        materials for use on roads within the boundaries of the former borough of High
d   Wycombe and had to be easily accessible in times of emergency . . .'

Then the minister dealt with alternative depots at different sites which were not relied
on in this court by the appellant.

The minister accepted those submissions in para 5. It was not necessary for the
minister to go further and insist on evidence of the acreage of each activity proposed by
e the county council in order to check its submissions. There were other relevant
considerations than mere acreage, for example, the access to the various sites and the
security of the pulveriser installation. It is impossible to say that the minister was wrong
in taking into account the material put before him by the county council or that because
he failed to take into account the exact acreage of the various sites his decision was
thereby vitiated.

f   The Secretary of State and the Divisional Court both rejected the submission of bad
faith on the part of the county council. Bad faith was however relied on but not pressed
in this court and we think the Divisional Court were right to reject it. At the same time
we cannot help thinking that it was foolish of the county council to threaten to cut off the
appellant's telephone and unwise of them not to serve another notice under s 25 after the
dismissal of the county court proceedings, and seek to obtain possession under Part II of
the Act as they did in the case of Mr Jackman. But those matters were all before the
g Secretary of State and it is impossible on judicial review to disturb his finding that the
county council genuinely required this site for their purposes.

Finally there was an application on behalf of the appellant to admit fresh evidence
which the Divisional Court had refused to admit. Like the Divisional Court we
considered the evidence de bene esse. What are the principles on which fresh evidence
h should be admitted on judicial review? They are: (1) that the court can receive evidence
to show what material was before the minister or inferior tribunal (see per Lord Denning
MR in *Ashbridge Investments Ltd v Minister of Housing and Local Government* [1965] 3 All ER
371 at 374, [1965] 1 WLR 1320 at 1327); (2) where the jurisdiction of the minister or
inferior tribunal depends on a question of fact, or where the question is whether essential
procedural requirements were observed, the court may receive and consider additional
evidence to determine the jurisdictional fact or procedural error (see de Smith's Judicial
j Review of Administrative Action (4th Edn, 1980, pp 140–141 and cases there cited));
(3) where the proceedings are tainted by misconduct on the part of the minister or
member of the inferior tribunal or the parties before it. Examples of such misconduct
are bias by the decision-making body, or fraud or perjury by a party. In each case fresh
evidence is admissible to prove the particular misconduct alleged (see *R v West Sussex*

Quarter Sessions [1973] 3 All ER 289 at 298, 301, [1974] QB 24 at 39, 42 per Orr and
Lawton LJJ).

There was discussion at the bar as to the situation where a party deliberately suppressed
material facts with the intention of misleading the minister. If that were the situation
then it would be for the court to consider whether the conduct of that party could be
described as fraudulent so as to permit the admission of fresh evidence.

It is said that there is a distinction between cases such as the *West Sussex* case where
certiorari was sought to quash the decision of an inferior tribunal after a hearing, and
cases such as the present where it is sought to quash the decision of the minister where
there has been no hearing. We can find no such distinction and the remarks of the
majority in the *West Sussex* case are quite general in their application to certiorari.

Reliance was placed by counsel for the appellant on the case of *Secretary of State for
Education v Metropolitan Borough Council of Tameside* [1976] 3 All ER 665, [1977] AC
1014. In that case fresh evidence was admitted to the Court of Appeal by consent.
Certain passages in the judgment of Scarman LJ in the Court of Appeal and in the
speeches of Lord Wilberforce and Lord Diplock in the House of Lords were particularly
relied on by counsel for the appellant (see [1976] 3 All ER 665 at 675, 681–682, 695,
[1977] AC 1014 at 1030, 1047, 1064). It was said that those statements support the
proposition that if the minister is misled by the failure of one party falling short of fraud
to put before him evidence which should have been put before him, and on which he
would probably have come to a different conclusion to that to which he came on the
evidence which was put before him, then the court on judicial review should admit that
evidence as fresh evidence. It was said that to fail to do so would be a breach of natural
justice.

The *Tameside* case was a very special case. In effect the minister was himself reviewing
the decision of the local authority and his decision was analogous to the position of the
court on judicial review. The evidence was admitted in the Court of Appeal by
consent. The case is not authority for the proposition relied on by counsel for the
appellants. Indeed there are indications in the speeches in the House of Lords to the
contrary (see [1976] 3 All ER 665 at 685–686, [1977] AC 1041 at 1052 per Lord
Wilberforce):

> 'To rephrase the question: on 11th June 1976 (this is the date of the direction, and
> we are not entitled to see what happened thereafter) could it be said that the
> authority were acting unreasonably in proceeding with a selection procedure which
> was otherwise workable, in face of the possibility of persistent opposition by
> teachers' unions and individual teachers, or would *the only* (not "the more")
> reasonable course have been for the authority to abandon their plans? This is I
> think the ultimate factual question in the case. And I think that it must be
> answered in the negative, ie that it could not be unreasonable, in June 1976, and
> assuming that the Secretary of State did not interefere, for the authority to put
> forward a plan to act on their approved procedure.' (Lord Wilberforce's emphasis.)

And Lord Russell said ([1976] 3 All ER 665 at 704, [1977] AC 1014 at 1076):

> 'The question whether the Secretary of State was justified in his conclusion that
> the proposals of the local authority were unreasonable falls to be decided at the date
> of his conclusion—11th June—that is common ground. I would not, however,
> subscribe to the view that facts subsequently brought forward as then existing can
> properly be relied on as showing that the proposals were not unreasonable, unless
> those facts are of such a character that they can be taken to be within the knowledge
> of the department.'

If there is doubt as to the construction of those words of Lord Russell, we agree, save in
one respect, with the construction put on them by the reporter in the headnote ([1977]
AC 1014 at 1016):

'Facts subsequently brought forward as existing on June 11 could not properly be relied on as showing that the authority's proposals were not unreasonable unless they were of such a character that they could be taken to have been within the knowledge of the Secretary of State.'

The words 'the department' used by Lord Russell at the end of his speech are distinguishable from the words 'the Secretary of State' used by the reporter at the end of the headnote, unless those words are to be interpreted as meaning 'the Secretary of State or his department'. The converse of Lord Russell's proposition as stated by him is that fresh evidence may be admitted of facts within the knowledge of the department though unknown to the minister at the time of his decision. This is an example of one of the classic reasons for interfering with the ministerial decision within *Associated Provincial Picture Houses Ltd v Wednesbury Corpn*, namely that such facts are plainly facts which the minister should have taken into account. If he failed to do so, fresh evidence of the facts within the knowledge of the department could be admitted as a ground for quashing his decision.

This court is bound by the majority judgments in *R v West Sussex Quarter Sessions* which formed the ratio decidendi of the case. *Secretary of State for Education v Metropolitan Borough of Tameside* is not authority for the proposition that the circumstances in which fresh evidence on judicial review may be admitted can be extended beyond the categories laid down in *R v West Sussex Quarter Sessions*.

There is nothing in the fresh evidence in this case to bring it within any of the categories of evidence which may be admitted on judicial review. We agree with the Divisional Court that the fresh evidence is not admissible. But we do not agree with the test proposed by the Divisional Court:

'So long as a minister or a tribunal has balanced the factors and weighed the evidence before him or it, no superior court should intervene unless it is plain that there has been such manifest failure to administer justice that the decision is perverse.'

We have already stated the principles on which fresh evidence may be admitted on judicial review.

Although it is true that there are certain mistakes in the statements of fact in the judgment of the Divisional Court, we do not think that those mistakes affected the conclusion at which the court arrived. We think that they were right to refuse the application for a writ of certiorari, although for the reasons which we have stated in this judgment. The appeal is accordingly dismissed.

Appeal dismissed.

Solicitors: *A Banks & Co* (for the appellant); *Treasury Solicitor*; *D U Pullen*, Aylesbury (for the county council).

Patricia Hargrove   Barrister.

National Westminster Bank Ltd v Stockman

QUEEN'S BENCH DIVISION
RUSSELL J
18th AUGUST 1980

Execution – Charging order – Land – Interest in land – Property held legally and beneficially by joint tenants – One of joint tenants a judgment debtor – Whether charging order may be made in respect of debtor's interest in land – Charging Orders Act 1979, s 2.

Section 2(1)[a] of the Charging Orders Act 1979 extends the availability of charging orders for securing payment of money due under a judgment or order to beneficial interests in the proceeds of sale of land held under trusts for sale and accordingly permits a charging order to be made on the debtor's interest in real property, such as an interest in a matrimonial home, which is held under a trust for sale (see p 801 *f*, post).

Irani Finance Ltd v Singh [1970] 3 All ER 199 distinguished.

Notes
For charging orders on land and interests in land, see 17 Halsbury's Laws (4th Edn) para 557.

For the Charging Orders Act 1979, s 2, see 49 Halsbury's Statutes (3rd Edn) 769.

Case referred to in judgment
Irani Finance Ltd v Singh [1970] 3 All ER 199, [1971] Ch 59, [1970] 3 WLR 330, 21 P & CR 843, CA, Digest (Cont Vol C) 342, *1628Aa*.

Interlocutory appeal
The plaintiffs, National Westminster Bank Ltd, appealed against the order of Master Ritchie on 19th June 1980 refusing their ex parte application for a charging order nisi to be made against the beneficial interest of the defendant, Hugh Stockman, in the property known as 12 Priory Gardens, Old Basing, Basingstoke, Hampshire to satisfy a judgment dated 30th August 1978 obtained by the plaintiffs against the defendant for £11,604 and £49 costs. By an order made by Mustill J on 11th July the notice of appeal was served on the defendant. The appeal was heard in chambers but judgment was given by Russell J in open court. The facts are set out in the judgment.

G A Mann for the plaintiffs.
David G M Marks for the defendant.

RUSSELL J. This is an appeal against the refusal of Master Ritchie to make a charging order nisi in respect of property at 12 Priory Gardens, Old Basing, Basingstoke. The plaintiffs obtained judgment against the defendant in default of defence in the sum of £11,604·10 together with costs on 30th August 1978. The ex parte application for the order nisi was dismissed by the master on 19th June 1980. I was told that apparently he was not satisfied that the provisions of the Charging Orders Act 1979, and in particular s 2 of that Act, enabled the order to be made. On 11th July 1980 the matter came on appeal before Mustill J, who ordered that notice of appeal should be served on the defendant. Consequently I have had the advantage of argument from counsel for the defendant as well as from counsel for the plaintiffs.

The facts can be stated very shortly. The judgment was in respect of moneys owing by the defendant to the plaintiffs in an overdrawn bank account. The defendant's matrimonial home was held by him and his wife, as so often happens, under a trust for

---

a   Section 2, so far as material, is set out at p 801 *e*, post

sale. The conveyance of the house to the defendant and his wife was a conveyance to them as joint tenants both legally and beneficially.

I have been referred to s 35 of the Administration of Justice Act 1956 and to the judgments of the Court of Appeal in *Irani Finance Ltd v Singh* [1970] 3 All ER 199, [1971] Ch 59. Section 35(1) of the 1956 Act provided:

> 'The High Court and any county court may, for the purpose of enforcing a judgment or order of those courts respectively for the payment of money to a person, by order impose on any such land or interest in land of the debtor as may be specified in the order a charge for securing the payment of any moneys due or to become due under the judgment or order.'

The judgment of the court in the *Irani* case, delivered by Cross LJ, traced the history of charges in favour of judgment creditors on the land of judgment debtors. I need not do so. The ratio of the judgment was that the words 'interest in land' to be found in s 35 did not include interests under trusts for sale of land. Such interests were not interests in land but interests in the proceeds of the sale of land. Those equitable interests, therefore, were not caught by the provisions of s 35 and no charging order could be made.

Section 35 of the 1956 Act has now been repealed by s 7 of the Charging Orders Act 1979. The short point for my consideration is whether s 2 of the 1979 Act has removed the limitations of s 35 of the 1956 Act, as interpreted by the Court of Appeal in the *Irani* case, so as to permit charges on the interests of those, such as the defendant in the instant case, who hold real property under the terms of a trust for sale. Section 2 of the 1979 Act, so far as it is relevant, provides:

> '(1) . . . a charge may be imposed by a charging order only on—(a) any interest held by the debtor beneficially—(i) in any asset of a kind mentioned in subsection (2) below, or (ii) under any trust . . .
> '(2) The assets referred to in subsection (1) above are—(a) land . . .'

Is the defendant caught by these words? In my judgment it was plainly the intention of Parliament that the availability of charging orders should be extended to cover cases in which the interest sought to be charged is a beneficial interest in the proceeds of sale of land held under a trust for sale. I think that that object has been achieved by the plain wording of s 2, despite the interesting arguments to the contrary advanced by counsel for the defendant. There are various safeguards available to the debtor when application is made to make the order absolute and to his wife whose position can be protected in the event of any application by the creditor which would have the effect of defeating the purpose for which the trust was established. These, however, are not matters before me. I shall allow the appeal and grant the charging order nisi.

Appeal allowed. Charging order nisi granted.

Solicitors: *Wilde Sapte* (for the plaintiffs); *Ward Bowie*, Basingstoke (for the defendant).

K Mydeen Esq   Barrister.

R v Crown Court at St Albans, ex parte Cinnamond

QUEEN'S BENCH DIVISION

DONALDSON LJ AND KILNER BROWN J

2nd JULY 1980

Crown Court – Supervisory jurisdiction of High Court – Sentence – Excessive sentence – Decision of Crown Court wrong in law or in excess of jurisdiction – Crown Court imposing sentence within statutory limits but exceeding normal discretionary sentence for offence – 18 months' disqualification for offence of careless driving – Whether imposition of sentence 'wrong in law or in excess of jurisdiction' – Whether sentence harsh and oppressive or so far outside normal sentence as to constitute error of law – Courts Act 1971, s 10(2).

The applicant, who had previous convictions for motoring offences, was convicted in a magistrates' court of two offences, namely driving with excess alcohol in his blood, for which he was disqualified for holding a driving licence for 18 months with a further three months' disqualification under the totting-up provisions, and driving without due care and attention (ie careless driving), for which he was disqualified for three months under the totting-up provisions, the periods of disqualification to run consecutively. The applicant appealed to the Crown Court against both convictions. That court allowed the appeal against conviction for driving with excess alcohol on a technical ground, but dismissed the appeal against conviction for careless driving and substituted for the three months' disqualification under the totting-up provisions a sentence of 18 months' disqualification for the offence itself with a further three months' disqualification under the totting-up provisions. The sentence of 18 months' disqualification was within the discretionary limits of disqualification for careless driving prescribed by s 93(2)[a] of the Road Traffic Act 1972. The applicant applied to the Divisional Court for, inter alia, an order of certiorari to quash the sentence of 18 months' disqualification on the ground that it was 'wrong in law or in excess of [the Crown Court's] jurisdiction', within s 10(2)[b] of the Courts Act 1971 because, even taking into account the applicant's previous convictions, to impose a disqualification of 18 months for careless driving went considerably beyond the period of disqualification imposed by courts throughout the country for that offence.

Held – (1) A discretionary sentence was 'wrong in law or in excess of jurisdiction' within s 10(2) of the 1971 Act if it was harsh and oppressive or so far outside the normal sentence imposed for the offence as to enable the Divisional Court in the exercise of a jurisdiction analogous to its jurisdiction in respect of administrative decisions to hold that the imposition of the sentence must have involved an error of law (see p 804 j to p 805 c and h, post); *Associated Provincial Picture Houses Ltd v Wednesbury Corpn* [1947] 2 All ER 680 and *Fleming v MacDonald* 1958 JC 1 applied.

(2) Although some disqualification for the applicant's offence of careless driving was merited in the circumstances, to impose a sentence of 18 months' disqualification, when the conviction for driving with excess alcohol, for which that very period of disqualification had been imposed, had been quashed, involved so great a disparity with the normal range of sentences for careless driving as to constitute an error of law, if not an excess of jurisdiction. Accordingly the Crown Court's decision imposing 18 months' disqualification for the careless driving would be quashed, but in the exercise of its power

---

a   Section 93(2), so far as material, provides: 'Where a person is convicted of an offence [of careless driving contrary to s 3 of the Road Traffic Act 1972] the court may order him to be disqualified for such period as the court thinks fit.'

b   Section 10(2) provides: 'Any decision [of the Crown Court other than certain decisions not material to this report] may be questioned by any party to proceedings on the ground that it is wrong in law or is in excess of jurisdiction.'

under s 16(1)[c] of the Administration of Justice Act 1960, the Divisional Court would substitute a disqualification of six months together with an additional, consecutive disqualification of three months under the totting-up provisions (see p 805 *f* to *j*, post).

Notes

For appeals from the Crown Court, see 11 Halsbury's Laws (4th Edn) para 700.

For the discretion of the court as to punishment and for matters to be considered in fixing punishment, see ibid paras 481, 483.

For the Administration of Justice Act 1960, s 16, see 7 Halsbury's Statutes (3rd Edn) 725.

For the Courts Act 1971, s 10, see 41 ibid 298.

For the Road Traffic Act 1972, s 93, see 42 ibid 1744.

Cases referred to in judgments

Associated Provincial Picture Houses Ltd v Wednesbury Corpn [1947] 2 All ER 680, [1948] 1 KB 223, [1948] LJR 190, 177 LT 641, 112 JP 55, 45 LGR 635, CA, 45 Digest (Repl) 215, 189.

Fleming v MacDonald 1958 JC 1, 33 Digest (Repl) 309, *1258.

Application for judicial review

Kevin Patrick Cinnamond applied for orders of (i) mandamus requiring the Crown Court sitting at St Albans (his Honour Judge Anwyl-Davies QC) to state a case for the opinion of the High Court in respect of its decision on 17th October 1979 to allow the applicant's appeal against his conviction by the Watford Magistrates' Court on 1st May 1979 of driving with a blood alcohol concentration over the prescribed limit but to dismiss his appeal against his conviction on the same date of driving without due care and attention and to increase the sentence for that offence from three months' to 21 months' disqualification, and (ii) certiorari to quash the disqualification. The facts are set out in the judgment of Donaldson LJ.

Nigel Fricker QC and *Stephen Martin* for the applicant.
The respondent was not represented.

DONALDSON LJ. In this case the applicant applies for judicial review to quash a decision of the Crown Court at St Albans given on 17th October 1979.

The applicant was convicted before the Watford magistrates on 1st May 1979 of two motoring offences. The first was driving with excess alcohol for which he was fined £150, his licence was endorsed and he was disqualified for 18 months and for a further three months under the totting-up provisions. The second charge of which he was convicted was driving without due care and attention. As far as that was concerned, he was fined £50, his licence was endorsed and a three months' disqualification was imposed under the totting-up provisions, those disqualifications being consecutive.

The facts were that he had driven his car, a Mercedes, along the north orbital road at Garston in Hertfordshire. No other vehicle was involved, but his car left the road and hit a lamp post on the central reservation. He had been breathalysed with a positive reaction. He had then given a sample of blood and on analysis it had emerged that he had 172 mg of alcohol per 100 ml of blood; in other words over twice the permitted limit.

His defence, as far as the alcohol offence was concerned, was first that he was not the driver of the car and second that his arrest had been unlawful because the medical practitioner in whose charge he was on admission to hospital had not been notified that the police wished him to undertake a breath test.

---

c   Section 16(1), so far as material, provides: 'Where a person who has been sentenced for an offence by a magistrates' court or, on appeal against conviction or sentence . . . applies to the High Court for an order of certiorari . . . the High Court may, instead of quashing the conviction, amend it by substituting for the sentence passed any sentence which the magistrates' court had power to impose . . .'

He appealed against both convictions and the Crown Court allowed the appeal against
the first charge, that relating to driving with excessive alcohol, not on the grounds that
he was not the driver but on the grounds that the requirements of s 8(2) of the Road
Traffic Act 1972 in relation to the medical practitioner had not been satisfied. As counsel
on his behalf very fairly said, it was a technical defence, but it was a good defence and it
succeeded.

As far as the second charge was concerned, driving without due care and attention, the
appeal against conviction was dismissed. The Crown Court then proceeded to consider
the sentence in relation to driving without due care and attention. They substituted for
that sentence (of three months' disqualification) a sentence of 18 months' disqualification
together with three months' disqualification under the totting-up provisions. They also
ordered him to pay the costs of both appeals so that, in effect, whereas when he was in
front of the magistrates he was sentenced to two years' disqualification, he was now faced
with 21 months' disqualification but the whole of that 21 months was attributed to the
driving without due care and attention, whereas the magistrates had said that that
offence only attracted three months' disqualification under the totting-up procedure.

The basis on which the application is made to this court is that the Crown Court erred
in law in imposing that sentence or, alternatively, it exceeded its jurisdiction.

Let it be said straight away that, so far as is known, this is the first case in which in
England a sentence by a Crown Court has been challenged in this court in circumstances
such as these. When I say 'circumstances such as these' I mean in circumstances in which
there is no doubt that the sentence imposed by the Crown Court was within the limits
permitted in terms by the statute. I say that because there is a power to disqualify in
relation to careless driving and there is no limitation on the period which can be
imposed. In terms of the statutory jurisdiction there could have been a disqualification
here for life, but of course that did not happen.

The question arises: what is the jurisdiction which this court is being invited to
exercise if it is not that the Crown Court has no jurisdiction in the strict sense which I
have indicated?

Counsel for the applicant has been of the greatest possible assistance to us in exploring
what our jurisdiction is. The starting point is, I think, the power of the Crown Court to
state a case under s 10 of the Courts Act 1971 in respect of any judgment or order of that
court other than a judgment or order relating to a trial on indictment and also other than
certain orders made under statutes which are immaterial. The power of that court to
state a case for the opinion of this court is in response to an application which is made on
the ground that the decision of the Crown Court is wrong in law or is in excess of
jurisdiction.

When this matter came before the Divisional Court previously, on the application for
leave, it was indicated to the applicant that he should proceed by judicial review rather
than case stated, which would have been the alternative procedure, in order to minimise
the delay and bearing in mind the fact that his disqualification had been imposed in
October 1979 and had not been suspended. I treat this as if it could equally well have
come before the court by case stated.

That then raises the question of what is meant by 'wrong in law' or 'in excess of
jurisdiction'. In relation to excess of jurisdiction, is this court confined to the exercise of
looking to the statute in any particular case and seeing whether the sentence is in excess
of that which the statute permits?

Here again we have had great help from counsel for the applicant because he has
referred us to a Scottish case, *Fleming v MacDonald* 1958 JC 1. It appears that in Scotland,
where there is an appeal by case stated under the Summary Jurisdiction (Scotland) Act
1954 in relation to the imposition of a sentence of imprisonment or indeed any other
sentence, the court will intervene if it is satisfied not only that the sentence is wrong but
that it is, to use the words used by the judges in those cases, 'harsh and oppressive'. If
authority is needed for that proposition, it is to be found in *Fleming v MacDonald* 1958 JC
1 at 2, per the Lord Justice-General (Lord Clyde).

For my part, I think that this court is empowered to exercise a similar jurisdiction,
probably subject to rather similar restrictions, namely that it is not sufficient to decide

that the sentence is severe, perhaps even unduly severe or surprisingly severe. It is

a necessary to decide that it is either harsh and oppressive or, if those adjectives are thought to be unfortunate or in any way offensive, that it is so far outside the normal discretionary limits as to enable this court to say that its imposition must involve an error of law of some description, even if it may not be apparent at once what is the precise nature of that error.

It seems to me that the jurisdiction which this court is empowered to exercise in this

b field can be considered analogous to the jurisdiction which it exercises in relation to the Crown and government departments where, on the tests in *Associated Provincial Picture Houses Ltd v Wednesbury Corpn* [1947] 2 All ER 680, [1948] 1 KB 223, it examines a decision and says that no reasonable authority could have reached this decision without a self-misdirection of some sort and therefore is satisfied that there has been some such misdirection.

c I turn, against that background, to consider the position which has arisen in this case. Of course the applicant is aggrieved at having appealed and ended up worse than when he started, or almost worse than when he started, because whilst it is true that his disqualification period was reduced by three months he had to pay all the costs of the appeal, including that part of the appeal in respect of which he was successful. But that is not as such a ground for intervening.

d What is said by counsel for the applicant, however, is this. While he accepts that the Crown Court was fully entitled to take account of the fact that he had been drinking to the extent that had been proved by the evidence and that this was an aggravating factor in the careless driving case, whilst it was fully entitled to take account of his previous record, which was bad (he had been convicted in August 1975 on a drunk-in-charge count when he had been disqualified for 12 months and fined £250, and since then he

e had had a very minor case of speeding), whilst it could take account of all those matters, still on a charge of careless driving, as contrasted with reckless driving, to impose a disqualification of as long as 18 months meant that the Crown Court was going very considerably beyond the range of penalties which are imposed up and down the country in the case of careless driving.

In support of that proposition he drew attention to the suggestions published in April

f 1975 by the Magistrates' Association which have received the approval of Lord Widgery CJ and Lord Elwyn-Jones LC, which are set out in Appendix III to Wilkinson's Road Traffic Offences (9th Edn, 1977, pp 881–885) and which suggest that perhaps for an average case of careless driving there would be endorsement but no disqualification at all. This is very far from being the average case of careless driving, bearing in mind the applicant's record. Disqualification was well merited, but 18 months' disqualification,

g particularly in the circumstances in which he succeeded in obtaining the quashing of a conviction in respect of which that very period of disqualification had been imposed, and quite rightly imposed, seems to me to involve so great a disparity with the normal range as to constitute an error of law, if not an excess of jurisdiction.

I would, therefore, quash this determination by the Crown Court, but I would go on to exercise the power which lies in this court under s 16 of the Administration of Justice

h Act 1960 to vary a sentence on certiorari, and I would substitute a disqualification of six months for the careless driving, together with an additional and consecutive disqualification of three months under the totting-up provisions.

KILNER BROWN J. I agree.

j *Certiorari granted to quash sentence of 18 months' disqualification and period of six months' disqualification substituted for offence of driving without due care and attention. Order for costs made in Crown Court not quashed.*

Solicitors: *Penman, Johnson & Ewins*, Watford, for the applicant.

N P Metcalfe Esq   Barrister.

Searose Ltd v Seatrain (UK) Ltd   *a*

QUEEN'S BENCH DIVISION (COMMERCIAL COURT)
ROBERT GOFF J
13th, 16th FEBRUARY 1981

Injunction – Interlocutory – Danger that defendant may transfer assets out of jurisdiction –   *b*
Injunction restraining removal of assets out of the jurisdiction – Unidentified assets – Unidentified
bank accounts – Costs incurred by third party in ascertaining whether asset to which injunction
applies is in his possession – Undertaking by plaintiff to bear costs of third party incurred in
ascertaining assets to which injunction applies.

Where a Mareva injunction is sought in respect of an asset which is not identified with   *c*
precision (eg money held in an unidentified bank account) the court may require the
plaintiff to give an undertaking to pay the reasonable costs incurred by any person, other
than the defendant, to whom notice of the terms of the injunction is given in ascertaining
whether any asset to which the order applies is within his possession or control. Although
primarily directed to protecting banks from expenses in tracing unidentified accounts,
such an undertaking may be required to protect other third parties similarly affected (see   *d*
p 807 *b c h* and p 808 *b* and *d* to *g*, post).

    Dictum of Lord Denning MR in *Prince Abdul Rahman Bin Turki Al Sudairy v Abu-Taha*
[1980] 3 All ER at 412 followed.

Notes
For an injunction restraining the disposition of property, see 24 Halsbury's Laws (4th   *e*
Edn) para 1018, and for cases on the subject, see 28(2) Digest (Reissue) 1091–1094, 918–
960.

Case referred to in judgment
Prince Abdul Rahman Bin Turki Al Sudairy v Abu-Taha [1980] 3 All ER 409, [1980] 1 WLR
1268, CA.   *f*

Application
By a writ issued on 12th February 1981 the plaintiff, Searose Ltd (trading as European
Container Services) claimed against the defendant, Seatrain UK Ltd, damages for breach
of contract made between the parties in or about or since 1975 and/or to be implied from
a course of dealing between them. By an ex parte application the plaintiff applied for an   *g*
injunction restraining the defendant from disposing of its assets within the jurisdiction,
save in so far as such assets exceeded £44,000 and, in particular, any moneys in any bank
account of the defendant with Williams & Glyn's Bank Ltd, 38 Moseley Street,
Manchester. The application was heard in chambers but judgment was delivered by
Robert Goff J in open court. The facts are set out in the judgment.   *h*

David Hunt for the plaintiff.
The defendant was not represented.

Cur adv vult

  j

16th February. **ROBERT GOFF J** read the following judgment: On Friday, 13th
February 1981, the plaintiff applied ex parte in chambers for a Mareva injunction to
restrain the defendant from disposing of its assets within the jurisdiction, save in so far
as such assets exceeded the sum of £44,000, which was the amount of the plaintiff's
claim against the defendant for damages for breach of contract. I granted the injunction;

but, since the application raised one matter which may be of general interest concerning
a this rapidly developing jurisdiction, I propose to repeat my judgment, so far as it
concerns the matter, in open court. The plaintiff has agreed to my taking this course.

The matter in question is this. The plaintiff asked that the Mareva injunction should
specify, in particular, any moneys in any bank account of the defendant with Williams
& Glyn's Bank Ltd, 38 Moseley Street, Manchester. I informed the plaintiff that, in the
circumstances, I was only prepared to grant the injunction if it gave an undertaking to
b pay the reasonable costs incurred by any person (other than the defendant) to whom
notice of the terms of the injunction was given in ascertaining whether or not any asset
to which the order applied was within his possession or control. I did so for the following
reasons.

In *Prince Abdul Rahman Bin Turki Al Sudairy v Abu-Taha* [1980] 3 All ER 409 at 412,
[1980] 1 WLR 1268 at 1273 Lord Denning MR said: 'When there is a Mareva injunction
c of this kind, if the people who are notified of it are put to any expense in regard to it, that
expense must be paid by the plaintiff.' Now it may well be that, in giving this guidance,
Lord Denning MR had particularly in mind the effect of Mareva injunctions on banks.
It is well known to the judges who sit in the Commercial Court that, as Mareva
injunctions have come to be granted more frequently, the banks in this country have
received numerous notices of injunctions which have been granted. Sometimes the
d injunction identifies the bank account in question; sometimes it identifies the branch of
a bank at which the defendant is said to have a bank account; sometimes it identifies the
bank and no more; sometimes it does not even identify the bank. Now, where the
particular account is identified I do not think the bank can reasonably complain. Every
citizen of this country who receives notice of an injunction granted by the court will risk
proceedings for contempt of court if he acts inconsistently with the injunction; and the
e bank, like any other citizen, must avoid any such action. But where the particular
account is not identified the situation is somewhat different. I do not think it is right
that the bank should incur expense in ascertaining whether the alleged account exists,
without being reimbursed by the plaintiff for any reasonable costs incurred. Banks are
not debt-collecting agencies: they are simply, in this context, citizens who are anxious
not to contravene an order made by the court, an order which has been obtained on the
f application of, and for the benefit of, the plaintiff. Even where the particular branch of
the bank is identified, some expense is likely to be incurred in ascertaining whether the
defendant has an account at the branch. But where the branch is not identified the bank
will be put in a very difficult position. It is, I think, well known that Barclays Bank has
over 3,000 branches in this country, and Lloyds Bank has over 2,000 branches. Are they
to circulate all their branches? If they did so, it would involve them in great expense;
g moreover such an exercise cannot, in ordinary circumstances, reasonably be expected of
them.

It seems to me that this problem can be solved, in accordance with the guidance given
by Lord Denning MR in *Prince Abdul Rahman's* case, by requiring the plaintiff to give an
undertaking in the terms which I have indicated. The effect of this undertaking will be
that a bank to whom notice of an injunction is given can, before taking steps to ascertain
h whether the defendant has an account at any particular branch, obtain an undertaking
from the plaintiff's solicitors to pay their reasonable costs incurred in so doing. The bank
will then be protected; moreover the plaintiff's solicitors will no doubt be encouraged to
limit their inquiry to a particular branch, or to certain particular branches.

It is possible that a practice may develop under which, in ordinary circumstances, the
clearing banks charge a standard fee where the branch of the bank is identified, and
j charge another standard fee per branch to be searched if no branch is identified. If
reasonable standard fees can be established to the satisfaction of the taxing masters, a
great deal of time and money may be saved hereafter on the taxation of costs.

I have certain other comments to make.

First, the costs of the search must in the first instance be borne by the plaintiff, on
whose ex parte application the injunction has been granted. Whether he will be able to

obtain an indemnity from the defendant will depend on any order as to costs which is thereafter made between the parties to the litigation.

Second, the undertaking required of the plaintiff must be so drawn as to affect only costs incurred by a person other than the defendant (to whom notice of the injunction is given) but not costs incurred by the defendant himself (on whom the order is served).

Third, although I have in this judgment dwelt on the position of banks, because they are most likely to be affected, the undertaking so given could, if appropriate, be equally effective to protect other third parties similarly affected.

Last, may I say this. It is, I believe, now generally recognised that the Mareva jurisdiction has filled a gap in the court's powers which badly needed to be filled. In the Commercial Court, certainly, a very large number of these injunctions are granted each year. But care must be taken to ensure that such injunctions are only given for the purpose for which they are intended, viz to prevent the possible abuse of the defendant removing assets in order to prevent the satisfaction of a judgment in pending proceedings; and likewise care must be taken to ensure that such injunctions do not bear harshly on innocent third parties. If these principles are not observed, a weapon which was forged to prevent abuse may become an instrument of oppression.

It follows that, first, an order for a Mareva injunction should not be sought in terms wider than are reasonably required in the circumstances of the case. Second, any asset in respect of which an order for Mareva injunction is sought should be identified with as much precision as is reasonably practicable. Third, as regards any asset to which the order applies but which has not been identified with precision in the form of order proposed (eg money held in an unidentified bank account), the plaintiff may be required to give an undertaking to pay reasonable costs incurred by any person (other than the defendant) to whom notice of the terms of the injunction is given in ascertaining whether or not any asset to which the order applies, but which has not been identified in it, is within his possession or control.

Of course, in many cases (for example where, as is usually the case, the plaintiff is unable to identify assets of the defendant which are known to be greater in value than the sum in respect of which he seeks a Mareva injunction) it will be appropriate for the court to give the Mareva injunction in the now hallowed form, under which the defendant is restrained from removing from the jurisdiction or otherwise disposing of any of his assets within the jurisdiction, and in particular a specific asset or assets, save in so far as the value of such assets exceeds a certain sum. But if an injunction is given in such terms the court may require, and indeed in my judgment should ordinarily require, that the plaintiff gives an undertaking in the form I have indicated.

In the present case, I have required the plaintiff to give such an undertaking as a condition of the grant of the injunction. It is right that I should record that the plaintiff made no objection to this; indeed the plaintiff regarded it as entirely reasonable.

Finally I should state that I have not considered in this case the position which may arise where a third party incurs expense by reason of the fact that, through the imposition of a Mareva injunction of which he is given notice, he is unable to part with the possession of a chattel (eg an aircraft) which has been entrusted to him by the defendant. This point will no doubt be considered in some future case in which it arises for decision.

Order accordingly.

Solicitors: *Lawrence-Jones & Co* (for the plaintiff).

K Mydeen Esq   Barrister.

a

McLoughlin v O'Brian and others

COURT OF APPEAL, CIVIL DIVISION

STEPHENSON, CUMMING-BRUCE AND GRIFFITHS LJJ

18th, 19th, 20th, 21st NOVEMBER, 16th DECEMBER 1980

b   *Negligence – Duty to take care – Driver of motor vehicle – Duty to other road users and owners of property – Foreseeable harm – Nervous shock – Plaintiff suffering nervous shock on hearing that family involved in road accident – Plaintiff at home at time of accident – Whether duty of care owed to plaintiff by driver causing accident.*

Damages – Personal injury – Nervous shock – Plaintiff's family killed or badly injured in road
c   *accident caused by defendant's negligence – Plaintiff at home at time of accident – Plaintiff informed of accident and going to hospital – Plaintiff suffering nervous shock as a result – Whether defendant owing duty of care to plaintiff – Whether plaintiff's injury reasonably foreseeable – Whether as matter of policy court would not impose duty of care on defendant to plaintiff.*

d   The plaintiff's husband and three children were involved in a road accident caused by the negligence of the defendants. One of the plaintiff's children was killed and her husband and other two children were badly injured. At the time of the accident the plaintiff was at home two miles away. She was told of the accident by a neighbour and was taken to hospital where she saw the injured members of her family and the extent of their injuries and shock and heard that her daughter had been killed. As a result of hearing,
e   and seeing the results of, the accident the plaintiff suffered severe and persisting nervous shock. The plaintiff claimed damages against the defendants for the nervous shock, distress and injury to health caused by the defendants' negligence. The judge dismissed her claim on the grounds that her injury was not reasonably foreseeable. The plaintiff appealed.

f   **Held** – The appeal would be dismissed for either of the following reasons—
    (1) (Per Stephenson LJ) It was reasonably foreseeable that the plaintiff was likely to be affected by the defendants' negligence, despite the fact that she was not at or near the scene of the accident at the time or shortly afterwards; and, since the only injury a person in her position could suffer was nervous shock, her injury was also reasonably foreseeable as being a consequence of the defendants' negligence. Accordingly the defendants were
g   under a prima facie duty of care to the plaintiff and were in breach of that duty. However, as a matter of policy and having regard to the fact that the duty of care in negligence had to stop somewhere, the court would not impose a duty of care on a negligent defendant beyond that owed to persons at or near the scene of the accident at or near the time it occurred (see p 811 *e*, p 814 *h j*, p 815 *c*, p 817 *c* to *g j*, p 818 *a b* and *g* to p 820 *j* and p 822 *g*, post); dicta of Lord Pearce in *Hedley Byrne & Co Ltd v Heller &*
h   *Partners Ltd* [1963] 2 All ER at 615 and of Lord Wilberforce in *Anns v London Borough of Merton* [1977] 2 All ER at 498 applied.
    (2) (Per Griffiths LJ) Even though the plaintiff's nervous shock was a reasonably foreseeable consequence of the defendants' negligence, in accordance with precedent and social policy the duty of care owed by a driver of a motor vehicle was limited to persons and owners of property on the road or near it who might be directly affected by the
j   driver's negligent driving, and accordingly the defendants did not owe a duty of care to the plaintiff because she had not been in the physical proximity of the accident when it occurred (see p 811 *e*, p 822 *j*, p 824 *g h*, p 826 *g h* and p 827 *c d* and *g* to p 828 *a* and *e*, post); *Hambrook v Stokes Brothers* [1924] All ER Rep 110, *Donoghue v Stevenson* [1932] All ER Rep 1 and *Bourhill v Young* [1942] 2 All ER 396 considered.

Notes
For liability for nervous shock, see 34 Halsbury's Laws (4th Edn) para 8, and for cases on *a*
the subject, see 17 Digest (Reissue) 145–147, 377–391.

For remoteness of damage, see 12 Halsbury's Laws (4th Edn) para 1127, and for cases
on the subject, see 36(1) Digest (Reissue) 63–65, 306–307, 227–236, 1232–1236.

Cases referred to in judgments
Abramẕik v Brenner (1967) 65 DLR (2d) 651, 62 WWR 332, 17 Digest (Reissue) 152, *283. *b*
Andrews v Williams [1967] VR 836.
Anns v London Borough of Merton [1977] 2 All ER 492, [1978] AC 728, [1977] 2 WLR 1024,
    141 JP 526, 75 LGR 555, HL, 1(1) Digest (Reissue) 128, 721.
Benson v Lee [1972] VR 879, 17 Digest (Reissue) 151, *277.
Best v Samuel Fox & Co Ltd [1952] 2 All ER 394, [1952] AC 716, HL, 36(1) Digest (Reissue)
    21, 71. *c*
Boardman v Sanderson [1964] 1 WLR 1317, CA, 17 Digest (Reissue) 145, 378.
Bourhill (or Hay) v Young [1942] 2 All ER 396, [1943] AC 92, 111 LJPC 96, 167 LT 261,
    1942 SC(HL) 78, HL; affg 1941 SC 395, 17 Digest (Reissue) 146, 388.
Chadwick v British Transport Commission [1967] 2 All ER 945, [1967] 1 WLR 912, 17
    Digest (Reissue) 147, 390.
Dillon v Legg (1968) 29 ALR 3d 1316. *d*
Donoghue (or M'Alister) v Stevenson [1932] AC 562, [1932] All ER Rep 1, 101 LJPC 119, 37
    Com Cas 350, 147 LT 281, 1932 SLT 317, HL, 36(1) Digest (Reissue) 144, 562.
Dulieu v White & Sons [1901] 2 KB 669, [1900–3] All ER Rep 353, 70 LJKB 837, 85 LT
    126, DC, 17 Digest (Reissue) 146, 385.
Hambrook v Stokes Brothers [1925] 1 KB 141, [1924] All ER Rep 110, 94 LJKB 435, 132 LT
    707, CA, 17 Digest (Reissue) 145, 377. *e*
Hedley Byrne & Co Ltd v Heller & Partners Ltd [1963] 2 All ER 575, [1964] AC 465, [1963]
    3 WLR 101, [1963] 1 Lloyd's Rep 485, HL, 36(1) Digest (Reissue) 24, 84.
Heron II, The, Koufos v C Cẕarnikow Ltd [1967] 3 All ER 686, [1969] 1 AC 350, [1967] 3
    WLR 1491, [1967] 2 Lloyd's Rep 459, HL, Digest (Cont Vol C) 882, 1754a.
Hinẕ v Berry [1970] 1 All ER 1074, [1970] 2 QB 40, [1970] 2 WLR 684, CA, 17 Digest
    (Reissue) 147, 391.
Home Office v Dorset Yacht Co Ltd [1970] 2 All ER 294, [1970] AC 1004, [1970] 2 WLR *f*
    1140, [1970] 1 Lloyd's Rep 453, HL, 36(1) Digest (Reissue) 27, 93.
Hughes v Lord Advocate [1963] 1 All ER 705, [1963] AC 837, [1963] 2 WLR 779, 1963 SC
    31, 1963 SLT 150, HL, 36(1) Digest (Reissue) 64, 234.
King v Phillips [1953] 1 All ER 617, [1953] 1 QB 429, [1953] 2 WLR 526, CA, 17 Digest
    (Reissue) 147, 389.
Lambert v Lewis [1980] 1 All ER 978, [1980] 2 WLR 299, [1980] 1 Lloyd's Rep 311, [1980] *g*
    RTR 152, CA.
Marshall v Lionel Enterprises Inc (1971) 25 DLR (3d) 141, [1972] 2 OR 177, 17 Digest
    (Reissue) 152, *284.
Morris v West Hartlepool Steam Navigation Co Ltd [1956] 1 All ER 385, [1956] AC 552,
    [1956] 1 WLR 177, [1956] 1 Lloyd's Rep 76, HL, 34 Digest (Repl) 243, 1778. *h*
Overseas Tankship (UK) Ltd v Morts Dock & Engineering Co Ltd, The Wagon Mound (No 1)
    [1961] 1 All ER 404, [1961] AC 388, [1961] 2 WLR 126, [1961] 1 Lloyd's Rep 1, [1961]
    ALR 569, PC, 36(1) Digest (Reissue) 63, 227.
Polemis and Furness Withy & Co Ltd, Re [1921] 3 KB 560, [1921] All ER Rep 40, 90 LJKB
    1353, 126 LT 154, 15 Asp MLC 398, 27 Com Cas 25, CA, 17 Digest (Reissue) 135, 313.
R v Sheppard [1980] 3 All ER 899, [1980] 3 WLR 960, HL. *i*
Schneider v Eisovitch [1960] 1 All ER 169, [1960] 2 QB 430, [1960] 2 WLR 169, 17 Digest
    (Reissue) 85, 24.
Spartan Steel & Alloys Ltd v Martin & Co (Contractors) Ltd [1972] 3 All ER 557, [1973] QB
    27, [1972] 3 WLR 502, CA, 17 Digest (Reissue) 149, 403.
Videan v British Transport Commission [1963] 2 All ER 860, [1963] 2 QB 650, [1963] 3
    WLR 374, CA, 36(1) Digest (Reissue) 120, 461.

Wagon Mound, The, (No 2), Overseas Tankship (UK) Ltd v Miller Steamship Co Pty Ltd [1966]
a   2 All ER 709, [1967] 1 AC 617, [1966] 3 WLR 498, [1966] 1 Lloyd's Rep 657, [1967]
ALR 97, [1966] 1 NSWR 411, PC, 36 (1) Digest (Reissue) 65, 236.

Cases also cited

Chester v Waverley (1939) 62 CLR 1.
Chapman v Hearse (1961) 106 CLR 112.
b   *Dodd Properties (Kent) Ltd v Canterbury City Council* [1980] 1 All ER 928, [1980] 1 WLR
433, CA.
Duwyn v Kaprielian (1978) 94 DLR (3d) 424.
Owens v Liverpool Corpn [1938] 4 All ER 729, [1939] 1 KB 394, CA.

Appeal

c   The plaintiff, Rosina McLoughlin, appealed against the judgment of Boreham J on 11th
December 1978 dismissing her claim against the defendants, Thomas Alan O'Brian, A E
Docker & Sons Ltd, Raymond Sygrove, and Ernest Doe & Sons Ltd for damages for
shock, distress and injury to her health. The facts are set out in the judgment of
Stephenson LJ.

d   *Michael Ogden QC* and *Jonathan Haworth* for the plaintiff.
Michael Turner QC and *John Leighton Williams* for the defendants.

Cur adv vult

16th December. The following judgments were read.

e

STEPHENSON LJ. I am authorised to say that Cumming-Bruce LJ, who is not able
to be here this morning, agrees with both the judgments which are about to be delivered.
    On 23rd October 1978 Boreham J decided that the plaintiff had no claim against the
four defendants for shock, distress and injury to her health and gave judgment for the
defendants. He also refused the plaintiff leave to present a petition of appeal to the House
f   of Lords pursuant to the 'leap-frogging' provision of s 12 of the Administration of Justice
Act 1969.
    The facts and circumstances which give rise to this claim and appeal are these. The
plaintiff is the wife of Thomas McLoughlin and was the mother of four children. On
19th October 1973 her elder son George, then aged 17, was driving his father and his two
young sisters, Kathleen aged 7 and Gillian aged nearly 3, in a motor car along the A604
g   road from Cambridge to Haverhill when it collided with a motor lorry owned by the
second defendants and driven by the first defendant. The lorry had just collided with
another motor lorry owned by the fourth defendants and driven by the third
defendant. There is no dispute that the collision with the motor car was caused by the
negligence of the defendants and that they were responsible in law for the injuries
thereby caused to Mr McLoughlin and the three children in the motor car with him.
h   Those injuries were: to George, injuries to his head and face, including cerebral
concussion, fractures of both scapulae and bruising and abrasions; to Kathleen,
concussion, a fracture of the right clavicle, bruising, abrasions and shock; to Gillian, such
serious injuries that she died almost immediately. But the defendants deny that they
owed the plaintiff any duty of care or that they broke any duty by the negligent driving
which injured her husband and children. Her injuries were of a different kind and were
j   pleaded as—

    'shock, distress and injury to health, loss and damage. The Plaintiff was born on
the 23rd June 1933. She suffered severe shock, organic depression, and a change of
personality. Symptoms include recurrent headaches, irritability, coughs, loss of
voice, loss of appetite, poor sleeping, depression and fatigue, lapse of memory and
loss of concentration, an irrational fear of the unknown, and perpetual myoclonus

of the left orbital muscles. The above has severely affected her abilities as a wife and mother. She has been and remains under medical treatment.'

The nature and extent of those injuries are not admitted, but the court is asked to assume that the plaintiff has developed, and received medical treatment for, a condition of nervous shock, as distinct from grief or sorrow, and the mental distress which that causes, and is a woman of reasonable fortitude and normal susceptibility to such shock. The condition for which she claims damages from the defendants was caused in the following way.

The accident took place at about 4 pm. The plaintiff was then at the family home on the same A604 road at Sawston, about two miles from the scene of the accident. The first she heard of the accident was the bells of a passing ambulance some time in the late afternoon. About 6 pm a Mr Pilgrim came and told her that there had been an accident, that he thought George was dying, that he did not know about Gillian and that he did not know where her husband was. He then drove her a distance of about eight or ten miles to Addenbrooke's Hospital in Cambridge. There she saw her other son Michael, 11 years old, apparently uninjured but crying, who told her that Gillian was dead. She was then taken down a passage past windows through which she could see Kathleen, crying, looking terrible, covered in some black stuff, her face all cut and oil all over her hair and face. She was then taken on down the passage, where she could hear a scream and loud shouting which she knew came from George, to see her husband. He was sitting with his head in his hands, covered in oil or something, with mud all over the floor. When he saw her, he limped across the room and started crying but was too dazed to talk. She could still hear George shouting and ranting and laughing. A doctor took her to see him and told her, 'Don't be too frightened by what you might see.' She saw him, only one side of his face and body uncovered and still shouting. She took his hand and managed to make him understand she was there before he lost consciousness. Then she went back to Kathleen. She had lacerations to her face which had been treated and her arm was strapped or bandaged; she did not speak but kept crying and clinging to her mother and would not let her go, 'and she was like this for weeks and weeks'. Then Mr Pilgrim drove her and her husband and Kathleen home.

It would be difficult to resist the conclusion that at least some part of the plaintiff's subsequent physical and mental condition was caused by what the judge called the 'harrowing experience' of being told what she was by Mr Pilgrim and of seeing and hearing what she did at the hospital. The question for the court is whether the defendants are legally liable to compensate her for her condition. The statement of claim sets out the facts of the two collisions, alleges that the collision with the motor car was caused by the defendants' negligence, then alleges that the injuries and death of those in the motor car were caused by that negligence and finally alleges, in para 7, amplified at the court's suggestion by amendment on the hearing of the appeal:

> 'At about 6 p.m. on the said date the Plaintiff was informed of the accident by one Pilgrim, and told that members of her family were involved and had been injured. She thereupon went to Addenbrookes Hospital, Cambridge where she was told that her child Gillian McLoughlin was dead. She there saw heard and spoke to her husband Thomas McLoughlin and her children George and Kathleen McLoughlin, who were suffering from the aforesaid injuries. As was reasonably foreseeable by reason of the matters aforesaid the Plaintiff has suffered shock distress and injury to health, loss and damage.'

Then follow the particulars of injuries which I have already read.

Claims for damages for injury by shock to A from physical injury caused to B by C's negligence have been adjudicated by the courts in a number of reported cases both in this country and elsewhere. The judge reviewed a good number of them. He concluded from them that his decision depended on the answer to the basic question: would the hypothetical reasonable bystander have foreseen the risk of injury by shock to this *a* plaintiff if the defendants failed to exercise reasonable care in the driving of their motor vehicles on the highway at the material place and time?

He answered it in the defendants' favour in these words:

b 'I feel bound by principle and what I conceive to be good sense, if not constrained by authority, to conclude that in such circumstances [as those of this case] injury to the mother is too remote a possibility to come within the ambit of the foresight of the reasonable bystander. Sorrow and hurt of the feelings and grief he would doubtless foresee but not, I think, injury by shock.'

That conclusion is challenged on three grounds succinctly stated in the notice of appeal as follows:

c '1. That the Learned Judge was wrong in deciding that the Respondent owed no duty to the Appellant to avoid exposing her to risk of injury by shock.

'2. That it was reasonably foreseeable that the Appellant might suffer injury from shock (a) as a result of being told of the death of her child and of injuries to other members of her family, and (b) as a result of what she saw and heard when she visited the injured members of her family in hospital.

d '3. That the Respondent was in breach of his duty of care towards the Appellant and is liable for such injury by shock as the Appellant suffered.'

Those grounds have been ably elaborated by counsel for the plaintiff in the course of taking us through many of the relevant authorities. At the end of all the arguments we have heard I have come to the conclusion that there are two questions, not one, to be answered. I take them from the speech of Lord Wilberforce in *Anns v London Borough of Merton* [1977] 2 All ER 492 at 498, [1978] AC 728 at 751–752:

e

f 'Through the trilogy of cases in this house, *Donoghue v Stevenson* [1932] AC 562, [1932] All ER Rep 1, *Hedley Byrne & Co Ltd v Heller & Partners Ltd* [1963] 2 All ER 575, [1964] AC 465 and *Home Office v Dorset Yacht Co Ltd* [1970] 2 All ER 294, [1970] AC 1004, the position has now been reached that in order to establish that a duty of care arises in a particular situation, it is not necessary to bring the facts of that situation within those of previous situations in which a duty of care has been held to exist. Rather the question has to be approached in two stages. First one has to ask whether, as between the alleged wrongdoer and the person who has suffered damage there is a sufficient relationship of proximity or neighbourhood such that, in the reasonable contemplation of the former, carelessness on his part may be likely to cause damage to the latter, in which case a prima facie duty of care arises. Secondly, if the first question is answered affirmatively, it is necessary to consider whether there are any considerations which ought to negative, or to reduce or limit the scope of the duty or the class of person to whom it is owed or the damages to which a breach of it may give rise . . .'

g

The first of Lord Wilberforce's questions is much the same as what the judge called the *h* basic question. The second arises if he answered the first wrongly and is in this form: if the hypothetical reasonable bystander could have foreseen the risk of injury by shock to this plaintiff, should logic nevertheless give way to common sense and should policy exclude her claim to be paid for this consequence of the defendants' negligence on the highway?

It has long been the law of England that a person driving a vehicle on a highway owes *j* a duty to take reasonable care not to injure other persons on the highway or to injure property adjoining the highway: see *Best v Samuel Fox & Co Ltd* [1952] 2 All ER 394 at 398, [1952] AC 716 at 731 per Lord Goddard.

As long ago as the beginning of this century the courts of this country recognised that a person on or near a highway might suffer not only injury to life or limb or health by impact with a vehicle negligently driven on the highway into collision with him or her,

but also injury to life or limb or health by fear for his or her safety caused by the threat
of such impact or collision: see *Dulieu v White & Sons* [1901] 2 KB 669, [1900–3] All ER
Rep 353.

Medical science recognised that such injury could be produced by the shock and fear
naturally suffered in such circumstances, and the law recognised that it was mere chance
whether the negligence creating that situation resulted in actual impact and its
consequences to life and limb and health or the apprehension of such impact and the
consequences of such apprehension, or both.

Once recognise that carelessness causing injury by shock or fright is actionable and you
must sooner or later decide whether fear for a person's own safety alone is actionable or
whether and in what circumstances fear for another's safety which produces the same
injury by shock in the frightened person is not actionable also. A quarter of a century
later this court had to decide that very question. In *Hambrook v Stokes Brothers* [1925] 1
KB 141, [1924] All ER Rep 110 Sargant LJ was of the opinion that fear for another's safety
would never in any circumstances be actionable, but the majority, consisting of Bankes
and Atkin LJJ, held that a mother on the highway in the vicinity of that part of the
highway where negligent driving of a motor lorry had injured her child could recover
damages for the injury inflicted on her by the shock of seeing the injured child
immediately after being knocked down by the lorry, but not for the injury inflicted by
the shock of being first told about the incident. Such was clearly the opinion of Atkin LJ,
and I think Bankes LJ also.

But, if the injury by shock to a mother's health when she is at or near the scene of the
accident which injures her child is an injury for which the wrongdoer who caused the
accident is legally liable, two more questions will sooner or later have to be answered.

1. How close does the relationship or tie between the person injured by impact and
the person injured by shock have to be? Parent and child, husband and wife, brother and
sister, grandparent and grandchild, sweethearts, lifelong friends? Do adoption and
illegitimacy come into consideration?

2. How close to the point of impact in time and place do the two have to be? Does the
person injured by shock have to be within sight or sound of the collision on or near the
highway where it takes place when it takes place? A wife or mother may be nowhere
near the scene of the accident but may suffer injury to health from shock when she hears
the news from a friend or a policeman, or by telephone or cable, or sees the husband or
child in hospital, or the corpse of her husband or child in the mortuary, or reads of the
accident in a newspaper, or hears of it on the wireless or sees it on television. By chance
the plaintiff in this case was not in the car in which her family were injured, nor on the
same part of the A604. By chance she lived far enough away to be told of the accident
before she saw and heard for herself some of its consequences in the hospital. Do the two
miles which separated her from the scene of the collision, or the one or two hours which
separated the time of the collision from the time when she first heard of it or reached the
hospital, absolve the defendants from legal liability to compensate her and deprive her
of the right to claim compensation from them?

It is a striking fact that the authorities to which we have been referred, decisions in
English, Scottish, Canadian, Australian and American cases, enable us to answer the first
question of the necessary natural or social bond with some certainty in the plaintiff's
favour, but the second question of the necessary temporal and spatial proximity against
her, though with less certainty. As the cases stand, there is no reported decision of any
person recovering damages for injury by shock who has not been at or near the scene of
the accident at the time or shortly afterwards and there are strong indications that a
person who was not there or thereabouts at the time, or was told of it later or saw its
results later in another place, would be outside the ambit of the wrongdoer's
responsibility.

The law has not drawn the line of legal responsibility firmly at the point where the
plaintiff who is mentally shocked is in danger of being physically shocked by the
negligent act of the defendant, like Mrs Dulieu and possibly Mrs Hambrook. Some such

consideration may have influenced the trial judge and the judges of this court to dismiss
a the claim of a mother who heard from her upstairs window in a side street her child
scream when the defendant's taxicab backed into him: see *King v Phillips* [1953] 1 All ER
617, [1953] 1 QB 429. But that case was distinguished by the trial judge in *Boardman v
Sanderson* [1964] 1 WLR 1317 and this court affirmed his decision in holding that a
father, who was in no danger of being run over by another defendant's reversing motor
car, could recover damages for shock caused by hearing his son scream and then seeing
b him with his foot trapped under a wheel of the car. Similarly the Supreme Court of
California held by a majority of four to three in *Dillon v Legg* (1968) 29 ALR 3d 1316 that
a judge was wrong to strike out the claim to damages of a mother who witnessed a road
accident to her child at a safe distance from the place where the defendant's automobile
struck and killed her child. She did not have to be within the zone of danger or risk of
physical impact herself, although the majority thought it would require legislation to
c override a judgment given only five years earlier and to put her outside that zone.

So the duty which a person on the highway owes to the person he runs down is not
always or necessarily the same as the duty he owes to the person who suffers shock as a
result of the running down of that other, and the liability of the person on the highway
to the person who suffers shock may be a secondary or derivative liability.

But the furthest away from the accident that any court has allowed a plaintiff to be
d who has succeeded in establishing such secondary liability is to be found in three
decisions at first instance: one of a judge of the High Court of Ontario, where the
plaintiff came from 'nearby' and saw the injured body of her husband on the highway
'shortly after' he had been injured: see *Marshall v Lionel Enterprises Inc* (1971) 25 DLR (3d)
141; another of a judge of the Supreme Court of Victoria, where the plaintiff ran from
her home 100 yards away after being told at once by one son of injury to another, saw the
e unconscious son on the road (what the judge called 'the immediate aftermath of the
accident'), went with him in the ambulance and shortly after arrival at the hospital was
informed that he was dead: see *Benson v Lee* [1972] VR 879; the third the decision of
Waller J in *Chadwick v British Transport Commission* [1967] 2 All ER 945, [1967] 1 WLR
912. There the plaintiff's husband was no relation of any person injured in the Lewisham
railway accident, but he came from his home 200 yards away to the rescue of many
f injured passengers at the scene of the accident and what he saw and heard in the course
of his efforts in rescuing at the scene of the accident was such a harrowing experience that
he became psychoneurotic until his death from causes unconnected with the accident.
The judge rejected a submission in the present case by counsel for the plaintiff that she
was a rescuer or in the same category as a rescuer, and counsel for the defendants submits
that there is no special category of rescuer, or if there is the judge was right in holding
g that she did not fall within it. I consider this point after discussing the general principles
which the judge drew from the authorities in formulating what he called the basic
question.

The first principle is the well-known principle of liability to neighbours in law which
Lord Atkin formulated in *Donoghue v Stevenson* [1932] AC 562 at 580, [1932] All ER Rep
1 at 11.

h The second principle is the principle of liability for reasonably foreseeable damage
which Viscount Simonds restated in giving the judgment of the Judicial Committee in
Overseas Tankship (UK) Ltd v Morts Dock & Engineering Co Ltd, The Wagon Mound (No 1)
[1961] 1 All ER 404 at 413–414, 415, [1961] AC 388 at 423, 426. Both principles go back
a long way before those dates, but in those two judgments they received authoritative
recognition and clarification.

j In *Bourhill v Young* [1942] 2 All ER 396, [1943] AC 92 the House of Lords denied
damages to a fishwife in an Edinburgh street who suffered nervous shock from the
sound, and possibly sight, of the results of a collision between a motor cycle and a car on
a part of the highway not far from where she stood but far enough to put her in no
personal danger. Their Lordships applied Lord Atkin's test in differing language. My
duty to my neighbour is owed, said Lord Atkin, to all persons 'so closely and directly

affected by my act that I ought reasonably to have them in contemplation as being so affected'.

Lord Thankerton said ([1942] 2 All ER 396 at 399, [1943] AC 92 at 98):

'. . . I shall confine myself to the question of the range of duty of a motor cyclist on the public road towards other passengers on the road. Clearly this duty is to drive the cycle with such reasonable care as will avoid the risk of injury to such persons as he can reasonably foresee might be injured by failure to exercise such reasonable care. It is now settled that such injury includes injury by shock, although no direct physical impact or lesion occurs. If then the test of proximity or remoteness is to be applied, I am of opinion that such a test involves that the injury must be within that which the cyclist ought to have reasonably contemplated as the area of potential danger which would arise as the result of his negligence, and the question in the present case is whether the appellant was within that area.'

Lord Russell quoted Lord Atkin's words in *Donoghue v Stevenson* and Lord Jamieson's words in the instant case that the driver's duty was 'limited to persons so placed that they may reasonably be expected to be injured by the omission to take such care' (see [1942] 2 All ER 396 at 401, 402, [1943] AC 92 at 101, 102).

Lord Macmillan cited the same words, and added ([1942] 2 All ER 396 at 403, [1943] AC 92 at 104):

'The duty to take care is the duty to avoid doing or omitting to do anything the doing or omitting to do which may have as its reasonable and probable consequence injury to others, and the duty is owed to those to whom injury may reasonably and probably be anticipated if the duty is not observed.'

Lord Wright also quoted Lord Atkin and Lord Jamieson, and made the distinction between the 'primary' or 'original' negligence of the motor cyclist against the owner of the car he ran into and his 'secondary' or 'derivative' negligence towards the plaintiff and applied the test whether the hypothetical reasonable man viewing the position ex post facto or—

'the reasonable hypothetical observer could reasonably have foreseen, the likelihood that anyone placed as the appellant was, could be affected in the manner in which she was.'

(See [1942] 2 All ER 396 at 404–406, [1943] AC 92 at 106–114.)

Lord Porter, after repeating Lord Atkin's words, said that if no complainant—

'was in such a position that direct physical injury could reasonably be anticipated to them or their relations or friends, normally I think no duty would be owed: and, if in addition no shock was reasonably to be anticipated to them as a result of the defender's negligence, the defender might, indeed, be guilty of actionable negligence to others but not of negligence towards them.'

(See [1942] 2 All ER 396 at 409, [1943] AC 92 at 117.)

So the motor cyclist, who was killed in the collision which frightened the plaintiff, was replaced by a reasonable hypothetical observer reviewing the scene ex post facto who with the knowledge of all the circumstances would not, in the opinion of the Law Lords, have foreseen that the plaintiff would suffer any injury, including shock.

All their formulations of the duty owed by the defendant are tinged with the assumption of local proximity, for that was all which on the facts of the plaintiff's situation they had to consider. Indeed, the defendant's counsel conceded that there might be no liability where a shocked plaintiff was an extravagant distance away from the scene of the accident (see [1943] AC 92 at 97). Nothing therefore was decided in *Bourhill's* case any more than in *Hambrook's* about a plaintiff far from the scene of the accident who never went near it. But there is also no indication that the defendant's duty might extend to such a plaintiff, except what can be derived from applying the test of

what was reasonably foreseeable by the hypothetical observer. At the date of that
a decision, as when *Hambrook's* case was decided, the rule laid down in *Re Polemis* [1921] 3
KB 560, [1921] All ER Rep 40 prevailed that, while reasonable foreseeability defined the
ambit of persons to whom a duty of care was owed, directness, not reasonable
foreseeability, was the criterion by which liability for damage from breach of duty was
decided. There is to my mind no clear indication that that doctrine had any effect on
these two decisions, but it may have coloured the courts' approach to both *Hambrook's* and
b *Bourhill's* cases.

The judgment of the Privy Council in *The Wagon Mound (No 1)* put an end to the *Re
Polemis* doctrine and extended the test of reasonable foreseeability to damage as well as
duty. Not only has the person who complains of a breach of duty to be reasonably
foreseeable as being affected by it but the damage he suffers has to be reasonably
foreseeable. The wrongdoer does not have to foresee the precise kind of injury or
c damage which may result from his breach of duty: see *Hughes v Lord Advocate* [1963] 1
All ER 705, [1963] AC 837; but the only kind of injury or damage which can affect a
person who is not present at or near to the tortfeasor when he causes an accident and
consequential injury and damage by his failure to take reasonable care is injury and
damage by nervous shock. So there is, as the judge saw in framing his basic question,
only one object which has to be reasonably foreseeable: the person injured, not the injury
d and damage; because, if the first is reasonably to be contemplated, so is the second, and,
if the duty is owed to the plaintiff and broken, liability necessarily follows; there is here,
as Lord Sumner might have put it, no culpability without compensation. Is it then
reasonably foreseeable that injury by shock may result from a piece of negligent driving
on a road to a person who is not within sight or sound of the accident which the driving
causes, but is later on and further off affected by what he hears and sees of the accident
e and its consequences, as this plaintiff is assumed to have been? My answer would be
Yes. It may be that medical science would regard the sort of injury by shock which the
plaintiff suffered as less likely to occur than it would have been if she had been within
sight and sound of the collision with the family's car. But, whatever evidence there
might be about that, I cannot think that the ordinary man, whose opinion of what is
reasonably foreseeable is what matters, would regard a normal loving mother, who
f experienced what the plaintiff experienced, as unlikely to be affected as she was. He
might consider her *more* likely to be made ill in this way if she suffered the anxiety of not
knowing the true facts and not being able to help for some time. The risk of her being
made ill by the shock of Mr Pilgrim's bad news, of Michael's bad news and of what she
then saw and heard at the hospital would, in my opinion, strike the hypothetical
reasonable observer as just as great as, or at best not substantially less than, the risk of her
g suffering the same mental injury had she been in or near the collision.

There is, of course, an element of almost outrageous unreality in applying to such a
case as this the conception of risks weighed and balanced against proportionate
precautions, which is stated, for instance, by Lord Reid in *Morris v West Hartlepool Steam
Navigation Co Ltd* [1956] 1 All ER 385 at 399, [1956] AC 552 at 574 and in *The Wagon
Mound (No 2)* [1966] 2 All ER 709 at 718, [1967] 1 AC 617 at 642. A driver of a motor
h car does not, before deciding to overtake another vehicle or to break a speed limit, weigh
up the risk of injuring or maiming other persons on the road, let alone the risk of some
near relation of the persons he may injure suffering consequential injury by shock miles
away, though if even a few drivers made that calculation the roads might be much safer
and motor insurance cover much less expensive. Nevertheless, that is the calculation
which the hypothetical observer would have to make in the case of an industrial accident
j when considering whether it resulted from a breach of an employer's or occupier's duty
to persons to whom a duty is admittedly owed. A driver who owes a duty to drive with
such reasonable care as will avoid the risk of injury to such persons as he can reasonably
foresee might be injured by failure to exercise such reasonable care must be assumed to
conduct the same sort of balancing operation; and the fact that there is no precaution
which a driver could take, except the precaution of driving carefully and not overtaking

or speeding, does not alter the driver's duty to take reasonable care not to injure by shock persons who are so closely or directly affected by his careless driving as to be likely to be thereby injured. The question is what would the driver have foreseen *if* he had thought about the consequence of his driving carelessly *and* if he had known that the first consequence would be injuring persons whose wife and mother was not with them. Would he not expect her to be told of the accident, to go to them, possibly in hospital, at the earliest opportunity, to be severely distressed and perhaps to suffer from nervous illness as a result?

The intervention of a messenger bringing the bad news to this wife and mother, as Mr Pilgrim did, seems to me the very kind of thing which would be likely to happen after an accident of this sort. I cannot therefore regard the distinction between the direct perception of an accident or its consequences and learning of them from another as important, and on this point I prefer the views of Paull J in *Schneider v Eisovitch* [1960] 1 All ER 169, [1960] 2 QB 430 and of Lush J in *Benson v Lee* [1972] VR 879 to those of the Lords Justices in *Hambrook v Stokes* and of the Saskatchewan Court of Appeal in *Abramazik v Brenner* (1967) 65 DLR (2d) 651. I would think it contrary to common sense if not illogical to make a negligent driver liable to a person who suffers from shock on recovering consciousness and learning of the death of a near and dear relation, only if the sufferer is rendered unconscious by the same negligent driving which caused the other's death (as in *Schneider's* case) and not if the sufferer was not physically injured in the collision caused by his negligent driving (as in *Benson's* case), which seems to have been the opinion of the Supreme Court of Victoria in *Andrews v Williams* [1967] VR 836.

The duty owed to rescuers seems to rest on the same basis of a natural and foreseeable reaction to injury being caused to others. The courts are doubtless concerned not to discourage benevolence and altruism, and they could not discourage natural affection if they tried. It is partly at least because a wrongdoer ought to expect that good Samaritans will rush to the rescue of the injured that he is legally liable for injury which they may suffer in the course of rescue. Ought he not also to expect that a person bound by particular ties of love and affection beyond a general love of humanity will go to help and comfort those he knows and loves as soon as possible, whether that is at the scene (as in *Videan v British Transport Commission* [1963] 2 All ER 860, [1963] 2 QB 650) or as here in the nearest hospital? If Mr Chadwick had decided or been asked to go to a Lewisham hospital in order to help the victims of that railway accident, would that difference have prevented him (or his widow) from recovering damages for the results to his health?

I think it would, but not because his conduct and his injury would be any less reasonably foreseeable; the reason I would give is contained in the answer which I shall give to the second question raised by the plaintiff's claim in this action.

I have considered whether it can be said that there is no prima facie duty of care owed by a driver on the road to a person in the position of the plaintiff, although her existence and the occurrence of her injury are reasonably foreseeable in any ordinary sense of those words. Just as the duty of an occupier is owed to visitors to his premises and occupiers of adjoining premises so the duty of a road user is owed to others on or near the road, and it may be said that that duty is the only duty and ought not to be extended to others beyond the highway and its environs any more than an employer's duty should be extended to shocked wives of workmen injured by his negligence. And it may be said that persons outside that geographical area are not so 'closely or directly' affected by a driver's actions as to be his neighbours. But Lord Atkin, in a judgment which opened a wide door to a far-reaching increase of claims, used those words to include a consumer (claiming, incidentally, damage for injury by shock) who was one of a large class whose members might be far away from the defendant and the time and place when and where he manufactured the article or put it into circulation. I appreciate that there is there a directness of contact between the unexamined article and the injured consumer which is absent here. Here there intervene injuries to others resulting from the negligent act or omission, as well as reports from others of what the negligent act or omission has caused. But these interventions, if they can be so regarded, do not, in my judgment, limit the vision or imagination of the hypothetical observer or make the ultimate effect on the plaintiff not reasonably foreseeable. It is always injuries to others, or the fear of what injuries to others there may be, which causes injury by shock to an otherwise uninjured person, whether he or she be a bystander or a rescuer or a close relation. It may be said that those injuries must be seen or feared at or near the scene of the accident which caused or might reasonably be thought to have caused them, and that the basis for the decisions in *Chadwick's* case, *Marshall's* case and *Benson's* case is that injury by shock was the effect of the accident and the injuries to others combined, whereas in such a case as the present the absence of the injured from the scene breaks up the combination of the accident and its immediate aftermath and makes the plaintiff's injury by shock a consequence not of the accident (except perhaps in so far as it has been reported to her) but of the injuries in isolation.

This seems to me an artificial analysis of the real cause of the plaintiff's injury and one which cannot have the effect of removing her injury from the defendants' responsibility for it without reverting to the rule in *Re Polemis* and considering that, though she herself is closely and directly affected by his negligence, her injury is too remote or indirect for the defendants to be liable for it.

To restrict the ambit of the duty owed by those responsible for driving carefully on a highway to those who are injured by shock when themselves on or near the highway would be to exclude from the mind of the hypothetical reasonable observer knowledge of now foreseeable medical facts or to attribute to his mind's eye enlightened by progressive awareness of mental illness an abnormal degree of myopia. It is easy to exaggerate what Lord Diplock has called in *R v Sheppard* [1980] 3 All ER 899 at 903, [1980] 3 WLR 960 at 965 'the hypothetical powers of observation, ratiocination and foresight of consequences possessed by this admirable but purely notional exemplar . . .', but I find it impossible to consider this plaintiff and her injury too far fetched to be within the contemplation of reasonable men applying their minds to natural and probable consequences of their careless driving.

Another possibility is that the plaintiff is not herself outside the ambit of the defendants' duty and negligence but that her injury is. That seems to have been in the judge's mind when he said:

> 'But even if it could be said that the plaintiff came within the ambit of the defendants' acts, was the possibility of her suffering injury by shock then reasonably foreseeable?'

And again when he concluded in words I have already quoted—

> 'that in such circumstances injury to the mother is too remote a possibility to come within the ambit of the foresight of the reasonable bystander.'

But, even if the judge is not in the final passage making the mistake of excluding from the reasonable bystander's knowledge the fact that the plaintiff was two miles away, this can only mean that the negligent driver ought to contemplate the possibility of injury to a person in the position of the plaintiff but not the possibility of injury to her by shock. Injury by shock is, however, the only possible injury to a person in her position, as I have already pointed out, and so, if injury to her ought to be reasonably foreseen, this injury to her ought to be so, unless it is medically 'too remote a possibility'. But, again, for the second time, I state my opinion that the reasonable bystander would not regard injury by shock to a wife and mother who had the experiences she had as too remote to be foreseeable by him. It would come within the modern rule of tort as stated by Lord Reid in *The Heron II, Koufos v C Czarnikow Ltd* [1967] 3 All ER 686 at 692, [1969] 1 AC 350 at 385–386:

> 'The defendant will be liable for any type of damage which is reasonably foreseeable as liable to happen even in the most unusual case, unless the risk is so small that a reasonable man would in the whole circumstances feel justified in neglecting it . . .'

I am therefore constrained to answer the judge's basic question, not as he did in the negative, but in the affirmative and to hold that the hypothetical reasonable bystander would have foreseen the risk of injury by shock to this plaintiff if the defendants failed to exercise reasonable care in the driving of their motor vehicles on the highway at the material place and time.

That is not, in my opinion, however, the end of the matter because the appeal raises another question not apparently argued, or argued so fully, below or considered separately by the judge; it is the second question stated by Lord Wilberforce in *Anns's* case. Although the facts of the defendants' situation are not within those of previous situations in which a duty of care has been held to exist, in my judgment there was between her and the two defendant drivers a sufficient relationship of proximity or neighbourhood such that in their reasonable contemplation carelessness on their part might be likely to cause damage; and therefore a prima facie duty of care arose. I am also of opinion that the damage which she suffered of injury by nervous shock from being told of the injuries to her family and seeing and hearing them and their results by her own unaided senses was the very kind of damage that these defendants' carelessness was likely to cause.

It may be difficult to determine how widely neighbourhood extends, as Lord Pearson put it in *Home Office v Dorset Yacht Co* [1970] 2 All ER 294 at 321, [1970] AC 1004 at 1005. I gratefully adopt Lord Pearce's opinion in *Hedley Byrne & Co Ltd v Heller & Partners Ltd* [1963] 2 All ER 575 at 615, [1964] AC 465 at 536 that the question 'depends ultimately on the courts' assessment of the demands of society for protection from the carelessness of others'.

Lord Wilberforce's second question must therefore be asked, and I would answer it, not without some reluctance, by saying that considerations of policy ought to take this sort of injury to this class of person out of the scope of the duty by limiting that scope to those on or near the highway at or near the time of the accident caused by the defendant's carelessness.

That is my assessment of the demands of society referred to by Lord Pearce. I conclude that they do not require that the defendants should be held liable to pay damages to the plaintiff. Ask me why, and I find some difficulty in stating a convincing reason. It is largely a matter of what may be called pretentiously 'judicial instinct' that the duty of the negligent driver, and the negligent employer and occupier of land and buildings, must stop somewhere; and I would stop it where it has been stopped for many years in the courts of this island, of the United States of America, of Australia and of Canada, although that has the effect of depriving by chance a plaintiff, who has by the defendants' carelessness been subjected to a dreadful ordeal, of any right to monetary compensation.

But the courts have recognised that in an imperfect world there cannot be perfect compensation and that judicial limits must be placed on who can recover damages for the fault of another and what damages they can recover; there must be restraint in doing justice to the wronged out of fairness to wrongdoers, even when they are insured. These considerations have so far prevailed in excluding heads of economic loss from a defendant's liability, on the ground of remoteness or of policy, as this court pointed out in *Lambert v Lewis* [1980] 1 All ER 978 at 1006, [1980] 2 WLR 299 at 331. I need not repeat more of what was said there than that—

> 'There comes a point where the logical extension of the boundaries of duty and damage is halted by the barrier of commercial sense and practical convenience.'

Counsel for the plaintiff has argued with some force that the policy grounds for excluding such a claim as the plaintiff's are not very strong. They are a multiplication of claims to burden the courts, and the economic consequences of such claims if successful, mainly in increasing accident insurance premiums; the difficulty of defining the class or classes of persons who can bring such claims, and the difficulty of deciding whether the plaintiffs suffer from psychiatric illness resulting from shock as distinct from the effects of grief, whether the plaintiffs' complaints of illness are genuine and whether the illness in fact results from the accident and injuries caused by the defendants' negligence or breach of duty.

These latter difficulties are already well known to the courts and the medical profession. The functional overlay, malingering, the illness pre-existing or caused otherwise, are all familiar problems. The argument from the opening of the door to fraudulent claims has been well dispatched by the Supreme Court of California in *Dillon v Legg* (1968) 29 ALR 3d 1316 at 1323. And counsel for the defendants very properly does not rely on that difficulty. But there is more force in the difficulty of defining the class, connected as it is with the number of potential claims and their economic consequences if the door is opened. This difficulty has been met by two pieces of legislation in Australia which have defined the class in the same way.

By s 4 of the New South Wales Law Reform (Miscellaneous Provisions) Act 1944 the State legislature provided:

'(1) The liability of any person in respect of injury caused after the commencement of this Act by an act, neglect or default by which any other person is killed, injured or put in peril, shall extend to include liability for injury arising wholly or in part from mental or nervous shock sustained by—(*a*) a parent or the husband or wife of the person so killed, injured or put in peril; or (*b*) any other member of the family of the person so killed, injured or put in peril where such person was killed, injured or put in peril within the sight or hearing of that member of the family . . .

'(5) In this section—"Member of the family" means the husband, wife, parent, child, brother, sister, half-brother, or half-sister or the person in relation to whom the expression is used. "Parent" includes father, mother, grandfather, grandmother, stepfather, stepmother and any person standing in loco parentis to another. "Child" includes son, daughter, grandson, granddaughter, stepson, stepdaughter and any person to whom another stands in loco parentis.'

There are substantially identical provision in ss 24 and 22 of the Law Reform (Miscellaneous Provisions) Ordinance 1955 applicable to the Australian Capital Territory, Part VII of which deals with injury arising from mental or nervous shock. The marginal note to s 24 shows that in that legislation the liability in respect of such injury by a default by which another person is injured was regarded as an extension of liability for such injury.

I think it is an extension, made by legislation. One court seems to have been of opinion that it could be made by the courts. The Supreme Court of California has laid down guidelines (in the judgment of Tobriner J with which the majority of the court concurred in *Dillon v Legg*) which appear to leave to juries decision of the question whether injury by shock is foreseeable according to the relationship of the person injured to the victim of the accident and the distance he is from the scene of it when injured.

The American Law Institute's Restatement, Torts, Second, ch 16, § 436, p 457, allows liability for physical harm to another resulting from emotional disturbance where that harm 'results from his shock or fright at harm or peril to a member of his immediate family occurring in his presence', to which is appended a caveat that the Institute expresses no opinion whether such liability 'may apply where bodily harm to the other results from his shock or fright at harm or peril to a third person who is not a member of his immediate family, or where the harm or peril does not occur in his presence'. On the caveat there is this comment (pp 460–461):

'Because of the absence of sufficient decisions, the Caveat leaves open the question of any possible liability . . . where the third person is not a member of the plaintiff's immediate family, or the harm or peril to the third person does not occur in the presence of the plaintiff. Thus no opinion is expressed as to whether the rule may apply where the plaintiff suffers shock at an injury to a mere stranger, or where he does not witness the injury to his child, but is informed about it afterward. Since the defendant has violated an original duty to the plaintiff, the argument may be advanced that the defendant should not be relieved of liability when that harm is brought about in the unusual way. However, where a stranger is involved, or where the plaintiff does not witness the harm or peril to a member of his family, there may be sufficient uncertainty as to the genuineness or seriousness of the emotional disturbance to justify, as a matter of administrative policy, a denial of liability.'

So far then all these courts have stopped short of this plaintiff and her claim and confined the duty of such defendants as these to exclude them from liability. They have never been asked to extend the confines to include liability to such as the plaintiff, but that very fact suggests that the boundary stands where the whole legal profession has assumed and acted on the assumption that it stands.

I think there is much to be said for the view of the majority of the Supreme Court of California in *Dillon v Legg* that it is a question of fact whether each particular plaintiff claiming to have suffered injury by shock from a defendant's negligence comes in or outside the proper confines and that it is for each judge and jury to extend the boundary when they think it sensible to do so. That would be in accordance with Lord Wright's opinion in *Bourhill's* case [1942] 2 All ER 396 at 406, [1943] AC 92 at 110 that the thing should stop not where lawyers have drawn a fixed line but 'where in the particular case the good sense of the jury, or of the judge, decides'. But it would not, in my judgment, be in accordance with the consensus of legal opinion to be collected from the authorities or with good sense and wise policy or ultimately reason and justice. It must be for the judge to rule the boundary line as a matter of law as definitely as he can, even if he leaves hard cases without a remedy. In concluding that the court must leave the bounds where policy has so far set them and rule the plaintiff out of the area of legal liability, I derive some comfort from reflecting that to encourage such claims as this would not only be oppressive to the careless in many activities and to their insurers, but would also do a grave disservice to many sufferers from nervous shock and mental injury, which may be exacerbated and prolonged or even made incurable by the anxieties of litigation. There may still be borderline cases, but I would leave it to Parliament, and not to judges or juries, to go beyond what Australian legislatures have done and extend the boundaries of liability further than they are now fairly well fixed.

It is not open to this court to shorten the boundaries and reduce the area of liability to that laid down in *Dulieu v White & Sons* [1901] 2 KB 669, [1900–3] All ER Rep 353, but counsel for the defendants reserves the right to ask higher authority to follow the opinion of Sargant LJ in *Hambrook v Stokes Brothers* [1925] 1 KB 141, [1924] All ER Rep 110 and reimpose that restriction.

I would dismiss the appeal.

GRIFFITHS LJ. On the afternoon of 19th October 1973 the plaintiff was in her home when a neighbour came to tell that her family had been involved in an appalling motor accident. One child had been killed and others badly injured. The neighbour rushed her to Addenbrooke's Hospital. There she found a most distressing scene. Her husband was injured and weeping, Kathleen was still covered in blood and dirt, the eldest son, only 17, who had been driving, was injured and hysterical, and Gillian, her youngest child, was dead.

The impact of these events caused the plaintiff to fall ill. We are to assume that it was more than grief: it was a recognisable psychiatric illness. The judge thought that the average man would not foresee that a mother exposed to such a catastrophic afternoon might suffer a shock that would cause a psychiatric illness. I am afraid that I cannot agree with him. I think that it is readily foreseeable that a significant number of mothers exposed to such an experience might break down under the shock of the event and suffer illness.

As the plaintiff's illness was a foreseeable consequence of being told of the injuries to her family and of seeing them in hospital it is submitted that the lorry drivers whose bad driving caused the accident are liable to compensate her for that illness. It is submitted

that liability for nervous shock depends on foreseeability of nervous shock and, as a
a foreseeable consequence of the bad driving was nervous shock to the mother on hearing
of the accident and seeing its consequences, it follows that the lorry drivers must pay her
damages. This result is said to flow from applying Lord Atkin's test of foreseeability in
Donoghue v Stevenson [1932] AC 562, [1932] All ER Rep 1 to determine the duty owed by
the lorry drivers to the plaintiff coupled with the test of foreseeability of the type of
damage suffered in *The Wagon Mound (No 1)* [1961] 1 All ER 404, [1961] AC 388.
b Counsel for the plaintiff submits that both tests are satisfied because it was foreseeable
that the mother would be affected by the bad driving as she would be told of the accident
and go to the hospital, and having regard to the gravity of the consequences it was
foreseeable that she would suffer nervous shock.

It is, I think, clear that if the judge had thought that it was foreseeable that the plaintiff
would have suffered nervous shock, a term which I use throughout as meaning a
c recognisable illness as opposed to grief or emotional upset, he would have accepted this
argument and found in her favour. If the argument is right it will certainly have far-
reaching consequences, for it will not only apply to road traffic accidents. Whenever
anybody is injured it is foreseeable that the relatives will be told and will visit them in
hospital, and it is further foreseeable that in cases of grave injury and death some of those
relatives are likely to have a severe reaction causing illness. Of course, the closer the
d relationship the more readily it is foreseeable that they may be so affected, but if we just
confine our consideration to parents and children and husbands and wives, it is clear that
the potential liability of the tortfeasor is vastly increased if he has to compensate the
relatives as well as the immediate victims of his carelessness. No case has been cited to us
in which our courts have given such a remedy. We have been shown many
Commonwealth decisions, but in none is it suggested that the common law provides
e such a remedy. But it is interesting to note that in Australia a number of the states and
territories have provided for such a remedy by statute, an indication to my mind that it
was not considered by Australian jurists to be available at common law.

The test of foreseeability is not a universal touchstone to determine the extent of
liability for the consequences of wrongdoing. There are many examples of situations in
which it is foreseeable that a careless act will cause damage or loss for which no remedy
f lies at common law. Let me give an example analogous to the present situation. Take
the case of the young wife whose husband is gravely injured by an accident at work and
rendered impotent and childless; it is surely foreseeable that she may suffer a psychiatric
illness as a result of strain imposed by the deprivation of his sexual and mental
companionship; but for this loss of consortium, as the law calls it, she has no cause of
action: see *Best v Samuel Fox & Co Ltd* [1952] 2 All ER 394, [1952] AC 716. In that case
g the husband was a steel erector who had been injured owing to the negligent operation
of an overhead travelling crane in the defendants' factory. The wife failed, not because
her illness was not foreseeable, but because the House of Lords held that the defendants
owed her no duty. Lord Morton said ([1952] 2 All ER 394 at 400, [1952] AC 716 at 734–
735):

> *'. . .* it has never been the law of England that an invitor, who has negligently but
h unintentionally injured an invitee, is liable to compensate other persons who have
suffered, in one way or another, as a result of the injury to the invitee. If the injured
man was engaged in a business, and the injury is a serious one, the business may
have to close down and the employees be dismissed. A daughter of the injured man
may have to give up work which she enjoys and stay at home to nurse a father who
has been transformed into an irritable invalid as a result of the injury. Such
j examples could easily be multiplied. Yet the invitor is under no liability to
compensate such persons, for he owes them no duty and may not even know of
their existence. There is thus no general principle of English law which would
entitle the appellant to succeed in the present case.'

But suppose in *Best v Samuel Fox & Co Ltd* the wife had suffered nervous shock as a
result of being told about her husband's injury, or later seeing his suffering, it cannot

surely be supposed she would have recovered damages for that illness as opposed to the illness caused by loss of consortium. She would fail because she was owed no duty by those who injured her husband.

Lord Goddard in his speech had this to say of road traffic accidents ([1952] 2 All ER 394 at 398, [1952] AC 716 at 731):

'But what duty was owed here by the employers of the husband to the wife? If she has an action in this case, so must the wife of any man run over in the street by a careless driver. The duty there which gives rise to the husband's cause of action arises out of what may for convenience be called proximity; the driver owes a duty not to injure other persons who are using the road on which he is driving. He owes no duty to persons not present except to those whose property may be on or adjoining the road which it is his duty to avoid injuring.'

In *King v Phillips* [1953] 1 All ER 617 at 623, [1953] 1 QB 429 at 441 Denning LJ expressed the duty of the driver as owed to everyone in the vicinity and in pointing out the limits of the duty he said:

'Some cases seem plain enough. A wife or mother who suffers shock on being told of an accident to a loved one cannot recover damages from the negligent party on that account.'

In considering liability for nervous shock it is not sufficient just to ask the question: was nervous shock a foreseeable consequence of the defendants carelessness? Foreseeability has to be considered at two stages in the inquiry. Firstly it is relevant to the existence of a duty of care, and at this stage of the inquiry the fact that nervous shock is foreseeable as a consequence of the defendant's action does not necessarily lead to the conclusion that the defendant owed a duty of care to the plaintiff. However, once it is decided that the defendant did owe a duty to the plaintiff and was in breach of it then the defendant's liability for nervous shock caused by that breach of duty will depend solely on whether nervous shock was a foreseeable consequence of the breach. It was of this second use of 'foreseeability' to test whether the type of damage suffered was recoverable that Viscount Simonds was speaking in *The Wagon Mound (No 1)* ([1961] 1 All ER 404 at 415, [1961] AC 388 at 426) when he said:

'As DENNING, L.J., said in *King* v. *Phillips* ([1953] 1 All ER 617 at 623, [1953] 1 QB 429 at 441) ". . . there can be no doubt since *Hay (or Bourhill)* v. *Young* that the test of *liability for shock* is foreseeability of *injury by shock.*" Their Lordships substitute the word "fire" for "shock" and indorse this statement of the law.' (Viscount Simonds's emphasis.)

Did the lorry drivers owe a duty of care to the plaintiff in her home two miles away from the scene of their bad driving? In my judgment they did not. It is a curious feature of the development of this branch of the law that almost all the reported decisions are concerned with accidents on the highway; perhaps it is because insurance made them worth pursuing. However that may be, although the decisions do show a gradual widening of the scope of the remedy, the common thread running through all the judgments is the concept of physical proximity to the accident, as a necessary ingredient to create the duty of care owed by the driver.

In *Dulieu v White* [1901] 2 KB 669, [1900–3] All ER Rep 353 a barmaid suffered shock causing her to give premature birth to a child as a result of the defendant's negligent driving of a pair-horse van into the public house. Kennedy J stated the duty thus ([1901] 2 KB 669 at 671–672, [1900–3] All ER Rep 353 at 355):

'The driver of a van and horses in a highway owes a duty to use reasonable and proper care and skill so as not to injure either persons lawfully using the highway, or property adjoining the highway, or persons who, like the plaintiff, are lawfully occupying that property.'

But he limited the remedy to those who suffered shock from the fear of immediate injury to their own persons.

In *Hambrook v Stokes Brothers* [1925] 1 KB 141, [1924] All ER Rep 110 the Court of
a Appeal extended the remedy to cover a mother on the highway who suffered shock
through fear of injury not to herself but to her child. The defendant negligently allowed
a lorry to run away downhill. It passed a mother who had just left her children round
a bend in the road. Seeing the lorry career past her and round the bend in the road, it was
alleged that she suffered shock through fear for her children's safety and this shock
caused her death. In the action by her husband for damages under the Fatal Accidents
b Act 1846 the judge left the jury to decide the question: was the death of the wife the
result of shock produced by fear of harm to herself? The Court of Appeal ordered a new
trial. Bankes LJ said ([1925] 1 KB 141 at 152, [1924] All ER Rep 110 at 114):

> '... the plaintiff would establish a cause of action if ... the death of his wife
> resulted from the shock occasioned by the running away of the lorry, that the shock
> resulted from what the plaintiff's wife either saw or realized by her own unaided
c > senses, and not from something which some one told her, and that the shock was
> due to reasonable fear of immediate personal injury either to herself or her children.'

Atkin LJ's judgment is of particular importance in view of the submission that the
application of his celebrated definition of a legal neighbour in his speech in *Donoghue v
Stevenson* [1932] AC 562, [1932] All ER Rep 1 leads to the conclusion that liability for
d nervous shock depends on foreseeability for nervous shock. He said ([1925] 1 KB 141 at
156, [1924] All ER Rep 110 at 115–116):

> 'It appears to me that if the plaintiff can prove that her injury was the direct result
> of a wrongful act or omission ... she can recover whether the wrong is a malicious
> and wilful act, is a negligent act, or is merely a failure to keep a dangerous thing in
e > control, as for instance a failure to keep a wild beast under control ... I agree that
> in the present case the plaintiff must show a breach of duty to her, but this she shows
> by the negligence of the defendants in the care of their lorry ... The duty of the
> owner of a motor car in a highway is not a duty to refrain from inflicting a
> particular kind of injury upon those who are in the highway. If so, he would be an
> insurer. It is a duty to use reasonable care to avoid injury to those using the
f > highway. It is thus a duty owed to all wayfarers, whether they be injured or not;
> though damage by reason of the breach is essential before a wayfarer can sue.'

He emphasised that the problem of whether the mother could recover from the shock
she suffered depended on the extent of the duty owed to her, and he concluded his
judgment by saying ([1925] 1 KB 141 at 159, [1924] All ER Rep 110 at 117):

g
> 'No doubt at the trial all the facts will be carefully investigated, including the
> possibility that the shock received by the mother was in no way caused by the sight
> or sound of the accident and apprehension of danger to the child or children, but
> solely to the report of the injury to the daughter, made to her by the third person.'

Sargant LJ, in a dissenting judgment, agreed with the test proposed by Kennedy J in
h Dulieu v White limiting recovery to cases of shock suffered as a result of fear of personal
injury to oneself. That is a test which counsel for the defendants reserves the right to
argue is correct before the House of Lords.
Had the present case come before Atkin LJ at the time he heard *Hambrook v Stokes
Brothers* the plaintiff would have failed because he would have held that as she was not on
or near the highway at the time of the accident the lorry drivers owed her no duty of
j care. Her injury was not the *direct* consequences of the lorry drivers' negligence: it was
a consequence of becoming aware of the results of their negligence. It is as well to
remind oneself of the answer Lord Atkin gave in *Donoghue v Stevenson* [1932] AC 562 at
580, [1932] All ER Rep 1 at 11 to the question, 'Who, then, in law is my neighbour?':

> 'The answer seems to be—persons who are so closely and directly affected by my
> act that I ought reasonably to have them in contemplation as being so affected when
> I am directing my mind to the acts or omissions which are called in question.'

If in a case subsequent to *Donoghue v Stevenson* the plaintiff had not been the consumer of the contents of the snail infested ginger beer bottle, who was clearly closely and directly affected by the presence of the snail, but her mother in another town who fell ill on being told of her daughter's experience, I venture to believe that Lord Atkin would have been surprised to learn that his dictum had been interpreted as creating a duty of care owed by the manufacturer to that mother. I believe he would have held as he did in *Hambrook v Stokes Brothers* that the mother was not so closely and directly affected by the negligence of the manufacturer as to create the necessary duty of care to found the tort of negligence.

In *Bourhill v Young* [1942] 2 All ER 396, [1943] AC 92 an Edinburgh fishwife standing behind a tram 45 feet away from a collision between a car and a motor cycle caused by the bad driving of the motor cyclist failed to recover for the nervous shock she claimed to have suffered as a result of hearing the collision and seeing its aftermath. All the members of the House of Lords were agreed that the motor cyclist owed no duty to her. As I read their speeches the concept of physical proximity to the bad driving is an essential element in founding the duty of care. Lord Thankerton limited the duty to 'the area of potential danger which would arise as a result of his negligence' and in the context in which that passage appears he is clearly referring to a physical area (see [1942] 2 All ER 396 at 399, [1943] AC 92 at 98). Lord Russell and Lord Macmillan approved the statement of the duty stated by Lord Jamieson (1941 SC 395 at 429):

> 'No doubt the duty of a driver is to use proper care not to cause injury to persons on the highway or in premises adjoining the highway, but it appears to me that his duty is limited to persons so placed that they may reasonably be expected to be injured by the omission to take such care.'

Lord Russell said ([1942] 2 All ER 396 at 402, [1943] AC 92 at 102):

> 'The pursuer was not in my opinion "so placed" or (to use the language of LORD MACKAY in this case) she has: ". . . totally failed to bring herself into any relationship to the cyclist which infers a duty of care in driving owed by him towards her."'

Lord Wright spoke of the duty being owed towards every person who came within the range of foreseeable danger, or within the ambit of the act. He said that the appellant 'was completely outside the range of the collision'. Lord Porter's speech is couched in wider terms, but it contains this passage speaking of the duty owed to persons in or near the street along which a car is negligently driven ([1942] 2 All ER 396 at 409, [1943] AC 92 at 117):

> 'If no one of them was in such a *position* that direct physical injury could reasonably be anticipated to them or their relations or friends, normally I think no duty would be owed . . .' (My emphasis.)

Bourhill v Young gives no support for the view that the plaintiff was owed a duty of care by these lorry drivers; on the contrary it is a powerful, if not conclusive, authority that she was not.

Since *Bourhill v Young* there have been four reported decisions on nervous shock resulting from a road accident; in three the plaintiff recovered, and in one she failed. In the three cases in which the plaintiff recovered he or she was either actually involved in the accident, as in *Schneider v Eisovitch* [1960] 1 All ER 169, [1960] 2 QB 430, or very close to it, as in *Boardman v Sanderson* [1964] 1 WLR 1317, where the father recovered for the shock of injury to his child which occurred in a yard outside the office into which the driver of the car knew that the father had gone, and in *Hinz v Berry* [1970] 1 All ER 1074, [1970] 2 QB 40, where a mother picking bluebells beside the road recovered damages for the shock of hearing and seeing the immediate result of an accident in which her husband was killed and her children injured when a motor car ran them down as they made tea beside the family dormobile on the other side of the road. But in *King v Phillips* [1953] 1 All ER 617, [1953] 1 KB 429 a mother in her house 70 yards from the accident failed to recover even though she heard her child scream as a taxi backed over his tricycle. The judge said the line had to be drawn somewhere and that the mother was owed no duty by the taxi driver, and the Court of Appeal upheld him.

We were also referred to a case arising out of the Lewisham train disaster, *Chadwick v British Transport Commission* [1967] 2 All ER 945, [1967] 1 WLR 912. Mr Chadwick went to help in the rescue of the victims trapped in the wrecked train. He worked all night and as a result of his experiences developed a psychiatric illness. It was held that as the defendants' negligence had caused the disaster they owed a duty to those who went to the rescue of the victims. Rescuers are drawn by the wrongdoer's negligence to the scene of his wrongful acts and it is foreseeable that they may there suffer injury from the physical situation that has been created. Mr Chadwick might have been injured by a wrecked carriage collapsing on him as he worked among the injured. A duty of care is owed to a rescuer in such circumstances but I am quite unable to include in the category of rescuers to whom a duty is owed a relative visiting victims in hospital, as counsel for the plaintiff invited us to do.

Every system of law must set some bounds to the consequences for which a wrongdoer must make reparation. If the burden is too great it cannot and will not be met, the law will fall into disrepute, and it will be a disservice to those victims who might reasonably have expected compensation. In any state of society it is ultimately a question of policy to decide the limits of liability. As the tort of negligence has developed over the last century the judges have felt their way forward towards acceptable frontiers within which to confine the liability. They strive to be fair to the victims but also not to impose a crushing burden on those who perhaps through a moment's inattention have set in train a disastrous sequence of events. Sometimes the judges go too far, as in *Re Polemis* [1921] 3 KB 650, [1921] All ER Rep 40, when they held that a man should be held liable for all the direct consequences of his negligence no matter how unforeseen or unforeseeable they might be. It was soon demonstrated that this was too harsh and unreasonable a rule and it was abandoned in favour of the rule that he should only be held liable for damage that he could foresee as a likely consequence of his action: see *The Wagon Mound (No 1)*. But even some forms of foreseeable damage will place a burden on the wrongdoer so great that it is out of all proportion to his moral responsibility and which there is no prospect of his being able to meet. The workman digging a hole in the road who accidentally but carelessly hits an electric cable causing a power cut can foresee that many factories may lose production and profit as a result of the failure of the electricity supply, but the result is so disproportionate to the act and the chance of such huge damages being met so remote, the law, as a matter of policy, gives no remedy to the factory owners for such pure economic loss; the judges say it is too remote, or as a matter of policy it should not be recoverable: see *Spartan Steel & Alloys Ltd v Martin & Co (Contractors) Ltd* [1972] 3 All ER 557, [1973] QB 27.

The development of the concept of the duty of care in negligence is one means by which the common law seeks to hold a reasonable balance in society between the wrongdoer and those who suffer as a consequence of his wrongdoing. Although the common law is continually developing and adapting to meet the changing pattern of the society it serves, there must be some degree of certainty about the remedies it gives, for otherwise no lawyer will be able to advise his client and no one will know where he stands. Where the decided cases show the emergence and establishment of well-recognised bounds to the duty of care owed in a given situation, such as by those who drive negligently, a judge should not, in my view, lightly depart from those bounds. He should not be tempted to do so unless he perceives some compelling reason why the policy of the law should change. He should remember that hard cases often make bad law.

I regard the decided cases as establishing that the duty of care of the driver of a motor vehicle on the road is limited to persons and owners of the property on the road or near to it who may be directly affected by the bad driving. It is not owed to those who are nowhere near the scene. It may be said that it is illogical that a mother who sees her children injured at the scene of the accident can recover for the shock but not the mother who sees them injured when she is called to hospital. There are two answers: firstly, the line has to be drawn somewhere, and, secondly, that in drawing the line it was no doubt realised that it is inherently more likely that those present at the accident will suffer *a* shock than those who have time to prepare themselves.

I am not persuaded that there are sound reasons why the law should strive to extend the scope of the duty.

There is no legal remedy for the emotional distress and grief suffered as a result of the injury or death of a relative or friend, but these can be painful experiences. We speak of people being grief stricken, and time being the only healer. Would it really be wise to *b* introduce into this common experience of mankind the possibility of some monetary solatium for their suffering if they are able to persuade a judge that the suffering is due in part to shock, not grief. It will obviously be a very difficult question to determine and I venture to question how much good it will in most cases do for the sufferer. A modest sum of money may be recovered but I suspect the recovery of health may be seriously delayed by the litigation. Both at the Bar and on the Bench I have listened to doctors and *c* particularly psychiatrists saying in cases of psychiatric illness that no further recovery is to be expected until the litigation is finished. I have often heard medical opinion suggest that litigation prolongs symptoms of psychiatric illness, making it more deepseated and difficult to treat. May we not by giving the remedy aggravate the illness? Surely health is better than money. The doubts I have about the wisdom of so radical an extension of the remedy for nervous shock, as the plaintiff's argument proposes, convince me that if *d* it is to be done it would be better allowed by statute than by a leap forward by the common law. There should be an opportunity for public debate to count the costs, and in particular to inquire of the medical profession whether such a remedy will in their opinion be in the best interests of the patients. If it is at the end of the day thought desirable by society to extend the remedy it can be done by a simple statute on the lines of those in force in Australia. *e*

I, too, would dismiss this appeal.

Appeal dismissed. Leave to appeal to the House of Lords granted.

Solicitors: *Vinters*, Cambridge (for the plaintiff); *Hextall, Erskine & Co*, Horsham (for the defendants).

Patricia Hargrove   Barrister.

Practice Direction

SUPREME COURT TAXING OFFICE

Costs – Taxation – Value added tax – Solicitor acting on his own behalf – Matter arising out of *g* *solicitor's practice – No supply of services – Value added tax not chargeable – Value added tax not to be claimed or allowed on taxation.*

1. A problem has recently arisen on the Practice Direction issued on 9th March 1973 ([1973] 1 All ER 974, [1973] 1 WLR 438) as varied by the Practice Direction issued on 28th January 1974 ([1974] 1 All ER 848, [1974] 1 WLR 217) which dealt generally with *h* the incidence of value added tax ('VAT') on the taxation of costs.

2. Where a solicitor acts in litigation on his own behalf in a matter arising out of his practice he is not treated for the purposes of VAT as having supplied services and therefore no VAT is chargeable on the bill of that solicitor.

3. Consequently where such a bill is presented for agreement or taxation VAT should not be claimed and should not be allowed on taxation. *j*

4. This Direction is made with the agreement of the Senior Registrar of the Family Division and the Admiralty Registrar, and is issued with the concurrence of the Lord Chancellor.

E J T MATTHEWS
Chief Taxing Master.

19th February 1981

Neilson v Laugharne

COURT OF APPEAL, CIVIL DIVISION

LORD DENNING MR, OLIVER AND O'CONNOR LJJ

11th, 12th, 13th NOVEMBER, 17th DECEMBER 1980

Discovery – Privilege – Production contrary to public interest – Class of documents – Statements taken by police in statutory investigation into complaints by member of public – No assurance of confidentiality given to makers of statements – Statements usable in disciplinary or criminal proceedings – Complainant bringing civil action against police – Whether plaintiff entitled to discovery of statements taken by police in investigation – Whether statements protected as a class by public interest privilege – Whether sufficient confidentiality attaching to documents to attract public interest privilege – Whether disclosure of statements in civil litigation likely to impede statutory purpose of police investigations – Police Act 1964, s 49.

Discovery – Legal professional privilege – Dominant purpose for which documents coming into existence – Statutory police investigation into complaints by plaintiff – Statements taken by police in statutory investigation – Investigation caused by plaintiff's letter to police before action – Whether statements taken by police in investigation protected from disclosure in plaintiff's subsequent action against police – Whether dominant purpose for taking statements statutory investigation or to obtain legal advice and provide evidence for plaintiff's threatened action – Police Act 1964, s 49.

Pursuant to a search warrant, the police searched the plaintiff's house for drugs while he was away. When the plaintiff got home he contacted the police, alleging that his house had been burgled. He was asked to come to the police station for questioning where he was held for five hours, although no charge was brought against him. The plaintiff consulted his solicitors, who on 7th August 1978 wrote a letter before action to the chief constable stating that they had been instructed by the plaintiff to bring proceedings for damages for trespass, damage to property, false arrest, wrongful imprisonment and assault. The chief constable, pursuant to the procedure laid down in s 49[a] of the Police Act 1964 for the investigation of a complaint by a member of the public against the police, decided to hold an investigation into the plaintiff's complaints. During the investigation the police took statements from several persons, including the plaintiff. Under the statutory procedure no assurance of confidentiality was given to the makers of the statements. The report of the investigation was considered by the Director of Public Prosecutions, as required by s 49, and the Police Complaints Board who respectively decided that there were no grounds for criminal or disciplinary proceedings against any police officer. The plaintiff nevertheless began civil proceedings in the county court against the chief constable claiming damages for trespass, negligence, false imprisonment and assault, and sought for the purpose of the action discovery of the statements taken in the investigation. The chief constable claimed that the statements were of a class protected from production to the plaintiff (i) by virtue of legal professional privilege and (ii) because their disclosure would be injurious to the public interest. Affidavits in support of the chief constable's objection asserted that the statements were confidential and that their confidentiality should be maintained to ensure full and frank co-operation by police officers in a s 49 investigation, and that the dominant purpose of the investigation was to obtain evidence for use in the plaintiff's threatened action. The county court judge, reversing the registrar, held that the statements were protected from disclosure by legal professional privilege but expressed doubt whether they were protected by public interest privilege. The plaintiff appealed. At the hearing of the appeal the chief constable contended (i) that the statements were entitled to legal professional privilege because the complaint which led to the investigation was in the

---

[a] Section 49, so far as material, is set out at p 832 *j, post*

form of a letter before action and therefore the investigation served the dual purpose of carrying out the statutory procedure under s 49 and providing evidence for use in the threatened litigation, and (ii) that the statements were also entitled to 'class' privilege on the ground of public interest. The plaintiff contended, inter alia, that they were not entitled to 'class' privilege on the ground of public interest because their use in disciplinary and criminal proceedings envisaged by the statutory procedure prevented a general claim of confidentiality being made, and that the most that could be claimed was 'contents' privilege, ie that particular statements could be withheld from production on the ground that they contained information which it was not in the public interest to disclose.

Held – (1) The statements were not protected from disclosure by legal professional privilege because the dominant purpose of the police in taking the statements was to carry out the statutory duty under s 49 of the 1964 Act to investigate the plaintiff's complaints and not to obtain legal advice in regard to his threatened action or for use in that action (see p 833 *j* to p 834 *a*, p 836 *j*, p 837 *b* to *g* and p 842 *c* to *e*, post); *Waugh v British Railways Board* [1979] 2 All ER 1169 applied.

(2) Statements taken in a s 49 investigation were, however, entitled to protection from disclosure as a class on the ground of public interest privilege for the following reasons—

(a) (per Lord Denning MR and O'Connor LJ) although the confidentiality attaching to the statements was not absolute, since no assurance of confidentiality was given and they could be used in certain proceedings, nevertheless sufficient confidentiality attached to them to make that one of the factors to be taken into account by the court, together with the need for candour by, and co-operation from, police officers in a s 49 investigation, in balancing the competing public interests for and against disclosure (see p 834 *a b*, p 835 *f g* and p 842 *f g*, post);

(b) (per Oliver and O'Connor LJJ) the test whether public interest privilege protected from disclosure statements taken in a s 49 investigation was not whether the statements were absolutely confidential but whether the likely consequence of a general right to their disclosure in civil litigation, in the context of the statutory purpose of s 49 that there should be full investigation of complaints against the police, would be to impede the carrying out of the statutory purpose of an investigation under s 49 so that disclosure would be contrary to the public interest (see p 838 *a* to *c* and *e* to *g*, p 839 *a* to *d j*, p 840 *a* to *d* and p 842 *f g*, post).

(3) Since the statements were of a confidential nature, their disclosure in civil litigation would be likely to impede the statutory purpose of s 49 by inhibiting police officers from giving full and frank co-operation in an investigation; and, if the statements were merely entitled to 'contents' privilege, that would impose an unduly heavy burden on police authorities and would impede the statutory procedure. It followed, therefore, that the public interest in protecting the statements as a class from disclosure in civil litigation outweighed the public interest in disclosing them in such litigation and the appeal would accordingly be dismissed (see p 836 *a b g h*, p 840 *f g* and p 842 *h* to p 843 *a*, post); dicta of Lord Reid and Lord Salmon in *Rogers v Secretary of State for the Home Office* [1972] 2 All ER at 1061, 1071, of Lord Cross in *Alfred Crompton Amusement Machines Ltd v Customs and Excise Comrs (No 2)* [1973] 2 All ER at 1184, of Lord Edmund-Davies in *D v National Society for the Prevention of Cruelty to Children* [1977] 1 All ER at 618 and *Gaskin v Liverpool City Council* [1980] 1 WLR 1549 applied.

Per Lord Denning MR. In cases where 'class' privilege is claimed the courts themselves should very rarely inspect the documents (see p 836 *f*, post).

Notes

For withholding documents from production on the ground that disclosure would be injurious to the public interest, see 13 Halsbury's Laws (4th Edn) paras 86–91, and for cases on the subject, see 18 Digest (Reissue) 154–160, 1265–1301.

For legal professional privilege, see 13 Halsbury's Laws (4th Edn) paras 71–73, and for
cases on the subject, see 18 Digest (Reissue) 99–102, 741–757.
For the Police Act 1964, s 49, see 25 Halsbury's Statutes (3rd Edn) 363.

Cases referred to in judgments

Burmah Oil Co Ltd v Bank of England (Attorney General intervening) [1979] 3 All ER 700,
[1980] AC 1090, [1979] 3 WLR 722, HL, Digest (Cont Vol E) 184, 1277a.
Conway v Rimmer [1967] 2 All ER 1260, [1967] 1 WLR 1031, CA; rvsd [1968] 1 All ER
874, [1968] AC 910, [1968] 2 WLR 998, HL, 18 Digest (Reissue) 155, 1273.
Crompton (Alfred) Amusement Machines Ltd v Customs and Excise Comrs (No 2) [1973] 2 All
ER 1169, [1974] AC 405, [1973] 3 WLR 268, HL, 18 Digest (Reissue) 102, 756.
D v National Society for the Prevention of Cruelty to Children [1977] 1 All ER 589, [1978] AC
171, [1977] 2 WLR, HL; rvsg [1976] 2 All ER 993, [1978] AC 171, [1976] 3 WLR 124,
CA, Digest (Cont Vol E) 185, 1301b.
Duncan v Cammell Laird & Co Ltd [1942] 1 All ER 587, [1942] AC 624, 111 LJKB 406, 166
LT 366, HL, 18 Digest (Reissue) 155, 1272.
Gaskin v Liverpool City Council [1980] 1 WLR 1549, CA.
Grosvenor Hotel, London, Re, (No 2) [1964] 3 All ER 354, [1965] Ch 1210, [1964] 3 WLR
992, CA, 18 Digest (Reissue) 157, 1279.
Rogers v Secretary of State for the Home Department, Gaming Board for Great Britain v Rogers
[1972] 2 All ER 1057, [1973] AC 388, [1972] 3 WLR 279, 136 JP 574, HL, Digest (Cont
Vol D) 267, 2835c.
Science Research Council v Nassé, BL Cars Ltd (formerly Leyland Cars) v Vyas [1979] 3 All ER
673, [1980] AC 1028, [1979] 3 WLR 762, [1979] ICR 921, HL; affg [1978] 3 All ER
1196, [1979] QB 144, [1978] 3 WLR 754, [1978] ICR 1124, CA, Digest (Cont Vol E)
186, 1301c.
Waugh v British Railways Board [1979] 2 All ER 1169, [1980] AC 521, [1979] 3 WLR 150,
[1979] IRLR 364, HL, Digest (Cont Vol E) 183, 943 (1).

Cases also cited

Lannon v Oxford (11th February 1980, unreported) Liverpool County Court.
Lonrho Ltd v Shell Petroleum Co Ltd [1980] 1 WLR 627, HL; affg [1980] QB 358, [1980] 2
WLR 367, CA.
R v Cheltenham Justices, ex parte Secretary of State for Trade [1977] 1 All ER 460, [1977] 1
WLR 95, DC.

Interlocutory appeal

The plaintiff, George Richard Neilson, appealed against the judgment of his Honour
Judge Sellers given in the Preston County Court on 6th June 1980 in favour of the
defendant, Albert Laugharne, the Chief Constable of Lancashire, setting aside the order
of Mr Registrar Proctor dated 8th May 1980 which required the chief constable to
disclose the documents itemised in part 3 of the first schedule to his revised list of
documents, being statements made for the purpose of an inquiry pursuant to s 49 of the
Police Act 1964 and the report of the investigating officer, Detective Superintendent
Rimmer, made pursuant to s 49. The grounds of the appeal were (1) that the documents
were statements prepared pursuant to an inquiry under s 49 of the 1964 Act, (2) that
having regard to the totality of the evidence the judge was wrong in law in holding that
the dominant purpose for the preparation of the statements was litigation and wrong in
holding that the statements were privileged from discovery by reason of having been
prepared for the purposes of litigation and (3) that the judge was wrong in law and
exercised wrong principles in refusing to order discovery of the documents. The chief
constable served a respondent's notice that, while seeking to uphold the order dated 6th
June 1980 on the grounds on which that order was made, he would contend on the
appeal that the order should be affirmed on the additional grounds (1) that the documents
for which discovery was sought were made in confidence and (2) that disclosure of them

would be injurious to the public interest. The facts are set out in the judgment of Lord
Denning MR.

E Somerset Jones QC and *Anthony H Edwards* for the plaintiff.
Richard Clegg QC, John J Rowe and *Peter Susman* for the chief constable.

Cur adv vult

17th December. The following judgments were read.

LORD DENNING MR. George Neilson has brought an action against the police. He
wants to see some of their papers. Can he do so? In July 1978 George Neilson was living
at 131 Burleywood, Skelmersdale, Lancashire. He went away for a few days. While he
was gone, the police on 5th July 1978 went to magistrates and got a search warrant under
s 23 of the Misuse of Drugs Act 1971. No doubt the police had reasonable grounds for
suspecting that controlled drugs were on the premises. In pursuance of the warrant, two
detectives, one a man, the other a woman, got into the house. They opened a sliding
window panel and climbed in. They searched for drugs, but found none. They did
notice, however, that the electricity meter had been tampered with. The lead seals were
missing. They thought that someone might have been dishonestly abstracting electricity
without paying for it, contrary to s 13 of the Theft Act 1968.

On 9th July 1978 George Neilson returned home. He saw that someone had been
in. Soon afterwards two detectives called to see him. He was ready with a complaint.
He told them that, whilst he had been away, his house had been burgled and that several
articles had been stolen, including one valued at £150. The detectives asked him to
come to the police station. He went with them. There he was asked questions about the
missing articles; also about drugs and electricity. He was there for five or six hours.
During the interview he said he had to take tablets for his heart and wanted them.
Someone went and got them for him. He complained that they were too slow about
it. Eventually he made a written statement. He withdrew the allegation that his house
had been burgled or anything stolen. He went home. No charge was brought against
him. Presumably the police had not enough evidence to warrant it.

Most men in George Neilson's position would have considered themselves lucky to
have got away with it so easily. But not so George Neilson. He turned round on the
police and made all sorts of allegations against them. He went to solicitors and got legal
aid. His solicitors wrote to the chief constable a letter dated 7th August 1978, a letter
before action:

'We are instructed to bring proceedings against you for damages for trespass,
damage to our Client's property and belongings, false arrest, wrongful imprisonment
and assault. Unless we have heard from you within the course of the next 7 days
that you are prepared to compensate our Client adequately, we are instructed to
bring proceedings against you without further warning.'

Stopping there for a moment, if the chief constable had taken the ordinary course in
litigation, if he had interviewed the witnesses and taken statements from them, all the
statements would have been covered by legal professional privilege. They would be
prepared for the dominant purpose of litigation (see *Waugh v British Railways Board*
[1979] 2 All ER 1169, [1980] AC 521).

1 *The police investigation*
But the chief constable did not take that course. Instead he regarded himself as bound
to cause an investigation to be held within the police force. This was done by reason of
s 49 of the Police Act 1964 which says:

'(1) Where the chief officer of police for any police area receives a complaint from
a member of the public against a member of the police force for that area he shall
. . . forthwith record the complaint and cause [the complaint] to be investigated.

'(3) On receiving the report of an investigation under this section the chief
officer of police, unless satisfied from the report that no criminal offence has been
committed, shall send the report to the Director of Public Prosecutions.'

The object of that statute was to ensure that if a policeman had done anything wrong,
the appropriate proceedings should be taken against him. Either criminal proceedings,
if it were a criminal offence by the policeman, or disciplinary proceedings, if it were a
disciplinary offence. Or no proceedings if there was no offence.

In pursuance of his duty under s 49, the chief constable wrote on 5th September 1978
to George Neilson's solicitors:

'I have decided to call for an investigation under the provisions of Section 49 of
the Police Act 1964, and to this end have appointed Detective Superintendent
Rimmer to act as Investigating Officer in this matter. Mr. Rimmer will be
contacting you and your Client in due course. The question of compensation will
be considered at the conclusion of the investigation.'

The investigation was held. The police took statements from several persons. We are
not told who they were, but it is easy to surmise. I expect they took a statement from the
informer who suggested that there were dangerous drugs to be found in the house; from
the two detectives who executed the search warrant; from the electricity people; and
from George Neilson himself. These statements were taken between 13th December
1978 and 7th March 1979. Then on 12th March 1979 Det Supt Rimmer made his
report. This was sent to the Director of Public Prosecutions. He decided that the
evidence did not justify the institution of criminal proceedings against any police
officer. The report was then sent to the Police Complaints Board. This was in accordance
with s 2 of the Police Act 1976. The complaints board decided that there was no reason
why disciplinary charges should be brought against any police officer. These decisions
were communicated to George Neilson and his solicitors. Put into plain language, there
was no ground for either criminal or disciplinary proceedings against the police.

2 *The civil action*

Nevertheless, George Neilson's solicitors decided to bring a civil action for damages
against the police. They got a civil aid certificate and issued a plaint in the county court
against the chief constable. They delivered particulars of claim for damages not
exceeding £2,000. Lists of documents were ordered. The chief constable inserted this
item:

'Statements (excepting that of plaintiff) made for purpose of enquiry pursuant to
Section 49 of the Police Act 1964 from 13th December 1978 to 7th March 1979.'

The chief constable objected to produce these statements on the grounds: '(i) that to do
so would be injurious to the public interest; and (ii) that they are subject to legal
professional privilege.' These objections were supported by two affidavits. One by a
common law clerk who asserted that the dominant purpose of the inquiry by Det Supt
Rimmer was to obtain evidence for the defence of the action. The other was by the
deputy chief constable that the statements were confidential, and that their confidentiality
should be maintained so as to ensure the co-operation of those concerned.

The registrar of the county court ordered production of the statements. He held there
was no legal professional privilege. The claim for public interest privilege was not
pressed before him. The judge upheld the claim for legal professional privilege; but was
very doubtful whether there was any public interest privilege.

3 *Legal professional privilege*

Since the decision in *Waugh v British Railways Board* [1979] 2 All ER 1169, [1980] AC
521, we have to look for the dominant purpose of the police in taking the statements.
On this point I am not prepared to accept the affidavit of the common law clerk. To my
mind it is clear that there were two purposes. One was to carry out the statutory duty to
investigate required by s 49 of the Police Act 1964. The other was to be able, in due

course, to deal with the letter before action. Of these two, the dominant purpose was to
carry out the duty under s 49. *After* that was done, then, and *then only*, was the question *a*
of compensation to be considered. Seeing that litigation was not the dominant purpose,
there is no legal professional privilege available here.

4 The intended use of the statements

No one could suggest that these statements were so confidential that they could never
be used in any legal proceedings. It was clearly contemplated that they might be used by *b*
the police in these ways.

If one or both of the detectives was charged with a criminal offence, the statements
could be used just as any other statements taken by the police are used in a prosecution.
There would be no 'class' privilege in respect of them; although there might be a
'contents' privilege, as, for instance, to keep secret the name of an informer.

Likewise, if one or both of the detectives was charged with a disciplinary offence, the *c*
statements could be used. The complainant would be present and would hear all that
was said by the witnesses. There would be no 'class' privilege, but there would be a
'contents' privilege in respect of any information 'which, in the public interest, ought not
to be disclosed to a member of the public': see reg 20(2)(*b*) of the Police (Discipline)
Regulations 1977, SI 1977 No 580.

Some reference was made to s 9 of the Police Act 1976, but that is of no relevance. It *d*
is only concerned with the staff of the Police Complaints Board. At any rate, seeing that
confidentiality was not absolute, the question is whether it was sufficient to entitle the
police to withhold production in civil proceedings.

5 Public interest privilege

There have been many cases lately on public interest privilege. They fall into two *e*
distinct categories.

(i) The old 'Crown privilege'

Until the year 1973 we spoke only of 'Crown privilege'. It was held that a government
department could intervene in a suit between two litigants and claim, *on the ground of
public interest*, that documents in the hands of one of the litigants should not be *f*
produced. The objection had to be taken by the minister himself or by the head of the
department, or some highly placed official in an affidavit giving his reasons. His affidavit
was, as a rule, conclusive. It was often said that the privilege could not be waived by the
Crown, even though it would be to its advantage to do so. And that the judge might take
the objection himself. The leading cases are *Duncan v Cammell Laird & Co Ltd* [1942] 1
All ER 587, [1942] AC 624; *Re Grosvenor Hotel, London* [1964] 3 All ER 354 at 358–363, *g*
[1965] Ch 1210 at 1241–1247; *Conway v Rimmer* [1967] 2 All ER 1260, [1967] 1 WLR
1031; on appeal [1968] 1 All ER 874, [1968] AC 910; *Rogers v Secretary of State for the
Home Department* [1972] 2 All ER 1057 at 1065–1066, [1973] AC 388 at 406 per Lord
Pearson; *Burmah Oil Co Ltd v Bank of England* [1979] 3 All ER 700, [1980] AC 1090. I do
not think that that kind of 'public interest' privilege applies here. There is no affidavit
by the Home Secretary as there was in *Conway v Rimmer* and *Rogers v Secretary of State for* *h*
the Home Department. There is here only an affidavit by the deputy chief constable. I
should not regard him as 'highly placed' for the purpose.

(ii) The modern 'public interest'

Since 1978 there has been rapidly developed another 'public interest' privilege. This
is a privilege which is asserted, not by a government department, but by one of the *j*
litigants himself. It need not be supported by any affidavit of any minister or highly
placed official. And it can be waived. I remember well that in *D v National Society for the
Prevention of Cruelty to Children* [1976] 2 All ER 993, [1978] AC 171, it was strongly
argued by counsel for the plaintiff in that case that there was no such public interest
privilege apart from the traditional 'Crown privilege', and his argument was accepted by
Scarman LJ; see [1976] 2 All ER 993 at 1003–1005, [1978] AC 171 at 195–197. But it did

not prevail. We extended it to protect the name of the person who informed the
a National Society for the Prevention of Cruelty to Children. It was in the public interest
that it should not be disclosed. The seed of this modern public interest was sown by Lord
Cross in *Alfred Crompton Amusement Machines Ltd v Customs and Excise Comrs (No 2)* [1973]
2 All ER 1169 at 1184, [1974] AC 405 at 433, when he said on behalf of himself and all
the other Law Lords in that case:

b   ' "Confidentiality" is not a separate head of privilege, but it may be a very material
consideration to bear in mind when privilege is claimed *on the ground of public
interest*. What the court has to do is to weigh on the one hand the considerations
which suggest that it is *in the public interest* that the documents in question should be
disclosed and on the other hand those which suggest that it is in the public interest
that they should not be disclosed and to balance one against the other.' (My
emphasis.)

c   That seed was sown in the old field of 'Crown privilege', but it fell also on the new field
with which the Crown was not concerned. It bore fruit in the pair of cases *Science
Research Council v Nassé* and *Leyland Cars v Vyas* in this court ([1978] 3 All ER 1196,
[1979] QB 144) and in the House of Lords ([1979] 3 All ER 673, [1980] AC 1028). The
decision was ostensibly based on the rule that the court has a general discretion to order
d discovery, coupled with the qualification that 'discovery shall not be ordered if and in so
far as the court is of opinion that it is not necessary either for fairly disposing of the
proceedings or for saving costs'. In applying that rule, this court, as I believe, and most
of the members of the House of Lords, had regard to the public interests involved. We
applied the words of Lord Edmund-Davies in *D v National Society for the Prevention of
Cruelty to Children* [1977] 1 All ER 589 at 618, [1978] AC 171 at 245:

e   '. . . where a confidential relationship exists . . . *and* . . . disclosure would be in
breach of some ethical or social value involving the public interest, the court has a
discretion to uphold a refusal to disclose relevant evidence provided it considers
that, *on balance, the public interest* would be better served by excluding such
evidence.' (My emphasis.)

f   Very recently we applied this principle in *Gaskin v Liverpool City Council* [1980] 1 WLR
1549. We held that a local authority was not bound to disclose the case notes and records
relating to a child in care. We drew a parallel between child care privilege and legal
professional privilege.
    This modern development shows that, on a question of discovery, the court can
consider the competing public interests involved. The case is decided by the court
g holding the balance between the two sides. One of them is asserting that, in the interest
of justice, the documents should be disclosed. The other is asserting that, in the public
interest, they should not be disclosed. Confidentiality is often to be considered. So is the
need for candour and frankness. So is the desirability of co-operation. Or any other
factors which present themselves. On weighing them all the judge decides according to
which side the balance comes down. Once it is decided that the public interest is in
h favour of non-disclosure, the decision is regarded as a precedent for later situations of the
same kind. So the body of law is built up. As Lord Hailsham said in *D v National Society
for the Prevention of Cruelty to Children* [1977] 1 All ER 589 at 605, [1978] AC 171 at 230:
'The categories of public interest are not closed, and must alter from time to time
whether by restriction or extension as social conditions and social legislation develop.'

j *6 Holding the balance*
    On the one hand we have a man who is suing the police for damages. He has got legal
aid and demands to see all the statements taken by the police. He, or rather his solicitors,
want to see the police statements so as to find out something, if they can, to back him
up. On the other hand there are the police who, for aught that appears, apart from the
plaintiff's complaint, have acted perfectly properly. Statements were taken on the basis
that they were to be used for a private investigation, to see if the police had acted

improperly in any way; and, if they had acted improperly, to be used in criminal or disciplinary proceedings against the police. No improper conduct by the police was *a* disclosed at all.

Yet now the plaintiff wants to see the statements for another purpose altogether: to help him make out a case for damages. I cannot think it can be right to let him do this. Some of the statements may contain the names of informers which should be kept secret anyway. I cannot think it incumbent on the police, or the court, to go through all these statements, or to consider the contents of them, so as to assert a 'contents' privilege. *b* It is in the public interest that the whole 'class' should be privileged from disclosure to the plaintiff.

If the plaintiff has any case at all, he must make it out on his own showing, supported by witnesses whom he can find himself. He should not be allowed to delve through these statements so as to make out a case, which he would not otherwise have.

c

Inspection of documents

It is not necessary for us to inspect the documents ourselves. Nor is it desirable. The plaintiff might well feel a grievance if the court decided against him on its own view of the documents, without his seeing them. As Viscount Simon LC said in *Duncan v Cammell Laird & Co Ltd* [1942] 1 All ER 587 at 594, [1942] AC 624 at 640–641:

> '. . . it is a first principle of justice that the judge should have no dealings on the *d* matter in hand with one litigant save in the presence of and to the equal knowledge of the other.'

And as Megaw LJ said in *Gaskin v Liverpool City Council* [1980] 1 WLR 1549 at 1555:

> '. . . inspection . . . should not be undertaken lightly or ill-advisedly. It may put *e* upon the court a burden which it is extremely difficult, perhaps in some circumstances impossible, to discharge fairly and satisfactorily.'

I have a feeling that the Burmah shareholders might have felt it unfair that the House of Lords should have looked at the documents themselves and said: 'They are relevant but we don't think they help much one way or the other': see *Burmah Oil Co Ltd v Bank of England* [1979] 3 All ER 700 at 716, 722, 727, [1980] AC 1090 at 1122, 1130, 1136. In *f* all 'class' cases, I think the court should very rarely inspect the documents themselves. Ex hypothesi there may be nothing in their contents to object to. At any rate, in this case, I do not think it would be proper to inspect the documents.

Conclusion

In my opinion the statements taken in pursuance of s 49 are privileged from *g* production in a way analogous to legal professional privilege, and child care privilege. This case bears a striking resemblance to *Gaskin*'s case. It looks like a 'fishing expedition'. Legal aid is being used by complaining persons to harass innocent folk who have only been doing their duty. The complainants make all sorts of allegations, often quite unjustified, and then use legal machinery to try to manufacture a case. We should come down firmly against such tactics. We should refuse to order production. *h*

OLIVER LJ. This appeal raises two questions.

First, are the statements taken in the instant case in the course of an inquiry instituted pursuant to s 49 of the Police Act 1964 protected from inspection on discovery in civil proceedings by legal professional privilege?

Second, and if they are not, are they protected from inspection on the grounds of *j* public policy?

The county court judge, reversing the order of the district registrar, held them to be protected on the ground of legal professional privilege, but speaking for myself I am quite clear that his judgment cannot be supported on this ground. The section lays down a mandatory procedure which is to be followed when a complaint is received regarding the conduct of a police officer. It requires the complaint to be investigated and a report *a*   made, but there is nothing whatever in the section to suggest that the statements are to be taken or the report prepared for the purpose of obtaining legal advice. The absence of this essential element is sought to be supplied in the instant case by reliance on the fact that the complaint which triggered off the inquiry took the form of what was clearly intended to be a letter before action. And thus, it is said, the inquiries which followed served a dual purpose. They carried out the statutory purpose of complying with the provisions of the section to which I have referred; but they also served the purpose of *b*   providing witnesses' statements for the proposed defendant's solicitors. The test is not in dispute. It is to be found in the decision of the House of Lords in *Waugh v British Railways Board* [1979] 2 All ER 1169, [1980] AC 521, and it is whether the dominant purpose for which the document in question came into existence was for obtaining advice or for use in the threatened litigation. Despite the persuasive submissions of counsel for the chief constable, I am quite clearly of the view that that test cannot be *c*   satisfied on the facts of the instant case and this is, in my judgment, demonstrated by the letter of 5th September 1978 which was addressed to the plaintiff personally and is contained in the papers before the court. This informs the plaintiff that it has been decided to call for an investigation under the section and that Det Supt Rimmer will shortly be calling on him for the purposes of that investigation. Now if, as counsel for the chief constable submits, the dominant purpose of Det Supt Rimmer's inquiries really *d*   was to provide material for the threatened civil proceedings, this was a very tricky letter indeed, for it involved, in effect, inviting the prospective plaintiff in those proceedings to make a statement to a representative of the proposed defendant for the purpose of the preparation of the defendant's case under the guise of carrying out a statutory inquiry. Let me say straight away that I am perfectly certain that so shabby a design never for one moment crossed the mind of the writer of this letter. I am quite sure that he never *e*   intended anything of the sort and that the letter meant and was intended to mean exactly what it said. And this, as I would have expected, is exactly what Mr Moody, the deputy chief constable, says in his affidavit. There is, however, in the defendant's evidence an affidavit by a clerk in the employment of the defendant's solicitors which formally suggests that the dominant purpose of the production of the statements was for use in the threatened litigation. This really cannot stand against the contemporary correspondence *f*   and the direct evidence of the person responsible for instituting the inquiry.

For my part, therefore, I am quite satisfied that the claim for legal professional privilege cannot be sustained and if the matter depended on this alone, I would allow the appeal and reverse the decision of the judge.

There remains, however, the question of public interest. The submission of counsel for the plaintiff is that, in the absence of any claim to withhold a particular document on *g*   the ground that it contains material of a specific type the disclosure of which would be contrary to the public interest (a matter on which no evidence at all has been tendered), the defendant cannot sustain any claim to protection. In the evidence, the claim has been expressed as a 'class' claim, but counsel for the plaintiff submits that this is not made out. In particular he points out that there can be no general claim for confidentiality in relation to the statements of which discovery is sought, since the contemplation of the *h*   section itself and the provisions of the Police (Discipline) Regulations 1977, SI 1977 No 580, indicate that they may be used, either in disciplinary proceedings at which the complainant himself is entitled to be present, or in a criminal prosecution. The ground of protection put forward in the defendant's evidence, namely that disclosure in civil proceedings will be likely to deter officers from making statements to the investigating officer, cannot, therefore, he submits, be supported, for if the maker of the statement *j*   knows, as he must be presumed to, that his statement will be used in criminal or disciplinary proceedings as a basis of evidence, it would be illogical to suggest that their possible use in civil proceedings would act as a deterrent. The 'confidentiality' argument must, he submits, therefore fail. There is, in any event, no privilege in confidentiality as such. It is only if a breach of confidentiality can be demonstrated to have adverse public consequences that protection can be claimed.

If the matter depended solely on whether a particular statement could be said to be, in

general, 'confidential', I would be disposed to agree that there is much to be said for this
conclusion, although it does not seem to me to follow that, because all or some of the *a*
material in statements taken in pursuance of the statutory purpose may form the basis
of witnesses' testimony in subsequent proceedings, this necessarily involves the disclosure
of the statements themselves. But for my part I do not think that 'confidentiality' in this
broad sense is the exclusive test. What, as it seems to me, one has to look at is the likely
consequences of a general right to disclosure in civil litigation in the context of the
statutory purpose sought to be achieved by the section, and to ask, first, whether these *b*
likely consequences support the contention that such disclosure would be contrary to the
public interest, and, second, if so, whether that interest is a consideration of such
importance as to outweigh the public interest in disclosure.

Every case of this kind depends ultimately on balancing the public interest in the
administration of justice, which demands the disclosure of all relevant material, against
a competing public interest in withholding that material. Immunity from disclosure, as *c*
Lord Salmon observed in *Rogers v Secretary of State for the Home Department* [1972] 2 All
ER 1057 at 1071, [1973] AC 388 at 412, is not lightly to be extended to classes of
documents other than those always recognised by the courts as entitled to immunity, but
the boundaries of immunity are not to be regarded as immutably fixed:

> 'The principle is that whenever it is clearly contrary to the public interest for a
> document or information to be disclosed, then it is in law immune from disclosure. *d*
> If a new class comes into existence to which this principle applies then that class
> enjoys the same immunity.'

In that case the House of Lords upheld the claim to privilege because, in the circumstances
of the case, disclosure would impede the carrying out by the Gaming Board of its
statutory functions. In that particular case, the disclosure would have involved disclosing *e*
the identity of informants with the probable result that they would, on future occasions,
be less likely to come forward. Now although it cannot, as counsel for the plaintiff points
out, be contended here that statements made to the investigating officer in pursuance of
his inquiries under s 49 of the Police Act 1964 are made under any assurance of
confidentiality, it does seem to me that nevertheless the same principle applies. The
statements are volunteered for a particular purpose, namely the statutory inquiry. No *f*
doubt the consequence is accepted, as it must be, that the inquiry may lead to a
prosecution or to a disciplinary inquiry in which the maker of the statement may be
called to give evidence of some or all of the matters contained in his statement and that
the statement may, therefore, to this extent fall to be used if such proceedings ensue. But
I do not think that it follows from that that disclosure of the statements for the quite
alien purpose of use in civil litigation would not inhibit those whose co-operation is *g*
required if the inquiry is to be sensibly and usefully conducted. And it is this which, as
it seems to me, is the critical test.

This is not simply a matter of inconvenience or the possibility of abuse. The danger
was touched on in the course of the argument that the liability of documents of this sort
to be disclosed on discovery might encourage those whose brushes with the police might
have given them a sense of grievance to launch speculative proceedings in the hope of *h*
uncovering evidence which might assist them in making good a civil claim; and the
suggestion implicit in this is that the documents ought therefore as a matter of public
policy to be protected from discovery. Speaking for myself, I am unimpressed by this
argument, which amounts to no more than saying that because discovery may be abused
it must therefore be inhibited altogether. A claim to protect a class of documents on the
ground of public policy must, I believe, be based on a firmer foundation than that merely *j*
of deterring a particular type of litigant. A citizen who has had past misunderstandings
with the law is no more entitled to litigate than any other citizen; but he is no less
entitled and there is no presumption that his grievance is speculative or groundless. The
possibility of groundless claims cannot therefore, in my judgment, be the touchstone for
determining whether relevant documents shall be produced. That possibility, if a

relevant consideration at all, is, I think, relevant only in so far as it bears on what, in my
a judgment, is the true test, namely whether the production of these documents is likely
to impede the carrying out of the public statutory purpose for which they are brought
into existence.

The purpose of the legislature in enacting the section was to ensure that all complaints
against police officers are fully and properly investigated and that, if the inquiries raise
the possibility that a criminal offence has been committed, the matter shall be referred
b to the Director of Public Prosecutions. The question therefore, as it seems to me, must
be this: will liability to disclosure in civil proceedings of statements taken in the course
of such inquiry adversely affect the attainment of the legislature's purpose? It seems to
me that it will in a number of ways. Take first the position of police officers who are
asked to co-operate on the inquiry. They may themselves be potential defendants and,
if they are, would clearly be disinclined to provide statements which might subsequently
c be used to found civil claims against them. They may be called on to provide information
about the activities of superior officers under whose command they are going to have to
continue to serve in future. They may well be willing, in the performance of their duty,
to do this and to accept that they may be called on to give evidence if a prosecution or
disciplinary proceedings follow. But the complaints which have to be investigated under
the Act are not restricted to those which may lead to prosecution or disciplinary
d proceedings. They cover things as trivial as minor incivility and as serious as assault.
Will officers freely co-operate in assisting in inquiries into the conduct of their superiors
if they know that, quite regardless of whether a prosecution or disciplinary proceedings
ensue, not only the fact that they have participated in the inquiry, but the very statements
which they have made, are liable to come to the knowledge of the officer whose conduct
is under investigation and under whom they may have to continue to serve by disclosure
e as a result of discovery in civil proceedings?

Statements may have to be taken from relatives or associates or neighbours of the
complainant, statements which may well, in the event, be adverse to the claim which he
seeks to assert, and which may result in a decision that disciplinary proceedings or
prosecution shall not be instituted. Are such persons likely to be willing to offer free and
truthful co-operation in investigations under the section, if they know that any
f statements which they make are liable to be disclosed to the complainant in any civil
proceedings which he may be minded to commence?

Finally, there is the position of the complainant himself. Counsel for the plaintiff, in
the course of his argument, stressed the unfairness of a position in which, in effect, the
defendant got a proof of the plaintiff's evidence in advance whilst he was deprived of the
opportunity of seeing the defendant's evidence. But this seems to me to be an argument
g in favour of, rather than against, the protection which is sought. There is no compulsion
on the complainant to co-operate in the inquiry. Having made his complaint, he may
refuse to give a statement to the investigating officer, and he is, I should have thought,
very much more likely to do so if he thinks that any statement which he makes may be
quoted against him in any civil proceedings which he has in contemplation. If, however,
these statements are protected from disclosure in any proceedings, that consequence will
h be avoided. If public policy prevents disclosure, it prevents it, in my judgment, in all
circumstances except to establish innocence in criminal proceedings. It is not like legal
professional privilege, which is the personal right of the party entitled to it and can be
waived (see *Rogers v Secretary of State for the Home Department* [1972] 2 All ER 1057 at
1066, 1070, [1973] AC 388 at 407, 412 per Lord Simon and Lord Salmon respectively).
As a consequence, therefore, although no doubt the complainant's statement may be
j included in counsel's brief and may form the basis on a cross-examination, it cannot be
used as evidence to controvert anything which the complainant's witnesses may say (see
Alfred Crompton Amusement Machines Ltd v Customs and Excise Comrs (No 2) [1973] 2 All ER
1169 at 1184, [1974] AC 405 at 434 per Lord Cross). Thus, it seems to me that here again
the protection sought in this case would assist the proper carrying out of the statutory
purpose if it is allowed, and impede it if it is refused.

Moreover there has to be borne in mind the immense burden on police authorities up and down the country if, in every case in which civil proceedings are instituted, every *a* statement made on an inquiry under the section has to be scrutinised and, if appropriate, made the subject matter of a 'contents' claim.

If, however, these documents have to be disclosed, the authorities would either have to face this burden or seek to procure, so far as possible, that investigating officers so conduct their inquiries as to ensure that the written record of statements made to them contains no material the disclosure of which might be injurious (for instance by *b* containing sources of information). An inquiry cannot be properly or fully conducted if the investigating officer has constantly to be keeping an eye on the possible consequences of public disclosure in civil proceedings.

Of course it must be recognised that there will be, among the statements taken, some, perhaps many, perhaps even the majority, which, in the event, could be disclosed without the fear of the sort of consequences to which I have referred. What seems to me *c* to be an important factor, however, is the effect on the conduct of the statutory function of carrying out the inquiry of the police authority's being obliged in every case to shoulder the additional burden of ensuring the innocuous nature of individual statements. This, to my mind, strongly points to the desirability of a class, rather than a contents protection. A similar point arose in *Rogers v Secretary of State for the Home Department* [1972] 2 All ER 1057 at 1061, [1973] AC 388 at 401, where Lord Reid said: *d*

> 'It is possible that some documents coming to the board could be disclosed without fear of such consequences. But I would think it quite impracticable for the board or the court to be sure of this. So it appears to me that, if there is not to be very serious danger of the board being deprived of information essential for the proper performance of their difficult task, there must be a general rule that they are not bound to produce any document which gives information to them about an *e* applicant.'

Lord Morris in that case is to much the same effect (see [1972] 2 All ER 1057 at 1064–1065, [1973] AC 388 at 405).

Taking all these considerations into account, I think that there is a very real danger that the prospect of disclosure on discovery of material gathered in the course of such an *f* inquiry will inhibit the proper conduct of the inquiry and thus frustrate the purpose of the legislature in making statutory provision for it. In my judgment, therefore, the public interest requires that these documents should be protected as a class, and I accordingly concur in the conclusion of Lord Denning MR. I agree that the appeal should be dismissed.

g

O'CONNOR LJ. On 7th July 1978 police officers acting under a valid search warrant entered the plaintiff's home at 131 Burleywood, Skelmersdale in Lancashire. The plaintiff was away from home; the warrant had been obtained on suspicion that the plaintiff was in possession of and/or dealing in drugs. No drugs were discovered, but in the search the police officers noticed that the seals of the electricity meter were broken; the electricity was on and they suspected that the meter had been tampered with so that *h* electricity was being extracted without payment. The plaintiff returned home during the evening of 8th July and immediately telephoned to the police to report that his home had been burgled. Uniformed officers went out to see him and told him that the CID would come the next day. About midday on 9th July CID officers came to the plaintiff's home and asked him to come with them to the police station; when they arrived at the police station they arrested him on suspicion of stealing electricity. The plaintiff was *j* held in custody for some five hours before he was bailed, and during that time he was questioned about the electricity, about drugs and also about his complaints that some of his property had been damaged and some had disappeared. Thereafter the plaintiff consulted his solicitors, and on 7th August they wrote a letter to the defendant, who is the chief constable for the Lancashire constabulary; it is necessary to refer to that letter in full:

'We act for Mr. Neilson who instructs that on or about 7th July 1978 Officers of
a your Constabulary stationed at Skelmersdale, forced an entry into his premises in
order to make a search whilst he was absent on a short holiday. Before our Client
left, he had secured all the doors and windows. We are instructed that after your
Officers left the premises they did not secure them properly or at all, and
furthermore, caused certain damage to property belonging to our Client. Our
Client returned to the premises at or shortly before midnight on the 8th July 1978
b to discover the damage whereupon he telephoned Skelmersdale Police Station and
the Police constable called at the premises and told our Client that he would ask
Officers of the C.I.D. to call the following day. The following day Officers of the
C.I.D. did call but promptly required our Client to attend Skelmersdale Police
Station with them and upon arrival there he was told that he was under arrest and
was placed in a cell where he was detained for about 6 hours. Furthermore, our
c Client's motor vehicle was wrongfully and without justification impounded. We
are further instructed that despite the fact that our Client told your Officers that he
suffered from a heart condition for which he had to take tablets regularly which had
been prescribed to him by his doctor, and despite the fact that he became unwell
whilst in police custody, your Officers were reluctant to supply him with the tablets
which were at his home and only did so grudgingly after some 2 hours, during
d which time our Client was suffering increasingly from the effects of his heart
condition, which we are told, was either brought on or aggravated by the conduct
of your Officers which we have referred to earlier in this letter. We are instructed
to bring proceedings against you for damages for trespass, damage to our Client's
property and belongings, false arrest, wrongful imprisonment and assault. Unless
we have heard from you within the course of the next 7 days that you are prepared
e to compensate out Client adequately, we are instructed to bring proceedings against
you without further warning. In fairness to the Officers concerned in this matter
and to you we wish to make it clear that our reference to assault refers only to the
failure to supply our Client with his tablets for his heart condition promptly when
requested to do so. There is no suggestion by our Client that there was any other
form of assault.'

f The letter received a formal acknowledgment on 10th August, and on 5th September the
deputy chief constable wrote to the plaintiff:

'Dear Sir

'COMPLAINTS AGAINST THE POLICE

g 'I refer to the above and have to inform you that I have decided to call for an
investigation under the provisions of Section 49 of the Police Act 1964.
'To this end I decided to appoint Det. Superintendent Rimmer to act as
Investigating Officer in this matter. Mr. Rimmer will be contacting you in due
course.

'Yours faithfully,
h   Deputy Chief Constable.'

The investigation was carried out during the next few months; statements were taken
from various people, including one from the plaintiff in November 1978. The statutory
machinery for dealing with complaints against the police was gone through, and on 27th
March 1979 the Director of Public Prosecutions wrote to the plaintiff to tell him that,
j having considered the report made by Det Supt Rimmer, no criminal proceedings were
to be instituted. On 15th May 1979 the Police Complaints Board informed the plaintiff's
solicitors that they had considered the case and accepted the decision of the deputy chief
constable not to institute any disciplinary charges.
On 30th April 1979 the plaintiff commenced proceedings in the Preston County
Court. By his amended particulars of claim the plaintiff claimed damages for trespass,
negligence, false imprisonment and assault. The pleadings having been completed, the

chief constable delivered a revised list of documents in December 1979. He claimed
privilege for the documents listed in parts 1, 2 and 3 of the first schedule. This appeal is *a*
concerned with the claim for privilege in respect of documents listed in part 3 of the first
schedule, which reads as follows:

'1. Statements (excepting that of plaintiff) made for the purpose of enquiry
pursuant to Section 49 of the Police Act 1964 from 13th December 1978 to 7th
March 1979.
'2. Report of Detective Superintendent Rimmer on enquiry pursuant to Section *b*
49 of the Police Act 1964. Date—12th March 1979.'

The claim for privilege for these documents was made in the following terms:

'The grounds on which I object to produce the said documents are: (i) that to do
so would be injurious to the public interest, and (ii) that they are subject to legal
professional privilege.'   *c*

The district registrar ordered inspection of the statements but refused inspection of the
report. On appeal the county court judge reversed that decision and refused inspection
of the statements on the grounds that they were protected by legal professional
privilege. The basis for the claim was an assertion in an affidavit sworn by a law clerk in
the defendant's solicitors' office to the effect that these statements were taken for the *d*
purpose of contesting the anticipated litigation at the suit of the plaintiff or at all events
that that was the dominant purpose for which they had come into existence. The
dominant purpose is the test laid down by the House of Lords in *Waugh v British Railways
Board* [1979] 2 all ER 1169, [1980] AC 521. I cannot accept this assertion. I think it is
quite clear that the dominant purpose in taking these statements was the s 49 inquiry,
and I think that is made quite certain by the fact that a statement was taken from the *e*
plaintiff himself.

In the alternative the defendant claims public interest privilege for the statements.
The basis for this claim is found in the affidavit of Mr Moody, the deputy chief constable;
in effect he says that the s 49 inquiry would be prejudiced if persons approached to make
statements thought that such statements might at some future time be used in civil
litigation and revealed to parties thereto. For my part I am sure that this is right. We *f*
were told that there are a great many complaints every year which have to be investigated
under the s 49 procedure ranging from trivial complaints to very serious allegations.
The complaints may come from honest citizens; on the other hand they also come from
criminals. The reasons for protecting such statements have been set out by Lord Denning
MR and Oliver LJ and I do not wish to add to them. I agree with what each of them has
said.   *g*

Counsel on behalf of the plaintiff submitted that this was not a case for a 'class'
privilege but at best one for a 'contents' privilege. He submitted that anybody making
a statement must be deemed to know that it might be used in criminal proceedings
against a police officer, or, alternatively, in disciplinary proceedings. In addition he
submitted that even if the statements should be protected whilst the inquiry was pending
there were no grounds for doing so once the inquiry was complete, as is the position in *h*
the present case. At first sight this submission seems attractive, but in my judgment
there are grounds of public policy which show that it must be rejected.

When statements are taken in confidence pursuant to the s 49 procedure, it is in the
public interest that full information should be forthcoming. Full information may be
much wider than that which can be evidence in a criminal case or indeed in disciplinary
proceedings. If 'class' privilege is not accorded to this material, then an immense burden *j*
will be put on the police to sift the material to make sure that the 'contents' privilege is
claimed.

Lastly, as the law now stands since the decision of the House of Lords in *Burmah Oil Co
Ltd v Bank of England (Attorney General intervening)* [1979] 3 All ER 700, [1980] AC 1090,
the court will balance the privilege against the duty to see that justice is done to the

plaintiff, and in some circumstances will look at the material in order to decide how this
a discretion should be exercised. In the present case there are no grounds for doing this.
I would dismiss the appeal.

Appeal dismissed. Leave to appeal to the House of Lords refused.

Solicitors: *Reynolds, Porter, Chamberlain,* agents for *Williams, Elsby & Co,* Bootle (for the
b plaintiff); *Brian Hill* (for the chief constable).

Sumra Green   Barrister.

c   # Scarfe v Adams and another

COURT OF APPEAL, CIVIL DIVISION
CUMMING-BRUCE, O'CONNOR AND GRIFFITHS LJJ
1st, 2nd, 3rd, 4th DECEMBER 1980

*d Sale of land – Conveyance – Parcels – Reference to plan – Conveyance of land and building in
separate lots – Large building divided into two halves – Transfer deeds not defining boundary but
referring to plan – Scale of plan too small to show precise boundary – Transfer deeds referring
to dividing wall as party wall – Whether boundary insufficiently identified – Whether extrinsic
evidence admissible to determine boundary.*

*e Sale of land – Conveyance – Parcels – Reference to plan – Large scale plan required if plan alone
to be used to describe boundary.*

An old estate, standing in 82 acres and including a manor house, cottages, a coach-house,
barns and outbuildings, was put up for sale at auction in separate lots. The coach-house
was split into two lots, each with some land. The northern half, put up for sale as lot 6,
consisted of a range of stables, a store room and a double garage with vacant possession
f on the ground floor and a flat with a protected tenant on the first floor. The southern
half, put up as lot 5, consisted of a range of stables and store rooms on the ground floor
and a first floor flat, all with vacant possession. The auction particulars contained an
architect's drawings showing planning consent to reconstruct each half as a separate
residence. At the auction the plaintiff bought lot 6 and the defendants bought lot 5. The
g plaintiff completed her purchase by deed of transfer a month after the auction and the
defendants completed by deed of transfer a month later. Each deed of transfer described
the land conveyed by reference to a plan bound therewith. The plans had a scale of
1:2500 and contained captions stating that they were published for the convenience of
purchasers only, that their accuracy was not guaranteed and that they were expressly
excluded from any contract. The only reference in the plaintiff's transfer deed to the
h division between her part of the coach-house and lot 5 was a covenant stating that it was
agreed and declared that the dividing wall between the land conveyed and lot 5 was a
party wall and was maintainable as such. No such wall was shown on the plan because
its scale was too small. The defendants' deed of transfer contained no reference in its text
to boundaries with lot 6, but the charge certificate on the register contained a note
referring to the covenant relating to the party wall in the plaintiff's deed. A dispute arose
j about the location of the boundary between the two halves of the coach-house. The
plaintiff contended that the boundary was the line of an existing wall dividing the
northern half of the coach-house from the southern half. Such a division, although it did
not divide the coach-house into two equal halves, was in accordance with the architect's
drawings included with the auction particulars. The defendants contended that the
boundary was indicated by an extension of a dotted line relating to rights of way shown

on the plan bound with the plaintiff's deed which divided the coach-house into two equal halves and that dividing walls were irrelevant to the issue of the boundary within the house or the division of the land.

Held – It was a well-established principle that if the terms of a transfer of land or an interest therein clearly defined the land or interest transferred extrinsic evidence was not admissible to contradict the transfer, and in such a case if the transfer did not truly express the bargain between vendor and purchaser the only remedy was by way of rectification of the transfer; but if the terms of the transfer did not clearly define the land or interest transferred extrinsic evidence, including any auction particulars forming the basis of the contract of sale, was admissible so that the court might do the best it could to arrive at the true meaning of the parties on a fair consideration of the language used. Since it was quite apparent from a perusal of the plaintiff's deed of transfer and the plan bound up with it that the property transferred by that deed from the vendor to the purchaser was not identified with any certainty, and since the plan was useless for telling how the boundary was to pass through the house, the court would admit in evidence the auction particulars which showed clearly that lots 5 and 6 were to be divided along the line of the existing party wall and not by reference to the dotted line shown on the plan bound with the plaintiff's deed. The court would make a declaration accordingly (see p 847 j, p 848 d to g, p 849 a to p 850 c and h to p 851 j and p 852 a, post).

Per Curiam. Although a general description of the property, and reliance on a small scale Ordnance map, may once have been sufficient for the purpose of conveying to a single purchaser a whole great property, together with its surrounding land, such description and such a plan is likely to be wholly inappropriate to achieve, without uncertainty and resulting confusion, the conveyance of the small divided parts of big buildings or to define the boundaries between the small gardens and courtyards of the adjoining plots into which the vendor has divided the land round the house. For such purposes it is absolutely essential that each parcel conveyed should be described in the conveyance or transfer deed with such particularity and precision that there is no room for doubt about the boundaries of each, and for such purposes, if a plan is intended to control the description, a small scale Ordnance map is worse than useless (see p 845 f to j, p 851 a and p 852 b c and f to h, post).

Per O'Connor LJ. If a house is to be divided and a plan is to form part of the material describing the boundary, it is essential that there be a large-scale plan of the house showing the rooms and the walls, particularly when there is reference in the deed to a party wall between the property being transferred and property which is to be transferred to another purchaser (see p 851 a, post).

Notes

For the description and plan of properties conveyed, see 34 Halsbury's Laws (3rd Edn) 349, para 601, and for cases on the subject, see 40 Digest (Repl) 298–301, 2486–2504.

For the definition of boundaries in conveyances, see 4 Halsbury's Laws (4th Edn) para 834, and for cases on the subject, see 7 Digest (Reissue) 309–311, 2136–2157.

Cases referred to in judgments

Eastwood v Ashton [1915] AC 900, 84 LJ Ch 671, 113 LT 562, HL, 17 Digest (Reissue) 427, 1889.

Grigsby v Melville [1973] 3 All ER 455, [1974] 1 WLR 80, 26 P & CR 182, CA, Digest (Cont Vol D) 279, 114b.

Kingston v Phillips [1976] Court of Appeal Transcript 279.

Neilson v Poole (1969) 20 P & CR 909, 7 Digest (Reissue) 311, 2157.

Cases also cited

Laybourn v Gridley [1892] 2 Ch 53.

Lyle v Richards (1866) LR 1 HL 222.

Mitchell v Mosley [1914] 1 Ch 438, CA.
a Smout v Farquharson [1972] Court of Appeal Transcript 381.
Willson v Greene (Moss, third party) [1971] 1 All ER 1098, [1971] 1 WLR 635.

Appeal

The plaintiff, Sylvia Margaret Scarfe, appealed against the decision of Mr Derek Holden sitting as a deputy circuit judge in the Guildford County Court on 10th December 1979
b whereby he dismissed the plaintiff's claims for declarations, injunctions or damages, and granted the defendants, John David Adams and his wife Marilyn Diane Adams, a declaration on their counterclaim that the boundary between the properties known respectively as no 1 and no 2 The Coach House, Rake Manor Estate, Milford, Surrey was as shown on a plan annexed to the defendants' defence, and whereby he granted an injunction restraining the plaintiff, by herself, her servants or agents from committing
c acts of trespass or preventing the defendants from using the whole of their premises. The plaintiff further sought an injunction restraining the defendants by themselves, their servants or agents from entering on the plaintiff's land. The facts are set out in the judgment of Cumming-Bruce LJ.

Dennis Levy for the plaintiff.
d Quintin Iwi for the defendants.

CUMMING-BRUCE LJ. The judgment that I am about to deliver should be regarded as a cautionary tale to be marked and digested by every conveyancing solicitor and legal executive. It is very seldom these days that it is practicable for people to reside in large houses that they have inherited from their ancestors. So now big houses are often
e divided into a number of separate houses or flats, and sold off by a common vendor to a number of separate purchasers. Each of the purchasers probably buys part of the original house, and part of the land around it, as freehold, with rights over and obligations to purchasers of some or all of the other parts of the original house and land. Such transactions call for special attention to detail on the part of conveyancing solicitors. Though a general description of the property, and reliance on a small scale Ordnance
f map, may once have been sufficient for the purpose of conveying to a single purchaser a whole great property, together with its surrounding land, such a description and such a plan is likely to be wholly inappropriate to achieve, without uncertainty and resulting confusion, the conveyance of the small divided parts of big buildings or to define the boundaries between the small gardens and courtyards of the adjoining plots into which the vendor has divided the land round the house.
g   The facts of the present case are really very simple, but I hope that this judgment will be understood by every conveyancing solicitor in the land as giving them warning, loud and clear, that a conveyancing technique which may have been effective in the old days to convey large property from one vendor to one purchaser will lead to nothing but trouble, disputes and expensive litigation if applied to the sale to separate purchasers of a single house and its curtilage divided into separate parts. For such purposes it is
h absolutely essential that each parcel conveyed shall be described in the conveyance or transfer deed with such particularity and precision that there is no room for doubt about the boundaries of each, and for such purposes if a plan is intended to control the description, an Ordnance map on a scale of 1:2500 is worse than useless. The plan or other drawing bound up with the deed must be on such a large scale that it clearly shows with precision where each boundary runs. In my view the parties to this appeal are the
j victims of sloppy conveyancing for which the professional advisers of vendor and purchasers appear to bear the responsibility. We are not concerned in this appeal with determining or apportioning that responsibility. This court has to try to reduce to order the confusion created by the conveyancers.
     These observations are not at all original. I have only repeated in my own language what fell from Buckley, Roskill and Goff LJJ four years ago in their judgments in *Kingston*

v Phillips [1976] Court of Appeal Transcript 279. It is, I think, unfortunate that the case did not get into the law reports. It may well be that the law reporters will think it *a* unnecessary to report the rest of this judgment, though it illustrates the kind of trouble that this unworthy conveyancing is liable to cause. But I express the hope that at least this introduction to my judgment will find its way into the law reports.

The Rake Manor Estate is at Milford in West Surrey. Standing in 82 acres was a manor house, also a second considerable residence, three cottages, a coach-house and garage with two flats above the stables, and a group of barns and outbuildings. The owners decided *b* to split the property up and sell it off by sale at auction in separate lots. We are concerned with the Coach House. This was to be split into two, each with some adjacent land, with rights of access to each part over the drive which runs from the manor house to the road. The northern half with half an acre of land was put up for sale as lot 6. The ground floor thereof was a range of stables, store room and double garage. On the first floor was a flat, with sitting room, kitchen, three bedrooms and a bathroom and water closet. This *c* flat was let to a protected tenant, Mrs Napier, so that the lot was put up for sale subject to the tenancy, with vacant possession of the ground floor. The southern half, with two acres of land, was put up for sale as lot 5. The ground floor likewise was a range of stables and storage rooms. Above them was a flat, consisting of sitting room, kitchen, two bedrooms, bathroom and water closet. Vacant possession was offered of the whole of lot 5, as there was no tenant in the flat. Before the sale of the Coach House, the vendor *d* applied for and obtained detailed planning consent to convert each half into a separate country residence, with consent to conversion in accordance with an architect's drawings available to the scrutiny of prospective purchasers. These drawings showed that the planning authority had consented to the reconstruction of each half into separate residences such that each house could have living rooms, kitchen and garage on the ground floor, and four bedrooms and a bathroom above them. *e*

The auction took place on 14th November 1978. The plaintiff, the appellant in this court, bought lot 6. The defendants, the respondents here, bought lot 5.

This is registered land. The plaintiff completed the purchase of lot 6 on 12th December 1978 by deed of transfer. The defendants likewise completed by deed of transfer on 10th January 1979.

The plaintiff's deed of transfer is entitled 'Transfer of Part imposing fresh restrictive *f* covenants'. The vendor transferred—

'the land shown and coloured blue on the plan bound up within and known as The Coach House Rake Manor Milford being part of the land comprised in the title above mentioned TOGETHER WITH the benefit of the rights easements and other matters mentioned in the First Schedule hereto but EXCEPT AND RESERVED as mentioned in the Second Schedule hereto.' *g*

That purports to be the description of the parcel transferred. It reveals very little. So one turns hopefully to the plan. But the scale is 1:2500. The caption reads: 'This Plan is published for convenience of Purchasers only. Its accuracy is not guaranteed and it is expressly excluded from any contract.' There are five parcels of land marked blue. No mention of a coach-house. But if you had been at the auction you would look for the *h* blue land marked '6'. There you can decipher a tracing of a building, which, if you know the land, but not otherwise, you would recognise as the rough outline of the northern end of the Coach House. Adjacent to it, coloured green, is a similar rough outline that can be recognised as marking the site of the south end of the Coach House. If you had been at the auction, but not otherwise, you would realise that that was the lot sold as '5'.

On the plan the drive is shown. At one end is marked letter A at the point where it *j* opens into Station Lane. And on the drive you can see letter C. These letters evidently are intended to be the letters referred to in cl (b) of the first schedule to the transfer deed: 'Rights of access over the drive on Lot 1 between the points marked A–C on the said plan.' There are three thickly marked lines like hyphens in a line running from the letter C towards the diagram indicating the Coach House. On the copy exhibited they

end at letters PT and the ring encircling the figure 5, but other less strongly printed
a marks continue over the diagram of the house and on in a westerly direction to end at the
corner of a diagram representing Lake Cottage. North of that dotted line the colour is
blue. South the colour is green.

   Astonishingly, the only reference in the transfer deed itself to the division between the
plaintiff's house and lot 5 is to be found in the transferee's covenant (g), which reads: 'It
is hereby agreed and declared that the dividing wall between the land hereby transferred
b and Lot 5 aforesaid is a party wall and is maintainable as such.' You look in vain on the
plan for that dividing wall, because no internal walls or partitions of any kind are shown
on it. They could not be drawn accurately on the plan as the scale is far too small.

   Nor does the plan indicate the boundary of the flat of which Mrs Napier was the sitting
tenant on the first floor of the land transferred to the plaintiff. Yet there is reference to
it in the transfer deed. See transferee's covenant (c): 'To maintain the pipes from the
c bathroom and kitchen of the flat forming part of the property hereby transferred.'

   When the defendants completed their purchase of lot 5, the text of their transfer deed
was as uninformative as the plaintiff's deed. The description of the land transferred
reads:

> 'the land shown and edged with red on the plan bound up within and known as
d The Coach House Milford Witley . . . being part of the land comprised in the Title
> above-mentioned . . . subject to rights of way for access over the drive coloured
> green on the said plan . . .'

There is a plan annexed. This plan shows a line from a point marked C on the drive
ending at the same corner of the cottage now called Lake Cottage. There is a heavy red
marking on the south side of the line. The scale is again 1:2500. There is no reference
e in the text of the transfer deed to boundaries with lot 6, but on the charge certificate on
the register there is a note, which reads as follows:

> 'NOTE:—A Transfer of land adjoining the northern boundary of the Coach House
> dated 18 December 1978 by Patricia Jane Gommes on the direction of Asmarley
> Properties Limited to [the plaintiff] contains the following agreement and
> declaration:—"It is hereby agreed and declared that the dividing wall between the
f land hereby transferred and Lot 5 aforesaid is a party wall and is maintainable as
> such". REMARK:—Lot 5 referred to is the land in this title.'

   This dispute and the ensuing expensive litigation has occurred because the plaintiff
claims that by her transfer deed the division between her house and the defendants'
house was the line of the wall dividing the north half from the south half, while the
g defendants claim that the dotted line shown on her Ordnance plan running from C on
the drive to the corner of Lake Cottage is the boundary between them. The defendants
say that that line cuts the Coach House clean in half, and that dividing walls are irrelevant
to the issue of the boundary within the house or division of the house.

   As the plaintiff completed first, the question is: what did the vendors transfer to the
plaintiff? If she is right as a matter of construction of her deed with the plan bound up,
h and if the defendants are right on the construction of their deed, the vendors have
purported to transfer to the defendants part of the Coach House which they had already
transferred to the plaintiff. This is because the wall which on 12th December 1978
divided much of the northern half of the Coach House from the southern half is several
feet south of a line drawn through the middle of the Coach House.

   Though I have up to now given an outline of the facts which give rise to the dispute,
j I wish to make it plain that the question raised in these proceedings is only the proper
construction to the plaintiff's transfer deed. And the starting point is that extrinsic
evidence is not admissible as an aid to its construction unless the relevant provisions of
the deed are uncertain, contradictory or ambiguous. Counsel for the plaintiff submits
that this deed is uncertain, contradictory and ambiguous. Counsel in the court below
invited the judge to admit evidence as to facts and circumstances from which the

common intention of vendor and purchaser was to be collected in order to understand the true meaning of the deed which they made, and the true effect of the plan to which *a* they referred as showing the land transferred. The judge admitted extrinsic evidence de bene esse but he decided that there was no such uncertainty or ambiguity as to make it right to admit that evidence as an aid to construction.

The learned deputy judge founded his conclusion on his confidence that the plan correctly indicated the point C as the point at which a peg had been placed by one Plumb two months before the auction, in order to determine the right of way from the land on *b* lot 6 to the drive, and also to make a boundary between lots 5 and 6, to show where the garden was going. With respect to the deputy judge, I find it difficult to share his confidence in the inference to be drawn from the notation of point C on the Ordnance plan. In his evidence-in-chief Plumb said that he did not deduce the position of point C from the boundaries of lots 5 and 6. He had with him a 25-inch plan, which was never identified or exhibited. He seems to have had a straight line on that plan which he was *c* using, and seems to have placed the peg at the point where that line bisected the drive. He does not suggest that he was in any way concerned with the correct division of the house between lots 5 and 6, but only with the gardens and the means of access. He was not concerned at all with the boundary of the land on the other side of the house. But it is clear to me that lines to run from the house to the drive on the west side and from the house to Lake Cottage on the east side must have as their points of origin the two ends *d* of the dividing line within the house. There is nothing in the deed to suggest that the division of the Coach House was to be controlled by the prior determination of means of access to the drive or of the boundaries of the garden on the one side and the courtyard on the other. It would be absurd to impute to the vendor such an intention unless there were strong internal indications thereof on the face of the deed. The same criticism is relevant to the importance ascribed by the deputy judge to the fact that the division of *e* the courtyard on the western side of the Coach House was to end at a corner of Lake Cottage.

Where description of the parcels is totally imprecise, and there is no explicit definition of the division of the house to be found in the description of the parcels, it is appropriate to examine the rest of the instrument to see if there is to be found any aid to the meaning of the deed in relation to the division of the house. I find two clear indications: (1) in *f* covenant (c) the parties clearly contemplate by their language that the flat forms part of the property transferred; (2) in covenant (g) it was agreed and declared that the dividing wall between the land transferred and lot 5 was a party wall. But a line bisecting the Coach House into two equal parts (a) would transfer part of the tenanted flat in lot 6 to lot 5 and (b) would not run through or within several feet of any dividing wall. That suggests that there is something wrong in treating the line marked from C to Lake *g* Cottage as controlling the division of the house.

Counsel for the defendants, in answer, submits that covenant (c) is only concerned with maintenance of pipes from the kitchen and bathroom of the flat, and may have been consistent with an intention to divide the landlord's rights over the tenanted flat and to secure to lot 5 the reversion of part of it. As to covenant (g) he submits that it was clumsily drafted, and was meant to contemplate a future dividing wall, after the *h* purchasers had reconstructed the house. He relies also on those words of cll (c) and (d) which clearly contemplate that a hopper head and manhole (4) shall be in lot 5.

The learned deputy judge said that he derived most assistance from the cases of *Grigsby v Melville* [1973] 3 All ER 455, [1974] 1 WLR 80 and *Neilson v Poole* (1969) 20 P & CR 909. The judge was wrong in thinking that *Grigsby* was an action for rectification. The decision was founded on the determination that, as a matter of construction, the deed *j* was clear, certain and unambiguous, so that there was no room for extrinsic evidence about the inconvenient consequences. *Neilson v Poole* was a case in which Megarry J as a matter of construction of the conveyance with plan attached, decided that it was uncertain and that therefore it was right to admit and consider extrinsic evidence. Having done so, Megarry J decided that the conveyance as a whole and the dividing line on the plan showed that the dividing line was along a line drawn on the plan, and the other conveyances supported the conclusion. I have difficulty in understanding how the decision of either case or the reasoning of Megarry J supported the deputy judge's conclusion.

We have had the advantage of citation of quite a number of well-known authorities. I find it unnecessary to analyse them, because of my view of the construction of the deed and its plan. I find its meaning uncertain, contradictory and ambiguous on the definition of boundaries between lots 6 and 5. The cases appear to establish beyond peradventure that if such is the situation on scrutiny of the instrument and accompanying plan, extrinsic evidence is admissible. Where I differ from the learned deputy judge is on the question whether, on reading the deed and studying the plan, the court is compelled to decide that there is uncertainty, contradiction and ambiguity in the deed. As I do not differ from the learned deputy judge on the law, save that I do not find that the cases he relied on support his conclusion, it is unnecessary to investigate further the history of the cases which have been cited to this court.

My conclusion is that when the text of the transfer deed is read as a whole, and is compared with the consequences of a division of the house along the line dotted on the Ordnance plan, the deed with its plan is seen to be ambiguous, uncertain and contradictory, such that extrinsic evidence is admissible to resolve the doubts to which the deed gives rise. I reach this conclusion independently of any difficulty which may flow from the fact that the plan which the conveyancer bound up with the deed to show the land bore the caption: 'Note.—This Plan is published for the convenience of the Purchaser only. Its accuracy is not guaranteed and it is expressly excluded from any contract.'

The extrinsic evidence called de bene esse before the judge pointed, in my view, overwhelmingly to a common intention of the plaintiff and the vendor that the division of the house should accord with the division delineated on the architect's plan which was in a folder containing the auctioneer's particulars of sale. The extrinsic evidence of the circumstances from which the true meaning of the deed may be discovered include the contract entered into between vendor and purchaser, founded as it was on the offer in the particulars of sale of lot 6 which the purchaser accepted. As I understood it, counsel for the defendants did not seek to argue that that contract did not contemplate sale of a part which included on the first floor the whole of the tenanted flat, and below, divided as shown on the architect's drawing, which was an essential condition of planning consent. The learned judge made a finding that the plaintiff intended to purchase lot 6 as shown in the architect's plan and described in the particulars. Having regard to those particulars and the fact that purchasers were invited to bid in reliance on the detailed planning consents in case they wished to avail themselves thereof, the evidence of intention common to vendor and purchaser to divide the Coach House along the line of the dividing wall between the two flats on the first floor and the wall beneath them on the ground floor as far as the corridor is, in my view, strong persuasive evidence that the ambiguity, uncertainty and contradiction appearing on the face of the deed and the plan bound up therewith should be resolved by construing the deed to accord with the parties' intentions.

So as a matter of construction I read the transfer deed with plan bound up as transferring that part of the Coach House which begins at the northern end thereof and continues to the wall dividing the flats on the first floor at the date of transfer, and the wall beneath them, notionally extended through the existing corridor to the outside wall. This boundary is, however, subject to the insert into lot 6 represented by a fireplace on the ground floor. I would make a declaration as to the boundary of the Coach House in lot 6 with lot 5 accordingly.

If this was an action for rectification of the transfer deed, which it is not, I would make a consequential revision of cl (c) of the transfer deed, as it is clear, as soon as the hopper head is seen from the ground, that it is on the wall of the flat in lot 6, and the drafting in the deed is simply another example of this slapdash conveyancer's method to describe it as on the wall of lot 5.

That brings me to the boundaries of the land outside. I take the view that it is clear that the deed contemplated a straight line at right angles to the eastern outer wall of the Coach House running from the line of division of the house down to the drive. As point *a* C was placed as a consequence of pegging the wrong line, this point is a few feet further down the drive than as shown on plan B, and the boundary of the gardens must be declared accordingly. The plaintiff gets a little bigger garden.

The problem of the western courtyard has been resolved by concession and agreement. The parties sensibly agreed (without prejudice to their conflicting submissions on the boundary within the Coach House) that, if the boundary within the *b* house is as the plaintiff contends, the boundary in the courtyard should follow the dog-leg shown on the architect's drawing, continuing as a straight line to the corner of Lake Cottage.

For these reasons, I would move that the appeal be allowed. A declaration should be granted that the boundaries between the plaintiff's land and the defendants' land are as I have stated above. This declaration should be precisely drafted in minutes of order. *c* The second declaration sought is consequential and should be granted.

The negative injunction claimed as the third relief should, in my view, be made, unless the defendants are prepared now to give an undertaking to the same effect.

There should be an order that the defendants pull down and remove a fence referred to in the particulars of claim. The question arises as to how much time should be given to the defendants to move this fence. We heard in this court that behind the fence, on *d* the defendants' side, there are plants and shrubs which will also have to be moved off the land now held to be the land of the plaintiff. Clearly the parties should agree a reasonable period of time to enable the unfortunate defendants not only to move their fence but to move the plants which they have probably taken a lot of trouble already in putting nicely in the right places. If the parties cannot agree on the period of time this court should, in my view, decide what that period should be. It has to be a reasonable time, because as it *e* is not only a matter of moving the fence but also a matter of moving the plants, the defendants should be given a reasonable period of time to undertake this tiresome work.

This court has not the material to decide the question of damages, which the judge on his findings did not have to consider. I am afraid that that issue will have to go back to the county court if the parties do not agree. In the circumstances, I would think that it would probably be better that the issue of damages should be tried by another judge. *f*

In conclusion, I would say this. These parties have bought their houses. They have to live together as next-door neighbours. The male defendant convinced himself, as the judge held, on the correctness of his own view. As a result, he acted in a way which was troublesome to the plaintiff. Hard feelings inevitably were generated and I strongly suspect that everybody lost their tempers. The parties should try to appreciate that their troubles, and the terrible expense to which they have been put, were not caused by the *g* other's malice or obstinacy, but by the misfortune that the conveyancers concerned did not draft the plaintiff's deed with proper particularity and used a plan wholly inappropriate for the purpose of controlling the description of the land transferred. After such passions have inevitably been aroused it is very difficult to begin again as good neighbours. But unless the parties can achieve that commendable end their future as neighbours is likely to continue to be very unhappy. *h*

For those reasons, I would allow the appeal and propose orders on the lines that I have stated.

O'CONNOR LJ. I agree that the appeal should be allowed and the orders suggested by Cumming-Bruce LJ be made, for the reasons given by him and also for those about to be given by Griffiths LJ. *j*

I only wish to add, very shortly, for myself that a perusal of the plaintiff's deed of transfer, with the plan bound up with it, makes it quite apparent that the property being transferred by that deed from the vendor to the purchaser is not identified with any certainty. The short point really is that the plan is quite useless for telling one how the boundary is to pass through the house. The house is drawn in outline on a scale which

is quite useless for telling one where the line is to be. If a house is to be divided and a plan
is to form part of the material describing the boundary, it is essential that there should
be a large-scale plan of the house showing the rooms and the walls. That is particularly
so when there is reference in the deed, as there is in the present case, to a party wall
between the property being transferred and property which is to be transferred to
another purchaser, in this case the defendants.

Once that situation is established, extrinsic evidence is to be available. Like Cumming-
Bruce LJ, once one looks at the particulars of sale, in my judgment, there is no possibility
of any doubt as to where the line should pass through the house, was intended to pass
through the house and, as the order which we are making declares, will from now on
pass through the house.

GRIFFITHS LJ. Although we have had the benefit of a fairly extensive citation of
authority, I do not find it necessary to review those authorities, as I regard the legal
principle to be applied in this appeal as well established and the cases cited as illustrations
of the practical application of that principle. The principle may be stated thus: if the
terms of the transfer clearly define the land or interest transferred extrinsic evidence is
not admissible to contradict the transfer. In such a case, if the transfer does not truly
express the bargain between vendor and purchaser, the only remedy is by way of
rectification of the transfer. But, if the terms of the transfer do not clearly define the land
or interest transferred, then extrinsic evidence is admissible so that the court may (to use
the words of Lord Parker in *Eastwood v Ashton* [1915] AC 900 at 913) 'do the best it can
to arrive at the true meaning of the parties upon a fair consideration of the language
used'. The same case makes it clear that the admissible extrinsic evidence will include
the auction particulars which formed the basis of the contract of sale.

The learned deputy county court judge concluded that he could not admit extrinsic
evidence because he thought there was no ambiguity in the language of the transfer or
the plan. I cannot agree with him. The plan is immediately suspect, because, owing to
its small scale, it is wholly inadequate to be used for the purpose of transferring part of
a building which was the principal object of the transfer. The Coach House is only
diagrammatically indicated on the plan; no attempt has been made to trace its true
outlines. This is not surprising. It would not have been a practical exercise to
superimpose them on such a small-scale Ordnance sheet. The plan appears to divide the
diagrammatic representation of the Coach House into two equal halves. But if this is
done it transfers a part only of the kitchen and a part only of the bathroom of the top flat,
which is on the face of it a fairly surprising state of affairs. The transfer must, however,
be read as a whole and in the transfer one finds that the purchaser is under a duty 'to
maintain the pipes from the bathroom and the kitchen of the flat forming part of the
property', and, reading further, that the wall of the kitchen and bathroom are declared
to be a party wall, for it is provided 'It is hereby agreed and declared that the dividing wall
between the land hereby transferred and Lot 5 aforesaid is a party wall and is
maintainable as such'. But if the plan is right there is no party wall. On the face of the
transfer all is confusion and extrinsic evidence is clearly admissible.

Once the extrinsic evidence is admissible, the position is as plain as a pikestaff. The
auction particulars show that the purchaser of lot 6 gets that part of the Coach House that
comprises the first floor flat at present let to a tenant and that part of the stabling below
it together with the north wing comprising a garage and a store room. The purchaser of
lot 5 gets the other flat on the first floor, with vacant possession, and the corresponding
part of the ground floor of the building at its southern end. How a purchaser of lot 5
could have persuaded himself in the face of these particulars that he was purchasing the
geometric half of the building passes my understanding. It is true that there is a mistake
in the special conditions of sale which describes a drainage hopper which is in fact on the
wall of lot 6 as being on the wall of lot 5 and the same error is made in respect of a
manhole, and these errors were carried into the transfer. But these are obvious mistakes

and carry no weight whatever when balanced against the description of lots 5 and 6 in the particulars of sale.

For the reasons which have been given so much more fully by Cumming-Bruce LJ, I agree that this appeal must be allowed and that the boundary between the properties be declared in the terms set out in his judgment, together with the necessary consequential orders of this court.

I wish now to add a few general observations. I am afraid we have seen little of the art of conveyancing in this case. These days more and more large buildings are being divided and sold in different lots for separate occupation. This calls for careful and skilful conveyancing. I do not know if it is a widespread practice in such transactions to rely on a small-scale Ordnance map without any adequate description of the property in the transfer, as was done in this case. But if it is, the sooner it stops the better. I mention this because the facts of an unreported decision of this court in 1976, *Kingston v Phillips* [1976] Court of Appeal Transcript 279, bear a remarkable similarity to the facts of this case. It was a case involving the sale of part of a country house, and the parcels clause read:

'The vendor as beneficial owner hereby conveys unto the purchaser all that piece or parcel of land being part of the Chicklade House Estate at Chicklade in the County of Wiltshire all which premises are by way of identification only more particularly delineated on the plan annexed hereto and thereon coloured pink And also all that dwellinghouse together with the outbuildings thereto erected thereon or on some part thereof being part of Chicklade House.'

Buckley LJ, who speaks with far greater authority than I do on these matters, had this to say:

'It will be observed that the parcels as there set out are really almost devoid of any particularity; all that is said about the property conveyed is that it is part of the Chicklade Estate and part of the dwelling house thereon. Unhappily, the plan which was annexed to that conveyance is wholly inadequate to perform the function which the draftsman of the conveyance seems to have contemplated that it would. It is a very dangerous practice for a conveyancer to frame a conveyance with parcels which are not adequately described. Perhaps the most important feature of all the features of a conveyance is to be able to identify the property to which it relates; and, if the draftsman of the conveyance chooses to identify the property solely by reference to a plan, it is of the utmost importance that he should make use of the plan which is on a scale sufficiently large to make it possible to represent the property and its boundaries in precise detail, giving dimensions and any other features which may be necessary to put beyond doubt the subject matter of the conveyance.'

It is perhaps a pity that that case was unreported and so was not brought to the attention of conveyancers. I can only express the hope that those words of Buckley LJ and the observations of Cumming-Bruce LJ in the present case may be drawn speedily to the attention of the profession.

Appeal allowed. Declaration as to boundaries between plaintiff's and defendants' properties as indicated by Cumming-Bruce LJ. Injunction restraining defendants from entering on plaintiff's property. Interim injunction made by judge below discharged. Issue of damages to go back to county court before a different judge.

Solicitors: *Reynolds, Porter, Chamberlain* (for the plaintiff); *Williams & Williams*, Beckenham (for the defendants).

Mary Rose Plummer   Barrister.

Practice Direction

EMPLOYMENT APPEAL TRIBUNAL

Employment Appeal Tribunal – Practice – Appeals – Appeals out of time – Institution of appeals – Appeals not appearing to disclose arguable points of law – Interlocutory applications – Meetings for directions – Right to inspect and copy certain documents – Listing of cases – Admissibility of documents – Complaints of bias – Exhibits and documents for use at hearing.

The Practice Direction dated 3rd March 1978 ([1978] 2 All ER 293, [1978] 1 WLR 573) as amended on 22nd February 1979 ([1979] 1 All ER 640, [1979] 1 WLR 289) is hereby revoked and replaced by the following.

1. The Employment Appeal Tribunal Rules 1980, SI 1980 No 2035, came into operation on 1st February 1981.

2. By virtue of para 17(2) of Sch 11 to the Employment Protection (Consolidation) Act 1978 the Employment Appeal Tribunal has power, subject to the 1980 rules, to regulate its own procedure.

3. Where the 1980 rules do not otherwise provide, the following procedure will be followed in all appeals to the Employment Appeal Tribunal.

4. *Appeals out of time*—(a) by virtue of r 3(1) of the 1980 rules every appeal under s 136 of the Employment Protection (Consolidation) Act 1978 or s 4 of the Employment Act 1980, to the Employment Appeal Tribunal shall be instituted by serving on the tribunal, within 42 days of the date on which the document recording the decision or order appealed from was sent to the appellant, a notice of appeal as prescribed in the 1980 rules. (b) Every notice of appeal not delivered within 42 days of the date on which the document recording the decision or order appealed from was sent to the appellant must be accompanied by an application for an extension of time, setting out the reasons for the delay. (c) Applications for an extension of time for appealing cannot be considered until a notice of appeal has been presented. (d) Unless otherwise ordered the application for extension of time will be considered and determined as though it were an interlocutory application. (e) In determining whether to extend the time for appealing, particular attention will be paid to the guidance contained in *Practice Note (Marshall v Harland & Wolff Ltd)* [1972] ICR 97 and to whether any excuse for the delay has been shown. (f) It is not necessarily a good excuse for delay in appealing that legal aid has been applied for, or that support is being sought e g from the Equal Opportunities Commission or from a trade union. In such cases the intending appellant should at the earliest possible moment, and at the latest within the time limit for appealing, inform the registrar, and the other party, of his intentions, and seek the latter's agreement to an extension of time for appealing. (g) Time for appealing runs from the date on which the document recording the decision or order of the industrial tribunal was sent to the appellant, notwithstanding that the assessment of compensation has been adjourned, or an application has been made for a review. (h) In any case of doubt or difficulty, notice of appeal should be presented in time, and an application made to the registrar for directions.

5. *Institution of appeal*—(a) Subject to r 3(2) of the 1980 rules, if it appears to the registrar that a notice of appeal or application gives insufficient particulars or lacks clarity either as to the question of law or the grounds of an appeal, the registrar may postpone his decision under that rule pending amplification or clarification of the notice of appeal, as regards the question of law or grounds of appeal, by the intended appellant. (b) An appellant will not ordinarily be allowed to contend that 'the decision was contrary to the evidence' or that 'there was no evidence to support the decision', or to advance similar contentions, unless full and sufficient particulars identifying the particular matters relied

on have been supplied to the appeal tribunal. (c) It will not be open to the parties to reserve a right to amend, alter or add to any pleading. Any such right is not inherent and may only be exercised if permitted by order for which an interlocutory application should be made as soon as the need for alteration is known.

6. *Special procedure*—(a) Where an appeal has not been rejected pursuant to r 3(2) but nevertheless the appeal tribunal considers that it is doubtful whether the grounds of appeal disclose an arguable point of law, the president or a judge may direct that the matter be set down before a division of the appeal tribunal for hearing of a preliminary point to enable the appellant to show cause why the appeal should not be dismissed on the ground that it does not disclose a fairly arguable point of law. (b) The respondent will be given notice of the hearing but since it will be limited to the preliminary point he will not be required to attend the hearing or permitted to take part in it. (c) If the appellant succeeds in showing cause, the hearing will be adjourned and the appeal will be set down for hearing before a different division of the appeal tribunal in the usual way. (d) If the appellant does not show cause, the appeal will be dismissed. (e) The decision whether this procedure will be adopted in any particular case will be in the discretion of the president or a judge.

7. *Interlocutory application*—(a) On receipt of an interlocutory application the registrar will submit a copy of the application to the other side, and will indicate that if it is not intended to oppose the application it may be unnecessary for the parties to be heard and that the appropriate order may be made in their absence. Where the application is opposed the registrar will also in appropriate cases give the parties an opportunity of agreeing to the application being decided on the basis of written submissions. (b) Save where the president or a judge directs otherwise, every interlocutory application to strike out pleadings or to debar a party from taking any further part in the proceedings pursuant to r 16 or r 21 will be heard on the day appointed for the hearing of the appeal, but immediately preceding the hearing thereof.

8. *Meeting for directions*—On every appeal from the decision of the certification officer, and, if necessary, on any other appeal or application, so soon as the answer is delivered, or, if a cross-appeal, the reply, the registrar will appoint a day when the parties shall meet on an appointment for directions and the appeal tribunal will give such directions, including a date for hearing, as it deems necessary.

9. *Right to inspect the register and certain documents and to take copies*—Where, pursuant to the direction dated 31st March 1976 (not reported), a document filed at the Employment Appeal Tribunal has been inspected and a photographic copy of the documents is bespoken, a copying fee of 25p for each page will be charged.

10. *Listing of cases*
A. *England and Wales*—(a) When the respondent's answer has been received and a copy served on the appellant, the case will be put in the list of cases for hearing. At the beginning of each calendar month a list will be prepared of cases to be heard on specified dates in the next following calendar month. That list will also include a number of cases which are liable to be taken in each specified week of the relevant month. Parties or their representatives will be notified as soon as the list is prepared; litigants in person will be notified by recorded delivery. When cases in the list with specified dates are settled or withdrawn cases warned for the relevant week will be substituted and the parties notified as soon as possible. (b) A party finding that the date which has been given causes serious difficulties may apply to the listing officer before the 15th of the month in which the case first appears in the list. No change will be made unless the listing officer agrees, but reasonable efforts will be made to accommodate parties in difficulties. Changes after the 15th of the month in which the list first appears will not be made other than on application to the President of the Employment Appeal Tribunal; arrangements for the making of such an application should be made through the listing officer. (c) Other cases

may be put in the list by the listing officer (with the consent of the parties) at shorter notice, e g where other cases have been settled or withdrawn or where it appears that they will take less time than originally estimated. Parties who wish their cases to be taken as soon as possible and at short notice should notify the listing officer. (d) Each week an up-to-date list for the following week will be prepared including any changes which have been made (in particular specifying cases which by then have been given fixed dates). (e) The monthly list and the weekly list will appear in the daily cause list and will also be displayed in room 6 at the Royal Courts of Justice and at 4 St James's Square, London SW1. It is important that parties or their advisers should inspect the weekly list as well as the monthly list. (f) If cases are settled or to be withdrawn notice should be given at once to the listing officer so that other cases may be given fixed dates.

B. *Scotland*—When the respondent's answer has been received and a copy served on the appellant both parties will be notified in writing that the appeal will be ready for hearing in approximately six weeks. The proposed date of hearing will be notified to the parties three or four weeks ahead. Any party who wishes to apply for a different date must do so within seven days of receipt of such notification. Thereafter a formal notice of the date fixed for the hearing will be issued not less than 14 days in advance. This will be a peremptory diet. It will not be discharged except by the judge on cause shown.

11. *Admissibility of documents*—(a) Where, pursuant to r 15 or r 19, an application is made by a party to an appeal to put in at the hearing of the appeal any document which was not before the industrial tribunal, including a note of evidence given before the industrial tribunal (other than the chairman's notes), the application shall be submitted in writing with copies of the document(s) sought to be made admissible at the hearing. (b) The registrar will forthwith communicate the nature of the application and of the document(s) sought to be made admissible to the other party and, where appropriate, to the chairman of the industrial tribunal, for comment. (c) A copy of the comment will be forwarded to the party making the application by the registrar who will either dispose of it in accordance with the 1980 rules or refer it to the appeal tribunal for a ruling at the hearing. In the case of comments received from the chairman of the industrial tribunal a copy will be sent to both parties.

12. *Complaints of bias etc*—(a) The appeal tribunal will not normally consider complaints of bias or of the conduct of an industrial tribunal unless full and sufficient particulars are set out in the grounds of appeal. (b) In any such case the registrar may inquire of the party making the complaint whether it is the intention to proceed with the complaint, in which case the registrar will give appropriate directions for the hearing. (c) Such directions may included the filing of affidavits dealing with the matters on the basis of which the complaint is made or for the giving of further particulars of the complaint on which the party will seek to rely. (d) On compliance with any such direction the registrar will communicate the complaint together with the matters relied on in support of the complaint to the chairman of the industrial tribunal so that he may have an opportunity of commenting on it. (e) No such complaint will be permitted to be developed on the hearing of the appeal unless the appropriate procedure has been followed. (f) A copy of any affidavit or direction for particulars to be delivered thereunder will be communicated to the other side.

13. *Exhibits and documents for use at the hearing*—(a) The appeal tribunal will prepare copies of all documents for use of the judges and members at the hearing in addition to those which the registrar is required to serve on the parties under the 1980 rules. It is the responsibility of parties or their advisers to ensure that all documents submitted for consideration at the hearing are capable of being reproduced legibly by photographic process. (b) In Scotland a copy of the chairman's notes will not be supplied to the parties except on application to the appeal tribunal on cause shown. In England and Wales copies will only be sent to the parties if in the view of the appeal tribunal all or part of such notes are necessary for the purpose of the appeal or on application to the tribunal on

cause shown. A chairman's notes are supplied for the use of the appeal tribunal and not for the parties to embark on a 'fishing' expedition to establish further grounds of appeal. (c) It is the duty of parties and their solicitors to ensure that only those documents which are relevant to the point of law raised in the appeal, and which are likely to be referred to, are included in the documents before the tribunal. (d) It will also be the responsibility of the parties or their advisers to ensure that all exhibits and documents used before the industrial tribunal, and which are considered to be relevant to the appeal, are sent to the appeal tribunal immediately on request. This will enable the appeal tribunal to number and prepare sufficient copies, together with an index, for the judges and members at least a week before the day appointed for the hearing. (e) A copy of the index will be sent to the parties or their representatives prior to the hearing so that they may prepare their bundles in the same order.

SLYNN J

17th February 1981   President.

Compania Financiera Soleada SA and others v Hamoor Tanker Corpn Inc
The Borag

COURT OF APPEAL, CIVIL DIVISION
LORD DENNING MR, SHAW AND TEMPLEMAN LJJ
16th, 17th, 18th, 19th DECEMBER 1980

Contract – Damages for breach – Remoteness of damage – Interest charges – Causation – Mitigation – Ship's managers arresting ship in breach of contract with owners – Owners arranging bank guarantee to secure release of ship – Amount of guarantee added to owners' overdraft and owners charged interest thereon – Owners claiming interest from managers – Whether interest too remote – Whether interest caused by arrest – Whether interest expended by owners in mitigation of managers' breach.

Under a management agreement made in 1969 the managers agreed to manage the operation of a vessel for the owners in return for a stipulated fee. The owners also agreed to reimburse the managers for any extra expenses incurred. In 1971 the managers incurred heavy expenditure on repairs and survey and duly demanded reimbursement from the owners. When the owners failed to make prompt payment, the managers, without informing the owners, caused the vessel to put into port at Cape Town while en route from Spain to the Arabian Gulf, and there, in breach of the agreement, had the vessel arrested under a writ in rem. In order to obtain release of the vessel by providing security for payment of the amount alleged to be due to the managers, the owners arranged for their bank to provide a guarantee in return for which the vessel was released 14 days later. The owners operated their business on a substantial overdraft and the bank in addition to debiting their account with commission for arranging the guarantee also debited the full amount of the guarantee itself against the account. The owners consequently incurred compound interest charges of $US95,000 on the full amount of the guarantee from 1974 to 1976. Following the vessel's release the owners claimed compensation from the managers for the wrongful arrest including reimbursement of the $95,000 interest on the guarantee. The managers refused to pay and the dispute was referred to arbitration. The umpire held that the owners were entitled to damages in respect of the commission charged by the bank in arranging the guarantee, but not in respect of the interest on the amount of the guarantee, since it resulted from the owners' financial policy in running their business on a substantial overdraft and was therefore too remote to be recoverable. On a special case stated by the umpire the judge held that the interest was money expended by way of mitigation of the managers' wrongful act and, the principles of causation and remoteness not being applicable, it was recoverable as a matter of course. The managers appealed to the Court of Appeal.

Held – The relationship of the parties, whether the equivalent of trustee and beneficiary or not, was irrelevant to deciding the essential question in issue, which was the proper compensation to be awarded to the owners for the wrongful arrest of the vessel and for obtaining its release, which in turn raised the question of whether the interest on the guarantee was a reasonable expense incurred by the owners in obtaining the guarantee. The owners' claim for the interest was a claim for damages for wrongful arrest rather than a claim for reimbursement of money expended in mitigation, and as such, whether it was expressed in terms of causation (on the basis that the liability to pay interest was not caused by the arrest) or remoteness of damage, the interest was not recoverable since it related to the owners' own particular arrangements with their bank (which were unknown to the managers), were not in the contemplation of the parties and were not reasonably foreseeable as flowing from the arrest; and (per Templeman LJ) whatever principle was invoked, whether that of causation or mitigation, the interest was a wholly unreasonable expense to incur and the managers were not liable for it. The appeal would accordingly be allowed and the umpire's award would be restored (see p 860 *h j*, p 861 *d* to p 862 *b e f* and *j*, p 863 *b* to *e* and p 864 *c* to *j*, post).

Notes

For remoteness and measure of damages in contract, see 12 Halsbury's Laws (4th Edn) paras 1127, 1174–1176, and for cases on the subject, see 17 Digest (Reissue) 135–159, 312–449.

Cases referred to in judgments

Dodd Properties (Kent) Ltd v Canterbury City Council [1979] 2 All ER 118, [1980] 1 WLR 433; rvsd [1980] 1 All ER 928, [1980] 1 WLR 433, CA.
Liesbosch, Dredger (Owners) v Owners of Steamship Edison [1933] AC 449, 102 LJP 73, sub nom *The Edison* [1933] All ER Rep 144, 149 LT 49, 18 Asp MLC 380, 38 Com Cas 267, 45 Ll L Rep 123, HL, 17 Digest (Reissue) 103, *113*.
Moore v DER Ltd [1971] 3 All ER 517, [1971] 1 WLR 1476, [1971] 2 Lloyd's Rep 359, [1972] RTR 97, CA, 17 Digest (Reissue) 132, *301.*
Parsons (H) (Livestock) Ltd v Uttley Ingham & Co Ltd [1978] 1 All ER 525, [1978] QB 791, [1977] 3 WLR 990, [1977] 2 Lloyd's Rep 522, CA, Digest (Cont Vol E) 172, *110a.*
Radford v De Froberville [1978] 1 All ER 33, [1977] 1 WLR 1262, 35 P & CR 316, Digest (Cont Vol E) 173, *141a.*

Cases also cited

Barclays Bank Ltd v Quistclose Investments Ltd [1968] 3 All ER 651, [1970] AC 657, HL.
Bunge SA v Kruse [1977] 1 Lloyd's Rep 492, CA.
Cairnsmore, The, The Gunda [1921] 1 AC 439, PC.
Edwards (Inspector of Taxes) v Bairstow [1955] 3 All ER 48, [1956] AC 14, HL.
Garnac Grain Co Inc v H M F Faure & Fairclough Ltd [1968] AC 1130, HL.
Hadley v Baxendale (1854) 9 Exch 341, [1843–60] All ER Rep 461.
Heron II, The, Koufos v C Czarnikow Ltd [1967] 3 All ER 686, [1969] 1 AC 350, HL.
Intertradex SA v Lesieur-Tourteaux SARL [1978] 2 Lloyd's Rep 509, CA.
Livingstone v Rawyards Coal Co (1880) 5 App Cas 25, HL.
Pioneer Shipping Ltd v BTP Tioxide Ltd, The Nema [1980] 3 All ER 117, [1980] QB 547, CA.
Roper v Johnson (1873) LR 8 CP 167.
Royal Greek Government v Minister of Transport (1949) 83 Ll L Rep 228.
Victoria Laundry (Windsor) Ltd v Newman Industries Ltd [1949] 1 All ER 997, [1949] 2 KB 528, CA.

Interlocutory appeal

The claimants, Compania Financiera Soleada SA, Netherlands Antilles Ships Management Corpn Ltd and Dammers and Van Der Heide's Shipping and Trading Co Ltd ('the managers'), appealed against so much of the judgment of Mustill J on 22nd June 1979 whereby he held, on an award in the form of a special case stated by the umpire, Mr Ralph E Kingsley, that Hamoor Tanker Corpn Inc ('the owners'), the respondents to the arbitration, were entitled to recover from the managers the sum of $US95,940·78 being interest charged by the National Bank of Kuwait Ltd, the owners' bankers, on the amount of a guarantee provided by the bank to enable the owners to secure the release of the vessel Borag following its arrest at Cape Town at the instance of the managers, who had been appointed managers of the vessel by the owners by agreement dated 19th April 1969. The facts are set out in the judgment of Lord Denning MR.

Kenneth Rokison QC and *Julian Cooke* for the managers.
David Johnson QC and *Peter Rawson* for the owners.

LORD DENNING MR. In this case a vessel was wrongfully arrested. It was afterwards released on the owner providing security. The question is: what is the proper measure of compensation for the owner?

The facts of the case are set out in the judgment of Mustill J ([1980] 1 Lloyd's Rep 111). So I need only state sufficient of them today to set the scene.

The owners of the vessel, the Borag, were a Liberian or Monrovian company. They were quite inexperienced in the management of vessels of that type. They therefore employed a company called Compania Financiera Soleada SA to manage the vessel. A management agreement was made in 1969 whereby the managers were to manage the vessel with the utmost care, as if they themselves were the owners of it, as if they were managing it in their own interests, managing it 'as a dedicated paterfamilias'.

The managers managed the vessel from 1969 to 1971. They were financed by the owners, who put them in funds at the beginning of each month. In addition, when extra expenses had been incurred, the managers would recoup them, on proper vouchers being produced.

Then in 1971 a special situation arose. The Borag entered into dry dock at Cadiz for repairs and survey. The account came to much more than was anticipated. The managers required to be put in funds to meet these extra expenses; and, of course, they wanted their monthly payment at the beginning of each month. But unfortunately, at the beginning of December, the managers had not been paid anything to meet the expenses. In particular they had not received the monthly advance for December 1971. The managers were disturbed about this. So they made a demand on the owners for payment; otherwise, they said, they would take steps on their own behalf to see that they received payment. That was in December 1971. I should say that a little time later the owners did pay the agreed sum of $US55,000 by way of the monthly payment; and said that they would pay any extra amount against vouchers. But this was too late for the managers, because meanwhile the managers decided to protect their interests as best they could. They did it in a most unfortunate way.

The vessel was at Cadiz. She was due to go round the Cape to the Gulf. She put in at Dakar on the way. The managers had arranged for one of their employees, Mr Van Brakel, to sail with the ship to Dakar. He was subsequently instructed to remain on board while the vessel went round the Cape. The usual practice was that the vessel would not go into the port at Cape Town (because she might be arrested). She would only stop outside to pick up mail, and then continue on her voyage to the Gulf. Instead, on this occasion, on Mr Van Brakel's instructions, the vessel did put into the port of Cape Town. The captain kept it quiet. He did not tell the owners anything about it. Mr Van Brakel told him to keep it quiet. So the vessel put into the port at Cape Town unbeknown to the owners. The managers there applied to the South African courts to arrest the ship in rem because, they said, they had these moneys due to them. The vessel was arrested in Cape Town on 17th December 1971. The owners were very upset. The conduct of the managers was a subterfuge. It was completely unjustified.

After the arrest, the owners took steps to get the vessel released. Their agents at Cape Town took the matter up, but they were very dilatory about it. Banks in Cape Town, Kuwait and the like had to be communicated with. At all events, it was a fortnight before the vessel was eventually released on 30th December 1971. So she was held up in Cape Town for 14 days owing to the wrongful arrest. As it happened, the 14 days were four days longer than they should have been. If the owners' agents had acted as promptly and expeditiously as they should have, the vessel would only have been under arrest for ten days. At all events, the vessel was out of action for at least 14 days by reason of the wrongful arrest.

All sorts of trouble arose, repudiation and cancellation of the arrangement and the like, which we need not go into at all. These matters were thrashed out in the course of a London arbitration of tremendous length. The hearing lasted 17 days, with leading counsel on both sides, and so forth. But I need not go into all the details because the umpire (Mr Kingsley) who heard the case held, after going through all the accounts, that the amount due from the owners to the managers was $US113,908·65. He was ready to award that sum as a final award in favour of the managers. The managers were entitled to that sum on the final statement of account, subject to this one point, on which the umpire stated a special case for the opinion of the court: what sum should be allowed to the owners as compensation for the wrongful arrest?

The owners' claim for compensation was put under three main heads. (1) The first was a pefectly legitimate head. It was the overheads and expenses thrown away by reason of the arrest and delay whilst the vessel was held up in Cape Town. The salaries of the crew, insurance and the like were all clearly expenses consequent on the wrongful arrest. (2) There was also a claim for the cost of providing the security and obtaining the release of the vessel. (3) In addition there was a claim for the loss of the profit the vessel would have made but for the wrongful arrest.

We are not concerned with the claim for overheads and expenses, because that has been settled in the sum of about $US30,000. Nor are we concerned with loss of profit, because it turned out that this was not a profit-making concern. What we are concerned about are the expenses of and incidental to obtaining the release of the vessel. They were divided into two main parts. The first was the cost of actually getting the guarantee and the bank charges incurred in doing it. That came to roughly $US30,000. We are not concerned with that. We are concerned with an interest charge coming to some $US95,000 as part of the expense of getting the vessel released.

The way in which the owners say they incurred that expense is very strange. It is so complicated that the umpire had to hear a lot of evidence in an attempt to sort it out. I will read the paragraphs of the award which deal with it. Paragraph 11(34) provides:

'The Bank Guarantee put up to procure the vessel's release from arrest was arranged by Owners through the National Bank of Kuwait ... The guarantee was actually furnished by the United Bank of Kuwait Limited against a counter-guarantee from the N.B.K. The N.B.K. was not required to provide a deposit with the United Bank of Kuwait Ltd. as counter-security for the guarantee.'

Paragraph 11(35) provides:

'Total commission charges made by the N.B.K. to the Owners amount to the agreed figure of Kuwait Dinars 9,208·07 or US Dollars 32,044·08 ...'

Then comes para 11(36) which deals with the point:

'In addition to the bank charges or commission mentioned above under paragraph 35 the N.B.K. raised interest charges against the Owners. Most of the December 1977 Hearing was taken up with controversy regarding this issue. On the very involved and detailed evidence I find that the interest charges arose from the fact that the Owners and their associated companies operated on the basis of a very substantial bank overdraft (finding this method of conducting their business convenient in view of their policy of making long-term investments abroad) and that consequently the N.B.K. found it right and necessary to increase the current overdraft by the amount of the Guarantee. The Managers were not informed by the Owners of the incurring of this interest charge; nor could they reasonably have *a* foreseen that as a result of their demand for the establishment of a Bank Guarantee the payment of interest charges, in addition to bank charges or commission, would flow as a natural and foreseeable consequence.'

It sounds very complicated; but the net result of it was that the owners were debited in their overdraft with the full amount of the sum guaranteed, and they had to pay interest on it. Not only simple interest, but compound interest. In other words, they had to pay *b* interest on the full amount involved, in contrast to a small sum used as a guarantee.

The whole question in the case is: can the owners recover this interest charge of such a large amount (it ran from 1971 to 1976) and not merely the cost of providing a guarantee which might never be called on? That is the real point in the case.

The umpire held that the compound interest was not a consequence of the guarantee which was established to procure the vessel's release from arrest; but it flowed from the *c* owners' financial policy in the conduct of their business. So he knocked that out. As to the overdraft, he said this, at para 12(c):

'The Owners are entitled to damages in respect of their reasonable foreseeable and naturally flowing costs and expenses of obtaining the vessel's release from wrongful arrest.' *d*

Paragraph 12(d) provides:

'The interest charges raised by the N.B.K. against Owners are not recoverable as damages naturally and foreseeably flowing from the wrongful arrest of the vessel and the Owners' efforts to secure the vessel's release from such arrest.'

On those findings, the umpire disallowed the interest charges, he disallowed the *e* compound interest point, and made his award accordingly.

The case was stated by the umpire for the opinion of the court. Mustill J reversed the decision of the umpire. He held that the owners could recover the whole of the interest charges. That would mean that the managers would get nothing. Their claim on the final award would be outweighed by the owners' claim for compensation. Now there is an appeal to us. *f*

Many points have been canvassed. I will try to deal with them shortly. First, the relationship between the owners and the managers. There was certainly a breach of duty under that relationship, whatever it was. It was said by counsel for the owners that it was equivalent to a relationship of a trustee and a beneficiary. The wrongful arrest was a breach of trust by the managers. Accordingly the compensation should be on the basis on which a trustee is made liable to account. He referred us to a passage in Underhill's *g* Law Relating to Trusts and Trustees (13th Edn, 1979, p 702) where the author says: 'Liability for breach of trust can be more extensive than liability for damages for tort or breach of contract.' But, if you read the whole passage, it seems to me plain that the author is dealing with that special aspect of a trustee's position when the trust funds are depleted or diminished in some way, and it is a question of the trustee recouping *h* them. The damages with which we are concerned in this case do not result from any intermeddling with trust property. There is no question of recoupment or restitution of money which has been done away with. It is simply damages for breach of duty. Whatever the relationship was, whether it was the special relationship between trustee and beneficiary or whether it was fiduciary or whether it was breach of contract, the whole question here is: what is to be the compensation for the wrongful act of arrest? I do not think any help is to be derived by putting the relationship into one or other *j* category. The whole question is: what is the proper compensation for the wrongful arrest of this vessel and her subsequent release?

The second point which arose was: what is the proper category into which to put the claim for the overdraft interest? Is its proper heading 'damages for wrongful arrest'? Or is it 'moneys expended in mitigation of damage'?

The umpire regarded it as a question of damages, expenditure recoverable as damages for a wrongful act. Whereas the judge, in his careful judgment, refused to treat it as damages. 'That is the wrong legal category,' he said. 'This is money expended by way of mitigation of another person's wrongful act to which different principles apply as to foreseeability, burden of proof, and the rest of it.'

I can understand that in some cases that distinction may be useful and valuable; but for myself, when expenditure is incurred as a result of a wrongful act, the common law has always looked on it as damages. I need not go through all the cases. In a personal injury case the medical expenditure incurred is regarded as damages. In damage to property, if you have a lorry or motor car which has been damaged and put out of action, the cost of providing a substitute is not regarded as sums expended in mitigation. It is always regarded as sums recoverable by way of damages for the wrongful act.

The distinction fades into nothingness in most cases. In *Moore v DER Ltd* [1971] 3 All ER 517, [1971] 1 WLR 1476 a car was damaged beyond repair. The test applied was: what was reasonable expenditure to make good the damage? Oliver J makes a useful analysis in *Radford v De Froberville* [1978] 1 All ER 33 at 44, [1977] 1 WLR 1262 at 1272. He points out that often there is nothing in it: it is virtually the same inquiry. There is the recent case of *Dodd Properties (Kent) Ltd v Canterbury City Council* [1979] 2 All ER 118, [1980] 1 WLR 433, where some of the cases were gone into. It seems to me, as a matter of common sense and common law, that expenditure made to obtain the release of a vessel from arrest should be regarded as an item of damages, and not as mitigation. It is the natural way of dealing with it.

The judge admitted that this was an attractive argument, but on the whole he felt that he could not accede to it. But it seems to me that it is the right way of dealing with it. It is damages, not mitigation.

Next there was the question of causation or remoteness. I would agree that the overdraft interest was in a sense a consequence of the unlawful arrest. It flowed from it in the sense that, if there had been no unlawful arrest, the overdraft would not have been incurred. But, as we all know, it is not every consequence of a wrongful act which is the subject of compensation. The law has to draw a line somewhere. That has nowhere been better stated than by Lord Wright in *The Edison* [1933] AC 449 at 460, [1933] All ER Rep 144 at 158:

> 'The law cannot take account of everything that follows a wrongful act; it regards some subsequent matters as outside the scope of its selection, because "it were infinite for the law to judge the cause of causes," or consequences of consequences ... In the varied web of affairs, the law must abstract some consequences as relevant, not, perhaps on grounds of pure logic but simply for practical reasons.'

That is the question in this case. Although the overdraft interest may be a consequence of the initial unlawful arrest, is it such a consequence that ought to be visited in damages? On this point (I do not care whether you call it 'causation' or whether you call it 'remoteness') causation and remoteness are two different ways of stating the same question: is the consequence sufficiently closely connected with the cause as to be the subject of compensation or not? To my mind causation and remoteness here are the same.

Counsel for the owners referred to the recent case of *H Parsons (Livestock) Ltd v Uttley Ingham & Co Ltd* [1978] 1 All ER 525, [1978] QB 791. In that case I drew a distinction between loss of profit cases on the one hand and damage or expenditure on the other. This comes into the damage and expenditure line and not into the loss of profit line.

As to the damage and expenditure cases, it seems to me that the rules we have laid down as to causation (whether it is sufficiently proximate to be a consequence or not) or remoteness (whether it is naturally and reasonably flowing from the breach or not) come down to the same thing. If applied, the judge himself would say that the managers were not liable. He said in his judgment:

> 'If it were appropriate to regard the bank interest as a direct item of damage, there would be much to be said for the view that it had reference to some particular arrangements of the owners which were unknown to the managers and not

communicated to them, and which were not therefore in the contemplation of the
parties at the time when they made the contract, and that accordingly they represent
an item which must be disallowed.'

So on that approach to the case, which I think is the right approach, the judge would have
come to the same view as the umpire.

It comes back to what Templeman LJ said in the first hour or two of hearing this
appeal: they are entitled to all the reasonable expenditure which they incurred as a result
of the wrongful arrest and getting the ship released; but not unheard of overdraft interest
of this kind.

In the circumstances the question of remission to the arbitrator does not apply. I
would only say this: the question of expenses incurred in respect of mitigation was fully
argued before the umpire. But he did not make any findings on it. He was content to
rest himself on the findings which I have already mentioned. Each of the parties wanted
to serve notice of motion to remit. The managers wanted to put in a notice of motion
saying how unreasonable was the so-called mitigation, and it should not be allowed. The
owners wanted to put in another motion to get a finding that it was reasonable. Pages
and pages were taken up in the notices of motion. The judge refused to go into them.
He thought that there had been too much delay in the matter. But it seems to me that,
if the umpire was at fault in not dealing with mitigation, it was his fault and not that of
either of the parties. If it was necessary, in order to do justice, to have findings on that
point, I should have thought it would have been very desirable to remit the matter to the
umpire for him to determine those outstanding points; especially as in the last paragraph
of his case stated he says in effect that, if anything was wanting, he would ask the court
to remit the award to him so as to enable him to redraft it.

In the circumstances it seems to me that it is quite unnecessary and undesirable to
remit the award to the umpire. It virtually comes to this: it seems to me that the umpire
directed himself properly. He thought that the interest charges were too remote, too
unreasonable, too unforeseeable altogether to be properly counted as a head of
compensation. That seems to me to be a very sensible and correct way of dealing with
it. It is not a matter in which the court should interfere.

I would therefore allow the appeal and restore the decision of the umpire.

SHAW LJ. I agree; and what I add is only a postscript to the judgment which has just
been delivered by Lord Denning MR. The arguments developed before the umpire as
to the respective concepts of causation, foreseeability and mitigation of damage assumed
almost the character of a debate on some philosophical abstraction. It is small wonder
that the umpire, in the elucidation of the problems with which he was confronted, made
an analysis which enabled him to arrive at an award seemingly based on only one of those
concepts. After all, he was called on to deal with a practical commercial situation and not
with a hypothetical exercise in jurisprudence elaborated by incursions into the law of
trusts. He looked at the whole matter as should a man of business who was sufficiently
informed in regard to the broad legal principles involved in breach of contract and the
right and reasonable basis for compensation for the damage occasioned by a particular
breach.

Although the umpire made no express reference to mitigation of damage, he must
have recognised the question of reasonableness as intruding itself into the determination
of what the damage arising from the breach was. Whether the costs of the guarantee
were incurred in mitigation of damage or constituted the actual damage might have
some consequence as to where lay the burden of proving what is reasonable or
unreasonable. But the answer to that problem ought not to affect the ultimate result in
any quantitative sense. As I read the award, the umpire had all the material basic
considerations in mind when reaching his decision. His resolution of the interrelated
problems was not only tenable but just in the light of the facts found by him; and they
were adequate to support a just result in legal as well as in mercantile terms.

With all respect to the judge, whose knowledge and experience in this field can hardly be surpassed, I venture to think that he was deflected from a relatively straight road into a legalistic labyrinth. If one returns to the straight road, there is no need to look for further elucidation of the facts, and therefore no occasion to remit the award to the umpire.

For the reasons which have been stated by Lord Denning MR, I too would allow the appeal and restore the award of the umpire.

TEMPLEMAN LJ. I also agree. The managers, in breach of contract, arrested the owners' vessel to secure payment of the owners' debts. The managers became liable for the reasonably foreseeable damages suffered by the owners as a result of that breach of contract. Counsel for the owners relied on cl 2 of the management agreement, which imposes on the managers a particularly onerous standard of duty. Rightly or wrongly the owners were then allowed to call evidence as to what the clause meant and as to the parties' discussions about its meaning when they were negotiating the agreement; and rightly or wrongly the gloss has been put on the clause that it imposed on the managers the duties of trustees. So be it; but that does not mean that the contractual laws of measurement of damages or mitigation can be thrown out of the window and that the owners, who can only be described as odd beneficiaries under a trust, can play ducks and drakes with the trustees when it comes to running up damages for breach of the duty imposed on the managers. In my judgment, in the circumstances of this case, cl 2 does not make any difference to the amount of money which the managers must find for their now admitted breach of contract.

Approaching the consequences of that breach of contract with the spectacles adopted by the managers, it was reasonably foreseeable that the owners would seek to procure the release of their vessel arrested in breach of contract, and for this purpose they might obtain a guarantee for payment of their debt, and they would incur expense in obtaining a guarantee. That expense, if reasonable, would be recoverable as foreseeable damages.

Approaching the case with the slightly different coloured spectacles put on by the owners, the obtaining of a guarantee was a reasonable form of mitigation. The reasonable expenses of obtaining a guarantee must be recoverable whichever pair of spectacles is adopted, either as being foreseeable damages or as being expenses of mitigation.

The owners paid a commission and bank charges to obtain a guarantee from their bankers. The umpire held that the commission and the bank charges were recoverable from the managers. Subsequently to the grant of the guarantee, the bankers debited an overdraft account of the owners with interest, compounded by quarterly rests, on the maximum sum secured by the guarantee. The owners submitted to and accepted liability for these interest charges down to 1976 but not beyond that date. The umpire held that these interest charges were not recoverable from the managers.

The owners had ample opportunity in the course of the arbitration to explain and justify their submission to interest charges in respect of money which they had never borrowed. Paragraphs 79 to 87 of the findings of fact requested by the owners were designed to establish that it was reasonable and necessary for the owners to incur and pay the interest charges. Conversely, the managers had ample opportunity in the course of the arbitration to establish that the interest charges were wholly unreasonable or, alternatively, partly unreasonable. Paragraphs 56 to 82 of the findings of fact requested by the managers were designed to establish that it was unreasonable for the owners to incur and pay the interest charges.

It is inconceivable that the umpire overlooked the necessity of making up his mind on these problems and overlooked the necessity of deciding in brief whether it was reasonable or unreasonable for the owners to incur these interest charges.

It was thus the task of the umpire to determine whether or not the interest charges were reasonable. This was not a difficult path for an umpire to follow. Unfortunately the umpire was plunged into a murky pool and was urged to distinguish between the shallow end of mitigation of damages, the middle depths of causation of damages, and the deep end of remoteness of damages. It is not surprising that the umpire reported the results of his journey, and short-circuited the requests for detailed findings of fact, and avoided the legal arguments to which he had been subjected, and avoided everything except the ultimate answer, namely that the interest charges were not reasonably foreseeable damages suffered by the owners as a result of the managers' breach of contract. In taking this shortcut, the umpire exposed himself to the accusations of the owners, to which we have been subjected, that he failed to ask himself the right question.

The learned judge plunged into the same pool and failed to discern that on any footing the umpire had provided a relevant and decisive answer. That answer is to be found in the umpire's award in paras 11(36) and 11(37), in para 12(c) and (d), and in the ultimate para 13(e). In short, he gave the ultimate answer that the interest charges were not damages naturally and foreseeably flowing from the wrongful arrest of the vessel.

The judge succeeded in holding that the interest charges were recoverable damages, although the only relevant finding of the umpire was that the interest charges were not foreseeable. The judge in his judgment said that the umpire's finding that the interest charges were unforeseeable did not justify the inference that the incurring of the interest charges was due to the owners having adopted an unreasonable form of mitigation. In my judgment, the inference of the umpire's award is irresistible that the interest charges were wholly unreasonable and should never have been incurred either as a head of damage or as part of a reasonable form of mitigation. The umpire, who found that the interest charges were not recoverable because they were not foreseeable, must have concluded that the bank charges and commission were recoverable because they were foreseeable. The only possible distinction between the bank charges and commission which were recoverable and the interest charges which were irrecoverable lies in the fact that the interest charges were wholly unreasonable and must have been found so by the umpire. The umpire must have thought that the owners could and should have adopted a form of mitigation which was reasonable, either by refusing to pay the interest charges to their bankers, or by seeking a guarantee elsewhere or by some other available form of securing the release of the vessel more cheaply.

The umpire found that the owners submitted to the interest charges because, as Lord Denning MR has quoted, they 'operated on the basis of a very substantial bank overdraft (finding this method of conducting their business convenient . . .)', and he held that 'the interest charges . . . are not recoverable as damages naturally and foreseeably flowing from the wrongful arrest'. To reach this conclusion, he must have determined that the interest charges were unreasonable and unnecessary; and, although as between the owners and their bank it may have suited the owners in their business interests and having regard to their relationship with their bankers to suffer this interest, nevertheless as between the owners and the managers the interest charges were wholly unreasonable and should not have been incurred.

Whatever principle is invoked, whether it be the principle of causation or mitigation, the acid test in the present circumstances must have been reasonableness; and, if the interest charges were unreasonable, they were not damages for which the managers are liable. I agree with counsel for the owners that in some circumstances different principles may require different tests and produce different results, but in the present case, if the interest charges were unreasonable, they were too remote; they were not caused by the breach; they were not part of a reasonable form of mitigation; all these matters hang together. In view of the fact that the umpire found that the interest charges were not recoverable and were not damages which were foreseeable, I have no doubt that he concluded that the interest charges were wholly unreasonable for the purpose of any and every principle which had been canvassed before him. As I said, he avoided all the detailed questions he was asked to find on and all the theoretical aspects of the matter and simply ruled that the interest charges were not recoverable.

I too would restore the umpire's award.

Appeal allowed. Award of umpire restored. Leave to appeal to the House of Lords refused.

Solicitors: *Holman, Fenwick & Willan* (for the managers); *Hedleys* (for the owners).

Sumra Green   Barrister.

a

W T Ramsay Ltd v Inland Revenue Commissioners
Eilbeck (Inspector of Taxes) v Rawling

b HOUSE OF LORDS

LORD WILBERFORCE, LORD FRASER OF TULLYBELTON, LORD RUSSELL OF KILLOWEN, LORD ROSKILL AND LORD BRIDGE OF HARWICH

26th, 27th, 28th, 29th JANUARY, 2nd, 3rd, 4th FEBRUARY, 12th MARCH 1981

c
Capital gains tax – Tax avoidance scheme – Self-cancelling transactions – Circular contracts – Scheme designed to produce allowable loss matched by capital gain which is not liable to tax – Property revolved in circle so that neither gain nor loss produced for taxpayer – Transactions in scheme not a sham – Whether transactions in scheme required to be considered individually – Whether scheme to be treated as a nullity if it produces neither gain nor loss to taxpayer.

d
Capital gains tax – Disposal of assets – Debt – Debt on a security – Security – Need for document or certificate issued by debtor – Loan by taxpayer company to subsidiary – Loan not secured on assets of subsidiary – Taxpayer company provided with statutory declaration by director of subsidiary recording acceptance of loan offer – Whether loan a 'debt on a security' – Finance Act 1965, Sch 7, paras 5(3)(b), 11(1).

e
Capital gains tax – Settlement – Interest in settled property – Tax avoidance scheme – Taxpayer purchasing reversionary interest – Interest split into two parts – Part appointed to another settlement and later sold at a non-taxable profit – Taxpayer selling remainder of interest at a loss – Profit matching loss – Whether taxpayer selling whole of reversionary interest despite decrease in value of assets in interest – Whether appointed assets remaining part of reversionary interest – Finance Act 1965, Sch 7, para 13(1).

f In two appeals the question arose whether tax avoidance schemes consisting of a number of separate transactions, none of which was a sham, but which were self-cancelling, had the effect of producing a loss which was allowable as a deduction for the purpose of assessing capital gains tax. In each case the scheme included a transaction designed to produce a loss to be offset against a gain previously made by the taxpayer which would otherwise be taxable, while another transaction produced a matching gain which was not liable to tax.

g In the first appeal the taxpayer acquired on 23rd February 1973 the whole of the issued shares of C Ltd for £185,034. On the same day the taxpayer offered and C Ltd accepted two loans ('loan L1' and 'loan L2') to C Ltd, each of £218,750, repayable at par after 30 and 31 years respectively. C Ltd was entitled to make earlier repayment if desired, and was obliged to do so if it went into liquidation. If either loan were repaid before its *h* maturity date, it had to be repaid at par or at its market value, whichever was higher. Both loans carried interest at the rate of 11% per annum but the taxpayer had the right, exercisable on one occasion only, to decrease the interest rate on one of the loans and increase correspondingly the interest rate on the other. The offer was accepted orally by C Ltd and afterwards the taxpayer was provided with a statutory declaration, made by one of C Ltd's directors, recording C Ltd's acceptance of the offer. The £437,500 was *j* duly advanced by the taxpayer to C Ltd from funds made available by a finance house. On 2nd March 1973 the taxpayer reduced the interest on loan L1 to nil and increased the interest rate on loan L2 to 22%, and sold loan L2 to M Ltd for £391,481, which was its approximate market value, thus making a capital profit of £172,731 on the sale of loan L2. In due course, after further loan and share transactions, loan L1 was repaid at par and the taxpayer company incurred a capital loss of £175,647 in respect of the sale of shares in C Ltd. In computing its corporation tax for the accounting period ended 31st May 1973 the taxpayer claimed, inter alia, that loan L2 was not a 'debt on a security' within paras 11(1)[a] and 5(3)(b)[b] of Sch 7 to the Finance Act 1965, because it had not been evidenced in a document as security, and that the capital profit of £172,731 arising on the sale thereof was therefore not a chargeable gain. The Special Commissioners held that loan L2 was 'loan stock or similar security', within para 5(3)(b), that its disposal was therefore a disposal of a 'debt on a security', within para 11(1), and that accordingly the gain arising on its sale was not exempt from liability to tax. The judge ([1978] 2 All ER 321) allowed an appeal by the taxpayer on the ground that the essential feature of a security as defined in para 5(3)(b) was a document or certificate issued by a debtor which would represent a marketable security or which would enable it to be dealt in and if necessary converted into shares or other securities and that, since no such document had been issued by C Ltd to the taxpayer as security for the loan, the loan was not a 'debt on a security' for the purpose of para 11(1). On appeal by the Crown, the Court of Appeal ([1979] 3 All ER 213) held that loan L2 had all the characteristics of loan stock since it was evidenced by a document or security, namely the statutory declaration, which was similar to a loan certificate usually furnished by a debtor company, and the loan could therefore be converted into shares. The court accordingly held that the gain arising on the disposal of loan L2 was not exempt from liability to tax. The taxpayer appealed to the House of Lords.

In the second appeal the taxpayer had made chargeable gains of £355,094 on the sale of shares and purchased a tax avoidance scheme from T Ltd, a Jersey company, with the object of eliminating his liability to capital gains tax. The scheme involved the creation of a settlement in Jersey with the taxpayer as the beneficiary of the reversionary interest therein and the use of an existing Gibraltar settlement having a trust fund of £600,000. The Gibraltar settlement contained a special power of appointment under which the trustees of the settlement had power, inter alia, to advance any part of the capital of the trust fund to (a) the reversioner and (b) the trustees of any other settlement under which the reversioner had an interest falling into possession at the time of such advance. At all material times the trust fund of the Gibraltar settlement was held by T Ltd on behalf of the trustees of that settlement and the only beneficiaries under that settlement, other than the taxpayer, were two Jersey companies associated with T Ltd, namely P Ltd and G Ltd. On 24th March 1975 the taxpayer purchased the reversionary interest under the Gibraltar settlement for £543,600, which was lent to him by T Ltd at 13½% interest per annum. On the following day at the taxpayer's request the trustees of the Gibraltar settlement exercised the power of appointment to advance to the trustees of the Jersey settlement the sum of £315,000 out of the funds of the Gibraltar settlement. The Gibraltar trustees directed T Ltd to make the necessary payments. Subsequently, on 3rd April, the taxpayer sold his reversionary interest in the Gibraltar settlement to G Ltd for £231,130 which went direct to T Ltd in part discharge of the debt owed to it by the taxpayer. On the same day the taxpayer also sold his reversionary interest in the Jersey settlement, of which he was the original beneficiary, to T Ltd for £312,100. That sum was retained by T Ltd by way of further part discharge of the loan made by it to the taxpayer. The balance of £370 outstanding was paid by the taxpayer to discharge the loan made by T Ltd. The taxpayer claimed that the sale of the Gibraltar reversion to G Ltd for £231,130 produced a loss of £312,470 (being the difference between the £543,600 paid for the reversion and the £231,130 received from G Ltd) which could be offset against his chargeable gains and that he was exempt under para

---

a   Paragraph 11(1), so far as material, provides: 'Where a person incurs a debt to another . . . no chargeable gain shall accrue to that (that is the original) creditor on a disposal of the debt, except in the case of the debt on a security (as defined in paragraph 5 of this Schedule).'

b   Paragraph 5(3), so far as material, provides: 'For the purposes of this paragraph . . . (b) "security" includes any loan stock or similar security . . . of any company, and whether secured or unsecured.'

13(1)^c of Sch 7 to the Finance Act 1965 from capital gains tax on the profit of £312,100 made on the sale of the Jersey reversion because it was the disposal of a reversionary interest by a person who had not acquired or derived title from a person who had acquired the interest for money consideration. The Revenue assessed the taxpayer to capital gains tax on the basis that the loss of £312,470 on the sale of the Gibraltar reversion was not an allowable deduction. The taxpayer appealed to the General Commissioners who upheld the taxpayer's claim that the purchase and sale of the Gibraltar reversion were to be considered as a separate transaction in isolation from the other transactions and that as such it had produced an allowable loss. On appeal by the Crown the judge ([1979] STC 16) reversed the commissioners' decision. The taxpayer appealed to the Court of Appeal ([1980] 2 All ER 12) who held (per Buckley and Donaldson LJJ) that since the appointment by the Gibraltar trustees was made under a special power the taxpayer's interest in the Jersey reversion remained subject to the Gibraltar settlement and part of the taxpayer's interest in the Gibraltar reversion, and (per Templeman LJ) that a circular contract or series of interdependent contracts which revolved the same property in a circle could not be divided into separate transactions and the profit or loss arising, if any, was to be judged by comparing the position at the start and at the finish of the circle. The Court of Appeal accordingly dismissed the taxpayer's appeal and he appealed to the House of Lords.

Held – The appeals would be dismissed for the following reasons—

(1) It was the task of the Revenue and the courts to ascertain the legal nature of any transaction to which it was sought to attach a tax or tax consequence, and if the legal nature was that which emerged from a series or combination of transactions which were intended to operate as such, it was the series or combination of transactions rather than the individual transactions to which regard was to be had. Accordingly, where a taxpayer used a scheme comprising a number of separate transactions with the object of avoiding tax, the Revenue and the courts were not limited to considering the genuineness or otherwise of each individual step or transaction in the scheme, but could consider the scheme as a whole and if it was found that the composite transaction produced neither a gain nor a loss it could be treated as a nullity for tax purposes. Applying that principle in each case, the only conclusion consistent with the intentions of the parties and with the documents taken as a whole was that there was an integrated and interdependent series of transactions which (apart from a small loss of £370 in the second case) had produced neither a gain nor a loss, and in those circumstances it would be wrong and a faulty analysis to pick out and segregate for tax purposes the one transaction that produced the loss. Accordingly, in each case the scheme was to be treated as a nullity for tax purposes (see p 871 *d* to *j*, p 872 *d f g*, p 873 *b* to *e*, p 874 *j*, p 877 *f* to *h*, p 881 *c* to *f* and p 883 *a* and *e f*, post); *Chinn v Collins*, p 189, ante, dictum of Lord Wilberforce in *Inland Revenue Comrs v Plummer* [1979] 3 All ER at 779 applied; dissenting judgment of Eveleigh LJ in *Floor v Davis* [1978] 2 All ER 1079 approved; *Inland Revenue Comrs v Duke of Westminster* [1935] All ER Rep 259 distinguished.

(2) In the first appeal loan L2 was in any event a 'similar security' to loan stock since it was an interest-bearing loan for a long fixed period which could only be redeemed at the higher of face value or market value, and as such could be dealt in and have a market value. Accordingly it was a 'debt on a security' rather than a mere debt for the purposes of para 5(3)(*b*) of Sch 7 to the 1965 Act. It therefore did not come within the exemption

---

c Paragraph 13(1) provides: 'No chargeable gain shall accrue on the disposal of an interest created by or arising under a settlement (including, in particular, an annuity or life interest, and the reversion to an annuity or life interest) by the person for whose benefit the interest was created by the terms of the settlement or by any other person except one who acquired, or derives his title from one who acquired, the interest for a consideration in money or money's worth, other than consideration consisting of another interest under the settlement.'

from chargeable gains applying to mere debts (see p 875 *h* to p 876 *b*, p 879 *e* to *j*, p 882 *j* and p 883 *a* and *e f*, post).

(3) In the second appeal, the taxpayer's interest in the Gibraltar reversion did not remain the same regardless of any change in the assets comprising the reversion, since the balance of £255,390 remaining after the Gibraltar trustees had exercised the power of appointment was not the whole fund in which the taxpayer had bought an interest. Consequently, the sale of the Gibraltar reversion for £231,130 was not the sale of the reversion which the taxpayer had originally purchased but merely a sale of the balance remaining after the exercise of the power of appointment. Alternatively, following the exercise of the power of appointment the taxpayer's reversionary interest in the Jersey settlement was to be regarded as part of his interest in the Gibraltar settlement (see p 877 *h* to p 878 *b*, p 880 *d* to *f*, p 882 *j* and p 883 *a* and *e f*, post).

Per Curiam. The distinction between a 'debt on a security' and an ordinary unsecured 'debt' for the purposes of para 11(1) of Sch 7 to the 1965 Act does not necessarily depend on the existence or otherwise of a document or certificate embodying the obligation to repay, nor (per Lord Wilberforce) on whether the debt can be converted into shares or other securities, since (per Lord Fraser) the true distinction is between a simple unsecured debt and a debt in the nature of an investment which can be dealt in and purchased as an investment (see p 875 *f* to *h*, p 879 *b c* and p 883 *a* and *e f*, post); *Cleveleys Investment Trust Co v Inland Revenue Comrs* 1971 SC 233 and *Aberdeen Construction Group Ltd v Inland Revenue Comrs* [1978] 1 All ER 962, explained.

Decisions of Court of Appeal in *W T Ramsay Ltd v Inland Revenue Comrs* [1979] 3 All ER 213 and in *Eilbeck (Inspector of Taxes) v Rawling* [1980] 2 All ER 12 affirmed.

Notes

For the treatment of a debt on a security for the purposes of capital gains tax, see 5 Halsbury's Laws (4th Edn) para 104.

For capital gains tax in relation to settled property, see ibid paras 45–48.

For the Finance Act 1965, Sch 7, paras 5, 11, 13, see 34 Halsbury's Statutes (3rd Edn) 953, 956, 957.

For the year 1979–80 and subsequent years of assessment paras 5, 11 and 13 of Sch 7 to the 1965 Act have been replaced by ss 82, 134 and 58 of the Capital Gains Tax Act 1979 respectively.

Cases referred to in opinions

Aberdeen Construction Group Ltd v Inland Revenue Comrs [1978] 1 All ER 962, [1978] AC 885, [1978] 2 WLR 648, 1978 SC (HL) 72, [1978] STC 127, HL; *varying* 1977 SC 265, [1977] STC 302, CS, Digest (Cont Vol E) 304, *145 2e(iii)*.

Black Nominees v Nicol (Inspector of Taxes) [1975] STC 372, 50 Tax Cas 229, 54 ATC 99, [1975] TR 93, Digest (Cont Vol D) 461, *1121a*.

Chinn v Collins (Inspector of Taxes), *Chinn v Hochstrasser (Inspector of Taxes)* p 189, ante, [1981] 2 WLR 14, [1981] STC 1, HL.

Cleveleys Investment Trust Co v Inland Revenue Comrs 1971 SC 233, 47 Tax Cas 300, 50 ATC 230, [1971] TR 205, CS.

Federal Comr of Taxation v Westraders Pty Ltd (1980) 30 ALR 353.

Floor v Davis (Inspector of Taxes) [1979] 2 All ER 677, [1980] AC 695, [1979] 2 WLR 830, [1979] STC 379, [1979] TR 163, HL; *affg* [1978] 2 All ER 1079, [1978] Ch 295, [1978] 3 WLR 360, [1978] STC 436, CA, Digest (Cont Vol E) 302, *145 2(i)*.

Gilbert v Internal Revenue Comr (1957) 248 F 2d 399.

Inland Revenue Comrs v Duke of Westminster [1936] AC 1, [1935] All ER Rep 259, 19 Tax Cas 490, 104 LJKB 383, 153 LT 223, HL, 28(1) Digest (Reissue) 507, *1845*.

Inland Revenue Comrs v Plummer [1979] 3 All ER 775, [1980] AC 896, [1979] 3 WLR 689, [1979] STC 793, HL, Digest (Cont Vol E) 290, *866d*.

Inland Revenue Comrs v Wesleyan and General Assurance Society [1948] 1 All ER 555, 30 Tax Cas 11, [1948] LJR 948, [1948] TR 67, 41 R & IT 182, HL; *affg* [1946] 2 All ER 749, 30 Tax Cas 11, 176 LT 84, CA, 28(1) Digest (Reissue) 264, *860*.

Knetsch v United States (1960) 364 US 361.
MacRae v Internal Revenue Comr (1961) 34 TC 20; affd 294 F 2d 56.
Mangin v Inland Revenue Comr [1971] 1 All ER 179, [1971] AC 739, [1971] 2 WLR 39, [1970] TR 249, PC, 28(1) Digest (Reissue) 543, 1322.
Rubin v United States (1962) 304 F 2d 766.
Snook v London and West Riding Investments Ltd [1967] 1 All ER 518, [1967] 2 QB 786, [1967] 2 WLR 1020, CA, Digest (Cont Vol C) 416, 21b.

Appeals

W T Ramsay Ltd v Inland Revenue Comrs

The taxpayer, W T Ramsay Ltd, appealed against the decision of the Court of Appeal (Lord Scarman, Ormrod and Templeman LJJ) ([1979] 3 All ER 213, [1979] STC 582) on 24th May 1979 allowing an appeal by the Crown against the decision of Goulding J ([1978] 2 All ER 321, [1978] STC 253) on 2nd March 1978 allowing the taxpayer's appeal against a decision of the Special Commissioners, dated 30th January 1976, whereby, on an appeal by the taxpayer against an assessment to corporation tax in the sum of £176,552 for the period ended 31st May 1973, the commissioners held that a loan made by the taxpayer to Caithmead Ltd was a 'debt on a security' within the meaning of the Finance Act 1965, Sch 7, paras 5(3)(b), 11(1), and that a chargeable gain accrued to the taxpayer when it disposed of a loan to Masterdene Finance Ltd on 2nd March 1973. The facts are set out in the opinion of Lord Wilberforce.

Eilbeck (Inspector of Taxes) v Rawling

The taxpayer, D M E Rawling, appealed against the decision of the Court of Appeal (Buckley, Templeman and Donaldson LJJ) ([1980] 2 All ER 12, [1980] STC 192) on 14th February 1980 dismissing his appeal against a decision of Slade J ([1979] STC 16) dated 17th July 1978 allowing an appeal by way of case stated by the Crown from the determination of the Commissioners for the General Purposes of the Income Tax for the division of North Birmingham allowing the taxpayer's appeal against an assessment to capital gains tax in the sum of £355,094 made on him for the year 1974–75. The facts are set out in the opinion of Lord Wilberforce.

D C Potter QC and *David C Milne* for W T Ramsay Ltd.
C N Beattie and *Hilda Wilson* for Mr Rawling.
Peter Millett QC and *Brian Davenport QC* for the Crown.

Their Lordships took time for consideration.

12th March. The following opinions were delivered.

LORD WILBERFORCE. The first of these appeals is an appeal by W T Ramsay Ltd, a farming company. In its accounting period ending 31st May 1973 it made a 'chargeable gain' for purposes of corporation tax by a sale-leaseback transaction. This gain it desired to counteract, so as to avoid the tax, by establishing an allowable loss. The method chosen was to purchase from a company specialising in such matters a ready-made scheme. The general nature of this was to create out of a neutral situation two assets one of which would decrease in value for the benefit of the other. The decreasing asset would be sold, so as to create the desired loss; the increasing asset would be sold, yielding a gain which it was hoped would be exempt from tax.

In the courts below, attention was concentrated on the question whether the gain just referred to was in truth exempt from tax or not. The Court of Appeal ([1979] 3 All ER 213, [1979] STC 582), reversing the decision of Goulding J ([1978] 2 All ER 321, [1978] STC 253), decided that it was not. In this House, the Crown, while supporting this decision of the Court of Appeal, mounted a fundamental attack on the whole of the scheme acquired and used by the taxpayer. It contended that it should simply be disregarded as artificial and fiscally ineffective.

Immediately after this appeal there was heard another taxpayer's appeal, *Eilbeck* (*Inspector of Taxes*) *v Rawling*. This involved a scheme of a different character altogether, but one also designed to create a loss allowable for purposes of capital gains tax, together with a non-taxable gain, by a scheme acquired for this purpose. Similarly, this case was decided, against the taxpayer, in the Court of Appeal ([1980] 2 All ER 12, [1980] STC 192) on consideration of a particular aspect of the scheme: and similarly, the Crown in this House advanced a fundamental argument against the scheme as a whole.

I propose to consider first the fundamental issue, which raises arguments common to both cases. This is obviously of great importance both in principle and in scope. I shall then consider the particular, and quite separate arguments, relevant to each of the two appeals.

I will first state the general features of the schemes which are relevant to the wider argument.

In each case we have a taxpayer who has realised an ascertained and quantified gain: in *Ramsay* £187,977, in *Rawling* £355,094. He is then advised to consult specialists willing to provide, for a fee, a preconceived and ready made plan designed to produce an equivalent allowable loss. The taxpayer merely has to state the figure involved, ie the amount of the gain he desires to counteract, and the necessary particulars are inserted into the scheme.

The scheme consists, as do others which have come to the notice of the courts, of a number of steps to be carried out, documents to be executed, payments to be made, according to a timetable, in each case rapid (see the attractive description by Buckley LJ in *Rawling* [1980] 2 All ER 12 at 16, [1980] STC 192 at 197). In each case two assets appear, like particles in a gas chamber with opposite charges, one of which is used to create the loss, the other of which gives rise to an equivalent gain which prevents the taxpayer from supporting any real loss, and which gain is intended not to be taxable. Like the particles, these assets have a very short life. Having served their purpose they cancel each other out and disappear. At the end of the series of operations, the taxpayer's financial position is precisely as it was at the beginning, except that he has paid a fee, and certain expenses, to the promoter of the scheme.

There are other significant features which are normally found in schemes of this character. First, it is the clear and stated intention that once started each scheme shall proceed through the various steps to the end; they are not intended to be arrested half-way (cf *Chinn v Collins* (*Inspector of Taxes*) p 189, ante). This intention may be expressed either as a firm contractual obligation (it was so in *Rawling*) or as in *Ramsay* as an expectation without contractual force.

Second, although sums of money, sometimes considerable, are supposed to be involved in individual transactions, the taxpayer does not have to put his hand in his pocket (cf *Inland Revenue Comrs v Plummer* [1979] 3 All ER 775, [1980] AC 896, [1979] STC 793 and *Chinn v Collins* (*Inspector of Taxes*). The money is provided by means of a loan from a finance house which is firmly secured by a charge on any asset the taxpayer may appear to have, and which is automatically repaid at the end of the operation. In some cases one may doubt whether, in any real sense, any money existed at all. It seems very doubtful whether any real money was involved in *Rawling*; but facts as to this matter are for the commissioners to find. I will assume that in some sense money did pass as expressed in respect of each transaction in each of the instant cases. Finally, in each of the present cases it is candidly, if inevitably, admitted that the whole and only purpose of each scheme was the avoidance of tax.

In these circumstances, your Lordships are invited to take, with regard to schemes of the character I have described, what may appear to be a new approach. We are asked, in fact, to treat them as fiscally a nullity, not producing either a gain or a loss. Counsel for Ramsay described this as revolutionary, so I think it opportune to restate some familiar principles and some of the leading decisions so as to show the position we are now in.

1. A subject is only to be taxed on clear words, not on 'intendment' or on the 'equity' of an Act. Any taxing Act of Parliament is to be construed in accordance with this

principle. What are 'clear words' is to be ascertained on normal principles; these do not
a confine the courts to literal interpretation. There may, indeed should, be considered the
context and scheme of the relevant Act as a whole, and its purpose may, indeed should,
be regarded: see *Inland Revenue Comrs v Wesleyan and General Assurance Society* [1946] 2
All ER 749 at 751, 30 Tax Cas 11 at 16 per Lord Greene MR and *Mangin v Inland Revenue
Comrs* [1971] 1 All ER 179 at 182, [1971] AC 739 at 746 per Lord Donovan. The relevant
Act in these cases is the Finance Act 1965, the purpose of which is to impose a tax on
b gains, less allowable losses, arising from disposals.

2. A subject is entitled to arrange his affairs so as to reduce his liability to tax. The fact
that the motive for a transaction may be to avoid tax does not invalidate it unless a
particular enactment so provides. It must be considered according to its legal effect.

3. It is for the fact-finding commissioners to find whether a document, or a transaction,
is genuine or a sham. In this context, to say that a document or transaction is a 'sham'
c means that, while professing to be one thing, it is in fact something different. To say that
a document or transaction is genuine, means that, in law, it is what it professes to be, and
it does not mean anything more than that. I shall return to this point.

Each of these three principles would be fully respected by the decision we are invited
to make. Something more must be said as to the next principle.

4. Given that a document or transaction is genuine, the court cannot go behind it to
d some supposed underlying substance. This is the well-known principle of *Inland Revenue
Comrs v Duke of Westminster* [1936] AC 1, [1935] All ER Rep 259, 19 Tax Cas 490. This
is a cardinal principle but it must not be overstated or over-extended. While obliging the
court to accept documents or transactions, found to be genuine, as such, it does not
compel the court to look at a document or a transaction in blinkers, isolated from any
context to which it properly belongs. If it can be seen that a document or transaction was
e intended to have effect as part of a nexus or series of transactions, or as an ingredient of
a wider transaction intended as a whole, there is nothing in the doctrine to prevent it
being so regarded; to do so is not to prefer form to substance, or substance to form. It is
the task of the court to ascertain the legal nature of any transactions to which it is sought
to attach a tax or a tax consequence and if that emerges from a series or combination of
transactions, intended to operate as such, it is that series or combination which may be
f regarded. For this there is authority in the law relating to income tax and capital gains
tax: see *Chinn v Collins (Inspector of Taxes)* and *Inland Revenue Comrs v Plummer*.

For the commissioners considering a particular case it is wrong, and an unnecessary
self-limitation, to regard themselves as precluded by their own finding that documents
or transactions are not 'shams' from considering what, as evidenced by the documents
themselves or by the manifested intentions of the parties, the relevant transaction is.
g They are not, under the *Duke of Westminster* doctrine or any other authority, bound to
consider individually each separate step in a composite transaction intended to be carried
through as a whole. This is particularly the case where (as in *Rawling*) it is proved that
there was an accepted obligation, once a scheme is set in motion, to carry it through its
successive steps. It may be so where (as in *Ramsay* or in *Black Nominees Ltd v Nicol
(Inspector of Taxes)* [1975] STC 372) there is an expectation that it will be so carried
h through, and no likelihood in practice that it will not. In such cases (which may vary in
emphasis) the commissioners should find the facts and then decide as a matter
(reviewable) of law whether what is in issue is a composite transaction or a number of
independent transactions.

I will now refer to some recent cases which show the limitations of the *Duke of
Westminster* doctrine and illustrate the present situation in the law.
j   1. *Floor v Davis (Inspector of Taxes)* [1978] 2 All ER 1079, [1978] Ch 295, [1978] STC
436, CA; affd [1979] 2 All ER 677, [1980] AC 695, [1979] STC 379, HL. The key
transaction in this scheme was a sale of shares in a company called IDM to one company
(FNW) and a resale by that company to a further company (KDI). The majority of the
Court of Appeal thought it right to look at each of the sales separately and rejected an
argument by the Crown that they could be considered as an integrated transaction. But

Eveleigh LJ upheld that argument. He held that the fact that each sale was genuine did not prevent him from regarding each as part of a whole, or oblige him to consider each step in isolation. Nor was he so prevented by the *Duke of Westminster* case. Looking at the scheme as a whole, and finding that the taxpayer and his sons-in-law had complete control of the IDM shares until they reached KDI, he was entitled to find that there was a disposal to KDI. When the case reached this House it was decided on a limited argument, and the wider point was not considered. This same approach has commended itself to Templeman LJ and has been expressed by him in impressive reasoning in the Court of Appeal's judgment in *Rawling*. It will be seen from what follows that these judgments, and their emerging principle, commend themselves to me.

2. *Inland Revenue Comrs v Plummer*. This was a prearranged scheme, claimed by the Revenue to be 'circular', in the sense that its aim and effect was to pass a capital sum round through various hands back to its starting point. There was a finding by the Special Commissioners that the transaction was a bona fide commercial transaction, but in this House their Lordships agreed that it was legitimate to have regard to all the arrangements as a whole. The majority upheld the taxpayer's case on the ground that there was a commercial reality in them: as I described them they amounted to 'a covenant, for a capital sum, to make annual payments, coupled with security arrangements for the payments' (see [1979] 3 All ER 775 at 781, [1980] AC 896 at 909, [1979] STC 793 at 798), and I attempted to analyse the nature of the bargain with its advantages and risks to either side.

The case is no authority that the court may not in other cases and with different findings of fact reach a conclusion that, viewed as a whole, a composite transaction may produce an effect which brings it within a fiscal provision.

3. *Chinn v Collins (Inspector of Taxes)*. This again was a prearranged scheme, described by the Special Commissioners as a single scheme. There was no express finding that the parties concerned were obliged to carry through each successive step; but the commissioners found that there was never any possibility that the appellant taxpayers and another party would not proceed from one critical stage to another. I reached the conclusion, on this finding and on the documents, that the machinery, once started, would follow out its instructions without further initiative and the same point was made graphically by Lord Russell (see p 196, ante). This case shows, in my opinion, that although the separate steps were 'genuine' and had to be accepted under the *Duke of Westminster* doctrine, the court could, on the basis of the findings made and of its own analysis in law, consider the scheme as a whole and was not confined to a step by step examination.

To hold, in relation to such schemes as those with which we are concerned, that the court is not confined to a single step approach, is thus a logical development from existing authorities, and a generalisation of particular decisions.

Before I come to examination of the particular schemes in these cases, there is one argument of a general character which needs serious consideration. For the appellants it was said that to accept the Crown's wide contention involved a rejection of accepted and established canons, and that, if so general an attack on schemes for tax avoidance as the Crown suggest is to be validated, that is a matter for Parliament. The function of the courts is to apply strictly and correctly the legislation which Parliament has enacted; if the taxpayer escapes the charge, it is for Parliament, if it disapproves of the result, to close the gap. General principles against tax avoidance are, it was claimed, for Parliament to lay down. We were referred, at our request, in this connection to the various enactments by which Parliament has from time to time tried to counter tax avoidance by some general prescription. The most extensive of these is the Income and Corporation Taxes Act 1970, s 460ff. We were referred also to well-known sections in Australia and New Zealand (Australia, the Income Tax Assessment Act 1936, s 260; New Zealand, the Income Tax Act 1976, s 99, replacing earlier legislation). Further, it was pointed out that the capital gains tax legislation (starting with the Finance Act 1965) does not contain any provision corresponding to s 460. The intention should be deduced therefore, it was said, to leave capital gains tax to be dealt with by 'hole and plug' methods; that such

schemes as the present could be so dealt with has been confirmed by later legislation as
a to 'value shifting' (see the Capital Gains Tax Act 1979, s 25ff). These arguments merit
serious consideration. In substance they appealed to Barwick CJ in the recent Australian
case of *Federal Comr of Taxation v Westraders Pty Ltd* (1980) 30 ALR 353 at 354–355.

I have a full respect for the principles which have been stated but I do not consider that
they should exclude the approach for which the Crown contends. That does not
introduce a new principle: it would be to apply to new and sophisticated legal devices the
b undoubted power and duty of the courts to determine their nature in law and to relate
them to existing legislation. While the techniques of tax avoidance progress and are
technically improved, the courts are not obliged to stand still. Such immobility must
result either in loss of tax, to the prejudice of other taxpayers, or to Parliamentary
congestion or (most likely) to both. To force the courts to adopt, in relation to closely
integrated situations, a step by step, dissecting, approach which the parties themselves
c may have negated would be a denial rather than an affirmation of the true judicial
process. In each case the facts must be established; and a legal analysis made; legislation
cannot be required or even be desirable to enable the court to arrive at a conclusion which
corresponds with the parties' own intentions.

The capital gains tax was created to operate in the real world, not that of make-
believe. As I said in *Aberdeen Construction Group Ltd v Inland Revenue Comrs* [1978] 1 All
d ER 962 at 996, [1978] AC 885 at 893, [1978] STC 127 at 131, it is a tax on gains (or, I
might have added, gains less losses), it is not a tax on arithmetical differences. To say that
a loss (or gain) which appears to arise at one stage in an indivisible process, and which is
intended to be and is cancelled out by a later stage, so that at the end of what was bought
as, and planned as, a single continuous operation, is not such a loss (or gain) as the
legislation is dealing with is in my opinion well, and indeed essentially, within the
e judicial function.

We were referred, on this point, to a number of cases in the United States of America
in which the courts have denied efficacy to schemes or transactions designed only to
avoid tax and lacking otherwise in economic or commercial reality. I venture to quote
two key passages, not as authority, but as examples, expressed in vigorous and apt
language, of a process of thought which seems to me not inappropriate for the courts in
f this country to follow. In *Knetsch v United States* (1960) 364 US 361 the Supreme Court
found that a transaction was a sham because it—

> 'did not appreciably affect the [taxpayer's] beneficial interest . . . there was
> nothing of substance to be realised by [him] from his transaction beyond a tax
> deduction . . . the difference between the two sums was in reality the fee for
> providing the facade of "loans".'

g

In *Gilbert v Internal Revenue Comr* (1957) 248 F 2d 399 Learned Hand J (dissenting on the
facts) said:

> 'The Income Tax Act imposes liabilities upon taxpayers based upon their financial
> transactions . . . If, however, the taxpayer enters into a transaction that does not
> appreciably affect his beneficial interest except to reduce his tax, the law will
h disregard it . . .'

It is probable that the United States courts do not draw the line precisely where we
with our different system, allowing less legislative power to the courts than they claim
to exercise, would draw it, but the decisions do at least confirm me in the belief that it
would be an excess of judicial abstinence to withdraw from the field now before us.
j   I will now try to apply these principles to the cases before us.

W T Ramsay Ltd v Inland Revenue Comrs
This scheme, though intricate in detail, is simple in essentials. Stripped of the
complications of company formation and acquisition, it consisted of the creation of two
assets in the form of loans, called loan 1 and loan 2, each of £218,750. These were made
by the taxpayer, by written offer and oral acceptance, on 23rd February 1973 to one of

the intra-scheme companies, Caithmead Ltd. The terms are important and must be set out. They were: (a) loan 1 was repayable after 30 years at par and loan 2 was repayable after 31 years at par, in each case with the proviso that Caithmead could (but on terms) make earlier repayment if it so desired and would be obliged to do so if it went into liquidation; (b) if either loan were repaid before its maturity date, then it had to be repaid at par or at its market value on the assumption that it would remain outstanding until its maturity date, whichever was the higher; (c) both loans were to carry interest at 11% per annum payable quarterly on 1st March, 1st June, 1st September and 1st December in each year, the first such payment to be on 1st March 1973; (d) the taxpayer was to have the right, exercisable once and once only, and then only if it was still the beneficial owner of both loan 1 and loan 2, to decrease the interest rate on one of the loans and to increase correspondingly the interest rate on the other. A few days later, on 2nd March 1973, the taxpayer, under (d) above, increased the rate of interest on loan 2 to 22% and decreased that on loan 1 to zero. The same day the taxpayer then sold loan 2 (which had naturally increased in value) for £391,481. This produced a 'gain' of £172,731 which the taxpayer contends is not a chargeable gain for corporation tax purposes (as to this, see below). Loan 2 was later transferred to a wholly-owned subsidiary of Caithmead and extinguished by the liquidation of that subsidiary. On 9th March 1973 Caithmead itself went into liquidation, on which loan 1 was repayable, and was repaid to the taxpayer. The shares in Caithmead, however, for which the taxpayer had paid £185,034, became of little value and the taxpayer sold them to an outside company for £9,387. So the taxpayer made a 'loss' of £175,647. It may be added, as regards finance, that the necessary money to enable Ramsay to make the loans was provided by a finance house on terms which ensured that it would be repaid out of the loans when discharged. The taxpayer provided no finance.

Of this scheme, relevantly to the preceding discussion, the following can be said.

1. As the tax consultants' letter explicitly states 'the scheme is a pure tax avoidance scheme and has no commercial justification in so far as there is no prospect of T [the prospective taxpayer] making a profit; indeed he is certain to make a loss representing the cost of undertaking the scheme'.

2. As stated by the tax consultants' letter, and accepted by the Special Commissioners, every transaction would be genuinely carried through and in fact be exactly what it purported to be.

3. It was reasonable to assume that all steps would, in practice, be carried out, but there was no binding arrangement that they should. The nature of the scheme was such that once set in motion it would proceed through all its stages to completion.

4. The transactions regarded together, and as intended, were from the outset designed to produce neither gain nor loss: in a phrase which has become current, they were self-cancelling. The 'loss' sustained by the taxpayer, through the reduction in value of its shares in Caithmead, was dependent on the 'gain' it had procured by selling loan 2. The one could not occur without the other. To borrow from *Rubin v United States* (1962) 304 F 2d 766 approving the Tax Court in *MacRae v Internal Revenue Comr* (1961) 34 TC 20 at 26, this loss was the mirror image of the gain. The taxpayer would not have entered on the scheme if this had not been so.

5. The scheme was not designed, as a whole, to produce any result for the taxpayer or anyone else, except the payment of certain fees for the scheme. Within a period of a few days, it was designed to and did return the taxpayer except as above to the position from which it started.

6. The money needed for the various transactions was advanced by a finance house on terms which ensured that it was used for the purposes of the scheme and would be returned on completion, having moved in a circle.

On these facts it would be quite wrong, and a faulty analysis, to pick out, and stop at, the one step in the combination which produced the loss, that being entirely dependent on, and merely a reflection of, the gain. The true view, regarding the scheme as a whole, is to find that there was neither gain nor loss, and I so conclude.

Although this disposes of the appeal, I think it right to express an opinion on the *a* particular point which formed the basis of the decisions below. This is whether the gain made on 9th March 1973 by the sale of loan 2 was a chargeable gain. The assumption here, of course, is that it is permissible to separate this particular step from the whole.

The taxpayer claims that the gain is not chargeable on the ground that the asset sold was a debt within the meaning of the Finance Act 1965, Sch 7, para 11. In that case, since the taxpayer was the original creditor, the disposal would not give rise to a chargeable gain. The Crown on the other hand contends that it was a debt on a security, within the
b meaning of the same paragraph, and of para 5(3)(*b*) of the same schedule. In that case the exemption in favour of debts would not apply.

The distinction between a debt and a debt on a security, and the criteria of the difference, have already been the subject of consideration in the Court of Session in *Cleveleys Investment Trust Co v Inland Revenue Comrs* 1971 SC 233, 47 Tax Cas 300 and *Aberdeen Construction Group Ltd v Inland Revenue Comrs* 1977 SC 302, [1977] STC 302, and
c in this House in the latter case ([1978] 1 All ER 962, [1978] AC 885, [1978] STC 127). I think it no overstatement to say that many learned judges have found it baffling, both on the statutory wording and as to the underlying policy. I suggested some of the difficulties of para 11 and of the definition in para 5(3)(*b*) of the same schedule in the *Aberdeen Construction Group Ltd* case and I need not recapitulate them. Such positive indications as have been detected are vague and uncertain. It can be seen, however, in
d my opinion, that the legislature is endeavouring to distinguish between mere debts, which normally (though there are exceptions) do not increase but may decrease in value, and debts with added characteristics such as may enable them to be realised or dealt with at a profit. But this distinction must still be given effect to through the words used.

Of these, some help is gained from a contrast to be drawn between debts simpliciter, which may arise from trading and a multitude of other situations, commercial or
e private, and loans, certainly a narrower class, and one which presupposes some kind of contractual structure. In the *Aberdeen Construction Group Ltd* case [1978] 1 All ER 962 at 968, [1978] AC 885 at 895, [1978] STC 127 at 133 I drew the distinction between—

> 'a pure unsecured debt as between the original borrower and lender on the one hand and a debt (which may be unsecured) which has, if not a marketable character, at least such characteristics as enable it to be dealt in and if necessary converted into
f shares or other securities.'

To this I would now make one addition and one qualification. Although I think that, in this case, the manner in which loan 2 was constituted, viz by written offer, orally accepted together with evidence of the acceptance by statutory declaration, was enough to satisfy a strict interpretation of 'security', I am not convinced that a debt, to qualify as
g a debt on a security, must necessarily be constituted or evidenced by a document. The existence of a document may be an indicative factor, but absence of one is not fatal. I would agree with the observations of my noble and learned friend Lord Fraser, in relation, in particular, to the *Cleveleys Investment Trust Co* case. Secondly, on reflection, I doubt the usefulness of a test enabling the debt to be converted into shares or other securities. The definition in para 5(3)(*b*) is, it is true, expressed to be given for the
h purposes of para 3 which is dealing with conversion; but I suspect that it was false logic to suppose that, because of this, 'securities' are to be so limited, and in any event I doubt whether the test supposed, if a necessary one, is useful, for even a simple debt can, by a suitable contract, be converted into shares or other securities.

With all this lack of certainty as to the statutory words, I do not feel any doubt that in this case the debt was a debt on a security. I have already stated its terms. It was created
j by a contract the terms of which were recorded in writing; it was designed, from the beginning, to be capable of being sold, and, indeed, to be sold at a profit. It was repayable after 31 years, or on the liquidation of Caithmead. If repaid before the maturity date, it had to be repaid at par or market value, whichever was the higher. It carried a fixed, though (once) variable, rate of interest.

There was much argument whether with these qualities it could be described as 'loan stock' within the meaning of para 5(3)(*b*) of Sch 7. I do not find it necessary to decide

this. The paragraph includes within 'security' any 'similar security' to loan stock; in my opinion these words cover the facts. This was a contractual loan, with a structure of *a* permanence such as fitted it to be dealt in and to have a market value. That it had a market value, in fact, was stated on 1st March 1973 by Messrs Hoare & Co Govett Ltd, stockbrokers. They then confirmed that an 80% premium would be a fair commercial price having regard to the prevailing levels of long term interest rates. I have no doubt that, on these facts, loan 2 was a debt on a security and therefore an asset which, if disposed of, could give rise to a chargeable gain.   *b*
I would dismiss this appeal.

Eilbeck (Inspector of Taxes) v Rawling
The scheme here was quite different from any of the others which I have discussed. It sought to take advantage of para 13(1) of Sch 7 to the Finance Act 1965; this exempts from capital gains tax any gain made on the disposal of, inter alia, a reversionary interest *c* under a settlement by the person for whose benefit the interest was created or by any other person except one who acquired the interest for consideration in money. The scheme was, briefly, to split a reversion into two parts so that one would be disposed of at a profit but would fall under the exemption and the other would be disposed of at a loss but could be covered by the exception. Thus there would be an allowable loss but a non-chargeable gain.   *d*
The scheme involved the use of a settlement set up in Gibraltar, another settlement set up in Jersey, and six Jersey companies, namely, to use their short titles, Thun, Goldiwill, Pendle, Tortola, Allamanda and Solandra, which were part of the same organisation, under the same management and operating from the same address. The Gibraltar settlement was made in 1973 by one Isola of a sum of £100. When the taxpayer came into the scheme in 1975 the fund consisted of £600,000, all of which was said to be *e* deposited in Jersey with Thun. The trusts were to pay the income to one Josephine Isola until 19th March 1976. Subject thereto the fund was to be held in trust for the settlor, Isola, his heirs and assignees. There was a power in cl 5 of the settlement to advance any part of the capital of the trust fund to the reversioner or to the trustees of any other settlement. But it was a necessary condition, in the latter case, that the reversioner should be indefeasibly entitled to a corresponding interest under such other settlement *f* falling into possession not later than the vesting day (19th March 1976) under the Gibraltar settlement. On the exercise of any such power a compensating advance had to be made to the income beneficiary.
On 20th March 1975 the settlor's reversionary interest was assigned to Pendle. On 24th March Thun agreed to lend the taxpayer £543,600 to enable him to buy the Gibraltar settlement reversion and agreed with the taxpayer that Tortola would, if *g* required within six months, introduce to the taxpayer a purchaser for the reversion. Pendle then agreed to sell and the taxpayer to buy the reversion for £543,600 and this sale was completed. So the taxpayer (conformably with para 13(1)) had acquired a reversion for consideration in money. The taxpayer directed Thun to pay the £543,600 to Pendle: he also charged his reversionary interests under the Gibraltar settlement and under the Jersey settlement, next mentioned, to Thun to secure the loan of £543,600.   *h*
The Jersey settlement was executed, as found by the General Commissioners, as part of the scheme. It was dated 21st March 1975 and made by the taxpayer's brother for £100 with power to accept additions. The trustee was Allamanda. The trustee was to apply the income for charitable or other purposes until the 'Closing Date' and subject thereto for the taxpayer absolutely. The closing date was fixed on 24th March 1975 as a date not later than 19th March 1976, the vesting date under the Gibraltar settlement (the *j* exact date seems not to be proved).
On 25th March 1975 the taxpayer requested the Gibraltar trustee to advance £315,000 to the Jersey settlement, to be held as capital of that settlement. On 27th March the Gibraltar trustee appointed £315,000 accordingly, and also appointed £29,610 to compensate the income beneficiary, which had become Goldiwill. These appointments were given effect to by Thun transferring money in Jersey to Allamanda, the Jersey

a trustee, and Goldiwill. So the taxpayer was now a person for whose benefit a reversion had been created under the Jersey settlement (see again para 13(1)). There was left £255,390 unappointed in the Gibraltar settlement.

On 1st April the taxpayer requested Thun to cause Tortola to nominate a purchaser of his interest under the Gibraltar settlement and on 3rd April Tortola nominated Goldiwill. Also on 3rd April the taxpayer agreed to sell his reversion under the Gibraltar settlement to Goldiwill for £231,130; the agreement recited that the trust fund then

b consisted of £255,390. The taxpayer assigned his reversion accordingly. This is the transaction supposed to create the loss. Also on 3rd April the taxpayer agreed to sell his reversion under the Jersey settlement to Thun for £312,100. The agreement recited that the trust fund then consisted of £315,100. Payment for these various transactions was effected by appropriations by Thun. The price for the two reversions (£231,130 and £312,100) making £543,230 due to the taxpayer was set off against the loan of £543,600

c made by Thun, leaving a balance due to Thun of £370. The taxpayer paid this and Thun released its charges. The only money which passed from the taxpayer was the £370, £3,500 procuration fee and £6,115 interest.

Of this scheme the following can be said.

1. The scheme was a pure tax avoidance scheme, designed by Thun and entered into by the taxpayer for the sole purpose of manufacturing a loss matched by a corresponding

d but exempt capital gain. It was marketed by Thun as a scheme available to any taxpayer who might purchase it, the sums involved being adapted to the purchaser's requirements.

2. Every individual transaction was, as found by the General Commissioners, carried through and was exactly what it purported to be.

3. It was held by the judge and not disputed by the Court of Appeal that, by its agreement with the taxpayer, Thun agreed to procure the implementation of all the steps comprised in the scheme and was in a position to obtain the co-operation of the associated

e companies Pendle and Goldiwill.

4. The scheme was designed to return all parties within a few days to the position from which they started, and to produce for the taxpayer neither gain nor loss, apart from the expenses of the scheme, the gain and the loss being 'self-cancelling'. The loss could not be incurred without the gain, because it depended on the reversion under the

f Gibraltar settlement being diminished by the appointed sum of £315,000 which produced the gain. The taxpayer would not have entered into the scheme unless this had been the case.

5. The scheme required nothing to be done by the taxpayer except the signing of the scheme documents, and the payment of fees. The necessary money was not provided by the taxpayer but was 'provided' by Thun on terms which ensured that it would not pass

g out of its control and would be returned on completion having moved if at all in a circle.

On these facts, it would be quite wrong, and a faulty analysis, to segregate, from what was an integrated and interdependent series of operations, one step, viz the sale of the Gibraltar reversion on 3rd April 1975, and to attach fiscal consequences to that step regardless of the other steps and operations with which it was integrated. The only conclusion, one which is alone consistent with the intentions of the parties, and with the

h documents regarded as interdependent, is to find that, apart from a sum not exceeding £370, there was neither gain nor loss and I so conclude.

Although this disposes of the appeal I think it right to deal with the particular point which, apart from the judgment of Templeman LJ, formed the basis of the decisions below. This is whether the sale of the reversion under the Gibraltar settlement on 3rd April 1975 gave rise to an allowable loss if regarded in isolation. I regard this, with all

j deference, as a simple matter. What was sold on 3rd April 1975 was the taxpayer's reversionary interest in £255,390; for this the taxpayer received £231,130 certified by Solandra to be the market price. Not only was this the fact (the trust fund at that time was of that amount) but the agreement for sale specifically so stated. It recited that the vendor, the taxpayer, was beneficially entitled to the sole interest in reversion under the Gibraltar settlement, 'being a Settlement whereof the trust fund presently consist [sic] of £255,390'. What he had bought, on the other hand, for £543,600 was a reversionary interest in £600,000, subject to the trustee's power to advance any part to him or to a settlement in which he had an equivalent reversionary interest. After the advance of £315,000 was made (effectively to the taxpayer, so that to this extent he had got back part of his money), all he had to sell was the reversionary interest in the remainder; this he sold for its market price. Alternatively, if the £315,000 is to be considered as in some sense still held under the Gibraltar settlement, the sale on 3rd April 1975 to Goldiwill for £231,130 did not include it. On no view can he say that he sold what he had bought; on no view can he demonstrate any loss. I think that substantially this view of the matter was taken by Buckley and Donaldson LJJ, and I agree with their judgments.

I would dismiss this appeal.

LORD FRASER OF TULLYBELTON. My Lords, each of these appeals raises one separate question of its own and one wider question common to both. I shall consider the separate questions first.

W T Ramsay Ltd v Inland Revenue Comrs

The taxpayer is a farming company. During its accounting period ended 31st May 1973 it sold the freehold of its farm, and made a gain of £187,977 which was chargeable for corporation tax purposes, on the same principles as it would have been charged to capital gains tax in the case of an individual.

Having taken expert advice, the taxpayer entered into a scheme to create a capital loss which could be set off against that chargeable gain. The essence of the scheme was that the taxpayer acquired two assets, one of which increased in value at the expense of the other, and both of which were then disposed of. The asset which decreased in value consisted of shares in a company called Caithmead Ltd, and the loss on that asset was intended to be allowable for corporation tax purposes, and therefore available to be set off against the gain on the farm. If that part of the scheme is considered by itself, it worked as intended and produced an allowable loss. The asset which increased in value was a loan to Caithmead Ltd. It was one of two loans, and was referred to as 'loan 2', and it was intended to be exempt from corporation tax on chargeable gains. The question in this appeal is whether that intention has been successfully realised.

The answer depends entirely on whether loan 2 was 'the debt on a security' in the sense of the Finance Act 1965, Sch 7, para 11(1). If it was, the gain on its disposal was chargeable. If it was not, the gain is not chargeable. The very unusual terms on which loan 2 was made by the taxpayer to Caithmead Ltd have been described by my noble and learned friend Lord Wilberforce and I need not repeat them.

The expression 'the debt on a security' is not one which is familiar to either lawyers or, I think, business men. Its meaning has been considered in two cases to which we were referred. In *Cleveleys Investment Trust Co v Inland Revenue Comrs* 1971 SC 233 at 244, 47 Tax Cas 300 at 318 Lord Cameron pointed out that whatever else it may mean it 'is not a synonym for a secured debt', and that is generally agreed. Lord Migdale thought that it meant 'an obligation to pay or repay embodied in a share or stock certificate . . .' (see 1971 SC 233 at 243, 47 Tax Cas 300 at 315). Lord Migdale's view was accepted by all the learned judges of the First Division in *Aberdeen Construction Group Ltd v Inland Revenue Comrs* 1977 SC 265, [1977] STC 302, but when the *Aberdeen* case reached this House the existence of a certificate was not treated as the distinguishing feature of the debt on a security. Lord Wilberforce expressed the view that the distinction was—

'between a pure unsecured debt as between the original borrower and lender on the one hand and a debt (which may be unsecured) which has, if not a marketable character, at least such characteristics as enable it to be dealt in and if necessary converted into shares or other securities.'

(See [1978] 1 All ER 962 at 968, [1978] AC 885 at 895, [1978] STC 127 at 133.)

Lord Russell said that loan stock 'suggests to my mind an obligation created by a
a company of an amount for issue to subscribers for the stock, having ordinarily terms for
repayment with or without premium and for interest' (see [1978] 1 All ER 962 at 975,
[1978] AC 885 at 903, [1978] STC 127 at 140). No disapproval of the observations in the
Court of Session was expressed, and I expressed general agreement with them. The
authors of the scheme in this appeal may have had these observations in mind when they
devised the scheme, as they went to some trouble to avoid having any certificate or
b voucher of the debt, and relied instead on a statutory declaration setting out the terms
and conditions of the loan.

Further consideration has satisfied me that the existence of a document or certificate
cannot be the distinguishing feature between the two classes of debt. If Parliament had
intended it to be so, that could easily have been stated in plain terms and there would
have been no purpose in using the strange phrase 'the debt on a security' in para 11(1) of
c Sch 7, or in referring to the 'definition' of security in para 5. The distinction in para 11(1)
is, I think, between a simple unsecured debt and a debt of the nature of an investment,
which can be dealt in and purchased with a view to being held as an investment. The
reason for the provision that no chargeable gain should accrue on disposal of a simple
debt by the original creditor must have been to restrict allowable losses (computed in the
same way as gains: see the Finance Act 1965, s 23, which was the relevant statute in 1973)
d because the disposal of a simple debt by the original creditor or his legatee will very
seldom result in a gain. No doubt it is possible to think of cases where a gain may result,
but they are exceptional. On the other hand it is all too common for debts to be disposed
of by the original creditor at a loss, and if such losses were allowed for capital gains tax it
would be easy to avoid tax by writing off bad debts, for example those owed by
impecunious relatives. But debts on a security, being of the nature of investments, are
e just as likely to be disposed of by the original creditor at a gain as they are at a loss, and
they are subject to the ordinary rule.

The features of the debt loan 2 in the present case which in my opinion take it out of
the class of simple debts into the class of debts on a security are these. First and foremost,
the debtor was not bound to repay it for 31 years. Such a long fixed term is unusual for
a debt, but it is typical of loan stock (a term which I use hereafter to include similar
f securities). Second, the debtor was entitled to repay it sooner, and bound to repay it on
liquidation, but in either of these cases only at the higher of face value or market value,
market value being calculated on the assumption that it would remain outstanding for
the full period of 31 years. Conditions of that sort are very unusual when attached to a
debt, but are characteristic of loan stock. Third, it bore interest and thus produced
income to the creditor, as an investment such as loan stock normally does but as debts
normally do not. For example, the debt owed by a subsidiary company to its parent
g company in the *Aberdeen* case did not carry interest. It is to be observed that para 11(1)
refers not to loan but to 'debt' and thus includes ordinary trade debts which rarely carry
interest. Fourth, being a long term interest-bearing debt, it possessed the characteristics
of marketability. Indeed, loan 2 was created only in order to be sold at a profit and it was
so sold. It could have been sold and assigned in part like loan stock, although an action
h to enforce payment might have required the concurrence of the original creditor.

If loan 2 had been surrendered and its proceeds used to pay for shares, it could in a
loose sense be said to have been 'converted' into shares or a new loan. But it was no more,
and no less, convertible than a simple debt, and I do not consider that convertibility is a
distinguishing factor of a loan on a security.

Counsel for Ramsay said that loan stock had to be capable of being 'issued' and
j 'subscribed for' and the loan 2 did not satisfy these requirements. But I agree with
Templeman LJ that loan 2 was in fact issued and subscribed for although the processes
were simple because only one lender was involved.

For these reasons I agree with the Court of Appeal that loan 2 fell within the description
of a debt on a security and that the taxpayer's gain on disposal of it was chargeable. I
would dismiss this appeal on that ground.

Eilbeck (Inspector of Taxes) v Rawling

This is another scheme designed to eliminate or reduce a capital gain. In this case the gain arose from sales of shares and amounted to about £355,000. Again, the details of the scheme have been explained by my noble and learned friend Lord Wilberforce, and I refer only to its essential elements. On 24th March 1975 the taxpayer acquired for £543,600 an asset, consisting of the reversionary interest under a settlement made in Gibraltar and administered by a trustee in Gibraltar. The taxpayer claims that on 3rd April 1975 he sold the same asset for £231,130 thereby making a loss of £312,470. The reason why the sale price was so much lower than the cost price of what is said to be the same asset only ten days earlier was that the trustee, in the exercise of a power under cl 5(2) of the settlement, had appointed £315,000 out of the capital trust fund to the trustees of another settlement. The other settlement had been made in Jersey and was administered by a trustee in Jersey. (The geographical location of these trusts is entirely irrelevant to the question raised in this appeal, which would be the same if both trusts had been in England.) The taxpayer maintains that the reduction in the amount of the Gibraltar trust fund, and hence the value of his reversionary interest in it, did not affect the continuing identity of the fund or of his interest. He says that his interest was in the assets of the fund, as they existed from time to time, and that it remains the same interest notwithstanding a change in the individual assets or in their value.

My Lords, I do not accept that contention. No doubt it would have been correct if the fall in value of the Gibraltar trust fund had been brought about merely by a fall in the value of its component assets, for instance, if the total value of the trust investments had fallen, or even if some of the investments had been altogether lost. But the position is entirely different in this case where the trust fund was divided into two parts, of which one was handed over to the Jersey trustee and the other was retained by the Gibraltar trustee. The retained fund was not the whole fund in which the taxpayer had bought an interest. It was only part of the fund and the reversionary interest in the retained part was only part of the reversionary interest which the taxpayer had bought. If the fund had been invested in stocks and shares, or other assets, it would have been necessary to apportion the assets to one or other part of the fund. This would have been more obvious if the retained fund had been sold before the appointment in favour of the Jersey settlement had been made; in that case the sale would expressly have been of part only of the total fund. It follows therefore that the taxpayer's claim to have sustained a loss measured by the difference between the cost of the whole reversionary interest and the price realised for part of it must fail.

That is enough to negative the taxpayer's claim as put forward, but I would go further and would adopt the analysis by Buckley LJ of the true position. In the circumstances of this case, where the appointment by the Gibraltar trustee was made under a special power, I agree with Buckley and Donaldson LJJ that the taxpayer's reversionary interest in the appointed fund is properly to be regarded as part of his interest in the Gibraltar fund. Buckley LJ (but not Donaldson LJ) assumed that the 'closing date' appointed by the trustee of the Jersey settlement was the same as the 'vesting day' under the Gibraltar settlement, that is 19th March 1976. There is no finding to that effect and we were told that the 'closing date' probably was 6th May 1975. But the identity of dates was not essential to the reasoning on which Buckley LJ proceeded. The position was that, after the appointment, the appointed fund was held by the Jersey trustee for purposes which, although in some respects different from those of the Gibraltar settlement (the tenant for life being different and the closing date probably being different), were within the limits laid down in the Gibraltar settlement. In particular the reversioner was the same and the closing date was not later than the vesting date in the Gibraltar settlement. If the difference had not been within the permitted limits, the appointment would of course not have been intra vires the Gibraltar trustee. Accordingly, the true price realised on disposal of the taxpayer's interest was in my opinion the sum of the price of the retained fund in Gibraltar (£231,130) and of the appointed fund in Jersey (£312,100), amounting to £543,230. His loss was therefore about £370.

For these reasons I would dismiss this appeal.

The wider question: was there a disposal in either of these cases?

a   The Crown maintains that it is entitled to succeed in both these appeals on the wider ground that in neither case should the disposal of the loss-making asset be considered separately from the scheme of which it formed part. On behalf of the taxpayer in each case reliance was placed on the finding by the Special Commissioners that the various steps in the scheme were not shams. The meaning of the word 'sham' was considered by Diplock LJ in *Snook v London and West Riding Investments Ltd* [1967] 1 All ER 518 at 528,

b [1967] 2 QB 786 at 802, where he said that—

> 'it means acts done or documents executed by the parties to the "sham" which are intended by them to give to third parties or to the court the appearance of creating between the parties legal rights and obligations different from the actual legal rights and obligations (if any) which the parties intend to create.'

c   Thus an agreement which is really a hire-purchase agreement but which masquerades as a lease would be a sham. Although none of the steps in these cases was a sham in that sense, there still remains the question whether it is right to have regard to each step separately when it was so closely associated with other steps with which it formed part of a single scheme. The argument for the Crown in both appeals was that that question should be answered in the negative and that attention should be directed to the scheme

d as a whole. This question must, of course, be considered on the assumption that the taxpayer would have been entitled to succeed on the separate point in each case.

    In my opinion the argument of the Crown is well founded and should be accepted. Each of the taxpayers purchased a complete prearranged scheme, designed to produce a loss which would match the gain previously made and which would be allowable as a deduction for corporation tax (capital gains tax) purposes. In these circumstances the

e court is entitled and bound to consider the scheme as a whole: see *Inland Revenue Comrs v Plummer* [1979] 3 All ER 775 at 779, [1980] AC 896 at 907, [1979] STC 793 at 797 and *Chinn v Collins (Inspector of Taxes)* p 189, ante. The essential feature of both schemes was that, when they were completely carried out, they did not result in any actual loss to the taxpayer. The apparently magic result of creating a tax loss that would not be a real loss was to be brought about by arranging that the scheme included a loss which was

f allowable for tax purposes and a matching gain which was not chargeable. In *Ramsay* the loss arose on the disposal of the taxpayer's shares in Caithmead Ltd. In *Rawling* it arose on the disposal of the taxpayer's reversionary interest in the retained part of the Gibraltar settlement. But it is perfectly clear that neither of these disposals would have taken place except as part of the scheme, and, when they did take place, the taxpayer and all others concerned in the scheme knew and intended that they would be followed by other

g prearranged steps which cancelled out their effect. In *Rawling* the intention was made explicit as the supplier of the scheme, a company called Thun Holdings Ltd, bound itself contractually, if the scheme was once embarked on, to carry through all the steps. There is, therefore, no reason why the court should stop short at one particular step. In *Ramsay* the supplying company, Dovercliffe Ltd, did not undertake any contractual obligation to carry the scheme through, but there was a clear understanding between the taxpayer and

h Dovercliffe that the whole scheme would be carried through; that was why the taxpayer had purchased the scheme. The absence of contractual obligation does not in my opinion make any material difference.

    The taxpayer in both cases bought a complete scheme for which he paid a fee. Thereafter he was not required to produce any more money, although large sums of money were credited and debited to him in the course of the complicated transactions

j required to carry out the scheme. The money was lent to the taxpayer at the beginning of the scheme, by Thun in the *Rawling* case and by a finance company, Slater Walker, in the *Ramsay* case, and was repaid to the lender at the end. The taxpayer never at any stage had the money in his hands, nor was he ever free to dispose of it otherwise than in accordance with the scheme. His interest in the assets, the shares and loans in the *Ramsay* case and the trust funds in the *Rawling* case, were charged in favour of the lenders by way of security, so that he was never in a position to require the price of any asset that was sold to be paid to him. Throughout the whole series of transactions the money was kept within a closed circuit from which it could not escape.

In *Rawling* there was not even any need for real money to be involved at all. On 24th March 1975 Thun agreed to lend the taxpayer £543,600 to enable him to purchase the reversionary interest in the Gibraltar settlement. On the same day the taxpayer agreed to purchase and Pendle (a subsidiary company of Thun) agreed to sell the reversionary interest to him and assign it to him, and the taxpayer directed Thun to pay the £543,600 to Pendle. The taxpayer never handled the money, and presumably the payment to Pendle was effected by an entry in the books of Thun, though it was not proved that such an entry was made. When the taxpayer sold his reversionary interest in the Gibraltar settlement to another subsidiary of Thun, it was already charged to Thun in security and the purchase price was paid by the subsidiary to Thun, again presumably by an entry in Thun's books. His reversionary interest in the Jersey settlement was sold direct to Thun and the balance of Thun's original loan to the taxpayer was extinguished. There was apparently no evidence before the special commissioners that Thun actually possessed the sum of £543,600 which they lent to the taxpayer to set the scheme in motion, not to mention any further sums that they may have lent to other taxpayers for other similar schemes which may have been operating at the same time, and it might well have been open to the Special Commissioners to find that the loan, and all that followed on it, was a sham. But they have not done so. In *Ramsay* 'real' money in the form of a loan from Slater Walker was used so that a finding of sham in that respect would not have been possible.

Counsel for the taxpayer naturally pressed on us the view that if we were to refuse to have regard to the disposals which took place in the course of these schemes, we would be departing from a long line of authorities which required the courts to regard the legal form and nature of transactions that have been carried out. My Lords, I do not believe that we would be doing any such thing. I am not suggesting that the legal form of any transaction should be disregarded in favour of its supposed substance. Nothing that I have said is in any way inconsistent with the decision in the *Duke of Westminster* case [1936] AC 1, [1935] All ER Rep 259, 19 Tax Cas 490 where there was only one transaction, the grant of an annuity, and there was no question of its having formed part of any larger scheme. The view that I take of this appeal is entirely consistent with the decision in *Chinn v Collins (Inspector of Taxes)*, and it could in my opinion have been the ground of decision in *Floor v Davis* in accordance with the dissenting opinion of Eveleigh LJ in the Court of Appeal with which I respectfully agree. In that case the taxpayer wished to dispose of shares in a company to an American company called KDI at a price which would have produced a large chargeable gain. In order to avoid the liability to capital gains tax he adopted a scheme which involved the incorporation of another company, FNW, to which he transferred his shares in order that they could subsequently be transferred by FNW to KDI. Eveleigh LJ said ([1978] 2 All ER 1079 at 1089, [1978] Ch 295 at 313, [1978] STC 436 at 446):

'I see this case as one in which the court is not required to consider each step taken in isolation. It is a question of whether or not the shares were disposed of to KDI by the taxpayer. I believe that they were. Furthermore, they were in reality at the disposal of the original shareholders until the moment they reached the hand of KDI, although the legal ownership was in FNW. I do not think that this conclusion is any way vitiated by *Inland Revenue Comrs v Duke of Westminster*. In that case it was sought to say that the payments under covenant were not such but were payments of wages. I do not seek to say that the transfer to FNW was not a transfer. The important feature of the present case is that the destiny of the shares was at all times under the control of the taxpayer who was arranging for them to be transferred to the American company. The transfer to FNW was but a step in that process.'

In my opinion the reasoning contained in that passage is equally applicable to the present appeals.

Accordingly I would refuse both appeals on the additional ground that the relevant asset in each case was not disposed of in the sense required by the statutes.

LORD RUSSELL OF KILLOWEN. My Lords, I find myself in full agreement with what has fallen from my noble and learned friends Lord Wilberforce and Lord Fraser, both on the features peculiar to these cases and on the general principles enunciated by them. I cannot hope for and will not attempt any improvements.

I am however unable to resist the temptation to add a brief comment on the *Rawling* case. That comment is that I wholly fail to comprehend the contention that the taxpayer sustained a loss (unless it be £370). The moneys advanced into the Jersey settlement, out of the Gibraltar settlement funds in which the taxpayer had acquired an absolute reversionary interest, conferred on him an absolute reversionary interest in the advanced funds which could not fall into possession later than it would have done under the Gibraltar settlement. The power of advancement was so framed that no other outcome was possible. Thus the taxpayer remained absolutely entitled in reversion to the funds. When the taxpayer sold his interest in the remaining unadvanced fund he sold only part of his reversionary interest. If the sequence of events had been the sale of his reversionary interest in £255,390 to Goldiwill, followed by advancement of the remaining £315,000 into the Jersey settlement, nobody could begin to suggest that there was a loss made on the sale to Goldiwill. This to my mind demonstrates the absurdity of the suggestion that a loss was incurred by the taxpayer by a reverse of that sequence. There was a further power under the Gibraltar settlement to advance directly into the taxpayer's pocket, and it was found necessary to the taxpayer's claim of a loss that, if that had happened, there would nevertheless have been the loss asserted on the disposal of his reversionary interest in the remainder to Goldiwill. That cannot possibly be right.

LORD ROSKILL. My Lords, I have had the advantage of reading in draft the speeches of my noble and learned friends Lord Wilberforce and Lord Fraser in these two appeals. I agree entirely with what my noble and learned friends have said and for the reasons they give I would dismiss both appeals.

LORD BRIDGE OF HARWICH. My Lord, I have had the advantage of reading in draft the speech of my noble and learned friend Lord Wilberforce. I am in complete and respectful agreement with it and cannot usefully add anything to it; accordingly I, too, would dismiss both these appeals.

Appeals dismissed.

Solicitors: *Slowes* (for W T Ramsay Ltd); *J Memery & Co* (for Mr Rawling); *Solicitor of Inland Revenue.*

Rengan Krishnan Esq   Barrister.

R v Brentford Justices, ex parte Wong

QUEEN'S BENCH DIVISION

DONALDSON LJ AND MUSTILL J

15th JULY 1980

Magistrates – Information – Time limit for laying information – Information laid just within time limit but decision to prosecute not taken until later – Delay in service of summons – Whether abuse of process of court – Whether magistrates having discretion to dismiss summons – Magistrates' Courts Act 1952, s 104.

On 30th January 1978 the applicant was involved in a road accident. On 28th July, which was just two days before the expiry of the six months' period permitted by s 104[a] of the Magistrates' Courts Act 1952 for the institution of proceedings in respect of an offence, the police laid an information alleging, inter alia, that the applicant had been driving without due care and attention. The police had not, however, finally decided by 28th July whether to prosecute and waited until October before sending the applicant a letter informing him that he would be prosecuted. The summons was not served until 7th December. On 25th April 1979, when the case came on for hearing, the applicant asked the magistrates to decline to hear it on the grounds (i) that the delay was prejudicial to him since the matter depended on the recollection of witnesses, and (ii) that for the police to lay an information at the last possible moment in order to give them longer than the statutory six months to decide whether to prosecute amounted to an abuse of the process of the court. The magistrates accepted the applicant's arguments on the merits but stated that they had no power to exercise a discretion not to hear a case where all the statutory requirements had been complied with. They adjourned the hearing and the applicant applied to the High Court for an order of prohibition forbidding them continuing the hearing.

Held – Magistrates had a discretion to refuse to hear a summons if the prosecution amounted to an abuse of the process of the court. Since the object of s 104 of the 1952 Act would be frustrated if a prosecutor could postpone, without reasonable excuse, the decision whether to prosecute merely by laying an information within the prescribed time limit, the magistrates were entitled to conclude that there had been an abuse of the process of the court because the police had deliberately attempted to gain time by laying the information and that there was no excuse for their delay in serving the summons (see p 887 c and f to p 888 a, post).

R v Fairford Justices, ex parte Brewster [1975] 2 All ER 757, *Director of Public Prosecutions v Humphrys* [1976] 2 All ER 497 and *R v Newcastle upon Tyne Justices, ex parte John Bryce (Contractors) Ltd* [1976] 2 All ER 611 considered.

Notes

For limitation of time within which an information should be laid, see 29 Halsbury's Laws (4th Edn) para 291.

For the Magistrates' Courts Act 1952, s 104, see 21 Halsbury's Statutes (3rd Edn) 273.

As from a day to be appointed s 104 of the 1952 Act is to be replaced by s 127(1) of the Magistrates' Courts Act 1980.

Cases referred to in judgments

Director of Public Prosecutions v Humphrys [1976] 2 All ER 497, [1977] AC 1, [1976] 2 WLR 857, 140 JP 386, 63 Cr App R 95, [1976] RTR 339, HL, Digest (Cont Vol E) 210, 472c.

---

a   Section 104 is set out at p 885 *f*, post

Garfield v Maddocks [1973] 2 All ER 303, [1974] QB 7, [1973] 2 WLR 888, 137 JP 461, 57
 Cr App R 372, DC, Digest (Cont Vol D) 637, *1333Aa.*
Mills v Cooper [1967] 2 All ER 100, [1967] 2 QB 459, [1967] 2 WLR 1343, 131 JP 349, 65
 LGR 275, DC, Digest (Cont Vol C) 337, *472b.*
R v Fairford Justices, ex parte Brewster [1975] 2 All ER 757, [1976] QB 600, [1975] 3 WLR
 59, 139 JP 574, DC, Digest (Cont Vol D) 631, *463a.*
R v Newcastle upon Tyne Justices, ex parte John Bryce (Contractors) Ltd [1976] 2 All ER 611,
 [1976] 1 WLR 517, 140 JP 440, [1976] RTR 325, DC, Digest (Cont Vol E) 397, *441a.*

Application for judicial review
Chiang Hoong Wong applied with the leave of the Divisional Court of the Queen's
Bench Division given on 22nd May 1979 for an order prohibiting the Brentford justices
from further proceeding with the trial of the applicant, inter alia, on a charge of driving
without due care and attention, contrary to s 3 of the Road Traffic Act 1972. The facts
are set out in the judgment of Donaldson LJ.

Peter Digney for the applicant.
Robin Bailey for the prosecutor.

DONALDSON LJ. This is an application for judicial review in the nature of
prohibition brought on behalf of the applicant in respect of proceedings before the
Brentford justices.
    On 30th January 1978 the applicant was involved in a road traffic accident on the
Staines Road, and the prosecution case was that at that time he was driving without due
care and attention and that his vehicle had not got an MoT certificate.
    We are not concerned directly with the merits of the prosecution case. The important
thing is that the accident happened on 30th January 1978, and it was on 28th July of the
same year that an information was laid by the police prosecutor. It is said that that
information was laid as a protective measure because, under s 104 of the Magistrates'
Courts Act 1952, it is provided:

    'Except as otherwise expressly provided by any enactment, a magistrates' court
    shall not try an information or hear a complaint unless the information was laid, or
    the complaint made, within six months from the time when the offence was
    committed, or the matter of complaint arose.'

    On 28th July the police prosecutor had still not reached a firm decision whether or not
to prosecute. I do not suggest, because I do not know, that that was because the police
prosecutor was in two minds whether this was an appropriate case in which to prosecute,
or whether he was still making inquiries as to the availability of witnesses, or whether
(since this is a Metropolitan Police case, and the Metropolitan Police Force being of the
size it is) there were administrative difficulties in getting the facts together and putting
it before somebody who had authority to prosecute.
    That does not really matter. The fact is (and this is accepted) that on 28th July there
had been no irrevocable decision to prosecute.
    Having laid the information and obtained the summonses, the prosecutor then
retained them, deliberately not serving them until October, when apparently a letter was
sent to the applicant telling him that he would be prosecuted. But even then the
summonses were not served. They were served on 7th December 1978.
    They finally came on for hearing on 25th April 1979. According to the affidavits filed
by the applicant's solicitor (and these will have been filed, I apprehend, on the prosecutor
and the Brentford justices either of whom could have challenged them if they wished)
what happened was this. The applicant's counsel asked the court to decline to hear the
matter—

    'on the grounds that the delay was prejudicial to the applicant in a matter of this
    sort that depends on the recollection of witnesses and that for the police to lay an

information on the last possible day in order to give them longer than the statutory 6 months to decide whether or not to prosecute amounted to an abuse of the process of the court.'

The affidavit continued as follows:

'The court after retiring stated that they were prepared to hear the matter but they would give the applicant the opportunity of going to the High Court to seek an order of prohibition forbidding them so to do. In answer to a question from counsel for the applicant the chairman stated that they accepted counsel's arguments on the merits of the matter and would be minded to decline to hear the case but they felt that they had no power to exercise a discretion not to hear a case if all the statutory requirements were complied with, and only the High Court could exercise such discretion.'

The issue which we have to decide is whether the magistrates had a discretion to decline to hear the summonses, or, if they had not, whether we have a discretion to issue an order of prohibition.

There is no authority directly in point, but we have been referred to three decisions as giving us some guidance as to the way in which we should act. The first, logically but not in point of time, is *R v Newcastle upon Tyne Justices, Ex parte John Bryce (Contractors) Ltd* [1976] 2 All ER 611, [1976] 1 WLR 517. In that case there was an application to amend a summons after the six months' period had expired, and it was not suggested that there was any injustice to the defence. May J, who was giving the judgment with which the other two judges agreed, said ([1976] 2 All ER 611 at 614, [1976] 1 WLR 517 at 520):

'In my view the six months' limitation provision in the 1952 Act is to ensure that summary offences are charged and tried as soon as reasonably possible after their alleged commission, so that the recollection of witnesses may still be reasonably clear, and so that there shall be no unnecessary delay in the disposal by magistrates' courts throughout the country of the summary offences brought before them to be tried. It is in this context that their power to permit the amendment of an information [under s 100 of the 1952 Act] referred to by Lord Widgery CJ [in *Garfield v Maddocks* [1973] 2 All ER 303 at 306, [1974] QB 7 at 12] is to be exercised; it must be exercised judicially; it must be exercised so as to do justice between the parties. But where it can be so exercised, where an information can be amended, even to allege a different offence, so that no injustice is done to the defence, I for my part can see no reason why the justices should not so exercise it even though the amendment is allowed after the expiry of the six months' period from the commission of the alleged offence.'

Then we go to *R v Fairford Justices, ex parte Brewster* [1975] 2 All ER 757, [1976] QB 600 and there the informations were laid and the summonses were issued, but they were incorrect in form. After the six months' period had expired fresh summonses were issued based on the same information. Lord Widgery CJ said ([1975] 2 All ER 757 at 759–760, [1976] QB 600 at 604):

'For my part this important point can be disposed of in this way. I cannot believe that this situation is such that whatever the delay, and however unreasonable and however great the prejudice to the defendant, yet delay is wholly irrelevant when it occurs between the laying of the information and the issue of the summons. There must be power in the court to control excesses of this kind as there is in most other similar features of procedure, and I do not for a moment think that the courts are powerless in that regard. But having regard to authority, or the lack of it perhaps is more important here, and having regard to the fact that in the present case there is really no suggestion whatever of prejudice on the part of the applicant *a* as defendant, it seems to me that in the present case it is quite impossible for us to hold that the delay in this matter, which I have described in some detail, is sufficient to deprive the justices of jurisdiction and thus to authorise us to order prohibition against them.'

It is to be noted that there Lord Widgery CJ is saying that, where delay is of such an order as to cause the court in justice to refuse to carry on with the hearing, the delay is *b* a matter which goes to jurisdiction, the jurisdiction of the justices. He does not say that it is not for the justices to determine whether the delay had been inordinate.

One further case should be referred to, and that is the decision of the House of Lords in *Director of Public Prosecutions v Humphrys* [1976] 2 All ER 497 at 527–528, [1977] AC 1 at 46. That case deals with issue estoppel, which of course is quite a different matter, but there is some helpful guidance to be obtained from the speech of Lord Salmon *c* where, after referring to a statement by Lord Parker CJ in *Mills v Cooper* [1967] 2 All ER 100 at 104, [1967] 2 QB 459 at 467 that 'every court has undoubtedly a right in its discretion to decline to hear proceedings on the ground that they are oppressive and an abuse of the process of the court', Lord Salmon joins with others of the Law Lords in suggesting that that may be too wide a statement of principle for this reason:

d 'I respectfully agree with my noble and learned friend, Viscount Dilhorne, that a judge has not and should not appear to have any responsibility for the institution of prosecutions; nor has he any power to refuse to allow a prosecution to proceed merely because he considers that, as a matter of policy, it ought not to have been brought.'

That is the basic justification for disagreeing with the very wide statement of discretion *e* in the quotation that I have read. He goes on to say:

'It is only if the prosecution amounts to an abuse of the process of the court and is oppressive and vexatious that the judge has the power to intervene.'

For my part, I think that it is open to justices to conclude that it is an abuse of the process of the court for a prosecutor to lay an information when he has not reached a *f* decision to prosecute. The process of laying an information is, I think, assumed by Parliament to be the first stage in a continuous process of bringing a prosecution. Section 104 of the 1952 Act is designed to ensure that prosecutions shall be brought within a reasonable time. That purpose is wholly frustrated if it is possible for a prosecutor to obtain summonses and then, in his own good time and at his convenience, serve them. Of course there may be delays in service of the summonses due perhaps to the evasiveness *g* of the defendant. There may be delays due to administrative reasons which are excusable, but that is not so in this case.

Here, as I understand it, there was a deliberate attempt to gain further time in which to reach a decision. It is perhaps hard on the prosecutor to characterise that as an abuse of the process of the court because I am sure there was no intention by the prosecutor to abuse the process of the court. He thought he could legitimately do this. For my part, *h* I do not think that he can. In such a case I think it is open to the magistrates to say, 'This is an abuse of process. We, therefore, decline jurisdiction and we dismiss the summonses'. But I think it is a matter which has to be investigated by magistrates.

The magistrates in this case had an opportunity to do so, but they did not realise it. We can make an order which will give them another opportunity to investigate the matter. They have in fact already indicated that they would be minded to exercise this *j* jurisdiction in favour of the applicant if they had it. In my judgment, they have it, and I would be very far from discouraging them from exercising it in the way which they meant to exercise it, on two grounds: first, because if I was sitting as a magistrate I would unhesitatingly exercise it in that way; and, second, because through no fault of the prosecutor or of the applicant, two years have now elapsed and that is an additional reason, if there is any doubt in the matter, for resolving it in favour of the applicant by dismissing the summonses.

a

MUSTILL J. I agree.

Order accordingly.

Solicitors: *Underwood & Co* (for the applicant); *Solicitor, Metropolitan Police* (for the prosecutor).

b

Sepala Munasinghe   Barrister.

Re Keeler's Settlement Trusts   *c*
Keeler and others v Gledhill and others

CHANCERY DIVISION
GOULDING J
25th JULY, 13th OCTOBER 1980

d

Trust and trustee – Remuneration of trustee – Order of court – Circumstances in which court will exercise jurisdiction to award remuneration – Director-trustee – Settlement comprising shares in companies – Trustees of settlement appointed directors of companies – Whether trustee-directors entitled to retain director's fees – Whether court having jurisdiction to authorise future retention of director's fees.

e

The trustees of a settlement owned all the shares in one company and the majority of the shares in another company, both of which had subsidiary companies. The settlement authorised the trustees to be appointed directors of the companies, but although it contained provision allowing a trustee to charge for professional services it made no provision for trustees who were directors of the companies to retain fees and remuneration from their directorships. Four trustees who were directors applied to the court for an order authorising them to retain fees and remuneration already received as directors and empowering them to retain such fees and remuneration in the future. Two of the trustee-directors were sons of the settlor, one being managing director of one of the companies and a director of the other, while the other was a director of one of the companies and managing director of a wholly-owned subsidiary. There was evidence from the settlor that both sons were actively engaged in the affairs of the companies of which they were directors, and although they had not received remuneration as directors of the companies owned by the trust they had both received substantial remuneration as directors of the subsidiary companies. The third trustee director was the settlor's wife. She had never performed any substantial duties as a director. The fourth trustee director had acted as the companies' auditor before being appointed a director of one of the companies and had been paid a fee in respect of his directorship.

f

g

h

Held – (1) Under its inherent jurisdiction to allow a trustee to retain remuneration, for which he would otherwise be accountable to the trust fund, if that remuneration was acquired as the result of exceptional effort and skill the court could, if the facts justified it, allow the two sons to retain remuneration already received by them as directors of subsidiaries of the companies controlled by the trust and an inquiry would (if desired) be directed to determine the amount, if any, they were entitled to retain and a similar inquiry would be directed in respect of the companies' former auditor. However, having regard to the fact that a trustee who was a director was required to exert on behalf of the trust the effort and skill which a prudent man of business would in general

j

a undertake in the management of his own investments, the inquiry would be restricted to ascertaining what was a fair remuneration for any effort and skill applied by the sons and former auditor in performing the duties of their directorships over and above the effort and skill ordinarily required of a director of a similar company appointed to represent the interests of a substantial shareholder. In the case of the settlor's wife, however, no inquiry would be directed since she had performed no substantial duties as a director (see p 892 *j* to p 893 *a* and *f* to *j*, p 894 *b* to *d f* to *h* and p 895 *a b f* to *h*, post);

b *Re Macadam* [1945] 2 All ER 664 and dicta of Walton J in *Re Duke of Norfolk's Settlement Trusts* [1978] 3 All ER at 921–922, 925 applied.

(2) The court also had jurisdiction in exceptional cases to allow a trustee-director to retain future remuneration if it was plainly expedient in the interests of the trust for the directorship to be held by the trustee and the additional duties imposed on the trustee were such that he could not fairly be expected to undertake them without receiving

c appropriate remuneration. However, since there was no evidence that the particular case was exceptional, the application would be stood over to allow the parties to file additional evidence if they so wished (see p 893 *b c*, p 895 *h j* and p 896 *a*, post); dictum of Walton J in *Re Duke of Norfolk's Settlement Trusts* [1978] 3 All ER at 924–925 applied.

Per Curiam. Although the court will be reluctant to sanction the retention of remuneration by a trustee-director unless application is made as soon as he begins to hold

d both offices concurrently, that principle need not be rigorously applied where the person concerned has been ignorant of his liability to account (see p 893 *d e*, post).

Notes

For remuneration of trustees, see 38 Halsbury's Laws (3rd Edn) 958–961, paras 1659–1662, and for cases on the subject, see 47 Digest (Repl) 251–255, 2207–2235.

e ### Cases referred to in judgment

Duke of Norfolk's Settlement Trusts, Re [1978] 3 All ER 907, [1979] Ch 37, [1978] 3 WLR 655, Digest (Cont Vol E) 638, 2219c.

Francis, Re, Barrett v Fisher (1905) 74 LJ Ch 198, 92 LT 77, 40 Digest (Repl) 716, 2093.

Freeman's Settlement Trusts, Re (1887) 37 Ch D 148, 57 LJ Ch 160, 57 LT 798, 40 Digest (Repl) 855, 3306.

f *Macadam, Re, Dallow and Moscrop v Codd* [1945] 2 All ER 664, [1946] Ch 73, 115 LJ Ch 14, 173 LT 395, 62 TLR 48, 47 Digest (Repl) 366, 3293.

Marshall v Holloway (1820) 2 Swan 432, 36 ER 681, LC, 47 Digest (Repl) 255, 2230.

Masters, Re, Coutts & Co v Masters [1953] 1 All ER 19, [1953] 1 WLR 81, 47 Digest (Repl) 253, 2219.

Worthington (deceased), Re, ex parte Leighton v Macleod [1954] 1 All ER 677, [1954] 1 WLR

g   526, 23 Digest (Reissue) 59, 733.

Application

By a summons dated 13th June 1980 the plaintiffs, Charles Richard Keeler, John Davis Keeler, Dawn Henrietta Wood, Paul Godfrey Peter Keeler and David James Keeler applied for (1) an order authorising Charles Richard Keeler, John Davis Keeler and

h Mamie Eileen Keeler, being the trustess of a settlement made by Charles Henry Keeler, to retain for their own use and benefit all fees and remuneration received by them in connection with their directorships of Keeler Holdings Ltd or Tregassow Farming Operations Ltd or any subsidiary company thereof and for Wallace Henry Duncan Campbell to retain for his own use and benefit all fees and remuneration received directly by him or indirectly by his firm as auditor of such companies, and (2) an order

j authorising the trustees and their successors to retain any fees or remuneration which they might receive in the future in connection with the directorships of, or employment by, companies controlled by the trust created by the settlement. The defendants were the settlor, the Attorney General and 18 named beneficiaries of the settlement, including 15 minors. The application was heard in chambers but judgment was given in open court. The facts are set out in the judgment.

Michael Hart QC for the plaintiffs and the trustees.
Henry Harrod for the minor beneficiaries.
R C Bailey, solicitor, for one of the adult beneficiaries and the settlor.
The other defendants did not appear.

Cur adv vult

13th October. **GOULDING J** read the following judgment. These proceedings are
about the trusts of a settlement dated 31st October 1951 made, for the benefit of his
family, by Charles Henry Keeler, a successful man of business in the field of optical goods
and instruments. The summons now before me is dated 13th June 1980. It seeks to
obtain two orders from the court.

The first is an order authorising four named applicants, who are the present trustees
of the settlement, to retain for their own benefit all fees and remuneration received by
them respectively in connection with their respective directorships, or in one case for
acting as auditor, of Keeler Holdings Ltd or of Tregassow Farming Operations Ltd or of
any subsidiary of either of those companies. The trustees control both the named
companies, holding the majority of the issued shares of Keeler Holdings Ltd and the
whole of the issued shares of Tregassow Farming Operations Ltd. It is convenient to
mention at once that a former company called Keeler Holdings Ltd, which had been
under the control of the trustees of the settlement since 1964, was put into liquidation
in 1973 and was then in effect replaced by the company now bearing the name. For the
purposes of this judgment I shall ignore that change of corporate identity and shall use
the name Keeler Holdings Ltd to denote indifferently the holding company for the time
being controlled by the trustees of the settlement.

The second order requested by the summons relates not to the past but to the future,
and is couched in extremely wide terms. I will read it verbatim from the summons:

> 'An Order that any of the Trustees for the time being of the above-mentioned
> Settlement or of any appointment made thereunder who may hereafter be or
> become a director or the holder of any other office or employment in any company
> any of whose shares shall form part of the Trust Fund (as defined in the said
> Settlement) or which may be controlled by any company any of whose shares shall
> form part of the Trust Fund (as so defined) shall be entitled to retain for his own use
> and benefit any fees or remuneration received by him in connection with such
> office or employment notwithstanding that his appointment to or retention of such
> office or employment may be directly or indirectly due to the exercise or non-
> exercise of any votes in respect of any shares forming part of the said Trust Fund.'

The application has been argued at chambers, where the summons was supported by
all parties, including the guardian ad litem of the minor beneficiaries. I wish however
to give judgment in court, in view of the difficulty I have encountered in deciding the
matter.

It comes before the court in an extraordinary way. No one has made any demand on
the trustees to account to the trust estate for the remuneration they have had, nor, I
think, have they admitted that they are liable to account, unless indeed their conduct in
taking out the summons constitutes such an admission. Moreover, no present intention
is disclosed that any existing trustee should retire or any new trustee be appointed. The
present application is in fact made in consequence of earlier proceedings concerning the
settlement which came before Brightman J early in 1977. According to the trustees'
evidence, the judge observed that, although the trustees controlled the Keeler group of
companies, there was no power in the settlement authorising them to retain remuneration
received in connection with their directorships. In an endeavour to assist them the
judge, at the request of the plaintiffs named in the originating summons, included a
special direction in his order of 14th March 1977, by which order he approved elaborate
terms of compromise of a question that had arisen regarding the powers of appointment

contained in the settlement. The special direction gave liberty to the parties to apply for
a the purpose of seeking authority for the trustees for the time being of the settlement to
retain directors' fees and other remuneration received by them from any company in
which shares had been or were or might thereafter be held by them as such trustees.
That is the source of the present application.

It is put forward in reliance on the inherent jurisdiction of the court. No arrangement
is proposed under the Variation of Trusts Act 1958, and it is conceded (as I think, rightly)
b that the desired relief cannot be given under s 57 of the Trustee Act 1925.

The settlement contains little that is relevant for present purposes. It recites among
other things the transfer, by the settlor to the original trustees, of a holding of shares in
C Davis Keeler Ltd, a company bearing the same name as, and possibly identical with,
one of the present subsidiaries of Keeler Holdings Ltd. Clause 4 of the settlement directs
the investment of trust money in the names or under the control of the trustees, and
c concludes with the following proviso:

> 'Provided that if one or more of the Trustees is at the request of the Trustees
> appointed or to be appointed as Director of any Company in which the Trustees
> have an interest sufficient shares in such Company to qualify such Trustee or
> Trustees as a director or directors of the Company may be transferred into the sole
> name or names of such Trustee or Trustees as the case may be.'
d

Clause 8 empowers the trustees to invest the trust fund in the purchase, or on the
security, of property of any nature whatsoever. Clause 9 declares that no part of the trust
fund shall be lent to or applied for the benefit of the settlor or any wife of the settlor in
any circumstances whatsoever. Clause 12 of the settlement, the final clause, is a
professional charging clause. It reads as follows:

e
> 'Any Trustee being a Banker Accountant Solicitor or other person engaged in any
> profession or business shall be entitled to be paid all usual professional and other
> charges for business transacted and acts done by him or any partner of his in
> connection with the trusts hereof (whether in the course of his profession or
> business or not) including acts which a Trustee not being in any profession or
> business could have done personally and a Trust Corporation hereafter appointed to
f
> act as a Trustee hereof shall be entitled to charge remuneration at such rate or scale
> as may be agreed at the date of appointment between the Trust Corporation and the
> person or persons making the appointment.'

Thus it appears from cl 4 that the draftsman of the settlement envisaged the possibility
of a trustee holding a directorship for the good of the trust, but was not instructed to
g modify the usual equities arising from such a situation.

The settlement has in effect been varied by the before-mentioned terms of compromise
approved by Brightman J and certain deeds of appointment executed in pursuance
thereof. I observe in passing that the terms of compromise authorised the trustees to
appoint any part of the trust fund or the income thereof in favour of any descendant of
the settlor notwithstanding that he or she might be one of the trustees.

h   The settlor recently swore an affidavit containing the following paragraph:

> 'When I established the settlement my chief concern was to have as trustees
> persons in whom I could have complete confidence. For that reason I selected
> Wallace Henry Duncan Campbell, who has been a life-long friend of mine. When
> my sons had acquired the necessary business experience they became trustees for the
> same reason. It seemed natural to me that members of the family should act as
j
> trustees of the family trust, and the fact that they were also concerned with the
> running of the family businesses made their appointment as trustees seem more
> rather than less appropriate to me. I will emphasise that my sons who are both
> trustees and directors are actively engaged in the affairs of the companies in which
> they are, respectively, directors.'

That evidence, I think, can do no more than induce a benevolent scrutiny of the present application. It is not suggested by counsel that there is any case for rectification of the settlement.

a

What then are the jurisdiction and the judicial duty of the court as regards the two kinds of relief sought, namely the exoneration of trustees from any equitable obligation to account for past remuneration obtained in connection with their office and the anticipatory release of such obligations as regards future remuneration? In that regard counsel have called my attention to three reported authorities: *Re Macadam* [1945] 2 All ER 664, [1946] Ch 73, *Re Masters* [1953] 1 All ER 19, [1953] 1 WLR 81 and *Re Duke of Norfolk's Settlement Trusts* [1978] 3 All ER 907, [1979] Ch 37. It is important, I think, to notice that these authorities fall into two classes. The first of them, like the present case, was concerned with the receipt by trustees of remuneration for acting in a collateral office as directors of a company. The two later cases were, on the other hand, applications to allow trustees to receive remuneration, or an increased remuneration, from the trust estate for performing the duties of the trusteeship itself.

b

c

In *Re Macadam* Cohen J held that certain trustees were in the circumstances of the case accountable for directors' fees received by them and left over the question whether they might be allowed to retain them, in whole or in part, presumably under the inherent jurisdiction of the court. He said ([1945] 2 All ER 664 at 672, [1946] Ch 73 at 82):

> 'If I can be satisfied (and that is the point I have not considered) that they were the best persons to be directors, I do not think it would be right for me to expect them to do the extra work for nothing.'

d

In *Re Masters* Danckwerts J commented on *Re Macadam*, in which he had been junior counsel for the trustees, and said that to his knowledge the course suggested by Cohen J was adopted and the remuneration was in fact authorised. He said so in delivering a judgment which authorised a trust corporation to charge for acting as administrator and trustee of an intestate's estate.

e

I observe in passing that two of the reports of the *Macadam* case (115 LJ Ch 14 at 21 and 62 TLR 48 at 52) suggest that the question reserved by Cohen J was in fact ultimately disposed of by compromise.

In the *Duke of Norfolk* case Walton J carefully reviewed the earlier authorities on the whole subject of the court's inherent jurisdiction to allow remuneration to trustees, including *Re Macadam* and *Re Masters*. After reading much of Danckwert J's judgment, Walton J continued ([1978] 3 All ER 907 at 921–922, [1979] Ch 37 at 54):

f

> 'It is therefore quite plain that Danckwerts J considered he was following *Marshall v Holloway* (1820) 2 Swan 432, 36 ER 681 and *Re Freeman's Settlement Trusts* (1887) 37 Ch D 148. In this latter case, the authorisation of remuneration was effected, as we have already seen, at the same time as the appointment of the trustees by the court. I therefore do not think that Danckwerts J thought he was in any way enlarging the inherent jurisdiction of the court. I would also comment that *Re Macadam, Dallow v Codd* [1945] 2 All ER 664, [1946] Ch 73 is a case where a trustee was being asked to account to the trust for an unauthorised profit he had made as a result of being a trustee, but as a result of extra work, his activities as a director, which were not strictly any part of his duties as a trustee. In these circumstances, Cohen J held that if he was satisfied that the trustee was the best person to be a director, he would allow retention of some or the whole of the fees. This seems plainly to be in a different category of case. The trustees having become accountable to the trust fund, the question is, for what sum are they accountable? And that sum must, on plainest principles of equity, be moulded so as to take account of any exceptional effort or skill shown in acquiring the sum in respect of which they are accountable in the first place.'

g

h

j

That then must be my criterion in deciding the first part of the summons. If and so far as the trustees are in principle accountable (and that is the hypothesis on which the

summons has been framed) I am to take account of any exceptional effort or skill shown
a in acquiring the remuneration in question. I shall have occasion to amplify those words
in a few minutes.

None of the authorities cited gives explicit guidance on the court's anticipatory
jurisdiction to allow a director-trustee to retain *future* remuneration for his own
benefit. In my opinion, however, the court does possess such jurisdiction, exercisable in
harmony with the principles that Walton J found applicable to the court's jurisdiction to
b authorise the remuneration of a trustee for his duties as such. They are set out at [1978]
3 All ER 924–925, [1979] Ch 58. In adapting them by analogy to the particular
anticipatory jurisdiction now under examination, and remembering the different source
of the remuneration, I am accordingly of opinion that this must be treated as an
exceptional jurisdiction, to be exercised sparingly, and that the court will only exercise
it (save perhaps in some wholly exceptional case) if satisfied that it is plainly expedient in
c the interests of the trust for the directorship in question to be held by a trustee, and that
the additional duties imposed on the trustee are such that he cannot fairly be expected to
undertake them without retaining an appropriate remuneration. The appropriate
remuneration must be determined by the court in the interest of the trust; it will not
necessarily be the whole of that paid by the company for the director's services. In
further conformity with Walton J's principles (see particularly [1978] 3 All ER 907 at
d 919, [1979] Ch 37 at 50–51), it is no doubt right to say that the court will be reluctant to
sanction the retention of remuneration by a director-trustee unless application is made
as soon as he begins to hold both offices concurrently, but I do not myself think that that
principle need be rigorously applied where the individual concerned has been ignorant
of his liability to account. It is patent on the face of a trust instrument whether any or
what remuneration is offered to a trustee as such; it is not, however, necessarily apparent
to a layman that he will be bound in conscience to hand over a collateral compensation,
e obtained in consequence of his trusteeship, but paid for services actually rendered to a
third party.

Having stated the law, as I understand it from the authorities cited by counsel, I turn
to apply it to the facts of the present case, and first to the question of remuneration
already received. The test I have taken from the judgment of Walton J is whether any
f exceptional effort or skill was shown in acquiring the remuneration. That was his
formulation in the *Duke of Norfolk* case [1978] 3 All ER 907 at 921–922, [1979] Ch 37 at
54. He paraphrased it by speaking of—

> 'those cases where the trustees are held to be accountable for profits which they
> have made out of the trust, but are in general allowed to keep that proportion of the
> profits so made (doubtless, in many cases, the whole) which results from their own
g > exertions above and beyond those expected of a trustee . . .'

(See [1978] 3 All ER 907 at 925, [1979] Ch 37 at 59.)

I do not think that any and every effort or skill applied by a trustee in executing the
office of a company director is to be regarded as exceptional or unexpected for this
purpose, certainly not in the present case, where it is made perfectly clear by cl 4 of the
h settlement that a trustee may be proposed for appointment as a director of any company
in which the trustees have an interest. The director-trustee, in my judgment, may in a
proper case be allowed to retain reasonable remuneration for effort and skill applied by
him in performing the duties of the directorship over and above the effort and skill
ordinarily required of a director appointed to represent the interests of a substantial
shareholder. The latter is something that a prudent man of business would in general
j undertake in the management of his own investments, and so in my view is in general
an exertion reasonably expected of a trustee. Compare the observation of Upjohn J in *Re
Worthington* [1954] 1 All ER 677 at 679, [1954] 1 WLR 526 at 529, cited in the *Duke of
Norfolk* case.

The first two trustee applicants named in the summons are Charles Richard Keeler, the
eldest son of the settlor, and John Davis Keeler, his second son. The settlor emphasises,

in his recent affidavit from which I have already quoted, that these applicants are, as he says, actively engaged in the affairs of the companies of which they are respectively a directors, but I have no evidence of the scale or intensity of their activity.

Mr C R Keeler has been a director of Keeler Holdings Ltd since 1965, its managing director since 1969, and is also a director of Tregassow Farming Operations Ltd. He has received no remuneration from either of those companies, but has over the years received very substantial director's fees from subsidiaries of Keeler Holdings Ltd. If, after an opportunity for reflection, his counsel so desires, I will direct in the case of this applicant b the following account and inquiries. 1. An inquiry what directorships of companies the plaintiff Charles Richard Keeler has acquired or retained by virtue of his position as a trustee of the settlement, and for what respective periods (down to the date of this order) he has held or has so retained the same. 2. An account of (a) the director's fees and other remuneration received by the said plaintiff from the said directorships respectively during the said respective periods and (b) any other director's fees or remuneration c received by the said plaintiff (down to the date of this order) by virtue of his position as a trustee of the settlement. 3. An inquiry how much (if anything) of the said respective fees and remuneration ought to be retained by the said plaintiff as a fair remuneration for the effort and skill applied by him in performing the duties of his respective directorships over and above the effort and skill ordinarily required of a director of (in each case) a similar company appointed to represent the interests of a substantial shareholder regard d being had to the benefit resulting to the trust and to all other relevant circumstances.

The formulation of inquiry no 1 is founded on the words used by Cohen J in *Re Macadam* [1945] 2 All ER 664 at 672, [1946] Ch 73 at 82. I have drawn part (b) of account no 2 to meet the possible case of a trustee whose holding of a directorship owes nothing to the trust, but whose emoluments are nevertheless awarded or obtained by virtue of the voting power of the trust investment. Inquiry no 3 is an attempt to apply e the general principles enunciated by Walton J in the *Duke of Norfolk* case.

Mr J D Keeler is a director of Tregassow Farming Operations Ltd, but has not been remunerated as such. He has been managing director of Tregassow Agriculture Ltd since 1961, and from that appointment he has received substantial emoluments. He became a trustee in 1970. Tregassow Agriculture Ltd was then a subsidiary of Keeler Holdings Ltd; it became a subsidiary of Tregassow Farming Operations Ltd on the group f reconstruction in 1973. In his case I will, if desired, direct the following account and inquiries: 4. An inquiry for what period or periods if any (down to the date of this order) the plaintiff John Davis Keeler has held the office of managing or other director of Tregassow Agriculture Ltd by virtue of his position as a trustee of the settlement. 5. An account of the director's fees and other remuneration received by the said plaintiff from such directorship (a) during the said period or periods (if any) or (b) otherwise by virtue g of his position as a trustee of the settlement. 6. An inquiry how much (if anything) of the said fees and remuneration ought to be retained by the said plaintiff as a fair remuneration for the effort and skill applied by him in performing the duties of his said directorship over and above the effort and skill ordinarily required of a director of a similar company appointed to represent the interests of a substantial shareholder regard being had to the benefit resulting to the trust and to all other relevant circumstances. h

It appears that under a revocable deed of appointment Mr J D Keeler is at present beneficially entitled to any income derived from the issued share capital of Tregassow Farming Operations Ltd, which itself owns the whole issued share capital of Tregassow Agriculture Ltd. That circumstance however does not absolve him from accounting for his remuneration, if otherwise liable to do so, first, because it is not possible in my judgment summarily to equate an annual expense of a wholly-owned subsidiary j company with potential contemporaneous dividend of its holding company, second, because there is some authority for saying that remuneration recovered from an accountable trustee is a *capital* asset of the trust fund (see *Re Francis* (1905) 74 LJ Ch 198) and, third, because Mr J D Keeler's before-mentioned beneficial interest was only appointed to him on 29th March 1977.

The third trustee applicant named in the summons is Mamie Eileen Keeler, the settlor's wife. The only relevant company (in fact two successive companies) from which she has received emoluments is Keeler Holdings Ltd; she has held unremunerated directorships in some others. Her directorship of Keeler Holdings Ltd was first acquired before the execution of the settlement, and she has been paid on a comparatively modest scale. The evidence does not suggest that she has ever performed any substantial duties and I infer from its silence that she has not, for the present application has clearly been prepared at leisure and with highly skilled advice. I therefore see no utility in making any order relating to Mrs Keeler. In any case cl 9 of the settlement, so long as it remains unvaried, may present an obstacle to her application, since the sums (if any) for which Mrs Keeler is accountable are in equity already part of the trust fund which, under cl 9, is not to be applied for her benefit in any circumstances whatsoever.

Finally comes the applicant Wallace Henry Duncan Campbell. He is a chartered accountant and an old friend of the settlor, who appointed him to be one of the trustees of the settlement on the making thereof. He was not as that time, it would appear, a director of any of the relevant companies. He and his partners then and subsequently acted as auditors and accountants to the various companies in the Keeler group and also gave them what the evidence describes as 'tax, secretarial and financial advice'. I see no reason to doubt that their usual charges for all that business were covered by cl 12 of the settlement. The wording of the clause shows, in more than one place, that the bounds of a trustee's professional activity are not to be tightly drawn. The parenthesis contained in cl 12 makes it clear that an accountant-trustee can properly charge for advice which transcends the limits of the accountancy profession. Moreover the words 'charges for business transacted . . . in connection with the trusts hereof' are wide enough to cover charges for company audit work obtained through the auditor's position as trustee. It would, in my judgment, be an unreasonable interpretation that would permit a person in that situation to retain money from the trust estate itself for auditing the trust accounts, yet make him account, because of a connection with his trusteeship, for fees paid by a company out of its own money for auditing the company's accounts. On 17th December 1973, however, Mr Campbell, who had earlier in the year retired from his firm, was appointed a director of Keeler Holdings Ltd, and he has since received a fee of £1,000 per annum in respect of that office. On the evidence it seems reasonably plain without inquiry that Mr Campbell acquired this directorship by virtue of his position as a trustee and is prima facie accountable for his emoluments as such, which are not expressly mentioned in the summons. The evidence does not describe his services as a director, and I do not know whether he has had occasion to exert any exceptional effort or skill. However, in view of his professional qualifications and long experience of the companies, I will, if desired, direct the following inquiry. 7. An inquiry how much (if anything) of the director's fees of £1,000 per annum received since 17th December 1973 by defendant Wallace Henry Duncan Campbell as a director of Keeler Holdings Ltd ought to be retained by him as a fair remuneration for the effort and skill applied by him in performing the duties of his said directorship over and above the effort and skill ordinarily required of a director of a similar company appointed to represent the interests of a substantial shareholder regard being had to the benefit resulting to the trust and to all other relevant circumstances.

It will be clear from what I have said about the court's jurisdiction and judicial duty that I do not think myself able, on the present evidence, to make any order on the second part of the summons, which asks for carte blanche regarding the future emoluments of the present trustees and their successors in the trust. Such prospective plenary indulgence is, in my judgment, far outside the inherent jurisdiction of the court. It could be conferred only by a statutory variation of the settlement. I feel much doubt whether any more limited relief, limited that is to be a named person or persons, a named company or companies, a defined period, and a maximum sum of money, can in the present case be justified, for I see on the evidence nothing really exceptional in the circumstances proved. There must be hundreds of trusts where trustees hold the capital of family companies for the benefit of members of a particular family without any special clause about directors' fees. Probably the commonest arrangement is for the family's

professional advisers or business friends to act as trustees, in close and informal
consultation (when expedient) with senior members of the family actively directing the *a*
companies.

However, in case a special necessity can be made out, I will, if requested, stand over the
second part of the summons with liberty to the parties to restore it at chambers and to file
additional evidence.

I propose to give counsel a short time in which to advise their clients and to take
instructions, so that they may tell me how much they desire of the relief that I have said *b*
I am willing to give. I shall of course welcome verbal improvements to the draft
accounts and inquiries which I offer. I am well aware that the taking of such accounts
and inquiries may possibly raise questions of principle in this not very well charted
region of equity. They will have to be dealt with if and when they occur.

I shall also have to provide an opportunity for submissions on costs. In the ordinary
way the costs of an application like this, seeking exceptional personal advantages for *c*
trustees, ought (whatever the outcome) to be borne by them in exoneration of the trust
estate. In the present case, however, I cannot help thinking that the court, by including
a special liberty to apply in the order dated 14th March 1977, has in a sense invited the
application, probably taking the view that it is in the true interest of the trust to
investigate and settle the whole matter as soon as possible. Thus it is arguable that the
costs of all parties to the summons, taxed on a common fund basis, might justly be raised *d*
and paid out of the capital of the trust estate, pro rata according to value as between
severed funds. But I shall of course be receptive also to any arguments to the contrary
that may be addressed to me on behalf of beneficiaries.

No order at date of report.

Solicitors: *Linklaters & Paines* (for the plaintiffs and the trustees and for the defendants).

Evelyn M C Budd   Barrister.

Taylor Fashions Ltd v Liverpool Victoria Trustees Co Ltd
Old & Campbell Ltd v Liverpool Victoria Trustees Co Ltd

CHANCERY DIVISION

OLIVER J

22nd, 23rd, 24th, 25th, 26th, 29th, 30th JANUARY, 27th FEBRUARY 1979

Estoppel – Representation – Mistake – Representor's subsequent knowledge of mistake – Relevance – Lease containing option to renew – Option void and unenforceable for want of registration – Lessors and lessees both unaware of invalidity – Lessors –aware of lessees' expenditure of money in expectation of being able to exercise option – Whether lessors entitled to refuse to accept lessees' exercise of option – Whether lessors estopped from relying on invalidity of option.

Estoppel – Conduct – Encouragement – Representee's conduct influenced by representor's encouragement or representation – Lessors encouraging lessees to believe option to renew lease was valid and to spend money on the faith of that belief – Option invalid – Whether unconscionable for lessors to take advantage of invalidity of option.

The second plaintiffs owned the freehold of commercial premises comprising two shops, each on five floors. In 1948 they leased one shop (no 22) to a third party for a term of 28 years with an option to renew for a further 14 years if, at his own expense, the tenant installed a lift. The option was not registered under the Land Charges Act 1925. Shortly after, the second plaintiffs sold the freehold of the premises to the defendants, who were adjoining owners, and took a lease back on the other shop (no 21) for a term of 42 years from 1948 subject to the defendants having the right to determine the lease of no 21 if the tenant of no 22 failed to exercise his option. The defendants were given notice of the terms of the lease to the third party and the option to renew. In 1958 the third party sold its lease of no 22 to the first plaintiffs, who installed a lift at a cost of £5,000 in expectation of their being entitled to exercise the option. The installation of the lift was known to and acquiesced in by the defendants. In 1963 the second plaintiffs wished to expand. They took a lease on an adjoining shop (no 20) from the defendants and spent some £12,000 altering the frontage and internal layout to combine nos 20 and 21 into a single shop. In order that the leases of both shops should coincide it was agreed that the lease of no 20 should be for 14 years with an option to renew for a further 14 years but subject to the defendants having the right to determine the lease if the tenant of no 22 failed to exercise his option. In 1976 the first plaintiffs served a notice exercising the option to renew the lease of no 22 but the defendants claimed that it was void for want of registration and that the leases of nos 20 and 21 were also affected by that invalidity. The defendants accordingly served notices to quit on both plaintiffs who applied to the court for specific performance and declaratory relief. The plaintiffs contended (i) that the first plaintiffs' option was not void for want of registration, and (ii) that, even if it was, the defendants were estopped from relying on the invalidity, having regard to the expenditure in installing a lift made by the first plaintiffs with the defendants' concurrence and to the assertion of the existence of the option in the leases granted by the defendants to the second plaintiffs over nos 20 and 21. The defendants contended that the doctrine of estoppel did not apply because the estoppel alleged was proprietory estoppel or estoppel by acquiescence and, for such an estoppel to arise, it was an essential prerequisite that the representor knew what his rights were and that the representee was acting in the belief that those rights would not be enforced, and thus such an estoppel did not arise where both parties were acting under a mistake as to the representor's rights.

Having decided that he was bound by authority to hold that the option was void as
against the defendants for want of registration, the judge then considered the question   *a*
whether the defendants were estopped from relying on the invalidity of the option.

Held – (1) The doctrine of estoppel by acquiescence was not restricted to cases where the
representor was aware both of what his strict rights were and that the representee was
acting in the belief that those rights would not be enforced against him. Instead, the
court was required to ascertain whether in the particular circumstances it would be
unconscionable for a party to be permitted to deny that which, knowingly or   *b*
unknowingly, he had allowed or encouraged another to assume to his detriment.
Accordingly, the principle could apply where, at the time when the expectation was
encouraged, both parties (and not just the representee) were acting under a mistake of
law as to their rights. Whether the representor knew of the true position was merely one
of the factors relevant to determining whether it would be unconscionable for him to be
allowed to take advantage of the mistake (see p 911 *j* to p 912 *a*, p 913 *b* to *e*, p 915 *j* to   *c*
p 916 *a* and p 918 *g h*, post); *Ramsden v Dyson* (1866) LR 1 HL 129, *Willmott v Barber*
(1880) 15 Ch D 96, *Plimmer v Mayor of Wellington* (1884) 9 App Cas 699, *Sarat Chunder
Dey v Gopal Chunder Lala* (1892) LR 19 Ind App 203, *Hopgood v Brown* [1955] 1 All ER
550, *Inwards v Baker* [1965] 1 All ER 446, *E R Ives Investments Ltd v High* [1967] 1 All ER
504, *Crabb v Arun District Council* [1975] 3 All ER 865 and *Shaw v Applegate* [1978] 1 All
ER 123 considered.   *d*
    (2) Although both the first plaintiffs and the defendants had mistakenly assumed that
by installing the lift the first plaintiffs would then have been entitled to exercise the
option to renew their lease, on the facts there was nothing to suggest that the defendants
had in any way created or encouraged the first plaintiffs' mistaken belief, or that the first
plaintiffs had installed the lift on the faith of their belief that they had a valid option,
since they had not shown that they would not have installed the lift if they had known   *e*
of the true position. The first plaintiffs' claim for specific performance therefore failed
(see p 905 *b* to *h*, p 918 *h* to p 919 *e*, p 920 *a* to *d* and p 922 *j*, post); dicta of Lord Eldon
LC in *Dann v Spurrier* (1802) 7 Ves at 235–236 and of Fry J in *Willmott v Barber* (1880) 15
Ch D at 106 applied.
    (3) The defendants were, however, estopped from asserting the invalidity of the   *f*
option against the second plaintiffs because the defendants were to be taken as having
represented both in 1948 and in 1963 in the leases offered to the second plaintiffs that the
option granted to the first plaintiffs, and on which the second plaintiffs' prospects for
renewal depended, was a valid option, and, further, the defendants had in 1963
encouraged the second plaintiffs to incur expenditure and alter their position irrevocably
by taking additional premises on the faith of the supposition that the option was valid.
In those circumstances it would be inequitable and unconscionable for the defendants to   *g*
frustrate the second plaintiffs' expectation which the defendants had themselves
created. The second plaintiffs were accordingly entitled to specific performance (see
p 907 *b* to *f*, p 920 *d* to p 921 *j* and p 922 *j* to p 923 *a*, post).

Notes
For estoppel by representation, see 21 Halsbury's Laws (4th Edn) 72–74, 145–149, and   *h*
for cases on the subject, see 21 Digest (Repl) 364–387, 1103–1195.
    For options to renew a lease, see 23 Halsbury's Laws (3rd Edn) 473, para 1094, and for
cases on the subject, see 31(1) Digest (Reissue) 278–282, 2301–2335.
    For the Land Charges Act 1925, see 27 Halsbury's Statutes (3rd Edn) 685.
    As from 29th January 1973 the 1925 Act was, so far as relevant, replaced by the Land
Charges Act 1972.   *j*

Cases referred to in judgment
Armstrong v Sheppard & Short Ltd [1959] 2 All ER 651, [1959] 2 QB 384, [1959] 3 WLR
    84, 123 JP 401, CA, 46 Digest (Repl) 393, 355.
Attorney General v Balliol College, Oxford (1744) 9 Mod Rep 407, 88 ER 538, LC, 31(1)
    Digest (Reissue) 170, 1458.

Bank Negara Indonesia v Philip Hoalim [1973] 2 MLJ 3.

Beesly v Hallwood Estates Ltd [1960] 2 All ER 314, [1960] 1 WLR 549; *affd* [1961] 1 All ER 90, [1961] Ch 105, [1961] 2 WLR 36, CA, 21 Digest (Repl) 377, *1135*.

Cairncross v Lorimer (1860) 3 LT 130, 7 Jur NS 149, 3 Macq 827, HL, 21 Digest (Repl) 411, *1318*.

Central London Property Trust Ltd v High Trees House Ltd [1956] 1 All ER 256, [1947] KB 130, [1947] LJR 77, 175 LT 332, 21 Digest (Repl) 376, *1133*.

Crabb v Arun District Council [1975] 3 All ER 865, [1976] Ch 179, [1975] 3 WLR 847, CA, Digest (Cont Vol D) 312, *1250a*.

Craine v Colonial Mutual Fire Insurance Ltd (1920) 28 CLR 305; *affd* sub nom *Yorkshire Insurance Co Ltd v Craine* [1922] 2 AC 541, [1922] All ER Rep 505, 91 LJPC 226, 128 LT 77, PC, 21 Digest (Repl) 472, *1664*.

Dann v Spurrier (1802) 7 Ves 231, 32 ER 94, LC, 31(1) Digest (Reissue) 67, *499*.

De Bussche v Alt (1878) 8 Ch D 286, [1874–80] All ER Rep 1247, 47 LJ Ch 381, 38 LT 370, 3 Asp MLC 584, LJJ, 21 Digest (Repl) 476, *1666*.

Eaglesfield v Marquis of Londonderry (1875) 4 Ch D 693, 34 LT 113; *on appeal* (1876) 4 Ch D 708, CA; *affd* (1878) 38 LT 303, HL, 35 Digest (Repl) 10, *45*.

Eaves, Re, Eaves v Eaves [1939] 4 All ER 260, [1940] Ch 109, 109 LJ Ch 97, 162 LT 8, CA, 49 Digest (Repl) 885, *8287*.

Electrolux Ltd v Electrix Ltd (1954) 71 RPC 23, CA, 46 Digest (Repl) 59, *336*.

Greene v Church Comrs for England [1974] 3 All ER 609, [1974] Ch 467, [1974] 3 WLR 349, 29 P & CR 285, CA, Digest (Cont Vol D) 754, *925ab*.

Gregory v Mighell (1811) 18 Ves 328, 34 ER 1, 31(1) Digest (Reissue) 67, *500*.

Grundt v Great Boulder Pty Gold Mines Ltd [1948] 1 All ER 21, [1948] Ch 145, [1948] LJR 1100, CA, 9 Digest (Reissue) 561, *3367*.

Hollington Brothers Ltd v Rhodes [1951] 2 All ER 578n, 31(1) Digest (Reissue) 181, *1515*.

Hopgood v Brown [1955] 1 All ER 550, [1955] 1 WLR 213, 219 LT 165, 40 Digest (Repl) 300, *2502*.

Inwards v Baker [1965] 1 All ER 446, [1965] 2 QB 29, [1965] 2 WLR 212, CA, Digest (Cont Vol B) 242, *1552a*.

Ives (E R) Investments Ltd v High [1967] 1 All ER 504, [1967] 2 QB 379, [1967] 2 WLR 789, CA, Digest (Cont Vol B) 619, *925c*.

Jackson v Cator (1800) 5 Ves 688, [1775–1802] All ER Rep 592, 31 ER 806, LC, 28(2) Digest (Reissue) 1011, *385*.

Kammins Ballrooms Co Ltd v Zenith Investments (Torquay) Ltd [1970] 2 All ER 871, [1971] AC 850, [1975] 3 WLR 287, 22 P & CR 74, HL, 31(2) Digest (Reissue) 953, *7757*.

Kitney v MEPC Ltd [1978] 1 All ER 595, [1977] 1 WLR 981, 35 P & CR 132, CA, Digest (Cont Vol E) 502, *904ac*.

Moorgate Mercantile Co Ltd v Twitchings [1975] 3 All ER 314, [1976] QB 225, [1975] 3 WLR 286, CA; *rvsd* [1976] 2 All ER 641, [1977] AC 890, [1976] 3 WLR 66, [1976] RTR 437, HL, Digest (Cont Vol E) 211, *1109a*.

Muller v Trafford [1901] 1 Ch 54, 70 LJ Ch 12, 31(2) Digest (Reissue) 743, *6134*.

National Enterprises Ltd v Racal Communications Ltd [1974] 3 All ER 1010, [1975] Ch 397, [1975] 2 WLR 222, [1975] 1 Lloyd's Rep 225, CA, Digest (Cont Vol D) 42, *691c*.

Onward Building Society v Smithson [1893] 1 Ch 1, 62 LJ Ch 138, 68 LT 125, 2 R 106, CA, 21 Digest (Repl) 325, *798*.

Plimmer v Mayor of Wellington (1884) 9 App Cas 699, 53 LJPC 105, 51 LT 475, PC, 11 Digest (Reissue) 129, **98*.

Ramsden v Dyson (1866) LR 1 HL 129, 12 Jur NS 506, HL, 31(1) Digest (Reissue) 68, *506*.

Robins, Re, Holland v Gillam [1928] Ch 721, [1928] All ER Rep 360, 97 LJ Ch 417, 139 LT 393, 40 Digest (Repl) 700, *1958*.

Rogers v Hosegood [1900] 2 Ch 388, 69 LJ Ch 652, 83 LT 186, CA, 40 Digest (Repl) 340, *2769*.

Sarat Chunder Dey v Gopal Chunder Lala (1892) LR 19 Ind App 203, ILR 20 Calc 296, 56 JP 741, PC, 21 Digest (Repl) 383, *1170*.

Shaw v Applegate [1978] 1 All ER 123, [1977] 1 WLR 970, 35 P & CR 181, CA, Digest (Cont Vol E) 336, 235a.

Smith, Re, Vincent v Smith [1930] 1 Ch 88, 99 LJ Ch 27, 142 LT 178, 40 Digest (Repl) 700, 1959.

Stiles v Cowper (1748) 3 Atk 692, 26 ER 1198, LC, 40 Digest (Repl) 830, 3060.

Svenson v Payne (1945) 71 CLR 531.

Willmott v Barber (1880) 15 Ch D 96, 49 LJ Ch 792, 43 LT 95, 31(2) Digest 703, 5748.

Adjourned summons

By a summons dated 19th October 1976 the first plaintiffs, Taylor Fashions Ltd ('Taylors'), sought as against the defendants, Liverpool Victoria Trustees Co Ltd, the determination of, inter alia, the question whether the defendants were estopped from denying that Taylors were entitled to exercise an option to renew a lease at 22 Westover Road, Bournemouth, notwithstanding that, at the date the defendants' predecessors acquired the reversion of the original lease, the option was not registered pursuant to the Land Charges Act 1925. By a summons dated 22nd October 1976 the second plaintiffs, Old & Campbell Ltd ('Olds'), sought as against the defendants a declaration that two notices dated 23rd June 1976 purporting to determine Olds's tenancies of 20–21 Westover Road, Bournemouth under s 25 of the Landlord and Tenant Act 1954 were null and void on the grounds that (i) in respect of 20 Westover Road Olds had validly exercised their option to renew a lease dated 22nd March 1963, and (ii) in respect of 21 Westover Road that the defendants' right to determine the tenancy had not arisen.

Richard Scott QC and *John Trenhaile* for Taylors.
Michael Essayan QC and *Robert Reid* for Olds.
Peter Millett QC and *Geoffrey Jaques* for the defendants.

Cur adv vult

27th February.   **OLIVER J** read the following judgment: I have before me two summonses, both concerned with some commercial premises in Bournemouth known as 20, 21 and 22 Westover Road. The defendants in each case are the same, namely the trustees of the Liverpool Victoria Friendly Society, who are the freeholders of the premises and the plaintiffs' landlords. The plaintiffs in the first summons are Taylors Fashions Ltd (to whom I will refer as 'Taylors') and they are the tenants of 22 Westover Road. In the second summons the plaintiffs are Old & Campbell Ltd (to whom I will refer as 'Olds') and they are the tenants of nos 20 and 21. The relevant background facts are common to both cases and the question at issue is the exercisability of an option contained in the demise of no 22 to renew the term for a further 14 years after the expiry of the original term in 1976. The defendants claim that the option is void against them for want of registration under the provisions of the Land Charges Act 1925 although they accept that, apart from this point, the relevant conditions for the exercise of the option have been fulfilled and that a proper notice to exercise the option has been given in due time. Consequent on the claimed invalidity of the option, the defendants have served on the plaintiffs respectively notices under the Landlord and Tenant Act 1954 in respect of all three premises, they having declined to renew the leases of nos 20 and 22 and having purported to exercise a right to break the lease of no 21, a right which arose only on the non-exercise by Taylors of the option in relation to no 22. The plaintiffs' riposte to this consists of claims for new leases under the 1954 Act and those claims are the subject matter of the summonses, but they have not yet been adjourned into court pending the determination of the plaintiffs' primary claims which are for specific performance and appropriate declaratory relief.

The defendants' case is not one which impresses itself on one immediately as overburdened with merit and the first impression is not significantly improved by a closer examination of the background. But, if they are right in law and if there is no

equity which assists the plaintiffs, it is no part of a judge's function to seek to impose on
a party to litigation his own idiosyncratic code of commercial morality. In saying that
I would not wish to be thought to be voicing a criticism of those who have the conduct
of the defendants' affairs. Those who undertake a fiduciary responsibility for the
management of the affairs of others are not always free to follow their own personal
inclinations in the performance of that responsibility.

I turn, therefore, to a more detailed consideration of the background facts relevant to
the dispute.

Numbers 21 and 22 together consist of a building of four storeys and a basement in a
favoured part of Bournemouth's shopping area, and both premises are used as retail
clothing stores. Prior to 1949 the freehold of the building was owned by Olds and they
carried on there at no 21 the business of gentlemen's tailoring and outfitting, and at no
22 the business of a ladies' fashion store which was conducted as a separate department
under the style 'Madame Campbell'. In 1948 it seems that they were minded to raise
further finance by disposing of the ladies' fashion business and also by disposing of the
freehold of the premises on the footing that the purchaser would grant them a lease back
of no 21 and would grant to the purchaser of the ladies' fashion business a lease of no 22.

In fact the agents who were instructed to offer the premises for sale offered them as
already subject to leases of nos 21 and 22 which were described in the original offer letter
as already having been granted. A letter offering the premises to the defendants was sent
in the middle of October 1948, at which time Olds were already in negotiation with a
purchaser for the business carried on in no 22.

Olds' agents had offered the freehold subject to leases of both parts for 28 years from
25th December 1948, but the terms negotiated with the purchasers of the ladies' fashion
business (a Mr and Miss Murray) in fact provided for the term to be extended to 42 years
if the tenants installed a lift in the premises.

On 5th November 1948 Olds entered into a formal agreement with the Murrays for
the grant to them of a lease of no 22 (less the basement) and the upper floors of no 21 on
the terms of a draft lease. Nothing turns on the terms of that agreement but it should,
perhaps, be mentioned that it contained a pre-emption clause obliging the tenants to
offer the premises back to Olds before disposing of them to anyone else and a similar
right of pre-emption if the landlords disposed of their proposed lease.

Pursuant to that agreement a lease was, on the same date, concluded between Olds and
the Murrays. The premises were described as no 22 but the demise was by reference to
a plan which included the upper floors over no 21. The lease contains the usual
definitions of landlord and tenant as including their respective successors and assigns and
it granted the Murrays a term of 28 years in no 22 from 25th December 1948 at an
annual rent of £2,850.

The only provisions of the document to which I need refer are those contained in cll
2(8) and (11) and 4(2), (3) and (5).

Clause 2(8) was a provision that the tenant agreed—

> 'Not without the previous consent in writing of the Landlords (such consent not
> to be unreasonably withheld) to erect or to permit or suffer to be erected any other
> building upon the demised premises nor to make or to permit or suffer to be made
> any alteration in or external projection on the front of or additions to the demised
> premises or cut maim or injure or permit or suffer to be cut maimed or injured any
> of the walls or timbers thereof.'

Clause 2(11) was a covenant—

> 'Not to assign underlet or part with possession of the demised premises or any part
> thereof without the written consent of the Landlords such consent however not to
> be unreasonably withheld in the case of a respectable and responsible person.'

The critical clauses are cll 4(2), 4(3) and 4(5) which are in these terms. Clause 4(2)
provides:

'*Neither* party shall without the consent in writing of the other (such consent not to be unreasonably or vexatiously withheld) make structural alterations to the *a* existing shop windows and shop fronts of the premises belonging to the Landlords and the premises hereby demised to the Tenants.'

Clause 4(3) provides:

'*At* any time during this demise the Tenants at their own expense may instal a lift to all floors of the building and the cost of such installation and all maintenance shall be borne by the Tenants and no compensation or any other payment whatsoever in *b* respect of such lift shall be made by the Landlords to the Tenants on the determination of this Lease for any reason.'

Then cl 4(5) provides:

'*If* the Tenants shall instal a lift in the premises hereby demised then the Landlords will on the written request of the Tenants made six calendar months before the *c* expiration of the term hereby created and if there shall not at the time of such request be any existing breach or non-observance of any of the covenants on the part of the Tenants hereinbefore contained at the expense of the Tenants grant to them a lease of the demised premises for the further term of fourteen years from the expiration of the said term and containing the like covenants and provisoes as are herein contained with the exception of the present clause for renewal the Tenants *d* on the execution of such renewed lease to execute a counterpart thereof And the rent reserved in such renewed lease shall be the same as that reserved hereby or such larger rental as shall be agreed between the parties at the time of such renewal or failing such agreement shall be a rental representing the fair market value at that time certified by an arbitrator appointed for that purpose by the President for the time being of the Bournemouth Chamber of Trade But in no event shall the rent *e* reserved in such renewed lease be less than that reserved hereby.'

Meanwhile negotiations were continuing between Olds and the defendants for the sale and purchase of the freehold and a letter of 30th November 1948 from the defendants to the vendors' agents shows the basis on which the defendants' offered price of £88,000 was being fixed. It seems that, at that time, the defendants had not appreciated that the lease to the Murrays had actually been granted because the letter treats its terms as still *f* being open to negotiation, although in another place it speaks of it as 'Messrs. Murray's existing Lease'. Three paragraphs of that letter are important as showing the state of mind of the defendants at the time. Their offer was stated to be 'subject to the following conditions'. Condition 2 (which related to the lease of no 22) concluded with these words:

'That the tenants are responsible for all structural and interior and exterior repairs *g* and decorations and also for the fire insurance premium payable on the premises demised to them. The minimum sum upon which the premium is to be payable is £50,000 plus two years loss of rent and Architects' fees. These tenants are also, subject to their installing a lift in the premises, to have the option for a further fourteen years at a rental to be agreed at the time of the exercising of the option, but *h* such rent not to be less than that payable in the Lease referred to above.'

Condition 3 was that Olds themselves should take a 42-year lease of the ground floor of no 22 and concludes thus:

'The Landlords are to have an option to terminate the Lease at the 28th year in the event of the tenants of No. 22 not exercising their option, for a further fourteen years.'   *j*

Condition 5 shows that the defendants then believed that the completion of the purchase and the grant of both leases were to be simultaneous. It is in these terms:

'The Society [that is the defendants] is to have the right of revision where possible and final approval of the two Leases and heating Agreement which are to be executed before the completion of the purchase.'

The defendants' misapprehension was corrected on 2nd December in a letter in which
a the vendors' agents explained that the Murrays' lease had already been completed but
expressed the view that they would probably agree to its modification to include the
insurance provision which the purchasers desired to have included. With that letter they
enclosed a copy of the Murrays' lease.

A formal sale agreement was concluded, the only significant feature of which was that
Olds retained their right of pre-emption as against the Murrays. The transaction between
b Olds and the defendants was completed on 31st March 1949 and, before completing, the
defendants' solicitors made, as one would expect, a search in the Land Charges Register
which showed no subsisting entries. This was not surprising. The view of the legal
profession at that time, based no doubt on the notes in the then current edition of
Wolstenholme and Cherry's Conveyancing Statutes (12th Edn, 1932), was that an option
to renew, being a covenant which touched and concerned the land and therefore ran
c with the reversion, did not require to be registered under the Land Charges Act 1925 in
order to bind a purchaser of the reversion on a lease. Prior to completion and in order to
accommodate the defendants' desire that the insurance to the premises should cover two
years' loss of rent a modification to this effect was indorsed on the lease and executed by
Olds and by the Murrays. That was done on 31st March 1949. The conveyance was
made expressly subject to the lease to the Murrays and was in these terms:

d
> '. . . subject also to a Lease of a part of the property hereby assured dated the Fifth
> day of November One thousand nine hundred and forty eight and made between
> the Vendor of the one part and Charles Gilbert Murray and Leah Elfreda Murray of
> the other part as modified by a Memorandum endorsed on the said Lease and dated
> the Twenty first day of March One thousand nine hundred and forty nine but with
> the benefit of the rent thereby reserved and the covenants on the part of the Lessees
e
> and conditions therein contained And also subject to and with the benefit of Clause
> 10 of an Agreement also dated the Fifth day of November One thousand nine
> hundred and forty eight and made between the Vendor of the one part and the said
> Charles Gilbert Murray and Leah Elfreda Murray of the other part.'

Clause 10 of the agreement related to certain alterations which the tenants of no 22
f were entitled to make to the premises and in particular provided for the landlords to
afford facilities for the installation of the lift and to surrender part of the space in the
basement to enable it to be installed.

The conveyance also refers expressly to a lease 'intended to bear even date with and to
be executed immediately after these presents'. That was, of course, the proposed lease of
no 21 to Olds which was granted on completion. That document demised no 21 to Olds
g for a term of 42 years from 25th December 1948 at a rent of £1,200 per annum and the
only part of it to which I need refer is cl 4(3) and (4) which is in the following terms:

> '(3) *If* the Tenants of the adjoining premises coloured pink on the plan No. 1
> attached hereto and known as No. 22 Westover Road Bournemouth aforesaid shall
> not exercise their option to have granted to them by the Landlords a further term
h
> of fourteen years after the expiration of the Lease to them of the said adjoining
> premises for twenty eight years from the Twenty fifth day of December One
> thousand nine hundred and forty eight then the Landlords shall have the option to
> determine this present demise at the end of the Twenty eighth year of the term
> hereby granted by giving notice in writing thereof to the Tenants at least twenty
> five clear weeks prior to the expiration of the Twenty eighth year of the term hereby
j
> granted whereupon this present demise and everything herein contained shall cease
> and be void but without prejudice to the rights and remedies of either party against
> the other in respect of any antecedent claim or breach of covenant and Provided that
> in the case of such option being exercised by the Landlords the Tenants shall not be
> required to paint the interior of the premises.
> '(4) *If* the Tenants of the said adjoining premises coloured pink or plan No. 1
> attached hereto and known as No. 22 Westover Road Bournemouth aforesaid shall

instal a lift in the said adjoining premises and for the purpose of such installation it
is essential that the well of the lift shaft shall be constructed below the ground floor   *a*
level of the said adjoining premises then the Tenants will afford all necessary and
essential facilities for such installation and construction and will if so required
surrender such part of the basement premises hereby demised as may be essential to
permit the proper construction of the well of the lift shaft . . . '

Then there are certain provisos about the space which has to be left which I do not think   *b*
I need read.

The next relevant event was that on 25th April 1958 the Murrays agreed to sell to
Taylors the goodwill, fixtures, fittings and lease of the ladies' outfitters business at no
22. Olds were agreeable to the sale and did not exercise their right of pre-emption. That
sale, of course, required also the defendants' consent and such consent was duly given by
a licence dated 5th August 1958, on which date the lease of no 22 was duly assigned to   *c*
Taylors. Nothing turns on the contents of the documents.

Almost at once Taylors set about carrying out extensive improvements to the premises
for which purpose they applied for and received the landlords' consent. A new shop
front was installed. They also prepared plans and obtained estimates for the installation
of a lift in the premises and the removal and replacement of partitioning, in particular
in the upper floors which appear previously to have been used as a residential flat. It is   *d*
not in dispute that this involved a substantial expenditure and some interruption of
business while the work was going on. Of particular importance was the installation of
the lift which, according to Mr Taylor's evidence, involved a total expenditure of over
£5,000. All this work, he told me, and I have no reason to doubt it, was done in the
belief that there was a valid and enforceable option which would provide Taylors with a
total term of 32 years. One curious feature of the case is that, although correspondence   *e*
has been traced relating to the shop front and the partition, there is no trace of
correspondence between Taylors or their architects and the defendants relating to the
lift. It is, I think, beyond doubt that the defendants knew that the lift was going to be
installed before the work was done, but no trace of any correspondence or memoranda
has been found in their surveying department files and their general files for the relevant
period have been destroyed in a routine clear-out. Mr Wilson, the present manager of   *f*
the estate department, who was not there at the material time, very fairly said that he
would have expected a record to exist in the estate department files and that the
defendants would have been consulted about the position of the lift. Mr Old told me
(and he was not cross-examined with regard to this) that he was in fact telephoned by the
defendants and informed that the lift was going to be installed. They wanted to ensure
that he was ready to carry out his undertaking to provide the necessary facilities. There   *g*
is also in evidence, first, a bill from Taylors' architects which covers 'Submitting drawings
and calculations to ground landlord to obtain Estate approval for the work' and, second
a plan of the building which was in the defendants' possession and which shows a site for
the lift, although not in the position in which it was finally installed. There can, in my
judgment, be no doubt at all that the defendants knew, before the work was done, that
Taylors were going to instal the lift and that they were agreeable to its being installed in   *h*
the place in which it was in fact installed. More controversial is the evidence of Mr
Taylor of a meeting on the site about a month before the work was done at which,
among others present, was a representative of the defendants. Although the defendants
have no record of this I think that it is inherently likely that it took place (indeed with
a major undertaking of this sort it would be surprising if it did not) and Mr Taylor's
evidence is supported by Mr Old, who also recollects a representative from the defendants   *j*
being present. The purpose of the meeting was to arrive at a final conclusion as to the
positioning of the lift in order to avoid cutting steel and to ensure that there was
sufficient headroom left below for the tenants of no 21. Now Mr Taylor's recollection is
that at that meeting he had the lease with him and that he said something to the effect
that the option would justify the cost of the installation. I am bound to say I have some
reservations about accepting this. It seems an improbable remark for Mr Taylor to make

in the context of what the persons present had gathered to discuss. It was not mentioned
a at all in Mr Taylor's affidavit evidence in support of the summons and did not come to
light until it was mentioned in a letter to the defendants' solicitors of 20th June 1978.
It is not supported by Mr Old, who has no recollection of it. I am quite certain that Mr
Taylor was doing his best to help the court but I cannot resist a suspicion that, in straining
his memory to recollect an event some twenty years ago, he may have convinced himself
that he actually then mentioned what is now, of course, clearly very much in his mind.
b I find myself unable, therefore, to find as a fact that the option was at that time
specifically brought by Mr Taylor to the mind of some representative of the defendant,
but at the same time it seems to me, as a matter of common sense, that having regard to
their knowledge of the contents of the lease it must have been known to the defendants
that the existence of the option would be at least a relevant consideration in Taylors'
undertaking the work and that they were carrying it out and expending money in the
c supposition and expectation that it was a necessary prelude to the exercise of the option
which, when the work was done, they would then be in a position to exercise if they
wished to and thus acquire the additional 14-year term which they or their predecessors
had been promised by the lease.

I cannot, however, find as a fact on the evidence before me that Taylors would not have
done the work if they had then been told that the option might be successfully contested
d so that they would have to rely on such rights only as they had under the Landlord and
Tenant Act 1954. They might or they might not. It is not a point which was in anyone's
mind. They had been advised when they purchased, Mr Taylor told me, that the option
was valid and that if they put in the lift they would be compensated by being able to
demand a new term of 14 years at a fixed rent. There was, he said, an underlying
assumption in his mind that the option was valid and would be exercised and nobody
e corrected it. That, of course, is not surprising for nobody on either side then had any idea
that the option might be capable of being resisted on any ground other than the failure
of the conditions on which it was to be exercised.

My findings are therefore: (1) that Taylors did the work and incurred the expenditure
in the expectation that (subject to the performance of the condition of complying with
the lessees' covenants) they would be able, if they wanted it, to obtain a further 14-year
f term at a rent calculated as provided in the lease, (2) that the fact that Taylors had this
expectation must have been known to the defendants, as also it must have been known
to them that the expectation was at least one factor which would have been taken into
consideration by Taylors in determining whether or not to insure the expenditure, (3)
that the doing of the work was known to and acquiesced in by the defendants (who in
fact had no right to object to it) and that they co-operated to the extent of ascertaining
g that their other tenants, Olds, did not object and of taking part in discussions regarding
the siting and construction of the lift, (4) that, at the time of the discussions and when the
work was done, the defendants did not suspect and had no reason to suspect that they
might have any reason for challenging the validity of the option, and (5) that if Taylors
had known that there were grounds for challenging the option they *might* (but not
certainly would) have taken a different course of action.

h The next relevant event in the chronology was something which had nothing to do
with any of the parties. It was the decision of Buckley J in *Beesly v Hallwood Estates Ltd*
[1960] 2 All ER 314, [1960] 1 WLR 549 to the effect that an option to renew contained
in a lease was registrable as a land charge under the Land Charges Act 1925 and was void
as against a purchaser of the reversion if not registered. It is common ground that the
significance of this in its impact on the parties to the transactions which I have described
j was not, at the time, appreciated by anybody.

That unconsciousness in fact endured for a number of years. At the end of 1962 Mr
Old, whether at his instance or that of the defendants is not clear, was engaged in
discussions with the defendants with a view to the enlargement of Olds' premises, either
by taking a lease of the adjoining properties nos 19 and 20 (which were also owned by the
defendants) and surrendering the lease of no 21 or by taking a lease of no 20 and effecting
alterations which would result in nos 20 and 21 becoming a single shop. It seems that

the latter appeared the more practical suggestion and in November 1962 the defendants offered Olds a lease of no 20 at a rent of £3,500 for 14 years with an option to renew for *a* a further 14. It is evident from the correspondence that the defendants wanted, so far as possible, to ensure that nos 19, 20 and 21 presented a uniform appearance which would allow them to be let in the future as a single unit and that this involved some fairly costly alterations to the shop front and internal layout and the removal of the internal division between nos 20 and 21. In a letter to the defendants' agents of 1st December 1962 Mr Old remarked: 'This is no 14 year project and is aimed at providing the landlord with as *b* nearly genuine a double unit as possible, the scrapping of our existing windows and much of our internal lay-out.' It is clear that he also became concerned that, if he was to take a lease of no 20 it should be tied in with the lease of no 21 so that he would not be left after 14 years with a lease of one but not the other. Similarly, he was sensible of the possibility that the defendants might be prejudiced if Taylors left at the end of 14 years, without extending their term, when the landlords might be left with premises which *c* might not be altogether easy to let on their own.

What was finally arranged was that the lease of no 20 should be for 14 years with an option to renew for a further 14 years and the defendants' unawareness of any question of the invalidity of Taylor's option is shown by a letter to their own solicitors of 7th February 1963 in which they gave the following instructions with regard to the term of the proposed lease of no 20. They say: *d*

'Term, 14 years from 25th December 1962 with the tenant having the option of a further 14 years subject to the Society having the right to determine the lease at the end of 14 years on the same terms as those granted to the lessor under the lease of No. 21 Westover Road. The leases of Nos. 21 and 22 Westover Road are enclosed and you will note the Society's right to determine is dependent on whether or not the tenants of No. 22 Westover Road exercise their option.' *e*

Correspondence ensued between the parties' solicitors and a draft lease was prepared, cl 4 of which provided for the tenants to have an option to renew if Taylors exercised their option in the lease of no 22. The expectation of the parties appears very clearly from the following passage from a letter dated 19th February 1963 from Olds' solicitors to the defendants' solicitors: *f*

'Clause 4. Although in practice our respective clients will no doubt be in close touch before any question of notice arises, it is suggested that the tenant should have a suitable period for consideration whether to exercise the present option, after expiry of the period within which (if at all) the Landlord must give notice to determine the lease of No. 21. Would it not in fact be simpler to enter into a lease for 28 years determinable after 14 years, which would achieve the same object *g* without the complication of another option and would secure uniformity with No. 21?'

That suggestion was in fact rejected and it was said that the lease of no 21 must stand on its own. In the result the lease of no 20 was executed on 22nd March 1963 and Olds expended money in altering and adapting the premises so as to make them integral with *h* no 20. It should be said, in fairness, that a substantial contribution to that work was also made by the defendants and the main work paid for by Olds was on the shop fronts and the fittings to no 20. Again, I need not refer to any of the terms of the lease other than the option clause which was in these terms:

'THE Landlords will at the written request of the Tenant made at least four months before the expiration of the term hereby created and if there shall not at the *j* time of such request be any existing breach or non-observance of any of the convenants on the part of the Tenants hereinbefore contained and if the option in respect of Number 22 Westover Road hereinafter referred to shall not have been exercised [I pause there to remark that it is common ground that that is a mistake and that it should read: 'hereinafter referred to *shall* have been exercised'] at the expense of the Tenant grant to him a Lease of the demised premises for the further

term of Fourteen Years from the expiration of the said term at the same rent as is
herein reserved until the Twenty fifth day of December One thousand nine hundred
and eighty three and thereafter at the yearly rent of Four Thousand Pounds and
containing the like covenants and provisoes as are herein contained with the
exception of the present convenant and option for renewal the Tenant on the
execution of such renewed Lease to execute the counterpart thereof and to pay to
the Landlords the Landlords legal costs and surveyors fees in connection with the
grant of such renewed lease PROVIDED ALWAYS that this option shall not be exercised
and the term hereby created shall not be renewed if the Tenants of the neighbouring
premises known as Number 22 Westover Road shall not exercise their option to
have granted to them by the Landlords a further term of Fourteen Years after the
expiration of the Lease to them of the said neighbouring premises for Twenty eight
years from the Twenty fifth day of December One thousand nine hundred and forty
eight.'

Mr Old, in his evidence, was quite definite that if he had known at the time that he
was getting a 14-year term without the possibility of a renewal under the option he
would not have taken on the lease of no 20. The negotiations would, he said, have been
on an entirely different basis. He also told me that the whole operation in 1963 involved
a cost of about £12,000. At that time, Taylors had put in the lift and Mr Old entertained
a fair certainty that they would want to exercise their option to continue. In the light of
this evidence, which I accept, it is, I think, clear that in committing themselves to the
lease of no 20 and incurring the expenditure that this involved, Olds were relying on the
continued exercisability of the option to Taylors in the lease of no 22 and that, had they
been told that that underlying assumption was invalid, they would not have so acted.
The lease itself, of course, and the negotiation leading up to it were based on the option
being then exercisable and indeed no sensible meaning can be given to the provisions of
cl 4, which I have read, on any other hypothesis. Equally it is clear, and it is common
ground, that the expectation of the availability of the option was shared by the defendants
themselves. It was not until 1975 that it came to their notice that there might be a
question whether it was void against them for want of registration.

On 7th June 1976 Taylors served notice exercising the option to renew and it is not in
dispute that if the option was then enforceable against the defendants that notice was a
good notice of exercise. They now claim specific performance of that option and there
is a similar claim by Olds for specific performance of the option in the 1963 lease and an
appropriate declaration as regards the clause in the 1949 lease.

The points which arise for decision therefore, are these. (1) Is Taylors' option, as the
defendants claim and as the plaintiffs contest, void as against the defendants for want of
registration? (2) If it is, are the defendants estopped as against Taylors from relying on
this ground of invalidity having regard to the expenditure by Taylors made with the
defendants' concurrence in 1959 and 1960? (3) If the option is indeed unenforceable
against the defendants, has it nevertheless been 'exercised' for the purposes of the break
and renewal clauses in the lease to Olds? (4) If it has not, are the defendants estopped as
against Olds from relying on the invalidity of an option which their own grants assert to
be subsisting?

The first of these questions has been the subject matter of previous decisions to which
I shall have to refer, but counsel for Taylors submits that I am not bound by them and
presents an argument which so far as I know has not been presented at any rate in this
form in any of the previous cases. He puts the case thus. The Land Charges Act 1925
(which was the statute in force at the material time) was concerned with the registration
of interests in land or equitable burdens on land and was designed to substitute
registration as a land charge for the equitable doctrine of notice in those cases where,
prior to 1925, the binding effect of the interest on a subsequent purchaser depended on
notice. The 1925 Act, of course, also applies to certain statutory or legal interests (for
instance, a puisne mortgage) but the important point for counsel is that it applies to
interests in land, not to merely contractual rights, or, in those cases where it does apply

to merely contractual burdens, it applies only to those which prior to 1925 depended for their enforceability against subsequent purchasers on the doctrine of notice (eg restrictive *a* covenants). The 1925 Act provides, in s 10, that interests or obligations of this sort may be registered as land charges of the appropriate class, and class C defines estate contracts as including 'a valid option of purchase, a right of pre-emption or any other like right'. Section 13(2) provides that a land charge of this type—

'shall . . . be void as against a purchaser of the land charged therewith, or of any *b* interest in such land, unless the land charge is registered in the appropriate register before the completion of the purchase.'

That means, counsel submits, that it is void as a land charge, ie as an interest in or incumbrance on the land, even if the purchaser has notice of the interest, and one sees this reflected in ss 198 and 199 of the Law of Property Act 1925 which provide *c* respectively that registration shall constitute actual notice and that a purchaser shall not be prejudicially affected by notice of a registrable charge if it is not registered. But, counsel submits, none of this touches contractual obligations which, by statute and quite independently of any equitable doctrine of notice, bind a purchaser as an integral part of the land purchased. The obligation resting on a reversioner under an option to renew in a lease is one of the obligations which, ever since the statute 32 Hen 8 c 34 (Grantees of *d* Reversions, 1540), has run with the land and remained binding at law quite regardless of any question of notice. It binds the reversioner not because it is an interest in land, although it may incidentally create one, but because it is a contractual obligation statutorily annexed to the land to which the Land Charges Act 1925 has no application. Indeed, it is expressly provided in s 6 of the Law of Property Act 1925 that nothing in Part I of that Act (and this must I think be referring particularly to the provisions of s *e* 1(3)) affects prejudicially the right to enforce, inter alia, lessor's covenants the burden of which run with the reversion.

There is, I think, a logic in counsel's submissions, which accord with the view of the original authors of Wolstenholme and Cherry, with what Harman J thought was the policy of the legislation in *Hollington Brothers Ltd v Rhodes* [1951] 2 All ER 578n and with the practice of the legal profession up to 1960. This view of the matter moreover derives *f* some support from the analysis of the anomalous nature of covenants running with the land contained in the judgment of Farwell J in *Muller v Trafford* [1901] 1 Ch 54. They are not executory in nature but bind the land from their inception and 'pass with it in much the same way as title deeds' (see *Rogers v Hosegood* [1900] 2 Ch 388 at 394). But, whatever might have been my view of the matter if it were still res integra, it is not so in fact and the judgment of Buckley J in *Beesly v Hallwood Estates Ltd* [1960] 2 All ER 314, *g* [1960] 1 WLR 549 is direct authority for the proposition that an unregistered option for renewal in a lease is void and unenforceable against a purchaser for money or money's worth of the reversion. That case is no less an authority because the actual decision in favour of the plaintiff was based on an entirely different point and was affirmed by the Court of Appeal on that ground (see [1961] 1 All ER 90, [1961] Ch 105). It has been adopted as correct, although apparently without argument, by the Court of Appeal in *h* *Greene v Church Comrs for England* [1974] 3 All ER 609, [1974] Ch 467 and *Kitney v MEPC Ltd* [1978] 1 All ER 595, [1977] 1 WLR 981, although in neither case was counsel's point argued. Nor indeed is it clear that the case before Buckley J was argued in this way. Counsel submits that I am not bound by *Beesly's* case and that, on the authority of *National Enterprises Ltd v Racal Communications Ltd* [1974] 3 All ER 1010, [1975] Ch 397, the existence of two Court of Appeal decisions where the specific point was not argued *j* does not preclude me from declining to follow it. That may be so, but nevertheless *Beesly's* case was a considered judgment on a difficult point of statutory interpretation and it has been followed and acted on for the past 18 years. Quite apart from judicial comity and from the respect that I would feel for any decision from that source, I am mindful of the remarks of Maugham J in *Re Smith, Vincent v Smith* [1930] 1 Ch 88 at 99, remarks, I should add, which were also made in the context of the 1925 property legislation. He said:

a
'I take this opportunity of repeating what I have said on previous occasions, that where a learned judge, after consideration, has come to a definite decision on a matter arising out of this exceedingly complicated and difficult legislation, it is very desirable that the Court should follow that decision, and accordingly I should be strongly inclined, whatever my own view was, to follow what I take to be the positive decision of Tomlin J. [in *Re Robins* [1928] Ch 721 at 736, [1928] All ER Rep 360 at 364].'

b
In my judgment, *Beesly's* case must be taken as representing the law and I would not feel at liberty, at this level, to depart from it now, even were I so minded to do.

I approach the case, therefore, on the footing that, whatever the parties may have thought, the option was in fact void as against the defendants (although of course still contractually binding as between the original parties) from the moment when they completed their purchase. This brings me to the second and fourth questions which I
c
have postulated above. As regards the general principles applicable I can treat the two questions together, although there are certain circumstances peculiar to Olds and some additional arguments of law in their case to which I shall have to refer later on. The starting point of the arguments of counsel for both plaintiffs on estoppel is the same and was expressed by counsel for Olds in the following proposition: if A, under an expectation created or encouraged by B that A shall have a certain interest in land, thereafter, on the
d
faith of such expectation and with the knowledge of B and without objection by him, acts to his detriment in connection with such land, a court of equity will compel B to give effect to such expectation.

This is a formulation which counsel for the defendants accepts but subject to one important qualification, namely that at the time when he created and encouraged the expectation and (I think that he would also say) at the time when he permitted the
e
detriment to be incurred (if those two points of time are different) B not only knows of A's expectation but must be aware of his true rights and that he was under no existing obligation to grant the interest.

This is the principal point on which the parties divide. Counsel for the plaintiffs contend that what the court has to look at in relation to the party alleged to be estopped is only his conduct and its result, and not, or, at any rate, not necessarily, his state of
f
mind. It then has to ask whether what that party is now seeking to do is unconscionable. Counsel for the defendants contends that it is an essential feature of this particular equitable doctrine that the party alleged to be estopped must, before the assertion of his strict rights can be considered unconscionable, be aware both of what his strict rights were and of the fact that the other party is acting in the belief that they will not be enforced against him.
g
The point is a critical one in the instant case and it is one on which the authorities appear at first sight to be divided. The starting point is *Ramsden v Dyson* (1866) LR 1 HL 129, where a tenant under a tenancy at will had built on the land in the belief that he would be entitled to demand a long lease. The majority in the House of Lords held that he would not, but Lord Kingsdown dissented on the facts. There was no or certainly no overt disagreement between their Lordships as to the applicable principle, but it was
h
stated differently by Lord Cranworth LC and Lord Kingsdown and the real question is how far Lord Cranworth LC was purporting to make an exhaustive exposition of principle and how far what he stated as the appropriate conditions for its application are to be treated, as it were, as being subsumed sub silentio in the speech of Lord Kingsdown. Lord Cranworth LC expressed it thus (at 140–141):

j
'If a stranger begins to build on my land supposing it to be his own, and I, perceiving his mistake, abstain from setting him right, and leave him to persevere in his error, a Court of equity will not allow me afterwards to assert my title to the land on which he had expended money on the supposition that the land was his own. It considers that, when I saw the mistake into which he had fallen, it was my duty to be active and to state my adverse title; and that it would be dishonest in me to remain wilfully passive on such an occasion, in order afterwards to profit by the mistake which I might have prevented. But it will be observed that to raise such an

equity two things are required, first, that the person expending the money supposes himself to be building on his own land; and, secondly, that the real owner at the *a* time of the expenditure knows that the land belongs to him and not to the person expending the money in the belief that he is the owner. For if a stranger builds on my land knowing it to be mine, there is no principle of equity which would prevent my claiming the land with the benefit of all the expenditure made on it. There would be nothing in my conduct, active or passive, making it inequitable in me to assert my legal rights.' *b*

So here, clearly stated, is the criterion on which counsel for the defendants relies. Lord Kingsdown stated the matter differently and rather more broadly, although in the narrower context of landlord and tenant. He says this (at 170–171):

'The rule of law applicable to the case appears to me to be this: If a man, under a verbal agreement with a landlord for a certain interest in land, or, what amounts to the same thing, under an expectation, created or encouraged by the landlord, that *c* he shall have a certain interest, takes possession of such land, with the consent of the landlord, and upon the faith of such promise or expectation, with the knowledge of the landlord, and without objection by him, lays out money upon the land, a Court of equity will compel the landlord to give effect to such promise or expectation. This was the principle of the decision in *Gregory* v. *Mighell* ((1811) 18 Ves 328, 34 ER *d* 1), and, as I conceive, is open to no doubt.'

So here, there is no specific requirement, at any rate in terms, that the landlord should know or intend that the expectation which he has created or encouraged is one to which he is under no obligation to give effect.

Counsel for the defendants does not, nor could he in the light of the authorities, dispute the principle. What he contends is that even if (which he contests) this is a case *e* where the defendants could be said to have encouraged the plaintiffs' expectations (and that is not necessarily the same as having encouraged or acquiesced in the expenditure) the principle has no application to a case where, at the time when the expectation was encouraged, both parties were acting under a mistake of law as to their rights.

There is, he submits, a clear distinction between cases of proprietary estoppel or estoppel by acquiescence on the one hand and promissory estoppel or estoppel by *f* representation (whether express or by conduct) on the other. In the latter case, the court looks at the knowledge of the party who has acted and the effect on him of his having acted. The state of mind of the promisor or representor (except to the extent of knowing, either actually or inferentially, that his promise or representation is likely to be acted on) is largely irrelevant. In the former case, however, it is essential, counsel submits, to show that the party alleged to have encouraged or acquiesced in the other party's belief himself *g* knew the true position, for if he did not there can be nothing unconscionable in his subsequently seeking to rely on it. Counsel for the defendants concedes that there may be cases which straddle this convenient dichotomy, cases which can be put either as cases of encouragement or proprietary estoppel on Lord Kingsdown's principle or as estoppel by representation, express or implied. But, he submits, the party alleging the estoppel must, whichever way he elects to put his case or even if he runs them as alternatives, *h* demonstrate the presence of all the essential ingredients of whatever type of estoppel he relies on. He cannot manufacture a third and new hybrid type of estoppel by an eclectic application of some of the ingredients of each. So, if he wishes to put his case as one of estoppel by representation, he must, for instance, show an unequivocal representation of existing fact. Equally, if he wants to rely on the circumstances of the case as raising a proprietary estoppel arising from acquiescence in his having acted on an erroneous *j* supposition of his legal rights, then he must accept the burden of showing that the error was known to the other party.

So far as proprietary estoppel or estoppel by acquiescence is concerned, he supports his submission by reference to the frequently cited judgment of Fry J in *Willmott v Barber* (1880) 15 Ch D 96 which contains what are described as the five 'probanda'. The actual case was one where what was alleged was a waiver by acquiescence. A lease contained a covenant against assigning, subletting or parting with possession without the lessor's

consent and the lessee had let a sublessee into possession of part of the land under an
a agreement with him which entitled him to occupy that part for the whole term and
conferred an option to purchase the remaining land for the balance of the term
outstanding when the option was exercised. The sublessee built on the land and the head
landlord was aware that he was in possession and was expending money. It was,
however, proved that he did not then know that his consent was required to a subletting
or assignment. The question arose between the sublessee and the head landlord when
b the sublessee tried to exercise his option over the remaining land and found himself met
with the response that the head landlord refused consent to the assignment. The case
was, on the judge's finding of fact, one simply of acquiescence by standing by and what
was being argued was that the landlord was estopped by his knowledge of the plaintiff's
expenditure on the part of the land of which the plaintiff *was* in possession from
withholding his consent to an assignment of that part of which he was not. It having
c been found as a fact that the landlord did not, at the time of the plaintiff's expenditure,
know about the covenant against assignment and that there was nothing in what had
passed between them to suggest either that the landlord was aware that the plaintiff was
labouring under the belief that no consent was necessary or to encourage that belief, Fry
J dismissed the plaintiff's claim. It has to be borne in mind, however, in reading the
judgment, that this was a pure acquiescence case where what was relied on was a waiver
d of the landlord's rights by standing by without protest.

It was a case of mere silence where what had to be established by the plaintiff was some
duty in the landlord to speak. The passage from the judgment most frequently cited is
where Fry J said this (at 105–106):

'A man is not to be deprived of his legal rights unless he has acted in such a way
as would make it fraudulent for him to set up those rights. What, then, are the
e elements or requisites necessary to constitute fraud of that description? In the first
place the plaintiff must have made a mistake as to his legal rights. Secondly, the
plaintiff must have expended some money or must have done some act (not
necessarily upon the defendant's land) on the faith of his mistaken belief. Thirdly,
the defendant, the possessor of the legal right, must know of the existence of his
own right which is inconsistent with the right claimed by the plaintiff. If he does
f not know of it he is in the same position as the plaintiff, and the doctrine of
acquiescence is founded upon conduct with a knowledge of your legal rights.
Fourthly, the defendant, the possessor of the legal right, must know of the plaintiff's
mistaken belief of his rights. If he does not, there is nothing which calls upon him
to assert his own rights. Lastly, the defendant, the possessor of the legal right, must
have encouraged the plaintiff in his expenditure of money or in the other acts which
g he has done, either directly or by abstaining from asserting his legal right. Where
all these elements exist, there is fraud of such a nature as will entitle the Court to
restrain the possessor of the legal right from exercising it, but, in my judgment,
nothing short of this will do.'

Counsel for the defendants submits that when one applies these five probanda to the
h facts of the instant case it will readily be seen that they are not all complied with. In
particular, he submits, the fourth probandum involves two essential elements, viz (i)
knowledge by the possessor of the legal right of the other party's belief and (ii) knowledge
that that belief is mistaken. In the instant case the defendants were not aware of their
inconsistent right to treat the option as void and equally they could not, thus, have been
aware that the plaintiffs' belief in the validity of the option was a mistaken belief.

j The alternative approach via estoppel by representation is not, he submits, open to the
plaintiffs in this case because so far as Taylors were concerned the defendants made no
representation to them at all and so far as Olds were concerned the representation of the
continuing validity of the option, if there was one at all, was a representation of law.

Now, convenient and attractive as I find counsel's submissions as a matter of argument,
I am not at all sure that so orderly and tidy a theory is really deducible from the
authorities, certainly from the more recent authorities which seem to me to support a
much wider equitable jurisdiction to interefere in cases where the assertion of strict legal

rights is found by the court to be unconscionable. It may well be (although I think that
this must now be considered open to doubt) that the strict *Willmott v Barber* probanda are *a*
applicable as necessary requirements in those cases where all that has happened is that the
party alleged to be estopped has stood by without protest while his rights have been
infringed. It is suggested in Spencer Bower and Turner on Estoppel by Representation
(3rd Edn, 1977, para 290) that acquiescence, in its strict sense, is merely an instance of
estoppel by representation and this derives some support from the judgment of the
Court of Appeal in *De Bussche v Alt* (1878) 8 Ch D 286 at 314. If that is a correct analysis *b*
then, in a case of mere passivity, it is readily intelligible that there must be shown a duty
to speak, protest or interfere which cannot normally arise in the absence of knowledge
or at least a suspicion of the true position. Thus for a landowner to stand by while a
neighbour lays drains in land which the landowner does not believe that he owns (see
Armstrong v Sheppard & Short Ltd [1959] 2 All ER 651, [1959] 2 QB 384) or for a
remainderman not to protest at a lease by a tenant for life which he believes he has no *c*
right to challenge (see *Svenson v Payne* (1945) 71 CLR 531) does not create an estoppel.
Again, where what is relied on is a waiver by acquiescence, as in *Willmott v Barber* itself,
the five probanda are no doubt appropriate. There is, however, no doubt that there are
judicial pronouncements of high authority which appear to support as essential the
application of all the five probanda over the broader field covering all cases generally
classified as estoppel by 'encouragement' or 'acquiescence' (see, for instance, the speech of *d*
Lord Diplock in *Kammins Ballrooms Co Ltd v Zenith Investments (Torquay) Ltd* [1970] 2 All
ER 871 at 895, [1971] AC 850 at 884).

   Counsel for the plaintiffs submits, however, that it is historically wrong to treat these
probanda as holy writ and to restrict equitable interference only to those cases which can
be confined within the strait-jacket of some fixed rule governing the circumstances in
which, and in which alone, the court will find that a party is behaving unconscionably. *e*
Whilst accepting that the five probanda may form an appropriate test in cases of silent
acquiescence, he submits that the authorities do not support the absolute necessity for
compliance with all five probanda, and, in particular, the requirement of knowledge on
the part of the party estopped that the other party's belief is a mistaken belief, in cases
where the conduct relied on has gone beyond mere silence and amounts to active
encouragement. In Lord Kingsdown's example in *Ramsden v Dyson*, for instance, there *f*
is no room for the literal application of the probanda, for the circumstances there
postulated do not presuppose a 'mistake' on anybody's part, but merely the fostering of
an expectation in the minds of *both* parties at the time but from which, once it has been
acted on, it would be unconscionable to permit the landlord to depart. As Scarman LJ
pointed out in *Crabb v Arun District Council* [1975] 3 All ER 865 at 877, [1976] Ch 179 at
195, the 'fraud' in these cases is not to be found in the transaction itself but in the *g*
subsequent attempt to go back on the basic assumptions which underlay it.

   Certainly it is not clear from the early cases that the courts considered it in all cases an
essential element of the estoppel that the party estopped, although he must have known
of the other party's belief, necessarily knew that that belief was mistaken. Thus in *Stiles
v Cowper* (1748) 3 Atk 692, 26 ER 1198 a remainderman was held to be estopped from
setting up the invalidity of a lease granted by the life tenant in excess of his powers after *h*
he had accepted rent for some years and allowed the tenant to lay out money on
building. Lord Hardwicke LC there said:

> 'Though the acceptance of rent under a lease by issue in tail, will bind them,
> where they claim *per formam doni* from the lessor, yet this alone will not bind the
> remainder-man in tail, who claims the leasehold estate by purchase, but is a
> circumstance however in favor of the lessee; and when the remainder-man lies by, *j*
> and suffers the lessee or assignee to rebuild, and does not by his answer deny that he
> had notice of it, all these circumstances together will bind him from controverting
> the lease afterwards.'

   There is no suggestion in the report that at the time of the expenditure and the receipt
of rent the remainderman knew that the lease was invalid. Indeed the statement in the
report that he 'thought it proper' to receive rent rather suggests the contrary.

In *Jackson v Cator* (1800) 5 Ves 688, [1775–1802] All ER Rep 592 it does not appear that
a either party was under any misapprehension as to the legal position, although this may
have been a case of promissory estoppel.

   In *Gregory v Mighell* (1811) 18 Ves 328, 34 ER 1, the case relied on by Lord Kingsdown
in formulating his proposition, the defendant was estopped from claiming that the
plaintiff's possession was non-consensual so as to render it unavailable as an act of part
performance. Here again this does not seem to have been a unilateral misapprehension
b as to what the legal position was when possession was taken. Nor, in my judgment, is
any such essential condition deducible from the cases following *Ramsden v Dyson* and
particularly from the more modern authorities. The fact is that acquiescence or
encouragement may take a variety of forms. It may take the form of standing by in
silence whilst one party unwittingly infringes another's legal rights. It may take the
form of passive or active encouragement or expenditure or alteration of legal position on
c the footing of some unilateral or shared legal or factual supposition. Or it may, for
example take the form of stimulating, or not objecting to, some change of legal position
on the faith of a unilateral or a shared assumption as to the future conduct of one of other
party. I am not at all convinced that it is desirable or possible to lay down hard and fast
rules which seek to dictate, in every combination of circumstances, the considerations
which will persuade the court that a departure by the acquiescing party from the
d previously supposed state of law or fact is so unconscionable that a court of equity will
interfere. Nor, in my judgment, do the authorities support so inflexible an approach,
and that is particularly so in cases in which the decision has been based on the principle
stated by Lord Kingsdown. Thus in *Plimmer v Mayor of Wellington* (1884) 9 App Cas 699
at 700 the stated case makes it clear that the respondent, who sought to raise the estoppel,
knew the state of the title at the date when he incurred the expenditure. There was
e simply a common supposition that he would not be summarily turned out.

   Now *Plimmer's* case cannot, I think, be explained as being one of estoppel by
representation or of promissory estoppel, for the interest arising by estoppel was treated
as giving rise to a cause of action which enabled the respondent to claim compensation.
Nor was it so treated by their Lordships of the Privy Council. Giving the opinion of the
Board Sir Arthur Hobhouse, having quoted the passage from Lord Kingsdown's speech
f to which I have referred, says this (at 711–713):

   'This case of *Ramsden v. Dyson* was strongly pressed in argument against the
   conclusion to which their Lordships have come, and it was said that Lord
   Cranworth's judgment, which represented the opinion of the majority, lays it down
   that an equity of the sort now relied on cannot be raised unless the occupant who
   improves the land believes it to be his own, and the owner of the improved land
g   knows of that mistaken belief. But there was no disagreement among the judges on
   the principles of law laid down in that case. Only Vice-Chancellor Stuart first, and
   after him Lord Kingsdown, drew from the evidence inferences of fact at variance
   with those drawn by the majority of the House, and so brought out a different legal
   conclusion . . . In the present case, the equity is not claimed because the landowner
h   has stood by in silence while his tenant has spent money on his land. This is a case
   in which the landowner has, for his own purposes, requested the tenant to make the
   improvements . . . Is it to be said that, when he had incurred the expense of doing
   the work asked for, the Government could turn round and revoke his licence at
   their will? Could they in July, 1856, have deprived him summarily of the use of the
   jetty? It would be in a high degree unjust that they should do so, and that the
j   parties should have intended such a result is, in the absence of evidence, incredible
   . . . Their Lordships consider that this case falls within the principle stated by Lord
   Kingsdown as to expectations created or encouraged by the landlord, with the
   addition that in this case the landlord did more than encourage the expenditure, for
   he took the initiative in requesting it.'

   Again in *Sarat Chunder Dey v Gopal Chunder Lala* (1892) LR 19 Ind App 203 at 214 Lord
Shand in giving the opinion of the Board said this:

'. . . their Lordships think it right to say that it would make no difference in the effect to be now given to the plea of estoppel against a purchaser under the mortgage *a* sale, though it clearly appeared that *Ahmed*, when he acted as he did in the mortgage transaction, was under the belief that the hiba was a valid deed which he could not set aside; nor is it of any moment that he neither contemplated committing any fraud, nor, in fact, committed any fraud by his acts or representations . . . The learned Counsel who argued the present case on either side were agreed that the terms of the *Indian Evidence Act* did not enact as law in *India* anything different from *b* the law of *England* on the subject of estoppel, and their Lordships entirely adopt that view. The law of this country gives no countenance to the doctrine that in order to create estoppel the person whose acts or declarations induced another to act in a particular way must have been under no mistake himself, or must have acted with an intention to mislead or deceive. What the law and the Indian statute mainly regard is the position of the person who is induced to act; and the principle on *c* which the law and the statute rest is that it would be most inequitable and unjust to him that if another, by representation made, or by conduct amounting to a representation, has induced him to act as he would not otherwise have done, the person who made the representation should be allowed to deny or repudiate the effect of his former statement, to the loss and injury of the person who acted on it. If the person who made the statement did so without full knowledge, or under *d* error, *sibi imputet*. It may, in the result, be unfortunate for him, but it would be unjust, even though he acted under error, to throw the consequences on the person who believed his statement and acted on it as it was intended he should do.'

Although counsel for the defendants submits that this was a case simply of estoppel by representation, I do not think that I can accept that except to the extent that proprietary estoppel of the type envisaged in Lord Kingsdown's exposition is a branch of estoppel by *e* representation, as, indeed, I believe that it is. It is true that in the passage which I have read the Board refers to representation by conduct, but the representation in the case before the Board was clearly one of law, or at least of private rights under the law, namely the validity of a particular deed, and was no different in quality from that representation which was made to Olds in the instant case, namely that there was a subsisting option exercisable vis-à-vis the defendants. *f*

That appears clearly from this passage from the opinion of the Board (at 212–213):

'. . . these actings on the part of *Ahmed* . . . amounted to a distinct declaration by him to the lender that the hiba in favour of *Arju Bibi* was a valid deed, or in any view, that, if the document was open to legal objections *Ahmed*, as the person entitled to challenge the deed, waived his right to do so, and consented for his interest to *g* represent and to hold the hiba as valid, and consequently as giving a legal right to *Arju Bibi*, as the proprietor, to grant the mortgage. There was a distinct representation by *Ahmed* professing to act as his mother's attorney, that she was owner in possession, having a good title to create a valid mortgage affecting the lands. It is, in their Lordships' opinion, impossible to take any other view of the effect of *Ahmed*'s conduct in the whole transaction, and particularly his signing the *h* mortgage and taking payment of the money; and it is equally clear that the transaction was concluded on the footing of that representation, and that the creditor was thereby induced to lend the money on the security of the mortgage.'

The statement of Lord Shand to which I have referred was adopted and applied by Isaacs J in *Craine v Colonial Mutual Fire Insurance Co* (1920) 28 CLR 305 and in this passage in his judgment he drew the clear distinction between the sort of considerations *j* applicable to a case of waiver and those applicable to a case of estoppel. He said (at 327):

'When its true foundations are stated, it will be seen that estoppel is separated from waiver in point of principle by a very broad line of demarcation. First of all, the law of estoppel looks chiefly at the situation of the person relying on the estoppel; next, as a consequence of the first, the knowledge of the person sought to be estopped is immaterial; thirdly, as a further consequence, it is not essential that the person sought to be estopped should have acted with any intention to deceive; fourthly, conduct, short of positive acts, is sufficient.'

Then he quotes the passage from Lord Shand to which I have already referred.

Counsel for the defendants meets this by the submission that the case was, again, one of estoppel by representation and that this merely underlines the clear distinction which he seeks to draw between proprietary estoppel by acquiescence or encouragement on the one hand and estoppel by representation and promissory estoppel on the other. It is, of course, true that the case was treated as one of representation of fact, namely the insurers intention to treat as legally valid a claim which was in fact open to legal objection, but this merely shows again, I think, how narrow is the line between representations of fact and law. In a sense, most representation of law can be approached on the footing that, whatever the law may be, it is the existing intention of the party making the representation to treat the law, as it is represented to be, as the conventional basis for the particular transaction which he has in mind. And, indeed, when the case went to the Privy Council, the judgment of the Board delivered by Lord Atkinson suggests that their Lordships were treating it as a matter of indifference whether the representation was that the claim made actually was valid (a question of law) or that it was the insurers' intention to treat it as valid (a question of fact): see *Yorkshire Insurance Co Ltd v Craine* [1922] 2 AC 541 at 553, [1922] All ER Rep 505 at 512.

The principles applied by the Board in *Sarat Chunder Dey v Gopal Chunder Lala* were applied by Clauson LJ in *Eaves v Eaves* [1939] 4 All ER 260, [1940] Ch 109 to a case where a widow had acquiesced in the disposition of a trust fund on the footing that her remarriage was lawful. There is nothing in the report to suggest that she knew at the time that it was, in fact, void and, indeed, it was not declared void until 12 years later. So here again, if the case be treated as one of representation, the representation was one of law. Equally, if it be treated as one of acquiescence, it was acquiescence without knowledge of the true legal position. Nevertheless, we find Clauson LJ saying this ([1939] 4 All ER 260 at 264–265, [1940] Ch 109 at 117–118):

> 'It is well settled that if a party has so acted that the fair inference to be drawn from his conduct is that he consents to a transaction to which he might quite properly have objected, he cannot be heard to question the legality of the transaction as against persons who, on the faith of his conduct, have acted on the view that the transaction was legal: *Cairncross* v. *Lorimer* ((1860) 3 LT 130). The principle applies even if the party whose conduct is in question was himself acting without full knowledge or in error: *Sarat Chunder Dey* v. *Gopal Chunder Lala*. In the circumstances of the present case the defendant was left by the plaintiff to act, and did in fact act, on the view that the winding up of the trust was a completely legal transaction, leaving the fund in his hands as his own for him to spend, and it appears to me to be contrary to all principle that the plaintiff should now be heard to question the legality of the transaction.'

The dichotomy of counsel for the defendants does, it is fair to say, derive some small support from the judgment of Evershed MR in *Hopgood v Brown* [1955] 1 All ER 550, [1955] 1 WLR 213 where he refers to Fry J's formulation of the requisites of estoppel in *Willmott v Barber* as addressed and limited to cases of estoppel by acquiescence and as not intended as a comprehensive formulation of the necessary requisites of estoppel by representation. That, however, does not necessarily imply his acceptance of the proposition that all the probanda are applicable to every case of estoppel by acquiescence, and it seems clear from his earlier pronouncement in *Electrolux Ltd v Electrix Ltd* (1954) 71 RPC 23 at 33 that that was not, indeed, his view.

Furthermore, the more recent cases indicate, in my judgment, that the application of the *Ramsden v Dyson* principle (whether you call it proprietary estoppel, estoppel by acquiescence or estoppel by encouragement is really immaterial) requires a very much broader approach which is directed to ascertaining whether, in particular individual circumstances, it would be unconscionable for a party to be permitted to deny that which, knowingly or unknowingly, he has allowed or encouraged another to assume to his detriment rather than to inquiring whether the circumstances can be fitted within the confines of some preconceived formula serving as a universal yardstick for every form of unconscionable behaviour.

So regarded, knowledge of the true position by the party alleged to be estopped becomes merely one of the relevant factors (it may even be a determining factor in certain cases) in the overall inquiry. This approach, so it seems to me, appears very clearly from the authorities to which I am about to refer. In *Inwards v Baker* [1965] 1 All ER 446, [1965] 2 QB 29 there was no mistaken belief on either side. Each knew the state of the title, but the defendant had been led to expect that he would get an interest in the land on which he had built and, indeed, the overwhelming probability is that that was indeed the father's intention at the time. But it was not a mere promissory estoppel, which could merely be used as a defence, for, as Lord Denning MR said ([1965] 1 All ER 446 at 449, [1965] 2 QB 29 at 37): 'It is for the court to say in what way the equity can be satisfied.' The principle was expressed very broadly both by Lord Denning MR and by Danckwerts LJ. Lord Denning MR said:

> '... but it seems to me, from *Plimmer's* case ((1884) 4 App Cas 699 at 713–714) in particular, that the equity arising from the expenditure on land need not fail "merely on the ground that the interest to be secured has not been expressly indicated ... the court must look at the circumstances in each case to decide in what way the equity can be satisfied." ... All that is necessary is that the licensee should, at the request or with the encouragement of the landlord, have spent the money in the expectation of being allowed to stay there. If so, the court will not allow that expectation to be defeated where it would be inequitable so to do.'

Danckwerts LJ said ([1965] 1 All ER 446 at 449–450, [1965] 2 QB 29 at 38):

> 'It seems to me that this is one of the cases of an equity created by estoppel, or equitable estoppel, as it is sometimes called, by which the person who has made the expenditure is induced by the expectation of obtaining protection, and equity protects him so that an injustice may not be perpetrated.'

An even more striking example is *E R Ives Investments Ltd v High* [1967] 1 All ER 504, [1967] 2 QB 379. Here, again, there does not appear to have been any question of the persons who had acquiesced in the defendant's expenditure having known that his belief that he had an enforceable right of way was mistaken. Indeed, at the stage when the expenditure took place, both sides seem to have shared the belief that the agreement between them created effective rights. Nevertheless the successor in title to the acquiescing party was held to be estopped. Lord Denning MR said this ([1967] 1 All ER 504 at 507–508, [1967] 2 QB 379 at 394):

> 'The right arises out of the expense incurred by the defendant in building his garage, as it is now, with access only over the yard: and the Wrights standing by and acquiescing in it, knowing that he believed he had a right of way over the yard. By so doing the Wrights created in the defendant's mind a reasonable expectation that his access over the yard would not be disturbed. That gives rise to an "equity arising out of acquiescence". It is available not only against the Wrights but also their successors in title. The court will not allow that expectation to be defeated when it would be inequitable so to do. It is for the court in each case to decide in what way the equity can be satisfied ...'

It should be mentioned that the Wrights themselves clearly also believed that Mr High had a right of way, because when they came to sell they sold expressly subject to it. So, once again, there is an example of the doctrine of estoppel by acquiescence being applied without regard to the question of whether the acquiescing party knew that the belief of the other party in his supposed rights was erroneous.

Counsel for both plaintiffs have also drawn my attention to the Privy Council decision in *Bank Negara Indonesia v Philip Hoalim* [1973] 2 MLJ 3 where again it seems that the misconception of the legal position which gave rise to the assurance creating the estoppel seems to have been shared by both parties. This is, however, rather a case of promissory estoppel than of the application of the *Ramsden v Dyson* principle.

More nearly in point is *Crabb v Arun District Council* [1975] 3 All ER 865, [1976] Ch

179, where the plaintiff had altered his legal position in the expectation, encouraged by
a the defendants, that he would have a certain access to a road. Now there was no mistake
here. Each party knew that the road was vested in the defendants and each knew that no
formal grant had been made. Indeed, I cannot see why in considering whether the
defendants were behaving unconscionably it should have made the slightest difference
to the result if, at the time when the plaintiff was encouraged to open his access to the
road, the defendants had thought that they were bound to grant it. The fact was that he
b had been encouraged to alter his position irrevocably to his detriment on the faith of a
belief, which was known to and encouraged by the defendants, that he was going to be
given a particular right of access, a belief which, for all that appears, the defendants
probably shared at that time.

The particularly interesting features of the case in the context of the present dispute
are, first, the virtual equation of promissory estoppel and proprietary estoppel or estoppel
c by acquiescence as mere facets of the same principle and, second, the very broad approach
of Lord Denning MR and Scarman LJ, both of whom emphasised the flexibility of the
equitable doctrine. It is, however, worth noting that Scarman LJ adopted and applied the
five probanda in *Willmott v Barber* which he described as 'a valuable guide'. He considered
that those probanda were satisfied and it is particularly relevant here to note again the
fourth one, namely that the defendant, the possessor of the legal right must know of the
d plaintiff's mistaken belief. If Scarman LJ had interpreted this as meaning, as counsel for
the defendants submits that it does mean, that the defendant must know not only of the
plaintiff's belief but also that it was mistaken, then he could not, I think, have come to
the conclusion that this probandum was satisfied, for it seems clear from the recital of the
facts by Lord Denning MR that, up to the critical moment when the plaintiff acted, *both*
parties thought that there *was* a firm assurance of access. The defendants had, indeed,
e even erected a gate at their own expense to give effect to it. What gave rise to the
necessity for the court to intervene was the defendants' attempt to go back on this
subsequently when they fell out with the plaintiff. I infer therefore that Scarman LJ
must have construed this probandum in the sense which counsel for the plaintiffs urge
on me, namely that the defendant must know merely of the plaintiff's belief which, in
the event, turns out to be mistaken.

f   Finally, there ought to be mentioned the most recent reference to the five probanda
which is to be found in *Shaw v Applegate* [1978] 1 All ER 123, [1977] 1 WLR 970. That
was a case where the plea of estoppel by acquiescence failed on appeal, but is significant
that two members of the court expressed serious doubt whether it was necessary in every
case of acquiescence to satisfy the five probanda. Buckley LJ said this ([1978] 1 All ER 123
at 130–131, [1977] 1 WLR 970 at 977, 978):

g
'As I understand that passage [and there he is referring to the passage from the
judgment of Fry J in *Willmott v Barber* to which I have already referred], what the
learned judge is there saying is that where a man has got a legal right, as the
plaintiffs have in the present case, being legal assignees of the benefit of the covenant
binding the defendant, acquiescence on their part will not deprive them of that
h legal right unless it is of such a nature and in such circumstances that it would really
be dishonest or unconscionable of the plaintiffs to set up that right after what has
occurred. Whether in order to reach that stage of affairs it is really necessary to
comply strictly with all five tests there set out by Fry J may, I think, still be open to
doubt, although no doubt if all those five tests were satisfied there would be shown
to be a state of affairs in which it would be dishonest or unconscionable for the
j owner of the right to insist on it. In *Electrolux Ltd v Electrix Ltd* (1954) 71 RPC 23
at 33 Evershed MR said: "I confess that I have found some difficulty—or should find
some difficulty if it were necessary to make up my mind and express a view
whether all five requisites which Fry, J., stated in the case of *Willmott v. Barber* must
be present in every case in which it is said that the plaintiff will be deprived of his
right to succeed in an action on the ground of acquiescence. All cases (and this is a
trite but useful observation to repeat) must be read in the light of the facts of the
particular case." So I do not, as at present advised, think it is clear that it is essential

to find all the five tests set out by Fry J literally applicable and satisfied in any particular case. The real test, I think, must be whether on the facts of the particular case the situation has become such that it would be dishonest or unconscionable for the plaintiff, or the person having the right sought to be enforced, to continue to seek to enforce it.'

And Goff LJ referred again to the judgment in *Willmott v Barber* and said ([1978] 1 All ER 123 at 132, [1977] 1 WLR 970 at 980):

'But for my part, I share the doubts entertained by Evershed MR in the *Electrolux* case whether it is necessary in all cases to establish the five tests which are laid down by Fry J, and I agree that the test is whether, in the circumstances, it has become unconscionable for the plaintiff to rely on his legal right.'

So here, once again, is the Court of Appeal asserting the broad test of whether in the circumstances the conduct complained of is unconscionable without the necessity of forcing those incumbrances into a Proscrustean bed constructed from some unalterable criteria.

The matter was expressed as follows by Lord Denning MR in *Moorgate Mercantile Co Ltd v Twitchings* [1975] 3 All ER 314 at 323, [1976] QB 225 at 241:

'Estoppel is not a rule of evidence. It is not a cause of action. It is a principle of justice and of equity. It comes to this. When a man, by his words or conduct, has led another to believe in a particular state of affairs, he will not be allowed to go back on it when it would be unjust or inequitable for him to do so. Dixon J [in *Grundt v Great Boulder Pty Gold Mines Ltd* (1937) 59 CLR 641 at 674] put it in these words: "The principle upon which estoppel *in pais* is founded is that the law should not permit an unjust departure by a party from an assumption of fact which he has caused another party to adopt or accept for the purpose of their legal relations." In 1947, after the *High Trees* case, I had some correspondence with Dixon J about it, and I think I may say that he would not limit the principle to an assumption of fact, but would extend it, as I would, to include an assumption of fact or law, present or future. At any rate, it applies to an assumption of ownership or absence of ownership. This gives rise to what may be called proprietary estoppel. There are many cases where the true owner of goods or of land has led another to believe that he is not the owner, or, at any rate, is not claiming an interest therein, or that there is no objection to what the other is doing. In such cases it has been held repeatedly that the owner is not to be allowed to go back on what he has led the other to believe. So much so that his own title to the property, be it land or goods, has been held to be limited or extinguished, and new rights and interests have been created therein. And this operates by reason of his conduct—what he has led the other to believe—even though he never intended it.'

The inquiry which I have to make therefore, as it seems to me, is simply whether, in all the circumstances of this case, it was unconscionable for the defendants to seek to take advantage of the mistake which, at the material time, everybody shared, and, in approaching that, I must consider the cases of the two plaintiffs separately because it may be that quite different considerations apply to each.

So far as Taylors are concerned there seem to me to be two difficulties in counsel's way. In the first place, whilst it is, no doubt, true that at the time when the work of putting in the lift was commenced with the defendants' knowledge and co-operation, co-operation at least to the extent of entering into discussions with regard to the siting of the lift, all parties shared the common belief that there was a valid an enforceable option, it is difficult to see how that belief had been in any way created or encouraged by the defendants. It arose so far as Taylors were concerned because they had previously taken an assignment of the Murrays' lease and had been, as Mr Taylor told me in his evidence, assured on that occasion by their solicitors that the option was valid and subsisting. When they came to instal the lift they were simply doing what was contemplated by the lease itself, and although it would have been obvious to anyone who knew the contents of the lease that the installation was a necessary or precondition to the exercise of the option, which Taylors might or might not wish to exercise when the term came to an

a end in 18 years' time, I can find nothing in the defendants' conduct which can properly
be said to have encouraged Taylors to believe in the validity of the option to any greater
extent than they had already been encouraged to do so by what they had previously been
told by their legal advisers. It must be remembered that, although the original
contemplation had been that the defendants might themselves grant the lease to the
Murrays, that was overtaken by events. They came into the picture, therefore,
fortuitously perhaps, merely as purchasers of the reversion on an existing lease and
b subject to all its expressed obligations so far as enforceable against them. The installation
of a lift was not something which they could prevent or control except possibly to the
extent to which their consent might have been necessary to the cutting of walls or
timbers. It was something which was expressly provided for in the lease and which,
although a condition precedent to the coming into existence of the option to renew, by
no means necessarily signified an intention that it would be exercised at the end of the
c term. So far as acquiescence pure and simple is concerned the defendants could not
lawfully object to the work and could be under no duty to Taylors to communicate that
which they did not know themselves, namely that the non-registration of the option
rendered it unenforceable. So far as encouragement is concerned, it is not in my
judgment possible fairly to say that the mere presence of the defendants' representative
at a site meeting 'encouraged' Taylors in their belief that the option was valid. No doubt
d it did nothing to *discourage* such a belief, but their representative would, I venture to
think, have been present even if Taylors had already made up their minds that the option
was not going to be exercised. It was referable to cl 4(3) of the lease which gave Taylors
the right to make the installation, not to cl 4(5) which conferred the option if the
installation was made.

The second difficulty in counsel's way seems to me to be this. The work which was
e carried out was work which was referable to the unexpired term which Taylors then held
and was no doubt undertaken with a view to making the premises more attractive and
convenient for customers of the business which, after all, was going to be carried on for
another 18 years before any question of exercising the option even arose. By that time,
the initial expense would long since have been written off by normal depreciation.
Taylors believed that the option was a valid option, that is to say that they had, potentially,
f a longer term than they had in fact. But what is there to indicate that the work was
undertaken 'on the faith of' that belief rather than merely 'in' that belief? Much the
same point arose in *Willmott v Barber* (1880) 15 Ch D 96 at 106 where Fry J felt unable to
say that the expenditure was incurred on the faith of the option rather than on the faith
of the plaintiff's existing possession of the land on which the building took place.
Counsel for the defendants has reminded me of Lord Eldon LC's remarks in *Dann v*
g *Spurrier* (1802) 7 Ves 231 at 235–236, 32 ER 94 at 95–96:

> 'It is upon the Plaintiff to prove, not merely to raise a probable conjecture, but to
> shew upon highly probable grounds a case of bad faith and bad conscience against
> the Defendant ... this Court will not permit a man knowingly, though but
> passively, to encourage another to lay out money under an erroneous opinion of
h > title; and the circumstance of looking on is in many cases as strong as using terms
> of encouragement; a lessor knowing and permitting those acts, which the lessee
> would not have done, and the other must conceive he would not have done, but
> upon an expectation, that the lessor would not throw an objection in the way of his
> enjoyment. Still it must be put upon the party to prove that case by strong and
> cogent evidence; leaving no reasonable doubt, that he acted upon that sort of
j > encouragement. [And as regards the actual case before him he said:] ... in order to
> give a person a larger interest in the property than he derives under the instrument
> making his title, it must be shewn, that with the knowledge of the person, under
> whom he claims, he conceived, he had that larger interest; and was putting himself
> to considerable expence, unreasonable, compared with the smaller interest; and
> which the other party observed, and must have supposed incurred under the idea,
> that he intended to give that larger interest, or to refrain from disturbing the other
> in the enjoyment. The Plaintiff has failed in that; and has relied on the Defendant.'

Then he held that the bill could not be sustained.

I refer also to the judgment of Lord Hardwicke LC in *Attorney General v Balliol College* **a** (1744) 9 Mod Rep 407 at 411, 88 ER 538 at 540. Mr Taylor very frankly said that it was assumed all along that here was a lease with an option to renew and that, for obvious reasons, no separate consideration was given to the desirability of the expenditure if the option was not available. It is conceivable that Taylors might not have done the work, although I find it difficult to believe that they would have contemplated operating a ladies' store on three floors in a fashionable Bournemouth shopping centre for 18 years **b** without the convenience of a lift. It is conceivable that, if they had known the true position, they might have sought to renegotiate a fresh option with the defendants rather than rely on their rights under the Landlord and Tenant Act 1954. But what Mr Taylor was unable to say was that they would not have done the work if they had not thought that the option was available, much less that the defendants were or must have been aware that they would not have done it.   **c**

Whilst, therefore, it may not seem very admirable for the defendants to avail themselves of a technicality which runs counter to the common assumption entertained by all the parties to the transaction, that is what the law permits them to do; and I cannot find, in the circumstances of this case, and even given the flexibility of the equitable principles, that Taylors have discharged the burden of showing that it is dishonest or unconscionable for them to do so. I must, therefore, dismiss Taylors' claim for specific **d** performance of the option, although I do so with some regret.

Turning now to the case of Olds, the position appears to me to be very different. First, the defendants obtained the freehold from them at a price which, whatever the defendants' views as to the materiality of the length of the term, was calculated so far as Olds were concerned on the footing that the break clause was to operate and the term of the lease back to be reduced from 42 to 28 years only in the event of the non-exercise by **e** Taylors of an option which was assumed to be, and must be taken as having been represented by the defendants to be, subsisting at the time when the lease was granted. Clearly that was the assumption, and it cannot, I think, be disputed when the correspondence is examined that the defendants knew that that was the assumption. Their counsel's retort is that if and so far as the reference to Taylors' option in Olds' lease constitutes a representation it is one of law which cannot found an estoppel. There seem **f** to me to be two answers to this. In the first place, it seems to me that what the break clause in the Olds' lease is representing is that Taylors have, at the date when the lease is granted, a subsisting option which they are at liberty to exercise so as to extend their term. If it does not mean that then the condition on which the break clause was to operate is otiose. But that, as it seems to me, is a representation of fact.

It is an assertion of the private rights subsisting between the defendants and the **g** adjoining tenants although it may involve an inseparable conclusion of law as to the enforceability of those rights. If it means, as counsel suggests, merely that the lease of the adjoining premises contains an option provision which may or may not be enforceable (as to which the representee must make up his own mind) then I think that he finds himself in great difficulty with the construction point raised by counsel for Olds and which I shall have to consider a little later.   **h**

Second and in any event, counsel for Olds puts his case alternatively on the *Ramsden v Dyson* principle. Here Olds were encouraged by the defendants to alter their legal position irrevocably on the faith of the belief of expectation, of which the defendants knew and which they themselves fostered by the terms of the lease, that they would be getting a term which was to be cut down only on a particular supposition, namely that Taylors would be either unwilling or would disentitle themselves from exercising their **j** option.

But it is, I think, unnecessary for counsel to rely solely on the transaction in 1949. The 1963 transaction presents an even clearer picture, because Olds were encouraged by the defendants to expend a very large sum on the premises and to take a lease of the adjoining premises on the faith of the expectation, encouraged by the defendants, that they would be entitled to renew in a particular event which, whether it was probable or not, Olds were at least invited to believe was possible. That they acted on that supposition

cannot I think be doubted. One has only to refer to Mr Old's statement in the
a correspondence leading up to the lease that 'this is no 14 year project'. Nor, equally, can
it be doubted that the defendants were aware of, and indeed shared, that supposition.
Again, I do not think that it really matters whether the case is put as one of estoppel by
acquiescence or of estoppel by representation. Clause 4 of the 1963 lease, in its entirety,
is without sense except on the footing that the reference to the tenants of the
neighbouring premises known as no 22 Westover Road exercising 'their option to have
b granted to them by the Landlords [ie by the defendants] a further term' is construed as
a reference to an option between those tenants and the defendants subsisting and still
capable of being exercised at the date of the lease. On any other footing the clause never
could have any sphere of operation at all. Again it seems to me that this is not a
statement of law but a representation of a present fact as regards the existence of a private
right between Taylors and the defendants from which, no doubt, there is to be drawn the
c conclusion that the option gives rise to certain legal consequences.
    As Jessel MR said in *Eaglesfield v Marquis of Londonderry* (1875) 4 Ch D 693 at 703:

'It is not the less a fact because that fact involves some knowledge or relation of
law. There is hardly any fact which does not involve it. If you state that a man is
in possession of an estate of £10,000 a year, the notion of possession is a legal notion,
d   and involves knowledge of law; nor can any other fact in connection with property
be stated which does not involve such knowledge of law. To state that a man is
entitled to £10,000 Consols involves all sorts of law. Therefore this is a statement
of fact, and nothing more; and I hold the argument to be wholly unfounded which
maintained that it was a statement of law.'

e   It would, in my judgment, be most inequitable that the defendants, having put
forward Taylors' option as a valid option in two documents, under each of which they are
the grantors, and having encouraged Olds to incur expenditure and to alter their position
irrevocably by taking additional premises on the faith of that supposition, should now be
permitted to resile and to assert, as they do, that they are and were all along entitled to
frustrate the expectation which they themselves created and that the right which they
f themselves stated to exist did not, at any material time, have any existence in fact.
    It was suggested to Mr Old that he was, after all, taking a chance on any view of the
matter when he took on the leases and incurred the expenditure, for Taylors might not
have exercised their option or they might have disentitled themselves from doing so by
failing to observe the covenants in the lease or giving notice in due time. And of course
that is right. But he knew the Murrays and had reserved a right of pre-emption which
g enabled him to purchase their lease himself if he did not approve of their proposed
assignee; and he knew Taylors and was prepared to tie his own lease to theirs on his own
estimate, which seems to have been fully justified, of the likelihood of their wishing to
renew. That was the position which he was prepared to accept. What he was not
prepared to accept and what clearly, to the defendants' knowledge if they had thought
about it, he would not have accepted was a position where there was no chance at all of
h Taylors exercising their option because they did not have one.
    Accordingly, in my judgment, although they would, of course, be perfectly entitled
to rely on any supervening ground of invalidity of the option occurring after 1963, the
defendants are estopped from now relying on a ground of invalidity existing at the date
when they represented the option to be valid. Although so far as Taylors are concerned
the exercise has not been effective, I think that the defendants must equally be estopped
j from denying that they have, so far as Olds are concerned, effectively exercised the
option. It follows that Olds' claim for specific performance succeeds.
    That is sufficient to conclude the case but I ought perhaps to mention two further
points. First, whether the defendants be estopped by representation or as a result of the
application of Lord Kingsdown's principle, I am far from persuaded that they are not also
estopped by their own deeds. Estoppel by deed, it is suggested in Spencer Bower and
Turner (3rd Edn, 1977, para 174), is merely a variety of what is described as 'estoppel, by
convention' and is summarised thus (in para 157):

'This form of estoppel is founded, not on a representation of fact made by a representor and believed by a representee, but on an agreed statement of facts *a* the truth of which has been assumed, by the convention of the parties, as the basis of a transaction into which they are about to enter. When the parties have acted in their transaction upon the agreed assumption that a given state of facts is to be accepted between them as true, then as regards that transaction each will be estopped against the other from questioning the truth of the statement of facts so assumed.'   *b*

Normally, of course, an estoppel by deed arises from the recitals but that is not, as I read the authorities, an essential feature. It may be created by a clear and distinct averment in the operative part. Counsel for the defendants relies on *Onward Building Society v Smithson* [1893] 1 Ch 1 as establishing that such an averment cannot be spelt out by implication from language which is not clear. That counsel for Olds accepts; but *c* implication is one thing, necessary implication is another. Here, where the 1963 deed speaks of the tenants of no 22 exercising 'their option to have granted to them' a new lease, it is not simply a matter of inference that they have, at the date of the deed, such an option. It is, as it seems to me, a necessary inference that they have, if the clause is to be given any sensible operation at all. If it does not mean that, if it means merely that those tenants have, in their lease, a form of words which may confer no right on them *d* at all to get a new lease, then I think this puts counsel for the defendants in grave difficulty as regards the question of construction which counsel for Olds has raised. It is unnecessary, in the view which I have taken of the case, for me to decide the point, but I am bound to say that I find it difficult to construe the clause as a whole as other than a clear statement of the conventional basis on which both parties were then approaching the transaction between them.   *e*

Second, I ought to say a word about the point which counsel for Olds put as his primary point, namely that as a matter of construction of the two leases to Olds the references to the tenants of no 22 'exercising' their option to have granted to them a new lease are references simply to those tenants taking the necessary steps to give them a contractual right to the grant of a new lease. He points out that, even though Taylors may not have the right to a new lease against the defendants, the option remained *f* capable of giving rise to contractual obligations between the original parties. Counsel's courage failed him at this point because he shrank from actually asserting that Taylors' option notice had actually done that for fear of prejudicing his position in some other proceedings which, I understand, are pending between Taylors and his clients. He does, however, submit that for the purpose of the clauses in Olds' lease it is a sufficient 'exercise' if Taylors, being entitled to do so as against their original lessor, serve a proper *g* notice.

Counsel for the defendants submits that 'exercise' must here mean an effective exercise actually entitling the tenant of no 22 to a new term, and he points to the surrounding circumstances from which it is clear that the intention of the parties was to ensure that, if the tenants of no 22 left at the end of their term, the landlords would not be left with premises which might be difficult to let if they could not also get possession of the *h* adjoining ground floor, being no 21. If he is wrong, counsel boldly claims rectification. I must say that I should require considerable persuasion before I could be induced to exercise a discretionary equitable remedy for the unmeritorious purpose of enabling one party to take advantage of a common mistake; but it does not, in my judgment, arise, because I feel bound to accept counsel's construction of the document purely as a matter of construction. The difficulty which then lies in his way, however, is that, allowing it *j* to be the right construction of the deed that 'exercise' means 'effective exercise' then, in my judgment, he has to accept the corollary that there is then the clearest representation on the face of the deed that an effective exercise is possible.

In the result, therefore, the claim of Taylors for specific performance must be dismissed and there will be in favour of Olds a delcaration as regards the non-operation of the break

clause in the 1949 lease and a decree of specific performance of the renewal option in the
a   1963 lease.

Orders accordingly.

Solicitors: *Jacobs & Reeves*, Bournemouth (for Taylors); *Allin & Watts*, Bournemouth (for
Olds); *J Tickle & Co* (for the defendants).
b

Evelyn M C Budd   Barrister.

Amalgamated Investment & Property Co Ltd
c   # (in liquidation) v Texas Commerce International Bank Ltd

QUEEN'S BENCH DIVISION (COMMERCIAL COURT)

ROBERT GOFF J

d   31st OCTOBER, 1st NOVEMBER, 3rd, 5th, 6th, 7th, 10th, 12th, 13th, 17th, 19th DECEMBER
1979, 16th MAY 1980

*Estoppel – Representation – Law – Representation that transaction having legal effect which it
does not in fact have – Representation causing or contributing to representee's error as to his legal
rights – Representee deprived of opportunity to renegotiate transaction – Whether unconscionable*
e   *for representor to take advantage of mistake – Whether effect of estoppel to enforce gratuitous
promise – Whether estoppel giving effect to transaction which would otherwise be void.*

*Estoppel – Conduct – Encouragement – Representee's conduct influenced by representor's
encouragement or representation – Representee mistakenly believing transaction to have legal
effect – Representor encouraging and reinforcing that belief – Whether unconscionable for*
f   *representor to take advantage of representee's mistake.*

An English property company arranged with an English merchant bank that the bank
should lend it $3m on the security of properties in England owned by the company and
should also lend $3,250,000 ('the Nassau loan') to a wholly-owned Bahamian subsidiary
of the company on the security of an office building in Nassau owned by the subsidiary
and a guarantee provided by the English company. Under the guarantee, in consideration
g   of the bank from time to time making loans or advances or giving credit to the Bahamian
subsidiary, the English company convenanted to pay the bank on demand all moneys at
any time owing or payable to the bank by the subsidiary. In order to circumvent
Bahamian restrictions on foreign banks trading in the Bahamas, the bank purchased an
'off the shelf' Bahamian subsidiary ('the Bahamian bank') and the Nassau loan was
h   effected by the bank making a loan to the Bahamian bank which in turn advanced the
same sum to the company's Bahamian subsidiary. The mortgage of the Nassau building
was executed between the Bahamian bank and the subsidiary, but the guarantee was
never amended and remained a guarantee by the English company in respect of money
owing to the bank rather than to the Bahamian bank. In the course of dealings between
the parties, however, it was apparent that both the bank and the English company
j   mistakenly believed the guarantee to be binding and effective and to cover the liability
of the English company in respect of the Nassau loan. The mistake originated in the
bank but the company, by its course of conduct, represented to the bank, and encouraged
it to believe, that the guarantee was binding and effective and covered the Nassau loan
and thereby confirmed and reinforced the bank's mistaken belief. Some time later the
English company got into financial difficulties and was ordered to be compulsorily

wound up. Both the bank and Bahamian bank exercised their respective powers as
mortgagees and sold the English properties owned by the English company and the *a*
Nassau building. That left some $750,000 outstanding on the Nassau loan while the
bank held a credit balance of about the same amount after the sale of the English
properties. The bank thereupon applied its credit balance to discharge the amount
owing on the Nassau loan and claimed that under the guarantee it was entitled to do
so. The liquidator of the English company issued a writ seeking a declaration that the
English company was under no liability to the bank under the guarantee in respect of the *b*
amount still owing on the Nassau loan. The bank contended (i) that the Bahamian bank
was no more than a nominee of the bank and the relationship between the two was so
close that the guarantee ought to apply to the Nassau loan made by the Bahamian bank,
and (ii) that the English company was estopped from contending that the guarantee did
not cover its subsidiary's liability to the Bahamian bank, because the English company
had actively acquiesced in and encouraged the bank's assumption that it had certain legal *c*
rights against the company and it would be unjust or unconscionable for the company
subsequently to deny the existence of those rights.

Held – (1) On the natural and ordinary meaning of the guarantee it applied only to
money due, owing or payable to the bank and not to money owing to the Bahamian
bank, however close the relationship between the two banks might have been (see p 929 *d*
b to *e*, post).

(2) On the question of estoppel, the doctrine of equitable estoppel was not confined to
certain defined categories, and where the estoppel alleged arose out of a situation where
both parties proceeded on the same mistaken assumption the inquiry which the court
had to make was whether in all the circumstances it was unconscionable for the
representor to seek to take advantage of the mistake (see p 935 *f* and p 936 *c* to *e*, post); *e*
Taylor Fashions Ltd v Liverpool Victoria Trustees Co Ltd p 897, ante, applied.

(3) Where the estoppel alleged was founded on active encouragement or representations made by the representor, it was only unconscionable for the representor to enforce
his strict legal rights if the representee's conduct was influenced by the encouragement
or the representation. However, it was not necessary for the encouragement or
representation to have been the initial cause of the representee's conduct in order to be *f*
unconscionable but merely that his conduct was so influenced by the encouragement or
representation that it would be unconscionable for the representor to enforce his legal
rights. The representations to the bank by the English company that the guarantee was
a binding and effective guarantee by the company and covered the Nassau loan so
influenced the bank in continuing to rely on the guarantee as providing enforceable
collateral for the Bahamian subsidiary's debt that it was unconscionable for the company *g*
to take advantage of the bank's error, and the company was therefore estopped from
asserting the invalidity of the guarantee (see p 936 *e* to *h* and p 938 *f* to p 939 *b* and *h*,
post); dictum of Bowen LJ in *Edgington v Fitzmaurice* [1881–5] All ER Rep at 862 and
Taylor Fashions Ltd v Liverpool Victoria Trustees Co Ltd p 897, ante, applied.

(4) Where there was a representation by one party to another that a transaction
between them had an effect which in law it did not have, an estoppel arose if it was then *h*
unconscionable for the representor to go back on his representation because it had caused
or contributed to the representee's error as to his true legal rights or deprived him of the
opportunity to renegotiate the transaction to render it legally enforceable in terms of the
representation. Moreover, the estoppel arose despite the fact that the effect of the
estoppel in the circumstances was to reduce the representor's rights or increase his
obligations and would thus enforce what was in effect a gratuitous promise. Accordingly, *j*
the mere fact that the effect of an estoppel would be to give effect to a gratuitous promise
did not prevent the English company from being estopped from asserting the invalidity
of the guarantee, since by confirming the bank's erroneous belief that the guarantee was
binding and effective in respect of the Nassau loan the English company had contributed
to the bank's error as to the legal effect of the guarantee and to the bank's failure to seek
to correct it (see p 937 *e* to p 938 *b* and p 939 *b c* and *h*, post); *Sarat Chunder Dey v Gopal
Chunder Lala* (1892) LR 19 Ind App 203, *Calgary Milling Co Ltd v American Surety Co of*

New York [1919] 3 WWR 98 and *De Tchihatchef v Salerni Coupling Ltd* [1931] All ER Rep
a 223 applied.

(5) Where an estoppel related to the legal effect of a transaction between the parties,
the estoppel would be enforced even if the underlying transaction would, but for the
estoppel, be devoid of legal effect, since it was not necessary in such a case for the
underlying relationship to constitute a binding legal relationship. Accordingly, the fact
that the guarantee was not in law a binding contract did not prevent the representations
b that it had contractual effect giving rise to an estoppel (see p 938 *c* to *e* and p 939 *c d* and
h, post); *Sarat Chunder Dey v Gopal Chunder Lala* (1892) LR 19 Ind App 203, *Spiro v Lintern*
[1973] 3 All ER 319 and *Taylor Fashions Ltd v Liverpool Victoria Trustees Co Ltd* p 897, ante,
applied; *Hughes v Metropolitan Railway Co* [1874–80] All ER Rep 187 considered.

(6) The English company could not claim that if the guarantee were enforced it would
be denied the right of subrogation against the Bahamian subsidiary, since any right of
c subrogation would only have been to the mortgage on the Nassau building and that
security had already been realised and applied in partial discharge of the debt (see p p 939
g h, post); dicta of Lord Cranworth LC in *Ramsden v Dyson* (1866) LR 1 HL at 152 and of
Bramwell LJ in *Simm v Anglo-American Telegraph Co* (1879) 5 QBD at 203 considered.

Notes
d For estoppel by conduct, see 16 Halsbury's Laws (4th Edn) paras 1609–1619, and for cases
on the subject, see 21 Digest (Repl) 411–461, *1310–1601*.

Cases referred to in judgment
Calgary Milling Co Ltd v American Surety Co of New York [1919] 3 WWR 98, 48 DLR 295,
    PC, 7 Digest (Reissue) 375, *2161*.
Central London Property Trust Ltd v High Trees House Ltd (1946) [1956] 1 All ER 256,
e   [1947] KB 130, [1947] LJR 77, 175 LT 332, 21 Digest (Repl) 376, *1133*.
Combe v Combe [1951] 1 All ER 767, [1951] 2 KB 215, CA, 12 Digest (Reissue) 219, *1411*.
Crabb v Arun District Council [1975] 3 All ER 865, [1976] Ch 179, [1975] 3 WLR 847, CA,
    Digest (Cont Vol D) 312, *1250a*.
De Bussche v Alt (1878) 8 Ch D 286, [1874–80] All ER Rep 1247, 47 LJ Ch 381, 38 LT 370,
    3 Asp MLC 584, LJJ, 21 Digest (Repl) 476, *1666*.
f *De Tchihatchef v Salerni Coupling Ltd* [1932] 1 Ch 330, [1931] All ER Rep 233, 101 LJ Ch
    209, 146 LT 505, 21 Digest (Repl) 376, *1132*.
Edgington v Fitzmaurice (1885) 29 Ch D 459, [1881–5] All ER Rep 856, 65 LJ Ch 650, 53
    LT 369, 50 JP 522, CA, 9 Digest (Reissue) 122, *642*.
Hughes v Metropolitan Railway Co (1877) 2 App Cas 439, [1874–80] All ER Rep 187, 46
    LJCP 583, 36 LT 932, 42 JP 421, HL, 21 Digest (Repl) 392, *1221*.
g *Ramsden v Dyson* (1866) LR 1 HL 129, 12 Jur NS 506, HL, 21 Digest (Repl) 453, *1551*.
Sarat Chunder Dey v Gopal Chunder Lala (1892) LR 19 Ind App 203, ILR 20 Calc 296, 56
    JP 741, PC, 21 Digest (Repl) 383, *1170*.
Simm v Anglo-American Telegraph Co, Anglo-American Telegraph Co v Spurling (1879) 5 QBD
    188, 49 LJQB 392, 42 LT 37, 44 JP 280, CA, 21 Digest (Repl) 388, *1196*.
Spiro v Lintern [1973] 3 All ER 319, [1973] 1 WLR 1002, CA, Digest (Cont Vol D) 315,
h   *1585a*.
*Taylor Fashions Ltd v Liverpool Victoria Trustees Co Ltd, Old & Campbell Ltd v Liverpool
    Victoria Trustees Co Ltd*, p 897, ante.
Willmott v Barber (1880) 15 Ch D 96, 49 LJ Ch 792, 43 LT 95, 31(2) Digest (Reissue) 703,
    5748.

j ### Action
By a writ issued on 9th January 1979 the plaintiff, Amalgamated Investment and
Property Co Ltd (in liquidation) ('AIP'), claimed against the defendant, Texas Commerce
International Bank Ltd ('the bank'), a declaration that AIP was under no liability to the
bank either under a guarantee dated 28th September 1970 executed by AIP to the bank
at its request or in any other way in respect of sums outstanding and owing by
Amalgamated (New Providence) Property Ltd ('ANPP'), a wholly-owned subsidiary of
AIP. The facts are set out in the judgment.

Andrew Morritt QC and *John G C Phillips* for AIP.
Anthony D Colman QC, Konrad Schiemann and *Mark Hapgood* for the bank.   a

Cur adv vult

16th May. **ROBERT GOFF J** read the following judgment: This case is concerned
with the question whether the plaintiff gave a binding and effective guarantee to the
defendant bank or, alternatively, the question whether the plaintiff is estopped from
denying that they gave such a guarantee. If either question is answered in the   b
affirmative, the plaintiffs cannot complain that the defendant bank was not justified in
appropriating, as it did, part of the proceeds of sale of certain mortgaged properties in
satisfaction of such guarantee.

The plaintiffs, Amalgamated Investment and Property Co Ltd ('AIP'), are a property
company incorporated in this country. AIP is now in liquidation, being the subject of a
compulsory winding-up order dated 3rd May 1976. AIP held, either directly or through   c
subsidiaries, a substantial number of properties, both in this country and overseas.
Among those properties was an office block in Nassau, which was owned by a wholly-
owned subsidiary of AIP incorporated in the Bahamas, Amalgamated (New Providence)
Property Ltd ('ANPP'). AIP was controlled by a Mr Gabriel Harrison, who was chairman
of AIP. He died in October 1974. The secretary of AIP was at all material times a Mr
Noel Foster. Mr Freeman was a director of AIP from 1971 until January 1976. Shortly   d
after joining, he was appointed assistant managing director; but he resigned as full-time
director in June 1974, to become managing director of another company, though he
remained a director in a non-executive capacity until January 1976.

The defendants are a merchant banking company incorporated in this country. I shall
refer to the defendants as 'the bank'. The bank was originally called the Burston and
Texas Commerce Bank, being partially owned by an English company controlled by a   e
Mr Burston, and partly by a Texan bank called the Texas Commerce Bank. In February
1975 the Texas Commerce Bank bought out the Burston interest, and the name of the
bank was then changed to Texas Commerce International Bank. In February 1975 a Mr
Nolan became managing director of the bank, succeeding a Mr Robinson; Mr Nolan had
been a director of the bank since 1972. He was succeeded as managing director by a Mr
Oldfield in February 1977. Mr Oldfield had joined the bank in an administrative   f
capacity in 1972, being concerned then with the loan portfolio; he became a manager in
December 1973, and a director in June 1976.

The facts of the case are very largely undisputed. The story starts in 1969. At that
time a wholly-owned subsidiary of AIP, called Gleniston Garden Estate Ltd (which I shall
refer to as 'Gleniston'), was developing a site which Gleniston owned in Nassau, erecting
on the site an office building which was called the Harrison building. Gleniston had   g
charged the Harrison building to their bankers, Barclays DC & O, to secure a bridging
loan. On 11th July 1969, following negotiations, a Mr Stokes, the then managing
director of the bank, wrote to Mr Harrison offering to make available to Gleniston a
facility of $3m for a period of five years, to be taken up in full by 30th June 1970, and to
be secured by a mortgage on the Harrison building and a guarantee by AIP. It was
intended that the advance should be applied in discharge of Barclays' bridging loan,   h
thereby ensuring that the bank would have a first charge over the Harrison building. On
15th July 1969 Mr Harrison accepted this offer, and exchange control permission was
obtained from the Bank of England and from the authorities in Nassau. On 15th
September 1969 AIP executed a guarantee in favour of the bank in respect of all moneys
due to the bank from Gleniston.

In January 1970 AIP entered into fresh negotiations with the bank for another advance,   j
to be secured on properties in the United Kingdom. On 27th January the bank offered
to make an advance of $2m for a period of five years, secured on the relevant properties,
the facility to be increased to $3m if a revaluation of the secured properties indicated a
sufficient margin; on 2nd February the offer was accepted by AIP. The advance of $2m
was made, secured by a mortgage dated 27th February; on 20th March, following a
revaluation of the properties, the advance was increased to $3m. I shall refer to this loan
as the 'UK loan', and to the loan in respect of the Harrison building as the 'Nassau loan'.

Meanwhile the Nassau loan was proceeding. In the spring of 1970 Barclays agreed to
a extend the period of its bridging loan to Gleniston until 31st December 1970. In May
1970 Mr Harrison expressed the desire to transfer the Harrison building, together with
the relevant loan facilities, from Gleniston to ANPP. To this proposal Barclays agreed;
and on 23rd September 1970 the bank also agreed and, at the same time, agreed to
increase the Nassau loan to $3,250,000 (following a valuation of the Harrison building
dated 1st September 1970, under which the building was valued at $5,100,000). On
b some date unknown to me the Harrison building must have been transferred from
Gleniston to ANPP. In consequence of this change, on 28th September 1970, AIP
provided the bank with a new form of guarantee securing advances to ANPP, the
previous guarantee securing advances to Gleniston being cancelled. This is the guarantee
which is the subject matter of the present proceedings. It was in a standard form of the
bank's. It was addressed by AIP (referred to in the guarantee as 'the Guarantor') to the
c bank (referred to in the guarantee simply as 'you'); and it was expressed to be 'in
consideration of your from time to time making or contributing loans or advances to or
otherwise giving credit or affording banking facilities' to ANPP (referred to in the
guarantee as 'the Principal'). The crucial provision of the guarantee was in the following
terms:

d 'The Guarantor will pay to you on demand all moneys which now are or shall at
any time or times hereafter be due or owing or payable to you on any account
whatsoever by the Principal . . .'

In November 1970 the bank agreed with Barclays to pay the Nassau loan direct to
Barclays' New York branch, for account of their branch in Nassau, for the credit of ANPP,
subject to the proviso that the mortgage on the Harrison building had then been
e completed and was held by the bank's solicitor's in escrow.

I come now to the event which is the source of all the difficulties in the present case.
In November 1970 the bank had instructed lawyers in the Bahamas (Messrs McKinney,
Bancroft & Hughes) to act on their behalf in respect of the proposed loan. Shortly before
14th December 1970 the bank cabled these Bahamian lawyers to arrange for the
mortgage to be in favour of 'one of your unused companies, this company to be a wholly
f owned subsidiary of our bank'. The reason for this change was that Bahamian legislation
did not permit a foreign bank to trade in the Bahamas without first obtaining permission
to do so; and it was to avoid this complication that the bank decided to use the medium
of a Bahamian subsidiary. So the lawyers took a company off the shelf; this became a
wholly-owned subsidiary of the bank called Portsoken Properties Ltd (which I shall refer
to as 'Portsoken'). They also set about amending the draft mortgage on the Harrison
g building, so that it became a mortgage in favour of Portsoken. Exchange control
permission was obtained from the Bahamian authorities permitting Portsoken to lend
US dollars without having to convert them into Bahamian dollars or into sterling, and
permitting them to repay US dollars to the bank. Then at the end of the year the
transaction was implemented. $3,250,000 were transferred by the bank to Barclays'
New York branch for account of their Nassau branch in favour of ANPP. At the same
h time the bank opened an account in its books in the name of Portsoken (though this was
at some time annotated in manuscript 're ANPP'); the opening debit in this account was
in the sum of $3,250,000. The bank advised AIP and ANPP of a debit to ANPP's account
of $3,250,000; this communication was acknowledged by AIP. In the books of the bank
it is plain that this transaction was treated as an advance by the bank to Portsoken, and
a further advance by Portsoken to ANPP. There was the account opened by the bank in
j the name of Portsoken, to which I have already refered; there is no evidence of any
account being opened by the bank in the name of ANPP. Likewise, the loan was treated
by ANPP as being a loan to it by Portsoken, not by the bank. In the minutes of a board
meeting of ANPP, dated 31st December 1970, it was recorded that the meeting
considered a report by the chairman that Portsoken had agreed to lend $3,250,000 to
ANPP to be secured by a mortgage on the Harrison building, and that the board
approved the granting of the mortgage to Portsoken. In fact the mortgage, dated 31st
December 1970, was duly executed under seal and was expressed to be between ANPP

and Portsoken, the covenant to repay capital and interest being a covenant to repay Portsoken. In due course, arrangements were made for the interest to be paid into the *a* account of Portsoken with the bank; though subsequently these arrangements were varied, and interest was paid through a bank in New York for the account of the bank. Since the interest payable by ANPP to Portsoken and by Portsoken to the bank was at the same rate, there was no differential; but the interest so received by the bank was always credited in the bank's books to the account of Portsoken with the bank. The audited accounts of the bank and of Portsoken are also consistent with a loan by the bank to *b* Portsoken, and a further loan by Portsoken to ANPP. But there was a crucial defect in these arrangements. The guarantee furnished by AIP to the bank was not amended; it remained a guarantee in respect of money due or owing or payable *to the bank*, not to Portsoken.

Although I shall have in due course to consider in some detail the events which occurred between 1970 and 1976, I propose at this stage to go straight to 1976. By this *c* time AIP were in serious financial difficulties. The interest instalment due on the Nassau loan at the end of December 1975 had not been fully paid. On 19th March 1976 the bank appointed a receiver of the properties in the United Kingdom charged to the bank by AIP and its subsidiaries in respect of advances made by the bank; and five days later Portsoken appointed a receiver of the Harrison building, which was the subject of the mortgage in Portsoken's favour. On 3rd May 1976 AIP was ordered to be wound up *d* compulsorily. At that date the bank had already called on AIP under its guarantee of 28th September 1970 to pay the unpaid balance of the Nassau loan, which was by then $2,750,000. Over a year later, on 26th May 1977, the liquidator of AIP replied asserting that, on the documents available to him, there was no liability on AIP under the guarantee in respect of the loan to ANPP. Meanwhile, however, the Harrison building had been sold, and the proceeds applied in discharge of the Nassau loan, leaving a balance *e* outstanding of about $750,000. Likewise, the UK properties mortgaged to secure advances by the bank to AIP and its subsidiaries were also sold and applied in discharge of such advances; this left a balance in the bank's hands of approximately the same amount as the sum outstanding on the Nassau loan, and the bank purported to apply the credit balance in discharge of the balance of the Nassau loan. This course was challenged by the liquidator; and on 9th January 1979 a writ was issued by AIP (in liquidation) *f* claiming a declaration that AIP was under no liability to the bank under the guarantee or otherwise in respect of the sums outstanding by ANPP under the loan to ANPP.

A defence was served by the bank on 12th February 1979, in which it was contended that the loan to ANPP was a loan by the bank, and that therefore AIP was liable under its guarantee in respect of the unpaid balance of the loan. This defence was subsequently amended to allege that, if the loan was made by Portsoken, then Portsoken advanced the *g* money as agent for the bank or, alternatively, that, on a true construction, the guarantee was applicable to the loan; or, finally, that AIP was estopped from contending that it was not liable under its guarantee in respect of the unpaid balance of the loan. On the basis of this defence, the trial began on 31st October 1979; but on the second day of the trial counsel for the bank informed me that substantial further documents were available on the issue of estoppel, and I acceded to an application by the bank for an adjournment of *h* the hearing, on appropriate terms as to costs.

The trial was resumed on 3rd December 1979. Entirely new points of defence had been served by the bank. The new defence maintained the contention that the Nassau loan had been made by the bank; but that contention was soon abandoned. In the outcome, two contentions alone were advanced by the bank. The first was that Portsoken 'held the mortgage and its rights under the mortgage deed in respect of the payment of *j* principal and interest by ANPP to the order, use and benefit' of the bank and that, therefore, the principal and interest outstanding in respect of the Nassau loan were moneys due or owing or payable to the bank under the guarantee. The second was that AIP was estopped from contending that the guarantee did not cover the liability of ANPP in respect of the Nassau loan.

With the first of these two contentions I can deal quite shortly. In the couse of argument, it transpired that the bank was not contending that Portsoken was in any way constituted a trustee for the bank; the contention was rather that, on a true construction, the guarantee should be held to be applicable to the Nassau loan made in the present case. The facts relied on by the bank were as follows: (1) Portsoken was simply a shell company acquired by the bank for the purposes of 'channelling' the mortgage to the bank; (2) Portsoken was simply a fronting company, which made no profit; (3) Portsoken had no administrative function in relation to the Nassau loan to ANPP; (4) the bank exercised complete control over Portsoken; (5) in reality, Portsoken had no power to take any action in relation to the Nassau loan, save at the direction of the bank; and (6) if the bank had at any time called for an assignment of the debt, that assignment would have been forthcoming as and when required.

From these facts, submitted counsel for the bank, the relationship between Portsoken and the bank was so close that the guarantee should be held applicable to the Nassau loan, really because Portsoken was no more than a nominee or fronting company or creature of the bank. I am bound to say that I find this argument unpersuasive. The words of the guarantee are clear, and under them the guarantee was applicable only to moneys due or owing or payable to the bank. It is plain, on the evidence before me, that the Nassau loan was advanced not by the bank, but by Portsoken; no part of the loan was ever due or owing or payable to the bank; the creditor was always Portsoken. I can see no reason for departing from the natural and ordinary meaning of the words of the guarantee; certainly, the facts relied on by counsel in support of his contention do not justify any such departure. The fact that the bank chose, for its own purposes, to substitute Portsoken as the lender in a transaction under which it had originally been intended that the bank should be the lender does not enable the bank thereafter to say that a guarantee given previously, guaranteeing payment of sums due or owing or payable to the bank, was applicable to the changed transaction, however close the relationship between the bank and the new lender may have been. In truth, there is no substance in the point, and I have no hesitation in rejecting it.

I turn, therefore, to the estoppel point, which is what, in its developed form, the whole case is about. After the new pleadings and further discovery, this point assumed much more substantial dimensions; and, before I can consider it, it is necessary for me to set out in some detail the facts, derived from the documents before the court and the oral evidence given by Mr Freeman, Mr Nolan and Mr Oldfield, on which the bank sought to build its argument.

I have already referred to the fact that there were two major advances by the bank or a subsidiary of the bank to AIP or a subsidiary of AIP: first, the loan of $3,250,000 by Portsoken to ANPP secured on the Harrison building in Nassau, which I have called 'the Nassau loan'; and, second, the advance of $3m by the bank to AIP secured on properties in the UK, which I have called 'the UK loan'. It was, of course, the Nassau loan to which the guarantee, which is the subject matter of these proceedings, was believed by all concerned to apply. However, the UK loan plays a substantial part in the story, because it was in relation to that loan that certain developments took place which show both parties, AIP and the bank, acting in the common belief that the guarantee applied to the Nassau loan.

The story of these developments begins in June 1974. On 27th June AIP sought the bank's consent to the release of one of the UK properties (30–30A St George's Street, Hanover Square, London W1) in exchange for two other properties; about a month later, on 25th July, the bank agreed in principle to the substitution, but only after an up-to-date valuation of the proposed substitute properties. Next, in September 1974, AIP asked the bank for a further facility of $250,000 to finance a development in Toronto; the bank reacted favourably to this request, but subject to a revaluation of all properties available to secure all facilities. On 25th September 1974 a meeting took place at the bank, attended by Mr Noel Foster, the secretary of AIP, and Mr Nolan (then a director of the bank, though shortly thereafter, in February 1975, to become managing director). At the meeting, the bank agreed to the substitution and the further advance, subject to up-to-date valuations of the Harrison building and the UK properties, and to further security being provided if the total sum to be advanced exceeded two-thirds of the value of all the properties which were charged to the bank to secure the advances. This was in accordance with the bank's policy of requiring 150% cover for all such loans. About three weeks later, on 18th October 1974, the bank wrote to AIP formally offering the further facility *a* of $250,000; but this was in fact never taken up. I should record that it was in October 1974 that Mr Gabriel Harrison died.

On 4th November 1974, following a telephone conversation on 1st November, Mr Robinson (then the managing director of the bank) wrote to Mr Foster agreeing to the release of the deeds of 30–30A St George's Street, against a cash deposit of £500,000 (which was to come out of the proceeds of sale of the property). The letter continued: *b*

> 'This money will be held in the name of Amalgamated Investment & Property Co. Ltd. as security for its own direct liabilities and its guarantee liabilities on account Amalgamated (New Providence) Property Co. Ltd. It is understood that the cash balance will be released as soon as we have established, by means of up to date valuations, that the liabilities of Amalgamated Investment & Property Co. Ltd. to *c* ourselves, both direct and by way of guarantee, do not exceed 66⅔% of the value of our security. To the extent that there is any shortfall, we are conscious that you have agreed that you will provide additional deed security . . .'

The reference to AIP's 'guarantee liabilities' can only have been a reference to the supposed guarantee of the loan of $3,250,000 to ANPP. Mr Oldfield (then a manager of *d* the bank) told me that he was party to drafting the letter; his understanding of the situation, which originated from somebody else within the bank, was that although the charge of the Harrison building had been provided to Portsoken, Portsoken having been interjected into the transaction simply as a vehicle for that purpose, the loan had been made by the bank itself to ANPP and the guarantee was therefore binding and effective. Four days later, Mr Foster returned a copy of Mr Robinson's letter *e* countersigned, confirming his approval of its terms. It is plain from this that Mr Foster too understood AIP's guarantee of the loan to ANPP to be binding and effective.

On 12th November Mr Foster sent the bank a valuation of the Harrison building dated 25th October 1974 in the sum of $3,200,000. Although this was nearly equal to the amount of the Nassau loan, ie $3,250,000, it followed that the property was by no means adequate to produce anything like the amount of the loan having regard to the very high *f* cost of realising property in the Bahamas; on a sale at $3,200,000 the net recovery would only have been $2,700,000 to $2,800,000. Obviously, too, the valuation was far too low for a charge on this property alone to secure the Nassau loan, having regard to the bank's policy of having 150% cover. On the same day, 12th November, the sum of £500,000 was deposited by AIP with the bank, thus enabling the deeds of 30–30A St George's Street *g* to be released.

On Christmas Eve Mr Foster telephoned the bank and informed it that the interest payment due on 29th December could not be paid. The bank agreed to accept $82,000 at that stage; the balance of $166,000 was to be paid later, and was not in fact paid until April 1975. This was not the first occasion on which interest had been paid late; there had been late payments of instalments of interest due in December 1972, June and *h* December 1973 and June 1974.

Then, on 15th January 1975, Mr Oldfield discovered that the charges provided by AIP did not constitute security for AIP's supposed guarantee of the Nassau loan to ANPP. This was drawn to his attention by a securities clerk at the bank. The bank required 'all moneys' charges, ie that each charge should secure all moneys due to the bank. When he discovered this problem Mr Oldfield telephoned Mr Foster, and they agreed on the *j* telephone to put the matter right. This agreement could only have been on the basis that both Mr Oldfield and Mr Foster believed that AIP's guarantee was binding and effective. Both of them were aware that at that time the bank was awaiting valuations of certain UK properties; their intention was that, as and when the bank took fresh charges, these should be expanded to secure AIP's liability as surety for ANPP. On 27th January Mr Foster wrote to Mr Oldfield, attaching further valuations of UK properties. The letter continued:

a
'I am attaching a summary of thirteen valuations submitted and, subject to your acceptance, would suggest that 83 Endell Street be added to the fixed properties already charged to secure the U.K. advance of U.S.$3m and that Kingsley Lodge and Kirkgate, Wakefield be charged to support our guarantee of your advance of U.S.$3¼m. to our Bahamian subsidiary. Assuming the other properties meet with your approval, I would like to retain the three small properties [these were specified] which we now hope to sell . . . I look forward to hearing from you when you have considered the position.'

b

Once again, this letter can only have been written on the basis that AIP's guarantee of the Nassau loan was binding and effective; and the letter is consistent with a belief on the part of Mr Foster that the loan had been advanced by the bank itself.

c
During the first six months of 1975 there were numerous telephone conversations between Mr Oldfield and Mr Foster. A recurrent theme of these conversations was that Mr Foster desired to recover the cash deposit of £500,000 to relieve AIP's cash flow problems, but that the bank was adamant that it should not be released until the bank was satisfied with the securities, on the basis of up-to-date valuations. Furthermore, at the end of February 1975, the UK loan matured (the Nassau loan did not mature until the end of December 1975). Because of its liquidity problems, AIP was unable to repay the UK loan on its maturity date; and on 25th March Mr Foster informed Mr Nolan on the telephone that AIP could not repay the UK loan before June 1976 and the Nassau loan before 1978. On 9th April Mr Foster attended a meeting at the bank. The meeting was called at his request, his purpose being to obtain release of the £500,000 deposit and renewal of the UK loan. At this time Mr Foster was well aware that the bank required 150% cover for its advances. The proposed all moneys charge (to cover in addition AIP's liability as surety for ANPP) was at least touched on, as was a proposal by the bank to convert the UK loan into a sterling loan. Mr Oldfield's note of the meeting contains the following passage (which I have every reason to believe is accurate):

d

e

f
'We have recently had discussions with the company with a view to switching the U.S.$3 million facility into sterling and agreement in principle has been reached, the repayment being approved by the Bank of England in its original letter of sanction dated 16th January 1970. As part of this exercise we have asked Messrs. Ziman & Co. [the bank's solicitors] to prepare a draft supplemental deed to the present mortgage forms covering the properties charged as collateral so as to ensure that not only will this collateral be held in cover of the new sterling loan, but also may be looked to in support of the guarantee of AIPC for the New Providence loan.'

g
The reference to the 'New Providence loan' is clearly a reference to the Nassau loan. The meeting led to the formal extension of the UK loan, and agreement that it should be converted into sterling. On the following day the new draft deed was sent by the bank to AIP. On 16th June the bank sent AIP a formal facility letter agreeing to an extension of the UK loan to 30th April 1976 on condition, inter alia, (1) that it would be switched into sterling, (2) that the bank would continue to have a first legal charge on certain properties, and would require a first legal charge on certain additional properties, and (3) that—

h

i
'the total market value (as determined by valuers acceptable to the Bank) of all collateral held by the Bank in regard to advances to either yourselves or your subsidiary Amalgamated (New Providence) Property Limited will at all times remain in excess of 150% of the total amount of such outstanding advances. Subject to this condition you will be entitled to the release of part of the collateral.'

The valuations of the properties to be charged underline the fact that the bank was requiring security from AIP large enough to cover its guarantee liabilities in respect of the Nassau loan to ANPP. A copy of the letter was returned countersigned by Mr Foster. On 23rd June the supplemental deed to the original charge was returned duly executed by AIP and its subsidiaries, signed by Mr Freeman as director and Mr Foster as

secretary of each company. By the supplemental deed, all the properties were charged to
secure not only the UK loan but also—   *a*

> 'all other amounts which now are or shall at any time or times hereafter be due
> or owing or payable to the Bank on any account whatsoever by [AIP] either solely
> or jointly with any other person firm or company and whether as principal debtor
> or as surety for any other person firm or company . . .'

The interest payment due at the end of June was again late, only part being paid on the *b*
due date, the remainder being paid later by agreement. On 2nd July AIP and a subsidiary
executed two further charges on two further properties, under which the subsidiary
covenanted to pay to the bank—

> 'all such sums of money as now are or shall from time to time be owing . . . by
> [AIP] or by [AIP] jointly with any other or others in partnership or otherwise and
> whether as principal or surety to the Bank, [and charged the property] by way of *c*
> legal mortgage with the payment to the Bank of all moneys payable to the Bank
> hereunder . . .'

Next, on 8th July, the bank, having received securities which on the basis of the
valuations of the properties secured were sufficient to cover all the sums advanced to AIP
and AIP's liability as surety for ANPP and having received charges on such properties *d*
expressed to cover all such liabilities of AIP, released the deposit of £500,000 to AIP.

On 1st August AIP paid a first instalment of £300,000 in reduction of the UK loan.
On 5th August AIP asked for the release of a charge on property in Derby; and on 8th
September a meeting took place at the bank, attended by Mr Foster and Mr Freeman, in
the course of which the repayment of the Nassau loan was discussed. The discussion
obviously proceeded on the assumption that the bank had AIP's guarantee (duly secured) *e*
for the Nassau loan, since the discussion included a proposal that the Harrison building
might be sold for $2,600,000 (which, allowing for expenses, was far less than the amount
of the Nassau loan). At the end of the meeting it was agreed, inter alia, that the Harrison
building should be put on the market, and that new valuations should be obtained of the
UK properties charged to secure the bank's advances. Later, on 22nd October, Mr
Freeman confirmed to Mr Nolan on the telephone that the sale of the Harrison building *f*
was proceeding on the lines discussed at the meeting.

During the autumn of 1975 the financial position of AIP deteriorated. At a meeting
held at the bank on 30th October a proposed moratorium was discussed. On 3rd
November a sum of $650,000 was received in part payment of the Nassau loan, and was
credited by the bank to the account of Portsoken, leaving a balance of $2,858,000
outstanding. On 5th December Mr Oldfield wrote to AIP agreeing to postponement of *g*
payment of the outstanding principal and interest of the UK loan to 19th December
1975. The interest due at the end of December was not then paid; a quarter ($50,000)
was paid on 5th January 1976, but the balance was never paid. In the spring of 1976
matters came to a head in the manner I have already described.

Such was the sequence of events between 1974 and 1976 on which the bank relied in
support of its plea of estoppel. Furthermore, on the basis of the documentary evidence *h*
and the oral evidence given by Mr Freeman, Mr Nolan and Mr Oldfield, I make the
following further findings of fact.

First , both organisations, the bank and AIP, were organisations of good repute and of
integrity, each having complete trust in the other. All the witnesses who gave evidence
were gentlemen of integrity, who gave their evidence with complete frankness; and I
have no doubt that Mr Foster was likewise a gentleman of integrity, who was most *j*
anxious to assist the bank in every way, and would never have been guilty of anything
remotely resembling sharp practice vis-à-vis the bank.

Second, both the officers of the bank directly concerned, Mr Nolan and Mr Oldfield,
believed at all material times that AIP's guarantee was binding and effective and covered
the liability of ANPP in respect of the Nassau loan. This was because they understood,
mistakenly, that the money had been advanced by the bank to ANPP, whereas it had in

fact been advanced by Portsoken. The source of their error lay in the bank itself; the
a mistake of both Mr Nolan and Mr Oldfield derived its origin not from anything said or
done by any person acting on behalf of AIP, but from documents held by the bank or
from persons within the bank.

Third, the officers of AIP most concerned, in particular Mr Foster but also Mr Freeman,
believed that AIP's guarantee was likewise binding and effective. Mr Freeman's
information about the transaction was somewhat sketchy; but Mr Foster was much more
b directly concerned. In all probability, the basis of Mr Foster's belief was that the money
had in fact been advanced by the bank; in particular, the supplemental deeds entered
into by AIP in June and July 1975 to provide charges on real property to secure the
guarantee appear to have been drawn up on the assumption that the advances had been
made by the bank. There is no evidence which persuades me to hold that Mr Freeman's
or Mr Foster's mistaken belief derived from anything said or done on behalf of the bank;
c it is more probable that their mistaken belief had an origin independent of the bank,
though after the question of securities to support AIP's guarantee was raised by the bank
in January 1975 the mistake of each, the bank and AIP, must have operated to reinforce
the mistaken belief of the other.

Fourth, by their whole course of conduct AIP, and in particular Mr Foster, represented
to the bank and encouraged the bank to believe that AIP's guarantee was binding and
d effective and covered the Nassau loan with the effect that, after the supplemental deed of
23rd June 1975, the guarantee was secured by charges on real property. The following
incidents are particularly relevant as constituting such course of conduct: (1) on 12th
November 1974 Mr Foster returned to the bank countersigned Mr Robinson's letter of
4th November 1974, an action which, having regard to the terms of the letter (which I
have already quoted), must have indicated Mr Foster's understanding that AIP's guarantee
e in respect of the Nassau loan was binding and effective; (2) on 15th January 1975, in his
telephone conversation with Mr Oldfield, Mr Foster agreed to arrange that AIP's
guarantee of the Nassau loan should be secured by charges on real property. Again, Mr
Foster thereby indicated to the bank his understanding that AIP's guarantee was binding
and effective; (3) Mr Foster's letter of 27th February 1975, from which I have already
quoted, was plainly to the same effect; (4) at the meeting on 9th April 1975, which I
f have already described, which led to the formal extension of the UK loan, there was a
discussion of the supplemental deed to the existing mortgages to ensure that the collateral
would, inter alia, secure AIP's guarantee of the Nassau loan; (5) in June 1975 Mr Foster
returned countersigned the bank's facility letter dated 16th June 1975 agreeing to an
extension of the UK loan on terms which plainly presupposed that AIP's guarantee of the
Nassau loan was binding and effective and would be secured by charges on real property;
g (6) on 23rd June 1975, pursuant to the foregoing arrangements, AIP executed the draft
supplemental deed which was in its terms wide enough for this purpose; on 2nd July
1975 AIP executed two further deeds which were likewise so effective.

Fifth, although the bank's erroneous belief that AIP's guarantee was so binding and
effective originated in its own office, I am satisfied that AIP's course of conduct influenced
the bank, and in particular Mr Oldfield, in the sense that it operated to confirm and
h reinforce his mistaken belief. This is a point to which I shall return later in this
judgment.

Sixth, encouraged by the conduct of AIP, the bank itself adopted a course of conduct
which was detrimental to its interests. In particular, it allowed the loans to remain
outstanding, despite opportunities to call them in, for example, when the interest
payment on the Nassau loans was not duly paid at the end of December 1974 or at the
i end of June 1975, and when the UK loan matured in February 1975. Furthermore, it
accepted the supplemental deeds as security for the Nassau loan, and on 8th July 1975
released to AIP the deposit of £500,000 made in November 1974.

Seventh, if at any time before the winding-up order the matter had come to light, I
have no doubt whatsoever that Mr Foster would immediately have arranged for AIP to
put the matter right.

I come now to the submissions of the parties. In considering those submissions, I am

conscious of the fact that the liquidator of AIP is adopting an attitude which, had the
company not been in liquidation, would never have been adopted by the directors of the
company. The point taken by the liquidator is a technical one, and to some extent
unmeritorious. But persons in that position have duties to perform, and it is sometimes
necessary for them to take points which others would be reluctant to take; and they are
entitled, like all others, to have each point considered and decided in accordance with the
established principles of law. To the submissions of the parties on the applicable
principles I now turn.

For the bank, counsel relied on a broad principle which he stated as follows. Where
a defendant conducts his affairs in reliance on the plaintiff's active acquiescence in, or
encouragement of, the defendant's assumption, made known to the plaintiff, that the
defendant has certain contractual or other rights of a non-proprietary nature against the
plaintiff and it would be unjust or unconscionable for the plaintiff now to deny the
existence of such rights, the plaintiff will be estopped from so doing. In the present case,
he submitted, the words and conduct of AIP and in particular of Mr Foster constituted
not merely acquiescence in, but encouragement of, the bank's known assumption that
it had rights against AIP in the nature of a guarantee or indemnity, secured by a charge
on real estate; and, having regard to the manner in which the bank was influenced by
such encouragement, it would be unconscionable for AIP now to deny the existence of
such rights. In the alternative, counsel put his case on the basis of representations by AIP
to a like effect, on the faith of which the bank acted so that it would now be
unconscionable for AIP to go back on its representations.

Counsel for AIP launched a frontal attack on these submissions. He submitted that
the first proposition formulated by counsel for the bank infringed three principles: it
presupposed no contract of which equity could grant specific performance; it permitted
the enforcement of a promise unsupported by consideration; and it gave a pecuniary
remedy for innocent misrepresentation. He proceeded, after a meticulous examination
of the authorities, himself to formulate the law relating to equitable estoppel in a series
of five propositions, as follows.

(1) Where either O encourages T to believe that he, O, will confer on T a certain
interest in his, O's, property, or O, knowing that T mistakenly believes that he, T, has a
certain interest in property belonging to O, stands by and says nothing, and T, in reliance
on O's encouragement or his own mistaken belief respectively, spends money on O's
property, O may be estopped from asserting his strict legal rights. See *Ramsden v Dyson*
(1866) LR 1 HL 129 and other authorities.

(2) Where O, having the right to object to a particular transaction which he knows T
proposes to carry out, does not object and T carries it out, O is thereafter estopped from
objecting because he assented to the act in question. See *De Bussche v Alt* (1878) 8 Ch D
286 at 314, [1874–80] All ER Rep 1247 at 1253 per Thesiger LJ, and other authorities.

(3) Where parties agree on a certain state of fact, for the purpose of a certain future
specific transaction, then in an action to enforce that transaction neither can assert facts
contrary to the agreement (though otherwise where the proceedings are not on the
agreement).

(4) Where O sees T acting in the mistaken belief that O is under some binding
obligation to him, or in a manner consistent only with the existence of such obligation,
and for reasons which are not within the knowledge of T but are within the knowledge
or means of knowledge of O, O is not under that obligation, O is under a duty to T to
disclose the non-existence of that obligation. If O does not do so, and T acts to his
detriment, O may be estopped. See *Spiro v Lintern* [1973] 3 All ER 319, [1973] 1 WLR
1002.

(5) Last there is the familiar principle of promissory estoppel founded on *Hughes v
Metropolitan Railway Co* (1877) 2 App Cas 439, [1874–80] All ER Rep 187 and *Central
London Property Trust Ltd v High Trees House Ltd* [1956] 1 All ER 256, [1947] KB 130. The
principle was not formulated by counsel. But I understand it to presuppose the existence

of a legal relationship between the parties, one of whom represents to the other that he
a will not enforce his strict legal rights against the other under that relationship; if on the
faith of that representation the representee so acts or desists from acting that it will be
inequitable in all the circumstances for the representor to go back on his representation,
he may be precluded from doing so.

Now counsel for AIP submitted that the present case fell within none of these
categories of equitable estoppel. It did not fall into the first category because the case was
b not concerned with property; furthermore, there was no suggestion that AIP ever
encouraged the bank to believe that AIP would grant the bank a right in future, or that
AIP was aware of the bank's mistake. Plainly, he said, the case fell into neither the second
nor the third categories. It did not fall into the fourth category, which presupposes
knowledge or means or knowledge of the mistaken party's mistake; nor did it fall into
the fifth category, which presupposes an existing legal relationship between the parties,
c whereas here there was none, the so-called guarantee of AIP being no more than a piece
of paper, an offer by AIP which never matured into a contract, because the bank itself
never made the advance which would, if given, have both constituted an acceptance and
furnished the required consideration.

Now I have to say at once that, despite its meticulous scholarship, I find this approach
difficult to accept. Of all doctrines, equitable estoppel is surely one of the most
d flexible. True, from time to time distinguished judges have enunciated statements of
principle concerning aspects of the doctrine, as, for example, the statements of Lord
Cranworth LC in *Ramsden v Dyson* (1866) LR 1 HL 129 at 140–141, of Thesiger LJ in *De
Bussche v Alte* (1878) 8 Ch D 286 at 314, [1874–80] All ER Rep 1247 at 1253 and of Fry
J in *Willmott v Barber* (1880) 15 Ch D 96 at 105–106, concerning what is usually called the
doctrine of acquiescence; the statement of Lord Kingsdown in *Ramsden v Dyson* LR 1 HL
e 129 at 170–171, on what may be called the doctrine of encouragement; and the
statements of Lord Cairns LC in *Hughes v Metropolitan Railway Co* (1887) 2 App Cas 439
at 448, [1874–80] All ER Rep 187 at 191 and of Denning J in *Central London Property
Trust Ltd v High Trees House Ltd* [1956] 1 All ER 256 at 258, [1947] KB 130 at 134, on
promissory estoppel. But all these have been statements of aspects of a wider doctrine;
none has sought to be exclusive. It is no doubt helpful to establish, in broad terms, the
f criteria which, in certain situations, must be fulfilled before an equitable estoppel can be
established; but it cannot be right to restrict equitable estoppel to certain defined
categories, and indeed some of the categories proposed are not easy to defend. Thus, in
Snell on Equity (27th Edn, 1973, ch 7), the learned editors isolate two categories of
equitable estoppel, promissory estoppel and proprietary estoppel. It may be possible
nowadays to identify the former with some degree of precision; but the latter is much
g more difficult to accept as a separate category. The cases concerned appear to derive from
two distinct principles the principle stated by Lord Cranworth LC in *Ramsden v Dyson*,
and the principle stated by Lord Kingsdown in the same case, the former being concerned
with an estoppel precluding a person, who stands by and allows another to incur
expenditure or otherwise act on the basis of a mistaken belief as to his rights, from
thereafter asserting rights inconsistent with that mistaken belief (commonly called the
h doctrine of acquiescence) and the other being concerned with an estoppel precluding a
person, who has encouraged another to improve his, the encourager's, property in the
expectation that he will receive an interest in it, from denying that he is entitled to that
interest (see LR 1 HL 129 at 170). It is to be observed that the first of these principles
appears to be directed towards preventing a person from fraudulently taking advantage
of another's error, whereas the latter appears to derive rather from encouragement or
i representation. As a separate category, proprietary estoppel may perhaps be regarded as
an amalgam of doubtful utility; and it is not surprising to find that the use of this term
has been the subject of some criticism (see, eg, Spencer Bower on Estoppel by
Representation (3rd Edn, 1977, para 308)). Indeed there are cases, in particular cases
concerned with the acquisition of easements, and with the legal effect of contracts, which
are not easy to accommodate within any of the current classifications. It is not therefore

surprising to discover a tendency in the more recent authorities to reject any rigid classification of equitable estoppel into exclusive and defined categories. The authorities *a* on the subject have recently been reviewed by Oliver J in his judgment in two related actions, *Taylor Fashions Ltd v Liverpool Victoria Trustees Co Ltd* and *Old & Campbell Ltd v Liverpool Victoria Trustees Co Ltd* p 897, ante, and on the basis of his analysis of the cases, which I gratefully adopt, he rejected an argument founded on rigid categorisation. The argument was that a clear distinction must be drawn between cases of proprietary estoppel and estoppel by acquiescence on the one hand and promissory estoppel or *b* estoppel by representation (whether express or by conduct) on the other; and that in the former class of case it was essential that the party alleged to be estopped himself knew the true position (ie that he knew that the other party was acting under a mistake as to his rights) the fourth of the five criteria laid down by Fry J in *Willmott v Barber* 15 Ch D 96 at 105 as necessary to establish estoppel by acquiescence. Oliver J, however, while recognising that the strict *Willmott v Barber* criteria may be necessary requirements in *c* cases where all that has happened is that the party alleged to be estopped has stood by without protest while his rights have been infringed, concluded that the recent authorities supported a much wider jurisdiction to interfere in cases where the assertion of strict legal rights is found by the court to be unconscionable. The cases before him were concerned with a situation where both parties had proceeded on the same mistaken assumption; and he concluded that the inquiry which he had to make was simply *d* whether, in all the circumstances of the cases before him, it was unconscionable for the defendants to seek to take advantage of the mistake which, at the material time, all parties shared.

In my judgment, in the case before me, the inquiry which I have to make is precisely the same. But before I turn to consider the facts of the case before me, there are certain general observations which I wish to make. *e*

First, the case advanced before me by the bank is not one of simple acquiescence by AIP in the mistaken belief of the bank; it is founded on active encouragement by AIP or representations by AIP, encouragement and representations which I have already found were in fact given and made by AIP to the bank. Now, in my judgment, where an estoppel is alleged to be founded on encouragement or representation, it can only be unconscionable for the encourager or representor to enforce his strict legal rights if the *f* other party's conduct has been influenced by the encouragement or representation.

Second, it is, in my judgment, no bar to a conclusion that the other party's conduct was so influenced that his conduct did not derive its origin only from the encouragement or representation of the first party. There may be cases where the representee has proceeded initially on the basis of a belief derived from some other source independent of the representor, but his belief has subsequently been confirmed by the encouragement or *g* representation of the representor. In such a case, the question is not whether the representee acted, or desisted from acting, solely in reliance on the encouragement or representation of the other party; the question is rather whether his conduct was so *influenced* by the encouragement or representation (I take the word 'influenced' from the judgment of Bowen LJ in *Edgington v Fitzmaurice* (1885) 29 Ch D 459 at 484, [1881–5] All ER Rep 856 at 862) that it would be unconscionable for the representor thereafter to *h* enforce his strict legal rights. Such a conclusion appears to be consistent with the decision of Oliver J in *Old & Campbell Ltd v Liverpool Victoria Trustees Co Ltd*. The point can also be illustrated by a hypothetical example. Let it be supposed that A and B are neighbours, and that A proposes to build a wall on what is in fact B's land, though both parties mistakenly believe it to be A's. A invites B's co-operation in the building of the wall, for example, by providing a means of access over his land for the purposes of *j* building work or by supporting an application for planning permission. B co-operates as requested, and the wall is built at A's expense. In such circumstances, it may well be unconscionable for B thereafter to assert his strict legal rights.

Third, it is in my judgment not of itself a bar to an estoppel that its effect may be to enable a party to enforce a cause of action which, without the estoppel, would not exist. It is sometimes said that an estoppel cannot create a cause of action, or that an estoppel can only act as a shield, not as a sword. In a sense this is true, in the sense that estoppel

is not, as a contract is, a source of legal obligation. But, as Lord Denning MR pointed out
a in *Crabb v Arun District Council* [1975] 3 All ER 865 at 871, [1976] Ch 179 at 187, an
estoppel may have the effect that a party can enforce a cause of action which, without the
estoppel, he would not be able to do. This is not, of course, true of all estoppels. Thus
a promissory estoppel derived from *Hughes v Metropolitan Railway Co* (1887) 2 App Cas
439, [1874–80] All ER Rep 187 is concerned with a representation by a party that he will
not enforce his strict legal rights; of its very nature such an estoppel cannot enable a party
b to enforce a cause of action. But in other cases an estoppel may do so, as for example in
cases of estoppel by acquiescence. Moreover (subject to one limitation, to which I shall
shortly refer) I can see no reason, in logic or in authority, why such a cause of action
should not consist of a contractual right. Thus in *Spiro v Lintern* [1973] 3 All ER 319,
[1973] 1 WLR 1002 a husband who had not authorised his wife to agree to sell his house
was held to be estopped from denying that his wife had such authority, with the effect
c that a purchaser from his wife was enabled to enforce against him a contract by his wife
for the sale of the house. It is true that that case may be treated as a case of estoppel by
acquiescence; but the Court of Appeal held that on the facts of the case the husband's
failure to disclose to the purchaser that his wife had acted without his authority amounted
to a representation by conduct that she had that authority. Furthermore, in two cases the
Privy Council has held that a representation by a party as to the legal effect of an
d agreement can give rise to an estoppel, with the consequence that the representee's rights
under the agreement are effectively enlarged: see *Sarat Chunder Dey v Gopal Chunder Lala*
(1892) LR 19 Ind App 203 and *Calgary Milling Co Ltd v American Surety Co of New York*
[1919] 3 WWR 98, the latter of which was applied by Luxmoore J in *De Tchihatchef v
Salerni Coupling Ltd* [1932] 1 Ch 330, [1931] All ER Rep 233. I observe in passing that it
is difficult to accommodate these cases within any of the five categories formulated by
e counsel for AIP.
Fourth, however, what I have said has to be reconciled with the general principle that
a purely gratuitous promise is unenforceable at law or in equity. At law and in equity,
generally speaking, a promise is only enforceable as a contractual obligation if it is
supported by consideration; and neither law nor equity will perfect an imperfect gift.
Furthermore, even if a purely gratuitous promise is acted on by the promisee, generally
f speaking such conduct will not of itself give rise to an estoppel against the promisor; such
an estoppel would be inconsistent with the general principle that purely gratuitous
promises will not be enforced: see *Combe v Combe* [1951] 1 All ER 767, [1951] 2 KB 215.
It was suggested to me that that case provided authority that no cause of action in
contract could be created by an estoppel. But that, in my judgment, is too sweeping a
proposition; it is inconsistent with authorities I have already cited, in particular the two
g decisions of the Privy Council referred to in the preceding paragraph. Indeed, there are
at least three groups of cases where estoppels may be enforced despite infringement of
this general principle; and I do not suggest that this list is exhaustive. The basis of all
these groups of cases appears to be the same: that it would despite the general principle
be unconscionable in all the circumstances for the encourager or representor not to give
effect to his encouragement or representation. The first group concerns cases where
h equity would regard it as fraudulent for the party against whom the estoppel is alleged
not to give effect to his encouragement or representation; an example of such a case is
where, on the principle stated by Lord Kingsdown in *Ramsden v Dyson* (1886) LR 1 HL
129 at 170, a party has encouraged another in the expectation that he shall have an
interest in the encourager's land, and the other party has, on the faith of that
encouragement, expended money on that land. The second group consists of cases
j concerned with promissory estoppel, in which one party represents to another that he
will not enforce his strict legal rights under a legal relationship between the parties. The
representation may be no more than a gratuitous promise; but it may nevertheless be
unconscionable for the representor to go back on it, because a representee may reasonably
be expected to act in reliance on such a forbearance, without going to the extent of
requiring a contractual variation. The third group concerns cases where one party has
represented to the other that a transaction between them has an effect which in law it
does not have. In such a case, it may in the circumstances be unconscionable for the

representor to go back on his representation, despite the fact that the effect is to reduce his rights or to enlarge his obligations and so give effect to what is in fact a gratuitous *a* promise; for the effect of the representation may be to cause or contribute to the representee's error or continued error as to his true legal rights, or to deprive him of an opportunity to renegotiate the transaction to render it legally enforceable in terms of the representation. Illustrations of such cases are to be found in the two Privy Council cases, and the decision of Luxmoore J which I have already cited. Such cases are very different from, for example, a mere promise by a party to make a gift or to increase his obligations *b* under an existing contract; such a promise will not generally give rise to an estoppel, even if acted on by the promisee, for the promisee may reasonably be expected to appreciate that, to render it binding, it must be incorporated in a binding contract or contractual variation, and that he cannot therefore safely rely on it as a legally binding promise without first taking the necessary contractual steps.

My fifth observations is this. Where, as in cases of promissory estoppel, the estoppel *c* is founded on a representation by a party that he will not enforce his legal rights, it is of course a prerequisite of the estoppel that there should be an existing legal relationship between the parties. But where, for example, the estoppel relates to the legal effect of a transaction between the parties, it does not necessarily follow that the underlying transaction should constitute a binding legal relationship. In such a case the representation may well, as I have already indicated, give rise to an estoppel although the *d* effect is to enlarge the obligation of the representor; and I can see no reason in principle why this should not be so, even if the underlying transaction would, but for the estoppel, be devoid of legal effect. Certainly the doctrine of consideration cannot of itself provide any insurmountable obstacle to this conclusion; for, whether the representation consists (as in the case of a promissory estoppel) of a forbearance or consists of a representation as to the legal effect of a transaction, it will in any event constitute an inroad on that *e* doctrine. An example of an estoppel giving rise to a binding obligation when none before existed is to be found in *Spiro v Lintern* [1973] 3 All ER 319, [1973] 1 WLR 1002, in which it was held that the purchaser could enforce a contract against the husband who would not, apart from the estoppel, have been under any obligation to him; and both *Sarat Chunder Dey v Gopal Chunder Lala* and *Old & Campbell Ltd v Liverpool Victoria Trustees Co Ltd* provide illustrations of estoppels which rendered effective otherwise *f* ineffective transactions.

In the light of these observations, I turn to examine the facts of the present case. First, as I have already held, there were numerous representations by Mr Foster on behalf of AIP to the bank that the guarantee given by AIP constituted a binding and effective guarantee by AIP to the bank (which was ultimately secured by a charge on real property) covering the Nassau loan to its subsidiary, ANPP. *g*

Second, I am satisfied that the representations of Mr Foster did indeed influence the bank in persisting in their conduct in relying on AIP's guarantee as providing enforceable collateral for ANPP's debt. True, the source of the bank's error lay in its own administration. Indeed, Mr Oldfield frankly admitted in his own evidence that, before Mr Foster made any representations to the bank, he was in no doubt that the Nassau loan was advanced to ANPP by the bank, not by Portsoken. However, later in his evidence he *h* said that by reason of the conduct of AIP (he had in mind in particular his various conversations with Mr Foster, and AIP's letter of 27th January 1975) his belief was reinforced. On the basis of this evidence, I asked counsel for AIP what the position would have been if Mr Foster, instead of being a man of complete integrity who shared Mr Oldfield's mistake, had fraudulently confirmed Mr Oldfield in his error. Would not the court be entitled to conclude that, having regard to the dealings between the parties, *j* Mr Foster's conduct had sufficiently influenced Mr Oldfield's conduct to render him liable in deceit? To that question I received no satisfactory answer; and I am satisfied that the answer should have been in the affirmative, for it is surely sufficient that the representor's conduct contributed to lulling the representee into a state of false security. Likewise, in all the circumstances, I am satisfied that Mr Foster's conduct, though of *a* course completely innocent, so influenced Mr Oldfield's conduct as to render it unconscionable on the part of AIP now to take advantage of the bank's error. Such a conclusion is, I would add, consistent with the decision of Oliver J in *Old & Campbell Ltd v Liverpool Victoria Trustees Co Ltd*, in which he held that the defendants were estopped from asserting the invalidity of an option, although (as I read the case) the error of the plaintiffs did not originally derive from the representations or encouragement of the defendants.

b   Third, I am satisfied that to hold that AIP is estopped from denying the invalidity of its guarantee is permissible, despite the general principle that neither law nor equity will enforce a purely gratuitous promise. For, by confirming the bank's erroneous belief that the guarantee was binding and effective and covered the Nassau loan, AIP contributed to the continuance of the bank's error as to the true legal effect or, rather, lack of legal effect of that document, and to the bank's failure to take the opportunity of putting matters *c* right.

Fourth, it makes no difference, in my judgment, that the guarantee was not of itself, in law, a binding contract. I accept the analysis of counsel for AIP that in strict law it was of itself no more than a piece of paper, a standing offer which, unaccepted, had long since lapsed. But, for the reasons I have already given, I can see no reason why, in principle, a representation that such a non-contractual document had a certain contractual effect *d* should be incapable of giving rise to an estoppel precluding the representator from thereafter going back on that representation where, as in the present case, it would be unconscionable for him to do so.

There remains, however, one further argument advanced on behalf of AIP, with which I must deal. Counsel submitted, on the basis of dicta of Lord Cranworth LC in *Ramsden v Dyson* (1866) LR 1 HL 129 at 152 and of Bramwell LJ in *Sims v Anglo-American* *e* *Telegraph Co* (1879) 5 QBD 188 at 203, that an estoppel will not be enforced unless there is reciprocity; here, he said, there was none, because if AIP was estopped from asserting the invalidity of the guarantee, the bank would obtain the benefit of the guarantee but AIP would not get the benefit of subrogation rights which it would have had if the money had in fact been advanced by the bank and the guarantee had been binding. Now, I can understand the force of such an argument in certain cases. No doubt, he who *f* comes to equity must do equity; and it might well be contrary to principle that a party should, by virtue of the doctrine of equitable estoppel, obtain the benefit of rights without incurring the burden of corresponding obligations which he would have incurred if the rights had been enforceable without the aid of the doctrine of estoppel. But I cannot see that this is so in the present case. If the guarantee had been binding, then any right of subrogation would have been to securities enforceable against the principal *g* debtor, ie against ANPP, which could only have been the mortgage over the Harrison building. But that security was in fact realised and the proceeds paid in partial discharge of the debt; so that no further benefit would have accrued to AIP by virtue of such right of subrogation, and I cannot therefore see that the lack of any such right on the part of AIP should preclude the bank from relying on the estoppel against AIP.

For these reasons, I accept the bank's submission that AIP is estopped from contending *h* that the guarantee does not cover the liability of ANPP in respect of the Nassau loan. It is, I understand, not in dispute that if this is so AIP is precluded from asserting that the bank was not entitled to apply the proceeds of sale of the UK properties, charged to it under the deeds I have referred to, in discharge of AIP's obligations under the guarantee. It follows that AIP is not entitled to the declaratory relief for which it asks.

j *Judgment for the bank.*

Solicitors: *Allen & Overy* (for AIP); *Nabarro Nathanson* (for the bank).

K Mydeen Esq   Barrister.

R v Uxbridge Justices, ex parte   *a*
Commissioner of Police of the Metropolis

QUEEN'S BENCH DIVISION
DONALDSON LJ AND KILNER BROWN J
2nd JULY 1980

b

Police – Property in possession of police – Delivery to owner – Costs of application for order for delivery to owner – Jurisdiction of justices to make order for costs – Justices having power to award costs where proceedings initiated by way of complaint – Whether 'application' by claimant for order for delivery of property to him properly made by way of complaint – Whether justices having power to order police to pay costs – Police (Property) Act 1897, s 1(1) – Magistrates' Courts Act 1952, s 55(1).   *c*

The applicant claimed a sum of money which came into the possession of the police during a criminal investigation. The applicant applied, by way of complaint, to magistrates for an order under s 1(1)ᵃ of the Police (Property) Act 1897 that it should be handed over to him. The magistrates made the order and, in the purported exercise of their power under s 55(1)ᵇ of the Magistrates' Courts Act 1952, awarded him £350 costs against the police. The police sought an order of certiorari to quash the order for costs on the ground that the magistrates had no jurisdiction to make such an order on an 'application' under s 1(1) of the 1897 Act because their power under s 55 of the 1952 Act was limited to proceedings initiated by complaint and an application under s 1(1) of the 1897 Act was not a complaint.   *d*

e

Held – Since on an application under s 1(1) of the 1897 Act magistrates were usually being asked to exercise a judicial function, i e to determine rights of property between parties, and the procedure by complaint was the appropriate method of initiating proceedings where magistrates were required to exercise a judicial function, it followed that the application had rightly been made by way of complaint, because there was a lis *f* between the applicant and the police (as the holders of the property) to be determined by the magistrates. The magistrates were therefore entitled under s 55 of the 1952 Act to order costs against the police on the applicant's complaint under s 1(1) of the 1897 Act. Accordingly the order of certiorari would be refused (see p 942 *a* to *c* and *f g j*, post).

Per Curiam. Where the police are in possession of property but have no means of knowing who is entitled to it and apply to magistrates for an order under s 1(1) of the *g* 1897 Act, it is arguable that there is in those circumstances no lis between the police and anybody else, and that the magistrates are acting not in a judicial but in a regulatory capacity when making an order under s 1(1) authorising the police to take some action (see p 942 *d j*, post).

h

a   Section 1(1), so far as material, provides: 'Where any property has come into the possession of the police in connection with their investigation of a suspected offence . . . a court of summary jurisdiction may, on application, either by an officer of police or by a claimant of the property, make an order for the delivery of the property to the person appearing to the magistrate or court to be the owner thereof, or, if the owner cannot be ascertained, make such order with respect to the property as to the magistrate or court may seem meet.'   j

b   Section 55(1), so far as material, provides: 'On the hearing of a complaint, a magistrates' court shall have power in its discretion to make such order as to costs—(a) on making the order for which the complaint is made, to be paid by the defendant to the complainant . . . as it thinks just and reasonable . . .'

a Observations on the factors to be taken into account by magistrates when deciding how to exercise their jurisdiction under s 55 of the 1952 Act (see p 942 g to p 943 a, post).

Notes

For property in the possession of the police, see 29 Halsbury's Laws (4th Edn) para 422, and for costs between parties in magistrates' courts, see ibid para 392.

b For the Police (Property) Act 1897, s 1, see 25 Halsbury's Statutes (3rd Edn) 280.

For the Magistrates' Courts Act 1952, s 55, see 21 ibid 231.

As from a day to be appointed s 55 of the 1952 Act is to be replaced by s 64 of the Magistrates' Courts Act 1980.

Application for judicial review

The Commissioner of Police of the Metropolis applied, with the leave of the Divisional *c* Court of the Queen's Bench Division, given on 5th April 1979, for an order of certiorari to quash an order made by the Uxbridge justices on 11th January 1979 whereby they directed that the applicant should pay the costs of the respondent, Sukh Deo Prasad, in the sum of £350. The facts are set out in the judgment of Donaldson LJ.

Laurence A Marshall for the applicant.
d Michael Harington for the respondent.

DONALDSON LJ. This is a very curious dispute which has arisen between the Commissioner of Police of the Metropolis and the respondent concerning some currency which came into the hands of the Commissioner of Police in circumstances to which the Police (Property) Act 1897 applies.

e Section 1 of that Act gives magistrates power to make orders with respect to property in the possession of the police. That is the sidenote. Subsection (1) provides that, where any property has come into the possession of the police in connection with any criminal charge or under various statutes, a court of summary jurisdiction may, on application either by an officer of police or by a claimant of the property, make an order for the delivery of the property to the person appearing to the magistrate or court to be the *f* owner thereof, or, if the owner cannot be ascertained, make such order with respect to the property as to the magistrate or court may seem meet.

The respondent claimed this property and the magistrates made an order in his favour. Then the question arose whether there was any power in the magistrates' court to award costs against the police or indeed against anybody else in favour of the applicant.

Magistrates' courts have no power at common law to make any order for costs. If the *g* magistrates in this case, who did make an order for costs, were acting with jurisdiction, that jurisdiction is to be found in s 55 of the Magistrates' Courts Act 1952. That section gives power to a magistrates' court to make an order for costs 'on hearing of a complaint'.

The problem reduces itself to this: if either an officer of police or a claimant of property makes application under the Police (Property) Act 1897, are those proceedings properly brought by way of complaint or should they be by way of application or notice *h* of motion or some other form of initiating process? If they are properly brought by complaint, there is power to award costs under s 55 of the 1952 Act. If it has to be brought in some other way, there being no other statutory power to order costs which could be applicable in this case, there is no power to order costs.

We are told that the Justice of the Peace, admirable journal though it is, has averted to this question on three occasions and has twice come down on one side of the fence and *j* once on the other, so that I am not sure that takes the matter very much further.

I think we have to approach this on the basis of principle and I am impressed by counsel's argument for the respondent that magistrates have two different functions: a judicial function and a regulatory function. The most obvious example of their regulatory function is in relation to the Licensing Acts. He submits that in relation to their regulatory function one has to find special provisions as to costs, the procedure by complaint being inappropriate, but that the procedure by complaint is appropriate to *a* initiate proceedings calling on magistrates to exercise a judicial function.

I think that is right. I then turn again to the Police (Property) Act 1897, and it seems to me that under s 1 the magistrates are usually being asked to exercise a judicial function. They are being asked to determine rights of property, albeit on a nisi basis, because under s 1(2) any party who claims to be entitled to possession of property which has been delivered to somebody else pursuant to an order made under the Act is entitled *b* within six months to apply to some other court of appropriate jurisdiction, and the magistrates' order does not act as any bar to whatever order that court sees fit to make. But, subject to that, it is essentially a judicial function.

I said 'usually' because there is one case in which it does not appear to be a judicial function. Normally there will be a claimant who says that the property is his. There may be several claimants all of whom say the property is theirs. Then there will be a lis *c* between the claimants inter se and between the claimants and the police as the holder of the property, and that lis will be determined for the time being by the magistrates' order. But one could get a case, as the statute contemplates, in which the police are in possession of property, but have no means of knowing who, if anybody, is entitled to the property. They then go to the magistrates and say, 'What do we do with this property?' The order which will be made by the magistrates will be their authority for *d* doing whatever the order requires. But there it can be argued that there is no lis between the police and anybody else, and the magistrates perhaps could be said not to be acting in a judicial capacity. They are acting in a regulatory capacity authorising the police to take some action.

I was at one time a little concerned that we should have the position in which, if the police apply, there being no claimant to the property, they should be unable to get costs *e* because it would be inappropriate to begin such proceedings by complaint (it would clearly be by application), whereas if there was a claimant on the horizon, either he or the police ought to proceed by complaint because, as I say, it would be a judicial proceeding. But although I think it is untidy that the logic of what I have been saying should lead to that result, it has no practical significance because of course, if there is no other party, no defendant to the complaint, there is nobody against whom the police *f* could get costs anyway.

Subject to that, I think that this is a judicial function. It is therefore appropriate to be brought by way of complaint. It being brought by way of complaint, there is jurisdiction to award costs under s 55 of the 1952 Act, but of course magistrates will no doubt exercise their discretion whether to award costs and will take account of the conduct of the police who may or may not contest a claim. They will no doubt take very full *g* account of the fact that the police, as the involuntary bailees of the property, have to get some form of authority to hand it over to anyone. If they are doing no more than acceding to an application or 'interpleading', they may well think that it will be wholly inappropriate that they should be asked to pay any costs at all. If they contest the claim and fail, that is a different matter, but if they are interpleading then I think the magistrates have a discretion and it would be an unusual case in which it was appropriate *h* to make an order for costs.

KILNER BROWN J. I agree. I think the matter can further be tested in this way, as Donaldson LJ has indicated. Suppose that the application is made by a claimant of the property and the police sensibly think that it is a bogus application. They may be *j* compelled to come to court and put the matter before the justices on the basis that this is a bogus application. In those circumstances I would have thought that the police would be entitled to their costs, though only if the justices in their discretion felt that the police intervention was proper and they were forced to intervene. As Donaldson LJ has pointed out, in circumstances such as this one ought to leave it to the good sense of the *a* justices to decide whether or not there should be an order for costs and, if so, what amount.

Application refused.

Solicitors: *R E T Birch* (for the applicant); *Edward Mackie & Co*, Ealing (for the respondent).

b   N P Metcalfe Esq   Barrister.

Guilfoyle v Home Office

c COURT OF APPEAL, CIVIL DIVISION

LORD DENNING MR, O'CONNOR LJ AND SIR JOHN MEGAW

18th, 19th NOVEMBER, 11th DECEMBER 1980

Prison – Prisoner – Letters – Correspondence with legal adviser – Power of governor to read or stop correspondence – Power curtailed where prisoner a party to legal proceedings and
d corresponding about them with legal adviser – Prisoner lodging petition with European Commission of Human Rights alleging interference with correspondence with legal adviser – Whether prisoner 'a party to . . . legal proceedings' by reason of lodging petition with commission – Prison Rules 1964 (SI 1964 No 388), r 37A(1).

The governor of the prison where the plaintiff was imprisoned refused to allow the
e plaintiff to correspond with his solicitor until he identified his complaint. The solicitor, on behalf of the plaintiff, lodged a petition with the European Commission of Human Rights complaining of violation of those articles in the Convention for the Protection of Human Rights entitling everyone to a fair hearing and to the right to respect for their correspondence. The commission had not at that stage decided whether the petition was admissible. The plaintiff sought a declaration against the Home Office that by lodging
f a petition with the commission he had become 'a party to . . . legal proceedings' within r 37A(1)[a] of the Prison Rules 1964, and was accordingly entitled to the privilege conferred by r 37A(1) of not having his correspondence with his legal adviser in connection with the proceedings read or stopped by the governor under r 33(3)[b] of those rules. The Home Office submitted that lodging a petition with the commission did not make the plaintiff a party to legal proceedings and that therefore the governor was entitled under r 33(3) to
g read and stop his correspondence with his solicitor. The judge dismissed the plaintiff's claim and he appealed.

Held – The appeal would be dismissed for the following reasons—
    (1) 'Legal proceedings' in r 37A(1) of the 1964 rules meant proceedings before a court or body which exercised judicial functions or which had power to make an enforceable
h adjudication, as distinct from bodies which exercised advisory, administrative or quasi-judicial functions, and, since the commission was purely an investigative body and did not exercise any judicial functions, proceedings before it were not 'legal proceedings' (see p 946 *g* to *j*, p 947 *j* to p 948 *c* and p 949 *j* to p 950 *a*, post); dicta of Lord Diplock in *Re Racal Communications Ltd* [1980] 2 All ER at 637–638 and of Lord Scarman in *Attorney General v British Broadcasting Corpn* [1980] 3 All ER at 181–182 applied.
j   (2) Moreover, the plaintiff was not by reason of his petition to the commission 'a party' to proceedings because (per Lord Denning MR) a petitioner only became a party when the commission accepted his petition as admissible so that the other party (ie the

---

a   Rule 37A(1) is set out at p 946 *e f*, post
b   Rule 33(3) is set out at p 946 *d e*, post

state against whom violation of the convention was alleged) was called on to answer the petition, or (per O'Connor LJ and Sir John Megaw) because an individual could never be *a* a party to proceedings before the commission for violation of the convention. It followed that, since the plaintiff was not 'a party to . . . legal proceedings' within r 37A(1), his correspondence could be read and stopped by the prison governor under r 33(3) (see p 946 j, p 947 b c and e f, p 948 a to c and p 949 f and j to p 950 a, post).

Notes   *b*
For letters to and from a prisoner, see 30 Halsbury's Laws (3rd Edn) 611, para 1175.
    For the European Commission of Human Rights and for applications thereto, see 18 Halsbury's Laws (4th Edn) paras 1629–1660.
    For the Prison Rules 1964, rr 33, 37A, see 18 Halsbury's Statutory Instruments (Third Reissue) 20, 22.

                                                                                        c
Cases referred to in judgments
Attorney General v British Broadcasting Corpn [1980] 3 All ER 161, [1980] 3 WLR 109, HL.
Gouriet v Union of Post Office Workers [1977] 3 All ER 70, [1978] AC 435, [1977] 3 WLR 300, 141 JP 552, Digest (Cont Vol E) 168, 3776a.
McIlkenny v Chief Constable of the West Midlands [1980] 2 All ER 227, [1980] QB 283, [1980] 2 WLR 689, CA.   *d*
Racal Communications Ltd, Re [1980] 2 All ER 634, [1980] 3 WLR 181, HL.

Cases also cited
Ahmad v Inner London Educational Authority [1978] 1 All ER 574, [1978] QB 36, CA.
Boaler, Re [1915] 1 KB 21, [1914–15] All ER Rep 1022, CA.
Runciman & Co v Smyth & Co (1904) 20 TLR 625, DC.   *e*
Sugden v Sugden [1957] 1 All ER 300, [1957] P 120, CA.

Appeal
This was an appeal by the plaintiff, Patrick Guilfoyle, from the order of Peter Pain J made on 4th July 1979 dismissing his claim made by originating summons for a declaration against the Home Office, the defendants, that as a serving prisoner who had made an *f* application to the European Commission on Human Rights (alleging breach of the European Convention for the Protection of Human Rights) he was a party to legal proceedings within r 37A(1) of the Prison Rules 1964 and entitled to correspond with his legal adviser in accordance with r 37A(1). The facts are set out in the judgment of Lord Denning MR.

                                                                                        g
Andrew Collins and *Donald Anderson* for the plaintiff.
Nicholas Bratza for the Home Office.

                                                                           Cur adv vult
                                                                                        h
11th December. The following judgments were read.

LORD DENNING MR. In November 1974 bombs were planted in two public houses in Birmingham. Twenty-one people were killed and 161 injured. I described it in *McIlkenny v Chief Constable of West Midlands* [1980] 2 All ER 227, [1980] QB 283. Patrick Guilfoyle was in prison on remand at the time. On 2nd May 1975 he was sentenced to *j* imprisonment totalling 12 years, and on 6th February 1977 to imprisonment totalling 15 years.
    Guilty as he was of a grave offence, he makes complaint of his treatment *after* he was arrested and before he was tried. He says that he and his companions in crime were assaulted by prison officers while he was at Winson Green prison in Birmingham in

1974. It looks as if they did get a little bit of rough handling by someone or other. They were bruised and received black eyes, but nothing more. It may have been done when they were trying to escape, or when they were refusing to do as they were told. At all events, their complaints have been fully investigated in this country. There was an internal inquiry by the governor of the prison. There was a Home Office inquiry by the Chief Constable of Lincolnshire. There was a trial of the prison officers before judge and jury. If any of the prison officers did anything wrong, no doubt disciplinary proceedings would have been taken against them.

Yet, despite all these investigations here, Patrick Guilfoyle has the audacity to seek to complain to the European Commission of Human Rights. He wants to lodge a petition to the commission claiming that he has been a victim of a violation by the United Kingdom of the rights set forth in the Convention for the Protection of Human Rights and Fundamental Freedoms (Cmnd 8969). He wants to obtain redress for the assaults which he alleges were made on him. He does not tell which article has been violated by the United Kingdom. But I expect he is relying on art 3 which says that 'No one shall be subjected to torture or to inhuman or degrading treatment or punishment'.

1. The European Commission and the European Court

Hereinafter I will speak of the European Commission of Human Rights as 'the European Commission', and of the European Court of Human Rights as 'the European Court'. The United Kingdom have accepted the jurisdiction of the European Court and the right of individual petitions to the European Commission, and this has just been renewed for a further period of five years.

(i) The European Commission

The position is that any person may lodge a petition to the European Commission claiming to be a victim of a violation of the rights set forth in the convention (art 25). The European Commission may accept his petition or reject it as inadmissible (art 27). If it accepts his petition, it holds an investigation and a hearing, which can be attended by counsel (art 28). It makes a report to the Committee of Ministers (art 31). They decide whether there has been a violation or not (art 32). But they take no action themselves to bring a case before the court.

(ii) The European Court

The European Court is quite separate and apart from the European Commission. No individual can bring a case before the European Court. Even if the European Commission have said in their report that there was a violation of human rights, the only persons who can bring a case before the European Court are the European Commission themselves, or one of the states themselves (art 48). The case is brought against the state which is alleged to have been guilty of a violation and not against any individual. But the European Court can require the state to make just satisfaction to the injured party (art 50).

2. The steps taken by Patrick Guilfoyle

Now in order to proceed before the European Commission Patrick Guilfoyle wants to write to his solicitor in this country. He wants to do this: to write a letter privately, which the prison governor is not at liberty to see, and to receive a reply, which the governor is not to see. He says that this is permitted under the Prison Rules 1964, SI 1964 No 388. The question in this case is whether the prison rules do so permit. This is how the point developed: on 11th January 1977 Patrick Guilfoyle wrote to his solicitor:

> 'Dear Sir,
>   'I received a letter from my mother. She told me that I should write to you regarding the epesode [sic] in Winson Green. I am quite prepared to meet you and give you a statement. I will leave the decision up to you. As you must know what I write in these letters are cencered [sic]. I thing [sic] if you get in touch with the

governor he will arrange a visit from you, as you are acting for me in the case. I will finish here. Hoping to hear from you. I hope you get this letter.

'P. J. Guilfoyle.'

On 24th February 1977 the solicitor sent a letter to Patrick Guilfoyle enclosing a green form for legal aid for him to complete, so as to enable the solicitor to visit him and give advice. That letter was not passed on to Patrick Guilfoyle. It was stopped.

The solicitor then on 24th March 1977 lodged a petition with the European Commission. The solicitor considered that the stopping of his letter to Patrick Guilfoyle was a breach of the convention. The petition complained of a violation of arts 6(1) and 8 of the convention. Article 6(1) entitles everyone to a fair and public hearing. Article 8 gives to everyone the right to respect for his correspondence. No decision has yet been taken by the commission in respect of the petition. It has not accepted it as admissible.

3. *The Prison Rules 1964*

No difficulties arise about an interview by the solicitor with Patrick Guilfoyle. He can hold an interview out of hearing, but in the sight of a prison officer. A question has arisen, however, about correspondence. The governor says that he can read any letter from Patrick Guilfoyle to his solicitor or vice versa. But the solicitor says that the governor cannot read it or stop it. The governor relies on r 33(3) of the Prison Rules 1964 which says:

'Except as provided by these Rules, every letter or communication to or from a prisoner may be read or examined by the governor or an officer deputed by him, and the governor may, at his discretion, stop any letter or communication on the ground that its contents are objectionable or that it is of inordinate length.'

The solicitor relies on r 37A(1) of the rules (inserted by SI 1972 No 1860). It says:

'A prisoner who is a party to any legal proceedings may correspond with his legal adviser in connection with the proceedings, and unless the Governor has reason to suppose that any such correspondence contains matter not relating to the proceedings it shall not be read or stopped under Rule 33(3) of these Rules.'

4. *'A party to any legal proceedings'*

In order to invoke r 37A(1), it is necessary for Patrick Guilfoyle to be 'a party to any legal proceedings'. That is the crucial point in the case. When Patrick Guilfoyle's solicitor lodged a petition with the European Commission (complaining of an alleged violation by the United Kingdom of his rights), did Patrick Guilfoyle then become 'a party to any legal proceedings'? To decide this question, it is necessary to find out what are 'legal proceedings'. To my mind the solution is to be found in the distinction between courts of judicature, that is, courts of law which exercise judicial functions: and arbitrations, tribunals and other bodies which exercise advisory, administrative or quasi judicial functions. This distinction was drawn by Lord Scarman in *Attorney General v British Broadcasting Corpn* [1980] 3 All ER 161 at 181–182, [1980] 3 WLR 109 at 135 and by Lord Diplock in *Re Racal Communications Ltd* [1980] 2 All ER 634 at 637–638, [1980] 3 WLR 181 at 185–186, and is in conformity with the amended r 37A(4) of the 1964 Rules (added by SI 1976 No 503). Translated into the affairs of the European Convention, the proceedings in the European *Court* of Human Rights are 'legal proceedings' because that court exercises judicial functions: but the proceedings in the European *Commission* are not, because the commission exercises no judicial function. They only make a report on the facts and state their opinion. They make no order at all, nothing which can be enforced by anyone.

Even if proceedings in the European Commission could be considered to be 'legal proceedings', when does an applicant become a 'party' to the legal proceedings? I think an applicant only becomes a 'party' when his application is accepted as admissible by the commission such that the other party is to be called on to answer it. To take some

parallels from our municipal jurisdiction. A vexatious litigant may not institute legal
proceedings except by the leave of the High Court: see s 51 of the Supreme Court of
Judicature (Consolidation) Act 1925. He does not become a 'party' when he applies for
leave. It is only when leave is given and he starts proceedings that he becomes a 'party'.
A mental patient cannot start proceedings against a mental institution except by leave of
the High Court: see s 141 of the Mental Health Act 1959. He does not become a 'party'
when he applies for leave. A person who complains of a public nuisance cannot start an
action except with the consent of the Attorney General in relator proceedings: see *Gouriet
v Union of Post Office Workers* [1977] 3 All ER 70, [1978] AC 435. He does not become a
'party' at any stage.

In my opinion, therefore, Patrick Guilfoyle is not a 'party to any legal proceedings'
within r 37A(1) of the 1964 Rules. The letters to and from his solicitor come within
r 33(3). They can be read and examined by the governor. Such an examination is
contemplated by the European Agreement relating to Persons participating in
Proceedings of the European Commission and Court of Human Rights (Cmnd 4699
(1969)) which came into force on 17th April 1971. Article 3 provides for the right of
legal advisers to correspond with their clients, but adds:

> '2. As regards persons under detention, the exercise of this rule shall in particular
> imply that: (a) if their correspondence is examined by the competent authorities, its
> despatch and delivery shall nevertheless take place without undue delay and without
> alteration . . .'

Although the letters to and from a legal adviser are liable to be read and examined by
the governor, he does not stop them if they are in connection with a petition by the
prisoner to the European Court of Human Rights. It was so stated by the Home
Secretary in answer to a question in the House of Commons.

Conclusion

In my opinion the Home Office, the governor and all concerned have acted very
properly. They have been guilty of no violation of human rights whatever. It is very
right and proper that the governor should be able to read and examine any letter
between Guilfoyle and his solicitor relating to the petition to the European Commission,
but he does not stop them. I would dismiss the appeal accordingly.

O'CONNOR LJ. The plaintiff is a prisoner sentenced to terms of 12 years and 15 years
in 1975 and 1977. In 1974 he was being held on remand in Winson Green prison in
Birmingham. He claims that he was the victim of assault at the time when the
Birmingham bombers were brought into that prison. In 1977 the prison governor
refused to allow the plaintiff to communicate with his solicitor by letter until he had
identified his complaint as required by standing orders. The governor was well within
his rights under the Prison Rules 1964, SI 1964 No 388: see rr 33 and 34 and in particular
r 34(8). Thereupon his solicitors, and I must assume on his instructions, had a petition
drafted, and in March 1977 sent it to the European Commission of Human Rights in
Strasbourg submitting that this lawful exercise of discretion by the governor was a
breach of arts 6 and 8 of the European Convention for the Protection of Human
Rights. Although 3½ years have elapsed, the commission has not yet said whether it
proposes to admit the petition and investigate the complaint.

This case, however, is not concerned with the merits or demerits of the petition. As
soon as the petition was sent off, the plaintiff claimed that he had become 'a party to any
legal proceedings' within the meaning of r 37A of the Prison Rules 1964 and that he was
entitled to the privilege conferred by para (1) of that rule. The Home Office say that
sending a petition to the European Commission of Human Rights does not make a
person 'a party to legal proceedings'. This case is brought by the plaintiff claiming a
declaration that he is 'a party to any legal proceedings'. Peter Pain J has held that he is
not. I agree with the judge. I do not think that the meaning of these six words presents

any difficulty. In my judgment, legal proceedings are proceedings brought before a court, tribunal, body, call it what you will, which has power to make an enforceable adjudication. This the European Commission of Human Rights cannot do. It is an investigative body; it reports to the Committee of Ministers; it can make recommendations; it can bring proceedings in the European Court. In that court the plaintiff could not be a party: no individual can. It is only the Commission and member states who can be parties in that forum.

It was submitted on behalf of the plaintiff that we should give a wide construction to this phrase because it was said the restriction imposed by a strict construction was at least against the spirit of the convention. I cannot accept the validity of this submission. The European Agreement of May 1969 (Cmnd 4699), to which the United Kingdom is a party, expressly recognises that persons in prison must expect to have their correspondence read.

I agree that the appeal should be dismissed.

SIR JOHN MEGAW. Parturiunt montes... At the outset it seemed that this case was concerned with possibly important issues as to human rights and that we were being asked to hold that the Home Office, albeit mistakenly rather than from any consciously bad motive, were interfering with the fundamental rights of prisoners in breach of treaty obligations undertaken by this country. But by the end of the argument it was apparent that no important question of principle as to fundamental human rights is involved. It is a simple question of the construction of six words in one paragraph of the Prison Rules 1964, SI 1964 No 388, as amended. The six words are 'a party to any legal proceedings'. Whichever of the submissions as to the question of construction is correct, it does not involve the consequence that there has been, or might be, an infringement by the United Kingdom of its treaty obligations as to the observance of human rights.

Lest it be thought that what I have said in the preceding paragraph involves implied adverse criticism by me of counsel, I would say at once that that is not so. Both counsel presented their respective arguments, I thought, with complete fairness, admirable clarity, thoroughness without prolixity, and with firm resistance of any temptation to take bad points or to overstress the significance of marginal points.

Counsel for the plaintiff made it clear from the outset that he did not contend that any of the Prison Rules 1964 to which we were referred were ultra vires. Nor did he contend that the European Convention for the Protection of Human Rights and Fundamental Freedoms, though it is a treaty binding as such on the United Kingdom in international law, is a part of the law of England and enforceable as such by English courts. But, more than that, he did not contend that the Prison Rules involved any breach of any principle of the convention, if r 37A(1) were to be construed in the way in which he submitted it ought to be construed.

In those circumstances, the only question of general principle affecting human rights which could have been involved in this case was the question whether, as counsel for the plaintiff submitted, if r 37A(1) ought to be interpreted by the court in the way in which the Home Office submitted that it should be interpreted, then there might be a conflict between that rule, so interpreted, and the convention. Counsel for the plaintiff submitted that, if there were two possible interpretations of the rule, one of which was consistent with the provisions of the human rights convention, and the other of which was in conflict with those provisions, the court should be disposed to prefer the interpretation which was consistent with this country's treaty obligations, as contained in the convention. That, if the facts had justified it, would have been a powerful argument and could be said to have involved a question of some importance as a matter of principle in the sphere of human rights.

The principle of the convention which counsel submitted might be infringed by the Home Office's interpretation of r 37A(1) was that, once a petition had been received by the European Commission of Human Rights from an individual complainant who is a prisoner, fundamental human rights require that the prison authorities should not be

permitted to read any correspondence passing between the prisoner and his legal advisers
with reference to the petition. Unfortunately for this submission of counsel for the
plaintiff, the existence of this fundamental human right seems to be precluded by, and
to be irreconcilable with, the European Agreement relating to Persons participating in
Proceedings of the European Commission and Court of Human Rights (Cmnd 4699).
That agreement was made in London on 6th May 1969. It was ratified by the United
Kingdom on 24th February 1971. It is published by Her Majesty's Stationery Office in
the Treaty Series (TS 44 (1971)). The provisions of art 3, paras 1 and 2(a), whether
interpreted by the ordinary English, or by any other, method, carry the inevitable
implication that it is not an infringement of a human right that correspondence by
prisoners ('persons under detention') with the commission and the court may be
'examined by the competent authorities'. It is not realistic to suppose that examination
of correspondence between a prisoner and his legal advisers would be an infringement of
a fundamental human right, when examination of his correspondence with the
commission itself is not an infringement.

So the case shrinks to this little measure. Is the plaintiff 'a party to any legal
proceedings' within the meaning of those words in r 37A(1) by reason of the fact that he
petitioned the European Commission of Human Rights on 21st March 1977 and that his
claim to be the victim of a violation of provisions of the convention by the government
of the United Kingdom is still pending before the commission? If he were, then the
Prison Rules 1964, more generous in this respect than what is required by the treaty
provisions as to fundamental human rights, would make it wrong for his correspondence
with his legal adviser to be read by the prison authorities unless the governor of the
prison had reason to believe that the correspondence contained matters not relating to
the proceedings. As I have said, whether the plaintiff is or is not 'a party to any legal
proceedings', the fact that his correspondence with his solicitors is read and, subject to the
decision of this appeal, will continue to be read by the prison authorities (though they
assert no right to stop letters provided they do indeed relate to the petition) raises no
arguable issue of infringement of provisions as to human rights to which this country
has subscribed by treaty. So we pass to a relatively dull and technical question of
construction, the answer to which may in some degree affect the plaintiff's legal rights,
but not, whatever the answer is to the question of construction, any fundamental human
right.

On that narrow issue, my conclusion is that on the true construction of r 37A(1) the
plaintiff is not a person who is a party to legal proceedings by reason of his petition to the
commission. It was conceded, as I think rightly and necessarily, by counsel for the
plaintiff that if the claim initiated by the plaintiff's petition, having at some date in the
future been reported on by the commission, were to be brought before the European
Court of Human Rights, the plaintiff would not be a party to the proceedings before the
court. Therefore at that stage r 37A(1) would undoubtedly not apply to him. Rule 33(3)
would apply. But, counsel for the plaintiff submits, that does not prevent the plaintiff
from being a party to legal proceedings during the present stage when the petition is
before the commission, either because the stage of consideration by the commission is
itself, separately, to be regarded as a set of 'proceedings', or because the whole process
before the commission, possibly before the Council of Ministers, and before the Court of
Human Rights is collectively to be regarded as one set of 'legal proceedings'.

It appears to me that, in order to decide whether the transaction initiated by the
petition to the commission is or is not 'legal proceedings', one must look at the whole of
the potential transaction from its initiation through to its outcome in the way of a
binding decision as to the right or rights asserted to have been infringed and as to
whether or not there has been an infringement. One may not divide the contemplated
transaction into separate 'proceedings' for the purpose of considering whether, in the
separate phases, they are properly described as 'legal' and whether or not a person is 'a
party'. Where, as here, the person cannot, not 'may not', but 'cannot', be a party to the
'proceedings' through to the end, to the decision-making stage, whether by the Council

of Ministers or by the European Court of Human Rights, it does not appear to me to be permissible to describe that person as being a party to those proceedings, however 'legal' those proceedings, viewed in their totality, may be. A person cannot be a party to legal proceedings if he is necessarily evanescent before the proceedings can come to fruition by way of decision.

In my opinion, Peter Pain J was right to refuse to grant the declaration. I should add that if I had taken the other view I should have thought that the declaration asked for is too wide. It would, in the light of counsel's proper and necessary concession, have to provide a limitation of time, so that the entitlement under r 37A would cease when the commission made its report.

Appeal dismissed. Leave to appeal to the House of Lords refused.

Solicitors: *Gamlens*, agents for *George E Baker & Co*, Guildford (for the plaintiff); *Treasury Solicitor*.

Frances Rustin   Barrister.

R v Rent Officer for Camden, ex parte Ebiri

QUEEN'S BENCH DIVISION
DONALDSON LJ AND FORBES J
27th OCTOBER 1980

Rent restriction – Rent – Determination of fair rent – Jurisdiction – Rent officer – Jurisdiction to determine whether there is a tenancy within the Rent Acts – Allegation by tenant that tenancy protected – Contention by landlord that tenancy was a holiday letting only – Rent officer satisfied that tenancy was protected tenancy – Whether rent officer under a duty to determine fair rent before court has decided whether there was a protected tenancy.

In May 1980 the tenants of a flat applied to a rent officer to register a fair rent for the premises. The landlords contended that the rent officer had no jurisdiction because the tenancy was not a protected tenancy but merely a holiday letting. The tenants initiated proceedings in the county court to determine the true nature of the tenancy. Meanwhile the rent officer arranged a preliminary meeting between the parties for 28th July and at the meeting he investigated the question whether the tenancy was protected and heard evidence from the parties. He concluded that the tenancy was not a holiday letting and that he had jurisdiction to proceed, but instead of doing so immediately he adjourned the meeting until 12th August to give the landlords time to apply for a judicial review if they so wished. The landlords took no steps to stop him proceeding but said that he was acting ultra vires in doing so because he was pre-empting the court's decision. At the meeting on 12th August the rent officer maintained that he had jurisdiction to proceed but said that it would be inappropriate in the circumstances for him to do so, so he adjourned the meeting sine die. The tenants applied for a judicial review in the form of an order of mandamus requiring him to determine and register a fair rent for the flat.

Held – Although on an application to register a fair rent a rent officer could not determine conclusively a disputed question whether there was a protected tenancy, since only the court could do that, he nonetheless had a duty to consider the question and to inquire into the facts. If, after hearing the evidence, he was satisfied that there was a protected tenancy, he was bound to proceed to determine and register a fair rent for the premises since he only had a discretion not to proceed if he was doubtful whether a protected tenancy existed. It followed that, since the rent officer was in no doubt that the tenancy was a protected tenancy, he was obliged to proceed to determine and register a fair rent for the flat. Accordingly the order of mandamus would be granted (see p 952 j to p 953 g and p 954 a and e f, post).

R v Rent Officer for Kensington and Chelsea, ex parte Noel [1977] 1 All ER 356 distinguished.

Per Curiam. A rent officer's discretion might extend to not proceeding in a case in which he is certain or virtually certain in his own mind that there is a protected tenancy but knows that within 24 hours it is going to be decided by a court of competent jurisdiction (see p 953 d e and g, post).

Notes

For the duty of a rent officer to consider whether he has jurisdiction in an application to register a fair rent in respect of an occupation of premises, see Supplement to 23 Halsbury's Laws (3rd Edn) para 1571B.

Cases referred to in judgments

R v Rent Officer for the London Borough of Brent, ex parte Ganatra [1976] 1 All ER 849, [1976] QB 576, [1976] 2 WLR 330, 140 JP 290, 31 P & CR 276, DC, Digest (Cont Vol. E) 384, 8416a.

R v Fulham, Hammersmith and Kensington Rent Tribunal, ex parte Zerek [1951] 1 All ER 482, [1951] 2 KB 1, 115 JP 132, 49 LGR 275, DC, 31(2) Digest (Reissue) 1044, 8238.

R v Rent Officer for Kensington and Chelsea, ex parte Noel [1977] 1 All ER 356, [1978] QB 1, [1977] 2 WLR 797, 33 P & CR 49, DC, Digest (Cont Vol E) 385, 8660a.

Case also cited

R v Croydon and South West London Rent Tribunal, ex parte Ryżewska [1977] 1 All ER 312, [1977] QB 876, DC.

Application for judicial review

The applicants, Cyril Ifeanyi Ebiri and Bekky Ebiri, applied for judicial review in the form of an order of mandamus directed to J McW Smith, a rent officer for the London Borough of Camden, requiring him to determine and register a fair rent for Flat 3, 105 York Way, London N 7, in accordance with para 5 of Sch 11 to the Rent Act 1977. The facts are set out in the judgment of Donaldson LJ.

David Watkinson for the applicants.
Simon D Brown and *John Laws* for the respondent.

DONALDSON LJ. In this matter the applicants, Mr Cyril Ebiri and Bekky Ebiri, apply for judicial review in the form of an order of mandamus addressed to the rent officer for the London Borough of Camden. The relief which the applicants seek is to require the rent officer to determine and to register a fair rent for certain premises within his area.

The history of the matter is this. The two applicants took a tenancy of the premises at Flat 3, 105 York Way, London N7, in November 1979. In May 1980 they applied to have a fair rent registered. A copy of the application was forwarded by the rent officer in the usual and required way to the landlords, Sherman Securities Ltd, and the landlords by a letter dated 18th June took the point that this was not a protected tenancy but was a holiday let and so was outwith the jurisdiction of the rent officer.

As soon as that letter was received by the applicants or very shortly afterwards they started proceedings in the county court in order to determine whether or not this was a protected tenancy, the applicants of course contending that it was and the landlords contending that it was not.

The rent officer meanwhile had arranged for a preliminary consultation between the parties to take place on 28th July, and at that meeting he went into the question of whether or not this was a protected tenancy. It was not a case, as was the position in *R v Rent Officer for Kensington and Chelsea, ex parte Noel* [1977] 1 All ER 356, [1978] QB 1 of merely having submissions from agents or representatives of the parties. The parties gave evidence. There was a statement from the tenants. A Mr Sherman represented the limited company landlord and Mr Sherman cross-examined the tenants.

At the end of the proceedings the rent officer said:

'In the light of what I have heard this afternoon, I have come to the conclusion that this is not a holiday let, but an ordinary regulated tenancy. In the light of the reference and Mr Ebiri's statement, I feel I have jurisdiction to proceed. I have cases where I decide straight away that there is a holiday let and adjourn them sine die for the tenant to prove it in court. Sometimes I have never heard any more, or the courts have confirmed it. In this instance there is no doubt in my mind, and I do feel that I can proceed.'

Having done that, he then proceeded to fix 12th August as being the date for the consultation when representations were to be made by both parties as to the amount of the fair rent, rather than proceeding straight away, to be in order to give the landlords opportunity to apply for judicial review if they wished to prevent him proceeding further and also to prepare any arguments they might want to advance to him about the exact level of rent.

The landlords took no steps to prohibit him from proceeding, and the parties met again before the rent officer on 12th August. Meanwhile the landlords had written to the rent officer on 4th August saying this:

'You will recall that despite the pending County Court proceedings to decide whether the occupancy of the above flat is a protected tenancy, you made your own decision that it is so. The fact that the letting agreement describes the tenancy as ". . . a holiday letting only", is prima facie evidence that it is until the Court decides otherwise under section 141 of the Rent Act 1977. We feel that you are pre-empting the decision of the Court and acting beyond your powers in proceeding with the application for the registration of a fair rent until the Court has determined whether a protected tenancy exists. In those circumstances we feel that the consultation proposed for 12th August should not be proceeded with.'

On 12th August the rent officer referred to that letter. He said that in his view the letter constituted 'new evidence' and that in the light of that and other factors he considered that it would be wiser for him not to register a rent. He said he would adjourn the consultation sine die. The representative of the tenants argued that that was not the right course and that the rent officer ought to register a rent. The rent officer said that he still thought he had jurisdiction to do so but that he would not in fact register a rent. He did not say so, but clearly he thought he was acting within the scope of his discretion and he said, somewhat incorrectly, that no one could compel him to register a rent.

The proceedings then went on by the tenants' representative urging the rent officer to give detailed reasons and drawing his attention to the fact that there might be rights vested in the tenants which would be lost if there was any delay as a result of orders being made bringing parts of the Housing Act 1980 into operation. I need not pursue exactly how that could operate. No orders have yet been made and it is unlikely that they will be made until the end of November. But it clearly was a factor which he was entitled to take into consideration if and in so far as he had a discretion in the matter.

The rent officer adhered to his view that he would not register the rent, but he did proceed to hear argument on what should be the level of rent which would be fixed if and when he was prepared to register it.

The facts end with a letter from the rent officer to the tenants' representative simply saying:

'Following the meetings held at this office on the 28th July and 12th August last, from the information made available to me and in view of the fact that application has been made to the Court for a Declaration I am adjourning this case pending the decision of the Court. No doubt you will let me know the outcome.'

In my judgment, it is the duty of a rent officer to consider what his jurisdiction is in a cases in which he has an application which depends on a disputed question whether the particular contractual arrangement between landlord and tenant or landlord and licensee is or is not a protected tenancy. He has to consider it but he cannot determine it. He has no jurisdiction to determine it on a final and binding basis, subject to appeal as between the parties. His jurisdiction is like that of an arbitrator. It stems from an assumption, namely, in the case of an arbitrator there is an agreement to refer; in the case of a rent officer determining a fair rent on an assumption that there is a protected tenancy.

b Somebody else has to decide whether that assumption is valid, if the matter is to be determined in a final and binding way. But this is very far from meaning of course that every case where there is a doubt is to be referred to the courts. The duty of the rent officer, I think it is clear from such cases as *Noel's* case, to which I have referred, and *R v Fulham, Hammersmith and Kensington Rent Tribunal, ex parte Zerek* [1951] 1 All ER 482, [1951] 2 KB 1, which is referred to in *Noel's* case, is to inquire as to the facts. If he is

c satisfied that there is not a protected tenancy he has no problem. He just does not proceed further until it has been determined by a court of competent jurisdiction that there is a protected tenancy. If he is satisfied that there is a protected tenancy (and, note, I say 'satisfied' and not 'decided' because he has no jurisdiction to decide), in my judgment, he must proceed. It is only if he is in doubt whether there is or is not a protected tenancy that he has a discretion whether to proceed or not to proceed. That is putting the

d position, I accept, in somewhat black and white terms, and his discretion might extend to not proceeding in a case in which he is certain or virtually certain in his own mind that there is a protected tenancy, but within 24 hours he knows it is going to be decided by a court of competent jurisdiction. I would not dissent from the view that in that highly unusual and marginal case he may have a discretion to postpone deciding the matter for 48 hours to get just beyond the decision. But the broad position, as I see it, is that he is

e obliged to proceed if he is satisfied.

What is unusual about this case is that the rent officer was satisfied. He expressed himself as being satisfied that this was a protected tenancy. He remained satisfied at all times and it is not possible to attack his satisfaction, as it was possible in *Noel's* case. There it was said that the rent officer could not be satisfied because he did not have any evidence on which to be satisfied. There was evidence in this case and he was satisfied. Let me

f make it clear in order that nobody should be influenced by anything that I say that he may have been wholly wrong in being so satisfied. That is a matter which the county court judge will have to determine eventually, but he was satisfied and, being satisfied, I think it was his duty to go ahead and register this rent. If he does not do so and there is any delay in the county court deciding the matter, it looks as if these applicants will suffer a real diminution in their rights. But quite apart from that, I think that was the

g rent officer's duty. Accordingly, I would let an order go requiring him to determine and to register whatever fair rent he determines.

FORBES J. I agree and I would only desire to add one short point because of a matter which arose in the course of argument. Of course in these cases the rent officer is often asked to determine a preliminary issue of fact: is this a protected tenancy or not? Such

h a determination is not conclusive, as Donaldson LJ has pointed out. The attitude which the rent officer ought to adopt is, I think, very shortly set out in the judgment of Slynn J in *Ex parte Noel* [1977] 1 All ER 356 at 361, [1978] QB 1 at 8 explaining the decision in *R v Rent Officer for the London Borough of Brent, ex parte Ganatra* [1976] 1 All ER 849, [1976] QB 576:

j 'What I understand Park J to have said was that, if the rent officer having gone into the matter found that he was in doubt whether there was jurisdiction so that he was not himself able to determine the matter, he should leave it so that the parties could take the matter to the county court if they so chose.'

Originally on behalf of the rent officer it was argued in this case that, although the rent officer initially decided on this preliminary issue that it was in fact a protected tenancy, he subsequently changed his mind, but this argument has now been abandoned. The argument now is that the rent officer was indeed satisfied that it was a protected tenancy but nevertheless decided it was inappropriate to proceed at once to determine to register the rent. In my judgment, he was wrong about that, as Donaldson LJ has said. However, during the course of the original discussion on the argument whether he had changed his mind, the effect of *Ex parte Noel* was said to be this: that the rent officer was precluded from deciding the question of whether it was a protected tenancy or not whenever the allegation was made that the tenancy documents were a sham; and in all those cases, so it was argued or said, he should always leave it to the county court. In my view, *Ex parte Noel* cannot be so read. It is clear to me that when one looks at the judgment of Slynn J what he started with was that the rent officer was entitled to conclude that there was a protected tenancy, but that in this particular case, *Ex parte Noel*, he went about it the wrong way. He attempted to decided that issue on submissions. Slynn J said ([1977] 1 All ER 356 at 363, [1978] QB 1 at 9–10):

> 'In my judgment it is quite impossible to resolve a matter of this kind merely on the basis of submissions made and arguments put before a rent officer by the solicitors for the parties. An allegation was made that the document was a cloak or a sham, that it was a device to avoid the effect of the Rent Acts. That is a matter which could only properly be dealt with by the hearing of oral evidence, and if required by subsequent cross-examination ... In my judgment the procedure which was adopted on this occasion is not at all satisfactory and the rent officer was not, because of the procedure adopted, in a position to come to a determination of this kind in the way that he did.'

As I say, I read that as simply an indication that in that particular case the rent officer went about it the wrong way because he attempted to deal with a question which involved fraud or something of that kind, at any rate that the document was a sham, not on oral evidence at all but on submissions by solicitors, and one could not determine a matter of that kind merely on such submissions. But where the rent officer goes into the matter and hears evidence, as he did in this case, and hears cross-examination of the applicants, it seems to me there is nothing in *Ex parte Noel* which prevents him, if he wishes, from determining that question, as indeed he did in this case. I agree with Donaldson LJ that the order should go in the way he has indicated.

Order of mandamus granted.

Solicitors: *Nicolas Madge* (for the applicants); *Treasury Solicitor*.

Jacqueline Charles   Barrister.

South Oxfordshire District Council v Secretary of State for the Environment

QUEEN'S BENCH DIVISION
WOOLF J
28th NOVEMBER, 5th DECEMBER 1980

Town and country planning – Permission for development – Material consideration – Time-expired permission – New application – Whether time-expired permission a material consideration to be taken into account – Town and Country Planning Act 1971, s 29(1).

In 1957 the applicants obtained permission from the local planning authority to build a bungalow on a site in a largely undeveloped part of the countryside. Under para 19[a] of Sch 24 to the Town and Country Planning Act 1971, planning permission granted before

---

[a] Paragraph 19, so far as material, is set out at p 956 *g h*, post

a 1st April 1969, if not implemented before the beginning of 1968, was deemed to have been granted subject to a condition that the development had to begin before 1st April 1974. By virtue of s 43(2)(b)[b] of the 1971 Act 'the digging of a trench which is to contain the foundations . . . of a building' amounted to the commencement of development. By 1st April 1974 the only construction on the site was the erection of a temporary builder's hut and the digging of some trenches. The applicants later applied to the planning authority for permission to erect two bungalows on the site, one of which was to be of

b the same design as that for which permission had been given in 1957 and the other of a different design. The planning authority refused permission and served an enforcement notice requiring the removal of the builder's hut. The applicants appealed to the Secretary of State, who appointed an inspector to inquire into the matter. The inspector, believing the 1957 planning permission still to be valid, recommended that planning permission be granted for the two new bungalows, but indicated that he would not have

c done so but for the existence of the 1957 planning permission. The Secretary of State found that no development relating to the 1957 planning permission had been begun before 1st April 1974 because the trenches did not amount to the commencement of development within s 43(2)(b) since they were in fact intended not for the bungalow for which permission had been given but for a different bungalow utilising the trenches already dug, and that therefore the 1957 planning permission had lapsed. The Secretary

d of State nonetheless regarded the 1957 planning permission as a 'vitally material consideration' to be taken into account under s 29(1)[c] of the 1971 Act when deciding whether fresh planning permission should be granted. He agreed with the inspector that planning permission should be given for the two new bungalows and allowed the appeals. The planning authority appealed, contending that, where a development had not been commenced before the time limit expired, on a fresh application the earlier

e planning permission was not a relevant consideration to be taken into account under s 29(1).

Held – When considering a fresh application for planning permission, a planning authority was not bound by a previous planning permission which had expired, but it was not obliged to disregard the pre-existing permission entirely since the pre-existing permission might still be a relevant or material consideration, but if so it was to be taken

f into account properly and not given more weight than was appropriate. Although the Secretary of State's decision in relation to the trenches was a perfectly proper decision because the trenches were not intended for the house for which permission had been given, on the facts, the Secretary of State had erred in regarding the 1957 planning permission as a 'vitally material consideration' and in all the circumstances his decision to allow the appeals would be quashed as being wrong in law (see p 957 *j* to p 958 *b* and

g p 960 *c* to *h*, post).

Peak Park Joint Planning Board v Secretary of State for the Environment [1979] JPL 618 considered.

Spackman v Secretary of State for the Environment [1977] 1 All ER 257 distinguished.

Notes

h For planning permission relating to development, see 37 Halsbury's Laws (3rd Edn) 269, para 370, for authorised development, see ibid 278–279, paras 377–378, and for cases on the subjects, see 45 Digest (Repl) 325–327, 335–340, 6–12, 33–55.

For the Town and Country Planning Act 1971, ss 29, 43, Sch 24, para 19, see 41 Halsbury's Statutes (3rd Edn) 1619, 1636, 1992.

j *b* Section 43, so far as material, provides:
  '(1) For the purposes of sections 41 and 42 of this Act, development shall be taken to be begun on the earliest date on which any specified operation comprised in the development begins to be carried out.
  '(2) In subsection (1) of this section "specified operation" means . . . (b) the digging of a trench which is to contain the foundations, or part of the foundations, of a building . . .'
  c Section 29(1), so far as material, is set out at p 957 *a*, post

Cases referred to in judgment

Peak Park Joint Planning Board v Secretary of State for the Environment [1979] JPL 618.

Pyx Granite Co Ltd v Minister of Housing and Local Government [1959] 3 All ER 1, [1960] AC 260, [1959] 3 WLR 346, 123 JP 429, 58 LGR 1, 10 P & CR 319, HL, 45 Digest (Repl) 336, 37.

Spackman v Secretary of State for the Environment [1977] 1 All ER 257, 33 P & CR 430, Digest (Cont Vol E) 595, 55f(i).

Appeal

By a notice of motion dated 26th January 1979, South Oxfordshire District Council ('the planning authority') applied under s 245 of the Town and Country Planning Act 1971 for an order to quash planning permissions granted on 18th December 1978 by the respondent, the Secretary of State for the Environment, to the applicants, Faherty Brothers Ltd, pursuant to s 36 of the 1971 Act, for the erection of a bungalow, and the planning permission granted pursuant to s 88(5)(a) of the 1971 Act for the temporary retention of a building which was the subject of an enforcement notice. The facts are set out in the judgment.

David Latham for the planning authority.
Simon D Brown for the Secretary of State.
R M K Gray for the applicants.

Cur adv vult

5th December. **WOOLF J** read the following judgment: In this application under s 245 of the Town and Country Planning Act 1971, the appellants, who are the planning authority for South Oxfordshire, are seeking to quash the decision of the Secretary of State contained in a letter dated 18th December 1978, in which, in respect of three appeals, the Secretary of State decided to quash an enforcement notice which the planning authority had served on the applicants, and to grant conditional planning permission for the retention of the building which was the subject matter of the enforcement notice, and to allow the applicants' two appeals against the refusal of the planning authority to grant them planning permission.

There is one point of planning law of general application raised, on which both the planning authority and the Secretary of State indicate they would welcome guidance.

The point arises out of the provisions which are now contained in Sch 24 to the Town and Country Planning Act 1971. Paragraph 19 of that schedule provides:

'. . . every planning permission granted or deemed to have been granted before 1st April 1969 shall [subject to exceptions which are not relevant here] if the development to which it relates had not been begun before the beginning of 1968, be deemed to have been granted subject to a condition that the development must be begun not later than the expiration of five years beginning with 1st April 1969.'

The effect of that provision is that unless the development is begun before 1st April 1974 the planning permission can no longer be relied on as permitting the development to which it referred. It re-enacts, as a transitional provision, the time limit as to the validity of planning permissions first introduced by the 1968 Act. Similar provisions dealing with planning permissions granted under the Town and Country Planning Act 1971 are contained in s 41 to s 44 of that Act. In particular s 43 defines when a development is to be taken to be begun for the purpose of s 41 and s 42 and para 19 of Sch 24.

On behalf of the planning authority it is contended that where development is not commenced before the time limit expires, on a fresh planning application the earlier planning permission is no longer a relevant consideration which it is permissible to take into account in deciding whether or not to grant the fresh application.

In deciding whether or not to grant planning permission, the planning authority is
a required by s 29(1) of the 1971 Act to 'have regard to the provisions of the development
plan . . . and to any other material considerations', and it is submitted that a time-expired
planning permission cannot be a material consideration. In support of this submission
counsel for the planning authority relies on the only previous relevant authority which
is *Peak Park Joint Planning Board v Secretary of State for the Environment* (27th April 1977).
a report of which appears in the Journal of Planning Law ([1979] JPL 618), and the
b transcript of which is before me. The judgment is that of Sir Douglas Frank whose
opinion as to planning matters I treat with very great respect because of his unrivalled
experience. In that case Sir Douglas was dealing with a decision by an inspector on behalf
of the Secretary of State in which the inspector, in dealing with an appeal against the
refusal of planning permission, purported to apply circular 17/69 of the Minister of
Housing and Local Government in deciding an application for planning permission
c where there was a previous time-expired permission. The circular dealt with the position
where applications are made to, in effect, renew planning permissions before they
became time-expired and stated:

> 'As a general rule such applications should be refused only where (a) there has
> been some material change of planning circumstances since the permission was
> granted, eg a change in planning policy for the area or in the relevant highway
d > considerations, (b) continued failure to begin the development will contribute
> unacceptably to the uncertainty about the future pattern of development, or (c) the
> application is premature because the permission still has a reasonable time to run.'

As Sir Douglas rightly pointed out, the reliance on the circular was, on the facts of that
case, misconceived because, unlike the circular, it did not concern a planning permission
e which was not time-expired. Sir Douglas did, however, go on to say:

> 'Of course nobody I would have thought would dispute that the existing planning
> permission is something which has to be taken into account. But the whole purpose
> of the amendment to the law introduced by s 38 of the 1968 Act, now ss 41 and 42
> of the 1971 Act, is to as it were remove stale longstanding planning permissions
f > from any consideration, to prevent them inhibiting the planning authority in their
> decision-making process. I therefore think that paragraph is not a planning policy
> consideration. If anything it is some form of administrative policy unrelated to
> planning, and if it is unrelated to planning questions, then following the well
> known principle enunciated in *Pyx Granite Co Ltd v Minister of Housing and Local
> Government* [1959] 3 All ER 1, [1960] AC 260 it is ultra vires. This view I find
g > supported by a reference to s 29 of the 1971 Act where it is provided that in dealing
> with a planning application the local planning authority shall have regard, so far as
> material to the application, to any other material considerations (that is other than
> the development plan). But as I have said the consideration must be material to
> planning, and I do not think that having regard to permissions which no longer
> have any effect is a planning consideration. And if the matter rested there on the
h > question of planning policy, then I would have had little hesitation in quashing the
> decision, but in my judgment it does not end there.'

The case Sir Douglas was dealing with was a special one because he dismissed the
appeal, taking the view that the inspector, on the way the appeal was argued before him,
had no alternative to dealing with the matter in the way in which he did. It may be,
therefore, that Sir Douglas did not intend his remarks to be regarded as having general
j effect. If they were intended to be of general effect, I am bound to say that I have
difficulty in agreeing with the views expressed.
The effect of the changes made by the 1968 Act, now embodied in ss 41 and 42 of the
1971 Act, is to get rid of out of date permissions and to allow a planning authority, if it
wants to do so, to prevent development by refusing permission in respect of development
for which permission previously existed. A planning authority is thus in no way bound

by a previous planning permission which has expired. However, the fact that it is in no way bound, does not mean that it is forced wholly to disregard that pre-existing *a* permission. That there was a pre-existing permission may still be a relevant or material circumstance which a planning authority is permitted to take into account, though it must do so properly and, as it is unlikely to be of great moment, not give it more weight than appropriate. For example, it is not unreasonable for a planning authority to want to be consistent in its consideration of planning applications, and taking into account a planning permission which has expired and considering whether there has been any *b* change of circumstances on a fresh application may assist in achieving consistency. I would regard a planning permission which has expired as still being part of the planning history of the site. In my view, it is not without significance that the planning authority can impose a special time limit which will then override the time limit provided for by the Act. If it does so, by the time a fresh application is made there could have been a change of circumstances which made the special time limit inappropriate. In such *c* circumstances a developer should be entitled to ask the planning authority to take into account on a fresh application the fact that if the original planning authority had known that that would prove to be the position, that time limit would not have been imposed and the fresh application would not have been necessary. If it could be relevant to have regard to a planning permission which has expired because of a special time limit, it should be permissible in the appropriate circumstances to have regard to planning *d* permission which has expired because of a statutory time limit.

Before leaving the *Peak Park* case, it is right that I should say that I see no reason why the general policy set out in the circular should be regarded as ultra vires and I would therefore reserve the question whether or not the criticism of that policy set out in the *Peak Park* case is justified.

It follows that I do not accept the planning authority's general contention as to the law. *e*
This, however, is not sufficient to dispose of the application. It is necessary to consider the specific decision of the Secretary of State on the facts of this case.

The enforcement notice related to a temporary builder's hut which the applicants justified solely on the ground that it was needed for the erection of a bungalow which was the subject of a planning permission granted on 8th February 1957. If that planning permission was still valid, then the enforcement notice would have to be quashed *f* because the hut would be permitted development under class 4 of Sch 1 to the Town and Country Planning General Development Order 1977, SI 1977 No 289. It was therefore necessary for the Secretary of State to decide whether as a matter of fact the development in respect of which the permission had been granted on 8th February 1957 had been begun before the end of March 1974. The applicants contended that it had been so begun because trenches had been dug which fulfilled the requirements of s 43(1) and *g* (2)(*b*) of the 1971 Act. While trenches had been dug, they had unfortunately not been for the bungalow to which the planning permission related but for a different bungalow which had been designed so that 'it is possible to re-orientate the trenches actually dug so that one wall more or less coincides with where the corresponding wall of the 1957 bungalow ought to be'. The Secretary of State did not consider this was sufficient for the provisions of s 43. He accordingly decided that the planning permission had expired on *h* 1st April 1974.

The Secretary of State went on to consider the two appeals from the decision of the planning authority to refuse permission for bungalows on the same site, and the deemed planning application for permission to retain the building which is the subject of the enforcement notice. One of the bungalows which was the subject of the appeal was of the same design as the bungalow which had been the subject matter of the earlier *j* planning permission. The other differed.

In his decision letter the Secretary of State quoted what the Inspector had concluded with regard to the planning merits of the s 36 appeals, which was as follows:

'On the planning merit of Section 36 appeals the inspector has concluded: "Turning to the Section 36 appeals, this is an area of largely undeveloped country, well away from any recognisable settlement. Although visually a bungalow here would not be unduly prominent; and when seen from any distance to the south would probably be dominated by the bigger house (Hadden House) standing above and to the north of it, it would certainly intensify such residential development as there is. Forgetting, temporarily, the history of the site it would be difficult to distinguish a dwelling here from other dwellings nearby which other people might apply to build. It could lead to other applications which could not justly be resisted. However, I conclude that there is already a valid planning permission on the site, and it would therefore be inconsistent to reject the first Section 36 appeal because the bungalow concerned is identical with the one for which I consider permission exists. But since this bungalow is in my view banal and unsuitable, every encouragement to build a more suitable dwelling should be given. The bungalow in the second Section 36 appeal is, I consider, a major improvement on that for which permission exists. I consider, therefore, that both appeals should be allowed." He recommended that permission should be granted.'

He then went on:

'10. These conclusions are not accepted insofar as they relate to the validity of the planning permission which had already been given on the site in 1957. It is noted that the 1957 conditional planning permission was granted by the former Wallingford Rural District Council acting on behalf of the former Berkshire County Council. It is further noted that following local government re-organisation measures of 1974 the present council took over the administration of planning functions in the former rural district area and adopted the policies of the former council. An application for a design of dwelling different from that approved in the 1957 permission was still outstanding and was not determined by the new council until the changeover date for the new council which coincided with the expiry date for planning permissions granted before the passing of the 1968 Act. The development plan for the area had not changed since the 1957 permission and at the time of these applications remained in force for the area as did some of the planning policies of the former local planning authorities which were taken over by the new council in 1974. The character of the area too remains what it was for many years, that is predominantly rural and agricultural with the bulk of Hadden House standing on higher ground above the appeal site when viewed from the south. Taking into account the history of the case which is considered to be a vitally material consideration in this instance and bearing in mind that the character of the area has not changed in the intervening years since 1957, the Inspector's conclusion that the bungalows "would not be unduly prominent when seen from any distance to the south and would probably be dominated by the bigger house (Hadden House) standing above and to the north of it" is accepted. In the special circumstances of this case the view is taken, in agreement with the Inspector that planning permission should be granted on these appeals.

'11. The Inspector's remarks on the design and the council's remarks recorded in the report about their preference for the "second" design of bungalow is however drawn to your client's attention.'

The first thing which is to be noted about the Secretary of State's decision is that he has granted a planning permission for a bungalow, the design of which the inspector concluded was 'banal and unsuitable'. It is understandable that the inspector should have recommended that permission should be granted for that bungalow because he took the view that there was already an existing planning permission for such a bungalow so there would not be any adverse effect in granting further permission. However, the Secretary of State had already concluded there was no longer an existing planning permission and therefore there was not that justification for granting planning permission in what was largely undeveloped countryside. As the Secretary of State apparently did not disagree with the inspector's view of the design of that bungalow, and as the applicants would have been quite content with planning permission for the second bungalow, I am bound to say that I am at a loss to understand why planning permission for a building of the original bungalow design was granted. Counsel for the Secretary of State, with his usual candour, confessed that he was equally surprised. It does suggest that there was some error in reasoning by the person responsible for making the decision of the Secretary of State in this case.

I also find it difficult to understand the reference that the decision should be granted on the appeals in agreement with the view taken by the inspector. It is true that the inspector did recommend that planning permission should be granted but it is reasonably clear that he only did so because of his erroneous conclusion that the original permission was still in existence. The reference by the inspector to largely undeveloped country and intensification of residential development and other applications seems clearly to indicate that the inspector was adverse to the granting of planning permission but for the pre-existing permission which he regarded as still valid.

Next it is to be noted that the Secretary of State says that the history is 'a vitally material consideration'. The reference to history must be because of the expired planning permission; as I have indicated such an expired planning permission can be a relevant consideration but I find it very difficult to see how it could ever be regarded in the context of this case as being 'a vitally material consideration'. While the weight to be given to a particular consideration is for the Secretary of State such a conclusion indicates that either the person responsible for making the decision on behalf of the Secretary of State misdirected himself, or he was acting perversely. In either event his decision was wrong in law. It is therefore not necessary for me to decide which is the appropriate label to apply. I suspect, however, that the person responsible for the decision has failed to appreciate the distinction between a situation where there is an existing planning permission which is still valid, and the position where there was a former planning permission which is no longer valid because it became time expired. I say this because the very words 'vitally material consideration' appear in *Spackman v Secretary of State for the Environment* [1977] 1 All ER 257 at 261 per Willis J. In *Spackman* it was a previous planning permission which was still in existence, which Willis J regarded as a 'vitally material consideration'.

I was referred to *Spackman's* case by counsel for the applicants because I was asked on behalf of the applicants if the matter was going back to the Secretary of State to indicate the Secretary of State's approach to the question of the trenches was wrong, bearing in mind that decision. I do not, I am afraid, agree. As far as the trenches are concerned, it seems to me that the Secretary of State's decision was a perfectly proper one, and, indeed, probably the only possible one, bearing in mind the facts of this case. *Spackman's* case is quite different because the trenches which were dug in the wrong position were intended for the house for which permission had been given, and not a property of different design.

It follows that I quash the Secretary of State's decision to grant planning permission for both bungalows and also quash his decision to grant permission for the retention of the hut.

Decision of the Secretary of State quashed.

Solicitors: *Sherwood & Co* (for the appellants); *Treasury Solicitor*; *Francis & Parkes*, Reading (for the second respondents).

K Mydeen Esq   Barrister.

R v Caldwell

HOUSE OF LORDS

LORD WILBERFORCE, LORD DIPLOCK, LORD EDMUND-DAVIES, LORD KEITH OF KINKEL AND LORD ROSKILL

10th, 11th DECEMBER 1980, 19th MARCH 1981

Criminal law – Damage to property – Recklessness whether property would be destroyed or damaged – Recklessness – Whether defence of drunkenness available – Criminal Damage Act 1971, s 1(1).

Criminal law – Damage to property – Damage to property with intent to endanger life or being reckless whether life would be endangered – Reckless – Whether defence of drunkenness available – Criminal Damage Act 1971, s 1(2).

The respondent had done some work for the owner of a hotel as the result of which he had a quarrel with the owner, got drunk and set fire to the hotel in revenge. The fire was discovered and put out before any serious damage was caused and none of the ten guests in the hotel at the time was injured. The respondent was indicted on two counts of arson under s 1(1) and (2)[a] of the Criminal Damage Act 1971. At his trial he pleaded guilty to the lesser charge of intentionally or recklessly destroying or damaging the property of another, contrary to s 1(1), but pleaded not guilty to the more serious charge under s 1(2) of damaging property with intent to endanger life or being reckless whether life would be endangered. He claimed that he was so drunk at the time that the thought that he might be endangering the lives of the people in the hotel had never crossed his mind. The trial judge directed the jury that drunkenness was not a defence to a charge under s 1(2) and he was convicted. On appeal, the Court of Appeal allowed the appeal on the ground that the mental element of intention or recklessness in regard to endangering life referred to in s 1(2)(b) was a matter of specific intent going beyond the actus reus and therefore had to be established as a separate ingredient of the offence, and drunkenness could accordingly be a good defence. The Crown appealed to the House of Lords.

Held (Lord Wilberforce and Lord Edmund-Davies dissenting on the reasoning)—When used in a criminal statute such as the 1971 Act the term 'reckless' was used not as a term of legal art but in the popular or dictionary sense of meaning 'careless, regardless or heedless of the possible harmful consequences of one's acts'. As such the term encompassed both a decision to ignore a risk of harmful consequences flowing from an act which the accused had recognised as existing and also a failure to give any thought to whether there was any risk in circumstances where, if any thought were given to the matter, it would be obvious that there was. Accordingly, the restricted form of recklessness which formed an ingredient of crimes of malice and subjective or objective tests of recklessness were not relevant to determining the issue of recklessness under the 1971 Act. Thus a person was guilty of recklessly destroying or damaging property belonging to another, contrary to s 1(1) of the 1971 Act, if (a) he committed an act which created an obvious risk that property would be destroyed or damaged and (b) when he committed the act he either gave no thought to the possibility of there being any such risk or, having recognised that there was some risk involved, he nevertheless had gone on to commit the act. And a person was guilty of recklessly endangering the life of another by intentionally or recklessly destroying or damaging property, contrary to s 1(2), if (a) what he did amounted to an offence under s 1(1), either because he actually intended to destroy or damage the property or was reckless (in the sense described above) whether it might be destroyed or damaged and (b) he was reckless (in a similar sense) whether the

---

a   Section 1 is set out at p 863 e f, post

life of another might be endangered. It followed, therefore, that, where a person was accused of an offence under s 1 of the 1971 Act and the charge was framed so as to charge *a* the person only with intending to destroy or damage the property of another under s 1(1) or intending by the destruction or damage of property to endanger the life of another under s 1(2), evidence of self-induced intoxication could be relevant to the accused's defence; but, where the charge was, or included, a reference to the accused's being reckless whether property belonging to another would be destroyed or damaged under s 1(1) or being reckless whether the life of another would be endangered by the *b* destruction or damage of property under s 1(2), evidence of self-induced intoxication was irrelevant. Accordingly, it was irrelevant that the respondent had failed to give any thought to the risk of endangering the lives of residents in the hotel because of his self-induced intoxication. Since, however, it made no practical difference to the respondent whether the appeal were dismissed or not, the appeal would be dismissed (Lord Wilberforce and Lord Edmund-Davies concurring in dismissing the appeal because they *c* agreed with the Court of Appeal) (see p 963 *b c*, p 964 *a* to *c*, p 966 *e f*, p 967 *a b* and *j* to p 968 *e*, p 972 *b* and *g* and p 973 *c* to *e*, post).

Director of Public Prosecutions v Majewski [1976] 2 All ER 142 applied.

R v Briggs [1977] 1 All ER 475, *R v Parker* [1977] 2 All ER 37, *R v Stephenson* [1979] 2 All ER 1198 and *R v Orpin* [1980] 2 All ER 321 overruled.

d

Notes
For the offence of destroying or damaging property, see 11 Halsbury's Laws (4th Edn) para 1306, and for cases on the subject, see 15 Digest (Reissue) 1439–1440, 12,690–12,693.

For the Criminal Damage Act 1971, s 1, see 41 Halsbury's Statutes (3rd Edn) 409.

e

Cases referred to in opinions
Director of Public Prosecutions v Majewski [1976] 2 All ER 142, [1977] AC 443, [1976] 2 WLR 623, 140 JP 315, 62 Cr App R 262, HL; *affg* [1975] 3 All ER 296, [1977] AC 443, [1975] 3 WLR 401, 139 JP 760, 62 Cr App R 5, CA, 14(1) Digest (Reissue) 54, 258.
Lederer v Hitchins [1961] WAR 99.
R v Briggs [1977] 1 All ER 475, [1977] 1 WLR 605, 63 Cr App R 215, CA, 15 Digest *f* (Reissue) 440, 12,691.
R v Cunningham [1957] 2 All ER 412, [1957] 2 QB 396, [1957] 3 WLR 76, 121 JP 451, 41 Cr App R 155, CCA, 15 Digest (Reissue) 1198, 10,292.
R v O'Driscoll (1977) 65 Cr App R 50, CA, Digest (Cont Vol E) 126, 251a.
R v Orpin [1980] 2 All ER 321, [1980] 1 WLR 1050, 70 Cr App R 306, CA.
R v Parker [1977] 2 All ER 37, [1977] 1 WLR 600, 63 Cr App R 211, CA, 15 Digest *g* (Reissue) 1440, 12,692.
R v Stephenson [1979] 2 All ER 1198, [1979] QB 695, [1979] 3 WLR 193, 143 JP 592, 69 Cr App R 213, CA, Digest (Cont Vol E) 161, 12,692a.
R v Venna [1975] 3 All ER 788, [1976] QB 421, [1975] 3 WLR 737, 140 JP 31, 61 Cr App R 310, CA, 15 Digest (Reissue) 1175, 9993.

h

Appeal
On 24th May 1979 the respondent, James Caldwell, was convicted at the Central Criminal Court before Miss Recorder Southworth QC and a jury, on two counts of arson, namely without lawful excuse damaging the property of another intending to damage it or being reckless whether it would be damaged and intending to endanger the life of another or being reckless whether the life of another would be endangered, contrary to *j* s 1(2) of the Criminal Damage Act 1971 (count 1) and without lawful excuse damaging property of another intending to damage it or being reckless whether it would be damaged, contrary to s 1(1) of the 1971 Act (count 2). He was sentenced to three years' imprisonment on count 1, no sentence being passed on count 2. He appealed to the Court of Appeal, Criminal Division (Lord Widgery CJ, Eveleigh LJ and O'Connor J), which allowed his appeal on count 1 on 31st March 1980 and quashed his conviction on

that count but imposed a sentence of three years' imprisonment on count 2. The court
a refused an application by the Crown for leave to appeal to the House of Lords but
certified, under s 33(2) of the Criminal Appeal Act 1968, that the following point of law
of general public importance was involved in its decision: whether evidence of self-
induced intoxication could be relevant to (i) whether the defendant intended to endanger
the life of another and (ii) whether the defendant was reckless whether the life of another
would be endangered within the meaning of s 1(2)(b) of the 1971 Act. On 3rd July the
b House of Lords gave the Crown leave to appeal. The facts are set out in the opinion of
Lord Diplock.

Neil Denison QC and *Kay Blundell-Jones* for the Crown.
Martin Thomas QC and *David Thomas* for the respondent.

c Their Lordships took time for consideration.

19th March. The following opinions were delivered.

LORD WILBERFORCE. My Lords, I would dismiss the appeal and answer the
certified questions as suggested by my noble and learned friend Lord Edmund-Davies.

d
LORD DIPLOCK. My Lords, the facts that gave rise to this appeal are simple. The
respondent had been doing work for the proprietor of a residential hotel. He considered
that he had a grievance against the proprietor. One night he got very drunk and in the
early hours of the morning he decided to revenge himself on the proprietor by setting
fire to the hotel, in which some ten guests were living at the time. He broke a window
e and succeeded in starting a fire in a ground room floor; but fortunately it was discovered
and the flames were extinguished before any serious damage was caused. At his trial he
said that he was so drunk at the time that the thought that there might be people in the
hotel whose lives might be endangered if it were set on fire had never crossed his mind.
    He was indicted at the Central Criminal Court on two counts of arson under s 1(1) and
(2) respectively of the Criminal Damage Act 1971. That section reads as follows:

f   '(1) A person who without lawful excuse destroys or damages any property
        belonging to another intending to destroy or damage any such property or being
        reckless as to whether any such property would be destroyed or damaged shall be
        guilty of an offence.
        '(2) A person who without lawful excuse destroys or damages any property,
        whether belonging to himself or another—(a) intending to destroy or damage any
g   property or being reckless as to whether any property would be destroyed or
        damaged; and (b) intending by the destruction or damage to endanger the life of
        another or being reckless as to whether the life of another would be thereby
        endangered; shall be guilty of an offence.
        '(3) An offence committed under this section by destroying or damaging property
        by fire shall be charged as arson.'

h
    Count 1 contained the charge of the more serious offence under s 1(2) which requires
intent to endanger the life of another or recklessness whether the life of another would
be endangered. To this count the respondent pleaded not guilty. He relied on his self-
induced drunkenness as a defence on the ground that the offence under sub-s (2) was one
of 'specific intent' in the sense in which that expression was used in speeches in this
j House in *Director of Public Prosecutions v Majewski* [1976] 2 All ER 142, [1977] AC 443.
Count 2 contained the lesser offence under s 1(1) to which the respondent pleaded guilty.
    The recorder directed the jury that self-induced drunkenness was not a defence to
count 1, and the jury convicted him on this count. The recorder sentenced him to three
years' imprisonment on count 1 but passed no sentence on count 2, the lesser offence, to
which he had pleaded guilty. On appeal the Court of Appeal held that her direction to
the jury as to the effect of self-induced drunkenness on the charge in count 1 was

wrong. They set aside the conviction on that count; but left the sentence of three years' imprisonment unchanged as they considered it to be an appropriate sentence on count 2. So it was only a Pyrrhic victory for the respondent; but it left the law on criminal damage and drunkenness in a state of some confusion.

The question of law certified for the opinion of this House was:

> 'Whether evidence of self-induced intoxication can be relevant to the following questions—(a) Whether the defendant intended to endanger the life of another; and (b) Whether the defendant was reckless as to whether the life of another would be endangered, within the meaning of Section 1(2)(b) of the Criminal Damage Act 1971.'

The question recognises that under s 1(2)(b) there are two alternative states of mind as respects endangering the life of another, and that the existence of either of them on the part of the accused is sufficient to constitute the mens rea needed to convert the lesser offence under s 1(1) into the graver offence under s 1(2). One is intention that a particular thing should happen in consequence of the actus reus, viz that the life of another person should be endangered (this was not relied on by the Crown in the instant case). The other is recklessness whether that particular thing should happen or not. The same dichotomy of mentes reae, intention and recklessness, is to be found throughout the section: in sub-s (1) and para (a) of sub-s (2) as well as in para (b); and 'reckless' as descriptive of a state of mind must be given the same meaning in each of them.

My Lords, the Criminal Damage Act 1971 replaced almost in their entirety the many and detailed provisions of the Malicious Damage Act 1861. Its purpose, as stated in its long title was to *revise* the law of England and Wales as to offences of damage to property. As the brevity of the Act suggests, it must have been hoped that it would also simplify the law.

In the 1861 Act, the word consistently used to describe the mens rea that was a necessary element in the multifarious offences that the Act created was 'maliciously', a technical expression, not readily intelligible to juries, which became the subject of considerable judicial exegesis. This culminated in a judgment of the Court of Criminal Appeal in *R v Cunningham* [1957] 2 All ER 412 at 414, [1957] 2 QB 396 at 399 which approved, as an accurate statement of the law, what had been said by Professor Kenny in his Outlines of Criminal Law (1st Edn, 1902):

> '. . . in any statutory definition of a crime "malice" must be taken . . . as requiring either (i) an actual intention to do the particular *kind* of harm that in fact was done, or (ii) recklessness as to whether such harm should occur or not (i.e. the accused has foreseen that the particular kind of harm might be done, and yet has gone on to take the risk of it) . . .'

My Lords, in this passage Professor Kenny was engaged in defining for the benefit of students the meaning of 'malice' as a term of art in criminal law. To do so he used ordinary English words in their popular meaning. Among the words he used was 'recklessness', the noun derived from the adjective 'reckless', of which the popular or dictionary meaning is 'careless, regardless, or heedless of the possible harmful consequences of one's acts'. It presupposes that, if thought were given to the matter by the doer before the act was done, it would have been apparent to him that there was a real risk of its having the relevant harmful consequences; but, granted this, recklessness covers a whole range of states of mind from failing to give any thought at all to whether or not there is any risk of those harmful consequences, to recognising the existence of the risk and nevertheless deciding to ignore it. Conscious of this imprecision in the popular meaning of recklessness as descriptive of a state of mind, Professor Kenny, in the passage quoted, was, as it seems to me, at pains to indicate by the words in brackets the particular species within the genus, reckless states of mind, that constituted 'malice' in criminal law. This parenthetical restriction on the natural meaning of recklessness was necessary to an explanation of the meaning of the adverb 'maliciously' when used as a term of art in the description of an offence under the Malicious Damage Act 1861 (which was the

matter in point in *R v Cunningham*); but it was not directed to and consequently has no
a bearing on the meaning of the adjective 'reckless' in s 1 of the Criminal Damage Act
1971. To use it for that purpose can, in my view, only be misleading.

My Lords, the restricted meaning that the Court of Appeal in *R v Cunningham* had
placed on the adverb 'maliciously' in the Malicious Damage Act 1861 in cases where the
prosecution did not rely on an actual intention of the accused to cause the damage that
was in fact done called for a meticulous analysis by the jury of the thoughts that passed
b through the mind of the accused at or before the time he did the act that caused the
damage, in order to see on which side of a narrow dividing line they fell. If it had crossed
his mind that there was a risk that someone's property might be damaged but, because
his mind was affected by rage or excitement or confused by drink, he did not appreciate
the seriousness of the risk or trusted that good luck would prevent its happening, this
state of mind would amount to malice in the restricted meaning placed on that term by
c the Court of Appeal; whereas if, for any of these reasons, he did not even trouble to give
his mind to the question whether there was any risk of damaging the property, this state
of mind would not suffice to make him guilty of an offence under the Malicious Damage
Act 1861.

Neither state of mind seems to me to be less blameworthy than the other; but, if the
difference between the two constituted the distinction between what does and what does
d not in legal theory amount to a guilty state of mind for the purposes of a statutory
offence of damage to property, it would not be a practicable distinction for use in a trial
by jury. The only person who knows what the accused's mental processes were is the
accused himself, and probably not even he can recall them accurately when the rage or
excitement under which he acted has passed, or he has sobered up if he were under the
influence of drink at the relevant time. If the accused gives evidence that because of his
e rage, excitement or drunkenness the risk of particular harmful consequences of his acts
simply did not occur to him, a jury would find it hard to be satisfied beyond reasonable
doubt that his true mental process was not that, but was the slightly different mental
process required if one applies the restricted meaning of 'being reckless as to whether'
something would happen, adopted by the Court of Appeal in *R v Cunningham*.

My Lords, I can see no reason why Parliament when it decided to revise the law as to
f offences of damage to property should go out of its way to perpetuate fine and
impracticable distinctions such as these, between one mental state and another. One
would think that the sooner they were got rid of the better.

When cases under s 1(1) of the new Act, in which the Crown's case was based on the
accused having been 'reckless as to whether . . . property would be destroyed or damaged',
first came before the Court of Appeal, the question as to the meaning of the expression
g 'reckless' in the context of that subsection appears to have been treated as soluble simply
by posing and answering what had by then, unfortunately, become an obsessive question
among English lawyers: is the test of recklessness subjective or objective? The first two
reported cases, in both of which judgments were given off the cuff, are *R v Briggs* [1977]
1 All ER 475, [1977] 1 WLR 605 and *R v Parker* [1977] 2 All ER 37, [1977] 1 WLR
600. Both classified the test of recklessness as subjective. This led the court in *R v Briggs*
h [1977] 1 All ER 475 at 477–478, [1977] 1 WLR 605 at 608 to say: 'A man is reckless in
the sense required when he carries out a deliberate act knowing that there is some risk
of damage resulting from that act but nevertheless continues in the performance of that
act.' This leaves over the question whether the risk of damage may not be so slight that
even the most prudent of men would feel justified in taking it, but it excludes that kind
of recklessness that consists of acting without giving any thought at all to whether or not
j there is any risk of harmful consequences of one's act, even though the risk is great and
would be obvious if any thought were given to the matter by the doer of the act. *R v
Parker*, however, opened the door a chink by adding as an alternative to the actual
knowledge of the accused that there is some risk of damage resulting from his act and his
going on to take it, a mental state described as 'closing his mind to the obvious fact' that
there is such a risk (see [1977] 2 All ER 37 at 40, [1977] 1 WLR 600 at 604).

R v Stephenson [1979] 2 All ER 1198, [1979] QB 695, the first case in which there was

full argument, though only on one side, and a reserved judgment, slammed the door
again on any less restricted interpretation of 'reckless' whether particular consequences   *a*
will occur than that originally approved in *Briggs*. The appellant, a tramp, intending to
pass the night in a hollow in the side of a haystack, had lit a fire to keep himself warm;
as a result of this the stack itself caught fire. At his trial, he was not himself called as a
witness but a psychiatrist gave evidence on his behalf that he was schizophrenic and
might not have had the same ability to foresee or appreciate risk as a mentally normal
person. The judge had given to the jury the direction on the meaning of reckless that   *b*
had been approved in *R v Parker*. The argument for the appellant on the appeal was that
this let in an objective test whereas the test should be entirely subjective. It was
buttressed by copious citation from previous judgments in civil and criminal cases where
the expressions 'reckless' or 'recklessness' had been used by judges in various contexts.
Counsel for the Crown expressed his agreement with the submissions for the appellant.
The judgment of the court contains an analysis of a number of the cited cases, mainly in   *c*
the field of civil law. These cases do not disclose a uniform judicial use of the terms; and
as respects judicial statements made before the current vogue for classifying all tests of
legal liability as either objective or subjective they are not easily assignable to one of those
categories rather than the other. The court, however, reached its final conclusion by a
different route. It made the assumption that although Parliament in replacing the 1861
Act by the 1971 Act had discarded the word 'maliciously' as descriptive of the mens rea   *d*
of the offences of which the actus reus is damaging property, in favour of the more
explicit phrase 'intending to destroy or damage any such property or being reckless as to
whether any such property would be destroyed', it nevertheless intended the words to be
interpreted in precisely the same sense as that in which the single adverb 'maliciously'
had been construed by Professor Kenny in the passage that received the subsequent
approval of the Court of Appeal in *R v Cunningham*.   *e*

My Lords, I see no warrant for making any such assumption in an Act whose declared
purpose is to revise the then existing law as to offences of damage to property, not to
perpetuate it. 'Reckless' as used in the new statutory definition of the mens rea of these
offences is an ordinary English word. It had not by 1971 become a term of legal art with
some more limited esoteric meaning than that which it bore in ordinary speech, a
meaning which surely includes not only deciding to ignore a risk of harmful   *f*
consequences resulting from one's acts that one has recognised as existing, but also failing
to give any thought to whether or not there is any such risk in circumstances where, if
any thought were given to the matter, it would be obvious that there was.

If one is attaching labels, the latter state of mind is neither more nor less 'subjective'
than the first. But the label solves nothing. It is a statement of the obvious; mens rea is,
by definition, a state of mind of the accused himself at the time he did the physical act   *g*
that constitutes the actus reus of the offence; it cannot be the mental state of some non-
existent, hypothetical person.

Nevertheless, to decide whether someone has been 'reckless' whether harmful
consequences of a particular kind will result from his act, as distinguished from his
actually intending such harmful consequences to follow, does call for some consideration
of how the mind of the ordinary prudent individual would have reacted to a similar   *h*
situation. If there were nothing in the circumstances that ought to have drawn the
attention of an ordinary prudent individual to the possibility of that kind of harmful
consequence, the accused would not be described as 'reckless' in the natural meaning of
that word for failing to address his mind to the possibility; nor, if the risk of the harmful
consequences was so slight that the ordinary prudent individual on due consideration of
the risk would not be deterred from treating it as negligible, could the accused be   *j*
described as 'reckless' in its ordinary sense if, having considered the risk, he decided to
ignore it. (In this connection the gravity of the possible harmful consequences would be
an important factor. To endanger life must be one of the most grave.) So to this extent,
even if one ascribes to 'reckless' only the restricted meaning, adopted by the Court of
Appeal in *Stephenson* and *Briggs*, of foreseeing that a particular kind of harm might
happen and yet going on to take the risk of it, it involves a test that would be described

in part as 'objective' in current legal jargon. Questions of criminal liability are seldom
a solved by simply asking whether the test is subjective or objective.

In my opinion, a person charged with an offence under s 1(1) of the 1971 Act is
'reckless as to whether or not any property would be destroyed or damaged' if (1) he does
an act which in fact creates an obvious risk that property will be destroyed or damaged
and (2) when he does the act he either has not given any thought to the possibility of
there being any such risk or has recognised that there was some risk involved and has
b none the less gone on to do it. That would be a proper direction to the jury; cases in the
Court of Appeal which held otherwise should be regarded as overruled.

Where the charge is under s 1(2) the question of the state of mind of the accused must
be approached in stages, corresponding to paras (a) and (b). The jury must be satisfied
that what the accused did amounted to an offence under s 1(1), either because he actually
intended to destroy or damage the property or because he was reckless (in the sense that
c I have described) whether it might be destroyed or damaged. Only if they are so satisfied
must the jury go on to consider whether the accused also either actually intended that the
destruction or damage of the property should endanger someone's life or was reckless (in
a similar sense) whether a human life might be endangered.

Turning now to the instant case, the first stage was eliminated by the respondent's plea
of guilty to the charge under s 1(1). Furthermore he himself gave evidence that his
d actual intention was to damage the hotel in order to revenge himself on the proprietor.
As respects the charge under s 1(2) the prosecution did not rely on an actual intent of the
respondent to endanger the lives of the residents but relied on his having been reckless
whether the lives of any of them would be endangered. His act of setting fire to it was
one which the jury were entitled to think created an obvious risk that the lives of the
residents would be endangered; and the only defence with which your Lordships are
e concerned is that the respondent had made himself so drunk as to render him oblivious
of that risk. If the only mental state capable of constituting the necessary mens rea for
an offence under s 1(2) were that expressed in the words 'intending by the destruction or
damage to endanger the life of another', it would have been necessary to consider
whether the offence was to be classified as one of 'specific' intent for the purposes of the
rule of law which this House affirmed and applied in *Director of Public Prosecutions v*
f *Majewski* [1976] 2 All ER 142, [1977] AC 443; and this it plainly is. But this is not, in my
view, a relevant inquiry where 'being reckless as to whether the life of another would be
thereby endangered' is an alternative mental state that is capable of constituting the
necessary mens rea of the offence with which he is charged.

The speech of Lord Elwyn-Jones LC in *Majewski*, with which Lord Simon, Lord
Kilbrandon and I agreed, is authority that self-induced intoxication is no defence to a
g crime in which recklessness is enough to constitute the necessary mens rea (see [1976] 2
All ER 142 at 150–151, [1977] AC 443 at 474–475). The charge in *Majewski* was of
assault occasioning actual bodily harm and it was held by the majority of the House,
approving *R v Venna* [1975] 3 All ER 788 at 794, [1976] 1 QB 421 at 428, that recklessness
in the use of force was sufficient to satisfy the mental element in the offence of assault.
Reducing oneself by drink or drugs to a condition in which the restraints of reason and
h conscience are cast off was held to be a reckless course of conduct and an integral part of
the crime. Lord Elwyn-Jones LC accepted as correctly stating English law the provision
in § 2.08(2) of the American Model Penal Code:

> 'When recklessness establishes an element of the offence, if the actor, due to self-
> induced intoxication, is unaware of a risk of which he would have been aware had
> he been sober, such unawareness is immaterial.'
j

So, in the instant case, the fact that the respondent was unaware of the risk of
endangering the lives of residents in the hotel owing to his self-induced intoxication
would be no defence if that risk would have been obvious to him had he been sober.

My Lords, the Court of Appeal in the instant case regarded the case as turning on
whether the offence under s 1(2) was one of 'specific' intent or 'basic' intent. Following
a recent decision of the Court of Appeal by which it was bound, *R v Orpin* [1980] 2 All

ER 321, [1980] 1 WLR 1050, it held that the offence under s 1(2) was one of specific
intent in contrast to the offence under s 1(1) which was of basic intent. This would be *a*
right if the only mens rea capable of constituting the offence were an actual intention to
endanger the life of another. For the reasons I have given, however, classification into
offences of specific and basic intent is irrelevant where being reckless whether a particular
harmful consequence will result from one's act is a sufficient alternative mens rea.

My Lords, the recorder's summing up was not a model of clarity. Contrary to the
view of the Court of Appeal she was right in telling the jury that in deciding whether the *b*
respondent was reckless whether the lives of residents in the hotel would be endangered,
the fact that, because of his drunkenness, he failed to give any thought to that risk was
irrelevant; but there were other criticisms of the summing up made by the Court of
Appeal which your Lordships very properly have not been invited to consider, since it
makes no practical difference to the respondent whether the appeal is allowed or not.
Since it is not worth while spending time on going into these criticisms, I would dismiss *c*
the appeal.

I would give the following answers to the certified questions: (a) if the charge of an
offence under s 1(2) of the Criminal Damage Act 1971 is framed so as to charge the
defendant only with 'intending by the destruction or damage [of the property] to endanger
the life of another', evidence of self-induced intoxication can be relevant to his defence;
(b) if the charge is, or includes, a reference to his 'being reckless as to whether the life of *d*
another would thereby be endangered', evidence of self-induced intoxication is not
relevant.

LORD EDMUND-DAVIES. My Lords, I respectfully concur in holding that this
appeal must be dismissed. I nevertheless consider that one of the certified questions
should be answered in a manner contrary to that favoured by a majority of your   *e*
Lordships. And I believe that the reason for my arriving at a different conclusion is of
some importance and that it should be explored.

We are concerned with a charge of arson in contravention of s 1(2) of the Criminal
Damage Act 1971, which needs to be seen in its statutory setting. Section 1 is in the
following terms: *f*

'(1) A person who without lawful excuse destroys or damages any property
belonging to another intending to destroy or damage any such property or being
reckless as to whether any such property would be destroyed or damaged shall be
guilty of an offence.

'(2) A person who without lawful excuse destroys or damages any property,
whether belonging to himself or another—(a) intending to destroy or damage any   *g*
property or being reckless as to whether any property would be destroyed or
damaged; and (b) intending by the destruction or damage to endanger the life of
another or being reckless as to whether the life of another would be thereby
endangered; shall be guilty of an offence.

'(3) An offence committed under this section by destroying or damaging property
by fire shall be charged as arson.'   *h*

In considering the section, there are two matters of particular importance. (1) What
constitutes 'recklessness' in the criminal law? (2) What is the mens rea of the offence
commonly (and understandably) known as 'aggravated arson' in s 1(2)(b)? I turn to these
questions forthwith.

(1) Recklessness   *j*
The words 'intention' and 'recklessness' have increasingly displaced in statutory crimes
the word 'maliciously', which has frequently given rise to difficulty in interpretation. In
R v Cunningham [1957] 2 All ER 412 at 414, [1957] 2 QB 396 at 399 Byrne J in the Court
of Criminal Appeal cited with approval the following passage which has appeared in
Kenny's Outline of Criminal Law from its first edition in 1902 onwards:

a '... in any statutory definition of a crime "malice" must be taken not in the old vague sense of "wickedness" in general, but as requiring either (i) an actual intention to do the particular *kind* of harm that in fact was done, or (ii) recklessness as to whether such harm should occur or not (i.e. the accused has foreseen that the particular kind of harm might be done, and yet has gone on to take the risk of it). It is neither limited to, nor does it indeed require, any ill-will towards the person injured.'

b Byrne J's comment was laconic and unqualified: 'We think that this is an accurate statement of the law ... In our opinion, the word "maliciously" in a statutory crime postulates foresight of consequence.' My Lords, my noble and learned friend Lord Diplock somewhat dismissively describes Professor Kenny as having been 'engaged in defining for the benefit of students the meaning of "malice" as a term of art in criminal law', adding:

c   'To do so he used ordinary English words in their *popular* meaning. Among the words he used was "recklessness", the noun derived from the adjective "reckless", of which the popular or dictionary meaning is "careless, regardless, or heedless of the possible harmful consequences of one's acts". It presupposes that, *if* thought were given to the matter by the doer before the act was done, *it would have been apparent to him* that there was a real risk of its having the relevant harmful consequences
d   ... This parenthetical restriction on the natural meaning of recklessness was necessary to an explanation of the meaning of the adverb "maliciously" when used as a term of art in the description of an offence under the Malicious Damage Act 1861 (which was the matter in point in *R v Cunningham*); but it was not directed to and consequently has no bearing on the meaning of the adjective "reckless" in s 1 of
e   the Criminal Damage Act 1971.' (Emphasis added.)

I have to say that I am in respectful, but profound, disagreement. The law in action compiles its own dictionary. In time, what was originally the common coinage of speech acquires a different value in the pocket of the lawyer than when in the layman's purse. Professor Kenny used lawyers' words in a lawyers' sense to express his distillation of an important part of the established law relating to mens rea, and he did so in a manner
f accurate not only in respect of the law as it stood in 1902 but also as it has been applied in countless cases ever since, both in the United Kingdom and in other countries where the common law prevails: see, for example, in Western Australia, *Lederer v Hitchins* [1961] WAR 99, and, in the United States of America, Jethro Brown's General Principles of Criminal Law (2nd Edn, 1960, p 115). And it is well known that the 1971 Act was in the main the work of the Law Commission, who defined recklessness by saying:

g   'A person is reckless if, (a) knowing that there is a risk that an event may result from his conduct or that a circumstances may exist, he takes that risk, and (b) it is unreasonable for him to take it, having regard to the degree and nature of the risk which he knows to be present.'

h (See Working Paper no 31, Codification of the Criminal Law: General Principles: The Mental Element in Crime (16th June 1970).)

It was surely with this contemporaneous definition and the much respected decision of *R v Cunningham* in mind that the draftsman proceeded to his task of drafting the 1971 Act.

It has therefore to be said that, unlike negligence, which has to be judged objectively, recklessness involves foresight of consequences, combined with an objective judgment
j of the reasonableness of the risk taken. And recklessness in vacuo is an incomprehensible notion. It *must* relate to foresight of risk of the particular kind relevant to the charge preferred, which, for the purpose of s 1(2), is the risk of endangering life and nothing other than that.

So, if a defendant says of a particular risk, 'It never crossed my mind', a jury could not on those words alone properly convict him of recklessness simply because they considered that the risk *ought* to have crossed his mind, though his words might well lead to a finding of negligence. But a defendant's admission that he 'closed his mind' to a *a* particular risk could prove fatal, for 'A person cannot, in any intelligible meaning of the words, close his mind to a risk unless he first realises that there is a risk; and if he realises that there is a risk, that is the end of the matter' (see Glanville Williams, Textbook of Criminal Law (1st Edn, 1978, p 79)).

In the absence of exculpatory factors, the defendant's state of mind is therefore all-important where recklessness is an element in the offence charged, and s 8 of the *b* Criminal Justice Act 1967 has laid down that:

> 'A court or jury, in determining whether a person has committed an offence,— (a) shall not be bound in law to infer that he intended *or foresaw* a result of his actions by reason only of its being a natural and probable consequence of those actions; but (b) shall decide whether he did intend *or foresee* that result by reference *c* to all the evidence, drawing such inferences from the evidence as appear proper in the circumstances.' (Emphasis added.)

My Lords, it is unnecessary to examine at length the proposition that ascertainment of the state of mind known as 'recklessness' is a *subjective* exercise, for the task was expansively performed by Geoffrey Lane LJ in *R v Stephenson* [1979] 2 All ER 1198, [1979] QB 695. And, indeed, that was the view expressed by the learned recorder herself *d* in the instant case when, citing *R v Briggs* [1977] 1 All ER 475 at 477, [1977] 1 WLR 605 at 608, she directed the jury at one stage in these terms:

> 'It may be the most useful function that I can perform if I read to you the most recent (I hope) definition of 'recklessness' . . . by a superior court . . . A man is reckless . . . when he carries out a deliberate act, knowing that there is some risk of *e* damage resulting from that act, but "nevertheless continues in the performance of that act . . ." That came, in fact, in a case of a straight arson and damage to property, but in this case you would probably feel that you had to add after the words to fit this section of the Act "some risk of damage to life" . . . because that is what we are concerned with. I see both counsel nod assent to that. So, we can stay on common ground.' *f*

(2) The 'mens rea' of aggravated arson

The first count charged the respondent with 'Arson contrary to Section 1(2) and (3) of the Criminal Damage Act 1971', and the particulars of the offence were in the following terms:

> 'James Caldwell on the 23rd day of December 1978 without lawful excuse you *g* damaged by fire a window frame and curtains at the Hydro Hotel . . . belonging to another intending to damage the said property or being reckless as to whether any such property would be damaged *and* intending by the said damage to endanger the life of another or being reckless as to whether the life of another would be thereby endangered." (Emphasis added.)

h

My Lords, the very layout of s 1 makes clear that a state of mind over and beyond that essential for a conviction under s 1(1) has to be established before the graver crime created by s 1(2) can be brought home. The latter has features both of an offence against property *and* an offence against the person, and a special 'intent' or a special 'recklessness' is involved, a state of mind 'ulterior' to the 'basic' intent or recklessness which is sufficient for s 1(1). And 'intention' and 'recklessness' are more than birds of a feather; they are *j* blood-brothers; so much so that Austin included 'recklessness' within the term 'intention' (see Jurisprudence (4th Edn, vol 1, pp 436, 441, 442)). As James LJ said in *R v Venna* [1975] 3 All ER 788 at 794, [1976] QB 421 at 429: 'In many cases the dividing line between intention and recklessness is barely distinguishable.' So in *R v O'Driscoll* (1977) 65 Cr App R 50 at 55, where the charge was one of manslaughter caused by setting fire

to a house, Waller LJ, giving the judgment of the Court of Appeal, Criminal Division,
a said:

> '. . . we are of the opinion in this case that the unlawful act relied on by the
> learned judge of damaging the building of another by fire involved a basic intent
> . . . It would have been different in our view if the intent had involved the question
> of danger to the life of others, as in subsection (2) of section 1 of the Criminal
> Damage Act 1971, because that would not be inherent in the *actus reus* if there was
> *b* an intention to endanger the life of another or recklessness as to whether the life of
> another would be endangered or not. As I have already stated, in our view this was
> a crime of basic intent . . . and therefore the defence of drunkenness does not avail
> at all: see D.P.P. v. MAJEWSKI ([1976] 2 All ER 142, [1977] AC 443].'

And in *R v Stephenson* [1979] 2 All ER 1198 at 1204, [1979] QB 695 at 704, where the
c charge was laid under s 1(1), Geoffrey Lane LJ said:

> 'There is no doubt that the subjective definition of "recklessness" does produce
> difficulties. One of them, which is particularly likely to occur in practice, is the case
> of the person who by self-induced intoxication by drinks or drugs deprives himself
> of the ability to foresee the risks involved in his actions. Assuming that by reason
> of his intoxication he is not proved to have foreseen the relevant risk, can he be said
> *d* to have been "reckless"? Plainly not, unless cases of self-induced intoxication are an
> exception to the general rule. In our judgment the decision of the House of Lords
> in *Director of Public Prosecutions v Majewski* makes it clear that they are such an
> exception. Evidence of self-induced intoxication such as to negative mens rea is a
> defence to a charge which required proof of a "specific intent", but not to a charge
> of any other crime. The Criminal Damage Act 1971, s 1(1) involves no specific
> *e* intent: see *R v O'Driscoll*. Accordingly, it is no defence under the 1971 Act for a
> person to say that he was deprived by self-induced intoxication of the ability to
> foresee or appreciate an obvious risk.'

That Geoffrey Lane LJ was referring in his final sentence only to s 1(1) of the Act is made
clear by its context, and in *R v Orpin* [1980] 2 All ER 321 at 323–324, [1980] 1 WLR 1050
f at 1054 Eveleigh LJ said:

> 'The mental element, intention or recklessness, in the second part of sub-s (2) is
> an aggravating circumstance which adds to the gravity of the actus reus which is
> defined in the first part of that subsection. Although the proof of that additional
> element will often involve evidence as to possible or actual danger to life, *the*
> *g* *additional aggravating factor lies in the mind.* It is the mental attitude to the
> consequences of an actus reus. It goes beyond the actus reus itself, and is therefore
> to be treated as a specific intent which has to be established as an ingredient of the
> offence. That being so, evidence of intoxication *is* relevant as one of those matters
> to be taken into consideration in determining whether or not the necessary mental
> element existed. There is nothing inconsistent in treating an offence under sub-s
> *h* (1) as a crime of basic intent and an offence under sub-s (2) as one of specific intent.
> It is only the second part of sub-s (2) which introduces a specific intent. The same
> words are used to denote the attitude of mind, but in the one case there is an act
> stipulated corresponding to the mental state and manifesting its existence, whilst in
> the other there is no such act.' (Emphasis added.)

But the trial judge here unfortunately failed to differentiate between the different
j types of arson embraced by s 1 of the 1971 Act by directing the jury without qualification
that 'arson is an offence of basic intent'. This led her, in purported pursuance of
Majewski, to conclude that—

> 'it is no defence for the accused, by reason of self-induced intoxication, to say that
> he was senseless and so had neither "intent" nor "recklessness" with regard to what

he was doing . . . One basic, simple act of setting fire to the curtains, with a view to
igniting the building, is what is relied on for the commission of the offence . . . if *a*
a person . . . sets out with intent to set fire to something, that is a positive, basic act,
and he has with him the equipment to do it, he cannot then be allowed to say,
"Well, yes, I meant to set fire to *that*, but that's all."'

In my judgment, the Court of Appeal, Criminal Division, was right in holding that
this direction contained two errors. In the first place, despite her earlier, correct *b*
directions as to the subjective nature of the 'recklessness' test, the recorder invited the
jury to hold recklessness established if *they* considered that it was '. . . a fair likelihood that
. . . if the wind was in the right direction, perhaps, to fan the flames rather than peter
them out, it might have got a good hold of the furniture in the room . . .' That was
undoubtedly a direction that the 'recklessness' of the accused's action was to be judged
objectively. And the second error lay in directing the jury without qualification that (a) *c*
all arson is an offence of basic intent and, consequently, that (b) since *Majewski* it matters
not if, by reason of the defendant's self-intoxication, he may not have foreseen the
possibility that his admittedly unlawful actions endangered life.

Something more must be said about (b) having regard to the view expressed by my
noble and learned friend Lord Diplock that the speech of Lord Elwyn-Jones LC in
Majewski 'is authority that self-induced intoxication is no defence to a crime in which *d*
recklessness is enough to constitute the necessary mens rea'. It is a view which, with
respect, I do not share. In common with all the Law Lords hearing that appeal, Lord
Elwyn-Jones LC adopted the well-established (though not universally favoured)
distinction between basic and specific intents. *Majewski* related solely to charges of
assault, undoubtedly an offence of basic intent, and Lord Elwyn-Jones LC made it clear
that his observations were confined to offences of that nature (see [1976] 2 All ER 142 at *e*
149, 150, 151–152, [1977] AC 443 at 473, 474, 475, 476). My respectful view is that
Majewski accordingly supplies no support for the proposition that, in relation to crimes
of specific intent (such as that in s 1(2)(b) of the 1971 Act), incapacity to appreciate the
degree and nature of the risk created by his action which is attributable to the defendant's
self-intoxication is an irrelevance. Lord Elwyn-Jones LC was dealing simply with crimes
of basic intent, and in my judgment it was strictly within that framework that he *f*
adopted the view expressed in the American Penal Code (which he referred to at [1976]
2 All ER 142 at 151, [1977] AC 443 at 475), and recklessness as an element in crimes of
specific intent was, I am convinced, never within his contemplation.

For the foregoing reasons, the Court of Appeal was in my judgment right in quashing
the conviction under s 1(2)(b) and substituting a finding of guilty of arson contrary to
s 1(1) and (3) of the 1971 Act. It follows, therefore, that I agree with learned counsel for *g*
the respondent that the certified point of law should be answered in the following
manner: 'Yes, evidence of self-induced intoxication can be relevant both to (a) whether
the defendant *intended* to endanger the life of another, and to (b) whether the defendant
was *reckless* whether the life of another would be endangered, within the meaning of s
1(2)(b) of the Criminal Damage Act 1971.'

My Lords, it was recently predicted that 'There can hardly be any doubt that *all* crimes *h*
of recklessness except murder will now be held to be crimes of basic intent within
Majewski' (see Glanville Williams, Textbook of Criminal Law (1978, p 431)). That
prophecy has been promptly fulfilled by the majority of your Lordships, for, with the
progressive displacement of 'maliciously' by 'intentionally or recklessly' in statutory
crimes, that will surely be the effect of the majority decision in this appeal. That I regret,
for the consequence is that, however grave the crime charged, if recklessness can *j*
constitute its mens rea the fact that it was committed in drink can afford no defence. It
is a very long time since we had so harsh a law in this country. Having revealed in
Majewski my personal conviction that, on grounds of public policy, a plea of drunkenness
cannot exculpate crimes of basic intent and so exercise unlimited sway in the criminal
law (see [1976] 2 All ER 142 at 168–170, [1977] AC 443 at 495–497), I am nevertheless

unable to concur that your Lordships' decision should now become the law of the land.
a   For, as Eveleigh LJ said in *R v Orpin* [1980] 2 All ER 321 at 324, [1980] 1 WLR 1050 at
1054:

> '... there is nothing inconsistent in treating intoxication as irrelevant when
> considering the liability of a person who has willed himself to do that which the law
> forbids (for example, to do something which wounds another), and yet to make it
> relevant when a further mental state is postulated as an aggravating circumstance
b   making the offence even more serious.'

By way of a postscript I would add that the majority view demonstrates yet again the
folly of totally ignoring the recommendations of the Butler Committee (Report on
Mentally Abnormal Offenders (Cmnd 6244 (1975)), paras 18, 53–58).

My Lords, I would dismiss the appeal.

c
LORD KEITH OF KINKEL. My Lords, I am in entire agreement with the reasoning
contained in the speech of my noble and learned friend Lord Diplock, which I have had
the benefit of reading in draft. I would answer the certified questions in the manner
which he proposes, and dismiss the appeal.

d   **LORD ROSKILL.** My Lords, I had prepared an opinion of my own in this appeal but
having had the advantage of reading in draft the speech of my noble and learned friend
Lord Diplock I am satisfied that no useful purpose would be served by delivering that
speech.   I agree in every respect with what my noble and learned friend has said in his
speech and with his proposed answers to the questions certified.   For the reasons he gives
I agree that this appeal should be dismissed.

e
Appeal dismissed.

Solicitors: *R E T Birch* (for the Crown); *Gordon & James Morton* (for the respondent).

Mary Rose Plummer   Barrister.

R v Lawrence

HOUSE OF LORDS
LORD HAILSHAM OF ST MARYLEBONE LC, LORD DIPLOCK, LORD FRASER OF TULLYBELTON, LORD
ROSKILL AND LORD BRIDGE OF HARWICH
5th, 9th FEBRUARY, 19th MARCH 1981

*Road traffic – Reckless driving – Causing death by reckless driving – Reckless – Mens rea –
Mental element required – Proper direction to be given to jury – Road Traffic Act 1972, ss 1, 2
(as substituted by the Criminal Law Act 1977, s 50(1)).*

The actus reus of the offence of driving recklessly, contrary to ss 1 and 2[a] of the 1972 Act,
is not merely driving without due care and attention but driving in a manner that creates
an obvious and serious risk of causing physical injury to any other road user or substantial
damage to property. The mens rea of the offence is driving in such a manner without
giving any thought to the risk or, having recognised that it exists, nevertheless taking the
risk. It is for the jury to decide whether the risk created by the accused's driving was
both obvious and serious, the standard being that of the ordinary prudent motorist as
represented by themselves (see p 977 j to p 978 a and p 982 a to c and f to p 983 g, post).

R v Caldwell p 961, ante, applied.

R v Murphy (William) [1980] 2 All ER 325 overruled.

Allan v Patterson 1980 SLT 77 approved.

Observations on the need for brevity in summing up to a jury and in the conduct of
Crown Court trials generally (see p 975 f to j, p 977 e to h, p 979 b c and p 983 d to g, post).

Notes

For causing death by reckless driving and for reckless driving, see 33 Halsbury's Laws
(3rd Edn) 622–623, paras 1047–1048.

For the Road Traffic Act 1972, ss 1, 2 (as substituted by the Criminal Law Act 1977,
s 50(1)), see 47 Halsbury's Statutes (3rd Edn) 1221.

Cases referred to in opinions

Allan v Patterson 1980 SLT 77, [1980] RTR 97.

R v Caldwell p 961, ante, HL.

R v Evans [1962] 3 All ER 1086, [1963] 1 QB 412, [1962] 3 WLR 1457, 127 JP 49, 61 LGR
32, 47 Cr App R 62, CCA, 45 Digest (Repl) 87, 298.

R v Murphy (William) [1980] 2 All ER 325, [1980] QB 434, [1980] 2 WLR 743, [1980]
RTR 145, CA.

R v Sheppard [1980] 3 All ER 899, [1980] 3 WLR 960, HL.

R v Stephenson [1979] 2 All ER 1198, [1979] QB 695, [1979] 3 WLR 193, 143 JP 592, 69
Cr App R 213, CA, Digest (Cont Vol E) 161, 12,692a.

Appeal

On 18th March 1980 the respondent, Stephen Richard Lawrence, was convicted at the
Crown Court at Ipswich before Mr Michael Weisman, sitting as a deputy circuit judge,
and a jury of causing death by reckless driving, contrary to s 1 of the Road Traffic Act
1972, as substituted by s 50(1) of the Criminal Law Act 1977. He was sentenced to six
months' imprisonment and disqualified for holding a driving licence for three years. He
appealed to the Court of Appeal, Criminal Division (Watkins LJ, Boreham and
Hodgson JJ) which allowed his appeal on 20th May 1980 and quashed his conviction.
On 23rd May the court refused an application by the Crown for leave to appeal to the
House of Lords but certified, under s 33(2) of the Criminal Appeal Act 1968, that the

---

a Sections 1 and 2 are set out at p 981 b c, post

following points of law of general public importance were involved in its decision: (1)
a was mens rea involved in the offence of driving recklessly; (2) if yes, what was the mental
element required; and (3) was the following a proper direction on a charge of driving
recklessly: 'A driver is guilty of driving recklessly if he deliberately disregards the
obligation to drive with due care and attention or is indifferent whether or not he does
so and thereby creates a risk of an accident which a driver driving with due care and
attention would not create'? On 24th July the House of Lords gave the Crown leave to
b appeal. The facts are set out in the opinion of Lord Hailsham LC.

D H *Penry-Davey* for the Crown.
A *Arlidge* for the respondent.

Their Lordships took time for consideration.

c
19th March. The following opinions were delivered.

LORD HAILSHAM OF ST MARYLEBONE LC. My Lords, the question in this
appeal is whether the conviction on 18th March 1980 of the respondent for causing death
by reckless driving should be restored. In my opinion it should not, both on the grounds
d on which it was quashed by the Court of Appeal, and on the more general ground about
to be formulated by my noble and learned friend Lord Diplock, with whose conclusions
and reasoning I wish to be wholly and unequivocally associated. If I proceed with a few
observations of my own about the course of the proceedings, it is because I wish to draw
some lessons from them regarding the general conduct of trials on indictment, and not
because I wish to repeat in other words what my noble and learned friend is about to say.
e   My Lords, it is notorious that there has grown up a serious backlog of cases for trial in
the Crown Court, and this is particularly the case in the South East and London. This
backlog has been a source of particular anxiety to me in both my terms of office, as I
know it is currently to the present Lord Chief Justice. The causes of it are complex, and
the remedies are therefore not particularly simple. But, so long as it persists, the whole
system of trial by jury, and the regard in which it is rightly held, are adversely affected.
f   My Lords, it is a truism to say that justice delayed is justice denied. But it is not merely
the anxiety and uncertainty in the life of the accused, whether on bail or remand, which
are affected. Where there is delay the whole quality of justice deteriorates. Our system
depends on the recollection of witnesses, conveyed to a jury by oral testimony. As the
months pass, this recollection necessarily dims, and juries who are correctly directed not
to convict unless they are assured of the reliability of the evidence for the prosecution
g necessarily tend to acquit as this becomes less precise, and sometimes less reliable. This
may also affect defence witnesses on the opposite side. In the instant case, an accident
took place unexpectedly in a matter of seconds. The evidence at the trial included the
testimony of witnesses, present on the occasion, none of whom could have been expecting
a moment before it occurred that they were to be confronted with a desperate tragedy,
to the sequence of events in which in 11 months' time they would be expected to testify
h on oath.
Part of the delay in bringing cases to trial is due to the increase in the volume of
indictable crime brought to the Crown Court. But part also is due to the increasing
prolixity in the conduct of cases when they actually come to be heard. It cannot be too
often stressed that verbose justice is not necessarily good justice. There is virtue, both
from the point of view of the prosecution and from the point of view of the defence, in
j incisiveness, decisiveness and conciseness, not only in addressing juries but in the general
conduct of a case, the examination and cross-examination of witnesses, the submission of
legal argument, and in summing up. A long trial is not necessarily a better one if a
shorter one would have sufficed. It is these considerations which lead me to analyse the
course of events in the present appeal, and not any desire to expand on or to qualify the
reasoning of my noble and learned friend.

The course of events was as follows. On 13th March 1980 in the Crown Court at
Ipswich the respondent (defendant) in these proceedings was arraigned on an indictment *a*
of great simplicity. It read as follows:

'Stephen Richard Lawrence is charged as follows:—
'Statement of Offence:—
'Causing death by reckless driving, contrary to section 1 of the Road Traffic Act
1972.
'Particulars of Offence:—   *b*
'STEPHEN RICHARD LAWRENCE, on the 13th day of April 1979 at Lowestoft in the
County of Suffolk, caused the death of Yvonne Letittia Crowther, by driving a
motor vehicle on a road, namely, Victoria Road, recklessly.'

I pause at this stage only to point out that, owing to the delays which have mounted up
in the South East and London, this simple case has taken a whole year less one month to *c*
come on for trial. That it took this length of delay to bring it on for trial is, of course, no
criticism of the judge, counsel or solicitors in the present case. It is the cumulative result
of the length and number of other cases with which your Lordships have not been
concerned.

The trial pursued its course during 13th (Thursday), 14th (Friday) and 17th (Monday)
March 1980. The learned judge commenced his summing up on Tuesday, 18th *d*
March. After this summing up and an interchange between the two counsel and the
judge the jury retired at 11.28 am. They returned at 2.15 pm after deliberating for 2
hours and 47 minutes, when they were given a majority verdict direction. At 2.32 pm
the jury delivered a note to the learned judge requesting further directions on the
meaning of 'driving recklessly'. There was a further interchange between judge and
counsel in the absence of the jury. At 3.15 pm the jury were summoned back and given *e*
a further direction. At 3.43 pm the jury convicted the respondent by a verdict of eleven
to one, and after the usual procedure the learned judge sentenced the respondent to six
months in prison and three years' disqualification.

On 20th May 1980 the whole trial aborted, because the Court of Appeal quashed the
conviction on the grounds that both directions left 'so much unclear as to render the
jury's verdict unsafe and unsatisfactory'. So other cases in the Crown Court at Ipswich *f*
were delayed by the judge, time consumed to no purpose during the better part of a
week. But that has not been the end of the matter. At the request of the prosecution the
Court of Appeal certified the three questions as of 'general public importance':

'1. Is mens rea involved in the offence of driving recklessly? 2. If yes, what is the
mental element required? 3. Is the following on a charge of driving recklessly a
proper direction: "A driver is guilty of driving recklessly if he deliberately disregards *g*
the obligation to drive with due care and attention or is indifferent as to whether or
not he does so and thereby creates a risk of an accident which a driver driving with
due care and attention would not create"?'

These three questions form the substance of the appeal. In certifying them the Court of
Appeal refused leave to appeal. This was given subsequently by the Appeal Committee *h*
of your Lordships' House, possibly because the question of 'recklessness' in criminal cases
was already before your Lordships in another context in *R v Caldwell* p 961, ante, in
which judgment has just been delivered.

I mention these facts because, altogether apart from the merits of the appeal, with
which my noble and learned friend Lord Diplock intends to deal, I think there are lessons
to be learned from these proceedings which ought urgently to be studied since they are *j*
directly relevant to the serious delays to which I have now drawn attention.

The facts of the case can be stated in stark simplicity. On 13th April 1979 at
approximately 8.30 pm, a husband and wife, Mr and Mrs Crowther, decided to drive
their van to an off-licence in Lowestoft in order to buy some soft drink for the
children. They arrived at their destination at approximately 9 pm. Their van was

parked on the opposite side of the road to the off-licence. Mr Crowther stayed in the van. Mrs Crowther crossed the road and entered the off-licence. When she came out, she stopped at the kerb. Her husband saw her blow him a kiss, and that was the last time he saw his wife alive. In crossing the road to return to the van there was a collision between herself and the second of two motor cyclists. The cycle involved in the collision was driven by the respondent. Mrs Crowther was killed instantaneously. Her body was carried 45 yards on the front of the cycle before the cycle stopped.

At the trial one solitary dispute of primary fact emerged. This was the speed at which the cycle was travelling. The prosecution led evidence intended to show that the cycle was travelling at a grossly excessive speed. Apart from the measurements on the road, there were witnesses of the accident, forensic evidence that the speedometer was jammed at 77 mph and as to the implications of this, and police evidence regarding the account of the accident by the accused.

By contrast, the accused gave evidence and called witnesses who testified that the true speed only was 30 to 40 mph, technically illegal, since the area was built up, possibly careless, but most improbably reckless.

Given the nature of the case, one would hardly think that the case presented much difficulty for a jury to try or for the judge to sum up in a manner calculated to lead them to a just and safe conclusion. If they were satisfied with the prosecution evidence to the extent required by the burden of proof in criminal cases they could hardly fail to convict. If they thought the defence evidence raised a reasonable doubt they could hardly fail to acquit. In the event they convicted by a majority, and their verdict was set aside as unsafe and unsatisfactory on the ground that the two directions on recklessness were so unclear. Neither the result, nor the delay in bringing the matter to trial, nor the course of the proceedings ought to afford any of us who are concerned in the administration of justice in any capacity much cause for satisfaction.

It has been said before, but obviously requires to be said again. The purpose of a direction to a jury is not best achieved by a disquisition on jurisprudence or philosophy or a universally applicable circular tour round the area of law affected by the case. The search for universally applicable definitions is often productive of more obscurity than light. A direction is seldom improved and may be considerably damaged by copious recitations from the total content of a judge's notebook. A direction to a jury should be custom-built to make the jury understand their task in relation to a particular case. Of course it must include references to the burden of proof and the respective roles of jury and judge. But it should also include a succinct but accurate summary of the issues of fact as to which a decision is required, a correct but concise summary of the evidence and arguments on both sides, and a correct statement of the inferences which the jury are entitled to draw from their particular conclusions about the primary facts. In the present instance there was only one issue of primary fact, the speed at which the cycle was travelling, and I doubt whether a direction could have been faulted if the jury had simply been told that if they were satisfied that the prosecution had proved that the accused had been travelling at a grossly excessive speed they were entitled to infer that he had been driving recklessly and as a result had caused Mrs Crowther's death, that if so they should convict, and that if they were not so satisfied they should acquit. As it is, I feel sure that the Court of Appeal were correct in their belief that the jury may well have been so bemused with the effect of the summing up that their verdict was unsafe and unsatisfactory, and that, if only for this reason, the appeal must fail. The verdict cannot be restored.

There is, however, a second reason why, in my judgment, the appeal by the prosecution must fail. Of the three questions of law certified by the Court of Appeal, I have no doubt that all three must be answered in the sense proposed by my noble and learned friend Lord Diplock. Since it follows from this that the third of these questions is answered in the negative, the learned judge's direction which broadly followed the formula contained in it was wrong in law. For this he can hardly be blamed since the formula broadly corresponds with that proposed by Eveleigh LJ in R v Murphy (William)

[1980] 2 All ER 325, [1980] 1 QB 434 (then just reported), which, to the extent described in detail by my noble and learned friend, must be considered overruled. I also associate *a* myself with my noble and learned friend's affirmative answer to the first question, and the formulation of his answer to the second, with the reasoning leading up to which I also agree. Though it does not directly affect the three questions posed I share the distate for the obsessive use of the expressions 'objective' and 'subjective' in crime. In all indictable crime it is a general rule that there are objective factors of conduct which constitute the so-called 'actus reus', and a further guilty state of mind which constitutes *b* the so-called 'mens rea'. The necessity for this guilty state of mind has been increasingly emphasised of recent years (cf *R v Sheppard* [1980] 3 All ER 899, [1980] 3 WLR 960), and this I regard as a thoroughly praiseworthy development. It only surprises me that there should have been any question regarding the existence of mens rea in relation to the words 'reckless', 'recklessly' or 'recklessness'. Unlike most English words it has been in the English language as a word in general use at least since the eight century AD almost *c* always with the same meaning, applied to a person or conduct evincing a state of mind stopping short of deliberate intention, and going beyond mere inadvertence, or, in its modern though not its etymological and original sense, mere carelessness. The Oxford English Dictionary quotes several examples from Old English, many from the Middle English period, and many more from modern English. The word was familiar to the Venerable Bede, to Langland, to Chaucer, to Sir Thomas More and to Shakespeare. In its *d* alternative and possibly older pronunciation, and etymologically incorrect spelling (wretchless, wretchlessly, wretchlessness) it was known to the authors of the Articles of religion printed in the book of Common Prayer. Though its pronunciation has varied, so far as I know its meaning has not. There is no separate legal meaning to the word. This retains its dictionary sense, adequately, I believe, expounded by my noble and learned friend Lord Diplock. It is, of course, true that, in a legal context, the state of *e* mind described as 'reckless' is discussed in connection with conduct objectively blameworthy as well as dangerous, while in common speech it is possible to conceive (for instance in the context of the winner of a military decoration in circumstances in which he is reckless of his own safety) of the use of the word without a blameworthy connotation. Now that my noble and learned friend has given it a lucid legal interpretation I trust that it will cause no more trouble to the profession, academics or *f* juries. I also associate myself with what he has said about the Scottish case of *Allan v Patterson* 1980 SLT 77. *R v Stephenson* [1979] 2 All ER 1198, [1979] QB 695 was discussed before us, but in view of what has just been said before your Lordships in *R v Caldwell* p 961, ante there is nothing I can usefully add, except that I respectfully accept the view of the majority in that case. Since the days of Noah, the effects of alcohol have been known to induce the state of mind described in English as recklessness, and not to inhibit it, and *g* for that matter to remove inhibitions in the field of intention, and not to destory intention. But that is a different question.

In the result the appeal fails.

LORD DIPLOCK. My Lords, on Good Friday, 13th April 1979, after night had fallen, the respondent ('the driver') was riding his motor cycle along an urban street in *h* Lowestoft. The street was subject to a 30 mph speed limit and there was a good deal of other traffic using it at the time. The driver ran into and killed a pedestrian who was crossing the road to return from an off-licence shop to her car which was parked on the opposite side of the street. The driver was in due course tried on indictment for the offence of causing her death by driving a motor vehicle on a road recklessly, contrary to s 1 of the Road Traffic Act 1972. *j*

Apart from the very tragic consequences of this accident the case that the jury had to try was about as simple and straightforward as any case can be in which the charge is one of driving recklessly. The only question of fact that was in issue was the speed at which the driver was travelling immediately before the impact. The prosecution's case was that the motor cycle was being driven at between 60 and 80 mph and probably much nearer to the latter. The case for the defence was that the speed of the motor cycle was no more than 30 or, at most, 40 mph and probably nearer to the former.

All that the jury had to do was to make up their minds whether, on that evidence, they were satisfied beyond reasonable doubt that the driver was in fact driving along this urban street, on which it was not disputed there was a good deal of other traffic, at a speed somewhere between 60 and 80 mph. If they were so satisfied, even the defence did not suggest that any sensible jury could come to any other conclusion than that he was driving recklessly; whereas, if they thought that his own estimate of his speed at 30 to 40 mph might be right, they ought to have found him not guilty, for the prosecution had not relied on any other aspect of his driving as constituting recklessness, apart from excessive speed.

I find it difficult to conceive that so simple a case could have taken more than a single day to try 20 years ago when, as a High Court judge, I was trying cases of the then newly-created offence of causing death by dangerous driving. I warmly endorse what Lord Hailsham LC has said about the tortoise pace at which cases in the Crown Court are nowadays so frequently allowed to amble on. It makes the trial itself a less effective and reliable means of achieving a just result and is one of the main causes of the long delays between committal and trial which are nothing short of a disgrace to our legal system.

In the course of his summing up the deputy circuit judge gave to the jury a direction as to what amounted in law to 'driving recklessly'. This direction the Court of Appeal described with justification, but also with the utmost sympathy, as confused. And so it was, because it sought to combine the very recent definition of 'driving recklessly' in s 2 of the Road Traffic Act 1972 that had been given by Eveleigh LJ in *R v Murphy (William)* [1980] 2 All ER 325, [1980] QB 434 ('the *Murphy* definition') with the definition of 'reckless' in s 1(1) of the Criminal Damage Act 1971 that had been given by Geoffrey Lane LJ in *R v Stephenson* [1979] 2 All ER 1178, [1979] QB 695. This latter definition has been the subject of disapproval by this House in the immediately preceding appeal, *R v Caldwell* p 961, ante.

The jury too must have found the direction confusing for, after three and a half hours' retirement, they sought further elucidation from the judge. In substance he repeated to them the *Murphy* direction and, after a further short retirement, the jury, by a majority of eleven to one, brought in a verdict of guilty.

The *Murphy* direction is in the following terms:

'A driver is guilty of driving recklessly if he deliberately disregards the obligation to drive with due care and attention or is indifferent whether or not he does so and thereby creates a risk of an accident which a driver driving with due care and attention would not create.'

Whether the *Murphy* direction is correct or not is the subject of the third question of law involved in the instant case that the Court of Appeal, in giving leave to appeal, has certified as being of general public importance. The other two are: '1. Is mens rea involved in the offence of driving recklessly? 2. If yes, what is the mental element required?'

To answer these question necessitates in the first instance a brief reference to the legislative history of those road traffic offences that had for so many years prior to 1977 been popularly known as 'careless driving' and 'dangerous driving' respectively.

The history starts with s 1 of the Motor Car Act 1903, which drew no distinction between driving 'recklessly' or 'negligently' or 'in a dangerous manner', so far as the gravity of the offence was concerned. It was in the following terms:

'(1) If any person drives a motor car on a public highway recklessly or negligently, or at a speed or in a manner which is dangerous to the public, having regard to all the circumstances of the case, including the nature, condition and use of the highway, and to the amount of traffic which actually is at the time, or which might reasonably be expected to be, on the highway, that person shall be guilty of an offence under this Act . . .'

This remained the law until it was repealed by the Road Traffic Act 1930, which made
separate offences of dangerous driving and careless driving. The former was the more
serious offence; it was triable on indictment as well as summarily and the penalties that
could be imposed included imprisonment and were heavier than those for careless
driving, which was triable summarily only.

The description of the offence of dangerous driving was:

'**11.**—(1) If any person drives a motor vehicle on a road recklessly, or at a speed
or in a manner which is dangerous to the public, having regard to all the
circumstances of the case, including the nature, condition, and use of the road, and
the amount of traffic which is actually at the time, or which might reasonably be
expected to be, on the road . . .

'**12.**—(1) If any person drives a motor vehicle on a road without due care and
attention or without reasonable consideration for other persons using the road . . .'

To these were added by s 8 of the Road Traffic Act 1956 the new offence of causing death
by reckless or dangerous driving, the manner of driving involved in this offence being
the same as under s 12(1) of the Road Traffic Act 1930.

These descriptions of the offences were reproduced in ss 1 and 2 and in s 3 respectively
of the Road Traffic Act 1972. Dangerous driving continued to be triable on indictment
as well as summarily; careless driving remained triable summarily only.

Although the adverb 'recklessly' as descriptive of a manner of driving has been there
ever since the single offence was split up into two of which one was treated as much
graver than the other, the practice so far as living memory goes had been to charge
defendants with driving 'at a speed or in a manner which is dangerous to the public' and
not with driving 'recklessly'. This is why the offence became popularly known as
dangerous, not as reckless, driving; and juries, when the trial was on indictment, were
instructed to consider whether in their judgment the defendant was driving in a manner
that was dangerous to the public. It was not thought necessary to confuse them by
talking about 'subjective' and 'objective' tests, although before 1963 they might have
been told that to convict of dangerous driving they must be satisfied that the way in
which the defendant was driving was something worse than a mere failure to show
proper consideration for other people using the road or some minor misjudgment of the
situation or momentary lack of attention. As a Queen's Bench judge I used so to direct
juries myself, in trying cases of causing death by dangerous driving.

By its decision in *R v Evans* [1962] 3 All ER 1086, [1963] 1 QB 412, however, the Court
of Criminal Appeal for practical purposes abolished the difference between the standard
of driving in careless driving and that involved in dangerous driving where danger to the
public did in fact result. At the trial of Evans the judge had directed the jury ([1962] 3
All ER 1086 at 1087, [1963] 1 QB 412 at 413–414):

'. . . in law it is now well settled that if the driving is in fact dangerous, and that
dangerous driving is caused by some carelessness on the part of the accused, then
however slight the carelessness, that is dangerous driving.'

This summing up was approved on appeal. The court said ([1962] 3 All ER 1086 at 1088,
[1963] 1 QB 412 at 418):

'If a man in fact adopts a manner of driving which the jury think was dangerous
to the other road users in all the circumstances, then on the issue of guilt it matters
not whether he was deliberately reckless, momentarily inattentive or even doing his
incompetent best.'

This merging of the standards of defective driving that was to amount to the offences
of careless and dangerous driving respectively, leaving the only difference between the
two offences that in the latter danger to the public had in fact been caused, led to an
increase in the number of cases in which the prosecution charged the defendant with
dangerous driving and the defendant, with his driving licence at stake, almost invariably
elected to be tried by jury.

My Lords, your Lordships may take judicial notice of the fact that the amendment of ss 1 and 2 of the Road Traffic Act 1972 by s 50 (1) of the Criminal Law Act 1977, which followed on the Report of the Interdepartmental Committee on the Distribution of Criminal Business between the Crown Court and Magistrates' Courts in 1975 (Cmnd 6323), was to restore the difference in culpability between driving offences which attracted the severer penalties which could be imposed for offences under s 2 of the Road Traffic Act 1972, and so justified the right of the accused to elect trial by jury, and the offences under s 3 which did not attract penalties severe enough to justify any such right of election, and by this means to reduce the load of business in the Crown Court.

The amendment took the form of substituting for ss 1 and 2 of the Road Traffic Act 1972 the following new sections:

'**1.** A person who causes the death of another person by driving a motor vehicle on a road recklessly shall be guilty of an offence.

'**2.** A person who drives a motor vehicle on a road recklessly shall be guilty of an offence.'

The elimination of the reference to driving at a speed or in a manner dangerous to the public was obviously intended to remove the overlap between the offence in s 2 which gave a right to trial by jury and the lesser offence in s 3 that did not, which had resulted from the decision in *R v Evans*. Section 3 creates an absolute offence in the sense in which that term is commonly used to denote an offence for which the only mens rea needed is simply that the prohibited physical act (actus reus) done by the accused was directed by a mind that was conscious of what his body was doing, it being unnecessary to show that his mind was also conscious of the possible consequences of his doing it. So s 3 takes care of this kind of inattention or misjudgment to which the ordinarily careful motorist is occasionally subject without its necessarily involving any moral turpitude, although it causes inconvenience and annoyance to other users of the road. So there is no reason why your Lordships should go out of your way to give to the new s 2 a wide ambit that would recreate the former overlap with s 3.

My Lords, this House has very recently had occasion in *R v Caldwell* p 961, ante, to give close consideration to the concept of recklessness as constituting mens rea in criminal law. The conclusion reached by the majority was that the adjective 'reckless' when used in a criminal statute, ie the Criminal Damage Act 1971, had not acquired a special meaning as a term of legal art, but bore its popular or dictionary meaning of careless, regardless, or heedless of the possible harmful consequences of one's acts. The same must be true of the adverbial derivative 'recklessly'.

The context in which the word 'reckless' appears in s 1 of the Criminal Damage Act 1971 differs in two respects from the context in which the word 'recklessly' appears in ss 1 and 2 of the Road Traffic Act 1972, as now amended. In the Criminal Damage Act 1971 the actus reus, the physical act of destroying or damaging property belonging to another, is in itself a tort. It is not something that one does regularly as part of the ordinary routine of daily life, such as driving a car or a motor cycle. So there is something out of the ordinary to call the doer's attention to what he is doing and its possible consequences, which is absent in road traffic offences. The other difference in context is that in s 1 of the Criminal Damage Act 1971 the mens rea of the offences is defined as being reckless whether particular harmful consequences would occur, whereas in ss 1 and 2 of the Road Traffic Act 1972, as now amended, the possible harmful consequences of which the driver must be shown to have been heedless are left to be implied from the use of the word 'recklessly' itself. In ordinary usage 'recklessly' as descriptive of a physical act such as driving a motor vehicle which can be performed in a variety of different ways, some of them entailing danger and some of them not, refers not only to the state of mind of the doer of the act when he decides to do it but also qualifies the manner in which the act itself is performed. One does not speak of a person acting 'recklessly', even though he has given no thought at all to the consequences of his act, unless the act is one that presents a real risk of harmful consequences which anyone acting with reasonable prudence would recognise and give heed to. So the actus reus of the offence under ss 1 and 2 is not simply driving a motor vehicle on a road, but driving it in a manner which in fact creates a real risk of harmful consequences resulting from it. Since driving in such a manner as to do no worse than create a risk of causing inconvenience or annoyance to other road users constitutes the lesser offence under s 3, the manner of driving that constitutes the actus reus of an offence under ss 1 and 2 must be worse than that; it must be such as to create a real risk of causing physical injury to someone else who happens to be using the road or damage to property more substantial than the kind of minor damage that may be caused by an error of judgment in the course of parking one's car.

The *Murphy* direction, as it seems to me, is defective in this respect before one comes to any question of mens rea. By referring to the duty to drive with 'due care and attention', which is a direct quotation from s 3, it makes the standard of driving that must be maintained, in order to avoid the more serious offence of driving recklessly, the same as in the less serious offence under s 3 and thus perpetuates the very mischief which the 1977 amendments were intended to remedy. For when a decision has to be made whether to prosecute a driver for an offence under s 2 instead of under s 3 the only material available to the prosecution is evidence of what the driver actually did, the actus reus of the offence. The prosecution has no way of knowing at that stage, when the choice of charge has to be made, what was the state of mind of the driver when or immediately before he did it. It can only infer this from what the driver was seen to do and any statement that he may have made.

I turn now to the mens rea. My task is greatly simplified by what has already been said about the concept of recklessness in criminal law in *R v Caldwell*. Warning was there given against adopting the simplistic approach of treating all problems of criminal liability as soluble by classifying the test of liability as being either 'subjective' or 'objective'. Recklessness on the part of the doer of an act does presuppose that there is something in the circumstances that would have drawn the attention of an ordinary prudent individual to the possibility that his act was capable of causing the kind of serious harmful consequences that the section which creates the offence was intended to prevent, and that the risk of those harmful consequences occurring was not so slight that an ordinary prudent individual would feel justified in treating them as negligible. It is only when this is so that the doer of the act is acting 'recklessly' if, before doing the act, he either fails to give any thought to the possibility of there being any such risk or, having recognised that there was such risk, he nevetherless goes on to do it.

In my view, an appropriate instruction to the jury on what is meant by driving recklessly would be that they must be satisfied of two things: first, that the defendant was in fact driving the vehicle in such a manner as to create an obvious and serious risk of causing physical injury to some other person who might happen to be using the road or of doing substantial damage to property; and, second, that in driving in that manner the defendant did so without having given any thought to the possibility of there being any such risk or, having recognised that there was some risk involved, had none the less gone on to take it.

It is for the jury to decide whether the risk created by the manner in which the vehicle was being driven was both obvious and serious and, in deciding this, they may apply the standard of the ordinary prudent motorist as represented by themselves.

If satisfied that an obvious and serious risk was created by the manner of the defendant's driving, the jury are entitled to infer that he was in one or other of the states of mind required to constitute the offence and will probably do so; but regard must be given to any explanation he gives as to his state of mind which may displace the inference.

My Lords, in *Allan v Patterson* 1980 SLT 77, Lord Emslie in the High Court of Justiciary did apply the label 'objective' to the test of whether a driver was driving recklessly within the meaning of s 3 of the Act. While for reasons set out in greater detail in my speech in *R v Caldwell* I think it is desirable in all cases of criminal liability to avoid the use of this label, I do not think that, having regard to the likelihood that the jury will

draw the inference to which I have referred, the practical result of approaching the
question of what constitutes driving recklessly in the way that was adopted by the Lord
Justice-General in *Allan v Patterson* is likely to be any different from the result of
instructing a jury in some such terms as I have suggested above. The same Act applies
to both countries; it would be unfortunate if the interpretation put on it by the Scottish
courts differed from that put on it by the courts in England and Wales.

I would give the following answers to the questions certified by the Court of Appeal:
1. mens rea is involved in the offence of driving recklessly; 2. the mental element
required is that, before adopting a manner of driving that in fact involves an obvious and
serious risk of causing physical injury to some other person who may happen to be using
the road or of doing substantial damage to property, the driver has failed to give any
thought to the possibility of there being any such risk, or, having recognised that there
was some risk involved, has none the less gone on to take it; 3. the *Murphy* direction is
wrong in the respects referred to earlier.

Since the deputy circuit judge gave to the jury what was substantially the *Murphy*
direction itself and also a somewhat confused version of it and both of these stated the
law too unfavourably to the driver, this appeal must in my view be dismissed.

LORD FRASER OF TULLYBELTON. My Lords, I have had the advantage of
reading in draft the speeches of my noble and learned friends Lord Hailsham LC and
Lord Diplock, and I agree with them. I would dismiss this appeal.

LORD ROSKILL. My Lords, I have had the advantage of reading in draft the speeches
of my noble and learned friends Lord Hailsham LC and Lord Diplock. I agree that this
appeal fails for the reasons given by my noble and learned friend Lord Diplock in his
speech. On the wider issues with which my noble and learned friends Lord Hailsham
LC and Lord Diplock deal, I wish to express my respectful concurrence with what they
have said. I would only add that but for the tragedy involved in this case, the charge
would have been one of reckless driving which could and very probably would have been
heard in a magistrates' court. It is difficult to believe that any magistrates' court would
not have dealt with this case if not in a morning at least within one full day and reached
the correct answer, whatever it might be.

LORD BRIDGE OF HARWICH. My Lords, I have had the advantage of reading in
draft the speeches of my noble and learned friends Lord Hailsham LC and Lord Diplock.
I fully agree with them both. Accordingly I too would dismiss this appeal.

Appeal dismissed. Certified questions answered in form indicated in Lord Diplock's opinion.

Solicitors: *Sharpe, Pritchard & Co*, agents for M F C *Harvey*, Ipswich (for the Crown);
Goldkorm, Davies & Co, agents for *Norton, Peskett & Forward*, Lowestoft (for the
respondent).

Mary Rose Plummer Barrister.

Carmel Exporters (Sales) Ltd v Sea-Land Services Inc

QUEEN'S BENCH DIVISION
ROBERT GOFF J
7th, 8th, 9th OCTOBER, 7th NOVEMBER 1980

Practice – Acknowledgment of service – Notice of intention to contest proceedings – Summons by defendant applying for order setting aside writ alleging court lacking jurisdiction – Non-compliance with rules for application – Failure to state 'grounds' of application in summons – Failure to serve supporting affidavit with summons – Failure to apply within prescribed time limit for extension of time for serving affidavit – Whether summons a nullity – Whether acknowledgment of service amounting to submission to jurisdiction – Whether court having discretion to treat failure to comply with rules as irregularities and to allow summons to proceed – Whether requirement to 'apply to the Court' within prescribed period requiring only issue of summons within prescribed period – RSC Ord 2, r 1(1)(2), Ord 12, r 8(1)(2)(3)(4).

A dispute over bills of lading arose between the plaintiffs, an English company, and the defendants, who carried on business outside the jurisdiction. On 30th July 1979 the plaintiffs' solicitors wrote to the defendants' English solicitors asking if they were willing to accept service of a writ on behalf of the defendants. On 6th August the defendants' solicitors replied disputing the plaintiffs' claim but stating that if proceedings were to be served they had 'no doubt that we shall be instructed to accept service' and proposing that any proceedings should be directed to them. On 11th June 1980 the plaintiffs issued and served a writ in the new form claiming damages against the defendants for breach of contract and misrepresentation. On 23rd July the defendants' solicitors duly completed and returned to the court the acknowledgment of service which stated that the defendants intended to contest the proceedings. Within 14 days of that notice of intention to defend, the defendants' solicitors issued and served a summons on the plaintiffs, pursuant to RSC Ord 12, r 8(1)[a], applying for an order setting aside the writ. The summons merely stated that the court 'does not have jurisdiction in this matter'. The return date of the summons, originally specified as 29th July, was revised to 7th October. The summons was served without the copy affidavit required by r 8(4) in support verifying the facts on which the application was based, although a supporting affidavit was served on the plaintiffs on 17th September and the summons and affidavit together were re-served on them on 23rd September. The plaintiffs submitted that the application should be dismissed because (i) the summons failed to comply with Ord 12, r 8, because it did not state 'the grounds of the application' as required by r 8(3), a copy affidavit in support was not served with the summons as required by r 8(4), and the defendants had failed to apply for an extension of time for serving the affidavit within 14 days of the notice of intention to defend, as required by r 8(2), and therefore, by virtue of r 8(7), the defendants were to be treated as having submitted to the jurisdiction, and (ii) the defendants had submitted to the court's jurisdiction by virtue of their solicitors' letter of 6th August 1979. It was conceded by the plaintiffs that there was no basis for the English court to assert jurisdiction in the case, and there was no evidence that the plaintiffs had suffered prejudice by reason of the defendants' procedural errors.

Held – The application to set aside the writ would be granted for the following reasons—
(1) Although the defendants had failed to comply with the requirement of RSC Ord 12, r 8(3) that the summons should state the 'grounds' of the application, since merely to state that the court lacked jurisdiction did not constitute 'grounds' for an application, and

---

a Rule 8 is set out at p 988 *c* to *j*, post

had also failed to comply with the requirement of r 8(4) that a supporting affidavit be
a served with the summons, those failures were to be treated, by virtue of RSC Ord 2,
r 1(1)[b], merely as irregularities and not as nullifying the defendants' summons, and
under Ord 2, r 1(2) the court had a discretion to allow the summons to proceed despite
those procedural failures. Moreover, since the defendants' application, even though
deficient, had been 'made' within the prescribed period of 14 days from the notice of
intention to defend, within r 8(2), the court was not precluded by r 8(2) from exercising
b its discretion under Ord 2, r 1(2) to allow the summons to proceed, and the defects in
procedure were not such that the court was required to exercise its discretion under
Ord 2, r 1(2) by setting aside the summons. In all the circumstances, therefore, the court
was entitled to, and would, exercise its discretion by giving the defendants leave to
amend their summons to state the grounds of their application and leave to proceed with
the summons despite the late service of the supporting affidavit (see p 989 g, p 990 f to
c j, p 991 b to d and f to h and p 993 g, post); dictum of Lord Denning MR in *Harkness v
Bell's Asbestos and Engineering Ltd* [1966] 3 All ER at 845–846 applied.
    (2) The indication by the defendants' solicitors in their letter of 6th August 1979 that
they expected that they would be instructed to accept service of any proceedings did not
constitute submission by the defendants to the court's jurisdiction (see p 992 c to e and
p 993 g, post).
d   Per Curiam. (1) It appears likely that the requirement in RSC Ord 12, r 8(1) that a
defendant wishing to dispute the court's jurisdiction shall 'apply to the Court' within 14
days of notice of intention to defend is to be construed as requiring only that the
summons or motion should be issued within that time, but the point should be drawn
to the attention of the Rule Committee for clarification (see p 993 b c, post).
    (2) Reconsideration should also be given by the Rule Committee to the inflexible
e fetter imposed by Ord 12, r 8(2) on the court's discretion under Ord 3, r 5 to extend the
time for doing any act in proceedings under Ord 12, r 8(1) (see p 993 f g, post).

Cases referred to in judgment

Bonnell v Preston (1908) 24 TLR 756, CA, 50 Digest (Repl) 384, 991.
Harkness v Bell's Asbestos and Engineering Ltd [1966] 3 All ER 843, [1967] 2 QB 729, [1967]
f   2 WLR 29, CA, 50 Digest (Repl) 251, 54.

Cases also cited

Brayhead (Ascot) Ltd v Berkshire County Council [1964] 1 All ER 149, [1964] 2 QB 303, DC.
Howard v Secretary of State for the Environment [1974] 1 All ER 644, [1975] QB 235, CA.
Keymer v Reddy [1912] 1 KB 215, CA.
Revici v Prentice Hall Inc [1969] 1 All ER 772, [1969] 1 WLR 157, CA.
g *Schafer v Blyth* [1920] 3 KB 140.

Summons

By a summons dated 2nd July 1980 the defendants, Sea-Land Services Inc, a company
carrying on business in the Netherlands, applied pursuant to RSC Ord 12, r 8(1), for an
order that the writ issued on 11th June 1980 by the plaintiffs, Carmel Exporters (Sales)
h Ltd, an English company, claiming damages against them for breach of contract and/or
misrepresentation in regard to certain bills of lading, be set aside on the ground that the
court did not have jurisdiction in the matter. The plaintiffs opposed the application on
the grounds (i) that the defendants had failed to comply with Ord 12, r 8(4) and (ii) that
through their solicitors they had submitted to the jurisdiction. The summons was heard
in chambers but judgment was delivered in open court. The facts are set out in the
j judgment.

Peter Gross for the defendants.
Michael Brindly for the plaintiffs.

b   Rule 1 is set out at p 990 c to f, post

Cur adv vult

a

7th November. **ROBERT GOFF J** read the following judgment: There is before the court an application on behalf of the defendants, Sea-Land Services Inc, for an order that the writ issued by the plaintiffs, Carmel Exporters (Sales) Ltd, be set aside on the ground that the court has no jurisdiction in the matter. The application raises some questions of general interest concerning the new procedure, and in particular concerning the new b
RSC Ord 12, r 8. I have therefore agreed, at the request of the parties, to deliver my judgment in open court.

The matter arises as follows (I take the facts from the affidavit evidence before me). It appears that the plaintiffs, who carry on business in this country, entered into an agreement on 15th/16th December 1978 for the purchase of six containers of Iranian cumin seeds from an Iranian company, Hassas Export Co Ltd, of Teheran, at a price of c
$2,498 per metric ton c & f Rotterdam. The containers were, it seems, to be shipped from Iran in two instalments: three in December 1978, and three in January 1979. At about the same time as they entered into their purchase contract with Hassas Export, the plaintiffs on-sold the goods to a Colombian buyer, fob Rotterdam, shipment January or, latest, first week February 1979. Bills of lading were issued in respect of the six containers. These bills were in the defendant's form, and appear to have been signed on d
their behalf; the defendants are a company carrying on business in the Netherlands. Three bills were dated 24th December 1978, relating to carriage on the Seabridge (a feeder vessel) and (as the plaintiffs contend) the San Pedro (an ocean-going vessel); and three bills were dated 3rd January 1979, relating also to carriage on the Seabridge and (as the plaintiffs contend) the Pioneer (another ocean-going vessel). The bills contain a demise clause, and are expressly governed by the law of the United States of America. It e
seems that the goods were not shipped from Iran in either December 1978 or January 1979. The plaintiffs took up the documents and paid for the goods, though they do not appear to have done so until April 1979; however it appears that their buyers must have rejected the documents, and that the plaintiffs were left with the goods on their hands. The market having fallen, they are now claiming damages from the defendants, on the grounds of breach of contract and/or misrepresentation. f

A dispute has arisen between the parties with regard to the bills of lading. The plaintiffs contend that the bills are shipped bills, whereas the defendants contend that they are received for shipment bills. It appears that the words 'On Board' are stamped on the bills; but the defendants contend that this was done without their authority. Furthermore, the defendants say that the bills relate only to the carriage on the Seabridge, and that the Seabridge was neither owned by, nor demise chartered to, the defendants. g

On the evidence before the court, it is plain that the only connection which the disputes have with this country is that the plaintiffs happen to be an English company. The plaintiffs put their case against the defendants first of all on the basis of breach of either a written contract or an oral contract. The written contract can only be that evidenced by the bills of lading, which have no connection with this country at all. If there was an oral contract, there is no evidence before the court that any such contract h
could conceivably have been governed by English law, or have had any connection with this country at all. There is no evidence that either contract was broken in this country. In the alternative, the plaintiffs put their case on the basis of an alleged misrepresentation, which apparently relates to the words 'On Board' having been stamped on the bills; though this can only have taken place in Iran, and there is once again no connection with this country at all. In truth there is no possible basis on which, in the present case, the j
English court could have asserted jurisdiction over the disputes between the parties; and indeed the plaintiffs have not suggested otherwise.

Even so, the plaintiffs oppose the defendants' application. They do so on two grounds. First, they say that the defendants' application must fail, because they have not complied with the relevant provisions of the new RSC Ord 12, r 8 (as substituted by RSC

(Writ and Appearance) 1979, SI 1979 No 1716). Second, they say that the defendants
a through their solicitors have submitted to the jurisdiction of the court.

Before I turn to consider these two submissions, I must outline the course which the
proceedings have taken to date. The writ was issued, with a general endorsement, on
11th June 1980. This was of course a writ in the new form. Thereafter the defendants'
solicitors duly completed and on 23rd June returned to the court an acknowledgment of
service in the new form. The acknowledgment of service identified the defendants,
b stated that the defendants intended to contest the proceedings, and gave the name and
address of the defendants' solicitors. On 2nd July the defendants' solicitors issued the
summons which is now before me. The return date originally specified in the summons
was 29th July; the relief asked for was simply 'an order that the writ issued on 11th June
1980 be set aside on the grounds that this Honourable Court does not have jurisdiction
in this matter'. The summons was served on the plaintiffs' solicitors, without any
c affidavit in support, by post, and was received by the plaintiffs' solicitors on 4th July. So
both issue and service of the summons took place within 14 days of the defendants'
acknowledgment of service, in which their solicitors gave notice of their intention to
defend the proceedings. The affidavit in support of the defendants' application was not
in fact served on the plaintiffs' solicitors until 17th September, having been posted to
them the day before; on 23rd September, the summons and affidavit together were re-
d served on the plaintiffs' solicitors. On 7th October, the revised return date for the
hearing of the summons, the matter came before the court for argument.

I shall consider first the plaintiffs' submission that the defendants' application must
fail, on the ground that they have not complied with the relevant provisions of RSC
Ord 12, r 8. For this purpose, it is necessary for me to set out in outline the new
procedure, and in detail the relevant provisions of Ord 12, r 8.
e   Under the old procedure, once a writ had been served on a defendant, if a defendant
failed to enter an appearance within the time limited for appearance the plaintiff was
entitled (subject to certain exceptions) to enter final judgment against the defendant for
a sum not exceeding that claimed in the writ and for costs. On the other hand, if the
defendant did enter an appearance, he thereby not only showed his intention to defend
the suit but also submitted himself to the jurisdiction of the court. If a defendant wished
f to challenge the jurisdiction of the court, there were two courses open to him. First he
might, with the leave of the court, enter a conditional appearance in the action. This had
the effect of preventing the plaintiff from entering judgment in default of appearance,
while maintaining the defendant's right to object to the jurisdiction of the court, or
indeed to any irregularity in the issue or service of the writ. However, subject to that
right, a conditional appearance was a complete appearance to the action for all
g purposes. Accordingly, on the expiration of the relevant time, if no application had been
made by the defendant to set aside the proceedings, or he had made such an application
and it had been dismissed, the appearance stood as unconditional and the plaintiff could
proceed with the action. So, if a defendant wished to avoid submitting to the jurisdiction,
his safer course was not to enter a conditional appearance, but to take the second course
open to him, which was to apply before entering an appearance for an order setting aside
h the proceedings. This was of course the usual application made by a party outside the
jurisdiction, served with proceedings by virtue of leave given under RSC Ord 11, if that
party did not wish to submit to the jurisdiction.

Such in outline was the old procedure. Under the new procedure, much has changed;
but for present purposes the most important change is that the step of 'appearance' has
been abolished. In its place, we now have the step of 'acknowledgment of service'; but
j the two steps are by no means the same. Nowadays, every writ for service must be
accompanied by a form of acknowledgment of service; and it is the duty of each
defendant who wishes to acknowledge service of the writ, and to defend the action, to
complete (either himself or by his solicitor) the form in accordance with the directions
set out on it, and then to return it to the appropriate court office. If he fails to do so
within the prescribed time, then judgment in default of acknowledgment of service may

be entered against him. But, although the acknowledgment of service may operate as a
statement of intention to defend the proceedings, nevertheless it does not operate as a   *a*
waiver of any irregularity in the issue or service of the writ. This is expressly stated in the
new RSC Ord 12, r 7, which provides as follows:

> 'The acknowledgment by a defendant of service of a writ or notice of a writ shall
> not be treated as a waiver by him of any irregularity in the writ or notice or service
> thereof or in any order giving leave to serve the writ or notice out of the jurisdiction   *b*
> or extending the validity of the writ for the purpose of service.'

Moreover, not only has the step of 'appearance' been abolished, but the practice of
entering a conditional appearance has likewise been abolished. Instead, we find a new
procedure for disputing the jurisdiction of the court. This procedure is set out in RSC
Ord 12, r 8, which, since it lies at the heart of the dispute now before me, I propose to set
out in full in this judgment. Rule 8 provides as follows: *c*

> '(1) A defendant who wishes to dispute the jurisdiction of the court in the
> proceedings by reason of any such irregularity as is mentioned in rule 7 or on any
> other ground shall give notice of intention to defend the proceedings and shall,
> within 14 days thereafter, apply to the Court for—(a) an order setting aside the writ
> or service of the writ or notice of the writ on him, or (b) an order declaring that the   *d*
> writ or notice has not been duly served on him, or (c) the discharge of any order
> giving leave to serve the writ or notice on him out of the jurisdiction, or (d) the
> discharge of any order extending the validity of the writ for the purpose of service,
> or (e) the protection or release of any property of the defendant seized or threatened
> with seizure in the proceedings, or (f) the discharge of any order made to prevent
> any dealing with any property of the defendant, or (g) a declaration that in the   *e*
> circumstances of the case the court has no jurisdiction over the defendant in respect
> of the subject matter of the claim or the relief or remedy sought in the action, or
> (h) such other relief as may be appropriate.
> '(2) Order 3, rule 5, shall apply in relation to the period of 14 days mentioned in
> paragraph (1) with the modification that the said period may be extended by the
> Court only on an application made before the expiration of the period.   *f*
> '(3) An application under paragraph (1) must be made—(a) in an Admiralty
> action in rem, by motion; (b) in any other action in the Queen's Bench Division, by
> summons; (c) in any other action, by summons or motion, and the notice of motion
> or summons must state the grounds of the application.
> '(4) An application under paragraph (1) must be supported by an affidavit
> verifying the facts on which the application is based and a copy of the affidavit must   *g*
> be served with the notice of motion or summons by which the application is made.
> '(5) Upon hearing an application under paragraph (1), the Court, if it does not
> dispose of the matter in dispute, may give such directions for its disposal as may be
> appropriate, including directions for the trial thereof as a preliminary issue.
> '(6) A defendant who makes an application under paragraph (1) shall not be
> treated as having submitted to the jurisdiction of the court by reason of his having   *h*
> given notice of intention to defend the action; and if the Court makes no order on
> the application or dismisses it, the notice shall cease to have effect, but the defendant
> may, subject to rule 6(1), lodge a further acknowledgment of service and in that case
> paragraph (7) shall apply as if the defendant had not made any such application.
> '(7) Except where the defendant makes an application in accordance with
> paragraph (1), the acknowledgment by a defendant of service of a writ or notice of   *j*
> a writ shall, unless the acknowledgment is withdrawn by leave of the Court under
> Order 21, rule 1, be treated as a submission by the defendant to the jurisdiction of
> the Court in the proceedings.'

It follows that a defendant who wishes to dispute the jurisdiction of the court under
this rule, either by reason of any such irregularity as is mentioned in r 7, or on any other

ground, must take the following steps. First, he must give notice of intention to defend
a the proceedings. That of course he does by completing in the appropriate manner the
form of acknowledgment of service, and by returning it to the appropriate court office.
Next, within 14 days thereafter, he must apply to the court for the order which he seeks;
this application must, if made in an action in the Queen's Bench Division (other than an
Admiralty action in rem), be made by summons; and it must in any event state the
grounds of the application, and be supported by an affidavit verifying the facts on which
b the application is based, a copy of which must be served with the summons by which the
application is made. However, it is important to remember that, in relation to the
period of 14 days after notice of intention to defend the proceedings within which the
defendant has to make his application to the court, Ord 3, r 5 (which enables the court
to extend or abridge the period within which a person is required by the rules to do any
act in any proceedings) applies, but subject to an important modification, namely that
c the period of 14 days may be extended by the court only on an application made before
the expiration of that period. This is indeed a rigid and draconian provision, which
could have very harsh consequences: nobody in court on the argument before me was
aware of any other comparable provision in the Rules of the Supreme Court.

It is against this background that I come to the first submission of the plaintiffs, viz,
that the defendants' application must fail, because they had not complied with the
d relevant provisions of Ord 12, r 8. They said that the defendants had failed to comply
with the rule in two respects. First, their summons, though issued and served within 14
days of their giving notice of intention to defend the proceedings, did not state the
grounds of the application as required by r 8(3); second, no copy of the affidavit was
served with the summons as required by r 8(4). It followed, they submitted, that the
defendants, having failed to make an application as required by the rule within the
e specified period of 14 days, and having failed to apply within that period for an extension
of time under Ord 3, r 5, could no longer dispute the jurisdiction of the court, and must
be treated as having submitted to the jurisdiction of the court by virtue of Ord 12, r 8(7).

It is clear that, whatever meaning is to be attached to the words 'apply to the Court' in
Ord 12, r 8(1), the defendants did make such an application within the specified period
of 14 days after they gave notice of intention to defend the proceedings, because they not
f only issued their summons but also obtained a return date and served the summons on
the plaintiffs' solicitors within the specified period. But it is equally clear that they failed
to comply both with the requirement that the summons so issued and served should
state the grounds of their application, and with the requirement that a copy of the
affidavit in support should be served with the summons. The latter point is conceded.
As to the former, the only ground stated in the summons is that 'this Honourable Court
g does not have jurisdiction in this matter'. That is plainly not enough; every application
under Ord 12, r 8(1) is an application whereby the defendant disputes the jurisdiction of
the court, and merely to reiterate that bald fact cannot constitute the 'grounds for the
application' required by r 8(3) to be stated in the summons.

In these circumstances, counsel's submission on behalf of the plaintiffs was simple. He
said that the defendants' failure to comply with either of these two requirements had the
h effect that the defendants failed to do what was required of them within the 14-day
period specified in r 8(1); and that it was now too late, because of the requirement of
r 8(2), to put the matter right.

I must confess that I contemplate the consequences of this submission with dismay.
I put on one side the fact that the plaintiffs' submission in the present case is entirely
without merit, since it is conceded that the case has no connection whatsoever with this
j country and so is not a case in which the English courts could assert any jurisdiction, and
there is no evidence of the plaintiffs having suffered any prejudice by reason of the
defendants' procedural errors. But looking at the matter simply as a point on the
construction of the rules, the effect of the plaintiffs' submission is that, if any mistake is
made as to the form of a defendant's application, for example, a notice of motion is issued
instead of a summons or vice versa, or the grounds are not stated in the summons (even
though the plaintiff may already know what they are) or the copy affidavit is not served

with the summons, even though the plaintiff may know all the relevant facts which are to be relied on, then once the 14-day period has expired without the matter being put *a* right or at least an application being made under Ord 3, r 5, the court is powerless to assist the defendant. The possible injustice can be highlighted by taking extreme examples: for example, where the grounds are stated not in the summons but in a letter with which the summons is enclosed; or where a copy of the supporting affidavit is sent not with the summons, but in a separate letter which reaches the plaintiff's solicitors the day before the summons is served; or where the plaintiff's solicitors notice the procedural *b* error, but lie low and say nothing until the 14-day period expires. That the court should be powerless to intervene to ensure that justice is done in such cases as these is surely unthinkable.

In my judgment, the short answer to the whole problem lies in the wide powers now conferred on the court under RSC Ord 2, r 1. That rule provides as follows:

'(1) Where, in the beginning or purporting to begin any proceedings or at any *c* stage in the course of or in connection with any proceedings, there has, by reason of any thing done or left undone, been a failure to comply with the requirements of these rules, whether in respect of time, place, manner, form or content or in any other respect, the failure shall be treated as an irregularity and shall not nullify the proceedings, any step taken in the proceedings, or any document, judgment or order therein. *d*

'(2) Subject to paragraph (3), the Court may, on the ground that there has been such a failure as is mentioned in paragraph (1), and on such terms as to costs or otherwise as it thinks just, set aside either wholly or in part the proceedings in which the failure occurred, any step taken in those proceedings or any document, judgment or order therein or exercise its powers under these rules to allow such amendments (if any) to be made and to make such order (if any) dealing with the *e* proceedings generally as it thinks fit.

'(3) The Court shall not wholly set aside any proceedings or the writ or other originating process by which they were begun on the ground that the proceedings were required by any of these rules to be begun by an originating process other than the one employed.'

It will at once be observed that, on a straightforward reading of Ord 2, r 1(1), there *f* have in the present case been in connection with proceedings, by reason of something left undone, two failures by the defendants to comply with the requirements of Ord 12, r 8. It would appear to follow, first, that each of such failures shall be treated as an irregularity; second, that neither shall nullify the step taken by the defendants in the proceedings, viz their application for an order that the plaintiffs' writ be set aside; and, third, that the court has a discretion either to set aside the defendants' application or to *g* exercise its power under the rules to allow such amendment to be made or to make such order dealing with the proceedings generally as it thinks fit. Such an approach is supported by the observations of Lord Denning MR in *Harkness v Bell's Asbestos and Engineering Ltd* [1966] 3 All ER 843 at 845–846, [1967] 2 QB 729 at 735–736 where he said of the then new RSC Ord 2, r 1:

'This new rule does away with the old distinction between nullities and *h* irregularities. Every omission or mistake in practice or procedure is henceforward to be regarded as an irregularity which the court can and should rectify so long as it can do so without injustice. It can at last be asserted that "it is not possible . . . for an honest litigant in Her Majesty's Supreme Court to be defeated by any mere technicality, any slip, any mistaken step in his litigation" [see *Re Pritchard (deceased)* *j* [1963] 1 All ER 873 at 879, [1963] Ch 502 at 518 per Lord Denning MR].'

On this approach, since the plaintiffs have suffered no prejudice by reason of the defendants' errors, I would of course not hesitate, in the exercise of my discretion, to give leave to the defendants to amend their summons to state the grounds of their application, and to proceed with their application despite the late service of their affidavit in support.

Counsel for the plaintiffs submitted that this course was not open to me. He first
a submitted that the defendants did not apply to the court within 14 days of giving notice
of intention to defend the proceedings as required by Ord 12, r 8(1), because their
summons, though issued and served within that time, stated no grounds as required by
Ord 12, r 8(3); accordingly, no application for an extension of time having been made
before the expiry of the 14-day period as required by r 8(2), the court was precluded by
the rules from assisting the defendants. In my judgment, that is not right. The
b defendants did apply to the court within the specified time, though their application was
in one respect deficient in point of content. Since the defendants did apply to the court
within the specified time, Ord 12, r 8(2), does not act as a fetter on the court's power to
do justice in the present case, Next, counsel for the plaintiffs sought to invoke the old
distinction between mandatory and directory requirements; and further submitted that,
having regard in particular to the imperative words of Ord 12, r 8, both of the
c requirements with which the defendants failed to comply were mandatory, with the
consequence that the court either could not or should not exercise its discretion under
Ord 2, r 1(2) in the defendants' favour. Again, I cannot accept this submission. I very
much doubt if the imperative terms of the relevant provisions of Ord 12, r 8 would even
under the old law have led to their being categorised as mandatory; but even if that were
so, counsel's submission would, of course, entirely defeat the purpose of the present RSC
d Ord 2, r 1(2), and detract from the breadth of the discretion conferred by that rule.
Counsel for the plaintiffs then referred me to a number of situations in which the defect
in procedure is so fundamental that the court will, he submitted, always set aside the
relevant proceedings or step in the proceedings: for example, where a writ has not been
served as required by the rules, or notice of discontinuance has been given without leave
where leave was needed; or a writ has, without leave to renew, been served more than 12
e months after its issue; or a judgment in default has been irregularly signed. The present
case fell, he submitted, within the same category. Let it be assumed, he submitted, that
by virtue of Ord 2, r 1(2) the defendants' application was not a nullity; nevertheless, the
court must exercise its discretion under that rule to set the application aside. Again, I
cannot accept this submission. I do not doubt that there are defects in procedure so
fundamental that the court will invariably exercise its power to set aside the relevant
f proceedings or step in the proceedings; though even in such a case there is usually no
draconian provision of the Rules of the Supreme Court, equivalent to Ord 12, r 8(2), to
prevent the party in error from curing his mistake by then proceeding in accordance
with the rules. But I do not for one moment accept that the defects in procedure in the
present case fall into this category. It is only necessary for me to point out that, if the
grounds of the defendants' application had been set out in a letter to the plaintiffs'
g solicitors enclosing the summons, and a copy of the affidavit in support had not been
served with the summons but had been served the next day but still within the 14-day
period, counsel for the plaintiffs' argument could have been precisely the same. Plainly
this cannot be right.

It follows that I am unable to accede to any of the plaintiffs' arguments on this point;
I therefore exercise my power to give leave to the defendants to amend their summons
h to state the grounds of their application, and to proceed with it despite the late service of
their affidavit in support.

I turn next to the plaintiffs' second submission, which is that the defendants'
application should be dismissed on the ground that the defendants, through their
solicitors, have submitted to the jurisdiction of the court. In support of this submission,
the plaintiffs rely on certain correspondence, prior to the issue of the writ, which passed
j between the plaintiffs and the defendants' solicitors, and which culminated in the
following exchange. On 30th July 1979 the plaintiffs wrote a letter to the defendants'
solicitors which ended as follows:

'We must ask you to deal with this matter expeditiously, and if your clients are
not willing to settle this on a friendly basis, we must ask you to answer the last

paragraph of our letter of the 24th July, namely, if you are willing to accept service
on behalf of your clients, when we will instruct our solicitors to issue proceedings.
We are leaving this matter open until the 6th August which should give you
sufficient time to communicate with your clients.'

On 6th August, the defendants' solicitors replied, still disputing the plaintiffs' claim,
and their letter ended as follows:

'If you wish to serve proceedings we have no doubt that we shall be instructed to
accept service of them. Please therefore direct any such proceedings to us.'

The writ was issued over ten months later, on 11th June 1980. By that date, the new
procedure had come into force; and the defendants' solicitors then completed the form
of acknowledgment of service, as I have indicated.

In my judgment, the short answer to this point is that on no view could this exchange
of correspondence amount to a submission to the jurisdiction. It is not even a case where
the defendants' solicitors write, stating with authority that they have authority to accept
service, and then do so; it is simply a case of an indication by the defendants' solicitors
that they themselves expected, indeed had no doubt, that they *would* be instructed to
accept service, and proposed that, on that basis, proceedings should be directed to
them. On no view, in my judgment, could such an indication constitute a submission
by the defendants to the jurisdiction of the English court. I therefore reject this
submission. In these circumstances it is unnecessary for me to burden this judgment
with consideration of other arguments advanced by the defendants, in particular the
argument that acceptance of service by a defendant's solicitors, even with the authority
of their client, does no more than establish the fact and time of service, and in no way
amounts to a submission to the jurisdiction or precludes the defendant from thereafter
seeking to set aside the proceedings on the ground that the English court has no
jurisdiction in the matter. Such arguments are of course open to the defendants, if the
matter should be taken further.

Before leaving the case, there are two matters to which I wish to draw attention. First,
in the course of the argument before me, it appeared that there is some doubt as to what
is meant by the words 'apply to the Court' in RSC Ord 12, r 8(1). Does this mean that the
defendant should have simply issued his summons or notice of motion? Or that he
should have issued it and obtained a return date? Or that he should have issued it and
served it? The answer to this question is not altogether clear, and I have to say that the
notes to the new rule in the Supreme Court Practice betray a somewhat ambivalent
attitude. Thus in para 12/7–8/6, when referring to the tight time-scale in Ord 12, r 8, it
is stated that this is designed so that the plaintiff should know at an early stage whether
or not the defendant intends to dispute the jurisdiction of the court or to object to any
irregularity and, if so, on what ground. Such a rationalisation is more consistent with a
requirement that a summons or notice of motion should have been issued and served
within the 14-day period; and some support for this construction is perhaps to be derived
from the wording of Ord 12, r 8(4), which requires the copy affidavit in support to be
served with the notice of motion or summons by which the application *is made*. On the
other hand, turning again to para 12/7–8/6, reference is there made to a defendant
applying within the 14-day period for an extension of time, if he is unable to *issue* his
summons or motion within the 14 days. This more limited requirement is more
consistent with the traditional approach, under which a distinction is drawn between an
application to the court, which constitutes the issue of the relevant process, and the
service of that process on the respondent. A clear example of this approach is to be found
in the new Ord 73, r 5 concerned with certain applications relating to arbitration
proceedings (to remit or set aside an award, or to direct an arbitrator to state his reasons),
which provides that: 'An application to the Court . . . must be made, and the summons
or notice must be served, within 21 days . . .' Furthermore, it was stated in para 12/8/2
of the Supreme Court Practice 1979 (in relation to the old practice that an application to
the court to set aside proceedings, after a conditional appearance, must be made within

a the time limited by the court: see the old RSC Ord 12, r 7) that the application to the court would be in time if the notice or summons was *issued* within the specified time. It is true that the authority cited in support of this proposition (*Bonnell v Preston* (1908) 24 TLR 756) did not in fact support it; even so, this appears to have been the accepted understanding of the old practice, and it was against this background that the new Ord 12, r 8 was drafted. The point does not arise for decision in the present case; but there must be a likelihood that the requirement in the new Ord 12, r 8(1) of application to the

b court within 14 days will be construed in the same sense, ie as requiring only that the summons or motion should be issued within that time. Since there is, however, some doubt as to the true construction of these words, and since it was argued before me that such a construction would not achieve the purpose expressed in para 12/7–8/6, I think it desirable for the point to be drawn to the attention of the Rule Committee so that they can, if they think fit to do so, clarify or amend the words of the rule.

c   Second, I wish to return to the requirement in the new Ord 12, r 8(2) that an application under Ord 3, r 5 for an extension of the 14-day period within which an application to the court under r 8(1) has to be made, must be made before the expiration of the 14-day period. The exceptional rigidity of this requirement contrasts forcibly with the flexibility which is now generally characteristic of the Rules of the Supreme Court, and which enables the court to ensure that justice is done. No doubt short time

d limits are sometimes desirable; a recent example of this is the period of 21 days now required under Ord 73, r 5 for the commencement and service of proceedings to challenge arbitration awards. But the imposition of the guillotine in Ord 12, r 8(2) appears to be contrary to the trend in our rules, which is to ensure so far as possible that parties do not fall into procedural traps, and to give the court power to deal with the situation if they do so. The widening some years ago of the court's powers under Ord 2,

e r 1 to deal with failures to comply with the rules, provides a vivid illustration of this trend. It is not difficult to see how, due to error, oversight or even illness in a busy solicitor's office, the 14-day period in r 8(1) might be allowed to pass without an application being made under Ord 3, r 5 for an extension of time. I must confess that it seems strange that the court should be deprived of any power to remedy the situation, especially where the plaintiff has suffered no prejudice, as for example where the point

f at issue has already been developed in correspondence. I therefore wish respectfully to suggest to the Rule Committee that reconsideration might be given to the inflexible fetter imposed by Ord 12, r 8(2) on the court's discretion under Ord 3, r 5, bearing in mind that the exercise of any discretion which the court has to extend time will always take into account the purpose of the time limit and the need for finality in any particular case.

g   In the result, I accede to the defendants' application and order that the plaintiffs' writ issued on 11th June 1980 be set aside.

Application to set writ aside granted. Leave to appeal.

Solicitors: *Sinclair, Roche & Temperley* (for the plaintiffs); *Ince & Co* (for the defendants).

K Mydeen Esq   Barrister.

Liverpool and District Hospital for Diseases of the Heart v Attorney General

CHANCERY DIVISION

SLADE J

9th, 10th, 31st OCTOBER 1980

Company – Compulsory winding up – Liquidator – Powers – Distribution of surplus assets – Charitable association – Memorandum expressly prohibiting distribution of surplus assets among members on winding up and directing transfer of assets to similar institution with similar objects – No similar provision in articles of association – Whether companies legislation applicable to distribution of charitable company's assets – Whether members 'entitled' to surplus assets or having 'rights and interests' in company – Whether assets to be distributed among members – Companies Act 1948, ss 265, 302.

Charity – Company – Jurisdiction of court – Charitable association under legal obligation to apply assets for exclusively charitable purposes – No trust in strict sense in relation to assets but company in analogous position to trustee – Whether jurisdiction to direct cy-près scheme – Whether jurisdiction dependent on existence of strict trust.

In 1927 a company ('the association') was incorporated as a charitable association under the Companies Acts with the objects, set out in its memorandum of association, of providing a hospital for the treatment of heart diseases and promoting and procuring research work into such diseases. Clause 3 of the memorandum provided that the incorporation of the association should not diminish or impair the authority, inter alia, of the Chancery Division over its council of management or other governing body; cl 4 provided that the association's income and property should be applied solely towards the promotion of its objects and that no portion thereof should be paid or transferred directly or indirectly by way of dividend, bonus, or otherwise by way of profit to the members of the association; and cl 9 provided that on the winding up or dissolution of the association any property remaining after satisfying its debts and liabilities 'shall not be paid to or distributed among the members of the Association, but shall be given or transferred to some other institution . . . having objects similar to the objects of the Association . . . such institution . . . to be determined by the Members of the Association . . . or in default thereof by [a] High Court judge' having jurisdiction in the matter. The association's articles provided for life members, annual members and honorary members. The articles did not contain any provision corresponding to cl 9 of the memorandum. In pursuance of its objects the association administered a hospital and a research institute. In 1948 the hospital became vested in the Minister of Health by virtue of the National Health Service Act 1946 and the association ceased to have any connection with it. Thereafter the association's functions in respect of the research institute gradually petered out. The association last filed an annual return in 1968. In February 1978 the Attorney General, pursuant to s 30(1) of the Charities Act 1960, petitioned the court for a winding-up order in respect of the association and on 20th March the court made a compulsory winding-up order. On the winding up the association was found to have surplus assets. It was not clear whether any members of the association were still alive. The liquidator took out a summons asking for directions whether the surplus assets were to be distributed among the association's members, if any, or whether, in accordance with cl 9 of the memorandum, they were to be transferred to another institution with similar objects and, if the former, for directions as to any members' respective rights and interests in the association and, if the latter, for directions for a cy-près scheme. The liquidator, on behalf of the members, submitted (i) that s 265[a] of the Companies Act 1948 prevailed over cl 9 of the memorandum and that the surplus assets

---

a   Section 265 is set out at p 1002 *a*, post

were to be distributed among the members in accordance with s 265, read with s 302[b] of
a the 1948 Act, since 'the articles' did not 'otherwise provide', within s 302, as they did not
contain any provision corresponding to cl 9 of the memorandum, and (ii) that, if the
assets did not fall to be dealt with under ss 265 and 302, the court had no jurisdiction to
interfere in the association's affairs and therefore no jurisdiction to direct a cy-près
scheme, because the assets were not subject to a strict trust. The Attorney General
submitted (i) that the provisions of the 1948 Act for the application of a company's assets
b on a winding up did not apply to a company established for exclusively charitable
purposes because such a company held its assets solely as trustee and not as beneficial
owner, (ii) even if the assets fell to be dealt with under ss 265 and 302, the members were
not entitled under those sections to distribution of the assets among themselves, and (iii)
the court had jurisdiction to direct a cy-près scheme.

Held – (1) A company formed under the 1948 Act for exclusively charitable purposes
c was not a trustee of its corporate assets in the strict sense, although it was in a position
analogous to a trustee, because the mere fact that its assets could be applied only for the
charitable purposes set out in its memorandum did not make the company a trustee of
those assets in the strict sense, since the concept of a company incorporated under the
1948 Act which was incapable of holding assets beneficially but which was nevertheless
capable of incurring liabilities was inconsistent with the general intention of the 1948
d Act. Furthermore under the 1960 Act[c] a charity could exist without a concomitant trust
in the strict sense. Accordingly the surplus assets fell to be dealt with under s 265 of the
1948 Act, read with s 302 of that Act (see p 1006 *h*, p 1007 *g* to *j* and p 1008 *a b*, post);
dictum of Lord Parker in *Bowman v Secular Society Ltd* [1916–17] All ER Rep at 17–18
applied; *Re Dominion Students Hall Trust* [1947] Ch 183, *Re French Protestant Hospital*
[1951] 1 All ER 938, *Soldiers', Sailors' and Airmen's Families Association v Attorney General*
e [1968] 1 All ER 448 and *Construction Industry Training Board v Attorney General* [1972] 2
All ER 1339 considered.

(2) However, because of the express direction in cl 9 of the memorandum that on
dissolution of the association its surplus assets were to be transferred to another charitable
institution, the members of the association were not entitled to distribution amongst
themselves of the surplus assets, even though the articles did not provide that the assets
f should not be so distributed, since, in view of cl 9 of the memorandum, which overrode
the provisions of the articles, it could not be said that the members were 'entitled' to the
surplus assets within s 265 or that they had any 'rights and interests' in the association
within s 302. Moreover, by virtue of s 20(1)[d] of the 1948 Act the members were deemed
to have contracted with the association on the basis of the memorandum, as well as the
articles, and, by necessary implication of law, cl 9 of the memorandum was deemed to
g be included in the articles for the purpose of s 265. Furthermore, the association had
been incorporated on the express footing of cl 9 of the memorandum and therefore its
provisions were binding on the liquidator and the court and could not be overridden by
ss 265 and 302 (see p 1008 *g* to p 1009 *c*, post); *Re Merchant Navy Supply Association Ltd*
[1947] 1 All ER 894 distinguished.

(3) The court had jurisdiction to intervene in the affairs of a charitable company even
h though a trust in the strict sense did not exist in relation to its assets. All that was
required to confer jurisdiction on the court was that the company should be obliged
under the terms of its constitution to apply its assets for exclusively charitable purposes,
for the basis of the court's jurisdiction over charities was the existence of a person or body
against whom the court, if necessary, could act in personam. Since under the terms of
its constitution the association's assets were at all times held subject to a legally binding
j obligation to apply them for exclusively charitable purposes, the court had jurisdiction

---

b   Section 302, is set out at p 1002 *b*, post
c   See, eg, ss 28(8), 46
d   Section 20(1), so far as material, provides: 'Subject to the provisions of this Act, the memorandum
      . . . shall, when registered, bind the company and the members thereof to the same extent as if [it]
      . . . had been signed and sealed by each member, and contained covenants on the part of each
      member to observe all the provisions of the memorandum . . .'

to direct a cy-près scheme in accordance with cl 9 of the memorandum (see p 1009 *j* to
p 1010 *e* and *j* to p 1011 *a*, post); *Re Dominion Students' Hall Trust* [1947] Ch 183, dictum   *a*
of Buckley J in *Re Vernon's Will Trusts* [1971] 3 All ER at 1064–1065 and *Construction
Industry Training Board v Attorney General* [1972] 2 All ER 1339 applied.

Notes

For distribution of a company's assets, see 7 Halsbury's Laws (4th Edn) paras 1310, 1322,
and for cases on the subject, see 10 Digest (Reissue) 1091–1092, 6702–6708.

For the court's jurisdiction over charities in relation to limited companies, see 5   *b*
Halsbury's Laws (4th Edn) para 717.

For the Companies Act 1948, ss 20, 265, 302, see 5 Halsbury's Statutes (3rd Edn) 134,
318, 337.

For the Charities Act 1960, ss 28, 30, 36, see 3 ibid 627, 630, 634.

Cases referred to in judgment
                                                                                                    c
Ashbury Railway Carriage and Iron Co v Riche (1875) LR 7 HL 653, 44 LJ Ex 185, 33 LT
    450, Ex Ch, 9 Digest (Reissue) 674, 4021.
Attorney General v Haberdashers' Co (1834) 1 My & K 420, 39 ER 741, LC, 8(1) Digest
    (Reissue) 299, 405.
Attorney General v Magdalen College, Oxford (1847) 10 Beav 402, 7 Hare 564n, 16 LJ Ch
    391, 10 LTOS 85, 11 Jur 681, 50 ER 637, 8(1) Digest (Reissue) 455, 2054.   *d*
Ayerst (Inspector of Taxes) v C & K (Construction) Ltd [1975] 2 All ER 537, [1976] AC 167,
    [1975] 3 WLR 16, [1975] STC 345, 54 ATC 141, HL, Digest (Cont Vol D) 492, 1664a.
Bowman v Secular Society Ltd [1917] AC 406, [1916–17] All ER Rep 1, 86 LJ Ch 568, 117
    LJ 161, HL, 8(1) Digest (Reissue) 302, 427.
Construction Industry Training Board v Attorney General [1972] 2 All ER 1339, [1973] Ch
    173, [1972] 3 WLR 187, CA, 8(1) Digest (Reissue) 291, 359.   *e*
Dominion Students' Hall Trust, Re, Dominion Students' Hall Trust v Attorney General [1947]
    Ch 183, [1947] LJR 371, 176 LT 224, 8(1) Digest (Reissue) 391, 1233.
Faraker, Re, Faraker v Durell [1912] 2 Ch 488, [1911–13] All ER Rep 488, 81 LJ Ch 635,
    107 LT 36, CA, 8(1) Digest (Reissue) 351, 833.
Finger's Will Trusts, Re, Turner v Ministry of Health [1971] 3 All ER 1050, [1972] Ch 286,
    [1971] 3 WLR 775, 8(1) Digest (Reissue) 353, 847.   *f*
*French Protestant Hospital, Re, Governors and Directors of the Hospital for Poor French
    Protestants and their descendants residing in Great Britain v Attorney General* [1951] 1 All
    ER 938, [1951] Ch 567, 13 Digest (Reissue) 261, 2332.
Lucas (deceased), Re, Sheard v Mellor [1948] 2 All ER 22, [1948] Ch 424, [1948] LJR 1914,
    CA, 8(1) Digest (Reissue) 351, 834.
Manchester Royal Infirmary, Re, Manchester Royal Infirmary v Attorney General (1889) 43   *g*
    Ch D 420, 59 LJ Ch 370, 62 LT 419, 8(1) Digest (Reissue) 430, 1690.
Merchant Navy Supply Association Ltd, Re, [1947] 1 All ER 894, 177 LT 386, 10 Digest
    (Reissue) 1151, 7165.
Soldiers', Sailors' and Airmen's Families Association v Attorney General [1968] 1 All ER 448,
    [1968] 1 WLR 313, 8(1) Digest (Reissue) 430, 1693.
Vernon's Will Trusts, Re, Lloyds Bank Ltd v Group 20 Hospital Management Committee   *h*
    (Coventry) [1971] 3 All ER 1061, [1972] Ch 300, [1971] 3 WLR 796, 8(1) Digest
    (Reissue) 353, 846.
Von Ernst et Cie SA v Inland Revenue Comrs [1980] 1 All ER 677, [1980] 1 WLR 468, CA.

Cases also cited

Hickman v Kent or Romney Marsh Sheep Breeders' Association [1915] 1 Ch 881, [1914–15] All
    ER Rep 900.   *j*
Inland Revenue Comrs v Yorkshire Agricultural Society [1928] 1 KB 611, [1927] All ER Rep
    536, CA.
Southern Foundries (1926) Ltd v Shirlaw [1940] 2 All ER 445, [1940] AC 701, HL.

Adjourned summons

By an originating summons dated 25th March 1980 issued by the Official Receiver as
liquidator of the Liverpool and District Hospital for Diseases of the Heart ('the

a

association') certain relief was sought by the Official Receiver in regard to the distribution of the surplus assets of the association on its compulsory winding up. The respondent to the summons was the Attorney General. The terms of the relief sought and the facts are set out in the judgment.

Mary Arden for the Official Receiver.
John Mummery for the Attorney General.

b

Cur adv vult

31st October. **SLADE J** read the following judgment: This is an application by the Official Receiver as liquidator of a company known as Liverpool and District Hospital for Diseases of the Heart, which is now in liquidation. The summons asks for certain directions concerning the distribution of its assets.

The company (which I will call 'the association') was incorporated on 13th May 1927

c

under the Companies Acts 1908 to 1917 as a company limited by guarantee, the word 'Limited' being omitted from its name by licence of the Board of Trade.

Its memorandum of association was signed by seven subscribers. Clause 1 stated its name. Clause 2 provided that its registered office should be situated in England. At the date of its dissolution, its registered office was in fact situated at premises in Liverpool. Clause 3 provided:

d

'The Association is a Charitable Association and the objects for which the Association is established are the following objects (so far as such objects may be properly objects of a charitable Association) . . .'

There then followed 29 numbered sub-paragraphs of which I think I need only read the first and seventh:

e

'(1) To provide, maintain and manage a hospital or hospitals for the treatment of patients suffering from diseases or ailments of the heart and any such other accommodation as may seem expedient for the treatment, care and training of any such patients . . .
'(7) To promote and procure to be carried out investigation and research work as to the cause and cure of diseases and ailments of the heart and other diseases and

f

ailments of any kind . . .'

Clause 3 of the memorandum of association concluded with two provisos, the second of which included a provision to the effect that the incorporation of the association should not diminish or impair any control or authority exercisable by the Chancery Division, the Court of Chancery of the County Palatine of Lancaster, the Charity

g

Commissioners or the Board of Education over its council of management or other governing body or any trustees of the association. Clause 4 of the memorandum began with the following words:

'The income and property of the Association whencesoever derived shall be applied solely towards the promotion of the objects of the Association as set forth in this Memorandum of Association and no portion thereof shall be paid or transferred

h

directly or indirectly by way of dividend, bonus or otherwise howsoever by way of profit to the members of the Association.'

There followed a proviso to cl 4 which is, I think, wholly immaterial for present purposes.

Clause 5 stated:

j

'No addition, alteration or amendment shall be made to or in the regulations contained in the Articles of Association for the time being in force unless the same shall have been previously submitted to and approved by the Board of Trade.'

Clause 6 stated:

'The fourth and fifth paragraphs of this Memorandum contain conditions on which a Licence is granted by the Board of Trade to the Association in pursuance of section 20 of the Companies (Consolidation) Act 1908.'

Clause 7 stated that the liability of the members was limited. Clause 8 contained, in effect, an undertaking by each member of the association to contribute to the assets of the association in the event of a liquidation during his membership or within one year thereafter, for payment of the debts and liabilities and other items there mentioned, such amount as might be required not exceeding £1.

Clause 9 stated:

'If upon the winding-up or dissolution of the Association there remains, after the satisfaction of all its debts and liabilities, any property whatsoever, the same shall not be paid to or distributed among the members of the Association, but shall be given or transferred to some other institution or institutions having objects similar to the objects of the Association, and which shall prohibit the distribution of its or their income and property amongst its or their members to an extent at least as great as is imposed on the Association under or by virtue of Clause 4 hereof, such institution or institutions to be determined by the Members of the Association at or before the time of dissolution, or in default thereof, by the Vice-Chancellor of the County Palatine of Lancaster or such Judge of the High Court of Justice as may have or acquire jurisdiction in the matter, and if and so far as effect cannot be given to the aforesaid provision, then to some charitable object.'

Articles 2 to 14 of the association's articles of association dealt with its membership as follows, references therein to 'the council' meaning its council of management:

'2. For the purpose of registration the number of Members of the Association is declared not to exceed 500, but the Council may from time to time register an increase of members.

'3. The subscribers to the Memorandum of Association of the Association and such other persons as shall be admitted as members by the Council shall be Members of the Association and shall be entered in the Register of Members accordingly.

'4. The power of admitting Members of the Association shall be vested in the Council but shall be exercised by the Council in accordance with any regulations or directions issued and subject to any restrictions or conditions imposed as regards any particular class of Members or otherwise by the Association in General Meeting. Every member must before being admitted sign a written consent to become a member in such form as the Council shall approve.

'5. There shall be three classes of Members of the Association namely Life Members, Annual Members, and Honorary Members.

'6. The subscribers to the Memorandum of Association shall be Life Members.

'7. Every individual person who shall contribute £10 or upwards at one time by way of donation to the Association or who shall be nominated by any body which shall contribute £10 or upwards at one time by way of donation to the Association shall be eligible if willing to become a Life Member.

'8. Any person who shall contribute 10s. or upwards at one time by way of subscription to the Association shall be eligible if willing to become an Annual Member.

'9. Any person who shall render service to the Association otherwise than by the contribution of money shall be eligible if willing to become an Honorary Member.

'10. An Honorary Member shall be exempt from liability for any subscription. An Annual Member shall be liable to pay to the Association an Annual Subscription of not less than 10s.

'11. An Honorary Member shall cease to be a Member at the end of any year (other than the year during which he was admitted as an Honorary Member) unless during such year his membership shall have been confirmed by the council.

'12. An Annual Member shall cease to be a Member at the end of any year if the annual subscriptions payable by him for such year and also for the last preceding year shall both be in arrear.

'13. Annual Subscriptions shall be treated as becoming due on the 1st February in each year.

a   '14. Any member shall forthwith cease to be a Member (a) if he shall die, or (b) if he shall resign by giving a notice in writing to the Association of his intention so to do.'

Article 15 conferred on the council the power to determine a member's membership subject to certain conditions.

Significantly for present purposes, the articles of association contain no provision corresponding with cl 9 of the memorandum of association.

b   Before 5th July 1948, which was 'the appointed day' for the purposes of the National Health Service Act 1946, the association administered a hospital known as 'the Liverpool and District Hospital for Diseases of the Heart'. It also administered an establishment known as 'the Institute of Research for the Prevention of Disease', which was associated with the hospital, though it did not confine itself to diseases of the heart. Subclauses 3(1) and (7) of its memorandum of association would appear to have given the requisite *c*   authority for these activities.

By virtue of the National Health Service Act 1946, the hospital became vested in the Minister of Health by a scheme made on 5th July 1948 by the Liverpool Regional Hospital Board under s 11 of the 1946 Act and approved by the Minister of Health. The administration and control of the hospital, which had by then moved to new premises, became vested in the North Wirral Hospital Management Committee. The hospital *d*   took the new name of 'the Caldy Manor Hospital'. After implementation of the scheme, the association ceased to run it or to have any connection with it. It did, however, continue to carry on limited functions relating to research into the cause and cure of heart diseases and ailments. It appears that the assets which it held in connection with these activities were not treated as vesting in the Minister, who made no claim to them. It also appears that for some years an accountant, Mr James Henderson, acted as treasurer *e*   of the so-called Institute of Research for the Prevention of Disease, though he did not direct its activities. He has supplied the Official Receiver with some helpful information about the institute in a memorandum and in correspondence. From this it appears that, at all material times, separate accounts were produced in respect of the activities of the hospital and of the institute and indeed that the two sets of activities were administered by different persons. However, after the association lost the hospital, its activities carried *f*   on under the name of the institute gradually dwindled and in due course petered out. It last filed an annual return on 6th December 1968. Attached to this return was a certified copy of accounts of what was described in the accounts themselves as 'Liverpool Heart Hospital's Institute of Research'. The balance sheet which formed part of these accounts showed net assets of £7,573·25. Though the actual accounts themselves were headed in the manner in which I have indicated, they were presented by Mr Henderson *g*   and the then secretary of the association as being the accounts of the association itself. Mr Henderson has explained to the Official Receiver that, though in the past the possible incorporation of the institute as a separate body had been discussed, nothing ever came of this. Though the frequent references to the institute in the documents give rise to some possibility of confusion, I can see no reason to conclude that the assets held by the association at the date of its dissolution were held on any special trusts. On the evidence *h*   I conclude that they were held merely for its general purposes as set out in its memorandum of association. Accordingly I shall deal with the application now before me on this footing.

On 16th February 1978, pursuant to s 30(1) of the Charities Act 1960, the Attorney General presented a petition to this court for a winding-up order in respect of the association. Among the matters particularly relied on in support of this petition were *j*   the fact that the association had failed to file any annual returns since 6th December 1968, that it no longer carried out the activities of a research institute and appeared unlikely to resume them, and further that certain moneys were payable to it under the will of the late Edith Hellon, in respect of which the trustees of the will had been unable to obtain a receipt from the association. On 20th March 1978, Oliver J made the usual compulsory winding-up order in respect of the association. As a result of the first meeting of its creditors and contributories, Mr H W J Christmas, one of the Official Receivers attached to the court, is the liquidator. The present application is supported by an affidavit sworn by Mr Christmas, in which he states that all accounts and books in his possession concern only that part of the association's functions referring to the institute of research and that he assumes that all documents relating to the hospital were handed over to the National Health Service in 1948.

The submission of a statement of affairs was dispensed with pursuant to an order of the court dated 17th October 1978. The liquidator confirms that no liabilities have been notified or become known to him during the course of his liquidation and that to the best of his knowledge the association had no liabilities. Despite appropriate advertisement by him, no proofs of debts have been lodged. At the date of the winding up, the association's assets comprised certain investments and deposit accounts, together with an interest under Edith Hellon's will. All these assets have now been realised. The liquidator's evidence is that as at 5th December 1979 the funds of the association totalled £14,727. Subject therefore to the costs, charges and the expenses of the liquidation, the assets now representing these funds and interest thereon constitute the surplus assets of the association.

Prima facie, having regard to cl 9 of the association's memorandum of association, such assets do not fall to be paid or distributed among the members of the association, but must be given or transferred to some other institution or institutions of the nature referred to in cl 9, namely:

'... such institution or institutions to be determined by the Members of the Association at or before the time of dissolution, or in default thereof by the Vice-Chancellor of the County Palatine of Lancaster or such Judge of the High Court of Justice as may have or acquire jurisdiction in the matter, and if and so far as effect cannot be given to the aforesaid provision, then to some charitable object.'

The liquidator's evidence is that, to the best of his knowledge and belief, there has been no determination by the members of the association as to the institution or institutions to which the assets of the association should be given or transferred and, indeed, that it is not clear whether the association still has any members at all. The absence of any surviving members would not be entirely surprising. For there is no evidence that any subscriptions have been made to the association for a number of years or that there has been in existence a council of management, which could confirm the continuing membership of honorary members. It would therefore appear that there can no longer be any annual or honorary members of the association and that the only remaining members, if any, would be life members, since after careful inquiries it appears that all the original subscribers to the memorandum are either dead or untraceable. It further appears that the only continuing life members would be those who both were qualified by donation, as provided by art 7, and had signed written consents to become members, as provided by art 4. The evidence contained in the liquidator's affidavit of 15th April 1980 and the exhibits thereto shows that he has made careful inquiries in relation to the existence of members and that no person has come forward to claim membership. In particular Mr Henderson, though with full knowledge of these proceedings, has not sought to assert any rights as a member.

The summons

For reasons which will appear, and notwithstanding the provisions of cl 9 of the association's memorandum of association, the liquidator has been advised that there is doubt as to who is entitled to its surplus assets. Accordingly, on 25th March 1980, he issued the summons which is now before me, joining the Attorney General as respondent. The substantive relief sought by it is as follows:

'1. That directions may be given as to whether the assets of the Association remaining after satisfaction of its liabilities and the payment of the costs charges and expenses of its liquidation (including the remuneration of the Liquidator) are to be distributed among the members of the Association according to their rights and interests in the Association or are in accordance with Clause 9 of the Memorandum a of Association thereof to be given or transferred either to some other institution or institutions having objects similar to the objects of the Association and which shall prohibit the distribution of its or their income and property amongst its or their members to an extent at least as great as is imposed on the Association under or by virtue of Clause 4 of the Memorandum of Association thereof or to some other charitable object.

b '2. If the assets are to be distributed to the members as aforesaid, that directions may be given as to their respective rights and interests in the Association and as to the settlement of a list of contributories.

'3. If the said assets are to be given or transferred to some other institution or institutions as aforesaid, that a scheme may be settled for the administration of the Association and the endowments thereof upon the footing that the trusts thereof have failed and that the property and funds thereof ought to be applied cy-près.'

c No member of the association has been joined as a party to the proceedings, because it has not proved possible to ascertain any such person. The liquidator's personal attitude in the proceedings is, of course, an entirely neutral one; he merely desires the protection of directions of the court. Counsel for the Official Receiver, however, came prepared to submit argument to the court on behalf of the class of members, if any, if so requested by the court, in opposition to the arguments put forward on behalf of charity by counsel

d for the Attorney General. In response to my request, she has submitted full and helpful argument, for which I am grateful. The amount of the moneys at stake in the present proceedings is relatively small. I am satisfied that the interests of the members, if any, have been more than adequately represented and that, even in their absence, the proceedings are properly constituted.

e *The issues*

The summons gives rise to some interesting problems concerning the legal consequences of the winding up of a charitable company incorporated under the Companies Acts. It is surprising that they have apparently not been determined before. Perhaps the reason is that, as counsel for the Attorney General told me, this was the first company to be wound up by the court on an application made by the Attorney

f General under s 30(1) of the Charities Act 1960.

When the respective arguments are set side by side, it seems to me that substantially they resolve themselves to the following three issues. (A) Are the surplus assets in question property of the association, which falls to be dealt with by the liquidator in accordance with s 265 of the Companies Act 1948? (B) If the answer to question (A) be Yes, are the members entitled to such surplus assets by virtue of s 265? (It is, I think,

g common ground that this section constitutes the only footing on which they can claim such entitlement.) (C) If the members are not entitled to such surplus assets, has the court jurisdiction to order a cy-près scheme and, in the exercise of its discretion, should it do so?

h *Issue (A)*

The Companies Act 1948 contains a large number of provisions relating to the application of a company's assets on a winding up. Though it expressly recognises that a company may be formed under the Act for promoting charity (see, for example, s 19(1)), it does not expressly exempt charitable companies from these provisions. Accordingly, counsel for the Official Receiver submitted that they apply in their full

j force in relation to the assets vested in the association at the date of its winding up; and indeed all her submissions, put forward on behalf of members, are based on this premise.

Section 257(1) of the 1948 Act provides, inter alia, that as soon as may be after making a winding-up order, the court shall 'cause the assets of the company to be collected, and applied in discharge of its liabilities'. After the process of collection of assets and discharge of liabilities has been completed on a winding up by the court, the net remaining assets of the company fall to be dealt with in accordance with s 265, which provides:

'The court shall adjust the rights of the contributories among themselves and distribute any surplus among the persons entitled thereto.'   *a*

Counsel for the Official Receiver has submitted that s 265 applies in the present case and that the members are 'the persons entitled' to the surplus, within the meaning of this section. It is common ground that light is thrown on the meaning of the phrase just quoted by s 302, which contains the following provisions for the application of a company's assets on a voluntary winding up:

> 'Subject to the provisions of this Act as to preferential payments, the property of   *b*
> a company shall, on its winding up, be applied in satisfaction of its liabilities pari
> passu, and, subject to such application, shall, unless the articles otherwise provide,
> be distributed among the members according to their rights and interests in the
> company.'

It would be a paradoxical result if the ultimate distribution of the net assets of a   *c*
company on a winding up by the court had to be effected in favour of different persons from those who would take on a voluntary winding up; and indeed counsel for the Attorney General has not so contended. As Lord Diplock said in *Ayerst v C & K Construction Ltd* [1975] 2 All ER 537 at 540, [1976] AC 167 at 176:

> '. . . the essential characteristics of the scheme for dealing with the assets of the   *d*
> company do not differ whichever of these procedures is applicable.'

Accordingly, counsel for the Official Receiver has submitted, under s 265, when read in conjunction with s 302, the net assets of the association in the present case must 'unless the articles otherwise provide' be distributed among 'the members according to their rights and interests in the company'.

The expression 'articles' is defined by s 455(1) of the 1948 Act as meaning 'the articles   *e*
of association of a company as originally framed or as altered by special resolution . . .'
The definition, however, is not in terms wide enough to include a company's memorandum of association. The articles of the association in the present case do not in terms 'otherwise provide' within the meaning of s 302, because they contain no provision corresponding with cl 9 of the memorandum. I understand that the articles of association of charitable companies limited by guarantee, incorporated under the Companies Acts,   *f*
in many, perhaps most, instances expressly repeat the provisions of the relevant clause of the memorandum, prohibiting the distribution of assets to members on a winding up and providing for their transfer to similar charitable institutions. It is the absence of such a provision in the association's articles which has led to the principal doubts in the present case, giving rise to the issue of the summons. Correspondingly, it is this point on which counsel for the Official Receiver primarily relies in supporting the claims of   *g*
members.

I confess that counsel's submissions, based on s 265 of the Companies Act 1948, at first sight struck me as somewhat startling. For they necessarily presuppose that members of the association are capable of having 'rights and interests in the company', within the meaning of s 302, and of being 'persons entitled thereto', for the purpose s 265, even though the association's memorandum contains (a) provisions expressly prohibiting the   *h*
distribution of the company's assets to members, both during its existence and on a winding up and (b) further provisions expressly directing the transfer of the company's assets to similar charitable institutions on a winding up.

However, the decision of Vaisey J in *Re Merchant Navy Supply Association Ltd* [1947] 1 All ER 894 may be said to be direct authority for the proposition that provisions of type   *j*
(a) will not by themselves prevent members from taking in reliance on s 302. In that case, a private company's memorandum had provided that its income and property should be applied solely towards the promotion of its objects and that no portion thereof should be transferred by way of dividend, bonus or otherwise to members of the company, but the memorandum and the articles contained no provision dealing with the manner of application of surplus assets on a winding up. The company went into voluntary liquidation. Questions then arose as to the application of its surplus assets,

having regard to s 247 of the Companies Act 1929, which corresponded with s 302 of the
a 1948 Act. Vaisey J held that if, contrary to his view, the provision in the memorandum
on its true construction prohibited the payment of surplus assets to members on a
winding up, it was inoperative, because it attempted to exclude the express provisions of
s 247, without substituting any alternative provision. He said this ([1947] 1 All ER 894
at 895):

> *b* 'Counsel for the Attorney-General has argued that this is a case in which the
> surplus profits ought to go to the Crown as being *bona vacantia*, because the only
> other claimants are subject to the prohibitive clause which provides that they are
> not entitled to any profit. It may well be that such was the intention of those who
> formed the company at a very critical moment of the war, but, if it was the
> intention, they should have put in an express provision to deal with the surplus
> assets in a winding up, *e.g.*, the common form provision which is to be found in the
> *c* memorandum and articles of a company limited by guarantee and registered
> pursuant to s. 18 of the Act of 1929, without the word "limited"—in other words,
> the form, sanctioned by the Board of Trade, which says that on winding up any
> surplus assets shall be transferred to some organisation having comparable objects.
> I find nothing of that kind here, and in all the circumstances it seems to me that
> s. 247 must prevail, with the result that I must declare that the surplus assets of the
> *d* company, after satisfying costs, ought to be distributed among the members of the
> company according to their rights and interests in the company.'

Vaisey J thus implicitly assumed in his judgment that the members of the company
had 'rights and interests in the company'. Similarly, in the present case, counsel for the
Official Receiver has submitted that s 265 of the 1948 Act must prevail over the
memorandum and that the net assets of the association ought now to be distributed
e among its members, according to their rights and interests.

Faced with these submissions on behalf of the members, counsel for the Attorney
General, submitted one proposition which at first sight I found as startling as the contrary
submission founded on s 265. This was to the effect that the statutory provisions for the
application of a company's assets on a winding up do not apply at all in relation to any
assets held by a charitable company, on the grounds that all such assets whatsoever are ex
f hypothesi held by the company solely as trustee and not beneficially. I must deal with
this submission, before turning to the other points on which counsel affirmatively bases
his case.

Though s 265 does not define the 'surplus' there referred to, and s 302 does not define
'the property of a company' there referred to, the two phrases in their context can, in my
judgment, include only those items of property which under the general law are available
g for the discharge of a company's liabilities. Thus they will include assets of which the
company is beneficial owner, even though the legal title may be vested in other
trustees. They will not, however, comprise assets of which the company at the date of its
liquidation was merely a trustee (in the strict sense) for third parties or for charitable
purposes, even though the legal title may have been vested in it. This much, I think, is
clear.

h Counsel for the Attorney General has submitted that a company established for
exclusively charitable purposes ex hypothesi holds its general corporate assets as trustee
for the general purposes set out in its memorandum of association. In this context he
referred me to a number of authorities, though I do not think he suggested that any of
them conclusively decide the point in his favour.

In *Re Manchester Royal Infirmary* (1889) 43 Ch D 420, a corporation incorporated under
j a special Act of Parliament held its funds for charitable purposes. North J held that the
funds were trust funds vested in it as a 'trustee' within the meaning of the Trust
Investment Act 1889. Since, however, the provisions of the special Act of Parliament
appear to have imposed an express trust on the corporation in regard to the assets
received by it, the case is of little assistance in the present context.

More pertinently, *Re Dominion Students' Hall Trust* [1947] Ch 183 concerned a charitable
company limited by guarantee which maintained a hostel for male students of the

overseas dominions of the British Empire, the benefits of which were restricted to dominion students of European origin. The company asked by summons for the *a* sanction of a scheme by which the charity might be administered as part of a wider charity for the benefit of all such students, regardless of their origin. It also asked by petition for confirmation of a special resolution to alter its memorandum of association in an appropriate manner with respect to its objects. Though the report does not indicate that the assets held by the company were subject to any special trusts, the argument presented to the court on behalf of the charity (at 185) was to the effect that the case was *b* one in which the court could 'administer the trusts of the charity cy-près'. Evershed J said (at 186) that he had thought it right to be particularly careful to see that he had jurisdiction to authorise the scheme and to sanction the petition. He then referred to the general principle that funds given by a testator for particular charitable purposes cannot be applied cy-près by the court, unless it has been shown to be impossible to carry out the testator's intention. He concluded, however, that the case before him fell within the *c* broad description of 'impossibility', illustrated by certain earlier decisions to which he referred. He did not specifically advert to the question whether the charity held its assets on trust, but seems implicitly to have accepted the assumption that trusts existed, simply by virtue of the fact that the objects of the company were charitable; and indeed he referred (at 187) to the corporation as 'the trust'. This case, therefore, does lend some support, albeit not conclusive support, to counsel for the Attorney General's proposition. *d*

In *Re French Protestant Hospital* [1951] 1 All ER 938, [1951] Ch 567 a charitable corporation had been established by Royal Charter. Its directors purported to introduce a byelaw designed to enable them to receive remuneration for services rendered. Danckwerts J held that the directors, though not themselves technically trustees, were in the same fiduciary position as trustees in respect of the affairs of the corporation and accordingly were debarred from introducing the new byelaw by the principle of law *e* which precludes trustees from making a profit out of their trust. So far as the report shows, the terms of the corporation's charter created no express trust in respect of the assets to be held by it. Danckwerts J, however, seems to have assumed that such a trust existed, for he expressed the view that—

> 'it would be a great change if it were thought proper for such a general provision *f* to be inserted in a document regulating charitable trusts, particularly on the motion of the trustees themselves.'

(See [1951] 1 All ER 938 at 941, [1951] Ch 567 at 572.)

Again, therefore, this case lends some, but by no means conclusive, support for counsel for the Attorney General's submission.

In *Soldiers', Sailors' and Airmen's Families Association v Attorney General* [1968] 1 All ER *g* 448, [1968] 1 WLR 313 questions arose as to the nature and extent of the powers of investment of the charity concerned, having regard to the Trustee Investments Act 1961. Cross J said this in the course of his judgment ([1968] 1 All ER 448 at 450, [1968] 1 WLR 313 at 317):

> 'One starts with this, that the plaintiff . . . which is a chartered corporation, is a charitable corporation and accordingly is in the position of a trustee with regard to *h* its funds. That was submitted by counsel for the Attorney-General and conceded by counsel for the Association.'

Since the existence of the trusteeship to which Cross J referred in this case was based on a concession of counsel, I think it is of limited assistance for present purposes.

Much more significant is the decision of the Court of Appeal in *Construction Industry* *j* *Training Board v Attorney General* [1972] 2 All ER 1339, [1973] Ch 173. In that case the question was whether the board was a charity within the meaning of s 45(1) of the Charities Act 1960. This subsection defines 'charity' as meaning—

> 'any institution, corporate or not, which is established for charitable purposes and is subject to the control of the High Court in the exercise of the court's jurisdiction with respect to charities . . .'

It was conceded that the purposes for which the board was established were charitable
a purposes. Substantially, therefore, the only question for the court was whether the board
was 'subject to the control of the High Court in the exercise of the Court's jurisdiction
with respect to charities', within the meaning of s 45(1). The majority of the Court of
Appeal (Buckley LJ and Plowman J, Russell LJ dissenting) held that it was so subject.
Much of the judgments in that case concerned the construction and effect of the particular
provisions of the constitution of the board and of various provisions of the Charities Act
b 1960. I do not think I need to refer to those passages. However, Buckley LJ made some
general observations in relation to the jurisdiction of the courts to regulate the proper
application of funds devoted to charitable purposes ([1972] 2 All ER 1339 at 1347–1348,
[1973] Ch 173 at 186–187):

> 'Where the Crown invokes the assistance of the courts for such purposes, the
> jurisdiction which is invoked is, I think, a branch of the court's jurisdiction in
c > relation to trusts. In such cases the relief granted often takes the form of an order
> approving a scheme for the administration of the charity which has been laid before
> the court, but this is not the only way in which the court can exercise jurisdiction
> in respect of a charity or over charity trustees. The approval of a scheme of this
> nature is, so far as I am aware, a form of relief peculiar to charities, but it does not
> constitute relief of a kind given in the exercise of a jurisdiction confined to giving
d > relief of that sort. The court could, for instance, restrain trustees from applying
> charitable funds in breach of trust by means of an injunction. In the case of a
> charity incorporated by statute this might, as was suggested in the present case, be
> explained as an application of the doctrine of ultra vires, but I do not think that this
> would be a satisfactory explanation, for a similar order on unincorporated trustees
> could not be so explained. Or, by way of further example, the court could order
e > charity trustees to make good trust funds which they had misapplied, or could order
> them to account, or could remove or appoint trustees, or could exercise any other
> kind of jurisdiction available in the execution of trusts other than charitable trusts.
> In every such case the court would be acting on the basis that the property affected
> is not in the beneficial ownership of the persons or body in whom its legal ownership
> is vested but is devoted to charitable purposes, that is to say, is held on charitable
f > trusts.'

Later in his judgment Buckley LJ expressed the conclusion that the funds from time to
time in the hands of the board were held 'on a statutory trust for exclusively charitable
purposes' (see [1972] 2 All ER 1339 at 1348, [1973] Ch 173 at 187). Plowman J, though
in a brief judgment appears to have agreed with this conclusion (see [1972] 2 All ER 1339
g at 1349–1350, [1973] Ch 173 at 188–189).
  Buckley LJ made some further observations on the subject in a recent decision of the
Court of Appeal in *Von Ernst et Cie SA v Inland Revenue Comrs* [1980] 1 All ER 677, [1980]
1 WLR 468. This case concerned capital transfer tax and the decision ultimately turned
on the proper meaning to be given to the phrase 'benefit' and 'beneficially entitled', as
these expressions were used in para 3(2) of Sch 7 to the Finance Act 1975. Buckley LJ said
h ([1980] 1 All ER 677 at 687–688, [1980] 1 WLR 468 at 479–480):

> 'We were referred to certain authorities which give support to the view that a
> company incorporated for exclusively charitable purposes is in the position of a
> trustee of its funds or at least in an analogous position. The authorities were in *Re
> French Protestant Hospital* [1951] 1 All ER 938, [1951] Ch 567, *Soldiers', Sailors' and
> Airmen's Families Association v Attorney-General* [1968] 1 All ER 448, [1968] 1 WLR
j > 313, *Construction Industry Training Board v Attorney-General* [1972] 2 All ER 1339,
> [1973] Ch 173 and *Re Finger's Will Trusts* [1971] 3 All ER 1050, [1972] Ch 286. In
> the first two of these cases it seems to me that it was assumed, rather than decided,
> that a corporate charity was in the position of a trustee of its funds. In the third, the
> question was what was meant by the words "in the exercise of the court's jurisdiction
> with respect to charities" in the Charities Act 1960, s 45(1). In the course of my
> judgment in that case I certainly did express the view that the court would exercise

its jurisdiction over corporate charities on the basis that their assets were held on charitable trusts and it appears to me that Plowman J, as I understand his very short judgment, agreed with me in that respect. *Re Finger's Will Trusts* turned on a question of whether or not a bequest to a charitable corporation, which ceased to exist in the testatrix's lifetime, demonstrated a general charitable intention capable of permitting a cy-près application. I do not think that it is a decision which is of assistance for present purposes.'

Buckley LJ, however, continued:

'On this part of the case as on the earlier part, I do not think that authority helps us much. We have to construe para 3(2).'

The remainder of his judgment made it plain that he reached his decision on the basis of his interpretation of the particular words of para 3(2) and not on the broader basis that a corporate charity is, ex hypothesi, in the position of a trustee of its funds.

It is significant that in *Von Ernst et Cie SA v Inland Revenue Comrs* [1980] 1 All ER 677 at 687, [1980] 1 WLR 468 at 479 Buckley LJ described the earlier authorities referred to by him as giving support to the view that—

'a company incorporated for exclusively charitable purposes is in the position of a trustee of its funds or *at least in an analogous position.*' (The emphasis is my own.)

It is also significant that, in the same case, Bridge LJ had said that, for the purposes of his own judgment, he assumed the correctness of a submission by the Crown that—

'a company formed under the Companies Acts, though its objects may be exclusively charitable, is nevertheless not a trustee of its assets.'

(See [1980] 1 All ER 677 at 684, [1980] 1 WLR 468 at 475.)

The third member of the court, Templeman LJ, expressed no view on this particular point.

The expressions 'trust' and 'trust property' may be, and indeed have been, used by the court in rather different senses in different contexts. Examples of cases where the court has used the expression otherwise than in their strict traditional sense are to be found in Lord Diplock's review of certain earlier authorities in *Ayerst v C & K (Construction) Ltd* [1975] 2 All ER 537 at 542–543, [1976] AC 167 at 179–180. In a broad sense, a corporate body may no doubt aptly be said to hold its assets as a 'trustee' for charitable purposes in any case where the terms of its constitution place a legally binding restriction on it which obliges it to apply its assets for exclusively charitable purposes. In a broad sense it may even be said, in such a case, that the company is not the 'beneficial owner' of its assets. In my judgment, however, none of the authorities on which counsel for the Attorney General has relied (including the decision in *Construction Industry Training Board v Attorney General* [1972] 2 All ER 1339, [1973] Ch 173) establish that a company formed under the Companies Act 1948 for charitable purposes is a trustee in the strict sense of its corporate assets, so that on a winding up these assets do not fall to be dealt with in accordance with the provisions of s 257ff of that Act. They do, in my opinion, clearly establish that such a company is in a position *analogous to that of a trustee* in relation to its corporate assets, such as ordinarily to give rise to the jurisdiction of the court to intervene in its affairs; but that is quite a different matter. The conclusion that a company incorporated for charitable purposes is not a trustee in the strict sense of its corporate assets, in my judgment, derives strong support from the following considerations.

First, there is the decision of the House of Lords in *Bowman v Secular Society Ltd* [1917] AC 406, [1916–17] All ER Rep 1. This was a case where a testator left his residuary estate outright to a society. Among the questions which arose was whether a trust was created for the purposes of the society. Lord Parker said ([1917] AC 406 at 440–441, [1916–17] All ER Rep 1 at 17–18):

'The only possible argument in favour of the testator's intention to create a trust rests upon this: The society is a body corporate to which the principle of your

Lordships' decision in *Ashbury Railway Carriage and Iron Co.* v. *Riche* ((1875) LR 7 HL
653) is applicable. Its funds can only be applied for purposes contemplated by the
memorandum and articles as originally framed or altered under its statutory
powers. A gift to it must, it may be said, be considered as a gift for those purposes,
and therefore the society is a trustee for those purposes of the subject-matter of the
gift. This argument is, in my opinion, quite fallacious. The fact that a donor has
certain objects in view in making a gift does not, whether he gives them expression
or otherwise, make the donee a trustee for those objects. If I give property to a
limited company to be applied at its discretion for any of the purposes authorized
by its memorandum and articles, the company takes the gift as absolutely as would
a natural person to whom I gave a gift to be applied by him at his discretion for any
lawful purpose. The case of *Attorney-General* v. *Haberdashers' Co.* ((1834) 1 My & K
420, 39 ER 741) is an express authority on this point. A gift of a fund on trust to pay
the income thereof in perpetuity to a society, whether corporate or otherwise,
might possibly, if the objects of the society were charitable, be established as a
charitable gift, exempt from objection on the ground that it created a perpetuity.
But it is one thing to establish a gift (which would otherwise fail) on the ground that
it is charitable, and quite another thing to avoid a gift which would otherwise be
good on the ground that it creates an unenforceable trust. If a gift to a corporation
expressed to be made for its corporate purposes is nevertheless an absolute gift to the
corporation, it would be quite illogical to hold that any implication as to the donor's
objects in making a gift to the corporation could create a trust. The argument, in
fact, involves the proposition that no limited company can take a gift otherwise
than as trustee. I am of opinion, therefore, that the society, being capable of
acquiring property by gift, takes what has been given to it in the present case, and
takes it as absolute beneficial owner and not as trustee.'

Lord Dunedin and Lord Buckmaster similarly stated that no trust existed (see [1917]
AC 406 at 435, 478 [1916–17] All ER Rep 1 at 14, 38). Though that decision itself did
not concern a charitable company, the observations of Lord Parker already cited were in
terms wide enough to include charitable companies and, as appears from this passage, the
existence of such companies was specifically present to his mind. I think it fair to assume
that if he had considered that different principles applied in respect of charitable
corporations, he would have been likely to qualify his generally expressed observations.
It is significant that so far as appears from the reports the *Bowman* decision was not even
referred to in argument either in the *Construction Industry Training Board* case or in *Von
Ernst et Cie SA v Inland Revenue Comrs*.

Second, the concept of a company incorporated under the Companies Act 1948 which
is incapable of holding any asset whatsoever beneficially but is nevertheless fully capable
of incurring liabilities in its own name and on its own behalf would seem to me
inconsistent with the general intention of the legislature, as appearing from the Act. It
would likewise be a remarkable result if, as counsel for the Attorney General contends,
its creditors on a winding up could never resort to its assets by reference to the statutory
scheme of distribution provided for by the Act, even if they might still have some right
of resort by reference to principles of trust law.

Third, as counsel for the Official Receiver pointed out, there are a number of
definitions in the Charities Act 1960 which presuppose that a charity can exist without
a concomitant trust in the strict sense. Thus s 28(8) defines 'charity proceedings' as
meaning—

'proceedings in any court in England or Wales brought under the court's
jurisdiction with respect to charities, or brought under the court's jurisdiction with
respect to trusts in relation to the administration of a trust for charitable purposes.'

Section 46 defines 'trusts' in relation to a charity as meaning:

'the provisions establishing it as a charity and regulating its purposes and
administration, whether those provisions take effect by way of trust or not . . .'

Section 45(2) contains a provision expressly excluding from the definition of 'charity' for the purposes of the Act 'any ecclesiastical corporation . . . in respect of the corporate property of the corporation . . .' The latter provision presupposes that, but for it, a 'charity' within the meaning of the Act would be capable of existing, even in respect of the corporate property of an ecclesiastical corporation.

For all these reasons, I accept counsel for the Official Receiver's submission that the assets held by the association at the date of the dissolution constituted assets of the association and that the net assets now fall to be dealt with in accordance with s 265 of the 1948 Act.

Issue (B)

I now have to consider whether the members (if any) can claim any rights in such assets by virtue of s 265 of the 1948 Act, in the manner submitted by counsel for the Official Receiver. Counsel for the Attorney General submitted that on any footing the answer to this question must be in the negative. As I have said, it is common ground that s 265 falls to be construed in conjunction with s 302. The decision of Vaisey J in *Re Merchant Navy Supply Association Ltd* [1947] 1 All ER 894 is authority for the proposition that these sections are by themselves capable of conferring statutory rights on members of a company to share in its surplus assets on a winding up, under the statutory scheme of distribution, even though neither its memorandum nor its articles expressly confer any rights on members to participate in this manner. Indeed, it is authority for the proposition that this result may ensue even if the company's memorandum expressly prohibits the distribution of assets to members both during its existence and after a winding up.

Nevertheless, any distribution of surplus assets under s 265 has to be effected among 'the persons entitled thereto' and, under s 302, among 'the members according to their rights and interests in the company'. It is one thing to hold that members may have 'rights and interests in the company' on its liquidation, within the meaning of s 302 (as Vaisey J implicitly held in the *Merchant Navy Supply Association* case), or that persons may be 'entitled' to its surplus assets for the purpose of s 265, even though its memorandum of association, without expressly directing distribution to other designated persons, expressly prohibits the distribution of any assets to members on a winding up. While I think it unnecessary to express any opinion whether Vaisey J's decision was correct on its particular facts, it is clearly arguable that a mere prohibitive provision of the nature contained in the company's memorandum of association in that case is not by itself capable of abrogating any statutory rights which members of the company would otherwise enjoy under s 265 or s 302. In my judgment, however, it would be quite another thing to hold that members may be 'entitled' for the purposes of s 265, or that they may have 'rights and interests in the company' for the purpose of s 302, even though a company's memorandum of association expressly directs that the surplus assets shall be transferred to other designated persons. The wording of s 302 makes it clear that an express direction to such effect contained in a company's articles of association would be capable of operating to deprive members of any benefits which they might otherwise enjoy on a liquidation by virtue of that section. A fortiori, in my judgment, an express direction to such effect in a company's memorandum of association would produce this result. If it should be asked why the legislature omitted any express reference in s 302 to a company's memorandum of association, my answer would be that such reference could reasonably have been considered unnecessary. As is stated in Halsbury's Laws of England:

'The articles are subordinate to the memorandum; any clause in them, if and so far as it is at variance with the memorandum, is to that extent overruled by it and inoperative, the memorandum being the charter of the company and defining its powers . . .'

(See 7 Halsbury's Laws (4th Edn) para 122.)

In my judgment, having regard to s 20(1) of the 1948 Act, the members of the association must be deemed to have contracted with the association on the basis of the

a memorandum, no less than the articles. I think that, by necessary implication of law, the provisions of cl 9 of the association's memorandum can properly be deemed to be included in its articles for the purposes of s 265. Even if that conclusion is incorrect, however, on any footing the members of the association, in the events which have happened, cannot in my judgment be said to be 'entitled' to its surplus assets, within the meaning of s 265, or to have any 'rights and interests in the company' within the meaning of s 302. The association has been incorporated, with all the privileges attached

b to incorporation, on the footing expressly stated in its memorandum of association that on a dissolution the surplus assets are to be transferred not to members but to other charitable institutions to be selected in the manner specified in cl 9. The provisions of cl 9 are, in my judgment, binding both on the liquidator and the court and are not capable of being overridden by s 265 or s 302. For these reasons the claims put forward on behalf of members in the present case must, in my judgment, fail.

c *Issue (C)*

It is, however, still necessary to consider whether the court has jurisdiction to order a cy-près scheme, as sought by the Attorney General, and if so whether in the exercise of its discretion it should do so. Counsel for the Official Receiver submitted that the court's jurisdiction to intervene in the affairs of a charity is always dependent on the existence

d of a trust. In this context, she referred to *Attorney General v Magdalen College, Oxford* (1847) 10 Beav 402, 50 ER 637 in which Lord Langdale MR held that the court had no jurisdiction to give the relief asked, on an information for the reformation of alleged abuses in the management of a school established by the founder of the college. The provisions of the college's statutes which regulated its government included a provision for a visitor, who thereby was given certain powers to enforce the statutes. Lord

e Langdale MR said ((1847) 10 Beav 402 at 410–411, 50 ER 637 at 640):

'The college has, no doubt, a very important duty to perform with reference to the school, and the performance of that duty may be enforced by proper authority; but, unless it be a duty founded on a trust which this Court can execute, the performance of the duty is not to be enforced here.'

f The court came to the conclusion that there was no evidence of a trust 'as the word is understood in this Court' and that the proper remedy was through the visitor, not the court (see (1847) 10 Beav 402 at 410, 50 ER 637 at 640). Counsel for the Official Receiver relied on this case as authority for the proposition that a trust (by which she meant a trust in the strict sense) has to exist before the court has jurisdiction to intervene in the affairs of a charity.

g I think, however, that *Re Dominion Students' Hall Trust* and *Construction Industry Training Board v Attorney General* are authority for the proposition that the court may have jurisdiction to intervene in the affairs of a company, even though a trust in the strict sense does not exist in relation to its assets. At least so far as appears from the facts as set out in the reports, a trust in this sense existed in neither of these cases. Though in the other cases relied on by counsel for the Attorney General (such as the *French Protestant*

h *Hospital* case), the court referred to the existence of a trust, they were, in my judgment, using the word 'trust' in the wider sense to which I have referred. In this context the learned editors of Halsbury's Laws of England make this significant comment:

'The court's jurisdiction has always been said to depend on the existence of a trust, but a limited company or other corporation is capable of being subject to the court's charity jurisdiction and therefore of being a charity for the purposes of the Charities

j Act 1960: see ss. 30, 45 (1). For the purposes of this rule the word "trust" may, perhaps, have a rather wider meaning than usual.'

(See 5 Halsbury's Laws (4th Edn) para 717, n 8.)

In my judgment the so-called rule that the court's jurisdiction to intervene in the affairs of a charity depends on the existence of a trust, means no more than this: the court has no jurisdiction to intervene unless there has been placed on the holder of the assets in question a legally binding restriction, arising either by way of trust in the strict traditional sense or, in the case of a corporate body, under the terms of its constitution, which obliges him or it to apply the assets in question for exclusively charitable purposes; for the jurisdiction of the court necessarily depends on the existence of a person or body who is subject to such obligation and against whom the court can act in personam so far as necessary for the purposes of enforcement. Nevertheless, it should be added for the sake of clarity, even when these conditions are fulfilled, the particular terms of the trust or constitution in question may operate substantially or partially to oust the jurisdiction of the court (see s 45(1) of the Charities Act 1960 and *Construction Industry Training Board v Attorney General* [1972] 2 All ER 1339 at 1343–1344, [1973] Ch 173 at 181–182 per Russell LJ). *Attorney General v Magdalen College, Oxford* was, in my judgment, one such case.

Counsel for the Official Receiver's submission that the court never has jurisdiction to intervene in the affairs of a charitable company unless the assets are held subject to a trust in the strict sense would involve the conclusion, as she recognised, that the court would *never* have jurisdiction to intervene in relation to the corporate assets of a charitable company formed under the Companies Acts. With due respect to the argument, this suggested conclusion has, I think, only to be stated to demonstrate the fallacy of the premise.

In the present case, as I have indicated, I do not think that the assets of the association were held by it subject to a trust in the strict sense. Nevertheless, under the terms of its constitution, they were at all times held subject to a legally binding obligation, which bound it to apply them for exclusively charitable purposes. It can therefore fairly be said that the position of the association in relation to its assets has at all times been analogous to that of a trustee for charitable purposes. This in my judgment suffices to give rise to the jurisdiction of the court to order a cy-près scheme in the events which have happened. Buckley J in referring to an incorporated charity in *Re Vernon's Will Trusts* [1971] 3 All ER 1061 at 1064–1065, [1972] Ch 300 at 304 said:

'The guild was, however, incorporated for exclusively charitable purposes, and its memorandum of association was so framed that its funds could never be distributed among its members and that in a winding-up any surplus assets would continue to be applied for objects similar to those of the incorporated guild. Whether and how far it would be right to regard the funds of the incorporated guild as subject to a charitable trust, I do not pause to consider beyond pointing out that any assets which it took over from the unincorporated guild would appear to have been subject to such a trust. Trust or no trust, however, it is true to say that the assets of the incorporated guild were all effectually dedicated to charity. In no circumstances— at least without the intervention of Parliament—could any of those funds have been used otherwise than for charitable purposes of the kind for which the guild existed so long as those purposes remained practicable. Even if those purposes ceased to be practicable, the charity would not cease to exist, although its funds would be applied cy-près. Such a charity, considered as a charity and apart from the mechanism provided for the time being and from time to time for holding its property and managing its affairs, could never cease to exist except by exhaustion of all its assets and cessation of its activities. A change merely in its mechanical aspect could not involve the charity ceasing to exist. The principle of the decisions in *Re Faraker, Faraker v Durell* [1912] 2 Ch 488, [1911–13] All ER Rep 488 and *Re Lucas (decd), Sheard v Mellor* [1948] 2 All ER 22, [1948] Ch 424 is, in my judgment, equally applicable to an incorporated charity of this kind as to a charity constituted by means of a trust. In such cases the law regards the charity, an abstract conception distinct from the institutional mechanism provided for holding and administering the fund of the charity as the legatee . . .'

In my judgment, the same principles are applicable in the present case. There is here no question of the particular provisions of the association's constitution ousting the jurisdiction of the court. On the contrary, it expressly recognises and adopts that jurisdiction (see cll 3 and 9 of its memorandum of association). The charity created by *a* the incorporation of the association has not ceased to exist merely by virtue of its winding up. Clause 9 of the memorandum in terms contemplated that, in the event of a winding up, its assets should be applied cy-près by being given or transferred to an institution or institutions having similar objects and to be selected by the court in default of any determination by the members. In my judgment, the court, in the exercise of its jurisdiction over charities, can and should give effect to this provision by directing a cy-près scheme.

b
Conclusion
    Other interesting points have been canvassed in argument concerning the relationship between the Companies Acts and the Charities Act 1960, in particular the provisions of s 5 of the Companies Act 1948, which would appear to give even a charitable company the power to alter its objects, and the provisions of s 30(2) of the Charities Act 1960,
c relating to the effect of such an alteration. However, I have not thought it necessary to deal with these points.
    In the final result, in answer to question 1 of the summons, I propose to direct that the assets of the association remaining after satisfaction of its liabilities and the payment of the costs, charges and expenses of its liquidation (including the remuneration of the liquidator) are, in accordance with cl 9 of the memorandum of association thereof, to be
d given or transferred to some other institution or institutions which shall have objects similar to the objects of the association and shall prohibit the distribution of its or their income and property among its or their members to an extent at least as great as was imposed on the association under or by virtue of cl 4 of its memorandum of association. No directions fall to be given under para 2 of the summons. Under para 3, I propose to direct a scheme for the administration of the association and the endowments
e thereof on the footing that the trusts thereof have failed and that the property and funds thereof ought to be applied cy-près.
    [After hearing counsel on the directions which should be given in relation to such a scheme, his Lordship continued:] Counsel for the Attorney General has invited me to settle a scheme for the administration of the assets of the association here and now, following my judgment. He has adduced in evidence an affidavit of Mr M E Mead, a
f solicitor who has had the conduct of this matter on behalf of the Attorney General. Mr Mead in this affidavit draws attention to the British Heart Foundation which is a national charity and, as its memorandum shows, has objects similar to objects of the association, in particular to the objects of the association which related to research into diseases of the heart. Mr Mead's evidence is that the foundation is the only charity appearing in the Charities Digest 1980 (which is a standard reference book for the major charities
g operating in the United Kingdom) as being concerned with research into heart diseases. Its memorandum of association contains a prohibition corresponding with that contained in cl 4 of the association's memorandum. Mr Mead has quite rightly drawn to the court's attention that Mr Henderson, the former accountant of the association, suggested that as the moneys which now form the assets of the association were probably contributed locally, a local charity in the Liverpool district ought to benefit. He has suggested the
h Liverpool School of Tropical Medicine. I have no doubt that this body is an excellent institution but, as Mr Mead points out, the evidence shows that research into heart diseases is only a very small part of the total work undertaken by that school. In all the circumstances, I accept the submission made on behalf of the Attorney General that the British Heart Foundation would be an eminently suitable recipient for the funds of the association. I propose, therefore, to direct that the assets of the association be transferred
j to the British Heart Foundation.

Determination and directions accordingly.

Solicitors: *Herbert Smith & Co* (for the Official Receiver); *Treasury Solicitor.*

Jacqueline Metcalfe   Barrister.

Holloway v Cross

QUEEN'S BENCH DIVISION
DONALDSON LJ AND HODGSON J
19th NOVEMBER 1980

Trade description – False trade description – Meaning of trade description – Indication of history including previous ownership or use – Previous use – Motor car – Mileage – Mileage recorded on odometer substantially less than actual mileage – Trader unaware of true mileage – Trader estimating mileage and including it in contract of sale – Estimated mileage substantially less than actual mileage – Whether estimate a false trade description – Trade Descriptions Act 1968, ss 2(1), 3(3).

A car dealer bought a car registered in 1973. Its odometer recorded that the car had done 716 miles but it had in fact done 73,000 miles. A prospective purchaser asked the dealer what the car's true mileage was. The dealer told him that he did not know (which was true) but that he would make inquiries. Subsequently, when completing an invoice for the sale of the car to the purchaser, the dealer asked him what his estimate of the car's true mileage was and when the purchaser refused or was unable to make any suggestion the dealer, using his knowledge of the motor trade and of the general condition of the car and of the information in a trade guide to car prices, suggested that the car had done about 45,000 miles which the purchaser accepted. The dealer wrote 'Recorded mileage indicator reading is 716 estimated 45,000' on the invoice and gave the purchaser a warranty document (issued by an insurance company) which only applied to cars which had done less than 60,000 miles. The dealer was charged with supplying, in the course of his trade or business, a car to which a false trade description had been applied, contrary to s 1(1)(b) of the Trade Descriptions Act 1968. The magistrates held that his estimate of the car's mileage was, by virtue of s 3(3)[a] of the 1968 Act, deemed to amount to a false trade description because it was likely to be taken as an indication of the history of the car. He was convicted and appealed, contending that in the circumstances his estimate was not a false trade description but merely an expert opinion, albeit a wrong opinion, given in response to the purchaser's inquiry.

Held – Even if the dealer's estimate had not been a 'false trade description' within s 2(1)[b] of the 1968 Act, which was debatable since it had been an indirect indication of the previous use of the vehicle the dealer's estimate was likely to have been taken as an indication of the history of the car, since there would have been no point in the purchaser asking for the dealer's opinion as to the mileage of the car unless he wished to obtain an indication of the actual mileage, and as such it was false to a material degree and so was deemed to amount to a false trade description by virtue of s 3(3) of the 1968 Act. Accordingly the dealer had been rightly convicted and his appeal would be dismissed (see p 1014 h to p 1015 b, post).

Notes

For false trade descriptions, see Supplement to 38 Halsbury's Laws (3rd Edn) para 820A.3.

For the Trade Descriptions Act 1968, ss 1, 2, 3, see 37 Halsbury's Statutes (3rd Edn) 949, 950, 952.

Case stated

This was an appeal by way of a case stated by the justices for the county of Kent acting in and for the petty sessional division of Medway in respect of their adjudication as a magistrates' court sitting at Chatham on 16th August 1978 whereby they convicted the

---

a   Section 3(3) is set out at p 1014 b, post

b   Section 2(1), so far as material, is set out at p 1013 j, post

appellant, Henry James Holloway, of offences under s 1(1)(*a*) and (*b*) of the Trade
a Descriptions Act 1968 on an information preferred by the respondent, Michael David
Cross of the Trading Standards Department, Gillingham, which alleged that on 1st
October 1977 at Wainscott, Kent the appellant in the course of a trade or business applied
to a Triumph 2·5 PI motor car, registration no HRN 670L, a false trade description as to
use, namely that the estimated mileage was 45,000 miles, contrary to s 1(1)(*a*), and that
on the same day he supplied to a purchaser a motor car to which a false trade description
b as to use was applied, contrary to s 1(1)(*b*). The facts are set out in the judgment of
Donaldson LJ.

Daniel Worsley for the appellant.
Gregory Stone for the respondent.

DONALDSON LJ. This is another of the odometer cases. Mr Holloway, who is a
c motor trader, appeals by case stated against his conviction by the magistrates for Kent
sitting at Chatham on 16th August 1978.

The charges were the usual charges under ss 1(1)(*a*) and 1(1)(*b*) of the Trade Descriptions
Act 1968 of applying a false trade description to any goods in the course of trade or
business and supplying or offering to supply goods to which a false trade description is
applied.
d The facts were these. The appellant had bought a Triumph motor car which had been
first registered in 1973. The mileage was, in fact, in excess of 70,000. When he bought
it the odometer reading was slightly over 700 miles. The purchaser saw the car and
asked the appellant what its correct mileage was. He was told by the appellant, as was the
fact, that he did not know. However, the appellant also said that he would make
inquiries. Apparently it was necessary to do some minor repairs on the car and the
e purchaser came back, with a view to buying the car, on 1st October 1977. He and the
appellant co-operated in completing a document known as a 'used car invoice'.

The appellant asked the purchaser what was the purchaser's estimation of the car's
mileage but, perhaps not surprisingly, the purchaser was unable or declined to make any
suggestions initially. The appellant then asked the purchaser if he thought that a figure
of 45,000 miles sounded correct. This was accepted by the purchaser on the basis, no
f doubt, that it sounded correct, and the invoice was completed by the appellant to read
'Recorded mileage indicator reading is 716 estimated 45,000'.

The magistrates found that the purchaser would not have bought the motor car if he
had known its true mileage was 73,000. They found that the figure of 45,000 miles was
an average figure for a vehicle of this make, age and appearance, and that the method of
calculating mileage, that is to say on the basis of make, age and appearance, is not always
g accurate or reliable. The magistrates went on to find that on the same occasion, when
delivery was being taken and this invoice was being made up, the appellant gave the
purchaser a warranty document issued by an insurance company, which applied to cars
under six years of age, which of course this car was, but only if they had covered less than
60,000 miles.

They found that the appellant, in putting forward the estimate of 45,000 miles, used
h his knowledge of the motor trade and the general condition of the car and the
information given in Glass's Guide. On that evidence, the magistrates came to the
conclusion that the description 'estimated 45,000 miles' did not come within s 2 of the
Trade Descriptions Act 1968 and so was not a trade description as such. Therefore, so far
as s 2 was concerned, there could have been no application of a false trade description.

However, they held that it was within the extension to the concept of a false trade
j description, which is provided by s 3(3). Let me therefore refer briefly to those two
sections. Section 2(1) provides:

> 'A trade description is an indication, direct or indirect, and by whatever means
> given, of any of the following matters with respect to any goods or parts of goods,
> that is to say . . . (*j*) other history including previous ownership or use.'

What was said below, and has extensively been repeated here, is that inasmuch as this statement was a mere statement of the appellant's opinion, it could not come within s 2. *a* Section 3(3), however, reads as follows:

'Anything which, though not a trade description, is likely to be taken for an indication of any of those matters and, as such an indication, would be false to a material degree, shall be deemed to be a false trade description.'

The magistrates accepted that what was said and done was not an application of a trade *b* description in the strict sense of the words but as being within the extended meaning provided by s 3(3).

They went on to explain that view in the following words, taken from the case stated:

'The indication was false to a material degree as set out in s 3(1) of the 1968 Act because the difference between the true mileage (73,000) and 45,000 was very large, *c* notwithstanding the fact that 45,000 was an alleged estimated figure; the likely impact of the words used was to mislead as to the true mileage of the car, bearing in mind all the circumstances inter alia: (a) The appellant had promised to find out the true mileage; (b) The fact that the appellant put forward 45,000 as an accurate estimate; (c) That a warranty document was also given by the appellant to the witness May which expressly related to cars under 60,000 miles; (d) The words were *d* not used in circumstances which suggested that no reliance should be placed on them; (e) One of the implications of the words used was that the mileage of the car was average when this was not so; and (f) One reason why the estimate was given was for the purposes of the warranty company, who would also have been misled by them.'

The question which is left for the opinion of this court is: *e*

'Whether the appellant's opinion, based on the condition and general appearance of the car, concurred in by the purchaser that it had travelled some 45,000 miles, expressed in the invoice as 'estimated 45,000 miles' in the absence of any evidence or suggestion by the prosecution that the said estimate was not made bona fide, amounted in law to a false trade description.' *f*

Counsel for the appellant, who has argued this appeal with conspicuous moderation and clarity, submits that this 'estimated 45,000' was neither a trade description within s 2 nor within the extension in s 3(3). His argument is really very simple. What it amounts to is this. The purchaser was interested to find out, since the matter was in doubt, what was the information of the appellant as to the mileage of the car. Taking the facts as a *g* whole, the purchaser knew perfectly well that the appellant did not know what the mileage was. All he wanted was an expert opinion. He got an expert opinion, and it was a bona fide expert opinion. That, he says, is the end of the matter. He adds for good measure that it is entirely irrelevant that there was an insurance company in the background or that the warranty document was given. He says that the charge relates solely to the application of the words 'estimated 45,000 miles'. *h*

In my judgment that is an undue simplification. If it is a valid argument in relation to s 2(1) and that the words, taken in the circumstances in which they were used, do not fall within s 2(1), which, I may say, is somewhat debatable, bearing in mind that 2(1) relates to an indication 'direct or indirect', it seems to me almost clear beyond argument that if this was not a trade description it was likely to be taken by the purchaser as an indication of the history of the vehicle and, of course, if so taken was false to a material *j* degree. There cannot have been any point in asking the opinion of the seller as to the mileage which seems to have been done, except with a view to obtaining an indication of what its mileage was in fact. Once I have said that, I have, I think really said everything that need be said. That was the conclusion of the magistrates. In my judgment they were entitled to reach that conclusion. I would personally have been

slightly surprised if they had reached any other conclusion. I would, therefore, answer
a the question of law by saying that the words complained of did amount, in law, to a false
trade description within the meaning of s 3(3).

HODGSON J. I agree. I would only add this. Speaking personally, I am far from
satisfied that the prosecution were right to concede that this expression of opinion was
not an indirect indication of previous use directly within s 2. Had that been the way the
b prosecution had put the case, and had the magistrates come to a decision on s 2, then I
would go this far with counsel for the appellant: that many of the findings of fact would
have been quite irrelevant because s 1 creates an offence of strict liability which can only
be got out of by a special defence set out under s 24. But, once the prosecution were
going on s 3(3), it was then necessary for the magistrates to decide whether what was said
was likely to be taken for an indication, and in deciding that I think they were right to
c take into account the matters, or at least many of the matters, on which they made
findings of fact.

Appeal dismissed.

Solicitors: *Redfern & Stigant*, Chatham (for the appellant); *W G Hopkin*, Maidstone (for the
d respondent).

N P Metcalfe Esq Barrister.

Storer v Wright and another
e
COURT OF APPEAL, CIVIL DIVISION
LORD DENNING MR, BRIGHTMAN LJ AND SIR GEORGE BAKER
5th, 6th, 26th NOVEMBER 1980

Legal aid – Taxation of costs – Review of taxation – Jurisdiction of court to order review – Law
f *Society refusing to give authority for review of taxation by judge – Solicitor applying to judge to*
have taxation reviewed as on ordinary non-legal aid taxation – Whether legal aid costs able to be
taxed and reviewed under ordinary procedure – Whether judge able to review legal aid taxation
without Law Society's authority to have taxation reviewed – RSC Ord 62, r 35 – Legal Aid
(General) Regulations 1971 (SI 1971 No 62), reg 23(7).

g Solicitors who acted for a legally-aided client submitted a bill of costs for taxation
following the dismissal of their client's action. The taxing master disallowed a number
of items relating to solicitors' and counsels' fees. The solicitors obtained leave from the
area committee under reg 23(6)(*b*)[a] of the Legal Aid (General) Regulations 1971 to carry
in an objection to the taxation. The taxing master heard the objection and disallowed
the items. The solicitors then applied to the Law Society under reg 23(7)[b] for authority
h to have the taxation reviewed by a judge but the Law Society, who considered that the
items of expenditure involved had not been justified, refused to give authority. The
solicitors appealed direct to a judge for a review of the taxation under RSC Ord 62, r 35[c]
in the same manner as on a review of an ordinary non-legal aid taxation. The Law
Society contended that a legal aid taxation could not be reviewed under Ord 62, r 35, and
that before it could be reviewed by a judge under reg 23(7) the Law Society's authority
j was required. The judge held that he had no jurisdiction to hear the appeal without the
authority of the Law Society. The solicitors appealed.

---

a Regulation 23(6), so far as material, is set out at p 1024 *d*, post
b Regulation 23(7), so far as material, is set out at p 1024 *e*, post
c Rule 35, so far as material, is set out at p 1022 *c*, post

Held – Because the review of a legal aid taxation was inquisitorial and administrative in character in contrast to an ordinary taxation which was adversarial in character, the two *a* systems of taxation were mutually exclusive. Legal aid taxation was confined to the procedure prescribed by reg 23 of the 1971 regulations and could not be carried out under the procedure for non-legal aid taxation prescribed by RSC Ord 62, rr 33 to 35. Accordingly, since the Law Society had properly refused to give their authority under reg 23(7) for a review and that decision could not be impugned, the judge had rightly decided that he had no jurisdiction to entertain the solicitors' application. The appeal *b* would accordingly be dismissed (see p 1017 *h*, p 1018 *a d*, p 1019 *c* to *g*, p 1020 *c d* and *g* to *j*, p 1021 *b j*, p 1022 *a* and *c* to *f*, p 1024 *h j* and p 1026 *a* and *f*, post).

Notes

For the Legal Aid (General) Regulations 1971, reg 23, see 5 Halsbury's Statutory Instruments (Fourth Reissue) 354.   *c*

As from 1st January 1981 the 1971 regulations have been replaced by the Legal Aid (General) Regulations 1980, SI 1980 No 1894.

Cases referred to in judgments

Collins v Royal Arsenal Co-operative Society Ltd (1962) 106 Sol Jo 818, 50 Digest (Repl) 496, 1764.

Giles v Randall [1915] 1 KB 290, [1914–15] All ER Rep 285, 84 LJKB 786, 112 LT 271, *d* CA, 51 Digest (Repl) 933, 4733.

Hammond v Hammond [1957] 3 All ER 16, [1957] P 349, [1957] 3 WLR 395, 50 Digest (Repl) 496, 1762.

Hanlon v Law Society [1980] 2 All ER 199, [1980] 2 WLR 756, HL; *varying* [1980] 1 All ER 763, [1980] 2 WLR 756, CA.

McCullie v Butler [1961] 2 All ER 554, [1962] 2 QB 309, [1961] 2 WLR 1011, 50 Digest *e* (Repl) 500, 1779.

Page v Page [1953] 1 All ER 626, [1953] Ch 320, [1953] 2 WLR 432, CA, 50 Digest (Repl) 495, 1758.

Rolph v Marston Valley Brick Co Ltd [1956] 2 All ER 50, [1956] 2 QB 18, [1956] 2 WLR 929, 50 Digest (Repl) 499, 1775.

Sutton v Sears [1959] 3 All ER 545, [1960] 2 QB 97, [1959] 3 WLR 791, 50 Digest (Repl) *f* 496, 1763.

Cases also cited

Brown v Brown [1952] 1 All ER 1018, CA.
Eaves v Eaves [1955] 3 All ER 849, [1956] P 154.
Neill v Glacier Metal Co Ltd [1963] 3 All ER 477, [1965] 1 QB 16.   *g*
Saltmarsh v Saltmarsh [1952] 2 All ER 6, DC.

Appeal

This was an appeal by the plaintiff's solicitors, Messrs Kingsford, Dorman & Co, against the decision of Neill J, sitting with assessors, on 9th July 1980 on the hearing of the solicitors' application for a review of the legal aid taxation of their costs, that the court *h* had no jurisdiction to entertain the application for review and that the application should be dismissed. The facts are set out in the judgment of Lord Denning MR.

Richard Fernyhough for the solicitors.
Duncan Matheson for the Law Society.

                                                   Cur adv vult *j*

26th November. The following judgments were read.

LORD DENNING MR. Peter Storer jumped off the pier at Swanage into the water. He hit some obstruction underneath. His leg was so badly injured that it had to be amputated. He said it was the fault of his instructors. He was on a diving course for one

a week run by the Divers Down Diving School. He said they ought to have been aware of
the danger and warned him not to dive or jump into the water at that place or at that
time. The accident happened on 7th September 1973. He was granted a civil aid
certificate on 22nd August 1974. A writ was issued on 19th December 1975. The action
was tried by Thompson J for four days from 8th to 11th November 1977. The judge
dismissed the claim altogether. He said it was the man's own fault. But he added that,

b if he had awarded damages, they would have been £40,000. The man was legally
aided. So the defendants got no costs out of him. They had to pay their own costs. That
was hard on them: all the result of legal aid. The man himself did not have to pay his
own costs. They were to be taxed and paid by the legal aid fund.

The man's solicitors, having lost the case, then brought in a bill of costs for payment
by the legal aid fund. It included the fees payable to leading counsel and junior counsel

c and solicitors' fees. One item in the bill related to a view which was held at Swanage pier,
together with a conference there. It was held in September 1977, four years after the
accident. The locus in quo was different in that the sea bed may well have been at a
different level and some civil engineering work (in operation at the date of the accident)
had been completed. It was attended by counsel, and by solicitors, as well as a diving
expert and a surveyor. It must have cost a lot of money. On taxation, the taxing master

d disallowed counsel's fees for attending the conference and view, and also the solicitors'
fees and expenses in connection with that view. He thought that a prudent solicitor with
a private client would not have expended that big a sum without his client's agreement
in advance, and that it was doubtful if the area committee would have authorised it if
they had been asked. There were other items too which the taxing master disallowed.
Such as counsel's fees for a conference in April 1976, on the ground that the taxing

e master could find nothing to show that any conference ever took place, and part of
leading counsel's brief fee (claimed at £550 but taxed at £350).

The solicitors were aggrieved, on their own account and for counsel, at the disallowing
of those items. They carried in objections. The taxing master adhered to his opinion.
He disallowed the items and gave his answers to the objections.

The solicitors then wanted to appeal to the judge. They asked the Law Society for

f authority to do so. The Law Society refused. So the solicitors went to the judge. They
appealed to him, asking that the cost of the view and other items should be allowed. But
the judge held that he had no jurisdiction to hear the appeal. He said that if the Law
Society had authorised it, he would have had jurisdiction, but, as the Law Society had not
authorised it, he had no jurisdiction.

g

1. *Ordinary taxations*

'Taxation of costs' is a technical term. All that it means is the allowing, or disallowing,
by an officer of the court, of the charges made by a solicitor for the work he has done.
The High Court has inherent jurisdiction to order a taxation or to review it. It also has

h jurisdiction under the Solicitors Act 1974, ss 56 to 75.

In all ordinary cases (other than legal aid taxation) the taxation is conducted on an
adversarial basis. The bill is put forward by one party, and contested by another. There
are two principal bases of taxation. (a) Taxation on the 'party and party' basis means that
the taxing officer must consider the matter as if a losing party had been ordered to pay
costs to a winning party. The taxing officer must allow only such costs as were necessary

j or proper for the attainment of justice. It is of great importance to litigants who are
unsuccessful that they should not be oppressed by having to pay an excessive amount of
costs. (b) Taxation on a 'common fund' basis means that the taxing officer should be
more generous. He should allow the solicitor a reasonable amount in respect of all costs
reasonably incurred (see RSC Ord 62, r 28(4)) and only disallow such as are unreasonably
high or unreasonably incurred.

2. *Legal aid taxations*

A legal aid taxation is different from all others, in that there is no one to oppose it. It is not adversarial, but inquisitorial. The taxing master is the inquisitor. The Legal Aid Act 1974 says in s 10(1) that 'a solicitor who has acted for a person receiving legal aid shall be paid for so acting out of the legal aid fund . . .' But who is to challenge his bill? There is no one to contest the amount at all. If the client has lost the case, and has a nil contribution, he is not concerned in the least with the amount that the solicitor charges. If he has won the case, and awarded damages, he may be much concerned, because the solicitor gets a charge, for his costs, on the amount of damages recovered. The higher the solicitor's bill, the less his damages. But the client is never represented in the taxation or even told about it.

Schedule 2, para 4, to the 1974 Act says that on a legal aid taxation—

'costs shall be taxed . . . according to the ordinary rules applicable on a taxation as between solicitor and client where the costs are to be paid out of a common fund . . .'

That only means on the same basis as would be applied if it were a taxation on a 'common fund' basis, that is, a reasonable sum in respect of costs reasonably incurred. That paragraph does not bring in the rule of the Supreme Court about review by a judge contained in Ord 62, r 35.

Seeing that there is no one to oppose, it seems to me that, on a legal aid taxation, it is the duty of the taxing officer to bear in mind the public interest. He should himself disallow any item which is unreasonable in amount or which is unreasonably incurred. In short, whenever it is too high, he must tax it down. Otherwise, the legal aid system could be much abused by solicitors and counsel. Not that it was abused in this case. But there is the possibility of it unless closely watched. I cannot help remarking that, in a legally-aided case, counsel's fees are not marked on the brief. Nor is there any negotiation about them between counsel's clerk and the solicitor. The barrister's clerk claims the fee at what he thinks the case is worth. Solicitors' fees are often left to a subordinate in the office or even to an outside costs clerk who may claim to be paid commission on the amount of the bill as drawn by him, not as taxed by the taxing master. Unless the principals keep close watch, there is a temptation for the clerks to claim fees that are unreasonably high. I do not suggest that they do so. But there is a temptation for them to say: 'It will be knocked down; 10% comes off anyway. It is a legally-aided case. The fund will pay.' If the costs are passed without inquiry, the fund will suffer. The public will have to pay more than they should. Very often the legal aid certificate is expressed in such wide terms as to give the solicitors a 'blanket' authority to conduct the proceedings, covering all items concerned in the course of it, without going to the area committee for specific authority: see, for instance, *Hanlon v Law Society* [1980] 2 All ER 199, [1980] 2 WLR 776. No doubt the certificate in the present case covered everything done in preparation for trial and of the trial itself. In any such case it is of the first importance that the taxing officer should go through all the items and see that there is no overcharging in any respect. Lawyers must not think that, on getting a certificate for legal aid, they have a blank cheque to draw on the legal aid fund as if it were a client with a bottomless purse ready to pay for everything the lawyer can think of. The only safeguard against abuse is the vigilance of the taxing master. He has a difficult task. With no one to oppose it, he has to take much of the solicitor's word for granted, as to the work done. It would be easy for him to let everything through without question. But he must resist that easy course. He must be a watchdog. He must bark when there is anything that arouses his suspicions.

Reverting now to the present case, the taxing officer disallowed various items, such as the cost of the view of the site and of the conference with counsel. The solicitors, on their own behalf and on behalf of counsel, were entitled to apply to the area committee for authority to carry in objections: see the Legal Aid (General) Regulations 1971, SI 1971 No 62, reg 23(6)(b). The area committee gave authority. The solicitors carried in

objections. The taxing master answered them. He gave detailed reasons for his
a disallowance of the various items.

The solicitors then, on their own behalf and on behalf of counsel, applied to the Law
Society for authority to have the taxation reviewed by a judge: see reg 23(7) of the 1971
regulations. It was considered by a very responsible sub-committee, consisting of Mr
Wegg-Prosser, Mr MacDonald and Mr Taylor. They had access to all the papers. They
refused to give authority. Nevertheless, the solicitors and counsel sought to appeal to the
b judge. Neill J held that, as the authority of the Law Society had not been given, he had
no jurisdiction to hear the appeal. But he gave leave to appeal to this court.

This question has been the subject of much discussion and much difference of opinion.
I do not think it would be useful to go through all the cases. Devlin J in *Rolph v Marston
Valley Brick Co Ltd* [1956] 2 All ER 50, [1956] 2 QB 18 drew attention to many
problems. The regulations were amended to deal with them. It is quite plain to my
c mind that one of the objects of the amendments was to make the decision of the taxing
master final and binding on both solicitors and counsel. They had to accept it, unless, in
the first place, authority was given by the area committee to carry in objection, in which
case the taxing master was to give his answers, and unless, in the second place, authority
was given by the Law Society to apply to the judge, in which case the judge would review
the taxation. In the absence of such authority, at each stage, the solicitors and counsel
d had to accept the decision of the taxing master. If authority were given, the expenses of
the appeal to the judge would be payable out of the legal aid fund; but, if it were not
given, that was the end of the matter.

It was suggested that it was unfair, that it was contrary to natural justice, for the Law
Society to have the last word. They manage the legal aid fund, and are interested in
protecting it. That is true. But the Law Society are also concerned with protecting the
e interests of their members, and of counsel, to see that they are properly paid for work
done. On balance, I should have thought their concern on behalf of their members and
of counsel would outweigh their concern for the legal aid fund. At any rate their two
rival interests cancelled one another out. The role of the Law Society was administrative.
So long as they acted fairly, their decision should not be disturbed. There was nothing
unfair here. I must say that, on reading the answers of the taxing master, I think he dealt
f with the matter most carefully and sensibly. I would commend him for his vigilance.
Having formed the opinion that these items were unreasonably incurred, he was quite
right to disallow them. And the Law Society were quite right to refuse authority for a
review.

I would, therefore, dismiss this appeal.

g **BRIGHTMAN LJ.** The question at issue is whether the solicitor of a legally-aided
person, on behalf of himself or on behalf of counsel, can apply to a judge for the review
of a taxing officer's certificate without obtaining the authority of the Law Society,
provided that he does so at his own risk as to costs, or whether an application for such a
review can only be made under the Legal Aid Regulations with the authority of the Law
Society.

h There are two main categories of costs: first, where the taxation is inter partes in the
sense that the purpose of the taxation is to quantify the costs payable to a litigant either
by his opponent or out of a fund, and, second, where the taxation is for the purpose of
quantifying the costs payable by a client to his own solicitor. Provision is made for both
species of taxation by RSC Ord 62, rr 28 to 32. These rules are grouped under the cross-
heading 'Assessment of Costs', and set out the four bases on which costs are taxed:

j   A. Party and party basis: r 28(2).
       B. Common fund basis: r 28(3). (This is simply a party and party taxation on a more
          generous scale.)
       C. Solicitor and own client basis: r 29. (This is virtually a full indemnity basis.)
       D. Trustee basis: r 31. (This is also substantially an indemnity basis, but the formula
          used in r 31 is a little different from that used in r 29.)

On a taxation of costs whether inter partes (i e between litigants, basis A, B or D) or on basis C (not between litigants) there will be adversaries appearing, or with an opportunity to appear, before the taxing master. I speak at the moment only of a non-legal aid taxation. In the case of a party and party taxation, there will for example be the plaintiff, appellant, applicant or petitioner on the one side and the defendant or respondent on the other side. In the case of a common fund taxation (which used to be called a 'solicitor and client' taxation) the adversarial groupings will be (or in theory are) exactly the same (in a non-legal aid case) as in a party and party taxation. In the case of a trustee taxation, the adversaries will normally be (or in theory are) the trustee-litigant on the one side and the beneficiary-litigant on the other side. In these three cases the solicitor and his client will always be on the same side. In the case of a taxation as between a solicitor and his own client, the adversaries will normally be the solicitor on the one side and his client on the other side. (This basis of taxation is occasionally adopted, at least in the Chancery Division, by special agreement between the parties although the taxation is proceeding between one litigant and another.)

The feature of all such taxations is that there are adversaries: the person liable to pay the costs, who is interested to see that the taxed costs are not erroneously high, and the recipient of the costs, who is interested to see that the taxed costs are not erroneously low. Only in the case of a solicitor and own client taxation is the solicitor on a different side from his client.

For the purpose of assessing the sums to be paid out of the legal aid fund to the solicitor and counsel of an assisted person, the Legal Aid and Advice Act 1949 adopted the principle of taxation on the common fund basis (then called the 'solicitor and client' basis, not to be confused with 'solicitor and own client' basis): see Sch 3, para 4(1). Any other basis might have been adopted. The same principle and the same wording appear in para 4(1) of Sch 2 to the Legal Aid Act 1974. The wording employed in both Acts is as follows:

'. . . costs shall be taxed for the purposes of this Schedule according to the ordinary rules applicable on a taxation as between solicitor and client where the costs are to be paid out of a common fund in which the client and others are interested . . .'

The words 'as between solicitor and client' have no significance apart from indicating that the basis of the taxation is the common fund basis. They are simply the old way of expressing what is now called a 'common fund' taxation. They do not indicate that the basis of taxation is that applicable as between a client and the solicitor acting for him. That is a 'solicitor and own client' taxation. The potential confusion between these two conventional descriptions was pointed out by Buckley LJ in *Giles v Randall* [1915] 1 KB 290 at 295, [1914–15] All ER Rep 285 at 286. The nomenclature but not the substance was altered in 1959 to avoid this confusion.

The 'common fund' taxation, which is obligatory in the case of a legal aid taxation, possesses a startling anomaly. Unlike all other taxations, there are no adversaries as a general rule. The taxation is inquisitorial or administrative in its nature, rather than adversarial. The solicitor of the assisted person carries in his bill of costs which includes the proposed fees of counsel. There is no one to oppose the solicitor. There is an investigation by the taxing master, rather than a decision by the taxing master between two rival submissions. This is unique. (A comparable situation does arise exceptionally in the Chancery Division in so-called non-hostile litigation where the same solicitors may quite properly be acting for all parties. This however is not a real exception to the general rule.)

Having regard to the fact that a legal aid taxation has this unusual feature of being conducted on administrative rather than on adversarial lines, it should not come as any surprise to discover that the regulations for a review of this unusual taxation differ from the regulations for a review of a non-legal aid taxation.

The review of a non-legal aid taxation is governed by RSC Ord 62, rr 33 and 34. These

two rules are grouped under the cross-heading 'Review'. Under r 33 the applicant for a
a review delivers written objections to his adversary and to the taxing officer. His
adversary may deliver written answers to the applicant and to the taxing officer. The
adversary is entitled to be heard, whether he has delivered written answers or not. The
taxing officer makes his decision and gives his reasons in writing if so required. Under
r 35 either the applicant or his adversary, if dissatisfied, may apply by inter partes
summons to the judge. The judge, either sitting alone or with assessors, may order the
b taxing officer's certificate to be amended or remit the matter to the same or another
taxing officer for taxation.

The review of a legal aid taxation, on the other hand, is dealt with by reg 23(6) to (11)
of the Legal Aid (General) Regulations 1971, SI 1971 No 62. Under para (5) where the
assisted person's solicitor is dissatisfied with any decision of the taxing officer on a legal
aid taxation, the solicitor can apply to the area committee for authority to carry in
c objections. If the area committee give authority, the solicitor may carry in objections
accordingly. It is then the duty of the solicitor to place before the taxing officer all
matters which are proper to be taken into account on the consideration of the
objections. There is no express provision at this stage for the appearance of any
adversary. In fact the only persons whose interests might be adversely affected by a
decision in favour of the solicitor-applicant would be the legal aid fund, the liability of
d which may be increased, and his client who may be burdened by a greater contribution
(up to the client's maximum contribution) or by a larger charge on the property
recovered. In other words, either the client is disinterested or his interest is opposed to
that of the solicitor as in the case of a 'solicitor and own client' taxation. If the solicitor
or counsel is dissatisfied with the decision of the taxing officer on any matter to which
objection has been taken, the solicitor may apply to the Law Society for authority to have
e the taxation reviewed: see para (7). If the Law Society give authority, the solicitor can
thereupon apply to the judge to review the taxation. Again it is the duty (under the
rules) of the solicitor to place before the judge all matters which are properly to be taken
into account on the review. In the case of a review by a judge, however, provision is
made by reg 24 for the intervention of another solicitor appointed by the Lord
Chancellor. At this stage the procedure could for the first time become adversarial.

f In the instant case the legally-aided person was an unsuccessful plaintiff in a personal
injuries action. The legal aid taxation was completed on 5th July 1978. Objections were
lodged on 6th October. This step was taken with the authority of the area committee
under reg 23(6). The taxing master dealt with the objections and gave written reasons
on 9th April 1979, after some delay which was not in any way the fault of the taxing
master. On 25th April the solicitor applied to the Law Society under paras (7) and (9) of
g reg 23 for authority to have the taxation reviewed by a judge. That authority was
refused on 12th June 1979.

The solicitor nevertheless applied by summons to the judge for a review. He
purported to be acting under RSC Ord 62, r 35, although he had previously been acting
under reg 23 of the 1971 regulations. He claimed to be entitled to make his application
under this rule as he was willing to proceed at his own risk as to costs.

h The question on this appeal is whether Neill J was correct in deciding that he had no
jurisdiction to review the taxation in the absence of the authority of the Law Society. He
held that a solicitor dissatisfied with the decision of the taxing officer to disallow an item
on review has no right to proceed, even at his own risk in costs, under Ord 62, r 35.

In my judgment a person who desires to have the taxation of a bill of costs reviewed
by a judge must be able to point to the rule or regulation which permits such a review
j to take place. In the instant case there are only two such rules or regulations to which the
applicant can point. One is RSC Ord 62, r 35. The other is reg 23(7) of the Legal Aid
(General) Regulations 1971. If neither is applicable, then there is no right to a review by
a judge, and a judge would have no jurisdiction to conduct such a review. So the
question is: can the applicant bring himself within r 35 or within reg 23(7)? If not, this
appeal must fail.

The immediate difficulty which confronts the applicant under reg 23(7) is that that
provision requires the applicant to have the authority of the Law Society, and the *a*
applicant does not possess such authority. It has been refused. There is nothing in the
provision to suggest that he can proceed in the absence of such authority. So reg 23(7)
does not assist him.

Can he then proceed under the 'review' rules of Ord 62? The solicitor claims that he
can, at his own risk as to costs. This claim calls for consideration from two aspects. First,
does r 35 fit the case, according to the wording of the rule? Second, if so, can the solicitor *b*
of a legally-aided person avail himself of the 'review' provisions of the Rules of the
Supreme Court, or is he confined to the comparable provisions of the 1971 regulations?

On the strict language of the rule, r 35 cannot have any application. It is expressed
only to apply to a case where the taxing master has made a decision—

> 'to allow or to disallow any item in whole or in part on review under rule 33 or
> 34, or with the amount allowed in respect of any item by a taxing officer on any *c*
> such review . . .'

In the instant case there has been no review under r 33 or r 34 of Ord 62. There has
been a review under a different provision, namely reg 23(6) of the 1971 regulations. So
the applicant is not within the rule. Furthermore, this wording of r 35 affords some
indication that rr 33 to 35 of Ord 62 and the review provisions of regs 23 to 25 of the *d*
1971 regulations are mutually exclusive.

Indeed it would be odd if, on the occasion of a review by a judge of a legal aid taxation,
provision were to exist for intervention by the Lord Chancellor to protect the legal aid
fund in a case where the assisted person's solicitor is the applicant with the authority of
the Law Society but not in a case where he is the applicant without any such authority,
for the interest of the legal aid fund and therefore of the Lord Chancellor in supporting *e*
the decision of the taxing officer is identical in each case.

I also agree with the judge that it would be cumbersome and unsatisfactory to have
two separate rights to obtain a review existing side by side. I see nothing unfair or
surprising in this conclusion. A legal aid taxation for the benefit of the solicitor and
counsel of an assisted person is not like an ordinary taxation. I would expect the system
to have its own rules. I would not expect two procedures to exist side by side, with the *f*
solicitor having a right to choose between them, and the right to switch from one to the
other as is sought to be done in this case.

I would dismiss the appeal.

SIR GEORGE BAKER. From the publication of the report of the Rushcliffe
Committee in May 1945 (Report of the Committee on Legal Aid and Legal Advice in *g*
England and Wales, Cmd 6641) to the passing of the Legal Aid and Advice Act 1949 on
30th July 1949, described at the time as 'the charter of the little man to the British Courts
of Justice' (see 459 HC Official Report (5th Series) col 1227), many lawyers were
apprehensive not only that remuneration would be subject to the 15% (now 10%)
deduction in the High Court which the legal profession accepted as their contribution to
success but that fees would be at a lower level than those in non-legally-aided litigation. *h*
That could have been fatal and at best highly detrimental to the success of the scheme,
for many of the best qualified in both branches of the profession would not have joined
the panels. That was no fanciful fear, for habits of thought about 'poor persons procedure'
were deeply ingrained. Those whose incomes did not exceed £2 a week gross could in
some cases obtain, but often at considerable outlay to the lawyer, the services of solicitors
and barristers without remuneration. There was a token fee of one guinea for counsel in *j*
some divorce cases involving servicemen, a scheme which was expanded after the Act to
cases conducted by the Law Society's divorce department. The fee remained at one
guinea for some time. In criminal cases until about 1960 the maximum inclusive fee for
a Queen's Counsel was 15 guineas but only if the trial judge certified that the case was of
exceptional length and difficulty.

The history is all to be found in detail in *Legal Aid* by Eric Sachs QC, one of the
a members of the original Legal Aid Committee of the Law Society and later Sachs LJ and
published early in 1951 with a foreword by Viscount Jowitt LC who mentioned (at p vii)
the then 'financial crisis'. There was then no appeal under the Rules of the Supreme
Court from a taxing master on quantum. Small wonder that the 'vital necessity of
adopting standards which can be accepted as reasonable' was stressed in the book (see
especially pp 36–38 and 138).
b   The provision in Sch 3, para 4(1), to the 1949 Act, which is now Sch 2, para 4(1), to the
Legal Aid Act 1974, is that—

> 'costs shall be taxed for the purposes of this Schedule according to the ordinary
> rules applicable on a taxation as between solicitor and client where costs are to be
> paid out of a common fund . . .'

c (Usually now referred to as 'on a common fund basis'.)
    From October 1950, when legal aid first became available, to 1956 it was normal
practice for a judge to review taxations, and there are many reported cases where this was
done in legal aid cases apparently under RSC 1883, Ord 65, r 27(41), as it then was. It is
unnecessary to refer to them save to note that there were references to the obligation,
which had been recognised in the Legal Aid (General) Regulations 1950, SI 1950 No
d 1359, reg 18(3), on the court to direct a taxation as between solicitors and client in
accordance with Sch 3 to the 1949 Act.
    In *Page v Page* [1953] 1 All ER 626 at 629, [1953] Ch 320 at 326 Evershed MR put it
thus:

> 'As a matter of practice (and, perhaps, also as a matter of law) the taxing master
> cannot, or cannot properly or effectively, tax the costs of any party to a proceeding
e > unless he is directed so to do by Act of Parliament or unless there is an order of the
> court similarly so directing him.'

The importance of this will become apparent shortly.
    Then in 1956 in *Rolph v Marston Valley Brick Co Ltd* [1956] 2 All ER 50, [1956] 2 QB
18 Devlin J, having made various findings dismissing an application by the plaintiffs'
f solicitors for an order directing that the costs of an unsuccessful summons for a review
of taxation as between solicitors and client should be taxed, doubted whether there was
jurisdiction because the solicitors had no authority from the client to lodge the original
appeal.
    In *Hammond v Hammond* [1957] 3 All ER 16, [1957] P 349 Karminski J, following the
reasoning of Devlin J, held that he had no jurisdiction to hear an application for a review
g in a legally-aided case brought in the name of the assisted person, who could neither
suffer nor benefit from the result, but in fact brought by the solicitor for the benefit of
the legal advisers.
    Then in *Sutton v Sears* [1959] 3 All ER 545, [1960] 2 QB 97 (heard on 9th October
1959) McNair J refused to follow Devlin J or Karminski J, and reviewed the taxation on
the ground that the right arose out of the relationship between the solicitor and his client
h which was a right expressly preserved by the 1949 Act.
    Finally, in *McCullie v Butler* [1961] 2 All ER 534, [1962] 2 QB 309 (heard on 10th May
1961 on objections before the Legal Aid (General) Regulations 1960, SI 1960 No 408)
Diplock J followed McNair J.
    So far as I can discover the Law Society sought to support the judges having jurisdiction
in all the cases.
j   So in 1960 complex and formidable problems faced the Law Society, who were
responsible for legal aid and had to administer the fund, and by the Lord Chancellor,
who had, inter alia, the power to make regulations (now by s 20 of the Legal Aid Act
1974). Justice had to be done to (a) the assisted person, who may or may not have a
financial interest in the result of a review depending on whether there is a balance of his
contribution (if any) still available, or property recovered over which there is a lien or

charge, (b) counsel and solicitors whose remuneration has been disallowed or reduced, and (c) the legal aid fund provided by the taxpayers.

The solution provided was reg 20 of the Legal Aid (General) Regulations 1960 of which most is now in the Legal Aid (General) Regulations 1971. However reg 20(8) was omitted from subsequent regulations.

The scheme of procedure is now to be found in reg 23 of the 1971 regulations. Briefly it is this.

(a) The assisted person is relieved of any liability, whether or not he is financially interested, to contribute—

'to the fund on account of the costs of any proceedings arising under paragraphs (6) to (11) or regulation 25 [that is for present purposes objections on review or appeal] or in consequence of any order made thereon . . .'

and an increase in the net liability of the fund is not to be a charge on property recovered or preserved in the legally-aided proceedings: see reg 23(5)(b).

(b) The assisted person's certificate even if discharged or revoked is to cover such proceedings the costs of which are to be paid out of the fund: see reg 23(5)(a).

(c) Where the assisted person's solicitor is dissatisfied with any decision of the taxing officer on the (common fund) taxation he—

'shall apply to the appropriate *area committee* for authority to carry in objections to the taxation and if the *area committee* give authority, the solicitor may thereupon carry in objections in accordance with rules of court . . .'

See reg 23(6)(b).

(d) Where the solicitor is dissatisfied with the decision of the taxing officer on any matter to which objection has been taken he 'shall apply to The Law Society for authority to have the taxation reviewed, and, if the Society give authority, the solicitor may thereupon apply to a judge . . .': see reg 23(7).

(e) If counsel is dissatisfied, the solicitor has a duty to report and if authority is given by the area committee or the Law Society to act as if he were himself the dissatisfied person: see reg 23(9).

(f) Finally reg 25(1) provides for appeals with the authority of the Law Society from the judge.

There are also provisions for the Lord Chancellor to appoint a solicitor to intervene.

Where an application is made under the regulations to carry in objections or to review, the fact that it is done by the solicitor in the name of the client is now immaterial, for the assisted person has no concern or potential liability. The use of his name is merely a convenience to identify the case. In the present case, however, the solicitor who had acted for Mr Storer, an unsuccessful assisted party, applied to the area committee under reg 23(6)(b) for authority to carry in objections to the common fund taxation. Authority was given. The objections were heard by Master Martyn who allowed some but disallowed four relating to counsel's fees and one relating to the solicitor's charges. He gave reasons. The solicitor applied to the Law Society for authority to go to the judge to review the five items. The Law Society, having seen the master's reasons, refused. They told the solicitor that the expense involved was not justified. Having seen the master's reasons and the original note that 'the taxing master has given the case full and adequate consideration' I fail to see how the sub-committee could have reached any other conclusion. I cannot accept the suggestion that the solicitor's case had not been heard. The taxing master referred to it in some detail; if the solicitor had wished or been able to expand the case he could have put further material before the Law Society. But the solicitor sought a review from the judge. Neill J held he had no jurisdiction to entertain the application but gave leave to appeal to this court.

The first argument is that reg 23(7) should be read to mean that if the Law Society refuse authority the solicitor may nevertheless appeal to the judge to review. I reject this. It is contrary to the plain words and disregards the history and purpose of reg 23.

Such a construction would mean that the solicitor need not apply at all either to the area
a committee or to the Law Society. To suggest that on an unauthorised application the
solicitor may be at some risk on costs because reg 23(5)(*a*) would not apply is but part of
the consequences. Regulation 23(5)(*b*), which is at the heart of the matter, relieves the
assisted person from financial risk in, but only in, 'proceedings arising under paragraphs
(6) to (11) or regulation 25', which deals with 'Appeal from review of taxation'
Unauthorised proceedings would not be under reg 23(6) to (11) or reg 25. So to retain
b the protection the words 'with or without authority' would have to be inferred so that
the sub-paragraph would read 'proceedings with or without authority under paragraphs
(6) to (11)' etc. Not only would that make nonsense of the whole regulation but it would
resurrect the conflict of interest between solicitor and legally-assisted client with all the
attendant problems which became apparent by 1960.

We have been supplied, as was Neill J, with the transcript of a judgment of Glyn-
c Jones J on 19th July 1962 in *Collins v Royal Arsenal Co-operative Society Ltd* 106 Sol Jo
818. For myself I am sorry it was not fully reported for, in reaching the conclusion that
he had no jurisdiction to entertain an unauthorised review, he dealt convincingly and
conclusively with most of the arguments now addressed to us. Our attention has been
drawn to reg 20(8) of the 1960 regulations, which reads:

d 'No costs shall be allowed on taxation in respect of any step for which, under the
provisions of this Regulation or Regulation 22, the authority of the appropriate Area
Committee or the Law Society is required, unless such authority was obtained
before the step was taken,'

as recognising the existence of a right in the solicitor to apply without authority. It was
omitted from the 1962 regulations (SI 1962 No 148) and I share a view expressed by
e Glyn-Jones J that it was inserted from an excess of caution in an attempt to cover
unforeseen difficulties.

Then it is said that, as reg 24(2) of the 1971 regulations requires the Law Society to
notify the Lord Chancellor when they give authority to apply to a judge with the name
and address of the assisted person's solicitor, the provision in reg 24(3) that the assisted
person's solicitor shall inform the Law Society if he applies to a judge to review and the
f Law Society shall notify the Lord Chancellor with his name and address, is consistent
only with an unauthorised application. Although no satisfactory explanation was given
to us, I think reg 24(3) is dealing with the application to the Law Society and reg 24(3)
with the later stage of the application to the judge. Regulation 23(6) is mentioned in reg
24(3) and I am unimpressed with the argument.

I now come to the argument that a solicitor is entitled when acting in a legally-aided
g case to apply to the court for a review of taxation according to the ordinary rules
applicable on a taxation as between solicitor and client on a common fund basis and that
reg 23 is ultra vires in so far as it purports to preclude a solicitor from applying for a
review without the authority of the Law Society.

The crucial words are 'ordinary rules applicable on a taxation as between solicitor and
client' which are in para 4(1) of Sch 2 to the 1974 Act and also in RSC Ord 62, r 28(4).
h There are also references in the regulations to 'taxation as between party and party': see,
for example, reg 23(4). These words define the scale on which costs are to be allowed,
whether a particular item is to be allowed and if so how much, 'the common fund basis
being a more generous basis than [a party and party basis]': see Ord 62, r 28(4). They do
not identify or prescribe a particular tribunal for taxation or the procedure to be
followed. 'A taxation as between' differs from 'a taxation between' used, for example, in
j reg 14(3). So I agree with Neill and Glyn-Jones JJ.

There are as it were two roads along which a taxation may go: that controlled by the
Rules of the Supreme Court and the Solicitors Act 1974 is one. That is the non-assisted
route. The other is the legal aid route for which the court gives the order for the journey
(see *Page v Page* [1953] 1 All ER 626 at 629, [1953] Ch 320 at 326 per Evershed MR) and
the Legal Aid Regulations say how it is to be made. A saving reference to the Rules of

the Supreme Court (for example in reg 23(1)) does not mean that the journeys must be the same in all respects and it is necessary to remember that only the client can start the journey on the non-assisted route. The solicitor presents his bill; the client, if he wants to challenge it, applies for a solicitor and client or own client or common fund taxation. Until he does there is as it were no lis. In my opinion all of reg 23 is intra vires and must be followed to found jurisdiction.

But it is said that the regulations deny natural justice in two ways. First, that the Law Society as general administrators of legal aid (see s 15 of the Legal Aid Act 1974) are acting as judges in their own cause when refusing authority. Second, that counsel is being deprived of an inherent right if no appeal lies to the judge. As to the former, the edifice of legal aid was built and rebuilt in part with the experience of its operation with an intricate system of checks and balances, of swings and roundabouts described, as I have said earlier, to secure justice and sometimes a compromise for at least three classes, litigants, lawyers and taxpayers, whose interests are often different. The Law Society acting through committees with representatives of the Bar as well as very experienced solicitors must be trusted to take an objective view here as elsewhere. Were it otherwise the whole scheme would be in danger of collapse.

As to counsel, they never had a right to taxation or review, for their fees had been paid (at least in theory) before a solicitor and client or common fund taxation. In legally-assisted cases they are deemed to have been paid and the only right, if it is a right, of counsel is to go along the road under the shelter of the solicitor's umbrella given to him by reg 23(9). That he cannot appeal to the judge without the authority of the Law Society is no more a denial of natural justice than were the pre-legal aid poor persons arrangements under which counsel was often actually out of pocket. His remedy now is as it was then: to say that he is not prepared to undertake such cases. But with the swings and roundabouts I doubt if anyone today is likely to withdraw from the legal aid panels because he or she cannot appeal to a judge. There is no more substance in the natural justice argument than there would be if it were put forward by a dissatisfied potential litigant (and there are many) refused a certificate for proceedings by the area committee whose decision is by reg 10(6) final on that matter.

I would dismiss this appeal.

Appeal dismissed.

Solicitors: *Kingsford, Dorman*; *David Edwards*, Secretary, Legal Aid (for the Law Society).

Frances Rustin   Barrister.

a R v Gateshead Justices, ex parte Tesco Stores Ltd
R v Birmingham Justices, ex parte D W Parkin Construction Ltd and others

b QUEEN'S BENCH DIVISION
DONALDSON LJ, FORBES AND BINGHAM JJ
18th, 26th FEBRUARY 1981

Magistrates – Jurisdiction – Trial of information – Duty of considering information delegated by justices' clerk to his assistant – Assistant considering information against accused within time limit *c* *for instituting proceedings – Accused appearing before justices after expiry of time limit – Whether information validly laid before assistant – Whether justices having jurisdiction to try information – Magistrates' Courts Act 1952, s 1(1) – Justices' Clerks' Rules 1970 (SI 1970 No 231), r 3.*

d On 6th February 1979, which was within the six-month time limit for the institution of proceedings in respect of an offence under the Food and Drugs Act 1965, a local authority sent an information to a magistrates' court alleging that on 17th August 1978 the applicants had committed an offence under that Act. In accordance with the prevailing practice, which had been generally adopted by magistrates' courts to ease the workload of justices and justices' clerks, the information was considered forthwith not by a justice of the peace or by the justices' clerk but by a senior assistant in the justices' clerk's office, *e* who had been specifically authorised by the clerk to consider informations on his behalf. The assistant decided that the information was in order and gave it to another senior assistant in the clerk's office to type and issue the summons. On 15th June 1979, when the case came on for hearing by the justices, the applicants contended that the court had no jurisdiction because the information had not been validly laid before a justice of the peace or the justices' clerk, in accordance with s 1[a] of the Magistrates' Courts *f* Act 1952 and r 3[b] of the Justices' Clerks' Rules 1970, before the expiry of the time limit prescribed by the 1955 Act and it was too late at that stage to lay a further information. The justices held that an information laid before a member of the clerk's staff was validly laid and went on to hear the information and convict the applicants. The applicants applied for an order of certiorari to quash the justices' decision.

g **Held** – The acts of considering an information and deciding whether a summons should be issued were judicial and not administrative and were therefore not functions which could be delegated. Each information had to be considered and each summons had to be individually authorised either by a justice of the peace or by the clerk to the justices acting as a justice of the peace because they were the only persons empowered by s 1 of the 1952 Act and r 3 of the 1970 rules to act in that regard. Furthermore, the summons *h* could not be issued on the authority of anyone except the particular justice of the peace or clerk to the justices who had considered the particular information on which it was based. It followed that the practice adopted in the magistrates' court was wrong and that the information against the applicants had not been validly laid before the expiry on 16th February 1979 of the time limit imposed by the 1955 Act for the institution of proceedings. Accordingly on 15th June 1979 the justices had had no jurisdiction to *j* adjudicate on the information and their decision would be quashed (see p 1031 *e*, p 1032 *g* to *j* and p 1033 *d* to *j*, post).

---

a   Section 1, so far as material, is set out at p 1031 *b* to *d*, post
b   Rule 3 is set out at p 1032 *e*, post

Dixon v Wells (1890) 25 QBD 249 and *R v Brentford Justices, ex parte Catlin* [1975] 2 All ER 201 considered.

Per Curiam. There are some ways in which the task of justices and their clerks can be legitimately lightened by suitable administrative assistance; for example, batches of informations having similar characteristics, such as those emanating from offices of specialist prosecutors, such as trading standards officers, can be placed before a single individual, and unusual informations, either in terms of the nature of the offence or of the facts alleged, can be identified by assistants to the clerk to the justices and placed before him or before specially qualified or experienced justices for consideration. Once the bundles of informations and summonses have been considered by a justice of the peace or by the clerk to the justices, authority can be given for others to affix the signature of the person who has considered the informations and authorised the issue of the summons (see p 1033 *j* to p 1034 *b*, post).

Notes
For the issue of a summons on the laying of an information, see 29 Halsbury's Laws (4th Edn) para 321, and for cases on the subject, see 33 Digest (Repl) 208, 460–461.

For the Magistrates' Courts Act, s 1, see 21 Halsbury's Statutes (3rd Edn) 185.

For the Justices' Clerks' Rules 1970, r 3, see 13 Halsbury's Statutory Instruments (Third Reissue) 77.

Cases referred to in judgment
Dixon v Wells (1890) 25 QBD 249, 59 LJMC 116, 62 LT 812, 54 JP 725, 17 Cox CC 48, DC, 33 Digest (Repl) 208, 460.
R v Brentford Justices, ex parte Catlin [1975] 2 All ER 201, [1975] QB 455, [1975] 2 WLR 506, 139 JP 516, DC, Digest (Cont Vol D) 631, 476a.

Case also cited
R v Fairford Justices, ex parte Brewster [1975] 2 All ER 757, [1976] QB 600, DC.

Applications for judicial review

R v Gateshead Justices, ex parte Tesco Stores Ltd

Tesco Stores Ltd applied with the leave of the Divisional Court of the Queen's Bench Division given on 28th November 1980 for an order of certiorari to quash the order of the Gateshead Magistrates' Court made on 15th June 1979 convicting the applicant on an information laid by Mr Peter Parkes on behalf of the Gateshead Borough Council alleging that the applicant had committed an offence under s 2 of the Food and Drugs Act 1955. The facts are set out in the judgment of the court.

R v Birmingham Justices, ex parte D W Parkin Construction Ltd and others

D W Parkin Construction Ltd, Denis William Parkin and John Taylor applied, with the leave of the Divisional Court of the Queen's Bench Division given on 1st November 1979, for an order of certiorari to quash the adjudication of the Birmingham Magistrates' Court on 2nd October 1979 whereby the company was convicted and fined £1 for the offence on 19th January 1977 of failing to pay a Class 1 contribution under the Social Security Act 1975 in respect of an employee earner in its employment, contrary to s 146 of that Act, and was ordered (i) to pay £35·46 under s 150 of the 1975 Act in respect of the unpaid contribution which was the subject of the offence and (ii) to pay £24,472·47 under s 151 of the 1975 Act in respect of its failure to pay other contributions due under that Act. The facts are set out in the judgment of the court.

W R H Crowther QC and *David Paton* for Tesco Stores Ltd.
M K Lee for D W Parkin Construction Ltd and its co-applicants.

Roger Henderson QC for Gateshead borough council.
a *Simon D Brown* for the Department of Health and Social Security.
Richard Wakerley for the Gateshead and Birmingham justices.

Cur adv vult

26th February. **DONALDSON LJ** read the following judgment of the court: The
b judgment which I am about to read is that of the court. On 19th January 1977 D W
Parkin Construction Ltd failed to pay a Class 1 contribution due under the Social Security
Act 1975 in respect of a Mr Brian King and, in consequence, on 2nd October 1979 the
company was convicted by the Birmingham justices of an offence contrary to s 146 of
that Act.
   On 17th August 1978 Mrs Eileen Thomas went to the supermarket of Tesco Stores Ltd
c in Ellison Street, Gateshead, and was sold a packet of biscuits. One of the biscuits
contained a cigarette filter tip and, in consequence, on 15th June 1979 Tescos were
convicted by the Gateshead justices of an offence under the Food and Drugs Act 1955.
   The common factor between these cases may not be readily apparent. It is an allegation
that in neither case had the justices any jurisdiction to adjudicate, because at no material
time were the informations laid before a person authorised to consider them. We say 'at
d no material time' because *R v Brentford Justices, ex parte Catlin* [1975] 2 All ER 201, [1975]
QB 455 is authority for the proposition that the appearance of the defendant before the
court can and usually will remedy any prior deficiencies with regard to the laying of an
information or the making of a complaint or the issue of a summons, since the
production of the purported summons to the magistrate in court will usually itself meet
the requirements for laying an information or making a complaint, and the presence of
e the defendant renders the summons unnecessary. But this is not true where, as in the
instant cases, the defendant first appears before the court after the expiry of the time
limited by statute for the laying of the information.
   In the case of D W Parkin Construction Ltd, the relevant statutory provision was s 147
of the Social Security Act 1975; the time limit was 12 months from the date of the
offence and this expired on 18th January 1978, whereas the appearance before the
f justices was on 2nd October 1979. In the case of Tesco Stores Ltd, the time limit was six
months from the date of the offence and this expired on 16th February 1979, whereas the
appearance before the justices was on 15th June 1979.
   Both companies now apply for judicial review and for orders quashing their respective
convictions. In the case of D W Parkin Construction Ltd, two directors, Mr Denis Parkin
and Mr John Taylor, join in the application because the conviction of the company may
g expose them to personal liability to pay arrears of national insurance contributions due
from the company and amounting to no less than £24,507·93.

D W Parkin Construction Ltd
   On 15th December 1977 Mr Brian Thomas of the Department of Health and Social
Security delivered a written information to the Brimingham Magistrates' Court alleging
h the offence under the Social Security Act 1975. It is not certain who considered it. The
information itself bears the facsimile signature of Mr Mountford, the clerk to the
Birmingham justices, but this is not of itself indicative of the fact that it was ever
considered or seen by Mr Mountford. Mr Mountford's account of the matter is as
follows:

   '... I am satisfied that Mr. Brian Thomas applied to the Court Clerk responsible
j for the issue of process on the 15th December, 1977, for the sole purpose of laying
   this information. Whether this information was later submitted to me, I do not
   know. My attention is given to some informations, others are dealt with by senior
   members of staff on my instructions. However, irrespective of whether I personally
   considered this information; or whether it was considered by a senior and competent

member of my staff acting under my specific direction, authority, and control, followed by the signing of the information (by way of affixing the facsimile of my *a* signature, whether by me or a senior officer authorised on that behalf by me) in my opinion it is correctly laid. Following the *Brentford Justices Ex parte Catlin* decision, I was advised that the procedure of granting process which we now operate is legally correct, and in my opinion this information is in order.'

In saying that he was so advised, Mr Mountford was referring to a circular issued in 1975 by the council of the Society of Justices' Clerks. This circular, so far as is material, *b* provided as follows:

'. . . every information must, at the very least, be examined to ascertain:—(i) that an offence known to law is alleged, and (ii) that it is not out of time, and (iii) that the court has jurisdiction, and (iv) that the informant has any necessary authority to prosecute. This examination of every information and the subsequent action to *c* complete the grant of process may be done in one of four ways:—
'*Grant of summons by a justice of the peace or the justices' clerk.*—(a) by a justice personally with the justices' clerk or a well-qualified assistant to assist him; or (b) by the justices' clerk personally; or (c) by a justices' clerk's assistant who then presents the informations to a justice or the justices' clerk and states formally that they are in order, so the justice or justices' clerk can formally receive the informations and *d* authorise the grant of process; the process will either be signed by the justices or justices' clerk, or the assistant will be given authority to affix the facsimile signature stamp of the justice or justices' clerk; or
'*Grant of summons by the justices' clerk only.*—(d) by a senior and competent justices' clerk's assistant (the assistant shall sign in the name of the clerk or affix a facsimile of the clerk's signature to the summons) acting without the immediate personal *e* involvement of the justices' clerk, but only under his specific direction, authority and control.'

Tesco Stores Ltd
On 6th February 1979 the director of legal services for the borough council of Gateshead posted an information to the clerk to the Gateshead justices. This was collected *f* from the post office on 7th February by Mr T Cook. Mr Cook was a junior assistant of the clerk to the justices, Mr John Griffiths. What happened next was the subject of an investigation by Mr Griffiths. He was faced with the problem that this was merely one of many informations, but we accept his conclusions as being likely to be correct. He says that the information would have been given to a Mr J White on the same day. Mr White was the listing officer and one of Mr Griffiths's senior assistants, specially *g* authorised by him to examine and to accept or reject informations on Mr Griffiths's behalf. Mr White considered the information and decided that it was in order. He then passed it to another of Mr Griffiths's assistants, Mr C Smith, for him to type and issue the summons. It is impossible to say quite when Mr White considered the information, but it must have been on or before 16th February 1979, because thereafter he was on leave. In the normal course of events he would have noted the date on the information, but this *h* was omitted in this instance.

By an unfortunate accident Mr Smith when issuing the summons showed the information as having been laid on 19th February 1979, that being the date when he received the information and thereafter he changed this to 6th February 1979, which was the date on which it was signed by the director of legal services. Clearly neither date is correct since an information is laid when it is considered by a person authorised to do *j* so. The only relevance of the fact that wrong dates were mentioned is that it put Tescos on inquiry and these proceedings ensued.

Mr Griffiths, like Mr Mountford, relied on the circular from the council of the Society of Justices' Clerks in establishing this procedure for dealing with informations.

The laying of informations and the issue of summonses

a We now turn to consider the problem which is central to these applications, namely before whom may informations be laid and who is empowered to decide whether or not to issue summonses.

Section 1 of the Magistrates' Courts Act 1952, so far as material, provides as follows:

b
'*Issue of summons to accused or warrant for his arrest.*—(1) Upon an information being laid before a justice of the peace for any county that any person has or is suspected of having committed an offence, the justice may, in any of the events mentioned in subsection (2) of this section—(a) issue a summons directed to that person requiring him to appear before a magistrates' court for the county to answer to the information . . .

c
'(2) A justice of the peace for a county may issue a summons or warrant under this section—(a) if the offence was committed or is suspected to have been committed within the county; or (b) if it appears to the justice necessary or expedient, with a view to the better administration of justice, that the person charged should be tried jointly with, or in the same place as, some other person who is charged with an offence, and who is in custody, or is being or is to be proceeded against within the

d
county; or (c) if the person charged resides or is, or is believed to reside or be, within the county; or (d) if under any enactment a magistrates' court for the county has jurisdiction to try the offence; or (e) if the offence was committed outside England and Wales . . .   Provided that where the offence charged is not an indictable offence—(i) a summons shall not be issued by virtue only of paragraph (c) of subsection (2) of this subsection . . .'

In 1952 there was no other authority for anyone to consider informations or
e complaints or to issue summonses. The wording of the section 'may . . . issue a summons' and 'if it appears to the justice necessary or expedient with a view to the better administration of justice' makes it clear that the power was discretionary and that the discretion had to be exercised by the justice acting judicially and therefore personally, since the judicial function can never be delegated.

This is in line with the law as it was prior to the enactment of the 1952 Act. In *Dixon*
f *v Wells* (1890) 25 QBD 249 a summons was held to be invalid when the complaint was considered by two justices and the summons was signed by a third justice who had not considered the complaint. It is not uninteresting in the context of the present applications to find Lord Coleridge CJ saying (at 254):

'It is said that it has become a general practice for the magistrates' clerk to hear complaints without any written or other information, fill up a form of summons,
g   obtain the signature of any magistrate, and so cause a man to be summoned, and perhaps exposed to a heavy penalty, although the magistrate signing the summons may not have ascertained whether there was a primâ facie case against the person summoned. If it be, indeed, the practice to sign a summons without hearing an information, and for one person to hear the information and another to sign the summons, a practice more loose or likely to lead to injustice, especially in matters
h   relating to perishable articles which require to be dealt with quickly, I can hardly conceive. In the present case, if the magistrate who signed the summons had heard the information, he might have thought that no primâ facie case had been made out, and have declined to issue the summons.'

The same point was made in *R v Brentford Justices, ex parte Catlin* [1975] 2 All ER 201
j at 207, [1975] QB 455 at 464 by Lord Widgery CJ. He said:

'It must however be remembered that before a summons or warrant is issued the information must be laid before a magistrate and he must go through the judicial exercise of deciding whether a summons or warrant ought to be issued or not. If a magistrate authorises the issue of a summons without having applied his mind to

the information then he is guilty of dereliction of duty and if in any particular
justices' clerk's office a practice goes on of summonses being issued without *a*
information being laid before the justice at all, then a very serious instance of
maladministration arises which should have the attention of the authorities without
delay.'

In 1970 a change was made. It may well be that this change was prompted by the
increasing work load of the justices and that a further change is now due. However that
may be, in 1970 the Lord Chancellor made the Justices' Clerks' Rules 1970, SI 1970 No *b*
231. These rules were made under s 15 of the Justices of the Peace Act 1949 as extended
by s 5 of the Justices of the Peace Act 1968.

The power under the 1949 Act was limited to making 'rules for regulating and
prescribing the procedure and practice to be followed in magistrates' courts and by
justices' clerks'. A 'justices' clerk' was defined by s 44, not very helpfully, as 'a clerk to the
justices for a petty sessions area', but the Act, by s 20, also prescribed qualifications for *c*
new candidates for the office of a justices' clerk as being those of a barrister or solicitor of
not less than five years' standing. Section 5 of the 1968 Act extended this power to—

'make provision enabling things authorised to be done by, to or before a single
justice of the peace, to be done instead by, to or before a justices' clerk; and any
enactment or rule of law regulating the exercise of any jurisdiction or powers of *d*
justices of the peace, or relating to things done in the exercise or purported exercise
thereof, shall apply in relation to the exercise or purported exercise thereof by virtue
of this subsection by the clerk to any justices as if he were one of those justices.'

Rule 3 of the Justices' Clerks' Rules 1970 was in the following terms:

'The things specified in the Schedule to these Rules, being things authorised to be *e*
done by, to or before a single justice of the peace for a petty sessions area may be
done by, to or before the justices' clerk for that area.'

Then the schedule provided:

'1. The laying of an information or the making of a complaint other than an
information or complaint substantiated on oath. *f*
'2. The issue of any summons, including a witness summons . . .'

There are other provisions to which I need not refer.

For the applicants it is submitted that reading the rules with the enabling power, it is
clear that the only person authorised to act as a justice of the peace, although he is not
one, is *the* clerk to the justices for the area, ie Mr Mountford in relation to the
Birmingham area and Mr Griffiths in relation to the Gateshead area. Furthermore, since *g*
the clerk is acting as a justice, he must act personally and cannot delegate any of his duties
or discretions.

In parenthesis we should add that whilst there was power under s 19 of the Justices of
the Peace Act 1949, and now under s 25 of the 1979 Act, to appoint more than one
justices' clerk for a particular area, each of whom would be *the* justices' clerk for this *h*
purpose, no such appointment appears to have been made in the case of the Birmingham
and Gateshead areas.

An information is not 'laid' within the meaning of the Magistrates' Courts Act 1952,
and is certainly not 'laid before a justice of the peace' unless it is laid before and
considered by either a justice of the peace or the clerk to the justices acting as a justice of
the peace pursuant to the 1970 rules and, incidentally, no summons can be issued by any *j*
other person or without a prior judicial consideration by that person of the information
on which the summons is based.

In the case of D W Parkin Construction Ltd, the information was 'laid' before and
considered by one or other of two unidentified assistants of Mr Mountford, who were no

doubt senior and competent but were not the clerk to the justices, nor, so far as is known,
even qualified for that office. In the case of Tesco Stores Ltd, the information was 'laid'
before and considered by Mr White, to whom the same considerations apply. It follows,
as the applicants submit, that the Birmingham and Gateshead justices acted without
jurisdiction in trying the informations and that their decisions should be quashed.

Three arguments to the contrary are advanced on behalf of the prosecutors and the
justices. First, it is submitted that in reality the consideration of an information and the
issue of a summons is normally a purely administrative function, and that it is only in an
insignificant minority of cases that there is really anything to consider or any materials
on which a judicial discretion could be exercised. We would accept that it is rare for the
issue of a summons to be refused, but it does happen from time to time and rightly so.
No doubt most prosecutions are brought by experienced and responsible prosecuting
authorities, who are well aware of the requirements of the law and take pains to make
sure that the informations are in order and that the cases are fit to be tried. But not all
prosecutions are brought by experienced and responsible prosecuting authorities. And
even in the case of such authorities, the requirement that a justice of the peace or the
clerk to the justices acting as a justice of the peace shall take personal responsibility for
the propriety of taking so serious a step as to require the attendance of a citizen before a
criminal court is a constitutional safeguard of fundamental importance. We have no
doubt that this function is judicial. We agree with that part of the advice of the council
of the Society of Justices' Clerks which affirms that every information must at the very
least be examined to ascertain: (i) that an offence known to law is alleged, (ii) that it is not
out of time, (iii) that the court has jurisdiction, and (iv) that the informant has any
necessary authority to prosecute. This is not an administrative function and still less is
it a purely clerical function which is really what is implied in this submission.

Second, it is submitted that since s 19 of the Justices of the Peace Act 1949 contemplates
that the clerk to the justices shall have a staff who should work under his direction and
s 118 of the Magistrates' Courts Act 1952 contemplates that there may be more than one
clerk to the justices for a petty sessional area, one being treated as the deputy to the other,
the statutory framework clearly involves a degree of delegation by the clerk. We agree,
but the clerk has many non-judicial duties and, in the absence of the clearest possible
words, there is no reason whatsoever for concluding that he alone in the whole judicial
system is empowered to delegate his judicial functions.

Third, it is submitted that if the applicants are correct in their submissions, the
administration of justice will grind to a halt because justices and clerks to justices, if
unassisted, cannot possibly process the number of informations and complaints now
being laid and made. In this context we were referred to evidence given to the Royal
Commission on Criminal Procedure, which suggests that in some parts of the country
the process of delegation has been taken to the point where there is a degree of integration
between the police and the staff of magistrates' courts, the police preparing the paperwork
not only in connection with the informations laid by them but also in relation to the
corresponding summonses.

The short answer to this is that if the practice is unlawful, expedience will not make
it lawful. Fiat justitia ruat coelum. The long answer is that we doubt whether the
system would grind to a halt, although it would undoubtedly be subjected to severe
strain. Although each information must be considered and each summons must be
authorised individually by a justice or by the justices' clerk, or, where more than one, by
one of the justices' clerks, and each must bear the signature of the person who considered
the information, their task can be considerably lightened by suitable administrative
assistance. Thus batches of informations having similar characteristics, eg those
emanating from the offices of specialist prosecutors such as trading standards officers, can
be assembled and placed before a single individual, thus lightening the task of
consideration. Again unusual informations, either in terms of the nature of the offence
or of the facts alleged, can be identified by assistants to the clerk to the justices and placed

before him or before specially qualified or experienced justices for consideration. And the task of signing can be performed vicariously by the use of a facsimile signature on a rubber stamp (*R v Brentford Justices, ex parte Catlin*). Bundles of informations and summonses can be considered by a justice or by the clerk to the justices and, thereafter, authority can be given for others to affix the signature of the person who has considered the informations and authorised the issue of the summonses.

The advice given by the council of the Society of Justices' Clerks was, we are told, approved informally before it was issued, and until these applications were made there was no suggestion that it was misconceived. In the circumstances it was natural that the clerks to the Birmingham and Gateshead justices should have organised their offices in the way revealed by these applications and we do not doubt that many, and possibly most, other clerks to justices do likewise, particularly in petty sessional divisions with a large case load. But that said, we have no doubt that this advice was misconceived and should no longer be followed.

One other thing should be said. Our judgment, if accepted, or affirmed on any appeal, must lead to a major reorganisation in the practices of magistrates' courts, but this is not to say that many or any defendants other than the applicants can complain that they were convicted without jurisdiction. Such a complaint could only be made where the defendant appeared before the court after the expiry of the time limit for trying an information, and then only if it appeared that the information had not in fact been considered by a qualified person. It will be difficult, if not impossible, now to discover whether this was the case unless, as happened here, those who complained took the point on the occasion of their appearance in court.

Orders of certiorari granted ; decisions of the justices quashed.

Solicitors: *Alsop, Stevens, Batesons & Co* (for Tesco Stores Ltd); *Sidney Mitchell & Co* (for D W Parkin Construction Ltd and its co-applicants); *Sharpe, Pritchard & Co*, agents for *Peter Parkes*, Gateshead (for Gateshead borough council); *Solicitor to the Department of Health and Social Security*; *Basil P Mellon & Co* (for the Gateshead justices); *F H Wilson* (for the Birmingham justices).

Sepala Munasinghe Esq   Barrister.

Church of Scientology of California v Customs and Excise Commissioners

COURT OF APPEAL, CIVIL DIVISION
STEPHENSON, BRIGHTMAN LJJ AND DAME ELIZABETH LANE
22nd APRIL 1980

COURT OF APPEAL, CIVIL DIVISION
STEPHENSON, OLIVER LJJ AND SIR JOHN WILLIS
16th JULY 1980

Value added tax – Supply of goods or services – Supply in the course of a business – Business – Body incorporated to propagate religion or religious philosophy – Courses provided to further that aim – Sale of books and other merchandise relating to the religious philosophy – Whether goods and services supplied in the course of a business carried on by the taxpayer – Finance Act 1972, s 2(2).

European Economic Community – Reference to European Court – Request for preliminary ruling concerning interpretation of Community law – Question to be referred by appellate court – Framing of question – Question based on assumption of fact not in issue before court of first instance – Whether proper for appellate court to refer question to European Court in absence of finding of fact by court of first instance – EEC Treaty, art 177.

Court of Appeal – Ground of appeal – Contention not raised in court of first instance – Contention forming basis of question sought to be referred to Court of Justice of the European Communities – Assumption of fact not included in findings of fact by court of first instance – Whether Court of Appeal entitled to treat decision of court of first instance as containing expressly or by necessary implication particular finding of fact – Whether Court of Appeal able to refer question to European Court in absence of particular finding of fact – Whether Court of Appeal should remit case to court of first instance for it to make particular finding of fact.

The taxpayer was incorporated in California with the object of propagating 'the religious faith of Scientology' and pursued that object in the United Kingdom by providing 'auditing' and 'training' courses and by selling books and other merchandise relating to scientology. The taxpayer was assessed to value added tax under s 2(2)[a] of the Finance Act 1972 for the period 1st April to 31st August 1973 on the basis that it was carrying on business in the United Kingdom and was making taxable supplies of goods and services in the course of that business. The taxpayer appealed to a value added tax tribunal, contending that the courses provided by it were education of a kind provided by a university otherwise than for profit within item 1(b)[b] of Group 6 of Sch 5 to the 1972 Act and accordingly there was no taxable supply within s 2(2)(a), and further that it was not carrying on any business and accordingly the goods and services supplied by it were not supplied in the course of a business carried on by it within s 2(2)(b). The tribunal found that the taxpayer was carrying on the business of propagating scientology as a commodity consisting of the training and auditing courses and the books and other merchandise relating to scientology, and dismissed the appeal. The judge affirmed that decision. The taxpayer appealed to the Court of Appeal, but prior to the hearing of the appeal, by

---

a   Section 2(2), so far as material, provides: 'Tax on the supply of goods or services shall be charged only where—(a) the supply is a taxable supply; and (b) the goods or services are supplied by a taxable person in the course of a business carried on by him ...'

b   Item 1, so far as material, exempts from value added tax 'The provision of education if ... (b) it is of a kind provided by a school or university and is provided otherwise than for profit.'

motion, sought a reference by the Court of Appeal under art 177ᶜ of the EEC Treaty to the Court of Justice of the European Communities for a preliminary ruling on a point *a* that had not been raised either before the value added tax tribunal or before the judge on the hearing of the appeal therefrom, namely whether, under EEC law or under s 2(2)(*b*) of the 1972 Act construed in the light of EEC law, a body propagating a religion or religious philosophy could be regarded as carrying on a business and so treated as a taxable person.

b

Held – (1) The questions for reference to the European Court were framed in the taxpayer's notice of motion on the assumption that the taxpayer was a non-profit-making religious or philosophical body, although there was no clear finding to that effect in the decision of the value added tax tribunal. The court was therefore not justified in treating that decision as containing expressly or by necessary implication an actual finding of fact that the taxpayer was such a body. Since questions to be referred to the European Court *c* should be framed in a manner appropriate to the particular circumstances of the case before the member state, the court was not in a position to frame questions that would exactly meet the circumstances of the case until the arguments on the substantive appeal had been presented (see p 1038 *g* to *j* and p 1039 *c d* and *f* to *j*, post.)

(2) The court could not remit the matter to the value added tax tribunal to make a finding, on the evidence as it had been before it, on the new issue of whether the taxpayer *d* was genuinely a religious or philosophical body because that evidence, and the cross-examination of witnesses, had been directed to the issues then being argued, and it would be quite unreal to ask the tribunal to determine the new issue without reopening the whole of the evidence and, if necessary, giving both sides an opportunity to call further evidence. Moreover, it would not be right for the court itself to determine the new issue on the basis that there was a question to be referred in the absence of any finding of fact *e* which would necessarily make that question relevant, since (a) if the court concluded that there was a question for reference the matter would still not be able to go on for want of the appropriate finding of facts or (b) if the court concluded that there was no case for reference the taxpayer might then proceed to the House of Lords and persuade it that there was a case for reference in which case the difficulty of there being no appropriate finding of facts would again arise (see p 1041 *d* to *g* and *j*, post). *f*

(3) Having regard to the manifest inconvenience of remitting the matter to the value added tax tribunal for a complete reopening and reargument of the new issue and to the fact that it was not argued below but was raised for the first time in the notice of appeal, it was appropriate for the court to dismiss the motion for reference and the appeal, and leave it to the taxpayer to raise the point in fresh proceedings relating to other outstanding assessments (see p 1041 *h j*, post). *g*

Per Curiam. As a general rule no question should be submitted to the Court of Justice of the European Communities based on an assumption which does not coincide with the facts which have been found or agreed (see p 1039 *j*, post).

Notes

For supplies relating to education which are exempt from value added tax, see 12 *h* Halsbury's Laws (4th Edn) para 901.

For references to the Court of Justice of the European Communities, see Supplement to 39A Halsbury's Laws (3rd Edn) para 32.

j

---

c Article 177, so far as material, provides: 'The Court of Justice shall have jurisdiction to give preliminary rulings concerning . . . (*b*) the validity and interpretation of acts of the institutions of the Community . . . Where such a question is raised before any court or tribunal or a Member State, that court or tribunal may, if it considers that a decision on the question is necessary to enable it to give judgment, request the Court of Justice to give a ruling thereon . . .'

a
For the Finance Act 1972, s 2, Sch 5, Group 6, see 42 Halsbury's Statutes (3rd Edn) 164, 223.

For the EEC Treaty, art 177, see 42A ibid 436.

Section 2 of the 1972 Act was substituted by s 14 of and Sch 6, para 1, to the Finance Act 1977 as from 1st January 1978, and Sch 5 to the 1972 Act was substituted by art 4 of and Sch 2 to the Value Added Tax (Consolidation) Order 1978, SI 1978 No 1064, as from 4th September 1978.

b

Application for reference

The Church of Scientology of California ('the taxpayer') sought, by notice of motion, a reference by the Court of Appeal to the Court of Justice of the European Communities under art 177 of the EEC Treaty requiring a preliminary ruling whether, having regard c to the adherence of the United Kingdom to the European Economic Community and to the incorporation of Community law into the law of the United Kingdom, arts 4 and 6 of the Second Council Directive of 11th April 1967 (Dir 67/228/EEC) applied to exclude from turnover taxes the supply of goods and services provided by a non-profit-making religious or philosophical body. The facts are set out in the judgment of Brightman LJ.

d *Louis Blom-Cooper QC* and *Philip Lawton* for the taxpayer.
Patrick Medd QC and *Simon D Brown* for the Crown.

BRIGHTMAN LJ delivered the first judgment at the invitation of Stephenson LJ. This is a motion by the Church of Scientology of California ('the taxpayer') for an order e that the questions set out in the schedule to the notice of motion relating to the value added tax regulations of the European Economic Community be referred to the Court of Justice of the European Communities for a preliminary ruling under art 177 of the EEC Treaty. Under that article this court has a discretion to make such a reference if it considers that a decision on the questions, or any of them, is necessary to enable the court to give judgment. The questions scheduled to the notice of motion, five in number, f have been informally superseded by three proposed questions handed to us by counsel for the taxpayer during the course of the argument as preferred alternatives, and I need only deal with the revised version.

The facts, shortly, are as follows. The motion was launched by the taxpayer pending the hearing of an appeal concerning an assessment to value added tax. The taxpayer was incorporated in California in 1954. It was conducting its activities in the United g Kingdom at the time when the value added tax system of taxation came into operation in this country, 1st April 1973, and I understand that the taxpayer is still so engaged. The Commissioners of Customs and Excise, the respondents to the motion and to the appeal, took the view that the taxpayer was liable to be registered as a taxable person and made an assessment on the taxpayer for the first period, 1st April 1973 to 31st August 1973. That assessment was made in 1974 and was appealed. Assessments for subsequent h periods will probably depend on the outcome of this appeal and the fate of the first assessment.

To summarise the position under the Finance Act 1972, the liability of a person to pay value added tax depends on his being a taxable person and registrable accordingly under the Act. A taxable person is one who makes, or intends to make, taxable supplies of goods or services in the course of a business carried on by him. 'Business' is defined in j s 45 as including any trade, profession or vocation.

The taxpayer is engaged in the propagation of scientology. Scientology is said, in the report of the proceedings before the London Value Added Tax Tribunal ([1977] VATTR 278 at 282), to be the discovery of a Mr Hubbard and it claims to be 'a religion or a religious philosophy containing spiritual counselling procedures intended to assist an individual to attain spiritual freedom'.

The assessment was appealed before the London tribunal which dismissed the appeal on 29th November 1977. The tribunal considered that it ought to regard scientology 'as *a* if it were a commodity consisting of the training and auditing courses and the books on Scientology, E-Meters and Sundry Merchandise sold by the UK Branch' (at 297).

The tribunal found that there were sufficient hallmarks of a business or commercial activity to compel it to hold that the taxpayer was carrying on a business for value added tax purposes, namely the business of propagating scientology. The taxpayer appealed to the High Court and that appeal was dismissed on 12th January 1979 ([1979] *b* STC 297).

The taxpayer now seeks to pray in aid the EEC regulations which require member states to introduce a common system of value added tax. The requirement is contained in the First Council Directive of 11th April 1967 (Dir 67/227/EEC) on the 'harmonisation of legislation of Member States concerning turnover taxes'. The Second Council Directive (Dir 67/228/EEC) of the same date is concerned with the structure and *c* procedures for application of that common system. Article 4 of the Second Directive, read with Annex A, contains a definition of taxable person which, as a matter of phraseology, is not identical with that subsequently adopted by the legislation of this country, namely the Finance Act 1972 to which I have already made reference. Article 4 and the relevant part of Annex A reads as follows:

> '"Taxable person" means any person who independently and habitually engages *d* in transactions pertaining to the activities of producers, traders or persons providing services, whether or not for gain.'

and

> 'The expression "activities of producers, traders, or persons providing services" is to be understood in a wide sense and to cover all economic activities, including, *e* therefore, activities of the extractive industries, agriculture and the professions . . .'

The submission of the taxpayer on the motion is that (i) under the EEC regulations or alternatively (ii) under the Finance Act 1972, construed in the light of the EEC regulations, it is arguable that as a matter of law a body propagating a religion or religious philosophy is not to be regarded as carrying on a business so as to be treated as *f* a taxable person, and that this arguable question is one which this court ought, in its discretion, to refer to the European Court for a preliminary ruling prior to the appeal. The taxpayer moves this court for a reference accordingly.

Speaking for myself, I take the view that a decision on the motion ought to be deferred until the arguments on the appeal have been presented. This court can then see whether a reference to the European Court is necessary, or desirable, and in particular what *g* precise form the questions, if any, ought to take.

One of the two difficulties I feel in adopting the course sought by counsel for the taxpayer is that both the effective questions are framed on the assumption that the taxpayer is a non-profit-making religious or philosophical body. I see however no clear finding to that effect in the decision of the tribunal. There is a statement at the beginning of the decision that scientology is, or claims to be, a religion or religious *h* philosophy (see [1977] VATTR 278 at 282), but that clearly is not a finding that the taxpayer is such a body. There is also a statement, which I think can properly be treated as a finding of fact, that the Internal Revenue Service of the United States of America treats the church as a tax exempt, religious, non-profit-making organisation. But that is not a finding of fact by the tribunal which reflects its own conclusion that the taxpayer is a religious or philosophical body. Counsel for the taxpayer also sought to rely on such *j* statement as a ground for saying that the burden of proof as to its status was shifted from the taxpayer to the Crown. I cannot myself take that view at all. There is a reference (at 295) to the dissemination of the religious philosophy of scientology which earlier (at 293) had been described by the tribunal as the 'religious philosophy of Mr Hubbard'. Later (at 295) there is, to my mind, the only important passage on this topic which I will read:

'The final matter for our consideration is whether the [taxpayer] provided the training and auditing courses at Saint Hill Manor and the Books, E-Meters and Sundry Merchandise relating to Scientology "in the course of a business" carried on by it, so as to become liable to account for tax on such supplies. On this aspect we do not accept the submission by [counsel for the taxpayer] that, as Scientology is to be regarded as a religion or a religious philosophy, the establishment at Saint Hill Manor is to be compared with a religious teaching foundation, and such a foundation would not normally be described as carrying on a business, even though it charged fees to its students. In our opinion an establishment can provide the study of a religion or a religious philosophy as a business in the same way as a study of a language or any other branch of knowledge.'

I have this comment on the passages that I have read, that, if it was essential to the taxpayer's case that it should be recognised by the tribunal as a religious or philosophical body, it is surprising that there was no direct finding by the tribunal to that effect, or any record in the tribunal's decision that this fact was conceded by the Crown. In my view the observations quoted above may merely have reflected the view of the tribunal that, even if (without so deciding) the taxpayer could be described as a religious or philosophical body, nevertheless it would be a taxable person within the meaning of the Finance Act 1972. As at present advised, I would not feel justified in treating the decision of the tribunal as containing expressly or by necessary implication an actual finding of fact that the taxpayer is a religious or philosophical body.

As a general rule, no question should in my view be submitted to the European Court based on an assumption which does not coincide with the facts which have been found or agreed.

A somewhat similar point arises in relation to the subsidiary assumption in question 2, namely that the goods and services of the taxpayer are not supplied in competition with any commercial profit-making concern. I doubt whether that assumption coincides with any finding of the tribunal, having regard to the statement which reads as follows (at 297): 'In the "auditing" courses the UK branch was competing with trained and partly-trained psychologists and psychiatrists who operated professionally.' That statement was made in the context of the view held by the tribunal that the operations of the taxpayer in the United Kingdom were partly of a therapeutic nature.

My other difficulty is this. It is important that the questions, if any are to be submitted to the European Court, should be framed in a manner appropriate to the particular circumstances of the case before the member state. Until the arguments on the appeal have been presented, so that I really understand all that we are talking about, I feel a complete lack of confidence in my own ability to frame questions that will be found exactly to meet the circumstances of the case. No question falling short of that standard ought, in my view, to be submitted to the European Court. I think that the instant case is one in which the need for, and scope of, any reference to the European Court will be more readily discernible when the appeal has been argued than before it has been argued.

For the reasons which I have stated, I myself would wish the motion to stand over pending argument on the appeal, with a view to the motion being restored at such time, if any, as the need for a reference becomes apparent to the court. It is a matter for the discretion of the court and that is how I would like to see the discretion exercised. I, therefore, propose that the motion be stood over for the time being.

DAME ELIZABETH LANE. I entirely agree with what Brightman LJ has said and with the reasons he has given for the view he holds and which I share that this motion should be stood over until the time he suggests.

STEPHENSON LJ. I also agree with the reasoning and the result of Brightman LJ's judgment and have nothing to add.

Motion stood over for the hearing of the appeal.

Appeal

The taxpayer appealed against the order of Neill J ([1979] STC 297) made on 12th January *a*
1979 whereby he dismissed an appeal by the taxpayer against a decision of the London
Value Added Tax Tribunal (chairman Lord Grantchester QC) ([1977] VATTR 278) that
the taxpayer was carrying on a business for the purposes of value added tax within s
2(2)(*b*) of the Finance Act 1972. The facts are set out in the judgment of Oliver LJ.

Louis Blom-Cooper QC and *Philip Lawton* for the taxpayer.   *b*
Patrick Medd QC and *Simon D Brown* for the Crown.

OLIVER LJ delivered the first judgment at the invitation of Stephenson LJ. This is an
appeal by the Church of Scientology of California ('the taxpayer') from a decision of
Neill J ([1979] STC 297) delivered on 12th January 1979 in which he dismissed the
taxpayer's appeal from a previous decision of the London Value Added Tax Tribunal *c*
([1977] VATTR 278) given on 29th November 1977, upholding the assessment of the
taxpayer to value added tax under s 2 of the Finance Act 1972 in respect of services
provided and merchandise sold between April 1973 and August 1973. The sum involved
is something of the order of £21,000.

The taxpayer's contentions before the value added tax tribunal were that the taxpayer
was, first of all, an exempted person as defined by the 1972 Act, in that it was engaged in *d*
the provision of education of the kind provided by a university, second, that the supply
of services and goods was not in the course of the business carried on by the supplier, and,
third, that the services and goods were not supplied for profit. All those contentions
were rejected.

Contentions 1 and 3 were not pursued before the learned judge and the main
argument before him appears to have centred on contention 2, and summarising it in its *e*
broadest possible terms it was that, inasmuch as the taxpayer was a religious or
philosophical body and that it was seeking to do nothing more than to expound and
communicate the tenets of its religion or philosophy, that (a) was not a business and (b)
could not be a business. The learned judge rejected those contentions.

The notice of appeal from his decision was given on 20th March 1979. That notice
specified various grounds of appeal on which it was urged that the learned judge had *f*
erred in law. Counsel for the taxpayer does not seek to support those grounds in their
original form, and there is, as I understand it, no question but that, so far as this
assessment is concerned (I say nothing of any other assessments), this appeal must be
dismissed unless the grounds can be expanded in the manner envisaged in an amended
notice of appeal which was dated 6th February 1980. By that amendment the taxpayer
sought to raise an entirely new ground of argument which was not advanced before the *g*
tribunal, nor before Neill J, and I state it in the most general terms because it has not been
fully developed before us. But in summary it amounts to this, that the Second Council
Directive of the European Economic Community of 11th April 1967 (Dir 67/228/EEC),
arts 4 and 6(2) and Annex B as interpreted by the jurisprudence of the Community have
the effect that a body which is a religious body is not to be regarded as carrying on a
business, that that directive, having been intended to produce uniformity as regards *h*
value added tax throughout the Community, overrides or takes precedence over local
legislation and that the effect of the directive is to confer a right on individual subjects of
the member states so that the taxpayer is able to resist the assessments made. That is
probably a great over-simplification of the argument, but as I understand it that is
broadly what it comes to and I think it is sufficient for the present purposes.

The amended notice having been given, the taxpayer came before this court on 22nd *j*
April 1980 on a motion by which it sought an order referring to the European Court
certain questions which it was thought would provide an authoritative answer and
which would enable this court to determine the appeal. That motion was adjourned to
come on with the present appeal because this court considered that until the hearing of
the appeal the court did not have sufficient facts before it to enable it to see what, if any,
questions required to be formulated, and it was thought that that could not be done
pending the hearing of the appeal.

The matter now comes before us on the substantive appeal and counsel for the
a taxpayer concedes that this European Community point, if I may so express it, is crucial
to his success. He asks us to remit the case to the value added tax tribunal because,
although that tribunal apparently made an underlying assumption, and indeed it appears
that counsel were content to accept it for the purpose of the points then being argued,
that the Church of Scientology was a religious or philosophical body, there was no
finding to that effect. There was considerable evidence of what the activity of the body
b consisted of, but that was directed to the questions which were then being canvassed,
namely whether the body was providing a university-style education and whether it was
carrying on a business.

The choices before us are, as it seems to me, threefold: firstly, to remit the case to the
value added tax tribunal, as counsel for the taxpayer asks us to; secondly, to listen to and
give judgment on an argument which counsel for the Crown is prepared to put before
c us that, in any event, this is not a case in which there should be any referral to the
European Court and that the matter is in fact so clear that there is nothing in the
European point of counsel for the taxpayer at all; and, thirdly, to dismiss the appeal.

As regards the first of those possible courses, counsel for the taxpayer has asked us to
remit the matter to the value added tax tribunal to find, on the evidence as it was before
it, whether the taxpayer was genuinely a religious or philosophical body because that is,
d in effect, a sine qua non for his success. But that does not seem to me to be a course which
we could possibly take. The evidence called before the value added tax tribunal is
directed to the issues then being argued, and the cross-examination of witnesses was, no
doubt, also directed to those issues as they then stood. In my judgment it would be quite
unreal to ask the tribunal to determine that matter without reopening the whole of the
evidence and if necessary giving both sides an opportunity to call further evidence.

Equally, I do not feel that it would be right that we should proceed to determine the
e matter on the basis that this court decides once and for all whether there is a question to
be referred in the absence of any finding of fact which would necessarily make that
question relevant. There would be only one or two effects of that if we did it. Firstly, if
we came to the conclusion that there was a question for reference, the matter would still
not be able to go on for want of the appropriate finding of facts. If we concluded that
f there was no case for reference, as counsel for the Crown would persuade us, then the
taxpayer might proceed to the House of Lords and counsel for the taxpayer might
persuade them that there was indeed a case for reference, and the same difficulty would
arise. So that does not seem to me to be a convenient course.

The choice therefore, as it seems to me, is between referring the matter back to the
value added tax tribunal with a direction to open the whole matter again, or to dismiss
g this appeal and leave it to the taxpayer to ventilate the point which it wants to raise in
entirely fresh proceedings relating to one or other of the very numerous other subsequent
assessments which are outstanding. Having regard to what seems to me to be the
manifest inconvenience of remitting the matter to the tribunal for a complete reopening
and reargument and to the fact that this was a point which was never argued below and
was raised for the first time on the amended notice of appeal in February of this year, I
h feel compelled to the conclusion that the appropriate course would be the last one which
I have mentioned, and I would accordingly dismiss the appeal.

STEPHENSON LJ. I agree and have nothing to add.

SIR JOHN WILLIS. I agree and have nothing to add.

Appeal and motion dismissed.

Solicitors: *Stephen M Bird*, East Grinstead (for the taxpayer); *Solicitor for the Customs and
Excise.*

Bebe Chua   Barrister.

Home Office v Commission for Racial Equality

QUEEN'S BENCH DIVISION

WOOLF J

2nd, 3rd, 14th OCTOBER 1980

Race relations – Discrimination – Duty of commission to eliminate discrimination – Commission proposing to investigate immigration control with a view to eliminating discrimination against coloured immigrants – Whether investigation connected with commission's duties – Whether commission's duty limited to elimination of discrimination expressly made unlawful by legislation – Whether enforcement of immigration control amounting to provision of goods, facilities and services – Whether commission having power to conduct investigation – Race Relations Act 1976, ss 20(1), 43(1)(a).

Race relations – Discrimination – Duty of commission to promote equality of opportunity and good race relations – Commission proposing to investigate immigration control – Whether promotion of equality of opportunity and good race relations restricted to areas where unlawful discrimination – Whether inquiry into immigration control would promote good race relations – Race Relations Act 1976, s 43(1)(b).

Race relations – Application of race relations legislation to Crown – Discrimination by Crown in immigration control – Whether Crown activities within scope of legislation – Race Relations Act 1976, s 75(1).

The Commission for Racial Equality believed that the Immigration Act 1971 was being applied more harshly to coloured immigrants than to white immigrants and informed the Home Office that, pursuant to the commission's general duties under s 43(1)[a] of the Race Relations Act 1976 and its power under s 48(1)[b] of that Act to conduct a formal investigation for any purpose connected with carrying out those duties, the commission proposed to conduct an investigation into the arrangements for enforcing the 1971 Act, with the aim of working towards the elimination of discrimination and promoting equality of opportunity among immigrants and good race relations. For the purpose of the investigation the commission wished to examine Home Office documents, to interview immigration officers and to conduct sample surveys of refusals of entry into the United Kingdom or refusals to vary leave to enter or remain. The commission did not intend to challenge the government's overall immigration policy. The Home Office issued a summons seeking (i) a declaration that the proposed investigation was ultra vires the commission's powers under the 1976 Act, and (ii) the determination of the question whether the commission had any power under the 1976 Act to investigate the manner of discharging government functions. The commission counterclaimed for declarations that it had power under the 1976 Act to conduct a formal investigation into acts done in administering immigration control and that the duty to work towards the elimination of discrimination in s 43(1)(a) of the 1976 Act was not restricted to discrimination in the fields of conduct specified in Parts II to IV of that Act.

Held – (1) On the true construction of s 75[c] of the 1976 Act, the 1976 Act bound the Crown in regard to acts and omissions similar to, but not necessarily the same as, acts which could amount to unlawful discrimination, and the scope of s 75 was not restricted

---

a Section 43, so far as material, is set out at p 1044 h, post
b Section 48, so far as material, is set out at p 1044 j, post
c Section 75, so far as material, is set out at p 1047 h, post

to acts expressly made unlawful discrimination by the Act. Accordingly, the treatment
a of a coloured immigrant in a wholly different manner from a white immigrant would
be an act to which s 75 applied (see p 1048 *a* to *e*, post).

(2) The proposed investigation was not connected with carrying out the commission's
duty under s 43(1)(*a*) of the 1976 Act to work towards 'the elimination of discrimination',
for that referred to the elimination of discrimination which was made unlawful by the
Act, and by ss 1 and 2^{*d*} of the Act discrimination was unlawful only in 'circumstances
b relevant for the purposes of any provision' of the Act and thus only where it was expressly
made unlawful under Parts I to IV of the Act, which did not include the control of
immigration. In any event the enforcement of immigration control did not amount to
discrimination in the provision of 'goods, facilities or services' within s 20(1)^{*e*} of the 1976
Act (see p 1048 *j* to p 1049 *e*, post); *Kassam v Immigration Appeal Tribunal* [1980] 2 All ER
330 applied.

c (3) However, the proposed investigation was connected with carrying out the
commission's duty under s 43(1)(*b*) of the 1976 Act to promote equality of opportunity
and good race relations, because (i) that duty was not restricted to areas where there was
unlawful discrimination under the Act, and (ii) an inquiry into immigration control
could be beneficial in promoting good race relations. Furthermore, bearing in mind that
it was a function of the commission to encourage harmonious community relations, it
d could not be assumed that Parliament did not intend the commission to have power to
inquire into the field of immigration (see p 1049 *h* to p 1050 *b*, post).

(4) Although, therefore, the commission had power under the 1976 Act to conduct
the proposed investigation, in view of its limited power under s 50^{*f*} of the Act to obtain
information, which was dependant on the Secretary of State's authorisation, and since if
the investigation was to proceed it could only result in recommendations for changes in
e the law, the proposed investigation was not likely to interfere with the functioning of
government (see p 1048 *f g* and p 1050 *c d*, post).

Notes
For the powers and duties of the Commission for Racial Equality, see Supplement to 4
Halsbury's Laws (4th Edn) para 1042B.13.
f   For the Race Relations Act 1976, ss 1, 2, 20, 43, 48, 50, 75, see 46 Halsbury's Statutes
(3rd Edn) 395, 396, 410, 425, 429, 430, 452.

---

g *d* Sections 1 and 2, so far as material, are set out at p 1049 *b*, post
e Section 20(1), so far as material, provides: 'It is unlawful for any person concerned with the
provision (for payment or not) of goods, facilities or services to the public or a section of the public
to discriminate against a person who seeks to obtain or use those goods, facilities or services—(*a*)
by refusing or deliberately omitting to provide him with any of them; or (*b*) by refusing or
deliberately omitting to provide him with goods, facilities or services of the like quality, in the like
manner and on the like terms as are normal in the first-mentioned person's case in relation to other
h members of the public or (where the person so seeking belongs to a section of the public) to other
members of that section.'
f Section 50, so far as material, provides:
       '(1) For the purposes of a formal investigation the Commission, by a notice in the prescribed
form served on him in the prescribed manner—(*a*) may require any person to furnish such written
information as may be described in the notice, and may specify the time at which, and the manner
and form in which, the information is to be furnished; (*b*) may require any person to attend at such
j time and place as is specified in the notice and give oral information about, and produce all
documents in his possession or control relating to, any matter specified in the notice.
       '(2) Except as provided by section 60, a notice shall be served under subsection (1) only where—
(*a*) service of the notice was authorised by an order made by the Secretary of State; or (*b*) the terms
of reference of the investigation state that the Commission believe that a person named in them
may have done or may be doing [certain specified acts] . . .'

Cases referred to in judgment

Kassam v Immigration Appeal Tribunal [1980] 2 All ER 330, sub nom *R v Immigration Appeal Tribunal, ex parte Kassam* [1980] 1 WLR 1037, CA.

R v Immigration Appeal Tribunal, ex parte Anluwalia (22nd February 1979, unreported), DC.

Summons

By a summons dated 14th November 1979 the Home Office sought as against the Commission for Racial Equality the following relief: (1) a declaration that it would be ultra vires the commission's powers to conduct (as it proposed) a formal investigation into the immigration service under ss 48 to 52 of the Race Relations Act 1976 with the following (or any like) terms of reference: to inquire into the arrangements made for the enforcement of the Immigration Act 1971 with special reference to equality of treatment afforded to persons of different racial groups entering or seeking to enter the United Kingdom for any purpose or seeking variations of the conditions of leave to remain therein; and (2) the determination of the question whether the commission had any, and if so what, powers under the 1976 Act to investigate the manner of discharge by the Crown of the functions of government. By a counterclaim dated 28th November 1979 the commission sought declarations that it had power under the 1976 Act to conduct a formal investigation into acts done in the administration of immigration control and that the duty imposed on it by s 43(1)(a) of the 1976 Act 'to work towards the elimination of discrimination' was a duty to work towards the elimination of all racial discrimination in the United Kingdom and was not restricted to discrimination in the fields of conduct specified in Parts II to IV (inclusive) of the 1976 Act. The facts are set out in the judgment.

Peter Scott QC and *Simon D Brown* for the Home Office.
John R MacDonald QC and *I A MacDonald* for the commission.

Cur adv vult

14th October. **WOOLF J** read the following judgment: The Race Relations Act 1976 is Parliament's third attempt at legislating in the delicate area of race relations. The Act provides for the establishment of the Commission for Racial Equality, the defendant in these proceedings. The commission replaces both the Race Relations Board, which had the job of policing or enforcing the previous legislation, and the Community Relations Commission which, under the previous legislation, was responsible for encouraging harmonious community relations.

Although the members of the commission are appointed by the Secretary of State for Home Affairs, it is expressly provided in Sch 1 to the Act that the commission is not an emanation of the Crown but a corporate body.

The commission's duties are expressly set out in s 43(1) of the Act as being threefold:

'(a) to work towards the elimination of discrimination; (b) to promote equality of opportunity, and good relations, between persons of different racial groups generally; and (c) to keep under review the working of this Act and, when they are so required by the Secretary of State or otherwise think it necessary, draw up and submit to the Secretary of State proposals for amending it.'

In addition to those duties, s 48(1) provides that:

'Without prejudice to their general power to do anything requisite for the performance of their duties under section 43(1), the Commission may if they think fit, and shall if required by the Secretary of State, conduct a formal investigation for any purpose connected with the carrying out of *those duties*.' (My emphasis.)

'Those duties' are the three duties I have just recited.

In these proceedings the Home Office contends that those provisions do not entitle the commission to conduct a formal investigation into the manner of discharge by the Crown of the functions of government, and, in particular, to make an inquiry into the arrangements made for the enforcement of immigration control.

The evidence is confined to affidavits from Mr David Lane, chairman of the commission, and correspondence between the commission and the Home Office, and the facts giving rise to these proceedings can be summarised as follows.

The commission believes that there is a widespread feeling among members of the coloured communities and especially those originating from the Indian sub-continent that the immigration laws and immigration controls operate more harshly on them than on other immigrants of a different ethnic origin. The commission has therefore, from time to time, written to the Home Secretary and other officers of the Home Office expressing its concern and seeking a reassurance with regard to certain aspects of policy. Of particular concern to the commission was the case of the Asian lady who was required to undergo a gynaecological examination at Heathrow Airport as part of the investigation to see whether or not she was entitled to leave to enter this country.

On 7th May 1979 the chairman of the commission wrote to the present Home Secretary and, under the heading 'Immigration Control Procedure', expressed the hope that he would respond positively to the requests which the commission had made to his predecessor shortly before the election. That letter quoted an extract from an earlier letter dated 18th April 1978 which read as follows:

'We accept the necessity for firm control of immigration by the Government. We in no way condone illegal immigration or overstaying or bogus marriages, and we support all fair and reasonable measures that can be taken to deal effectively with such abuses. It is essential, however, that the policy and practice of immigration control should be non-discriminatory and should be consonant with Britain's humane and liberal traditions and with her international obligations. Immigration policy is directly bound up with the task of building a multi-racial society based on equal and civilised treatment for all its inhabitants.'

The letter went on to raise again the question of the gynaecological examination of the Asian lady. It recited the fact that the Home Secretary's predecessor had been asked to take further action, and in particular, to hold an independent inquiry, and also stated that the commission had resolved to hold an investigation itself if it was not satisfied with the Home Secretary's stance.

On 12th June 1979 the commission wrote to the Minister of State at the Home Office in the following terms:

'Nationality law and immigration policy
We should be interested to learn more of the Government's intentions. With regard to immigration control procedures and our request for an independent inquiry, the Commission had a long discussion last week. We considered carefully your letter of 21 May and the Home Secretary's view that decisions about an inquiry should await clarification of the House of Commons Select Committe arrangements in the new Parliament. A Select Committee inquiry could of course be valuable and we would be ready to cooperate with it, although its nature would probably be different from the type of investigation which we ourselves have had in mind. We feel, however, that the need for reassurance about the fair operation of the system is pressing and that the delay involved in waiting for a Select Committee decision is undesirable. We still believe that the ideal course would be for the Home Secretary himself to establish an independent inquiry (on the lines suggested in my letter of 7 May), and the Commission asked me to try to arrange a meeting with you in order to discuss this possibility further. In view of this, we decided not to embark on any investigation ourselves before the end of June, and if by that time you felt in a position to set up an inquiry, we would not go ahead with our own. However, if

you feel unable to do so, we decided that we would then proceed to conduct a formal investigation with the following terms of reference: "To inquire into the arrangements for the enforcement of the Immigration Act 1971 with special reference to equality of treatment afforded to persons of different racial groups entering or seeking to enter the United Kingdom for any purpose or seeking variations of the conditions of leave to remain therein. The term 'racial group' has herein the meaning assigned to it in section 3 of the Race Relations Act 1976". The Commission asked me to emphasise that, in embarking on an investigation, we would not be challenging the Government's overall immigration policy but would be concerned with the arrangements made for its application, particularly from the point of view of non-discrimination.'

On 9th July 1979 the commission informed the Home Office that it was embarking on a formal investigation with terms of reference virtually identical to those set out in the letter of 12th June 1979.

The correspondence then continued with the Home Office indicating that it had been legally advised by the Attorney General that the proposed investigation would be outside the purpose for which the commission was by law established, and the commission indicating that it had received advice to the contrary from leading counsel.

Neither side being prepared to alter its view, these proceedings were commenced.

In the proceedings the Home Office seeks—

'(1) . . . a Declaration that it would be ultra vires the Defendants' powers to conduct (as they propose) a formal investigation into the Immigration Service purportedly under the provisions of Sections 48–52 of the Race Relations Act 1976 with the following (or any like) terms of reference: "To inquire into the arrangements made for the enforcement of the Immigration Act 1971 with special reference to equality of treatment afforded to persons of different racial groups entering or seeking to enter the United Kingdom for any purpose or seeking variations of the conditions of leave to remain therein. The term 'racial group' has herein the meaning assigned to it in Section 3 of the Race Relations Act 1976."

'(2) . . . the determination of the Court on the following question, namely whether the Defendants have any, and if so what, powers under the Race Relations Act 1976 to investigate the manner of discharge by the Crown of the functions of Government (in contra-distinction to such acts of the Executive as by Sections 75 and 76 of the Act are expressly made subject to the application of the Act).'

The commission has also sought relief in the form of the following declarations:

'(1) A declaration that the Defendants have power under the Race Relations Act 1976 to conduct a formal investigation into acts done in the administration of immigration control.

'(2) A declaration that the duty imposed on the Defendants by section 43(1)(a) of the Race Relations Act 1979 "to work towards the elimination of discrimination" is a duty to work towards the elimination of all racial discrimination in the United Kingdom and is not restricted to discrimination in the fields of conduct specified in parts II to IV (inclusive) of the Race Relations Act 1976.'

As the Home Office is contending that the proposed investigation is ultra vires the commission, it is relevant to see what Mr Lane had to say about the form which the investigation would take. In his first affidavit which was sworn on 27th November 1979 he stated:

'The aim of the investigation proposed by the Commission is in accordance with the Commission's general duties under Section 43 of the Race Relations Act 1976, and in particular with its duties to work towards the elimination of discrimination and promote equality of opportunity and good relations between persons of different racial groups generally. In proposing such an investigation the Commission

a
has in mind its powers under Section 51, if necessary or expedient, to recommend changes in a person's policies or procedures and its power to make recommendations to the Secretary of State for changes in the law.'

In his second affidavit which was sworn on 11th September 1980 Mr Lane said:

b
'The Commission's investigation would go into great detail and would last longer than a parallel inquiry by the said Sub-Committee. It would examine, among other things, sample surveys of refusal of entry or refusal to vary leave to enter or remain. It would hope to examine Home Office documents, papers and instructions, to interview officials, to hold discussions at ports of entry, and to examine casework records of such bodies as the United Kingdom Immigrants Advisory Service ("UKIAS") and the Joint Council for the Welfare of Immigrants ("JCWI"). Such detailed examination would have to be carried out in large part by members of the Commission's staff, acting under the supervision of the Commissioners appointed to conduct the said investigation.'

c

d
Further insight as to what was causing concern to the commission appears from its notes of 7th May 1979, that is, delays in dealing with applications, standard of proof, various aspects of discriminatory treatment and a number of other matters including the operation of the appeal system. Clearly the commission has in mind a wider ranging investigation, but not one, according to the letter of 12th June 1979 which challenges the overall immigration policy.

In opening the case on behalf of the Home Office counsel contended that it was inconceivable that Parliament could have intended the commission to have the power to embark on an investigation of this sort. In his submission, the documents to which I

e
have referred indicated that it would involve investigating the acts of the Home Secretary himself, immigration officers, police officers, adjudicators, the Immigration Appeal Tribunal, the Lord Chancellor and the High Court in respect of the exercise of its prerogative powers. He stressed that all these bodies were involved directly or indirectly in the enforcement of immigration control. He pointed out that if the commission was entitled to look into immigration, it would also be entitled to look into the working of

f
the police, the Customs and Excise, and the Inland Revenue. He drew attention to the fact that the commissions's powers under the Race Relations Act 1976 were almost the same as those of the Equal Opportunities Commission under the Sex Discrimination Act 1975 and if the Commission for Racial Equality could look into the functions of government, the Equal Opportunities Commission would also be entitled to do so.

Bearing in mind those submissions it is convenient at the outset to consider the extent

g
to which the Act binds the Crown. In this respect the earlier Race Relations Act 1968 was quite clear. Section 27(1) simply stated: 'This Act binds the Crown.' The present Act deals with the matter quite differently. Section 75 provides:

h
'(1) This Act applies—(a) to an act done by or for purposes of a Minister of the Crown or government department; or (b) to an act done on behalf of the Crown by a statutory body, or a person holding a statutory office, as it applies to an act done by a private person.
'(2) Parts II and IV apply to—(a) service for purposes of a Minister of the Crown or government department, other than service of a person holding a statutory office; or (b) service on behalf of the Crown for purposes of a person holding a statutory office or purposes of a statutory body; and (c) service in the armed forces,

j
as they apply to employment by a private person, and shall so apply as if references to a contract of employment included references to the terms of service . . .'

It is not necessary for me to set out the whole of the remaining provisions of s 75.

In relation to sub-s (1) it was contended on behalf of the Home Office that that only applies to acts which could be done by a private person. It was accepted that the combined effects of sub-ss (1) and (2) meant that, if the Crown unlawfully discriminated in the employment field, then the Act would be enforceable against the Crown.

So if it discriminated in the engagement of immigration officers the Act would have an application in the immigration field. However, apart from discrimination which was expressly made unlawful under the Act, the Home Office contended that it did not apply to the Crown or government departments.

Thus, in the course of argument, counsel for the Home Office contended that if an immigration officer treated coloured immigrants in a wholly different manner from the way in which he treated white immigrants this would not be an act to which s 75 referred, because it was not an act capable of being done by an individual.

I cannot accept this restricted interpretation of s 75. It is true that only an immigration officer and not a private person can purport to exercise immigration control. However, the type of act to which I have just made reference is one which a private person in a different capacity is quite able to perform, for example a doorkeeper at a nightclub, and so it seems to me that that would be an act falling within s 75. After all it is only a government department who can engage immigration officers. A private individual cannot do that. But the Home Office concedes that such an engagement would be an act within s 75.

Nonetheless, the wording used in s 75 was clearly intended to have a more restricted effect than the wording contained in the previous Act. It appears to me that an act for the purposes of s 75, which is defined in s 78 as including a deliberate omission, means some act which, while not necessarily the same, is one similar to the kind of act which can amount to unlawful discrimination under the Act of 1976. It does not, in my view, include activities of the sort involved in formulating and expressing government policy, or the hearing of cases before the courts and tribunals. I draw attention to the contrast between the word 'act' and the word 'functions' used in s 71.

However, my view as to the proper interpretation of s 75 only plays a limited part in resolving the issues between the parties. Section 75 does not give any direct help as to what is the proper subject matter for inquiry by the commission. It only assists as to the extent which the Act can be enforced against the Crown. As to this the commission on its own has only extremely limited powers. While the commission has wide powers to hold a formal investigation, its ability to require persons to furnish written information or to attend to give oral information is very limited unless the Secretary of State is in agreement with the steps which it proposes to take. Section 50(1) enables the commission to serve a notice requiring information to be given but, with an exception which is not relevant here, such notice can only be served where it is authorised by the Secretary of State or the investigation is one where the commission believes that the person named has been guilty of unlawful conduct under the Act. The result, therefore, is that in the case of the proposed investigation in question, or any investigation into a like subject, unless the Secretary of State were prepared to make an order giving the necessary authority the commission would be without teeth and would not be able to get any information from anyone who is not prepared to volunteer it. The fears expressed by counsel for the Home Office, to which I referred at the outset, must be judged in the light of this real restriction on the commission's powers.

The section of the Act which is at the heart of the dispute between the parties is s 43. Section 48 makes it clear that formal investigations must be for a purpose connected with the carrying out of the three duties set out in s 43, which I have already cited. So it is necessary to decide whether the proposed investigation is connected with the carrying out of those duties.

The duty specified in s 43(1)(a) refers to the elimination of discrimination. Counsel for the Home Office, in my view rightly, contends that this means the elimination of discrimination which is made unlawful by the Act. The Act does not make all discrimination unlawful. Subject to s 20 to which I will make reference hereafter, it is common ground that the existence of immigration control and the enforcement of that immigration control is not discrimination made unlawful by the Act. As such

immigration control involves discrimination, counsel for the Home Office argues that it
a cannot have been intended that it should be the duty of the commission to work for its
elimination bearing in mind it is authorised by the Immigration Act 1971.

The reasons why immigration control is not discrimination for the purposes of the Act
are as follows. Discrimination is defined in s 3(3) of the 1976 Act as any discrimination
falling within s 1 or s 2 of the Act. Both ss 1 and 2, in defining discrimination, do so in
respect of 'any circumstances relevant for the purposes of any provision of this Act'.
b Although counsel for the commission argued strongly to the contrary, I am satisfied that
the use of this reference to 'any circumstances relevant for the purposes of any provision
of this Act' confines the definition of discrimination to discrimination which is expressly
made unlawful under Parts II to VI of the Act.

This was the view taken by the Court of Appeal in *R v Immigration Appeal Tribunal, ex
parte Kassam* [1980] 2 All ER 330, [1980] 1 WLR 1037 as to the interpretation of the
c similar provisions of the Sex Discrimination Act 1975 and also of Eveleigh LJ in *R v
Immigration Appeal Tribunal, ex parte Anluwalia* (22nd February 1979, unreported) in
relation to that Act. While I accept those cases were only concerned in deciding what was
unlawful discrimination, I would apply the same reasoning to the interpretation of the
word 'discrimination' in s 43(1)(*a*).

Enforcement of immigration control could only give rise to unlawful discrimination
d for the purposes of the Act if the activity in question fell within s 20(1), that is, if it
amounted to discrimination in the provision of 'goods, facilities or services'.

In the *Kassam* case the Court of Appeal concluded that the words 'facilities' and
'services' did not cover the giving of leave to enter or remain by the Secretary of State
under the Immigration Act 1971, and, while reserving his position if there should be an
appeal, counsel for the commission accepts that, in view of that decision, I am bound to
e treat discrimination in the immigration field as not being discrimination made unlawful
by the Act. It follows that the commission is not entitled to rely on s 43(1)(*a*).

Omitting for the moment s 43(1)(*b*) and turning to s 43(1)(*c*), which deals with the
duty to keep under review the working of the Race Relations Act 1976, on the evidence
before me the commission cannot rely on s 43(1)(*c*) since, so far as the commission is
concerned about the working of any Act, it is the Immigration Act 1971 and not the
f 1976 Act.

There remains s 43(1)(*b*) which is the duty under s 43 which was relied on by Mr Lane
in his first affidavit. In dealing with this part of s 43 counsel for the Home Office divided
his submissions into two parts. First of all he dealt with the words 'to promote equality
of opportunity' and said this was merely the obverse of the 'elimination of discrimination',
and therefore the arguments which I have just dealt with in relation to discrimination
should lead to the same conclusions about the promotion of equality of opportunity.
g While I had reservations about this part of counsel's submissions and questioned whether
there was not some difference, his submission is supported by the terms of ss 47(1) and
51(1) and, were it not for the additional words in s 43(1)(*b*) referring to the promotion of
'good relations' as well as equality of opportunity, I would have concluded that s 43(1)(*b*)
only refers to the promotion of equality of opportunity in an area where discrimination
h would be unlawful. However, I do not consider that this limited view of s 43(1)(*b*) can
apply to the duty to promote good relations. The contrast between the wording in
ss 47(1) and 51(1) and that in s 43(1)(*b*) is significant. It is interesting to see that the same
dual reference to equality of opportunity and good relations appears in ss 44(1) and 70(1).

I consider the explanation for the reference to good relations in s 43(1)(*b*) is the fact that
the commission combines the duties of its two predecessors. The elimination of
j discrimination and the promotion of equal opportunity reflects the duties of the old
board. The duty to promote good relations is a reflection of the duty which was
contained in s 25 of the Race Relations Act 1968, which required the Community
Relations Commission to encourage the establishment of, and assist others to take steps
to secure the establishment of, harmonious community relations.

The commission takes the view that an inquiry into the control of immigration could be beneficial in promoting good relations between racial groups. Such an investigation seems to me to be an investigation which the commission could properly regard as **a** having this result and as being connected with the carrying out of its duty under s 43(1)(*b*). Immigration clearly has a very real impact on race relations. A country which has had no immigration, in consequence of which the persons concerned are all of the same colour, race, nationality and ethnic or national origins, does not require a Race Relations Act. Immigration control is bound up with problems as to the ability of this country to absorb different racial groups. Bearing in mind the dual functions of the **b** commission, I cannot accept that Parliament must be assumed to have intended, as the Home Office contends, that the field of immigration should be a no-go area for the commission.

Nor do I accept that the consequences of my conclusion are as drastic as the Home Office submitted. I have already indicated that unless the Secretary of State is prepared to supply it with teeth, the commission has limited powers to obtain information. This **c** limitation may mean that without the Home Office's co-operation the investigation is not worthwhile. However, if the investigation proceeds, with or without that co-operation, the only result will be that the commission may be able to make recommendations to the Secretary of State for changes in the law or otherwise and to publish or make its report available for inspection. Results hardly likely to substantially interfere with the functioning of government.　　　　　　　　　　　　　　**d**

[His Lordship, having heard submissions on the point, then decided not to make any declarations.]

Applications refused.

Solicitors: *Treasury Solicitor ; Bindman & Partners* (for the commission).　　　　**e**

K Mydeen Esq　　Barrister.

f

Westminster City Council v Monahan and others

COURT OF APPEAL, CIVIL DIVISION
LAWTON, EVELEIGH LJJ AND SIR DAVID CAIRNS　　　　　　　　　　　　　　**g**
19th JANUARY 1981

Land – Summary proceedings for possession – Order for possession – Abridgment of time for making order – Urgency – Procedure for applying for abridgment of time – Application to be made to judge hearing summons – Plaintiff serving properly constituted summons and establishing clear right to possession of premises against defendant – Summons heard by Queen's Bench judge **h** *before five clear days after date of service of summons – Judge taking view case not one of urgency – Judge dismissing summons – Whether judge should have adjourned summons until five days elapsed before making final order – RSC Ord 113, r 6(1).*

On 7th January 1981 the defendants occupied vacant premises in a block of property as a protest against the local authority's plan to redevelop the site. The defendants had no **j** right or title to the premises. On 7th January the local authority started summary proceedings for possession against them by issuing an originating summons under RSC Ord 113. Their affidavit in support of the summons stated that the premises were vacant and were due to be demolished very shortly but did not state why it was necessary to act promptly in the matter. The local authority wished to abridge the time for getting *a* possession, on the ground of urgency, and took the view that under Ord 113, r 6(1)^a it was necessary for them to apply to a judge, prior to the hearing of the summons, for leave to serve short notice of the summons. Accordingly, on 8th January they applied to Russell J for leave to serve the summons for hearing on 14th January. Russell J, who had before him the local authority's affidavit that the premises were shortly to be demolished, gave leave to serve short notice of the summons to be returnable on 14th January. The defendants obtained affidavits from members of the local authority and others stating

b that redevelopment of the site was undesirable and was unlikely to take place in the current financial climate. When the summons came on for hearing on 14th January before Lawson J, he accepted that the defendants had no right or title to occupy the premises, but took the view that there was little likelihood of the redevelopment scheme proceeding and that the case was not one of urgency. He therefore set aside Russell J's order for short notice of the summons under Ord 113, and dismissed the summons. The

c local authority appealed, contending that although Lawson J was entitled on 14th January to refuse to make a final order on the summons by virtue of r 6(1) of Ord 113 because the evidence of urgency was inadequate and five clear days from the date of service of the summons had not elapsed, nevertheless, as the local authority's affidavits clearly established that they were entitled to possession of the premises, he ought not to have dismissed the summons but ought to have adjourned it until the necessary time had

d elapsed before making a final order. The defendants contended that on 14th January the judge was entitled to dismiss the summons altogether or, alternatively, was entitled to refuse to make an order thus leaving the local authority to restore the summons at a later date.

Held – Where there was a properly constituted summons under RSC Ord 113 and clear

e evidence that the defendant had no answer to it but the judge was not satisfied of the urgency of the case and therefore was not entitled under r 6(1) to allow abridgment of the time specified therein for making a possession order, the practice in the Queen's Bench Division ought to be the same as that in the Chancery Division, namely that the judge should adjourn the matter until the time specified in r 6(1), ie five clear days from the date of service of the summons, had elapsed before making a final order on the

f summons. It followed that since the local authority had a clear case for possession and the defendants had no answer to it, the judge ought not to have dismissed the summons on 14th January but ought to have adjourned it until five clear days from the date of service of the summons had elapsed. In the circumstances the court would make the order which could have been made at first instance once the five-day period had elapsed. Accordingly the appeal would be allowed (see p 1055 *d* to *h* and p 1056 *d* to *g*, post);

g *Practice Direction* [1970] 3 All ER 240 applied.

Per Curiam. Where an applicant for a possession order under Ord 113 wishes to abridge the time for getting the order because of urgency, the application to abridge the time should be made to the judge who hears the summons, who alone is concerned with the issue of urgency, and should not be made to any other judge prior to the hearing of the summons. An application in regard to abridgment of time can however be made

h prior to the hearing for the administrative purpose of obtaining an order that the summons should be accepted for listing before a judge although five clear days from the date of service of the summons have not elapsed (see p 1055 *a* to *c* and p 1056 *f g*, post).

Notes

For summary proceedings for possession of land, see Supplement to 32 Halsbury's Laws

j (3rd Edn) para 606A, and for cases on the subject, see Digest (Cont Vol D) 1069–1071, 5588–5596.

Case referred to in judgments

Mercy v Persons Unknown (1974) 231 Estates Gazette 1159, CA.

---

a   Rule 6(1) is set out at p 1054 *h*, post

Cases also cited

Greater London Council v Jenkins [1975] 1 All ER 354, [1975] 1 WLR 155, CA.
Orpen Road (9), Stoke Newington, Re [1971] 1 All ER 944, [1971] 1 WLR 166.

Appeal

By an originating summons dated 7th January 1981 the plaintiffs, Westminster City
Council, brought proceedings under RSC Ord 113 against the defendants, James
Monahan, Brian Lake, G Kirk and persons unknown, for an order for possession of
premises at 51 Charing Cross Road, London WC2, on the grounds that they were entitled
to possession of the premises and that the defendants were in occupation of them
without licence or consent. On 8th January 1981 Russell J gave the plaintiffs leave to
serve short notice of the summons, making the summons returnable on 14th January
1981. On 14th January Lawson J set aside Russell J's order for short notice and dismissed
the plaintiffs' application for possession under RSC Ord 113. The plaintiffs appealed and
by notice dated 14th January applied for an order abridging the time for setting down
the appeal and for an expedited appeal, and further applied for hearing of the appeal
forthwith if the court should order an expedited appeal. The facts are set out in the
judgment of Lawton LJ.

Peter Mottershead QC and *Philip Newman* for the plaintiffs.
David Watkinson for the defendants.

LAWTON LJ. This is an application by the Lord Mayor and citizens of the City of
Westminster against James Monahan, Brian Lake, a woman called Kirk, and persons
unknown, to expedite the hearing of an appeal from an order made by Lawson J in
chambers on 14th January 1981. The application went on to ask that, if the application
to expedite the hearing was granted, the court should hear the appeal forthwith. We do
expedite the hearing and we have today heard the appeal. The appeal is one of some
importance, because it has revealed some misunderstanding about the effect of RSC Ord
113.

On the west side of Charing Cross Road, in the City of Westminster, there is a block
of property known as Sandringham West. It consisted at one time of about 200 flats and
at street level a number of shops. One of these was known as no 51 and was the shop of
an antiquarian bookseller. The Westminster City Council have plans for the
redevelopment of the site of Sandringham West. These plans have been the subject
matter of acute controversy, not only within the council chamber itself but amongst
others who are interested in the development of that part of the City of Westminster. By
a majority, the City of Westminster have resolved to go on with their redevelopment
plan. Some of those who were in the minority and some of their supporters outside the
council are concerned about the decision to redevelop the site at the present time. No
doubt there are many reasons why the redevelopment of the site is being opposed, but
one of them is a pragmatic one, that in these days of financial stringency the money is not
available to redevelop and, if the first step towards redevelopment is taken, namely
demolition of the existing building, there will be left on the site in the foreseeable future
what has been described by counsel as a hole alongside the road and no doubt an
unsightly one.

The defendants in this case were amongst those who were bitterly opposed to the
decision of the Westminster City Council to redevelop the site. On or about 7th January
1981 they occupied the vacant bookseller's shop at no 51. The tenant of that shop had
given up possession to the Westminster City Council earlier that month. During the
course of 7th January 1981 the Westminster City Council sent workmen to no 51 to
secure the premises pending demolition. When they arrived they found the defendants
in occupation and the defendants intimated to them that they intended to remain there
all round the clock. The workmen reported back to the chief executive of the
Westminster City Council. As a result, he decided to start proceedings by way of

originating summons under RSC Ord 113 for an order for possession against the
a defendants. It was clear to him, and it has been clear to us, that the defendants had no
title whatsoever to be in possession of no 51. They were there as protesters against the
decision of the Westminster City Council to go on with the redevelopment of this site.
They were not even homeless people seeking somewhere to live. What they were doing
was making a gesture for the purpose of attracting attention to what the Westminster
City Council were doing.

b   An originating summons under Ord 113 has to be supported by evidence. A law clerk
named Jones was given the task of drafting the necessary affidavits and swearing them.
I have some sympathy with Mr Jones because he was not fully qualified as a lawyer and
he had to take steps to do what he could to get the matter before the court as quickly as
possible. What he did was to deal with the bare essentials of the matter so far as the
Westminster City Council were concerned. He did not deal in his affidavit with any of
c the background matter and in particular he did not give any reasons why it was necessary
to act promptly for the purposes of getting possession of no 51. He took the view, and
those behind him took the view, having regard to the wording of Ord 113, r 6, that it
would be necessary to get the leave of a judge to give what is commonly known as 'short
notice' of the originating summons. As a result, an application was made by counsel to
Russell J on 8th January 1981 for leave to serve the originating summons for hearing on
d 14th January 1981. We have been told in the course of the hearing today that counsel
told Russell J that the demolition contractors would be moving in by the end of the
month to start the demolition of Sandringham West. Russell J gave leave to serve short
notice of the originating summons. In due course it came on for hearing on Wednesday
14th January before Lawson J.

        By that time the defendants had obtained affidavits from a number of people, some of
e whom were members of the Westminster City Council, in which they expressed their
opinion about the undesirability of developing Sandringham West and what they
considered to be the unlikely chance of the development going ahead in the present
financial climate. There was nothing whatsoever in these affidavits to show that the
defendants had, or claimed to have, any right or title to be in occupation of no 51.

        When the case was called on before Lawson J in chambers, it took a somewhat unusual
f course, because, according to the affidavit of Mr Jones and, indeed, to the affidavit of Mr
Lake, which was put in on behalf of the defendants, the judge started by dealing with
what one might call the general merits of the redevelopment scheme of the Westminster
City Council. He took the view, on such information as was before him in the affidavits,
that there was not much likelihood of this redevelopment scheme going forward, having
regard to the difficulties existing at the present time over public finance. In those
g circumstances, he asked why the Westminster City Council wanted to go on with their
originating summons for possession. After some discussion with counsel, most of which
seems to have been irrelevant, the judge did get down to the point which was for him to
deal with, namely whether there was any evidence on the affidavits which would entitle
him, on Wednesday 14th January 1981, to make a final order. He came to the conclusion
that there was no such evidence on the affidavits.

h   Counsel, who today has appeared on behalf of the Westminster City Council, has
accepted that the evidence of urgency was inadequate. In those circumstances, the judge
clearly was entitled to refuse to make a final order there and then for possession of
no 51. But what the affidavits did disclose and what the judge, from what he said, clearly
accepted was that the defendants had no right or title to be in no 51 at all. In other
words, save for the fact that there was no urgency about the matter, the plaintiffs clearly,
j on their affidavits, had established a right to an order for possession but not a right to
have that order made on 14th January 1981.

        The judge made an order in these terms: 'that the order of the Hon. Mr Justice Russell
herein of the 8th January 1981 as to short notice to be set aside, and the application under
Order 113 be dismissed.' It is against that order in that form that the Westminster City
Council have appealed to this court. The argument has been that, having regard to the

fact that the originating summons was taken out in the right kind of case, was properly
served and supported by affidavits, and all the evidence therein showed that the *a*
Westminster City Council had a right to the order, the judge should not have dismissed
the originating summons under RSC Ord 113 but should have adjourned the matter in
order to ensure that the necessary time elapsed before a final order was made.

The defendants, on the other hand, have submitted that the judge was entitled to
dismiss the originating summons altogether; alternatively, if he was not entitled to
dismiss it altogether, he was entitled to refuse to make any order on 14th January 1981, *b*
leaving the Westminster City Council to restore the originating summons before either
the same judge or another judge at a later date.

The course of events, as I indicated at the beginning of my judgment, reveals a certain
confusion of thought about the way in which RSC Ord 113 operates. It is now necessary
for me to examine Ord 113 in some detail. The jurisdiction given by Ord 113 came into
existence in 1970 as a result of the gap in the law which was revealed by a series of *c*
squatter cases which had occurred in the two or three years before 1970. These cases had
shown that there was difficulty in getting speedy possession of property when it had been
occupied by trespassers. The objects of Ord 113 were twofold. The first was to provide
a procedure whereby an order for possession could be obtained even though the property
owner did not know the names of the trespassers; and the second was so that the time lag
between starting proceedings and getting an order for possession could be very *d*
considerably shortened. The intention was that the new procedure should be used in a
particular type of case. That type of case is defined in r 1, which is in these terms:

> 'Where a person claims possession of land which he alleges is occupied solely by
> a person or persons (not being a tenant or tenants holding over after the termination
> of the tenancy) who entered into or remained in occupation without his licence or
> consent or that of any predecessor in title of his, the proceedings may be brought by *e*
> originating summons in accordance with the provisions of this order.'

As I understand that rule, it means this, that a property owner faced with squatters can
decide for himself whether he wishes to proceed for recovery of his property by writ in
the ordinary way or whether he wishes to proceed by way of the summary proceedings
described in r 1. The summary proceedings described in r 1 are, however, confined to a *f*
particular type of case and if a property owner decides to use the procedure prescribed by
r 1 he has to comply with the other provisions of the order. He must use the form of
originating summons prescribed by the rule. The affidavit in support must contain the
matters to which r 3 applies. He must serve the originating summons in accordance
with r 4. Rule 4(3) provides: 'Order 28, rule 3, shall not apply to proceedings under this
order.' RSC Ord 28, r 3 is a rule which deals with the amount of time that must be given *g*
by way of notice to a defendant. So what r 4 is doing is getting rid of the time limits set
out in Ord 28, r 3. It takes the new procedure out of that particular rule. It does not take
the new procedure out of other rules in Ord 28, including r 5 dealing with adjournments.

Then Ord 113, r 6(1) which is the relevant one for the purposes of this appeal, provides
as follows:

> 'A final order shall not be made on the originating summons except by a judge in *h*
> person and shall, except in case of urgency and by leave of the court, not be made
> less than five clear days after the date of service.'

Then r 6(2) deals with the form of the order for possession.

It is Ord 113, r 6 which has caused the difficulty in this case and has seemingly caused
difficulty in other cases, because the idea has got around that, if it is thought necessary to *j*
abridge the time for getting an order for possession because of urgency, and it may well
be in some cases that an order for possession is required very urgently indeed, what can
be done is to go to a judge before the date of the hearing and ask him to abridge the time
because of urgency. That seems to have been the intention in this case. The plaintiffs
went to Russell J. If that judge did think he was abridging time because of urgency (and

I doubt whether he did), he would have been deciding an issue in the absence of the
a defendants and without their being heard. But on my reading of Ord 113, r 6(1) it is the
judge who makes the final order who is concerned with the issue of urgency, no one
else. It follows, therefore, save for an administrative purpose to which I shall refer in a
moment, that going to another judge, who is not going to hear the summons, to certify
that there is urgency, is not the right procedure to follow. But for an administrative
reason it may be necessary to go to another judge. The reason is this. In the ordinary
b way, so we were told, the listing clerks will not accept an originating summons for
hearing before a judge except with a minimum of five days' notice. They will, however,
of course, accept such a summons on less than five days' notice if a judge so orders. It
follows, therefore, that when a property owner wishes to bring an originating summons
to the attention of the judge before five clear days, it will be necessary for him to go to
a judge for the purpose of getting the listing clerks to accept the originating summons
c for listing. That was the real purpose of the application which was made to Russell J.

When the matter comes before the judge on the hearing of the originating summons,
he has to decide, first, whether the originating summons has been properly issued,
whether the evidence in support of it is adequate, and if he is so satisfied, then he will
make the final order. But he must not make the final order unless at least five clear days
have elapsed, save when the case is one of urgency. It follows that if, in a particular case,
d the summons is properly constituted, the evidence is clear and there is no possible answer
to the summons, but the judge is of the opinion that it is not a case of urgency, what he
should do is to adjourn the matter until such time as five clear days have elapsed.

This seems to be the practice in the Chancery Division, according to a Practice
Direction dated 31st July 1970 ([1970] 3 All ER 240, [1970] 1 WLR 1250). Paragraph 6
of that Practice Direction is as follows:

e   'An application for abridgment of time for the purposes of r 6(1) shall be made to
the judge at the hearing in court and if the judge does not allow such abridgment
the matter shall be adjourned to such date as the judge shall direct.'

It seems to me that the practice in the Queen's Bench Division should be the same as
in the Chancery Division; in other words, if everything is in order except that the judge
f is not satisfied about urgency, he should do what judges in the Chancery Division do,
namely adjourn the matter so that at least five clear days have elapsed before the final
order is made.

In deciding in that way I am not for one moment suggesting that the judge can never
dismiss an application under RSC Ord 113. He clearly can. If the case does not come
within the ambit of Ord 113 he can dismiss it. If there is something wrong with the
g service he can dismiss it. If it is clear that matters have been joined in the summons
which ought not to be there he can dismiss it. If there is an issue to be tried and on the
trial of the issue it appears that the plaintiff has not got the case which he said he had then
clearly the judge should dismiss it. But when, as in this case, the plaintiffs' case is as clear
as anything could be and the defendants have not got the beginnings of an answer, in my
judgment it would be wrong to dismiss the summons out of hand. The proper course
h would be to adjourn it.

It was said on behalf of the defendants, who in this court have made no attempt to
make any claim of right to be in possession of these premises, that the judge could have
done what was done in *Mercy v Persons Unknown* (1974) 231 Estates Gazette 1159, namely
refuse to make an order, thereby leaving the plaintiffs to restore the summons before the
same judge or another judge. It is necessary now for me to say something about the
j decision in *Mercy's* case because it was a case relied on strongly by the defendants in this
appeal. That was a case in which a property owner sought to get squatters out of his
property using the summary procedure under Ord 113. The originating summons was
issued on 22nd May 1974. The hearing took place on 24th May 1974. In other words,
seven clear days had not elapsed, as the rules then required. The judge made an order for
possession. There was, in the judgment of this court, no evidence of urgency and, as a

result, the court discharged the order for possession. The basis on which it discharged the order for possession is clear from one sentence in the judgment of Lord Denning MR. It is to this effect: 'It was not a proper case for the judge to make a final order on that Friday, the 24th May. On that ground I think the appeal should be allowed and the order of the judge set aside.' Stephenson LJ gave judgment to substantially the same effect. I agreed with the judgments delivered by Lord Denning MR and Stephenson LJ.

When this case was first brought to our attention I was of the opinion that we might find ourselves bound by it for the purposes of this appeal unless it could be distinguished. In order to make certain what had happened the court sent for, and looked at, the form of order which was made. The order was in these terms: 'It is ordered that this appeal be allowed and the order of the Honourable Mr. Justice Bristow set aside.' It follows that in Mercy's case all that the court was doing was setting aside an order made by Bristow J when there had not been seven clear days between the taking out of the summons and the making of the final order. It was not a case where the proceedings for all purposes under Ord 113 had been dismissed.

Counsel for the defendants in this court conceded that in Mercy's case what could have happened would have been for the property owner to have gone back after seven clear days had passed and asked the court to reconsider the matter; and, having regard to the fact that there was no evidence that the squatters had any right to be on the premises, it is probable that an order would have been made. He asked us to adopt the same course here: to adjudge that no order should have been made on 14th January 1981, leaving the plaintiffs to go back and ask for an order at some later date. For my part, I can see no sense in taking that course, because had they gone back all that would have happened would have been that they would have got their order. In the circumstances of this case it seems to me that the proper course for this court to take, bearing in mind the provisions of s 27 of the Supreme Court of Judicature (Consolidation) Act 1925, is for this court to make the order which could have been made at first instance once five clear days had elapsed.

In those circumstances, I would allow the appeal.

EVELEIGH LJ. I agree. Mr Jones seems to have thought that it was sufficient to say that the premises were due to be demolished very shortly. Not surprisingly, particularly in view of the other affidavits filed in the case, the judge did not regard that information as sufficient to justify him making an order as a matter of urgency. I agree, for the reasons stated by Lawton LJ, that the judge, however, should not have dismissed the case but should have adjourned it.

I too agree, for the reasons stated, that this appeal should be allowed.

SIR DAVID CAIRNS. I also agree that the appeal should be allowed and the order made as indicated by Lawton LJ, for the reasons which have already been given.

Appeal allowed. Order for possession granted.

Solicitors: *D P Flynn* (for the plaintiffs); *Jane Wright* (for the defendants).

Mary Rose Plummer   Barrister.

Infabrics Ltd and others v Jaytex Ltd

HOUSE OF LORDS

LORD WILBERFORCE, LORD EDMUND-DAVIES, LORD FRASER OF TULLYBELTON, LORD SCARMAN AND LORD ROSKILL

17th, 18th, 19th FEBRUARY, 26th MARCH 1981

Copyright – Infringement – Artistic work – Fabric design – Publication – What amounts to publication – Wholesale shirt manufacturer importing shirts bearing plaintiff's design – Wholesaler selling shirts to retailers for sale to public – Whether 'publishing' work referring to first publication only – Whether sale by wholesaler to retailers 'publication' – Whether publication taking place whenever reproductions of work issued to public – Copyright Act 1956, ss 3(5)(b), 49(2)(c).

Copyright – Infringement – Damages – Damages for infringement and conversion – Cumulative or alternative – Whether there can be an 'infringing copy' if no infringement – Copyright Act 1956, s 18(1).

Copyright – Infringement – Damages – Conversion – Design used on shirts – Measure of damages – Copyright Act 1956, s 18(1).

The respondents ('Infabrics') made printed fabrics for use in manufacturing shirts and owned the copyright in a fabric design known as 'the P design'. In March 1974 their representative visited the appellants ('Jaytex'), who were wholesalers in shirts, and showed to a director of Jaytex a portfolio of designs which included the P design. In July 1974, while in Hong Kong buying for Jaytex, the director was shown by a Hong King textile company some two thousand fabric designs, including the P design. The director did not recollect that Infabrics had shown him the design and he selected it and other designs from the Hong Kong company for the manufacture of shirts to be imported into the United Kingdom. The shirts were shipped from Hong Kong between 21st November 1974 and 24th February 1975. Infabrics discovered shirts bearing the P design on offer for sale in London and on 21st February 1975 wrote to Jaytex claiming to be the owners of the copyright in the design. Jaytex replied that they had purchased the fabric in good faith in Hong Kong without knowledge that any copyright was being infringed. On 6th May Infabrics issued a writ against Jaytex claiming damages under ss 17 and 18[a] of the Copyright Act 1956 for infringement of copyright and for conversion. Infabrics relied, inter alia, on the 'publication' of the design when the shirts were offered for sale in London as constituting an infringement of copyright under s 3(5)(b)[b] of the 1956 Act. Such an infringement, if proved, being a primary infringement the defence of lack of knowledge of the copyright was not available to Jaytex. The judge held, inter alia, that the sale and distribution of the shirts by Jaytex in the United Kingdom did not amount to infringement by 'publishing' the design, within s 3(5)(b). Infabrics appealed, contending, inter alia, that for the purpose of s 3(5)(b) 'publishing' included publication at any time of a copyright work whether it was previously published or not. Jaytex contended that 'publishing' was restricted to the first publication of a work so that the act of publishing converted a hitherto unpublished work into a published work, and, since the P design had already been published by Infabrics, Jaytex could not be said to have 'published' it. The Court of Appeal ([1980] 2 All ER 669) held that publishing was not restricted to the first publication of a previously unpublished work, that Jaytex had therefore published the design and in consequence of the infringement were liable in conversion, under s 18(1), for the value of all the shirts bearing the design sold by them. Jaytex appealed to the House of Lords.

---

a Section 18, so far as material, is set out at p 1068 c, post

b Section 3(5), so far as marterial, is set out at p 1060 d, post

Held – The appeal would be allowed for the following reasons—

(1) Having regard to the fact that the long-established distinction in copyright law *a* between published and unpublished works had not been changed by the 1956 Act, on the true construction of s 3(5)(*b*) of that Act infringement by 'publishing the work' meant making available to the public a work which was previously unpublished and accordingly excluded sales or the issue of reproductions to the public unless such sale or issue was the first publication of the work. On the basis that Infabrics had already made the P design public in the United Kingdom it followed that Jaytex had not 'published' the *b* design within s 3(5)(*b*) and had not committed a primary infringement of the design when they sold the shirts manufactured in Hong Kong (see p 1061 *b g h*, p 1062 *c* to *f* and *j* to p 1063 *b*, p 1065 *d*, p 1066 *h* to p 1067 *d h j* and p 1069 *d e*, post).

(2) The remedy of conversion provided for in s 18(1) of the 1956 Act was alternative to, or cumulative with, the remedy of damages and depended on proof of infringement. Thus if a plaintiff failed to establish infringement, he had no independent *c* cause of action in conversion. Infabrics having failed to establish infringement, they were not entitled to damages for conversion (see p 1062 *f g* and *j* to p 1063 *b*, p 1068 *e* to *h* and p 1069 *d e*, post); *Caxton Publishing Co Ltd v Sutherland Publishing Co Ltd* [1938] 4 All ER 389 applied.

Per Curiam. (1) Section 49(2)(*c*)[c] of the 1956 Act is not a definition of 'publishing' for the purposes of s 3(5)(*b*) but instead deals with the subsistence of copyright and the time *d* of publication (see p 1061 *a b*, p 1062 *j* to p 1063 *b*, p 1065 *g h*, p 1066 *a* to *c* and p 1069 *d e*, post).

(2) The measure of damages in conversion under s 18(1) is the value of the 'infringing copies' within s 18(3) on the basis that the plaintiff is entitled to damages as if he were the owner of the articles. The fact that the infringing design might have been placed on articles of considerable value such as gold medallions is irrelevant (see p 1062 *g* to p 1063 *e* *b* and p 1068 *j* to p 1069 *b* and *d e*, post).

Decision of the Court of Appeal [1980] 2 All ER 669 reversed.

Notes

For copyright in an artistic work, and for infringement of copyright by publication, see 9 Halsbury's Laws (4th Edn) paras 842, 916, and for cases on infringement of copyright *f* in an artistic work, see 13 Digest (Reissue) 125–127, *1031–1054*.

For innocence as a defence to an action for infringement of copyright and for conversion or detention of an infringing copy, see 9 Halsbury's Laws (4th Edn) para 938.

For damages for conversion, see ibid para 948.

For the Copyright Act 1956, ss 3, 17, 18, 49, see 7 Halsbury's Statutes (3rd Edn) 135, 163, 165, 204.

g

Cases referred to in opinions

Caxton Publishing Co Ltd v Sutherland Publishing Co Ltd [1938] 4 All ER 389, [1939] AC 178, 108 LJ Ch 5, 160 LT 17, HL; *affg* [1936] 1 All ER 177, [1936] Ch 323, 105 LJ Ch 150, 154 LT 367, CA, 13 Digest (Reissue) 145, 146, *1198, 1201*.

Van Dusen v Kritz [1936] 2 KB 176, 105 LJKB 498, 155 LT 258, 13 Digest (Reissue) 142, *h* *1178*.

Appeal

By a writ dated 6th May 1975 the plaintiffs, Infabrics Ltd ('Infabrics'), who were manufacturers of printed fabrics, Angela Jean Hill, a textile designer and colour consultant trading as ABCD, and Jane Higgison, a freelance fabric designer, brought an action against the defendants, Jaytex Ltd (sued as Jaytex Shirt Co Ltd) ('Jaytex'), seeking *j* an injunction restraining Jaytex from infringing the plaintiffs' copyright in an artistic work, namely a fabric design known as 'Past the post', an inquiry as to the damages suffered by the plaintiffs by reason of Jaytex's acts of infringement, damages for

---

c   Section 49(2) is set out at p 1063 *g* to *j*, post

a conversion and delivery up or destruction of all infringing material in Jaytex's possession, custody or control. On 19th May 1978 Whitford J ([1978] FSR 451) gave judgment, holding that the importation into the United Kingdom, and the offering for sale, selling and distribution after 5th March 1975, of shirts bearing the Past the post design constituted infringement of the plaintiffs' copyright and directed an inquiry as to the damages for infringement of copyright and for conversion from 5th March 1975. On Jaytex giving an undertaking against future infringements, the judge did not grant the

b plaintiffs an injunction. Infabrics appealed against the limitation of their remedy to acts done after 5th March 1975. On 11th February 1980 the Court of Appeal (Buckley and Donaldson LJJ) ([1980] 2 All ER 669, [1980] Ch 282) allowed their appeal holding that the acts of importation and sale by Jaytex before 5th March 1975 constituted infringement by 'publishing' and accordingly that Jaytex were liable also in damages in conversion. Jaytex appealed to the House of Lords with leave of the Court of Appeal.

c The facts are set out in the opinion of Lord Wilberforce.

Geoffrey Everington QC and *John Drysdale* for Jaytex.
Thomas Blanco-White QC and *Michael Fysh* for Infabrics and the other respondents.

d Their Lordships took time for consideration.

26th March. The following opinions were delivered.

LORD WILBERFORCE. My Lords, this appeal is concerned with an artistic work designed by the third respondent, the copyright in which belongs to the first respondents

e ('Infabrics'), and which is claimed to have been infringed by the appellants ('Jaytex').
The work consists of an attractive drawing in colours of three racehorses with jockeys engaged in a close finish at a winning post, this drawing being repeated at spaced intervals. It has become known as 'Past the post' though that point had in fact not been reached.

Put very shortly, the essential facts are that a representative of Jaytex saw the design in

f Hong Kong at the premises of a company called Textile Alliance Ltd and selected it from a number of others. Jaytex then ordered a quantity of cloth to be printed with the design and arranged with a shirt maker, also in Hong Kong, to make it up into shirts and export them to the United Kingdom. Jaytex then arranged for the shirts to be put on the market and sold by retailers. They sold well in the King's Road, Chelsea.

The claim as framed and as presented at the trial was based on infringement of

g copyright by importation from Hong Kong and sale in this country of shirts made from cloth bearing the Past the post design which would have infringed the copyright if the cloth had been made in the United Kingdom. It was based on s 5 of the Copyright Act 1956 which requires, as a condition of liability for infringement, knowledge that the making of the cloth constituted an infringement of the copyright or would have done so if the cloth had been made in the United Kingdom.

h Jaytex denied any such knowledge and the trial took place on that issue. It was held by Whitford J that until 5th March 1975, a fortnight after a warning letter had been sent, Jaytex had no such knowledge, but that after that date they had. Jaytex accepted the latter finding, and an inquiry as to damages was ordered.

In their speech in reply, after Jaytex's case had been closed, counsel for Infabrics contended for the first time that Jaytex were liable for infringement on the basis of

j 'publishing' the work, under ss 1 and 3(5)(*b*) of the Act. They obtained leave to amend their statement of claim by inserting the following paragraph:

> '5. Further or alternatively the defendants have infringed the said copyright work [sic] by publishing the same by their aforesaid acts of sale and distribution of shirts bearing the said design.'

The reference to 'aforesaid acts' is to those acts of sale and distribution in the United Kingdom as to which Whitford J had held that Jaytex were not liable for infringement on the ground of lack of knowledge. In view of the late stage at which this claim was introduced, no additional evidence was called to support it. In particular, and this may well have been fatal, no evidence was called, or was available, that the artistic work was unpublished at the date of the alleged publication by Jaytex.

On appeal to the Court of Appeal Infabrics did not dispute the finding of the judge that Jaytex did not have the necessary knowledge for liability under s 5. The Court of Appeal, however, was persuaded to hold that the acts of importation and sale nevertheless constituted infringement by publishing. Because of this infringement they held that Jaytex were liable for damages in conversion under s 18 of the 1956 Act, the measure of damages being the value of the shirts.

The immediately relevant sections of the 1956 Act as to 'publishing' are ss 1, 3(5)(b) and 49(2). Section 1 lays the basis for copyright and of infringement by reference to certain acts, to be later specified, which are exclusively reserved to the owner of the copyright. It is important to notice that both the exclusive rights, of which the copyright consists, and any infringement of those rights, extend to the United Kingdom and any other country to which the relevant provisions of the Act extend. The territorial area, which may be referred to as 'the territory' includes Hong Kong.

The section dealing with artistic works is s 3 (literary, dramatic and musical works are dealt with in s 2). By s 3(5) the acts restricted by the copyright in an artistic work are '(a) reproducing the work in any material form [not relied on]; (b) publishing the work . . .' There is no definition of 'publishing' in this section, and there are great difficulties in extracting the meaning of the word from the rest of the Act.

There are three suggested meanings. The first (accepted by the Court of Appeal) is that publishing consists of the issue of reproductions of the work to the public. The second (contended for by Infabrics) is that publishing is what is done by a publisher. The third (contended for by Jaytex) is that publishing means making public, in the territory, a work which had not previously been made public in the territory. I shall examine these in order.

1. The interpretation of the Court of Appeal is based on s 49(2)(c) of the 1956 Act which reads, together with the introductory and closing words of s 49(2):

> 'With regard to publication, the provisions of this subsection shall have effect for the purposes of this Act, that is to say . . . (c) subject to the preceding paragraphs, a literary, dramatic or musical work, or an edition of such a work, or an artistic work, shall be taken to have been published if, but only if, reproductions of the work or edition have been issued to the public . . . and in determining for the purposes of paragraph (c) of this subsection, whether reproductions of a work or edition have been issued to the public, the preceding subsection shall not apply.'

Reference back to sub-s (1) of the section unfortunately leads to an intricate piece of drafting which can only be approximately summarised by saying that reproduction includes reproduction of a substantial part of a work, but even this is qualified by a proviso referring to several other sections. It is this labyrinthine quality, which pervades the whole Act, that makes it so extraordinarily difficult to interpret. However, I think that we can take it that para (c) applies only to the issue of reproductions of the whole work.

The question then is whether the Court of Appeal was right in treating s 49(2)(c) as a definition of 'publishing' in s 3(5)(b). Infabrics did not support this approach, and I think that this was inevitable. In the first place, if the interpretation were right, it would follow that a retail seller of a copyright work would be regarded as publishing it, a novel consequence and one contrary to the well-accepted distinction between primary and secondary infringement. Moreover, it would be difficult to reconcile with the requirement of knowledge which s 5 imposes with regard to selling. Would a selling publisher be entitled to the defence of ignorance or not? More importantly, perhaps, if

s 49(2)(c), together with the closing words, were to apply to 'publishing' in s 3(5)(b), it
a would not be an infringement under s 1(2) to publish a substantial part of the work. This
would be paradoxical, and also contrary to s 49(1) as above summarised. In my opinion,
the correct view of s 49(2)(c), on which I think both sides agree, is that it is not a
definition of 'publishing' for the purposes of the Act (it is indeed not cast in the form of
a definition) but is a provision relating to the words in s 3(3) (and similarly in s 2(2))
'Where an original work has been published, then . . copyright shall subsist in the
b work . . .' In other words, it is dealing with subsistence of copyright, and stating a rule
as to the time of publication, a matter of importance in relation to the subsistence of
copyright. The conclusion, through this regrettably opaque reasoning, is that the Court
of Appeal's approach cannot be supported.

2. Infabric's contention is that publishing means what a publisher does. I should say
of this, first, that even if this were correct there would still be difficulties in the way of
c Infabrics. As I have explained, evidence which might have borne directly on the question
whether what Jaytex did amounts to publishing in this sense was not called and I think
it far from clear, on the existing material, that Jaytex did anything amounting to
publishing, sc acting as publishers of the design.

But in any event I cannot accept the meaning offered. In relation to copyright,
whether under common law or statute, 'publishing' and 'publication' are fundamental
d expressions meaning making available to the public, and it would take a great deal of
contextual restraint to force them into a narrower and special meaning. Counsel for
Infabrics ingeniously tried to overcome this initial difficulty by deriving the word
'published' in the Copyright Act 1911 (the predecessor of the 1956 Act) from the Berne
Copyright Convention of 1886 (C 5167) with reference to which the 1911 Act was no
doubt drafted. The word there used in the French authentic text and translated by
e 'published' is 'édité', a word which seems to suggest what is done by an éditeur, ie a
publisher. But even in the convention the word is used in various contexts with various
meanings, and so is 'published' in the 1911 Act. Indeed, s 1(3) provides that for the
purposes of the Act publication means the issue of copies to the public. So I do not think
that the convention indication is a strong one.

In the 1956 Act itself, counsel for Infabrics was able to point to some contexts in which
f 'publishing' or 'publisher' may refer to what is done by a 'publisher'. The clearest of these
is s 7(7). But that section does not apply to artistic works, and has to be regarded as a
special compartment on its own: it relates to libraries and archives. Section 15, again, is
of a specialised character: it relates to published editions of literary, dramatic or musical
works. It may be true that in relation to such productions, ie to editions of literary,
dramatic or musical works, the person who gives the work to the public would normally
g be a 'publisher', but I find that insufficient reason for imposing that meaning on
'publishing' etc throughout the Act. In my opinion this suggested meaning cannot stand
before the strong prima facie meaning which must exist, in the context of copyright, to
interpret publication as making available to the public something unpublished.

3. The submission of Jaytex is, for these reasons, prima facie convincing. All through
the history of copyright, under the common law, and through the legislation over 280
h years, there has been the well-known contrast between unpublished works and published
works. The distinction lies at the roots of the law. The 1911 Act was drafted wholly in
line with these traditional concepts. Section 1(1)(a) and (b) deals respectively with a
published work and an unpublished work. Under s 1(2) the position is clear. Copyright
is the sole right to produce or reproduce the work in any material form etc, and 'if the
work is unpublished, to publish the work or any substantial part thereof', and by s 1(3)
j publication 'means the issue of copies of the work to the public'. By s 2 infringement is
linked to the rights defined in s 1, so publication *of an unpublished work* is infringement.
The position is then perfectly plain: if that Act applied to the present case, Jaytex could
not be guilty of infringement by publishing. The question is whether the 1956 Act has
changed this. As with all other questions, the complexity and obscurity of the Act makes
any answer difficult and a certain answer impossible. It is at least permissible to start

from the point that (a) it is unlikely that the law as to and the distinction between *a*
published and unpublished works would have been changed without some clear
indication, and (b) it is implausible that a person who escapes secondary infringement
liability through lack of knowledge should be condemned for primary infringement
irrespective of knowledge. The result of the contention of Infabrics indeed would be to
take away almost entirely the protection, in respect of lack of knowledge, given by s 5(3)
and (4) notwithstanding that these provisions substantially reproduce the terms of s 2(2)
of the 1911 Act conferring similar protection. As against this, and the main difficulty for *b*
Infabrics, there is the unqualified reference in s 3(5)(*b*) to 'publishing' contrasted with the
reference in the 1911 Act of s 1(2) to publishing the work if unpublished.

The explanation of this change suggested by Infabrics, and which I accept, is this.
There has been significant change in the 1956 Act, as compared with the 1911 Act,
regarding the scope of copyright. Under s 1(1) of the 1911 Act copyright subsisted in a
published work only if the work was published within the countries to which the Act *c*
extended ('the territory'). So 'publishing' in that context clearly meant making public in
the territory a work not previously made public in the territory.

Section 3(3)(*b*) of the 1956 Act enabled copyright of, inter alia, an artistic work to
subsist even though the work was published not in the territory, if the author was a
qualified person. This made it inappropriate to preserve in s 3(5)(*b*) an express condition
that the work must have been unpublished, since if such words had been inserted, the *d*
qualified person above referred to could not have prevented publication in the territory
or sued for infringement in the event of such publication. When however it is a matter
of dealing with infringement, the relevant provisions (in s 1(1) and (2)) are concerned
only with publication in the territory. In such a context, in accordance with the accepted
meaning of the words, publishing can only mean making public what had not previously
been made public in the territory. Since it is not shown that the design in this case had *e*
not previously been so made public, the case based on publishing must fail. In my
opinion, therefore, Infabrics fail to establish any infringement as regards acts done before
5th March 1975. Two other points remain.

First: *conversion.* In my opinion it is clear that, if a plaintiff fails to establish
infringement, he has no independent cause of action in conversion. The terms of ss 17
and 18, contained in Part III of the 1956 Act, headed 'Remedies for Infringements of *f*
Copyright', demonstrate that conversion is a remedy, alternative to, or (to some extent)
cumulative with, the remedy of damages for infringement and depends on proof of
infringement. Consequently damages for conversion cannot be claimed as regards acts
prior to 5th March 1975.

Second: *measure of damages.* This arises under s 18. The Court of Appeal held that, in
this case, the measure of damages in conversion must be the value of the shirts, which *g*
were clearly the 'infringing copies' (see s 18(3)). In my opinion, the wording of s 18(1)
of the 1956 Act admits of no other solution; particularly, it does not admit of measuring
the damages by reference to the increase in value of the shirts through the addition of the
design, or by the value of the shirts less the cost of the substrate or the work put into the
making. A plaintiff is entitled to such damages as would be recoverable if he were the
owner, and under the general law these are equivalent to the value. *h*

The result in this case is not manifestly unjust or exorbitant, but I appreciate that in
other imaginable instances very harsh results might follow. The section seems to have
developed from one originally intended to deal with copies from plates, and extended to
other reproducing media listed in sub-s (3). It may well not have been thought out in
relation to industrial designs, when the substrate may be of much greater value than the
design imposed. It would seem to merit consideration. *j*

In the result I would allow the appeal and restore the order made by Whitford J. The
costs should be reserved over the inquiry as to damages.

LORD EDMUND-DAVIES. My Lords, for the reasons developed in the speeches of
my noble and learned friends Lord Wilberforce and Lord Scarman, which I have had the

advantage of reading in draft, I also would allow this appeal and restore the order of
a Whitford J. I would reserve the costs to be dealt with at the inquiry as to damages.

LORD FRASER OF TULLYBELTON. My Lords, I have had the advantage of
reading in draft the speeches of my noble and learned friends Lord Wilberforce and Lord
Scarman and I agree with them. For the reasons explained by them I would allow this
appeal.

b
LORD SCARMAN. My Lords, the appellants, Jaytex Ltd, who are makers and
importers of shirts and blouses, were the defendants to an action in which the respondents
alleged infringement of copyright and claimed damages. The acts relied on as an
infringement of copyright were the importation into the United Kingdom and the
subsequent sale, or offer for sale, to the public of shirts manufactured in Hong Kong.
c The respondents, Infabrics, alleged that they owned the copyright in the design printed
on the fabric of which the shirts were made. For the purposes of this appeal it matters
not which of the respondents owned the copyright. The design was the original artistic
work of the third respondent, who, under an arrangement made by and with the second
respondent, transferred her rights to Infabrics Ltd, the first respondents. Two matters
may, therefore, in the interests of simplicity of exposition, be put aside: the rights, inter
d se, of the respondents and the application (under s 31) of the Copyright Act 1956 to
territories other than the United Kingdom.
   Save in respect of the last importation, which Jaytex admit was an infringement under
s 5 of the 1956 Act, Infabrics failed at the trial before Whitford J but succeeded in the
Court of Appeal. Jaytex now appeal to your Lordships' House.
   The appeal raises questions of importance in copyright law, of which the most
e important is that of the true construction of s 3(5)(b) of the 1956 Act. The subsection
designates the acts which, being restricted to the owner of copyright in an artistic work,
constitute, if committed in the United Kingdom (or other territories to which the Act
extends) without his licence, an infringement of copyright. They are four: (a) reproducing
the work in any material form; (b) publishing the work; (c) including the work in a
television broadcast, and (d) including the work in a television programme to be
f transmitted to subscribers to a diffusion service.
   The 1956 Act contains no definition of 'publishing the work' unless, as the Court of
Appeal thought, s 49(2)(c) provides a definition. Since this appeal cannot be decided
without also deciding whether the Court of Appeal was right or wrong so to treat the
provision in that paragraph, I set out sub-s (2) of the section in full:

g
> 'With regard to publication, the provisions of this subsection shall have effect for
> the purposes of this Act, that is to say,—(a) the performance, or the issue of records,
> of a literary, dramatic or musical work, the exhibition of an artistic work, the
> construction of a work of architecture, and the issue of photographs or engravings
> of a work of architecture or of a sculpture, do not constitute publication of the
> work; (b) except in so far as it may constitute an infringement of copyright, or a
> contravention of any restriction imposed by section forty-three of this Act, a
h publication which is merely colourable, and not intended to satisfy the reasonable
> requirements of the public, shall be disregarded; (c) subject to the preceding
> paragraphs, a literary, dramatic or musical work, or an edition of such work, or an
> artistic work, shall be taken to have been published if, but only if, reproduction of
> the work or edition have been issued to the public; (d) a publication in the United
> Kingdom, or in any other country, shall not be treated as being other than the first
j publication by reason only of an earlier publication elsewhere, if the two publications
> took place within a period of not more than thirty days; and in determining, for the
> purposes of paragraph (c) of this subsection, whether reproductions of a work or
> edition have been issued to the public, the *preceding subsection shall not apply.*'

   In the case of a s 3(5) infringement (sometimes referred to as 'a primary infringement')
ignorance of the existence of copyright is no defence. But in the cases of a s 5

infringement it is. Section 5 provides that copyright is infringed by any person who, without the licence of the owner of the copyright, imports, sells, lets for hire, or *a* distributes for purposes of trade in the United Kingdom any article, if to his knowledge the making of the article constituted an infringement, or would have done so if it had been made in the United Kingdom. Section 5 infringements are sometimes described as 'secondary infringements'. Knowledge that the article infringes copyright is an essential ingredient of the infringement.

The mere recital of these statutory provisions reveals the importance to traders of this *b* appeal. If selling an article, the making or importation of which was an infringement, is itself the publication of the artistic work reproduced on the article, the seller will be liable for the 'primary' infringement of publishing the work and deprived of the safeguard provided to honest traders by s 5. It will be of no avail to him that he imported or sold the article in ignorance of the fact of infringement. In the trial judge's opinion 'this cannot have been intended' (see [1978] FSR 451 at 468) and he held that sale was not *c* an offence included in the prohibitions to be found in s 3(5). The Court of Appeal recognised the difficulty but, treating s 49(2)(c) of the Act as a definition clause, felt itself constrained to conclude that selling to the public was publication as there defined, ie the issuing of copies to the public.

The findings of fact are these. In March or, at the latest, very early April 1974, Mr Jaffa of Infabrics showed Mr Ripper (and some others) of Jaytex a number of designs suitable *d* for shirts including the design in question. It is a repetitive design of three horses racing neck-and-neck toward and past the winning post; and it became known as the 'Past the post' design. The judge, however, found that the design 'really made no great impression on Mr Ripper's mind' at the time. In July 1974 Mr Ripper went to Hong Kong. At the premises of Textile Alliance Ltd ('TAL') he was shown two thousand or more designs, some already printed on fabrics and some as drawings on a card. One of them was the *e* 'Past the post' design. He made a selection which included Past the post. He had no detailed recollection of the design (though it 'struck a bell'), and it never occurred to him that he had seen it a few months earlier in England. He gave instructions for TAL to deliver a substantial quantity of fabric printed with the design to Hong Kong shirtmakers to be made up into shirts. TAL then printed the fabric (or the bulk of it, for some was already printed) and, after an interval, delivered it to the shirt makers. The shirts were, *f* in accordance with the instructions of Jaytex, dispatched to the United Kingdom, where Jaytex arranged for their sale and distribution to retailers.

There were four shipments from Hong Kong: 21st November and 1st December 1974 and 10th January and 24th February 1975. Importation into the United Kingdom would have taken place some five weeks after shipment.

Early in 1975 Infabrics discovered that shirts bearing the design were on sale in the *g* King's Road, Chelsea. On 21st February 1975 they wrote to Jaytex claiming to be the owners of the copyright. It is accepted that in respect of the last shipment there was a s 5 infringement, importation having been made after the lapse of a reasonable time for inquiries following on the notice of 21st February 1975 (see *Van Dusen v Kritz* [1936] 2 KB 176). Whatever the result of the appeal, therefore, there has to be an inquiry into damages. On the result of the appeal will depend whether the inquiry relates to all four *h* importations or only the last. Whitford J, holding that there had been no infringement by publishing, ordered an inquiry limited to the last importation. The Court of Appeal, holding that by importing the shirts and arranging for their sale to the public Jaytex had published the design in the United Kingdom, ordered an inquiry as to damages in respect of all the shirts sold.

Three questions fall to be considered by the House: (1) whether, when the shirts were *j* put on sale in the United Kingdom, Jaytex infringed Infabrics's copyright by 'publishing the work', a question of construction of s 3(5)(b) of the 1956 Act; (2) whether conversion damages can be recovered in respect of 'infringing copies' even where no act of infringement can be shown to exist, a question of construction of s 18 of the Act; (3) the measure of conversion damages.

a   It is no longer suggested, in view of the findings of fact, that there was any infringement by reproduction or (save for the last shipment) by any commercial dealing covered by s 5. It is, therefore, now common ground that Infabrics must fail on the issue of infringement (save for the last shipment) unless they can make good the submission, which the Court of Appeal accepted, that selling (or arranging for the sale) to the public of an infringing article is 'publishing the work'. The topic is one of the least explored in copyright law. It is devoid of authority; and the Act is tortuous and obscure in its use of

b   the words 'publish' and 'publication'. To add to the difficulties, it is necessary before turning to the law to clarify a factual obscurity which may well be due to the belated appearance of the point (by amendment of the statement of claim) as an afterthought after trial had begun. The question of fact, not directly dealt with in evidence, is this: did Infabrics, the owners (as they claim) of the copyright, themselves publish the design in the United Kingdom before Jaytex put their shirts on sale to the public? For, if they did,

c   then, on one view as to the meaning of s 3(5)(*b*), the sales by Jaytex, being subsequent to Infabrics's publication, were not an infringement under the paragraph. Certainly Infabrics have not proved that the design was unpublished in the United Kingdom before the Jaytex 'publication' (as they seek to characterise the sales). Such evidence as there is suggests strongly that shirts bearing the design and made by Infabrics were on sale before Jaytex put theirs on sale. In my opinion, it would not be right to treat the design as unpublished prior to Jaytex putting their shirts on sale to the public. If there

d   be any doubt, the burden of proof is on Infabrics; and they have not discharged it. I shall, therefore, proceed on the basis that Infabrics were the first to make the design public in the United Kingdom. They were the first to put shirts bearing the design on sale to the public. There is no evidence to suggest that they were not.

I turn now to construe s 3(5)(*b*) of the 1956 Act. The Court of Appeal, treating

e   s 49(2)(*c*) as a definition clause, applied it to s 3(5)(*b*) and held that an artistic work is to be taken to have been published if copies of the work are issued to the public. It held that selling the shirts to the public was the issuing of copies of the design to the public. Whitford J, though he refused to treat the paragraph as a definition clause, considered it an indication of what the words 'publishing the work' meant, but refused, because of the anomalous consequences of so doing, to hold that sales or the other commercial dealings

f   covered by s 5 were in themselves 'publishing the work'.

If the Court of Appeal was correct to treat s 49(2)(*c*) as definitive, it was surely correct in holding that to put articles bearing a reproduction of the artistic work on sale to the public must be taken to constitute a publishing of the work. Even if the paragraph is no more than an indication, as Whitford J thought, it is, in my judgment, quite impossible to disregard, as the judge did, so strong an indication because of the anomalous

g   consequences of following it.

But is s 49(2)(*c*) intended either as a definition or as an aid to the interpretation of s 3(5)(*b*)? Notwithstanding the sidenote to the section, I think it is clear that it is not. Subsection (1), as its proviso shows, is concerned with infringement and so does apply to the acts which s 3(5)(*b*) prohibits. But sub-s (2), counsel for Jaytex has persuasively submitted, deals not with infringement but with subsistence of copyright. Subsection

h   (2)(*a*), he submits, protects the owner of copyright, by providing that he is not to be taken as having published the work merely by doing any acts specified in para (*a*), though doing them without his licence would certainly constitute infringement. Similarly, he submits that the true effect of para (*b*) is that an owner of copyright will not have lost the great advantage of his work being unpublished merely by a colourable publication not intended to satisfy the reasonable requirements of the public, though such a publication,

j   if it was a reproduction, adaptation or copy of a substantial part of the work, would be an infringement. This view of the two subsections is strengthened by the concluding words of sub-s (2), which provide that in determining for the purposes of para (*c*) whether the reproductions of a work have been issued to the public, sub-s (1) which deals with infringement shall not apply. The force of the submission is, however, to some extent, diminished by the opening words of sub-s (2) and by the way in which para (*b*) is drafted.

I find, however, that this analysis of s 49(1) and (2) makes sense. It certainly induces a doubt whether para (c) is intended to define, or indicate, the meaning to be attributed to *a* 'publishing', in the context of s 3(5). It is, I think, significant that counsel for Infabrics was not prepared to support the Court of Appeal's view that s 49(2)(c) is a definition clause. He took a different position. He submitted that the purpose of sub-s (2)(c) was merely to determine the moment of publication, i e when copies were issued to the public. He refused to treat s 49(2)(c) as definitive, even though to do so would have supported his clients' case.   *b*

I have come to the conclusion that the Court of Appeal erred in treating s 49(2)(c) as a definition of publication. Counsel's analysis of sub-ss (1) and (2) appears to me accurate, and I accept counsel's submission for Infabrics as to the purpose of para (c).

Counsel for Infabrics submitted that to discover what was meant in s 3(5)(b) by 'publishing the work' it was necessary to look at the 1956 Act as a whole and, in particular, to note the various contexts in which the verb 'publish' and the noun *c* 'publication' are used. You will find, he submitted, that, when the Act refers to 'publishing' or 'publication', it means publishing in a business sense. 'Publishing is what a publisher does' was his succinct summary of his argument. He then drew attention to the facts and submitted that what Jaytex did in Hong Kong and England was the equivalent of what a publisher does in finding a manuscript and arranging for its printing, binding and distribution for sale. The ingenuity of the submission (no hint of *d* which is to be found in the pleadings) is that it avoids the anomaly of having to hold that any and every sale to the public of an article bearing a design which infringes copyright is a publication of the design. If he be right, a sale is only a publication if it be the final act in a combined operation analogous to the business of publishing. In the instant case, the combined operation was that of selecting the design, arranging for manufacture and importation of the shirts, and putting them on sale to the public in the United Kingdom. *e*

Counsel supported his submission by references to a number of sections in the Act which deal with publication of a work, notably ss 7(7), 15(2) and 20(4)(b).

In this way counsel for Infabrics managed to support the decision of the Court of Appeal, but not the reasoning. I find, however, his approach to the question of construction unacceptable. When construing words and phrases in an Act dealing with a subject as complex and varied as copyright, it is perilous, in the absence of clear *f* guidance in the Act, to assume that in respect of every element or aspect of the subject ordinary English words, which have many applications, are used consistently to express only one particular application. That they should be construed as bearing the same generic meaning I accept. Publish is to make public. This meaning the words 'publish', 'publishing' and 'publication' will always have. But the context will determine, for example, whether the words 'publish' and 'publication' refer exclusively to a first *g* publication or include subsequent publications, whether they mean an event such as the act or occasion of being published or are used to indicate a state of affairs, i e the state of a work having been published (being in the 'public domain') as contrasted with being unpublished. The contexts within the Act where the words are found are so various, and frequently so far removed from the context of s 3(5)(b), that I reject counsel's approach based on a study of the various provisions to which he referred us.   *h*

I have come to the conclusion that the correct approach to the construction of s 3(5)(b) is to construe it in the light of the provisions with which it is closely linked. Section 3, read as a whole and in its relationship with s 1, is the clue. Copyright means the exclusive right to do the restricted acts. Publishing the work is a restricted act. Making public a hitherto unpublished work is certainly an act of publishing the work. Does the word 'publishing' when used in s 3(5)(b) mean any more than that? Counsel for Infabrics *j* submits that it means much more. But I find it intrinsically unlikely that Parliament, without expressly saying so, intended to apply the meaning for which he contends to the publishing of an artistic work. It would be strange if Parliament, legislating for the protection of original artistic works, should apply, sub silentio, the analogy of book publishing to the publication of an artistic work. Possible? Yes. Likely? No.

Unpersuaded that such a meaning is likely, I turn to s 3 itself. I am at once impressed

a with the distinction drawn between an unpublished and a published work. Section 3(2) provides that copyright shall subsist in every original artistic work, which is unpublished, provided the author was 'a qualified person' (put generally, a British subject or resident or a person domiciled in the United Kingdom or a country to which the Act extends: see s 1(5) of the Act). If, however, the work has been published anywhere in the world, certain other conditions have to be met, though, if the first publication took place in the

b United Kingdom (or other country to which the Act extends) the author, even if an unqualified person, has copyright: see s 3(3). Thus a qualified person has a very important right: no one, without his permission, may publish his work in the United Kingdom (or other country to which the Act extends) if unpublished in that territory.

When one turns to s 3(5) itself, the prohibition on reproduction of the work (or a substantial part of it: see s 49(1)) which one finds in para (*a*) takes care of publication of

c the work after its first publication. It is logical, sensible and just that the subsection should also contain a specific protection for unpublished work, provided always that its author can show that copyright subsists in the work (as he can if he is a qualified person). This, in my view, is the purpose of para (*b*). It involves no more than giving the generic meaning of 'publish' to the word 'publishing' and holding that the paragraph refers to the publishing of what was previously unpublished. But this view raises the

d query: why does the paragraph contain no reference to the work being unpublished?

This is, I think, a difficulty. The absence of any reference to the work being 'unpublished' together with the reference to 'first publication' in sub-s (3) might seem to indicate that 'publishing the work' refers not only to a first publication in the United Kingdom but includes subsequent publications. But, if this view be adopted, one is inescapably driven either to the far-fetched characterisation of publication of an artistic

e work for which counsel for Infabrics contends or to the anomaly that all sales to the public of an article reproducing the work (like the shirts in this case), since they make the work public, are 'publishing the work', in which event the s 5 safeguards for honest traders are largely worthless.

The reason for the omission in s 3(5)(*b*) becomes clear when one looks at the Copyright Act 1911. Section 1(2) of that Act included in its definition of copyright the right 'if the

f work is unpublished, to publish the work or any substantial part thereof'. Some such words would have been included in s 3(5)(*b*), it can be argued, had Parliament intended to limit its operation to unpublished works. Counsel for Jaytex provided the answer. The 1956 Act has extended the subsistence of copyright. It can now subsist in a work which has been published, though not published in the United Kingdom (or other country to which the Act extends). To have repeated in s 3(5)(*b*) the reference which one

g finds in s 1(2) of the 1911 Act to unpublished work would have failed to protect the qualified person's right to first publication in the United Kingdom. The reference, therefore, had to be omitted.

There are, of course, important differences between the 1911 Act and the 1956 Act; and the long title of the 1956 Act describes it as an Act, inter alia, 'to make new provision in respect of copyright'. But there are also important similarities and a real consistency

h in approach of the two Acts to basic matters of principle. I do not find in the extensions of copyright introduced by the 1956 Act any indication that, where copyright subsists, the right of the qualified person to restrict the making public of work which is unpublished is of any less concern to the law now than it was in 1911. For these reasons, therefore, I accept the Jaytex's submission that 'publishing the work' in s 3(5)(*b*) means making public in the United Kingdom or other country to which the Act extends a work

j hitherto unpublished in that territory. The restriction, of course, inures to the benefit only of one who can prove that pursuant to s 3(2) of the Act copyright subsists in the work.

For these reasons I would allow the appeal on the question of infringement. Since Infabrics have failed to establish that the design was unpublished when Jaytex put their shirts on sale, they are unable to establish that the Jaytex sales were a 'primary' infringement under s 35(5)(b). I would add that on this view of the paragraph some sales, but only some (and they are likely to be few), can constitute the infringement of 'publishing the work'.

A sale will constitute such an infringement only if it is a first publication in the United Kingdom. No other sales in the United Kingdom can or will infringe unless they are caught by s 5 (or, because of their circumstances, constitute a reproduction by the seller of the design).

I turn now to the two questions on damages. Section 17 of the 1956 Act provides that in an action for infringement relief by way of damages shall be available: see sub-s (1). Subsection (2) provides that, if it be proved or admitted that the defendant was not aware, and had no reasonable grounds for suspecting, that copyright subsisted in the work, the plaintiff shall be entitled not to damages but only to an account of profits.

Section 18(1) provides that the owner of a copyright shall be entitled—

> 'to all such rights and remedies, in respect of the conversion or detention . . . of any infringing copy . . . as he would be entitled to if he were the owner of every such copy . . .'

Subsection (2) provides, in terms comparable with s 17(2), a defence of lack of knowledge (if proved or admitted) either that copyright subsisted or that the articles converted were infringing copies. Subsection (3) defines 'infringing copy' in terms which would seem to indicate that conversion damages are recoverable in some situations in which no act of infringement has been proved.

The perplexities of the two sections and their relationship to each other were explored in depth by Buckley LJ in the Court of Appeal, and I respectfully agree with his conclusions. The difficulties, I think, are more of policy than of interpretation, and are not amenable to cure by judicial decision.

First, it was submitted that on the true construction of s 18(3) there can be an 'infringing copy' without an act of infringement. If this be right, a remarkable consequence must follow: if the shirts fall within the definition of 'infringing copy' contained in the subsection, Infabrics may be able to recover damages even though they can prove no act of infringement. In *Caxton Publishing Co Ltd v Sutherland Publishing Co Ltd* [1938] 4 All ER 389, [1939] AC 178, which was, of course, decided under the 1911 Act, three members of this House clearly expressed their view that there could never be a claim for conversion of infringing copies which had come into existence without any act of infringement. I would apply that view to s 18 of the current Act. Any other conclusion appears to me absurdly unjust. The fallacy of the argument to the contrary, which is based on the hypothetical provision in s 18(3) for importation (itself an echo of a similar provision in s 5(2) and (3)), is that it treats s 18 as substantive law creating a cause of action. But the section (together with s 17) appears in Part III of the Act which is cross-headed 'Remedies for Infringements of Copyright'. The two sections provide remedies, and should not be construed as doing anything else. An act of infringement must, therefore, be proved before damages under either section are recoverable.

This view of s 18 disposes of the claim for 'conversion damages' in respect of the first three importations. It is, therefore, unnecessary to consider Infabrics's submission that because the design was clearly modern, if not contemporary, Jaytex cannot rely on a s 18(2) defence. They submit that the defence of unawareness, or no reasonable grounds for suspicion, of the existence of copyright, which ss 17(2) and 18(2) afford, is not available to Jaytex because of the wide application of the Act and the length of time for which copyright endures. So long as any such proposition be treated not as law but as an application of common sense, I do not demur.

A more troublesome point on s 18 is the measure of damages. In cases, like the present, of industrial design, damages for infringement under s 17 are often small. Limited (in the absence of special circumstances) to the depreciation in value of the copyright, they can be minimal. In the present case Infabrics paid only a few pounds for the design. But damages for conversion can be very great. If the industrial application

of the infringing copy is a success, damages are recoverable as if the owner of the
a copyright was the owner of every infringing copy sold: see s 18(1). And what if the
infringing copy be engraved on a silver chalice or a gold medallion? The language of the
subsection is, I think, clear: it bestows on the owner of the copyright the rights and
remedies to which at common law an owner of goods is entitled for their conversion. It
treats the owner of the copyright as if he were the owner of the infringing copies. Since
at common law the damages for conversion are ordinarily measured by reference to the
b value of the goods converted, I would not think it legitimate to construe the subsection
otherwise, though the result will be injustice in some cases. If the possibility of excessive
damages is to be eliminated, legislation will be needed, for the language of the subsection
permits of no other construction.

Finally, the remedies under ss 17 and 18 are, as were their predecessors in ss 6 and 7 of
the 1911 Act, cumulative, not alternative. The reasoning of Lord Wright MR in
c *Sutherland Publishing Co Ltd v Caxton Publishing Co Ltd* [1936] 1 All ER 177 at 179, 180–
182, [1936] Ch 323 at 334, 336–338 when that case was in the Court of Appeal is as
applicable to ss 17 and 18 of the 1956 Act as it was to the two sections in the 1911 Act.
Overlapping must be avoided. 'Each claim must receive its appropriate evaluation. It
must be left to the good sense of the tribunal which assesses the damages to avoid giving
excessive damages' (see [1936] 1 All ER 177 at 181, [1936] Ch 323 at 337).

d   For these reasons I would allow the appeal and restore the order of Whitford J. There
will be an inquiry into damages in respect of the final importation. Costs will be
reserved to be dealt with at the inquiry.

LORD ROSKILL. My Lords, I have had the advantage of reading in draft the speech
of my noble and learned friends Lord Wilberforce and Lord Scarman. For the reasons
e they give I agree that this appeal should be allowed.

Appeal allowed.

Solicitors: *Miller, Clayton & Co* (for Jaytex); *Birkbeck, Montagu's & Co* (for Infabrics and the
other respondents).

Mary Rose Plummer   Barrister.

Beer v Bowden

COURT OF APPEAL, CIVIL DIVISION
BUCKLEY, GEOFFREY LANE AND GOFF LJJ
1st, 2nd APRIL 1976

Landlord and tenant – Lease – Rent review clause – Rent payable on review to be fixed by agreement between the parties – Rent not to be less than original rent payable under lease – No arbitration clause or other machinery for fixing rent in default of agreement – Parties failing to agree rent on rent review – Whether court could imply term that market rent was payable in order to give business efficacy to lease – Whether in absence of agreement original rent payable under lease continuing to be payable.

Under the terms of a lease demising premises for a term of 14 years from 25th March 1968 the rent payable by the tenant was to be £1,250 per annum for the first five years and was to be reviewed every five years thereafter, the new rent to be 'such rent as shall . . . be agreed between the Landlords and the Tenant but no account shall be taken of any improvements carried out by the Tenant in computing the amount of the increase, if any, and in any case [the rent shall be] not less than the yearly rental' of £1,250 payable under the lease. The parties failed to agree on the new rent at the end of the first five years and the landlord issued an originating summons seeking determination of the questions whether, on the true construction of the rent review clause, the rent payable during the second five-year period was the proper and reasonable rental for the premises having regard to their market value on 25th March 1973, and, if so, whether the proper and reasonable rental was £2,850. The judge held that the tenant was liable to pay a fair rent as at 25th March 1973 excluding tenant's improvements, provided that it was not to be less than £1,250, and that the rent for the remainder of the term was to be similarly determined on 25th March 1978. The tenant appealed, contending that either on the true construction of the rent review clause or by an implied term of the lease the rent continued to be £1,250 per annum in default of agreement, and that a term that a fair rent was payable could not be implied as there was no arbitration clause or other machinery for fixing the rent in the absence of agreement in the lease.

Held – The appeal would be dismissed for the following reasons—
   (1) On the true construction of the rent review clause the 'rent [to] be agreed' by the parties was a fair rent excluding the tenant's improvements, provided however that in the event of depreciation in the value of the premises the rent was not to be reduced below £1,250 per annum. The clause could not mean that in default of agreement the rent was to continue at the rate of £1,250 per annum because such a construction would render the clause inoperative since the tenant would never agree to pay a higher rent (see p 1073 c to f, p 1975 j and p 1076 c e g h, post).
   (2) Since there was a subsisting lease and it was conceded that some rent was payable in default of agreement, the court could, despite the absence of an arbitration clause, imply a term to fill the gap in the lease where there was no agreement on the new rent, in order to give business efficacy to the lease, and, since the parties clearly intended that a fair rent should be fixed by agreement on the rent reviews, the court would imply a term that in the absence of agreement the rent payable during the second five years should be the fair market rent excluding tenant's improvements (see p 1074 d e h, p 1075 g to j and p 1076 c to j, post); *Foley v Classique Coaches Ltd* [1934] All ER Rep 88 applied.

Notes
For rent review agreements, see 23 Halsbury's Laws (3rd Edn) 539, para 1197.

Cases referred to in judgments

a   *Foley v Classique Coaches Ltd* [1934] 2 KB 1, [1934] All ER Rep 88, 103 LJKB 550, 151 LT 242, CA, 40 Digest (Repl) 359, 2880.

Kenilworth Industrial Sites Ltd v E C Little & Co Ltd [1975] 1 All ER 53, [1975] 1 WLR 143, 29 P & CR 141, CA; *affg* [1974] 2 All ER 815, [1974] 1 WLR 1069, 28 P & CR 263, Digest (Cont Vol D) 580, 3952c.

King's Motors (Oxford) Ltd v Lax [1969] 3 All ER 665, [1970] 1 WLR 426, 21 P & CR 507,
b   31(1) Digest (Reissue) 277, 2300.

Moorcock, The (1889) 14 PD 64, [1886–90] All ER Rep 530, 58 LJP 73, 60 LT 654, 6 Asp MLC 373, CA, 12 Digest (Reissue) 781, 5395.

Appeal

By an originating summons the plaintiffs, Anthony Wilders Beer, William Paul Elliott
c   de Beer and Michael Wills de Beer ('the landlords'), sought the determination of the court on the questions (1) whether on the true construction of clause 1 of a lease dated 17th July 1968 made between them and the defendant, Harold Herbert Bowden ('the tenant'), in regard to premises known as 54–56 Torbay Road, Paignton, Devon, and of a memorandum to the lease dated 17th May 1971, the rental payable under the lease for the period between 25th March 1973 and 24th March 1978 was a proper and reasonable
d   rent having regard to the market value of the premises on 25th March 1973, and (2) if so, whether the sum of £2,850 per annum represented a proper and reasonable rent. On 12th June 1975 Foster J gave judgment for the plaintiffs on the summons and ordered that the tenant was liable between 25th March 1973 and 24th March 1978 to pay a rental representing what the demised premises were reasonably worth on 25th March 1973 on a demise for a term of five years therefrom, provided that no account was taken of any
e   improvements carried out by the tenant, and the rental was not to be less than £1,250 per annum. The judge ordered similar provisions to apply to the rental payable from 25th March 1978 to the end of the term. The tenant appealed. The facts are set out in the judgment of Goff LJ.

Ellen Solomons for the landlords.
f   *Geoffrey Jaques* for the tenant.

GOFF LJ delivered the first judgment at the invitation of Buckley LJ. This is an appeal from a judgment of Foster J dated 12th June 1975, given in proceedings commenced by originating summons, raising questions as to the effect of the provision as to rent in a lease, dated 17th July 1968, of premises known as 54–56 Torbay Road, Paignton, in the
g   county of Devon.

The appellant was the defendant in the proceedings and tenant under the lease. It is not necessary, I think, to read any part of the lease other than some parts of cl 1, by which clause the premises were demised for a term of ten years from 25th March 1968. The clause then reads—

h   'paying therefor as follows:— Until the 24th day of March 1973 (yearly and proportionately for any fraction of a year) the rent of £1,250 per annum and from the 25th day of March 1973 such rent as shall thereupon be agreed between the Landlords and the Tenant but no account shall be taken of any improvements carried out by the Tenant in computing the amount of increase, if any, and in any case not less than the yearly rental payable hereunder such rent to be paid in advance
j   by four equal quarterly payments on the four usual quarter days.'

The term of ten years was increased in 1971 to fourteen years by a memorandum endorsed on the lease which reads as follows:

'Memorandum. In consideration of the covenants on the part of the Tenant contained in the within-written Lease the Landlords agree that the term of years contained in Clause 1 of the within-written Lease shall be read and construed as if the term of fourteen years were substituted therein in the place of ten years and the *a* reference in the said Clause to a rent review in respect of the rent to be charged for the said premises from the 25th day of March 1975 shall be read and construed as if there were also inserted reference to a rent review for the rent to be charged for the said premises from the 25th day of March 1978 but that in all other respects the covenants conditions and agreements in the within-written Lease shall remain in full force.' *b*

At the end of the first five years, the parties failed to agree on a new rent. In these circumstances, the landlords issued an originating summons, which was amended before the hearing, and, in its amended form, posed two question in these terms:

'1. Whether upon the true construction of Clause 1 of a Lease made the 17th day of July 1968 between the Plaintiffs as Landlords and the Defendant as Tenant of *c* premises known as 54 and 56 Torbay Road aforesaid and of the memorandum to the said Lease dated the 17th day of May 1971 the rental payable under the said Lease (subject only to the provisions of Part II of the Counter-Inflation Act 1973 and orders made thereunder) between the 25th days of March 1973 and 1978 is a proper and reasonable rental having regard to the market value of the said premises on the 25th day of March 1973. 2. If yes, whether the sum of £2850 per annum represents *d* such a proper and reasonable rental.'

It is not absolutely plain what happened at the hearing, because the judge came to the conclusion that he had decided something which was not in accordance with the submissions of either party, and on that account he made no order as to costs. But, as far as I can gather, except that he imported the restriction that one should not take account of tenant's improvements in ascertaining the market value of the premises, he did in fact *e* (though perhaps by a different route) accept the submission which was being made on behalf of the landlords, or at any rate arrived at the same result.

In reply, it appears to have been suggested on behalf of the landlords that if the true view were that no rent was reserved at all for the second five years, then the lease was or had become void for uncertainty. That submission arose in that way only, and it was not *f* submitted on behalf of the tenant, nor has it been submitted before us, that the lease was or became void.

The actual order which the judge made was as follows:

'This Court doth declare upon the true construction of Clause 1 of the said Lease [then it is described by its date and parties] and of a Memorandum [which is also described] that the [tenant] is liable to pay to the [landlords] (a) between 25th March *g* 1973 and 24th March 1978 (subject only to the provisions of Part II of the Counter-Inflation Act 1973 and orders made thereunder) a rental representing what the demised premises at 54 and 56 Torbay Road Paignton Devon were reasonably worth on 25th March 1973 on a demise for a term of 5 years therefrom provided that (i) in computing such amount no account shall be taken of any improvements carried out by the [tenant] and (ii) the said rental shall not be less than £1,250 per annum *h* and (b) between 25th March 1978 and 24th March 1982 a rental representing what the said premises are reasonably worth on 25th March 1978 on a demise for a term of 4 years therefrom subject to the same provisos as are set out in sub-paragraphs (i) and (ii) of paragraph (a) of this Order.'

The expression used there, 'what the said premises are reasonably worth', must, I *j* think, mean what would be a fair rental value for the premises. I cannot see any other meaning which could be attributed to it. I think one should also point out that, of course, so far as para (b) of that order is concerned, it will only become operative subject to any agreement which the parties may make with regard to the rent for the last four years.

The landlords are content to stand on the order, but they have served a respondents'

a notice in which, should this court be of opinion that the order ought to be reversed or varied, they seek to make certain submissions as to the proper order and to revive the alternative contention that the lease might be void.

Counsel for the tenant, who has taken every point here which could be taken on behalf of the tenant, has put forward as his first submission an argument that the words in cl 1, 'and in any case not less than the yearly rental payable hereunder', on their true

b construction, mean 'and in default of agreement the yearly rental payable hereunder', that is, £1,250. He says that cl 1 is really in three parts: first, it reserves a rent of that amount for the first five years; second, it provides that the rent for the second five years shall be as the parties agree; and, third, so construing the words I have mentioned, he says it provides that in default of agreement the rent shall continue to be £1,250. He treats the words, 'but no account shall be taken of any improvements carried out by the Tenant

c in computing the amount of increase, if any' as if they were in parenthesis, but he does not take into that parenthesis the further words, 'and in any case not less than the yearly rental payable hereunder'.

I think, for my part, that that is an impossible construction. It is not, on the scheme of the clause as a whole, in my view, the natural meaning of the words; and, if one is to treat any part of it as in parenthesis, I think the provision about rent is as much in the

d parenthesis as the provision about tenant's improvement. But, secondly, that construction would make the clause futile, because, if in default of agreement the rent was to continue to be £1,250, obviously the tenant would never agree to pay more, however much the premises might appreciate in value, and conversely, in the unlikely event of them depreciating, the landlord clearly would not agree to accept less. All that that clause was doing, as it seems to me, was setting out the basis on which it was contemplated that the

e parties would seek to agree on the rent to become payable at the end of the first five years. I think 'such rent as shall thereupon be agreed' must be 'such fair rent'. It does not make sense otherwise. So the basis was that it was to be a fair rent, not taking into account improvements made by the tenant himself, and in the perhaps unlikely event of depreciation, the rent was not to be reduced below £1,250. Accordingly, in my judgment, that submission fails.

f Then counsel for the tenant seeks to obtain the same result by a different method, by implying a covenant that in the absence of an agreement the rent shall be £1,250. In approaching that argument, it must be observed first, as I have said, that the tenant does not suggest that the lease ever was or has become void for uncertainty. If he had done so, I think he would have been in difficulties, but it is not necessary to pause to consider that further, because he has not done so, and the court has to approach this problem on the

g footing that there is a subsisting lease. Second, he concedes (and, in my judgment, rightly) that he cannot stay on there and pay no rent at all. Quite apart from the fact that one would naturally lean towards that conclusion, he has quite fairly indicated that there are provisions in the lease which support it and indeed render it inevitable. He has referred us to the covenant for quiet enjoyment and the provision about cesser or suspension of rent in the event of damage to the premises by fire.

h That being so, we have to imply some term defining what the rent is to be. He submits that there are two alternatives: one £1,250; the other, a fair market rent for the premises; of course, subject to the qualification about tenant's improvements. Given, therefore, that some implication has to be made, I asked him on what in the lease he founded the implication that the rent should be £1,250. His answer was: 'I say, look at the two alternatives, look at such authorities as there are, and where market rent is

j implied they show that there must be something in the nature of an arbitration clause to fix a rent. Here there is nothing to justify implication of market rent.' He said: 'If the landlord wants to get an increased rent, there must be something in the lease clearly giving him the right to that advantage.' Buckley LJ has suggested that that might be improved on in this way: cl 1 shows there must be at least £1,250 and there is no clear machinery for imposing a higher rent. Whichever way you look at it, I can see no

justification whatever for accepting the alternative implied term which crystallises and
fixes the rent for the residue of the 14 years at the sum of £1,250.

The authorities on which counsel for the tenant relied were, first, *King's Motors
(Oxford) Ltd v Lax* [1969] 3 All ER 665, [1970] 1 WLR 426. But that case, in my
judgment, is wholly distinguishable and does not really assist at all. That was a case of an
option to renew, and the exercise of the option could operate, if at all, only to create a
contract. Valid contract it could not be, because an essential term, namely the rent, was
neither agreed nor ascertainable. That, in my judgment, poses an entirely different
problem from that which arises where one starts with the premise that there is a
subsisting lease which creates an estate in the land and with the premise that the court
must imply some term, because it is conceded that rent is payable.

The second authority, *Foley v Classique Coaches Ltd* [1934] 2 KB 1, [1934] All ER Rep 88
is relied on by both sides. The landlords in the court below relied on it in support of
implying a fair rent by analogy with what was there implied, a reasonable price. But
counsel for the tenant relies on it because he says it shows that one could only make an
implication of that character if assisted by the presence of an arbitration clause. It is fair
to say that if one looks only at the judgment of Maugham LJ he did appear to be relying
substantially on the arbitration clause in arriving at his conclusion (see [1934] 2 KB 1 at
16, [1934] All ER Rep 88 at 94). But I do not think that is the true ratio of the case.
Where you have got an arbitration clause, then if you imply a term that there shall be a
reasonable price (as it was in that case) or a fair rent (as it would be in this), any dispute
as to what is reasonable or fair falls within the arbitration clause; and, if you have not got
one, it falls to be resolved by the court. But, in my judgment, the presence or absence of
an arbitration clause does not matter. I would refer to a passage in the judgment of
Scrutton LJ where, whilst it is true he referred to an arbitration clause, he put the matter
as one of general principle. He said ([1934] 2 KB 1 at 10, [1934] All ER Rep 88 at 91):

> 'In the present case the parties obviously believed they had a contract and they
> acted for three years as if they had; they had an arbitration clause which relates to
> the subject-matter of the agreement as to the supply of petrol, and it seems to me
> that this arbitration clause applies to any failure to agree as to the price.'

That is what it applies to. Then he goes on:

> 'By analogy to the case of a tied house there is to be implied in this contract a term
> that the petrol shall be supplied at a reasonable price and shall be of reasonable
> quality. For these reasons I think the Lord Chief Justice was right in holding that
> there was an effective and enforceable contract, although as to the future no definite
> price had been agreed with regard to the petrol.'

Greer LJ said ([1934] 2 KB 1 at 11, [1934] All ER Rep 88 at 92):

> 'I think the words of Bowen L.J. in *The Moorcock* ((1889) 14 PD 64, [1886–90] All
> ER Rep 530) are clearly applicable to a case of this kind, and that in order to give
> effect to what both parties intended the Court is justified in implying that in the
> absence of agreement as to price a reasonable price must be paid, and if the parties
> cannot agree as to what is a reasonable price then arbitration must take place.'

So, again, one implies a term on general principles, and then only turns to the
arbitration clause to resolve any dispute arising on the implied term.

The third and last authority on which counsel for the tenant relied was *Kenilworth
Industrial Sites Ltd v E C Little & Co Ltd* [1974] 2 All ER 815 at 817–818, [1974] 1 WLR
1069 at 1071 where Megarry J said:

> 'First, the lease reserves no rent beyond the first five years. The question is not
> one of the landlord having an option to displace an agreed rent for the later years of
> the term. If no new rent is ever ascertained, then as a matter of obligation under the
> terms of the lease, no rent at all is reserved for the last 16 years of the term. Counsel

a for the tenant repudiated any idea that the tenant could remain rent-free after the first five years, and accepted and asserted that the tenant must pay rent at the rate initially reserved, namely, £2,980 a year. This, however, is not what the lease says, and counsel had to rely on a term to this effect being implied in the lease. Such a term, however, would be entirely contrary to the mechanism laid down by cl 5, and would have to be a term implied if, and only if, the landlord failed to operate cl 5 according to its tenor. There seem to me to be considerable difficulties in implying

b a conditional term of this kind.'

But, of course, Megarry J did not have the problem whether anything should be implied and, if so, what, before him, because there was a clause which gave the landlord a right to require an increase in rent to be ascertained in accordance with certain prescribed machinery. The point in *Kenilworth's* case was that the landlord failed to serve notice to start that machinery working within the time prescribed. The question at issue

c was whether time was of the essence and he was therefore too late or not. The judge held that he was within time. Therefore, the machinery operated, and there was no necessity to imply anything, or room for doing so.

That case went to the Court of Appeal, and it is unnecessary to refer to the judgments there except for one passage, where what I have just been saying is clearly pointed out by

d Megaw LJ. He there said ([1975] 1 All ER 53 at 55, [1975] 1 WLR 143 at 146):

'But, says counsel for the tenants, it is proper and necessary to imply into this lease the provision that if the landlords fail within the stated time to give the notice seeking agreement or arbitration, then the rent which was payable in the preceding period shall continue to be the rent to be paid during the succeeding five years. For myself, I am quite unable to see that there is any valid basis for implying such a term

e in this lease. It would, in my judgment, be inconsistent with the express provisions of cll 1 and 5, whether read separately or together. Moreover, the provisions of the second proviso cannot, in my judgment, be ignored, and if they are not ignored there is no reason for implying such a term.'

That was because the proviso said that the landlord was not to fail in the exercise of

f ascertainment of the new rent merely because he was out of time.

Therefore, as it seems to me, the authorities do not assist counsel for the tenant. On the contrary, they are against him, because the nearest case to the present one is *Foley's* case, where the court did imply a reasonable price, and did so, as I think, quite clearly without having to rely on the arbitration clause. At all events, in my judgment, such a clause is not essential. Therefore, one is left with the two alternatives which have been posed.

g Now, the court must imply a term in order to give business efficacy to the contract, and I ask myself: why should it choose the alternative which is inconsistent with the basis which the parties showed they contemplated, rather than the one that implements it? Really, counsel for the tenant is attempting by an implied term to get himself back into the first submission, that of an implied agreement fixing a rent in default of agreement, and his second argument produces the same futility. It is quite obvious from cl 1 that the

h parties intended that the rent should be increased if the premises appreciated in value, and none the less so although they used the words 'if any'. They clearly contemplated also, as it seems to me, that the rent should be increased to such amount as would be a fair rent for the premises excluding tenant's improvements. They failed to agree. There is a hiatus. As the judge rightly held, that hiatus has to be filled by an implied term, and

j it seems to me quite obvious that one must imply the alternative which gives effect to that clearly expressed intention of the parties.

In my judgment, therefore, the judge was right; and I would dismiss the appeal.

GEOFFREY LANE LJ. I agree. Had this been a contract of sale or an ordinary commercial contract of some sort, there would be a great deal to be said for the view that from the date of the first rent review in March 1973 the contract was void for uncertainty, the parties having failed to agree on a vital term of the contract. But here there is a *a* subsisting estate, and a subsisting estate in land, the lease, which is to continue until 1982, 14 years from the date of the lease itself. It is conceded by the tenant that some rent must be paid in respect of these premises by the tenant, and therefore it follows that the court must imply something, some term which will enable a rent to be fixed.

Counsel for the tenant submits that on the face of the agreement and on the true construction of it, the landlord has failed to stipulate for anything more than the original *b* rent of £1,250 per annum, and that therefore the court should fix that amount as the proper rent for the next period. Counsel concedes that if that is the case, then on the further review which is due to take place in 1978, exactly the same thing will happen and the tenant will be in the happy position of paying a rent for the whole of the rest of the term which is well below the market value. That is plainly a highly undesirable result on any view, because it would mean in effect that the court would be implying an unfair *c* rent. But, for the reasons which have been set out by Goff LJ, that is not a tenable construction of the terms of the lease.

The court should, if it can, give effect to the intention of the parties as exhibited from the terms of the agreement itself. That intention was quite clearly to fix at these moments of review a fair rent by agreement between the parties, subject to the provisos which they set out. *d*

Now, in the absence of such agreement, the court, as is made quite clear from the decision of this court in *Foley v Classique Coaches* [1934] 2 KB 1, [1934] All ER Rep 88, must try to produce the same effect for the parties. It seems to me that the judge's order in this case produces precisely that desirable effect.

For those reasons, as well as those already advanced by Goff LJ, I too would dismiss this appeal. *e*

BUCKLEY LJ. I agree. It appears to me that the introduction by implication of a single word in the clause in the lease relating to the rent to be payable solves the problem of this case; that is, the insertion of the word 'fair' between the words 'such' and 'rent'. If some such implication is not made, it seems to me that this would be a completely inoperative rent review provision, because it is not to be expected that the tenant would *f* agree to an increase in the rent if the rent to be agreed was absolutely at large. Clearly the parties contemplated that at the end of five years some adjustment might be necessary to make the position with regard to the rent a fair one, and the rent review provision with which we are concerned was inserted in the lease to enable such an adjustment to be made. The suggestion that on the true construction of the clause it provides that the rent shall continue to be at the rate of £1,250 a year unless the parties otherwise agree would, *g* in my opinion, render the provision entirely inoperative, because, as I say, one could not expect the tenant voluntarily to agree to pay a higher rent.

For the reasons which have been developed by Goff and Geoffrey Lane LJJ in the two judgments which they have delivered, I am in agreement that this appeal should be dismissed, the judge having, I think, arrived at the right conclusion.

h

Appeal dismissed.

Solicitors: *Scott, Son & Chitty*, Epsom (for the landlords); *Boxall & Boxall*, agents for *R Hancock & Son*, Callington (for the tenant).

Diana Brahams   Barrister.

a
Thomas Bates & Son Ltd v Wyndham's (Lingerie) Ltd

COURT OF APPEAL, CIVIL DIVISION
BUCKLEY, EVELEIGH AND BRIGHTMAN LJJ

b 13th, 14th, 17th, 18th, 19th, 20th, 21st NOVEMBER 1980

*Landlord and tenant – Lease – Rectification – Common intention of parties – Unilateral mistake
– Lease not giving effect to parties' common intention due to landlord's mistake – Tenant aware
of mistake at date of execution of lease – Mistake contrary to landlord's interest and beneficial to
tenant's interest – Tenant not drawing landlord's attention to mistake – Failure by landlord to
c provide machinery in rent review clause for fixing rent in default of agreement between parties
– Whether landlord entitled to rectification of clause – Whether standard of proof of common
intention higher than balance of probability.*

*Estoppel – Deed – Rectifiable deed – Common intention of parties – Unilateral mistake – Lease
– Mistake by lessor in drafting lease – Lessee aware of mistake – Conditions under which estoppel
d arising – Whether lessee estopped from resisting rectification of lease.*

*Landlord and tenant – Lease – Rent review clause – Rent payable on review to be rent agreed
between parties or fixed by arbitration in default of agreement – Whether rent on review to be
reasonable rent as between parties or market rent.*

e In December 1957 the tenants took an assignment of a lease of premises which had been
executed in 1956. The lease contained an option giving the tenants the right on the
expiration of the lease to take a further seven or fourteen years' lease 'at a rent to be agreed
between the landlords and the tenants but in default of such agreement at a rent to be
fixed by [an] arbitrator'. The tenants exercised the option and in 1963 were granted a
new lease for seven years. The 1963 lease contained an option for the grant of a further
f seven-year term on terms similar to the option in the 1956 lease. On 4th May 1970 the
tenants gave the landlords formal notice exercising the option. Negotiations followed
between the parties and in September 1970 the tenants accepted the landlords' offer of a
14-year lease at an exclusive rent of £2,350 per annum for the first five years and subject
to review every five years thereafter. The 1970 lease was prepared by the landlords who
by an oversight omitted to include provision for the fixing of rent by arbitration in
default of agreement on a rent review and the rent review clause merely stated that the
g rent for the rent review periods was to be 'such rents as shall have been agreed between
the lessor and the lessee'. It had not been agreed by the parties that the reference to
arbitration should be omitted, and the tenants although aware of the omission at the
time they executed the new lease did not bring it to the landlords' attention. When the
rent came up for review at the end of the first five years the landlords realised their
omission and suggested to the tenants that the rent for the next five-year period should
h be £5,000 per annum, that being in the landlords' opinion a market rent, and that if the
parties failed to agree the rent should be fixed by an arbitrator. The tenants rejected both
the proposed rent and the referral of the matter to arbitration. The landlords brought an
action claiming (i) a declaration that the rent payable on the rent reviews was to be the
market rent for the premises, and (ii) rectification of the rent review clause to provide for
determination of the rent by arbitration in default of agreement. The tenants
j counterclaimed for a declaration that either the premises were to be held rent free for the
remainder of the lease or the rent was to be £2,350 for the remainder. The judge
granted the landlords' declaration that the rent on review was to be a market rent,
ordered rectification of the rent review clause in the terms requested by them, and
dismissed the tenants' counterclaim. The tenants appealed. At the hearing of the appeal

the tenants, while conceding that because of previous authority[a] they could not contend
that the rent should continue to be £2,350 and that in default of agreement a reasonable   *a*
rent was payable, nevertheless contended that the judge had been wrong to order
rectification of the rent review clause. The landlords for their part conceded that if the
order for rectification were to stand it was to be read as an agreement to arbitrate and not
as an agreement to abide by a valuation, and on that footing the rent to be fixed by the
arbitrator was to be such rent as would be reasonable for the particular parties to agree on
having regard to all the considerations which would have affected their negotiations for   *b*
a new rent, rather than a market rent as ordered by the judge.

Held – (1) Where two parties to an instrument had a common intention and it was
shown (a) that the plaintiff erroneously believed that the instrument gave effect to that
intention, (b) that the defendant knew that it did not because by reason of the plaintiff's
mistake the instrument contained or omitted something, (c) that the defendant failed to   *c*
bring the mistake to the plaintiff's notice, and (d) that the mistake would benefit the
defendant or (per Eveleigh LJ) merely that it would be detrimental to the plaintiff, the
court was entitled to conclude that the defendant's conduct was such that it would be
inequitable to allow him to resist, or that he should be estopped from resisting,
rectification of the instrument to give effect to the common intention, despite the fact
that the mistake was not at the time of the execution of the instrument a common   *d*
mistake but rather a unilateral mistake. It was not necessary for the plaintiff to show that
the defendant was guilty of sharp practice (see p 1085 *f g*, p 1086 *a* to *d*, p 1090 *a* to *c f g*
and p 1091 *a b*, post); *A Roberts & Co Ltd v Leicestershire County Council* [1961] 2 All ER 545
and dictum of Russell LJ in *Riverlate Properties Ltd v Paul* [1974] 2 All ER at 660 applied.

(2) The parties had a common intention to include in the rent review clause in the
1970 lease provision for arbitration in default of agreement similar to that in the 1963   *e*
lease, especially (per Buckley LJ) since under the option in the 1963 lease the tenants had
a contractual right to have the rent in the sixth and seventh years of the 1970 lease
determined by arbitration in default of agreement. The omission of provision for
arbitration in the rent review clause occurred as the result of the landlords' mistake and
was contrary to their interests. Furthermore, although the tenants had realised the
landlord's mistake they had not drawn it to the landlord's attention. The landlords were   *f*
accordingly entitled to rectification of the rent review clause in the 1970 lease by the
insertion therein of provision for reference to arbitration in default of agreement on the
rent payable on the rent reviews (see p 1084 *d* to *g*, p 1086 *f* and *j* to p 1087 *b*, p 1089 *c*
d and *j* to p 1090 *a c d f g* and p 1091 *b*, post).

(3) Since the rent review clause referred to such rent 'as shall have been agreed'
between the parties, and not to the rent 'agreed for the demised premises', the rent to be   *g*
agreed under the clause or to be fixed by the arbitrator in default of agreement was to be
the rent which it would be reasonable for the particular parties to agree having regard to
all the circumstances (such as tenant's expenditure on improvements) which were
relevant to their negotiations for a new rent, and was not to be a rent assessed objectively
on the basis of the market rent at which the premises might reasonably be expected to
be let. It followed that the judge's declaration that the rent was to be the market rent,   *h*
was incorrect (see p 1087 *f* to *h*, p 1088 *e* to *j*, p 1089 *c d* and p 1090 *c d* and *f g*, post);
Ponsford v HMS Aerosols Ltd [1978] 2 All ER 837 distinguished.

Per Buckley and Brightman LJJ. The standard of proof required to establish the
common intention of the parties in a rectification action is the ordinary civil standard of
the balance of probability although (per Buckley LJ) a high standard of such proof might
be required in the circumstances and (per Brightman LJ) as the alleged common   *j*

intention necessarily contradicts the written instrument, strong evidence will be required
a   to counteract the evidence of the instrument (see p 1085 *b* to *d* and p 1090 *g* to *j*, post).

Notes
For the considerations affecting rectification, see 26 Halsbury's Laws (3rd Edn) 914–917,
paras 698–1704, and for cases on unilateral mistake, see 35 Digest (Repl) 138, *309–316*.
b   For rent review clauses, see 23 Halsbury's Laws (3rd Edn) 539, para 1197.

Cases referred to in judgments
Beer v Bowden p 1070, ante, CA.
Hornal v Neuberger Products Ltd [1956] 3 All ER 970, [1957] 1 QB 247, [1956] 3 WLR
     1034, CA, 35 Digest (Repl) 39, *332*.
c   *Ponsford v HMS Aerosols Ltd* [1978] 2 All ER 837, [1979] AC 63, [1978] 3 WLR 241, 38
     P & CR 270, [1979] RVR 19, HL, Digest (Cont Vol E) 364, *3952f*.
Riverlate Properties Ltd v Paul [1974] 2 All ER 656, [1975] Ch 133, [1974] 3 WLR 564, 28
     P & CR 220, CA, Digest (Cont Vol D) 688, *273a*.
Roberts (A) & Co Ltd v Leicestershire County Council [1961] 2 All ER 545, [1961] Ch 555,
     [1961] 2 WLR 1000, 59 LGR 349, 35 Digest (Repl) 138, *316*.
d   *Sykes (F & G) (Wessex) Ltd v Fine Fare Ltd* [1967] 1 Lloyd's Rep 53, CA.

Cases also cited
Bottomley v Ambler (1877) 38 LT 545, CA.
British Bank for Foreign Trade v Novimex [1949] 1 All ER 155, [1949] 1 KB 623, CA.
Brown v Gould [1971] 2 All ER 1505, [1972] Ch 53.
e   *Churchward v Ford* (1857) 2 H & N 446, 157 ER 184.
Clerk v Palady (1598) Cro Eliz 859, 78 ER 1085.
Collins v Collins (1858) 26 Beav 306, 53 ER 916.
Courtney and Fairbairn Ltd v Tolaini Brothers (Hotels) Ltd [1975] 1 All ER 716, [1975] 1
     WLR 297, CA.
f   *Dempster (R & J) v Motherwell Bridge & Engineering Co* 1964 SLT 353.
Dungey v Angore (1794) 2 Ves 304, 30 ER 644, LC.
Foley v Classique Coaches Ltd [1934] 2 KB 1, [1934] All ER Rep 88, CA.
Hillas & Co Ltd v Arcos Ltd (1932) 147 LT 503, [1932] All ER Rep 494, HL.
Joscelyne v Nissen [1970] 1 All ER 1213, [1970] 2 QB 86, CA.
Kenilworth Industrial Sites v E C Little & Co [1975] 1 All ER 53, [1975] 1 WLR 143, CA.
King's Motors (Oxford) v Lax [1969] 3 All ER 665, [1970] 1 WLR 426.
g   *Liverpool City Council v Irwin* [1976] 2 All ER 39, [1977] AC 239, HL.
May & Butcher Ltd v R (1929) [1934] 2 KB 17 n, [1929] All ER Rep 679, HL.
Moorcock, The (1889) 14 PD 64, [1886–90] All ER Rep 530, CA.
Prenn v Simmonds [1971] 3 All ER 237, [1971] 1 WLR 1381, HL.
Reade v Johnson (1591) Cro Eliz 242, 78 ER 498.
h   *Trollope & Colls v North West Metropolitan Regional Hospital Board* [1973] 2 All ER 260,
     [1973] 1 WLR 601, HL.
United Scientific Holdings v Burnley Borough Council [1977] 2 All ER 62, [1978] AC 904, HL.

Appeal
The plaintiffs, Thomas Bates and Son Ltd ('the landlords'), brought an action against the
j   defendants, Wyndham's (Lingerie) Ltd ('the tenants'), seeking (1) a declaration that on
the true construction of a lease dated 17th December 1970 made between the landlords
and the tenants in relation to factory premises at Church Road, Harold Wood, Havering,
the rents during the rent review periods provided for in the lease should be the market
rents for the premises, (2) rectification of the lease to provide for determination of the

rents by a single arbitrator in default of agreement between the parties, (3) alternatively, a declaration that the lease was void and/or rescission of the lease, (4) in the further *a* alternative, a declaration that the tenants were liable to pay a proper sum for use and occupation of the premises from 15th November 1975, and (5) an inquiry into the market rent during the first rent review period or, alternatively, an inquiry into what was the proper sum for the use and occupation of the premises from 15th November 1975. The tenants counterclaimed for a declaration that from 15th November 1975 the demised premises were held by them for the residue of the unexpired term of the lease *b* rent free; alternatively, the rent reserved by the lease from 15th November 1970 to the expiry of the lease was £2,350 per annum. By a judgment given on 6th June 1979 Michael Wheeler QC sitting as a deputy judge of the High Court declared that on the true construction of the lease the rents during the rent review periods in the lease should be the market rent for the premises, and ordered rectification of the lease to provide that in default of agreement between the parties as to the rents payable they were to be *c* determined by a single arbitrator to be appointed by the president of the Royal Institution of Chartered Surveyors. The deputy judge dismissed the counterclaim. The tenants appealed seeking an order that the rents reserved by the lease for the period 15th November 1980 to the expiry of the lease was £2,350 per annum; alternatively that no rent was reserved during that period. The facts are set out in the judgment of Buckley LJ.

d

Edward Nugee QC and *Joseph Harper* for the tenants.
Robert Wakefield for the landlords.

BUCKLEY LJ. This is an appeal from a decision of Michael Wheeler QC, sitting as a *e* deputy judge in the Chancery Division on 6th June 1979.

The issues in the case relate to a rent review clause contained in a lease dated 17th December 1970 and made between the plaintiffs as lessors and the defendants as lessees. The subject matter was some factory premises at Hornchurch in Essex. In order to understand the issues it is necessary to go back in history a little while.

In the year 1956, by a lease dated 20th August 1956, the plaintiffs (whom I shall call *f* 'the landlords') let to predecessors of the defendants (and I will call the defendants 'the tenants') the factory premises in question for a term of seven years from 1st September 1956 at a yearly rent of £650. That lease contained, in cl 5, an option provision in the following terms:

> 'That the lessor will on the written request of the lessee made six months before *g* the end of the term hereby created and if at the time of such request there shall not be any existing breach or non-observance of any of the covenants on the part of the lessee hereinbefore contained at the expense of the lessee grant to the lessee a lease of the demised premises for a further term of seven or fourteen years from the expiration of the said term at a rent to be agreed between the lessor and the lessee but in default of such agreement at a rent to be fixed by a single arbitrator appointed *h* by the President for the time being of the Royal Institution of Chartered Surveyors and containing the like covenants and provisos as are herein contained.'

The term under that lease was in due course assigned to the tenants, and when the time for the exercise of the option drew near Mr Bates, the managing director of the landlords, wrote a letter to the tenants, for the attention of a Mr Avon, who was the *j* director of the tenants who at all times has handled matters relating to this leasehold property on behalf of the tenants, a letter drawing attention to the fact that the time had come to consider a renewal of the lease, and Mr Bates said in that letter that the landlords would require an addition of £125 per annum, bringing the rent up to £775 per annum for the seven years from the expiration of the then current lease.

Stimulated by that communication, Mr Avon, on behalf of the tenants, gave a formal
a notice exercising the option on 19th February 1963, requesting the landlords to grant to
the tenants a renewed lease of the premises for the further term of 14 years from the
expiration of the current term, 'at a rent to be agreed between us [quoting from the
notice] but in default of such an agreement, at a rent to be fixed by a single arbitrator
appointed by the President of the Royal Institution'.

In response to that Mr Bates wrote in reply saying that in fact the landlords would
b require rather more rent than he had stated in his earlier letter: £850 a year. In
consequence of which there were some oral communications, and on 11th March 1963
Mr Bates wrote to Mr Avon confirming offers which he had made orally for a further
seven year term at £800 a year, and proposing that the landlords should construct certain
additional buildings on the property, in consideration of which there would be a further
rent of another £800 a year during the ensuing seven year period.

c   Those terms were accepted by the tenants, and on 29th November 1963 the parties
entered into a new lease for a term of seven years from 15th November 1963 at a yearly
rental of £1,600; and that lease contained an option clause in precisely the same terms as
the option clause in the 1956 lease, save that it only granted an option for a further seven
years and not for seven or 14 years as had been the case in the 1956 lease.

Time went by and the year 1970 arrived when the time was approaching for the
d exercise of the option in the 1963 lease, and we find that on the 14th April 1970 the
landlords wrote a letter to the tenants drawing their attention to this fact, in consequence
of which Mr Avon, on 4th May, signed and sent to the landlords a formal notice
exercising the option contained in the 1963 lease, and by that notice he requested the
landlords to grant a renewed lease of the premises for a further term of seven years from
the expiration of the then current term 'at a rent to be agreed between us, but in default
e of such agreement at a rent to be fixed by a single arbitrator appointed by the President
for the time being of the Royal Institution', and so on. The language of that notice
followed the language of the option clause contained in the 1963 lease.

As has been pointed out in argument, the effect of that notice was to change the legal
relationship between the parties and to bring into existence a contract for the grant of a
further term of seven years at a rent to be agreed or, in default of agreement, to be fixed
f by an arbitrator.

The landlords wrote back to the tenants on 7th May indicating that the rent they
would require would be £2,600 per annum for the first three years of the new term of
seven years, the rental thereafter to be reviewed and agreed for the remainder of the
term. Those words are taken from the letter of 7th May 1970. So being then under a
contractual obligation to grant a new lease for seven years at a rent to be agreed or in
g default of agreement to be fixed by an arbitrator, they proposed agreeing the rent for part
of that term only, leaving the remainder of the term the subject of a further review and
agreement at a later date.

On 3rd August (that is to say, rather later than the letter I have just referred to of 7th
May), there having been some oral communications in the meantime and Mr Avon
having paid a visit to the landlords' offices to discuss the matter, the landlords wrote
h saying that they were prepared to grant a lease for a further period of 14 years from the
expiration of the then current term, with a clause for rent reviews at the end of the fifth
and tenth years of the term, the rental for the first period of five years to be £2,350 per
annum exclusive of rates.

To that letter Mr Avon replied on 17th August 1970 that the tenants were reluctantly
prepared to accept the figure of £2,350, but he said that they were not in agreement with
j rent reviews after five and ten years but were willing to accept a clause for a rent review
at the end of the seventh year. That was, in effect, a counter-offer to the offer which had
been put forward in the letter of 3rd August 1970.

The landlords replied on 18th August insisting on rent reviews after five and ten year
intervals, and on 20th August, following some telephonic communication, they again
wrote insisting on the rent reviews, and that letter has a postscript: 'Whilst your present

lease provides for a further seven years' renewal, the question of the rent review period is something quite separate and distinct.'

It seems to me that the landlords there are saying: we recognise your right under the exercise of the option; you are entitled to a term of seven years at a rent to be agreed or in default of agreement to be fixed by an arbitrator, but we are not at the moment prepared to agree any rent beyond the first five years.

On 22nd September the tenants' solicitors, Messrs Nabarro Nathanson, wrote indicating that the tenants, subject to formal exchange of the lease, accepted the offer of a new lease for a term of 14 years from 15th November 1970, at the exclusive rent of £2,350 per annum, subject to review at the expiration of the fifth and tenth years of the new term.

It seems to me that it is implicit in that that the rent, at any rate in respect of the two years next following the initial five years of the term under the new lease, would be fixed by agreement or, in default of agreement, by an arbitrator appointed under the provisions to that effect in the option clause.

The lease and counterpart were then executed and exchanged. The lease had not been prepared by the landlords' legal advisers; it was prepared under the instructions of Mr Bates and was typed by Mr Bates's secretary, Miss Cannon. The lease so prepared and executed demised the property to the tenants for a term of 14 years from 15th November 1970, and now I quote from the document itself:

'Yielding And Paying therefor during the first Five Years of the said term unto the Lessor the yearly rent of Two Thousand Three Hundred and Fifty pounds and for the next period of five years of the said term and the final period of four years of the said term such rents as shall have been agreed between the Lessor and the Lessee such rents to be paid clear of all deductions by equal monthly payments on the First day of each month in advance.'

and then there is a provision that the tenants should also pay the costs of insurance but we are not concerned with that.

The lease contains an option clause in, I think, the same terms as the option clause which was contained in the 1963 lease except that any further lease to be granted under the option in the 1970 lease was not to be required to contain an option clause. It will be observed that in the reddendum there is no reference to arbitration in default of agreement.

At a later stage when the time for fixing the rent from the end of the first five years of the term onwards became imminent, the landlords became aware of this and wrote a letter, signed by Mr Foley who was the property manager for the landlords, to the tenants as follows:

'As you will be aware under the terms of your lease the rent of this property is due to be reviewed, effective from 15th November, 1975, and this letter is intended to be a formal notice advising you of our intention to review the rent. The lease has no specific note how the rent may be settled should your company and ourselves fail to agree upon a figure and I suggest that the matter be settled by an independent arbitrator. I therefore enclose an agreement in duplicate and shall be obliged if you will sign the top copy and return it to me.'

As a result of that, and a hastener written on 2nd May 1975, a telephone conversation took place on 6th May 1975, in the course of which Mr Avon said he was not prepared to sign any such agreement. Mr Foley then got into contact with the landlords' own solicitors, who advised him that because the rent review clause did not contain some means of definitely settling the new rent eg by arbitration following appointment by the president of the Royal Institution of Chartered Surveyors, should the parties to the lease not agree, the review clause would be unenforceable at law and the rent could remain the same until the lease expired.

Nothing further seems to have taken place immediately with regard to that, but there

was later a telephone conversation between Mr Avon and Mr Foley, to which I shall have
a   to refer again later, in which Mr Avon said (or is said by Mr Foley to have said) that he had
been aware of the implications of the clause from the day the lease was signed; that he
might be prepared to pay a slightly higher rent, but not nearly so high a rent as the
landlords were in fact then proposing.

It seems to me clear that the omission of any reference to arbitration in default of
agreement in the reddendum of the lease of 1970 must have been due to a mistake on the
b   part of Mr Bates, under whose instructions, as I have said, that lease was prepared. The
omission was one which was clearly contrary to the landlords' interests. The only
possible legal consequences which have been suggested in the course of argument are,
first, that no rents having been agreed in respect of any period after the first five years of
the 14-year term, no rent would be payable after the end of that five year period.
Counsel for the tenants, although he did not in the course of his argument altogether
c   abandon the idea that that might be the legal consequence of the omission, frankly and
very properly admitted that it could not have been in the contemplation of the parties
that there would be any period during the term of this lease when no rent would be
payable at all, and it is inconceivable that that could have been the parties' real intention.

Secondly, it has been suggested that as no rent other than the rent of £2,350 per
annum would have been agreed, that rent should continue in force until some other rent
d   should be agreed by the parties. It seems to me that such a proposition is absolutely
contrary to the clear intention of the rent review provision. The rent review provision
was clearly a provision insisted on by the landlords because they wanted the matter
reviewed at the end of five years and wanted a new rent to be then arrived at. If merely
by withholding consent or agreement to a new rent the tenants could stultify the
revision clause and ensure that the original rent of £2,350 should continue to be payable,
e   the whole purpose of the rent revision clause would be destroyed or frustrated. I cannot
believe that it could have been Mr Bates's intention that the lease in the form in which
he framed it should have had that effect.

Thirdly, it has been suggested that in respect of the period after the first five years, and
in default of agreement between the parties, the rent would have to be fixed by a process
of litigation involving the implication of the parties' intentions, and it has been suggested
f   that by implication the rent ought either to be the market rent, that is to say the rent for
which this property would be let in the open market, or such rent as this particular
landlord and this particular tenant would agree having regard to all the matters which
would affect them in arriving mutually at a rent which the one was content to accept and
the other was content to pay, which would very possibly be markedly different from a
market rent, and it seems to me inconceivable that the landlords would have been
g   content to rely on fixing a rent by a process of implication in that way without it being
at all clear in what way the court would view the matter and how the rent to be so
ascertained should be assessed.

The only other possible legal consequence of the omission that has been suggested at
all, either in the course of argument or in the course of the evidence given before the trial
judge, was that the clause was entirely inoperative because of the omission and because
h   either it amounted to no more than an agreement to agree, or it amounted to a provision
which contained such defective machinery that it could not be carried into practical
effect. It will be seen that advice on those lines was what was received by Mr Foley. It
seems also to have been the advice received by Mr Avon.

Mr Foley gave evidence before the deputy judge, but Mr Avon did not. The deputy
judge was somewhat critical of Mr Avon for not giving evidence. That was, no doubt,
j   a matter which rested not so much in Mr Avon's discretion as in the discretion of those
who were conducting the case on the part of the tenants. The judge, in the course of his
judgment, made the following finding:

> 'In evidence before me Mr Foley amplified this note [he is referring to a note
> written on the letter of 23rd September to which I have already referred]. I think

it probable that in his oral evidence Mr Foley may to some extent have telescoped two telephone conversations with Mr Avon into one. His evidence, which was given with care and which I accept without hesitation, was to the following effect. He said that he quoted a new rent to Mr Avon of, he thought, about £5,000 per annum; that Mr Avon seemed amused and, when asked what he thought, said he might pay £100 or £200 more. Mr Foley said he realised that Mr Avon's figure bore no relation to the market value but he felt that he (Foley) was in a slightly ticklish position and said he would refer the position to Bates's solicitors; that Mr Avon then said that he (Foley) must be aware as he (Avon) was that the rent revision clause as drawn was inoperative and that he (Avon) had been aware of this at the time the lease was entered into because it had been brought to his notice by Wyndham's solicitors.'

The deputy judge, in the course of his judgment, spoke critically of Mr Avon in that respect and said that, in his judgment, Mr Avon's conduct amounted to sharp practice. As the judge had not heard any evidence from Mr Avon we cannot tell in what circumstances Mr Avon acted as he did, or under what advice he acted as he did. It is clear that he was at that time in contact with and receiving advice from the tenants' solicitors, and for my part I do not feel it necessary to associate myself with that stricture on the part of the judge on Mr Avon's conduct. Nevertheless the fact emerges that when the tenants executed the 1970 lease they did so realising the omission of any reference to arbitration in default of agreement in the review clause and without drawing the attention of the landlords to that omission in any way.

The only reasonable conclusion, it appears to me, that can be drawn from the documents is that the lease was executed, in the form in which it was with regard to the terms of the review clause, as a consequence of a mistake on Mr Bates's part, for at the time when the lease was prepared and put forward the tenants had a contractual right to have the rent, at any rate in respect of the sixth and seventh years of the term, agreed or, in default of agreement, determined by an arbitrator appointed by the president of the Royal Institution of Chartered Surveyors. No doubt the grant of the lease displaced the contract which had arisen as a result of the exercise of the option, but the terms of that contract relating to fixing the rent in respect of the first seven years of the term which was granted by the 1970 lease remained in force up to the execution of the lease and that, in my judgment, affords a strong indication that until, at any rate, Mr Avon realised the omission of any reference to arbitration, it was the mutual intention of both parties that the rent to be paid under the lease after the first five years should be a rent which was agreed between the parties or, in default of agreement, ascertained by arbitration.

Mr Bates did not give evidence because unhappily he had died in January 1973. That was a date a considerable number of months after the issue of the writ but before the trial. No written statement of Mr Bates made during his lifetime was adduced in evidence under the Civil Evidence Act 1968. We are told by counsel, but we have got no other evidence of the fact, that Mr Bates did not make any written statement. So there was no evidence of any kind emanating from him.

But there was the evidence of Miss Cannon. Miss Cannon's evidence, in my view, in no way negatives the possibility or probability that the omission of a reference to arbitration was due to a mistake on Mr Bates's part. Her evidence, taking it quite shortly and generally, is to the effect that she typed the lease; that she did it in accordance with instructions which she received from Mr Bates; but there is nothing in her evidence which establishes one way or the other whether Mr Bates, in giving his instructions, was himself labouring under a mistake. If, as Mr Avon thought was the position, the clause in the way in which it was drawn was an inoperative clause, it seems to me to be absolutely manifest that it must have been so framed as the result of a mistake, for one cannot believe that any landlord would put into a lease a clause which he intended to be inoperative.

Counsel for the tenants has said that there is no evidence as to what Mr Bates's
a intention was, and he stressed that in cases of rectification a high standard of proof is
required by the court. Indeed, in some cases the standard has been equated with the
criminal standard of proof, 'beyond all reasonable doubt'. I think that the use of a variety
of formulations used to express the degree of certainty with which a particular fact must
be established in civil proceedings is not very helpful and may, indeed, be confusing.
The requisite degree of cogency of proof will vary with the nature of the facts to be
b established and the circumstances of the case. I would say that in civil proceedings a fact
must be proved with that degree of certainty which justice requires in the circumstances
of the particular case. In every case the balance of probability must be discharged, but in
some cases that balance may be more easily tipped than in others.

In *Hornal v Neuberger Products Ltd* [1956] 3 All ER 970 at 973, [1957] 1 QB 247 at 258
Denning LJ said:

c   'The more serious the allegation the higher the degree of probability that is
        required; but it need not, in a civil case, reach the very high standard required by
        the criminal law.'

That, in my judgment, encapsulates the law about the standard of proof required in civil
proceedings applicable to all civil proceedings, and is as applicable to cases of rectification
d as to any other kind of civil action.

The landlords claim rectification in the present case on the basis of a principle
enunciated by Pennicuick J in *A Roberts & Co, Ltd v Leicestershire County Council* [1961] 2
All ER 545 at 551–552, [1961] Ch 555 at 570:

        'The second ground rests on the principle that a party is entitled to rectification
        of a contract on proof that he believed a particular term to be included in the
e   contract and that the other party concluded the contract with the omission or a
        variation of that term in the knowledge that the first party believed the term to be
        included . . . The principle is stated in SNELL'S PRINCIPLES OF EQUITY (25th Edn, 1960,
        p 569) as follows: "By what appears to be a species of equitable estoppel, if one party
        to a transaction knows that the instrument contains a mistake in his favour but does
        nothing to correct it, he (and those claiming under him) will be precluded from
f   resisting rectification on the ground that the mistake is unilateral and not common".'

Of course if a document is executed in circumstances in which one party realises that
in some respect it does not accurately reflect what down to that moment had been the
common intention of the parties, it cannot be said that the document is executed under
a common mistake, because the party who has realised the mistake is no longer labouring
under the mistake. There may be cases in which the principle enunciated by Pennicuick J
g applies although there is no prior common intention, but we are not, I think, concerned
with such a case here, for it seems to me, on the facts that I have travelled through, that
it is established that the parties had a common intention down to the time when Mr
Avon realised the mistake in the terms of the lease, a common intention that the rent in
respect of any period after the first five years should be agreed or, in default of agreement,
fixed by an arbitrator.

h   The principle so enunciated by Pennicuick J was referred to with approval in this court
in *Riverlate Properties Ltd v Paul* [1974] 2 All ER 656 at 660, [1975] Ch 133 at 140, where
Russell LJ, reading the judgment of the court, said:

        'It may be that the original conception of reformation of an instrument by
        rectification was based solely on common mistake: but certainly in these days
j   rectification may be based on such knowledge on the part of the defendant: see for
        example *A Roberts & Co Ltd v Leicestershire County Council*. Whether there was in any
        particular case knowledge of the intention and mistake of the other party must be
        a question of fact to be decided on the evidence. Basically it appears to us that it
        must be such as to involve the lessee in a degree of sharp practice.'

In that case the lessee against whom the lessor sought to rectify a lease was held to have had no such knowledge as would have brought the doctrine into play. The reference to   *a* 'sharp practice' may thus be said to have been an obiter dictum. Undoubtedly I think in any such case the conduct of the defendant must be such as to make it inequitable that he should be allowed to object to the rectification of the document. If this necessarily implies 'some measure' of sharp practice, so be it; but for my part I think that the doctrine is one which depends more on the equity of the position. The graver the character of the conduct involved, no doubt the heavier the burden of proof may be; but,   *b* in my view, the conduct must be such as to affect the conscience of the party who has suppressed the fact that he has recognised the presence of a mistake.

For this doctrine (that is to say the doctrine of *A Roberts v Leicestershire County Council*) to apply I think it must be shown: first, that one party, A, erroneously believed that the document sought to be rectified contained a particular term or provision, or possibly did not contain a particular term or provision which, mistakenly, it did contain; second, that   *c* the other party, B, was aware of the omission or the inclusion and that it was due to a mistake on the part of A; third, that B has omitted to draw the mistake to the notice of A. And I think there must be a fourth element involved, namely that the mistake must be one calculated to benefit B. If these requirements are satisfied, the court may regard it as inequitable to allow B to resist rectification to give effect to A's intention on the ground that the mistake was not, at the time of execution of the document, a common   *d* mistake.

Counsel for the tenants has drawn attention to a number of other departures in the language of the 1970 lease from the language of the corresponding clauses of the 1963 lease, and he says that this lease was not, or should not be regarded as having been, granted in pursuance of the exercise of the option, but as a newly negotiated lease, the negotiations no doubt being prompted by the exercise of the option, but the new lease   *e* not flowing from the exercise of the option. I, with respect to counsel's argument, do not find very much force in that contention. The parties were of course at liberty to modify the terms of their lease in any way they mutually agreed and none of these variations to which I am now referring has any bearing on the review clause or the language employed in it. It seems to me, as I have already said, that the omission from the review clause of any reference to arbitration was one which was clearly contrary to the landlords' interests,   *f* one which must have occurred as a result of a mistake on the part of Mr Bates.

The judge disposed of the matter on this aspect in three numbered paragraphs:

'(i) That I cannot regard Miss Cannon's evidence as proving that Mr Bates was not making a mistake in omitting a longstop provision for arbitration of some sort; (ii) that although Miss Cannon said that she thought there had been other Bates leases which contained the same type of rent review provision as the 1970 lease, none was   *g* produced, and I cannot accept that any reasonable businessman would deliberately have adopted such a potentially defective provision; and (iii) that the provision for an option to renew the 1970 lease in cl 5 (which was in similar terms to the options in Wyndham's earlier leases) showed perfectly clearly that the parties recognised the necessity for a longstop for rent fixing purposes and that it is reasonable to suppose   *h* that it was a provision in these terms which Bates mistakenly omitted and which Wyndham's (through Mr Avon) deliberately allowed to go uncorrected.'

I have already dealt with Miss Cannon's evidence. With regard to the judge's paragraph (ii), I agree that it is highly improbable that Mr Bates would have purposely adopted a form of clause which was so disadvantageous as the review clause is with the omission of   *j* any reference to arbitration.

With regard to paragraph (iii), I would myself prefer to relate this point, not to cl 5 of the 1970 lease, but to the exercise of the option under the 1963 lease and the contract which arose from its exercise. The point is, I think, precisely the same point. It is that the parties must have had present to their minds the desirability, and indeed the

obligation of the landlords in relation at any rate to the first seven years of the new term,
a to arrive at a rent which was not necessarily a rent which had to be at the same rate
throughout the term, but they had to arrive at a rent which was agreed between them
or, in default of agreement, was one determined by arbitration.

There was no precedent for a review clause contained in the 1963 lease, for the 1963
lease did not provide for any rent review; and it is not difficult to believe that a layman
like Mr Bates, in preparing the 1970 lease, failed to detect the shortcoming of the review
b clause as he had framed it, and failed to apply his mind to the difficulties which would
arise if no provision was made for reference to arbitration.

On these findings to which I have just referred, the judge rectified the lease. The form
of the order provides as follows:

'THIS COURT DOTH DECLARE that upon the true construction of the Lease dated 17th
December 1970 and made between the Plaintiffs and the Defendants comprising
c factory premises at Church Road, Harold Wood in the London Borough of Havering
the rents during the period of five years from the 15th November 1975 and the
period of four years from the 15th November 1980 should be the market rent for
the said premises. AND THIS COURT DOTH ORDER that the said Lease be rectified so that
in the reddendum thereof after the words "such rents as shall have been agreed
between the Lessor and the Lessee" there be inserted the words "or shall in default
d of such agreement be determined by a single arbitrator to be appointed by the
President for the time being of the Royal Institution of Chartered Surveyors".'

So far as rectification is concerned, the language which the judge has adopted follows
the language used in the option clauses in this case, except that he used the word
'determined' instead of 'fixed', and perhaps it would have been better if the word had
e been 'fixed'.

If the lease is so rectified the question arises: by what measure is an arbitrator to fix the
rent if the parties do not agree? Counsel for the landlords initially contended that the
arbitrator so-called would act not as an arbitrator but as a valuer. He based that argument
on the use of the words 'shall have agreed' and the word 'fixed' in the review clause. On
that basis he submitted that the rent should be the market rent for the property, on the
f authority of a decision of the House of Lords in *Ponsford v HMS Aerosols Ltd* [1978] 2 All
ER 837, [1979] AC 63. Subsequently he conceded that the clause must be read as an
agreement to arbitrate and not as an agreement to abide by a valuation. On that footing
he agreed that, on the true construction of the clause, the rent should be such as it would
have been reasonable for this landlord and this tenant to have agreed under the lease. It
would consequently be proper for the arbitrator to take into account all considerations
which would affect the mind of either party in connection with the negotiation of such
g a rent, as, for example, past expenditure by the tenant on improvements.

In my judgment, counsel for the landlords was right to make that concession and to
have accepted that the present case falls within the reasoning of the minority of the
House of Lords in *Ponsford v HMS Aerosols* and not within the reasoning of the majority
in that case. The review clause which was there under consideration was a review clause
h in a lease which provided for a yearly rent of £9,000—

'during the first seven years of the said term and during the second and third
seven years of the term . . . the sum of NINE THOUSAND POUNDS aforesaid or such sum,
whichever be the higher, as shall be assessed as a reasonable rent for the demised
premises for the appropriate period such assessment to be made in the following
manner that is to say: (a) Such assessment as shall be agreed between the parties
j hereto in writing [and there were certain provisions as to the date by which that
agreement should be reached] (b) In the event of the parties hereto failing to reach
such agreement as aforesaid on or before the dates appointed . . . then the reasonable
rent for the second and third periods shall be fixed or assessed by an independent
surveyor . . .'

That form of clause, as it seems to me, focuses attention on what is there described as 'a reasonable rent for the demised premises' for the appropriate period, and that expression is first used without any reference to agreement between the parties to the lease at all. It then goes on to provide that such assessment (that is to say, the fixing of the amount of the rent so to be charged) shall be either agreed or, in default of agreement, arrived at by valuation by an independent surveyor. That form of wording, in my judgment, certainly affected the views of the majority of the House of Lords in that case. Lord Dilhorne said ([1978] 2 All ER 837 at 842, [1979] AC 63 at 77):

'The rent payable by the tenants will of course be rent for the demised premises, but as I see it the task of the surveyor is not to assess what would be a reasonable rent for the tenants to pay but what is a reasonable rent for the premises.'

Lord Fraser said ([1978] 2 All ER 837 at 847, [1979] AC 63 at 83):

'In my opinion the words point unambiguously to the result contended for by the landlords, and they mean the reasonable rent assessed on an objective basis, without reference to the particular landlord or the particular tenant or to the history of how the premises came to be built or paid for.'

Lord Keith said ([1978] 2 All ER 837 at 850, [1974] AC 63 at 86):

'In my opinion the words "a reasonable rent for the demised premises" simply mean "the rent at which the demised premises might reasonably be expected to let".'

Lord Wilberforce and Lord Salmon took a contrary view. They thought that what had to be ascertained was what would be reasonable between the particular parties to the transaction. However, they were in the minority on the construction of that particular rent review clause. But it appears to me that the terms of the clause there under consideration were noticeably different in important respects from the clause which we have, which refers to nothing other than such rent as the parties shall have agreed. Consequently I think that counsel for the landlord was well advised in making the concession which he made.

Counsel for the tenants, on the other hand, who had argued in the earlier stages of the appeal that in default of agreement the rent should continue after the review date at the original rate of £2,350 per annum, conceded that in the light of a decision of this court in *Beer v Bowden* p 1070, ante, he could no longer support that argument. That again was a concession which I think he was constrained to make. The decision in *Beer v Bowden* was only brought to the attention of counsel and, through counsel, to the attention of the court late in the course of the argument.

So the parties are now at one that, on the true construction of the clause as rectified, the rent is to be fixed by the arbitrator at such amount as it would be reasonable for the parties to agree having regard to all such considerations as I have mentioned. This is not the construction adopted by the judge, who, as appears from the terms of his order, implied a term that the rent to be agreed should be the market rent. His attention had not, of course, been drawn to the decision of this court in *Beer v Bowden*. As I understand the position, neither party now contends that the judge's view in that respect is right, and I myself am satisfied that the market rent would not provide a proper standard to adopt in the present case. In my judgment, in default of agreement between the parties, the arbitrator would have to assess what rent it would have been reasonable for these landlords and these tenants to have agreed under this lease having regard to all the circumstances relevant to any negotiations between them of a new rent from the review date.

If I were wrong on the point of rectification, then, on construction and by a process of implication, the rent to be ascertained in default of agreement must, I think, be a fair rent as between the landlords and the tenants. It would be most unjust that the landlords

should receive no rent because of failure of the parties to agree. The landlords have
a granted a 14-year term and the court must endeavour to fill any gap in the terms of the
lease by means of a fair and reasonable implication as to what the parties must have
intended their bargain to be. See in this connection the decision of this court in *F & G
Sykes (Wessex) Ltd v Fine Fare Ltd* [1967] 1 Lloyd's Rep 53, which was a case very different
on its facts from the present, but in which the court explained the function of any court
of construction where parties have embarked on any commercial relationship but under
b terms that are not altogether adequate to cover the eventualities. The court would
ascertain by inquiry what rent the landlord and the tenant, as willing negotiators anxious
to reach agreement, would arrive at for each of the two rent review periods. In short, the
standard would be the same, as I see it, as would have to be adopted by an arbitrator
under the clause if it is rectified in the way in which I consider that it should be rectified.

For these reasons I think that the judge, while he came to the wrong conclusion on the
c matter of market rent, reached the right conclusion on the matter relating to
rectification. I would accordingly uphold that part of his order which directed
rectification, though I would substitute the word 'fixed' for 'determined', purely as a
matter of pedantry, I think. It is for consideration whether, in those circumstances, any
declaration is really required to be included in the order at all. That is a matter on which,
perhaps, we can hear submissions at a later stage. I would dispose of the matter in that
d way.

EVELEIGH LJ. The correspondence, beginning with 4th May 1970, contained
references to rent reviews. The first reference specifically was:

> 'at a rent to be agreed between us, but in default of such agreement, at a rent to
> be fixed by a single arbitrator appointed by the President for the time being of the
e > Royal Institution of Chartered Surveyors . . .'

The letter of 7th May from the tenants' solicitors accepting the proposed lease for 14
years said merely:

> 'at the exclusive rent of £2,350 per annum, subject to review at the expiration of
> five and ten years of the new term.'
f

Quite clearly that letter was written on the basis that the nature of the review was
understood. It is inconceivable that a solicitor would confirm an agreement and ask for
a draft lease which would, of course, reflect that agreement, as they in fact did, if such an
important matter had not been resolved. The word 'review' was clearly shorthand. I
take the letter of 7th May from the landlords to the tenants in the same way. The phrase
g there used is 'thereafter to be reviewed and agreed for the remainder of the term'. If
anyone had asked the parties at that time how the review would take place, I am quite
convinced that the answer would have been that the machinery contemplated had
already been put forward by Mr Avon of Wyndhams in his letter of 4th May, to which
the letter of the 7th May was a reply.

I see nothing in the words of the other letters written in the course of negotiations
h between the parties to indicate that the review machinery first referred to was being
abandoned in favour of something else. I find it particularly difficult to conclude, as the
tenants contend, that it was being replaced by a vague gentleman's agreement. The fact
that the parties ultimately agreed on a lease of different duration from that originally
agreed, and containing other terms not in the lease of 1963, in no way alters my
conclusion. Certain important changes were specifically discussed. The machinery for
j rent review as opposed to the length of the period was treated without further
discussion. The only reasonable conclusion, in my opinion, must be that the parties were
negotiating on the basis that rent review in default of agreement was to be as indicated
in the letter of 4th May. I therefore think that there was a common intention that the
rent should be fixed by a single arbitrator in default of agreement.

I also think that the evidence established that Mr Avon knew that the lease did not contain the appropriate clause, and knew that Mr Bates intended that it should. Where a party is aware that the instrument does not give effect to the common intention of the parties as communicated each to the other, there may well be an inference of sharp practice or unfair dealing. In my opinion, this will not always be so. I do not think that it is always necessary to show sharp practice. In a case like the present if one party alone knows that the instrument does not give effect to the common intention and changes his mind without telling the other party, then he will be estopped from alleging that the common intention did not continue right up to the moment of the execution of the clause. There is no need to decide whether his conduct amounted to sharp practice. I think he might at that time have had no intention of taking advantage of the mistake of the other party. I do not think that it is necessary to show that the mistake would benefit the party who is aware of it. It is enough that the inaccuracy of the instrument as drafted would be detrimental to the other party, and this may not always mean that it is beneficial to the one who knew of the mistake.

I agree that the lease should be rectified in the way indicated by Buckley LJ and I agree with the order which he proposes. I should just add that I, too, regard this case as different from *Ponsford v HMS Aerosols Ltd* [1978] 2 All ER 837, [1979] AC 63. There the reference was specifically to the demised premises and that is an important difference. Lord Keith said ([1978] 2 All ER 837 at 849, [1979] AC 63 at 85):

> 'At first impression the words "reasonable rent for the demised premises" suggest that what has to be ascertained is simply the rent which is reasonable for the premises as such in their actual state, the situation being viewed entirely objectively. "The demised premises" must mean the demised premises as improved, by virtue of both of the ordinary law and the passage I have quoted from the licence agreement. So on this view any contribution the improvements might have made to the rental value would have to enter into the assessment.'

And he also clearly attached importance to the words 'demised premises' in the passage which Buckley LJ has just read.

For those reasons I agree that the lease should be rectified in the terms stated, and I further agree with the interpretation of 'reasonable rent' that Buckley LJ has given.

BRIGHTMAN LJ. I agree that the order of the deputy judge should stand, subject to minor variation, for the reasons given by Buckley LJ.

I wish to say a few words only on two points. First as regards the standard of proof. The standard of proof required in an action of rectification to establish the common intention of the parties is, in my view, the civil standard of balance of probability. But as the alleged common intention ex hypothesi contradicts the written instrument, convincing proof is required in order to counteract the cogent evidence of the parties' intention displayed by the instrument itself. It is not, I think, the standard of proof which is high, so differing from the normal civil standard, but the evidential requirement needed to counteract the inherent probability that the written instrument truly represents the parties' intention because it is a document signed by the parties.

The standard of proof is no different in a case of so-called unilateral mistake such as the present. The mistake in the instant case was unilateral and not common only because the tenants became aware of the implications of the review clause on the eve of the execution of the new lease. That consideration, as it seems to me, leads to no different conclusion in relation to the standard of proof required in a rectification action.

The other point I want to touch on briefly is this. In his judgment the judge said:

> '. . . the parties recognised the necessity for a longstop for rent fixing purposes and . . . it is reasonable to suppose that it was a provision in these terms which [the

landlords] mistakenly omitted and which [the tenants] (through Mr Avon) deliberately allowed to go uncorrected. In my judgment this was sharp practice . . .'

I would not be prepared to assume, on the evidence, that Mr Avon was consciously guilty of sharp practice. Nor is such an assumption necessary for the landlords' case. As I indicated, I take the view that there was a common intention on both sides to extend to the new lease the rent assessment arrangements contained in the covenant for renewal in the expiring lease. The discrepancy between the formula in the expiring lease and the formula in the engrossment of the new lease was not observed by Mr Avon until it was pointed out by his solicitor. I am not willing to assume that the reputable firm of solicitors acting for him would have allowed him to execute the lease in any circumstances which they saw to be dishonest. If the judgment is intended to contain a finding of sharp practice on the part of Mr Avon, I would respectfully wish to disagree with the learned judge on such a finding. I do not think this would be justified.

As I have said, I agree that the judge's order should, with the slight variation mentioned, stand.

Order of deputy judge directing rectification upheld.

Solicitors: *Chethams* (for the tenants); *Tolhurst & Fisher*, Southend-on-Sea (for the landlords).

Diana Brahams   Barrister.

I Congreso del Partido   *a*

COURT OF APPEAL, CIVIL DIVISION
LORD DENNING MR AND WALLER LJ
3rd, 4th, 5th, 9th, 10th, 11th, 12th JULY, 1st OCTOBER 1979

Constitutional law – Foreign sovereign state – Immunity from suit – Exceptions – Commercial *b*
transaction – Admiralty – Action in rem – Ship owned by foreign sovereign state – Ordinary
trading ship – Foreign sovereign state defaulting in commercial transaction for foreign policy
reasons – Ship owned by Republic of Cuba – Ship used for commercial purposes – Ship delivering
cargo from Cuba to Chile pursuant to contract – Diplomatic relations between Cuba and Chile
severed – Ship diverted from Chile and cargo disposed of elsewhere on orders of Cuban government
– Action in rem against ship brought by cargo owners in respect of non-delivery of cargo – *c*
Whether Republic of Cuba entitled to claim immunity from suit.

Early in 1973 a Cuban state enterprise, Cubazucar, agreed to sell to a Chilean company
a quantity of sugar to be delivered in monthly instalments between January and October
1973. The August instalment was dispatched on two ships, the Playa Larga and the
Marble Islands. Both ships were under voyage charter to Cubazucar from Mambisa, *d*
another Cuban state enterprise. Although Cubazucar and Mambisa were not departments
of the government of Cuba, they were both under the direct control of the Cuban
government. Mambisa was described in the charterparty as the owner of the Playa Larga
and was the demise charterer of the Marble Islands. On 11th September, while the Playa
Larga was in the course of discharging her cargo at Valparaiso in Chile, and the Marble
Islands was still on the high seas bound for Chile, the government in Chile, which had *e*
been on friendly terms with the Cuban government, was overthrown and replaced by a
new government which the Cuban government found to be politically repugnant.
Diplomatic relations between the two countries were severed and Cuba decided to have
no further commercial dealings with Chile. The Cuban government ordered the Playa
Larga to leave Valparaiso immediately and the Marble Islands not to go to Chile. The
Playa Larga returned to Cuba with the remainder of her cargo and the Marble Islands *f*
went to North Vietnam. The cargoes on both ships were then disposed of by Mambisa.
In September 1975 Mambisa, acting on behalf of the Republic of Cuba, took delivery in
England of a new ship, the Congreso, which was an ordinary trading ship registered in
the name of the Republic of Cuba and was intended to be operated and managed by
Mambisa. After Mambisa had taken delivery of the Congreso, the plaintiffs, the Chilean
owners of the cargoes of sugar on board the Playa Larga and the Marble Islands, brought *g*
actions in rem, pursuant to s 3(4)(b)*ᵃ* of the Administration of Justice Act 1956, against
the Congreso as a ship beneficially owned by the Republic of Cuba, which, the plaintiffs
claimed, would have been liable on claims in actions in personam for damages for
conversion and/or breach of contract for non-delivery of the cargoes under s 1(1)(g) and
(h)*ᵇ* of that Act. The Congreso was subsequently arrested in England. The Republic of
Cuba moved to have the plaintiffs' writs set aside on the ground that it was entitled to *h*

---

a Section 3(4), so far as material, provides: 'In the case of any . . . claim arising in connection with a
     ship, where the person who would be liable on the claim in an action in personam was, when the
     cause of the action arose, the owner or charterer of, or in possession or in control of, the ship, the
     Admiralty jurisdiction of the High Court may (whether the claim gives rise to a maritime lien on
     the ship or not) be invoked by an action in rem against—(*a*) that ship, if at the time when the
     action is brought it is beneficially owned as respects all the shares therein by that person; or (*b*) any *j*
     other ship which, at the time when the action is brought, is beneficially owned as aforesaid.'
b Section 1(1), so far as material, provides: 'The Admiralty jurisdiction of the High Court shall be as
     follows, that is to say, jurisdiction to hear and determine any of the following questions or claims
     . . . (*g*) any claim for loss of or damage to goods carried in a ship; (*h*) any claim arising out of any
     agreement relating to the carriage of goods in a ship or to the use or hire of a ship . . .'

invoke sovereign immunity in respect of the proceedings. At the hearing of the motion
a the plaintiffs contended that when a sovereign state engaged in commerce or descended
into the market place it could not later claim sovereign immunity in regard to any
default by it in its transactions. The Republic of Cuba, while conceding that it was not
entitled to absolute immunity from suit, contended that it was entitled to claim
immunity in the circumstances because its action in preventing delivery of the sugar to
the Chilean consignees was done in the exercise of its sovereign authority (jus imperii)
b as part of its foreign policy. The judge ([1978] 1 All ER 1169) upheld the republic's claim
to sovereign immunity and the plaintiffs appealed.

Held – (1) In actions in personam, as in actions in rem, a restrictive rather than an
absolute doctrine of sovereign immunity applied, so that a trading vessel owned by a
foreign sovereign state could be arrested in an action in personam for a trading debt,
c subject however to any claim for sovereign immunity founded on an act done in the
exercise of sovereign authority (jus imperii) (see p 1100 f, p 1101 d to f and p 1107 e,
post); *The Porto Alexandre* [1918–19] All ER Rep 615 and *The Philippine Admiral* [1976] 1
All ER 78 considered.

(2) Whether an act of a sovereign state was jure imperii entitling it to immunity or
merely jure gestionis depended on the nature of the act rather than its purpose and (per
d Waller LJ) on whether the foreign state acted in the exercise of its sovereign authority or
as a private person. Applying that test, the question was (per Lord Denning MR)
whether the dispute before the court brought into question the legislative or international
transactions of the foreign government or (per Waller LJ) whether the whole activity in
dispute was commercial in nature and the foreign state's action was in no way concerned
with sovereignty (see p 1102 a to f, p 1107 e, p 1108 d and p 1109 b c, post); dictum of
e Lord Denning in *Rahimtoola v HEH the Nizam of Hyderabad* [1957] 3 All ER at 463–464,
Claim against the Empire of Iran (1963) 45 ILR 57 and *Victory Transport Inc v Comisaria
General de Abastecimientos y Transportes* (1964) 336 F 2d 354 applied.

(3) (Per Waller LJ, Lord Denning MR dissenting) The decision to prevent the cargoes
of sugar being delivered to their Chilean consignees was a governmental act by the
Republic of Cuba resulting from a political decision in the field of foreign policy which
f bore no relation to commercial interests and the Republic of Cuba was accordingly
entitled to sovereign immunity in respect of the plaintiffs' claims. The court being
evenly divided, the decision appealed against would be affirmed (see p 1109 d to f and h,
post).

Decision of Robert Goff J [1978] 1 All ER 1169 affirmed.

g **Notes**

For sovereign immunity from suit, see 8 Halsbury's Laws (4th Edn) para 410, and for
cases on the subject, see 1(1) Digest (Repl) 54–56, 358–366.

For sovereign immunity and actions in rem and in personam in Admiralty
proceedings, see 1 Halsbury's Laws (4th Edn) paras 304, 310, and for cases on those
subjects, see 1(1) Digest (Reissue) 219–223, 238–232, 1240–1251, 1292–1305.

h For the Administration of Justice Act 1956, ss 1, 3, see 1 Halsbury's Statutes (3rd Edn)
21, 26.

The immunity from the jurisdiction of the courts which foreign sovereign states can
claim is now regulated by the State Immunity Act 1978.

Cases referred to in judgments

j *Aksionairnoye Obschestvo A M Luther v James Sagor & Co* [1921] 3 KB 532, [1921] All ER
Rep 138, 90 LJKB 1202, 125 LT 705, CA, 11 Digest (Reissue) 344, 23.

Alfred Dunhill of London Inc v Republic of Cuba (1976) 425 US 682, 48 US L Ed 2d 301, 96
S Ct 1854 (US Supreme Court).

Anglo-Iranian Oil Co Ltd v Jaffrate, The Rose Mary [1953] 1 WLR 246, 11 Digest (Reissue)
730, 491.

Banco Nacional de Cuba v Sabbatino (1964) 376 US 398.
Carey v National Oil Corpn (1978) 453 F Supp 1097.
Charkieh, The (1873) LR 4 A & E 59, 42 LJ Adm 17, 28 LT 513, 1 Asp MLC 581, 1(1) Digest (Reissue) 57, *373.*
Claim against the Empire of Iran (1963) 45 ILR 57.
Compania Naviera Vascongada v Steamship Cristina [1938] 1 All ER 719, [1938] AC 485, 107 LJP 1, 159 LT 394, 19 Asp MLC 159, HL, 1(1) Digest (Reissue) 228, *1297.*
Czarnikow (C) Ltd v Centrala Handlu Zagranicznego 'Rolimpex' [1978] 1 All ER 81, [1978] QB 176, [1977] 3 WLR 656, [1977] 2 Lloyd's Rep 201, CA; *affd* [1978] 2 All ER 1043, [1979] AC 351, [1978] 3 WLR 274, [1978] 2 Lloyd's Rep 305, HL, Digest (Cont Vol E) 525, *2748b.*
Helbert Wagg & Co Ltd, Re, Re Prudential Assurance Co Ltd [1956] 1 All ER 129, [1956] 1 Ch 323, [1956] 2 WLR 183, 2 Digest (Reissue) 295, *1663.*
Industria Azucarera Nacional SA and Compania de Refineria de Azucar de Vina del Mar v Empresa de Navigación Mambisa, The Imias (1st November 1973) (Civil No 7902) US District Court for the District of the Canal Zone.
Paley (Princess Olga) v Weisz [1929] 1 KB 718, [1929] All ER Rep 513, 98 LJKB 465, 141 LT 207, CA, 11 Digest (Reissue) 717, *412.*
Parlement Belge, The (1880) 5 PD 197, [1874–80] All ER Rep 104, 42 LT 273, 4 Asp MLC 234, CA, 1(1) Digest (Reissue) 220, *1244.*
Philippine Admiral (Owners) v Wallem Shipping (Hong Kong) Ltd, The Philippine Admiral [1976] 1 All ER 78, [1977] AC 373, [1976] 2 WLR 214, [1976] 1 Lloyd's Rep 234, PC, 1(1) Digest (Reissue) 229, *1301.*
Porto Alexandre, The [1920] P 30, [1918–19] All ER Rep 615, 89 LJP 97, 122 LT 661, 15 Asp MLC 1, 1 Ll L Rep 191, CA, 1(1) Digest (Reissue) 228, *1298.*
Rahimtoola v HEH the Nizam of Hyderabad [1957] 3 All ER 441, [1958] AC 379, [1957] 3 WLR 884, HL, 1(1) Digest (Reissue) 60, *389.*
Schooner Exchange, The v McFaddon (1812) 7 Cranch 116.
Spacil v Crowe (1974) 489 F 2d 614.
Thai-Europe Tapioca Service Ltd v Government of Pakistan, Ministry of Food and Agriculture, Directorate of Agricultural Supplies (Imports and Shipping Wing) [1975] 3 All ER 961, [1975] 1 WLR 1485, [1976] 1 Lloyd's Rep 1, CA, 1(1) Digest (Reissue), 54, *362.*
Trendtex Trading Corpn v Central Bank of Nigeria [1977] 1 All ER 881, [1977] QB 529, [1977] 2 WLR 356, [1977] 1 Lloyd's Rep 581, CA; *rvsg* [1976] 3 All ER 437, [1976] 1 WLR 868, 1(1) Digest (Reissue) 59, *382.*
Uganda Co (Holdings) Ltd v Government of Uganda [1979] 1 Lloyd's Rep 481.
United States of America v Dollfus Mieg et Cie SA [1952] 1 All ER 572, [1952] AC 582, HL, 1(1) Digest (Reissue) 60, *388.*
Victory Transport Inc v Comisaria General de Abastecimientos y Transportes (1964) 336 F 2d 354.
Ysmael (Juan) & Co Inc v Government of the Republic of Indonesia [1954] 3 All ER 236, [1955] AC 72, [1954] 3 WLR 531, [1954] 2 Lloyd's Rep 175, PC, 1(1) Digest (Reissue) 231, *1304.*

Cases also cited

Adams v National Bank of Greece SA [1960] 2 All ER 421, [1961] AC 255, HL.
Arantzazu Mendi, The [1939] 1 All ER 719, [1939] AC 256, HL.
Bank Voor Handel en Sheepvaart NV v Administrator of Hungarian Property [1954] 1 All ER 969, [1954] AC 584, HL.
Berizzi Bros Co v SS Pesaro (1925) 271 US 562.
Blad's Case (1673) 3 Swan 603, 36 ER 991, PC.
Brunswick (Duke) v King of Hanover (1848) 2 HL Cas 1, 9 ER 993, HL.
Buttes Gas & Oil Co v Hammer (No 2), Occidental Petroleum Corpn v Buttes Gas & Oil Co [1975] 2 All ER 51, [1975] QB 557, CA.

Charent, The [1942] Nytt Jurisdisk Arkiv 1, Supreme Court of Sweden.

a   *Chilean Copper Corpn, Decision denying third party attachment of copper sold by* (Superior Court of Hamburg, 22nd January 1973) 12 ILM 251.

Danish State Railways in Germany, Re (1953) 20 ILR 178.

Deutsche Bank und Disconto Gesellschaft v Banque des Marchands de Moscou (1932) 107 LJKB 386, CA.

Ditta Campione v Ditta Peti Nitrogenmuveh and Popular Hungarian Republic (1974) Rivista di
b   Diretto Internazionale privato e processuale (14th November 1972, no 3368, Corte di Cassazione).

Duff Development Co Ltd v Government of Kelantan [1924] AC 797, [1924] All ER Rep 1, HL.

Flota Maritima Browning de Cuba SA v SS Canadian Conqueror (1962) 34 DLR (2d) 628.

Fried Krupp AG, Re [1917] 2 Ch 188.

Gagara, The [1919] P 95, [1918–19] All ER Rep 369.

c   *Jassy, The* [1906] P 270.

Jupiter, The [1924] P 236, [1924] All ER Rep 405, CA.

Jurisdiction over Yugoslav Military Mission (30th October 1962), Federal Constitutional Court, Federal Republic of Germany.

Kahan v Federation of Pakistan [1951] 2 KB 1003, CA.

Krol v Bank Indonesia (1958) 26 ILR 180.

d   *Lecouturier v Rey* [1910] AC 262, HL.

Maredelanto Compania Naviera SA v Bergbau-Handel GmbH, The Mihalis Angelos [1970] 3 All ER 125, [1971] QB 164, CA.

Mighell v Sultan of Johore [1894] 1 QB 149, [1891–4] All ER Rep 1019, CA.

National American Corpn v Federal Republic of Nigeria and Central Bank of Nigeria (1978) 448 F Supp 622.

e   *Oppenheimer v Cattermole (Inspector of Taxes), Nothman v Cooper (Inspector of Taxes)* [1975] 1 All ER 538, [1976] AC 249, HL.

Republic of Peru v Dreyfus Brothers & Co (1888) 38 Ch D 348.

Republic of the Philippines (13th December 1977, 2 BVM 1/76), Federal Constitutional Court, Federal Republic of Germany.

Republic of Mexico v Hoffman (1945) 324 US 30.

f   *Secretary of State in Council of India v Kamachee Boye Sahaba* (1859) 13 Moo PCC 22, 19 ER 388, PC.

Société Anonyme Dhlellemes et Masurel v Banque Centrale de la République de Turquie (1963) 45 ILR 85.

Victoria Nyanza, Re certain craft captured on the [1919] P 83.

Wadsworth v Queen of Spain, De Haber v Queen of Portgugal (1851) 17 QB 171, 8 State Tr NS
g   53, 117 ER 1246.

Young v The Scotia [1903] AC 501, PC.

Youssef M Nada Establishment v Central Bank of Nigeria (District Court Frankfurt/M, file No 3/8 o 14/76, announced 25th August 1976).

h   **Interlocutory appeal**

The plaintiffs, the owners of the cargo lately laden on board the vessels Marble Islands and Playa Larga, appealed against the decision of Robert Goff J ([1978] 1 All ER 1169, [1978] QB 500) given on 23rd January 1977 setting aside their writs and all subsequent proceedings in their actions against the owners of the vessel I Congreso del Partido on the grounds that the owners of that vessel were the government of the Republic of Cuba
j   which was entitled to claim, and had claimed, sovereign immunity from the court's jurisdiction. The facts are set out in the judgment of Lord Denning MR.

Robert Alexander QC, Bernard Rix and *Rosalyn Higgins* for the plaintiffs.
Thomas H Bingham QC and *Brian Davenport* for the Republic of Cuba.

Cur adv vult

a

1st October. The following judgments were read.

LORD DENNING MR.

1. *The organisation of Cuba*

The Republic of Cuba is organised on lines with which we are becoming familiar in these courts. The commerce of the country is not in private hands. It is entrusted by the *b* government to state trading enterprises. The sugar trade is in the hands of an enterprise called Empresa Exportadora de Azucar ('Cubazucar'). The shipping is in the hands of another called Empresa de Navegación Mambisa ('Mambisa'). These state enterprises are very like the Polish state organisation Rolimpex which was considered by us and by the House of Lords in *C Czarnikov Ltd v Centrala Handlu Zagranicznego 'Rolimpex'* [1978] 1 All ER 81, [1978] QB 176; [1978] 2 All ER 1043, [1979] AC 351. The state owns the sugar, *c* but Cubazucar buys and sells it. The state owns the ships, but Mambisa has possession and control of them. Each of these state trading organisations must comply with the overall directions of the government; but on day-to-day matters each makes its own decisions about its commercial activities. Neither of them is a department of the government of Cuba. But each is subject to the control of the government and must do as it says.

d

Similarly with Chile. It has a state trading enterprise which holds the majority of shares in a company called Industria Azucarera Nacional SA ('Iansa').

2. *The contracts*

In 1973, when the two countries were on very friendly terms, Cubazucar of Cuba made a contract with Iansa of Chile. Under it Cubazucar was to sell nearly 130,000 *e* metric tons of sugar to Iansa by eight shipments of 10,000 to 20,000 tons each. It was an ordinary commercial contract. The price was $US176·53 per ton, c and f free out to a Chilean port. The purchasers Iansa were to open an irrevocable and confirmed letter of credit payable in Cuba. On shipping the sugar, Cubazucar would take the bills of lading to the National Bank of Cuba and get payment against the shipping documents.

We are concerned here with two of the shipments of sugar. The one of 10,476 tons by *f* a vessel called the Playa Larga. She flew the Cuban flag. She was owned by the Republic of Cuba, but chartered to Mambisa, who sub-chartered her by a voyage charter to Cubazucar. The second of 10,890 tons by a vessel called Marble Islands. She flew the Somali flag and was owned by a Liechtenstein corporation. She was under demise charter to Mambisa, who had sub-chartered her on a voyage charter to Cubazucar.

g

3. *The coup d'état*

On 11th September 1973 there was a coup d'état in Chile. President Allende was killed. His government was overthrown and was replaced by a new government formed by President Pinochet. It was of a very different complexion. From extreme left to extreme right. The Cuban government say that there was violence specially directed at them. Their embassy was attacked. Their vessel, the Playa Larga, was shelled. Their *h* ambassador had to leave for his own safety. They regarded it as a major international incident. It was debated by the Security Council in the United Nations on 17th and 18th September 1973. The Cuban government broke off diplomatic relations with Chile. It froze all Chilean assets. It ordered its vessel to leave. On 27th September 1973 the Cuban government passed a law forbidding all dealings with Chile. It was 'a deliberate act of International policy' and was expressed to take effect from 11th September 1973. *j*

4. *The ships get away*

On the morning of 11th September 1973 the Playa Larga had arrived in Chile and was lying at anchor in the port of Valparaiso. The Chileans had put on board four large cranes for unloading sugar. They belonged to a Chilean corporation, Compania de

Refineria de Azucar de Vina del Mar ('Crav'). She had already discharged part of the
cargo amounting to 2,569 tons, and had on board the remaining part of 7,907 tons, yet
to discharge for delivery to Lansa. She was at anchor awaiting instructions to return to
berth to complete discharging. After the coup d'état the Cuban government gave urgent
instructions to the master. She weighed anchor and started to leave the port with sugar,
cranes and all. The Chileans did their best to stop her. She had no port clearance. They
transmitted radio messages telling her to stop. They sent out a helicopter and a
destroyer. They fired warning shots. But she got away.

The next day, on her way northwards, the Playa Larga met the other vessel, the Marble
Islands. She was at sea a day's journey from Valparaiso. She had on board a cargo of
10,890 tons of sugar. It was also destined for the Chilean importers, Iansa. But she also
had had urgent orders from the Cuban government. Instead of going on to Valparaiso,
she turned round and went northwards in company with the Playa Larga. Together they
sailed north for three days, covering 1,500 miles and then put into Callao, the port for
Lima in Peru. The Chilean ambassador to Peru sent his naval attaché to the vessels. He
asked the captains to discharge the sugar at Callao. Both categorically refused. The
Cuban ambassador made his weight felt. He gave instructions that under no
circumstances was the sugar to be unloaded in Callao.

Five days later the Playa Larga left Callao on her own. She made her way up the coast
of South America, through the Panama Canal, across the Caribbean Sea till she reached
Cuba. She discharged her cargo of sugar there on 5th October 1973, ie 3½ weeks after
leaving Valparaiso. The Cuban authorities took possession of the sugar and supplied it
to their own people in Cuba for their own use.

The Marble Islands had a more exciting time. She stayed at Callao a further week.
Then she left on 27th September 1973 and went north, hoping to go through the
Panama Canal on the way to Cuba. But when she got to Balboa at the Pacific end of the
Canal the Chilean importers Iansa got her arrested by the United States authorities in the
Canal Zone, because of their claim to the sugar. The master was not the sort of man to
submit to this interference. Nor was the Cuban government. He broke arrest, and sailed
off to the west. He went on for days and days across the wide stretches of the Pacific. No
doubt he put into some port for bunkers. Perhaps to Yokohama or Hong Kong. Then
across the South China Sea until he reached a country friendly to Cuba. It was North
Vietnam. He berthed at Haiphong, the port for Hanoi. It was on 6th November 1973,
nearly six weeks after he had left Callao. At Haiphong he unloaded her cargo of sugar.
The Cuban authorities presented it to the people of Vietnam as a gift. Meantime, whilst
she was crossing the Pacific, on 13th October 1973, she had been purchased from her
Liechtenstein owners by the Republic of Cuba.

5. The ownership of the sugar

The Chilean importers Iansa were very angry about all this. The sugar in both ships
belonged to them. They had paid for it and got the shipping documents. They had
opened letters of credit which had been honoured. The payment for the cargo on the
Playa Larga had been made and the documents received on 29th August 1973, long
before the coup d'état. They had also paid for the cargo in the Marble Islands. Their
correspondent bank in Paris had paid on 14th September 1973 in the belief that the
documents for the Marble Islands had been presented by Cubazucar on 11th September
1973, before the coup d'état.

Beyond all doubt Iansa had paid for both cargoes and Cubazucar had received the
payment. The owners of the four large cranes, the Chilean corporation Crav, were
equally angry. They had lost their cranes beyond recall.

6. The arrest of the Imias

The Chileans then discovered that the Imias, a vessel owner by the Cuban government
(and run by Mambisa), was passing through the Panama Canal zone. The Chilean
importers and crane owners determined to get her. They issued writs in the United

States Canal Zone District Court against Mambisa claiming more than $US4m. They served the Imias with a writ of foreign attachment and arrested her. The Cuban *a* government claimed her release on the ground of sovereign immunity. The United States Department of State conceded it, whereupon the District Court allowed her to go free: see *Spacil v Crowe* (1974) 489 F 2d 614. A well-informed commentator suggests that 'diplomatic and political considerations were deemed to be of overriding importance'; see Professor Monroe Leigh, 'Sovereign Immunity—The Case of the "Imias"' (1974) 68 American Journal of International Law 280–289. *b*

7. *The arbitration*

In November 1974 Iansa commenced arbitration proceedings against Cubazucar before the Sugar Association in London. They were so protracted that an award was not made until 18th April 1978. The arbitrators then made an award in the form of a special case. It has not yet come before the court for decision. *c*

In the course of the arbitration the arbitrators inquired closely into the circumstances in which the cargoes were diverted. They found that the decisions were taken during the morning of 11th September 1973 at a high level in the Cuban government; and that Cubazucar were involved in and party to those decisions. They found that at that time, on 11th September 1973, the documents for the Marble Islands had not been presented for payment; that at that very time Cubazucar and their bankers, the National Bank of *d* Cuba ('NBC'), knew that the Marble Islands had been diverted; and nevertheless thereafter with knowledge of her diversion, presented documents for payment; and got payment from them. The arbitrators found that Cubazucar and NBC were parties to an attempt (which as things turned out proved successful) to obtain payment for the sugar on board the vessel, well knowing that there was no likelihood that the cargo would be delivered to Iansa. *e*

We allowed the arbitrators' award to be put before us on the footing that their findings were in no way binding on the Republic of Cuba and that we would only look at them for what they were worth. The telexes set out in the award go far to support those findings. So much so that I think we should have regard to them in so far as they are relevant to the issue we have to decide. *f*

8. *The sister ship, I Congreso del Partido, comes on the scene*

Meanwhile, whilst the arbitration was going its slow length along, Iansa saw an opportunity of getting redress in another way. They discovered that a new vessel was being built at a yard in Sunderland, here in England. She was being built for a Liberian company; but, whilst she was still on the stocks, the Liberian company had assigned the benefit of the contract to the Cuban state shipping enterprise, Mambisa. On 3rd *g* September 1975 she completed her sea trials. On 5th September 1975, ie two days later, Mambisa took delivery of her on behalf of the Republic of Cuba. She was named I Congreso del Partido ('the Congreso'), and was entered in the Cuban registry in the name of the Republic of Cuba as owners of her. She was a trading vessel and intended for use for trading.

Iansa were quick to seize the opportunity. Within four days they started an action in *h* rem here in England, and arrested the Congreso. A few weeks later they started two more actions in rem and rearrested her. In due course security was given. She was released from arrest and went trading for Cuba. So the dispute has been transferred from the ship to the security.

9. *These actions* *j*

In these actions the plaintiffs were described as 'The owners of cargo lately laden on board the ship or vessel "Playa Larga" [or "Marble Islands" as the case may be]'; and the defendants as 'The owners . . . [of] the ship or vessel "I Congreso del Partido"'.

For some time in these actions the plaintiffs Iansa sought to make Mambisa liable; and this was canvassed extensively before the judge. But all that has disappeared now. Only two actions remain in being. The plaintiffs now only seek to make the Republic of Cuba

a   liable. They say that the Republic of Cuba were the owners of the Playa Larga and the
Marble Islands, and that they have claims against the Republic of Cuba for the loss of the
cargoes on those vessels, and that the Republic of Cuba were liable in personam for
them. So much so that the Admiralty Court has jurisdiction to determine the claims in
personam under ss 1(1)(g) and (h) and 3(1) of the Administration of Justice Act 1956.
They go on to say that, at the time when the actions were brought in late 1975, the new

b   vessel, the Congreso, was beneficially owned by the Republic of Cuba, and that in
consequence the Admiralty jurisdiction can be invoked by an action in rem against the
Congreso by virtue of s 3(4)(b) of the 1956 Act.

10. *The effect of s 3(4)(b) of the 1956 Act*
In applying s 3(4)(b) you have first to consider the position at the time *when the cause of*

c   *action arose* in connection with the offending ship. You have then to discover *a person*
who would be 'liable on the claim in an action in personam'. Having discovered him,
you have to consider the position *at the time when the action is brought.* You have then to
inquire whether that person at that time beneficially owned any other ship (a sister ship)
besides the offending ship. If there is such a person, you can invoke the Admiralty
jurisdiction of the High Court against that sister ship.

d   Now in this case the plaintiffs say that the Cuban government were that person. They
say that that government was liable in personam at the time when the cause of action
arose; and that that government were the beneficial owners of that sister ship, the
Congreso, at the time when the action was brought.
It is quite clear that the Cuban government owned the Congreso at the time when the
actions were brought. So the inquiry is only whether the Cuban government were liable

e   in personam at the time when the cause of action arose.

11. *The liability in personam*
On that analysis, it seems to me that we can put on one side any complication about
the sister ship. The legal position is just the same as it would be if the Playa Larga on her

f   way back had put into Kingston, Jamaica, and had been arrested there; or if the Marble
Islands had put into Hong Kong after 13th October 1973 and had been arrested there.
At those times would the Cuban government be liable in personam for the claims of the
Chileans? I think the Cuban government would be and for these reasons.
First, so far as the Playa Larga is concerned, the Chilean importers have a claim for
damages for breach of contract. It arises out of the bill of lading dated 9th August

g   1973. That says in express terms that this contract of carriage is entered into with 'the
owner of the above-named ship'. The consignee was named as Industria Azucarera
Nacional SA (Iansa). The owners were the Cuban government. The failure to deliver at
Valparaiso was clearly a breach of contract unless excused by some defence such as
frustration or force majeure.
Furthermore, so far as the Playa Larga is concerned, the Chilean importers, Iansa, have

h   claims in tort against the Cuban government for detinue or conversion of the sugar,
starting with the carrying of it off to Callao, then the refusal to deliver at Callao, and
eventually the disposal of it in Cuba.
Second, so far as the Marble Islands is concerned, their claim is solely in tort for detinue
or conversion. The Cuban government only became owners of the vessel on 13th
October 1973 when she was crossing the Pacific; but they clearly converted the sugar

j   when she reached Haiphong on 6th November 1973. They unloaded it and presented it
to the people of Hiaphong as a gift.
So the Cuban government are to my mind clearly a person who would be liable on the
claim in an action in personam when the cause of action arose. Save for this one point,
and it is the great point in the case: is the Cuban government entitled to claim sovereign
immunity, so as to deprive the court of any jurisdiction in the matter?

12. *The restrictive doctrine of sovereign immunity*

Until a few years ago this case would have been covered by *The Porto Alexandre* [1920] **a**
P 30, [1918–19] All ER Rep 615. It was there held by the Court of Appeal that, in an
action in rem, a trading vessel owned by a sovereign state was immune from arrest, even
when it incurred ordinary trading debts or liabilities. In that case it was for salvage.
That was in the days when this country adopted and applied the absolute doctrine of
sovereign immunity. But it was not followed by the Privy Council in *The Philippine*
Admiral [1976] 1 All ER 78, [1977] AC 373. It was there held that, in an action in rem, **b**
a trading vessel owned by a sovereign state could be arrested for a trading debt. In that
case it was for goods supplied and disbursements made for the ship. Strangely enough,
however, the Privy Council confined themselves to actions in rem. They seem to have
thought that, in actions in personam, a foreign sovereign was still absolutely entitled to
invoke the doctrine of sovereign immunity (see (1976) 1 All ER 78 at 95–96, [1977] AC
373 at 402–403). Such was the view of Lawton and Scarman LJJ in *Thai-Europe Tapioca* **c**
Service Ltd v Government of Pakistan [1975] 3 All ER 961, [1975] 1 WLR 1485 and of
Donaldson J in *Uganda Co (Holdings) Ltd v Government of Uganda* [1979] 1 Lloyd's Rep
481. In *Trendtex Trading Corpn v Central Bank of Nigeria* [1977] 1 All ER 881, [1977] QB
529, however, Shaw LJ and I took a different view. I said of the restrictive theory ([1977]
1 All ER 881 at 891, [1977] QB 527 at 556–557):

> 'It covers actions in personam. In those actions, too, the restrictive theory is more **d**
> consonant with justice. So it should be applied to them. It should not be retained
> as an indefensible anomaly.'

My view has been reinforced by several important events. First, the United States of
America has passed the Foreign Sovereign Immunities Act 1976 adopting the restrictive
theory. Second, the United Kingdom has passed the State Immunity Act 1978 also **e**
adopting it. Third, the United Kingdom has ratified the European Conventions of 1926
and 1972 also adopting it (see the International Convention for the Unification of Certain
Rules concerning the Immunity of State-owned Ships 1926 (Misc 2 (1938); Cmd 5672)
and the European Convention on State Immunity 1972 (Misc 31 (1972); Cmnd 5081).

In view of these developments I think it plain that the absolute doctrine is no longer
part of international law. The restrictive theory holds the field in international law, and **f**
by reason of the doctrine of incorporation it should be applied by the English courts, not
only in actions in rem but also in actions in personam. The difficulty lies, however, in
applying it to the various situations which arise.

13. *State trading vessels*

Ships of war, and ships of a sovereign state 'destined for its public use', have always **g**
been considered to be absolutely immune from arrest. Even if they were involved in a
collision with a merchantman, they could not be arrested in rem; nor could the sovereign
be sued in personam. Such was established in the United States in the great case of *The*
Schooner Exchange v McFaddon (1812) 7 Cranch 116 and in England in *The Parlement Belge*
(1880) 5 PD 197, [1874–80] All ER Rep 104, though the position now is modified in
regard to collisions etc by the Brussels Convention of 1926. **h**

That doctrine about warships was wrongly extended in *The Porto Alexandre* [1920] P
30, [1918–19] All ER Rep 615 to state trading vessels. But now that that case is no longer
law, I am of opinion that we can go back to the law as stated by that great international
lawyer Sir Robert Phillimore over 100 years ago in *The Charkieh* (1873) LR 4 A & E 59.
That vessel was owned by the Khedive of Egypt. She was used as an ordinary merchant
trading vessel. She was in collision in the Thames. Sir Robert Phillimore said (at 99– **j**
100):

> 'No principle of international law, and no decided case, and no dictum of jurists
> of which I am aware, has gone so far as to authorize a sovereign prince to assume the
> character of a trader, when it is for his benefit; and when he incurs an obligation to

a a private subject to throw off, if I may so speak, his disguise, and appear as a sovereign, claiming for his own benefit, and to the injury of a private person, for the first time, all the attributes of his character . . . assuming the privilege to exist, it has been waived with reference to this ship by the conduct of the person who claims it.'

This view of international law is strongly supported by the Brussels Convention of 1926. Article 1 says:

b 'Sea-going ships owned or operated by States, cargoes owned by them, and cargoes and passengers carried on State owned ships, as well as the States which own or operate such ships and own such cargoes shall be subject, as regards claims in respect of the operation of such ships or in respect of the carriage of such cargoes, to the same rules of liability and the same obligations as those applicable in the case of privately-owned ships, cargoes and equipment.'

c Article 3 makes an exception in the case of ships of war etc.

Similar provisions are contained in the Foreign Sovereign Immunities Act 1976 (90 Stat 2891), § 1605(a), (b) in the United States, and in our State Immunity Act 1978. I refer especially to s 10(2) which says:

d 'A State is not immune as respects—(a) an action in rem against a ship belonging to that State; or (b) an action in personam for enforcing a claim in connection with such a ship, if, at the time when the cause of action arose, the ship was in use or intended for use for commercial purposes.'

So, in regard to state trading vessels, I take it that when a sovereign chooses to go into the markets of the world so as to let out his vessel for hire or to carry goods for freight, just like an ordinary private shipowner for commercial purposes, then he clothes himself *e* in the dress of an ordinary ship's captain. He is liable to be sued on his contract or for his wrongs in the courts of any country which has jurisdiction in the cause. He cannot renounce the jurisdiction by a plea of sovereign immunity. He can, of course, plead frustration, or force majeure, if and in so far as they afford a defence. But he must face the music. He seeks like an actor to run behind the arras and come out saying: 'Look, I *f* am no longer a ship's captain. I wear the crown of a king. You cannot sue me.' That he should not be allowed to do.

If this view be correct, there is no need to go further, at any rate so far as the Playa Larga is concerned. The Cuban state owned her and used her, or permitted her to be used, for the carriage of sugar on an ordinary trading voyage. The Cuban state cannot avail themselves of sovereign immunity in respect of any loss of or damage to cargo arising out of or in consequence of that trading, no matter what the cause be of that loss *g* or damage.

14. *Sovereign authority*

It was submitted, however, by counsel for the Republic of Cuba that, in these cases and in all others, the sovereign can claim immunity when the acts which caused the loss or *h* damage were done by him in the exercise of his sovereign authority, or, as it is put in Latin, jure imperii, as distinct from jure gestionis. This is a very elusive test. As to what acts fall within it is anyone's guess. As Terence says in Phormio 454: 'Quot homines tot sententiae: suo quoique mos' (So many men, so many opinions: his own a law to himself) (see Phormio 454).

But, however elusive the test, counsel for the Republic of Cuba submits that action in *j* the foreign relations or diplomatic field falls squarely within the category of 'sovereign governmental acts'. In the present case, he said, the acts done by the government of Cuba were taken in the foreign relations field following a violent military coup against the government of a close ally, and were therefore sovereign governmental acts, jure imperii.

On this point we were referred to masses of cases and textbooks in many languages of many countries and to masses of affidavits by professors of international law all over the

world. I stand amazed at the time and money which the parties have expended on this
case.

15. The nature of the act, not its purpose
One thing seems to be reasonably clear. Immunity depends on the nature of the act
and not on its purpose. After much research I declared in *Rahimtoola v HEH the Nizam of
Hyderabad* [1957] 3 All ER 441 at 463–464, [1958] AC 379 at 422, in a passage which
counsel for the Republic of Cuba was good enough to commend:

> '... at the present time sovereign immunity should not depend on whether a
> foreign government is impleaded, directly or indirectly, but rather on the nature of
> the dispute. Not on whether "conflicting rights have to be decided," but on the
> nature of the conflict. Is it properly cognizable by our courts or not? If the dispute
> brings into question, for instance, the legislative or international transactions of a
> foreign government, or the policy of its executive, the court should grant immunity
> if asked to do so, because it does offend the dignity of a foreign sovereign to have the
> merits of such a dispute canvassed in the domestic courts of another country; but if
> the dispute concerns, for instance, the commercial transactions of a foreign
> government (whether carried on by its own departments or agencies or by setting
> up separate legal entities), and it arises properly within the territorial jurisdiction of
> our courts, there is no ground for granting immunity.'

The only qualification I need make to that passage today is that the phrase about
'territorial jurisdiction of our courts' has no application to an action in rem against a
foreign state owned trading ship, for the reasons stated by Robert Goff J in the present
case (see [1978] 1 All ER 1169 at 1197–1198, [1978] QB 500 at 534).

Subject to that qualification, that passage has virtually been adopted by Parliament in
the State Immunity Act 1978 in s 3(1) in relation to commercial transactions: and in
s 14(2) in regard to separate legal entities.

Whenever that passage comes to be applied, you must remember that there is always
some action taken or omitted by the foreign government or by one of their separate legal
entities which gives rise to the dispute. Sovereign immunity depends on the nature of
that action: not on the purpose or intent or motive, use whichever word you like, with
which it is done. To prove this I would take the old chestnut. All the pundits say that
when a government department places an order for boots for the army it is acting jure
gestionis, not jure imperii; but when it places an order for guns it is jure imperii. I
cannot accept that distinction. Suppose the navy department of a foreign government
orders a helicopter for military purposes and their agriculture department orders a like
helicopter for surveying the fields. In neither case is the foreign government entitled to
sovereign immunity. The seller is not concerned with the purpose for which the
helicopter is required. Likewise with a gun. The seller is not concerned whether the
foreign government want it to kill an enemy or to fire a salute or to train recruits.
Whenever a foreign government order goods or services of a trader, they ought to pay for
them, no matter for what purpose they intend to use them. Especially in these days
when foreign governments order many goods and engage many services in the name of
their state trading enterprises. If they refuse to take delivery, they ought to pay damages,
unless they have some defence such as frustration or force majeure.

This view is supported by the case of *Claim against the Empire of Iran* (1963) 45 ILR 57
at 60 in which the Federal Constitutional Court of West Germany considered many
authorities in many countries and said:

> 'As a means for determining the distinction between acts *jure imperii* and *jure
> gestionis* one should rather refer to the nature of the State transaction or the resulting
> legal relationships, and not to the motive or purpose of the State activity.'

Finally, in the Foreign Sovereign Immunities Act 1976 of the United States in
§ 1603(d) it says: 'The commercial character of an activity shall be determined by

reference to the nature of the course of conduct or particular transaction or act, rather
a than by reference to its purpose.'

16. *Actions such as nationalisation, requisition and confiscation*
We were referred to many actions which undoubtedly attract sovereign immunity by
their very nature. Such as the familiar case where a foreign government, by legislative
measures, nationalise property or a business situated in their own country, no matter
b whether it is the property or business of their own nationals or others, providing they are
ready to pay compensation to those affected: see *Aksionairnoye Obschestvo A M Luther v
James Sagor & Co* [1921] 3 KB 532, [1921] All ER Rep 138, *Princess Olga Paley v Weisz*
[1929] 1 KB 718, [1929] All ER Rep 513, *Re Helbert Wagg & Co Ltd* [1956] 1 All ER 129
at 140, [1956] 1 Ch 323 at 348–349 and *Carey v National Oil Corpn* (1978) 453 F Supp
1097. Next, the equally familiar case where a foreign government, by legislative or
c executive measures, requisitions the property of their own subjects for the public use of
that country, even though the property may not be inside their territory at the time,
provided again that they are ready to pay compensation for the hire of it (see *The Cristina*
[1938] 1 All ER 719, [1938] AC 485); or the case which sometimes occurs where a
foreign government take possession of the property of others, for safe custody, without
confiscating it (see the 51 bars in *United States of America v Dollfus Mieg et Cie SA* [1952] 1
d All ER 572, [1952] AC 582); or the cases where there is a custodian of enemy property.
In all those cases the sovereign is entitled to immunity.
But confiscation or expropriation by a foreign government of the property of aliens
resident there, without compensation, is contrary to international law; and the foreign
government have no immunity in respect of it: see the 13 bars in *United States of America
v Dollfus Mieg et Cie SA* [1952] 1 All ER 572, [1952] AC 582, *Anglo-Iranian Oil Co Ltd v
e* *Jaffrate, The Rose Mary* [1953] 1 WLR 246, the dissenting judgment of White J in *Banco
Nacional de Cuba v Sabbatino* (1964) 376 US 398 and the European cases he cites in *Alfred
Dunhill of London Inc v Republic of Cuba* (1976) 425 US 682 at 709–710.
In all those cases the action by the government comes 'out of the blue' so as to injure
the individual or deprive him of his property. Those cases have no application here
because the transactions originated with the government themselves. It was the initial
f trading step which enabled them to do what they did.

17. *The nature of the act here*
In the case of the Playa Larga the origin of all that happened was a simple commercial
transaction by which the government of Cuba agreed to carry sugar to Chile and deliver
it to the Chilean importers. When the Playa Larga got to Valparaiso and failed or refused
g to deliver the cargo of sugar there, and afterwards refused at Callao, that was a plain
repudiation and breach of that contract. Such an act, a plain repudiation of a contract,
cannot be regarded as an act of such a nature as to give rise to sovereign immunity. It
matters not what was the purpose of the repudiation. If it had been done for economic
reasons, as, for instance, because the market price of sugar had risen sharply, it could not
possibly have given rise to sovereign immunity. If it had been done for humanitarian
h reasons, as, for instance, because the Cuban government were short of sugar for their
own people, or wanted to give it to the people of North Vietnam, equally it could not
possibly have given rise to sovereign immunity. It was in fact done out of anger at the
coup d'état in Chile, and out of hostility to the new regime. That motive cannot alter the
nature of the act. Nor can it give sovereign immunity where otherwise there would be
none. It is the nature of the act that matters, not the motive behind it. This is supported
j by the decision itself in *Trendtex Trading Corpn v Central Bank of Nigeria* [1977] 1 All ER
881, [1977] QB 529, and the parallel decisions in Germany and the United States. No one
suggested that the policy of the new Nigerian government afforded any answer. It is also
supported by the reasoning of four wise judges of the United States Supreme Court in
Alfred Dunhill of London Inc v Republic of Cuba (1976) 425 US 682 at 695, who held that 'the
concept of an act of state should not be extended to include the repudiation of a purely

commercial obligation owed by a foreign sovereign or by one of its commercial instrumentalities'. That case concerned the United States doctrine of act of state, which *a* is similar to our doctrine of sovereign immunity.

In the case of the Marble Islands the origin of all that happened was a simple commercial transaction by which one of the state organisations of Cuba agreed to carry sugar to Chile and deliver it to the Chilean importers. The Cuban government induced their state organisation to repudiate that contract and ordered it to carry the sugar to North Vietnam. The Cuban government then bought the vessel and, by their conduct, *b* adopted the repudiation as their own. They continued the repudiative act and went on to carry the sugar to North Vietnam and handed it to the people there. The nature of the transaction was again the repudiation of a purely commercial obligation. Its purpose was twofold: to show their hostility to Chile and to help the people of Vietnam. But the purpose does not matter. The act by its very nature was an act of repudiating a binding commercial obligation. Such an act does not give rise to sovereign immunity. *c*

Conclusion

I would not leave this important case without a word of tribute to Robert Goff J who tried the case. Many of the points argued before him have not been reargued before us, because the parties accepted his decision on them. The one point on which I do differ from him is that he regards the diversion of the two cargoes as 'essentially an act of *d* foreign policy', whereas I regard it as essentially a repudiative breach of contract. Foreign policy afforded only the motive for the act. It did not affect the nature of it. When the government of a country enter into an ordinary trading transaction, they cannot afterwards be permitted to repudiate it and get out of their liabilities by saying that they did it out of high governmental policy or foreign policy or any other policy. They cannot come down like a god on to the stage, the deus ex machina, as if they had nothing *e* to do with it beforehand. They started as a trader and must end as a trader. They can be sued in the courts of law for their breaches of contract and for their wrongs just as any other trader can. They have no sovereign immunity. I would allow the appeal accordingly.

WALLER LJ. In these actions Robert Goff J on 27th January 1977 held that the *f* Republic of Cuba, as owner of the Congreso, were entitled to invoke sovereign immunity. The plaintiffs appeal against that decision on the grounds, among others, that the ship was a commercial ship on a commercial venture and accordingly is not entitled to immunity. The judgment of the judge is reported ([1978] 1 All ER 1169, [1978] QB 500), and it is convenient to refer to parts of that to save repetition.

Save for one matter, I see no reason to differ from any of the provisional findings of fact *g* made by the judge (see [1978] 1 All ER 1169 at 1175–1181, [1978] QB 500 at 506–513). I agree with the judge's finding that the decision by the government that the Playa Larga should leave Valparaiso was taken partly out of concern for the safety of the ship. We were invited at the hearing of this appeal to consider an award in arbitration proceedings between Iansa and Cubazucar; I do not consider it would be proper to incorporate findings by arbitrators in proceedings where the parties were different. I am of opinion, *h* however, that sufficient information is before us to say that the decision was also influenced by the deterioration of relations between Cuba and Chile which culminated in the termination of diplomatic relations within 24 hours.

I do not find it necessary to repeat here the details of the proceedings before Robert Goff J which are fully set out in his judgment (see [1978] 1 All ER 1196 at 1181–1183, [1978] QB 500 at 513–517). This appeal relates to the second and third actions there *j* mentioned.

Before dealing with the essential issues in this dispute, Robert Goff J had to consider whether or not he was bound by the decision in *The Porto Alexandre* [1920] P 30, [1918–19] All ER Rep 615. The Privy Council in *The Philippine Admiral* [1976] 1 All ER 78 at

89, [1977] AC 373 at 395, considered the principles to be applied in actions in rem when

a sovereign immunity was claimed. Lord Cross quoted the well-known passage from the speech of Lord Atkin in *The Christina* [1938] 1 All ER 719 at 720–721, [1938] AC 485 at 490, setting out the doctrine of sovereign immunity:

> 'The foundation for the application to set aside the writ and arrest of the ship is
> to be found in two propositions of international law engrafted on to our domestic
> law which seem to me to be well-established and to be beyond dispute. The first is
b > that the courts of a country will not implead a foreign sovereign. That is, they will
> not by their process make him against his will a party to legal proceedings, whether
> the proceedings involve process against his person or seek to recover from him
> specific property or damages. The second is that they will not by their process,
> whether the sovereign is a party to the proceedings or not, seize or detain property
> which is his, or of which he is in possession or control.'

c
Lord Cross thereafter considered a number of other cases which I do not here repeat and set out his conclusion (see [1976] 1 All ER 78 at 95–96, [1977] AC 373 at 402–403). Robert Goff J came to the conclusion that he was not bound by the decision in *The Porto Alexandre*. The contrary was not argued before this court. I entirely agree with the reasoning of the judge.

d Were it not for this conclusion, the plaintiffs would have been in an impossible position because in *The Porto Alexandre* the Court of Appeal held that *The Parlement Belge* (1880) 5 PD 197, [1874–80] All ER Rep 104 had decided that any ship owned by or in the possession of a foreign sovereign enjoys immunity in an English court irrespective of the use to which it is put. The present case therefore presents an entirely new problem and one which did not arise in *The Philippine Admiral*. Robert Goff J stated it as follows

e ([1978] 1 All ER 1169 at 1189, [1978] QB 500 at 524):

> 'It was common ground between the parties that, where a plaintiff proceeds by
> way of an action in rem against an ordinary trading ship, then even though such
> vessel is the property of a foreign sovereign he cannot have the writ set aside on the
> ground of sovereign immunity where the claim arises out of the ordinary operations
> of the vessel as a trading vessel ... It must also follow ... that the position would
f > be the same if the vessel arrested was an ordinary trading vessel in the ownership of
> a foreign sovereign, and that vessel was the sister ship of another ordinary trading
> vessel in the same ownership out of whose ordinary trading operations the claim
> arose ... But the question which arises in the present case, and did not arise in *The
> Philippine Admiral*, is this: what if the claim, in respect of which an ordinary trading
> vessel belonging to a foreign sovereign is arrested, arises as a result of a governmental
g > act of that sovereign? In those circumstances should the English court set aside the
> proceedings on the ground that the foreign sovereign is impleaded?'

Counsel for the plaintiffs submitted that when the sovereign engages in commerce or, as he put it, descends into the market place, and is the owner of a vessel which is an ordinary trading vessel no claim for immunity can arise and that it is inappropriate to

h examine the motive for the breach. Counsel for the Republic of Cuba, while accepting that the restrictive doctrine of sovereign immunity applies, submitted that the fundamental principle was to refuse jurisdiction where the defendant is a friendly foreign government and the dispute concerns the sovereign public acts of that government.

We have been referred to a very large number of decisions both in the United States

j of America, which, like Britain, adopted until comparatively recently the absolute doctrine of sovereign immunity, and from other countries in Europe which have for very many years adopted the restrictive doctrine of sovereign immunity. None of the decisions is directly in point. In no case has the commercial character of the vessel and the non-commercial sovereign act of the state been in such conflict as in the present case.

In *Rahimtoola v HEH the Nizam of Hyderabad* [1957] 3 All ER 441 at 463–464, [1958] AC 379 at 422 Lord Denning, when dealing with the resolution of conflict of authority, said: *a*

'Faced with an inconsistency between two lines of cases, the only course is to see which is more consistent with the principle. For this I go back, as UPJOHN J did, to the words of that great international lawyer SIR ROBERT PHILLIMORE in *The Charkieh* ((1873) LR 4 A & E 59 at 97) who, after a full review of the authorities, said this: "The object of international law, in this as in other matters, is not to work injustice, not to prevent the enforcement of a just demand, but to substitute negotiations *b* between governments, though they may be dilatory and the issue distant and uncertain, for the ordinary use of courts of justice in cases where such use would lessen the dignity or embarrass the functions of the representatives of a foreign state ..." Applying this principle it seems to me that at the present time sovereign immunity should not depend on whether a foreign government is impleaded, directly or indirectly, but rather on the nature of the dispute. Not on whether *c* "conflicting rights have to be decided," but on the nature of the conflict. Is it properly cognizable by our courts or not? If the dispute brings into question, for instance, the legislative or international transactions of a foreign government, or the policy of its executive, the court should grant immunity if asked to do so, because it does offend the dignity of a foreign sovereign to have the merits of such a dispute canvassed in the domestic courts of another country; but if the dispute concerns, for *d* instance, the commercial transactions of a foreign government (whether carried on by its own departments or agencies or by setting up separate legal entities), and it arises properly within the territorial jurisdiction of our courts, there is no ground for granting immunity.'

Of the many cases cited which together show the approach of other countries to the *e* question of sovereign immunity I only wish to quote two. The first is the case of *Claim against the Empire of Iran* (1963) 45 ILR 57, decided by the Federal Constitutional Court of the Federal Republic of Germany in April 1963. Although the facts there were very different from the present case, the court considered with great care the application of the doctrine of sovereign immunity in a number of different countries. There are observations in the *Empire of Iran* case 45 ILR 57 at 64–81 cited from decisions of courts *f* in different countries which are helpful in showing the approach made in those countries when distinguishing between acta jure imperii and acta jure gestionis. In Belgium the Court of Appeal of Ghent in 1879 said:

'When however the state having regard to the needs of the community does not limit itself to its political role but acquires and owns property, concludes contracts, becomes a creditor or debtor or even engages in trade, it is not acting in the sphere *g* of public authority but as a civil or private person.'

(See 45 ILR 57 at 64.)

The Austrian Supreme Court asserted jurisdiction over Turkey in respect of a claim for payment for certain building work carried out at the Turkish Embassy in Vienna and said: *h*

'In private law actions which in no way touched on the sovereignty of the State claimed against, the foreign State also had to be subject to Courts of the State where the business was situated.'

(See 45 ILR 57 at 66.)

And in another Austrian case also cited the court, following the decision just quoted, *j* examined 'whether the plaintiff is claiming against the sued State on the strength of a private law relationship or one in its sovereign domain' and said:

'In order to decide whether a private or sovereign act was involved, the act (which was carried out by organs of the State) is to be judged not by its aim or its purpose;

whether an act of one or the other sort is involved "is to be determined" from the nature of the legal proceeding, *i.e.* "from the inherent internal character of the transaction or from the legal relations created".'

(See 45 ILR 57 at 66.)

And a quotation in relation to the Greek courts was:

'State immunity is limited to activities which a State engages in as a sovereign political power and does not extend to matters which arise from activities—such as the administration of property—which in no way concern its sovereignty.'

(See 45 ILR 57 at 68.)

And later in the judgment in the *Empire of Iran* case the court said this (at 80):

'As a means for determining the distinction between acts *jure imperii* and *jure gestionis* one should rather refer to the nature of the State transaction or the resulting legal relationships, and not to the motive or purpose of the State activity. It thus depends on whether the foreign State has acted in exercise of its sovereign authority, that is in public law, or like a private person, that is in private law.'

And lastly (at 81):

'National law can only be employed to distinguish between a sovereign and non-sovereign activity of a foreign State in so far as it cannot exclude from the sovereign sphere, and thus from immunity, such State dealings as belong to the field of State authority in the narrow and proper sense, according to the predominantly-held view of States.'

These quotations do lend support to the argument that the act which causes the claim has to be examined and that the claim for sovereign immunity is defeated when the whole activity is commercial and the act is in no way concerned with sovereignty.

The second case to which I would refer is *Victory Transport Inc v Comisaria General de Abastecimientos y Transportes* (1964) 336 F 2d 354 at 360, heard in the United States Court of Appeals Second Circuit. In giving judgment Smith J said this:

'The purpose of the restrictive theory of sovereign immunity is to try to accommodate the interest of individuals doing business with foreign governments in having their legal rights determined by the courts, with the interest of foreign governments in being free to perform certain political acts without undergoing the embarrassment or hindrance of defending the propriety of such acts before foreign courts.'

At that time, which was 1964, the United States was moving from a position of absolute immunity to a position of restrictive immunity.

Our attention was also called to the International Convention for the Unification of certain Rules concerning the Immunity of State-owned Ships (the Brussels Convention); Misc 2 (1938); Cmd 5672. Although the United Kingdom was party to this convention and signed in 1926, the convention had not been ratified at the time of the events in the present case. However it was cited to us as showing the state of international law at the relevant time. By art 1:

'Sea-going ships owned or operated by States, cargoes owned by them, and cargoes and passengers carried on State-owned ships, as well as the States which own or operate such ships and own such cargoes shall be subject, as regards claims in respect of the operation of such ships or in respect of the carriage of such cargoes, to the same rules of liability and the same obligations as those applicable in the case of privately-owned ships, cargoes and equipment.'

And by art 3(1):

'The provisions of the two preceding Articles shall not apply to ships of war, State-owned yachts, patrol vessels, hospital ships, fleet auxiliaries, supply ships and other vessels owned or operated by a State and employed exclusively at the time when the cause of action arises on Government and non-commercial service, and such ships shall not be subject to seizure, arrest or detention by any legal process nor to any proceedings *in rem*.'

It was said on the one hand that these two articles were evidence of international law and supported the argument that there was no sovereign immunity for a merchant vessel. On the other hand, the provisions of art 3 show that the signatories intended to preserve sovereign immunity in proper cases. Counsel for the Republic of Cuba also relied on the writings of foreign lawyers to support the view that the convention did not exclude sovereign immunity in a proper case. See also Professor O'Connell's article on the Foreign Sovereign Immunities Act 1976 in the United States in which he argued that an exception for jure imperii must be implied to that statute (Proceedings of the Conference of International Law Association, 17th November 1978, p 12).

We have also had for our consideration a number of affidavits of foreign lawyers which I have found of considerable assistance in considering the many international authorities cited to us. These opinions emphasise that the court will not grant immunity where a commercial vessel involved in a private law activity is subject to a private law claim, for example collision damage. But they do suggest that, if the claim for sovereign immunity is founded on an act said to be jure imperii, then the nature of the act must be examined.

The background to the Republic of Cuba's case is that prior to September 1973 they had friendly commercial and diplomatic relations with 'the democratically elected government of Chile' but that according to the then Cuban ambassador to Chile, on 11th September 1973, the military junta overthrew by force the government of Chile and publicly announced that it had severed diplomatic relations with the government of Cuba. It was on 11th September that the Playa Larga was ordered to leave Valparaiso and on 12th September that the Marble Islands was ordered to go to Peru. Both vessels arrived at the Peruvian port of Callao on 15th September. Both ships refused to unload there, the Playa Larga left on 20th September for Cuba and the Marble Islands left on 27th September, and ultimately arrived at Haiphong, Vietnam, on 6th November. In Cuba, Law No 1256 was enacted on 27th September but expressed to take effect from 11th September. On 16th October the Republic of Cuba became the owner of the Marble Islands. Both cargoes had been sold or otherwise disposed of.

The claim in respect of the cargo on the Marble Islands is in tort, being damages for detention or conversion or breach of duty. There was no contractual relationship between the Republic of Cuba and the plaintiffs. The claim in respect of the cargo on the Playa Larga is in contract and tort, the claim in tort being the same as in the case of the Marble Islands and the breach of contract being breach of the contract in the bill of lading which was signed by the master. Although there are differences of detail between the case of the Marble Islands and that of the Playa Larga it is clear, in my opinion, that in each case the cause of the failure to deliver was the reaction of the Republic of Cuba to the coup d'état in Chile. Our attention has been called to differences between the affidavits filed on each side but none of these differences is sufficient to offset the basic facts which I have set out above.

Counsel for the plaintiffs, in support of his submission that the Republic of Cuba are to be judged as an operator of commercial vessels for commercial purposes, emphasised that they have a nationalised corporation, Mambisa, which owns ships and a state-owned enterprise, Cubazucar, for the export of sugar. They also own merchant ships other than through Mambisa. The republic are therefore heavily involved in commerce and accordingly when action of the republic prevents commercial contracts being fulfilled either because of tortious interference or because of breach of contract no further facts *a* can be proved to establish sovereign immunity. If there is any defence it should be raised at trial.

Counsel for the Republic of Cuba submits that the court must look at the basic facts which have prevented the cargoes from being delivered to Iansa. They do not merely show a colourable case of state interference. It is not a mere assertion. It is at the very least an arguable case (see per Lord Somervell in *Rahimtoola v HEH the Nizam of Hyderabad* [1957] 3 All ER 441 at 456, [1958] AC 379 at 410 and see also *Juan Ysamael & Co Inc v* *b* *Government of the Republic of Indonesia* [1954] 3 All ER 236, [1955] AC 72). It is essentially a political act of foreign policy. It appears from the many authorities cited that not every country draws the line between acta jure imperii and acta jure gestionis in the same place, but I draw the inference from the passages which are quoted in the *Empire of Iran* case (1963) 45 ILR 57, that one way of posing the question is to ask whether the state has acted in exercise of its sovereign authority or as a private person. And, if there is borne *c* in mind the passage quoted above from *Victory Transport Inc v Comisaria General de Abastecimientos y Transportes* (1964) 336 F 2d 354 at 360, the Republic of Cuba clearly have an interest in being free to perform political acts without undergoing the embarrassment or hindrance of defending the propriety of such acts before foreign courts. I do not read the affidavits of foreign lawyers as doing anything to dispel this approach; on the contrary some, at any rate, give such a view clear support.

d In my opinion in this case it was the act of the government of the Republic of Cuba which prevented these cargoes from being delivered. I do not think it is possible to say that the act was clearly commercial in its nature. It was not like the *Empire of Iran* case, a mere refusal to foot the bill for the work done. It was not like *Trendtex Trading Corpn v Central Bank of Nigeria* [1977] 1 All ER 881, [1977] QB 529, where there was a cancellation of contracts because too much had been ordered. No suggestion has been *e* made that it was in the commercial interests of the Republic of Cuba to cease trading with Chile. On the contrary, it was a political decision, a foreign policy decision which bore no relation to commercial interests. The dispute would bring into question 'legislative or international transactions of a foreign government, or the policy of its executive' (see per Lord Denning in *Rahimtoola v HEH the Nizam of Hyderabad* [1957] 3 All ER 441 at 463–464, [1958] AC 379 at 422). I am of opinion therefore that subject to *f* certain subsidiary points with which I must deal the Republic of Cuba are entitled to claim sovereign immunity in these two cases.

It is submitted by the plaintiffs that sovereign immunity will not be granted if the act on which the claim is based is contrary to international law, ie either confiscatory without compensation or discriminatory. I entirely agree with Robert Goff J's view thereon (see [1978] 1 All ER 1169 at 1195–1196, [1978] QB 500 at 531–532) and I do not *g* wish to add anything on the point.

The final point taken by counsel for the plaintiffs is that the Republic of Cuba are not in possession of the Congreso. Again I entirely accept the judgment of Robert Goff J on this point (see [1978] 1 All ER 1169 at 1188–1189, [1978] QB 500 at 522–523). I would only add that the view which he has expressed is in accordance with that of Lord Wright in *The Christina* [1938] 1 All ER 719 at 731–732, [1938] AC 485 at 507–508 and the Privy *h* Council in *The Philippine Admiral* [1976] 1 All ER 78 at 96–97, [1977] AC 373 at 404. I would dismiss this appeal.

Appeal formally dismissed. Leave to appeal to the House of Lords granted.

Solicitors: *Bischoff & Co* (for the plaintiffs); *Coward Chance* (for the Republic of Cuba).

Sumra Green   Barrister.

Planmount Ltd v Republic of Zaire

QUEEN'S BENCH DIVISION
LLOYD J
29th APRIL 1980

Constitutional law – Foreign sovereign state – Immunity from suit – Exceptions – Commercial transaction – Action in personam – Contract to repair ambassador's official residence in England – Repairers receiving only part of contract price for work – Action to recover balance – Contract made before State Immunity Act 1978 came into force – Whether defence of sovereign immunity available – State Immunity Act 1978, ss 3, 10.

Under a contract dated 10th January 1978 (ie before the State Immunity Act 1978 came into force) the plaintiffs agreed to carry out certain building work for the Republic of Zaire at the official London residence of its ambassador. The plaintiffs were paid only part of the contract price for the work and issued a writ against the Republic of Zaire claiming the balance. A master gave the plaintiffs leave to serve the writ outside the jurisdiction. The Republic of Zaire applied to have the writ set aside on the ground that it was an independent sovereign state and as such entitled to sovereign immunity. The plaintiffs submitted that the doctrine of sovereign immunity did not apply to a state's commercial transactions. The Republic of Zaire contended that as the contract had been made before the 1978 Act came into force, it was protected because (i) prior to the Act the doctrine of absolute sovereign immunity still prevailed in relation to actions in personam and it was only in relation to actions in rem that there had been any relaxation, and (ii) it was clear from the way in which the 1978 Act was drafted that the law in relation to actions in personam had not been changed until the Act came into force, for while s 10, which applied to actions in rem, was given retrospective effect, s 3[a], which created an exception to the general rule of immunity in the case of commercial transactions, applied only to transactions entered into after the Act came into force.

Held – (1) On a true analysis of the authorities prior to the 1978 Act, a foreign sovereign state was not entitled to absolute sovereign immunity in English courts either in actions in rem or in actions in personam but could only invoke the doctrine in respect of governmental acts. A foreign sovereign state's commercial transactions were therefore not protected (see p 1112 f g and p 1114 a b, post); *Trendtex Trading Corpn Ltd v Central Bank of Nigeria* [1977] 1 All ER 881, *Hispano Americana Mercantil SA v Central Bank of Nigeria* [1979] 2 Lloyd's Rep 277 and *I Congreso del Partido* p 1092, ante, followed; *Thai-Europe Tapioca Service Ltd v Government of Pakistan* [1975] 3 All ER 961, *The Philippine Admiral* [1976] 1 All ER 78 and *Uganda Co (Holdings) Ltd v Government of Uganda* [1979] 1 Lloyd's Rep 481 considered.

(2) There was no presumption that, by legislating, Parliament intended to change the law, and the mere fact that some provisions in a statute had been given retrospective effect could not give rise to an inference that if the retrospective provisions confirmed or codified existing law the other provisions were intended to change it. In any event neither s 3 nor s 10 of the 1980 Act was retrospective (see p 1114 b c, post).

---

a   Section 3, so far as material, provides:
'(1) A State is not immune as respects proceedings relating to—(a) a commercial transaction entered into by the State; or (b) an obligation of the State which by virtue of a contract (whether a commercial transaction or not) falls to be performed wholly or partly in the United Kingdom
. . .
'(3) In this section "commercial transaction" means—(a) any contract for the supply of goods or services . . . (c) any other transaction or activity (whether of a commercial, industrial, financial, professional or other similar character) into which a State enters or in which it engages otherwise than in the exercise of sovereign authority . . .'

a (3) The defence of sovereign immunity was accordingly not available to the Republic of Zaire because it was not acting in a governmental but in a private or commercial capacity when it entered into the contract with the plaintiffs. It followed that the case was a proper one for service of the writ out of the jurisdiction under RSC Ord 11, r 1(*f*) (see p 1114 *f* to *j*, post).

Notes
b For sovereign immunity from suit, see 8 Halsbury's Laws (4th Edn) para 410, 18 ibid, para 1548, and for cases on the subject, see 1(1) Digest (Reissue) 54–59, 358–382.
For the State Immunity Act 1978, ss 3, 10, see 48 Halsbury's Statutes (3rd Edn) 90, 94.

Cases referred to in judgment
Claim against the Empire of Iran (1963) 45 ILR 57.
c *Compania Naviera Vascongada v SS Cristina* [1938] 1 All ER 719, [1938] AC 485, 107 LJP 1, 159 LT 394, 19 Asp MLC 159, HL, 1(1) Digest (Reissue) 228, *1297*.
Hispano Americana Mercantil SA v Central Bank of Nigeria [1979] 2 Lloyd's Rep 277, CA.
I Congreso del Partido [1978] 1 All ER 1169, [1978] QB 500, [1977] 3 WLR 778, [1977] 1 Lloyd's Rep 536; *on appeal* p 1092, ante, [1980] 1 Lloyd's Rep 23, CA, 1(1) Digest (Reissue) 230, *1302*.
d *Miliangos v George Frank (Textiles) Ltd* [1975] 3 All ER 801, [1976] AC 443, [1975] 3 WLR 758, [1967] 1 Lloyd's Rep 201, HL; *affg* [1975] 1 All ER 1076, [1975] QB 487, [1975] 2 WLR 555, [1975] 1 Lloyd's Rep 587, CA, Digest (Cont Vol D) 691, *64c*.
Philippine Admiral (Owners) v Wallem Shipping (Hong Kong) Ltd, The Philippine Admiral [1976] 1 All ER 78, [1977] AC 373, [1976] 2 WLR 214, [1976] 1 Lloyd's Rep 234, PC, 1(1) Digest (Reissue) 229, *1301*.
e *Thai-Europe Tapioca Service Ltd v Government of Pakistan* [1975] 3 All ER 961, [1975] 1 WLR 1485, 1 Lloyd's Rep 1, CA, 1(1) Digest (Reissue) 54, *362*.
Trendtex Trading Corpn Ltd v Central Bank of Nigeria [1977] 1 All ER 881, [1977] QB 529, [1977] 2 WLR 356, [1976] 1 Lloyd's Rep 1, CA; *rvsg* [1976] 3 All ER 437, [1976] 1 WLR 868, 1(1) Digest (Reissue) 59, *382*.
Uganda Co (Holdings) Ltd v Government of Uganda [1979] 1 Lloyd's Rep 481.

f ### Appeal
The plaintiffs, Planmount Ltd, appealed against the decision of Master Bickford-Smith, given on 9th January 1980, whereby he ordered that service out of the jurisdiction of a writ, issued on 16th May 1979 against the defendants, the Republic of Zaire, be set aside. The appeal was heard in chambers but judgment was delivered in open court.
g The facts are set out in the judgment.

John Jarvis for the plaintiffs.
Anthony Hoolahan QC and *Thomas Shields* for the defendants.

h **LLOYD J.** In this action the plaintiffs, a small firm of builders, claim against the Republic of Zaire the balance of an account due for building work done on the ambassador's official residence in The Bishop's Avenue, Hampstead. The defendants seek to set aside service of the writ on the ground that the Republic of Zaire is an independent sovereign state and is therefore entitled to sovereign immunity. Since the point is one of some general interest I was asked to give my judgment in open court.
j Prior to January 1978, the plaintiffs had, according to their evidence, done a number of small building jobs for the defendants at the residence in Hampstead and at the embassy in Chesham Place. Then, on 10th January 1978, the plaintiffs agreed to carry out substantial works at the residence. The contract is in writing. It was signed, on behalf of the Embassy of the Republic of Zaire, by the ambassador himself. The contract price was £54,400. The work was to start the next day and was to be completed by 12th

May 1978. There were agreed variations amounting to £8,096·66 in all. The defendants have paid £47,800 leaving a difference of £14,696·66 which the plaintiffs claim in these *a* proceedings.

The writ, with the statement of claim indorsed, was issued on 16th May 1979. The master gave leave, ex parte, to serve out of the jurisdiction in August 1979. But on 9th January 1980 he set aside service of the writ and stayed all further proceedings on the ground, as he put it, that the plaintiffs would have great difficulty in overcoming the obstacle of absolute immunity. Counsel for the defendants sought to support the *b* master's decision on two grounds. In the first place he argued that prior to the passing of the State Immunity Act 1978, the rule of absolute immunity still prevailed in the case of actions in personam. It was only in the case of actions in rem that there had been any relaxation. He relied on *Compania Naviera Vascongada v SS Cristina* [1938] 1 All ER 719, [1938] AC 485, *The Philippine Admiral* [1976] 1 All ER 78, [1977] AC 373, *Thai-Europe Tapioca Service Ltd v Government of Pakistan* [1975] 3 All ER 961, [1975] 1 WLR 1485 and *c* *Uganda (Holdings) Ltd v Government of Uganda* [1979] 1 Lloyd's Rep 481, in which Donaldson J followed the *Thai-Europe* case rather than the subsequent decision of the Court of Appeal in the *Trendtex Trading Corpn Ltd v Central Bank of Nigeria* [1977] 1 All ER 881, [1977] QB 529.

Second, counsel sought support for his argument from the provisions of the State Immunity Act 1978 itself. That Act does not apply directly to this case since it only came *d* into force on 22nd November 1978, some ten months after the contract between the plaintiffs and the defendants. But according to counsel's argument the clear inference from the way the Act was drafted is that Parliament was changing the law in respect of actions in personam, but not in respect of actions in rem; for s 3, which creates an exception to the general rule of immunity in the case of commercial transactions, only applies to transactions entered into after the coming into force of the Act; whereas s 10, *e* which applies to actions in rem, applies to causes of action arising before the coming into force of the Act. This shows, so it was said, that whereas s 10 was confirming or codifying existing law, s 3 was creating new law.

As to counsel's first argument, it seems to me that the matter is concluded by the decision of the Court of Appeal in *Trendtex*. That case established, by a majority consisting of Lord Denning MR and Shaw LJ, the restrictive theory of sovereign *f* immunity as part of English law. In other words, a foreign state is entitled to sovereign immunity in respect of its governmental acts but not in respect of its commercial transactions. *Trendtex* was itself an action in personam. It is impossible to treat the judgments of the majority in that case as being confined to actions in rem. It is true that Donaldson J in the *Uganda* case regarded the decision in *Trendtex* as being irreconcilable with the previous decision of the Court of Appeal in *Thai-Europe*. But the *Uganda* case is *g* not the latest pronouncement in this field. The point has been considered afresh on at least two occasions by the Court of Appeal.

In *Hispano Americana Mercantil SA v Central Bank of Nigeria* [1979] 2 Lloyd's Rep 277 the question before the Court of Appeal was very similar to that in *Trendtex*, namely whether the plaintiffs were entitled to a Mareva injunction against the Central Bank of Nigeria. It was argued that the position had been changed since *Trendtex* by the State *h* Immunity Act 1978. That argument was rejected. It was held that the Act was not retrospective. With regard to *Trendtex*, Lord Denning MR said (at 279):

'Apart from those two grounds, it seems to me that the international law remains as I stated it in the *Trendtex* case. We had before us a decision of the Provincial Court of Frankfurt in which (in a precisely similar case to ours) an injunction had *j* been granted: and in the *Trendtex* case (operating as we thought in accordance with international law as it then stood) we granted an injunction. It seems to me that the latest statutes of the U.S. and of our Parliament are not sufficient to alter the international law as we stated it. It was suggested that the decision in *Trendtex* was per incuriam. But we have again been referred to the authorities on what would a   amount to per incuriam: and especially to what was said by myself in *Miliangos v. George Frank (Textiles) Ltd* ([1975] 1 All ER 1076, [1975] QB 487) ... and by Lord Simon of Glaisdale when the case reached the House of Lords ([1975] 3 All ER 801, [1976] AC 443. All I would say about that is that *Trendtex* was not decided per incuriam. On the point of the injunction, as well as the point of sovereign immunity in regard to the Central Bank of Nigeria, *Trendtex* governs this case. It is precisely in point on an almost identical situation. The proper course for this

b   Court to take is simply to follow *Trendtex* and hold that there is no sovereign immunity and that a *Mareva* injunction should go pending the ultimate decision.'

Waller and Cumming-Bruce LJJ agreed with Lord Denning MR.
The second case is *I Congreso del Partido* [1978] 1 All ER 1169, [1978] 1 QB 500. That was an action in rem. But what was said by Robert Goff J, at first instance is nevertheless relevant to the present case. After analysing the previous authorities, including *The*

c   *Philippine Admiral* and *Trendtex*, he said ([1978] 1 All ER 1169 at 1191, [1975] QB 500 at 526):

> 'The result of the decision in *The Philippine Admiral* appears, therefore, to have been that the law was committed to two irreconcilable propositions. The first proposition was that, in the case of actions in personam, a foreign sovereign is
d   absolutely entitled to invoke the doctrine of sovereign immunity. The second proposition was that, in the case of actions in rem against an ordinary trading ship, a foreign sovereign who owns the ship may, through execution on his property, effectively be held liable on a claim in personam. The anomaly can only be entirely avoided in one of two ways; either, as in English law before *The Philippine Admiral*, by adopting the absolute doctrine of sovereign immunity in respect of both actions
e   in personam and actions in rem, or, as in most foreign jurisdictions (many of which, though they distinguish between rights in rem and rights in personam, do not have separate categories of actions in rem and actions in personam), by applying the restrictive doctrine to all actions, limiting sovereign immunity to the case of an actus jure imperii as opposed to an actus jure gestionis. The result of *Trendtex Trading Corpn v Central Bank of Nigeria* is that, subject to any appeal to the House of
f   Lords, the restrictive doctrine of sovereign immunity is now applicable in all cases and so the anomaly has been removed.'

On appeal from that decision of Robert Goff J the Court of Appeal was divided as to the result (see p 1092, ante). But Lord Denning MR and Waller LJ were agreed as to the applicable principles. After referring to the *Thai-Europe* case [1975] 3 All ER 961, [1975] 1 WLR 1485 and the *Uganda* case [1979] 1 Lloyd's Rep 481 Lord Denning MR continued
g   (see p 1100, ante):

> 'In *Trendtex* ... however, Shaw LJ and I took a different view. I said of the restrictive theory: "It covers actions in personam. In those actions, too, the restrictive theory is more consonant with justice. So it should be applied to them. It should not be retained as an indefensible anomaly." My view has been reinforced by several important events.'

h   Lord Denning MR then refers to the Foreign Sovereign Immunities Act of the United States of America, the State Immunity Act 1978 and the fact that the United Kingdom had ratified the European Conventions of 1926 and 1972 and then continued:

> 'In view of these developments I think it plain that the absolute doctrine is no
j   longer part of international law. The restrictive theory holds the field in international law, and by reason of the doctrine of incorporation it should be applied by the English courts, not only in actions in rem but also in actions in personam.'

Waller LJ did not, I think, expressly approve the passage I have quoted from the judgment of Robert Goff J, but it is clear from the whole tenor of his judgment that he

was in substantial agreement with the judgment below; and there is certainly nothing
to suggest in his judgment that he thought there was still a distinction between actions   *a*
in rem and actions in personam. Both the *Hispano* case and the *Congreso* case are, I
understand, on their way to the House of Lords. Unless the House of Lords decide
otherwise, it seems to me to have been clearly established by successive decisions in the
Court of Appeal that prior to the passing of the State Immunity Act 1978, a foreign state
had no absolute immunity in the English courts, whether the action be in rem or in
personam.   *b*

As for counsel's second argument, I was not convinced that there is any relevant
distinction between s 3 and s 10 of the State Immunity Act 1978. It is clear that s 3 is not
retrospective; no more I think is s 10; but even if it were, it would not be legitimate to
infer that Parliament was intending to change the law by s 3. Parliament is of course
presumed to know the state of the law. But there is no presumption that, by legislating,
Parliament intends to change the law; and I do not see why that inference should be   *c*
drawn in relation to one provision of an Act merely because other provisions in the same
Act are said to have been given retrospective effect.

Assuming I am right that the defendants never had absolute immunity in English law,
the only remaining question is whether, on the facts of the present case, the defendants
were acting in a governmental capacity or whether they were acting in a private or
commercial capacity. That is a question which often gives rise to difficulty, as it did in   *d*
the *Congreso* case; but it gives rise to no such difficulty in the present case. On the facts
alleged by the plaintiffs this is a simple case of the defendants' 'mere refusal to foot the
bill for the work done', to use the language of Waller LJ, in the *Congreso* case (see p 1109,
ante).

An almost identical question came before the Constitutional Court of the Federal
Republic of Germany in *Claim against the Empire of Iran* (1963) 45 ILR 57. In that case a   *e*
firm of builders in Cologne carried out certain repairs to the central heating system in the
Iranian Embassy on the instructions of the ambassador. They claimed DM292. The
question was whether the Iranian Empire could be sued. It was referred to the
Constitutional Court. The court held, after an exhaustive review of the decisions in
many other jurisdictions, that the contract for repairs was to be regarded as a non-
sovereign function of the foreign state (see at 81). The *Empire of Iran* case is quoted   *f*
extensively in both the judgments of the Court of Appeal in the *Congreso* case. To my
mind, it is hard to imagine a clearer case of an act or transaction of a private or
commercial nature than the repairs to the ambassador's residence. The case is on all fours
with the *Empire of Iran* case. It follows that the defence of sovereign immunity is not
available. No other ground for setting aside service of the writ has been advanced in the
evidence or relied on by counsel. In my judgment this is a proper case for service out of   *g*
the jurisdiction under RSC Ord 11, r 1(*f*).

According to the note to the master's judgment, he thought there might be some
difficulty in effecting service. But I see no difficulty. Section 12 of the State Immunity
Act 1978 provides for service on foreign states through the Foreign and Commonwealth
Office. That section applies to any proceedings instituted after 22nd November 1978
even though the proceedings relate to matters which occurred before 22nd November   *h*
1978 (see s 23(3) and (4)). These proceedings were not instituted until 16th May 1979.
Accordingly s 12 applies. For the reasons I have endeavoured to give I would allow the
appeal and give the plaintiff leave to serve out of the jurisdiction in accordance with s 12
of the 1978 Act.

Appeal allowed.   *j*

Solicitors: *Arram, Fairfield & Co* (for the plaintiffs); *H Davies & Co* (for the defendants).

K Mydeen Esq   Barrister.

a

Swales v Cox

QUEEN'S BENCH DIVISION
DONALDSON LJ AND HODGSON J
13th NOVEMBER 1980

b   *Arrest – Arrest without warrant – Power of police to enter place (if need be by force) to effect arrest – Place – Private dwelling house Whether request for permission to enter precondition of entry – Criminal Law Act 1967, s 2(6).*

Arrest – Arrest without warrant – Power of police to enter place (if need be by force) to effect arrest – Force – What constitutes force – Criminal Law Act 1967, s 2(6).

c

Two police officers, who had reasonable grounds for suspecting that C had committed an arrestable offence, followed him to the respondent's house. C, knowing that they were behind him, dashed in and shut the door. In the purported exercise of their power under s 2(6)[a] of the Criminal Law Act 1967 to enter any place (if need be by force) for the purpose of arresting a person without a warrant, the police officers opened the door and *d* went in. They saw the respondent and told him that they were police officers pursuing C. The respondent said that they had no right to barge in and tried to stop them leaving the house with C. The respondent was subsequently charged with obstructing the police in the execution of their duty, contrary to s 51(3) of the Police Act 1964. He was convicted and appealed to the Crown Court which held (i) that a police officer's statutory power of entry under s 2(6) of the 1967 Act, like his right of entry at common law, could *e* be lawfully exercised only after there had first been a demand to enter followed by a refusal of the demand, (ii) that, as the police officers had not asked for permission to enter the respondent's house, they were trespassers and so could not be on the premises in the lawful execution of their duty, and (iii) that accordingly the respondent could not be guilty of an offence under s 51(3) of the 1964 Act. On a case stated by the Crown Court at the request of the police,

f **Held** – (1) Section 2 of the 1967 Act was intended to provide a comprehensive code relating to the rights of a police officer to enter a place without a warrant in the circumstances to which s 2(4) and (5) applied, ie where he suspected that an arrestable offence had been or was about to be committed. In those circumstances he had an unqualified right to enter under s 2(6) but if he used force and his use of it was subsequently questioned he had to prove that its use was in fact necessary, because the *g* words 'by force' in s 2(6) were qualified by the phrase 'if need be' (see p 1119 *b g* and p 1120 *c*, post).

(2) In s 2(6) the word 'force' meant the application of energy to an obstacle with a view to removing it. In the case of a door, 'force' was used if the door was open and it was necessary to use energy to open it further, or if the door was closed and the handle was *h* turned from the outside and the door was eased open (see p 1119 *c* to *e* and p 1120 *c*, post).

(3) The case would be remitted to the Crown Court with a direction to continue with the hearing of the respondent's appeal and to consider the question whether in all the circumstances it was necessary for the police officers to use force (see p 1120 *b c*, post).

Per Curiam. Vis-à-vis entering a private dwelling house, the position of a police officer armed with a warrant to arrest is no different from that of an officer acting *j* without a warrant under s 2 of the 1967 Act. He too can rely on the powers under s 2(4) and (6) to enter without asking for permission (except in so far as permission is necessary before he is going to use force) because the warrant shows that he has reasonable cause to believe (1) that an arrestable offence has been committed and (2) that the person named in the warrant is guilty of an offence (see p 1119 *h* to p 1120 *c*, post).

---

a   Section 2, so far as material, is set out at p 1118 *g* to *j*, post

Notes

For the Police Act 1964, s 51(3), see 25 Halsbury's Statutes (3rd Edn) 364.

For the Criminal Law Act 1967, ss 2(4)(5)(6), 3(1)(2), see 8 Halsbury's Statutes (3rd Edn) 553, 554.

Case stated

This was a case stated by his Honour Judge D Herrod QC sitting with justices in respect of their adjudication at the Crown Court at Leeds.

On 6th March 1979 at Leeds Magistrates' Court the respondent, James Swales, was convicted of an offence of wilfully obstructing Peter Simpson, a police constable acting in the execution of his duty, contrary to s 51(3) of the Police Act 1964. The respondent appealed against the conviction to the Crown Court at Leeds.

The court heard the appeal on 16th July 1979 and gave judgment on 27th July 1979.

It was contended by the appellant that the respondent was guilty of wilfully obstructing the police in the execution of their duty on the basis that the police were empowered to enter on the premises, by force if necessary, in pursuance of the provisions of s 2(4) and (6) of the Criminal Law Act 1967.

The way the appellant put his case was that the police had followed Ian Charles to the home of the respondent they knew he was in the house; they had reasonable cause to suspect that he was guilty of an arrestable offence; they had power to arrest him without warrant; and they were empowered to open the closed door and enter the respondent's home for the purposes of arresting Charles pursuant to the authority conferred on them by sub-ss (4) and (6).

It was contended by the respondent that although the police were empowered to enter on the premises, that power could only be lawfully exercised after there had first been a demand to enter the premises followed by a refusal of that demand; that in the absence of any such demand and refusal their right to enter was void ab initio and they were trespassers; that they could not, therefore, be on the premises in the lawful execution of their duty; and that the respondent could not be guilty of the criminal offence of obstructing them in the lawful execution of their duty.

The court was of opinion that:

(1) Power to enter premises at common law was subject to a prior demand and refusal.

(2) Section 2(6) of the Criminal Law Act 1967 does not give the police power to enter on premises where there was no prior demand and refusal because (a) s 2 of the Criminal Law Act 1967 did not repeal or replace the provisions of the common law; (b) the new power of entry created by sub-ss (4) and (6) of s 2 of the 1967 Act is subject to a prior demand to enter and a refusal of that demand; (c) had Parliament intended to change the existing principles of common law it should and would have expressed that intention in plain terms whereas no such words appear in s 2 of the Act.

Apart from the court's findings on the principal submission in the case, it was necessary to deal with the further submission made by the appellant that the old common law rules related only to the entry into premises by force; that they had no application to a peaceful entry; and that when the officers in this case made their entry to the home of the respondent they did so merely by opening a closed door, which was a peaceful entry.

The opinion of the court was that 'entry by force' means entering on premises without an invitation to do so.

For all the reasons stated above, the court took the view that the entry of the police on the respondent's premises was unlawful and the respondent could not be guilty of the offence of obstructing them in the lawful execution of their duty and accordingly allowed the respondent's appeal.

The question for the opinion of the High Court was (i) whether the police are empowered under the provisions of s 2(6) of the Criminal Law Act 1967 to enter premises where there has been no prior demand and refusal to enter, and (ii) whether an entry to premises by opening a closed door amounts to an entry by force.

John D Topham for the appellant.
Gordon Lakin for the respondent.

DONALDSON LJ. This is an appeal by a prosecutor by way of case stated. It raises
a matters of fundamental importance to the law of England and matters which are also of
very considerable interest. If I may say so, it has been very well argued on both sides.

The case was stated by his Honour Judge Herrod sitting with justices and is in respect
of their decision at the Crown Court at Leeds allowing an appeal by Mr Swales against his
conviction of obstructing a police constable acting in the execution of his duty, contrary
to s 51(3) of the Police Act 1964. The point of the appeal concerned the circumstances
b in which a police officer was entitled to enter a private dwelling house without first
asking for permission to do so.

Let me first give the facts, which I can take from the excellent judgment delivered by
the judge at the end of the hearing of the appeal. He put the facts as follows:

c 'At 6.30 pm on Thursday, 5th October 1978, two police officers were keeping
observations on a house in Kirkstall Road, Leeds, which was occupied by a young
man called Ian Charles. The police had reasonable grounds for believing that Ian
Charles had committed an offence of burglary, and that is why they were keeping
observations on his home. The officers were wearing uniform trousers, but they
were not wearing headgear of any kind, and instead of uniform jackets, they were
wearing ordinary anoraks. They saw Ian Charles approaching the house, though
d they themselves moved towards the house. Charles turned and saw the officers. He
began to run away and he was chased by the officers, who shouted more than once:
"Stop, police." Charles did not stop. Indeed, he ran to a nearby house where he was
seen to enter through the kitchen door and he closed the door behind him. When
the officers got to the door they tried to open it, but they were prevented from
doing so by Charles, who was holding the handle on the inside. Eventually he let
e go of the handle, and when he did so the officers opened the door and went inside
the kitchen. Inside the kitchen were three people in addition to Charles, and the
officers noticed that Charles had gone to the back of the kitchen. One of those
inside the kitchen was the owner of the house, Mr James Swales. He said to the
police: "Who are you, and what do you mean by forcing your way into my
house?" When he spoke those words Mr Swales was standing between Charles and
f the officers. One of the officers told him that they were police and that they were
in pursuit of Charles, whom they believed to be a wanted person. With this the
officers tried to move towards Charles, but Mr Swales blocked their path. Mr Swales
asked the officers for their names. They gave him their names, and Mr Swales
began to write them down on a newspaper which was lying on the kitchen table.
As he did that, the officers made their way past Mr Swales and approached Charles,
g each of the officers taking hold of one of his arms. They then tried to remove him
from the house. As they began to move towards the door, Mr Swales also took hold
of Charles. He was told not to do so, as he was obstructing the officers in their
duty. Mr Swales replied: "I don't care, I am going to inform the chief constable in
the morning. I'll see that you are done. You have no right to barge in here." Pc
Simpson replied: "We are in pursuit of a wanted person and we have in law a power
h of entry into your house." Despite this, Mr Swales stood in the doorway of the
kitchen blocking the exit of the officers, who by this time were having to struggle
with Charles. As they pushed past Mr Swales, some plastic ribbon blinds became
entangled round the head of Charles and the blinds were damaged. Mr Swales
shouted after the police: "You bastards will pay for this." The officers then took
Charles to the police car, where they confirmed his identity, and he was removed to
j the police station. He was afterwards charged with the offence of burglary [which
is of course an arrestable offence]. Later that evening the police returned to the
home of Mr Swales, cautioned him, and informed him of the offence which he had
committed. Mr Swales replied: "Well, I didn't know you were police." [Again I
would add that was plainly untrue.] In evidence, Pc Simpson [who was the only
officer to be called, although the other one was tendered] said that he believed that
he had a power of entry in pursuit of a criminal without first asking for permission

to enter the house. He said that this was what he had been taught at the police training school and that in his view, he was acting perfectly lawfully and in accordance with the powers conferred on the police by the Criminal Law Act of 1967.' *a*

That indeed is the issue. If these police constables were not authorised to enter by the Criminal Law Act 1967, they had no authority to enter at all, and it would follow that they were not acting in the execution of their duty. Mr Swales, however anti-social his conduct may have been, was in law entitled to obstruct them in what they were doing *b* in the house.

I say that the issue turns entirely on the Criminal Law Act 1967 because it is conceded in this case that the judge of the Crown Court correctly analysed the position at common law which existed prior to the 1967 Act and since, unless altered by that Act as follows: that there was power of entry into premises at common law and, if necessary, power to break doors to do so in four cases, but in four cases only, that is to say by a constable or *c* a citizen in order to prevent murder, by a constable or a citizen if a felony had in fact been committed and the felon had been followed to a house, by a constable or a citizen if a felony was about to be committed, and would be committed, unless prevented, and by a constable following an offender running away from an affray. In any other circumstances there was no power to enter premises without a warrant, and, even in these four cases where there was power not only to enter but to break in in order to do *d* so, it was an essential precondition that there should have been a demand and refusal by the occupier to allow entry before the doors could be broken.

What is said on behalf of the respondent in this case is that all that the 1967 Act did was to substitute the concept of an arrestable offence for a felony and that the law, with that substitution, remains the same. It follows that there can never be a right in a police constable to enter premises without a warrant unless he first asks for permission to enter *e* and is refused.

For my part, I do not think that that is the position. The 1967 Act is expressed to be in its long title—

'An Act to amend the law of England and Wales by abolishing the division of crimes into felonies and misdemeanours and to amend and simplify the law in *f* respect of matters arising from or related to that division or the abolition of it . . . and for purposes connected therewith.'

This appeal turns on the provisions of ss 2(4), (5) and (6) and 3. Section 2(4) reads as follows:

'Where a constable, with reasonable cause, suspects that an arrestable offence has *g* been committed, he may arrest without warrant anyone whom he, with reasonable cause, suspects to be guilty of the offence.'

Subsection (5) reads:

'A constable may arrest without warrant any person who is, or whom he, with reasonable cause, suspects to be, about to commit an arrestable offence.' *h*

Subsection (6) reads:

'For the purpose of arresting a person under any power conferred by this section a constable may enter (if need be, by force) and search any place where that person is or where the constable, with reasonable cause, suspects him to be.'

Section 3(1) provides: *j*

'A person may use such force as is reasonable in the circumstances in the prevention of crime, or in effecting or assisting in the lawful arrest of offenders or suspected offenders or of persons unlawfully at large.'

Subsection (2) provides:

a
'Subsection (1) above shall replace the rules of the common law on the question when force used for a purpose mentioned in the subsection is justified by that purpose.'

In my judgment, Parliament in 1967 was intending to provide a comprehensive code on the rights of a constable to enter a place (be it noted not 'premises' but 'a place', which

b is the word used in s 2(6)) in circumstances in which a constable with reasonable cause suspected that an arrestable offence had been committed or a constable, again with reasonable cause, suspected that an arrestable offence was about to be committed. The code provided that he might enter without qualification but not that he might use force without qualification. If he had to use any force, then it is governed by the phrase which occurred in parenthesis, '(if need be . . .)'.

c First of all, let me define what I think is meant by 'force'. In the context of outside premises of course there is no problem about force unless there is a gate or something of that sort. The constable simply enters the place and is authorised to do so by sub-s (6). But if he meets an obstacle, then he uses force if he applies any energy to the obstacle with a view to removing it. It would follow that, if my view is correct, where there is a door which is ajar but it is insufficiently ajar for someone to go through the opening

d without moving the door and energy is applied to that door to make it open further, force is being used. A fortiori force is used when the door is latched and you turn the handle from the outside and then ease the door open. Similarly, if someone opens any window or increases the opening in any window, or indeed dislodges the window by the application of any energy, he is using force to enter, and in all those cases a constable will have to justify the use of force.

e The first hurdle which he will have to overcome in justifying force will be by providing an answer to the question: 'Why did you not ask to be allowed in?' That 'an Englishman's home is his castle' is perhaps a trite expression, but it has immense importance in the history of this country, and it still has immense importance. Anybody who seeks to enter by force has a very severe burden to displace. There will undoubtedly be cases where it can be displaced. One has only to think of the cases which occasionally

f do arise where a criminal is at large and the public, for example, are warned not to approach him because he is known to be a very dangerous man. If a constable is following such a man into premises, it may be essential for his own protection that he shall give no warning of his approach by asking the leave of the criminal to enter the premises. That of course is an extreme case, and there will be all sorts of other circumstances in between.

g For my part, I think it would be wholly wrong to add to the provisions of the statute. The statute says that force can be used 'if need be'. All I am saying is that those words are of immense weight and importance, and if the question arises 'Was it necessary?' the constable will have to prove that it really was necessary before he will be able to justify an entry by force in the sense which I have indicated.

There remains one further matter which I should mention. In the course of argument

h it was said that, if we were to reach the conclusion that I favour, it would produce this very odd result. There is nothing in the 1967 Act which alters the powers of a constable who is acting with a warrant. Section 2 is dealing with a constable acting without a warrant. So it is said one is left with the common law rules. Accordingly the unfortunate constable who is armed with a warrant to arrest must ask the permission of the occupier to enter before he can enter any premises, unless he is within the four exceptions to

j which I have referred. For my part, I do not accept that that is the law. The constable in those circumstances, in my judgment, is entitled to say, 'I have here a warrant for the arrest of the particular individual concerned. That provides me with reasonable cause for believing two things; first, that an arrestable offence has been committed [I am assuming of course that the warrant is issued in respect of an arrestable offence]; and, second, that

the person named in the warrant is guilty of the offence'. That meets the conditions of
s 2(4). In those circumstances he is able to rely on his powers under s 2(4) and (6) and to
enter without asking for permission, save in so far as permission is necessary because he
is going to use force and therefore he has to satisfy the precondition that it was necessary
to use force. But he is in no worse position because he has a warrant. He can use the
warrant to meet the preconditions of s 2(4) and therefore he is in exactly the same
position as a constable who has not got a warrant.

For those reasons I think that the Crown Court came to a decision which is different
from the decision that I would give. The Crown Court came to the conclusion that the
entry of the police was unlawful and that accordingly Mr Swales could not be guilty of
the offence of obstructing them in the lawful execution of their duty. If my view of the
section is right, then in the circumstances of this case the real issue was: did the police
officers need to use force? For the avoidance of doubt, let me make it clear that in this
case we have been concerned solely with the statutory power of entry of police officers
under s 2(6) of the Criminal Law Act 1967, which only arises in aid of the power of arrest
under sub-ss (4) and (5). We have not been concerned with the common law.

HODGSON J. I agree.

*Case remitted to the Crown Court with a direction to continue the hearing and to consider the
question of whether in all the circumstances there was a need to use force.*

*The court refused leave to appeal to the House of Lords but certified under s 1(2) of the
Administration of Justice Act 1960 that the following point of general public importance was
involved in the decision: whether on the true construction of s 2(6) of the Criminal Law Act 1967
in circumstances to which the subsection applies a police officer may enter without a prior refusal
or permission to enter.*

Solicitors: *Hewitt, Woollacott & Chown,* agents for M D Shaffner, Wakefield (for the
appellant); *Pearlman Grazin & Co,* Leeds (for the respondent).

April Weiss   Barrister.

a   # Savjani v Inland Revenue Commissioners

COURT OF APPEAL, CIVIL DIVISION
LORD DENNING MR, TEMPLEMAN AND DUNN LJJ
21st JANUARY 1981

b   *Race relations – Unlawful discrimination – Provision of goods, facilities or services – Services –*
Advice to taxpayer enabling him to claim tax relief to which he is entitled – Taxpayer entitled to
tax relief in respect of child – Taxpayers claiming relief normally only required to produce short
form of birth certificate relating to child – Taxpayer advised and required to produce full birth
certificate because he came from India – Inland Revenue having policy that all persons from
Indian subcontinent required to produce full certificate for child when first claiming tax relief –
c   *Whether Inland Revenue policy unlawful discrimination – Whether Inland Revenue providing*
'services' to public in disseminating and giving advice on entitlement to claim tax relief – Race
Relations Act 1976, s 20(1).

The plaintiff was born in India and in 1970 came to England where his son was born in
1976. His wife was given a short form of birth certificate for the child which gave only
d   the child's name, sex and date of birth. The plaintiff was entitled to claim tax relief in
respect of the child and in November 1976 was advised by the local tax inspector's office
that as he came from India he had to produce a full birth certificate for the child, showing
his and his wife's names and where they came from, in order to claim the relief, and that
the short form of certificate was insufficient. The full certificate cost £2·50. The
plaintiff queried the need to produce a full certificate and took up the matter with the
Commission for Racial Equality who alleged that the Inland Revenue, by in requiring
e   the plaintiff to produce a full certificate, were unlawfully discriminating against him.
The Inland Revenue replied that it was their policy that taxpayers from the Indian
subcontinent who claimed tax relief for a child were required to produce a full certificate
for the child even though other claimants for the relief were only required to produce
the short form of certificate. On 15th June 1977 the plaintiff again visited the local tax
f   office to claim the relief and was again advised and required to produce a full birth
certificate for his child. Since he then knew that he would not have been so treated had
he not been of Indian origin, he felt humiliated. He brought an action against the Inland
Revenue Commissioners claiming a declaration that the commissioners had unlawfully
discriminated against him on racial grounds, contrary to s 20(1)(b)^a of the Race Relations
Act 1976, by requiring and advising him on account of his origins to produce at his own
expense a full certificate for his child in order to claim tax relief when other taxpayers
g   were only required to produce a short form of certificate. He also claimed damages. The
judge dismissed the claim on the ground that, although the giving of advice by the
Inland Revenue to taxpayers was a 'service' within s 20(1) of the 1976 Act and refusal to
give advice to a person because of his race would amount to unlawful discrimination
within s 20(1)(a), where advice was actually given to a taxpayer the contents of the advice
h   could not amount to unlawful discrimination. The plaintiff appealed. On the appeal the
commissioners submitted that, as the advice which their officer gave to the plaintiff was

---

a   Section 20, so far as material, provides:
    '(1) It is unlawful for any person concerned with the provision (for payment or not) of goods,
    facilities or services to the public or a section of the public to discriminate against a person who
    seeks to obtain or use those goods, facilities or services—(a) by refusing or deliberately omitting to
j   provide him with any of them; or (b) by refusing or deliberately omitting to provide him with
    goods, facilities or services of the like quality, in the like manner and on the like terms as are
    normal in the first-mentioned person's case in relation to other members of the public or (where
    the person so seeking belongs to a section of the public) to other members of that section.
    '(2) The following are examples of the facilities and services mentioned in subsection (1) . . . (g)
    the services of any profession or trade, or any local or other public authority.'

incidental to the commissioners' statutory duty to collect taxes and give the statutory tax reliefs, the advice was not within the scope of s 20 of the 1976 Act.

Held – The Inland Revenue were providing 'services' to the public within s 20(1) of the 1976 Act when performing the duties laid on them by s 10[b] of the Income and Corporation Taxes Act 1970 and s 42[c] of the Taxes Management Act 1970 to make a deduction from tax liability for a dependent child and to repay any consequential overpayment of tax, and in disseminating and giving advice to taxpayers to enable them to claim that tax relief. Accordingly, if a tax inspector or the Inland Revenue Board made it more difficult on racial grounds for a particular taxpayer to obtain the relief than they did for other taxpayers, they were discriminating against him in the provision of the service of enabling the tax relief to be claimed, contrary to s 20(1)(b) of the 1976 Act. It followed that the plaintiff was entitled to the declaration claimed and to damages. The appeal would accordingly be allowed (see p 1124 j to p 1125 b e, p 1126 c to j and p 1127 d e h, post).

Kassam v Immigration Appeal Tribunal [1980] 2 All ER 330 distinguished.

Per Lord Denning MR and Templeman LJ. The production of a full birth certificate in certain circumstances when tax relief for a dependent child is claimed can be made lawful by an arrangement sanctioned by a minister of the Crown under s 41(2)[d] of the 1976 Act (see p 1125, c d and p 1127 b c, post).

Notes

For the meaning of unlawful discrimination, see 4 Halsbury's Laws (4th Edn) para 1035.

For the Income and Corporation Taxes Act 1970, s 10, see 33 Halsbury's Statutes (3rd Edn) 43.

For the Taxes Management Act 1970, s 42, see 34 ibid 1288.

For the Race Relations Act 1976, ss 20, 41, see 46 ibid 410, 424.

Case referred to in judgments

Kassam v Immigration Appeal Tribunal [1980] 2 All ER 330, [1980] 1 WLR 1037, CA.

Appeal

By amended particulars of claim dated 28th January 1980 the plaintiff, Prabhudas Savjani, claimed against the defendants, the Commissioners for Inland Revenue ('the commissioners') (1) a declaration that on 15th June 1977 the commissioners unlawfully discriminated against him on racial grounds, contrary to s 20(1)(b) of the Race Relations Act 1976, by requiring and advising him, on account of his national origins, to obtain and produce at his own expense, a certified copy of an entry in a register of births in order to claim tax relief for a dependent child, whereas the commissioners normally required or advised taxpayers who claimed tax relief for a dependent child to produce only a short form of birth certificate; and/or (2) damages limited to £100. The commissioners by their defence denied unlawful discrimination. By a judgment given on 15th August 1980 his Honour Judge Heald sitting in the Nottingham County Court dismissed the plaintiff's claim on the ground that there had been no unlawful discrimination since the plaintiff had not been refused advice and the advice given to him was given in the course of carrying out the commissioners' statutory functions. The plaintiff appealed. The grounds of the appeal were that on the agreed facts put before the judge he ought to have held that the commissioners provided facilities or services to the public or a section of the public, within s 20(1) of the 1976 Act, and that they had discriminated against the plaintiff on racial grounds in providing such facilities or services contrary to the provisions of the 1976 Act. By a respondent's notice the commissioners, while seeking to uphold the judgment on the grounds on which it was entered, contended that it

---

b   Section 10, so far as material, is set out at p 1123 d, post
c   Section 42, so far as material, is set out at p 1125 j, post
d   Section 41 (2), so far as material, is set out at p 1125 b, post

should be affirmed on the following ground also, namely that the judge ought to have
a accepted the commissioners' submission that they were not persons concerned with the
provision of facilities or services within s 20(1) of the 1976 Act and that the fact that they
gave advice and information incidental to the performance of their statutory functions
did not bring them within the aim or purview of s 20. The facts are set out in the
judgment of Lord Denning MR.

b John Macdonald QC and Peter Susman for the plaintiff.
Alan Moses for the commissioners.

LORD DENNING MR. Mr Prabhudas Savjani was born in India. He came to this
country in 1970. He is married. His wife came from Kenya. They have a son, born on
15th May 1976 at the Royal Infirmary at Leicester. He is named Neil Prabhudas
c Savjani. His mother registered his birth. She was given a short certificate of birth. It
only gave the name of the child, its sex and the date of birth.
   The father was entitled to tax relief in respect of his child. That is provided by s 10 of
the Income and Corporation Taxes Act 1970, which says:

   'If the claimant proves—(a) that there is living at any time within the year of
   assessment a child of his ... he shall ... be entitled ... to a deduction from the
·d   amount of income tax with which he is chargeable ...'

or in a proper case repayment of tax which he has already paid.
   So Mr Savjani would be entitled to tax relief in respect of this child. He went along to
the office of the inspector of taxes in Leicester. At that office there are ample facilities for
people to obtain advice and information as to their tax position. There were five
e interview booths in this particular room at Lillie House in Leicester. Chairs were
provided for members of the public waiting to be interviewed. In another room there
were two interview booths and chairs for members of the public. We have been shown
a series of pamphlets which have been issued by the income tax authorities in which they
give advice as to the relief different categories of claimants are entitled to. On the back
of the pamphlet entitled 'Income Tax PAYE' there is a notice saying:

f   'Remember—if you want help ask at any tax office or PAYE Enquiry Office. You
   will find addresses in the telephone book under "Inland Revenue".'

Mr Savjani went to the office of the inspector of taxes on 26th November 1976 in order
to claim tax relief in respect of his son. He took the short form of birth certificate. A
clerk looked up a file and found that Mr Savjani, the father of the child, had been born
g at Kanakpur in India. Thereupon the clerk said to him: 'It is no good your bringing the
short form of birth certificate which only gives the name and sex of the child and the date
of birth: you must bring the full birth certificate which gives the name of the child's
father and mother and where they came from.'
   Mr Savjani said that, when he was told that, he felt very humiliated and upset, because
he knew that, if he had been born in England, he would not have had to produce a full
h birth certificate in regard to his child. The short form would have been sufficient, which
cost him nothing. But the full birth certificate cost £2·50. So Mr Savjani paid £2·50 and
got the full birth certificate and produced it to the Revenue authorities. When he did so,
he was granted relief and received a repayment of tax.
   The matter was taken up by the Commission for Racial Equality. They said that the
officers of the Inland Revenue had been guilty of unlawful discrimination contrary to the
j Race Relations Act 1976. An agreed statement of facts was put before the judge, and has
now been put before us. I will read the material paragraph from the agreed facts which
the Inland Revenue Commissioners said was their policy:

   'At all material times the [commissioners] had a policy in relation to the proof of
   claims that each taxpayer originating from the Indian sub-Continent (including one
   who had come to the United Kingdom from another country such as Kenya) when

claiming tax relief for the first time for a child born in the United Kingdom should
be required to produce a certified copy of the entry in the Register of Births relating
to such child in proof of his claim. Normally, and as a general rule, such certified
copies were not required from other claimants for this relief. This requirement was
embodied in written instructions issued by the Inland Revenue Officers.'

So it is plain that instructions went out from the Inland Revenue officers that, in
respect of a child whose parent or parents were born in the Indian subcontinent, they
were not to be satisfied with the short form of birth certificate. The applicant had to
provide the full form, with the names and place of birth of the father and mother.
Correspondence passed between the Race Relations Board and the Inland Revenue. On
17th May 1977 the Inland Revenue wrote to the Race Relations Board, saying:

'... In the case of claimants who are immigrants, we are bound to consider a
report made to Parliament by the Public Accounts Committee in 1968. The
Committee found that fraudulent claims to personal reliefs had been made upon an
extensive scale by immigrants from the Indian sub-continent and that the claim had
frequently been supported by false documents. Following this report we were
obliged to introduce more stringent checks upon claims by immigrants. In the case
of children born in the United Kingdom, these have included the inspection of the
full birth certificate which enables the child allowance entitlement of the claimant
to be verified by reference to original evidence of the names of the father and
mother.'

So there it is. It is a policy rule laid down by the Inland Revenue. In respect of
children whose parents were born on the Indian subcontinent, they require the
production of the full birth certificate.

The question is whether or not there was unlawful discrimination. The judge held
that there was not. Now there is an appeal to this court.

I need not go into all the sections of the Race Relations Act 1976 except to say, first:
this was plainly a discrimination. On racial grounds this father was treated less
favourably than other fathers. But the question is: was it an unlawful discrimination?
To answer that, one has to look to s 20 of the 1976 Act:

'It is unlawful for any person concerned with the provision (for payment or not)
of goods, facilities or services to the public or a section of the public to discriminate
against a person who seeks to obtain or use those goods, facilities or services—(a) by
refusing or deliberately omitting to provide him with any of them [and so forth].'

The whole question is whether in this case the Revenue authorities were providing
'facilities or services' within that section. Examples are given in s 20(2). One example is
'(c) facilities by way of banking or insurance or for grants, loans, credit or finance';
another is '(g) the services of any profession or trade, or any local or other public
authority'. The Revenue authorities are clearly a 'public authority'. The question is
whether they are providing 'service' to people like the father in this case, who came to
claim tax relief.

The judge drew a distinction between the giving of advice and the advice itself. He
said that the commissioners would be guilty of discrimination if they said, 'We will only
give advice to white people and not to coloured people'. But that they were not guilty
if they said to a coloured person, 'We advise you to bring a full birth certificate'. He held
that the giving of advice was a 'service'; but not the actual advice itself.

To my mind the distinction which was drawn is too fine by far. Under the Taxes
Management Act 1970 the Revenue are entrusted with the care and management of
taxes. They provide a service to the public in collecting tax. They also provide a service
to a section of the public in so far as they give relief from tax or make repayments of tax
or, I would add, give advice about tax. Those are all most valuable services which the
Revenue authorities provide to the public as a whole and to sections of the public. It
seems to me that the provisions for granting relief, giving advice, and the advice which

is given, are the provision of services. As Templeman LJ indicated in the course of
argument: would it be right for the Revenue authorities to issue a circular saying the
people born in England need not worry about full certificates, the Revenue would take
their word, but they would require them in the case of someone coming from the
subcontinent of India? It seems to me that such a circular would be the provision of a
service. It would be discrimination in the provision of a service to the public.

I can understand the difficulty of the Revenue authorities in dealing with the
problem. To what extent should they insist on the production of birth certificates?
There is a way out given by s 41(2) of the Race Relations Act 1976:

> 'Nothing . . . shall render unlawful any act whereby a person discriminates against
> another . . . if that act is done—(a) in pursuance of any arrangements made . . . by
> or with the approval of . . . a Minister of the Crown.'

If the appropriate minister of the Crown should think that arrangements should be made
for insisting in certain circumstances on the production of a full birth certificate, that
could be made perfectly lawful by an arrangement sanctioned by the minister under
s 41. It seems to me that that would be the right way to do it. The minister should take
responsibility for it. He can be asked questions in Parliament about it. That is the way
in which the problem can be solved.

Another alternative would be this: let the inspector ask any claimant for a full birth
certificate, irrespective of his colour or race, if he thinks the circumstances are sufficiently
suspicious to call for one.

I would only mention *Kassam v Immigration Appeal Tribunal* [1980] 2 All ER 330,
[1980] 1 WLR 1037, which was before another division of this court. In that case
discrimination was alleged against the immigration authorities. The court held that, in
dealing with people coming in under the immigration rules, the immigration authorities
were not providing 'services' within the meaning of the Sex Discrimination Act 1975.
This case is very different. The Revenue are providing 'services' in regard to relief from
tax or repayment of tax. Those services come within the provisions of the Act. If there
is discrimination in the carrying out of those services, it is unlawful.

I think, therefore, that the appeal should be allowed.

TEMPLEMAN LJ. The Race Relations Act 1976 undoubtedly poses and is continually
posing a large number of administrative difficulties both for the Crown and for large
organisations; and in the present instance the Inland Revenue are to be treated with
sympathy rather than criticism. Undoubtedly their task will be made more difficult by
the Act if it applies to them. On the other hand, the Act was brought in to remedy very
great evil. It is expressed in very wide terms, and I should be very slow to find that the
effect of something which is humiliatingly discriminatory in racial matters falls outside
the ambit of the Act. Nevertheless, of course, one must look at the Act and construe its
provisions.

I begin with the Board of Inland Revenue which by s 1 of the Inland Revenue
Regulation Act 1890 was brought into existence by Her Majesty the Queen as persons
'for the collection and management of inland revenue'; and by s 13(1) of that Act the
board were directed to 'collect and cause to be collected every part of inland revenue, and
all money under their care and management'. By s 10 of the Income and Corporation
Taxes Act 1970 a taxpayer who proves that he has an infant child and that he has custody
of and maintains the child at his own expense is entitled to a deduction from his tax
liability and a repayment of any consequential overpayment of tax which he has already
suffered. By s 42 of the Taxes Management Act 1970 any claim by a taxpayer must be
made to the Board of Inland Revenue, primarily to an inspector; and by sub-s (7):

> 'The inspector or the Board may give effect to any claim by discharge of tax or, on
> proof to the satisfaction of the inspector or the Board that any tax has been paid by
> the claimant by deduction or otherwise, by repayment of tax.'

So in every case the inspector has to be satisfied by the taxpayer that he is entitled to the relief.

By the combined effect of ss 1, 3, 20 and 75 of the Race Relations Act 1976 it is unlawful for any person, and that includes the Board of Inland Revenue and an inspector of taxes, concerned with the provision of goods, facilities or services to the public to discriminate against any person on the ground of his ethnic or national origin by treating him less favourably by refusing to provide him with services on the terms normally extended to others.

As counsel submitted on behalf of the commissioners, the board and the inspector are performing duties, those duties laid on them by the Act which I have mentioned, but, in my judgment, it does not necessarily follow that the board and the inspector are not voluntarily or in order to carry out their duty also performing services for the taxpayer. The duty is to collect the right amount of revenue; but, in my judgment, there is a service to the taxpayer provided by the board and the inspector by the provision, dissemination and implementation of regulations which will enable the taxpayer to know that he is entitled to a deduction or a repayment, which will entitle him to know how he is to satisfy the inspector or the board if he is so entitled, and which will enable him to obtain the actual deduction or repayment which Parliament said he is to have. For present purposes, in my judgment, the inspector and the board provide the inestimable services of enabling a taxpayer to obtain that relief which Parliament intended he should be able to obtain as a matter of right subject only to proof.

Now if the inspector or the board make it more difficult for a taxpayer who is entitled to relief and who does satisfy all the conditions, to obtain that relief than they do for other taxpayers, they are discriminating in the provision of the service to the public and the service to him of enabling tax relief to be obtained.

Counsel for the commissioners submitted that the Race Relations Act 1976 does not apply to the Inland Revenue at all, but he naturally and wisely recoiled from the suggestion that the inspector of taxes might decline to interview a taxpayer if the taxpayer were coloured. He made forcibly the submission that, when the board decides for sensible reasons that a higher standard of proof is required from taxpayers who come from the Indian subcontinent, the board are not providing a service to that taxpayer; they are carrying out their duty to the Crown. As I have already indicated, it does not seem to me that the two concepts are mutually exclusive. The board and the inspectors perform their duty and carry out a service and, in my judgment, it is a service within the meaning of s 20 of the Race Relations Act 1976.

Counsel for the commissioners relied on *Kassam v Immigration Appeal Tribunal* [1980] 2 All ER 330, [1980] 1 WLR 1037, where this court had to consider the very different case of the powers of the Secretary of State under the Immigration Act 1971. In relation to those powers, wide discretions are conferred on the Secretary of State. Ackner LJ said in that case ([1980] 2 All ER 330 at 335, [1980] 1 WLR 1037 at 1043):

'In my judgment, when the Secretary of State is exercising his discretion in relation to powers granted to him by the Immigration Act 1971, he is not providing a "facility" within the meaning of [the similar, almost identical, Sex Discrimination Act 1975].'

In the present case, as I have indicated, subject to the question of proof, the taxpayer is absolutely entitled to the relief which he prays; and the Inland Revenue performs the service of enabling him to get the relief to which he is absolutely entitled. Accordingly, I do not think the *Kassam* case stands in the way of our reaching the conclusion which I have mentioned.

As Lord Denning MR has pointed out, while the 1976 Act outlaws discrimination of the kind which has appeared in this case, the Act recognises that there may arise administrative and other difficulties of the kind set out in the letter from Sir William Pile dated 17th May 1977, when he made the point that the actions of the Inland Revenue are not inspired by any desire to make life more difficult for those of non-Anglo-Saxon

origin; they are inspired by their duty to collect the right amount of tax and by the
a evidence that amongst the immigrants from the Indian subcontinent there are false
claims which must be exposed. I fully accept that the motives of the Inland Revenue in
this case are perfectly above board and proper; they have never been concealed. The
board do not wish to discriminate. What they wish to do is to make quite sure they get
the right amount of tax. The Race Relations Act 1976 itself recognises that some kind
of discrimination may need to be authorised; and, as Lord Denning MR has pointed out,
b s 41(2)(*a*) confers power on the appropriate minister. If he thinks it right to do so, if he
considers that all the difficulties pointed out by Sir William Pile are so extreme and that
the kind of discrimination which is now in question is necessary in order that the proper
amount of revenue shall be obtained, and honest taxpayers shall not be exploited by those
who are dishonest, the minister can approve the arrangements whereby the present
practices of the Revenue or something like it, perhaps something milder, are
c sanctioned. Of course the minister will be accountable to Parliament, and there can be
discussions about whether these wholesale precautions are really necessary. This is a
politicians' problem rather than a civil service problem, and it is on the politicians that
the responsibility should be left, in my judgment, of providing any exceptions to the
wide words of the Race Relations Act 1976 and the obvious intention by that Act to burn
out what has been the serious evil of racial discrimination.

d   Accordingly, in my judgment, the appeal should be allowed. The judge was faced
with the *Kassam* case and he drew the arguable distinction between advice and decision.
I recognise the force of that point in the same way as I recognise the force of the
argument submitted by counsel for the commissioners. But, balancing these things, I
have in my mind no doubt that for the purposes of s 20 the Board of Inland Revenue and
the inspectors are providing services and must therefore have regard to the 1976 Act. As
e Lord Denning MR has said, it is a short, interesting and not easy point which was well
argued by counsel on behalf of the plaintiff and by counsel on behalf of the
commissioners. I agree that the appeal should be allowed.

DUNN LJ. I have felt more difficulty than Lord Denning MR and Templeman LJ in
deciding that in the action they took in relation to the plaintiff's claim for child benefit
f the commissioners were providing services to the public or a section of the public. If
they were not, then, however discriminatory the practice set out in Sir William Pile's
letter of 17th May 1977 might be, it would not be unlawful under s 20 of the Race
Relations Act 1976. I find considerable force in the argument of counsel for the
commissioners that, in considering the proof required to support the plaintiff's claim to
tax relief, the inspector was concerned with his statutory duty under the Taxes
g Management Act 1970 and the Income and Corporation Taxes Act 1970 and was not
concerned with the provision of any services, even though the statutory duty involved
the giving of advice. Counsel for the commissioners submitted that all the inspector was
concerned with was to decide the correct amount of tax payable by the plaintiff since,
under the 1970 Act, child benefits fell to be deducted from the total tax payable.
    However, having heard the judgments of Lord Denning MR and Templeman LJ, I am
h not prepared to dissent from them; though, in agreeing that the appeal should be
allowed, I do so with some doubt and hesitation.

*Appeal allowed; declaration in form asked; damages of £25 awarded. Leave to appeal to the
House of Lords.*

Solicitors: *Bindman & Partners* (for the plaintiff); *Solicitor of Inland Revenue.*

Sumra Green Barrister.

Hulley v Thompson

QUEEN'S BENCH DIVISION
WALLER LJ AND STEPHEN BROWN J
12th MAY 1980

Supplementary benefit – Benefit paid for requirements of person whom another person is liable to b
maintain – Recovery of expenditure from relative liable for maintenance – Complaint against
father for order requiring him to pay sums in respect of benefit paid to mother for children –
Father divorced from mother – When divorce granted consent order made by court providing
that father should not pay any maintenance to mother for children but should transfer his half-
share in the matrimonial home to mother – Father's resources sufficient to pay maintenance for
children – Whether commission entitled to recover expenditure for children from father – c
Whether father a person 'liable to maintain' children notwithstanding terms of consent order –
Supplementary Benefits Act 1976, ss 17(1), 18(1).

The father of two children was divorced from the mother. When the divorce was
granted a consent order was made that the father should not pay any maintenance to the
mother for herself or for the children but should transfer to the mother his half share, d
worth £12,500, in the matrimonial home. The Supplementary Benefits Commission
paid benefit to the wife for the children. The father was earning between £55 and £77
a week. The commission made a complaint against him under s 18(1)[a] of the
Supplementary Benefits Act 1976, as the person liable to maintain the children under
s 17(1)[b] of that Act, seeking to recover from him such sums in respect of the benefit paid
as the court considered appropriate. The magistrates decided that in exercising their e
discretion to make an order under s 18(1) the terms of the consent order were a relevant
consideration and that having regard to the consent order no order should be made
against the father. The commission appealed. The father submitted that the transfer of
his half-share in the house to the mother under the consent order was to be treated for the
purpose of the complaint as being made in lieu of his liability to maintain the children.

Held – The father remained a person 'liable to maintain' his children within s 18(1) of f
the 1976 Act notwithstanding the terms of the consent order, for the consent order did
not avoid his liability to maintain them under s 17(1) of that Act. Since prima facie his
resources were sufficient to meet that liability the magistrates had wrongly exercised
their discretion under s 18(1) in refusing to make an order against him and the case
would be remitted to them for reconsideration on the basis that he was a person liable to g
maintain the children for the purpose of s 17(1). Accordingly, the appeal would be
allowed (see p 1130 *d* to *j* and p 1131 *c* to *e*, post).

Notes

For the liability of a spouse to maintain his children under the social security legislation,
see 24 Halsbury's Laws (4th Edn) para 507. h
    For recovery of benefit from liable relatives, see Supplement to 27 Halsbury's Laws
(3rd Edn) para 965.
    For the Supplementary Benefits Act 1976, ss 17, 18, see 46 Halsbury's Statutes (3rd
Edn) 1060, 1061.

Case referred to in judgments

Diss Urban Sanitary Authority v Aldrich (1877) 2 QBD 179, 46 LJMC 183, 36 LT 663, 41 JP j
    549 DC, 33 Digest (Repl) 311, *1352*.

---

a   Section 18(1) is set out at p 1130 *b*, post
b   Section 17(1) is set out at p 1130 *a*, post

Case also cited

a *National Assistance Board v Parkes* [1955] 3 All ER 1, [1955] 2 QB 506.

Case stated

This was an appeal by Michael Donald Hulley, an officer of the Supplementary Benefits Commission, by way of case stated by the justices for the county of Derby acting in and

b for the petty sessional division of High Peak in respect of their adjudication as a domestic court sitting at Buxton on 21st June 1978 whereby they dismissed a complaint dated 27th February 1978 preferred by the appellant against the respondent, Frank Thompson, in which the appellant applied for an order under s 18 of the Supplementary Benefits Act 1976 that the respondent, being the father of Christopher David Thompson and Anne Lorraine Thompson whom he was liable to maintain under s 17 of the 1976 Act, pay to

c the Secretary of State for Social Services such sum as the court considered appropriate. The facts are set out in the judgment of Waller LJ.

Simon D Brown for the appellant.
T B Hegarty for the respondent.

d

WALLER LJ. This is an appeal by way of case stated from a decision of the justices for the county of Derby, High Peak petty sessional division, in respect of an adjudication made on 21st June 1978.

A complaint had been preferred by the appellant, an officer of the Supplementary Benefits Commission, against the respondent, as father of two children whom he was

e liable to maintain pursuant to s 17 of the Supplementary Benefits Act 1976, that benefit had been paid for those children and continued to be paid. The Supplementary Benefits Commission were applying for an order under s 18 of the Supplementary Benefits Act 1976 for the respondent to pay such sums as the court considered appropriate.

The respondent was the father of two children born on 28th May 1965. He was the person liable to maintain the children. He was divorced at the Derby County Court.

f When the decree was granted there was an order by consent ordering that the respondent should not pay any maintenance to the petitioner for either herself or for any children of the family, and within two months of the date of the order that the respondent should transfer to the petitioner all his interest in the matrimonial home. There was a further provision about the proceeds of a policy of insurance and about the enforcement of arrears, and a statement that the approximate value of the property transferred was some

g £25,000 free of mortgages (that was in 1976), that the respondent's net wage was between £55 and £70 weekly and that benefit had been paid by the Department of Health and Social Security for both children.

The justices, having found those facts, came to the conclusion that they had a discretion whether or not they made an order, and they declined to make an order, ordering the appellant to pay costs.

h The first thing I should say is this. The justices purported to decline to make the order on the basis of a case called *Diss Urban Sanitary Authority v Aldrich* (1877) 2 QBD 179. But having looked at that case, in my view it gives no authority whatever to the conclusion to which the justices came in this case. So we have to approach it on the basis of the facts found.

It is submitted on behalf of the respondent that the discretion given by s 18 of the 1976

j Act is a very wide discretion and that the justices were entitled to take into account the agreement that had been made in the county court, which had provided that the wife would not make a claim for maintenance for the children. It was submitted that the transfer by the respondent of the half share in the house was in the nature of a capital sum which this court should infer was in lieu of maintenance not only for the wife, but for the children.

Section 17 of the Supplementary Benefits Act 1976 reads:

'(1) For the purposes of this Act—(a) a man shall be liable to maintain his wife and *a* his children; and (b) a woman shall be liable to maintain her husband and her children . . .'

Section 18(1) reads:

'Where supplementary benefit is paid or claimed to meet requirements which are, or include, those of a person whom another person is, for the purposes of this *b* Act, liable to maintain (in this section referred to respectively as "the dependant" and "the liable relative") the Commission may make a complaint against the liable relative to a magistrates' court for an order under this section.'

Section 18(3) reads:

'On the hearing of a complaint under subsection (1) above the court shall have *c* regard to all the circumstances and, in particular, to the resources of the liable relative, and may order him to pay such sum, weekly or otherwise, as it may consider appropriate.'

It was under s 18(1) that this complaint was made, and it is submitted by counsel for the respondent that s 18(3) gives a discretion to the justices sufficiently wide to justify the *d* decision which they made in this particular case.

In my judgment the liability of both wife and husband is unambiguously set out in s 17(1) of the 1976 Act. That indicates that each of them is liable for the maintenance of their children and while there may be cases where, as between husband and wife, other arrangements might be made, in the case of children it is difficult to see how a consent arrangement can avoid the husband's or wife's liability to maintain the children. *e*

In this case the Supplementary Benefits Commission have paid benefit to the wife in respect of the children. It follows from that that the wife herself must have been entitled to benefit for the children. In those circumstances the question must arise what is the father doing in respect of his liability, because prima facie he would be responsible for all that which the wife was unable herself to provide. Counsel for the respondent submits that the respondent has provided for that liability by the capital sum of half his share in *f* the house which he transferred to the wife.

In my judgment it is quite impossible to take that simplistic view. The justices should have been considering how much the husband could pay towards the maintenance of the children. Prima facie he should be paying the balance of that which the wife was unable to pay. But it may well be that on consideration some deduction should be made in the circumstances of the case, which would take into consideration the whole of the terms *g* of the consent order in the county court.

In my judgment the justices came to the wrong conclusion in exercising the discretion which they did, and this case must go back to be reconsidered. They should reconsider this case on the basis that the respondent is liable to maintain these two children. Prima facie the amount he is earning, £55 to £70 per week, does include resources sufficient to enable him to meet his responsibility to maintain these children. Is there something in *h* the light of the order made in the county court which would reduce that responsibility in any way? It may be that they could come to either conclusion: either there is nothing to reduce it or there is something to reduce it. That would be a matter for them. I would send this case back with that indication.

j

STEPHEN BROWN J. I agree that this appeal should be allowed.

The Supplementary Benefits Act 1976, by s 17(1), makes it clear that it is a continuing liability on the part of a man to maintain his children. The facts found by the justices in this case indicate that the children were not in fact being maintained by either the father or the mother, at any rate to the extent necessary for their ordinary welfare, since they

found that benefit had been paid by the Department of Health and Social Security for
a both children to the mother.

It would appear that the present unfortunate situation arises in large measure from the
rather extraordinary order which was made at the Derby County Court in November
1976 when there was a financial settlement between the father and the mother of these
children consequent on their divorce. It was then ordered that the respondent 'do not
pay any maintenance to the petitioner for either herself or any children of the family'.
b A transfer to the petitioner, as she was then, of the respondent's share in the matrimonial
home was ordered by consent, but this was not a provision for the children, although it
is true that it resulted in them having a roof over their heads. It is unfortunate that a
consent order of that kind is on the record, since it may later mislead a court having to
consider an application of this kind. Certainly no provision was made in the terms of
that order for the maintenance of the children.

c   That being so, the liability undoubtedly falls on the respondent, as it does on the
mother, to maintain these children. It seems to me that the justices have really
considered the consent order made at Derby County Court as being rather in the nature
of a bar to their making any order of the kind sought on this occasion. They do not
record it as being a bar, but merely say that in their discretion, which they seem to think
was absolute, they decided they need not make any order of any kind.

d   Having regard to the facts which they found, particularly as to the income of the
respondent, it would appear that the respondent should be able to provide something
towards the maintenance of his children.

The justices should consider the financial circumstances. I do not consider that the
fact that in the past a transfer of property order has been made between the father and the
mother should obscure the continuing obligation of the father to maintain his
e children. Accordingly I agree that this case must be sent back to the justices to consider
the matter in the light of the circumstances obtaining and, as s 18(3) stipulates, in the
light of the resources of the liable relative, in this case both the father and the mother.

Appeal allowed; case remitted.

Solicitors: *Solicitor to the Department of Health and Social Security* (for the appellant); *Lomax,
Geddes & Co*, Manchester (for the respondent).

Dilys Tausz   Barrister.

R v Barrington

COURT OF APPEAL, CRIMINAL DIVISION
DUNN LJ, PHILLIPS AND DRAKE JJ
13th, 28th NOVEMBER 1980

*Criminal evidence – Similar facts – Circumstances in which similar fact evidence admissible –
Evidence of facts relating not to similar offence but to similar surrounding circumstances –
Accused charged with indecent assault – Similar fact evidence which does not include evidence
disclosing actual commission of similar offence – Evidence revealing facts strikingly similar to
circumstances surrounding offence charged – Whether evidence admissible.*

The accused was charged on indictment with indecently assaulting the complainants,
three young girls, at X's house. The prosecution alleged that he had lured the
complainants to the house on the pretext that they were required as baby-sitters but that
he had, in fact, wanted them for his own sexual purposes, because, once there, he had
shown them pornographic pictures, asked them to pose for photographs in the nude and
indecently assaulted them. The complainants gave evidence to that effect. The accused
contended that the evidence was a tissue of lies and that each complainant had her own
private motive for concocting a story against him. In order to show that the complainants
were telling the truth and that the accused was operating a system, the prosecution
called, with the leave of the judge, three young girls, B, S and A, who said that they, too,
had been lured to the house on the pretext of baby-sitting and then shown pornographic
pictures and asked to pose for photographs in the nude. Not one of them, however, said
that the accused had indecently assaulted her. The accused was convicted. He appealed,
contending that the evidence of B, S and A was incapable of amounting to similar fact
evidence because it did not include evidence of the commission of offences similar to
those with which he had been charged, and accordingly should not have been admitted.

Held – Evidence of similar facts which did not include evidence disclosing the
commission of an offence similar to that charged but which related solely to the
surrounding circumstances could be admitted if it was evidence of facts which were
strikingly similar to those surrounding the commission of the offence charged. The
evidence of B, S and A had therefore been properly admitted because (a) it revealed
features which were strikingly similar to the circumstances surrounding the commission
of the offences charged and was of positive probative value in determining the truth of
the charges against the accused in that it tended to show that he was guilty of the offences
charged, and (b) because there was no suggestion that it should have been excluded on
the ground that its prejudicial effect outweighed its probative value (see p 1141 e to g,
post).

R v Scarrott [1978] 1 All ER 672 applied.

Notes
For similar fact evidence in criminal cases generally, see 11 Halsbury's Laws (4th Edn)
paras 375, 376.

    For similar fact evidence in indecent assault cases, see ibid para 381, and for cases on
the subject, see 14(2) Digest (Reissue) 509–521, 4167–4299.

Cases referred to in judgment
Boardman v Director of Public Prosecutions [1974] 3 All ER 887, [1975] AC 421, [1974] 3
    WLR 673, 139 JP 52, 60 Cr App R 165, HL, 14(2) Digest (Reissue) 527, 4296.
Director of Public Prosecutions v Kilbourne [1973] 1 All ER 440, [1973] AC 729, [1973] 2
    WLR 254, 137 JP 193, 57 Cr App R 381, HL, 14(2) Digest (Reissue) 526, 4295.

Noor Mohamed v R [1949] 1 All ER 365, [1949] AC 182, PC, 14(2) Digest (Reissue) 510, *4177.*

a
R v Doughty [1965] 1 All ER 560, [1965] 1 WLR 331, 129 JP 172, 42 Cr App R 110, CCA, 14(2) Digest (Reissue) 525, *4278.*

R v Horry [1949] NZLR 791, CA.

R v Johannsen (1977) 65 Cr App R 101, CA.

R v Novac (1976) 65 Cr App R 107, CA.

b
R v Scarrott [1978] 1 All ER 672, [1978] QB 1016, [1977] 3 WLR 629, 142 JP 198, 65 Cr App R 125, CA, Digest (Cont Vol E) 139, *4299a.*

R v Smith (1915) 84 LJKB 2153, [1914–15] All ER Rep 262, 114 LT 239, 80 JP 31, 25 Cox CC 271, 11 Cr App R 229, CCA, 14(1) Digest (Reissue) 397, *3352.*

Appeal

c
On 15th November 1979, the appellant, Brian John Barrington, was convicted in the Crown Court at Bristol, before Milmo J, on three counts of indecent assault and on one count of attempting sexual intercourse with a girl under 16. He was sentenced to a total of three years' imprisonment. He was subsequently given leave by O'Connor J to appeal against his conviction. The facts are set out in the judgment of the court.

d
David Lane for the appellant.
Patrick Whelon for the Crown.

Cur adv vult

e
28th November. **DUNN LJ** read the following judgment of the court: This appeal once again raises the question as to the admissibility of what is called similar fact evidence, especially in sexual cases. In particular it raises the question of whether evidence of similar facts falling short of similar offences with which an accused is charged can ever be admissible.

On 15th November 1979, at the Crown Court at Bristol, before Milmo J, the appellant and Constance May Meredith were arraigned on an amended indictment containing ten

f
counts. The appellant was involved in nine of the counts. Three counts charged him with rape; two counts charged him with unlawful sexual intercourse with a girl under 13 years of age; one count (count 10) charged him with unlawful sexual intercourse with a girl under 16 years of age, and three counts charged him with indecent assault. The counts charging unlawful sexual intercourse were alternatives to the counts charging rape. He pleaded not guilty to all the counts. He was found guilty on three charges of indecent assault; not guilty as charged, but guilty of attempt, on count 10; and not guilty

g
on the remaining counts.

On 29th November he was sentenced as follows: count 4 (indecent assault on a girl aged 11 years) three years' imprisonment; count 7 (indecent assault on a girl aged 13 years) 18 months' imprisonment concurrent; count 9 (indecent assault on a girl aged 13 years) 12 months' imprisonment concurrent; count 10 (attempted sexual intercourse

h
with a girl under 16) nine months' imprisonment concurrent. Total imprisonment, three years. The appellant was also ordered to pay the prosecution costs not exceeding £500 and to pay the whole of the defence costs.

He now appeals against conviction by leave of the single judge, who observed for the attention of counsel and the full court: 'I have given leave because I think the full court should consider the directions on corroboration. But for that issue I would have refused

j
leave.' The single judge refused the appellant's application for leave to appeal against sentence and his renewal of that application has been refused by the full court.

Constance May Meredith, aged 29, was indicted jointly with the appellant on three counts of indecent assault and by herself on a single count charging assault occasioning bodily harm (she beat one girl, Sally, with a cane causing weals). Meredith pleaded guilty to all the counts against her and she was sentenced to a total of 18 months' imprisonment. She has not applied for leave to appeal. After her arrest she eventually made a full confession and volunteered to give evidence for the prosecution, which she did.

The case for the Crown at the trial was that the appellant and Meredith combined together to induce young girls to go into Meredith's house, ostensibly for the purpose of baby-sitting, but in reality for the sexual purposes of the appellant. For that purpose they operated and put into effect a system which emerged through the evidence.

In her evidence Meredith said that at the end of 1978 she was working as a casual waitress at a hotel. She there met the appellant who was a travelling salesman engaged in the sale of heating apparatus. He told her that he was in fact Terry Nation and that he was the script-writer of the television series Dr Who. She believed him and became sexually involved with him. Within a few days he moved from the hotel to her house, even though the house was described as a dirty, squalid and ill-furnished place. He asked Meredith to procure young girls for him for sexual purposes, the younger the better. He assured her that if they were under 16 years of age he would not have sexual intercourse with them, but would only play with them. He offered to give her £50 per girl and in addition he said that he would take out £30,000 worth of computer shares for her daughter (then aged 2½ years) whom he would also send to a private school. At the time Meredith was very short of money and heavily in debt and she agreed to his request. He suggested also that Meredith train as a masseuse so that she could persuade the girls to allow her to massage them.

Anita, aged 15 years, gave evidence. She was the first girl to be procured and was readily available. She had been employed by Meredith as a baby-sitter since the summer of 1978. She was still so employed and she was sexually experienced. The appellant told her that he was the writer of books, like Dr Who, under the name Terry Nation. He showed her a number of pornographic books. One evening after Meredith left the room the appellant committed various acts of indecency on Anita, and attempted to have intercourse with her. She struggled and he did not succeed. Anita's evidence was the basis of his conviction on count 10. Anita said that she returned to baby sit once after that. The appellant offered her £200 if she would pose for some photographs. He did not say what kind of photograph, but from what he had done to her she had a good idea what type he wanted.

Early in 1979, Susan, aged 11, took over the job of baby-sitting from Anita. She was paid £1 a night for her services. Susan said that one evening Meredith fell asleep and the appellant then took her, Susan, upstairs to Meredith's bedroom. He told her to take her skirt and jumper off and, although she did not want to, she did so, because she was frightened. He then pushed her onto the bed and got on top of her. She tried to push him off but she could not. He then committed various acts of indecency on her. When giving evidence she did not mention sexual intercourse. She did not say that the appellant had had, or had tried to have, sexual intercourse with her, neither did she say that he had not. She was not cross-examined about it but merely asked general questions on the basis that all her evidence was untrue. The incident ended when Meredith came upstairs. Meredith said that when she arrived upstairs, Susan was lying across the bed with her pants and socks off and the appellant was on top of her, moving up and down as if he were trying to have intercourse with her. Susan appeared to be upset and after she had gone home, the appellant apologised.

Despite his apologies, the same sort of thing occurred on another evening, the only difference being that on the later occasion Susan did not seem upset. She continued to baby-sit for a week or two, and during that time she frequently had her bottom smacked and caned by the appellant. On one occasion after a bath Meredith massaged Susan's back, and while she was doing so the appellant came into the room and took over the massage. He turned her onto her face and massaged her back. He then turned her onto her back and there followed various acts of indecency by both the appellant and Meredith on Susan.

Sally, aged 13, succeeded her sister Susan as Meredith's baby-sitter. On one occasion, *a* after she had had a bath, Meredith massaged her and while she was doing so the appellant came into the room. Sally was frightened and the appellant went downstairs. Later that same day Sally had another bath by request and afterwards the appellant took photographs of her in the nude, in various poses, including indecent ones. He told her that she would get £200 for them. When she later saw the photographs she was scared that someone else might see them, or that they might be put in books. Frequently she, Meredith and the appellant were together in the bedroom, nude, and indulging in sexual practices.

b This happened on more than one occasion, and afterwards when she went downstairs the appellant would smack or cane her bottom. Similar acts occurred on every occasion that she went baby-sitting for Meredith. On one occasion in the bedroom she took a photograph of Meredith and the appellant in the nude.

It was suggested in cross-examination of Meredith and each of the three girls that the whole of their evidence was a tissue of lies and that the three girls had put their heads

c together to concoct a false story against the appellant, whose conduct had been such that it should not have excited any criticism at all. At the conclusion of their evidence, there was an application by counsel for the Crown to call three other girls, whose statements were annexed to a notice of additional evidence. In support of his application counsel said:

d 'It was put to Sally, the last girl, I think, in effect, that the girls had put their heads together and knew what each was saying and that each had their own private motives for making up these lies. The prosecution say that is not right and the truth of what the girls say can be judged by seeing the picture as a whole. It was a course of conduct which occurred with three further girls who, I suggest, were in the pipeline for further offences had not the matter blown up early in March. Certainly,

e they were being introduced to the house, shown sexual matters, introduced to sexual matters, in this course of conduct hoping that the girls would be amenable.'

Counsel for the defence objected. He said:

'My Lord, I respectfully submit that the evidence of Bernadette and of the two other girls should be excluded. I have analysed their respective witness statements and may I state my conclusions first and then show your Lordship how I arrive at

f them. My first proposition is this, and if I may call Anita and the two sisters "the complainants", and if I may call Bernadette and the two other sisters "the girls", for shortness and brevity of distinction, my Lord; the evidence of the three girls, Bernadette and the two other sisters, and it is their witness statements as they stand, do not corroborate the evidence of the three complainants in the material allegations of rape and or indecent assault.'

g Later counsel said:

'If these girls were to give evidence the prejudicial effect of their evidence would outweigh their probative value.'

After further argument the judge ruled the evidence of the three other girls as

h admissible, giving his reasons in the following terms:

'In my judgment this evidence is admissible and it is admissible on two grounds which can be stated quite shortly. One is that it is evidence, and it is for the jury to say what weight is to be given to it, it is evidence that to the knowledge of the defendant, girls were being recruited for immoral purposes, as one tests that by

j showing them these photographs, for immoral purposes under the cover of being required for baby-sitting. It is evidence for the jury to consider whether it was not for the immoral gratification of the defendant that these girls were being recruited for that alleged purpose. Secondly, because the leave was given and the court was pressed to give leave for the girls to be interrogated, or for one of the girls to be cross-examined, on matters which would not otherwise have been allowed under the

recent Act to be cross-examined, because the suggestion was that the allegation
which these girls were making about this man were emanations of their own dirty
minds, fabrications which had nothing to do with anything with which he was
connected or that he had in any way taken any part in the matters complained of.
I admit this evidence on these grounds.'

The three other girls accordingly gave evidence. Their names were Bernadette, aged
13, and two sisters, Shirley, aged 15, and Anne, aged 16. It appeared that whilst Sally was
still employed as baby-sitter by Meredith, the appellant and Meredith saw the three girls
in a café in Gloucester with a view to engaging a new baby-sitter. They were obviously
schoolgirls, dressed in school uniform. The appellant asked them what they were doing
and they told him that they were playing truant. He went out to buy some film and
when he returned he drove them all back to the house in his car.

Bernadette said that the appellant told them that he was Terry Nation. He was smartly
dressed. When they got to the house they were shown photographs of nude women by
the appellant and by Meredith and they were asked if they would like to have their
photographs taken. At that stage, she, Bernadette, went out to keep an appointment
with a social worker. When she came back she was shown photographs, decent ones, of
Shirley and Anne clothed. She went to the bedroom with Meredith to have her
photograph taken. One was taken of her fully clothed and then she agreed to have
photographs of her taken in the nude. Four were taken of her in indecent positions and
they were shown to the appellant. She was paid £2 for them. She was shown
photographs of girls being whipped and other photographs, including an obscene one of
part of the appellant's body. She was offered a job as a baby-sitter and she was paid £5 for
two days' work.

Anne said that at the house they were shown by the appellant magazines containing
pornographic photographs. They were also shown other photographs by both Meredith
and the appellant, including the obscene one of the appellant. It was suggested that she,
Anne, should be photographed. She agreed to be photographed with her clothes on but
she refused to be photographed in the nude, even though she was told that there was a
prize of £200 and both the appellant and Meredith tried to persuade her that she could
do with the money. Baby-sitting was not mentioned to her at the house, although that
was supposed to be why they had gone there and she was not offered a job as a baby-sitter.

Shirley gave evidence which did not differ in any essential way from that of her
sister. She said that the appellant told them that he produced films like The Persuaders
and The Saint and talked about the film stars he knew. At the house she also was shown
the indecent photographs. She had her photograph taken clothed, but she refused to
have any nude photographs taken although she was told about the £200 prize. She, like
her sister, heard nothing more about the baby-sitting. No photographs of any of the girls
were found by the police. Meredith said they had been destroyed when the investigation
started.

The appellant did not give evidence and no other evidence was called by the defence.
It was submitted that all the allegations against the appellant were lies. He had not done
any of the things alleged against him and he had not indulged in any improper
behaviour. He did not show the girls any improper books or photographs. If they had
seen any they must have obtained them themselves. The whole case was a wicked
conspiracy by the girls.

In his summing up the judge said:

'No evidence as we know was called by the defence, but I think I can fairly
summarise what the defence in this case has been as indicated by the speech from
counsel. It is that the defendant never committed any of the offences charged, and
that the evidence given in respect of those offences are lies from start to finish. He
never indulged in any improper behaviour or did any of the things which are
alleged against him as having taken place in that house. So far as the pictures are
concerned, it is said that the girls could have got their hands on these pictures, and

a I say: "How did they get to know what was in these pictures?"; and then, members of the jury, it is further suggested, and it is for you to say whether there is a vestige of support for this or not, that this is a gigantic conspiracy, a wicked diabolical conspiracy by these girls for some ulterior reason which I think counsel said it was not for him to suggest a motive and he could not do so and was not going to do so.'

The judge dealt with the similar fact evidence and said:

b 'There is a body of evidence which you have had in this case which can be described and called "similar fact" evidence, evidence of system. It relates, members of the jury, primarily to the evidence of Bernadette and the two other sisters, coupled with the evidence of the three girls against whom offences are alleged. Bernadette and the other sisters do not give any direct evidence of the charges in the indictment, and moreover, members of the jury, the evidence they give does not *c* pretend to prove that the accused committed or even attempted to commit on them the offences charged in the indictment. . . These girls' evidence is relevant in so far as it goes to show that Brian Barrington was at the material time using the same technique and methods of luring girls into no 49 for the purpose of performing acts of physical indecency with them.'

d The judge then listed six pieces of evidence which he left to the jury as capable of constituting similar fact evidence. First the baby-sitting proposition. Second, the boasting claims to the girls about his position as a script-writer of well-known television programmes, and a friend of the stars. Third, Meredith was described as a professional photographer. Fourth, the evidence about the £200 prize for nude photographs. Fifth, the evidence that all the girls were shown pornographic pictures and pornographic magazines. And, sixth, the technique, as the judge described it, that was employed to try *e* to get the girls to strip eventually for nude photographs. The judge concluded:

'And you may think that the nude photographs were merely part of the leading to what is said to be the eventual indecent assaults of various kinds and descriptions.'

The judge then went on to deal with the question of corroboration. He said this:

f 'If you are satisfied that the evidence of these girls, coupled with the other girls or even taken by themselves (it is really "taken by themselves" I ought to say), taken to prove that there was an intention on the part of this defendant to get these girls into the house, one after the other, for indecent purposes that could amount to corroboration. It is for you to say whether it does or whether it does not.'

g The judge, at the end of his summing up, came back to that and said:

'There is what I will refer to as the similar fact evidence, the evidence of system, and that is the evidence of Bernadette and the two other sisters. You know what I am referring to, and that I have directed you could be corroboration. It is for you to decide whether it is in fact corroboration, and members of the jury, the prosecution have submitted to you or they have not put that matter before you as *h* corroboration; they have only put it as evidence of similar facts.'

Counsel for the appellant made no complaint about the direction as to the evidence of the three other girls being capable of corroborating the evidence of the complainants if the evidence of the three other girls was admissible. Indeed in the light of the remarks of Lord Cross in *Director of Prosecutions v Kilbourne* [1973] 1 All ER 440 at 464, [1973] AC *j* 729 at 760, it would have been impossible for him to have done so. Lord Cross said:

'Once the "similar fact" evidence is admitted—and it was common ground that it was properly admitted in this case—then of necessity it "corroborates"—ie strengthens or supports— the evidence given by the boy an alleged offence against whom is the subject of the count under consideration.'

But counsel for the appellant submitted that the evidence of the other girls should not have been admitted at all. None of the other girls gave evidence of an indecent assault, or any other act of indecency on their person. Indeed their evidence related to events after Susan and Sally had been to the house. It was accordingly incapable of amounting to similar fact evidence. Although other grounds were put forward in the notice of appeal, this was the only ground relied on in this court.

Counsel for the appellant referred us first to *R v Doughty* [1965] 1 All ER 560 at 562, [1965] 1 WLR 331 at 334 where Lord Parker CJ said this:

'It is to be observed in the present case that, while it might be said that there was evidence capable of being treated in a sinister respect and held to be indecent assault, the acts to which the small girls had spoken were certainly equally consistent with what one might call a paternal or avuncular interest. It is not without interest that neighbours came, and particularly the mother of Carol, and said that she knew this man, that he was highly respected, and that she absolutely trusted her childern with him, and that he undoubtedly was very fond of children. That there was evidence of familiarity in the sense of a paternal or avuncular interest is undoubted. The evidence that it was not merely for that but in order to satisfy lust was tenuous to a degree. Further, it is to be observed that, even if the acts complained of were capable of being interpreted as indecent, it was quite a different form of indecency in regard to physical acts to that spoken to by the girls who were the subject of the counts. In the circumstances, this court is satisfied that, where the evidence of indecency is tenuous to a degree and where, even if held to be indecent, it is a different form of indecency, then the court can only exercise its discretion in one way, by excluding that evidence, the reason being that its prejudicial value is quite overwhelming. It is well-known that this court is very reluctant ever to interfere with the discretion of a trial judge. They will in the ordinary way only do so if he has erred in principle. The court feels, however, that, in the circumstances as I have indicated them, this discretion could properly only be exercised in one way, by excluding the evidence. That being so, and this evidence being clearly directed to both counts—both that dealing with Carol as well as that dealing with Shirley—the only proper course the court can take is to quash both convictions.'

Nobody could say that the evidence of the three other girls in this case disclosed no more than a paternal or avuncular interest on the part of the appellant and we do not feel that we are assisted by *R v Doughty*.

Counsel for the appellant also referred us to more recent and well-known authorities on the admissibility of similar fact evidence. They are *Boardman v Director of Public Prosecutions* [1974] 3 All ER 887, [1975] AC 421, *R v Johannsen* (1977) 65 Cr App R 101, *R v Novac* (1976) 65 Cr App R 107 and *R v Scarrott* [1978] 1 All ER 672, [1978] QB 1016. He also referred us to Cross on Evidence (5th Edn, 1979, p 356) and to *R v Horry* [1949] NZLR 791. In that case—

'The evidence the admission of which was complained of was, first, that of two women, who, as well as the complainant, had each replied to the accused's newspaper advertisement and had (separately) met him by appointment; each had had an interview with him broadly similar to that between the accused and the complainant, except that in the case of these two women there was no suggestion of any attempt to kiss or to assault; and, secondly, the evidence of a Detective-sergeant (to whom the accused was well known as one who had many convictions), who saw him meet and converse with one of these two women. It was contended that the evidence of the two women served merely to show that they, too, had been deceived, which was not an offence, and was irrelevant; that such evidence merely created in the minds of the jury prejudice against the accused; and that the evidence of the Detective-sergeant, in so far as it revealed the accused was known to him and that the Detective-sergeant troubled to keep him under observation, implied previous

offences, and so prejudiced the accused from obtaining a fair trial. The admissibility
of the two young women's evidence was argued in Chambers before trial, when it
was sought to justify its being led on the grounds (i) that it was indicative of system,
and (ii) that it assisted in the establishment of the identity of the accused as the
person against whom [the complainant's] allegations were directed. The learned
Judge ruled that the evidence was admissible on the latter ground.'

On appeal to the Court of Appeal, Gresson J said (at 793):

'Dealing first with the question as to whether this evidence was properly
admitted: in order to be admissible, it must be relevant. It contributed nothing
towards establishing that the accused improperly kissed or assaulted S.L., which was
the offence with which he was charged, and, in so far as it revealed deception
practised upon other young women, it was prejudicial. But it had relevance on the
question of identity, and this, on the depositions, was in issue no less than whether
a kiss was forced on an unwilling recipient.'

Having cited a large number of authorities, the learned judge said (at 798):

'It was in the light of these authorities that Callan, J., had to rule. As the matter
then stood, the evidence, being relevant to the issue of identity, was admissible, but,
from counsel's assurance that identity would not be disputed, it became clear that
identity would not in fact be the subject of contention. Evidence that goes to an
issue not really in contest, and merely prejudices the accused, should be excluded.'

The judge then referred to the then recent decision of the Privy Council in *Noor Mohamed
v R* [1949] 1 All ER 365, [1949] AC 182 and said that decision—

'has established beyond all question that there is such a discretionary power. But
in this case the question goes deeper, and is whether the evidence is admissible at all,
since the issue to which it relates no longer exists. Its sole justification is to establish
identity, and that the Crown is no longer called upon to do... Our view is,
therefore, that the learned Judge should have disallowed the evidence, not as a
matter of discretion, but because it was inadmissible as irrelevant.'

So if the question of identity had remained in issue, the evidence would have been
relevant to that issue and would have been admitted notwithstanding that it did not
disclose the commission of any offence.

In all the cases so far cited, except *R v Doughty* and *R v Horry*, the evidence of similar
facts included evidence of the commission of an offence similar to that with which the
accused was charged. Counsel could find no case in which it did not and the evidence
was held admissible.

Finally counsel relied on a passage in the current edition of Archbold's Pleading,
Evidence and Practice in Criminal Cases (40th Edn, 1979, para 1324), under the heading
'Proximity', which is in the following terms:

'(1) The decisions of the Court of Appeal are not consistent on another point,
namely whether the "striking similarity" must relate to the commission of the
offence as opposed to the surrounding circumstances. In *R. v. Novac and others*
((1976) 65 Cr App R 107) the facts were very like those in *Johannsen* ((1977) 65 Cr
App R 101) ...'

Archbold then cites a passage from *R v Novac* 65 Cr App R 101 at 112:

'If a man is going to commit buggery with a boy he picks up, it must surely be
a commonplace of such an encounter that he will take the boy home with him and
commit the offence in bed. The fact that the boys may in each case have been
picked up by Raymond [one of the appellants] in the first instance at amusement
arcades may be a feature more approximating to a "unique or striking similarity."
... It is not, however, a similarity in the commission of the crime. It is a similarity

in the surrounding circumstances and is not, in our judgment, sufficiently proximate to the commission of the crime itself to lead to the conclusion that the repetition of this feature would make the boys' stories inexplicable on the basis of coincidence.' **a**

Archbold then continues:

'(2) In R. v. *Scarrott* ([1978] 1 All ER 672, [1978] QB 1016) the court were faced with the apparent conflict between the approach of the differently constituted **b** courts in R. v. *Johannsen* and R. v. *Novac and others* to barely distinguishable facts. After referring to the use by the court in R. v. *Novac and others* of "the rather strange word . . . 'proximate'" the court made it plain that they preferred the approach of the court in R. v. *Johannsen*. They said that "it would be wrong . . . to elevate the passage" (cited in (1), *ante*) ". . . into a statement of law." They also pointed out that "in one of the most famous of all cases dealing with similar fact evidence, the *Brides* **c** *in the Bath* case [R v *Smith* (1915) 84 LJKB 2153, [1914–15] All ER Rep 262] the court had regard to the facts that the accused man married the women, and that he insured their lives. Some surrounding circumstances have to be considered in order to understand either the offence charged or the nature of the similar fact evidence which it is sought to adduce and in each case it must be a matter of judgment where the line is drawn."' **d**

Counsel submitted that evidence to be admissible must be probative of an indecent assault, not merely of an intention to commit an indecent assault. And inasmuch as none of the three other girls had in fact said that they had been indecently assaulted their evidence was not probative of the charges of indecent assault on the three complainants.

Counsel for the appellant submitted that evidence of similar facts to be admissible must relate to the facts of an offence similar to that with which the appellant was **e** charged, and not to the surrounding circumstances, which he submitted were too remote. He conceded however that if the evidence of the three other girls had included evidence of indecent assault, then their evidence, including the evidence of surrounding circumstances, would have been admissible, even though Susan had not been introduced by photographs, although Sally was photographed in the nude.

Counsel for the Crown sought to support the ruling of the judge that the evidence of **f** the three other girls was admissible on the basis that the principal issue in the case was whether the appellant had lured all six girls to the house for a sexual purpose, or whether, as the defence alleged, the purpose was an innocent one, namely baby-sitting, and that the evidence tended to rebut that defence. In our judgment the admission of the evidence can certainly be supported on that ground. But admission of the evidence can be supported on another and wider ground. **g**

It is well established that, although evidence of a disposition or propensity to commit the offence with which the accused is charged is not admissible, evidence may in certain circumstances be led of similar facts tending to show that the accused is guilty of the offence charged. Such evidence has it appears hitherto only been admitted where it has disclosed the commission of similar offences although it has also included the surrounding circumstances. In some cases the similarity of the surrounding circumstances has been **h** stressed more than the similarity of the mode of commission of the offences themselves. Surrounding circumstances include the preliminaries leading up to the offence, such as the mode and place of the initial approach and the inducement offered or words used.

The two sets of facts must be looked at as a whole. In R v *Scarrott* the very point with which we are concerned was raised although it was not necessary for the decision because **j** there was evidence of the commission of an offence. Scarman LJ, giving the judgment of the court, said ([1978] 1 All ER 672 at 679–680, [1978] QB 1016 at 1025–1026):

'Counsel for the appellant has based a submission . . . that, to be admissible, the similar fact evidence must reveal features of a striking similarity with the offence

a
itself, not its surrounding circumstances. He submits that is all that the rather strange word that Bridge LJ used [in *R v Novac* (1977) 65 Cr App R 107 at 112] "proximate" means. In our view, we are here in that area of judgment on particular facts from which the criminal law can never depart. Plainly some matters, some circumstances, may be so distant in time or place from the commission of an offence as not to be properly considered when deciding whether the subject-matter of similar fact evidence displays striking similarities with the offence charged. On the

b
other hand, equally plainly, one cannot isolate, as a sort of laboratory specimen, the bare bones of a criminal offence from its surrounding circumstances and say that it is only within the confines of that specimen, microscopically considered, that admissibility is to be determined. Indeed, in one of the most famous cases of all dealing with similar fact evidence, "the brides in the bath case", *R v Smith*, the court had regard to the facts that the accused man married the women and that he insured

c
their lives. Some surrounding circumstances have to be considered in order to understand either the offence charged or the nature of the similar fact evidence which it is sought to adduce and in each case it must be a matter of judgment where the line is drawn. One cannot draw an inflexible line as a rule of law... We therefore have to reach a judgment on the evidence of this particular case, and to determine whether the evidence adduced, that is the similar fact evidence adduced,

d
possesses such features that it is a proper exercise of judgment to say that the evidence is logically probative, that it has positive probative value in assisting to determine the truth.'

We accept and follow the reasoning of Scarman LJ in *R v Scarrott*. The various facts recited by the judge in this case as constituting similar facts were so similar to the facts of the surrounding circumstances in the evidence of the complainants that they can

e
properly be described as 'striking'. That they did not include evidence of the commission of offences similar to those with which the appellant was charged does not mean that they are not logically probative in determining the guilt of the appellant. Indeed we are of opinion that taken as a whole they are inexplicable on the basis of coincidence and that they are of positive probative value in assisting to determine the truth of the charges against the appellant, in that they tended to show that he was guilty of the offences with

f
which he was charged.

In deciding whether or not to admit similar fact evidence the judge will always assess whether the prejudice caused outweighs the probative value of the evidence. In this appeal counsel has not suggested that if the evidence is admissible it should be excluded on the ground that it is prejudicial. We are satisfied that the evidence was properly admitted and accordingly, for the reasons we have given, the appeal is dismissed.

g

Appeal dismissed.

The court refused leave to appeal to the House of Lords but certified, under s 33(2) of the Criminal Appeal Act 1968, that the following point of law of general public importance was involved in the decision: whether evidence of similar facts falling short of similar offences with which an accused is charged can ever be admissible.

Solicitors: *Taynton & Son*, Gloucester (for the appellant); *Director of Public Prosecutions*.

Sepala Munasinghe Esq   Barrister.

Thermo Engineers Ltd and others v Ferrymasters Ltd and others

QUEEN'S BENCH DIVISION (COMMERICAL COURT)

NEILL J

8th, 9th, 10th, 11th, 22nd SEPTEMBER 1980

Carriers – Contract – Loss or damage to goods – Determination of carrier's liability – Carriage on same vehicle throughout journey – Carriage involving other means of transport – When carriage by road ceasing and other means of transport commencing – Act or omission of carrier by road – Event which could only have occurred in the course of other means of transport – Carriage of machinery on trailer from England to Denmark – Road carrier contracting to arrange carriage for whole journey – Machinery damaged when trailer being loaded onto ship by stevedores – Whether damage occurring during carriage by 'other means of transport' – Whether damage caused by act or omission of 'carrier by road' – Whether damage caused by 'event which could only have occurred in the course of and by reason of carriage by ... other means of transport' – Carriage of Goods by Road Act 1965, Sch, arts 2(1), 17(2), 23(4), 25(1).

The defendants, who were carriers, agreed by a contract of carriage made in 1975 to transport a heat exchanger worth £19,807 from the plaintiffs' factory in England to a purchaser in Denmark. The heat exchanger, a substantial piece of equipment weighing about 5,000 kg, projected about half a metre above the trailer on which it was loaded when ready for transport. The defendants arranged for sub-contractors to take the trailer to Felixstowe docks and for shipment of the trailer to Copenhagen on a vessel under a bill of lading dated 3rd November 1975. At the docks the loading of the trailer on board ship was taken over by the dock stevedores who recorded that the heat exchanger exceeded the height of the trailer by about two feet. The stevedores drove the trailer across the stern loading ramp between the dock and the ship and then attempted to manoeuvre the trailer into the lower cargo deck. The upper part of the heat exchanger hit the deckhead and was extensively damaged. The stevedores were familiar with the vessel but in any event the height of the lower deck was prominently displayed on a pillar at the entrance to the deck. When the heat exchanger reached Denmark it was rejected by the purchaser and returned to the plaintiffs who managed to salvage parts worth £1,920 from it. The plaintiffs brought an action against the defendants claiming the sum of £17,887, being the difference between the value of the heat exchanger and the salvaged parts. The plaintiffs alleged that the defendants were in breach of contract and/or in breach of their duty in performing their contract of carriage. The question arose whether the defendants' liability was to be determined under the Convention on the Contract for the International Carriage of Goods by Road 1965 ('CMR') as set out in the schedule to the Carriage of Goods by Road Act 1965. The plaintiffs contended that by virtue of CMR art 2(1)[a] the defendants were liable under CMR art 17(1)[b], even though the journey involved both land and sea transport, because the goods had remained on the same vehicle for the whole journey. The defendants contended that the carriage was outside CMR because of the proviso to art 2(1) since (i) the damage occurred during carriage by 'other means of transport' (ie during the sea carriage), (ii) the damage 'was not caused by an act or omission of the carrier by road' and (iii) the damage was caused 'by some event which could only have occurred in the course of and by reason of the carriage by [the] other means of transport'. The defendants further contended that if CMR did apply, art 17(2) relieved the defendants of liability because they had used due diligence and the damage was caused through circumstances which they could not avoid and the consequences of which they were unable to prevent.

---

a   Article 2 is set out at p 1146 g to j, post

b   Article 17, so far as material, is set out at p 1149 f, post

Held – (1) CMR did not apply to determine the defendants' liability because the carriage
a fell within the exception contained in the proviso to CMR art 2(1) for the following
reasons—

(a) Having regard to the fact that CMR was intended to be consistent with other
international conventions, for the purposes of art 2(1) when a road vehicle was loaded
onto a ship for further carriage in the course of the same journey the point where
carriage by road ceased and carriage by sea commenced was, as a general rule, to be
b determined by the Hague Rules. Accordingly, carriage by road did not continue up
until the time the vehicle was secured in the vessel since under the Hague Rules carriage
by sea included the operation of loading a vessel. Since the damage to the heat exchanger
occurred during the loading of the vessel it therefore occurred, for the purposes of the
proviso to art 2(1), during carriage by 'other means of transport' and not during carriage
by the carrier by road (see p 1147 *c* to *f*, post); *Pyrene Co Ltd v Scindia Steam Navigation Co*
c *Ltd* [1954] 2 All ER 158 applied.

(b) In order to achieve the purpose of art 2(1) the words 'carrier by road' were to be
construed narrowly and not as imposing a wide responsibility on the road carrier, even
though as a general rule a road carrier who undertook to carry goods abroad in a vehicle
was liable under CMR for the acts or omissions of sub-carriers who carried the goods
other than by road. On a restricted construction of art 2(1) the damage 'was not caused
d by an act or omission of the carrier by road' since it was caused not by anyone involved
in the carriage by road but by those involved in loading the vessel, namely the stevedores
and the ship's officers (see p 1147 *h j* and p 1148 *e*, post).

(c) In determining for the purposes of art 2(1) whether damage was caused by an 'event
which could only have occurred in the course of and by reason of the carriage by [the]
other means of transport' the question was not whether the damage could only have
e occurred in the course of the other means of transport but whether the event causing the
damage could only have occurred in the course of the other means of transport. Since
the event which caused the damage, namely the collision with the deckhead in the course
of loading the vessel, could only have occurred in the course of and by reason of the
carriage by 'other means of transport', the proviso to art 2(1) applied to exempt the
defendants from the general provisions of CMR (see p 1148 *g h* and p 1149 *d*, post).

f (2) Since CMR did not apply to the carriage of the heat exchanger from Felixstowe to
Copenhagen, the defendants' liability was to be determined, by virtue of the proviso to
art 2(1), in the manner in which it would have been determined if there had been merely
a contract for the carriage of the exchanger by sea in accordance with 'the conditions
prescribed by law'. At the time of the contract of carriage, ie November 1975, the Hague
Rules prescribing conditions for carriage by sea provided, under art 5, for a carrier to
increase his liabilities under the Hague Rules provided such increase in liability was
g embodied in a bill of lading. Having regard to the terms of the bill of lading, the
defendants' liability fell to be determined not in accordance with the Hague Rules but in
accordance with such conditions as the plaintiffs could and would have agreed with a
carrier by sea in November 1975 if a separate contract had been made for the carriage of
the machinery from Felixstowe to Copenhagen (see p 1148 *j* to p 1149 *d*, post).

h Per Curiam. (1) The provision in CMR art 17(2) relieving a carrier of liability if the
loss, damage or delay is caused through circumstances 'which the carrier could not avoid'
does not refer merely to loss, damage or delay 'which the carrier could not avoid by the
exercise of reasonable care'; the words 'which the carrier could not avoid' are to be given
their full meaning (see p 1150 *a*, post).

(2) Where damage to goods renders the goods as a whole unacceptable refund of
j carriage charges under CMR arts 23(4)^c and 25(1)^d is to be made in full since the fact that

---

c   Article 23(4), so far as material, provides: '. . . the carriage charges . . . incurred in respect of the
carriage of the goods shall be refunded in full in case of total loss and in proportion to the loss
sustained in case of partial loss, but no further damages shall be payable.'

d   Article 25(1) provides: 'In case of damage, the carrier shall be liable for the amount by which the
goods have diminished in value, calculated by reference to the value of the goods fixed in
accordance with article 23, paragraphs 1, 2 and 4.'

the goods may have a scrap value does not render the loss a partial loss. Furthermore a claim for return freight of the damaged goods is also in principle recoverable (see p 1150 *a* *c* to *f*, post).

Notes

For the convention on the international carriage of goods by road, see 5 Halsbury's Laws (4th Edn) paras 417–418.

For the Carriage of Goods by Road Act 1965, Sch, arts 2, 17, 23, 25, see 28 Halsbury's *b* Statutes (3rd Edn) 443, 449, 451, 452.

Cases referred to in judgment

Buchanan (James) & Co Ltd v Babco Forwarding and Shipping (UK) Ltd [1977] 3 All ER 1048, [1978] AC 141, [1977] 3 WLR 907, [1978] 1 Lloyd's Rep 119, [1978] RTR 59, [1978] 1 CMLR 156, HL; *affg* [1977] 1 All ER 518, [1977] QB 208, [1977] 2 WLR 107, [1977] *c* 1 Lloyd's Rep 234, [1977] RTR 457, [1977] 2 CMLR 455, CA, Digest (Cont Vol E) 36, 1435.
Fothergill v Monarch Airlines Ltd [1980] 2 All ER 696, [1980] 3 WLR 209, HL.
Kühne & Nagel v Transports Internationaux Van Mieghem (1974) 9 ETL 330.
Pyrene Co Ltd v Scindia Steam Navigation Co Ltd [1954] 2 All ER 158, [1954] 2 QB 402, [1954] 2 WLR 1005, [1954] 1 Lloyd's Rep 321, 41 Digest (Repl) 273, 593. *d*
Tatton (William) & Co Ltd v Ferrymasters Ltd [1974] 1 Lloyd's Rep 203.

Action

By a writ dated 3rd November 1976 the plaintiffs, Thermo Engineers Ltd and Anhydro A/S, claimed against the defendants, Ferrymasters Ltd and Anglo Overseas Transport Co Ltd, damages pursuant to arts 23 and 25 of the Convention on the Contract for the *e* International Carriage of Goods by Road ('CMR'), set out in the schedule to the Carriage of Goods by Road Act 1965, for breach of contract and/or breach of duty in the loading, handling, custody, care and discharge of an air heater battery and its carriage between Aylesbury, Buckinghamshire, and Copenhagen. The facts are set out in the judgment.

Richard Aikens for the plaintiffs. *f*
Jonathan Mance for the defendants.

Cur adv vult

22nd September. **NEILL J** read the following judgment: I am concerned in this case *g* with the Carriage of Goods by Road Act 1965 and with the Convention on the Contract for the International Carriage of Goods by Road set out in the schedule to that Act (which I shall refer to respectively as 'the 1965 Act' and 'CMR'.)

The action arises out of a contract for the carriage of a steam heat exchanger from the premises of the first plaintiffs, Thermo Engineers Ltd, at Aylesbury, to the premises of the second plaintiffs, Anhydro A/S, in Copenhagen. The contract was made between *h* Thermo Engineers and the first defendants, Ferrymasters Ltd. The second defendants named in the writ, who carry on business as shipping and forwarding agents, have not been served with the proceedings and it is not necessary for me to say any more about them.

Most of the facts are not in dispute and there has been put before the court an agreed statement setting out an account of the main events. In addition I heard oral evidence *j* from three witnesses, Mr Mitchell who was called on behalf of the plaintiffs, and Mr Driver and Mr Clarke who were called on behalf of Ferrymasters.

Thermo Engineers manufacture heat exchangers. In 1975 they sold a heat exchanger to Anhydro in Copenhagen. Ferrymasters agreed to transport the heat exchanger to Copenhagen. On 31st October 1975 the heat exchanger was loaded at Aylesbury onto a

trailer belonging to Ferrymasters. A box of spares and some pipes were loaded as well.
a The trailer had a superstructure but it was not sheeted. The height from the ground to
the bed of the trailer was 1·05 metres. The height from the bed to the top of the
superstructure was 2·87 metres. The total height of the trailer itself was therefore 3·92
metres. For the purpose of loading, the heat exchanger was divided into two parts which
were loaded one in front of the other. Each part had dimensions of about 3·7 metres in
length by 1·3 to 1·5 metres in width by 3·265 to 3·33 metres in height. It will be
b apparent therefore that the height of the load exceeded the height of the superstructure
by about half a metre. In the agreed statement of facts this excess is stated to be about 1 ft
3 in to 2 ft. The agreed photographs give a clear picture of the trailer and its
superstructure and of the two parts of the load. The total weight of the heat exchanger
and the spares and pipes was 5,100 kg.

Ferrymasters sub-contracted the carriage from Aylesbury to their own premises at
c Felixstowe to Eastern Roadways of Norwich. The trailer reached Felixstowe on 31st
October. On the next day, Saturday, 1st November, the trailer was taken by Mr Driver,
a shunter driver employed by Ferrymasters, to Felixstowe Docks. Before he left
Ferrymasters' premises Mr Driver was given a shipping note by the yard foreman. This
shipping note directed Mr Driver to go to a compound at the docks. Mr Driver took the
trailer to the compound. He went to the office of the Felixstowe Dock and Railway Co
d Ltd (I shall call that company 'the dock company') and handed in the shipping note. A
checker employed by the dock company came out with Mr Driver and inspected the
load. The checker brought with him a document called an equipment condition and
receipt form. The checker filled in the form and in the section headed 'Damage to Cargo'
he wrote these words: 'Machinery loaded thro' framework. Too high'. The form
contained a printed sketch of a trailer which was there to enable the checker to indicate
e the position of any damage. The checker drew some lines on the sketch and wrote above
it the words '2 foot high up'. The form, which was in triplicate, was then initialled by
the checker and dated '1.11.75'. Mr Driver signed his name in the appropriate space on
the form. He was then given one of the three copies, which he took back to
Ferrymasters. The other copies were kept in the office of the dock company, one copy
being intended for the shippers' agents. There was no evidence, however, that that copy
f reached the shipping company before the ship was loaded.

The trailer remained in the custody of the dock company over the weekend. On
Monday, 3rd November the trailer was taken to be loaded onto a ship called the Orion.
Ferrymasters had made a contract of carriage with Tor Line AB. This contract is
evidenced by a bill of lading dated 3rd November. The Orion was a ship which operated
between Felixstowe and Denmark during 1975, and the contract between Tor Line AB
g and the owners of the vessel was produced in court. It is clear that the ship had made a
number of journeys from Felixstowe before 3rd November 1975 and it is not in dispute
that employees of the dock company who acted as stevedores were familiar with the
dimensions and layout of the vessel.

I should refer now to para 10 of the agreed statement of facts. It is there recorded that
on 3rd November Mr Ford, an employee of the dock company, driving a Tugmaster
h vehicle, pushed the trailer in reverse onto the Orion on the directions of another
employee, Mr Maule, a dock foreman with the dock company, with the assistance of
other such employees and/or with the assistance of the ship's crew. Mr Maule had
directed Mr Ford to take the trailer to a space Mr Maule had selected in the lower cargo
deck of the vessel forward of the entrance ramp. The statement of facts continues:

j   'The height between the lower cargo deck and the second cargo deck is shown on
the inboard pillar facing the stern of the vessel, in large letters, as 4.2 metres. The
top part of the goods struck the deckhead at the lower end of the ramp. The trailer
and the goods were taken off the vessel and later reloaded on board the vessel at the
after end of the lower cargo deck. The goods and trailer were carried there to
Copenhagen, Denmark, without further incident.'

And then in para 14: 'Because the goods were damaged on arrival in Copenhagen, they were rejected by Anhydro A/S.' It is not in dispute that the second plaintiffs were *a* entitled to reject the goods. The statement of facts continues in para 16:

'Thermo Engineers Ltd [that is the first plaintiffs] arranged to have the goods returned to their premises at Aylesbury, where they salvaged such parts of the cargo which were capable of being used by them in the manufacture of other similar goods, or otherwise.'

b

The net salved value of the goods was £1,920 and the value of the goods at the time they were accepted for carriage was £19,807. The primary claim, therefore, is for £17,887, being the difference between the value of the goods when accepted for carriage and the net salved value.

The issues to be considered can be listed as follows. (1) Is the liability of Ferrymasters to be determined in accordance with the general provisions of CMR or are some other *c* provisions applicable by reason of CMR art 2? (2) If the general provisions of CMR do not apply, how is the liability of Ferrymasters to be determined? (3) If the general provisions of CMR do apply, can Ferrymasters rely on CMR art 17(2)? (4) If Ferrymasters are liable in accordance with the general provisions of CMR what sums can the plaintiffs recover in respect of freight?

It is common ground that unless the general provisions of CMR are excluded by art 2 *d* the rights of the parties are to be determined in accordance with those provisions. It is also common ground that in construing CMR I should follow the guidance given in the speeches in the House of Lords in *James Buchanan & Co Ltd v Babco Forwarding & Shipping (UK) Ltd* [1977] 3 All ER 1048, [1978] AC 141 and in *Fothergill v Monarch Air Lines Ltd* [1980] 2 All ER 696, [1980] 3 WLR 209. I must therefore give 'a purposive construction to the convention looked at as a whole': see per Lord Diplock in *Fothergill*'s case [1980] 2 *e* All ER 696 at 704, [1980] 3 WLR 209 at 221. In the context of the construction of CMR I was also referred to parts of the English text of a commentary on it written by Professor Roland Loewe of Austria in about 1975. This commentary was mentioned by Roskill LJ in the *Buchanan* case [1977] 1 All ER 518 at 524, [1977] QB 208 at 216 and is printed in 11 European Transport Law 311. In addition my attention was drawn to four cases concerning CMR decided in Germany, Holland and Belgium, and I was provided with *f* translations of the relevant reports in European Transport Law. Finally, I should mention that I had the benefit of being given a copy of the French text of CMR.

I turn now to CMR art 2 which is in these terms:

'1. Where the vehicle containing the goods is carried over part of the journey by sea, rail, inland waterways or air, and, except where the provisions of article 14 are *g* applicable, the goods are not unloaded from the vehicle, this Convention shall nevertheless apply to the whole of the carriage. Provided that to the extent that it is proved that any loss, damage or delay in delivery of the goods which occurs during the carriage by the other means of transport was not caused by an act or omission of the carrier by road, but by some event which could only have occurred in the course of and by reason of the carriage by that other means of transport, the *h* liability of the carrier by road shall be determined not by this Convention but in the manner in which the liability of the carrier by the other means of transport would have been determined if a contract for the carriage of the goods alone had been made by the sender with the carrier by the other means of transport in accordance with the conditions prescribed by law for the carriage of goods by that means of transport. If, however, there are no such prescribed conditions, the liability of the *j* carrier by road shall be determined by this Convention.

'2. If the carrier by road is also himself the carrier by the other means of transport, his liability shall also be determined in accordance with the provisions of paragraph 1 of this article, but as if, in his capacities as carrier by road and as carrier by the other means of transport, he were two separate persons.'

a It will be seen that the first sentence of art 2 establishes the general rule that where goods remain on the same vehicle for the whole journey the provisions of CMR will apply even though the journey involves, for example, a sea crossing. This general rule, however, does not cover cases of loss, damage or delay in delivery of the goods where the following cumulative conditions are satisifed: (a) the damage etc occurred during the carriage by the other means of transport; (b) the damage etc was not caused by an act of omission of the carrier by road; and (c) the damage etc was caused by some event which *b* could only have occurred in the course of and by reason of the carriage by that other means of transport.

In the present case counsel for the plaintiffs has contended that the general provisions of CMR apply and that none of these conditions has been satisfied. I must therefore examine the conditions in turn.

It will be remembered that the damage occurred at the moment when the upper part *c* of the heat exchanger struck the deckhead of the lower 'tween deck of the Orion. Counsel for the plaintiffs argued that at that moment the carriage by sea had not yet begun, and that it was only when the effective means of carriage had ceased to be by the wheels of the trailer, and the trailer and its load were secured in the ship, that the carriage by road could be said to have ceased. Counsel for the defendants, on the other hand, argued that carriage by sea includes the operation of loading. He referred me to the *d* Hague Rules (see the Carriage of Goods by Sea Act 1924, Sch, and the Carriage of Goods by Sea Act 1971, Sch) and the decision of Devlin J in *Pyrene Co Ltd v Scindia Steam Navigation Co Ltd* [1954] 2 All ER 158, [1954] 2 QB 402.

With respect, I am unable to accept the argument of counsel for the plaintiffs that the road transport continued until the trailer and its load were secured in the ship. There is force in the submission of counsel for the defendants that CMR was intended to fit in *e* with other conventions, and I incline to the view that as a general rule the first condition of art 2 will be satisfied where it is proved that sea carriage as understood in the Hague Rules has begun. I recognise, however, that there may be cases where the exact line between two successive means of transport will be difficult to draw. I must concern myself with the facts of the present case. Here I am satsified that the damage occurred during the carriage by the other means of transport. At the relevant time the loading *f* was well advanced, and, as can be seen from the sketch plan drawn by Mr Clarke, the trailer had already passed across the outboard ramp and across the line of the stern.

I turn to the second condition. In reaching a decision about this condition it is necessary to have regard to the terms of CMR art 3. Article 3 provides, under the heading 'Persons for whom the Carrier is Responsible', as follows:

g 'For the purposes of this Convention the carrier shall be responsible for the acts and omissions of his agents and servants and of any other persons of whose services he makes use for the performance of the carriage, when such agents, servants or other persons are acting within the scope of their employment, as if such acts or omissions were his own.'

I am satisfied on examination of CMR as a whole that as a general rule a carrier by road *h* who has undertaken to carry goods by a vehicle from this country to a place abroad will be liable for the acts or omissions of sub-carriers who perform the sea carriage or air carriage, or as the case may be. This conclusion is consistent with ss 1 and 14(2) of the 1965 Act. I consider, however, that in art 2 the words 'carrier by road' have to be construed in such a way as to impose a narrower responsibility. A construction which imposed a wide responsibility on the carrier by road would, in my view, be contrary to *j* the purposes which para (1) of art 2 seeks to achieve. It would also be inconsistent with para (2) of that article.

The main argument of counsel for the plaintiffs on the second condition, however, was put forward on the basis that the words 'act or omission of the carrier by road' did not include any default by a sub-carrier by another means of transport. He submitted (a) that Ferrymasters were negligent in failing to warn the stevedores and the ship's officers that the load was of an unusual height and that it projected above the frame of the trailer. Such a warning, he said, should have been given in the loading list or by some other *a* means, (b) that the dock company, who knew of the excess height, were the agents of Ferrymasters (in their capacity as carriers by road) for the purpose of receiving and marshalling the goods to be shipped, and that they failed in their duty to pass on their knowledge, both within their own organisation and to third parties, to those who carried out the loading. In my view there are simple and commonsense answers to both these submissions.   *b*

The stevedores and the ship's officers knew the height of the lower deck. Indeed, the height '4·2 metres' was displayed in large letters on an inboard pillar facing the stern. It is to be remembered that the Orion had been sailing from Felixstowe nearly every week since the previous May. According to the evidence of Mr Clarke the height of the lower deck on the Orion was less than the average height of decks used for this kind of traffic. It was also established that though most trailers, including 12-metre trailers such as the *c* plaintiffs' trailer, are less than 4·2 metres in height there is no standard height for the framework of a trailer. Moreover, though, in Mr Clarke's words, it is 'not too common' for out-of-gauge goods to be loaded onto this sort of trailer it is not unknown. It is to be noted that the loading list had no column in which to show the height of any trailer or of any load. Furthermore, the trailer itself with its frame had a height of 3·92 metres, and this height might well have been increased during loading by reason of the *d* adjustment of the fifth wheel. Unfortunately the stevedores and the ship's officers involved in the loading did not give adequate attention to the fact that this was a low deck. The height of the trailer and its load (which was not covered in any way) was obvious. The top of the load was flat and quite broad. I am not concerned here with a narrow or barely visible projection. Looking at all these circumstances I do not see that Ferrymasters or the dock company, in any capacity other than as stevedores, were in *e* breach of any duty of care or that any act or omission of these companies, as persons involved in the carriage by road, caused the damage. The damage was caused by those directly involved in the loading.

I come to the third condition. The wording of this part of art 2 is not easy to construe. Counsel for the plaintiffs submitted that this condition would be satisfied only by an event which was peculiar to the relevant means of transport, for example, the *f* wetting of goods by sea water in the case of carriage by sea. An overhead obstruction, said counsel, is not a peril peculiarly associated with the sea; a similar incident could have occurred on land if, for example, the trailer had collided with a low bridge or the entrance to a garage. I see the force of this argument but I am not persuaded by it. One is concerned to consider not whether the loss or damage could only have occurred in the course of the other means of transport but whether the event could only have so *g* occurred. It seems to me that any adequate description of the relevant events in this case would have to include a statement to the effect that a collision with the bulkhead of a ship had taken place in the course of loading the ship. Such an event could only have occurred in the course of, and by reason of, the carriage by sea. I therefore consider that the third condition is satisfied.

I must turn now to the second issue. Where the conditions set out in the proviso in *h* para 1 of art 2 are satisfied the liability of the carrier by road is determined not by CMR but—

> 'in the manner in which the liability of the carrier by the other means of transport would have been determined if a contract for the carriage of the goods alone had been made by the sender with the carrier by the other means of transport in accordance with the conditions prescribed by law for the carriage of goods by that *j* means of transport.'

Counsel for the defendants argued that in the context of the present case the liability of Ferrymasters is to be determined in accordance with the Hague Rules as being the conditions prescribed by law in force in November 1975. Counsel for the plaintiffs, on the other hand, relied on the fact that art 5 of the Hague Rules allows a carrier to increase

a his responsibilities and liabilities under the rules provided such increase is embodied in the bill of lading. I was referred to the bill of lading and, in particular, to cll 11 and 13. At this stage I am not asked to determine what the plaintiffs can recover if the general provisions of CMR do not apply. The parties may be able to agree a figure. But if they cannot do so the determination of the compensation recoverable may involve the consideration of a number of arguments, for example, as to the meaning of 'gold value'

b in art 9 of the Hague Rules, and whether or not the free market value of gold is the appropriate yardstick, arguments which, so far, have been merely adumbrated. For the moment I am being asked to decide only the preliminary question: is the compensation to be determined in accordance with art 4, r 5, and art 9 of the Hague Rules, or do the 'conditions prescribed by law' in CMR, art 2, para 1 extend to such conditions as the sender and the sea carrier could legally, and would, have agreed in November 1975?

c   I have come to the conclusion that, having regard to art 5 of the Hague Rules and the terms of the bill of lading, the argument of counsel for the plaintiffs is to be preferred. Accordingly, in determining the compensation payable, it will be necessary to consider what conditions could and would have been agreed. I can therefore summarise my findings as follows: (1) that the conditions set out in CMR, art 2, para 1 have been satisfied and (2) that the compensation payable to the plaintiffs is to be calculated in

d accordance with such conditions as they could, and would, have agreed with a carrier by sea in November 1975 if a separate contract for the carriage of the heat exchanger alone from Felixstowe to Copenhagen had been made.

It is therefore unnecessary for me to express a view on the other issues. Nevertheless, I think it is right that I should state my conclusions on the arguments directed to CMR arts 17, 23 and 25.

e   Counsel for the defendants argued that if the provisions of CMR applied to the plaintiffs' claim Ferrymasters were relieved from liability by reason of art 17, para 2. I should read the first two paragraphs of art 17. This article is in Chapter 4 under the heading 'Liability of the Carrier':

f   '1. The carrier shall be liable for the total or partial loss of the goods and for damage thereto occurring between the time when he takes over the goods and the time of delivery, as well as for any delay in delivery.

'2. The carrier shall however be relieved of liability if the loss, damage or delay was caused by the wrongful act or neglect of the claimant, by the instructions of the claimant given otherwise than as a result of a wrongful act or neglect on the part of the carrier, by inherent vice of the goods or through circumstances which the carrier could not avoid and the consequences of which he was unable to prevent . . .'

g   It is clear from para 1 of art 17 that prima facie the liability of the carrier by road extends throughout the period of carriage, that is, in the present case, from Aylesbury to Copenhagen. The question for consideration is whether Ferrymasters are relieved from liability under para 2 by being able to prove that the damage was caused through circumstances which they could not avoid and the consequences of which they were

h unable to prevent.

Counsel for the defendants argued that the concluding words of para 2 mean that a carrier can escape liability if he proves that he used due diligence. Counsel for the plaintiffs, on the other hand, contended that the words were equivalent to a force majeure. He drew my attention in support of this contention to one of the four cases to which I referred earlier in general terms, *Kühne & Nagel v Transports Internationaux Van*

j *Mieghem* (1974) 9 ETL 330, a decision of the Tribunal de commerce in Brussels. I have already said that I consider that the general effect of art 3 when considered in the light of the 1965 Act and CMR as a whole is to make the carrier by road responsible for the acts of sub-carriers. The damage here was caused by those responsible for loading the trailer onto the Orion. In my view these persons were plainly persons of whose services Ferrymasters were making use for the performance of the carriage. I am therefore satisfied that, even if the standard envisaged by art 17, para 2 is one of due diligence, Ferrymasters would not be able to escape liability. I am inclined to the view, however, that the words 'through circumstances which the carrier could not avoid' allow a more limited relief from liability than would have been the case if words such as 'by the exercise of reasonable care' had been added. Both the English and the French texts show that the court is concerned to inquire: was the damage caused through circumstances which the carrier *could not* avoid? The words I have emphasised should be given their full meaning.

I come finally to submissions based on arts 23 and 25. Counsel for the defendants argued (a) that as the heat exchanger retained a scrap value the sum recoverable for the carriage to Copenhagen (£580) should be reduced proportionately in accordance with art 23, para 4 and art 25, para 1, and (b) that the plaintiffs could not recover the cost of transporting the damaged goods backs from Denmark to Aylesbury because such a charge was not incurred in respect of the relevant carriage. I can deal with these arguments quite shortly. In my judgment, it is important to have regard to the fact that though the heat exchanger had some scrap value the damage was such as to render the whole unit unacceptable. The loss of part of a consignment does not provide a satisfactory parallel. I therefore consider that if the compensation were to be calculated in accordance with CMR the whole £580 would be recoverable.

The claim for the return freight involves different considerations, but in my judgment this sum also is recoverable in principle, though it would be necessary for the plaintiffs to prove that the sum claimed was a proper and reasonable charge. In the *Buchanan* case Lord Wilberforce approved Master Jacob's decision that customs duty was recoverable because it was chargeable having regard to the way in which the goods had been carried (see [1977] 3 All ER 1048 at 1054, [1978] AC 141 at 154). Moreover in the Court of Appeal in that case Lord Denning MR expressed the view that return carriage is recoverable and disapproved of the decision by Browne J on this point in *William Tatton & Co Ltd v Ferrymasters Ltd* [1974] 1 Lloyd's Rep 203. Roskill LJ agreed with Lord Denning MR (see [1977] 1 All ER 518 at 524, 528, [1977] QB 208 at 215, 220). If, therefore, I had held CMR to apply I would have allowed in principle the claims for return freight set out in para 6 of the amended points of claim.

Order accordingly.

Solicitors: *Clyde & Co* (for the plaintiffs); *Herbert Smith & Co* (for the defendants).

K Mydeen Esq   Barrister.

Williams v Home Office

QUEEN'S BENCH DIVISION
MCNEILL J
17th, 29th JANUARY 1980

Discovery – Privilege – Production contrary to public interest – Class of documents – Documents relating to government policy – Communications to and from ministers and senior public servants – Communications relating to formulation of policy – Plaintiff claiming damages in respect of treatment in prison – Plaintiff's claim arising out of policy to isolate particular prisoners – Home Secretary claiming public interest immunity in respect of documents relating to policy to isolate prisoners – Plaintiff's claim involving rights of citizen and liberty of subject – Plaintiff having arguable case of unlawful interference with his rights – Whether Home Secretary's claim to privilege valid.

The plaintiff, a long-term prisoner, brought an action against the Home Office claiming damages for false imprisonment and a declaration that the Home Office had acted ultra vires in respect of his detention in an experimental 'control unit' set up within the prison system to isolate and control prisoners who were considered to be troublemakers. As a matter of policy, detention in the control unit was for a minimum period of 180 days in two stages, each lasting 90 days. During the first stage the prisoner was denied almost all association with other prisoners and during the second stage he was permitted only limited association with other prisoners. Detention in the control unit was authorised by the Home Secretary under r 43(2)[a] of the Prison Rules 1964 which provided for the Home Secretary to authorise a prisoner's removal from the association of other prisoners 'for a period not exceeding one month' and to renew that authority 'from month to month'. The plaintiff claimed that by instituting a predetermined policy of a minimum of 180 days' detention in the control unit the Home Secretary thereby fettered his duty under r 43(2) to review the situation before renewing the authority for the plaintiff's detention each month.

In the course of discovery of documents in the action the Home Office disclosed documents amounting to some 6,800 pages. However, the Home Office objected to the disclosure of 23 documents on the ground that they consisted of communications to and from ministers, and records of meetings with ministers or between officials, all of which related to the formulation of policy on the control unit. The Home Secretary issued a certificate claiming public interest privilege in respect of the 23 documents on the grounds that they came within the class of documents relating to the formulation of government policy, and it was necessary for the proper functioning of the public service that they should be withheld from production because their production would inhibit freedom of expression between ministers and inhibit officials from giving full and uninhibited advice to ministers. The plaintiff applied for production of the disputed documents in order that he might inspect them. At the hearing of the application the Home Secretary contended that the question whether he had acted ultra vires was a question of law in which the court would have to decide whether what was done to the plaintiff was lawful or unlawful according to the Prison Act 1952 and the 1964 rules, and that the Home Office's policy was irrelevant and discovery of documents relating to it was unnecessary.

Held – (1) Public interest privilege could not be claimed on the ground that the candour of ministers and officials might be inhibited. Accordingly the Home Office could not claim privilege from production of the documents on that ground (see p 1155 c d and g, post); *Conway v Rimmer* [1968] 1 All ER 874 applied.

(2) The plaintiff's action did not turn merely on a question of law, namely whether the

---

a   Rule 43(2) is set out at p 1156 d, post

control unit scheme was ultra vires the 1952 Act and the 1964 rules, but extended to
issues of expert opinion and fact, namely whether the manner in which monthly
extensions were made under r 43(2) of the 1964 rules removing the plaintiff from the
association of other prisoners was unconscionable or unreasonable. Furthermore the
plaintiff's action involved the rights of the citizen and the liberty of the subject. The
plaintiff had an arguable case that there had been an unlawful interference with his
rights and there was a more than reasonable probability that the disputed documents
were likely to contain material that supported his case. That had to be balanced against
the fact that disclosure might lead to ill-informed criticism of the Home Office, although
some protection against that would be afforded by the implied undertaking imposed on
a party to whom documents were disclosed that they were not to be used for any purpose
other than the action (see p 1158 a to c, p. 1159 b to f, p 1160 g h and p 1161 b, post);
dictum of Lord Reid in *Conway v Rimmer* [1968] 1 All ER at 888, *Riddick v Thames Board
Mills Ltd* [1977] 3 All ER 677 and *Burmah Oil Co Ltd v Bank of England* [1979] 3 All ER 700
considered.

(3) Weighing the factors for and against disclosure in the balance, the public interest
of justice prevailed and the court would inspect the documents to see whether they
ought to be disclosed to the plaintiff. Having inspected the documents, six of them
would wholly or partly be ordered to be disclosed (see p 1161 b to d, post).

Notes

For withholding documents from production on the ground that disclosure would be
injurious to the public interest, see 13 Halsbury's Laws (4th Edn) paras 86–91, and for
cases on the subject, see 18 Digest (Reissue) 154–160, 1265–1301.

For treatment of prisoners and prison discipline, see 30 Halsbury's Laws (3rd Edn)
611–615, paras 1177–1184.

For the Prison Rules 1964, r 43, see 18 Halsbury's Statutory Instruments (Third
Reissue) 24.

Cases referred to in judgment

Burmah Oil Co Ltd v Bank of England (Attorney General intervening) [1979] 3 All ER 700,
[1980] AC 1090, [1979] 3 WLR 722, HL, Digest (Cont Vol E) 184, 1277a.
Church of Scientology of California v Department of Health and Social Security [1979] 3 All ER
97, [1979] 1 WLR 723, CA, Digest (Cont Vol E) 181, 495c.
Conway v Rimmer [1968] 1 All ER 874, [1968] AC 910, [1968] 2 WLR 998, HL; *subsequent
proceedings* [1968] 2 All ER 304, [1968] 2 WLR 1535, HL, 18 Digest (Reissue) 155,
1273.
D v National Society for the Prevention of Cruelty to Children [1977] 1 All ER 589, [1978] AC
171, [1977] 2 WLR 201, HL, Digest (Cont Vol E) 185, 1301b.
*R v Hull Prison Board of Visitors, ex parte St Germain, R v Wandsworth Prison Board of
Visitors, ex parte Rosa* [1979] 1 All ER 701, [1979] QB 425, [1979] 2 WLR 42, 143 JP
411, 68 Cr App R 212, CA, Digest (Cont Vol E) 488, 6a.
Riddick v Thames Board Mills Ltd [1977] 3 All ER 677, [1977] QB 881, [1977] 3 WLR 63,
CA, Digest (Cont Vol E) 180, 495b.

Application for production of documents

The plaintiff, Michael Sidney Williams, sought an order under RSC Ord 24, r 13(2) for
the production for inspection of certain documents in the possession of the defendant,
the Home Office, in connection with an action brought by the plaintiff claiming damages
for false imprisonment and a declaration that the defendant had acted ultra vires. By a
certificate dated 13th November 1979 the Secretary of State for the Home Department
objected to the production of 23 documents on the ground of public interest
immunity. On 9th January 1980 Master Elton by an order made by consent on the
restored summons for directions ordered that the matter be referred to the judge under
Ord 32, r 12. The application was heard in chambers but judgment was given by
NcNeill J in open court. The facts are set out in the judgment.

Stephen Sedley and *Michael Beloff* for the plaintiff.
Philip Vallance for the Home Office.

Cur adv vult

a   29th January. **McNEILL J** read the following judgment: The plaintiff seeks an order for the production for the purposes of inspection of a number of documents which have been disclosed in the defendant's list of documents and which are listed in a schedule to a certificate of Her Majesty's Secretary of State for the Home Department dated 13th November 1979.

b   By that certificate the Secretary of State expresses the opinion that production of the documents would be injurious to the public interest. I am required to decide whether or not the documents are privileged from production under what is now called 'public interest immunity'.

Consideration of the question proceeds on the basis that by disclosure of the documents in the schedule their relevance to the issues in the case is conceded by the Home Office:
c   see, for example, Lord Edmund-Davies in *Burmah Oil Co Ltd v Bank of England* [1979] 3 All ER 700 at 717, [1980] AC 1090 at 1125:

> 'A party to litigation who seeks, as here, to withhold from disclosure to the other party documents which being included in their list or affidavit of documents are ex concessis relevant to the litigation has . . . a heavy burden of proof.'

d   This reflects the view previously expressed by Lord Edmund-Davies in *D v National Society for the Prevention of Cruelty to Children* [1977] 1 All ER 589 at 615, [1978] AC 171 at 242:

> 'It is a serious step to exclude evidence relevant to an issue, for it is in the public interest that the search for truth should, in general, be unfettered. Accordingly, any
e   hindrance to its seeker needs to be justified by a convincing demonstration that an even higher public interest requires that only part of the truth should be told.'

Against that, I remind myself that the certificate of the Secretary of State raises, at the very least, a prima facie case for some fetters on the search for truth. Until the decision of the House of Lords in *Conway v Rimmer* [1968] 1 All ER 874, [1968] AC 910 indeed it
f   would have been regarded as conclusive. Even now, there are certain classes of document which ought not to be disclosed whatever their content may be (see per Lord Reid [1968] 1 All ER 874 at 888, [1968] AC 910 at 952). Lord Pearce put it in this way ([1968] 1 All ER 874 at 906, [1968] AC 910 at 980):

> 'There is not and never has been any doubt that the High Court will not order the production of any document where this would imperil the State or harm the public
g   interest as a whole. It has normally accepted the Minister's word on such a point.'

Lord Upjohn, dealing with the 'contents' rather than the 'class' cases, said ([1968] 1 All ER 874 at 914, [1968] AC 910 at 993):

> 'First, with regard to the "contents" cases there is, I think, no dispute and it does
h   not strictly arise in this case. A claim made by a Minister on the basis that the disclosure of the contents would be prejudicial to the public interest must receive the greatest weight . . .'

The present case, as will appear when I set out the terms of the certificate, is a 'class' and not a 'contents' case, subject possibly to the exception of one document. In 'class' cases, the House of Lords made it clear in *Conway v Rimmer* (I quote from the headnote ([1968]
j   AC 910 at 911) which fairly summarises the effect of the speeches) that 'When there is a clash between the public interests (1) that harm should not be done to the nation or the public service by the disclosure of certain documents and (2) that the administration of justice should not be frustrated by the withholding of them, their production will not be ordered if the possible injury to the nation or the public service is so grave that no other interest should be allowed to prevail over it, but, where the possible injury is substantially less, the court must balance against each other the two public interests involved'.

For the purposes of this exercise the court may in a proper case inspect the documents;

if the court could not without inspection decide whether the balance of public interests lay for or against disclosure there should be such inspection; it would seem that, if the *a* court were minded to inspect, the Crown should be given an opportunity to appeal. In the present case, however, counsel for the Crown has conceded that if I decide to inspect there will be no appeal against that decision.

There are two further preconditions to inspection. Firstly, the court must only inspect with the possibility of ordering production in mind if production 'is necessary either for disposing fairly of the cause or matter or for saving costs': see RSC Ord 24, r 13(1). Not *b* all relevant documents necessarily satisfy that test. Secondly, there must be a reasonable probability (see the words of Lord Keith in the *Burmah Oil* case [1979] 3 All ER 700 at 726, [1980] AC 1090 at 1137) that the documents contain material which would give substantial support to a contention in an issue in the cause.

It is now necessary to turn to the documents in question, to the Secretary of State's certificate and to the issues in the action. I say at once that this is not a case in which the *c* claim for immunity is based on matters of state policy such as foreign affairs, defence or the like, what was conveniently in argument referred to as 'high policy', where it might well be that the certificate would be accepted without more.

The relevant passages in the certificate are as follows:

> '3. I have formed the opinion that the production of the documents would be *d* injurious to the public interest for the reasons set out below. They consist of communications between to or from ministers (including ministers' personal secretaries acting on behalf of ministers) relating to the formulation of policy on control units, records of meetings attended by ministers and concerned with the formulation of such policy and communication between officials commenting on submissions to ministers in connection with the formulation of policy. I would emphasise that immunity is not being claimed in the particular circumstances of *e* this case in respect of documents recording policy already formulated, for example in the form of briefing material for ministers. On the contrary I understand that a wealth of such documentation has already been produced. [I interpolate to say that this is undoubtedly so. Counsel for the plaintiff accepted that the disclosed documents with his instructions were in a bundle at least a foot in height, and it is a relevant consideration that there has already been extensive discovery, including *f* the production of a large number of memoranda of or communications between junior officials.]
>
> '4. Of the documents, those originating in August and September, 1973 relate to the formulation of policy as to the nature and purpose of control units and as to their regime. Those originating in May and June, 1974 relate to the formulation of policy in relation to the imminent introduction of control units. Those originating *g* in October and November, 1974 relate to the formulation of policy in connection with the possible alteration of the regime of the control units. Those originating in May, June, September and October, 1975 relate to the formulation of policy as to whether or not the control unit facility at Wakefield should be closed.
>
> '5. It is in my opinion necessary for the proper functioning of the public service that the documents should be withheld from production. They are all documents *h* falling within the class of documents relating to the formulation of Government policy. As appears from the description of the documents in the schedule such policy was decided at high level. It is in my view contrary to the public interest that details of the views of ministers and officials contained in such a class of document should be revealed and it is inconsistent with the need for full and uninhibited advice from officials to ministers that such a class of documents should be produced. *j*
>
> '6. I would like to further describe the note from the Parliamentary Under-Secretary of State, Dr. Shirley Summerskill to the Secretary of State, Mr. Roy Jenkins dated 6th November, 1974. This note is a record of a visit she made to the control unit at Wakefield Prison, her observations on the visit and her suggestions for consideration as to possible variations in the regime. Insofar as this note, as I accept,

does not in its entirety relate to the formulation of policy I consider its production

a would be contrary to the public interest as being inconsistent with the need for freedom of expression between ministers at all times.'

At an earlier stage in this judgment I indicated that immunity for all the documents in question was sought on the basis that, with one possible exception, they came under a 'class' and not a 'contents' immunity; the possible exception was the document last

b mentioned, that is in para 6 of the Secretary of State's certificate dealing with Dr Summerskill's visit to Wakefield. While, as the Secretary of State accepts, this is not a document relating in its entirety to the formulation of policy the claim for immunity is in my view based on the class of document described as those where there is 'a need for freedom of expression between ministers'; it is not, therefore, in my view a 'contents' claim, or indeed 'a possible exception' in the sense in which I previously used those

c words; it is protected, if at all, by a 'class' immunity.

So far as that phrase 'freedom of expression' used in para 6 of the certificate and the phrase in para 5 of the certificate 'the need for full and uninhibited advice from officials to ministers' are concerned the preponderance of opinion in *Conway v Rimmer* was opposed to the use of 'candour' as a ground for granting immunity in a case where without that ground production would be ordered (see [1968] 1 All ER 874 at 888, 891,

d 904, 909 and 914, [1968] AC 910 at 952, 957, 976, 984 and 993 per Lord Reid, Lord Morris, Lord Hodson, Lord Pearce and Lord Upjohn). In the *Burmah Oil* case (although Lord Wilberforce in his dissenting speech thought that 'candour' as a ground for immunity has 'received an excessive dose of cold water' (see [1979] 3 All ER 700 at 707, [1980] AC 1090 at 1112)), Lord Keith thought it had 'little weight, if any', and went on to say ([1979] 3 All ER 700 at 724, [1980] AC 1090 at 1132):

e 'The notion that any competent or conscientious public servant would be inhibited at all in the candour of his writings by consideration of the off-chance that they might have to be produced in litigation is in my opinion grotesque. To represent that the possibility of it might significantly impair the public service is even more so. Nowadays the state in its multifarious manifestations impinges closely on the lives and activities of individual citizens. Where this has involved a

f citizen in litigation with the state or one of its agencies, the candour argument is an utterly insubstantial ground for denying him access to relevant documents.'

Lord Scarman thought that candour in the advice offered to ministers was a factor which could legitimately be put into the balance, while questioning whether, save in documents which concerned the national safety, affected diplomatic relations or related to some state secret of high importance, there was anything so important in 'secret

g government' that it must be protected even at the price of injustice in the courts (see [1979] 3 All ER 700 at 733–734, [1980] AC 1090 at 1145).

Accordingly, putting candour on one side, I turn to the other ground of immunity claimed in para 5 of the Secretary of State's certificate, that is to say that it is contrary to the public interest that details of the views of ministers and officials contained in such a class of document should be revealed.

h Some outline of the issues in the cause is necessary.

On 23rd February 1971 the plaintiff was sentenced to a term of 14 years' imprisonment at Glamorgan Assizes. He therefore became subject to the provisions of the Prison Act 1952 and the Prison Rules 1964, SI 1964 No 388. He served some part of his sentence at Her Majesty's Prison at Wakefield.

j Some time in 1974 the Home Office designated some part of that prison as a 'control unit', and the plaintiff was detained in the control unit for 180 days between 23rd August 1974 and 18th February 1975. Some brief reference to the purpose of the control unit is necessary. It was a segregated part of the prison set out, putting it in broad terms, for the reception and detention of prisoners who, among other things, were thought deliberately to set out to disrupt the regime of the prison itself.

In these proceedings, the plaintiff claims, in effect, that his detention in the control unit was unlawful, involving as he contends it did, among other things, cellular confinement other than was permitted by the 1964 rules, an undue deprivation of the *a* society of others, contrary to the 1952 Act and the rules and cruel and unusual punishment in breach of the Bill of Rights (1688); further he contends that the institution of the control unit and its regime were outwith the powers of the Home Office. Additionally, he alleges breaches of the rules of natural justice, and the pleadings raise issues of fact as to the circumstances of his detention.

In particular, the plaintiff contends that the regime for the control unit was in breach *b* of the 1964 rules in requiring him to be held in and under the regime of the control unit for two stages of detention, the first of 90 days without association and the second of 90 days with restricted association: see r 43, as amended, of the 1964 rules which reads as follows:

'(1) Where it appears desirable, for the maintenance of good order or discipline or in his own interests, that a prisoner should not associate with other prisoners, either *c* generally or for particular purposes, the governor may arrange for the prisoner's removal from association accordingly.

'(2) A prisoner shall not be removed under this Rule for a period of more than 24 hours without the authority of a member of the board of visitors, or of the Secretary of State. An authority given under this paragraph shall be for a period not exceeding one month, but may be renewed from month to month.' *d*

The plaintiff by his statement of claim and in particular by his reply contends, and counsel on his behalf did not shrink from asserting, that the Home Office 'used' (or more accurately 'misused') r 43 to avoid the necessity of legislation or formal amendment of the rules by purporting to comply with 28-day renewals when it was at all material times intended and contemplated that the plaintiff should be deprived of association or of full *e* association throughout the 180-day period of the control unit regime.

It is to be noted that what happened in the plaintiff's case is in no sense, and this is conceded by the Home Office, covered by the disciplinary code laid down in the rules. By formal admission the Home Office accepts that the plaintiff 'was not detained in the said control unit as a result of his being accused of any specific disciplinary offence . . .' Moreover, the Home Office does not by the pleadings set up any justification for the *f* deprivation of association, taking the stand that the control unit and its regime were a lawful exercise of the Home Office's powers under the Act and rules.

The scheme itself is set out in a circular instruction CI 35/1974, dated 17th June 1974 and issued by the Home Office. A copy of the instruction has been disclosed and is before me. Reference to paras 11 to 15 inclusive appears prima facie to support the contention that a 90 plus 90 day period was intended or contemplated as the period of the regime *g* and, by an addendum of 27th August 1974, 'The references to periods of three months should be corrected to read 90 days'. Annex D to CI 35/1974, also dated 27th August 1974, being 'Notes for Convicted Prisoners in Control Units', states at para 4 that:

'Stage 1 will normally last 90 days subject to the requirements under Rule 43 for periodic renewal of the application of the Rule. If you have been civil, co-operative and have worked diligently during Stage 1, you may expect to move to Stage 2 after *h* 90 days. If at any time you fail to work without good reason or cause any sort of trouble, you will return to the beginning of Stage 1 and start all over again before becoming eligible for Stage 2.'

Those concluding words later came to be considered as the reverter rule.

A similar reference to '90 days subject again to the renewal requirements of Rule 43' *j* is included in the description of stage 2 in para 5. Annex E to the same circular (again dated 27th August 1974) reads:

'(1) Prisoners transferred to control units would always be made subject to the provisions of Rule 43. (2) Authority will be given by the control units committee

a
on behalf of the Secretary of State when a prisoner is allocated to one of the control units. (3) In order that this authority can be renewed as required by the provisions of Rule 43(2) a return of all prisoners in a control unit should be submitted to P3 on Form 1299 not less than four working days before the end of each month.'

In effect, the plaintiff says, for the words 'may be renewed from month to month' in r 43(2) the Home Office has, without parliamentary or other authority, substituted the words 'shall be renewed until at least 90 (or 180) days have been served', that is to say at
b
least two mandatory and not discretionary renewals.

Following a parliamentary question, the scheme was further amended on 28th November 1974 (by which date the plaintiff had completed, or substantially completed, his first stage of 90 days); in particular, I note the following amendment by insertion of a new paragraph in annex E as follows:

c
'It will be open to the Board of Visitors, the Governor or [a medical officer] to make representations to headquarters during the process of monthly renewal or at any other time if they consider that circumstances have arisen which necessitate the removal of a prisoner from the unit.'

I also observe that, in a disclosed answer to the parliamentary question, the then
d
Secretary of State said this:

'... the existing instructions provide that a person who misbehaves should automatically recommence the prescribed period in the control unit, regardless of the time he has already spent there. I have decided that these should be modified to give the governor and the board of visitors discretion as to the extent to which a prisoner should revert.'

e
This answer is reflected in amendments to paras 12 and 13 of the scheme and to paras 4 and 5 of annex D.

On this material, one view could well be that at the least the Secretary of State had fettered the discretion which he ought to exercise monthly under r 43(2) on each proposed renewal of authority to remove a prisoner from association by intending or
f
contemplating what was in reality a 90-day or even a 180-day order, with, until the amendments of November 1974, automatic reverter to the beginning in the event of misbehaviour, and with no opportunity for intervention by the board of visitors, governor or medical officer even if circumstances had arisen which necessitated the removal of a prisoner from the unit. If this were sufficient on the presently disclosed material no further discovery would be necessary for disposing fairly of the cause.

g
It is contended on behalf of the Home Office that as the real issue here is one of law, the court being asked to decide whether or not the scheme was ultra vires the 1952 Act and the 1964 rules, further discovery is unnecessary. The court, it is said, simply has to look at the documents in the light of the Act and the rules to arrive at a conclusion on this point. As counsel for the Home Office put it, the question for the court is not what the Secretary of State or his advisors thought to be the true purpose of the scheme for control
h
units and their regime but was what was done to this plaintiff lawful or not, having regard to the true character of the control unit and its regime as appears from the scheme and the 1952 Act and the 1964 rules. There is, he said, no issue of fact as to what actually was done to the plaintiff. Moreover, he says, it would not take the plaintiff any further if it were shown not merely that the Home Office acted wrongfully but that it did so for the wrong reason.

j
Counsel for the Home Office further argues that this case is distinguishable from *Conway v Rimmer*, where there was an issue of fact for trial as to malice, and the *Burmah Oil* case, where there was an issue of fact for trial whether or not a sale of stock was unconscionable and procured in breach of duty. Accordingly, expressions of opinion in those cases are by no means conclusive in the present case and, as he repeated, where there was no issue of fact.

There is, however, as is accepted on both sides, and whether or not there is any issue of fact, an issue of professional opinion; both sides have been advised by experts in the field of penology and have exchanged reports. These go, I am told, inter alia, into such issues as that which the plaintiff pleads as *undue* deprivation of association and to *cruel and unusual punishment*. Moreover, there *are* issues of fact, not the least of which is the manner in which, if not the reasons for which, the Secretary of State (or the control units committee on his behalf after 27th August 1974) exercised, and was intended to exercise, the power or duty to renew at monthly intervals the authority to remove the plaintiff from association purportedly under r 43(2) of the 1964 rules in the special circumstances of the control unit regime.

In this context, there are passages in the speeches of their Lordships in the *Burmah Oil* case which support the contention that there should be production here. Lord Salmon, having pointed out that the only issues of fact were 'whether the Bank's insistence on buying Burmah's BP stock units below the market price and with no profit sharing scheme of any kind was "unconscionable, inequitable and unreasonable" and whether this transaction was "procured by the Bank acting in breach of its duty of fair dealing and taking an unfair and unconscionable advantage of Burmah . . .", went on to say ([1979] 3 All ER 700 at 714, [1980] AC 1090 at 1120):

'Whether unconscionable conduct of this kind would carry any legal liability can be decided only at the trial of the action . . . If, however, during the Bank's discussions with the government immediately prior to the conclusion of the agreement for the purchase of the BP stock the Bank had said anything to suggest that in its view the terms of the purchase insisted on by the government were unconscionable this would strongly support Burmah's assertion that those terms were indeed unconscionable. The known fact that the Bank had already stated, in effect, that the terms were unfair and unreasonable suggests that it may well be that it stated that the terms were also unconscionable. If the Bank did so, it would be strong evidence to support Burmah's case on the facts. No one can tell without looking at the documents referring to the discussions between the Bank and the government what was said by the Bank at these discussions.'

Lord Edmund-Davies said ([1979] 3 All ER 700 at 718, [1980] AC 1090 at 1126):

'. . . it could . . . prove a valuable reinforcement of Burmah's case if they could establish by means of some of the withheld documents that the Bank had itself committed themselves to the view that the terms finally presented to Burmah were tainted by those unconscionable features of which Burmah complained.'

Lord Keith put it in this way ([1979] 3 All ER 700 at 726, [1980] AC 1090 at 1135–1136):

'. . . I have come to the conclusion that a reasonable probability exists of finding the documents in question to contain a record of the views of the responsible officials of the Bank of England expressed in such terms as to lend substantial support to the contention that the bargain eventually concluded with Burmah was unconscionable. I do not agree that the issue of unconscionability is to be treated entirely objectively. If it were to be proved, for example, that the Deputy Governor of the Bank strongly protested that the terms of the bargain were unconscionable but was overborne by the government, that would in my view be strong evidence in Burmah's favour.'

Lastly of these quotations, Lord Scarman used these words ([1979] 3 All ER 700 at 731, [1980] AC 1090 at 1142):

'Burmah's case is not merely that the Bank exerted pressure: it is that the Bank acted unreasonably, abusing its power and taking an unconscionable advantage of the weakness of Burmah. On these questions the withheld documents may be very *a*   revealing. This is not "pure speculation". The government was creating the pressure; the Bank was exerting it on the government's instructions.'

It was accepted that the documents in the *Burmah* case were 'high level', and concerned with the formulation of policy; they included communications between, to and from ministers and between, to and from senior officials of the Treasury, the Department of Energy and the Bank. The House of Lords nevertheless (by a majority of four to one) held that there should be inspection of them. Having inspected them, I observe, it was
b   decided that none contained matters of such evidential value as to make disclosure necessary for fairly disposing of the cause.

Finally, the present case is one in which the rights of the citizen and the liberty of the subject is in issue, at least that limited right of personal freedom protected by the 1952 Act and the 1964 rules which is preserved to a prisoner serving a lawful sentence of imprisonment: see the words of Shaw LJ in *R v Hull Prison Board of Visitors* [1979] 1 All
c   ER 701 at 716–718, [1979] QB 425 at 455–456.

If the plaintiff has an arguable case for saying, and at this interlocutory stage that is all that I need to consider, that there has been an unlawful interference with his rights as a citizen given by statute or rules thereunder on the part of the Home Office it is a strong argument in his favour when balancing the respective public interests involved in this sort of case. He has such a case. He may not win at trial but he should not be barred
d   from a fair trial on all the relevant material unless the public interest immunity claimed in the certificate prevails.

That public interest is not said to be one of high policy: it is concerned with details of prison administration. There is said to be the formulation of policy on a high level, involving indeed as appears from the schedule, two successive Secretaries of State, two Ministers of State and one Parliamentary Under-Secretary, as well as senior officials; but
e   I observe that in effect the same level of ministers and officials is concerned here as in the *Burmah Oil* case.

If not based on 'candour', for the reasons already mentioned, I have to consider whether or not the claim for immunity based on what Lord Reid spoke of in the following terms in *Conway v Rimmer* [1968] 1 All ER 874 at 888, [1968] AC 910 at 952
f   should prevail here:

> 'To my mind the most important reason is that such disclosure would create or fan, ill-informed or captious public or political criticism. The business of government is difficult enought as it is, and no government could contemplate with equanimity the inner workings of the government machine being exposed to the gaze of those ready to criticise without adequate knowledge of the background and
g   perhaps with some axe to grind.'

Lord Keith, however, in the *Burmah Oil* case [1979] 3 All ER 700 at 725, [1980] AC 1090 at 1134, dealing with this passage, recognised that the public interest that justice should be done might—

h   > 'demand, though no doubt only in a very limited number of cases, that the inner workings of government should be exposed to public gaze, and there may be some who would regard this as likely to lead, not to captious or ill-informed criticism, but to criticism calculated to improve the nature of that working as affecting the individual citizen.'

Lord Scarman thought this to be a factor—
j
> 'legitimately to be put into the balance which has to be struck between the public interest in the proper functioning of the public service (ie the executive arm of government) and the public interest in the administration of justice.'

(See [1979] 3 All ER 700 at 734, [1980] AC 1090 at 1145.)

It is interesting to observe that Lord Scarman went on to postulate that the court's power to inspect should only be used if the court is in doubt:

'Where documents are relevant (as in this case they are), I would think a pure "class" objection would by itself seldom quieten judicial doubts, particularly if, as here, a substantial case can be made out for saying that disclosure is needed in the interest of justice.'

Despite that spur to judicial intervention, I propose to approach my decision on the basis that I should first, if satisfied that I should do so, inspect the documents.

In favour of inspection, it is said that it would tend to the fair disposal of the cause if, for example, the recorded opinion of a senior official in the department, than whom there can be few better versed in penology, accorded with the opinion of one or other of the expert witnesses whom I have mentioned on, for example, the normality or propriety of continuing deprivation of association over and above the statutory period renewable under the rules of 28 days (was it recognised in the documents as undue, cruel or unusual?) or again if, for example, the documents disclosed a plain intention to 'misuse' the rules by purporting to import into the scheme the 28-day renewal when a minimum 90-day regime was intended or contemplated, for, at the very least, this would bear on discretion if and when the court had to consider the granting of declaratory relief as sought. Or if, for example, the documents contained what was in effect an admission by a senior official that the plaintiff's claim for relief was well founded.

Some support for the view that such material might be found is contained in the Secretary of State's parliamentary answer already mentioned: some additional support might be found in investigating how r 43(3) of the 1964 rules was to operate under the control unit regime. That paragraph says this:

'The governor may arrange at his discretion for such a prisoner as aforesaid [that is a prisoner removed from association] to resume association with other prisoners, and shall do so if in any case the medical officer so advises on medical grounds.'

How was that paragraph to operate under the control unit regime? Was the governor's discretion there set out wholly removed prior to November 1974, and if so by what authority and in what manner?

In addition, I was shown a document, one of the documents for which immunity was sought but which (or a copy of which) came into the possession of the plaintiff's solicitors. The Treasury Solicitor was informed of this and counsel for the Home Office agreed that I might read the document and make such use of it, if any, as I thought fit. For identification it is the document in the schedule dated 7th May 1974 described as 'Submission Hewlings to PUS (Petersen) Parliamentary Under-Secretary of State (Summerskill) and Secretary of State (Jenkins)'. I have read the document. In my view it reinforces to the point of certainty the view which I had tentatively reached that as a matter of reasonable probability the documents were likely to contain material supportive of the plaintiff's case. I refer in that document, for example, to a passage which refers to the normal constraints of punishment being ineffective, to another dealing with deprivation to a large extent of such normal enjoyments as free association, and to a third which mentions the delicate ground of prisoners' rights, privileges and liberties.

The risks attendant on inspection and production as postulated by Lord Reid (see [1968] 1 All ER 874 at 888, [1968] AC 910 at 952) are in any event minimised in two ways. Firstly, if after inspection the court orders production, the order may provide for production of part only of a document, the remainder being sealed up or otherwise obscured. Secondly, it is plain from the decision of the Court of Appeal in *Riddick v Thames Board Mills* [1977] 3 All ER 677, [1977] QB 881 if it was not plain before, that a party who disclosed a document was entitled to the protection of the court against any use of the document otherwise than in the action in which it is disclosed. As Lord Denning MR put it ([1977] 3 All ER 677 at 687, [1977] QB 881 at 896):

a 'The courts should, therefore, not allow the other party, or anyone else, to use the document for any ulterior or alien purpose . . . In order to encourage openness and fairness, the public interest requires that documents disclosed on discovery are not to be made use of except for the purposes of the action in which they are disclosed.'

Undoubtedly this applies to litigants and their legal advisers: see also the references in *Church of Scientology of California v Department of Health and Social Security* [1979] 3 All ER 97 at 101–102, 116, [1979] 1 WLR 723 at 729, 746. Much of the reservation expressed

b by Lord Reid to which I have referred would in my view be met by adherence to what was said by the Court of Appeal in *Riddick's* case, reasserting what indeed had been the law previously.

Having weighed all these various factors in the balance, I have come to the conclusion that the public interests of justice, including as they do here the rights of the citizen, and that liberty of a prisoner preserved for him by the statute and rules, must be the

c prevailing interest and that I should inspect the withheld documents. Accordingly I have asked the Treasury Solicitor to provide the documents for that purpose.

The Treasury Solicitor provided the withheld documents in a sealed envelope which I opened only after completing the final draft of my judgment above. Having inspected the documents and applying the principles which I have outlined above I consider that the following documents or parts of documents should be produced for inspection and

d I so order. I take the description of each document from the schedule to the Secretary of State's certificate. There are six documents to which I refer.

1. 13th August 1973. Submission Hewlings to PUS (Petersen) and Minister of State (Colville).

2. 7th May 1974. This is the document referred to in my judgment which is already in the hands of the plaintiff's solicitors. If and in so far as it is necessary to do so, I order

e that it be produced for inspection.

3. 16th October 1974. Note of meeting held by Secretary of State with officials reviewing policy.

4. 21st October 1974. Note of further meeting held by Secretary of State with Parliamentary Under-Secretary of State and officials reviewing policy.

5. 29th September 1975. Minute from Morris to Beck and others enclosing draft

f submission to the Secretary of State: 'The review: paragraph 2' only. The remainder of the minute to be covered or omitted.

6. 30th September 1975. The paragraph referred to in no 5 above is repeated in this minute, and to the same extent only that minute is to be produced for inspection with the remainder covered or omitted. I say at once that what is ordered to be produced for inspection there is no more than duplication of what is ordered to be produced under

g no 5.

That is the extent of the production which I order.

Order accordingly.

Solicitors: *Harriet Harman* (for the plaintiff); *Treasury Solicitor.*

K Mydeen Esq   Barrister.

Attorney General ex rel Tilley v London Borough of Wandsworth

a

CHANCERY DIVISION

HIS HONOUR JUDGE MERVYN DAVIES QC SITTING AS A JUDGE OF THE HIGH COURT
6th, 7th, 17th MARCH 1980

b

COURT OF APPEAL, CIVIL DIVISION
LAWTON, BRANDON AND TEMPLEMAN LJJ
4th FEBRUARY 1981

Child – Care – Local authority – Duty to diminish need to receive children into care – Duty to provide advice, guidance and assistance to promote child's welfare – Specific power to provide **c** *'assistance in kind' – Local authority passing resolution that where parents of children intentionally homeless it should not provide assistance with accommodation – Whether 'assistance' including provision of accommodation – Whether specific power to provide 'assistance in kind' not including provision of accommodation and cutting down any general power to provide accommodation – Whether resolution invalid – Whether resolution amounting to fetter on authority's duty to diminish need to take children into care by providing accommodation for* **d** *family – Children and Young Persons Act 1963, s 1(1).*

Section 1(1)[d] of the Children and Young Persons Act 1963 imposed on local authorities the duty to promote children's welfare by providing advice, guidance and 'assistance' in order to diminish the need to receive children into care under the Children Act 1948, and specifically empowered a local authority to provide 'assistance in kind' or, in exceptional *e* circumstances, in cash. The social services committee of a local authority passed a resolution, subsequently confirmed by the full council, that in cases where the housing department of the authority had determined that a family with young children were intentionally homeless for the purpose of the Housing (Homeless Persons) Act 1977 and subsequently the family approached the authority's social services department assistance with accommodation would not be provided under the provisions of the 1963 Act, *f* although consideration would be given to receiving the children of the family into care if the circumstances warranted it. In practice exceptions were made by the social services department in applying the resolution. The Attorney General at the relation of a ratepayer and member of the local authority's council sought a declaration as against the local authority that the resolution was invalid and could not be implemented because it amounted to a limitation on the exercise by the authority of its duty under s 1(1) of the *g* 1963 Act. The judge held that s 1(1) of the 1963 Act empowered a local authority to give assistance in the form of accommodation for a child and its parents and that the resolution fettered that discretion. Accordingly he granted the declaration sought. The local authority appealed.

Held – The appeal would be dismissed for the following reasons—   *h*
  (1) Since the purpose of s 1(1) of the 1963 Act was to diminish the need to receive children into care under the 1948 Act when the parents had no proper accommodation for their children, the general power to provide 'assistance' contained in that section included the power to provide accommodation for a child and its parents. Accordingly, even if the specific power in s 1(1) to provide 'assistance in kind' did not include the provision of accommodation, it did not cut down the general power to provide accommodation (see *j* p 1170 *f* to *j* and p 1171 *g h*, post).
  (2) On a proper exercise of the powers contained in s 1(1), the parents' intentional homelessness was only one factor to be taken in account in considering what the best way

---

a   Section 1(1), so for as material, is set out at p 1170 *c d*, post

was in which the powers under s 1(1) should be exercised in a child's interest. It followed
a that the local authority's resolution was invalid because it laid down a policy which fettered
its powers under s 1(1) in such a way that the facilities offered to a child under that section
did not depend on the particular circumstances of the child or its family but on the general
policy not to provide accommodation under s 1(1) when the parents of a child were
intentionally homeless under the 1977 Act, and because (per Lawton and Brandon LJJ) the
policy contained no exceptions (see p 1171 *b* to *h*, post).

b

Notes

For the establishment by a local authority of a social services committee for the discharge
of the authority's functions under, inter alia, the Children and Young Persons Act 1963, see
24 Halsbury's Laws (4th Edn) para 854.

For the Children and Young Persons Act 1963, s 1, see 17 Halsbury's Statutes (3rd Edn)
c 701.

As from 1st April 1981 s 1 of the 1963 Act is replaced by s 1 of the Child Care Act 1980.

Cases referred to in judgments

Associated Provincial Picture Houses Ltd v Wednesbury Corpn [1947] 2 All ER 680, [1948] 1 KB
223, [1948] LJR 190, 177 LT 641, 112 JP 55, 45 LGR 635, CA, 45 Digest (Repl) 215, 189.
d Secretary of State for Education and Science v Metropolitan Borough of Tameside [1976] 3 All ER
665, [1977] AC 1014, [1976] 3 WLR 641, 75 LGR 190, HL, Digest (Cont Vol E) 194, 33c.
Stringer v Minister of Housing and Local Government [1971] 1 All ER 65, [1970] 1 WLR 1281,
68 LGR 788, 22 P & CR 255, [1970] RVR 481, Digest (Cont Vol D) 918, 46b.

Action

e By an amended writ and statement of claim issued on 30th July 1979 the Attorney General
at the relation of Tracey Sandra Helen Tilley, a councillor of the defendant local authority,
the London Borough of Wandsworth ('the local authority'), and a ratepayer within the local
authority's area, alleged that by a resolution passed by the local authority's social services
committee on 4th July 1979 the local authority resolved not to comply with its duty to
consider the provision of housing or cash for housing in respect of children whose parents
f were intentionally homeless within the meaning of s 17 of the Housing (Homeless Persons)
Act 1977, and claimed (1) a declaration that the local authority was not entitled to exclude
consideration of the provision of housing or cash for housing in order to promote the
welfare of children by diminishing the need to receive them into care, pursuant to s 1 of
the Children and Young Persons Act 1963, on the ground that the children were living
with persons determined by the local authority to be 'intentionally homeless' within s 17
g of the 1977 Act, and (2) a declaration that the resolution passed by the local authority's
social services committee on 4th July 1979 was unlawful and that the local authority was
not entitled to implement or give effect to it. The facts are set out in the judgment of his
Honour Judge Mervyn Davies QC.

John Macdonald QC and *Andrew Bano* for the plaintiff.
h Michael Beloff for the local authority.

Cur adv vult

17th March. **HIS HONOUR JUDGE MERVYN DAVIES QC** read the following
j judgment: This is a relator action in which a local authority, the London Borough of
Wandsworth, are the defendants. The relator is Mrs Tracey Tilley who is a ratepayer of the
borough. Mrs Tilley is, and has been since 1971, a member of the council of the borough.
She was from December 1973 to May 1978 the chairman of the council's social services
committee. On 4th July 1979 that committee passed a resolution which was confirmed by
the council on 24th July 1979. Paragraph (a) of the resolution reads as follows:

'That in those cases where intentional homelessness had been determined by the Council in respect of a family with young children and, subsequently, an approach is made to the Social Services Department, it be decided that assistance with alternative housing be not provided under the provisions of the Children and Young Persons Act 1963 although consideration be given to the reception into care of the children should their circumstances so warrant it and that the whole matter be reviewed by Committee in three months time.'

The claim in the action is in effect for a declaration that that resolution is invalid and ought to have no effect. The resolution refers to a review in three months time. In fact no such review took place. I understand that that was due to this action being started before there was an opportunity for such review. Paragraph 5 of the amended statement of claim in setting out the resolution omits the words at the end, 'and that the whole matter be reviewed etc.'

I will refer to the legislation that gave rise to the passing of that resolution. I mention first the Housing (Homeless Persons) Act 1977 because it is that Act that gives rise to the phrase 'intentional homelessness' that is included in the resolution. The Housing (Homeless Persons) Act 1977 imposes certain duties on local authorities, including the defendant local authority, with respect to persons who are homeless. It is not necessary to set out the specific provisions of the Act. It suffices to say that the Act distinguishes between persons who are homeless intentionally and persons who are homeless otherwise than intentionally. Intentional homelessness is defined in s 17 of the Act. An example of a case of intentional homelessness is the man who in receipt of a sufficient income wilfully refuses to pay his rent and is in consequence evicted. The duty of the local authority with respect to the father of a family unintentionally homeless is to provide accommodation for him and his family. On the other hand, the father (or mother) of a family intentionally homeless is not in so favourable a position. In this case the local authority are simply obliged (a) to furnish advice and appropriate assistance (see s 4(2)) and (b) to secure that accommodation is made available for the homeless family's occupation for such period as the local authority consider will give him a reasonable opportunity of himself securing accommodation for his occupation (see s 4(3)). This duty of securing accommodation may be performed by the local authority making accommodation of its own available, or by securing that the homeless one obtains accommodation from some other person, or by giving him such advice and assistance as will secure that he obtains accommodation from some other person (see s 6). It follows that a family intentionally homeless may be placed by the local authority in temporary accommodation. But when the time comes that the local authority regard the homeless ones as having had a reasonable opportunity of securing their own accommodation, they may be evicted by the local authority from their temporary refuge. If they are so evicted and have nowhere else to go, then they are homeless without any duties owed to them under the Act by the local authority. Section 12 of the Act says that a local authority when administering the 1977 Act is to have regard to such guidance as may from time to time be given by the Secretary of State. The Secretary of State has given such guidance in a code that was before me. I am satisfied that the defendant local authority has had full regard to this code. They are not necessarily bound by its terms but they are obliged to have regard to the code.

Section 1 of the Children Act 1948 (which is being replaced by s 2 of the Child Care Act 1980) imposes on a local authority the duty to receive children into care in certain circumstances. Thus a child whose parents are in certain circumstances prevented from providing for the child's proper accommodation is to be received into care. Section 1 of the Children and Young Persons Act 1963 (which is being replaced by another provision which is in like terms, that is by s 1 of the Child Care Act 1980) provides, so far as material, as follows:

'(1) It shall be the duty of every local authority to make available such advice, guidance and assistance as may promote the welfare of children by diminishing the a need to receive children into or keep them in care under the Children Act 1948, the principal Act [ie the Children and Young Persons Act 1933] . . . or to bring children before a juvenile court; and any provisions made by a local authority under this subsection may, if the local authority think fit, include provision for giving assistance in kind or, in exceptional circumstances, in cash . . .

'(3) Where any provision which may be made by a local authority under subsection (1) of this section is made (whether by that or any other authority) under

b any other enactment the local authority shall not be required to make the provision under this section but shall have power to do so . . .'

The section may have been enacted following some remarks in para 20 of the Report of the Committee on Children and Young Persons (the Ingleby Report; Cmnd 1191) published in October 1960. The purpose of the section is to avoid the need to receive

c into care if the welfare of the child will better be promoted by the giving of advice, guidance or assistance. In exceptional circumstances assistance by way of cash is contemplated.

The defendants are the local authority for the purposes of the Acts I have mentioned. Its housing committee operates the Housing (Homeless Persons) Act 1977 and its social services committee, a statutory committee under the Local Authority Social Services Act

d 1970, operates the Children Acts.

I now turn to the circumstances in which the resolution dated 4th July 1979 came to be passed. I had before me an agreed bundle. This includes (i) a report dated 27th June 1979 by Mr Lister, the chairman of the social services committee, (ii) a note concerning that report, (iii) the minutes of the meeting of the social services committee held on 4th July 1979, (iv) the agenda (in part) for the council meeting to be held on 24th July

e 1979. The relator and Mr Leo Goodman who is the director of social services at Wandsworth gave evidence for the plaintiff. The defendants called no evidence.

Mr Lister's report shows that in June 1979 there were three recent cases of families with children regarded as intentionally homeless. They were evicted after the machinery of the 1977 Act had been operated. It is feared that the number of such families so evicted may increase, perhaps considerably. The average cost of maintaining an average

f family in bed and breakfast accommodation in Wandsworth is £76 a week. A family evicted in the way I have mentioned is not, as I have said, able to call in aid the 1977 Act, that is to say, immediately after eviction from temporary accommodation provided under the 1977 Act the family are not entitled, if they have no place to go to, to be given a further or second period of temporary accommodation under the 1977 Act. In this situation the family will go, or be advised to go, to the social services department of the

g council. There they will ask for help.

Before July 1979 the view in Wandsworth was that such a family could, in an appropriate case, be given assistance under s 1 of the 1963 Act. The assistance could be the provision of bed and breakfast accommodation for the family at the expense of the defendants. The reasoning behind this is that the children stand in peril of being received into care in that the parents cannot provide accommodation: see s 1 of the 1948

h Act. In this situation it is the duty of the local authority under s 1 of the 1963 Act to make available such assistance as may promote the welfare of the children by diminishing the need to receive them into care. In an exceptional circumstance such as intentional homelessness the assistance may be in cash expended in bed and breakfast accommodation for the whole family. In this way, so the reasoning proceeds, the welfare of the children is promoted in that they are kept with their parents instead of being received into care.

j Whether or not in a particular case assistance is to be given in this way under s 1 of the 1963 Act is of course dependent on the responsible officer of the social services department being satisfied on the particular case that the welfare of the child or children does in fact require that the child or children remain with its or their parents rather than being received into care. Although Mr Lister's report refers to three recent cases I was not told how many intentionally homeless families in all had been given bed and breakfast accommodation in this way before July 1979. Nor do I know how many such families have since been given such accommodation. But I gather that the number has *a* at all times been small.

The problem of how to deal with intentionally homeless families who after eviction from temporary accommodation provided under the 1977 Act ask the social services department for help was considered at the meeting of the social services committee held on 4th July 1979. There was considerable discussion as the minutes show. The Lister recommendation, subject to the addition of the words concerning review, was accepted *b* and the resolution was passed in the terms I have set out. No doubt the committee was influenced by para 5 of Mr Lister's report which suggests (a) that to afford bed and breakfast facilities achieves little in the long term interest of the families as affording only a limited respite, and (b) that to afford bed and breakfast accommodation nullifies the efforts of the housing department to help the families to help themselves. It may be supposed that the resolution was passed with, as well, economy in mind. That may not *c* be so. Mr Goodman said a child in care costs the council £140 a week unless it is fostered when the cost is perhaps £17 to £24 a week. The relator, Mrs Tilley, said that the resolution marked a change in the council's policy. She contended that the new policy meant that the 1977 Act was improperly influencing the right administration of the Children Acts. In cross-examination she agreed that the social services department would in implementing the resolution be prepared to consider exceptions to the rule laid *d* down by the resolution. In his cross-examination Mr Goodman accepted that para 4 of the amended defence was true. Paragraph 4, as far as material, reads:

> 'The Social Services Department and/or the Defendants have at all material times since the said notification implemented and continued to implement the policy contained in the said resolution, but have been and are prepared to listen to any applicant for assistance therefrom as to why an exception should be made to the said *e* policy in the case of the said applicant.'

The first submission of counsel for the local authority was that a local authority has no power under s 1 of the 1963 Act to provide assistance by way of housing or bed and breakfast accommodation or of cash for such accommodation. If this submission is upheld some surprising consequences ensue. First, a local authority may not under s 1 *f* provide accommodation for anyone, whether intentionally or unintentionally homeless, so that the local authority have acted unlawfully in the past in affording accommodation under s 1 to anyone. Secondly, that the resolution now under consideration was without effect in that the local authority were resolving not to exercise a power or duty which they do not have. Thirdly, the general view prevailing in local authority and government departments as to the providing of accommodation under s 1 is wrong. Although *g* counsel for the plaintiff is concerned to see the resolution of 4th July 1979 set aside it is not surprising that he did not ask that the resolution be set aside on this ground. The attitude of counsel for the plaintiff was that the council can use s 1 to provide accommodation but that the council cannot resolve to use s 1 in the way indicated in the resolution. Accordingly, I must deal with the submission of counsel for the local authority. He accepted the consequences I have mentioned but rightly maintained that *h* such consequences were no ground for rejecting his submission.

I understand that the word 'assistance' is nowhere defined in any of the Children Acts. Counsel for the local authority says that s 1 must be construed in its plain and ordinary meaning, so that the phrase 'assistance in kind' must mean the provision of goods or services or things as opposed, as he said, to real property. Goods or services are concepts distinct from accommodation or housing. The phrase 'assistance . . . in cash' *j* must take its colour, he says, from assistance in kind so that cash can only be given for the purchase of things or goods or services and not for accommodation. He drew attention to ss 12 and 43 of the National Assistance Act 1948 as they stood when the 1963 Act was passed. The 1948 Act may be helpful but not, I think, authoritative in construing s 1 of the 1963 Act. I see that the Local Authority Social Services Act 1970 which established

local authority social services committees has several references to the National Assistance
a Act 1948. Section 12(2) of the 1948 Act enacted that references in Part II of the Act to the
giving of assistance in kind included references to the issuing of orders for the free
provision of goods or services. Section 43 of the 1948 Act defined 'assistance' as the word
is used in that section. It embraced both assistance in kind and the provision of
accommodation under Part III of the 1948 Act (Part III is the forerunner of the 1977
Act). Accordingly, it is said that since the 1948 Act distinguished assistance in kind from
b assistance by way of the provision of accommodation it may be inferred that assistance
in kind when used in s 1 of the 1963 Act does not include assistance by way of the
provision of accommodation.

I do not accept counsel's submission. I have three considerations in mind. First,
reading s 1 of the 1963 Act in isolation I would certainly understand that if assistance in
kind may be given then assistance by way of housing or bed and breakfast accommodation
c may be given. The phrase 'in kind' does not seem to me to involve the idea of movables
or services and nothing else. The phrase simply means in specie, or without substitution:
see the Shorter Oxford Dictionary. Section 12(2) of the 1948 Act emphasised this by
saying that assistance in kind 'includes', not 'means', the provision of goods and
services. Second, one sees that the purpose of s 1 of the 1963 Act is to diminish the need
to receive children into care. One of the occasions when children are received into care
d is when their parents have no accommodation for them: see the Children Act 1948,
s 1. Accordingly, one would suppose that s 1 of the 1963 Act was intended to allow of
a local authority providing accommodation for children. Third, even if one assumes that
'assistance in kind' does exclude assistance by the giving of accommodation the use of the
phrase 'assistance in kind' in s 1 of the 1963 Act does not mean that one must read the
word 'assistance' where it first appears in the section as limited to assistance in kind or in
e cash. The words after the semicolon in sub-s (1) are to my mind explanatory or enlarging
words rather than restrictive in any way of the meaning of the word 'assistance' when it
first appears in the section. Accordingly I am satisfied that one form of assistance that a
local authority may provide under s 1 of the 1963 Act is the placing of a child with its
parents in accommodation, and either in accommodation which the local authority owns
or in accommodation owned by someone else for which the local authority pays.
f Whether or not any such placing takes place, and, if so, for how long, is of course to be
decided on the facts of a particular case and in this regard the welfare of the child will be
a principal but not the only consideration.

I now turn to the submission of counsel for the plaintiff. Put very briefly his
submission was that if the local authority may provide accommodation for families
under s 1 of the 1963 Act then it is ultra vires for the local authority to resolve to refuse
g accommodation for families who are intentionally homeless; and particularly if they
decide on this course while remaining ready to provide accommodation under the Act
for other families. The resolution, he said, frustrates the policy and objects of s 1 of the
1963 Act in that the resolution cuts out one of the courses open to the council in dealing
with the children of intentionally homeless parents.

Section 1 of the 1963 Act imposes a duty and confers a discretion on the local
h authority. The resolution in effect declares that in carrying out that duty and exercising
that discretion the council will not make living accommodation available for a specified
class of families. Accordingly the council has declared a policy which it will follow in
carrying out the provisions of the 1963 Act. That is to say there is a policy that whenever
any case of an intentionally homeless family is before the social services committee it will
not afford accommodation under the 1963 Act for that family. As I understand, a
j decision of this kind by a local authority may, within strict limits, be reviewed by the
courts. In *Associated Provincial Picture Houses Ltd v Wednesbury Corpn* [1948] 1 KB 223 at
233–234, cf [1947] 2 All ER 215 at 685 Lord Greene MR said:

'. . . I will summarize once again the principle applicable. The court is entitled to
investigate the action of the local authority with a view to seeing whether they have

taken into account matters which they ought not to take into account, or, conversely, have refused to take into account or neglected to take into account matters which *a* they ought to take into account. Once that question is answered in favour of the local authority, it may still be possible to say that, although the local authority have kept within the four corners of the matters which they ought to consider, they have nevertheless come to a conclusion so unreasonable that no reasonable authority could ever have come to it. In such a case, again, I think the court can interfere.'

b

See also *Secretary of State for Education and Science v Metropolitan Borough of Tameside* [1976] 3 All ER 665 at 695, [1977] AC 1014 at 1065 where Lord Diplock refers to Lord Greene MR's judgment.

In *Stringer v Minister of Housing and Local Government* [1971] 1 All ER 65, [1970] 1 WLR 1281, Cooke J had under consideration an agreement whereby a local planning authority undertook to discourage land development within the bounds of its powers within a *c* specified area. The learned judge said ([1971] 1 All ER 65 at 72, [1970] 1 WLR 1281 at 1289):

> 'It seems to me that the intention of this agreement was to bind the authority to disregard considerations to which, under the terms of the section, it is required to have regard. I think the agreement was ultra vires the authority for those reasons.' *d*

In light of these authorities it seems to me that I may examine the resolution to see whether the local authority has thereby bound itself to make future decisions in individual cases under the 1963 Act without taking into account some of the considerations that under the Act ought to be taken into account. If the local authority has bound itself in that way the resolution is clearly bad. I think the local authority has *e* so bound itself. I say that because when the local authority, acting by its social services committee or by its responsible social services officer, is considering a particular case of a child whose parents are prevented from providing for his proper accommodation the local authority have a duty under the 1948 Act to receive the child into care. At the same time the local authority must consider pursuant to the 1963 Act whether any assistance given under that Act will promote the child's welfare by diminishing the need to receive *f* him into care. Since assistance under the 1963 Act includes the provision of accommodation it is plain that in every case where there is a family without a home for whatever reason, the local authority is obliged to consider whether the welfare of the child requires that some attempt be made to keep the family together. The local authority should on each occasion ask, should this child be taken from its homeless parents and received into care, or does his welfare require that, if some accommodation *g* can be found for his family, that he remain with his parents? It may very well be, in many cases, that the interests of a child will be much better served by its being received into care. However, this question as to what is best to be done must, as I see it, be asked on every occasion when the local authority, acting by its responsible officer, is considering a receiving into care in respect of a child of homeless parents. The resolution dated 4th July 1979 means that consideration of the question I have mentioned will not be taken *h* into account in respect of the children of the intentionally homeless. The resolution is therefore, for the reasons I have stated, invalid.

Counsel for the local authority pointed out that a policy laid down by a resolution such as this will be operated in a sensible fashion and that plainly the policy would not be adhered to in each and every case. He referred to Mr Goodman's acceptance of para 4 of the amended defence which I have read. Further he said, as I understand it, that at least *j* one family had been considered for accommodation since the date of the resolution despite being a family who by the terms of the resolution are debarred from being given any accommodation. I fully accept that the social services committee are likely to allow of exceptions to the rule they have made. That being so I must refer to some observations of Cooke J in the *Stringer* case [1971] 1 All ER 65 at 80, [1971] 1 WLR 1281 at 1298:

a
'It seems to me that the general effect of the many relevant authorities is that a Minister charged with the duty of making individual administrative decisions in a fair and impartial manner may nevertheless have a general policy in regard to matters which are relevant to those decisions, provided that the existence of that general policy does not preclude him from fairly judging all the issues which are relevant to each individual case as it comes up for decision.'

b
The question therefore arises whether the resolution, despite being invalid in its actual wording, nevertheless is to be regarded, in the light of the evidence about exceptions being allowed, as a mere statement of general policy. I do not think the resolution can be so regarded. In the *Stringer* case [1971] 1 All ER 65 at 79, [1971] 1 WLR 1281 at 1297 Cooke J said that the question is whether the existence of such a policy as the minister had in that case disabled the minister from acting fairly on the consideration of a particular appeal. So the question here is whether or not the existence of the resolution

c
will disable the social services committee from acting fairly when considering the future of a child of intentionally homeless parents. My view is that while the resolution stands the committee would be much influenced by the policy it lays down and so much so as to raise a doubt whether any decision reached could be said to be a fair decision. The mere existence of the resolution means that in operating s 1 of the 1963 Act there would be differentiation between children according to the conduct of their parents. Children

d
in general are unaffected by the resolution and automatically have the full benefit of s 1. Children of the intentionally homeless will, while the resolution stands, expressly have to claim the full benefit of s 1. I therefore do not think the resolution can be supported as being a mere statement of general policy.

It follows that the plaintiff succeeds in the action. There will be a declaration as in para 2 of the amended statement of claim. I do not think that any declaration as in para 1 is

e
necessary.

Judgment for the plaintiff. Declaration accordingly.

Appeal

f
The local authority appealed to the Court of Appeal.

Michael Beloff for the local authority.
John Macdonald QC and *Andrew Bano* for the plaintiff.

TEMPLEMAN LJ delivered the first judgment at the invitation of Lawton LJ. This

g
is an appeal from a decision of his Honour Judge Mervyn Davies QC sitting as an additional judge of the Chancery Division and delivered on 17th March 1980. The judge declared ultra vires a resolution which was passed by the social services sub-committee of the council of the London Borough of Wandsworth ('the local authority') on 4th July 1979 and confirmed by the full council on 24th July 1979.

The resolution was:

h
'That in those cases where intentional homelessness had been determined by the Council in respect of a family with young children and, subsequently, an approach is made to the Social Services Department, it be decided that assistance with alternative housing be not provided under the provisions of the Children and Young Persons Act 1963 although consideration be given to the reception into care of the children should their circumstances so warrant it and that the whole matter

j
be reviewed by Committee in three months time.'

The learned judge decided that it is not open to the local authority to lay down that certain discretions and duties which are available and are imposed on the local authority by the Children and Young Persons Act 1963 shall not be carried out.

The Housing (Homeless Persons) Act 1977 introduces the notion of intentional

homelessness. Under that Act local authorities are under a duty to provide
accommodation for families with children and their duties vary when the homelessness *a*
of the parents is intentional or unintentional. In the case of unintentional homelessness,
a local authority is under a duty to provide permanent accommodation. In the case of
intentional homelessness, and that could occur, for example, if a parent rashly gave up
property which he owned or of which he had a lease, or behaved so badly that he was
evicted as being a nuisance or in breach of covenant, then the duty of the local authority
is much more limited. The local authority need not provide permanent accommoda- *b*
tion. It must give the parent advice and assistance to find somewhere else for himself,
and it has to give him temporary accommodation while he can look round and find some
place for himself and his family.

The Children and Young Persons Act 1963 deals with individual children. Section
1(1) of the Act provides:

> 'It shall be the duty of every local authority to make available such advice, *c*
> guidance and assistance as may promote the welfare of children by diminishing the
> need to receive children into or keep them in care under the Children Act 1948
> . . . and any provisions made by a local authority under this subsection may, if the
> local authority think fit, include provision for giving assistance in kind or, in
> exceptional circumstances, in cash.'

d
Under s 1 of the Children Act 1948 a child may be taken into care where it appears to
a local authority, inter alia, that his parents through incapacity or any other circumstances,
are prevented from providing for his proper accommodation, maintenance and
upbringing. So in the case of a child, if his parents cannot provide him with proper
accommodation, maintenance and upbringing the local authority can take that child
into care; in other words, remove him from his parents and put him with foster parents *e*
or in a home. The Children and Young Persons Act 1963, s 1(1), imposes on the local
authority a duty to diminish the need to take a child into care, in other words a duty to
see, if possible, that the child can stay with his parents or, perhaps, with some other
relations, by such advice, guidance and assistance as the local authority may think
appropriate. The resolution which is now in question says that alternative housing be
not provided under the provisions of the 1963 Act, but consideration should be given to *f*
taking the children of intentionally homeless parents into care.

Counsel for the local authority sought to uphold that resolution in two ways, one
oblique and one direct. His oblique way was to say that, as a matter of construction, it
is not open to a local authority under the 1963 Act to provide assistance by way of
housing, because the express powers which are conferred on a local authority refer to the
'giving of assistance in kind or, in exceptional circumstances, in cash'. He says that *g*
'assistance in kind' does not include providing accommodation and that, therefore, cash
cannot be provided to pay for accommodation. But, in my judgment, that is a
misconstruction of the 1963 Act. The Act is dealing with children who are taken into
care under the Children Act 1948. That can happen, as I have already indicated, if the
parents are unable to provide accommodation for the child, and the 1963 Act provides
that if there is lack of accommodation the local authority must try and deal with the *h*
situation by some other method than by taking the child into care. To my mind the
word 'assistance' in s 1(1) of the 1963 Act clearly includes the provision of accommodation
and then provides that the general powers of a local authority shall include specific
powers. The specific powers do not cut down the general powers of the local authority
in the way which counsel for the local authority argues and which would prevent that
authority from diminishing the need to receive children into care by providing them *j*
with accommodation or by paying for accommodation.

Construction being out of the way, we have to consider whether the local authority
can properly order its committees and its officials not to provide alternative housing
under the 1963 Act in the case of children of parents who are intentionally homeless. On
well-recognised principles public authorities are not entitled to fetter the exercise of a

discretion or to fetter the manner in which they are empowered to discharge the many
a duties which are thrust on them.   They must at all times, in every particular case,
consider how to exercise their discretion and how to perform their duties.

Although the resolution appears to be mandatory and to prevent alternative housing
being provided under the 1963 Act, nevertheless counsel for the local authority said, and
the judge accepted that there was evidence, that exceptions were in practice made to the
resolution.   On a question of ultra vires the practice of making exceptions is irrelevant,
b but for my part, even if the resolution had provided for exceptions and even if, as counsel
urged, this was a general policy and not a mandatory order, the resolution would not get
rid of the vice that a local authority, dealing with individual children, should not make
a policy or an order that points towards fettering its discretion in such a way that the
facilities offered to the child do not depend on the particular circumstances of that child,
or of its family, but follow some policy which is expressed to apply in general to cases.
c The fact of the matter is that intentional homelessness can take many forms and can be
arrived at for a great many reasons.   Children's needs, and their welfare, depend on a
variety of factors.   When the local authority are considering the exercise of their powers
and duties under the 1963 Act one of the factors they must take into account is the
history of the family, including any history of intentional homelessness.   The local
authority must not take intentional homelessness into account for the purpose of
d punishing the child or punishing the parents of the child, but must take it into account
in asking 'What is the best way, in the interests of this child, of exercising the powers
which are given to us?'   If, of course, there is a history of a parent who continually
changes homes and causes great stress and worry to a child it may be that the local
authority will say 'In those circumstances, we think we had better take the child into
care'.   On the other hand, if the intentional homelessness still enables the family to be
e brought up as a family under one roof, or does not require the child to be taken into care,
the local authority may come to a different conclusion.

In what was, if I may say so, a careful and lucid judgment, the judge dismissed the
construction of the 1963 Act for which counsel for the local authority contended; the
judge correctly applied the principle that local authorities are not allowed to fetter their
discretions and duties, and he reached a conclusion which I cannot fault save for this, that
f I am not myself persuaded that even a policy resolution hedged around with exceptions
would be entirely free from attack.   Dealing with children, the discretion and powers of
any authority must depend entirely on the different circumstances of each child before
them for consideration.

Accordingly, I would dismiss this appeal.

g **BRANDON LJ.**   I agree with the judgment just delivered by Templeman LJ, but I
would like to make one reservation.

I am satisfied that this resolution lays down a policy without any exceptions at all and
is invalid.   Whether a resolution which laid down some general policy with a number of
specified exceptions would also be invalid is not a question which falls for decision by this
court today, and I would prefer to reserve my opinion in respect of such a resolution to
h a case where it does arise for decision.

LAWTON LJ.   I agree that the appeal should be dismissed and I share Brandon LJ's
reservation on the point which he has mentioned.

Appeal dismissed.

Solicitors: *Susan G Smith* (for the local authority); *Wilford McBain* (for the plaintiff).

Mary Rose Plummer   Barrister.

R v Landy and others

COURT OF APPEAL, CRIMINAL DIVISION

LAWTON LJ, MICHAEL DAVIES AND BINGHAM JJ

4th, 5th, 8th, 9th, 10th, 11th, 12th DECEMBER 1980, 12th JANUARY 1981

Criminal law – Conspiracy – Conspiracy to defraud – Dishonesty of accused main ingredient of offence – Particulars of offence to be given in indictment – Direction to be given to jury.

Criminal law – Trial – Summing up – Attributes of summing up – Summing up should be clear, concise and intelligible and follow a plan.

Criminal law – Trial – Pre-trial review – Purpose of review – Papers to be placed before trial judge for the review well before date of review.

An indictment charged the defendants, who were directors of a bank, with conspiracy to defraud. The particulars of the offence given in the indictment stated that between certain dates the defendants conspired together and with others to defraud such companies and persons as might lend to, or deposit funds with, the bank by 'falsely representing' that the bank's business was being conducted in an honest and proper manner, by knowingly employing the funds 'to the prejudice of' lenders and depositors and contrary to the bank's best interests, by fraudulently concealing that the funds were being so employed, 'and by divers other false and fraudulent devices'. The particulars did not show how the false representations were made, how the funds were employed to the prejudice of the bank and its customers or the nature of the concealment. Although defence counsel attempted to get further particulars of the alleged offence, he was told that he would get all the information he needed from Crown counsel's opening speech. The case was complicated and the papers in it massive. Although there was a pre-trial review before the trial judge he was provided with the papers only a day or two before the review and could not in that time sufficiently master them to make the review worthwhile. The trial lasted 90 days; 73 days were taken up with the Crown's opening speech, counsel's submissions and the evidence, and the remaining 17 days with the Crown's closing speech which lasted 4 days, defence counsel's closing speeches which lasted 7 days, and the judge's summing-up which lasted 6 days. The summing up was seriously defective because the judge failed to direct the jury clearly that they had to be sure that the defendants had agreed dishonestly to act in the manner alleged, and treated evidence from which fraud could be inferred as if it were proof of fraud. The summing up was also so diffuse that it was likely to confuse the jury. The defendants were convicted and appealed. At the hearing of the appeal the Crown conceded that the summing up was seriously defective but submitted that the court should apply the proviso to s 2(1)[a] of the Criminal Appeal Act 1968 on the ground that if the jury had been properly directed they would have convicted the defendants.

Held – (1) The offence of conspiracy to defraud was one of dishonesty, that being the all-important ingredient of the offence, and the dishonesty to be proved was dishonesty in regard to the defendants' actual beliefs and intentions in the particular circumstances. Accordingly, in directing the jury the judge was required to stress that ingredient of

---

[a] Section 2(1), so far as material, provides: 'Except as provided by this Act, the Court of Appeal shall allow an appeal against conviction if they think—(a) that the verdict of the jury should be set aside on the ground that under all the circumstances of the case it is unsafe or unsatisfactory . . . and in any other case shall dismiss the appeal: Provided that the Court may, notwithstanding that they are of opinion that the point raised in the appeal might be decided in favour of the appellant, dismiss the appeal if they consider that no miscarriage of justice has actually occurred.'

dishonesty and should have directed the jury that what mattered was the state of mind

a of the defendants themselves and not what reasonable men in their circumstances would have believed or intended, although what reasonable men would have believed might help the jury to decide what the defendants' beliefs were. Furthermore, the jury should have been directed that whilst a defendant's assertion that he had acted honestly throughout a transaction had to be considered, like any other piece of evidence, if the jury were satisfied that throughout the transaction in question a defendant had, or might

b have acted honestly, he was entitled to be acquitted (see p 1181 *e* to *h* and p 1184 *a*, post).

(2) The entitlement of a defendant to a fair trial meant that he was entitled (a) to have the jury clearly and correctly directed as to the law to be applied and (b) to have all the defences which were open to him fairly put to the jury. Since the trial judge had failed to tell the jury in clear and precise terms that they had to be sure that each defendant had agreed to act dishonestly, and had thereby deprived each defendant of having his defence

c that he had been honest but careless fairly put to the jury, the defendants had not had a fair trial. In those circumstances the verdicts were unsatisfactory and it could not be said that no miscarriage of justice had occurred. Accordingly, the proviso to s 2(1) of the 1968 Act could not be applied. It followed that the appeals would be allowed and the convictions quashed (see p 1181 *j*, p 1182 *f*, p 1183 *a* to *c* and *f* to *j* and p 1184 *a*, post).

Per Curiam. (1) At a pre-trial review the judge, who should normally be the trial

d judge, should take the initiative to ensure that all unnecessary detail is omitted from the case. He cannot do this unless he is given the papers well before the review hearing, so that he has time to read and analyse them, and if he has not been given the papers in time he may think it right to postpone the review (see p 1178 *c d*, post).

(2) Although the particulars in an indictment charging conspiracy to defraud do not have to contain the same detail as is required in a statement of claim in an action for

e damages for conspiracy to defraud, the particulars in the indictment should be such as will enable the defendants and the trial judge to know the nature of the Crown's case from the face of the indictment and will prevent the Crown from shifting its ground during the trial without applying for leave to amend the indictment. The words 'and by divers other false and fraudulent devices' are outdated and should no longer be used in an indictment. Furthermore, the terms 'falsely representing' and 'to the prejudice of' are

f too imprecise and likely to confuse a jury (see p 1178 *h* to p 1179 *a* and *f*, post); *R v Feely* [1973] 1 All ER 341 explained.

(3) Counsel's closing speeches should not be prolix and a summing up should be clear, concise and intelligible. If it is overloaded with detail, whether of fact or law, and follows no obvious plan it will not have the attributes it ought to have (see p 1179 *h* and p 1183 *b*, post).

g **Notes**

For conspiracy to defraud and for the indictment in conspiracy to defraud, see 11 Halsbury's Laws (4th Edn) paras 61–62, and for cases on an indictment for conspiracy, see 14(1) Digest (Reissue) 129–132, 877–912.

For the judge's summing up, see 11 Halsbury's Laws (4th Edn) para 297.

h **Cases referred to in judgment**

R v Feely [1973] 1 All ER 341, [1973] QB 530, [1973] 2 WLR 201, 132 JP 157, 57 Cr App R 312, CA, 15 Digest (Reissue) 1263, *10,830*.

R v Moon [1969] 3 All ER 803n, [1969] 1 WLR 1705, 133 JP 703, CA, 14(2) Digest (Reissue) 811, *6984*.

j *R v Sinclair* [1968] 3 All ER 241, [1968] 1 WLR 1246, 132 JP 527, 52 Cr App R 618, CA, 15 Digest (Reissue) 1400, *12,271*.

Stafford v Director of Public Prosecutions [1973] 3 All ER 762, [1974] AC 878, [1973] 3 WLR 719, 58 Cr App R 256, HL, 14(2) Digest (Reissue) 786, *6695*.

Welham v Director of Public Prosecutions [1960] 1 All ER 805, [1961] AC 103, [1960] 2 WLR 669, 124 JP 280, 44 Cr App R 124, HL, 14(1) Digest (Reissue) 253, *1860*.

Cases also cited

Boggeln v Williams [1978] 2 All ER 1061, [1978] 1 WLR 873, DC.
R v Allsop (1976) 64 Cr App R 29, CA.
R v Badjan (1966) 50 Cr App R 141, CCA.
R v Barnes (1970) 55 Cr App R 100, CA.
R v Cordrey, R v Carvello (14th March 1980, unreported), CA.
R v Diggin [1980] Crim LR 656, CA.
R v Greenfield [1973] 3 All ER 1050, [1973] 1 WLR 1151, CA.
R v Greenstein [1976] 1 All ER 1, [1975] 1 WLR 1353, CA.
R v Griffiths (1974) 60 Cr App R 14, CA.
R v Hallatt (26th February 1980, unreported), CA.
R v Lawrence (20th May 1980, unreported), CA.
R v Mansell (27th June 1980, unreported), CA.
R v Muff (2nd November 1979, unreported), CA.
R v Penny (3rd October 1980, unreported), CCC.
R v Prater [1960] 1 All ER 298, [1960] 2 QB 464, CCA.
R v Sheppard (14th January 1974, unreported), CA.
Scott v Comr of Police for the Metropolis [1974] 3 All ER 1032, [1975] AC 819, HL.

Appeals

On 25th July 1979 at the Central Criminal Court before his Honour Judge Abdela QC and a jury the appellants, Harry Landy, Arthur Malcolm White and Charles Kaye, were convicted, on count 1 of an indictment, of conspiracy to defraud and sentenced as follows: Landy to five years' imprisonment, and a fine of £350,000 (12 months' imprisonment consecutive in default) with an order to pay £100,000 towards costs and an order under s 188 of the Companies Act 1948 for five years; White to four years' imprisonment and a fine of £5,000 (or 12 months' imprisonment in default) with an order to pay £2,000 towards costs and an order under s 188 of the 1948 Act for five years; and Kaye to 12 months' imprisonment suspended for two years with an order to pay £2,500 towards costs. Landy and White were also convicted on counts 2 and 3 of the indictment of conspiracy to utter forged documents for which each was sentenced to three years' imprisonment concurrent to the sentences imposed under count 1. Kaye was acquitted on counts 2 and 3. All three appellants appealed against conviction on the ground, inter alia, that the summing up was defective because, in particular, the judge failed to direct the jury clearly on the ingredients of conspiracy to defraud and because his summing up was so diffuse that it was likely to confuse the jury. The facts are set out in the judgment.

John Hazan QC and *James Goudie* for Landy.
John Alliott QC and *Robin Laurie* for White.
Richard Du Cann QC and *Henry Grunwald* for Kaye.
Allan Green and *Robert Rhodes* for the Crown.

At the conclusion of the argument Lawton LJ announced that appeals would be allowed and the convictions quashed and that the court would give its reasons at a later date.

12th January. **LAWTON LJ** read the following judgment of the court: The appellants, Harry Landy, Arthur Malcolm White and Charles Kaye, appeal by leave of this court against their convictions at the Central Criminal Court on July 25 1979, after a trial lasting 90 days before his Honour Judge Abdela QC. All three were convicted on a count charging them with conspiracy to defraud; Landy and White were also convicted on two counts charging them with conspiracy to utter forged documents. Kaye was acquitted on those counts. Landy was sentenced to five years' imprisonment for the conspiracy to defraud. He was also fined £350,000 for that offence with a further 12 months'

imprisonment in default of payment and ordered to pay £100,000 towards the costs of
a the prosecution. He was also sentenced to concurrent terms of three years' imprisonment
on each of the counts of conspiracy to utter forged documents. White was sentenced to
four years' imprisonment for the conspiracy to defraud and concurrent terms of three
years for the conspiracies to utter forged documents. He was also fined £5,000 on the
count charging conspiracy to defraud and was ordered to pay £2,000 towards the legal
aid costs of his defence. Kaye was sentenced to 12 months' imprisonment suspended for
b two years and ordered to pay a contribution of £2,500 towards the legal aid costs of his
defence.

On 12th December 1980 we adjudged that the convictions of all three appellants
should be quashed on the ground that the verdicts had been unsatisfactory. We stated
that we would give our reasons later and we are today doing so.

The case centred round Landy. He was born in 1911. In 1935 he married the
c daughter of a wealthy man named Williams who had extensive interests, including one
in banking acquired later and known as the Palestine British Bank. Soon after his
marriage Landy became involved in his father-in-law's business interests and by about
1968 he was a director of 156 companies and had himself become a wealthy man. He
became a managing director of the Palestine British Bank in 1953. This bank had been
founded in Palestine in 1942 and had a London branch. From 1962 onwards its premises
d were on two floors of the Williams National House in Holborn Viaduct. In 1968 the
London branch was incorporated as the Israel British Bank (London) Ltd. It was a
wholly-owned subsidiary of the parent bank which was from about 1962 known as Israel
British Bank (Tel Aviv). This bank was managed by another of Williams's sons-in-law
named Bension. We shall refer to the Tel Aviv bank as 'IBBTA' and the London bank as
'IBBL'. Until his death in 1971 Williams was chairman of both banks. During the
e period with which this case is concerned IBBL was primarily a bankers' bank, that is to
say, most of its business was international and consisted of borrowing from and lending
to other banks but it had a few private depositors, mostly charities and members of, or
connected with, the Williams family or the Williams group of companies. Outwardly
IBBL was run like any other secondary bank based in London. It was recognised as an
authorised bank and depository by the Bank of England for the purposes of the Exchange
f Control Act 1947. Without this recognition it could not have carried on its international
banking business.

IBBTA was run differently. It had its international banking side but it dealt in
commodities, futures, securities, gold and silver on what was described later by the
liquidator of IBBL as an enormous scale. Indeed such was the scale of its dealing activities
that the Bank of Israel, which in that country occupies a position and performs a function
g akin to that of the Bank of England, was displeased with what was going on as being
inconsistent with normal banking activities and took steps, seemingly unsuccessfully, to
stop Bension doing what he was doing, which was to do IBBTA's dealings through a
group of companies which had been formed, mostly in Liechtenstein, from the late
1940s onwards by Williams or persons connected with him. Two companies, Mobilia
and Investment and Building Trust (IBT), had been founded by Landy, the first in 1951,
h the other in 1962. The beneficiaries of IBT were stated to be Landy and Williams's four
daughters. Why Bension wanted to do IBBTA's dealings through these Liechtenstein
companies was never established. During the period covered by the indictment, that is
from 30th September 1968 to 12th July 1974, he may have wanted to hide what he was
doing from the Bank of Israel.

Bension used IBBL as a source of finance for these dealings. He would borrow money
j from IBBL, asking that it should be credited to IBBTA's account with another bank
outside the United Kingdom. He would then use this money for dealing in the name of
one of the Liechtenstein companies. IBBL, however, would not debit IBBTA but the
Liechtenstein companies of Bension's choice. The full details of Bension's dealings and
of the profits and losses made have never been discovered. Attempts by IBBL's liquidator
to find out have been unsuccessful. It is known, however, that substantial profits were

made from dealings in gold and silver through a Liechtenstein company called Denver Finance Establishment. IBBL debited the Liechtenstein companies with the interest *a* payable on the loans requested by Bension in their names but the liquidator was unable to find any evidence that any profits which may have been obtained from Bension's dealings, and there were probably substantial ones from some of them, ever reached IBBL, Landy, his wife or any of the Williams group of companies based in Great Britain. There was a lot of documentary evidence showing that over many years and particularly between 1968 and 1974 Landy gave instructions to the so-called trustees of *b* the Liechtenstein companies, who were little more than registrars. These instructions were mostly of a formal kind and were usually given at Bension's request. Landy never went to Liechtenstein and there was no evidence that he took an active part in Bension's dealings.

He did, however, know that Bension was managing IBBTA in a way which met with the disapproval of the Bank of Israel. On 12th January 1969 Landy had been present at *c* a meeting in Israel which had been attended by the governor of the Bank of Israel, Dr Heth, who was an examiner of that bank, Bension and others connected with IBBTA. The governor and Dr Heth made it clear to the two joint managing directors of IBBTA, who were Landy and Bension, although the latter was the active one, that the Bank of Israel was disturbed first by the size of the indebtedness of the Williams group of companies to IBBTA as the security for loans seemed to be inadequate, second by various *d* management deficiencies for which Bension carried responsibility, and, third, by auditing deficiencies which had concealed IBBTA's true liquidity position and showed that bank as being stronger than it was. IBBTA's position was serious. At the end of 1968 there had been a deficiency of £(I)37m in collateral securities. The Williams group of companies owed £(I)28m, which was covered by no more than a guarantee.

The Bank of Israel's expressions of disapproval did not curb Bension's activities nor stop *e* IBBL from providing finance for them. By 1970 IBBTA required help from the Bank of Israel. A loan of £(I)12m by that bank to IBBTA was arranged on terms, the important one for the purposes of this case being that no credit whatsoever should be given to the Williams group of companies, which included IBT and Mobilia which Landy had established, without Dr Heth's prior authority. This agreement was disregarded. IBBL continued to finance IBBTA through the Liechtenstein companies. *f*

In October 1972 the Supreme Court in Israel, when dismissing an appeal by IBBTA in a civil case (referred to in the evidence as the Gutwirth case) had stated that IBBTA was unfit to act as a bank or trustee. On 7th November 1972 the governor of the Bank of Israel, accompanied by Dr Heth, had a meeting with Landy and Bension. At the trial there was some difference of recollection as to what had been said at this meeting. The details may not be all that important; but what is clear is that Landy left the meeting *g* knowing that the governor disapproved of Bension and the way he was running IBBTA. On 15th November 1972 Landy had a private meeting with the governor. According to Landy the governor said that Bension had not acted fraudulently but he had gone as far as he could within the law, he was too speculative and needed restraining. After this conversation Dr Heth joined them and, according to his recollection, Landy said the agreement made in December 1970 would be honoured. It *h* was not. The only step which IBBL seems to have taken to safeguard its position in relation to the advances to the Liechtenstein companies was to ask IBBTA for guarantees, and letters of pledge, in respect of two Liechtenstein companies. They were given. The guarantees were not in the usual form used by banks and it is probable that they would not have been enforceable in law. The pledges were nothing more than pieces of paper. At one stage, one of the Liechtenstein companies did deposit some securities but *j* they were no longer available when IBBL's liquidator took over. None of the usual banking inquiries were made as to what was being pledged and about the supporting titles.

Even if the guarantees given by IBBTA had been enforceable the loans made to the

Liechtenstein companies exceeded them and were at a higher level in 1973 than they had
a been in 1971, $80m as against $40m.

Apart from the kind of transaction to which we have referred and which were the core
of the Crown's case there was evidence of a number of banking malpractices. There was
an inadequate spread of risk. Some Liechtenstein companies were debited with large
loans without evidence that they were the borrowers. IBBTA's account was credited
with repayments when those of Liechtenstein companies should have been. These
b wrong creditings were no mere bookkeeping errors or even malpractices. They operated,
and probably were intended to operate, to improve IBBTA's appearance of liquidity.
IBBL's balance sheet was made to give a better impression than the true figures did by
means of end of year transfers, the so-called window-dressing of accounts. Substantial
loans were made or overdrafts allowed to Landy and to members of the Williams family
or Williams companies without interest being charged or security given. By July 1974
c two-thirds of IBBL's sterling advances, nearly £5m, were to the Williams family or the
Williams companies. The advances were concealed in the accounts on audit dates by
temporary credits. Landy's own indebtedness in July 1974 on an interest free overdraft
was £1m. We do not consider it necessary for the purposes of this judgment to give any
more details of these banking irregularities. In our opinion the trial would have been
easier for the judge to conduct and the issues clearer for the jury if the prosecution had
d omitted some of them from their case.

We must, however, refer specifically to one kind of banking transaction which had
irregular features, namely the discounting of bills of exchange in respect of what
purported to be a series of dealings in diamonds. These dealings were part of the
evidence on the conspiracy to defraud count, and the subject of the conspiracy to utter
forged document counts. Landy was the director of a small Williams company called E
e Posen & Co Export Ltd ('Posen'). During 1972, 1973 and the first half of 1974 two Israeli
companies, S J Birmback and I Sussman and Syndiam purported through Posen to sell ·
diamonds to two Liechtenstein companies, named Nargin and Secmex, which were
Williams companies. Bills of exchange were drawn and discounted by IBBL. No
diamonds were sold. The first of the Israeli companies had gone out of business and the
second did not exist. The invoices which were used for the purposes of getting Bank of
f England authorisation for the discounting were forged. All these dealings looked odd
commercially because they were always for about the same weight of diamonds and the
amounts of the bills were always much the same, varying between £48,000 and
£42,000. IBBL got little out of these transactions and on occasions waived the discount
charges. Between March and July 1974, 45 bills matured and payment became
overdue. Not until 10th July 1974 was anything done to get payment on these bills.
g They were never met. IBBL lost over £2m.

All through 1973 and the first half of 1974 the Bank of Israel became more and more
concerned about the way IBBTA was being conducted. On 9th July 1974, with the
consent of the Israeli government, they seized it, whatever that may mean in Israeli
law. This put IBBL in difficulty. On 11th July 1974 IBBL suspended all payments.
Various investigations were carried out. In August 1974 IBBL presented its own petition
h for winding-up. The Official Receiver was appointed provisional liquidator and partners
in Price Waterhouse & Co were appointed special managers. On 2nd December 1974 a
compulsory winding-up order was made and in January 1975 joint liquidators were
appointed from the same firm of accountants.

When IBBL stopped payments it owed £37m to 85 banks, £4m to members of the
Williams family and to companies in the Williams group, and £1.8m to other
j depositors. It was owed £31m by four Liechtenstein companies and one Swiss company,
£2m on bills of exchange discounted by Posen and £5m by members of the Williams
family and companies in the Williams group. Most of these debts were thought to have,
and indeed proved to have, little value. The deficit in July 1974 was about £38m; but
since then considerable sums have been obtained from Landy and the Williams

interests. All small depositors and charities have been repaid in full. The larger creditors are likely to be paid a dividend of about 40p in the £.

Landy, White and Kaye were arrested in April 1977. After committal proceedings which lasted 31 days, they were committed for trial at the Central Criminal Court together with one Peter Lynn, who had been a partner in IBBL's auditors and who was acquitted on the indictment, and one Joseph Bloomberg who died before the trial started on 1st March 1979.

Before the trial started there was a pre-trial review before Judge Abdela. A full-scale review was certainly needed. However it was only a day or two before the review that the judge was provided with the papers, which were massive, and a copy of the opening speech of leading counsel before the committing justices. The review produced no worthwhile result. This was not the fault of the judge. He could not be expected to master this complicated case in the time available to him. Had he been able to do so we have no doubt that he would have done some extensive pruning. That would be an important object of a pre-trial review in cases of this kind. Prosecuting counsel who have been immersed in the details of a case for months sometimes do not appreciate the difficulty which a judge and a jury may have in assimilating the evidence. At the pre-trial review the judge (and he should normally be the one who is going to try the case) should be ready and willing to take the initiative to ensure that all unnecessary detail is omitted. This he cannot do unless he is given the papers well before the review hearing and has time to read and analyse them. If he is not he may think it right to postpone the review. We are sure that a robust pre-trial review in this case would have resulted in a shorter and more satisfactory trial.

The particulars set out under count 1 of the indictment were as follows:

> 'Harry Landy, Arthur Malcolm White, Charles Kaye, Joseph Bloomberg and Peter Lynn on divers days between the 30th day of September 1968 and the 12th day of July 1974 conspired together and with the late Walter Nathan Williams, Joshua Bension and the late Isaac Cohen [an officer of IBBTA] to defraud such corporations, companies, partnerships, firms and persons as might lend funds to or deposit funds with Israel British Bank (London) Limited by falsely representing that the business of Israel British Bank (London) Limited was being conducted in an honest and proper manner, by knowingly employing such funds to the prejudice of the said lenders and depositors and contrary to the best interests of the Israel British Bank (London) Limited, by fraudulently concealing that the said funds were being so supplied, and by divers other false and fraudulent devices.'

Counsel for the Crown told us that he drafted this indictment with that used in *R v Sinclair* [1968] 3 All ER 241, [1968] 1 WLR 1246 in mind. It is a form which is commonly used, particularly at the Central Criminal Court. In simple cases it may be adequate but in a complicated case it is not because it lacks particularity. There was nothing to show how the false representations were made or how the funds were employed to the prejudice of IBBL and its customers or what was the nature of the concealment. Junior counsel for Landy asked for particulars at the beginning of the committal proceedings, the committal charge being the same as count 1 of the indictment. He was told that he would get all the information he needed from the opening speech of leading counsel for the Crown. Attempts to get particulars at later stages of the case were met with the same answer. We were told by counsel that this is the answer almost always given by prosecuting counsel. In our judgment particulars should have been given and for these reasons: first, to enable the defendants and the trial judge to know precisely and on the face of the indictment itself the nature of the Crown's case, and second to stop the Crown shifting its ground during the course of the case without the leave of the trial judge and the making of an amendment. The words 'and by divers other false and fraudulent devices' are a relic of the past and should never again appear in an indictment. In criticising the form of indictment used in this case, we should not be taken to be adjudging that particulars of conspiracies to defraud should be

set out in the same kind of detail as would be required in a statement of claim in an action
a for damages for conspiracy to defraud. What is wanted is conciseness and clarity.

In our opinion the particulars of the count charging conspiracy to defraud should have
been in some such terms as these:

'PARTICULARS OF OFFENCE

'HARRY LANDY, ARTHUR MALCOLM WHITE, CHARLES KAYE and PETER LYNN on divers
days between the 30th day of September 1968 and the 12th day of July 1974
b conspired together and with the late Walter Nathan Williams, Joshua Bension and
the late Isaac Cohen to defraud such corporations, companies, partnerships, firms
and persons as might lend funds to or deposit funds with Israel British Bank
(London) Ltd ("the bank") by dishonestly (1) causing and permitting the bank to
make excessive advances to insubstantial and speculative trading companies
incorporated in Liechtenstein and Switzerland, such advances being inadequately
c secured, inadequately guaranteed and without proper provision for payment of
interest, (2) causing and permitting the bank to make excessive advances to its
parent company in Tel Aviv, such advances being inadequately secured, inadequately
guaranteed and without proper provision for payment of interest, (3) causing and
permitting the bank to make excessive advances to individuals and companies
connected with the said Walter Nathan Williams and his family, such advances
d being inadequately secured, inadequately guaranteed and without proper provision
for payment of interest, (4) causing and permitting the bank's accounts and Bank of
England returns to be prepared in such a way as (a) to conceal the nature, constitution
and extent of the bank's lending and (b) to show a false and misleading financial
situation as at the end of the bank's accounting years, (5) causing and permitting the
bank to discount commercial bills when (a) there was no underlying commercial
e transaction (b) the documents evidencing the supposed underlying transactions
were false and (c) the transactions were effected in order to transfer funds to the
bank's parent company in Tel Aviv.'

Such particulars would have avoided such terms as 'falsely representing' and 'to the
prejudice of' which are imprecise and likely to confuse juries and would have made
f everyone aware of what the Crown were alleging.

The first 73 days of the trial were taken up with Crown counsel's opening speech,
submissions and evidence. The last days of winter passed into high summer. By the
beginning of July the jury must have had the evidence well in mind. What they wanted
at that stage of the case was a clear and concise summary of what each party was putting
forward. What they got was 11 days of counsels' speeches followed by 6 days of
g summing up. Crown counsel's speech went on for 4 days, the speeches of defending
counsel taking up 7 days. We have no reason for thinking that counsel were unduly
prolix by the standards of present day forensic fashion. The fault lies partly in the
fashion but also in the present tendency to overload cases. The great advocates of the past
did not find it necessary to address juries at such great length. We can see no good reason
for such prolixity nowadays. If the object of a closing speech is to ensure that the jury
h keep in mind when considering their verdict the points which counsel wish to bring out,
they are unlikely to do so if, as in the case of counsel's speech for the Crown, they heard
it three weeks before.

The case which the judge had to sum up came to this. For some six years, IBBL
siphoned money to IBBTA which was used by Bension for speculative dealings through
the Williams Liechtenstein companies. In the case of the Posen transactions there was
j not even speculation, just fraud. The inference was that Bension was behaving as he did
partly for his own benefit and partly for that of the Williams interests, which included
Landy's interest. In order to effect the siphoning various banking malpractices were
used, together with much concealment of what was going on. The Crown submitted
that all three appellants must have known what was going on and were actively engaged
first in ensuring that money did go to IBBTA for what they must have known were

purposes which put at risk IBBL's customers, and second in concealing what was happening. Landy was in charge of IBBL. From 1971 he had been the chairman of both   *a* IBBTA and IBBL. During the period covered by the indictment, and at a time when he knew of the disquiet felt by the Bank of Israel about the way Bension was behaving and managing IBBTA's business, he attended board meetings in Tel Aviv. He took no effective steps to ensure that IBBTA performed the agreement made with the Bank of Israel in December 1970 and connived at its breach. He knew that some of IBBL's staff were disturbed about the irregularities and that one of them, an accountant named   *b* Coxall, disapproved so strongly at what was going on that he resigned his appointment as from 31st December 1972. Further Landy took advantage of his position to get an interest-free and unsecured overdraft from IBBL of about £1m.

The case against White was of the same general kind as that against Landy but was not as strong. He had joined the London branch of IBBL in 1964. He was then 32. He had had several years of experience of merchant banking in London behind him. He became   *c* a director of IBBTA in 1967 and of IBBL in 1968 when it was incorporated. He did not attend board meetings in Tel Aviv. He was in charge of IBBL's foreign exchange department and in that capacity he gave instructions relating to the raising of the finance which was debited to the Liechtenstein companies but went to IBBTA. His department was also concerned with discounting bills of exchange. He knew that some members of IBBL's staff, in particular Coxall, were disturbed about the banking irregularities and   *d* accounting malpractices which were going on but continued to allow them to do so. The Crown submitted that he was willing to further the fraudulent aims of both Landy and Bension because they had made it worthwhile for him to do so. Besides his salary, which in 1974 was £12,000 per annum, he had been given various facilities, including one for share dealing in Tel Aviv and a Swiss Bank account into which IBBTA paid between £90,000 and £100,000 as commission based on IBBL's net profits and a percentage of all   *e* funds remitted to IBBTA from IBBL including the money which was debited to the Liechtenstein accounts.

The Crown's case against Kaye was much the same in nature as that against White but he was lower down the executive ladder in IBBL. He had started his working career as a clerk. After war service he got a job as a bookkeeper and cashier with the London branch of the Palestine British Bank. He was made a director of IBBL in July 1970 and   *f* by 1974 was earning about £5,200 per annum. At all material times he was in charge of IBBL's general banking business. In that capacity he knew what was being lent to the Williams family interests and that the Posen bills were being discounted. Although he had no professional qualifications as an accountant, after Coxall's resignation in December 1972 he became IBBL's chief accountant and in that capacity signed Bank of England returns of foreign currency positions which inaccurately described the advances to the   *g* Liechtenstein companies as 'deposits with and advances to banks abroad'. Coxall, who was Kaye's predecessor as chief accountant, had refused to sign returns in this form and his concern over this deception of the Bank of England had been one of the reasons for his resigning his position with IBBL. Kaye knew of the irregularities and malpractices which had caused Coxall to be disturbed and to resign but he was prepared to go on helping Landy to manage IBBL in a way which led to the closing of the bank. One of the   *h* strongest pieces of evidence against Kaye was his own admission when giving evidence about a 'window-dressing operation' to which he was a party that it could be considered dishonest and disgraceful conduct on the part of an authorised bank. A little earlier he had said that 'window-dressing' was 'certainly unethical and technically improper'.

Landy's defence can be summed up in a short phrase. He claimed to have been honest but careless. He said that at the material times he was a very wealthy man, which was   *j* true. He trusted Bension, who was his brother-in-law, and had no reason not to do so. The Bank of Israel had had its suspicions about Bension's behaviour as a banker but had not suggested before July 1974 that he should be stopped operating as such. Further it had had far better opportunities than he had had to learn what was going on because from 1973 onwards it had had its officers supervising inside IBBTA. Neither he nor the

Williams interests in the United Kingdom had made anything out of Bension's
a dealings. There had been no risk for IBBL in making unsecured loans to either him or
the Williams interests because all the borrowers were well able to repay and after the
crash did so. Landy claimed that he had given little of his time to the affairs of either
IBBTA or IBBL. He had many other interests, both business and charitable, which
occupied most of his working hours. He knew little about banking being by training
and experience a dealer in property.

b White's defence was that he had been honest, loyal and over-trusting. Although he
was a director of IBBTA he knew little about what was going on in Tel Aviv. Whenever
queries arose about the regularity of transactions between IBBL and IBBTA he had
spoken to Landy and had accepted whatever he had been told. He had had no concern
with the preparation of the yearly accounts and balance sheets and only signed them after
Landy had agreed them with the auditors.

c Kaye's defence was much the same. He was able to say, with truth, that he knew far
less than White about what was going on. Unlike White he received nothing more than
his salary, which was modest.

All three defences can be described as 'confessions and avoidance'. Few of the primary
facts were in issue; the documents spoke for themselves. What was in issue was the
honesty of the three defendants. There could be no doubt that all three defendants,
d particularly Landy, had failed lamentably to perform their duties as directors, with the
result that IBBL had crashed. Had they been sued in misfeasance proceedings it is
probable, indeed almost certain, that judgment would have been given against them.
Misfeasance, however, is not necessarily dishonesty, but may be evidence from which
dishonesty can be inferred.

What the Crown had to prove was a conspiracy to defraud which is an agreement
e dishonestly to do something which will or may cause loss or prejudice to another. The
offence is one of dishonesty. This is the all-important ingredient which must be stressed
by the judge in his directions to the jury and must not be minimised in any way. There
is always a danger that a jury may think that proof of an irregularity followed by loss is
proof of dishonesty. The dishonesty to be proved must be in the minds and intentions
of the defendants. It is to their states of mind that the jury must direct their attention.
f What the reasonable man or the jurors themselves would have believed or intended in
the circumstances in which the defendants found themselves is not what the jury have
to decide; but what a reasonable man or they themselves would have believed or
intended in similar circumstances may help them to decide what in fact individual
defendants believed or intended. An assertion by a defendant that throughout a
transaction he acted honestly does not have to be accepted but has to be weighed like any
g other piece of evidence. If that was the defendant's state of mind, or may have been, he
is entitled to be acquitted. But if the jury, applying their own notions of what is honest
and what is not, conclude that he could not have believed that he was acting honestly,
then the element of dishonesty will have been established. What a jury must not do is
to say to themselves: 'If we had been in his place we would have known we were acting
dishonestly, so he must have known he was.' What they can say is: 'We are sure he was
h acting dishonestly because we can see no reason why a man of his intelligence and
experience would not have appreciated, as right-minded people would have done, that
what he was doing was dishonest.' In our judgment this is the way *R v Feely* [1973] 1 All
ER 341, [1973] QB 530 should be applied in cases where the issue of dishonesty arises.
It is also the way in which the jury should have been directed in this case, but,
unfortunately, they were not.

j There were three basic defects in the summing up: first, the trial judge failed to direct
the jury clearly that they had to be sure that each of the defendants had agreed dishonestly
to act in the way the Crown alleged; second, on occasions he treated inferences from the
evidence as if they were rules of law; and, third, the summing up was so diffuse that it
was likely to confuse the jury. As the Crown accepted in this court that the summing up
was seriously defective, and contested the appeal largely on the question whether the

proviso to s 2(1) of the Criminal Appeal Act 1968 should be applied, it is unnecessary to set out in detail the passages in the summing up about which complaint has been made **a** on behalf of the appellants. A few examples will suffice.

Early in his summing up the judge said:

> '. . . I think it is only right that I should try and help you if I can in relation to the approach that I invite you to make about the words "to defraud" and "prejudice", because to defraud is in fact to act to the prejudice of another's right. If anyone may be prejudiced in any way by the fraud that is enough to constitute the intent to **b** defraud. If anyone may be prejudiced, and it is important to remember this: that an intent to risk possible injury to another's right is sufficient intent to prejudice . . .'

More followed on the same lines. By this direction dishonesty was taken out of the concept of defrauding, and that which could be evidence of defrauding, as by acting to **c** the prejudice of another's right, was treated as if it *constituted* (the judge's word) an intent to defraud. Crown counsel understandably was concerned about this direction. The next day, when the court sat, and in the absence of the jury, he invited the judge's attention to *R v Sinclair* [1968] 3 All ER 241, [1968] 1 WLR 1246 and the approval by this court in that case of the trial judge's use of the words 'deliberate dishonesty'. Judge Abdela seemed somewhat reluctant to accept what was being suggested to him. He **d** concluded this interruption by saying: 'Very well, and I will certainly deal with it in the appropriate time.' He went on with his summing up all that day. The next day, which was now two days after he gave what was clearly a misdirection in law to the jury, he said this:

> 'I am indebted to learned counsel, who have pointed out to me that a part of my direction to you at the outset of this case may have led you to apply probably an **e** unsatisfactory test of the defendants' state of mind when considering whether or not their conduct, or the conduct of any one of them, was dishonest. Let me make it clear. To prove fraud it must be established that the conduct was deliberately dishonest.'

The words 'may have led you to apply probably an unsatisfactory test' were inapt to **f** describe what had happened. He had directed the jury to apply a wrong test and should have said so specifically and have gone on there and then in clear terms which would have been incapable of being misunderstood to direct them what the law was: see *R v Moon* [1969] 3 All ER 803n, [1969] 1 WLR 1705. What he did do was to continue as follows:

> 'Now what sort of test should be applied as to whether the conduct was **g** dishonest? It is fraud if it is proved that there was a taking of a risk which there was no right to take, which would cause detriment or prejudice to another, and you will ask and inquire: have the prosecution proved and established that? Because the test of dishonesty is what we call a subjective one, that is to say, it is a question of the state of mind of the accused person.'

h

What the judge was doing was making the same mistake as he had made earlier in his summing up, treating evidence from which fraud could be inferred as if it were proof of fraud; and he made his direction more confusing by tacking onto the end of it a reference to a subjective test, which may have been a new and strange concept for many, probably most, of the jurors and which had no connection with what he had just said to them. At the very end of his summing up, in what he intended to be a helpful summary of the **j** issues, he once again left the jury with the impression that they could find each of the appellants guilty on the first count if they had taken a risk with the assets of IBBL, in a manner which they knew to be contrary to the best interest of that bank and to the prejudice of lenders or depositors, and the jury thought that such conduct was dishonest.

During this long summing up the jury were never told in clear and precise terms that
a they had to be sure that each of the appellants had agreed to act dishonestly. The
complaint about the diffuseness of the summing up arises from its length, the lack of an
obvious structure and the judge's propensity to instruct the jury on the law relating to
peripheral matters such as the duties of directors and the recording in accounts of loans
to directors. A summing up should be clear, concise and intelligible. If it is overloaded
with detail, whether of fact or law and follows no obvious plan, it will not have any of the
b attributes it should have. This summing up suffered from the fact that the judge was
over-conscientious. He seems to have decided that the jury should be reminded of nearly
all the details of the evidence and directed as to every facet of the law which applied. He
must have spent hours preparing his summing up but in the end he got lost in the trees
and missed the wood.

We turn to the directions given by the judge on the two counts charging conspiracy
c to utter forged documents, the Posen counts. There was much overlap between these
counts and that charging conspiracy to defraud. The Posen transactions were part of the
means by which Bension got money from London to Tel Aviv. We doubt whether any
useful purpose was served by adding the Posen counts to the indictment. On their face
there was nothing to show whom the alleged conspirators intended to defraud. The
Crown's case, based on *Welham v Director of Public Prosecutions* [1960] 1 All ER 805, [1961]
d AC 103, was that the intention was to defraud the Bank of England by inducing that
body to give permission for the remission of funds to Israel by producing forged invoices
as evidence of genuine commercial transactions. If there were a conspiracy it could also
have been to defraud IBBL. When the judge started his summing up on these counts, he
seems to have thought that the conspiracy alleged was one to defraud IBBL and directed
the jury accordingly. At the end of the day, and in the absence of the jury, counsel for
e the Crown pointed out that the Crown was alleging an intent to defraud the Bank of
England. The next day the judge invited the jury's attention to the limited way in which
the Crown had put its case. The judge gave a new direction but it fell somewhat short
of what this court in *R v Moon* [1969] 3 All ER 803n, [1969] 1 WLR 1705 said should be
done when a judge has to make a correction but in other respects it was satisfactory. Had
this part of the summing up stood by itself we should have upheld the convictions of
f Landy and White on these two counts. They were, however, not much more than part
of the Crown's case on count 1. The judge himself referred to 'a considerable amount of
overlap'. It follows, in our judgment, that the defects in the summing up on count 1
were bound to spill over onto the Posen counts so as to make convictions on those counts
unsatisfactory if that on count 1 was adjudged unsatisfactory.

Most of the argument in this court was directed to the application of the proviso to
g s 2(1) of the Criminal Appeal Act 1968. Counsel for the Crown took us through the
evidence in detail and invited us to adjudge, following the dictum of Viscount Dilhorne
in *Stafford v Director of Public Prosecutions* [1973] 3 All ER 762 at 766, [1974] AC 878 at
893 that if the jury had been properly directed it would inevitably have come to the same
conclusion. Counsel for Landy submitted that when there has been a fundamental
misdirection, as he said there had been in this case, the proviso should never be applied.
h We do not intend in this judgment to express any opinion as to when the proviso can be
applied and when it cannot. We are concerned with the facts of this case and nothing
more. The appellants were entitled to a fair trial. Nowadays that means that they were
entitled to have the jury clearly and correctly directed as to the law to be applied and to
have all defences fairly open to them put to the jury. In this case, for the reasons we have
stated, the jury were not directed correctly or clearly as to the law, and this was not on a
j minor matter but on the issue which went to the heart of the case, namely what was
meant by 'defraud'. Because of this, each appellant lost his chance of having his defence
(honest but careless) fairly put to the jury. It follows that two essentials of a fair trial were
missing. In such circumstances the verdicts must be unsatisfactory and if they are it
cannot be said that no miscarriage of justice has actually occurred.

It was for these reasons that we allowed the appeals and quashed the convictions.

Appeals allowed. Convictions quashed.

Solicitors: *D J Freeman & Co* (for Landy); *Harold Stern & Co* (for White); *Whitelock & Storr* (for Kaye); *Director of Public Prosecutions.*

N P Metcalfe Esq   Barrister.

Practice Note

CHANCERY DIVISION

Bankruptcy – Practice – Petition – Petition based on bankruptcy notice – Affidavit showing result of search of bankruptcy notice file – Affidavit not required where petition presented in court which issued bankruptcy notice.

Hitherto the practice has been that, where a bankruptcy petition is presented which is founded on a bankruptcy notice, an affidavit showing the result of a search of the bankruptcy notice file has been required to be filed on behalf of the creditor. Where the bankruptcy notice has been issued by the court to which the petition is presented, this requirement serves no useful purpose.

Directions have already been given by the Chief Registrar that no such affidavit will in future be required on the creditor's behalf in such cases. It will, however, continue to be the responsibility of persons filing bankruptcy petitions to inspect the bankruptcy notice file in order to ascertain whether there has been any application to set aside the bankruptcy notice.

By the direction of the judges of the Chancery Division exercising bankruptcy jurisdiction.

RICHARD HUNT
25th March 1981   Chief Bankruptcy Registrar.

a   # Lambert and another v Lewis and others

HOUSE OF LORDS

LORD DIPLOCK, LORD ELWYN-JONES, LORD FRASER OF TULLYBELTON, LORD SCARMAN AND LORD
BRIDGE OF HARWICH

10th MARCH, 8th APRIL 1981

b *Tort – Contribution between joint tortfeasors – Claim by defendant against third party –*
Defective trailer coupling supplied by dealer to vehicle owner for use with trailer – Coupling
unsafe for purpose for which it was designed by manufacturer – Continued use of coupling by
owner after he ought to have known of defective condition – Defective coupling causing trailer to
break away from vehicle and cause accident resulting in death and injury to occupants of another
c *vehicle – Whether continued user of defective coupling by owner breaking chain of causation*
between dealer's breach of warranty in supplying defective coupling and accident – Liability of
owner, dealer and manufacturer inter se.

The plaintiff was injured and her husband was killed when their car was hit by a trailer
which had become detached from a Land-Rover belonging to a farmer. The plaintiff
d brought an action for damages against the farmer, the dealers who had supplied the
trailer coupling and the manufacturers of the coupling. The farmer brought third party
proceedings against the dealers, and the dealers in turn brought fourth party proceedings
against the manufacturers. The trial judge found that the coupling was defective in
design and dangerous in use on the public highways and that the defects were readily
foreseeable by an appropriately skilled engineer considering the problem. He further
e found that part of the coupling on the farmer's Land-Rover had been missing and that
the farmer must have been aware of the fact. He accordingly apportioned liability at
75% for the manufacturer and 25% for the farmer. He acquitted the dealers of all
negligence. In the third party proceedings brought by the farmer against the dealers
seeking, in reliance on warranties of fitness implied by s 14 of the Sale of Goods Act 1893,
an indemnity for the damages for which he was liable to the plaintiff, the judge held that
f the defects in design were breaches of warranty for which the farmer would have been
entitled to nominal damages but that the damage for which the farmer had been held to
be liable was caused by his own negligence in continuing to use a broken coupling. The
judge consequently dismissed both the third party and the fourth party proceedings.
The farmer appealed to the Court of Appeal against the judge's finding of negligence
against him, and also appealed against the dismissal of his claim for an indemnity against
the dealers in the third party proceedings. The dealers, as a precaution, appealed against
g the dismissal of their fourth party proceedings against the manufacturers. The Court of
Appeal ([1980] 1 All ER 978) dismissed the farmer's appeal against the judge's finding of
negligence against him, but allowed his appeal in the third party proceedings against the
dealers on the ground that, there being no break in the chain of causation between the
manufacturers' negligence, consisting in the defective design of the coupling, and the
plaintiff's damage, there could be no such break between the dealers' breach of warranty,
h likewise consisting in the defective design of the coupling, and the farmer's loss
occasioned by his share of the liability for the plaintiff's damage. The Court of Appeal
also dismissed the dealers' appeal in the fourth party proceedings against the
manufacturers. The dealers appealed to the House of Lords in respect of the Court of
Appeal's decisions in the third party and the fourth party proceedings.

j **Held** – (1) Where a person was held liable to a stranger for negligent failure to take a
certain precaution, and he sought to recover over from someone with whom he had a
contract on the ground that his liability to the stranger was caused by a breach of
warranty by the other contracting party, he was entitled to recover over only if, by that
contract, the other contracting party had warranted that he need not take the very

precaution for the failure to take which he was held liable in law to the stranger. Since
the trial judge had found that there was no express warranty of the quality of the   *a*
coupling or its fitness for the purpose of towing trailers, the farmer was forced to rely on
the implied warranty under s 14(1) of the 1893 Act that the coupling as fitted to the
Land-Rover would be reasonably fit for towing trailers, which in the context included a
warranty that it might be used on a public highway without danger to other users of the
road. Although that implied warranty related to the coupling at the time of delivery
under the contract of sale in the state in which it was delivered and for a reasonable time   *b*
thereafter so long as it remained in the same apparent state as that in which it was
delivered, apart from normal wear and tear, once it had become apparent to the farmer
that the locking mechanism of the coupling was broken, and consequently that it was no
longer in the same state as when it was delivered, that brought to an end any warranty
by the dealers of the coupling's continued safety in use on which the farmer was entitled
to rely. It followed, therefore, that the farmer's claim against the dealers' failed in limine   *c*
(see p 1190 *j* to p 1191 *f* and p 1192 *e* to *h*, post); dictum of Winn LJ in *Hadley v Droitwich
Construction Co Ltd* [1967] 3 All ER at 914 applied.

(2) The farmer's liability arose, not from the defective design of the coupling but from
his own negligence in failing, when he knew that the coupling was damaged, to have it
repaired or to ascertain if it was still safe to use. Since the issue of causation on which the
farmer's claim against the dealers depended was whether the farmer's negligence resulted   *d*
directly and naturally, in the ordinary course of events, from the dealers' breach of
warranty, which manifestly it did not, it followed that the Court of Appeal was wrong
to conclude that there was no break between the dealers' breach of warranty and the
farmer's loss occasioned by his share of the liability for the plaintiff's damage (see p 1191
g and p 1192 *e* to *h*, post).

(3) It followed that the dealers' appeal in the third party proceedings brought by the   *e*
farmer would be allowed; and, since there was no liability for the dealers to pass on to the
manufacturers, the dealers' appeal in the fourth party proceedings against the
manufacturers would be dismissed (see p 1191 *j* to p 1192 *a* and *d* to *h*, post).

Per Curiam. (1) The citation of a plethora of authorities which apply a well-established
principle of law that has been clearly stated in the leading case on the subject and
paraphrase it to illustrate the particular facts there in issue, apart from being time- and   *f*
cost-consuming, presents the danger of so blinding the court with case law that it has
difficulty in seeing the wood of legal principle for the trees of paraphrase (see p 1189 *h* to
p 1190 *a* and p 1192 *e* to *h*, post).

(2) Where economic loss suffered by a distributor in the chain between a manufacturer
and the ultimate consumer consists of a liability to pay damages to the ultimate consumer
for physical injuries sustained by him, or consists of a liability to indemnify a distributor   *g*
lower in the chain of distribution for his liability to the ultimate consumer for damages
for physical injuries, such economic loss may yet be held to be recoverable from the
manufacturer (see p 1192 *c* to *h*, post).

Decision of the Court of Appeal [1980] 1 All ER 978 reversed in respect of the third
party proceedings and affirmed in respect of the fourth party proceedings.

h

Notes

For contribution and indemnity between joint and several tortfeasors, see 37 Halsbury's
Laws (3rd Edn) 137–141, paras 247–250.

For the Sale of Goods Act 1893, s 14, see 30 Halsbury's Statutes (3rd Edn) 14.

As from 18th May 1973 s 14 of the 1893 Act was substituted by the Supply of Goods
(Implied Terms) Act 1973, s 3. As from 1st January 1980 s 14 of the 1893 Act has been   *j*
replaced by the Sale of Goods Act 1979, Sch 1, para 6 in relation to contracts made before
18th May 1973, by Sch 1, para 5, to the 1979 Act in relation to contracts made on or after
18th May 1973 and before a day to be appointed, and by s 14 of the 1979 Act in relation
to contracts made on or after the appointed day.

Cases referred to in opinions

a   *Donoghue v Stevenson* [1932] AC 562, [1932] All ER Rep 1, 101 LJPC 119, 37 Com Cas 350, 1932 SC (HL) 31, 1932 SLT 317, HL, 36(1) Digest (Reissue) 144, 562.

Hadley v Droitwich Construction Co Ltd [1967] 3 All ER 911, [1968] 1 WLR 37, CA, 3 Digest (Reissue) 498, 3282.

Mowbray v Merryweather [1895] 2 QB 640, [1895–9] All ER Rep 941, 65 LJQB 50, 73 LT 459, 59 JP 804, 14 R 767, CA, 36(1) Digest (Reissue) 95, 365.

b   **Appeal**

Lexmead (Basingstoke) Ltd ('the dealers') appealed against the decision of the Court of Appeal (Stephenson, Roskill and Lawton LJJ) ([1980] 1 All ER 978, [1980] 1 WLR 683) on 1st May 1979 whereby in third party proceedings brought by Donald Richard Lewis (the owner of a Land-Rover and trailer) ('the farmer') against the dealers and arising out of an action brought by the plaintiffs, Iris Frances Lambert (on her own behalf and as c   administratrix of the estates of her husband George Charles Lambert and her son Kirby George Lambert both deceased) and Tracy Frances Lambert (an infant suing by her mother and next friend Iris Frances Lambert), against the defendants, the farmer, Hugh Francis Larkin (the driver of the Land-Rover at the material time), B Dixon-Bate Ltd (the manufacturers of a towing coupling by which the trailer was attached to the Land-Rover) d   ('the manufacturers') and the dealers, the Court of Appeal allowed an appeal by the farmer against the decision of Stocker J on 11th November 1977 whereby he dismissed the farmer's claim in the third party proceedings. · The dealers also appealed against the further decision of the Court of Appeal (Stephenson, Roskill and Lawton LJJ) ([1980] 1 All ER 978, [1980] 1 WLR 683) on 24th May 1979 whereby in fourth party proceedings brought by the dealers against the manufacturers and also arising out of the plaintiffs' e   action it dismissed the dealers' appeal against the decision of Stocker J on 11th November 1977 whereby he dismissed the dealers' claim in the fourth party proceedings. The facts are set out in the opinion of Lord Diplock.

Michael Turner QC, Patrick Phillips QC and *Timothy Lamb* for the dealers.
Roy Beldam QC and *R F Nelson* for the farmer.
f   *Piers Ashworth QC* and *R Livesey* for the manufacturers.

Their Lordships took time for consideration.

8th April. The following opinions were delivered.

g   **LORD DIPLOCK.** My Lords, this appeal arises out of a traffic accident, with tragic consequences, which took place as long ago as September 1972. A trailer carrying rubble became detached from a Land-Rover belonging to the first defendant, the first respondent to this appeal ('the farmer'), which was being driven by his servant along a road in Farnborough. The trailer careered across the road and hit a car coming in the opposite direction. In it were the plaintiff, her husband who was driving, and their two children. Her husband and son were killed; the plaintiff and her daughter suffered h   relatively minor injuries. It has never been suggested that the husband was in any way to blame for the accident.

The plaintiff, acting on behalf of herself and as next friend of her daughter, and also as administratrix of the estates of her husband and her son, brought an action for damages against the farmer and also the driver of the Land-Rover. (There is no need for j   any further mention of the latter.) She subsequently joined, as additional defendants, the appellants to this appeal ('the dealers'), who had sold the trailer coupling to the farmer and fitted it on the Land-Rover, and the second respondents to this appeal ('the manufacturers') who had manufactured the coupling. The farmer brought third party proceedings against the dealers and the dealers in turn brought fourth party proceedings against the manufacturers. The appeal to your Lordships House is brought in these third and fourth party proceedings alone.

Damages had been agreed at £45,000 before the action eventually came on for trial before Stocker J in October 1977. The only issue was how the liability for the agreed damages should be allocated between the various defendants. The hearing lasted ten days, much of the time being spent on expert engineering evidence about the design and manufacture of the coupling and the cause of its having become detached at the time of the accident.

The clear and careful judgment of Stocker J (which is reported at [1978] 1 Lloyd's Rep 810 and to which reference can be made) contains a detailed description of the mechanical nature of the coupling. For the purposes of this appeal, however, I do not find it necessary either to repeat or paraphrase it here. What matters is his finding of fact, which was that the coupling was defective in design and dangerous in use on the public highway and that these defects were readily foreseeable by an appropriately skilled engineer considering the problem. He accordingly found the manufacturers liable to the plaintiff for negligence in having supplied and put into circulation for use without intermediate examination a coupling that was 'defective in design and dangerous in use'.

The coupling was designed for use interchangeably with trailers fitted with either cup-shaped or ring-type means of attaching them to the towing vehicle. The trailer with which the farmer always used it had a cup-shaped means of attachment. The defect in design was that all that prevented the coupling coming apart when a trailer with a cup-shaped means of attachment was being towed was a locking mechanism operated by a handle attached to a spindle, and the safety of this device depended on the integrity of the spindle which was hidden from view inside a metal casing. The handle protruded below the bottom of the coupling and was liable to be struck or jarred or even broken in the course of normal use, with the likelihood of causing the spindle to be distorted or sheared. This would have had the effect of causing the lock to fail and permitting the coupling to come apart. This was something that might happen without the driver of the vehicle being aware of it at the time that it occurred.

On the judge's findings, this was what had happened in the instant case. When the accident occurred, both the handle and the spindle were missing. The casing of the locking mechanism was full of dirt and it was this dirt alone that had prevented the lock itself from falling off entirely. The judge was satisfied by the expert evidence that the coupling must have been in this condition for between three and six months before the accident and that the farmer who knew that the handle operated the locking mechanism must have been aware that the handle at least, which, unlike the spindle, was clearly visible, had been broken off throughout that period. He found the farmer negligent in that—

> 'he continued to use this coupling over a period of months in a state in which it was plainly damaged without taking steps to have it repaired or even to ascertain whether or not it was safe to continue to use it in such condition.'

As between the manufacturer and the farmer, the judge apportioned the liability as to 75% to the manufacturer and 25% to the farmer. He acquitted the dealers of all negligence. They had purchased a coupling made by reputable manufacturers and the defect in design would not be apparent on reasonable examination.

In the third party proceedings brought by the farmer against the dealers the farmer sought an indemnity for damages for which he was liable to the plaintiff. He relied on the warranties implied under s 14(1) and (2) of the Sale of Goods Act 1893 (which was in force in its unamended form at the relevant time) that the coupling should be reasonably fit for the purpose for which it was supplied, viz towing trailers with a Land-Rover, and that it should be of merchantable quality. The judge held that because of its defect in design which made it dangerous in use, there were breaches of both warranties for which the farmer would be entitled to nominal damages at least if he had claimed them; but the

judge held that the damages for which he had found the farmer liable were caused by his
a own negligence in continuing to use a coupling which he knew was broken without
taking steps to have it repaired or to ascertain whether it was safe. He held that the
principle in *Mowbray v Merryweather* [1895] 2 QB 640, [1895–9] All ER Rep 941, on
which the farmer had relied, was subject to the limitation stated by Winn LJ in *Hadley
v Droitwich Construction Co Ltd* [1967] 3 All ER 911 at 914, [1968] 1 WLR 37 at 43.

This limitation, in the view of Stocker J, made it impossible for the farmer to rely on
b either of the implied warranties of fitness or of merchantability as enabling him to
recover from the dealers the damages he was liable to pay the plaintiff for his own
negligence. The only negligence of which the farmer had been found guilty was that
when he knew that the coupling was damaged, because the handle had been broken off,
he continued for months to use it in that damaged state without having it repaired or
even ascertaining whether or not it was safe to continue to use it in that condition. The
c dealers had not impliedly warranted that if the coupling should be broken when in use
the farmer need take neither of these elementary and obvious precautions once he knew
that it was in a damaged condition.

My Lords, I shall be reverting to these two authorities when I come to deal with the
proceedings in the Court of Appeal. The judge's decision that the farmer had no claim
against the dealers made moot the dealers' claim against the manufacturers in the fourth
d party proceedings. The judge accordingly dismissed them; but it is nevertheless
convenient at this point to mention how that claim was framed. The dealers had not
bought the coupling direct from the manufacturers but from one of several wholesalers
with whom they dealt; owing to a defective system of store-keeping records they could
not tell which. So they were unable to identify an immediate seller against whom they
in their turn could rely on the implied warranties of fitness or merchantability. They
e based their claim against the manufacturers in the alternative on a collateral warranty,
negligent misstatement and thirdly, but it would seem a trifle mutedly, on ordinary
negligence of the kind dealt with in *Donoghue v Stevenson* [1932] AC 562, [1932] All ER
Rep 1.

The farmer appealed against the judge's finding of negligence against him. This
appeal was dismissed by the Court of Appeal (Stephenson, Roskill and Lawton LJJ)
f ([1980] 1 All ER 978, [1980] 1 WLR 683) and no more need be said about it. The farmer
also appealed against the dismissal of his claim for an indemnity against the dealers in the
third party proceedings. The dealers, as a precaution in case they should be held liable
to the farmer, appealed against the dismissal of their fourth party proceedings against the
manufacturers.

The argument before the Court of Appeal lasted a broken period of seven days. The
g farmer's appeal in the third party proceedings against the dealers for an indemnity in
respect of the damages for which he was liable to pay to the plaintiff was allowed; the
dealers' appeal in the fourth party proceedings against the manufacturers was
dismissed. On appeal to this House by the dealers against both these judgments of the
Court of Appeal, counsel estimated that the hearing here would also take at least seven
days, and that in the course of argument it would be necessary to cite a very large number
h of authorities, both English and foreign, to your Lordships.

My Lords, the respect which under the common law is paid to precedent makes it
tempting to the appellate advocate to cite a plethora of authorities which do no more
than illustrate the application to particular facts of a well-established principle of law that
has been clearly stated in what, by consensus of Bench and Bar and academic writers, has
come to be treated as the leading case on the subject. In those cases that are no more than
j illustrative, however, there are likely to be found judicial statements of the principle that
do not follow the precise language in which the principle is expressed in the leading case,
but use some paraphrase of it that the judge thinks is specially apt to explain its
application to the facts of the particular case. The citation of a plethora of illustrative
authorities, apart from being time- and cost-consuming, presents the danger of so
blinding the court with case law that it has difficulty in seeing the wood of legal principle

for the trees of paraphrase. This, I cannot help thinking, is what must have happened in the instant case.

    The farmer's case against the dealers, by the time it reached the Court of Appeal, was based exclusively on breach of a contractual warranty. So the question of legal principle involved is: in what circumstances can a party, A, to a contract, who has been found liable for breach of a duty of care owed by him to a stranger, X, to the contract, recover from the other party, B, to the contract as damages for breach of warranty the amount of the damages for negligence which A himself has been ordered to pay to X? The question was said by Lord Esher MR to have arisen for the first time in the leading case of *Mowbray v Merryweather* [1895] 2 QB 640, [1895–9] All ER Rep 941. Apart from the brief exegesis by Winn LJ in *Hadley v Droitwich Construction Co Ltd* [1967] 3 All ER 911, [1968] 1 WLR 37, this is the only authority to which I see any need to refer. In *Mowbray v Merryweather* the contractual warranty relied on by the plaintiffs was an implied one of fitness for purpose in similar terms to the implied warranty under s 14(1) of the Sale of Goods Act 1893, in casu that tackle supplied by the defendants to the plaintiffs for use by the latter's employees in unloading a ship was reasonably fit for use for that purpose by those employees with safety to themselves. A chain forming part of the tackle was defective; as a result of this defect it broke and injured an employee of the plaintiffs. The defect could have been discovered by the plaintiffs on reasonable examination. Their failure to examine it constituted the negligence for which damages against them were awarded to the injured employee. The argument that the plaintiffs' allowing it to be used without examination was not the natural result of the defendants' breach of warranty of fitness for purpose invoked from Lord Esher MR an interlocutory observation that underlines the elementary justice of the principle of law that the Court of Appeal was about to lay down: 'The question', he said, 'is whether the plaintiffs are not entitled to say that they were misled into their breach of duty towards the workman by the warranty' (see [1895] 2 QB 640 at 641). In Lord Esher MR's judgment the successful contention of the plaintiff, which he expressly approved, was stated in the following terms ([1895] 2 QB 640 at 643; cf [1895–9] All ER Rep 941 at 942):

> 'The plaintiffs say that they took the chain on the faith of the warranty and gave it to their workmen to use; while being so used it broke, because it was not in accordance with the warranty: that was the sole cause of its breaking; and the natural result was that this workman was injured; and he thereupon sued the plaintiffs in respect of his injuries, and they were compelled to pay him the amount which they now seek to recover from the defendant. It is true that he could not have recovered unless, as between himself and the plaintiffs, the plaintiffs had been guilty of want of care; but the plaintiffs say that, as between themselves and the defendant, they were not bound to examine the chain because the defendant had warranted it sound, that they had a right to rely on that warranty, and did rely on it, and the defendant cannot rely on a duty to use due care which was owed, not to him, but to the workman.'

What was said by Winn LJ in *Hadley v Droitwich Construction Co Ltd* [1967] 3 All ER 911 at 914, [1968] 1 WLR 37 at 43 but expressly disapproved by the Court of Appeal in the instant case is, in my view, correct and does no more than state a limitation that is plainly implicit in the ratio decidendi of *Mowbray v Merryweather*:

> '... in a case where A has been held liable to X, a stranger, for negligent failure to take a certain precaution, he may recover over from someone with whom he has a contract only if, by that contract, the other contracting party has warranted that he *need not*—there is no necessity to—take the very precautions for the failure to take which he has been held liable in law to [X].' (Winn LJ's emphasis.)

So in order to see whether the farmer's claim against the dealers falls within this principle the first inquiry to be made is: what are the terms of the warranty which it is claimed was broken? Stocker J had found that there was no *express* warranty of the a   quality of the coupling or its fitness for the purpose of towing trailers, so the farmer was driven to rely on the implied warranties under s 14(1) and (2) of the Sale of Goods Act 1893 (in its unamended form), both of which were clearly applicable to his contract with the dealers. It is, however, only necessary to refer to the warranty under sub-s (1), that the coupling as fitted to the Land-Rover should be reasonably fit for towing trailers fitted with either cup-shaped or ring-type means of attachment. Fitness in this context plainly includes a warranty that it may be so used on a public highway without danger to other

b   users of the road.

      The implied warranty of fitness for a particular purpose relates to the goods at the time of delivery under the contract of sale in the state in which they were delivered. I do not doubt that it is a continuing warranty that the goods will continue to be fit for that purpose for a reasonable time after delivery, so long as they remain in the same apparent state as that in which they were delivered, apart from normal wear and tear. What is a

c   reasonable time will depend on the nature of the goods, but I would accept that in the case of the coupling the warranty was still continuing up to the date, some three to six months before the accident, when it first became known to the farmer that the handle of the locking mechanism was missing. Up to that time the farmer would have had a right to rely on the dealers' warranty as excusing him from making his own examination of the coupling to see if it were safe; but, if the accident had happened before then, the

d   farmer would not have been held to have been guilty of any negligence to the plaintiff. After it had become apparent to the farmer that the locking mechanism of the coupling was broken, and consequently that it was no longer in the same state as when it was delivered, the only implied warranty which could justify his failure to take the precaution either to get it mended or at least to find out whether it was safe to continue to use it in that condition would be a warranty that the coupling could continue to be safely used to

e   tow a trailer on a public highway notwithstanding that it was in an obviously damaged state. My Lords, any implication of a warranty in these terms needs only to be stated to be rejected. So the farmer's claim against the dealers fails in limine. In the state in which the farmer knew the coupling to be at the time of the accident, there was no longer any warranty by the dealers of its continued safety in use on which the farmer was entitled to rely.

f   The Court of Appeal reasoned that, since there was no break in the chain of causation between negligence of the manufacturers, which consisted in the defective design of the coupling, and the plaintiff's damage, there could be no such break between the dealers' breach of warranty, which likewise consisted in the defective design of the coupling, and the farmer's loss occasioned by his share of the liability for the plaintiff's damage. With respect, this reasoning was erroneous. The farmer's liability arose not from the defective

g   design of the coupling but from his own negligence in failing, when he knew that the coupling was damaged, to have it repaired or to ascertain if it was still safe to use. The issue of causation, therefore, on which the farmer's claim against the dealers depended was whether *his* negligence resulted directly and naturally, in the ordinary course of events, from the dealers' breach of warranty. Manifestly it did not.

      My Lords, it does not appear that consideration of whether the implied warranty of

h   fitness of the coupling would be reasonably understood by the parties to the contract as continuing notwithstanding the obvious damage to its locking mechanism played a conspicuous part in the argument before the Court of Appeal. It does not feature prominently in the farmer's printed case before this House. So it is understandable that the Court of Appeal did not deal with it specifically, although it may be that an argument on these lines was in the Lords Justices' minds when, in allowing the farmer's appeal

j   against the dealers in the third party proceedings, they felt it necessary to express their disapproval of the statement of Winn LJ in *Hadley v Droitwich Construction Co Ltd* which I have already cited. This, in my view, correctly states the principle of law applicable to the farmer's claim against the dealers for breach of warranty and, for the reasons I have given, is fatal to its success. I would accordingly allow the dealers' appeal in the third party proceedings.

This makes it unnecessary for your Lordships to go on to deal with the dealers' appeal in the fourth party proceedings against the manufacturers. There is no liability for the dealers to pass on to the manufacturers; so on this ground the appeal must be dismissed. Your Lordships accordingly have heard no argument on any of the three alternative grounds on which, if they had been liable to their buyer, the dealers would have sought to pass on that liability to the manufacturers with whom they were in no direct contractual relationship. The simplest ground was that which was based on the duty which, as was first held authoritatively by this House in *Donoghue v Stevenson* [1932] AC 562, [1932] All ER Rep 1, lies on a manufacturer of an article sold by him in circumstances which make it unlikely that a distributor or ultimate purchaser will subject the goods to such inspection before use as would reveal a dangerous defect, and to take reasonable care that the article is free from any defect likely to cause injury to the user. The Court of Appeal rejected this ground of liability because, in its view, it was bound by authority to hold that what may conveniently be referred to as the *Donoghue v Stevenson* principle was restricted to damage by physical injury but did not extend to purely economic loss. While in the absence of argument it could not be right to express any final view, I should not wish the dismissal of the dealers' appeal to be regarded as an approval by this House of the proposition that where the economic loss suffered by a distributor in the chain between the manufacturer and the ultimate consumer consists of a liability to pay damages to the ultimate consumer for physical injuries sustained by him, or consists of a liability to indemnify a distributor lower in the chain of distribution for his liability to the ultimate consumer for damages for physical injuries, such economic loss is not recoverable under the *Donoghue v Stevenson* principle from the manufacturer.

I should therefore allow the dealers' appeal in the third party proceedings and dismiss their appeal in the fourth party proceedings.

LORD ELWYN-JONES. My Lords, I have had the advantage of reading in draft the speech of my noble and learned friend Lord Diplock. I fully agree with it and with the order he proposes.

LORD FRASER OF TULLYBELTON. My Lords, I have had the advantage of reading in advance the speech prepared by my noble and learned friend Lord Diplock, and I agree with it. For the reasons given by him I would allow the dealers' appeal in the third party proceedings and dismiss their appeal in the fourth party proceedings.

LORD SCARMAN. My Lords, I have had the advantage of reading in draft the speech delivered by my noble and learned friend Lord Diplock. I agree with it, and for the reasons he gives I would allow the dealers' appeal in the third party proceedings and dismiss their appeal in the fourth party proceedings. I also agree with the order proposed by my noble and learned friend as to costs.

LORD BRIDGE OF HARWICH. My Lords, I have had the advantage of reading in draft the speech of my noble and learned friend Lord Diplock. I fully agree with it and with the order he proposes.

Appeal in third party proceedings allowed. Appeal in fourth party proceedings dismissed.

Solicitors: *Young, Jones, Hair & Co* (for the dealers); *Stevensons* (for the farmer); *Hextall Erskine & Co*, agents for *Laces & Co*, Liverpool (for the manufacturers).

Mary Rose Plummer   Barrister.

a

Attorney General's Reference (No 4 of 1979)

COURT OF APPEAL, CRIMINAL DIVISION

LORD LANE CJ, BOREHAM AND GIBSON JJ

b   9th, 10th JUNE, 14th JULY 1980

Criminal law – Handling stolen goods – Stolen goods – Proof that goods were stolen – Thief paying into bank account money honestly obtained and money obtained by deception – Thief giving accused cheque drawn on account – No means of identifying sum against which cheque drawn – Accused assuming that cheque represented her share of money obtained by deception – Whether
c   *jury could infer from belief of accused that cheque represented 'stolen goods' – Theft Act 1968, ss 22, 24(2)(a).*

A thief, who was a fellow employee of the accused, had a bank account into which she paid cheques that she received from their employer. Those cheques represented (i) sums earned by, and due to, her fellow employees, which she was required to pay to them, (ii)
d   sums earned by her and (iii) sums obtained by her from the employer by deception. The thief handed to the accused a cheque for £288·53 drawn on the account. At that time each of the categories of the sums paid in was greater in total than the balance of £641·32 in the account. The accused was charged with dishonestly receiving stolen goods knowing or believing the same to be stolen goods, contrary to s 22[a] of the Theft Act 1968. She admitted that she knew that the thief had obtained sums from their employer
e   by deception and, when asked whether the cheque paid to her was her share, replied that she supposed that it was. The judge ruled that, as it was impossible to identify from which of the three categories of money in the thief's account the cheque in favour of the accused had been drawn, there was no evidence on which the jury could conclude that it amounted to 'stolen goods' within the meaning of s 24(2)(a)[b] of the 1968 Act. He accordingly directed the jury to acquit the accused. The Attorney General referred to the
f   court the question whether, in the circumstances, the jury were entitled to infer from the intention or belief of the parties that the payment received by the accused out of the mixed fund represented stolen goods within s 24(2)(a).

Held – (1) As both a cheque obtained by deception and a balance in a bank account came within the extended definition of 'goods' in ss 4(1)[c], 24(4) and 34(2)(b)[d] of the 1968
g   Act, the cheques which the thief had obtained by deception and the balance in her bank account could, to the extent of the value of the tainted cheques, be goods which directly represented stolen goods in the hands of the thief as being the proceeds of the disposal or realisation of the goods stolen, within s 24(2)(a) of that Act. However, in order to prove dishonest handling by the accused, it was necessary for the prosecution to establish both that at the material time the thief's bank account in fact comprised, at least in part, the
h   proceeds of the stolen goods and also that the accused received, at least in part, such proceeds (see p 1198 c to f, post).

---

a   Section 22 provides:

    '(1) A person handles stolen goods if (otherwise than in the course of the stealing) knowing or believing them to be stolen goods he dishonestly receives the goods, or dishonestly undertakes or assists in their retention, removal, disposal or realisation by or for the benefit of another person, or
j   if he arranges to do so.

    '(2) A person guilty of handling stolen goods shall on conviction on indictment be liable to imprisonment for a term not exceeding fourteen years.'

b   Section 24, so far as material, is set out at p 1197 j to p 1198 a, post
c   Section 4(1), so far as material, is set out at p 1198 b, post
d   Section 34(2), so far as material, is set out at p 1198 b, post

(2) The fact that the thief's bank account was a mixed one, containing sums honestly obtained by her as well as the sums dishonestly obtained by her, might make it difficult but it did not make it impossible to prove that at least part of what she paid to the accused represented the proceeds of stolen goods. However, the accused's admission that she regarded the cheque as 'her share' was admissible only as to her knowledge that the payment represented stolen goods and as to her honesty in receiving the money, and could not establish that the payment to her did or could represent stolen goods. To prove that the prosecution had to show that the payment could, by reference to the payments in and out of the account, be a payment representing stolen goods, and the accused could not make a valid and admissible admission as to that unless she had personal knowledge of the working of the thief's bank account. It followed that the jury were not entitled to infer from the intention or belief of the accused that the cheque represented 'stolen goods' within s 24(2)(a) (see p 1199 a to h, post); *Surujpaul called Dick v Reginam* [1958] 3 All ER 300 applied.

Per Curiam. It may perhaps be that a payment can be proved to have been a payment of money representing stolen goods, even where there was enough honest money in the account to cover the payment, if there is proof, direct or by way of necessary inference, of the intention of the paying thief to pay out the stolen money (see p 1199 g, post).

Semble. The receipt of a thief's cheque, drawn in circumstances wherein it is plain that it must serve to transfer the proceeds of stolen goods, constitutes receiving stolen goods on the ground that such a cheque directly or indirectly represents the stolen goods within s 24(2)(a) (see p 1198 j, post).

Notes

For obtaining property by deception, see 11 Halsbury's Laws (4th Edn) para 1278 and for cases on the subject, see 15 Digest (Reissue) 1386–1387, 12131–12137.

For the meaning of stolen goods, see 11 Halsbury's Laws (4th Edn) para 1290.

For the Theft Act 1968, ss 4, 22, 24, 34, see 8 Halsbury's Statutes (3rd Edn) 784, 796, 797, 804.

Cases referred to in judgment

Attorney General's Reference (No 2 of 1975) [1976] 2 All ER 753, [1976] 1 WLR 710, 62 Cr App R 255, CA, 15 Digest (Reissue) 1037, 8984.

Surujpaul called Dick v Reginam [1958] 3 All ER 300, [1958] 1 WLR 1050, 42 Cr App R 266, PC, 14(1) Digest (Reissue) 101, 672.

Reference

This was a reference by the Attorney General, under s 36 of the Criminal Justice Act 1972, for the opinion of the Court of Appeal on a point of law arising in a case where the accused had been acquitted on the direction of the trial judge on an indictment containing one count charging the accused with dishonestly receiving certain stolen goods knowing or believing them to be stolen goods, contrary to s 22 of the Theft Act 1968. The terms of the reference and the facts are set out in the judgment of the court.

A J D Nicholl for the Attorney General.
Malcolm Lee for the respondent.

Cur adv vult

14th July. **LORD LANE CJ** read the following judgment of the court: This reference by the Attorney General arises out of a case in which the respondent ('the accused') was indicted on one count which alleged that she dishonestly received certain stolen goods, namely a cheque for £288·53, knowing or believing the same to be stolen goods.

After a submission on behalf of the accused at the end of the prosecution case, the trial judge directed the jury to acquit. There was no issue as to the receipt by the accused of

the cheque, nor was it in dispute that the person who paid the cheque had previously
a obtained sums of money by dishonest deception, but the judge ruled that there was no
evidence that the cheque so paid to the accused was in law stolen goods.

The facts of the case were these. Over a period of six months in 1976 and 1977, a
fellow employee of the accused obtained by deception from their employer certain
cheques. It is convenient, for brief reference, to refer to that fellow employee as 'the
thief'. The thief paid those fraudulently obtained cheques into her bank account.

b   During the same period the thief also paid into her bank account other cheques which
she had lawfully received from her employer and which represented, firstly, amounts
earned by and due to fellow employees which she was required to pay on to those
employees, and, secondly, sums lawfully earned by the thief. The total of the sums paid
into the bank account by the thief as sums dishonestly obtained by deception from the
employer was £859.

c   The thief had duly paid out to the other employees the amounts she had received for
such payments.

On the date when the thief handed to the accused the cheque for £288·53, the state of
the thief's bank account was a credit balance of £641·32.

The total amount lawfully received into the account by the thief for payment to other
employees, which had been paid out to them, exceeded that balance of £641·32. The
d total amount lawfully received by the thief in respect of her own earnings and paid into
the account had also exceeded £641·32. The court has no information as to the nature
or purpose of other disbursements made from the account by the thief and assumes that
there was no evidence.

There was evidence that the accused had admitted that she knew of the obtaining by
deception of the £859 by the thief. It is said that there was evidence from which it
e would have been open to the jury to conclude that, for the continued deceptions of the
thief to succeed, the co-operation, or at least acquiescence, of the accused was necessary.
Whatever the reason it was thought more appropriate to charge her with handling than
with obtaining by deception.

The accused was asked about the cheque paid to her by the thief. One question asked
of her was this: 'Was that your share?' She replied: 'I suppose it was.' She added,
f according to the evidence which the jury was invited to consider: 'I suppose you could
call it guilt but I haven't touched it.'

The judge at trial was invited to rule that there was no evidence on which the jury
could conclude that the cheque given to the accused by the thief amounted in law to
stolen goods within the meaning of the Theft Act 1968.

Two points were taken on behalf of the accused by counsel. First, that the offence of
g handling stolen goods could not be committed with reference to a stolen thing in action,
or to a thing in action representing stolen goods and, secondly that on the evidence
before the court the offence of handling stolen goods could not be proved.

As to the first point, the judge rejected the submission. As to the second, the judge
ruled that, since the thief's bank account had been fed by payments in the three
categories described above, namely (i) sums lawfully obtained for payment on to other
h employees, (ii) sums lawfully obtained as money earned by the thief, and (iii) the
£859·70 dishonestly obtained by deception, it was impossible for the prosecution to
prove that the payment made to the accused was in law stolen goods.

In reaching his conclusion the judge said this:

'I have to consider whether or not the cheque which the thief paid to the accused's
j   account indirectly represents the stolen goods in the hands of the thief. It is very
tempting to say that if the drawer of the cheque and the recipient of the cheque
intend that the money represented by the cheque shall represent that part of the
choses in action owed by the bank to the account holder which is stolen money that
that is sufficient for these purposes. But in my view the [1968 Act] does not say
that. It does not imply it and I consider that, as I have to construe this part and every

part of the Act strictly, if Parliament had intended to provide for such a case it would have said so.'

It is from this conclusion on the second point that the point of law referred to this court arises. The point of law referred to us under s 36(1) of the Criminal Justice Act 1972 is as follows:

'Where a payment is made out of a fund constituted by a mixture of money amounting to stolen goods within the meaning of Section 24 of the Theft Act 1968, and money not so tainted, or of a bank account similarly constituted, in such a way that the specific origin of the sum paid cannot be identified with either portion of the fund, is a jury entitled to infer that the payment represented stolen goods within the meaning of Section 24(2) of the Act, from the intention of the parties that it should represent the stolen goods or a share thereof?'

Before dealing with the substance of the question as it arose in the instant case as a point of law, it is necessary to emphasise that the power given to the Attorney General to refer a point of law to this court is a power to refer a point of law which actually arose in a real case. There is no power to refer theoretical questions of law, however interesting or difficult. As was said in this court by James LJ in *Attorney General's Reference (No 2 of 1975)* [1976] 2 All ER 753 at 765, [1976] 1 WLR 710 at 714:

'A reference of a point of law under s 36 of the 1972 Act is not a reference in the abstract but is in relation to the case in which the point has arisen.'

The point of law as referred begins with reference to a fund constituted by a mixture of money. There was no mixture of money in this case. The question continues with reference to a bank account constituted by a mixture of money. The court will deal with that part of the question, although we do not suggest that a mixed fund of money in specie would necessarily require to be treated in any different manner.

The point of law as stated also refers to the fact that the bank account of the thief in this case had been fed with money of the three types stated: sums honestly received for onward payment to other employees; sums honestly received by and for the thief herself; and stolen money, ie the proceeds of cheques obtained by fraud. At the time of payment of the cheque for £288·53 to the accused, that sum could not be objectively identified as coming from any one of the three types of money. So much is obvious from the nature of a bank account in which the balance is stated, for the purposes of the banker and of the customer, as the sum of the various credits and debits. At the trial, the attitude of the prosecution was, as stated by the judge, that it was impossible to say what part of the money in the thief's account represented stolen goods, and the prosecution therefore submitted that the intention of the parties, ie of the paying thief and of the receiver of the payment, must be looked at as at the time when the money passed. The question referred to us assumes, in conformity with that attitude, that, apart from proof of what any party to the payment *said* about her intention at the time of payment, it was impossible to demonstrate that the balance in the account at the time of payment, or the particular payment made, was to be regarded, for the purposes of the prosecution, as having originated from any particular type of money in the account.

The submissions which have been made can be summarised as follows. Counsel for the accused, who has appeared to support the ruling made by the judge, has submitted that the offence of handling cannot be committed with reference to a thing in action, at least so far as concerns handling by receiving. He made it clear that this was not the main point of his argument and he did no more than raise the point for the court's consideration. He referred us to passages in Smith on the Law of Theft (4th Edn, 1979) and in Smith and Hogan on Criminal Law (4th Edn, 1978) in which the point was discussed.

The main submission developed by counsel for the accused was that, where a bank account was made up of a mixture of credit, some lawfully obtained and some dishonestly

obtained, as in this case, the receipt of a payment or part of that mixed fund cannot be
demonstrated as being in law the receipt of stolen goods. Once the identity of the
dishonestly obtained, or stolen, money is destroyed by mixing in the account with
untainted money, that identity as stolen money cannot be subsequently revived by any
evincing or proof of intention on the part of the holder of the account or of the recipient
of a payment. This conclusion was, said counsel, a consequence in law of the nature of
money.

Counsel on behalf of the Attorney General on the reference has submitted that a chose
in action was capable of being stolen goods within the meaning of s 24(2) of the 1968
Act, ie as—

'other goods which directly or indirectly represent . . . the stolen goods in the
hands of the thief as being the proceeds of any disposal or realisation . . . of the goods
stolen . . .'

Next, he submitted that the receipt of a payment out of a mixed bank account, like that
of the thief in this case, could be proved by admissible evidence to constitute the receipt
of stolen goods if it could thereby be shown that the intention of the thief, in making
payment out of the mixed fund, was to pay to the receiver all or part of that part of the
mixed fund which represented the stolen goods in the hands of the thief.

Counsel for the Attorney General contended that the matter should be approached by
examining first whether, on the evidence of the payments in and out of the account, it
was possible that, as at the date of the payment in question, that payment could constitute
part of the mixed fund which represented the stolen goods. If that is shown to be
possible (he argued as at the date that the cheque is drawn) then, according to his
submission, it is necessary to consider whether by admissible evidence it is demonstrated
that the thief, in paying the money, intended the payment to be part of the mixed fund
which represented the stolen goods. If a prima facie case to that effect is made out the
jury must be allowed to consider the whole case, and, if they think right, to reach the
conclusion that the payment received represented stolen goods within the meaning of
s 24(2) of the 1968 Act. If they could reach that conclusion, of course, the jury would
have to consider the other essential issues whether the defendant knew or believed the
payment to represent stolen goods and whether she received the payment dishonestly.

Perhaps because it was thought that admissible and effective evidence of the intention
of the thief in making any such payment might rarely be available, counsel contended
that the rules of common law and equity, which relate to the principle of trading
property, and the rules of equity relating to the right of a beneficiary under a trust to
trace trust assets which have passed through the bank account of a trustee to a volunteer
were of assistance to his submissions.

He said that the 1968 Act was enacted by reference to and against the background of
the general law of property, that the rules of common law and equity which relate to
tracing and restitution supported the general argument that the nature of a payment out
of a mixed fund could be determined by reference to the intention of the payer, and that
a jury should be directed in such a case as this to consider those rules of law and equity
and have regard to them in deciding whether the money paid out of the mixed fund
bank account by the thief was proved to have been part of the money dishonestly
obtained by the thief. Reference was made to a number of cases.

We can begin the statement of our opinion on the point of law referred to us by
observing that the cheque which the accused was alleged to have received was, plainly,
not part of the goods originally stolen or obtained. In order to succeed, therefore, the
prosecution had to bring the case within the terms of s 24(2) of the 1968 Act, which
defines the scope of offences relating to the handling of stolen goods. The relevant
provisions of s 24(2) read as follows:

'. . . references to stolen goods shall include . . . (a) any other goods which directly
or indirectly represent or have at any time represented the stolen goods in the hands'

of the thief as being the proceeds of any disposal or realisation of the whole or part of the goods stolen . . .'

By s 24(4) the reference to 'goods which have been stolen' includes goods which have been obtained by deception.

It was submitted that the language of s 24(2)(a) afforded some support for the first point made on behalf of the accused, namely that a thing in action cannot be handled by receiving within s 22 of the 1968 Act. By s 34(2)(b), however, the interpretation section of this Act, '"goods", except in so far as the context otherwise requires, includes money and every other description of property except land, and includes things severed from the land . . .' Further, by the combined effect of ss 4(1) and 34(2), '"Property" includes money and all other property, real or personal, including things in action . . .'

In our judgment therefore it is clear from that extended definition of 'goods' that a cheque obtained by deception constitutes stolen goods for the purposes of ss 22 and 24 of the 1968 Act.

Next, it is clear that a balance in a bank account, being a debt, is itself a thing in action which falls within the definition of goods and may therefore be goods which directly or indirectly represent stolen goods for the purposes of s 24(2)(a).

Further, where, as in the present case, a person obtains cheques by deception and pays them into her bank account, the balance in that account may, to the value of the tainted cheque, be goods which 'directly . . . represent . . . the stolen goods in the hands of the thief as being the proceeds of any disposal or realisation of the . . . goods stolen . . .' within the meaning of s 24(2)(a).

If, however, the prosecution is to prove dishonest handling by receiving, it is necessary to prove that what the handler received was in fact the whole or part of the stolen goods within the meaning of s 24(2)(a). To prove that, the prosecution must prove (i) that at the material time, namely, at the time of receipt by the handler, in such a case as this, the thief's bank balance was in fact comprised, at least in part, of that which represented the proceeds of stolen goods, and (ii) that the handler received, at least in part, such proceeds.

In some cases no difficulty will arise. For example, if the thief opened a new account and paid into it only dishonestly obtained cheques, then the whole balance would constitute stolen goods within the meaning of s 24(2)(a). If then the thief transferred the whole balance to an accused, that accused would, in our opinion, have received stolen goods.

By the same reasoning, if at the material time the whole of the balance in an account consisted only of the proceeds of stolen goods, then any cheque drawn on that account would constitute stolen goods within s 24(2)(a).

We have no doubt that when such a cheque is paid, so that part of such a balance in the thief's account is transferred to the credit of the receiver's account, the receiver has received stolen goods because he has received a thing in action which '. . . directly represents . . . the stolen goods in the hands of the thief . . . as being the proceeds of . . . realisation of the . . . goods stolen . . .'

The same conclusion follows where the receiver directly cashes the cheque drawn on the thief's account and receives money from the paying bank.

The allegation in this case was that the accused received stolen goods when she received the thief's cheque. Counsel for the accused, in the course of argument, was disposed to accept a suggestion from a member of the court that a cheque drawn by the thief, directed to her bank, and intended to enable the accused to obtain transfer of part of the thief's credit balance, or cash, might not itself be stolen goods within the meaning of s 24(2)(a). This point is not necessary for decision on the point of law referred to us and it has not been fully argued. It appears to us that there is much to be said in favour of the proposition that receipt of such a cheque, drawn in circumstances wherein it is plain that it must serve to transfer the proceeds of stolen goods, would constitute receiving stolen goods on the grounds that such a cheque would directly or indirectly represent the stolen goods within s 24(2)(a).

The difficulties arise for the prosecution where, as in the present case, the stolen
a cheques are paid into a mixed account containing sums honestly obtained. In our
opinion the difficulties are of proof and not of principle.

The mere fact that stolen cheques have been paid into a mixed account will often
render more difficult proof that at least part of what was received by an accused from that
account represented the stolen goods in the hands of the thief as being the proceeds of the
goods stolen. It does not preclude such proof.

b In some circumstances proof may be simple. For example, a particular account, into
which it is proved that stolen cheques were paid, may have been little used with few
cheques drawn on it. It might readily be demonstrated that the sum paid to the accused
was in excess of that part of the balance which could possibly represent the proceeds of
honest cheques. In such circumstances the accused would be shown to have received
stolen goods within s 24(2)(a).

c In the present case the prosecution sought such proof, as to the nature of the payment
received by the accused, from the statement which the accused made as to her
understanding and intention when the payment was made. She had said that she
regarded the payment to her as 'her share'. In our opinion, such an admission could not
by itself prove either that part of the thief's bank balance did or could represent stolen
goods within s 24(2)(a), or that part of such stolen goods was received by the accused.
d Her admission was, of course, plainly admissible on the issue of her knowledge that the
payment represented stolen goods, and as to her honesty in receiving the money. On the
issue of fact, however, whether the cheque received by her represented stolen goods, the
primary rule is that an accused can only make a valid and admissible admission of a
statement of fact of which the accused could give admissible evidence: see *Surujpaul
called Dick v Reginam* [1958] 3 All ER 300, [1958] 1 WLR 1050. It is not necessary in this
e case to examine the limits of, or the extent of any exceptions from, that primary rule.

In our opinion counsel for the Attorney General was right in his submission when he
acknowledged that the prosecution must, in such a case as this, prove in the first place
that any payment out of a mixed account *could*, by reference to payments in and out, be
a payment representing stolen goods. Unless she had personal knowledge of the working
of the thief's account, the accused could make no valid admission as to that.

f It is to be noted that the point of law referred to us contains the words 'is a jury entitled
to infer . . . from the intention of the parties . . .?' The use of the plural 'parties' is
misleading. There was no direct evidence in this case of what the intention of the thief
might have been, only of that of the receiver. It may perhaps be that a payment can be
proved to have been a payment of money representing stolen goods, even where there
was enough honest money in the account to cover the payment, if there is proof direct
g or by way of necessary inference of the intention of the paying thief to pay out the stolen
money. That problem can be decided when it arises. It does not do so here. The
prosecution did not advance their case on such a basis.

The only question arising on the facts here is whether a jury is entitled to infer that the
payment represented stolen goods within s 24(2)(a) of the 1968 Act from the intention
or belief of the receiver that it should or did. The answer is No.

h
Determination accordingly.

Solicitors: *Director of Public Prosecutions*; *Pickering & Butters*, Stafford (for the respondent).

Denise Randall   Barrister.

Note

a

Biggins v Secretary of State for the Environment and another

and other appeals

b

QUEEN'S BENCH DIVISION
WOOLF J
27th MARCH 1981

*Practice – Dismissal of action for want of prosecution – Applications to quash certain orders or c
decisions of a minister or government department – Applications affecting other parties as well
as immediate parties to applications – Undesirability of leaving applications outstanding
indefinitely – Applications to be entered in Special Paper List – Applications to be dismissed if not
prosecuted without delay – RSC Ord 94.*

Appeals

d

At the direction of the Queen's Bench Division of the High Court, eleven appeals, viz (1)
Biggins v Secretary of State for the Environment and another, (2) *E & H Langman (Welling) Ltd
v Secretary of State for the Environment and another*, (3) *Ready Mixed Concrete (Lincolnshire)
Ltd v Secretary of State for the Environment and another*, (4) *Coyne v Secretary of State for the
Environment and another*, (5) *Parpas v Secretary of State for the Environment and another*,
(6) *Watneys London Ltd v Secretary of State for Transport*, (7) *Ashcroft and another v Secretary* e
of State for the Environment and another, (8) *Harrison v London Rent Assessment Committee*,
(9) *Vesclare Holdings Ltd and another v London Borough of Waltham Forest and another*,
(10) *Oldroyd v Secretary of State for the Environment and another* and (11) *Roberts v Secretary
of State for Social Services*, being appeals which were entered on various dates between
1975 and 1978 but in which no further steps had been taken, were by ex parte motion
listed for hearing on 27th March 1981 with a view to their being dismissed for want of f
prosecution. The appeal in *Ashcroft v Secretary of State for the Environment* was disposed
of by consent.

Simon D Brown for the respondents.
The appellants did not appear or were not represented.

g

WOOLF J. Each of the appeals which were listed and which have been called before me
were appeals to the High Court under the provisions of RSC Ord 94.

Order 94 indicates the general nature of the appeals which are dealt with under that
Order. It provides in r 1(1):

> 'Where by virtue of any enactment the High Court has jurisdiction, on the h
> application of any person, to quash any order, scheme, certificate or plan, any
> amendment or approval of a plan, any decision of a Minister or government
> department or any action on the part of a Minister or government department, the
> jurisdiction shall be exercisable by a single judge of the Queen's Bench Division.'

Many of the appeals which are dealt with under that Order affect not only the j
immediate parties to the appeal but other persons as well. The appeals are, therefore,
ones which it is undesirable to leave outstanding indefinitely.

The cases which were listed today and which have been called on were all appeals
which were entered between 1975 and 1978. Thereafter there had been complete
inactivity.

Accordingly, in February of this year letters were written to the solicitors of the
a appellants in these terms:

> 'I am writing at the direction of the Court to draw your attention to this matter
> which was entered in this office on [and then it gave the date]. If it is your client's
> intention to proceed with this appeal you should inform this office as soon as
> possible. If it is intended to withdraw this appeal you should complete and return
> the enclosed form of withdrawal. If no reply is received within 10 days of the date
b > of this letter this appeal will be listed for hearing without further notice with a view
> to it being dismissed for want of prosecution.'

No reply was received in any of the cases which were listed, and accordingly a letter
was subsequently written to all the parties following the lack of response in these terms:

> 'I write at the direction of the Court to inform you that this matter will be listed
c > for hearing on Friday the 27th March 1981 at 10.30 a.m. with a view to its being
> dismissed for want of prosecution.'

With the exception of one case in the list (*Ashcroft v Secretary of State for the Environment*)
which is now being disposed of by consent, in each of the other cases the court will order
that they will be dismissed for want of prosecution.

d The court having taken that course, it is appropriate on this occasion to remind the
profession of the new arrangements which have been made to deal with appeals of this
sort. These are now entered in the new Special Paper List administered by the Head
Clerk of the Crown Office. There are exceptions. Those are preliminary issues, points
of law, motions to commit, motions for judgment and motions under RSC Ord 73
released by the Commercial Judge. The cases which I have referred to as exceptions
e continue to be administered by the Clerk of the Lists.

In the case of appeals such as the ones that were listed this morning, a considerable
backlog had developed, as was the case with the Divisional Court List. This backlog has
in the past led to substantial delay in the disposal of those appeals.

Happily under the new arrangements the position is considerably improved. It is
expected that in the near future the normal time for disposal of such appeals will be
f within three months. It is hoped that urgent cases will be dealt with quicker than that.

Such a satisfactory position will require the co-operation of both sides of the profession.
I am sure that that co-operation will be forthcoming and I recognise that, initially, the
speedy disposal will place a burden on the profession. At the same time as I recognise
that that co-operation will be forthcoming I should give a warning that, if in fact cases are
not prosecuted, the same course which was adopted today will be adopted in the future
g where appropriate and the cases will be listed by the court so that consideration can be
given to their dismissal for want of prosecution.

Appeals dismissed.

Solicitors: *Treasury Solicitor.*

Sepala Munasinghe Esq   Barrister.

Dunlop v Woollahra Municipal Council   *a*

PRIVY COUNCIL

LORD DIPLOCK, LORD SIMON OF GLAISDALE, LORD EDMUND-DAVIES, LORD SCARMAN AND LORD BRIDGE OF HARWICH

12th, 13th, 14th JANUARY, 23rd FEBRUARY 1981

Tort – Action on the case – Unlawful act – Action for loss or harm suffered as inevitable consequence of defendant's unlawful, intentional and positive act – Legal advice subsequently proving wrong – Whether loss or harm suffered as result of invalid act also giving rise to cause of action.

Negligence – Duty to take care – Action taken as result of legal advice – Local authority passing invalid resolution affecting plaintiff – Resolution passed on legal advice – Whether authority in breach of duty of care to plaintiff not to pass ultra vires resolution.

Negligence – Duty to take care – Breach of rules of natural justice – Local authority breaching rules of natural justice – Whether breach of rules of natural justice amounting to breach of duty of care owed to person affected.

Public office – Abuse of – Ingredients of tort – Misfeasance a necessary element.

In December 1972 the appellant purchased a property in a residential area using a bank loan to finance the purchase. The appellant, in conjunction with the owners of two adjoining properties, hoped to obtain planning consent for the erection of one or more 8-storey buildings of residential flats on the site and then sell the site to a development company at a price greatly enhanced by the planning consent. The local planning authority ('the council') were opposed to the proposed development, and on the advice of their solicitors, passed two resolutions, one restricting the building of residential flats on the site to three storeys and the other imposing a building line restriction requiring any new building on the site to be set back a certain distance from the boundary. Both resolutions were, on legal advice, passed in the form of building restrictions imposed by the council acting in their capacity as the local authority rather than as planning restrictions imposed by a planning authority. The appellant obtained declarations that both resolutions were invalid and void. In particular, the resolution restricting the number of storeys was held to be ultra vires, while the resolution imposing the building line restriction was held to be invalid because the appellant had not been given the opportunity to which, so it was held, he was entitled of presenting objections before the resolution was passed. The judge specifically found that the council had not acted mala fide in passing the resolutions. By reason of a slump in the property market in the period between the passing of the resolutions and the appellant's obtaining the declarations the appellant was not able to sell his property at the price he originally envisaged and was forced to incur overdraft charges, rates and taxes for a further two years before he could find a buyer at an acceptable price. The appellant brought an action against the council claiming damages for the loss suffered as a result of the invalid resolutions. He contended that he had a cause of action against the council for (i) trespass on the case in that he had suffered loss as the inevitable consequence of the unlawful, intentional and positive acts of the council, (ii) negligence in that the council had failed to take reasonable care by seeking proper legal advice before passing the resolution restricting the number of storeys and had failed to take reasonable care to give him a proper hearing before passing the building line resolution, and (iii) abuse of public office by the council in passing the resolutions. The trial judge dismissed the appellant's claim and he appealed to the Privy Council.

Held – The appeal would be dismissed for the following reasons—

a (1) The principle of law that a person was entitled to recover damages in an action on the case for loss or harm suffered as the inevitable consequence of the unlawful, intentional and positive act of another only applied if the act was illegal or forbidden by law and did not apply to an act which was merely null and void and incapable of affecting legal rights. The council's resolutions being merely invalid and not unlawful, the appellant's claim for damages on the case failed (see p 1208 *h* to p 1209 *c* and p 1210 *c*,

b post); *Beaudesert Shire Council v Smith* (1966) 120 CLR 145 considered.

(2) The appellant's claim in negligence failed because—

(a) assuming the council owed the appellant a duty of care to ascertain whether the resolution restricting the number of storeys was within their statutory power to pass (and it was doubtful whether such a duty of care existed), no breach of that duty had been proved since the council had received advice, albeit wrong advice, from qualified

c solicitors; and in any event prior to the decision that the resolution was invalid the question whether the council had power to pass the resolution was so evenly balanced that giving advice either way would not have amounted to negligence (see p 1209 *d* to g and p 1210 *c*, post);

(b) the failure by a public authority to give a person an adequate hearing before exercising a statutory power which affected him or his property was not by itself a breach

d of a duty of care giving rise to damages, because the effect of the failure was merely to render the exercise of the power void, and the person affected, being just as able as the public authority to deduce that fact, was entitled to ignore it since it was incapable of affecting his legal rights (see p 1209 *h* to p 1210 *a* and *c*, post).

(3) Misfeasance was a necessary element in the tort of abuse of public office, and, in the absence of malice, the passing by a public authority of a resolution which was devoid

e of legal effect when the authority had no prior knowledge of the invalidity was not conduct capable of amounting to misfeasance. The appellant's claim that the council had abused their public office therefore failed (see p 1210 *b c*, post).

Notes

For actions on the case, see Supplement to 30 Halsbury's Laws (3rd Edn) para 549A.22.

f For negligence by a public authority in relation to its statutory functions, see 34 Halsbury's Laws (4th Edn) paras 4, 7.

For abuse of public office, see 30 Halsbury's Laws (3rd Edn) 702–705, paras 1346–1347.

Cases referred to in judgment

g *Beaudesert Shire Council v Smith* (1966) 120 CLR 145, HC of Aust.

Dunlop v Council of the Municipality of Woollahra [1975] 2 NSWLR 446.

Grand Central Car Park v Tivoli Freeholders [1969] VR 62.

Kitano v The Commonwealth (1973) 129 CLR 151.

Mogul Steamship Co v McGregor, Gow & Co [1892] AC 25, [1891–4] All ER Rep 263, 61 LJQB 295, 66 LT 1, 56 JP 101, 7 Asp MLC 120, HL; *affg* (1889) 23 QBD 598, 58 LJQB

h 465, 61 LT 820, 53 JP 709, 6 Asp MLC 455, CA, 12 Digest (Reissue) 288, 2087.

Appeal

Dr Roger Massie Dunlop appealed, pursuant to leave granted by the Supreme Court of New South Wales, against a final judgment of the Common Law Division of that court given by Yeldham J on 28th July 1978 dismissing an action brought by the appellant, as

j plaintiff, against the respondents, the Council of the Municipality of Woollahra, as defendants, for damages for losses suffered by the appellant in consequence of two invalid resolutions passed by the council on 10th June 1974 in purported exercise of their powers under ss 308(1) and 309(4) of the Local Government Act 1919 (NSW). The facts are set out in the judgment of the Board.

A B Shand QC, B Rayment (both of the New South Wales Bar) and *R Toulson* for Dr Dunlop.
Murray Wilcox QC and *P D McClellan* (both of the New South Wales Bar) for the council.   *a*

LORD DIPLOCK. The action in which this appeal to Her Majesty in Council is brought by the unsuccessful plaintiff ('Dr Dunlop') is the sequel to a previous action *Dunlop v Council of the Municipality of Woollahra* [1975] 2 NSWLR 446 between the self-same parties tried before Wootten J, in which the plaintiff was successful. From that *b* judgment the defendant ('the council') did not appeal. Both that action and the present action arose out of two resolutions which the council passed on 10th June 1974 in purported exercise of their powers under ss 308 and 309 respectively in Part XI of the Local Government Act 1919 to fix a building line for Dr Dunlop's property at 8 Wentworth Street, Point Piper, and to regulate the number of storeys which might be contained in any residential flat building erected on that property.   *c*

In the first action Dr Dunlop sought and obtained from Wootten J on 26th September 1975 declarations that each of the resolutions was invalid and void, the resolution fixed a building line because a procedural requirement as to giving notice to Dr Dunlop had not been satisfied and the resolution regulating the number of storeys because it was ultra vires. The judge expressly rejected Dr Dunlop's allegation that in passing the resolutions the council were not acting bona fide.   *d*

In the instant case, which was tried by Yeldham J, Dr Dunlop claimed to recover from the council damages which he alleged he had sustained as a result of the invalid resolutions during the period from the passing of the resolutions on 10th June 1974 to 25th October 1975, this being the last day on which the council might have appealed against the judgment of Wootten J. In the present action the council are estopped from contending that either of the resolutions was valid, since those were issues that had been *e* decided against them by the judgment in the previous action against which they had not appealed. Dr Dunlop in his turn is prevented, by a similar issue estoppel, from asserting that in passing the resolutions the council were acting mala fide. This being so he put his cause of action arising from the passing of the invalid resolutions in three different ways: (1) as trespass on the case within the principle laid down in *Beaudesert Shire Council v Smith* (1966) 120 CLR 145 ('the *Beaudesert* claim'); (2) as negligence; and (3) as abuse of public *f* office. Yeldham J held that Dr Dunlop had no right of action sounding in damages under any of these three heads. He accordingly dismissed the action and gave judgment for the council. It is against this judgment that the instant appeal is brought.

The relevant facts up to the date of the resolutions are set out in extensive detail in the judgment of Wootten J. They are summarised again in the judgment of Yeldham J, which contains a detailed statement of the relevant facts subsequent to that date. Their *g* Lordships will accordingly content themselves with as brief a summary as is compatible with a proper understanding of the ways in which the three causes of action relied on by Dr Dunlop were put and the reasons why Yeldham J rejected each of them.

The area in which Wentworth Street is situate is subject to the provisions of the Woollahra Planning Scheme Ordinance prescribed by the Governor under Part XIIA of the Local Government Act 1919. Under this scheme the council were the responsible *h* authority. Point Piper was in an area which was zoned for use for residential purposes. The residential zones under the scheme are divided into classes according to the nature of the development permitted (a) without the approval of the responsible authority, (b) only with their approval and (c) not at all. Any development which involved building, however, before it was undertaken would require the approval of the council, not in their capacity as responsible authority under the scheme, but as council of the area for the *j* purposes of Part XI of the Local Government Act 1919, B which is headed 'Building regulation'. It is convenient to speak of approval by the council given as responsible authority under the scheme as 'planning permission' and approval given by them under Part XI of the Act as 'building permission'.

The classes of residential zones under the scheme which are relevant for present
a purposes are those numbered 2(*a*), 2(*b*) and 2(*c*). Dr Dunlop's property in Wentworth
Street formed part of a small triangular area that was zoned 2(*c*), but was surrounded by
areas that were zoned 2(*a*). The relevant difference between these zones is that in zones
2(*a*) and 2(*b*) buildings containing residential flats that are more than three storeys high
are absolutely prohibited, whereas in zone 2(*c*) residential flat buildings of more than
three storeys may be erected but only with the planning permission of the council, and
b subject to the proviso that in that part of the zone 2(*c*) in which Wentworth Street is
situated their total height above sea level does not exceed 235·5 feet.

The scheme came into operation in December 1972, and in the same month Dr
Dunlop, who had an interest in 10 Wentworth Street under a family trust, bought the
next door property, no 8, with a view to selling it for development in conjunction with
no 10 and no 12, which was owned by a Mr Howarth. In January 1973 Dr Dunlop, the
c trustees of no 10 and Mr Howarth entered into conditional contracts with a development
company for the sale of these three properties, the condition being that within a limited
time planning permission should have been obtained for the erection on the three
properties of a multi-storey flat building. An application for planning permission to
erect two 8-storey tower buildings was made by the development company in February
1973. Planning permission was refused by the council in September 1973. Against that
d refusal the development company appealed to the Local Government Appeals Tribunal
under Part XIIB of the Local Government Act 1919. The appeal was dismissed by that
tribunal on 6th May 1974 and the development company rescinded its contract with Dr
Dunlop and the other vendors on 23rd May 1974.

In rejecting the appeal on the grounds that the development company's proposal for
two 8-storey buildings would be an overdevelopment of the site, that it would be out of
keeping with the existing character of Wentworth Street and that the provisions for car
e parking were unsatisfactory, the tribunal indicated its opinion that some residential flat
development on a reduced scale should be allowed and that this need not be limited to
three storeys.

On receipt of this decision the council were advised by their solicitors that if on sound
planning grounds they wanted to limit flat buildings erected on 8, 10 and 12 Wentworth
f Street to a maximum of three storeys they should, as the council of the area, exercise their
power under s 309(4) of the Local Government Act 1919 to regulate the number of
storeys in any residential flat building on those properties at no more than three. The
council's planning officer supported this proposal on planning grounds and repeated a
recommendation that she had made previously that, in the same capacity as the council
of the area, they should exercise their powers under s 308 to fix an appropriate building
g line for the three properties.

These recommendations were accepted and at a meeting of the council on 10th June
1974 the two resolutions complained of were passed. At some time before this date there
had been a meeting between Dr Dunlop and representatives of the council at which his
future plans for the development of his property were discussed. He was then informed
of the council's proposal to exericse their power under s 309(4), but no specific mention
h was made of any proposal to fix a building line under s 308.

On being notified of these resolutions by the council Dr Dunlop employed an architect
to examine whether a development involving flat buildings limited to three storeys
would be worthwhile from the financial point of view having regard to the price that he
had paid for 8 Wentworth Street. By the end of June 1974 the architect advised him that
it would not, and shortly after Dr Dunlop started his first action against the council for
j declarations that the two resolutions were invalid on the ground that he was entitled to
prior notice of the council's proposal to pass the resolutions and an opportunity to put his
case against them, which he alleged was not afforded him, and, in the case of the
resolution regulating the number of storeys, that it was void on the additional ground
that it was ultra vires because it was inconsistent with cl 44 of the Woollahra Planning

Scheme Ordinance. This action came on for hearing in July 1975 and, as already mentioned, judgment in Dr Dunlop's favour was given on 26th September 1975.

In the meantime while that action was still pending Dr Dunlop, on 24th November 1974, submitted a fresh application to the council for planning permission for the erection of a residential flat building of eight storeys on 8 Wentworth Street alone. This application was refused by the council by resolution of 14th July 1975. Twelve reasons were given for this refusal of which only one, the sixth, was based on the council's resolutions of 10th June 1974. Against this refusal Dr Dunlop did not exercise his right of appeal to the Local Government Appeal Tribunal, because he recognised that independently of the resolutions of 10th June 1974 there were other respects in which the development proposed in this application was unsatisfactory.

In April 1976, some six months after the judgment of Wootten J and the expiry of the council's time for appealing from it, Dr Dunlop engaged a fresh architect who on 27th July 1976 submitted to the council a fresh application for planning permission in respect of 8 Wentworth Street alone. This application was for a 7-storey building containing residential flats. The council approved this application in December 1976. Dr Dunlop then put 8 Wentworth Street on the market; but he was unable to find a buyer for it at a price that he was willing to accept until 18th August 1977.

By then Dr Dunlop had started his second action against the council, in which this appeal is brought. In each of the three ways in which he puts his cause of action against the council proof of actual damage resulting from the conduct complained of is an essential element in the cause of action. To succeed on the *Beaudesert* claim the damage suffered must also be the 'inevitable consequence' of such conduct. The only act of the council relied on as resulting in actual damage to Dr Dunlop is the passing of the two resolutions on 10th June 1974. He makes no complaint about the refusal of his application for planning permission lodged in November 1974. Before examining the ways in which his cause of action is pleaded it is, in their Lordships' view, convenient to consider briefly what would have been the legal effect on his property of the two resolutions if they had been valid.

Part XI of the Local Government Act 1919 dealing with building regulation is earlier in date than Part XIIA dealing with town and country planning schemes. For the most part it is concerned with the need to obtain the specific approval of the council of an area for the erection or alteration of a particular building, but it does, by s 308, confer on the council of an area a more general power to fix building lines for any part of their area, and, by s 309, a power to obtain proclamations declaring parts of their area to be residential districts, and also to regulate the number of storeys which may be contained in flat buildings erected anywhere in their area. Planning schemes made under Part XIIA (though they need not do so) contain provisions which have the same effect as the fixing of a building line, or the regulating of the number of storeys which may be contained in residential flat buildings. The effect of building lines and regulation of the number of storeys is restrictive only; they confer no positive right on the owner of any property to build up to the building line or up to the maximum number of storeys. He still requires specific planning permission and building permission to do this on his particular property, and such permission may be withheld. Prima facie restrictions imposed by the council of an area under ss 308 and 309 and those imposed under a planning scheme are cumulative. The development for which the owner of the property applies for building permission must comply with both: s 310(a) so provides. Section 342(G)(4), however, provides that a scheme made under Part XIIA may (though it need not do so) suspend the operation of any provision of the Act, including ss 308 and 309, to the extent that the provision or any action taken under it is inconsistent with any of the provisions of the scheme.

The effect of the resolutions, if valid, would thus have been to impose on the development of 8, 10 and 12 Wentworth Street restrictions additional to those contained in the scheme itself; and, although the council could remove them at any time at or

before an application for building permission was sought, their Lordships would accept
a that the existence of valid regulations in the terms of those passed by the council on 10th
June 1974 would reduce the market value of no 8 as land ripe for development.

However, by the end of September 1975, the resolutions had been held by Wootten J
to be invalid; but Dr Dunlop did not sell 8 Wentworth Street until some years after their
invalidity had been established and the value of his property restored. His claim for
damages was accordingly based on the contention that, during the period between the
b passing of the resolutions and the date on which the declaration of their invalidity by
Wootten J was no longer subject to appeal, he was deprived of the opportunity of selling
his property at its true value. The property had been bought by him on overdraft and he
claims as damages moneys paid during that period by way of interest on the overdraft
and rates and taxes on the property, together with a small sum paid to his architect for
examining whether a viable development of the property in conformity with the
c resolutions was possible.

Yeldham J did not find it necessary to decide whether Dr Dunlop had proved that he
had in fact suffered any damage, even on this basis. The bottom had dropped out of the
property market in 1974 and he did not in fact find a purchaser at a price that he was
willing to accept until August 1977 despite the continuing overdraft charges and rates
and taxes. The learned judge was satisfied that even if some damnum could have been
d established it would have been damnum sine injuria. Since, as will appear, their
Lordships agree with him that no actionable wrong on the part of the council had been
established, they do not find it necessary to decide whether or not the persuasive
argument on behalf of the council that Dr Dunlop failed to prove that he had suffered
any damage, let alone any inevitable damage, as a result of the passing of the resolutions
ought to be accepted.

e Their Lordships accordingly now turn to the paragraphs of the statement of claim
which contain the three different ways in Dr Dunlop's cause of action is put. (Paragraph
10 has been omitted; it contained an allegation of mala fides which was not open to Dr
Dunlop because of the issue estoppel resulting from Wootten J's judgment, and was very
properly abandoned.)

f
'9. On 10th June 1974 [the council] unlawfully and intentionally passed certain
resolutions in respect of the premises 8–12 Wentworth Street, Point Piper and each
of them which purported to have the effect of limiting the number of storeys of
buildings on the said land to three and also purported to fix certain boundary set-
backs in respect of buildings to be erected on the said land . . .

g
'11. The resolution as to the number of storeys on the land was contrary to the
Council's prescribed planning scheme ordinance.

'12. The resolution as to the boundary set-backs was unlawful being in breach of
[the council's], duty to act fairly as required by the Local Government Act.

'13. [Dr Dunlop] suffered loss as the inevitable consequence of the unlawful
intentional and positive acts of [the council] referred to in and about the passing of
h the said resolutions in that inter alia he was delayed in putting his land to its highest
and best economic use and also had to pay interest, expenses, and legal costs until
such time as the unlawful resolutions referred to above were set aside by the
Supreme Court . . .

'15. Further, in the alternative to paragraphs 13 and 14 above, [the council] was
under a duty to [Dr Dunlop] to perform its duties under Parts XI and XIIA of the
j Local Government Act in dealing with building and development controls with
respect to the said land, in a reasonable, careful and responsible manner but [the
council] in and about passing the said resolutions acted unreasonably, negligently
and irresponsibly whereby [Dr Dunlop] suffered the loss and damage referred to in
paragraph 13 above.

'15A. Further, in the alternative, [the council] was a public corporate body which occupied a public office and was incorporated by a public statute and which had power to and did exact revenue from ratepayers in its area under the Local Government Act to enable it to perform its public duties and [the council] abused its said office and public duty under the said Statute by purporting to pass each of the said resolutions with the consequence that damage was occasioned to [Dr Dunlop].'

The Beaudesert claim

Paragraph 13 is clearly based on the words used by the High Court in *Beaudesert Shire Council v Smith* (1966) 120 CLR 145 at 156 to lay down a broad principle of law which the three members of the court considered could be extracted from eight English cases, mostly old, which they had previously cited:

'... it appears that the authorities cited do justify a proposition that, independently of trespass, negligence or nuisance but by an action for damages upon the case, a person who suffers harm or loss as the inevitable consequence of the unlawful, intentional and positive acts of another is entitled to recover damages from that other.'

Their Lordships understand that they are not alone in finding difficulty in ascertaining what limits are imposed on the scope of this innominate tort by the requirements that in order to constitute it the acts of the tortfeasor must be 'positive', having as their 'inevitable consequence' harm or loss to the plaintiff and, what is crucial in the instant case, must be 'unlawful'. The eight cases referred to as a solid body of authority for the proposition appear to be so miscellaneous in character that they throw no further light on the matter. Nor, although *Beaudesert* was decided some 14 years ago, has it been clarified by judicial exegesis in the Australian courts, or followed in any other common law jurisdiction. It has never been applied in Australia in any subsequent case. In *Kitano v The Commonwealth* (1973) 129 CLR 151 Mason J, whose reasons for judgment were later adopted by the Full Court of the High Court of Australia, expressed the view that an act done in breach of a statutory duty in respect of which the statute neither expressly nor by implication provides a civil remedy in damages is not necessarily 'unlawful' within the meaning of the *Beaudesert* principle although it clearly is unlawful in the ordinary sense of that term. A plaintiff, said Mason J (at 175), 'must show something over and above what would ground liability for breach of statutory duty if the action were available', but what that something more was he did not attempt to identify. He held that the plaintiff, Kitano, did not bring himself within the *Beaudesert* principle because, inter alia, 'he had not succeeded in showing that the act was tortious (and not merely a contravention of the statute)'. In *Grand Central Car Park v Tivoli Freeholders* [1969] VR 62 McInerney J held that carrying on a trade without a permit in contravention of a statute did not fall within the epithet 'unlawful' in the formulation of the *Beaudesert* principle.

In the instant case Yeldham J did not find it necessary to embark on a general consideration of what kinds of act were intended by the authors of the judgment in *Beaudesert* to be included in the expression 'unlawful'. The only acts relied on were the passing of two invalid resolutions; so what he was concerned with, and what their Lordships are concerned with, was a specific question: whether an act which in law is null and void and so incapable of affecting any legal rights is, *for that reason only*, included in that expression. The learned judge found no difficulty in answering that question in the negative. He pointed out that in the *Beaudesert* judgment the principle is stated twice, once before the citation of the old authorities relied on (at 152) and once after (at 156), and that in the earlier statement the word 'unlawful' is replaced by 'forbidden by law'. He went on to cite a number of English cases in which the distinction between unlawfulness or illegality on the one hand and invalidity on the other is clearly drawn.

Of these their Lordships need only mention *Mogul Steamship Co Ltd v McGregor, Gow & Co*, both in the Court of Appeal ((1889) 23 QBD 598) and in the House of Lords ([1892] AC 25, [1891–4] All ER Rep 263). The rejection of one of the appellant's arguments in that case turned on this very distinction.

It is true, as Lord Halsbury LC pointed out in the above-cited case, that prior to 1892 the word 'unlawful' had sometimes been used to describe acts that were void and incapable of giving rise to legal right or obligation; but this extended use of the expression he condemned as inaccurate and so far as their Lordships are aware it has not been used in that extended sense in any subsequent English judgments. Their Lordships have no doubt that in using the expression 'unlawful' in *Beaudesert* the High Court intended it to be understood in what for the past 90 years has been its only accurate meaning. Their Lordships accordingly agree with Yeldham J that Dr Dunlop fails on his *Beaudesert* claim.

Negligence

The basis of Dr Dunlop's allegation of negligence by the council in passing the resolution regulating the number of storeys that might be contained in any flat building on 8, 10 and 12 Wentworth Street at not more than three was that they owed him a duty to take reasonable care to ascertain whether such a resolution was within their statutory powers. The breach of this duty of care that was alleged was the council's failure to seek proper detailed legal advice.

After discussing a number of Australian, English and Canadian cases Yeldham J felt considerable doubt, which their Lordships share, as to the existence of any such duty of care owed to Dr Dunlop, but he found it unnecessary to go into this interesting jurisprudential problem since he was clear that even assuming the existence of such a duty no breach of it had been proved. The council's resolution of 10th June 1974 limiting the number of storeys was passed on the initiative and advice of their solicitors, as a lawful means of preventing the erection of residential flat buildings of more than three storeys on the properties in question if they were satisfied that this was desirable on planning grounds. What more could the council be reasonably expected to do than to obtain the advice of qualified solicitors whose competence they had no reason to doubt? It is true that Wootten J held that the legal advice which the council had received from their solicitors had been wrong; but it is only fair to the reputation of the solicitors who gave it to add that, until that judgment made the matter res judicata between the parties, the question of law, which turned on the construction to be placed on two clauses in the planning scheme and in particular on whether or not a restriction on the maximum number of storeys in residential flat buildings was inconsistent with a restriction on the maximum height above sea level of all buildings, was an evenly balanced one and, in their Lordships' view, to answer it either way at any time before that judgment could not have amounted to negligence on the part of a solicitor whose advice was sought on the matter.

As respects the resolution which purported to fix the building lines the only ground on which Wootten J held this to be void was because the council had failed to give Dr Dunlop the kind of hearing to which he was entitled before they passed it, and, in particular, because he should have been specifically informed, but was not, that the council were contemplating exercising their powers under s 308 to fix building lines. This question too was not an easy one, as is shown by the fact that it took Wootten J 20 closely reasoned pages of his judgment and the citation of some two score of authorities to reach the conclusion that he did. Yeldham J held that failure by a public authority to give a person an adequate hearing before deciding to exercise a statutory power in a manner which will affect him or his property cannot by itself amount to a breach of a duty of care sounding in damages. Their Lordships agree. The effect of the failure is to render the exercise of the power void and the person complaining of the failure is in as good a position as the public authority to know that that is so. He can ignore the purported exercise of the power. It is incapable of affecting his legal rights.

In agreement with Yeldham J their Lordships are of opinion that the claim in negligence fails too.

a

Abuse of public office

In pleading in para 15A of the statement of claim that the council abused their public office and public duty Dr Dunlop was relying on the well-established tort of misfeasance by a public officer in the discharge of his public duties. Yeldham J rightly accepted that the council as a statutory corporation exercising local governmental functions were a *b* public officer for the purposes of this tort. He cited a number of authorities on the nature of this tort, to which their Lordships do not find it necessary to refer, for they agree with his conclusion that, in the absence of malice, passing without knowledge of its invalidity a resolution which is devoid of any legal effect is not conduct that of itself is capable of amounting to such 'misfeasance' as is a necessary element in this tort. So, in their Lordships' view, the claim as framed in para 15A also fails.   *c*

Their Lordships will humbly advise Her Majesty that this appeal should be dismissed. Dr Dunlop must pay the council's costs.

Appeal dismissed.

Solicitors: *Reynolds, Porter, Chamberlain* (for Dr Dunlop); *Young, Jones, Hair & Co* (for the council).

Mary Rose Plummer   Barrister.

Williams v Home Office (No 2)

QUEEN'S BENCH DIVISION

TUDOR EVANS J

25th–29th FEBRUARY, 3rd–7th, 10th–14th, 17th–21st, 24th, 25th MARCH, 9th MAY 1980

Prison – Prison conditions – Removal from association – Control unit – Legality – Unit established in ordinary prison to deal with troublemakers – Prisoners in unit not allowed to associate with one another – Strict regime imposed – Whether Secretary of State having power to set up control unit – Whether detention of prisoners in unit justifiable – Whether regime in unit a 'cruell and unusuall punishment' and contrary to Bill of Rights – Prison Act 1952, s 12(1) – Prison Rules 1964 (SI 1964 No 388), r 43.

False imprisonment – Prisoner serving sentence – Removal from association – Control unit – Unit established in ordinary prison to deal with troublemakers – Prisoners in unit not allowed to associate with one another – Strict regime imposed – Whether detention in unit unlawful – Prison Act 1952, s 12(1) – Prison Rules 1964 (SI 1964 No 388), r 43.

Natural justice – Prison – Control unit – Prisoner transferred from ordinary prison to control unit – Control unit involving separation from other prisoners and strict regime – Whether Secretary of State under duty to inform prisoner of reason for transfer and give him opportunity of making representations.

In accordance with a circular instruction issued by the Secretary of State for Home Affairs, a special control unit was established in 1974 at Wakefield Prison as a means of containing and controlling prisoners who were considered to be troublemakers and inducing them to realise that it was in their own interests to improve their behaviour. The regime in the unit was divided into two stages, each lasting 90 days. During stage 1 a prisoner was confined mainly to his cell and was denied almost all association with other prisoners. He was not obliged to work but the 90 days under stage 1 did not start to run until he did so. During stage 2 the prisoner was allowed a degree of association with the other prisoners in the unit. If he failed to work or caused trouble during stage 2, he reverted to stage 1 and was required to complete a further period of 90 days' good behaviour before qualifying for re-entry to the second stage. Once he had completed a full period of 180 days he qualified for return to normal prison life. In 1974 the governor of the prison where the plaintiff was serving a term of 14 years' imprisonment imposed on him in 1971 requested that he be transferred to the control unit. The plaintiff had not been charged with any disciplinary offence under the Prison Rules 1964 but he was considered by the governor to be a totally subversive and dedicated troublemaker. On 20th August the governor's request was considered and approved by the control unit committee, acting for the Secretary of State under r 43(1)[a] of the 1964 rules, which provided for the removal of a prisoner from association with other prisoners where it was considered desirable in the interests of good order and discipline. On 23rd August the plaintiff was transferred to the control unit. A card in his cell informed him in general terms why he had been transferred to the unit and told him of his right to make requests and complaints. The control unit committee did not meet to consider his case again until 10th February 1975 when they authorised his release to normal prison life on 18th February (ie 180 days after he had entered the unit). Shortly afterwards the control unit was closed down. In 1980 the plaintiff was released from prison on parole. He brought an action against the Home Office claiming damages for false imprisonment in respect of the 180-day period he spent in the control unit, and a declaration that the Home Office had acted ultra vires and unlawfully in setting up and operating the control

---

a   Rule 43, so far as material, is set out at p 1228 *b c*, post

unit pursuant to the circular instruction. He contended that his imprisonment was
unlawful during his detention in the control unit (i) because the nature of the
imprisonment there was different from and worse than that in the remainder of the
prison system and was in breach of the 1964 rules, (ii) because the Home Office could not
rely on s 12(1)^b of the Prison Act 1952 to justify his detention in the unit since s 12(1)
merely empowered the Secretary of State to confine him to prison and was not concerned
with the nature of the imprisonment, (iii) because the Secretary of State, acting through
the control unit committee, had no power to act under r 43(1) of the 1964 rules since the
only person who could do so was a prison governor, (iv) because, even if the Secretary of
State had power to act under r 43, the plaintiff's detention was in any event unlawful
after his first month in the unit since there was no review of his case in accordance with
r 43(2), (v) because the regime in the unit was punitive in character and contrary not only
to the policy and object of the 1952 Act and the 1964 rules but also to the Bill of Rights
which prohibited the infliction of 'cruell and unusuall punishments', which, he
submitted, was to be interpreted as meaning 'cruel or unusual punishments', and (vi)
because, contrary to the rules of natural justice, the plaintiff had not been specifically told
why he was being transferred to the unit nor was he given an opportunity of making
representations why he should not be detained there.

Held – (1) The action for damages for false imprisonment would be dismissed for the
following reasons—

(a) the sentence imposed on the plaintiff in 1971 and s 12(1) of the 1952 Act justified
his confinement in any prison (see p 1241 a b, post);

(b) the Secretary of State had power to act under r 43 of the 1964 rules and that power
had been properly exercised for one month from 20th August 1974 by the agency which
he adopted for that purpose, ie the control unit committee (see p 1228 j to p 1229 b,
post);

(c) although r 43(2) required a review at the end of one month of the position of a
prisoner who had been removed from association with other prisoners under r 43(1), the
fact that the control unit committee had not complied with r 43(2) did not affect the
lawfulness of the plaintiff's detention in the unit (see p 1231 d e j, post);

(d) furthermore, the lawfulness of his detention could not be affected by the
conditions of his detention since they were a matter for the Secretary of State and a
prisoner's safeguard against unacceptable conditions lay in his right under the 1964 rules
to complain to the prison governor or to the Secretary of State (see p 1227 c and p 1241
e, post); R v Hull Prison Board of Visitors, ex parte St Germain [1979] 1 All ER 701 applied;

(e) on its true construction the Bill of Rights only prohibited the infliction of
punishments which were both cruel and unusual, and on the evidence the regime in the
control unit was in fact neither a cruel nor an unusual punishment (see p 1235 b c h,
p 1244 c d h, p 1245 e f and p 1246 c g, post); McCann v R (1975) 68 DLR (3d) 661 and R
v Miller and Cockriell (1977) 70 DLR (3d) 324 considered;

(f) in the circumstances the rules of natural justice did not require the plaintiff to be
given notice of the specific reason why he was being transferred to the control unit or an
opportunity to make representations why he should not be detained there; the rules of
natural justice merely required that the control unit committee should act fairly when
considering the application to transfer the plaintiff to the control unit and that it had
done (see p 1247 g to j, post).

(2) The claim for a declaration would also be dismissed because the Secretary of State
was entitled to act under r 43 of the 1964 rules, the action for damages for false
imprisonment had failed and any breach of the 1964 rules did not affect the validity of
the plaintiff's detention in the control unit, and in any event, the declaration would be
of no practical value since there was no evidence that the Secretary of State intended to
reopen the control unit (see p 1248 e to j, post); Merricks v Nott-Bower [1964] 1 All ER 717
applied.

---

b Section 12(1) is set out at p 1217 j, post

Notes

a For treatment of prisoners and prison discipline, see 30 Halsbury's Laws (3rd Edn) 611, paras 1177–1184.

For the Prison Act 1952, s 12, see 25 Halsbury's Statutes (3rd Edn) 835.

For the Prison Rules 1964, SI 1964 No 388 r 43, see 18 Halsbury's Statutory Instruments (Third Reissue) 24.

Cases referred to in judgment

b *Admiralty Lords Comrs v Aberdeen Steam Trawling & Fishing Co Ltd* 1909 SC 335, 46 SLR 254, 1 SLT 2, 22 Digest (Reissue) 99, *551.

Arbon v Anderson [1943] 1 All ER 154, [1943] KB 252, 112 LJKB 183, 168 LT 24, 37 Digest (Repl) 446, 52.

Attorney General v Wilts United Dairies (1922) 91 LJKB 897, 127 LT 822, 38 TLR 781, HL; *affg* 37 TLR 884, CA, 25 Digest (Repl) 153, 638.

c *Becker v Home Office* [1972] 2 All ER 676, [1972] 2 QB 407, [1972] 2 WLR 1193, CA, Digest (Cont Vol D) 729, 33b.

Bono v Saxbe (19th April 1977, unreported) US District Court of Illinois.

Carltona Ltd v Comrs of Works [1943] 2 All ER 560, CA, 17 Digest (Reissue) 490, 131.

Chic Fashions (West Wales) Ltd v Jones [1968] 1 All ER 229, [1968] 2 QB 299, [1968] 2 WLR 201, 132 JP 175, CA, 14(1) Digest (Reissue) 215, 1573.

d *Clonce v Richardson* (1974) 379 Fed Supp 338.

Cobbett v Grey (1849) 4 Exch 729, 8 State Tr NS 1075, 19 LJ Ex 137, 14 LTOS 182, 14 JP 56, 154 ER 1409, 38 Digest (Repl) 60, 329.

Congreve v Home Office [1976] 1 All ER 697, [1976] QB 629, [1976] 2 WLR 291, CA, Digest (Cont Vol E) 586, 40c.

Devala Provident Gold Mining Co, Re (1883) 22 Ch D 593, 52 LJ Ch 434, 48 LT 259, 1(2) e Digest (Reissue) 827, 5352.

Durayappah v Fernando [1967] 2 All ER 152, [1967] 2 AC 337, [1967] 3 WLR 289, PC, Digest (Cont Vol C) 811, *420b.

Ghani v Jones [1969] 3 All ER 1700, [1970] 1 QB 693, [1969] 3 WLR 1158, 134 JP 166, CA, 11 Digest (Reissue) 745, 608.

Guilfoyle v Home Office p 943, ante, [1981] 2 WLR 223, CA.

f *Holroyd v Doncaster* (1826) 3 Bing 492, 11 Moore CP 440, 4 Dow & Ry MC 537, 4 LJ OSCP 178, 130 ER 603, 33 Digest (Repl) 387, 6.

Lavender (H) & Son Ltd v Minister of Housing and Local Government [1970] 3 All ER 871, [1970] 1 WLR 1231, Digest (Cont Vol C) 967, 51d.

Liversidge v Anderson [1941] 3 All ER 338, [1942] AC 206, 110 LJKB 724, 166 LT 1, HL, 17 Digest (Reissue) 467, 28.

g *McCann v R* (1975) 68 DLR (3d) 661, 29 CCC 2d 337, Digest (Cont Vol E) 489, *29b.

Merricks v Nott-Bower [1964] 1 All ER 717, [1965] 1 QB 57, [1964] 2 WLR 702, 128 JP 267, CA, 18 Digest (Reissue) 160, 1300.

Osborne v Milman (1886) 17 QBD 514; *on appeal* 18 QBD 471, 56 LJQB 263, 56 LJQB 263, 56 LT 808, 51 JP 437, 14(1) Digest (Reissue) 13, 22.

Payne v Home Office (2nd May 1977, unreported).

h *R v Gaming Board for Great Britain, ex parte Benaim* [1970] 2 All ER 528, [1970] 2 QB 417, [1970] 2 WLR 1009, 134 JP 513, CA, Digest (Cont Vol C) 397, 352Aa.

R v Hull Prison Board of Visitors, ex parte St Germain [1979] 1 All ER 701, [1979] QB 425, [1979] 2 WLR 42, 68 Cr App R 212, CA, Digest (Cont Vol E) 488, 6a.

R v Miller and Cockriell [1975] 6 WWR 1, 63 DLR (3d) 193, 24 CCC (2d) 401; *on appeal* 70 DLR (3d) 324, 31 CCC (2d) 177, Digest (Cont Vol E) 144, *4455.

j *R v Secretary of State for Home Affairs, ex parte Bhajan Singh* [1975] 2 All ER 1081, [1976] QB 198, [1975] 3 WLR 225, 139 JP 676, CA, 2 Digest (Reissue) 213 1223.

R v Skinner [1968] 3 All ER 124, [1968] 2 QB 700, [1968] 3 WLR 408, 132 JP 484, 52 Cr App R 599, CA, Digest (Cont Vol C) 930, 322q.

Ridge v Baldwin [1963] 2 All ER 66, [1964] AC 40, [1962] 2 WLR 935, 127 JP 295, 61 LGR 369, HL, 37 Digest (Repl) 195, 32.

Rookes v Barnard [1964] 1 All ER 367, [1964] AC 1129, [1964] 2 WLR 269, [1964] 1
    Lloyd's Rep 28, HL, 45 Digest (Rcpl) 580, *1464.*

Russell v Duke of Norfolk [1949] 1 All ER 109, CA, 25 Digest (Reissue) 502, 4387.

Scavage v Tateham (1601) Cro Eliz 829, 78 ER 1056, 38 Digest (Repl) 95, 682.

Solway, The (1885) 10 PD 137, 54 LJP 83, sub nom *Burt v Livingstone, The Solway,* 53 LT
    680, 5 Asp MLC 482, 22 Digest (Reissue) 99, 680.

Swan v Miller [1919] 1 IR 151.

Waddington v Miah [1974] 2 All ER 377, [1974] 1 WLR 683, 138 JP 497, 59 Cr App Rep
    149, HL; *affg* sub nom *R v Miah* [1974] 1 All ER 110, [1974] Crim LR 430, CA, 2
    Digest (Reissue) 224, *1240.*

Yorke v Chapman (1839) 10 Ad & El 207, 2 Per & Dav 493, 8 LJQB 282, 3 Jur 1147, 113
    ER 89, 21 Digest (Repl) 290, *575.*

Action

The plaintiff, Michael Sidney Williams, brought an action against the defendant, the
Home Office, claiming (i) damages for false imprisonment in respect of the period from
23rd August 1974 to 18th February 1975 which he spent in the part of Wakefield Prison
known as the control unit, and (ii) a declaration that in setting up and operating the
control unit pursuant to Circular Instruction CI 35/1974 the defendant acted ultra vires
and unlawfully. The facts are set out in the judgment.

Stephen Sedley and *Michael Beloff* for the plaintiff.
Hugh Carlisle QC and *Philip Vallance* for the defendant.

Cur adv vult

9th May. **TUDOR EVANS J** read the following judgment: In this action, the plaintiff
claims damages, including an award of exemplary damages, for the tort of false
imprisonment. The action relates to a period of 180 days which the plaintiff spent
between 23rd August 1974 and 18th February 1975 in a part of Wakefield Prison known
as the control unit whilst he was serving a sentence of 14 years' imprisonment. The
plaintiff sues the Home Office alleging that the tort was committed against him by his
detention in the unit. The plaintiff also asks for a declaration that the circular instruction
(CI 35/1974) by which the control unit was set up and operated was ultra vires the
defendant and unlawful. A circular instruction is a means whereby instructions are
given from the headquarters of the Prison Department at the Home Office to governors
of prisons. The control unit was established on the authority of the Secretary of State.
The Home Office is the appropriate department nominated to be the defendant in this
type of proceedings.

    On 17th February 1971 the plaintiff, who is now aged 39, was convicted at Glamorgan
Assizes on one of three counts in an indictment charging him with armed robbery of a
bank in Cardiff. His sentence of 14 years was an extended sentence. The plaintiff served
his sentence in various prisons. In August 1974 the governor of Hull Prison described
the plaintiff as a 'high notoriety category A prisoner' and as 'a totally subversive and
dedicated troublemaker'. The control unit was established as a means of containing and
controlling prisoners who were considered to be troublemakers in prisons and it was the
assessment of the plaintiff as such which caused his transfer to the unit. In essence, as I
shall explain in greater detail later, it is the plaintiff's case that the onus in the tort of false
imprisonment rests on the defendant to justify the detention of the plaintiff in the
regime at the control unit and that they are unable to do so because of the nature of the
imprisonment and for other reasons. I must therefore begin by considering the
background of the events which led to the setting up of the unit and why the plaintiff
was sent there.

    The evidence in this case shows that for some time there had been considerable
concern and anxiety among the administrators of prisons at the influence which

troublemakers were exercising on prison life. In 1968 a subcommittee of the Advisory
a Council on the Penal System, under the chairmanship of Professor Radzinowicz, had
recommended the setting up of segregation units at dispersal prisons for violent prisoners
or for those who were able to disrupt prison life because of their ability to dominate and
manipulate other prisoners. The system of dispersal prisons was also recommended by
the Radzinowicz committee: see the report of the Advisory Council on the Penal system,
'the Regime for Long Term Prisoners in Conditions of maximum security'. It was a
b system whereby long-term prisoners were dispersed throughout the prison system.
Both recommendations were adopted.

In 1972 there was widespread disruption and disorder in a large number of prisons,
which was described by Mr B A Emes, a witness called for the defendant. Mr Emes is
now the head of the P5 division of the prison department at the Home Office with the
rank of assistant controller. He has had a very long experience of prison administration.
c He joined the prison service in 1957 and has spent all his time thereafter in the prison
service, except for a period of four years. He has been a governor, class I. According to
Mr Emes, in 1972 there were a number of passive demonstrations in prisons. News of
the demonstrations spread rapidly from prison to prison. In August 1972 there was a
one day national prison strike by prisoners in over 20 prisons. Thereafter, there were
fewer demonstrations, but they changed in character. Whereas they had been passive
d and fairly good natured, they now become violent. In the autumn of 1972 there was an
attempt at a mass escape at Gartree Prison, which resulted in a battle between the staff
and the escaping prisoners and which caused very substantial damage and a total
temporary breakdown of control in the prison.

Against that background, a working party was set up to consider the question of
control in the dispersal prisons. Mr Emes was a member of the working party. Whilst
e the working party committee recommended the continuation of segregation units as a
means of removing disruptive prisoners from ordinary prison life, it was of the opinion
that segregation units had not been wholly effective for a number of reasons. Among the
reasons was the fact that the segregation units were not sufficiently insulated or isolated
from the main part of the prison. Thus the inmates were still able to influence the
prisoners in the main prison. The committee therefore recommended that special
f control units should be set up in dispersal prisons, physically separate and insulated from
the main prison, and that prisoners who were allocated to it should not come from the
prison in which the unit was situated. The accountable divisions of the prison
department at the Home Office were given the task of producing a scheme for control
units.

Mr Emes was then a member of P2 division and as such was concerned in formulating
g the scheme. The purpose, the nature and the details of the control units are contained in
an instruction, CI 35/1974, which was circulated on 17th June 1974. It was approved by
the Secretary of State.

There were to be two control units; one was to be at Wakefield and the other at
Wormwood Scrubs, although the latter was never opened. The units operated as follows:
a governor who had in his prison a prisoner whom he considered should be sent to the
h unit requested the regional director of prisons to consider the case. If the director
approved the request, he sent it to a control unit committee which had been set up to
consider applications at headquarters on the authority of the Secretary of State. The
committee had to consider each case and it had to be satisfied that the prisoner involved
met the criteria necessary for admission.

On 20th August 1974 the committee considered five cases. Two were rejected, but
j three, the plaintiff, a Mr McMullan and a Mr Masterson, were approved. They were
transferred from their prisons to the control unit at Wakefield on 23rd August 1974.
The plaintiff left the unit on 18th February 1975. He was then transferred to another
prison. He was granted parole in March 1980. He expects to be released from his
sentence in July next.

It is now necessary to describe in outline the nature of the regime in the control unit. The aims of the unit were twofold: first, to relieve the dispersal prisons for limited periods from the pressures and strains caused by prisoners who deliberately set out to undermine and disrupt life in the prisons in which they were held. This aim was called during the course of the hearing giving the prison system 'a breather'. The second aim was to create a framework which would help the prisoner to realise that it was in his own interest to mend his ways. The latter was to be achieved by removing the prisoner to the unit until such time as he was able to show his willingness to sustain good behaviour for a substantial period of time.

To these ends, the regime was divided into two stages. Originally, as appears in CI 35/1974, each stage was to last for three months, but these periods were amended on 27th August 1974 to 90 days each. At stage 1, the prisoner did not associate with other prisoners, save when he had one hour's exercise a day. In fact, as I shall consider later, the plaintiff exercised alone for the first month. The prisoners were not obliged to work. As appears from para 23 of CI 35/1974 refusal to work was not to be treated as a disciplinary offence, because this would lead to a confrontation between the prisoner and the staff which the regime was designed to avoid. If the prisoner worked he was paid for it, but if he did not, time did not start to run. He could only qualify for stage 2 if he worked.

At stage 2 the prisoner was allowed a degree of association with other prisoners in the unit. He was allowed to associate at work and for leisure or educational purposes as I must consider again later. At stage 2 if the prisoner failed to work or attempted to cause trouble, he reverted to stage 1, and he was then required to start again and to complete a further continuous period of 90 days' good behaviour before qualifying for entry into stage 2.

If the prisoner completed a full period of 180 days he qualified for return to normal location in a dispersal prison. The test for a return to normal location was 'the fact of demonstrable and sustained good behaviour and constructive effort in the unit'. A welfare officer and an educational officer were available in the unit. A prison medical officer was responsible for the physical and mental health of the prisoners. There was a system of privileges. The prisoner was allowed the use of the library. He was allowed a visitor once a month. There were visits from the board of visitors and members of other interested external organisations.

When the prisoner was admitted to his cell, a cell information card informed him why, in general terms, he had been transferred to the unit, the purpose of the unit, the details of the regime, his right to make requests and complaints, his privileges, and other matters I shall mention later.

Before I consider the legal basis of the plaintiff's claim, I shall mention the plaintiff's personal background up to the time of his admission to the unit. Following his conviction the plaintiff was made a category A prisoner in March 1971. The system of dividing prisoners into categories was adopted as the result of a recommendation by the late Earl Mountbatten of Burma, who in 1966 held an inquiry into prison escapes and security (see Cmnd 3175 (1966)). He recommended that prisoners should be classified into four categories. Category A prisoners are those whose escape would be highly dangerous to the public or the police or to the security of the state. Category B prisoners are those for whom the very highest conditions of security are not necessary, but for whom escape must be made very difficult. Category C prisoners are those who cannot be trusted in open conditions, but who do not have the ability to make a determined attempt to escape and for whom basic security conditions are sufficient, and category D prisoners are housed in open prisons without danger.

After conviction, the plaintiff served his sentence in seven prisons, three of which were dispersal prisons. As I have already mentioned, by August 1974 the plaintiff was considered to be a dedicated troublemaker. From May to 10th August 1974 he served his sentence in Hull Prison. On the latter date he was transferred to Durham Prison for 14 days for segregation under r 43 of the Prison Rules, SI 1964 No 388. Rule 43 has figured very largely in this case, and I must refer to its exact language later, but it provides an administrative power, in the interests of good order and discipline, to a   remove a prisoner, either generally or for particular purposes, from association with other prisoners.

The plaintiff's transfer to Durham was made pursuant to a circular instruction (CI 10/1974) which had been issued on the recommendation of the working party which had reported in March 1973. This provided for the removal of a prisoner from his normal prison location for a 'cooling off' period of 14 days. It was used, in the language of the circular instruction—

b   '... for a troublemaker who needs to be removed from normal location because of an imminently explosive situation caused by either his actual or impending disruptive behaviour, and for whom placement in the segregation unit is inappropriate or impractical, either because the prisoner would still be able to exercise a disruptive influence from his segregation unit ... or because the extent to which the prisoner provides a focal point for prisoner unrest would mean that the
c   mere act of placement in the segregation unit could have a provocative and explosive effect on the rest of the establishment.'

The grounds of application by the governor of Hull for the plaintiff's transfer from Durham to the control unit were based on an assessment of the plaintiff's present behaviour which included the extent of actual or feared disruption and of the likely
d   consequences of his continued presence in his then conditions. The governor wrote:

'Williams is a high notoriety, Category "A" prisoner, and an amalgam of his physical capacity to intimidate with his influence among similar sophisticated prisoners, has lent a ready effectiveness to his activities. His continued presence in normal dispersal conditions must inevitably, it would seem, result in an extension of the already long and formidable history of subversion and disruption to good
e   order that has been his chosen role.'

The immediate cause of the application is described in these terms:

'9.8.74 (Hull) Williams is again demonstrating his deeply rooted and anti-authority attitude and is observed moving from group to group sowing the seeds of discontent. (I doubt that he has it in him to be any different.) He has contributed
f   largely to changing a composed wing to a seething mass of resentment and rebellion.'

With that outline of the events leading to the plaintiff's admission to the control unit, I shall now consider the nature of the plaintiff's claim for damages and declaratory relief. As I have said, each claim is centred on the nature of the regime in the unit and the circumstances which caused the plaintiff to be transferred to it.
g   Counsel for the plaintiff makes these submissions, which I shall enumerate:

1. Any detention of a plaintiff against his will is the tort of false imprisonment unless the defendant can show lawful authority. The onus is on the defendant to justify the detention and to prove that it was lawful.

2. The defendant seeks to justify the detention of the plaintiff in the unit by relying
h   on the sentence of the court passed in 1971, on the terms of the Prison Act 1952 and on the Prison Rules 1964, as amended. The rules were made by the Secretary of State pursuant to his powers under s 47(1) of the Act. The plaintiff submits that the defendant cannot justify the detention by the sentence of the court; that merely justified his presence in a prison.

The relevant section of the Act is s 12(1) which, in so far as the language is material,
j   provides: 'A prisoner ... may be lawfully confined in any prison.' Counsel submits that the detention cannot be justified by the subsection. It is only a defence to an action, the basis of which is concerned with the location or place of imprisonment. It is not concerned with any tortious act done to a prisoner inside a prison. Section 12(1), submits counsel, is not concerned with the nature of the imprisonment, which is the central feature of the plaintiff's case.

3. Counsel starts with the general proposition that although detention in a prison may be lawful it can become unlawful if the mode or nature of the imprisonment changes. Thus there can in law be a tortious imprisonment during the currency of a lawful imprisonment. He submits that on the evidence the nature or quality of the plaintiff's imprisonment in the control unit was of a different and worse nature than was practised in the remainder of the prison system. The facts which the plaintiff asks me to find are set out in para 14 of a submission of fact which counsel has drafted. I shall refer to them in item 8 below.

4. The defendant cannot justify the plaintiff's detention under the Prison Rules because there were breaches of the rules. Counsel accepts that there is ample authority that a plaintiff cannot rely on a breach of the rules to establish or support a cause of action: see *Arbon v Anderson* [1943] 1 All ER 154, [1943] KB 252, *Becker v Home Office* [1972] 2 All ER 676, [1972] 2 QB 407, *R v Hull Prison Board of Visitors, ex parte St Germain* [1979] 1 All ER 701, [1979] QB 425 and *Payne v Home Office* (2nd May 1977, unreported), a decision of Cantley J to which I shall have to refer later when I consider the issue of natural justice which is raised by the plaintiff.

But, although the plaintiff cannot support his action by relying on a breach of the rules, it is submitted that the defendant cannot justify the detention of the plaintiff in a regime which constituted a breach of the rules. On this part of the case I shall have to consider the status of the Prison Rules and whether any breaches of them can have any effect of the lawfulness of the plaintiff's detention. In para 5 of the amended defence it is pleaded:

'The plaintiff was detained as part of his said term of imprisonment in accordance with the Prison Act 1952 and/or the Prison Rules 1964 . . . as amended and in particular Rules 1, 2, 3 and 43 thereof under the lawful authority of the Secretary of State and such detention was lawful.'

Notwithstanding the express reliance by the defendant on the rules, if there was any breach of the rules, but the rules are found in law to be irrelevant to the question whether the plaintiff's detention was lawful, then in my judgment the defendant is not bound by the pleading and I am not precluded from deciding whether the plaintiff's detention was lawful.

The Prison Rules which are material have to be considered from two points of view: first, relating to the authority to detain the plaintiff in the unit and, secondly, relating to the nature (that is, the conditions) of the regime. I shall first consider the nature of the plaintiff's case with respect to the Prison Rules in that order.

5. The transfer of the plaintiff from Hull to the unit and his detention there for 180 days was made by the control unit committee acting for the Secretary of State under r 43 of the Prison Rules, to which I have already referred. The plaintiff makes three submissions. First, that on a proper construction of r 43 the Secretary of State has no power to act under the rule. It is submitted that the only person who has power to act under the rule is the governor of a prison exercising an 'on the spot' jurisdiction. Therefore, it is argued, since the Secretary of State had no power, the detention was ultra vires and unlawful from beginning to end. The defendant cannot justify the detention, and I should declare that CI 35/1974, by which the regime was set up and operated, was ultra vires and unlawful.

Second, if the Secretary of State had power there was a failure to comply with the procedure laid down in r 43(2). It is argued that initial detention can only be for 24 hours, but may be authorised for one month by the Secretary of State and that thereafter it may be renewed from month to month. It is submitted that the renewal procedure involves a fresh consideration and a fresh exercise of the authority to detain, but that in fact the Secretary of State decided in advance to detain the plaintiff for 180 days and that the authority to detain month by month was issued automatically by the control unit committee without a fresh consideration of the plaintiff's case, and therefore without any exercise of discretion. Put shortly, counsel submits that the process of renewal must a　involve a review. The result of these two submissions, if acceptable, is that if the Secretary of State had no power under r 43 the detention was unlawful from the beginning, but if he did have power the detention was unlawful after the first month.

The third argument relating to power to detain under r 43 is that when CI 35/1974 was circulated there was no reference in it to the fact that the plaintiff was transferred to and was being detained in the control unit on an exercise of an authority under r 43. This was not carried out until 27th August 1974 when, by Annex E, the circular
b　instruction was amended. It is therefore argued that there was a lacuna in the authority and that on any view the detention of the plaintiff between 23rd and 27th August was unjustified and unlawful.

I shall now consider the breaches of the Prison Rules alleged in relation to the nature of the imprisonment. It is submitted on evidence which I shall consider later that the essential nature of the penal system of this country for very nearly a hundred years has
c　been based upon the concept of rehabilitation. Thus r 1 requires the training and treatment of convicted prisoners to encourage them to lead good and useful lives. The plaintiff relies on para 14 of CI 35/1974 in which it is stated: 'The regime of the unit is not directed towards providing "treatment": there is no expectation that it will cure prisoners of wanting to stir up trouble; only demonstrate to them that it does not pay to do so.'

d　The plaintiff also relies on the report of the working party of March 1973, in which (for example in para 126(ii)) the authors recommended that the control unit should be large enough to provide for positive treatment and work. It is submitted that the working party report was 'the brief' to which the divisions responsible for producing CI 35/1974 had to work, but that they did not do so. Thus there was a breach of r 1. It is also submitted that there was a breach of r 2(1) which provides that order and discipline
e　shall be maintained with firmness, but with no more restriction than is required for safe custody and well-ordered community life.

Rule 43, which, as I have said, provides inter alia for the total withdrawal of association for a prisoner, and thus, in effect, for confinement to his cell, has to be read with r 2(1) in mind, according to the submission of the plaintiff. It is said that the regime in the control unit involved 23 hours a day in his cell for the plaintiff with an almost total loss
f　of human company, although I shall consider the facts later. Moreover, the regime provided for a minimum of 180 days with the risk of reversion. Professor Taylor, one of the plaintiff's expert witnesses, said that only the governor has power under r 43 and he always adopts a flexible approach to the exercise of his power. He watches the situation and when he judges it to be right he frees the prisoner from r 43 regime. Thus it is submitted that there was a breach of r 2(1).

g　The plaintiff also relies on the absence in the working party report of any reference to isolation and reversion. He also relies on the recommendation in the working party report to trial periods whereby the prisoner would be released to ordinary prison population and moved back again if the experiment were to fail.

The third breach which is alleged relates to r 2 (2) and (3). These provide in effect that the prison staff shall influence prisoners by good example, that they should encourage
h　self-respect and a sense of responsibility in prisoners and that they should enlist the prisoners' willing co-operation. But the plaintiff submits that the staff in the unit were told to be, and were in fact, 'coolly neutral' or 'coolly professional'. They were cold and unresponsive. Such an attitude is said to be unheard of in English penal policy and practice.

The plaintiff again relies on the contents of the working party report in which it is said
j　that a significant constructive element can be built into the regime if the staff see the prisoners as individuals needing help and therefore deserving of some special tolerance. The plaintiff further submits that there were breaches of r 3(3), which provides that a prisoner shall not be deprived unduly of the society of other persons, and of r 28, which provides that arrangements shall be made to allow prisoners to work, where possible, outside cells and in association with one another. These two rules are said to confer a

right to association. It is submitted that the regime in the unit constituted a breach of
these rules so far as stage 1 is concerned.

The plaintiff further alleges that there was a breach of rr 47 and 56, which provide for
awards (that is punishments) for offences against discipline. I should explain that the
removal of a prisoner from association with other prisoners in the interests of good order
and discipline under r 43 is not a punishment for an offence. It is an administrative
action which does not confer on the prisoner an opportunity to be heard in opposition to
the proposed action. Rules 47 to 56 are concerned with offences against discipline and,
within the language of the rules, the prisoner involved has the right to be heard and the
right to present his case. He also has a statutory right to present his case when charged
with an offence: see s 47(2) of the 1952 Act.

The plaintiff submits that at stage 1 he was in effect given cellular confinement for 90
days, which is the type of punishment given for an offence against discipline and that he
was given a punishment in excess of the maximum of 56 days which could have been
awarded for a proved offence. The plaintiff relies on the words, which I have already
read, in which the governor of Hull Prison described the plaintiff as 'moving from group
to group sowing the seeds of discontent'. The plaintiff submits that this was evidence of
an incitement to mutiny which is an offence under r 52(1)(a), for which the maximum
penalty is 56 days. It is said that the plaintiff was being punished for this offence under
the guise of r 43. Thus the plaintiff's time in the unit, at least at stage 1, was a
punishment within a punishment and cannot be justified. The regime itself, argues the
plaintiff, was punitive in character. He seeks to put in evidence a number of documents,
which I shall consider later, which he argues are evidence against the defendant and
probative of his submission.

Finally, it is said that the regime was contrary to the policy and object of the Prison Act
and Rules, the purpose of which is to promote the reform of prisoners. I think that this
argument really states in different language the arguments I have already outlined with
respect to rehabilitation.

6. The plaintiff's next ground for submitting that the detention cannot be justified
and is therefore unlawful is based on a provision in the Bill of Rights (1688) prohibiting
the infliction of 'cruell and unusuall punishments'.

Counsel correctly points out that the Bill of Rights is a bulwark of the constitution in
protecting the liberty of the subject and that it has, at least twice, successfully been
invoked by the courts in modern times and once very recently. The cases are: *Attorney
General v Wilts United Dairies Limited* (1922) 91 LJKB 897 and *Congreve v Home Office*
[1976] 1 All ER 697, [1976] QB 629. Both cases are concerned with the provision that
there shall be no taxation without the grant of Parliament.

According to the plaintiff's submission, the proper reading of the provision in the Act
leads to the construction that the Act prohibits cruel *or* unusual punishment. The
plaintiff relies on the judgment of Heald J in *McCann v R* (1975) 68 DLR (3d) 661, a case
decided in British Columbia on similar language in the Canadian Bill of Rights 1960.
Heald J followed a dissenting judgment of McIntyre J in the Court of Appeal in British
Columbia in the case of *R v Miller and Cockriell* [1975] 6 WWR 1. There was an appeal
in the last case after the decision in *McCann* and the nine members of the Supreme Court
of Canada held that the proper construction of the words 'cruel and unusual' was not
disjunctive (see 70 DLR (3d) 324). The plaintiff submits that on the facts of the present
case the regime was either cruel or unusual. He asks me, in reaching that conclusion, to
compare the facts found with respect to control units in *McCann* and in two American
cases: *Bono v Saxbe* (19th April 1978, unreported) in the Eastern District of Illinois and
Clonce v Richardson (1974) 379 Fed Supp 338. The two American cases were concerned
with United States' legislation prohibiting cruel and unusual punishments.

Counsel on both sides have made a comparison of the features of the control units in
the North American cases and the present case. Many of the facts relied on in support of
the argument that the regime offended the Bill of Rights are the same as those advanced

in support of the submission that the imprisonment in the unit was of a different nature
a from that in the remainder of the prison system.

Assuming the facts and the construction for which the plaintiff contends, it is argued
that it is against the law of this country to inflict a cruel or unusual punishment. Counsel
accepts that the plaintiff does not have a cause of action for damages for breach of the Bill
of Rights, but he argues that unless such a punishment is authorised by the Prison Act,
either expressly or by necessary implication, then such a punishment is unlawful. That
b being so, the regime was unlawful and it cannot be justified so as to defeat the
presumption of tort which arises from a detention of the plaintiff against his will. If the
cruel or unusual punishment is not justifiable under the Prison Act, it is said that it
cannot be justified under r 43 of the 1964 rules. The rule is merely a part of delegated
legislation and, if such legislation conflicts with an Act of Parliament, the Act prevails
and the delegated legislation is pro tanto void.

c   7. The next ground on which the plaintiff argues that the detention in the unit cannot
be justified and is unlawful is based upon the principles of natural justice. An application
of these principles is said to have required that the plaintiff should have been told why
he was being transferred to the unit and that he should have had the opportunity to
make representations why he should not be sent there.

As appears from paras 1, 2 and 3 of the list of facts in item 8 below which counsel for
d the plaintiff asks me to find, I am asked to find as a fact that the plaintiff was given no
notice of the reasons for putting him in the unit and no opportunity to contest them. I
am asked to find that the plaintiff knew the general but not the specific reason alleged
against him.

I am further asked to find that the specific reasons for his transfer were: (a) specific
allegations of indiscipline and incitement to mutiny, in respect of which no charges were
e brought; and (b) a general allegation of sowing the seeds of discontent, in respect of
which it is said that the defendant conceded there was insufficient evidence.

The plaintiff does not suggest that the principles of natural justice required that he
should be given a hearing, but that he should have been given the chance to make
representations.

The plaintiff further argues that the principles of natural justice arise because the
f Secretary of State had no power to transfer the plaintiff to the unit under r 43, and no
power to detain him. If he did, the detention was unlawfully continued because of a
failure to comply with the provisions of r 43 concerning renewal.

Generally, counsel submits that when considering the application of the rules of
natural justice to the particular facts and circumstances of this case, I should bear in mind
that the plaintiff's liberty, although attenuated, was being further and drastically
g restricted. Counsel submits that prisoners are not outlaws and that where a decision by
an authority adversely affects a prisoner's liberty or well-being the decision should not be
taken without giving him the opportunity to oppose it.

Counsel has referred to many authorities on this part of the case, amongst which was
R v Hull Prison Board of Visitors, ex parte St Germain [1979] 1 All ER 701, [1979] QB
425. That was a case in which the Court of Appeal held that the decision of a board of
h visitors when performing a judicial act was capable in law of being the subject of judicial
review. Counsel relies particularly on the observations of Shaw LJ ([1979] 1 All ER 701
at 716, [1979] QB 425 at 455):

> 'Now the rights of the citizen, however circumscribed by a penal sentence or
> otherwise, must always be the concern of the courts unless their jurisdiction is
> clearly excluded by some statutory provision.'

j
It is submitted that when deciding whether a decision offends the principles of natural
justice, I have to consider the adverse effect of the decision from the point of view of the
individual affected by it and not from the point of view of the authority imposing it. In
other words, it is wrong to approach the application of the principles of natural justice

bearing in mind that the particular decision was desirable or advantageous or was convenient to the authority.

a

Finally, counsel argues that if there was a breach of the principles of natural justice then the decision to send the plaintiff to the unit was void and his detention there cannot be justified.

8. The facts which I am asked to find are contained in the list of facts submitted by counsel for the plaintiff. I shall for the moment refer only to those listed under para 14(e) (i) to (xiii). The suggested facts are these: (i) there was no association at all for the first *b* month of the plaintiff's stay in the unit and none, except at exercise, for the remainder of the 90 days of stage 1; (ii) the attitude of the staff was deliberately distant. This relates to the issue of the 'coolly professional' attitude of the staff, to which I have referred; (iii) the visits to the plaintiff when he was in the unit did not afford him any company. As I shall consider when I turn to the evidence, the plaintiff was visited by his sister, Mrs Newall. It is said that the visits were affected by the oppressive presence of the prison *c* staff. The plaintiff was visited frequently by such visitors as the board of visitors, the Under-Secretary of State, members of Parliament, visiting magistrates, priests and others. He was visited by the no 1 governor on 20 occasions, by the deputy governor on 20 occasions, and by the prison medical officer daily. It is said that none of these visits were social visits and that they did not afford the plaintiff company and companionship; (iv) there was no visual relief in the cell: (v) there was no auditory relief. These suggested *d* facts refer to the evidence that the walls of the cell were dull in colour, that the plaintiff could only see the sky through the cell window, and that he was not allowed a radio. The lack of visibility from the cell and the lack of a radio is said to have amounted to a sensory deprivation which, together with other features of the regime, was damaging to the plaintiff's nervous stability; (vi) there was insufficient daylight by which to read. The plaintiff invites me to assess this fact (if proved) in association with r 11(a) of the United *e* Nations Minimum Standard Rules (Cmd 7662 (1949)) that windows shall be large enough to enable prisoners to read or work by natural light; (vii) the only work available was dull and repetitious; (viii) the plaintiff was subject to surveillance and searches by the prison staff. It is said that the plaintiff was watched when he was using the lavatory and shower and that he and his cell were too frequently searched; (ix) there was no chance of remission; (x) there was a continuing threat of reversion for misconduct falling short of *f* a disciplinary offence or, in effect, as a second penalty for a proved offence or for refusal to work. Counsel submits that the risk of reversion was punitive in nature; (xi) stage 2 of the regime was little different from stage 1, partly because of the small number of prisoners, but also partly because the effect of stage 1 on the plaintiff was such that he preferred to retreat to his cell to avoid the surveillance of the staff. This part of the case will involve assessment of the undoubted fact that at stage 2 when the plaintiff could *g* have associated with his two fellow prisoners he often preferred to work in his cell; (xii) the plaintiff was held in solitary confinement for 23 hours a day at stage 1; (xiii) the plaintiff did not know specifically why he was in the unit. I also noted in the course of the submissions on behalf of the plaintiff some of the facts which I shall now list: (xiv) the lack of possessions; (xv) the silence in the unit. I shall, of course, have to consider evidence on which it is alleged that the plaintiff underwent stress. This issue is not *h* confined to the issue of damages.

With respect to the issue of damages, the plaintiff claims a compensatory and an exemplary award. There are two features of the claim for compensatory damage: first, damages for the mere fact of the unlawful detention, which is said to have amounted to false imprisonment. Secondly, it is submitted that the award should include a sum to compensate the plaintiff for the effect on him of his time in the unit. According to the *j* plaintiff, the regime in the unit at times frightened, depressed and disorientated him. He still becomes, as he put it in evidence, 'very paranoic'. He called a psychiatrist, Dr Woolf, who first examined him on 17th August 1978, over four years after the plaintiff had left the unit. In evidence he described the plaintiff as having 'minor neurotic symptoms' and he expressed the opinion that when the plaintiff was in the unit he would only have had such symptoms.

In support of his claim for an award of exemplary damages, the plaintiff relies on the
a speech of Lord Devlin in *Rookes v Barnard* [1964] 1 All ER 367, [1964] AC 1129. Lord
Devlin referred to the various categories of conduct which should be met with an award
of exemplary damages and which included 'oppressive, arbitrary or unconstitutional
action by the servants of the government' (see [1964] 1 All ER 367 at 410, [1964] AC
1129 at 1226). Counsel has submitted that this is a bad case of its kind and that I should
award substantial damages under this head to punish and deter such conduct.

b   The regime, it is said, was oppressive because it bore harshly on the plaintiff in that it
isolated him beyond what the law allowed; it was arbitrary because it had no legal
basis. Moreover, the decision to send the plaintiff to the unit was considered behind the
plaintiff's back. It was unconstitutional because it was introduced by an internal
document (CI 35/1974) which was not sanctioned by the Prison Act, it was not sanctioned
by the Prison Rules and it offended the Bill of Rights and the rules of natural justice. It
c is said that the regime was introduced secretly and without advanced publicity. When
the nature of the regime was described in answer to a Parliamentary question, there was
no reference to the fact that the inmates would be deprived of human company.

It is argued that the Home Office was warned that the regime was inexcusable. The
plaintiff relies on a large number of documents some of which were disclosed as the
result of the order of McNeil J in *Williams v Home Office* p 1151, ante, after a contested
d issue of public interest immunity, but I shall have to consider the evidential status of
these documents on a number of issues of fact later on. The defendant submits that I
should disregard them, because they are not evidence.

With respect to the declaration, the plaintiff puts forward these grounds. The control
unit was set up pursuant to CI 35/1974. In doing so, the defendant acted ultra vires and
unlawfully. There was no power to set up the regime under r 43, and what was done was
e in breach of the Prison Rules, the Bill of Rights and the principles of natural justice as
they ought to be applied in this case.

I shall now outline the argument of the defendant. First, the defendant relies on the
sentence of the court passed in 1971 and the provision of s 12(1) of the 1952 Act to justify
the plaintiff's presence in the control unit. It is argued that the plaintiff was lawfully
sentenced and that, by s 12(1) of the Act, the Secretary of State is empowered lawfully to
f confine the plaintiff in any prison. Therefore it cannot be unlawful to have confined the
plaintiff as a part of his sentence in the control unit. The plaintiff replies that s 12(1)
merely justifies taking the plaintiff to the unit. It cannot justify what was done to him
whilst he was there, as I have already explained.

Second, it is submitted on behalf of the defendant that the plaintiff is really
complaining of the conditions of his detention, and that the conditions of detention are
g a matter for the Secretary of State alone. It is accepted that a prisoner is able to exercise
legal rights when in prison. If, for example, he were to suffer personal injury as the
result of the negligence of a fellow prisoner or a member of the staff, he could sustain an
action for damages. What he cannot do, having exhausted his legal rights to appeal, is to
challenge the lawfulness of his detention. The defendant submits that there were no
breaches of the Prison Rules, but that, even if there were, such breaches do not affect the
h lawfulness of the detention which, as I have said, is covered by the sentence of the court
and s 12(1) of the 1952 Act. Counsel for the defendant submits that the Prison Rules are
not mandatory; they are regulatory only. The plaintiff cannot sue on them and, in the
same way, a breach is irrelevant to the question whether the plaintiff was lawfully
detained.

Third, it is submitted that the Bill of Rights is not relevant to the action for damages.
j If I reject the defendant's primary contention that the detention of the plaintiff was
lawful under the sentence of the court and the Act, then the Bill of Rights is superfluous
to the plaintiff's argument. If, on the other hand, I accept the defendant's argument that
the detention was lawful and that the conditions of confinement are irrelevant to the
question whether the plaintiff was lawfully detained, then the defence is made out and
the Bill of Rights is also irrelevant.

Counsel further submits that the language of the Bill of Rights is clear in intent, that it means what it says and that it prohibits the infliction of cruel *and* unusual punishments. He submits that the regime was not cruel and unusual or either. He relies on similar and, in some respects, what he describes as more restrictive regimes in the English penal system by way of comparison.

Fourth, it is submitted that the content of natural justice only required that the control unit committee should have considered the application to transfer the plaintiff fairly, and it is not disputed that the committee did act fairly.

I need not refer, at the moment, to the defence on the facts or to the argument of the defendant on damages.

With respect to the claim for declaration, counsel accepts that I have jurisdiction to make a declaration, but he submits that I should not do so for these reasons. First, the plaintiff has no enforceable rights either under the Prison Act or the Prison Rules or the Bill of Rights and that I should not grant a declaration except in pursuance of an enforceable legal right. Second, a declaration has never been made in relation to the Prison Rules except by consent. Counsel has referred me to the decision of Peter Pain J in *Guilfoyle v Home Office* (see p 943, ante).

Third, it is contrary to policy to grant a declaration on the facts of this case. The argument is one of policy and convenience. It is argued that if I find that there is no liability in tort, I should, if I were to grant a declaration, give the plaintiff by the back door what I have denied him at the front. I should be encouraging disgruntled prisoners, past and present, to come to court. Administration and discipline would be undermined.

Fourth, the granting of a declaration would serve no useful purpose. The control unit was closed in October 1975 by a circular instruction cancelling CI 35/1974. The plaintiff left the unit five years ago. It is submitted that in reality the unit will never return and it would be wrong to grant a declaration of mere academic interest.

I must now consider the questions of law and fact which arise. Counsel for the plaintiff is undoubtedly right in his first submission that to detain a plaintiff against his will is prima facie tortious and that, unless the detention can be justified, the tort of false imprisonment is made out. I need only refer to two cases. In *Holroyd v Doncaster* (1826) 3 Bing 492, 130 ER 603 it was held that '. . . it was . . . clear that a party who took upon himself to imprison another was primâ facie guilty of trespass, the onus of justifying which rested entirely with himself'. There are similar observations in *Liversidge v Anderson* [1941] 3 All ER 338, [1942] AC 206.

I must therefore approach the issue of liability asking myself the question whether the defendant can justify the detention of the plaintiff in the control unit at Wakefield. Before I consider this question by reference to the Prison Act, the Prison Rules, the Bill of Rights and the principles of natural justice and the facts, I must consider the authorities cited on behalf of the plaintiff for the general proposition that, although a detention in a prison may be lawful, it can become unlawful if the nature or quality of the imprisonment changes. The change in the nature or quality of the imprisonment alleged relates, as I have said, to the conditions of imprisonment in the unit when compared with the nature or quality of imprisonment in the remainder of the prison system.

A number of cases have been cited by counsel for the plaintiff to which I shall refer, but I should say at once that, as I understand these cases, they do not support the proposition for which they are advanced. They are all concerned with the detention of a prisoner in a place not authorised by law. They all derive from a time when there were particular prisons or types of prisons appropriate for the circumstances which caused the prisoner to be sent there. Thus, if a civil debtor was committed to prison for non-payment of debt he had to be sent to a place of detention for civil debtors. He could not be placed in a prison for the detention of criminals. If he was, there could be no lawful justification for the detention, which was therefore unlawful. All the cases cited have this feature of detention in the wrong 'place'.

The first case is *Scavage v Tateham* (1601) Cro Eliz 829, 78 ER 1056. The plaintiff alleged that he was falsely imprisoned for 18 days. The defendant pleaded lawful justification. He, as a justice of the peace, had detained the plaintiff in his own house on suspicion of having committed a robbery. It was held that the detention could not be justified and was tortious for two reasons. First, because the defendant had authority to

a detain the plaintiff only for a period of three days. Second, because he had no power to detain the plaintiff in his own house. His power was limited to confining suspects in the common gaol for surrender at gaol delivery. The first ground of the decision was detention for a time longer than authorised by law. It is still a well recognised principle in the tort of false imprisonment, but it is irrelevant here. The second ground was detention in the wrong place, that is one not authorised by law. The defendant had no

b legal power to detain the plaintiff in the place in question.

The second case is *Yorke v Chapman* (1839) 10 Ad & El 207, 113 ER 80. The plaintiff had been committed to the Queen's Bench prison for debt. Whilst in prison he was alleged to have assaulted a prison watchman. The marshal of the prison then transferred the plaintiff to another part of the prison known as the 'strongroom'. The plaintiff sued the marshal for assault and false imprisonment. There was a motion to stay the

c proceedings on the ground that the marshal had statutory power to detain prisoners in the strongroom, that the plaintiff's grievance was only that he had been detained in one room rather than another and that the plaintiff's only remedy was to exercise his statutory right to petition the judges for compensation. Denman CJ held that the plaintiff's rights were not confined to the statutory remedy and that he had no power to stay the proceedings.

d *Yorke v Chapman* is authority for the proposition that if a plaintiff was lawfully detained in the type of prison appropriate to his circumstances he might have a cause of action if, without justification, he was transferred to another type of prison for other offenders, albeit that the second prison was within the same building. This state of the law as it existed up to and including the nineteenth century has to be contrasted with the present power of the Secretary of State by virtue of s 12(1) of the 1952 Act.

e The third case on which the plaintiff relies is *Osborne v Milman* (1886) 17 QBD 514. The plaintiff was committed to prison for having practised as a solicitor when he was not qualified to do so. He was taken to Holloway Prison, placed on the criminal side and treated as a convicted criminal 'not sentenced to hard labour'. He brought an action for false imprisonment. He claimed that he had not been convicted of any criminal offence and that his detention on the criminal side of the prison could not be justified. Denman

f J agreed and awarded him damages. He held that the plaintiff was not 'a convicted criminal person' and that there was no statutory power to detain the plaintiff on the criminal side.

Counsel for the plaintiff submitted that *Osborne v Milman* showed that the tort in that case consisted both of being put in the wrong 'place' and in objectionable conditions on the criminal side. On that assumption he argues that the plaintiff in the present case was

g placed in the control unit in breach of r 43 (his detention therefore being unauthorised) and in conditions which, like the criminal side in *Osborne v Milman*, were worse for him than they otherwise would have been. But I do not agree that the tort in *Osborne v Milman* consisted both in the detention in the wrong place and in objectionable conditions. There is no doubt that the conditions for the plaintiff in *Osborne v Milman* were not as agreeable as they would have been if the plaintiff had been detained in the

h proper place, but that was not part of the tort. The conditions were the consequence of the tort and not the cause of it. Whether a breach of r 43 can have any effect on the lawfulness of the detention of the plaintiff in the present case turns on the effect in law of a breach or non-compliance with the rules.

The fourth case on which the plaintiff places much reliance is *Cobbett v Grey* (1850) 4 Exch 729, 154 ER 1409. The plaintiff had been committed to the Queen's Bench prison

j for not paying the costs arising out of a suit in the Court of Chancery. Whilst he was in custody in the appropriate part of the prison, called no 2, the judgment creditor obtained an order compelling the plaintiff to file a schedule of his property. The plaintiff failed, or was said to have failed, to produce it. He was then removed to a part of the prison set aside for class 1 debtors, that is, for those who had failed to provide a schedule when ordered. The conditions on that side were alleged to be 'more confined, dark and unsalubrious'. He moved for habeas corpus, but that failed, Wilde CJ observing: 'If the keeper of the prison is acting improperly in placing him in the particular part of the prison of which he complains the ordinary means of redress for the wrong are open to him.'

The plaintiff then sued the Secretary of State, Sir George Grey, and the prison keeper,   *a* named Hudson, for damages for false imprisonment and assault. The action was tried by Pollock CB and a jury. After legal argument, he directed a verdict for the defendant. The plaintiff moved for a new trial. Numerous issues, not relevant here, were argued but Parke B said (4 Exch 729 at 736, 154 ER 1409 at 1412): 'The removal of a person from one part of a prison to another, in which by law he ought not to be confined, is primâ   *b* facie a trespass.' This passage is entirely in keeping with the other cases that a detention could only be justified by detention in the place prescribed by law.

Counsel for the plaintiff argued as he did with respect to *Osborne v Milman* that the conditions in *Cobbett v Grey* were worse for the plaintiff and that therefore the case is authority for the proposition that imprisonment may become unjustifiable and unlawful by reason of such conditions. But, for the reasons which I gave when considering *Osborne*   *c* *v Milman*, I do not accept that the conditions of imprisonment were relevant to liability in tort.

Counsel for the plaintiff relied on the dissenting judgment of Pollock CB in *Cobbett v Grey*. He, in accordance with the practice of the time, sat in the Exchequer Chamber notwithstanding his having tried the action. He said (4 Exch 729 at 744–745, 154 ER at 1415–1416):   *d*

'. . . a gaoler who violates certain rules which are given to him by the Secretary of State with respect to the classification of prisoners, is not liable to an action of trespass for violating those rules, at the suit of each prisoner. He may be responsible to the authorities who have given those directions, but it is his duty to confine the prisoners; and if he does simply confine the prisoners, and confines them in a wrong place, a prisoner has no action of trespass against him. It would be a different thing   *e* if fetters were put on, or any other personal hardship used; but the prisoners are merely confined within the four walls, within which four walls it is his duty to confine them.'

Counsel relies on the reference to fetters. He argues that the opinion was being expressed that lawful detention in the four walls of a prison can become unlawful   *f* because the nature (that is, the conditions) of imprisonment have changed. But as I understand Pollock CB, he was simply saying that the use of fetters as a means of detention would not be authorised by law. It may also be that he had in mind that it would be an assault.

This point appears to have been made by Alderson B. He was one of the majority opinion, but he referred to the use of fetters. He said (4 Exch 729 at 742, 154 ER 1409   *g* at 1415):

'I quite agree that, as against the defendant Hudson, there is no doubt, if a party chooses by force or threats of force to compel a prisoner to move from one part of a prison to another, that is properly the subject of an action of trespass, just as much as the putting an additional fetter upon the prisoner which by law he is not entitled to do.'   *h*

The final authority on this part of the case to which counsel refers and in which he finds support for the general proposition is *Arbon v Anderson* [1943] 1 All ER 154, [1943] KB 252. Counsel for the defendant referred to the headnote in the All England Law Reports ([1943] 1 All ER 154 at 155) where the facts are more fully set out. The plaintiff and others were detained during the last war pursuant to powers under reg 18B of the   *j* Defence (General) Regulations 1940. They brought an action against the Secretary of State based on breaches of the Prison Rules. One of the principal complaints was the lack of facilities for association. Goddard LJ sitting as an additional judge in the Queen's Bench Division, rejected the plaintiff's claim, holding that there had been no breach of the Prison Rules, but he added, obiter dicta, that such a breach, if proved, could not found a cause of action. Goddard LJ considered *Cobbett v Grey* and observed that it related to 'imprisonment in the wrong place'. He then considered *Osborne v Milman* and said a ([1943] 1 All ER 154 at 156, [1943] KB 252 at 254–255): 'But both these cases relate to the nature of the imprisonment. Here the prisoners were lawfully imprisoned and the questions relate to the conditions of their imprisonment.'

Counsel for the plaintiff submitted that the reference in this passage to the 'nature of the imprisonment' means that Goddard LJ was of the opinion that the earlier cases were not only dealing on the issue in tort with the wrong place of confinement, but with the nature of the imprisonment in the sense of the conditions of the imprisonment. I do not b read the judgment in this way. I think that Goddard LJ was merely saying that the nature of the imprisonment was tortious because it was in a place not authorised by law.

That all the cases cited by the plaintiff are authority for this limited proposition is the view of modern textbook writers: see Salmond on Torts (17th Edn, 1977, p 123) and Clerk and Lindsell on Torts (14th Edn, 1975, para 684) under the heading 'Imprisonment in the wrong place'. I hold that there is no authority in modern law to support the c plaintiff's submission that although a detention may be lawful it can become unlawful if the nature (meaning the conditions) of the imprisonment changes.

It seems to me that on this part of the case I am ultimately concerned with these questions of law: (i) on a proper construction of s 12(1) of the 1952 Act, does the subsection lawfully justify the detention of a prisoner in a prison? (ii) what, if at all, is the relevance of the conditions of imprisonment to the lawfulness of the detention? (iii) d what, if at all, is the relevance of a breach or non-compliance with the Prison Rules with respect to the issue of lawful detention?

If these questions are answered favourably to the defendant, then the imprisonment in the control unit would be justified, subject of course to the plaintiff's arguments with respect to the Bill of Rights and natural justice. But, on this hypothesis I would still have to decide whether the Secretary of State had power under r 43 and whether he complied e with any such power. Moreover, I should, on any view, have to decide issues of fact in case a different view prevailed on the answers to these questions in a higher court.

I shall therefore consider whether the Secretary of State had power to segregate prisoners under r 43 and whether, if he did, there was a compliance with the power. I shall then consider the argument that on any view of the construction of r 43 there was a lacuna in the authority between 23rd and 27th August 1974. Finally, I shall consider f the evidence and make findings of fact before I answer what seems to me to be the essential three questions on this part of the case.

An issue of fact arises whether any Secretary of State has exercised powers under r 43 before it was done in the case of CI 35/1974. The plaintiff's two expert witnesses, Professor Taylor and Dr Thomas, gave evidence on this issue. Professor Taylor is the Professor of Sociology in the University of York. He said that he was familiar with the g conditions of the operation of r 43. According to Professor Taylor, when jurisdiction is exercised it is the governor's decision. Dr Thomas is a reader in the University of Nottingham and has worked to some extent in the English prison system. In 1960 he was an assistant governor class I. He then served at Feltham Borstal as an assistant governor. In 1964 he taught at the Staff College at Wakefield. In 1967 he became a lecturer in social studies at the University of Hull. Dr Thomas has advised governments h in Australia about their penal systems. He has had no experience of day-to-day life in English prisons since 1967 and he has never held a position in a dispersal prison.

Dr Thomas said in evidence that in the English prison system it is always the governor who puts a man on r 43, although in cross-examination he agreed that there was an occasion when the Secretary of State in 1967 required that all long-term ordinary class prisoners should be placed under r 43 automatically on initial reception in prison after j sentence. This was done by CI 49/1967. According to Mr Emes, the Secretary of State has power to segregate prisoners under r 43 and he has given such instructions to governors, although it is done rarely. He referred to CI 49/1967 as an example. Those instructions were cancelled in 1974. Another example where the Secretary of State has exercised a power to order segregation, according to Mr Emes, was in the case of the 'cooling off' provision under CI 10/1974. That is the provision whereby the plaintiff was transferred from Hull Prison to Durham on 10th August 1974, as I have already considered.

Although in the day-to-day life in prison it is the governor who exercises the jurisdiction to segregate a prisoner from association with other prisoners, there is no doubt, and I find, that the Secretary of State has in the past asked governors to segregate prisoners under r 43. But the fact that the Secretary of State has exercised such a power does not, of course, prove that he has any such power to do so under the rule. The plaintiff contends that on a proper construction of the rule he has no such power.

Rule 43 provides:

'(1) Where it appears desirable, for the maintenance of good order or discipline or in his own interests, that a prisoner should not associate with other prisoners, either generally or for particular purposes, the governor may arrange for the prisoner's removal from association accordingly.

'(2) A prisoner shall not be removed under this Rule for a period of more than 24 hours without the authority of a member of the board of visitors, or of the Secretary of State. An authority given under this paragraph shall be for a period not exceeding one month, but may be renewed from month to month.

'(3) The governor may arrange at his discretion for such a prisoner as aforesaid to resume association with other prisoners, and shall do so if in any case the medical officer so advises on medical grounds.'

Counsel for the plaintiff submits that the natural meaning of the words of r 43(1) is that where it appears desirable to the governor, he may arrange for the prisoner's removal from association and that the rule only makes sense if it appears desirable to the person who is going to make the arrangement. He further submits that the natural meaning of r 43(1) and (2) read together is that the governor, having exercised his discretion to remove a prisoner, can only do so for a period of 24 hours. If he wishes to maintain the regime for a longer period he must obtain the authority of the board of visitors or the Secretary of State.

Thus, according to counsel, there is a two-tier system; the governor has to decide whether it is a proper case to make the arrangement, but his power is limited in time and may be continued only with other authority. In other words, according to the plaintiff, the governor initiates the process, and its continuance beyond 24 hours is subject to the safeguard of the authority of the board of visitors or the Secretary of State. The latter act is a supervisory safeguard. Any other view, submits counsel, leads to the conclusion that the Secretary of State, having initiated the process himself, can authorise its continuance. Moreover, since by para (3) the governor has a discretion to remove a prisoner from r 43, and indeed he must do so if the prison medical officer so recommends, according to counsel for the plaintiff it is not sensible or possible to suppose that the power to put the prisoner into a r 43 regime is given to separate hands.

Counsel for the defendant submits that para (1) does not in its opening words state to whom it may appear desirable that the prisoner shall be placed on a r 43 regime. He contends that it may appear desirable to someone other than the governor and that, if it appears desirable to the Secretary of State or anybody authorised by him (for example, the regional director of prisons or the control unit committee), the governor may be informed that it is desirable for the prisoner to be subject to r 43, in which case the governor may arrange to segregate the prisoner. According to him, the governor, by reason of the language of r 43(3), continues in such cases to have an overriding discretion to release a prisoner and must do so if so advised by the prison medical officer.

It is quite clear that r 43 provides an administrative power to remove a prisoner wholly or in part from association with other prisoners and that in the vast majority of cases it is the governor who uses the power in the ordinary day-to-day life of the prison. I do not think that the initial exercise of power can only be for 24 hours. Rule 43(2) provides that a prisoner shall not be removed without the authority of the board of visitors or the Secretary of State for more than 24 hours. It seems to follow that if an authority is given the prisoner may initially be removed for more than 24 hours, but not for more than one month.

There may therefore be an authority by the Secretary of State in the first instance to

remove for one month. It would therefore not be correct to hold that the role of the
a Secretary of State is simply confined to supervising the exercise of the governor's power
only after a period of 24 hours. But if the Secretary of State can give an initial authority
for a month, is he precluded from initiating the process? Is this process simply confined
to the governor? I do not think so. The language of r 43(1) is not sufficiently precise to
lead to a construction that the initial exercise of power is confined to the governor. It
would be surprising if the Secretary of State, who by statute is responsible for prisons and
b prisoners, could not tell a governor of a prison that a prisoner or a class of prisoners ought
to be segregated in a r 43 regime. The language of r 43 plainly leaves an over-all and
continuing discretion on the governor to release a prisoner. If, having put a prisoner on
r 43 at the suggestion of the Secretary of State, the circumstances changed and the
governor deemed it desirable to release the prisoner back into the general prison
population, he plainly could do so: see r 43(3).

c   In this case the evidence shows, and I find, that the plaintiff was in fact continuously
supervised. The governor visited him 20 times; the deputy governor also visited him 20
times; the assistant governor 1, Mr Papps, visited him 15 times. The plaintiff was visited
by the board of visitors who, by s 4(2) of the 1952 Act, have an obligation, inter alia, to
visit prisons and examine the treatment and conduct of prisoners and to see that the
provisions of the Act and rules are complied with. Dr Pollitt was the prison medical
d officer. He, or the other medical officer on duty, visited the control unit every day,
usually between 9 and 10 am.
       It was Dr Pollitt's evidence, which I accept, that if he had had any medical ground to
advise the release of the plaintiff or the other two men in the unit, Mr Masterson and Mr
McMullan, he would have done so. He said that he had no medical cause for concern in
the case of any of them, but this is a matter which I must consider later.

e   As I have already said, the Secretary of State has an over-all responsibility for prisons
and prisoners. Section 1 of the 1952 Act confers on him all the powers and jurisdiction
in relation to prisons and prisoners which, before the Prison Act 1877, were exercisable
by other authorities. It is clear that he is ultimately responsible for prisoners, including
their control. By s 47(1) of the 1952 Act the Secretary of State has power to make rules
for the regulation and management of prisons and other places of detention and, amongst
f other matters, for the classification, discipline and control of prisoners. It was in
pursuance of this power that the 1964 rules were made. I do not think that it can be said
that he is unable to exercise power under the rules made by him and approved by
Parliament. I hold that the Secretary of State has power to act under r 43 and that the
power was properly exercised for one month from 20th August 1974 by the agency
which he had appointed for that purpose, the control unit committee.

g   Before I consider the argument of the plaintiff with respect to the renewal of authority
after the first month, I should mention alternative arguments put forward by counsel for
the defendant. He submitted that in fact it was the governor of Hull who acted in the
case of the plaintiff under r 43 and that in effect the plaintiff's detention was in pursuance
of an arrangement made by the governor.
       In the memorandum sent by the governor of Hull to the regional director dated 12th
h August 1974, the governor requested the transfer of the plaintiff to the control unit.
Counsel argues that the documents show that the governor of Hull was fully acquainted
with the plaintiff's history and that by making the request to the regional director, who
passed it on to the control unit committee, he was making the arrangement. This is an
ingenious argument, but I do not think that it is correct on the facts. The governor
merely requested the plaintiff's transfer. He did not exercise the discretion to transfer
j or to make the arrangement. This was done by the control unit committee.
       Mr Emes was present as an observer at the meeting of the committee on 20th August
1974. He said in evidence in chief that the committee considered the ground rules or
criteria for admission at two meetings. According to Mr Emes, the committee considered
each case and applied the criteria correctly. On this evidence it was not the governor who
made the arrangement. He selected the candidate. The regional director made an initial
judgment of the suitability of the application. The control unit committee then
exercised its discretion afresh and they made the arrangement.

Counsel made further alternative submissions on this part of the case which I shall consider briefly. He submitted that if I were to find that there was non-compliance with *a* r 43 then the plaintiff's removal from Hull to Wakefield was in pursuance of and was justifiable by s 12(2) of the 1952 Act which provides:

'Prisoners shall be committed to such prisons as the Secretary of State may from time to time direct; and may by direction of the Secretary of State be removed during the term of their imprisonment from the prison in which they are confined *b* to any other prison.'

It is argued that I should reach the conclusion that the Secretary of State was entitled to arrange to transfer the plaintiff from Hull to Wakefield under this subsection. But as I understand it, the subsection merely provides power to commit to a prison and to move a prisoner from prison to prison. I do not think that the plaintiff's detention in the *c* control unit could be said to be made pursuant to this power.

A further alternative argument is based on r 3 of the 1954 rules. This rule relates to the classification of prisoners. It provides that prisoners shall be classified in accordance with any directions of the Secretary of State having regard to their age, temperament and record and with a view to maintaining good order and discipline and facilitating training and furthering the training and treatment of convicted prisoners. The argument is that *d* the plaintiff, as an intractable troublemaker, was being reclassified on the directions of the Secretary of State and sent to the unit. The purpose of the reclassification was a consideration of the training and treatment of other prisoners affected by the plaintiff's activities.

But the evidence is that the Secretary of State was throughout purporting to act under r 43, not only in relation to initial detention, but also with respect to the renewal of the *e* detention month by month. In the documents disclosed as a result of the order of McNeil J there is no suggestion that the Secretary of State was acting, or ever had it in mind to act, under r 43.

I shall now consider the question of the meaning of the provision for renewal of authority within r 43(2). As I mentioned earlier counsel for the plaintiff submits that the paragraph requires a fresh consideration of the facts of the case before each monthly *f* authority to renew was given. On this construction there must be a review involving an exercise of discretion. It is submitted that on the facts there was a predetermined policy to detain the plaintiff for the period of stages 1 and 2.

Counsel has cited a number of authorities for the proposition that where a minister of the Crown has a statutory discretion he cannot fetter its exercise by a pre-existing policy. Counsel cited *H Lavender & Son Ltd v Minister of Housing and Local Government* *g* [1970] 3 All ER 871, [1970] 1 WLR 1231. In that case the minister had a predetermined policy in relation to planning permission, and it was held by Willis J that, although he might have a policy, he was obliged to exercise his statutory discretion by giving a genuine and unfettered consideration to an application for planning permission. He could not fetter his discretion in advance by a predetermined policy.

Counsel submitted that this principle in relation to property rights applies with *h* greater force to cases where the personal liberty of the subject is concerned, and in this context he cited *Chic Fashions (West Wales) Ltd v Jones* [1968] 1 All ER 229, [1968] 2 QB 299 and *Ghani v Jones* [1969] 3 All ER 1700, [1970] 1 QB 693. He laid particular emphasis on the observations of Lord Denning MR in the latter case, where he said ([1969] 3 All ER 1700 at 1706, [1970] 1 QB 693 at 709): 'A man's liberty of movement is regarded so highly by the law of England that it is not to be hindered or prevented except on the *j* surest grounds.'

Counsel submits that these observations apply to a prisoner so that his liberty within the prison system should not be cut down. It is said that the plaintiff was, at least at stage 1 of the regime, restricted from the freedom of movement he would otherwise have had, by a predetermined policy to deny him the ordinary period in prison of associating with other prisoners. Counsel submits further that on the facts the control unit committee simply renewed the plaintiff's detention under the r 43 regime automatically.

a Counsel for the defendant submits that on the facts the minister did not have a predetermined policy to retain the plaintiff in the unit for the full period of 180 days and that the governor of Wakefield Prison always had the discretion to release the plaintiff. This policy to detain him for at least 180 days was made in advance, but the discretion to release if appropriate circumstances arose was not fettered. Moreover, counsel submits that the question which has to be asked when considering renewal of the authority is whether anything had changed since the initial decision to detain. If nothing had

b changed then the authority might be renewed. In other words, the defendant invites me to approach the question of renewal on the basis that initially the control unit committee considered all the facts of the plaintiff's case and decided that he should be detained for stages 1 and 2 of the regime. At the end of each month nothing had changed and therefore the authority to renew was issued.

I am asked to approach the question of renewal in a commonsense way and on the

c basis that since nothing had changed it would be unrealistic to hold that the committee should have reconsidered all the facts. It is pointed out that in practice in prison life there are certain categories of offenders who are detained in a state of non-association for very long periods without a fresh consideration of the facts when the authority is renewed. These prisoners are certain types of sexual offenders whose presence in prison, because of the nature of their offence, is unacceptable to the general prison population or to certain

d other types of prisoners. Such sexual offenders request isolation from the general population under r 43. They are called 'own request men'.

So far as the facts of this part of the case are concerned, I find that there was a predetermined policy to detain the plaintiff for the period of each stage of the regime, but that that policy did not preclude the release of the plaintiff if circumstances required it. CI 35/1974 did not expressly or, in my judgment, by necessary implication take away

e the governor's discretion under r 43(3). I have already made certain findings on this part of the case. But equally, it seems to me that the renewal was automatic.

Mr Allum, who was the unit manager, said in evidence that London kept in touch with the unit through the governor and that when the unit was opened there was a series of staff meetings to discuss problems in the unit. Mr Allum added that he and Mr Waugh, who was the principal officer in the unit, met monthly to monitor progress in

f the unit. Mr Allum's evidence is far too imprecise to justify a finding that the control unit committee was given information on which it exercised its discretion to renew the detention.

Mr Emes, when cross-examined, said that he accepted that the plaintiff was not mentioned in the minutes of the committee from August 1974 to January 1975 because the full committee did not consider his case. He did say that a Mr Smith, who was a

g member of the committee, was in regular contact with the governor and through him with Mr Allum, but this is hearsay evidence and in any event it does not show that the question of renewal was considered.

Counsel for the plaintiff asks me to find, and I do find (i) that no request for renewed authority was received by the Home Office from the governor of Wakefield in relation to the plaintiff during his period in the unit until the application for his discharge was

h made at the end of January 1975, (ii) that the control unit committee did not discuss or consider the plaintiff between 20th August 1974 and 4th February 1975, (iii) that on 4th February 1975 the committee authorised the plaintiff's release on 18th February 1975, subject to any intervening reversion.

The question I have to decide is whether it is a compliance with the rule to renew the authority automatically. In my judgment, the renewal of authority under r 43(2) does

j require a consideration of the state of the relevant facts before there is renewal. The language of the provision in the rule that the authority shall not exceed one month, but may be renewed from month to month, suggests to me that the renewing authority should at least look at what had happened in the preceding month. That was not done on my findings of fact. The committee did not on the evidence even ask themselves the limited question: has anything changed? I therefore find that there was not a compliance with the renewal procedure, but whether it affects in any way the lawfulness of the plaintiff's detention is a matter I must consider later.

[His Lordship then considered the facts on which the plaintiff relied in support of his
claims that there had been breaches of the Prison Rules and that the imprisonment in the
control unit was different and worse than that in the remainder of the prison system and
was contrary to the Bill of Rights. His Lordship found that a prisoner was not 'unduly'
deprived of the society of other persons for the period of stage 1 because the deprivation
was not excessive, and there had therefore been no breach of r 3(3) of the Prison Rules.
His Lordship further found that the instructions to the prison staff in the control unit to
avoid confrontations with prisoners were not contrary to the Prison Rules because an
objective designed to prevent a prisoner being put on a charge or to persuade him to co-
operate with the regime was not contrary to the Prison Rules. His Lordship then
considered whether the control unit regime was a punishment for the plaintiff and
found that the decision to transfer the plaintiff to the control unit was an administrative
and non-punitive decision taken to relieve the prison system. His Lordship further
found that the conditions in the control unit were significantly different from conditions
of punishment by cellular confinement. His Lordship continued:]

In support of his submission that the regime in the control unit was, and was seen to
be, punitive in character by the accountable divisions of the Home Office responsible for
producing CI 35/1974, counsel for the plaintiff relies on some of the documents disclosed
as a result of the order of McNeil J in *Williams v Home Office* p 1151, ante.

There are seven documents, some of which relate to the issue of the punitive nature of
the regime and the issue of the Bill of Rights. Counsel submits that the contents of these
documents amount to admissions or are corroborative of the plaintiff's case that the
character of the regime was punitive, that it involved a deprivation of human contact
and that the regime was harmful. It is submitted that the contents of the documents are
receivable in evidence as admissions and that it is then a question for me to determine the
weight to be given to the documents, balancing them against other evidence. In broad
terms, the contents of the documents relate to the plaintiff's case as I have described it.
They all express opinions about the regime.

Mr Emes agreed in cross-examination that there was concern at all levels of the Home
Office that the common usage of the term punitive in the sense of disagreeable might
result in the control unit being interpreted as a punishment and that there was a
similarity between the circumstances of some aspects of some types of punishment and
the control unit.

Counsel for he plaintiff submitted that the documents amount to admissions that the
regime was punitive in character on three grounds. First, it is submitted that the
members of the various departments who expressed the opinions were privies of the
Crown. Privity is said to arise because they were members of the Home Office, which
itself represents the Crown's interest in the prison system. I am satisfied that this cannot
be a valid ground for an admission in this case. The members of the prison department
were not the privies of the Crown. The principle in question in any event seems to me
to be confined to cases involving property interests, as junior counsel for the defendant
submitted, referring to 17 Halsbury's Laws (4th Edn) para 68 and Phipson on Evidence
(12th Edn, 1976, para 707).

Second, counsel submits that the contents of the documents amount to admissions
because they were made by persons who were the alter ego of the Secretary of State. The
principle by which the documents amount to admissions is, according to this argument,
that a minister does not delegate his power through a civil servant, but always acts
through him on the legal assumption that the civil servant and he are one in law. Thus
the hand and mouth of the civil servant are those of the Secretary of State, and what they
write and say are his words.

Counsel submits that the Secretary of State is charged with running prisons, which he
does through the responsible and senior members of the Prison Department. He relies
on a general observation in Wade on Administrative Law (4th Edn, 1977, p 314): 'Legally
and constitutionally the act of the official is the act of the minister, without any need for
specific authorisation in advance or ratification afterwards.'

Junior counsel, replying for the defendant, submits that of necessity civil servants
perform two functions. There are constitutional occasions when the civil servant will

sometimes be the alter ego of the minister. The minister cannot perform all his activities
a and therefore the doctrine is that when the civil servant does what it is the minister's
duty to do, he is the minister. Counsel referred me to *Carltona Ltd v Comrs of Works*
[1943] 2 All ER 560. I need not repeat the facts. Lord Greene MR said (at 563):

> 'In the administration of government in this country the functions which are
> given to ministers ... are functions so multifarious that no minister could ever
> personally attend to them ... The duties imposed upon ministers and the powers
b > given to ministers are normally exercised under the authority of the ministers by
> responsible officials of the department.'

These words were repeated in *R v Skinner* [1968] 3 All ER 124, [1968] 2 QB 700 to which
counsel referred.

That, submits counsel for the defendant, is the true basis of the alter ego doctrine. But
c civil servants perform a second function, which is simply their ordinary work. They are
not then the alter ego of the minister. Counsel submits that when the various civil
servants were expressing the opinions to be found in the relevant documents, they were
merely doing so in the course of their ordinary work, and they were not expressing the
opinions of the Secretary of State. I entirely agree with that submission. It would, I
think, be surprising if whenever a civil servant expressed a written or spoken opinion in
d the course of his work that constituted an admission by the Secretary of State.

The third ground on which it is argued by counsel for the plaintiff that the contents
of the documents are receivable as admissions is that the civil servants expressing the
opinions were the agents of the Secretary of State. The defendant objects that an
admission by an agent can only be evidence if it is made to a third party. None of the
contents of the documents were made to third parties. They are all internal
e documents. Counsel for the plaintiff submits that there is no rule of law that to be
receivable in evidence as an admission a statement must be made to a third party. He
submits that the one authority in which it was held that the admission must be to a third
party before it can be received in evidence was wrongly decided.

I have been referred by both counsel to the leading textbook writers. In Cross on
Evidence (5th Edn, 1979, p 525), the author writes: 'The statement of the agent which
f is tendered as an admission must, on the preponderance of authority, have been made to
a third person, not to the principal.' *Re Devala Provident Gold Mining Company* (1883) 22
Ch D 593 is cited in support of that proposition. The editors of Phipson on Evidence
(12th Edn, 1976, paras 728, 730) express the same opinion and state that *The Solway*
(1885) 10 PD 137, in which it was held that a statement to a principal is in law receivable
as an admission even though not made to a third party, was wrongly decided. 17
g Halsbury's Laws (4th Edn) para 72 seems to me to support the general proposition.

In *Re Devala* a shareholder applied to have his name removed from the register of
shareholders on the ground that he had been induced to become a shareholder by a
material misrepresentation in the company's prospectus. The only evidence that the
representation was untrue was a statement made by the chairman of the company at a
shareholder's meeting. Fry J held that the statement was not admissible because the
h chairman was not acting as an agent in a transaction between the company and a third
party. He said (22 Ch D 593 at 596):

> 'It appears to me, however, that it is not admissible, for it was made by the agent,
> not in a transaction between the company and a third party, but at a meeting of the
> company. It is the case of an agent making a report to his own principal, and, in my
> view, when an agent is making a confidential report to his principal the report is not
j > admissible evidence in favour of a third party.'

Fry J did not in the course of his judgment give reasons for this conclusion.

In *The Solway* Hannen P held that a letter from the master of a ship to her owners was
admissible in evidence. The letter was not written to a third party. The case is directly
at variance with *Re Devala*. Hannen P said (10 PD 137 at 138):

> 'It seems to me that this case comes within a leading rule of the law of evidence,

for it is clear that the log of a vessel is admissible in evidence by the other side, to shew what entries have been made by the agent of the owners of the vessel on which the log is kept. This letter comes within the same rule . . .'

The Solway is therefore clear authority that an admission to be receivable in evidence need not be made to a third party. If this is the law then the various memoranda and other documents are receivable by me, even though they are internal and were not made to third parties.

The Solway was considered by Lord Dunedin in *Admiralty Lords Comrs v Aberdeen Steam Trawling and Fishing Co Ltd* 1909 SC 335. He pointed out (at 340) that a ship's log is admissible in evidence by the provisions of the Merchant Shipping Act and not at common law, and that therefore the admission of the letter as evidence in *The Solway* by analogy with the admissibility of a ship's log was misconceived.

In *Swan v Miller* [1919] 1 IR 151 a majority in the Irish Court of Appeal refused to follow *The Solway*. The document in *Swan v Miller* was a letter written by an agent to his principal. The court held that the letter could not be treated as an admission by the principal in his dealing with a third party. O'Connor LJ said (at 183): 'The notion that a principal should be bound by what his agent says to him seems to me to have no warrant whatever, in law or sense.'

The preponderance of authority, direct and persuasive, is in favour of the defendant's submission. It seems to me that to be receivable in evidence an admission by an agent must be made to a third party. As counsel pointed out it is not an unreasonable conclusion to limit the admissibility of such evidence to the area in which the agent is representing his principal in his dealings with a third party. When an agent is talking to his principal, submits counsel, he is not making a statement in the course of his agency.

It seems to me that the rule which I have considered is well entrenched in principle, that there is long-standing authority to support it and that the proposition is sustainable in principle and reason. I therefore follow *Re Devala* and hold that the documents are not receivable as admissions, but with one exception which I shall mention in a moment. Nor do I think that they can be received as corroborative of the plaintiff's case.

The one document which needs separate consideration is an unsigned note of a meeting held on 21st October 1974 between the Secretary of State, the Under-Secretary of State and various members of the prison department. The Secretary of State is recorded as referring to the various criticisms which were being made of the control unit and expressed concern that an allocation to the unit was an administrative matter, although it had many of the features of punishment. The note continues:

'In the course of the discussion it was explained that while allocation to a Control Unit or withdrawal from association under Rule 43 had, in their effects upon the individual, many of the features of punishment and were related to things the prisoner had done, they were not punishments in the sense of being specific penalties for specific proven offences against the Prison Rules. They were measures taken to remove a person from association because of a continuing pattern of behaviour—usually evidenced to some extent by proved offences—in order to enable prison life to continue satisfactorily.'

Counsel for the defendant submitted that the document is hearsay by some unknown person and that if the plaintiff wished to produce this evidence he should call the maker or rather the Secretary of State. But this is a document produced on discovery containing remarks attributable to the Secretary of State. I do not think it would be right to ignore it, but what weight I give to it is another matter. It seems to me on the evidence I have heard that the reply given to the Secretary of State is an accurate summary of r 43 segregation. The note does not state how the Secretary of State replied to the advice he was given. At the meeting various changes were made in the machinery for allocation of prisoners to the unit and the renewal procedure, and CI 35/1974 was amended accordingly.

The question I have to decide is whether the regime was punitive in character. Mr Allum agreed in cross-examination that the regime might appear punitive to a prisoner

in the same way as a prison might appear punitive to a member of the public. Mr Emes
a agreed that one of the reasons for isolation was to make it sufficiently disagreeable so that
it would be worthwhile for a man to work his passage. He said that it was known that
the prisoner would find the regime disagreeable. The intention was to ensure that he did
not continue to make a nuisance of himself in the prison system. He said that there were
two elements in the regime: first, to teach the prisoner that it was not going to pay him
to go on being a troublemaker and, secondly, to make him not want to go back. In this
b sense, according to Mr Emes, there was an element of deterrence, but he added that
many things can be deterrent without being a punishment. For him punishment is the
response to a proven act.

   I do not think that the regime was devised to punish the prisoners; nor do I think that
the plaintiff was in fact being punished when he was sent there. As I have already said,
punishment is not within the ambit of r 43. If this rule were used merely as a device to
c punish a particular prisoner, it would be highly improper and there would be a breach
of the rule, although with what legal effect I have yet to consider. Junior counsel for the
defendant pointed out that, objectively viewed, a punishment regime and a r 43 regime
can appear to be close together. If a prisoner is beaten up and the governor strongly
suspects, but is unable to prove, that a particular prisoner is responsible, he would be
fully entitled to place the suspect on r 43, not to punish the prisoner, but to prevent a
d repetition of the incident in the interests of good order and discipline.

   Finally, I should add, with respect to the other documents that I have considered, that
even if I had admitted them I should have given them little weight. They are expressions
of opinion given without the advantage which I have had of hearing very lengthy
argument and the fullest evidence. Some of them were given before the final version of
CI 35/1974 appeared at a time when considerable inter-divisional discussion was taking
e place as to the ethos of the regime in the unit and the means of carrying it out.

   Counsel for the plaintiff invites me to find that the punitive character of the regime
is shown by what counsel has called a 'harsh and degrading character' of Mr McMullan's
punishment in the unit. This is a reference to the fact that Mr McMullan was on three
occasions given a punishment award for offences against discipline, the details of which
I shall mention later. He was placed in the strong box of the control unit. There was
f only a concrete block in the cell as a bed, with a mattress. He said in evidence that he had
to sit on the floor to eat. These conditions were undoubtedly very severe, but they were
punishments for an offence and they do not, in my judgment, show that the regime in
the control unit itself was punitive.

   Whilst I am considering the documents, I should say that Mr Emes was asked a
number of questions about various working documents, memoranda and documents
g recording the results of discussions, most of which relate to the stage when the nature
and the details of the regime were being worked out. Some of the views expressed were
individual views. For example, a Mr Chambers expressed the view that the control unit
should not have the features of special security wings. Mr Emes said that Mr Chambers
was expressing his own view, but I did not understand Mr Emes to accept in any way that
the control unit was comparable with the special security wings, though that was the
h view of Professor Taylor. These are all individual views. I have to make up my own
mind about the nature and character of the regime on all the evidence I have heard. On
the evidence I do not think that the regime was punitive in character.

   I must now consider the specific facts which the plaintiff asks me to find in para 14 of
counsel's list of facts. I summarised these submissions in item 8 when I outlined the
nature of the plaintiff's case. I shall now follow the same order. All these submissions
j of fact are intended to prove that the control unit regime constituted imprisonment of
a different and worse nature than the remainder of the prison system, and this in turn is
part of the submission, that being of a different nature, the imprisonment in the unit
cannot be justified and that the regime offended the Bill of Rights. I have already held
that there is no authority which supports the proposition in relation to the nature of the
imprisonment.

   [His Lordship then stated his findings on the specific submissions made on behalf of
the plaintiff, as follows:]

(i) (a) *No association whatever for the first month.* This is factually true. I am satisfied, and I find, that the solitary exercise for the first month was not intentionally or deliberately inflicted on the plaintiff. There are, as I have said, many occasions when men are deprived of association in prison life in r 43 regimes. The unit, in my judgment, was not of a different or worse nature than the remainder of the prison system on this aspect of the facts.

(b) *Apart from exercise there was no association at all for 90 days.* This is factually accurate.

(ii) *The attitude of the staff was deliberately distant.* I have already considered this issue and made findings of fact. I find that in practical terms there was no difference between the unit and the remainder of the system, save that the plaintiff was required to make the initial approach. That was the only difference, and it had little effect in practice.

(iii) *Visits did not afford the plaintiff company, nor would visits by available specialists have done so.* There is no doubt on the evidence that in ordinary prisons in practice the staff do sometimes bend the rules and allow prisoners and their visitors to talk unhindered and alone, but rule 33(3) and (4) provide that every visit to a prisoner shall take place within the sight and hearing of a prison officer, unless the Secretary of State otherwise directs. The fact that the rules may be stretched in other prison locations does not mean that the conditions in the control unit were of a different nature and worse than in other prisons.

No doubt visiting conditions did not afford the plaintiff as much company as at Parkhurst. The evidence shows that the plaintiff had a considerable number of visits from the board of visitors and other interested organisations. They were not, of course, social visits, although certainly they broke up the plaintiff's day.

The point which is made on this part of the case is that the plaintiff was without human companionship and therefore his imprisonment was of a different nature and worse than practised in the remainder of the prison life. No one does or could claim that stage 1 was not disagreeable. Mr Emes, as I have said, accepted that the purpose was to make it sufficiently disagreeable to persuade a prisoner that it would not be worthwhile to return. Rule 43 regimes are practised in the remainder of the prison system, and when a prisoner is totally deprived of association, he does unfortunately lack human company.

Later I shall consider the defendant's submission that in fact the deprivation of human company at stage 1 had little effect on the plaintiff because when he had the chance to associate with Mr McMullan and Mr Masterson who were fellow prisoners at stage 2, he elected not to do so.

(iv) and (v) *There was no visual and no auditory relief.* This submission relates to conditions in the plaintiff's cell and the fact that he was deprived of a radio. The evidence from Mr Emes, which I accept, shows that when a man is on r 43 in a segregation unit he is not allowed a radio. This is confirmed by the segregation unit rules. Even 'own request' men segregated for their own protection are not allowed radios.

I cannot therefore find that the lack of auditory relief made the imprisonment of a different and worse nature than in the rest of the prison system. But I think that the lack of visual relief outside the cell probably did. As to the complaint of the colour of the cell, apart from the plaintiff's evidence, there is very little evidence as to its effect.

The question is whether on the facts there is any evidence that the plaintiff suffered sensory deprivation. The prison medical officer, Dr Pollitt, gave evidence on this issue. Dr Pollitt's evidence will be material when I consider the evidence of the effect of the regime on the plaintiff later. But Dr Pollitt wrote a report on 29th August 1975, in which he said:

'I understand that it has been suggested in some circles that prisoners in the Control Unit are subject to sensory deprivation or psychological pressures. As somebody who has visited the Control Unit regularly and on many occasions, I cannot accept either of these suggestions.'

a In the witness-box Dr Pollitt confirmed the accuracy of this passage. I thought that Dr Pollitt was an excellent and clear witness. He said that his report was true and was based on his own observation. I accept that evidence and I accept that there was no evidence of sensory deprivation.

(vi) *There was insufficient light by which to read.* The plaintiff said in evidence that because there was a mesh over the window there was no daylight and it was necessary to have the
b light on all day. I do not recollect any evidence as to the means of lighting in other prison locations.

This issue was also related to a complaint which the plaintiff made that he was unable to control the lighting in his cell and that it was liable to be switched fully on at night after lights were put out.

On my finding, the light was not on at night. In deciding the issues on this part of the
c case, I have regard to r 11(a) of the Standard Minimum Rules, which provides that windows shall be large enough to read or to work by natural light. But on the whole of the evidence I do not think this issue is really one of substance.

(vii) *The only work was dull and repetitious.* According to the plaintiff, he sewed mail bags in his cell at stage 1. At stage 2 he was allowed to work outside his cell, and at first he did so, sticking envelopes. I understood from his evidence that he did not care for this work
d and that he changed back to sewing mail bags. He said that in ordinary prison he worked in association in a large workshop or outside the prison, that the atmosphere was relaxed and that he was not watched.

But the plaintiff was undergoing a r 43 regime involving, at stage 1, limited association. In these circumstances I am not able to follow how he could work in ordinary prison conditions. No doubt sewing mail bags is dull and repetitious and it is
e of a different and worse nature than practised in the rest of the system when a prisoner is not on r 43 segregation.

(viii) *The plaintiff was subject to surveillance and searches by the prison staff.* These complaints relate to the searching of the plaintiff and his cell and to an allegation that he was watched
f whilst using the shower and, particularly, the lavatory. I find as a fact that the system of accompanying prisoners to the lavatory was not different in nature and worse than the remainder of the system. It is necessary to carry out searches in the prison system for security reasons and to ensure compliance with the rules. As the plaintiff said men in prison do sometimes secrete things in lavatories for other prisoners, and, according to the entry in the history sheet for 31st August 1974, the plaintiff was discovered attempting to secrete tobacco for Mr Masterson in the washing recess.
g By r 39(1) of the Prison Rules the frequency of searches depends on the governor. I am not satisfied that the frequency of searching was different from the remainder of the prison system.

(ix) *There was no possibility of remission of the term spent in the control unit for good conduct, whether under r 56 (punishment) or r 43(3).* The question I am asked to answer in this
h context is whether the regime in the unit was of a different and worse nature than the remainder of the system. If in framing the question in this way counsel is making the comment that under r 56 a prisoner undergoing punishment can earn remission, that is factually correct. The plaintiff was not undergoing punishment. He was detained under r 43 for the maintenance of good order and discipline. Although there is no remission as such under r 43, the governor does, as Mr Emes agreed in cross-examination, take a
j prisoner off the regime as soon as he considers that it is right to do so. The decision, according to Mr Emes, is arrived at after a review of wide-ranging factors, some of which are not directly related to the immediate behaviour of the prisoner.

Rule 43(3) confers, as I have said, a discretion on the governor to allow a prisoner to resume association. From what I understand of the evidence, it is not remission of a punishment for an offence. CI 35/1974 did not remove the governor's right to exercise his discretion to remove the plaintiff from the regime, although there was clearly a policy decision that, so long as the plaintiff remained healthy, he would remain in the regime. *a*

Clearly, the regime had in this respect different features from the ordinary system, but, for the reasons I gave when I considered Mr Emes's evidence in relation to the alleged breaches of the rules, I do not think that it was worse than the rest of the system. But it is right that there was no provision for remission in the regime in the unit.

b

(x) *There was continuing threat of repeated and indefinite prolongation of the term in the unit (a) for misconduct falling short of a disciplinary offence, (b) as a second penalty for a disciplinary offence charged and proved and (c) for refusal to work.* It is clear from the language of CI 35/1974 that if a prisoner refused to work and if he attempted to cause trouble he would revert to stage 1. The circular instruction envisaged that if a man repeatedly misbehaved he would revert. In that sense there was a risk of repeated and indefinite prolongation *c* of the regime within the terms of the sentence.

As I mentioned earlier, it is clear from Mr Emes's evidence that men do spend long periods on r 43, and it is also clear from the evidence that if a prisoner is on r 43 and misbehaves he is likely to remain on the regime. To that extent the regime in the unit seems to me not to be dissimilar.

The purpose of the provision that if a man misbehaved he would revert was to attempt *d* to persuade him to co-operate and behave himself. It is, in my judgment, not accurate on the evidence to say that the risk of reversion made the regime in the control unit worse than that practised in the remainder of the system. The onus was put on the prisoner and he knew, as appears from the cell information card, that if he behaved himself he would be released from the regime after a fixed period.

Counsel submits that the effect of reversion on top of a punishment for an offence *e* against prison discipline operated as a second penalty. In a sense it did, but again, as I understand the evidence, if a man undergoing a r 43 regime commits an offence he is liable to be punished for that offence and, as I understand the prison system, he is likely to continue on r 43.

(xi) *That stage 2 was in practice little different from stage 1, partly because of the small number f of prisoners, but partly because of the impact on the plaintiff's personality which made him want to retreat from surveillance to his cell.* In order to explain this submission, I should say that at stage 2 when the plaintiff was able to associate with Mr McMullan and Mr Masterson he often preferred to work and did work in his cell. The defendant submits that if the plaintiff was or felt so deprived of human company at stage 1 it is surprising that he forewent the opportunity to mix with his fellow prisoners on every possible occasion that *g* he could.

The plaintiff's answer to this is that the solitary confinement at stage 1 had such an effect on him that he preferred to be in his cell rather than work with the other prisoners under the surveillance of the staff.

The reference in counsel's submission to the small number of prisoners is a reference to the fact that only three prisoners, the plaintiff, Mr McMullan and Mr Masterson, were *h* in the unit at one time. That is a matter of mere chance. It is only relevant when I come to consider the complaint concerning the silence in the unit in due course.

The question which is now raised involves the evidence concerning the effect of the regime on the plaintiff. As I understand the question submitted by counsel, it is argued that, because of the impact of the regime on the plaintiff, it was of a different and worse nature than the remainder of the prison system. I shall now consider the evidence *j* bearing on the effect of the regime on the plaintiff at both stages. It is also relevant on the issue of damages.

In essence, it is the plaintiff's case that the isolation and lack of human company, together with the threat of reversion and the attitude of the staff, bore so harshly on him that it caused him at times to be frightened, depressed and disorientated. He said in evidence in chief that it was in the back of his mind at stage 1 that he would not get out of the regime. He did not know how much of it he could stand.

a
When cross-examined he said that the prison department attacked his brain. He said that he used to sit in his cell having 'mental gymnastics', that this had continued for five years and that it still occasionally happened. In evidence in chief he described himself as still getting very paranoid. When he is sitting in a room with people he says that he feels they are looking at him or talking about him and he has to leave the room.

b
[His Lordship then considered the medical evidence called on behalf of both the plaintiff and the defendant and continued:] There is no doubt on the evidence that at stage 2 the plaintiff very frequently refused association with Mr McMullan and Mr Masterson. The fact is amply documented in the history sheets. The entries also show that the prison officers making the entries very frequently refer to the fact that the plaintiff was laughing, joking, in good humour and lighthearted. I have already read some of the many entries.

Other typical entries are these:

c
'20.12.74 Very cheerful to-day, declined association p.m. and evening. 24.12.74 The usual Williams to-day, always a laugh and a joke. Declined assoc. 21.1.75 Continues to amble his way through his time here. Very pleasant with staff today worked in cell all day. 14.2.75 Refused associated work and evening, he continues to work extremely well in his cell. Always ready for a laugh with any of the staff . . .'

d
Both Mr Waugh and Mr Allum stated in evidence, as I mentioned earlier, that the entries which they made are accurate. The plaintiff's answer to these two features of the history sheet are: first, that he was so affected by the regime in the unit that he preferred the security of his cell and, second, that although the 20 or so prison officers accurately recorded what they saw he was merely, as I have said, putting on a brave face to conceal his true feelings and to get through the regime as best he could.

e
Dr Woolf said in evidence that people do retreat to what they regard as a safe situation, even though it is one which is very unpleasant. Dr Leigh agreed that a patient may not only be uncomplaining, but that he may put on a falsely brave face. I of course accept Dr Woolf and Dr Leigh that such situations can arise, but I am entirely satisfied that that was not the position in this case. I find it impossible to accept that the plaintiff was able to deceive all the prison officers as to his true feelings.

f
I bear in mind that I have not seen the prison officers give evidence, but the entries are, in my judgment, strong in their effect. Moreover, Mr Allum made what sounded to me a telling and truthful answer when he said in cross-examination that the plaintiff was not play-acting. He added: 'We saw the true Williams.' I accept the evidence of Mr Allum and that of Mr Waugh as to the accuracy of their entries in the history sheets.

g
According to Mr Allum, the plaintiff had association until 5th December 1974, when he left the workroom despite being told to stay. He was put on a report. The plaintiff agreed that he was dealt with leniently. After that he was permitted to work in his cell, which was his wish. The trouble, according to Mr Allum, was caused because the plaintiff and Mr Masterson did not get on. Mr Allum said that he permitted the plaintiff to work in his cell because to force two people to work together could cause confrontation.

h
The plaintiff denied that he refused association because of trouble with Mr Masterson. He said that he chose to stay in the cell rather than sit, as he put it, and be ogled at by the prison officers. He disputed a number of the entries in the history sheets, saying that they were not accurate or true. As I understand his evidence, he said that the entries showing that he had put on weight when in the unit were not accurate.

j
I reject the plaintiff's evidence. I accept the evidence of Mr Allum as to the reason why the plaintiff refused association. I find as a fact that the refusal was wholly unconnected with the conditions in the regime or the plaintiff's reaction to it.

I regret to have to say that I did not find the plaintiff a convincing witness. I am not satisfied that the conditions of isolation, the lack of human company, the threat of reversion or the fact, as I have found it, that the plaintiff had to make the running in his relationship with the prison officers had the slightest effect on the plaintiff's nervous or mental health. I am not satisfied that the plaintiff has mildly neurotic symptoms today attributable to his time in the unit.

In answer to the plaintiff's submission which I am presently considering, I find that a
desire to avoid surveillance played no part in the plaintiff's decision to work in his cell at   *a*
stage 2. I have considered the other issues of fact implicit in the submission. It also
follows from my findings of fact that if the damages fall to be considered I should only
be able to award compensatory damages for the fact of unlawful detention.

(xii) *That the plaintiff was held in solitary confinement for 23 hours a day at stage 1.* It is the
fact that the plaintiff had no association at stage 1, save at exercise, and that he worked in
his cell. The evidence shows, and I find, that at no point during stage 1 did more than   *b*
two hours pass without interruption. In my judgment, the regime was not different in
nature and worse in the unit than in the rest of the prison system for a prisoner
undergoing a r 43 regime of non-association. As I have already found, many prisoners
undergo a similar regime for long periods.

(xiii) *That the plaintiff did not know specifically why he was in the unit.* Counsel for the   *c*
plaintiff asked me to find that the regime was of a different nature and worse than the
remainder of the prison system for this reason. The plaintiff's prison record and related
documents were admitted as such. Counsel for the defendant has submitted that it is not
credible that the plaintiff did not know his past record and why he was being transferred
to Wakefield. I agree that it is incredible that the plaintiff did not know his past
record. One entry reads: '5.8.74. (Hull) Took part in a passive all wing sit-in   *d*
demonstration lasting hours. Reported to work after representatives had been seen by
D/Gov. A ringleader.' The plaintiff may not have been told the specific details of the
conduct which led to his transfer to the control unit, but I am quite sure he knew of
them.

There were two further matters which I noted in counsel's submission of fact in the
course of argument.   *e*

(xiv) *Lack of possessions.* I have already referred to the nature of the possessions which the
plaintiff was allowed, and, in my judgment, the nature and extent of them cannot be
reasonably criticised.

(xv) *Silence in the unit.* The plaintiff said in the course of his evidence in chief that it was   *f*
very quiet in the unit. He said that you could hear a pin drop. He somewhat
inconsistently complained that the prison officers used to walk about with heavy boots,
making a noise, and that they used to whistle. This, according to the plaintiff, was done
to annoy the prisoners. He said that this noise happened constantly.

When he gave evidence, Mr Allum stated that the unit was designed to receive more
than three prisoners. It was in fact designed to receive about 20. Mr Waugh said that it   *g*
was not his intention to keep the unit quiet. He agreed in cross-examination that if there
had been more than three prisoners there would have been more noise. When he
opened the plaintiff's case to me, counsel submitted that there was an enforced silence.
I do not find that that submission is supported by the evidence. No doubt the unit was
quiet, but I accept Mr Waugh's explanation for this.

h

I must now consider the questions which seem to me to be crucial on this part of the
plaintiff's case, apart from the argument based on the Bill of Rights and natural justice.
The questions are these: (i) On a proper construction of s 12(1) of the 1952 Act, does the
subsection lawfully justify the detention of a prisoner in a prison? (ii) What, if at all, is
the relevance of the conditions of imprisonment to the lawfulness of the detention? (iii)
What, if at all, is the relevance of a breach or non-compliance with the Prison Rules with   *j*
respect to the issue of lawful detention?

Section 12(1) of the Act empowers the Secretary of State lawfully to confine a prisoner
in any prison. Counsel for the plaintiff submits, as I understand him, that the subsection
is concerned only with the place of imprisonment and not with any tortious act done
within it. This means that the subsection is not capable of justifying the detention of a
prisoner when the nature of the imprisonment differs from that in the remainder of the
system and where there is a breach of the Prison Rules.

In my judgment, the sentence of the court and the provisions of s 12(1) always afford
a a defence to an action of false imprisonment. The sentence justifies the fact of
imprisonment and the subsection justifies the confinement of a prisoner in any prison.
How then can it be unjustifiable and unlawful to confine him there? I accept the
submission of counsel for the defendant that the sentence of the court and the provisions
of s 12(1) provide a defence to this action, subject to the arguments based on the Bill of
Rights and natural justice.

b Counsel for the defendant raised a further argument based on s 14(2) and (3), which
I shall mention briefly. These subsections provide:

'(2) No cell shall be used for the confinement of a prisoner unless it is certified by
an inspector that its size, lighting, heating, ventilation and fittings are adequate for
health . . .
c '(3) A certificate given under this section in respect of any cell may limit the
period for which a prisoner may be separately confined in the cell and the number
of hours a day during which a prisoner may be employed therein.'

Counsel's submission, as I understood it, is that since s 14(3) provides that a certificate
may limit the period for which a prisoner may be separately confined, it presupposes that
he may be confined for an unlimited number of hours if there is no certificate.
d Therefore, since there was no certificate in respect of the plaintiff, he could be indefinitely
confined even for 24 hours a day in the cell. It is submitted that s 14(3) is express
Parliamentary authority for an indefinite confinement. I cannot accept this argument.
Section 14 of the Act has all the appearance of a health and welfare provision, and, in my
judgment that is all it is dealing with.

The next question is whether the lawfulness of the detention can be affected by the
conditions of the detention. I do not think so. The question of the conditions of
e imprisonment is a matter for the Secretary of State. The check or safeguard against
unacceptable conditions in the present state of the law lies in the prisoner's rights under
the rules to complain to the governor or the Secretary of State. Counsel for the plaintiff
submits that if this is right it means that a prisoner is without remedy even though he
is subjected to a regime which is harsh and unpleasant.

f There is in fact in the administration of prisons of this country ample safeguard against
abuse. As I have already said, s 4(2) of the Act provides comprehensively for supervision
of the conduct of prison officers, the treatment and conduct of prisoners and all matters
concerning the management of prisons. The subsection provides a duty in terms that
officers of the Secretary of State shall ensure compliance with the Prison Act and rules.
Conditions vary from prison to prison, according to the category of the prisoner and his
behaviour in prison.
g The position of a prisoner in prison is shown by passages from two cases. In *R v Hull
Prison Board of Visitors, ex parte St Germain* [1979] 1 All ER 701 at 725, [1979] QB 425 at
466 Waller LJ said:

'There are many administrative decisions made within prisons which would not
be capable of review and which would have as serious consequences to the prisoner
as some findings of a board of visitors. Section 12 of the Prison Act 1952 allows the
h Secretary of State to confine "in any prison" and to remove from one prison to
another. Prisoners may be categorised A, B or C, and the consequences may be very
different, for example the difference between a top-security prison and an open
prison. A prisoner may be segregated under r 43. This would be an administrative
decision with serious consequences but one which could not be reviewed by a court.'

j In *Payne v Home Office* (2nd May 1977, unreported) the plaintiff contended that before
being put into category A he should, in accordance with the principles of natural justice,
have been informed of what was alleged against him and that he should have been given
the opportunity of answering it. Cantley J said:

'What is the situation of a convicted prisoner? He is someone who, for an offence
against the law, is obliged to undergo lawful confinement whether he likes it or
not. He may be lawfully confined in any prison and some prisons are more pleasant

or less disagreeable than others. He may be removed from the prison where he is to another prison which may be much less congenial or much less convenient from his point of view. The duty of the prison authorities is to keep him in custody for the appropriate period and to take care not to allow him to escape. It is not for the prisoner to choose the place or the conditions of his confinement. The Prison Rules provide in very considerable detail for humane and constructive treatment of prisoners and for giving them various privileges, but they do not confer any rights upon them. The prisoner's safeguards against abuse are provided by complaint to the governor or by petition to the Secretary of State.'

I respectfully adopt the observations in both of these cases and apply them here. Nor, in my judgment, is the result in any way affected by a breach of the Prison Rules. The nature of the rules has been considered in many cases.

In *Arbon v Anderson* [1943] 1 All ER 154 at 156–157, [1943] KB 252 at 255 Goddard LJ having said that the rules do not confer any rights on prisoners, observed:

'It would be fatal to all discipline in prisons if governors and warders had to perform their duty always with the fear of an action before their eyes if they in any way deviated from the rules. The safeguards against abuse are appeals to the governor, to the visiting committee, and finally to the Secretary of State, and those in my opinion, are the only remedies.'

In *Becker v Home Office* [1972] 2 All ER 676 at 682, [1972] 2 QB 407 at 418 Lord Denning MR said:

'If the courts were to entertain actions by disgruntled prisoners, the governor's life would be made intolerable. The discipline of the prison would be undermined. The Prison Rules are regulatory directions only. Even if they are not observed, they do not give rise to a cause of action.'

The observations in both of these cases were concerned with the question whether a prisoner could sue for a breach of the rules, but they indicate the nature of the rules. In my judgment, a breach of the rules is not relevant to the question, can the defendant justify in law the detention of the plaintiff. The defendant pleads the sentence of the court, the Prison Act and Rules in the amended defence. Reliance on the rules was unnecessary. It is the sentence of the court and the Act that are relevant to the issue of lawful detention and not the rules.

Counsel for the plaintiff submits that in this case there was an imprisonment within an imprisonment, that is to say, a tortious imprisonment within the currency of a lawful imprisonment. I find the concept hard to apply. The tort of false imprisonment consists of a complete deprivation of liberty for any time, however short, without lawful excuse: see, for example, Clerk and Lindsell on Torts (14th Edn, 1975, para 681).

When the plaintiff, as he did on occasions, had association during stage 2 with Mr McMullan and Mr Masterson the restraints on his freedom of movement were no different from his ordinary life in prison. When at stage 1 he left his cell to slop out or to fetch his food or to go to the library or to go on exercise, either alone or with his fellow prisoners, which type of imprisonment prevailed? Was it the tortious or the lawful imprisonment? I find it difficult to see how the concept of false imprisonment has any application in a case such as this.

Counsel submits that the defendant cannot justify the detention of the plaintiff in the regime in the control unit, because the nature of the regime offended the provision in the Bill of Rights 1688 prohibiting the infliction of cruel and unusual punishments. It is agreed that the plaintiff's presence in the unit at Wakefield was part of the sentence passed upon him in 1971 and that in that sense it was therefore a part of his punishment. The argument has been concentrated upon the meaning of the words 'cruel and unusual' and whether the regime as a matter of fact was either or both, dependent on the construction which I adopt.

The preamble to the Act refers to 'illegal and cruel punishments', but counsel submits that I should disregard the preamble because the meaning of the enacting words is clear.

On behalf of the plaintiff it is submitted that the clause may have two meanings: (i) that it is only a punishment which is both cruel and unusual, which must not be inflicted; or (ii) that the clause may be read disjunctively with the result that the Act prohibits the infliction of cruel punishment and, separately, the infliction of unusual punishments.

On the latter reading, if the regime in the unit was either cruel or unusual there would be a breach of the Act. As I have said, it is argued on behalf of the plaintiff that such a regime is not authorised by the 1952 Act and, if it is authorised by the rules, then the Bill of Rights must prevail, and the regime is accordingly unjustifiable and unlawful.

Counsel for the plaintiff submits that if the words 'cruel and unusual' are used conjunctively, that would mean that it would be lawful to inflict a cruel punishment in present day England, provided such a punishment was inflicted commonly. It is argued that such a construction would be absurd and that it can never be legal to inflict a cruel punishment. Therefore the proper construction is to read the statutory words disjunctively so as to prohibit either a cruel or an unusual punishment.

I am not sure that that argument is correct. I suppose it may be said that it depends on the point of view. Some people regard long terms of imprisonment as cruel, common though they may be and necessary to protect the community.

Counsel relies on the judgment of Heald J in *McCann v R* (1975) 68 DLR (3d) 661. That was a case concerned with the special control units in the British Columbia Penitentiary. The plaintiffs claimed declaratory relief in respect of their time in the units on the ground that the regime offended the Canadian Bill of Rights, which prohibits 'cruel and unusual treatment or punishment'.

Heald J followed the dissenting judgment of MacIntyre J in *R v Miller and Cockriell* [1975] 6 WWR 1. That case was an appeal from a conviction for murder of a police constable and the resulting sentence of death. One of the grounds of appeal was that punishment of death for murder was 'cruel and unusual' within the meaning of the Canadian statute and therefore prohibited by law. The majority opinion read the words conjunctively and held that the punishment of death was not unusual.

McIntyre J, dissenting, considered that the words the statute should be read disjunctively. He said (at 67):

'The words employed to describe the forbidden punishment are conjunctive in form, that is, cruel *and* unusual. Confusion has resulted at times from the use of the two words. While there is a suggestion of a differing view in England, in American judicial and academic writing on the subject, which is the principal source of material on this point, the words have generally been construed disjunctively . . . It has been suggested that the use of the word "unusual" was inadvertent in the English Bill of Rights and the general trend of opinion suggests that it has been given a limiting or controlling influence on the word "cruelty". In my view, then, it is permissible and preferable to read the words "cruel" and "unusual" disjunctively so that cruel punishment, however usual . . . could come within the prescription.'

Neither counsel has been able to trace authority or academic writing in this country which shows a differing view, favouring the conjunctive construction.

Adopting the disjunctive construction and applying the test of 'cruel' alone, Heald J in *McCann v R* found that the conditions in the special control unit were cruel and contrary to the Canadian Bill of Rights. Counsel for the plaintiff asks me to follow the same reasoning of construction, and, by comparing the facts in this case with the facts in *McCann v R* and two American cases, to reach the same conclusion about the unit at Wakefield.

Counsel for the defendant pointed out that in *R v Miller and Cockriell* there was an appeal to the Supreme Court (70 DLR (3d) 234). The court unanimously rejected the disjunctive construction and, indeed, as appears from the judgment of Laskin CJC (at 331), in the course of the argument for the appellants, counsel said that he would not insist on the disjunctive construction and, as Laskin CJC pointed out, in effect abandoned the point.

Two approaches to the construction of the words 'cruel and unusual' recommended themselves to the Supreme Court. One view was expressed by Laskin CJC and three of the judges agreed with him. Laskin CJC said (at 332):

> 'The various judgments in the Supreme Court of the United States, which I would not discount as being irrelevant here, do lend support to the view that "cruel and unusual" are not treated there as conjunctive in the sense of requiring a rigidly separate assessment of each word, each of whose meanings must be met before they become effective against challenged legislation, but rather as interacting expressions colouring each other, so to speak, and hence to be considered together as a compendious expression of a norm. I think this to be a reasonable appraisal . . .'

Ritchie J, with whom four of the judges agreed, said (at 345): 'In my opinion the words "cruel and unusual" . . . are to be read conjunctively and refer to "treatment or punishment" which is both cruel and unusual.'

There is a fully developed body of case law in Canada, but no authority in this country. I can find no reason for construing the words 'cruel and unusual' in a disjunctive sense. The words are clear in their meaning and show an intention to prohibit punishments which are both cruel and unusual.

In my judgment, the regime in the control unit was not unusual when compared with other regimes in the English penal system. The characteristics of the regime in the unit were not dissimilar from the regimes in the segregation unit instituted as the result of the Radzinowicz report. As I have already held, prisoners spend long periods in segregation in such units. It is not unusual for men on r 43 to spend long periods with non-association. Mr Emes said that there is a segregation unit in every dispersal prison.

Counsel for the plaintiff asks me to hold that the regime in the unit was unusual in the lay sense that even in segregation units prisoners served shorter sentences with the possibility of remission, that prisoners on r 43 were held for the shortest practicable time and that their cases were reviewed; that association might be permitted and that normal relations with prison officers continued. He submits that no civilised society had been shown to have similar units, save those outlawed in Canada and the United States.

It is true that men might serve shorter sentences with remission in the segregation units and on r 43, but it is not uncommon for them to serve long periods and much longer than in the control unit. It is true that on r 43 association may be allowed, but equally on the facts it is commonly not allowed. It is also true that prisoners and staff often have favourable relationships, but Mr Waugh, who is a prison officer of great experience, while accepting that officers do develop relationships with prisoners, said that this is not so in segregation units. I accept Mr Waugh's evidence.

In any event, I am satisfied that in fact both the plaintiff and Mr McMullan rapidly developed easy relations with the prison officers, as the history sheets and the evidence of Mr Allum shows. Mr Waugh said that he did not believe that there was any extra 'cool professionalism' in the attitude of the staff. The only difference was that the inmates had to make the first move.

As to the question whether other countries have similar units, I have yet to consider whether the facts found in the case of the control units in the Canadian and United States cases are comparable. I do not think that the unit at Wakefield was unusual and on that finding there was not a breach of the Bill of Rights.

I heard lengthy argument on the issue whether the Wakefield unit was 'cruel'. Counsel for the plaintiff asks me to find that the standard set for prisons by r 31 of the United Nations Standard Minimum Rules adopts the standard set for civil society by the Bill of Rights 1688, the Universal Declaration of Human Rights (UN 2 (1949); Cmd 7662) and the European Convention of Human Rights and Fundamental Freedoms (TS 71 (1953); Cmd 8969).

Rule 31 of the Standard Minimum Rules provides: 'Corporal punishment, punishment by placing in a dark cell, and all cruel, inhuman or degrading punishments shall be completely prohibited as punishments for disciplinary offences.'

Article 3 of the European Convention of Human Rights provides: 'No one shall be subjected to torture or to inhuman and degrading treatment or punishment.' The language is similar to that of the Bill of Rights.

Counsel for the plaintiff has, on this part of the argument, referred me to *Waddington*
a *v Miah* [1974] 2 All ER 377, [1974] 1 WLR 683, and *R v Secretary of State for Home*
Affairs, ex parte Bhajan Singh [1975] 2 All ER 1081, [1976] QB 198 as to the approach
which I should adopt towards the Minimum Standard Rules and the European
Convention. I need only refer to a sentence in the judgment of Lord Denning MR in
the latter case, where he said ([1975] 2 All ER 1081 at 1083, [1976] QB 198 at 207):
'The court can and should take the convention into account. They should take it into
b account whenever interpreting a statute which affects the rights and liberties of the
individual.'

I take into account the provisions when considering whether the regime in the unit
was 'cruel'. Counsel for the plaintiff suggested a formula which I should adopt when
approaching the question whether the regime was cruel. He said that there is an
irreducible minimum below which the court, reflecting public standards of morality,
c will not allow society to sink, whatever the pressures may be to take the relevant steps.
Thus, granted the urgent need to deal with troublemakers and subverters in prison, some
steps might fall below an acceptable minimum. Above that level there may be conduct
towards prisoners which is cruel because it is disproportionate. Counsel submits that if
the conduct called into question does not fall below the minimum level then I must
balance what was done against the need for doing it. Apart from these standards, the test
d for what is cruel is objective. I should look at the regime as it was and ask myself
whether it was cruel in relation to the sort of person who was in the unit, that is the
inveterate troublemaker.

Counsel for the defendant accepted this approach and I shall do so. I have no doubt
that the regime did not fall below the irreducible minimum, judged by contemporary
standards, of public morality. That the authorities felt that something had to be done to
e deal with troublemakers is only too plain from the report of the working party and the
evidence of Mr Emes, which I have accepted.

Was what was done 'cruel'? There are two comparative standards: one within the
English prison system and the other in the North American cases. Judged by the
standards of the English prison system, I do not think that the regime in the unit was
cruel. The report of the Radzinowicz committee, which was approved by the whole of
f the Advisory Council on the Penal System, recommended a regime which in many ways
is not unlike the control unit. Although men might be released after a short time, the
committee clearly envisaged that prisoners might be in the segregation unit for a long
time and (see para 166) that it would not have been necessary to have found them guilty
of a specific offence.

In the working party report of March 1973 the possibility was recognised that prisoners
g 'will have to spend long periods, perhaps even until discharge, in the special units'. The
privileges available in the segregation unit would be more limited than in the control
unit, and the prisoner should have none of the minor amenities of life, save letters and
visits. In the control unit the prisoner had extensive possessions and the right to have
tobacco. He was, it is true, denied the right to have a radio, but that is also the provision
in the segregation unit. Comparing the control unit with the segregation unit, I do not
h think that the latter was cruel.

When he gave evidence, Professor Taylor made a comparison of features in the special
control unit in *R v McCann* and *Clonce v Richardson* (1974) 379 Fed Supp 338, and he
expressed the opinion that there was a similarity between the control unit and the
regimes in the North American penitentiaries.

I am thus asked to say that the control unit regime was cruel. I have been provided
j with the details of the facts in another case, *Bono v Saxbe* (19th April 1978, unreported)
heard in the Eastern District of Illinois. Professor Taylor said that he had read the details
of the facts in *Saxbe*, but he said that in terms of comparison the facts were less
effective. But if I am to compare the regime in the control unit with *McCann* and *Clonce*
in order to decide whether the regime in the control unit was cruel, I do not follow why
I should not compare the control unit with the facts in *Saxbe*.

As I said earlier, counsel have prepared a very helpful table comparing the features at
Wakefield with the features of the units in *McCann*, *Clonce* and *Saxbe*. The facts are

extremely detailed. It is not possible to refer to them other than in outline. I have read
them and I bear them fully in mind.

While some features were better (for example in *Clonce* at the equivalent of stage 2 the
prisoner was allowed a radio and even television) my impression is that the features at
Wakefield were better than in the other cases. In *McCann* the light was left on for 24
hours, being dimmed at night. The prisoners had exercise only for 30 to 40 minutes a
day and always taken indoors. There was no furniture in the cell, except a cement slab,
bedding, a WC and a hand basin. The prisoners had to sleep with their heads near the
toilet bowl. But above all, they were in the unit, on the whole, for very much longer
periods. The plaintiff *McCann* spent a total of 1,471 days in the unit, of which the longest
continuous period was 754 days. Another plaintiff, named Oag, spent 682 days in the
unit, of which 573 were continuous. The prisoners were locked in their cells for 23½
hours a day.

I bear all the comparative details in mind, including those in *Clonce* and *Saxbe*, but they
do not displace my conclusion that the regime in the Wakefield unit was not cruel.

Counsel for the plaintiff submitted that I should find that there were reasonable
alternatives to the control unit. The only alternatives suggested in the evidence were
transfer of the plaintiff to another prison or a period on r 43 in the dispersal prison or a
system of trial periods in the unit, the latter being rejected for reasons given by Mr Emes,
which I have accepted. But the expedients of transfer and removal from association had
already been tried and had failed. In para 8 of CI 35/1974 it is said that the normal
alternatives of transfer and non-association will have been tried before the prisoner was
to be transferred to the unit.

Although Dr Thomas was highly critical of the control unit, he nevertheless was a
supporter of the 'fortress' principle for the detention of long term prisoners,
recommended in 1966 in the report of the Mountbatten Committee. This would have
involved a concentration of long term prisoners in one prison. It was not adopted, as I
understand it, because of the inevitably repressive nature of the regime and its
consequential effect on staff/inmate relationships. It was feared that the prisoners would
see their incarceration as 'the end of the road'.

Presumably, therefore, Dr Thomas would not regard the rejected regime of the
'fortress' as cruel, and yet he condemns the regime at Wakefield.

I am asked to consider objectively what was the effect of the regime on the sort of
prisoners, the plaintiff, Mr McMullan and Mr Masterson, who were in the unit. As I
have held, I am not satisfied that the regime had any ill effect upon them. There are no
other prisoners by whose reaction I can judge the effect of the regime.

I bear in mind the whole of my findings of fact with respect of the regime at stages 1
and 2, the feature of reversion and the attitude of the staff, in reaching my conclusion
that the regime was not cruel.

Finally, there is the issue of natural justice. I have been referred to very many
authorities on this difficult branch of the law, but I need refer only to one of them,
R v Gaming Board for Great Britain, ex parte Benaim [1970] 2 All ER 528, [1970] 2 QB 417,
for the principles which I must apply. Lord Denning MR said ([1970] 2 All ER 528 at
533, [1970] 2 QB 417 at 430):

> 'It is not possible to lay down rigid rules as to when the principles of natural
> justice are to apply: nor as to their scope and extent. Everything depends on the
> subject-matter; see what Tucker LJ said in *Russell v Duke of Norfolk* [1949] 1 All ER
> 109 and Lord Upjohn in *Durayappah v Fernando* [1967] 2 All ER 152, [1967] 2 AC
> 337. At one time it was said that the principles only apply to judicial proceedings
> and not to administrative proceedings. That heresy was scotched in *Ridge v Baldwin*
> [1963] 2 All ER 66, [1964] AC 40 . . .'

I have therefore to consider the extent of the application of the principles in relation
to the subject matter of this case. Counsel for the defendant did not dispute that the
principles of natural justice applied, but he submitted that they only extend to making
sure that the control unit committee acted fairly when considering the application to
transfer the plaintiff to the unit.

a Counsel for the defendant urges that in cases where the administrative jurisdiction under r 43 is exercised it is inconceivable that prisoners should be given an opportunity to make representations against the procedure proposed. He submits that it would undermine the whole basis of administrative decisions under r 43 if the prisoners were allowed to make representations why they should not be deprived of association under the rules. There is, of course, a clear distinction between jurisdiction under r 43 and the hearing of an offence under rr 47 to 56. In the latter case the prisoner has a statutory

b right to be heard and there is full provision under the rules.

Counsel for the defendant invites me to adopt the approach which Cantley J took in *Payne v Home Office* (2nd May 1977, unreported). That, as I have said, was a case in which the plaintiff sought to invoke the principles of natural justice in relation to his classification as a Category A prisoner. He submitted that he ought to have been informed of what was being alleged against him and allowed to put his own case.

c Having considered all the cases, including *R v Gaming Board of Great Britain, ex parte Benaim* the legislative framework in which the legislator was working and the scope and objective of the proceedings, Cantley J held that it was inappropriate that a prisoner should have the right to be heard in relation to classification. He held that the legislation did not contemplate that a prisoner should be given the details relevant to his classification or to make representations as to how he should be classified. The duty was,

d in the circumstances, confined to acting fairly when classifying prisoners.

Counsel submits that if a prisoner has no right to make representations about his classification, then a prisoner in r 43 cases should not be allowed to do so.

I have earlier reviewed in some considerable detail the approach which counsel for the plaintiff submits that I should adopt. He argues that the Secretary of State had no power to act under r 43 and that, if he had such a power, the procedure for renewal was not

e followed. In the latter context counsel submits that the basic modicum of fairness was not followed because the renewal of the plaintiff's detention under the control unit regime was automatic. According to this argument, it would be unrealistic to hold that the plaintiff had the safeguard of complaining to the governor; he could do nothing. Nor would it be realistic to hold that the plaintiff had the safeguard of complaining to the Secretary of State; he would be being a judge in his own cause.

f It seems to me that Parliament, as reflected in the Prison Act and the Prison Rules, drew a clear distinction between r 43 cases and cases of offences against discipline. In the former case the prisoner has no voice in the decision which is to be taken. When a man is transferred to a segregation unit he is not able to make any representation. In para 166 of the Radzinowicz report it is said that before transferring a prisoner to a segregation unit it is not necessary for them to have been guilty of an offence, and it therefore follows

g that there is no right to be heard or to make any representation against the decision.

It is true that in this case the renewal procedure was followed automatically and without considering whether there had been any change in the plaintiff's position. On the evidence, and my finding, there was no change. I do not think that the fact that the control unit failed to follow the procedural steps shows that they acted unfairly or that they should have given the plaintiff the right to make representations. The plaintiff

h could, as he knew and as appears from the cell information card, have petitioned the Secretary of State. There is no evidence to suggest that the Secretary of State would not have considered any petition of the plaintiff fully and fairly.

In all the circumstances of this case, I do not consider that the principles of natural justice required that the plaintiff should have been given notice of what was intended and the opportunity to make representations that he should not be transferred to the

j unit. Such a step is not within the contemplation of the Prison Act or the Prison Rules and would be damaging to the exercise of the administrative power under r 43. Nor do I think that the principles of natural justice required that he should have had the opportunity to make representations when his detention was renewed month by month.

I hold that the principles of natural justice required the control unit committee to consider the request to transfer the plaintiff to the unit fairly and in accordance with the prescribed criteria. It is not suggested that the committee failed in that respect.

For all the reasons I have given, I hold that the detention of the plaintiff in the control unit at Wakefield from 23rd August 1974 to 20th February 1975 was lawfully justified and that the action in tort fails. It is therefore not necessary for me to consider the issue of damages. I should say that counsel for the plaintiff asked me to assess the damages in the event of the action failing, but I do not consider that it would be appropriate to do so. I have found that there is, on the issue of compensatory damages, no element of nervous and mental suffering. I do not think that it is realistic to value something which I have found did not exist. The element of unlawful detention in compensatory damages did not exist. On any view, in my judgment, it could not have existed at stage 2 when the plaintiff was free to associate with his fellow prisoners.

So far as the claim for exemplary damages is concerned, it is said that the defendants acted in an arbitrary way because they acted unlawfully. I have found that the defendant did act lawfully, although there was a non-compliance with the Prison Rules, the breach of which did not have any legal effect. It is said that the defendants acted oppressively because the regime bore harshly on the inmates subjected to it. As I have held, on the authorities to which I have referred, prison conditions unfortunately do vary, according to the category and behaviour of the prisoner. It is said that the Secretary of State acted unconstitutionally because he had no power to do what he did. I have held that the Secretary of State was lawfully entitled to act.

Counsel for the plaintiff submitted that the regime was not made public because the authorities did not publish what they intended to do, but circulated the regime by a circular instruction. As I said at the beginning of my judgment, a circular instruction is the means by which instructions are passed from headquarters to governors in the field. As I understand the practice, this is the way in which such regimes are established. It was done in the case of the 'cooling off' procedure by CI 10/1974.

Counsel made a number of other submissions on the issue of exemplary damages, but, since the issue of damages does not arise, I do not think it necessary to consider them.

With respect to declaratory relief, I have a discretion whether to make an order. In this case, in the exercise of my discretion, I do not consider that I should make a declaration for these reasons: first, I have held that the Secretary of State had power to act under r 43; second, the action of false imprisonment has failed and any breach of the rules did not go to the validity of the plaintiff's detention. The highest point of the plaintiff's case could, in my judgment, have been that there was a breach of the Prison Rules which are regulatory and not mandatory. Third, and most important, it is well established that it is inappropriate to grant declarations which are academic and of no practical value. In *Merricks v Nott-Bower* [1964] 1 All ER 717 at 721, [1965] 1 QB 57 at 67 Lord Denning MR stated the approach which should be adopted to the granting of declarations. He said: 'If a real question is involved, which is not merely theoretical, and on which the court's decision gives practical guidance, then the court in its discretion can grant a declaration.'

The control unit at Wakefield was closed in October 1975 and the plaintiff left it in February of that year. The chances of its return seem to me on the evidence to be very remote. It is true that at the very end of his cross-examination Mr Emes said that in 1975 the Secretary of State had retained the option to reopen the unit. This was made in answer to a Parliamentary question. Mr Emes said that he had no knowledge of any intention to reopen the control units. No one can, of course, say what a Secretary of State may decide to do at some future time, but on all the present information I think that a declaration would be of no practical use.

For the reasons I have given, the claims for damages and a declaration must fail.

Action dismissed.

Solicitors: *Harriet Harman* (for the plaintiff); *Treasury Solicitor.*

K Mydeen Esq Barrister.

End of Volume 1